CODE OF VIRGINIA
1950

With Provisions for Subsequent Pocket Parts

ANNOTATED

Prepared under the Supervision of

The Virginia Code Commission

BY

The Editorial Staff of the Publishers

VOLUME 10

2004 Replacement Volume

(Includes Acts of the 2004 Regular and Special Sessions.)

LexisNexis

P.O. Box 7587, Charlottesville, VA 22906-7587

4906011

ISBN 0-8205-8604-8

www.lexisnexis.com

Customer Service: 1-800-833-9844

(Pub.49005)

User's Guide

In order to assist both the legal profession and the lay person in obtaining the maximum benefit from the Code of Virginia, a User's Guide has been included in Volume 1. This guide contains comments and information on the many features found within the Code of Virginia intended to increase the usefulness of this set of laws to the user. See Volume 1 of this set for the complete User's Guide.

Suggestions, comments, or questions about the Code of Virginia or this Replacement Volume are welcome. You may call us toll free at (800) 833-9844, fax us toll free at (800) 643-1280, email us at Customer.Support@LexisNexis.com, or write Code of Virginia Editor, LexisNexis, P.O. Box 7587, Charlottesville, Virginia 22906-7587.

For an online bookstore, technical and customer support, and other company information, visit LexisNexis' Internet home page at **http://www.lexis.com.**

Table of Contents

VOLUME 10

Table of Titles

TITLE

IN ADDITION, THIS PUBLICATION CONTAINS

Table of Comparative Sections

Showing Sections of the Code of 1919 and Acts Subsequently Codified, as They Appear in Michie Code of 1942 and Michie Supplement of 1948, and Corresponding Sections of the Code of 1950.

Michie Code Section	Code 1950 Section
1	1-1
2	1-10
3	1-11
4	1-12
5	1-13
5a	1-13
5b	1-15
6	1-16
7	1-17
8	1-6
9	7-1
10	7-2
11	7-3
12	7-4
13	7-5
14	7-6
15	7-7
16	7-8
16a	Omitted
17	7-17
17a	Repealed by Acts 1936, p. 612
18	7-18
19	7-19
19a-19b	Repealed by Acts 1936, p. 612
19c	7-21
19d	7-25
19e	7-24
19f	7-20
20	7-10
21	7-11
22	7-12
23	7-13
24	7-14
25	7-15
26	7-16
27	7-26, 7-28, 7-29
28	7-27
29	7-30
30	7-31
31	7-32
32	7-33
33	7-34
33a	7-36
33b	7-31
34	57-1
35	57-2
36	57-3

Michie Code Section	Code 1950 Section
37	57-4
38	57-7
38a	57-16
39	57-8
40	57-9
41	57-10
42	57-11
43	57-12
44	57-13
45	57-14
46	57-15
46a	57-17
46b	18-231.1
47	57-19
47a	40-63
48	57-20
49	57-21
49a	57-18
50	57-22
51	57-23
52	57-24
53	57-25
53a	57-28 to 57-30
54	57-36
55	57-37, 57-38
56	57-26
57	57-27
58	Repealed by Acts 1946, p. 408
58a	57-39
59	57-31 to 57-35
59a	57-40 to 57-47
60	57-5
61	57-6
61a	Omitted
61a(1)	10-133,10-134
61b, 61c	Omitted
62	1-18
63	1-19
64	1-20
65	1-21
66	55-1
67	1-14
68	24-1
69	24-2
70	24-3
71	24-4
72	24-5
73	24-6

Michie Code Section	Code 1950 Section
74	24-7
75	24-8
76	24-9
77	24-10
78	24-11, 24-12, 24-15
79	24-14, 24-15
80	24-13
81	24-16
82	24-17 to 24-20
82a	24-21
83	24-22
83a	24-24, 24-25
83b	24-25 to 24-27
83c	24-28
84	24-29 to 24-31
85	24-32
86	24-52 to 24-54
86a	24-57
86b	24-58
86c	24-59
86d	24-60
86e	24-61, 24-62
86f	24-63
86g	24-64
86g(1)	24-119
86g(2)	24-119
86h	24-119
87	24-34
88	24-35, 24-36
89	24-37 to 24-41
90	24-91
90a	24-92
91	24-93
92	24-42
93	24-67 to 24-73
94	Repealed by Acts 1946, p. 484
94a	24-84
94b	24-83.1
95	24-83
96	24-65
97	24-66
98	24-74 to 24-82.1
99	24-94, 24-95
100	24-85 to 24-88
101	24-89
102	24-90
103	24-112
104	24-113, 24-114

Michie Code Section	Code 1950 Section
105	24-115
106	24-116
107	24-96 to 24-101
107a	24-102 to 24-105
107b	24-106 to 24-111
108	24-117
108a	24-118
109	24-120 to 24-122
110	24-123
111	24-124
112	24-125
113	24-126
114	24-127
115	24-128
116	24-129
117	Repealed by Acts 1928, p. 239
118	24-148
119	24-149
120	24-150, 24-151
121	24-152
122	24-153
123	24-154
124	24-155
125	24-156
126	15-527, 63-320, 63-321
127	24-157
128	24-158
129	17-118.1, 24-160 to 24-167
130	24-143
131	24-159
132	24-142
133	24-144
134, 135	Omitted
136	24-145
136a	24-147.1
137	24-147
138	24-145
139	24-146
140	24-136
141	24-137
142	24-180
143	24-44
144	24-46 to 24-51, 24-179
145	24-45
145a	24-181
146	24-138
147	24-139
148	24-193, 24-194, 24-195 to 24-197
148a	24-194.1
149	24-198, 24-199
150	24-255, 24-256
151	24-257
152	24-182, 24-183
153	24-216
154	24-33, 24-130 to 24-135
154a	24-234
155	24-213 to 24-215, 24-217
156	24-218 to 24-222
157	Repealed by Acts 1948, p. 706
157a	24-290.1 to 24-290.6
158	24-43, 24-223 to 24-229
159	24-230 to 24-233
160	24-185
161	24-186, 24-187
162	24-244 to 24-247, 24-252
162a	24-291 to 24-318
163	24-236, 24-237
164	24-250
165	24-238
166	24-251
167	24-188, 24-239, 24-240
168	24-170, 24-176
169	Repealed by Acts 1946, p. 318
170	24-177
171	24-241
172	24-242
173	24-243, 24-248, 24-249
174	24-253
175	24-254
176	24-184, 24-258
177	24-259 to 24-264
178	24-265
179	24-266
180	24-267 to 24-269
181	24-270
182	24-200 to 24-203, 24-271 to 24-274
183	24-275
184	24-276, 24-277
185	24-278 to 24-281
186	24-282
187	24-205
188	Repealed by Acts 1946, p. 484
189	24-283
190	24-284
191	24-285 to 24-289
192	24-290
193	24-189
194	24-190
195	24-191
196	24-192
197	24-140
197a	24-141
198	24-204
199	24-206
200	24-55, 24-207 to 24-209
201	24-210
202	24-319
203	24-321 to 24-325
204	24-326
205	24-327 to 24-331
206	24-332
207	24-333
208	24-334 to 24-336
209	24-337
210	24-320
211	24-338
212	24-339
213	24-340
214	24-341
215	24-342
216	24-343
216a	24-344
217	24-345
218	Repealed by Acts 1946, p. 322
219-220	Repealed by Acts 1922, p. 878
220(1)-220(14)	Omitted
220(15)-220(40)	Repealed by Acts 1945, p. 11
220(41)-220(57)	Omitted
221	24-346
222	24-348
223	24-349
224	24-353 to 24-357, 24-407
225	24-359, 24-360
226	24-361, 24-362
227	24-347, 24-363 to 24-366
228	24-367, 24-368
229	24-369 to 24-373
230	24-374, 24-375
231	24-406
232	Repealed by Acts 1942, p. 511
233	Omitted
234	24-402
235	24-405
236	24-376
237	24-377, 24-408
238	24-378 to 24-382
239	24-383 to 24-386
240	24-387
241	24-388
242	24-389
243	24-390
244	24-404
245	24-396
246	24-350
246a	24-391
246b	24-235, 24-392
247	24-393 to 24-395

Michie Code Section	Code 1950 Section
248	24-351, 24-352, 24-358, 24-397
249	Repealed by Acts 1942, p. 539
249a	24-398 to 24-401
250	24-403
251	24-440
252	24-441
253	24-442, 24-443
254	24-444
255	24-445
256	24-446, 24-447
257	24-448
258	24-449
259	24-419 to 24-422
260	24-178, 24-423
261	24-424
262	24-425
263	24-426
264	24-427, 24-428
265	24-429
266	Repealed by Acts 1946, p. 487
267	24-430 to 24-438
268	24-439
268(1)	24-409 to 24-415
268(2)	24-416
268(3)	24-417, 24-418
268a	24-211
268b	24-212
268c	24-450
268d	24-451
268e	24-452
268f	24-453
268g	24-454
268h	24-455
269	49-1
270, 271	Repealed by Acts 1926, p. 318
272	49-2
273	49-3
274	49-4
275	49-5
275a	49-6
276	49-7
276a	Omitted
277	49-8
278	49-9
278a	49-10
279	49-12
279a	2-11
280	49-13
281	49-14
282	49-15
283	49-16
284	49-17
285	49-18
285a	Omitted
286	49-19
287	49-20
288	49-11, 49-21
289	2-26
290	2-27, 2-28
291	2-29
291a	2-30
291b	2-28
291c	2-31
291d	Omitted
292	2-32
293	2-33
294	30-1
295	30-2
296	30-3
297	30-4
298	30-5
299	30-6
300	30-7
301	30-8
302	30-9
303	30-10
304	30-11
305	30-12
306	30-13
307	30-14
308	30-15
309	30-16
309a-309b	Repealed by Acts 1938, p. 27
310	30-17
311	30-18
311a	9-53 to 9-60
312	30-19
312a	30-20
312b	30-21
312c	30-22
312d	30-23
312e	30-24
312f	30-25
312g	30-26
312h	30-27
312i	30-28
313-317	Repealed by Acts 1930, p. 974
318	2-37
319	2-36
320	2-38
320a	Omitted
321	2-40
321a	2-40.1
322	9-49 to 9-52
322a	2-43
322b	2-45
322c	2-42
323-324	Repealed by Acts 1932, p. 884
325	2-7, 2-8
326	2-9
327	2-10
328	2-11
329	2-12
330	2-13
331	Omitted
332	2-14 to 2-16, 52-23, 52-24
333	Omitted
334	2-63
335	2-145
336	Omitted
336a	2-39
337	Repealed by Acts 1932, p. 884
338	2-17
339	2-18
340	2-146
341	2-147
342	2-148
342a	2-24
342b	2-23
342c	Repealed by Acts 1940, p. 344
342d	2-5, 2-6, 8-268
343	2-59
344	2-60
345	2-61
345a	54-1
346	2-64
347	Repealed by Acts 1938, p. 238
347(1)-347(2)	Repealed by Acts 1938, p. 238
347(3)	42-13, 42-14
347(4)	2-245, 42-15
347(5)	42-16
347(6)	42-17
347(7)	Repealed by Acts 1938, p. 238
347(8)	42-18
347(9)	42-19
347(10)	Omitted
347(11)	42-23
348	42-33
349	42-42
350	42-43
351	42-13, 42-34 to 42-41, 42-44, 42-45, 42-47 to 42-49
352	42-50, 42-51
353	42-58, 42-59
354	42-60, 42-61
355	42-62, 42-63
355a	Repealed by Acts 1936, p. 116
355b	Omitted
356	42-52
357	42-53
358	42-54
358a	Omitted
359	42-44, 42-45
360	42-46
361	42-55 to 42-57
362	42-20 to 42-22

Michie Code Section	Code 1950 Section
363	54-261 to 54-272
364	42-1 to 42-3
365	42-4 to 42-12
365(½)	42-24 to 42-32
365(1)	2-237
365(2)	2-236
366-367	Repealed by Acts 1936, p. 116
368-371	Omitted
372	Repealed by Acts 1936, p. 76
373-374	Omitted
374a	285 to 2-93, 2-94 to 2-97, 14-14
374b	59-16 to 59-18
374c	8-714
375-378	Repealed by Acts 1936, p. 76
378a	Repealed by Acts 1934, p. 74
378b	2-98 to 2-102
378c	2-103
378d	2-104 to 2-108, 2-112
378e	2-104
378f	2-109 to 2-111
378g	2-113
378h	2-114
378i	2-115
378j	2-116
379	Omitted
380	2-212
381	2-213, 2-214
382	2-219
383	2-220 to 2-222
384	2-223
385	2-226
385a	2-227
386	2-228
387	2-229
388	2-230
389	2-231
390	2-232
391	2-233
392	2-234
393	2-235, 2-238
394	2-2, 2-239 to 2-241
395	2-242, 2-243
396	2-244
397	2-47
398	2-224
399	2-225
400	2-245
401	2-246
401a	2-247
401b	2-249 to 2-254
401c	2-255, 2-256
401d	2-257 to 2-259
401e	2-260, 2-261
401e1	2-259.2
401f	2-262

Michie Code Section	Code 1950 Section
401g	2-263
401h	2-264
401i	2-265
401j	2-215
401k	2-216
401l	2-217
401m	2-266
401n	2-267
401o	2-218
401p	2-248
401q	2-268
402	2-66
403	2-67
403a	2-41
404	2-68
405	2-69
406	2-70
407	2-71
407a	Omitted
408	2-72
409	Repealed by Acts 1936, p. 53
410	2-73
410a	41-1
410b	2-74
410c	2-77.1 to 2-77.9
411	2-75
412	2-76
413	2-77
414	41-2
415	41-44
416	41-12
417	41-9
418	41-3
419	41-4
420	41-15, 41-16
421	41-8.1
422	41-17
423	41-18
424	41-19
425	41-20
426	41-21
427	41-22
428	41-23
429	41-24
430	41-25
431	41-26
432	41-27
433	41-28
434	41-29
435	41-30
436	41-31
437	41-32
438	41-33
439	41-34
440	41-35
441	41-36
442	41-37
443	41-38
444	41-45 to 41-47
445	41-48

Michie Code Section	Code 1950 Section
446	41-49
447	41-50
448	41-51
449	41-52
450	41-53
451	41-54
452	41-55
453	41-56
454	41-57
455	41-58
456	41-59
457	41-39
458	41-40
459	41-8
460	41-11
461	41-13
462	41-10
463	41-41
464	41-42
465	41-43
466	Omitted
467	41-5
468	41-6
469	41-7
470	41-14
471	41-60
472	41-61
473	41-62
474	41-63
475	41-64
476	41-65
477	41-66
478	41-67
479	41-68
480	41-69
481	41-70
482	41-71
483	41-72
484	41-73
485	41-74
486	41-75
487	41-76
488	41-77
489	55-168
490	55-169
491	55-170
492	55-171
493	55-172
494	55-173
495	55-174
496	55-175
497	55-176
498	55-177
499	55-178
500	55-179
501	55-180
502	55-181
503	55-182
504	55-183
505	55-184
506	55-185

Michie Code Section	Code 1950 Section
507	55-186
508	55-187
509	55-188
510	55-189
511	55-190
512	55-191
513	55-192
514	55-193
515	55-194
516	55-195
517	55-196
518	55-197
519	55-198
520	55-199
521	55-200
522	55-201
523	10-84, 10-85
524	10-85
525	10-32
526	10-33, 10-34
527	10-34
527a	10-68 to 10-74
528	Omitted
529	10-41, 10-115
530	10-37
531	10-38
532	10-42
533	10-40
534	10-35
535	10-88
536	10-36
536a	10-48 to 10-50
537	10-87
538	10-89
539	10-86
540	10-55
541	10-46, 10-56 to 10-58, 10-60, 10-90
541a	10-59
542	10-47
542a	10-61
543	10-43
544	10-44
545	10-62
545a	10-63
546	10-65
546a	10-64
546b	10-66
547	10-67
548	10-45
549	10-39
549a	Repealed by Acts 1948, p. 1004
549a1	10-75 to 10-83
549b	10-51 to 10-54
549(1)	58-838.1
549(2)	58-838.2 to 58-838.4
549(3)	58-838.5
549(4)	58-838.6
549(5)	58-838.7

Michie Code Section	Code 1950 Section
549(6)	58-838.8
549(7)	58-838.9
549(8)	58-838.10
549(9)	58-838.11
549(10)	58-838.12
549(11)	58-838.13
549(12)	58-838.14
549(13)	58-838.15
549(14)	58-838.16
549(15)	58-838.17
549(16)	58-838.18
549(17)	58-838.19
549(18)	58-838.20
550, 551	Omitted
552	2-128
553	2-129
554	2-130
555	2-131
556	Omitted
557	2-132
558	2-133
559	2-140
560	2-141
561	2-144
562	2-142
563	2-134
564	2-135
565	2-138, 2-139
565a	2-136, 2-137, 2-143
565b	Repealed by Acts 1926, p. 938
566	54-84 to 54-88
567	54-89 to 54-91
568	54-92
569	54-93
570	54-94
571	54-95 to 54-99
572	54-100
572a	54-101, 54-102
573	2-117
574	2-118
575	2-119
576	2-120
577	2-121
578	2-122
579	2-123
580	2-124
580a	30-29
580b	30-30
580c	30-31
580d	30-32
580e	30-33
580f	30-34
580(1)	54-2
580(2)	54-3
580(3)	54-4 to 54-9
580(4)	54-10
580(5)	54-11
580(6)	54-12 to 54-14
580(7)	54-15
580(8)	54-16

Michie Code Section	Code 1950 Section
580(a1)	9-1
580(a2)	9-2
580(a3)	9-3
580(a4)	9-4
580(a5)	9-5
580(a6)	9-6
580(b1)-580(b3)	Repealed by Acts 1946, p. 399
581	9-7
582	9-11
582a	9-12
583	9-10
584	9-8
585	9-9
585(1)-585(4)	Repealed by Acts 1938, p. 238
585(4)a	Omitted
585(5)-585(9)	Repealed by Acts 1938, p. 238
585(10)-585(14)	Omitted
585(15)-585(32)	Repealed by Acts 1930, p. 49
585(33)	Omitted
585(34)	10-2, 10-4 to 10-6
585(34a)	10-2
585(35)	10-7
585(36)	10-8
585(37), 585(38)	Omitted
585(39)	10-9, 10-116
585(40)	10-10
585(41)	10-11
585(42), 585(43)	Omitted
585(44)	10-13, 10-14
585(45), 585(46)	Omitted
585(47)	10-21
585(47)a	10-21.3
585(47)b	10-21.1
585(48)	10-17
585(49)	10-15
585(50), 585(51)	Omitted
585(51)a	10-21.2
585(51)b	9-16, 9-17
585(51)c	9-18, 9-19
585(51)d	9-20
585(51)e	9-21
585(51)f	9-22 to 9-25
585(51)g	9-26
585(51)h	9-27, 9-28
585(51)i	9-29
585(51)j	9-35
585(51)k	9-30
585(51)l	9-31
585(51)m	9-32
585(51)o	9-36
585(51)p	9-37 to 9-39
585(51)q	9-40
585(51)r	9-41, 9-42
585(51)s	9-43
585(51)t	9-44
585(51)u	9-45, 18-319
585(51)v	9-46

Michie Code Section	Code 1950 Section
585(51)w	9-47
585(51)x	9-48
585(51)y	2-25
585(52)-585(58)	Omitted
585(58a)	7-22
585(58b)	10-99
585(58c)	10-100
585(58d)	10-101, 10-102
585(58e)	10-104
585(58f)	10-103
585(58g)	10-105
585(58h)	10-106, 10-107
585(58i)	10-108
585(58j)	10-109
585(58k)	10-110
585(58l)	10-111
585(58m)	10-112
585(58n)	Omitted
585(59)	2-34
585(60)	2-47
585(61)	2-58
585(62)	44-11, 44-13
585(63)	2-65, 2-66
585(64)	9-7
585(65)	Omitted
585(66)	2-1
585(66a)	2-3, 2-4
585(67)	Omitted
585(68)	2-149, 2-160
585(69)	2-7, 2-8, 2-150, 2-152 to 2-154, 2-155, 2-159, 2-160, 2-161, 2-162, 2-163, 2-166, 2-167, 2-168, 2-175, 2-176, 2-189, 2-200 to 2-205, 14-15
585(70)	2-246, 2-265
585(71)	Omitted
585(71a)	46-23 to 46-26, 52-1 to 52-4
585(71b)	15-555.1, 52-4.1
585(72)	2-125 to 2-127, 2-134
585(73), 585(74)	Omitted
585(75)	23-61
585(76)	Omitted
585(77)	54-53
585(78), 585(79)	Omitted
585(80)	40-1, 45-1
585(81), 585(82)	Omitted
585(83)	3-138
585(84)	28-11, 28-12, 29-3, 29-5 to 29-8, 29-11
585(85)	Omitted
585(86)	Repealed by Acts 1942, p. 630
585(87)	63-3

Michie Code Section	Code 1950 Section
585(88)	63-365, 63-371
585(89)	Omitted
585(89a)	37-53 to 37-60
585(90)	Repealed by Acts 1930, p. 53
585(91)	Repealed by Acts 1930, p. 676
585(92)	Repealed by Acts 1930, p. 53
585(93)	65-9, 65-127
585(94)	2-35
585(94a)	9-66 to 9-68
585(95)	2-78
585(96)	2-79
585(97)	2-81
585(98)	2-82
585(99)	2-83
585(100)	2-84
585(101)	2-80
585(a1)-585(a4)	Omitted
585(b1)	9-61
585(b2)	9-62
585(b3)	9-63
585(b4)	9-64
585(b5)	9-65
586	Repealed by Acts 1928, p. 1226
587	55-26
587a	55-31
587b	55-32
588	55-27
589	55-28
590	55-29
591	55-30
592	55-33
593	55-34
594, 595	Repealed by Acts 1928, p. 1226
596-600	Repealed by Acts 1932, p. 884
601	22-17
602	22-18
603, 604	Repealed by Acts 1932, p. 884
605, 606	Repealed by Acts 1920, p. 494
607	Repealed by Acts 1932, p. 884
608	22-26, 22-28
609	22-19, 22-276
610	22-202
610a-610g	Repealed by Acts 1928, p. 1226
611	22-1, 22-2
611a	Omitted
612	22-11 to 22-15
613	22-29
614	22-53, 22-143
615	22-30, 22-37
616	22-36
617	22-296 to 22-298

Michie Code Section	Code 1950 Section
618	22-299 to 22-306
619, 620	Omitted
621	22-310
622	22-311
623	22-312
624	22-140
625	22-319 to 22-324
626	22-330
627	22-21
628	22-40
629	22-16, 22-20
630	22-22 to 22-24
631	22-25
631a	22-27
632	22-101
633	22-102
634	22-103
635	22-104
636	22-105
637	22-106
638	22-107
639	22-108
640	22-109
641	22-110
642	22-111
643	22-112
644	22-113
644(1)	22-68, 22-69
644a-644r	Repealed by Acts 1928, p. 1227
645	22-114
645a	22-115
646	22-116
647	22-117
648	22-145
649	22-31 to 22-34, 22-38
650	22-35
651	22-32, 22-38, 22-39
652	22-36.1
653, 653a	Repealed by Acts 1942, p. 682
653a1	22-60 to 22-67
653a2	22-42, 22-43, 22-99, 22-100
653a3	22-141
653a4	22-83
653b	Omitted
654	Omitted
655	22-45 to 22-48.1, 22-49 to 22-52, 22-70
656	22-71, 22-78, 22-210
657	22-122 to 22-125
658	22-121
659	22-54
660	22-72, 22-203 to 22-206
660a	22-211
661	22-79
662	22-136

Michie Code Section	Code 1950 Section
663	22-229, 22-231
664	22-207 to 22-209, 22-230
664a	Repealed by Acts 1948, p. 73
665	Repealed by Acts 1942, p. 108
666	22-239
667	22-57
668	Repealed by Acts 1942, p. 108
668a	22-55
669	22-149
670	22-7
671	22-152 to 22-158
671a	Repealed by Acts 1928, p. 1226
671b	22-160
672	22-189 to 22-201
673	22-167
674	22-188
674(1)	22-188
674a-674f	Omitted
674g	22-168 to 22-172
674h	22-173
674i	22-174
674j	22-175
674k	22-176
674l	22-177
674m	22-178
674n	22-188
675	22-120
676	22-144, 22-147
676a	Repealed by Acts 1928, p. 1226
677	22-148
678	22-161
678a	Repealed by Acts 1948, p. 90
678b	22-5, 22-139, 22-139.1
678c	22-162
679	22-6
680	22-221
681	22-8, 22-9
681a-681e	Repealed by Acts 1928, p. 1226
682	22-218, 22-219, 22-222
683	22-251 to 22-255
683a	22-279
683a1	22-280
683a2	22-281
684	22-257 to 22-263
685	22-264 to 22-267
686	22-256, 22-268 to 22-273
686a	22-274
687	22-275
687a	22-142
688	22-233 to 22-238

Michie Code Section	Code 1950 Section
688a	22-240
689	22-248
690	22-249
691	22-250
692	Omitted
693	22-220
694	22-277
695	22-223 to 22-227
696	Omitted
697	22-228
698	22-126 to 22-130
698a	Repealed by Acts 1945, p. 58
698b	Omitted
699	22-131
700	22-132, 22-133
701	22-137
702	22-134
703	22-138
703a	Repealed by Acts 1928, p. 1226
704	22-118
705	22-241 to 22-247
706	22-119
707	22-135
708	22-213
709	22-214
710	22-215
711	22-216
712	22-59
713	22-163
714	22-212
715	22-3, 22-58, 22-146, 22-166, 22-217, 22-232, 22-283
716	22-164
717	22-165
718	22-159
718a	22-179
718b	22-180
718c	22-181, 22-182
718d	22-183, 22-184
718e	22-185
718f	22-186
718g-718l	22-187
719-740a	Repealed by Acts 1928, p. 1226
740b	22-10
740c	Repealed by Acts 1928, p. 1227
741	22-278
742-756e	Repealed by Acts 1928, p. 1226
757-773	Repealed by Acts 1928, p. 1226
773a	Omitted
773b	Repealed by Acts 1928, p. 1226
774	22-3
775	22-4
776	22-44

Michie Code Section	Code 1950 Section
777	22-94
778	22-95, 22-96
779	22-35, 22-48.2
780	22-89
781, 782	Repealed by Acts 1942, p. 108
783	22-132, 22-139
784, 785	Omitted
786	22-90 to 22-93, 22-97, 22-98, 22-206
786(1)	22-284
786(2)	22-285
786(3)	22-287
786(4)	22-288
786(5)	22-289
786(6)	22-290
786(7)	22-291
786(8)	Omitted
786(9)	22-292
786(10)	22-293
786(11)	22-294
786(12)	22-286
786(13)	22-295
786(14)	22-307
786(15)	Omitted
786(16)	22-308, 22-309
786(17)	22-313
786(18)	22-314
786(19)	22-315
786(20)	22-316
786(21)	22-317
786(22)	22-318
787-805	Repealed by Acts 1942, p. 500
806	23-62, 23-69
807	23-70 to 23-72
808	23-73
809	23-74
810	23-75
811	23-76
812	23-77
813	23-78
814	23-79
815	23-80
816	23-64
817	23-63
817a	Repealed by Acts 1936, p. 449
818	23-66
819	Repealed by Acts 1928, p. 1032
820	23-67
821	23-65
822	23-81
823	23-82
824	23-83
825	23-84
826	23-85
827	23-68
828	10-92.1

Michie Code Section	Code 1950 Section
829	10-91, 10-92.1
830	10-93
830a	10-98
831	10-94
832	10-95
833	10-96
833a	23-86
833b	23-87
833c	23-88
833d	23-89
833e	23-90
833f	23-91
834	23-92
835	23-93 to 23-97
836	23-98
837	23-99
838	23-109
839	23-100
840	23-101
841	23-102
842	23-103
843	Repealed by Acts 1930, p. 974
844	23-104
845	23-105
845a	23-106
846	23-108
847	23-109
848	23-110
849	23-107
850	23-111
851	23-112
852	23-113
853	23-136, 23-137
854	Repealed by Acts 1936, p. 449
855	23-140
856	23-130
857	23-131
858	Repealed by Acts 1936, p. 449
859	23-115 to 23-117
860	23-114
861	23-118, 23-119
862	23-120
863	23-121
864	23-122 to 23-126
865	23-128
866	23-127
867	23-141
868	23-138, 23-139
869	23-133, 23-134
869(1)	3-152
870	3-153
870a	3-151
871	3-154 to 3-156
871a	3-157
871b	3-158
871c	3-159
871d	3-160
872	3-161

Michie Code Section	Code 1950 Section
873	3-162, 3-163
874	3-164, 3-165
875	3-166, 3-167
876	3-168
877	3-169
878	3-170
879	3-171, 3-172
880	3-173
881	3-174
882	3-175 to 3-177
882a	3-178
883-884a	Omitted
884b	Repealed by Acts 1938, p. 969
885	3-179
886	3-180, 3-181
887	3-182
888	3-183
889	3-184, 3-185
890	3-186, 3-187
891	3-188
892	3-189
893	3-190
894-905	Omitted
905(1)	3-191
905(2)	3-192
905(3)	3-193
905(4)	3-194, 3-195
905(5)	3-196
905(6)	3-197
905a	Omitted
906	Repealed by Acts 1932, p. 884
907	3-565
908	3-566
909	3-568
910	3-569 to 3-575
911	3-576
912	3-577
913	3-578
914	3-584 to 3-588
915	3-589
916	3-590
917	3-591
918	3-592 to 3-594
919	3-579, 3-583
920	3-582
920a	Repealed by Acts 1938, p. 984
921, 922	Omitted
923	3-40, 3-41
924	3-42, 3-43
925	3-44
925a	23-129, 23-147 to 23-155
926-930	Repealed by Acts 1920, p. 492
931, 932	Omitted
933	23-132
934	23-47
935	23-41 to 23-44

Michie Code Section	Code 1950 Section
936	23-39, 23-40, 23-44, 23-46
937	23-48
938	Repealed by Acts 1936, p. 449
938a	23-45
938b	23-49
939	23-54
939a	Omitted
940, 941	Repealed by Acts 1932, p. 844
942	23-55, 23-56
943	23-57, 23-58
944	23-59
945	Repealed by Acts 1936, p. 449
946	23-60
947	23-165
948	23-166
949, 950	Repealed by Acts 1930, p. 769
951	23-167
952	Repealed by Acts 1930, p. 769
953	Repealed by Acts 1936, p. 449
954	23-169
955, 956	Repealed by Acts 1930, p. 769
957	23-170
958-965	Repealed by Acts 1930, p. 768
966	23-171
967	23-172
968	Repealed by Acts 1930, p. 769
969	23-174
969a	23-173
969b	23-168
970	23-156
970a	23-164
971	23-157
972	23-158
973	23-159
974	23-160
975	23-161
976	23-162
977	23-163
978	Repealed by Acts 1940, p. 284
978a	63-162 to 63-169
978a1	63-204.1 to 63-204.24
978b	23-164
978c	Repealed by Acts 1926, p. 86
978d-978h	23-164
979	23-175
980	23-176
981	23-177
982	23-178

Michie Code Section	Code 1950 Section
983	23-180
984	Repealed by Acts 1940, p. 274
985	23-179
986	23-1
987	Repealed by Acts 1926, p. 868
988	23-3
989	23-2
990	23-5
991	23-6
992	23-6
992(1)-992(13)	23-30
992(14)	23-9
993	23-31
994	23-32
995	23-33
996	23-34
997	23-35
997a	Omitted
997b	23-37
997c	23-38
998	Repealed by Acts 1932, p. 884
999	23-4
1000	23-51
1001	23-52
1002	23-53
1003	23-50
1003a	23-8
1003b-1003g	Omitted
1003h	22-325
1003i	22-326
1003j	22-327
1003k	22-328
1003l	22-329
1003l(a)	23-7
1003l(b)	23-10 to 23-13
1004	37-1 to 37-7, 37-183
1005	37-1, 37-37
1005a	37-17 to 37-22
1006	37-26 to 37-35, 37-59, 37-60, 37-232
1006a	37-34, 37-36
1006b	37-38 to 37-42
1006c	37-254 to 37-260
1006d	37-91.2
1007	37-9, 37-12
1008	37-10 to 37-12
1008a	32-136
1009	Repealed by Acts 1938, p. 372
1010	37-42, 37-44 to 37-46
1011-1012	Repealed by Acts 1938, p. 372
1013-1014a	Omitted
1014b	37-47 to 37-51
1015	37-8
1016	37-43
1017	37-61 to 37-65
1018	37-66, 37-67, 37-121
1019	37-68 to 37-70
1020	37-71 to 37-74, 37-126, 37-132
1020a	37-78
1021	37-75
1022	37-76 to 37-78
1023	37-79
1024	37-83 to 37-85
1025	37-86
1026	37-86.1, 37-86.2
1027	37-87 to 37-89
1028	37-90
1029	37-122 to 37-125
1030	37-91
1031	37-113 to 37-118
1032	37-103, 37-104
1033	37-105, 37-106
1034	37-107, 37-108
1035	37-109 to 37-112
1035a	37-99 to 37-101
1035b	37-102
1036	37-119, 37-120
1037	37-127
1037a	37-128
1037b	37-129
1037c	37-130
1037d	37-131
1038	37-92
1039	37-215.1
1040	37-133
1041	37-135
1042	37-132, 37-133
1043	37-134
1044	37-97
1045	37-93
1046	37-94
1047	37-95, 37-96
1048	37-82, 37-92
1049	37-80, 37-81
1050	37-136, 37-139.1, 37-142, 37-152
1050a	37-141
1051	37-138
1052	37-139
1053	37-136 to 37-139.1, 37-143 to 37-145
1054	37-146 to 37-150, 37-151
1055	8-689.1
1056	8-689.2
1057	8-689.3
1058	37-125.1 to 37-125.3, 37-153
1058a	37-125.4, 37-125.5
1058b	37-125.6 to 37-125.12
1058c	37-125.13
1058d	37-125.14
1059	37-13, 37-52
1060	37-227
1061	37-15
1062	37-16
1063	37-228
1064	37-229
1065	37-230
1066	37-178, 37-226
1067	37-182
1067a	37-179, 37-181
1068	37-154 to 37-156
1069	37-175
1070	37-157 to 37-159, 37-163
1071	37-160 to 37-162
1072	37-164 to 37-166
1073	37-167 to 37-170
1074	37-171 to 37-174
1075	37-176, 37-177
1076	37-184
1077	37-186 to 37-191
1078	37-194
1079	37-193, 37-195 to 37-199
1079a	37-195 to 37-197
1080	37-200 to 37-206
1080a	37-140
1081	37-207
1082	37-208, 37-209
1083	37-210
1084	37-225
1085	37-211 to 37-213
1086	37-214, 37-215
1087	37-216
1088	37-217, 37-218
1089	37-182.1
1090	37-224
1091	37-219 to 37-223
1092	37-191, 37-192
1093	37-185
1094	37-180
1095	37-14
1095a	37-98
1095b	37-247
1095c	37-248
1095d	37-249, 37-250
1095e	37-251
1095f	37-252
1095g	37-253
1095h	37-231
1095i	37-233 to 37-242
1095j	37-243
1095k	37-244
1095l	37-245
1095m	37-246
1095(1)	37-23
1095(2)	37-24
1095(3)	37-25
1096	9-13
1097	9-14

Michie Code Section	Code 1950 Section
1098	9-15
1099	3-1
1100	3-2
1101	3-3
1102	3-4
1103	3-5
1104	3-7
1105	3-8, 14-19
1106	3-9 to 3-12
1107	3-13
1108	Omitted
1109	3-15
1110	3-82 to 3-85
1111	3-86, 3-87
1112	3-88
1113	3-89
1114	3-90, 3-91
1115	3-92, 3-93
1116	Repealed by Acts 1920, p. 107
1117	3-94
1118	3-95 to 3-97
1119	3-98 to 3-101
1120	3-102 to 3-113
1121	3-114
1122	3-115, 3-116
1123	3-117
1124	Omitted
1125	3-80
1126-1131	Repealed by Acts 1920, p. 107
1132	3-118 to 3-123
1133	3-124, 3-125
1134	3-126 to 3-132
1135	3-133, 3-134
1136	3-135, 3-136
1137	3-137
1137(1)	Omitted
1137a-1137i	Repealed by Acts 1948, p. 939
1137j	3-198
1137k	3-199 to 3-208.11
1137l	3-208.31 to 3-208.38
1137m	3-208.39
1137n	3-208.19 to 3-208.30
1137o	3-208.12 to 3-208.16
1137p	3-208.40 to 3-208.43
1137q	3-208.44, 3-208.45
1137r	3-208.46
1137s	3-208.47
1137t	3-208.17
1137u	3-208.18
1138-1153	Repealed by Acts 1924, p. 138
1153(1)	3-209
1153(2)	3-210
1153(3)	3-211
1153(4)	3-212
1153(5)	3-213
1153(6)	3-214
1153(7)	3-215
1153(8)	3-216
1153(9)	3-217
1153a, 1153b	Repealed by Acts 1946, p. 575
1153b1	Repealed by Acts 1942, p. 315
1153b2	Repealed by Acts 1946, p. 575
1153c	Repealed by Acts 1946, p. 575
1153d	Repealed by Acts 1936, p. 718
1153e-1153k	Repealed by Acts 1946, p. 575
1153l	Repealed by Acts 1930, p. 565
1153m-1153q	Repealed by Acts 1946, p. 575
1154	3-219
1154a-1154j	Repealed by Acts 1946, p. 575
1154k	3-218
1154l-1154n	3-220
1154o	3-221
1154p	3-222
1154q	3-223
1154r	3-224
1154s	3-225
1154t	3-226
1154u	3-227
1154v	3-228
1154(1)	3-281, 59-77
1155-1158	Repealed by Acts 1932, p. 884
1159	3-282
1160	3-323 to 3-328
1161	3-329
1162	3-330
1163	3-331
1164	3-332
1165	3-333
1166	3-334
1167	3-335
1168	3-281.1
1169	3-337
1170	3-341
1171	3-342
1172	3-343
1173	3-452 to 3-460
1174-1182	3-322
1183	3-647
1184	3-322
1185	3-283
1186	3-338
1187	3-339
1188	3-340
1189	3-322
1190	3-321
1190(a)	3-306
1190(b)	3-307
1190(c)	3-308
1190(d)	3-309
1190(e)	3-310
1190(f)	3-311
1190(g)	3-312
1190(h)	3-313
1190(i)	3-314
1190(j)	3-315
1190(k)	3-316
1190(l)	3-317
1190(m)	3-318
1190(n)	3-319
1190(o)	3-320
1190(p)	Omitted
1191, 1192	Omitted
1192a	3-690 to 3-697
1193, 1194	Omitted
1195	3-698
1196	3-699
1196a	3-477
1196b	3-478
1196c	3-479
1196d	3-481
1196e	3-482
1196f	Omitted
1197	3-344
1197a	3-471
1197b	3-472
1197c	3-473
1197d	3-474
1197e	3-475
1197f	3-476
1198	3-700 to 3-702
1199	3-703
1200	3-704
1201	3-705
1202, 1203	Omitted
1204	3-345
1205	3-401
1206	3-402
1207	3-403
1208	3-404 to 3-408
1209	3-409
1210	3-410, 3-411
1211	3-412
1211a-1211i	Repealed by Acts 1934, p. 239
1211j-1211v	Repealed by Acts 1948, p. 1041
1211v(1)	3-384 to 3-395
1211v(2)	3-396
1211v(3)	3-397
1211v(4)	3-398
1211v(5)	3-399
1211v(6)	3-400
1211v(7)	3-400.1
1211v(8)	3-400.12

Michie Code Section	Code 1950 Section
1211v(9)	3-400.2 to 3-400.11
1211v(10)	3-400.13
1211v(11)	3-400.14
1211v(12)	3-400.15
1211v(13)	3-400.16
1211v(14)	3-400.17 to 3400.19
1211v(15)	3-400.20
1211v(16)	3-400.21
1211v(17)	3-400.22
1211v(18)	3-400.23
1211v(19)	3-400.24
1211v(20)	3-400.25
1211v(21)	3400.26, 3400.27
1211(22)	3-400.28
1211v(23)	3-400.29
1211v(24)	3-400.30, 3-400.31
1211v(25)	3-400.32
1211v(26)	3-400.33 to 3-400.35
1211v(27)	3-400.36
1211v(28)	3-400.37
1211v(29)	3-400.38
1211v(30)	3-400.39
1211w	3-346
1211x	3-347 to 3-351
1211y	3-352 to 3-364
1211z	3-365
1211aa	3-366
1211bb	3-369 to 3-371
1211cc	3-367, 3-368
1211dd	3-372
1211ee	3-373
1211ff	3-374
1211gg	3-375 to 3-378
1211hh	3-379
1211ii	3-380
1211jj	3-381
1211kk	3-382
1211ll	Omitted
1211mm	3-383
1211nn	3-416, 3-417
1211oo	3-418
1211pp	3-419
1211qq	3-421
1211rr	3-422
1211ss	3-423
1211tt	3-424
1211uu	3-388, 3-393
1211vv	3-394
1211ww	3-395, 3-418, 3-420
1211xx	3-461 to 3-470
1212	3-413
1213	3-414
1214	3-415
1215	3-425 to 3-451
1216, 1217	Repealed by Acts 1934, p. 829
1218	3-303
1219	3-304
1220	3-305
1221	3-648 to 3-659
1222	3-660 to 3-665, 3-671
1223	3-336
1223a	3-567
1224-1225	Repealed by Acts 1938, p. 984
1226	Repealed by Acts 1928, p. 353
1227	Repealed by Acts 1938, p. 984
1227a	3-285 to 3-301.1, 3-480, 3-656, 3-666 to 3-671, 3-706, 28-196
1227b	3-302
1228	Omitted
1228a	61-59
1228b	61-60
1228c	61-63
1228d	61-64
1228e	61-65
1228f	61-66
1228g	61-67
1228h	61-68, 61-69
1228i	61-70
1228j	61-71
1228k	61-72
1228l	61-73
1228m	61-74
1228n	61-77
1228o	61-61, 61-62
1228p	61-75
1228q	61-76
1228(1)	61-78
1228(2)	61-79
1228(3)	61-80
1228(4)	61-81
1228(5)	61-82
1228(6)	61-83
1228(7)	61-84
1228(8)	61-85
1228(9)	61-86
1228(10)	61-87
1228(11)	61-88
1228(12)	61-89
1228(13)	61-90
1228(14)	61-91, 61-92
1228(15)	61-93
1228(16)	61-94
1228(17)	Omitted
1228(18)	29-155.1
1229	3-610 to 3-612
1230	3-613
1231	3-614 to 3-617
1232	3-618
1233	3-619
1234	3-620
1235	3-621
1236	3-622
1237	3-623 to 3-625
1238	3-626
1239	3-627 to 3-633
1240	3-634
1241	3-635 to 3-638
1242	3-640
1243	Repealed by Acts 1918, p. 483
1244	3-641
1245	3-642
1246	3-643
1247	3-644
1248	3-645
1249	3-646
1249a	3-639
1249b	3-677
1249c	3-678
1249d	3-679
1249e	3-680
1249f	3-681
1249g	3-682
1249h	3-683
1249i	3-684
1249j	3-685
1249k	3-686
1249l	3-687
1249m	3-688
1249n	3-689
1249o	Omitted
1250	3-526
1251	3-527
1252	3-528
1253	3-529
1254	3-530
1255	3-532
1256	3-533
1257	3-534
1258	3-535 to 3-541
1259	3-542, 3-543
1260	3-544 to 3-550
1261	3-551 to 3-553
1262	3-554
1263	3-555 to 3-559
1264	3-560 to 3-562
1265	3-563, 3-564
1265(1)	13-249
1265(2)	13-248
1265(3)	13-254
1265(4)	13-255
1265(5)	13-256
1265(6)	13-260
1265(7)	13-263
1265(8)	13-257, 13-258, 13-264
1265(9)	13-258
1265(10)	13-261

Michie Code Section	Code 1950 Section
1265(11)	13-265
1265(12)	13-266
1265(13)	13-267
1265(14)	13-269 to 13-277
1265(15)	13-268
1265(16)	13-262
1265(17)	13-278
1265(18)	13-285
1265(19)	13-288
1265(20)	13-251
1265(21)	13-289
1265(22)	13-286
1265(23)	13-287
1265(24)	13-252
1265(25)	13-279
1265(26)	13-284
1265(27)	Omitted
1265(28)	13-250
1265(29)	13-290
1265(29)a	13-259
1265(30)	13-291
1265(31)	13-292
1265(32)	13-253
1265(33)	13-280
1265(34)	13-281
1265(35)	13-282
1265(36)	13-283
1265(37)	3-531
1265(38)	3-45, 3-46
1265(39)	3-47 to 3-51
1265(40)	3-52, 3-53, 3-54
1265(40a)	3-52, 3-52.1
1265(41)	3-55
1265(42)	3-56 to 3-59
1265(43)	3-68 to 3-76
1265(44)	3-77
1265(45)	3-78
1265(46)	3-79
1265(47)	3-67
1265(48)	3-60 to 3-62
1265(49)	3-63
1265(50)	3-64 to 3-66
1265(51)	Omitted
1266	Repealed by Acts 1927, p. 117
1267	3-139 to 3-142
1268	3-143 to 3-146
1269	3-147 to 3-150
1270	Omitted
1271	Repealed by Acts 1927, p. 117
1272	54-787
1273	54-786
1274	54-776 to 54-781
1275	54-782 to 54-785
1276	Repealed by Acts 1948, p. 1031
1276a	54-788
1276b	54-788.1
1276c	54-789.1
1276d	54-789.2, 54-789.3
1276e	54-789.4
1276f	54-789.5 to 54-789.7
1276g	54-789.8
1277	54-789
1278	54-790
1279	54-791
1280	3-81
1281	3-6
1282	3-14
1283	3-595
1284	3-596
1285	3-597
1286	3-598
1287, 1288	Omitted
1289	3-16
1289a	3-32
1289b	3-33, 3-34
1289c	3-35
1289d	3-36
1289e	3-37
1289f	3-38
1289g	3-581
1289h	3-28
1289i	3-29
1289j	3-30
1289k	3-31
1289l	10-116, 10-117, 23-135
1289m	3-39
1289(1)	3-17
1289(2)	3-18
1289(3)	3-19
1289(4)	3-20
1289(5)	3-21
1289(6)	3-22
1289(7)	3-23
1289(8)	3-24
1289(9)	3-25
1289(10)	3-26
1289(11)	3-27
1289(12)	Omitted
1289(13)	21-1
1289(14)	21-2
1289(15)	21-3
1289(16)	21-6 to 21-10
1289(17)	21-12 to 21-32
1289(18)	21-33 to 21-41
1289(19)	21-42 to 21-52
1289(20)	21-53 to 21-64
1289(20a)	21-11
1289(20b)	21-65
1289(21)	21-66 to 21-81
1289(22)	21-82
1289(23)	21-83 to 21-89
1289(24)	21-90 to 21-105
1289(25)	21-4
1289(26)	21-5
1289(27)	21-106 to 21-112
1289(28), 1289(29)	Omitted
1290	61-4
1291	61-5
1292	61-6
1293	61-7
1294	61-8
1295	61-9
1296	61-10
1297	61-11
1298	61-12
1299	61-13
1300	61-14
1301	61-15
1302	61-16
1303	61-17
1304	61-18
1305	61-19
1306	61-20
1307	61-21
1308	61-22
1309	61-23
1310	61-24
1311	61-25
1312	61-26
1313	61-27
1314	61-28
1315	61-29
1316	61-30
1317	61-31
1318	61-32
1319	61-33
1320	61-34
1321	61-35
1322	61-36
1323	61-37
1324	61-38
1325	61-39
1326	61-40
1327	61-41
1328	61-42
1329	61-43
1330	61-44
1331	61-45
1332	61-46
1333	61-47
1334	61-48
1335	61-49
1336	61-50
1337	61-51
1338	61-52
1339	61-53
1340	61-54
1341	61-55
1342	61-56
1343	61-57
1344	61-58
1345	61-2
1346	61-3

Michie Code Section	Code 1950 Section
1347	61-1
1348	61-95
1349	61-96
1350	61-97
1351	61-98
1352	61-99
1353	61-100
1354	61-101
1355	61-108
1356	61-102
1357	61-103
1358	61-104
1359	61-105
1360	61-106
1361	61-107
1361a	61-146
1361b	61-147
1361c	61-148
1361d	61-149
1361e	61-150
1361f	61-151
1361g	61-152
1361h	61-153
1362	61-109
1363	61-110
1364	61-111
1365	61-112
1366	61-113
1367	61-114
1368	61-115
1369	61-116
1370	61-117
1371	61-118
1372	61-119
1373	61-120
1374	61-121
1375	61-122
1376	61-123
1377	61-124
1378	61-125
1379	61-126
1380	61-127
1381	61-128
1382	61-129
1382a	61-154, 61-155
1383	61-130
1384	61-131
1385	61-132
1386	61-133
1387	61-134
1388	61-135
1389	61-136
1390	61-136
1391	61-137
1392	61-138
1393	61-139
1394	61-140
1395	61-141
1396	61-142
1397	61-143
1398	61-144

Michie Code Section	Code 1950 Section
1399	61-145
1399(1)	3-229 to 3-239
1399(1a)	3-240 to 3-256
1399(2)-1399(26)	3-257
1400-1410	3-284
1410a	3-672 to 3-676
1411	3-284
1411a	59-61 to 59-70
1412-1443	3-284
1443a	Repealed by Acts 1928, p. 1289
1443b	Omitted
1443c-1443k	Repealed by Acts 1928, p. 1289
1443(1)	59-41
1443(2)	59-46 to 59-48
1443(3)	59-42 to 59-45
1443(4)	59-49, 59-50
1443(5)	59-51
1443(6)	59-53
1443(7)	59-48
1443(8)	59-54, 59-55
1443(9)	59-52
1443(10)	59-56
1443(11)	59-57, 59-58
1443(12)	59-59
1443(13)	59-60
1443(14)	59-162
1443(15)	59-163
1443(16)	59-164
1444	59-200
1445	59-201, 59-202
1446	59-203
1447	59-204
1448	59-205
1449	59-206
1450	59-207
1451	59-208
1452	59-209
1453	59-210, 59-211
1454	59-212
1454(1)	3-258
1454(2)	3-259 to 3-261
1454(3)	3-262
1454(4)	3-263
1454(5)	3-264 to 3-267
1454(6)	3-268
1454(7)	3-269
1454(8)	3-271, 3-272
1454(9)	3-273
1454(10)	3-274 to 3-277
1454(11)	3-278 to 3-280.1
1454(12)	3-270
1455	59-177, 59-178
1456	59-179
1457	59-180
1458	59-181 to 59-183
1458a	59-184
1459	59-185
1460	59-187
1461	59-186

Michie Code Section	Code 1950 Section
1462	59-188
1463	59-189
1463a	59-191, 59-192
1463b	59-193
1463c	59-194
1463d	59-195
1463e	59-196
1463f	59-197
1463g	59-198
1463h	59-199
1463i	59-2
1463j	59-3
1463k	59-4
1463l	59-5
1463m	59-6
1463n	59-7
1463o	59-8
1463p	59-1
1463(1)	59-9
1463(2)	59-10 to 59-12
1463(3)	59-13
1463(4)	59-14
1463(5)	59-15
1463(6)	59-19
1464-1470	Repealed by Acts 1924, p. 321
1471	Repealed by Acts 1924, p. 137
1472-1485	Repealed by Acts 1924, p. 321
1485(1)	59-95
1485(2)	Repealed by Acts 1926, p. 115
1485(2)a	59-82
1485(3)	59-96 to 59-98
1485(4)	59-99, 59-100
1485(5)	59-85 to 59-88
1485(5a)	59-80, 59-81
1485(5b)	59-106 to 59-114
1485(6)	59-89
1485(7)	59-90
1485(8)	59-92
1485(9)	59-93
1485(10)	59-94
1485(11)	59-83, 59-140
1485(12)	59-136
1485(13)	59-137
1485(13½)	59-73 to 59-75
1485(14)	59-101, 59-102
1485(14½), 1485(14½)a	Repealed by Acts 1946, p. 274
1485(15)	59-125
1485(16)	59-128
1485(17)	59-126, 59-127
1485(17½)	59-103, 59-104
1485(18)	59-105
1485(18½)	59-129
1485(19)	59-120 to 59-124

Michie Code Section	Code 1950 Section
1485(20)	59-131 to 59-133
1485(21)	59-130
1485(22)	59-72
1485(23)	59-138, 59-139
1485(24)	59-71
1485(25)	59-78, 59-79, 59-84, 59-91
1485(26)	Omitted
1485(27)	59-134, 59-135
1485(28)-1485(31)	Repealed by Acts 1946, p. 274
1485(31a)	59-115 to 59-119
1485(32)	3-507
1485(33)	3-508
1485(34)	3-509
1485(35)	3-510
1485(36)	3-511
1485(37)	3-512
1485(38)	3-506
1485(39)	3-483
1485(40)	3-484 to 3-487
1485(41)	3-488 to 3-491
1485(42)	3-492
1485(43)	3-493
1485(44)	3-494
1485(45)	3-495
1485(46)	3-496
1485(47)	3-497, 3-498
1485(48)	3-499
1485(49)	3-500
1485(50)	3-501
1485(51)	3-502, 3-503
1485(52)	3-504
1485(53)	3-505
1485(54)	3-605
1485(55)	3-606
1485(56)	3-607, 3-608
1485(57)	3-609
1485(58)	3-599
1485(59)	3-600
1485(60)	3-601
1485(61)	3-602
1485(62)	3-603
1485(63)	3-604
1485(64)	3-513
1485(65)	3-514
1485(66)	3-515, 3-516
1485(67)	3-517
1485(68)	3-518
1485(69)	3-519
1485(70)	3-520
1485(71)	3-521
1485(72)	3-522
1485(73)	3-523
1485(74)	3-523.1, 3-524
1485(75)	3-525
1485(76)	Omitted
1485(77)	3-525.1

Michie Code Section	Code 1950 Section
1485(78)	3-525.2 to 3-525.5
1485(79)	3-525.6 to 3-525.10
1485(80)	3-525.11
1485(81)	3-525.12
1485(82)	3-525.13
1485(83)	3-525.14, 3-525.15
1485(84)	3-525.16
1485(85)	3-525.17
1485(86)	3-525.18, 3-525.19
1486	32-1 to 32-5
1487	32-6 to 32-15
1488	32-16
1489	32-23 to 32-30
1490	32-31
1491	32-10, 32-17, 32-22, 32-311, 32-312
1492	32-32 to 32-34
1493	32-35 to 32-37
1494	32-38
1495	32-39
1496	32-40
1497	32-41, 32-42
1498	32-43 to 32-47
1499	32-17, 32-18
1500	32-52
1501	32-19
1502	32-20, 32-21
1503	32-50
1504	32-51
1505	32-51, 32-57, 32-83
1506	32-296
1507	32-313
1508	32-314
1509	32-315
1510	32-316
1511	32-317
1512	32-318
1513	32-319
1514	32-320
1514a	32-321
1514a1	32-297
1514a2	32-298
1514a3	32-299
1514a4	32-300
1514a5	32-301
1514a6	32-302
1514a7	32-303
1514a8	32-304
1514a9	32-305
1514a10	32-306
1514a11	32-307
1514a12	32-308
1514a13	32-309
1514a14	32-310
1514b	Omitted
1514b1	62-10

Michie Code Section	Code 1950 Section
1514b2	62-12
1514b3	62-11
1514b4	62-13
1514b5	62-15 to 62-17, 62-22
1514b6	62-18
1514b7	62-19
1514b8	62-20, 62-21
1514b9	62-23
1514b10	62-22
1514b11	62-24
1514b12	62-29, 62-30
1514b13	62-41
1514b14	62-27
1514b15	62-39
1514b16	62-40
1514b17	62-26
1514b18	62-28
1514b19	62-25
1514b20	62-34 to 62-38
1514b21	62-42
1514b22	62-33
1514b23	62-31
1514b24	62-14
1514b25	62-32
1514b26	Omitted
1514b27	32-365
1514b28	32-366
1514b29	32-367
1514b30	32-368, 32-369
1514b31	32-370
1514b32	32-371
1514b33	32-372
1514b34	32-373
1514b35	32-374
1514b36	32-375
1514b37	32-376
1514b38	32-377
1514b39	32-378
1515	32-48
1515a	32-49
1515b	32-53
1516	32-84
1516a	32-85
1517	32-60
1518	32-55
1519	32-56
1520	48-1 to 48-6
1521	48-7
1522	48-8
1523	48-9
1524	48-10, 48-11
1525	48-12
1526	48-13
1527	48-14
1528	48-15
1529, 1530	Repealed by Acts 1928, p. 1226
1531	32-58
1532	Omitted
1533	32-71

Michie Code Section	Code 1950 Section
1534	32-72
1535	32-73
1536	32-74
1537	32-75
1538	32-76
1539	32-77
1540	32-78
1541	32-79
1542	32-80
1543	32-81, 32-82
1543a	32-104
1544	32-61
1545	32-62
1545a	32-64 to 32-68, 35-55
1546	32-88
1547	32-89
1548	32-86
1549	32-87
1550	32-69
1550a	Omitted
1551, 1552	Repealed by Acts 1930, p. 664
1553	29-203
1554	32-70
1554a	32-59
1554b	32-90
1554c	32-91
1554d	32-92
1554e	32-93, 32-94
1554e1	32-95
1554f	32-96
1554g	32-98
1554h	32-99
1554i	32-100
1554j	32-101
1554k	32-97
1554l	32-102
1554m	32-103
1554n	32-105
1554o	32-106
1554p	32-107
1554q	32-108
1554r	32-109
1554s	32-110
1554t	32-111
1554u	32-112
1554(1)	32-291
1554(2)	32-292
1554(3)	32-293
1554(4)	32-294
1554(5)	32-292, 32-294
1554(5a)	32-293.1
1554(5b)	32-295
1554(6)	Omitted
1554(7)	Repealed by Acts 1948, p. 1107
1554(8)	32-276 to 32-278
1554(9)	32-279
1554(10)	32-280
1554(11)	32-281
1554(12)	32-282
1554(13)	32-283
1554(14)	32-284
1554(15)	32-285
1554(16)	32-286
1554(17)	32-287
1554(18)	32-288
1554(19)	32-289
1554(20)	Omitted
1554(21)	32-290
1554(22)	32-212
1554(23)	32-213
1554(24)	32-214
1554(25)	32-215 to 32-219
1554(26)	32-220 to 32-222
1554(27)	32-223
1554(28)	32-224
1554(29)	32-225 to 32-230
1554(30)	32-236 to 32-257
1554(31)	32-258
1554(32)	32-231
1554(33)	32-261 to 32-264
1554(34)	32-265 to 32-270
1554(35)	32-271
1554(36)	32-272
1554(37)	32-273
1554(38)	32-274
1554(39)	32-275
1554(40)	32-259
1554(41)	32-260
1554(42)	32-232
1554(43)	32-233
1554(44)	32-234
1554(45)	Omitted
1554(46)	32-235
1554(47)	32-196
1554(48)	32-197
1554(49)	32-198
1554(50)	32-199
1554(51)	32-200
1554(52)	32-204
1554(53)	32-201
1554(54)	32-202
1554(55)	32-203
1554(56)	32-205
1554(57)	32-206
1554(58)	32-207
1554(59)	32-208
1554(60)	32-209
1554(61)	32-210
1554(62)	32-211
1554(63)	32-211.1
1554(64)	32-211.2
1555	32-130, 32-131
1556	32-132
1557	32-133
1558	32-133
1559	32-54
1560	32-135
1560(1)	32-138 to 32-141
1560(2)	32-142 to 32-144
1560(3)	32-145
1560(4)	32-146
1560(5)	32-147
1560(6)	32-148
1560(7)	32-149 to 32-152
1560(8)	32-153, 32-154
1560(9)	32-155
1560(10)	32-156, 32-157
1560(11)	32-158 to 32-160
1560(12)	32-161
1560a-1560l3	21-120
1560m	21-113
1560n	21-114, 21-115
1560o	21-118
1560p-1560s	21-139
1560s1	21-117
1560s2	Omitted
1560s3	21-119
1560s4	21-116
1560t-1560z	21-120
1560z1	21-122
1560z2	21-123
1560z3	21-124
1560z4	21-125
1560z5	21-126
1560z6	21-127 to 21-136
1560z7	21-137, 21-138
1560aa-1560gg	21-139
1560hh	21-141
1560ii	21-142
1560jj	21-145 to 21-153
1560kk	21-154 to 21-167
1560kk1	21-203 to 21-213
1560ll	21-168
1560mm	21-169 to 21-171
1560nn	21-180 to 21-186
1560oo	21-189 to 21-195, 21-197, 21-198
1560pp	21-200
1560qq	21-201
1560rr	21-177
1560ss	21-172
1560tt	21-173
1560uu	21-175
1560vv	21-176
1560ww	21-178
1560xx	21-179
1560yy	21-174
1560zz	21-187
1560aaa	21-188
1560bbb	21-214 to 21-217
1560ccc	21-218 to 21-222
1560ddd	21-196
1560eee	21-199

Michie Code Section	Code 1950 Section
1560fff	21-143
1560ggg	21-144
1560hhh	21-202
1560iii	21-223
1560iii1	21-224
1560iii2	21-225
1560iii3	21-228 to 21-236
1560iii4	21-237 to 21-247
1560iii5	21-248
1560iii6	21-249 to 21-251
1560iii7	21-260 to 21-266
1560iii8	21-269 to 21-275, 21-277, 21-278
1560iii9	21-280
1560iii10	21-282
1560iii11	21-257
1560iii12	21-252
1560iii13	21-253
1560iii14	21-255
1560iii15	21-256
1560iii16	21-258
1560iii17	21-259
1560iii18	21-254
1560iii19	21-267
1560iii20	21-268
1560iii21	21-283 to 21-286
1560iii22	21-287 to 21-289
1560iii23	21-276
1560iii24	21-279
1560iii25	21-226
1560iii26	21-227
1560iii27	21-281
1560iii28	21-290
1560jjj-1560ooo	Repealed by Acts 1940, p. 735
1560ppp-1560vvv	21-291
1560www	62-62, 62-63
1560xxx	62-64 to 62-67
1560yyy	Omitted
1561	32-322
1562	32-323
1563	32-324
1564	32-325, 32-326
1565	32-341
1566	32-342
1567	32-343, 32-344
1568	32-345
1569	32-346
1570	32-347
1571	32-348
1572	32-349
1572a	32-353.1 to 32-353.3
1573	32-350
1574	32-351
1575	32-327 to 32-329, 32-352
1575a	32-353
1576	32-330
1577	32-331 to 32-334
1578	32-335
1579	32-336
1580	32-337
1581	32-340
1582	32-339
1583	32-338
1584	Repealed by Acts 1948, p. 818
1584a	Omitted
1584(1)	35-25
1584(2)	35-26
1584(3)	35-27
1584(4)	35-28, 35-29
1584(5)	35-30
1584(6)	35-31
1584(7)	35-32 to 35-34
1584(8)	35-35 to 35-37
1584(9)	35-38
1584(10)	35-39
1584(11)	35-40
1584(12)	35-41
1584(13)	35-42
1584(14)	35-15
1584(15)	35-16
1584(16)	35-17
1584(17)	35-18, 35-19
1584(18)	35-20
1584(19)	35-21
1584(20)	35-22
1584(21)	35-23, 35-24
1585	35-1
1586	35-2
1587, 1588	Repealed by Acts 1948, p. 994
1589	35-4
1590	35-5
1591	Repealed by Acts 1922, p. 24
1592	35-6
1593	35-7
1594-1596	Repealed by Acts 1948, p. 1083
1597	35-8
1598	Repealed by Acts 1948, p. 1083
1599	35-9
1600, 1601	Repealed by Acts 1948, p. 1083
1602	35-10
1603	35-11
1604	35-12
1605	35-13
1606	35-14
1607	35-3
1607a	Repealed by Acts 1943, p.1083
1607a1	32-63
1607b	35-55
1607c	35-58, 35-60
1607d	35-56, 35-57, 35-59
1607e	35-54
1607f	35-54
1607f1	35-61 to 35-63
1607f2	35-64
1607f3	35-65 to 35-78
1607g	35-43
1607h	35-44 to 35-50
1607i	35-51
1607j	35-52
1607k	35-53
1608	54-274
1609	54-273
1610	54-282 to 54-292, 54-300, 54-303
1611	54-293 to 54-295
1612	54-297 to 54-299, 54-301, 54-302
1613	54-305 to 54-307
1613a	54-280
1614	54-281, 54-308
1614a	Omitted
1615	54-277
1615a	Omitted
1616	54-279, 54-304, 54-309
1617	54-310 to 54-312
1618	54-313 to 54-315
1618a	54-315.1 to 54-315.4
1619	54-316 to 54-321
1619a	54-321.1
1620	54-296
1621	54-276 to 54-276.6
1621a	54-276.7, 54-276.8
1622	54-275
1623	54-322 to 54-325
1624	54-368
1625	54-370 to 54-374
1626	54-375
1627	54-376 to 54-381
1628	54-381
1629	54-382, 54-383
1630	54-384, 54-393
1631	54-394
1632	54-395
1633	54-385
1634	54-386, 54-387
1635	54-388 to 54-392
1636	54-396
1637	54-396, 54-397, 54-398
1638	54-369
1639	54-278
1639a	54-147.1, 54-278.1, 54-397.1
1639b	54-103, 54-104
1639c	54-105
1639d	54-106 to 54-108
1639e	54-109
1639f	54-110, 54-111
1639g	54-112

Michie Code Section	Code 1950 Section
1640	54-146, 54-147
1641	54-141, 54-172, 54-174, 54-195
1642	54-153 to 54-160
1643	54-161 to 54-163
1644	54-175 to 54-177
1645	54-178
1646	54-168 to 54-171, 54-173
1647	54-179, 54-180
1648	54-181, 54-182
1649	54-187
1650	54-189 to 54-194
1651	Omitted
1652	54-146, 54-167, 54-196, 54-197
1653	54-168, 54-183 to 54-186, 54-188, 54-198, 54-199
1654	54-148 to 54-150, 54-152, 54-164 to 54-166, 54-200
1654(1)	54-487
1654(2)	54-488
1654(3)	54-489
1654(4)	54-490, 54-491
1654(5)	54-492 to 54-495
1654(6)	54-496
1654(7)	54-497, 54-498
1654(8)	54-499
1654(9)	54-500 to 54-504
1654(10)	54-505, 54-506
1654(11)	54-507
1654(12)	54-508
1654(13)	54-509
1654(14)	54-510
1654(15)	54-511
1654(16)	54-512
1654(17)	54-513
1654(18)	54-514
1654(19)	54-515
1654(20)	54-516
1654(21)	54-517
1654(22)	Omitted
1654(23)	54-518
1654(24)	Omitted
1654(25)	54-519
1655	54-401
1656	54-402
1657	54-474
1658	Repealed by Acts 1948, p. 89
1659	54-470
1660	54-471
1661	54-523
1662	54-399
1663	54-461
1663a	54-462
1664	54-463 to 54-465
1664a	54-466, 54-467
1664b	54-468
1664c	54-469
1664d	54-472
1664e	54-473
1665	54-400
1666	54-404 to 54-409
1667	54-410 to 54-412
1668	54-412
1669	54-413
1670	54-414
1671	54-416, 54-416.1, 54-418
1672	54-415
1673	54-421, 54-423, 54-429
1674	54-430, 54-432 to 54-433
1675	54-522
1676	54-428
1677	54-426
1678	54-427
1679	54-419
1680	54-424
1681	54-429, 54-478, 54-481 to 54-483, 54-486
1682	54-417, 54-475 to 54-480
1682a	54-520
1683	54-431
1684	54-420, 54-421
1685	54-422
1686	54-425
1687	54-420
1688	54-423
1689	Repealed by Acts 1924, p. 702
1690	54-480.1
1691	54-484, 54-485
1692	54-524
1693	Omitted
1693a	54-457 to 54-460
1694-1698	Omitted
1698a	54-440, 54-441
1698b	54-441
1698c	54-442 to 54-444
1698d	54-443, 54-445
1698e	54-446
1699	54-403
1700	54-434
1701	54-521
1702	54-474
1702(1)	54-447 to 54-456
1702a	54-435
1702b	54-436
1702c	54-437
1702d	54-438, 54-439
1702e	54-201
1702f	54-202 to 54-207
1702g	54-208, 54-211 to 54-213
1702h	54-209, 54-210
1702i	54-214
1702j	54-215
1702k	Omitted
1702l	54-216
1702m	32-113
1702n	32-114
1702o	32-115
1702p	32-116
1702q	32-117
1702r	32-118
1702s	32-119
1702t	32-120
1702u	32-121
1702v	32-122
1702w	32-125
1702x	32-123, 32-125
1702y	32-124
1702z	32-126, 32-127
1702aa	32-128
1702bb	32-129
1702cc	Omitted
1703	54-326
1704	54-327 to 54-334
1705	54-335 to 54-343, 54-356, 54-360
1706	54-344, 54-345
1707	54-346 to 54-349
1708	54-350, 54-351
1709	Omitted
1710	54-352
1711	54-353, 54-354
1712	54-355, 54-357, 54-358
1713	54-359, 54-361
1714	54-362
1714a	54-363 to 54-367
1715	54-223
1715(1)	54-218
1716	54-224 to 54-227
1717	Repealed by Acts 1936, p. 229
1718	54-228
1719	54-229 to 54-239
1719a	54-241 to 54-243
1720	54-248, 54-249
1720a	54-244 to 54-246
1720b	54-255
1720c	54-257 to 54-260
1721	54-247, 54-250, 54-251
1721a	54-252 to 54-254
1722	54-219, 54-231
1723	54-256
1724	54-218
1724a	54-259, 54-260
1725	54-240
1726	54-217
1726a	54-234
1726b	Omitted
1726c	54-217

Michie Code Section	Code 1950 Section
1726d	Omitted
1727	54-220 to 54-222
1728	Repealed by Acts 1940, p. 28
1729	Omitted
1730	32-355
1731	32-356
1732	32-357
1733	32-358, 32-359
1734	32-360 to 32-362
1735	32-363
1736	32-364
1736(1)	54-574
1736(2)	54-575
1736(3)	54-576
1736(4)	54-577
1736(5)	54-578
1736(6)	54-579
1736(7)	54-580
1736(8)	54-581
1736(9)	54-582
1736(10)	54-583
1736(11)	54-584
1736(12)	54-585
1736(13)	54-586
1736(14)	54-587
1736(15)	54-588
1736(16)	54-589
1736(17)	54-590
1736(18)	54-591
1736(19)	54-592
1736(20)	54-593
1736(21)	54-594
1736(22)	54-595
1736(23)	54-596
1736(24)	54-597
1736(25)	54-598
1736(26)	54-599
1736(27)	54-600
1736(28)	54-601
1736(29)	54-602
1736(30)	54-603
1736(31)	54-604
1736(32)	54-605
1736(33)	54-606
1736(34)	54-607
1736(35)	54-608
1736(36)	54-609
1736(37)	54-610
1736(38)	54-611
1736(39)	54-612
1736(40)	54-613
1736(41)	54-614
1736(42)	54-615
1736(43)	54-616
1736(44)	54-617
1736(45)	54-618
1736(46)	54-619
1736(47)	54-620
1736(48)	54-621
1736(49)	54-622
1736(50)	54-623
1736(51)	54-624
1736(52)	54-625
1736(53)	54-626
1736(54)	54-627
1736(55)	54-628
1736(56)	54-629
1736(57)	54-630
1736(58)	54-631
1736(59)	54-632
1736(60)	54-633
1736(61)	54-634
1736(62)	54-635
1736(63)	54-636
1736(64)	54-637
1736(65)	54-638
1736(66)	54-639
1736(67)	54-640
1736(68)	54-641
1736(69)	54-642
1736(70)	54-643
1736(71)	54-644
1736(72)	54-645
1736(73)	54-646
1736(74)	54-647
1736(75)	54-648
1736(76)	54-649
1736(77)	54-650
1736(78)	54-651
1736(79)	54-652
1736(80)	54-653
1736(81)	54-654
1736(82)	54-655
1736(83)	54-656
1736(84)	54-657
1736(85)	54-658
1736(86)	54-659
1736(87)	54-660
1736(88)	54-661
1736(89)	54-662
1736(90)	54-663
1736(91)	54-664
1736(92)	54-665
1736(93)	54-666
1736(94)	54-667
1736(95)	54-668
1736(96)	54-669
1736(97)	54-670
1736(98)	54-671
1736(99)	54-672
1736(100)	54-673
1736(101)	54-674
1736(102)	54-675
1736(103)	54-680
1736(104)	54-677
1736(105)	54-676
1736(106)	54-679
1736(107)	54-678
1736(108)	54-681
1736(109)	54-682
1736(110)	54-683
1736(111)	54-684
1736(112)	54-685
1736(113)	54-686
1736(114)	54-687
1736(115)	54-688
1736(116)	54-689
1736(117)	54-690
1736(118)	54-691
1736(119)	54-692
1736(120)	54-693
1736(121)	54-694
1736(122)	54-695
1736(123)	54-696
1736(124)	54-697
1736(125)	54-698
1736(126)	54-699
1736(127)	54-700
1736(128)	54-701
1736(129)	54-702
1736(130)	54-703
1736(131)	54-704
1736(132)	54-705
1736(133)	54-706
1736(134)	54-707
1736(135)	54-708
1736(136)	54-709
1736(137)	54-710
1736(138)	54-711
1736(139)	54-712
1736(140)	54-713
1736(141)	54-714
1736(142)	54-715
1736(143)	54-716
1736(144)	54-717
1736(145)	54-718
1736(146)	54-719
1736(147)	54-720
1736(148)	54-721
1736(149)	54-722
1736(150)	54-723
1736(151)	54-724
1736(152)	54-725
1736(153)	54-726
1736(154)	54-727
1736(155)	54-728
1736(156)	54-729
1737	21-292 to 21-294
1738	21-295 to 21-305
1739	21-306
1740	21-307 to 21-309
1741	21-310
1742	21-311
1743	21-312
1744	21-313
1745	21-314
1746	21-315 to 21-322
1747	21-323
1748	21-324
1749	21-325
1750	21-326 to 21-332
1751	21-333

TABLE OF COMPARATIVE SECTIONS

Michie Code Section	Code 1950 Section
1752	21-334
1753	21-335
1754	21-336
1755	21-337
1756	21-338 to 21-344
1757	21-345
1758	21-346
1759	21-347
1760	21-348
1761	21-349 to 21-356
1762	21-357
1763	21-358
1764	21-359
1765	21-360
1766	21-361
1767	21-362
1768	21-363
1769	21-364
1770	21-365
1771	21-366 to 21-389
1771a	21-390 to 21-392
1772	21-393, 21-394
1773	21-395
1774	21-396 to 21-401
1775	Omitted
1776	21-402 to 21-408
1777	21-409 to 21-411
1777a	21-412 to 21-422
1778	21-423
1779	21-424
1780	21-425
1781	Omitted
1782	62-183
1783	62-43
1783a	62-44
1784	62-45
1785	62-46
1786	62-47 to 62-49
1787	62-50
1788	62-51, 62-52
1789	62-53
1790	62-54, 62-55
1791	62-56
1792	62-57
1793	62-58
1794	62-59
1795	62-60
1796	62-61
1796a	18-327
1796b	18-328
1797	40-2
1798	40-3
1799	40-4, 40-5
1800	40-6
1801	40-7
1802	40-8, 40-9
1803	40-10 to 40-14
1804	40-15
1805	40-16
1806	40-17 to 40-19
1807	40-33
1808	40-34 to 40-38
1808a	40-96, 40-96.1
1808a1	Omitted
1808b	40-97 to 40-98.1
1808c	40-100 to 40-100.5
1808d	40-101
1808e	40-102
1808f	40-103
1808g	40-104
1808h	40-121
1808i	40-105
1808j	40-113
1808k	40-106
1808l	40-107
1808m	40-109 to 40-111
1808n	40-108
1808o	40-99, 40-114, 40-116, 40-118
1808p	40-115 to 40-117, 40-122
1808q	40-119
1808r	40-120
1808s	40-39 to 40-43
1809-1816	Repealed by Acts 1922, p. 855
1816a	40-112
1817	40-22
1818	40-23 to 40-25
1819	40-26 to 40-28
1820	40-29
1821	40-62
1822	40-44
1823	40-45
1824	40-46
1825	40-47
1826	40-48
1827	40-49
1828	40-52, 40-53
1829	40-54
1830	40-55 to 40-58
1831	Repealed by Acts 1922, p. 607
1831a	40-60
1832	40-59
1833	40-50
1834	40-51
1834a	40-61
1834b	40-20
1835	45-1 to 45-3
1836	45-4 to 45-6
1837	45-18 to 45-23
1838	45-24
1839	45-25
1840	45-26
1841	45-27
1842	45-28
1843	45-29
1844	45-30
1845	45-31
1846	45-32
1847	45-33
1848	45-34
1849	45-9
1850	45-10
1851	45-11
1852	45-54
1853	45-55
1854	45-56
1855	45-57, 45-58
1856	45-35
1857	45-36
1858	45-37
1859	45-38
1860	45-39
1861	45-59
1862	45-60
1863	45-40
1864	45-41
1865	45-42
1866	45-61
1867	45-62
1868	45-63
1869	45-64
1870	45-65
1871	45-67
1872	45-68
1873	45-69
1874	45-70
1875	45-71
1876	45-72
1877	45-73 to 45-75
1878	45-76
1879	45-43
1880	45-46 to 45-49
1881	45-50
1882	45-51
1883	45-52
1884	45-53
1885	45-77
1886	45-78 to 45-81
1887	45-12
1887a	45-13
1887b	45-14
1887c	45-82
1887d	45-83
1887e	45-44
1887f	45-45
1887g	45-84
1887h	45-88, 45-89
1887i	45-90
1887j	45-85
1887k	45-86
1887l	45-87
1887m	45-7
1887n	45-16
1887o	45-17
1887p	45-15
1887q	45-8
1887r	45-66

Michie Code Section	Code 1950 Section
1887(1)	65-1
1887(2)	65-2
1887(2a)	65-3
1887(2b)	65-4
1887(2c)	65-6
1887(2d)	65-7
1887(2e)	65-54
1887(2f)	65-42
1887(2g)	65-43
1887(2h)	65-44, 65-45
1887(2i)	Repealed by Acts 1948, p. 479
1887(2j)	65-46
1887(2k)	65-47
1887(2l)	65-48
1887(2m)	65-49
1887(2n)	65-50
1887(2o)	65-32
1887(2p)	Omitted
1887(3)	Omitted
1887(4)	65-20
1887(4a)	65-20
1887(5)	65-22, 65-23
1887(6)	65-33
1887(7)	65-34
1887(8)	65-21
1887(9)	65-24
1887(10)	65-36
1887(11)	65-99
1887(12)	65-5, 65-37 to 65-39, 65-108
1887(13)	65-8
1887(14)	65-35
1887(15)	65-25
1887(16)	65-102
1887(17)	65-40
1887(18)	Omitted
1887(19)	65-41
1887(20)	65-26 to 65-31
1887(21)	65-78
1887(22)	65-79
1887(23)	65-82
1887(24)	65-83
1887(25)	65-84
1887(26)	65-85
1887(27)	65-86
1887(28)	65-88
1887(29)	65-59
1887(30)	65-51
1887(31)	65-52
1887(32)	65-53
1887(33)	65-60
1887(34)	65-55
1887(35)	65-56
1887(36)	65-57
1887(37)	65-58
1887(38)	65-61
1887(39)	65-62
1887(40)	65-63 to 65-66
1887(41)	65-67
1887(42)	65-68
1887(43)	65-69
1887(44)	65-70
1887(45)	65-71
1887(46)	65-72
1887(47)	65-95
1887(48)	65-73, 65-74
1887(49)	65-75
1887(50)	65-76
1887(51)	65-77
1887(52)	65-9
1887(52a)	51-18 to 51-21
1887(53)	14-26, 65-10 to 65-12
1887(54)	65-13 to 65-15
1887(55)	65-16 to 65-18, 65-91.1
1887(56)	65-19
1887(57)	65-90
1887(58)	65-91
1887(59)	65-92
1887(60)	65-93
1887(61)	65-94
1887(62)	65-96
1887(63)	65-97
1887(64)	65-87
1887(65)	65-98
1887(66)	65-89
1887(67)	65-115 to 65-119
1887(68)	65-100
1887(69)	65-101 to 65-103
1887(70)	65-104
1887(71)	65-80, 65-81
1887(72)	65-105
1887(73)	65-107
1887(74)	65-109, 65-110
1887(75)	65-106, 65-111 to 65-114, 65-120 to 65-128
1887(76), 1887(77)	Omitted
1887(78)	65-127
1887(79)	Omitted
1887(80)	65-129
1887(81)	65-130
1887(82)	65-131
1887(83)	65-132
1887(84)	65-133
1887(85)	65-134
1887(86)- 1887(92)	Omitted
1887(93)	60-1
1887(94)	60-2 to 60-17, 60-18 to 60-23
1887(95)	60-41 to 60-45, 60-47.1
1887(96)	60-17.1 to 60-17.3, 60-46 to 60-46.5
1887(97)	60-47
1887(98)	60-48 to 60-57
1887(99)	60-45.1, 60-58 to 60-76.1
1887(100)	60-82 to 60-84
1887(101)	60-90 to 60-94
1887(102)	60-26 to 60-28
1887(103)	60-29 to 60-40
1887(104)	60-85 to 60-88
1887(105)	60-95 to 60-101
1887(105a)	60-102 to 60-105
1887(106)	60-77 to 60-81
1887(107)	60-106 to 60-108
1887(108)	60-112 to 60-117
1887(109)	60-109 to 60-111
1887(110)	60-24
1887(111)	60-25
1887(112)	40-21
1887(113)	40-68
1887(114)	40-69
1887(115)	40-70
1887(116)	40-71
1887(117)	40-72
1887(118)	40-73
1887(119)	40-74
1887(120)	40-75
1887(121)	40-76
1887(122)	40-77
1887(123)	40-78
1887(124)	40-79
1887(125)	40-80
1887(126)	40-81
1887(127)	40-82
1887(128)	40-83
1887(129)	40-84
1887(130)	40-85
1887(131)	40-86
1887(132)	40-87
1887(133)	40-88
1887(134)	40-89
1887(135)	40-90
1887(136)	40-91
1887(137)	40-92
1887(138)	40-93
1887(139)	40-94
1887(140)	40-95
1888-1902	Repealed by Acts 1922, p. 156
1902a	63-23
1902b-1902e	Omitted
1902f	63-28 to 63-32
1902g	63-47
1902h	63-33
1902i	63-39
1902j	Omitted
1902k	63-289 to 63-293
1902l	Omitted
1902m	63-61 to 63-65
1902n	63-71, 63-72

Michie Code Section	Code 1950 Section
1902n1	63-73
1902o	63-80, 63-81, 63-86 to 63-99
1903	63-34, 63-48, 63-49
1903a	53-281 to 53-287
1904	Omitted
1904(1)	63-101
1904(2)	63-6, 63-15 to 63-22
1904(3)	63-10 to 63-12
1904(4)	63-13, 63-24 to 63-26, 63-43, 63-44
1904(5)	63-38 to 63-42, 63-46
1904(6)	63-50 to 63-52, 63-53 to 63-60
1904(7)	63-66 to 63-70
1904(8)	63-75 to 63-79, 63-82 to 63-85
1904(9)	63-27, 63-74
1904(10)	63-115
1904(11)	63-116
1904(12)	63-117
1904(13)	63-118 to 63-122
1904(14)	Repealed by Acts 1948, p. 1111
1904(15)	63-126
1904(16)	63-123
1904(17)	63-124
1904(18)	63-127, 63-128
1904(19)	63-129
1904(20)	63-130
1904(21)	63-131 to 63-134
1904(22)	63-125
1904(23)	63-135, 63-136
1904(24)	63-137 to 63-140
1904(25)	63-141
1904(26)	63-142
1904(27)	63-143
1904(28)	63-144 to 63-148
1904(29)	63-150
1904(29a)	63-152
1904(30)	63-149
1904(31)	63-153 to 63-156
1904(32)	63-151
1904(33)	63-157, 63-158
1904(34)	63-159 to 63-161
1904(35)	63-170 to 63-176
1904(36)	63-178
1904(37)	63-177
1904(38)	63-179
1904(39)	63-180
1904(40)	63-181
1904(41)	63-182 to 63-186
1904(42)	Repealed by Acts 1948, p. 1111
1904(43)	63-190
1904(44)	63-187
1904(45)	63-188
1904(46)	63-191, 63-192
1904(47)	63-193
1904(48)	63-194
1904(49)	63-195 to 63-198
1904(50)	63-189
1904(51)	63-199, 63-200
1904(52)	63-201 to 63-204
1904(53)	63-205
1904(54)	63-206 to 63-212
1904(55)	63-213 to 63-215
1904(55a)	63-216
1904(56)	63-217 to 63-220
1904(57)	63-102
1904(58)	63-103
1904(59)	63-104
1904(60)	63-105
1904(61)	63-106
1904(62)	63-107
1904(63)	Repealed by Acts 1940, p. 613
1904(64)	63-108
1904(65)	63-109 to 63-111
1904(66)	63-112
1904(67)	Repealed by Acts 1940, p. 613
1904(68)	63-100
1904(68a)	63-113
1904(69)	63-114
1904(70)	63-222
1904(71)	63-223
1904(72)	63-224
1904(73)	63-225
1904(74)	63-226
1904(75)	63-227
1904(76)	63-228
1904(77)	63-229
1904(78)	63-230
1904(79)	63-231
1905	63-259 to 63-266
1906	63-257, 63-258
1907	63-267, 63-268
1908	63-269, 63-270
1909	63-271 to 63-276
1910	63-277 to 63-283
1911	63-284, 63-285
1912	63-286, 63-287
1913	63-288
1914	63-294 to 63-296
1915	63-297, 63-298
1916	63-299
1917	63-300
1918	63-301, 63-302
1919	63-304
1920	63-305
1921	63-306
1922	63-307
1922a	53-266 to 53-271
1922b	53-272 to 53-276
1922c	53-277
1922d	53-278
1922e	53-279
1923	18-6
1924	63-303
1925-1930	Repealed by Acts 1922, p. 847
1930a	Repealed by Acts 1940, p. 524
1930b	32-162 to 32-167
1930c	63-374 to 63-378
1931-1935	Repealed by Acts 1922, p. 152
1935(1)	63-232
1935(2)	63-233
1935(3)	63-234 to 63-236
1935(4)	63-237, 63-238
1935(5)	63-239
1935(6)	63-240
1935(7)	63-241
1935(8)	63-242
1935(9)	63-243
1935(10)	63-244
1935(11)	63-245
1935(12)	63-246
1935(13)	63-247
1935(14)	63-248
1935(15)	63-249
1935(16)	63-250
1935(17)	63-252
1935(18)	63-253
1935(19)	63-251
1935(20)	63-254
1935(21)	63-255
1935a-1935k	Repealed by Acts 1942, p. 336
1935k1	63-256
1935l-1935aa	Repealed by Acts 1938, p. 669
1936	20-61, 20-62
1936a	20-63
1937	20-64, 20-65
1937a	20-66
1937b	20-70
1937c	20-67 to 20-69
1938	20-71
1939	20-72 to 20-79
1940	20-80
1941	20-81, 20-82
1942	20-83, 20-84
1943	20-85
1944	20-86, 20-87
1944a	20-88
1945	16-130, 16-131

Michie Code Section	Code 1950 Section
1945a	16-132.1
1946	16-138
1947	16-151
1947a	16-132
1948	16-133, 16-143, 16-152
1948a	16-134, 16-135, 16-153
1948b	16-156
1949	16-139
1950	16-140, 16-141, 16-144, 16-157
1950a	16-142
1951	16-150
1951a	16-148
1951b	16-155
1951c	16-149
1951d	16-145
1951e	16-147
1951f	16-146
1952	16-136, 16-154
1953	16-137
1953a	16-158
1953b	16-161
1953c	16-171
1953d	16-159, 16-165
1953e	16-162, 16-163, 16-166, 16-172
1953f	16-164
1953g	16-167
1953h	16-169
1953i	16-170
1953j	16-168
1953k	16-160
1953l, 1953m	Omitted
1953n	Repealed by Acts 1932, p. 151
1953o	Repealed by Acts 1932, p. 137
1954-1959	Repealed by Acts 1926, p. 78
1960	53-19
1961	63-370
1961a	63-367
1961b, 1961c	63-366
1962-1969	Repealed by Acts 1922, p. 673
1969a	33-1 to 33-6
1969b	33-6, 33-7
1969c	33-9
1969d	33-10
1969e	33-5, 33-12, 33-17 to 33-22
1969e(⅛)	33-114, 33-115
1969e(¼)	33-23
1969e(¼a)	33-24, 33-45
1969e(¼b)	33-25
1969e(½)	33-121
1969e(1)	Omitted
1969e(1½)	33-123
1969e(2)	33-16
1969e(2¼)	33-132
1969e(2½)	33-36
1969e(3)	33-125
1969e(4)	33-116, 33-117
1969e(4½)	33-118
1969e(5)	33-173
1969f	33-13, 33-14
1969g	33-32
1969h	33-99 to 33-104
1969i	33-105 to 33-107
1969j	Omitted
1969j(1)	33-57
1969j(2)	33-59 to 33-67
1969j(3)	33-68
1969j(4)	33-70
1969j(5)	33-73
1969j(6)	33-74
1969j(7)	33-75
1969j(8)	33-58
1969j(9)	33-117.1
1969k	33-110
1969l	33-109
1969l(1)	33-135
1969m	33-15
1969n, 1969o	Omitted
1969p	33-11
1970-1972	33-140
1972(1)	33-111
1972a	Repealed by Acts 1926, p. 389
1972b-1973	Omitted
1973a	33-130
1973b	33-131
1974, 1975	Repealed by Acts 1922, p. 673
1975a	Omitted
1975b	33-30
1975c	Omitted
1975d	33-31
1975e	33-33
1975f	33-34
1975g-1975p	Omitted
1975q, 1975r	Repealed by Acts 1944, p. 175
1975r1	33-209 to 33-214
1975s	33-76
1975t	33-77 to 33-79
1975t1	33-81
1975u-1975y	Omitted
1975z	33-113.1
1975aa	33-69
1975bb	33-8
1975cc-1975ff	Omitted
1975gg	33-108
1975hh	33-44
1975ii	33-46, 33-47
1975jj	33-138
1975kk	33-48, 33-49
1975ll	33-51
1975mm	33-56
1975nn	33-52
1975oo	33-141
1975pp	33-113
1975pp(1)	33-137
1975pp(2)	33-113.2
1975pp(3)	33-50.1
1975qq, 1975rr	Omitted
1975ss	33-53 to 33-55
1975ss(1)	33-26
1975ss(2)	33-82 to 33-88
1975ss(3)	33-89
1975ss(4)	33-27
1975ss(5)	33-50
1975tt	Omitted
1975uu	33-122
1975vv	33-124
1975ww	33-80
1975xx	33-85
1975yy	33-37 to 33-43
1975zz	33-90 to 33-95
1975aaa	33-133, 33-134
1976-1982	Repealed by Acts 1928, p. 568
1983	Repealed by Acts 1932, p. 47
1984-1986	Repealed by Acts 1928, p. 568
1987	Repealed by Acts 1932, p. 47
1988-2001	Repealed by Acts 1928, p. 568
2002	Omitted
2003-2014	Repealed by Acts 1928, p. 568
2014a-2014c	33-139
2014d	33-140
2014e	33-72, 33-140
2015-2039	Repealed by Acts 1928, p. 568
2039(1)	33-140
2039(2)	33-142, 33-143
2039(3)	33-144, 33-145
2039(4)	33-146, 33-147
2039(5)	33-148 to 33-152
2039(6)	33-153
2039(7)	33-154
2039(8)	33-155
2039(9)	33-156 to 33-158
2039(9a)	33-155.1
2039(10)	Repealed by Acts 1942, p. 380
2039(11)-2039(15)	33-140
2039(16), 2039(17)	Omitted
2039(18)	33-140
2039(19)	62-139, 62-140
2039(20)	33-140
2039(21)	33-159, 33-160
2039(22)	33-97
2039(23)	33-126
2039(24)	33-127

Michie Code Section	Code 1950 Section
2039(25)	33-128
2039(26)	33-119
2039(27)	33-120
2039(28)	Repealed by Acts 1942, p. 429
2039(29)	33-161
2039(30)	33-140
2039(31)	33-140
2039(32)	33-98
2039(33)	33-129
2039(34)-2039(46)	33-140
2039(47)	Omitted
2040	33-183
2041	33-184
2042	33-185
2043	33-186
2044	33-187, 33-188
2045	33-189
2046	33-190
2047	33-191
2048	33-192
2049	33-193
2050	33-194 to 33-200
2051	33-201
2052	33-171
2053	33-162
2054	33-174
2055	33-175
2056	33-176
2057	33-177, 33-178
2057a	33-168
2058	33-163
2059	33-167
2060	33-179
2061	33-180
2062	33-165
2063	33-169
2064	33-170
2065	33-181
2066	33-182
2067	33-215
2068	33-216
2069	33-217
2070	Repealed by Acts 1944, p. 5
2071	33-164
2072	33-166
2072(1)	33-221
2072(2)	33-224
2072(3)	33-222
2072(4)	33-223
2072(5)	33-225, 33-226
2072(6)	33-226
2072(7)	33-172
2072(8)	33-218 to 33-220
2072(9)	33-227
2072(10)	33-229
2072(11)	33-237
2072(12)	33-228
2072(13)	33-230
2072(14)	33-231
2072(15)	33-232
2072(16)	33-233
2072(17)	33-234
2072(18)	33-236, 33-238 to 33-242
2072(19)	33-243
2072(20)	33-244
2072(21)	33-245, 33-246
2072(22)	33-248
2072(23)	33-247
2072(24)	33-250
2072(25)	33-249
2072(26)	33-235
2072(27)	33-251
2072(28)	33-252
2072(29)	33-253
2072(30)	33-254
2072(31)	33-255
2072(32)	Omitted
2072(33)	33-202 to 33-208
2073	53-58, 53-61 to 53-66, 53-100
2073a	53-67 to 53-72
2073b	53-73
2074	53-110
2075	53-101 to 53-102.1, 53-104, 53-164
2076	53-111
2077	53-112
2078	53-114
2079	53-115
2080	53-113
2081	53-116
2082	53-117
2083, 2084	Omitted
2085	51-118
2086	53-119
2087	53-120
2088	53-121
2089	53-122
2090-2092	Omitted
2093	53-123.1
2094	53-105 to 53-108
2095	53-221
2096	53-103
2096a	53-109
2096b	53-123
2097-2108	Omitted
2108a-2108g	Repealed by Acts 1930, p. 79
2109-2122	33-140
2122a-2124	Omitted
2124a-2124m	33-140
2124n	Omitted
2124o	33-267 to 33-269.1
2124p	33-256
2124q	33-257
2124r	33-258
2124s	33-259
2124t	33-260
2124u	33-261 to 33-266
2125-2132	Repealed by Acts 1932, p. 884
2132a	Repealed by Acts 1932, p. 673
2133-2143	Repealed by Acts 1932, p. 884
2143a, 2143b	Repealed by Acts 1932, p. 673
2144	Omitted
2144a	Repealed by Acts 1932, p. 673
2145	Repealed by Acts 1932, p. 884
2145(1)-2145(14)	Repealed by Acts 1932, p. 673
2145(14)a	Repealed by Acts 1940, p. 683
2145(15)-2145(56)	Repealed by Acts 1932, p. 673
2145(56$^1/_2$)	Repealed by Acts 1930, p. 849
2145(57)	Repealed by Acts 1928, p. 1020
2145(58)-2145(72)	Repealed by Acts 1932, p. 673
2145(72)a	Omitted
2145(73)-2145(76)	Repealed by Acts 1932, p. 673
2146-2147	Repealed by Acts 1942, p. 423
2148	Repealed by Acts 1932, p. 884
2149-2153	Repealed by Tax Code
2154	Repealed by Acts 1932, p. 884
2154(1)-2154(21)	Repealed by Acts 1926, p. 258
2154(22)-2154(31)	Repealed by Acts 1932, p. 399
2154(32)-2154(36)	Repealed by Acts 1926, p. 278
2154(37)	Omitted
2154(38), 2154(39)	Repealed by Acts 1926, p. 278
2154(39$^1/_2$)	Omitted
2154(39)a-2154(39)e	Repealed by Acts 1932, p. 673
2154(39)e1	46-37
2154(39)f, 2154(39)g	Repealed by Acts 1932, p. 673

Michie Code Section	Code 1950 Section
2154(39)g1	Omitted
2154(40)	33-270
2154(41)	33-271
2154(42)	33-272
2154(43)	33-273
2154(44)	33-274
2154(45)	33-276
2154(46)	33-277
2154(47)	33-275
2154(48)	Omitted
2154(49)	46-1
2154(50)	Omitted
2154(51)	46-29 to 46-31
2154(51a)	46-40, 52-7
2154(52)	46-27
2154(53)	46-38, 46-39, 52-8 to 52-10
2154(54)	52-6
2154(54a)	33-11.1, 46.41, 52-11
2154(55)	46-14
2154(56)	46-15 to 46-17
2154(57)	46-32 to 46-36
2154(58)	52-5
2154(59)	46-42, 46-43
2154(60)	46-46 to 46-48, 46-67
2154(60a)	46-45
2154(61)	46-49 to 46-51
2154(62)	46-141
2154(63)	46-52
2154(64)	46-68 to 46-74, 46-77 to 46-79, 46-83
2154(65)	46-75
2154(66)	46-80
2154(67)	46-96 to 46-99
2154(68)	46-101, 46-102
2154(68a)	46-100
2154(69)	46-105 to 46-109
2154(70)	8-67.1 to 8-67.3, 46-110 to 46-125
2154(70a)	8-67.1, 8-67.2
2154(71)	46-44
2154(72)	46-82
2154(73)	46-62, 46-103, 46-104
2154(74)	46-84 to 46-92
2154(74a)	46-93, 46-94
2154(75)	46-95
2154(76)	46-53
2154(77)	46-6
2154(78)	46-54, 46-359
2154(79)	46-56 to 46-58, 46-60, 46-61, 46-379
2154(79)a	46-55
2154(80)	46-2
2154(81)	46-4, 46-5
2154(82)	46-154 to 46-161
2154(82a)	46-162 to 46-170
2154(82a1)	46-171 to 46-173
2154(82b)	46-176
2154(82c)	46-153
2154(82d)	46-175
2154(82e)	46-64, 46-65
2154(83)	58-643 to 58-683
2154(83a)	46-142 to 46-151
2154(83b)	46-152
2154(83c)	46-21, 46-22
2154(83d)	46-174
2154(84)	46-179
2154(84a)	46-177
2154(84b)	46-178
2154(85)	46-63
2154(86)	46-66
2154(87)	46-81
2154(88)	Repealed by Acts 1942, p. 645
2154(89)	46-76
2154(90)	46-7
2154(91)	46-8 to 46-10
2154(92)	46-11
2154(93)	46-12
2154(94)	46-3
2154(95)	46-13
2154(96)	46-180
2154(97)	46-181
2154(98)	46-183
2154(99)	46-200 to 46-206
2154(99a)	46-213
2154(100)	46-184 to 46-186
2154(100a)	46-214
2154(101)	46-207
2154(102)	46-187
2154(103)	46-188
2154(104)	46-189
2154(105)	46-190
2154(106)	Repealed by Acts 1944, p. 609
2154(107)	46-17.1 to 46-17.4, 46-405, 46-406
2154(108)	46-208 to 46-211
2154(108a)	8-646.3 to 8-646.8
2154(109)	46-212
2154(110)	46-215
2154(111)	46-216
2154(112)	46-220
2154(113)	46-221
2154(114)	46-222
2154(115)	46-223
2154(116)	46-224 to 46-226
2154(117)	46-227
2154(118)	46-228
2154(119)	46-229
2154(120)	46-230
2154(121)	46-231, 46-232
2154(122)	46-233 to 46-237
2154(123)	46-238, 46-239, 46-244
2154(124)	46-240
2154(125),	46-241, 46-242
2154(126)	46-243 to 46-250
2154(127)	Repealed by Act 1938, p. 159
2154(128)	46-251
2154(129)	46-252
2154(130)	46-253
2154(131)	46-254, 56-407, 56-409
2154(132)	46-255
2154(133)	46-256 to 46-259
2154(133a)	46-260 to 46-262
2154(134)	46-263
2154(135)	46-217
2154(136)	46-218
2154(137)	46-219
2154(138)	46-309, 46-310
2154(139)	46-192
2154(140)	46-191
2154(141)	46-264 to 46-275
2154(142)	46-276 to 46-279
2154(143)	46-280
2154(144)	46-281
2154(145)	46-282
2154(146)	46-283 to 46-287
2154(147)	46-288
2154(148)	46-289 to 46-293
2154(149)	46-294
2154(150)	46-295 to 46-298
2154(151)	46-304
2154(152)	46-305 to 46-308
2154(153)	46-302, 46-303
2154(154)	46-311 to 46-315
2154(155)	46-316
2154(156)	46-317 to 46-322, 46-323, 46-324
2154(156a)	46-322.1
2154(157)	46-325
2154(158)	46-326 to 46-330
2154(159)	46-331 to 46-333
2154(160)	46-334 to 46-335.1

Michie Code Section	Code 1950 Section
2154(160a)	46-336 to 46-338.1
2154(161)	46-339
2154(162)	46-340
2154(162a)	46-341
2154(163)	46-342
2154(164)	46-299 to 46-301
2154(165)	46-18
2154(166)	46-19
2154(167)	46-193, 46-194
2154(168)	46-195 to 46-197
2154(168a)	46-197.1
2154(169)	46-20, 46-198, 46-199
2154(170)	46-343
2154(171)	Omitted
2154(172)	46-348 to 46-350
2154(173)	46-351, 46-352
2154(174)	46-353 to 46-358.1
2154(175)	46-182
2154(176)	46-361, 46-364
2154(177)	46-362
2154(178)	46-363
2154(179)	46-347, 46-365, 46-376, 46-377
2154(180)	46-366
2154(181)	46-367
2154(182)	46-368 to 46-373, 46-378
2154(183)	46-374
2154(184)	46-375
2154(185)-2154(187)	Repealed by Acts 1948, p. 495
2154(188)	46-360
2154(189)	Omitted
2154(190	8-646.2
2154(191)	46-380
2154(192)	46-381
2154(193)	46-382
2154(194)	46-383
2154(195)	46-384
2154(196)	Omitted
2154(197)	46-385
2154(198)	Omitted
2154(199)	46-346
2154(200)	46-345
2154(201)	46-344
2154(202)	Omitted
2154(203)	Omitted
2154(204)-2154(208)	Repealed by Acts 1944, p. 609
2154(209)	58-686, 58-687
2154(210)	58-693 to 58-701
2154(211)	58-695, 58-702 to 58-708
2154(212)	58-709, 58-710
2154(213)	58-692.1, 58-711 to 58-714
2154(214)	58-730
2154(215)	58-715, 58-716
2154(216)	58-717
2154(216a)	Repealed by Acts 1944, p. 28
2154(216b)	58-717
2154(216c)	58-719
2154(216d)	58-720
2154(217)	58-721 to 58-723
2154(218)	58-724
2154(219)	58-725
2154(220)	58-726
2154(221)	58-727
2154(222)	58-728
2154(222a)	46-126 to 46-133.1
2154(223)	58-729
2154(224)	58-688
2154(225)	58-690
2154(226)	58-691
2154(227)	58-692
2154(228)	58-689
2154(229), 2154(230)	Omitted
2154(230a)	33-31
2154(230b)	58-731
2154(230c)	58-732
2154(230d)	58-733
2154(230e)	58-744
2154(230f)	58-734 to 58-741
2154(230g)	58-746
2154(230h)	58-745
2154(230i)	58-748
2154(230j)	58-742
2154(230k)	58-749, 58-750
2154(230l)	58-747
2154(230m)	58-751
2154(230n)	58-752
2154(230o)	58-743
2154(230p)	58-753
2154(230q)	58-755
2154(230r)	58-756
2154(230s)	58-754
2154(230t)	58-757
2154(230u), 2154(230v)	Omitted
2154(231)	46-28
2154(232)	8-646.1
2154(233)	52-12
2154(234)	52-13
2154(235)	52-14
2154(236)	52-15
2154(237)	Omitted
2154(238)	33-298
2154(239)	33-299
2154(240)	33-300, 33-301
2154(241)	33-303 to 33-305
2154(242)	33-306
2154(243)	33-307 to 33-313
2154(243a)	33-314
2154(244)	33-316
2154(244a)	33-318
2154(245)	33-315
2154(246)	33-317
2154(247)	33-280, 33-319
2154(248)	33-322
2154(249)	33-320
2154(250)	33-302
2154(251)	33-321
2154(252)	33-323
2154(253)	33-324
2154(a1)	46-386
2154(a2)-2154(a4)	46-387
2154(a5)	Repealed by Acts 1948, p. 438
2154(a6)	46-492
2154(a7)	46-493
2154(a8)	46-494
2154(a9)	46-495
2154(a10)	46-496
2154(a11)	46-497
2154(a12)	46-498
2154(a13)	46-499, 46-500
2154(a14)	46-501
2154(a14)a	46-390, 46-496.1
2154(a15)	46-394
2154(a16)	46-416, 46-417
2154(a17)	46-418, 46-419
2154(a18)	46-420 to 46-422
2154(a19)	46-423
2154(a20)	46-425
2154(a21)	46-424
2154(a22)	46-59
2154(a23)	46-426, 46-427
2154(a24)	46-428
2154(a25)	46-429
2154(a26)	46-430
2154(a27)	46-431
2154(a28)	46-432
2154(a29)	46-434
2154(a30)	46-433
2154(a31)	46-435
2154(a32)	46-436
2154(a33)	46-437
2154(a34)	46-438
2154(a35)	46-439
2154(a36)	46-440
2154(a37)	46-441
2154(a38)	46-442 to 46-444
2154(a39)	46-445

Michie Code Section	Code 1950 Section
2154(a40)	46-448, 46-449
2154(a41)	Omitted
2154(a42)	46-397
2154(a43)	45-402
2154(a44)	46-398 to 46-400
2154(a45)	46-401
2154(a46)	45-404
2154(a47)	45-407, 45-408
2154(a48)	46-409, 46-410
2154(a49)	46-411, 46-412
2154(a50)	46-413
2154(a51)	46-17.1, 46-405
2154(a52)	46-403
2154(a53)	46-452
2154(a54)	46-414
2154(a55)	46-446
2154(a56)	46-447
2154(a57)	46-392
2154(a58)	46-450
2154(a59)	46-451
2154(a60)	45-453
2154(a61)	46-454
2154(a62)	46-457
2154(a63)	46-458
2154(a64)	46-395
2154(a65)	45-455
2154(a66)	45-456
2154(a67)	45-459
2154(a68)	45-460
2154(a69)	46-461, 46-462
2154(a70)	46-463
2154(a71)	46-464
2154(a72)	46-465
2154(a73)	46-466
2154(a74)	46-467
2154(a75)	46-468, 46-469
2154(a76)	46-470
2154(a77)	46-471
2154(a78)	46-472, 46-473
2154(a79)	46-474
2154(a80)	46-475, 46-476
2154(a81)	46-477, 46-478
2154(a82)	46-479
2154(a83)	46-480
2154(a84)	46-481
2154(a85)	46-482
2154(a86)	46-483
2154(a87)	46-484
2154(a88)	46-485
2154(a89)	46-415
2154(a90)	46-396
2154(a91)	46-393
2154(a92)	46-486
2154(a93)	46-487
2154(a94)	46-488
2154(a95)	46-489, 46-490
2154(a96)	46-491
2154(a97)	46-391
2154(a98)	46-389
2154(a99)	46-388

Michie Code Section	Code 1950 Section
2154(b1)	46-502
2154(b2)	46-503
2154(b3)	46-510
2154(b4)	46-512 to 46-514
2154(b5)	46-515, 46-516
2154(b6)	46-517 to 46-519
2154(b7)	46-520
2154(b8)	46-511
2154(b9)	46-521
2154(b10)	46-522
2154(b11)	46-523
2154(b12)	46-524
2154(b13)	46-508
2154(b13a)	46-536 46-537
2154(b14)	46-525
2154(b15)	46-526 to 46-531
2154(b16)	46-504 to 46-506
2154(b17)	46-507, 46-508
2154(b18)	46-532
2154(b19)	46-533
2154(b20)	46-534
2154(b21)	46-535
2154(b22)	46-538
2154(b23)	46-539
2154(b23)a	46-540
2154(b23)b	46-540
2154(b24)	46-509
2155	Repealed by Acts 1928, p. 346
2156	2-176
2157	2-177
2158	2-178 to 2-183, 2-191
2158a	2-192
2158	2-187
2159	2-186
2160	2-184
2161	2-185
2162	2-188
2163-2171	Repealed by Acts 1928, p. 346
2171a	Omitted
2172	2-165
2173	2-193
2174	2-196
2175	2-194
2176	2-199
2177	2-164, 2-193
2178	2-195
2179	2-198
2180	2-197
2181	2-206
2182, 2183	Repealed by Acts 1928, p. 346
2184	2-207 to 2-209
2185	2-210

Michie Code Section	Code 1950 Section
2186	2-171
2187	2-172
2188	2-174
2189	2-170
2190	2-169
2191	2-173
2192	2-164
2193	Repealed by Acts 1928, p. 346
2194	2-158
2195	Repealed by Acts 1928, p. 346
2196	2-156
2196(1)	2-154.1
2197, 2198	Repealed by Acts 1928, p. 346
2199	2-157
2200	Repealed by Acts 1928, p. 346
2201	Repealed by Tax Code
2202-2204	Repealed by Acts 1928, p. 346
2205-2208	Repealed by Tax Code
2209	Repealed by Acts 1926, p. 991
2210-2212a	Repealed by Tax Code
2213-2216	Repealed by Acts 1924, p. 574
2217-2225	Repealed by Tax Code
2225a-2225j	Repealed by 1926, p. 252
2225(1)-2225(12)	Repealed by Tax Code
2226-2227	Repealed by Acts 1922, p. 512
2228-2258	Repealed by Tax Code
2259-2262	Repealed by Acts 1924, p. 572
2263-2298	Repealed by Tax Code
2299	Repealed by Acts 1924, p. 589
2300-2306a	Repealed by Tax Code
2306b	51-2
2306c	3-580
2307-2313	Repealed by Tax Code
2313a	Repealed by Acts 1926, p. 955
2314, 2315	Repealed by Tax Code
2316-2323	Omitted
2323a-2324	Repealed by Acts 1930, p. 664

Michie Code Section	Code 1950 Section
2324a-2324i	Repealed by Acts 1936, p. 486
2325, 2326	Repealed by Acts 1930, p. 664
2327-2336	Repealed by Tax Code
2337	Repealed by Acts 1928, p. 1344
2338, 2339	Repealed by Tax Code
2340	Repealed by Acts 1924, p. 589
2341-2347	Repealed by Tax Code
2347a-2347c	Omitted
2348	Repealed by Tax Code
2349	Repealed by Acts 1928, p. 1344
2349a-2359	Repealed by Tax Code
2359a-2359d	Repealed by Acts 1926, p. 897
2359e-2366	Repealed by Tax Code
2366a	54-1.1, 54-1.2
2367-238	Repealed by Tax Code
2384a	54-810
2384b	58-381
2384c	54-811
2384d	54-814
2384e	54-815
2384f	54-816
2384g	54-817
2384h	54-818
2384i	54-809, 54-812, 54-813, 54-819, 54-820
2384j	54-823
2384k	54-820
2384l	54-824
2384m	54-821
2384n	54-822
2384o	54-795
2384p	54-796, 54-797, 54-802, 58-371.1
2384q	54-798, 54-799
2384r	54-800
2384s	54-801
2384t	54-803 to 54-805
2384u	54-806
2384v	54-807
2384w	54-808
2385-2388	Repealed by Tax Code
2388a	Repealed by Acts 1940, p. 493
2389-2392d	Repealed by Tax Code
2392e	58-1152
2392f	Omitted
2393-2396	Repealed by Tax Code
2397	Repealed by Acts 1926, p. 258
2398-2400	Repealed by Tax Code
2401-2403	Repealed by Tax Code
2404	2-62
2405-2429	Repealed by Tax Code
2430-2431	Omitted
2432-2450c	Repealed by Tax Code
2451-2453	Repealed by Acts 1940, p. 342
2454	58-1023
2454a	58-1024
2455	Repealed by Acts 1918, p. 635
2456	58-1025
2456a	Repealed by Tax Code
2457	58-1110 to 58-1112
2458	58-1113 to 58-1116
2459	58-1117
2460	58-1029 to 58-1031
2461	58-1032
2462	58-1033
2463	58-1034
2464	58-1035
2465	58-1036
2466	Repealed by Acts 1920, p. 19
2467	Repealed by Acts 1940, p. 342
2468	58-1037
2469	58-1038
2470	58-1039
2471	58-1040
2472	58-1041
2473	Repealed by Acts 1940, p. 342
2474	58-1042
2475	58-1043
2476	58-1044
2477	58-1045
2478	58-1046
2479	58-1047
2480	58-1048 to 58-1050
2481	58-1051
2482	58-1052 to 58-1058
2483	58-1059
2484	58-1060
2485	58-1061
2486	58-1062
2487	58-1063
2488	58-1064, 58-1065
2489	58-1067 to 58-1071
2490	58-1072
2491	58-1073 to 58-1075
2492	58-1076
2493	58-1077
2494	58-825
2495	58-1083 to 58-1097
2495a	10-34.1, 10-34.2
2496	58-1098
2497	58-1099
2498	58-1026
2499	58-1078
2500	58-1079 to 58-1081
2501	58-1027, 58-1028
2502	58-1022, 58-1082
2503	58-1101 to 58-1106
2503a	58-1107
2503a1	58-1108
2503b	58-1066
2503c	58-1109
2503d	58-1100
2504	41-4, 41-78
2505	41-79
2506	41-80
2507	41-81
2508	41-82
2509	41-83
2510	8-758
2511	8-759
2512	8-760
2513	8-761
2514	8-762
2515	Omitted
2516	8-763
2517	8-764
2518	8-765
2519	8-766
2520	8-767
2521	8-768
2521a	8-427, 8-428
2522	8-769
2523	8-770
2524	8-771
2525	8-772
2526	8-773
2527	8-774
2528	8-775
2529	8-776
2530	8-777
2531	8-778
2532	8-779
2533	Repealed by Tax Code
2534	8-780
2535	8-781
2536	8-782
2537	8-783
2538	8-784
2539	8-785
2540	8-786
2541	8-787
2542	8-788
2542a	10-16

Michie Code Section	Code 1950 Section
2543	19-299
2544	19-300, 19-301
2545	19-302
2546	19-331 to 19-335
2547	19-327
2548	Repealed by Tax Code
2549	19-319
2550	19-310
2551	19-311
2552	19-312
2553	19-313
2554	19-323
2555	19-325
2556	Omitted
2557	19-336
2558	19-324
2559	19-320
2560	19-321
2561	19-322
2562	19-326
2563	19-314
2564	19-315
2565	19-316
2566	19-317
2567	19-318
2568	19-328
2569	19-337
2570	19-338
2571	19-339
2572	19-340
2573	19-341
2574	19-342
2575	19-329
2576	19-330
2577	19-298
2577a	2-48
2577b	2-49
2577c	2-50
2577d	2-51
2577e	2-52
2577f	2-53
2577g	2-54
2577h	2-55
2577i	2-56
2577j	2-57
2577k	2-46, 14-18
2577l	15-575, 15-576
2577m	15-577
2577m(1)	15-578
2577m(2)	15-579, 15-584
2577m(3)	15-580
2577m(4)	15-582
2577n	15-583
2577o	15-585
2578	8-752
2579	8-753
2580	8-754
2581	8-755
2582	8-756
2583	8-757
2584-2602	2-270
2603	Omitted
2604-2606	Repealed by Tax Code
2607-2611	Omitted
2612	2-283
2613	2-284
2614-2617	Repealed by Tax Code
2618	2-285
2619, 2620	Repealed by Tax Code
2621	Omitted
2622	2-287
2623	2-292
2624	2-293
2624a	2-151, 2-288 to 2-291, 56-45
2625	2-294
2626	2-295
2627	2-296
2628	2-271
2629	2-272
2630, 2631	Omitted
2632	2-273
2633	2-274
2634	2-275
2635	2-276
2636	2-277
2637	2-278
2638	2-279, 2-280
2639	2-281
2640	2-269
2641	Omitted
2641a	2-282
2641(1)-2641(11)	2-270
2642-2672a	51-1
2672b-2672d	23-7.1
2672(1)	51-31
2672(2)	51-32
2672(3)	51-38 to 51-42
2672(4)	51-43, 51-44
2672(5)	51-45
2672(6)	51-46 to 51-49
2672(6a)	51-50
2672(7)	51-60 to 51-67
2672(8)	51-97 to 51-99.1
2672(9)	51-100 to 51-105
2672(10)	51-108
2672(11)	51-109
2672(12)	51-106, 51-107
2672(13)	51-71
2672(14)	51-81 to 51-86
2672(15)	51-72
2672(16)	51-87 to 51-96
2672(17)	51-73
2672(18)	51-74
2672(19)	51-75
2672(20)	51-76 to 51-80
2672(21)	51-68
2672(22)	51-69
2672(23)	51-70
2672(24)	51-33, 51-34
2672(24a)	51-52 to 51-59
2672(24b)	51-114.1
2672(25)	51-110
2672(25a)	Omitted
2672(26)	51-51
2672(27)	51-35
2672(28)	51-111
2672(29)	51-36
2672(30)	51-30
2672(31)	51-37
2672(32)	Omitted
2672(33)	51-25
2672(34)	51-26
2672(35)	51-27
2672(36)	51-28
2672(37)	51-22 to 51-24
2672(38)	51-29
2673-2673	Repealed by Acts 1930, p. 973
2673(1)	44-1
2673(2)	44-2
2673(3)	44-3
2673(4)	44-4
2673(5)	44-5
2673(6)	44-6
2673(7)	44-7
2673(8)	44-8
2673(9)	44-9
2673(10)	44-10
2673(11)	44-12, 44-14, 44-19
2673(12)	44-11
2673(13)	44-13, 44-15, 44-23
2673(14)	44-24
2673(15)	44-25
2673(16)	44-26
2673(17)	44-27
2673(18)	44-28
2673(19)	44-29
2673(20)	44-30
2673(21)	44-31
2673(22)	44-32
2673(22a)	44-32.1
2673(23)	44-33
2673(24)	44-34
2673(25)	44-35
2673(26)	44-36
2673(27)	44-37
2673(28)	44-38
2673(29)	44-39
2673(30)	44-40
2673(31)	44-41
2673(32)	44-42
2673(33)	44-43
2673(34)	44-44
2673(35)	44-45
2673(36)	44-46
2673(37)	44-47

Michie Code Section	Code 1950 Section
2673(38)	44-48
2673(39)	44-49
2673(40)	44-50
2673(41)	44-51
2673(42)	44-52
2673(43)	44-54
2673(44)	44-53
2673(45)	44-55 to 44-58, 44-63
2673(46)	44-59
2673(47)	44-60
2673(48)	44-61
2673(49)	44-62
2673(50)	44-63
2673(51)	44-67
2673(52)	44-68
2673(53)	44-69
2673(54)	44-70, 44-71
2673(55)	44-72
2673(56)	44-73
2673(57)	44-74
2673(58)	44-66
2673(59)	44-64
2673(60)	44-65
2673(61)	44-75
2673(62)	44-76
2673(63)	44-77
2673(64)	44-78
2673(65)	44-79
2673(66)	44-80
2673(67)	44-81
2673(68)	44-82
2673(69)	44-83
2673(70)	44-84
2673(71)	44-85
2673(72)	44-86
2673(73)	44-87, 44-88
2673(74)	44-89
2673(75)	44-90
2673(76)	44-91
2673(77)	44-92
2673(78)	44-93
2673(79)	44-94
2673(80)	44-95
2673(81)	44-96
2673(82)	44-97
2673(83)	44-98
2673(84)	44-99
2673(85)	44-100
2673(86)	44-101
2673(87)	44-102
2673(88)	44-103
2673(89)	44-104
2673(90)	44-105
2673(91)	44-106
2673(92)	44-107
2673(93)	44-108
2673(94)	44-109
2673(95)	44-110
2673(96)	44-111

Michie Code Section	Code 1950 Section
2673(97)	44-112
2673(98)	44-113
2673(99)	44-114
2673(100)	44-115
2673(101)	44-116
2673(102)	44-117
2673(103)	44-118
2673(104)	44-119
2673(105)	44-120
2673(106)	Omitted
2673(107)	44-122
2673(108)	44-121
2673(109)	44-123, 44-124
2673(110)	44-125
2673(111)	44-126 to 44-128
2673(112)	44-129
2673(113)	44-130
2673(114)	44-131
2673(115)	44-132
2673(116)	44-133
2673(117)	44-134, 44-135
2673(118)	44-136
2673(119)	44-137
2673(120)	44-138
2673(121)	44-139
2673(122)	Omitted
2673(123)	44-140
2673(124)	44-204
2673(125)	Omitted
2673(126)	44-141
2673(127)	44-142
2673(128)	44-143
2673(129)	44-144
2673(130)	44-145
2673(131)	44-146
2673(132)	44-147
2673(133)	44-148
2673(134)	44-149
2673(135)	44-150
2673(136)	44-151
2673(137)	44-152
2673(138)	44-153
2673(139)	44-154
2673(140)	44-155
2673(141)	44-156
2673(142)	44-157
2673(143)	44-158
2673(144)	44-159
2673(145)-2673(151)	44-207
2673(152)-2673(179)	Omitted
2673(180)	44-205
2673(181)	44-206
2673(182)	44-207
2673(183)	Omitted
2673(184)	44-207
2674	15-27
2675	15-28

Michie Code Section	Code 1950 Section
2676	15-29
2677	15-30
2678	15-31
2679	15-32
2680	15-33
2681	15-34
2682	15-35
2683	15-36
2684	15-37
2684a	15-162
2684b	15-163
2684c	15-164
2684d	15-165 to 15-168
2684e	15-169
2684f	15-170 to 15-174
2684g	15-220
2684h	15-221
2684i	15-222
2684j	15-223 to 15-226
2684k	15-227, 15-228, 15-229
2684l	15-231
2684m	Omitted
2685	15-38 to 15-42
2685a, 2685b	Omitted
2686	15-3
2687	15-55
2688	15-56 to 15-58
2689	15-59
2690	15-60
2691	15-61
2692	15-62
2693	15-63
2694	15-64, 15-65
2695	15-19.1
2695(1)	15-763
2695(2)	15-777
2695a-2695g	Repealed by Acts 1936, p. 116
2695h	40-65, 40-66
2695i	40-67
2696	15-475, 15-476
2697	15-477
2698	15-478 to 15-480, 15-482
2698a	2-7, 2-8, 15-483
2699	15-481, 15-482
2700	15-484
2701	15-485
2702	15-486
2702a	15-490
2702b	15-491
2702c	15-492
2702d	15-493
2702e	15-494 to 15-496
2702f	15-497 to 15-499
2703	15-487
2704	15-488
2704a	15-489
2705	15-500 to 15-502

Michie Code Section	Code 1950 Section
2706	15-503
2707	15-504, 15-505
2708	15-508
2709	15-709, 22-150
2709a	15-21, 22-56
2710	15-4, 15-232
2711	15-241, 15-242
2712	15-233
2713	15-234
2714	15-242
2715	15-243
2716	15-526, 63-319
2717	15-244, 15-245
2718	15-240
2719	15-246
2720	Repealed by Tax Code
2721	Repealed by Acts 1920, p. 587
2721a	Repealed by Tax Code
2722	15-247
2722a	15-248, 22-53
2723	15-506, 15-692, 63-328
2724	15-253, 15-254
2724a	15-256
2724b	15-255
2725	15-693
2725a	15-263
2725b	15-539 to 15-541
2725c	15-542, 15-543
2725d	15-544, 15-545
2725e	15-546 to 15-549
2726	15-711
2726a	Repealed by Acts 1948, pp. 325, 740
2726a1	14-164
2726b-2726l	Repealed by Acts 1940, p. 115
2726m-2726y	Repealed by Acts 1942, p. 597
2726z	14-164.2
2726z1	14-164.3
2727	15-249 to 15-251
2727a	15-659 to 15-662
2727b	15-252
2728	15-9
2728a	Omitted
2728b	59-141 to 59-143
2729	15-20
2729a	Repealed by Acts 1930, p. 664
2729b	Repealed by Acts 1930, pp. 665, 737
2730	63-221
2730a	63-334
2730b	63-336

Michie Code Section	Code 1950 Section
2730c	15-724 to 15-726
2731	15-694
2732	15-12
2733	15-573
2733a	51-114
2734	15-11
2734a	Omitted
2734b	21-426
2734c	15-706
2734d	15-17
2734e	15-24, 21-118.1, 22-151
2734f	22-282
2734g	32-134.1
2734h	15-16.1
2735	15-630
2735a	15-645
2735b	15-646
2735c	15-647
2735d	15-648
2735e	15-649
2735f	15-650
2735g	15-651
2735h	15-652
2735i	15-653
2735j	15-654
2735k	15-655
2735l	15-656
2735m	15-657
2735n	15-658
2736	Repealed by Acts 1926, p. 55
2737	15-265
2738	15-601
2739	15-602
2740	15-603
2741	15-604
2741a	15-589
2741a1	15-590
2741a2	15-22, 15-23
2741b	15-605
2742	15-696
2742a	Repealed by Acts 1932, p. 482
2742b	15-778
2743	15-8, 27-3, 27-25
2743a	15-15
2743b	15-10
2743c	15-759
2743d	15-712
2743e	15-511
2743f	15-886 to 15-890
2743g	27-28
2743h	15-705
2743i	15-705
2743j	15-704
2743k	15-713
2743l	Omitted
2743m	27-4, 27-27, 27-27.1, 27-39
2744	15-235

Michie Code Section	Code 1950 Section
2745	15-43
2746	15-44
2747	15-45, 15-46
2748	15-47
2749	15-48
2750	15-49
2751	15-50
2752	15-51
2753	15-52
2754	15-53
2755	15-54
2756	15-264
2757	15-720 to 15-723
2757a	15-761
2757a1	15-762
2757b-2757i	Repealed by Acts 1932, p. 888
2757(j)	15-759.2
2757(j1)	15-738, 15-739
2757(k)-2757(q)	15-759.2
2758	Repealed by Tax Code
2759	15-257
2760	15-258
2761	15-259
2762, 2763	Repealed by Tax Code
2764	15-260
2765	15-261
2766	15-236
2767	Repealed by Tax Code
2768	Repealed by Acts 1927, p. 127
2769	Repealed by Acts 1948, p. 115
2769a	14-55 to 14-59
2770	Repealed by Acts 1934, p. 550
2770a	15-237
2771	15-262
2772	Repealed by Acts 1948, p. 296
2772a	15-707
2773	15-238, 15-239
2773a	Repealed by Acts 1930, p. 21
2773(1)-2773(9)	15-755
2773(9a)	Repealed by Acts 1946, p. 263
2773(9b)	15-757
2773(10)	15-345
2773(11)	15-346
2773(12)	15-347
2773(13)	15-348

Michie Code Section	Code 1950 Section
2773(14)	15-349
2773(15)	15-350
2773(15a)	15-351
2773(16)	15-352
2773(16a)	15-352.1
2773(17)	15-353
2773(17a)	15-353.1
2773(18)	15-354
2773(18a)	15-355
2773(18b)	22-84 to 22-88
2773(18c)	22-88.1, 22-88.2
2773(19)	15-356
2773(20)	15-357
2773(21)	15-358
2773(22)	15-359
2773(23)	15-360
2773(23a)	15-361
2773(24)	15-266
2773(25)	15-267 to 15-271
2773(26)	15-272
2773(27)	15-273
2773(28)	15-274 to 15-277
2773(29)	15-278 to 15-280
2773(30)	15-281 to 15-283
2773(31)	15-284
2773(32)	15-285, 15-286
2773(33)	15-287
2773(34)	15-288
2773(35)	15-289
2773(36)	15-290
2773(37)	15-291
2773(38)	15-292, 22-80 to 22-82
2773(39)	15-293
2773(40)	15-294
2773(41)	15-295
2773(42)	15-296
2773(43)	15-297
2773(44)	15-298
2773(45)	15-299
2773(46)	15-300
2773(47)	15-301
2773(48)	15-302
2773(49)	15-303
2773(50)	15-304
2773(51)	15-305
2773(52)	15-306
2773(53)	15-307, 15-308 to 15-310
2773(53a)	15-307.1
2772(54)	15-311 to 15-313, 33-140
2773(55)	15-314, 15-315
2773(56)	15-316
2773(57)	15-317
2773(58)	15-318
2773(59)	15-319
2773(60)	15-320
2773(61)	15-321
2773(62)	15-322
2773(63)	15-323
2773(64)	15-324, 22-41, 22-80 to 22-82
2773(65)	15-325
2773(66)	15-326
2773(67)	15-327
2773(68)	15-328
2773(68a)	15-328.1
2773(69)	15-329
2773(70)	15-330
2773(71)	15-331
2773(72)	15-332
2773(73)	15-333
2773(74)	15-334
2773(75)	15-335
2773(76)	15-336
2773(77)	15-337
2773(78)	15-338, 15-339
2773(79)	15-340 to 15-343
2773(79a)	15-344
2773(79b)	15-362
2773(79c)	15-363
2773(79d)	15-364
2773(79e)	15-365
2773(79f)	15-366
2773(79g)	15-367
2773(79h)	15-368
2773(79i)	15-369
2773(79j)	15-370
2773(79k)	15-371
2773(79l)	15-372
2773(79m)	15-373
2773(79n)	15-374
2773(79o)	15-375
2773(79p)	15-376
2773(79q)	15-377
2773(79r)	15-378
2773(79s)	15-379
2773(79t)	15-380
2773(79u)	15-381
2773(79v)	15-382
2773(79w)	15-383
2773(79x)	15-384
2773(80)	15-916
2773(81)	15-917
2773(82)	15-918, 15-919
2773(83)	15-920
2773(84)	15-921
2773(85)	15-922
2773(86)	15-924
2773(87)	15-923
2773(88)	15-925
2773(89)	15-926
2773(90)	15-915
2773(91)	15-891
2773(92)	15-892
2773(93)	15-893
2773(94)	15-894
2773(95)	15-895
2773(96)	15-896
2773(97)	15-897
2773(98)	15-898
2774, 2774a	Repealed by Tax Code
2775	15-581
2775a	Omitted
2776-2793	Repealed by Tax Code
2794	63-322
2795	63-256, 63-326
2796	63-327
2797	63-325
2798	63-323
2799	63-324
2800	63-330
2801	63-331
2802	63-332
2803	63-333
2804	63-337
2805	63-322
2806	Repealed by Acts 1936, p. 16
2806a, 2806b	Omitted
2807	63-329
2808	63-338
2809	63-339
2810	63-340
2810a	63-341
2811	63-342 to 63-344
2812	63-345
2812a	63-308
2812b	63-309
2812c	63-310
2812d	63-311
2812e	63-312
2812f	63-313
2812g	63-314
2812h	63-315
2812i	63-316
2812j	63-317
2812k	63-318
2813	Omitted
2814	15-524
2815	Repealed by Acts 1946, p. 601
2816	15-510
2817	15-509
2818	Repealed by Acts 1946, p. 601
2818a	Omitted
2819	Repealed by Acts 1946, p. 601
2820	18-21
2821	15-512
2822	15-514

Michie Code Section	Code 1950 Section
2823	8-4.1, 8-4.2
2824	15-513
2825	15-515
2826	15-516
2827	15-517
2828	15-518
2829	15-519
2830	8-421.1
2831	8-421.2
2832	8-422.1
2833	Repealed by Acts 1932, p. 343
2834	8-422.2
2835	15-520
2836	15-521
2837	15-522
2838	15-523
2838a	15-525
2839	15-528
2840	15-529
2841	15-530
2842	15-531
2843	15-533
2844	15-532
2845	15-534
2846	15-535
2847	15-536
2848	15-537
2849	15-538
2849(1)	55-287, 55-288
2849(2)	55-289
2849(3)	55-290
2849(4)	55-291
2849(5)	55-292, 55-293
2849(6)	55-294
2849(7)	55-295
2849(8)	55-296
2849(9)	Omitted
2849(10)	55-297
2850	47-1
2850a	47-2
2851	47-3
2852	47-4
2853	47-5 to 47-7
2854	15-686, 15-688 to 15-691
2854a	15-737
2855	15-687, 53-132
2856	53-138
2857	53-149
2858	53-150
2859	53-148
2860	53-151
2861	53-152
2862	53-153
2863	53-154 to 53-160
2864	53-161
2865	15-693.1, 53-129
2866	15-693.1, 53-130
2867	15-693.1, 53-131
2868	53-137, 53-143, 53-144, 53-168
2869	53-162
2870	53-172
2871	53-169
2872	53-139, 53-142
2873	53-140
2874	53-141
2875	53-145
2876	53-145, 53-146
2877-2879	53-183.1
2880	53-167
2880a	53-195, 53-197 to 53-199
2880b	53-200
2880c	53-201
2880d	53-202
2880e	Omitted
2880f	53-203
2880g	53-204
2880h	Omitted
2880i	53-196
2880j	53-204.1
2880k	15-855
2880l	15-856
2880m	15-857
2880n	15-858
2880o	15-859
2880p	15-860
2880p1	15-861
2880q	15-862
2880r	15-863
2880s	15-864
2880t	15-865
288u	15-866
2880v	15-867, 15-867.1
2880w	15-868
2880x	15-869
2880y	15-870
2880z	15-871
2880aa	15-872
2880bb	15-873
2880cc	15-874
2880dd	15-875
2880ee	15-876, 15-876.1
2880ff	15-877
2880gg	15-878
2880hh	15-879
2880ii	15-880 to 15-882
2880jj	15-883
2880kk	15-884
2880ll	15-885
2880mm	15-844
2880nn	15-845
2880oo	15-846
2880pp	15-847
2880qq	15-848
2880rr	15-849
2880ss	15-850
2880tt	15-851
2880uu	15-852
2880vv	15-853
2880ww	15-854
2880xx	62-117.1
2880yy	62-117.2
2880zz	62-117.3
2880aaa	62-117.4
2880bbb	62-117.5
2881	15-66 to 15-68
2882	15-69
2883	15-70
2884	15-71
2885	15-76, 15-77
2885a	15-75
2885b	15-72 to 15-74
2886	15-83, 15-84
2887	15-85
2888	15-86
2889	15-87
2890	15-88
2891	15-85 to 15-89
2892	15-90
2893	15-91 to 15-93
2894	15-94
2895	15-95
2896	15-96
2897	15-97
2898	15-98
2899	15-99
2900	15-100
2901	15-101
2902	15-102
2903	15-103
2904	15-104
2905	15-105
2906	15-106
2907	15-107
2908	15-83
2909	15-108, 15-109
2910	15-110
2911	15-111
2912	15-112
2913	15-113
2914	15-114
2915	15-115
2916	15-116
2917	15-117
2918	15-118
2919	15-119
2920	15-120
2921	15-121
2922	15-122
2923	15-123
2924	15-124
2925	15-455 to 15-458, 15-462 to 15-464
2926	15-459
2927	15-460
2928	15-461
2929	15-465
2930	15-466 to 15-469
2931	15-470

Michie Code Section	Code 1950 Section
2932	15-471
2933	15-442, 15-471
2934	15-472
2935	15-428
2936	15-426.1
2937	15-427
2938	15-430
2939	15-431
2940	15-432
2941	15-433
2942	15-434
2943	15-435
2944	15-436, 15-437
2945	15-438 to 14-440
2946	15-386
2947	15-441
2948	15-443, 15-444
2949	15-388, 15-429, 15-445, 15-446
2950	15-447
2951	15-448 to 15-454
2952	15-394
2953	15-1
2954	15-473
2955	15-474
2956	15-125, 15-126
2957	15-130 to 15-132
2958	15-127 to 15-128.1, 15-133 to 15-136, 15-141
2958a, 2958b	Omitted
2959	15-148
2960	15-142, 15-143
2961	15-137
2962	15-138, 15-140, 15-151, 15-152
2963	15-139
2964	15-144
2965	15-145
2966	15-150
2967	15-149
2968	15-129, 15-146, 15-147
2969	15-153
2970	15-154
2971	15-155 to 15-157
2971(1)	15-158 to 15-161
2971(2)	15-175
2971(3)	15-176
2971(4)	15-177
2971(5)	15-178, 15-179
2971(6)	15-180
2971(7)	15-181
2971(8)	15-182, 15-183
2971(9)	15-184
2971(10)	15-185
2971(11)	15-186
2971(12)	15-187
2971(13)	15-178, 15-188
2971(14)	15-189
2971(15)	15-190
2971(16)	15-191
2971(17)	15-192
2971(18)	15-193, 15-194, 15-203.1
2971(19)	15-195, 15-197
2971(20)	15-198
2971(21)	15-199
2971(22)	15-200
2971(23)	15-201
2971(24)	15-202
2971(25)	15-203
2971(26)	15-207
2971(27)	15-204
2971(28)	15-205
2971(29)	15-206
2971(30)	15-208
2971(31)	15-209
2971(32)	15-195, 15-203.1
2971(33)	15-196
2971(34)	15-210
2971(35)	15-211
2971(36)	15-212
2971(37)	15-213
2971(38)	15-214
2971(39)	15-215
2971(40)	15-216
2971(41)	15-217
2971(42)	15-218, 15-219
2972	15-385
2973	15-78
2974	15-79
2975	15-8 to 15-82
2976	15-19
2977	15-765
2978	15-396, 15-397
2979	15-398
2980	15-399
2981	15-400
2982	15-393
2983	15-401
2984	15-402
2985	15-403, 15-404
2986	15-405
2987	15-387
2988	15-390 to 15-392
2989	15-415
2990	15-416
2991	15-557
2991a	Repealed by Acts 1936-37, p. 45
2991b	52-16 to 52-19
2992	15-417
2993	15-418
2994	24-168
2995	24-56
2996	24-174, 24-175
2997	24-23
2998	24-173
2999	24-171, 24-172
3000	24-172
3001	24-169
3002	15-422
3003	15-423
3004	15-424
3005	15-559
3006	15-560
3007	15-413
3008	15-414
3009	Repealed by Acts 1920, p. 19
3010	15-407 to 15-409
3011	Omitted
3012	15-406
3013	15-410 to 15-412
3014	15-774
3015	15-775
3015a	15-776
3016	15-727
3017	15-716
3018	15-728
3019	15-729
3020	15-730 to 15-732
3021	15-733
3022	15-734
3023	15-735
3024	15-736
3025	Omitted
3026	15-389
3027	53-189 to 53-194
3028	15-419 to 15-421
3029	15-425
3030	15-6
3030a	15-695
3030b	15-702, 15-703, 15-771
3030c	15-18
3031	51-715
3031a	15-708
3032	15-7
3032a	15-714
3032b	15-697 to 15-700
3032c	15-552, 27-1
3033	15-6, 15-556, 27-2, 59-76
3034	15-2, 15-5, 15-16, 15-668
3034a	15-14
3034b	15-554
3034c	32-134
3035	51-112
3035a	15-561, 27-40
3035b	15-25
3035c	Repealed by Acts 1948, p. 95
3035c1	15-24.1, 27-38
3035d	51-115
3035e	51-116
3035f	51-117
3035g	51-118
3035h	51-119
3035i	51-120

Michie Code Section	Code 1950 Section
3035j	51-121
3035k	51-122
3035l	51-124
3035m	51-123
3035n	51-125
3035o	51-126, 51-126.1
3035p	51-127
3035q	Omitted
3035r	51-113
3036	15-767
3037	15-768
3038	15-769
3039	15-770
3040	15-747
3041	15-773
3042	15-749 to 15-754
3042a	15-667
3043-3053	Omitted
3054	15-740
3055	15-741
3056	15-742
3057	15-743
3058	15-744
3059	15-745
3060	15-746
3061	53-163
3062	Repealed by Tax Code
3063	15-558
3064	15-717 to 15-719
3065	15-701
3065a	15-772
3065b	15-748
3066	Repealed by Tax Code
3067	15-669 to 15-671
3068	15-672, 15-673
3069	15-674
3070	15-675
3071	15-676
3071a	15-678
3071b	15-677
3072, 3073	Repealed by Tax Code
3074	42-1 to 42-3
3074a	5-29
3074b	5-30
3074c	5-31
3074d	5-32
3074e	5-33
3074f	5-34 to 5-37
3074g	5-38
3074h	5-39
3074i	Omitted
3075-3077	Repealed by Tax Code
3078	15-395
3078a	15-26
3078b	63-335
3078c	15-13
3078d	15-679 to 15-685

Michie Code Section	Code 1950 Section
3079	15-591, 15-592
3080	15-593
3081	Omitted
3081a	15-594
3082	15-595
3083	15-596
3083a	15-597
3083(1)	15-587
3083(2)	15-588
3084	15-598
3085	15-623
3086	15-624
3087	15-625
3088	15-626
3089	15-599
3090	15-600
3090a	15-627 to 15-629
3090b	15-631
3090c	15-632
3090d	15-633
3090e	15-634
3090f	15-635
3090g	15-636
3090h	15-637
3090i	15-638
3090j	15-639
3090k	15-640
3090l	15-641
3090m	15-642
3090n	15-643
3090o	15-644
3090p	15-663 to 15-666
3091	15-586
3091a-3091n	15-590.1
3091o	15-606
3091p	15-607
3091q	15-608
3091r	15-609 to 15-612
3091s	15-613
3091t	15-614
3091u	15-615
3091v	15-616
3091w	15-617
3091x	15-618
3091y	15-619
3091z	15-620
3091aa	15-621
3091bb	15-622
3091cc	Omitted
3091(1)	15-819
3091(2)	15-820
3091(3)	15-821
3091(4)	15-822
3091(5)	15-823
3091(6)	15-824
3091(7)	15-825
3091(8)	15-826
3091(9)	15-827
3091(10)	15-828
3091(11)	15-829
3091(12)	15-830

Michie Code Section	Code 1950 Section
3091(13)	15-831
3091(14)	15-832
3091(15)	15-833
3091(16)	15-834
3091(17)	15-835
3091(18)	15-836
3091(19)	15-837
3091(20)	15-838
3091(21)	15-839
3091(22)	15-840
3091(23)	15-841
3091(24)	15-842
3091(25)	Omitted
3091(26)	15-843
3091(27)	15-899
3091(28)	15-900
3091(29)	15-901 to 15-903
3091(30)	15-904
3091(31)	15-905
3091(32)	15-906
3091(33)	15-907
3091(34)	15-908
3091(35)	15-909
3091(36)	15-910
3091(37)	15-911 to 15-913
3092	39-1, 39-2
3093	16-1
3094	16-124
3095	16-127
3095a	16-128
3095b	16-125
3096	16-126
3097	16-84
3098	16-85
3099	16-86
3100	16-87
3101	16-88
3101a	16-2
3102	16-90, 16-91, 16-93
3103	16-96
3104	16-101
3105	16-92
3105a	16-97
3106	16-102 to 16-107, 16-121
3107	16-98 to 16-100
3108	16-108
3109	16-109
3109a	16-89
3110	Repealed by Acts 1934, p. 344
3111	16-110
3111a	39-3
3112	16-111
3112a	16-113
3113	16-119
3114	16-118
3115	16-117
3116	16-94

Michie Code Section	Code 1950 Section
3117	16-95
3118	16-115
3118a	16-116
3119	16-122, 16-123
3120	16-120
3120a	16-3
3120b	16-114
3121	27-8, 27-23, 27-24
3122	27-9
3123	27-11
3124	27-12
3125	27-13
3126	27-6, 27-7
3127	27-14
3128	27-15
3129	27-16
3130	27-17
3131	27-18
3132	27-19
3133	27-20
3134	27-21
3135	27-22
3136	27-10
3137	27-30
3137a	Repealed by Acts 1948, p. 994
3138	27-31 to 27-33, 27-35
3139	27-34
3140	27-36, 27-37
3141	Repealed by Acts 1948, p. 994
3142	27-51
3143	27-52
3144	27-53
3144a	27-41
3144b	27-42
3144c	27-43
3144d	27-44
3144e	27-45
3144f	27-46
3144g	27-47
3144h	27-48
3144i	27-49
3144j	27-50
3144k	27-29
3144l-3144r	Omitted
3144s	27-26
3144t-3144w	Omitted
3144x	27-5.1
3145	27-54
3145a	54-18 to 54-21
3145a1	27-63
3145a2	27-64
3145a3	27-65
3145a4	27-66 to 27-68
3145a5	27-69
3145a6	27-71
3145a7	27-72
3145a8	27-73
3145a9	27-74
3145a10	27-75
3145a11	27-76
3145a12	27-77
3145a13	27-78, 27-79
3145a14	27-80
3145a15	27-81
3145a16	27-82
3145a17	27-70
3145a18	27-83
3145a19	27-84
3145a20	27-85
3145b	54-22, 54-23, 54-25
3145c	54-26
3145d	54-24
3145e	54-30 to 54-32
3145f	54-27
3145g	54-28, 54-29
3145h	54-37
3145i	54-36
3145j	54-33
3145k	54-34
3145l	54-17, 54-39
3145m	54-38
3145n	Omitted
3145o	54-35
3145p	2-259.1, 15-710
3145q	54-40
3145r	54-41
3145(1)	36-1
3145(2)	36-2
3145(3)	36-3
3145(4)	36-4
3145(4a)	36-40
3145(4b)	36-41
3145(4c)	36-42
3145(4d)	36-43
3145(4e)	36-44
3145(4f)	36-45
3145(4g)	36-46
3145(4h)	36-36
3145(4i)	36-38
3145(4j)	36-39
3145(4k)	36-47
3145(4l)	36-23
3145(4m)	36-18
3145(4n)	36-24
3145(4o)	36-35
3145(4p)	36-37
3145(4q)	36-25
3145(4r)	36-20
3145(5)	36-11 to 36-15
3145(6)	36-16
3145(7)	36-17
3145(8)	36-19
3145(8a)	36-48
3145(8b)	36-49
3145(8c)	36-50
3145(8d)	36-51
3145(8e)	36-52
3145(8f)	36-53
3145(8g)	36-54
3145(8h)	36-55
3145(9)	36-21
3145(10)	36-22
3145(11)	36-24
3145(12)	36-27
3145(13)	36-28
3145(14)	36-29
3145(15)	36-30
3145(16)	36-31
3145(17)	36-32
3145(18)	36-33
3145(19)	36-26
3145(20)	36-5
3145(21)	36-6
3145(22)	36-7
3145(23)	36-8
3145(24)	36-9
3145(25)	36-34
3145(26)	36-10
3145(26a)	36-65 to 36-69
3145(27)	36-56
3145(28)	36-58
3145(29)	36-59
3145(30)	36-60
3145(31)	36-61
3145(32)	36-62
3145(33)	36-64
3145(34)	36-57
3145(35)	36-63
3145(36)	Omitted
3146	28-13 to 28-25, 28-33
3146a	28-4
3146b	28-28
3147	28-30, 28-31
3148	28-27
3148a	28-248 to 28-250, 28-251 to 28-253
3149	28-34 to 28-40
3150	28-208, 28-209
3150a	28-212
3151	28-217
3151a	28-29
3152	28-6
3153	28-7, 28-26
3154	28-98, 28-118
3154a	28-3
3155	28-1
3156	28-2
3157	28-129
3157a	10-22
3157b	10-23
3157c	10-24
3157d	10-25
3157e	10-26
3157f	10-27
3157g	10-28
3157h	10-29

Michie Code Section	Code 1950 Section
3157i	10-30,10-31
3157j	28-254
3157k	28-255
3158	28-42
3159	28-61
3160	28-43
3161	28-44
3162	28-46
3163	28-45
3164	28-85, 28-86
3165	28-47
3166	28-48, 28-87
3167	28-60
3168	28-49
3169	28-68 to 28-75
3170	28-81 to 28-83
3171	28-84
3172	28-88
3172a	28-89
3173	28-50
3174	28-51
3175	28-67
3176	28-62
3177	28-63
3178	28-64
3179	28-65
3180	28-66
3181	28-76 to 28-80
3182	28-90
3183	28-91
3184	28-52 to 28-54
3184a	28-55
3185	28-59
3186	28-58
3187	28-56
3188	28-206, 28-210
3189	28-57
3189a	28-244 to 28-247
3190	28-127
3191	28-122
3192	28-123
3193	28-124, 28-187
3194	28-128
3195	28-126
3196	28-132
3197	28-187
3198	28-133
3199	28-125
3200	28-113 to 28-116
3201	28-186
3202	28-121
3202a	28-98.1
3203	28-197
3204	28-191
3205	28-198
3205a	28-242
3206	28-243
3207	28-136
3208	28-92 to 28-97
3209	28-99
3210	28-137
3211	28-141
3212	28-142 to 28-146
3213	28-213
3214	28-147 to 28-156
3215	28-157
3216	28-100 to 28-109
3217	28-158
3218	28-110
3219	28-111
3220	28-112, 28-195
3221	28-188
3222	28-140
3223	28-139
3224	28-138
3225	28-218
3226	28-117
3227	28-120
3228	28-203
3229	28-201
3230	28-204
3231	28-200
3232	28-32
3233	28-119
3234	28-5
3235	28-41
3236	28-211
3237	28-214
3238	28-215
3239	28-208, 28-209
3240	28-216
3241	28-9
3242	28-134
3243	28-1
3244	28-131
3244a	28-8
3245	28-192
3246	28-189
3247	28-193
3248	28-211
3249	28-185
3250	28-207
3251	28-210
3252	28-199
3253	28-159
3254	28-160
3255	28-161
3256	28-162
3257	28-163
3258	28-164
3259	28-165
3260	28-166, 28-167
3261	28-168
3262	28-169
3263	28-202
3264	28-194
3265	28-170 to 28-177
3266	28-178
3267	28-180
3267a	28-179
3268	28-181
3269	28-182
3270	28-183
3271	28-184
3272	28-190
3273	28-130
3274	28-135
3275	28-10
3276	Omitted
3277	28-205
3278-3298c	Repealed by Acts 1936, p. 650
3299	28-219 to 28-231
3299a	28-232
3300	28-233
3301	28-234
3302	28-235
3303	28-236
3304	28-238
3305	28-237
3305a	28-239
3305b	28-240
3305c	28-241
3305(1)	29-1
3305(2)	29-4
3305(3)	29-9, 29-10
3305(4)	29-11
3305(5)	29-12
3305(6)	29-50
3305(6a)	29-38 to 29-49
3305(6b)	29-2
3305(7)	29-65
3305(8)	29-13 to 29-16
3305(9)	33-23.1
3305(10)	Omitted
3305(11)	29-17
3305(12)	29-18
3305(13)	29-19
3305(14)	29-20 to 29-22
3305(14a)	29-23
3305(15)	29-24 to 29-29
3305(16)	29-30 to 29-35
3305(17)	29-36
3305(18)	29-37
3305(19)	29-51 to 29-56
3305(19a)	29-81 to 29-92
3305(19b)	29-121 to 29-124
3305(19c)	Omitted
3305(19d)	29-78
3305(20)	29-66, 29-67
3305(21)	29-61 to 29-64
3305(22)	29-57 to 29-60
3305(23)	29-53 to 29-55, 29-75
3305(24)	Repealed by Acts 1936, p. 148
3305(25)	29-80
3305(25a)	29-79, 29-117 to 29-120
3305(26)	29-75
3305(27)	29-76

Michie Code Section	Code 1950 Section
3305(28)	29-77
3305(29)	29-68
3305(30)	29-69 to 29-74
3305(31)	29-74
3305(32)	29-93 to 29-102
3305(33)	29-103 to 29-116
3305(34)	29-125 to 29-129
3305(34a)	29-129.1
3305(35)	29-130
3305(36)	29-132, 29-143
3305(36a)	29-144
3305(36b)	29-145
3305(36c)	29-145.1
3305(37)	29-133 to 29-142
3305(37a)	Omitted
3305(38)	29-146
3305(39)	29-131
3305(39a)	Omitted
3305(40)	29-148, 29-149
3305(41)	29-150
3305(42)	29-151
3305(42a)	29-152
3305(43)	29-153
3305(44)	29-155
3305(45)	29-154
3305(46)	29-156
3305(46a)	29-157
3305(47)	29-158
3305(48)	29-161 to 29-164
3305(49)	29-159
3305(49a)	29-160
3305(50)	29-165 to 29-170
3305(51)	29-171
3305(52)	29-172
3305(53)	29-173
3305(54)	29-174 to 29-176
3305(55)	29-177
3305(56)	29-178
3305(57)	29-179
3305(58)	29-180
3305(59)	29-181
3305(60)	29-182
3305(61)	29-183
3305(62)	29-184
3305(63)	29-185 to 29-187
3305(64)	29-188
3305(65)	29-189
3305(66)	29-190
3305(67)	29-191
3305(68)	29-192
3305(69)	29-193
3305(69a)	29-194
3305(70)	29-195
3305(70a)	29-196
3305(71)	29-197
3305(71a)	29-198
3305(72)	29-199
3305(73)	29-200
3305(74)	29-201
3305(75)	29-202, 29-203
3305(76)	29-204
3305(77)	29-205
3305(78)	29-206
3305(79)	29-207
3305(80)	29-208
3305(81)	29-209
3305(82)	29-213
3305(82a)	29-211
3305(83)	29-210
3305(84)	Omitted
3306-3315a	Repealed by Acts 1930, p. 664
3316	Repealed by Acts 1928, p. 721
3317-3330	Repealed by Acts 1930, p. 664
3330a	Omitted
3330b-3339	Repealed by Acts 1930, p. 664
3339a	29-212
3339b-3360a	Repealed by Acts 1930, p. 664
3360b	29-147
3360c-3365a	Repealed by Acts 1930, p. 664
3366	29-214 to 29-216
3367	29-217 to 29-219
3368	29-220
3369	29-221
3370	29-222
3371	29-223
3372	29-224
3373	29-225
3374	29-226
3375	29-227
3376	29-228
3377	29-229
3377a-3377p	Repealed by Acts 1930, p. 664
3378	17-33
3379	17-34
3380	17-35
3381	17-36
3382	Repealed by Acts 1934, p. 428
3382a	17-49
3383	17-39, 17-48
3384	17-38
3385	17-37, 17-40
3386	17-44
3386a	17-46
3387	17-45
3387a	17-47
3387b	17-59.1
3388	17-41, 17-43
3389	17-53
3390	17-55
3391	17-78
3392	17-59
3392a	14-126, 17-88 to 17-91
3393	17-60 to 17-66
3393a	17-68, 17-69
3393b	17-67
3394	17-79
3395	17-80
3396	17-81
3397	17-82
3398	17-83
3399	17-70
3400	17-71, 17-72
3401	17-77
3402	55-66.6
3403	17-50 to 17-52
3404	17-56
3405	17-57, 17-103
3406	17-58
3407	14-123, 17-54
3407a	55-137.1
3407a1	55-137.2
3407b	17-42
3408	54-42
3408a	Omitted
3409	54-67
3409a	54-68
3410	54-53, 54-54
3411	54-63, 54-64
3412	54-56
3413	54-55 to 54-57, 54-62
3414	54-65
3415	54-66
3416	54-58
3417	54-59
3418	54-60
3419	54-61
3419a	54-61.1
3420	54-72
3421	54-43
3422	54-44
3422a	Repealed by Acts 1938, p. 772
3423	54-73
3424	54-74
3424a	54-76
3424b	54-77
3425	54-75
3425a	54-47
3426	54-45
3426a	Repealed by Acts 1938, p. 213
3426b	54-80
3426c	54-81
3426d	Omitted
3426e	54-79

Michie Code Section	Code 1950 Section
3426f	54-78
3426g	54-82, 54-83
3427	54-46
3428	54-69
3428a	14-99
3429	54-70
3430	54-71
3430a	54-48 to 54-50
3430b	54-51
3430c	54-52
3431	14-9
3431a	14-10
3432	14-11
3433	Repealed by Acts 1936, p. 76
3434	14-12, 14-13
3435	14-15
3436	Omitted
3437	14-16, 14-17
3438, 3439	Omitted
3440	14-25
3441	14-19
3442	14-20
3443	14-21
3444	Repealed by Acts 1930, p. 974
3445	Repealed by Acts 1936, p. 116
3446	Omitted
3447	14-22
3448	14-23
3449	14-24
3450-3452	Omitted
3453	14-27
3454	14-28 to 14-29.1
3455	14-30
3456	14-31
3457	14-32
3458	14-33
3459	14-34
3460	14-35
3461	14-36
3462	14-37
3462a	Repealed by Acts 1944, p. 474
3463	14-38
3464	51-12 to 51-14
3465	14-39, 14-41, 14-42
3466	Repealed by Acts 1938, p. 335
3466a	14-43, 14-44
3466b	14-45
3467	14-46
3467a	14-47
3468	Repealed by Acts 1938, p. 335
3469	14-48
3470	Repealed by Acts 1938, p. 335
3471	14-49
3472	14-1

Michie Code Section	Code 1950 Section
3473	14-5
3474	14-6
3475	14-7
3476	14-3
3477	14-4
3477a	14-2
3477b	14-66
3477c	14-68, 14-70
3477d	14-69
3477e	14-69
3477f	14-71
3477f1	14-70, 14-71
3477g	14-74, 14-75
3477h	14-60, 14-61
3477i	14-62
3477j	14-63
3477k	14-64
3477l	14-65
3477m	14-76 to 14-78
3477n	14-80
3477o	14-145
3477p	14-79
3478	14-13, 14-114, 14-115
3479	14-144
3480	14-143
3481	14-135
3481a	14-8
3482	14-142
3483	14-109
3484	14-123
3485	14-124
3486	8-482, 8-497.1, 14-40, 14-129
3487	14-106, 14-116 to 14-121
3487a	Omitted
3487(1)	14-81 to 14-84
3487(2)	Omitted
3487(3)	14-86
3487(4)	14-87 to 14-89
3487(5)	14-90
3487(6)	14-91, 14-92, 53-173
3487(7)	14-93
3487(8)	53-165, 53-166, 53-170, 53-171, 53-174 to 53-176
3487(9)	53-178 to 53-183, 53-184 to 53-186
3487(10)	14-94
3487(11)	14-95, 53-187
3487(12)	53-188
3488	14-104,14-105
3489	14-107
3490	14-108
3491	14-101
3492	14-100
3493	14-98

Michie Code Section	Code 1950 Section
3494	14-165
3495	14-166 to 14-168
3496	14-169
3497	14-170
3498	14-171
3499	14-172
3500	14-173
3501	14-110
3502	14-166
3503	14-85
3504	14-96
3505	14-130, 14-131
3506	14-125
3507	14-136 to 14-140
3508	14-122
3509	Omitted
3510	53-135.1, 53-162.1
3511	14-97
3512	14-186
3512a	14-192
3513	14-111
3514	14-103
3515	Omitted
3516	14-145 to 14-153, 14-155, 14-156 to 14-161
3516a	14-155
3516b	14-162, 14-163
3516b1-3516d	Omitted
3516d(1)	14-73
3516d(2)	14-72
3516e	Omitted
3516f	14-154
3516g, 3516h	Omitted
3516i	14-113
3516j-3516m	Repealed by Acts 1940, p. 675
3516m1, 3516m2	14-155.1
3516m3	53-177
3516n	14-67
3516o	14-112
3516(1)	14-155
3516(2)	14-155.3
3516(3)	14-155.2
3517	14-180
3518	14-181
3519	14-182
3520	14-183
3521	14-184
3522	14-185
3523	14-176
3524	8-511.1
3525	14-175
3526	14-177
3527	14-174
3528	14-178
3528a	14-179
3529	14-187
3530	14-188, 14-189

Michie Code Section	Code 1950 Section
3531	14-190
3532	14-191
3533	14-193
3534	14-194
3535	14-195
3536	14-196
3537	14-197
3538	8-869
3539	8-872
3540	8-868.1
3541	8-874 to 8-879
3542	8-901
3543	8-902
3544	8-903
3545	8-904
3546	8-905
3547	8-880 to 8-885
3548	8-886
3549	8-893
3550	8-894 to 8-898
3551	8-899
3552	8-900
3553	8-870
3554	8-871
3555	8-887 to 8-892
3556-3561	Repealed by Acts 1922, p. 869
3562	8-873
3563	18-223
3564	55-202
3565	55-203
3566	55-204
3567	55-205
3568	55-206
3569	55-207
3570	55-208
3571	55-209
3572	55-210
3573	62-1
3573a	62-3
3574	62-2
3575	62-4
3576	62-5
3577	62-6
3578	62-7, 62-8
3579-3581	59-213
3581a	62-9
3581(1)	62-68 to 62-70
3581(2)	62-71, 62-72
3581(3)	62-73
3581(4)	62-74, 62-75
3581(5)	62-76 to 62-81
3581(6)	62-82
3581(7)	Omitted
3581(8)	62-83, 62-84
3581(9)	62-94
3581(10)	62-85
3581(11)	62-86
3581(12)	62-87
3581(13)	62-88
3581(14)	62-89

Michie Code Section	Code 1950 Section
3581(15)	62-90, 62-91
3581(16)	62-92, 62-93
3582	62-95
3583	62-96
3584	62-97
3585	62-98
3586	62-99
3587	62-100
3588	62-101
3589	62-102
3590	62-103
3591	62-104
3592	62-105
3593	62-106
3594	54-837
3594a	54-838
3595	54-839
3596	62-158
3597	62-159
3598	62-160
3599	62-161
3600	62-162
3601	62-163
3602	62-164
3603	62-165
3604	62-166
3605	62-167
3606	62-168
3607	62-169
3608	62-170
3609	62-171
3610	62-172
3611	62-173
3612	62-174
3613	54-527 to 54-529
3614	54-530
3615	54-536, 54-538, 54-539, 54-541
3615a	54-537, 54-540
3616	54-537, 54-542
3617	54-525, 54-555, 54-556
3618	54-550
3619	54-551
3620	54-543, 54-557
3621	54-548, 54-571
3622	54-572
3623	54-544, 54-546, 54-558
3624	Repealed by Acts 1942, p. 717
3625	54-547, 54-552
3626	54-545, 54-546
3627	54-549
3628-3629	Repealed by Acts 1944, p. 426
3630	54-567
3631	54-564

Michie Code Section	Code 1950 Section
3632	Repealed by Acts 1944, p. 426
3633	54-554
3634	54-553
3635	54-566
3636	54-570
3637	54-533
3638	54-534
3639	54-535
3640	54-531, 54-532
3641	Repealed by Acts 1944, p. 426
3642	54-573
3643	54-560
3644	54-561
3645	54-559, 54-565
3646	54-569
3647	54-526, 54-568
3648	62-148
3649	62-149
3650	62-150
3651	62-151
3652	62-152
3653	62-153
3654	62-154
3655	62-155
3656	62-156
3657	62-157
3658	62-138
3659	62-144
3660	62-143
3661	62-145
3662	62-146
3663	62-147
3664	62-122
3665	62-124
3666-3668	Repealed by Acts 1922, p.117
3669	62-141
3670-3677	Repealed by Acts 1922, p. 117
3678	62-123
3679	62-125
3680	62-126
3681	62-127
3682	62-128
3683	62-129
3684	62-130
3685	62-131
3686	62-132
3687	62-133
3688	62-134
3689	62-135
3690	62-136
3691	62-137
3692	Omitted
3692a	Repealed by Acts 1926, p. 412
3692(1)-3692(3)	Omitted

Michie Code Section	Code 1950 Section
3692(4)	62-111
3692(5)	62-112
3692(6)	62-113
3692(7)	62-114
3692(8)	62-115, 62-116
3692(9), 3692(10)	Omitted
3692(11)	62-117
3692(11a)	62-119
3692(11b)	62-118
3692(11c)	62-120
3692(11d)	62-121
3692(12)	Omitted
3692(13)	10-122, 10-123
3692(14)	10-124
3692(15)	10-125
3692(16)	Omitted
3692(17)	10-126
3693	12-1, 13-1, 56-1
3694	12-9
3694a	Repealed by Acts 1926, p. 49
3695	12-10
3696	12-11
3697	12-5
3698, 3698a	Omitted
3699	12-39
3700	12-40
3701	12-38
3702	12-12
3703	12-41
3704	Repealed by Tax Code
3705	12-42
3706	12-43
3707	12-44
3708	12-45
3709	56-35
3710	56-36
3711	12-54
3712	56-37
3713	55-38
3714	13-157
3715	12-39, 12-46
3716	12-14, 12-20, 56-114
3716(a)	12-16
3717	56-41
3718	56-128
3719	56-42
3720	56-129
3721	56-43
3722	12-52
3723	12-57
3724	12-58
3725	12-49
3726	12-18, 12-19, 12-53, 12-54
3727	12-17
3728	12-21
3729	12-55
3730	12-56
3731	12-59
3732	12-62
3733	12-51, 12-61
3734	12-63
3735	12-64
3736	56-110
3737	56-131
3738	56-136
3739	56-137
3740	56-138
3741	56-141
3742	12-3
3743	12-50
3744	12-60
3745	12-22
3746	12-23
3746a	13-212
3747	12-24
3747a	12-25
3748	Repealed by Tax Code
3749	12-6
3750	12-7
3751	12-4
3752	12-13
3753	Omitted
3754	12-2
3755	12-15
3756	12-26
3757	13-67, 13-68
3758	33-136
3759	12-27
3760	12-28
3761	12-29
3762	12-30
3763	12-31
3764	12-32
3765	12-33
3766	12-8
3767	12-47
3768	12-34
3769	12-35
3770	12-48
3771	56-39
3772	12-37
3773	12-36
3774	56-104
3774(1)	14-25
3774a	54-562, 54-563
3774b	56-76
3774c	56-77
3774d	56-78
3774e	56-79
3774f	56-80
3774g	56-81
3774h	56-81
3774i	56-82
3774i1	56-83
3774i2	56-84
3774i3	56-85
3774j	56-86
3774k	56-87
3774l	56-88
3774m	56-89
3774n	56-91
3774o	56-90
3774p	Omitted
3774q	56-92
3775	51-15, 51-17
3775(1)	51-16, 51-17
3775(2)-3775(7)	Repealed by Acts 1930, p. 714
3775a	5-1
3775b	5-2
3775c	5-10.5
3775d	5-10.1
3775e	5-12
3775f	5-10.4
3775g	5-5
3775h	5-6
3775i	5-10.2
3775j	5-10.3
3775k	5-13
3775l	5-8
3775m	5-11
3775n	5-10
3775o-3775s	Repealed by Acts 1942, p. 534
3775t	5-3
3775u	5-4
3775v	5-40
3775w	5-7
3775x	5-9
3775y	5-14
3775z	5-41
3775aa	5-15 to 5-19
3775aa1	5-42 to 5-46
3775bb	5-20
3775cc	5-21
3775dd	5-22
3775ee	5-23
3775ff	5-24
3775gg	5-25
3775hh	5-26
3775ii	5-27
3775jj	5-28
3775kk	5-39.1 to 5-39.3
3776	13-2
3776a	13-6
3777	13-19
3777a	13-20
3778	13-30, 13-31
3779	13-34
3780	13-35 to 13-37
3780a	13-87
3780b	Omitted
3780c	13-91
3780d	Omitted

Michie Code Section	Code 1950 Section
3780e	58-462
3780f, 3780g	Omitted
3781	13-92 to 13-95
3782	13-22
3783	13-96
3784	13-21
3785	13-29
3786	13-190
3787	13-10
3788	13-97
3789	13-200
3789a	13-209
3790	13-208
3791	13-202
3792	13-87 to 13-90
3793	13-103
3794	13-105
3795	13-197
3796	13-189
3797	13-192
3798	13-203
3799	13-193
3800	13-194, 13-195
3801	13-196
3802	13-198
3803	13-204
3804	13-205
3805	13-210
3806	13-33
3807	13-98
3808	13-199
3809	13-60
3810	13-61 to 13-65, 13-70
3810a	13-69
3810a1	13-70
3810b	13-65
3811	13-77 to 13-82
3812	13-72
3813	13-73
3813a	13-75
3813b	13-76
3814	13-74
3815	13-71
3816	13-207
3817	13-28
3818	13-104
3819	13-104
3820	13-9, 13-32, 13-213
3820a	13-83 to 13-86
3821	13-40 to 13-42
3822	13-43 to 13-45, 13-47 to 13-54
3822a	13-47 to 13-54
3822b	13-46
3823	13-55
3824	13-57
3825	13-58
3826	13-59
3827	13-56
3828	56-349
3829	13-191
3830	13-7
3831	13-66
3832	25-233
3833	12-63.1
3834	13-4
3835	Repealed by Tax Code
3836	13-18
3837	13-100
3838	13-101
3839	13-102
3839a	13-105.1
3840	13-206
3841	13-3
3842	13-5
3843	13-99
3844	13-219
3845	13-214, 13-215
3846	13-216
3846a	13-214, 13-217
3847	13-8, 13-211
3848	13-211, 13-218
3848(1)	Repealed by Tax Code
3848(2)	13-166
3848(3)	13-167
3848(4)	13-168
3848(5)	13-169
3848(6)	13-170
3848(7)	13-171
3848(8)	13-172
3848(9)	13-173
3848(10)	13-174
3848(11)	13-175
3848(12)	13-176
3848(13)	13-177
3848(14)	13-178
3848(15)	13-179
3848(16)	13-180
3848(17)	13-181
3848(18)	13-182
3848(19)	13-183
3848(20)	13-184
3848(21)	13-185
3848(22)	13-186
3848(23)	13-187
3848(24)	13-165
3848(25)	13-165
3848(26)	13-188
3848(27)-3848(46)	Omitted
3848(47)	13-110
3848(48)	13-106
3848(49)	13-111, 13-112
3848(50)	13-113 to 13-127, 13-158
3848(51)	13-128 to 13-132, 13-154, 13-159 to 13-163
3848(51a)	6-235 to 6-241
3848(52)	13-109, 13-137 to 13-142
3848(53)	13-134
3848(54)	13-135
3848(55)	13-144
3848(55)a	13-145
3848(55)b	13-146
3848(55)c	13-147
3848(55)d	13-148
3848(56)	13-133
3848(57)	13-151
3848(58)	13-136
3848(59)	13-143
3848(60)	13-149
3848(61)	13-150, 13-155
3848(62)	13-152
3848(63)	13-153
3848(64)	13-164
3848(65)	13-107
3848(66)	13-108
3848(67)	32-168 to 32-177
3848(68)	32-178 to 32-194
3848(69)	32-195
3848(70)	6-550
3848(71)	6-551
3848(72)	6-552
3848(73)	6-553
3848(74)	6-554
3848(75)	6-555
3848(76)	6-556
3848(77)	6-557
3848(78)	6-558
3848(79)	6-559
3848(80)	6-560
3848(81)	6-561
3848(82)	6-562
3848(83)	6-563
3848(84)	6-564
3848(85)	6-565
3848(86)	6-566
3848(87)	6-567
3848(88)	6-568
3848(89)	Omitted
3849	13-23
3850	13-24
3851	13-25 to 13-27
3852	13-39
3853	13-201
3854	13-11 to 13-17
3855	13-238 to 13-246
3855a	13-247
3856	56-339
3857	56-340, 56-345 to 56-348, 56-450
3857a	56-111, 56-345 to 56-348, 56-450
3858	56-355

Michie Code Section	Code 1950 Section
3859	56-343
3859a	13-38
3860	56-356
3861	56-357
3862	56-358
3863	56-344
3864	56-370
3865	56-47
3866	56-48
3866a	56-49
3867	56-53
3868	56-50
3869	56-52
3870	56-51
3871	56-54
3872	13-220
3873	13-221
3874	13-222 to 13-224
3874a	13-225
3875	13-226 to 13-230
3875a	13-231
3876	13-232
3877	13-233
3878	13-234
3879	13-235
3879a	13-236
3880	13-237
3881	56-1
3882	56-14
3883	56-16
3884	56-17 to 56-22
3885	56-23 to 56-32
3885a	56-15
3886	56-364
3887	56-34
3888	56-33
3889	56-44
3890	56-45
3891	56-8
3892	Repealed by Acts 1932, p. 427
3893	56-46
3894	56-5
3895	56-9
3896	56-10
3897	56-11
3898	56-12
3899	56-13
3900	56-2
3901	56-3
3902	56-6
3903	56-7
3903(1)	56-4
3904	56-96, 56-97, 56-103
3905	56-94
3906	56-93
3907	56-112
3908	56-98
3909	56-100
3910	56-102

Michie Code Section	Code 1950 Section
3911	56-99
3912	56-105
3913	56-106
3914	56-95
3915	56-116
3916	56-117
3917	56-118
3918	56-107
3919	56-108
3920	56-101, 56-109
3921	56-113
3922	56-133
3923	56-134
3923a	56-135
3924	56-139
3925	56-140
3926	56-119, 56-120
3927	56-115
3928	Omitted
3928a	56-123
3928b	56-124
3929	56-121
3930	56-119
3931	56-125
3932	56-130
3933	56-126
3934	56-127
3935	56-132
3935(1)	56-142
3935(2)	56-143
3935(3)	56-144, 56-204
3935(4)	12-54, 56-145, 56-146
3935(5)	12-10, 56-203
3935(6)	56-147 to 56-156
3935(7)	56-157 to 56-160
3935(8)	56-161
3935(9)	56-162 to 56-166
3935(10)	56-167
3935(11)	56-168, 56-169
3935(12)	56-170 to 56-174, 56-199
3935(13)	56-176 to 56-186
3935(14)	56-187 to 56-190
3935(15)	12-6, 56-191
3935(16)	56-198
3935(17)	56-200
3935(18)	56-196
3935(19)	56-175
3935(20)	56-197
3935(21)	56-195, 56-201
3935(22)	56-192, 56-193
3935(23)	12-63
3935(24)	12-64
3935(25)	56-194
3935(26)	56-205

Michie Code Section	Code 1950 Section
3935(27)	56-202
3935(28)	56-206
3936	56-361
3937	56-371
3938	56-372
3938a	56-374
3939	56-445
3940	56-377
3941	56-378
3942	56-385
3943	56-383
3944	56-324.1, 56-353, 56-354
3945	Repealed by Acts 1928, p. 1115
3945a	56-382
3946	56-429
3947	56-430
3948	56-431
3949	56-432
3950	56-433
3951	56-434
3952	56-427
3953	56-359
3954	56-435
3955	56-341
3956	56-386
3957	56-350
3958	56-414
3959	56-416
3960	56-415
3960a	Omitted
3961	56-351
3962	56-396
3963	56-397
3964	56-398
3965	56-399
3966	56-400
3967	56-401
3968	56-402
3969	56-380, 56-403
3970	56-417
3971	56-360
3972	56-363
3973	56-405
3974	56-365
3974a	56-366 to 56-368.1
3974b	56-369
3975	56-379
3976	56-413
3977	56-380
3978	56-390
3979	56-389, 56-391
3980	56-392
3981	56-394
3982	56-395
3983	56-393
3984	56-375
3985	56-406
3985a	56-408

Michie Code Section	Code 1950 Section
3986	56-409
3986a	56-411
3987	56-412
3988	56-448
3989	56-418
3990	56-376
3991	56-426
3992	56-428
3993	56-447
3994	56-436
3995	56-437
3996	56-438
3997	56-439
3998	56-410
3999	56-362
4000	56-342
4001	56-440
4002	56-446
4003	56-449
4004	56-384
4005	56-373
4006	56-387
4006a	56-388
4007	56-404
4008	56-442
4009	56-443
4010	56-444
4011	56-381
4012	56-420
4013	56-421
4014	56-422
4015	56-423
4016	56-424
4017	56-425
4018	56-352
4019	56-419
4019a	56-441
4020	56-207
4021	56-208
4022	56-452
4023	56-453
4024	56-454
4025	56-455, 56-456
4026	56-457
4027	56-266
4028	56-267
4029	56-268
4030	56-267, 56-269
4031	56-122
4032	56-271
4033	56-270
4034	56-272
4035	56-458, 56-466
4036	56-484
4037	56-460, 56-461, 56-467
4038	56-459, 56-462, 56-466
4039	56-463
4040	56-464
4041	56-465

Michie Code Section	Code 1950 Section
4042	56-469
4043	56-470
4044	56-471
4045	56-472
4046	56-473
4047	56-474
4048	56-475
4049	56-468
4050	56-476
4051	56-477
4052	56-478
4052a	56-478.1
4053	56-482
4054	56-481
4055	56-479
4056	56-480
4057	56-483
4057(1)	56-231
4057(2)	56-210
4057(3)	56-209
4057(4)	56-211
4057(5)	56-212
4057(6)	56-213
4057(7)	56-222
4057(8)	56-223
4057(9)	56-224
4057(10)	56-225
4057(11)	56-217
4057(12)	56-218
4057(13)	56-219
4057(14)	56-220
4057(15)	56-221
4057(16)	56-214
4057(17)	56-226
4057(18)	56-227
4057(19)	56-215
4057(20)	56-216
4057(21)	56-228
4057(22)	56-229
4057(23)	56-230
4057(24)	56-255
4058	56-256
4059	56-257
4060	56-258
4061	56-256
4062	56-259
4063	56-260
4064, 4065	Repealed by Acts 1927, p. 125
4065a	56-40
4066	56-234, 56-236 to 56-241
4067	56-232
4068	56-233
4069	56-246
4070	56-248, 56-249
4071	56-235
4071a	56-242 to 56-245
4072	56-247
4072a	56-250 to 56-252
4073	56-253

Michie Code Section	Code 1950 Section
4073a	56-261
4073b	56-262
4073c	56-263
4073d	56-264
4073e	Omitted
4073f	56-265
4073g	56-254
4073h	56-451
4073(1)	56-55
4073(2)	56-56
4073(3)	56-58
4073(4)	56-59
4073(5)	56-60 to 56-63
4073(6)	56-69
4073(7)	56-65
4073(8)	56-66
4073(9)	56-70
4073(10)	56-67
4073(11)	56-57
4073(12)	56-71, 56-72
4073(13)	56-73
4073(14)	56-74
4073(15)	56-64
4073(16)	56-55, 56-58, 56-75
4074-4097a	33-136
4097b-4097y	Omitted
4097y(1)	56-273
4097y(2)	56-274
4097y(3)	56-275, 56-337
4097y(4)	12-54, 56-276, 56-277
4097y(5)	12-10, 56-336
4097y(6)	56-278 to 56-287
4097y(7)	56-273, 56-288 to 56-290, 56-291.1 to 56-291.3, 56-291.9 to 56-291.12, 56-299.1
4097y(7a)	56-291.13
4097y(8a)	56-291
4097y(9)	56-292 to 56-296.1
4097y(10)	56-297
4097y(11)	56-298
4097y(12)	56-299, 56-300 to 56-303, 56-333
4097y(13)	56-305 to 56-315
4097y(13a)	56-324, 56-335
4097y(13b)	12-6, 56-320
4097y(13c)	56-332
4097y(13d)	56-334
4097y(13e)	56-325
4097y(13f)	56-304
4097y(13g)	56-331
4097y(13h)	56-324, 56-335

Michie Code Section	Code 1950 Section
4097y(13i)	56-321, 56-322
4097y(13j)	12-63
4097y(13k)	12-64
4097y(13l)	56-323
4097y(13m)	56-338
4097y(14)	46-134
4097y(15)	46-135
4097y(16)	46-136
4097y(17)	46-137
4097y(18)	46-138 to 46-138.2
4097y(19)-4097y(21a)	Omitted
4097y(22)	46-139
4097y(23), 4097y(24)	Omitted
4097y(25)	46-140
4097y(26), 4097y(27)	Omitted
4097z	56-326
4097aa	56-327
4097bb	56-328
4097cc	56-330
4097dd	56-329
4097ee	Repealed by Acts 1946, p. 459
4097ff	58-503, 58-627 to 58-637
4097(1)	56-338.1
4097(2)	56-338.2
4097(3)	56-338.3 to 56-338.5
4097(4)	56-338.16 to 56-338.18
4097(5)	56-338.8 to 56-338.11
4097(6)	56-338.12, 56-338.13
4097(7)	56-338.14
4097(8)	56-338.15
4097(9)	56-338.7
4097(10)	56-338.6
4098-4149	Repealed by Acts 1928, p. 1339
4149(1)	6-6
4149(2)	6-7, 6-8
4149(3)	6-9
4149(3a)	6-29.1
4149(4)	6-133, 6-134
4149(5)	6-133
4149(6)	6-13
4149(7)	6-24
4149(7a)	6-25
4149(8)	6-18
4149(9)	6-14 to 6-17
4149(10)	6-18 to 6-21
4149(10a)	6-2
4149(11)	6-10
4149(12)	6-22
4149(13)	6-23, 6-51
4149(14)	6-26 to 6-29
4149(15)	6-31, 6-32
4149(16)	6-33
4149(17)	6-34, 6-35
4149(18)	6-36
4149(19)	6-37
4149(20)	6-38
4149(21)	6-39
4149(22)	6-44
4149(23)	6-43, 6-45, 6-46
4149(24)	6-47
4149(25)	6-67, 6-68
4149(26)	6-135
4149(27)	6-136
4149(28)	6-137
4149(29)	6-3
4149(30)	6-49
4149(31)	6-50
4149(32)	6-48
4149(33)	6-52
4149(34)	6-54
4149(35)	6-53
4149(36)	6-56
4149(37)	6-55
4149(38)	6-264
4149(39)	6-72
4149(40)	6-71
4149(41)	6-539, 6-540
4149(42)	6-73
4149(43)	6-74
4149(43a)	6-75
4149(44)	6-129 to 6-131
4149(45)	6-62
4149(46)	6-63
4149(47)	6-76
4149(48)	6-77
4149(48a)	6-78, 6-79
4149(49)	6-64 to 6-66
4149(50)	6-80
4149(51)	6-82
4149(52)	6-105 to 6-118
4149(52a)	6-81
4149(52b)	6-69
4149(52c)	6-58 to 6-61
4149(53)	6-119
4149(54)	6-128
4149(55)	6-120, 6-121
4149(56)	6-122 to 6-127
4149(56a)	6-4
4149(57)	6-132
4149(58)	6-83
4149(59)	6-84
4149(60)	6-85
4149(61)	6-86
4149(62)	6-87
4149(63)	6-88
4149(64)	6-89
4149(65)	6-90
4149(66)	6-11, 6-91
4149(67)	6-92
4149(68)	6-93
4149(69)	6-94 to 6-103
4149(69a)	6-103.1
4149(70)	6-104
4149(71)	Repealed by Acts 1930, p. 31
4149(71)a	64-133
4149(72)	6-57
4149(72a)	6-30
4149(73)	6-12
4149(73a)	6-70
4149(73b)	6-40 to 6-42
4149(73c)	6-138
4149(73d)	6-139
4149(74), 4149(75)	Omitted
4149(76)	6-5
4149a	6-263
4149b	6-265 to 6-270
4149c	6-271
4149d	6-272
4149e	6-273
4149f	6-264.1
4150	6-342
4151	6-343
4152	6-344
4153	6-345
4153(1)	6-569
4153(2)	6-570
4153(3)	6-571
4153(4)	6-572
4153(5)	6-573
4153(6)	6-574
4153(7)	6-575
4153(8)	6-576
4154-4167	Repealed by Acts 1932, p. 108
4167(1)-4167(28)	Repealed by Acts 1946, p. 767
4168	Repealed by Tax Code
4168(1)	6-242, 6-244, 6-245, 6-251
4168(2)	6-243, 6-244, 6-249
4168(3)	6-248
4168(4)	6-252
4168(5)	6-250
4168(6)	6-253
4168(7)	6-254
4168(8)	6-255
4168(9)	6-246
4168(10)	6-257
4168(11)	6-258
4168(11½)	6-256
4168(11½)a	6-260
4168(11½)b	6-261
4168(11½)c	6-262

Michie Code Section	Code 1950 Section
4168(11½)d	6-259
4168(11½)e	6-247
4168(12)	6-202
4168(13)	6-204, 6-205, 6-207
4168(14)	6-208
4168(15)	6-203
4168(16)	6-209
4168(17)	6-213
4168(18)	6-229 to 6-232
4168(19)	6-218
4168(20)	6-219
4168(21)	6-220
4168(22)	6-221
4168(23)	6-222
4168(24)	6-214
4168(25)	6-215
4168(26)	6-216
4168(27)	6-223
4168(28)	6-224
4168(29)	6-210
4168(30)	6-225
4168(31)	6-226
4168(32)	6-227
4168(33)	6-228
4168(34)	6-211
4168(35)	6-217
4168(36)	6-206
4168(37)	6-212
4168(37)a	6-233
4168(37)b	6-234
4168(37)c	Repealed by Acts 1936, p. 68
4168(38)-4168(57)	Repealed by Acts 1944, p. 567
4168(58)-4168(67)	Repealed by Acts 1946, p. 269
4168a-4168p	Repealed by Acts 1942, p. 521
4168a1	6-274
4168a2	6-275
4168a3	6-321
4168a4	6-322
4168a5	6-279
4168a6	6-280
4168a7	6-281
4168a8	6-282, 6-337
4168a9	6-284
4168a10	6-285
4168a11	6-286
4168a12	6-287
4168a13	6-288
4168a14	6-289
4168a15	6-309
4168a16	6-296
4168a17	6-299
4168a18	6-300
4168a19	6-283
4168a20	6-290
4168a21	6-291
4168a22	6-292
4168a23	6-293
4168a24	6-294
4168a25	6-295
4168a26	6-323 to 6-326
4168a27	6-327, 6-328
4168a28	6-329
4168a29	6-330
4168a30	6-331
4168a31	6-332, 6-333
4168a32	6-334
4168a33	6-310
4168a34	6-297
4168a35	6-298
4168a36	6-311
4168a37	6-301, 6-302
4168a38	6-303
4168a39	6-304
4168a40	6-305
4168a41	6-306
4168a42	6-307
4168a43	6-308
4168a44	6-312
4168a45	6-313
4168a46	6-314
4168a47	6-315
4168a48	6-338
4168a49	6-316
4168a50	6-317
4168a51	6-318
4168a52	6-319
4168a53	6-320
4168a54	6-335
4168a55	6-336
4168a56	6-278
4168a57	Omitted
4168a58	6-276
4168a59	6-277
4168a60, 4168a61	Omitted
4168b1	6-140
4168b2	6-141
4168b3	6-142
4168b4	6-143
4168b5	6-144
4168b6	6-145
4168b7	6-148
4168b8	6-149
4168b9	6-153
4168b10	6-150
4168b11	6-151
4168b12	6-152
4168b13	6-155
4168b14	6-156
4168b15	6-168
4168b16	6-169
4168b17	6-170
4168b18	6-171
4168b19	6-172
4168b20	6-173
4168b21	6-174
4168b22	6-175
4168b23	6-176
4168b24	6-177
4168b25	6-178
4168b26	6-146
4168b27	6-154
4168b28	6-191
4168b29	6-192
4168b30	6-193
4168b31	6-179
4168b32	6-180
4168b33	6-181
4168b34	6-182
4168b35	6-183
4168b36	6-184
4168b37	6-185
4168b38	6-186
4168b39	6-187
4168b39a	6-188
4168b40	6-194 to 6-196
4168b41	6-197
4168b42	6-198
4168b43	6-199
4168b44	6-200
4168b45	6-201
4168b46	6-159
4168b47	6-189
4168b48	6-190
4168b49	6-160
4168b50	6-158
4168b51	6-161
4168b52	6-162
4168b53	6-163
4168b54	6-164
4168b55	6-165
4168b56	6-166
4168b57	6-167
4168b58	6-147
4168b59	6-157
4168b60, 4168b61	Omitted
4169	38-2
4170, 4171	Omitted
4172	12-7
4173-4175	Omitted
4176	38-2
4177	38-31
4178	38-125
4179	38-126
4180	38-132 to 38-136
4181	38-30
4182	38-124
4183	38-129
4184	27-55
4184a	38-127
4185	Repealed by Acts 1948, p. 487
4186	27-56, 27-57

Michie Code Section	Code 1950 Section
4187	27-58
4188	27-59
4189	27-60
4190	27-61
4191	Omitted
4192	27-62
4193	Omitted
4194	38-17
4195	38-18 to 38-20
4196	38-21
4197, 4198	Omitted
4199	38-128
4200	38-1
4201	38-27
4202	38-28
4203	38-32
4204	38-29, 38-36, 38-38
4204a	38-4
4205	38-33
4206	38-47
4207	38-34
4208	38-35
4209	38-22
4210	38-57
4211	38-39 to 38-46
4212	38-48
4213	38-49
4214	38-50
4215	38-138
4216	38-51
4217	38-52
4218	38-53
4218a	38-37
4219	38-227
4219a	38-115 to 38-118
4219b	38-119 to 38-121
4220	38-7
4220a	38-10
4221	38-11
4221a	38-59
4222	38-61, 38-62, 38-64 to 38-66, 38-362, 38-363
4223	38-68
4224	38-69
4225	38-70
4225a	38-109 to 38-114
4226	38-58
4226a	38-100 to 38-108
4227	38-8
4227a	38-9
4227b	38-240 to 38-246
4228	38-365, 38-366
4228a	Repealed by Acts 1926, p. 372
4229	38-122
4230	38-123
4231	38-24
4232	38-25
4233	38-12, 38-13
4234	38-26

Michie Code Section	Code 1950 Section
4234a	38-71 to 38-79
4235	38-59, 38-80 to 38-89
4235a	38-60
4235b	38-59, 38-90 to 38-99
4235c	38-67
4235d	38-364
4236	Omitted
4237	38-54
4238	38-55
4239	38-56
4240	38-3
4241	38-23
4241a	38-6
4242	38-138
4243	38-139
4244	38-140
4245	38-141
4246	38-142
4246a	38-5
4246b	38-137
4246c	27-5
4246d	38-130
4246e	38-131
4246f	38-14 to 38-16
4247	38-413
4248	38-369
4248a	38-368
4249	38-414
4250	38-370
4251	38-415
4251a	38-420 to 38-423
4251b	38-424 to 38-426
4251c	38-371 to 38-373
4251c(1)	38-374, 38-375
4251c(2)	38-376 to 38-383
4251c(3)	38-384, 38-385
4251d	38-386
4251e	38-387
4251f	38-388
4252	38-416
4253	38-417
4254	38-418
4255	38-419
4256	38-389
4257	38-390 to 38-396
4257a	38-4.1 to 38-4.4
4258	Repealed by Acts 1936, p. 783
4258a	38-397 to 38-403
4258b	38-404, 38-405
4258c	38-406, 38-407
4258d	38-408
4258e	38-409, 38-410
4258f	38-411
4258f(1)	38-412
4258g	Repealed by Acts 1940, p. 502
4258h	38-428

Michie Code Section	Code 1950 Section
4258i	38-427, 38-429 to 38-431
4258j	38-432
4258k	38-433
4258l	38-434 to 38-439
4258(1)	38-143
4258(2)	38-145
4258(3)	38-146
4258(4)	38-147
4258(5)	38-149
4258(6)	38-150
4258(7)	38-151, 38-152
4258(8)	38-153
4258(9)	38-154
4258(10)	38-155
4258(11)	38-148
4258(12)	38-156
4258(13)	38-157
4258(14)	38-158
4258(15)	38-144
4259	38-445 to 38-448
4260	38-461 to 38-463
4261	38-464
4262	38-454
4263	38-440
4264	38-441
4265	38-442, 38-455 to 38-458
4266	38-459
4267	38-453
4268	38-465
4269	38-460
4270	38-450 to 38-452
4271	38-466
4272	38-443, 38-444, 38-449
4273	38-254
4274	38-255
4275	38-256
4276	38-257
4277	38-283
4278	38-284
4279	38-280
4280	38-282
4280a	38-286 to 38-293
4281	38-301 to 38-303
4282	38-307
4283	38-306
4284	38-264 to 38-268, 38-276, 38-277
4285	38-269
4286	38-270
4287	38-271
4288	38-272 to 38-275
4289	38-259
4290	38-260
4291	38-278
4292	38-285
4293	38-279

Michie Code Section	Code 1950 Section
4294	38-304, 38-305, 38-316 to 38-318
4295	38-294
4296	38-295 to 38-300
4297	38-319
4298	38-261
4299	38-320
4300	38-321
4301	38-322
4302	38-258
4302a	38-281
4302b	38-308
4302c	38-309, 38-310
4302d	38-311
4302e	38-312
4302f	38-313
4302g	38-314
4302h	38-315
4303	38-262
4304	38-263
4304a	38-323
4304b	38-324 to 38-326
4304c	38-327
4304d	38-328
4304e	38-329
4304(1)	38-467
4304(2)	38-479, 38-480
4304(3)	38-488 to 38-490
4304(4)	38-484
4304(5)	38-485, 38-486
4304(6)	38-493
4304(7)	38-487
4304(8)	38-478
4304(9)	38-481
4304(10)	38-483
4304(11)	38-482
4304(12)	38-468 to 38-470
4303(13)	38-471
4304(14)	38-472
4304(15)	38-473 to 38-475
4304(16)	38-492
4304(17)	38-491
4304(18)	38-494
4304(19)	38-476
4304(20)	38-477
4304(21)	38-496
4304(22)	38-495
4304(23)	8-61
4304(24)	8-62
4305	38-159 to 38-161, 38-167, 38-176
4305a	38-177 to 38-186
4305b	38-187 to 38-189
4305c	38-190
4305d	38-172
4305e	38-191
4305f	38-162
4305g	38-192
4305h	38-193
4306	Omitted
4307	38-168, 38-169
4308	38-173
4309	38-174
4310	38-170, 38-171
4311	38-228
4312	Repealed by Acts 1923, p. 53
4313	38-163 to 38-165
4314	38-166
4314a-4314r	Repealed by Acts 1928, p. 1119
4314(1)-4314(17)	Repealed by Acts 1948, p. 799
4314(18)	Repealed by Acts 1942, p. 640
4314(19)	38-194 to 38-199
4314(20)	38-200 to 38-206
4314(21)	38-207
4314(22)	38-208 to 38-211
4314(23)	38-212
4314(24)	38-213
4314(25)	38-214
4314(26)	38-215
4314(27)	38-216
4314(28)	38-217
4314(29)	38-218
4314(30)	38-218.1
4314(31)	38-218.2
4314(32)	38-218.3 to 38-218.5
4314(33)	38-218.6
4314(34)	38-218.7
4314(35)	38-218.8
4314(36)	38-218.9, 38-218.10
4314(37)	38-218.11, 38-218.12
4315	38-219 to 38-221
4316	38-222
4317	38-223
4318	38-224
4319	38-225
4320	38-226
4321	Omitted
4322	38-229
4323	38-230
4324	38-231
4325	38-232
4325a	38-233 to 38-237
4326	38-175
4326a	38-238
4326b	38-239
4326b1-4326b6	Repealed by Acts 1948, p. 790
4326b7	38-497
4326c	38-498
4326d	38-499
4326e	38-500 to 38-502
4326f	38-503
4326g	38-504
4326h	38-505
4326i	38-506
4326j	38-507
4326k	38-508
4326l	38-509
4326m	38-510
4326n	38-511
4326o	38-512
4326p	38-513
4326q	38-514
4326r	38-515, 38-516
4326s	38-517
4326t	38-518
4326u	38-519
4326v	38-520
4326w	38-521, 38-522
4327	38-523
4328	38-524
4328a	38-525
4329	38-529
4330	38-530
4331	38-531
4332	38-532, 38-533
4333	38-534
4334	38-535
4335	38-536 to 38-539
4336	38-526
4337	38-528
4338	38-540
4339	38-527
4340	38-541, 38-542
4340a	38-543, 38-544
4340b	38-545
4340c	38-546
4340d	38-547
4340e	38-548
4340f	38-558 to 38-562
4340g	38-563
4340h	38-550
4340i	38-564
4340j	38-549
4340k	58-502
4340l	38-551 to 38-557
4341	38-330
4342	38-336
4343	38-337
4344	38-334, 38-335
4345	38-346
4346	38-332, 38-333
4347	38-347
4348	38-348
4349	38-338 to 38-342

Michie Code Section	Code 1950 Section
4350	38-343, 38-344
4350a	38-345
4350(1)	Omitted
4350(2)	38-331
4350(3)	Repealed by Acts 1948, p. 790
4350(4)	Omitted
4350(5)	38-349
4350(6)	38-247, 38-248
4350(7)	38-253.20 to 38-253.25
4350(8)	38-253.15 to 38-253.26
4350(9)	38-253.5 to 38-253.15
4350(10)	38-253.34
4350(11)	38-253.35
4350(12)	38-251, 38-252
4350(13)	38-253.16 to 38-253.19
4350(14)	38-249
4350(15)	38-253.40
4350(16)	38-253.36 to 38-253.39
4350(17)	38-253.41
4350(18)	38-250
4350(19)	38-253.2 to 38-253.4
4350(20)	38-253.42
4350(21)	38-253, 38-253.1
4350(22)	38-253.43 to 38-253.45
4350(23)	38-253.67 to 38-253.71
4350(24)	38-253.72 to 38-253.79
4350(25)	38-253.51 to 38-253.61
4350(26)	38-253.80
4350(27)	38-253.81
4350(28)	38-253.62
4350(29)	38-253.47, 38-253.48
4350(30)	38-253.63 to 38-253.66
4350(31)	38-253.46
4350(32)	38-253.86
4350(33)	38-253.82 to 38-253.85
4350(34)	38-253.87
4350(35)	38-253.88
4350(36)	38-253.49, 38-253.50
4351	38-350
4352	38-351, 38-352
4353	38-356
4353a	38-357
4354	38-361, 58-501
4354a	38-63
4355	38-354
4356	38-358
4357	38-353
4357a	38-359
4358	38-355
4359	38-360
4359(1)	50-1
4359(2)	50-2
4359(3)	50-3
4359(4)	50-4
4359(5)	50-5
4359(6)	50-6
4359(7)	50-7
4359(8)	50-8
4359(9)	50-9
4359(10)	50-10
4359(11)	50-11
4359(12)	50-12
4359(13)	50-13
4359(14)	50-14
4359(15)	50-15
4359(16)	50-16
4359(17)	50-17
4359(18)	50-18
4359(19)	50-19
4359(20)	50-20
4359(21)	50-21
4359(22)	50-22
4359(23)	50-23
4359(24)	50-24
4359(25)	50-25
4359(26)	50-26
4359(27)	50-27
4359(28)	50-28
4359(29)	50-29
4359(30)	50-30
4359(31)	50-31
4359(32)	50-32
4359(33)	50-33
4359(34)	50-34
4359(35)	50-35
4359(36)	50-36
4359(37)	50-37
4359(38)	50-38
4359(39)	50-39
4359(40)	50-40
4359(41)	50-41
4359(42)	50-42
4359(43)	50-43
4359(44), 4359(45)	Omitted
4359(46)	50-44
4359(47)	50-45
4359(48)	50-46
4359(49)	50-47
4359(50)	50-48
4359(51)	50-49
4359(52)	50-50
4359(53)	50-51
4359(54)	50-52
4359(55)	50-53
4359(56)	50-54
4359(57)	50-55
4359(58)	50-56
4359(59)	50-57
4359(60)	50-58
4359(61)	50-59
4359(62)	50-60
4359(63)	50-61
4359(64)	50-62
4359(65)	50-63
4359(66)	50-64
4359(67)	50-65
4359(68)	50-66
4359(69)	50-67
4359(70)	50-68
4359(71)	50-69
4359(72)	50-70
4359(73)	50-71
4359(74)	50-72
4359(75)	50-73
4359(76)	Omitted
4359(77)	54-749
4359(78)	54-730 to 54-732, 54-734
4359(79)	54-737 to 54-747
4359(80)	54-750
4359(81)	54-751
4359(82)	54-752
4359(83)	54-733, 54-753, 54-761.1
4359(84)	54-762
4359(85)	54-763 to 54-764.1
4359(86)	54-770 to 54-775
4359(87)	54-765
4359(88)	54-735, 54-736, 54-748
4359(89)	Omitted
4359(90)	54-766
4359(91)	Omitted
4359(91a)	54-767 to 54-769
4359(92)-4359(102)	Repealed by Acts 1947, p. 46
4359(103)	54-113, 54-128
4359(104)	54-114 to 54-117
4359(105)	54-118
4359(106)	54-119, 54-121, 54-122
4359(107)	54-123
4359(108)	54-120, 54-121
4359(109)	54-124
4359(110)	54-125 to 54-127
4359(111)	54-129 to 54-131

Michie Code Section	Code 1950 Section
4359(112)	54-132 to 54-136
4359(113)	54-137
4359(114)	54-142, 54-143
4359(115)	54-138
4359(116)	Omitted
4359(117)	54-139, 54-140
4359(118)	54-141
4359(118a)	54-144
4359(118b)	54-145
4359(119)	54-113
4360	25-1
4361	25-2
4362	25-3 to 25-6
4363	25-7
4364	25-8, 25-9
4365	25-10, 25-11
4366	25-12 to 25-15
4367	25-16
4368	25-17
4369	25-18 to 25-20
4370	25-21
4371	25-23
4372	25-24
4373	25-25
4374	25-26
4375	25-27
4376	25-28
4377	25-29 to 25-31
4378	25-32
4379	25-33 to 25-35
4380	25-36, 25-37
4381	25-38
4382	25-39 to 25-41
4383	25-42, 25-43
4384	25-45, 25-46
4384a	56-458.1
4385	25-232
4385a	33-71
4386	25-44
4387	25-22
4387a	25-47 to 25-55
4388	Omitted
4388a	25-56
4388b	25-57
4388c	25-58
4388d	25-59
4388e	25-60, 25-61
4388f	25-62 to 25-66
4388g	25-67 to 25-69
4388h	25-70 to 25-84
4388i	25-85, 25-86
4388j	25-87 to 25-95
4388k	25-96 to 25-100
4388l	25-101 to 25-104
4388m	25-105
4388n	25-106 to 25-111
4388o	25-112
4388p	25-113
4388q	25-114
4388r	25-115
4388s	25-116
4388t	25-117
4388u	25-118
4388v	25-119
4388(1)	25-120
4388(2)	25-121
4388(3)	25-122
4388(4)	25-123
4388(5)	25-124 to 25-126
4388(6)	25-127 to 25-131
4388(7)	25-132 to 25-138
4388(8)	25-139 to 25-151
4388(9)	25-152 to 25-166
4388(10)	25-167 to 25-168
4388(11)	25-169 to 25-177
4388(12)	25-178 to 25-183
4388(13)	25-184 to 25-187
4388(14)	25-188
4388(15)	25-189 to 25-194
4388(16)	25-195
4388(17)	25-196
4388(18)	25-197
4388(19)	25-198
4388(20)	25-199
4388(21)	25-200
4388(22)	25-201
4388(23)	25-202
4388(24)	25-203
4388(25)	25-204
4388(26)	25-205
4388(27)	25-206
4388(28)	25-207
4388(29)	25-208 to 25-215
4388(30)	25-216
4388(31)	25-217
4388(32)	25-218
4388(33)	25-219 to 25-221
4388(34)	25-222
4388(35)	25-223
4388(36)	25-224
4388(37)	25-225
4388(38)	25-226
4388(39)	25-227
4388(40)	25-228
4388(41)	25-229
4388(42)	25-230
4388(43)	25-231
4388(44)	45-99 to 45-103
4388(45)	45-104
4388(46)	45-105
4388(47)	45-94 to 45-98
4389	18-350
4390	18-351
4391	18-352
4391a	18-352.1
4392	18-353
4392a	Repealed by Acts 1932, p. 68
4392b	18-354
4392c	18-355
4392d	18-356
4392e	18-357
4392f	18-358
4392g	18-359
4392h	18-360
4393	18-30
4394	18-31
4395	18-32
4396	18-33
4397	18-34
4398	18-35
4399	18-67
4400	18-69
4401	18-68
4402	18-70
4403	18-80
4404	18-81
4405	18-163
4406	18-232
4407	18-43
4407a	18-44
4407b	18-45
4408	18-46
4409	18-47
4410	18-48
4410a	18-49
4411	18-50
4412	18-51
4413	18-52, 18-53
4414	18-54 to 18-55.1
4415	18-56
4416	18-57
4417	18-58
4418	18-59
4419	18-60
4420	18-61
4421	18-62
4422	18-63
4423	18-64
4424	18-65
4425	18-66
4426	18-319
4426a	18-320
4427	18-321
4427a	18-339
4427b	18-72
4427c	18-36

Michie Code Section	Code 1950 Section
4427d	18-37
4427e	18-38
4427f	18-39
4427g	18-40
4427h	18-41
4427i	18-42
4427j	18-73
4428	18-148, 18-149
4429	18-150
4430	18-151
4431	18-152
4432	18-153
4433	18-154
4434	18-155
4435	18-156, 18-157
4436	18-158
4436a	Omitted
4437	18-159
4438	18-160
4439	18-161, 18-162
4439a	18-221
4440	18-164, 18-165
4440a	Repealed by Acts 1946, p. 164
4441	Omitted
4441(1)	62-178 to 62-181
4442	18-166
4443	18-167
4444	18-168
4445	Repealed by Acts 1930, p. 664
4445a	Repealed by Acts 1928, p. 1026
4445b	Repealed by Acts 1928, p. 1339
4446	Omitted
4446(1)	18-217
4447	18-170
4447a	Repealed by Acts 1932, p. 59
4447b	18-188
4448	18-169
4449	18-203
4449a	59-153 to 59-155
4449b	59-145 to 59-152
4449c	59-165 to 59-168
4449d	59-156 to 59-161
4450	18-204
4451	18-171
4452	18-172
4453	18-174
4454	18-175
4454a	18-176
4455	18-178
4455a	18-177
4456	18-179
4457	18-173
4457a	Repealed by Acts 1928, p. 1339
4458	18-271
4459	18-180
4459a	18-181
4459b	18-184
4460	18-185
4460a	18-347
4460a1	18-190
4460b	18-191
4461	18-199
4462	18-200
4463	18-201
4463a	18-202
4464	18-182
4464a	18-183
4465	18-156
4465a	18-189
4465b	18-192 to 18-198
4465c	33-325 to 33-327
4466	18-222
4467	18-216
4467a	18-233 to 18-235
4468	18-205
4469	18-206
4470	18-207
4471	18-208
4472	18-209
4473	18-210
4474	18-211
4475	18-212
4476	18-213
4477	18-214
4477a	Omitted
4477b	18-186, 18-187
4478	18-215
4479	18-224
4480	18-236
4480a	18-225
4480b	18-226
4481	18-227
4482	18-228
4482a	18-229
4482b	18-229.1
4483	18-230
4483a	18-231
4483b	18-7
4484	18-22
4485	18-23
4486	19-273
4487	18-24
4488	18-25
4489	18-26
4490	18-27
4491	18-28
4492	18-29
4493	18-237
4494	18-238
4495	18-239
4496	18-240
4497	18-241
4498	18-242
4499	18-245
4500	18-246
4501	18-247
4502	18-243
4503	18-244
4504	18-248
4504a	18-248.1
4505	18-249
4506	18-250
4507	18-251
4508	18-252
4508a	18-253
4509	18-254
4510	18-262
4511	18-263
4512	18-264
4513	18-265
4514	18-266
4515	18-267
4516	18-268
4517	18-269
4518	18-270
4519	18-259
4520	18-260
4521	18-255
4522	18-256
4523	18-257
4524	18-258
4525	18-272
4526	18-261
4527	18-124
4528	18-125
4529	18-126
4530	18-127
4531	18-128
4532	18-129
4533	18-130
4533a	18-131
4534	18-146
4535	18-147
4535a	18-135 to 18-145
4536	18-132
4536a	18-133
4537	18-134
4537a	18-273
4537b	18-344
4537c	18-335
4538	20-41
4539	20-42
4540	20-40, 20-58
4541	20-33
4542	20-28
4543	18-82
4544	18-83
4545	18-84
4546	20-59
4547	20-60
4548	18-87
4548a	18-85
4548b	18-86
4548c	18-87
4548d	18-88
4548e	18-89

Michie Code Section	Code 1950 Section
4548f	18-90 to 18-93
4548g	18-94 to 18-96
4549	18-113
4550	18-119
4551	18-98
4552	18-120
4553	18-121
4554	18-99
4555	18-100, 18-101
4556	18-102
4557	18-103
4558	18-104
4559	18-105
4560	18-106
4561	18-107
4561a	18-108
4561b	18-122
4562	18-109
4563	18-110
4564	18-111
4565	18-112
4566	18-123
4567	Omitted
4567a	18-218 to 18-220
4568	18-114
4569	18-115
4570	18-329
4571	18-330
4572	18-331
4573	18-332
4574	18-333
4575	18-334
4576	18-116
4577	18-117
4578	18-118
4578a	18-71
4579	18-97
4580	18-21
4580(1)	4-119
4580(2)	4-120
4580(3)	4-121
4580(4)	4-122
4580(5)	4-123
4580(6)	4-124
4580(7)	4-125
4580(8)	4-126
4581-4675	Repealed by Acts 1934, p. 135
4675(1)	4-1
4675(2)	4-2
4675(3)	4-3 to 4-6
4675(4)	4-7, 4-8
4675(4a)	4-10
4675(4b)	4-9
4675(5)	4-11
4675(6)	4-12
4675(7)	4-13
4675(8)	4-14
4675(9)	4-15
4675(9a)	4-16
4675(10)	4-17

Michie Code Section	Code 1950 Section
4675(11)	4-18
4675(12)	4-19
4675(14)	4-20
4675(15)	4-21
4675(16)	4-22
4675(17)	4-23
4675(17a)	4-24
4675(18)	4-25
4675(18a)	4-26
4675(18b)	4-27
4675(18c)	4-28
4675(18d)	4-29
4675(19)	4-30
4675(20)	4-31
4675(21)	4-32
4675(22)	4-33
4675(23)	4-34
4675(23a)	4-35
4675(24)	4-36
4675(25)	4-37
4675(25a)	15-553
4675(26)	4-38
4675(26a)	4-39
4675(27)	4-40
4675(28)	4-41
4675(28a)	4-42
4675(28b)	4-43
4675(29)	4-44
4675(30)	4-45
4675(31)	4-46
4675(31a)	4-47
4675(31b)	4-45.3
4675(31c)	4-45.2
4675(32)	4-48
4675(33)	4-49
4675(34)	4-50
4675(35)	4-51
4675(35a)	4-52
4675(36)	4-53
4675(37)	4-54
4675(38)	4-55
4675(38a)	4-56
4675(39)	4-57
4675(40)	4-58
4675(40a)	4-59
4675(41)	4-60
4675(41a)	4-61
4675(41b)	4-61.1
4675(41c)	4-61.2
4675(42)	4-62
4675(42a)	4-63
4675(43)	4-64
4675(44)	4-65
4675(45)	4-66
4675(46)	4-67
4675(47)	4-68
4675(48)	4-69
4675(48a)	4-70
4675(49)	4-71
4675(49a)	4-72
4675(49b)	4-73

Michie Code Section	Code 1950 Section
4675(49c)	4-74
4675(50)	4-75
4675(50a)	4-76
4675(51)	4-77
4675(52)	4-78
4675(53)	4-79
4675(54)	4-80
4675(55)	4-81
4675(56)	4-82
4675(57)	4-83
4675(58)	4-84
4675(58a)	4-85
4675(58b)	4-86
4675(59)	4-87
4675(60)	4-88
4675(61)	4-89
4675(61a)	4-90
4675(61b)	4-91
4675(62)	4-92
4675(62a), 4675(62b)	Omitted
4675(63)	4-94
4675(64)	4-95
4675(65)	4-96
4675(66)	4-98
4675(67), 4675(68)	Omitted
4675(69)	4-96
4675(69a)	4-93
4675(70)	4-99
4675(71)	4-100
4675(72)	4-101
4675(73)	4-102
4675(74)	4-103
4675(75)	4-104
4675(76)	4-105
4675(77)	4-106
4675(78)	4-107
4675(79)	4-108
4675(80)	4-109
4675(80a)	4-110
4675(81)	4-111
4675(82)	4-112
4675(83)	4-113
4675(83a)	4-114
4675(83b)	4-97
4675(84)	4-115
4675(85)	4-116
4675(86)	4-117
4675(87)	Omitted
4675(88)	4-118
4675(89)	Omitted
4675(90) to 4675(117)	Repealed by Acts 1934, p. 135
4676	18-284
4677	18-285
4678	18-286
4679	18-287
4680	18-288
4681	18-289

Michie Code Section	Code 1950 Section
4682	18-281
4683	18-282
4684	18-283
4685	18-290
4686	18-278
4687	18-297
4688	18-298
4689	18-299
4690	18-300
4691	18-280
4692	18-279
4693	18-301
4693a	18-303
4694	18-302
4694a	18-291 to 18-296
4695	18-304
4696	18-305
4697	18-306
4697a	18-313
4697b	18-314 to 18-317
4697c	18-318
4698	18-307
4699	18-308
4700	18-309
4701	18-310
4702	18-311
4703	18-312
4704	18-276
4705	18-277
4705a	64-50
4706	18-342
4707	18-343
4708	61-116
4709	18-349
4710	18-346
4711	Repealed by Tax Code
4711a	40-64
4712	18-336
4713	18-337
4714	18-322
4715	18-323
4716	18-324
4717	18-325
4718	18-326
4718a	18-275
4719	18-341
4719a	Repealed by Acts 1932, p. 673
4720	18-345
4721	18-348
4721a	18-338
4722	Repealed by Acts 1932, p. 884
4722a	15-553, 18-75 to 18-79
4722(1)	50-74 to 50-78, 59-169 to 59-176
4722(2)	18-340
4722(3)	18-74
4722(4)	Omitted
4722(4a)	59-214 to 59-219
4722(5)	59-20, 59-21
4722(6)	59-22
4722(7)	59-23
4722(8)	59-24, 59-25
4722(9)	59-26
4722(10)	59-27, 59-28
4722(11)	59-29
4722(12)	59-30
4722(13)	59-31
4722(14)	59-32
4722(15)	59-33
4722(16)	59-34
4722(17)	59-35
4722(18)	59-36, 59-37
4722(19)	59-38
4722(20)	Omitted
4722(21)	59-39, 59-40
4723-4729	Repealed by Acts 1946, p. 324
4730	33-279
4731	33-297
4732	Repealed by Acts 1946, p. 104
4733	33-283
4734	33-290, 33-291
4735	33-292
4736	33-284
4737	33-286
4738	33-287
4739	33-285
4740	Repealed by Acts 1920, p. 486
4741	33-281, 33-282
4741a	Repealed by Acts 1938, p. 435
4742	33-293
4743	33-294, 33-295
4744	33-296
4745	33-288
4745a	33-289
4746	62-182
4747	62-184
4748	62-185
4749	62-186
4750	62-188
4751	62-189
4752	62-187
4753	62-191
4754	62-190
4755	62-142
4756	62-175 to 62-177
4757	33-278
4758	18-1
4759	19-266
4760	19-264
4761	19-216
4762	55-4
4763	18-2
4764	18-3
4765	18-4
4766	18-5
4767	18-8
4768	19-3
4769	19-194
4770	19-195
4771	19-196
4772	19-197
4773	19-230
4774	19-231
4775	19-232
4776	19-167, 19-221
4777	19-217
4778	19-238
4779	19-239
4780	19-240
4781	19-241
4782	19-265
4783	19-267.1
4784	19-267
4785	19-268
4786	19-269
4787	19-234
4788	19-235
4788a	53-288, 53-289
4788b	53-290
4788c	53-230 to 53-237
4788d	53-238 to 53-240
4788e	53-241
4788f	53-242 to 53-249
4788g	53-250
4788h	53-251
4788i	Repealed by Acts 1944, p. 45
4788j	53-252 to 53-256
4788k	53-257 to 53-261
4788l	53-262
4788m	53-263
4788n	53-265
4788o-4788s	Omitted
4789	18-9
4790	18-10
4791	18-11
4792	18-12
4793	18-13
4794	18-14
4795	18-15
4796	18-16
4797	15-562 to 15-565
4797a	15-556, 15-563
4798	15-567
4799	15-568
4800	15-569
4801	15-570
4802	15-571
4803	15-572

Michie Code Section	Code 1950 Section
4803a-4803g	Repealed by Acts 1932, p. 791; 1934, p.16; 1945, p. 36
4803h-4803j	15-574
4804	18-17, 18-18
4805	18-19, 18-20
4806-4808	Repealed by Acts 1946, p. 601
4809	Repealed by Acts 1926, p. 461
4810-4818a	Repealed by Acts 1946, p. 601
4818(1)	Omitted
4818(2)	19-15
4818(3)	19-16
4818(4)	19-17
4818(5)	19-18
4818(6)	19-19
4818(7)	19-20
4818(8)	19-21
4818(9)	19-22, 32-345
4818(10)	19-23
4818(11)	19-24
4818(12)	19-25
4818(13)	19-26
4818(14)	19-27
4818(15)	64-125
4819	19-28
4820	19-29
4821	19-31
4822	19-32
4822a	19-30
4822b	19-31
4822c	19-32
4822d	19-33
4822e	19-34
4822f	19-28, 19-29
4823	19-71
4824	19-72
4824a	19-72.1
4825	19-73
4825a	18-274, 19-74, 19-75
4825b	19-76
4826	19-77
4827	19-78
4827a	52-20, 52-21
4827b	52-22
4828	19-88
4829	19-90
4829a	19-89
4830	19-93
4831	19-94
4832	19-91
4833	19-96
4834	19-98
4835	19-93, 19-100
4836	19-97
4837	19-95
4838	19-99

Michie Code Section	Code 1950 Section
4839	19-80
4840	19-114
4841	19-85
4842	19-79
4843	19-82
4844	19-83
4845	19-84
4846	19-101
4847	19-86
4848	19-81
4849	19-12
4850	19-13
4851	19-122
4852	19-123
4853	19-125
4854	19-124
4855	19-126
4856	19-127
4857	19-128
4858	19-129
4859	19-130
4860	19-132
4861	19-133
4862	19-134
4863	19-135
4864	19-131
4865	19-140
4866	19-136
4867	19-147, 19-148
4868	19-233
4869	19-141
4870	19-142
4871	19-143
4872	19-220
4873	19-144
4874	19-145
4875	19-146
4876	19-149
4877	19-150
4878	19-151
4879	19-139
4880	19-137
4881	19-152
4882	19-153
4883	19-154
4884	19-155
4885	19-156
4886	19-157
4887	19-87
4888	19-138
4889	19-158
4890	19-159
4891	19-9
4892	19-160
4893	19-161, 19-164, 19-169
4894	19-214
4895	19-171 to 19-177
4895a	19-178
4896	19-179, 19-180
4897	19-170

Michie Code Section	Code 1950 Section
4898	19-183
4899	19-185
4899a	19-186
4900	19-166, 19-182
4901	19-187
4902	19-188,19-189
4902a	19-190
4902b	19-191
4903	19-192
4904	19-184
4905	19-218
4906	19-219
4907	19-215
4908	19-201
4909	19-202 to 19-207
4910	19-208 to 19-210
4911	19-211
4912	19-212
4913	19-213
4914	19-198
4915	19-199
4916	19-200
4917	19-2
4918	19-222
4919	19-223
4920	19-224
4921	19-225, 19-226
4922	19-227
4923	19-228
4924	19-229
4925	19-272
4926	19-165
4927	19-168, 19-181
4928	19-193
4928(1)	19-242
4928(2)	19-243 to 19-246
4928(3)	19-247 to 19-249
4928(4)	19-250
4928(5)	19-251
4928(6)	19-252
4928(7)	53-301 to 53-304
4929	19-253
4930	19-254
4931	19-255
4932	19-256
4933	19-257
4934	19-258
4935	19-259, 19-260
4936	Repealed by Acts 1938, p. 138
4937	19-261
4938	19-262
4939	19-263
4940	19-274
4941	19-275
4942	19-276
4943	19-277
4943a	19-278

Michie Code Section	Code 1950 Section
4944	19-279
4945	19-280
4946	19-281
4947	19-282
4948	19-270
4949	19-303
4950	19-304
4951	19-305, 19-306
4952	19-307
4952a	19-308
4953	19-309
4954	19-283
4955	19-284
4956	19-285
4957	19-287
4958	19-289
4959	19-290
4960	19-286, 19-288, 19-291
4961	19-293
4962	19-294
4963	19-295
4964	19-296
4965	19-297
4966	19-292
4967	19-162
4968	Omitted
4969	19-236, 19-237
4970	19-4 to 19-6
4970a	19-7
4971	19-8
4972	19-102
4973	19-103 to 19-105
4973a	19-106 to 19-108
4974	19-109
4975	19-110
4976	19-111
4977	19-112
4978	19-113
4979	19-119
4980	19-116
4980a	19-115
4981	19-117
4981a	19-118
4982	19-120
4983	19-121
4984	Repealed by Acts 1926, p. 461
4985	19-10
4986	19-11
4987	16-4
4987a	16-45, 16-51, 16-55, 16-59
4987b	16-56, 16-57, 16-68, 16-83
4987c	16-42, 16-52 to 16-54
4987d	16-58
4987e	14-50 to 14-54
4987f	Repealed by Acts 1942, p. 189
4987f1	16-66, 16-81, 16-82
4987f2	16-69, 16-75
4987f3	16-70
4987f4	16-66, 16-71, 16-72.1
4987f5	14-141, 16-129.1, 39-4
4987f6	16-129
4987f7	16-80
4987f8	16-72, 16-73, 16-74
4987g	16-60, 16-61, 16-62 to 16-64, 16-83, 19-71
4987g(1)	Omitted
4987g(2)	16-61.1
4987h	16-76
4987i	16-77
4987j	16-78, 16-79
4987k	16-46
4987l	16-43, 16-44, 16-67
4987m	14-54, 14-132 to 14-134
4987n	Omitted
4987o	16-47 to 16-49
4987p	Omitted
4988-4988p	Repealed by Acts 1936, p. 628
4988(1)-4988(29)	Repealed by Acts 1936, p. 629
4988(30)	16-112
4988(31)-4988(43)	Repealed by Acts 1936, p. 629
4989	16-6 to 16-10
4990	16-10
4991	16-11
4992	16-5
4992(1)-4992(5)	Omitted
4992(6)	53-4, 53-5
4992(7)	Omitted
4992(8)	53-206
4992(9)	53-205
4992(10)	53-8, 53-9
4992(11)	53-133 to 53-135
4992(12)	53-136
4992(13)	53-147
4992(14)	53-264
4992(15)	53-220
4992(16)	53-99
4992(17)	53-10 to 53-17
4993	53-20
4994	53-21
4995	53-22
4996	53-23
4997	53-24
4997a	53-40
4997b	37-91.1, 53-313 to 53-315, 63-346
4998	53-305, 53-306
4999	53-307
5000	53-308
5001	53-309
5002	53-310
5003	53-311
5004	53-312
5005	53-25
5006	53-43
5007	53-44 to 53-46
5008	53-29
5008a	53-41
5009	53-51
5009a	Repealed by Acts 1932, p. 151
5009b	53-74
5010	53-32
5011	53-36
5012	53-48 to 53-50
5013	53-59
5014	53-57
5015	53-56
5016	53-27
5016a	53-55
5017	53-209 to 53-216
5018	53-217
5019	53-207, 53-208
5020	53-27, 53-218
5021	53-219
5022	53-54
5023	53-53
5024	53-52
5025	53-60
5026	53-26
5027	53-3
5028	53-18
5029	53-75
5030-5035	Omitted
5036	Repealed by Acts 1928, p. 564
5037-5039	Omitted
5040	53-39
5041	Omitted
5042	53-38
5043	53-226
5044	Repealed by Acts 1944, p. 349
5044a	53-225
5045	53-222
5045a	53-223
5046	53-37
5047	53-76, 53-77
5047a	53-78
5047b	Omitted
5048	53-79
5048a	53-220.1
5048b	53-224
5048c	Repealed by Acts 1948, p. 849

Michie Code Section	Code 1950 Section
5048d	53-28
5048e	53-30
5048f	53-31
5048g	Repealed by Acts 1928, p. 562
5048h	53-227
5048i	53-33
5048j	53-6, 53-7
5048k	53-34
5048l	53-35
5048m	53-47
5048n	53-42
5049	53-291
5050	53-292
5051	53-293
5052	53-294
5053	53-295
5054	53-296
5055	53-297
5056	53-298
5057	53-299
5058	53-300
5058a	53-299.1
5058(1)	53-80
5058(2)	53-81
5058(3)	53-82
5058(4)	53-83 to 53-85
5058(5)	53-86
5058(6)	53-87
5058(7)	Omitted
5058(8)	53-88, 53-89
5058(9)	53-90
5058(10)	63-372
5058(11)	53-91, 53-97
5058(12)	53-92
5058(13)	53-98
5058(14)	53-93 to 53-96
5058(15)	53-124 to 53-128
5058(16)	63-373
5059	19-35
5060	19-36
5061-5067	Repealed by Acts 1940, p. 486
5068	19-1
5069	19-271
5070	2-44
5070a	19-37
5070b	19-38
5070c	19-39
5070d	19-40
5070e	19-41, 19-42
5070f	19-43
5070g	19-44
5070h	19-45
5070i	19-46
5070j	19-47
5070k	19-48
5070l	19-49, 19-50
5070m	19-51
5070n	19-52

Michie Code Section	Code 1950 Section
5070o	19-53
5070p	19-54
5070q	19-55
5070r	19-56
5070s	19-57
5070t	19-58
5070u	19-59
5070v	19-60
5070w	19-61 to 19-63
5070x	19-64
5070y	19-65
5070z	19-66
5070aa	19-67
5070bb	19-68
5070cc	19-69
5070dd	Omitted
5070ee	19-70
5071	20-13
5072	20-14, 20-15
5073	20-37
5073a	20-1 to 20-12
5074	20-16, 20-17, 20-20 to 20-22
5075	20-19
5076	20-20
5077	20-29
5077a	20-30
5078	20-49
5079	20-23
5080	20-23, 20-25
5081	20-26
5082	20-31
5083	20-27
5084	20-38
5085	20-38
5086	20-39
5087	20-43, 20-57
5088	20-45
5088a	20-46
5088b	20-45, 20-47
5089	20-40, 20-44, 20-58
5090	20-48
5091	20-56
5092	20-18
5093	20-24
5094	20-32
5095	20-34
5096	20-35
5097	20-36
5098	20-18
5099	Repealed by Acts 1932, p. 884
5099a	20-50 to 20-55
5100	20-89
5101	20-89
5102	20-90
5103	20-91 to 20-93
5104	20-95
5105	20-96 to 20-98
5106	20-99 to 20-101
5106a	20-102

Michie Code Section	Code 1950 Section
5107	20-103
5108	20-104
5108a	20-105
5109	20-106
5110	20-94
5111	20-107 to 20-113
5111a	20-114, 20-115
5112	20-116
5112a	20-117
5113	20-118
5114	20-119
5115	20-120 to 20-121.1
5116	20-122
5116a	20-123
5117	64-27
5118	64-28
5119	64-30
5120	64-31
5121	64-32, 64-33
5122	64-34
5123	64-35
5124	64-36
5125	64-37, 64-38
5126	64-39
5127	64-40
5128	64-41
5129	64-29
5130	64-42
5131	55-269
5132	55-270
5133	55-271
5133a	55-277
5133a1	55-272
5133a2	55-273
5133a3	55-274
5133a4	55-275
5133b	55-276
5133c	55-253
5133d	55-254
5133e	55-255
5133e1	55-255.1
5133f	55-256
5133g	55-257
5133h	55-258
5133i	55-259
5133j	55-260
5133k	55-261
5133l	55-262
5133m	55-263
5133n	55-264
5133o	55-265
5133p	55-266
5133q	55-267
5133r	55-268
5134	55-35 to 55-37
5135	55-40
5136	55-44
5137	55-45
5138	55-46
5139	55-47

Michie Code Section	Code 1950 Section
5139a	64-20 to 64-22, 64-25, 64-26
5139b	64-23
5140	64-24
5141	55-2
5142	55-3
5143	55-22
5144	8-93.1
5145	55-23
5145a	55-56
5146	55-5
5147	55-6, 55-7
5147a	55-9
5148	55-10
5149	55-11
5150	55-12
5151	55-13
5152	55-14
5153	55-15
5154	55-16
5155	55-17
5156	55-18
5157	55-19
5158	64-43
5159	55-20
5160	55-21
5161	8-703.1, 8-703.2
5162	55-48
5163	55-49
5164	55-75
5165	55-57
5166	55-58
5167	55-59, 55-60
5167a	55-61
5167a1	55-62
5167b	55-65
5167b1	55-66
5167c	55-63
5167d	55-64
5168	55-50
5169	55-51
5170	55-67
5171	55-68
5172	55-69
5173	55-70
5174	55-71
5175	55-72
5176	55-73
5177	55-74
5178	55-76
5179	55-77
5180	55-226
5181	55-78
5182	55-79
5183	55-53
5183a	55-54
5183b	55-55
5184	55-80
5185	55-81
5186	55-82
5187	55-83 to 55-86
5188	55-87
5189	55-88 to 55-90
5190	55-91
5191	55-92
5191a	55-93
5191b	55-94
5192	11-1
5193	55-95
5194	55-96
5194a	55-100
5195	55-97
5196	55-98
5197	55-99
5198	55-101
5199	55-102
5200	55-103, 55-104
5201	55-105
5202	55-52
5202a	Repealed by Acts 1946, p. 269
5203	55-107
5204	55-106
5205	55-113
5205a	55-115
5206	55-114
5207	55-113, 55-120
5207a	55-123
5207b	55-124
5207b1	55-125
5207c	55-126
5208	55-119
5208a	55-135
5208b	55-136
5209	55-121, 55-137
5209a	55-128
5209b	55-126
5209c	55-122
5209d	55-127
5209e	55-130
5209f	55-129
5209g	55-131
5209h	55-132
5209i	55-133
5209j	55-134
5209k	55-130
5210	55-116 to 55-118
5210a	55-108
5211	55-41
5212	55-109, 55-110
5213	55-111
5214	Omitted
5214a	17-84
5214b	17-85
5214c	17-87
5214d	14-127, 17-86
5214e	14-102
5214f	17-92
5215	55-43
5216	55-138
5216a	55-139
5216b	55-140
5216c	55-141
5216d	55-142
5217-5219	Repealed by Acts 1946, p. 642
5220	15-766
5221-5222o	Repealed by Acts 1946, p. 642
5222p	15-796
5222q	15-797
5222r	15-798
5222s	15-799 to 15-801
5222t	15-802
5222u	15-803
5222v	15-804
5222w	15-805
5222x	15-806
5222y	15-807
5222z	15-808
5222aa	15-809
5222bb	15-810 to 15-812
5222cc	15-813
5222dd	15-814
5222ee	15-815
5222ff	15-816
5222gg	15-817, 15-818
5223	55-151
5224	55-152
5224a	55-143 to 55-150
5225	55-112
5225a	15-779
5225b	15-780 to 15-782
5225c	15-783 to 15-788.1
5225d	15-789, 15-790
5225e	15-791
5225f	15-792, 15-793
5225g	15-794
5225h, 5225i	Omitted
5225j	15-794.1
5225k	15-794.2, 15-794.3
5226	64-47
5227	64-48
5228	64-49
5229	64-51
5229a	64-57
5229b	64-56
5230	64-52
5231	64-55
5232	64-58
5233	64-59
5234	64-60
5235	64-61
5236	64-62
5237	64-63
5238	64-64
5239	64-65
5240	64-66
5241	64-67
5241a	64-68
5242	64-69
5243	64-70
5244	64-53

Michie Code Section	Code 1950 Section
5245	64-54
5246	64-71
5247	64-72
5248	64-89
5249	64-73, 64-74
5250	64-82
5251	64-88
5252	64-83
5253	64-75
5254	64-76
5255	64-77
5256	64-78
5257	64-79
5258	64-80
5259	64-81, 64-84, 64-85
5260	64-86
5261	64-87
5262	64-90
5263	64-91
5263a	64-92
5264	64-1
5265	64-2
5266	64-3
5267	64-4
5268	64-5
5269	64-6
5270	64-7
5271	64-8
5272	64-9
5273	64-11
5273a	Repealed by Acts 1928, p. 1340
5274	64-18
5275	64-12
5276	64-13 to 64-16
5277	64-19
5278	64-17
5278a	64-102
5278a1	64-119
5278a2	64-93 to 64-100
5278b	55-156
5278c	55-157, 55-158
5278d	55-159, 55-160
5278e	55-161
5278f	55-162
5278g	55-164
5278h	55-165
5278i	55-163, 55-166
5278j	55-167
5279	8-690
5280	8-691
5281	8-692 to 8-696
5282	8-698
5283	8-699
5284	8-700
5285	8-701
5285a	8-697
5286	8-702
5286a	8-703
5287	45-91
5288	45-92
5289	45-93
5290	28-256
5291	28-257
5292	28-258
5293	21-428
5294	21-429
5295	21-430
5296	21-431
5297	21-432
5298	40-133
5299, 5300	Omitted
5301	40-134
5302	40-135
5303	40-138
5304	40-136
5305	40-137
5306	40-139
5307	40-140
5308	40-141
5309	40-142
5310	40-143
5311	40-144
5312	40-145
5313	40-146
5313(1)	40-123
5313(2)	40-131
5313(3)	40-124
5313(4)	40-125
5313(5)	40-126
5313(6)	40-127
5313(7)	40-128, 40-129
5313(8)	40-130
5313(9)	Repealed by Acts 1942, p. 230
5313(10)	40-132
5314	31-2
5315	31-3
5316	31-4
5317	31-5
5318	31-6
5319	31-7
5320	31-1, 31-8, 31-9, 31-15
5321	31-10
5321a	31-11.1, 37-150.1
5322	31-11
5323	31-12
5324	31-13
5325	26-39
5326	8-677, 31-14
5327	31-15
5328	31-16
5329	31-17
5330	31-18
5331	8-87
5331a	8-629
5332	8-169
5332a	32-137
5333	Repealed by Acts 1942, p. 259
5333a	63-347
5333b	63-348
5333b1	63-364
5333c	63-349, 63-350
5333d	63-351
5333e	63-352, 63-353, 63-355
5333f	63-354
5333g	63-356
5333h	63-357, 63-358
5333i	63-359
5333j	63-360
5333k	63-361
5333l	63-362
5333m	63-363
5334	8-674
5334a	8-678 to 8-680, 8-682, 8-685, 8-686, 8-688, 8-694
5335	8-675, 8-676
5336	8-678
5337	8-679
5337a	8-680
5338	Omitted
5338a	55-42
5338b	8-681
5339	8-309
5340	8-682, 8-683
5341	8-684
5342	8-685
5343	8-751
5344	8-686
5345	8-687
5346	8-688
5347	8-689
5348	Repealed by Acts 1926, p. 898
5349	64-122
5349a	64-123
5350	26-60
5351	26-61
5352	26-62, 26-63
5353	26-64
5354	26-65
5355	26-66
5356	26-67
5357	64-128
5358	64-112
5359	64-113
5360	64-114
5361	64-103
5362	64-104, 64-105
5363	64-106
5364	64-107
5365	64-108
5366	64-109
5367	64-110
5368	64-111
5369	64-115
5370	64-116
5371	64-117
5371a	26-4

Michie Code Section	Code 1950 Section
5372	64-129
5373	64-130
5374	64-124
5375	64-118
5376	64-126
5377	64-131, 64-142, 64-156
5377a	64-131.1
5377b	64-131.2
5378	64-138
5379	64-127
5380	64-143
5381	64-144
5382	64-145
5383	64-146
5384	64-134
5385	64-135
5386	64-157
5387	64-158
5388	64-159
5389	64-160
5390	64-147
5391	64-148
5392	64-149
5392a	55-25
5393	64-136
5393a	Repealed by Acts 1934, p. 247
5393b	64-139, 64-140
5393c	64-132, 64-137
5394	64-141
5395	64-171
5396	64-172
5397	64-173, 64-173.1
5398	64-174
5399	64-175
5400	64-176
5400a	26-59
5400b	26-68
5400c	26-69
5400d	26-70
5400e	26-71
5401	26-8, 26-9
5402	26-10
5402a	26-11
5403	26-12 to 26-14
5404	26-15
5405	26-16
5406	26-5
5407	26-6
5408	26-17, 26-18
5409	26-19
5409a	26-20
5410	Repealed by Acts 1946, p. 327
5411	26-21
5412	26-22
5413	26-23
5414	26-24
5415	26-25, 26-26
5416	26-2
5417	26-3
5418	26-47
5419	26-46
5420	64-161
5421	64-162
5422	64-163
5423	26-27
5424	26-28, 26-29
5425	26-30
5426	26-31
5427	26-32
5428	26-33, 26-35 to 26-37
5429	26-34
5430	26-38
5431	26-40 to 26-45
5432	26-56
5433	26-7
5434	64-164
5435	64-165
5436	64-166
5437	64-167
5438	64-168
5439	64-169
5439a	64-170
5440	8-171 to 8-173
5440a	8-515
5440b	64-150 to 64-155
5440(1)	55-278
5440(2)	55-279
5440(3)	55-280
5440(4)	55-281
5440(5)	55-282
5440(6)	55-283
5440(7)	55-284
5440(8)	55-285
5440(9)	55-286
5440(10)	Omitted
5441	55-38
5442	55-39
5443	55-8
5444	64-10
5445	8-789 to 8-791
5446	8-792
5447	8-791, 8-793
5448	55-225
5449	8-794
5450	8-795
5451	8-796
5452	8-797
5453	8-798
5454	8-799
5455	8-800
5456	8-801
5457	8-802
5458	8-803
5459	8-804
5460	8-805
5461	8-806
5462	8-807
5463	8-808
5464	8-809
5465	8-810
5466	8-811
5467	8-812
5468	8-813
5469	8-814
5470	8-815
5471	8-816
5472	8-817
5473	8-818
5474	8-819
5475	8-820
5476	8-821
5477	8-822
5478	8-823
5479	8-824
5480	8-825, 8-826
5481	8-827
5482	8-828
5483	8-829
5484	8-830
5485	8-831
5486	8-832
5487	8-833
5488	8-834
5489	8-835
5490	8-836 to 8-841
5491	8-842
5492	8-843
5493	8-844
5494	8-845
5495	8-846
5496	8-847
5497	8-848
5498	8-849
5499	8-850
5500	8-851
5501	8-852
5502	8-853
5503	8-854
5504	8-855
5505	8-856
5505a	8-906 to 8-910
5506	55-211
5507	55-212
5508	55-213
5509	55-214
5510	55-215
5511	55-216
5512	55-217
5513	55-218
5514	55-220
5515	55-221
5516	55-222
5517	55-223
5518	55-224
5519	55-227
5520	55-228
5521	55-229
5522	55-230

Michie Code Section	Code 1950 Section
5523	55-231
5524	55-233
5525	55-234
5526	55-235
5527	55-236
5528	55-237
5529	55-238
5530	55-239
5531	55-240
5532	55-241
5533	55-242
5534	55-243
5535	55-244
5536	55-245
5537	55-246
5538	55-247
5539	55-248
5539(1)	44-162
5539(2)	44-160
5539(3)	44-161
5539(4)	44-163, 44-164
5539(5)	44-167 to 44-174
5539(6)	44-175, 44-176
5539(7)	44-177 to 44-180
5539(8)	44-181
5539(9)	44-183
5539(10)	44-184
5539(11)	44-193, 44-194
5539(12)	44-195 to 44-203
5539(13)	44-187 to 44-192
5539(14)	44-161, 44-165, 44-185
5539(15)	44-186
5539(16)	44-182
5539(17)	44-166
5540	55-249
5541	55-250
5542	55-251
5543	55-252
5544-5546	Omitted
5547	55-219
5548	6-339
5549	6-340
5550	6-341
5551	6-346
5552	6-347
5553	6-348
5554	6-349
5555	6-350
5556	6-351
5557	6-352
5557a	Repealed by Tax Code
5558	11-14
5559	11-15
5560	11-16
5561	11-2
5562	11-3
5562a	11-4
5563	6-353
5564	6-354
5565	6-355
5566	6-356
5567	6-357
5568	6-358
5569	6-359
5570	6-360
5571	6-361
5572	6-362
5573	6-363
5574	6-364
5575	6-365
5576	6-366
5577	6-367
5578	6-368
5579	6-369
5580	6-370
5581	6-371
5582	6-372
5583	6-373
5584	6-374
5585	6-375
5586	6-376
5587	6-377
5588	6-378
5589	6-379
5590	6-380
5591	6-381
5592	6-382
5593	6-383
5594	6-384
5595	6-385
5596	6-386
5597	6-387
5598	6-388
5599	6-389
5600	6-390
5601	6-391
5602	6-392
5603	6-393
5604	6-394
5605	6-395
5606	6-396
5607	6-397
5608	6-398
5609	6-399
5610	6-400
5611	6-401
5612	6-402
5613	6-403
5614	6-404
5615	6-405
5616	6-406
5617	6-407
5618	6-408
5619	6-409
5620	6-410
5621	6-411
5622	6-412
5623	6-413
5624	6-414
5625	6-415
5626	6-416
5627	6-417
5628	6-418
5629	6-419
5630	6-420
5631	6-421
5632	6-423
5633	6-424
5634	6-425
5635	6-426
5636	6-427
5637	6-428
5638	6-429
5639	6-430
5640	6-431
5641	6-432
5642	6-433
5643	6-434
5643a	Repealed by Acts 1928, p. 1339
5644	6-435
5645	6-436
5646	6-437
5647	6-438
5648	6-439
5649	6-440
5650	6-441
5651	6-442
5652	6-443
5653	6-444
5654	6-445
5655	6-446
5656	6-447
5657	6-448
5658	6-449
5659	6-450
5660	6-451
5661	6-452
5662	6-453
5663	6-454
5664	6-455
5665	6-456
5666	6-457
5667	6-458
5668	6-459
5669	6-460
5670	6-461
5671	6-462
5672	6-463
5673	6-464
5674	6-465
5675	6-466
5676	6-467
5677	6-468
5678	6-469
5679	6-470
5680	6-471
5681	6-472
5682	6-473
5683	6-474
5684	6-475

Michie Code Section	Code 1950 Section
5685	6-476
5686	6-477
5687	6-478
5688	6-479
5689	6-480
5690	6-481
5691	6-482
5692	6-483
5693	6-484
5694	6-485
5695	6-486
5696	6-487
5697	6-488
5698	6-489
5699	6-490
5700	6-491
5701	6-492
5702	6-493
5703	6-494
5704	6-495
5705	6-496
5706	6-497
5707	6-498
5708	6-499
5709	6-500
5710	6-501
5711	6-502
5712	6-503
5713	6-504
5714	6-505
5715	6-506
5716	6-507
5717	6-508
5718	6-509
5719	6-510
5720	6-511
5721	6-512
5722	6-513
5723	6-514
5724	6-515
5725	6-516
5726	6-517
5727	6-518
5728	6-519
5729	6-520
5730	6-521
5731	6-522
5732	6-523
5733	6-524
5734	6-525
5735	6-526
5736	6-527
5737	6-528
5738	6-529
5739	6-530
5740	6-531
5741	6-532
5742	6-533
5743	6-534
5744	6-535
5745	6-536
5746	6-537
5747	6-538
5748	6-539, 6-540
5749	6-541
5750	6-542
5751	6-543
5751a	6-543.1
5751b	Repealed by Acts 1928, p. 1339
5752	6-544
5753	6-545
5754	6-546
5755	6-547
5756	6-548
5757	6-549
5758	2-19, 2-20
5758a	2-21
5758b	2-22
5758c, 5758d	Omitted
5759	8-509
5760	6-422
5760a	11-8
5761	8-92, 11-9
5762	8-93
5763	11-10
5764	11-11
5765	11-12
5766	11-13
5767	38-367
5767a	11-5 to 11-7
5768	8-94
5769	8-95
5770	8-518
5771	49-22
5772	2-190
5773	2-184, 49-24
5774	49-25
5775	49-26
5776	49-23
5777	49-27
5778	49-28, 49-29
5779	8-627
5779(1)	11-17, 11-18, 11-20 to 11-22
5779(2)	11-19
5780	8-649
5781	8-630
5782	8-650
5783	8-651
5784	8-647
5785	8-652
5786	8-633
5787	8-634 to 8-637
5788	8-638
5789	8-639
5790	8-628, 8-640
5790a	8-170
5791	8-641
5792	8-642
5793	8-643
5794	8-644
5795	8-645
5796	8-646
5796a	8-654
5796b	8-632.1
5797	8-586, 8-587
5798	8-588
5799	8-589
5800	8-591
5801	8-593
5802	8-592
5803	8-594
5804	8-590
5805	8-5
5806	8-6
5807	8-7
5808	8-8
5809	8-31
5810	8-13
5811	8-14 to 8-16
5812	8-25, 8-26, 8-512
5813	8-28
5814	8-29
5815	8-17
5816	8-18
5817	8-10
5818	8-24
5819	8-22
5820	8-19
5821	8-27
5822	8-9
5823	8-30
5824	8-32
5825	8-23, 8-33
5826	8-34
5826a	8-20
5827	8-11
5827a	8-21
5827b	55-24
5827c	8-12
5828	8-36
5829	8-35
5830	8-37
5831	8-704
5832	8-705
5833	8-706
5834	8-707
5835	8-708
5836	8-709
5837	8-710
5838	8-711
5839	8-712
5840	8-713
5841	8-857
5842	8-858
5843	8-859
5844	8-860
5845	8-861
5846	8-862 to 8-864
5847	8-865
5848	8-596
5849	8-598

Michie Code Section	Code 1950 Section
5850	8-597
5851	8-599
5852	8-600
5853	8-603
5854	8-601
5855	8-602
5856	8-604
5857	8-605
5858	8-606
5859	8-607
5860	8-609
5861	8-608
5862	17-93, 17-94
5863	17-95
5864	17-96
5865	17-97
5865a	Omitted
5866	17-99
5867-5869	Repealed by Acts 1938, p. 138
5870	17-110, 17-111
5871	Repealed by Acts 1938, p. 138
5872	17-98
5873	17-104 to 17-107
5874	17-108
5875	17-109
5876	Repealed by Acts 1924, p. 391
5877	17-112
5878	42-13
5879	17-113
5880	17-115
5881	17-115
5882	17-114
5883	17-116
5884	17-100
5885	17-101
5886	17-102
5887	17-117
5887a	17-117, 17-119, 17-127
5887b	Omitted
5888	17-119
5889	17-120, 17-121
5889a	17-122
5890	17-123
5891	17-124
5892	Omitted
5893	17-127, 17-128
5893a-5893c	Omitted
5893d-5893f	17-127
5893g, 5893h	Omitted
5893i	17-127
5893j	Omitted
5893k - 5893m	17-127
5894	17-129
5895	17-130
5896	17-131 to 17-133
5897	17-134
5898	17-7
5898a	Repealed by Acts 1938, p. 140
5898b	14-45.1
5899	17-8
5900	17-9
5901	17-10
5901a	17-11
5902	17-12
5903	14-164.1
5904	17-125
5904a-5904c	16-50
5904d	Repealed by Acts 1932, p. 772
5904e-5904i	16-50
5905	17-135, 17-136
5905a	17-135, 17-136
5905b	17-137.1
5906	17-138
5907	17-137
5908	17-143
5909	17-144
5910	17-139
5910a	17-140 to 17-142
5911	17-118
5911a	17-196 to 17-208
5911b	Repealed by Acts 1938, p. 354
5912	17-145, 17-146
5913	17-153
5914	17-154
5915	17-155
5916	17-156
5917	17-157
5918	17-158
5919	17-159
5920	17-161
5921	17-162
5922	17-164
5923	17-165
5924	17-166 to 17-169
5925	17-152
5926	17-163
5927	17-149
5928	17-147
5929	17-150
5930	17-151
5930a	14-128
5931	Omitted
5932	17-148
5933	17-160
5933a	17-170 to 17-182
5934	17-185
5935	17-186
5936	17-187
5937	17-188, 17-189
5938	17-190
5939	Omitted
5940	17-191
5941	17-192
5942	17-193
5943	17-184
5943a	17-183
5944	17-194
5945	17-195
5946	17-209
5947	17-210
5948	17-211
5949	17-212,17-213
5950	17-214
5951	17-215
5952	17-216
5953	17-217
5954	17-218
5955	17-219
5956	17-220
5957	17-221
5958	16-40.1, 17-1
5959	17-21
5960	8-1.1
5960a	8-86.1
5961	17-6
5962	17-27
5962a	17-28 to 17-31
5963	17-13
5964	17-14
5965	17-15
5966	17-16
5967	17-17
5968	17-18
5969	17-19
5970	17-22, 17-23
5971	17-24
5972	17-25
5973	17-26
5974	17-32
5975	17-3
5976	17-4
5977	17-5
5978	17-2
5978a	51-3 to 51-7
5978b	51-9 to 51-11
5978c	51-8
5979	17-73
5980	17-74
5981	17-75
5982	17-76
5983	8-577.1
5984	8-174, 8-175
5985	8-178
5986	8-180
5987	8-181
5988	8-182
5989	8-183
5990	8 184
5991	8-185, 8-186
5992	8-187 to 8-189
5993	8-190
5994	8-191
5995	8-179
5996	8-192
5997	8-194

Michie Code Section	Code 1950 Section
5998	8-176, 8-195
5999	8-196
6000	8-199, 8-200
6001	8-201
6002	8-202
6003	8-218
6004	8-203
6005	8-197
6006	8-198
6007	8-204
6008	8-205
6009	8-206
6010	8-207, 8-208
6011	8-177
6012	8-193
6013	8-216
6014	8-215
6015	16-12
6016	16-18
6017	16-14
6018	16-15
6019	16-16
6020	16-19, 39-5
6021	39-6
6021a	16-13
6022	16-17, 16-17.1
6023	16-24
6024	16-25
6025	16-26
6026	16-27
6027	16-28
6028	16-29
6029	1634
6030	16-35
6031	16-36
6032	1637
6033	16-38
6034	16-39
6035	16-20 to 16-23
6036	16-30
6037	16-31
6038	16-32
6039	16-33
6040	16-40
6040a-6040f	Repealed by Acts 1936, p. 629
6041	8-51 to 8-53
6042	8-54, 8-55
6043	8-76
6043a	8-653
6044	8-715
6045	8-716
6046	8-717 to 8-723
6046a	Omitted
6047	8-724
6048	8-211
6049	8-38
6050	8-39
6051	8-40
6052	8-41
6053	8-42

Michie Code Section	Code 1950 Section
6054	8-43
6055	8-44
6056	8-47
6057	8-50
6058	8-66
6059	8-48
6060	8-49
6061	8-45, 8-46
6061a	8-46.1
6062	8-56 to 8-58
6062(a)	8-69
6062(b)	8-70
6063	8-59
6064	8-60
6064a	8-63
6065	8-64
6066	8-65
6067	8-67
6068	8-68
6069	8-71
6070	8-72
6071	8-73 to 8-75
6071a	8-77
6072	8-78
6073	8-79
6073a	8-80
6073b	8-81
6074	8-82
6075	8-83
6076	8-84
6077	8-85
6078	8-86
6079	8-132
6080	8-89
6081	8-106
6082	8-105
6083	8-104
6084	8-138
6085	8-102
6086	8-866
6087	8-648
6088	8-508
6089	8-867
6089(1)	8-868
6090	8-510
6091	8-111
6092	8-112
6093	8-113
6094	8-516
6095	8-117
6096	8-126
6097	8-125
6097a	8-136
6098	8-88
6099	8-90
6100	8-91
6101	8-97
6102	8-96
6103	8-118
6104	8-119
6105	8-133

Michie Code Section	Code 1950 Section
6106	8-369
6107	8-134
6108	8-135
6109	8-107
6110	8-103
6111	8-101
6112	8-137
6113	8-100
6114	8-108
6115	8-99
6116	8-120
6117	8-140
6118	8-109
6119	8-110
6120	8-124
6121	8-213
6122	8-121
6123	8-122
6124	8-98
6125	8-114
6126	8-115
6127	8-116
6128	8-123
6129	8-131
6130	8-355
6130a	8-356 to 8-366
6131	8-345
6132	8-346
6133	8-511
6134	8-347
6135	8-351
6136	8-130
6137	8-139
6138	8-127
6139	8-128, 8-129
6140	8-141
6140a	8-578
6140b	8-580
6140c	8-581
6140d	8-582
6140e	8-579
6140f	8-583
6140g	8-584
6140h	8-585
6141	8-236
6142	8-237
6143	8-238
6143a	8-750
6144	8-239 to 8-240.1
6145	8-241
6146	8-242
6147	8-247
6148	8-243
6149	8-244
6150	8-245, 8-246
6151	8-226
6152	8-227
6153	8-228
6154	8-229, 8-230
6155	8-231
6156	8-232

Michie Code Section	Code 1950 Section
6157	8-233, 8-234
6158	8-235
6159	8-503
6160	8-504
6161	8-505
6162	8-506
6163	8-507
6164	8-145
6165	8-146
6166	8-147
6167	8-148
6168	8-149, 8-150
6169	8-151
6170	8-152
6171	8-153
6172	8-154
6173	8-155
6174	8-156
6175	8-157
6176	8-158
6177	8-159
6178	8-248
6179	8-249, 8-250
6180	8-251
6181	8-252
6182	8-253
6183	8-254
6184	8-255
6185	8-256
6186	8-257
6187	8-258
6188	19-92
6189	8-263
6190	8-264
6191	8-265
6192	8-270
6192a	8-273
6193	8-270
6194	8-274
6195	8-275
6196	8-276
6197	8-266, 8-269
6198	8-267
6199	8-278
6200	8-279
6201	8-280
6202	8-281
6203	8-282
6204	8-283
6204a	8-284
6205	8-271
6206	8-272
6207	8-277
6208	8-285
6209	8-286
6210	8-287
6211	8-288
6212	8-289
6213	8-290
6214	8-291
6215	8-292

Michie Code Section	Code 1950 Section
6216	8-293
6217	8-296 to 8-298
6218	8-299, 8-300
6219	8-301
6220	8-302
6221	8-303
6222	8-294
6223	8-295
6224	8-328, 8-329
6225	8-304
6226	8-305
6227	8-306
6228	8-307, 8-308
6228a	8-310
6229	8-311
6230	8-312
6231	8-313
6232	8-314
6233	8-315
6234	8-316
6235	8-317 to 8-319
6236	8-320 to 8-323
6237	8-324 to 8-326
6238	8-237
6239	64-101
6239a	55-154, 55-155
6240	8-631
6240a	8-632
6241	8-209
6242	8-517
6243	8-160 to 8-162, 8-164
6243a	8-163
6244	19-163
6245	8-165 to 8-168
6246	8-214
6247	8-212
6248	55-153
6249	8-210
6250	8-217
6251	8-352
6252	8-330
6253	8-331 to 8-341
6253a	8-342
6254	8-225
6255	8-219
6256	8-220
6257	8-221
6258	8-222
6259	8-223
6260	8-224
6261	8-353
6262	8-513
6263	8-367
6264	8-368
6265	8-514
6266	8-655
6266a	64-44 to 64-46
6267	8-656
6268	8-657
6269	8-658

Michie Code Section	Code 1950 Section
6270	8-659, 8-660
6271	8-661
6272	8-662
6273	8-663
6274	8-664
6275	8-665
6276	8-666
6277	8-667
6278	8-668
6279	8-669
6280	8-725
6281	8-726
6282	8-727
6283	8-728, 8-729
6284	8-730
6285	8-731
6286	8-732
6287	8-733
6288	8-734
6289	8-259
6290	8-260
6291	8-741
6292	8-742
6293	8-743
6294	8-261
6294a	8-735 to 8-740
6295	8-262
6296	8-670, 8-671
6297	8-672
6298	26-48, 26-49
6298a	26-54
6299	26-50
6300	26-51
6301	26-1
6302	26-52
6303	26-53
6304	26-55
6304a	26-57
6304b	26-58
6305	8-354
6306	8-673
6307	8-370
6308	8-371
6309	8-372
6310	8-744, 8-745
6311	8-746
6312	8-747
6313	8-748
6314	8-749
6315	8-612
6316	8-613
6317	8-614 to 8-617
6318	8-611
6319	8-610
6320	8-618
6321	8-619
6322	8-620, 8-621
6323	8-622
6324	8-623
6325	8-624

Michie Code Section	Code 1950 Section
6326	Repealed by Acts 1922, p. 769
6327	8-625
6328	8-626
6329	8-485
6330	8-487
6331	8-487
6332	8-488
6333	8-348
6334	8-349
6335	8-350
6336	8-462
6337	8-463, 8-464
6338	8-465
6339	8-466
6340	8-467
6340a	8-468
6341	8-469
6342	8-470
6343	8-471
6344	8-472
6345	8-473
6346	8-474
6347	8-475
6348	8-476
6349	Repealed by Acts 1920, p. 416
6350	8-490
6351	8-477
6352	8-478
6353	8-479
6354	8-480
6355	8-489
6356	8-499
6357	8-481
6358	8-483
6359	8-483
6360	8-484
6361, 6362	Repealed by Acts 1938, p. 138
6363	8-491
6364	8-492
6365	8-493, 8-494
6366	8-495
6367	8-496
6368	8-497
6369	8-498
6370	8-502
6371	8-501
6372	8-500
6373	8-1
6374	8-3
6375	8-4
6376	8-2
6377	8-595
6378	8-519
6379	8-520
6380	8-521
6381	8-522
6382	8-523
6383	8-524, 8-525

Michie Code Section	Code 1950 Section
6383a	8-565
6384	8-538
6385	8-539
6386	8-526
6387	8-527, 8-528
6388	8-530
6389	8-533 to 8-536
6390	8-537
6391	8-547
6392	8-529
6393	8-545
6394	8-540
6395	8-541
6396	8-548
6397	8-549
6398	8-550, 8-551
6399	8-552
6400	8-553
6401	8-531
6402	8-554
6403	8-555, 8-556
6404	8-557
6405	8-558, 8-559
6406	8-542
6407	8-560
6408	8-546
6409	8-532
6410	8-561
6411	8-562
6412	8-563
6413	8-543
6414	8-544
6415	8-564
6416	8-566
6417	8-567
6418	8-568
6419	8-569
6420	8-570
6421	8-571, 8-572
6422	8-573
6423	8-574
6424	8-575, 8-576
6425	8-575, 8-577
6426	43-1 to 43-3
6427	43-4, 43-5
6427a	43-6
6428	43-7, 43-8
6429	43.9, 43-10
6429a	43-11, 43-12
6429b	43-13
6430	43-14
6431	43-15
6432	43-16
6433	43-17
6434	43-18
6435	43-19
6436	43-20, 43-21
6437	43-22, 43-23
6437a	43-70
6437b	43-71
6438	43-24

Michie Code Section	Code 1950 Section
6439	43-25
6440	43-26
6441	Repealed by Acts 1920, p. 28
6442	43-64
6443	43-33
6444	43-31
6445	43-32
6446	43-41, 43-42
6447	43-43
6448	43-62
6449	43-34
6450	43-35
6451	43-36
6451a	43-63
6451b	43-37
6451c	43-38
6451d	43-39
6451e	43-40
6452	43-27
6453	43-28
6454	43-29
6454a	43-44 to 43-61
6455	43-30
6456	43-67 to 43-69, 55-66.2 to 55-66.5, 55-66.7
6457	43-65, 55-66.1
6457a	55-60.1
6458	43-66
6459	8-343
6460	8-344
6461	8-373, 8-374
6462	8-375
6463	8-377
6464	8-378
6465	8-380, 8-381
6466	8-382
6467	8-383
6468	8-376
6468a	8-385
6469	8-142, 8-143
6469a	8-144
6470	8-386 to 8-389
6471	8-390
6471a	8-379
6472	8-391
6473	8-392
6474	8-393
6475	8-394
6476	8-395
6477	8-396
6478	8-397
6479	8-398
6480	8-399, 8-400
6481	8-401
6482	8-405
6483	8-402, 8-403
6484	8-404
6485	8-406, 8-411, 8-412
6486	8-413

Michie Code Section	Code 1950 Section
6487	8-415
6488	8-420
6489	8-421
6490	8-422
6491	8-416, 8-417
6492	8-423
6493	8-418
6494	8-419
6495	8-424
6496	8-425
6497	8-407
6498	8-408
6499	8-410
6500	8-409
6501	8-431 to 8-433
6502	8-434
6503	8-435
6504	8-436
6505	8-437
6506	8-438
6507	8439
6508	8-440
6508a	8-435, 8-437
6509	8-441, 8-442
6510	8-443 to 8-446
6511	8-447
6512	8-448
6513	8-449
6514	8-426
6515	8-429
6515a	8-430
6516	8-407
6517	8-414
6518	8-450
6519	55-232
6520	8-451
6521	8-452
6522	8-453
6523	8-454
6524	8-455
6525	8-456
6526	8-457
6527	8-458
6528	8-459
6529	8-460
6530	8-461
6531	34-4, 34-5
6532	34-6
6533	34-7
6534	34-8
6535	34-9
6536	34-10
6537	34-11
6538	34-12
6539	34-13
6540	34-14
6541	34-15
6542	34-16
6543	34-17
6544	34-18
6545	34-19
6546	34-20
6547	34-21
6548	34-22
6549	34-23
6550	34-24
6551	34-25
6552	34-26
6553	34-27
6554	64-120
6555	34-29
6555a	40-30 to 40-32
6556	34-30, 34-31
6557	34-32
6558	34-33
6559	8-449.1
6560	8-449.2
6561	8-449.3
6562	64-121
6563	34-3
6564	34-28
6565	34-2
6566	34-1
6567	1-2, 1-3
6567a	8-384
6568	1-7
6569	1-4
6570	1-8, 1-9
6571	1-5
6571a-6571e	Omitted
6571f	17-222, 17-223
6571g	17-224
6571h	17-225
6571i	17-226, 17-227

Table of Tax Code Sections

SHOWING SECTIONS OF THE TAX CODE AND CORRESPONDING SECTIONS OF THE CODE OF 1950.

Tax Code Section	Code 1950 Section
1	Omitted
2	58-1
3	58-2
4	Omitted
5	58-2
6	58-5 to 58-8
7	58-9
8	58-10
8a	58-851
9	22-138.1
9a	Repealed by Acts 1932, p. 43
9b	58-11
10	58-28, 58-29
11	58-30, 58-31
12	58-32
13	58-46
14	58-33
15	58-35
16	58-36 to 58-38
17	58-39
18	58-40
19	58-41 to 58-43
20	58-44
21	58-47
22	58-49 to 58-51
23	58-77
24	58-78, 58-102
25	58-81 to 58-83
26	58-84
27	58-79
28	58-85
29	58-86
30	58-87, 58-88
30a	58-86.1, 58-88.2 to 58-88.4
31	58-89, 58-90, 58-91
32	58-92
33	58-93 to 58-96
34	58-97
35	58-80
36	58-98
36a	58-99
37	58-100
38	58-88.1, 58-101
39	58-103
40	58-104
41	58-105
42	58-106, 58-110
43	58-107
44	58-108
45	58-109
46	58-112 to 58-114
47	58-115, 58-116
48	58-111
49	58-117
50	58-118 to 58-121
51	58-122 to 58-127
52	58-128
53	58-88.1, 58-130
54	58-131 to 58-132
55	58-133
56	58-134
57	58-135
58	58-136 to 58-139
59	58-140
60	58-141 to 58-143
61	58-144, 58-145
62	58-146, 58-147
63	58-148
64	58-149
65	58-150
66	58-151
67	13-68.1, 13-211.1, 58-129
68	58-405
69	8-353.1, 8-509.1, 55-64.1, 58-406
69a	55-64.1
70	58-408
71	58-409
72	58-407
73	58-410 to 58-413, 58-418
73a	58-416
73b	58-419
73c	58-417
74	58-414
75	58-422
76	58-415
77	58-420
78	58-421
79	58-423
80	58-426, 58-427
81	58-428 to 58-433
82	58-424
83	58-425
84	58-434 to 58-437
85	58-438
86	58-440
87	58-441
88	58-439
89	58-465
90	58-466, 58-467, 58-470 to 58-472
91	58-468, 58-473 to 58-477.1
92	58-479
93	58-480, 58-481
94	58-482
95	58-485
96	58-469
97	58-484
97a	58-483
97b	58-478
98	58-152 to 58-157
98a	58-192
99	58-159
100	58-160
101	58-161
102	58-166
103	58-167 to 58-169
104	58-170
105	58-171, 58-172
106	58-173
107	58-174, 58-175
108	58-176 to 58-179
109	58-180, 58-181
110	58-182
111	58-183
112	58-184
113	58-185
114	58-186
115	58-162, 58-163
116	58-187
117	58-165
118	58-188
119	58-164
119a1	58-217.1
119a2	58-217.2
119a3	58-217.3
119a4	58-217.4
119a5	58-217.5
119a6	58-217.6
119a7	58-217.6
119a8	58-217.7
119a9	58-217.8
119a10	58-217.9
119a11	58-217.10
119a12	58-217.11
119a13	58-217.12
119a14	58-217.13
119a15	58-217.14

Tax Code Section	Code 1950 Section
120	58-189 to 58-191, 58-193 to 58-209
120(1)	58-218 to 58-220
120(2)	58-221
120(3)	58-222
120(4)	58-223 to 58-225
120(5)	58-226
120(6)	58-227 to 58-229
120(7)	58-230, 58-231
120(8)	58-232, 58-233
120(9)	58-234
120(10)	58-235
120(11)	58-236
120(12)	58-237
120(13)	58-158
120(14)	58-238
120(15)	Omitted
120a	58-210
120b	58-211 to 58-213
120c	58-214
120d	58-215, 58-216
120e	58-217
121	58-54 to 58-63
122	58-64, 58-65
123	58-52
124	58-53
125	58-66 to 58-70
126	58-71 to 58-76
127	58-239, 58-240
127(1)	58-266.3
127(2)	58-266.2
128	Omitted
129	58-241 to 58-243
130	58-244
131	58-245
132	58-246
133	58-247
134	58-248
135	58-249
136	58-250 to 58-252
137	58-253
138	58-254
139	58-255
140	58-256
141	58-257
142	58-258
143	58-259
144	58-260
145	58-261
146	58-262
147	58-263
148	58-264
149	58-265
150	58-266
151	58-267
152	58-268
153	58-276 to 58-282
153a	58-283
154	58-284
155	58-269
156	58-270

Tax Code Section	Code 1950 Section
157	58-271 to 58-275
158	58-370
159	58-371
160	54-792
161	54-793
162	54-794
163	58-285
164	58-286
165	58-287
166	58-288
166a	58-371.2
167	58-372
168	Repealed by Acts 1938, p. 350
169	Repealed by Acts 1930, p. 862
170	58-290
171	58-291
171a	58-292
172	58-373
173	58-374
174	58-293
175	58-289
176	58-297 to 58-303.1
176a	58-294
176b	58-295
176c	58-296
177	58-375
178	58-376
179	Repealed by Acts 1930, p. 862
179a	58-377
179b	58-377.1
180	58-378
181	58-380
181a	Repealed by Acts 1930, p. 862
182	54-825 to 54-835, 58-382
182a	54-836, 58-383
183	58-384
184	58-385
185	58-386
185½	58-379
186	58-387
186a	58-387.1
187	58-388
188	58-304 to 58-317, 58-318 to 58-339, 58-833
188a	Repealed by Acts 1934, p. 196
188b	58-304.1, 58-317.1
189	58-389
189a	Omitted
190	58-362 to 58-369.1
190a	58-390
191	54-840 to 54-842, 54-844 to 54-852, 54-854 to 54-859, 58-392
191a	54-853
191a1	54-843

Tax Code Section	Code 1950 Section
191b	Repealed by Acts 1944, p. 157
192	58-340 to 58-345
192a	58-354
192b	58-346 to 58-353
193	58-393
194	58-394
194a	58-395
195	58-396
196	58-398
197	58-399
198	58-355 to 58-361.1
198a	58-397
199	58-400
200	58-401
201	58-402
202	58-403
203	58-391
204	58-404
205	58-442
206	58-443
207	58-444
208	13-35, 58-445 to 58-447
209	58-448, 58-449
210	58-450 to 58-455
211	58-456 to 58-460
212	58-461
213	58-463
214	58-464
215	58-524 to 58-533, 58-537 to 58-539
215a	58-534, 58-535
216	58-515 to 58-523, 58-536, 58-540, 58-541
216a	58-588 to 58-601
216b	58-646 to 58-659
217	58-542 to 58-545
217a	58-618 to 58-626
218	58-548 to 58-552, 58-554, 58-555
219	58-546 58-547, 58-553
220	58-556 to 58-562
221	58-570 to 58-573, 58-576, 58-577
222	58-574, 58-575
223	58-565 to 58-569
224	58-563, 58-564
225	58-581 to 58-584, 58-586, 58-587
226	58-578
227	58-579, 58-580, 58-585
228	58-604, 58-607 to 58-614
229	58-602, 58-603, 58-605, 58-606, 58-615 to 58-617
229a	58-504 to 58-509

Tax Code Section	Code 1950 Section
230	58-660 to 58-671
231	58-510
232	58-514
233	58-511
233a	58-681 to 58-685
234	58-512
235	58-672 to 58-678
235a	58-679, 58-680
236	58-513
237	58-486 to 58-493, 58-495, 58-496
238	58-497, 58-498
239	58-499, 58-500
240	58-494
241	58-758
242	58-776 to 58-780, 58-782 to 58-784, 58-785 to 58-789, 58-794
242a	58-764
242b	58-776, 58-784.1, 58-785
243	58-793
244	58-790
245, 246	Repealed by Acts 1930, p. 878
247	58-791, 58-792
247(1)	58-792.1
248, 249	Repealed by Acts 1930, p. 878
250	58-759
251	58-760, 58-762, 58-763
251a	58-770, 58-815
252	58-796
253	58-804
254	58-805
255	58-806
256	58-807
257	58-808
258	58-809
259	58-810
260	58-811
261	58-812
262	58-765
262a	58-766
263	58-813
264	58-771
265	58-773
265a	58-772
265b	58-772.1
266	58-814
267	58-797
268	58-798
269	58-799
270	58-800
271	58-801
272	58-802
273	58-803

Tax Code Section	Code 1950 Section
274	Repealed by Acts 1940, p. 342
275	58-774, 58-775
276	58-816, 58-817
277	58-818 to 58-821
278	58-822 to 58-824
279	58-761
280	58-826, 58-827
281	58-828
282	58-767
282a	Repealed by Acts 1942, p. 115
282b	58-768
283	58-829, 58-830
284	58-831
285	58-832
286	58-835 to 58-837
287	58-838
288	58-839
289	58-840
290	58-841
291	58-842
292	58-843
293	58-844
294	58-845
295	58-846
296	58-266.1
297	58-847 to 58-849
298	58-850
299	15-10.1
300	58-852
301	58-853
302	58-854
303	58-855
304	58-856
305	58-857
306	58-858
307	58-859, 58-860
308	58-861
309	58-862
309a	58-863
310	58-864
310a	58-865, 58-866
310b	58-867
310c	58-868
310d	58-869
310e	58-870 to 58-872
310f	58-873
310g	58-874
310h	58-875
310i	Omitted
311-314	Repealed by Acts 1946, p. 371
315	58-876, 58-877
316	58-878
317	58-879 to 58-883
318	58-884
319	58-885
320	58-886
321	58-887, 58-888
322	58-889

Tax Code Section	Code 1950 Section
323	58-890
324	58-891
325, 326	Omitted
327	58-892, 58-893
328	Repealed by Acts 1932, p. 418
329	Omitted
330-343	Repealed by Acts 1946, p. 371
344	58-895 to 58-902, 58-914
345	58-903, 58-904
346	58-905 to 58-910
347	58-911, 58-912
348	58-913, 58-915
348a	Omitted
348b	58-769
348c	Omitted
349	58-916
350	58-938 to 58-941, 58-943 to 58-945, 58-947 to 58-952
350a	58-942
350b	58-946
351	58-917
352	58-918
353	58-926
354	58-919
355	58-920
356	58-921
357	58-923
358	58-922
359	58-925
360	58-924
361	58-927, 58-928
362	58-929
363	58-930
363a	Omitted
364	58-931
365	58-932
366	58-953 to 58-957
367	58-933 to 58-935
368	58-936
369	58-958
370	58-959
371	58-960
372	58-961 to 58-965
372a	Omitted
372b	58-966
373	Repealed by Acts 1933, p. 61
373a, 373a1	Omitted
373b	58-968
374	58-973
375	58-974
376	58-975
377	58-976, 58-977
378	58-1001 to 58-1005
379	58-1006
380	58-1007, 58-1008
381	58-1009

Tax Code Section	Code 1950 Section
382	58-1010
383	58-1011
384	58-1012
385	58-1013
386	58-981, 58-982
387	58-978
388	58-979, 58-980
389	58-983
390	58-984, 58-985, 58-987
391	Repealed by Acts 1940, p. 342
392	58-988
393	58-989
394	58-990, 58-991
394a	58-990
394b	58-986
395	58-992 to 58-996
396	58-997
396a	Repealed by Acts 1936, p. 33
396b	58-990
396c	58-998
397-401	Repealed by Acts 1930, p. 770
402	58-999

Tax Code Section	Code 1950 Section
402a	58-1000
403	58-1014 to 58-1020
403a	58-1021
404	58-967
405	58-937
406	58-969 to 58-972
407	58-1118 to 58-1121
408	58-1122 to 58-1128
409	58-1129
410	58-1130 to 58-1132, 58-1134 to 58-1136
410a	58-1133
411	58-1137, 58-1138
412	58-1139
413	58-1141 to 58-1144
414	58-1145 to 58-1151
414a	58-795
415	58-1153 to 58-1157
416	58-1158
417	58-1159
417a	58-1140
418	58-1160, 58-1161
419	58-1162
420	58-1163
421	58-1164
422	58-1165

Tax Code Section	Code 1950 Section
423	58-1166
424	58-4
424a	58-27
425	58-20 to 58-22, 58-834
426	Repealed by Acts 1934, p. 290
427	58-18
428	58-23
429	58-24, 58-25
430	58-26
431	58-45
432	58-48
433	58-2
434	58-3
435	58-12 to 58-16
435a	58-19
435b	Repealed by Acts 1944, p. 319
435c	58-17
436-438	Omitted
439	43-41, 43-43
440	58-34
441	Omitted

Table of Reorganization Provisions of 1948

Showing Sections of the Reorganization Provisions of 1948 and Corresponding Sections of the Code of 1950.

R. P. Section	Code 1950 Section
1-1	1-1
1-2	1-2
1-2.1	1-2.1
1-3	1-3
1-4	1-4
1-5	1-5
1-6	1-6
1-7	1-7
1-8	1-8
1-9	1-9
2-1	2-1
2-4	2-2
2-5	2-3, 2-4
2-65	2-65
2-66	2-66
2-67	2-67
2-68	2-68
2-69	2-69
2-70	2-70
2-71	2-71
2-72	2-72
2-73	2-73
2-74	2-74
2-75	2-75
2-75.1	2-75.1
2-75.2	2-75.2
2-76	2-76
2-77	2-77
2-78	2-78
2-79	2-79
2-80	2-80
2-81	2-81
2-82	2-82
2-83	2-83
2-84	2-84
2-117	2-117
2-118	2-118
2-119	2-119
2-120	2-120
2-121	2-121
2-122	2-122
2-123	2-123
2-124	2-124
2-145	2-145
2-146	2-146
2-147	2-147
2-148	2-148
2-149	2-149
2-149.1	2-149.1
2-149.2	2-149.2
2-150	2-150
2-151	2-151
2-152	2-152
2-153	2-153
2-154	2-154
2-155	2-155
2-156	2-156
2-157	2-157
2-158	2-158
2-159	2-159
2-160	2-160, 2-160.1
2-161	2-161
2-161.1	2-161.1
2-162	2-162
2-163	2-163
2-164	2-164
2-165	2-165
2-166	2-166
2-167	2-167
2-167.1	2-167.1
2-168	2-168
2-169	2-169
2-170	2-170
2-171	2-171
2-172	2-172
2-173	2-173
2-174	2-174
2-175	2-175
2-176	2-176
2-177	2-177
2-178	2-178
2-179	2-179
2-180	2-180
2-181	2-181
2-182	2-182
2-183	2-183
2-184	2-184
2-185	2-185
2-186	2-186
2-187	2-187
2-188	2-188
2-189	2-189
2-190	2-190
2-191	2-191
2-192	2-192
2-193	2-193
2-194	2-194
2-195	2-195
2-196	2-196
2-197	2-197
2-198	2-198
2-199	2-199
2-200	2-200
2-201	2-201
2-202	2-202
2-203	2-203
2-204	2-204
2-205	2-205
2-206	2-206
2-207	2-207
2-208	2-208
2-209	2-209
2-210	2-210
2-211	2-211
2-213	2-212
2-214	2-213, 2-214
2-215	2-215
2-216	2-216
2-217	2-217
2-218	2-218
2-219	2-219
2-220	2-220
2-221	2-221
2-222	2-222
2-223	2-223
2-224	2-224
2-225	2-225
2-226	2-226
2-227	2-227
2-228	2-228
2-229	2-229
2-230	2-230
2-231	2-231
2-232	2-232
2-233	2-233
2-234	2-234
2-235	2-235
2-236	2-236
2-237	2-237
2-238	2-238
2-239	2-239
2-240	2-240
2-241	2-241
2-242	2-242
2-243	2-243
2-244	2-244
2-245	2-245
2-246	2-246
2-247	2-247
2-248	2-248
2-249	2-249
2-250	2-250
2-251	2-251

R. P. Section	Code 1950 Section
2-252	2-252
2-253	2-253
2-254	2-254
2-255	2-255
2-256	2-256
2-257	2-257
2-258	2-258
2-259	2-259
2-259.1	2-259.1
2-260	2-260
2-261	2-261
2-262	2-262
2-263	2-263
2-264	2-264
2-265	2-265
2-266	2-266
2-267	2-267
2-268	2-268
2-269	2-269
2-270	2-270
2-271	2-271
2-272	2-272
2-273	2-273
2-274	2-274
2-275	2-275
2-276	2-276
2-277	2-277
2-278	2-278
2-279	2-279
2-280	2-280
2-281	2-281
2-282	2-282
2-283	2-283
2-284	2-284
2-285	2-285
2-286	2-286
2-287	2-287
2-288	2-288
2-289	2-289
2-290	2-290
2-291	2-291
2-292	2-292
2-293	2-293
2-294	2-294
2-295	2-295
2-296	2-296
3-209	3-209
3-210	3-210
3-211	3-211
3-212	3-212
3-213	3-213
3-214	3-214
3-215	3-215
3-216	3-216
3-217	3-217
3-218	3-218
3-219	3-219
3-220	3-220
3-221	3-221
3-222	3-222
3-223	3-223

R. P. Section	Code 1950 Section
3-224	3-224
3-225	3-225
3-226	3-226
3-227	3-227
3-228	3-228
6-550	6-550
6-551	6-551
6-552	6-552
6-553	6-553
6-554	6-554
6-555	6-555
6-556	6-556
6-557	6-557
6-558	6-558
6-559	6-559
6-560	6-560
6-561	6-561
6-562	6-562
6-563	6-563
6-564	6-564
6-565	6-565
6-566	6-566
6-567	6-567
6-567.1	6-567.1
6-568	6-568
9-7	9-7
9-8	9-8
9-9	9-9
9-10	9-10
9-11	9-11
9-12	9-12
9-49	9-49
9-50	9-50
9-51	9-51
9-52	9-52
9-52.1	9-52.1
10-1	10-1
10-2	10-2
10-3	10-3
10-4	10-4
10-5	10-5
10-6	10-6
10-7	10-7
10-8	10-8
10-8.1	10-8.1
10-9	10-9
10-10	10-10
10-11	10-11
10-12	10-12
10-12.1	10-12.1
10-12.2	10-12.2
10-12.3	10-12.3
10-13	10-13
10-14	10-14
10-15	Omitted
10-16	10-21
10-17	10-21.1
10-17.1	10-16
10-18	10-21.3
10-18.1	Omitted
10-19	10-17

R. P. Section	Code 1950 Section
10-20	10-15
10-21	10-21.2
10-21.1	10-18
10-21.2	10-19
10-21.3	10-20
10-22	10-22
10-23	10-23
10-24	10-24
10-25	10-25
10-26	10-26
10-27	10-27
10-28	10-28
10-29	10-29
10-30	10-30
10-31	10-31
10-32	10-32
10-33	10-33
10-34	10-34
10-34.1	10-34.1
10-34.2	10-34.2
10-35	10-35
10-36	10-36
10-37	10-37
10-38	10-38
10-39	10-39
10-40	10-40
10-41	10-41
10-42	10-42
10-43	10-43
10-44	10-44
10-45	10-45
10-46	10-46
10-47	10-47
10-48	10-48
10-49	10-49
10-50	10-50
10-51	10-51
10-52	10-52
10-53	10-53
10-54	10-54
10-55	10-55
10-56	10-56
10-57	10-57
10-58	10-58
10-59	10-59
10-60	10-60
10-61	10-61
10-62	10-62
10-63	10-63
10-64	10-64
10-65	10-65
10-66	10-66
10-67	10-67
10-68	10-68
10-69	10-69
10-70	10-70
10-71	10-71
10-72	10-72
10-73	10-73
10-74	10-74
10-75	10-75

TABLE OF REORGANIZATION PROVISIONS OF 1948

R. P. Section	Code 1950 Section
10-76	10-76
10-77	10-77
10-78	10-78
10-79	10-79
10-80	10-80
10-81	10-81
10-82	10-82
10-83	10-83
10-84	10-84
10-85	10-85
10-86	10-86
10-86.1	10-86.1
10-87	10-87
10-88	10-88
10-89	10-89
10-90	10-90
10-90.1	10-90.1
10-91	10-91
10-92	10-92
10-92.1	10-92.1
10-93	10-93
10-94	10-94
10-95	10-95
10-96	10-96
10-97	10-97
10-99	10-99
10-100	10-100
10-101	10-101
10-102	10-102
10-103	10-103
10-104	10-104
10-105	10-105
10-106	10-106
10-107	10-107
10-108	10-108
10-109	10-109
10-110	10-110
10-111	10-111
10-112	10-112
10-113	10-113
10-113.1	10-113.1
10-113.2	10-113.2
10-114	10-114
10-115	10-115
10-116	10-116
10-117	10-117
10-118	10-118
10-119	10-119
10-120	10-120
10-121	10-121
10-122	10-122
10-123	10-123
10-124	10-124
10-125	10-125
10-126	10-126
10-127	10-127
10-128	10-128
10-129	10-129
10-130	10-130
10-131	10-131
10-132	10-132
14-60	14-60
14-61	14-61
14-62	14-62
14-63	14-63
14-64	14-64
14-65	14-65
18-135	18-135
18-136	18-136
18-137	18-137
18-138	18-138
18-139	18-139
18-140	18-140
18-141	18-141
18-142	18-142
18-143	18-143
18-144	18-144
18-145	18-145
19-14	19-14
19-15	19-15
19-16	19-16
19-17	19-17
19-18	19-18
19-19	19-19
19-20	19-20
19-21	19-21
19-22	19-22
19-23	19-23
19-24	19-24
19-25	19-25
19-26	19-26
19-27	19-27
24-24	24-24
24-25	24-25
24-26	24-26
24-27	24-27
24-28	24-28
27-30 to 27-35	Repealed by Acts 1948, p. 994
27-36	27-51
27-37	27-52
27-38	27-53
27-39	27-54
32-291	32-291
32-292	32-292
32-293	32-293
32-294	32-294
32-295	Repealed by Acts 1948, p. 1108
32-296	32-296
32-354	32-354
32-355	32-355
32-356	32-356
32-357	32-357
32-358	32-358
32-359	32-359
32-360	32-360
32-361	32-361
32-362	32-362
32-363	32-363
32-364	32-364
41-1	41-1
41-2	41-2
41-3	41-3
41-4	41-4
41-5	41-5
41-6	41-6
41-7	41-7
41-8	41-8
41-8.1	41-8.1
41-9	41-9
41-10	41-10
41-11	41-11
41-12	41-12
41-13	41-13
41-14	41-14
41-15	41-15
41-16	41-16
41-17	41-17
41-18	41-18
41-19	41-19
41-20	41-20
41-21	41-21
41-22	41-22
41-23	41-23
41-24	41-24
41-25	41-25
41-26	41-26
41-27	41-27
41-28	41-28
41-29	41-29
41-30	41-30
41-31	41-31
41-32	41-32
41-33	41-33
41-34	41-34
41-35	41-35
41-36	41-36
41-37	41-37
41-38	41-38
41-39	41-39
41-40	41-40
41-41	41-41
41-42	41-42
41-43	41-43
41-44	41-44
41-45	41-45
41-46	41-46
41-47	41-47
41-48	41-48
41-49	41-49
41-50	41-50
41-51	41-51
41-52	41-52
41-53	41-53
41-54	41-54
41-55	41-55
41-56	41-56
41-57	41-57
41-58	41-58
41-59	41-59
41-60	41-60
41-61	41-61

R. P. Section	Code 1950 Section
41-62	41-62
41-63	41-63
41-64	41-64
41-65	41-65
41-66	41-66
41-67	41-67
41-68	41-68
41-69	41-69
41-70	41-70
41-71	41-71
41-72	41-72
41-73	41-73
41-74	41-74
41-75	41-75
41-76	41-76
41-77	41-77
41-78	41-78
41-79	41-79
41-80	41-80
41-81	41-81
41-82	41-82
41-83	41-83
42-58	42-58
42-59	42-59
42-60	42-60
42-61	42-61
42-62	42-62
42-63	42-63
42-63.1	42-64, 42-65
44-8	44-8
44-9	44-9
44-10	44-10
44-11	44-11
44-12	44-12
44-13	44-13, 44-14
44-14	44-15
44-15	44-16
44-17	44-17
44-18	44-18
44-19	44-19
44-20	44-20
44-21	44-21
44-22	44-22
44-23	44-23
44-24	44-24
44-112	44-112
44-113	44-113
44-114	44-114
44-123	44-123
44-124	44-124
44-127	44-125
44-128	44-126 to 44-128
44-129	44-129
44-130	44-130
44-131	44-131
44-132	44-132
44-133	44-133
44-134	44-134
44-135	44-135
44-136	44-136
44-137	44-137
44-138	44-138
44-139	44-139
44-140	44-140
51-30	51-30
51-31	51-31
51-32	51-32
51-33	51-33
51-34	51-34
51-35	51-35
51-36	51-36
51-37	51-37
51-38	51-38
51-39	51-39
51-40	51-40
51-41	51-41
51-42	51-42
51-43	51-43
51-44	51-44
51-45	51-45
51-46	51-46
51-47	51-47
51-48	51-48
51-49	51-49
51-50	51-50
51-51	51-51
51-52	51-52
51-53	51-53
51-54	51-54
51-55	51-55
51-56	51-56
51-57	51-57
51-58	51-58
51-59	51-59
51-60	51-60
51-61	51-61
51-62	51-62
51-63	51-63
51-64	51-64
51-65	51-65
51-66	51-66
51-67	51-67
51-68	51-68
51-69	51-69
51-70	51-70
51-71	51-71
51-72	51-72
51-73	51-73
51-74	51-74
51-75	51-75
51-76	51-76
51-77	51-77
51-78	51-78
51-79	51-79
51-80	51-80
51-81	51-81
51-82	51-82
51-83	51-83
51-84	51-84
51-85	51-85
51-86	51-86
51-87	51-87
51-88	51-88
51-89	51-89
51-90	51-90
51-91	51-91
51-92	51-92
51-93	51-93
51-94	51-94
51-95	51-95
51-96	51-96
51-97	51-97
51-98	51-98
51-99	51-99
51-100	51-100
51-101	51-101
51-102	51-102
51-103	51-103
51-104	51-104
51-105	51-105
51-106	51-106
51-107	51-107
51-108	51-108
51-109	51-109
51-110	51-110
51-111	51-111
52-1	52-1
52-2	52-2
52-3	52-3
52-4	52-4
52-5	52-5
52-6	52-6
52-7	52-7
52-8	52-8
52-9	52-9
52-10	52-10
52-11	52-11
52-11.1	52-11.1
53-1	53-1
53-11	53-2
53-12	53-3
53-14	53-4, 53-5
53-15	53-6, 53-7
53-16	53-8, 53-9
53-17	53-10 to 53-17
53-18	53-18
53-19	53-19
53-20	53-20
53-21	53-21
53-22	53-22
53-23	53-23
53-24	53-24
53-25	53-25
53-26	53-26
53-27	53-27
53-28	53-28
53-29	53-29
53-30	53-30
53-31	53-31
53-32	53-32
53-33	53-33
53-34	53-34
53-35	53-35

TABLE OF REORGANIZATION PROVISIONS OF 1948

R. P. Section	Code 1950 Section
53-36	53-36
53-37	53-37
53-38	53-38
53-39	53-39
53-40	53-40
53-41	53-41
53-42	53-42
53-43	53-43
53-44	53-44
53-45	53-45
53-46	53-46
53-47	53-47
53-48	53-48
53-49	53-49
53-50	53-50
53-51	53-51
53-52	53-52
53-53	53-53
53-54	53-54
53-55	53-55
53-56	53-56
53-57	53-57
53-58	53-58
53-59	53-59
53-60	53-60
53-61	53-61
53-62	53-62
53-63	53-63
53-64	53-64
53-65	53-65
53-66	53-66
53-67	53-67
53-68	53-68
53-69	53-69
53-70	53-70
53-71	53-71
53-72	53-72
53-73	53-73
53-74	53-74
53-75	53-75
53-76	53-76
53-77	53-77
53-78	53-78
53-79	53-79
53-80	53-80
53-81	53-81
53-82	53-82
53-83	53-83
53-84	53-84
53-85	53-85
53-86	53-86
53-87	53-87
53-89	53-88, 53-89
53-90	53-90
53-91	53-91
53-92	53-92
53-93	53-93
53-94	53-94
53-95	53 95
53-96	53-96
53-97	53-97

R. P. Section	Code 1950 Section
53-98	53-98
53-99	53-99
53-100	53-100
53-101	53-101
53-102	53-102
53-102.1	53-102.1
53-103	53-103
53-104	53-104
53-105	53-105
53-106	53-106
53-107	53-107
53-108	53-108
53-109	53-109
53-110	53-110
53-111	53-111
53-112	53-112
53-113	53-113
53-114	53-114
53-115	53-115
53-116	53-116
53-117	53-117
53-118	53-118
53-119	53-119
53-120	53-120
53-121	53-121
53-122	53-122
53-123	53-123
53-123.1	53-123.1
53-124	53-124
53-125	53-125
53-126	53-126
53-127	53-127
53-128	53-128
53-129	53-129
53-130	53-130
53-131	53-131
53-132	53-132
53-133	53-133
53-134	53-134
53-135	53-135
53-135.1	53-135.1
53-136	53-136
53-137	53-137
53-138	53-138
53-139	53-139
53-140	53-140
53-141	53-141
53-142	53-142
53-143	53-143
53-144	53-144
53-145	53-145
53-146	53-146
53-147	53-147
53-148	53-148
53-149	53-149
53-150	53-150
53-151	53-151
53-152	53-152
53-153	53-153
53-154	53-154
53-155	53-155

R. P. Section	Code 1950 Section
53-156	53-156
53-157	53-157
53-158	53-158
53-159	53-159
53-160	53-160
53-161	53-161
53-162	53-162
53-162.1	53-162.1
53-163	53-163
53-164	53-164
53-165	53-165
53-166	53-166
53-167	53-167
53-168	53-168
53-169	53-169
53-170	53-170
53-171	53-171
53-172	53-172
53-173	53-173
53-174	53-174
53-175	53-175
53-176	53-176
53-177	53-177
53-178	53-178
53-179	53-179
53-180	53-180
53-181	53-181
53-182	53-182
53-183	53-183
53-183.1	53-183.1
53-184	53-184
53-185	53-185
53-186	53-186
53-187	53-187
53-188	53-188
53-189	53-189
53-190	53-190
53-191	53-191
53-192	53-192
53-193	53-193
53-194	53-194
53-195	53-195
53-196	53-196
53-197	53-197
53-198	53-198
53-199	53-199
53-200	53-200
53-201	53-201
53-202	53-202
53-203	53-203
53-204	53-204
53-204.1	53-204.1
53-205	53-205
53-206	53-206
53-207	53-207
53-208	53-208
53-209	53-209
53-210	53-210
53-211	53-211
53-212	53-212
53-213	53-213

R. P. Section	Code 1950 Section
53-214	53-214
53-215	53-215
53-216	53-216
53-217	53-217
53-218	53-218
53-219	53-219
53-220	53-220
53-220.1	53-220.1
53-221	53-221
53-222	53-222
53-223	53-223
53-224	53-224
53-225	53-225
53-226	53-226
53-227	53-227
53-228	53-228
53-229	53-229
53-232	53-230
53-233	53-231
53-234	53-232
53-235	53-233
53-236	53-234, 53-235
53-237	53-236, 53-237
53-238	53-238
53-239	53-239
53-240	53-240
53-241	53-241
53-242	53-242
53-243	53-243
53-244	53-244
53-245	53-245
53-246	53-246
53-247	53-247
53-248	53-248
53-249	53-249
53-250	53-250
53-251	53-251
53-252	53-252
53-253	53-253
53-254	53-254
53-255	53-255
53-256	53-256
53-257	53-257
53-258	53-258
53-259	53-259
53-260	53-260
53-261	53-261
53-262	53-262
53-263	53-263
53-264	53-264
53-265	53-265
53-266	53-266
53-267	53-267
53-268	53-268
53-269	53-269
53-270	53-270
53-271	53-271
53-272	53-272
53-273	53-273
53-274	53-274
53-275	53-275
53-276	53-276
53-277	53-277
53-278	53-278
53-278.1	19-214.1, 53-278.1
53-279	53-279
53-280	53-280
53-281	53-281
53-282	53-282
53-283	53-283
53-284	53-284
53-285	53-285
53-286	53-286
53-287	53-287
53-288	53-288
53-289	53-289
53-290	53-290
53-291	53-291
53-292	53-292
53-293	53-293
53-294	53-294
53-295	53-295
53-296	53-296
53-297	53-297
53-298	53-298
53-299	53-299
53-300	53-300
53-301	53-301
53-302	53-302
53-303	53-303
53-304	53-304
54-860	54-860
54-861	54-861
54-862	54-862
54-863	54-863
54-864	54-864
54-865	54-865
54-866	54-866
54-867	54-867
54-868	54-868
59-177	59-177
59-178	59-178
59-179	59-179
59-180	59-180
59-181	59-181
59-182	59-182
59-183	59-183
59-184	59-184
59-185	59-185
59-186	59-186
59-187	59-187
59-188	59-188
59-189	59-189
59-189.1	59-189.1
59-190	59-190
59-191	59-191
59-192	59-192
59-193	59-193
59-194	59-194
59-195	59-195
59-196	59-196
59-197	59-197
59-198	59-198
59-199	59-199
62-107	62-107
62-108	62-108
62-109	62-109
62-110	62-110
62-111	62-111
62-112	62-112
62-113	62-113
62-114	62-114
62-115	62-115
62-116	62-116
62-117	62-117
63-1	63-1
63-2	63-2
63-3	63-3
63-4	63-4
63-5	63-5
63-6	63-6
63-7	63-7
63-8	63-8
63-9	63-9
63-10	63-10
63-11	63-11
63-12	63-12
63-13	63-13
63-14	63-14
63-15	63-15
63-16	63-16
63-17	63-17
63-18	63-18
63-19	63-19
63-20	63-20
63-21	63-21
63-22	63-22
63-23	63-23
63-24	63-24
63-25	63-25
63-26	63-26
63-27	63-27
63-28	63-28
63-29	63-29
63-30	63-30
63-31	63-31
63-32	63-32
63-33	63-33
63-34	63-34
63-35	63-35, 63-36
63-36	63-37
63-37	63-38
63-38	63-39
63-39	63-40, 63-41
63-40	63-42
63-41	63-43
63-42	63-44, 63-45
63-43	63-46
63-44	63-47
63-45	63-48
63-46	63-49
63-50	63-50

TABLE OF REORGANIZATION PROVISIONS OF 1948

R. P. Section	Code 1950 Section
63-51	63-51
63-52	63-52
63-53	63-53
63-54	63-54
63-55	63-55
63-56	63-56
63-57	63-57
63-58	63-58
63-59	63-59
63-60	63-60
63-61	63-61
63-62	63-62
63-63	63-63
63-64	63-64
63-65	63-65
63-66	63-66
63-67	63-67
63-68	63-68
63-69	63-69
63-70	63-70
63-71	63-71
63-72	63-72
63-73	73-73
63-74	63-74
63-75	63-75
63-76	63-76
63-77	63-77
63-78	63-78
63-79	63-79
63-80	63-80
63-81	63-81
63-82	63-82
63-83	63-83
63-84	63-84
63-85	63-85
63-86	63-86
63-87	63-87
63-88	63-88
63-89	63-89
63-90	63-90
63-91	63-91
63-92	63-92
63-93	63-93
63-94	63-94
63-95	63-95
63-96	63-96
63-97	63-97
63-98	63-98
63-99	63-99
63-100	63-100
63-101	63-101
63-102	63-102
63-103	63-103
63-104	63-104
63-105	63-105
63-106	63-106
63-107	63-107
63-108	63-108
63-109	63-109
63-110	63-110
63-111	63-111

R. P. Section	Code 1950 Section
63-112	63-112
63-113	63-113
63-114	63-114
63-115	63-115
63-116	63-116
63-117	63-117
63-118	63-118
63-119	63-119
63-120	63-120
63-121	63-121
63-122	63-122
63-123	63-123
63-124	63-124
63-125	63-125
63-126	Repealed by Acts 1948, p. 1111
63-127	63-126
63-128	63-127, 63-128
63-129	63-129
63-130	63-130
63-131	63-131
63-132	63-132
63-133	63-133
63-134	63-134
63-135	63-135
63-136	63-136
63-137	63-137
63-138	63-138
63-139	63-139
63-140	63-140
63-141	63-141
63-142	63-142
63-143	63-143
63-144	63-144
63-145	63-145
63-146	63-146
63-147	63-147
63-148	63-148
63-149	63-149
63-150	63-150
63-151	63-151
63-152	63-152
63-153	63-153
63-154	63-154
63-155	63-155
63-156	63-156
63-157	63-157
63-158	63-158
63-159	63-159
63-160	63-160
63-161	63-161
63-162	63-162
63-163	63-163
63-164	63-164
63-165	63-165
63-166	63-166
63-167	63-167
63-168	63-168
63-169	63-169
63-170	63-170
63-171	63-171

R. P. Section	Code 1950 Section
63-172	63-172
63-173	63-173
63-174	63-174
63-175	63-175
63-176	63-176
63-177	63-177
63-178	63-178
63-179	63-179
63-180	63-180
63-181	63-181
63-182	63-182
63-183	63-183
63-184	63-184
63-185	63-185
63-186	63-186
63-187	63-187
63-188	63-188
63-189	63-189
63-190	Repealed by Acts 1948, p. 1111
63-191	63-190
63-192	63-191, 63-192
63-193	63-193
63-194	63-194
63-195	63-195
63-196	63-196
63-197	63-197
63-198	63-198
63-199	63-199
63-200	63-200
63-201	63-201
63-202	63-202
63-203	63-203
63-204	63-204
63-205	63-205
63-206	63-206
63-207	63-207
63-208	63-208
63-209	63-209
63-210	63-210
63-211	63-211
63-212	63-212
63-213	63-213
63-214	63-214
63-215	63-215
63-216	63-216
63-217	63-217
63-218	63-218
63-219	63-219
63-220	63-220
63-221	63-221
63-222	63-222
63-223	63-223
63-224	63-224
63-225	63-225
63-226	63-226
63-227	63-227
63-228	63-228
63-229	63-229
63-230	63-230
63-231	63-231

R. P. Section	Code 1950 Section
63-232	63-232
63-233	63-233
63-234	63-234
63-235	63-235
63-236	63-236
63-237	63-237
63-238	63-238
63-239	63-239
63-240	63-240
63-241	63-241
63-242	63-242
63-243	63-243
63-244	63-244
63-245	63-245
63-246	63-246
63-247	63-247
63-248	63-248
63-249	63-249
63-250	63-250
63-251	63-251
63-252	63-252
63-253	63-253
63-254	63-254
63-255	63-255
63-256	63-256
63-257	63-257
63-258	63-258
63-259	63-259
63-260	63-260
63-261	63-261
63-262	63-262
63-263	63-263
63-264	63-264
63-265	63-265
63-266	63-266
63-267	63-267
63-268	63-268
63-269	63-269
63-270	63-270
63-271	63-271
63-272	63-272
63-273	63-273
63-274	63-274
63-275	63-275
63-276	63-276
63-277	63-277
63-278	63-278
63-279	63-279
63-280	63-280
63-281	63-281
63-282	63-282
63-283	63-283
63-284	63-284
63-285	63-285
63-286	63-286
63-287	63-287
63-288	63-288
63-289	63-289
63-290	63-290
63-291	63-291
63-292	63-292
63-293	63-293
63-294	63-294
63-295	63-295
63-296	63-296
63-297	63-297
63-298	63-298
63-299	63-299
63-300	63-300
63-301	63-301
63-302	63-302
63-303	63-303
63-304	63-304
63-305	63-305
63-306	63-306
63-307	63-307
63-347	63-347
63-348	63-348
63-349	63-349
63-350	63-350
63-351	63-351
63-352	63-352
63-353	63-353
63-354	63-354
63-355	63-355
63-356	63-356
63-357	63-357
63-358	63-358
63-359	63-359
63-360	63-360
63-361	63-361
63-362	63-362
63-363	63-363
63-364	63-364
63-365	63-365
63-366	63-366
63-367	63-367
63-368	63-368
63-369	63-369
63-370	63-370
63-371	63-371
63-372	63-372
63-373	63-373
63-374	63-374
63-375	63-375
63-376	63-376
63-377	63-377
63-378	63-378

Table of Acts Through 1948 Not Previously Codified

SHOWING ACTS PASSED AT THE SESSIONS OF THE GENERAL ASSEMBLY HELD DURING THE YEARS 1918 THROUGH 1948, WHICH ARE CODIFIED IN THE CODE OF 1950, BUT WHICH WERE NOT CODIFIED IN MICHIE CODE OF 1942 OR MICHIE SUPPLEMENT OF 1948, AND CORRESPONDING SECTIONS OF THE CODE OF 1950.

Acts Year and Page	Code 1950 Section
1918, p. 752	22-253
1922, p. 184	24-119
1922, p. 641	22-253
1922, p. 862	22-188
1926, p. 530	19-92.1
1927, p. 192	2-270
1927, p. 210	33-112
1928, p. 324	23-30
1928, p. 1214	22-253
1930, p. 29	22-253
1930, p. 862	17-20
1932, pp. 884, 885	23-142 to 23-146
1933, p. 29	60-89
1933, pp. 83-92	23-14 to 23-29
1934, p. 14	15-574
1934, p. 55	22-188
1934, pp. 271, 272	9-78 to 9-84
1934, p. 292	15-760
1936, p. 81	24-119
1936, pp. 336-338	9-78 to 9-84
1936, p. 342	2-270
1936, p. 377	51-114
1936, p. 440	58-769
1936, p. 522	23-77.1
1936, p. 550	33-28, 33-29
1936-37, p. 28	23-19
1936-37, p. 141	22-188
1938, p. 11	15-551
1938, p. 16	58-894
1938, p. 117	58-769
1938, p. 321	22-188
1938, pp. 486, 487	23-142 to 23-146
1940, pp. 135-137	32-379 to 32-387
1940, p. 298	16-65
1942, p. 194	58-769
1942, p. 343	58-769
1942, p. 346	58-769
1942, p. 433	38-523.1
1942, p. 519	58-769
1942, p. 531	23-36

Acts Year and Page	Code 1950 Section
1942, p. 592	46-153.1, 58-645
1944, p. 10	22-10
1944, p. 12	24-119
1944, p. 70	58-769
1944, p. 293	15-550
1944, p. 304	58-769
1944, p. 348	58-768.1
1944, p. 357	15-574
1944, p. 432	59-144
1944, p. 436	24-119
1944, p. 437	51-127.10, 51-127.11, 51-127.13 to 51-127.15, 51-127.17, 51-127.19 to 51-127.21, 51-127.25 to 51-127.29
1944, p. 443	21-120
1944, p. 449	24-119
1944, p. 621	24-119
1944, p. 636	15-507
1945, pp. 41, 42	56-291.4 to 56-291.8
1945, p. 49	2-93.1
1945, p. 61	22-253
1945, p. 82	15-758
1946, p. 20	58-894
1946, p. 64	21-121, 21-140
1946, p. 65	56-291.4, 58-769
1946, p. 94	7-23
1946, p. 113	21-427
1946, p. 166	17-126
1946, pp. 183-187	23-14, 23-15, 23-18 to 23-21
1946, p. 200	15-764
1946, p. 201	24-119
1946, p. 233	15-574
1946, p. 234	51-114
1946, p. 245	3-579.1
1946, p. 246	58-769
1946, p. 258	15-756
1946, p. 296	58-769
1946, p. 297	15-914
1946, p. 339	4-45.1

Acts Year and Page	Code 1950 Section
1946, p. 402	58-769
1946, p. 424	23-36
1946, p. 469	51-114
1946, p. 476	51-114
1946, p. 651	7-23
1946, p. 652	21-120
1946, p. 716	15-795
1947, p. 13	51-114
1947, p. 58	58-769
1947, p. 60	15-551
1947, p. 61	51-114
1947, p. 63	24-119
1947, p. 64	21-139
1947, p. 70	58-769
1947, p. 74	56-291.4, 56-291.5
1947, p. 76	58-781
1947, p. 144	4-45.1
1948, p. 55	21-291.1
1948, p. 59	17-83.1
1948, p. 74	24-119
1948, p. 77	58-986.1
1948, p. 78	24-119
1948, p. 91	51-114
1948, p. 102	58-769
1948, p. 115	21-120
1948, p. 118	21-139
1948, p. 129	15-26.1
1948, p. 174	15-24.2
1948, p. 276	62-67.1, 62-67.2
1948, pp. 281, 282	62-67.3 to 62-67.10
1948, p. 326	58-784
1948, p. 337	15-761.1
1948, p. 333	15-756, 15-761.1
1948, p. 352	28-88.2
1948, p. 418	42-60.1
1948, p. 491	32-386
1948, pp. 497-500	9-69 to 9-77
1948, pp. 500, 518	24-119
1948, p. 560	28-57.1
1948, p. 567	28-88.1

Acts Year and Page	Code 1950 Section
1948, p. 584	28-90.1, 58-784
1948, p. 587	30-14.1
1948, p. 689	15-222.1 to 15-222.3
1948, p. 692	15-230, 15-231.1, 15-231.2
1948, p. 693	15-231.3, 15-705
1948, p. 718	15-759.1
1948, p. 729	15-26.1
1948, pp. 729, 730	15-927 to 15-936
1948, p. 731	28-250.1
1948, p. 807	24-119
1948, p. 853	22-253
1948, p. 905	15-574
1948, p. 958	63-52.1
1948, p. 1007	15-795
1948, p. 1083	23-36
1948, p. 1085	23-36.1
1948, p. 1119	22-20.1

Table of Acts Codified Subsequent to 1948

ACTS 1950

Acts 1950 Page	Code 1950 Section
3	8-1.2, 30-14.3
4	21-121.1, 21-140.1
6	30-22.1, 63-204.14
7	27-29.1, 30-14.2
8	15-241
9	15-605
10	58-778
12-15	22-146.1 to 22-146.9
16	3-82, 3-83, 22-146.10, 22-146.11
17	3-89
18	3-95, 3-116
19	8-11, 18-55.1
20-24	1-13 to 1-13.34
25	14-116
26	15-705.2
28	15-94.1
29-33	45-145 to 45-157
33	63-367
35	15-130, 58-863
36	18-131
37	18-317
39	37-97
40	59-61 to 59-70R
41-46	59-61.1 to 59-61.11
47	42-66, 59-61.12
48	10-133R, 10-134R, 15-574.1, 42-67
50	39-4
51	46-259.1
52	17-7
54	46-279.1, 46-306, 56-232
55	54-765, 56-234
56	58-1104
58	10-76, 10-79, 10-80, 10-83
59	58-897.1
60	6-543.1, 6-543.2, 58-769, subsec. (8)R
61	6-543.3, 58-12
66	61-156 to 61-158
67	29-194.1, 61-159, 61-160
68	8-76, 8-794
69, 70	17-228 to 17-231
70	8-388
71	14-87, 15-239
72	20-104
73	54-280.1
73, 74	54-308.1 to 54-308.4
75	54-324, 54-325, 58-266.3
76	21-3
77	21-6
78	8-38
80	14-57
83	58-371.2
84	46-216
86	32-181
87	32-379
89	51-47, 51-48
91	57-39.1
92	28-122.1
93	6-232
94	17-119.1, 46-193
96	8-701.1
97	15-480
98	54-274
99	14-51
101	2-29
102	22-253.1
103	51-62
107	15-336
108	15-306.1
108, 109	32-104.1 to 32-104.4
110	54-273
111	54-282, 54-284
112	54-301 to 54-303, 54-308
113	15-10
114	19-29
116	58-376
123	15-362, 15-370
124	15-372
125	15-376
126	15-383
130	45-94 to 45-105R
130-144	45-106 to 45-144
145	33-228
147	33-234, 33-251
149	22-133.1, 29-65
150	52-7
151	15-220
152	22-126, 22-128
152, 153	27-86 to 27-90
154	27-85.1, 52-9.1, 52-91.2
155	58-266.1, 58-266.2
156	45-80, 45-81, 58-266.3
157	33-155, 65-54
161	23-50.1, 23-50.2
161, 162	33-50.2 to 33-50.5
163	58-320, 58-399R
164	24-193, 24-194
165	24-225, 24-265
166, 167	28-243.26 to 28-243.33
168	28-243.21 to 28-243.33
169	28-243.1, 28-243.24, 28-243.25
170-176	28-243.2 to 28-243.20
176	15-850
178	15-850.1
179	38-371
181	38-366.1
183	15-781
184	63-69.1, 63-69.2
185	33-113.2, 63-69-3
187	32-388 to 32-390, 55-248.1
188	44-160 to 44-203R
221	46-40
224	58-834.1
225	10-34.2
226	22-161
227	3-501, 38-192R
228	3-284R, 3-322R, 15-356.1
229	28-198.1, 46-31, 46-171 to 46-173R
230	24-251
231	38-397
238	38-398, 38-412
239	54-836.1
240	46-64
241	38-189
242	2-27.1, 2-28R, 38-495
243	32-276, 32-278
244	32-285, 32-288, 46-142
245	24-130, 24-207
246	15-590.2, 15-590.3, 24-290.1
247	2-128 to 17-137.4
249	46-165, 46-361, 46-377R
251	46-63
252	63-28
253	24-220
258, 259	2-38.1 to 2-38.3
284	24-92
315	15-555
316	15-24.1R, 27-38R, 58-839
317	58-844
318	29-36.1

Acts 1950 Page	Code 1950 Section
319	21-120
322	58-341
323	15-504.1
349	29-209
353	54-165, 54-181
354	3-360.1
355	22-164.1
356	22-164.2, 26-6, 53-140
357	58-534
360	2-291.1, 60-63
361	24-119
366	23-19
368	56-273
370	56-274
372	8-174, 8-178
374	8-182
377	38-221
379	38-203
380	38-213
381	24-118, 38-253.26, 38-253.33, 38-557
385	13-78
386, 387	13-35, 13-35.1
388	8-61, 8-62, 8-65
389	11-17
390	15-678.1
392	29-205
393	28-212
394	10-21
395	15-167
396	15-268
397	15-340
398	15-360
399	15-495
400	33-48.1
401	33-49.1, 33-49.2, 58-730
403	38-253.21
404	13-265, 38-65
405	3-150.1
406	29-202
407	46-65, 56-337.1
408-410	9-88 to 9-95
410	58-943.1
411	15-481, 29-129.1
412-416	15-551.1 to 15-551.11
423	59-214
437	58-375.1
440	8-378.1, 18-161
441	29-155.2, 29-155.3, 63-348.1
442	18-74, 29-155.4, 29-155.5
443	15-67, 17-136
444, 445	15-551.12 to 15-551.15
445	18-302
446	20-49
447	19-11, 53-184
448	14-181
449	8-468.1, 54-762
451	22-240.1
452, 453	22-43 to 22-43.3
453	33-279.1
454	14-155.4, 14-155.5
455	8-59.1
456	16-91
457	26-48
458	33-173.1
459	8-669, 13-190
460	55-36
461	13-46
462	13-47, 24-182
463	15-504, 24-183
464	1-13.35
465	1-13.36, 22-67
467	8-692, 64-18
468-470	54-864 to 54-868
471	28-88.4
472	22-152, 22-153, 28-88.5
473	22-154
474	51-114, subsec. (5)R, 54-432, 54-433
475	56-261.1
476	13-245, 33-38, 33-39
477	17-69.1, 22-175
478	13-96.1, 56-407
480	46-327, 59-101.1
481	56-232
483	18-160
484, 485	32-337 to 32-337.3
486	1-13.37, 22-151.1
487	15-900
488	15-824
489	15-825, 56-261.2
490	15-64, 22-67
588-595	56-485 to 56-508
596	58-769
597	58-1118
598	58-1130 to 58-1132
599-601	56-265.1 to 56-265.9
602	35-62.1
603	15-705, 32-293.1, 32-294
604	8-279.1, 8-279.2
606	9-85, 9-86, 64-173
607	9-87
612	19-73
613	20-61
614	14-123
618	17-127.1
619	29-52, 59-220, 59-221
620	8-67.1
621	19-165, 46-155
624	63-119
625	46-160, 46-168
626	46-138, 63-356.1
627	29-52
628	56-47
630	56-334
632	2-155.1, 57-5
633	16-70
634	20-121, 63-373
635	58-404.1
636	40-62.1, 40-62.2
637	13-247.1, 14-66
639	28-90.1R, 46-447.1
640	8-266, 58-792.2
641	63-67.1 to 63-67.3
659	19-23, 58-14, 58-16
660	58-153, 58-626.1
662	29-202, 58-306
663	22-277
664	2-132, 8-288
665	46-328
665-690	16-172.1 to 16-172.84
690	16-130 to 16-172R, 46-264, 63-257 to 63-288R, 63-294 to 63-307R
691	46-210, 46-317
692	2-138
693	46-45
694	15-362, 15-370
695, 696	15-372 to 15-374
696	15-382.1
698	46-261, 46-262, 46-297
699	46-298
700	29-184.1, 58-776.1, 58-776.2
701	6-234, 58-776.3, 58-776.4
703	59-20
704	59-30R, 59-40
722	15-793
723	15-803, 15-814
724	26-59, 33-156 to 33-158R
725	15-766
726	33-141
727	33-76 to 33-18R
727-737	33-76.1 to 33-76.24
737	51-98
738	56-209
739	56-224, 56-226
740	15-504.1, 55-13.1
741	18-282.1, 20-71.1

TABLE OF ACTS CODIFIED SUBSEQUENT TO 1948

Acts 1950 Page	Code 1950 Section
773	58-769
774, 775	20-88.1 to 20-88.11
776	14-97
818	26-37
819	24-194.1R, 24-194.2
849	15-274.1
850	46-247
851	15-748, 58-897
866	29-150.1
869	21-120
872	14-57
876	4-61
877	4-81
879	4-59
880	46-209
881	46-212
882	46-213R, 46-214R, 46-219.1, 51-110.1
883-886	51-128 to 51-142
886	54-751
888	19-78.1, 46-454, 52-20
889	15-891R, 15-891.1, 15-891.2, 15-892 to 15-898R
890, 891	15-891.3 to 15-891.9
891	29-151
892	46-204
893	58-316
894	58-346, 58-354
895	58-115.1, 64-122
896	15-717.1, 15-717.2, 56-367
897, 898	53-278.2 to 53-278.4
898	58-638.1
899	37-1.1, 37-3
900	37-7, 37-9, 37-14
901	37-16, 37-17, 37-24, 37-26, 37-32, 37-34.1, 37-39, 37-40
902	37-41, 27-42, 37-42.1, 37-46, 37-47, 37-53, 37-61
903	37-63, 37-67, 37-81, 37-83 to 37-85
904-907	37-68 to 37-80
908	37-81, 37-83 to 37-85, 37-86.1, 37-86.2
909-912	37-87 to 37-96
913	37-98, 37-99, 37-102
914	37-103, 37-105, 37-108
915	37-109 to 37-111, 37-113
916	37-119, 37-121 to 37-125
917, 918	37-125.1 to 37-127
919	37-128, 37-132 to 37-133
920-922	37-134 to 37-140
923	37-141, 37-143, 37-145
924	37-153 to 37-154, 37-158
925	37-176 to 37-178, 37-180 to 37-182
926	37-182.1 to 37-185
927	37-186, 37-187, 37-189, 37-190
928	37-192, 37-194, 37-195
929	37-196, 37-200 to 37-205
930-932	37-206 to 37-216
933	37-219, 37-221 to 37-224
934	37-225, 37-226, 37-231, 37-241, 37-249
935	37-254 to 37-255, 37-257.1, 37-257.2
936	29-163, 37-43R, 37-82R, 37-179R, 37-258
937	23-159, 23-163.1
938	46-338.1
939	53-109, 53-109.1
940, 941	24-118.1 to 24-118.3
941	46-257
942	46-250, 58-721
944	33-179, 56-414
945	58-988, 58-989
946	51-52, 58-992 to 58-995R
947	22-280.1, 43-53
948	8-628.1
949	46-418
950	58-145.1
951, 952	22-166.1 to 22-166.4
953	2-218.1, 2-221, 22-166.5, 22-166.6
954	22-228
955	2-232
956	2-239.1
957	2-240, 2-246
958	2-218R, 2-239R, 2-241R, 2-247, 63-220.1
965-968	58-86.2 to 58-86.5
968	16-50
971	14-163.1
973	14-164R, 22-107.1
974	15-338, 22-107.2
976	28-136
978	28-209
979	28-3, 28-217
980	28-45
981	28-47, 28-50.1, 28-50.2
982	18-147.1, 46-326
983-987	54-200.1 to 54-200.22
987	15-152.1, 28-123
988	28-158
990	28-7, 54-109
991	54-110
993	38-178, 38-179
994	38-184 to 38-186
995	38-190
996	38-49
997	22-37
998	22-20.1R, 22-109, 22-211R, 38-428
1005-1010	3-209 to 3-211
1012-1015	3-213 to 3-215
1016	38-225, 58-346, 58-352
1017	58-772.1
1018	28-51
1019	15-766.1, 19-94.1
1020	15-766.2
1028-1031	3-228.1 to 3-228.12
1031	2-181
1032	38-218.10
1033	38-253.43, 38-253.44
1145	15-795
1147	28-88.1, 28-88.3
1164	11-6
1165	21-116.1
1166	17-41
1216	23-51, 23-52
1220	51-114
1244-1248	15-705.3, 15-714.1 to 15-714.9
1266	58-780, 58-782, 58-783
1267	58-784, 58-784.2 to 58-785
1268	58-795.1
1269	58-774.1, 58-774.2, 58-777R, 58-779R, 58-781R, 58-784.1R
1270	56-355.1, 58-775R
1271	2-244
1272, 1273	23-135.1 to 23-135.5
1273	29-188.1

Acts 1950 Page	Code 1950 Section
1289-1292	23-35.1 to 23-35.13, 23-36R, 23-36.1R
1294	56-366
1295	58-78
1298	58-81
1303	58-82, 58-84
1304	58-98
1306	58-105
1307	58-119, 58-120
1308	58-121.1, 58-122
1309	58-81, 58-99R, 58-100R
1311	22-101.1, 22-101.2
1312	18-74.1
1312-1330	15-764.1 to 15-764.32
1520, 1521	46-249.1 to 46-249.4
1521	51-110
1522	51-31
1524	51-47
1525	51-62
1526	51-82
1527	51-99
1528	51-101
1591	15-231.4
1596	28-4.1, 37-75
1597	46-436
1599-1603	59-10 to 59-19.1
1603	58-402
1604	46-503, 58-402.1
1607	15-222.3
1608	15-224
1609	15-222.4
1610	6-148
1610-1614	16-739.1 to 16-739.6

ACTS 1952

Acts 1952 Chapter	Code 1950 Section
1	51-30 to 51-111R, 51-111.68
2	51-111.1 to 51-111.8
4	24-120, 24-121, 24-213, 24-349, 24-356, 24-359, 24-365, 24-387, 24-389, 24-390, 24-397, 24-402 to 24-406
5	17-127
8	53-220
11	15-591
12	11-20
13	29-209
14	65-16
15	51-111.72 to 51-111.74
16	15-253
17	33-26
19	22-306.1
20	58-776.5
22	6-205
23	6-76
24	6-93R
25	6-78
26	21-118.2
28	16-88, 16-172.9
29	51-29.1 to 51-29.7
30	60-14
32	58-86.4
34	17-79
35	62-117.6, 62-117.7
36	15-24.3
37	15-338
38	58-266.3
39	58-851.1
41	33-7
43	15-24.2
47	51-111.73, 51-111.74
48	51-111.2
49	15-360.1
50	58-12
51	58-81
52	28-243.34 to 28-243.63
53	28-243.1 to 28-243.33R
54	19-123
55	29-184.2
56	2-20.1
57	16-82
58	16-19
59	51-112
60	8-636
61	62-106.1 to 62-106.9, 62-107 to 62-117R
62	63-183
68	6-12.1
70	6-253
71	63-355
72	22-79
74	23-9.1
75	6-26, 6-29.1
76	6-83 to 6-90R
77	8-56
78	29-163, 29-163.1
79	19-32
80	55-275
81	58-85.1
82	58-1141
83	23-7.1
84	58-397
87	22-149
88	13-192
89	14-135
90	6-196
91	14-155.4
93	27-27.1
95	59-218
96	29-140.1
97	28-50.1R
99	56-405
100	20-91, 20-121
101	13-190
102	30-19.2
103	8-750, 8-751
104	19-124
108	57-26
109	55-125
111	2-22.1
112	15-485
113	21-118
114	8-178
115	20-46
117	15-11
118	3-27.1 to 3-27.5
119	2-80
120	2-29
121	44-141 to 44-142.2, 44-144 to 44-145.6, 44-146.1
122	8-296
123	33-76.21
124	33-76.5
125	15-778
126	58-1038
127	33-76.12
128	63-5.1
129	8-182
131	4-40, 4-108
132	55-186 to 55-186.2
133	20-37.1
134	58-391
135	58-644
136	58-412
137	46-340
139	23-31
140	13-229.1
141	19-188
142	53-211, 53-213
143	23-35.3
144	58-51R
145	58-984
146	14-123
147	54-795
148	56-65.1
149	64-127.1
150	2-55
153	25-56 to 25-119R
154	63-309
155	54-212
156	14-153R, 14-154R
157	51-111.9 to 51-111.67
158	24-92
159	15-240
160	24-402
162	15-352.4
164	58-776.1

Acts 1952 Chapter	Code 1950 Section
166	13-273.1
168	15-287, 15-289
169	46-64
170	22-67
171	53-11, 53-13
172	23-1.1
175	3-1
177	28-20, 28-33.1
178	28-77.1
179	28-249, 28-251
180	28-25.1
181	28-201.2
183	3-209 to 3-211, 3-214
184	60-14, 60-22, 60-42, 60-47, 60-67, 60-68, 60-72, 60-73.1, 60-77.1
185	41-1, 41-3 to 41-7R, 41-8.2, 41-10 to 41-38R, 41-40 to 41-67R, 41-78 to 41-83R, 41-84 to 41-89
186	38.1-644.1, 38.1-644.2
187	15-485.1
188	37-77, 46-414
189	4-102
190	58-496R, 58-497 to 58-502
191	58-64
192	46-45.1
194	8-200
195	29-36.1
196	26-40
197	55-89, 55-90
198	15-352, 15-352.2, 15-353, 15-355.2
200	36-19.1
202	21-116.1
203	15-274.1
205	65-48, 65-49
209	24-121
210	37-257.2R
211	54-305, 54-306
212	24-352
213	23-95
214	17-135
217	53-151
219	18-231.1
220	15-310.1
221	15-861.1
222	15-10.1:1
223	33-255.1 to 33-255.22
224	46-154
225	2-64.1 to 2-64.8
226	65-51, 65-52, 65-62, 65-67, 65-68
227	54-1
228	24-118.5 to 24-118.9
229	58-773.1
230	54-422
231	14-56
232	19-168
233	53-278.1
234	8-1.2, 30-5
235	19-164
236	17-211
237	46-341
240	18-302
241	28-201.1
242	15-304
243	15-371.1
244	55-131, 55-134
245	51-127.1 to 51-127.8
246	15-334.1
248	8-511.1
249	8-694
250	33-114.1
251	46-199
252	8-703
253	58-292
254	16-123.4
255	19-241.1
256	18-8
257	34-30
261	58-295.1
262	17-127.3
264	53-142.1
266	58-769
267	15-222.4
268	15-762
269	15-757
270	18-113
271	58-406
272	23-110
273	22-247R
274	22-242R
275	18-313
276	30-29, 30-31
277	15-16.3
279	22-251
280	22-71
281	58-629 to 58-629.2
282	24-3
283	21-133
284	16-62
285	19-172
286	17-43
287	63-67.3R, 63-68
288	28-52.1
289	15-5.1
290	18-335.1, 18-335.2
291	30-14.4
293	53-306, 58-152, 58-156, 58-159, 58-161.1, 58-161.2, 58-163R, 58-171R, 58-172R, 58-173, 58-176, 64-151
295	15-250
296	58-640
297	53-295
298	18-89.1
299	18-302.1
300	21-120
303	16-78
304	15-253
305	3-80 to 3-117R, 3-117.1 to 3-117.33
306	46-48.1
307	51-18.1
308	3-602 to 3-604
309	19-189
310	9-16, 9-29
312	14-51
313	20-49
316	22-43.3R
317	38-1 to 38-564R, 38.1-1 to 38.1-31.1, 38.1-32 to 38.1-734
318	19-21 to 19-26
319	62-194
320	58-645R
322	14-155.7
323	58-1021.1
326	11-2.1
327	15-504
328	15-125 to 15-152.1R, 15-152.2 to 15-152.28
329	64-121.1
330	24-290.3, 24-290.4
331	14-86, 14-95
332	15-676
333	15-789
334	16-14, 16-29, 16-30, 16-81, 16-91
335	15-487.1
336	15-487
337	33-111
338	29-108
339	29-210
340	29-184.1
341	24-68
342	46-328
343	51-111.70
345	33-107
346	15-273
347	14-57
348	19-214.1
349	19-166, 19-167R
350	57-33
351	62-193
352	46-541
353	51-111.71
355	29-55
357	46-542
358	62-192

Acts 1952 Chapter	Code 1950 Section
359	44-147, 44-151, 8-674 to 8-676, 8-678 to 8-680, 8-682, 8-685 to 8-689.1, 8-689.4
362	51-111.69
363	21-427
364	58-851.3
366	29-68.1
367	29-202
369	15-795
370	55-59, 55-65.1
371	15-605.1 to 15-605.13
372	56-291.8:1
375	55-24
376	56-476.1
377	8-444, 8-445
378	8-628.1
379	22-128.1
381	15-16.2
382	15-560.1
384	8-67.4
385	65-85
386	58-643
387	3-538, 59-112R, 59-114 to 59-114.3
390	53-61
391	54-758
392	2-200.1
393	58-398
395	46-104.2
396	46-363
397	46-377.1
398	56-366R, 56-366.1, 56-367R, 56-368R
399	56-369
400	56-406.1
401	15-714.1 to 15-714.5
403	46-326
404	46-176
405	63-5.2
406	58-687, 58-692.2, 58-710.1 to 58-710.3, 58-713, 58-717
407	58-78
408	56-212
409	63-51, 63-53.1, 63-56, 63-58, 63-61, 63-62, 63-63R, 63-64, 63-69, 63-71 to 63-73, 63-75, 63-75.1, 63-80
410	58-639, 58-639.1
411	56-382
412	10-82
413	15-291
414	58-36
415	46-158
416	10-21.1
417	10-74.1 to 10-76
418	46-166.1
419	16-172.1, 16-172.4, 16-172.6, 16-172.7, 16-172.9, 16-172.11, 16-172.17, 16-172.23, 16-172.25, 16-172.28, 16-172.30, 16-172.31, 16-172.33, 16-172.38, 16-172.39, 16-172.42 to 16-172.44, 16-172.49, 16-172.51, 16-172.52, 16-172.60, 16-172.65 to 16-172.67, 16-172.69 to 16-172.71, 16-172.73R, 16-172.75, 16-172.77 to 16-172.80
420	63-359.1
421	51-127.21
422	15-7.1
423	58-839
424	13-61
427	36-4, 36-4.1, 36-19.2
429	18-43, 18-50R
430	15-764.2
431	8-276.1
432	34-29
433	57-12
434	17-41
436	15-290
437	63-356.2
438	8-373
439	55-139.1
440	15-551.11:1
441	58-371.2
442	15-590.1:1
443	15-350.1
446	14-145
447	58-78.1
448	54-451
449	63-194
450	54-869 to 54-872
451	54-457 to 54-460R, 54-487, 54-499, 54-516
452	58-387.1
453	18-147.1
454	46-334
455	46-305
457	17-153
459	14-155.1
460	58-266.3
461	58-61
462	58-838.19
463	19-74
464	55-88.1, 55-96.1
465	15-233
466	46-322.2
467	18-78
469	55-66.4
470	65-18.1
471	58-1107
472	15-6.1
474	15-355.1
475	18-236R, 46-3
476	38.1-31.2
477	62-31R
478	62-41
479	14-66.1, 14-68.1, 14-69.1, 14-70, 14-71.1
480	37-34.2
481	24-45.1
482	23-107
483	18-349.1 to 18-349.4
484	29-153.1, 29-153.2
485	33-240
486	58-570 to 58-577
487	8-300.1
488	24-319, 24-321
489	24-393 to 24-395.3, 24-431, 24-434 to 24-436
491	4-58
492	37-125.1, 37-125.14, 37-125.15
493	52-11.1
494	42-24 to 42-27, 42-29, 42-30, 42-32
496	4-2
497	56-49
498	46-45, 46-348
499	33-123.1
500	15-295
501	58-284.1
502	23-50
503	42-2, 42-3, 42-8
504	42-4 to 42-7, 42-9, 42-10, 42-12
505	33-45
506	17-111.1, 17-111.2
507	58-851.2
508	46-5
509	24-345.1 to 24-345.15
510	20-88
514	58-946.1
516	20-88.1 to 20-88.11R, 20-88.12 to 20-88.31
517	14-163.1
518	14-155
519	14-155.6
520	18-17
521	15-791.1
522	8-71
523	24-373
524	24-23.1 to 24-23.4
525	40-22.1
526	14-155
527	58-863

Acts 1952 Chapter	Code 1950 Section
528	58-299, 32-117 to 32-119, 32-122, 32-124, 32-126, 32-128, 32-129
531	16-123 to 16-123.3
532	58-355, 63-124, 63-138, 63-149.1, 63-159, 63-188, 63-202, 63-215, 63-218
534	58-638.2
535	4-25, 4-33, 4-38
536	46-52
537	46-104.1
538	46-17.1
539	58-180
540	24-37
542	24-118.4
543	58-85.2
544	46-409, 46-421, 46-422.1 to 46-424
545	46-11
546	54-790.1
547	54-788.2
549	63-362
550	63-348
551	65-4
552	22-141
553	54-60 to 54-62.2
555	21-118.3
557	53-135.1
558	63-372R, 63-373R, 63-373.1
559	18-305.1, 19-11, 19-29
562	15-899
563	18-160, 18-161
565	65-43R, 65-44, 65-45R
566	14-66
567	54-210 to 54-210.2
568	51-15
569	15-352.3
570	53-299.1
571	6-14, 6-15R, 6-15.1 to 16-15.3, 6-16R, 6-17R, 6-20, 13-40
572	33-11
573	29-131
575	22-188
576	33-288.1
579	3-221
580	15-766
581	24-216, 24-252
583	22-5
584	20-61.1
585	58-946
586	15-239
587	51-112
588	29-209
589	29-209
591	15-351
592	35-64.1 to 35-64.6
593	22-48
594	18-153
595	15-926.1
597	56-142, 56-143
598	58-1109.1
599	58-288.1
601	58-478.1
602	46-259.2
603	65-42
605	27-65
606	22-166.2, 22-166.3, 22-166.7
608	29-2.1, 29-3, 29-5, 29-27, 29-28, 29-34.1, 29-34.2, 29-56, 29-114.1, 29-125, 29-128, 29-128.1, 29-144
609	55-286.1
610	15-353.1
611	15-354.1
612	16-50
613	56-51.1
614	63-48R, 63-49R
615	22-43.4
616	14-193
617	8-310
618	18-106
619	29-129.1
620	30-19.1
626	21-119.1
630	58-942
632	56-338.19 to 56-338.39, 58-731, 58-732, 58-734 to 58-735.2, 58-736, 58-737, 58-739 to 58-744, 58-745R, 58-746 to 58-753.2, 58-754.1, 58-755
634	22-208
635	58-776.6
636	58-769, subsec. (3)R
637	1-15, 15-24.2
638	28-98.2
639	22-316
641	23-35.1, 23-35.3 to 23-35.5
642	17-30.1
643	28-158
644	63-293
646	17-137.2
647	28-70
648	28-190.1
649	28-38, 28-39
650	28-137.1
651	23-36.2
652	46-267, 46-269, 46-271
653	28-10.1
654	28-196.2
657	10-90.2 to 10-90.9
658	8-906, 8-908
659	21-11
660	46-376
662	28-196.1
666	46-195.1, 46-211R, 46-212, 46-215.1, 46-226, 46-231, 46-238, 46-347.1, 46-347.2, 46-378, 46-416.1
667	3-424.1 to 3-424.8
668	13-238
669	4-112
670	46-394
671	46-203, 46-209, 46-220, 46-220.1, 46-222, 46-256
672	3-707
673	28-240
674	40-64
675	46-22.1
676	28-143
677	58-404.01
679	58-412.1
680	29-1.1
681	8-67.1
682	46-105.2
683	3-579.2
684	2-4.1
686	33-255.23
687	58-293
688	15-825
690	54-276.7
691	37-231, 37-231.1
692	20-72
693	18-290
694	15-20.1
695	33-119
696	56-509 to 56-528
697	40-75 to 40-95R, 40-95.1 to 40-95.6
698	54-306.1
699	8-435
700	37-61.2, 37-62
701	14-187
702	62-11, 62-23, 62-33
703	9-1 to 9-6R, 9-6.1 to 9-6.14, 54-2 to 54-16R
704	33-193
705	9-23, 32-336
707	23-9.2
710	56-417.1
711	58-838
714	14-87
715	62-14.1

ACTS 1952, EX. SESS.

Acts 1952, Ex. Sess. Chapter	Code 1950 Section
2	4-112
3	56-49.1
5	3-117.25
6	51-127.21, 51-127.25
10	15-240
14	55-132.1
16	46-210
17	24-14
18	24-12
21	2-27.2
22	32-336
23	17-136.1
26	14-155.6R
27	14-155.8
28	24-194.3, 24-194.4
29	58-769
31	22-119.1

ACTS 1954

Acts 1954 Chapter	Code 1950 Section
1	30-15.1
2	18-17
3	15-152.8
4	58-484.1
5	14-134.1
7	56-384
8	17-83.2 to 17-83.4
10	57-26
11	6-55
13	46-242.1
14	17-145, 17-147, 17-149 to 17-154, 17-163, 17-164, 17-169 to 17-169.4, 17-170 to 17-182R
15	46-234
17	58-715
20	38.1-495.1 to 38.1-495.5
21	4-86
23	8-59
24	13-78.1, 13-79
25	29-169
26	19-241.1
27	16-172.9
34	46-308
35	10-64.1
38	28-93.1
43	28-158
44	46-302
45	8-188 to 8-190
46	15-320
48	15-250
49	15-688
55	14-163.1
57	46-318
58	46-272
59	46-1
60	46-99.1
62	23-50
63	28-204.1
65	58-12
68	21-121.1, 21-140.1
71	2-259.2, 15-712, 22-9, 22-262, 63-162, 63-204.1
74	18-165
80	58-769
81	15-527
82	3-706
83	17-118.1
87	4-80.1
88	33-76.6
90	58-780.1
91	15-240
92	23-4.1
93	59-106.1, 59-107 to 59-111R, 59-113R, 59-114R, 59-114.1
94	15-20.2
95	14-156
99	14-193
100	63-165
101	15-574.2
102	15-353
107	4-80
108	56-527
109	33-213
110	4-79, 4-115
111	28-204.2
113	46-532
114	46-279
115	15-705.2
120	29-52.1
122	56-406.1, 56-409R, 56-410R
123	46-361
124	15-353.2
126	51-127.1
127	29-184
129	57-19
130	29-202
131	18-329
132	17-19.1
134	27-54.1 to 27-54.4
135	21-117.1
136	14-124
137	46-255
138	14-123
139	51-132, 51-134 to 51-136.2, 51-139 to 51-142
140	8-272
141	53-272
142	32-292
143	34-29, 34-30
144	19-181, 19-183
145	55-26
146	57-41 to 57-43R
147	4-61.1, 4-89, 4-118.1
148	22-9.1 to 22-9.3
150	15-692.1
151	15-351
152	29-188.1, 19-194.1
153	15-705
154	23-98
155	29-165, 29-166
156	29-165.1
157	62-106.5, n.
158	46-138.2R, n.
159	15-859
160	6-23.1
161	38.1-659, 38.1-673, 38.1-677, 38.1-680
162	13-231.1
163	15-615.1
164	19-186
165	17-7
167	8-73.1
168	46-195
169	8-370
170	7-25.1
171	44-117.1
174	46-193
175	17-27
176	28-48
177	28-178
178	28-136
179	28-10.1
180	29-36.1
181	15-243
182	58-178, 58-179, 64-127
183	15-253
184	58-895.1
185	23-77.1
186	18-224
188	13-19.1, 56-4R
189	58-643, 58-643.1, 58-646 to 58-659R
191	45-0.1 to 45-1, 45-3 to 45-6, 45-8 to 45-12.1, 45-13R, 45-14, 45-14.1, 45-15R, 45-16 to 45-18, 45-20, 45-23 to 45-27, 45-29, 45-31 to 45-35, 45-36R, 45-37R, 45-38, 45-39, 45-42, 45-43, 45-44R, 45-45R, 45-45.1, 45-46 to 45-53R, 45-53.1 to 45-53.8, 45-54 to 45-60R, 45-60.1 to 45-60.5, 45-62 to 45-68R, 45-68.1 to 45-72, 45-74, 45-75, 45-76R, 45-77,

Acts 1954 Chapter	Code 1950 Section
	45-77.1, 45-79, 45-81 to 45-83, 45-85.1 to 45-86, 45-88
193	53-195
194	37-75
195	16-172.75
196	16-50
197	46-418.1
198	2-4.2
201	32-353
203	60-20, 60-22, 60-25.1, 60-42, 60-45, 60-46, 60-47, 60-49, 60-67 to 60-71, 60-73, 60-73.1, 60-75
204	46-183.1, 46-183.2
205	58-960
206	22-67
207	58-486
208	15-239
209	58-776.7
210	46-101
211	46-96
212	38.1-202.1
213	46-418
214	28-201.1
215	28-46.1
216	28-91.1
217	46-310.1
218	56-366.2
219	58-293
220	22-43.1
221	4-45, 4-46
222	46-427.1
223	15-20.3
224	63-73.1
225	46-209
226	58-730.1
228	29-132, 29-136
229	19-202
230	38.1-397
231	38.1-44
232	38.1-167
233	65-9
234	20-107
236	18-348.1
237	54-398.1 to 54-398.28
238	8-751
239	62-192
241	51-111.27, 51-111.31
243	14-57
244	46-212
246	15-555, 65-4
247	18-165.1
249	16-51
250	58-811.1
251	14-135
252	8-182
253	58-847
254	8-524.1, 8-526
255	15-666.12
256	63-318.1
257	22-153, 22-154
258	63-59
259	63-222 to 63-224.4, 63-225R, 63-226R, 63-227
261	22-120.2
262	63-366, 63-368, 63-369
263	38.1-381.1
264	15-686
265	63-67.1
266	2-244
268	57-7
269	63-66.1
270	16-172.63
271	46-414.1
273	2-20.1
274	51-29.8 to 51-29.18
277	58-963, 58-964
278	58-681
279	11-23
280	29-61, 29-62
281	29-202
282	63-35
284	16-172.71
285	16-172.68
286	15-241
287	14-133
289	22-72
290	63-101
291	22-7.1, 22-97
293	46-419
295	1-13.10:1
296	23-77.2
297	15-239
298	56-237
299	15-22
300	58-784.2
301	4-31, 4-105
304	17-41
305	29-90
309	57-12
310	46-273
311	27-25.1
312	46-342
313	46-215.2
314	15-666.1 to 15-666.11
315	16-172.29
317	58-758
319	33-229, 33-251, 33-253
320	13-39.1 to 13-39.5
321	15-16.4, 21-134.1, 21-134.2
323	15-487
324	21-120
325	15-607, 15-621.1
326	22-21
328	2-19
329	8-277.1
330	62-9.1 to 62-9.4
331	2-228, 2-232, 2-240
332	15-739.1
333	6-422, 8-1.2, 8-44, 8-46.1, 8-51, 8-67.2, 8-67.4, 8-74, 8-76, 8-96 to 8-99, 8-102, 8-105, 8-106, 8-109, 8-114 to 8-116, 8-118, 8-133, 8-134, 8-152, 8-153, 8-160, 8-161, 8-165, 8-166, 8-211, 8 212, 8-220, 8-238, 8-268, 8-304, 8-347, 8-386, 8-455, 8-487, 8-490, 8-509, 8-513, 8-514, 8-517, 8-519 to 8-522, 8-524, 8-527, 8-547, 8-557, 8-567, 8-579, 8-629, 8-632, 8-638, 8-640, 8-652, 8-791, 8-792, 8-796, 8-800 to 8-803, 8-805, 8-814, 8-818, 8-821, 8-825, 8-827 to 8-829, 8-867, 58-1014, 16-19, 58-1016
334	22-35
335	58-732, 58-734.1, 58-739.2, 58-739.3, 58-744, 58-744.1, 58-748.1:1
336	19-168
337	29-209
338	4-34.1
339	29-188, 29-194, 29-195, 29-196, 29-213.1 to 29-213.4
341	46-134 to 46-140R, 46-142 to 46-151R, 46-153R, 46-153.1R, 56-279.1, 56-304 to 56-304.12, 58-627
342	22-8.2R
343	23-70, 23-71
344	56-338.2
345	46-491.1
346	32-335
347	24-449
349	33-111
351	4-26
352	28-124
353	42-9
354	56-265.1
356	46-241.1
360	16-77
362	16-55
363	38.1-29.1

Acts 1954 Chapter	Code 1950 Section
364	46-313
365	2-42.1
366	8-58
367	28-103
368	28-170
370	65-92
372	56-413.1, 56-413.2
373	46-543 to 46-545
374	33-136R
375	24-45
377	46-197.2
378	46-431, 46-437, 46-455, 46-460, 46-474, 46-492
379	8-432.1, 8-443 to 8-445, 34-29
380	46-201
381	46-203
382	15-739.7 to 15-739.13
383	38.1-287.1
384	15-668.1
385	22-126
386	38.1-283
387	26-68.1
388	38.1-309
389	20-93
390	8-628.2
391	22-100.1 to 22-100.12
392	54-656
393	46-413
394	23-50.3
395	54-429
396	54-415, 54-416, 54-440
397	23-19
398	31-6
399	37-141
400	15-570
401	46-209.1
402	18-114
403	46-294.1
404	51-111.69, 51-111.70
406	18-75.1, 18-76
407	3-52.1R, 3-64 to 3-79R, 3-79.1 to 3-79.18
409	27-29.1
410	15-691.1
411	15-574
412	37-48.1
413	18-214.1
414	23-35.1, 23-35.3, 23-35.5, 23-35.6
415	54-120
416	8-196.1
417	15-589.1
418	35-3.1
419	56-222
421	15-791
422	46-336
424	33-289R
425	58-266
427	8-653
428	54-113, 54-129, 54-145.1
429	32-337, 32-337.1, 32-337.3
430	64-101
431	40-74.1 to 40-74.5
432	51-127.21
433	46-256.1
434	58-450
435	46-541
436	46-317.1
437	3-590
439	51-29.1
441	3-594.1
442	14-155.9
443	14-31
445	37-125.14
446	28-196.2
447	28-111
448	28-112.1
450	65-93
451	56-54.1
452	14-85
453	3-79.19 to 3-79.27
454	46-365
455	15-754.1 to 15-754.8
456	26-10.1
457	33-120.1
458	46-209
459	62-183.1
460	51-111.54
461	8-873.1 to 8-873.3
462	15-777.1
463	58-851.1
464	64-119.1
465	58-851
466	55-139.2
467	51-111.3:1
468	31-5
469	19-269.1
470	14-195.1
471	12-6
473	56-47
474	22-296
476	22-112
478	24-277.1
479	32-293.2
480	58-780
481	20-61, 20-62, 20-63, 20-88
482	20-88.15:1, 20-88.20:1 to 20-88.22:1
483	58-965.1
484	4-52, 4-53, 4-55, 4-57, 4-75, 4-81
485	4-42, 4-109.1
486	11-9.1
487	10-3
488	58-838
489	63-348 to 63-349, 63-351 to 63-353, 63-355, 63-358, 63-361, 63-362R
490	4-101.1, 4-104
491	46-64
493	58-780
494	63-96
495	63-115, 63-141, 63-179
496	40-35
497	51-111.10
498	58-943.2
499	13-83, 13-86
500	58-968
501	3-706.1, 3-706.2
502	58-784.4
503	18-146.1
504	4-56
505	40-35
506	3-598.1 to 3-598.6
507	63-53
508	32-40.1 to 32-40.3
509	58-1162.1
510	58-77
511	24-321, 24-324, 24-330, 24-339, 24-340.1
512	4-61
513	24-213
515	58-772.1
516	58-81.1
517	58-266.4
518	65-41, 65-90
520	33-255.2, 33-255.4, 33-255.7 to 33-255.9, 33-255.14 to 33-255.16
521	24-194.2
522	58-359
523	24-345.3, 24-345.8
524	58-412
525	56-232
526	8-750
527	16-172.4, 16-172.6, 16-172.9, 16-172.13, 16-172.15, 16-172.16, 16-172.84
528	58-78.1
529	15-8
530	24-120
531	16-40.2
532	58-78, 58-81
533	58-1141
534	33-50.1

Acts 1954 Chapter	Code 1950 Section
535	15-161.1 to 15-161.3
536	15-38, 15-40 to 15-42
537	58-78
538	46-416.2
539	24-338.1
540	15-705.3
541	56-51.1
543	13.231:1, 8-54 to 8-56
544	8-128R
545	8-49
546	8-140.1, 8-140.2, 8-715R, 8-716R
547	8-67.3
548	19-299
549	8-789
550	8-759, 8-761, 8-773
551	8-4.1
552	8-198
553	8-240
554	15-764.12
556	54-276.6
557	55-59
558	10-83.1 to 10-83.3
567	29-55.1
569	54-225R
570	54-244, 54-245
572	42-66.1, 42-66.2
573	63-85
574	16-70
575	46-65
576	33-173.1
577	20-61.1
578	33-228
582	63-293.1
584	15-786
585	46-31
587	58-940
588	33-298, 33-302, 33-303, 33-308 to 33-310, 33-312, 33-314, 33-315R, 33-317, 33-321
589	8-24
590	64-23
591	54-62.2
592	15-719.1
593	8-45R, 8-46R, 8-48R, 8-82 to 8-86R, 8-100R, 8-101R, 8-103R, 8-104R, 8-107R, 8-108R, 8-110R, 8-112R, 8-113R, 8-117R, 8-121R, 8-125 to 8-127R, 8-132R, 8-136R, 8-137R, 8-151R, 8-210R, 8-222R, 8-242R, 8-243R, 8-330 to 8-342R, 8-345R, 8-351R, 8-474R, 8-481R, 8-488R, 8-492R, 8-508R, 8-515R, 8-516R, 8-565R, 8-717 to 8-719R, 8-722 to 8-724R, 8-790R, 8-806 to 8-808R, 8-868R
594	46-64
595	16-172.61
596	17-127.4
597	53-251.1
598	8-388
599	16-172.42
600	26-40
601	26-7.1 to 26-7.3
602	11-8
603	63-127, 63-191
604	8-5
605	8-122, 8-122.1, 8-124R, 8-310
606	8-836 to 8-838, 8-841
607	8-628R, 8-628.1
608	8-239 to 8-239.2
609	8-793
610	8-346R, 8-510, 8-511, 8-720R, 8-721R
611	8-244
612	8-719.1R
613	34-32
614	8-641, 8-642, 8-645, 8-646
615	8-432
616	8-466 to 8-468R, 8-468.1, 8-469R, 8-470R, 8-471, 8-472R
617	8-241
618	8-348
619	8-245, 8-246
620	8-399, 8-409R
621	8-144R, 8-154
622	8-528
623	29-52
624	8-437
625	54-443 to 54-445
626	54-277R, 54-293, 54-300, 54-305, 54-306, 54-306.2 to 54-308, 54-310
627	54-316, 54-317
628	54-318, 54-320
629	14-71
630	46-22.1
632	29-15
633	22-120.1, 51-111.24
634	51-12, 51-13
635	51-3, 51-4, 51-7, 51-15, 51-18, 51-19, 51-20
636	58-105.1
637	11-24 to 11-29
638	22-7, 22-33, 22-43, 22-43.1, 22-62, 22-98, 22-122, 22-204, 22-218, 22-223, 22-253.1
639	19-248
641	53-19.1 to 53-19.4
642	21-292, 21-192.1, 21-295, 21-297, 21-298R, 21-300, 21-306, 21-313R, 21-314, 21-320R, 21-334, 21-337, 21-338, 21-344, 21-346 to 21-349, 21-351 to 21-353, 21-355 to 21-361, 21-363 to 21-367, 21-372, 21-381 to 21-385, 21-388, 21-389, 21-393, 21-394, 21-396, 21-398 to 21-400, 21-402, 21-405, 21-408 to 21-418, 21-420 to 21-424, 21-426
643	51-111.29, 51-111.41
644	58-320
645	15-937 to 15-958
646	32-9
647	22-188.2
648	14-66
651	4-78.1
652	14-77, 15-10.1, 58-916
653	46-212.1
654	65-51, 65-52, 65-62, 65-68
655	58-773
657	14-181
658	14-42R, 14-155.10
659	63-119, 63-145, 63-209
660	8-38
661	14-155
662	14-66
663	28-137.1
664	64-151
666	32-120.1, 32-123R, 32-124R, 32-125, 32-129
667	62-106.1 to 62-106.3, 62-106.7, 62-106.8, 62.106.10 to 62-106.19
668	37-1 to 37-2, 37-4 to 37-6, 37-85, 37-97.1, 37-136 to 37-136.2, 37-137, 37-138R, 37-139, 37-139.1, 37-181, 37-182, 37-183, 37-185 to 37-189, 37-192, 37-201R, 37-212, 37-213, 37-226R, 37-231
669	56-265.10 to 56-265.13
670	21-3, 21-6, 21-11, 21-29, 21-31, 21-32, 21-43, 21-45, 21-65
671	22-139.1
672	58-86.4
673	2-54, 30-19.01

Acts 1954 Chapter	Code 1950 Section
674	29-194, 29-197.1
675	22-166.4R, 22-166.5R, 22-166.8 to 22-166.13
676	58-766
677	38.1-299
678	16-172.77
679	32-329
680	16-172.80
681	63-379 to 63-385
682	4-2
683	14-86
684	3-676.1 to 3-676.5
686	29-145.1
688	3-213
690	24-107
691	24-55, 24-77, 24-118.10
692	6-174.1, 6-175.1, 6-189.1
693	33-191.1
694	29-161
695	29-35.1, 29-35.2
696	3-513, 3-524
697	3-506 to 3-512R, 3-512.1 to 3-512.7
698	32-312.1
699	45-106, 45-107R, 45-107.1 to 45-122, 45-124, 45-126 to 45-131, 45-139 to 45-141, 45-144
700	29-37.1
701	57-2.1
702	1-14
703	24-120
704	33-255.45 to 33-255.66, n.
705	33-255.24 to 33-255.44, n.
706	9-77.1
707	54-83.1
709	4-10, 8-204, 14-5 to 14-5.5, 14-30, 14-46R, 14-47, 14-57, 14-58R, 14-186, 14-187, 19-193, 22-67, 54-58
710	62-14.1

ACTS 1956

Acts 1956 Chapter	Code 1950 Section
3	17-136, n.
4	17-117, 17-119
6	17-117, n.
7	17-135, 17-136
8	17-119.1
9	19-106 to 19-108
10	14-124.1
11	23-88
12	23-76
14	46-376
15	55-197
16	15-823
17	15-701
18	55-136
19	17-69.1
20	17-127.10
21	17-127.5
22	4-5
23	4-78
24	17-41
25	15-13
26	58-371.2
27	15-671
28	33-172.1
29	22-175
30	23-168
31	23-157
32	58-769.1
34	58-797, 58-798
35	46-322.1
36	46-312.1, 46-316
37	3-1
38	2-20.1
39	33-27
41	27-29
42	15-24.4
45	6-29.1
46	59-120
47	46-333.1
48	54-352
49	54-349
51	29-55.1
53	4-51
54	4-112.1
55	17-127.6
56	46-262
57	58-266.6
59	26-9, 26-22
60	37-25.1 to 37-25.6
61	58-838.5, 58-838.8
63	27-5.2
64	8-67.1
65	64-58R
66	46-64
68	29-57, 29-62
69	58-86.2 to 58-68.5R, 58-91, 58-94, 58-106, 58-108 to 58-113, 58-117, 58-126, 58-504, 58-513R, 58-524, 58-526, 58-530, 58-531, 58-556, 58-557, 58-560, 58-565, 58-566, 58-568, 58-570, 58-576, 58-581, 58-586, 58-588, 58-590, 58-591, 58-607, 58-610, 58-613, 58-622, 58-878, 58-961, 58-966, 58-978
70	4-57.1
71	6-279, 6-285, 6-286, 6-290, 6-301, 6-302, 6-309, 6-310, 6-316 to 6-317, 6-320, 6-323, 6-338
72	52-4.1
74	3-359.1
75	10-74.2, 10-75 to 10-79.1, 10-80R, 10-81 to 10-83
77	3-79.3
78	33-50.2
79	65-93
80	43-29
81	6-51
82	6-264.1
83	26-40
84	2-181, 2-183R, 58-944
85	46-44.1
86	46-328.1
87	33-1
88	56-304.2:1
89	56-300
90	6-207, 6-213, 6-214, 6-217, 6-218, 6-223 to 6-226, 6-229
91	33-116.1
92	33-12
93	20-121.01
95	15-43, 15-45
97	32-200
98	51-111.10
101	54-430
103	17-127.7
104	63-15
105	37-27
106	33-76.11
107	58-838.5:1
108	2-20.1
109	64-1
110	19-92.1
112	33-255.24 to 33-255.41, n.
113	33-255.45 to 33-255.66, n.
114	46-5.1
116	15-761.2
117	27-26
120	46-503
121	16.1-177, 16.1-177.1
122	16.1-205
123	5-16
125	63-25
126	63-51, 63-52, 63-52.1R, 63-53, 63-53.1, 63-56, 63-58
127	63-289R, 63-290R, 63-291, 63-292
128	46-317.2
131	56-334

Acts 1954 Chapter	Code 1950 Section
132	46-156
133	16.1-164
134	46-198
135	28-204.3
136	20-121.2
138	33-224
139	21-120
140	22-12
141	46-334
142	28-204.4
144	54-762
145	54-738
146	54-758
147	54-749
149	6-361
151	18-349.5 to 18-349.8
152	33-57
153	15-324
154	33-317, n.
156	8-182
158	33-228, 33-245, 33-252
159	26-13
160	8-514.1
161	33-136.1
162	29-197
163	54-200 to 54-200.02
164	46-254 to 46-254.2, 56-407R, 56-408, 56-414
165	54-442
166	29-184.1
167	42-63
168	42-30
169	42-45
170	28-4.2
172	38.1-302
173	38.1-281
175	6-32R
176	6-122, 6-123, 6-197, 6-230, 6-257
178	29-126
180	29-145.2
181	38.1-286
182	18-17
183	16.1-208
184	2-154.1, 2-288, 2-291R, 2-292R, 2-293R, 2-297, 2-298, 15-21, 15-22R, 15-589R, 15-590R, 15-605.10, 15-615.1, 15-638, 15-652, 22-56R, 22-102, 23-32, 23-81, 32-254R, 33-255.24 to 33-255.44, n. 33-255.45 to 33-255.66, n. 51-125, 51-127.26
185	37-136.1
186	19-3
187	63-349, 63-354
188	58-478
189	15-574.1
191	14-155.4
192	46-241.1
193	14-51, 14-52, 14-52.1R
194	16.1-198, 16.1-199, 16.1-201
195	15-15.1
196	15-555.1
197	15-766.3
199	27-24
200	15-319, 15-328.2
202	58-984
203	57-19
204	18-225.1
206	18-82
207	62-106.2
208	19-72.2
209	6-348.1
210	56-377
211	33-255.24 to 33-255.44, n., 33-255.45 to 33-255.66, n.
212	15-27 to 15-37R
213	22-280
214	14-5.2, 14-5.3
215	46-335.1, 46-338.1R, 46-338.2
216	46-215.2
217	2-60, 14-123, 15-67, 17-54
218	15-8
219	58-793 to 58-795
220	54-217 to 54-260R, 54-260.1 to 54-260.63
221	33-125
222	46-416.2
223	9-11
224	19-92
225	54-496 to 54-498
226	31-19 to 31-25
227	55-88, 55-90, 55-92
228	2-236
229	62-69
230	6-55.1
231	64-147
234	38.1-108
235	24-207
236	54-750
237	22-277
238	14-56, 14-57
239	24-118.4
241	58-413
242	58-266.1
243	65-51, 65-52, 65-62, 65-68
245	15-9.1
246	15-13.1
247	63-309
252	54-58
254	23-100.1
255	58-766
256	54-50
259	32-334.1
260	32-353
267	62-148 to 62-157R
268	32-186 to 32-195R, 32-195.1 to 32-195.20
269	33-74
270	28-12
271	28-45
273	15-739.8, 15-754.3
274	29-188.1
275	29-147.1
277	15-323, 15-328.1
278	62-3.1
279	6-234
280	44-75, 44-78
282	15-901
283	65-4
284	3-600, 3-602 to 3-603.1
286	9-77.2
287	63-367 to 63-369
289	18-146 to 18-147, 18-304
290	54-832
292	46-45
293	28-170
296	59-114.4
297	24-118.5, 24-119
298	2-62.1, 2-135.1
299	58-450
300	63-348, 63-351, 63-356.1
301	8-482
302	15-354.2
303	18-221
304	64-38.1
305	58-154, 58-220
306	58-249
307	8-160, 8-165
308	3-598.1, 3-598.4, 3-598.6
310	3-295R
311	23-9.3 to 23-9.14
313	28-98.1
316	53-247
317	22-67
318	29-90
320	15-692.2
321	22-142
322	17-127.11
323	36-44, n.
324	22-9.2:1
326	17-127.8
327	36-47.1
329	15-686
331	18-188.1
332	17-127.9
335	55-152
336	15-795
336	29-21, 29-22

Acts 1954 Chapter	Code 1950 Section
338	29-209
340	18-231.2
341	47-1
342	53-272
343	29-110
344	53-312.1
345	53-82
346	17-118.1, 24-164
347	8-477
348	58-769.1
349	15-320
350	58-153
351	65-115
352	56-338.14
353	56-304.2
354	46-22
355	58-638, 58-639
356	38.1-123, 38.1-124
357	28-172.1
358	65-114.1 to 65-114.5
359	15-590.1:2
360	38.1-472
361	22-126
362	58-310, 58-326
363	51-111.18
364	46-212
365	22-60
366	2-20.1
367	58-633.1
368	58-638.1
369	16.1-202.1 to 16.1-202.9
370	24-194.3
372	58-919.1
373	23-14
374	58-784.2
375	29-136
376	3-584, 3-589
377	58-64
378	24-44, 24-45
379	15-626
380	2-79
381	46-318
382	24-345
383	58-769.1
384	4-109
385	40-104
386	53-19R, 53-27 to 53-31R, 53-35R, 53-36R, 53-41R, 53-44R, 53-46R, 53-49R, 53-51 to 53-54R, 53-56R, 53-58R, 53-59R, 53-88R, 53-101R, 53-105R, 53-106R, 53-110 to 53-113R, 53-121R, 53-123R, 53-127R, 53-132R, 53-148R, 53-153R, 53-196R, 53-218R
387	2-92
388	18-261.1
389	54-278
390	23-9.2
392	24-24
394	35-16.1
395	24-213
396	32-1
397	54-142
398	24-456
399	43-17
400	63-293.2
401	15-756
402	8-577.1
403	14-155.11
405	16.1-178, 16.1-181
408	26-16.1, 26-35.1
409	15-220
411	54-432.3
412	32-337, 32-337.1, 32-337.3
414	21-427.1
415	63-81.1
416	19-29
417	38.1-406, 38.1-435
418	4-41
419	29-36.1
422	23-181
423	6-54
424	2-40
425	16.1-158
426	55-66.5
427	24-119.1
428	13-1 to 13-292R, 13.1-1 to 13.1-527
429	56-75
430	40-74.4
431	38.1-64, 38.1-65, 38.1-71, 38.1-74, 38.1-75, 38.1-80, 38.1-81, 38.1-82R, 38.1-83, 38.1-495.5, 38.1-551, 38.1-579, 38.1-589, 38.1-666, 38.1-667
432	8-38, 8-59, 8-60, 8-61R, 8-62R, 8-65
433	6-10, 6-12.1R, 6-20, 6-146, 6-152, 6-164, 6-204, 6-206, 6-236, 6-242, 6-250, 6-251
434	56-485 to 56-508
435	56-339 to 56-344R, 56-345 to 56-347, 56-349 to 56-351R, 56-355R, 56-356 to 56-358R, 56-370R
436	56-232
437	56-209 to 56-231, 56-47R, 56-48R, 56-49, 56-49.1 to 56-51R, 56-51.1, 56-52 to 56-54.1R
439	58-431, 58-445, 58-446R, 58-447, 58-452R, 58-453R, 58-459, 58-463
440	60-6R, 60-6.1, 60-8R, 60-8.1, 60-12, 60-14, 60-20, 60-22, 60-25, 60-39, 60-42, 60-45, 60-45.2, 60-46, 60-47, 60-63, 60-64, 60-67, 60-68, 60-70, 60-76.1, 60-76.2, 60-81, 60-83, 60-96 to 60-98
441	51-111.70
442	17-136
443	40-109
444	3-117.2 to 3-117.4, 3-117.6 to 3-117.8, 3-117.19, 3-117.21, 3-117.29, 3-117.30, 3-117.32
445	37-75
446	8-289.1
447	29-3
448	64-68.1
449	58-266.3, 58-266.5
450	56-338.29, 56-338.32, 56-338.34, 56-338.36
451	33-4
452	16.1-213.1 to 16.1-213.7
453	28-249
454	57-20
455	14-75
458	51-111.54
460	9-26
461	15-20.4
462	33-191.1
463	40-109
465	22-9.3
466	29-162
467	65-101
469	15-20
470	29-184.3
471	21-291
472	15-714.5, 15-714.10
473	32-292, 32-293.1
474	15-714.9
475	58-627 to 58-629, 58-632, 58-634.1
476	46-328, 46-334, 46-336R, 46-339
477	46-162, 46-165, 46-166, 46-168
478	58-12
479	65-4
480	15-10.1
481	14-155

Acts 1954 Chapter	Code 1950 Section
482	32-84R, 32-85R, 32-85.1 to 32-85.6
483	46-326, 46-328
486	62-43
487	15-766
488	18-338.1
490	29-148
491	10-127
492	18-361 to 18-366, 56-133 to 56-135R
493	37-125.1, 37-125.15, 37-135.1
494	56-338.40 to 56-338.48
495	58-514.1
497	15-916
498	24-118.5
499	32-312.1
500	58-223, 58-238
501	58-141
502	58-1118
503	8-365
504	58-138
505	46-257
506	19-120
507	3-610, 3-611, 3-613 to 3-615, 3-617, 3-619 to 3-624, 3-625R, 3-626 to 3-630, 3-630.1R, 3-631, 3-632R, 3-633R, 3-634 to 3-638, 3-640
508	54-401
509	59-140.1
510	59-128.1
511	43-63.1
512	8-397
513	58-78
516	20-1
517	3-642 to 3-646R, 3-646.1 to 3-646.15
518	3-677 to 3-689R, 3-689.1 to 3-689.14
519	4-105
520	4-25
521	4-37
522	4-114, 4-114.1
523	4-31
524	58-362
525	24-323, 24-327, 24-328, 24-330, 24-334, 24-337
527	58-494
528	3-327, 3-328
529	3-310, 32-117, 32-119, 32-120.1, 32-122.1, 32-122.2, 32-128, 32-129
532	22-141
533	46-238
534	65-39
535	20-100
536	64-123
537	16.1-175 to 16.1-177
538	9-16.1
539	33-111
541	38.1-301.1 to 38.1-301.9
543	28-226
544	24-129.1
549	46-64
552	15-231.4:1 to 15-231.4:78, n.
554	15-220, 15-221, 15-222.3, 15-224, 15-230, 15-231.3
555	16-1 to 16-172.84R, 16.1-1 to 16.1-202, 16.1-203 to 16.1-213, 16.1-214 to 16.1-217
556	14-132 to 14-134, 14-134.1R, 14-135, 14-136, 14-137R
557	18-75.1 to 18-75.3
558	43-33
560	51-111.36, 51-111.40, 51-111.42, 51-111.46, 51-111.50, 51-111.55, 51-111.57, 51-111.60, 51-111.64
561	51-111.2 to 51-111.3:1, 51-111.5
562	51-134 to 51-136
563	25-18.1
564	63-127, 63-191
565	33-70
567	40-96, 40-100.6
568	46-45
570	46-64
571	18-113.1
572	14-85
573	14-155.12
574	14-163.1
575	8-170
577	18-252, 18-253
578	63-126, 63-150, 63-190, 63-213
580	33-64
581	58-770.1
582	15-239, 33-160
583	15-239
584	54-44.1
586	28-123
587	18-225
588	21-118
590	15-414
591	22-57.1, 22-83.1, 22-84 to 22-88.1R
593	51-111.41
594	8-138.2
595	8-138.1
596	19-121.1
597	46-158.1
598	58-1142
599	58-71
600	46-212.2
602	55-144, 55-146, 55-148
603	14-71.2
604	14-69.2
605	14-70.1
606	14-68.2
607	56-448
608	63-106, 63-109
609	14-86
611	57-7
612	58-546 to 58-555
613	58-82
614	58-105
615	36-8, 36-9, 36-11
616	10-117.1
617	29-184.2
618	58-412.2
620	22-35
621	34-30
622	6-78
623	63-107
624	44-142.1
625	3-425 to 3-451R, 3-451.1 to 3-451.17
626	56-406.2
627	38.1-257.1
629	58-396.1
630	14-66, 14-66.1R
632	62-94.1 to 62-94.12
633	22-37
634	58-987
635	22-101.1:1, 22-101.2
636	15-754.1
637	34-5, 34-26, 34-27
639	46-265
640	46-275
641	63-101, 63-105
642	55-154
643	36-5
644	23-35.9
645	30-29, 30-31
646	62-11
647	1-15.1
648	46-410
650	28-143
651	46-305
652	51-111.57
653	25-234
654	21-2, 21-6, 21-10, 21-11, 21-45, 21-54 to 21-57, 21-59 to 21-62, 21-64
655	15-739.7
656	22-241, 22-242
658	24-37
660	26-45.1

Acts 1954 Chapter	Code 1950 Section
661	3-676.6
663	58-306
664	15-8
665	46-363
666	46-105.01
667	63-138.1, 63-202.1, 63-218.1
668	21-112.1 to 21-112.20
669	15-9.1
670	22-10.1
671	22-100.3, 22-100.7, 22-100.9, 22-100.12
672	15-18
673	33-255.45 to 33-255.56, n.
674	55-59
676	33-279, 33-317
677	58-354.1 to 58-354.7
678	38.1-21, 38.1-360
679	29-202
681	53-206.1 to 53-206.11
682	56-287.1 to 56-287.3
683	3-648, 3-659 to 3-661
684	29-145.1
686	46-209.2
687	19-283
688	19-273.1
689	23-76
690	51-111.67
691	21-120
692	38.1-542
693	29-171.1
694	15-16.5
695	24-194.2
696	22-324.1
697	56-338.2
698	46-342
699	17-30.1
700	46-204
701	58-960
702	46-207.1
703	46-413
705	46-155
706	55-125
707	33-255.24 to 33-255.44, n.
708	46-109.1 to 46-109.10
709	29-153
710	15-237
711	37-34.3
713	55-134.1
714	33-191.1
715	14-68

ACTS 1956, EX. SESS.

Acts 1956, Ex. Sess. Chapter	Code 1950 Section
1	24-345.3
2	2-262
4	14-163.1
5	22-67
7	15-504
8	14-57
10	14-132
11	8-38
14	37-125.5
15	24-194.3
16	58-12
17	16.1-43
18	15-563
19	17-127.6
23	58-387.1
27	38.1-474
30	7-34.1
31	18-349.9 to 18-349.16
32	18-349.17 to 18-349.24
33	54-74, 54-78, 54-79
34	30-35, n.
35	18-349.25 to 18-349.30
36	18-349.31 to 18-349.37
37	30-35 to 30-41
38	58-792.1
39	22-159
40	15-8
43	15-239
44	22-67
45	18-75.2
46	19-29
47	54-52.1
48	17-127.12
49	15-707
50	15-666.2, 15-666.3
53	65-7.1
55	46-546 to 46-553
56	22-115.19, n.
57	22-115.1 to 22-115.9
58	22-115.10 to 22-115.19
59	22-253.2
60	22-72, 22-72.1
61	22-205
62	22-115.20
63	22-56.1
64	51-111.10, 51-111.38:1 to 51-111.38:3
65	2-86.1
66	22-5
67	15-577, 22-117, 22-125 to 22-127.1, 22-129, 22-138
68	22-188.3 to 22-188.15
69	22-188.30 to 22-188.40
70	22-232.1 to 22-232.16

ACTS 1958

Acts 1958 Chapter	Code 1950 Section
1	2-57.1
2	2-75.1
4	53-295
5	64-25
7	15-406.1
8	20-14.1
9	15-5.1
10	46.1-254
11	56-56
12	16.1-115
13	8-59
14	55-66.3
15	23-49.1
17	23-19
18	51-127.26
19	6-185
20	6-183
21	6-225
23	2-182
24	2-299
25	6-348.1
26	6-188
27	38.1-479
28	38.1-195
29	30-6
30	3-220
31	58-321.1
32	58-770.1
33	58-769.1
34	58-84.1
35	58-839
36	60-68
38	29-81
39	29-209
41	22-188.41 to 22-188.45
42	24-37, 24-39
43	40-34
44	22-32
45	22-130.1 to 22-130.4
46	15-10.1:2
47	2-4.2, 23-9.1
48	15-861.1
51	15-926.1
56	35-42.1

Acts 1958 Chapter	Code 1950 Section
58	8-316.1 to 8-316.3
60	14-163.1
61	27-26.1 to 27-26.3
65	15-739.8
66	8-114
67	8-257
69	54-129
70	58-292
71	58-1152.1
72	58-829.1
74	6-76
76	51-127.15
77	58-811.1
79	4-42
82	36-11, 36-13, 36-17, 36-47
83	36-7.1
84	54-751 to 54-751.2
85	9-78, 9-80 to 9-82, 9-84
86	11-20, 11-23
87	58-687, 58-693, 58-695, 58-713, 58-723, 58-730.2
88	13.1-301.1, 13.1-301.2
89	54-95
90	23-50
91	33-279.2
94	3-228.4, 3-228.10
96	17-195.1 to 17-195.6
97	15-764.25
99	15-508
100	15-504
101	15-230
102	2-297
103	2-20.1
104	6-192.1
110	3-347, 3-348, 3-349R, 3-373, 3-377
112	15-291
114	18-187.1 to 18-187.3
116	36-5, 36-22
118	29-169
119	2-36
121	17-119, 17-119.1
122	58-335, 58-341
123	15-18.1
124	2-1, 2-160, 2-160.1, 2-162, 2-211 to 2-213, 2-215 to 2-217, 2-218.1, 2-219 to 2-230, 2-232 to 2-238, 2-239.1, 2-240, 2-242 to 2-247, 2-249 to 2-255, 2-257, 2-258, 2-259.2, 2-260, 2-262, 2-263, 2-265 to 2-268, 53-68, 53-69, 53-73
125	59-177 to 59-189.1R, 59-189.2 to 59-189.17
126	56-304.3
127	51-29.1
128	15-754.1, 15-754.3
129	58-792.1
130	56-304.9
133	32-147, 32-161
134	4-79
139	6-91, 6-153, 6-204, 6-244
140	22-166
142	31-10
143	17-221.1 to 17-221.17
145	29-54.1
146	15-20
147	29-139.1
148	3-513 to 3-515, 3-517, 3-518, 3-520
149	3-512.8 to 3-512.20
153	29-158.1
154	37-61.1, 37-64, 37-99, 37-102, 37-109, 46.1-427, 46.1-439
155	59-120
157	58-665, 58-666
158	37-92.1
159	4-115
160	24-182, 24-183R
161	54-273 to 54-275, 54-276.6, 54-281.1, 54-281.2, 54-295.1 to 54-295.7, 54-296 to 54-298, 54-301.1, 54-302, 54-308.5, 54-309 to 54-311, 54-313, 54-315.1, 54-317, 54-319, 54-319.1, 54-322 to 54-324
162	22-112
163	18-98.1 to 18-98.3
164	40-97, 40-100.3
165	29-132, 29-133
166	18-225
167	2-19
168	59-214.1, 59-218, 59-220R, 59-221R
169	20-97
170	18-159
171	36-4.1
172	29-61
173	62-106.7
174	62-106.1, 62-106.2, 62-106.4, 62-106.6, 62-106.8, 62-106.12, 62-106.14
175	28-204.5
176	4-118.1
177	4-105
178	4-114
179	23-135.8 to 23-135.11
180	38.1-70.1 to 38.1-70.4
182	28-93
183	28-124
184	28-123
186	10-61.1
187	65-4
189	14-156
190	15-10
191	15-13.2
192	4-44
193	4-111
194	4-55
195	63-53.1
196	15-766
197	62-117.1
199	2-75
200	6-38
201	56-274.1
203	58-258
204	28-204.1:2
206	14-155.1
207	15-351
208	8-218
209	16.1-15
210	16.1-84
211	16.1-112
212	19-121.1
213	8-67.5
214	55-19
215	8-596, 8-598
216	8-180
217	34-29
218	55-125
219	18-70
220	55-106.1
221	8-35, 8-396, 8-397
222	6-191.1, 6-193.1, 6-194.1 to 6-196
223	9-48.1 to 9-48.5
224	14-28.1, 14-28.2
225	8-24.1
227	19-50, 19-285
228	17-216
229	19-186
230	15-574.3
231	8-288
232	3-197.1 to 3-197.12
233	32-60
234	8-353.1R, 8-509.1R
235	2-90, 2-90.1
236	65-96
238	58-115.2

Acts 1958 Chapter	Code 1950 Section
239	63-73.1
240	54-526R, 54-545R
241	5-47 to 5-61
242	33-290A, 33-291R, 56-412.1, 56-412.2
243	3-666.1, 33-295R
244	13.1-400.1 to 13.1-400.8
245	18-341.1
248	15-482
249	53-251
250	53-149R, 53-154 to 53-160R, 53-162.1R, 53-177R, 53-189 to 53-194R, 53-200R
253	54-52.1
254	22-166.3
257	15-360
259	59-8.1 to 59-8.9
261	15-870, 15-870.1, 15-873.1
262	15-15
263	15-20.5
264	15-25.1
265	8-178
267	51-114
268	15-114
269	4-15
270	4-61
271	8-703.1
272	19-120
273	56-275.1
274	22-276
275	54-275.1
277	37-144.1
279	15-8
280	15-42.1
281	26-40
282	38.1-381
283	6-103.1
284	15-739.7
285	56-274
286	14-132, 14-136
287	18-313
288	3-35
290	62-3
291	15-241
292	19-7.1
293	22-231.1
294	54-276.7
295	16.1-115
296	32-337
297	37-34.3
298	32-22
299	28-204.1:1
300	22-204
301	22-285, 22-286
302	28-201.3
303	8-204, 19-193
305	58-1063
306	45-17.1 to 45-17.4
307	58-1107
309	24-345.3
310	18-229.01
312	58-81
313	58-643, 58-643.1R
314	58-790, 58-804
315	29-145.1
316	33-15.1
317	33-47.1
318	29-122
319	22-188.46 to 22-188.49
320	14-155
321	40-109
322	46.1-397, 46.1-398
323	46.1-281.1
324	53-109.1
325	63-379, 63-380, 63-382, 63-385
326	17-127, 17-127.1, 17-127.13, 17-127.14
328	15-77.1 to 15-77.76
329	15-65.1 to 15-65.3
330	1-13.22
331	14-155.4
332	15-229
333	24-3, 24-11, 24-12, 24-14
335	9-105
336	63-369.1
337	2-22.2
338	8-208.1, 19-135.1, 19-193.1
339	58-769
340	14-56R, 14-56.1
341	14-57
342	62-43, 62-44
344	16.1-194 to 16.1-197
345	33-57.1
346	37-75
349	14-86
350	63-373.1
351	24-23.1, 24-23.4, 24-345.7
352	18-6
353	16.1-162
354	16.1-209
355	15-480
356	51-111.54
357	18-76
359	33-113.2
360	15-709.1
361	58-12
363	2-66.1
364	23-1
365	14-56
367	51-111.31, 51-111.36
368	51-114.2
369	33-317
370	2-49
371	14-68
372	20-61.1
373	30-35 to 30-41R, 30-42 to 30-51
374	15-861
375	22-67
376	16.1-201
377	18-301
378	15-152.25
379	16.1-43.1
380	8-293
382	15-668.2
384	2-262
385	44-145.3
386	37-96
387	8-636
388	63-105
389	15-918, 15-919, 15-921, 15-923
391	46.1-82
392	64-57.1
393	44-1, 44-2, 44-5, 44-6, 44-8 to 44-10, 44-13, 44-15, 44-19, 44-24 to 44-30, 44-32 to 44-33, 44-34R, 44-35 to 44-41, 44-43 to 44-46, 44-49 to 44-51, 44-54, 44-75, 44-76, 44-78, 44-81 to 44-84, 44-86, 44-87, 44-90, 44-91R, 44-92R, 44-93, 44-95R, 44-96, 44-98, 44-99, 44-102, 44-104, 44-105R, 44-106 to 44-108, 44-111 to 44-113, 44-116, 44-117, 44-117.1R, 44-118R, 44-119, 44-120
394	4-85
395	4-28
398	3-676.1 to 3-676.3, 3-676.4:1, 3-676.4:2, 3-676.5
399	16.1-137
400	15-764.12
401	15-749
402	15-764.12, 15-764.13
403	56-222
404	54-17

Acts 1958 Chapter	Code 1950 Section
407	46.1-167.1 to 46.1-167.6
408	54-789.3
409	21-29, 21-31, 21-31.1
410	21-10
411	21-112.21
412	10-114
413	62-9.1
414	2-29
415	58-362, 58-367.2
416	64-138
417	34-29
418	13.1-282
419	51-111.18
420	29-144.1
421	37-6.1
422	2-232
423	57-12
424	55-52
425	14-181
426	42-25
427	10-1, 10-3, 10-5, 10-6, 10-8.1, 10-12, 10-13, 10-14, 10-118 to 10-120, 10-121R, 10-128, 10-130
428	58-795
430	8-449.1
431	58-823
433	63-246
434	36-11.1
435	55-88
436	15-333, 15-504.2
437	15-855
440	15-504
441	15-792.1
442	58-944, 58-947
443	29-551
444	29-144, 29-162, 29-163
445	29-121
446	37-48.1
447	18-70.1
449	28-95, 28-172.1
450	64-71.1
451	29-136.1
452	38.1-349
453	38.1-356.1
454	21-120
455	12-65 to 12-67
456	15-239
457	65-43.1, 65-44, 65-48
458	3-6.1
459	58-715, 58-719, 58-730, 58-730.1
460	15-792
461	54-298 to 54-300, 54-302, 54-306, 54-306.3, 54-309, 54-316, 54-317.1 to 54-319, 54-320, 54-321.2
462	14-77.1
464	61-78 to 61-82, 61-85, 61-86, 61-89, 61-91, 61-93
465	22-277
466	9-77.3
467	62-117.8 to 62-117.11
468	53-272, 53-275
469	38.1-286
470	8-633, 8-634
471	28-195
472	37-125.7, 37-125.15
473	37-155R
474	15-692.2
475	28-204.6
476	28-93.2
477	28-158
479	29-184.3
481	58-266.3
482	46.1-66, n.
483	3-209 to 3-219R, 3-219.1 to 3-219.13, 3-221
484	10-103, 15-714.10, 15-764.14
485	33-238, 33-240, 33-255.7
486	23-19
487	3-79.7
488	62-106.12
489	46.1-352.1
490	33-40.1
491	29-45
492	29-44
493	29-55
495	29-146
496	18-77, 46.1-417, 46.1-419, 46.1-420
498	9-96 to 9-99
499	22-306.1
500	22-232.1 to 22-232.3, 22-232.5, 22-232.7, 22-232.9R, 22-232.10, 22-232.17
501	46.1-1, 46.1-444, 46.1-450, 46.1-467, 46.1-472, 46.1-485, 46.1-504
503	9-77.3
505	2-124.1
506	13.1-93, 13.1-118, 13.1-133, 13.1-256, 13.1-280, 13.1-294, 13.1-311.1
507	15-555.2
508	62-195
509	65-97
510	58-359
511	58-355
513	42-26
514	29-148
515	22-64
516	8-10.1
518	36-27
519	63-106, 63-119, 63-145, 63-183, 63-209
520	8-42.1
521	21-120
522	54-145.2
523	5-24.1
525	38.1-477.2
526	16.1-24
527	58-393, 58-393.1
528	8-327.1
529	38.1-477.1
530	58-476.1
531	58-371.2
533	36-4
534	2-135.1
535	54-516
537	58-784.2
538	8-182
540	44-114.1 to 44-114.4
541	46-1 to 46-553R, 46.1-1 to 46.1-167, 46.1-168 to 46.1-281, 46.1-282 to 46.1-344, 46.1-347 to 46.1-352, 46.1-353 to 46.1-364, 46.1-366 to 46.1-555
542	2-87, 4-20, 33-11.1, 52-11, 53-16.1, 56-334
543	18-220.1 to 18-220.5
544	22-278R, 22-280R, 22-281R, 33-283R, 44-101R
545	27-25.1
546	32-70.1, 33-294R
547	33-109
548	33-281R, 33-282R, 33-284 to 33-286R, 33-292R, 33-293R, 33-296R
549	35-64R
550	52-4.2
551	54-399, 54-400 to 54-402R, 54-403.1, 54-406, 54-407, 54-410, 54-411, 54-414, 54-415, 54-417, 54-418R, 54-420, 54-422, 54-423.1, 54-424, 54-425R, 54-425.1 to 54-426.1, 54-429R, 54-430R,

Acts 1958 Chapter	Code 1950 Section
	54-431 to 54-432.2, 54-433, 54-434R, 54-434.1, 54-434.2, 54-435 to 54-439R, 54-440 to 54-441.1, 54-447, 54-448, 54-452, 54-463, 54-471, 54-478 to 54-480, 54-484 to 54-486, 54-499
552	15-18, 33-279.3
553	7-33.1
554	33-32
555	14-133
556	37-34.2:1 to 37-34.2:7
557	31-19 to 31-25R, 31-26 to 31-36
558	64-139
559	58-811.2
560	9-100 to 9-104
561	5-14.1 to 5-14.3
562	58-445, 58-447, 58-448R, 58-458, 58-463
564	13.1-10, 13.1-12, 13.1-17, 13.1-20, 13.1-21, 13.1-26, 13.1-32, 13.1-49, 13.1-55, 13.1-58, 13.1-63, 13.1-64, 13.1-66, 13.1-67, 13.1-92, 13.1-104, 13.1-106, 13.1-110, 13.1-115, 13.1-115.1, 13.1-120, 13.1-123, 13.1-134, 13.1-204, 13.1-209, 13.1-211, 13.1-214, 13.1-231, 13.1-255, 13.1-269, 13.1-272, 13.1-273, 13.1-276, 13.1-278, 13.1-278.1, 13.1-285, 13.1-295, 13.1-316, 13.1-337, 13.1-345, 13.1-517
565	13.1-135, 13.1-296
566	12-22R, 12-23R, 12-57.1
568	65-51, 65-52, 65-62, 65-68
569	23-107
570	58-117
571	33-39
572	53-122
573	33-101, 33-105, 33-106, 33-107R
574	54-784.1 to 54-786, 54-789.4
575	29-184.2
576	24-53, 24-68, 24-71
577	59-114.5 to 59-114.9
578	16.1-87, 16.1-91
579	59-191 to 59-195, 59-198
580	24-364.1
581	33-70R, 33-70.1 to 33-70.11, 33-74R
582	51-111.70
583	33-252
584	33-114
585	58-1141, 58-1142
586	2-4.3
587	9-29, 9-38
588	21-121
589	33-36.1 to 33-36.9
590	58-65.1
591	58-78
592	3-595 to 3-598R
593	3-139R, 3-139.1 to 3-139.5, 3-140R, 3-141R, 3-143 to 3-150R
594	3-151, 3-154, 3-155, 3-158 to 3-161, 3-164, 3-171, 3-172
595	37-62.1
596	38.1-75
597	38.1-64, 38.1-65
598	18-348.2
600	46.1-345
601	14-179
602	58-1024
603	19-297.1
604	40-36
605	24-84R, 24-114, 24-135, 24-210, 24-285
606	18-239.1, 18-239.2
607	29-151
608	30-10
609	29-145.1
610	37-38.1
611	52-23, 52-24
612	46.1-342
613	58-766
614	59-153 to 59-155.3
615	2-139, 15-583
616	16.1-206.1
617	15-454
619	18-147.1
620	15-8.1
621	24-145
623	19-103
624	51-136.1
625	58-730
626	46.1-167
627	56-529 to 56-530, n.
628	22-218 to 22-220
629	59-106.1
630	11-23.1
631	22-188.12
632	22-130.3, 22-130.4
635	22-206
636	32-391 to 32-405
637	20-63
638	62-94.1, 62-94.3, 62-94.4
639	32-406 to 32-410, 54-574 to 54-729R
640	15-586 to 15-666.12R, 15-666.13 to 15-666.68, 22-167 to 22-188.2R
641	16.1-176

ACTS 1959, EX. SESS.

Acts 1959, Ex. Sess. Chapter	Code 1950 Section
1	22-115.10, 22-115.12, 22-115.13, 22-115.15R, 22-115.19
2	22-251 to 22-275R
4	18-151.1 to 18-151.5
5	28-218.1 to 28-218.3
6	22-115.21
9	6-51
10	46.1-155
11	2-20.1
12	15-707
13	24-119
14	29-184.2
15	38.1-286
16	29-202
17	24-345.3
18	15-20.8
20	33-308
21	46.1-280
22	46.1-65, 46.1-66
23	46.1-155
24	33-191.1
25	29-184.1
27	23-91.1, n.
28	28-218.1 to 28-218.3
30	24-119
31	16.1-201
32	22-188.50, 22-188.51
33	37-34.2:1, n.
34	22-108, 22-110
35	15-707
36	15-16.1
38	56-291.4
39	30-47
40	32-392
41	55-119
42	38.1-381
43	38.1-456, 38.1-465, 38.1-465.1, 38-1-466, 38.1-468.1
45	15-666.16
46	15-666.69 to 15-666.76

Acts 1959, Ex. Sess. Chapter	Code 1950 Section
47	51-111.24
48	22-120.1R
49	22-294.1 to 22-294.3
50	23-38.1
51	58-921, 58-925, 58-928
52	58-839, 58-844, 58-846.1
53	22-115.1 to 22-115.14R, 22-115.16 to 22-115.21R, 22-115.22 to 22-115.28
54	14-56.1
55	46.1-65
56	58-769.1
57	13.1-94, 13.1-128
58	51-112
59	51-111.54
60	23-91.1 to 23-91.4
61	23-19
62	8-182
63	19-92.1
64	17-41
65	2-20.1
66	2-20.1
68	22-161.1 to 22-161.5
69	15-288, 15-320, 15-353, 15-370, 15-395, 15-551.3, 15-575 to 15-577, 15-579, 15-582R, 15-584, 15-585
70	38.1-381
71	22-232.18 to 22-232.31
72	22-275.1 to 22-275.25
73	58-78
74	22-188.30 to 22-188.40R
75	22-188.41 to 22-188.45R
76	22-188.46 to 22-188.49R
77	22-188.3 to 22-188.15R
78	22-89 to 22-90
79	22-55, 22-60, 22-72, 22-73, 22-78, 22-97, 22-120.3 to 22-120.5, 22-121 to 22-125R, 22-126, 22-127, 22-127.1R, 22-128, 22-129R, 22-130, 22-131R, 22-132, 22-133, 22-139R, 22-139.1R, 22-141
80	22-21.1
81	22-194R, 22-196R, 22-219
82	29-184.2, 29-184.4
83	58-355
84	30-13, 30-14
85	37-34.2:1, n.
86	46.1-276
87	54-500
88	54-445
89	54-504
90	46.1-280
91	46.1-343
92	55-134.1
94	54-1
95	36-19.3

ACTS 1960

Acts 1960 Chapter	Code 1950 Section
1	15-65.1, n.
5	55-59
6	15-668.1
10	54-1
11	54-31
12	54-788.1
14	15-854.1
16	8-54, 8-76
17	14-133
19	20-121
20	13.1-434 to 13.1-436
21	13.1-424 to 13.1-433
22	6-79.1
23	6-78
24	2-20.1
25	17-41
27	6-76
29	6-357
30	29-184.2
31	38.1-436
33	15-241
34	15-237
35	8-639
36	21-118
39	2-29
43	19.1-115
44	15-574.2
45	55-276
46	29-184.1:1
47	3-249
48	22-43.1
49	58-884
50	15-16.1
53	15-9.2
54	60-92, 60-94.1, 60-96
56	23-49.1
58	58-822 to 58-824
59	58-355, 58-362
60	58-67.1
61	45-26, 54-24, 54-98, 54-260.13, 54-295.7, 54-341, 54-395, 54-398.12, 54-741, 54-789
62	6-12R, 6-245
63	6-255
64	6-251
65	6-351.1
66	21-291R, 21-291.2

Acts 1960 Chapter	Code 1950 Section
67	38.1-482.1 to 38.1-482.16
68	56-334
69	14-155
71	13.1-513, 13.1-514.1
73	26-17
74	6-348
75	46.1-3
76	20-79
77	19.1-211
78	8-135.1
79	46.1-64, 46.1-158R, 46-1-158.1
80	13.1-140 to 13.1-155
81	43-4.1
82	17-46
83	15-555.2
84	2-175
85	8-780 to 8-788R
86	54-446.1
87	15-239
88	53-97R
89	65-38 to 65-39.1
90	54-58
92	15-666.48, 15-666.52
93	58-943.3, 58-945
94	19.1-196
95	58-792.1
97	18.1-173
98	18.1-173.1
99	18.1-15.1
100	62-106.7, 62-106.8
101	4-85
102	16.1-176.1
103	16.1-178.2
104	4-22
105	55-24
106	14-133
107	58-792.3
108	20-91
110	46.1-357
111	38.1-192
112	38.1-286R
113	46.1-216
114	8-293
115	38.1-291
116	38.1-208
117	38.1-363.1
119	46.1-12, 46.1-58, 46.1-107
120	46.1-290, 46.1-301
121	46.1-36
122	46.1-291.1
123	46.1-163
124	54-446
125	46.1-293, 46.1-308, 46.1-308.1, 46.1-311, 46.1-313
126	29-148
127	38.1-381.1

Acts 1960 Chapter	Code 1950 Section
128	29-55.2
129	29-145.1
131	29-158.2
132	8-654.1
133	37-1.1, 37-5
134	37-37
136	60-10, 60-26, 60-42, 60-44, 60-45.2, 60-47, 60-67, 60-68, 60-70 to 60-73.1, 60-75, 60-76.2
138	51-111.55
140	29-194.2
141	46.1-14
142	42-55
144	16.1-43.2
145	15-688
146	17-79
147	30-5
148	18.1-272
149	65-4
150	54-793R, 54-794R, 58-285R, 58-286, 58-287 to 58-288.1R
151	46.1-253
152	15-870.1R, 15-873.1R
153	46.1-193
154	15-884
156	46.1-255, 46.1-256, 46.1-265, 46.1-267, 46.1-268, 46.1-287
157	46.1-351
159	46.1-197
161	57-26
164	10-8.1, 10-118, 10-119, 10-130
167	15-557
168	15-11
170	29-202
172	46.1-180
173	29-161.1
174	15-453
175	16.1-16
176	15-13
177	46.1-378
178	46.1-382
179	46.1-413
180	23-14, 23-39 to 23-42, 23-44, 23-45, 23-47, 23-48R, 23-49, 23-49.1
182	14-56.1
183	54-89, 54-93
184	32-294
185	35-3.1
186	35-25
187	23-93, 23-94
188	46.1-167.1 to 46.1-167.5
189	38.1-605R, 38.1-608R, 38.1-622R
191	58-19.1 to 58-19.5
192	17-153.1
194	17-119, 17-119.1
195	18.1-160
196	61-132
198	14-5.2
199	17-126.1
200	46.1-423
201	46.1-383
202	51-28.1
203	15-15.2
204	46.1-3
205	14-155.13
206	63-373.1
207	63-78, 63-96
208	21-6, 21-29, 21-37, 21-38, 21-41
209	46.1-167.7
211	15-707.1
212	15-574.3
214	13.1-214
215	2-161.1R, 2-211.1, 2-222, 2-267
216	2-259
217	22-67R, 22-67.1
218	46.1-342.1
222	22-133, 22-141
223	46.1-343
224	6-348.2
225	15-16
226	18.1-340.1
228	28-148
230	36-19.3R
231	58-687
232	40-35
233	18.1-227 to 18.1-236.3
234	42-26
235	42-28
236	14-181
237	2-128
238	18.1-261, 18.1-263, 18.1-265, 18.1-266
239	58-831.1, 58-831.2
240	2-164R, 2-171R, 2-174, 2-193
242	59-101.2
243	46.1-149
244	10-76 to 10-77, 10-81, 10-83
245	2-22.2R, 2-22.3
246	62-183
247	3-348
248	32-148, 32-153, 32-154
249	58-86.1:1
250	3-541
251	1-13.36
252	46.1-121
253	3-451.14
254	54-750
255	8-390
256	46.1-250
257	62-190
262	37-10 to 37-12R
263	37-34.2:6, 37-34.2:7
264	19.1-28
266	2-300 to 2-305
267	18.1-358 to 18.1-358.2
268	54-273
269	10-79.1
271	33-3
272	38.1-472, 38.1-472.1, 38.1-473R, 38.1-474R, 38.1-475 to 38.1-477, 38.1-477.1 to 38.1-478R, 38.1-479, 38.1-480, 38.1-481R
273	38.1-424, 38.1-424.1, 38.1-426 to 38.1-428.4
274	8-393
275	20-61
276	6-35
277	38.1-301.6R
278	14-132, 14-136
279	64-140
280	46.1-334
281	38.1-296
282	14-163.1
283	3-619
284	16.1-92
285	55-130
286	53-198.1
287	65-10.1
288	24-68
289	38.1-91
290	38.1-296
291	38.1-92.1
292	38.1-659
293	38.1-378
294	38.1-44
295	15-250
296	13.1-204
297	65-49
298	65-66
299	65-90
300	13.1-242.1
301	8-169
302	8-170
303	8-480.1
304	32-411 to 32-414
305	32-220, 32-222
306	15-707
307	1-13.35

Acts 1960 Chapter	Code 1950 Section
308	33-75.1 to 33-75.4
309	15-901
310	65-85
311	14-155
312	15-678.1
313	15-764.10
314	16.1-176
315	56-304.11
318	9-42
319	9-23
320	9-16.1
321	40-34
322	46.1-428
324	29-184
325	56-338.8, 56-338.12, 56-338.14
328	58-81
329	58-268
330	55-210.1 to 55-210.29
331	16.1-178, 63-73, 63-241, 63-351
332	51-111.41:2
333	54-298, 54-299, 54-310
334	54-307, 54-308, 54-308.5, 54-310, 54-310.1
335	58-476 to 58-476.6, 58-477 to 58-478.1R, 58-481, 58-483R
336	40-126, 40-127
339	58-32
340	35-3
342	51-29.7:1
343	58-792.4
346	58-524, 58-526
347	7-33.1
348	51-111.41:3
349	58-411
351	9-105
352	33-15.1
354	2-22.4
355	29-184.3
356	54-260.25
357	32-195.1, 32-195.2, 32-195.6R, 32-195.7R, 32-195.8, 32-195.16
358	18-1 to 18-366R, 18.1-1 to 18.1-170, 18.1-172 to 18.1-188, 18.1-190 to 18.1-226, 18.1-237 to 18.1-271, 18.1-273 to 18.1-340, 18.1-341 to 18.1-358, 18.1-359 to 18.1-429
359	15-20.4
360	15-548
361	16.1-26, 16.1-27
362	16.1-124, 16.1-125, 16.1-127
363	20-48
364	46.1-350, 46.1-351, 46.1-362, 46.1-417, 46.1-421
365	53-276R
366	19-1 to 19-342R, 19.1-1 to 19.1-102, 19.1-104 to 19.1-122, 19.1-123 to 19.1-145, 19.1-147 to 19.1-163, 19.1-164 to 19.1-259, 19.1-260 to 19.1-297, 19.1-299 to 19.1-373
367	14-96
368	14-132
369	14-140
370	15-25.1
371	15-571
372	16.1-90
373	16.1-129
374	17-163
375	52-21
376	53-142
378	23-36.2
379	54-60, 54-61, 54-61.1R, 54-62, 54-62.1, 54-66
380	24-119, subsection (1) (c)R
382	15-384.10 to 15-384.78, n.
383	24-345.3
384	8-868.2
385	37-128
386	37-125.1, 37-125.5
387	37-230.1
388	16.1-158
389	19.1-163.1
390	63-101
391	46.1-267, 46.1-285, 46.1-319
392	58-757.1 to 58-757.27
393	4-15.1
395	63-369.1
396	58-12
397	46.1-180, n.
398	58-715, 58-732, 58-733, 58-744, 58-753.3
399	20-118
400	51-111.22, 51-111.27, 51-111.31 to 51-111.33
401	58-128, 58-373, 58-443, 58-461R
402	6-140 to 6-201R, 6-201.1 to 6-201.63
403	4-40, 4-108
404	51-112
405	14-68.3
406	33-298, 33-302, 33-317 to 33-317.3, 33-321
407	14-51, 14-52
411	53-188
412	15-243
413	29-184.2
414	58-811.1
415	14-69.3
416	14-71.3
417	14-70.2
418	58-829, 58-829.2, 58-829.3
421	54-441
423	42-19.1
424	46.1-357
426	8-511
427	24-131, 24-370
428	26-20.1
430	15-764.12
432	53-103
434	40-96, 40-97, 40-100, 40-100.4:1, 40-100.6, 40-101, 40-102, 40-104 to 40-111, 40-114, 40-116, 40-118
435	14-50
436	56-284
437	19.1-122.1
438	6-348.3
439	23-35.3, 23-35.5
440	63-135, 63-136, 63-157, 63-158, 63-199, 63-200, 63-212
441	54-44.2
442	58-18R, 58-128, 58-129, 58-131 to 58-131.18, 58-134, 58-148, 58-151, 58-418
443	56-451.1
444	65-85
445	9-16.2
446	9-44.1
447	9-44.2
448	22-115.22 to 22-115.28R, 22-115.29 to 22-115.35
449	53-293
450	53-109.1
451	32-322 to 32-353.3R, 32-353.4 to 32-353.31
452	58-494
453	15-16.1

Acts 1960 Chapter	Code 1950 Section
457	46.1-110.1, 46.1-110.2
458	58-712
459	54-50.1
460	22-107.1
461	22-115.36, 22-115.37
462	38.1-381
463	22-119
464	22-20
465	18.1-359
466	8-386
467	19.1-154
468	8-111.1
469	8-288
472	15-740 to 15-746R
473	32-392
474	15-152.9
475	51-21.1
476	4-33, 4-104
478	16.1-143.1
480	33-255.24 to 33-255.44, n.
482	17-41
483	15-220
484	64-126
485	14-155.14
486	51-114.2
487	15-555
488	24-150
490	36-19.4
491	33-57.2 to 33-59.1, 33-60R, 33-60.1 to 33-60.3, 33-62R, 33-62.1, 33-63R, 33-63.1, 33-64 to 33-65.1, 33-67 to 33-67.2
492	58-17R
493	19.1-259.1
494	23-9.2:1
496	37-254, 37-258.1 to 37-258.3, 37-259, 37-260
497	15-65.4, 15-77.77
498	34-29
499	58-716
500	62-174.1 to 62-174.19
501	36-55.1
502	8-441
503	38.1-314.1 to 38.1-314.16
504	8-270
505	14-86, 14-86.1
507	32-10.1 to 32-10.3
508	58-425 to 58-427, 58-434, 58-435, 58-440, 58-441
510	46.1-190
511	46.1-367, 46.1-437
513	15-285, 15-290
514	14-66.2
515	15-20.8
516	15-20.6
517	28-39, 28-43 to 28-45.01, 28-57.1, 28-61, 28-71, 28-93.1, 28-95, 28-99, 28-100, 28-102R, 28-103, 28-108, 28-110, 28-123, 28-124, 28-136 to 28-137.1, 28-141, 28-142, 28-144R, 28-157, 28-162.1, 28-163R, 28-264R, 28-170 to 28-172, 28-178, 28-187, 28-188, 28-191, 28-195, 28-201.1, 28-201.4
518	7-1.1
519	15-152.26
520	59-227 to 59-235
521	54-767
522	6-51
523	58-371.2
524	15-891.3
525	15-891.10
526	58-951
527	64-70
528	15-6
529	15-93
530	24-158
531	22-141, 22-141.1
532	56-285R, 56-338.50 to 56-338.64
533	15-15.3
534	15-692.3
535	3-203.1, 3-203.2, 3-205, 3-208.1, 3-208.7, 3-208.8:1, 3-208.22, 3-208.31
536	29-57
537	29-129.1, 29-132
538	29-130.1
539	9-6.2, 29-126
540	29-32
541	29-37, 29-68.1
543	58-153
544	56-405
545	15-7.2
546	33-117.2 to 33-117.4
547	58-1142, 58-1152.1
548	18.1-55
550	15-152.12
551	17-119, 17-221.1, 17-221.4, 17-221.7, 17-221.10, 17-221.14
553	62-1
554	58-266.2, 58-266.3
556	65-51, 65-52, 65-62, 65-68
557	38.1-291
558	38.1-108
559	51-131
561	21-120
562	21-121.2, 21-140.2
563	15-666.29
564	15-666.32:2
565	55-58.1
566	29-53, 29-54, 29-55
567	15-923
568	29-122
569	8-157, 8-158
570	46.1-225
571	43-34
572	8-182
573	58-1010
574	56-281
575	30-19.2
576	14-132.1
577	19.1-32.1
578	59-222 to 59-226
580	65-85
581	14-135, 14-143
582	28-57.2
583	15-524
584	14-145
587	8-639
588	2-20.1
589	26-40
590	29-135, 29-136, 29-138, 29-150
591	46.1-328
592	10-14.1
593	36-11.2
594	29-5
598	63-127.1
599	54-513
600	62-2.1
601	15-508
602	9-77.3
603	58-628, 58-629, 58-711, 58-715, 58-730, 58-747, 58-757.01
604	51-111.10, 51-111.11, 51-111.16, 51-111.29, 51-111.34, 51-111.38, 51-111.38:3, 51-111.38:10 to 51-111.38:16, 51-111.41:1, 51-111.46, 51-111.47, 51-111.55 to 51-111.59, 51-111.62, 51-111.63, 51-111.67:1 to 51-111.67:13
606	15-8
607	4-112.2

Acts 1960 Chapter	Code 1950 Section
608	4-73.1
609	58-101, 58-121

ACTS 1962

Acts 1962 Chapter	Code 1950 Section
1	15-65.2, 15-77.73
2	2-20.1
3	17-119.2
6	60-69
7	17-127.15
8	33-279.3
9	19.1-32.1
10	8-227, 8-422.1, 8-460, 8-461, 55-230, 55-237
11	3-592
12	60-42, 60-45.2, 60-47, 60-68
13	54-1
14	13.1-62
15	18.1-102
16	56-419.1
19	15-350.2
20	37-75
22	52-21
23	15-707
25	58-27.1
26	21-121.2, 21-140.2
29	3-117.19
30	54-445.1
31	54-499, 54-499.1
35	46.1-343
38	6-49.1, 6-51
39	55-66.3
41	57-12
42	18.1-21
43	51-111.67:4 to 51-111.67:6
44	13.1-2, 13.1-18, 13.1-74
45	54-147, 54-147.2, 54-167, 54-187
46	17-127.16
47	6-201.49
48	53-57.1
49	51-28.2
50	51-111.24
51	63-28
52	9-48.6
54	15-504, 15-508
55	14-8.1
57	3-384 to 3-400.39R, 3-400.40 to 3-400.107, 3-416 to 3-424.8R
60	3-451.1, 3-451.5 to 3-451.7, 3-451.11R, 3-451.11:1
62	4-79
64	36-47.1

Acts 1962 Chapter	Code 1950 Section
66	40-1 to 40-12, 40-17R, 40-18, 40-20, 40-21, 40-22.1, 40-23R, 40-24, 40-25 to 40-29R, 40-33 to 40-37, 40-38R, 40-44, 40-44.1, 40-45 to 40-54R, 40-54.1, 40-55, 40-58, 40-59R, 40-60R, 40-61 to 40-61.3
67	56-529 to 56-530, n.
69	23-14, 23-39 to 23-42, 23-47, 23-49 to 23-49.20
70	65-43.1
71	60-14, 60-18, 60-21.1
73	58-695
74	23-7
75	9-29.1
76	15-666.32:1, 15-666.32:3
77	22-42
78	23-135.8
79	4-115
80	37-25.6, 37-125.1, 37-125.5, 37-125.6, 37-125.7R, 37-125.15
81	23-35.9
82	54-95
83	60-68
84	46.1-339
85	46.1-329
86	46.1-154
87	46.1-206
89	46.1-299
90	29-188, 29-190
91	63-218R, 63-218.1R
92	46.1-159
93	58-767
94	27-25.1
95	58-355
96	33-136.2
97	15-239
100	24-277.2, 24-277.3
101	57-3
102	13.1-24.1, 13.1-212.1
103	58-1048, 58-1051
104	1-13.27
106	29-158.3
107	8-182
108	16.1-130, 16.1-138
109	43-27.1, 43-53.1
110	8-417
111	26-16.1R, 26-35.1R, 26-37
113	46.1-330
114	17-127.6
115	64-108
118	18.1-146.1
121	46.1-252.1
125	46.1-198.1

Acts 1962 Chapter	Code 1950 Section
126	3-709.1 to 3-709.23
127	54-274
128	54-315.1
129	58-12
130	15-764.12
131	58-413
132	15-508.1
134	29-184.3
136	29-184, 29-185
137	58-985
138	60-115 to 60-117
139	38.1-438
141	29-144.5
142	53-299.1
143	53-274
145	38.1-674
146	46.1-284, 46.1-313, 46.1-314
148	26-20
149	58-822
150	58-757.1, n.
151	4-15.1
152	43-2
153	5-10.6, 5-10.7
154	38.1-480
156	55-58.1
157	3-583.1 to 3-583.8
159	13.1-147
161	63-162
162	46.1-343
163	15-20.3:1
166	43-70, 43-71
168	15-505
169	55-6
170	6-201.13, 6-201.29, 6-201.32
171	64-119
172	38.1-659
173	6-54
174	58-795
175	46.1-248
176	33-298, 33-317.1, 33-317.3R
177	22-107.3
178	2-66.1R, 2-77.10 to 2-77.12
179	11-20, 11-23
180	58-1038
181	22-288
182	4-40, 4-108
183	22-207
184	3-16.1 to 3-16.4
185	24-45
186	53-293
188	23-7.1
189	15-9.2
192	46.1-343.1
193	14-163.1
194	22-29.1 to 22-29.14
195	22-29.15
196	17-119.1

Acts 1962 Chapter	Code 1950 Section
197	46.1-332
198	32-167.1 to 32-167.6
199	29-171.1
200	4-84.1
201	24-45.1
202	21-400.1
203	15-714.12
204	21-280.1
205	23-20.1
206	15-764.16
207	21-200.1
208	21-130.1
209	15-739.3:1
210	4-15.2
212	21-29
213	21-10
214	46.1-45
215	58-78
217	14-56.1
218	15-241
219	12-41.1
220	15-666.64
221	56-347
222	56-49
223	22-67.1R, 22-67.2
224	31-10
225	18.1-238.1
226	29-184.5
227	14-185, 14-187
228	33-191.1
229	29-145.1
230	24-314
231	16.1-35.1
232	15-552.1
233	17-28
234	15-562
235	2-86.2
236	58-797, 58-798
237	17-117, 17-118, 17-119, 17-127.17
238	55-136
239	13.1-102.1, 13.1-265.1
240	18.1-200 to 18.1-202
241	22-97.1
242	20-107
243	42-19.2
244	47-1
245	51-111.57
246	46.1-315, 46.1-320
247	2-29
248	58-732
249	58-687
250	8-47, 8-66, 8-66.1
251	32-415 to 32-422
253	12-65, 12-66, 38.1-21, 38.1-252
254	46.1-357
255	46.1-298
256	2-5, 42-58.1, 42-59.1
257	32-91
260	24-300, 24-305, 24-307
261	46.1-375.1
262	2-66.2
263	38.1-165.1
264	57-39.2 to 57-39.7, n.
265	15-152.29
266	38.1-221
267	6-79.2
268	6-426.1
270	60-46
272	23-91.5 to 23-91.8
273	33-228, 33-234
274	23-135.12 to 23-135.16
275	10-125.1, 10-126
276	51-19, 51-25
277	54-873 to 54-898
278	58-266.5
279	58-266.3
280	23-135.17 to 23-135.21
281	58-884
282	58-806
283	15-686
284	1-13.3:1
285	17-7.1
286	17-119.1
287	17-122
288	20-91
289	18.1-228
290	20-118
291	51-111.70:1
292	14-86
293	42-19.3
295	64-18
297	63-44, 63-101, 63-106, 63-110
298	3-708.1 to 3-709, 59-71 to 59-106.1R, 59-114.1 to 59-140.1R
299	58-520.1
300	37-34.2:7
301	55-109.1
302	18.1-58, 46.1-16, 46.1-62, 46.1-177, 46.1-192, 46.1-305, 46.1-350, 46.1-351, 46.1-398, 46.1-495
303	33-58.1
304	54-295
305	58-81.2
306	57-16
307	46.1-193, 46.1-194
308	32-85.4
309	54-292.1
310	15-666.27:1
313	46.1-280
315	1-13.35
316	16.1-199, 16.1-200
317	58-735.4
318	58-744.1
319	58-750
320	58-747
321	58-735.3
322	58-726
323	58-722
324	58-689
325	58-754
326	53-135.1, 53-251.2
327	53-266, 53-266.1, 53-268, 53-271, 53-272, 53-278, 53-278.5, 53-279
328	37-34.3
331	58-153
333	15-7.3
335	21-134.1
336	36-49
337	9-67
338	64-54
339	65-14
340	65-92
341	33-113.2
343	18.1-421
344	59-21.1
345	30-42, 30-44, 30-45
346	62-106.8:1
348	33-38
350	55-61.1
351	33-255.44:1 to 33-255.44:9, n.
352	40-118
354	10-8.1, 10-13, 10-118 to 10-120R
355	10-12, 10-122R, 10-124R, 10-125R, 10-128, 10-130 to 10-132
356	2-34, 2-57.01
357	46.1-309.1
358	58-702
359	58-704
360	33-255.45 to 33-255.66R
361	16.1-94
362	20-23
363	63-119, 63-145
364	2-306 to 2-309
366	19.1-42
367	55-125
368	46.1-34.1, 46.1-59, 46.1-78, 46.1-368, 46.1-375, 46.1-378, 46.1-384, 46.1-516, 46.1-523, 46.1-535
369	16.1-178
370	53-122.1

Acts 1962 Chapter	Code 1950 Section
371	6-27.2
373	23-19, 23-21, 23-22, 23-26
374	19.1-262
375	65-96
376	40-64.1
377	37-33
378	1-13.38
379	17-221.1 to 17-221.5, 17-221.7, 17-221.8, 17-221.9R, 17-221.10, 17-221.11R, 17-221.12R, 17-221.13, 17-221.14R
380	58-263.1
381	15-26.1
382	46.1-249
383	24-323, 24-324
384	14-155
385	4-22
386	14-155.1, 14-155.4R
388	8-355, 8-358
389	54-42.1
390	46.1-115
391	55-88.1, 55-96.1, 58-297
392	62-106.5, n.
393	15-714.13 to 15-714.28
394	54-276
395	32-275.1 to 32-275.3
396	35-42.2 to 35-42.8
397	29-55.4
399	15-254, 15-255R, 15-288, 15-320, 15-551.3, 15-580
400	15-14, 15-15R, 15-15.2R
401	15-233
402	15-20.7
403	63-119, 63-145, 63-183
404	6-26 to 6-27.1
405	17-15, 17-18
406	28-1 to 28-258R, 28.1-1 to 28.1-94, 28.1-95 to 28.1-101, 28.1-102 to 28.1-226
407	15-766.1 to 15-766.3R, 15-779 to 15-854.1R, 15-855 to 15-870R, 15-871 to 15-873R, 15-874 to 15-890R, 15-891.1 to 15-891.10R, 15-899 to 15-913R, 15-915 to 15-926.1R, 15-961 to 15-969.3
408	15-551.11
409	17-41
411	18.1-241
412	58-81, 58-84
413	14-85
414	18.1-119.1
415	17-153
417	51-111.55
418	8-750.1
419	17-30.1, 17-30.2
420	29-121, n.
421	23-9.2:1
422	24-71
423	58-715
424	46.1-423.1, 46.1-423.2
426	25-1 to 25-46R, 25-46.1 to 25-46.34
427	51-111.41:1
428	22-331 to 22-344
430	8-636
431	46.1-180.2
432	51-3
437	63-291, 63-293
438	51-111.58:1
439	14-62, 14-86, 14-95, 14-145
441	14-5.2
444	16.1-116, 16.1-118
445	17-46, 17-46.1
446	19.1-336
448	55-63
449	54-276.9
450	54-446.2
451	32-423 to 32-427
452	55-17.1
453	4-15
454	51-136
456	59-10
457	38.1-381
458	46.1-411
461	58-180, 58-199
464	11-9.2
465	8-750, 8-751
466	8-289.2
469	29-2.1, 29-14, 29-34, 29-55, 29-57, 29-77, 29-116, 29-131, 29-132, 29-138, 29-140, 29-140.1, 29-142, 29-143, 29-148, 29-149, 29-153, 29-161, 29-162 to 29-167, 29-169, 29-172, 29-175, 29-176
471	46.1-231
472	29-184.2
473	58-757.2, 58-757.9, 58-757.27
475	24-118.1, 24-118.2, 24-118.5 to 24-118.7R, 24-118.8 to 24-118.10
476	8-654.3
477	58-766.1
478	29-126
479	27-26.4
480	15-574.4
482	22-235.1, 46.1-357, 46.1-380
483	8-653
484	6-577 to 6-585
485	51-127.15, 51-127.17, 51-127.21, 51-127.25
486	58-266.3
487	15-9.1
488	24-118.4
489	15-688
490	58-266.6
491	63-59
492	15-20.8
493	15-481.1
494	15-668.2
495	18.1-238.2
496	15-666.41
497	21-118
499	19.1-137
501	14-5.3
502	58-919.2
503	65-51, 65-52, 65-62
504	15-574.3
505	18.1-89
506	18.1-288
507	38.1-31.3
508	58-962
509	28.1-101.1
510	14-86, 14-95
511	15-668.2, 15-717.1
512	46.1-267
513	19.1-6
514	29-184.6
515	42-18, 42-19
516	57-7, 57-8, 57-10 to 57-15
517	51-111.41
518	58-399.1
519	19.1-84
520	29-144.1R, 29-144.2 to 29-144.4, 29-145R
522	15-504
523	15-414
524	24-158
525	18.1-74.1
526	29-52
527	56-406.1
528	56-406.2
529	6-201.26
530	65-4
532	4-25
533	4-2

Acts 1962 Chapter	Code 1950 Section
534	2-4.4
535	46.1-43, 46.1-45
536	24-9, 24-46, 24-55.1, 24-56, 24-68, 24-83.1, 24-101, 24-107, 24-114, 24-130, 24-134, 24-148, 24-182, 24-252, 24-277.4, 24-285, 24-321, 24-345.2, 24-345.5, 24-345.8, 24-345.9, 24-351, 24-401
537	40-20.1
538	56-368.1
542	51-111.67:2
543	14-125.1
544	22-276.1
545	8-654.2
546	14-132, 19.1-337
547	14-27
549	6-314
550	33-136.1
551	32-310
552	33-255.1, 33-255.2, 33-255.4, 33-255.7 to 33-255.9, 33-255.14, 33-255.16
553	58-302.1
554	21-120
555	15-354.3
556	59-8.3
557	20-88
558	15-666.18:1
559	32-22
561	19.1-299R
562	38.1-170, 38.1-456, 38.1-464, 38.1-465, 38.1-465.2, 38.1-466, 38.1-467, 38.1-468.2
563	15-666.77
564	6-51
566	6-201.26:1
567	38.1-674
568	8-373
569	24-194.2
570	64-121
571	21-118.4
572	14-86
573	64-71.1
574	46.1-65
575	46.1-335
576	26-59
577	2-272R, 2-278R, 2-279R, 2-279.1, 23-29
578	58-838
579	58-1104
580	15-12
581	15-8.2
583	15-854.2
584	21-291.2
585	51-134
586	58-629.1
587	18.1-15.2
588	65-49
589	8-143
590	38.1-442
591	15-16.6
593	18.1-119.2
595	15-240
596	15-338
597	24-194.3
598	19.1-13
600	15-10.1:2
601	15-707
603	63-349, 63-351, 63-354 to 63-356
605	33-191.1
607	8-749
609	51-28.2
610	23-40, 23-49.1
611	9-77.3
612	58-103, 58-104, 58-113, 58-151.1 to 58-151.35
613	6-129.1, 6-130, 6-131
614	6-130
616	4-90.1
617	1-15, 15-24.2R, 15-24.3
618	32-47.1 to 32-47.8, n.
619	35-42.2 to 35-42.8
620	18.1-354
621	63-140.1 to 63-140.16
622	16.1-218 to 16.1-221
623	15.1-1 to 15.1-9, 15.1-10, 15.1-11, 15.1-13, 15.1-14 to 15.1-18, 15.1-19, 15.1-20, 15.1-21 to 15.1-26, 15.1-27 to 15.1-29, 15-1-30 to 15.1-32, 15.1-34 to 15.1-37, 15.1-38 to 15.1-44, 15.1-45 to 15.1-73, 15.1-74 to 15.1-124, 15.1-126 to 15.1-131, 15.1-132 to 15.1-143, 15.1-144 to 15.1-159, 15.1-160 to 15.1-175, 15.1-176 to 15.1-184, 15.1-185 to 15.1-190, 15.1-191 to 15.1-235, 15.1-236 to 15.1-238, 15.1-239 to 15.1-249, 15.1-250 to 15.1-322, 15.1-323 to 15.1-364, 15.1-368 to 15.1-376, 15.1-377 to 15.1-380, 15.1-504 to 15.1-515, 15.1-516 to 15.1-518, 15.1-519 to 15.1-522, 15.1-527 to 15.1-546, 15.1-547 to 15.1-650, 15.1-652 to 15.1-675, 15.1-676 to 15.1-686, 15.1-687 to 15.1-695, 15.1-697 to 15.1-809, 15.1-810 to 15.1-908, 15.1-910 to 15.1-1007, 15.1-1009 to 15.1-1148, 15.1-1228 to 15.1-1238, 15.1-1239 to 15.1-1270, 15.1-1310 to 15.1-1341
625	18.1-55, 18.1-59
626	62-174.2, 62-174.4 to 62-174.8, 62-174.10, 62-174.11, 62-174.13, 62-174.14, 62-174.18
627	55-79.1 to 55-79.33
628	16.1-210
629	35-38
631	54-112.1 to 54-112.25
633	18.1-329 to 18.1-331
634	13.1-6.1
635	24-14
636	28.1-94.1
637	62-2.1, 62-3
638	24-12
639	54-83.2 to 54-83.28

ACTS 1963, EX. SESS.

Acts 1963, Ex. Sess. Chapter	Code 1950 Section
2	24-17 to 24-17.2, 24-18.1, 24-28.1, 24-67, 24-67.1, 24-78, 24-79, 24-87.1, 24-119.2, 24-120 to 24-124, 24-128.1
3	33-3

ACTS 1964

Acts 1964 Chapter	Code 1950 Section
1	17-117, 17-119, 17-119.1, 17-135
2	17-127.11
3	60-2, 60-8.1, 60-12, 60-42, 60-43, 60-45.2, 60-68, 60-69
4	58-386R
5	6-482

TABLE OF ACTS CODIFIED SUBSEQUENT TO 1948

Acts 1964 Chapter	Code 1950 Section
7	8-489
8	2-244
9	16.1-221, 17-226, 17-228 to 17-231
10	17-57, 17-58
11	19.1-29.1
12	20-83.1
13	15.1-364
14	58-739.3
15	46.1-199
16	46.1-262
17	4-45.1
18	17-127.15
19	58-61
20	46.1-237, 46.1-238
27	15.1-534
28	64-121
29	62-106.5, n.
30	15.1-20.1
31	15.1-11
32	15.1-25
33	57-3
34	8-628.1
36	15.1-70
38	38.1-362.1 to 38.1-362.6
40	23-91.9 to 23-91.12
41	27-87, 27-88
42	46.1-31, 58-692.2R, 58-748.1R
43	24-64.1
46	15.1-225
48	23-115
50	23-147 to 23-155R, 23-155.1 to 23-155.10
52	58-465.1, 58-465.2, 58-470.1, 58-470.2, 58-471, 58-473, 58-480.1, 58-484.1
53	58-85.3
54	32-298, 37-254
55	31-26 to 31-29
56	54-325
57	55-123
58	6-34
60	29-209
61	29-202
63	58-757.1, n.
64	15.1-687
65	27-54.1
68	58-355, 23-165R, 23-165.1 to 23-165.9, 23-166 to 23-170, 23-171R, 23-172R, 23-173
71	2-262
72	38.1-301.3, 38.1-301.7
74	29-153.1, 29-153.2
75	6-220, 6-221, 6-227 to 6-229
79	10-45 to 10-47, 10-55, 10-57 to 10-59, 10-61, 10-61.1, 10-62, 10-67
80	58-638.2
81	9-29.1
83	51-20
85	4-15.1
87	46.1-374
88	63-44
89	22-29
90	23-29
91	23-9.15 to 23-9.20
92	63-183
93	32-292
94	65-51, 65-52, 65-62, 65-68
96	51-111.52:1
97	23-54 to 23-61R, 23-164.1 to 23-164.9
99	20-123R, 32-353.32, 32-353.33, 63-359R
100	22-83R, 22-83.1
101	54-398.15, 54-398.27
102	23-9.2:1
103	46.1-2
106	46.1-308.2 to 46.1-308.8
108	17-5, 17-134
111	57-39.2 to 57-39.7, n.
112	51-3
113	56-291.4
115	28.1-41
116	65-53
117	51-111.41:2
118	46.1-193
119	22-209
121	32-195.21 to 32-195.35
122	58-715
123	58-98
124	18.1-410
125	2-48, 2-77.10 to 2-77.12
128	3-208.48 to 3-208.59
129	55-115
130	18.1-269
132	20-87.1
133	15.1-190
135	16.1-143.1 to 16-1-143.7
138	15.1-152
139	63-348.1
140	53-37
142	46.1-93
143	16.1-201
145	3-583.1
146	22-29.10
147	38.1-735 to 38.1-745
148	38.1-200
149	38.1-183.1
150	6-78, 6-79R, 6-79.1R
151	6-201.29
152	42-66, 42-66.3 to 42-66.5
153	3-576.1
157	62-187.1
158	32-411 to 32-414R, 32-414.1 to 32-414.19
159	23-182 to 23-191
160	29-57
161	32-197, 32-200
163	3-13.1, 3-13.2
164	23-91.5 to 23-91.7
165	21-121.3, 21-122, 21-140.3
166	22-67.2
167	8-690
169	64-90
171	19.1-6.1
172	26-4
173	15.1-143.1
174	22-280.2
175	6-201.26:1
176	58-381.1
177	59-19.1
178	58-16.1
179	58-713
180	58-687
181	58-693
182	58-735.1
183	58-732
185	46.1-375.1
186	51-111.56, 51-111.57
187	22-318
188	56-281.1
189	15.1-73
190	65-53
191	15.1-341
192	22-218.3
193	22-83.2
194	46.1-421
195	56-232, 56-234, 56-241
196	7-25.3
198	58-12
200	17-119.1
201	54-74
202	15.1-995, 15.1-1053
203	42-9
204	3-609.1

Acts 1964 Chapter	Code 1950 Section
205	46.1-7
207	29-139
209	65-95
210	4-25
211	17-221.18 to 17-221.29
212	17-137.5
213	22-9.3
214	3-710 to 3-729
215	4-22
216	27-40.1, 27-40.2
217	58-588, 58-597, 58-598
218	46.1-65, 46.1-78, 46.1-149, 46.1-150, 46.1-154, 46.1-155, 46.1-156, 46.1-157, 46.1-162, 46.1-164
219	6-63R, 6-71 to 6-75R, 6-341, 6-353 to 6-421R, 6-423 to 6-558R, 8-13, 8-94, 8-114, 8-223, 8-517, 8-593, 8-654.3R, 8.1-101 to 8.1-208, 8.2-101 to 8.2-725, 8.3-101 to 8.3-805, 8.4-101 to 8.4-504, 8.5-101 to 8.5-117, 8.6-101 to 8.6-111, 8.7-101 to 8.7-603, 8.8-101 to 8.8-406, 8.9-101 to 8.9-507, 8.10-101 to 8.10-104, 11-5 to 11-7R, 13.1-401 to 13.1-423R, 43-27R, 43-28R, 43-44 to 43-61R, 55-83 to 55-86R, 55-88 to 55-94R, 55-96, 55-98R, 55-99R, 55-143 to 55-151R, 56-120R, 56-121R, 56-126R, 56-127R, 61-1 to 61-52R
220	13.1-320
222	58-306
223	51-111.55
224	18.1-158
225	54-763
226	54-100
227	2-27.1, 44-8, 44-11, 44-17, 44-20, 44-21, 44-23, 44-25, 44-27, 44-30, 44-31, 44-33, 44-41, 44-43 to 44-45, 44-48, 44-49, 44-80, 44-93, 44-115, 44-135, 44-204
228	56-265.4:1
230	46.1-427, 46.1-428R, 46.1-429
231	19.1-227 to 19.1-231, 19.1-234, 19.1-239
232	16.1-178
233	20-45, 20-47
234	9-7
235	10-83.01
236	6-201.29:1
237	24-60.1
238	19.1-186.1, 19.1-186.2
239	46.1-179.1 to 46.1-179.3, 46.1-383.2, 18.1-56R, 18.1-57, 18.1-59
240	18.1-55R, 18.1-55.1
241	15.1-257
242	15.1-26.1
243	21-121.2, 21-140.2
244	26-49
245	15.1-516
246	8-182
247	46.1-179.1 to 46.1-179.3
249	15.1-538
251	46.1-380
252	56-304.1
253	46.1-19, 46.1-19.1, 46.1-20
254	33-136.1
255	58-628, 58-711, 58-744
256	33-35.1 to 33-35.7, 33-113 to 33-115R
257	33-48.1, 33-49
258	33-35
259	33-32
260	33-23.1 to 33-23.5
261	33-57.1
262	33-117.2, 33-117.3
263	33-75.5 to 33-75.11
264	2-4.2
265	33-2, 33-3, 33-12
266	46.1-190
267	46.1-16.1
268	8-180
269	15.1-238
272	43-63
273	20-113
274	39-4.1
275	51-111.70:1
276	22-324.1 to 22-329R, 22-330.1 to 22-330.11
278	15.1-41
279	15.1-493
280	58-86.1:2
281	58-795.2
284	54-276.7
285	54-311.1
286	46.1-335
289	14.1-200.1
290	58-76
291	25-232
294	25-122
296	58-774.2
297	9-62R, 9-63R, 10-21.3R
298	37-15
299	37-96
302	2-47
303	2-268.1 to 2-268.8, 42-53 to 42-55R
304	15.1-249.1
306	3-239.1 to 3-239.11
307	15.1-13.1
308	58.811.1
309	8-386, 8-390R, 55-96
311	58-721, 58-749
312	15.1-9.1
313	15.1-9
314	6-422, 11-1, 55-95, 55-96, 55-152
315	40-118.3
316	40-20.2
317	54-276.4
318	40-20.1
319	46.1-187
320	33-255.44:1 to 33-255.44:9, n.
321	14.1-11.1
322	37-71.2, 37-204.1
323	58-384
324	42-32.2
325	42-32.1
326	12-57.1
327	35-25, 35-29, 35-42.1
328	2-57.01
331	8-81.1 to 8-81.5
332	54-50
333	8-24.2
334	46.1-309.1
336	56-304.9
337	55-141
338	43-4.1
340	54-112.1 to 54-112.4, 54-112.11 to 54-112.16, 54-112.21, 54-112.26, 54-112.27
341	54-456.1, 54-456.2
342	56-200
344	21-120
345	29-114.2
346	62-174.15
347	42-12.1 to 42-12.5, n.
348	33-191.1
349	46.1-3.1
350	28.1-147
352	13.1-3, 13.1-17

Acts 1964 Chapter	Code 1950 Section
353	33-36.10
354	46.1-339
355	38.1-602, 38.1-606
356	8-293
358	23-14
359	63-82
360	29-77.1
361	58-61
362	7-25.2
363	20-91
366	65-85
367	2-299
369	58-86.1:3
371	18.1-329
372	18.1-131.1 to 18.1-131.8
373	15.1-376.1
374	33-172.1
375	46.1-516
376	33-138
377	55-154
378	36-48.1, 36-49.1, 36-50.1, 36-51.1, 36-52.1, 36-55
380	33-45
381	17-199.1
383	33-59
384	55-127
386	14-1 to 14-197R, 13.1-1 to 14.1-11, 14.1-12 to 14.1-200, 14.1-201
387	8-825.1
388	46.1-209
389	33-67.3
390	64-57.1
391	46.1-3.2
392	58-223, 58-238
393	28.1-52, 28.1-58, 28.1-74, 28.1-79, 28.1-82, 28.1-89, 28.1-92, 28.1-93, 28.1-101, 28.1-101.1R, 28.1-108, 28.1-109, 28.1-116, 28.1-120, 28.1-124, 28.1-128, 28.1-134, 28.1-140, 28.1-146, 28.1-165, 28.1-174
394	18.1-358
395	46.1-383.1
396	46.1-351.1, 46.1-351.2
397	4-40, 4-108
399	58-1053.1
400	18.1-159
402	39-7
403	15.1-536
404	1-13.35
405	23-192 to 23-213
406	2-1
407	51-111.67:3
408	46.1-193
409	51-111.41:1
410	55-93
411	16.1-44
412	13.1-93.1
413	15.1-125
414	46.1-58
415	15.1-135, 15.1-136
416	5-10.1
417	13.1-76
418	13.1-30
419	13.1-41.1
421	53-219
422	63-17
423	58-411, 58-412, 58-419R
424	58-266.1
425	58-516, 58-517, 58-519, 58-524, 58-531, 58-534R, 58-535R
426	15.1-13.2
427	15.1-29.1
428	22-37
429	63-349, 63-352 to 63-356, 63-360
430	58-418
433	46.1-423.1
434	18.1-237
435	8-654.2
436	32-9
438	6-348.4
439	42-19.4
440	23-14, 23-31
441	29-140
442	51-10
443	8-628.2
444	37-61
445	29-52
446	15.1-73.2
447	22-331, 22-332, 22-334, 22-336 to 22-340, 22-341, 22-342R, 22-343, 22-344
448	64-126
449	29-188.1
451	29-57, 29-58
452	8-305
453	18.1-119.1
454	58-103, 58-104.1
455	46.1-353
457	8-313
458	26-10.1
459	63-348
460	63-138.1, 63-202.1
461	24-118.8
462	35-38.1
463	6-570 to 6-574
464	26-46.1 to 26-46.3
465	31-10
466	55-210.15
467	15.1-966, 15.1-967
468	58-3.1
469	58-1145.1
470	58-12.1
472	58-833
473	8-200
474	29-80
475	62-46 to 62-51, 62-53, 62-54, 62-56 to 62-58, 62-60.1, 62-61
476	3-151 to 3-178R, 3-178.1 to 3-178.21, 3-178.23, 3-178.24
477	38.1-381
478	29-81
479	54-145.2
480	62-106.5, n.
483	37-1.1, 37-61
484	8-178
485	39-3
486	6-67R, 6-68R
487	33-70.6
488	58-797, 58-798
489	15.1-9.2
490	22-43
492	29-184.2
493	57-12
494	20-88.20
495	13.1-256.1
496	22-7.2
497	15.1-607
498	15.1-475
499	35-16.1
500	8-170
501	55-59
502	8-157
503	40-109
504	40-97, 40-118.1, 40-118.2, 40-119
505	40-96.1
506	16.1-115
507	29-57.1
508	15.1-37.2
511	30-20 to 30-28R, 30-28.1 to 30-28.11
512	21-3, 21-6 to 21-14, 21-17, 21-18, 21-20 to 21-23, 21-26 to 21-31.1, 21-33, 21-34, 21-36, 21-38, 21-41, 21-43, 21-45, 21-47, 21-49, 21-51, 21-53, 21-61, 21-65, 21-88, 21-89, 21-92, 21-93, 21-101, 21-103, 21-106 to 21-112.4, 21-112.6 to 21-112.14, 21-112.17, 21-112.19, 21.112.20
513	10-54.1
514	8-357
515	24-37
516	16.1-208

Acts 1964 Chapter	Code 1950 Section
517	21-116, 21-118.4
518	51-3
520	21-291.2
521	15.1-246, 15.1-247
522	46.1-229
523	56-259, 56-260.1
524	39-8 to 39-13
525	21-112.22
526	24-318.1 to 24-318.8
528	15.1-456
529	58-86.1:4
530	58-851.4
531	54-52
532	29-23.01
533	17-30.1
534	57-35.1 to 57-35.10
535	15.1-495
536	24-3
537	24-23.1 to 24-23.3
538	24-97
539	24-134
540	24-134.1
541	24-135
542	24-290.3
543	24-334.1
544	24-345.5
545	24-351, 24-356
547	15.1-430
548	58-769.1
549	29-144.5
550	17-127.18
551	12-41, 13.1-123, 13.1-124, 13.1-285
552	29-202
553	57-20
554	3-691, 3-692, 3-694, 3-696
555	8-272
557	24-321, 24-330
558	33-228
560	18.1-409
562	29-65
564	15.1-365, 15.1-478, 15.1-481, 15.1-483, 15.1-484, 15.1-491
565	33-142, 33-144, 33-146, 33-148 to 33-151, 33-153, 33-154
568	54-276.9
569	59-216
570	55-114.1
571	56-276
572	56-304, 56-304.4, 56-304.6:1, 56-304.6:2, 56-304.12
574	46.1-94
575	38.1-262.1
576	58-371.2
577	18.1-238
578	3-513 to 3-514

Acts 1964 Chapter	Code 1950 Section
579	46.1-115
580	13.1-236
582	32-364.1
583	58-355
584	58-769.1
585	38.1-257.1
586	15.1-534
587	3-525.20 to 3-525.38
588	19.1-114
589	18.1-222, 18.1-223, 18.1-224R
590	25-46.28
591	54-729.1
592	24-18.2
593	24-245
594	51-111.67:4
596	38.1-264
597	23-9.3
598	16.1-178
599	15.1-116
600	29-168
601	57-3
602	65-32
603	65-4
605	38.1-108, 38.1-113
607	23-30.1 to 23-30.22
608	24-52.1
609	3-525.11
610	20-46
611	46.1-45
612	38.1-381.2
613	46.1-184
614	46.1-192.1
615	24-350.1
616	24-359, 24-397, 24-402
617	46.1-357
618	46.1-1
619	33-303, 33-308, 33-322
620	58-766, 58-766.1
621	56-416
622	54-78, 54-79, 54-80R, 54-81R, 54-82, 54-83, 54-83.1:1 to 54-83.1:4
623	18.1-74.1:1 to 18.1-74.1:3, 59-21.1R
624	28.1-100
625	9-77.3
626	56-529 to 56-530, n.
627	3-609.2 to 3-609.21
628	46.1-302
629	58-919.3
630	15.1-1342, n.
631	15.1-1342 to 15.1-1372
632	15.1-431
635	23-14, 23-15, 23-19, 23-21, 23-22, 23-26
636	20-79
637	24-277.2

Acts 1964 Chapter	Code 1950 Section
640	37-1.1, 37-6R, 37-61, 37-61.1, 37-62 to 37-64, 37-69, 37-71.3, 37-71.4, 37-72, 37-75, 37-78, 37-79, 37-99, 37-100, 37-102, 37-103, 37-105 to 37-109, 37-110R, 37-110.1R, 37-111, 37-113 to 37-117, 37-118R, 37-119, 37-126, 37-128, 37-130 to 37-131, 37-136.1, 37-154R, 37-156 to 37-168R, 37-171 to 37-178R, 37-180 to 37-187R, 37-189R, 37-190R, 37-193 to 37-200R, 37-202 to 37-204R, 37-205 to 37-209R, 37-212R, 37-214 to 37-215.1R, 37-217 to 37-222R, 37-224R, 37-225R, 37-230.2
644	58-797
645	15.1-686.1R, 15.1-686.2
646	1-15
647	29-184.3
648	20-91
649	4-80.2
650	29-184.5
651	14.1-184, 17-30.2
652	29-208.1
653	29-184
654	62-174.5 to 62-174.7, 62-174.13:2, 62-174.15, 62-174.17, 62-174.18, 62-192R, 62-193R, 62-195
655	29-184.4
656	14.1-74
657	19.1-241.1 to 19.1-241.6

ACTS 1964, EX. SESS.

Acts 1964, Ex. Sess. Chapter	Code 1950 Section
1	24-14
2	24-12
3	15.1-9
5	24-13.1, n.
6	58-733
7	46.1-105.1
8	23-38.1R
9	51-111.38:1
10	58-19.1 to 58-19.5R
11	22-294.1 to 22-294.3R

Acts 1964, Ex. Sess. Chapter	Code 1950 Section
12	22-115.31, 22-115.32, 22-115.34
13	22-115.36R, 22-115.37R
14	22-21.1R
15	22-159R
16	36-49.2
17	38.1-301.1
20	55-136
21	16.1-202.5
22	46.1-154, 46.1-155
23	33-57.3
24	28.1-227
25	14.1-46
26	42-19.4
27	24-194

ACTS 1965, EX. SESS.

Acts 1965, Ex. Sess. Chapter	Code 1950 Section
1	24-3

ACTS 1966

Acts 1966 Chapter	Code 1950 Section
2	56-529 to 56-530, n.
4	58-963.1
5	3-598.7 to 3-598.11
6	27-5.4
7	54-349
8	10-57.1
9	3-219.2 to 3-219.4, 3-219.6, 3-219.9 to 3-219.10, 3-219.12, 3-219.14
10	56-338.20
11	33-43.1 to 33-43.5
14	23-41, 23-49.1
16	14.1-74
18	23-49.11 to 23-49.17, 23-49.20 to 23-49.22
19	16.1-115
20	54-96
21	54-112.19, 54-112.26, 54-112.27
22	14.1-116
23	17-224
24	17-127.16
25	54-58
26	54-30, 54-31
27	54-83.15, 54-83.19
28	54-757 to 54-761, 54-765
29	54-861, 54-864, 54-867, 54-868
30	60-42, 60-43, 60-46, 60-47, 60-49, 60-57, 60-68
33	15.1-538
36	46.1-357
37	46.1-309.1, 46.1-310, 46.1-314
38	14.1-164
41	10-100, 10-101, 10-106, 10-107
42	58-753.1
43	63-162
44	15.1-376.1
46	38.1-187
47	15.1-694
48	44-146.2 to 44-146.12
53	40-14, 40-15
54	2-34, 2-38.1 to 2-38.3R, 2-45.1 to 2-45.5, 2-46, 2-47, 2-57.01 to 2-57.04, 2-65 to 2-66, 2-66.2, 2-77 to 2-77.2, 2-77.7, 2-77.8, 2-81, 10-123R, 10-125.1R, 10-126R, 55-297
58	58-792.1
59	46.1-330
60	29-188.1
61	46.1-121
64	65-51, 65-52, 65-62, 65-68
65	33-57
66	33-50.2
68	23-91.1 to 23-91.4R, 23-91.14 to 23-91.17, 23-91.20 to 23-91.23
69	22.10.2
71	17-117.1, 17-127.10, 17-135, 17-137.1, 17-137.6
75	40-95.7, 40-95.8
76	40-61.2
77	40-12
78	1-13.22, 1-13.35, 1-13.36
79	1-13.30
80	18.1-175.1
81	36-49.1, 36-51.1, 36-52.1
82	22-67.2
84	58-769.2
85	46.1-193, 46.1-196, 46.1-345
86	2-98 to 2-116R
87	38.1-301.1
88	40-24
89	40-20.3
90	40-1.1
91	40-35
92	40-95.2, 40-95.3
93	55-60
94	23-50
95	14.1-11.2
97	15.1-51, 15.1-52
98	54-306, 54-308
100	3-708.33
101	38.1-349
102	7-1 to 7-36R, 7.1-1 to 7.1-38
103	32-364.1
104	14.1-11.3
105	63-44
106	9-104.1
107	63-140.2
108	63-115
110	55-275
111	51-111.52:1
112	63-135, 63-136, 63-157, 63-158, 63-199, 63-200, 63-212
115	24-141
116	24-182
117	50-18, 50-35
118	8-13
119	50-32
120	20-63
121	33-35.4
122	46.1-255
125	14.1-144
127	15.1-239
128	46.1-215
130	46.1-400
131	13.1-39
132	15.1-511.1
134	27-1 to 27-3
135	17-119.1
136	6-559 to 6-568R
137	55-125, 55-131
138	17-119.1
139	17-208.1
140	15.1-19.1
141	17-119.1
142	17-119.1
143	17-119.1
144	17-119.1
145	16.1-43
147	51-111.54
148	17-111.1
149	57-15.1
150	22-218.2
151	58-304 to 58-339R, 58-418, 58-441.1 to 58-441.51
152	14.1-46
153	54-775.1 to 54-775.9, 54-864, 54-867, 54-868
154	54-112.16
155	54-112.11:1
157	54-60, 54-61
158	51-3, 51-8 to 51-11R, 51-12, 51-15, 51-16R, 51-18, 51-28.1, 51-28.2R, 51-28.3

Acts 1966 Chapter	Code 1950 Section
159	32-22
161	15.1-223, 15.1-224
162	23-35.9
163	17-137.7
164	32-378.1 to 32-378.4
165	46.1-295.1
166	54-280.1R, 54-282, 54-292, 54-306.1R, 54-308.1 to 54-308.4R, 54-316, 54-317, 54-317.2, 54-318.1, 54-319, 54-320
167	15.1-90.1
168	51-29.1, 51-29.7:1
169	63-204.25 to 63-204.30
170	15.1-335
171	54-481
173	28.1-93
174	51-111.10, 51-111.41, 51-111.41:1, 51-111.43, 51-111.45 to 51-111.47, 51-111.49, 51-111.53, 51-111.55 to 51-111.57, 51-111.58:1, 51-111.60, 51-111.62, 51-111.67:4 to 51-111.67:6, 51-111.70:1, 51-114.2
175	51-111.10
176	10-21.4 to 10-21.12
177	23-9.2:2
178	33-255.44:11 to 33-255.44:32, n.
179	32-112.1 to 32-112.9
181	46.1-167.1, 46.1-167.3, 46.1-167.4
182	38.1-381
183	46.1-436.1
184	38.1-361.1
185	38.1-70.9 to 38.1-70.12
186	13.1-501, 13.1-514
187	3-228.13 to 3-228.22
189	21-127.1
190	15.1-377
192	37-33
193	54-399
194	54-445.1
196	46.1-34.1
197	58-1052
198	9-6.7
199	21-121.2:1
200	65-4
201	15.1-73.3
202	15.1-492
203	21-292
204	58-78.2
205	58-447R
206	9-77.3
207	18.1-411
208	22-235.1
210	8-746
211	8-180
212	8-441, 39-4
213	52-7
214	18.1-38, 18.1-39
216	57-8
217	14.1-112, 14.1-113
218	13.1-237
219	6-201.22:1
220	51-29.8
221	5-9.1
222	2-87, 29-37.2
223	18.1-119.3
224	16.1-216
225	42-19.4
226	24-118.4
227	8-300, 8-300.1
228	2-36.1
231	58-851
232	17-127.17R
233	16.1-201
235	17.127.5
236	14.1-122
237	16.1-214
238	46.1-417
239	15.1-995
240	19.1-246.1
241	22-7.1
242	31-26, 31-27, 31-29
244	58-151.31
245	15.1-156
246	16.1-33
247	18.1-100 to 18.1-103, 18.1-119, 18.1-119.1, 19.1-252, 19.1-253
248	15.1-33, n.
249	2-11
250	17-41
251	55-197
252	28.1-96
253	15.1-444.1
254	64-90
255	15.1-623
256	15.1-496
258	63-52
259	63-167.1
260	55-13.2
261	38.1-35
262	38.1-30.1
263	38.1-114
264	58-486
265	38.1-36.1
266	38.1-182, 38.1-199, 38.1-200, 38.1-202.1, 38.1-207, 38.1-208, 38.1-215, 38.1-216
267	58-98.1
268	8-211.1
269	15.1-37.3, 15.1-509R
270	15.1-31
272	14.1-103
273	22-149
274	64-147
276	32-195.10:1
278	29-55.2
279	14.1-53
280	15.1-535
281	2-1, 2-77.10 to 2-77.12
283	54-260.7
284	54-260.32
285	6-352.1 to 6-352.5
286	29-65
287	58-98
289	38.1-4, 38.1-183.2, 38.1-408, 38.1-443
290	15.1-510.1 to 15.1-510.6
291	54-729.1
292	18.1-200.1
293	63-179
294	28.1-50
295	44-93
296	3-197.1 to 3-197.7, 3-197.10, 3-197.11
297	46.1-3
298	46.1-450
299	38.1-264
300	53-9, 53-291, 53-293R
301	15.1-73.2
302	27-54.1
303	15.1-8
304	15.1-646
307	30-32
308	57-12, 57-16
309	14.1-56
310	37-150.1
311	58-769.1
312	15.1-515.1R
313	23-4.1
314	64-83
315	9-77.3
318	15.1-572
320	8-182
321	58-371.2
322	10-12.1
323	8-158R
324	26-27
325	64-117
326	26-10, 26-10.1
327	26-46.2
328	26-3
329	26-8
330	64-72.1
331	64-144
332	8-750
333	26-15
334	64-126
335	26-33, 64-161,

Acts 1966 Chapter	Code 1950 Section
	64-162, 64-169
336	26-12.1
337	26-12
338	26-12.2
339	8-751
340	26-2
341	53-296
342	38.1-348.2 to 38.1-348.4
343	13.1-89
344	15.1-430, 15.1-486, 15.1-489, 15.1-490
345	12-41.2
346	64-138
347	8-272
348	17-14.1, 17-18
349	8-305, 8-310R
350	46.1-226
351	51-127.10, 51-127.11, 51-127.17, 51-127.18, 51-127.20, 51-127.21, 51-127.25, 51-127.26
352	58-81
353	33-353.27
354	63-279 to 63-381, 63-382R, 63-383
355	24-60.1
356	4-15.1
357	4-40, 4-108
358	58-737.1:1
359	35-64.1 to 35-64.5
360	20-61
361	18.1-91
362	8-301
363	19.1-84, 54-440, 54-446.3 to 54-446.13
364	14.1-73
365	46.1-171.1
366	33-22.1
368	37-34.2:7
369	33-3.1
370	65-96
371	37-16.2
373	46.1-335
374	58-851.6
375	46.1-369
376	46.1-413
377	46.1-439
378	33-116.1
379	3-40 to 3-44R, 3-44.1 to 3-44.8
380	58-851.7
381	3-609.15
382	40-63
383	36-27.1
384	14.1-86
385	17-27
386	58-1107
387	13.1-290.1
388	65-85
390	15.1-11.1
391	15.1-230
392	8.2-716
393	8.3-110
394	8.9-105
395	8.9-401
396	8-94
397	11-1
398	55-58.1
399	55-95
400	55-96
401	55-96.1R
402	44-24.1
403	17-79.1
404	16.1-118.1
405	15.1-504, 15.1-522
406	14.1-166
408	4-75
409	14.1-143
410	63-69.1 to 63-69.3R
411	29-184.3
412	9-841.1 to 9-841.4
413	29-148
415	5-24.2
416	8-669
417	65-87
418	36-49.1
419	15.1-1345, 15.1-1348, 15.1-1353, 15.1-1358
420	18.1-312
421	15.1-506.1
422	18.1-69.1
423	63-101
424	15.1-534
425	64-57.2
426	53-99.1
427	41-8.3
428	29-193
429	15.1-16.1
430	53-295
431	4-22
432	15.1-528
433	3-269.1 to 3-269.6
434	8-10.2
435	27-5.3
436	8-791
437	20-63
438	33-155
439	8-654.4
440	62-53.1
441	64-71.2
442	29-209
443	11-20.1
444	57-38.1
445	18.1-238.3
446	18.1-158, 18.1-158.1
447	38.1-205
449	20-98
450	8-65
452	8-752
453	24-312, 24-314
454	18.1-130
455	15.1-491
456	63-145
457	38.1-99
458	43-33
459	38.1-381
460	19.1-241R, 19.1-241.1 to 19.1-241.3
461	10-151 to 10-158
462	23-51, 23-52
463	15.1-589, 15.1-589.1
464	15.1-723, 15.1-724, 15.1-729, 15.1-757, 15.1-763, 15.1-769, 15.1-771, 15.1-779, 15.1-787, 15.1-789R, 15.1-790R, 15.1-791
465	10-13
466	13.1-21
467	23-75
468	62-106.5, n.
469	46.1-234.1
470	33-133, 33-134
471	29-121, n.
472	8-263.1
473	29-159.1, n.
474	18.1-117.1
475	42-9
476	15.1-135
477	10-3
478	63-59
480	15.1-503.1
481	15.1-495.1, n.
482	53-128.1 to 53-128.5
483	53-247
484	33-136.3
485	33-279.3
488	58-78
489	10-146 to 10-150
490	46.1-295.2
491	63-291.1
492	55-125, 55-127, 55-136
493	29-122
494	33-328 to 33-331
495	15.1-522, 15.1-544
496	8-199
497	10-17.10 to 10-17.30
498	58-944
499	34-4.1
500	16.1-53.1
501	14.1-58
502	46.1.-343.2
504	65-46
505	55-66.4
506	55-257
507	42-9

Acts 1966 Chapter	Code 1950 Section
509	16.1-202.3, 16.1-202.4
510	10-3
511	46.1-192.2
512	25-46.21:1
513	33-64.1
514	15.1-501
516	18.1-236.2, 18.1-236.4
517	8-329.1
518	8-67.1
519	64-119.2
520	64-119.1
521	14.1-128, 19.1-109, 19.1-110, 19.1-116, 19.1-124
522	19.1-296
523	38.1-381.3
525	10-159 to 10-166
526	3-347, 3-347.1, 3-347.2, 3-348, 3-351
527	29-57
528	37-121.1 to 37-121.3
529	32-8.1
530	63-106
531	15.1-623, 15.1-623.1
532	8-654.1:1
533	46.1-412, 46.1-417.1
534	32-197
535	3-6.1R, 3-16.5 to 3-16.9, 3-117.8, 3-117.32, 3-627, 3-628, 3-631, 32-40.2 58-715, 58-730
538	64-71.1
539	58-514.2
540	58-587.1, 58-617.2
541	58-512.1
542	58-851.5
543	56-273
544	58-728
545	46.1-165
546	46.1-350
547	27-37
548	46.1-167.4
549	46.1-362
550	46.1-64.1
551	23-175 to 23-181R, 23-181.1 to 23-181.10
552	56-247
554	58-86.1:5
555	63-309
556	22-29
557	8.5-117, 8.9-312
558	46.1-69 to 46.1-77, 46.1-80, 46.1-87
559	58-1009
560	23-30.1 to 23-30.22, n.
561	10-17.1 to 10-17.9, 10-114R
562	58-359, 58-363R, 58-364R, 58-367.2
563	22-208.1
564	58-716
565	14.1-58
566	14.1-56
567	53-104
568	46.1-167.3
569	8.9-302
570	32-30.1
571	23-9
572	23-18
573	23-9.10
574	15.1-184.1
575	56-274
576	5-1 to 5-61R, 5.1-1 to 5.1-9, 5.1-10 to 5.1-36, 5.1-37 to 5.1-76
577	63-307.1 to 63-307.4
578	18.1-74.2
579	19.1-295.1 to 19.1-295.6
580	38.1-88 to 38.1-91, 38.1-93 to 38.1-95, 38.1-95.1, 38.1-97
581	1-15
582	58-12
583	8-636
584	6-1 to 6-585R, 6.1-1 to 6.1-76, 6.1-78 to 6.1-146, 6.1-148 to 6.1-329, 6.1-331 to 6.1-351
585	46.1-198
586	46.1-169.1
587	58-685.10 to 58-685.25, 58-685.26, n.
588	37-36.1
589	46.1-350
590	22-232.1 to 22-232.8R, 22-232.10 to 22-232.17R, 22-232.18 to 22-232.31R
591	46.1-441.1
592	46.1-296.1
593	63-72.1
594	45-0.1 to 45-157R, 45.1-1 to 45.1-161
595	46.1-369
596	15.1-456
597	14.1-155.1
598	3-672 to 3-676R, 3-676.1 to 3-676.6R, 3-676.7 to 3-676.22, 3.1-872 to 3.1-884R
599	63-107
600	6-62.1, 64-131.1
601	22-37
603	40-100, 40-117, 40-118.3
604	22-276.1
605	22-223, 22-228
606	22-72.2
607	46.1-183, 46.1-184
608	46.1-150
609	22-307.1
610	54-83.2
611	58-397.1
612	15.1-504
613	46.1-225
614	40-24.1
615	46.1-3.2
616	23-14
617	54-882, 54-882.1
618	58-412
621	56-232, 23-30.1 to 23-30.22, n., 23-31
622	4-79, 4-115
623	38.1-70.13
624	15.1-609.1, 15.1-644.1
625	58-81.3
626	63-106.1
627	17-119
628	51-128 to 51-142R, 51-143 to 51-158
629	31-11.1, 31-11.2
630	54-52.3
631	46.1-383
632	10-135 to 10-145
634	54-749, 54-750, 54-758, 54-764.1, 54-771
635	18.1-55.1
636	18.1-56.1, 18.1-57
637	14.1-55 to 14-1.58, 14.1-62.1
638	53-230, 53-234, 53-238, 53-243, 53-245, 53-251.1, 53-252
639	46.1-179
640	23-35.3
641	62-2.1
642	28.1-97
643	46.1-1
644	33-288.1
645	23-133, 23-135.1, 23-135.2, 23-135.3R, 23-135.4 to 23-135.6
646	23-164.10
647	23-159.1
648	62-106.8:2
649	8.9-402
650	64-119
651	15.1-1373 to 15.1-1390
653	54-758
654	46.1-45, 46.1-280
655	46.1-267, 46.1-285

Acts 1966 Chapter	Code 1950 Section
656	28.1-116
657	54-1-2.1 to 54-102.14, 54-103 to 54-112R, 54-273 to 54-275, 54-276.6, 54-281.3, 54-282, 54-284, 54-287, 54-296, 54-297, 54-298, 54-309.1, 54-313, 54-315.1, 54-317, 54-317.1, 54-318, 54-319, 54-322 to 54-324, 54-864
658	3-598.12 to 3-598.19
659	19.1-239
663	33-298, 33-317, 33-317.1
664	46.1-267, 46.1-285
665	63-141
667	45.1-162 to 45.1-179
668	24-277.1, 24-277.2, 24-277.3, 24-277.4
669	19.1-19.1 to 19.1-19.4, 19.1-260R
670	15.1-135, 52-4.1
671	14.1-190
673	8-289.1
674	14.1-153
675	58-78.3
676	2-117 to 2-124.1R, 30-28.12 to 30-28.20
677	2-1 to 2-309R, 2.1-1 to 2.1-38, 2.1-39 to 2.1-51, 2.1-52 to 2.1-64, 2.1-65 to 2.1-82, 2.1-83 to 2.1-339
679	23-192 to 23-213R, 23-214 to 23-231
681	58-355
683	55-79.2, 55-79.3, 55-79.4, 55-79.7, 55-79.9, 55-79.11, 55-79.13, 55-79.14, 55-79.34 to 55-79.38
684	28.1-18, 28.1-48, 28.1-61, 28.1-65, 28.1-73, 28.1-74, 28.1-75R, 28.1-86R, 28.1-87, 28.1-89, 28.1-91, 28.1-98, 28.1-109, 28.1-120, 28.1-124, 28.1-137, 28.1-139, 28.1-165, 28.1-167, 28.1-179, 28.1-183, 28.1-204 to 28.1-226R
685	23-30.1 to 23-30.22R, 23-30.23 to 23-30.38
686	3-228.3 to 3-228.9, 3-228.11
687	46.1-193.1
688	14.1-50, 14.1-51, 14.1-66
689	2-57.05 to 2-57.015
690	58-4.1, 58-4.2
691	22-72
694	46.1-190, 46.1-423
695	28.1-59
696	28.1-58
697	23-9.2:1
698	9-106 to 9-106.02, 9-106.05 to 9-106.08
699	46.1-199, 46.1-225, 46.1-226, 46.1-285
701	19.1-186.1
702	3-1 to 3-729R, 3.1-1 to 3.1-22, 3.1-23 to 3.1-275, 3.1-276 to 3.1-296, 3.1-297 to 3.1-348, 3.1-349 to 3.1-426, 3.1-427 to 3.1-763, 2.1-764 to 3.1-884, 3.1-885 to 3.1-1010
703	14.1-17, 14.1-18, 14.1-23, 14.1-24 to 14.1-28R
704	14.1-73
706	46.1-230
707	23-49.1
709	16.1-173
711	4-118.2
712	46.1-252.1
714	24-37
715	19.1-228, 19.1-230, 19.1-230.1, 19.1-231, 19.1-234, 19.1-235, 19.1-237, 19.1-239.1
717	2.1-1, n., 3.1-1, n., 5.1-1, n., 6.1-1, n., 7.1-1, n., 45.1-1, n.
718	9-67, 9-68

ACTS 1968

Acts 1968 Chapter	Code 1950 Section
1	46.1-296, 46.1-296.1
3	62-106.7
4	55-125, 55-127, 55-136
5	16.1-77
6	15.1-51
7	4-28, 4-61, 4-71, 4-98.1 to 4-98.12, 4-98.13, 4-98.14, 4-98.16, 4-98.17
8	65-51, 65-52, 65-62, 65-68
9	60-22, 60-42, 60-46, 60-62.1, 60-68
10	54-42.1
11	4-15.1
12	58-151.13
13	58-486 to 58-492, 58-498, 58-502.1 to 58-502.10
14	58-149R, 58-150R, 58-151, 58-151.36 to 58-151.41
15	58-514.3 to 58-514.12
19	63-167.2
21	15.1-9.1:2
23	15.1-19.2
24	15.1-133
25	18.1-349.1
26	63-179
27	54-102.5
28	54-874
29	54-756R, 54-761.1
30	54-102.2
31	54-775.8
32	54-775.3
33	17-126.2
35	63-359.1
36	44-54.1 to 44-54.3
37	58-12
38	33-75.9
39	33-35.4, 33-50.2
40	10-36
41	58-749
42	13.1-48, 13.1-230
43	63-165.1, 63-204
44	8-4.3
45	54-112.19
46	46.1-45
47	46.1-16.1
49	3.1-754, 3.1-756
50	58-721
51	12-45
56	6.1-68.1
57	24-3, 24-12, 24-14
59	6.1-22
60	51-112
61	6.1-57
62	21-121, 21-140.2
63	58-1104
64	3.1-1011 to 3.1-1017, 3.1-1019
65	26-40.1
66	8-689
67	56-224.1
69	61-1 to 61-160R, 61.1-1 to 61.1-61
71	32-137
73	10-76
74	54-60, 54-61, 54-62.1, 54-62.2
76	54-775.7
77	54-35, 54-37
79	10-8.1
80	15.1-710
81	32-364.2
83	57-39
85	3.1-22.3
86	62.187.1

Acts 1968 Chapter	Code 1950 Section
87	13.1-36
88	3.1-646.1, 3.1-646.2
89	46.1-225, 46.1-226, 46.1-267, 46.1-285
90	24-164
92	6.1-318, 6.1-319
93	23-49.2 to 23-49.10R, 23-50 to 23-50.3R, 23-50.4 to 23-50.14
94	18.1-349
95	18.1-349
96	58-396
97	24-28, 24-118.1
98	46.1-40.1
99	46.1-299
100	56-493
102	19.1-339
103	8-24.2
104	3.1-951
105	53-208
106	40-24.1
107	17-117, 17-118, 17-119, 17-127.7
108	23-222
109	13.1-77
110	13.1-50
111	13.1-68, 13.1-69
112	13.1-94
113	54-145.11 to 54.145.20
114	13.1-73
115	13.1-76
116	13.1-93, 13.1-256
118	11-9.3
119	13.1-528 to 13.1-540, 13.1-541, n.
121	2.1-56
122	42-34, 42-35
123	19.1-114
124	1-13.39
125	38.1-706
126	10-5
127	56-223
128	53-4
131	60-94.1
132	53-42
133	17-137.8
134	17-153.1
135	17-154.1
136	17-119.1
137	17-195.1 to 17-195.6
138	44-78
139	22-57.2
140	3.1-846 to 3.1-866R, 3.1-867, 3.1-868, 3.1-869R, 3.1-870R, 3.1-871
141	24-55, 24-207
142	3.1-763.14 to 3.1-763.17, 3.1-764, 3.1-765, 3.1-767 to 3.1-769, 3.1-769.1 to 3.1-769.4, 3.1-770.1 to 3.1-770.3
143	24-118
144	46.1-441.2
145	46.1-295.3
146	46.1-187
147	51-29.8
148	46.1-326.1
149	21-6
151	46.1-414
152	53-38
153	16.1-200
154	33-39.1
155	46.1-255
156	46.1-98R, 46.1-98.1
157	15.1-159.2 to 15.1-159.7
158	24-194.3
159	54-762
160	2.1-51.6
162	33-109
163	46.1-321
164	46.1-278, 46.1-278.1, 46.1-279R, 46.1-280
165	46.1-231, 46.1-234, 46.1-241
166	46.1-167.8 to 46.1-167.13
167	46.1-383
168	46.1-26.1
169	62-190
170	33-173.1, 33-245
171	46.1-309.1, 46.1-310, 46.1-314
172	46.1-275, 46.1-281.1, 46.1-282, 46.1-293, 46.1-295.1, 46.1-308, 46.1-311
175	56-405.1
176	46.1-369
177	51-111.54
178	22-138.1, 22-218, 22-218.1R, 22-220, 22-223, 22-275.1 to 22-275.5, 22-275.13, 22-275.15, 22-275.18, 22-275.23, 22-275.24R, 22-275.25R
180	51-127.20, 51-127.25, 51-127.26
181	3.1-807, 3.1-809, 3.1-814, 3.1-821
182	15.1-995.1
183	56-274
184	46.1-342
185	24-57
187	46.1-93, 46.1-96
188	46.1-68.1
191	58-441.49:1
194	21-254
197	6.1-138
199	38.1-381
202	51-29.19
203	46.1-343
205	6.1-361
206	58-960
208	33-255.24 to 33-255.44, n.
210	9-106
211	54-789
212	54-775.3
213	54-741
214	54-112.9
215	54-24
216	54-398.12
217	54-98
218	46.1-345
220	58-998
221	33-136.3
222	53-23.1
223	2.1-38, 2.1-51.2, 2.1-63.1 to 2.1-63.8, 2.1-64, 2.1-64.1 to 2.1-64.3R, 55-297
224	15.1-1400 to 15.1-1415, 15.1-1420 to 15.1-1441, 15.1-1450, 15.1-1451, n., 15.1-1452, 15.1-1500 to 15.1-1505
225	14.1-44, 16.1-123, 16.1-124, 16.1-158, 17-32.1
226	56-405
227	33-58
228	52-11.2
229	18.1-260
230	33-317
232	33-70.6
233	24-220
234	15.1-301
235	29-55.4
236	65-43.1
237	28.1-196
238	38.1-295.1
239	19.1-261R
240	33-279.3
241	13.1-6
242	29-103
243	46.1-188
244	8-503
245	20-88.26
246	46.1-113, 46.1-115
248	8-182
249	18.1-78.6
250	9-61, 9-64R, 9-65R

Acts 1968 Chapter	Code 1950 Section
251	8-906, 8-908, 8-909
252	54-295
253	14.1-164
254	13.1-149
255	6.1-157
256	6.1-156
257	55-70
258	58-863.1
259	58-1030.1
260	16.1-98
261	22-161
262	40-24
263	40-39 to 40-43R
264	40-96, 40-97
266	38.1-98.1
267	6.1-158
268	24-64.1
269	15.1-547
270	6.1-58.1
271	54-802
272	40-20
273	40-123
274	40-35
275	21-121.4
276	22-9.2:1
277	40-100.4:1
278	40-109
279	15.1-478.1
280	40-61.3
281	22-21
282	38.1-424
283	6.1-25
284	24-290.3
285	46.1-1
286	58-120.1
287	16.1-217.1
289	58-792.5
290	15.1-456
291	58-847
292	38.1-348.5
294	15.1-518
295	22-330.12 to 22-330.15, 22-330.16, n.
297	55-125.1
298	53-126.6
300	15.1-327.1
301	53-100.1
302	53-213.1
303	53-37
304	53-133.1
305	19.1-46.1
306	3.1-701, 3.1-716
308	58-81.1
309	29-163.2
310	45.1-56, 45.1-63
311	10-17.10, 10-17.18, 10-17.21, 10-17.26
312	36-49.1
313	33-70.7

Acts 1968 Chapter	Code 1950 Section
314	32-414.4
315	15.1-982, 15.1-1002
316	9-112 to 9-115
318	20-14, 20-14.1, 20-16, 20-17 to 20-19R, 20-20, 20-26, 20-34 to 20-36R, 20-50 to 20-60R, 32-353.34
319	55-154
320	43-32
321	58-685.11
323	6.1-328
324	6.1-330, 6.1-330.2R, 6.1-330.4R
325	6.1-5.1
326	20-121
327	32-242
328	15.1-533, 15.1-534R
330	15.1-137.1
331	63-5.3
332	18.1-417.1
333	46.1-328
334	46.1-55
335	46.1-413, 46.1-413.1
336	29-209
337	54-341
338	46.1-155
339	38.1-196.1
340	18.1-415.1
342	58-111
343	58-151.25
344	15.1-827
345	58-466.1
346	63-349
347	65-53
348	19.1-214
349	18.1-425, 18.1-427
350	18.1-365
351	22-53.1
352	19.1-338
354	15.1-431
355	15.1-1248 to 15.1-1251
356	54-729.01 to 54-729.018
357	53-103
358	17-30.1
359	8-596.1
360	17-31R
361	16.1-33
362	18.1-82
363	15.1-1359
366	46.1-351.1, 46.1-351.2
368	33-138
369	46.1-124
370	54-52.2
371	32-1
375	15.1-783

Acts 1968 Chapter	Code 1950 Section
376	16.1-43.2
377	65-85
378	15.1-591R
379	6.1-71
380	8-685
381	8-694
382	26-1.1
383	37.1-136
384	64-127
385	64-161
386	8-38
387	17-222, 17-224 to 17-226
388	46.1-179.01
389	32-30.1
390	17-127, 17-127.19
391	18.1-70.1
392	58-355
393	33-287
395	43-33
396	32-418
397	17-144.1
398	18.1-81.1
399	26-60, 26-66
400	18.1-9
401	18.1-319
403	58-157, 58-164
404	24-397
406	14.1-20
407	15.1-489
408	15.1-73.3
409	15.1-28
410	38.1-389.1
411	32-195.20:1, 38.1-348.1
412	8-690
413	29-209
414	2.1-118
415	25-232.1
416	15.1-286
417	15.1-236
418	15.1-262
419	15.1-28.1
420	15.1-1067.1, n.
421	46.1-555.1 to 46.1-555.8
422	15.1-508
423	15.1-11, 15.1-11.2
425	15.1-514
426	42-9
427	18.1-212
428	51-3
429	14.1-119
430	32-310.1 to 32-310.8
431	19.1-42
432	22-276.2
433	22-235.1
434	26-36.1
435	16.1-157
436	16.1-143.2

Acts 1968 Chapter	Code 1950 Section
437	16.1-143.3
438	6.1-352 to 6.1-360, 46.1-545, 54-846
439	15.1-523 to 15.1-525, 18.1-129 to 18.1-146.1R, 59-1 to 59-235R, 59.1-1 to 59.1-195
440	29-188.1
441	23-35.9
442	58-919.2, 58-919.3
443	26-64
444	23-9
445	22-249
446	22-206
447	15.1-432
449	15.1-1342, n.
450	15.1-550
451	16.1-154
452	14.1-41
454	22-37
455	20-97
456	8-73
457	16.1-92
458	51-111.52:1
459	15.1-514.1
460	18.1-247 to 18.1-253R, 18.1-254R, 18.1-254.1 to 18.1-254.12
462	58-77
463	46.1-181
465	63-14, 63-15, 63-20, 63-28, 63-29 to 63-32R, 63-33
466	63-68, 63-72.1, 63-73, 63-103, 63-106
467	63-56, 63-82
468	20-45, 20-46, 37.1-156
475	22-55.1
476	46.1-387.1 to 46.1-387.12
477	37-1 to 37-260R, 37.1-1 to 37.1-202
478	63-127, 63-127.1, 63-191
479	2.1-340 to 2.1-346
480	18.1-119.1R, 18.1-125.2 to 18.1-125.10
481	14.1-184, 19.1-241.5
482	8-603
483	20-113
484	8-54, 20-99
485	8-636
486	17-30.1:1
487	8-596
488	14.1-166, 14.1-167
489	6.1-249, 6.1-271, 6.1-272, 6.1-276, 6.1-277, 6.1-280, 6.1-282, 6.1-285 to 6.1-288, 6.1-291, 6.1-294, 6.1-301
490	8-229
492	52-7
493	46.1-177.1
494	46.1-349, 46.1-350
495	16.1-129.2
496	16.1-220
497	46.1-198, 46.1-198.2
498	46.1-172
499	2.1-64.22
500	51-28.3
501	22-97
502	37.1-3
503	44-93
505	54-388
508	51-153
511	7.1-21.1
512	53-299.1
513	18.1-69.2
514	26-46.2
515	64-174
516	56-457.1 to 56-457.10
517	32-22
518	18.1-125.1
519	33-303, 33-308
520	18.1-216
521	54-424
522	29-65
523	10-92.01
524	38.1-408.1
525	53-206.9 to 53-206.11
526	9-100, 9-101.1, 9-102, 9-103, 9-104.1, 9-104.2
527	29-121, n.
530	18.1-88.1
532	23-174.1 to 23-174.9
533	10-145.1
534	56-259
535	25-46.20, 33-63.1
536	9-48.1 to 9-48.6R, 9-48.7, n.
537	19.1-19.2
538	33-255.44:11 to 33-255.44:32, n.
539	2.1-304.1
540	54-414
542	62-63, 62-65, 62-67
543	15.1-491
545	23-49.21, 23-49.22R
546	22-9.1:1 to 22-9.1:6
548	58-710.2, 58-710.3, 58-739.3, 58-748.2
549	6.1-63
550	3.1-796.1 to 3.1-796.11
551	15.1-1358.1 to 15.1-1358.3
552	18.1-282.1 to 18.1-282.4
553	38.1-442.1
554	15.1-20.2
556	15.1-1250
557	2.1-257
558	2.1-268
559	38.1-746 to 38.1-755
560	6.1-196 to 6.1-198, 6.1-200, 6.1-201, 6.1-202R, 6.1-204, 6.1-205R, 6.1-206, 6.1-207, 6.1-208R, 6.1-208.1 to 6.1-208.5, 6.1-209 to 6.1-211, 6.1-214R, 6.1-216 to 6.1-219, 6.1-222.1R, 6.1-226
561	46.1-421
562	2.1-38, 2.1-51.2, 2.1-64.15 to 2.1-64.21
563	16.1-9, 16.1-20
564	22-345 to 22-347
565	54-83.9, 54-83.19
566	33-133.1
567	9-84.01 to 9-84.06
568	43-2 to 43-4, 43-4.1, 43-6R, 43-8, 43-10, 43-11, 43-12R, 43-13, 43-13.1, 43-14R, 43-14.1, 43-20, 43-21, 43-23.1, 43-23.2
569	15.1-73.2
570	13.1-3, 13.1-3.1
572	19.1-86
573	54-33
574	6.1-333
575	46.1-190, 46.1-191.1
576	58-46.1
577	14.1-42.1
578	16.1-217.1 to 16.1-217.4, 32-291 to 32-296R, 63-1 to 63-385R, 63.1-1 to 63.1-5, 63.1-6 to 63.1-28, 63.1-29 to 63.1-71, 63.1-72 to 63.1-74, 63.1-75 to 63.1-96, 63.1-97 to 63.1-140, 63.1-142 to 63.1-248

Acts 1968 Chapter	Code 1950 Section
579	15.1-187
581	16.1-173
582	54-317, 54-417, 54-445, 54-481, 54-487
583	46.1-252
584	63-51
585	63-232 to 63-235, 63-237, 63-239, 63-241
586	63-110.1
588	38.1-347.1
589	14.1-73.1
590	53-222
591	14.1-143
592	32-57.1
593	58-763, 58-764, 58-764.1
594	32-63.1
595	15.1-491
596	14.1-46
597	54-795
598	3.1-722.1 to 3.1-722.11
599	8-435
600	14.1-42
601	33-47.2
602	15.1-164
603	53-147
604	54-152, 54-165, 54-169, 54-173, 54-181, 54-200.8, 54-200.16
605	43-34, 46.1-56, 46.1-88, 46.1-93
606	6.1-48.1
607	14.1-80
608	18.1-254.01
609	4-98.18 to 4-98.20
610	58-359
611	15.1-190
612	10-136
613	15.1-1232
614	22-127
615	8-317
617	51-111.67:1
618	14.1-17
619	58-266.1
621	46.1-140 to 46.1-148R
622	54-83.5, 54-83.8
623	4-22
624	58-769
625	15.1-504
626	55-200
627	58-877
628	58-863
629	58-81
630	58-1145
631	58-769.3
632	8-204
633	38.1-730 to 38.1-732
634	15.1-1132
635	15.1-67
636	58-78
637	58-578, 58-581, 58-582, 58-588, 58-590, 58-593, 58-594, 58-602, 58-607 to 58-610, 58-612
638	58-441.49:2
639	8-304, 8-305, 8-791, 8-879, 14.1-123, 14.1-127R, 14.1-128, 14.1-132R, 14.1-137, 14.1-156, 14.1-156.1, 14.1-160, 15.1-153, 16.1-75.1, 18.1-239, 18.1-247 to 18.1-251, n., 19.1-16, 19.1-18, 19.1-20, 19.1-100.1, 19.1-101, 19.1-102, 19.1-104 to 19.1.107, 19.1-110, 19.1-124, 19.1-125, 19.1-131, 19.1-138R, 19.1-283, 19.1-319, 24-157, 39-1 to 39-13R, 39.1-1 to 39.1-25, 49-3, 49-4, 55-113, 55-202
640	46.1-413.2
641	46.1-1, 46.1-193
642	46.1-357, 46.1-357.2, 46.1-365, 46.1-368, 46.1-370.1, 46.1-373, 46.1-375, 46.1-375.2, 46.1-379, 46.1-380R, 46.1-380.1, 46.1-380.2
643	22-205
647	51-151
648	51-146
649	29-55
650	16.1-143.2
651	23-35.1, 23-35.3 to 23-35.5, 23-35.7, 23-35.8
652	15.1-493
653	46.1-1, 46.1-286.1 38.1-569 to 38.1-638R, 38.1-638.1 to 38.1-638.61
655	15.1-264
656	64-1 to 64-176R, 64.1-1 to 64.1-187
657	19.1-233, 19.1-239
658	16.1-143.1
659	28.1-116, 33-69, 62-1 to 62-195R, 62.1-1 to 62.1-194.1, 62.1-195, 62.1-196
660	65-1 to 65-134R, 65.1-1 to 65.1-137
661	18.1-268.1 to 18.1-268.9
662	18.1-235.1, 18.1-236.1
665	20-88
666	63-105, 63-110, 63-115, 63-140.2:1, 63-205
667	63-115, 63-141, 63-179
668	63-88, 63-135, 63-136, 63-141, 63-157, 63-158, 63-199, 63-200
669	63-7, 63-35, 63-36
670	63-5.1R, 63-5.2, 63-10, 63-26, 63-38, 63-39, 63-46, 63-47R
672	29-184.2, 29-184.3
673	29-52
674	54-315.1
675	18.1-312
677	64.1-102
678	21-120
679	9-77.3
680	15.1-526
681	29-194
683	2.1-54 to 2.1-56, 2.1-58 to 2.1-60
684	15.1-444.1
685	46.1-1, 46.1-444, 46.1-450, 46.1-472, 46.1-485, 46.1-504
686	15.1-63
687	15.1-1374, 15.1-1379, 15.1-1382
688	62-106.5, n.
689	13.1-205, 13.1-205.1
691	22-207R, 22-208R, 22-217.1 to 22-217.8
692	29-121, n.
693	56-304.1, 56-304.2:1, 56-304.4 to 56-304.6, 56-304.6:1, 56-304.6:2, 56-304.7, 56-304.9, 56-304.11, 56-304.12
694	15.1-1130, 15.1-1131, 15.1-1131.1
695	15.1-9.1:1
696	36-11
698	32-195.36

Acts 1968 Chapter	Code 1950 Section
	to 32-195.50
699	55-201.1
700	33-57
701	18.1-272
702	22-95
704	15.1-2
705	15.1-1246.1
706	8-47.1
708	54-112.12, 54-112.16, 54-112.19
709	54-83.7, 54-83.9, 54-83.12, 54-83.15
710	36-52.2
711	14.1-5, 14.1-9
712	46.1-416.1
713	19.1-46
714	15.1-431
715	54-260.60
716	20-37.2
717	2.1-106.1 to 2.1-106.8
719	23-92 to 23-94
720	56-265.3
721	38.1-381
722	19.1-19.6, 52-4.1R
723	8-266
724	19.1-19.3
725	51-111.70:1
726	23-9.2:1
727	6.1-41.1
728	4-80.2
729	58-441.14, 58-441.51
730	46.1-289
731	22-67.2
732	17-30
733	13.1-75, 13.1-78
734	45.1-180 to 45.1-197
735	15.1-448
736	51-111.67:2
737	5.1-2, 5.1-23, 52-8
738	60-1 to 60-117R, 60.1-1 to 60.1-74, 60.1-75 to 60.1-134
739	22-20
740	9-107 to 9-111
741	6.1-326
742	58-792
743	40-104, 40-118.3
744	5.1-25.1 to 5.1-25.4
745	28.1-179
746	28.1-1, 28.1-2, 28.1-2.1, 28.1-3 to 28.1-5
747	28.1-83, 28.1-89, 28.1-91, 28.1-108, 28.1-116, 28.1-119, 28.1-124, 28.1-132, 28.1-134, 28.1-137, 28.1-160
748	28.1-48 to 28.1-50, 28.1-51.1, 28.1-53
749	28.1-23
750	28.1-173.2
751	62-194
752	45.1-162, 45.1-163, 45.1-165, 45.1-167, 45.1-168
753	23-159.1R
754	6.1-234
756	46.1-169.1
757	58-412
759	38.1-381.4
760	52-4.2
761	4-98.12:1
762	4-73.2
763	4-56
764	29-184.7, n.
765	22-218.4
766	54-308.6, 54-309
767	32-423
769	14.1-58.1
770	46.1-287.1
771	4-15.3
772	7.1-10
773	5.1-83 to 5.1-88
774	15.1-73.4
775	35-64.5
778	58-54
780	5.1-77 to 5.1-82
781	63-115, 63-116, 63-118, 63-119, 63-123, 63-127, 63-127.1, 63-132, 63-140.5, 63-140.9, 63-141, 63-142, 63-144, 63-145, 63-149, 63-179, 63-180, 63-181, 63-183, 63-187, 63-191, 63-208, 63-209, 63-214, 63-216
782	8-581.1
783	32-220
784	2.1-111
785	28.1-165, 28.1-173, 28.1-173.1
786	55-59
788	2.1-33
789	19.1-227
790	23-37.1 to 23-37.5
791	6.1-125
792	18.1-380.1, 18.1-380.2
793	15.1-31
794	7.1-15
796	54-276.9
797	15.1-724, 15.1-727, 15.1-729, 15.1-734, 15.1-735, 15.1-737, 15.1-763, 15.1-769, 15.1-770, 15.1-773, 15.1-779, 15.1-783, 15.1-784, 15.1-785, 15.1-787, 15.1-791
800	15.1-131
801	27-2, 27-3.1
802	17-140.1
803	54-426.1
807	58-12

ACTS 1969, EX. SESS.

Acts 1969, Ex. Sess. Chapter	Code 1950 Section
1	15.1-486
2	18.1-253.1, 18.1-253.2
3	22-217.3
4	14.1-9, 14.1-19
5	24-251
7	15.1-125
8	10-17.18, 10-17.19
9	58-12
10	15.1-1149 to 15.1-1151, 15.1-1151.1, 15.1-1152 to 15.1-1164
13	30-13
14	37.1-134
17	14.1-72
18	14.1-42
19	18.1-70.1
20	19.1-218
21	56-529, n., 56-530, n.
22	23-30.01
24	30-19.1, 30-19.3
25	22-61, 22-68
26	32-195.15

ACTS 1970

Acts 1970 Chapter	Code 1950 Section
1	2.1-326.1 to 2.1-326.3
2	58-449R
3	13.1-124
4	13.1-91, 13.1-117, 13.1-254, 13.1-279
5	58-462
6	58-457R
7	8-135.1
8	18.1-164
10	8-170
11	46.1-193.1
12	55-59
13	6.1-66
14	6.1-64
15	6.1-12
16	46.1-291
17	46.1-262.1
18	46.1-293

Acts 1970 Chapter	Code 1950 Section
19	46.1-309.1
20	46.1-310
21	46.1-319
22	46.1-293.1
23	46.1-282
24	46.1-275
25	46.1-314
26	46.1-308
27	46.1-311
28	46.1-278
29	46.1-172
30	56-338.65 to 56-338.84
31	10-37
32	56-304.13, 56-627
33	56-274
34	56-290.1
35	46.1-380.2
36	46.1-115.1
37	15.1-1047.1
38	6.1-319.1, 6.1-328
39	55-60
40	33-67.3R, 33-75.01 to 33-75.011
41	46.1-357
42	6.1-61
43	55-232
44	56-219
45	38.1-755R, 38.1-755.1
46	37.1-65
47	3.1-32, 3.1-33, 3.1-35, 3.1-36, 3.1-37R, 3.1-38R
48	3.1-546 to 3.1-562R, 3.1-562.1 to 3.1-562.10
49	3.1-463 to 3.1-530R, 3.1-530.1 to 3.1-530.9
50	63.1-142
52	6.1-299
53	38.1-756
54	22-7.1, 22-7.2
55	14.1-42.2
56	43-32
57	58-946.1
59	46.1-176
60	2.1-109
61	17-41
62	53-278.2, 53-278.3
63	19.1-228
64	18.1-356R, 18.1-357R
65	64.1-57
66	46.1-49
67	19.1-296
68	46.1-167.4
69	54-273, 54-274, 54-281, 54-281.2, 54-282, 54-284, 54-295.7, 54-296 to 54-299, 54-301, 54-302, 54-306, 54-307, 54-308, 54-308.5, 54-309, 54-310, 54-310.1, 54-311.1, 54-313, 54-315.1, 54-317, 54-319, 54-322 to 54-324
70	64.1-15R
71	22-72
72	32-70.1
73	26-40
74	38.1-196.2
75	2.1-327
76	55-139 to 55-139.2R, 55-142.1 to 55-142.9
77	13.1-542 to 13.1-556
78	29-184.1:2
79	29-144.2, 29-145.1
80	18.1-119.1:1
82	29-65
83	58-12
85	58-1104.1
86	3.1-637, 3.1-640
87	16.1-173
88	22-61
89	14.1-137
90	17-119.1
91	17-119.1
92	17-119.1
94	57-24.1
95	6.1-47
98	23-114, 23-116, 23-118, 23-122, 23-124, 23-126 to 23-131
99	46.1-172
101	19.1-19.1R, 19.1-19.1:1
102	58-151.21
103	46.1-172.1 60.1-47, 60.1-48, 60.1-52, 60.1-53, 60.1-59, 60.1-61, 60.1-70, 60.1-80, 60.1-129
110	33-57.1
111	3.1-360.1 to 3.1-360.8
112	29-184.2, 29-184.3R
113	4-89
114	53-38
115	54-112.29
116	54-326 to 54-367R, 54-367.1 to 54-367.37
117	23-9.3
118	19.1-19.2
119	4-98.2
120	4-98.10
121	19.1-300
122	17-5
123	63.1-103
124	21-127.1
126	22-79.1 to 22-79.6
127	13.1-50
128	23-9.2:1
132	28.1-136
134	15.1-125
136	1-13.40
138	62.1-132, n.
139	15.1-526.1
140	61.1-46.1
141	58-465.1
142	14.1-11.1
143	15.1-1005
144	15.1-223
145	38.1-424
146	38.1-183.2
147	38.1-198
148	29-136.1R
149	29-207, 29-208
150	32-290.1 to 32-290.3
152	18.1-173.2
153	14.1-11R, 14.1-11.3R, 14.1-11.4
154	22-53.1
155	22-32
156	22-72.1, 22-97.1
157	58-443
158	55-210.6:1
159	46.1-382
160	46.1-3.01
161	15.1-364.1, 15.1-482.1
162	22-275.4:1
163	46.1-173
165	46.1-268
166	23-4.1
169	46.1-280
170	30-14, 30-14.2
171	62.1-128, 62.1-129, 62.1-131 to 62.1-133, 62.1-135
172	15.1-1054
173	3.1-74, 3.1-75R, 3.1-75.1, 3.1-76R, 3.1-76.1, 3.1-77R, 3.1-77.1, 3.1-78R, 3.1-80R, 3.1-81R, 3.1-81.1, 3.1-82, 3.1-92R, 3.1-92.1, 3.1-93R, 3.1-95 to 3.1-98R, 3.1-102, 3.1-103
174	3.1-188.1 to 3.1-188.19
175	3.1-296.11 to 3.1-296.21
176	3.1-531.1, 3.1-535.1
179	14.1-144
180	15.1-1131.1
182	25-232.1
184	13.1-3
185	14.1-46
186	38.1-252
187	27-4, 27-6R, 27-6.1, 27-7, 27-8,

Acts 1970 Chapter	Code 1950 Section
	27-8.1, 27-9 to 27-11, 27-12R, 27-13, 27-14, 27-15R, 27-15.1, 27-15.2, 27-16R, 27-17, 27-18R, 27-19 to 27-21, 27-23R, 27-23.1 to 27-23.10, 27-24 to 27-29.1R, 27-30, 27-32, 27-32.1, 27-34, 27-34.1, 27-36, 27-39, 27-41, 27-43, 27-46, 27-83, 27-84
188	38.1-199.1
189	22-89.2
190	46.1-255, 46.1-257
191	19.1-19.3
192	46.1-45
193	22-348 to 22-350
194	29-153.1, 29-153.2
195	54-826, 54-827, 54-829
196	15.1-11.1
197	23-9.2:3
198	63.1-164
199	54-145.13 to 54-145.15
200	59.1-148.1, 59.1-148.2
201	11-19
202	2.1-82.1, 2.1-93, 2.1-94, 2.1-106.7
203	9-11
204	18.1-228, 18.1-235
205	15.1-694
208	29-184.8
209	15.1-181
211	15.1-510.1
212	15.1-510.3, 15.1-510.6
213	22-330.11
214	23-86, 23-89, 23-90
215	22-33.1
216	15.1-493
217	54-861, 54-864, 54-867, 54-868
218	15.1-791
219	15.1-28.1
220	58-78
222	36-49.1, 36-53
223	15.1-1131.1
224	52-11.2
225	2.1-272, 2.1-286, 15.1-8, 15.1-862, 15.1-880
227	38.1-389.2
228	9-24 to 9-28, 9-29.1, 9-34, 9-40, 9-43
230	26-5.1
231	58-266.1
232	16.1-158, 32-137
233	63.1-53
234	6.1-327
235	6.1-158
236	6.1-138
237	6.1-157
238	46.1-351.2
239	29-129.1
240	62.1-170
241	8-76
242	58-450
243	56-452R, 56-453R
244	64.1-123, 64.1-124, 64.1-130
245	45.1-183
246	14.1-164R, 14.1-164.1
247	15.1-589.2
248	64.1-29
250	14.1-182
251	26-49
252	53-133.1
253	21-120
254	29-11
255	54-58
256	29-57.2
257	46.1-252.2
258	56-234, 56-234.1
259	51-111.52:1
260	2.1-87, 14.1-13
262	2.1-38, 2.1-51.2, 2.1-109.1 to 2.1-109.5
263	46.1-296, 46.1-296.1
264	33-279.1
265	56-265.1
266	46.1-301
267	42.1-75
268	15.1-172
269	46.1-354.1
270	6.1-2.1
271	15.1-131.3
272	8-792
273	35-19, 35-24, 35-42, 35-64.5
274	29-77
275	53-275
276	56-508.1 to 56-508.7
277	58-730.3
278	20-88
279	8-76
280	37.1-38.1 to 37.1-38.4
281	4-118.2
282	15.1-510.5:1
283	46.1-284
284	20-61
285	15.1-133
286	13.1-514
287	46.1-93
288	56-277.1
289	64.1-105.1
290	3.1-884.1 to 3.1-884.16R, 3.1-884.17 to 3.1-884.36
291	41-1 to 41-89R, 41.1-1 to 41.1-20
292	46.1-394R, 46.1-444
293	23-9.6
294	23-9.10:1
296	64.1-57
297	4-84
298	46.1-525.1
299	19.1-32.1
300	46.1-172.01
301	46.1-264.1
302	4-2
303	15.1-1403
305	12-68 to 12-83
307	55-257
308	25-46.29 to 25-46.31
309	4-2
310	3.1-796.12 to 3.1-796.28
311	20-91
312	11-20, 11-23
313	58-55.1
315	7.1-7.2
316	14.1-41, 14.1-42
317	16.1-143.3
319	54-113, 54-115, 54-115.1, 54-119, 54-120, 54-124, 54-126, 54-127, 54-129 to 54-134, 54-138, 54-140 to 54-142, 54-145.1, 54-145.2, 58-298
321	40-1 to 40-146R, 40.1-1 to 40.1-11, 40.1-22 to 40.1-54, 40.1-55 to 40.1-126
322	33-1 to 33-331R, 33.1-1 to 33.1-46, 33.1-47 to 33.1-115, 33.1-117 to 33.1-132, 33.1-133 to 33.1-345, 33.1-347 to 33.1-385
323	63.1-38.1, 63.1-59.1
324	11-30 to 11-34
325	58-829, 58-851
326	63.1-240
327	63.1-248
328	63.1-96
329	4-28
330	58-404.2
331	2.1-63.4:1, 9-100 to 9-104.2R
332	15.1-432 to 15.1-436R
333	38.1-740
334	9-84.07
335	54-83.7
336	19.1-227.1
337	46.1-192
338	46.1-181.1
339	53-220.1

Acts 1970 Chapter	Code 1950 Section
340	53-98R, 53-99R
341	53-394
342	7.1-7.1
343	7.1-4.1
344	25-46.35
345	25-46.32, 33-65
346	37.1-195 to 37.1-198, 37.1-200 to 37.1-202
347	46.1-349
348	6.1-132.1
350	55-154
351	4-15
352	8-744.1
353	18.1-107.1
354	8-267.1
355	8-685
356	18.1-80.1
357	29-112.1
358	15.1-66.1, 15.1-66.2
360	4-60
361	63.1-116
362	20-27
363	56-265.8:1
364	58-71, 58-72
365	14.1-124
366	8-1.3, 16.1-25R
367	42.1-45
368	58-284.2
369	58-151.8:1
370	38.1-293.1
371	19.1-137
372	9-107
373	53-133.1
374	18.1-253.3
375	15.1-261.1
376	3.1-189, 3.1-198.1, 3.1-217, 3.1-217.1 to 3.1-217.3, 3.1-227, 3.1-233.1, 3.1-241
377	57-38.1
378	38.1-355
379	14.1-149
380	15.1-27.1
381	18.1-88, 18.1-88.1, 18.1-89
382	14.1-144.1
383	37.1-34.1
384	23-38.2
385	54-260.13
386	11-2.2
387	16.1-150
390	19.1-100.2
391	32-386.1
393	54-375.1
394	4-73.2, 4-112.1
395	8-358
396	6.1-129
397	6.1-171
398	6.1-155.1
399	6.1-131

Acts 1970 Chapter	Code 1950 Section
400	3.1-722.1, 3.1-722.9, 3.1-722.12, 3.1-722.13
401	58-1104
402	8-272
403	33-35.5
404	17-228
405	36-25
406	29-11.1
407	53-304.1 to 53-304.8
408	3.1-328
409	58-685.13
411	58-766
414	20-121.3
415	33-11
416	19.1-87.1
419	53-133.2
420	58-61
421	8-629.1
422	2.1-64.15
423	18.1-236.5
424	26-36.1
425	64.1-140
426	64.1-121
427	15.1-506.1
428	34-26, 34-27, 34-29, 34-30R
429	19.1-320
430	54-74
431	3.1-684.1 to 3.1-684.19
432	3.1-646.3
433	10-55
434	15.1-23.1
435	35-8
436	15.1-466
437	32-197
438	16.1-178
439	32-8.1
440	58-804
441	21-121, 21-140.2
442	18.1-400.1 to 18.1-400.6
443	58-76.1
444	15.1-1250
445	23-8.1
446	2.1-288
448	14.1-38
449	15.1-1357, 15.1-1358, 15.1-1362
450	59.1-67.1 to 59.1-67.3
451	22-275.4
452	15.1-29.2
453	15.1-14
454	15.1-1310
455	15.1-995
456	2.1-341, 2.1-344
457	3.1-22.5
458	58-753.1, 58-753.1:2, 58-753.1:3, 58-757
459	20-79

Acts 1970 Chapter	Code 1950 Section
460	32-364.1R, 32-364.3 to 32-364.11
462	24-1 to 24-456R, 24.1-1 to 24.1-281
463	2.1-238R, 2.1-239R, 2.1-347 to 2.1-358, 3.1-240R, 4-5R, 4-80R, 4-80.1R, 9-8R, 15.1-67 to 15.173.3R, 15.1-111R, 15.1-123R, 15.1-444.1R, 15.1-618R, 15.1-656R, 15.1-717R, 15.1-780R, 15.1-1328R, 15.1-1354R, 18.1-411R, 21-164R, 21-244R, 22-213R, 28.1-18R, 32-224R, 36-16R, 37.1-37R, 56-142 to 56-206, n., 56-336R, 58-1034R
464	62.1-69.1 to 62.1-69.4
465	63.1-40 to 63.1-42, 63.1-44
466	9-61R, 9-65.1 to 9-65.14
467	63.1-41
468	10-167 to 10-175
469	10-17.9:1, 10-17.10, 10-17.18
470	65.1-21, 65.1-28, 65.1-46, 65.1-47R, 65.1-48R, 65.1-51, 65.1-52, 65.1-54 to 65.1-57, 65.1-65, 65.1-71, 65.1-75.1, 65.1-83R, 65.1-84R, 65.1-88, 65.1-88.1, 65-1-95, 65.1-105, 65.1-106, 65.1-117.1, 65.1-118, 65.1-127
473	2.1-257
475	64.1-75.1
476	51-111.18, 51-111.37, 51-111.38:10 to 51-111.38:16R, 51-111.41:1, 51-111.45, 51-111.47, 51-111.49, 51-111.53 to 51-111.55, 51-111.57, 51-111.58, 51-111.58:1, 51-111.60, 51-111.60:1, 51-111.62, 51-111.67:7, 51-111.70:1, 51-111.70:2
477	14.1-17
478	30-28.12, 30-28.13
479	30-28.1, 30-28.1:1, 30-28.2, 30-28.3, 30-28.5, 30-28.8
480	21-2 to 21-6, 21-10, 21-12R, 21-12.1,

Acts 1970 Chapter	Code 1950 Section
	21-12.2, 21-13, 21-13.1, 21-14, 21-17, 21-19R, 21-20, 21-21R, 21-22R, 21-23, 21-24 to 21-26R, 21-27, 21-27.1, 21-27.2, 21-28 to 21-30, 21-31R, 21-31.1R, 21-31.2, 21-31.3, 21-33 to 21-37, 21-39, 21-40, 21-42 to 21-57, 21-59, 21-61, 21-62, 21-64 to 21-68, 21-72, 21-75 to 21-80, 21-82 to 21-84, 21-86, 21-88 to 21-90, 21-92, 21-93, 21-95, 21-100, 21-101, 21-103, 21-105, 21-109 to 21-111, 21-112.2 to 21-112.4, 21-112.4:1, 21-112.5 to 21-112.10, 21-112.12, 21-112.13
481	46.1-170
486	62.1-194
489	58-685.11
491	36-49.1
493	8-210.1
494	38.1-381
495	54-85, 54-86, 54-89, 54-95, 54-102
496	22-9, 22-9.1, 22-9.2, 22-9.2:1, 22-55.1, 22-228, 22-275.5, 22-275.12 to 22-275.14
498	22-67.2
499	4-24
500	8-178, 8-182
501	20-107, 20-109.1
503	33-35.8
504	18.1-246.1
505	15.1-37.2
506	32-365 to 32-367, 32-370, 32-372 to 32-374, 32-378, 32-378.1 to 32-378.4
507	46.1-350, 46.1-387.2, 46.1-387.8
508	18.1-62, 18.1-62.1 to 18.1-62.3
509	58-371.2
510	46.1-179.01
511	18.1-54.1
512	58-757.28
513	54-260.37
514	54-751.1
515	46.1-184
516	18.1-216.1
517	65.1-53
519	54-762
521	46.1-169.1, 46.1-190, 46.1-287, 46.1-288R
522	14.1-112
523	17-126.2
524	15.1-131.2
525	22-223
526	22-249
527	13.1-529, 13.1-531, 13.1-534
529	15.1-889.1
530	15.1-29.3
531	54-276.10
532	38.1-4, 38.1-183.1
534	58-880R
536	6.1-44
537	29-202
538	20-121.01
539	2.1-109.01 to 2.1-109.07
540	58-151.13
541	4-89
542	14.1-166, 14.1-167
543	23-165.10
544	4-107
545	4-37
546	2.1-110, 2.1-114
547	58-266.1
548	46.1-380.2
549	13.1-205
551	14.1-53
552	8-74
553	14.1-123, 14.1-128
554	32-240.1
555	36-49.1
556	9-96
557	2.1-20.1
558	8-225.1
559	16.1-218 to 16.1-220
560	18.1-236.6, 18.1-236.7
561	7.1-35
562	58-12
563	54-750, 54-758, 54-762
564	38.1-70.9 to 38.1-70.12R, 38.1-381.5
565	15.1-292
566	8-751
567	64.1-56
568	64.1-9R
569	14.1-125
570	15.1-376.1
571	54-524.110 to 54-524.132
572	15.1-299
573	15.1-486.1
574	8-302
575	51-178
576	6.1-234.1, 6.1-330
577	32-364.2:1
578	32-120.1
579	29-83, 29-87
580	58-81
581	15.1-504
582	58-930
583	15.1-334, 15.1-336R
584	21-113
585	11-23.2 to 11-23.4
588	58-151.36
589	18.1-87
590	56-529, n., 56-530, n.
591	21-11R, 21-11.1 to 21-11.15
593	53-295
595	38.1-92, 38.1-92.1
596	36-49.1
597	21-120
598	15.1-1378, 62.1-160, 62.1-162
599	51-127.15, 51-127.21
600	16.1-158, 16.1-176
601	23-155.6, 23-164.5, 23-187
602	63.1-93, 63.1-94, 63.1-99.1
603	2.1-5, 2.1-6
604	46.1-45.1
605	54-50
606	10-145.2 to 10-145.8, 42-1 to 42-67R, 42.1-1 to 42.1-28, 42.1-30, 42.1-31, 42.1-33 to 42.1-44, 42.1-46 to 42.1-58, 42.1-60 to 42.1-70, 42.1-72 to 42.1-74
607	54-729.2 to 54-729.24
608	58-81
609	23-19, 23-30.01 to 23-30.03
610	28.1-36, 28.1-167
611	15.1-135
614	33-70.10
615	22-9.1:4
616	6.1-361R, 6.1-362, 6.1-363
617	15.1-1240, 15.1-1244, 15.1-1246.1R, 15.1-1250, 15.1-1252, 15.1-1261, 15.1-1269.1
618	56-98R, 56-98.1, 56-99R, 56-99.1, 56-100R, 56-100.1
619	3.1-758 to 3.1-762, 3.1-762.1, 3.1-763
620	23-38.3 to 23.38.10
621	62.1-3, 62.1-3.1
622	18.1-55.1
623	54-1
624	23-49.14
625	3.1-779, 3.1-781, 3.1-785 to 3.1-787, 3.1-790 to 3.1-792, 3.1-795, 3.1-796

Acts 1970 Chapter	Code 1950 Section
627	4-25, 4-30, 4-33, 4-38, 4-98.3, 4-98.19
628	36-11.1:1
629	28.1-49R, 28.1-49.1
630	20-62, 53-47
631	46.1-103.1
632	46.1-53
635	38.1-238
636	38.1-79
637	23-9.11
638	62.1-14 to 62.1-44.1R, 62.1-44.2 to 62.1-44.33
639	32-195.21, 32-195.25, 54-147, 54-152, 54-172, 54-184, 54-200.1, 54-200.2
640	19.1-233
641	29-184.7, n.
642	8-654.5
643	65.1-70
644	29-91
645	32-9, 32-9.1
646	54-83.15
648	53-2, 53-3, 53-5 to 53-7R, 53-9, 53-10 to 53-16R, 53-16.1, 53-17R, 53-18, 53-20, 53-21, 53-22R, 53-23, 53-32R, 53-34, 53-39, 53-40, 53-43R, 53-50, 53-57, 53-60 to 53-62, 53-64, 53-65R, 53-66R, 53-67, 53-73, 53-75, 53-76, 53-76.1 to 53-76.3, 53-77R, 53-78R, 53-79, 53-80 to 53-83R, 53-84, 53-85R, 53-86R, 53-89, 53-90R, 53-91R, 53-92, 53-93R, 53-94 to 53-96, 53-98, n., 53-99, n., 53-99.1R, 53-100, 53-102.1, 53-103, 53-104, 53-107 to 53-109, 53-109.1, 53-114 to 53-120, 53-122, 53-122.1, 53-124 to 53-126R, 53-128R, 53-135.1, 53-136, 53-140, 53-142.1, 53-145, 53-146, 53-161, 53-163, 53-164, 53-166, 53-167R, 53-179, 53-183.1R, 53-184, 53-195, 53-198, 53-201, 53-206, 53-206.1 to 53-206.3, 53-206.6, 53-206.8, 53-208, 53-213, 53-217R, 53-219, 53-221, 53-223, 53-224, 53-225R, 53-227 to 53-229, 53-231 to 53-234, 53-236, 53-293 to 53-242, 53-244, 53-247, 53-249 to 53-251, 53-251.2, 53-253, 53-254, 53-257, 53-258, 53-260 to 53-266, 53-268, 53-278R, 53-279, 53-280R, 53-291, 53-292, 53-294, 53-301, 53-305, 53-314
649	40-20
650	18.1-346, 19.1-84, 54-399R, 54-403R, 54-403.1R, 54-404 to 54-417R, 54-419 to 54-424R, 54-425.1 to 54-428R, 54-431 to 54-433R, 54-434.1R, 54-434.2R, 54-440 to 54-446.13R, 54-447 to 54-456.2R, 54-461 to 54-524R, 54-524.1 to 54-524.109
651	10-100
652	18.1-126, 18.1-126.1
653	23-35.9
654	15.1-73.4
655	58-829.3
656	38.1-311
657	51-146, 51-148, 51-150, 51-151, 51-153, 51-155, 51-156, 51-157.1
658	58-81
660	16.1-201
661	54.112.1 to 54-112.4, 54-112.11:1, 54-112.12, 54-112.14, 54-112.15, 54-112.19, 54-112.21, 54-112.28
662	44-1, 44-4, 44-16, 44-27, 44-28, 44-30, 44-33
663	9-6.2
665	22-330.17 to 22-330.35
667	28.1-51.2
668	59.1-21.1 to 59.1-21.6
669	20-88.13, 20-88.15, 20-88.15:1, 20-88.16, 20-88.16:1, 20-88.18 to 20-88.20, 20-88.20:2, 20-88.21, 20-88.22, 20-88.22:01, 20-88.22:1, 20-88.23, 20-88.23:1 to 20-88.23:3, 20-88.24, 20-88.25, 20-88.26:1, 20-88.28:1 to 20-88.28:4, 20-88.30, 20-88.30:1 to 20-88.30:7
670	2.1-64.29 to 2.1-64.31
671	54-17R, 54-17.1
672	63.1-221, 63.1-221.1, 63.1-236
673	37.1-64, 37.1-66R, 37.1-67, 37.1-69R, 37.1-70, 37.1-71, 37.1-78.1, 37.1-79 to 37.1-84R, 37.1-86R, 37.1-89
674	21-118.4
675	58-685.12
676	4-37, 4-114
678	14.1-73, 14.1-73.1
679	14.1-55 to 14.1-58, 14.1-58.1R, 14.1-62.1R
680	8-67.2
681	22-285
682	2.1-21
683	46.1-95
684	33-70.2
685	9-116
686	4-62, 4-73, 4-112
687	2.1-181, 2.1-187, 51-111.52:3, 56-45
688	4-15.1
689	32-424
690	16.1-199
691	22-37
692	40-61.2, 40-61.3
693	14.1-113
694	14.1-143
695	6.1-117.1
696	22-276.1, 46.1-373, 46.1-380.2
698	51-111.52:2
699	32-353.22
700	27-5.1
701	62.1-44.34
702	33-255.24 to 33-255.44, n.
703	15.1-1403
704	38.1-569 to 38.1-638, n.
705	46.1-351.1, 46.1-351.2
706	53-206.12
707	5.1-83 to 5.1-88R, 5.1-88.1 to 5.1-88.5
708	5.1-89 to 5.1-151, 56-142 to 56-206R
711	18.1-367.1 to 18.1-367.6
713	8-887
714	55-29.1 to 55-29.3
715	64.1-22
716	40-9.1 to 40-16R, 40-18R, 40-18.1 to 40-18.10, 40-19R
717	5.1-1, 5.1-4, 5.1-5, 5.1-7.1, 5.1-9.1,

Acts 1970 Chapter	Code 1950 Section
	5.1-16.1, 5.1-21.1, 5.1-25, 5.1-36, 5.1-44, 5.1-48, 5.1-51 to 5.1-53
718	16.1-217.1
719	55-118.1 to 55-118.9
720	40-64.2, 40-64.3
721	63.1-62, 63.1-87, 63.1-97R, 63.1-97.1, 63.1-99R, 63.1-100, 63.1-101R, 63.1-102R, 63.1-104, 63.1-105, 63.1-107, 63.1-110, 63.1-111R, 63.1-120, 63.1-122, 63.1-202
722	14.1-72
723	4-25
724	46.1-387.2, 46.1-387.4, 46.1-387.5
725	15.1-1374
726	28.1-82, 28.1-85.1, 28.1-91R, 28.1-92, 28.1-109, 28.1-110, 28.1-119.1, 28.1-120, 28.1-160, 28.1-165, 28.1-167, 28.1-189R
727	4-22
728	23-223 to 23-225, 23-227 to 23-231
729	56-325, 56-326 to 56-328R, 56-329, 56-330
730	56-142 to 56-206, n.
731	56-390 to 56-404R
732	60.1-111
734	4-38
735	23-35.3
736	46.1-184
739	58-81
741	51-21.1, n.
744	46.1-351.1, 46.1-351.2
745	2.1-33
748	58-851.2
749	22-332, 22-334, 22-344, 22-344.1, 22-344.2
750	15.1-945
751	15.1-1028, 15.1-1030, 15.1-1041, 15.1-1050, 15.1-1061, 15.1-1066, 15.1-1070, 15.1-1077, 15.1-1093, 15.1-1119, 15.1-1140
752	58-157
753	63.1-127.1, 63.1-128 to 63.1-130R, 63.1-132R, 63.1-133R, 63.1-133.1
754	46.1-30
755	16.1-201
756	4-4
757	10-161, 10-162
758	37.1-106
759	2.1-38, 2.1-51.2, 2.1-64.23 to 2.1-64.28
761	20-113
762	58-27.2
764	59.1-68.01
765	16.1-201
766	38.1-756.1, 38.1-757 to 38.1-774
768	54-573.1, 54-573.17, 54-864
769	10-90.10 to 10-90.19, 58-838.5, 58-838.7
770	58-838.1, 58-838.2, 58-838.4, 58-838.5:1, 58-838.8 to 58-838.10
771	54-859.1 to 54-859.14, 54-861, 54-864, 54-867, 54-868
772	58-54, 58-54.1
773	58-664
774	51-111.67:4
775	54-864, 54-899 to 54-915
776	63.1-92
777	3.1-18.1 to 3.1-18.3
778	51-179
779	51-3 to 51-7R, 51-12 to 51-15R, 51-17 to 51-21.1R, 51-22 to 51-28.1R, 51-28.3R, 51-29R, 51-29.1 to 51-29.7:1R, 51-29.8 to 51-29.19R, 51-111.10, 51-160 to 51-177
780	59.1-68.2
781	2.1-133.1 to 2.1-133.3
782	44-142.2, 44-145.2
783	39.1-15, 49-4
784	4-40 to 4-42, 4-43R, 4-44
785	4-108, 4-109, 4-109.1, 4-109.2, 4-110R, 4-111

ACTS 1971, EX. SESS.

Acts 1971, Ex. Sess. Chapter	Code 1950 Section
1	2.1-345, 4-4, 5.1-77, 5.1-125, 8-581.1, 8-653, 13.1-400.6, 13.1-519, 13.1-535, 15.1-53, 15.1-276, 15.1-277, 15.1-322, 15.1-324, 15.1-372, 15.1-670, 15.1-674, 15.1-677, 15.1-685, 15.1-850, 15.1-894, 15.1-1061, 15.1-1349, 17-116, 19.1-35, 19.1-346, 21-243, 22-29.5, 22-29.10, 22-151.1, 28.1-6, 30-14.2, 33.1-92, 38.1-54, 38.1-60, 38.1-104, 38.1-133, 38.1-279, 38.1-765, 39.1-7, 54-118, 56-64, 56-338.7, 56-338.71, 56-374, 58-404.1, 58-465.2, 58-597, 58-684, 58-824, 58-953, 58-956, 58-973, 59.1-92
2	8-1.2, 8-494R
3	58-772, 58-804
4	58-864, 58-881
5	58-963.1
6	58-1021
7	65.1-4, 65.1-19
8	33.1-355
9	56-8.1
10	58-27.3, 58-49R, 58-50R
11	58-844, 58-851.1
12	58-978, 58-987 to 58-989
13	58-1118, 58-1141, 58-1162, 58-1163R
14	1-4
15	54-911, 54-912
16	49-1
17	5.1-136
18	15.1-664, 15.1-667, 15.1-668
19	15.1-721
20	15.1-727
21	25-52
22	30-1
23	56-1
24	56-38
25	56-457R
26	5.1-33
27	17-118, 17-120, 17-139
28	19.1-246
29	19.1-328 to 19.1-330, 19.1-332 to 19.1-334, 19.1-338, 19.1-339
30	56-97, 56-107, 56-129
31	56-239, 56-240
32	56-320
33	58-9
34	3.1-8
35	15.1-819
36	15.1-1047.1,

Acts 1971, Ex. Sess. Chapter	Code 1950 Section
	15.1-1135
37	54-563
38	56-35, 56-36
39	56-37, 56-41R, 56-42R, 56-43
40	56-462
41	58-519, 58-603
42	15.1-559 to 15.1-561, 15.1-567, 15.1-568
43	2.1-153
44	38.1-379.1 to 38.1-379.3
45	58-503.1
46	58-540R, 58-541R, 58-616R, 58-617R, 58-672, 58-676R, 58-677R, 58-679
47	58-822, 58-823
48	58-45.1
49	1-12, 1-13.2, 1-13.5:1, 1-13.21, 1-13.26, 1-13.27:1, 1-13.29, 1-13.38, 1-13.41
50	17-3R, 17-3.1, 17-4R, 17-5
51	17-93, 17-94, 17-99 to 17-102, 17-104 to 17-109R, 17-112
57	2.1-60
60	58-61
63	15.1-63
64	15.1-307, 15.1-308, 15.1-323
65	15.1-589, 15.1-623
66	15.1-757, 15.1-760, 15.1-761
67	15.1-792
68	15.1-991
69	22-234
70	65.1-10
71	30-13
87	22-29.6
88	51-111.10, 51-111.18, 51-111.41:1, 51-111.57, 51-111.67:2
89	51-111.67:4
90	58-617.2
91	10-17.10, 10-17.18:1, 10-17.18:2, 10-17.23:1 to 10-17.23:3, 10-17.24 to 10-17.27R
93	22-67.2
94	54-524.2, 54-524.89, 54-524.101
95	14.1-112
98	13.1-204
99	15.1-228, 15.1-229
100	22-1R, 22-1.1
101	22-146.1 to 22-146.11R
102	22-221R, 23-10 to 23-13R
103	36-70 to 36-85
104	56-338.17, 56-338.18, 56-338.37, 56-338.38, 56-338.83, 56-338.84
106	30-28.1:1
107	19.1-19.3
108	9-111
109	16.1-196
110	53-8
111	54-306
114	56-529, n., 56-530, n.
115	26-40
116	24.1-12R, 24.1-12.1
117	13.1-77
118	24.1-4R, 24.1-4.1
119	24.1-1, 14.1-23, 24.1-36 to 24.1-39, 24.1-41, 24.1-45.1, 24.1-47, 24.1-72.1 to 24.1-72.9, 24.1-81, 24.1-86, 24.1-90, n., 24.1-91, 24.1-100, 24.1-101, 24.1-111, 24.1-112, 24.1-117, 24.1-119, 24.1-134, 24.1-135, 24.1-166, 24.1-168, 24.1-172, 24.1-174, 24.1-185, 24.1-188, 24.1-203, 24.1-227 to 24.1-230
120	24.1-14R, 24.1-14.1
121	2.1-303
122	14.1-41, 14.1-42
124	9-106
125	2.1-177
126	15.1-239
127	22-29.15 22-101, 22-101.1R, 22-101.1:1R, 22-101.2R, 22-102
129	30-19
131	24.1-81
133	58-16.2
135	3.1-1
137	2.1-33
138	63.1-44
139	2.1-210
140	15.1-965.1 to 15.1-965.8
141	33.1-132
143	2.1-33
148	2.1-179.1
149	17-127.13
150	35-64.3
152	15.1-145
153	36-19
154	2.1-37.1 to 2.1-37.18
155	2.1-118, 2.1-257, 2.1-316, 4-56, 9-107, 14.1-68 to 14.1-70, 14.1-72, 14.1-73, 14.1-75 to 14.1-80, 14.1-85 to 14.1-87, 14.1-89, 14.1-96, 14.1-101, 14.1-105, 14.1-111, 14.1-125, 14.1-136, 15.1-41, 15.1-42, 15.1-48, 15.1-51, 15.1-74, 15.1-75, 15.1-77, 15.1-86, 15.1-87, 15.1-90.1, 15.1-134, 15.1-796, 15.1-796.1, 15.1-824, 15.1-825, 15.1-989, 15.1-993, 15.1-1020, 15.1-1104, 25-46.33, 25-173, 25-202, 30-10, 30-44, 30-46, 30-47, 35-31, 37.1-71, 37.1-73 to 37.1-75, 37.1-78, 37.1-125, 37.1-130, 37.1-137, 43-14.1, 43-34, 46.1-351.1, 46.1-351.2, 58-37, 58-41, 58-43, 58-69, 58-181, 58-991, 58-1001, 58-1003 to 58-1005, 58-1086, 64.1-131, 64.1-132, 65.1-13
156	14.1-29 to 14.1-32, 14.1-52, 14.1-120, 14.1-181, 14.1-182, 17-17, 17-18, 64.1-114, 65.1-93, 65.1-98
157	12-1 to 12-83R, 12.1-1 to 12.1-43
158	15.1-700, 15.1-706, 15.1-720, 15.1-729, 15.1-742, 15.1-808, 15.1-987, 15.1-988, 15.1-992, 15.1-998, 15.1-1021
159	15.1-821
160	22-19.1, 22-21.2
161	22-72, 22-97, 22-100.1, 22-100.2R, 22-100.3, 22-100.6, 22-100.7, 22-100.9, 22-100.12R
162	22-116, 22-117, 22-126R, 22-126.1, 22-127, 22-128, 22-130R, 22-138.1R, 22-141R, 22-141.1R

Acts 1971, Ex. Sess. Chapter	Code 1950 Section
163	22-156, 22-161.1 to 22-161.5R
164	22-307R, 22-315
165	24.1-82, 24.1-83R
169	58-760.1
170	54-524.107:1
171	58-77 to 58-86.1:5R, 58-87 to 58-98.1R, 58-101 to 58-148R, 58-151R, 58-151.01 to 58-151.0111, 58-151.2, 58-151.3, 58-151.11, 58-151.14, 58-151.19, 58-151.21, 58-151.28, 58-151.31, 58-515.39
172	58-769.4 to 58-769.151:1, 58-769.16, n., 58-804
173	55-29.1 to 55-29.6
174	13.1-3
175	13.1-205
176	2.1-348, 2.1-349, 2.1-349.1, 2.1-353, 2.1-356, 22-206R
177	52-11.2
179	10-90.10 to 10-90.19R, 10-90.20 to 10-90.29, 58-838.5R, 58-838.5:2, 58-838.7R, 58-838.7:1
180	2.1-358
181	37.1-183R, 37.1-183.1
182	37.1-179
183	32-137
185	51-111.10, 51-111.41:1, 51-111.54, 51-111.67:2
186	15.1-545, 15.1-546, 15.1-546.1R
187	58-12.2
188	14.1-46
189	18.1-200, 18.1-200.1R, 18.1-201
190	65.1-88.2
191	18.1-230
192	58-681
193	58-847
194	14.1-17R, 14.1-17.1
195	58-27.4
196	58-77
197	62.1-44.15:1
198	22-330.18
199	15.1-37.4 to 15.1-37.8
200	15.1-571, 15.1-571.1, 15.1-572 to 15.1-581R
201	15.1-787, 15.1-788, 15.1-788.1
202	15.1-803, 15.1-806
203	22-11, 22-12R, 22-12.1, 22-13, 22-19
204	24.1-29, 24.1-33
205	24.1-41, 24.1-42, 24.1-47, 24.1-48, 24.1-127R, 24.1-128R, 24.1-182
206	24.1-152, 24.1-154
209	10-21.1
210	54-524.109:1 to 54-524.109:8
211	2.1-268.1
212	58-404.2, n.
213	58-757.28, n.
214	58-76.1, n.
215	58-49, n.
216	38.1-381
217	58-266.3
218	23-7.1
219	54-113.1
221	58-792
222	24.1-253
223	15.1-40.1, 15.1-40.2
224	15.1-170, 15.1-176 to 15.1-180, 15.1-185, 15.1-185.1, 15.1-186, 15.1-187, 15.1-190, 15.1-190.1, 15.1-225
225	22-3.1, 22-30, 22-32, 22-34R, 22-38, 22-43, 22-43.1R, 22-43.2R, 22-43.4R, 22-61
226	24.1-167, 24.1-183
227	56-8.2
228	16.1-162
231	23-35.1 to 23-35.3, 23-35.7, 23-35.8
232	58-12.3
234	15.1-1032.1
235	60.1-3, 60.1-11, 60.1-12, 60.1-14, 60.1-14.1, 60.1-14.2, 60.1-26, 60.1-27, 60.1-44, 60.1-51, 60.1-51.1, 60.1-52.1 to 60.1-52.3, 60.1-59, 60.1-79, 60.1-84, 60.1-89, 60.1-89.1, 60.1-99, 60.1-100
236	14.1-67, 14.1-82
238	15.1-131
239	2.1-106.6:1
240	14.1-18.1
241	22-29.10, 22-29.15
245	2.1-210, 15.1-599 to 15.1-561, 15.1-567, 15.1-568, 26-40, 54-306, 54-524.109:1 to 54-524.109:8, 58-45.1, 58-77, 62.1-44.15:1
246	24.1-14.1
247	24.1-358, 24.1-22, 24.1-52, 24.1-126, 24.1-143, 24.1-166, 24.1-168, 24.1-185, 24.1-199, 24.1-229, 24.1-258
249	46.1-423.3
250	19.1-347.1 to 19.1-347.5, 19.1-351
251	18.1-254.1 to 18.1-254.4, 18.1-254.5R, 18.1-254.5:1
253	14.1-125
254	15.1-796
255	18.1-62.2
257	37.1-109
261	58-151.21
262	19.1-148
263	8-178, 8-182
264	24.1-40
265	24.1-41, 24.1-72.5 to 24.1-72.9R, 24.1-88, 24.1-133, 24.1-229

ACTS 1972

Acts 1972 Chapter	Code 1950 Section
1	58-12.4
2	33.1-268
3	46.1-278
4	46.1-184
5	30-14.4, 30-15.1
6	46.1-262.1
7	46.1-267
8	46.1-291.1
10	58-1024
11	63.1-47
13	2.1-1
14	58-919.1
15	54-295.7, 54-308.6, 54-310
16	54-128
17	4-98.11
18	23-38.11 to 23-38.18, 23-38.19, n.
19	23-38.20 to 23-38.29
21	24.1-4.1R, 24.1-4.2
23	60.1-111
26	51-111.54
33	46.1-191
35	23-47, 23-49
36	32-301
39	46.1-296
41	15.1-504

Acts 1972 Chapter	Code 1950 Section
43	14.1-33
47	46.1-444
48	23-132R
49	50-74
50	63.1-204
51	23-50.6
52	18.1-19
53	18.1-79
54	53-61, 53-67, 63.1-110.1
55	53-38
56	28.1-38R
57	54-749
58	53-184
59	53-37.1
60	16.1-198, 16.1-200
61	46.1-154.2
62	33.1-38, 33.1-74
63	46.1-248
64	46.1-304
65	33.1-345, 33.1-346
66	46.1-301
67	46.1-35.1
69	14.1-9
71	56-245.1
73	2.1-167, 8-750.1, 15.1-117, 15.1-127, 15.1-765, 15.1-768, 16.1-178, 16.1-199, 16.1-205, 16.1-210, 16.1-211, 22-275.22, 32-310.8, 58-923, 63.1-67.1, 63.1-87, 63.1-92, 63.1-220, 63.1-225, 63.1-228
74	32-6.1 to 32-6.3
75	4-89
76	4-89
77	46.1-158.1
78	3.1-531
79	33.1-55
80	46.1-149.1
82	17-127.16
84	13.1-556
85	55-79.17
86	22-72.1, 22-97.1, 46.1-169.2
88	58-2
89	46.1-193
90	3.1-746
91	39.1-14.1
92	32-353.34
93	58-463
94	32-1
95	54-102.14
96	64.1-157
97	19.1-349
98	3.1-290
100	38.1-382.1
102	19.1-300

Acts 1972 Chapter	Code 1950 Section
103	54-74
104	8-441, 8-441.1
105	46.1-180.3
107	19.1-32.1, n.
110	38.1-371.1, 38.1-371.2
111	16.1-208.1
113	6.1-352 to 6.1-360R
114	2.1-21
115	38.1-366
116	64.1-87.1
117	51-111.41:1
118	51-111.55
119	10-138.1
120	3.1-763.15
122	2.1-93
123	13.1-50
124	36-47.2
125	18.1-81.1
126	18.1-78.6
127	53-128.7 to 53-128.10
128	17-41
129	22-70
130	55-106, 55-113
131	54-43
132	3.1-951
133	29-65
134	3.1-250 to 3.1-255, 3.1-257 to 3.1-259
135	9-109.1, 9-111, 53-168.1
136	23-216
137	22-61
138	4-17, 4-19, 4-23, 4-59
139	18.1-408.1 58-166, 58-167, 58-169, 58-176, 58-177, 58-198 to 58-201
141	15.1-827
143	4-78
145	3.1-127 to 3.1-134R, 19.1-296R, 19.2-297R, 19.1-300 to 19.1-311R, 53-21.1, 53-75.1 to 53-75.8, 53-166.1, 53-183.2, 53-183.3, 53-184.1, 53-184.2, 53-228.1, 53-316 to 53-323
146	46.1-264.1
147	63.1-40
148	51-111.41:1
149	29-54.1
150	27-54.2
151	51-111.24, 51-11.68:1, 51-149, 51-165R, 51-165.1, 51-166

Acts 1972 Chapter	Code 1950 Section
152	58-514.6
153	58-502.4
154	45.1-32
155	30-19.1
156	63.1-171.1 to 63.1-171.7
158	33.1-355
159	8-685
160	14.1-42.2
161	15.1-1250
162	15.1-770
163	10-76.1, 10-77, 10-79, 10-79.1, 10-81.1, 10-83.01
164	15.1-158.1, n.
165	54-30, 54-31
167	42.1-57
168	4-61
169	25-46.17:1
170	14.1-163
171	14.1-137
172	2.1-5
173	37.1-132, 37.1-133R
174	36-49.1
175	53-19.1, 53-19.2 to 53-19.4R
176	53-79
177	16.1-185
178	4-30, 4-31, 4-34, 4-104 to 4-106, 4-113
179	54-91.1
180	13.1-543, 13.1-549.1
181	54-83.1:5 to 54-83.1:25, 54-864
185	58-834
186	58-54.1, 58-55, 58-57, 58-58, 58-65.1
187	6.1-112
188	23-38.5
189	6.1-63, 6.1-64
190	6.1-73.1
191	6.1-71, 6.1-153, n.
192	6.1-201, 6.1-216, 6.1-217
193	26-64
194	54-276.101
195	6.1-94
196	8.8-102
198	23-37.1, 23-37.3 to 23-37.5
199	18.1-265, 18.1-268.7
200	46.1-65
201	17-119
202	14.1-158
203	6.1-31.1, 6.1-31.2

Acts 1972 Chapter	Code 1950 Section
204	39.1-8, 39.1-9
205	2.1-227
206	45.1-180, 45.1-181, 45.1-183
207	58-685.19
208	46.1-80
209	26-36.1
210	23-9.3
211	46.1-94
212	17-127.20
214	13.1-554.1
215	14.1-53
216	8-4.1:1
217	59.1-45
218	15.1-152
219	21-120
220	15.1-293.1
221	21-118.5 to 21-118.8
222	21-120
223	2.1-109.01, 2.1-109.03, 2.1-109.04
224	22-60
225	14.1-78, 19.1-308
226	3.1-621
227	51-178
228	56-277.1
229	65.1-54 to 65.1-56, 65.1-65, 65.1-70, 65.1-71, 65.1-88, 65.1-99
230	46.1-52
231	58-153
232	5.1-104
233	56-338.20
234	46.1-184
235	45.1-23
236	21-137R, 21-137.1, 21-137.2
237	40.1-51.5 to 40.1-51.19, 59.1-168 to 59.1-176R
238	51-176
240	2.1-229
241	40.1-30
242	40.1-48
243	40.1-25
244	27-5.1
245	22-218, 22-218.2, 22-223
246	27-70
247	14.1-144
248	22-236R, 22-236.1
249	46.1-75
250	58-57, 58-61
252	27-23.1
255	6.1-320
256	15.1-89
267	46.1-2, 46.1-3
273	38.1-381.5
274	9-85
275	6.1-40
276	14.1-200.2
278	46.1-192.2
279	32-104.5 to 32-104.10
280	55-66.3
281	5.1-90.1
282	9-106.03, 9-106.04
285	8-327.2
286	46.1-188
287	15.1-506.1
288	58-838.5:1
289	37.1-49 to 37.1-54R, 37.1-54.1
290	33.1-223.1
291	58-31
292	46.1-347
293	53-151
294	62.1-79.1, 62.1-79.2
295	19.1-234
296	3.1-722.16 to 3.1-722.28
297	56-320
298	16.1-158.1
299	46.1-90.1
300	46.1-72, 46.1-128
301	46.1-41, 46.1-51
302	58-685.13
303	46.1-115
304	4-98.12:2
305	62.1-77.1
306	55-154
307	38.1-756
308	30-29
310	58-151.02, 58-151.03, 58-151.032, 58-151.032:1, 58-373
311	58-46
312	32-353.33
313	32-367
314	14.1-11.1
315	58-760.1
316	58-27, 58-166, 58-167, 58-238, 58-838.8, 58-838.9
318	56-304.7
319	22-9.3
320	52-4.3
321	26-45.2
322	16.1-144
323	32-137
324	54-734
325	58-838.21
326	26-20.1
327	8-229
328	58-157
329	29-230 to 29-237
330	16.1-201
331	58-219
332	64.1-73
338	58-617.2
339	6.1-344, 6.1-349, 6.1-350.1
340	58-844, 58-851.1
341	37.1-67
342	37.1-105
343	42.1-70
345	58-381, 58-393.1
346	46.1-352
347	15.1-517.1
348	53-179
349	59.1-17, 59.1-18, 59.1-19R
350	58-48.1 to 58-48.5
351	58-26.1
352	58-829.4, n.
353	46.1-525.1
354	16.1-190
355	58-441.18, 58-441.20, 58-441.21, 58-441.27, 58-441.27:1
356	2.1-33
357	15.1-364
358	19.1-296
359	22-276.1
360	15.1-608
361	8-676, 8-679
362	46.1-7
363	58-44.1
364	18.1-318.1
365	16.1-202.3
366	19.1-111.1
367	8-210.1R, 8-210.2
368	8-703
369	46.1-205
370	15.1-1241 to 15.1-1244.1
371	10-21.1
373	46.1-14
374	5.1-47, 5.1-48
375	46.1-555.7
376	4-108 to 4-109.2
377	4-40 to 4-42
378	46.1-51, 46.1-87
379	22-9
380	46.1-471
381	29-117
382	37.1-111
383	37.1-117
384	58-728
385	46.1-267.1
386	46.1-170
387	63.1-51
389	16.1-29
390	14.1-52
391	54-42
392	32-365 to 32-367,

Acts 1972 Chapter	Code 1950 Section
	32-370, 32-372, 32-373, 32-378 to 32-378.4
393	33.1-72
394	18.1-44
396	33.1-90
397	8-791
398	62.1-3.01
399	59.1-53.1, 59.1-53.2
400	6.1-234.1
401	28.1-8, 28.1-20
402	46.1-2
403	2.1-81.1 to 2.1-81.4
404	10-176
405	2.1-33
406	46.1-413
408	8-67.2, 46.1-2, 46.1-28, 46.1-72, 46.1-77, 58-726, 58-747
410	38.1-299
411	26-12.1
412	62.1-167, 62.1-168, 62.1-170, 62.1-172, 62.1-173, 62.1-177, 62.1-196
413	10-21.3:1
414	29-57.1:1, 29-64
415	62.1-164
416	44-100
417	25-26.36
418	56-296.1R
419	46.1-383
420	59.1-47
421	18.1-236.7
423	62.1-134, 62.1-135, 62.1-137, 62.1-140
424	28.1-65
425	13.1-75
426	22-73
427	46.1-105.2
428	15.1-155
429	32-195.3:1 to 32-195.5:2, 32-195.8:1 to 32-195.8:3
430	16.1-202.3
431	32-11.1, 54-276.11
432	54-729.10, 54-729.13, 54-729.18, 54-729.25
433	46.1-1, 46.1-444, 46.1-450, n., 46.1-472, 46.1-504
434	22-33
435	46.1-167.5
436	25-46.2:1, 25-120 to 25-231R
437	56-304.1
438	54-145.2
439	46.1-341
440	45.1-8
441	8-268
442	46.1-400, 46.1-402, 46.1-451
443	3.1-790
444	54-56
445	46.1-299
446	46.1-330
447	61.1-22 to 61.1-37R
448	59.1-21.2 to 59.1-21.5, 59.1-21.7
449	64.1-188 to 64.1-196
450	55-79.2
451	31-27
452	58-546 to 58-555R
454	46.1-184
456	15.1-766
457	3.1-296.1 to 3.1-296.3, 3.1-296.5, 3.1-296.6, 3.1-296.10:1
458	55-115
459	58-587.1, 58-617.2
460	20-61
461	19.1-146
462	22-74
463	46.1-395
464	65.1-4
465	58-151.066, 58-151.078
466	36-12, 36-22, 36-27, 36-30, 36-49
468	29-184.1:2, n.
469	18.1-74.1:1
470	15.1-708
471	46.1-181.2
472	28.1-1
473	46.1-104.1
474	16.1-129.3, 46.1-179, 46.1-179.2
475	63.1-225
476	37.1-43
477	46.1-178
478	58-1010.1
479	8-374
480	40.1-80, 40.1-81R, 40.1-81.1, 40.1-84, 40.1-93, 40.1-95, 40.1-97R
481	32-139.1
482	20-109, 20-109.1
484	18.1-15R, 18.1-15.2R, 18.1-15.3
485	11-17 to 11-20, 11-22, 11-23
486	58-412
487	53-213, 53-213.01
488	59.1-178 to 59.1-180, 59.1-182.1, 59.1-188.1, n.
489	46.1-247
490	33.1-24.1, 33.1-41, 33.1-43, 33.1-46.1, 33.1-288, 46.1-380.2, 58-628, 58-629, 58-711, 58-715, 58-730, 58-730.3, 58-733, 58-744, 58-753.1:2
491	16.1-118
492	32-310.4
493	35-38
494	2.1-236, 2.1-255, 2.1-257, 2.1-259, 2.1-263R, 2.1-265, 2.1-266R, 2.1-266.1, 2.1-267, 2.1-270, 2.1-280, 2.1-283R, 2.1-291
496	44-12
497	3.1-962.1
498	37.1-194 to 37.1-198
499	3.1-588 to 3.1-610R, 3.1-610.1 to 3.1-610.21
500	32-353.27
501	17-70
502	46.1-357.2
503	2.1-243.1
504	32-6
505	56-338.51
506	2.1-270.1
508	15.1-503.1
509	29-122
510	14.1-18.1
511	22-72
512	22-318.1
514	3.1-953
515	23-9.11
516	53-278.1
517	6.1-327.1
518	16.1-218
519	56-259
520	29-11.1
521	46.1-343
522	46.1-180
523	22-330.17 to 22-330.19, 22-330.21, 22-330.33
524	9-65.12, 9-65.14
525	4-98.17
526	6.1-234.1
527	38.1-482.1, 38.1-482.3, 38.1-482.4, 38.1-482.7
528	46.1-258
529	51-127.10, 51-127.11, 51-127.13, 51-127.15, 51-127.17, 51-127.18:1, 51-127.20, 51-127.21, 51-127.23,

Acts 1972 Chapter	Code 1950 Section
	51-127.25, 51-127.27, 51-127.30
530	38.1-638.29, 38.1-638.31, 38.1-638.32
531	3.1-4, 3.1-19 to 3.1-22R
532	29-202
533	25-46.4:1, 25-46.4:2
534	56-304.6:1
535	54-60
536	63.1-90.1
537	38.1-255.1, 56-234.2
538	46.1-375, 46.1-375.2R
539	28.1-116
540	63.1-175, 63.1-195 to 63.1-197, 63.1-209
541	38.1-287
542	23-7.1
543	63.1-85.1 to 63.1-85.7
544	15.1-1242, 15.1-1249
546	46.1-193
547	17-143
548	58-510
549	8-266, 14.1-90, 15.1-38, 15.1-41, 15.1-48, 15.1-50, 15.1-51, 15.1-91 to 15.1-102R, 15.1-620, 15.1-659, 15.1-713R, 15.1-740, 15.1-753, 17-74, 19.1-20, 22-149, 58-511, 58-1048, 58-1091
550	23-14, 23-91.14 to 23-91.17R, 23-91.24 to 23-91.33
551	14.1-52.1
552	46.1-167.1, 46.1-167.3, 46.1-167.4
553	46.1-193
554	51-111.60:3
555	42.1-23.1
556	19.1-42
557	21-5.1, 21-5.2, 21-10
558	32-57.1
559	36-55.7 to 36-55.23
560	56-338.19
561	13.1-557 to 13.1-574
562	15.1-19.3
563	58-151.011, 58-151.031
564	14.1-63, 14.1-79
565	58-46, 58-151.098R, 58-151.099, 58-151.0100R, 58-151.0101R, 58-151.28, 58-441.43R
566	2.1-299.1, 2.1-299.2
567	40.1-1, 40.1-2, 40.1-6, 40.1-22 to 40.1-24, 40.1-26, 40.1-40, 40.1-46, 40.1-48, 40.1-49, 40.1-51
568	51-111.10, 51-111.37, 51-111.46, n., 51-111.55, 51-111.57, 51-111.58:1, 51-111.60:2, 51-144, 51-147, n., 51-151, 51-153, 51-156, 51-159, 51-161, 51-164, 51-168, 51-170, 51-170.1, 51-173
570	58-381.1
571	56-529, n., 56-530, n.
572	15.1-11.1
573	53-84, 53-104, 53-133.2, 53-138, 53-169, 53-205R
574	2.1-53
575	18.1-358.4
576	46.1-231
577	13.1-544.1
578	54-276.9
579	13.1-124.1, 13.1-286.1
580	13.1-15, 13.1-16R, 13.1-17, 13.1-19, 13.1-20, 13.1-53
581	22-37 2.1-111, 2.1-155, 2.1-156
582	2.1-111, 2.1-155, 2.1-156, 2.1-162R, 2.1-172, 2.1-330, 30-18R
583	20-46
584	32-30.2
585	16.1-107, 16.1-112
586	17-127.3
587	46.1-50.1
588	14.1-153
589	15.1-115
590	37.1-110
591	36-86 to 36-96
592	58-983, 58-1024
593	15.1-535
594	14.1-46
595	15.1-1403
596	15.1-116
597	7.1-21
598	59.1-121, 59.1-124, 59.1-127, 59.1-130
599	15.1-1410
600	20-14.2
601	58-266.5
602	40.1-44.1, 40.1-51.1 to 40.1-51.4
603	22-9.1, 22-9.1:01 to 22-9.1:06, 22-9.1:4, 22-9.2:1
604	22-230R, 22-230.1, 22-230.2, 22-231R
605	46.1-105.3
606	13.1-45, 13.1-48, 13.1-54
607	27-40.1 to 27-40.3
608	46.1-193
609	46.1-1, 46.1-30, 46.1-45 to 46.1-46, 46.1-55, 46.1-58, 46.1-59, 46.1-61 to 46.1-64, 46.1-96, 46.1-97, 46.1-101 to 46.1-103, 46.1-106 46.1-108, 46.1-109 46.1-112, 46.1-149 46.1-165, 46.1-167.1, 46.1-167.5
610	14.1-46
611	8-362
612	65.1-52
613	22-57
614	54-750
615	65.1-71.1
616	58-760.1
617	14.1-55 to 14.1-58, 14.1-73
618	59.1-41.1 to 59.1-41.6
619	65.1-23, 65.1-28, 65.1-50, 65.1-51, 65.1-56.1, 65.1-60, 65.1-65.1, 65.1-74, 65.1-90
620	2.1-358, 15.1-51, 15.1-813R, 24.1-1, 24.1-23 to 24.1-26, 24.1-31, 24.1-35.1, 24.1-46, 24.1-48, 24.1-53, 24.1-60, 24.1-72.2, 24.1-72.4, 24.1-89, 24.1-105, 24.1-107, 24.1-109, 24.1-111, 24.1-119, 24.1-124, 24.1-133, 24.1-143, 24.1-150, 24.1-151, 24.1-166, 24.1-169, 24.1-176, 24.1-177, 24.1-185, 24.1-190, 24.1-203, 24.1-207, 24.1-213, 24.1-216, 24.1-227 to 24.1-229, 24.1-232, 24.1-251, 24.1-253, 24.1-257, 24.1-258, 24.1-260, 24.1-277

Acts 1972 Chapter	Code 1950 Section
621	24.1-228, 24.1-231
622	24.1-253
623	22-67.2
624	15.1-51
626	14.1-112
627	14.1-112
629	37.1-199, 37.1-200, 37.1-201R, 37.1-202R
630	9-120 to 9-124
631	55-125, 55-125.1, 55-127, 55-130, 55-131, 55-134, 55-134.1, 55-136
632	9-116 to 9-119
634	22-331 to 22-338, 22-340, 22-343, 22-344, 22-344.1R, 22-344.2, 22-344.3
635	37.1-1, 37.1-123
636	6.1-327
637	58-587.1
638	46.1-167.1, 46.1-167.4, 46.1-449R, 46.1-450R, 46.1-453R, 46.1-455 to 46.1-458R, 46.1-459, 46.1-463, 46.1-469
639	14.1-16, 37.1-1, 37.1-21, 37.1-24, 37.1-29 to 37.1-33, 37.1-35, 37.1-36, 37.1-49 to 37.1-54, n., 37.1-64, 37.1-65, 37.1-68, 37.1-71, 37.1-76, 37.1-78, 37.1-85, 37.1-94, 37.1-95, 37.1-97, 37.1-98, 37.1-102, 37.1-104.2, 37.1-121 to 37.1-124, 37.1-126, 37.1-128, 37.1-145, 37.1-148, 37.1-151, 37.1-153, 37.1-156, 37.1-158, 37.1-160, 37.1-162, 37.1-166, 37.1-168, 37.1-170
640	46.1-301.1
641	2.1-51.1 to 2.1-51.5R, 2.1-51.7 to 2.1-51.12
642	18.1-417.2
644	28.1-108, 28.1-109, 28.1-134
645	8-266
646	3.1-722.1, 3.1-722.4, 3.1-722.9, 3.1-722.10, 3.1-722.14, 3.1-722.15
647	14.1-112
648	58-797
650	33.1-319, n.
651	32-8.2
652	56-46.1
653	3.1-45, 15.1-604, 15.1-613R, 15.1-613.1, 15.1-711R, 15.1-711.1
654	17-49R
655	13.1-549
656	15.1-510.7
657	56-49
658	37.1-24.1
659	63.1-124
660	9-47
662	22-89, 22-95, 22-100.13
663	22-140.1
665	22-60
666	6.1-362, n.
667	58-12, 58-12.4 to 58-12.11
670	15.1-136.1 to 15.1-136.7
672	16.1-164
673	8-711.1
674	15.1-506.1
676	23-38.10:1
677	6.1-327
678	6.1-328
679	4-25, 4-98.2
680	58-441.6, 58-685.13
681	8-490.1
682	54-573.2
683	13.1-514
684	13.1-400.1, 13.1-400.9
685	58-687, 58-691.1, 58-693, 58-700R, 58-709, 58-713, 58-717, 58-721, 58-723, 58-728, 58-735, 58-746, 58-749, 58-749.2
686	23-30.39 to 23-30.58
689	7.1-2
690	10-187 to 10-196
691	4-98.2, 4-98.18, 4-98.19
692	60.1-61
693	13.1-144.1, 13.1-145, 13.1-147, 13.1-148, 13.1-149.1, 13.1-153
694	58-16.3
695	15.1-495
696	65.1-98
697	23-9.2:2R, 23-9.2:4
698	46.1-547 to 46.1-547.2, 46.1-550.1, 46.1-550.2
699	22-283.1
700	46.1-6
701	56-281
702	46.1-191.2
703	37.1-67
704	15.1-239
705	19.1-190
707	15.1-729
708	14.1-40R, 14.1-41, 14.1-42, 14.1-42.1, n., 14.1-43R, 14.1-44, n., 16.1-1 to 16.1-8R, 16.1-9, n., 16.1-10 to 16.1-19R, 16.1-20, n., 16.1-21 to 16.1-24R, 16.1-26 to 16.1-28R, 16.1-29, n., 16.1-30 to 16.1-32R, 16.1-33, n., 16.1-34R, 16.1-35R, 16.1-35.1, n., 16.1-36 to 16.1-42R, 16.1-43, n., 16.1-43.1R, 16.1-43.2, n., 16.1-44, n., 16.1-45 to 16.1-53R, 16.1-53.1, n., 16.1-54 to 16.1-69R, 16.1-69.1 to 16.1-69.52, 16.1-70.1, 16.1-139, 16.1-141, 16.1-143R, 16.1-143.1 to 16.1-144, n., 16.1-145 to 16.1-149R, 16.1-150, n., 16.1-151 to 16.1-153R, 16.1-153.1, 16.1-154, 16.1-157, 16.1-203 to 16.1-206, 16.1-206.1R, 16.1-207, 16.1-208, 16.1-210 to 16.1-213, 17-222, 17-225.1, 51-111.10, 51-111.10:1, 51-111.67:2, 51-161, 51-176, n., 51-176.1
709	17-127.7
710	32-423 to 32-424.1, 32-425R, 32-426, 32-427
711	62.1-13.1 to 62.1-13.20
712	15.1-1032.1
713	20-61.1
714	63.1-40
715	58-774
716	14.1-73.2
717	4-26, 4-33, 4-98.18, 4-104
718	63.1-53, 63.1-92, 63.1-107, 63.1-116, 63.1-117, 63.1-120, 63.1-172
719	8-204, 14.1-5, 14.1-18.1, 14.1-19, 14.1-105, 14.1-111, 14.1-189, 14.1-190, 19.1-218, 19.1-275, 19.1-315
720	8-88.1

Acts 1972 Chapter	Code 1950 Section
721	58-151.092R, 58-175R, 58-182 to 58-185R, 58-225R, 58-234 to 58-237R, 58-441.37R, 58-1118 to 58-1119, 58-1120R, 58-1121R, 58-1131R, 58-1132, 58-1134, 58-1135R, 58-1137, 58-1138, 58-1160
722	56-107
723	46.1-57
725	18.1-63
727	18.1-358, 18.1-358.1R, 18.1-358.2R, 18.1-358.3, 18.1-359
728	10-8.1, 10-17.1 to 10-17.9R, 62.1-44.35 to 62.1-44.44
729	46.1-167.4
730	15.1-158.1, n.
731	14.1-50, 14.1-55, 14.1-64
732	22-19.1, n.
733	36-50.1
734	15.1-540
735	2.1-326.2
736	54-524.104:2
737	40.1-12, 40.1-13, 40.1-16, 40.1-17, 40.1-18.1, 40.1-19
738	25-46.35R, 25-235 to 25-254, 33.1-132.1 to 33.1-132.11R
739	6.1-31
740	6.1-23, 26-45.1
741	3.1-15, 3.1-88, 3.1-90, 3.1-91, 3.1-122, 3.1-123, 3.1-258, 3.1-363, 3.1-401, 3.1-403, 3.1-797, 3.1-801, 3.1-828, 3.1-835, 3.1-844, 3.1-891, 4-90, 18.1-55.1, 19.1-36, 19.1-38, 19.1-39, 19.1-44, 32-17, 32-31.1 to 32-31.8, 54-524.77, 59.1-159, 59.1-165, 62.1-44.15
742	25-46.34
743	15.1-131.4
745	22-29.2, 22-29.4, 22-29.6 to 22-29.8, 22-29.11
746	22-141.2
747	24.1-90
748	9-31R
749	14.1-19, 14.1-20
751	37.1-67, 37.1-73
753	16.1-35.1, 16.1-87
754	63.1-133.2 to 63.1-133.6
756	18.1-55.1
757	18.1-56.1R, 18.1-57, 18.1-59
758	54-524.102
761	22-220.1
762	8-631.1
763	2.1-85, 2.1-88, 2.1-106.2, 2.1-106.3:1, 2.1-106.7, 27-71, 57-5
764	60.1-3, 60.1-40, 60.1-47, 60.1-58, 60.1-65, 60.1-77, 60.1-80, 60.1-89, 60.1-99, 60.1-126, 60.1-127
765	33.1-95, 33.1-98, 33.1-99R, 33.1-101 to 33.1-105R, 33.1-107 to 33.1-115R, 33.1-124, 33.1-127, n., 33.1-132
766	9-125 to 9-138
767	15.1-239, 15.1-241
768	63.1-106
769	58-371.2
770	58-16.2
771	54-113
772	32-364.6
773	53-21.2
774	10-177 to 10-186
775	32-9
776	58-1127, 58-1128
777	33.1-320, n.
778	32-112.10 to 32-112.19
779	28.1-46.1 to 28.1-46.3
780	58-943.3
781	10-17.10, 10-17.14, 10-17.18, 10-17.19, 10-17.29, 10-17.30
782	36-12, 36-22, 36-27, 36-49
783	15.1-1374, 15.1-1375, 15.1-1378
784	45.1-4, 45.1-12, 45.1-12.1, 45.1-14, 45.1-15, 45.1-68, 45.1-104
785	10-8.1, 45.1-162 to 45.1-179R, 45.1-198 to 45.1-220
786	8-266
787	47-1
788	64.1-57
789	15.1-486
790	15.1-540
791	15.1-1357, 15.1-1358.1R, 15.1-1358.2
792	40.1-57.1
794	1-20, 24.1-134
795	58-766.2
796	6.1-126 to 6.1-193R, 6.1-195.1 to 6.1-195.76
797	54-260.1 to 54-260.63R, 54-260.64 to 54-260.76
798	54-318.2, 54-524.2, 54-524.16, 54-524.17, 54-524.19, 54-524.21, 54-524.22R, 54-524.22:1, 54-524.23, 54-524.31, 54-524.33 to 54-524.35, 54-524.40, 54-524.42R, 54-524.43R, 54-524.47, 54-524.47:2 to 54-524.47:4, 54-524.53, 54-524.56, 54-524.58:1 to 54-524.59:1, 54-524.63R, 54-524.64R, 54-524.67, 54-524.68, 54-524.70R, 54-524.71R, 54-524.72, 54-524.74R, 54-524.75 to 54-524.77, 54-524.79 to 54-524.84R, 54-524.84:1 to 54-524.84:13, 54-524.101R, 54-524.101:1 to 54-524.101:3, 54-524.103 to 54-524.104:1
799	18.1-346
800	19.1-32.2 to 19.1-32.5
801	51-111.52:4
803	2.1-20.1
805	54-146, 54-147, 54-147.2, 54-148R, 54-150, 54-152, 54-153, 54-156 to 54-158, 54-163, 54-164R, 54-165, 54-167, 54-170 to 54-173, 54-174R, 54-175 to 54-182, 54-185 to 54-187, 54-188R, 54-189 to 54-189.2, 54-190 to 54-194R, 54-195 to 54-199, 54-200.01, 54-200.02, 54-200.1, 54-200.2, 54-200.4 to 54-200.7, 54-200.9 to 54-200.12, 54-200.14 to 54-200.16, 54-200.17R, 54-200.18 to 54-200.23
807	40.1-109
809	15.1-702
812	54-784.1, 54-786.1, 54-788.3, 54-788.4, 54-789.1, 54-789.2, 54-789.4 to 54-791
813	58-515, 58-516R, 58-516.1, 58-517R, 58-518, 58-519,

Acts 1972 Chapter	Code 1950 Section
	58-521R, 58-522 to 58-527, 58-529 to 58-531, 58-533R, 58-537, 58-538, 58-542 to 58-545R, 58-560, 58-563 to 58-569R, 58-578, 58-584, 58-588, 58-589R, 58-592, 58-593, 58-594R, 58-595R, 58-596, 58-597, 58-598R, 58-600R, 58-602, 58-604R, 58-605, 58-607, 58-610, 58-612, 58-622
814	15.1-1405
815	15.1-702
816	55-258
817	46.1-235
818	15.1-493
819	46.1-252.01
820	15.1-712
821	21-11.3, 21-11.9, 21-11.10
822	30-19.4
823	18.1-62.1, 18.1-273, 20-48, 20-49, 32-137, 32-353.19, 32-364.2:1R, 37.1-65, 40.1-25, 44-3, 46.1-170, 46.1-357, 63.1-222, 63.1-225, 63.1-236
824	1-13.42, 3.1-972, 28.1-41, 32-303, 40.1-13, 40.1-80, 40.1-84, 40.1-100, 40.1-104, 40.1-110, 47-3, 47-4R, 54-28, 54-60, 54-61R, 54-89, 54-170, 54-174, n., 54-200.9, 54-260.23, n., 54-260.27, n., 54-305, 54-306, 54-308, 54-308.5, 54-308.6, 54-382, 54-398.15, 54-398.18R, 54-524.21, 54-524.123, 54-729.03, 54-750, 54-788.1, 54-869.6, 54-910, 59.1-138, 60.1-14, 63.1-149
825	1-13.42, 6.1-207, 8-15, 8-654.1, 8-654.1:1, 8-686, 11-8, 26-50, 31-9, 34-10, 34-24, 38.1-638.28, 38.1-638.29, 55-44, 57-9, 58-20, 64.1-27, 64.1-47, 64.1-70, 64.1-71, 64.1-90, 65.1-76
826	9-139 to 9-143
827	58-151.02, 58-151.013, 58-151.015, 58-151.016, 58-151.023, 58-151.024, 58-151.032, 58-151.062, 58-151.067, 58-151.0111, 58-151.2, 58-151.13, 58-151.23
828	15.1-545, 15.1-546
829	36-97 to 36-119
830	36-55.24 to 36-55.52
831	58-757.01
832	1-13.42, 6.1-207, 8-15
833	28.1-48
834	54-729.016:1
835	16.1-164
836	38.1-43.5, 38.1-174, 38.1-220, 38.1-221 to 38.1-223R, 38.1-225 to 38.1-240R, 38.1-241, 38.1-242, 38.1-243 to 38.1-248R, 38.1-250R, 38.1-252, 38.1-256 to 38.1-258R, 38.1-262.1R, 38.1-279.1 to 38.1-279.28, 38.1-342.1, 38.1-362.4
837	15.1-504
839	14.1-183
840	62.1-44.19:1, n., 62.1-44.19:2, n.
841	51-111.67:5
842	46.1-497 to 46.1-499, 46.1-501, 46.1-502
843	54-524.47:1
844	46.1-291.1
845	20-61
846	2.1-133.2
847	23-35.1, 23-35.2, 23-35.4, 23-35.5R, 23-35.5:1, 23-35.6, 23-35.8
848	40.1-29
849	4-22
850	15.1-23.1
851	46.1-15.1, 46.1-15.2, 46.1-89.1
852	15.1-788
854	15.1-729, n.
855	21-11.16 to 21-11.19
856	8-86.1, 14.1-29, 14.1-30, 14.1-32, 14.1-120, 14.1-182, 17-99, 58-74
857	6.1-319.1
858	58-266.2R, 58-266.3R, 58-578, 58-603, 58-606
859	38.1-380.1, 46.1-497.1
860	30-52 to 30-55
861	23-14, 23-86 to 23-91R, 23-91.34 to 23-91.44
862	58-628, 58-712, 58-744
863	15.1-967
864	23-38.30 to 23-38.44
865	62.1-2
866	62.1-3

ACTS 1973

Acts 1973 Chapter	Code 1950 Section
1	46.1-357
2	23-38.12, 23-38.13, 23-38.15 to 23-38.18
3	58-757.8
4	29-11.1
5	46.1-301.1
6	8-653
7	2.1-114
8	46.1-177
9	17-28
10	54-20
11	19.1-87.1
12	59.1-147
13	40.1-80, 40.1-83, 40.1-99 to 40.1-101, 40.1-105, 40.1-106, 40.1-108, 40.1-109, 40.1-112
14	28.1-109
15	18.1-110
16	4-56
17	2.1-63.4:1
18	16.1-133
19	28.1-42
20	9-6.2
21	28.1-48
23	62.1-3
24	23-38.20 to 23-38.29R, 23-38.45 to 23-38.52, 23-38.53, n.
25	46.1-167.1, 46.1-167.3, 46.1-167.4
26	25-46.22
27	18.1-70.1
28	32-195.8, 38.1-31.2, 38.1-342.2
29	36-49.1
30	15.1-719R, 24.1-1, 24.1-18, 24.1-19, 24.1-23, 24.1-29, 24.1-43, 24.1-45, 24.1-46, 24.1-50, 24.1-53, 24.1-60, 24.1-84, 24.1-88, 24.1-89R, 24.1-101, 24.1-111, 24.1-129, 24.1-143, 24.1-144, 24.1-146, 24.1-164, 24.1-166, 24.1-167, 24.1-172, 24.1-209, 24.1-228, 24.1-232, 24.1-240, 24.1-246.1, 24.1-247, 24.1-251, 24.1-257,

Acts 1973 Chapter	Code 1950 Section
	24.1-277
33	56-406
35	21-112.1, 21-112.18, 21-112.20:1
38	53-166.1
42	63.1-116.1
45	55-222.1, n.
50	13.1-36
54	17-45
55	23-185
56	46.1-302.1
57	30-19
58	46.1-302.2
59	53-295
60	54-751
62	46.1-343.3
63	22-69
64	54-524.101:2
65	62.1-13.14:1, 62.1-13.18:1
66	46.1-287.2
67	46.1-171.2
69	2.1-20.1
71	15.1-364
72	46.1-172.02
75	58-817
76	37.1-36
77	37.1-382
78	37.1-195
79	40.1-58.1
83	23-107
86	54-83.2, 54-83.4, 54-83.6, 54-83.8
87	6.1-195.40
88	6.1-195.5:1
89	6.1-195.63:1
90	54-382
93	58-769.8
94	64.1-57
97	22-19.1
98	19.1-92.1
99	22-223
101	22-21.3, 22-55
103	15.1-29.4
104	29-202
105	54-274
106	23-38.20 to 23-38.29R, 23-38.45 to 23-38.52, 23-38.53, n.
107	33.1-126
108	8-468.1
109	33.1-221.1
111	6.1-2.2
112	29-184.2
113	29-194
114	53-38
115	37.1-47
117	15.1-431
118	18.1-257
119	28.1-67, 28.1-69
120	29-162.1, 29-162.2
121	38.1-168
122	63.1-55
123	55-154
124	15.1-51
125	33.1-41, 33.1-43, 33.1-43.1
126	14.1-53
127	38.1-181
128	6.1-195.29
129	29-202
130	19.1-112, 19.1-113
131	18.1-213 to 18.1-215
132	33.1-80
133	6.1-195.33
134	22-56.1
135	15.1-1249
136	13.1-544.1
137	46.1-202.1
139	58-55.1
140	58-27.2
143	16.1-118.1
144	15.1-179
147	59.1-21.4 to 59.1-21.6
148	28.1-9
149	54-524.76
152	58-784.5
153	22-67.2
156	6.1-195.47
158	46.1-229
159	14.1-112
160	15.1-437
161	55-106.2
162	46.1-295.3
163	15.1-704
164	46.1-425
165	46.1-95
166	33.1-91
167	55-268.1 to 55-268.10
168	2.1-17.1
169	15.1-466
170	22-276.1
171	18.1-346
172	2.1-359 to 2.1-370
173	38.1-121, 65.1-104
174	58-685.19
175	14.1-155.1
176	15.1-1403
177	8-266
178	2.1-213, 38.1-108
179	62.1-44.15:1
180	14.1-70
181	22-218.2
182	46.1-104.1
183	46.1-328, 46.1-332
184	29-65
186	22-149
190	46.1-105.4
191	29-11.2
193	15.1-879
194	46.1-45.2
195	15.1-44
197	33.1-46.2
198	58-151.013, 58-151.023, 58-151.032, 58-151.032:1, 58-151.097
199	3.1-997
200	3.1-657
201	63.1-44, 63.1-47, 63.1-47.1, 63.1-51, 63.1-92, 63.1-120
202	33.1-319, n.
204	53-213.1
205	23-30.41, 23-30.58
207	46.1-44, 58-685.11
208	53-213, 53-213.01
209	58-769.5 to 58-769.8, 58-769.10, 58-769.12
210	58-792.01
211	15.1-242, 15.1-249
212	32-112.10 to 32-112.19R 32-112.20 to 32-112.23
214	46.1-383.3
215	33.1-251, 33.1-252, 33.1-285
216	14.1-73.2
217	64.1-77
218	17-54
219	2.1-127
220	22-161
221	16.1-201
222	37.1-67
223	22-217.9
224	58-441.15
225	38.1-381
227	63.1-172 to 63.1-175, 63.1-177, 63.1-179 to 63.1-182
228	54-145.20
229	33.1-185
231	15.1-1348
232	2.1-328.1
233	53-133.1
234	53-37.1
235	9-109.2
236	8-449.1
237	2.1-106.8
238	15.1-1272, 15.1-1275, 15.1-1276, 15.1-1279 to 15.1-1281, 15.1-1286
239	6.1-330, 6.1-330.5
240	2.1-96
241	2.1-299.1
242	30-5
245	22-164
246	29-193
247	8-24.2

Acts 1973 Chapter	Code 1950 Section
248	56-529, n., 56-530, n.
249	8-40
250	38.1-173.1, 38.1-173.2
251	10-17.18 to 10-17.18.2, 10-17.29
252	32-364.3:1
253	53-231, 53-234, 53-236, 53-240, 53-241, 53-243, 53-244, 53-250, 53-257, 53-258, 53-260, 53-264, 53-265
254	65.1-113.1
256	2.1-114, 15.1-7.1
257	6.1-39
259	32-104.11
260	44-141 to 44-146.1R, 44-146.13 to 44-146.28
261	3.1-311
262	56-240, 56-241, 56-245
263	2.1-339.1 to 2.1-339.3
264	63.1-25.1, 63.1-78.1, 63.1-92
266	51-111.41:2
267	30-42 to 30-51R
268	51-111.41:1
269	58-441.27
270	15.1-503.1R, 15.1-503.2
271	15.1-702
273	11-4.1
274	15.1-686
275	22-60
276	16.1-217.1
277	8-629
278	58-757
279	58-151.13
280	58-1130
281	58-31
282	58-66, 58-155, 58-156, 58-166, 58-167, 58-173, 58-179.1, 58-193.1, 58-207, 58-230, 58-238
284	54-1, 54-63, 54-65
285	31-26, 31-29, 31-32
286	15.1-491
287	15.1-9.1, 15.1-9.2R
288	46.1-235
289	15.1-136.2
290	51-151
294	38.1-380.1, 46.1-497.1
295	2.1-63.4:2, 2.1-63.4:3
296	54-260.70, 54-260.72
297	2.1-20.1, 65.1-4
298	2.1-107, 2.1-108
299	22-56.1
300	22-220.1
301	55-218.1
302	16.1-199
303	36-55.1 to 36-55.6
305	56-338.2
306	56-273
307	56-46.1
308	19.1-221.1
310	33.1-141
311	22-19.1, n.
312	14.1-46
313	58-441.3
315	20-61
316	14.1-184.1, 19.1-241.7 to 19.1-241.12
317	43-63
318	6.1-327, 6.1-327.1, 6.1-330.1
319	32-9.1
320	15.1-43.1
321	58-847
322	2.1-257, 2.1-259, 30-5, 30-19.5, 30-28.12 to 30-28.14, 30-28.16, 30-28.19, 30-28.20, 30-33, 51-111.10
323	58-151.0111
324	15.1-1345
325	58-847
326	18.1-268.7
327	9-144, 9-145
328	33.1-348
329	14.1-46
330	53-21.1, 53-76.3, 53-103, 53-104
331	58-628, 58-712, 58-744
332	15.1-18.1:1
334	15.1-431
335	2.1-255
336	58-64.1
337	32-137
338	8-676
340	23-8.2, 23-9.10
341	55-59
342	15.1-903, 19.1-328 to 19.1-1334R, 19.1-338 to 19.1-341R, 19.1-347.5R, 19.1-347.6, 53-103, 53-221R
343	4-25
345	58-151.013
346	20-61
349	4-22
350	62.1-3.02
353	26-40
354	8-725
355	55-269R, 55-269.1, 55-271, 55-272R, 55-272.1, 55-273 to 55-275, 55-277
357	32-364.4:1
358	36-87 to 36-93
360	33.1-70.1, 33.1-225.1
361	62.1-3
364	32-31.3
366	9-47
368	22-151.2
369	29-114.2, 29-114.4
371	46.1-183.1
372	36-94, 36-95, 36-95.2, 36-95.3
373	29-197
374	55-79.9
375	55-79.4, 55-79.7, 55-79.13, 55-79.21:1, 55-79.21:2
376	56-478R
377	56-35
378	56-480
379	54-903, 54-910, 54-912, 54-912.1
380	15.1-504
381	62.1-172, 62.1-177
382	62.1-13.5
383	63.1-56.1
384	10-17.107 to 10-17.112
385	8-24
386	46.1-321
387	2.1-37.17:1
388	62.1-13.2, 62.1-13.5
389	46.1-16.1
390	38.1-381
391	54-169, 54-187, 54-200.8
392	15.1-1357.1
393	15.1-42.1
394	46.1-442
395	15.1-11.1
396	46.1-380.2, 46.1-438
397	56-265.3
398	8-42.1R
399	18.1-15.3
400	54-524.104:2
401	2.1-116, 3.1-36, 3.1-277, 6.1-94, 8-4.1, 8-147, 8-148, 8-577.1, 8-638, 10-59, 15.1-139, 19.1-148, 19.1-308, 23-35.9, 23-35.11

Acts 1973 Chapter	Code 1950 Section
	to 23-35.13, 23-36.2, 23-142, 31-9, 32-56, 32-423, 36-57, 44-1, 44-3, 44-4, 44-12, 44-55, 44-59, 44-62 to 44-64, 44-69, 44-82, 44-100, 44-114.4, 52-9.1, 53-75.7, 53-183.2, 54-283, 55-3, 55-117, 56-419.1, 64.1-127, 65.1-65, 65.1-65.1, 65.1-66, 65.1-69, 65.1-74, 65.1-76
402	15.1-14
403	53-291
405	58-766
406	17-40, 63.1-221
407	14.1-72
408	8-586, 8-588, 8-591
409	19.1-137
410	58-963, 58-964
411	28.1-120.1
412	58-412
413	4-89
414	6.1-345
415	14.1-11.1
416	32-9.1
417	62.1-44.34:1, 62.1-44.34:2
418	45.1-206
419	32-211.3 to 32-211.16
420	46.1-550.3
421	2.1-21
423	59.1-21.8 to 59.1-21.18
425	40.1-1 to 40.1-2.1, 40.1-6, 40.1-22, 40.1-25, 40.1-28, 40.1-38, 40.1-42, 40.1-43, 40.1-44R, 40.1-44.1, 40.1-46, 40.1-48, 40.1-49R, 40.1-49.1, 40.1-51.1, 40.1-51.1:1, 40.1-51.2, 40.1-51.3:1, 40.1-51.6, 40.1-69, 40.1-113
426	25-245
427	18.1-358, 18.1-358.3, 18.1-358.4R
428	32-195.10:1, 38.1-347.1
429	22-37
430	33.1-90
431	9-84.5 to 9-84.10
433	58-76.1, n.
434	33.1-346.1
435	22-330.18, 22-330.33
436	65.1-56.1, 65.1-65.1, 65.1-65.2
437	14.1-11.4
438	58-12, 58-12.5, 58-12.7 to 58-12.10, 58-12.11, n., 58-12.12 to 58-12.16, 58-12.18, 58-12.19
439	8-58, 8-174 to 8-208.1R, 8-208.2 to 8-208.38, 19.1-148, 19.1-150, 19.1-194 to 19.1-219R
440	16.1-77, 16.1-88, 16.1-133.1, 16.1-158, 16.1-164, 16.1-173, 16.1-176, 16.1-176.1R, 16.1-176.2, 16.1-177.1, 16.1-178, 16.1-189, 16.1-195 to 16.1-197, 16.1-210
441	13.1-68
442	19.1-89.1 to 19.1-89.10
443	10-93, 10-98, 10-117.1R, 62.1-44.83 to 62.1-44.107
444	58-16.2
446	58-45, 58-70, 58-174, 58-176, 58-178, 58-224, 58-1118, 58-1118.1, 58-1140.1, 58-1160
447	54-524.104:1
448	59.1-102.1 to 59.1-102.7
449	15.1-89R
450	62.1-44.43
451	38.1-748.1, 38.1-749
452	2.1-330 to 2.1-335R, 30-52 to 30-55R, 30-56 to 30-63
453	27-63, 27-64, 27-70 to 27-70.2, 27-72, 27-75, 27-76, 27-79 to 27-79.8, 27-81, 27-83, 27-85, 27-85.2
454	6.1-13
455	46.1-314.1
456	33.1-320, n.
457	46.1-50, 58-685.13:1
458	58-151.013
459	18.1-57
460	56-273, 56-274
461	2.1-342 to 2.1-345
462	32-214, 32-261, 32-262, 32-265, 32-266, 32-269, 32-271 to 32-271.8, 32-272 to 32-275R
463	18.1-316, 18.1-340
465	2.1-1, 37.1-1, 37.1-1.1
466	19.1-228
467	58-762, 58-983, 58-990, 58-1000.1, 58-1020, 58-1024, 58-1027 to 58-1033R, 58-1035 to 58-1117R, 58-1117.1 to 58-1117.11
468	54-524.65
469	22-21.4
470	54-524.101:5
473	54-524.101:4
474	15.1-136.2
476	13.1-246.1
477	32-298
478	15.1-1241, 15.1-1244, 15.1-1245, 15.1-1246, 15.1-1248
479	54-524.17, 54-524.77, 54-524.84:4, 54-524.101:1
480	15.1-466, 15.1-510.7R
482	63.1-112
483	8-315.1
484	13.1-549.2, 54-42.2, 54-42.3, 54-48, 54-875.1
485	19.1-102, 19.1-106, 19.1-109.1 to 19.1-109.9, 19.1-110R, 19.1-111R, 19.1-116R, 19.1-122R, 19.1-122.1R, 19.1-124R, 19.1-126R, 19.1-127, 19.1-135R, 19.1-145
486	21-89.1 to 21-89.15
487	54-734, 54-762 to 54-763, 54-764R, 54-764.1R, 54-764.2 to 54-764.5
488	30-19.3
489	14.1-46
491	22-249
492	43-33
495	46.1-45
496	58-760.1
497	58-341, 58-342, 58-381.1
498	46.1-282.1
499	15.1-134, 51-122, 51-127.20
501	32-379.1
502	19.1-85
504	38.1-43.5, 38.1-174, 38.1-220, 38.1-221 to 38.1-223R, 38.1-225 to 38.1-240R, 38.1-241, 38.1-242, 38.1-243 to 38.1-248R, 38.1-250R, 38.1-252, 38.1-256 to 38.1-258R,

Acts 1973 Chapter	Code 1950 Section
	38.1-262.1R, 38.1-279.1 to 38.1-279.28R, 38.1-279.29 to 38.1-279.57, 38.1-342.1, 38.1-362.4, 38.1-750
505	38.1-178.1 to 38.1-178.9, 38.1-178.10, n.
506	31-27 to 31-29, 31-32, 31-33
507	2.1-111, 2.1-155, 2.1-156, 2.1-172
508	33.1-46.1, 33.1-97
509	8.1-105, 8.1-201, 8.2-107, 8.5-116, 8.9-102 to 8.9-106, 8.9-114, 8.9-203 to 8.9-205, 8.9-301, 8.9-302, 8.9-304 to 8.9-308, 8.9-312, 8.9-313, 8.9-318, 8.9-401 to 8.9-406, 8.9-408, 8.9-501, 8.9-502, 8.9-504, 8.9-505, 8.11-101 to 8.11-108, 55-152R
510	25-46.20
511	18.1-55.1
512	30-19.4
513	15.1-172, 15.1-177, 15.1-199
514	54-274
515	57-12
517	46.1-154
519	14.1-73
520	23-7
521	15.1-1249
522	58-266.1:1
523	15.1-228 to 15.1-232, 15.1-234, 51-111.10, 51-111.18, 51-111.20, 51-111.22, 51-111.24, 51-111.27, 51-111.30:1, 51-111.31, 51-111.34, 51-111.41:1, 51-111.41:2, 51-111.52:1, 51-111.52:2, 51-111.52:4, 51-111.52:5, 51-111.55 to 51-111.57, 51-111.58:1, 51-111.60:2, 51-111.67:7, 51-144, 51-151 to 51-153, 51-156, 51-159, 51-161, 51-163.1, 51-164, 51-168 to 51-170.1, 51-173, 51-174.1, 51-180
524	2.1-98, 9-67, 9-85, 9-89, 9-96, 9-107, 22-9.3, 22-346, 30-29
526	18.1-256
527	54-734
528	15.1-1374, 15.1-1378, 15.1-1382, 15.1-1384
529	54-273 to 54-275, 54-276.4, 54-281.2, 54-281.4 to 54-282, 54-287, 54-290 to 54-291.1, 54-295, 54-295.6, 54-297 to 54-299, 54-300.1, 54-300.2, 54-306.3 to 54-307, 54-308, 54-308.5, 54-308.6, 54-310, 54-311, 54-317, 54-317.2, 54-318R, 54-318.3, 54-319R, 54-320, 54-321
530	28.1-57.1
531	14.1-19.1
532	22-9.1:4
533	46.1-252.3
534	56-334
535	9-6.15 to 9-6.22
536	5.1-41.1
537	59.1-68.2, 59.1-68.3
538	9-54 to 9-55.1, 9-56R, 9-57, 9-58R, 9-60R
539	30-19.6
540	30-19.7
541	9-120 to 9-124
542	65.1-23, 65.1-24R, 65.1-26, 65.1-28, 65.1-54, 65.1-55, 65.1-65, 65.1-66, 65.1-69, 65.1-71, 65.1-88
543	27-39, 27-40.1 to 27-40.2
544	8-142, 8-208.1R, 8-373, 8-377, 14.1-33, 14.1-144.1, 15.1-19, 15.1-1014R, 15.1-1015R, 15.1-1030, 17-7, 17-7.1, 17-11R, 17-26, 17-103, 17-111.1, 17-116.1 to 17-116.4, 17-119R, 17-119.1R, 17-119.1:1, 17-119.1:2, 17-120, 17-122 to 17-123, 17-127 to 17-127.16R, 17-127.18 to 17-127.20R, 17-127.21, 17-129, 17-135 to 17-169.4R, 17-183 to 17-221.8R, 17-221.10R, 17-221.13R, 17-221.15 to 17-221.29R, 17-226, 19.1-161R, 19.1-194 to 19.1-219R, 26-8 to 26-10.1, 26-11R, 26-12, 46.1-367
545	8-524, 8-538, 8-564, 8-566, 14.1-44.1 to 14.1-44.5, 14.1-85, 14.1-86, 14.1-125, 14.1-128, 14.1-129R, 14.1-137, 14.1-156, 14.1-156.1R, 14.1-160, 15.1-662, 15.1-720, 15.1-755, 15.1-787, 15.1-934R, 15.1-991, 16.1-75.1R, 19.1-32.1R, 19.1-374 to 19.1-400, 24.1-89R, 39.1-1 to 39.1-25R, 51-111.10, 51-111.67:2
546	14.1-40R, 14.1-41, 14.1-42, 14.1-42.2 to 14.1-44R, 15.1-63, 16.1-1 to 16.1-69R, 16.1-69.1 to 16.1-69.19, 16.1-69.20R, 16.1-69.21 to 16.1-69.33, 16.1-69.35 to 16.1-69.52, 16.1-70.1, 16.1-139, 16.1-141, 16.1-143 to 16.1-153R, 16.1-153.1, 16.1-154, 16.1-203 to 16.1-206, 16.1-206.1R, 16.1-207, 16.1-208, 16.1-210 to 16.1-213, 17-222, 51-111.10, 51-111.10:1, 51-111.67:2, 51-161, 51-163, 51-176R, 51-176.1, 51-177
547	16.1-69.33
548	54-524.55R, 54-524.106

ACTS 1974

Acts 1974 Chapter	Code 1950 Section
1	16.1-69.6:1
3	16.1-69.18, 16.1-69.41R
4	44-146.14, 44-146.16 to 44-146.19, 44-146.21, 44-146.22, 44-146.24, 44-146.28, 44-146.29, n.

Acts 1974 Chapter	Code 1950 Section
6	58-942
18	22-217.8
23	2.1-63.1
24	7.1-40
25	58-218.1
26	63.1-223, 63.1-224
27	2.1-82.1, 2.1-88R, 2.1-88.1, 2.1-90R, 2.1-91R, 2.1-91.1, 2.1-96, 2.1-106.3:1
28	15.1-136.2
29	23-41
30	58-412
31	58-687, 58-715, 58-717, 58-721, 58-749, 58-753.1
32	58-302.2
33	58-769.8
34	58-769.6, 58-769.10
40	23-9.10:2
41	27-52
42	17-119.1:2
43	17-119.1:2
44	2.1-1, 2.1-51.9, 2.1-64.23, 2.1-121, 8-300, 8-300.1, 9-121, 9-141, 15.1-710, 15.1-768, 16.1-141, 16.1-178 to 16.1-178.2, 16.1-181, 16.1-198, 16.1-202.5, 16.1-203, 16.1-205, 16.1-206, 16.1-211, 16.1-212, 18.1-200, 18.1-201, 18.1-202, 19.1-28, 19.1-295.1, 19.1-295.6, 19.1-296, 20-48, 20-49, 20-87.1, 20-88.15:1, 23-35.3, 23-35.5:1, 32-137, 32-148, 32-155, 32-356, 37.1-57, 37.1-97, 37.1-123, 53-1 to 53-4R, 53-8R, 53-9R, 53-16.1R, 53-18R, 53-19.1R, 53-19.5 to 53-19.38, 53-21.1, 53-50, 53-75.1, 53-75.8, 53-76.1, 53-76.3, 53-89, 53-96, 53-103, 53-104, 53-128.1, 53-128.6, 53-128.7, 53-133.2, 53-173, 53-184, 53-213.01, n., 53-230, 53-238, 53-241 to 53-245, 53-247, 53-249, 53-250, 53-261, 53-264, 53-266, 53-268, 53-279, 53-285, 53-296, 53-324 to 53-333, 54-112.29, 56-137, 56-138, 63.1-1R, 63.1-1.1, 63.1-2, 63.1-4, 63.1-5.1, 63.1-7, 63.1-14, 63.1-15, 63.1-25.1, 63.1-28R, 63.1-29R, 63.1-30R, 63.1-32, 63.1-47.1, 63.1-56.1, 63.1-85.1, 63.1-87, 63.1-92, 63.1-93, 63.1-97.1, 63.1-134, 63.1-135, 63.1-137, 63.1-138, 63.1-239 to 63.1-248R
45	2.1-1, 2.1-51.9, =cc2 2.1-64.23, 2.1-121, 8-300, 8-300.1, 9-121, 9-141, 15.1-710, 15.1-768, 16.1-141, 16.1-178 to 16.1-178.2, 16.1-181, 16.1-198, 16.1-202.5, 16.1-203, 16.1-205, 16.1-206, 16.1-211, 16.1-212, 18.1-200, 18.1-201, 18.1-202, 19.1-28, 19.1-295.1, 19.1-295.6, 19.1-296, 20-48, 20-49, 20-87.1, 20-88.15:1, 23-35.3, 23-35.5:1, 32-137, 32-148, 32-155, 32-356, 37.1-57, 37.1-97, 37.1-123, 53-1 to 53-4R, 53-8R, 53-9R, 53-16.1R, 53-19.1R, 53-19.5 to 53-19.38, 53.21.1, 53-50, 53-75.1, 53-75.8, 53-76.1, 53-76.3, 53-89, 53-96, 53-103, 53-104, 53-128.1, 53-128.6, 53-128.7, 53-133.2, 53-173, 53-184, 53-213.01, n., 53-230, 53-238, 53-241 to 53-245, 53-247, 53-249, 53-250, 53-261, 53-264, 53-266, 53-268, 53-279, 53-285, 53-296, 53-324 to 53-333, 54-112.29, 56-137, 56-138, 63.1-1R, 63.1-1.1, 63.1-2, 63.1-4, 63.1-5.1, 63.1-7, 63.1-14, 63.1-15, 63.1-25.1, 63.1-28R, 63.1-29R, 63.1-30R, 63.1-32, 63.1-47.1, 63.1-56.1, 63.1-85.1, 63.1-87, 63.1-92, 63.1-93, 63.1-97.1, 63.1-134, 63.1-135, 63.1-137, 63.1-138, 63.1-239 to 63.1-248R
46	46.1-104.1
47	46.1-32.1
48	46.1-30
49	46.1-442
51	29-184.2
52	33.1-268
53	15.1-1357.2
54	32-195.5:1, 32-195.5:2
55	29-121, n.
56	29-126, 29-127
57	29-5
58	29-34.1
59	29-1.1, 29-2
60	29-163.2
62	37.1-98.1
63	51-127.9
65	23-7.2
66	37.1-84.2
67	32-1
68	53-180
69	53-214
70	53-227
71	13.1-54
72	13.1-91
73	56-491, 56-492
74	3.1-329
75	6.1-22
77	6.1-195.41
78	58-441.7
79	58-397.2
80	58-979
81	6.1-68
82	2.1-326.2
83	27-76, 27-84
84	42.1-35
85	28.1-69, 28.1-70
86	13.1-514
87	38.1-381
88	46.1-497
89	28.1-228, 28.1-229
90	15.1-503.2
91	2.1-55
92	62.1-3
93	28.1-101.2
94	51-122
95	38.1-348.1, 38.1-360
96	10-17.31 to 10-17.106R, 28.1-36.1 to 28.1-36.12R, 29-23.2 to 29-23.10R, 45.1-180.1R, 45.1-197.1R, 62.1-13.2:1R, 62.1-13.4:1R, 62.1-13.5:1R, 62.1-44.45 to 62.1-44.82R
97	28.1-52
98	58-470
99	15.1-440
100	15.1-431
101	29-144.4
102	29-38
103	15.1-19.3
105	29-65
106	6.1-213
107	29-65
108	29-140

Acts 1974 Chapter	Code 1950 Section
109	29-121, n.
110	19.1-246.1
111	37.1-88
112	21-291.2
113	19.1-84, 54-524.101:5
114	19.1-109.1
115	6.1-197
116	6.1-200.1
117	6.1-216
118	64.1-189
119	14.1-46
120	63.1-39
121	53-278.1
122	8-586
123	20-100R
124	9-65.14
125	9-109:3
126	26-8.1
127	53-144, 53-185
128	53-109
129	46.1-49
130	55-136
131	50-37.1, 50-37.2, 50-74
132	15.1-1272, 15.1-1274
133	58-812
134	58-46
135	15.1-51
136	58-381.1
137	36-49.1
138	57-15
139	8-685
140	64.1-121
141	10-90.26
142	46.1-3
143	6.1-212
145	46.1-339, 46.1-343, 46.1-343.1
146	9-6.4, 9-6.7, 9-67
148	62.1-141
150	46.1-99, 46.1-106, 46.1-154
151	9-6.19
153	55-275
154	22-235.1
155	8-628.3
156	26-2
157	54-260.72
159	58-444
160	22-220.1, 22-249
161	15.1-1357
162	23-9.2:4
163	20-99.1
164	54-260.73
165	14.1-11.5, n.
166	43-33
167	56-420
168	15.1-163.1
169	15.1-381
170	46.1-63, 46.1-101, 46.1-149, 46.1-154.1, 46.1-167.1
171	46.1-59
172	8-223
173	2.1-352
174	6.1-227.1
175	6.1-232.1
176	6.1-231, 6.1-232
177	58-441.27:1
178	58-151.072, 58-151.073
179	58-792.01
180	58-374
181	6.1-195.65
183	6.1-2
184	6.1-94
185	9-6.4
186	58-155
187	6.1-329R
188	46.1-547.1
189	46.1-516, 46.1-523
190	8.9-104
191	22-38
192	58-443
193	58-450
194	54-367.16, 54-367.22, 54-367.25
195	40.1-22, 40.1-51.5, 40.1-51.7, 40.1-51.9, 40.1-51.9:1, 40.1-51.10, 40.1-51.11:1
196	58-266.1
197	8-669
198	60.1-88.1
199	22-275.1
200	19.1-106.1
201	65.1-52, 65.1-56.1
202	58-441.24
203	8-208.34
204	10-91, 10-92, 10-92.1, 10-93 to 10-96, 10-98R
205	53-273
206	52-232
207	19.1-160
210	46.1-35.1
211	56-304.1
212	46.1-380.2
213	46.1-127
214	46.1-124
215	46.1-42.1
216	10-46.1, 10-46.2
217	46.1-298
218	46.1-265
219	46.1-279.1
220	8-208.33
222	46.1-190
223	46.1-357
224	58-943.2
225	14.1-33
226	15.1-1266
227	22-335
228	16.1-133
229	15.1-51
230	46.1-248
231	2.1-226
232	2.1-219
233	59.1-102.1 to 59.1-102.7R
234	14.1-117, 14.1-118
235	46.1-155
236	29-210
237	62.1-44.21, 62.1-44.32
238	55-154
239	16.1-88.1
240	53-250
241	19.1-100
242	33.1-288
243	8-208.16
244	38.1-659, 38.1-676
246	15.1-326, 15.1-329, 15.1-331, 15.1-341, 15.1-345, 15.1-347
247	58-471, 58-484
248	58-151.0111
249	38.1-249
250	23-9.2:1
252	46.1-343
253	13.1-520.1, 13.1-527.1 to 13.1-527.3
254	40.1-53
257	54-260.73:1
258	22-67.2
259	10-152, 10-158
260	15.1-7.1
261	6.1-319.2
262	9-121
263	36-55.34, 36-55.37, 36-55.41
264	60.1-52
265	21-89.3
266	16.1-181
267	4-25, 4-31, 4-33
269	6.1-364 to 6.1-369
270	10-17.107 to 10-17.112
271	14.1-55 to 14.1-58, 14.1-73
272	34-1, 34-10 to 34-12, 34-15 to 34-17, 34-23, 34-24, 34-31, 34-32, 40.1-21, 40.1-34 to 40.1-38R, 40.1-122
273	37.1-199
274	62.1-3.03
276	15.1-1249
277	29-55.3

Acts 1974 Chapter	Code 1950 Section
278	20-97
279	17-41
280	6.1-362.1
281	58-151.065
282	15.1-262
283	40.1-84
284	6.1-195.34
285	13.1-50
286	6.1-32.1 to 6.1-32.10
287	33.1-78.1
288	2.1-327, 2.1-329
290	6.1-320, 6.1-321, 6.1-330
291	13.1-95
292	6.1-2.3, 6.1-2.4
293	58-848, 58-851.8
294	58-851.6, 58-851.7
295	2.1-328.1
296	37.1-156 to 37.1-171R, 37.1-171.1
297	3.1-684.13, 14.1-20, 16.1-69.6, 17-116.1, 17-119.1:1, 17-126.2, 22-67.2, 33.1-268, 62.1-13.2
298	36-104
299	29-32.1, 29-32.2
300	32-414.11
301	37.1-1
302	29-2.1, 29-132 to 29-134, 29-140, 29-142, 29-143, 29-146
303	22-330.17, 22-330.33 to 22-330.35
304	2.1-257, 2.1-267, 2.1-268
305	15.1-9.1:1
306	58-1026.1
308	35-64.3
309	58-847
310	9-106.1 to 9-106.5
311	20-107
312	45.1-180, 45.1-181, 45.1-182 to 45.1-188, 45.1-190R, 45.1-191, 45.1-193, 45.1-194, 45.1-195, 45.1-197, 45.1-197.2
313	28.1-59
314	65.1-106
315	65.1-94
316	22-19.1, n.
317	23-14, 23-31, 23-49.11 to 23-49.13, 23-49.15 to 23-49.18, 23-49.20, 23-49.21
318	54-872.1, 54-872.2
319	33.1-62
320	58-151.032
321	13.1-3
322	6.1-117.1
323	45.1-89, 45.1-104, 45.1-221 to 45.1-225
324	6.1-324.1
325	15.1-526.2
326	46.1-157.1
327	28.1-183.2
328	63.1-110
329	63.1-55.1
330	15.1-29.5, 18.1-358R, 18.1-358.3R, 18.1-359 to 18.1-363R, 18.1-363.1, 40.1-28.1 to 40.1-28.5
331	46.1-342
332	2.1-341, 2.1-342, 2.1-344, 2.1-345
333	16.1-69.33
334	27-34.2
335	37.1-84.1
336	22-330.36 to 22-330.47
337	63.1-222
338	58-797
339	15.1-867.1
342	18.1-371.1 to 18.1-371.4
346	25-46.22
347	46.1-1, 46.1-52.1, 46.1-184, 46.1-206.1, 46.1-222, 46.1-229.1, 46.1-229.2, 46.1-231.1, 46.1-247, 46.1-277, 46.1-299, 46.1-340, 46.1-368.1
348	10-156
349	17-79.2
350	6.1-39
351	37.1-67R, 37.1-67.1
352	58-797
353	14.1-44.2:1, 51-111.10, 51-111.10:1, 51-111.18, 51-111.22:1, 51-111.31, 51-111.32, 51-111.36, 51-111.37, 51-111.41:1, 51-111.46, 51-111.47, 51-111.54, 51-111.55, 51-111.57, 51-111.58:1, 51-111.60, 51-111.60:4, 51-111.63 to 51-111.66, 51-111.67:1, 51-111.67:2, 51-111.67:4, 51-111.67:6, 51-111.67:13R, 51-144, 51-146, 51-147, 51-151, 51-153, 51-156, 51-161, 51-164, 51-168, 51-170, 51-173, 51-176.1, 51-177R
354	2.1-51.9, 10-181, 10-183, 10-184R, 10-184.1, 10-185
355	8-96.1
356	14.1-18, 14.1-18.1, 30-19.4
358	16.1-196
359	46.1-45.3
360	46.1-442
361	46.1-332
362	58-1141, 58-1142, 58-1145, 58-1152.1
363	29-52, 29-53, 29-54, 29-55, 29-55.1, 29-55.2R, 29-56, 29-84, 29-110, 29-122, 29-123R, 29-124R
365	46.1-199, 46.1-226
366	37.1-96
367	9-146 to 9-148
368	46.1-296
369	8-208.10, 24.1-23
370	14.1-112
371	6.1-249, 6.1-271, 6.1-271.1, 6.1-272R, 6.1-277, 6.1-280, 6.1-285 to 6.1-288, 6.1-291, 6.1-294
372	46.1-178.1
373	8.9-204.1
374	13.1-504
375	11-4.2
376	9-111.1
377	9-107
378	58-444
379	14.1-143
380	13.1-514
381	13.1-518.1
382	13.1-505
385	62.1-3
386	58-266.5
387	58-837
388	5.1-51, 58-692, 58-711, 58-713.1, 58-715, 58-716, 58-730, 58-732 to 58-735.2, 58-736, 58-737, 58-740 to 58-741.1, 58-743, 58-744, 58-746, 58-749, 58-750, 58-753.1, 58-753.1:1, 58-753.3R, 58-755, 58-757
389	58-441.34
390	8-296.1
391	19.1-191
392	6.1-349

Acts 1974 Chapter	Code 1950 Section
393	6.1-319.3
394	22-41 to 22-41.7
395	63.1-291 to 63.1-298
397	58-626.1
398	15.1-527.1, n.
399	4-45
400	46.1-64
401	15.1-1054
402	37.1-24.2
403	46.1-254.1
404	37.1-194
405	40.1-28.6
406	15.1-16.2
407	15.1-889
409	13.1-501, 54-730
410	46.1-104.1
411	54-175
412	46.1-387.9:1
413	63.1-249 to 63.1-273, 63.1-274, n., 63.1-275 to 63.1-289, 63.1-290, n.
414	63.1-133.2 to 63.1-133.6R, 63.1-133.7 to 63.1-133.14, 63.1-133.15, n.
415	63.1-87, 63.1-103R
416	55-79.39 to 55-79.103
417	63.1-53
418	63.1-105
419	63.1-196
420	2.1-51.9, 2.1-63.4:1R, 2.1-371 to 2.1-373
421	63.1-231
422	63.1-108, 63.1-109
423	14.1-11.4
424	55-58.1
425	58-1140.1
426	58-766.3
427	58-760.1
428	24.1-1, 24.1-23, 24.1-31, 24.1-35, 24.1-35.1, 24.1-41, 24.1-43, 24.1-45, 24.1-46, 24.1-48, 24.1-55, 24.1-65, 24.1-67, 24.1-101, 24.1-107, 24.1-113, 24.1-122, 24.1-137, 24.1-155, 24.1-163, 24.1-165, 24.1-166, 24.1-183, 24.1-203, 24.1-207, 24.1-209, 24.1-222, 24.1-224, 24.1-227 to 24.1-229, 24.1-231 to 24.1-234, 24.1-247
429	14.1-53
430	11-4.1
431	5.1-5, 58-441.6, 58-685.27 to 58-685.38
432	2.1-121
433	36-99, 36-105
434	28.1-52.1, n., 28.1-57.1R
435	8.7-209
436	32-4
437	36-99.1
438	58-266.1
439	51-127.11, 51-127.15, 51-127.16, 51-127.17, 51-127.20, 51-127.24, 51-127.30
440	58-730.3
441	9-123.1
442	15.1-136.6
443	19.1-42
444	8-636R, 8-636.1
445	58-829
446	32-310.1:1, 32-310.2
447	54-524.102
448	58-456
449	15.1-7.1
450	58-355
452	13.1-93.1, 13.1-253, 13.1-256.1
453	46.1-26.1, 46.1-197R, 46.1-362, 46.1-365, 46.1-383, 46.1-383.1R, 46.1-387.2, 46.1-400, 46.1-417, 46.1-419R, 46.1-420R, 46.1-423, 46.1-436, 46.1-514.1 to 46.1-514.20
454	46.1-78, 46.1-555.7, 46.1-555.9
455	46.1-190, 46.1-286.1
456	54-42, 54-48
457	46.1-250.1
458	55-230, 55-232.1, 55-232.2
459	54-25
460	4-2, 4-4, 4-7, 4-11, 4-22, 4-28, 4-34, 4-40, 4-45.1R, 4-46, 4-57, 4-60, 4-62, 4-63, 4-72, 4-73.1R, 4-73.2R, 4-75, 4-79, 4-80.2, 4-95R, 4-98.1, 4-98.2, 4-98.11, 4-98.19, 4-104, 4-108, 4-112.1, 4-112.2R, 4-115
461	51-111.67:14 to 51-111.67:20, 51-111.67:21, n.
462	33.1-1 to 33.1-6, 33.1-8 to 33.1-14, 33.1-16, 33.1-17, 33.1-19, 33.1-22
463	23-38.54 to 23-38.60
464	16.1-208, 20-61, 20-63 to 20-72, 20-76R, 20-77 to 20-81, 20-83.1, 20-84, 20-87, 20-88.13, 20-88.20:2, 20-88.31, 63.1-90.1
465	14.1-52
466	19.1-8, 60.1-6, 60.1-8, 60.1-12 to 60.1-14, 60.1-26, 60.1-47, 60.1-51.1, 60.1-58, 60.1-61, 60.1-69, 60.1-72, 60.1-74, 60.1-75, 60.1-79 to 60.1-81, 60.1-85, 60.1-86, 60.1-89, 60.1-94, 60.1-132 to 60.1-134
467	3.1-426, 3.1-426.1, 3.1-436R, 3.1-437, 3.1-437.1, 3.1-441, 3.1-452, 3.1-454 to 3.1-457R, 3.1-462R
468	46.1-351.1
469	58-12, 58-12.20 to 58-12.34
470	15.1-821
471	2.1-64.23 to 2.1-64.26, 2.1-64.27R
472	58-757.29
473	20-79
474	58-730.3
475	32-386
476	53-325
477	46.1-99, 58-685.11 to 58-685.13, 58-685.14 to 58-685.20, 58-685.24, 58-685.25
478	56-250, 56-251R, 56-252R
479	13.1-501, 13.1-504 to 13.1-506
480	22-9 to 22-9.1:03R, 22-9.1:04, 22-9.1:05 to 22-9.3R, 22-10.3 to 22-10.13, 22-55.1R, 22-275.5
481	16.1-129.3R, 19.1-92.1
482	22-37
483	52-1, 52-8.1
484	14.1-44.2, 16.1-69.33, 19.1-382, 19.1-383, 19.1-384, 19.1-386, 19.1-387, 19.1-389, 19.1-390R, 19.1-392 to 19.1-395, 51-111.10, 51-111.10:1, 51-111.67:2, 51-161, 51-163
485	58-757.01
486	13.1-93.1, 13.1-100, 13.1-256.1
487	46.1-65.1

Acts 1974 Chapter	Code 1950 Section
488	63.1-92, 63.1-92.1, 63.1-93, 63.1-120
489	63.1-239 to 63.1-248, n.
490	2.1-124
491	63.1-123
492	63.1-96
493	63.1-223
494	20-13.1
496	53-19.22:1
497	4-2, 4-61
498	56-46.1
499	63.1-133.16 to 63.1-133.28
500	38.1-301.4
501	63.1-183.1
502	53-184
503	63.1-47.1, 63.1-93, 63.1-120
504	63.1-25.2, 63.1-122, 63.1-123
505	63.1-239 to 63.1-248, n.
506	53-21.1
507	63.1-223, 63.1-226, 63.1-238.1 to 63.1-238.5
508	16.1-69.35:1, n.
509	37.1-7
510	58-834
512	15.1-136.2
513	16.1-173
514	15.1-25
515	17-79
516	40.1-51.3:2
517	2.1-209, 2.1-210
518	32-139.1
519	29-202
521	15.1-437
522	55-96
523	14.1-112
524	17-28
525	40.1-79, 40.1-80, 40.1-82, 40.1-84
526	15.1-490
527	9-126
528	46.1-193
529	15.1-1357.3
530	15.1-478
531	2.1-24.1
532	8-501
533	53-213, 53-213.01R
534	54-1.3 to 54-1.13, 54-17.1, 54-18, 54-24R, 54-26, 54-27 to 54-36R, 54-39R, 54-40R, 54-83.1:5, 54-83.1:6R, 54-83.1:11 to 54-83.1:25R, 54-83.2, 54-83.3R, 54-83.4R, 54-83.6 to 54-83.21R, 54-83.22, 54-83.23 to 54-83.26R, 54-83.27, 54-84, 54-89 to 54-91R, 54-92 to 54-100R, 54-102.2, 54-102.3, 54-102.4 to 54-102.13R, 54-112.1, 54-112.3, 54-112.6R, 54-112.7, 54-112.8, 54-112.9 to 54-112.25R, 54-112.26, 54-112.27R, 54-112.28R, 54-145.12, 54-145.14 to 54-145.19R, 54-145.20, 54-267, 54-268, 54-271, 54-398.3, 54-398.8R, 54-398.10, 54-398.11 to 54-398.17R, 54-398.19 to 54-398.26R, 54-398.28R, 54-524.111, 54-524.116, 54-524.117 to 54-524.132R, 54-573.4 to 54-573.17R, 54-729.03, 54-729.2, 54-729.3, 54-729.5, 54-729.7 to 54-729.12R, 54-729.14R, 54-729.16 to 54-729.25R, 54-735R, 54-736R, 54-741 to 54-743R, 54-747R, 54-748R, 54-750 to 54-754R, 54-755R, 54-757 to 54-761.1R, 54-762 to 54-763R, 54-764.2 to 54-764.4R, 54-765R, 54-770 to 54-772R, 54-775.1R, 54-775.2 to 54-775.4, 54-775.5R, 54-775.6R, 54-775.8R, 54-775.9R, 54-784.1R, 54-785R, 54-786.1, 54-787R, 54-788, 54-788.1 to 54-791R, 54-859.3R, 54-859.4, 54-859.5 to 54-859.14R, 54-860, 54-861, 54-864, 54-868R, 54-869, 54-870, 54-872, 54-902R, 54-905R, 54-906R, 54-908 to 54-915R
535	18.1-340
536	54-49, 54-51
537	46.1-267
539	15.1-1032.1, n.
540	46.1-229.3, n.
541	46.1-229
542	46.1-357
543	33.1-75.1
544	23-9.3 to 23-9.5, 23-9.6R, 23-9.6:1, 23-9.7R, 23-9.9, 23-9.11R, 23-9.12R, 23-9.14
545	59.1-9.1 to 59.1-9.17, 59.1-9.18, n., 59.1-22 to 59.1-41R
546	62.1-145
547	15.1-491
548	4-98.9, 4-98.10
550	15.1-535, 15.1-540
551	8-646.1
552	8-629.2
553	53-206.1
554	46.1-198
555	54-317.2
556	46.1-343
557	6.1-61, 26-40
558	19.1-243
559	46.1-179.1
560	65.1-54, 65.1-55, 65.1-56.1, 65.1-65, 65.1-65.1, 65.1-71
561	8-441.2
562	32-8.3
564	38.1-335.2
565	6.1-195.2, 6.1-195.19
566	15.1-1357
568	46.1-547
569	17-41
570	15.1-431
571	14.1-73.2
572	8.1-208, 11-4.3
573	45.1-201 to 45.1-205, 45.1-207, 45.1-208.1
574	18.1-372 to 18.1-379R, 57-40 to 57-47R, 57-48 to 57-68
575	19.1-19.3
577	52-25 to 52-30
578	6.1-370 to 6.1-379
579	27-40.2
580	46.1-335
581	20-104.1, 20-105
583	53-222.1
584	16.1-197
585	16.1-194, 16.1-199
586	54-524.101:1
587	6.1-226.1 to 6.1-226.13, 6.1-226.14, n.
589	46.1-2.1
590	15.1-89.1, n.
591	18.1-55.1
592	14.1-44.3
593	58-66.1
594	2.1-107 to 2.1-109R, 2.1-109.6 to 2.1-109.8
597	54-42.1 to 54-42.3

Acts 1974 Chapter	Code 1950 Section
598	15.1-505
600	54-901
601	3.1-632, 3.1-634
602	62.1-194.1:1
603	62.1-194
604	46.1-167.4
605	46.1-368
606	20-37.2
607	38.1-380.2
608	54-52
610	36-47.1
611	8-208.21
612	16.1-69.44
613	16.1-92
614	58-76.1, n.
615	18.1-120
616	6.1-60
617	19.1-150
618	19.1-148
619	32-31.7
620	16.1-166, 16.1-172, 63.1-204, 63.1-225
621	46.1-65
622	36-97
623	15.1-241
625	25-46.20
627	14.1-84
628	32-9.1
629	64.1-7.1
630	18.1-203
631	32-8.2
632	23-35.1
633	15.1-131.5
634	2.1-291
635	30-19.1
636	58-151.13
638	15.1-545, 15.1-545.1, 15.1-546
639	32-137
640	19.1-239
641	16.1-204
642	3.1-796.29 to 3.1-796.38
643	6.1-328
644	15.1-23.2, 15.1-23.3, 59.1-68.4, 59.1-68.5
645	16.1-198 to 16.1-202.3, 63.1-239 to 63.1-248, n.
646	15.1-51
647	3.1-107 to 3.1-126R, 3.1-126.1 to 3.1-126.13
648	16.1-70.1
649	18.1-308
650	2.1-326.2
651	45.1-202, 45.1-212, 45.1-212.1
652	18.1-223
654	23-35.9 to 23-35.13
655	15.1-11

Acts 1974 Chapter	Code 1950 Section
656	58-769.3:1, n.
657	20-88
658	15.1-560.2
659	64.1-57
660	60.1-13, 60.1-14, 60.1-100
661	37.1-20.1
662	13.1-36
663	54-740
664	46.1-330
665	6.1-4, 6.1-19, 6.1-22 to 6.1-32, 6.1-51.1, 6.1-54, 6.1-55, 6.1-78, 6.1-114, 6.1-122, 6.1-123, 6.1-125
666	16.1-98
667	37.1-105
668	36-55.7 to 36-55.23R, 36-55.28, 36-97, 36-107, 36-108, 36-110, 36-111, 36-113, 36-120 to 36-130
669	8-629.3
670	26-65
671	16.1-69.40, 16.1-194
672	64.1-105.2
673	16.1-205, 16.1-207
674	54-74.1
675	2.1-352
676	46.1-33, 46.1-383.2R, 46.1-494
678	54-112.4R, 54-112.4:1, 54-112.4:2, 54-112.5R
679	18.1-63.1
680	55-222.1R, 55-248.2 to 55-248.40
682	58-151.013
683	11-20.2
684	54-30
685	54-731 to 54-731.2, 54-749, 54-750, 54-751, 54-751.1, 54-753, 54-754.1, 54-755, 54-757, 54-758, 54-759.1, 54-761.2, 54-762, 54-762.2, 54-762.3, 54-763, 54-764.4, 54-767, 54-770, 54-775
686	40.1-13, 45.1-15, 54-28, 54-60, 54-89, 54-260.70, 54-306.4R, 54-308.5, 54-308.6, 54-398.15, 54-524.21, 54-729.03, 54-750, 54-788.1, 54-859.6

ACTS 1975

Acts 1975 Chapter	Code 1950 Section
2	4-98.18
3	18.2-242.1, 59.1-68.02
5	16.1-69.9
6	15.1-1357
7	15.1-1353
8	30-16.1
9	63.1-1.1:1
10	14.1-20
11	44-146.2 to 44-146.12R, 44-146.14, 44-146.16 to 44-146.19, 44-146.12, 44-146.22, 44-146.24, 44-146.28
12	28.1-172
13	15.1-528.1, n.
14	18.1-1 to 18.1-429R, 18.2-1 to 18.2-508
15	18.1-1 to 18.1-529R, 18.2-1 to 18.2-508
16	46.1-167.1
17	46.1-63.1
18	46.1-159
19	58-46.2
20	58-939
21	46.1-410
22	58-959
23	58-266.1
24	46.1-380.1
25	46.1-105.4
26	58-715
27	65.1-52
28	64.1-189, 64.1-192
29	3.1-188.20 to 3.1-188.31
30	15.1-66.3
31	15.1-131.6
32	15.1-1047.2
34	6.1-200.2
35	6.1-216
36	1-13.27:2
37	17-54
39	53-290.1 to 53-290.10
40	17-119.1:2
41	16.1-69.6:1
42	2.1-124
43	59.1-68.2 to 59.1-68.5
44	6.1-100.1, 6.1-195.70:1
45	58-884
46	58-151.013
47	58-829, 58-851
48	58-851
49	58-151.13
50	58-151.032
51	58-790
52	58-441.27, 58-441.27:1R
53	63.1-279
54	63.1-256

Acts 1975 Chapter	Code 1950 Section
55	58-587.1, 58-617.2
56	8-94.1
57	58-943.3
58	17-70
59	15.1-561
63	38.1-381.5
67	54-1.13R, 54-1.14
68	38.1-299
69	38.1-480
70	40.1-28.4
73	6.1-195.4, 6.1-195.22:1
74	15.1-381
75	13.1-501, 13.1-514
76	15.1-133
77	56-114R
78	36-21
79	6.1-195.49:1
80	6.1-5.2
81	6.1-5.1
82	38.1-397
83	15.1-1404
84	8-427
85	3.1-722.24
86	56-288
87	51-178
88	13.1-92, 13.1-93, 13.1-115.1
89	56-282.1
95	36-55.1 to 36-55.6
98	15.1-503.2
99	15.1-491
100	15.1-51
101	16.1-69.9:3
102	3.1-203, 3.1-217.2, 3.1-217.3R, 3.1-222, 3.1-233.1, 3.1-238
103	23.9.15 to 23-9.18, 23-9.19R, 23-9.20R, 23-9.21
104	46.1-330
105	46.1-65
106	54-367.3, 54-367.4, 54-367.12
107	58-712
108	46.1-198.1
109	15.1-1276
110	15.1-911, 15.1-912
111	23-94
113	63.1-277
114	46.1-181.3
115	3.1-741.1
117	46.1-237, 46.1-238R, 46.1-239R, 46.1-240
118	8-750.1
119	20-15
120	50-75
121	63-1-92
122	56-274
123	56-281
124	46.1-64
125	63.1-51
126	10-17.21
128	16.1-166
129	6.1-195.54
130	6.1-195.57
131	15.1-1032.1, n.
132	14.1-5, 14.1-18.1 14.1-19
133	18.2-343
134	46.1-423.3
135	3.1-47 to 3.1-49, 3.1-52
136	8-5.1
138	46.1-178.2
139	22-330.37, 22-330.43
140	22-228
143	15.1-778.1, 15.1-779
145	15.1-285
146	58-996
147	22-40.1
148	58-153.1, 58-155
149	10-92.2
150	22-37
151	58-919.2
152	29-3
153	29-65
155	38.1-279.33
162	14.1-46
163	38.1-183.2
164	38.1-381.1
166	58-293
167	28.1-128
168	29-209
170	38.1-313, 38.1-482.10
171	46.1-66.1
172	29-184.2
173	27-34.2
174	58-766
175	38.1-738
176	15.1-7.1, 63.1-26
178	53-330
179	15.1-1348
180	42.1-29 to 42.1-29.2
181	46.1-254.2
182	8-373
184	38.1-733.1
185	28.1-139, 28.1-139.1
186	28.1-117R
187	46.1-229
188	51-179
189	25-46.9
190	63.1-48
191	46.1-178
192	26-20.1
193	8-208.33, 8-208.34, 8-208.38
195	9-96, 9-97
196	23-38.45, 23-38.46, 23-38.49
197	37.1-89
198	37.1-34.1
199	28.1-87
200	37.1-194
201	46.1-178.1
202	46.1-193.1
203	60.1-52.4
204	62.1-44.33
205	46.1-179.1
206	46.1-105.5
207	63.1-124
208	2.1-257
209	2.1-358
210	56-304
211	5.1-116, 5.1-118
212	56-300
214	15.1-1135, 15.1-1139, 15.1-1140, 15.1-1147
215	38.1-455, 38.1-456, 38.1-465.1, 38.1-465.2
216	27-34.3
217	59.1-21.2, 59.1-21.4
218	54-50
220	32-211 to 32-211.8
221	57-49, 57-60, 57-65, 57-69
222	9-111
223	58-797
224	4-37.1
225	8.9-403 to 8.9-406
226	14.1-112
227	16.1-108
228	16.1-115
229	55-66.7
230	59.1-74
231	2.1-1
232	30-28.11R
233	58-769.6
234	58-963
235	8-789, 8-791, 8-791.1, 55-232, 55-237
236	12.1-15
237	37.1-67.1
238	54-734
240	46.1-354.1
241	2.1-49
242	33.1-90.1
243	58-372.1
244	53-213.1, 53-251
245	32-31.3
246	40.1-25.1
247	32-31.7
248	16.1-197, 63.1-56
249	58-64
250	36-75
251	21-118.4
252	37.1-36
253	15.1-827, 15.1-827.1
254	15.1-1376
255	33.1-151

Acts 1975 Chapter	Code 1950 Section
257	58-1142, 58-1148, 58-1152.2
259	58-1000.2
260	3.1-14
261	47-1
262	38.1-638.18, 38.1-638.31, 38.1-638.34, 38.1-638.45
263	10-181
266	53-222.1R
267	32-353.4, 32-353.21
268	62.1-13.2, 62.1-13.5, 62.1-13.20
269	18.2-102.1
270	6.1-273
272	51-114, 51-127.9
273	15.1-156
275	9-67, 9-68
277	14.1-105.1
279	62.1-44.15:1
280	65.1-88
281	32-195.8, 38.1-348.6, 38.1-360
282	10-138.2
283	3.1-796.29, 3.1-796.30
284	55-63, 55-65, 55-66
285	58-371.2
286	16.1-208.1, 53-278.3
287	63.1-87
288	29-184
289	59.1-9.9
290	15.1-135.1
291	46.1-267.2
292	53-262
294	32-8.4
295	32-276.1, 32-280 to 32-281.1, 32-286
296	51-111.31
297	40.1-49.1
298	16.1-133.1
299	63.1-195
300	63.1-39
301	63.1-253
302	63.1-251.1, 63.1-276.1
303	46.1-547.2
304	46.1-516
305	46.1-550.1, 46.1-550.2, 46.1-550.4
306	51-111.67:4
307	2.1-341, 2.1-342
308	22-72, 22-97, 22-217.5, 22-217.6, 22-217.8:1
309	51-111.67:4
310	38.1-740
311	63.1-25.2, 63.1-53, 63.1-133.13, 63.1-133.14, 63.1-133.17 to 63.1-133.19, 63.1-133.21, 63.1-133.23, 63.1-250, 63.1-256, 63.1-261, 63.1-275, 63.1-279 to 63.1-282, 63.1-285 to 63.1-288
312	2.1-342
313	2.1-353
314	55-248.5, 55-248.10
315	37.1-23.1
316	53-230 to 53-234
317	10-146 to 10-150
318	42.1-72 to 42.1-73.1, 42.1-74.1
319	38.1-381.5
320	63.1 112, 63.1-127.2
321	9-141
322	53-38
323	2.1-156, 2.1-157 to 2.1-159R, 2.1-196R, 2.1-196.1
324	30-58R, 30-58.1
325	2.1-54, 2.1-60, 2.1-61
326	56-65.2
327	15.1-44.2
328	22-72, 22-97
329	46.1-547
330	65.1-4.1
331	9-65.2:1
333	2.1-349
334	14.1-44.2, 16.1-69.5, 16.1-69.9:1, 16.1-69.11, 16.1-69.14, 16.1-69.18, 16.1-69.32, 16.1-69.33, 16.1-69.39, 16.1-69.45, 16.1-69.47, 16.1-69.47:1, 16.1-69.51, 16.1-87, 16.1-91, 16.1-154, 16.1-162, 16.1-218
335	62.1-44.15
336	63.1-58.1
337	63.1-120
338	28.1-81.1
339	62.1-44.15:2
341	16.1-217.1 to 16.1-217.4R, 63.1-248.1 to 63.1-248.17
342	46.1-315.1, n.
343	37.1-128.1
345	36-96
350	38.1-371.2
358	56-232 56-249.1, 56-250
359	8-208.14:1, 8-208.17
360	51-111.10:2
361	2.1-114
362	33.1-223
363	55-79.01 to 55-79.06
364	63.1-223, 63.1-226, 63.1-228 to 63.1-232
365	65.1-99, 65.1-129, 65.1-134, 65.1-138 to 65.1-145
366	2.1-349.1
367	36-106
368	63.1-33, 63.1-54
369	8-324.1
370	8-320, 8-324
371	53-278.1
372	2.1-121, 2.1-122
373	62.1-44.19:1, 62.1-44.19:2, n.
374	58-758.1
375	55-17.1
376	58-12.41
377	3.1-193 to 3.1-194.2, 3.1-211.1, 3.1-212.1, 3.1-212.2, 3.1-249.1 to 3.1-249.21
378	15.1-37.3:1, 15.1-37.3:2
379	14.1-38
380	43-17.1
381	15.1-1405
382	46.1-1, 46.1-444, 46.1-472, 46.1-504
383	2.1-351
386	63.1-196
387	14.1-73.2
388	63.1-124.1
389	8-608.1
390	2.1-51.7, 2.1-51.9, 2.1-52, 2.1-53, 2.1-113
392	15.1-1032.1
393	2.1-114.1
394	36-97, 36-99
395	9-32R
396	23-14
397	23-31
398	6.1-2.5
399	23-9.10:3
400	23-38.11, 23-38.12, 23-28.14 to 23-38.17
401	29-121, n.
402	29-65
403	13.1-322
404	15.1-526.2
405	15.1-1367
406	63.1-56, 63.1-207, 63.1-208R, 63.1-219.1 to 63.1-219.6
407	13.1-9
408	4-2, 4-25, 4-30, 4-89
409	29-121, n.
411	7.1-25R, 7.1-25.1
412	33.1-75
413	4-98.17
415	55-79.41, 55-79.43, 55-79.44, 55-79.47, 55-79.49, 55-79.51 to

Acts 1975 Chapter	Code 1950 Section
	55-79.54, 55-79.58, 55-79.61, 55-79.63, 55-79.67, 55-79.72, 55-79.74, 55-79.79 to 55-79.80:1, 55-79.84, 55-79.87 to 55-79.89, 55-79.93, 55-79.94, 55-79.97, 55-79.100
417	58-341
418	8-654.6
419	54-729.26
420	58-833.1
421	54-132, 54-133
422	9-107
423	58-12:42
424	58-685.30
425	54-524.2
426	46.1-1
427	30-6, 30-7
429	62.1-177.1
430	16.1-190
431	62.1-3
432	45.1-33.1 to 45.1-33.6
433	37.1-67.1
434	22-29.2, 22-29.6
435	8-654.7
437	63.1-172
438	63.1-123
439	63.1-198
440	46.1-254.1
441	9-121
442	30-28.1, n., 30-27.7, 30-28.9R, 30-28.9:1
443	22-127
444	15.1-267
445	33.1-242
446	65.1-56
447	65.1-54, 65.1-55, 65.1-56.1, 65.1-65, 65.1-65.1, 65.1-71
448	6.1-2.2 to 6.1-2.4R, 6.1-195.17R, 6.1-195.34, 6.1-195.36R, 6.1-195.37R, 6.1-215R, 6.1-217, 6.1-234, 6.1-234.1R, 6.1-311 to 6.1-328R, 6.1-330R, 6.1-330.1R, 6.1-330.3R, 6.1-330.5R, 6.1-330.6 to 6.1-330.48, 6.1-362 to 6.1-363R, 8-223, 11-4.2R
449	7.1-22
450	65.1-56
451	51-111.52:4
452	14.1-46, 15.1-809.2
453	29.194.1
455	36-48
456	63.1-289.1
457	40.1-28.7
458	46.1-418
460	29-121, n.
461	63.1-221
463	58-12.16, 58-12.35 to 58-12.40
464	22-10.11
465	16.1-173
466	34-4, 34-13, 34-18, 34-19, 34-21, 34-26
467	62.1-13.13, 62.1-13.16
468	22-67.2
469	17-60, 17-60.1, 55-66.3 to 55-66.7
470	42.1-23
471	65.1-52, 65.1-87
472	65.1-99.1
473	63.1-171.3
474	63.1-42
475	32-31.9 to 32-31.22
476	19.2-163.1 to 19.2-163.4
478	8-646.9
479	54-147, 54-149, 54-152, 54-173, 54-175.1 to 54-177, 54-180, 54-181, 54-184, 54-187, 54-189, 54-189.1, 54-200.5, 54-200.11
480	4-72R, 4-72.1
481	4-75
482	4-46
483	4-98.2, 4-98.10, 4-98.18, 4-98.19
484	23-41, 23-43R
485	21-5.3
486	15.1-1370
487	32-31.5:1, 32-31.6
488	9-106.1 to 9-106.5R, 9-106.6 to 9-106.22
489	15.1-1375
490	21-118.4
491	2.1-353.1
492	18.2-390
493	18.2-488
494	58-757.01
495	19.1-1 to 19.1-400R, 19.2-1 to 19.2-392
499	58-355, 58-396
500	1-13.25, 11-3, 13.1-2, 13.1-2.1, 13.1-3.1, 13.1-6, 13.1-10, 13.1-14, 13.1-15, 13.1-17 to 13.1-19, 13.1-21 to 13.1-23, 13.1-24.1 to 13.1-26, 13.1-30, 13.1-32, 13.1-34, 13.1-39.1 to 13.1-41.1, 13.1-45, 13.1-47, 13.1-49, 13.1-53R, 13.1-54, 13.1-56 to 13.1-58, 13.1-61, 13.1-63, 13.1-64, 13.1-67, 13.1-68, 13.1-69.1, 13.1-70, 13.1-72 to 13.1-81, 13.1-85, 13.1-86, 13.1-89, 13.1-91, 13.1-93, 13.1-95, 13.1-104 to 13.1-106, 13.1-110, 13.1-111, 13.1-115, 13.1-120, 13.1-121, 13.1-123, 13.1-125, 13.1-128, 13.1-134, 13.1-203, 13.1-204.1, 13.1-205R, 13.1-205.1 to 13.1-207.2, 13.1-209, 13.1-210, 13.1-212.1, 13.1-213, 13.1-217, 13.1-224, 13.1-225, 13.1-228, 13.1-230, 13.1-231, 13.1-234, 13.1-237, 13.1-243, 13.1-245, 13.1-247R, 13.1-252, 13.1-256.1, 13.1-257, 13.1-267 to 13.1-269, 13.1-273, 13.1-274, 13.1-278, 13.1-282, 13.1-285, 13.1-286, 13.1-287, 13.1-290, 13.1-295, 13.1-514, 55-119, 55-136, 56-64R
501	2.1-63.01 to 2-63.03
502	9-6.7, n., 9-6.15 to 9-6.20, 9-6.21R
503	9-6.1 to 9-6.14R, 9-6.14:1 to 9-6.14:20
504	58-831.1, 58-831.2
505	3.1-692
506	15.1-978
507	18.2-216, 59.1-44
508	54-273, 54-274, 54-275, 54-276.4, 54-276.5, 54-276.7, 54-276.9, 54-276.10, 54-280R, 54-281.2, 54-281.4, 54-281.5, 54-282, 54-284, 54-290.1, 54-291, 54-295 to 54-295.3, 54-295.6, 54-295.7, 54-298, 54-299, 54-300R, 54-300.2, 54-300.3, 54-301 to 54-303R, 54-304, 54-305, 54-306R, 54-308.5, 54-308.6, 54-309.1, 54-310, 54-310.1R, 54-311.1,

Acts 1975 Chapter	Code 1950 Section
	54-312, 54-315.1 to 54-315.3, 54-317, 54-318.1, 54-319.1R, 54-321.1, 54-321.2, 54-323
509	2.1-64.32 to 2.1-64.38
510	9-7
512	54-273, 54-274.1
513	22-10.11
514	9-11, 9-12
515	2.1-36R, 14.1-134, 15.1-63 to 15.1-66R, 24.1-1, 24.1-18, 24.1-19, 24.1-22 to 24.1-26, 24.1-29, 24.1-32, 24.1-41.2, 24.1-43, 24.1-45, 24.1-45.1, 24.1-49, 24.1-50, 24.1-55 to 24.1-55.2, 24.1-59, 24.1-76 to 24.1-77, 24.1-78R, 24.1-79 to 24.1-79.10, 24.1-100.1, 24.1-101, 24.1-126, 24.1-129, 24.1-132, 24.1-144, 24.1-150 to 24.1-152, 24.1-163, 24.1-165 to 24.1-167, 24.1-172, 24.1-174, 24.1-217, 24.1-227 to 24.1-230, 24.1-232, 24.1-252 to 24.1-254.1, 24.1-255 to 24.1-258, 24.1-259R, 24.1-262, 24.1-277, 24.1-279
516	46.1-6
517	4-45, 4-98.12, 15.1-29.5, 15.1-40.2, 15.1-57, 15.1-58, 15.1-60, 15.1-180, 15.1-187, 15.1-274, 15.1-526.1, 15.1-559, 15.1-564, 15.1-583, 15.1-584, 15.1-589.1, 15.1-623.1, 15.1-676, 15.1-686, 15.1-686.2, 15.1-694, 15.1-695, 15.1-698, 15.1-723, 15.1-724, 15.1-784, 15.1-948, 15.1-1075, 15.1-1088, 15.1-1089, 15.1-1103, 15.1-1131, 15.1-1132, 15.1-1138, 15.1-1150, 15.1-1157, 15.1-1230, 15.1-1244, 15.1-1244.1, 15.1-1273, 15.1-1425, 22-79.4, 22-130.2, 22-130.3, 29-194.2
518	63.1-289.2
519	56-508.1
520	45.1-2, 45.1-40, 45.1-41, 45.1-104
521	15.1-495, 15.1-496 to 15.1-496.3
522	54-729.01 to 54-729.018R, 54-916 to 54-922
523	51-111.41:1
524	63.1-76 to 63.1-78, 63.1-79 to 63.1-83, 63.1-85, 63.1-87, 63.1-94, 63.1-100R, 63.1-104R, 63.1-107, 63.1-116 to 63.1-117, 63.1-127R, 63.1-131R
525	2.1-64.23 to 2.1-64.26
527	15.1-1165
528	63.1-195
529	29-144
530	40.1-28.8 to 40.1-28.12
531	3.1-722.22
532	36-49.1
533	46.1-111
534	15.1-29.6
535	55-248.41 to 55-248.48
536	36-55.25, 36-55.26, 36-55.28, 36-55.30, 36-55.31, 36-55.32, 36-55.33R, 36-55.33:1, 36-55.34R, 36-55.34:1, 36-55.35, 36-55.36, 36-55.38, 36-55.39, 36-55.44, 36-55.49
538	63.1-287
539	63.1-180, 63.1-213
540	32-31.5:2
541	58-829, 58-851
542	22-351 to 22-359
543	13.1-548
544	51-163
545	56-223
547	1-14R, 23-173, 55-26R, 56-114R, 58-790, 58-804
549	46.1-83.3
550	56-480.1
551	25-46.20
552	51-111.52:5
553	46.1-400, 46.1-401, 46.1-403
554	46.1-206
555	33.1-47.1
556	38.1-108, 38.1-113
557	20-65
558	22-275.3, 22-275.6
559	16.1-173
560	46.1-252.1, 46.1-252.1:1, n.
561	5.1-1
563	32-414,3, 32-414.4
564	32-6.4
565	54-281.5
566	36-94 to 36-95, 36-95.4
567	22-79.4
568	22-223, 37.1-96
569	18.2-399.1
570	57-35.3, 57-35.8:1
573	15.1-37, 15.1-37.1, 15.1-332.1, 15.1-875, 15.1-1250.1
574	15.1-503.2
575	2.1-33, 8-373, 15.1-9.1:2R, 15.1-137.1, n., 15.1-486.1, n., 15.1-491, 15.1-503.2, 15.1-522, 15.1-538, 15.1-646, 15.1-809.1R, 15.1-956, 22-83.2, n., 22-120.2, n., 22-128.1, n., 29-147.1, n., 29-194, 29-197.1, n., 36-19.1, n., 36-19.4, n., 36-27.1, n., 56-291, 4, 58-776.6, n., 58-792.3, n., 58-895, 58-896
576	18.2-336
577	46.1-347.1, 46.1-347.2
578	8-208.21
579	15.1-491
580	19.2-159.1
581	57-35.7, 57-35.9R
582	15.1-491
583	57-39.8 to 57-39.18
585	63.1-107, 63.1-107.1
586	2.1-358
587	18.2-268
588	53-291, 53-292R, 53-294
589	2.1-80R, 2.1-95 to 2.1-97R, 6.1-115 to 6.1-118R, 20-41R, 20-42R, 20-44R, 29-49R, 29-140.1R, 29-165 to 29-168R, 32-69R, 32-70.1R, 33.1-349R, 33.1-350R, 54-524.101:1 to 54-524.108R, 59.1-42 to 59.1-68.01R, 59.1-68.1R
590	18.2-311.1
591	14.1-69, 14.1-105 14.1-111, 14.1-121, 14.1-123, 14.1-125, 14.1-128R, 14.1-128.1, 14.1-200.1R, 15.1-148R
593	8-208.30R, 8-208.31R, 14.1-184R, 14.1-184.1R,

Acts 1975 Chapter	Code 1950 Section
	15.1-141R, 17-30.1:1R, 17-30.2R, 53-273 to 53-275R, 53-278.1 to 53-278.4R
594	18.2-308
595	2.1-36R, 15.1-63 to 15.1-66R, 24.1-78R, 24.1-79.1 to 24.1-79.10
596	63.1-249 to 63.1-251, 63.1-261, 63.1-270, 63.1-275 to 63.1-276, 63.1-277, 63.1-279 to 63.1-282, 63.1-285 to 63.1-288
597	51-111.10, 51-111.37, 51-111.47, 51-111.60, 51-111.67:2, 51-111.67:6, 51-144, 51-161
598	18.2-137
599	46.1-343
601	18.2-271.1
602	18.2-91
603	18.2-95
604	18.2-52
605	18.2-58
606	18.2-61 to 18.2-67
607	18.2-253, 54-524.78R, 54-524.101:1 to 54-524.108, n.
608	18.2-474.1
609	29-147.1R
610	51-111.22, 51-111.47
611	51-111.10, 51-111.41:1, 51-111.54, 51-111.67:2
612	58-14.1
613	58-14.2
614	58-792.01
615	58-792.02
616	58-33.1
617	58-33.2
618	58.817.1
620	58-512.1, 58-514.2, 58-760
621	58-266.1
622	58-785.1
623	58-33.3
624	18.2-53.1
625	36-124
626	2.1-374 to 2.1-376
627	59.1-21.19 to 59.1-21.24
628	18.2-53.1
629	15.1-528.1R, 15.1-966
630	53-250
631	9-109.3
632	4-96.1, n.
633	22-151.2, 22-280.1, 46.1-190, 46.1-287
635	15.1-36.1
636	15.1-676
637	53-331
638	53-333
639	22-275.26 to 22-275.28
640	17-30.1
641	15.1-427 to 15.1-431, 15.1-440, 15.1-446R, 15.1-446.1 to 15.1-450, 15.1-453, 15.1-454, 15.1-456, 15.1-457, 15.1-464 to 15.1-467, 15.1-469 to 15.1-475, 15.1-482, 15.1-482.1, 15.1-486, 15.1-486.1, n., 15.1-487R, 15.1-489, 15.1-495, 15.1-495.1R, 15.1-496, 15.1-497, 15.1-503.2
642	54-306.01
643	54-872.1, 54-872.2
644	20-4, 20-27, 20-29R, 20-38R, 20-38.1, 20-45R, 20-45.1, 20-45.2, 20-48, 20-49, 20-61, 20-67, 20-70, 20-71.1, 20-74, 20-75, 20-79, 20-83, 20-86, 20-87, 20-88, 20-88.23:3, 20-89R, 20-89.1, 20-91, 20-92R, 20-93 to 20-96, 20-99, 20-101R, 20-102 to 20-104, 20-107, 20-109, 20-110, 20-112 to 20-115, 20-119R, 20-120 to 20-121.01, 20-122
645	6.1-363.1, 54-44.1
646	58-16.2
647	53-67
648	54-102.14 to 54-102.23
650	52-8.1
651	22-230.3
652	8-211.1

ACTS 1976

Acts 1976 Chapter	Code 1950 Section
2	14.1-46
4	13.1-9, 13.1-10, 13.1-208, 13.1-209
5	46.1-66
6	46.1-267
7	46.1-179.2
8	46.1-357, 46.1-369
9	15.1-1054
10	59.1-1 to 59.1-9R
11	15.1-911, 15.1-953, 15.1-955, 15.1-957, 15.1-985, 21-123
12	24.1-43
14	33.1-351, 33.1-369, 33.1-370, 33.1-371, 33.1-374, 33.1-375
15	32-167.7, 54-274
16	22-330.20, 22-330.33
17	46.1-41.1, 46.1-355.1
18	22-74
19	23-38.55
20	46.1-35.1
21	23-40, 23-49.1, 23-49.23 to 23-49.33
22	2.1-64.18, 9-141, 22-29.4
23	22-8R
24	46.1-199, 46.1-226
25	23-155.4, 23-155.6
26	8-67.2
27	46.1-167.1
28	46.1-413
29	33.1-370
30	46.1-184
31	46.1-184
32	54-376, 54-393 to 54-394.1
33	63.1-173.1
34	28.1-172
35	3.1-667, 3.1-668, 3.1-670, 3.1-672, 3.1-674 to 3.1-679, 3.1-681
36	4-75
37	4-50, 4-55
38	29-65
39	53-250
40	46.1-410
41	37.1-194
42	16.1-158, 16.1-178
43	19.2-50
44	3.1-699.1
45	53-258
47	28.1-51.2R
48	46.1-379, 46.1-380.1, 46.1-380.2
49	29-184.2
50	8-277.1
51	62.1-44.34:1, 62.1-44.34:2
52	16.1-69.33
53	58-266.1:1, 58-774
54	18.2-359
55	58-769.11
56	16.1-69.6:1
57	46.1-375
58	58-769.6:1
59	46.1-42.1

Acts 1976 Chapter	Code 1950 Section
60	46.1-150
61	9-53, 9-57R, 9-57.1
62	46.1-441.1
63	33.1-225.2
64	4-2 to 4-4, 4-6, 4-6.1
65	46.1-302.3
66	54-851
67	4-31, 4-105
68	6.1-380
69	15.1-37 to 15.1-37.1:7, 15.1-332.1, 15.1-875, 15.1-1250.1
70	40.1-80
71	15.1-491
73	11-23
74	46.1-252.1
75	18.2-212
76	18.2-129
77	43-32
78	46.1-39
79	59.1-70
80	38.1-301.5
81	6.1-195.18
82	6.1-195.64
83	38.1-249R
84	13.1-3R
85	38.1-775 to 38.1-788, 38.1-789, n.
86	46.1-514.6, 46.1-514.11
87	59.1-68.3
88	10-144, 10-145.2, 10-145.3, 10-145.6
89	56-412.1
90	46.1-198.1
91	3.1-22.5, 3.1-126.5
92	15.1-702, 15.1-708
93	15.1-7.1
94	6.1-66
95	15.1-50
96	6.1-39
97	22-89.2R
98	22-275.11, 22-275.20
99	22-72.1, 22-97.1
103	22-234.1
104	59.1-78, 59.1-81 to 59.1-88
105	56-279.1, 56-291.13, 56-338.15, 56-338.35, 56-338.62, 56-338.81
106	56-338.41:1
107	56-457.8:1
108	56-297
109	56-304.14
110	56-293.1
111	38.1-472.1
112	30-28.18
113	62.1-154
114	19.2-8
115	8-577.1
116	22-276.1
117	36-55.28
118	8.4-104
119	10-6
120	2.1-259
121	38.1-381
122	38.1-381
123	22-276.1
124	17-116.2
125	2.1-82.1
126	16.1-69.6, 17-119.1:1
127	22-67.2
128	30-19.01
129	29-197.2, n.
131	30-15.2
132	18.2-249
133	17-127.21
134	4-25
135	46.1-16R, 46.1-16.01
136	4-79
137	36-99.2
138	19.2-34, 19.2-35, 19.2-37, 19.2-44, 19.2-44.1R
139	58-358R
140	19.2-175
142	19.2-57
143	46.1-471, 46.1-472
144	29-55.3:1
145	53-272
146	18.2-168
147	46.1-105.6
148	46.1-413.1
149	65.1-100R, 65.1-100.1
150	34-26
151	65.1-61
152	6.1-68
153	18.2-87.1
154	15.1-29.6
155	55-60
156	46.1-167.5, 46.1-397
157	11-2
158	46.1-387.9:2
159	13.1-113
160	6.1-330.41
161	15.1-66.1
162	9-108
163	19.2-68
164	3.1-704, 3.1-712
165	65.1-62
166	65.1-65, 65.1-70
169	4-98.12:2
170	30-13
171	29-65
172	33.1-223.2
174	15.1-773
175	15.1-683, 15.1-684
176	22-67.2
177	55-230
178	8-142
180	53-213.1
181	18.2-251
182	15.1-29.1:1
183	15.1-364.1
184	46.1-173
185	32-31.7:1
186	63.1-248.14
187	65.1-4.1
188	62.1-44.19:2, n.
189	23-14, 23-31
190	9-97.1
191	22-217.3
192	22-155R
193	32-423
194	15.1-604
196	46.1-555.9
197	51-127.16, 51-127.20, 51-127.21
198	2.1-68.1
199	15.1-48, 15.1-138.1, 15.1-144, 58-371.2
200	28.1-51.1
201	53-108R
202	6.1-219
203	6.1-208.4
204	6.1-212.1
205	6.1-207.1
206	15.1-131.5
207	11-20.2
208	33.1-75.1
209	53-220, 53-251
210	53-37.2, 53-38.1
211	7.1-13 to 7.1-18R, 7.1-18.1, 7.1-20, 7.1-21, 7.1-22
212	17-116.4
213	43-2
214	63.1-67.7
215	63.1-105.1
216	63.1-238.3 to 63.1-238.5
217	63.1-21
218	63.1-5R
219	13.1-10.1, 13.1-209.1
220	19.2-13
221	33.1-200.1
222	32-357, 32-361
224	22-285, 22-290
225	62.1-135
226	22-217.3
227	46.1-555.10
228	6.1-71
229	13.1-501
230	33.1-192.1,

Acts 1976 Chapter	Code 1950 Section
	33.1-386 to 33.1-389
231	19.2-67
232	53-299.2
233	18.2-414.1
234	29-52.2
236	3.1-249.1, n., 3.1-249.6, 3.1-249.8, 3.1-249.12, 3.1-249.13
238	8-623
239	15.1-158.1, n.
240	32-195.3:1
241	9-147
243	15.1-1263
244	18.2-415
245	19.2-187, 19.2-187.1
246	53-290.6
247	33.1-43
248	53-172
249	53-19.39
250	40.1-23, 59.1-137
251	15.1-29.7
252	19.2-76.1
253	43-23.1
254	54-872.3 to 54-872.5
255	28.1-87, 28.1-89, 28.1-92
256	28.1-108
257	55-59
258	19.2-182.1
259	38.1-70.13R, 46.1-513.1, 46.1-513.2, 46.1-514R
260	38.1-674
261	8-208.16
262	2.1-267, 2.1-268
263	6.1-195.34
264	46.1-172.03
265	56-484.1 to 56-484.3
266	44-123.1, 44-124R, 44-124.1, 44-125 to 44-128R, 44-135R, 44-135.1, 44-137
267	15.1-506.1
268	56-466
269	18.2-460, 19.2-271
270	15.1-466
271	19.2-66
272	17-126.3
273	18.2-163
274	53-94.1
275	38.1-279.36
276	38.1-279.38
277	54-42
278	38.1-279.34, 38.1-279.48R, 38.1-279.48:1
279	38.1-279.44R, 38.1-279.44:1 to 38.1-279.44:3, 38.1-279.56
280	51-111.52:5
281	32-260
282	22-217.7
283	22-275.7, 22-275.18, 22-275.19
284	13.1-50
285	19.2-298
286	53-183.2
287	19.2-310.1
288	40.1-51.10
289	6.1-364 to 6.1-369R
290	56-234
291	15.1-456
292	19.2-165.1
293	19.2-59
294	54-916, n.
295	53-38, 53-166.1
296	32-8.5, 32-8.6
297	6.1-363.1
299	2.1-373
300	53-250.1
301	15.1-40.2
302	18.2-308
303	15.1-37.3:3
304	60.1-14
305	18.2-215
306	16.1-69.32
307	16.1-69.35
308	8-208.33, 14.1-105, 14.1-111, 14.1-189, 14.1-190, 19.2-278, 25-46.22, 58-942
310	14.1-105, 14.1-105.1
311	58-1130
312	18.2-427
313	16.1-176
314	46.1-247
315	46.1-296
316	16.1-115
317	32-120, 32-120.1
318	18.2-192
319	16.1-69.7:1
320	46.1-423.4
321	16.1-190
322	46.1-230, 46.1-231
323	46.1-154.3
324	16.1-158
326	47-1
327	54-152, 54-163, 54-169, 54-173, 54-175.1, 54-181, 54-200.5, 54-200.8, 54-200.16
328	56-16.1
329	38.1-279.46
330	38.1-482.17 to 38.1-482.33
331	54-276.10
332	18.2-509
333	32-197
334	22-107.3, 22-113
335	54-872.3 to 54-872.5
336	19.2-390, 46.1-413
337	56-291.1
338	26-4
339	46.1-66, 46.1-97
340	6.1-58.2
341	12.1-15.1
342	38.1-348.6
343	28.1-52.2
344	14.1-112
345	20-79
346	56-406
347	16.1-158.2
348	63.1-248.3, 63.1-248.4
349	32-296.1
350	13.1-255, 13.1-256
351	18.2-302, 18.2-303.1, 18.2-305R
352	22-37
353	63.1-230.1
354	8-399
355	32-195.8, 38.1-348.7, 38.1-360
356	20-39, 20-40, 20-89.1
357	63.1-249 to 63.1-251, 63.1-252 to 63.1-258, 63.1-261 to 63.1-263, 63.1-265 to 63.1-273, 63.1-275 to 63.1-276, 63.1-277, 63.1-279 to 63.1-281, 63.1-285 to 63.1-287
358	54-524.65
359	46.1-421
360	2.1-349.1
361	46.1-224.1
362	46.1-516, 46.1-523, 46.1-550
363	46.1-525.1
364	16.1-199
365	63.1-209
366	63.1-236
367	63.1-228
368	46.1-360
369	46.1-547.2
370	15.1-486.1, n.
371	18.2-53.1
372	46.1-1
374	16.1-69.9, 16.1-69.11, 16.1-69.17:1, 16.1-69.19, 16.1-69.44, 19.2-345,

Acts 1976 Chapter	Code 1950 Section
	19.2-346, 37.1-89, 51-161
375	58-441.3
376	24.1-40.1 to 24.1-40.6
377	54-57R, 54-57.1
378	56-274
379	56-235.1
380	33.1-96
381	63.1-134.1 to 63.1-137, 63.1-139, 63.1-140
382	63.1-54.1
383	63.1-33
384	28.1-60, 28.1-65
385	14.1-5
386	35-14
387	16.1-115
388	43-70
389	29-194.1
390	43-71
391	33.1-72
392	28.1-48
393	53-76.1
394	18.2-480.1
395	8-59
396	46.1-188
397	53-19.36:1
398	15.1-571.1
399	44-1, 44-2, 44-5, 44-40, 44-40.1, 44-42 to 44-53
400	14.1-55 to 14.1-58
401	15.1-37.5:1
402	15.1-51
403	15.1-152
404	46.1-181.4
405	56-264.1
406	54-524.61
407	15.1-506.1, 22-56.2
408	57-65.1, 56-65.2R
409	15.1-491
410	46.1-104.1, 46.1-149.1
411	56-274
412	15.1-50
413	43-4
414	51-111.10:1
418	58-758.1
419	64.1-57
421	58-12.57
422	58-435
423	58-162
425	53-251
426	58-12.58
427	58-16.2
428	58-983
429	51-111.53
430	33.1-89
431	58-165.1, 58-218.2
433	64.1-123
434	58-730
435	26-20
436	58-151.035, 58-151.050:1, 58-151.050:2
437	64.1-57.1
438	58-12.55
439	58-66.1
440	58-633
441	4-96.1, n.
442	40.1-28.9
443	29-144.6
444	16.1-69.33, 16.1-69.35
445	16.1-69.51:1
446	15.1-29.5
447	4-25
448	16.1-202.3
449	15.1-11.3
450	58-687
451	2.1-257
453	46.1-528, 46.1-550.2
454	46.1-2
455	46.1-103.1R
456	58-1140.1, 58-1160
457	15.1-131
458	15.1-670 to 15.1-673R, 15.1-741 to 15.1-753R
459	16.1-69.44, 37.1-89
460	46.1-50, 46.1-104.1 46.1-105.4
461	9-49, 9-51
462	20-61, 53-135.1
463	9-113.1
464	16.1-178, 16.1-181.1
465	16.1-69.48
466	10-184.1 to 10-185
467	2.1-340.1, 2.1-341.1, 2.1-343, 2.1-344, 2.1-341.1
468	15.1-84.1
469	32-8.2
470	15.1-491
471	19.2-45
472	30-28.01, 30-28.1, 30-28.2 to 30-28.4, 30-28.5R, 30-28.5:1, 30-28.7, 30-28.8:2 30-28.9:1 30-28.10R, 30-28.10:1
473	56-335
474	30-32
475	53-38
476	53-37.1
477	15.1-381
478	58-769.8
483	15.1-1232
484	9-7, 10-136, 36-108
485	58-381.1
486	58-14.1
487	6.1-63, 6.1-195.34
488	15.1-1411
489	58-441.2
490	9-68
491	22-29.6
492	9-139
493	38.1-65.1
495	38.1-381.6
496	4-25, 4-33, 4-38
497	15.1-561, 15.1-561.1
498	19.2-311
499	4-80.2
500	46.1-105.4
501	46.1-321
502	8-47
503	18.2-31, 18.2-32
504	18.2-390, 18.2-391
505	46.1-31 to 46.1-31.2, 46.1-33R, 46.1-33.1, 46.1-413, 46.1-494R
506	18.2-287.1
507	56-248.1
508	56-338.85 to 56-338.92
510	36-19, 36-49.1
511	51-111.60
512	51.1-239
515	18.2-105, 18.2-105.1, 19.2-81
516	63.1-51
517	53-19.19
518	58-847
519	58-476.9
521	58-266.1
522	2.1-326.2
523	58-412
525	51-151
526	18.2-85
527	58-847
528	58-151.013
529	58-730.4, 58-753.4
530	58-715, 58-716, 58-753.1
531	6.1-375
532	58-806
533	2.1-196.1
534	58-744
535	6.1-195.35
536	8.9-402, 8.9-403
537	51-111.46
538	51-111.55 51-151, 51-168
539	51-111.41:1
540	51-111.41:4, 51-111.49
541	51-111.57, 51-111.62, 51-111.67, 51-153, 51-170
542	51-111.60
543	58-760.1
544	15.1-19.2
545	51-111.24,

Acts 1976 Chapter	Code 1950 Section
	51-111.52:1R, 51-111.52:4
546	55-26.1
547	58-837
548	57-39.8 to 57-39.13, 57-39.17 to 57-39.18
549	63.1-273
550	63.1-287
551	51-111.67:2
552	19.2-54, 19.2-57
553	19.2-159, 19.2-163
554	6.1-39.1, 6.1-39.2, 6.1-94
555	58-730.3
556	56-257.1
557	28.1-109.1
558	58-54.1
559	8-81.3, 14.1-103, 14.1-134, 38.1-706, 47-1, 47-2
560	58-829.1:1
561	17-60
562	38.1-3, 38.1-183.2, 38.1-404, 38.1-408, 38.1-443
563	58-1122
564	56-304.5
565	58-587.1, 58-617.2
566	15.1-1357
567	35-61, n., 35-62, n., 35-62.1, n., 35-63, n., 35-64.1, n., 35-64.2, n., 35-64.3, n., 35-64.4, n., 35-64.5, 35-64.6, n., 58-685.11, 58-685.12, 58-685.23, 58-766.2R, 58-829.3, 58-829.4R, 58-851
568	58-759.1, 58-759.2
569	18.2-341
570	19.2-81
571	9-144
572	19.2-390
574	29-202
576	32-21.6:1
577	18.2-104.1, 19.2-270.1
578	15.1-1032.1, n.
579	10-145.9, 62.1-3
580	2.1-121
581	51-111.31
582	15.1-505, 15.1-901
583	15.1-21
585	21-118
586	15.1-966
587	15.1-978
588	15.1-1165
589	16.1-222 to 16.1-225
590	14.1-46.01
591	60.1-26
592	18.2-335
593	2.1-348, 2.1-351, 2.1-353.1, 2.1-354, 2.1-358
594	44-146.21
595	14.1-73
596	29-184, 35-42.1
597	2.1-377 to 2.1-386
598	45.1-5, 45.1-21, 45.1-42
601	22-230.3
602	22-19.01, 30-19.02
603	65.1-136, 65.1-137
604	14.1-17.1
605	19.2-368.1 to 19.2-368.18
607	40.1-22, 40.1-22.1, 40.1-49.1R, 40.1-49.2, 40.1-51.1, 40.1-51.2, 40.1-51.4:1, 40.1-51.4:2
608	54-102.1 to 54-102.3R, 54-102.14R, 54-102.17, 54-775.2 to 54-775.4R, 54-775.7R, 54-864, 54-923 to 54-939, 54-941 to 54-946, 54-948
610	58-685.11, 58-685.12 to 58-685.13:1, 58-685.20
611	8-654.8 to 8-654.10, 8-911 to 8-922, 38.1-389.2
612	18.2-271.1, 46.1-417, 46.1-421
613	15.1-37.9
614	18.2-248, 18.2-250, 18.2-255, 54-524.2, 54-524.8, 54-524.11 to 54-524.13, 54-524.15, 54-524.17, 54-524.19, 54-524.21, 54-524.22:1, 54-524.23, 54-524.26, 54-524.27, 54-524.31, 54-524.34R, 54-524.34:1, 54-524.37, 54-524.39 to 54-524.41:2 54-524.44, 54-524.47, 54-524.48, 54-524.65, 54-524.67, 54-524.68, 54-524.72R, 54-524.73R, 54-524.84:1, 54-524.84:4, 54-524.84:6, 54-524.84:8, 54-524.84:10, 54-524.84:12, 54-524.84:13, 54-524.109:1
615	8-475, 8-476, 8-489, 19.2-321 to 19.2-323
616	24.1-4.2, 24.1-10, 24.1-14.1, 24.1-17, 24.1-23, 24.1-26.1, 24.1-35.1R, 24.1-36, 24.1-37, 24.1-46, 24.1-49, 24.1-59, 24.1-76, 24.1-88, 24.1-96.1, 24.1-105, 24.1-110, 24.1-114, 24.1-132.1, 24.1-135, 24.1-150, 24.1-165 to 24.1-167, 23.1-182, 24.1-187, 24.1-191, 24.1-196 to 24.1-198, 24.1-203, 24.1-227, 24.1-257, 24.1-258, 24.1-272, 24.1-277
617	15.1-239
618	53-165
619	15.1-458
620	19.2-8
621	62.1-44.15
622	10-17.23
623	32-6.4
624	32-9.1
625	19.2-393 to 19.2-397
626	62.1-44.18:1, 62.1-44.18:2
627	3.1-198, 3.1-221, 3.1-227, 3.1-232R, 3.1-233, 32-428 to 32-438
628	32-48
630	17-74 to 17-76
636	38.1-22.1, 38.1-279.31, 38.1-389.4
637	21-291.2
638	36-103
640	2.1-342
641	18.2-242.1
642	15.1-430, 15.1-431, 15.1-448, 15.1-450, 15.1-489, 15.1-494
643	54-524.109:9 to 54-524.109:18
644	54-524.93
645	59.1-21.14
646	15.1-1031
647	13.1-93.1
648	29-121, n.
649	63.1-195
650	15.1-44.1, 15.1-464
651	54-1.14, 54-869 to 54-871R
652	32-414.4:1, 32-414.4:2
653	21-89.5
654	51-111.30, 51-111.34, 51-111.37, 51-111.67:4, 51-156, 51-163, 51-170
655	65.1-56
656	13.1-514, 13.1-514.1

Acts 1976 Chapter	Code 1950 Section
657	32-424, 32-424.1
658	6.1-2.1, 6.1-13, 6.1-16, 6.1-55, n., 6.1-55.1, 6.1-56, 6.1-62, 6.1-69, 6.1-84, 6.1-86 to 6.1-88, 6.1-90, 6.1-92 to 6.1-94, 6.1-114, 6.1-125, 6.1-195.44, 6.1-195.47, 6.1-195.48, 6.1-195.65, 6.1-195.71, 6.1-213.1, 6.1-220, 6.1-221, 6.1-223.1, 6.1-226.7, 6.1-254, 6.1-298, 6.1-309
659	8-441, 8-441.3, 8-442, 20-78.1
660	29-68, 29-69 to 29-74, 29-163.1, 29-205 to 29-207, 29-209
661	62.1-44.19
662	15.1-1041.1
663	58-46-3
664	14.1-46
665	2.1-328.1
666	58-441.6
667	14.1-33, 14.1-38R, 16.1-69.44, 16.1-69.45, 16.1-69.47, 16.1-69.49
668	58-12.43 to 58-12.56
671	37.1-1, 37.1-2, 37.1-6, 37.1-9, 37.1-10, 37.1-13, 37.1-17, 37.1-19, 37.1-20.1 to 37.1-23, 37.1-24, 37.1-24.1R 37.1-29 to 37-1-34.1 37.1-35R, 37.1-36, 37.1-38, 37.1-38.1 to 37.1-38.4R, 37.1-39, 37.1-40, 37.1-42 to 37.1-43, 37.1-45R, 37.1-46R, 37.1-48, 37.1-54.1 to 37.1-57R, 37.1-58, 37.1-59R 37.1-60R, 37.1-61, 37.1-62R, 37.1-63 to 37.1-65, 37.1-67.1 to 37.1-68, 37.1-70 to 37.1-73, 37.1-76, 37.1-78, 37.1-78.1, 37.1-84.1, 37.1-84.2, 37.1-88 to 37.1-91, 37.1-97, 37.1-98, 37-1-99, 37.1-102R, 37.1-103 to 37.1-104.1, 37.1-106, 37.1-107, 37.1-109, 37.1-110, 37.1-117, 37.1-118, 37.1-120, 37.1-121, 37.1-123, 37.1-125, 37.1-126, 37.1-127R, 38.1-128R, 37.1-128.01 to 38.1-132, 37.1-134 to 37.1-138, 38.1-140R, 37.1-141, 37.1-148, 37.1-152, 38.1-153, 37.1-155, 38.1-171.1, 37.1-179 to 37.1-181, 37.1-183.1 to 37-1-189, 37.1-190 to 37.1-193R, 37.1-194, 37.1-195, 38.1-197 to 37.1-199
672	14.1-51.1
673	14.1-52
674	14.1-63
675	58-847, 58-963
676	58-760, 58-786, 58-787, 58-790
677	19.2-181
678	51-111.10, 51-161, 51-163
679	58-903
680	22-223, 22-228, 38.1-96, 58-441.48
681	22-1.1, 22-218, 22-218R, 22-218.2R, 22-220, 22-223, 22-275.1, 22-275.3, 22-275.6, 22-275.13, 22-275.18
682	22-275.26
683	15.1-49.1
684	21-118, 21-118.4
685	55-122, 55-123, 55-125 to 55-127, 55-129 to 55-132, 55-134 to 55-135, 55-137.1, 55-137.2
686	58-512.1
687	58-514.2
688	14.1-11.1
689	14.1-53
690	58-1152.1
691	18.2-271.1, 46.1-417, 46.1-421
692	22-275.4, 22-275.4:1, 22-275.11:1
693	4-15.1
694	58-151.013
695	4-40, 4-108
696	4-26, 4-37, 4-114
697	2.1-153
698	4-31, 4-37
699	51-111.10
700	4-98.2
701	56-234.3
702	4-2, 4-37
703	4-25
704	2.1-38.2
705	14.1-73.2
706	9-111
707	46.1-351.1
708	60.1-22.1, 60.1-47, 60.1-51.1, 60.1-52, 60.1-52.5, 60.1-61, 60.1-62, 60.1-74, 60.1-80
709	2.1-342, 2.1-344, 2.1-346
710	62.1-104.1, 62.1-105, 62.1-106
711	58-778.1
712	58-441.3
713	22-1.1, 22-218, 22-218.2R, 22-220, 22-223, 22-275.1, 22-275.3, 22-275.6, 22-275.13, 22-275.18
714	22-19.1, n.
715	2.1-118
716	58-834.1, 58-834.2
717	58-764, 58-776, 58-776.1, 58-776.5 to 58-776.7R, 58-778, 58-778.1, 58-780R, 58-780.1R, 58-782 to 58-784R, 58-784.2R, 58-784.3, 58-784.4R, 58-784.5, 58-792, 58-792.1 to 58-792.5R, 58-795, 58-795.1R
718	14.1-46
719	58-266.1, 58-355R, 58-356, 58-357, 58-359, 58-360, 58-361R, 58-361.1, 58-362R, 58-362.1R, 58-365 to 58-369.1R, 58-397 to 58-397.2R
720	58-151.067, 58-151.090
723	22-41.2
724	33.1-90.2
725	2.1-41.1
726	2.1-121, 2.1-122, 2.1-123R
728	2.1-177, 2.1-192, 58-28
729	2.1-51.7, 2.1-51.9, 2.1-51.13 to 2.1-51.15
730	2.1-51.8R, 2.1-51.8:1
731	2.1-39.1
732	2.1-51.7, 2.1-51.9, 2.1-51.16 to 2.1-51.18
733	2.1-51.7, 2.1-51.9, 2.1-51.19 to 2.1-51.21
734	2.1-51.7, 2.1-51.9, 2.1-51.22 to 2.1-51.24
735	14.1-18.2, 30-19.4
736	40.1-28.10
737	9-111.2, 15.1-36.1R, 54-729.1R, 54-729.27 to 54-729.34
738	56-247.1
739	37.1-217 to 37.1-224
740	19.2-81.2, 53-19.18:1

Acts 1976 Chapter	Code 1950 Section
741	2.1-64.23
742	56-249.2
743	2.1-51.7, 2.1-51.9, 2.1-51.11, 2.1-51.25 to 2.1-51.28
744	46.1-343
746	2.1-9R, 2.1-10R, 30-28.20R, 33.1-17R, 42-1-20 to 42-1-28R, 42.1-29 to 42.1-29.2R, 42.1-76 to 42.1-90
748	15.1-503.3
750	4-98.10
752	19.2-81.1
753	19.2-74
754	46.1-225
756	15.1-136.2, 53-19.18:1
757	10-197 to 10-213, 18.2-140
758	54-388, 54-396
759	2.1-243.1
760	2.1-52 to 2.1-63.03R, 2.1-63.1 to 2.1-63.4R, 2.1-63.4:2 to 2.1-63.8R, 2.1-109.1 to 2.1-109.5R, 2.1-387 to 3-1-419, 15.1-1402, 15.1-1406, 15.1-1411, 15.1-1424 to 15.1-1426, 15.1-1441, 15.1-1502 to 15.1-1504
761	2.1-114R, 2.1-114.2 to 2.1-114.8, 2.1-115R
762	15.1-160, 15.1-162
763	56-237, 56-237.1
764	58-441.6
765	8-629.2
766	15.1-1032.1
767	2.1-51.9, 9-120 to 9-124R, 32-365 to 32-378.4R, 37.1-24.1R, 37.1-203 to 37.1-216
768	4-98.2, 4-98.10
769	15.1-134
770	58-441.5:1, 58-441.6, 58-441.52
771	9-107R, 9-107.1, 9-108R, 9-108.1, 9-109, 9-109.4, 9-209.5, 9-111.3 to 9-111.14, 19-2-388 to 19.2-390
772	15.1-75.1, 15.1-136.2, 15.1-136.3, 15.1-136.4R, 15.1-136.4:1, 15.1-136.5R, 15.1-136.5:1, 15.1-136.6R, 15.1-136.6:1, 27-39, 27-40.1, 27-40.1:1, 51-119, 51-122 to 51-122.2, 65.1-47.1
773	33.1-346, 33.1-346.1
774	3.1-382.1
775	2.1-420, 2.1-421
777	58-519
778	58-514.2:1, 58-580, 58-603
781	58-151.013, 58-151.014:1

ACTS 1977

Acts 1977 Chapter	Code 1950 Section
1	24.1-40.3:1
2	8.01-671
3	54-740
4	17-119.1:1, 17-119.1:2
5	16.1-69.6, 16.1-69.6:1
6	19.2-159.1
7	62.1-45, 62.1-46, 62.1-47, 62.1-51, 62.1-53, 62.1-55, 62.1-57 to 62.1-59, 62.1-62
8	8.01-427.1
9	46.1-184
10	15.1-475
13	28.1-128
15	62.1-13.6, 62.1-13.7
18	37.1-205, 37.1-207
20	29-144.6
21	3.1-692, 3.1-722.4
25	16.1-69.16
26	62.1-104, 62.1-106, 62.1-107, 62.1-109, 62.1-111
27	37.1-220
28	15.1-51
30	24.1-1, 24.1-36
31	10-17.16
32	62.1-44.12, 62.1-44.15
33	28.1-3.1
34	53-252
35	28.1-167
36	63.1-42R, 63.1-43, 63.1-43.1
37	63.1-36
38	62.1-44.85, 62.1-44.87, 62.1-44.90, 62.1-44.91, 62.1-44.93, 62.1-44.95 to 62.1-44.100, 62.1-44.106
39	10-206
40	21-112.1, 21-112.2, 21-112.5, 21-112.12, 21-112.20
46	6.1-195.45
47	15.1-19.2
48	58-760.1
49	58-764.1
50	10-145.10
51	38.1-320, 38.1-322
52	57-35.2
53	57-39.10
54	57-35.3
55	38.1-283, 38.1-284
56	58-833
57	3.1-22.6 to 3.1-22.12
58	38.1-691, 38.1-703
59	56-247.1
60	20-99
63	18.2-77
65	15.1-431
66	15.1-295, 15.1-296
67	63.1-211.1
69	54-765.1 to 54-765.9, 54-767 to 54-769R
70	14.1-105.1
71	20-79
72	46.1-267
73	3.1-679
74	44-43 to 44-45, 44-46R, 44-53
76	55-47.1
77	56-338.41
78	38.1-381
79	15.1-131, 23-232 to 23-238
80	14.1-52
81	46.1-416.1
82	63.1-54.2
83	63.1-133.1
84	22-202R
85	22-300
86	54-524.22:1
87	23-7.1
88	37.1-196, 37.1-199
89	37.1-179
90	37.1-194
91	55-79.95
92	36-108
93	1-13.3:1
94	16.1-69.39:1
95	16.1-70.1
96	26-37
97	19.2-81
98	54-91.1
99	58-1141, 58-1142, 58-1145, 58-1146, 58-1152.1
100	36-124
101	47-1
102	20-14
103	18.2-191
104	2.1-114.1
105	63.1-172
106	53-290.1, 53-290.2, 53-290.5, 53-290.7 to 53-290.10
107	18.2-107, 18.2-472

Acts 1977 Chapter	Code 1950 Section
108	19.2-8
109	19.2-54, 19.2-57
110	6.1-61
111	13.1-514
112	38.1-380.1, 38.1-380.2, 46.1-497.1
113	65.1-103
114	55-297
116	15.1-19.3
120	17-47.1
123	13.1-36
124	15.1-506.1
125	56-249.3 to 56-249.5
126	15.1-50, 63.1-185
127	54-273, 54-275.2
134	32-31.4, n.
135	32-353.32, 32-353.33
136	36-19
137	15.1-1348
138	6.1-195.29
139	14.1-3.1
140	6.1-195.34
141	55-66.4
142	17-70.1
143	18.2-351
144	64.1-121
145	42.1-71
146	64.1-66.1
147	55-41
148	64.1-123.1
149	21-89.3
150	33.1-12
151	55-59
152	26-45R
153	58-60
154	38.1-781
155	32-300
156	1-13.1:1
157	22-106
158	32-220
159	32-238.1
160	6.1-60
161	54-388, 54-394, 54-396
162	23-9.2:4
163	46.1-547, 46.1-547.1, 46.1-550.1, 46.1-550.2, 46.1-550.4
164	46.1-105.7
165	11-2.3
166	46.1-65
167	29-52.2, 46.1-149.1
168	23-91.35
169	16.1-115, 16.1-118, 16.1-118.1
172	15.1-494
174	38.1-390, 38.1-390.1, 38.1-410.1
175	33.1-46.3
177	15.1-491
178	18.2-188
179	9-117, 9-118
180	22-286R
181	38.1-381.6
182	53-213
183	21-121.5
184	63.1-54.1
185	15.1-158.1, n.
186	3.1-14
187	53-19.18
188	38.1-381.7
189	37.1-98
190	6.1-58.2
191	37.1-197
192	8.01-42
193	54-524.2
194	18.2-56.1
195	17-126.3
196	46.1-167.3
197	17-120
198	19.2-34
200	15.1-686.3
202	8.01-581.3, 8.01-581.12:1
203	2.1-349
204	22-199
205	9-6.14:7
206	33.1-338
207	46.1-181.4R, 46.1-181.4:1
208	8.01-413
209	27-34.2:1
210	58-512.1, 58-760
211	58-834.1, n., 58-834.2, n.
212	58-476, 58-476.1
213	58-769.8
214	33.1-72
215	19.2-368.4 to 19.2-368.10, 19.2-368.12, 19.2-368.13
216	19.2-245
217	15.1-108
218	15.1-136.2
219	33.1-369
220	22-249
221	33.1-75.1
222	20-109
223	19.2-358
225	15.1-239
226	56-405.2, 56-405.3, 56-406R
227	15.1-548
228	15.1-446.1, 15.1-447
230	8.01-115
231	15.1-791
233	19.2-76.2
236	46.1-97
237	17-9
238	15.1-1374
239	4-96.1, n.
240	18.2-271.1
241	63.1-87, 63.1-106
242	2.1-206.1
243	58-151.080
244	58-151.067
245	58-685.29:1, 58-685.35R
246	58-151.074
247	58-441.6
248	58-494
249	64.1-92
250	58-151.31
251	17-95.1
252	46.1-1
253	34-26
254	55-66.4:1
255	38.1-367.1, 38.1-387.1
256	26-46.1
257	6.1-93
258	46.1-65.1
259	46.1-196
260	56.1-162
261	56-234.3, 56-234.4
262	28.1-170
263	62.1-44.23, 62.1-44.31, 62.1-44.32
264	38.1-443.1
265	58-76.2
267	46.1-176
268	58-985
269	15.1-262
271	21.291.2
276	21-118
277	15.1-1031.1 to 15.1-1031.3
278	4-79
279	2.1-383
280	4-2
281	23-38.55, 23-38.56, 23-38.57R, 23-38.58, 23-38.59
282	17-60
283	20-121.02
284	46.1-248
285	18.2-361
286	60.1-58
287	19.2-135
288	19.2-6
289	19.2-56
290	14.1-155.2
291	62.1-44.10, 62.1-44.26
292	2.1-94, n.
293	1-13.39:1
294	43-1
295	18.2-389
296	23-9.5, 23-14,

Acts 1977 Chapter	Code 1950 Section
	23-31, 23-164.1, 23-164.2, 23-164.4, 23-164.6, 23-164.7, 23-164.9, 23-164.10
297	58-151.013, 58-151.032
298	2.1-415R, 10-21.13
299	3.1-726
300	15.1-90.1
301	40.1-51.8
302	54-524.31, 54-524.59, 54-524.65, 54-524.67, 54-524.84:4, 54-524.84.6, 54-524.84.8, 54-524.84:10, 54-524.84:12, 54-524.84:13
303	21-120
304	18.2-64.1
305	24.1-72.10 to 24.1-72.15
306	15.1-567
307	15.1-1054
308	40.1-29
309	55-154
310	62.1-44.108 to 62.1-44.112
311	27-5.1
312	45.1-180, 45.1-180.2 to 45.1-180.4, 45.1-181, 45.1-182R, 45.1-182.1, 45.1-183, 45.1-184, 45.1-184.1, 45.1-184.2, 45.1-185, 45.1-186R, 45.1-186.1, 45.1-189R, 45.1-193R, 45.1-193.1, 45.1-195, 45.1-197, 45.1-197.2
313	38.1-280.1, 38.1-295R, 38.1-368, 38.1-700.1
314	55-59
315	44-41.1
316	22-5
317	38.1-44, 38.1-45, 38.1-48 to 38.1-48.10
318	38.1-314.6, 38.1-314.13, 38.1-320, 38.1-324, 38.1-325, 38.1-326R
319	23-9.5, 23-14, 23-31, 23-164.1, 23-164.2, 23-164.4, 23-164.6, 23-164.7, 23-164.9, 23-164.10
320	58-266.1
321	38.1-174
322	38.1-73R, 38.1-88, 38.1-89, 38.1-90, 38.1-95, 38.1-95.1, 38.1-97, 38.1-695, 38.1-695.1, 38.1-703
323	58-769.10
324	53-94.1
325	38.1-342.1
326	15.1-134, 15.1-649, 15.1-775, 18.2-85, 27-1, 27-15.1, 27-23.1, 27-39 to 27-46, 27-49, 37.1-148, 44-149, 44-152, 44-156, 44-157, 46.1-248, 46.1-250.1, 51-111.37, 65.1-4, 65.1-4.1
327	38.1-389.3
328	18.2-111.1
329	6.1-118.1, 18.2-181
330	60.1-12, 60.1-13, 60.1-14, 60.1-21, 60.1-26, 60.1-47, 60.1-48.1, 60.1-51.1, 60.1-52.3, 60.1-52.4R, 60.1-52.4:1, 60.1-52.5R, 60.1-52.5:1, 60.1-75, 60.1-80, 60.1-81, 60.1-82, 60.1-83, 60.1-84, 60.1-86.1, 60.1-89.1, 60.1-89.2, 60.1-100
331	52-8.2
332	19.2-45
333	64.1-87.1
334	27-30
335	19.2-68
336	56-235, 56-235.2, 56-235.3, 56-245
337	58-12.59
338	2.1-253, n., 2.1-271, n.
339	53-304.9, 53-304.10
340	46.1-40.1
341	23-9.2:1
342	23-38.32, 23-38.33, 23-38.36, 23-38.38
343	2.1-64.23
344	19.2-308.1, 53-251
345	65.1-99, 65.1-129, 65.1-134, 65.1-146 to 65.1-152
346	32-6.1 to 32-6.3R, 37.1-179, 37.1-183.1
347	2.1-554 to 2.1-559
349	54-175.2
351	37.1-199
352	2.1-236, n.
354	53-23
355	37.1-67.6
356	13.1-531, 13.1-534
357	9-108.1
358	22-10.13
359	54-295.2
360	16.1-225
361	58-12.60, 58-12.61
362	58-12.62
363	58-12.63
364	58-12.64
365	58-12.65, 58-12.66
366	23-7.3
367	58-12.67
368	58-12.68
369	58-12.69
370	58-12.63
371	58-12.70
372	58-12.71
373	58-12.72
374	58-12.73
375	58-12.74
376	9-111.2, 54-729.27 to 54-729.30
377	9-6.14:4, 10-22 to 10-31R, 18.2-287.1, 29-23.1R, 29-36.1R, 29-50R, 29-62, 29-65, 29-108.1, 29-114.2, 29-117, 29-121, n., 29-138, 29-140, 29-144.5, 29-144.6, 29-150.1R, 29-154, 29-155.1, 29-158, 29-159 to 29-160R, 29-169R, 29-263.2, 29-230 to 29-234
378	58-12.75
379	58-12.76
380	65.1-99
381	9-6.14:4, 15.1-1232 to 15.1-1232.2
382	43-32, 46.1-73
383	46.1-265
384	58-12.77
385	16.1-69.48
386	53-61
387	28.1-82
388	46.1-111
389	22-67.2
391	14.1-46, 14.1-46.01
392	29-52
393	22-276.1, 22-276.3

Acts 1977 Chapter	Code 1950 Section
394	25-46.8
395	3.1-733, 3.1-736 to 3.1-738.1
396	3.1-660, 3.1-684.16, 3.1-763.10, 3.1-792, 58-151.071, 58-151.077, 58-151.093, 58-151.13, 58-151.22, 58-151.23, 58-151.26, 58-151.38, 58-151.40, 58-177, 58-226, 58-425, 58-435, 58-441, 58-441.26, 58-441.27, 58-685.30, 58-838.14, 58-838.15, 58-1160, 58-1162
397	42.1-60, 42.1-62 to 42.1-66, 42.1-67 to 42.1-69R, 42.1-70
398	58-55.1
399	56-457.8
400	53-128.8, 53-128.9 to 53-128.15
401	57-63, 57-69
402	46.1-351.1, 46.1-351.2
403	15.1-785.1, n.
404	5.1-8
408	46.1-387.9:2
409	18.2-248
410	32-63.2
411	46.1-202.1
412	32-31.22
413	2.1-51.21, 23-9.5, 23-214 to 23-215, 23-223, 23-224, 23-226, 23-227
414	38.1-178.1, 38.1-178.1:1 to 38.1-178.1:7, 38.1-178.2, 38.1-178.3:1, 38.1-178.7, 38.1-178.8, 38.1-178.11 to 38.1-178.19
415	38.1-279.33
416	14.1-46, 14.1-46.01
417	23-7
418	58-61, 58-64
419	58-778
422	8.01-581.12:2
423	36-97, 36-99, 36-105, 36-114 to 36-116
424	10-150.1 to 10-150.10
426	38.1-311.1
427	55-248.3 to 55-248.5, 55-248.6:1, 55-248.7, 55-248.9, 55-248.11, 55-248.11:1, 55-248.21:1, 55-248.29, 55-248.34, 55-248.37
428	55-79.54, 55-79.58:1, 55-79.83, 55-79.84:1, 55-79.89, 55-79.90, 55-199
429	51-111.67:3
430	2.1-409, 2.1-410, 2.1-416 to 2.1-419R
431	36-55.31:1
432	40.1-28.9
433	30-19.8
434	65.1-106.1
435	13.1-224
436	56-237.2
437	32-120.2
438	40.1-11.1
439	4-25, 4-78
440	3.1-398
441	54-276.9
442	15.1-192 to 15.1-194
443	56-366.3
444	22-330.17, 22-330.22, 22-330.23, 22-330.25 to 22-330.29, 22-330.34
445	60.1-34, 60.1-52, 60.1-52.2, 60.1-60, 60.1-64, 60.1-71, 60.1-74, 60.1-74.1, 60.1-88, 60.1-91, 60.1-94, 60.1-96, 60.1-126
446	2.1-43
447	2.1-42.1
449	8.01-673, 14.1-112, 14.1-120, 58-71, 58-73, 58-74R
450	9-6.14:7, 9-6.14:9
451	8.01-345, 8.01-350R
452	3.1-610.22 to 3.1-610.28
453	58-760.1
454	8.01-511, 8.01-514
456	58-760.1
457	8.01-217
458	8.01-341, 8.01-341.1
459	9-6.14:9
460	8.01-52
462	8.01-606
463	14.1-112
464	55-248.13:1
465	19.2-360
466	6.1-61
467	56-304.2
468	45.1-271
469	22-330.16:1
470	33.1-233
471	32-428.1, 32-429, 32-430, 32-432, 32-433, 32-435R, 32-435.1 to 32-437
472	46.1-339.1
473	15.1-503.2, 15.1-503.3R
474	64.1-1
475	20-107
476	54-145.2
477	58-12.78
478	18.2-18, 18.2-31, 18.2-32
479	58-12.79
480	18.2-391.1
481	58-157
482	58-12.80, 58-12.81
483	14.1-189, 14.1-190, 19.2-278, 19.2-329
484	13.1-520
485	50-37.1, 50-37.2, 50-74
486	58-155.1
487	58-833.1
488	55-199
489	58-12.82
490	24.1-22, 24.1-41, 24.1-47, 24.1-48, 24.1-52, 24.1-72.1, 24.1-76, 24.1-133, 24.1-167, 24.1-183, 24.1-228, 24.1-229
491	30-28.1:1 to 30-28.4, 30-28.5:1, 30-28.6, 30-28.8:2R
492	17-110.1, 17-110.2, 18.2-10, 18.2-32, 19.2-264.2 to 19.2-264.5
493	14.1-5 to 14.1-5.3, 14.1-9.1
495	44-134.1
496	34-4, 34-4.1, 34-18, 34-19, 34-21, 34-26, 34-27
497	53-291
498	53-95R, 53-115R
499	53-296
500	27-83.1
501	42.1-77, 42.1-80, 42.1-82
503	63.1-110
504	58-441.6
505	2.1-8.1 to

Acts 1977 Chapter	Code 1950 Section
	2.1-8.8
506	23-2.1, 37.1-84.1:1, 53-19.15:1
507	58-978, 58-983
508	13.1-2.1
509	54-1.15
510	22-275.4:2
511	29-183 to 29-213R, 29-213.5 to 29-213.34
512	22-67.2
514	56-274
515	45.1-200
516	21-118, 21-118.4
517	14.1-7
518	54-168, 54-181, 54-195, 54-200.16
519	63.1-171.4
520	18.2-392
521	40.1-51.4:3
522	6.1-330.22R, 6.1-330.23
523	32-137
524	15.1-467
526	63.1-231, 63.1-232R
527	8.01-581.18
528	22-19.1, n.
529	38.1-50, 38.1-52, 38.1-53, 38.1-54, 38.1-55, 38.1-56, 38.1-56.1, 38.1-57.1
530	38.1-279.49:1
531	32-353.19, 32-353.32
533	58-712, 58-712.1
534	22-330.6:1
535	51-178
536	16.1-69.9
537	58-685.12, 58-685.13
538	63.1-251, 63.1-253, 63.1-264, 63.1-268, 63.1-286
539	8.9-402 to 8.9-406
540	53-63
542	2.1-41.2, 22-22
543	23-135.7:1 to 23-135.7:7
545	2.1-348
546	53-251
547	63.1-55.1 to 63.1-55.7
548	46.1-357
549	46.1-226
550	56-457.8:2, 56-457.9
551	14.1-143
552	46.1-357
553	18.2-55
554	15.1-66.1, n., 15.1-66.2R, 15.1-66.4
555	54-524.109:12, 54-524.109:14, 54-524.109:15, 54-524.109:17
556	63.1-236
557	15.1-27.1
558	18.2-258.1, 54-524.76R
559	16.1-139 to 16.1-217R, 16.1-226 to 16.1-329, 53-327.1, 53-329.1, 63.1-56, 63.1-195, 63.1-204, 63.1-206.1, 63.1-248.9, 63.1-248.12
560	2.1-549 to 2.1-553, 9-112R, 9-113R, 9-114R, 9-115R
561	58-16.4
562	63.1-55.8, 63.1-56
563	63.1-238.3
564	2.1-358
565	14.1-55, 14.1-56, 14.1-57, 14.1-58
566	15.1-430
567	63.1-195
568	54-276.7:1
569	63.1-196.2
570	53-251
571	63.1-56.1
572	9-113.1
573	58-404.2, n.
574	55-154.1
575	32-211.5 to 32-211.9, 32-211.12, 32-211.17
576	24.1-18
577	46.1-193
578	33.1-23.1 to 33.1-23.5, n., 33.1-24R, 33.1-24.1R, 33.1-28, 33.1-38R, 33.1-39, 33.1-40R, 33.1-41, 33.1-43, 33.1-44 to 33.1-46.1, 33.1-70R, 33.1-70.01, 33.1-70.1, 33.1-72, 33.1-73 to 33.1-75R, 33.1-75.2, 33.1-76 to 33.1-78.1R, 33.1-141, 58-730
579	54-864, 54-865, 54-949 to 54-956
580	59.1-79
581	56-306, 56-338.16, 56-338.36
583	55-169, 55-171 to 55-175, 55-180 to 55-183, 55-184R, 55-184.1, 55-185R, 55-186, 55-186.1, 55-189, 55-192, 55-193, 55-197, 55-200
584	15.1-8.1, 15.1-9.1, 15.1-9.1:1, 15.1-109, 15.1-286, 15.1-507, 15.1-558, 15.1-608, 15.1-643, 15.1-706, 15.1-822
585	14.1-122.1, 14.1-123, 16.1-69.40:1, 16.1-302, 18.2-8, 19.2-240, 19.2-241, 19.2-254.1, 19.2-258.1, 19.2-345, 19.2-353.2, 19.2-354, 46.1-1, 46.1-16.01, 46.1-178.01, 46.1-416.1, 46.1-423.3, 46.1-425
586	54-311.1, 54-311.2
587	46.1-44
588	2.1-521.1
589	59.1-21.20, 59.1-21.21R, 59.1-21.21:1, 59.1-21.22, 59.1-21.23 to 59.1-21.28
590	54-306.01
591	58-441.15
592	56-529, 56-530, n.
593	22-20
594	58-792.01
595	58-757.27, 58-757.29
596	2.1-130
597	9-65.1 to 9-65.14R, 23-239 to 23-253
598	3.1-776R, 3.1-796.39 to 3.1-796.57, 15.1-29.1R, 18.2-144, 18.2-397
600	53-19.26
601	9-65.2:1, n., 10-214
602	18.2-335
603	38.1-348.7
604	58-441.21:1
606	32-195.8, 38.1-348.7, 38.1-348.8, 38.1-360
607	32-195.8
608	36-124
609	10-199, 10-201, 10-203
611	58-55, 58-514.2:1

Acts 1977 Chapter	Code 1950 Section
612	58-151.013
613	2.1-414, 15.1-1411, 15.1-1412, 15.1-1424, 15.1-1502, 15.1-1504, 27-55, 27-56, 27-58 to 27-61, 27-64, 27-66R, 27-67, 27-68R, 27-70 to 27-70.2, 27-71R, 27-72, 27-73, 27-74 to 27-77R, 27-78 to 27-79.1, 27-79.3 to 27-79.5, 27-79.7, 27-80, 27-81, 27-83, 27-85 to 27-85.2, 36-55.27, 36-55.28, 36-55.51, 36-71, 36-73 to 36-77, 36-79 to 36-82, 36-84, 36-85, 36-97 to 36-99.1, 36-100, 36-102, 36-104, 36-105, 36-107, 36-108, 36-111, 36-113, 36-116, n., 36-118, 36-120 to 36-123R, 36-124, n., 36-125 to 36-130R, 36-131 to 36-139, 38.1-44
616	4-40, 4-108, 10-201.1, 10-206, 58-404.02
617	8-1 to 8-922R, 8.01-1 to 8.01-688
618	16.1-301
619	15.1-1374, 15.1-1375
620	2.1-257, n., 32-40.2, 51-111.5, 51-111.7, 51-111.10, 51-111.16, 51-111.18, 51-111.22:2, 51-111.24, 51-111.31, 51-111.37, 51-111.41:4, 51-111.52:4, 51-111.52:5, 51-111.53, 51-111.55, 51-111.58:1, 51-111.60:1, 51-111.67:2, 51-111.67:3, 51-111.67:4, 51-150, 51-163, 51-167, 51-168, 51-173, 65.1-47.1
621	8.01-66.1
623	14.1-53, 14.1-64, 15.1-50.1, 15.1-821
624	2.1-223.5R, 2.1-223.6, 2.1-543.1, 9-6.14:5, 11-2.01, 11-20, 11-23, 12.1-39, 12.1-42R, 14.1-69.1, 14.1-112 to 14.1-112.2, 14.1-113.1, 14.1-133.1, 14.1-178.1, 14.1-195.1 to 14.1-195.6, 15.1-80, 15.1-1360, 16.1-76, 16.1-77.1, 16.1-77.2, 16.1-88.01, 16.1-88.02, 16.1-91.1 to 16.1-92, 16.1-98, 16.1-106, 17-123, 17-123.1, 18.2-121.1, 18.2-216.1, 18.2-324.1, 18.2-504.1, 19.2-260, 19.2-264.1, 19.2-265.1, 19.2-267, 19.2-268.1, 19.2-269.1, 19.2-271.1, 19.2-271.2, 20-37.2R, 20-61.2, 20-96, 20-98R, 25-46.4:2R, 29-130.2, 41.1-16, 54-729.15, 55-155, 55-232, 55-298 to 55-335, 56-469, 56-474R, 58-1014, 58-1015R, 58-1130, 63.1-88.1, 64.1-30, 64.1-34, 64.1-89, 64.1-145, 65.1-98
625	23-8.2, 23-8.3
626	9-108.1, 9-111.3, 9-111.10, 9-111.12, 19.2-389
627	16.1-273, n.
628	56-338.85, n., 56-419.2
629	9-6.23
630	15.1-1032.1
631	56-67.1
632	46.1-343
633	54-524.77R, 54-524.77:1
634	63.1-55, 63.1-55.8, 63.1-56, 63.1-56.2
635	59.1-196 to 59.1-207
636	15.1-18
637	18.2-266
638	18.2-268, 18.2-269
639	32-137.1, 54-317.2R, 54-317.3 to 54-317.5, 54-321.3 to 54-321.8
640	9-16 to 9-17, 9-18R, 9-19, 9-20R, 9-21R, 9-30, 9-37, 9-44.1, 9-44.2, 54-1.4, 54-1.5R, 54-1.6R, 54-1.7 to 54-1.10, 54-1.12, 54-114, 54-115.1R, 54-122R, 54-124 to 54-127, 54-129, 54-131, 54-133, 54-144, 54-860R, 54-861, 54-862R, 54-863R, 54-864, 54-865, 63.1-299 to 63.1 308
641	15.1-136.2
642	16.1-330
643	53-334
644	46.1-342
645	63.1-56, 63.1-195, 63.1-207, 63.1-207.1
647	9-6.14:3
648	15.1-486.2
649	59.1-208 to 59.1-215
655	46.1-315.2, 46.1-317.1
656	2.1-398
657	64.1-19, 64.1-19.1
658	58-151.050
659	18.2-268
660	55-59, 55-62, 55-63
662	63.1-251, 63.1-252, 63.1-256, 63.1-271, 63.1-273, 63.1-276, 63.1-277, 63.1-281, 63.1-285, 63.1-288
663	58-151.13
664	14.1-143
665	22-100.3:1, 22-100.7:1
666	46.1-3.02
667	10-17.107 to 10-17.112
668	23-14, 23-156 to 23-164R, 23-181.1 to 23-181.10R, 23-254 to 23-260, 63.1-85.4
669	54-154, 54-156, 54-157
670	23-91.26, 23-91.27
671	46.1-254.1
672	2.1-38, 2.1-51.18:1, 2.1-51.18:2, 2.1-82 to 2.1-109.07R, 2.1-109.6 to 2.1-109.8R, 2.1-235 to 2.1-294R, 2.1-422 to 2.1-521, 2.1-522 to 2.1-543, 2.1-544 to 2.1-548, 22-331 to 22-344.3R, 30-28.16, 32-31.1 to 32-31.8R
673	15.1-1374
674	37.1-89
675	19.2-392.1 to 19.2-392.4
676	23-9.15 to 23-9.21R, 23-261 to 23-264

Acts 1977 Chapter	Code 1950 Section
677	2.1-341 to 2.1-343, 2.1-345
678	33.1-185, 33.1-190
679	45.1-101.1, 45.1-101.2
680	32-154
681	15.1-237, 15.1-1506 to 15.1-1513, 25-46.2:2, 33.1-89.1, 58-769.6
682	19.2-305, 19.2-305.1
683	4-45, 4-46
684	15.1-836.1, 15.1-915.1

ACTS 1978

Acts 1978 Chapter	Code 1950 Section
1	51-111.47
2	16.1-69.6:1
3	9-96
4	32-195.11, 32-195.12, 32-195.12:1, 32-195.13, 32-195.14R, 32-195.28 to 32-195.30, 32-195.31R, 32-195.43, 32-195.44, 32-195.44:1, 32-195.45, 32-195.46R, 38.1-44 to 38.1-48.1, 38.1-48.8, 38.1-85, 38.1-85.1, 38.1-105 to 38.1-106, 38.1-305, 38.1-556, 38.1-556.1, 38.1-638.20, 38.1-638.23, 38.1-638.23:1, 58-487, 58-489, 58-497, 58-498, 58-502.1, 58-502.2
6	42.1-36
7	2.1-21
8	9-91
9	15.1-131.3
10	32-137
11	15.1-50, 37.1-195
12	46.1-201
13	46.1-19.1R
14	2.1-363, 6.1-26, 6.1-29, 6.1-31, 6.1-55.1, 6.1-88, 6.1-195.4, 6.1-195.44, 6.1-232, 6.1-245, 6.1-293, 6.1-299, 12.1-16
15	15.1-246, 15.1-249.1
16	32-195.3:1
17	46.1-229.3, n.
19	2.1-116.1 to 2.1-116.9
20	38.1-25, 38.1-86, 38.1-89, 38.1-94, 38.1-95, 38.1-96, 38.1-97, 38.1-97.2
24	2.1-450.1
25	58-951
26	22-150
27	46.1-190, 46.1-205
28	54-729.29
29	46.1-154.3
32	2.1-51.9, 2.1-51.24
34	54-83.1:7, 54-83.1:8, 54-83.1:09, 54-83.1:9R, 54-83.1:10
35	56-278, 56-338.9R, 56-338.27R, 56-338.73
36	46.1-1
37	15.1-50, 15.1-1231, 16.1-316, 16.1-317
40	16.1-77, 16.1-92
41	65.1-4
42	16.1-119, 16.1-120, 16.1-122
43	33.1-225.3
44	46.1-514.8
46	20-105.1
47	46.1-2
48	46.1-553.1
49	58-972
50	58-441.6
51	58-402
52	2.1-210
53	2.1-329
54	58-1117.4
56	38.1-381.8
58	15.1-238.1
59	43-34
60	44-146.16
61	17-126.4
62	58-627
63	19.2-63.1
64	19.2-297
65	8.01-229
66	8.01-506, 16.1-103
67	58-151.013, 58-151.032
68	58-55
69	4-98.10
70	2.1-20.1
71	58-744
72	10-90.23, 10-90.26, 58-838.5:2, 58-838.7:1
73	58-717
74	58-716
75	8.01-391, 8.4-406
82	58-441.6
83	2.1-33, 15.1-50, 32-279
84	2.1-51.27, 2.1-407 to 2.1-410, 2.1-560 to 2.1-563
85	28.1-128, 28.1-128.1
87	46.1-198.1
88	2.1-51.9:1
89	15.1-667
90	8.01-320
91	46.1-198.1
92	45.1-213, 45.1-220.1 to 45.1-220.5
94	45.1-101 to 45.1-101.2, 54-276.9
95	15.1-50.01, n.
96	2.1-121
103	2.1-335.1 to 2.1-335.3
104	55-248.21:1
105	22-5
106	15.1-51
107	28.1-170
108	4-32, 4-79
113	15.1-51
115	15.1-285
116	58-765 to 58-766.1R
117	14.1-3.1, 19.2-353.2
118	45.1-27, 45.1-35, 45.1-41, 45.1-42, 45.1-81, 45.1-84, 45.1-85, 45.1-88, 45.1-89, 45.1-102, 45.1-103, 45.1-105
119	45.1-106, 45.1-108, 45.1-115R, 45.1-115.1
120	45.1-2, 45.1-4, 45.1-5, 45.1-8, 45.1-10, 45.1-16, 45.1-19, 45.1-20, 45.1-29R, 45.1-33.6R, 45.1-54, 45.1-56 to 45.1-58, 45.1-65, 45.1-67, 45.1-104
121	2.1-557.1
122	19.2-368.5
123	18.2-438
124	8.01-654
125	4-21
126	15.1-162
128	30-28.14R
129	54-765.9
130	18.2-256
131	19.2-305.1
132	8.01-328.1
133	16.1-69.33
134	46.1-413, 46.1-415R

Acts 1978 Chapter	Code 1950 Section
135	22-56.1:1
136	2.1-536, 2.1-538
137	9-107.1
138	36-87, 36-88, 54-731, 54-731.1, 54-749
139	2.1-482
140	22-220
141	15.1-8.1
142	16.1-284
143	63.1-73.1
144	33.1-185
145	33.1-23.4
146	63.1-67.7
147	22-217.4
148	15.1-521R
149	27-17.1
150	15.1-505
151	18.2-250
152	56-274
153	4-98.2, 4-98.18
155	58-829.5
156	38.1-167
157	58-151.21, 58-151.22
158	58-151.013
159	58-151.03, 58-580
160	54-162.1
161	58-46
162	32-154
163	15.1-26.2
164	23-9.2:1
165	8.01-418.1
166	58-151.067
167	58-181R, 54-181.1, 54-200.16R, 54-200.16:1
168	46.1-555.10
170	23-50.15
171	37.1-207
172	7.1-41
173	55-65.1
174	4-27
175	32-31.17
176	8.01-341
177	18.2-248, 18.2-250, 53-291
178	58-829
179	63.1-17
180	63.1-55.1:1
181	58-441.3
182	46.1-252.1
183	51-178
184	58-151.042
185	46.1-104.1
187	3.1-145, 33.1-147, 33.1-151, 33.1-152, 33.1-161, 33.1-162
188	46.1-66
189	36-55.40
190	4-25, 4-33, 4-38
191	58-12.56
192	58-12.83
193	40.1-28.5
194	46.1-179.01
195	2.1-204, 14.1-85, 14.1-192, 14.1-195.5, 14.1-195.6, 19.2-139, 19.2-175, 19.2-278, 19.2-334
196	58-12.84
197	27-5.5
198	9-53, 9-55.1
199	29-144.3
200	16.1-69.35, 51-178
201	46.1-105.3, 46.1-105.4
202	46.1-252.1, 46.1-551
203	46.1-550.3
204	22-5
205	46.1-400
206	40.1-117, 40.1-118, 40.1-120
207	58-441.15
208	28.1-82, 28.1-83
209	8.01-345
210	19.2-368.4
211	46.1-382
212	58-12.85
213	37.1-36R, 37.1-42.2
214	56-405
215	22-275.11:1
216	58-12.86
217	53-206.2
218	29-63, 29-64
219	2.1-1, 3.1-1, 3.1-2, 3.1-8, 3.1-14 to 3.1-16, 3.1-18 to 3.1-18.3
220	46.1-472, 46.1-485
221	46.1-514.13
222	45.1-21
223	46.1-550.1
224	54-524.65
225	22-330.6:2
226	33.1-346, 33.1-346.1
227	53-258
228	58-12.87
230	14.1-195.1
231	34-4, 34-4.1
232	56-484.2
233	46.1-291
234	55-79.97
235	15.1-504
236	56-491
237	8.01-615
238	60.1-74
239	24.1-184, 24.1-186, 24.1-186.1, 24.1-187
240	29-213.5, 29-213.6, 29-213.7, 29-213.8, 29-213.10, 29-213.11, 29-213.16, 29-213.19, 29-213.20, 29-213.24, 29-213.25, 29-213.26, 29-213.27, 29-213.31
241	27-78.1
242	15.1-232
243	2.1-353.1
244	63.1-309 to 63.1-314
245	18.2-189
246	6.1-330.15
247	54-187, 54-200.6
248	54-166, 54-187, 54-189.1, 54-189.2R, 54-195
249	14.1-33, 14.1-34
250	58-769.6, 58-769.8
251	15.1-28.1
252	28.1-144.1
253	34-1
254	46.1-330, 46.1-335
255	2.1-425
256	63.1-236
257	9-111.1, 9-111.1:1
258	24.1-165
259	46.1-296
260	2.1-37.7
262	8.01-581.12:2
263	46.1-370
264	15.1-19.4, 15.1-19.5
265	15.1-114R
266	46.1-294.1
267	3.1-610.25 to 3.1-610.28
268	15.1-11.4, 36-99.1
269	60.1-48.1
270	9-149 to 9-152
271	2.1-373
272	29-213.19
273	29-213.31
274	29-213.11
275	46.1-315
276	15.1-1375

Acts 1978 Chapter	Code 1950 Section
277	15.1-867.2
278	28.1-170
279	15.1-490
280	18.2-315
281	64.1-123.1
282	46.1-3.02
283	15.1-475
284	8.9-402, 8.9-403, 8.9-405, 8.9-406
285	8.9-402
287	62.1-132, n.
288	46.1-514.21
289	46.1-110
290	55-79.97
291	63.1-56.3
292	54-872.6 to 54-872.15, 63.1-299 to 63.1-308R
293	63.1-56.1
294	46.1-15.2, 46.1-82 to 46.1-84, 46.1-89.1, 46.1-157.1, 46.1-341
295	63.1-289.2
296	63.1-58.1
297	36-55.39
298	15.1-1260
299	33.1-221
300	46.1-184
301	4-96.2, n.
302	46.1-315.2
303	29-144.6
304	24.1-165
305	33.1-242
306	53-60R, 53-60.1
307	46.1-45
308	32-353.20, 32-353.28
309	53-325
310	16.1-286
311	46.1-267
314	2.1-51.29
315	55-25.1
317	2.1-432.1
318	6.1-195.39
319	14.1-46.01
320	15.1-430, 15.1-491.1 to 15.1-491.6
321	8.01-511
322	22-276.1
323	55-352 to 55-354
324	6.1-29
325	56-265.4:1, 56-265.4:2
326	59.1-71
327	26-5.2
328	19.2-265.2
329	11-17, 11-18, 11-20, 11-23
330	24.1-105
331	29-114.2
332	55-79.73, 55-79.74
333	17-47.2
334	8.01-261
335	46.1-551
336	8.01-274
337	33.1-150
338	55-286.1, 64.1-189, 64.1-192
339	8.01-506.1
340	8.01-341
341	53-290.1
342	44-41.1
343	18.2-425.1
344	8.01-126
345	55-232.1
346	64.1-123
347	28.1-59, 28.1-60, 28.1-61, 28.1-65, 28.1-81.1R
348	46.1-555.1
349	38.1-348.7, 38.1-348.8
350	19.2-389
351	6.1-195.34
352	18.2-271.1
353	46.1-383
354	19.2-249
355	40.1-51.8
356	58-12.88
357	46.1-267
358	28.1-59
359	18.2-209
360	36-48.1, 36-52.3
361	53-291
362	19.2-157
363	55-79.75
364	18.2-195
365	19.2-160
366	64.1-94
367	8.01-376
368	19.2-346
369	28.1-167
370	54-872.4
371	40.1-28.10
372	40.1-5
373	9-140, 9-143
374	15.1-29.7
375	38.1-348.9
376	23-49.25, 23-49.28
377	20-62
378	55-248.31
379	19.2-250
380	15.1-559
381	24.1-258
382	15.1-778.1
383	16.1-299
384	44-117
385	58-769.13
386	22-10.3, 22-10.4, 22-10.5, 22-10.7, 22-10.8, 22-10.11, 22-275.5R, 22-275.6
388	30-64 to 30-73
389	15.1-211
392	56-245.2, 56-245.3
393	58-837
394	12.1-31
395	58-847
396	3.1-11, 3.1-18.1, 3.1-685, 3.1-723
397	13.1-514
399	3.1-22.8
400	8.01-350.1
401	32-137
402	46.1-41
403	8.01-114
404	16.1-69.47:1
405	8.01-676
406	8.01-581.8
407	15.1-1260
408	54-276.7
409	2.1-384.1
410	19.2-241
411	15.1-898
412	20-97
413	19.2-368.18
414	8.01-262
415	8.01-364
416	8.01-421
417	8.01-420
418	8.01-537
419	8.01-76
420	2.1-33
421	16.1-76
422	8.01-1.1
424	46.1-252.1
425	58-418.1
426	8.01-427.1R
427	58-12.89
428	9-111.2, 54-729.29
429	16.1-466
430	22-97
431	14.1-50
432	58-404.2, n.
433	58-266.4
434	4-56
435	14.1-46, 14.1-46.01
436	4-56, 4-72.1, 4-84
437	23-7.3
438	6.1-330.16, 6.1-330.24
439	15.1-466
440	15.1-466
441	38.1-52, 38.1-371.2, 38.1-381.5

Acts 1978 Chapter	Code 1950 Section
442	14.1-19.2
443	18.2-77
444	58-152, 58-219
445	16.1-296
446	4-31
447	54-1.11
448	20-88.28:5
449	2.1-70R
450	21-89.5
451	53-319R, 53-319.1
452	2.1-37.3, 2.1-37.8
453	23-93, 23-94
454	32-211.18 to 32-211.23
455	2.1-51.18, 2.1-64.28:1 to 2.1-64.28:4
456	22-30R, 22-30.1
457	58-1123
459	57-35.5
460	15.1-684.1, 15.1-684.2, 15.1-686, 15.1-687
461	46.1-115
462	55-66.1:1
463	16.1-69.40, 19.2-37
465	54-318.1, 54-318.2, 54-321.2, 54-322
466	54-297, 54-298
467	19.2-390
468	64.1-19
469	15.1-37.2:1
470	52-5R
471	8.01-236
473	3.1-621
474	53-19.38:1
475	10-17.23
476	11-2.3
477	19.2-266
478	15.1-295
479	6.1-195.49:2
480	17-119.2
481	64.1-74
482	37.1-110
483	64.1-118
484	20-124
485	29-61
486	63.1-133.11, 63.1-133.12
487	33.1-72
488	22-67.2
489	45.1-2, 45.1-21 to 45.1-23, 45.1-25, 45.1-26
490	16.1-88.2
491	13.1-528, 13.1-531, 13.1-534
492	53-128.6
493	60.1-18 to 60.1-20R, 60.1-47, 60.1-53 to 60.1-57R, 60.1-80, 60.1-85, 60.1-86, 60.1-86.1R
495	44-146.19
496	32-195.8, 38.1-348.10, 38.1-360
497	63.1-155
498	33.1-320, n.
499	32-1
500	19.2-19 to 19.2-21, 19.2-24, 19.2-45, 19.2-73, 19.2-74, 19.2-123, 46.1-7
501	16.1-107
502	14.1-112
503	18.2-335
504	8.01-676
505	58-441.6
506	8.01-511
507	29-213.24
508	36-55.25, 36-55.30:1
509	32-364.6
510	55-336 to 55-348, 55-349, n., 55-350
511	30-74 to 30-77
512	32-211.6
513	3.1-796.39, 3.1-796.42, 3.1-796.44, 3.1-796.48
515	2.1-564 to 2.1-569
516	23-9.10
517	32-310.2R, 32-310.2:1, 32-310.2:2
518	22-1.1, 22-218, 22-218.1:1, 22-223, 22-275.1, 22-275.3
520	55-248.36
521	54-113
522	22-360 to 22-363
524	15.1-175.2
525	8.01-606
526	15.1-374, 15.1-1375
527	22-72.1, 22-97.1
528	54-1.16
529	229-19.1, n.
531	56-236.1
533	15.1-11
534	54-398.4R, 54-398.4:1
535	63.1-124
536	63.1-238.1, 63.1-238.3
537	15.1-133.1
538	9-26
539	54-776, 54-778R, 54-784.01 to 54-784.04, 54-786, 54-786.1R, 54-786.2 to 54-786.8, 54-788R
540	3.1-14, 3.1-290 to 3.1-292, 3.1-295, 3.1-297, 3.1-309, 3.1-315, 3.1-320, 3.1-325, 3.1-332, 3.1-635, 3.1-642, 3.1-648 to 3.1-650, 3.1-662, 3.1-678, 3.1-682, 3.1-684.13, 3.1-684.17, 3.1-763.7, 3.1-763.11, 3.1-789, 3.1-793, 3.1-796.26
541	8.01-581.19, 32-137.1, 54-317.3, 54-317.4, 54-321.5 to 54-321.7
542	57-35.9:1
543	15.1-491
544	22-230.3
545	2.1-505, 2.1-512, 2.1-513.1
546	28.1-109
547	15.1-158.1, n.
548	28.1-108, 28.1-109
549	3.1-796.41, 18.2-402
550	46.1-1, 46.1-444, 46.1-504
551	15.1-160, 15.1-162, 22-127
552	53-235
533	63.1-248.13
554	15.1-482.1
555	53-19.11
557	36-11
558	15.1-769
559	3.1-796.44, 3.1-796.47, 3.1-796.48, 3.1-796.54, 3.1-796.55, 18.2-144, 18.2-397, 29-213.5, 29-213.7, 29-213.8, 29-213.16, 29-213.24, 29-213.25, 29-214.26, 29-213.27, 29-213.31
560	54-729.33
561	54-276.9:1
562	63.1-55.5, 63.1-55.6
563	46.1-167.1, 46.1-167.4, 46.1-432, 46.1-513.1
564	8.01-512,

Acts 1978 Chapter	Code 1950 Section
	34-29, 63.1-257
565	42.1-48
566	20-88.18
567	20-14.2
569	52-9.1:1
570	2.1-398
571	10-201, 10-206, 10-208
572	14.1-46, 14.1-46.01
573	2.1-341
574	53-76
578	36-105
579	4-37, 4-80.2R, 4-118.3 to 4-118.19, 4-118.20, n.
580	2.1-488.1 to 2.1-488.6, 9-7R, 9-9 to 9-12R
581	36-99
583	28.1-93
584	15.1-456
585	62.1-13.6
586	20-63
587	15.1-28.2
588	14.1-73
589	29-213.23:1, n.
590	15.1-478
592	15.1-29.6
593	18.2-268
594	15.1-241
595	53-245
596	40.1-79, 40.1-95, 40.1-96, 40.1-98
597	24.1-257
598	62.1-182
599	24.1-257
600	18.2-334.1, 59.1-216 to 59.1-254
601	8.01-400.1, 8.01-406, 19.2-164
602	2.1-570 to 2.1-573
603	63.1-85.2, 63.1-85.4:1, 63.1-85.6
604	15.1-1509
605	14.1-123, 16.1-69.40:1, 16.1-69.40:2, 16.1-228, 16.1-302, 19.2-45, 19.2-254.1, 19.2-254.2, 19.2-258.1, 46.1-1, 46.1-2, 46.1-5, 46.1-7, 46.1-14, 46.1-76, 46.1-82, 46.1-83, 46.1-88, 46.1-90.1, 46.1-98.1, 46.1-104.1, 46.1-105.7, 46.1-116, 46.1-138, 46.1-160, 46.1-167.3, 46.1-167.5, 46.1-172.01, 46.1-172.02, 46.1-172.1, 46.1-193, 46.1-202.1, 46.1-229, 46.1-234.1, 46.1-254.2, 46.1-264.1, 46.1-282.1, 46.1-315, 46.1-341
606	2.1-51.18, 9-153 to 9-155, 27-67
607	2.1-51.18, 22-330.12 to 22-330.16:1R, 27-91 to 27-93
608	18.2-58
609	53-165
610	18.2-359
611	16.1-69.48, 16.1-69.49R
612	18.2-441.1
613	16.1-263
614	53-323
615	18.2-204.1
616	33.1-157
617	2.1-164, 15.1-1269.2, n.
618	18.2-295
620	53-315.1
621	47-2.1
622	54-316, 54-317
623	53-168
624	6.1-63
625	6.1-278
626	16.1-309
627	56-233.1
628	55-57.1
629	17-60.1
630	4-69
631	36-55.31:1
632	37.1-225 to 37.1-233
634	45.1-197.3 to 45.1-197.18
635	2.1-51.15, 22-330.1, 22-330.1:1, 22-330.4R, 22-330.4:1, 22-330.4:2, 22-330.4:3, 22-330.6R, 22-330.6:1, 22-330.9, 22-330.10, 22-330.11
636	56-249.6
638	19.2-213, 19.2-213.1
639	18.2-341
640	18.2-254
641	2.1-71.1
642	15.1-37.7, 15.1-1028, 15.1-1030, 15.1-1041, 15.1-1050, 15.1-1061, 15.1-1066, 15.1-1070, 15.1-1077, 15.1-1093, 15.1-1119, 15.1-1140
643	16.1-246, 16-1-247
644	58-769.8
645	58-769.8
646	58-266.1:2
647	20-31.1, 20-38.1, 20-61.1, 63.1-234R, 64.1-5R, 64.1-5.1, 64.1-5.2, 64.1-6R, 64.1-6.1, 64.1-7R, 64.1-8R, 64.1-8.1, 64.1-11, 64.1-16, 64.1-64, 64.1-71, 64.1-71.1
648	16.1-241
649	2.1-51.23:1
650	2.1-51.23, 33.1-12
651	33.1-390, 33.1-391
652	33.1-13
653	2.1-421, 2.1-454, 2.1-469 to 2.1-479R, 22-344.4 to 22-344.15
654	58-27.2
655	62.1-129
656	58-441.6, 58-685.13:2, 58-829
657	32-310.9 to 32-310.11
658	38.1-22.1, 38.1-790 to 38.2-809, 58-490
659	55-7
660	53-38, 53-38.01
661	18.2-433
662	46.1-547.1
663	58-757.01
664	58-12.90
665	58-441.6
666	14.1-75
667	53-316 to 53-318, 53-320R, 53-321R
668	58-199
669	15.1-37.3:4
670	13.1-559, 13.1-560, 13.1-561, 13.1-562, 13.1-563, 13.1-565, 13.1-566, 13.1-569, 13.1-569.1, 13.1-572, 59.1-21.18:1
671	63.1-206.1
672	63.1-124
673	58-628, 58-638 to 58-644R
674	13.1-544.2, 13.1-545.1

Acts 1978 Chapter	Code 1950 Section
675	18.2-118
676	8.01-319
677	58-180
678	32-9.2
679	36-19
680	58-12.91
681	13.1-223.1
682	27-23.1
683	6.1-2.1, 6.1-2.7, 6.1-11.1, 6.1-39, 6.1-40R, 6.1-41.1, 6.1-61, 6.1-62, 6.1-195.48, 6.1-195.57, 6.1-197, 6.1-381 to 6.1-388
684	16.1-223, 16.1-224
685	6.1-2.8
686	18.2-98.1
687	19.2-306
688	38.1-311.1
689	9-109
692	58-851.7
693	58-65
694	32-423
695	9-67, 9-68
696	38.1-131.1, 38.1-133.1
697	19.2-12
698	19.2-163.1 to 19.2-163.3, 19.2-163.5, 19.2-163.6
699	6.1-195.40
700	56-234.3
701	38.1-33 to 38.1-35, 38.1-212, 38.1-213
702	3.1-15, 3.1-410
703	36-97
704	58-12.92
705	54-524.84:10
706	58-441.3
707	54-276.9
708	46.1-149
710	18.2-300, 18.2-301R, 18.2-302R
711	15.1-242
712	18.2-165.1
713	19.2-392.3
714	58-64
715	18.2-308
716	19.2-305, 19.2-336
717	15.1-50, 15.1-1231, 16.1-316, 16.1-317
718	8.01-100, 8.01-103, 8.01-104R, 18.2-114.1, 18.2-209.1, 18.2-209.2

Acts 1978 Chapter	Code 1950 Section
719	14.1-155.3
720	19.2-159
721	19.2-59
722	3.1-562.6
723	56-218
724	56-224.1
725	15.1-165 to 15.1-167
726	2.1-206.1
727	45.1-4
728	6.1-55.1
729	45.1-7, 45.1-12, 45.1-13, 45.1-17, 45.1-26, 45.1-30, 45.1-34, 45.1-36, 45.1-37, 45.1-39, 45.1-40, 45.1-44, 45.1-48, 45.1-53.1, 45.1-59, 45.1-68, 45.1-69, 45.1-90, 45.1-98, 45.1-99.1
730	19.2-8, 63.1-195, 63.1-203, 63.1-204, 63.1-211.1, 63.1-220, 63.1-220.1, 63.1-221, 63.1-223, 63.1-225, 63.1-236
731	63.1-124.1
732	16.1-281
733	63.1-226.1
734	63.1-56, 63.1-204
735	63.1-204, 63.1-225
736	20-78.1
737	36-139
738	16.1-300
739	16.1-275, 16.1-279, 16.1-280, 53-329.1
740	16.1-242, 16.1-244, 16.1-246, 16.1-263, 16.1-279, 16.1-281 to 16.1-283, 16.1-300, 16.1-301
741	19.2-200, 19.2-206
742	23-35.1, 23-35.2
743	23-35.1, 23-35.3, 23-35.4, 23-35.5:1, 23-35.6
744	63.1-225
745	23-38.10:2 to 23-38.10:7
746	20-109, 20-109.1
747	63.1-248.3, 63.1-248.6
748	46.1-315.2
749	63.1-55.1, 63.1-55.2
750	63.1-220, 63.1-229
751	36-99.1, 36-137, 36-139
752	3.1-796.54

Acts 1978 Chapter	Code 1950 Section
753	2.1-51.30
754	63.1-47, 63.1-48
755	19.2-120, 19.2-121, 19.2-123 to 19.2-125, 19.2-130 to 19.2-132, 19.2-135, 19.2-136, 19.2-138, 19.2-143, 19.2-145, 19.2-150, 19.2-152
756	16.1-279
757	9-156 to 9-166
758	58-685.13
759	18.2-335
760	19.2-37
761	65.1-47.1
762	15.1-50
763	15.1-50, 21-27
764	59.1-225 to 59.1-260, 59.1-261, n.
765	10-213.1
766	58-685.13
767	9.01-229
768	27-40.1
769	57-122
770	2.1-482 to 2.1-484, 2.1-486, 2.1-504, 37.1-13, 37.1-14 to 37.1-18R
771	58-441.21:1R
772	58-266.1
773	58-441.48
774	58-760.1
775	58-155.1
776	58-760.1
777	58-760.1
778	24.1-1, 24.1-23, 24.1-29, 24.1-30, 24.1-31, 24.1-32, 24.1-36, 24.1-37, 24.1-41, 24.1-43, 24.1-53, 24.1-92, 24.1-126, 24.1-132, 24.1-133, 24.1-134, 24.1-140, 24.1-144, 24.1-166, 24.1-167, 24.1-168, 24.1-169, 24.1-172, 24.1-184, 24.1-185, 24.1-192, 24.1-224, 24.1-228, 24.1-229, 24.1-232, 24.1-233, 24.1-233.1, 24.1-253, 24.1-279
779	18.2-248, 18.2-250
780	58-760.1
781	19.2-76.2
782	58-162.1
783	58-151.032
784	58-151.032:2, 58-151.050:3, 58-441:6, 58-456, 58-514.2:2, 58-516.1R, 58-518,

Acts 1978 Chapter	Code 1950 Section
	58-519, 58-520R, 58-520.1R, 58-522, 58-523, 58-526R, 58-527R, 58-529 to 58-531, 58-539
785	58-151.032
786	58-603
788	58-760.1
789	58-1152.1
790	58-760.1
791	18.2-181
792	32-388
794	19.2-175
795	4-40, 4-108
796	58-151.03, 58-151.062
797	6.1-58.1
798	58-441.21:1R
799	58-266.1
801	13.1-76.1, 13.1-529, 13.1-531
802	2.1-392R, 2.1-393
803	18.2-63.1
804	13.1-92
805	58-55
807	18.2-187R, 18.2-187.1
808	14.1-19.1
810	2.1-342, 2.1-382
811	2.1-486
812	11-23.5
813	18.2-163
814	62.1-44.34:6
815	62.1-44.34:7
816	62.1-44.34R, 62.1-44.34:1 to 62.1-44.34:5
817	58-266.1
818	10-17.30:1
819	58-441.6
820	2.1-51.18, 2.1-51.24, 2.1-64.15 to 2.1-64.22R, 33.1-392 to 33.1-398
821	58-12.93
822	59.1-21.16:1
823	6.1-2.6
824	32-211.5, 32-439 to 32-448
825	19.2-390, 19.2-392
826	2.1-341, 2.1-346, 2.1-346.1
827	62.1-44.2, 62.1-44.15
828	13.1-553
829	46.1-410
830	16.1-269
831	8.01-294
832	15.1-36.2
833	54-524.2, 54-524.24, 54-524.47:3, 54-524.56, 54-524.59, 54-524.67:1, 54-524.69, n., 54-524.84:6
834	2.1-42.1, 9-6.23, 54-527
835	29-11.1, 29-238 to 29-248
837	3.1-22.13 to 3.1-22.21, 10-17.113 to 10-17.124, 10-21.1R, 10-38R
838	58-70, 58-218, n., 58-238.1 to 58-238.36
839	54-524.67:2
840	40.1-12 to 40.1-21R, 54-872.16 to 54-872.26
841	51-1R, 51-2R, 51-111.16, 51-111.24, 51-111.27, 51-111.28, 51-111.29, 51-111.33, 51-111.34, 51-111.41:4, 51-111.47, 51-111.50, 51-111.52:5, 51-111.55, 55-111.60, 51-111.67:4, 41-111.67:7, 51-146, 51-151, 51-161, 51-168, 65.1-4
843	58-829
844	2.1-114.5
845	2.1-114.5, 2.1-114.5:1 to 2.1-114.5:6, 15.1-7.1, 15.1-7.2
846	2.1-113, 2.1-113.1 to 2.1-113.3
847	2.1-353.2, 2.1-354, 2.1-354.1
848	58-12.79
849	54-260.68, 54-269.70, 54-260.70:1 to 54-260.70:3, 54-260.72, 54-260.73

ACTS 1979

Acts 1979 Chapter	Code 1950 Section
1	20-107, 20-121, 20-121.4
2	23-9.5
3	8.01-400
4	38.1-381.7
5	54-367.7R, 54-367.8, 54-367.11 to 54-367.13, 54-367.15R, 54-367.16R, 54-367.18R, 54-367.19, 54-367.21R, 54-367.22R, 54-367.24R, 54-367.25, 54-367.26, 54-367.31R, 54-367.32, 54-367.33R, 54-367.33:1, 54-367.34R, 54-367.35:1, 54-367.37R
6	17-119.1:2
7	16.1-69.6:1
8	54-260.71:1
9	56-234.5
10	22-79.4
11	2.1-37.13
12	55-59, 55-59.1 to 55-59.4, 55-62, 55-63, 55-106.3, 58-762
13	38.1-347.1, 38.1-348.7, 38.1-360, 38.1-824
14	14.1-103, 47-1R, 47-2
15	16.1-228
16	11-17
17	23-93
18	28.1-57, 28.1-67, 28.1-69R, 28.1-69.1, 28.1-70
19	2.1-206.1
20	46.1-30
23	15.1-41.1
25	46.1-206
27	24.1-30
28	23-9.10:1
29	22-10.13
30	19.2-245.1
31	8.01-329
32	58-151.050:1
33	58-151.26
34	19.2-76.1
35	15.1-1377
36	8.01-514
37	24.1-165
38	37.1-234 to 37.1-238
39	54-370, 54-375.1, 54-377.1, 54-379, 54-387R, 54-388, 54-388.1, 54-389R, 54-390R, 54-392R, 54-393 to 54-397.1, 54-398.01, 54-398.02
41	37.1-10
43	63.1-236
44	46.1-299
45	16.1-99
46	58-713, 58-721, 58-746, 58-749
47	38.1-354.1, 38.1-818
48	29-148.1
50	40.1-29
51	29-213.24

Acts 1979 Chapter	Code 1950 Section
52	6.1-54
53	6.1-56
54	37.1-1, 37.1-122, 37.1-179, 37.1-184
55	57-60, 57-63
56	45.1-93
57	6.1-13
58	6.1-49, 6.1-50
59	6.1-41
60	6.1-195.43
61	46.1-157
62	46.1-514.21, n.
63	3.1-907 to 3.1-917R
64	33.1-70.01
65	10-17.18:3
66	2.1-488.1
67	10-21.5
68	45.1-195
69	3.1-22.4
70	46.1-328
71	56-480.2
72	3.1-763.7, 3.1-763.9, 3.1-763.13R
73	63.1-177, 63.1-189, 63.1-190, 63.1-192
74	46.1-104.2
75	46.1-281.1R, 46.1-295.1R
76	6.1-195.21
77	6.1-195.22:2
78	6.1-330.42
79	6.1-195.12
80	65.1-2.1, 65.1-52
81	6.1-195.34
82	33.1-246.1
83	14.1-33; 14.1-34R, 14.1-64, 14.1-79 to 14.1-82, 14.1-84.1 to 14.1-84.7, 52-26, 52-28, 63.1-135
84	33.1-23.1, 33.1-23.1:1, 33.1-41, 33.1-43, 33.1-44, 33.1-80
85	15.1-945.1 to 15.1-945.6, 15.1-966 to 15.1-967.1, 15.1-970R, 15.1-971, 15.1-977.1 to 15.1-977.24, 15.1-978 to 15.1-982R, 15.1-982.1 to 15.1-983, 15.1-991, 15.1-994R, 15.1-997, 15.1-998, 15.1-1009, 15.1-1031.4, 15.1-1032.1, 15.1-1034 to 15.1-1036, 15.1-1038 to 15.1-1041, 15.1-1044 to 15.1-1047, 15.1-1055, 15.1-1055.1, 15.1-1058.1 to 15.1-1058.5, 15.1-1084, 15.1-1095, 15.1-1130R, 15.1-1130.1 to 15.1-1133, 15.1-1135, 15.1-1138, 15.1-1140, 15.1-1141, 15.1-1145, 15.1-1146R, 15.1-1146.1, 15.1-1147, 15.1-1148R, 15.1-1165R, 15.1-1166 to 15.1-1170
86	46.1-190
88	33.1-75.1
89	33.1-75.1
90	13.1-156 to 13.1-161
91	56-241.1
93	10-145.9
94	16.1-309.1
96	63.1-163
97	38.1-348.11, 38.1-360, 38.1-818
98	22-217.4, 22-217.4:1
99	13.1-3.1
100	46.1-1, 46.1-181.5
101	6.1-2.9
102	6.1-330.16
103	56-496
104	13.1-565
105	46.1-550.5
106	56-102, 56-102.1
107	2.1-557, 2.1-559.1 to 2.1-559.7
108	54-201 to 54-216R
109	53-19.22:2, 53-135.2
110	42.1-78
111	15.1-475
112	29-9
113	38.1-381
114	62.1-67
115	46.1-545
117	10-17.12
118	6.1-277
119	10-181
120	22-220.1
121	20-6
122	19.2-393, 19.2-394, 19.2-396, 19.2-397
123	52-11.1
124	46.1-375, 57-48
125	9-156
126	22-276.1
127	53-38
128	28.1-170
129	56-497
130	63.1-83
131	2.1-555, 2.1-558
132	46.1-551
133	58-44.2
134	58-404.02
135	2.1-329.1
136	23-9.5, 23-14, 23-31, 23-155.1 to 23-155.3, 23-155.7, 23-155.8, 23-155.10
137	31-26 to 31-29, 31-31
138	6.1-207.2
139	6.1-217
140	29-11.1
141	2.1-42.2
142	22-205.1, 22-205.2
144	23-91.32, n.
145	23 9.5, 23-14, 23-31, 23-155.1 to 23-155.3, 23-155.7, 23-155.8, 23-155.10
146	23-174.1 to 23-174.3, 23-174.5 to 23-174.7, 23-174.8R, 23-174.9R
147	2.1-64.33, 23-136 to 23-138, 23-165.1 to 23-165.7, 23-165.9 to 23-167, 23-168R, 23-169R, 23-170, 23-173R, 23-174
148	58-441.6
149	23-91.32, n.
151	2.1-206.1
152	58-769.11
153	58-503.2, 58-514.3
154	2.1-369
155	15.1-8
156	58-795.2
157	15.1-506.1
158	15.1-686
159	46.1-53.1
160	58-512.1, 58-514.2:2, 58-514.2:3, 58-760
165	6.1-195.47
173	2.1-190.1
175	13.1-43
176	38.1-367.1
177	22-5
178	58-12.48
179	58-769.10
180	58-769.8
181	15.1-320, 15.1-320.1
182	15.1-491
183	15.1-466
184	15.1-216
185	46.1-65
186	58-12.94
187	15.1-29.7
188	15.1-466
189	27-34.1
190	6.1-216
191	2.1-432.2
192	8.01-453

Acts 1979 Chapter	Code 1950 Section
193	44-146.16, 44-146.18, 44-146.23
194	19.2-163.1 to 19.2-163.6
195	58-759.1R, 58-759.2R, 58-760.2, 58-760.3
196	4-69
197	29-55.3:2
198	58-441.18
199	4-98.12
200	13.1-529 to 13.1-531
201	65.1-52, 65.1-53
202	16.1-254
203	53-207
204	37.1-65.1, 37.1-65.2, 37.1-67.5, 37.1-67.6, 37.1-89
205	58-411.6
206	15.1-547
207	29-213.11, 35-42.1, 63.1-171.2, 63.1-171.7
208	15.1-364.1
209	15.1-543
210	15.1-538
211	49-18.1
212	54-325.2:1
213	46.1-303
214	15.1-173
215	2.1-178, 2.1-179, 2.1-179.1R, 2.1-208R, 2.1-209, 2.1-210, 2.1-230R
216	33.1-356, 33.1-361, 33.1-365
218	63.1-196.4, 63.1-209
219	40.1-79, 40.1-80, 40.1-82R, 40.1-84, 40.1-86R, 40.1-87, 40.1-88, 40.1-92, 40.1-95, 40.1-100, 40.1-104, 40.1-105, 40.1-106 to 40.1-108R, 40.1-109, 40.1-110R, 40.1-112, 40.1-114
223	58-381.1
224	2.1-155.1
225	8.01-506
226	58-151.013, 58-151.032:1, 58-151.032:2
227	4-98.10
228	46.1-400
229	20-125 to 20-146
230	19.2-262
231	2.1-51.29R, 2.1-425.1
232	15.1-785.1, n.
233	14.1-50, 14.1-51, 14.1-55, 14.1-56
234	2.1-489 to 2.1-491
235	25-236
236	14.1-70
237	22-67.2
239	15.1-296
240	58-978, 58-979, 58-991
241	15.1-366
242	8.01-511 to 8.01-512.1, 8.01-515
243	2.1-521.1, 19.2-8, 36-55.27, 54-786.4, 55-347
244	46.1-154, 46.1-154.2R, 46.1-156, 46.1-157
245	15.1-40.3
249	56-240
250	18.2-76
251	15.1-467 to 15.1-469, n.
252	10-150.11 to 10-150.18, 18.2-142R
253	6.1-195.22
254	63.1-76
256	14.1-46R, 14.1-46.01
257	30-19.03
258	4-25
259	58-961
260	22-220.1
261	8.01-581.4 to 8.01-581.6
262	22-249
263	46.1-343
264	29-2.1, 29-6, 29-11, 29-13, 29-20, 29-24, 29-30, 29-32, 29-127, 29-128.1, 29-143, 29-161, 29-172, 29-177R, 29-213.17, 29-213.29, 29-213.30
265	24.1-122
266	2.1-127
267	16.1-299
268	19.2-81
269	8.01-343
270	56-338.51, 56-338.54
272	2.1-1, 2.1-51.24, 5.1-1 to 5.1-1.7, 5.1-2R, 5.1-2.1 to 5.1-2.4, 5.1-3R, 5.1-4 to 5.1-9.1, 5.1-10R, 5.1-21.1, 5.1-24 to 5.1-25.2, 5.1-25.4, 5.1-26 to 5.1-30R, 5.1-31, 5.1-40, 5.1-41, 5.1-44, 5.1-46 to 5.1-52, 5.1-54R, 5.1-55, 5.1-57, 5.1-71, 5.1-78, 5.1-79, 5.1-88.1 to 5.1-88.4, 5.1-89
273	15.1-1249
274	28.1-49, 28.1-52.2, 28.1-59, 28.1-70, 28.1-119 to 28.1-120, 28.1-133, 28.1-134, 28.1-163, 28.1-165, 28.1-179, 28.1-230 to 28.1-239
275	22-217.3
276	29-130.2
277	15.1-291
278	15.1-274.1
279	27-85.3 to 27-85.6
280	15.1-1240, 15.1-1249, 15.1-1250, 15.1-1269
281	16.1-283
282	55-70.1
283	2.1-394
284	58-514.2:1, 58-580, 58-581
286	19.2-299
287	29-56, 29-59
288	15.1-571.1
289	3.1-22.22 to 3.1-22.27
290	45.1-106.1, 45.1-198R, 45.1-199R, 45.1-200, n., 45.1-201 to 45.1-212.1R, 45.1-213, n., 45.1-214 to 45.1-220R, 45.1-220.1 to 45.1-220.5, n., 45.1-226 to 45.1-270
291	56-265.14 to 56-265.29
293	24.1-247R, 24.1-248R, 24.1-249, 24.1-250
294	2.1-41.2, 2.1-51.9, 23-9.9:1, 23-40, 23-49.1:1, 28.1-195, 28.1-197R, 28.1-197.1
295	2.1-336 to 2.1-339
296	54-83.1:8, 54-524.113
297	15.1-833 to 15.1-835, 15.1-836.1, 15.1-836.2, 15.1-838, 15.1-839, 15.1-908 to 15.1-910R, 15.1-911, n., 15.1-912, n., 15.1-913 to 15.1-915R, 15.1-915.1, n.
298	22-217.1,

Acts 1979 Chapter	Code 1950 Section
	22-217.5:1 to 22-217.6:1, 22-217.7:1 to 22-217.8:1
299	58-769.3:1, n.
300	9-88, 9-89, 9-91
301	2.1-353.2
302	45.1-194
303	15.1-238
304	3.1-796.56, 3.1-796.59 to 3.1-796.65, 59.1-200
306	59.1-21.10, 59.1-21.11, 59.1-21.13 to 59.1-21.15, 59.1-21.16:2
307	62.1-44.113 to 62.1-44.116
309	56-259
310	58-685.13:2
311	30-28.16
312	13.1-504
313	56-245.2, 56-245.3
314	2.1-51.21, 9-84.01R, 9-84.01:1, 9-84.03
315	45.1-73, 45.1-81, 45.1-87
316	2.1-37.8, 9-68, 9-126, 9-147, 14.1-18, 30-32, 30-56
318	2.1-167, 15.1-159.8
319	2.1-398, 2.1-399
320	2.1-398
321	33.1-72R, 33.1-72.1, 33.1-225.1
322	64.1-87.1
323	64.1-116
324	38.1-52
325	8.01-581.12:1R, 8.01-581.20
326	3.1-806 to 3.1-809, 3.1-810.1, 3.1-810.2, 3.1-814, 3.1-815R, 3.1-818R, 3.1-819, 3.1-821, 3.1-824R
327	54-83.22, 54-112.3
328	15.1-9.1:01, n.
329	24.1-46, 24.1-187, 24.1-222
330	9-145.1 to 9-145.4
331	8.01-261, 8.01-262
332	9-144
333	15.1-131.7, 15.1-142 to 15.1-142.2, 15.1-156, n., 15.1-157R, 15.1-158R, 15.1-158.1, n., 15.1-159R, 15.1-159.1R, 15.1-527.1, n.
334	10-181
335	19.2-73.1
336	18.2-147.1
337	58-16.2:1
338	16.1-250
339	63.1-222, 63.1-231
340	55-171, 55-200
341	38.1-342.2
342	64.1-124.1
343	12.1-30.1
345	8.01-511
346	57-39.10
347	63.1-248.6
348	18.2-370, 18.2-374.1, 40.1-100, 40.1-101, 40.1-113, 63.1-248.6
349	18.2-111
351	58-831, 58-831.01
352	15.1-11.4, 36-99.1
353	18.2-271.1
354	40.1-1, 40.1-39R, 40.1-41 to 40.1-43R, 40.1-45 to 40.1-48R, 40.1-49.2R, 40.1-49.3 to 40.1-49.7, 40.1-51.1, 40.1-51.1:1R, 40.1-51.2:1 to 40.1-51.3, 40.1-51.4R
355	2.1-116.10 to 2.1-116.14
356	8.01-53
357	5.1-103
358	3.1-382.1
359	58-758.1
360	43-3
361	46.1-211
362	15.1-51
363	18.2-50.1
364	19.2-187.01, 19.2-187.1
365	29-213.6
366	4-98.18
367	8.01-272
368	15.1-515.2
369	2.1-341, 2.1-344, 2.1-345
370	24.1-263
371	58-151.032, 58-151.032:2, n., 58-151.032:3
372	3.1-1020 to 3.1-1030
374	36-55.25, 36-55.30:1R, 36-55.33:2, 36-55.31, 36-55.33:1
375	6.1-63
376	6.1-2.7
377	15.1-1508, 15.1-1509, 15.1-1511 to 15.1-1513
378	19.2-390
379	13.1-518, 13.1-534, 13.1-567
382	2.1-536, 2.1-538
383	9-85 to 9-87
384	16.1-269
385	38.1-133.1
386	6.1-65.1
387	54-524.84:4, 54-524.84:6, 54-524.84:8, 54-524.84:10, 54-524.84:12
388	54-524.69
389	3.1-709, 3.1-713, 3.1-716, 3.1-718, 3.1-721
390	17-54
391	37.1-196
392	63.1-285
393	16.1-302
394	5.1-23, 5.1-145
395	15.1-466
396	54-276.12
397	6.1-330.27R, 6.1-330.27:1
398	54-941
399	38.1-348.7
400	18.2-341
401	46.1-550.6 to 46.1-550.14
402	27-34.2
403	2.1-467.2, 2.1-467.4, 2.1-467.5
404	58-151.02
405	56-136 to 56-138R
406	40.1-44.1, 40.1-128 to 40.1-134
407	6.1-72R, 6.1-73R, 6.1-77R, 6.1-125.1 to 6.1-125.16, 6.1-195.23R, 6.1-195.26R, 6.1-195.30R, 6.1-207, 6.1-208.2R, 6.1-208.5
408	54-1.3R, 54-1.4R, 54-1.7 to 54-1.12R, 54-1.14 to 54-1.16R, 54-1.17 to 54-1.42, 54-26.1, 54-83.1:011, 54-83.22:1, 54-91.2, 54-121, 54-127R, 54-132R, 54-573.18, 54-861R, 54-864 to 54-867R, 54-872R, 54-872.1 to 54-872.15R, 54-901.1, 54-935.1, 54-939.1, 54-943.1
409	2.1-427
410	47-4.1 to 47-4.8
411	53-251, 53-296R
412	43-7
413	18.2-254

Acts 1979 Chapter	Code 1950 Section
414	30-28.4, 30-28.5:1, 30-28.5:2
415	53-210, 53-211, 53-213, 53-216R, 53-251.3
416	15.1-1603 to 15.1-1634
417	3.1-428
418	62.1-13.5
419	14.1-73.2
420	18.2-334.2, 18.2-335R, 18.2-340.1 to 18.2-340.12
423	58-151.13:1
424	36-19.5
425	63.1-196.3
426	37.1-67.2, 37.1-67.3
427	33.1-206
428	46.1-82, 46.1-83
429	2.1-564
431	15.1-262, 15.1-376.1, 15.1-491.01, 15.1-847, 33.1-183.1, 58-773.2
432	21-89.6
433	9-152.1 to 9-152.5
434	44-146.30
435	18.2-247 to 18.2-255, 18.2-257 to 18.2-258.1, 54-524.2, 54-524.56, 54-524.84:4
436	58-685.11
437	38.1-455, 38.1-456, 38.1-465.1, 38.1-465.2, 38.1-470.1
438	20-122, 64.1-48
439	54-145.2
440	54-52
441	2.1-155.1
442	56-501.1
443	58-664
444	8.01-298
445	16.1-69.44
446	27-34.2:1
447	8.01-391
448	2.1-51.18:2
449	54-832
450	2.1-121
451	63.1-55.5, 63.1-55.6
452	16.1-115
453	63.1-248.10
454	22-37
455	2.1-38.1R, 2.1-64.29 to 2.1-64.31R
456	15.1-1026, 15.1-1029, 15.1-1030
457	38.1-367.2
458	38.1-366
459	65.1-10
460	29-121, n.
461	63.1-175
462	63.1-278
463	65.1-104R, 65.1-104.1 to 65.1-105, 65.1-108, 65.1-113.2, 65.1-115R, 65.1-116R, 65.1-135
464	8.01-319
465	14.1-85R, 19.2-334
466	30-19.2
467	18.2-308.1
468	19.2-160, 19.2-237
469	19.2-349
470	11-21
471	9-109.2:1, 9-109.3
472	40.1-11.1
473	58-785.1
474	18.2-308.2
475	30-19.4
476	54-872.23
477	56-119
478	46.1-61
479	18.2-204.1
480	19.2-389
481	16.1-309
482	2.1-114.5
483	63.1-195, 63.1-196
484	40.1-30
486	55-306, 55-316, 55-323, 55-327, 55-328, 55-330
487	58-972
488	20-96
489	36-75
490	9-75, 9-76
491	8.01-480
492	56-249.5R, 56-249.6
493	59.1-201
494	25-46.8, 25-46.28, 25-46.30, 25-46.31
495	16.1-97
496	8.01-460
498	8.01-582, 8.01-589
499	8.01-66
500	18.2-165.1
501	8.01-382
502	20-22, 20-24
503	15.1-131
504	44-20
505	32.1-88, 54-524, 109:18
506	59.1-207.1 to 59.1-207.6
507	15.1-267
508	2.1-422
509	2.1-204
510	16.1-69.40:1
511	16.1-69.40:3
512	2.1-420R, 2.1-421R
513	38.1-280 to 38.1-285R, 38.1-287 to 38.1-294R, 38.1-295.1 to 38.1-301.5R, 38.1-301.7 to 38.1-325R, 38.1-327R, 38.1-327.1 to 38.1-327.61
514	2.1-335.1
515	40.1-71
516	19.2-175
517	58-1152.1
518	19.2-123
519	2.1-437R, 2.1-437.1 to 2.1-437.3
520	19.2-138
521	8.01-66.1
522	15.1-40.1, 24.1-86
523	59.1-262 to 59.1-269
524	62.1-13.2
525	14.1-123, 19.2-353.3
526	46.1-334
527	17-59, 58-797
528	63.1-155
529	9-95.1 to 9-95.4
530	50-45.1
531	3.1-618
532	22-204
533	40.1-49.8
534	37.1-120R
535	22-19.1, n.
536	16.1-133
537	4-37, 4-62
538	14.1-51
539	58-12.95
540	58-12.96
541	58-12.97
542	43-3
543	58-760.1
544	58-760.1
545	58-760.1
546	58-12.98
547	58-12.99
548	58-12.100
549	58-12.101
550	58-12.102
551	58-12.103
552	58-12.104
553	58-12.105
554	58-12.106
555	58-441.6
556	58-441.3
557	58-441.6
558	58-441.6
559	58-61, 58-218, n., 58-238.13, n.,

Acts 1979 Chapter	Code 1950 Section
	58-238.19, 58-238.47, 64.1-160, 64.1-161
560	58-411
561	58-441.6
562	58-441.6
563	58-760.1
564	58-441.6
565	58-266.1
566	58-61
567	58-238.9
568	58-266.1
569	58-411
570	58-266.1
571	58-835
572	58-441.6
573	58-441.12
574	58-778
575	58-441.6
576	58-33.1, 58-829, 58-829.1:1, 58-829.2R, 58-829.5 to 58-829.7, 58-835, 58-836, 58-851, 58-851.7
577	58-33.1, 58-769.2, 58-769.3, 58-776 to 58-776.4, 58-778, 58-786, 58-787, 58-789, 58-792.02, 58-895, 58-895.1R, 58-896R, 58-897, 58-898 to 58-899, 58-913
582	18.2-31
583	19.2-54
584	19.2-56
585	18.2-112
592	2.1-116.1
594	14.1-123, 46.1-413
595	57-48 to 57-54, 57-56, 57-57, 57-59 to 57-61, 57-63, 57-65, 57-66, 57-67, 57-79
596	58-151.013
597	16.1-241
598	57-48, 57-55, 57-60
599	8.01-217
600	15.1-131.6
601	53-103
602	19.2-66 to 19.2-68
603	8.01-217
604	46.1-173
605	16.1-241, 16.1-305
606	28.1-124
607	33.1-20R
608	56-274
609	56-282
610	56-281.2
611	46.1-31

Acts 1979 Chapter	Code 1950 Section
612	8.01-217
613	9-6.14:4, 36-55.30, 36-55.30:3
615	16.1-262
616	4-79
617	56-249.2, 56-249.3
618	56-274
619	23-9.6:1
620	46.1-64
621	4-96.3
622	4-78
623	23-164.3, 23-164.5
624	22-56.3
625	53-238, 53-263R
626	57-60
627	15.1-50
628	16.1-241
629	60.1-26
630	16.1-327, 22-143, 23-1.1
631	40.1-26R
632	58-769.8
633	2.1-339.1
634	60.1-80, 60.1-88R, 60.1-88.01, 60.1-89.1, 60.1-89.2, 60.1-94
635	60.1-84
636	60.1-99
637	60.1-12, 60.1-14, 60.1-26
638	18.2-265R
639	58-151.0105, 58-151.0106
640	59.1-9.4
641	19.2-265.3
642	18.2-308 19.2-81.2, 53-39
643	15.1-38, 15.1-47
644	2.1-64-23
645	3.1-796.46, 18.2-399.1, 18.2-402, 29-213.19
646	18.2-253, 18.2-253.1
647	44-1, 44-2, 44-32.1
648	55-66.6
649	19.2-120, 19.2-318, 19.2-319
650	54-260.65
651	9-108.1
652	60.1-52.3
653	46.1-177
654	18.2-388
655	16.1-249
656	40.1-22
657	29-213.19
658	8.01-3
659	20-109.1
660	14.1-70, 15.1-48

Acts 1979 Chapter	Code 1950 Section
661	19.2-76
662	8.01-265
663	18.2-47
664	49-25, 49-26
665	8.01-345
666	63.1-209
668	16.1-89
669	37.1-110
670	28.1-46.1 to 28.1-46.4
671	9-141, 10-187 to 10-196R, 15.1-37.1:3, 15.1-37.1:6
672	2.1-391, 2.1-405R, 2.1-406R, 36-140
673	53-168
674	34-1
675	60.1-51.1, 60.1-58, 60.1-59, 60.1-132
676	53-168
677	9-139, 9-141, 9-143
678	2.1-373, 2.1-391, 2.1-397.1, 2.1-410, 2.1-483R, 2.1-552, 2.1-559, 9-143, 10-184.1, 37.1-207
679	19.2-74, 19.2-80
680	19.2-74
681	60.1-58
682	2.1-342
683	2.1-382, 2.1-383
684	2.1-342, 2.1-344
685	2.1-384, 9-111.11:1
686	2.1-342, 15.1-135.1
687	2.1-341
688	2.1-382
689	2.1-342, 2.1-382
690	58-1118.1
691	60.1-47
692	34-3.1
693	58-465, n., 58-485.1 to 58-485.20
694	58-1140
695	16.1-279
696	16.1-279
697	8.01-35.1
698	53-335 to 53-343

Acts 1979 Chapter	Code 1950 Section
699	16.1-138
700	16.1-233, 16.1-234, 16.1-310, 22-41.2, 53-19.20, 53-19.22:1, 53-21.2, 53-47, 53-92, 53-96, 53-195, 53-201, 53-206, 53-206.1, 53-206.8, 53-241.1 to 53-245, 53-262, 53-266, 53-268, 53-279, 63.1-248.16
701	16.1-246 to 16.1-248, 16.1-256, 16.1-260
702	16.1-279
703	53-262
704	18.2-175
705	9-109, 9-110
706	53-38, 53-166.1
707	37.1-73
708	19.2-20
709	58-628
710	58-757.01
711	32-1 to 32-448R, 32.1-1 to 32.1-309, 54-524.109:9 to 54-524.109:18R, 62.1-45 to 62.1-63R
712	18.2-186.1
713	8.01-225, 54-276.9R, 62.1-62, n., 62.1-63, n.
714	28.1-175.1, 28.1-177
715	54-276.10
716	18.2-510
717	18.2-267, 18.2-268
718	36-98
719	15.1-53, 15.1-282, 15.1-526.3, 15.1-611, 15.1-646, 15.1-1514 to 15.1-1602
720	54-260.74, 54-321, 54-325.1 to 54-325.8
721	38.1-810 to 38.1-862
722	8.01-66.2 to 8.01-66.11
723	3.1-796.58
724	57-39.19
726	38.1-362.1 to 38.1-362.6R, 38.1-362.7 to 38.1-362.9, 38.1-818
727	54-295, 54-298, 54-308.5, 54-311, 54-316 to 54-317.1, 54-321.2, 54-325.1
728	18.2-268
729	8.01-225, 54-276.9
730	23-31, 23-37R
731	30-59.1, 30-62R
732	58-12.107
733	58-958.1
734	2.1-114.5:1, 2.1-114.5:6, 15.1-7.1
735	19.2-135, 19.2-143
736	16.1-306
737	16.1-306

ACTS 1980

Acts 1980 Chapter	Code 1950 Section
1	15.1-51
2	58-792
3	14.1-46.01
4	63.1-68 to 63.1-75, 63.1-76, n., 63.1-77 to 63.1-85
5	45.1-27
6	10-92.2
8	15.1-51
9	46.1-14
10	46.1-432
11	15.1-51
12	2.1-51.23:1
13	46.1-289
14	46.1-267.2
16	15.1-108
17	33.1-391
18	63.1-106
19	63.1-112
20	63.1-106
21	46.1-303
23	46.1-31
24	46.1-105.5
25	46.1-149
26	46.1-526
27	46.1-528
28	29-153.2
29	46.1-38, 46.1-192, 46.1-351, 46.1-362, 46.1-423.1, 46.1-438
30	46.1-226
31	46.1-320
32	28.1-82
33	28.1-136
34	28.1-109
35	21-89.5, 21-89.7
37	46.1-45.2, 46.1-180.2
38	33.1-221
39	33.1-145, 33.1-151, 33.1-157
40	63.1-195, 63.1-207, 63.1-207.1, 63.1-219.6R
44	15.1-765, 15.1-776.1
45	15.1-966, 15.1-967, 15.1-967.2, 15.1-968R, 15.1-969, 15.1-972 to 15.1-976R
47	15.1-467, n., 15.1-468, n., 15.1-469, n.
48	62.1-148.1
49	58-46
50	2.1-328.2, n.
51	46.1-1
52	29-55.3:3
53	46.1-41.1
54	29-213.11
55	46.1-105.8
56	5.1-7.1R
58	15.1-550
59	5.1-39.1
62	15.1-768
64	15.1-155
67	15.1-1249
73	15.1-475
74	15.1-722, 15.1-724, 15.1-726, 15.1-727
75	58-769.7
76	6.1-330.18
79	15.1-686.2, 15.1-687, 15.1-687.1, 15.1-687.2
81	58-441.6
82	58-588, 58-597
84	58-510
85	51-111.60
86	15.1-1518
87	3.1-328
88	51-114
89	51-111.41:1, 51-111.41:4, 51-146
90	13.1-68, 13.1-69.1
91	17-119.1:2
93	16.1-69.6:1
95	11-17, 11-17.1
96	33.1-72.1
97	36-85.1
98	54-935
99	18.2-191, 18.2-193, 18.2-195
100	23-49.14

Acts 1980 Chapter	Code 1950 Section
	to 23-49.17
101	23-38.11,
	23-38.12, 23-38.14
	to 23-38.17
102	20-78.1
103	6.1-39
104	36-98
105	46.1-65,
	58-834
106	15.1-131.6
107	36-137
108	55-79.77
109	58-685.32
110	38.1-472.1
111	9-97
112	38.1-264
113	46.1-234.2
116	55-66.3
117	53-179
118	46.1-357.2
119	2.1-11R,
	2.1-11.1, 2.1-13R,
	2.1-14R, 2.1-16R
122	9-34,
	9-45
123	55-66.7
124	58-792.02
125	58-795.2
127	54-734
128	33.1-44
129	16.1-113
130	46.1-229.1
133	36-30,
	36-49, 36-49.1
134	19.2-200,
	19.2-206
135	51-112
136	51-111.2
137	51-111.50
138	51-179
139	19.2-46
140	18.2-162.1
141	33.1-345
142	56-442
	to 56-444R
143	55-125
144	15.1-1342, n.
145	14.1-112
146	14.1-70
147	33.1-46.4
148	26-15
149	18.2-105
150	54-524.2
151	30-19.4
153	9-141
154	20-23
155	20-49
156	38.1-747,
	38.1 748
157	54-273,
	54-274, 54-279,

Acts 1980 Chapter	Code 1950 Section
	54-296, 54-309,
	54-313, 54-315.1,
	54-317, 54-322
	to 54-324
158	54-925
159	15.1-1250
160	19.2-264.4
161	46.1-516
162	54-837
	to 54-839R
163	51-111.60:1
164	8.01-581.20
165	46.1-357
166	37.1-67.3
167	34-13
168	46.1-320
170	15.1-966.1
171	59.1-206
172	15.1-540
173	18.2-315R
174	18.2-104
175	18.2-95,
	18.2-96
176	37.1-67.6
177	17-223
178	17-229
179	18.2-253.1
180	54-524.35
181	6.1-198
182	6.1-200.3
183	8.01-416,
	16.1-88.1R
184	32.1-60
185	13.1-254
186	38.1-482.19,
	38.1-482.20,
	38.1-482.23
187	38.1-92,
	38.1-92.1
188	29-55.3:4
189	23-7.3
190	19.2-121
191	2.1-116.5
192	13.1-117
194	14.1-41 to
	14.1-42.1R, 16.1-69.9,
	16.1-69.9:2, 16.1-69.10,
	16.1-69.12, 16.1-69.47R
195	19.2-48
197	16.1-69.39:1
198	2.1-114.5
199	26-20.1
200	19.2-181
201	6.1-224.1
202	29-213.35
203	54-524.56
204	38.1-362.10
	to 38.1-362.16
205	38.1-435
207	6.1-216
208	6.1-195.11:1

Acts 1980 Chapter	Code 1950 Section
209	6.1-195.63:1R
210	6.1-216
211	6.1-259
212	15.1-262
213	55-200
214	9-145.1
215	15.1-285,
	15.1-286
216	13.1-529
217	16.1-293
218	28.1-119.1
220	15.1-543
221	2.1-344,
	18.2-31, 44-54.2,
	46.1-192, 58-12.103
222	13.1-505
223	10-223
	to 10-251
224	14.1-5
225	58-730.5,
	58-730.6
226	15.1-37.3:5
227	58-628,
	58-629, 58-711,
	58-715, 58-730,
	58-730.3, 58-744,
	58-753.1, 58-753.1:2,
	58-757
228	52-9
229	23-19.2:1R,
	23-38.61 to 23-38.69
230	56-274
232	52-1,
	52-8.1
233	18.2-278, n.
234	16.1-256
235	16.1-284
236	15.1-364
237	30-29
	to 30-34R
238	18.2-308
239	30-58.2
240	53-67
241	58-769.15
242	56-304.4
243	63.1-256,
	63.1-272
244	19.2-68
245	16.1-278
246	56-61
247	12.1-31
248	18.2-50.1
249	56-233
250	10-14.2
251	15.1-898
252	2.1-507
253	62.1-3
255	2.1-121,
	28.1-12.1
256	62.1-170
257	15.1-533

Acts 1980 Chapter	Code 1950 Section
258	15.1-161.1
259	56-236.1
260	53-103
261	45.1-209.1
262	58-730
263	58-985
264	64.1-92
265	6.1-55.1
266	58-272
267	55-19
268	63.1-229
269	2.1-125
270	54-524.65
271	29-138, 29-145.1, 29-155.2 to 29-155.4
272	54-872.20
273	2.1-51.30
274	56-304.1
275	33.1-351, 33.1-370
276	58-960
277	3.1-722.10
278	16.1-279
279	63.1-282 to 63.1-284R
280	63.1-238.3
281	18.2-204.2
282	58-664
283	56-227
284	63.1-195
285	18.2-250
286	38.1-776.1, 38.1-776.2, 38.1-778
287	54-524.65
288	54-524.16, 54-524.23, 54-524.26, 54-524.27, 54-524.31, 54-524.34:1, 54-524.40, 54-524.41:1, 54-524.44, 54-524.47:3
289	54-74, 54-74.1
290	58-761.1
291	3.1-135 to 3.1-157R, 3.1-188.20 to 3.1-188.23, 3.1-188.25, 3.1-188.26, 3.1-188.29, 3.1-188.31R, 3.1-188.31:1, 3.1-188.31:2, 3.1-188.32 to 3.1-188.49
292	64.1-122.1
293	55-210.3, 55-210.6:1, 55-210.9
294	56-265.4:3
295	16.1-283
296	4-90.2
297	4-98.10
298	15.1-508.1
299	4-31, 4-37, 4-118.11
300	53-128.16 to 53-128.21
301	29-11, 33.1-69.1
303	18.2-186.2
304	15.1-1377, 15.1-1391
305	21-89.3, 45.1-106, 45.1-115.1, 45.1-116, 45.1-139
306	5.1-2.2
307	3.1-814
308	3.1-292
309	9-109
310	55-154
311	30-28.5:2
312	62.1-3.01, 62.1-3.02
313	3.1-668, 3.1-669R, 3.1-669.1, 3.1-672R, 3.1-672.1, 3.1-676
314	58-829.1:1
315	63.1-14
316	3.1-777 to 3.1-796R, 3.1-796.01 to 3.1-796.020, 3.1-796.1 to 3.1-796.6, 3.1-796.9, 3.1-796.11:1 to 3.1-796.11:10
317	58-837, 58-874, 58-875
318	58-266.1
319	63.1-248.16
320	49-1
321	15.1-489
322	15.1-447
323	15.1-295
324	4-2, 4-25.1, 4-27
325	28.1-83
326	38.1-381
327	30-19.04
328	46.1-343
329	6.1-195.27:1
330	6.1-330.39
331	38.1-381
332	20-107
333	18.2-53.1
334	9-106.7
335	15.1-801
336	6.1-5.3
337	46.1-267, 46.1-285
338	16.1-69.25:1
339	18.2-460.1
340	18.2-397
341	13.1-39.1, 13.1-40
342	46.1-282.1
343	58-884
344	19.2-74.1
345	6.1-330.10
346	8.01-75
347	46.1-193
348	6.1-39.1, 6.1-39.2
349	19.2-232
350	6.1-195.4
351	6.1-195.13R, 6.1-195.13:1
352	6.1-195.22
353	6.1-195.39
354	46.1-226
355	46.1-254.1
356	14.1-44.4
357	2.1-440 to 2.1-442, 2.1-447, 2.1-458
358	15.1-478.2
359	46.1-104
360	58-804
361	55-31.1
362	19.2-54
363	58-769.10
364	45.1-198, n., 45.1-200.1, 45.1-201, n., 45.1-216, n., 45.1-220.1, n., 45.1-226, n., 45.1-234
365	42.1-86
366	46.1-179.1 to 46.1-179.3
367	58-685.29
368	21-11.18 to 21-11.20
369	28.1-195
371	58-597
372	15.1-1374
373	33.1-46.1
374	33.1-43.2
376	2.1-548.1 to 2.1-548.5
377	63.1-39, 63.1-44
378	10-17.23, 32.1-27, 62.1-44.32
379	15.1-466
381	15.1-466
382	58-831.2
383	63.1-44
384	56-249.6
385	58-681
386	55-79.79
387	28.1-4
388	45.1-41, 45.1-105
389	11-24 to 11-26, 11-27R, 11-28, 11-29
390	43-13

TABLE OF ACTS CODIFIED SUBSEQUENT TO 1948

Acts 1980 Chapter	Code 1950 Section
392	17-92
393	15.1-142.2, n., 15.1-527.1, n.
394	17-47.3
395	3.1-1031 to 3.1-1049
396	58-785.1
398	37.1-65.3
399	9-85
400	22.1-222
401	18.2-248.2
402	32.1-174.1, 32.1-174.2
403	11-17, 11-23
404	38.1-50, 38.1-51, 38.1-52R, 38.1-52.1 to 38.1-52.14, 38.1-53 to 38.1-56
405	33.1-75.1
406	60.1-79
407	4-69
408	60.1-61
409	64.1-21
410	32.1-46
411	8.01-35.1
412	58-412, 58-829, 58-829.2:1, 58-829.7, 58-831
413	3.1-276, 3.1-277, 3.1-283
414	58-758.1, n.
415	56-247.1
416	18.2-340.2, 18.2-340.3, 18.2-340.8
417	58-760.2, 58-760.3
418	4-15.01
419	8.01-225
420	15.1-536
421	65.1-4.2
422	2.1-376.1
423	19.2-270.2
424	63.1-135, 63.1-137, 63.1-140
425	54-729.27, 54-729.33, 54-729.34
426	60.1-61, 50.1-62
427	58-411
428	10-215 to 10-222
429	2.1-21, n.
430	6.1-330.20
431	6.1-330.20
432	18.2-340.9
433	54-1.2:1
434	16.1-69.32:1
435	6.1-330.20

Acts 1980 Chapter	Code 1950 Section
436	46.1-387.8
437	8.01-66.1
438	64.1-131
439	64.1-179
440	26-5.2
441	25-46.7, 33.1-229
442	45.1-2, 45.1-12, 45.1-20.1
443	65.1-106
444	65.1-153 to 65.1-163
445	57-55R, 57-55.1
446	56-238
447	16.1-218, 17-228
448	8.01-217
449	43-3
450	14.1-46.01
451	10-17.114
452	8.01-353
453	8.01-389
454	64.1-64
455	8.01-217
456	46.1-171
457	59.1-21.18:2 to 59.1-21.18:4
458	4-69.1, 4-79
459	18.2-200.1
460	15.1-31
461	56-291.3:6, n.
462	6.1-71, 64.1-123 to 64.1-125
463	60.1-23, 60.1-37R, 60.1-47, 60.1-52, 60.1-67R, 60.1-67.1, 60.1-80
464	40.1-51.15:1
465	1-15.2
466	9-146 to 9-148R
467	56-291.3:1 to 56-291.3:5, 56-291.4 to 56-291.8:1R
468	3.1-1050 to 3.1-1056, 4-119 to 4-126R
469	10-17.18, 46.1-41, 46.1-326.2 to 46.1-326.14, 52-4
470	32.1-67
471	59.1-68.6 to 59.1-68.8
472	18.2-498.1 to 18.2-498.5
473	4-24.1

Acts 1980 Chapter	Code 1950 Section
474	45.1-33.7 to 45.1-33.12
475	2.1-344
476	2.1-344
477	2.1-373.1
478	2.1-373.2
479	8.01-44.1
480	60.1-75, 60.1-84, 60.1-85, 60.1-91
481	2.1-114.5:1
482	2.1-114.5:1
483	15.1-292
484	46.1-485
485	53-214
486	46.1-309.1
487	23-35.5:1, 23-35.6
488	2.1-425.1R, 2.1-522 to 2.1-526R, 2.1-526.1 to 2.1-526.8
489	27-72, 27-78.1
490	4-98.1, 4-98.2, 4-98.7
491	43-4
492	19.2-74
493	58-769.8
494	29-52, 29-52.1R, 29-53R, 29-54, 29-54.1, 29-55, 29-56, 29-66, 29-68, 29-69, 29-94, 29-95, 29-96R, 29-96.1, 29-97R, 29-100, 29-101, 29-106 to 29-108.1R, 29-109, 29-111R, 29-111.1, 29-112R, 29-112.1R, 29-113, 29-114R, 29-114.1R, 29-118, 29-121R, 29-122, 29-154
495	55-248.11
496	19.2-8
497	58-811.1
498	27-34.4, 27-79.9
499	8.01-241
500	29-52
501	58-841
502	8.01-126, 55-248.31
503	32.1-164.1
504	53-307, 53-307.1
505	19.2-38, 19.2-38.1
506	18.2-47
507	64.1-180.1

Acts 1980 Chapter	Code 1950 Section
508	58-769.8, 58-769.8:1
509	6.1-330.44:1
510	45.1-246, 45.1-246.1
512	15.1-29.8
513	32.1-178
514	8.01-513
515	53-265.1
516	3.1-418.1
517	19.2-191
518	64.1-42
519	46.1-384.1
520	60.1-14
521	19.2-368.11, 19.368.18
522	60.1-14
523	46.1-6
524	4-33, 4-34, 4-98.18
525	2.1-513, 2.1-513.1R, 10-45.1 to 10-45.4
526	4-25, 4-33
527	16.1-241
528	4-25
529	16.1-241
530	16.1-232
531	19.2-311
532	40.1-28.10
533	54-60, 54-62, 54-62.1R, 54-62.2
534	18.2-346, 18.2-348, 18.2-355 to 18.2-358, 18.2-360
535	8.01-341
536	16.1-69.44
537	8.01-511, 8.01-512, 8.01-512.2
538	2.1-234.1 to 2.1-234.9
539	15.1-466.1
540	14.1-164.1
541	4-45, 4-46
542	9-111.9
543	4-45, 4-46, 4-96.3
544	8.01-606
545	15.1-33.1
546	55-337 to 55-339, 55-340.1, 55-342, 55-344
547	15.1-19.3
548	18.2-162
549	15.1-19
550	14.1-78
551	46.1-3
552	2.1-348
553	18.2-268
554	65.1-136
555	55-230, 55-230.1, 55-232 to 55-232.2, 55-237
556	37.1-225 to 37.1-228, 37.1-230
558	15.1-945.7
559	2.1-574 to 2.1-586, 7.1-36R, 15.1-186, 15.1-189, 15.1-228 to 15.1-232, 15.1-234, 15.1-262, 15.1-264, 15.1-265, 15.1-506.1, 15.1-571.1, 15.1-609, 15.1-609.1, 15.1-644, 15.1-644.1, 15.1-708, 15.1-770, 15.1-1003, 22-1 to 22-363R, 22.1-1 to 22.1-345, 23-1, 23-70 to 23-72, 23-115, 23-117, 23-258, 25-232, 46.1-380.2, 51-111.24, 57-60, 58-441.48
560	29-130.2
561	22.1-214.1
562	2.1-349.1
563	26-12.3
565	15.1-1500 to 15.1-1505R
566	53-166.1, 53-166.2
567	28.1-185.1, 62.1-184
568	46.1-387.5
569	58-776
570	22.1-199
571	54-740
572	16.1-266
573	19.2-56, 19.2-57
574	43-20
575	22.1-297
576	22.1-3
577	15.1-945.7
578	58-465 to 58-485R, 58-485.01 to 58-485.018, 58-485.1 to 58-485.20R
580	14.1-134R 14.1-168, 14.1-170, 47-1 to 47-7R, 47.1-1 to 47.1-33, 55-116 to 55-118R
581	38.1-327.7, 38.1-327.33
582	37.1-1, 37.1-2R, 37.1-3, 37.1-5, 37.1-6, 37.1-8R, 37.1-9R, 37.1-10 to 37.1-13, 37.1-20R, 37.1-20.1, 37.1-21R, 37.1-22 to 37.1-24, 37.1-24.2, 37.1-25R, 37.1-26R, 37.1-27 to 37.1-32, 37.1-34, 37.1-34.1R, 37.1-39, 37.1-42 to 37.1-42.2, 37.1-43R, 37.1-58, 37.1-61, 37.1-64 to 37.1-65.1, 37.1-67.1 to 37.1-67.3, 37.1-70, 37.1-71, 37.1-78, 37.1-95, 37.1-97 to 37.1-99, 37.1-121, 37.1-122, 37.1-124, 37.1-128.01, 37.1-128.02, 37.1-128.03R, 37.1-128.04, 37.1-128.1, 37.1-128.2, 37.1-132, 37.1-134.1, 37.1-138, 37.1-139, 37.1-141, 37.1-142, 37.1-179, 37.1-179.1, 37.1-180R, 37.1-181, 37.1-182, 37.1-183.1, 37.1-183.2, 37.1-185 to 37.1-187, 37.1-194 to 37.1-200, 37.1-203 to 37.1-209, 37.1-210 to 37.1-213R, 37.1-214, 37.1-215, 37.1-216R, 37.1-217 to 37.1-220, 37.1-223
583	37.1-99
584	32.1-122.1 to 32.1-122.4
585	53-19.35
586	46.1-351.1, 46.1-351.2
587	14.1-51, 14.1-73, 14.1-73.1R, 14.1-73.1:1 to 14.1-73.1:3, 14.1-73.2
588	14.1-50, 14.1-51, 14.1-51.1R, 14.1-52, 14.1-53, 14.1-55 to 14.1-58, 14.1-62, 14.1-64, 14.1-66, 14.1-73, 14.1-74
589	18.2-271.1
592	15.1-945.3, 15.1-945.4, 15.1-945.6, 15.1-945.7,

Acts 1980 Chapter	Code 1950 Section
	15.1-994.1, 15.1-1032.1, 15.1-1046, 15.1-1167
593	14.1-195.1
594	14.1-195.1
595	51-111.54, 51-111.67:2, 51-111.67:4 to 51-111.67:6
596	2.1-328, 51-111.24 to 51-111.24:8, 51-111.52:2R, 51 111.52:4R, 51-111.52:5R
597	63.1-315 to 63.1-319
598	43-33, 43-34
599	65.1-139, 65.1-140, 65.1-141R, 65.1-141.1, 65.1-142R, 65.1-142.1, 65.1-143R, 65.1-144
600	65.1-88, 65.1-96, 65.1-97
601	37.1-132
602	29-144.4:1
603	15.1-1261
604	15.1-486.1, n.
605	28.1-59
606	65.1-97
607	29-144.4:1
608	9-157, 9-161
609	28.1-109
610	58-441.6
611	58-441.6, 58-441.15
612	23-243, 23-244, 23-249
613	16.1-69.45
614	58-12.108, 58-12.109
615	2.1-541 to 2.1-548R, 17-111.3 to 17-111.7
616	54-145.11, 54-145.12
617	58-441.6
618	58-441.6, 58-685.31
620	2.1-51.27, 2.1-454, 2.1-563.1 to 2.1-563.12, 15.1-23.1
621	58-441.6
622	58-12.110 to 58-12.121
623	8.01-66.5, 801-66.6, 8.01-66.8
624	4-15.1R, 4-22.1, 4-24R
625	23-174.4
626	19.2-163, 19.2-326, 53-299.1
627	58-441.15
628	2.1-410
629	58-151.1
630	13.1-102.2, 13.1-265.2
631	58-441.6
632	14.1-155.4
633	58-48.6 to 58-48.8, 58-151.01, 58-151.32R, 58-435, 58-441.38, 48-441.41R, 58-685.34R, 58-757.1, 58-757.23, 58-838.17, 58-1117.20, 58-1118, 58-1118.1, 59-1119, 59-1119.1, 58-1130, 58-1134, 58-1136, 58-1137
634	54-113, 54-114, 54-115, 54-116, 54-117R 54-118R, 54-119, 54-120, 54-123 to 54-126, 54-128, 54-129R, 54-129.1 to 54-129.3, 54-130R, 54-131, 54-132.1, 54-133, 54-134 to 54-137R, 54-138 to 54-142, 54-143R, 54-144, 54-145R, 54-145.1R, 54-145.2
635	54-145.3 54-145.3:9
637	51-111.16, 51-111.67:4
638	51-111.16, 51-111.67:4
639	24.1-29, 24.1-32, 24.1-36, 24.1-37, 24.1-46, 24.1-48, 24.1-72.12, 24.1-92, 24.1-95, 24.1-105, 24.1-106, 24.1-109 to 24.1-111, 24.1-113.1, 24.1-115, 24.1-117, 24.1-133, 24.1-135, 24.1-151, 24.1-152, 24.1-154, 24.1-155, 24.1-165, 24.1-167, 24.1-168, 24.1-185, 24.1-189, 24.1-206.1, 24.1-219, 24.1-228, 24.1-229, 24.1-250, 24.1-251, 24.1-261
640	51-111.52:5, n.
641	51-2.1
642	51-111.60
643	51-111.67:12.1
644	51-111.47:1
645	51-111.59:1
646	51-111.16, 51-111.60
647	51-111.3
648	23-93
649	58-627
650	58-678, 58-692, 58-710.1 to 58-710.3R, 58-711
651	58-732 to 58-734.1, 58-738, 58-739.1, 58-739.2R, 58-739.3, 58-740 to 58-742, 58-744, 58-746 to 58-748, 58-748.2, 58-749, 58-749.1, 58-755
652	58-64
653	26-4
654	13.1-92
656	58-760.1
657	58-1142
658	23-8.1R, 23-8.3R, 23-9R, 23-265 to 23-276
659	6.1-14
660	62.1-13.21 to 62.1-13.28
661	58-787
662	62.1-69.5 to 62.1-69.20
663	58-847, 58-964, 58-1140.1, 58-1160, 58-1160.1
667	38.1-915 to 38.1-930
666	58-760.1
667	22.1-18, n.
668	58-603
670	27-87, 27-88, 27-90
671	10-90.1R, 10-90.26
672	2.1-206.1R, 2.1-225, 10-145.11
673	58-760.1
674	60.1-127
675	58-16.5
676	58-715, 58-744
677	45.1-195
678	2.1-342, 18.2-261, 54-950, 54-950.2, 54-953 to 54-955.1, 54-957

Acts 1980 Chapter	Code 1950 Section
	to 54-961
679	23-38.30 to 23-38.32, 23-38.33R, 23-38.33:1, 23-38.34R, 23-38.35, 23-38.36, 23-38.37R, 23-38.38 to 23-38.43
680	51-111.26
681	51-111.18
682	38.1-810 to 38.1-812, 38.1-813, n., 38.1-813.1 to 38.1-814, 38.1-816 to 38.1-818, 38.1-821, 38.1-822R, 38.1-822.1, 38.1-824 to 38.1-828, 38.1-834R, 38.1-835 to 38.1-848R, 38.1-849 to 38.1-862R, 38.1-892 to 38.1-914
687	2.1-532 to 2.1-590R, 2.1-541, n., 30-28.16, 30-34.1 to 30-34.10
695	15.1-50
696	56-265.15, 56-265.16, 56-265.18 to 56.265.20, 56-265.25
698	16.1-269
699	15.1-29.5
700	51-127.23
701	13.1-543
702	55-79.48
703	56-90.1
704	46.1-441.2, 46.1-514.17
705	8.01-636, 8.01-637
706	6.1-195.34
707	6.1-330.14R, 6.1-330.14:1
708	6.1-330.37
709	55-59
710	56-265.15
711	2.1-357
712	28.1-230
713	6.1-330.13R, 6.1-330.13:1
714	6.1-66
715	54-318.1
716	58-371.2
718	14.1-18
719	38.1-348.12, 38.1-360, 38.1-818, 38.1-835 to 38.1-848, n., 38.1-849 to 38.1-862, n.
720	38.1-813R, 38.1-863 to 38.1-890, 38.1-891, n.
721	5.1-1, 5.1-5, 5.1-6, 5.1-7, 5.1-8, 5.1-9.1 to 5.1-9.9, 5.1-11, 5.1-12, 5.1-23, 5.1-39, 5.1-56, n., 5.1-77 to 5.1-82R, 5.1-89, 5.1-103 to 5.1-106R, 5.1-145
722	51-111.10:01, 51-111.28:1, 51-111.46:1, 51-111.47:01, 51-111.55:1, 51-111.57:1
723	30-28.16
724	6.1-330.16
725	30-34.11 to 30-35.14
726	15.1-242
727	55-79.94
728	2.1-20.2 to 2.1-20.4, 2.1-64.4 to 2.1-64.14R, 2.1-64.23, 2.1-113.2, 3.1-5R, 3.1-427, 5.1-2.4R, 5.1-57, n., 9-95R, 9-105R, 9-107.1, 9-142, 9-153, 10-6, 10-17.13R, 10-20R, 10-21.6R, 10-90.1R, 10-90.22, 10-97R, 10-145.5R, 15.1-173, 15.1-945.2, 22.1-15R, 22.1-164, 22.1-575, 23-9.3, 23-9.10:1, 23-9.10:2, 23-30.25, 23-38.32, 23-217, 23-221.1R, 24.1-18, 28.1-8, 29-5R, 32.1-10R, 32.1-91R, 32.1-119, 32.1-233, 32.1-242, 33.1-5R, 36-110R, 36-138R, 37.1-9R, 40.1-22, 40.1-117, 45.1-10, 45.1-195, 46.1-26.1, 46.1-550.2, 51-111.18, 51-111.26, 53-19.26R, 54-1.29R, 54-162.1R, 54-260.69, 54-267R, 54-295, 54-295.7, 54-367.12, 54-375.1R, 54-524.15, 54-784.01R, 54-872.23, 54-954, 62.1-44.10R, 62.1-129, 63.1-17R, 63.1-76R, 63.1-85.6R
729	27-2.1
730	6.1-2.6R, 6.1-2.10 to 6.1-2.15
731	64.1-123.2
732	8.01-300
733	19.2-299
734	56-245.1:1
735	58-1145
736	58-266.1
737	18.2-255.1
738	55-79.74,

Acts 1980 Chapter	Code 1950 Section
	55-79.74:1, 55-79.94
739	16.1-86
740	63.1-223, 63.1-228
741	56-245.3
742	15.1-686.4
743	38.1-327.19, 38.1-327.28, 38.1-327.45
744	58-33
745	9-152.1 to 9-152.5
746	29-213.19
747	30-19.03
748	6.1-2.9:1
749	30-19.03
750	5.1-2.1, 5.1-2.2:1, 5.1-2.5 to 5.1-2.24, 5.1-56 to 5.1-76R
751	60.1-132
752	2.1-384
753	58-441.3, 58-441.6
754	2.1-341, 2.1-342, 2.1-344
755	58-441.34
756	58-441.6, 58-441.49:3
757	13.1-543, 13.1-549, 13.1-550, 54-1.18, 54-17.1, 54-18R, 54-18.1, 54-19, 54-23, 54-26, 54-26.2, 54-37, 54-874, 54-875
758	19.2-40R, 19.2-49R, 19.2-50, n., 19.2-51R
759	18.2-274 to 18.2-278R, 18.2-278.1 to 18.2-278.7, 56-338.20

ACTS 1981

Acts 1981 Chapter	Code 1950 Section
1	57-5
2	36-99
3	15.1-1378
4	14.1-44.2, 19.2-34, 19.2-35
5	19.2-48.1
6	8.01-320, 8.01-328.1
7	22.1-214
8	2.1-116
9	46.1-550.11
10	13.1-400.1
12	15.1-37.5, 15.1-37.5:1, 15.1-37.6, 15.1-788, 24.1-17, 24.1-17.1, 24.1-88
13	14.1-46.01
14	14.1-144.1
15	2.1-353.01
16	29-52, 29-92.1 to 29-92.7
17	46.1-291
18	2.1-328.3
19	33.1-345
20	53-251.3
21	2.1-1, 63.1-1.1 to 63.1-11, 63.1-13, 63.1-14, 63.1-24, 63.1-25.1, 63.1-25.2, 63.1-31
22	54-325.2
23	28.1-173.1
24	4-37, 4-62, 4-112, 4-112.1, 46.1-384.1
25	28.1-186, 38.1-203
26	16.1-69.6:1
27	17-119.1:2
28	60.1-14
30	54-524.84:6
31	19.2-8
32	45.1-4
33	10-93
34	54-733
35	2.1-344
36	2.1-185
37	6.1-278
38	6.1-278
39	40.1-51.11
40	8.01-44.1
41	22.1-299.1
42	38.1-348.13
44	15.1-292.1, n.
46	38.1-397R, 38.1-397.1
47	55-210.2 to 55-210.8, 55-210.10 to 55-210.14, 55-210.16R, 55-210.18 to 55-210.19, 55-210.21, 55-210.26, 55-210.27:1, 55-210.30
48	42.1-70
49	17-54
50	3.1-796.51
51	13.1-322
52	28.1-69.1, 28.1-83, 28.1-85, 28.1-96, 28.1-124, 28.1-128.1, 28.1-166, 28.1-167, 28.1-179
53	6.1-125.5
54	15.1-1508
55	6.1-244
56	6.1-234
57	13.1-205.1
58	13.1-544, 13.1-544.1
59	6.1-195.34
60	29-144.4
61	28.1-48
62	6.1-195.11
63	28.1-128.1
64	10-152, 10-158
65	6.1-69
71	40.1-129, 40.1-130, 40.1-132
72	28.1-82
73	58-48.2
74	60.1-68.1
75	63.1-195, 63.1-207, 63.1-207.1
76	45.1-186.2
77	15.1-10.1
78	15.1-1132
80	2.1-563.1
81	55-226.1
83	2.1-393
86	6.1-2.10
87	2.1-114.5:1
90	63.1-41
91	15.1-623
92	15.1-702
93	6.1-195.3:1
94	58-238.2
95	58-441.33
96	58-151.25, 58-151.26
97	58-151.067:1
98	64.1-160
99	60.1-70, 60.1-73
100	12.1-23
101	56-338.56, 56-338.57, 56-338.62
102	56-338.41:1, 56-338.44, 56-338.45
103	54-42.1
104	2.1-512
105	11-18, 11-20, 11-23
106	6.1-330.15
107	38.1-736 to

Acts 1981 Chapter	Code 1950 Section
	38.1-738, 38.1-740R, 38.1-740.1, 38.1-740.2, 38.1-741 to 38.1-743, 38.1-745
108	8.01-341.2
109	16.1-296
110	8.01-293
111	28.1-17
112	2.1-511
113	26-20.1
114	2.1-398
115	8.01-50
116	44-146.16, 44-146.17
117	54-740
119	28.1-139
120	15.1-42
122	15.1-9.1:1
123	63.1-248.2
124	15.1-274.1
125	46.1-105.7
127	62.1-69.19
128	28.1-154
129	8.01-76
130	3.1-726, 3.1-731, 3.1-733
131	45.1-90
132	54-1.18, 54-962 to 54-968
134	58-966
135	2.1-295 to 2.1-302R
137	54-112.2
138	28.1-128.01
139	15.1-166, 15.1-167
140	3.1-741.2
141	37.1-134.2
142	22.1-273
143	58-846.1
144	32.1-248
145	58-405, 58-685.12:1, 58-685.20, 58-685.23, 58-685.25, 58-833
146	55-79.80
147	6.1-330.24
148	55-248.31:1
149	25-247.1
150	8.01-353
151	51-111.67:4
152	14.1-101
153	58-1009
154	9-153 to 9-155.2, 27-91R to 27-93R
155	55-222
156	21-112.2, 21-112.11, 21-112.12R, 21-112.12:1, 21-112.13, 21-112.18
157	18.2-340.6
158	58-879, 58-884
159	16.1-135
161	19.2-163.1
162	3.1-678
163	46.1-184, 46.1-230
164	32.1-67
165	18.2-96.1
166	32.1-134.3
167	2.1-410, 2.1-457, 2.1-457.1
168	13.1-508
169	13.1-527.01
170	32.1-112
171	38.1-42.1
172	38.1-384, 38.1-387, 38.1-387.1
173	10-201.1
174	8.01-581.16
175	16.1-301
176	5.1-8
177	56-207R, 56-208R
178	58-1147
179	45.1-48
180	55-79.83
181	2.1-20.3
182	15.1-1232
183	64.1-87
184	16.1-256
185	22.1-212.1
186	18.2-214.1
187	46.1-339, 46.1-342, 46.1-343, 46.1-347
188	18.2-110
189	22.1-280.1
190	22.1-239
191	22.1-157
192	33.1-43
193	46.1-167.1, 46.1-167.4
194	46.1-357.2
195	18.2-271.1
196	30-19.3
197	18.2-80, 18.2-81, 18.2-97, 18.2-102, 18.2-150, 18.2-162, 18.2-165.1, 18.2-186, 18.2-187.1, 18.2-188, 18.2-195, 18.2-197, 19.2-289, 19.2-290
198	29-213.28
202	9-45.1
203	6.1-52
204	29-20, 58-151.072:1
205	59.1-198, 59.1-200
206	14.1-11.1
207	19.2-389
208	38.1-173.1
211	10-224 to 10-229, 10-231, 10-232, 10-234 to 10-236, 10-239 to 10-242, 10-245, 10-247
212	58-785.1
213	16.1-267
214	6.1-2.9:2
215	33.1-398R, 33.1-399
216	54-170
217	13.1-543
218	46.1-556 to 46.1-563
219	10-45.2 to 10-54.4, 44-134.1R
220	8.01-512
221	2.1-488.1
222	63.1-175, 63.1-178, 63.1-201
223	52-9
224	19.2-305.1
225	23-50.6
226	54-182R
228	1-13.11R
229	22.1-87
230	8.01-27.1, 18.2-181
231	16.1-218, 17-228
232	33.1-72.1
233	37.1-67.4
234	2.1-467.2, 42.1-19
235	19.2-297
236	58-829.5
237	46.1-422
238	52-8.3
239	26-46.1, 26-46.2
240	33.1-70.01
241	38.1-327.52
242	37.1-76
243	38.1-279.33, 38.1-279.33:1
244	13.1-505, 13.1-506
245	38.1-380.2, 38.1-382.1R
246	15.1-609, 15.1-644, 15.1-708, 15.1-770, 22.1-40, 22.1-44, 22.1-47, 22.1-75
247	65.1-65, 65.1-70
248	60.1-89, 60.1-89.2
249	60.1-124, 60.1-124.1
250	60.1-80
251	60.1-58, 60.1-132
252	60.1-88.1, 60.1-89
253	13.1-10.1R, 13.1-209.1R
254	15.1-33.2
255	18.2-186.1R, 32.1-310 to 32.1-321, 32.1-322, n.
256	15.1-33.3
257	23-38.12, 23-38.13,

Acts 1981 Chapter	Code 1950 Section
	23-38.15, 23-38.16
258	54-260.72, 54-260.74
259	63.1-204
260	3.1-191, 3.1-193, 3.1-194, 3.1-198, 3.1-198.1R, 3.1-202, 3.1-203, 3.1-206 to 3.1-208, 3.1-211, 3.1-215 to 3.1-222, 3.1-224 to 3.1-231, 3.1-233, 3.1-233.2, 3.1-235R, 3.1-236 3.1-242, 3.1-246, 3.1-248, 3.1-249, 3.1-249.8 to 3.1-249.10, 3.1-249.13
261	15.1-535
262	62.1-44.15:1
263	19.2-299
264	63.1-43.1
265	65.1-99.1
266	15.1-33.1
267	58-64
268	57-35.1
269	4-98.2
270	4-109.2R, 4-109.3
271	6.1-63, 6.1-64
272	38.1-35, 38.1-208, 38.1-212
273	18.2-340.1, 18.2-340.9
274	18.2-340.2, 18.2-340.9, 18.2-340.13
275	63.1-174.1
276	53-241.1
277	50-45
278	53-151
279	46.1-181.4:1
280	8.01-358
281	64.1-132.1 to 64.1-132.4
282	32.1-36
283	58-151.13
284	15.1-135.1
285	13.1-50
286	8.01-55
287	63.1-196.01
288	44-97.1
289	19.2-159.1
290	58-863.2
291	55-154.2
292	19.2-270.3
293	18.2-373
294	21-120
295	17-62, 20-23, 20-25, 20-26
296	15.1-50.1, 15.1-821
297	8.01-217
298	20-24
299	53-19.14:1
300	54-276.5
301	29-213.25
302	19.2-368.5:1
303	46.1-198.1
304	46.1-290
305	8 01-581.1
306	19.2-80.1
307	16.1-309.1
308	9-53, 9-55, 9-75.1, 62.1-67
309	36-137, 36-139
310	19.2-171 to 19.2-174, 19.2-179R, 19.2 181, 20-46
311	47.1-19
312	8.01-452.1
313	8.01-66.2
315	2.1-51.27, 2.1-391, 2.1-411 to 2.1-414R, 2.1-564 to 2.1-568, 9-55.1, 15.1-1406, 62.1-44.112
316	15.1-236, 25-46.7
317	38.1-865
318	63.1-230
319	23-123R, 23-129R
320	13.1-119, 13.1-135, 13.1-281, 13.1-296
321	33.1-75.3
322	38.1-348.12R, 38.1-348.12:1
323	33.1-150 to 33.1-154
324	15.1-29.9
325	36-98.1
326	5.1-7, 5.1-7.2, 5.1-25.1
327	8.01-581.7:1
328	60.1-52.3
329	1-12
330	6.1-208.4
331	15.1-11.4, 40.1-117
332	15.1-7.3
333	46.1-190
334	53-179
335	2.1-114.2:1
336	6.1-330.44
337	32.1-76
338	46.1-267
339	6.1-121R, 18.2-444.2
340	33.1-346
341	22.1-3
342	22.1-3, 22.1-5
343	6.1-62.1
344	32.1-87
345	6.1-277
346	32.1-162.1 to 32.1-162.6
347	13.1-514
348	15.1-466
349	55-248.11
352	55-248.11
353	55-248.11
354	32.1-188
355	46.1-105.9
356	13.1-514
357	32.1-83
358	14.1-47.1, 14.1-47.2
359	63.1-238.1, 63.1-238.3, 63.1-238.4
360	56-289
362	38.1-123 to 38.1-125R, 13.1-514
363	56-129.1
365	4-56
367	24.1-165
369	60.1-14, 60.1-51.1, 60.1-52.2
370	33.1-44
371	10-90.22R, 10-90.23R, 10-90.26R, 10-90.30 to 10-90.39
372	58-838.5:2, 58-838.7:1
373	6.1-330.10
374	60.1-14
375	60.1-14
376	18.2-308
377	2.1-380.1
379	11-23.6 to 11-23.10
380	53-133.1 to 53-133.4
381	4-15.2R, 4-15.3, n., 4-37.2, 4-98.4, 4-98.20, 4-112.3, 4-112.4, 4-114.2
382	19.2-73, 19.2-74, 19.2-74.1R, 19.2-82, 19.2-128, 46.1-178, 46.1-178.1, 46.1-179, 46.1-179.2
383	14.1-73
384	3.1-22.28, 3.1-22.29
385	56-232
386	19.2-328, 53-183.2
387	9-6.14:7, 9-6.14:9
388	32.1-283, 32.1-287
389	38.1-52.14R, 38.1-57.2 to 38.1-57.26, 38.1-57.27, n., 38.1-57.28
390	6.1-330.18
391	58-711, 58-744
392	53-209.1 to 53-209.6, 53-214, 53-215R, 53-220, 53-227R, 53-251, 53-251.2, 53-251.3
393	51-151, 51-168

Acts 1981 Chapter	Code 1950 Section
394	46.1-227
395	46.1-199, 46.1-226
396	51-162, 51-174.1
397	18.2-32, 18.2-61, 18.2-63, 18.2-63.1, 18.2-64R, 18.2-64.1, 18.2-65R, 18.2-66 to 18.2-67.10, 18.2-359, 18.2-361, 18.2-366, 18.2-370, 18.2-371
398	58-441.6
399	58-238.38
400	58-441.2
401	58-12.122 to 58-12.125
402	58-151.03, 58-151.013, 58-151.032 to 58-151.032:2, 58-151.033, 58-151.034, 58-151.036R, 58-151.037, 58-151.038 to 58-151.040R, 58-151.041 to 58-151.043, 58-151.045, 58-151.047, 58-151.048, 58-151.050:1 to 58-151.050:3, 58-151.079, 58-151.079:1, 58-151.0111
403	51-111.10:2, 51-111.10:3, 51-111.54, n.
404	16.1-77, 16.1-92
405	58-441.6, 58-685.39 to 58-685.50, 62.1-168, 62.1-186.1 to 62.1-186.24
406	14.1-73.1:1
407	4-22.1, 4-24.1R
408	58-19.6 to 58-19.21
409	58-441.6
410	4-24.1R, 4-25, 4-25.1, 4-89, 4-90
411	14.1-105
412	4-25
413	58-12.126 to 58-12.131
414	58-151.013
415	14.1-53, 14.1-58.2
416	58-441.3
417	33.1-251, 33.1-252, 33.1-285
418	15.1-427, 15.1-447, 15.1-490
419	58-266.1
420	58-441.16
421	58-1014
422	16.1-129.1
423	59.1-202
424	18.2-268
425	24.1-31, 24.1-40.3:1, 24.1-43, 24.1-55, 24.1-92, 24.1-99, 24.1-109, 24.1-111, 24.1-113.1, 24.1-126, 24.1-133 to 24.1-136, 24.1-141 to 24.1-144, 24.1-146, 24.1-150, 24.1-166, 24.1-176, 24.1-189, 24.1-190, 24.1-210, 24.1-222, 24.1-222.1, 24.1-227, 24.1-228R, 24.1-228.1, 24.1-229, 24.1-232, 24.1-234, 24.1-254.2, 24.1-255, 24.1-273, 24.1-277
426	8.01-281
427	2.1-121
431	58-758.1
432	58-485.04, 58-485.06, 58-485.08
433	58-943.3
434	58-760.1
435	63.1-235
436	58-919.2
437	58-834, 58-851.6
438	58-441.16
439	58-778
440	58-685.19
442	58-831.2
443	58-58
444	15.1-1357
445	58-829.8
446	9-6.14:21
447	54-1.18:1, 54-19, 54-20R, 54-21R, 54-83.1:8, 54-83.1:09R, 54-83.22, 54-85, 54-87R, 54-88R, 54-112.4:1R, 54-112.4:2, 54-115, 54-116R, 54-117R, 54-145.12, 54-262, 54-263R, 54-265R, 54-266R, 54-398.4:1, 54-398.6R, 54-398.7R, 54-524.113, 54-524.115R, 54-573.3, 54-729.4, 54-738, 54-859.2, 54-903, 54-904R, 54-907, 54-925, 54-933, 54-937, 54-924
449	8.01-195.1 to 8.01-195.8
450	21-11.21 to 21-11.29
451	8.01-220.1
452	6.1-254, 6.1-267, 6.1-267.1, 6.1-269, 6.1-299
453	43-32
454	16.1-241, 37.1-171.1R, 54-325.2, 54-325.3R to 54-325.6R, 54-325.9 to 54-325.15
455	55-79.94
456	2.1-342, 63.1-55.4
457	8.01-413
458	56-304.11
459	56-334
460	18.2-121.2
461	2.1-384
462	55-360 to 55-400
463	37.1-67.1
464	2.1-342, 2.1-384, 62.1-134.1
465	2.1-507
466	2.1-342
467	15.1-466.1
468	35-1 to 35-78R, 35.1-1, to 35.1-28
469	55-401 to 55-414, 55-415, n., 64.1-18R
471	2.1-344
472	19.2-163
473	6.1-330.16
474	19.2-368.11
475	16.1-241, 16.1-279
476	25-46.29 to 25-46.31, 33.1-128
478	51-111.67:2
479	51-111.5
480	55-79.41, 55-79.84:1, 55-79.98
482	22.1-32
483	15.1-768
484	64.1-171
485	14.1-79, 14.1-84.1 to

Acts 1981 Chapter	Code 1950 Section
	14.1-84.7
486	19.2-163
487	16.1-246, 16.1-279, 16.1-280, 16.1-287, 16.1-293, 16.1-300, 53-19.23, 53-134, 53-324 to 53-334
488	16.1-241
489	29-213.19
490	32.1-186
491	16.1-228, 16.1-241, 16.1-279
492	16.1-279
494	38.1-917
495	8.01-314
496	54-52.2:1
497	53-312.1
498	36-105
499	27-63, 27-64, 27-65R, 27-66.1, 27-69R, 27-70R, 27-70.1, 27-70.2R, 27-72, 27-73, 27-73.1, 27-78.1, 27-79, 27-79.1R to 27-79.8R, 27-79.9, 27-80, 27-81, 27-83, 27-83.1R, 27-84, 27-85R, 27-85.1R, 27-85.2
500	8.01-615
501	16.1-241
502	16.1-241
503	55-79.94
504	2.1-384
505	23-9.2, 23-30.01, 23-30.02
506	45.1-179.1 to 45.1-179.11, 56-265.1
507	29-213.19
508	29-213.19
509	32.1-180
510	16.1-241, 16.1-279
511	2.1-19
514	2.1-206, 4-22, 8.01-604, 8.01-605, 15.1-1041, 55-184.1, 55-186, 55-188 to 55-190, 55-192, 55-197, 55-200
516	54-42.2
517	23-4.2
518	55-154
519	59.1-70
520	6.1-94
521	6.1-221, 6.1-221.1
522	13.1-8, 13.1-123, 13.1-207.2, 13.1-285
523	13.1-120, 13.1-282
524	56-291.3:1
525	28.1-64, 28.1-72.1, 28.1-185
526	2.1-71
527	32.1-273
528	19.2-123
529	19.2-310, 19.2-390, 53-21.1
530	38.1-220, 38.1-279.31, 38.1-931 to 38.1-948
531	65.1-20
533	7.1-18.1
534	9-52.1
535	22.1-287
536	4-118.11
537	2.1-225, 10-145.11 to 10-145.13
538	54-729.28
539	55-248.35
540	22.1-256, 22.1-271
541	22.1-93
542	46.1-224.1
543	58-371.2
544	20-88.01
545	55-19.1
546	15.1-1511
547	2.1-164
548	3.1-796.48
549	29-213.17:1
550	45.1-20.2
551	15.1-151
552	15.1-51
554	21-118.4
555	54-941, 54-942
556	15.1-51
557	62.1-80.1
558	54-1.28:1
559	19.2-53, 19.2-54, 19.2-56
560	15.1-51
561	15.1-51
562	8.01-66.9
563	21-118.4
564	21-118, 21-118.4
565	4-98.7
566	4-15.3R
567	3.1-40 to 3.1-43, 3.1-44.1 to 3.1-46
568	18.2-371, 18.2-371.1
569	2.1-234.10 to 2.1-234.28
570	24.1-209, 24.1-221, 24.1-236R, 24.1-236.1, 24.1-237 to 24.1-243, 24.1-246.1R 24.1-249, 24.1-250
572	19.2-12
573	54-325.2
574	4-69.1R, 4-69.2
575	38.1-362.8:1 to 38.1-362.8:3, 38.1-362.13, 38.1-362.15, 38.1-362.17, 38.1-818, 38.1-818.1
576	16.1-82
577	3.1-27.36
578	3.1-27.36
579	28.1-49.1, 28.1-50
580	34-10 to 34-12R, 34-15R, 34-16R, 34-17, 34-23, 34-24, 64.1-11, 64.1-126R, 64.1-127R, 64.1-151.1 to 64.1-151.5, 64.1-154, 64.1-155, 64.1-157
581	54-859.15 to 54-859.27
582	62.1-44.32
583	2.1-234.6
584	15.1-239
585	46.1-1, 46.1-171, 46.1-171.1, 46.1-172.03, 46.1-173, 46.1-190, 46.1-208.1, 46.1-215.1, 46.1-217, 46.1-229, 46.1-229.01, 46.1-229.1, 46.1-229.2, 446.1-229.2:1, 46.1-235, 46.1-263, 46.1-227
586	4-37
587	19.2-12
588	6.1-330.37
589	2.1-41.2, 2.1-342, 2.1-384, 9-109, 62.1-128 to 62.1-132.19, 62.1-133R, 62.1-134R, 62.1-135R, 62.1-136, 62.1-137R, 62.1-140
590	62.1-140, 62.1-142, 62.1-143,

Acts 1981 Chapter	Code 1950 Section
	62.1-147, 62.1-147.1
591	55-59
592	19.2-368.4
593	18.2-204.1, 46.1-383.3, 46.1-385
594	46.1-383.3
595	51-127.10, 61-127.12
596	62.1-44.32
597	20-1
598	18.2-248.2R, 18.2-265.1 to 18.2-265.4
599	58-441.6
600	4-37
602	58-16.2
604	38.1-327.1, 38.1-327.13R, 38.1-327.33, 38.1-327.34, 38.1-327.36, 38.1-327.44, 38.1-327.45
605	38.1-44, 38.1-85
606	60.1-40.1, 60.1-47, 60.1-52, 60.1-75, 60.1-79 to 60.1-82, 60.1-83R, 60.1-84R, 60.1-84.1, n., 60.1-84.2, 60.1-85R, 60.1-85.1, n., 60.1-86R, 60.1-91
607	18.2-31
608	19.2-59.1
609	18.2-465.1
610	15.1-1250
611	15.1-486.2
612	55-269.1, 55-270, 55-271, 55-272.1, 55-273, 55-274, 55-275, 55-277
613	8.01-609
614	23-255, 23-260.1
615	8.01-676
619	46.1-397, 46.1-441.2
620	62.1-44.12, 62.1-44.14
621	58-60
622	40.1-79
623	14.1-46.01
624	46.1-326.3, 46.1-326.9, 46.1-326.14
625	58-760.2
626	46.1-291
627	55-416 to 55-421, 55-422, n., 55-423
628	17-116.1
629	58-151.032:4, 63.1-320 to 63.1-325
630	14.1-143R, 14.1-143.1, 14.1-144R, 14.1-145R, 14.1-148 to 14.1-150R, 14.1-152 to 14.1-155.1R, 14.1-155.3R, 14.1-155.4R
632	2.1-20.4, 2.1-64.23, n., 2.1-64.24 to 2.1-64.28R, 9-107.1, n., 9-108.1, n., 9-109, n., 9-109.1R, 9-109.2R, 9-109.2:1, n., 9-109.3, n., 9-109.4R, 9-109.5R, 9-110, n., 9-111 to 9-111.9R, 9-111.9, n., 9-111.10R, 9-111.11R, 9-111.11:1, n., 9-111.12 to 9-111.14R, 9-167, n., 9-168 to 9-196
633	62.1-44.38
634	53-19.40, 53-38
635	3.1-18.4 to 3.1-18.8
636	58-266.1
637	17-46, 17-46.1, 17-47.1 to 17-47.3R, 17-47.4, 42.1-77, 42.1-82, 42.1-91, 63.1-235
646	22.1-306

ACTS 1981, SP. SESS.

Acts 1981, Sp. Sess. Chapter	Code 1950 Section
1	6.1-330.18
2	24.1-14.1R, 24.1-14.2
4	25-46.34:1
5	24.1-12.1R, 24.1-12.2
6	38.1-381
7	6.1-330.18
8	24.1-4.2R, 24.1-4.3
10	25-46.34:1
12	24.1-12.2
13	60.1-51.1
14	24.1-14.2
15	20-25
16	24.1-12.2R, 24.1-12.3

ACTS 1982

Acts 1982 Chapter	Code 1950 Section
3	15.1-494
4	16.1-69.6:1
5	44-146.19
6	54-765.3
7	2.1-410
10	15.1-137.1, n.
11	37.1-128.1, 37.1-130, 37.1-132
12	2.1-574, 2.1-576, 2.1-579, 2.1-580, 2.1-583
13	59.1-201 to 59.1-203, 59.1-206
14	37.1-134.2
15	32.1-92R
16	32.1-241, 32.1-242, 32.1-244
17	15.1-865
18	23-9.2:4
19	15.1-270
20	15.1-29.4
21	22.1-214
23	37.1-196.1
24	60.1-67.1
25	60.1-14
27	29-55.3:3
29	29-130.2
30	15.1-9.1, n., 15.1-9:1, 15.1-680R
31	4-98.12
32	15.1-623, 15.1-623.1, 15.1-644
33	19.2-388, 19.2-390
35	52-21
36	36-139
38	15.1-138
39	15.1-456
40	19.2-66
41	32.1-310, 32.1-311R, 32.1-320
43	54-872.17
44	15.1-491
45	18.2-50.1
46	16.1-241
47	22.1-294

Acts 1982 Chapter	Code 1950 Section
48	15.1-51
50	37.1-1, 37.1-105, 37.1-110, 37.1-197, 37.1-202.1
51	35.1-25
53	32.1-102.1, n.
54	62.1-69.10
55	24.1-170, n.
56	13.1-400.1
57	17-119.1:2
59	58-16.5
60	59.1-915
61	15.1-1166
62	58-541.1, 58-664
63	13.1-400.1, 38.1-644.1
64	29-32, 29-32.1
65	4-67R
66	4-25, 4-28, 4-31, 4-32, 4-33, 4-38, 4-46, 4-49R, 4-51, 4-52, 4-62, 4-63, 4-112
67	46.1-167.7, 46.1-513.1
68	21-11.3
71	18.2-308
72	29-80
73	29-158
74	58-960
75	15.1-644
77	28.1-128.3
78	6.1-269R, 6.1-269.1
79	6.1-256R, 6.1-256.1
80	6.1-195.4
81	10-150.13, 10-150.14, 10-150.16, 10-150.17
82	65.1-52
83	40.1-109
84	40.1-28
85	46.1-65, 46.1-105.9
87	58-847, 58-964
88	46.1-104.1
89	32.1-112
90	46.1-279.01
91	16.1-260
92	46.1-326.2, 46.1-326.6
93	23-38.62, 23-38.66, 23-38.69
96	15.1-18.3
97	36-98.1, 36-98.2
98	60.1-38
99	3.1-763.9
100	3.1-610.1, 3.1-610.15
101	36-55.35
102	62.1-3
103	6.1-195.40R, 6.1-195.40:1, 6.1-195.40:2
104	13.1-36
105	8.01-461
107	56-248.1, 56-249.4
108	15.1-675, 15.1-675.1, 15.1-683, 15.1-687.3
109	2.1-180.1
110	2.1-328.4
111	6.1-39.2
112	6.1-79
113	36-96
114	58-862
115	63.1-223
116	28.1-229
117	45.1-194
118	45.1-104
119	4-98.2
120	56-224.1
121	28.1-128.2
122	4-118.12:1
123	58-760.1
125	14.1-47.2
126	3.1-684.20 to 3.1-684.40
127	28.1-46.4
128	65.1-88.1
129	38.1-816, 38.1-817
130	6.1-195.9
132	38.1-932, 38.1-934
133	40.1-80
134	40.1-81.1
135	40.1-85
136	40.1-87
137	40.1-112
138	24.1-90, n.
139	15.1-589
141	58-685.17:1 to 58-685.17:8
143	38.1-255.2
144	15.1-50
145	4-11, 4-98.14, 4-103
146	24.1-75
147	46.1-366
150	3.1-14
151	8.01-581.2, 8.01-581.9
152	36-55.32
153	16.1-104, 16.1-118, 16.1-118.1, 19.2-145
154	18.2-214.1
155	8.01-602, 8.01-603R, 8.01-604, 8.01-605
156	6.1-195.52, 6.1-195.70:1
157	46.1-157
158	33.1-390, 33.1-391
159	46.1-317.2
160	46.1-111
161	46.1-162
162	46.1-113
163	15.1-133.01
164	Art. II, § 2, n.
165	54-937
166	16.1-286
167	33.1-72.1
168	62.1-132.14
169	18.2-119
170	54-872.21
171	16.1-281, 16.1-282, 63.1-55, 63.1-56.2, 63.1-238.2, 63.1-238.3
172	3.1-796.6, 3.1-796.11:3, 3.1-796.11:4
173	15.1-550
174	4-79
175	36-55.39
176	36-55.33:1
177	33.1-8
178	63.1-321, 63.1-323 to 63.1-325
179	9-85
180	46.1-368, 46.1-375, 46.1-383.3
181	15.1-182, 15.1-183, 15.1-187, 15.1-188, 15.1-982.2
182	13.1-211, 13.1-217, 13.1-231
183	62.1-85
184	33.1-222
185	6.1-60R, 6.1-60.1
186	27-64, 27-72, 27-78.1
187	3.1-722.16, 3.1-722.19, 3.1-722.20, 3.1-722.20:1, 3.1-722.21 to 3.1-722.24, 3.1-722.27, 3.1-722.28
188	54-775R
189	46.1-336
191	7.1-40.1
192	63.1-133.12:1
194	29-144.5
195	55-79.80

Acts 1982 Chapter	Code 1950 Section
196	8.01-35.1
197	54-112.1 to 54-112.3, 54-112.4:2, 54-112.7, 54-112.8, 54-112.26 to 54-112.26:2, 54-112.29
198	32.1-102.1, n.
199	46.1-105.7
200	60.1-79.1
201	38.1-279.36
202	46.1-379
203	33.1-189.1
204	4-46
205	46.1-80, 46.1-81
206	55-79.50
207	54.1-41
208	6.1-195.35
209	6.1-195.34
210	23-4.2
211	6.1-195.51
212	58-12.131 to 58-12.143
213	44-208
214	4-37
215	32.1-75.1
216	15.1-27.1
218	33.1-75.2, 33.1-75.3
219	58-441.34
220	54-274
221	46.1-400
222	44-146.31 to 44-146.33
223	38.1-327.24, 38.1-480, 38.1-482.1, 38.1-482.2, 38.1-482.3R, 38.1-482.3:1, 38.1-482.4 to 38.1-482.6, 38.1-482.7R, 38.1-482.7:1, 38.1-482.8 to 38.1-482.13, 38.1-482.14R, 38.1-482.14:1, 38.1-482.15, 38.1-482.16R, 38.1-482.16:1, 38.1-482.16:2
224	6.1-195.57:1, 6.1-195.57:2
225	2.1-342, 2.1-384
226	38.1-279.33, 46.1-31
227	38.1-456
228	38.1-461, 38.1-462, 38.1-464 to 38.1-467
229	38.1-389.3R
230	55-58.2, 55-60, 55-96
231	36-55.44
232	62.1-182
233	6.1-2.9:3
234	45.1-41
235	36-55.44
236	62.1-179
237	60.1-51.1R, 60.1-51.2, 60.1-52.1, 60.1-52.6, 60.1-123
238	2.1-512.1, 10-17.115 to 10-17.124R, 29-238 to 29-247R
239	27-23.6
240	2.1-467, 2.1-467.6R
241	58-924.1
242	33.1-285
243	2.1-51.18:1R, 2.1-51.18:2R, 30-34.2, 30-34.2:1
244	19.2-354
245	3.1-582 to 3.1-587R
246	45.1-235
247	46.1-112
248	56-338.65
249	55-13.3
250	55-333
251	29-213.26
252	40.1-89
253	18.2-147.2
254	50-45.2
255	45.1-21
256	46.1-343
257	56-273, 56-274
258	22.1-288, 23-2.1:1
259	8.01-47
260	55-248.6, 55-248.21, 55-248.21:1, 55-248.23 to 55-248.25, 55-248.28, 55-248.31, 55-248.37
261	33.1-50, 33.1-268
262	13.1-514
263	6.1-63
264	38.1-327.3, 38.1-327.46
265	60.1-52
266	13.1-341
267	36-98, 36-99, 36-103, 36-105
268	18.2-341
269	45.1-272 to 45.1-285
270	53.1-151
271	19.2-128
272	19.2-81
273	55-79.94
274	19.2-66
275	59.1-270 to 59.1-284
276	18.2-248
277	55-424 to 55-506
278	54-524.56
279	15.1-29:3
280	55-298R, 55-298.1 to 55-298.5
281	15.1-11.4
282	63.1-124
283	23-141.1 to 23-141.5
284	3.1-754
285	59.1-9.10
287	46.1-357
288	4-78.1, 4-112.4
290	24.1-30, 24.1-43, 24.1-44
291	15.1-431
292	2.1-198, 58-973
293	15.1-466.01, 15.1-491.2
294	15.1-483.1
295	37.1-194
297	15.1-37.4
298	20-79.1, 20-113
299	18.2-340.3
300	62.1-13.2 to 62.1-13.5, 62.1-13.5:2, 62.1-13.6, 62.1-13.15, 62.1-13.15:2, 62.1-13.20
301	18.2-36, 18.2-270, 18.2-271, 18.2-271.1, 46.1-417
302	6.1-125.3
303	65.1-23.1
304	64.1-1, 64.1-11
305	20-15
306	20-103
307	20-61.1, 20-61.2
308	20-91
309	20-107R, 20-107.1 to 20-107.3
310	55-248.11
311	20-99.1

Acts 1982 Chapter	Code 1950 Section
312	20-109.1
313	8.01-328.1
314	36-99.1
315	8.01-341
316	4-98.10
317	46.1-49
318	2.1-51.30R, 2.1-526.2, 2.1-526.3, 2.1-526.5 to 2.1-526.11
319	60.1-58
320	33.1-386 to 33.1-388
321	46.1-550.3:1
322	32.1-76.1
323	55-248.13:2
324	58-151.014:2
325	2.1-21
326	65.1-56
327	65.1-40.1
328	6.1-55.1R
329	10-220
330	36-47
331	55-210.2, 55-210.3, 55-210.3:1, 55-210.8, 55-210.9, 55-210.12, 55-210.14, 55-210.18
332	58-1142
333	2.1-343
334	45.1-270.1 to 45.1-270.7
335	29-146
338	32.1-112.1
339	8.01-615
340	22.1-157
341	6.1-330.20
343	33.1-246.1, n.
344	40.1-79.1
345	2.1-51.15, 2.1-371 to 2.1-373.2, 22.1-222, 63.1-310
346	2.1-373.3 to 2.1-373.8, 32.1-76.1
347	2.1-20.4, 45.1-106 to 45.1-144R, 45.1-286 to 45.1-361
348	58-266.1
349	55-248.11
350	59.1-21.11
351	58-151.072:2
353	38.1-763
354	22.1-201
355	2.1-373.9
356	23-9.2:5
357	36-99.3
358	58-730.5
359	58-1147
360	51-111.54, n.
361	3.1-231
362	13.1-510
363	60.1-26, 60.1-58, 60.1-61, 60.1-91, 60.1-92
364	51-111.67:18
365	55-57.1
366	16.1-133
367	19.2-368.11
368	15.1-11.1
369	2.1-2
370	60.1-79
372	13.1-45, 13.1-226
373	64.1-73
374	15.1-1513.1 to 15.1-1513.8
375	13.1-126, 13.1-288
376	14.1-46.01, 15.1-778.1
378	8.01-413
379	23-135.7:8 to 23-135.7:13
380	18.2-167.1
381	15.1-364
382	18.2-96.1
383	65.1-105
384	8.01-316, 8.01-317, 8.01-319, 25-46.10
385	45.1-20
386	63.1-105
387	38.1-790, 38.1-793.1, 38.1-794, 38.1-796, 38.1-797
388	32.1-93 to 32.1-102R, 32.1-102.1 to 32.1-102.3, 32.1-102.4 to 32.1-102.11
389	29-213.24:1
390	46.1-172
391	43-13
392	8.01-401.1
393	38.1-189.1, 38.1-202.2, 38.1-216
394	46.1-516
395	36-4.1
396	Art. II, § 1, n.
397	8.01-195.3
400	3.1-819
401	54-524.22:1, 54-524.22:2
402	63.1-257
403	33.1-269, 33.1-277
405	8.01-449
406	51-111.54
407	13.1-504
409	2.1-232
410	65.1-98.1
411	6.1-80
412	40.1-49.4
413	58-16.2:2
414	2.1-114.7:1
415	3.1-621, 3.1-632, 3.1-637
416	40.1-113
417	3.1-18.4 to 3.1-18.8
418	33.1-23.01
419	9-169, 9-179, 9-180
420	55-66.4:1
421	2.1-564
422	51-11.24:5 to 51-111.24:7
423	51-111.41:3
424	13.1-512
425	9-6.14:9, 45.1-220.3, 45.1-230
426	58-266.1:3, n.
427	51-111.53, 51-111.56, 51-150, 51-152, 51-167, 51-169
428	6.1-195.13:1R, 6.1-195.13:2
429	6.1-81
430	38.1-171, 38.1-171.1, 38.1-173
431	52-4.3
433	15.1-686.4R, 58-835.1
434	46.1-309.1
435	37.1-67.4
436	58-58
437	55-168, 55-169
438	6.1-330.19R, 6.1-330.19:1
439	65.1-102
440	54-730
441	8.01-52
442	15.1-131.8
443	51-111.36
444	8.01-384.1, 19.2-164, 19.2-164.1
445	46.1-181.4:1
446	62.1-13.6, 62.1-13.7
447	21-118.4
448	2.1-114.5:1
449	2.1-342
450	38.1-380.1, 38.1-380.2, 46.1-497.1
451	16.1-266
452	2.1-342
453	55-171
454	37.1-89, 37.1-134.2
455	6.1-94,

Acts 1982 Chapter	Code 1950 Section
	6.1-195.65
456	64.1-197 to 64.1-206
457	58-760.1
458	19.2-303
459	2.1-51.9, 2.1-51.15
460	13.1-123, 13.1-124, 13.1-285, 13.1-286
461	28.1-59, 28.1-65, 28.1-65.1
462	18.2-247, 18.2-248, 18.2-248.3, 18.2-248.4, 18.2-249, 18.2-253, 18.2-255
462	15.1-1377, 15.1-1387
464	29-213.11
465	16.1-296
466	58-861
467	51-111.10 to 51.111.10:3, 51-111.16, 51-111.27, 51-111.28, 51-111.28:1, 51-111.41:1, 51-111.41:4, 51-111.46:1, 51-111.49, 51-111.55:1, 51-111.57:1, 51-111.59:1, 51-111.60:1, 51-111.65, 51-111.67:2, 51-111.67:4, 51-147, 51-148, 51-164, 51-165.1
468	62.1-13.20
469	15.1-1240, 15.1-1250.2, 15.1-1260
470	2.1-114.5:1
471	37.1-67.3
472	20-88
473	9-170
474	15.1-50.1
475	55-79.94
476	19.2-310
477	18.2-389
478	51-111.10, 51-111.10:01, 51-111.11, 51-111.16, 51-111.22, 51-111.38:1, n., 51-111.38:2, n., 51-111.38:3, n., 51-111.38:4, 51-111.38:5, 51-111.67:2
479	37.1-128.02
481	45.1-362 to 45.1-380
482	38.1-381.5
483	20-128
485	19.2-74
486	55-172, 55-180 to 55-183, 55-184.1, 55-186, 55-186.2, 55-190.1, 55-191
487	33.1-2
488	22.1-32
489	9-6.16 to 9-6.20
490	18.2-474.1
491	8.01-66.9
492	53.1-150
493	15.1-84.1, 15.1-117, 15.1-532, 15.1-547, 58-919.1
494	14.1-123
495	24.1-206.2
496	26-40
497	2.1-344, 2.1-347, 2.1-353.2, 2.1-354.1, 2.1-358
498	24.1-165
499	53.1-47, 53.1-48
500	19.2-74
501	32.1-74
502	18.2-83, 18.2-212, 18.2-431
503	46.1-176
504	Art. IV, § 6, n.
505	54-524.84:4, 54-524.84:8, 54-524.84:10
506	18.2-61
507	19.2-165.1
508	18.2-67.2
509	18.2-110
510	22.1-270, 22.1-271, 1R, 22.1-271.1, 22.1-271.2
511	32.1-238.1 to 32.1-238.5
512	46.1-525.1, 46.1-537
513	19.2-183
514	16.1-299
515	18.2-308.2
516	2.1-344
517	32.1-74
518	32.1-238.6 to 32.1-238.10
519	20-132
521	18.2-370.1
522	2.1-20.4
523	19.2-13
525	64.1-57
526	56-304.2
527	4-33, 4-38, 4-98.18, 4-104
528	58-151.063
529	58-12.144 to 58-12.147
530	58-151.26
531	18.2-340.9
532	58-12.149, 58-12.150
533	38.1-871R, 58-441.6
534	54-62, n.
535	19.2-390
536	58-860
537	8.01-400.2
538	2.1-20.4, 54-1.18, 54-792R, 54-795 to 54-808R, 54-809, 54-810, n., 54-813, 54-817R, 54-819, 54-824.1 to 54-824.30, 58-286, n., 58-289, n., 58-381, 58-371.1R
540	4-22, 4-22.1
541	58-685.13
543	46.1-254.2
544	18.2-340.3, 18.2-340.9, 18.2-340.14
545	55-79.40, 55-79.41, 55-79.41:1, 55-79.44, 55-79.49, 55-79.50, 55-79.54, 55-79.74:2, 55-79.74:3, 55-79.79
546	58-441.6
547	58-441.6
548	58-266.1
549	26-45.1, 64.1-57
550	55-171
551	64.1-57, 64.1-57.2
552	58-266.1
553	18.2-308
554	58-266.1
555	58-441.49
556	4-22.1
557	18.2-340.3
558	58-266.1
559	58-587.2
560	2.1-342
561	18.2-127
562	15.1-1261
563	5.1-2.7, 5.1-2.10
564	12.1-20
565	41.1-15, 55-186.2
566	25-46.22
567	15.1-1261
568	18.2-60.1, 18.2-60.2

Acts 1982 Chapter	Code 1950 Section
569	14.1-123, 14.1-125, 14.1-128.1R, 14.1-200.2R, 19.2-347
570	45.1-381, 45.1-382
571	6.1-200.4, 6.1-200.5
572	6.1-211
573	38.1-476.1
574	6.1-213
575	6.1-210
576	38.1-32.1
577	38.1-348.14, 38.1-818
578	22.1-18, n.
579	51-111.5
580	51-111.24:2
581	41-111.60, 51-122
582	2.1-116
583	62.1-104.1R, 62.1-105, 62.1-106, 62.1-115.1 to 62.1-115.10
584	56-249.6
585	65.1-88
586	38.1-356.01
587	6.1-330.15
588	64.1-179
589	14.1-52.1R, 14.1-143.1R, 14.1-143.2, 14.1-166R, 14.1-167R
590	13.1-553, 54-17.1, 54-25, 54-26.1, 54-37.1 to 54-37.3
592	20-88.01
593	6.1-70.1
594	18.2-255.2
596	36-19
597	17-79.3
598	54-367.1, 54-367.4, 54-367.6, 54-367.11 to 54-367.14, 54-367.19, 54-367.20, 54-367.25, 54-367.30, 54-367.32, 54-367.33:1, 54-367.33:2, 54-367.35, 54-367.36
599	32.1-287
600	14.1-84.2, 14.1-84.6:1
601	8.01-264, 8.01-265
602	54-50
603	3.1-684.9, 3.1-684.10, 3.1-684.12, 3.1-684.14
605	54-297 to 54-299, 54-300.1, 54-305, 54-306.3, 54-308.7
606	54-295.7R, 54-315.1, 54-321, 54-323, 54-324R
607	42.1-70
608	19.2-76.1
609	6.1-259, 6.1-267.1, 6.1-299.1
610	14.1-195.1, 14.1-195.2
611	16.1-115, 19.2-346
612	16.1-279
613	16.1-279
614	15.1-23.1
616	58-587.1, 58-617.2
617	46.1-115, 58-766.3
618	58-847
619	58-760, 58-769.3:2
620	58-1020.1
621	58-19.7, 58-19.9 to 58-19.15, 58-19.18 to 58-19.20
622	64.1-62.1, 64.1-62.2
623	58-835
624	58-769.8, 58-769.10:1
625	38.1-348.11
626	6.1-330.21
628	56-275.01, 56-279.1, 56-304.4
630	58-54.1, 58-55, 58-58, 58-64
631	2.1-164
632	28.1-51.1
633	6.1-226R, 6.1-236R, 54-42.1, 54-734, 54-792R, 54-796R, 54-810R, 54-813R, 54-836R, 54-822, 54-841 to 54-843, 54-844R, 58-151.013, 58-151.013:1, 58-151.032, 58-151.032:1, 58-151.032:2, 58-241 to 58-266R, 58-266.1, 58-266.7 to 58-266.10, 58-267 to 58-271R, 58-272, n., 58-273 to 58-284.2R, 58-286, 58-289 to 58-292R, 58-293, n., 58-294 to 58-298R, 58-299, 58-300R, 58-301R, 58-340, 58-341, n., 58-342 to 58-353R, 58-354.1 to 58-354.7R, 58-370 to 58-371.1R, 58-372R, 58-372.1, n., 58-373R, 58-374, 58-375 to 58-377R, 58-377.1, 58-378 to 58-381R, 58-381.1, n., 58-382 to 58-385R, 58-387 to 58-393R, 58-393.1, 58-394, 58-395R, 58-396, n., 58-396.1R, 58-398R, 58-399.1 to 58-401R, 58-402, n., 58-402.1 to 58-404.01R, 58-405, 58-406 to 58-410R, 58-411, n., 58-412, n., 58-412.1, 58-412.2, 58-413 to 58-417, 58-418R, 58-418.1, n., 58-420R, 58-422, 58-423, 58-580, 58-585R, 58-603, 58-829, 58-829.5, 58-831, 58-838.5R, 58-838.5:1
634	46.1-314.2 to 46.1-314.7
635	2.1-342
636	2.1-121, 16.1-238, 16.1-239, 16.1-275, 16.1-276, 16.1-294, 16.1-313, 16.1-322.1, 16.1-322.2, 18.2-31, 18.2-55, 19.2-303, 19.2-303.1, 19.2-310, 19.2-310.1R, 53-1 to 53-343R, 53.1-1 to 53.1-260, 58-441.6
637	15.1-40.1
638	38.1-381, 46.1-167.2
639	51-111.67:4
640	51-111.24:6, 51-111.24:7
641	58-16.2, 62.1-132.19, n.
642	38.1-380.2, 38.1-381
643	33.1-223
644	32.1-92.1
645	32.1-92.2
646	46.1-315,

Acts 1982 Chapter	Code 1950 Section
	46.1-315.2, 46.1-321, 46.1-321.1, 46.1-326.8
647	2.1-436R, 2.1-437.1 to 2.1-437.3R, 2.1-439R, 2.1-442, 2.1-443R, 2.1-448R, 2.1-449R, 2.1-450, 2.1-450.1, 2.1-451, 2.1-452R, 2.1-454R, 2.1-454.1, 2.1-458R, 2.1-459 to 2.1-463R, 2.1-483.1, 2.1-548.1 to 2.1-548.5R, 4-7, 11-17R, 11-17.1, n., 11-18 11-17, n., 11-18, n., 11-19R, 11-20, n., 11-20.1R, 11-20.2R, 11-21, n., 11-22R, 11-23, n., 11-23.1 to 11-23.5R, 11-35 to 11-80, 15.1-108, 15.1-109, 15.1-127, 15.1-287R, 15.1-605, 15.1-640, 15.1-712, 15.1-766, 22.1-141R, 24.1-113.1, 33.1-185, 33.1-186R, 33.1-187, n., 33.1-188R, 22.1-189R, 33.1-190, 33.1-192.1, 53.1-47, 53.1-49, 53.1-52
648	13.1-92
649	58-441.6
650	24.1-1, 24.1-17, 24.1-31, 24.1-32, 24.1-45, 24.1-46, 24.1-49.1, 24.1-53, 24.1-55.2, 24.1-59, 24.1-72.2, 24.1-72.13, 24.1-88, 24.1-90.1, 24.1-100.1, 24.1-105.1, 24.1-119, 24.1-126.1, 24.1-158 to 24.1-160, 24.1-165, 24.1-166.1, 24.1-167 to 24.1-169, 24.1-180, 24.1-185, 24.1-199, 24.1-203, 24.1-228.1, 24.1-250, 24.1-251, 24.1-257, 24.1-260, 24.1-261, 24.1-277
651	58-61
652	8.9-402 to 8.9-406
653	19.2-168.1, 19.2-169R, 19.2-169.1 to 19.2-169.7, 19.2-170 to 19.2-174R, 19.2-175, 19.2-176
654	18.2-53.1
655	46.1-387.2, 46.1-387.3
656	46.1-254.2
659	32.1-102.3:1
660	15.1-1403
661	2.1-1R, 2.1-1.1
662	15.1-1269.1
663	55-79.43, 55-79.94
664	38.1-747, 38.1-748
665	38.1-751
666	9-173.1, 9-173.2, 18.2-388
667	2.1-587 to 2.1-598
669	58-117.1
670	40.1-88
671	46.1-35.1, 46.1-55, 46.1-78, 46.1-149, 46.1-154, 46.1-339, 46.1-438, 46.1-514.12, 46.1-528, 46.1-550.8, 56-304.4, 58-627 to 58-629, 58-730.7 to 58-730.17
672	46.1-160
673	46.1-423.3, 46.1-425
674	8.01-295, 14.1-105, 14.1-105.1
677	23-38.56
678	22.1-154, 22.1-155
679	2.1-329
680	53.1-20.1
681	46.1-16.01, 46.1-159, 46.1-172, 46.1-174, 46.1-236R, 46.1-237, 46.1-287, 46.1-347
682	54-734
683	16.1-246
685	Art. II, § 2, n.
686	Art. II, § 1, n.
687	Art. IV, § 6, n.

ACTS 1982, SP. SESS.

Acts 1982, Sp. Sess. Chapter	Code 1950 Section
1	24.1-12.3

ACTS 1983

Acts 1983 Chapter	Code 1950 Section
1	16.1-69.6:1
2	17-119.1:2
3	45.1-283, 45.1-285.1 to 45.1-285.10
4	14.1-84.6:2, 15.1-1130.1, 15.1-1135
6	54-386.1, 54-386.2
8	55-246.1
9	3.1-27.2, 3.1-27.3, 3.1-27.5
11	15.1-504
12	15.1-496.1
13	60.1-88.01
14	60.1-14, 60.1-26, 60.1-52.3
16	60.1-79, 60.1-120
17	54-872.16, 54-872.17, 54-872.20, 54-872.23R, 54-872.23:1, 54-872.24
18	28.1-93
19	18.2-22
20	2.1-51.15, 9-138.1 to 9-138.4
21	16.1-133.1
22	58-12.151
23	58-12.152
25	54-1.2:2, 54-276.12R
26	24.1-12.3
27	36-19
28	54.37.3
29	58-12.153
30	15.1-184.1
31	58-12.154
32	22.1-128
33	15.1-364
34	46.1-551
35	58-12.155
36	58-835.1
37	58-1117.1
38	46.1-104.1
39	55-248.7
40	54-317.4
41	2.1-64.33, 2.1-64.38
42	29-213.23R
43	58-12.156
44	58-12.157, 58-12.158
48	44-146.18:1
50	54-291.1
51	15.1-51
52	15.1-1232.3
53	29-55.4
54	64.1-57.2
55	64.1-66.1
56	9-6.14:10
58	58-12.159
59	55-361, 55-374, 55-374.1, 55-378, 55-386, 55-390, 55-395, 55-400
60	55-79.97
61	38.1-381.6, 38.1-381.8
62	30-28.19R
63	23-91.5 to 23-91.12R
64	20-25
65	44-41.1
66	63.1-250, 63.1-252,

Acts 1983 Chapter	Code 1950 Section
	63.1-253
67	37.1-181
68	36-7
70	45.1-73
71	3.1-739R
72	8.01-225
73	45.1-255
74	44-20
75	62.1-186.3
76	15.1-51
77	45.1-261.1
78	28.1-172
80	15.1-1243, 15.1-1246
83	64.1-87.1, 64.1-87.2
84	9-55.1
85	46.1-326.8
87	62.1-13.6
88	16.1-296
89	58-58
90	58-984R, 58-985
91	18.2-172.1
92	45.1-240
93	45.1-249, 45.1-251
94	38.1-563
95	2.1-27.1
96	55-454
97	19.2-160
98	15.1-867.2
100	58-441.6
101	15.1-548
102	65.1-22
103	14.1-112, 14.1-112.2, 14.1-113, 14.1-114, 26-36, 55-66.7, 59.1-74
104	58-441.38
105	16.1-133
107	8.01-345
108	30-34.5
109	58-838.8
110	3.1-360.1 to 3.1-360.8R
111	45.1-89.1
112	56-274, 56-338.51
113	58-12.160
114	15.1-552
115	2.1-20.4, 54-1.18, 54-1.30, n., 54-924, 54-925 to 54-927R, 54-929, 54-949, n., 54-950, 54-950.2
116	54-321.2:1
117	2.1-328.5
119	24.1-252, 24.1-253, 24.1-254, 24.1-254.1, 24.1-255, 24.1-257, 24.1-258, 24.1-261
121	3.1-1027, 3.1-1027.1
123	40.1-79.1
124	55-58.2
125	38.1-381.5
126	62.1-170
127	33.1-8
128	16.1-69.21
129	18.2-54.1, 18.2-54.2
130	56-304.11
131	45.1-270.2 to 45.1-270.4
132	46.1-261, 46.1-268
133	63.1-171.8
134	45.1-234
135	16.1-69.40
136	8.01-28
137	3.1-637
138	15.1-308
139	64.1-105.2
140	58-70
142	3.1-796.41
143	38.1-526
144	58-829.9
145	22.1-60
146	33.1-90
147	55-376
148	23-216
149	16.1-69.6, 17-119.1:1
150	2.1-20.4, 54-933, 54-934R, 54-934.1
151	38.1-822.1R
152	15.1-778.1
153	63.1-174.01, 63.1-175, 63.1-196.5
154	9-97, 9-106 to 9-106.08R
155	15.1-1250.01
156	6.1-371
157	44-119
158	6.1-211
160	38.1-327.24, 38.1-471.1
161	58-763, 58-790, 8-792.02, 58-795.2, 58-812, 58-817.1
162	33.1-55
163	9-150
165	2.1-373
166	29-140
167	15.1-466
169	46.1-343.1
170	46.1-343
171	33.1-72.1
172	53.1-131.1
173	59.1-200
174	16.1-274
175	18.2-31
176	62.1-186.7
177	3.1-657
178	19.2-187
179	15.1-249.1
180	17-68
181	8.01-35.1
182	38.1-480
183	8.01-281
184	58-441.6
185	38.1-327.16, 38.1-327.24, 38.1-327.25, 38.1-327.28
186	53.1-45
187	18.2-388
188	24.1-168, 24.1-185
189	21-89.5
190	2.1-190, 13.1-156, 55-210.2, 55-210.3, 55-210.5, 55-210.7, 55-210.8:1, 55-210.8:2, 55-210.9:1, 55-210.10:2, 55-210.12, 55-210.12:1R, 55-210.13, 55-210.24, 55-210.24:1, 55-210.25
191	29-56, 29-59
192	15.1-11
193	6.1-13, 6.1-383, 6.1-389 to 6.1-397
194	6.1-381, 6.1-383, 6.1-383.1, 6.1-383.2, 6.1-384, 6.1-388
195	22.1-270
196	65.1-155
197	38.1-380.1
198	29-92.1, 29-92.4
199	58-12.161
200	58-12.162
202	15.1-945.4
203	46.1-326.1:1
204	8.9-301, 8.9-302, 8.9-306, 8.9-312, 8.9-313
205	58-12.163
206	19.2-81
207	18.2-268
208	8.01-581.3
209	59.1-177 to 59.1-188.1R
210	62.1-186.2
211	46.1-302.4

Acts 1983 Chapter	Code 1950 Section
212	4-84
213	32.1-238.6R,
	32.1-238.6:1
214	56-304.9
215	2.1-373
217	15.1-945.7,
	15.1-977.22:1
218	62.1-129
219	23-38.70,
	23-38.71
220	55-66.3:1,
	55-66.4:1
221	15.1-491.3
223	23-7
224	19.2-267.1
225	58-834.3
226	46.1-282
227	19.2-368.15
228	49-3
229	14.1-88,
	14.1-121,
	14.1-122.1
230	55-79.57
231	13.1-514
232	15.1-66.3
233	18.2-308.2
234	46.1-516
235	32.1-273.1
236	23-38.47
237	58-12.164
238	54-846,
	54-850
239	65.1-1
240	14.1-91R,
	32.1-249,
	32.1-250,
	32.1-251,
	32.1-252,
	32.1-256,
	32.1-257,
	32.1-258,
	32.1-259,
	32.1-260,
	32.1-261,
	32.1-262,
	32.1-263,
	32.1-264,
	32.1-269,
	32.1-270,
	32.1-271,
	32.1-272,
	32.1-273,
	32.1-274,
	32.1-275.1,
	32.1-276,
	32.1-276.1
241	55-248.21:1
242	35.1-9
243	53.1-154
244	55-248.5
245	33.1-278
247	2.1-27.2
248	46.1-213
249	58-12.165
250	6.1-81
251	35.1-26
252	58-266.5:1
253	20-103
254	19.2-76.2,
	19.2-76.3
255	58-1117.7
256	24.1-12.3
257	55-248.12
258	58-19.8
259	32.1-134.4
260	1-13.39R,
	9-66 to
	9-77.3R,
	9-77.4 to
	9-77.12
261	54-824.3
262	46.1-171.1
263	8.01-66.5,
	8.01-66.9
264	24.1-151
265	56-304.6
266	24.1-14.2
267	4-15
268	2.1-328.6
269	32.1-178
270	58-835.1
271	4-56
272	29-77
273	58-835.1
274	15.1-29.5
275	15.1-136.2
277	25-46.34:1, n.
278	8.01-508
279	46.1-423.3
280	16.1-241
281	46.1-295.3
282	57-63
283	29-130.2
284	56-291.3:6, n.
285	56-338.93 to
	56-338.103
286	54-524.31
287	65.1-56
288	65.1-57R
289	2.1-81.4,
	2.1-384,
	10-8.1
290	18.2-222
291	55-108
292	63.1-238.2
293	8.01-331,
	8.01-334R,
	14.1-139,
	14.1-168,
	16.1-302,
	17-59,
	17-70,
	17-70.1,
	17-79
294	3.1-885 to
	3.1-898R
295	9-6.14:9
296	46.1-314.3
297	8.01-324
298	2.1-41.2,
	62.1-129
299	28.1-47.1
300	6.1-198
301	6.1-210
302	6.1-212
303	62.1-132.11:1
304	58-33.4,
	58-769.15,
	58-774.1R,
	58-774.2,
	58-776.1,
	58-776.4R
	58-785,
	58-786,
	58-787R,
	58-789,
	58-795,
	58-895,
	58-897,
	58-898R,
	58-899,
	58-915
305	8.01-412.2 to
	8.01-412.7
306	28.1-121
307	28.1-47,
	28.1-48,
	28.1-57R,
	28.1-69.1,
	28.1-123,
	28.1-165
308	51-111.26:1,
	55-210.28:1,
	55-210.30
309	42.1-70
310	55-79.94,
	55-487
311	46.1-343.4
312	55-425
313	58-76.1, n.
317	14.1-75
318	28.1-23
319	15.1-162.1
320	64.1-11
321	33.1-75.3
322	45.1-181
323	7.1-8R,
	28.1-188R,
	28.1-188.1
324	62.1-186.2
325	33.1-75.3
326	14.1-63,
	14.1-79

TABLE OF ACTS CODIFIED SUBSEQUENT TO 1948

Acts 1983 Chapter	Code 1950 Section
327	22.1-312, 22.1-313
328	26-20.1
329	46.1-179.01
330	8.01-43
331	18.2-328
332	15.1-871
334	63.1-229
335	8.01-217
336	16.1-249, 16.1-284
337	18.2-423, 18.2-423.1
338	2.1-41.2, 62.1-129
339	33.1-46.2
340	4-28, 4-79, 4-98, 4-99
341	15.1-131.6:1
343	33.1-75.1
344	53.1-180, 53.1-181, 53.1-183, 53.1-184.1,
345	58-117.1, 58-117.10
346	65.1-4
347	36-47
348	24.1-23
349	16.1-256, 16.1-260
350	15.1-589
351	27-40.4, 51-122.01
352	15.1-36.2
353	38.1-42.2
354	22.1-312
355	42.1-70
356	45.1-23
357	2.1-116.1, 9-169, 65.1-47.1
358	16.1-238, 16.1-239, 16.1-275, 16.1-294, 16.1-313, 16.2-314, 16.1-322.1 to 16.1-322.4, 53.1-80, 53.1-81, 53.1-82, 53.1-83.1, 53.1-84, 53.1-85, 53.1-89R, 53.1-91, 53.1-95, 53.1-104, 53.1-104.1, 53.1-115, 53.1-115.1, 53.1-121
359	60.1-52
360	18-2-475, 18.2-476
361	15.1-50.1, 15.1-821
362	19.2-155
363	6.1-330.10
364	15.1-686, 15.1-687.4 to 15.1-687.7
365	18.2-268
367	8.9-302
368	50-68
369	50-45
370	8.1-380.1
371	38.1-37.1, 38.1-371.2, 38.1-381.1, 38.1-381.5
372	2.1-342, 2.1-379, 2.1-382, 58-46
373	19.2-169.1

Acts 1983 Chapter	Code 1950 Section
374	57-48, 57-52, 57-54, 57-55.1, 57-57, 57-59, 57-60, 57-61, 57-63
375	3.1-796.13, 3.1-796.15, 3.1-796.16, 3.1-796.17, 3.1-796.18, 3.1-796.19, 3.1-796.20, 3.1-796.25, 3.1-796.26
376	22.1-218.1
377	2.1-700
378	53.1-154.1
379	3.1-49
380	46.1-189
381	46.1-115
382	14.1-48, 14.1-50, 14.1-51, 14.1-52, 14.1-65, 14.1-66, 14.1-69.1R, 14.1-70, 14.1-71R, 14.1-72R, 14.1-76, 14.1-80, 14.1-81R, 14.1-84R
383	15.1-37.3:2
384	58-441.6
385	23-108
386	36-71, 46.1-1, 55-248.41, 58-685.11
387	6.1-195.8
388	16.1-69.40:1
389	16.1-305
390	15.1-11
391	36-55.37:1
392	15.1-491
393	13.1-220
394	19.2-392.2
395	54-524.67, 54-524.68
396	55-248.39
397	46.1-73
398	24.1-46
399	8.01-511, 8.01-512R, 8.01-512.1R, 8.01-512.3, 8.01-515, 8.01-516R, 8.01-516.1, 8.01-520
400	58-730.8
401	54-1.22:1
402	8.01-320
403	15.1-538
404	8.01-229, 8.01-380
405	55-248.34
407	14.1-105
408	13.1-529, 13.1-530
409	15.1-29.10
410	2.1-347 to 2.1-358R, 2.1-599 to 2.1-634
411	2.1-373.4 to 2.1-373.6
412	18.2-380, 18.2-381
413	17-116.01 to 7-116.014
414	58-441.3

Acts 1983 Chapter	Code 1950 Section
415	19.2-349
416	65.1-100.2
417	38.1-43.7 to 38.1-43.11
418	19.2-368.11
419	15.1-8
420	56-222
421	65.1-147
422	15.1-1250, 15.1-1263, 21-118.4
424	4-96
425	8.01-348
426	22.1-101, 2.1-701, 2.1-702
427	4-22
428	8.01-328.1
429	15.1-28.3
430	58-12.166
431	19.2-303
432	22.1-287.1
433	22.1-271.1, 22.1-271.2
434	15.1-236, 15.1-237, 15.1-238
435	47.1-4, 47.1-20.1, 47.1-23, 47.1-24
436	11-41.1
437	8.01-229
438	56-46.1
439	15.1-489, 15.490
440	63.1-85.2, 63.1-85.2:1, 63.1-85.4
441	38.1-949 to 38.1-954
442	15.1-510.2R 15.1-510.3R, 15.1-510.5R, 15.1-863R, 15.1-864R
443	56-99.2
444	15.1-496.2
445	18.2-224
446	6.1-195.22:3
447	6.1-195.34
448	38.1-21
449	63.1-127.2
450	6.1-195.70:1R 6.1-195.70:2
451	32.1-292
452	58-151.013, 58-151.032
453	6.1-11.2
454	6.1-25R, 6.1-26R, 6.1-27R, 6.1-28R, 6.1-29R, 6.1-30R, 6.1-30.1 to 6.1-30.3
455	33.1-72.1
456	54-524.65
457	38.1-35, 38.1-58, 38.1-168, 38.1-179 to 38.1-217R, 38.1-217.1 to 38.1-217.13, 38.1-217.14, n., 38.1-217.15 to 38.1-217.47

Acts 1983 Chapter	Code 1950 Section
457	38.1-682, 38.1-724, 38.1-818, 38.1-899, 51-111.67:7
458	46.1-178
459	8.01-69, 8.01-78
460	65.1-149
461	24.1-1, 24.1-7, 24.1-16, 24.1-90.1R, 24.1-133, 24.1-138, 24.1-139, 24.1-141, 24.1-154, 24.1-155, 24.1-165, 24.1-166, 24.1-184, 24.1-222, 24.1-227, 24.1-228.1, 24.1-229, 24.1-250, 24.1-282
462	2.1-342
463	30-28.1:1
464	38.1-347.2, 38.1-813.4
465	6.1-200.3
466	6.1-216
467	8.01-313, 8.01-316, 26-59
468	8.01-511, 16.1-279
469	65.1-52
470	24.1-45
471	65.1-88
472	58-151.013
473	46.1-384.1
474	16.1-279
475	62.1-171
476	15.1-50.2
477	53.1-1
478	31-15
479	6.1-299R
480	38.1-327.1, 38.1-327.3
481	20-79.1, 58-1010, 63.1-256, 63.1-272
482	55-176, 55-200
483	24.1-175, 24.1-195
484	56-457.8
485	8.01-577
486	38.1-763
487	6.1-70, 26-60
488	20-78.2
489	18.2-340.6
491	6.1-2.1
492	6.1-195.58
493	23-35.1
494	46.1-105.10
495	14.1-195.1
496	8.01-38, 8.01-581.15
497	2.1-51.31
498	58-1001, 58-1009
499	8.01-251, 14.1-123, 14.1-125, 16.1-69.52R, 16.1-69.53 to 16.1-69.58, 16.1-87R, 16.1-94.1, 16.1-95, 16.1-98, 16.1-100, 16.1-103, 16.1-104R, 16.1-114R, 16.1-116, 16.1-130R, 16.1-138R, 16.1-304R, 19.2-341, 19.2-347, n., 19.2-348, 19.2-349
500	6.1-282, 6.1-284
501	16.1-292
502	15.1-33.4
503	8.01-420.2
504	18.2-269 to 18.2-271.1, 46.1-421
505	8.01-420.3. 19.2-165
506	6.1-195.70
507	6.1-100, 6.1-100.1, 6.1-110.1 to 6.1-110.13
508	15.1-510.4
509	53.1-153
510	18.2-340.3
511	24.1-43
512	64.1-62.1
513	18.2-251
514	15.1-1374, 15.1-1377, 15.1-1378.1, 15.1-1378.2, 15.1-1379
515	46.1-153.1, 46.1-328, 46.1-330, 46.1-335, 46.1-335.1, 46.1-339, 46.1-343
516	13.1-514
517	13.1-510
518	15.1-236, 36-27.01
519	17-110.1, 19.2-264.3
521	22.1-221
522	2.1-20.4, 54-1.18, 54-824.1 to 54-824.4, 54-824.5R, 54-824.6R, 54-824.7, 544-824.8R, 54-824.9R, 54-824.9:1 to 54-824.9:3, 54-824.10 to 54-824.14R, 54-824.16R, 54-824.17, 54-824.18R, 54-824.19, 54-824.20R, 54-824.21, 54-824.22 54-824.30R, 15.1-1167R
523	15.1-1166R, 15.1-1167.1, 15.1-1168
524	18.2-374.1
525	15.1-137.2
526	56-508.5
528	54-317.5, 54-524.50R, 54-524.50:1, 54-524.58, 54-524.65, 54-524.66, 54-524.89, 54-524.90R, 54-955
529	18.2-308
530	15.1-490
531	6.1-125.3
532	54-325.8:1 to 54-325.8:12, 54-325.8:13, n.
533	32.1-102.1, 32.1-132
534	13.1-2.1, 56-508.4
535	18.2-265.1 to 18.2-265.3, 18.2-265.5
536	19.2-67
537	42.1-32.1 to 42.1-32.7
538	22.1-213, 37.1-1
539	2.1-33
540	2.1-21.1
541	19.2-299, 19.2-299.1
542	57-15
543	19.2-215.1 to 19.2-215.11
544	58-833, 58-833.1R
545	58-19.7, 58-19.17, 58-19.18
546	2.1-234.13, n.
547	58-664
549	58-758.1
550	58-266.8
551	58-48.6
552	58-405
553	58-55
554	58-266.1
555	58-405
556	58-760
557	58-441.6
558	15.1-1513.8
559	60.1-58
560	5.1-22
561	53.1-116
562	22.1-32
563	15.1-546
564	19.2-82
565	58-441.6
566	46.1-149, 46.1-167
567	8.01-581.13
568	16.1-279
569	54-1.28, 54-729.28
570	58-503, 58-503.1, 58-510, 58-511, 58-512.1, 58-514, 58-514.1, 58-522, 58-524, 58-525, 58-528, 58-529, 58-530, 58-531, 58-538, 58-539, 58-556, 58-557, 58-558, 58-559, 58-588, 58-590, 58-592, 58-597, 58-668, 58-669, 58-670, 58-671R,

Acts 1983 Chapter	Code 1950 Section
	58-672, 58-678, 58-679, 58-681, 58-682, 58-683, 58-685, 58-760, 58-764.1, 58-848, 58-915, 58-1117.20
571	6.1-330.42:1
572	59.1-273, 59.1-274, 59.1-279, 59.1-280, 59.1-281R
573	58-687
575	58-151.23, 58-151.40
576	15.1-142.2
577	46.1-347
578	18.2-51.1, 18.2-57.1
579	18.2-127
580	14.1-144.1, 17-116.1
582	32.1-65
583	14.1-105.1
584	18.2-340.7
586	46.1-68.1
588	17-111.3
589	2.1-703
590	44-93
591	28.1-185.2
592	46.1-181.4:1
593	11-35
594	15.1-1031.1 to 15.1031.3, 15.1-1034
595	15.1-37.4, n., 15.1-527.2, n.
596	33.1-320, n.
597	23-38.53:1 to 23-38.53:3
599	58-441.6
600	14.1-53, 14.1-55, 14.1-56, 14.1-57, 14.1-58, 14.1-58.2R, 14.1-61, 14.1-73, 14.1-74
601	9-6.14:7
602	18.2-308.3
603	28.1-165, 28.1-165.1, 28.1-166
604	63.1-55.1, 63.1-55.4
605	63.1-55.01
606	53.1-67
607	2.1-342, 15.1-201
608	4-37, 4-62, 4-63, 4-98.10, 4-112, 4-112.1, 46.1-368, 46.1-375, 46.1-383
609	15.1-466
610	58-959
611	8.9-401
612	54-524.67
613	15.1-316, 15.1-512.1
614	63.1-221
615	11-41.2
616	16.1-77, 16.1-77.1, 16.1-77.2, 16.1-88.2, 16.1-120
617	33.1-251, 33.1-252, 33.1-285
618	58-711, 58-744
619	32.1-164.2
620	33.1-26, n.
621	46.1-387.3

ACTS 1984

Acts 1984 Chapter	Code 1950 Section
1	8.01-511, 8.01-512.4, 8.01-512.5
2	10-145.12
3	62.1-169
4	28.1-107
5	9-6.14:3, 9-6.14:7R, 9-6.14:7.1, 9-6.14:9, 9-6.14:9.1 to 9-6.14:9.4, 9-6.14:22 to 9-6.14:25, 9-6.16, 9-6.17, 9-6.19, 9-6.20, 30-74 to 30-77, n.
6	29-138
7	44-40
10	32.1-186
11	62.1-44.15
12	54-315.2
13	28.1-49.1
14	3.1-296.1 to 3.1-296.10:1R
15	54-189
16	42.1-70
17	2.1-40
18	8.01-320
19	55-58.2, 55-96
20	15.1-1509, 15.1-1511
21	55-79.48
22	18.2-340.3
23	16.1-69.33
24	19.2-74, 46.1-416.1
25	16.1-91R
26	29-57, 29-58
27	55-79.82, 55-79.83
28	54-187
29	55-79.97
30	9-168, 9-186
31	18.2-265.3
32	19.2-303, 19.2-305, 19.2-305.1, 19.2-354
33	19.2-315
34	16.1-305
35	55-122, 55-123, 55-125 to 55-127, 55-129 to 55-132, 55-134 to 55-135, 55-137.1, 55-137.2
37	19.2-36
38	16.1-113
39	26-59
40	8.9-403, 8.9-404
41	19.2-37
42	37.1-138
43	53.1-129
44	16.1-275
45	54-129.1
46	54-281.7
47	46.1-111
48	8.01-44
50	8.01-345
51	54-965
52	4-56
53	4-26
54	63.1-38.1
55	63.1-196.4
56	2.1-563
57	54-729.27, 54-729.29, 54-729.30
58	2.1-703
59	28.1-184
61	18.2-503
63	57-12
64	46.1-3.02
65	15.1-51
66	54-299
67	2.1-583
68	4-32.1
69	13.1-92
70	63.1-206.1
71	16.1-282
72	54-325.2
73	46.1-373
74	63.1-195
75	54-321
76	63.1-87
77	16.1-316
78	55-248.31
79	54-325.8:2
81	54-318.3
82	54-1.18, 54-859.1 to 54-859.4R
83	54-872.17, 54-872.19, 54-872.21, 54-872.23:1
84	55-79.83
85	2.1-342
86	17-126.5
87	15.1-286
88	54-325.2:2
92	58-769.6, 58-769.8, 58-769.10
93	8.01-327.1
94	8.01-467
95	8.01-412.5
98	46.1-339.2
99	28.1-173
100	28.1-108, 28.1-112, 28.1-118.1

Acts 1984 Chapter	Code 1950 Section
101	11-9.1
102	55-79.72
103	55-79.97
104	2.1-38, 2.1-41.2
105	4-22
106	15.1-51
107	58-12.167
108	16.1-112
110	2.1-33
111	15.1-466
117	32.1-289.1
118	6.1-2.10
119	19.2-76.2
120	60.1-14
121	8.01-602, 55-210.2 to 55-210.2:2, 55-210.3R, 55-210.3:01, 55-210.3:02, 55-210.3:1R, 55-210.3:2, 55-210.4R, 55-210.4:01, 55-210.6:2, 55-210.8, 55-210.10R, 55-210.11:01, 55-210.11:1R, 55-210.12, 55-210.15, 55-210.16:1, 55-210.18, 55-210.19, 55-210.26R, 55-210.26:1
122	2.1-599
123	27-5.1
124	46.1-229.01
125	46.1-295.3
126	46.1-258
127	33.1-75.3
128	4-85
129	46.1-550.3:1
130	22.1-115
131	22.1-37
132	6.1-195.39
133	6.1-63
134	6.1-61
135	2.1-359, 2.1-360, 2.1-363, 2.1-363.1
136	6.1-195.11
137	28.1-197.1R
138	22.1-89.1
139	60.1-14
140	20-1 to 20-12R, 32.1-60
141	54-524.65
142	15.1-1231
143	46.1-555.6, 46.1-555.10
144	46.1-154
145	58-12.168
146	33.1-72.1
147	46.1-181.4:1
148	232.1-101
149	30-34.2:1
150	58-405, 58-829.1:1
151	2.1-612
152	2.1-627
153	58-151.013
154	58-587.1, 58-617.2
155	53.1-160
156	46.1-66
157	22.1-18
158	46.1-3.2
159	11-40.2
160	11-57, 11-58
161	14.1-5, 14.1-17.1, 14.1-18 to 14.1-18.2, 30-19.4
162	58-151.013
165	8.01-342
167	15.1-776.1
168	58-851.5:1
169	5.1-88.2
170	54-262, 54-268R, 54-268.1, 54-269R, 54-270R, 54-271, 54-271.1
171	58-405
172	6.1-17
173	31-29
174	37.1-48
175	15.1-364, 15.1-493
176	10-176
177	21-5.1, 21-5.2
178	45.1-21
179	36-99.4
180	4-33, 4-34, 4-37, 4-38, 4-98.18, 4-98.19
181	58-847
182	46.1-336.1
183	2.1-51.8:2
184	45.1-4
185	46.1-308.2 to 46.1-308.8R
186	54-524.84:4, 54-524.84:12
187	9-6.14:4, 28.1-24, 28.1-27
188	45.1-1.9
189	32.1-257, 32.1-271
190	46.1-3
191	56-304.7
192	54-524.84:4, 54-524.84:6
193	32.1-182
194	2.1-557, n., 2.1-559.1, n., 2.1-559.8
195	31-26, 31-27, 31-29
196	2.1-608
197	22.1-209.1
198	33.1-229
199	29-2.1
200	4-2, 4-7, 4-15, 4-15.01, 4-22.1, 4-25, 4-25.1, 4-28, 4-37, 4-45, 4-46, 4-64, 4-84, 4-89
201	54-731, 54-731.1, 54-732, 54-738, 54-740, 54-749
202	30-19.01R, 30-19.02R, 30-28.16
203	54-1.18, 54-729.2 to 54-729.26R
204	60.1-14, 60.1-26, 60.1-52.1, 60.1-52.3
206	44-41.1
208	16.1-279
209	37.1-1
216	15.1-28.4, 15.1-867.2R
217	24.1-97
218	32.1-70.1
219	32.1-261
220	54-83.22:2, 54-112.3:1
221	14.1-46.01:1
222	58-769.10
223	15.1-29.11
224	28.1-128.4
225	14.1-112
226	8.01-81
227	56-426R, 56-426.1
228	45.1-95
229	45.1-48
230	45.1-256
231	65.1-87
232	32.1-292
233	36-55.53 to 36-55.62
234	24.1-129, 24.1-218
235	10-216, 10-221, 10-222
236	45.1-5
237	45.1-12
238	15.1-491
239	15.1-1242, 15.1-1246, 15.1-1247
240	62.1-115.3
241	15.1-262
242	28.1-128.1
244	28.1-108
245	28.1-19R
246	62.1-3.01
247	58-266.1, 58-266.11
248	29-213.57, 29-213.58
251	58-12.169
252	2.1-341, 2.1-343.1, 2.1-346.1
253	53.1-191
254	29-213.73
255	15.1-1231
256	46.1-326.2
257	58-12.170

Acts 1984 Chapter	Code 1950 Section
258	46.1-114
259	28.1-108, 28.1-109, 28.1-112
260	58-12.171
261	58-12.172
262	58-12.173
263	46.1-326.8, 46.1-326.14
264	26-40
265	28.1-230
266	54-765.2 to 54-765.4, 54-765.8
267	58-760.1
268	57-48, 57-49, 57-51, 57-60, 57-61, 57-65
269	19.2-305.1, 58-19.7
270	54-145.3:1 to 54-145.3:6, 54-145.3:8
271	36-94
272	3.1-249.9
273	58-778, 58-895
275	2.1-429
276	58-835.1
277	37.1-67.3
278	19.2-249.1
279	11-37, 11-44, 11-48
280	46.1-314.2
281	55-507
282	19.2-299.1
283	54-730, 54-731.1, 54-731.3, 54-740, 54-765.2
284	10-138.2
285	15.1-482.1
287	56-46.1
288	28.1-20R
289	54-74
290	2.1-116
291	9-81
292	58-12.174
293	14.1-125
294	13.1-124.1, 13.1-286.1
295	13.1-126, 13.1-288
296	6.1-278
297	56-508.6
298	13.1-514
299	6.1-30.3
300	38.1-348.10:1, 38.1-348.11
301	13.1-26
302	6.1-195.29
303	6.1-195.77 to 6.1-195.95
304	6.1-330.41
305	58-835.1
306	58-12.175
307	58-703, 58-707, 58-735.1
308	46.1-65
309	26-20.1
310	58-12.176
311	38.1-21
312	56-235.2
313	53.1-67, 53.1-187
314	58-12.177
315	55-170.1 to 55-173, 55-175, 55-180, 55-182.1, 55-186 to 55-186.2, 55-192, 55-197, 55-200, 55-200.1
316	28.1-119.1
317	14.1-105
318	4-98.11
319	58-46
320	2.1-234.8
321	55-79.94, 55-487
322	44-146.32
323	45.1-244, 45.1-369.1
324	2.1-526.9
325	54-278.2
327	58-266.5:1
328	58-847.1
329	2.1-114.5:1
330	11-40
331	15.1-244
332	10-214R, 44-146.29:1, 44-146.29:2
333	55-374.1
334	13.1-504.1
335	6.1-387
336	58-12.155
337	45.1-4
338	56-291.3:7
339	64.1-74.1, 64.1-134
340	38.1-381.5
341	56-232
342	46.1-154.01
343	6.1-95, 6.1-97R, 6.1-98
344	6.1-195.65
345	46.1-180
346	6.1-195.5:1
347	55-79.79
348	63.1-323
350	36-19, 36-23, 36-47
351	6.1-216
352	6.1-200.6, 6.1-200.7
353	6.1-209
354	6.1-211
355	3.1-426.1
356	14.1-112
357	46.1-198
358	54-68R
359	54-50.1
360	18.2-308
361	32.1-164.3
362	14.1-103
363	17-126.6, n.
364	38.1-472.1
365	15.1-19.3
366	13.1-32
367	3.1-158 to 3.1-169R
368	6.1-195.22
369	18.2-341
370	58-685.29, 58-685.32
371	23-38.56
372	58-811.2
373	16.1-281
374	2.1-210, 2.1-226, 2.1-231, 2.1-328.7, 2.1-329
375	54-729.28
376	55-66.4:1
377	25-46.19
378	2.1-207
379	58-12.178
380	15.1-502R, 15.1-503
381	46.1-3
382	56-1, 56-265.4, 56-265.4:4
383	38.1-381.9
384	29-213.68:1
385	15.1-18.3
386	18.2-105.2
387	15.1-29.9
388	65.1-28
389	42.1-1
392	63.1-248.6
393	2.1-1.2
394	15.1-19.2:1
395	2.1-342
396	43-32, 43-33, 46.1-73
397	58-54.1
398	15.1-90.2
399	46.1-167.1, 46.1-167.3, 46.1-167.4, 46.1-513.1
400	46.1-267
401	32.1-164.1:1
402	63.1-314.1 to 63.1-314.7
403	2.1-457
404	46.1-1
405	58-12.179
406	13.1-2.1, 56-508.1, 56-508.4, 56-508.5
408	60.1-26
409	65.1-70
410	6.1-218
411	65.1-52

Acts 1984 Chapter	Code 1950 Section
412	10-145.11
413	22.1-346 to 22.1-349, 23-254 to 23-260.1R
414	65.1-49
415	22.1-277
416	9-144
417	62.1-172R, 62.1-172.1, 62.1-185
418	58-685.40, 62.1-186.1
419	58-441.6
420	55-248.11
421	2.1-155.3
422	23-7R, 23-7.4
423	58-12.180
424	32.1-103 to 32.1-111R, 32.1-120, 32.1-120.1, 32.1-121
425	37.1-65.1
426	46.1-308
427	55-79.87
428	58-64
429	55-375
430	2.1-20.1, 2.1-181R, 51-111.3, 51-111.5, 51-111.6, 51-111.10, 51-111.10:01, 51-111.24, 51-111.26, 51-111.27, 51-111.29, 51-111.30:1R, 51-111.36, 51-111.41:4, 51-111.46, 51-111.47:1, 51-111.50, 51-111.54 to 51-111.55:1, 51-111.58:2, 51-111.61, 51-111.63, 51-111.67:4, 51-111.68:1, 51-144, 51-146, 51-150, 51-151, 51-156.1, 51-161, 51-168, 51-173.1, 56-45
431	37.1-202.1
432	58-12.181
433	2.1-342, 32.1-239, 32.1-242, 32.1-244, 32.1-244.1, 32.1-245
434	54-113
435	16.1-279
436	22.1-254, 22.1-254.1
437	54-17.1
438	56-405.01, n.
439	56-405.02
440	9-145.5 to 9-145.7
441	38.1-380.3
442	6.1-330.27:1
443	8.01-581.2
444	3.1-426, 9-84.07, 10-17.14, 10-137, 15.1-945.2, 15.1-945.3, 21-7, 22.1-343, 22.1-344, 24.1-18, 42.1-13, 62.1-44.14
445	6.1-330.30
446	6.1-332.1
447	54-955.1
448	13.1-547, 13.1-549.3
449	56-265.4:3
450	36-19
451	15.1-200
452	55-154
453	56-234.3
454	56-234.3
455	55-374
456	20-107.1
457	32.1-163, 32.1-165, 32.1-166.1 to 32.1-166.10
458	60.1-48, 60.1-52, 60.1-52.2, 60.1-52.3, 60.1-58, 60.1-73, 60.1-74, 60.1-84.2, 60.1-132
459	15.1-28.5
460	55-248.49
461	9-46.1
462	30-28.7
463	28.1-23, 28.1-23.1
464	46.1-113, 46.1-162, 46.1-164, 46.1-526
465	3.1-170 to 3.1-176R
466	3.1-250 to 3.1-261R
467	33.1-75.1
468	60.1-47, 60.1-48, 60.1-79.1
469	4-17
470	54-26.1
471	58-835.1
472	8.01-37.1
473	2.1-344, 2.1-393
474	55-106.4
475	2.1-71
476	46.1-149, 46.1-373, 46.1-564 to 46.1-570
478	9-96, 9-97, 9-98R
479	15.1-796
480	24.1-17, 24.1-22.1, 24.1-29, 24.1-34, 24.1-43, 24.1-45, 24.1-46, 24.1-49, 24.1-49.01, 24.1-55, 24.1-76, 24.1-101, 24.1-105, 24.1-106, 24.1-109, 24.1-110, 24.1-119, 24.1-158 to 24.1-160, 24.1-166, 24.1-167, 24.1-206.2, 24.1-250, 24.1-253, 24.1-257, 24.1-257.1
481	23-38.61 to 23-38.65, 23-38.67, 23-38.69 to 23-38.69:3
482	8.01-220.2
483	22.1-32
484	46.1-254.3
485	15.1-162, 15.1-605
487	3.1-249.16
488	46.1-228.1
489	17-29, 17-30
490	53.1-131.1
491	19.2-56, 19.2-57
492	3.1-796.39 to 3.1-796.65R, 18.2-392 to 18.2-403R, 18.2-403.1 to 18.2-403.3, 29-213.5 to 29-213.34R, 29-213.36 to 29-213.100
493	8.01-225, 32.1-112.1R
494	8.01-581.13
495	58-12.99
496	37.1-197
497	32.1-157 to 32.1-162R
498	2.1-450, 9-141, 63.1-52, 63.1-53, 63.1-69, 63.1-69.1, 63.1-79, 63.1-82, n., 63.1-85, 63.1-87, 63.1-92, 63.1-94, n., 63.1-95, 63.1-97.1, 63.1-116.1, n.
499	16.1-251, 16.1-252
500	16.1-89
501	56-451.2
502	2.1-549, n., 2.1-552, 2.1-553.1
503	59.1-207.7, 59.1-207.8
504	55-37
505	37.1-197
506	16.1-123R, 16.1-123.1, 16.1-124R, 16.1-125R
507	63.1-65
508	33.1-252
511	58-587.2

Acts 1984 Chapter	Code 1950 Section
512	14.1-195.1
513	2.1-342, 2.1-344, 10-186.1 to 10-186.21, 32.1-178
514	53.1-141 to 53.1-143
515	9-168, 9-170, 9-173
516	53.1-60, 53.1-131
517	18.2-340.9
518	62.1-13.5:3, n., 62.1-13.25:1, n.
519	8.01-66.9:1
520	15.1-37.3:6
521	43-7
522	58-441.6
523	15.1-162.1
524	8.01-3, 9-77.11:01
525	15.1-292.2
526	54-77
527	29-213.68
528	10-145.12
529	58-12.182 to 58-12.184
531	58-16.2:2
532	2.1-342
533	15.1-140.1, 18.2-414.2
534	19.2-81
535	63.1-87, 63.1-124.1
536	8.01-405
537	20-120
538	9-168
539	46.1-199, 46.1-225, 46.1-226, 46.1-267
540	44-93
541	38.1-381
542	58-730.3
543	4-42, 9-169, 15.1-136.2, 33.1-252
544	46.1-192.1
545	46.1-149
546	58-12.185 to 58-12.187
547	58-685.37
548	32.1-164.1
549	38.1-327.36
550	3.1-796.11:4
552	15.1-1261
554	15.1-1250
555	54-524.65
556	62.1-13.21, 62.1-13.22, 62.1-13.25
557	8.01-479
558	24.1-12.3, n.
559	4-25.1, 4-30, 4-33, 4-98.18, 4-103, 4-104
560	55-378
561	9-173.3
562	56-46.1
563	10-145.12
564	14.1-63
565	8.01-129
567	16.1-247
568	65.1-135
569	8.01-401.2
570	16.1-69.21, 16.1-69.35, 16.1-69.44
571	18.2-460
572	55-376
573	55-57.1
574	6.1-330.16
575	32.1-164.2
577	8.01-225
578	63.1-124
579	9-6.24
580	37.1-239 to 37.1-241
582	59.1-10 to 59.1-21R, 59.1-68.2, 59.1-285 to 59.1-293
583	54-859.28
584	53.1-134
585	19.2-153
586	63.1-40, 63.1-43.1
587	18.2-473
588	15.1-28.6
589	37.1-207
590	2.1-1.1, 2.1-51.9, 10-8.1, 10-91 to 10-93R, 10-94, n., 10-95R, 10-96R, 10-214R, 23-135.7:7, 33.1-222, 40.1-1, 40.1-6, 40.1-11, 40.1-22, 45.1-1R, 45.1-1.1 to 45.1-1.8, 45.1-1.10, 45.1-2 to 45.1-4, 45.1-6 to 45.1-8, 45.1-15, 45.1-18, 45.1-21 to 45.1-24, 45.1-27, 45.1-31, 45.1-33 to 45.1-33.3, 45.1-33.5, 45.1-33.11, 45.1-40, 45.1-89, 45.1-101.2, 45.1-179.2, 45.1-180, 45.1-180.2, 45.1-180.3, 45.1-182.1, 45.1-197.2R, 45.1-197.18, 45.1-198 to 45.1-203, 45.1-207, 45.1-209.1, 45.1-212, 45.1-212.1R, 45.1-213, 45.1-220.3, 45.1-220.5, 45.1-221 to 45.1-223, 45.1-228 to 45.1-231, 45.1-232R, 45.1-234 to 45.1-237, 45.1-239, 45.1-241 to 45.1-244, 45.1-247, 45.1-248, 45.1-250 to 45.1-253, 45.1-255, n., 45.1-256, 45.1-260, 45.1-261.1, 45.1-262, 45.1-270.5, 45.1-270.7, 45.1-273, 45.1-279, 45.1-282, 45.1-285.3, n., 45.1-288, 45.1-289, 45.1-291, 45.1-294, 45.1-297, 45.1-312, 45.1-313, 45.1-325, 45.1-358, 45.1-361 to 45.1-363, 45.1-365, 45.1-366, 45.1-370, 45.1-376, 45.1-377R, 45.1-378, 45.1-382 to 45.1-391
592	18.2-427
594	16.1-264
595	27-7
597	33.1-320, n.
598	19.2-56
599	15.1-26.01
600	6.1-330.27:2
601	19.2-8, 55-79.58, 55-79.72, 55-79.74, 55-79.83, 55-79.84:1, 55-79.94
602	58-711, 58-744
603	4-58, 4-60, 4-75, 4-92
604	20-88.27
605	44-12
606	65.1-129, 65.1-135
607	19.2-187
608	65.1-87.1
609	8.01-328.1, 20-99
610	56-529, n., 56-530, n.
611	20-99.2
612	2.1-196.1, 2.1-203, 2.1-402, 2.1-438
613	8.1-201, 8.5-114, 8.8-102 to 8.8-108, 8.8-201 to 8.8-208, 8.8-301, 8.8-302, 8.8-304 to 8.8-321, 8.8-401 to 8.8-408, 8.9-103, 8.9-105, 8.9-203, 8.9-302, 8.9-304, 8.9-305, 8.9-309, 8.9-312, 13.1-20, 13.1-21, 13.1-75, 13.1-78
614	8.9-401
615	2.1-51.35 to 2.1-51.37
616	20-99

Acts 1984 Chapter	Code 1950 Section
617	15.1-550
618	19.2-243
619	19.2-368.2, 19.2-368.3, 19.2-368.13R
620	18.2-248.5
621	19.2-270.4
622	15.1-131.3
623	18.2-268, 18.2-271
625	18.2-330
626	63.1-272
627	54-260.65
628	63.1-55.3
629	32.1-76.1R, 32.1-76.3
630	46.1-65
631	16.1-228, 16.1-241, 16.1-253.1, 16.1-262, 16.1-279, 16.1-279.1, 16.1-296, 16.1-298
632	17-116.03
633	20-121.02
635	17-116.010
636	58-151.013
637	28.1-203
638	8.01-195.6, 8.01-195.7
639	45.1-90
640	38.1-934, 38.1-938, 38.1-939
641	2.1-5R, 2.1-6R, 2.1-8R, 2.1-483.1, 2.1-504, 2.1-504.1 to 2.1-504.5, 2.1-505, 2.1-506R, 2.1-507R, 2.1-509R, 2.1-510R, 2.1-511, 2.1-512
642	19.2-392.1, 19.2-392.2
643	53.1-116
644	27-15.1, 27-30, 27-36
645	16.1-241
646	8.01-537, 8.01-537.1, 8.01-540, 8.01-543, 8.01-550, 8.01-551, 8.01-552R, 8.01-553, 8.01-568
647	43-10
648	56-1.1
649	20-107.3
650	2.1-37.13
651	16.1-241, 20-107.2
652	63.1-256, 63.1-268.1
653	37.1-194
654	14.1-52.01
655	53.1-154
656	20-88.30:5
657	16.1-244
658	46.1-421
659	65.1-98
660	46.1-387.9:3
661	15.1-137.2, 15.1-138, 15.1-138.1, 15.1-139
662	51-111.26:2, 51-111.67:13.1, 51-111.67:17
663	37.1-142
664	38.1-482.4:1
665	16.1-241, 16.1-279
666	18.2-266, 18.2-268
667	18.2-262
668	53.1-150
669	16.1-241, 16.1-244
670	63.1-85.1R, 63.1-85.1:1 to 63.1-85.1:3, 63.1-85.2, 63.1-85.2:1, 63.1-85.3R, 63.1-85.3:1, 63.1-85.4, 63.1-85.4:1, 63.1-85.7
671	2.1-21
672	58-151.032, 58-151.032:1, 58-151.032:2
673	18.2-271, 46.1-421, 46.1-437, 46.1-514.9, 46.1-514.11 to 46.1-514.13:1, 46.1-514.15 to 46.1-514.17, 46.1-514.19
674	58-151.013, 58-151.014:1
675	4-40 to 4-42R, 4-108 to 4-109.1R, 4-111R, 10-139, 10-140, 10-142, 10-155R, 15.1-28.7, 19.2-152.1, 58-1 to 58-1166R, 58.1-1 to 58.1-3993
676	58-769.10
677	63.1-173.1R, 63.1-182.1
678	59.1-274
679	58-831
680	58-405
681	58-769.10, 58-769.10:1
682	58-151.2
683	58-441.6
684	18.2-247
685	36-88
686	38.1-381.9, 38.1-381.10
687	58-715, 58-753.1
688	9-91.1, 10-257.1
689	58-829
690	58-441.3
691	2.1-27.3
692	58-405
693	58-441.6
694	65.1-4.3
695	1-13.28:1, 1-13.28:2, 14.1-84.6:1, 15.1-977.19:1, 15.1-977.20 to 15.1-977.22, 15.1-977.22:2, 15.1-1135, 15.1-1135.1, 15.1-1141, 15.1-1141.1, 15.1-1146.1:1, 15.1-1147, 22.1-38.1, 46.1-65, 58-266.1, 58-441.49, 58-617.2
698	8.01-195.4, 8.01-195.6, 8.01-195.7
699	62.1-197 to 62.1-223
700	15.1-1374, 15.1-1375
701	17-116.01 to 17-116.07, 17-116.09 to 17-116.011, 17-116.014
702	14.1-125
703	1-13.27:3, 2.1-37.1, 2.1-116, 2.1-121, 2.1-124, 2.1-612, 4-31, 4-37, 8.01-20, 8.01-113, 8.01-429, 8.01-626, 8.01-645, 8.01-649, 8.01-651, 8.01-665, 8.01-669 to 8.01-671, 8.01-673, 8.01-674, 8.01-675R, 8.01-675.1 to 8.01-675.4, 8.01-676R, 8.01-676.1, 8.01-679, 8.01-681, 8.01-682, 8.01-684, 8.01-685, 8.01-686R, 8.01-687R, 10-17.28, 14.1-196, 15.1-258, 16.1-298, 17-13, 17-57, 17-111.6, 17-222, 17-228, 19.2-119, 19.2-124, 19.2-181, 19.2-317 to 19.2-321, 19.2-322R, 19.2-322.1, 19.2-323, 19.2-325 to 19.2-327, 19.2-368.8, 20-46, 21-105, 28.1-34, 29-228, 30-5, 32.1-102.7, n., 33.1-358, 37.1-186, 46.1-367, 46.1-387.10, 46.1-437, 46.1-543, 49-13, 49-22, 51-178, 53.1-78, 54-74, 54-74.1, 57-67, 58-689, 58-754, 58-1126, 58-1129, 60.1-67.1,

Acts 1984 Chapter	Code 1950 Section
	60.1-69, 60.1-71, 62.1-44.24, 62.1-44.30, 62.1-44.106, 63.1-237, 65.1-4, 65.1-93, 65.1-98
704	54-260.69
705	11-52
706	10-21.3:2
707	19.2-123
709	16.1-266, 16.1-267, 19.2-159, 19.2-159.1
710	54-275.1, 54-276.7:2
711	15.1-51
712	15.1-7.3
713	22.1-253.1 to 22.1-253.13
714	45.1-255R, 45.1-255.1
715	10-46, 10-54, 10-69, 58-838.5:2
716	56-249.6
717	55-418, 55-419
718	38.1-818
719	38.1-327.1, 38.1-327.46, 38.1-327.52, 38.1-327.55, 38.1-327.56, 38.1-327.58
720	2.1-51.7, 2.1-51.8:1, 2.1-51.9, 2.1-51.9:1, 2.1-51.10:1, 2.1-51.11R, 2.1-51.14 to 2.1-51.18, 2.1-51.22R, 2.1-51.23R, 2.1-51.23.1, 2.1-51.24R, 2.1-51.25 to 2.1-51.27, 2.1-51.28R, 2.1-51.31 to 2.1-51.34, 2.1-64.28:1, 2.1-64.28:3, 2.1-113, 2.1-113.1, 2.1-113.3, 2.1-114.3, 2.1-177 to 2.1-179, 2.1-192, 2.1-373.4, 2.1-387 to 2.1-389, 2.1-391, 2.1-407 to 2.1-410, 2.1-422, 2.1-423, 2.1-486, 2.1-559.1, 2.1-559.2, 2.1-560 to 2.1-563, 2.1-563.2, 2.1-563.3, 2.1-576, 2.1-578, 2.1-579, 5.1-1.1, 5.1-2.2, 9-153, 9-174, 9-176, 10-184.1, 15.1-173, 18.2-308, 19.2-81.2, 22.1-222, 33.1-393, 33.1-394, 33.1-397, 36-132, 36-133, 36-137, 37.1-10, 42.1-80, 44-146.18, 53.1-5, 53.1-29, 53.1-48, 54-1.25, 54-1.30, 54-1.31, 54-950.1, 54-952, 54-955.1, 58-19.8, 58-19.9, 58-19.13, 58-19.18, 58-19.21, 58-28, 59.1-21.16:2, 59.1-274, 59.1-275, 63.1-321, 63.1-323 to 63.1-325
721	56-55, 56-76, 56-241, 56-481.1, 56-482.1, 56-482.2
722	15.1-608
723	54-524.67:3
724	54-524.58:2
725	56-235.4, 56-249.6
726	55-287, 55-288R, 55-288.1 to 55-290, 55-292 to 55-296, 55-297.1, 55-297.2
727	54-306.1:1
728	2.1-704 to 2.1-713
729	58-151.013, 58-151.013:1, 58-405
730	32.1-74
731	3.1-27.37 to 3.1-27.50
732	21-120
733	54-62, n.
734	2.1-2R, 2.1-2.1, 2.1-64.38, 2.1-114.5:6, 2.1-114.8R, 2.1-234.13, 2.1-335.1, 2.1-488.2R, 2.1-488.2:1, 2.1-559R, 2.1-569R, 2.1-586, 3.1-18R, 3.1-18.7, 3.1-22.4, 3.1-27.35, 4-13, 9-26R, 9-84, 9-94R, 9-119R, 9-143, 9-152, 9-152.4, 9-155, 9-165R, 9-168, 9-186, 10-17.18, 10-164, 10-186, 10-232, 22.1-171, 23-1R, 23-1.01, 23-22, 23-30.36, 23-38.33:1, 23-38.64, 23-111R, 23-135.7:9, 23-135.7:13, 23-227, 23-253, 23-264R, 28.1-17R, 28.1-199, 29-19R, 32.1-14, 37.1-27, 37.1-218, 40.1-4R, 40.1-4.1, 40.1-6, 42.1-1, 44-23R, 53.1-14R, 53.1-31, 53.1-139, 53.1-189, 54-1.25, 54-1.33, 54-367.11, 54-379R, 54-524.20R, 54-955.1, 59.1-273, 60.1-34, 62.1-44.40, 62.1-44.88R, 62.1-139, 63.1-13R, 63.1-56, 63.1-82R, 63.1-85.4, 63.1-248.7, 63.1-295R
735	22.1-253.1 to 22.1-253.13
736	11-62.1 to 11-62.9
738	59.1-294 to 59.1-310
739	2.1-20.4, 2.1-51.9, 10-8.1, 10-17.114, 10-18, 10-19, 10-21.3:1, 10-21.3:3 to 10-21.3:8, 10-21.4 to 10-21.13R, 10-168 to 10-172, 10-173.1 to 10-173.7, 10-175, 10-176, 10-218, 15.1-1405, 19.2-16, 22.1-222, 33.1-62, 33.1-63, 33.1-223, 58-769.5, 58-769.7, 58-769.11, 58-769.12
740	32.1-102.1, 32.1-102.3, 32.1-102.6, 32.1-102.7R, 32.1-102.9
741	55-248.38:1
742	2.1-121, 22.1-312
743	44-146.16, 44-146.23
744	2.1-20.01
745	9-106.6 to 9-106.22R, 33.1-371, 44-146.30
746	2.1-1.1, 2.1-51.27, 2.1-114.5:1, 2.1-114.5:6, 2.1-407 to 2.1-410R, 2.1-445R, 2.1-445.1, 2.1-454.1, 2.1-457.1, 2.1-560 to 2.1-563.12R, 2.1-563.13 to 2.1-563.27, 15.1-7.1, 51-111.67:17
747	19.2-368.4
748	33.1-1, 33.1-2, 33.1-23.2
749	9-197 to 9-249
750	2.1-1.1, 2.1-38, 2.1-51.9, 2.1-64R, 2.1-384, 2.1-512.1, 2.1-548.6 to 2.1-548.14, 3.1-18.6, 3.1-22.8, 3.1-22.9, 3.1-249.13, 9-88 to 9-94R, 9-152.1, 9-152.2, 10-1R, 10-2R, 10-3, 10-6, n., 10-8 to 10-10R, 10-12, 10-12.1R,

Acts 1984 Chapter	Code 1950 Section
	10-13 to 10-14.1, 10-14.2R, 10-15, 10-17, 10-18, 10-21, 10-21.3:1, 10-21.4 to 10-21.13R, 10-32, 10-33, 10-34.1, 10-34.2, 10-41, 10-45.2, 10-46.1, 10-46.2, 10-90.31, 10-90.32, 10-90.36, 10-90.37, 10-94R, 10-100, 10-101, 10-128, 10-130, 10-136, 10-137.1, 10-138, 10-138.1, 10-139.1, 10-140R, 10-142R, 10-143R, 10-145.3R, 10-145.4R, 10-145.9R, 10-145.11, 10-145.12, 10-146 to 10-150R, 10-150.2 to 10-150.9, 10-150.16, 10-171, 10-181, 10-184.2, 10-198, 10-199, 10-212, 10-217 to 10-219, 10-252 to 10-262, 13.1-142, 15.1-1377, 21-6, 21-7, 28.1-230, 30-74, 32.1-242, 33.1-351, 58-760.2, 58-769.5, 58-769.7, 58-769.11, 58-769.12, 58-838.7:1, 62.1-44.35R
751	18.2-98.1R, 18.2-152.1 to 18.2-152.14
752	17-30.1, 19.2-165
753	36-99.5, 63.1-171.7
755	15.1-1412, n., 19.2-163, n., 19.2-326, n.
759	16.1-279
760	33.1-223.1, 33.1-391
761	54-260.74:1
762	15.1-1250.02
763	15.1-28.01, 15.1-28.1
764	11-35, 11-37, 11-45
765	44-1, 44-2.1, 44-4, 44-6, 44-87, 44-88, 44-96 to 44-100, 44-102, 44-104, 44-115
766	19.2-82
767	8.01-66.9
768	58-829.1
769	15.1-23.1
770	18.2-248.6
771	8.9-403 to 8.9-406, 12.1-21, 13.1-8, 13.1-124, 13.1-286, 13.1-505, 13.1-508 to 13.1-510, 13.1-512, 13.1-514, 13.1-525, 58-450, 59.1-70, 59.1-80, 59.1-82 to 59.1-84
772	23-185
773	59.1-207.9 to 59.1-207.14
774	55-419
775	24.1-132, 24.1-228.2
777	8.01-581.2 to 8.01-581.6, 8.01-581.10
778	2.1-1.1, 18.2-271.1, 32.1-114, 33.1-252, 33.1-392 to 33.1-399R, 37.1-218, 46.1-25, 46.1-40.2 to 46.1-40.6, 46.1-314.4, 46.1-368
779	2.1-38, 2.1-51.18, 2.1-64.28:4, 2.1-427, 9-170, 9-179, 14.1-73.2, 14.1-84.2, 14.1-84.6:1, 15.1-131, 19.2-81.2, 23-235, 27-34.2, 27-34.2:1, 54-729.27, 54-729.29, 54-729.30
780	8.01-313, 18.2-268, 46.1-1, 46.1-7, 46.1-25 to 46.1-26.1, 46.1-37, 46.1-40.1, 46.1-167.3 to 46.1-167.5, 46.1-167.7, 46.1-167.13, 46.1-172.02, 46.1-176, 46.1-177.1, 46.1-178.1, 46.1-191, 46.1-192.1, 46.1-250.1, 46.1-329, 46.1-347.1, 46.1-348 to 46.1-355, 46.1-357.2, 46.1-358 to 46.1-363, 46.1-366, 46.1-368 to 46.1-375.1, 46.1-376R, 46.1-377 to 46.1-379, 46.1-380.1, 46.1-380.2, 46.1-382, 46.1-383, 46.1-383.3, 46.1-384 to 46.1-385, 46.1-387.2, 46.1-387.9, 46.1-387.9:1, 46.1-396, 46.1-397, 46.1-405, 46.1-412, 46.1-413.1, 46.1-414, 46.1-417 to 46.1-418, 46.1-421, 46.1-423, 46.1-423.2 to 46.1-423.4, 46.1-424 to 46.1-426, 46.1-430, 46.1-436, 46.1-438, 46.1-441 to 46.1-442, 46.1-452, 46.1-459, 46.1-462, 46.1-469, 46.1-490, 46.1-491, 46.1-493, 52-9
781	2.1-1.1, 2.1-20.4, 2.1-51.15, 20-88, 32.1-74 to 32.1-76.3R, 32.1-312, 32.1-319, 32.1-320, 32.1-323 to 32.1-330, 63.1-55, 63.1-77, 63.1-78, 63.1-78.1R, 63.1-79 to 63.1-81, 63.1-82, n., 63.1-83, 63.1-85, 63.1-87, 63.1-92, 63.1-92.1, 63.1-94R, 63.1-116.1R, 63.1-123
782	9-250 to 266

ACTS 1985

Acts 1985 Chapter	Code 1950 Section
1	16.1-292
2	56-232, 56-234
3	38.1-327.9, 38.1-327.62 to 38.1-327.71
4	20-107.3
5	20-61.1
6	15.1-306.1
7	46.1-343
8	22.1-79
9	20-99.1
10	46.1-404, 52-4.2
11	46.1-282.2
12	24.1-4.3, 24.1-12.3
13	15.1-1511, 15.1-1513
15	29-122.1
17	63.1-172
18	63.1-204, 63.1-225
19	63.1-314.3
20	63.1-317.1
21	29-213.66
24	3.1-972
26	2.1-326
28	38.1-472.1
29	65.1-154
30	58.1-2653, 58.1-2655, 58.1-3201
31	58.1-2623, 58.1-2626
32	56-508.6
33	38.1-327.7
34	12.1-4
35	65.1-65
36	38.1-217.31
37	56-508.1, 56-508.4

Acts 1985 Chapter	Code 1950 Section
	to 56-508.6
38	56-508.8 to 56-508.14
39	38.1-381
40	40.1-51.6, 40.1-51.15
41	56-232, 56-232.1, 56-234
42	33.1-23.1 to 33.1-23.4, 33.1-23.5:1, 33.1-41R, 33.1-41.1, 33.1-43R, 33.1-43.1R, 33.1-45R, 33.1-80R, 33.1-81R, 33.1-83R
43	17-119.1:2
44	16.1-69.6:1
45	19.2-37
48	8.01-446.1
49	54-154
56	15.1-176
58	27-85.4
59	15.1-239
60	58.1-3968
62	58.1-3372R
63	15.1-827.1
64	58.1-3350
65	29-52.2
66	15.1-1167.2, 15.1-1168
67	9-6.14:4, 9-6.14:22, 9-6.16, 62.1-197, 62.1-199, 62.1-200, 62.1-203, 62.1-204, 62.1-206, 62.1-208, 62.1-216, 62.1-219, 62.1-221
68	62.1-186.7
69	55-79.94, 55-487
70	36-55.28
72	2.1-51.34, 2.1-234.29 to 2.1-234.34
73	57-1
74	11-40.2
75	55-79.74:1
77	2.1-33, 19.2-45
78	58.1-3
79	55-248.11
80	14.1-11.1
81	2.1-342
82	57-63
83	55-79.74, 55-462
84	9-106.23 to 9-106.27
85	2.1-373.4
86	32.1-269
87	37.1-98, 37.1-98.1R, 37.1-98.2
88	56-274, 56-274.1
89	55-248.11
90	46.1-441.1
91	46.1-3
92	8.01-40.1, 18.2-152.12
93	46.1-248
94	14.1-112
95	57-36, 57-37
96	54-281.1, 54-281.2, 54-295.1, 54-295.2, 54-295.6, 54-308.6, 54-309, 54-317
97	15.1-800
98	58.1-609
99	16.1-69.40
100	18.2-165.2
101	11-62.5, 11-62.7
102	28.1-203
103	44-93
104	21-114, 21-116
105	58.1-3503
106	37.1-67.6
107	55-79.46, 55-79.84:1, 55-79.92
108	15.1-533
109	15.1-1416
110	18.2-90
111	14.1-47.2
112	2.1-373.01
113	2.1-191
114	2.1-391
115	2.1-112
116	54-740
119	29-55
120	58.1-3706, 58.1-3712.1
121	23-38.62
123	46.1-66, 58.1-2402
124	10-173.8
125	28.1-85.1R, 28.1-124, 28.1-126R, 28.1-127
126	58.1-3650.149, n.
127	15.1-1412
128	10-198
129	51-111.6, 51-111.47, 51-111.47:01
130	33.1-190
131	58.1-3928, 58.1-3929R, 58.1-3930, 58.1-3937, 58.1-3938
132	19.2-38.1
133	16.1-69.51
134	58.1-811
137	23-7.1
138	15.1-729
139	22.1-145
140	14.1-84.2
141	2.1-701, 2.1-702
142	15.1-7.4
143	58.1-3650.173 to 58.1-3650.178, n.
144	58.1-2111.1, 58.1-2112, 58.1-2124.1, 58.1-2125
145	15.1-155
146	2.1-234.13, 3.1-22.4, 3.1-27.35, 9-84, 10-164, 10-232, 22.1-171, 23-1.01, 23-30.36, 23-38.33:1, 23-38.64, 23-227, 23-253, 62.1-139
148	46.1-190
149	62.1-69.6 to 62.1-69.13, 62.1-69.16 to 62.1-69.18, 62.1-69.20
150	15.1-18.2
151	60.1-35R, 60.1-132
152	60.1-14, 60.1-52.1, 60.1-52.3, 60.1-75
153	32.1-317
154	29-52
155	2.1-342
156	58.1-3511
157	32.1-122.2
158	22.1-215, 37.1-42.1
159	54-937
160	46.1-291
161	23-231.1
162	46.1-105.11
164	11-37, 11-41, 11-41.3, 11-64, 11-66, 11-70
165	28.1-172.1
166	28.1-167
167	58.1-2105, 58.1-2116
169	15.1-247
170	15.1-29.12, 15.1-867.1R
171	8.01-449, 8.01-450
173	3.1-4.1, 3.1-796.11:3
174	53.1-137, 53.1-165
175	53.1-159
176	19.2-263.1
177	8.01-320
179	23-7.4
180	28.1-165
181	28.1-172
182	18.2-56.1
183	16.1-244
184	19.2-270.1
185	46.1-105.12
186	57-35.1
187	56-46.2
188	8.01-359
189	64.1-1
190	58.1-3650.179 to 58.1-3650.182, n.
191	65.1-52
192	8.01-223.1
193	2.1-51.9, 2.1-51.21,

Acts 1985 Chapter	Code 1950 Section
	9-99.1, 10-260R
194	22.1-123
195	20-25
196	15.1-193
197	24.1-43, 24.1-97, 24.1-129
199	19.2-76.1
200	19.2-353.4
201	14.1-112
202	55-37
203	16.1-293, 16.1-294
204	58.1-106, 58.1-107
205	8.01-37.1
206	56-338.65
207	22.1-7, 22.1-214, 22.1-214.2, 37.1-10, 37.1-10.01
208	55-248.6:1
209	46.1-199, 46.1-226
210	16.1-281
211	16.1-299
212	2.1-20.01:1
213	8.01-262
214	8.01-378
215	37.1-142
216	8.01-606
217	26-17, 64.1-65, n.
218	46.1-221, 46.1-221.1
219	46.1-547
220	58.1-3506
221	58.1-322, 58.1-331, 58.1-345, 58.1-346, 58.1-381, 58.1-401 to 58.1-403, 58.1-431, 58.1-490, 58.1-492, 58.1-618, 58.1-700, 58.1-1117, 58.1-1710, 58.1-1727 to 58.1-1729, 58.1-1805, 58.1-1825, 58.1-1826, 58.1-2025, 58.1-2526, 58.1-3200, 58.1-3275, 58.1-3300, 58.1-3507, 58.1-3909 to 58.1-3911R
222	4-22, 4-22.1
223	15.1-136.3
224	3.1-81.1
225	2.1-701
226	22.1-148
227	22.1-101
228	32.1-283
229	63.1-25.1
230	19.2-368.18
231	46.1-441.2
232	46.1-350
233	38.1-816
234	38.1-482.4:1R, 38.1-482.4:2
235	46.1-550.3:1
236	51-111.67:1
237	3.1-796.25 to 3.1-796.27
238	64.1-21
241	58.1-3516
242	59.1-263
243	38.1-95
244	46.1-252.1
245	55-66.4:2
246	17-59
247	19.2-294.2, 53.1-218, 53.1-220.1
248	46.1-267
249	62.1-44.15
250	46.1-199
251	63.1-210.1
252	18.2-340.2
253	19.2-153
254	60.1-14
255	63.1-142
256	2.1-548.8
257	15.1-1357
258	58.1-3516
259	15.1-131.9, 52-31 to 52-34
260	16.1-228, 16.1-248R, 16.1-248.1 to 16.1-250.1, 16.1-255, 16.1-266, 16.1-277.1, 16.1-279, 16.1-284 to 16.1-285.1, 16.1-292
261	37.1-67.3
262	8.01-250.1
263	10-145.11
264	54-49.1
265	2.1-563.16
266	18.2-191 to 18.2-195
267	10-145.11
268	55-248.39
269	46.1-267
270	16.1-241
271	14.1-76, 14.1-80
272	52-6
273	32.1-69.1, 32.1-69.2
274	54-933.1
275	18.2-105
276	15.1-366
277	2.1-344
278	42.1-35, 42.1-39
279	18.2-380
280	18.2-25
281	4-79
282	56-46.1, 56-265.2
283	17-116.05
284	29-92.4
285	63.1-195, 63.1-204, 63.1-220, 63.1-220.1
286	11-54, 11-55
287	46.1-267
288	32.1-121.1
289	15.1-11.1
290	8.01-508
291	54-297, 54-298R, 54-299R, 54-300.1R, 54-300.3
292	46.1-387.9:3
293	63.1-133.1
294	55-210.2:1, 55-210.3:01, 55-210.3:2, 55-210.3:3, 55-210.9:1, 55-210.12, 55-210.18, 55-210.19, 55-210.24, 55-210.24:1
295	19.2-317.1
296	45.1-74
297	8.9-403
298	63.1-222
299	18.2-162
300	63.1-222
301	53.1-131
302	45.1-73
303	54-274, 54-310, 54-315.1
304	20-97
305	54-367.9
306	19.2-392
307	19.2-169.1
308	16.1-311, 16.1-312
309	37.1-199
310	8.01-269
311	15.1-11.4
312	38.1-4
313	32.1-271
314	55-248.5
315	2.1-155, 2.1-167, 15.1-167
316	54-281.4 to 54-281.6, 54-281.8, 54-281.9
317	15.1-1392
318	38.1-389.3:1
319	32.1-180
320	33.1-23.03
321	15.1-66.4, 15.1-131.6, 19.2-155, 19.2-328, 53.1-76, 53.1-94
322	18.2-152.3, 18.2-152.4, 18.2-152.6, 18.2-152.7, 18.2-152.10, 18.2-152.14
323	60.1-120
324	22.1-67
325	38.1-381
326	3.1-1021, 3.1-1022, 3.1-1025, 3.1-1030
327	54-276.1
328	54-325.2:2
330	8.01-35.1
331	45.1-364R, 45.1-364.1
332	22.1-217.1, 37.1-58.1

Acts 1985 Chapter	Code 1950 Section
333	46.1-149
334	22.1-270
335	32.1-127
336	54-524.50:1
337	54-306.1:2
338	32.1-178.1
339	6.1-60.1
341	2.1-553.2
342	15.1-37.3:6
343	27-23.1 to 27-23.5
344	36-88
345	64.1-57.1
346	10-113 to 10-117R, 10-168 to 10-170, 10-172, 10-173.2 to 10-173.4, 10-173.6, 10-173.7, 10-175, 10-176
347	54-274, 54-281.10 to 54-281.13
348	22.1-303
350	22.1-214.3
351	24.1-67
352	2.1-328.5, 2.1-328.8
353	18.2-340.9
354	3.1-699.1, 3.1-700.1, 3.1-722.5:1, 3.1-722.20:1
355	18.2-267
356	54-142
357	3.1-27.41
358	59.1-71
359	23-38.17:1, 23-38.18
360	19.2-389, 63.1-198 to 63.1-199
361	38.1-42.1
362	26-40
363	6.1-223.2
364	6.1-200.4
365	6.1-226.4, 6.1-226.6, 6.1-226.7
366	6.1-226.9
367	16.1-243
368	16.1-279
369	16.1-86.1, 17-30.3
370	38.1-217.21
371	17-116.05:1
372	32.1-247
373	54-147, 54-152
375	46.1-551
376	18.2-23.1
377	18.2-253.2
378	16.1-69.35:2
379	16.1-88.2
380	13.1-229, 38.1-39.1
381	42.1-70
382	56-484.2
384	63.1-195, 63.1 196
385	29-213.85
386	23-234
387	15.1-503.4:10, 15.1-833 to 15.1-836, 15.1-836.3, 15.1-837, 30-19.1
388	16.1-285
389	56-241.1, 56-241.2
390	37.1-128.1, 37.1-132
391	32.1-164.4
392	17-61, 43-4.1
393	18.2-268
394	18.2-311
395	45.1-95
396	19.2-164, 19.2-164.1
397	3.1-1, 3.1-8, 3.1-426, 9-84.07, 9-154, 10-17.14, 15.1-945.2, 15.1-945.3, 22.1-343, 22.1-344, 42.1-7R, 42.1-13, 62.1-44.14, 62.1-44.15, 63.1-85.2:1
398	18.2-152.5
399	26-40
400	38.1-522 to 38.1-549R, 38.1-549.1 to 38.1-549.24
401	38.1-753
402	26-30
403	54-318.3
404	56-209 to 56-211, 56-213 to 56-218, 56-222 to 56-224, 56-227 to 56-231.14
405	56-501, 56-501.01, 56-502
406	58.1-3912
407	22.1-1, 22.1-199, 22.1-256
408	29-213.92:1, 29-213.93
409	59.1-311 to 59.1-335
410	2.1-187, n.
411	32.1-287
412	32.1-297.1
414	57-39.2, n., 57-39.7, n.
415	15.1-687.8, 15.1-687.9
416	8.01-300, 15.1-508
417	15.1-499.1
418	54-74.01
419	9-6.25
420	18.2-221
421	2.1-20.4, 2.1-574 to 2.1-586R, 9-139 to 9-143R, 20-46R, 20-47R, 22.1-222R, 40.1-28.7R, 51.01-1 to 51.01-46, 63.1-171.1R, 63.1-171.2R, 63.1-171.4R, 63.1-171.6R, 63.1-171.7R
422	15.1-466
423	22.1-29.1
424	46.1-154.3
425	6.1-194.1 to 6.1-194.106, 6.1-195.1 to 6.1-195.76R
426	46.1-328, 46.1-330, 46.1-331, 46.1-335, 46.1-336
427	18.2-308
428	18.2-31
429	64.1-59, 64.1-62.3, 64.1-67R, 64.1-67.1, 64.1-87.1, 64.1-87.2
430	64.1-69.1
431	64.1-58R, 64.1-58.1, 64.1-60
432	64.1-63R, 64.1-63.1
433	8.01-261, 8.01-264, 8.01-506
434	20-147 to 20-154
435	18.2-477.1
436	18.2-465.1
437	46.1-181.4:1, 46.1-254.3
438	63.1-54.1, 63.1-54.2
439	50-8.1
440	33.1-70.1
441	22.1-309
442	20-107.3
443	44-146.18, 44-146.18:2
444	18.2-51.1
445	65.1-102
446	19.2-368.4, 19.2-368.9 to 19.2-368.11
447	2.1-1.1, 2.1-1.3 to 2.1-1.5, 2.1-51.9, 2.1-51.15, 2.1-51.18, 2.1-51.21, 2.1-51.27, 2.1-64.32, 2.1-114.5:3, 2.1-550, 2.1-559.1, 2.1-705, 3.1-32, 22.1-339, 22.1-340, 44-146.18, 46.1-1, 46.1-22, 63.1-85.1:2
448	2.1-1.6 to 2.1-1.9, 2.1-20.4, 2.1-51.9, 2.1-51.9:1, 2.1-51.15, 2.1-51.18, 2.1-64.36, 2.1-113.1, 2.1-116.11, 2.1-393, 2.1-486, 2.1-488.1, 2.1-550, 2.1-559.4, 2.1-700, 2.1-703, 3.1-22.4, 3.1-194.1,

Acts 1985 Chapter	Code 1950 Section
	3.1-249.13, 3.1-276, 3.1-287, 3.1-290, 3.1-308, 3.1-309, 3.1-319, 3.1-320, 3.1-618, 3.1-631, 3.1-634, 3.1-647, 3.1-648, 3.1-678, 3.1-684.13, 3.1-684.32, 3.1-763.6, 3.1-763.7, 3.1-796.013, 3.1-796.11:2, 3.1-796.13, 3.1-796.15, 3.1-1043, 4-2, 4-3, 4-6.1, 5.1-2.1, 9-16, 9-84.5, 9-95.1, 9-116, 9-138.1, 9-149, 9-152.1, 9-153.1, 9-156, 9-157, 10-17.10, 10-17.20, 10-21.3:4, 10-90.32, 10-135, 10-173.2 to 10-173.4, 10-173.6, 10-173.7, 10-186.3, 10-186.4, 10-217, 10-218, 10-256, 15.1-173, 21-3, 21-6, 22.1-299.1, 22.1-339, 22.1-341, 23-9.10 to 23-9.10:2, 23-135.7:7, 23-135.7:13, 23-141.3, 28.1-230, 32.1-79, 32.1-80, 32.1-89, 32.1-114, 32.1-122.1, 32.1-122.2, 32.1-233, 32.1-242, 32.1-328, 33.1-1, 40.1-2, 40.1-22, 42.1-32.7, 42.1-80, 45.1-5, 45.1-270.7, 45.1-295, 51-111.26:2, 51-111.67:17, 54-1, 54-1.18, 54-291.1, 54-295.1, 54-729.30, 54-737, 54-765.2, 54-934.1, 54-950, 54-951, 58.1-3239, 60.1-38, 62.1-153, 63.1-248.16
449	40.1-1, 40.1-40R, 40.1-50R, 40.1-51
450	46.1-321 to 46.1-321.2
451	64.1-123.3
452	46.1-105.13
453	65.1-99, 65.1-100.3
454	11-62.10
455	15.1-466
456	3.1-1057 to 3.1-1064
457	4-2, 4-22.1, 4-25.1
458	24.1-203 to 24.1-225
459	8.01-249
460	58.1-608
461	3.1-22.30 to 3.1-22.37
462	46.1-199, 46.1-225, 46.1-226, 46.1-267
463	58.1-2621, 58.1-2623, 58.1-2625
464	58.1-1803
465	58.1-322, 58.1-322.1, 58.1-402
466	58.1-332
468	58.1-608
469	58.1-608
470	58.1-2800R, 58.1-2801 to 58.1-2805, 58.1-2808, 58.1-2809, 58.1-2812R
471	58.1-608
472	58.1-608
473	58.1-602, 58.1-608
474	58.1-1712
477	58.1-608
478	15.1-945.2:1, 15.1-945.3, 15.1-945.7, 15.1-945.8, 15.1-977.20, 15.1-977.25, 15.1-1034, 15.1-1041, 15.1-1047.1, 15.1-1055, 15.1-1167.1, 58.1-3237
479	23-38.30 to 23-38.32, 23-38.33:1, 23-38.36:1, 23-38.38, 23-38.43
480	2.1-606
481	46.1-206, 46.1-209.1, 46.1-210
482	22.1-258
483	8.01-217
484	16.1-279
485	29-144.5:1
486	55-318, 55-321
487	22.1-296.1
488	16.1-260, 20-60.1 to 20-60.5, 20-61.2, 20-79.1, 20-88.26:1, 20-88.29:1, 53.1-60, 63.1-250 to 63.1-251, 63.1-252R, 63.1-252.1, 63.1-253R, 63.1-256 to 63.1-258, 63.1-264, 63.1-267.1, 63.1-268R, 63.1-271, 63.1-275.1R, 63.1-276, 63.1-277, 63.1-279R, 63.1-285, 63.1-287, 63.1-289.1
489	14.1-118.1, 17-59.2, 17-59.3
490	51-111.24:2, 51-111.27
491	22.1-208.1
492	8.01-264
493	22.1-32
495	58.1-3606, 58.1-3607
496	45.1-33.5:1 to 45.1-33.5:4
497	9-116, 9-116.1, 9-117R, 9-117.1, 9-117.2, 9-118R
498	59.1-21.11
499	8.01-424
500	45.1-89
501	10-173.9
502	2.1-20.1:1, 2.1-342, 9-254
505	2.1-51.21, 3.1-32 to 3.1-39R, 23-155.01 to 23-155.04
506	18.2-391
507	19.2-81
508	18.2-55
509	6.1-392
510	19.2-398
511	46.1-212.1
513	32.1-102.1
514	8.01-195.7
515	2.1-114.5:1, 15.1-7.1, 15.1-7.2
516	60.1-47
517	55-361R, 55-361.1 to 55-363, 55-365R, 55-365.1, 55-367 to 55-371, 55-373 to 55-376, 55-377R, 55-378R, 55-379, 55-380, 55-382, 55-386 to 55-390, 55-391R, 55-391.1, 55-392R, 55-392.1, 55-393R, 55-393.1, 55-394R, 55-394.1, 55-395R, 55-396, 55-399.1, 55-400
518	63.1-172
519	32.1-325
520	23-9.2:3, 23-38.12
521	34-17
522	12.1-20, 12.1-43, 13.1-1 to 13.1-300R, 13.1-601 to 13.1-998, 56-249.7
523	2.1-608
524	8.01-511
525	19.2-163
526	18.2-48.1
527	2.1-339.4 to 2.1-339.8
528	12.1-19, 13.1-82, 13.1-91, 13.1-117,

Acts 1985 Chapter	Code 1950 Section
	13.1-254, 13.1-279, 58.1-2021, 58.1-2806, 58.1-2810
529	8.01-460
530	24.1-49
531	58.1-3703
532	32.1-325
534	2.1-526.13 to 2.1-526.15, 2.1-526.17
535	32.1-325
536	4-118.6
537	54-1.2:3
538	19.2-265.4
539	58.1-3713, n.
540	16.1-246
541	62.1-13.5
542	4-118.21 to 4-118.41
543	58.1-3912
544	6.1-5, 6.1-382, 6.1-383.1, 6.1-392, 6.1-398 to 6.1-407
545	9-154, 38.1-44.1, 58.1-2508
546	28.1-49.1
547	46.1-105.14
548	20-99.1
549	4-118.4, 4-118.6:1 to 4-118.11, 4-118.14, 4-118.17R, 4-118.20:1
550	58.1-3284.1
551	4-98.12
552	6.1-208.6
553	15.1-491.7
554	38.1-955 to 38.1-971
555	18.2-477 to 18.2-479, 53.1-151, 53.1-203
556	58.1-3819
557	58.1-2652, 58.1-2658.1
558	15.1-28.02, 15.1-28.03
559	4-37, 4-62, 4-112, 4-112.1, 46.1-384.1
560	58.1-334, 58.1-432
561	46.1-279.01
562	33.1-75.3
563	60.1-52
564	32.1-325
565	2.1-605, 2.1-610, 11-74
566	59.1-274.1
567	55-248.9:1
568	63.1-238.3
569	18.2-248, 18.2-249
570	19.2-271.3
571	2.1-129, 9-86
572	23-7.4

Acts 1985 Chapter	Code 1950 Section
573	44-75
574	33.1-75.1
575	14.1-140.1
576	13.1-543
577	14.1-73.1:2
579	8.01-27.2
580	8.01-66.9
581	15.1-730.1
583	63.1-204.1
584	16.1-251, 16.1-252, 16.1-283
585	59.1-296 to 59.1-296.3, 59.1-306, 59.1-308, 59.1-308.1
586	15.1-836.1:1, 24.1-165.1
588	38.1-867, 38.1-876, 38.1-887
589	62.1-13.22
592	64.1-64R, 64.1-64.1, 64.1-65R, 64.1-65.1
593	22.1-4, 22.1-289
594	33.1-124
595	16.1-253
596	2.1-114.5:1, 2.1-116
597	18.2-268
599	63.1-92
600	46.1-341, 46.1-341.1
601	45.1-311
602	9-6.14:4, 9-6.14:4.1, 9-6.14:6R, 9-6.14:7.1, 9-6.14:8, 9-6.14:9.4, 9-6.14:10R, 9-6.14:20R, 9-6.14:22, 9-6.16
604	6.1-381, 6.1-383.1
605	54-305
606	38.1-818.2
607	12.1-19, 50-44R, 50-45R, 50-45.1R, 50-45.2R, 50-46 to 50-67R, 50-68R, 50-69 to 50-73R, 50-73.1 to 50-73.77
609	18.2-267, 18.2-268
612	45.1-88.1
613	32.1-177, 32.1-185.1
614	58.1-3650.116, n., 58.1-3650.183 to 58.1-3650.219, n.
615	28.1-49.1
616	38.1-327.15 to 38.1-327.17, 38.1-327.18R, 38.1-327.21, 38.1-327.22, 38.1-327.23R, 38.1-327.24, 38.1-327.25, 38.1-327.26R, 38.1-327.27R, 38.1-327.30, 38.1-327.31, 38.1-327.32R, 38.1-327.33, 38.1-327.34, 38.1-327.36, 38.1-327.39, 38.1-327.41R, 38.1-327.44 to 38.1-327.44:3
617	19.2-303.2
618	2.1-342

ACTS 1986

Acts 1986 Chapter	Code 1950 Section
1	13.1-752, n., 13.1-768, n., 13.1-914, n., 13.1-930, n., 58.1-2804, 58.1-2805, n., 58.1-2808 to 58.1-2811R
3	24.1-12.3
4	38.1-1, n.
5	55-248.11
6	36-55.30
7	9-97
8	46.1-104
9	62.1-115.1, 62.1-115.2, 62.1-115.5, 62.1-115.6, 62.1-115.8
10	46.1-555.9
11	56-245.3
12	33.1-163
13	54-367.11:1
14	46.1-164
15	12.1-17, 56-304.14R
16	46.1-485 to 46.1-486.1, 46.1-490
19	18.2-422
21	17-79.3
22	58.1-602
23	15.1-117
24	44-146.21
25	16.1-122
26	16.1-258
27	16.1-119
29	55-248.21:1
30	3.1-18.2
31	57-49
32	36-103
33	42.1-73.1
35	58.1-3110
36	8.01-375
37	36-70, 36-71R, 36-71.1 to 36-85.1, 36-85.2 to 36-85.15, 36-114
38	58.1-3812, 58.1-3814
39	58.1-1812
40	46.1-178.2
41	15.1-364
42	54-260.71:1
43	54-260.70, 54-260.72
44	58.1-3650.220, n.
45	16.1-114.1, 16.1-115R
46	8.01-418
51	58.1-3516
52	15.1-133
53	26-59
54	15.1-466

Acts 1986 Chapter	Code 1950 Section
55	57-39.1
57	18.2-308
58	58.1-3713
59	16.1-241
60	2.1-1.6, 2.1-20.4, 2.1-51.18, 9-153.1, 9-155, 27-34.2, 27-34.2:1, 27-72, 38.2-401
61	54-824.2, 54-824.3, 54-824.9:1
62	2.1-384
63	57-20
64	54-924, 54-928, 54-929, 54-930R, 54-932, 54-934.1R
67	46.1-291.01
69	46.1-125
70	4-98.2, 4-98.12
71	15.1-37.5
72	46.1-1, 46.1-328, 46.1-328.1, 46.1-330.1, 46.1-335
73	51-151
74	13.1-646
75	16.1-69.6:1
76	38.2-4300
77	23-38.70
78	17-119.1:2
80	63.1-195, 63.1-205.1
81	54-524.65
82	2.1-526.8:1
85	23-7.2
86	54-281.2, 54-317
87	54-278.1R
88	63.1-204
89	8.01-676:1
90	15.1-257
91	54-260.74
92	37.1-197
93	63.1-112, 63.1-124
94	4-31
95	16.1-259
96	15.1-377, 15.1-377.1
97	15.1-499.1
98	15.1-514.2
99	54-948R
100	54-929
101	4-37
102	4-118.23
103	4-79
104	37.1-185
106	15.1-29.13
107	58.1-608
108	29-213.87
109	64.1-157
110	32.1-292
111	14.1-47.2
112	51.01-11
113	4-78, 4-112.3
115	46.1-357.3
116	32.1-292
117	25-46.3:1, 25-232R, 25-232.01
118	57-39.2, n., 57-39.3, n.
120	10-145.11
122	6.1-194.85
123	46.1-65
124	46.1-267
125	62.1-170
126	46.1-547
127	46.1-267
128	9-170
129	60.2-623.1
130	4-22.1
131	4-15.01
132	8.01-457
133	36-98.1
134	37.1-67.4
135	32.1-127
136	32.1-69.1
137	2.1-326.2:1
138	7.1-40.2
139	15.1-137.3
141	55-184.2
142	2.1-113.1, 2.1-113.3
143	16.1-296
144	46.1-104.1, 46.1-254.2
145	62.1-193
146	6.1-218
147	6.1-212.1
149	11-35
150	63.1-135
151	63.1-138, 63.1-139
152	10-218, 10-220
153	28.1-46.4
154	37.1-96
155	1-13.4R, 1-13.23:1, 1-13.30, 1-13.34
156	30-19.6R
157	9-6.14:23
158	46.1-121
159	15.1-510.8
160	16.1-89, 16.1-131
161	46.1-550.10
162	36-55.37:1
163	46.1-547.01
164	15.1-1402, 15.1-1404, 15.1-1405
165	46.1-55
166	1-13.3:1, 17-41
167	17-59
168	28.1-108
169	29-213.57, 29-213.58
170	2.1-328.1, 2.1-328.9
171	28.1-109, 28.1-134
172	32.1-65 to 32.1-67
173	15.1-486.1, n.
174	15.1-29.5
175	59.1-142
176	37.1-198
177	65.1-147
178	54-200.7
179	15.1-687.10
180	2.1-127
182	29-164
183	15.1-14.1
184	28.1-44, 28.1-130, 28.1-133, 28.1-134, 28.1-179
185	54-933
186	46.1-107
187	59.1-296
188	10-45, 10-46.1, 10-46.2, 10-55 to 10-59, 10-61 to 10-65, 10-89, n., 27-54.1, 27-54.4, 27-54.5, 56-427, 56-449
189	9-161
190	4-25.1, 4-26, 4-30, 4-33, 4-98.18, 4-104
191	53.1-108
192	46.1-122
194	32.1-273
195	58.1-3506
196	51-112.1
197	59.1-167.1
198	54-260.74:1
200	3.1-388, 35.1-14.1
201	20-147 to 20-154
202	19.2-37
203	15.1-589.3
205	54-50
206	58.1-3916
207	54-524.31, 54-524.52R
208	15.1-437
209	62.1-115.4
210	59.1-336 to 59.1-341, 59.1-342, n., 59.1-343
211	40.1-51.5, 40.1-51.7, 40.1-51.8
212	11-35
213	63.1-55.4
214	58.1-3213
215	22.1-254.1
216	4-79
217	15.1-23.1
218	34-5
220	46.1-45.2
221	14.1-17.1, n., 14.1-79, n., 14.1-84.1R, 22.1-281, n., 37.1-96, n.,

TABLE OF ACTS CODIFIED SUBSEQUENT TO 1948

Acts 1986 Chapter	Code 1950 Section
	51-111.67:5, n., 63.1-138, 63.1-139, n.
222	45.1-27
225	45.1-5.1
226	46.1-44.1
227	8.01-581.1 to 8.01-581.4:2, 8.01-581.6, 8.01-581.7, 8.01-581.11:1
228	46.1-41, 46.1-326.14, 52-4
229	46.1-267
230	19.2-354
231	13.1-604, 13.1-605, 13.1-804, 13.1-805
232	13.1-630, 13.1-762, 13.1-829, 13.1-924
233	13.1-775
234	13.1-751, 13.1-754, 13.1-913, 13.1-916
235	14.1-79, 14.1-84.4
236	23-9.2:4
237	54-325.7, 54-325.8
238	8.01-66.9
239	1-17.1, 1-17.2
240	15.1-1540
241	24.1-22.1R, 24.1-59
243	58.1-2627
244	2.1-1.7, 2.1-703.1
245	15.1-11.1
246	46.1-138.1
247	42.1-40
248	24.1-33, 24.1-45.2
249	8.01-506.1
251	38.2-3542
252	20-121.02
253	8.01-378
254	28.1-83
255	49-3, 49-4
256	37.1-98
257	6.1-398
258	32.1-307
259	65.1-40.1
260	15.1-50, 22.1-30
263	8.01-320
264	16.1-299
265	38.2-4917
266	40.1-51.9:1, 40.1-51.10, 40.1-51.11:1, 40.1-51.15
267	58.1-353
268	8.01-679.1
269	6.1-60.1
270	2.1-327
271	58.1-3220, 58.1-3221
272	55-79.72
273	2.1-342, 28.1-23.2
274	37.1-234 to 37.1-236
275	8.01-293, 8.01-328.1
276	8.01-453
277	55-106.5
278	8.01-269
279	54-524.111, 54-524.112
280	2.1-179.2
281	16.1-228, 63.1-55, 63.1-55.8, 63.1-56, 63.1-195
282	22.1-92
283	46.1-314.2, 46.1-314.4
284	2.1-700
285	23-38.69:3
286	29-12.1, n.
287	46.1-370.01
288	2.1-526.12 to 2.1-526.17
290	53.1-16
291	2.1-342
292	15.1-262, n.
293	15.1-684.1, 15.1-687.11
294	17-6
295	16.1-256
296	8.01-66
297	9-210, 9-236 to 9-249R, 9-249.1
298	2.1-201R
299	55-142.1
300	63.1-198.1
301	2.1-600
302	30-66, 30-67, 30-70, 30-71, 30-73R
303	54-325.1
304	11-24, 11-25
305	64.1-2
306	23-51, 23-52, n., 23-53, n.
307	54-276.7, 54-311.3
308	16.1-228, 16.1-251 to 16.1-253, 63.1-248.2, 63.1-248.10
309	37.1-98
310	58.1-3650.221 to 58.1-3650.236, n.
311	58.1-608
312	14.1-47.2, 15.1-833, 15.1-925, 15.1-1130.2, 15.1-1135, 15.1-1135.1, 15.1-1138, 15.1-1141.2
315	29-213.74
316	54-826, 54-832, 54-841, 54-847, 54-851, 54-859.16, 54-859.17, 54-859.23
317	8.01-419
318	4-37
319	54-262
320	6.1-81
321	13.1-668, 13.1-851
322	58.1-520, 58.1-521, 58.1-525
323	56-265.13:1 to 56-265.13:7
324	55-79.42, 55-79.61, 55-79.90
325	59.1-344 to 59.1-352
326	8.01-508
327	19.2-80, 19.2-122R, 19.2-234
328	21-89.8
329	15.1-317.1, 15.1-1239.1
330	52-32
331	2.1-20.4, 32.1-163.1, 32.1-164.1:1, 32.1-164.4, 32.1-166.4, 32.1-166.6, 62.1-199
332	11-41
333	15.1-1167.1
334	6.1-71, 6.1-194.58, 6.1-208.4
335	2.1-51.9, 2.1-51.21
336	58.1-608
337	56-531 to 56-534
338	15.1-136.2
339	58.1-2707
340	21-122.1
341	8.01-114, 8.01-115, 8.01-118R, 8.01-119, 8.01-466, 8.01-477.1, 8.01-483, 8.01-487.1, 8.01-533, 8.01-546 to 8.01-546.2, 55-230, 55-232 to 55-232.2
342	29-144.6
343	58.1-3650.237 to 58.1-3650.239, n.
344	28.1-233, 28.1-238
345	54-786.5
346	55-108
347	15.1-1561
348	54-278.3
349	37.1-67.3, 37.1-78.1, 37.1-101
350	58.1-608
351	58.1-3916.1
352	57-2.01
353	58.1-3916
355	15.1-836.1:1
356	2.1-632
357	36-11
358	23-4.3, 23-4.4, 23-9.10:4
359	55-361.1, 55-362, 55-374
360	10-156, 10-158.1 to 10-158.20
361	29-92.4

Acts 1986 Chapter	Code 1950 Section
362	29-213.78 to 29-213.80, 29-213.82 to 29-213.84
363	13.1-301
364	38.2-1814, 38.2-1814.1
365	56-299
366	58.1-3516, n.
367	33.1-210
368	55-425
370	14.1-143.2
372	15.1-136.2
374	4-98.2, 4-98.7, 4-98.11, 4-98.18
375	3.1-73.1 to 3.1-73.4
376	38.2-231
377	54-274
378	65.1-46, 65.1-46.1
379	15.1-175
381	16.1-260, 16.1-279
382	16.1-279
383	2.1-342
384	2.1-20.4, 15.1-945.4
385	10-145.11
387	63.1-225
388	8.01-329
389	8.01-38, 8.01-243
390	3.1-22.8 to 3.1-22.10, 3.1-22.12
391	58.1-608
392	33.1-46.1
393	32.1-325
394	16.1-313, 16.1-322.1, 16.1-322.2, 53.1-95.1
395	65.1-23.1
396	8.01-264
397	20-91
399	64.1-161, 64.1-162, 64.1-164R
400	58.1-2101, 58.1-2112, 58.1-2131 to 58.1-2132.2, 58.1-2143, 58.1-2147, 58.1-2301, n.
401	32.1-164, 32.1-176.1 to 32.1-176.7, 36-97, 62.1-44.85, 62.1-44.92, 62.1-44.97, 62.1-44.100, 62.1-44.101R, 62.1-44.101:1
402	62.1-44.85, 62.1-44.87, 62.1-44.90, 62.1-44.91, 62.1-44.93, 62.1-44.96 to 62.1-44.100, 62.1-44.106, n.
403	8.01-264
404	38.2-4610R, 38.2-4610.1, 38.2-4611R, 38.2-4612R, 38.2-4613
405	16.1-69.6, 17-119.1:1
406	18.2-371.2
407	63.1-323, 63.1-324
408	3.1-452
409	18.2-308.2
411	58.1-608
412	58.1-608
414	18.2-48.1
415	62.1-203, 62.1-206, 62.1-209, 62.1-224 to 62.1-232
416	2.1-1.5, 63.1-326 to 63.1-330
417	46.1-330
418	6.1-330.19:1
419	32.1-64.1, 32.1-64.2
420	56-274
421	20-107.2
422	19.2-368.3, 19.2-368.4
424	59.1-285 to 59.1-293R
425	16.1-267, 19.2-163
427	36-98.3, 36-137, 36-139
428	55-222
429	27-5.1R, 27-94 to 27-101, 36-114, 36-118, 36-119.1
430	63.1-174.1
432	59.1-200
433	53.1-165
434	54-282 to 54-285, 54-290.2, 54-293, 54-295, 54-295.6, 54-311, 54-312, 54-313, 54-316, 54-317.3 to 54-317.5, 54-318.1, 54-318.3, 54-318.4, 54-321, 54-321.2, 54-325, 54-325.1
435	58.1-1720, 58.1-1724
436	51.01-10.1
437	63.1-195
438	15.1-1343, 15.1-1344, 15.1-1348, 15.1-1357
439	54-273
440	32.1-324, 32.1-324.1
441	32.1-325.1
442	15.1-1272, 15.1-1274, 15.1-1275, 15.1-1278, 15.1-1281, 15.1-1286.1
443	58.1-3650.240 to 58.1-3650.244, n.
444	58.1-3650.245, n.
445	18.2-308.1, 18.2-310
446	22.1-32
447	15.1-37.3:7
448	63.1-55.3
449	18.2-249
450	58.1-2626.1
451	18.2-308
452	53.1-83
453	18.2-248
454	8.01-38, 8.01-243
455	32.1-325
456	2.1-20.4
457	19.2-368.5, 19.2-368.7, 19.2-368.11R, 19.2-368.11:1, 19.2-368.17
458	8.01-250.1
460	18.2-51.2
461	20-108.1
462	55-66.3
463	54-524.84:4, 54-524.84:6, 54-524.84:10, 54-524.84:12
464	54-154, 54-156, 54-157, 54-290, 54-367.3 to 54-367.4:1, 54-371, 54-372, 54-375, 54-524.6, 54-524.7, 54-524.13, 54-777, 54-777.1, 54-784, 54-924, 54-928, 54-929, 54-930R, 54-932, 54-933, 54-933.2, 54-934.1R, 54-937, 54-937.1, 54-942, 54-942.1, 54-950.3
465	16.1-296
466	22.1-212.1
467	18.2-248.1
468	15.1-175, 15.1-209
469	2.1-342
470	63.1-229
471	18.2-268
472	19.2-368.17
473	15.1-1374, 15.1-1375
474	51-111.10 to 51-111.10:2, 51-111.15, 51-111.38, 51-111.41:1, 51-111.41:4, 51-111.47:1, 51-111.49, 51-111.53, 51-111.56 to 51-111.58:2,

Acts 1986 Chapter	Code 1950 Section
	51-111.59:1, 51-111.60, 51-111.62R, 51-111.67:3, 51-111.67:4, 51-111.67:10, 51-111.67:13.1, 51-111.68:1, 51-146, 51-150, 51-152, 51-153, 51-155, 51-156, 51-163, 51-167, 51-169, 51-170, 51-172, 51-173, 58.1-322
475	18.2-268
476	63.1-267.1
477	15.1-261.1, 15.1-262
478	37.1-67.1
479	17 119.1:2
480	60.1-1 to 60.1-134R, 60.2-100 to 60.2-635
481	63.1-231
482	63.1-231
483	15.1-475, 15.1-496.2
484	8.9-307, 18.2-115
485	18.2-249
486	22.1-32
487	63.1-55.3
488	2.1-512.1, 62.1-4
489	8.01-512.4
490	46.1-15.2, 46.1-15.3, 46.1-56, 46.1-85, 46.1-89.1, 46.1-520
491	58.1-2625
492	2.1-1.1, 2.1-1.3, 2.1-1.6, 2.1-1.7, 2.1-20.4, 2.1-51.7, 2.1-51.8:1, 2.1-51.8:2, 2.1-51.9, 2.1-51.38 to 2.1-51.40, 2.1-64.33, 2.1-425.2, 9-144R, 9-145R, 10-186.1 to 10-186.21R, 10-263 to 10-304, 10-305 to 10-312, 18.2-278.2 to 18.2-278.7R, 32.1-177 to 32.1-186R, 32.1-238.1 to 32.1-238.5R, 59.1-271
493	60.1-47
495	15.1-776.1R, 15.1-783.1, 15.1-783.2
497	15.1-821
498	10-100, 10-101, 10-103, 10-105, 10-106, 10-108 to 10-110, 10-112.1, 33.1-31, 33.1-32
499	22.1-253.8
500	6.1-2.9:4 6.1-194.2, 6.1-194.12, 6.1-194.23, 6.1-194.41, 6.1-194.91, 6.1-194.98
502	6.1-249, 6.1-252R, 6.1-278, 6.1-308, 6.1-309
503	18.2-370, 18.2-370.1
504	15.1-1399.1 to 15.1-1399.9
505	6.1-39 to 6.1-39.2R, 6.1-39.3, 6.1-39.4
506	8.01-229, 16.1-241, 16.1-309.1, 16.1-331 to 16.1-334
507	2.1-129, 9-86
508	58.1-2625
509	6.1-194.14, 6.1-194.41, 6.1-194.54, 6.1-194.69, 6.1-194.72, 6.1-194.91, 6.1-194.93, 6.1-194.95
510	54-937
511	8.01-581.1
512	55-66.4:2
513	42.1-32.7
514	30-19.1:1
515	58.1-322
516	18.2-61, 18.2-67.1 to 18.2-67.2:1, 19.2-218.1, 19.2-218.2
517	16.1-248.1
518	15.1-285
519	9-168
520	15.1-503.4:1 to 15.1-503.4:9
521	56-265.3
522	58.1-2625
523	8.01-434
524	64.1-87.1
525	55-19.2
526	64.1-16
527	46.1-167.1, 46.1-167.3
528	38.2-4300
529	13.1-842, 13.1-857, 13.1-912, 13.1-929
530	2.1-446, 46.1-198
531	54-25.1
532	13.1-814.1
533	20-107.3
534	8.01-195.2
535	19.2-168, 19.2-168.1, 19.2-169.5, 19.2-175, 19.2-264.3:1
536	2.1-504.4, 23-9.1
537	20-107.3, 20-108
538	14.1-112
539	10-37, 10-44, 10-69, 10-71, 10-74, 10-84, 10-90.4, 10-90.8R
540	13.1-730
541	58.1-3516
542	16.1-250
543	26-59
544	38.2-2204
545	58.1-608, 58.1-1404, 58.1-3840
546	9-6.25:1 to 9-6.25:3
547	2.1-1.6, 2.1-1.7, 2.1-1.9
548	65.1-99.1
549	23-38.30, 23-38.31, 23-38.32:1, 23-38.33:1, 23-38.44:1
550	32.1-325.2, 38.2-3500, 38.2-4214
551	32.1-313 to 32.1-315, 32.1-320, 32.1-321.1 to 32.1-321.4, 63.1-124
552	18.2-271.1
553	33.1-23.04, 46.1-78, 46.1-555.9, 58.1-2101, 58.1-2105, 58.1-2113, 58.1-2116, 58.1-2122, 58.1-2124, 58.1-2127.1 to 58.1-2127.7, 58.1-2146, 58.1-2300 to 58.1-2311R, 58.1-2701, 58.1-2706
554	2.1-526.8
555	22.1-253.1 to 22.1-253.3, 22.1-253.5 to 22.1-253.12
556	15.1-503.4:1 to 15.1-503.4:9
557	55-425
558	2.1-526.8, 24.1-31.1, 24.1-32, 24.1-33.1, 24.1-33.2, 24.1-43, 24.1-45.3, 24.1-46, 24.1-97, 24.1-132, 24.1-206.2R, 24.1-206.3, 24.1-257R, 24.1-257.2, 24.1-260
559	11-35, 11-41
560	2.1-526.12 to 2.1-526.17
561	47.1-4
562	38.1-1 to 38.1-971R, 38.2-100 to 38.2-4916
563	10-270.1, 10-279
564	2.1-1.6, 2.1-1.7, 2.1-20.4, 54 949, 54 950,

Acts 1986 Chapter	Code 1950 Section
	54-950.1, 54-951, 54-952R, 54-953 to 54-955.1, 54-956R, 54-957R, 54-960, 54-960.1
565	2.1-1.5, 2.1-1.6, 2.1-41.2, 42.1-1 to 42.1-3.1, 42.1-4R, 42.1-13, 42.1-79
566	10-266, 10-270
567	2.1-1.1, 2.1-1.3, 2.1-1.6, 2.1-51.9, 3.1-249.13, 10-31.1 to 10-31.7, 10-32, 10-33, 10-34.1 to 10-37, 10-39 to 10-41, 10-45.2 to 10-46.2, 10-50 to 10-52, 10-54 to 10-55, 10-57, 10-57.1, 10-68 to 10-74, 10-83.01, 10-84 to 10-84.2, 10-85 to 10-90R, 10-90.2, 10-90.3, 10-90.7, 10-90.9, 10-90.31, 10-90.32, 10-90.36, 10-90.37, 10-253, 56-426.1, 58.1-1609
568	53.1-120
570	46.1-282.1
571	13.1-758, 13.1-760, 13.1-762, 13.1-766, 13.1-766.1, 13.1-920, 13.1-922, 13.1-924, 13.1-928, 13.1-928.1
572	33.1-23.1
573	15.1-262, 15.1-526.4
574	36-91
575	22.1-253.1 to 22.1-253.3, 22.1-253.5 to 22.1-253.12
576	2.1-548.12, 2.1-548.15
577	59.1-21.2
578	18.2-425.1
579	18.2-268
580	18.2-271.2
581	54-944
583	55-9
584	8.01-195.2 to 8.01-195.8, 15.1-1364, 15.1-1371
585	18.2-374.1
586	55-248.42, 55-248.47, 55-248.50, 55-248.51
587	22.1-79.1
588	46.1-179.02, 46.1-341, 46.1-341.01 to 46.1-341.03, 46.1-341.1R, 46.1-342, 46.1-342.1, 46.1-347, 46.1-416.1
589	46.1-347
590	18.2-271.1
592	2.1-342
593	24.1-40.7 to 24.1-40.11
594	20-60.3, 20-60.5, 20-79.1, 63.1-53, 63.1-250 to 63.1-250.4, 63.1-252.1, 63.1-271, 63.1-287
595	15.1-687.12
596	18.2-374.2
597	23-30.24, 23-30.25, 23-30.27:1 to 23-30.29, 23-30.31
598	38.2-4900, 38.2-4902, 38.2-4904.1, 38.2-4905
599	8.01-411
600	24.1-162.1
601	8.01-249
602	10-304.1
603	2.1-1.5, 2.1-51.21, 9-97, 9-99.2 to 9-99.4
604	8.01-581.19:1
605	58.1-608, 58.1-610, 58.1-3840
606	19.2-310
607	46.1-31, 46.1-34.1, 46.1-414
608	10-136, 10-138, 10-141R, 10-258, 10-261
609	37.1-67.3, 37.1-197.1
610	2.1-429
611	44-93, 44-204
612	38.2-2217.1
613	46.1-1, 46.1-41.2
614	8.01-577, 8.01-578 to 8.01-580R, 8.01-581.01 to 8.01-581.016
615	2.1-703, 3.1-84, 3.1-101, 3.1-126.7, 3.1-126.10, 3.1-186, 3.1-248, 3.1-249.14, 3.1-270, 3.1-712, 3.1-770.3, 3.1-884.30, 3.1-933, 3.1-1052, 4-31, 4-37, 5.1-8, 9-6.14:4.1, 9-6.14:11, 9-6.14:12, 9-6.14:14.1,
	9-6.14:16, 9-6.14:22, 9-192, 10-17.23:1, 10-17.23:2, 10-17.23:3R, 10-90.6, 10-186.18, n., 21-89.10, 27-81, 28.1-29, 28.1-33, 32.1-102.11, 32.1-164.1, 32.1-175, 33.1-358, 33.1-366, 37.1-186, 40.1-51.16, 45.1-179.11, 45.1-196, 45.1-240, 45.1-251, 45.1-254, 45.1-378, 46.1-61, 46.1-367, 46.1-437, 46.1-539, 46.1-540 to 46.1-542R, 54-1.36R, 54-1.37, 54-1.38R, 54-320, 54-524.32, 57-67, 62.1-13.15, 62.1-44.24, 62.1-44.29, 62.1-44.106R, 62.1-115.6, 63.1-180, 63.1-213
616	49-7
618	15.1-708
619	58.1-3650.222, n., 58.1-3650.246, n.
620	15.1-800
621	23-7.5
622	13.1-617, 13.1-619, 13.1-635, 13.1-637, 13.1-764, 13.1-766, 13.1-817, 13.1-819, 13.1-834, 13.1-836, 13.1-926, 13.1-928
623	13.1-647
624	6.1-330.16, 6.1-330.47:1
625	18.2-308
626	15.1-609.1
627	63.1-198.1
628	6.1-194.20
629	19.2-169.6, 19.2-176, 37.1-67.1
630	46.1-516, 46.1-525
631	33.1-163.1
632	18.2-502
633	32.1-162.7 to 32.1-162.14
634	58.1-3919
635	18.2-266, 18.2-269
636	19.2-52, 19.2-56.1
637	10-271
638	6.1-58.2
639	46.1-400, 46.1-401, 46.1-402R, 46.1-403, 46.1-405R, 46.1-407, 46.1-409 to 46.1-411, 46.1-513.1R
640	52-8.4
641	18.2-308,

Acts 1986 Chapter	Code 1950 Section
	18.2-308.2, 18.2-310
643	14.1-79, n., 14.1-84.1, n., 14.1-143.2, n., 19.2-163.2, n., 19.2-326, n., 23-19, n., 28.1-46.4, n., 37.1-89, n., 58.1-600, n.
644	8.01-600

ACTS 1986, SP. SESS.

Acts 1986, Sp. Sess. Chapter	Code 1950 Section
1	20-60.5
2	51-173
3	20-60.5
4	51-173
6	58.1-1724
9	33.1-190
10	58.1-2402
11	46.1-149, 46.1-154, 58.1-2401, 58.1-2402, 58.1-2425
12	58.1-603, 58.1-604, 58.1-614, 58.1-622, 58.1-627, 58.1-628, 58.1-638, 58.1-639
13	2.1-1.1, 9-6.25:2, 33.1-1, 33.1-2, 33.1-12, 33.1-13, 33.1-23.03:1, 33.1-268, 33.1-269, 33.1-270, 33.1-277, 33.1-278, 33.1-279.1, 33.1-285, 33.1-287
14	8.01-653.1
15	33.1-23.03:1, n., 58.1-1724, 58.1-2105, 58.1-2113, 58.1-2116, 58.1-2122, 58.1-2124, 58.1-2146, 58.1-2701, 58.1-2706
16	8.01-653.1

ACTS 1987

Acts 1987 Chapter	Code 1950 Section
1	8.01-121
2	13.1-752, 13.1-768, 13.1-775, 13.1-914, 13.1-930, 13.1-936, 58.1-2804, 58.1-2805
3	60.2-604
4	46.1-181.4:1, 46.1-254.3
5	14.1-114, 16.1-274, 63.1-236.1
6	16.1-283
7	24.1-17
8	15.1-430, 15.1-491, 15.1-495
9	58.1-320 to 58.1-322, 58.1-323, n., 58.1-323.1, 58.1-323.2, 58.1-402, 58.1-478
10	38.2-205.1
11	2.1-234.13
13	51-111.55, 51-111.55:1, 51-111.60:1
14	51-111.55, 51-111.55:1, 51-111.60:1
15	3.1-249.22 to 3.1-249.26
16	16.1-69.6:1
22	14.1-44.4
29	15.1-687.13
30	21-291.2
32	44-40, 44-40.2
33	15.1-131.10
34	56-291.3:7
35	20-97
36	16.1-244
37	43-34
38	20-121
41	20-155
42	20-14.2
43	28.1-104
44	54-276.7, 54-311.3
45	10-181
46	3.1-937
47	32.1-166.1
48	29.1-529
49	51.01-11
50	51.01-21, 51.01-28
52	10-17.114, n.
54	2.1-1.1, 2.1-1.3, 2.1-1.6, 2.1-1.9, 2.1-20.4, 9-6.25:3, 29.1-102, n., 29.1-109, n.
55	9-6.14:5.1
56	1-17.1
57	21-291.1R
59	13.1-692.1, 13.1-700R, 13.1-700.1, 13.1-704, 13.1-870.1, 13.1-879R, 13.1-879.1, 13.1-883
61	15.1-18.3
62	62.1-13.6
63	2.1-373.4
65	22.1-98
66	62.1-193.1 to 62.1-193.3
67	62.1-193.1 to 62.1-193.3
70	8.01-375
71	2.1-343.2
72	2.1-450.1
73	2.1-328.1
74	23-30.36:1
75	15.1-1261
78	15.1-499.1
79	37.1-197
80	15.1-18.3
81	11-47.1
82	15.1-18.3
83	29.1-300.1 to 29.1-300.3
84	28.1-185
86	2.1-548.10, 2.1-548.11
87	16.1-77
88	17-116.01
89	29.1-339.1
90	28.1-165.1
91	11-47.1
92	1-13.3
93	16.1-77
94	29.1-346
95	29.1-101.1, 29.1-110, 29.1-302.1, 29.1-328, 29.1-332
96	19.2-169.6, 37.1-67.1
97	22.1-314
98	16.1-97R, 16.1-97.1
99	15.1-499.1
100	57-35.1
101	29.1-701, 62.1-168, n.
102	36-11
103	2.1-129, n.
104	55-101
105	55-332
106	46.1-212.1
107	4-98.2
108	18.2-308.2
109	23-9.2:3
110	54-129.3
111	55-248.52
112	56-529, n., 56-530, n.
113	60.2-116, 60.2-214, 60.2-219
114	60.2-519.1, 60.2-531, 60.2-532
115	59.1-274
116	8.01-66
117	62.1-199, 62.1-203
118	24.1-168
120	10-264
121	10-266
122	9-48.7R
123	30-34.6
124	30-19.3
125	19.2-276
126	29.1-301
127	28.1-172
128	30-34.4:1

Acts 1987 Chapter	Code 1950 Section
	to 30-34.7
129	24.1-203
130	19.2-389, 63.1-198.1 to 63.1-199
131	19.2-389, 63.1-198.1
132	62.1-44.15:3
133	62.1-199, 62.1-203
134	29.1-100
135	46.1-291.1
136	19.2-206
137	37.1-110
138	2.1-400
139	4-118.11, 4-118.31
140	13.1-858
141	17-222
143	23-95.1
144	9-168
145	56-129.1
146	46.1-105.7
147	46.1-551
148	46.1-550.3:2
149	20-25
150	6.1-217
151	46.1-1, 46.1-45.2
152	46.1-3.2, 46.1-181.5, 46.1-551
153	15.1-1349
154	46.1-357
155	8.01-341.2
156	33.1-72.1
157	32.1-233
158	15.1-1357
159	28.1-165.1
160	16.1-69.56 to 16.1-69.58
161	17-229
162	9-152
163	62.1-44.110 to 62.1-44.112
164	36-55.33:1, 36-55.34:1
165	40.1-6, 40.1-22, 40.1-117
167	36-94
169	15.1-686.2
170	12.1-21
171	20-96
172	6.1-94, 6.1-194.85
173	6.1-363.1
174	38.2-4614
175	19.2-319
176	11-37
177	13.1-860
178	18.2-104
179	2.1-1.7, 2.1-51.23:1R, 9-6.25:1
180	8.4-106
181	13.1-724
182	8.01-506
183	13.1-605, 13.1-616, 13.1-635, 13.1-756, 13.1-805, 13.1-816, 13.1-834, 13.1-918
184	56-141
185	56-128
186	55-9
187	2.1-328.10
188	22.1-128
189	8.01-337
190	20-78.2
191	13.1-722
192	30-5
193	8.01-43, 8.01-44
194	11-45
195	37.1-142
196	6.1-273
197	14.1-183
198	54-524.69
199	54-959.1
200	15.1-335
201	15.1-249.1
202	46.1-3.2
203	16.1-260
204	56-66
205	22.1-81
206	32.1-31
207	33.1-72.1
208	46.1-65
209	37.1-134.2
210	2.1-179
211	2.1-179
212	58.1-3516
213	65.1-4, 65.1-4.4, 65.1-6
214	30-34.10 to 30-34.10:3
215	51-111.28
216	15.1-1032.2
217	42.1-77, 42.1-79.1
218	11-37, 11-41.2, 11-41.2:1
219	2.1-1.7, 2.1-51.15, 9-6.25:1, 9-267 to 9-273
220	21-11.16:1
221	32.1-138 to 32.1-138.2
222	64.1-151.1
223	32.1-163.2
224	32.1-127
225	22.1-274.1
226	54-524.65
231	21-11.16:1
233	58.1-3516
234	10-197 to 10-213.1R, 10-253, 10-277 to 10-277.14
236	55-210.12, 55-210.13
237	56-304 to 56-304.2
238	19.2-356, 19.2-358
239	2.1-610, n.
240	22.1-289.1
241	19.2-294
242	2.1-179
243	46.1-65
244	58.1-3731
245	58.1-3226.1
246	4-118.27, 4-118.30
247	4-118.4, 4-118.7, 4-118.10
248	11-45
249	10-274
250	16.1-282
251	22.1-110
252	4-37, 4-114
253	15.1-730.2
254	36-55.25, 36-55.30, 36-55.33:2
255	8.01-38.1
256	8.01-341, 8.01-341.1
257	13.1-692.1, 13.1-700R, 13.1-700.1, 13.1-704, 13.1-870.1, 13.1-879R, 13.1-879.1, 13.1-883
258	3.1-249.9, 10-273
259	8.01-271.1
260	8.01-225
261	15.1-7.01
262	58.1-3650.247, n., 58.1-3650.248, n.
263	58.1-3650.249, n.
264	58.1-3650.250, n.
265	54-60
266	58.1-3650.251, n.
267	58.1-3650.252 to 58.1-3650.256, n.
268	58.1-3650.257 to 58.1-3650.259, n.
269	58.1-3650.260, n.
270	58.1-3650.261, n.
271	58.1-3650.262, n.
272	58.1-3650.263, n.
273	58.1-3650.264, n.
274	58.1-3650.265, n.
275	58.1-3650.266, n.
276	6.1-194.58
277	18.2-67.10
278	58.1-3650.267, n.
279	58.1-3650.268, n.
280	58.1-3650.269, n.
281	58.1-3650.270, n.
282	56-210, 56-217
283	6.1-371 to 6.1-373, 6.1-379, 6.1-380R

Acts 1987 Chapter	Code 1950 Section
284	58.1-3650.271, n., 58.1-3650.272, n.
285	18.2-308.4, n.
286	58.1-3650.273, n.
287	58.1-3650.274, n.
288	64.1-123.3
289	6.1-194.41
290	15.1-7.01
291	3.1-249.9, 10-273
292	2.1-27.4
293	58.1-3650.275, n.
294	8.01-229, 8.01-243, 8.01-243.1
295	56-531
296	6.1-125.3
297	6.1-60.1
298	46.1-291
299	56-303.1
300	58.1-3650.276, n.
301	58.1-3650.277, n.
302	58.1-3650.278, n.
303	58.1-3650.252, n.
304	58.1-3650.279, n.
305	50-73.61
306	15.1-1399.1 to 15.1-1399.9R, 15.1-1399.10 to 15.1-1399.17, 36-55.53 to 36-55.62R
307	15.1-1263
308	65.1-4.1
309	58.1-3650.280, n.
310	58.1-3650.281, n., 58.1-3650.282, n.
311	30-19.9
312	15.1-456
313	55-248.14
314	58.1-3650.283 to 58.1-3650.285, n.
315	46.1-291
316	58.1-3650.286, n.
318	58.1-3274
319	29.1-530.1
320	58.1-2623, 58.1-2625, n., 58.1-2626, 58.1-2643, n.
321	46.1-343
322	3.1-418.1
323	2.1-114.5:1
324	62.1-203, 62.1-233 to 62.1-241
325	38.2-613, 46.1-550.12
326	2.1-121
327	15.1-29.5
328	22.1-315
329	23-14, 23-35.1, 23-35.2
330	19.2-165.1
331	60.2-600, 65.1-82
332	46.1-551
334	46.1-387.9:3
335	6.1-194.71
337	56-218, 56-265.4:2
338	30-19.04
339	54-58
340	11-9.4
341	24.1-239
342	46.1-45.2
343	65.1-108
344	46.1-172.03
346	46.1-223
347	46.1-267
348	22.1-32
349	24.1-129, 24.1-130
350	24.1-12.3
351	6.1-62
352	6.1-32.6, 6.1-32.9, 6.1-39.3, 6.1-41.1
353	38.2-208
354	22.1-154
355	46.1-138.1
356	18.2-391
357	19.2-254
358	18.2-200.1, 54-113
359	22.1-296.1
360	55-218.1
361	55-248.13
362	58.1-3274
363	36-55.26
364	58.1-2623, 58.1-2625, n., 58.1-2626, 58.1-2643, n.
365	4-25
366	23-7.5
367	53.1-83
368	15.1-1377
369	2.1-429.4
370	46.1-267
371	22.1-207.1
372	46.1-341, 46.1-341.02, 46.1-341.03, 46.1-342, 46.1-342.1, 46.1-343.1
373	58.1-908
374	22.1-260
375	9-6.14:4.1, 32.1-81
376	58.1-2628
377	58.1-3110
378	8.01-606
379	54-179R, 54-313 to 54-315R, 54-385R
380	55-66.7
381	46.1-268
382	8.01-225
383	15.1-1364
384	15.1-379
385	56-76
386	46.1-535
387	55-248.21, 55-248.31
388	46.1-45.2
389	15.1-29.14
390	19.2-120
391	46.1-291.01
392	51-111.10, 51-111.10:01
393	46.1-254.2
394	46.1-387.6
395	55-79.79
398	32.1-325
399	15.1-15, 15.1-29.2
400	32.1-175.1
401	2.1-342
402	15.1-171.1, 22.1-79
403	32.1-71.1 to 32.1-71.4
404	15.1-481
405	32.1-264
406	46.1-343
407	54-880
408	2.1-1.1, 2.1-1.3, 2.1-1.6, 2.1-1.7, 2.1-1.9, 2.1-20.4, 9-6.25:1 to 9-6.25:3
409	46.1-387.9:2, 46.1-421
410	6.1-274
411	32.1-242
412	55-79.94
413	2.1-1.1, 2.1-1.3, 2.1-1.6, 9-6.25:2, 23-38.2, 29.1-313, 37.1-1, 37.1-1.1R, 37.1-1.2, 37.1-96, 46.1-427, 46.1-429
414	22.1-209.2
415	37.1-67.2
416	37.1-67.2
417	38.2-1330
418	27-72
419	15.1-735, 15.1-736.1, 15.1-763, 15.1-766
420	46.1-343
421	15.1-159.2, 15.1-159.5, 15.1-159.7
422	15.1-28.01
423	6.1-43, 6.1-44
424	20-109.1
425	13.1-545.1
426	22.1-343
427	32.1-77
428	55-248.4, 55-248.16
429	38.2-2201,

Acts 1987 Chapter	Code 1950 Section
	38.2-2202
430	22.1-29.1
431	13.1-760, 13.1-769.1, 13.1-922, 13.1-931.1, 38.2-1040
432	15.1-13, 15.1-1557, 15.1-1558
433	36-47
434	13.1-525.1, 13.1-561.1, 58.1-2804, 59.1-80.1, 59.1-95.1
435	15.1-7.3
436	62.1-13.16:1
437	2.1-1.8, 2.1-116.15 to 2.1-116.17
438	18.2-340.9
439	19.2-169.5, 19.2-264.3:1
440	33.1-75.1
441	15.1-1348
442	8.01-226
443	63.1-248.6
446	32.1-325
447	54-524.84:14
448	18.2-67, 18.2-67.01
449	8.01-329, 14.1-103
450	8.01-329
451	36-55.41, 36-55.51:1
452	45.1-287, 45.1-288, 45.1-293, 45.1-295 to 45.1-297, 45.1-299 to 45.1-302, 45.1-311, 45.1-313, 45.1-314, 45.1-320 to 45.1-322
453	10-17.114
455	65.1-88
456	11-41, 11-41.1
457	23-38.30, 23-38.33:1, 23-38.62:1, 23-38.66
458	2.1-1.5, 2.1-51.21, 42.1-1, 42.1-2, 42.1-54
459	8.01-329, 14.1-103
460	8.01-676.1
461	2.1-116.4
462	59.1-21.7:1, 59.1-200
463	15.1-23.2, 59.1-200
464	59.1-21.7:1, 59.1-198 to 59.1-201
465	18.2-271.1
466	46.1-105.15
467	46.1-105.16
468	45.1-270.3:1, 45.1-270.4, 45.1-270.5:1, 45.1-270.6
470	45.1-5, 45.1-5.1R
471	1-17.2
472	46.1-105.15
473	55-222, 55-248.9
474	11-37, 11-41.2, 11-41.2:1
475	65.1-88
476	3.1-684.13, 3.1-684.14, 3.1-1043, 3.1-1044
477	24.1-40.8, 24.1-40.9
478	24.1-45.2
479	56-55, 56-65.1
480	32.1-112, 32.1-113, 32.1-114, 32.1-116.1, 32.1-116.2, 32.1-148, 32.1-149, 32.1-153
481	10-145.12, 10-145.13
482	63.1-231
483	15.1-508, 15.1-554
484	58.1-15, 58.1-322, 58.1-323, 58.1-401, 58.1-402, 58.1-490, 58.1-492, 58.1-493, 58.1-936
485	28.1-101.3
486	24.1-90, n.
487	18.2-268
488	3.1-796.66 to 3.1-796.129, 15.1-28.5:1, 19.2-8, 29-1 to 29-248R, 29.1-100 to 29.1-609, 29.1-610, n., 29.1-611 to 29.1-746, 32.1-48.1 to 32.1-48.4, 62.1-5R, 62.1-166 to 62.1-186.24R, 62.1-196R
489	26-2
491	2.1-342
492	44-146.34 to 44-146.40
493	19.2-270.1
494	6.1-61
495	33.1-221.1:1, 56-451.2R
496	15.1-7.3:1, 15.1-506.1R
497	16.1-253, 16.1-253.1, 16.1-279.1
498	55-401
499	62.1-13.22, 62.1-13.28
500	51.01-44, 51.01-45
501	15.1-474.1, 15.1-474.2
502	10-271
503	8.01-413.1
504	64.1-62.1
505	29-32.1, n.
506	2.1-378, 22.1-295.1
507	29.1-301
509	2.1-116.9:1 to 2.1-116.9:5
510	24.1-162.1R, 24.1-202.1 to 24.1-202.10
511	2.1-198
512	38.2-2228.1
513	55-248.45
514	58.1-4000, n.
515	58.1-608
516	58.1-1402
517	2.1-526.18 to 2.1-526.22, 9-6.25:1, 55-297.2R
518	58.1-3650.287, n.
519	60.2-116, 60.2-214, 60.2-219
520	38.2-1030, 38.2-1037, 38.2-1800, 38.2-2701, 38.2-2806, 38.2-3503, 38.2-3523, 38.2-3702, 38.2-3912, 38.2-4307, 38.2-4508, 38.2-4805
521	38.2-1800 to 38.2-1803, 38.2-1805 to 38.2-1812, 38.2-1814 to 38.2-1819, 38.2-1821 to 38.2-1837, 38.2-1839 to 38.2-1845
522	54-273, 54-936
523	33.1-23.3
524	58.1-608
525	58.1-3211, 58.1-3215
526	38.2-2807
527	8.01-226.1
528	36-99.6, 62.1-44.34:8, 62.1-44.34:9
529	38.2-1601, 38.2-1603, 38.2-1606, 38.2-1608 to 38.2-1611, 38.2-1616
530	58.1-4000, n.
531	2.1-116, 18.2-334.3, 58.1-322, 58.1-460, 58.1-4000 to 58.1-4028
532	58.1-608
533	58.1-3617
534	58.1-3215
535	59.1-21.11
536	33.1-23.3
537	58.1-3919.1
538	46.1-309.2
539	60.2-212.1, 60.2-212.2
540	38.2-5000 to 38.2-5021

Acts 1987 Chapter	Code 1950 Section
541	58.1-608
542	2.1-191
543	54-273, 54-936
544	58.1-608
545	33.1-23.3, 33.1-44
546	58.1-3211
547	59.1-307
548	58.1-608
549	38.2-3408, 38.2-4221
550	58.1-3230, 58.1-3233, 58.1-3239, 58.1-3240
551	38.2-3408, 38.2-4221
552	15.1-1507 to 15.1-1513
553	9-29, 9-29.1
554	38.2-2802, 38.2-2804, 38.2-2806, 38.2-2807
555	54-145.3:1 to 54-145.3:8, 54-765.2 to 54-765.9
556	6.1-2, 6.1-2.7, 6.1-4, 6.1-5.1, 6.1-5.3, 6.1-6, 6.1-113, 6.1-194.6
557	38.2-3408, 38.2-4221
558	6.1-2, 38.2-400
559	65.1-102
560	65.1-56
561	57-49, 57-52.1, 57-55.2, 57-57, 57-59, 57-61, 57-61.1
562	54-145.3:5
563	15.1-503.2
564	15.1-7.3, 15.1-116
565	38.2-400, 38.2-1606, 38.2-1611.1, 38.2-1709, 38.2-3812, 38.2-4123, 38.2-4214, 38.2-4216R, 38.2-4216.1, 38.2-4217, 38.2-4222, 38.2-4223, 38.2-4225R, 38.2-4226, 38.2-4517, 38.2-4518, 38.2-4521, 58.1-2501, 58.1-2520
566	4-79
567	8.01-195.4, 8.01-259, 8.01-261, 8.01-621R, 8.01-638R, 54-76, 60.2-625
568	58.1-3503
569	15.1-37.3:8
570	58.1-3916
571	51-111.54
572	58.1-3510
574	28.1-4, 28.1-5
575	51-111.10:1, 51-111.10:3, 51-111.27, 51-111.33, 51-111.41:1
576	6.1-2.10, 6.1-2.13
577	6.1-2.10
578	63.1-196.4
579	54-145.4 to 54-145.10, 54-145.10:1 to 54-145.10:11
580	19.2-266
581	2.1-1.7, 2.1-342, 2.1-714 to 2.1-725, 9-6.25:2
582	58.1-3916
583	11-40
585	38.2-1039.1, 38.2-5100 to 38.2-5115
586	38.2-5200 to 38.2-5208
587	58.1-608
588	6.1-369.1 to 6.1-369.10
589	20-99.1
590	20-99.1
591	58.1-3510
592	18.2-308
593	2.1-27.5
594	8.01-288, 8.01-320, 8.01-327, 8.01-328.1, 20-99, 20-99.1
595	58.1-3916
596	6.1-408 to 6.1-431
597	20-60.3, 20-78.1, 20-107.2
598	16.1-243, 16.1-279
599	58.1-490, 58.1-492
600	23-38.16
601	2.1-178
602	19.2-163.2
603	18.2-134, 18.2-134.1
604	55-49.1, 55-66.5, 64.1-71.1
605	26-12.3
606	56-508.12
607	59.1-207.13
608	16.1-243
609	20-60.5, 63.1-250.1:1
610	54-84 to 54-102R, 54-102.24 to 54-102.35
611	58.1-492
613	2.1-179.2
614	58.1-403
615	58.1-322
616	2.1-234.13
617	58.1-3703
618	58.1-3703
619	51-111.67:15 to 51-111.67:20
620	16.1-243
621	19.2-163.2
622	6.1-330.6 to 6.1-330.46R, 6.1-330.47, n., 6.1-330.47:1R, 6.1-330.48, n., 6.1-330.49 to 6.1-330.90
623	6.1-330.10, n., 6.1-330.54
624	15.1-994.1, 16.1-69.6, 17-119.1:1
625	18.2-119
626	54-969 to 54-977
627	63.1-195
628	58.1-3231, 58.1-3237.1
629	15.1-29.15
630	6.1-330.10, n., 6.1-330.54
631	2.1-608, n.
632	16.1-228, 16.1-241, 16.1-248.1, 16.1-260, 16.1-264, 16.1-266, 16.1-279, 16.1-292, 46.1-357
633	10-61.1
634	6.1-194.107, 6.1-399.1
635	15.1-16.1
636	55-248.13
637	8.01-220.1:1
638	19.2-163
639	6.1-330.19:1, n., 6.1-330.20, n., 6.1-330.63, 6.1-330.78
640	63.1-250.3, 63.1-252.1, 63.1-256, 63.1-267.1, 63.1-268.1
641	33.1-124
642	32.1-325
643	40.1-49.8 to 40.1-49.12
645	8.01-229, 8.01-243, 8.01-243.1
646	15.1-1372.1 to 15.1-1372.16
647	38.2-4021
648	19.2-353.5
649	16.1-279, 20-74, 20-88.28:2, 20-88.30:6, 20-108, 20-112, 63.1-252.1
650	63.1-238.1 to 63.1-238.4
651	15.1-503.4:2.1
652	9-6.14:4.1
653	23-35.1, 23-35.3

Acts 1987 Chapter	Code 1950 Section
654	32.1-126.1, 63.1-198.01
655	38.2-400, 38.2-1606, 38.2-1611.1, 38.2-1709, 38.2-3812, 38.2-4123, 38.2-4214, 38.2-4216R, 38.2-4216.1, 38.2-4217, 38.2-4222, 38.2-4223, 38.2-4225R, 38.2-4226, 38.2-4517, 38.2-4518, 38.2-4521, 58.1-2501, 58.1-2520
656	36-99.7
657	8.9-307
658	20-60.3, 20-60.5, 20-79.1, 20-88.29:1, 63.1-249, 63.1-250.3
659	19.2-265.5
660	54-84 to 54-102R, 54-102.24 to 54-102.35
661	18.2-266, 18.2-268
662	15.1-1372.21 to 15.1-1372.36
663	18.2-271.1
664	8.01-44.2
666	32.1-229 to 32.1-229.2, 32.1-234R
667	16.1-286
668	53.1-151, 53.1-155, 53.1-156, 53.1-159
669	46.1-105.17
670	19.2-138 to 19.2-140R, 19.2-143
672	15.1-791.1 to 15.1-791.15
673	55-66.3
674	8.01-195.4
675	46.1-252.3, n.
676	19.2-299, 19.2-299.1
677	62.1-44.34:5, 62.1-44.34:10 to 62.1-44.34:12
678	13.1-501, 13.1-503, 13.1-504, 13.1-505 to 13.1-506, 13.1-515, 13.1-517, 13.1-518, 13.1-520, 13.1-521, 13.1-522, 38.2-1837 to 38.2-1845
679	8.01-243
680	24.1-12.3
681	63.1-238.1 to 63.1-238.4
682	8.01-271.1
683	6.1-277, 6.1-284R, 6.1-284.1
684	8.01-676.1
685	38.2-2205
686	54-1.18, 54-83.1:8.1, 54-83.1:10, 54-903.1, 54-950, 54-950.2, 54-950.2:1
688	9-202, 23-38.32, 62.1-129
689	18.2-213.1
690	58.1-2804
691	38.2-1306.1
692	63.1-198.1 to 63.1-199
693	63.1-197, 63.1-198.1, 63.1-198.2
694	20-109
695	46.1-339, 46.1-339.01
696	8.01-310, 46.1-35, 46.1-35.1, 46.1-44.2, 46.1-78, 46.1-95, 46.1-105, 46.1-105.2, 46.1-105.3, 46.1-105.4, 46.1-105.6, 46.1-105.10, 46.1-105.11, 46.1-105.13, 46.1-105.14, 46.1-157.2, 46.1-167, 46.1-381, 46.1-397, 46.1-438, 46.1-514.15, 46.1-529, 46.1-550.15, 58.1-2105, 58.1-2116, 58.1-2146, 58.1-2425
697	38.2-231, 38.2-1904, 38.2-1905.1, 38.2-1905.2, 38.2-1906, 38.2-1908 to 38.2-1910, 38.2-1912, 38.2-2003, 38.2-2005, 38.2-2006
698	2.1-1.7, 2.1-51.15, 9-6.25:2, 63.1-196.01, 63.1-196.1, 63.1-202, 63.1-202.1
699	37.1-62.1
700	16.1-253.2
701	27-32.2
702	50-37.1, 50-73.1, 50-73.2, 50-73.4, 50-73.5, 50-73.8, 50-73.11, 50-73.12, 50-73.14R, 50-73.15 to 50-73.21, 50-73.22R, 50-73.22:1 to 50-73.25, 50-73.28, 50-73.33 to 50-73.36, 50-73.38 to 50-73.40, 50-73.43, 50-73.47, 50-73.49 to 50-73.51, 50-73.54, 50-73.63, 50-73.64, 50-73.67, 50-73.77, 50-74, 59.1-69, 59.1-70
703	16.1-69.35
704	18.2-49.1
705	18.2-119
706	20-60.3, 20-60.5, 20-79.1, 20-88.29:1, 63.1-249, 63.1-250.3
707	17-116.05:1, 18.2-308
708	8.01-602
709	8.01-264
710	8.01-675.3, 17-116.05:1, 17-116.07, 19.2-398 to 19.2-409
711	58.1-3713.2
712	54-278.4
713	8.01-581.13, 8.01-581.16, 8.01-581.19, 8.01-581.19:1
714	6.1-330.19:1, n., 6.1-330.20, n., 6.1-330.63, 6.1-330.78
715	58.1-3703
717	15.1-466
718	2.1-360
719	37.1-71
720	18.2-433.1 to 18.2-433.3
721	46.1-343
722	23-9.2:6
723	14.1-84.1, n., 14.1-143.2, n., 28.1-46.4, n.

ACTS 1987, SP. SESS.

Acts 1987, Sp. Sess. Chapter	Code 1950 Section
1	2.1-457, 2.1-599 to 2.1-634R, 2.1-639.1 to 2.1-639.24, 2.1-639.30 to 2.1-639.61, 9-263, 10-17.12, 11-72 to 11-74, 24.1-167, 36-55.28, 45.1-4
2	54-60

ACTS 1988

Acts 1988 Chapter	Code 1950 Section
2	6.1-5.3, 6.1-194.6
3	6.1-194.39
4	6.1-194.69
5	6.1-194.85
6	24.1-227
7	56-420 to 56-425R
8	24.1-228.1
9	54-740
10	2.1-563.23

Acts 1988 Chapter	Code 1950 Section
11	46.1-341
12	54-749
13	59.1-296.1
14	10.1-1451, 52-8.4
15	55-79.58:1, 55-79.84:1, 55-79.88, 55-79.91, 55-79.92, 55-79.93
16	55-79.89
17	16.1-228, n., 16.1-241, n., 16.1-248.1, n., 16.1-260, n., 16.1-264, n., 16.1-266, n., 16.1-279, n., 16.1-292, n., 46.1-357, n.
19	29.1-505, 29.1-530.2, 29.1-548, 29.1-550, 29.1-552
20	10.1-416
21	10.1-413.1
22	16.1-69.6:1
23	2.1-234.13
24	59.1-200, 59.1-207.17 to 59.1-207.27
25	29.1-733.1
26	10.1-1305, 10.1-1307, 10.1-1308
27	28.1-119.1
29	38.2-510
30	44-146.30
31	33.1-75.1
32	38.2-1824, 38.2-1834
33	19.2-243
34	19.2-272
35	17-70
36	1-13.19
37	8.01-2
38	19.2-311
39	2.1-342
40	11-41
41	2.1-373.2
42	9-17, 54-1.18:1, 54-19, 54-83.22, 54-102.26, 54-115, 54-145.12, 54-155, 54-260.65, 54-262, 54-283, 54-295.2, 54-371, 54-398.4:1, 54-524.6, 54-738, 54-777, 54-824.4, 54-937, 54-942, 54-950.4, 54-963
43	33.1-221.1
44	51.01-3
45	5.1-6R, 5.1-9.4R, 5.1-12, 5.1-15, 5.1-18R, 5.1-19R, 5.1-25
46	9-170
47	16.1-275
48	54-729.29, 54-729.33, 54-729.34
49	14.1-112
50	19.2-56
51	55-96
52	14.1-112
53	63.1-222
54	20-16.1
55	36-99.5:1
56	44-146.32
57	2.1-511
58	59.1-325
60	32.1-198, 32.1-199R, 32.1-200
61	63.1-177, 63.1-210
62	55-248.31
63	4-98.12:2
64	54-189.1
65	27-34.2, 27-34.2:1
66	54-154, 54-950.3
67	2.1-1.7, 2.1-51.18, 2.1-51.40, 9-6.25:2, 9-274 to 9-280
68	55-248.7, 55-248.35
69	15.1-1372.7, 15.1-1372.7:1
70	5.1-46, 5.1-48R
71	17-116.02, 17-116.05:2
72	31-29
73	59.1-353 to 59.1-363
74	46.1-7
75	28.1-174
76	46.1-45
77	46.1-279.01
78	46.1-427
79	33.1-345, 46.1-229.4
80	33.1-90
81	46.1-326.2
82	46.1-343
84	33.1-75.1
85	32.1-135.1
87	22.1-212.2
88	22.1-146, 22.1-147
89	54-305
90	23-38.56
91	23-38.30, 23-38.33:1
92	63.1-85.5
93	63.1-85.4
94	23-38.70, 23-38.71
95	22.1-67
96	22.1-218
97	32.1-65, 32.1-66, 32.1-67, 32.1-67.1
98	37.1-67.1
99	32.1-325
100	55-142R, 55-142.01
101	22.1-101R, 22.1-101.1, 22.1-215
102	15.1-609
103	22.1-274.1
104	6.1-330.66:1
105	22.1-205, 46.1-368
106	19.2-353.5
107	46.1-1, 46.1-354.1, 46.1-370.2
109	15.1-37.3:3
110	3.1-395
112	22.1-98
113	55-142.1, 55-142.2, 55-142.3, 55-142.4, 55-142.7
114	22.1-79.1, n.
115	6.1-393
116	17-79.3
117	10.1-1400, 10.1-1402
118	2.1-329
119	53.1-120
120	43-32
121	55-66.7
122	2.1-128
124	23-7.4
125	63.1-68
126	63.1-142, 63.1-166
127	37.1-239R, 37.1-240R, 37.1-241R
128	63.1-133.8, 63.1-133.24
129	63.1-174.01, 63.1-196.5
130	32.1-36, 32.1-38
131	60.2-602
132	54-305, 54-306.3
133	9-155
139	9-173
140	2.1-440, 2.1-447, 2.1-451
145	6.1-330.77
147	6.1-269.1
148	15.1-514.2

Acts 1988 Chapter	Code 1950 Section
149	61.1-7 to 61.1-21R
150	8.3-106
151	2.1-342, 63.1-177, 63.1-209
152	6.1-200.3
153	38.2-4809, 38.2-4812
154	63.1-238.6 to 63.1-238.11
155	6.1-2.9
156	4-98.12
158	29.1-510, 29.1-533
159	8.01-47
160	45.1-288, 45.1-311.1
161	29.1-328
162	29.1-519
163	22.1-260
164	38.2-5019
165	16.1-253.1
167	62.1-44.3, 62.1-44.15, 62.1-44.23, 62.1-44.31
169	15.1-1260
170	6.1-63
171	6.1-73.1R
172	30-56
173	2.1-51.18, 2.1-51.40
174	2.1-548.10
175	29.1-521
176	29.1-738
177	1-15
178	38.2-1700
179	29.1-300.1
180	29.1-301
181	29.1-302.1
182	3.1-22.8, 3.1-22.10, 3.1-22.11
183	36-99.5
184	55-248.5, 55-248.21:1
185	38.2-4201, 38.2-4208, 38.2-4216.1, 38.2-4222
186	6.1-303
187	38.2-1814.1
188	38.2-2228.1
189	38.2-231, 38.2-2003
190	15.1-159.5
191	29.1-509
192	24.1-199
193	13.1-639
194	13.1-604.1, 13.1-712R
195	36-139.1
196	10.1-1135, 62.1-194.2

Acts 1988 Chapter	Code 1950 Section
197	8.01-675.4
198	63.1-195, n.
199	27-34.3, 27-61, 27-63R, 27-64R, 27-70.1R, 27-72R, 27-73.1R, 27-78.1, 27-79R, 27-80 to 27-84R, 27-97, 36-119.1, 63.1-178
200	58.1-802
201	54-126
203	32.1-164, 32.1-176.4
205	32.1-331
207	54-175.3
208	2.1-114.5
210	15.1-225
211	15.1-1374, 15.1-1375
212	37.1-205.1
213	14.1-47.2
214	30-28.18
215	32.1-325
216	22.1-271.2
217	36-19, 36-47
218	36-55.26
219	63.1-193
220	16.1-250, 16.1-277.1
221	63.1-236
222	51-111.53, 51-150, 51-167
223	51-111.7
224	51-111.55:1
225	37.1-67.3
226	36-55.28
227	43-34
228	18.2-371.1
229	38.2-1801
230	18.2-340.2, 18.2-340.3, 18.2-340.6, 18.2-340.7
231	56-245.3
232	23-38.45 to 23-38.50
233	56-265.3
234	22.1-17
235	56-282.1
236	59.1-270 to 59.1-277, 59.1-279 to 59.1-284
237	18.2-308.2
238	9-77.4
240	54-824.9:2
241	59.1-204.1
242	22.1-312
243	54-368
244	15.1-1372.26, 15.1-1372.35
246	23-9.2:3.1
247	23-38.72,

Acts 1988 Chapter	Code 1950 Section
	23-38.73
248	58.1-490
249	58.1-392, 58.1-393R, 58.1-394
250	29.1-303, 29.1-303.1, 29.1-303.2, 29.1-304, 29.1-305, 29.1-306, 29.1-309, 29.1-310, 29.1-311, 29.1-318, 29.1-343, 29.1-402, 29.1-409, 29.1-415, 29.1-416, 29.1-417
251	54-524.26
252	32.1-125.2
253	58.1-3661
254	2.1-373.4
255	49-1, 49-3
256	15.1-437
257	30-19.04
258	2.1-179
259	22.1-175
260	2.1-180
261	4-44, 4-65, 4-66, 4-99, 4-127 to 4-145, 4-144, n., 58.1-700 to 58.1-718R
262	58.1-2120.1, 58.1-2145
263	15.1-1416
264	15.1-28.01
265	29.1-742
266	54-524.57, 54-524.58, 54-955
267	2.1-20.3, n., 28.1-23
268	15.1-446.1
270	15.1-1032.2
271	54-25.1
272	58.1-2111
273	1-17.2, 2.1-20.01:2
274	15.1-173
275	6.1-211
276	58.1-2712
277	58.1-3226.1
278	58.1-3013
279	15.1-466
280	58.1-3282
281	11-24.1
282	58.1-3984
283	54-524.84:6, 54-524.84:8, 54-524.84:10
284	15.1-270
285	37.1-195
286	11-41.2:1
287	32.1-273
289	40.1-51.8, 40.1-51.10, 40.1-51.15, 40.1-51.16

Acts 1988 Chapter	Code 1950 Section
290	2.1-114.5:1, 2.1-114.5:2, 15.1-7.1, 15.1-7.2
291	24.1-143.1
292	58.1-1712
293	46.1-2
294	54-37.1
295	45.1-253, 45.1-362 to 45.1-380R
296	6.1-58.1, 6.1-59, 6.1-59.1
297	6.1-237
298	38.2-1046, 38.2-1047, 38.2-1048
299	10.1-416
300	10.1-413.1
301	45.1-88.1
302	38.2-1833
303	6.1-2, 6.1-415, 6.1-416, 6.1-416.1, 6.1-420
305	24.1-49
306	58.1-3965
307	46.1-192.1
308	28.1-101.4
309	6.1-200.2
310	10.1-812
311	6.1-2.9:5
312	55-170.1
313	28.1-87, 28.1-92, 28.1-93, 28.1-95
314	58.1-1404
315	28.1-173.1:1
317	7.1-40.3
318	24.1-143.1
319	22.1-303.1
321	8.01-379.1
322	57-48, 57-49, 57-52, 57-54, 57-55.1, 57-57, 57-61, 57-61.1
323	46.1-384
324	8.01-673
325	32.1-127, 32.1-127.1
326	46.1-309.2
327	18.2-308.2:1
328	62.1-44.15
329	30-34.2:1
330	38.2-513
331	58.1-531, 58.1-531.1
332	10.1-1410.1
333	38.2-300, 38.2-305
334	58.1-3213
335	38.2-1836, 38.2-1845
336	38.2-401

Acts 1988 Chapter	Code 1950 Section
337	16.1-113
338	13.1-504.2
339	46.1-267
340	27-95, 27-96, 27-97, 27-97.1, 40.1-23 to 40.1-25.1R
341	38.2-2804, 38.2-2806, 38.2-2807
342	55-19.3
343	11-9.2
344	46.1-309.2
345	64.1-57.1
346	64.1-67.2
347	26-40.2
348	6.1-18
349	59.1-207.28 to 59.1-207.33
350	8.01-353
351	46.1-267
352	44-75R, 44-75.1, 44-75.2, 44-78R, 44-78.1, 44-79R, 44-83
353	19.2-81
354	2.1-1.6, 2.1-20.4, 9-6.25:2, 54-1.18
355	18.2-248
356	15.1-29.16
358	18.2-108.1
359	18.2-308, 18.2-310, 18.2-311
360	65.1-4, 65.1-4.1
361	2.1-33
362	20-121.02
363	46.1-41, 46.1-79, 46.1-87, 46.1-88, 46.1-89, 46.1-90
364	9-6.14:4.1, 9-6.14:22, 9-6.14:23, 28.1-24, 36-55.30:3
365	65.1-104.2
366	19.2-270
367	36-11.1:1
368	6.1-125.3
369	15.1-1372.7, 15.1-1372.7:1
370	64.1-130
371	53.1-203
372	58.1-2402, 58.1-2403
373	15.1-11.5, 15.1-282
374	59.1-279
375	29.1-356
376	16.1-294
377	55-172, 55-175, 55-186,

Acts 1988 Chapter	Code 1950 Section
	55-200
378	55-210.2, 55-210.12, 55-210.13, 55-210.14R, 55-210.24:1, 55-210.24:2, 55-210.26:1, 55-210.27:1
379	58.1-604.1 to 58.1-604.3
381	58.1-2706
382	8.01-677.1
383	15.1-791, n.
384	29.1-300.1
385	29.1-356
388	55-142.1 to 55-142.4, 55-142.7
389	15.1-8.1
390	10.1-1500
391	17-116.013
392	15.1-29.15
393	54-145.3:1, 54-145.3:3
394	55-70.1
395	2.1-342
396	15.1-131.8
397	53.1-60, 53.1-131
399	32.1-57
400	54-524.67:4
401	15.1-791.6, 15.1-791.14
402	15.1-18.2
403	18.2-87
404	20-91, 20-121
405	13.1-605, 13.1-609, 13.1-615, 13.1-615.1, 13.1-616, 13.1-635, 13.1-752, 13.1-754, 13.1-756R, 13.1-768, 13.1-769.1, 13.1-775.1, 13.1-775.2, 13.1-805, 13.1-809, 13.1-815, 13.1-815.1, 13.1-816, 13.1-834, 13.1-914, 13.1-916, 13.1-918R, 13.1-930, 13.1-931.1, 13.1-936.1, 13.1-936.2, 58.1-2801 to 58.1-2807R, 58.1-2813R
406	19.2-368.4
407	63.1-248.6:1
408	15.1-486.1, n.
409	8.01-424
410	36-85.11
411	2.1-342
412	55-428
413	46.1-413.1
414	18.2-189
415	18.2-465.1
416	36-19
417	63.1-238.3

Acts 1988 Chapter	Code 1950 Section
418	32.1-127, 32.1-127.1
419	58.1-3730.1
420	8.01-438, 8.01-449, 8.01-453, 8.01-454, 8.01-484
421	58.1-812, 58.1-3801, 58.1-3803
422	58.1-3237
424	2.1-1.7, 2.1-20.4, 2.1-51.27, 2.1-563.28 to 2.1-563.35, 9-6.14:4.1, 9-6.25:2
425	54-42.01
426	8.01-397
427	46.1-34.1
428	18.2-248.5
429	58.1-811
430	58.1-3001, 58.1-3005
431	32.1-262, 63.1-230
432	15.1-7.3:1
433	8.01-27.2
434	10.1-1310.1, 10.1-1407.1, 62.1-44.15:4
435	2.1-121
436	15.1-458, 15.1-460, 15.1-462
437	18.2-67.2
438	15.1-447
439	15.1-489
440	56-265.1
441	32.1-176.5
442	13.1-646, 13.1-725, 13.1-725.1, 13.1-726, 13.1-726.1, 13.1-727, 13.1-727.1, 13.1-728R, 13.1-730
443	19.2-143
444	58.1-441
445	54-524.31
446	58.1-3516
447	32.1-70
448	20-97
449	15.1-609
450	29.1-525
451	46.1-65.2
452	46.1-1
453	16.1-293
454	18.2-268
455	19.2-74
456	58.1-3128.1
457	58.1-601
458	32.1-121.1
459	32.1-69.1, 32.1-70
460	18.2-295
461	2.1-328.11
462	58.1-3233

Acts 1988 Chapter	Code 1950 Section
463	58.1-3211
464	6.1-60.1
465	19.2-163
466	58.1-3211
467	40.1-22
468	18.2-268
469	24.1-167, 2.1-639.14:1
470	46.1-167.1, 46.1-167.4
471	46.1-551
472	19.2-163
473	19.2-152.1
474	29.1-300.1, 29.1-530.1
475	19.2-152.1
476	2.1-45
477	3.1-27.3, 3.1-27.6, 3.1-27.35
478	17-116.02
479	17-116.05:2
480	58.1-3703
481	15.1-491
482	19.2-271.2
483	45.1-295
484	15.1-27.1
485	59.1-198, 59.1-203
486	32.1-116.1:1
487	29.1-532
488	29.1-301
489	45.1-255.1R
490	10.1-413.2
491	8.01-581.9
492	8.01-42.1
493	18.2-308.1
494	19.2-187
495	20-85R, 20-86R, 20-87
496	18.2-181.1
497	18.2-128
498	2.1-234.9:1 to 2.1-234.9:7, 9-6.14:4.1
499	58.1-3703
500	55-248.13:1
501	16.1-253.2
502	20-79
503	8.01-268
504	32.1-325
505	8.01-66.2
506	16.1-97.1
507	51-178
508	19.2-346R, 19.2-353.5
509	19.2-345R
510	19.2-48.1
511	19.2-35
512	55-81
513	15.1-499.1
514	58.1-2702

Acts 1988 Chapter	Code 1950 Section
515	32.1-121.1
516	31-26 to 31-36R, 31-37 to 31-59
518	65.1-99
520	46.1-3.02
521	60.2-612
522	38.2-4221
523	38.2-300, 38.2-317
524	19.2-319
525	14.1-181
526	2.1-327, 51-111.24:1
527	16.1-269
528	24.1-43
529	38.2-2403
530	18.2-308.3
531	51-111.58:1, 51-156
532	15.1-686.2, 15.1-686.5 to 15.1-686.7
533	3.1-572 to 3.1-581R
534	59.1-200
535	6.1-194.96, 6.1-194.108
536	2.1-639.2, 6.1-194.2, 13.1-501
537	3.1-796.127
538	3.1-796.66, 3.1-796.85, 3.1-796.97:1, 3.1-796.98
539	8.01-465.1 to 8.01-465.5
540	51-111.58:1, 51-156, 51-173
541	16.1-223, 16.1-224, 16.1-225, 16.1-300, 16.1-305, 19.2-387
542	19.2-11.1
543	65.1-103
544	2.1-726 to 2.1-735, 8.01-66.2, 8.01-66.5, 8.01-66.9, 8.01-231, 23-38.10:4, 58.1-3, 58.1-520, 60.2-633, 65.1-102
545	65.1-148
546	55-66.3
547	6.1-125.3
548	38.2-2403
549	27-95, 27-98.1 to 27-98.5
550	18.2-31
551	38.2-3416, 38.2-3541, 38.2-3707
552	3.1-188.32, 3.1-188.36
553	8.01-582,

Acts 1988 Chapter	Code 1950 Section
	8.01-583, 8.01-585, 8.01-586, 8.01-617, 17-28.1
554	38.2-208
555	6.1-1.1, 6.1-114, 6.1-194.18
556	36-55.33:1
557	53.1-183
558	15.1-791.2, 15.1-791.6
559	46.1-387.8
560	9-170
561	13.1-692.1, 13.1-704, 13.1-870.1, 13.1-883
562	33.1-75.1
563	58.1-535
564	65.1-56
565	38.2-2206
566	8.01-220.1:1
567	22.1-32
568	46.1-45
569	10.1-1409
571	42.1-70
572	36-48, 36-49, 36-49.1
573	15.1-493
574	22.1-319, 22.1-320, 22.1-321, 22.1-322, 22.1-324, 22.1-327, 22.1-329, 22.1-332, 22.1-333
575	18.2-249
576	22.1-88
577	45.1-21, 45.1-22, 45.1-24, 45.1-41
578	38.2-2206
579	63.1-223
580	54-367.2
581	58.1-401
582	22.1-32
583	8.01-288, 8.01-327, 20-99.1R, 20-99.1:1
584	29.1-521.1
585	38.2-2206
586	38.2-2206
587	62.1-13.5
588	5.1-1, 5.1-88.1, 5.1-88.5R
589	59.1-9.15
590	10.1-1415, n.
591	36-48, 36-49, 36-49.1
592	29.1-747 to 29.1-774
593	18.2-136
594	38.2-2206
595	55-210.8:1
596	65.1-56
597	45.1-54
598	24.1-132
599	63.1-223, 63.1-228
600	28.1-179
601	36-11
602	55-248.5
603	59.1-207.11 to 59.1-207.16
604	65.1-149
605	29.1-205
607	56-338.65, 56-338.70
608	2.1-1.1, 2.1-1.3, 2.1-1.6, 2.1-20.4, 2.1-51.9, 9-6.25:2, 10.1-2100 to 10.1-2115
609	58.1-3650.288, n.
610	58.1-3650.289, n.
611	58.1-3650.290, n., 58.1-3650.291, n., 58.1-3650.292, n.
613	58.1-3650.293, n., 58.1-3650.294, n.
614	58.1-3650.295, n.
615	18.2-283.1
616	24.1-255, 24.1-257.3
618	58.1-3650.296, n.
619	58.1-3650.297, n.
620	20-107.1
621	2.1-114.5:1
622	58.1-3650.298, n.
623	8.01-581.21 to 8.01-581.23
624	24.1-229, 24.1-234
625	15.1-11.01
626	15.1-90.1R, 15.1-90.3, 15.1-90.4
627	10.1-1406
628	58.1-3650.289, n.
629	58.1-3650.299, n.
630	58.1-3650.300, n.
632	32.1-203
633	58.1-3650.301, n.
634	2.1-20.1
635	65.1-23.1
636	58.1-3650.296, n.
637	33.1-46.2
638	15.1-79
639	58.1-3650.288, n.
640	11-41
641	58.1-3650.302, n.
642	8.01-327
643	55-210.8:1, 55-210.25
644	8.01-195.9
645	22.1-253.1 to 22.1-253.13R, 22.1-253.13:1 to 22.1-253.13:8
646	2.1-51.13, 2.1-51.14, 2.1-51.15
647	58.1-3650.303, n.
648	15.1-7.5
649	56.49, 56-535 to 56-552
652	58.1-3650.304, n.
654	33.1-75.3
655	38.2-2210, 38.2-2212
656	46.1-105.18
657	58.1-3650.305, n.
658	58.1-3650.116
659	58.1-3650.306, n.
660	15.1-131.6:2
661	58.1-3650.307, n.
662	46.1-401
663	58.1-3650.308, n.
664	58.1-3650.309, n., 58.1-3650.310, n., 58.1-3650.311
665	38.2-2210
666	18.2-341
667	28.1-172R
668	54-524.17:1
669	46.1-339.01, 46.1-339.02
671	58.1-3650.312, n.
672	58.1-3650.313, n.
673	58.1-3650.314, n.
674	8.01-498
675	58.1-3650.315, n.
678	60.2-219
679	19.2-305.2
680	58.1-3650.316, n.
681	37.1-20.2
682	22.1-253.1 to 22.1-253.13R, 22.1-253.13:1 to 22.1-253.13:8
684	58.1-3650.317, n.
685	2.1-27.4
686	63.1-248.5, 63.1-248.5:1
687	36-137, 36-139, 36-141 to 36-151
688	19.2-135
689	9-160
690	10.1-560, 21-89.3, n.
691	24.1-229, 24.1-234
694	10.1-565, 10.1-566, 10.1-569, 21-89.7, n., 21-89.8, n., 21-89.11, n.
695	58.1-3230,

Acts 1988 Chapter	Code 1950 Section
	58.1-3231, 58.1-3233, 58.1-3234, 58.1-3237, 58.1-3241
696	10.1-1407R, 10.1-1408R, 10.1-1408.1
697	14.1-116
698	16.1-108, 16.1-112
699	58.1-3924
700	15.1-503.2
701	46.1-63, 46.1-101, 46.1-149, 46.1-551
702	58.1-3814.1
703	2.1-129
704	46.1-63, 46.1-97, 46.1-149, 46.1-321.2
707	2.1-1.5, 2.1-51.9, 10.1-2000 to 10.1-2012
708	22.1-98, n.
709	2.1-129, n.
710	28.1-59, 28.1-65, 28.1-65.1
711	8.01-229
712	46.1-198
713	37.1-105
714	24.1-241.1
715	29.1-530.1
716	2.1-1.6, 2.1-20.4, 9-6.25:2, 42.1-15.1, 42.1-51, 42.1-52, 54-1.18, 54-261 to 54-272R
718	52-8.4
719	2.1-129, n.
720	10.1-1009 to 10.1-1016
721	10.1-419
722	9-86, n.
723	2.1-526.12, 2.1-526.14, 2.1-526.17:1, 9-6.14:4.1, 32.1-126.1, 36-99.7, 55-79.94, 63.1-198.01
724	51-111.56
725	58.1-2702
726	58.1-3516
727	58.1-2662.1, 58.1-2662.2
728	15.1-1132
729	58.1-3510, n.
730	58.1-433, 58.1-2600
731	2.1-234.13
732	10.1-560 to 10.1-564, 21-89.3 to 21-89.6, n., 21-89.15R
733	15.1-493
734	24.1-257.2, 24.1-260
735	15.1-466
736	32.1-229, 32.1-229.01
737	54-273, 54-281.14 to 54-281.16, 54-368
738	58.1-811, 58.1-812
739	46.1-90.2
740	62.1-13.28
741	58.1-322, 58.1-330
742	19.2-349
743	58.1-322
744	19.2-81
745	20-107.3
746	20-107.3
747	20-107.3
748	19.2-368.2, 19.2-368.11:1, 19.2-368.18
749	16.1-309.1
750	19.2-349
751	46.1-291
752	19.2-81
753	18.2-249
754	22.1-253.13:7
755	58.1-322, 58.1-330
756	58.1-322
757	19.2-353.4
758	19.2-163.2
759	8.01-576.1 to 8.01-576.3
760	32.1-116.3
761	2.1-234.13
762	15.1-1344.1, 18.2-160.1
763	2.1-526.8, 10.1-501.1, 21-65.1, n.
764	19.2-309.1
765	2.1-1.1, 2.1-1.3, 2.1-1.6, 2.1-1.7, 2.1-20.4, 2.1-43, 2.1-51.15, 6.1-330.76, 9-6.14:4.1, 9-6.25:1, 9-6.25:2, 9-6.25:3, 9-16 to 9-48R, 13.1-545R, 18.2-502.1, 54-1 to 54-977R, 54.1-100 to 54.1-4111, 59.1-124, 59.1-127, 59.1-130
766	8.01-261, 60.2-114, 60.2-531, 60.2-623, 60.2-625
767	2.1-639.13
768	58.1-535
769	38.2-2900 to 38.2-2913
770	19.2-349, 19.2-353.2R, 19.2-353.3, 19.2-353.4R, 19.2-354, 19.2-358, 46.1-413, 46.1-423.3
771	16.1-289.1, 16.1-292, 16.1-298
772	15.1-1372.5, 15.1-1372.6, 15.1-1372.7, 15.1-1372.15, 15.1-1372.17, 15.1-1372.18
773	58.1-323.1
774	19.2-163.2
776	58.1-3245 to 58.1-3245.5
777	20-61.2, n.
778	8.01-195.7
779	18.2-224
780	2.1-526.8, 10.1-501.1, 21-65.1, n.
781	18.2-271.1, 18.2-271.2
782	20-61.1, n.
783	38.2-2900 to 38.2-2913
784	58.1-3713
785	19.2-309.1
786	4-98.16
787	19.2-177R, 19.2-177.1
788	58.1-4007
789	32.1-116.3
790	32.1-325
791	16.1-279, 16.1-283
792	16.1-260
793	18.2-308
794	16.1-228, 20-107.2
795	63.1-260R, 63.1-260.1
796	24.1-202.10
797	16.1-241
798	46.1-40.1:1, 46.1-383, 54-276.9:2
799	16.1-77, 16.1-122.1 to 16.1-122.7
800	10.1-814, n., 14.1-79, n., 14.1-84.1, n., 14.1-143.2, n., 19.2-326, n., 28.1-46.4, n., 32.1-102.1, n., 37.1-89, n., 46.1-326.2, n., 53.1-120, n.
801	8.01-195.7, 8.01-195.2 to

Acts 1988 Chapter	Code 1950 Section
	8.01-195.8, n., 15.1-1364, n., 15.1-1371, n.
802	54-145.4, 54-145.6, 54-145.7, 54-145.9, 54-145.10:2, 54-145.10:3, 54-145.10:4R, 54-145.10:5, 54-145.10:8, 54-145.10:10, 54-145.10:11
803	16.1-260
804	8.9-403 to 8.9-406
805	33.1-346, 46.1-315.1R
806	46.1-326.2 to 46.1-326.4, 46.1-326.6 to 46.1-326.11, 46.1-326.13, 46.1-326.14R, 52-4
807	54-145.10:6
808	46.1-351.1
809	51-111.41:1, 51-111.51, 51-111.58, 51-146, 51-155, 51-172
810	15.1-526.4
813	15.1-499.1
815	23-38.62:2
816	15.1-646, n.
817	58.1-345.1
818	8.01-351
819	58.1-346.1
820	9-6.14:4.1
821	2.1-1.6, 2.1-548.16 to 2.1-548.21, 9-6.25:1
822	58.1-3506
823	53.1-135, 53.1-139, 53.1-139.1
824	53.1-150
825	20-107.3
826	16.1-275, 16.1-280
827	54-62, n.
828	38.2-4800, 38.2-4806
829	11-41.2
830	2.1-234.13
831	38.2-301, 38.2-302
832	58.1-3650.318 to 58.1-3650.320, n.
833	15.1-1635 to 15.1-1650
834	2.1-234.4, 2.1-234.8, 2.1-327, 2.1-328, 2.1-328.1, 2.1-328.3, 2.1-328.5, 2.1-328.8, 2.1-328.9, 2.1-328.10, 2.1-328.12, 2.1-329.01, 15.1-207, 15.1-211, 15.1-1358,
	58.1-3156, 58.1-3157R
836	32.1-37.1, 54-260.74:2
837	11-41.3
838	52-8.5
839	2.1-1.1, 2.1-1.3, 2.1-1.6, 2.1-20.4, 2.1-51.27, 2.1-129R, 2.1-736 to 2.1-743, 9-6.23, 9-6.25:1, 9-85 to 9-87R, 23-7.1
840	38.2-3405
841	2.1-526.9, 2.1-526.9:1, 8.01-587, 8.01-588, 8.01-588.1, 8.01-589, 8.01-600, 8.01-600.1, 8.01-602, 14.1-143.2, 55-210.9:2
842	46.1-550.6
843	32.1-69.1, 32.1-70
844	33.1-12, 33.1-23.03:1, 33.1-23.03:3R, 33.1-268, 33.1-269, 33.1-276, 33.1-277, 33.1-279.1, 33.1-283, 33.1-285, 33.1-285.1
845	63.1-248.13:1
846	18.2-67.9
847	58.1-3833
848	2.1-526.1 to 21.526.10, 2.1-526.11:1
849	2.1-639.13 to 2.1-639.15, 2.1-639.15:1, 2.1-639.41
850	59.1-202
851	19.2-389, 22.1-296.2
852	19.2-349, 19.2-353.2R, 19.2-353.3, 19.2-353.4R, 19.2-354, 19.2-358, 46.1-413, 46.1-423.3
853	19.2-81
854	33.1-210.1
855	18.2-334.4, 19.2-66, 59.1-364 to 59.1-405
856	15.1-491, 15.1-491.5, 15.1-493, 15.1-497
857	8.01-581.21 to 8.01-581.23
858	18.2-271.1
859	18.2-271.1, 18.2-271.2, 18.2-272, 46.1-350
860	46.1-417, 46.1-417.1, 46.1-418R,
	46.1-438, 46.1-442, 46.1-466, 46.1-471, 46.1-514.4R
861	58.1-346.2
862	15.1-37.3:9
864	15.1-159.2
865	9-6.14.14:1, 46.1-1, 46.1-90.1R, 46.1-95R, 46.1-113 to 46.1-130R, 46.1-138R, 46.1-138.1R, 46.1-164R, 46.1-167.2, 46.1-516, 46.1-517, 46.1-517.1, 46.1-517.2, 46.1-520, 46.1-521R, 46.1-522, 46.1-523, 46.1-524R, 46.1-525, 46.1-525.01 to 46.1-525.012, 46.1-525.1 to 46.1-539R, 46.1-543R, 46.1-544R, 46.1-544.1 to 46.1-544.6, 46.1-545 to 46.1-547R, 46.1-547.3 to 46.1-547.10, 46.1-548, 46.1-549, 46.1-550.5:4 to 46.1-550.5:39, 46.1-550.1R, 46.1-550.2R, 46.1-550.4R, 46.1-550.5R, 46.1-550.5:1 to 46.1-550.5:3, 46.1-550.6, 46.1-550.7R, 46.1-550.7:1, 59.1-361
866	8.01-328.1, 20-49.1 to 20-49.8, 20-61.1R, 20-61.2R
867	20-61.3
868	62.1-3
869	15.1-499.1
870	54-524.65:1
872	53.1-151
873	17-116.05:1, 17-116.07, 19.2-177R, 53.1-40.1 to 53.1-40.8
874	54-278.3
875	23-9.2:6
876	15.1-12.1
878	8.01-328.1, 20-49.1 to 20-49.8, 20-61.1R, 20-61.2R
879	15.1-73.4, 15.1-778.1, 15.1-782
880	20-107.3
881	15.1-945.3, 15.1-945.7, 15.1-965.1, 15.1-965.9 to 15.1-965.27, 15.1-1167.1, 15.1-1168
882	63.1-204, 63.1-221, 63.1-223
883	8.01-676.1
884	8.01-195.3
885	16.1-316,

Acts 1988 Chapter	Code 1950 Section
	16.1-317
886	16.1-249
887	16.1-279, 20-107.2
888	2.1-1.5, 2.1-51.18, 9-6.23, 9-6.25:2, 18.2-271.1, 18.2-271.2
889	19.2-61 to 19.2-63, 19.2-63.1, 19.2-66 to 19.2-68, 19.2-69, 19.2-70.1 to 19.2-70.3
890	56-529, n., 56-530, n.
891	2.1-1.1, 2.1-1.3, 2.1-1.5, 2.1-1.6, 2.1-51.9, 2.1-342, 2.1-344, 2.1-548.8:1 to 2.1-548.8:3, 9-152.1 to 9-152.5R, 10-1 to 10-312R, 10.1-100 to 10.1-1901, 21-1 to 21-112.21R, 27-5.2R, 27-5.4R, 27-54.1 to 27-54.5R, 32.1-238.6:1 to 32.1-238.10R, 45.1-1.8R, 56-426.1R, 62.1-44.108 to 62.1-44.112R, 62.1-115.1 to 62.1-115.10R, 62.1-153R, 62.1-154R
892	63.1-248.13:1
893	4-25, 4-78
894	20-61.3
895	15.1-499.1
896	58.1-3275
897	46.1-401
898	63.1-55.4
899	58.1-333, 58.1-400.1, 58.1-401, 58.1-403, 58.1-430, 58.1-433, 58.1-472, 58.1-602, 58.1-608, 58.1-2600, 58.1-2605, 58.1-2608, 58.1-2621 to 58.1-2625R, 58.1-2628, 58.1-2629, 58.1-2631, 58.1-2633, 58.1-2640, 58.1-2647, 58.1-2648, 58.1-2650, 58.1-2651, 58.1-2660
900	63.1-248.13:1
901	2.1-1.7, 2.1-33, 9-6.25:1, 9-95.5 to 9-95.6
902	2.1-342
903	33.1-12, 33.1-23.03:1,
	33.1-23.03:3R, 33.1-268, 33.1-269, 33.1-276, 33.1-277, 33.1-279.1, 33.1-283, 33.1-285, 33.1-285.1
904	54-317, 54-524.34:2, 54-524.53
905	16.1-241, 16.1-279, 20-88.22, 20-88.22:01, 20-88.23
906	20-60.3, 20-60.5, 20-79.1, 20-79.2, 63.1-53, 63.1-250, 63.1-250.1 to 63.1-250.4, 63.1-251.1, 63.1-252.1, 63.1-254, 63.1-255, 63.1-256, 63.1-258.1 to 63.1-258.3, 63.1-260R, 63.1-260.1, 63.1-262, 63.1-264, 63.1-266, 63.1-267.1, 63.1-268.1, 63.1-270, 63.1-274.1 to 63.1-274.9, 63.1-275 to 63.1-290R
907	20-108.1, 20-108.2, 63.1-250.1, 63.1-251, 63.1-264, 63.1-264.1, 63.1-264.2, 63.1-286R

ACTS 1989

Acts 1989 Chapter	Code 1950 Section
1	11-56.1
2	28.1-36, 28.1-36.01, 28.1-183
3	15.1-18.3
4	37.1-132, 37.1-134.2
5	10.1-1207, 10.1-1213 to 10.1-1221
6	46.1-172
7	38.2-3408, 38.2-4221, 54.1-3000, 54.1-3005, 54.1-3013
8	8.01-460
9	58.1-608, n.
10	4-118.21, 4-118.42 to 4-118.61, 4-118.21 to 4-118.41R, 4-118.42
12	58.1-608, n., 58.1-623.1
13	58.1-608, n.
14	13.1-728.1 to 13.1-728.9
15	46.1-516
16	54.1-306
17	46.1-551
18	52-4
19	9-154, n., 38.2-401, n., 58.1-2508, n.
24	15.1-239
25	15.1-486.1, n.
26	29.1-509
27	15.1-494
28	2.1-187, 6.1-194.69, 46.1-389, 46.1-443, 46.1-465, 46.1-466, 46.1-472, 46.1-504, 46.1-514.6, 51-111.24:1, 51-111.52:3
29	58.1-3516
30	15.1-117
34	58.1-3920.1
35	15.1-1399.13, 15.1-1399.16
36	58.1-3516
37	11-41.2:1
38	58.1-3604
39	58.1-322, 58.1-322.2, 58.1-402
40	58.1-3215
41	51-111.18
42	4-25, 4-78, 4-112.3
43	17-119.1:2
44	16.1-69.6:1
45	54.1-2913, 54.1-2913.1
46	33.1-56
47	46.1-267
48	46.1-49, 46.1-49.1
49	15.1-1403
50	18.2-287.1
51	21-120
52	15.1-1510
53	2.1-429
54	9-6.14:4.1
55	31-4
56	2.1-342, 2.1-344
57	55-79.74:1
58	55-79.75
59	18.2-429
60	23-38.72 to 23-38.74
62	46.1-33.2
63	55-79.40
64	58.1-1204.1
65	46.1-291.01
66	32.1-285
67	32.1-325.3, 32.1-325.4
68	55-344
69	8.01-585
70	20-107.3
71	9-6.14:7.1,

Acts 1989 Chapter	Code 1950 Section
	9-6.14:9, 9-6.14:22, 9-6.14:24
72	18.2-340.4
73	32.1-5, 32.1-8, 32.1-13.1, 32.1-14
74	2.1-639.6
75	2.1-127
76	18.2-340.5
77	58.1-520, 58.1-531, 58.1-531.1, 58.1-535
78	56-338.20, 56-338.29
79	58.1-1724.1
80	58.1-3506
81	58.1-3001, 58.1-3005
82	14.1-53
83	15.1-1312
84	14.1-84.2, 14.1-84.3
85	42.1-48
86	58.1-3980, 58.1-3984
87	55-248.45
88	36-87 to 36-91
89	58.1-3220, 58.1-3221
90	27-97
91	29.1-302.2
92	22.1-302
93	23-7.1
94	22.1-94, 22.1-115
97	54.1-2301
98	23-7.2
99	58.1-3
100	22.1-303
101	23-38.56
102	22.1-129
103	9-154, n., 38.2-401, n., 58.1-2508, n.
104	60.2-528
105	23-9.6:1
106	22.1-218, 22.1-220
107	23-164.3
108	2.1-391, 60.2-113
109	63.1-248.6
110	46.1-49, 46.1-49.1
111	24.1-21
112	2.1-121.1, 15.1-37.5:2
113	18.2-340.2, 18.2-340.3, 18.2-340.6, 18.2-340.10, 18.2-340.12
114	2.1-21.2
115	56-334
121	8.01-195.4
130	32.1-225
131	54.1-2712
132	2.1-27.6
133	51.5-31
134	15.1-1032.2
135	22.1-343
136	22.1-344, 22.1-344.1
137	17-51
138	24.1-48, 24.1-72.10, 24.1-72.11
139	46.1-375
140	29.1-801
141	24.1-168, 24.1-185
142	18.2-502.2
143	33.1-75.3
144	60.2-524
145	59.1-391
146	8.01-581.1, 8.01-581.20
147	46.1-357.3
148	46.1-516
149	15.1-1342, n.
150	15.1-1357
151	38.2-3602R 38.2-3604, 38.2-3608, 38.2-3609,
152	13.1-605, 13.1-615, 13.1-617, 13.1-805, 13.1-815, 13.1-817
153	64.1-105
154	13.1-546.1
157	29.1-717.1, 29.1-717.2
158	64.1-123.1
159	54.1-106
160	2.1-373.2:1, 2.1-373.1, 2.1-373.2
161	36-55.33:1
162	6.1-2.7
163	47.1-4
164	45.1-293
165	2.1-1.1, 2.1-1.3, 2.1-51.40, 9-274, 9-275, 9-278, 9-279, 9-280
166	55-19.2
167	58.1-3127.1
168	52-4.3
169	19.2-299
170	19.2-269.2
171	15.1-246, 15.1-249.1
172	59.1-274, 59.1-275
173	63.1-174.1
174	15.1-503.2
175	59.1-148.3
176	51.5-9.1 to 51.5-9.3, 51.5-11, 51.5-14
177	15.1-186
178	15.1-1403.1, 15.1-1404.1
179	22.1-122, 22.1-122.1
180	15.1-590.1
181	51.5-3, 51.5-16, 51.5-18
182	16.1-305
183	16.1-306
185	56-495
186	14.1-104
187	46.1-547.6
188	56-245.3
189	9-292 to 9-296
190	2.1-21
191	63.1-238.3
192	24.1-229.1
193	32.1-138.3
195	32.1-324, n.
196	54.1-3900, n., 54.1-3925, n., 54.1-3926, n.
197	22.1-27
198	9-6.23
199	9-96, 9-97
200	57-12
201	38.2-3408, 38.2-4221
202	5.1-25.1
203	29.1-553
204	29.1-300.1
205	6.1-194.32:1
206	29.1-812, 29.1-813
207	20-121.02
208	29.1-310
209	8.01-420.4
210	15.1-37.3:10
211	56-5.1
212	8.01-391
213	29.1-338
214	63.1-236.1
215	10.1-1105
216	38.2-4310, 38.2-4311, 38.2-4317, 38.2-4317.1
217	29.1-344
218	62.1-44.23:1
219	62.1-44.38
220	56-304.11
221	38.2-4312
222	11-47.1, n.
223	58.1-1717
224	15.1-11.6
225	22.1-254.2

Acts 1989 Chapter	Code 1950 Section
226	10.1-1602
227	24.1-32
228	58.1-4007
229	16.1-69.40
230	6.1-2.6:1
231	11-47.1, n.
232	15.1-486.1, n.
233	9-169, 9-180
234	5.1-35, 5.1-41
235	11-45
236	38.2-1315
238	58.1-3916
239	6.1-254, 6.1-255
240	59.1-41.1, 59.1-41.2, 59.1-41.3, 59.1-41.4, 59.1-41.6
241	54.1-1106.1
242	14.1-50, 14.1-51, 15.1-159.9
243	38.2-2201, 38.2-2202
244	54.1-2105
245	58.1-300, 58.1-520, 58.1-540 to 58.1-549
246	58.1-3650.321, n., 58.1-3650.322, n., 58.1-3650.323, n.
247	58.1-3650.324, n.
248	58.1-3650.325, n.
249	58.1-3650.326, n.
250	58.1-3650.327, n.
251	58.1-3650.328, n.
252	58.1-3650.329, n.
253	58.1-3650.330 to 58.1-3650.354, n.
254	2.1-114.5, 2.1-114.5:1, 2.1-114.5:6, 15.1-7.2, 37.1-195
255	5.1-25.1
256	46.1-2
257	23-50.15:1
258	9-153.1, 27-5.5, 27-34.4, 27-66.1R, 27-73R, 27-78R, 27-78.1R, 27-79.9R, 27-85.2R, 27-95, 27-99, 35.1-8R, 36-105.1, 36-135, 36-139, 36-139.2 to 36-139.4, 63.1-196.3
259	18.2-340.9
260	11-61
261	9-156, 9-157, 9-157.1, 9-158, 9-160, 9-163
262	46.1-267
263	58.1-313
264	16.1-69.35
265	58.1-3713
266	4-10.1, 4-105, 4-114
267	63.1-74, 63.1-83.1
268	2.1-64.32, 2.1-64.32:1, 2.1-64.35
269	32.1-325
271	63.1-182.1
272	4-118.7, 4-118.16
273	2.1-591, 2.1-595
274	33.1-72.1
275	32.1-229, 32.1-229.01
276	46.1-401
277	22.1-211, 22.1-212, 63.1-196.02, 63.1-196.03
278	54.1-3000, 54.1-3005, 54.1-3007, 54.1-3009, 54.1-3022 to 54.1-3028
279	36-137, 36-139
280	36-55.63, 58.1-336, 58.1-435
281	15.1-1638
282	54.1-2964
283	32.1-229, 32.1-229.01
284	10.1-1415
285	15.1-18.4
286	33.1-221.1:2, 58.1-815
287	22.1-279.1, 22.1-280R
288	38.2-3708
289	58.1-461, 58.1-462, 58.1-470
290	46.1-172.04
291	58.1-3817
292	14.1-84.2
293	14.1-70
294	15.1-131.3
295	46.1-171.01
296	11-41, 11-41.1
297	46.1-326.1:2
298	53.1-17
299	9-6.14:4.1, 9-6.18
300	58.1-3378
301	55-248.31
302	46.1-410
303	33.1-23.3, 33.1-44
304	15.1-238, 15.1-238.1
305	33.1-223
306	2.1-1.6, 2.1-20.4, 9-6.25:1, 54.1-2956.1 to 54.1-2956.5
307	63.1-195, 63.1-205, 63.1-205.1R
308	46.1-550.5:39 to 46.1-550.5:41
309	11-37
310	63.1-321, 63.1-323, 63.1-324
311	4-31
312	65.1-4.5
313	65.1-99
314	58.1-3703, 58.1-3840, 63.1-149, 63.1-152, 63.1-156, 63.1-164
316	2.1-457
317	46.1-326.1:2
318	65.1-96, 65.1-97
319	65.1-2.1
320	24.1-227, 24.1-228.1
321	46.1-65
322	24.1-1
323	11-37
324	65.1-99
325	62.1-195.1
326	51.5-44
327	58.1-3
328	58.1-1724.1
329	58.1-3516
330	23-35.9 to 23-35.11, 23-35.12, 23-35.13
331	9-84.03
332	15.1-466
333	63.1-110
334	37.1-71
335	19.2-368.7, 19.2-368.11:1, 19.2-368.12
336	33.1-221
337	8.01-195.4
338	46.1-1, 46.1-104
339	60.2-219
340	15.1-29.17
341	40.1-49.4, 59.1-406 to 59.1-414
342	62.1-13.21, 62.1-13.22, 62.1-13.25
343	18.2-323.1
344	3.1-796.96
346	55-58.2
348	8.01-66
350	21-291.2
351	10.1-1202
352	15.1-687.14
353	15.1-686.2R, 15.1-686.3R

Acts 1989 Chapter	Code 1950 Section
354	15.1-687.15
355	15.1-765.1, 15.1-773, 15.1-783.1
356	63.1-43.1, 63.1-44, 63.1-44.1
357	15.1-1239, n.
358	2.1-340.1, 2.1-341, 2.1-342, 2.1-343, 2.1-343.1, 2.1-344, 2.1-344.1, 2.1-345, 2.1-346, 2.1-346.1
359	15.1-491, 15.1-493
360	62.1-13.5
361	38.2-5020
362	29.1-505.1
363	46.1-550.5:27
364	46.1-550.5:1
365	46.1-550.5:30
366	15.1-37.3:6
367	46.1-1, 46.1-21
368	16.1-241, 20-49.2
369	19.2-123
370	19.2-223
371	23-7.4
372	28.1-173
373	63.1-124.2
374	19.2-299.1
376	6.1-80
377	6.1-60.1
378	44-146.36
380	58.1-3713, 58.1-3713.3
381	38.2-1905.1, 38.2-1905.2, 38.2-2228.1
382	22.1-271.2, 32.1-46
383	55-248.34, 55-248.35
384	15.1-430, 15.1-491
385	19.2-160
386	19.2-305.2
387	26-12.3, 58.1-1712, 58.1-1714
388	13.1-514
389	62.1-44.15
390	58.1-3373
391	58.1-3833, 58.1-3840
392	22.1-205, 46.1-357
393	15.1-466
394	21-120
395	2.1-335.1
396	6.1-194.69
397	54.1-500 to 54.1-507, 54.1-509, 54.1-511, 54.1-512, 54.1-514, 54.1-516, 54.1-517
398	2.1-526.12, 2.1-526.14:1, 2.1-526.14:2, 32.1-126.1, 36-99.7, 55-79.94
399	51-111.24:2
400	58.1-3609, 58.1-3621
401	3.1-1033, 3.1-1042
402	46.1-154.3
403	15.1-466
404	15.1-11.1
405	15.1-23.1
406	9-138.1
407	15.1-496
408	13.1-528 to 13.1-541R
409	2.1-429
410	62.1-10, 62.1-11
411	6.1-411 to 6.1-413
412	30-28.15, 30-28.16, 30-28.18
413	2.1-1.6, 3.1-73.2, 3.1-73.3, 3.1-73.4R, 3.1-73.5, 9-6.25:2
414	44-1, 44-2.1R, 44-12, 44-13, 44-19, 44-54.4 to 44-54.12, 44-80, 44-81, 44-93, 44-115
416	37.1-134.3
417	58.1-1724
418	58.1-3245
419	13.1-858
420	27-97
421	16.1-69.40:2, 28.1-187, 29.1-335, 29.1-337, 29.1-354, 29.1-519, 29.1-520, 29.1-521, 29.1-526, 29.1-528, 29.1-603, 29.1-606
422	13.1-870.1, 13.1-870.2
423	53.1-80 to 53.1-83
424	29.1-600
426	8.01-42.2
427	29.1-302.1
428	28.1-94.1
429	58.1-2626.1
430	62.1-44.34:8 to 62.1-44.34:11
431	28.1-173.1:1
432	45.1-270.2, 45.1-270.3
433	32.1-127.2
434	32.1-127
435	38.2-1814, 38.2-1814.1, 38.2-1816, 38.2-1817, 38.2-1819, 38.2-1822, 38.2-1830, 38.2-1836
436	8.01-225.1
437	65.1-4.6
438	65.1-93
439	46.1-441.2
440	10.1-1411
441	45.1-390.1
442	11-47.2
443	32.1-116.3
444	46.1-423.3
445	17-47.4
446	8.01-195.3
447	15.1-489, 15.1-490, 15.1-491.02
448	56-265.16R, 56-265.16:1, 56-265.17, 56-265.18, 56-265.20, 56-265.25
449	15.1-489, 15.1-490, 15.1-491.02
450	8.01-269
451	16.1-122.1
453	19.2-163.2
454	32.1-176.5
455	19.2-13
456	22.1-166
457	51.5-4
458	19.2-187.01
459	37.1-84.1
460	9-173.4, 9-173.5
461	19.2-163.2
462	10.1-603.16 to 10.1-603.23
463	38.2-5001, n., 38.2-5020
464	22.1-32
465	13.1-333R, 13.1-333.1
466	64.1-5.1, 64.1-5.2
467	10.1-603.1 to 10.1-603.15
468	10.1-600, 10.1-601R, 10.1-602, 10.1-603, 10.1-658, 10.1-659
469	58.1-622
470	24.1-79.5
471	15.1-475
472	2.1-548.8:3
473	16.1-296
474	44-93
475	2.1-20.1:02
476	53.1-131.2
478	2.1-342,

Acts 1989 Chapter	Code 1950 Section
	2.1-344, 9-6.14:4.1, 58.1-4008, 58.1-4009, 58.1-4015, 58.1-4017, 58.1-4019, 58.1-4020, 58.1-4022, 58.1-4023
479	14.1-9.1R, 33.1-400 to 33.1-408
480	8.01-581.9
481	19.2-270.4
482	6.1-68.1
483	13.1-706
484	51-111.37, 51-111.41:1, 51-150, 51-151, 51-156, 51-157.1
485	15.1-498.1 to 15.1-498.10
486	18.2-49.1
487	38.2-3405
488	38.2-2228
489	51.5-4
490	54.1-4200 to 54.1-4202
491	18.2-313.1
492	26-31, 64.1-171, 64.1-173, 64.1-179
493	1-13.28:1
494	19.2-163.2
495	15.1-466, 15.1-475
496	65.1-101
497	10.1-600, 10.1-601R, 10.1-602, 10.1-603, 10.1-658, 10.1-659
498	10.1-603.16 to 10.1-603.23
499	10.1-603.1 to 10.1-603.15
500	29.1-509
501	2.1-119R
502	65.1-46.1, 65.1-52
503	19.2-163.2
504	22.1-32
505	29.1-509
506	18.2-460
507	22.1-132.1
509	16.1-244
510	54.1-2914, 54.1-3301, 54.1-3302, 54.1-3304.1
511	15.1-29.18
512	30-28.18
513	37.1-134.4
514	18.2-308.2
515	22.1-207.2, 22.1-254
516	22.1-305.1
517	32.1-102.1, 32.1-102.3:2 to 32.1-102.3:4
518	8.01-296
519	19.2-132
520	16.1-309
521	63.1-110
523	38.2-5001, 38.2-5004, 38.2-5005, 38.2-5006, 38.2-5007, 38.2-5008, 38.2-5009, 38.2-5011, 38.2-5016, 38.2-5018, 38.2-5019R, 38.2-5020, 38.2-5021
524	8.01-296
525	53.1-160
526	46.1-401
527	18.2-31
528	4-79R, 4-79.1
529	45.1-295, 45.1-301, 45.1-302, 45.1-304, 45.1-312, 45.1-313, 45.1-314, 45.1-316, 45.1-321, 45.1-322, 45.1-334, 45.1-336
530	18.2-501.1 to 18.2-501.5
531	18.2-308.2
532	15.1-446.1, 15.1-456
533	62.1-198, 62.1-199, 62.1-201, 62.1-204
534	37.1-71
535	26-59, 31-2, 31-8
536	53.1-23.1
537	56-469, 56-470, 56-475, 56-476, 56-476.1, 56-477
538	18.2-308
539	65.1-87.1
540	65.1-88
541	53.1-233, 53.1-234
542	18.2-308
543	38.2-1801
544	19.2-389, 22.1-296.2
545	16.1-243
546	18.2-373
547	2.1-380, 63.1-248.6
548	31-45
549	16.1-250
550	22.1-60
551	62.1-198, 62.1-199, 62.1-201, 62.1-204
552	65.1-55.1
553	3.1-1021, 3.1-1025, 10.1-209 to 10.1-217, 29.1-566
554	18.2-36.1, 18.2-269
555	58.1-3211
556	8.01-259, 8.01-261, 20-96
557	16.1-249
558	18.2-144.1
559	2.1-20.1
560	2.1-116
561	8.01-581.2
562	20-99.1:1
563	16.1-88.2
564	15.1-239
565	19.2-163
566	15.1-499.1
567	18.2-248.5
568	58.1-3211, 58.1-3212, 58.1-3213.1
569	19.2-152.1
570	18.2-213.1
571	53.1-120
572	40.1-27.1
573	33.1-46.2
574	18.2-36.1, 18.2-269
575	2.1-1.6, 2.1-20.4, 3.1-249.27 to 3.1-249.78, 3.1-189 to 3.1-249.26R, 9-6.25:2
576	13.1-320
577	13.1-323
578	20-108.2
579	20-108.2
580	18.2-248.6, 18.2-248.7
581	58.1-602
582	19.2-266
583	40.1-29
584	54.1-902
585	58.1-608
586	53.1-131
587	30-19.1:2
588	8.01-229
589	58.1-3510, 58.1-3510.1 to 58.1-3510.3, 58.1-3706
590	58.1-335
591	37.1-84.1, 37.1-89, 37.1-134.2R, 37.1-134.5, 54.1-2970
592	54.1-2984
593	36-27
594	47.1-21
595	14.1-112, 14.1-123
596	55-57.2

Acts 1989 Chapter	Code 1950 Section
597	16.1-218, 17-228
598	20-49.3
599	20-108.1, 20-108.2, 63.1-250.1, 63.1-264.2
600	55-19
601	9-6.14:11, 9-6.14:17
602	55-122, 55-123, 55-125, 55-125.1, 55-126, 55-127, 55-129, 55-130, 55-131, 55-132, 55-134, 55-134.1, 55-134.2, 55-135, 55-137.1, 55-137.2
603	11-41.2:1
604	18.2-264.1, 18.2-268
605	56-41.1
606	38.2-1331, 38.2-4214, 38.2-4230 to 38.2-4235
607	55-40, 64.1-19.1
608	62.1-44.34:7
609	13.1-941 to 13.1-944
610	18.2-268
611	8.01-324
612	55-246.1
613	2.1-51.14:1, 22.1-271.3, 23-9.2:3.2, 32.1-11.1, 32.1-11.2, 32.1-36, 32.1-36.1, 32.1-37.2, 32.1-39, 32.1-45.1, 32.1-55.1, 32.1-289.2
614	2.1-1.7, 2.1-20.4, 2.1-51.15, 2.1-553.2R, 9-6.25:2, 9-281 to 9.291
616	8.01-345
617	2.1-1.6, 2.1-1.7, 2.1-20.4, 9-6.25:2, 32.1-117 to 32.1-122R, 32.1-122.01 to 32.1-122.08, 32.1-122.4
618	32.1-27, 32.1-27.1, 32.1-123, 32.1-124, 32.1-125, 32.1-125.1, 32.1-126, 32.1-127, 32.1-127.01, 32.1-132, 32.1-135, 32.1-137, 32.1-331R
619	18.2-255.2
621	38.2-2206, 46.1-1, 46.1-400, 46.1-444, 46.1-472, 46.1-504
622	15.1-687, 15.1-687.01, 15.1-687.15, 15.1-687.16
623	10.1-1408.1, 15.1-11.02
624	8.01-66.9
625	56-273, 56-274, 56-338.104 to 56-338.126
626	6.1-194.69
627	62.1-44.32, 62.1-44.34:3, 62.1-44.34:7R, 62.1-44.34:10 to 62.1-44.34:13
628	16.1-279
629	58.1-347, 58.1-351, 58.1-450, 58.1-455, 58.1-1805, 58.1-1840
630	10.1-1422.1, 58.1-640 to 58.1-644
631	11-24, 57-35.1 to 57-35.10R, 57-35.11 to 57-35.34, 57-39.8 to 57-39.18R
632	8.01-345
633	2.1-1.6, 2.1-1.7, 2.1-20.4, 9-6.25:2, 32.1-117 to 32.1-122R, 32.1-122.01 to 32.1-122.08, 32.1-122.4
634	15.1-491.8
635	32.1-332 to 32.1-342
636	2.1-1.7, 2.1-20.1:01, 9-6.25:1
637	55-361.1, 55-368, 55-369, 55-370, 55-374, 55-380, 55-384
638	18.2-249
639	58.1-322, 58.1-322.2, 58.1-402
641	16.1-241.1, 16.1-296.1, 17-116.05:5, 20-96.1, 20-96.2
642	58.1-347, 58.1-351, 58.1-450, 58.1-455, 58.1-1805, 58.1-1840
644	46.1-330
645	46.1-1, 46.1-328.1, 46.1-330, 46.1-330.1
646	38.2-3418.1, 38.2-3607, 38.2-4319
647	63.1-195, 63.1-204, 63.1-211.1R, 63.1-220, 63.1-220.1 to 63.1-220.5, 63.1-221, 63.1-223, 63.1-225, 63.1-226, 63.1-228, 63.1-238.01, 63.1-238.02
648	58.1-3230
649	16.1-241.1, 16.1-296.1, 17-116.05:5, 20-96.1, 20-96.2
650	6.1-6.1, 6.1-60.1
651	6.1-369.1 to 6.1-369.10R, 59.1-335.1, 59.1-335.2, 59.1-335.5 to 59.1-335.10
652	53.1-37, 53.1-56, 53.1-59, 53.1-160
653	38.2-501, 38.2-3100.1, 38.2-3401, 38.2-4214, 38.2-4319, 38.2-4509
655	6.1-369.1 to 6.1-369.10R, 59.1-335.1 to 59.1-335.12
656	2.1-1.1, 2.1-1.3, 2.1-1.6, 2.1-51.9, 2.1-488.1, 2.1-548.13, 3.1-18.6, 9-6.25:1, 9-6.25:2, 10.1-100, 10.1-101, 10.1-103, 10.1-105, 10.1-114, 10.1-206, 10.1-400, 10.1-413.2, 10.1-419, 10.1-502, 10.1-707, 10.1-800 to 10.1-817R, 10.1-900 to 10.1-906R, 10.1-1001, 10.1-1003, 10.1-1121, 10.1-1202, 10.1-2200 to 10.1-2216, 10.1-2300 to 10.1-2306, 10.1-2400 to 10.1-2404, 15.1-1135, 28.1-101.4, 28.1-115, 28.1-147, 32.1-242, 33.1-31, 33.1-32, 33.1-62, 33.1-63, 33.1-223, 58.1-345.1, 58.1-3220, 58.1-3230, 58.1-3233, 58.1-3239, 58.1-3240
657	32.1-343 to 32.1-350, 63.1-134 to 63.1-141R
658	15.1-29.19
659	10.1-1900R,

Acts 1989 Chapter	Code 1950 Section
	10.1-1901R
660	2.1-20.4, 10.1-707
661	15.1-1372.22, 15.1-1372.23, 15.1-1372.33
662	65.1-104.3
663	18.2-308.5
664	2.1-20.1, 2.1-20.1:2
665	13.1-543, 13.1-544
666	56-235.4, 56-249.6
667	6.1-411, 6.1-422
668	2.1-180, n., 2.1-512, n., 10.1-2213, n., 14.1-79, n., 14.1-84.1, n., 14.1-143.2A, n., 19.2-326, n., 28.1-46.4, n., 32.1-102.1, n., 37.1-89, n., 46.1-326.2, n., 46.1-441.2, n., 53.1-120, n.
675	16.1-271
676	59.1-313, 59.1-317
677	9-6.14:16, 63.1-119
678	10.1-1127.1
679	55-508 to 55-516
680	18.2-128, 18.2-129R
681	8.01-35.1
682	18.2-255.2
683	53.1-240, 66-15
684	8.01-512.4, 11-24 to 11-29R, 37.1-142, 38.2-4021, 54.1-2800, 54.1-2803 to 54.1-2807, 54.1-2820 to 54.1-2825
685	46.1-342.1
686	46.1-550.5:27
687	2.1-457, 2.1-512
688	15.1-965.16, n.
689	59.1-200, 59.1-415 to 59.1-423
690	18.2-249, 19.2-386.1 to 19.2-386.13
691	16.1-279
692	29.1-416
693	54.1-1806
694	58.1-3506
695	2.1-1.7, 2.1-20.4, 2.1-51.15, 2.1-553.2R, 9-6.25:2, 9-281 to 9-291
696	32.1-176.5
697	15.1-491.2:1
698	8.01-66.1
699	32.1-127
700	23-135.7:14 to 23-135.7:19
701	58.1-2101, 58.1-2105, 58.1-2116
702	8.01-420.01
703	59.1-200, 59.1-424 to 59.1-428
704	42.1-63, 42.1-65
705	18.2-204.2, 18.2-269, 18.2-270, 18.2-271, 18.2-271.1, 19.2-258.1, 46.1-1, 46.1-15, 46.1-31, 46.1-167.5, 46.1-254.2, 46.1-351, 46.1-355, 46.1-355.1, 46.1-356, 46.1-357, 46.1-357.2, 46.1-365, 46.1-368, 46.1-370, 46.1-370.2R, 46.1-371, 46.1-372.1 to 46.1-372.32, 46.1-373, 46.1-374R, 46.1-375, 46.1-380.1, 46.1-380.2, 46.1-387.2, 46.1-392, 46.1-412.1, 46.1-413, 46.1-413.1, 46.1-417, 46.1-421, 46.1-563, 56-334
706	46.1-65
707	18.2-322.1
708	46.1-211.1
709	18.2-255.2
710	2.1-504.4
711	2.1-394.1, 10.1-812, 10.1-813, 10.1-814
712	46.1-169.2
713	58.1-816
714	25-238 to 25-247
715	15.1-14.2
716	37.1-67.1, 37.1-67.3
717	16.1-285.1
718	15.1-48.1
719	19.2-54, 19.2-56
720	62.1-44.15:5
721	62.1-242 to 62.1-253
722	46.1-326.7
723	9-156, 9-157, 9-157.1, 9-158, 9-160, 9-163
724	19.2-132.1
725	16.1-248.1, 16.1-274, 16.1-279, 16.1-292
726	19.2-81, 29.1-738 to 29.1-738.5
727	33.1-12, 33.1-345, 46.2-100 to 46.2-1610
728	38.2-231
729	8.01-581.13, 8.01-581.16, 8.01-581.19, 8.01-581.19:1, 8.01-581.20
730	8.01-581.1
731	16.1-279
732	58.1-608
733	2.1-1.1, 2.1-1.3, 2.1-1.6, 2.1-20.4, 2.1-51.18, 2.1-121, 2.1-700, 2.1-701, 2.1-703, 9-6.25:2, 9-168, 9-268, 9-271, 16.1-222, 16.1-228, 16.1-233, 16.1-238, 16.1-240, 16.1-241, 16.1-246, 16.1-275, 16.1-279, 16.1-284.1, 16.1-286, 16.1-287, 16.1-294, 16.1-295, 16.1-300, 16.1-309, 16.1-310, 16.1-311, 16.1-318, 18.2-64.1, 18.2-473, 18.2-477.1, 18.2-480.1, 20-48, 20-49, 22.1-340, 22.1-341, 23-35.3, 29.1-317, 36-99.4, 53.1-31, 53.1-237 to 53.1-260R, 54.1-2969, 63.1-248.16, 63.1-314.3, 66-1 to 66-35
734	9-6.14:16, 63.1-119
735	15.1-783.01
736	64.1-57
738	19.2-271
739	30-19.05, 30-19.1:3, 58.1-602, 58.1-608, 58.1-608.1, 58.1-610
740	16.1-279, 20-103, 20-107.2
741	23-7.1:01
742	58.1-3650.321 to 58.1-3650.324, n.
743	24.1-49
744	33.1-46.2

Acts 1989 Chapter	Code 1950 Section
745	52-4.4, 18.2-308.2:2
746	32.1-343 to 32.1-350, 63.1-134 to 63.1-140R
747	32.1-332 to 32.1-342
748	15.1-491.8
749	58.1-322, 58.1-330
751	6.1-13, 6.1-390, 6.1-391, 6.1-392.1, 6.1-394, 6.1-394.1, 6.1-397

ACTS 1989, SP. SESS.

Acts 1989, Sp. Sess. Chapter	Code 1950 Section
1	58.1-1823
2	58.1-1823
3	51-111.15, 51-112, 51-127.7, 51-180R, 58.1-322, 58.1-330
4	6.1-13, 6.1-392.1, 6.1-394.1
5	23-70, 23-72
6	58.1-1823
7	6.1-13, 6.1-392.1, 6.1-394.1
9	33.1-268, 33.1-269, 33.1-276, 33.1-277
11	33.1-268, 33.1-269, 33.1-276, 33.1-277

ACTS 1990

Acts 1990 Chapter	Code 1950 Section
1	2.1-51.16 to 2.1-51.18, 2.1-51.41 to 2.1-51.43, 9-95.6, 18.2-271.2, 33.1-1, 33.1-3, 33.1-407, 37.1-207, 44-146.18:2, 46.2-200, 46.2-223, 46.2-224, 46.2-1502, 66-2
2	62.1-44.15:5, n.
3	2.1-210, 2.1-329, 6.1-2.9:4, 6.1-194.2, 6.1-194.3, 6.1-194.12, 6.1-194.18, 6.1-194.23, 6.1-194.32 to 6.1-194.33, 6.1-194.41, 6.1-194.45, 6.1-194.48, 6.1-194.50, 6.1-194.53, 6.1-194.62, 6.1-194.69, 6.1-194.83, 6.1-194.87, 6.1-194.91, 6.1-194.94, 6.1-194.98, 6.1-194.100, 6.1-194.108, 6.1-195.86, 6.1-216, 6.1-226.8, 6.1-330.70, 8.01-583, 8.01-600, 15.1-1580, 26-40, 26-45.2, 38.2-1432, 51.1-122, 54.1-1119, 54.1-2113, 59.1-335.2
4	6.1-410, 6.1-428
5	13.1-501, 13.1-505
6	13.1-514
7	6.1-2.9, 6.1-2.9:1, 6.1-2.9:3
8	6.1-416
9	8.1-105, 8.4A-101 to 8.4A-108, 8.4A-201 to 8.4A-212, 8.4A-301 to 8.4A-305, 8.4A-401 to 8.4A-406, 8.4A-501 to 8.4A-507
10	38.2-1222 to 38.2-1224
11	11-41.2:1
12	10.1-1455
13	62.1-44.32
14	62.1-44.15:3
15	54.1-3425
18	15.1-291, 15.1-874
19	15.1-446.1, 15.1-489
20	46.2-1001
22	10.1-1201, n.
23	45.1-288, 45.1-318 to 45.1-320, 45.1-357.1 to 45.1-357.5
24	52-8.4
25	16.1-133
27	19.2-16
31	13.1-521, 13.1-570
32	6.1-420
34	56-304.13
36	33.1-75.3
38	15.1-600.1
39	46.2-1167
40	58.1-2403, n.
41	46.2-1572
42	58.1-3122.1
43	15.1-136.2, 15.1-136.3, 15.1-136.5:1, 15.1-136.6:1
44	15.1-18.3
45	46.2-100
46	58.1-3303
48	42.1-48
49	54.1-500, 54.1-501
50	2.1-526.12, 2.1-526.14:1
51	2.1-639.9
52	32.1-113
53	2.1-511
54	23-19
55	55-248.4
56	15.1-131.11
57	18.2-340.6
58	15.1-14
59	37.1-67.3
60	37.1-67.3
61	15.1-431
62	15.1-1167.1
63	14.1-46.01:1
64	64.1-87.1, 64.1-87.2
65	26-17.1
66	26-44.1
68	15.1-137.3
69	27-97
70	58.1-3406
71	2.1-133.4
72	54.1-907
73	54.1-500 to 54.1-503
74	19.2-317.1R
75	16.1-129.1R
76	19.2-169.6, 19.2-176
77	8.01-420.3
78	46.2-1222
79	46.2-604
80	8.01-6
82	18.2-248
83	46.2-1569
84	46.2-1581
85	63.1-274.4
87	15.1-50, 15.1-1377
88	14.1-112
89	8.9-403
90	13.1-509, 13.1-512, n.
91	23-7.1:01
92	45.1-1.5, 45.1-92R, 45.1-92.1, 45.1-286 to 45.1-361R, 45.1-361.1 to 45.1-361.40
94	37.1-71
95	44-146.17
96	18.2-340.6
97	15.1-447
98	9-168
99	8.01-413
100	19.2-390
101	63.1-236.1
102	32.1-81
103	32.1-122.02
104	54.1-3000, 54.1-3005
105	54.1-514
106	23-49.28
107	53.1-60, 53.1-131
108	4-30
109	16.1-86,

Acts 1990 Chapter	Code 1950 Section
	16.1-86.1R
110	16.1-292
111	22.1-30
112	16.1-69.6:1
113	17-119.1:2
114	17-119.1:2
115	29.1-307
117	58.1-608
120	3.1-22.35
121	46.2-1220
122	9-145.8 to 9-145.10, 9-145.9, n.
123	29.1-567
124	57-5
125	15.1-24.1
126	58.1-3713, n.
127	10.1-1102
128	58.1-3650.357, n.
129	58.1-3650.358, n.
130	58.1-3650.359, n.
131	58.1-3650.360, n.
132	58.1-3650.361, n.
133	58.1-3650.362, n.
134	58.1-3650.363, n.
135	58.1-3650.364, n.
136	58.1-3650.365, n., 58.1-3650.366, n.
137	58.1-3650.367, n.
138	58.1-3650.368, n.
139	58.1-3650.369, n.
140	58.1-3650.370, n.
141	58.1-3650.356, n.
142	58.1-3650.371, n.
143	58.1-3650.372, n.
144	58.1-3650.373, n., 58.1-3650.374, n.
145	58.1-3650.375, n.
146	58.1-2660, 58.1-2670
147	58.1-3650.376, n.
148	58.1-3650.377, n.
149	58.1-3650.378, n.
150	58.1-3650.379, n.
151	58.1-3510
152	58.1-3901
154	28.1-165
155	15.1-11.01
156	24.1-258
158	58.1-3213
159	46.2-342
160	33.1-190.1
161	46.2-1053
162	58.1-3111
163	58.1-2424
164	58.1-3510.1, 58.1-3510.3
165	58.1-3713.4
166	33.1-62, n.
167	46.2-1001
168	28.1-46.4
169	15.1-489
170	15.1-466
171	15.1-475
172	15.1-11.5:1
173	2.1-1.6, 9-6.25:1, 10.1-410.1
175	15.1-171.1
176	15.1-466
177	15.1-11
178	11-41.2:1
179	62.1-69.1 to 62.1-69.4R
180	56-540, 56-546
181	46.2-752
182	18.2-340.6
183	3.1-684.12, 3.1-684.14
184	15.1-29.9
185	53.1-106
186	15.1-381
187	46.2-752
188	46.2-752
189	22.1-98, n.
190	33.1-151, 33.1-152
191	32.1-102.3:2
192	63.1-85.4:1, 63.1-85.5
193	24.1-46
194	54.1-103
195	46.2-1142.1
196	10.1-1172, 33.1-355, 58.1-1610
197	46.2-1521, 46.2-1546, 46.2-1548, 46.2-1575 to 46.2-1578, 46.2-1601
198	33.1-166.1
199	24.1-176
200	24.1-229.1
201	24.1-31.1
202	63.1-220.2
203	33.1-253, n.
204	62.1-163
205	22.1-214
206	59.1-378
207	46.2-1207
208	55-48
209	53.1-131.2
210	10.1-1602
211	3.1-418.1
212	28.1-53
213	22.1-98, n.
214	24.1-217
215	54.1-1120
216	58.1-2704
217	2.1-342, 2.1-346, 16.1-77, 16.1-83, 16.1-106
218	46.2-341.4, 46.2-341.16, 46.2-341.20,
	46.2-341.21, 46.2-341.25, 46.2-341.26, 46.2-341.31, 46.2-936
219	9-6.14:14.1
220	53.1-151, n.
221	53.1-40.8, 53.1-40.9
222	3.1-796.116
223	38.2-3304
224	38.2-4300, 38.2-4303, 38.2-4307.1, 38.2-4310, 38.2-4315, 38.2-4317.1
225	10.1-415
226	40.1-51.8, 40.1-51.13, 40.1-51.19
227	13.1-647
228	13.1-654, 13.1-677
229	13.1-730
230	13.1-719
231	10.1-1307
234	38.2-5001
235	10.1-1321.1
236	38.2-3700
237	29.1-521
238	10.1-1300, 10.1-1303, 10.1-1307.1 to 10.1-1307.3, 10.1-1310.1, 10.1-1314.1, 10.1-1320.1
239	15.1-131.9
240	38.2-1300
241	38.2-2229
242	33.1-96
243	19.2-266
244	38.2-5018
245	58.1-2706, 58.1-2711
246	8.01-40.2
247	6.1-194.84:1
248	13.1-425
249	16.1-218, 17-228
250	46.2-1571
252	13.1-728.1, 13.1-728.2
253	1-13.35:1
254	15.1-600.1
255	3.1-418.1
256	37.1-62.1, n.
257	16.1-248.1
258	8.01-331, 16.1-69.55, 16.1-305 to 16.1-307, 17-28, 19.2-240
259	6.1-371, 6.1-372, 6.1-374, 6.1-375, 6.1-378.1, 6.1-379R

Acts 1990 Chapter	Code 1950 Section
260	6.1-363.1
261	6.1-277
262	55-19.3, n.
263	13.1-517, 13.1-566
264	55-34.1 to 55-34.19
265	38.2-502, 38.2-516
266	46.2-1233.1
267	13.1-662
268	38.2-3608
269	54.1-3313
270	54.1-3434.1 to 54.1-3434.4
271	59.1-369
272	59.1-364, n., 59.1-370.1
273	23-7.5, n.
274	37.1-67.6
275	38.2-1905
276	8.01-465.6 to 8.01-465.13
277	22.1-218
278	58.1-3730.1
279	16.1-88.2
280	8.01-229
281	38.2-310
282	13.1-695, 13.1-874
283	13.1-766.1, 13.1-928.1
284	38.2-3418.1
285	38.2-5200 to 38.2-5205, 38.2-5207, 38.2-5208
286	38.2-5206
287	15.1-466
288	37.1-207
289	58.1-811
290	38.2-1910
291	22.1-253.13:7
292	13.1-706
293	38.2-2114
294	58.1-302, n.
295	22.1-3.1, 22.1-288.1, 32.1-275.2, 52-31.1
296	58.1-3245 to 58.1-3245.2, 58.1-3245.4, 58.1-3245.5
297	63.1-236.1
298	15.1-37.3:11
299	15.1-1399.10, 15.1-1399.14, 15.1-1399.16, 15.1-1399.17
300	4-25.1, 4-33, 4-98.18, 4-104
301	38.2-3542, 38.2-4214, 38.2-4319
303	3.1-418.1
306	65.1-104.2
307	54.1-3205.1, 54.1-3215
308	63.1-55.3
309	54.1-3408
310	2.1-1.8, n., 2.1-116.15 to 2.1-116.17, n.
311	37.1-183.2, 37.1-189.1
312	15.1-1374, 15.1-1375
313	24.1-59
314	62.1-195.2
315	22.1-275.1
316	19.2-264.4
317	2.1-51.16 to 2.1-51.18, 2.1-51.41 to 2.1-51.43, 9-95.6, 18.2-271.2, 33.1-1, 33.1-3, 33.1-407, 37.1-207, 44-146.18:2, 46.2-200, 46.2-223, 46.2-224, 46.2-1502, 66-2
318	54.1-507
319	46.2-749
320	8.01-413
321	29.1-702, 29.1-702.1, 29.1-711
322	3.1-796.115
323	15.1-687.18
324	15.1-133.01:1
325	13.1-758, 13.1-920
326	15.1-1167.1
327	15.1-140.1, 18.2-414.2
328	55-66.4:1
329	46.2-1572.1
330	58.1-3516
331	38.2-4214.1, 38.2-4408.1, 38.2-4509.1
332	38.2-316
333	38.2-3126, 38.2-3127
334	38.2-4609
335	58.1-492
336	32.1-297.1, n.
337	13.1-671.1, 13.1-673
338	6.1-330.77, n., 6.1-330.84, n., 6.1-330.85, n., 6.1-330.86:1, n., 6.1-330.89, n.
339	56-484.2
340	6.1-2.10
341	15.1-1637 to 15.1-1642, 15.1-1645, 15.1-1646
342	32.1-163
343	50-37.1, 50-73.1, 50-73.11:1, 50-73.12, 50-73.13, 50-73.15, 50-73.24, 50-73.28, 50-73.51, 50-73.56, 50-73.57:1, 50-73.61, 50-74
344	59.1-338, 59.1-338.1
345	54.1-810R 54.1-812,
346	59.1-426
347	3.1-385.1 to 3.1-385.8
348	38.2-1309
349	58.1-608.1
350	2.1-1.1, 2.1-1.6, 2.1-20.4, 9-6.25:2, 66-1
351	59.1-402
352	4-96
353	2.1-563.32
354	9-182
355	8.01-391
357	59.1-426
358	63.1-248.16
359	59.1-148.3
360	10.1-1408.1
362	15.1-14.2
363	54.1-2806, 54.1-2813
364	2.1-548.15R, 28.1-22.1, 28.1-22.2
365	3.1-796.88, 3.1-796.92
366	59.1-400
367	2.1-548.13
368	40.1-51.4:3
369	3.1-1021, 3.1-1025, 29.1-563
370	3.1-188.27, 3.1-188.27:1
371	29.1-100
372	45.1-95
373	6.1-196 to 6.1-225, 6.1-225.1 to 6.1-225.63
374	17-59, 17-60, 17-79, 55-48, 55-58
376	19.2-163.2
377	19.2-163.2
378	19.2-163.2
379	32.1-135.2, 37.1-186.1, 54.1-2962.1
380	15.1-116
381	2.1-1.6, 9-6.25:1, 10.1-415.1
382	15.1-292.1, n., 15.1-295

Acts 1990 Chapter	Code 1950 Section
383	32.1-324.1
384	5.1-25.1, 15.1-489, 15.1-491.02
385	63.1-75.1, 63.1-142
386	9-272, 9-272.1
387	9-203, 9-204
388	22.1-302
389	32.1-325.1:1
390	4-25.1, 4-33, 4-98.18, 4-104
391	32.1-122.06
392	59.1-296 to 59.1-299, 59.1-306, 59.1-308 to 59.1-308.2
393	38.2-3419.1, 38.2-4214, 38.2-4319
394	32.1-335
395	11-45, 32.1-325
396	58.1-3650.380 to 58.1-3650.382, n.
397	10.1-411.1
399	58.1-608
400	58.1-3650.383, n.
402	4-98.2, 4-98.7
403	58.1-608
404	44-146.19
405	58.1-3650.384, n.
406	58.1-608
407	58.1-3650.385, n., 58.1-3650.386, n.
408	29.1-606
409	37.1-142, 64.1-190, 64.1-191, 64.1-193
410	56-265.13:6
411	22.1-132.1
412	8.9-403 to 8.9-406
413	18.2-308.6
414	8.01-582, 8.01-600
415	22.1-132.1
416	58.1-334, 58.1-337, 58.1-432, 58.1-436
417	65.1-52
418	46.2-100, 46.2-321, 46.2-687, 46.2-1061, 46.2-1131, 46.2-1168, 46.2-1220
420	13.1-559
421	15.1-116
422	2.1-1.6, 9-6.25:1, 10.1-415.1
423	13.1-638, 13.1-646
424	15.1-1135
425	34-34, 55-19
426	18.2-154
427	45.1-270.4:1
428	13.1-757
429	37.1-67.1
430	10.1-1418.1
431	56-265.13:6
432	23-7.1:01
433	59.1-296 to 59.1-296.3, 59.1-297 to 59.1-299, 59.1-306, 59.1-308 to 59.1-308.2
434	57-35.11, 57-35.11:1, 57-35.14, 57-35.19, 57-35.20, 57-35.24, 57-35.26, 57-35.27, 57-35.35
435	2.1-344
436	58.1-3821, n.
437	54.1-1118 to 54.1-1120, 54.1-1123
438	32.1-164
439	38.2-3419.1, 38.2-4214, 38.2-4319
440	32.1-335
441	54.1-2722
442	4-98.16
443	18.2-340.4
444	22.1-213
445	28.1-48
446	28.1-173R, 28.1-173.3
447	23-31
448	36-99.5:1
449	11-47.2, 15.1-11.5:01
450	22.1-290
451	22.1-89.2
452	18.2-102.2
454	18.2-138
455	46.2-752
456	59.1-390
457	9-77.4
458	2.1-1.1, 2.1-1.3, 2.1-51.15, 2.1-373.4, 2.1-700, 2.1-703.1, 9-6.25:2, 51.5-1, 51.5-2, 51.5-31, 51.5-33 to 51.5-37, 51.5-40, 51.5-46, 63.1-182.1, 63.1-314.3
459	2.1-1.6, 2.1-20.4, 9-6.25:2, 54.1-300, 54.1-2009 to 54.1-2011, 54.1-2013 to 54.1-2019
460	55-210.13
461	36-55.39
463	30-28.5:1
464	38.2-1805, 38.2-1809, 38.2-1816, 38.2-1817, 38.2-1836
465	9-6.25:1, 56-484.4 to 56-484.7
466	2.1-1.6, 2.1-20.4, 9-6.25:2, 46.2-1700 to 46.2-1703, 54.1-300, 54.1-1000 to 54.1-1003R
467	2.1-234.32, 2.1-234.34
468	32.1-163.3
469	15.1-1374
470	46.2-920.1
471	16.1-77
472	10.1-1406
473	15.1-499.1
474	19.2-316.1, 53.1-67.1
475	15.1-493
476	24.1-110, 24.1-167
477	38.2-3420 to 38.2-3424.1
478	32.1-102.3:2
479	58.1-3211
481	13.1-543
482	56-304 to 56-304.2, 56-304.11, 56-338.26
483	56-304.5, 58.1-2654, 58.1-2654.1
484	2.1-526.8
485	30-19.7R, 30-28.10:1R, 30-28.16
486	58.1-3211
487	38.2-1905.1, 38.2-1912
488	13.1-620, 56-232, 56-265.1, 56-265.4:5
490	2.1-114.5:1
491	10.1-560
492	58.1-3814.1
493	28.1-173.1
494	28.1-52
495	15.1-499.1
496	46.2-1168
498	38.2-5020, 38.2-5020.1
499	10.1-1400, 10.1-1402
500	15.1-37.5:1, 15.1-37.7, 15.1-788, 24.1-17R, 24.1-17.1R, 24.1-17.2, 24.1-17.3, 24.1-40.7, 24.1-40.9
501	15.1-326
502	46.2-1231 to 46.2-1233
503	38.2-1906.1
504	58.1-3211
505	33.1-252
506	62.1-198, 62.1-199,

Acts 1990 Chapter	Code 1950 Section
	62.1-204
507	58.1-322, 58.1-330R
508	46.2-694
509	33.1-252
510	18.2-127
511	53.1-150
512	54.1-400, 54.1-403, 54.1-412 to 54.1-415
513	15.1-2, n.
514	15.1-238
515	15.1-18.2, 15.1-18.3
516	2.1-234.9:1 to 2.1-234.9:4
517	22.1-65, 22.1-280.1
518	14.1-46.01
519	10.1-1415.1
520	10.1-1425.1 to 10.1-1425.5
521	28.1-45.1, 28.1-46R
522	46.2-1182
523	3.1-328
524	38.2-612
525	58.1-322, 58.1-330R
526	58.1-3650.387, n.
527	58.1-3650.388, n.
528	58.1-3650.389, n.
529	58.1-3650.390, n.
530	58.1-3650.391, n.
531	38.2-3407.1, 38.2-4214, 38.2-4319
532	58.1-3650.392, n.
533	58.1-3650.393, n.
534	38.2-5001, 38.2-5008
535	38.2-5002, 38.2-5008, 38.2-5009
536	9-268, 9-270, 9-271
537	63.1-26
538	2.1-340.1 to 2.1-343, 2.1-344, 53.1-136
539	46.2-1236, 46.2-1237
540	15.1-11.5:2
541	15.1-29.20
543	14.1-133.2
544	32.1-176.5
545	15.1-687.19
547	32.1-176.5
548	19.2-187.01
549	19.2-368.19 to 19.2-368.22
550	19.2-368.4
551	19.2-368.3
552	19.2-368.11:1
553	8.01-480, 58.1-3942
554	16.1-227
555	46.2-933
556	18.2-310
557	18.2-340.9
558	19.2-12
559	65.1-55
560	16.1-245.1
561	33.1-75.1
562	57-38.2
563	15.1-11.5:2
564	16.1-122.1, 16.1-122.3
565	16.1-77, n., 16.1-122.1, n.
566	17-27, 17-30
567	20-108.1
568	16.1-334, 16.1-334.1
569	20-121.4
570	11-2
571	46.2-1233, n.
572	19.2-265.1
573	46.2-1232, n., 46.2-1233, n.
574	10.1-1411
575	19.2-8
576	32.1-252
577	15.1-29.20
578	53.1-180
579	58.1-3321
580	62.1-44.34:11
581	62.1-44.34:11, 62.1-44.34:12
582	62.1-44.34:11
583	17-47.4
584	54.1-1505, 59.1-200
585	24.1-165.2
586	54.1-1200
587	11-33.1, 11-34
588	18.2-282
589	36-99.6:1
590	54.1-2404
591	15.1-491.8
592	59.1-189
593	36-85.3, 36-85.11, 36-99.8
594	18.2-308.2:2
595	13.1-543
596	38.2-1901, 38.2-1905.1, 38.2-1906, 38.2-1908, 38.2-1913, 38.2-1916 to 38.2-1916.2, 38.2-1923
597	38.2-1906, 38.2-1910, 38.2-1912
598	62.1-44.34:24 to 62.1-44.34:28
599	18.2-282
600	16.1-244
601	55-154.1R, n.
602	19.2-271
603	19.2-392.2
604	46.2-1231.1
605	15.1-37.3:12
606	65.1-147
607	2.1-20.1
608	15.1-11.5
609	15.1-37.3:12
610	65.1-56.1
612	22.1-132.1
613	33.1-252
614	40.1-118 to 40.1-121, 40.1-126
615	20-49.8
616	10.1-1425.6 to 10.1-1425.9
617	18.2-255.2
618	9-297 to 9-300
619	58.1-442
620	19.2-368.2
622	18.2-255.2
623	20-124
624	19.2-143
625	18.2-308.4
626	19.2-76.1
627	18.2-415
628	8.01-377.1
629	16.1-254
630	56-49
631	19.2-245.2
632	9-170
633	2.1-563.26, 15.1-456
634	9-297 to 9-300
635	16.1-246, 18.2-308.1, 19.2-81
636	20-107.3, n.
637	2.1-121
638	18.2-371.1
639	18.2-188.1
640	18.2-308
641	16.1-269
642	16.1-246
644	18.2-85
645	16.1-88.03
646	23-9.1:1
647	18.2-85
648	18.2-308
649	58.1-3650.394, n., 58.1-3650.395, n.
650	58.1-608
655	58.1-608
656	58.1-608, n.
657	58.1-608
659	58.1-1802.1
660	63.1-320, n.
661	32.1-176.5
662	55-79.74:1, 55-79.75, 55-79.97
663	18.2-152.4
664	15.1-439
665	43-32
666	58.1-1402, n.
667	58.1-3916
668	16.1-271
669	19.2-270.5, 19.2-310.2 to 19.2-310.7, 19.2-387, 53.1-23.1R
670	58.1-3734.1
671	58.1-3294
672	2.1-639.1, 15.1-491

Acts 1990 Chapter	Code 1950 Section
673	16.1-254
674	15.1-29.21
675	57-39.1
676	19.2-310, 53.1-20 to 53.1-21, 53.1-60, 53.1-131, 53.1-161, 53.1-184.2
677	58.1-3506
678	58.1-3
679	66-10, 66-30
680	23-7.4
681	54.1-3408.1
682	3.1-796.67:1
683	54.1-4011
684	53.1-151
685	15.1-430
686	46.2-1216
687	60.2-314, 60.2-519.2, 60.2-521, 60.2-633
688	2.1-511
689	33.1-223, 58.1-2111, 58.1-2113, 58.1-2146
690	58.1-3661
691	46.2-882
692	18.2-308.1:1, 18.2-308.2:1, 18.2-308.2:2, 19.2-390
693	58.1-3506
694	58.1-608, 62.1-145
695	58.1-3233
696	58.1-3916
697	19.2-175, 19.2-300, 19.2-301
700	58.1-905
701	19.2-311, 19.2-316, 53.1-63, 53.1-64, 53.1-66, 53.1-67, 19.2-312R
702	58.1-3916
703	36-99.5:1
704	16.1-228, 16.1-241, 16.1-279
705	58.1-3518
706	51.1-1000 to 51.1-1003
707	4-2, 4-25, 4-33, 4-38
708	15.1-466
709	58.1-338, 58.1-445.1
710	33.1-268, 33.1-269, 33.1-277
711	57-48, 57-49, 57-55.1R, 57-57, 57-59, 57-61, 57-61.1
712	2.1-179, 2.1-326.1
713	37.1-134.4
714	58.1-322, n.
715	58.1-1604, n., 58.1-1605, n., 58.1-1609 to 58.1-1611, n.
716	32.1-330
717	62.1-44.3, 62.1-44.5, 62.1-44.15, 62.1-44.23, 62.1-44.32
718	54.1-1706
719	15.1-482
720	18.2-255
721	2.1-342, 9-6.14:4.1, 32.1-331.1 to 32.1-331.5
722	15.1-1402, 15.1-1404, 15.1-1412, 15.1-1416.1, 36-140
723	59.1-284.1 to 59.1-284.6
724	8.01-416
725	46.2-1200.1
727	4-31, 4-105
728	37.1-67.1, 37.1-67.3
729	8.01-296
730	8.01-335
731	17-111.4
732	58.1-4007, 58.1-4017, 58.1-4021
733	2.1-20.4, 19.2-163.1
734	19.2-163.3
737	19.2-187
738	8.01-465.2, 14.1-112
739	17-111.6
740	63.1-73
741	8.01-326.1, 8.01-329
742	16.1-260
743	16.1-246
744	16.1-246, 18.2-308.1, 19.2-81
745	2.1-114.5:1
746	18.2-31
747	65.1-82
749	55-59.2
750	57-35.11, 57-35.11:1, 57-35.14, 57-35.19, 57-35.20, 57-35.24, 57-35.26, 57-35.27, 57-35.35
751	6.1-278
752	2.1-121, 9-173.6 to 9-173.13, 16.1-274
753	32.1-102.3:2
754	19.2-264.4
755	35.1-14.2
756	26-17.2
757	9-301 to 9-304
758	8.01-341, 8.01-345
759	15.1-1032.2
760	63.1-248.2
761	18.2-51.3
762	16.1-81
763	26-58
764	20-107.3, n.
765	9-271, 9-272
766	19.2-389, 22.1-296.2
767	8.01-296
768	19.2-310, 53.1-20 to 53.1-21, 53.1-60, 53.1-131, 53.1-161, 53.1-184.2
769	16.1-228, 16.1-251, 16.1-252
770	46.2-869
771	4-62, 4-112
772	59.1-207.11, 59.1-207.13, 59.1-207.15, 59.1-207.16
773	4-59, 4-101.1
774	59.1-371
775	16.1-279
776	59.1-310.1 to 59.1-310.6
777	32.1-36.1, 32.1-38
778	42.1-77 to 42.1-79, 42.1-80 to 42.1-82, 42.1-85 to 42.1-86.1
779	46.2-878
780	32.1-203
781	10.1-1400, 10.1-1408.1, 10.1-1411, 10.1-1422.2, 10.1-1455
782	64.1-57
783	54.1-4009, 54.1-4101
784	19.2-81
785	23-38.19:1, 23-38.19:2
786	46.2-1532.1
787	56-235.4
788	18.2-10, 18.2-11
789	65.1-88
790	44-97.1
791	2.1-121
792	22.1-199, n.
793	32.1-325
794	58.1-323.1, n.
795	38.2-3425 to 38.2-3430, 38.2-4214
796	23-7.1:01
797	16.1-279, 18.2-371, 22.1-17.1, 22.1-209, 22.1-209.1:1, 22.1-253.13:1, 22.1-254, 22.1-258, 22.1-262, 22.1-263, 22.1-265, 22.1-267, 22.1-274, 22.1-279R, 22.1-279.2, 22.1-280.1, 22.1-289, 22.1-344
798	37.1-67.3
799	29.1-509
800	22.1-290.1, 23-9.2:6R
801	63.1-195, 63.1-196,

Acts 1990 Chapter	Code 1950 Section
	63.1-196.1, 63.1-196.3, 63.1-198, 63.1-198.02 to 63.1-199, 63.1-201 to 63.1-202.1
802	38.2-3425 to 38.2-3430, 38.2-4214
803	22.1-217
804	32.1-126.2, 36-99.9
805	22.1-32
808	29.1-509
809	37.1-188.1
810	4-25.1
811	62.1-9.1, 62.1-13.4, 62.1-13.16:1, 62.1-13.18:2, 62.1-13.27:1
812	32.1-248.1
813	15.1-262, 15.1-480.1
814	15.1-486.2R, 15.1-486.3
815	2.1-234.13, 2.1-234.21
816	53.1-150
817	10.1-2212
818	54.1-2931
819	2.1-342, 32.1-112
820	22.1-253.13:1, 22.1-253.13:3 to 22.1-253.13:6, 22.1-253.13:8
821	58.1-816, n.
822	15.1-783.01
823	36-99.7, 54.1-500 to 54.1-502, 54.1-509, 54.1-511, 54.1-516, 54.1-517
824	11-62.1, 11-62.11
825	2.1-1.6, 2.1-384, 2.1-426, 2.1-427, 2.1-429, 2.1-429.1 to 2.1-429.3R, 2.1-431R, 2.1-432, 2.1-432.1, 2.1-432.2 to 2.1-434R, 2.1-434.1 to 2.1-434.12, 9-6.25:1, 18.2-253, 18.2-267, 18.2-268, 18.2-308, 19.2-187, 19.2-187.01, 29.1-738.2, 46.2-341.25, 46.2-341.26, 53.1-23.1, 54.1-3431
826	38.2-4214, 38.2-4319, 38.2-5300 to 38.2-5309
828	46.2-357, 46.2-360
830	36-55.63, 58.1-335, 58.1-336, 58.1-435
831	8.01-70, n., 8.01-71, n., 8.01-86, n., 8.01-157, n., 8.01-261, 31-45, 50-25, 55-20, 55-35, 55-40, n., 55-41, 55-42, n., 55-43, 55-44, 55-46, 55-52, 55-64, 55-79.48, 55-138, 55-269.1, 55-271, 55-275, n., 55-277, 55-403, 55-472, 58.1-3967, 64.1-1, 64.1-13, 64.1-14, 64.1-16 to 64.1-16.4, 64.1-19 to 64.1-44, n., 64.1-151.1 to 64.1-151.3, 64.1-151.6, 64.1-199
832	2.1-1.5, 2.1-20.4, 12.1-11.1, 14.1-39.1, 16.1-69.22:1, 17-7.01, 51-2.1 to 51-179R, 51.1-100 to 51.1-168, 51.1-200 to 51.1-209, 51.1-300 to 51.1-309, 51.1-400 to 51.1-405, 51.1-500 to 51.1-514, 51.1-600 to 51.1-605, 51.1-700 to 51.1-706, 51.1-800 to 51.1-823, 51.1-900, 65.1-10.1
833	9-145.11 to 9-145.15
834	15.1-491.8, 15.1-491.9
835	22.1-277.1
836	20-49.1, 20-60.5, 20-79.2, 32.1-261.1, 63.1-250.1, 63.1-274.6
837	53.1-95.2 to 53.1-95.24
838	65.1-4.1:1
839	22.1-253.13:1, 22.1-253.13:3 to 22.1-253.13:6, 22.1-253.13:8
840	15.1-486.4
841	58.1-3237
842	16.1-228, 16.1-279
843	58.1-3841
844	18.2-115.1
845	32.1-102.3:2
846	58.1-3833
847	58.1-3650.396, n.
849	58.1-2403, n.
853	58.1-3713.4
854	14.1-46.01:1
855	15.1-791.2, 15.1-791.6, 15.1-791.9, 15.1-791.11 to 15.1-791.14, 15.1-791.16, 15.1-1372.1 to 15.1-1372.6, 15.1-1372.7:1, 15.1-1372.8, 15.1-1372.10, 15.1-1372.12, 15.1-1372.13, 15.1-1372.18R, 15.1-1372.21 to 15.1-1372.26, 15.1-1372.28, 15.1-1372.30, 15.1-1372.32 to 15.1-1372.35
856	23-19
857	11-47.2, 15.1-11.5:01
858	58.1-3219 to 58.1-3219.3
859	32.1-336 to 32.1-339, 32.1-341
860	15.1-172, 15.1-175, 15.1-177, 15.1-177.1, 15.1-185, 15.1-199, 15.1-210.1
861	32.1-163, 32.1-164
862	58.1-3833
864	18.2-255
865	24.1-167
866	18.2-255
867	63.1-248.6:2
868	15.1-491, 15.1-491.2, 15.1-491.2:1
869	32.1-163, 32.1-164
870	52-8.4
871	58.1-3219 to 58.1-3219.3
872	15.1-172, 15.1-175, 15.1-177, 15.1-177.1, 15.1-185, 15.1-199, 15.1-210.1
873	32.1-336 to 32.1-339, 32.1-341
874	23-35.1 to 23-35.4, 23-35.5:1 to 23-35.8, 32.1-122.5 to 32.1-122.8
875	58.1-335R, n.
876	2.1-234.13
877	23-35.1 to 23-35.4, 23-35.5:1 to 23-35.8, 32.1-122.5 to 32.1-122.8
878	22.1-32
879	15.1-1372.21 to 15.1-1372.25, 15.1-1372.27 to 15.1-1372.29, 15.1-1372.32 to 15.1-1372.35
888	58.1-461, n., 58.1-462, n., 58.1-470, n.
889	58.1-608

Acts 1990 Chapter	Code 1950 Section
890	58.1-3822
891	46.2-1219.1
892	2.1-743, 2.1-744
893	38.2-1400, 38.2-1413
894	51-111.60:5, n., 51.1-169
895	15.1-527.3
896	16.1-279, 20-79.1 to 20-79.3, 63.1-250.3, 63.1-256, 63.1-258.1, 63.1-267.1, 63.1-268.1, 63.1-272
897	17-95.1, 17-116.05
898	8.01-225
899	19.2-353.3
900	46.2-1530
901	38.2-3411.1
902	15.1-291.1 to 15.1-291.11
903	18.2-340.1, 18.2-340.7
904	3.1-796.96:1
905	15.1-136.2, 15.1-136.3, 15.1-136.5:1, 15.1-136.6:1
906	15.1-465.1
907	59.1-21.9 to 59.1-21.13, 59.1-21.15, 59.1-21.16:2
908	60.2-229, 60.2-532, 60.2-602, 60.2-612
909	22.1-165, 22.1-166.1 to 22.1-168
910	58.1-316, 58.1-317
911	54.1-1100, 54.1-1101, 54.1-1103, 54.1-1105 to 54.1-1106.1, 54.1-1107R, 54.1-1107.1R, 54.1-1108 to 54.1-1112, 54.1-1114, 54.1-1115, 54.1-1118 to 54.1-1120, 54.1-1123, 54.1-1126
912	10.1-1455
913	18.2-346.1
915	63.1-314.3 to 63.1-314.6, 63.1-314.7R, 63.1-314.8
916	38.2-137, 38.2-401.1
917	62.1-44.34:1R to 62.1-44.34:6R, 62.1-44.34:11, 62.1-44.34:14 to 62.1-44.34:23, 62.1-195R
918	58.1-3967
919	10.1-1400, 10.1-1402, 10.1-1405, 10.1-1406, 10.1-1408.1, 10.1-1409, 10.1-1455
920	2.1-1.6, 2.1-20.4, 9-6.25:1, 54.1-2954.1 to 54.1-2956
923	58.1-3650.397, n.
926	9-305 to 9-309
927	37.1-110, 55-19, 55-19.1R
928	46.2-873
929	18.2-268, 29.1-738.2, 46.2-341.26
930	57-55.3
931	24.1-258.1, n.
932	4-2, 4-61, 4-78, 4-112.3
933	18.2-137
934	53.1-116, 53.1-124
935	58.1-3957
936	18.2-287.2
937	2.1-114.5:1, 2.1-116
938	55-171, 55-173, 55-175, 55-176, 55-182.1, 55-186, 55-187, 55-188R, 55-189, 55-190.1, 55-194
939	22.1-132.1
940	46.2-1516
941	6.1-330.85:1, n.
942	34-1, 34-3, 34-4 to 34-6, 34-13, 34-14, 34-17 to 34-19, 34-21, 34-26, 34-28.1, 38.2-3123
943	14.1-125, 16.1-82
944	18.2-310
945	44-146.19, 44-146.21
947	33.1-267 to 33.1-269, 33.1-271, 33.1-273, 33.1-276 to 33.1-279.1, 33.1-282 to 33.1-285, 33.1-287 to 33.1-291, 33.1-293
948	18.2-258, 18.2-258.01
949	18.2-271, 18.2-271.1, 46.2-389, 46.2-391
950	6.1-125.3, 63.1-256, 63.1-260.1
951	18.2-286.1
952	54.1-518 to 54.1-525
953	58.1-339, n.
954	46.2-1547, 46.2-1575
955	46.2-1014.1, 46.2-1055.1
956	36-55.30, 36-55.34:2, 36-55.36:1
957	18.2-62
958	32.1-43 to 32.1-45, 32.1-48.01 to 32.1-48.04, 32.1-51R, 32.1-52R
959	32.1-289 to 32.1-291, 32.1-292R, 32.1-292.1, 32.1-294R
960	38.2-1905, 38.2-2212
961	15.1-11.5
962	62.1-44.34:2 to 62.1-44.34:4
963	2.1-1.6, 9-6.25:1, 45.1-5, 45.1-5.2, 45.1-5.3, 45.1-104, 45.1-33.7R to 45.1-33.12R
964	46.2-105.1
965	18.2-388
966	54.1-2956.6 to 54.1-2956.8
967	45.1-361.41, 62.1-195.1
968	2.1-342, 9-6.14:4.1, 32.1-331.6 to 32.1-331.11
969	15.1-291.1 to 15.1-291.11
970	2.1-1.6, 9-6.25:1, 22.1-305.2, 22.1-299.1R
971	14.1-112, 14.1-123, 14.1-133.3, 15.1-131.12
972	2.1-457, n., 2.1-512, n.
973	15.1-466
974	46.2-882
975	16.1-241, 16.1-246, 16.1-275, 16.1-280, 16.1-335 to 16.1-348, 37.1-61, 66-20
976	19.2-8, 24.1-256, 24.1-262

ACTS 1990, SP. SESS.

Acts 1990, Sp. Sess. Chapter	Code 1950 Section
1	58.1-4021

ACTS 1991

Acts 1991 Chapter	Code 1950 Section
2	19.2-83.1
3	24.1-233.1
4	38.2-124, 38.2-2201
5	63.1-124.3
6	15.1-1374, 15.1-1375, 15.1-1378, 15.1-1379

Acts 1991 Chapter	Code 1950 Section
7	18.2-10
8	58.1-3109, 58.1-3903, 58.1-3980, 58.1-3984
9	24.1-254.1, 24.1-255, 24.1-257.1, 24.1-257.3
10	24.1-60
11	24.1-202.1 to 24.1-202.10R
12	15.1-18.2
13	18.2-248
16	15.1-640
19	8.01-380
20	17-119.1:2
23	8.01-195.2, 8.01-195.4, 8.01-195.5, 8.01-195.6, 8.01-195.8, 15.1-1371
24	8.01-465.14 to 8.01-465.25
25	15.1-505, 15.1-901
26	16.1-79
27	14.1-11.1
28	15.1-21
29	15.1-18.2
30	15.1-466
31	17-93.1, 17-116.01
32	32.1-246.1
33	63.1-55.3
34	63.1-56, 63.1-204
35	15.1-1416
36	15.1-646, n.
37	32.1-297.1
38	19.2-267
39	8.01-428
41	19.2-3.1, 19.2-82
42	24.1-49
43	19.2-299, 53.1-185
44	2.1-1.7, 2.1-335.1, 2.1-335.2, 2.1-335.3, 9-6.25:1
45	54.1-501
46	14.1-90
47	15.1-466
48	36-148.1
49	36-100
50	42.1-32.7
51	54.1-803R
53	27-97
54	27-4, 27-23.6
55	46.2-808
56	8.01-28
57	15.1-261.1
58	64.1-166
59	9-168
60	20-103, 20-107.2
61	58.1-3516
62	16.1-264
63	58.1-3211
64	18.2-272, 46.2-301
65	3.1-796.105
66	62.1-44.34:25
67	15.1-1513.3, 15.1-1513.9
69	58.1-3233
70	29.1-101
71	7.1-40.4
73	11-41
74	19.2-12
75	8.01-384.2
76	63.1-221
77	3.1-796.86
78	14.1-195.2
79	22.1-340
80	9-6.14:4.1, 23-9.6:2
81	8.01-420.4
82	29.1-702, 29.1-718
83	10.1-1504
84	2.1-1.6, 9-6.25:1, 9-6.25:2, 10.1-105 to 10.1-107, 10.1-206R, 10.1-603.1, n., 10.1-603.2, 10.1-603.4, 10.1-603.7, 10.1-1202
85	18.2-287.3
86	37.1-89
87	38.2-3538, 38.2-4229.1
88	38.2-1822
89	64.1-7.1
90	56-46.1
92	46.2-1571
93	32.1-5
94	32.1-127.2R
95	32.1-257.1, 32.1-261.1R
96	23-164.5
97	8.01-55, 8.01-424, 65.1-93
98	16.1-281, 16.1-282
99	29.1-529
100	46.2-1052
101	10.1-1424.1
102	54.1-2903, 54.1-2938R
103	38.2-3411.2, 38.2-4319
104	38.2-1904
105	46.2-1023
106	46.2-1150
107	46.2-1157
108	46.2-746.1
109	13.1-718
110	13.1-900
111	54.1-2947, 54.1-2948
112	13.1-675
113	46.2-749.1
114	62.1-13.28, n.
115	46.2-216.1
116	38.2-2212
117	46.2-1535
118	46.2-302
119	46.2-853
120	38.2-3603
121	3.1-796.112
123	12.1-18, 12.1-19, 12.1-20, 12.1-22R, 13.1-617, 13.1-817R
124	13.1-679, 13.1-680, 13.1-682, 13.1-695, 13.1-859, 13.1-860, 13.1-862, 13.1-874
125	13.1-752, 13.1-768, 13.1-914, 13.1-930
126	5.1-1.6, 5.1-7
127	6.1-1.1
128	12.1-15
130	54.1-306
131	18.2-271.1
132	13.1-852.1
133	32.1-46
134	32.1-122.6
135	16.1-77
136	24.1-49
137	24.1-91, 24.1-166, 24.1-167
138	22.1-199
139	22.1-207.2
140	22.1-30
141	54.1-3408
143	15.1-686.01, 15.1-687.4, 15.1-687.16, 15.1-687.20, 15.1-687.21
144	8.01-217
145	8.01-391
146	13.1-695
147	26-27
148	56-46.1
149	59.1-296
150	19.2-163.2
151	54.1-1105R, 54.1-1111
152	36-98.3, 40.1-128 to 40.1-134R

Acts 1991 Chapter	Code 1950 Section
153	40.1-49.4
154	59.1-415, 59.1-417
155	8.01-66.1
156	59.1-206
157	6.1-330.71
159	16.1-336, 16.1-338 to 16.1-341, 16.1-346, 16.1-346.1, 37.1-67.1
160	6.1-63 to 6.1-66
161	37.1-151.1, 37.1-155
162	19.2-73.1
163	22.1-30
164	58.1-3713
165	46.2-1012
166	65.1-38
167	46.2-214
168	13.1-1000 to 13.1-1069
169	46.2-1161.1
170	6.1-225.64
171	6.1-330.84, 6.1-330.85, 6.1-330.86:1, 6.1-330.89
172	15.1-295
173	58.1-346.3
174	54.1-4101, 54.1-4101.1
175	11-45
176	57-35.12
177	16.1-69.35
178	22.1-1, 22.1-19, 22.1-201, 22.1-204, 22.1-207, 22.1-208.1
179	58.1-346.4
181	54.1-2205, 54.1-2206
182	22.1-50
183	20-88.14, 20-88.26:1, 63.1-268.1
184	57-60
185	55-248.46, 55-248.50
186	2.1-114.5:1
187	58.1-3912
188	10.1-502
189	15.1-21.1, 15.1-965.24:1, 15.1-1131.1, 15.1-1135, 17-116.1, 17-117, 17-119.1:1, 17-126.7, 24.1-90.2, 52-11.2
190	3.1-27.5, 9-202, 10.1-1800, 10.1-2401
191	22.1-177
192	53.1-79.1
193	46.2-1075.1
194	15.1-320, 62.1-44.18, 62.1-44.18:1R, 62.1-44.19
195	32.1-11.3
196	32.1-11.4
197	64.1-96.1
198	15.1-486.4
199	59.1-21.11
200	29.1-534, 29.1-535
201	15.1-499.2
202	19.2-349
203	17-79
204	17-79
205	55-248.4
206	36-55.33:2
207	36-55.37:1
208	15.1-1405
209	10.1-1415.2
210	58.1-323.1
211	2.1-1.6, 2.1-51.9:1, 9-6.25:1
212	2.1-1.7, 9-6.25:1, 9-95.1 to 9-95.4R
213	2.1-342
214	9-6.14:14.1, 46.2-334, 46.2-1701.1, 46.2-1702 to 46.2-1707
215	38.2-2212.1
216	65.1-87.1
217	51.1-126
218	53.1-124
219	46.2-1221
220	59.1-142
221	46.2-1231
223	13.1-501, 13.1-504, 13.1-511, 13.1-512, 13.1-514
224	46.2-1313
225	50-73.5
226	19.2-194, 19.2-195
227	2.1-121.2
228	6.1-194.40, 13.1-716
229	19.2-299
230	6.1-194.109 to 6.1-194.154
231	15.1-1357
232	18.2-31
233	15.1-491.2:1
234	15.1-20.3 to 15.1-20.6, 15.1-53 to 15.1-62R
235	15.1-493
236	8.01-631.1
237	10.1-1411
238	18.2-57.2
239	62.1-44.15
240	58.1-3370
241	18.2-160.1
242	29.1-311
243	58.1-3968
244	20-99
245	2.1-234.9:1, 2.1-234.9:2
246	62.1-140
247	58.1-3506
249	60.2-528
250	33.1-72.1, 33.1-75.1
251	33.1-210.1R
252	6.1-24
253	58.1-3503
254	6.1-2.10
255	58.1-3503
256	8.01-26, 34-5, 34-28.1
257	8.01-424
258	16.1-322.5, 16.1-322.6, 16.1-322.7
259	20-97
260	15.1-151
261	38.2-1028, 38.2-1029, 38.2-1030, 38.2-1031, 38.2-1037, 38.2-1038, 38.2-1045, 38.2-1206, 38.2-1207, 38.2-1213
262	16.1-232
263	13.1-620, 56-232.2, 56-265.1
264	38.2-1316.1 to 38.2-1316.8, 38.2-1316R
265	15.1-292.3
266	36-107.1
267	58.1-3700
268	18.2-255.2
269	38.2-613.1
270	15.1-50.1, 15.1-821
271	58.1-3958
272	56-536, 56-539 to 56-544, 56-549, 56-551
273	22.1-298
275	65.1-88
277	65.1-4.1

Acts 1991 Chapter	Code 1950 Section
278	53.1-131.2
279	22.1-32
280	15.1-447
281	13.1-504, 13.1-505
282	6.1-32.2, 6.1-32.3, 6.1-32.8, 6.1-32.9, 6.1-399
283	38.2-1411.1
284	46.2-1001
285	28.1-120
286	58.1-3213
287	58.1-339.1, 58.1-437
288	15.1-466
289	10.1-1200, 10.1-1208, 10.1-1210
290	54.1-3200
291	54.1-403, 54.1-413, 54.1-414
292	38.2-2114.1
293	3.1-22.28
294	3.1-726, 9-6.14:4.1
295	18.2-371, n., 22.1-17.1, 22.1-209, 22.1-253.13:1, 22.1-254, 22.1-258, 22.1-262, 22.1-263, 22.1-265, 22.1-267, 22.1-274, 22.1-279R, 22.1-280.1, 22.1-289, 22.1-344
296	60.2-618
297	15.1-37.3:11R
298	22.1-129, 22.1-234
299	54.1-600 to 54.1-603, 54.1-604R, 54.1-606
300	59.1-200, 59.1-207.34 to 59.1-207.39
301	65.1-51
302	51.1-163
303	3.1-949.01
304	22.1-253.13:1
305	29.1-509
306	22.1-254.1
307	46.2-208
309	13.1-615
310	13.1-753, 13.1-915
311	13.1-775.1, 13.1-936.1
312	38.2-1300, 38.2-1301, 38.2-1310.1

Acts 1991 Chapter	Code 1950 Section
314	15.1-11.01
315	15.1-11.01
316	58.1-15, 58.1-347, 58.1-351, 58.1-450, 58.1-455, 58.1-475, 58.1-635, 58.1-1408, 58.1-1510, 58.1-3219.1
317	18.2-136
318	38.2-414
319	32.1-71
320	29.1-747 to 29.1-750
322	6.1-39.3
323	33.1-23.03:1, n., 58.1-2425, 58.1-638, n.
324	56-508.12
327	18.2-136
328	46.2-1052
330	58.1-3506
331	58.1-15, 58.1-347, 58.1-351, 58.1-450, 58.1-455, 58.1-475, 58.1-635, 58.1-1408, 58.1-1510, 58.1-3219.1
333	3.1-249.29
334	63.1-258.1
335	32.1-102.3:2.1
336	29.1-739
337	2.1-1.1, 2.1-1.3, 2.1-51.40, 9-274, 9-275, 9-278 to 9-280R
338	9-169, 19.2-12, 28.1-45.2
339	5.1-21.1
340	38.2-1700, 38.2-1704
341	2.1-548.8
342	19.2-389, 22.1-296.2
343	64.1-73
344	3.1-884.20, 3.1-884.21:1, 9-6.14:4.1
345	2.1-446, 9-170, 46.2-882
346	58.1-322, 58.1-344, 58.1-344.1, 58.1-355, 58.1-491.1, 58.1-905
347	2.1-739
348	3.1-796.66, 3.1-796.68, 3.1-796.119

Acts 1991 Chapter	Code 1950 Section
349	2.1-187
350	14.1-135
351	58.1-3650.395 to 58.1-3650.429, n.
352	65.1-155
353	33.1-41.1, 33.1-44
354	65.1-4.1
355	65.1-1 to 65.1-163R, 65.2-100 to 65.2-1310
356	38.2-515
357	55-210.3:01, 55-210.6R, 55-210.6:1, 55-210.24, 55-210.25
358	3.1-796.130 to 3.1-796.133
359	15.1-1032.2
360	10.1-110
361	58.1-322, 58.1-344, 58.1-344.1, 58.1-355, 58.1-491.1, 58.1-905
362	58.1-104, 58.1-332, 58.1-344, 58.1-453, 58.1-460, 58.1-472, 58.1-492, 58.1-1824, n.
363	11-4.1
364	63.1-220.2, 63.1-220.3
365	6.1-330.89
366	2.1-187
367	6.1-225.57
368	38.2-3115
369	38.2-232, 38.2-4214, 38.2-4319
370	18.2-270
371	38.2-1611.1, 38.2-1709
372	46.2-1220
373	56-338.104, 56-338.106, 56-338.107, 56-338.109, 56-338.110, 56-338.111:1, 56-338.112, 56-338.115, 56-338.118, 56-338.119, 56-338.122, 56-338.123, 56-338.126, 56-338.127
374	46.2-368
375	6.1-330.77:1
376	65.1-88
377	58.1-3650.430 to 58.1-3650.443, n.

Acts 1991 Chapter	Code 1950 Section
378	41.1-3, 41.1-4.1, 41.1-5
379	2.1-328, 51.1-603
380	3.1-796.98
381	51.1-800, 51.1-1003
382	52-8.4
383	53.1-1, 53.1-68, 53.1-75, 53.1-79, 53.1-90, 53.1-91, 53.1-92, 53.1-109, 53.1-110, 53.1-118, 53.1-122, 53.1-123, 53.1-124, 53.1-125, 53.1-126, 53.1-130
384	18.2-56.1
385	20-87.1
386	22.1-123
387	8.01-581.9
388	24.1-146
389	59.1-148.3
390	63.1-274.10
391	51.1-116
392	16.1-69.35, 16.1-227
393	58.1-3713, n.
403	16.1-69.16
404	29.1-738.01
405	13.1-663, 13.1-664.1
406	17-225, 17-227
409	29.1-744.1
410	53.1-159
411	28.1-47.1, 28.1-47.2
412	53.1-59
414	17-60.1, 55-66.3, 55-66.6
415	55-19.2R 55-19.3, 55-19.4
416	46.2-1001
417	38.2-1809
418	13.1-501, 13.1-504
419	17-119.1:2
420	19.2-72
421	9-173.7
422	15.1-239
423	53.1-151
424	18.2-175
425	4-33
426	4-2
427	19.2-181R, 19.2-182, 19.2-182.2 to 19.2-182.13
428	53.1-131.2
429	6.1-76R
430	58.1-3730
432	64.1-67.2
433	51.1-102, 51.1-802
434	50-73.17, 50-73.20, 50-73.67, 50-73.77
435	50-37.3
436	37.1-134.4
437	23-7.2
438	20-108
439	59.1-70
441	64.1-69.1
442	17-116.01
443	40.1-76R, 40.1-77R
444	15.1-501.1
445	58.1-3952
447	36-55.33:1, 36-55.34:1
448	58.1-3109
451	3.1-796.107
453	53.1-82
454	23-9.10:1, 32.1-71.2, 32.1-114, 32.1-279
455	8.01-581.1
456	58.1-104, 58.1-332, 58.1-344, 58.1-453, 58.1-460, 58.1-472, 58.1-492, 58.1-1824, n.
457	2.1-716, 2.1-717
458	11-2.3R
461	10.1-109
462	37.1-134.5
463	8.01-506
464	8.01-581.1
465	46.2-1025
467	15.1-687.22
468	4-37
469	10.1-560
470	2.1-639.6
471	58.1-3916
472	46.2-694
473	2.1-343.1
474	24.1-254.3
475	13.1-559, 13.1-561, 13.1-562, 13.1-563, 13.1-565, 13.1-570
476	15.1-321
477	19.2-188.1
478	58.1-3506
479	64.1-5.2
480	9-310, 22.1-253.13:2
481	58.1-3906
482	18.2-251
483	19.2-123
484	58.1-3916
485	2.1-198, 58.1-307
486	38.2-5020
487	10.1-411.1
488	9-6.14:7.1
489	8.01-262.1, 8.01-581.015
490	58.1-3233
491	18.2-271.1
492	54.1-2971.1
493	58.1-3916
494	46.2-1088.1
495	45.1-261.1, 45.1-270.3, 45.1-270.3:1R, 45.1-270.4, 45.1-270.4:1
496	16.1-260
497	2.1-526.14:1, 2.1-526.14:2, 55-79.41, 55-79.43, 55-79.57, 55-79.58, 55-79.59, 55-79.61, 55-79.69, 55-79.70, 55-79.72, 55-79.74:3, 55-79.77, 55-79.78, 55-79.80, 55-79.80:1, 55-79.82R, 55-79.84, 55-79.94, 55-79.97
498	3.1-6.1
499	40.1-29
500	55-248.41, 55-248.42, 55-248.44:1
501	18.2-444.2
502	18.2-165.1
503	8.01-28, 8.01-470, 16.1-88
505	52-8.4
506	18.2-53.1
507	50-74
508	6.1-330.54
509	58.1-3916
510	9-291.1
511	16.1-241, 16.1-260, 16.1-278.13, 16.1-279, 40.1-78, 40.1-79R, 40.1-79.01, 40.1-79.1, 40.1-80R, 40.1-80.1, 40.1-81.1, 40.1-83R, 40.1-84, 40.1-85, 40.1-87, 40.1-89, 40.1-90R, 40.1-91R, 40.1-92, 40.1-93,

Acts 1991 Chapter	Code 1950 Section
	40.1-95R, 40.1-96, 40.1-98R, 40.1-99R, 40.1-100, 40.1-100.1, 40.1-100.2, 40.1-101, 40.1-103, 40.1-105R, 40.1-109, 40.1-111R, 40.1-112, 40.1-113
512	19.2-123
513	15.1-495
514	32.1-176.4
515	18.2-308.2:2
516	46.2-1020
517	18.2-370.1
518	22.1-214
519	54.1-2957.01, 54.1-3303, 54.1-3401, 54.1-3408
520	25-46.3, 25-46.7, 25-46.9, 25-46.11, 25-46.17, 25-46.19, 25-46.20, 25-46.20:1 to 25-46.20:5, 25-46.21, 25-46.27, 25-46.29, 33.1-132, 33.1-238
521	15.1-28.01
522	54.1-115
523	22.1-3.1, 22.1-4R
524	54.1-2957.01, 54.1-3303, 54.1-3401, 54.1-3408
525	18.2-308.2:2
526	22.1-207.2
527	64.1-179
528	15.1-136.2, 23-7.1:01
529	15.1-50, 53.1-106
530	8.01-265
531	46.2-1185, 46.2-1187, 46.2-1187.1 to 46.2-1187.3
532	54.1-3408, 63.1-25.1, 63.1-174, 63.1-174.01, 63.1-174.1, 63.1-175, 63.1-177, 63.1-178.1, 63.1-179R, 63.1-179.1 63.1-180
533	15.1-136.2
534	8.01-511, 16.1-228, 16.1-253.2, 16.1-260, 16.1-274, 16.1-278.1 to 16.1-278.19, 16.1-279R, 16.1-286, 16.1-291, 16.1-292, 16.1-296, 16.1-298, 18.2-64.1, 18.2-119, 20-49, 20-78.1, 20-79.1, 20-79.2, 22.1-265, 37.1-97, 63.1-195, 63.1-226, 66-13, 66-17
535	5.1-12
536	8.1-105, 8.1-201, 8.2A-101 to 8.2A-532, 8.9-113, 46.2-640.1
537	18.2-56.2
538	15.1-466
539	54.1-2800
540	58.1-3703
541	15.1-362.1
542	19.2-76.1
543	22.1-168.1
544	58.1-612
545	20-107.2, 20-108.1, 20-108.2, 63.1-274.5, 63.1-274.6
546	18.2-186, 18.2-191, 18.2-195, 18.2-195.1, 18.2-195.2, 18.2-198.1
547	40.1-28.10
548	24.1-263.1
549	21-168, 21-176
550	22.1-140
551	2.1-1.6, 2.1-20.4, 9-6.25:2, 10.1-1408.2, 54.1-300, 54.1-2209 to 54.1-2212
552	55-248.5
553	22.1-79
554	2.1-179.3
555	2.1-1.6, 2.1-20.4, 9-6.25:2, 36-85.16 to 36-85.36
557	36-86 to 36-96R, 36-96.1 to 36-96.23
558	18.2-371.2
559	11-37
560	19.2-386.1, 19.2-386.3, 19.2-386.4, 19.2-386.9 to 19.2-386.12, 19.2-386.14
561	2.1-342, 32.1-102.1, 32.1-102.2, 32.1-102.3:2, 32.1-102.3:3, 32.1-102.3:4, 32.1-102.4, 32.1-102.6
562	2.1-51.39:1
563	2.1-1.1, 2.1-1.3, 2.1-1.6, 2.1-51.15, 2.1-116.16, 2.1-373.4, 2.1-397.1, 2.1-549 to 2.1-553.2R, 2.1-557, 2.1-559.1 to 2.1-559.8R, 2.1-700, 9-6.25:1, 9-116, 9-117.1R, 9-117.2R, 9-138.1, 9-138.3, 9-268, 9-270.1, 9-271, 9-285, 9-290, 22.1-279.2, 32.1-122.2, 51.5-1, 51.5-2, 63.1-248.16, 63.1-314.8
564	9-77.11:02, 54.1-3910
565	58.1-612
566	15.1-50, 53.1-106
567	53.1-106
568	15.1-50, 53.1-95.2, n., 53.1-106
569	22.1-132.1
570	18.2-287.4
571	2.1-342, n., 9-6.14:4.1, n., 32.1-331.6 to 32.1-331.11
572	58.1-3703
573	56-245.3
574	11-61
575	7.1-40.5
576	54.1-2105
577	14.1-125
578	2.1-179, 2.1-179.2
579	18.2-308.1
580	53.1-128, 53.1-129
581	19.2-119, 19.2-120, 19.2-121, 19.2-123, 19.2-124, 19.2-130, 19.2-132, 19.2-132.1R, 19.2-133R, 19.2-134, 19.2-136, 19.2-137, 19.2-144, 19.2-148, 19.2-149
582	15.1-29.22
583	54.1-2982, 54.1-2983, n.,

Acts 1991 Chapter	Code 1950 Section
	54.1-2984
584	9-6.14:12
585	19.2-123
586	18.2-340.6
587	2.1-1.6, 3.1-676, 3.1-677, 3.1-679, 3.1-684.41 to 3.1-684.58
588	20-107.2, 20-108.1, 20-108.2, 63.1-274.5, 63.1-274.6
589	54.1-1902, 54.1-1903
590	2.1-1.6, 9-6.25:1, 23-7.4, 23-8.2R, 23-9.2:3.2, 23-9.3, 23-9.6:1, 23-9.9, 23-9.10, 23-9.10:1, 23-9.10:3, 23-9.10:4, 23-38.10:3, 23-38.10:5R, 23-38.10:6, 23-261, 23-262R, 23-263R, 23-266
591	59.1-365, 59.1-369, 59.1-371, 59.1-375, 59.1-376, 59.1-377, 59.1-382, 59.1-383, 59.1-385, 59.1-387, 59.1-389, 59.1-390, 59.1-391, 59.1-392, 59.1-393, 59.1-404R, 59.1-405
592	24.1-165
593	53.1-106.1
594	9-145.16 to 9-145.20
595	63.1-195, 63.1-196.04
596	40.1-28.10
597	53.1-40.10
599	15.1-491.8, 15.1-491.9
600	20-156 to 20-165, 32.1-261, 32.1-289.1, 63.1-236.1
601	15.1-291.2
602	63.1-220.3, 63.1-221
603	24.1-228.1:1
604	9-6.14:16, n., 63.1-119, n.
605	3.1-919, 3.1-924.1, 3.1-936, 3.1-949.1 to 3.1-949.3, 3.1-966R, 3.1-966.1, 3.1-966.2, 59.1-200
606	22.1-257
607	29.1-556.1
608	59.1-200, 59.1-429 to 59.1-434
609	15.1-505, 15.1-901
611	32.1-257, 64.1-7.1
612	51.1-1000, 51.1-1003
613	54.1-1202
614	57-35.36
615	15.1-28.01
616	19.2-215.1
617	14.1-52
618	16.1-274
620	38.2-204R, 38.2-205R, 38.2-513, 38.2-514, 38.2-1811R, 38.2-1824
621	54.1-3806.1
622	46.2-752
623	17-119.1:2
624	58.1-3516
625	55-41
626	46.2-1581
627	9-6.23, 23-231.2 to 23-231.7
628	4-25, 4-118.4, 4-118.43
629	22.1-17.2, 54.1-3006.1
630	59.1-200, 59.1-429 to 59.1-434
631	52-11
632	20-107.3
633	19.2-270.3
634	11-41.2:1
635	8.01-582, 8.01-600, 58.1-3177
636	37.1-67.3
637	18.2-308
638	2.1-51.5:1
640	20-107.3
643	54.1-2900, 54.1-2956.9, 54.1-2956.10, 54.1-2956.11, 54.1-2965R
644	32.1-285, 63.1-248.6
645	2.1-116, 11-40, 51.1-126, 51.1-126.1
646	58.1-3506.1 to 58.1-3506.8
647	58.1-608
648	15.1-800
649	18.2-250, 18.2-250.1
650	54.1-3900
651	20-60.3, 20-60.5, 20-79.3, 63.1-250, 63.1-250.1, 63.1-252.1
652	17-79.1
653	44-93
654	46.2-1523, 46.2-1524, 59.1-200, 59.1-435 to 59.1-441
655	36-106
656	2.1-234.13
657	18.2-340.3
658	10.1-1402, n., 10.1-1408.1, n., 10.1-1455, n.
659	54.1-1102
660	11-41.2:1
661	15.1-7.1, 15.1-7.2
662	11-46.2, 40.1-135 to 40.1-138
663	38.2-508.1
664	19.2-163.7, 19.2-163.8
665	15.1-11.5:3, 15.1-879R
666	33.1-23.03:1, 33.1-268, 33.1-269, 33.1-272, 33.1-277, 58.1-638
667	55-508 to 55-514, 55-516
668	15.1-170 to 15.1-227R, 15.1-227.1 to 15.1-227.65, 15.1-235.1R, 15.1-545R, 15.1-545.1R, 15.1-546R, 15.1-812, 15.1-819, 15.1-826, 22.1-79
669	32.1-122.6:01, 54.1-3011.1, 54.1-3011.2
670	18.2-51.2
672	8.01-285, 8.01-299, 8.01-301, 8.01-306, 8.01-313, 12.1-19.1, 13.1-517, 13.1-566, 13.1-637, 13.1-758,

Acts 1991 Chapter	Code 1950 Section
	13.1-766, 13.1-767, 13.1-769, 13.1-836, 13.1-920, 13.1-928, 13.1-929, 13.1-931, 38.2-616, 50-73.7
673	15.1-11.03
674	8.01-249
675	52-8.2
676	29.1-305.1
678	38.2-508.1
679	2.1-512
680	19.2-270.2
681	11-41.2:1
682	22.1-146
683	28.1-53
684	55-182.1, 55-182.2
685	9-168
686	62.1-132.20
687	19.2-187.01
688	46.2-1063
689	14.1-133.2
690	4-46, 4-98.2, 4-98.3, 4-98.5, 4-98.12, 4-98.13
691	33.1-192.1, 33.1-386, 33.1-387
692	8.01-264
693	8.01-229
694	20-60.3, 20-60.5, 20-79.3, 63.1-250, 63.1-250.1, 63.1-252.1
695	32.1-162.7 to 32.1-316
696	16.1-278.9, 16.1-279
697	26-40
698	20-107.3, 20-112, 20-115
699	38.2-2205.1
700	51.1-505, 51.1-514
701	11-56.2
702	10.1-1300, 10.1-1309.1, 10.1-1410, 10.1-1428, 62.1-44.3, 62.1-44.15:1.1
703	15.1-292.4
704	55-361.1, 55-362, 55-368, 55-369, 55-370, 55-370.1, 55-374.1, 55-376, 55-381, 55-400
705	53.1-261 to 53.1-266
706	10.1-1603, 10.1-1610, 10.1-1618
707	40.1-2, n.
708	2.1-344
709	24.1-254.1, 24.1-254.3, 24.1-257.1, 24.1-257.2, 24.1-262, 24.1-263, 24.1-276, 24.1-277
710	4-78.1, 4-112.4, 6.1-119, 12.1-34, 15.1-332, 15.1-348, 15.1-505, 15.1-901, 15.1-1431, 18.2-91, 18.2-95, 18.2-270, 18.2-340, 18.2-389, 24.1-266, 24.1-270, 24.1-275, 24.1-278, 55-79.28, 57-59, 59.1-75
711	23-232, 23-233.1, 23-234, 23-234.1, 23-235, 23-236, 23-237
712	46.2-1529, 46.2-1546, 46.2-1548, 46.2-1549, 46.2-1549.1, 46.2-1550, 46.2-1550.1, 46.2-1550.2, 46.2-1551, 46.2-1552, 46.2-1557.1
713	33.1-23.03:1, 33.1-268, 33.1-269, 33.1-272, 33.1-277, 58.1-638
714	58.1-1825
715	16.1-241, 16.1-253.2 to 16.1-253.4, 19.2-81.3
716	18.2-308.2:2
717	46.2-1157
718	10.1-1311, 10.1-1316, 10.1-1402, 10.1-1406, 10.1-1418.1, 10.1-1455, 10.1-2500, 10.1-2501, 10.1-2502, 62.1-44.15, 62.1-44.32, 62.1-252
719	51.1-100, n., 51.1-101, n., 51.1-110, n., 51.1-125, n., 51.1-138, 51.1-142, n., 51.1-145, 51.1-155, 51.1-166, 51.1-200, n., 51.1-208
720	55-248.9
721	54.1-2820
722	8.01-229, 8.01-244

ACTS 1991, 1st SP. SESS.

Acts 1991, 1st Sp. Sess. Chapter	Code 1950 Section
1	58.1-608
5, 6	25-232.2
9	60.2-528
11	24.1-12.3R, 24.1-17.100 to 24.1-17.203
12	24.1-1
13	9-6.14:16, n., 63.1-119, n.
14	18.2-255.2
15	11-41.2:1
16	24.1-17.130, 24.1-17.167, 24.1-17.177
17	46.2-1141
18	24.1-14.2R, 24.1-17.4 to 24.1-17.47
20	24.1-17.164, 24.1-17.168, 24.1-17.170, 24.1-17.171, 24.1-17.173, 24.1-17.174 24.1-17.197, 24.1-17.202

ACTS 1991, 2nd SP. SESS.

Acts 1991, 2nd Sp. Sess. Chapter	Code 1950 Section
6	24.1-4.3R, 24.1-5R, 24.1-17.300 to 24.1-17.314

ACTS 1992

Acts 1992 Chapter	Code 1950 Section
1	55-290
2	65.2-512
3	40.1-51.10, 40.1-51.15:1
4	60.2-219

Acts 1992 Chapter	Code 1950 Section
5	60.2-226
6	56-493
7	38.2-501, 38.2-514
8	38.2-301
9	6.1-303
10	54.1-918
11	12.1-13
12	65.2-101
13	13.1-543
14	38.2-1045, 38.2-1049, 38.2-1051R, 38.2-4310, 38.2-4319
15	32.1-203
16	13.1-543
17	6.1-333
18	13.1-505
19	13.1-501, 13.1-525
20	38.2-1046, 38.2-4310
21	38.2-2601
22	38.2-4311
23	38.2-3407.1, 38.2-4306.1, 38.2-4319
24	6.1-112
25	59.1-119.1
26	29.1-812
27	10.1-1418.1
28	62.1-224
32	15.1-1637, 15.1-1646
33	46.2-920
34	46.2-1023
39	15.1-11.7
40	2.1-342
41	63.1-195, 63.1-196, 63.1-196.1, 63.1-196.3, 63.1-198, 63.1-198.02 to 63.1-199, 63.1-201 to 63.1-202.1
42	63.1-195, 63.1-196, 63.1-196.1, 63.1-196.3, 63.1-198, 63.1-198.02 to 63.1-199, 63.1-201 to 63.1-202.1
43	18.2-340.1, 18.2-340.3, 18.2-340.9
44	33.1-18
46	15.1-23.1
47	15.1-494
48	6.1-56
49	38.2-1813
50	38.2-301
51	6.1-194.69
52	54.1-501.1
53	23-41
54	19.2-254.1, 19.2-254.2
55	19.2-34
56	19.2-187
57	8.01-452.1
58	18.2-251, 18.2-259.1, 46.2-390.1
59	19.2-368.22
60	18.2-340.6
61	2.1-548.8:4
62	2.1-51.6:1
63	59.1-148.3
64	54.1-511
65	54.1-2105
66	64.1-73
67	55-220.1
68	6.1-63, 54.1-2010, 54.1-2012, 54.1-2013
69	55-510
70	54.1-3805.1
71	55-510
72	43-3, 55-79.46, 55-79.74:1, 55-79.75, 55-79.80:1, 55-79.83, 55-79.84
73	36-105
74	8.01-53
75	11-62.1, 11-62.2, 11-62.5
76	18.2-258.1
77	19.2-299
78	11-41.2:1
79	20-108.2, 63.1-264.2
80	19.2-163.3, 19.2-163.4
81	2.1-1.7, 2.1-51.18, 2.1-64.28:1 to 2.1-64.28:3, 9-6.25:3
82	3.1-1060
83	59.1-148.3
84	36-96.20, 54.1-2101, 54.1-2102R, 54.1-2103,
85	2.1-427
86	2.1-434.2
87	55-59
88	20-107.3
89	2.1-1.5
90	16.1-291
91	16.1-69.6:1
92	17-119.1:2
93	46.2-1025
94	33.1-71R
95	46.2-224, 46.2-1503
96	46.2-920, 46.2-1022
97	33.1-62, n.
98	46.2-100
99	46.2-105.2, 46.2-370
101	3.1-742.1, 3.1-742R, 3.1-743, 3.1-744R, 3.1-745 to 3.1-748.1
102	59.1-296
103	2.1-1.5, 9-6.25:3, 23-9.5, 23-14, 23-31, 23-49.1, 23-49.23 to 23-49.25, 23-49.27 to 23-49.29, 23-49.31 to 23-49.33
104	8.01-66.9, 32.1-347
105	11-40.3, 24.1-113.1
106	32.1-81
107	32.1-324, 32.1-325.3
108	5.1-1.6, 8.01-402, 33.1-23.03:1, 33.1-82, 33.1-90, 33.1-90.1R, 33.1-90.2, 33.1-185, 33.1-223,
109	46.2-389, 46.2-390, 46.2-391.1, 46.2-411, 46.2-417, 46.2-434, 46.2-490.1

Acts 1992 Chapter	Code 1950 Section
110	2.1-734,
	11-62.11
111	8.01-195.4,
	16.1-77,
	43-34,
	63.1-260.1
113	10.1-1140.1
114	3.1-249.31,
	3.1-249.45
115	46.2-1573
116	46.2-1569
117	59.1-299,
	59.1-306
119	46.2-1095,
	46.2-1098,
	46.2-1099
121	3.1-1,
	3.1-22.4,
	3.1-249.28,
	3.1-276,
	3.1-610.25,
	10.1-502
122	28.1-166
123	3.1-796.115
124	3.1-684.14
125	63.1-220.3
127	32.1-46
128	32.1-288
129	4-19
130	22.1-178,
	22.1-179R
131	22.1-254.1
132	2.1-1.6,
	9-6.25:1,
	22.1-253.13:1,
	22.1-253.13:5,
	22.1-290.1,
	22.1-293,
	22.1-294,
	22.1-298,
	22.1-299,
	22.1-304,
	22.1-305.2,
	22.1-316,
	23-231.2
134	46.2-1500
135	46.2-1571
136	6.1-51,
	6.1-111,
	6.1-112,
	6.1-113,
	6.1-194.86,
	6.1-194.95
137	54.1-2944
138	10.1-2213
139	38.2-4902,
	38.2-4910
140	38.2-2204
141	46.2-726,
	56-304
142	46.2-728.1,

Acts 1992 Chapter	Code 1950 Section
	46.2-728.2
143	2.1-1.7,
	9-6.25:2,
	9-320
	to 9-324
144	53.1-135,
	53.1-139,
	53.1-139.1R
145	10.1-1102
146	54.1-3221
147	65.2-512
148	46.2-1500,
	46.2-1519,
	46.2-1600
	to 46.2-1609
149	46.2-373,
	46.2-1156
150	2.1-342
151	22.1-343
152	54.1-500
153	2.1-343.1
154	3.1-81.1,
	3.1-105
155	13.1-301
156	6.1-411
157	13.1-518
158	13.1-561
159	46.2-1090.1
160	38.2-231,
	38.2-2113,
	38.2-2208
161	4-31,
	4-37,
	4-44,
	4-98.6,
	4-105,
	4-114
162	4-98.2,
	4-98.18,
	4-98.19
163	22.1-281,
	22.1-284
164	22.1-60
165	2.1-563.23,
	2.1-563.24,
	2.1-563.25,
	2.1-563.26
166	32.1-46
167	2.1-1.1,
	2.1-1.3,
	2.1-51.43,
	2.1-342,
	33.1-12,
	33.1-89.2,
	33.1-221.1:1,
	33.1-223.1,
	33.1-390R,
	33.1-391R
	33.1-391.1
	to 33.1-391.5,
	58.1-638,

Acts 1992 Chapter	Code 1950 Section
168	2.1-1.5
169	63.1-44
170	63.1-89.1
171	2.1-548.16
172	2.1-1.7,
	9-6.25:1,
	2.1-700R
173	9-173.5
174	22.1-275.1
175	22.1-122.1
176	23-49.22:1
	to 23-49.22:4
177	3.1-796.122,
	18.2-403.1,
	18.2-403.2,
	19.2-8
178	11-41.2:1
179	53.1-68
180	10.1-2205
181	2.1-467,
	2.1-467.1,
	2.1-467.2,
	2.1-467.5
182	22.1-50
183	10.1-414
184	10.1-560
185	53.1-115.2
186	62.1-248.1
187	23-232.1,
	23-234
188	53.1-145
189	63.1-124.2
190	63.1-58.2
191	18.2-53.1
192	56-265.15,
	56-265.16:1,
	56-265.17,
	56-265.20
193	55-59
194	47.1-30
195	59.1-148.3
196	53.1-180,
	53.1-181,
	53.1-185.1
197	15.1-11.04,
	15.1-857.1
198	29.1-302.3
199	20-60.3,
	63.1-251.2
200	2.1-342,
	9-6.14:4.1,
	32.1-331.1R
	to 32.1-331.11R
201	53.1-16
202	28.1-173.1:1,
	28.2-711
203	2.1-342,
	32.1-239,
	32.1-241
	to 32.1-245,
	32.1-244.1R

Acts 1992 Chapter	Code 1950 Section
204	22.1-132.1
205	32.1-116.1:2
206	53.1-106.1, n.
207	2.1-342
208	10.1-1450
209	22.1-209.2
210	38.2-102, 38.2-105.1, 38.2-106, 38.2-107.1, 38.2-1443.1, 38.2-3113.1, 38.2-3219
212	53.1-106
213	9-153.1
214	63.1-248.6
215	4-25, 4-98.3
216	9-6.14:22, 9-6.17, 9-77.7, 9-77.8, 9-77.10, 9-77.11, 9-77.11:01, 9-77.12
217	23-231.8 to 23-231.12
218	9-84.03
219	63.1-85.5R
220	4-11, 4-44
221	2.1-116.2
222	53.1-155, 2.1-1.6, 2.1-20.4, 9-6.25:2
223	36-85.16 to 36-85.36
224	6.1-90, 6.1-194.79
225	38.2-3600, 38.2-3608
226	46.2-752
227	46.2-749.2
229	15.1-37.3:6
230	38.2-2202
231	40.1-117
232	15.1-18.2, 15.1-18.3
234	18.2-374.1
235	28.1-173.2
237	29.1-344.1
238	8.01-27.1
239	28.1-136
240	8.01-581.20
241	38.2-4300
242	3.1-949.2, 3.1-969.1 to 3.1-969.15
243	54.1-1110
244	15.1-491.9
246	28.1-120
247	15.1-1250.01
248	18.2-258
249	14.1-125.1
250	29.1-702
252	14.1-120
253	14.1-120.1
254	29.1-601
255	33.1-23.5:2
256	10.1-2202
262	29.1-301
263	58.1-3819, 58.1-3833
264	58.1-2103
266	33.1-252
267	33.1-41.1
268	46.2-1220
269	46.2-1212
270	2.1-391
273	46.2-301
274	15.1-1651 to 15.1-1661
275	3.1-177.1, 3.1-178R to 3.1-188R
276	51.1-600 to 51.1-602, 51.1-604, 51.1-605
278	59.1-198, 59.1-200
279	46.2-900
282	54.1-518R to 54.1-525R
283	6.1-94, 6.1-194.85, 6.1-372, 6.1-392.1, 6.1-393, 6.1-412, 6.1-416
284	59.1-430
285	29.1-509
286	10.1-1408.1
287	58.1-3939.1
288	24.1-228.1
289	3.1-249.33
290	18.2-340.3
291	24.1-228.1:2
292	58.1-3013
293	24.1-143, 24.1-144
294	3.1-796.97:1
295	28.1-173.2
296	58.1-323.1
297	8.01-609
298	10.1-562, 10.1-566, 10.1-569, 15.1-499.1, 15.1-687.8
299	38.2-1700, 38.2-1705
300	10.1-1402, n., 10.1-1408.1, n., 10.1-1455, n.
301	59.1-280, 59.1-280, n.
302	62.1-44.34:23
303	2.1-1.6, 9-6.25:1, 10.1-1323 to 10.1-1326
304	9-160
305	58.1-3650.444, n., to 58.1-3650.478, n.
306	19.2-114
307	18.2-403.4
308	2.1-1.6, 9-6.25:1, 10.1-410.2
309	58.1-2704, 58.1-2706, 58.1-2707
310	18.2-110
311	23-38.19:2
312	8.01-342
313	58.1-338, n., 58.1-445.1, n.
314	58.1-608, 58.1-608, n.
315	Const., Art. X, § 8, n.
316	2.1-191.1 to 2.1-191.4
317	58.1-332
318	18.2-444.2
319	17-48R
320	58.1-323.1
322	36-96.1:1, 36-96.2, 36-96.3, 36-96.7, 36-96.13
323	46.2-749.2
324	45.1-361.41
325	36-55.63, 58.1-336, 58.1-435
326	2.1-180
327	2.1-207, 2.1-191R
328	18.2-340.3
329	24.1-146, 24.1-147
330	54.1-1100
331	2.1-511
332	33.1-320, n.
333	53.1-83.1, 53.1-85
334	32.1-127
335	15.1-687.13
336	22.1-132.1
337	54.1-2822
338	54.1-2011
340	24.1-222.2

Acts 1992 Chapter	Code 1950 Section
341	10.1-417
342	14.1-52
343	2.1-113.1,
	2.1-113.3
344	15.1-1513.3
345	62.1-44.34:21
346	58.1-3211
347	36-55.63,
	58.1-336,
	58.1-435
348	54.1-2112,
	54.1-2113
349	4-27,
	4-79.1,
	4-89
350	4-25,
	4-33,
	4-38
351	33.1-223.3
	to 33.1-223.9
352	18.2-162,
	18.2-162.1
353	15.1-431
354	22.1-42
355	46.2-752
356	36-99.5:1,
	58.1-608,
	63.1-172,
	63.1-174.01,
	63.1-182.1,
	63.1-194.1
	to 63.1-194.12
357	18.2-340.6
358	32.1-122.5:1
359	57-35.11:1,
	57-35.19,
	57-35.20,
	57-35.21:1,
	57-35.26,
	57-35.27
360	45.1-95
361	45.1-361.38
362	15.1-366
363	62.1-241.11,
	62.1-241.12
364	46.2-1030
365	6.1-54
366	6.1-60.1
368	11-41.2:1
369	58.1-339
370	15.1-21
372	15.1-11.2
373	55-50
374	29.1-332,
	29.1-333
375	3.1-311
376	56-88,
	56-88.1,
	56-265.13:7
377	12.1-21,
	13.1-617
378	62.1-218,
	62.1-230.1,
	62.1-239.1,
	62.1-241.1
	to 62.1-241.10
379	46.2-1024
380	15.1-466,
	15.1-491
381	2.1-391
382	58.1-3980,
	58.1-3984
383	58.1-3211
384	58.1-2402
385	58.1-461,
	58.1-462,
	58.1-470
386	58.1-3
387	16.1-69.35
388	58.1-2653,
	58.1-2655
389	33.1-223.3
	to 33.1-223.9
390	16.1-69.17,
	49-3
391	19.2-303,
	19.2-390
392	8.01-324
393	8.01-391
394	58.1-339.1R,
	58.1-437R
395	26-22R
396	8.01-433.1
397	58.1-3712.1, n.
398	53.1-223
399	58.1-3814
400	54.1-3811
401	58.1-461,
	58.1-462,
	58.1-470
403	43-32
404	58.1-610
405	46.2-1095,
	46.2-1098,
	46.2-1099
406	22.1-32
407	2.1-1.6,
	2.1-1.7,
	9-6.23,
	9-6.25:1,
	9-317
	to 9-319,
	32.1-122.1R
	to 32.1-122.4R
409	9-6.14:4.1,
	54.1-2957.01,
	54.1-2957.2
410	46.2-1025
411	54.1-2702
412	32.1-151,
	32.1-153,
	54.1-2901,
	54.1-2982,
	54.1-2987.1,
	54.1-2988,
	54.1-2989,
	54.1-2991
413	46.2-373
414	38.2-5020,
	54.1-106,
	54.1-2901,
	54.1-2927
415	58.1-610
417	51.1-502.1
418	15.1-1031.5
419	37.1-71
420	23-231.3
421	53.1-95.2,
	53.1-95.3
422	9-169,
	19.2-389,
	58.1-4006
423	18.2-325,
	18.2-326,
	18.2-334
424	2.1-114.5
425	24.1-40.7,
	24.1-40.7:1,24.1-40.8R,
	24.1-40.9R
	24.1-40.10,
	24.1-40.11,
426	2.1-1.5,
	10.1-202,
	10.1-1017
	to 10.1-1025,
	10.1-2213
427	55-243,
	55-248.34
428	2.1-51.17:1,
	32.1-127,
	37.1-182.1,
	54.1-2403.1
429	2.1-702
430	54.1-1300,
	54.1-1301,
	54.1-1302.1,
	54.1-1303
	to 54.1-1305.2,
	54.1-1308,
	54.1-1302R,
	54.1-1306R,
	54.1-1307R
431	55-70.1
432	9-84.03
433	24.1-48
434	23-38.71
435	19.2-8,
	36-106
436	23-49.22:1
	to 23-49.22:4
437	58.1-608
438	55-79.01
439	22.1-209.2

Acts 1992 Chapter	Code 1950 Section
441	16.1-316, 16.1-317
442	58.1-3650.479, n. to 58.1-3650.484, n.
443	2.1-639.42, 2.1-639.43
444	2.1-344
445	24.1-36, 24.1-37, 24.1-92
446	54.1-2105
447	24.1-252
449	58.1-4006, 58.1-4008, 58.1-4012 to 58.1-4014, 58.1-4019, 58.1-4020
450	55-514
451	55-248.11:1
452	32.1-134.2 to 32.1-134.4
453	15.1-965.28 to 15.1-965.41
454	8.01-156
455	36-139.5
456	36-99.6, 62.1-44.14, 62.1-44.34:11, 62.1-44.34:14, 62.1-44.34:15.1 to 62.1-44.34:20, 62.1-44.34:23
457	2.1-51.6:2
458	15.1-11.04
459	8.01-310, 46.2-502
460	6.1-13, 6.1-194.12
461	3.1-796.118
462	46.2-878.1
463	10.1-1426, 10.1-1427
464	10.1-1207, 29.1-101.2 to 29.1-101.9, 10.1-1213R to 10.1-1221R
465	15.1-498.2, 15.1-498.3, 15.1-498.4, 15.1-498.6, 15.1-498.7, 15.1-498.9, 15.1-498.10
466	65.2-510.1, 65.2-712
467	59.1-272
468	13.1-400.6, 13.1-519, 13.1-568, 38.2-1508
469	65.2-301
470	38.2-2121
471	13.1-688, 13.1-868
472	13.1-646
473	38.2-4229.1
474	38.2-2205
475	65.2-406
476	56-265.1, 56-265.4:5
477	40.1-51.20 to 40.1-51.22, 54.1-501, 54.1-507R
478	17-79.3
479	18.2-50.2, 18.2-50.1R
480	62.1-195.1
481	38.2-4300, 38.2-4302, 38.2-4303, 38.2-4316
482	60.2-603
483	55-305
484	16.1-285.1
485	19.2-358
486	18.2-91, 18.2-92
487	18.2-309
488	9-6.14:4.1, 10.1-1322, 10.1-1322.1, 10.1-1322.2
489	9-145.21 to 9-145.29
490	15.1-11.03
491	3.1-177.1, 3.1-178R to 3.1-188R
492	28.1-48.1, 28.2-208.1
493	8.2-310, 28.1-48, 28.1-48.2 to 28.1-48.6
494	58.1-608
495	8.01-381
496	16.1-245
497	16.1-69.33
498	14.1-90, 19.2-310.01
499	18.2-462.1
500	18.2-62
501	8.01-27.2
502	16.1-260
503	28.1-48, 28.1-48.2 to 28.1-48.5, 28.1-48.6
504	28.1-48.1
505	10.1-1402, n., 10.1-1408.1, n., 10.1-1455, n.
506	8.01-407
507	10.1-1410.1, n.
508	16.1-250, 16.1-250.1
509	16.1-242
510	18.2-308
511	58.1-3650.485, n. to 58.1-3650.502, n.
514	64.1-189, 64.1-192
515	36-99.10
516	20-49.1, 20-49.3, 20-49.4
517	15.1-431.1
518	51.1-165
519	58.1-460
520	18.2-130
521	55-405, 55-406
522	8.01-379.2, 19.2-263.2
524	15.1-765.1, 15.1-765.2, 15.1-768, 15.1-773
525	18.2-163, 18.2-187.1
526	18.2-57.2
527	16.1-260, 63.1-250.2
528	59.1-274
529	53.1-150
530	51.1-502
531	18.2-204.2, 46.2-347
532	8.01-335, 26-49, 43-70, 43-71, 55-66.5, 55-66.7, 55-66.1R, 55-106.3R
533	46.2-113
534	8.01-226.1
535	19.2-163.2
536	8.01-360
537	8.01-324
538	18.2-258
539	16.1-337, 16.1-341, 16.1-344, 16.1-345
540	18.2-85
541	40.1-51.23 to 40.1-51.41
542	16.1-260
543	20-108.1
544	11-9.5
545	59.1-200, 59.1-313, 59.1-318, 59.1-320R, 59.1-320.1, 59.1-323,

Acts 1992 Chapter	Code 1950 Section
	59.1-325
	to 59.1-329,
	59.1-330R
	59.1-330.1
	to 59.1-332,
	59.1-335
546	18.2-90
547	16.1-305,
	19.2-368.3
548	51.1-165
549	9-6.25:1,
	56-484.4
	to 56-484.7
550	55-59.2
551	18.2-369
552	6.1-48,
	6.1-48.1,
	6.1-194.14
553	46.2-1092
554	16.1-274
555	14.1-123,
	14.1-125
556	9-145.40
	to 9-145.44
557	19.2-266
558	14.1-123
559	18.2-271.1
560	18.2-271.2
561	18.2-268,
	46.2-341.26
562	18.2-224
563	20-99,
	20-99.1:1
564	8.01-384
565	16.1-107
566	15.1-131,
	37.1-67.1
567	8.01-420.2
568	46.2-361
569	9-169
570	38.2-1866
	to 38.2-1874
571	8.01-328.1
572	46.2-1500,
	46.2-1573.1
573	53.1-83.1,
	53.1-85
574	13.1-1002,
	13.1-1005,
	13.1-1008,
	13.1-1010.1,
	13.1-1011,
	13.1-1012,
	13.1-1022,
	13.1-1024,
	13.1-1024.1,
	13.1-1025,
	13.1-1028,
	13.1-1035,
	13.1-1039,
	13.1-1052,
	13.1-1054,
	13.1-1055,
	13.1-1067,
	13.1-1067.1,
	13.1-1100
	to 13.1-1123,
	38.2-1837,
	38.2-1838,
	38.2-1841,
	54.1-411,
	54.1-2000,
	54.1-2005,
	54.1-2007,
	54.1-2717,
	54.1-2718,
	54.1-3215,
	54.1-3902,
	54.1-3908,
	54.1-3909,
	54.1-3936,
	54.1-3937,
	58.1-811
575	13.1-603,
	13.1-720,
	13.1-722,
	13.1-729,
	13.1-730,
	13.1-766.1,
	13.1-1002,
	13.1-1005,
	13.1-1060,
	13.1-1067,
	13.1-1070
	to 13.1-1073,
	50-37.3,
	50-73.1,
	50-73.17,
	50-73.48:1
	to 50-73.48:4,
	50-73.57:2,
	58.1-811
576	19.2-121,
	19.2-123,
	19.2-131,
	19.2-134,
	19.2-135
577	46.2-742.1
578	9-182,
	9-183.1
	to 9-183.12,
	54.1-1900R
	to 54.1-1908R
579	58.1-1724
580	18.2-299,
	18.2-300,
	18.2-303,
	18.2-303.1,
	18.2-304,
	18.2-306,
	18.2-307
581	15.1-477
582	2.1-224,
	2.1-394,
	2.1-398,
	2.1-399,
	2.1-399.1
583	55-210.12,
	55-210.26:1
584	64.1-57
585	16.1-241,
	16.1-278.15,
	20-107.2
586	38.2-1800,
	38.2-3717
	to 38.2-3738,
	38.2-3700R
	to 38.2-3716R
587	18.2-62
588	38.2-212,
	38.2-1300,
	38.2-1301,
	38.2-1306.2,
	38.2-1307,
	38.2-1308,
	38.2-1310.1,
	38.2-1317
	to 38.2-1323,
	38.2-1329
	to 38.2-1332,
	38.2-1400,
	38.2-1401,
	38.2-1403,
	38.2-1405,
	38.2-1407,
	38.2-1411.1,
	38.2-1411.2,
	38.2-1413
	to 38.2-1418,
	38.2-1421,
	38.2-1422,
	38.2-1426
	to 38.2-1427.3,
	38.2-1429,
	38.2-1437,
	38.2-1437.1,
	38.2-1440,
	38.2-1441,
	38.2-1443,
	38.2-1445 to
	38.2-1447,
	38.2-1846
	to 38.2-1865,
	38.2-3127.1,
	38.2-3128,
	38.2-3139,
	38.2-3140,
	38.2-3143,
	38.2-3144,
	38.2-4230
	to 38.2-4234,
	38.2-5100
	to 38.2-5103,

Acts 1992 Chapter	Code 1950 Section
	38.2-5108,
	38.2-5109,
	38.2-1411R
589	15.1-37.2:1
590	8.01-581.13
591	22.1-253.13:1,
	22.1-253.13:3,
	22.1-253.13:6,
	22.1-253.13:7
592	2.1-1.6,
	2.1-51.27:1
	to 2.1-51.27:4,
	9-6.14:4.1,
	9-6.25:3,
	10.1-2215R,
	10.1-2216R
593	2.1-342
594	22.1-57.1
	to 22.1-57.5
595	54.1-401
596	15.1-486.1, n.
597	46.2-1168
598	46.2-870
599	32.1-176.4
600	15.1-518,
	15.1-865
601	58.1-608
602	58.1-3516
603	8.01-44.1,
	22.1-16.1,
	23-9.2:3.3,
	32.1-12.1,
	32.1-162.16
	to 32.1-162.20,
	37.1-24.01,
	37.1-84.1,
	51.5-5.1,
	53.1-5.1,
	53.1-36,
	54.1-2407,
	63.1-25.01,
	66-10.1,
	37.1-234R
	to 37.1-238R
604	53.1-131.2
605	2.1-27.7
606	11-2.4
607	63.1-223,
	63.1-226,
	63.1-228,
	63.1-229,
	63.1-231,
	63.1-236,
	63.1-236.1,
	63.1-228.1R
608	46.2-862
609	2.1-1.7,
	9-6.25:2,
	9-145.30
	to 9-145.34
610	54.1-3408
611	22.1-276.1
612	2.1-342,
	32.1-102.1,
	32.1-102.3:2,
	32.1-102.11,
	32.1-102.3:3R,
	32.1-102.3:4R
613	54.1-405
614	8.01-44.3,
	63.1-85.4:1
615	8.01-374.1
617	55-41,
	55-42.1,
	55-47.01,
	64.1-01,
	64.1-16.1,
	64.1-16.2,
	55-47R
618	9-275,
	9-276.1,
	9-277R
619	2.1-373.4
620	2.1-384
621	62.1-44.15:6,
	62.1-44.15:7,
	62.1-44.15:8
622	2.1-21
623	19.2-348,
	19.2-349
624	54.1-2105
625	58.1-3919.1,
	58.1-3934
626	9-299
627	9-6.25:2,
	9-6.25:3,
	9-268,
	51.5-31,
	51.5-33,
	51.5-34,
	51.5-35.1,
	51.5-37,
	51.5-38,
	51.5-40,
	51.5-46,
	51.5-35R
628	53.1-106
629	18.2-340.9
630	2.1-1.5,
	2.1-51.21,
	9-6.25:2,
	23-9.2:3,
	23-38.30
	to 23-38.32:1,
	23-38.33:1,
	23-38.34:1,
	23-38.34:2,
	23-38.35,
	23-38.36,
	23-38.36:1,
	23-38.38
	to 23-38.41,
	23-38.43,
	23-38.44:1
	to 23-38.44:3,
	23-38.61R
	to 23-38.69:3R
631	33.1-23.03:1, n.,
	46.2-206, n.,
	46.2-692,
	46.2-697.1,
	46.2-728.1,
	46.2-728.2,
	46.2-1558
632	58.1-3706,
	58.1-3732
633	44-146.40
634	2.1-1.7,
	9-6.25:2,
	51.5-47
	to 51.5-52
635	54.1-2820
636	58.1-3713, n.
637	18.2-308.2:2
638	15.1-11.5,
	15.1-11.5:1
640	10.1-2211
641	19.2-389,
	22.1-296.2
642	58.1-3506
643	2.1-1.6,
	3.1-73.6
	to 3.1-73.8,
	9-6.25:1
644	34-26,
	34-28
646	23-38.53:2
647	55-41,
	55-42.1,
	55-47.01,
	64.1-01,
	64.1-16.1,
	64.1-16.2,
	55-47R
648	14.1-105
649	15.1-11
650	19.2-8,
	36-106
651	55-66.7R
652	16.1-322.5
	to 16.1-322.7
653	13.1-301,
	13.1-309.1
654	53.1-261
	to 53.1-266
655	15.1-18.2
656	44-146.40
657	62.1-44.15:6
	to 62.1-44.15:8
659	9-6.14:14.1,
	54.1-105,
	54.1-109,
	54.1-110,

Acts 1992 Chapter	Code 1950 Section
	54.1-2400,
	54.1-2401,
	54.1-2917,
	54.1-2921,
	54.1-3010
660	37.1-128.02,
	37.1-128.1,
	37.1-132,
	37.1-133.1
661	63.1-202.1
662	20-88.02,
	20-88.01R
663	2.1-51.6:3
664	37.1-128.02,
	37.1-128.1,
	37.1-132,
	37.1-133.1
665	58.1-322
666	22.1-323
	to 22.1-323.2,
	22.1-328,
	37.1-181,
	37.1-182,
	63.1-175,
	63.1-177,
	63.1-178,
	63.1-196,
	63.1-196.1,
	63.1-196.4,
	63.1-201
667	54.1-3434.01
668	23-231.8
	to 23-231.12
669	58.1-3516
670	18.2-340.3
671	58.1-322, n.
672	2.1-20.01:1
673	22.1-227
674	34-29
675	10.1-1302
676	58.1-3713, n.
677	55-508
678	58.1-12,
	58.1-302,
	58.1-311,
	58.1-322,
	58.1-402,
	58.1-906,
	58.1-1823,
	58.1-2508
679	22.1-306,
	22.1-308,
	22.1-309,
	22.1-313
680	58.1-3506,
	58.1-3507
681	19.2-368.5,
	19.2-368.19
	to 19.2-368.21
682	32.1-102.3:2,
	32.1-102.4
683	58.1-3149,
	58.1-3919.1,
	58.1-3934
684	26-44.1
685	18.2-248
686	58.1-322
	58.1-438,
687	19.2-368.11:1
688	63.1-248.9
689	54.1-3319
690	51.1-100, n.,
	51.1-101, n.,
	51.1-110, n.,
	51.1-125, n.,
	51.1-142, n.
691	58.1-322
692	2.1-563.32,
	9-6.25:1,
	2.1-526.18R
	to 2.1-526.22R
693	6.1-194.7,
	8.1-201,
	8.1-207,
	8.2-511,
	8.3A-101
	to 8.3A-605
	8.4-101
	to 8.4-110,
	8.4-111,
	8.4-201
	to 8.4-204,
	8.4-205.1,
	8.4-206,
	8.4-207.1
	to 8.4-210,
	8.4-211.1
	to 8.4-214,
	8.4-301
	to 8.4-303,
	8.4-401
	to 8.4-403,
	8.4-405
	to 8.4-407,
	8.4-501
	to 8.4-504,
	8.3-101R
	to 8.3-805R
	8.4-109R,
	8.4-205R,
	8.4-207R,
	8.4-211R
694	51.1-305
695	15.1-1651
	to 15.1-1661
696	8.01-413
697	19.2-392.2
698	14.1-133.2
699	18.2-374.3
701	16.1-278.9
702	8.01-226.2
703	10.1-1410.1, n.
704	2.1-1.7,
	9-6.25:2,
	9-145.21
	to 9-145.29
705	18.2-308
706	2.1-1.6,
	2.1-20.4,
	9-6.25:2,
	54.1-106,
	54.1-2503,
	54.1-2600,
	54.1-2601,
	54.1-2602
707	18.2-308.4
708	18.2-255
709	55-248.41
	to 55-248.50:2
710	2.1-639.13
711	32.1-45.2
712	27-37.1
713	43-13,
	54.1-1100,
	54.1-1103,
	54.1-1106,
	54.1-1111
714	33.1-133
715	54.1-1100
716	16.1-278.15,
	20-107.2,
	20-108.1,
	20-108.2,
	34-34,
	51.1-102,
	51.1-802,
	63.1-250.1,
	63.1-251,
	63.1-256,
	63.1-270
717	54.1-2105,
	55-517
	to 55-525
718	19.2-389
719	8.01-324
720	8.01-417.1
721	8.01-44.4
722	18.2-271
723	18.2-248.01
724	18.2-255
725	18.2-110
726	18.2-53.1
727	18.2-308.1
728	16.1-247
729	15.1-138
730	10.1-1402, n.,
	10.1-1408.1, n.,
	10.1-1409, n.,
	10.1-1455, n.
731	8.01-226
732	16.1-286
733	6.1-2.13,
	38.2-4616

Acts 1992 Chapter	Code 1950 Section
734	54.1-3923, 54.1-3925 to 54.1-3925.3
735	18.2-280, 18.2-282, 18.2-308.1
736	16.1-278.9
737	18.2-248, 54.1-3401, 54.1-3401.1, 54.1-3435 to 54.1-3435.5, 54.1-3448, 54.1-3450, 54.1-3452, 54.1-3454, 54.1-3436R
738	18.2-279
739	55-59.1
740	53.1-32, 53.1-145, 53.1-185
741	9-145.45, 9-145.46
742	15.1-138, 16.1-228, 16.1-241, 16.1-253.4, 16.1-278.14, 16.1-278.15, 20-107.2
743	54.1-3405
744	16.1-69.6
745	18.2-374.1:1
746	19.2-389, 63.1-196.04, 63.1-198, 63.1-198.1
747	2.1-429, 3.1-801, 32.1-65, 32.1-72R
748	54.1-2981 to 54.1-2993, 37.1-134.4R,
749	14.1-125.1
750	15.1-7.3
751	10.1-1308, n., 10.1-1400, n., 10.1-1402, n., 10.1-1426, n.
752	37.1-67.3, 37.1-134.5
753	36-99.11, 46.2-1236, 46.2-1237
754	23-135.7:20, 36-55.27:1, 36-55.28, 36-55.63, 36-131, 36-135, 36-137, 36-139, 23-135.7:19R
755	2.1-51.14:1, 9-6.25:1, 9-6.25:2, 22.1-217, 22.1-284, 51.5-5, 51.5-7, n., 51.5-14, 51.5-15, 51.5-18, 51.5-21 to 51.5-23, 51.5-27 to 51.5-29, 63.1-68.1, 63.1-74, 63.1-74.1, 63.1-75.1, 63.1-77, 63.1-79, 63.1-81, 63.1-83, 63.1-85, 63.1-153, 63.1-155, 63.1-161 51.5-7R, 63.1-78R
756	18.2-247, 18.2-248
757	15.1-431
758	15.1-791.2, 15.1-791.3, 15.1-791.7, 15.1-791.13, 15.1-791.14, 15.1-791.16, 15.1-1372.1, 15.1-1372.2, 15.1-1372.2:1, n., 15.1-1372.3, 15.1-1372.4, 15.1-1372.5, 15.1-1372.6, 15.1-1372.7:1, 15.1-1372.8, 15.1-1372.10, 15.1-1372.12, 15.1-1372.13, 15.1-1372.17, 15.1-1372.37
759	54.1-2405
760	32.1-87, 54.1-3408
761	11-79.1, 11-79.2
762	38.2-2119
763	18.2-182.1, 58.1-216, 58.1-486, 58.1-637, 58.1-1005, 58.1-1008, 58.1-1017, 58.1-1614, 58.1-1618, 58.1-1816
764	36-99.11, 46.2-1236, 46.2-1237
765	11-61
766	55-226.2, 56-245.2, 56-245.3
767	38.2-5020
768	59.1-200, 59.1-207.40 to 59.1-207.44, 18.2-219R
769	2.1-328.1
770	2.1-20.1:2 to 2.1-20.1:4
771	2.1-1.7, 2.1-745, 2.1-761 to 2.1-768, 9-6.23, 9-6.25:1
772	54.1-2981 to 54.1-2993, 37.1-134.4R
773	10.1-1308, n., 10.1-1400, n., 10.1-1402, n., 10.1-1426, n.
774	10.1-1308, n., 10.1-1400, n., 10.1-1402, n., 10.1-1426, n.
775	10.1-218 to 10.1-225
776	3.1-684.43, 3.1-684.44, 3.1-684.46, 3.1-684.53
777	16.1-77, 40.1-49.3 to 40.1-49.7
778	9-292, 9-293, 9-294
779	36-98.01, 43-1, 43-3, 43-4, 43-4.01, 43-13.2
780	54.1-400

Acts 1992 Chapter	Code 1950 Section
	54.1-402.1, 54.1-406, 54.1-410
782	4-15
783	54.1-400 to 54.1-402.1, 54.1-406, 54.1-410
784	8.9-403, 8.9-405, 14.1-112, 50-75, 59.1-74
785	22.1-350 to 22.1-354
786	19.2-163.2
787	36-98.01, 43-1, 43-3, 43-4, 43-4.01, 43-13.2
788	9-145.35 to 9-145.38, 9-145.39
790	18.2-287.4
791	19.2-389, 22.1-296.2
792	8.01-335
793	9-6.14:4.1, 54.1-2952, 54.1-2952.1, 54.1-3303, 54.1-3401, 54.1-3408
794	46.2-752
795	64.1-16.3
796	8.01-195.4 to 8.01-195.7
797	59.1-284.7 to 59.1-284.12
798	11-46.2, 40.1-135 to 40.1-138
799	9-311 to 9-315
800	38.2-3431, 38.2-3432, 38.2-3540.1, 38.2-4214, 38.2-4319
801	10.1-2202 to 10.1-2205, 10.1-2206.1, 10.1-2206.2 10.1-2206R
802	13.1-603, 13.1-672.1 to 13.1-672.5, 13.1-672R
803	8.01-335
804	32.1-170 to 32.1-171.1, 32.1-174
805	46.2-1025
806	46.2-752
807	59.1-442 to 59.1-444
808	54.1-2406, 54.1-3405
809	54.1-2104
810	2.1-328, 5.1-88.2, 6.1-21, 6.1-195.86, 26-40, 26-40.01, 26-44, 26-45.1, 51.1-803, 54.1-1119, 54.1-2113
811	51.1-101, 51.1-102, 51.1-128, 51.1-142, 51.1-143, 51.1-156, 51.1-165, 51.1-303, 51.1-402
812	10.1-2500, 15.1-489, 45.1-361.1, 54.1-1100, 62.1-242, 62.1-254 to 62.1-270, 62.1-44.83R to 62.1-44.107R
813	24.1-17.109, 24.1-17.119, 24.1-17.128, 24.1-17.130, 24.1-17.137, 24.1-17.141, 24.1-17.186, 24.1-17.188, 24.1-17.189, 24.1-17.198, 24.1-17.199, 24.1-17.200, 24.1-17.202
814	16.1-88.03
815	51.1-206
816	65.2-801
817	8.01-249
818	9-311 to 9-316
819	62.1-44.34:8 to 62.1-44.34:13, 62.1-44.34:16
820	4-37, 58.1-3732.1, 59.1-364, 59.1-365, 59.1-368, 59.1-369, 59.1-375, 59.1-377, 59.1-378, 59.1-380 to 59.1-383, 59.1-391, 59.1-392, 59.1-396
821	Const., Art. X, § 8, n.
822	18.2-95, 18.2-96
823	15.1-227.70 to 15.1-227.82
825	46.2-1079
826	51.1-101, 51.1-155
827	15.1-291.2, 15.1-291.10
828	24.1-110
829	9-6.14:9
830	16.1-228, 16.1-247, 16.1-278.8, 16.1-278.9, 18.2-266, 18.2-267, 18.2-268.1 to 18.2-268.12, 18.2-269, 18.2-271, 29.1-738.2, 46.2-341.18, 46.2-341.22, 46.2-341.24, 46.2-341.25, 46.2-341.26:1 to 46.2-341.26:11, 46.2-341.27, 46.2-341.31, 46.2-936, 18.2-268R, 46.2-341.26R
831	32.1-71.1, 32.1-71.2, 32.1-71.4
832	64.1-67.2
833	18.2-251, 18.2-259.1, 46.2-390.1
834	58.1-3820, n., 58.1-3819
835	8.01-335
836	3.1-684.59 to 3.1-684.64, 28.2-100

Acts 1992 Chapter	Code 1950 Section
	to 28.2-1420
	28.1-1R,
	41.1-4.1R,
	62.1-1R
	to 62.1-4R,
	62.1-9.1R,
	62.1-13.1R,
	62.1-13.21R,
	62.1-194.1:1R
837	2.1-1.7,
	2.1-745
	to 2.1-759,
	9-6.25:1,
	16.1-278.5,
	16.1-286,
	16.1-294,
	22.1-101.1,
	37.1-197.1,
	63.1-55,
	63.1-248.6,
	66-14,
	66-35,
	2.1-700R,
	2.1-701R,
	2.1-702R,
	2.1-1.7, n.
838	46.2-384,
	46.2-386
839	11-41.2:1
841	2.1-1.6,
	2.1-20.4,
	9-6.25:2,
	54.1-2503,
	54.1-3710
	to 54.1-3716
842	58.1-3203
843	15.1-475
844	19.2-389,
	32.1-126.01,
	32.1-162.9:1,
	63.1-173.2,
	63.1-189.1,
	63.1-194.13
845	58.1-2103.1
846	9-310
848	9-156
	to 9-160,
	9-161.1,
	9-162.1,
	9-163,
	9-161R,
	9-162R
851	15.1-227.66
	to 15.1-227.69
852	18.2-254
853	10.1-1402
	to 10.1-1402.3
854	58.1-3967
855	24.1-168,
	24.1-185

Acts 1992 Chapter	Code 1950 Section
856	46.2-492,
	46.2-830.1
857	30-34.4:1,
	30-34.5
858	46.2-352,
	46.2-355
859	53.1-88,
	53.1-133.1
	to 53.1-133.9
860	20-108.1,
	20-108.2
861	19.2-316.1
862	18.2-36.1
863	14.1-133.2
864	46.2-1063
865	2.1-639.2
866	15.1-27.2
867	20-49.8
868	54.1-3314.1,
	54.1-3316
869	16.1-282
870	38.2-517
871	18.2-322.1
872	18.2-308.2:2
873	2.1-429,
	3.1-801,
	32.1-65,
	32.1-72R
874	24.1-17.301
	to 24.1-17.311,
	24.1-17.313
875	46.2-351
876	4-98.12:2
877	55-526,
	55-527
878	2.1-234.11,
	2.1-234.13
879	22.1-212.3,
	22.1-212.4,
	23-38.53:4
	to 23-38.53:7
880	2.1-1.7,
	2.1-745
	to 2.1-759,
	9-6.25:1,
	16.1-278.5,
	16.1-286,
	16.1-294,
	22.1-101.1,
	37.1-197.1,
	63.1-55,
	63.1-248.6,
	66-14,
	66-35,
	2.1-700R
	to 2.1-702R
881	19.2-77
882	38.2-517
883	18.2-323.01
884	16.1-340

Acts 1992 Chapter	Code 1950 Section
885	59.1-149
	to 59.1-167.3,
	59.1-158R
	to 59.1-161R
886	16.1-228,
	16.1-253.1,
	16.1-253.2,
	16.1-279.1,
	18.2-57.2,
	19.2-81.3,
	16.1-253.3R
887	2.1-1.1,
	2.1-1.3,
	2.1-1.7,
	2.1-51.9,
	5.1-8,
	9-6.25:2,
	10.1-1182
	to 10.1-1192,
	10.1-2501,
	10.1-2502,
	29.1-900,
	29.1-101.2
	to 29.1-101.9,
	29.1-103,
	62.1-195.1,
	62.1-201,
	62.1-218,
	3.1-18.7R,
	10.1-1200R
	to 10.1-1221R
888	18.2-60.3
889	58.1-3605.1,
	58.1-3603
890	54.1-2400
891	18.2-270,
	18.2-271,
	46.2-389,
	46.2-395,
	46.2-416.1
895	2.1-1.6,
	9-6.25:1,
	28.1-47,
	28.1-48.7
	to 28.1-48.15
897	22.1-227

ACTS 1992, SP. SESS.

Acts 1992, Sp. Sess. Chapter	Code 1950 Section
1	16.1-69.17,
	49-3
2	16.1-69.17,
	49-3
3	58.1-3237,
	58.1-3237.1
4	6.1-330.63,
	6.1-330.78
5	2.1-116

ACTS 1993

Acts 1993 Chapter	Code 1950 Section
1	55-79.73:1
2	22.1-348, 22.1-349
4	64.1-122.2
5	19.2-270.6
6	16.1-269
7	22.1-118
8	16.1-69.6:1
9	17-119.1:2
10	28.2-208, 28.2-208.1
11	28.2-226, 28.2-301, n., 28.2-502, n., 28.2-702
12	23-7.4, n.
13	10.1-1316, 10.1-1320
14	58.1-3211
15	32.1-87, 54.1-3408
16	8.01-156
17	32.1-126.01, 32.1-162.9:1, 63.1-173.2, 63.1-189.1, 63.1-194.13
18	62.1-44.34:23
19	10.1-104.1
20	62.1-44.34:11
21	56-235.5
22	58.1-2656
23	10.1-1455
24	46.2-203.1, 46.2-301, 46.2-355, 46.2-395, 46.2-416
25	58.1-3813
26	2.1-191.2
27	58.1-3954
28	58.1-322, n., 58.1-322.2, n., 58.1-402, n.
29	2.1-51.31
30	18.2-255.2
31	16.1-69.6:1
32	19.2-187.01
33	19.2-188.1, 19.2-310.2
34	18.2-322.1
35	33.1-125, 33.1-127, 33.1-129
36	55-344
37	58.1-339
38	54.1-3912
39	55-66.6
40	58.1-2702
41	58.1-3
42	58.1-2709
43	55-142.4
44	11-41.2:1
45	55-79.61
46	5.1-88.6
47	38.2-1414, 38.2-1427.3
48	19.2-389, 46.2-208, 63.1-248.8
49	58.1-3211
50	46.2-752
51	58.1-3967
52	46.2-340
53	46.2-336
54	58.1-460
55	38.2-1400
56	58.1-3822
57	46.2-1306.1
58	6.1-381
59	6.1-225.61
60	13.1-609, 13.1-809
61	13.1-620, 13.1-627
62	6.1-331
63	46.2-752
64	6.1-58.1
65	58.1-3703
66	58.1-3211
67	33.1-89
68	46.2-1139
69	46.2-1516
70	46.2-332, 46.2-341.4, 46.2-341.7, 46.2-341.10:1
71	33.1-72.1, 33.1-75.1
72	46.2-1314
73	46.2-1063
74	29.1-744.2
75	13.1-514, 13.1-514.1
76	58.1-3813
77	38.2-1601
78	58.1-3507
79	20-107.3
80	18.2-340.7
81	5.1-36, 5.1-41
82	33.1-46.2
83	46.2-703.1
85	32.1-176.4
86	46.2-1220
87	29.1-514
88	22.1-47.1 to 22.1-47.3
89	17-119.1:2
90	46.2-1571
91	58.1-3916
92	2.1-37.13, 2.1-37.17:1
93	58.1-3700
94	46.2-1164
95	14.1-112
96	55-512
97	32.1-36.1
98	46.2-878
99	58.1-608
100	58.1-3506
101	58.1-2707
102	58.1-3234
103	58.1-3017
104	58.1-3834
105	38.2-301, 38.2-302, 38.2-3324
106	3.1-388.1
108	52-8.4
109	11-47
110	2.1-703R, 2.1-759.1, 11-45, 22.1-218
111	54.1-1200, 54.1-1205
112	44-81
113	6.1-330.76, 13.1-619, 13.1-634, 13.1-819, 13.1-833, 13.1-1001.1, 13.1-1002, 13.1-1005, 13.1-1010.1, 13.1-1010.2, 13.1-1011, 13.1-1015, 13.1-1023, 13.1-1038.1, 13.1-1067, 13.1-1067.1R, 13.1-1071, 13.1-1072, 13.1-1102
114	15.1-227.67
115	3.1-685 to 3.1-688, 3.1-690, 3.1-690.1, 3.1-690.2
116	15.1-446.1
117	46.2-833.1
118	46.2-342
119	3.1-796.115
120	46.2-649.1
121	15.1-483.1
122	46.2-1519
123	46.2-1508
124	2.1-1.6, n.,

Acts 1993 Chapter	Code 1950 Section
	9-6.25:2, n., 36-85.17, n. to 36-85.21, n., 46.2-1500
125	46.2-1220
126	46.2-1078
127	46.2-706
128	15.1-431
129	54.1-111
130	38.2-508
132	38.2-3412R, 38.2-3412.1, 38.2-3413R
133	46.2-100
134	46.2-1157
135	51.1-102
136	58.1-3381
137	25-46.22
138	2.1-20.1
139	36-135
140	56-508.15, 56-508.16
141	7.1-10.1
142	38.2-1704
143	13.1-627
144	24.1-23
145	38.2-1801, 38.2-1813
146	59.1-372
147	38.2-4601.1, 38.2-4614
148	38.2-3431, 38.2-4319
149	58.1-3211
150	34-4.1, 34-6, 34-13, 34-14, 34-26, 34-27, 34-28.1
151	46.2-1102
152	38.2-508.2
153	60.2-611
154	58.1-608
155	2.1-188, 2.1-232
156	38.2-2124
157	58.1-3220.1
158	38.2-136, 38.2-1306.2, 38.2-1307, 38.2-1308, 38.2-1309, 38.2-1310R, 38.2-1322, 38.2-1323, 38.2-1331, 38.2-1334.1, 38.2-1334.2, 38.2-1341 to 38.2-1346, 38.2-4123, 38.2-4214, 38.2-4233, 38.2-4319, 38.2-4408, 38.2-4509
159	58.1-2402
160	24.1-97.1
161	22.1-118
162	2.1-1.7, 9-6.25:1, 9-145.47 to 9-145.49
163	58.1-3713
164	46.2-440
165	60.2-114.1
166	4-30
167	63.1-105
168	9-6.14:8.1
169	4-90.1
170	45.1-17
171	45.1-21
172	46.2-1089.1
174	3.1-735, 3.1-796.66, 3.1-796.68 to 3.1-796.70, 3.1-796.71, 3.1-796.73 to 3.1-796.74, 3.1-796.75, 3.1-796.83:1, 3.1-796.83:2, 3.1-796.107, 3.1-796.121, 3.1-796.128, 18.2-403.1 to 18.2-403.3
175	46.2-752
176	22.1-132.1
177	2.1-21
178	37.1-3
179	13.1-508
180	13.1-510
181	46.2-1099
182	6.1-8, 6.1-80
183	6.1-409, 6.1-412, 6.1-415, 6.1-416.1, 6.1-422, 6.1-425
184	6.1-363.1
186	6.1-60.1
187	58.1-3516.1
188	63.1-248.6:1
189	53.1-160
190	4-2, 4-25, 4-98.2
191	22.1-218
192	63.1-323
193	32.1-326.1
194	32.1-335, 32.1-338
195	53.1-150
196	38.2-414
197	32.1-122.6:02
198	55-79.99
199	54.1-2013.1
200	13.1-603
201	35.1-25
202	11-79
203	32.1-139R to 32.1-144R
204	29.1-529
205	2.1-342, 2.1-384
206	54.1-1706
207	22.1-132.1
208	8.01-412.4
209	29.1-344.1, 29.1-350
210	22.1-296.2
211	10.1-1422.1, 10.1-1422.3, 10.1-1422.4, 58.1-640, n., to 58.1-642, n., 58.1-643R, 58.1-644, n.
212	22.1-137
213	62.1-243
214	10.1-1400, 10.1-1408.1
215	10.1-1400
216	28.2-528
217	28.2-637R
218	28.2-540
219	28.2-226.1, 28.2-226.2, 28.2-240R, 28.2-241
220	22.1-36.1
221	4-59
222	2.1-25
223	11-41.01
224	36-55.44
225	63.1-196.5
226	2.1-514, 2.1-518R, 2.1-520
227	22.1-140
229	2.1-116.2
230	2.1-51.5:1
231	62.1-44.34:9, 62.1-44.34:23
232	2.1-1.7, n., 2.1-700, n., 2.1-701, n., 2.1-702, n., 2.1-746, n.,

Acts 1993 Chapter	Code 1950 Section
	2.1-750, n. to 2.1-758, n., 9-6.25:1, n., 16.1-278.5, n., 16.1-286, n., 16.1-294, n., 22.1-101.1, n., 37.1-197.1, n., 63.1-55, n., 63.1-248.6, n., 66-14, n., 66-35, n.
233	13.1-672.4, 13.1-672.5
234	46.2-649.2, 46.2-1179.1
236	9-145.30
237	28.2-242
238	28.2-503
239	62.1-195.1
240	57-55.2:1
241	28.2-302.1, 28.2-302.5, 28.2-302.10
242	11-41
243	29.1-739.1
244	6.1-33
245	28.2-227
246	60.2-114
247	45.1-22.1, 45.1-30.1, 45.1-65.1, 45.1-65.2
248	2.1-1.7, 2.1-51.21:1, 2.1-51.21:2, 2.1-51.40:1, 9-6.23, 9-6.25:1, 9-325 to 9-329
249	60.2-301, 60.2-302, 60.2-512, 60.2-532, 60.2-533, 60.2-612, 60.2-618
250	60.2-214
251	7.1-40.6
252	4-15
253	58.1-2101, 58.1-2116
254	45.1-361.1
255	46.2-749.3, 58.1-2101, 58.1-2116, 58.1-2117.1
257	38.2-1905.2
258	15.1-381
259	64.1-157
260	10.1-1152
261	56-304.15
262	54.1-3923
263	38.2-3411
264	10.1-2212
265	13.1-620, 56-1.2
266	15.1-1518
267	8.01-506.1
268	8.01-581.1
269	19.2-349
270	2.1-341, 2.1-342, 2.1-343.1, 2.1-344
271	38.2-3432
272	21-121.6
273	29.1-529
274	10.1-1422.5, 45.1-390.1R
275	29.1-742
276	45.1-361.41
278	46.2-871
279	18.2-340.9
280	65.2-101
282	11-41.2:1, n.
283	2.1-1.7, n., 2.1-700, n., to 2.1-702, n., 2.1-746, n., 2.1-750, n. to 2.1-758, n., 9-6.25:1, n., 16.1-278.5, n., 16.1-286, n., 16.1-294, n., 22.1-101.1, n., 37.1-197.1, n., 63.1-55, n., 63.1-248.6, n., 66-14, n., 66-35, n.
284	59.1-410
285	22.1-178
286	22.1-298
287	22.1-85
288	15.1-486.1
289	46.2-1531
290	46.2-711
291	46.2-351, 46.2-361
292	50-37.1, 50-37.3, 50-73.4, 50-73.11, 50-73.11:1, 50-73.11:2, 50-73.12, 50-73.13, 50-73.15, 50-73.17, 50-73.57, 50-73.77
293	22.1-5
294	22.1-304
295	19.2-182.2 to 19.2-182.6, 19.2-182.8 to 19.2-182.10, 19.2-182.12, 19.2-182.14 to 19.2-182.16, 37.1-151.1R
296	2.1-342
297	16.1-309.1
298	32.1-325
299	14.1-112
301	7.1-40.7
302	46.2-1313
303	2.1-639.2, 2.1-639.9, 2.1-639.13
304	51.1-142
305	38.2-4300
306	38.2-3500, 38.2-3525, 38.2-4214, 38.2-4319
307	38.2-322, 38.2-4214, 38.2-4319, 38.2-4509
308	1-13.9:1
309	58.1-3650.503 to 58.1-3650.520, n.
310	15.1-1415, 15.1-1440, 30-19.05, 58.1-609.1 to 58.1-609.13, 58.1-610, 58.1-629, 58.1-1720, 58.1-3510.1, 58.1-3510.3, 58.1-608R, 58.1-609R
311	8.01-109
312	16.1-69.19
313	19.2-387, 19.2-389, 19.2-391
314	53.1-127.1
315	32.1-45.1
316	58.1-2101, 58.1-2116
317	18.2-48
318	58.1-2102, 58.1-2104, 58.1-2109.1, 58.1-2115, 58.1-2120.1 to 58.1-2120.3, 58.1-2128.1, 58.1-2132.3, 58.1-2133 to

Acts 1993 Chapter	Code 1950 Section
	58.1-2136
319	19.2-217.1
322	18.2-286, 29.1-521.2
324	58.1-3516.1
326	58.1-3703
327	16.1-69.44
328	36-105
329	15.1-38
330	9-145.39:1 to 9-145.39:4
331	2.1-563.32
332	9-173.14, 9-173.15
333	2.1-373.1
334	14.1-101, 15.1-83.1, 15.1-84.1
335	32.1-127
336	35.1-10, 35.1-11, 35.1-14
337	32.1-122.6:02
338	63.1-220.3
339	63.1-133.29 to 63.1-133.40
340	33.1-69.01
341	24.1-258
342	54.1-3500
343	15.1-366
344	16.1-267, 16.1-343
345	14.1-195.1
347	32.1-102.3:2
348	19.2-389, 46.2-208, 63.1-248.8
349	33.1-152.1
350	19.2-73.1
351	22.1-319, 22.1-320, 22.1-322, 22.1-324, 22.1-327, 22.1-328, 22.1-333
352	22.1-30
353	62.1-44.34:15.1
354	59.1-274
355	24.1-174.1
359	15.1-295
361	22.1-280.2
364	32.1-60
365	55-510
366	6.1-302
367	15.1-518
368	16.1-69.9:4, 17-122.1
369	56-265.13:3
370	57-7R, 57-7.1, 57-15
371	58.1-602.1
372	58.1-3967
373	15.1-486.3
374	2.1-20.1:10 to 2.1-20.1:15
375	62.1-44.34:11, 62.1-44.34:12, 62.1-44.34:16
376	46.2-1600, 46.2-1602.1, 46.2-1603, 46.2-1603.2
377	19.2-264.3:2
378	65.2-805, 65.2-902
379	65.2-607
380	15.1-29.7
381	38.2-2206
382	55-248.6:1
383	15.1-1263
384	58.1-1805
385	8.01-516.1
386	14.1-112
387	53.1-80 to 53.1-82.3, 53.1-83R
388	58.1-2140 to 58.1-2143, 58.1-2145
389	45.1-98 to 45.1-98.4
390	10.1-1011
391	33.1-221.1:3, 33.1-268, 33.1-269, 33.1-277, 58.1-815.1, 58.1-816, 58.1-816.1
392	15.1-1031.1 to 15.1-1031.3
393	24.1-263
394	46.2-1231
395	15.1-791.3, 15.1-1372.3, 15.1-1372.23, 33.1-409 to 33.1-425
396	24.1-261
397	18.2-340.3, 18.2-340.9
398	15.1-1168.1, 15.1-1169
399	30-13
402	15.1-360.1
403	18.2-174.1
404	54.1-3002, 54.1-3010
405	46.2-1217, 46.2-1233.2
406	18.2-77
407	24.1-168, 24.1-185
408	51.1-206
409	46.2-1001
410	18.2-251
411	18.2-371
412	8.01-446
413	24.1-101
414	24.1-227, 24.1-228.1
415	9-168
416	18.2-264
417	20-111.1
418	18.2-66
419	6.1-2, 6.1-237.1 to 6.1-237.11, 13.1-620, 13.1-627, 6.1-237R, 6.1-238R to 6.1-242R
420	24.1-229.1
421	17-116.01:1
422	62.1-44.34:13
423	19.2-152.1
424	4-34
425	19.2-243
426	26-49, 55-59
427	55-220.1
428	8.01-420.4
429	17-41
430	59.1-369
431	19.2-76
432	6.1-2, 6.1-4, 6.1-17, 6.1-20, 6.1-21, 6.1-23, 6.1-32.11 to 6.1-32.30
433	4-11
434	19.2-368.18
435	16.1-228, 16.1-249
436	19.2-299.1
437	15.1-491.9
438	9-126
439	18.2-187.1, 18.2-190.1 to 18.2-190.4
440	18.2-67.8
441	8.01-396.1
442	45.1-2, 45.1-14, 45.1-21, 45.1-48, 45.1-52,

Acts 1993 Chapter	Code 1950 Section
	45.1-54 to
	45.1-56,
	45.1-60,
	45.1-62 to
	45.1-64,
	45.1-78,
	45.1-83 to
	45.1-85,
	45.1-98
443	63.1-248.3
444	46.2-309,
	46.2-323.1
445	14.1-118.1,
	17-59.2
446	14.1-53,
	15.1-821
447	19.2-265.01
448	19.2-303,
	19.2-390
449	18.2-303.1
450	18.2-361
451	18.2-308.2:2
452	19.2-265.01
453	59.1-443,
	59.1-444
454	55-17.1
455	3.1-14,
	59.1-200
456	10.1-1308,
	10.1-1402,
	62.1-44.15
458	22.1-296.2
459	10.1-1425.10 to
	10.1-1425.18
460	66-3,
	66-25.1
461	18.2-308.2:2,
	54.1-4201
462	19.2-183.1,
	19.2-262.1,
	19.2-263R
463	18.2-32
464	53.1-45,
	53.1-45.1,
	53.1-47
465	16.1-330.1,
	16.1-330.2
466	19.2-299
467	16.1-228,
	18.2-287.3R,
	18.2-308.2:1,
	18.2-308.7
468	16.1-299,
	16.1-301,
	16.1-306,
	16.1-307,
	18.2-308.2,
	19.2-388,
	19.2-389.1,
	19.2-390
469	10.1-1408.1
471	46.2-323,
	46.2-330,
	46.2-334,
	46.2-335,
	46.2-345,
	46.2-348
472	45.1-392
473	16.1-88.03
474	32.1-102.3:2
475	52-25.1
476	10.1-1408.1
477	52-8.4:1,
	54.1-4200,
	54.1-4201.1
478	16.1-88.03
480	24.1-29
481	8.01-195.3
482	16.1-278.9
483	56-414
484	19.2-386.11
485	53.1-151
486	18.2-308.2:2
487	66-3,
	66-25.1
488	53.1-45,
	53.1-45.1,
	53.1-47
489	19.2-183.1,
	19.2-262.1,
	19.2-263
490	18.2-32
491	53.1-151,
	53.1-199
492	19.2-299
493	18.2-308.2:2,
	54.1-4201
494	16.1-228,
	18.2-287.3R,
	18.2-308.7,
	18.2-308.2:1
495	9-145.37
496	10.1-1400,
	10.1-1408.1
497	15.1-1250.01
498	22.1-307,
	22.1-315
499	2.1-1.1,
	2.1-1.3,
	2.1-1.6,
	2.1-20.4,
	2.1-51.40,
	2.1-344,
	2.1-703.1,
	9-6.25:2,
	54.1-100.1,
	54.1-101,
	54.1-103,
	54.1-104,
	54.1-108,
	54.1-109,
	54.1-111 to
	54.1-114,
	54.1-200,
	54.1-201,
	54.1-300 to
	54.1-302,
	54.1-307,
	54.1-309,
	54.1-500,
	54.1-501,
	54.1-515,
	54.1-705,
	54.1-800,
	54.1-1100,
	54.1-1300,
	54.1-1302.1,
	54.1-1800,
	54.1-2019,
	54.1-2111,
	54.1-2112,
	54.1-2200,
	54.1-2201
500	18.2-58.1
501	46.2-323,
	46.2-330,
	46.2-334,
	46.2-335,
	46.2-345,
	46.2-348
502	53.1-20
503	46.2-1552.1
504	46.2-1550,
	46.2-1557.2
505	9-77.8,
	11-45
506	63.1-248.6
509	7.1-40.6
510	2.1-116
511	46.2-1138.2
512	18.2-62
513	18.2-334.2,
	18.2-340.1
514	46.2-360
518	46.2-361
519	58.1-3
520	20-108.1
521	2.1-1.6,
	9-6.25:1,
	10.1-208.1 to
	10.1-208.6
522	58.1-2627
523	8.01-249
524	64.1-67.2, n.
525	26-20.1
526	40.1-49.5
527	18.2-271.1
528	58.1-2670.1
529	58.1-2604
530	6.1-2.11,
	6.1-2.12
531	54.1-2808.1
532	57-35.14,

Acts 1993 Chapter	Code 1950 Section
	57-35.14:1, 57-35.20, 57-35.27
533	9-169, 46.2-217
534	20-60.3, 20-108.1, 63.1-251, 63.1-252.1
535	55-1
536	2.1-373.4
537	2.1-342, 9-6.14:4.1, 32.1-331.12 to 32.1-331.17
538	33.1-351, 33.1-353, 33.1-355, 33.1-356, 33.1-360, 33.1-361, 33.1-369, 33.1-370, 33.1-373
539	54.1-2013
540	32.1-102.3:2
541	58.1-322, n., 58.1-322.2, n., 58.1-402, n.
542	2.1-1.6, 2.1-20.4, 2.1-51.27, 2.1-739, 2.1-743, 2.1-744.1 to 2.1-744.6, 9-6.25:3
543	40.1-51.5, 40.1-51.8
544	40.1-51.10, 40.1-51.15
545	24.1-49, 24.1-50
546	24.1-36, 24.1-37
547	9-284
548	51.1-165
549	18.2-53.1, 18.2-67.2, 18.2-67.5, 18.2-67.10
550	19.2-76.1
551	9-6.14:9.1 to 9-6.14:9.3
552	2.1-342
553	63.1-220.3, 63.1-220.4, 63.1-223, 63.1-225, 63.1-229
554	14.1-52
555	54.1-2729
556	8.01-399
557	58.1-3516
559	58.1-3619
560	46.2-749.4
561	2.1-114.5
562	58.1-438.1
563	14.1-52
564	32.1-102.3:2, 32.1-102.3:2, n.
565	46.2-752
566	46.2-731
567	2.1-757
568	51.1-206
569	19.2-299.1
570	8.01-418.2
571	46.2-649.2, 46.2-1179.1
572	8.01-341
573	20-107.2
574	46.2-1219.1
575	18.2-188
576	60.2-229
577	57-49
579	46.2-829
580	55-331
581	26-12, 26-12.1
582	45.1-243, 45.1-258
583	57-49
584	58.1-3237.1
585	58.1-338, 58.1-445.1
586	46.2-1530
587	33.1-46.2
588	46.2-353, 46.2-354
589	16.1-306
590	18.2-67.3
591	46.2-1094
592	19.2-268.2
593	16.1-77, n., 16.1-122.1, n.
597	55-59.1
598	46.2-1233.1
599	20-107.2
600	40.1-29
601	3.1-796.67:2, 3.1-796.105, 3.1-796.120
602	63.1-251
603	16.1-273
604	3.1-919, 3.1-920, 3.1-921R, 3.1-922 to 3.1-928, 3.1-932 to 3.1-934, 3.1-936, 3.1-941.1 to 3.1-944, 3.1-947, 3.1-948R, 3.1-949, 3.1-949.1, 3.1-949.4, 3.1-950, 3.1-951R to 3.1-954R, 3.1-954.1, 3.1-955R, 3.1-956 to 3.1-958, 3.1-962R, 3.1-962.1, 3.1-965, 3.1-967
605	8.01-396.1
606	62.1-44.15:3
607	9-77.4
608	18.2-115.1
609	18.2-110, 18.2-346
610	8.01-413.01
611	15.1-1032.2
614	9-145.39:5 to 9-145.39:8
615	8.01-379.1
616	53.1-127.1
617	46.2-358
619	24.1-49, 24.1-50
620	14.1-53, 15.1-821
621	2.1-37.01, 15.1-49, 15.1-50R, 15.1-50.4, 15.1-50.5, 15.1-765.2, 44-146.19
622	9-169, 15.1-136.2, 56-334
623	29.1-417, 29.1-418, 29.1-422, 29.1-743
624	65.2-1203
625	46.2-749.3, 58.1-2101, 58.1-2116, 58.1-2117.1
626	36-108
627	38.2-3737
628	18.2-371.1
629	19.2-187.2
630	15.1-131.6:1
631	18.2-371.2
632	16.1-292

Acts 1993 Chapter	Code 1950 Section
633	20-107.2
634	55-79.94,
	55-248.18,
	55-487
635	14.1-195.1
636	19.2-119 to
	19.2-121,
	19.2-123
637	19.2-271.2
638	2.1-342,
	9-157.1,
	9-158,
	9-160,
	9-163,
	9-166.1 to
	9-166.7,
	11-45
639	24.1-257.1,
	24.1-257.2
640	58.1-301
641	
	24.1-1R to
	24.1-282R, 24.2-100 to
	24.2-1019
642	11-46.3
643	15.1-11.04,
	15.1-857.1
644	28.2-1208
645	16.1-305.1,
	16.1-309
646	58.1-608
647	58.1-608.1
649	30-19.04
651	15.1-11.04,
	15.1-857.1
652	2.1-7.1,
	15.1-945.3
653	2.1-1.7,
	2.1-51.21,
	2.1-51.21:3,
	2.1-51.21:4,
	9-6.25:1
654	22.1-251,
	22.1-252R
655	32.1-116.3
656	62.1-140,
	62.1-147
657	32.1-126.01,
	32.1-162.9:1,
	63.1-173.2,
	63.1-189.1,
	63.1-194.13
658	22.1-32
659	22.1-271.4
660	2.1-1.6,
	2.1-20.4,
	2.1-526.14,
	2.1-526.14:1R,
	2.1-526.14:2R,
	9-6.25:2,
	32.1-126.1,
	36-99.7,
	54.1-500,
	54.1-500.1,
	54.1-501,
	54.1-502 to
	54.1-505,
	54.1-506R,
	54.1-508R,
	54.1-509R,
	54.1-511R,
	54.1-512,
	54.1-513,
	54.1-515 to
	54.1-517,
	63.1-198.01
661	22.1-253.13:4
662	36-97,
	54.1-410
663	15.1-1399.18 to
	15.1-1399.25,
	45.1-246
664	32.1-11.2,
	32.1-36.1
665	2.1-1.7,
	2.1-51.21,
	2.1-51.21:3,
	2.1-51.21:4,
	9-6.25:1
666	16.1-311
667	55-79.41,
	55-79.46,
	55-79.53,
	55-79.54,
	55-79.71,
	55-79.72R,
	55-79.72:1,
	55-79.72:2,
	55-79.73,
	55-79.74:4,
	55-79.77,
	55-79.80,
	55-79.80:2,
	55-79.83,
	55-79.84:1,
	55-79.87
668	32.1-102.4
669	9-6.14:4.1,
	9-6.16,
	9-6.17,
	9-6.20,
	9-77.10:1
670	15.1-1248
671	44-146.16,
	44-146.19
672	15.1-491
673	46.2-341.26:2,
	46.2-341.28
674	18.2-308.2:01,
	18.2-308.2:2
675	29.1-717.3
677	46.2-357
678	54.1-2003
679	38.2-1614R
681	15.1-163,
	15.1-167
683	38.2-4900
684	29.1-519
686	59.1-296.2:1
687	46.2-361
688	18.2-268.7
689	26-17R,
	26-17.1R,
	26-17.2R,
	26-17.3 to
	26-17.10
690	15.1-1248
691	2.1-483.2
692	32.1-138.1
693	65.2-702
694	65.2-703
695	38.2-1815
696	24.1-17.115,
	24.1-17.126,
	24.1-17.130,
	24.1-17.131,
	24.1-17.133,
	24.1-17.154,
	24.1-17.156 to
	24.1-17.159,
	24.1-17.161 to
	24.1-17.164,
	24.1-17.170,
	24.1-17.174,
	24.1-17.175,
	24.1-17.191,
	24.1-17.192,
	24.1-17.196,
	24.1-17.198,
	24.1-17.202
697	23-165.4,
	23-165.5
698	22.1-207.3
699	2.1-51.38 to
	2.1-51.40,
	2.1-64.33,
	2.1-548.10,
	2.1-548.11,
	2.1-548.20,
	2.1-703.1,
	10.1-1100,
	59.1-271
700	32.1-326.1
701	55-19.5
702	8.01-66.12,
	8.01-225.1,
	8.01-581.13,
	8.01-581.16,
	8.01-581.18 to
	8.01-581.19:1
703	18.2-366
704	32.1-102.1 to
	32.1-102.3,

Acts 1993 Chapter	Code 1950 Section
	32.1-102.3:2, 32.1-102.4, 32.1-102.11, n.
705	32.1-48.02
707	15.1-492, n.
708	18.2-255.2
709	10.1-609.1
710	1-13.39:2
711	10.1-1322
712	24.1-17.5 to 24.1-17.10, 24.1-17.13, 24.1-17.14, 24.1-17.17, 24.1-17.19, 24.1-17.20, 24.1-17.22, 24.1-17.26, 24.1-17.29, 24.1-17.30, 24.1-17.32, 24.1-17.34, 24.1-17.36 to 24.1-17.41, 24.1-17.45, 24.1-17.46
713	57-27.1
714	15.1-28
715	24.1-251, 24.1-251.1
716	15.1-492, n.
717	54.1-1116R
718	2.1-1.6, 2.1-548.22 to 2.1-548.25, 9-6.25:1
719	65.2-102
720	2.1-341, 2.1-343
721	10.1-1308, n., 10.1-1400, n., 10.1-1402, n., 10.1-1426, n.
722	2.1-116.9:6
723	15.1-945.3
724	2.1-394
725	65.2-804
726	2.1-1.8, 2.1-116.18, 2.1-116.19, 9-6.23
727	18.2-340.9
728	32.1-176.4
729	18.2-255.2
730	22.1-19, 63.1-195, 63.1-196, 63.1-196.001, 63.1-196.01, 63.1-196.01:1, 63.1-196.03, 63.1-196.04, 63.1-196.1, 63.1-196.3, 63.1-196.3:1, 63.1-196.5, 63.1-198, 63.1-198.01, 63.1-198.02R, 63.1-198.03, 63.1-198.04, 63.1-198.1, 63.1-198.2, 63.1-199, 63.1-201, n., 63.1-201.1, 63.1-202, 63.1-202.1, 63.1-210.1, 63.1-211.2, 63.1-211.3
731	15.1-676, 15.1-700, 15.1-760.1, 15.1-808, 15.1-816, 15.1-830, 15.1-933
732	56-537, 56-543
733	15.1-362.1
734	15.1-431
735	9-6.15, n.
736	59.1-455 to 59.1-459
737	57-5
738	15.1-502.1
739	10.1-1321.1
740	22.1-289
741	59.1-274
742	22.1-19, 63.1-195, 63.1-196, 63.1-196.001, 63.1-196.01, 63.1-196.01:1, 63.1-196.03, 63.1-196.04, 63.1-196.1, 63.1-196.3, 63.1-196.3:1, 63.1-196.5, 63.1-198, 63.1-198.01, 63.1-198.02R, 63.1-198.03, 63.1-198.04, 63.1-198.1, 63.1-198.2, 63.1-199, 63.1-201, 63.1-201.1, 63.1-202, 63.1-202.1, 63.1-210.1 to 63.1-211.3
743	2.1-20.1:2 to 2.1-20.1:4
744	15.1-18.2
745	15.1-1511
746	18.2-268.2
747	18.2-460
748	18.2-308
749	62.1-44.15:6
750	2.1-342
751	2.1-1.8, 2.1-116.18, 2.1-116.19, 9-6.23
752	2.1-1.7, 2.1-51.21:1, 2.1-51.21:2, 2.1-51.40:1, 9-6.23, 9-6.25:1, 9-325 to 9-329
753	54.1-2956.9 to 54.1-2956.11
754	55-248.6
755	10.1-204
756	62.1-44.15:6
757	2.1-1.5, 2.1-51.43, 9-6.23, 18.2-271.2
758	15.1-446.1, 15.1-447, 15.1-489
759	8.01-419.1, 43-34
760	59.1-200, 59.1-445 to 59.1-454
761	15.1-1511
762	32.1-102.3:2
763	15.1-362.1
764	38.2-106, 38.2-107
765	22.1-138, 32.1-229.01:1
766	2.1-116, 52-6.1
767	54.1-2940, 54.1-3605
768	53.1-32, 53.1-32.1
769	8.01-226.3
770	15.1-430, 15.1-447, 15.1-503.2
771	15.1-1646, 15.1-1646.1

Acts 1993 Chapter	Code 1950 Section
772	9-6.14:9.1 to 9-6.14:9.3
773	3.1-249.27, 3.1-249.35, 3.1-249.46, 3.1-249.47, 3.1-249.49, 3.1-249.51 to 3.1-249.55, 3.1-249.58, 3.1-249.63, 3.1-249.64, 3.1-249.70, 3.1-249.77
774	6.1-330.72, 38.2-122.1, 38.2-233, 38.2-1601, 38.2-1902
775	3.1-796.128
776	24.1-254.1, 24.1-255, 24.1-257.1
777	22.1-132.1
778	16.1-334, 20-49
780	15.1-496.1
781	2.1-37.01, 15.1-49, 15.1-50R, 15.1-50.4, 15.1-50.5, 15.1-765.2, 44-146.19
782	15.1-7.3
783	22.1-32
784	54.1-2927
785	32.1-127.3
786	15.1-428.1, 15.1-457R
787	53.1-80 to 53.1-82.3, 53.1-83R
788	36-106
789	15.1-29.23
790	2.1-1.6, 3.1-22.38 to 3.1-22.52, 9-6.25:3
791	15.1-37.3:9
792	65.2-312
793	33.1-23.03:1, 33.1-268, 33.1-269, 33.1-272, 33.1-277, 58.1-638
794	32.1-176.4, 32.1-176.5
796	46.2-817
797	15.1-1416
800	46.2-1053
801	10.1-1425.8
802	33.1-70.01
803	58.1-321, 58.1-322
804	30-19.1:4
805	2.1-1.6, 3.1-22.38 to 3.1-22.52, 9-6.25:3
806	60.2-114, 65.2-903
807	51.5-3
808	46.2-1052, 46.2-1053
809	3.1-796.11:3 to 3.1-796.11:8, 3.1-796.11:10
810	54.1-3408
811	18.2-340.3, 18.2-340.6, 18.2-340.9
812	18.2-340.5
813	24.1-228.2:1
814	36-137
815	54.1-1100
816	54.1-2103
817	3.1-796.85 to 3.1-796.92, 3.1-796.96, 3.1-796.97, 3.1-796.128, 18.2-403.3
818	55-520
819	22.1-209.1:2, 22.1-257, 22.1-278
820	2.1-51R
821	58.1-3650.504 to 58.1-3650.506, n., 58.1-3650.510, n., 58.1-3650.512, n., 58.1-3650.521 to 58.1-3650.564, n.
822	13.1-308, 13.1-336
823	15.1-499.1
824	55-518
825	18.2-249
826	15.1-50.3, 15.1-821.1
827	55-510
828	4-25
829	15.1-29.24
830	10.1-104.1
831	18.2-308.4
832	23-38.53:6, 23-38.53:7
833	16.1-318
834	52-25.1
835	18.2-53.1
836	15.1-466
837	10.1-1410
838	15.1-1403
839	29.1-335
840	18.2-477.1
841	8.01-114 to 8.01-117, 8.01-119, 8.01-121, 8.01-261, 8.01-533, 8.01-534, 8.01-537, 8.01-537.1, 8.01-540, 8.01-541, 8.01-551, 55-230, 55-230.1, 55-232.1R
842	55-369, 55-370
843	23-7.1:02
844	8.01-229
845	18.2-159
846	15.1-466, 15.1-475
847	55-524
848	55-525
849	55-463, 55-492
850	15.1-1241, 15.1-1250.03, 15.1-1252, 15.1-1259
851	15.1-1372.6, 15.1-1372.7:1
852	18.2-63, 18.2-64.1
853	18.2-374.1:1
854	43-34.1
855	18.2-309
856	22.1-209.1:2, 22.1-257, 22.1-278
857	36-55.28
858	15.1-50.1
859	9-6.25:1, 9-330 to 9-333
860	15.1-131
861	18.2-308
864	15.1-466
865	58.1-345.1, 58.1-346, 58.1-346.1, n., 58.1-346.2, n., 58.1-346.3, n., 58.1-346.4, n.,
866	2.1-124, 3.1-1053,

Acts 1993 Chapter	Code 1950 Section
	3.1-1058,
	4.1-100 to
	4.1-517
	6.1-18,
	6.1-195.82,
	7.1-21.1,
	9-169,
	15.1-136.2,
	16.1-278.9,
	18.2-110,
	18.2-265.4,
	18.2-433,
	23-7.1:01,
	33.1-252,
	46.2-347,
	46.2-867,
	51.1-800,
	54.1-3443,
	58.1-1101,
	58.1-3259,
	58.1-3505,
	58.1-3507,
	58.1-3833
867	15.1-1348
868	40.1-57.2,
	40.1-57.3
869	9-6.25:1,
	9-6.25:2,
	54.1-2410 to
	54.1-2414,
	54.1-2503,
	54.1-2506,
	54.1-2510,
	54.1-2964
870	15.1-1372.6,
	15.1-1372.7:1
872	2.1-21
876	2.1-639.6
877	58.1-345.1,
	58.1-345.1, n.
878	22.1-57.3,
	22.1-57.3:1
879	40.1-57.2,
	40.1-57.3
880	58.1-346
881	56-304.16
882	18.2-308.2:1
883	2.1-342
884	15.1-489
885	46.2-1801 to
	46.2-1805
886	46.2-1801 to
	46.2-1805
887	20-15
888	18.2-308.8
889	16.1-305.1,
	16.1-309,
	22.1-3.2,
	22.1-132.1,
	22.1-277.2,
	22.1-278,
	22.1-289
890	58.1-346.1, n.,
	58.1-346.3, n.
891	Const.,
	Art. II, § 2, n.,
	Const., Art. II, § 3, n.,
	Const., Art. II, § 4, n.
892	Const., Art. IV,
	§ 14, n.
893	Const,
	Art. V, § 6, n.
894	15.1-33.2
895	14.1-18.2, n.,
	51.1-101,
	51.1-126.1,
	51.1-142,
	51.1-143,
	51.1-157,
	51.1-301,
	51.1-308,
	51.1-504
896	15.1-1377,
	15.1-1378
897	62.1-44.26
898	9-6.14:2,
	9-6.14:4.1,
	9-6.14:7.1,
	9-6.14:9,
	9-6.14:9.1,
	9-6.14:9.3,
	9-6.14:11,
	9-6.14:12,
	9-6.14:14.1
899	54.1-2103
900	55-79.84:1
901	30-28.1:2
903	22.1-3,
	22.1-254,
	22.1-256
905	8.01-576.4 to
	8.01-576.12
906	25-46.20
907	53.1-151
908	16.1-269
909	8.01-401.3
910	4-2,
	4-98.2
911	58.1-3210
915	27-23.1
916	2.1-20.1:01
917	46.2-351.1
918	58.1-3703,
	58.1-3706
919	18.2-271.1
920	18.2-259.1,
	46.2-390.1
921	24.1-254.1,
	24.1-255,
	24.1-257.1
922	63.1-110
923	63.1-75.1,
	63.1-142
924	46.2-906.1
925	10.1-560 to
	10.1-564,
	10.1-566,
	10.1-569,
	10.1-569.1
926	16.1-299,
	16.1-301,
	16.1-306,
	16.1-307,
	18.2-308.2,
	18.2-308.2:1,
	19.2-388,
	19.2-389.1,
	19.2-390
927	16.1-330.1,
	16.1-330.2
928	8.01-581.2 to
	8.01-581.4:1,
	8.01-581.5,
	8.01-581.7 to
	8.01-581.8,
	8.01-581.9R
929	8.01-217
	8.01-259,
	8.01-261
	8.01-320,
	8.01-353.01,
	14.1-112,
	14.1-113,
	14.1-114R,
	14.1-135.1,
	14.1-137R,
	16.1-69.5,
	16.1-69.6:1,
	16.1-69.7,
	16.1-69.8,
	16.1-69.9:01,
	16.1-69.9:1,
	16.1-69.10,
	16.1-69.12,
	16.1-69.21,
	16.1-69.22:1,
	16.1-69.35,
	16.1-69.37 to
	16.1-69.39,
	16.1-69.48,
	16.1-69.50,
	16.1-69.55,
	16.1-94,
	16.1-97.1,
	16.1-106,
	16.1-107,
	16.1-133,
	16.1-226,
	16.1-228,
	16.1-241,
	16.1-242 to
	16.1-244,
	16.1-260,

Acts 1993 Chapter	Code 1950 Section
	16.1-262 to
	16.1-264,
	16.1-266,
	16.1-272.1,
	16.1-272.2,
	16.1-278,
	16.1-278.2,
	16.1-278.3,
	16.1-278.12,
	16.1-278.13,
	16.1-278.15,
	16.1-278.18,
	16.1-278.20,
	16.1-289,
	16.1-292,
	16.1-296,
	16.1-296.2,
	16.1-297,
	16.1-298,
	16.1-300,
	16.1-302,
	16.1-305,
	16.1-306,
	16.1-306.1,
	17-7.2,
	17-116.05,
	20-49,
	20-49.2,
	20-79,
	20-96,
	20-99.1:1,
	20-107.3,
	20-113,
	22.1-87,
	22.1-214,
	22.1-214.1,
	31-8,
	31-15R to
	31-18R
	32.1-258,
	32.1-260,
	63.1-204.1,
	63.1-209,
	63.1-220.5,
	63.1-221,
	63.1-222,
	63.1-235,
	63.1-236,
	63.1-248.5:1,
	63.1-252.1,
	63.1-268.1,
	64.1-5.1
930	2.1-20.1,
	2.1-33,
	2.1-37.3,
	2.1-747,
	2.1-751,
	2.1-753,
	2.1-757,
	8.01-331,
	9-168,
	9-173.8,
	15.1-720,
	16.1-69.11,
	16.1-69.17,
	16.1-69.32,
	16.1-69.33,
	16.1-133.1,
	16.1-218,
	16.1-224,
	16.1-230,
	16.1-232 to
	16.1-236,
	16.1-240,
	16.1-241.1R,
	16.1-245 to
	16.1-247,
	16.1-253.4,
	16.1-254 to
	16.1-256,
	16.1-259,
	16.1-267,
	16.1-269 to
	16.1-273,
	16.1-275,
	16.1-277.1,
	16.1-278.4 to
	16.1-278.8,
	16.1-278.14,
	16.1-278.16,
	16.1-278.17,
	16.1-280,
	16.1-281,
	16.1-291,
	16.1-293,
	16.1-296, n.,
	16.1-299,
	16.1-307,
	16.1-309,
	16.1-314,
	16.1-316,
	16.1-317,
	16.1-328,
	16.1-331,
	16.1-339 to
	16.1-342,
	16.1-344,
	16.1-348,
	17-28,
	17-111.4,
	17-111.6,
	17-222,
	18.2-64.1,
	18.2-351,
	18.2-353,
	18.2-477.1,
	19.2-48.1,
	19.2-71,
	19.2-218.2,
	19.2-240,
	19.2-262,
	19.2-353.3,
	19.2-368.3,
	19.2-368.6,
	20-67,
	20-71.1,
	20-88,
	20-88.13,
	20-88.20:2,
	20-138 to
	20-140,
	22.1-257,
	22.1-262,
	22.1-268,
	22.1-279.2,
	37.1-1,
	37.1-64,
	37.1-97,
	40.1-28.9,
	46.2-334,
	46.2-336,
	46.2-386,
	46.2-1098,
	53.1-120,
	53.1-124,
	53.1-145,
	54.1-2969,
	63.1-56,
	63.1-57.1,
	63.1-204,
	63.1-220.3,
	63.1-248.2 to
	63.1-248.4,
	63.1-248.6,
	63.1-248.13,
	63.1-249,
	63.1-256,
	63.1-267.1,
	65.2-101
932	44-75.1,
	44-75.1:1
933	58.1-3713, n.,
	58.1-3713.1, n.
934	58.1-3700
935	15.1-159.7:1 to
	15.1-159.7:7
936	3.1-398.1
937	11-47.3
938	2.1-20.1:2 to
	2.1-20.1:4
939	2.1-526.9,
	8.01-600.1R
940	8.01-420.4
941	20-27
942	54.1-1115.1
943	59.1-274
944	9-6.14:7.1,
	10.1-1307.01,
	10.1-1402.01,
	62.1-44.15:01
945	8.01-424
947	22.1-269.1
948	10.1-1105,

Acts 1993 Chapter	Code 1950 Section
	10.1-1181.1 to 10.1-1181.7
949	46.2-706.1
950	38.2-4608, 38.2-4617, 38.2-4618
951	8.01-428
952	30-28.1, 30-28.2, 30-28.5:1, 30-28.7
953	63.1-133.1
954	4-98.12:2, 4-98.12:2, n.
955	63.1-248.6, 63.1-248.6:1, 63.1-248.7, 63.1-248.7:1, 63.1-248.8
956	55-509.1, 55-513, 55-515, 58.1-3284.1
957	2.1-373.1, 15.1-291.1, 32.1-37.1, 32.1-102.3:1, 32.1-102.3:2, 32.1-102.3:2.1, 32.1-162.7, 36-99.5:1, 36-139.3, 37.1-98, 54.1-3408, 58.1-608, 63.1-25.1, 63.1-172, 63.1-173R, 63.1-173.2, 63.1-173.3, 63.1-174, 63.1-174.001, 63.1-174.01, 63.1-174.1, 63.1-175, 63.1-177, 63.1-178.1, 63.1-179.1, 63.1-180 to 63.1-182.1
958	54.1-2105.1, 55-79.93:1, 55-504.1, 55-516.1, 55-528 to 55-530
959	3.1-796.66, 3.1-796.74, 3.1-796.94, 3.1-796.101, 3.1-796.126:1 to 3.1-796.126:7
960	38.2-3430 to 38.2-3433
961	18.2-128
962	63.1-236
963	2.1-384, 63.1-248.6:1
965	32.1-263, 32.1-283, 32.1-285, 32.1-285.1, 54.1-2807
966	20-27
967	9-252, 9-253, 9-263
970	16.1-107, 16.1-296
971	11-45, 32.1-325
972	16.1-278.9, 18.2-270
973	18.2-340.2:1, 18.2-340.6, 18.2-340.9
974	56-484.2
975	16.1-274, 63.1-51
976	15.1-805.1
977	3.1-796.93:1, 3.1-796.116, 3.1-796.117
978	19.2-264.5
979	59.1-274
980	14.1-133.2
981	16.1-260
982	15.1-1662 to 15.1-1675
983	24.1-17.301, 24.1-17.303, 24.1-17.313
984	46.2-1112, 46.2-1113
985	38.2-317, 38.2-1901, 38.2-1902, 38.2-1904, 38.2-1905.1, 38.2-1905.2, 38.2-1906, 38.2-1908, 38.2-1912, 38.2-1912.1, 38.2-1913, 38.2-1916, 38.2-1919, 38.2-1919.1, 38.2-2000.1, 38.2-2001, 38.2-2002, 38.2-2002.1, 38.2-2009R, 38.2-2014, 38.2-2015, 65.2-823
986	32.1-290, 32.1-290.1, 32.1-292.1, 32.1-295
987	36-11.1:1
988	9-156, 9-157, 9-159, 9-160,
989	63.1-133.1
990	32.1-325.01
991	54.1-2408, 54.1-2409, 54.1-2915, 54.1-2917
992	22.1-254.1
993	2.1-373.1, 15.1-291.1, 32.1-37.1, 32.1-102.3:1, 32.1-102.3:2, 32.1-102.3:2.1, 32.1-162.7, 36-99.5:1, 36-139.3, 37.1-98, 54.1-3408, 58.1-608, 63.1-25.1, 63.1-172, 63.1-173R, 63.1-173.2, 63.1-173.3, 63.1-174, 63.1-174.001, 63.1-174.01, 63.1-174.1 63.1-175, 63.1-177, 63.1-178.1, 63.1-179.1, 63.1-180, 63.1-181, 63.1-182, 63.1-182.1
994	2.1-429, n., 2.1-512, n., 14.1-79, n., 14.1-143.2, n., 19.2-326, n., 33.1-23.5:1, n., 33.1-41.1, n., 37.1-89, n., 53.1-120, n., 58.1-638, n.
995	46.2-1176 to

Acts 1993 Chapter	Code 1950 Section
	46.2-1187
996	24.1-165.3
997	10.1-1318
998	46.2-1176 to 46.2-1187

ACTS 1993, SP. SESS.

Acts 1993, Sp. Sess. Chapter	Code 1950 Section
1	2.1-234.13, 2.1-234.25, 2.1-234.28:1
2	46.2-1176 to 46.2-1187

ACTS 1994

Acts 1994 Chapter	Code 1950 Section
1	58.1-301
3	2.1-155.1R, 30-78 to 30-84
4	2.1-51.27, 51.1-100R to 51.1-124R, 51.1-124.1 to 51.1-124.10, 51.1-124.20 to 51.1-124.27, 51.1-124.30 to 51.1-124.35
5	6.1-32.18:1 to 6.1-32.18:3
6	6.1-32.25
7	6.1-21, 6.1-32.15, 6.1-32.30R, 6.1-67, 6.1-68, 6.1-71, 6.1-78 to 6.1-80, 6.1-111, 6.1-113
8	38.2-4705
9	38.2-2230
10	13.1-509
11	65.2-312
12	56-257.2
13	6.1-225.19
14	6.1-225.60
15	12.1-28
16	2.1-190.1, 2.1-234R
17	2.1-114.5
18	18.2-286, 29.1-521.2
19	16.1-300
20	9-168
21	16.1-292
22	9-145.21

Acts 1994 Chapter	Code 1950 Section
23	7.1-22
24	9-173.6
25	26-4
26	54.1-1502, 54.1-1503
27	8.01-342
28	2.1-1.6, 2.1-20.4, 9-6.25:1, 9-6.25:2, 40.1-51.3:1, 40.1-51.4:1, 40.1-51.4:2, 45.1-1 to 45.1-105R, 45.1-145 to 45.1-161R, 45.1-161.1, 45.1-161.2 to 45.1-161.24, 45.1-161.25 to 45.1-161.42, 45.1-161.43 to 45.1-161.98, 45.1-161.99 to 45.1-161.322
29	54.1-405
30	54.1-3900
31	23-231.8 to 23-231.10
32	8.01-266
33	7.1-40.2:1
34	4.1-103.1, 19.2-389
35	34-28.1
36	16.1-266, 16.1-266.1
37	8.01-277
38	8.01-581.2
39	8.01-424
40	8.01-512.3, 8.01-512.4
41	19.2-187
42	16.1-252
43	2.1-304.2 to 2.1-304.7, 9-6.25:1
44	36-139
45	9-182, 9-183.1 to 9-183.3, 9-183.8, 9-183.9
46	9-183.4
47	9-183.3
48	2.1-116, 58.1-4024
49	58.1-4020
50	46.2-357

Acts 1994 Chapter	Code 1950 Section
51	46.2-911R
52	33.1-190.2
53	54.1-3408
54	46.2-828
55	22.1-123
56	46.2-906.1
57	32.1-102.3:2
58	54.1-3001
59	18.2-68R to 18.2-70R
60	9-173.4R, 9-173.5R, 9-173.14R, 9-173.15R, 9-173.16 to 9-173.20
61	2.1-51.14:1, n., 9-6.25:1, n., 9-6.25:2, n., 51.5-5, n., 51.5-7R, 51.5-14, n., 51.5-15, n., 51.5-18, n., 51.5-21, n., 51.5-22, n., 51.5-23, n., 51.5-27, n., 51.5-28, n., 51.5-29, n.
62	32.1-46
63	9-305 to 9-309R
64	2.1-1.5, 2.1-45, 2.1-51.21, 2.1-116, 2.1-132, 2.1-451, 2.1-467, 2.1-467.2, 7.1-28, 8.01-673, 8.01-675.4, 9-6.25:2, 14.1-112, 16.1-306.1, 17-47.4, 17-60, 17-111.5, 24.2-926, 30-28.15, 30-34.5 to 30-34.7, 42.1-1, 42.1-2, 42.1-3.1, 42.1-8 to 42.1-11, 42.1-13, 42.1-15,

Acts 1994 Chapter	Code 1950 Section
	42.1-17 to 42.1-19, 42.1-41, 42.1-51, 42.1-54, 42.1-72, 42.1-78 to 42.1-79.1, 42.1-82, 42.1-83, 42.1-85, 42.1-86, 42.1-87, 42.1-88, 42.1-91, 53.1-24, 63.1-74.1, 63.1-235, 63.1-314.3, 64.1-94
65	33.1-252
66	33.1-252.1
67	33.1-386
68	22.1-300
69	46.2-920, 46.2-1029.1
70	54.1-2914
71	52-8.4
72	46.2-1532.1
73	46.2-1605
74	2.1-639.2
75	44-146.21
76	51.5-49
77	24.2-312, n.
78	10.1-2211
79	54.1-1115
80	55-518
81	2.1-1.7, 9-6.25:1, 51.5-9.01, 51.5-25.1, 63.1-70.1
82	63.1-61
83	55-210.18
84	36-55.44:1
85	2.1-51.27, 51.1-100 to 51.1-124R, 51.1-124.1 to 51.1-124.10, 51.1-124.20 to 51.1-124.27, 51.1-124.30 to 51.1-124.35
86	33.1-190.2
87	15.1-538
88	15.1-491.9
89	16.1-69.6:1, 17-119.1:2
101	30-28.5:1
102	53.1-106
103	54.1-3001
104	22.1-178, 46.2-1091
105	6.1-32.22, 6.1-48, 6.1-48.1, 6.1-194.14, 6.1-194.117
106	38.2-1800, 38.2-1814, 38.2-1824
107	63.1-172
108	3.1-796.87, 51.5-44
109	32.1-71.1 to 32.1-71.4R
111	32.1-122.6:1
112	28.2-1400, 28.2-1401, 28.2-1403, 28.2-1405, 28.2-1406, 28.2-1411, 28.2-1412, 28.2-1415
113	29.1-523, 29.1-525
114	8.01-581.1
115	3.1-796.93:1, 3.1-796.94
116	46.2-903
117	46.2-1077
118	46.2-1052
119	6.1-60.1
120	28.2-539
121	28.2-241
122	13.1-603
123	38.2-4705, 38.2-4706
124	28.2-200, 28.2-531
125	28.2-1306, 28.2-1406
126	63.1-198.3
127	46.2-746
128	53.1-20
134	7.1-40.8
138	38.2-3430, 38.2-3431, n., 38.2-3432, n., 38.2-3433, n.
139	58.1-461, n., 58.1-462, n., 58.1-470, n.
140	36-139
141	32.1-176.4
142	24.2-684
143	55-59.1
144	15.1-133.01
145	2.1-328.10, 2.1-328.13
146	32.1-45.2
147	58.1-461, n., 58.1-462, n., 58.1-470, n.
148	15.1-729
149	24.2-543
151	18.2-268.4
152	58.1-3520 to 58.1-3522
153	58.1-3952
154	46.2-1142
155	28.2-227
156	40.1-100
157	46.2-873
158	2.1-51.5:1
159	10.1-104.2
160	15.1-1399.18 to 15.1-1399.20, 15.1-1399.23
161	60.2-524
162	10.1-2212
163	28.2-302.7:1
164	58.1-438.1
165	15.1-33.2
166	15.1-18.2
167	15.1-11
168	3.1-796.113
169	10.1-1425.10, 10.1-1425.12, 10.1-1425.19
170	59.1-21.11:1
171	58.1-3506
172	55-79.97
173	58.1-3650.565 to 58.1-3650.577, n.
175	38.2-1866, 38.2-1868, 38.2-1869, 38.2-1871, 38.2-1874
176	46.2-800
177	15.1-896
178	46.2-1023
179	4.1-118
180	56-484.2
181	12.1-10
182	15.1-37.5
183	46.2-728.3
184	13.1-514.1
185	54.1-500 to 54.1-501, 54.1-503, 54.1-516, 54.1-517
186	58.1-1213
187	36-99.10R
188	63.1-105, 63.1-105.2
189	13.1-693, 13.1-872
190	15.1-1250.01

Acts 1994 Chapter	Code 1950 Section
191	23-30.28
193	15.1-1513.9
194	29.1-415
195	58.1-332
196	62.1-44.34:11, 62.1-44.34:16
197	19.2-305.1, 58.1-520
198	8.01-400
199	58.1-3235
200	32.1-330.1
201	6.1-2.16 to 6.1-2.18
202	38.2-3737
203	60.2-623
204	10.1-1322.3
205	10.1-115, 10.1-116 to 10.1-118, 10.1-224, 15.1-136.2, 18.2-51.1, 18.2-57.1, 19.2-16R
206	2.1-427
207	58.1-3912
208	58.1-900, n.
209	58.1-3341, 58.1-3940
210	58.1-3275
211	53.1-40.4
212	33.1-46.2
213	32.1-325.2, 38.2-508.3, 38.2-3405.1, 38.2-3407.2, 38.2-3411.2, 38.2-4214, 38.2-4319
214	36-105
216	33.1-223.3, 33.1-223.4, 33.1-223.6 to 33.1-223.8
217	13.1-301, 13.1-302 to 13.1-304, 13.1-305, 13.1-307, 13.1-309, 13.1-309.1, 13.1-311.1
218	46.2-1220, 46.2-1221
219	23-30.28
220	7.1-40.2:1
221	58.1-3506
222	30-19.05, 30-19.1:3, 58.1-608.2
223	16.1-282
224	38.2-4400, 38.2-4401, 38.2-4402R, 38.2-4402.1, 38.2-4404, 38.2-4405, 38.2-4408 to 38.2-4409, 38.2-4411
225	46.2-731
226	9-168
227	10.1-1322
228	46.2-742.2
229	57-26
230	32.1-45.1
231	2.1-179.2
232	22.1-296.2
233	33.1-269, 33.1-277
234	54.1-2906
236	32.1-45.1
237	9-6.14:4.1
238	38.2-2206, 65.2-309.1
240	24.2-713
241	46.2-351.1
242	55-518
244	29.1-521, 29.1-521.3
247	54.1-1404
248	65.2-524
249	63.1-124.1
250	24.2-405, 24.2-406, 24.2-418
251	15.1-26.2
252	58.1-3001, 58.1-3005
253	46.2-665
254	15.1-24
255	46.2-487
256	36-97, 36-99.6, 36-99.6:1R, 36-105
257	15.1-492, n.
258	22.1-323, 22.1-323.1
259	22.1-348
260	53.1-106.1, n.
261	3.1-14, 59.1-200
262	62.1-44.15:3
263	63.1-110
264	46.2-1313
265	18.2-60, 22.1-280.1
266	58.1-3506
267	58.1-3701
268	15.1-131.3, 15.1-159.7
269	53.1-129
270	53.1-95.7, 53.1-95.8, 53.1-106
271	65.2-101
272	22.1-167.1
273	19.2-83R
274	28.2-1302
275	27-97, 27-98, 27-99
276	9-145.30, 22.1-350
277	62.1-44.34:14, 62.1-44.34:15.1, 62.1-44.34:17
278	2.1-373.4
279	46.2-694
280	46.2-830
281	32.1-122.5:1, 32.1-122.6
282	56-281.2
283	54.1-3305
284	15.1-292.4
285	22.1-280.1
286	65.2-101
287	24.2-629, 24.2-712
288	32.1-164.5, 62.1-44.19:3
289	65.2-705
290	6.1-61
291	13.1-750, 13.1-767
292	58.1-3518.1
293	15.1-1054, 15.1-1167.1
294	38.2-4229.1
295	58.1-3967
296	54.1-3316
297	32.1-347
298	24.2-222, n., 24.2-223, n.
299	54.1-3434
300	54.1-3434.1, 54.1-3435.01, 54.1-3435.1
301	46.2-742.2
303	38.2-3431 to 38.2-3433, 38.2-3523
304	46.2-208
305	18.2-371.2
306	38.2-233
307	24.2-310
308	38.2-1300, 38.2-1301, 38.2-1301.1, 38.2-1306, 38.2-1306.1, 38.2-1320.1,

Acts 1994 Chapter	Code 1950 Section
	38.2-1331,
	38.2-1846,
	38.2-1855,
	38.2-1858,
	38.2-1863,
	38.2-4123
309	56-222
310	56-210,
	56-217,
	56-225
311	56-265.13:6.1
312	6.1-2,
	6.1-98R,
	6.1-373
313	56-265.13:5,
	56-265.13:6,
	56-265.13:7
314	56-141R
315	6.1-194.96,
	6.1-398
316	38.2-135,
	38.2-316,
	38.2-400,
	38.2-403,
	38.2-1024,
	38.2-1303,
	38.2-1800,
	38.2-1819,
	38.2-1822,
	38.2-1833,
	38.2-1834,
	38.2-1840,
	38.2-2223,
	38.2-2529,
	38.2-3100,
	38.2-3419.1,
	38.2-3500,
	38.2-3543.1,
	38.2-4802
317	15.1-25,
	15.1-1378
318	9-77.12
319	6.1-194.18
320	38.2-514,
	38.2-3407.3,
	38.2-3407.4,
	38.2-4214,
	38.2-4319
321	24.2-611,
	24.2-656
322	58.1-1410
325	58.1-609.8
326	18.2-128
327	64.1-134
328	8.01-401.1
329	10.1-410.2
330	6.1-194.136
331	6.1-194.123:1,
	6.1-194.149
332	15.1-898
333	65.2-802
334	54.1-404.1
335	9-182,
	9-183.1
336	19.2-9.1
337	18.2-268.7
338	16.1-278.9
339	18.2-61
340	3.1-722.1,
	3.1-722.1:1 to
	3.1-722.5,
	3.1-722.6R,
	3.1-722.6:1 to
	3.1-722.13
341	15.1-482
342	15.1-499.1,
	36-106
344	56-337.2
345	46.2-416
346	38.2-2231
347	56-484.2
348	13.1-759,
	13.1-763,
	13.1-921,
	13.1-925,
	13.1-1015,
	13.1-1040,
	13.1-1046
349	13.1-543,
	13.1-544,
	13.1-545.1,
	13.1-546,
	13.1-549.3R,
	13.1-1102,
	13.1-1103,
	13.1-1106,
	13.1-1107,
	13.1-1114R
350	50-2,
	50-6,
	50-15,
	50-18,
	50-34,
	50-36,
	50-40,
	50-43.1 to
	50-43.10
351	6.1-398,
	6.1-399,
	6.1-401R,
	6.1-402,
	6.1-404,
	6.1-406,
	6.1-407
352	56-16,
	56-429,
	56-433,
	56-436 to
	56-438,
	56-439.1
353	6.1-194.41,
	6.1-194.42,
	6.1-194.46,
	6.1-194.96 to
	6.1-194.98,
	6.1-194.100R,
	6.1-194.101R,
	6.1-194.103,
	6.1-194.105,
	6.1-194.106,
	6.1-194.108R,
	6.1-194.150
354	53.1-106
355	13.1-514.1
356	46.2-308
357	15.1-9.1:1
358	10.1-1321
359	18.2-266,
	18.2-266.1,
	18.2-267,
	18.2-268.2,
	18.2-268.3,
	18.2-268.4, n.,
	18.2-268.5,
	18.2-268.7 to
	18.2-268.10,
	18.2-269,
	18.2-271,
	18.2-271.1,
	46.2-301,
	46.2-301.1,
	46.2-341.24,
	46.2-341.27,
	46.2-391.2 to
	46.2-391.5
360	16.1-279.1,
	18.2-60.3
361	19.2-11.1,
	19.2-265.01
362	16.1-272,
	19.2-298.1 to
	19.2-298.3,
	19.2-390,
	19.2-390.1,
	46.2-323,
	53.1-116.1,
	53.1-160.1
363	18.2-266,
	18.2-266.1,
	18.2-267,
	18.2-268.2,
	18.2-268.3,
	18.2-268.4,
	18.2-268.5,
	18.2-268.7 to
	18.2-268.10,
	18.2-269,
	18.2-271,
	18.2-271.1,
	46.2-301,
	46.2-301.1,
	46.2-341.24,
	46.2-341.27,

Acts 1994 Chapter	Code 1950 Section
	46.2-391.2 to
	46.2-391.5
364	18.2-29
365	58.1-609.2,
	58.1-609.3,
	58.1-609.7 to
	58.1-609.9
366	65.2-312
367	3.1-1060
368	55-513
369	58.1-13.1
370	3.1-4,
	3.1-14
371	15.1-536
372	15.1-503.4
373	32.1-272 to
	32.1-273.1
374	38.2-3407.5,
	38.2-4214,
	38.2-4319
375	18.2-308,
	19.2-12,
	19.2-187,
	19.2-187.01
376	22.1-216,
	22.1-220
378	36-55.41
379	54.1-402.1
380	58.1-3650.565, n.,
	58.1-3650.567, n.,
	58.1-3650.568, n.,
	58.1-3650.573 to
	58.1-3650.576, n.,
	58.1-3650.578 to
	58.1-3650.609, n.
381	58.1-609.2,
	58.1-609.3,
	58.1-609.7 to
	58.1-609.9
382	43-1
383	23-231.8 to
	23-231.10
384	8.01-581.3
385	46.2-1569
386	58.1-3340
387	3.1-796.108,
	3.1-796.115
388	43-13.3
389	11-41.2:1
390	8.01-413,
	32.1-127.1:01,
	42.1-77,
	54.1-2403.2
391	10.1-202
392	2.1-51.8:3
393	64.1-121
394	52-25.1
395	32.1-169,
	32.1-172
396	46.2-1164
397	58.1-3732.2
398	18.2-387
399	64.1-123.2
400	59.1-199,
	59.1-200
401	17-116.01:1
402	55-248.11
403	18.2-259.1
404	3.1-796.134 to
	3.1-796.136
405	Va. Const., Art. IV,
	§ 14, n.
406	36-114
407	17-116.2,
	19.2-6
408	65.2-802
409	29.1-310
410	15.1-827
411	29.1-217
412	29.1-551
413	29.1-531
414	29.1-735.1,
	29.1-739.1
415	19.2-163.4
416	62.1-44.34:23
417	46.2-1220
418	46.2-1572.2
419	10.1-1425.8
420	15.1-14.2
421	15.1-466
422	64.1-206.1 to
	64.1-206.8
423	46.2-870
424	58.1-3220 to
	58.1-3221
426	33.1-46.2
427	18.2-51.1,
	18.2-57.1
428	19.2-390
429	58.1-811
430	9-331
431	15.1-1513.6
432	14.1-90,
	14.1-112,
	14.1-112.2R to
	14.1-118R,
	14.1-135R,
	14.1-178.1R,
	14.1-198,
	15.1-227.7,
	15.1-296,
	17-69.1,
	18.2-264.1R,
	19.2-147,
	19.2-353.3,
	19.2-390,
	21-118.4,
	26-36R,
	29.1-334,
	33.1-126R,
	43-42,
	43-43,
	43-69R,
	55-141,
	55-142.01,
	55-142.4,
	55-167,
	55-246,
	55-370,
	56-438,
	59.1-71,
	59.1-73R,
	59.1-104R,
	59.1-116R
433	3.1-40 to
	3.1-46.1R,
	23-132.1 to
	23-132.12,
	23-133 to
	23-135.7R,
	23-165.11
434	9-145.38R
435	58.1-3220 to
	58.1-3221
436	29.1-521,
	29.1-536
437	15.1-21.1
439	33.1-46.2
440	18.2-29
441	54.1-3904
442	2.1-483.1:1
443	58.1-1401.1
444	32.1-127.3
445	15.1-770
446	58.1-609.6
448	15.1-1664
449	15.1-133
450	2.1-639.9
451	19.2-163
452	13.1-627
453	22.1-92
454	17-119.1:2
455	46.2-840
456	46.2-1109,
	46.2-1112,
	46.2-1114,
	46.2-1116,
	46.2-1117,
	46.2-1126
457	23-232.2
458	15.1-28.1
459	33.1-41.1
460	62.1-44.34:17
461	10.1-1302,
	10.1-1401,
	62.1-44.9
462	65.2-601.1
463	55-79.74:1
464	7.1-40.8
465	10.1-572
466	32.1-332 to
	32.1-335,
	32.1-337,

Acts 1994 Chapter	Code 1950 Section
	32.1-338
467	59.1-148.4
468	18.2-67.5:1
469	46.2-834
470	33.1-221.1:3,
	58.1-815.1
471	24.2-304
472	2.1-51.39:2,
	2.1-769 to
	2.1-774,
	2.1-776 to
	2.1-778,
	2.1-785
473	15.1-23.1
474	2.1-504.2
475	55-415,
	64.1-97 to
	64.1-104R,
	64.1-104.1 to
	64.1-104.9
476	26-7.4,
	64.1-57
477	15.1-1250,
	15.1-1260
478	46.2-1522 to
	46.2-1527R,
	46.2-1527.1 to
	46.2-1527.8
479	2.1-567
480	2.1-27.8
481	54.1-800,
	54.1-805 to
	54.1-808R,
	54.1-807.1,
	54.1-808.1,
	54.1-809R,
	54.1-809.1,
	54.1-810.1,
	54.1-811 to
	54.1-825R,
	54.1-826,
	54.1-827
482	59.1-445 to
	59.1-449,
	59.1-453
483	55-70.1
484	58.1-520.1
485	2.1-342
486	2.1-1.7,
	9-6.23,
	9-6.25:1,
	9-145.50,
	9-145.51
487	53.1-60
488	58.1-322,
	58.1-1823
489	62.1-44.23
490	18.2-477.1
491	53.1-116.2,
	53.1-116.2, n.
492	28.2-707

Acts 1994 Chapter	Code 1950 Section
493	58.1-3
495	10.1-2212
496	17-30.1
497	19.2-165
498	14.1-112
499	16.1-309.1
500	16.1-69.25
501	6.1-63,
	6.1-65.1,
	6.1-66
502	52-25.1
503	38.2-1034,
	38.2-1225,
	38.2-1314,
	38.2-1401,
	38.2-4222,
	38.2-4517
504	15.1-561
505	15.1-11.2
506	18.2-340.1,
	18.2-340.2,
	18.2-340.3 to
	18.2-340.5,
	18.2-340.9,
	18.2-340.11
507	2.1-345
508	8.01-43,
	8.01-44
509	58.1-3376
510	24.2-901
511	18.2-374.1:1
512	56-553 to
	56-555
513	62.1-260,
	62.1-263
514	54.1-3710 to
	54.1-3716R
515	8.01-53
516	15.1-51
517	8.01-335
518	20-103,
	20-107.1,
	20-109
519	8.01-275.1
520	33.1-221.1:4,
	33.1-268,
	33.1-269,
	33.1-277,
	58.1-2146.1
521	16.1-279.1,
	18.2-60.3
522	38.2-3407.6,
	38.2-4214,
	38.2-4319
523	51.1-808
524	6.1-32.11,
	6.1-32.14:1,
	6.1-32.14:2,
	6.1-32.18,
	6.1-32.20,
	6.1-32.28

Acts 1994 Chapter	Code 1950 Section
525	15.1-37.3:13
526	65.2-101
527	58.1-2402,
	58.1-2423.1
528	46.2-752
529	55-248.11
531	58.1-2101
532	2.1-342
533	23-8.2:1
534	18.2-499
535	62.1-44.34:11
536	19.2-270.4
537	46.2-1566
538	8.01-446
539	15.1-1052
540	58.1-3971
541	28.2-208,
	28.2-550
542	16.1-309.1
543	19.2-267
544	29.1-509
545	18.2-259.1
546	19.2-358
547	8.01-241 to
	8.01-242
549	62.1-44.15:3
550	15.1-535,
	15.1-540
551	55-59
552	8.01-43,
	8.01-44
553	11-47.01
554	55-106
555	18.2-111
556	10.1-1418.2
557	15.1-1032.2
558	2.1-1.6,
	9-6.25:1,
	54.1-3505,
	54.1-3510 to
	54.1-3514,
	65.2-603
559	28.2-302.7
560	58.1-3812
561	40.1-51.4:4
562	64.1-73
563	55-7.1
564	2.1-20.1, n.,
	2.1-33, n.,
	2.1-37.3, n.,
	2.1-747, n.,
	2.1-751, n.,
	2.1-753, n.,
	2.1-757, n.,
	8.01-217, n.,
	8.01-259, n.,
	8.01-261, n.,
	8.01-320, n.,
	8.01-353.01, n.,
	9-168, n.,
	9-173.8, n.,

Acts 1994 Chapter	Code 1950 Section
	14.1-112, n.,
	14.1-113, n.,
	14.1-114, n.,
	14.1-135.1, n.,
	14.1-137, n.,
	15.1-720, n.,
	16.1-69.5, n.,
	16.1-69.6:1, n.,
	16.1-69.7, n.,
	16.1-69.8, n.,
	16.1-69.9:01, n.,
	16.1-69.9:1, n.,
	16.1-69.10, n.,
	16.1-69.12, n.,
	16.1-69.21, n.,
	16.1-69.22:1, n.,
	16.1-69.32, n.,
	16.1-69.33, n.,
	16.1-69.35, n.,
	16.1-69.37, n.,
	16.1-69.38, n.,
	16.1-69.39, n.,
	16.1-69.48, n.,
	16.1-69.50, n.,
	16.1-69.55, n.,
	16.1-94, n.,
	16.1-97.1, n.,
	16.1-106, n.,
	16.1-107, n.,
	16.1-133, n.,
	16.1-133.1, n.,
	16.1-218, n.,
	16.1-224, n.,
	16.1-226, n.,
	16.1-228, n.,
	16.1-230, n.,
	16.1-232, n.,
	16.1-233, n.,
	16.1-234, n.,
	16.1-235, n.,
	16.1-236, n.,
	16.1-240, n.,
	16.1-241, n.,
	16.1-241.1, n.,
	16.1-242, n.,
	16.1-243, n.,
	16.1-244, n.,
	16.1-245, n.,
	16.1-245.1, n.,
	16.1-246, n.,
	16.1-247, n.,
	16.1-253.4, n.,
	16.1-254, n.,
	16.1-255, n.,
	16.1-256, n.,
	16.1-259, n.,
	16.1-260, n.,
	16.1-262, n.,
	16.1-263, n.,
	16.1-264, n.,
	16.1-266, n.,
	16.1-267, n.,
	16.1-269, n.,
	16.1-270, n.,
	16.1-271, n.,
	16.1-272, n.,
	16.1-272.1, n.,
	16.1-272.2, n.,
	16.1-273, n.,
	16.1-275, n.,
	16.1-277.1, n.,
	16.1-278, n.,
	16.1-278.2, n.,
	16.1-278.3, n.,
	16.1-278.6, n.,
	16.1-278.7, n.,
	16.1-278.8, n.,
	16.1-278.12, n.,
	16.1-278.13, n.,
	16.1-278.14, n.,
	16.1-278.15, n.,
	16.1-278.16, n.,
	16.1-278.17, n.,
	16.1-278.18, n.,
	16.1-278.20, n.,
	16.1-278.80, n.,
	16.1-278.81, n.,
	16.1-289, n.,
	16.1-291, n.,
	16.1-292, n.,
	16.1-293, n.,
	16.1-296, n.,
	16.1-296.2, n.,
	16.1-297, n.,
	16.1-298, n.,
	16.1-299, n.,
	16.1-300, n.,
	16.1-302, n.,
	16.1-305, n.,
	16.1-306, n.,
	16.1-306.1, n.,
	16.1-309, n.,
	16.1-314, n.,
	16.1-316, n.,
	16.1-317, n.,
	16.1-328, n.,
	16.1-331, n.,
	16.1-339, n.,
	16.1-340, n.,
	16.1-341, n.,
	16.1-342, n.,
	16.1-344, n.,
	16.1-348, n.,
	17-7.2, n.,
	17-28, n.,
	17-111.4, n.,
	17-111.6, n.,
	17-116.05, n.,
	17-222, n.,
	18.2-64.1, n.,
	18.2-351, n.,
	18.2-353, n.,
	18.2-477.1, n.,
	19.2-48.1, n.,
	19.2-71, n.,
	19.2-218.2, n.,
	19.2-240, n.,
	19.2-262, n.,
	19.2-353.3, n.,
	19.2-368.3, n.,
	19.2-368.6, n.,
	20-49, n.,
	20-49.2, n.,
	20-67, n.,
	20-71.1, n.,
	20-79, n.,
	20-88, n.,
	20-88.13, n.,
	20-88.20:2, n.,
	20-96, n.,
	20-99.1:1, n.,
	20-107.3, n.,
	20-113, n.,
	22.1-87, n.,
	22.1-214, n.,
	22.1-214.1, n.,
	22.1-257, n.,
	22.1-262, n.,
	22.1-268, n.,
	22.1-279.2, n.,
	31-8, n.,
	31-15, n.,
	31-16, n.,
	31-17, n.,
	31-18, n.,
	32.1-258, n.,
	32.1-260, n.,
	37.1-1, n.,
	37.1-64, n.,
	37.1-97, n.,
	40.1-28.9, n.,
	46.2-334, n.,
	46.2-336, n.,
	46.2-386, n.,
	46.2-1098, n.,
	53.1-120, n.,
	53.1-124, n.,
	53.1-145, n.,
	54.1-2969, n.,
	63.1-56, n.,
	63.1-57.1, n.,
	63.1-204, n.,
	63.1-204.1, n.,
	63.1-209, n.,
	63.1-220.3, n.,
	63.1-220.5, n.,
	63.1-221, n.,
	63.1-222, n.,
	63.1-235, n.,
	63.1-236, n.,
	63.1-248.2, n.,
	63.1-248.3, n.,
	63.1-248.4, n.,

Acts 1994 Chapter	Code 1950 Section
	63.1-248.5:1, n., 63.1-248.6, n., 63.1-248.13, n., 63.1-249, n., 63.1-252.1, n., 63.1-256, n., 63.1-267.1, n., 63.1-268.1, n., 64.1-5.1, n., 65.2-101, n.
565	2.1-726
566	58.1-2113
567	54.1-3905
568	18.2-67.10
569	19.2-12
570	8.01-44.5
571	29.1-529
572	8.01-413
573	46.2-360, 46.2-391
574	36-105, 36-105.01
575	16.1-241, 18.2-49.1
576	16.1-122.1
577	3.1-22.5, 3.1-263 to 3.1-275.7, 9-6.14:4.1
578	59.1-207.16:1
579	19.2-294.2, 53.1-218
580	55-361.1, 55-362, 55-363, 55-364.1, 55-366 to 55-371, 55-374, 55-374.1, 55-375, 55-376, 55-379R, 55-380, 55-386, 55-390, 55-391.1
581	54.1-307.1
582	53.1-200
583	55-225.1, 55-225.2
584	33.1-124, 33.1-128
585	4.1-208, 4.1-209
586	65.2-313
587	29.1-738
588	2.1-548.8:01
589	33.1-221.1:5, 33.1-268, 33.1-269, 33.1-277, 58.1-815.2
590	58.1-322, 58.1-402
591	15.1-536
592	62.1-260, 62.1-263
593	15.1-10
594	15.1-10.1
595	58.1-609.5
596	22.1-79
597	33.1-221.1:3, 58.1-815.1
598	19.2-11.1, 19.2-265.01
599	15.1-1263
600	65.2-306
601	54.1-1100, 54.1-1103, 54.1-1106, 54.1-1108
602	15.1-1263
603	16.1-305
604	16.1-281, 16.1-282
605	10.1-603.2, 10.1-603.8
606	2.1-342
607	24.2-925
608	58.1-3221
609	38.2-3405
610	32.1-11.2
611	36-55.63, 58.1-336, 58.1-435, 58.1-609.7, 63.1-323
612	53.1-131.2
613	53.1-150
614	10.1-1408.1
615	15.1-1646, 15.1-1646.1R
616	8.01-581.1
617	15.1-132.1
618	22.1-253.13:1, 22.1-253.13:4
619	46.2-1231
620	18.2-369
621	2.1-399.1, 23-50.16, 23-77.3
623	30-13, 30-14
624	18.2-308.2:2
625	54.1-414, 54.1-415
626	19.2-12
627	15.1-295
629	15.1-291.2
630	3.1-796.94
631	58.1-3506
632	58.1-341.1
633	24.2-706
634	15.1-292
635	18.2-36.1
636	3.1-796.97:1
637	58.1-346.5
638	53.1-150
639	18.2-26
640	18.2-386.1
641	29.1-200
642	19.2-76.3
643	32.1-283.1, 63.1-209, 63.1-248.6, 63.1-248.9
644	9-156
645	9-166.3, 9-166.5, 9-166.7
646	13.1-722.1, 13.1-898.1
647	38.2-1316.2, 38.2-4811
648	9-156
649	3.1-22.5, 3.1-126.2R, 3.1-126.2:1 to 3.1-126.11, 3.1-126.12R, 3.1-126.12:1, 3.1-126.12:2, 3.1-126.12:3, 3.1-126.13R, 9-6.14:4.1
650	15.1-1416
651	8.01-581.1
652	56-265.1
653	2.1-114.5:1, 2.1-116
654	22.1-208.2
655	59.1-200
656	2.1-342.1, 24.2-107, 24.2-405, 24.2-407.1, 24.2-444, 24.2-706
657	54.1-3312
658	18.2-57, 18.2-121
659	53.1-131.2
660	11-71
661	2.1-1.5, 2.1-1.6, 2.1-41.2, 9-6.25:3, 11-35, 23-38.75, 23-38.76, 23-38.77 to 23-38.82,

Acts 1994 Chapter	Code 1950 Section
	23-38.83 to
	23-38.87,
662	33.1-269,
	33.1-277
663	2.1-639.33,
	2.1-639.4
664	8.01-512.2
665	63.1-274.6
666	9-6.25:1, n.,
	9-6.25:2, n.,
	22.1-217, n.,
	22.1-284, n.,
	63.1-68.1, n.,
	63.1-74, n.,
	63.1-74.1, n.,
	63.1-75.1, n.,
	63.1-77, n.,
	63.1-78, n.,
	63.1-79, n.,
	63.1-81, n.,
	63.1-83, n.,
	63.1-85, n.,
	63.1-153, n.,
	63.1-155, n.,
	63.1-161, n.
667	58.1-3245,
	58.1-3245.2,
	58.1-3245.4 to
	58.1-3245.5
668	54.1-3434.01
669	32.1-325.1:1
670	19.2-389
671	36-85.16,
	36-85.18,
	36-85.19,
	36-85.32,
	46.2-1522
672	66-11
673	16.1-296,
	20-88.12 to
	20-88.31R,
	20-88.32 to
	20-88.82
674	15.1-1646,
	15.1-1646.1R
675	63.1-248.6
676	46.2-871
677	Va. Const.,
	Art. II, § 2, n.,
	Va. Const.,
	Art. II, § 3, n.,
	Va. Const.,
	Art. II, § 4, n.
679	15.1-491.9
680	32.1-102.3:2
681	25-46.20,
	25-46.3, n.,
	25-46.7, n.,
	25-46.9, n.,
	25-46.11, n.,
	25-46.17, n.,
	25-46.19, n.,
	25-46.20:1, n.,
	25-46.20:2, n.,
	25-46.20:3, n.,
	25-46.20:4, n.,
	25-46.20:5, n.,
	25-46.21, n.,
	25-46.27, n.,
	25-46.29, n.,
	33.1-132, n.,
	33.1-238, n.
682	18.2-36.1
683	15.1-492, n.
684	62.1-202 to
	62.1-205,
	62.1-221,
	62.1-231.1,
	62.1-231.2,
	62.1-240.1,
	62.1-240.2,
	62.1-241.9:1,
	62.1-241.9:2
685	65.2-604
686	63.1-175
687	8.01-576.9 to
	8.01-576.11
688	53.1-131.2
689	22.1-146,
	22.1-148
691	44-146.40
692	55-19.5
693	22.1-201
694	53.1-133.01
695	15.1-475, n.
696	33.1-373
697	18.2-308
698	62.1-44.15,
	62.1-44.17:1
699	38.2-3418.1:1,
	38.2-4319
700	9-173.8,
	19.2-389,
	46.2-208,
	63.1-248.8
701	15.1-11.2:1
702	46.2-1573
703	10.1-560
704	63.1-248.7:2
705	15.1-497
706	18.2-103,
	18.2-104,
	19.2-297R
707	65.2-714
708	32.1-172
709	22.1-277.2
710	13.1-723
711	32.1-102.3:2
712	22.1-274
713	2.1-639.9
714	15.1-227.7 to
	15.1-227.9,
	15.1-227.24:1,
	15.1-227.45,
	15.1-227.55,
	15.1-227.64:1
715	53.1-71.1 to
	53.1-71.6
717	10.1-1322.4
718	20-49.9
719	16.1-241,
	20-107.2
720	53.1-131.2
721	22.1-280.2
722	54.1-2409.1
723	22.1-30,
	22.1-57.3
724	2.1-639.2,
	2.1-639.15,
	2.1-639.31,
	2.1-639.41
725	29.1-306
726	32.1-102.3:2
727	2.1-639.4:1,
	2.1-639.21,
	2.1-639.33
728	58.1-602.1, n.,
	58.1-608.1
729	63.1-250.1
730	19.2-295.2
731	18.2-311.2
732	2.1-155.1R,
	30-78 to
	30-84
733	2.1-639.15,
	2.1-639.41
734	46.2-882
735	2.1-639.36,
	2.1-639.41
736	37.1-67.3
737	15.1-1374
738	8.01-226.4
739	16.1-279.1,
	18.2-60.3
740	3.1-22.5,
	3.1-74 to
	3.1-106R,
	3.1-106.1 to
	3.1-106.4,
	3.1-106.5 to
	3.1-106.22,
	9-6.14:4.1
741	33.1-23.03:01
742	24.2-629,
	24.2-712
743	3.1-22.5,
	3.1-758,
	3.1-797 to
	3.1-828R,
	3.1-828.1 to 3.1-828.4,

Acts 1994 Chapter	Code 1950 Section
	3.1-828.5 to 3.1-828.17, 9-6.14:4.1
744	22.1-57.3:1, n.
745	15.1-491.03, 36-99.10:1
747	32.1-163, 32.1-163.1, 32.1-163.4 to 32.1-164.1:1, 32.1-166.6, 32.1-166.10, 32.1-176.4
748	9-6.14:11
749	54.1-2712
750	58.1-439
752	24.2-503.1, 24.2-929
753	29.1-600, 29.1-600.1, 29.1-608R
754	54.1-1100, 54.1-1103
755	2.1-51.15, 9-138.1
756	46.2-352
757	56-338.105, 56-338.107
758	2.1-639.16
759	15.1-1519, 15.1-1523, 15.1-1525, 15.1-1526
760	22.1-279.2
761	22.1-279.2
762	22.1-209.1:2
763	54.1-3446, 54.1-3448, 54.1-3452, 54.1-3454
764	20-60.3, 20-108.1, 63.1-252.1, 63.1-263.1
765	32.1-325.02
766	55-70.1
767	20-79.3, 63.1-250.1
768	58.1-439
769	16.1-278.15, 20-79, 20-103, 20-107.2, 20-124.1 to 20-124.6
770	Va. Const., Art. V, § 6, n.
771	33.1-252
772	18.2-61, 18.2-67.1 to 18.2-67.2:1
774	15.1-431
775	15.1-965.24:1
776	2.1-639.4:1, 2.1-639.21, 2.1-639.33
777	2.1-639.15, 2.1-639.41
778	54.1-2924.1, 54.1-3005, 54.1-3505, 54.1-3600, 54.1-3605, 54.1-3609, 54.1-3610, 54.1-3611, 54.1-3705
779	3.1-22.28, 3.1-22.29
780	14.1-51, 15.1-9, 15.1-50.1, 15.1-50.2, 15.1-821
781	15.1-486.5
782	22.1-296.2
783	46.2-1571
784	54.1-406
785	51.1-142, 51.1-155.1
786	22.1-127
787	54.1-2901
788	22.1-92
789	23-38.53:4 to 23-38.53:6, 22.1-212.3R, 22.1-212.4R, 23-38.53:7R
790	22.1-253.13:1, 22.1-253.13:4, n.
791	65.2-402
792	14.1-51, 15.1-9, 15.1-50.1, 15.1-50.2, 15.1-821
793	2.1-639.15, 2.1-639.41
794	18.2-61, 18.2-67.1 to 18.2-67.2:1
795	20-60.3, 63.1-252.2
796	32.1-257
797	32.1-102.3:2
798	15.1-486.5
799	22.1-203.1
800	58.1-105, 58.1-1813
801	9-6.14:4.1, 22.1-280.3
802	15.1-491
803	54.1-2900, 54.1-2956.6R, 54.1-2956.7R, 54.1-2956.8:1, 54.1-2956.8:2
804	65.2-306
805	15.1-292.4
806	55-66.01
807	8.01-383.1
808	22.1-289
809	46.2-1569.1
810	9-182, 9-183.1 to 9-183.3, 9-183.5, 9-183.7, 9-183.9, 9-183.12
811	19.2-348
812	55-66.1:01
813	16.1-241, 16.1-241.2
814	36-96.16 to 36-96.18
815	2.1-639.4, 2.1-639.33
816	Va. Const., Art. II, § 2, n., Va. Const., Art. II, § 3, n., Va. Const., Art. II, § 4, n.
817	Va. Const., Art. V, § 6, n.
818	Va. Const., Art. IV, § 14, n.
819	46.2-1105
820	9-77.8
821	51.1-303
822	17-47.4
823	2.1-234.11, 2.1-234.13
825	4.1-212, 4.1-230
826	4.1-212, 4.1-310
827	58.1-3503
828	19.2-264.3, 19.2-295.1, 19.2-297.1
829	2.1-483.1:1
830	9-173.8, 19.2-389, 46.2-208, 63.1-248.8
832	18.2-56.2
833	52-35
834	19.2-368.6, 19.2-368.14
835	16.1-305.1, 16.1-309,

TABLE OF ACTS CODIFIED SUBSEQUENT TO 1948

Acts 1994 Chapter	Code 1950 Section
	22.1-288.2,
	22.1-289
836	20-88.02:1
837	63.1-196.001,
	63.1-196.3:1
838	46.2-1176,
	46.2-1178,
	46.2-1180
839	2.1-342
840	63.1-248.3,
	63.1-248.4,
	63.1-248.6
841	19.2-349,
	19.2-353.3,
	19.2 354,
	46.2-391.1,
	46.2-395,
	53.1-131.2
842	14.1-112,
	14.1-113
843	2.1-1.7,
	9-6.23,
	9-6.25:1,
	9-145.50,
	9-145.51
844	4.1-309
845	2.1-341,
	19.2-11.2,
	19.2-269.2
846	2.1-42.3
847	22.1-32
848	29.1-531,
	29.1-547,
	29.1-553,
	29.1-567
849	46.2-499
850	9-170,
	15.1-131.8 to
	15.1-131.8:4
851	2.1-639.4,
	2.1-639.33
852	56-265.1,
	56-265.3:1
853	2.1-342,
	54.1-2506.1
854	2.1-757,
	16.1-278.20,
	22.1-7,
	22.1-101.1,
	22.1-209.2,
	22.1-213,
	22.1-214,
	22.1-215,
	22.1-216,
	22.1-218.1,
	22.1-220,
	22.1-221,
	22.1-254.1,
	32.1-69.1
855	56-556 to
	56-575
856	63.1-236,
	63.1-236.01
857	2.1-779 to
	2.1-794,
	30-28.01 to
	30-28.9:1R
858	9-6.23,
	63.1-25.3,
	63.1-133.41 to
	63.1-133.55
859	16.1-228,
	16.1-241,
	16.1-249,
	16.1-269R,
	16.1-269.1 to
	16.1-269.6,
	16.1-270,
	16.1-271,
	16.1-275,
	16.1-278.8,
	16.1-280,
	16.1-285.1,
	16.1-285.2,
	16.1-299,
	16.1-301,
	16.1-306,
	18.2-308.2,
	19.2-240,
	19.2-311,
	53.1-20,
	66-25.2
860	19.2-264.3,
	19.2-295.1,
	19.2-297.1
861	53.1-68
862	19.2-264.3,
	19.2-295.1,
	19.2-297.1
863	9-310
864	22.1-209.1:3
865	2.1-757,
	2.1-758,
	16.1-228,
	16.1-278.2,
	16.1-278.4,
	16.1-281,
	16.1-282,
	63.1-55.8,
	63.1-56,
	63.1-56.2 to
	63.1-57,
	63.1-67.2,
	63.1-195,
	63.1-204
866	46.2-100,
	46.2-731,
	46.2-739,
	46.2-1236R,
	46.2-1237,
	46.2-1238R
867	32.1-122.6,
	32.1-122.9,
	32.1-122.10,
	23-35.1 to
	23-35.7R,
	23-35.8R
868	9-173.4R,
	9-173.5R,
	9-173.14R,
	9-173.15R,
	9-173.16 to
	9-173.20
869	20-49.8,
	20-61.3
870	18.2-271.1
871	46.2-355
872	38.2-5001,
	38.2-5016,
	38.2-5017,
	38.2-5020
873	15.1-783.2
874	33.1-252
875	58.1-438.1
876	51.1-124.3
881	19.2-264.3,
	19.2-295.1,
	19.2-297.1
882	11-47.4,
	11-79
883	51.1-124.4,
	51.1-132,
	51.1-510
884	58.1-3965,
	58.1-3967
885	18.2-144.2
887	22.1-5
888	46.2-1500
889	6.1-370 to
	6.1-375,
	6.1-376R,
	6.1-377,
	6.1-378.1
890	56-265.15,
	56-265.15:1,
	56-265.16:1 to
	56-265.19,
	56-265.20R,
	56-265.21 to
	56-265.25,
	56-265.26R,
	56-265.30 to
	56-265.32
891	63.1-55.3
892	2.1-114.5:01
894	53.1-159
895	15.1-11.4R,
	36-99.1R,
	36-137, n.,
	54.1-1102,
	54.1-1117,
	54.1-1118,
	54.1-1128, 54.1-1129 to

Acts 1994 Chapter	Code 1950 Section
	54.1-1135
897	11-54
898	10.1-603.2,
	10.1-603.8
899	51.1-303
900	22.1-32
901	53.1-131.1
902	32.1-162.9
903	24.2-928
904	16.1-249
905	9-170,
	15.1-131.8 to
	15.1-131.8:4
906	63.1-144
907	16.1-253.1,
	16.1-253.4,
	16.1-279.1,
	18.2-308.1:2 to
	18.2-308.1:4,
	37.1-67.3,
	37.1-129
908	33.1-62, n.
910	3.1-829 to
	3.1-835,
	3.1-837,
	3.1-839,
	3.1-842 to
	3.1-845
911	54.1-500 to
	54.1-501,
	54.1-503,
	54.1-516,
	54.1-517
912	16.1-69.40:1
913	16.1-274.1,
	16.1-305.1,
	16.1-309,
	22.1-288.2,
	22.1-289
914	46.2-742,
	46.2-749.2:1,
	46.2-749.5
915	2.1-781.1,
	30-28.1:1R
917	64.1-66.1R,
	64.1-160,
	64.1-161,
	64.1-163,
	64.1-165,
	64.1-165.1
918	2.1-342,
	11-35,
	11-46,
	11-52,
	11-70,
	11-71
919	20-164,
	32.1-257,
	64.1-5.1,
	64.1-7.1R,
	64.1-8.1
920	10.1-2402,
	10.1-2404
921	53.1-233,
	53.1-234
922	46.2-1135
923	53.1-95.8,
	53.1-109
924	2.1-483.1
925	38.2-1905
926	19.2-316.1,
	53.1-67.1
927	33.1-252
928	15.1-291.1,
	15.1-291.2
929	55-66.4:1
931	2.1-341,
	19.2-11.2,
	19.2-269.2
932	15.1-321,
	58.1-1803,
	58.1-3916,
	58.1-3958
933	19.2-76
934	63.1-105.1
935	53.1-145
936	3.1-796.96
937	2.1-779 to
	2.1-794,
	30-28.01 to
	30-28.9:1R
938	9-6.14:7.1,
	9-6.14:9
939	37.1-1,
	37.1-195
940	63.1-196.001,
	63.1-196.3:1
941	32.1-138.4,
	32.1-138.5,
	63.1-177.1,
	63.1-177.2
942	63.1-236,
	63.1-236.01
944	10.1-1425.20 to
	10.1-1425.25
945	19.2-349,
	19.2-353.3,
	19.2-354,
	46.2-391.1,
	46.2-395,
	53.1-131.2
946	11-41.02
947	65.2-1006
949	16.1-228,
	16.1-241,
	16.1-249,
	16.1-269R,
	16.1-269.1 to
	16.1-269.6,
	16.1-270,
	16.1-271,
	16.1-275,
	16.1-278.8,
	16.1-280,
	16.1-285.1,
	16.1-285.2,
	16.1-299,
	16.1-301,
	16.1-306,
	18.2-308.2,
	19.2-240,
	19.2-311,
	53.1-20,
	66-25.2,
950	18.2-53.1
951	9-6.23,
	63.1-25.3,
	63.1-133.41 to
	63.1-133.55
952	20-88.02:1
953	53.1-95.8,
	53.1-109
954	2.1-114.5
955	42.1-77,
	42.1-79.1,
	42.1-80,
	42.1-82,
	42.1-83,
	42.1-87,
	42.1-91
956	54.1-2982,
	54.1-2987.1
957	45.1-361.29,
	62.1-195.1
958	54.1-2403.2
959	46.2-208 to
	46.2-210
960	65.2-402
961	58.1-3511
962	46.2-752,
	58.1-3511
963	38.2-3407.2,
	38.2-3407.3,
	38.2-4209.1,
	38.2-4209.2,
	38.2-4312.1,
	38.2-4312.2
964	3.1-320,
	3.1-321

ACTS 1994, Sp. Sess.

Acts 1994, Sp. Sess. Chapter	Code 1950 Section
1	38.2-2206, n.,
	65.2-309.1
2	58.1-1823
3	16.1-69.6:1
5	2.1-388, n.,
	51.1-124.22, n.,
	51.1-130,
	51.1-155,
	51.1-157,

Acts 1994, Sp. Sess. Chapter	Code 1950 Section
	51.1-206, 51.1-306, 51.1-308, 58.1-322, 58.1-1823
6	46.2-725.1, 46.2-750, 46.2-751, 46.2-1549.1
7	16.1-69.6:1
10	46.2-301.1

ACTS 1994, 2nd Sp. Sess.

Acts 1994, 2nd Sp. Sess. Chapter	Code 1950 Section
1	17-232 to 17-238, 18.2-10, 18.2-11, n., 19.2-152.2 to 19.2-152.7, 19.2-295.2, 19.2-297.1, 19.2-298.01, 19.2-299, 19.2-303.3, 19.2-305.3, 19.2-316.2, 19.2-316.3, 53.1-20, 53.1-20.1, 53.1-32.1, 53.1-40.01, 53.1-67.2 to 53.1-67.8, 53.1-116, 53.1-145, 53.1-150, 53.1-165.1, 53.1-180 to 53.1-184, 53.1-184.1R, 53.1-184.2 to 53.1-185.3, 53.1-187, 53.1-189, 53.1-191, 53.1-197.1, 53.1-202.1 to 53.1-202.4
2	17-232 to 17-238, 18.2-10, 18.2-11, n., 19.2-152.2 to 19.2-152.7, 19.2-295.2, 19.2-297.1, 19.2-298.01, 19.2-299, 19.2-303.3, 19.2-305.3, 19.2-316.2, 19.2-316.3, 53.1-20, 53.1-20.1, 53.1-32.1, 53.1-40.01, 53.1-67.2 to 53.1-67.8, 53.1-116, 53.1-145, 53.1-150, 53.1-165.1, 53.1-180 to 53.1-184, 53.1-184.1R, 53.1-184.2 to 53.1-185.3, 53.1-187, 53.1-189, 53.1-191, 53.1-197.1, 53.1-202.1 to 53.1-202.4
4	24.2-303, 24.2-304
5	36-49.1:1
6	11-41.2:1
7	2.1-1.6, 2.1-451.1 to 2.1-451.4, 9-6.23, 9-6.25:1, 53.1-10
8	22.1-257
10	36-49.1:1

ACTS 1995

Acts 1995 Chapter	Code 1950 Section
1	20-108.2
2	6.1-249, 6.1-256.1, 6.1-271R, 6.1-271.1R, 6.1-272.1, 6.1-277R, 6.1-278, 6.1-284.1, 6.1-285, 6.1-286, 6.1-287R, 6.1-288, 6.1-291
3	38.2-2114, 38.2-2212
4	65.2-101
5	2.1-526.9, 53.1-110
6	2.1-466, n., 2.1-467, n., 23-1.01, n.
7	16.1-241, 63.1-248.6:1
8	15.1-644
9	8.01-247.1, 8.01-248
10	3.1-14, 59.1-200
11	11-41.2:1
12	7.1-40.2:2
13	8.01-452.1
14	8.01-374.1, n.
15	54.1-3912
16	2.1-114.5:1
17	15.1-79
18	11-35
19	59.1-405.1
20	16.1-69.6:1, 17-119.1:2, n.
21	10.1-2202, 10.1-2202.1, 10.1-2204
22	56-265.4:4, 56-481.2
23	18.2-268.2
24	58.1-3371, 58.1-3373, 58.1-3374
25	9-6.14:7.1, 9-6.14:9.1, 9-6.14:9.3
26	54.1-2822.1
27	58.1-2403
28	10.1-2212
29	58.1-3518
30	2.1-526.8:1
31	18.2-266.1
32	9-145.51
33	36-85.17
34	51.5-33, 51.5-34R
35	56-265.4:4, 56-481.2
36	56-265.4:2
37	19.2-243
38	58.1-3
39	46.2-1001
40	23-49.25
41	17-225
42	46.2-906.1
43	54.1-308.1
44	27-86 to 27-90R
45	58.1-3813
46	46.2-711, 46.2-724
47	58.1-1823, n.
48	55-114.1,

Acts 1995 Chapter	Code 1950 Section
	55-115, 55-123, 55-125 to 55-127, 55-129 to 55-132, 55-134 to 55-135, 55-137.1, 55-137.2
49	44-75.1
50	58.1-2401
51	14.1-48, n., 14.1-69, 14.1-93, 14.1-95, 14.1-95.1, 14.1-105, 14.1-108, 14.1-109R, 14.1-111R, 14.1-111.1, 19.2-338, 55-248.31:1
52	51.1-505
53	36-135
54	46.2-878.1
55	33.1-46.2
56	22.1-75
57	16.1-69.35
58	15.1-11.03
59	15.1-33.4
60	38.2-1046, 38.2-1048, 38.2-1413, 38.2-1414, 38.2-1427.3, 38.2-1432, 38.2-2710, 38.2-4811
62	6.1-411, 6.1-417, 6.1-424
63	6.1-47
65	54.1-3917.1
66	46.2-1221
67	46.2-1801 to 46.2-1805, n.
68	38.2-3405
69	38.2-1000, 38.2-1001
70	13.1-604, 13.1-804, 13.1-1003, 50-73.17
71	46.2-1112
72	23-7.2:1
74	22.1-72
75	6.1-330.72
76	13.1-769, 13.1-931
77	29.1-309, 29.1-321
78	32.1-2, 32.1-11.3, 32.1-11.4
79	9-182, 9-183.1 to 9-183.3, 9-183.7, 9-183.9
80	38.2-4319
82	6.1-62
83	6.1-194.21
84	6.1-56
85	46.2-368
86	65.2-900
87	6.1-64
88	54.1-3408
89	2.1-51.40
90	2.1-1.6, 9-6.25:1, 32.1-241, 32.1-242R
91	46.2-752
92	46.2-920, 46.2-1023
93	54.1-3915.1, 54.1-3916
94	33.1-12
95	36-105
96	58.1-602
97	40.1-51.9, 40.1-51.10, 40.1-51.12, 40.1-51.15
98	2.1-548.9, 2.1-548.12
99	54.1-3804, n., 54.1-3805.2
100	58.1-438.1
101	58.1-609.3, 58.1-609.6, 58.1-609.7
102	58.1-609.4
103	3.1-249.27, 3.1-249.51, 3.1-249.53, 9-6.14:4.1
104	3.1-106.4 to 3.1-106.7, 3.1-106.9
105	33.1-75.3
106	46.2-1090
107	62.1-44.15:6
108	58.1-3981
109	10.1-1425.8
110	59.1-207.3
111	10.1-1101
112	2.1-133.6, 10.1-1453, 15.1-131.8, 15.1-131.8:1 to 15.1-131.8:4, 19.2-59.1, 23-7.1:01, 53.1-119
113	46.2-872
114	13.1-632, 13.1-831
115	10.1-1425.21, 10.1-1425.23
116	50-43.1, 50-43.7, 50-43.11, 50-43.12, 50-73.78, 54.1-3902
117	19.2-316.1, 53.1-67.1
118	46.2-208, 46.2-209
119	38.2-2701
120	40.1-6, n.
121	46.2-440, 46.2-441
122	46.2-1020
123	32.1-81
124	46.2-1933, 46.2-1936 to 46.2-1938, 46.2-2208
125	54.1-2105
126	46.2-666
127	58.1-811
128	9-205, 15.1-1399.15, 15.1-1399.16, 59.1-284.1, 59.1-284.2, 59.1-284.4, 59.1-284.5R
129	28.2-700, 28.2-705
130	29.1-738.2, 29.1-738.3
131	58.1-3516.1
132	46.2-102
133	6.1-194.33 to 6.1-194.37
134	46.2-749.3
135	10.1-1320
136	28.2-201
137	56-65.1
138	8.01-374.1, n.
139	6.1-363.1
140	6.1-32.11, 6.1-32.14, 6.1-32.14:1R, 6.1-32.14:2, 6.1-32.18, 6.1-32.19, 6.1-32.20, 6.1-32.23 to

Acts 1995 Chapter	Code 1950 Section
	6.1-32.28
141	46.2-1179.1
142	58.1-3506
143	58.1-3340
144	46.2-1220
145	46.2-341.21,
	52-8.4
146	46.2-1141
147	33.1-63, n.
149	52-11.3
150	56-529, n.
151	46.2-341.21,
	52-8.4
152	2.1-116, n.,
	2.1-116.20 to
	2.1-116.26
	2.1-391,
	9-169, n.,
	12.1-18, n.,
	23-9.2:3.1, n.,
	23-49.1, n.,
	23-50.7, n.,
	23-77.3, n.,
	23-217, n.,
	51.1-124.1, n.,
	51.1-124.27, n.,
	51.1-153,
	51.1-155,
	51.1-155.1,
	51.1-165,
	51.1-200,
	51.1-205,
	51.1-300, n.,
	53.1-1, n.,
	58.1-4008, n.,
	65.2-200, n.
155	1-13.2,
	1-13.29
156	2.1-133.5 to
	2.1-133.11,
	15.1-136.1 to
	15.1-136.3R,
	15.1-136.4:1R,
	15.1-136.5:1R,
	15.1-136.6:1R,
	15.1-136.7R
157	24.2-700
158	10.1-1322
159	15.1-1054, n.,
	24.2-312, n.
160	3.1-657
167	38.2-233,
	38.2-1800,
	38.2-1814,
	38.2-1824,
	38.2-3727,
	38.2-3737
168	13.1-1002,
	13.1-1012,
	13.1-1021.1,
	13.1-1022,
	13.1-1027,
	13.1-1029,
	13.1-1030,
	13.1-1032,
	13.1-1033R,
	13.1-1040,
	13.1-1046,
	13.1-1048,
	13.1-1117,
	59.1-69,
	59.1-70,
	65.2-101
169	28.2-302.3
170	57-49
171	58.1-609.6
173	15.1-227.66 to
	15.1-227.69R,
	58.1-608.3
174	15.1-600
175	6.1-2.9:6
176	10.1-2211
177	4.1-124
178	15.1-431
179	2.1-20.1:03
180	7.1-40.2:2
181	15.1-1420R to
	15.1-1441R
182	38.2-4300
184	10.1-1307.3
185	58.1-1823, n.
186	2.1-639.16
187	56-265.4:4,
	56-481.2
188	22.1-168.1
189	38.2-2206
190	2.1-751,
	2.1-753
192	24.2-123
193	36-19
194	2.1-1.8, n.,
	2.1-116.18, n.,
	2.1-116.19, n.,
	9-6.23, n.
195	33.1-1,
	33.1-3,
	33.1-4,
	33.1-8
196	4.1-338
197	24.2-659,
	24.2-668,
	24.2-670
198	15.1-37.3:14
199	55-268.1
200	58.1-602.1R
201	58.1-3818
202	58.1-338, n.,
	58.1-445.1, n.
203	58.1-1823, n.
204	58.1-609.3,
	58.1-1501,
	58.1-1505
205	57-49
206	11-47.3
207	15.1-28
208	13.1-514
209	3.1-796.128:1
210	15.1-1420 to
	15.1-1441R
211	64.1-13
212	59.1-385
213	13.1-514
214	65.2-714
215	36-55.39
216	10.1-1411
217	59.1-392
219	2.1-20.01:1,
	2.1-391
220	32.1-176.5
221	6.1-432 to
	6.1-443
222	4.1-320
223	33.1-1,
	33.1-3,
	33.1-4,
	33.1-8
224	53.1-1
225	31-6
226	38.2-2217,
	46.2-498
227	54.1-601,
	54.1-2103
228	55-248.38:1
229	58.1-3660
230	54.1-2933.1
231	24.2-417.1
232	22.1-208.2:1
233	22.1-168.1
234	24.2-123
235	13.1-514
236	29.1-744.1
237	65.2-813.1
238	12.1-17
239	58.1-3914,
	58.1-3921,
	58.1-3924,
	58.1-3961
240	15.1-37.3:14
241	29.1-703,
	29.1-703.1,
	29.1-703.2,
	29.1-710,
	29.1-717
242	59.1-89
243	36-139.3
244	22.1-211,
	22.1-212,
	63.1-196.02R,
	63.1-196.03R
245	13.1-514.1
246	22.1-273
247	58.1-2403
248	15.1-30R

Acts 1995 Chapter	Code 1950 Section
249	2.1-121.1, 15.1-37.4, 15.1-37.5 to 15.1-37.9R, 15.1-527.2R, 15.1-571.1, 15.1-803, 15.1-804R, 15.1-806R, 15.1-807R, 24.2-304.1 to 24.2-304.6, 24.2-306, 24.2-312
250	15.1-22R, 15.1-228R to 15.1-235R, 15.1-264R, 15.1-265R, 22.1-126.1 22.1-161.1 to 22.1-161.8, 23-3.1
251	15.1-871, 18.2-138.1
252	46.2-744
253	4.1-201, 4.1-310
254	46.2-335
255	57-33R
256	62.1-44.15:3
257	28.2-1001
259	38.2-3323
260	56-237.2, 56-501.01
261	20-108.1
262	63.1-44.1
263	2.1-563.31
264	15.1-458
265	45.1-161.64
266	65.2-714
267	38.2-2206, 65.2-309.1
268	8.01-249
269	45.1-361.21, 45.1-361.29
270	38.2-3412.1
271	55-66.4:1
272	65.2-101
273	16.1-266.1
274	22.1-209.01
275	59.1-385
276	58.1-612
277	54.1-2971.01, 54.1-3408.1
278	2.1-343.1
279	63.1-324
280	44-146.28:1
281	13.1-620, 56-508.1 to 56-508.14R
283	28.2-1000R
284	15.1-518, 15.1-518.2
285	15.1-1249
288	65.2-101
290	15.1-50.4, 22.1-30
291	15.1-132.2
294	63.1-124
295	2.1-51.6:4, 7.1-31.1
296	24.2-419, 24.2-420R, 24.2-420.1
297	19.2-17
298	59.1-408, 59.1-410, 59.1-411
299	2.1-342
300	51.1-142
301	6.1-5, 6.1-39.5, 6.1-43, 6.1-44.1 to 6.1-44.25, 58.1-1201
302	38.2-5001
303	58.1-811
304	16.1-346.1
305	53.1-80 to 53.1-82, 53.1-82.2, 53.1-82.3
306	18.2-126
307	51.1-124.22, 51.1-142, 51.1-146, 51.1-156, 51.1-163, 51.1-165, 51.1-168, 51.1-505, 51.1-803
309	54.1-2403.01
310	8.01-620
311	56-265.2, 56-265.2:1
312	57-60
313	63.1-44.1
314	24.2-405, 24.2-406, 24.2-418
315	23-38.76, n., 23-38.81, 23-38.82, 23-38.84
316	22.1-36.1
317	4.1-201, 4.1-310
318	22.1-208.1
319	65.2-502, 65.2-510
321	38.2-4135
322	13.1-553
323	60.2-526
324	65.2-406
325	6.1-225.35
326	6.1-225.20
327	54.1-2009, 54.1-2010
328	15.1-29.25
329	24.2-612.1
330	16.1-284.1
331	14.1-44.2
332	15.1-11.2:2
333	15.1-24, 32.1-332 to 32.1-335, 32.1-337, 32.1-338
334	15.1-1638
335	19.2-73.2
336	54.1-3926
337	46.2-335
339	15.1-29.3
340	18.2-31
341	11-4.4
342	8.01-581.014
343	54.1-3510
344	37.1-144
345	38.2-4300
346	30-19.1:2, 58.1-3605, 58.1-3650
347	16.1-260
349	15.1-29.7
350	46.2-342
351	15.1-491
352	19.2-243
353	2.1-20.1
354	33.1-221.1:4, 33.1-221.1:5R, 33.1-268, 33.1-269, 33.1-277, 58.1-815.2R, 58.1-2146.1
355	20-13.1R, 20-14
356	28.2-203.1
357	2.1-424, 2.1-563.16
358	14.1-5, 14.1-5.2
359	2.1-127, 15.1-1399.14, 23-38.30, 23-38.33:01, 23-38.33:1
360	51.1-512, 51.1-512.1
361	2.1-1.6, 2.1-739.1 to 2.1-739.4,

Acts 1995 Chapter	Code 1950 Section
	9-6.23, 9-6.25:1
362	2.1-342
363	64.1-45.1
365	58.1-439, 58.1-439.1
366	8.01-55
367	8.01-581.2
368	13.1-616, 13.1-816, 13.1-1005, 50-73.17
369	11-9.1, 11-9.6, 37.1-132.1
370	59.1-371
371	14.1-112, 14.1-123, 19.2-11.3
372	46.2-342
373	40.1-1, 40.1-51.1
374	4.1-305
375	19.2-353.5
376	29.1-816
377	55-516.2
378	14.1-44.2, 14.1-44.3
379	8.01-512.3
380	19.2-354
381	64.1-62.3
382	56-235.4
384	2.1-127, 15.1-1399.14, 23-38.30, 23-38.33:01, 23-38.33:1
385	58.1-604
386	15.1-466
388	15.1-466
389	15.1-466
390	46.2-1603.1, 46.2-1603.2
391	54.1-2730, 54.1-2731
392	9-6.25:1, n., 9-6.25:2, n., 22.1-217, n., 22.1-284, n., 63.1-68, 63.1-68.1, 63.1-74, n., 63.1-74.1, n., 63.1-75.1, n., 63.1-77, n., 63.1-78, n., 63.1-79, n., 63.1-81, n., 63.1-83, n., 63.1-85, n., 63.1-153, n., 63.1-155, n., 63.1-161, n., 63.1-68, n.
393	15.1-37.3:9
394	46.2-1603.1
395	58.1-3916, 58.1-3958
396	2.1-752, 2.1-754
397	58.1-3850
398	9-6.14:11, 9-6.14:12
399	2.1-512
400	2.1-382
401	63.1-195, 63.1-198
402	15.1-1241, 15.1-1250.03
403	2.1-639.6
404	22.1-291.1
405	8.01-606
406	22.1-19, n., 22.1-253.13:3, n.
407	15.1-136R, 19.2-392.01
408	15.1-132.2
409	19.2-389
410	18.2-429
411	13.1-637
412	46.2-752
413	19.2-81.3
414	15.1-1248
415	15.1-1248
416	33.1-72.1, 33.1-75.1
417	2.1-1.6, 9-6.25:1, 10.1-1414, 10.1-1415, 10.1-1416, 10.1-1422 to 10.1-1422.05, 58.1-1705, 58.1-1710
419	46.2-1149.1
420	38.2-3407.9, 38.2-4214, 38.2-4319
421	46.2-1571
422	58.1-401
423	58.1-4013
424	15.1-496.1
425	22.1-201, n.
426	46.2-301.1
427	18.2-10
428	20-115
429	16.1-260, 16.1-305.2, 22.1-288.2
430	16.1-305
431	15.1-478
432	46.2-750
433	19.2-81.3
434	8.01-446, 19.2-305.1
435	46.2-301.1
436	60.2-612, 60.2-613
437	19.2-187, 19.2-187.01
438	19.2-340, 19.2-341
439	18.2-52
440	14.1-112
441	19.2-354
442	10.1-1408.1
443	64.1-96.2 to 64.1-96.11
444	55-34.5
445	58.1-3903.1, 58.1-3980
446	38.2-4312.1
447	19.2-270.1, 19.2-270.2
448	16.1-290
449	46.2-752, 58.1-3511
450	63.1-25.01, n., 63.1-105, 63.1-105.1, 63.1-105.3 to 63.1-105.7, 63.1-133.41 to 63.1-133.55, 63.1-251
451	16.1-250
452	15.1-466
453	5.1-31, 5.1-36
454	56-232.3
455	32.1-162.8
456	4.1-215
457	15.1-466
458	46.2-1001
459	46.2-1225
460	46.2-752
461	27-1 to 27-4
462	30-19.1:5, 30-19.1:6
463	14.1-112, 14.1-134.1, 18.2-264.01, 37.1-129
464	2.1-51.17:01
465	19.2-81
466	56-484.2
467	9-311, n., 38.2-3407.7, 38.2-3407.8R, 38.2-4209.1, 38.2-4209.2R, 38.2-4312.1,

Acts 1995 Chapter	Code 1950 Section
	38.2-4312.2R
468	46.2-343
469	58.1-3516.1
470	8.01-66.2
471	19.2-74
472	58.1-401
473	46.2-1309
474	15.1-466
475	15.1-491
476	38.2-2206
477	46.2-1571
478	18.2-429
479	46.2-752
481	20-108.2
482	17-237
483	20-78.2, 63.1-267
484	20-88.32, 20-88.36, 20-88.67
485	19.2-303.4, 19.2-305, 19.2-335, 19.2-336
486	18.2-270.1, 18.2-270.2, 46.2-360, 46.2-391
487	22.1-32
488	23-7.2:1
489	37.1-67.3
490	9-173.12
491	32.1-314
492	46.2-833.01
493	18.2-128
494	15.1-499.1, 36-106
495	2.1-639.2, 2.1-639.14
496	3.1-796.96
497	4.1-100, 4.1-200, 4.1-208, 4.1-231, 4.1-233
498	32.1-34.1
499	2.1-342, 2.1-344, 9-6.14:4.1, 32.1-283.1
500	8.01-581.17
501	9-334, 9-335
502	19.2-295.2, 19.2-303.3, 19.2-316.2, 19.2-316.3, 53.1-67.4, 53.1-145, 53.1-180, 53.1-181, 53.1-183 to 53.1-185, 53.1-185.2, 53.1-185.3
503	8.01-654, 8.01-654.1, 17-97, 17-110.2, 19.2-163.7, 53.1-232.1
504	19.2-265.4
505	32.1-102.3:2
506	54.1-2957.01
507	58.1-400.1, 58.1-2600
508	22.1-79.2
509	54.1-106, 54.1-2701, 54.1-2901
510	10.1-603.16, 10.1-603.18 to 10.1-603.20, 10.1-603.22
511	18.2-308.1
513	22.1-129
514	56-265.2
515	60.2-229, 60.2-301, 60.2-531, 60.2-535, 60.2-619, 60.2-620, 60.2-622
516	9-6.14:4.1
517	16.1-296
518	4.1-100, 4.1-200, 4.1-208, 4.1-231, 4.1-233
519	32.1-45.3, 54.1-2971.1
520	2.1-759, 9-267, 63.1-248.2
521	22.1-79.2
522	38.2-3503, 38.2-3514.1, 38.2-3605, 38.2-4214, 38.2-4319
523	36-105
524	32.1-102.1
525	14.1-112
526	22.1-79.2
527	11-46, 11-70
528	9-334, 9-335
529	54.1-3307, 54.1-3408
530	2.1-7.2
531	54.1-106
532	32.1-288
533	22.1-209.1:2, 22.1-279.2R
534	32.1-36
535	46.2-334, 46.2-335
536	16.1-285.2
537	38.2-3418.2, 38.2-4319
538	18.2-248
539	58.1-638
540	15.1-486.4
542	58.1-638
543	40.1-51.20, 40.1-51.21, 54.1-501, 54.1-503
544	4.1-208, 4.1-209
545	33.1-23.03:4
546	19.2-164, 19.2-164.1
547	58.1-3965
548	11-41.2:1
549	4.1-227
550	8.01-66.2
551	19.2-44
552	19.2-215.1
553	58.1-3812, 58.1-3814
554	38.2-1868, 38.2-1869
555	8.01-267.1 to 8.01-267.9
556	46.2-809.1
557	58.1-3907
558	16.1-309.1
561	6.1-93
562	2.1-342, 2.1-343
563	4.1-227
564	10.1-1198, 10.1-1199
565	2.1-124
566	19.2-353.5
567	19.2-295.1
568	11-41.2:1
569	45.1-161.177, 45.1-161.179
570	4.1-208, 4.1-209
571	19.2-163
572	33.1-252
573	55-511, 55-512
574	19.2-295.2, 19.2-303.3, 19.2-316.2, 19.2-316.3,

Acts 1995 Chapter	Code 1950 Section
	53.1-67.4,
	53.1-145,
	53.1-180,
	53.1-181,
	53.1-183,
	53.1-184,
	53.1-185,
	53.1-185.2,
	53.1-185.3
576	33.1-23.03:4
577	18.2-308.1:5
578	18.2-253
579	2.1-42.3
580	55-248.31
581	54.1-1100,
	54.1-1103,
	54.1-1131
582	22.1-212.1:1
583	15.1-486.4
584	15.1-491
585	40.1-51.20,
	40.1-51.21,
	54.1-501,
	54.1-503
586	8.01-413
588	2.1-345
589	16.1-122.1
590	58.1-3812,
	58.1-3814
592	14.1-118.1
593	63.1-252.1
594	8.01-389
595	46.2-320,
	63.1-250.1
597	2.1-133.6,
	2.1-133.7,
	2.1-133.9,
	2.1-133.10
599	8.01-127.1
600	63.1-252.1
601	55-248.18
602	58.1-302
603	15.1-430,
	15.1-491
604	2.1-795,
	2.1-797 to
	2.1-799
605	51.1-505
606	58.1-3650.610 to
	58.1-3650.620, n.
608	54.1-2710
609	10.1-1429.1 to
	10.1-1429.3
610	3.1-796.66,
	29.1-417
611	19.2-38.1
612	2.1-20.1:2 to
	2.1-20.1:4
613	15.1-227.70 to
	15.1-227.77,
	15.1-227.83 to
	15.1-227.87
614	58.1-3713, n.
615	38.2-401
616	11-41.2:1
617	58.1-609.1,
	58.1-609.4,
	58.1-609.7 to
	58.1-609.10
618	58.1-3650.611, n.,
	58.1-3650.612, n.,
	58.1-3650.614, n.,
	58.1-3650.618, n.
	58.1-3650.621 to
	58.1-3650.649, n.
620	51.1-142
621	13.1-1062,
	13.1-1063,
	50-73.67,
	50-73.68
622	10.1-1429.1 to
	10.1-1429.3
623	54.1-2708.1
624	55-210.3:01,
	55-210.6:1
625	3.1-796.70
626	15.1-1231,
	15.1-1274
627	54.1-2710
628	19.2-11.4
629	15.1-227.70 to
	15.1-227.77,
	15.1-227.83 to
	15.1-227.87
630	4.1-215
631	32.1-126.3,
	36-99.9:1
632	32.1-102.3:2
633	15.1-362.1
634	15.1-1248
635	58.1-3713, n.
636	8.01-581.13
637	38.2-401
638	2.1-1.5,
	2.1-342,
	2.1-548.8, n.,
	2.1-548.26 to
	2.1-548.43
639	32.1-31, n.,
	35.1-18, n.,
	35.1-25, n.
641	32.1-102.3:2
642	18.2-128
643	56-257.3,
	56-265.1
644	54.1-3802
645	19.2-174.1,
	19.2-175,
	19.2-178,
	19.2-389
646	2.1-114.5:1
647	33.1-257,
	33.1-263R,
	56-39R,
	56-556 to 56-561,
	56-562R,
	56-563 to 56-573.2,
	56-574
648	59.1-460 to
	59.1-466
649	63.1-25.1,
	63.1-172,
	63.1-173.3,
	63.1-174,
	63.1-174.001,
	63.1-174.2
650	38.2-5600 to
	38.2-5603
651	15.1-11.2
652	38.2-2204
653	26-18
654	10.1-617,
	10.1-625,
	10.1-628,
	10.1-634.1
657	33.1-346,
	46.2-208
658	15.1-33.4
659	46.2-752
660	15.1-28.01, n.,
	15.1-28.04,
	15.1-28.1,
	15.1-1250.01
661	4.1-100
662	15.1-478
663	23-38.18
664	58.1-609.1,
	58.1-2100,
	58.1-2101,
	58.1-2103,
	58.1-2105 to
	58.1-2107,
	58.1-2111 to
	58.1-2112,
	58.1-2114 to
	58.1-2119,
	58.1-2120.2R,
	58.1-2120.3,
	58.1-2122 to
	58.1-2124.1,
	58.1-2126,
	58.1-2127.1 to
	58.1-2127.7R,
	58.1-2128 to
	58.1-2129,
	58.1-2131.2,
	58.1-2131.3,
	58.1-2133 to
	58.1-2135,
	58.1-2142,
	58.1-2142.1,
	58.1-2144 to
	58.1-2146.1,

Acts 1995 Chapter	Code 1950 Section
	59.1-21.16:2, 62.1-44.34:13
665	16.1-241
667	15.1-11.2:2
668	37.1-67.3
669	8.01-66.2
670	46.2-115, 46.2-676, 46.2-915.1, 46.2-1157
671	46.2-906.1
672	46.2-351.1, 46.2-489, 46.2-490, 46.2-490.2, 46.2-491, 46.2-495, 46.2-496R, 46.2-497R, 46.2-498 to 46.2-503, 46.2-505, 46.2-506
673	58.1-3220, 58.1-3221
674	20-103
675	18.2-371.2
676	46.2-208
677	9-6.14:7.1
678	26-59
679	58.1-3301
680	33.1-69.2
681	22.1-279.1
682	5.1-7, 5.1-8R, 5.1-88.7 to 5.1-88.10
683	15.1-132.1
684	26-59, 64.1-73
685	15.1-132.1
686	46.2-208
687	16.1-309.1, 19.2-11.01, 19.2-11.1, 19.2-265.01, 19.2-299, 19.2-299.1, 19.2-305.1, 53.1-133.02, 53.1-155, 53.1-160
688	33.1-69.2
690	5.1-7, 5.1-8R, 5.1-88.7 to 5.1-88.10
691	2.1-1.6, 3.1-1065 to 3.1-1080
692	51.1-153, 51.1-155, 51.1-155.1, 51.1-165, 51.1-205, 51.1-206
693	15.1-1676 to 15.1-1687
694	11-41.2:01, 53.1-261, 53.1-262, 53.1-265 to 53.1-267
695	32.1-102.3:2
696	2.1-752, 15.1-50.5, 16.1-233, 16.1-284.1, 16.1-286, 16.1-318, 16.1-322.5
698	16.1-309.2 to 16.1-309.10, 16.1-310 to 16.1-314R, 16.1-322.1, 16.1-322.2, 16.1-322.4
699	2.1-752, 15.1-50.5, 16.1-233, 16.1-284.1, 16.1-286, 16.1-318, 16.1-322.5
700	22.1-343, 23-38.53:8 to 23-38.53:10
701	66-3
702	36-49.1:1, 36-105
703	3.1-18.2, 59.1-199, 59.1-201, 59.1-201.1, 59.1-204, 59.1-204.1, 59.1-206, 59.1-207
712	58.1-609.8
713	19.2-163
714	20-79.2, 63.1-250.2, 63.1-250.3, 63.1-258.1
715	58.1-609.7
716	24.2-643
717	9-6.14:7.1
719	58.1-609.3, 58.1-609.6, 58.1-609.8, 58.1-609.10
720	19.2-299.1
721	51.1-155.1, 51.1-155.2
722	2.1-342, 15.1-765.2
723	58.1-1505, 58.1-2106, 58.1-2118
724	22.1-257, 22.1-277.01, 22.1-277.1, 22.1-278
725	53.1-10
726	59.1-204, 59.1-204.1, 59.1-207
727	46.2-1025
728	15.1-21.1, 15.1-1135, 15.1-1146.1:2, 22.1-57.1:1
729	32.1-46
730	2.1-116.1
731	19.2-389, 22.1-296.2
732	15.1-1400 to 15.1-1412.1, 15.1-1414R, 15.1-1416, 36-139.6, 36-139.7, 36-140R
733	14.1-52
734	2.1-20.1:2 to 2.1-20.1:4
735	9-336 to 9-339
736	9-6.14:9.1
737	2.1-1.6, 2.1-20.4, 9-6.25:2, 10.1-1408.2, 54.1-300, 54.1-2209 to 54.1-2212R
738	54.1-2506.2
739	10.1-1410
740	15.1-9.1:3
741	54.1-2105, n., 54.1-2130 to 54.1-2144
742	32.1-46
743	30-19.03, 30-19.03:1
744	9-6.14:14.1, 38.2-1902, 38.2-2217.1, 46.2-106, 46.2-200, 46.2-703, 46.2-757 to 46.2-769,

Acts 1995 Chapter	Code 1950 Section
	46.2-2000 to 46.2-2050, 46.2-2100 to 46.2-2114, 46.2-2200 to 46.2-2209, 46.2-2300 to 46.2-2312, 46.2-2400 to 46.2-2409, 46.2-2500 to 46.2-2519, 46.2-2600 to 46.2-2610, 52-8.4, 56-273, 56-273 to 56-277.1R, 56-278 to 56-287R, 56-287.1 to 56-287.3R, 56-288 to 56-290.1R, 56-291 to 56-291.3:7R, 56-291.9, 56-291.11, 56-291.13, 56-292 to 56-296R, 56-296.1 to 56-298R, 56-299 to 56-303.1R, 56-304 to 56-304.2 to 56-304.9, 56-304.11, 56-304.12 to 56-304.16R, 56-305R to 56-323R, 56-324 to 56-338R, 56-338.1 to 56-338.18R, 56-338.19 to 56-338.39R, 56-338.40 to 56-338.49R, 56-338.50 to 56-338.64R, 56-338.65 to 56-338.84R, 56-338.93 to 56-338.103R, 56-338.104 to 56-338.127R, 56-457.1 to 56-457.10R, 58.1-2114, 58.1-2700, 58.1-2700.1 to 58.1-2700.3, 58.1-2702, 58.1-2705 to 58.1-2709, 58.1-2711, 58.1-2712R, 58.1-2712.1
745	38.2-5300, 38.2-5400 to 38.2-5409
746	16.1-249, 16.1-269.5
747	46.2-725, 46.2-725.1R, 46.2-726, 46.2-728.3, 46.2-729R 46.2-732, 46.2-736.1 to 46.2-737, 46.2-739 to 46.2-749.2:1, 46.2-749.4, 46.2-749.6 to 46.2-749.11, 46.2-750
748	16.1-249
749	10.1-2116, 46.2-749.2
750	22.1-217, 22.1-241
751	58.1-2662.1, 58.1-2690, 58.1-3818.1 to 58.1-3818.7
752	16.1-301
753	32.1-102.3:2
754	32.1-127.1:02, 54.1-2403.3
755	22.1-257, 22.1-277.1
756	53.1-133.1 to 53.1-133.5
757	2.1-114.5:1, 2.1-116
758	9-266.1 to 9-266.19
759	8.01-47, 22.1-280.1
760	11-71.1
761	24.2-686
762	22.1-175.1 to 22.1-175.3
763	2.1-639.15, 2.1-639.41
765	9-157, n., 9-158, 9-158.1
766	53.1-32
767	2.1-1.5, 2.1-1.6, 2.1-20.4, 2.1-41.2, 9-6.25:3, 46.2-200, n., 46.2-1500, 46.2-1502R, 46.2-1503 to 46.2-1521, 46.2-1527.1 to 46.2-1530, 46.2-1532, 46.2-1533, 46.2-1536, 46.2-1539, 46.2-1541R, 46.2-1542 to 46.2-1549, 46.2-1550, 46.2-1551, 46.2-1553 to 46.2-1556, 46.2-1565.1, 46.2-1566, 46.2-1568, 46.2-1569, 46.2-1573, 46.2-1575 to 46.2-1577, 46.2-1582, 46.2-1900 to 46.2-1921, 46.2-1927 to 46.2-1991
768	53.1-183, 53.1-185.2
769	2.1-394.2
770	2.1-114.5:1 to 2.1-114.5:6R, 2.1-116.01 to 2.1-116.013, 8.01-418.2, 15.1-7.2, 15.1-687.16, 30-34.2:1, 63.1-26
771	54.1-1102, 54.1-1103, 54.1-1108.2 to 54.1-1112, 54.1-1114, 54.1-1115, 54.1-1118, 54.1-1119, 54.1-1126
772	16.1-241, 16.1-243, 16.1-262, 63.1-204, 63.1-220,

Acts 1995 Chapter	Code 1950 Section
	63.1-220.2 to 63.1-220.7, 63.1-221 to 63.1-223, 63.1-225, 63.1-225.1, 63.1-227, 63.1-229, 63.1-231, 63.1-233, 63.1-236 to 63.1-237
773	22.1-280.1
774	2.1-505, 23-4.01
775	58.1-433, n., 58.1-439.2, 58.1-439.3, 58.1-2600, n., 58.1-2626.1, n.
776	9-6.14:14.1, 46.2-731, 46.2-1237
777	54.1-2900, 54.1-2901
778	19.2-299, 53.1-155
779	58.1-333, n., 58.1-430, n., 63.1-320 to 63.1-325, n.
781	19.2-389, 22.1-296.2
783	9-336 to 9-339
784	54.1-1118, 54.1-1120
785	24.2-916, 24.2-917, 24.2-919, 24.2-922, 24.2-923, 24.2-928, 24.2-929
786	58.1-609.7 to 58.1-609.9, 58.1-1505, 58.1-2106, 58.1-2118, 58.1-2403
788	2.1-440, 51.1-124.20, 51.1-124.26, 51.1-124.30
789	38.2-135, 38.2-5500 to 38.2-5514
790	9-6.14:7.1
791	18.2-426, 18.2-429
792	59.1-271, 59.1-273, 59.1-274, 59.1-279 to 59.1-280.2, 59.1-282 to 59.1-284.01
793	10.1-1193 to 10.1-1197
794	2.1-526.8
796	15.1-1400 to 15.1-1412.1, 15.1-1414R, 15.1-1416, 36-139.6, 36-139.7, 36-140R
797	35.1-1, 53.1-68, 53.1-127
798	16.1-249, 16.1-269.5
799	16.1-77, 46.2-351.1 to 46.2-358, 46.2-360, 46.2-361
800	2.1-746
801	22.1-257, 22.1-277.01, 22.1-277.1, 22.1-278
802	16.1-249, 16.1-269.5
803	9-6.14:14.1, 38.2-1902, 38.2-2217.1, 46.2-106, 46.2-200, 46.2-703, 46.2-757 to 46.2-769, 46.2-2000 to 46.2-2050, 46.2-2100 to 46.2-2114, 46.2-2200 to 46.2-2209, 46.2-2300 to 46.2-2312, 46.2-2400 to 46.2-2409, 46.2-2500 to 46.2-2519, 46.2-2600 to 46.2-2610, 52-8.4, 56-273R, 56-274 to 56-291.3:7R, 56-291.9 to 56-291.13R, 56-292 to 56-303.1R, 56-304R, 56-304.1 to 56-304.16R, 56-304.12R, 56-304.13R, 56-304.15R, 56-304.16R, 56-305 to 56-338.127R, 56-457.1 to 56-457.10R, 58.1-2114, 58.1-2700 to 58.1-2700.3, 58.1-2702, 58.1-2705 to 58.1-2709, 58.1-2711, 58.1-2712R, 58.1-2712.1
804	16.1-309.1
805	9-6.14:14.1, 46.2-731, 46.2-1237
806	16.1-266.2
807	55-66.01, 55-66.1:01R
808	24.2-686
809	19.2-389, 22.1-296.2
810	63.1-248.3
811	2.1-110, n., 2.1-116, n., 2.1-116.20 to 2.1-116.26, 2.1-391, 9-169, n., 12.1-18, n., 23-9.2:3.1, n., 23-49.1, n., 23-50.7, n., 23-77.3, n., 23-217, n., 51.1-124.1, n., 51.1-124.27, n., 51.1-153, 51.1-155, 51.1-155.1, 51.1-165, 51.1-200, n., 51.1-205, 51.1-300, n., 53.1-1, n., 58.1-4008, n., 65.2-200, n.
812	2.1-1.5, 2.1-342, 51.5-53 to 51.5-59
813	54.1-2105, n.,

Acts 1995 Chapter	Code 1950 Section
	54.1-2130 to 54.1-2144
814	2.1-1.8, 2.1-800 to 2.1-803, 9-6.23, 9-6.25:2
815	2.1-1.3, 2.1-1.7, 2.1-20.4, 9-6.23, 9-6.25:1, 9-340 to 9-349
816	2.1-1.5, 2.1-1.6, 2.1-20.4, 2.1-41.2, 9-6.25:3, 46.2-200, n., 46.2-1500, 46.2-1502R, 46.2-1503 to 46.2-1521, 46.2-1527.1 to 46.2-1530, 46.2-1532, 46.2-1533, 46.2-1536, 46.2-1539, 46.2-1541R, 46.2-1542 to 46.2-1549, 46.2-1550, 46.2-1551, 46.2-1553 to 46.2-1556, 46.2-1565.1, 46.2-1566, 46.2-1568, 46.2-1569, 46.2-1573, 46.2-1575 to 46.2-1577, 46.2-1582, 46.2-1900 to 46.2-1921, 46.2-1927 to 46.2-1991
817	16.1-252, 16.1-290, 63.1-204.2, 63.1-204.3, 63.1-251.3
818	2.1-114.5:1 to 2.1-114.5:6R 2.1-116.01 to 2.1-116.013, 8.01-418.2, 15.1-7.2, 15.1-687.16, 30-34.2:1, 63.1-26
819	54.1-2106
820	54.1-3500, 54.1-3501, 54.1-3503 to 54.1-3506
821	53.1-32
822	3.1-763.5:1 to 3.1-763.5:8
823	10.1-2116, 46.2-749.2
824	18.2-60.3
825	24.2-686
826	16.1-241, 16.1-243, 16.1-262, 63.1-204, 63.1-220, 63.1-220.2 to 63.1-220.7, 63.1-221, 63.1-222, 63.1-223, 63.1-225, 63.1-225.1, 63.1-227, 63.1-229, 63.1-231, 63.1-233, 63.1-236 to 63.1-237
827	36-49.1:1, 36-105
828	32.1-116.01
829	18.2-308
830	15.1-132.1
831	58.1-4022
832	3.1-796.94, 10.1-569
833	33.1-320.1
834	18.2-67.5:2, 18.2-67.5:3, 19.2-297.1
835	24.2-106, 24.2-110
836	46.2-1176 to 46.2-1179, 46.2-1180 to 46.2-1182.1, 46.2-1183, 46.2-1187.2
837	2.1-1.5, 2.1-1.9, 2.1-51.27, 2.1-20.4, 2.1-342, 9-6.25:3, 18.2-334.2, 18.2-340.1 to 18.2-340.14R, 18.2-340.15 to 18.2-340.38
838	2.1-725
839	2.1-124, 18.2-374.1
840	16.1-309.2 to 16.1-309.10, 16.1-310R to 16.1-314R 16.1-322.1, 16.1-322.2, 16.1-322.4,
841	2.1-234.12, 2.1-234.13
842	22.1-57.3:3, 22.1-76
843	38.2-5110
844	15.1-131, 15.1-138, 19.2-169.6, 19.2-177.1, 37.1-67.01, 37.1-67.1, 37.1-67.2R, 37.1-67.3, 37.1-67.4, 37.1-71, 37.1-72, 37.1-88, 37.1-89, 37.1-134.5, 37.1-197, 37.1-197.1, 63.1-174.001
845	33.1-320.1
846	53.1-19
847	46.2-325, 46.2-335
848	24.2-106, 24.2-110
849	46.2-1529.1, 46.2-1530
850	2.1-1.6, 2.1-504, 9-6.25:1, 10.1-1108, 28.2-1200, 28.2-1201, 28.2-1301, 28.2-1401 to 28.2-1514, 41.1-3, 41.1-4R, 41.1-5, 41.1-16
851	46.2-1176 to 46.2-1183, 46.2-1187.2
852	16.1-241, 16.1-241.2, 22.1-1,

Acts 1995 Chapter	Code 1950 Section
	22.1-199.1,
	22.1-279.3,
	58.1-4022

ACTS 1996

Acts 1996 Chapter	Code 1950 Section
1	46.2-870
2	24.2-312, n.
3	4.1-406,
	4.1-505
4	Va. Const., Art. X,
	§ 11, n.
5	24.2-648
6	24.2-926
7	29.1-302.1
8	24.2-653,
	24.2-668,
	24.2-671
9	29.1-503R
10	38.2-1831,
	38.2-1843,
	38.2-1855,
	38.2-1863
11	38.2-3600,
	38.2-3606,
	38.2-3607,
	38.2-3608
12	38.2-316
13	6.1-62,
	6.1-194.21
14	6.1-194.78,
	6.1-194.144
15	56-265.13:6
16	6.1-2.1,
	6.1-2.9:4,
	6.1-194.87,
	6.1-232,
	6.1-250,
	6.1-330.48,
	6.1-381,
	13.1-514,
	13.1-620,
	13.1-627
17	6.1-406
18	56-235.5
19	56-76,
	56-77
20	62.1-224,
	62.1-229
21	46.2-1605
22	38.2-402,
	38.2-4319,
	58.1-2508
23	33.1-269
24	46.2-1001
25	6.1-47
26	6.1-13,
	6.1-33,
	6.1-39.3,
	6.1-194.12,
	6.1-194.114,
	6.1-194.131
27	6.1-60.1
28	53.1-27
29	46.2-1149.1
30	6.1-418
31	38.2-2228 —
	38.2-2228.1R
32	38.2-234,
	38.2-1306.1
33	Va. Const., Art. I,
	§ 8-A, n.
34	33.1-46.2
35	46.2-1178.1,
	46.2-1183
36	46.2-872,
	46.2-1139,
	46.2-1140,
	46.2-1141,
	46.2-1142,
	46.2-1143,
	46.2-1144,
	46.2-1145,
	46.2-1146,
	46.2-1147,
	46.2-1148,
	46.2-1149,
	46.2-1149.1
37	54.1-3307,
	54.1-3401,
	54.1-3437,
	54.1-3438,
	54.1-3439,
	54.1-3441
38	37.1-182.2
39	46.2-1115
40	Va. Const., Art. VI,
	§ 1, n.
41	38.2-3412.1
42	2.1-741
43	9-145.51
45	16.1-278.5
46	9-145.33:1
47	38.2-1317
48	56-265.13:7
49	54.1-1404
50	59.1-148.3
51	9-6.14:4.1
52	7.1-40.9
53	2.1-116
54	37.1-182.2
55	46.2-667
56	65.2-1000,
	65.2-1005
57	64.1-121
58	64.1-90
59	24.2-222, n.
60	19.2-307
61	2.1-1.6,
	54.1-1300—54.1-1308R,
	59.1-199
62	14.1-123
63	59.1-207.38
64	Va. Const., Art. II,
	§§ 1, 2, n.
65	64.1-184
66	2.1-133.6
67	32.1-46
68	56-484.4,
	56-484.5,
	56-484.6,
	56-484.7R
69	58.1-2101,
	58.1-2107,
	58.1-2111,
	58.1-2119,
	58.1-2122,
	58.1-2128
70	44-54.6
71	44-75.1
72	24.2-101,
	24.2-114,
	24.2-401,
	24.2-404.1,
	24.2-409.1,
	24.2-411.1,
	24.2-411.2,
	24.2-412,
	24.2-413,
	24.2-415.1,
	24.2-416.1—24.2-416.5,
	24.2-417,
	24.2-425,
	24.2-426,
	24.2-427,
	24.2-428,
	24.2-428.1,
	24.2-428.2,
	24.2-429,
	24.2-431,
	24.2-444,
	24.2-643,
	24.2-1002.1
73	24.2-101,
	24.2-114,
	24.2-401,
	24.2-404.1,
	24.2-409.1,
	24.2-411.1,
	24.2-411.2,
	24.2-412,
	24.2-413,
	24.2-415.1,
	24.2-416.1—24.2-416.5,
	24.2-417,
	24.2-425,
	24.2-426,
	24.2-427,
	24.2-428,
	24.2-428.1,
	24.2-428.2,
	24.2-429,

Acts 1996 Chapter	Code 1950 Section
	24.2-431,
	24.2-444,
	24.2-643,
	24.2-1002.1
74	10.1-1142
75	38.2-3407.1,
	38.2-4306.1
76	54.1-500
77	2.1-209,
	2.1-210,
	2.1-234.3,
	2.1-234.9:2,
	2.1-327,
	2.1-360,
	2.1-639.2,
	2.1-639.15,
	2.1-639.15:1,
	2.1-639.31,
	2.1-639.41,
	3.1-27.3,
	3.1-27.12,
	3.1-27.34,
	8.01-676.1,
	8.9-105,
	9-199,
	9-234,
	10.1-312,
	11-61,
	12.1-10,
	13.1-724,
	13.1-826,
	13.1-982,
	13.1-989,
	15.1-466,
	15.1-1624,
	18.2-113,
	29.1-101.3,
	36-55.30:2,
	36-55.44,
	36-96.1:1,
	36-143,
	38.2-1432,
	38.2-4700,
	55-66.3:1,
	55-344,
	58.1-403,
	58.1-3149,
	58.1-3706,
	58.1-3730,
	59.1-199,
	59.1-265,
	59.1-271,
	59.1-280,
	62.1-221,
	62.1-226,
	62.1-235,
	62.1-241.3,
	63.1-321,
	63.1-324
78	54.1-2210
79	56-265.15,
	56-265.15:1,
	56-265.19,
	56-265.24,
	56-265.31
80	6.1-84,
	6.1-194.79,
	6.1-194.145
81	38.2-1509,
	38.2-1514
82	46.2-1081
83	37.1-132.1
84	64.1-157
85	33.1-221
86	19.2-368.4,
	19.2-368.11:1
87	46.2-872,
	46.2-1139,
	46.2-1140,
	46.2-1141,
	46.2-1142,
	46.2-1143,
	46.2-1144 to
	46.2-1149.1
88	46.2-1237
89	46.2-752
91	46.2-1001
92	46.2-1042
93	64.1-149,
	64.1-150
94	2.1-563.31,
	9-145.52—9-145.56
95	60.2-633
96	54.1-1119,
	54.1-1120
97	2.1-1.5,
	9-6.25:1,
	9-350—9-353
98	2.1-20.01:1
99	15.1-18.3
100	46.2-1178.1,
	46.2-1183
101	33.1-223
102	29.1-306
103	23-31
104	10.1-1146R
105	2.1-1.7,
	9-6.25:1,
	10.1-630,
	10.1-631,
	15.1-227.4,
	15.1-227.5R,
	15.1-227.46R,
	22.1-161.6R,
	58.1-608.3
106	60.2-622
107	60.2-600,
	60.2-608.1
108	60.2-623
109	29.1-302.1
110	23-9.10R
111	9-266.5
112	19.2-37
113	2.1-373.1
114	33.1-145.1,
	56-44—56-46R,
	56-93—56-99.1R,
	56-100.1,
	56-101R,
	56-102,
	56-102.1—56-110R,
	56-111,
	56-112—56-116R,
	56-117,
	56-118,
	56-129R,
	56-129.1,
	56-130,
	56-131,
	56-132R,
	56-139R,
	56-266—56-272R,
	56-345R,
	56-345.1,
	56-348R,
	56-354,
	56-355.2,
	56-359—56-361R,
	56-362,
	56-363,
	56-364,
	56-365R,
	56-365.1,
	56-366.1,
	56-366.2R,
	56-366.3,
	56-368.1,
	56-369,
	56-371—56-382R,
	56-384—56-389R,
	56-405,
	56-405.01R,
	56-405.02,
	56-405.1,
	56-405.2,
	56-405.3R,
	56-406.1,
	56-406.2,
	56-411,
	56-413R,
	56-413.01,
	56-413.1,
	56-413.2R,
	56-417R,
	56-418R,
	56-419.1R,
	56-427R,
	56-428,
	56-445R,
	56-446,
	56-447—56-451R,
	56-451.1,
	56-454—56-456R

Acts 1996 Chapter	Code 1950 Section
115	54.1-2114
116	2.1-563.28,
	2.1-563.32,
	9-145.51
118	29.1-300.1,
	29.1-301,
	29.1-303.3
119	62.1-44.5
120	17-119.1:2
121	16.1-69.6:1
122	22.1-202
123	22.1-221
124	22.1-202
125	33.1-355
126	6.1-411
127	23-9.10R
128	33.1-221
129	10.1-2116
130	60.2-623
131	33.1-223
132	63.1-171.8R
133	22.1-216,
	22.1-218
134	23-218,
	40.1-118
135	23-231.3
136	28.2-708
137	44-135.1
138	33.1-252
141	46.2-1022
142	54.1-2806
143	33.1-269
144	46.2-1001
145	11-45,
	46.2-1097
146	46.2-1115
147	46.2-840R
148	5.1-7
149	33.1-41.1
150	22.1-17.3
151	29.1-300.1,
	29.1-301,
	29.1-303.3
152	9-6.14:4.1,
	54.1-2900,
	54.1-2957.1—
	54.1-2957.3R,
	54.1-3200,
	54.1-3207,
	54.1-3222—54.1-3224,
	54.1-3303,
	54.1-3401,
	54.1-3408
153	44-75.1:1
154	2.1-384,
	2.1-434.1—2.1-434.12R,
	9-170,
	9-196.1—9-196.12,
	18.2-267,
	18.2-268.9,
	19.2-310.2,
	46.2-341.25
155	2.1-20.1,
	32.1-325,
	38.2-3414.1,
	38.2-4319
156	56-235.2
157	33.1-145.1,
	56-102,
	56-111,
	56-117,
	56-118,
	56-129.1,
	56-130,
	56-131,
	56-345.1,
	56-354,
	56-355.2,
	56-362,
	56-363,
	56-365.1,
	56-366.1,
	56-366.3,
	56-368.1,
	56-369,
	56-405,
	56-405.02,
	56-405.1,
	56-405.2,
	56-406.1,
	56-406.2,
	56-411,
	56-413.01,
	56-428,
	56-446,
	56-451.1,
	56-44—56-46R,
	56-93—56-99.1R,
	56-100.1,
	56-101R,
	56-102.1—56-110R,
	56-112—56-116R,
	56-129R,
	56-132R,
	56-139R,
	56-266—56-272R,
	56-345R,
	56-348R,
	56-359—56-361R,
	56-364,
	56-365R,
	56-366.2R,
	56-371—56-382R,
	56-384—56-389R,
	56-405.01R,
	56-405.3R,
	56-413R,
	56-413.1,
	56-413.2R,
	56-417R,
	56-418R,
	56-419.1R,
	56-427R,
	56-445R,
	56-447—56-451R,
	56-454—56-456R
158	9-6.14:4.1,
	54.1-2900,
	54.1-3200,
	54.1-3207,
	54.1-3222—54.1-3224,
	54.1-3303,
	54.1-3401,
	54.1-3408,
	54.1-2957.1—
	54.1-2957.3R
159	38.2-1866,
	38.2-1867,
	38.2-1868R,
	38.2-1868.1,
	38.2-1869,
	38.2-1870,
	38.2-1871,
	38.2-1872,
	38.2-1873,
	38.2-1874
160	62.1-44.15:4
161	9-84.03
162	25-46.3, n.,
	25-46.7, n.,
	25-46.9, n.,
	25-46.11, n.,
	25-46.17, n.,
	25-46.19, n.,
	25-46.20, n.,
	25-46.20:1, n.,
	25-46.20:2, n.,
	25-46.20:3, n.,
	25-46.20:4, n.,
	25-46.20:5, n.,
	25-46.21, n.,
	25-46.27, n.,
	25-46.29, n.,
	33.1-132, n.,
	33.1-238, n.
163	22.1-253.13:1,
	22.1-254,
	22.1-254.01
164	2.1-116.010,
	2.1-116.011R,
	2.1-116.012,
	2.1-116.03,
	2.1-116.05,
	2.1-116.06,
	2.1-116.09,
	15.1-7.1,
	15.1-7.2,
	15.1-687.16
165	46.2-1801—
	46.2-1805R,
	46.2-2700—
	46.2-2703
166	54.1-3000,

Acts 1996 Chapter	Code 1950 Section
	54.1-3005, 54.1-3008, 54.1-3029
167	15.1-38, 15.1-40
168	2.1-342
169	3.1-1075
170	46.2-2011.1
171	46.2-502
172	46.2-878.2
173	36-96.21
174	2.1-133.6
175	60.2-618
176	54.1-500
177	9-291.1
178	65.2-711
179	2.1-1.6, 54.1-1300—54.1-1308R, 59.1-199
180	40.1-51.20, 54.1-500, 54.1-500.1, 54.1-501, 54.1-503, 54.1-505, 54.1-512, 54.1-514, 54.1-516, 54.1-517
181	65.2-801
182	60.2-618
183	54.1-3408
184	37.1-71
185	22.1-47.3
186	22.1-295
187	33.1-46.2
188	23-38.34:1
189	9-6.14:4.1, 9-6.14:14.1, 23-38.44:4
190	22.1-277.2
191	33.1-46.2
192	32.1-112.2
193	32.1-323.1
194	60.2-618
195	32.1-330.1
196	37.1-33
197	22.1-298
198	22.1-212.2:1
199	60.2-618
200	35.1-22
201	2.1-20.1, 32.1-325, 38.2-3414.1, 38.2-4319
202	32.1-176.5
203	23-31.1
204	23-38.34:1
205	9-6.14:4.1, 9-6.14:14.1, 23-38.44:4
206	38.2-2212
213	3.1-796.120
214	28.2-208, 28.2-228.1
215	23-9.6:1
216	8.1-105, 8.1-206, 8.4-104, 8.5-114, 8.8-101—8.8-108R, 8.8-201—8.8-208R, 8.8-301—8.8-321R, 8.8-401—8.8-408R, 8.8A-101—8.8A-116, 8.8A-201—8.8A-210, 8.8A-301—8.8A-307, 8.8A-401—8.8A-407, 8.8A-501—8.8A-511, 8.8A-601, 8.9-103, 8.9-105, 8.9-106, 8.9-115, 8.9-116, 8.9-203, 8.9-301, 8.9-302, 8.9-304, 8.9-305, 8.9-306, 8.9-309, 8.9-312, 13.1-424—13.1-433R
217	24.2-905
218	6.1-6.1, 6.1-47
219	47.1-19
220	60.2-114
221	29.1-530, n.
222	15.1-242, 15.1-247
223	24.2-671, 24.2-675
224	24.2-705
225	15.1-1032.2
226	19.2-353.5
227	10.1-2212
228	28.2-1205
229	28.2-700
230	53.1-27
231	17-79.3
232	38.2-5016
233	15.1-491.9
234	53.1-19
235	15.1-11.2
236	10.1-1400, 10.1-1408.1
237	38.2-231, 38.2-2114
238	13.1-708
239	38.2-2212
240	38.2-4806
241	22.1-208.2:2
242	6.1-330.60
243	6.1-330.71, 6.1-330.72
244	60.2-212
245	38.2-1612
246	13.1-730
247	22.1-221
249	3.1-796.68, 3.1-796.83:1, 18.2-403.1
250	38.2-1904, 38.2-2005, 65.2-101
251	24.2-405, 24.2-406, 24.2-418
252	65.2-510
253	24.2-706
254	56-46.1
255	50-73.49, 50-73.69
256	55-184.1
257	13.1-627
258	24.2-626
259	38.2-5300
260	6.1-125.15:1
261	11-40
262	38.2-3431
263	14.1-47.2
264	60.2-512
265	11-3, 13.1-1002, 13.1-1004, 13.1-1010.1, 13.1-1015, 13.1-1024, 13.1-1031, 13.1-1046, 13.1-1049, 13.1-1052, 13.1-1054, 13.1-1059, 13.1-1102, 13.1-1104, 13.1-1105, 13.1-1110, 13.1-1117, 13.1-1121, 50-73.11:1, 64.1-48
266	3.1-296.12, 3.1-296.13
267	59.1-410, 59.1-411
268	6.1-45
269	38.2-3432
270	24.2-505
271	24.2-627
272	56-484.2

Acts 1996 Chapter	Code 1950 Section
273	19.2-354
274	6.1-372
275	10.1-565
276	38.2-124, 38.2-2201
277	28.2-241
278	56-257
279	9-6.14:4.1, 15.1-1228, n., 15.1-1232
280	11-40
281	55-79.90
282	13.1-633, 13.1-832, 13.1-1067, 50-37.3
283	3.1-27.1—3.1-27.36R
284	53.1-45.1
285	10.1-1163, 10.1-1164, 10.1-1167, 10.1-1168, 10.1-1169
286	3.1-1050—3.1-1056R
287	2.1-335.2
288	53.1-121
289	2.1-343.1
290	10.1-1425.8
291	48-5, 48-11
292	50-1—50-43.12R, 50-73.75, 50-73.77, 50-73.78, 50-73.79, 50-74R
293	16.1-330.1
294	40.1-51.5, 40.1-51.9:2
295	24.2-701, 24.2-704
296	Va. Const., Art. IV, § 14, n.
297	24.2-684, 24.2-687, 30-19.10
298	36-55.33:2, 36-55.35, 36-55.37:1R, 36-55.40,
299	9-332
300	2.1-51.27:1
302	52-8.4
303	5.1-7
304	38.2-1230, 38.2-1231
305	60.2-533
306	6.1-80
307	46.2-498
308	24.2-110
309	4.1-227
313	15.1-362.1
314	29.1-529
315	58.1-498
316	58.1-214
317	64.1-120, 64.1-131
318	32.1-330.2
319	59.1-365
320	9-6.14:4.1
321	2.1-345
322	58.1-3518.1
323	34-3, 58.1-3112, 58.1-3129, 58.1-3912, 58.1-3919, 58.1-3940, 58.1-3941, 58.1-3965
324	58.1-3914
325	15.1-466
326	55-248.35
327	36-96.3
328	8.01-230
329	54.1-406
330	34-21, 34-29, 34-34
331	20-107.2, 20-109.1
332	8.01-343, 14.1-195.1
333	28.2-708
334	8.01-27.1
335	2.1-64.38
336	2.1-1.5, 23-231.8
337	15.1-965.22:1
338	30-34.10:2
339	9-310
340	46.2-1116
341	2.1-373.1
342	53.1-183
343	37.1-67.1, 37.1-67.3
344	14.1-112, 55-142.01
345	9-6.14:4.1
346	54.1-3913.1
347	46.2-1022
348	46.2-1220
349	15.1-965.22:1
350	56-235.6
351	3.1-796.97, 3.1-796.97:1
352	8.01-316, 8.01-317, 15.1-583, 15.1-1036, 20-104, 64.1-108, 64.1-109, 64.1-110, 64.1-179
353	15.1-475
354	58.1-3012
355	2.1-429
356	58.1-609.7
361	32.1-127
362	58.1-1803
363	58.1-520, 58.1-524, 58.1-525, 58.1-526, 58.1-527, 58.1-528, 58.1-530
364	2.1-211, 2.1-212—2.1-218R, 2.1-221, 2.1-222R, 58.1-3150, 58.1-3158
365	54.1-3200, 54.1-3211, 54.1-3220
366	2.1-1.6, 2.1-427, 2.1-428R, 2.1-429.4, 9-6.25:1
367	60.2-602
368	2.1-451.1—2.1-451.4R, 53.1-45.1, 53.1-45.2—53.1-45.5
369	36-96.21
370	58.1-9, 58.1-202.1
371	14.1-46.01
372	55-337, 55-342, 55-347, 55-374.1, 59.1-321, 55-339—55-340.1R, 55-345, 55-346R, 55-348R, 55-350R
373	38.2-2119
374	46.2-360
375	58.1-461, n., 58.1-462, n., 58.1-470, n.
376	58.1-609.7
377	8.01-249, n.
378	56-241.1
379	55-519
380	54.1-1102, 54.1-1110
381	58.1-2600,

Acts 1996 Chapter	Code 1950 Section
	58.1-2660
382	2.1-804—2.1-806
384	15.1-292
388	54.1-3001
389	46.2-1224.1
390	2.1-211, 2.1-212—2.1-218R, 2.1-221, 2.1-222R, 58.1-3150, 58.1-3158
391	58.1-1803
392	46.2-833.01
393	24.2-707
394	8.01-419
395	24.2-928
396	22.1-296.2
397	55-19
398	19.2-299.1
399	54.1-3908
400	22.1-227.01
401	58.1-322, 58.1-344, 58.1-344.1, 58.1-491.1, 58.1-905
402	19.2-164, 19.2-164.1
403	46.2-1028
404	4.1-225
405	24.2-901, 24.2-903, 24.2-904, 24.2-928
406	54.1-3408
407	54.1-3307, 54.1-3401, 54.1-3437, 54.1-3438, 54.1-3439, 54.1-3441
408	54.1-3303, 54.1-3401, 54.1-3408, 54.1-3410, 54.1-3411, 54.1-3422, 54.1-3426, 54.1-3435.2, 54.1-3443, 54.1-3446, 54.1-3463
409	45.1-243
410	45.1-243
411	32.1-127
412	37.1-195
413	58.1-520, 58.1-524, 58.1-525, 58.1-526, 58.1-527, 58.1-528, 58.1-530
414	46.2-362
415	46.2-351.2
416	20-60.5, 20-79.3
417	8.01-389
418	19.2-390.1
419	55-210.3:01
420	10.1-2212
421	15.1-499.1
422	46.2-1137
423	19.2-271.2
424	15.1-503.2
425	38.2-106, 38.2-106.1, 38.2-3113.2
426	15.1-491.9
427	8.01-449
428	19.2-389, 32.1-126.02
429	19.2-390
430	15.1-18.2
431	14.1-125.2
432	19.2-389
433	28.2-707
434	28.2-526, 28.2-530, 28.2-532
435	2.1-442
436	54.1-3200, 54.1-3211, 54.1-3220
437	2.1-328.14
438	54.1-603
439	18.2-266
440	15.1-7.2
441	11-40.1R
442	2.1-504.4
443	4.1-208, 4.1-209
444	58.1-346
445	19.2-305.3
446	46.2-1105
447	2.1-1.6, 2.1-427R, 2.1-428R, 2.1-429.4, 9-6.25:1
448	65.2-505
449	58.1-9, 58.1-202.1
450	15.1-497
451	15.1-491
452	15.1-466
453	46.2-1979
454	17-59
455	63.1-53
456	15.1-466
457	65.2-903
458	58.1-461, n., 58.1-462, n., 58.1-470, n.
459	58.1-609.7
460	11-37
461	57-48, 57-60, 57-61
462	58.1-4019.1
463	16.1-69.55, 16.1-306
464	15.1-1519
466	56-235.7
467	22.1-296.2
468	54.1-2926, 54.1-3422, 54.1-3423, 54.1-3424
469	2.1-342
470	54.1-2900, 54.1-2956.9
471	63.1-85.4
472	15.1-291.2
473	38.2-514.1
474	46.2-364, 46.2-706, 46.2-706.1, 46.2-707
475	2.1-1.6, 2.1-526.3, 2.1-526.4R, 2.1-526.5, 2.1-526.11:1, 9-6.25:1
476	56-479.1
477	58.1-3822
478	58.1-3203
479	58.1-609.7
480	58.1-3213
481	63.1-44
482	9-291.1
483	28.2-539
484	19.2-8
485	22.1-79
486	23-218, 40.1-118
487	63.1-198.03:1
488	Va. Const., Art. I, § 8A, n.
489	46.2-364, 46.2-706, 46.2-706.1, 46.2-707
490	54.1-3408
491	20-49.8, 20-108.1, 20-108.2, 63.1-250.1
492	2.1-1.7, 2.1-20.4, 2.1-51.15, 9-6.25:2,

Acts 1996 Chapter	Code 1950 Section
	9-268,
	9-271,
	9-281—9-291R,
	9-291.1,
	63.1-196.5,
	63.1-211.2,
	63.1-314.8
493	10.1-536
494	38.2-4610.2
495	63.1-87, n.,
	63.1-110, n.
496	54.1-2926,
	54.1-3422,
	54.1-3423,
	54.1-3424
497	58.1-439.4
498	36-55.26,
	36-55.30,
	36-55.30:2,
	36-55.38
499	30-19.05
500	2.1-51.33
501	8.01-293,
	8.01-466,
	8.01-511
502	63.1-171.8R
503	2.1-1.1,
	2.1-1.6,
	2.1-51.18,
	9-6.25:2,
	66-1,
	66-4
504	23-9.13:1
505	58.1-4019.1
506	46.2-1105
507	9-6.25:1
508	2.1-327,
	2.1-328,
	2.1-328.9,
	23-38.80,
	26-40,
	26-40.01,
	51.1-803
509	18.2-371.2
510	2.1-1.6,
	2.1-526.3,
	2.1-526.4R,
	2.1-526.5,
	2.1-526.11:1,
	9-6.25:1
511	32.1-325,
	63.1-97.1,
	63.1-107
512	46.2-1090
513	43-2
514	15.1-291.2
515	32.1-331.13
516	8.01-413.01
517	18.2-371.2
518	10.1-569
519	54.1-2925
520	58.1-339.2
521	58.1-339
522	22.1-253.13:1
524	6.1-420
525	46.2-1001
526	2.1-639.14
527	18.2-55
528	58.1-3907
529	58.1-3503
530	54.1-2910,
	54.1-2919,
	54.1-2920
531	32.1-102.3:2
532	54.1-2409.2
533	32.1-46
534	58.1-3603
535	9-145.2
536	58.1-3516
537	58.1-3506
538	8.01-296,
	8.01-325
539	19.2-297.1
540	18.2-60.3
541	9-183.1,
	9-183.2,
	9-183.3
542	19.2-390.1
543	9-183.2
544	19.2-305.4
545	19.2-11.1
546	19.2-11.01,
	19.2-265.01
547	10.1-1406.1
548	2.1-639.7:1,
	2.1-639.8
549	64.1-123,
	64.1-123.1,
	64.1-123.3,
	64.1-124,
	64.1-124.1,
	64.1-130,
	64.1-132.2,
	64.1-151.2,
	64.1-151.4
550	9-313, n.,
	9-315, n.,
	38.2-3431, n.
	38.2-3514.2,
	38.2-4214,
	38.2-4319
551	55-168,
	55-170.1,
	55-171,
	55-172,
	55-173,
	55-184.1,
	55-190
552	19.2-298.01
553	2.1-483.1:1,
	15.1-464
554	10.1-1429.4
555	15.1-495
556	53.1-116
557	55-527
558	4.1-100,
	4.1-103,
	4.1-104,
	4.1-119
559	8.01-384.1:1
560	36-55.39
561	15.1-50.3,
	15.1-821.1
562	46.2-752
563	15.1-826, n.
566	44-75.1:1
567	15.1-687.23
568	53.1-180
569	53.1-182.1
570	65.2-712
571	15.1-21, n.
572	15.1-1032.2
573	3.1-448,
	3.1-450,
	9-6.14:4.1,
	18.2-340.20,
	29.1-824,
	46.2-1163,
	46.2-1578,
	55-79.102,
	58.1-527,
	58.1-3230,
	59.1-373,
	60.2-625,
	62.1-111,
	63.1-165
574	24.2-542
575	58.1-2114,
	58.1-2144.1,
	58.1-2700,
	58.1-2700.1,
	58.1-2701,
	58.1-2702,
	58.1-2706,
	58.1-2711
576	9-183.2
577	46.2-817
578	2.1-346,
	2.1-346.1
579	15.1-7.2
580	36-55.63,
	58.1-336,
	58.1-435
581	58.1-3660.1
582	45.1-392
583	22.1-215
584	4.1-206,
	4.1-221.1,
	4.1-230,
	4.1-231,
	4.1-233
585	15.1-427,
	15.1-446.1,

Acts 1996 Chapter	Code 1950 Section
	15.1-447
586	24.2-908.1
587	66-14
588	17-41
589	2.1-1.1,
	2.1-1.3,
	2.1-51.21:3,
	2.1-51.40,
	2.1-342,
	2.1-548.6—2.1-548.25R,
	2.1-548.44
	—2.1-548.52,
	9-6.25:1,
	9-202,
	9-204,
	9-249.1,
	9-285,
	9-290,
	9-333,
	10.1-1425.7,
	15.1-1377,
	23-135.7:7,
	36-139.6,
	59.1-284.1,
	60.2-108—2.1-548.52, n.,
	63.1-133.41,
	63.1-133.45
590	2.1-51.6:1,
	2.1-51.6:2,
	2.1-51.40,
	2.1-384,
	2.1-548.29,
	2.1-548.29:01
	—2.1-548.29:03,
	2.1-548.32,
	2.1-548.43,
	9-6.14:4.1,
	9-145.39:2,
	9-145.39:7,
	9-275,
	9-276.1,
	13.1-983,
	13.1-985,
	15.1-18.4,
	15.1-1638,
	15.1-1653,
	15.1-1664,
	33.1-221.1:1,
	36-139.6,
	46.2-750
591	46.2-605,
	46.2-626R,
	46.2-1073,
	46.2-1074,
	46.2-1075
592	17-41
593	45.1-392
594	22.1-215
595	58.1-3660.1
596	4.1-206,
	4.1-221.1,
	4.1-230,
	4.1-231,
	4.1-233
597	66-14
598	2.1-51.6:1,
	2.1-51.6:2,
	2.1-51.40,
	2.1-384,
	2.1-548.29,
	2.1-548.29:01
	—2.1-548.29:03,
	2.1-548.32,
	2.1-548.43,
	9-6.14:4.1,
	9-145.39:2,
	9-145.39:7,
	9-275,
	9-276.1,
	13.1-983,
	13.1-985,
	15.1-18.4,
	15.1-1638,
	15.1-1653,
	15.1-1664,
	33.1-221.1:1,
	36-139.6,
	46.2-750
599	2.1-1.1,
	2.1-1.3,
	2.1-51.21:3,
	2.1-51.40,
	2.1-342,
	2.1-548.6—2.1-548.25R,
	2.1-548.44—2.1-548.52,
	9-6.25:1,
	9-202,
	9-204,
	9-249.1,
	9-285,
	9-290,
	9-333,
	10.1-1425.7,
	15.1-1377,
	23-135.7:7,
	36-139.6,
	59.1-284.1,
	60.2-108, n.,
	63.1-133.41,
	63.1-133.45
600	15.1-427,
	15.1-446.1,
	15.1-447
601	24.2-908.1
603	58.1-3506
604	4.1-100,
	4.1-208,
	4.1-209,
	4.1-231,
	4.1-233
605	58.1-3506
606	30-19.05,
	30-19.1:3
607	15.1-1638
608	8.01-293,
	8.01-466,
	8.01-511
609	2.1-341
610	38.2-3418.1
611	38.2-3418.1:2,
	38.2-4319
612	15.1-37.3:13
613	15.1-431
614	58.1-3
615	46.2-392
616	2.1-20.1, n.,
	2.1-33, n.,
	2.1-37.3, n.,
	2.1-747, n.,
	2.1-751, n.,
	2.1-753, n.,
	2.1-757, n.,
	8.01-217, n.,
	8.01-259, n.,
	8.01-261, n.,
	8.01-320, n.,
	8.01-331, n.,
	8.01-353.01, n.,
	9-168, n.,
	9-173.8, n.,
	14.1-112, n.,
	14.1-135.1, n.,
	14.1-137, n.,
	15.2-720, n.,
	16.1-69.5, n.,
	16.1-69.6:1, n.,
	16.1-69.7, n.,
	16.1-69.8, n.,
	16.1-69.9:01, n.,
	16.1-69.9:1, n.,
	16.1-69.10, n.,
	16.1-69.11, n.,
	16.1-69.12, n.,
	16.1-69.17, n.,
	16.1-69.21, n.,
	16.1-69.22:1, n.,
	16.1-69.32, n.,
	16.1-69.33, n.,
	16.1-69.35, n.,
	16.1-69.37, n.,
	16.1-69.38, n.,
	16.1-69.39, n.,
	16.1-69.48, n.,
	16.1-69.50, n.,
	16.1-69.55, n.,
	16.1-94, n.,
	16.1-97.1, n.,
	16.1-106, n.,
	16.1-107, n.,
	16.1-133, n.,
	16.1-133.1, n.,
	16.1-218, n.,
	16.1-224, n.,

Acts 1996 Chapter	Code 1950 Section
	16.1-226, n.,
	16.1-228, n.,
	16.1-230, n.,
	16.1-232, n.,
	16.1-233, n.,
	16.1-234, n.,
	16.1-235, n.,
	16.1-236, n.,
	16.1-240, n.,
	16.1-241, n.,
	16.1-241.1, n.,
	16.1-242, n.,
	16.1-243, n.,
	16.1-244, n.,
	16.1-245, n.,
	16.1-245.1, n.,
	16.1-246, n.,
	16.1-247, n.,
	16.1-253.4, n.,
	16.1-254, n.,
	16.1-255, n.,
	16.1-256, n.,
	16.1-259, n.,
	16.1-260, n.,
	16.1-262, n.,
	16.1-263, n.,
	16.1-264, n.,
	16.1-266, n.,
	16.1-267, n.,
	16.1-270, n.,
	16.1-271, n.,
	16.1-272, n.,
	16.1-272.1, n.,
	16.1-273, n.,
	16.1-275, n.,
	16.1-277.1, n.,
	16.1-278, n.,
	16.1-278.2, n.,
	16.1-278.3, n.,
	16.1-278.4, n.,
	16.1-278.5, n.,
	16.1-278.6, n.,
	16.1-278.7, n.,
	16.1-278.7, n.,
	16.1-278.8, n.,
	16.1-278.12, n.,
	16.1-278.13, n.,
	16.1-278.14, n.,
	16.1-278.15, n.,
	16.1-278.16, n.,
	16.1-278.17, n.,
	16.1-278.18, n.,
	16.1-278.20, n.,
	16.1-280, n.,
	16.1-281, n.,
	16.1-289, n.,
	16.1-291, n.,
	16.1-292, n.,
	16.1-293, n.,
	16.1-296, n.,
	16.1-296.2, n.,
	16.1-297, n.,
	16.1-298, n.,
	16.1-299, n.,
	16.1-300, n.,
	16.1-302, n.,
	16.1-305, n.,
	16.1-306, n.,
	16.1-306.1, n.,
	16.1-307, n.,
	16.1-309, n.,
	16.1-316, n.,
	16.1-317, n.,
	16.1-328, n.,
	16.1-331, n.,
	16.1-339, n.,
	16.1-340, n.,
	16.1-341, n.,
	16.1-342, n.,
	16.1-344, n.,
	16.1-348, n.,
	17-7.2, n.,
	17-28, n.,
	17-111.4, n.,
	17-111.6, n.,
	17-116.05, n.,
	17-222, n.,
	18.2-64.1, n.,
	18.2-351, n.,
	18.2-353, n.,
	18.2-477.1, n.,
	19.2-48.1, n.,
	19.2-71, n.,
	19.2-218.2, n.,
	19.2-240, n.,
	19.2-262, n.,
	19.2-353.3, n.,
	19.2-368.3, n.,
	19.2-368.6, n.,
	20-49, n.,
	20-49.2, n.,
	20-67, n.,
	20-71.1, n.,
	20-79, n.,
	20-88, n.,
	20-96, n.,
	20-99.1:1, n.,
	20-107.3, n.,
	20-113, n.,
	20-138, n.,
	20-139, n.,
	20-140, n.,
	22.1-87, n.,
	22.1-214, n.,
	22.1-214.1, n.,
	22.1-257, n.,
	22.1-262, n.,
	22.1-268, n.,
	31-8, n.,
	31-15, n.,
	32.1-258, n.,
	32.1-260, n.,
	37.1-1, n.,
	37.1-64, n.,
	37.1-97, n.,
	40.1-28.9, n.,
	46.2-334, n.,
	46.2-336, n.,
	46.2-386, n.,
	46.2-1098, n.,
	53.1-120, n.,
	53.1-124, n.,
	53.1-145, n.,
	54.1-2969, n.,
	63.1-56, n.,
	63.1-57.1, n.,
	63.1-204, n.,
	63.1-204.1, n.,
	63.1-209, n.,
	63.1-220.3, n.,
	63.1-220.5, n.,
	63.1-221, n.,
	63.1-222, n.,
	63.1-235, n.,
	63.1-236, n.,
	63.1-248.2, n.,
	63.1-248.3, n.,
	63.1-248.4, n.,
	63.1-248.5:1, n.,
	63.1-248.6, n.,
	63.1-248.13, n.,
	63.1-249, n.,
	63.1-252.1, n.,
	63.1-256, n.,
	63.1-267.1, n.,
	63.1-268.1, n.,
	64.1-5.1, n.,
	65.2-101, n.
617	2.1-51.17
618	55-509,
	55-509.2
619	25-233
620	36-115,
	36-135, n.
621	15.1-362.1
622	58.1-1101
623	53.1-95.8:1,
	53.1-109.1,
	53.1-109.2
624	58.1-322
625	51.1-142
626	4.1-305
627	33.1-254, n.
628	38.2-226.1
629	58.1-339.3,
	58.1-439.5
630	2.1-64.35
631	29.1-738.02,
	29.1-738.1,
	29.1-738.2
632	53.1-261
633	9-335
634	58.1-202,

Acts 1996 Chapter	Code 1950 Section
	58.1-307, 58.1-313, 58.1-1805, 58.1-1817, 58.1-1818, 58.1-1834, 58.1-1835, 58.1-1845
635	58.1-9
636	2.1-179, 2.1-179.3, 2.1-179.4, 2.1-179.5, 23-19
637	58.1-1823
638	9-6.14:4.1, 59.1-156
639	9-6.14:14.1, 46.2-1576
640	58.1-105, 58.1-112
641	15.1-965.24:2
642	59.1-284.13
643	58.1-202.2
644	15.1-1167.1
645	59.1-284.14
646	8.01-226
647	54.1-2002.1
648	45.1-181, 45.1-184.2
649	15.1-965.24:2
650	15.1-1167.1
651	59.1-284.14
652	59.1-284.13
653	58.1-202.2
654	58.1-1823
655	58.1-105, 58.1-112
656	2.1-179, 2.1-179.3, 2.1-179.4, 2.1-179.5, 23-19
657	58.1-9
658	9-6.14:14.1, 46.2-1576
659	45.1-181, 45.1-184.2
660	8.01-226
661	54.1-2002.1
662	51.1-155.1, 51.1-155.2
663	59.1-378.1
664	19.2-295.1
667	15.1-431
668	8.01-390
669	53.1-228.1
671	16.1-309.2, 16.1-309.3, 16.1-309.4, 16.1-309.6, 16.1-309.8
672	23-15, 23-17, 23-19, 23-30.24, 23-30.26, 23-30.28, 23-30.29, 23-30.29:1—23-30.29:3, 23-30.31
673	19.2-386.3
674	17-83.1:1—17-83.1:4
675	26-68.1, 64.1-105, 64.1-106, 64.1-107, 64.1-108, 64.1-109, 64.1-110, 64.1-112
676	19.2-222R
677	10.1-202
679	53.1-234
680	26-59, 64.1-73
681	26-15
682	16.1-309.2, 16.1-309.3, 16.1-309.4, 16.1-309.6, 16.1-309.8
683	11-35, 11-37
684	26-68.1, 64.1-105, 64.1-106, 64.1-107, 64.1-108, 64.1-109, 64.1-110, 64.1-112
685	30-19.03:1, 30-19.1:6
686	10.1-202
687	24.2-914.1
688	10.1-571
689	23-15, 23-17, 23-19, 23-30.24, 23-30.26, 23-30.28, 23-30.29, 23-30.29:1—23-30.29:3, 23-30.31
690	46.2-910
691	22.1-319, 22.1-320, 22.1-326, 22.1-329, 23 265, 23-266, 23-267, 23-268, 23-269, 23-271, 23-275
692	4.1-133
693	8.01-6, 8.01-6.1
694	63.1-320, n., 63.1-321, n., 63.1-322, n., 63.1-323, 63.1-324, n., 63.1-325, n., 58.1-333, n., 58.1-430, n.
695	33.1-46.2
696	14.1-136
698	8.01-43, 8.01-44
699	19.2-353.3, n.
700	14.1-7
702	2.1-1.7, 2.1-51.40, 9-6.25:2, 9-145.39:5, 9-274—9-280R
703	22.1-343, 53.1-59
704	38.2-508.4, 38.2-613
705	9-6.14:4.1
706	58.1-3713, 58.1-3713.01
707	54.1-1106, 54.1-1108, 54.1-1108.1, 54.1-1110.1
708	56-487, 56-493, 56-494, 56-501, 56-502
709	51.1-165.1
710	8.01-317, 58.1-3965, 58.1-3967
711	51.1-124.3, 63.1-73
712	58.1-3823
713	15.1-21.2
714	33.1-200.2
715	15.1-640, n., 58.1-3700, 58.1-3700.1, 58.1-3701, 58.1-3703, 58.1-3703.1, 58.1-3706, 58.1-3707R,

Acts 1996 Chapter	Code 1950 Section
	58.1-3708,
	58.1-3725R,
	58.1-3732
716	58.1-345.1
717	4.1-322
718	18.2-460
719	58.1-1823, n.
720	15.1-640, n.,
	58.1-3700,
	58.1-3700.1,
	58.1-3701,
	58.1-3703,
	58.1-3703.1,
	58.1-3706,
	58.1-3707R,
	58.1-3708,
	58.1-3725R,
	58.1-3732
721	65.2-101
722	3.1-562.6
723	3.1-531R,
	3.1-533,
	3.1-539,
	3.1-543R
724	3.1-563,
	3.1-571R
725	15.1-21.2
726	22.1-343,
	53.1-59
727	2.1-738
728	3.1-394,
	3.1-396
729	3.1-22.22—3.1-22.27R
730	4.1-305
731	51.1-124.3,
	63.1-73
732	58.1-3942
733	10.1-1171
734	10.1-1418.3
735	9-6.14:4.1
736	28.2-1308,
	33.1-223.2:1,
	62.1-44.15:5
737	62.1-44.34:8,
	62.1-44.34:9,
	62.1-44.34:10,
	62.1-44.34:11,
	62.1-44.34:12,
	62.1-44.34:13,
	62.1-44.34:14,
	62.1-44.34:15.1
738	58.1-345.1
739	58.1-337,
	58.1-436
740	15.1-1320,
	15.1-1324,
	15.1-1329,
	15.1-1332,
	15.1-1333,
	15.1-1334,
	15.1-1339.1,
	15.1-1340
741	54.1-1501
742	36-99.7
743	15.1-21.2
744	22.1-342.1
745	60.2-214,
	60.2-524, n.
746	63.1-274.10
747	19.2-389,
	63.1-197,
	63.1-198,
	63.1-198.1,
	63.1-199,
	63.1-248.7:2
748	32.1-127.3,
	54.1-106
749	16.1-88.2
750	59.1-378.1
752	37.1-135
753	18.2-461
755	2.1-116.08,
	16.1-227,
	16.1-228,
	16.1-241,
	16.1-248.1,
	16.1-248.2,
	16.1-249,
	16.1-255,
	16.1-256,
	16.1-260,
	16.1-261,
	16.1-263,
	16.1-269.1,
	16.1-269.3,
	16.1-269.4,
	16.1-269.6,
	16.1-272,
	16.1-274.1,
	16.1-278.8,
	16.1-278.8,
	16.1-284,
	16.1-284.1,
	16.1-285,
	16.1-285.1,
	16.1-285.2,
	16.1-290,
	16.1-293,
	16.1-299,
	16.1-299.1,
	16.1-301,
	16.1-302,
	16.1-302.1,
	16.1-303,
	16.1-305,
	16.1-305.1,
	16.1-307,
	16.1-308,
	16.1-309,
	16.1-309.4,
	18.2-473,
	19.2-3.1,
	19.2-38, n.,
	19.2-311,
	19.2-388,
	19.2-389.1,
	19.2-390,
	19.2-392.01,
	22.1-209.1:2,
	22.1-288.2,
	22.1-344,
	29.1-317,
	53.1-63.1,
	53.1-66,
	66-10,
	66-13,
	66-24
756	59.1-88,
	59.1-89
757	54.1-2810
758	45.1-256
759	22.1-60
760	19.2-368.18
761	46.2-619
762	54.1-3102.1
763	23-231.3
764	2.1-20.1:3
765	58.1-3220.01
766	54.1-3804.1
767	16.1-278.15,
	20-103,
	20-124.2
768	51.1-153
769	18.2-52.1
770	46.2-1224
771	16.1-241.2,
	22.1-279.3
772	9-316
773	10.1-559.1
	—10.1-559.11
774	45.1-161.8,
	45.1-161.10,
	45.1-161.31,
	45.1-161.49,
	45.1-161.55,
	45.1-161.57,
	45.1-161.59,
	45.1-161.62,
	45.1-161.63,
	45.1-161.64,
	45.1-161.68,
	45.1-161.73,
	45.1-161.80,
	45.1-161.88,
	45.1-161.89,
	45.1-161.91,
	45.1-161.108,
	45.1-161.112,
	45.1-161.113R,
	45.1-161.115,
	45.1-161.116,
	45.1-161.122,

Acts 1996 Chapter	Code 1950 Section
	45.1-161.123,
	45.1-161.128,
	45.1-161.133,
	45.1-161.135,
	45.1-161.139,
	45.1-161.141,
	45.1-161.142,
	45.1-161.144,
	45.1-161.145,
	45.1-161.147,
	45.1-161.150,
	45.1-161.151,
	45.1-161.152,
	45.1-161.156,
	45.1-161.160,
	45.1-161.162,
	45.1-161.164,
	45.1-161.166,
	45.1-161.167,
	45.1-161.168,
	45.1-161.169,
	45.1-161.181,
	45.1-161.186,
	45.1-161.187,
	45.1-161.190R,
	45.1-161.191,
	45.1-161.195,
	45.1-161.196,
	45.1-161.200,
	45.1-161.202,
	45.1-161.205,
	45.1-161.206,
	45.1-161.208,
	45.1-161.209,
	45.1-161.210,
	45.1-161.213,
	45.1-161.214,
	45.1-161.216,
	45.1-161.219,
	45.1-161.220,
	45.1-161.221,
	45.1-161.222,
	45.1-161.223,
	45.1-161.224,
	45.1-161.225,
	45.1-161.226,
	45.1-161.227,
	45.1-161.228,
	45.1-161.229,
	45.1-161.231,
	45.1-161.234,
	45.1-161.245,
	45.1-161.249,
	45.1-161.256,
	45.1-161.257,
	45.1-161.258,
	45.1-161.270,
	45.1-161.276,
	45.1-161.279,
	45.1-161.280,
	45.1-161.286,
	45.1-161.294,
	45.1-161.305
775	54.1-2901,
	63.1-174.3
776	38.2-3407.10,
	38.2-4214,
	38.2-4319,
	38.2-4509
777	33.1-351
778	15.1-291.2
779	54.1-2901,
	54.1-2952
780	63.1-248.5:1
781	32.1-13.1, n.
782	32.1-345,
	32.1-346,
	32.1-347
783	2.1-342
784	58.1-3
785	46.2-320
786	2.1-342
787	37.1-134.5
788	32.1-27.1,
	32.1-325
789	59.1-279.1
790	22.1-79
791	63.1-248.5:1
792	32.1-345,
	32.1-346,
	32.1-347
793	58.1-3
794	2.1-342
795	11-41.2:02,
	66-25.3—66-25.7
796	32.1-325
797	32.1-27.1
798	22.1-79
799	32.1-13.1, n.
800	37.1-134.5
801	38.2-1005.1,
	51.1-124.3, n.
802	44-135.1
804	53.1-29
805	44-75.1
806	19.2-390
807	53.1-150.1
808	48-5,
	48-11
809	19.2-316.1,
	53.1-67.1
810	29.1-302,
	29.1-302.1
812	2.1-41.2,
	42.1-13
813	63.1-248.5:1.01
815	18.2-461
816	58.1-609.3,
	58.1-609.4,
	58.1-609.8
817	46.2-817
818	9-6.14:4.1
819	2.1-1.7,
	9-6.25:1,
	10.1-630,
	10.1-631,
	15.1-227.4,
	15.1-227.5R,
	15.1-227.46R,
	22.1-161.6R,
	58.1-608.3
820	16.1-309.7
821	33.1-41.1
822	54.1-603
823	2.1-563.31,
	9-145.52—9-145.56
824	54.1-2210
825	29.1-306
826	36-55.63,
	58.1-336,
	58.1-435
827	11-41,
	11-59,
	11-61,
	11-79
828	16.1-297
829	7.1-42,
	22.1-212.1
830	58.1-3850
831	38.2-1005.1,
	51.1-124.3, n.
832	22.1-319,
	22.1-320,
	22.1-326,
	22.1-329,
	23-265,
	23-266,
	23-267,
	23-268,
	23-269,
	23-271,
	23-275
833	58.1-3819
834	35.1-22
835	2.1-234.11,
	2.1-234.13,
	2.1-234.25,
	53.1-82.2
836	63.1-248.5:1.01
837	58.1-338,
	58.1-445.1
838	53.1-29
839	55-19.4
840	22.1-304
841	18.2-270.1
842	28.2-507
843	46.2-1605
844	15.1-18.3
846	40.1-51.20,
	54.1-500,
	54.1-500.1,
	54.1-501,
	54.1-503,

Acts 1996 Chapter	Code 1950 Section
	54.1-505, 54.1-512, 54.1-514, 54.1-516, 54.1-517
847	36-49.1:1
848	63.1-105.1
849	32.1-102.3:2
850	15.1-144, 15.1-145, 15.1-151, 15.1-152, 15.1-153, 19.2-13, 19.2-17R
851	32.1-325.2
852	63.1-248.18
853	37.1-33
854	45.1-361.17, 45.1-361.21, 45.1-361.29, 45.1-361.30, 45.1-361.33, 45.1-361.35
855	2.1-342, 2.1-344
856	63.1-248.18
857	63.1-105
858	63.1-248.6
859	2.1-51.6:5, 2.1-51.6:1, 2.1-51.6:2R
860	28.2-1000, n.
861	15.1-1677, 15.1-1678, 15.1-1679, 15.1-1680, 15.1-1682, 15.1-1684, 15.1-1685, 15.1-1686
862	2.1-342, 2.1-344
863	63.1-248.6
864	32.1-326.2
865	46.2-391.2
866	9-170, 16.1-243, 16.1-245.1, 16.1-253, 16.1-253.1, 16.1-253.2, 16.1-253.4, 16.1-278.14, 16.1-278.14, 16.1-279.1, 16.1-296, 16.1-296.2, 16.1-298, 18.2-57.2, 18.2-60.3, 18.2-308.1:4, 19.2-81, 19.2-81.3, 19.2-81.4, 20-103
867	15.1-493
868	23-9.14:1
869	2.1-116.03, 2.1-116.05, 2.1-116.06, 2.1-116.09, 2.1-116.010, 2.1-116.011R, 2.1-116.012, 15.1-7.1, 15.1-7.2, 15.1-687.16
870	16.1-305, 19.2-389.1
871	11-41.2:1
873	15.1-644, 22.1-57.3, 24.2-226, 24.2-227, 24.2-228
874	58.1-439
875	23-220.1
876	18.2-31
877	15.1-687.24
878	23-7.2:1
879	16.1-278.15, 20-103, 20-124.2, 63.1-252.1
880	19.2-390.1
881	19.2-389, 37.1-20.2R, 37.1-20.3
882	20-88.32, 20-88.39, 20-88.48, 63.1-250.1
883	6.1-2.13, 6.1-2.13:1, 38.2-4614
884	16.1-278.15, 20-103, 20-124.2, 63.1-252.1
886	24.2-222, n.
887	8.01-9
888	55-79.80:3, 55-79.90
889	63.1-252.1, 63.1-252.2
890	54.1-2105
891	22.1-258, 22.1-261, 22.1-262, 22.1-263, 22.1-265
892	46.2-335
893	37.1-67.01, 37.1-67.1, 37.1-67.3, 37.1-89
894	46.2-335
895	55-66.3
896	58.1-3018
897	11-45, 15.1-1241
898	22.1-32
899	8.01-225, 32.1-111.1—32.1-111.15, 32.1-112, n., 32.1-148—32.1-156R
900	16.1-279.1
901	32.1-102.3:2, n.
902	2.1-1.7, 2.1-51.15, 2.1-342, 2.1-344, 9-6.25:2, 9-156—9-166.7R, 11-45, 32.1-122.02, 32.1-276.2—32.1-276.11, 32.1-335—32.1-337
903	54.1-2105
904	59.1-69
905	2.1-1.5, 2.1-20.1, 2.1-116, 2.1-342, 2.1-344, 9-156, 9-166.2, 23-50.11, 23-50.16:1—23-50.15:36, 23-232, 32.1-85, 51.1-126.1, 51.1-126.2,
906	Va. Const., Art. I, § 8-A, n.
907	Va. Const., Art. II, § 1, n., Va. Const., Art. II, § 2, n.
908	Va. Const., Art. IV, § 14, n.
909	Va. Const., Art. X, § 11, n.
910	Va. Const., Art. I, § 8A, n.
911	Va. Const., Art. VI, § 1, n.
913	18.2-258.02
914	2.1-116.08, 16.1-227, 16.1-228, 16.1-241,

Acts 1996 Chapter	Code 1950 Section
	16.1-248.1, 16.1-248.2, 16.1-249, 16.1-255, 16.1-256, 16.1-260, 16.1-261, 16.1-263, 16.1-269.1, 16.1-269.3, 16.1-269.4, 16.1-269.6, 16.1-272, 16.1-274.1, 16.1-278.8, 16.1-284, 16.1-284.1, 16.1-285, 16.1-285.1, 16.1-285.2, 16.1-290, 16.1-293, 16.1-299, 16.1-299.1, 16.1-301, 16.1-302, 16.1-302.1, 16.1-303, 16.1-305, 16.1-305.1, 16.1-307, 16.1-308, 16.1-309, 16.1-309.4, 18.2-473, 19.2-3.1, 19.2-38, n., 19.2-311, 19.2-388, 19.2-389.1, 19.2-390, 19.2-392.01, 22.1-209.1:2, 22.1-288.2, 22.1-344, 29.1-317, 53.1-63.1, 53.1-66, 66-10, 66-13, 66-24
915	59.1-365, 59.1-380, 59.1-383, 59.1-385, 59.1-392, n., 59.1-403
916	16.1-293, 22.1-254, 22.1-258, 22.1-265, 22.1-280.1
917	46.2-605, 46.2-626R, 46.2-1073, 46.2-1074, 46.2-1075
918	46.2-335
919	18.2-340.16, 18.2-340.19, 18.2-340.24, 18.2-340.33, 18.2-340.34, 18.2-340.37, 18.2-340.38, 58.1-3
920	46.2-676
921	33.1-46.2
922	46.2-725, 46.2-742, 46.2-749.2:1, 46.2-749.2:2—46.2-749.2:5
923	33.1-70.2
924	51.1-155.1, 51.1-155.2
925	20-88.32, 20-88.39, 20-88.48, 63.1-250.1
926	46.2-1801—46.2-1805R, 46.2-2700—46.2-2703
927	19.2-389, 37.1-20.2R, 37.1-20.3
928	46.2-351.2
929	19.2-81, 29.1-738, 29.1-738.4
930	51.5-55
931	23-7.1—23-7.3R, 23-7.4, 23-7.4:1—23-7.4:3
932	2.1-1.8, 2.1-800—2.1-803R, 9-6.23, 9-6.25:2, 9-350—9-354
933	2.1-116, 23-77.4, 51.1-126, 51.1-126.1, 51.1-126.2, 51.1-502.1, 51.1-502.2
934	54.1-309, n. 54.1-1102, 54.1-1118, 54.1-1128, 54.1-1129, 54.1-1130, 54.1-1131, 54.1-1132, 54.1-1133, 54.1-1134, 54.1-1135
935	2.1-457, 2.1-457.1R, 2.1-457.2, 2.1-457.3
936	58.1-333, n., 58.1-430, n., 63.1-320, n., 63.1-321, n., 63.1-322, n., 63.1-323, 63.1-324, n., 63.1-325, n.
937	8.01-399, 8.01-581.13, 8.01-581.19, 8.01-581.19:1, 19.2-169.5, 19.2-182.2, 19.2-182.5, 19.2-182.8, 19.2-182.9, 19.2-264.3:1, 32.1-135.2, 37.1-186.1, 54.1-2900, 54.1-2901, 54.1-2902, 54.1-2903, 54.1-2904, 54.1-2907, 54.1-2908, 54.1-2929, 54.1-2940, 54.1-3600, 54.1-3601, 54.1-3603, 54.1-3604, 54.1-3605, 54.1-3606, 54.1-3607R, 54.1-3608, 54.1-3612—54.1-3616
938	19.2-316.1, 53.1-67.1
939	51.1-143, 51.1-143.1, 51.1-801.1
940	32.1-126
941	32.1-321.3
942	11-41.2:02, 66-25.3—66-25.7
943	46.2-100, 46.2-212.1, 46.2-216.2,

Acts 1996 Chapter	Code 1950 Section
	46.2-324,
	46.2-332,
	46.2-334,
	46.2-335,
	46.2-402,
	46.2-416,
	46.2-499,
	46.2-606,
	46.2-698,
	46.2-738,
	46.2-1053
944	19.2-389,
	22.1-296.3
945	16.1-279.1
946	32.1-325
947	20-108.2,
	63.1-264.2
948	63.1-250.1
949	55-66.3,
	55-66.4:1
950	11-45,
	15.1-227.70,
	15.1-227.74,
	15.1-227.75,
	15.1-227.76,
	15.1-227.77,
	15.1-227.78,
	15.1-227.84,
	15.1-227.85,
	15.1-227.88,
	15.1-227.89
951	33.1-320.1R,
	33.1-320.2
952	2.1-384,
	2.1-434.1—
	2.1-434.12R,
	9-170,
	9-196.1—9-196.12,
	11-41.2:1, n.,
	18.2-267,
	18.2-268.9,
	19.2-310.2,
	46.2-341.25
953	11-41.2:1
954	58.1-4019
955	15.1-292.1
956	19.2-13
957	57-39.20—
	57-39.25
958	19.2-83.1
959	18.2-31,
	19.2-247
960	19.2-83.1,
	22.1-296.1,
	22.1-315
961	22.1-307
962	2.1-1.6,
	2.1-483.1:2,
	9-6.25:2,
	11-41.2:1R,
	11-41.2:2—
	11-41.2:5
963	6.1-2.9:7
964	22.1-254,
	22.1-258,
	22.1-261,
	22.1-262,
	22.1-263,
	22.1-265,
	22.1-280.1
965	11-41
966	59.1-435,
	59.1-436,
	59.1-437,
	59.1-440
967	38.2-3407.10,
	38.2-4214,
	38.2-4319
968	19.2-155
969	53.1-185.3
970	16.1-309.7
971	58.1-3508.1
972	30-19.1:4
973	19.2-120
974	22.1-199.1
975	58.1-4020
976	14.1-112,
	14.1-123,
	19.2-368.18
977	55-79.41,
	55-79.53,
	55-79.74,
	55-79.74:3,
	55-79.80,
	55-79.80:1
978	2.1-457.1R,
	2.1-457.2,
	2.1-457.3,
	2.1-457
979	62.1-44.34:8,
	62.1-44.34:10,
	62.1-44.34:11
980	8.01-399,
	8.01-581.13,
	8.01-581.19,
	8.01-581.19:1,
	19.2-169.5,
	19.2-182.2,
	19.2-182.5,
	19.2-182.8,
	19.2-182.9,
	19.2-264.3:1,
	32.1-135.2,
	37.1-186.1,
	54.1-2900,
	54.1-2901,
	54.1-2902,
	54.1-2903,
	54.1-2904,
	54.1-2907,
	54.1-2908,
	54.1-2929,
	54.1-2940,
	54.1-3600,
	54.1-3601,
	54.1-3603,
	54.1-3604,
	54.1-3605,
	54.1-3606,
	54.1-3607R,
	54.1-3608,
	54.1-3612—54.1-3616
981	23-7.4,
	23-7.4:1—23-7.4:3,
	23-7.1—23-7.3R
982	2.1-505, n.,
	23-4.01, n.
983	10.1-634.1
984	18.2-271.1
985	28.2-613
986	22.1-302
987	2.1-434.10
988	58.1-3
989	11-44.1,
	38.2-1812.1,
	38.2-1839
990	51.1-143,
	51.1-143.1,
	51.1-801.1
991	32.1-321.3
992	23-9.14:1
993	54.1-2100,
	54.1-2101,
	54.1-2106R,
	54.1-2106.1
994	46.2-100,
	46.2-212.1,
	46.2-216.2,
	46.2-324,
	46.2-332,
	46.2-334,
	46.2-335,
	46.2-402,
	46.2-416,
	46.2-499,
	46.2-606,
	46.2-698,
	46.2-738,
	46.2-1053
995	2.1-116,
	23-77.4,
	51.1-126,
	51.1-126.1,
	51.1-126.2,
	51.1-502.1,
	51.1-502.2
996	3.1-14
997	51.1-153,
	51.1-205
998	32.1-114.1
999	32.1-126
1000	16.1-293,
	22.1-17.1,

Acts 1996 Chapter	Code 1950 Section
	22.1-287, 22.1-289, 22.1-343, 22.1-344
1001	2.1-342
1002	8.01-501, 8.01-502
1005	10.1-1182, 10.1-1186
1006	54.1-1102, 54.1-1118, 54.1-1128, 54.1-1129, 54.1-1130, 54.1-1131, 54.1-1132, 54.1-1133, 54.1-1134, 54.1-1135
1007	46.2-391.2
1008	10.1-1142
1009	23-38.52
1011	46.2-334, 46.2-335
1012	9-6.14:4.1, 59.1-156
1013	46.2-320
1014	54.1-1109
1015	19.2-81, 29.1-738, 29.1-738.4
1016	2.1-440.1
1017	32.1-114
1018	33.1-320.1R
1019	11-35, 11-40, 11-41, 11-41.3R
1020	2.1-27.4
1021	15.1-1273, 15.1-1274, 15.1-1688—15.1-1705
1022	46.2-334, 46.2-335
1023	63.1-133.49
1024	2.1-746
1025	59.1-365, 59.1-380, 59.1-383, 59.1-385, 59.1-403
1026	46.2-692.1, 46.2-725, 46.2-735, 46.2-736.2, 46.2-742, 46.2-742.1, 46.2-742.2, 46.2-743, 46.2-746.3, 46.2-746.4, 46.2-746.6:1, 46.2-746.7, 46.2-748, 46.2-749, 46.2-749.2:2—46.2-749.2:5, 46.2-749.4, 46.2-749.7:1, 46.2-750
1027	46.2-1581
1028	54.1-2972
1029	20-108.2, 63.1-264.2
1030	51.1-145, 51.1-166
1031	2.1-51.12:1—2.1-51.12:3
1032	62.1-44.29, 10.1-1318, 10.1-1457, 62.1-44.29
1033	16.1-122.1, n.
1034	58.1-439.2
1035	46.2-334.1, 46.2-335, 46.2-335.1, 46.2-335.2, 46.2-498
1037	33.1-46.2
1038	11-45, 15.1-227.70, 15.1-227.74, 15.1-227.75, 15.1-227.76, 15.1-227.77, 15.1-227.78, 15.1-227.84, 15.1-227.85, 15.1-227.88, 15.1-227.89
1040	18.2-91
1041	22.1-32
1042	24.2-901, 24.2-908, 24.2-910, 24.2-1014
1043	46.2-1900, 46.2-1902R, 46.2-1903R, 46.2-1907, 46.2-1909—46.2-1912, 46.2-1916, 46.2-1918, 46.2-1919, 46.2-1927, 46.2-1930, 46.2-1931, 46.2-1933, 46.2-1942R, 46.2-1943, 46.2-1944, 46.2-1947—46.2-1953, 46.2-1955, 46.2-1956, 46.2-1961R, 46.2-1975—46.2-1977, 46.2-1979, 46.2-1985, 46.2-1988, 46.2-1992.85, 46.2-1993—46.2-1993.82
1044	2.1-1.5, 9-350—9-361
1045	15.1-1227.1—15.1-1227.5
1046	2.1-1.5, 2.1-20.1, 2.1-116, 2.1-342, 2.1-344, 9-156, 9-166.2, 23-50.11, 23-50.15:2—23-50.15:36, 23-232, n., 32.1-85, n., 51.1-126.1, n., 51.1-126.2, n.
1047	58.1-2402
1048	2.1-1.5, 9-350—9-361
1049	2.1-466
1050	32.1-102.1, 32.1-102.2
1051	8.01-512.3
1052	46.2-1900, 46.2-1902R, 46.2-1903R, 46.2-1907, 46.2-1909, 46.2-1910, 46.2-1911, 46.2-1912, 46.2-1916, 46.2-1918, 46.2-1919, 46.2-1927, 46.2-1930, 46.2-1931, 46.2-1933, 46.2-1942R, 46.2-1943, 46.2-1944, 46.2-1947, 46.2-1948, 46.2-1949,

Acts 1996 Chapter	Code 1950 Section
	46.2-1950, 46.2-1951, 46.2-1952, 46.2-1953, 46.2-1955, 46.2-1956, 46.2-1975, 46.2-1976, 46.2-1977, 46.2-1979, 46.2-1985, 46.2-1988, 46.2-1992—46.2-1992.85, 46.2-1993—46.2-1993.82
1053	46.2-1500
1054	63.1-249.1, 63.1-274.10
1055	15.1-1227.1—15.1-1227.5

ACTS 1997

Acts 1997 Chapter	Code 1950 Section
3	54.1-2729
5	46.2-357
6	19.2-120
7	10.1-1105, 10.1-1126.1
8	18.2-51.1, 18.2-57.1
9	46.2-100
10	19.2-76, 19.2-80
11	9-6.14:4, 9-6.14:7.2, 9-6.16, 9-6.18
12	15.1-320, 15.1-321, 15.1-1250, 15.1-1260, 15.1-1261, 21-118.4, 21-118.5
13	29.1-828, 29.1-829
15	65.2-400, 65.2-401
16	16.1-69.6:1
17	17-119.1:2
18	59.1-365, 59.1-380, 59.1-383, 59.1-385, 59.1-392, n.
19	46.2-1224
20	54.1-3401
21	10.1-2117—10.1-2134
22	2.1-51.12:1, n., 2.1-51.12:2
23	46.2-1017
24	6.1-39.5
25	46.2-1030
26	38.2-317
27	19.2-390
28	38.2-109
29	2.1-328.13
30	59.1-436
31	2.1-20.01
32	9-168
33	46.2-882
34	19.2-12
35	46.2-1001
36	46.2-1078
37	4.1-203
38	66-3.1
39	53.1-16
40	4.1-111
41	36-55.41
42	14.1-125
43	2.1-20.1
44	2.1-2.2
45	2.1-1.6, 9-6.25:1, 10.1-418.1
47	46.2-1302
48	33.1-403
49	33.1-41.1
50	6.1-194.79, 6.1-194.145
51	6.1-32.21
54	22.1-214
55	10.1-1308
56	38.2-3407.3
57	29.1-413, 29.1-415, 29.1-416, 29.1-417, 29.1-419
58	25-46.20
59	32.1-286
60	9-145.40—9-145.44R, 9-145.50
61	33.1-221.1R
62	58.1-3703
63	58.1-1840R
64	58.1-4007.1
65	46.2-1090.1
66	7.1-40.10
67	2.1-567
68	11-78.1
69	20-88.74
70	46.2-1139
71	58.1-3510.01
72	10.1-2211
73	2.1-329.1, n.
74	57-27.2, 57-39.1:1
77	58.1-3507, n., 58.1-3508.1
78	2.1-1.6, 9-6.25:1, 51.1-124.23
79	9-183.5
80	9-183.1, 9-183.2
81	20-156, 20-158
82	54.1-2108, 54.1-2113
83	11-74
84	2.1-639.16
85	11-35
86	54.1-2138
87	9-6.14:4.1, 9-6.14:7.1, 9-6.16, 9-6.17, 9-6.18, 9-6.19R
88	9-6.14:4.1, 46.2-1988, 46.2-1992.82, 46.2-1993.79
89	33.1-221
90	46.2-749.2:13
91	46.2-2401
93	33.1-90
94	46.2-726
96	46.2-1072, 46.2-1072.1
99	65.2-1201
100	24.2-644
101	58.1-609.4
102	2.1-1.6, 9-6.25:1, 9-196.2, 9-196.3R
103	22.1-296.1, 22.1-296.4
104	46.2-332, 46.2-1191
105	56-265.1
106	58.1-322, 58.1-402
107	54.1-2972
108	29.1-737, 29.1-742, 29.1-743R
109	9-6.14:4.1
110	56-46.3
111	6.1-5.1, 6.1-225.3:1
112	6.1-330.63, 6.1-330.78
113	6.1-282
114	24.2-422
115	62.1-44.15:6
116	54.1-2800
117	46.2-2700—46.2-2703R
118	58.1-4007.1
119	54.1-2138
120	18.2-51.1, 18.2-57.1
121	8.1-105, 8.2-403, 8.6-101—8.6-111R, 8.6A-101—8.6A-110
122	3.1-376, 3.1-378R
123	53.1-128
124	4.1-100
125	53.1-32.01, 53.1-133.01:1
126	4.1-124
127	53.1-116.3
128	6.1-330.60
129	6.1-331, 6.1-336, 6.1-338
130	10.1-1700
131	65.2-1203
132	57-22, 57-25
133	13.1-1103
134	53.1-129
135	8.01-452.1
136	18.2-324, 33.1-345
137	60.2-511
138	56-234.3
139	38.2-4312.3
140	19.2-305.3R

Acts 1997 Chapter	Code 1950 Section
141	6.1-39.4R, 6.1-39.4:1, 6.1-94
142	6.1-114
143	56-265.13:3
144	36-139.3
145	13.1-514.2
146	10.1-1163
147	19.2-59
148	56-265.1
149	46.2-1025, 46.2-1102
150	46.2-1201, 46.2-1202
151	16.1-266.2, n.
152	29.1-738.6
153	38.2-1901, 38.2-1903
154	62.1-44.15:6
155	10.1-1186.1, 62.1-44.17:2, 62.1-44.17:3
156	56-217
157	38.2-235
158	65.2-713
159	3.1-796.96, 3.1-796.119
160	38.2-1611.1, 38.2-1709, 38.2-2806
161	3.1-17.1
162	57-60
163	11-41.1
164	11-45.1
165	11-62.7
166	36-99.7
167	33.1-210.2
168	58.1-3850
169	19.2-389
170	38.2-2206
171	60.2-219
172	29.1-553
173	55-79.80:2, 55-513
174	51.1-602, 51.1-603, 51.1-603.1
176	11-47.3
177	19.2-389
178	15.1-965.10
179	3.1-991, 3.1-997, 3.1-1009R
180	6.1-330.55, 58.1-3018
181	9-351, 9-352
182	2.1-404
183	4.1-406, n., 4.1-407, 4.1-505, n., 4.1-506
184	58.1-339
185	29.1-217
186	46.2-100
187	2.1-304.3, 2.1-304.4, 2.1-304.6
188	50-73.11:1, 50-73.36, 50-73.38, 50-73.39R, 50-73.51, 50-73.83, 50-73.125, 50-73.130, 50-75—50-78R
189	60.2-219
190	13.1-603, 13.1-722, 13.1-766.1, 13.1-1002, 13.1-1010.1, 13.1-1010.2, 13.1-1010.3, 13.1-1011, 13.1-1014, 13.1-1023, 13.1-1029, 13.1-1030, 13.1-1038.1, 13.1-1040, 13.1-1046, 13.1-1060, 13.1-1064, 13.1-1067, 13.1-1070, 13.1-1072, 13.1-1073, 50-37.3, 50-73.1, 50-73.48:1, 50-73.48:3, 50-73.48:4, 50-73.57:2, 50-73.130
191	38.2-2206
192	58.1-3503
193	58.1-202.1
194	15.1-687.23
195	66-22.1
197	62.1-132.4
198	2.1-342
199	38.2-1905.1, 38.2-1905.2R, 38.2-1906
200	54.1-2101.1
202	60.2-528, 60.2-614, 60.2-618, 60.2-619
203	38.2-3408, 38.2-4221
204	9-183.2
205	55-58.2, 55-66.01
206	54.1-3307.1R
207	53.1-40
208	14.1-69
209	24.2-614
210	16.1-278.5
211	15.1-37.10
212	9-6.14:4.1, 40.1-51.9:1, 40.1-51.10, 40.1-51.10:1, 40.1-51.11:1, 40.1-51.15
213	51.1-803
214	26-17.4, 26-24
215	14.1-112, 14.1-123, 14.1-133.4, 15.1-159.7:1, n.
216	13.1-615, 13.1-752, 13.1-768, 13.1-775, 13.1-775.1, 13.1-815, 13.1-914, 13.1-930, 13.1-936, 13.1-936.1
217	13.1-852.1
218	54.1-3437.1
219	55-268.1
220	26-46.1
221	55-66.3
222	55-79.97, 55-484, 55-512, 55-530
223	9-349
224	17-79.3
225	65.2-704
226	13.1-671.1
227	54.1-2912.1
228	6.1-422
229	63.1-324
230	2.1-483.1:1
231	54.1-2101.1
232	2.1-116, 51.1-126.4, 51.1-502.3, 62.1-128, 62.1-129.1, 62.1-132.1, 62.1-132.6, 62.1-132.7, 62.1-147.2
233	22.1-32
234	15.1-362.1
235	18.2-31
236	15.1-11.5:3
237	2.1-505, n., 23-4.01, n.
238	54.1-3935
239	54.1-3900.01, 54.1-3936
240	9-145.47
241	20-109
243	16.1-122.4
244	58.1-3506
245	58.1-605
246	46.2-752
247	29.1-300.1, 29.1-302.1
248	32.1-111.4, 32.1-111.5
249	29.1-521
250	58.1-3503, 58.1-3504, 58.1-3506
251	58.1-3984
252	58.1-3812
253	16.1-77, n., 16.1-122.1—16.1-122.7, n.
254	64.1-161
255	10.1-2211
256	18.2-268.9
257	58.1-490
258	28.2-1210
259	28.2-613
260	10.1-1450, 46.2-341.9:1
261	21-119
262	55-254
263	64.1-66.2
265	33.1-69.01, n.
266	10.1-2103,

Acts 1997 Chapter	Code 1950 Section
	10.1-2104, 10.1-2106
267	29.1-301
268	10.1-1188
269	9-145.47
270	10.1-2211
271	32.1-36, 32.1-37, 32.1-38
272	54.1-3408
273	51.1-146, 51.1-510, 51.1-512, 51.1-512.1, 51.1-514
274	45.1-161.38
276	15.1-1710—15.1-1722
277	6.1-58.1
278	6.1-71, 6.1-194.58, 6.1-225.49
279	13.1-501, 13.1-504, 13.1-505, 13.1-505.1, 13.1-507, 13.1-514, 13.1-515, 13.1-518.1, 13.1-519, 13.1-522, 13.1-523.1
280	51.1-142
281	54.1-603
282	40.1-22.1
283	46.2-200, 46.2-438, 46.2-613, 46.2-649, 46.2-652, 46.2-653, 46.2-659R, 46.2-694, 46.2-694.1, 46.2-696, 46.2-697, 46.2-699R, 46.2-701, 46.2-712, 46.2-714, 46.2-726, 46.2-755, 46.2-759, 46.2-762, 46.2-769R, 46.2-917.2, 46.2-1128, 46.2-1129, 46.2-1142.1, 46.2-1149.2, 46.2-1156, 46.2-1157, 46.2-1168, 46.2-1175, 46.2-1552.1, 46.2-2100, 52-8.4, 52-8.4:2, 58.1-2401, 58.1-2402, 58.1-2403, 58.1-2425, 58.1-2700, 58.1-2702, 58.1-3703
284	28.2-102
285	45.1-241
286	3.1-796.105, 3.1-796.120
287	58.1-3817, 58.1-3818
288	65.2-600
289	13.1-514.1
290	38.2-613.01
291	38.2-3514.1
292	8.01-581.17
293	45.1-161.155
294	10.1-1400
295	2.1-342
296	65.2-709
297	38.2-4312
298	60.2-526, n.
299	7.1-43
300	58.1-2142.1
301	58.1-346.4:1
302	58.1-346.2:1
304	24.2-627
306	58.1-3813
307	58.1-609.6
308	23-21
309	2.1-112, 15.1-7.5, n.
310	2.1-313, 23-29, 2.1-304.1R, 2.1-305—2.1-312R, 2.1-314R, 2.1-315—2.1-317R, 2.1-318—2.1-326R
311	18.2-287.2
313	18.2-18, 18.2-31
314	58.1-3245.6—58.1-3245.11, 59.1-283
315	19.2-270.5
316	17-116.010
317	37.1-132
318	16.1-278.8
319	62.1-209
320	2.1-373
321	32.1-111.3
322	19.2-165.1
323	37.1-195
324	2.1-1.5, 23-231.8, 23-231.9, 23-231.10, 23-231.11, 23-231.12
325	17-40
326	3.1-884.21:2
327	58.1-3967
328	24.2-604
329	32.1-122.7
330	18.2-61
331	15.1-292.4
332	36-99, n.
333	8.01-420.5, 65.2-706.1
334	8.01-225
336	24.2-627
337	24.2-1002.01
338	10.1-1704, 10.1-1801.1, 10.1-1801.2
339	53.1-182.1, 53.1-183
340	53.1-106
341	18.2-308.2:2, 52-4.4
342	32.1-167, 32.1-176.1:1
343	8.1-105, 8.2-512, 8.5-101—8.5-117R, 8.5A-101—8.5A-118, 8.9-103, 8.9-104, 8.9-105, 8.9-106, 8.9-304, 8.9-305
344	46.2-357
345	19.2-298.01
346	24.2-401, 24.2-418, 24.2-651
347	2.1-752, 16.1-286, 16.1-309.3
349	8.01-220.1:2
350	58.1-438.1
352	36-105.2
353	10.1-1418.1, 10.1-1418.2
354	20-45.2
355	58.1-499
356	10.1-611.1
357	22.1-199.1
358	17-116.08, 19.2-317
359	32.1-325, n.
360	2.1-1.5, 2.1-1.6, 2.1-1.9, 9-6.23, 9-6.25:1, 22.1-346.1
361	2.1-1.5, 2.1-1.6, 2.1-1.9, 9-6.23, 9-6.25:1, 22.1-346.1
362	22.1-3.3
363	15.1-1242, 15.1-1250.03, 15.1-1257
364	2.1-787.1, 24.2-914, 24.2-914.1
365	20-45.2
366	22.1-32
367	9-78—9-84R, 23-253.1—23-253.7
371	16.1-305.1, 22.1-277.02
372	22.1-146
375	30-19.03:2
376	23-38.33:1, 23-38.34:1
377	38.2-2226
378	46.2-301.1
379	59.1-274
380	18.2-251
381	2.1-304.1:1
382	22.1-79
383	65.2-524
384	22.1-147
385	60.2-114, 60.2-512, 60.2-600, 60.2-608.2, 60.2-623
386	4.1-201
387	19.2-311
388	2.1-24.2, 57-2.01
389	54.1-2105
390	9-6.14:4.1,

Acts 1997 Chapter	Code 1950 Section
	45.1-161.3, n., 45.1-161.7, 45.1-161.8, 45.1-161.9, n., 45.1-161.19, 45.1-161.20, 45.1-161.22R, 45.1-161.42—45.1-161.56R, 45.1-161.57, 45.1-161.59, 45.1-161.60, 45.1-161.61, 45.1-161.62, 45.1-161.63, 45.1-161.64, 45.1-161.77, 45.1-161.78, 45.1-161.81, 45.1-161.82, 45.1-161.83, 45.1-161.89, 45.1-161.90, 45.1-161.102, 45.1-161.104R, 45.1-161.292:1—45.1-161.292:72, 45.1-161.293, 45.1-161.294, n., 45.1-161.296, 45.1-161.304, 45.1-305, n., 45.1-161.307, 45.1-161.309, 45.1-161.310, 45.1-161.311, 45.1-161.311:1, 45.1-161.311:2, n., 45.1-221, 45.1-225, 45.1-225.1—45.1-225.3
391	18.2-322.1R, 22.1-278.2
392	2.1-787.1, 24.2-914, 24.2-914.1
393	46.2-2313
394	22.1-199.1
395	8.01-513
396	58.1-346.3:1
397	63.1-174
398	58.1-3516.2
399	38.2-5016
400	13.1-708
401	8.01-66.1
402	9-364, 9-365
403	54.1-1128—54.1-1135
404	2.1-715, 2.1-716, 2.1-717, 2.1-725, 15.1-37.3:8, 15.1-783.1, 15.1-783.2
405	65.2-400, 65.2-401
406	1-13.7
407	6.1-93, 6.1-194.78, 6.1-194.144
408	22.1-3.3
409	60.2-535
410	65.2-813.2
411	15.1-870
412	63.1-116, 63.1-117, 63.1-118R, 63.1-119
413	14.1-118.1, 17-59.2
414	32.1-330.3, 38.2-226.1
415	9-298, 38.2-3431
416	15.1-292.01
417	55-79.80:2, 55-513
418	4.1-353
419	58.1-2506
420	63.1-204.3
421	45.1-361.27, 45.1-361.42
423	5.1-51, 46.2-206, 58.1-2146, 58.1-2425, 58.1-2701
424	8.01-262.1
425	4.1-100
426	38.2-4601.1
427	63.1-198
428	58.1-1822
429	24.2-707
430	16.1-301
431	46.2-888, 46.2-894, 46.2-896, 46.2-1200, 46.2-1212.1
432	2.1-27.9
433	58.1-3503, 58.1-3506
434	16.1-309.1
436	27-31, 27-32, 27-34.2
437	2.1-548.29, 23-220.2—23-220.4
438	24.2-653, 24.2-668
439	2.1-342, 2.1-344, 8.01-581.13, 9-6.14:4.1, 54.1-2400, 54.1-2505, 54.1-2515, 54.1-2516, 54.1-2517, 54.1-2518
440	63.1-250.1
441	16.1-263
442	2.1-27.9
443	53.1-133.03
444	22.1-296.2
445	18.2-138.1
446	32.1-111.10
447	24.2-303, 24.2-304
448	2.1-548.29, 23-220.2—23-220.4
449	32.1-290
450	24.2-707
451	2.1-27.4
452	16.1-309.1
453	54.1-2972
454	32.1-127
455	19.2-152.1
456	24.2-653, 24.2-668
457	58.1-3503, 58.1-3506
458	22.1-254.2
459	24.2-115
460	24.2-618, 24.2-620, 24.2-621
461	18.2-138.1
462	32.1-102.12
463	16.1-278.4, 16.1-278.6
464	24.2-705.1, 24.2-710
465	22.1-279.4
466	22.1-199.2, 22.1-253.13:1, 22.1-254.01
467	63.1-250.1
468	2.1-20.1
469	54.1-2923.1
470	32.1-272
471	30-4, 30-6, 30-7
472	18.2-271.1
473	46.2-320
474	56-458, 56-462
475	32.1-330.3, 38.2-226.1
476	19.2-120
477	58.1-346.1:1
478	46.2-301.1
479	46.2-1135
480	8.01-220.1:3
481	58.1-3916
483	2.1-563.16, n., 2.1-563.31, n., 46.2-200, n., 52-4, n.
484	46.2-1571
485	46.2-676
486	46.2-100, 46.2-307, 46.2-330, 46.2-342, 46.2-343, 46.2-345, 46.2-389, 46.2-390.1, 46.2-434, 46.2-692, 46.2-697.1, 46.2-717R
487	4.1-307
488	2.1-483.1, 11-35, 62.1-132.6
489	4.1-208, 4.1-209
490	9-145.45, 9-145.46R
491	2.1-20.01:1
492	19.2-163
493	46.2-332, 46.2-1191

Acts 1997 Chapter	Code 1950 Section
494	33.1-23.3
495	10.1-1411
496	46.2-755, 58.1-22, 58.1-526, 58.1-3128, 58.1-3916, 58.1-3921, 58.1-3922, 58.1-3924, 58.1-3928R, 58.1-3933, 58.1-3934, 58.1-3941, 58.1-3952, 58.1-3958
497	59.1-279
498	15.1-11.2:3
499	46.2-752
500	46.2-674
501	33.1-23.03:4
502	62.1-44.33
503	8.01-413.01, 38.2-2201
504	33.1-46.2
505	2.1-1.6, 9-6.25:1, 10.1-418.1
506	46.2-1220
507	46.2-1178
508	18.2-271.1
509	19.2-390
510	29.1-401
511	65.2-500, 65.2-502, 65.2-503, 65.2-518
512	10.1-1413.1
513	38.2-1816
514	18.2-31
515	56-458, 56-462
516	19.2-262
517	58.1-3, 59.1-271, 59.1-279, 59.1-280, 59.1-280.1, 59.1-280.2, 59.1-282.4
518	19.2-262, 19.2-262.1
519	62.1-44.19:4—62.1-44.19:8
520	10.1-1318, n., 10.1-1457, n., 62.1-44.29, n.
521	2.1-20.1
522	29.1-744
523	24.2-412, 24.2-421R, 24.2-705
524	15.1-483.1
526	53.1-145, 63.1-105.8
527	15.1-1240, 15.1-1241, 15.1-1250, 15.1-1252, 15.1-1258, 15.1-1259, 15.1-1260, 15.1-1268
528	19.2-368.2, 19.2-368.6
529	15.1-491
530	60.2-526, n., 60.2-533, 60.2-602
531	38.2-322
532	19.2-151
534	15.1-29.11
537	15.1-131.4
538	13.1-514
539	24.2-412, 24.2-421R, 24.2-705
540	8.01-73
541	16.1-299.2
542	18.2-258.1
543	15.1-491
544	40.1-28.10
545	15.1-483.1
546	53.1-128, 53.1-129
547	15.1-29.10
548	15.1-11.3
549	46.2-2013.1
550	15.1-29.15
551	8.01-382
552	32.1-126.3
553	46.2-368
554	15.1-1688, 15.1-1692, 15.1-1693, 15.1-1694, 15.1-1695, 15.1-1696, 15.1-1699, 15.1-1701, 15.1-1702, 15.1-1703, 15.1-1706—15.1-1709
555	18.2-355
556	54.1-2408.1, 54.1-2708, 54.1-2920, 54.1-3009, 54.1-3217R, 54.1-3317R, 54.1-3605, 54.1-3808R
557	19.2-188.2
558	37.1-67.3
559	46.2-1180
560	54.1-503
561	17-47.4
562	63.1-251.2
563	63.1-25.3
564	54.1-2400, 54.1-2401, 54.1-2919, 54.1-3010
565	8.01-249
566	54.1-3408
567	2.1-1.6, 2.1-342, 9-6.14:4.1, 32.1-73.1—32.1-73.4
568	32.1-102.3:2.2, 38.2-4900, n.
569	54.1-2400.01
570	15.1-494
572	36-49.1:1
573	15.1-1240, 15.1-1241, 15.1-1250, 15.1-1252, 15.1-1258, 15.1-1259, 15.1-1260, 15.1-1268
575	63.1-86.1
576	7.1-37
577	2.1-639.15, 2.1-639.41
579	8.01-446, 8.01-449, 17-60, 17-70.1, 55-66.4:2
581	62.1-44.15:4
582	3.1-796.93:1
583	38.2-1800.1, 38.2-1816, 38.2-1818, 38.2-1822, 38.2-1825, 38.2-1838, 38.2-1841, 38.2-1868.1, n., 38.2-1869, 38.2-1871
584	27-97, 27-99, 36-99.3
585	22.1-277, 22.1-277.2, 22.1-278
586	18.2-371.3
587	2.1-111.1, 3.1-796.94, 3.1-796.94:1, 3.1-796.94:2, 14.1-47.3, 15.1-1—15.1-1705R, 15.2-100—15.2-107, 15.2-200—15.2-208, 15.2-300—15.2-307, 15.2-400—15.2-418, 15.2-500—15.2-541, 15.2-600—15.2-642, 15.2-700—15.2-749, 15.2-800—15.2-858, 15.2-900—15.2-973, 15.2-1000, 15.2-1100—15.2-1130, 15.2-1200—15.2-1249, 15.2-1300—15.2-1310, 15.2-1400—15.2-1433, 15.2-1500—15.2-1543, 15.2-1600—15.2-1656, 15.2-1700—15.2-1753, 15.2-1800—15.2-1814, 15.2-1900—15.2-1906, 15.2-2000—15.2-2030, 15.2-2100—15.2-2159, 15.2-2200—15.2-2232, 15.2-2233, 15.2-2234, 15.2-2235, 15.2-2236, 15.2-2237—15.2-2328, 15.2-2400—15.2-2413, 15.2-2500—15.2-2513, 15.2-2600—15.2-2663, 15.2-2700—15.2-2709, 15.2-2800—15.2-2810, 15.2-2900—15.2-2908, 15.2-3000—15.2-3004, 15.2-3100—15.2-3109, 15.2-3200—15.2-3245, 15.2-3300—15.2-3308, 15.2-3400, 15.2-3401, 15.2-3500—15.2-3550,

Acts 1997 Chapter	Code 1950 Section
	15.2-3600—15.2-3605, 15.2-3700—15.2-3712, 15.2-3800—15.2-3834, 15.2-3900—15.2-3919, 15.2-4000—15.2-4005, 15.2-4100—15.2-4120, 15.2-4200—15.2-4222, 15.2-4300—15.2-4314, 15.2-4400—15.2-4407, 15.2-4500—15.2-4534, 15.2-4600—15.2-4618, 15.2-4700—15.2-4716, 15.2-4800—15.2-4815, 15.2-4900—15.2-4920, 15.2-5000—15.2-5005, 15.2-5100—15.2-5158, 15.2-5200—15.2-5218, 15.2-5300—15.2-5367, 15.2-5400—15.2-5431, 15.2-5500—15.2-5508, 15.2-5600—15.2-5616, 15.2-5700—15.2-5714, 15.2-5800—15.2-5819, 15.2-5900—15.2-5917, 15.2-6000—15.2-6015, 15.2-6100—15.2-6110, 15.2-6200—15.2-6214, 15.2-6300—15.2-6321, 21-134.01, 37.1-242—37.1-253
589	46.2-1030
590	38.2-137R, 38.2-401.1R, 58.1-2508
592	14.1-47.2
593	22.1-278.1
594	54.1-3446
595	18.2-251.2
596	22.1-209.1:2, n.
597	22.1-274
598	15.1-561
599	54.1-3029
600	32.1-102.1
601	15.1-249.1
602	15.1-162.1
603	16.1-253.1, 16.1-253.4, 16.1-279.1, 18.2-57.2, 19.2-81.3
604	15.1-159.7
605	20-103
606	9-173.8, 19.2-389
607	15.1-491.8, 15.1-491.9
608	22.1-277, 22.1-277.2, 22.1-278
609	32.1-290.1, 54.1-2982, 54.1-2984
610	30-19.1:7
611	2.1-1.7, 9-371, 9-372, 9-373, 36-139
612	10.1-1307.01
613	15.1-539.1
614	15.1-11.01
615	55-531—55-533
616	2.1-786
617	22.1-199.1
619	18.2-260.1
620	28.2-1000, n.
621	63.1-86.1
622	46.2-844
623	10.1-1186.2
624	9-6.14:4.1, 10.1-1197.1—10.1-1197.4, 10.1-2500, 10.1-2502
625	10.1-2117—10.1-2134
626	10.1-2117—10.1-2134
627	10.1-1422.4
628	10.1-1186.2
629	46.2-873
631	58.1-609.7, 58.1-609.8, 58.1-609.9, 58.1-609.10
634	59.1-280.1, 59.1-282.1
635	2.1-786
636	2.1-342
637	46.2-113
638	15.1-131
639	66-25.1
640	58.1-333, 58.1-430, 63.1-320, 63.1-321, 63.1-322, 63.1-323, 63.1-324, 63.1-325
641	2.1-341, 2.1-342, 2.1-344, 2.1-639.2, 2.1-639.9, 2.1-639.13, 51.1-124.20, 51.1-124.26, 51.1-151R
642	16.1-318, n.
643	18.2-67.4
644	53.1-68
645	10.1-1186.3
646	4.1-208
648	20-79.1, 63.1-250.3, 63.1-258.1
649	54.1-501
650	24.2-411
651	62.1-233, 62.1-234, 62.1-237, 62.1-238, 62.1-239, 62.1-239.1
652	2.1-429.01
653	63.1-251.4
654	16.1-296
655	22.1-209.1:4
656	2.1-20.1, 38.2-3407.5
657	16.1-299
662	4.1-208
663	20-79.1, 63.1-250.3, 63.1-258.1
664	16.1-296
665	62.1-233, 62.1-234, 62.1-237, 62.1-238, 62.1-239, 62.1-239.1
666	24.2-411
667	10.1-1186.3
668	15.1-131
669	59.1-280.1, 59.1-282.1
670	19.2-298.1, 19.2-390.1
671	32.1-325
672	19.2-298.1, 19.2-390.1
674	60.2-526, n., 60.2-533, 60.2-602
675	14.1-125.2
676	15.1-503.2
677	54.1-3401, 54.1-3435.2
679	32.1-351—32.1-353
680	8.01-335
681	55-7.2
682	8.01-413, 32.1-127.1:02R, 32.1-127.1:03, 54.1-2403.3
683	32.1-325
684	36-55.39
685	22.1-271.3
686	22.1-129, 22.1-199.1
687	63.1-55.3
688	32.1-122.10:01, 38.2-305, 38.2-4214, 38.2-4308, 38.2-4315, 38.2-4319
689	22.1-302
690	16.1-241, 20-124.1, 63.1-233
691	15.1-132.1, 18.2-51.4, 18.2-268.3, 18.2-270, 18.2-270.1, 19.2-11.01, 19.2-294.1, 19.2-299, 19.2-368.2, 19.2-389, 46.2-301, 46.2-301.1, 46.2-316, 46.2-341.18, 46.2-341.28, 46.2-351, 46.2-351.2, 46.2-384, 46.2-389, 46.2-391, 46.2-391.2, 46.2-391.4, 46.2-394, 46.2-395
692	9-6.14:21
693	8.01-341.1

Acts 1997 Chapter	Code 1950 Section
694	58.1-1
696	58.1-609.7
697	58.1-2101, 58.1-2122
698	54.1-2400.2, 54.1-2400.3, 54.1-2708.1R, 54.1-2910R, 54.1-3612R
700	15.1-37.3:6
701	58.1-3118, 58.1-3310
703	28.2-903.1, 29.1-554.1, 29.1-738
704	58.1-3211
705	58.1-3
706	46.2-391
707	56-235.4
708	16.1-241
709	18.2-31, 18.2-32.1, 18.2-51.2
710	58.1-3211, 58.1-3213
711	2.1-116, 2.1-116.09, 51.1-124.22, 51.1-124.27, 51.1-155.1
713	23-38.53:11
714	65.2-402
715	33.1-70.1
716	6.1-2.19—6.1-2.29
717	58.1-609.6
718	15.1-466
719	54.1-2712.1, 54.1-2726.1
720	54.1-3016.1
721	19.2-83.1, 19.2-389, 22.1-296.2, 22.1-315
722	32.1-45.2
724	58.1-3965, 58.1-3966, 58.1-3969
725	58.1-605
726	58.1-439.6
727	22.1-29
728	22.1-277.2
729	33.1-70.1
730	32.1-325
731	58.1-2101, 58.1-2114, 58.1-2118, 58.1-2135, 58.1-3941, 58.1-3942
732	58.1-3703.1
733	46.2-341.4, n., 46.2-803.1
734	22.1-277
735	58.1-609.8
737	15.1-466
738	15.1-491.001
739	15.1-887
740	33.1-72.1
741	15.1-11.03
742	15.1-364.2
743	15.1-1682, 19.2-389, 37.1-197.2
744	46.2-1052
745	15.1-23.1
746	23-38.53:11
747	18.2-47, 18.2-48, 18.2-472.1, 19.2-298.1, 19.2-298.2, 19.2-298.3, 19.2-298.4, 19.2-390, 19.2-390.1, 53.1-116.1, 53.1-160.1
748	38.2-3407.5:1
749	18.2-477.1
750	8.01-502.1
751	37.1-128.02, 37.1-128.1, 37.1-132
752	16.1-318
753	16.1-77, 16.1-92, 16.1-114.1
754	8.01-320
755	32.1-79, 32.1-87
756	58.1-2626.1, n.
757	58.1-3819
758	15.1-1374, 15.1-1375, 15.1-1378
759	45.1-361.9, 45.1-361.17, 45.1-361.19, 45.1-361.23, 45.1-361.29
760	55-79.84, 55-516
761	40.1-52
762	22.1-279.5
763	15.1-1374, 15.1-1375, 15.1-1378
764	58.1-3819
765	45.1-361.29
766	55-79.84, 55-516
767	Va. Const., Art. II, § 1, n.
768	Va. Const., Art. VI, § 10, n.
769	Va. Const., Art. X, § 6, n.
770	Va. Const., Art. VII, § 2, n.
771	Va. Const., Art. VI, § 10, n.
772	Va. Const., Art. VI, § 10, n.
773	46.2-1109, 46.2-1112
774	46.2-692.1, 46.2-698, 46.2-711, 46.2-724, 46.2-725, 46.2-729.1, 46.2-734.1, 46.2-739, 46.2-741, 46.2-742.2, 46.2-743, 46.2-746.4, 46.2-746.4:1, 46.2-746.5, 46.2-746.8, 46.2-746.10, 46.2-747.1, 46.2-748.2, 46.2-749.2:8—46.2-749.2:12, 46.2-749.4:1—46.2-749.4:3, 46.2-749.6:1, 46.2-749.7:2
775	53.1-20.1
777	2.1-342, 18.2-340.16, 18.2-340.18, 18.2-340.19, 18.2-340.20, 18.2-340.22, 18.2-340.23, 18.2-340.25, 18.2-340.26, 18.2-340.28, 18.2-340.30, 18.2-340.31, 18.2-340.32, 18.2-340.33, 18.2-340.34
778	15.1-687.25
779	18.2-128
780	46.2-1220
781	46.2-873
782	2.1-342
783	36-99.11, 46.2-100, 46.2-676, 46.2-731, 46.2-1237R, 46.2-1240—46.2-1259
784	4.1-309
785	2.1-1.5, 2.1-1.6, 2.1-116, 2.1-342, 2.1-344, 9-6.14:4.1, 9-6.25:3, 11-35, 23-38.75, 23-38.76, 23-38.77, 23-38.80, 23-38.81, 23-38.82R, 34-4, 58.1-322
786	58.1-439
787	58.1-3
788	23-105
789	59.1-284.15
790	16.1-252, 16.1-253, 16.1-266, 16.1-278.2, 16.1-281, 16.1-282, 16.1-282.1, 16.1-296, 16.1-296.2
791	9-155, 38.2-401
792	20-49.1, 20-49.3, 20-49.7, 20-49.9, 63.1-250.1:2, 63.1-274.10
793	46.2-1094, 46.2-1095

Acts 1997 Chapter	Code 1950 Section
794	20-91, 32.1-263, 32.1-267, 32.1-268, 46.2-320, 54.1-116, 63.1-250.1, 63.1-263.1
795	9-168, 17-234, 53.1-134
796	19.2-389, 20-60.3, 20-60.6, 20-87.1, 63.1-250, 63.1-250.1, 63.1-250.2:1, 63.1-252.1, 63.1-260.3, 63.1-274.6, 65.2-531, 65.2-903
797	20-88.32, 20-88.39, 20-88.41, 20-88.47, 20-88.48, 20-88.49, 20-88.50, 20-88.64, 20-88.64:1—20-88.64:5, 20-88.70, 20-88.71, 20-88.76, 20-88.77, 20-88.77:1, 20-88.77:2, 20-88.78
798	59.1-372
799	2.1-1.7, 32.1-297.1
800	46.2-844
801	2.1-124, 4.1-212, 4.1-222, 4.1-225, 4.1-401, 4.1-500, 6.1-5, 6.1-17, 6.1-32.5, 6.1-32.11, 6.1-70, 6.1-194.56, 6.1-195.78, 6.1-195.80, 6.1-225.48, 8.01-94, 8.01-229, 8.01-249, 8.01-338, 8.01-581.12, 8.01-606, 8.01-670, 8.3A-308, 8.4-405, 13.1-603, 13.1-662, 13.1-803, 14.1-90, 15.1-244, 15.1-369, 16.1-69.28, 17-28, 18.2-76, 19.2-141, 19.2-368.5, 19.2-390, 21-295, 21-310, 24.2-101, 24.2-404, 24.2-418, 24.2-427, 25-46.13, 25-46.28, 26-4, 26-5, 26-7, 26-7.1, 26-7.4, 26-17.10, 26-27, 26-45.2, 26-46, 26-60, 26-61, 26-62, 26-63, 26-66, 26-67, 29.1-801, 32.1-138, 37.1-87, 37.1-108, 37.1-109, 37.1-110, 37.1-111, 38.2-3415, 38.2-4200, 38.2-4500, 46.2-314, 46.2-322, 46.2-380, 46.2-1500, 46.2-1900, 46.2-1992, 46.2-1993, 50-73.28, 50-73.48, 50-73.109, 51.5-3, 53.1-40.1, 53.1-227, 54.1-601, 54.1-2409, 54.1-2915, 54.1-2916, 54.1-2917, 54.1-2970, 54.1-2983, 54.1-2992, 55-19, 55-29, 55-34.13, 55-118.5, 55-213, 55-276, 59.1-21.14, 59.1-347, 59.1-353, 62.1-117, 63.1-55.5, 63.1-107, 63.1-182.1, 64.1-57, 64.1-157, 64.1-180.1, 65.2-527, 65.2-528, 65.2-701
802	46.2-1993.3, 46.2-1993.67, 46.2-1993.67:1
803	2.1-1.5, 2.1-20.1:02, 23-9.4, 23-277—23-286, 51.1-124.36, n.
804	32.1-45.2
805	24.2-426R, 24.2-427
806	9-6.14:4.1, 32.1-122.6:03, 38.2-3407.11, 54.1-2506.1, 54.1-2950, 54.1-2952.1, 54.1-3303, 54.1-3401, 54.1-3408, 58.1-609.7
807	38.2-3430.1—38.2-3430.10, 38.2-3431, 38.2-3432R, 38.2-3432.1—38.2-3432.3, 38.2-3433, 38.2-3434—38.2-3437, 38.2-4214, 38.2-4216.1, 38.2-4217, 38.2-4229.1, 38.2-4306, 38.2-4319, 38.2-4322, 38.2-4323, 58.1-2501, n.
808	59.1-274, 59.1-279
809	8.01-225
810	63.1-202.01
811	10.1-2211
812	4.1-105, 18.2-371.2
813	9-6.23, 23-231.13—23-231.18
814	38.2-5700—38.2-5707
815	9-221, 9-228.1—9-228.4, 9-235
816	46.2-692.1, 46.2-698, 46.2-711, 46.2-724, 46.2-725, 46.2-729.1, 46.2-734.1, 46.2-739, 46.2-741, 46.2-742.2, 46.2-743, 46.2-746.4, 46.2-746.4:1, 46.2-746.5, 46.2-746.8, 46.2-746.10, 46.2-747.1, 46.2-748.2, 46.2-749.2:8—46.2-749.2:12, 46.2-749.4:1—46.2-749.4:3, 46.2-749.6:1, 46.2-749.7:2
817	2.1-1.6, 2.1-563.36—2.1-563.41, 9-6.23, 9-6.25:1
819	19.2-353.3
820	8.01-293
821	51.1-124.28
822	58.1-609.4, 58.1-609.6, 58.1-609.7, 58.1-609.8, 58.1-609.9, 58.1-609.10
824	58.1-609.6
825	2.1-155.3
826	22.1-3
827	22.1-253.13:5, 23-9.2:3, 23-9.8, 23-9.13:1
828	22.1-253.13:1, 22.1-253.13:2, 22.1-253.13:4, 22.1-254, 22.1-254.01
829	22.1-253.13:1
830	22.1-276.2, 22.1-277, 22.1-278
831	16.1-106, 16.1-298, 19.2-152.8—19.2-152.10
832	18.2-77, 18.2-79, 18.2-90, 18.2-91
833	18.2-57, 18.2-57.1R, 18.2-121
834	58.1-609.3
835	22.1-253.13:4
836	17-47, 17-74, 17-75, 17-76
837	4.1-309
838	2.1-342, 18.2-340.16, 18.2-340.18, 18.2-340.19, 18.2-340.20, 18.2-340.22, 18.2-340.23, 18.2-340.25, 18.2-340.26, 18.2-340.28, 18.2-340.30, 18.2-340.31, 18.2-340.32, 18.2-340.33,

Acts 1997 Chapter	Code 1950 Section
	18.2-340.34
839	54.1-3510, 54.1-3515, 65.2-603
840	53.1-20
841	46.2-325, 46.2-334, 46.2-335
842	26-1.2, 26-2, 26-3, 26-8.1, 26-12, 26-12.1, 26-15, 26-17.3, 26-17.8R, 26-18, 26-24, 26-32, 26-36.1R, 26-37, 26-39, 55-59.4
843	2.1-786
844	2.1-639.15, 2.1-639.41
845	9-6.14:4.1, 28.2-103, 28.2-1207, 62.1-44.15:5.1
846	58.1-3018
847	30-85—30-88
848	46.2-1500, 46.2-1508, 46.2-1521, 46.2-1900, 46.2-1908, 46.2-1921, 46.2-1992, 46.2-1992.6, 46.2-1992.19, 46.2-1993, 46.2-1993.6, 46.2-1993.19
849	58.1-3664
850	9-6.14:4.1, 10.1-1197.1—10.1-1197.4, 10.1-2500, 10.1-2502
851	63.1-202.01
852	58.1-439
853	46.2-755, 58.1-2401, 58.1-2402, 58.1-2425, 58.1-3510
855	54.1-2709, 54.1-2722
856	2.1-114.5
857	46.2-320, 63.1-263.1
858	2.1-1.6, 2.1-51.27, 2.1-454.1, 2.1-563.13, 2.1-563.15, 2.1-563.16, 2.1-563.23—2.1-563.27R, 2.1-563.27:1—2.1-563.27:8, 9-6.25:2, 15.1-23.1, 15.1-456
859	2.1-7.3
860	36-108, 36-115, n., 36-135
861	2.1-1.5, 2.1-1.6, 2.1-116, 2.1-342, 2.1-344, 9-6.14:4.1, 9-6.25:3, 11-35, 23-38.75, 23-38.76, 23-38.77, 23-38.80, 23-38.81, 23-38.82R, 34-4, 58.1-322
862	16.1-255, 16.1-260, 16.1-269.1, 16.1-269.6, 16.1-296, 19.2-310.3
863	11-35, 22.1-212.2:2
864	11-65, 11-66, 11-68, 11-70
865	33.1-128
866	8.01-226.2
868	9-6.14:4.1, 28.2-1307
869	32.1-45.1
870	9-228.5—9-228.8
872	58.1-3211
873	2.1-1.6, 3.1-1081—3.1-1103, 9-6.25:3
874	15.1-11.2:2
875	10.1-1408.1
876	24.2-940
877	29.1-712, 29.1-716, 29.1-717, 58.1-1401, 58.1-1404, 58.1-1405, 58.1-1410
878	2.1-1.5, 9-84.08, 9-84.09, 9-84.09:1, 9-84.09:2, 9-84.09:3, 9-84.09:4, 46.2-749.2:2, 58.1-346.6
879	8.01-220.1:2
880	46.2-1052
881	46.2-808.1, 46.2-830
882	4.1-105, 18.2-371.2
883	9-168, 17-234, 53.1-134
884	15.1-227.70, 15.1-227.75, 15.1-227.76, 15.1-227.78, 15.1-227.84, 15.1-227.85, 15.1-227.90, 15.1-227.91
885	2.1-1.6, 9-6.25:2, 10.1-1408.2, 54.1-500, 54.1-500.1, 54.1-501, 54.1-503, 54.1-516, 54.1-517, 54.1-1100, 54.1-1102, 54.1-1103, 54.1-1108.2, 54.1-1118, 54.1-1119, 54.1-1120, 54.1-1123, 54.1-1125, 54.1-1126, 54.1-1127, 54.1-1129, 54.1-1130, 54.1-1131, 54.1-1132, 54.1-1133, 54.1-1134, 54.1-1135, 54.1-2211, 54.1-2212
886	2.1-20.1:03, 2.1-20.1:04
887	55-511, 55-515.1
888	2.1-1.5, 2.1-20.1:02, 23-9.4, 23-277—23-286, 51.1-124.36
889	51.1-210
890	58.1-346.7
891	2.1-1.5, 2.1-20.1:02, 23-9.4, 23-277—23-286, 51.1-124.36
892	3.1-796.93:1
893	44-146.17, 44-146.18, 44-146.28
894	22.1-344, 53.1-10, 66-13
895	19.2-389, 20-60.3, 20-60.6, 20-87.1, 63.1-250, 63.1-250.1, 63.1-250.2:1, 63.1-252.1, 63.1-260.3, 63.1-274.6, 65.2-531, 65.2-903
896	20-49.1, 20-49.3, 20-49.7, 20-49.9, 63.1-250.1:2, 63.1-274.10
897	20-88.32, 20-88.39, 20-88.41, 20-88.47, 20-88.48, 20-88.49, 20-88.50, 20-88.64:1—20-88.64:5, 20-88.70, 20-88.71, 20-88.76, 20-88.77, 20-88.77:1, 20-88.77:2, 20-88.78
898	20-91, 32.1-263, 32.1-267, 32.1-268, 46.2-320, 54.1-116, 63.1-250.1, 63.1-263.1
899	22.1-212.2:1, 23-38.10:1
900	22.1-4.1
901	8.01-581.13,

Acts 1997 Chapter	Code 1950 Section
	38.2-3412.1, 54.1-2400.1, 54.1-3500, 54.1-3501, 54.1-3503, 54.1-3504, 54.1-3505, 54.1-3506, 54.1-3507, 54.1-3508
902	17-79.3
903	58.1-3703
904	36-99.11, 46.2-100, 46.2-676, 46.2-731, 46.2-1237R, 46.2-1240—46.2-1259
905	46.2-752
906	32.1-87, 54.1-3408
907	2.1-442
908	46.2-844
909	58.1-322
910	22.1-287
911	46.2-752, 58.1-3916
912	46.2-1220
913	38.2-3430.1—38.2-3430.10, 38.2-3431, 38.2-3432R, 38.2-3432.1—38.2-3432.3, 38.2-3433, 38.2-3434—38.2-3437, 38.2-4214, 38.2-4216.1, 38.2-4217, 38.2-4229.1, 38.2-4306, 38.2-4319, 38.2-4322, 38.2-4323, 58.1-2501
914	2.1-37.8:1, 2.1-37.17:1
915	24.2-651.1
916	18.2-308
917	2.1-563.31, 59.1-467—59.1-469
918	3.1-796.126:8—3.1-796.126:11
919	40.1-6
920	2.1-37.8:1
921	8.01-2, 8.01-68, 11-9.1, 13.1-506, 13.1-562, 14.1-112, 18.2-308, 18.2-308.1:2, 24.2-232, 26-6, 26-17.4, 26-30, 26-50, 26-59, 37.1-67.3, 37.1-89, 37.1-109, 37.1-128.01—37.1-134.5R, 37.1-134.6—37.1-134.22, 37.1-137.1—37.1-137.5, 37.1-144, 46.2-400, 54.1-2976, 58.1-3015, 63.1-55.6, 63.1-107, 65.2-525, n.
922	18.2-308
923	22.1-199.1

ACTS 1998

Acts 1998 Chapter	Code 1950 Section
1	24.2-302
2	16.1-69.6:1
3	17-119.1:2
4	22.1-163, 22.1-167.2
6	18.2-122R
7	9-145.48
8	18.2-144.1
9	6.1-249
10	6.1-370, 6.1-378.2
11	38.2-5701, 38.2-5702
12	38.2-512
13	9-326
14	14.1-125.2, n.
15	38.2-407
16	13.1-400.1, 13.1-400.3, 13.1-400.4, 13.1-400.4:1, 13.1-400.5, 38.2-1800, 38.2-1814, 38.2-1824
17	38.2-316
18	6.1-13
19	6.1-94, 6.1-194.85, 6.1-194.149
20	2.1-234.5, 2.1-329R, 2.1-360
21	2.1-234.5, 2.1-328.15, 2.1-329R, 2.1-360
22	13.1-501, 13.1-504
23	6.1-225.61:1
24	38.2-3430.2, 38.2-3430.4, 38.2-3430.6, 38.2-3431, 38.2-3432.1, 38.2-3432.2, 38.2-3432.3, 38.2-3435, 38.2-3514.2, 38.2-3531
25	38.2-3430.3:1
26	38.2-3431, 38.2-3433
27	2.1-1.6, 2.1-20.4, 9-6.25:2, 13.1-549, 13.1-1111, 22.1-140, 54.1-300, 54.1-400, 54.1-403, 54.1-407
28	62.1-44.15:5.2
29	54.1-2108
30	40.1-79.01
31	9-170
32	55-79.44, 55-79.52, 55-79.54, 55-79.57, 55-79.73, 55-79.73:1, 55-79.77, 55-79.97, 55-508, 55-511, 55-512, 55-514, 55-515.1, 55-515.2, 55-516.2
33	6.1-416.1
34	6.1-225.6
35	2.1-20.1
37	37.1-67.1
38	17-228
39	2.1-1.5, 2.1-179, 9-6.14:4.1, 15.2-5002, 23-9.2:3, 23-38.72, 23-38.30—23-38.44:4R
42	38.2-203, 38.2-1322, 38.2-1401, 38.2-4302, 38.2-4309, 38.2-4319, 38.2-4509
43	38.2-3418.3, 38.2-4319
44	6.1-298, 6.1-300
45	23-231.15, 23-231.16, 23-231.17
46	38.2-1866, 38.2-1868.1, 38.2-1869, 38.2-1872
47	38.2-514.2, 38.2-1800, 38.2-1814, 38.2-1815, 38.2-1824
48	6.1-58.2
49	38.2-3407.3
50	9-310
51	58.1-346.8
52	44-60, 65.2-101
53	9-183.3
54	16.1-309.6
55	23-231.15, 23-231.16, 23-231.17
56	2.1-20.1, 32.1-325, 38.2-3418.4, 38.2-4319
57	18.2-340.16, 18.2-340.33
58	2.1-1.7, 9-6.25:2, 9-145.21—9-145.29R
60	38.2-1026
61	23-38.75, 23-38.77
62	23-7.4:2
63	56-240
64	56-531
65	65.2-603
66	22.1-346
67	59.1-470—59.1-474
68	65.2-520
69	6.1-2.19, 6.1-2.20, 6.1-2.21, 6.1-2.23, 6.1-330.72
70	22.1-147
71	54.1-3925
72	22.1-253.13:4
73	22.1-138.1
74	58.1-3823
75	17-79.3
76	37.1-134.13:1
77	4.1-207
78	23-231.3, 23-231.4
79	23-7.4:2
80	63.1-47
81	18.2-140

Acts 1998 Chapter	Code 1950 Section
82	10.1-409
83	8.01-341
84	29.1-700, 29.1-747R, 29.1-749.1
85	23-38.75, 23-38.77
86	10.1-1422.03
87	62.1-44.34:11, 62.1-44.34:12, 62.1-44.34:13
88	28.2-705
89	6.1-330.72, 6.1-330.85
90	62.1-44.34:18
91	60.2-114, 60.2-623
92	56-265.2
93	10.1-104.3
94	65.2-525
95	65.2-705
96	22.1-205
97	9-151, 40.1-6
98	28.2-539
99	3.1-1060
100	65.2-512
101	54.1-3301, 54.1-3303
102	22.1-71
103	22.1-253.13:1
104	57-60, 57-63
105	54.1-3404, 54.1-3448, 54.1-3452
106	22.1-212.2, 22.1-253.13:6
107	63.1-252.1
108	60.2-114, 63.1-274.11
109	63.1-250.1:3
110	29.1-744.2
111	23-214, 23-215
112	54.1-3408, 63.1-73.1
113	19.2-389, 22.1-296.3
114	28.2-204.1
115	63.1-195, 63.1-211.3
116	18.2-250, 18.2-250.1
117	26-4, 26-12.3, 58.1-1712, 58.1-1714
118	2.1-399.1
119	54.1-3926
120	38.2-3418.3, 38.2-4319
121	11-35, 23-76.1
122	9-182, 9-183.1, 9-183.3, 9-183.4, 9-183.6, 9-183.7, 9-183.9, 9-183.11, 9-183.12
123	7.1-10.1
124	46.2-334.01, 46.2-495, 46.2-498
126	63.1-195
127	2.1-563.31, 59.1-467, 59.1-468, 59.1-469
128	22.1-202
129	32.1-138.6—32.1-138.15, 38.2-5400, 38.2-5401, 38.2-5300—38.2-5309R
130	37.1-197.2
131	22.1-208.2:1.1
132	11-35, 23-76.1
133	46.2-1052
134	46.2-1025
135	58.1-322, n., 58.1-322.2, n., 58.1-402, n.
140	40.1-51.4:4
141	38.2-2212
142	38.2-231, 38.2-2114, 38.2-2212
143	65.2-715
144	29.1-306, 29.1-519
145	45.1-226, n., 62.1-44.16, n.
146	38.2-3408, 38.2-4221
147	46.2-208, 46.2-382
148	38.2-3407.4:1
149	63.1-55.02
150	58.1-3818
151	Va. Const., Art. X, § 6, n.
152	24.2-506, 24.2-521, 24.2-543
153	24.2-928
154	38.2-3318R, 38.2-3318.1, 38.2-3319R, 38.2-3319.1, 38.2-3319.2, 38.2-3320R, 38.2-3320.1, 38.2-3321R, 38.2-3321.1, 38.2-3322R, 38.2-3322.1, 38.2-3322.2, 38.2-3323, 38.2-3324, 38.2-3331, 38.2-3521R, 38.2-3521.1, 38.2-3522R, 38.2-3522.1, 38.2-3523R, 38.2-3523.1, 38.2-3523.2, 38.2-3523.3, 38.2-3523.4, 38.2-3524R, 38.2-3525, 38.2-3526, 38.2-3533, 38.2-3543.1, 38.2-3543.2, 38.2-4214, 38.2-4319
155	32.1-248.2
156	10.1-1105, 10.1-1150.1—10.1-1150.6
157	40.1-112
158	54.1-3806.1
159	45.1-361.13
160	28.2-1400, 28.2-1403
161	28.2-102
162	6.1-2.19
163	50-73.2, 50-73.69, 50-73.78, 50-73.130, 50-73.133
164	38.2-1800, 38.2-1814, 38.2-1824
165	2.1-1.5, 56-484.8—56-484.11
166	38.2-401
167	10.1-409
168	10.1-112
169	54.1-2810, n.
172	10.1-2212, 58.1-3607
173	59.1-148.3
174	46.2-749.2:14
175	46.2-746.7
176	51.1-124.22
178	15.2-2119.1
179	29.1-529, 29.1-544
180	15.2-903
181	46.2-749.2:14
182	15.2-2114
183	8.01-66.5
186	Va. Const., Art. II, § 1, n.
187	24.2-115, 24.2-636
188	15.2-5156
189	4.1-103.01
190	17-95.1, 17-116.01:1
191	24.2-303
192	63.1-47
193	51.1-142
194	15.2-963
195	2.1-20.1:2, 2.1-20.1:3, 2.1-20.1:4
196	51.1-124.20, 51.1-124.26
197	58.1-2627, 58.1-2628
198	15.2-1802
199	8.01-654.1
200	19.2-298.01
201	58.1-4007.1
202	55-58.1
203	8.01-195.3
204	53.1-121
205	11-70
207	2.1-483.1:1
208	4.1-207
209	16.1-69.40:1
210	21-291.2
212	42.1-35
213	26-45.1
214	55-19
215	55-169

Acts 1998 Chapter	Code 1950 Section
216	28.2-1001
217	32.1-277, 32.1-281
219	33.1-56
220	58.1-3732.3
221	15.2-2245.1
222	9-97, 11-45
223	15.2-2119
224	15.2-2143
225	11-9.2
226	17-234
227	45.1-361.43, 45.1-361.44
228	45.1-361.35
229	45.1-361.29
230	38.2-1601, 38.2-1603, 38.2-1604, 38.2-1606, 38.2-1618, 38.2-1620, 38.2-1621, 38.2-1622
231	6.1-398, 6.1-399, 6.1-400R, 6.1-402R, 6.1-405R, 6.1-407R
232	57-60, 57-63
233	10.1-2211
234	64.1-16.1
235	58.1-3122.2, 58.1-3172.1
236	27-36
237	63.1-202
238	4.1-324
239	58.1-346.3:1
240	53.1-45
241	60.2-618
242	59.1-470—59.1-474
244	2.1-457.2, n.
245	2.1-116.09
246	24.2-506, 24.2-521, 24.2-543
247	62.1-44.15, n., 62.1-44.18:2, n.
248	10.1-109, n.
250	11-41.4
251	19.2-398
252	56-501R, 56-501.01R, 56-502
253	58.1-439.7, 58.1-439.8, 58.1-445.1R
254	24.2-700, 24.2-701
255	13.1-504
256	15.2-1512.1
257	2.1-20.1, 32.1-325
258	57-15
259	8.01-329, 14.1-103
260	55-248.6
261	54.1-2103
262	54.1-2103
263	2.1-116.03, 2.1-116.07
264	24.2-633, 24.2-634, 24.2-639
265	54.1-2106.1
266	16.1-107
267	2.1-505, n.
268	54.1-2105
269	55-243
270	24.2-669
271	54.1-1103
272	58.1-3665
274	58.1-3237
276	14.1-70
277	17-237
279	8.01-360
280	16.1-299.1, 19.2-310.2, 19.2-310.3, 19.2-310.4, 19.2-310.5
281	18.2-32
282	10.1-109, n.
283	58.1-346.8
284	46.2-749.2:14.1, 46.2-749.2:15, 46.2-749.2:16
285	46.2-604
286	46.2-746.11
287	22.1-178
288	46.2-746.11:1
289	32.1-102.1
290	14.1-70
291	58.1-332
292	58.1-332.1
293	46.2-746.11:2
294	46.2-746.11:3
295	46.2-746.11:4
297	46.2-746.11:5, 46.2-746.12
298	46.2-357
299	46.2-1172
300	46.2-1079
301	4.1-111
302	46.2-604
303	8.01-581.09, 8.01-581.010
305	14.1-70
307	14.1-70
308	22.1-226.1—22.1-226.4
309	22.1-32
311	53.1-129
313	15.2-2118
314	8.01-399
315	32.1-70, 32.1-70.1R
316	54.1-2943
317	9-313, n., 32.1-111.3
318	32.1-330.3, 38.2-226.2
319	54.1-2900, 54.1-2950.1, 54.1-2951R, 54.1-2951.1—54.1-2951.3
320	29.1-101, 29.1-101.01, 58.1-638
321	33.1-46.2
322	46.2-323, 46.2-335, 46.2-342, 46.2-345, 46.2-1191, 58.1-2403
323	46.2-666
324	15.2-2404
325	46.2-1503.3, 46.2-1521, 46.2-1527.1, 46.2-1527.2, 46.2-1527.3, 46.2-1527.5, 46.2-1581, 46.2-1921, 46.2-1992.19, 46.2-1993.19
326	54.1-2712.1, 54.1-2726.1
327	14.1-70
328	15.2-2143
329	33.1-400, 33.1-403
330	33.1-72.1, 33.1-75.1
331	34-6
332	58.1-3505
333	58.1-811
334	33.1-75.3
335	58.1-478
337	58.1-3812, 58.1-3814
338	33.1-72.1
339	54.1-3935
340	33.1-72.1, 33.1-75.1
341	33.1-75.3
342	33.1-75.3
345	15.2-705
346	15.2-2308
347	58.1-3732.4
349	58.1-803
350	53.1-121
351	22.1-217.01
352	58.1-342
353	19.2-298.01
354	24.2-114
355	22.1-277.02, 22.1-277.1
356	38.2-508.4, n.
357	11-41.2:3
358	58.1-1823
359	2.1-548.32
360	23-231.14, 23-231.16
361	58.1-3211, 58.1-3506.2
362	23-9.2:3
363	18.2-371.2
364	4.1-103.01
365	58.1-2500, 58.1-2510
367	58.1-439
368	24.2-309.1
369	15.2-705
370	46.2-733
371	58.1-339.2
372	58.1-339.2
373	23-38.78, 58.1-322
374	58.1-1823
375	58.1-3916
376	15.2-953

Acts 1998 Chapter	Code 1950 Section
377	23-7.4:1
378	14.1-112, n.
379	22.1-277
380	15.2-1541.1
381	46.2-749.7:3
382	24.2-919
383	2.1-27.10
384	55-519
385	15.2-2286
386	2.1-20.1
387	Va. Const., Art. VII, § 2, n.
388	65.2-1201
389	51.1-168
391	46.2-1224
392	26-48, 26-51
393	46.2-1508.1
394	3.1-796.90
395	22.1-32
396	23-214, 23-215
397	63.1-195, 63.1-211.3
398	18.2-340.16, 18.2-340.33
399	62.1-198, 62.1-199, 62.1-203, 62.1-204, 62.1-206, 62.1-207, 62.1-208, 62.1-209, 62.1-210, 62.1-213, 62.1-214, 62.1-215, 62.1-216, 62.1-216.1, 62.1-219
400	11-14
401	46.2-1179.1
402	8.01-8
403	46.2-1224
404	46.2-706, 46.2-708
405	19.2-389
407	51.1-155, 51.1-162, 51.1-207
408	51.1-142
410	26-48, 26-49, 26-51
411	46.2-892
412	22.1-296.2
413	15.2-1610
414	38.2-1403, 38.2-1413, 38.2-1414, 38.2-1415, 38.2-1421, 38.2-1423, 38.2-1433
415	29.1-521
416	24.2-914.1
417	46.2-1025
418	46.2-1510
419	46.2-1021
420	10.1-1176, 58.1-1604, 58.1-1605, 58.1-1609
421	46.2-1179.1
423	46.2-882
424	46.2-1224
425	15.2-1704
426	33.1-90
427	2.1-41.2, 2.1-342, 2.1-467, 2.1-467.2, 2.1-467.4, 2.1-467.5, 2.1-467.7, 2.1-467.8, 7.1-28, 7.1-29, 9-361, 15.2-1412, 28.2-1200, 41.1-1, 41.1-2, 41.1-5, 41.1-6, 41.1-7, 41.1-15, 42.1-1, 42.1-12, 42.1-13, 42.1-14, 42.1-15, 42.1-16, 42.1-18, 42.1-30, 42.1-31, 42.1-32.7, 42.1-77, 42.1-79, 42.1-79.1, 42.1-80, 42.1-81, 42.1-85, 42.1-86, 42.1-86.1, 42.1-88, 42.1-89, 55-186.2, 55-200, 58.1-3129, 58.1-3306
428	19.2-250
429	46.2-746.11:6, 46.2-746.12
430	46.2-492
431	65.2-604
432	13.1-1005, 13.1-1010.1, 13.1-1011.1, 13.1-1022, 13.1-1024, 13.1-1039, 13.1-1040.1, 13.1-1046, 13.1-1050.1, 58.1-1813, 63.1-325
433	2.1-504.2, n., 33.1-3, n.
434	16.1-248.2
435	22.1-254.1
436	19.2-81.5
437	46.2-502
438	2.1-116.07
439	46.2-872
440	19.2-163
441	33.1-41.1
442	36-55.30, 36-55.40, 36-55.44
443	29.1-700, 29.1-747R 29.1-748, 29.1-749
444	58.1-3823
445	19.2-389
446	37.1-65, 37.1-67.3
447	37.1-3
448	18.2-74.2
449	2.1-20.1:2, 23-50.16:5, 23-50.16:24, 23-50.16:24.1, 23-50.16:24.2, 23-50.16:32, 51.1-126.2R
450	32.1-127
451	19.2-163
452	55-246.1
453	2.1-373.4R
454	55-79.52, 55-79.80:3, 55-79.97
455	37.1-89
456	22.1-253.13:3
457	15.2-2244
458	54.1-3000, 54.1-3005
459	32.1-325
460	55-362, 55-366, 55-367, 55-368, 55-369, 55-370, 55-370.1, 55-371, 55-374, 55-374.1, 55-374.2, 55-375, 55-376, 55-380, 55-382, 55-386, 55-389, 55-391.1, 55-394.1, 55-396
461	55-248.38:1
462	55-248.11
463	55-79.97, 55-484, 55-512, 55-530
466	2.1-512
467	2.1-394, 2.1-394.1, 2.1-397.1, 2.1-399.1, 2.1-399.2
468	63.1-14, 63.1-15
469	54.1-2400
470	8.01-413, 32.1-127.1:01, 32.1-127.1:03, 42.1-77, 54.1-111, 54.1-2403.2, 54.1-2403.3, 54.1-3401, 54.1-3434, 54.1-3434.01
471	9-170
472	46.2-336
478	24.2-105.1
479	10.1-2202.2
480	5.1-2.16, 5.1-51, 5.1-52
481	58.1-609.5
482	16.1-69.25:1, 16.1-77, 16.1-88.01, 16.1-92, 16.1-122
483	23-9.2:3, 23-38.12
484	19.2-368.2, 19.2-368.3, 19.2-368.3:1, 19.2-368.5, 19.2-368.5:1, 19.2-368.6, 19.2-368.11:1
485	19.2-11.01, 19.2-264.4, 19.2-295.3
486	58.1-439.9
487	10.1-1011, 58.1-3205

Acts 1998 Chapter	Code 1950 Section
488	15.2-1535, 16.1-316
489	4.1-206, 4.1-231, 4.1-233
490	54.1-3415, 54.1-3422, 54.1-3423, 54.1-3424
491	58.1-339.4
492	58.1-608.3
493	8.01-225
494	63.1-249.1
495	16.1-69.25:1, 16.1-77, 16.1-88.01, 16.1-92, 16.1-122
496	54.1-2912.2
497	58.1-608.3
498	2.1-234.11, 2.1-234.12, 2.1-234.13, 2.1-234.14, 2.1-234.16, 2.1-234.20, 2.1-234.21, 2.1-234.23, 2.1-234.25, 2.1-234.27, 53.1-82.3
499	63.1-249.1
500	8.01-225
501	46.2-749.6:1.1
502	15.2-106
503	58.1-3714
504	2.1-234.11, 2.1-234.12, 2.1-234.13, 2.1-234.14, 2.1-234.16, 2.1-234.20, 2.1-234.21, 2.1-234.23, 2.1-234.25, 2.1-234.27, 53.1-82.3
505	32.1-64.1, 32.1-64.2
506	32.1-64.1, 32.1-64.2
507	2.1-124
508	46.2-738.1
509	29.1-748, n.
510	2.1-124
511	46.2-746.01
512	29.1-700, 29.1-747R, 29.1-749.2
513	32.1-64.1, 32.1-64.2
514	29.1-700, 29.1-738.03, 29.1-747R
515	29.1-700, 29.1-736, 29.1-747R, 29.1-801, 29.1-808, 29.1-808.1, 29.1-813, 29.1-818
516	58.1-3230, 58.1-3666
518	18.2-190.1—18.2-190.4
519	19.2-163.2
520	15.2-2308
521	16.1-305
522	46.2-380
523	9-170
524	2.1-1.6, 3.1-1104, 3.1-1105, 9-6.25:1
525	33.1-371.1
526	19.2-163.2
528	15.2-2308
529	58.1-1825, 58.1-3981, 58.1-3984
530	19.2-163.2
531	29.1-744.1
532	58.1-3818
533	29.1-700
534	2.1-757
535	4.1-210, 4.1-230, 4.1-231, 4.1-233
536	2.1-440.1
537	29.1-700, 29.1-744.1R, 29.1-747R, 29.1-748
538	16.1-309.8
539	2.1-1.6, 3.1-1104, 3.1-1105, 9-6.25:1
540	33.1-371.1
541	53.1-106
542	58.1-3916
543	62.1-132.20
544	58.1-609.8
545	46.2-1220
546	46.2-870
547	46.2-1304
548	33.1-253, n.
549	24.2-115.1, 24.2-712
550	16.1-242.1, 16.1-253, 16.1-281, 16.1-282, 16.1-282.1, 16.1-283, 16.1-296, 16.1-298
551	63.1-198, 63.1-198.1, 63.1-198.2, 63.1-198.3, 63.1-198.4, 63.1-199
552	63.1-172, 63.1-174.1
553	62.1-69.25—62.1-69.33
554	32.1-325
555	46.2-803.1
556	25-46.5
557	54.1-2900, 54.1-2954, 54.1-2954.1, 54.1-2955, 54.1-2956, 54.1-2956.01
558	32.1-325, 63.1-25
559	58.1-1823, n.
560	46.2-870
563	29.1-700, 29.1-747R, 29.1-749.3
564	54.1-2987.1
565	33.1-252
566	19.2-8
567	22.1-253.13:3
568	15.2-2118
569	18.2-60.4, 18.2-119, 18.2-308.1:4, 19.2-81.3, 19.2-152.8, 19.2-152.9, 19.2-152.10
570	18.2-60.3
571	32.1-325
572	24.2-115.1, 24.2-712
574	46.2-1304
576	16.1-249
577	8.01-654
578	10.1-1181.1, 10.1-1181.2
579	18.2-74.2
580	54.1-2914
581	63.1-198, 63.1-198.1, 63.1-198.2, 63.1-198.3, 63.1-198.4, 63.1-199
582	24.2-230, 24.2-232, 24.2-410, 37.1-134.6, 37.1-134.14, 37.1-134.15, 37.1-134.18, 37.1-137.2
583	15.2-912.1
584	8.01-424
585	15.2-2291
586	3.1-22.49
587	Va. Const., Art. VII, § 10, n.
589	9-96, 9-97
590	38.2-415, 52-36, 58.1-2508
591	2.1-399.1
592	20-49.8, 20-108.1
593	54.1-2900, 54.1-2956.1, 54.1-2956.4, 54.1-2956.5
594	37.1-67.1
595	22.1-89.3
596	8.01-243.2, 8.01-271.1, 8.01-410, 8.01-644.1, 53.1-60.1
597	54.1-3420.2
598	6.1-2.20
599	58.1-438.1
600	22.1-32
602	22.1-253.13:4, 22.1-199.2, 22.1-209.1:4, 22.1-253.13:1, 22.1-253.13:3, 22.1-253.13:4, 22.1-254.01
603	64.1-5.1
604	20-107.1, 20-109
605	28.2-1203
606	58.1-3661
607	8.01-424
608	59.1-365, 59.1-392
609	15.2-2230.1
610	8.01-424, 26-12, 26-15, 26-20.1, 55-59.4, 64.1-133R, 64.1-134, 64.1-135
611	37.1-67.01, 37.1-67.1
612	20-108.1
613	Va. Const., Art. VII, § 10, n.

Acts 1998 Chapter	Code 1950 Section
614	54.1-2961
615	19.2-76
616	20-103
617	55-527
618	20-108.2
619	9-6.14:4.1, 11-45, 59.1-364, 59.1-365, 59.1-369, 59.1-370, 59.1-371, 59.1-374, 59.1-389, 59.1-390, 59.1-391, 59.1-392
620	22.1-258
621	22.1-298
622	2.1-746, 9-6.23, 9-267, 9-268, 9-270, 9-271, 9-272
623	15.2-2257, 55-508, 55-509
624	8.01-622.1
625	38.2-3418.5, 38.2-4319
627	22.1-199.2, 22.1-209.1:4, 22.1-253.13:1, 22.1-253.13:3, 22.1-253.13:4, 22.1-254.01
628	54.1-2987.1
629	63.1-24, n.
630	54.1-2901, 54.1-2982, 54.1-2987.1
631	2.1-20.1, 32.1-325, 38.2-3418.6, 38.2-4319
633	56-247, n.
634	36-96.10, 36-96.11
636	2.1-7.4
637	54.1-3935
638	20-155
639	8.01-451
640	15.2-1215
641	3.1-418.1, 35.1-14.2
642	15.2-2293.1
643	15.2-2108.1
645	58.1-609.6
647	14.1-82.1
648	58.1-3927R, 58.1-3128, 58.1-3919, 58.1-3934, 58.1-3937R, 58.1-3939.1R, 58.1-3940, 58.1-3958, 58.1-3980
649	46.2-752, 58.1-3916
650	14.1-118.1
651	17-83.1:1—17-83.1:4
652	15.2-2108.1
653	32.1-325
654	46.2-746.8:1
655	22.1-277.01:1, 22.1-277.01:2
656	16.1-122.1
657	51.1-124.11, 51.1-159
658	51.1-602
660	51.1-144
661	51.1-126.5
662	18.2-308
663	46.2-833.01
664	36-106
665	2.1-1.7, 2.1-373, 2.1-373.02, 9-6.25:1
666	11-45
667	37.1-195
668	15.2-4203, 15.2-4207—15.2-4210
669	8.01-225.2
670	18.2-308
671	59.1-207.11, 59.1-207.13, 59.1-207.16:1
672	2.1-37.12:1, 2.1-37.12:2
674	51.1-155, 51.1-157, 51.1-206, 51.1-306
675	51.1-142
676	2.1-20.1:2, 2.1-20.1:3, 2.1-20.1:4, 51.1-142, 51.1-155.2, 51.1-165, 51.1-206
677	16.1-253.4
678	51.1-124.1, n.
679	18.2-340.32
680	37.1-48.1, 37.1-98, 37.1-194—37.1-199, 37.1-202.1, 37.1-242, 37.1-243, 37.1-245—37.1-248.1, 37.1-250—37.1-253
681	46.2-1571
682	46.2-1569
683	15.2-2232
684	16.1-253.1, 16.1-253.4, 16.1-279.1, 18.2-119, 19.2-81, 19.2-152.8, 19.2-152.9, 19.2-152.10
685	46.2-833.01
686	15.2-4203, 15.2-4207—15.2-4210
687	18.2-60
688	18.2-251
689	51.1-142
690	36-49.1:1
691	54.1-1115
692	45.1-241
693	36-139, 63.1-87, n., 63.1-110, n.
694	58.1-3713.01
695	45.1-161.292:2, 45.1-161.292:4, 45.1-161.292:7, 45.1-161.292:8, 45.1-161.292:15, 45.1-161.292:26, 45.1-161.292:29, 45.1-161.292:30, 45.1-161.292:32, 45.1-161.292:33, 45.1-161.292:35, 45.1-161.292:36, 45.1-161.292:37, 45.1-161.292:38, 45.1-161.292:44, 45.1-161.292:46, 45.1-161.292:47, 45.1-161.292:49, 45.1-161.292:50, 45.1-161.292:51, 45.1-161.292:54, 45.1-161.292:55, 45.1-161.292:56, 45.1-161.292:62, 45.1-161.292:63, 45.1-161.292:64, 45.1-161.292:66, 45.1-161.292:70, 45.1-161.292:71, 45.1-161.292:73, 45.1-161.294, 45.1-161.296, 45.1-161.305, 45.1-161.307, 45.1-225.1, 45.1-225.2
696	15.2-1800
697	11-45
698	2.1-20.1:05
699	2.1-20.1:04
700	10.1-2109
701	2.1-1.7, 2.1-51.21, 9-6.25:1, 9-329.1, 9-329.2
702	22.1-79.1
703	18.2-271.1, 32.1-73.2, 46.2-411
704	16.1-241.3, 63.1-248.3, 63.1-248.6
705	10.1-1454.1
706	3.1-461.1—3.1-461.4
707	56-77, 56-82, 56-209, 56-210, 56-212, 56-217, 56-217.1, 56-218, 56-225, 56-226, 56-229
708	2.1-1.6, 9-6.25:2, 54.1-2310—54.1-2342, 57-35.11R
709	2.1-20.1, 32.1-325, 38.2-3418.7, 38.2-4319
710	46.2-746.11:7
712	2.1-133.6, 2.1-133.7:1, 2.1-133.8, 2.1-133.9, 2.1-133.10
713	24.2-222
714	10.1-2109
715	9-365
716	16.1-241.3,

Acts 1998 Chapter	Code 1950 Section
	63.1-248.3, 63.1-248.6
717	10.1-1454.1
718	32.1-307, 54.1-2800, 54.1-2825, 54.1-2973
719	22.1-154—22.1-158
720	19.2-353.3
721	2.1-1.6, 9-6.25:2, 54.1-2310—54.1-2342, 57-35.11
722	8.01-44.5
723	8.01-513
724	2.1-1.7, 9-6.23, 9-6.25:1, 18.2-254, 37.1-203—37.1 207, 37.1-208R, 37.1-209R, 37.1-214R, 37.1-215R, 37.1-216R, 37.1-217R, 37.1-218R, 37.1-219, 37.1-223
725	22.1-208.01
726	38.2-2232
727	20-60.3, 20-79.1, 20-79.2, 20-79.3, 20-88.32, 20-88.64, 63.1-249, 63.1-249, 63.1-250, 63.1-250.3, 63.1-256, 63.1-257, 63.1-258.1
728	15.2-4905, 15.2-4907, 15.2-4917
729	58.1-3819
730	Va. Const., Art. VI, § 10, n.
731	19.2-353.3
732	2.1-639.15, 2.1-639.41, 2.1-786
733	58.1-3819
735	55-19.5
736	6.1-2.19
737	8.01-513
738	54.1-2820
739	54.1-500, 54.1-501, 54.1-503, 54.1-512, 54.1-513R, 54.1-516, 54.1-517
740	33.1-221.1:3, 58.1-815.1
742	56-458, 56-462, 56-468.1, 56-468.2, 56-458, n.
743	46.2-223
744	32.1-122.10:01, 38.2-4308, 54.1-114, 54.1-2400.2, 54.1-2400.3, 54.1-2909, 54.1-2910.1
745	60.2-114, 60.2-623
746	51.1-142, n., 51.1-143, n., 51.1-147, n., 51.1-155, 51.1-155.1
748	22.1-212.5—22.1-212.15
749	46.2-360, 46.2-361
750	8.01-129
751	55-514
752	15.2-1812
753	11-42, 11-63, 11-65, 11-70
754	43-13, 54.1-1100, 54.1-1101, 54.1-1103, 54.1-1106, 54.1-1108.2, 54.1-1111
755	36-97, 36-99
756	15.2-1215
757	2.1-37.17:1
758	56-458, 56-462, 56-468.1, 56-468.2
759	59.1-274.2, 59.1-280, 59.1-280.1, 59.1-280.2
760	63.1-248.9
761	33.1-221.1:3, 58.1-815.1
762	15.2-2108
763	46.2-749.2:13
765	30-19.1:8
766	Va. Const., Art. X, § 6, n.
767	Va. Const., Art. VII, § 10 n.
768	Va. Const., Art. VI, § 10, n.
769	Va. Const., Art. VII, § 2, n.
770	Va. Const., Art. II, § 1, n.
771	Va. Const., Art. VII, § 10, n.
772	32.1-25
773	19.2-158
774	51.1-513R, 51.1-1100—51.1-1140
775	63.1-58.2
776	53.1-116
777	2.1-343.1:1
778	10.1-202.1
779	16.1-122.1
780	10.1-107, 10.1-200, 10.1-200.1
781	63.1-251.4
783	14.1-112, 14.1-134.1, 16.1-273, 18.2-251, 18.2-251.01, 18.2-251.02, 18.2-252, 18.2-270.1, 18.2-271.3, 19.2-299, 19.2-299.2
784	2.1-1.5, 2.1-179, 9-6.14:4.1, 15.2-5002, 23-9.2:3, 23-38.30R, 23-38.72
785	19.2-298.1—19.2-298.4, 19.2-390.1, 19.2-390.2
786	9-96R, 9-99R, 23-287—23-290
787	2.1-1.6, 2.1-371, 2.1-373.10, 2.1-373.14, 9-6.25:1, 37.1-134.6, 37.1-134.14:1, 37.1-134.19
788	18.2-60
789	46.2-910
790	2.1-20.3, 2.1-20.4, 9-14, 9-371, 9-372—9-377, 14.1-18
791	9-97, 11-45
792	46.2-334.01, 46.2-495, 46.2-498
793	2.1-51.14
794	32.1-102.3:2, 32.1-102.3:2.1R, 32.1-102.4
795	32.1-176.5:1, 55-519, 62.1-44.15:4.1
796	54.1-3900, 54.1-3919, 54.1-3922, 54.1-3925.1, 54.1-3926, 54.1-3928, 54.1-3931
797	24.2-640
798	53.1-32
799	9-99.01, 9-99.02
800	22.1-253.13:1
801	15.2-2307
802	46.2-208, 46.2-819, 46.2-819.1
803	32.1-111.4, 32.1-111.5, 54.1-2901, 54.1-2982, 54.1-2987.1, 54.1-2988, 54.1-2989
804	2.1-37.17:1
805	62.1-44.15, 62.1-44.17:1
806	22.1-277.03
807	9-182, 9-183.1, 9-183.3, 9-183.4, 9-183.6, 9-183.7, 9-183.9, 9-183.11, 9-183.12
808	2.1-707, 2.1-708, 2.1-710.1—2.1-710.3
812	30-19.1:3, 58.1-609.1, 58.1-609.4, 58.1-609.6—58.1-609.10
813	51.1-142, 51.1-143
815	22.1-70.1
816	22.1 253.13:1

Acts 1998 Chapter	Code 1950 Section
817	3.1-796.66, 3.1-796.67:2, 3.1-796.68, 3.1-796.72, 3.1-796.83:2, 3.1-796.92, 3.1-796.93:1, 3.1-796.94, 3.1-796.96, 3.1-796.97:1, 3.1-796.101, 3.1-796.102, 3.1-796.104—3.1-796.108, 3.1-796.109R, 3.1-796.110—3.1-796.119, 3.1-796.121, 3.1-796.122, 3.1-796.124, 3.1-796.126:1, 3.1-796.126:7, 3.1-796.126:8, 3.1-796.126:10, 3.1-796.126:11, 3.1-796.127, 3.1-796.128
818	53.1-262
819	59.1-77R, 59.1-92.1—59.1-92.21
820	8.01-195.3
821	18.2-95, 18.2-108.1
822	51.1-126.6
823	15.2-1427
825	18.2-370.01
826	22.1-253.13:5, 22.1-298
827	46.2-1550, 46.2-1952, 46.2-1992.44
828	22.1-199.1
829	16.1-241, 16.1-349—16.1-355
830	16.1-249
831	19.2-354, 46.2-395
833	15.2-4305, 15.2-4307, 15.2-4308, 15.2-4309, 15.2-4313
834	19.2-298.1—19.2-298.4, 19.2-390.1, 19.2-390.2
835	33.1-375.1
836	62.1-44.34:18
837	10.1-1455, 10.1-2500
838	2.1-639.6
839	2.1-343.1:1
840	14.1-112, 14.1-134.1, 16.1-273, 18.2-251, 18.2-251.01, 18.2-251.02, 18.2-252, 18.2-270.1, 18.2-271.3, 19.2-299, 19.2-299.2
842	9-365.1
843	22.1-253.13:3
844	18.2-308.2:2
845	18.2-340.19, 59.1-369
846	18.2-308
847	18.2-308
848	54.1-4000—54.1-4005, 54.1-4006R, 54.1-4007R, 54.1-4008, 54.1-4009—54.1-4014, 59.1-200
849	46.2-746.11:8, 46.2-746.12:2
850	63.1-172, 63.1-179.1, 63.1-180
851	2.1-20.1
852	22.1-217, 22.1-253.13:5, 22.1-298
854	32.1-111.4, 32.1-111.5, 54.1-2901, 54.1-2982, 54.1-2987.1, 54.1-2988, 54.1-2989
855	58.1-3, 58.1-339.5
856	16.1-322.4
857	29.1-744.3
858	2.1-20.1, 32.1-325, 38.2-3418.7, 38.2-4319
860	63.1-196.002
861	8.01-383.1
862	2.1-37.12:1, 2.1-37.12:2
863	62.1-44.15, 62.1-44.17:1
864	15.2-2404
865	15.2-926
866	24.2-101, 24.2-803
867	32.1-305—32.1309R, 54.1-2800, 54.1-2803, n., 54.1-2818.1—54.1-2818.3
868	43-34
869	15.2-5136
870	22.1-288.2
871	22.1-274
872	2.1-20.2, 2.1-20.5—2.1-20.12, 2.1-38, 2.1-38.3, 2.1-68, 2.1-71.2, 2.1-180, 8.01-609.1, 8.01-618.1, 9-178.1, 9-178.2, 9-183.13—9-183.21, 12.1-12, 14.1-1 to 14.1-201R, 15.2-1414.1—15.2-1414.7, 15.2-1508.1—15.2-1508.4, 15.2-1537.1, 15.2-1605.1, 15.2-1608.1, 15.2-1608.2, 15.2-1609.1—15.2-1609.9, 15.2-1612.1, 15.2-1614.1, 15.2-1615.1, 15.2-1627.1, 15.2-1627.2, 15.2-1627.3, 15.2-1635.1, 15.2-1636.1—15.2-1636.19, 16.1-69.48:1—16.1-69.48:4, 17-1 to 17-238R, 17.1-100—17.1-131, 17.1-200—17.1-291, 17.1-300—17.1-329, 17.1-400—17.1-418, 17.1-500—17.1-524, 17.1-600—17.1-629, 17.1-700—17.1-709, 17.1-800—17.1-806, 19.2-46.1, 19.2-46.2, 19.2-47.1, 22.1-32, 22.1-296, 30-14.01, 30-19.11—30-19.20, 37.1-39, 37.1-42.3
873	36-96.6
874	58.1-322, 58.1-402
875	2.1-20.1, 32.1-325
876	2.1-196.2
877	38.2-401
878	22.1-209.1:5
879	22.1-18.1
880	36-27
881	9-6.25:1 9-300—9-333R, 9-341, 9-342, 9-343, 9-346
882	19.2-389, 37.1-197.2
883	46.2-341.4
884	20-49.1, 20-60.3, 20-60.6, 63.1-250.2:1
885	63.1-252.1, 63.1-252.2
886	8.01-452.1
887	18.2-31
888	46.2-100
890	22.1-212.5—22.1-212.15
891	32.1-5, 32.1-122.10:01, 32.1-137.1—

Acts 1998 Chapter	Code 1950 Section
	32.1-137.17, 38.2-511, 38.2-4214, 38.2-4301, 38.2-4302, 38.2-4307, 38.2-4308R, 38.2-4311R, 38.2-4312, 38.2-4316, 38.2-4319, 38.2-4509, 38.2-5400—38.2-5409R, 38.2-5800—38.2-5811
892	18.2-152.4
893	16.1-318, n.
894	58.1-3511
895	54.1-800—54.1-827R, 54.1-828—54.1-835
896	58.1-439.10
897	58.1-400.1, 58.1-2600, 58.1-2662.1
898	36-49.1:1
899	2.1-1.7, 2.1-51.21, 9-6.25:1, 9-329.1, 9-329.2
900	22.1-163, 22.1-167.2
901	22.1-199.1, 22.1-253.13:1
902	22.1-199.1, 22.1-199.2, 22.1-209.1:4, 22.1-253.13:1, 22.1-253.13:3, 22.1-253.13:7, 22.1-254.01, 22.1-278
903	22.1-199.3
904	22.1-274.01
905	33.1-23.03:2, 33.1-46.1, 58.1-638, 58.1-2425
906	15.2-1500
907	33.1-23.03:2, 33.1-46.1, 58.1-638, 58.1-2425
908	38.2-3407.12, 38.2-4214, 38.2-4319

ACTS 1998, SP. SESS.

Acts 1998 Chapter	Code 1950 Section
2	2.1-155, 9-311.1, 15.2-1636.20, 22.1-175.1—22.1-175.4, 46.2-208, 58.1-3523—58.1-3536, 58.1-3912, 58.1-3916.01

ACTS 1999

Acts 1999 Chapter	Code 1950 Section
1	62.1-44.17:1.1
2	38.2-1812.2
3	8.01-357
4	38.2-2204
5	51.1-513.1
6	44-146.27
7	44-146.27
8	28.2-1308, 33.1-223.2:1, 62.1-44.15:5
9	15.2-1627.3, 17.1-275.1 — 17.1-275.5, 17.1-281, 19.2-165, 19.2-354, 53.1-131.1, 53.1-150
10	17.1-507
11	16.1-69.6:1
12	58.1-608.1
14	2.1-118
15	9-99.4
16	26-17.4, 31-1 — 31-9, 31-10 — 31-13R, 31-14, 31-14.1, 31-18.1, 55-44, 55-45R
17	8.01-418.3
18	46.2-1025
19	54.1-2957.01, n.
20	38.2-5802
21	18.2-477.2
22	44-120.1
23	58.1-346.5, n.
24	42.1-53R
32	58.1-346.1:1
33	9-183.1
34	58.1-4019
35	9-299, n., 38.2-3418.10, 38.2-4319
37	54.1-202
38	64.1-16.1
39	36-49.1:1
40	57-61
41	2.1-379
43	16.1-318, n.
44	38.2-1840, 38.2-1841, 38.2-1847, 38.2-1859, 38.2-4802, 38.2- 4803
45	18.2-259.1
47	8.01-243.2
48	8.01-502.1
50	16.1-318, n.
51	2.1-68
52	58.1-3118
53	46.2-1601
54	16.1-260
55	54.1-1118, 54.1-1120
56	18.2-111.2
57	54.1-2017
58	16.1-277.1
59	38.2-1826, 38.2-1842, 38.2-1856, 38.2-1864, 38.2-4803.1, 38.2-5703
60	6.1-58.1
61	38.2-2811
62	6.1-330.77
63	6.1-225.2, 6.1-225.14, 6.1-225.16, 6.1-225.23, 6.1-225.23:1, 6.1-225.27, 6.1-225.53
64	22.1-70.2, 42.1-36.1
65	55-79.80:01, 55-248.18, 55-464.1
66	55-66.5
67	46.2-100
68	46.2-1001
69	7.1-40.11
70	2.1-20.01:1
71	46.2-1220
72	46.2-1025
73	8.01-262
74	26-17.9
75	46.2-1052
76	11-9.6
77	6.1-194.2, 15.2-2247, 46.2-100, 46.2-111, 46.2-653, 46.2-1115, 46.2-1500, 46.2-1900, 55-66.1:1, 55-248.4, 55-248.49, 58.1-2401, 58.1-2403, 58.1-2425, 59.1-207.2, 59.1-313
78	46.2-1217
79	60.2-513, 60.2-536, 60.2-619, 60.2-620
80	55-248.16
81	57-59
82	54.1-2106.1
83	13.1-543, 13.1-1102
84	58.1-1205, 58.1-1207, n.
85	29.1-569
86	38.2-1800, 38.2-1815, 38.2-1816, 38.2-1817, 38.2-1824, 38.2-1866, 38.2-3523.3, 38.2-4224, 38.2-4313
87	46.2-878.2
88	33.1-89
89	24.2-219, n., 24.2-223, n.
90	58.1-3123
91	62.1-44.34:16
92	13.1-514

Acts 1999 Chapter	Code 1950 Section
93	4.1-100
94	58.1-2706
95	6.1-194.12
96	8.9-402
97	38.2-1812
98	4.1-111, 4.1-119
99	58.1-3526
100	13.1-550, 13.1-552, 13.1-1115, 13.1-1117
101	13.1-847
102	13.1-658
103	58.1-106, 58.1-107, 58.1-108
104	62.1-204
105	54.1-2106.1
106	28.2-302.7, 28.2-302.7:1
107	28.2-302.5, 28.2-302.10:1
108	26-17.10
109	6.1-2.10, 6.1-2.13:1
110	10.1-609
111	51.1-126.5, 51.1-153, 51.1-155, 51.1-162, 51.1-165, 51.1-205, 51.1-207, 51.1-308, 51.1-505
112	4.1-230
113	3.1-796.115, 3.1-796.124
114	45.1-235
115	24.2-112
116	38.2-3540.1
117	24.2-408, 24.2-409
118	24.2-404.2, 46.2-208.1
119	62.1-44.34:13
120	24.2-922
121	9-77.11
122	45.1-361.22
123	58.1-3980
124	62.1-44.34:13
125	6.1-125.15
126	15.2-1242
127	11-41.2:3
128	24.2-228
129	38.2-517
130	8.01-262.1
131	53.1-109.01
133	17.1-252
136	15.2-708
138	58.1-602
141	58.1-608.3
142	46.2-870
144	51.1-1100, 51.1-1101, 51.1-1103, 51.1-1104, 51.1-1105, 51.1-1107, 51.1-1110, 51.1-1112, 51.1-1113, 51.1-1114, 51.1-1116, 51.1-1117, 51.1-1118, 51.1-1121, 51.1-1123 — 51.1-1129, 51.1-1131 — 51.1-1135.1
145	1-13.32, 2.1-7.4
146	58.1-15
148	15.2-1636.20
149	55-418
150	52-14
151	15.2-1518
152	58.1-339.2
153	8.01-341.1
154	24.2-443
155	10.1-572
156	58.1-606
157	15.2-4903
158	58.1-408
159	2.1-457.2
160	11-45
161	16.1-296.1R, 20-96.1, 20-96.2R
162	58.1-3245.1
163	17.1-252
164	2.1-27.11
166	46.2-871
171	4.1-100
174	15.2-901, 15.2-906
178	11-41
180	58.1-15
183	58.1-339.2
184	58.1-608.3
185	15.2-1636.20
186	58.1-408
187	58.1-602
188	46.2-1240
189	58.1-3523
190	58.1-3245.1
191	22.1-81
192	58.1-3128, 58.1-3921
193	64.1-136.1
194	11-45
195	33.1-375.1
196	55-9, 55-20.1, 55-21
197	64.1-57.2
198	8.01-582
199	46.2-2503, 46.2-2510.1, 46.2-2511.1
200	58.1-3509, 58.1-3704
201	10.1-1107
202	58.1-3, n., 58.1-3983.1, 58.1-3984
203	58.1-3715
204	29.1-536
205	58.1-3211
206	2.1-21, n.
207	10.1-1183
208	54.1-2012
209	3.1-796.122
210	58.1-346.9
211	46.2-676
212	46.2-613
213	58.1-339.2
215	29.1-109
216	58.1-3013
217	46.2-1575, 46.2-1576, 46.2-1985, 46.2-1986, 46.2-1992.79, 46.2-1992.80, 46.2-1993.76, 46.2-1993.77
219	24.2-632
220	10.1-1105
221	8.01-343
228	58.1-3822
229	58.1-609.2
230	11-35
231	55-248.11
232	46.2-1025
233	58.1-3819
234	58.1-3819
235	59.1-274
236	46.2-752
241	58.1-3819
242	58.1-3822
248	11-35
249	59.1-274
250	15.2-1127
251	36-106
252	64.1-73, 64.1-73.1
253	58.1-3819
254	29.1-112
255	29.1-327
256	45.1-161.8, 45.1-161.17, 45.1-161.32, 45.1-161.58, 45.1-161.59, 45.1-161.63, 45.1-161.64, 45.1-161.65, 45.1-161.66, 45.1-161.70, 45.1-161.77, 45.1-161.78, 45.1-161.80, 45.1-161.83, 45.1-161.87, 45.1-161.88, 45.1-161.108, 45.1-161.109, 45.1-161.114, 45.1-161.115, 45.1-161.116, 45.1-161.117, 45.1-161.118, 45.1-161.121, 45.1-161.123, 45.1-161.124, 45.1-161.129, 45.1-161.133,

Acts 1999 Chapter	Code 1950 Section
	45.1-161.134, 45.1-161.135, 45.1-161.140, 45.1-161.141, 45.1-161.143, 45.1-161.144, 45.1-161.147, 45.1-161.150, 45.1-161.151, 45.1-161.152, 45.1-161.158, 45.1-161.159, 45.1-161.162, 45.1-161.165, 45.1-161.170, 45.1-161.173, 45.1-161.181, 45.1-161.185R, 45.1-161.186, 45.1-161.187, 45.1-161.188, 45.1-161.189, 45.1-161.191, 45.1-161.192R, 45.1-161.193, 45.1-161.194, 45.1-161.195, 45.1-161.196, 45.1-161.197, 45.1-161.203, 45.1-161.207, 45.1-161.209, 45.1-161.210, 45.1-161.211, 45.1-161.213, 45.1-161.220, 45.1-161.221, 45.1-161.222, 45.1-161.227, 45.1-161.228, 45.1-161.230R, 45.1-161.231, 45.1-161.235, 45.1-161.249, 45.1-161.251, 45.1-161.256, 45.1-161.257, 45.1-161.258, 45.1-161.263, 45.1-161.266, 45.1-161.269, 45.1-161.270, 45.1-161.280, 45.1-161.282, 45.1-161.285, 45.1-161.290, 45.1-222, 45.1-224
257	10.1-2117, 10.1-2128, 10.1-2131, 10.1-2132
258	55-248.4
259	54.1-2010
260	58.1-3819
261	54.1-1120
262	54.1-1123
263	55-79.97
266	19.2-71
267	19.2-37
269	18.2-249
273	18.2-268.9
274	18.2-119.1
275	15.2-1717.1
276	38.2-3542
277	53.1-129
278	15.2-1738
279	46.2-1001
281	58.1-638
282	18.2-33
283	15.2-1605.1
284	51.1-124.12
285	58.1-322
286	19.2-298.01, 19.2-368.2, 30-19.1:5
287	33.1-223.2:2
288	13.1-730
289	58.1-3506
290	33.1-369
291	46.2-941
292	46.2-730
293	8.01-226.5
294	18.2-64.2, 18.2-67.4
295	15.2-2403
296	19.2-187
298	58.1-322
299	46.2-640, 58.1-3942
304	58.1-439.11
306	33.1-70.1
307	9-170, 18.2-268.6, n., 18.2-268.9, n., 19.2-188.1, n., 19.2-310.5, n.
308	46.2-205
310	33.1-223.2:3
311	15.2-2118
312	59.1-148.3
313	60.2-526, n.
314	65.2-604
315	33.1-190.3
317	58.1-332
318	33.1-82
319	16.1-69.9:3, 16.1-69.10, 17.1-507, 17.1-511
320	33.1-70.1
321	38.2-3407.3:1
322	19.2-112
323	46.2-941
324	8.01-44.5
325	4.1-206, 4.1-231, 4.1-233
326	8.01-425.1
327	54.1-4005, 54.1-4008, 54.1-4012
328	2.1-51.42, n.
329	46.2-649.1:1, 46.2-681R
330	46.2-342
331	6.1-2.9:8, 9-313, n.
332	33.1-13.1
333	36-105, 36-105.01
334	58.1-608.1
335	40.1-51.8, 40.1-51.19:1 — 40.1-51.19:5
336	7.1-40.11
337	15.2-4904
338	9-49
339	58.1-322, 58.1-402
341	36-105, 36-105.01
342	2.1-738
343	54.1-1128, 54.1-1129—54.1-1132, 54.1-1134, 54.1-1135
344	11-54
345	15.2-3209
346	3.1-17.1
347	15.2-5114, n.
348	18.2-246.1—18.2-248.6, 18.2-248.7R
349	17.1-805
350	16.1-269.2, 16.1-273, 16.1-278.8
351	18.2-130
352	15.2-1730.1
353	8.01-316
354	22.1-175.1—22.1-175.5
355	6.1-378.3
356	59.1-389
357	60.2-113
358	58.1-3506, 58.1-3902, 58.1-3912
359	55-248.4, 55-248.31:01
360	18.2-340.30
361	18.2-340.25
362	36-106
363	17.1-227.1
364	58.1-3813
365	58.1-322
366	58.1-611.1, 58.1-3833, 58.1-3840
367	18.2-61, 18.2-67.1, 18.2-67.2, 18.2-67.2:1
368	22.1-3
369	17.1-227.1
370	16.1-94.01
371	19.2-152.8, 19.2-152.9, 19.2-152.10
372	19.2-303.3, 53.1-181, 53.1-182, 53.1-182.1,

Acts 1999 Chapter	Code 1950 Section
	53.1-184.2R
373	6.1-330.77
374	24.2-1019
375	15.2-1505
376	3.1-796.106:1
377	22.1-253.13:1
378	26-17.4, 26-18, 26-19, 26-20
379	15.2-4902
380	4.1-111, n., 4.1-227, n.
381	23-38.56
382	55-248.25:1
383	19.2-389
384	2.1-114.5, 2.1-116, n.
385	2.1-20.1:5
386	15.2-2404, 15.2-2413
387	59.1-207.16
388	22.1-122.1
389	58.1-3958
390	55-248.4, 55-248.31:01
391	22.1-175.1—22.1-175.5
392	36-106
393	54.1-1106
394	22.1-5
395	22.1-266
396	58.1-1101, 58.1-3507
397	58.1-638
400	58.1-811
401	58.1-609.1
403	58.1-3967
404	58.1-339.6
405	33.1-191
407	51.1-142
408	15.2-4904
409	15.2-2021
410	36-49.1:1
411	56-576—56-595
412	2.1-1.1, 2.1-1.3, 2.1-1.7, 2.1-20.4, 2.1-51.27, 2.1-51.40, 2.1-51.44—2.1-51.50, 2.1-563.16, 2.1-563.17, 2.1-563.28—2.1-563.35R, 2.1-563.35:1—2.1-563.38, 2.1-563.40, 2.1-563.41, 9-6.14:4.1, 9-6.23, 9-6.25:1, 9-6.25:2, 9-145.50R, 9-145.51R, 9-145.53, 9-145.56, 9-253, 9-266.4, 9-361, 42.1-80
414	15.2-4904
415	56-210
416	13.1-657
417	15.2-2021
418	36-49.1:1
419	56-232
421	2.1-1.1, 2.1-1.3, 2.1-1.7, 2.1-20.4, 2.1-51.27, 2.1-51.40, 2.1-51.44—2.1-51.50, 2.1-563.16, 2.1-563.17, 2.1-563.28—2.1-563.35R, 2.1-563.35:1—2.1-563.38, 2.1-563.40, 2.1-563.41, 9-6.14:4.1, 9-6.23, 9-6.25:1, 9-6.25:2, 9-145.50R, 9-145.51R, 9-145.53, 9-145.56, 9-253, 9-266.4, 9-361, 42.1-80,
422	22.1-207.1
423	22.1-32
424	22.1-350, 22.1-352, 23-7.4:2, 23-14, 23-31, 23-91.20, 23-91.23, 23-231.2, 23-231.3, 23-231.4, 23-231.5
425	22.1-272.1
426	22.1-209.1:9
427	22.1-348
428	22.1-348
429	22.1-298
430	15.2-953
431	22.1-86.1
432	22.1-278.2
433	2.1-1.1, 2.1-1.3, 2.1-1.7, 2.1-20.4, 2.1-51.27, 2.1-51.40, 2.1-51.44—2.1-51.50, 2.1-563.16, 2.1-563.17, 2.1-563.28—2.1-563.35R, 2.1-563.35:1—2.1-563.38, 2.1-563.40, 2.1-563.41, 9-6.14:4.1, 9-6.23, 9-6.25:1, 9-6.25:2, 9-145.50R, 9-145.51R, 9-145.53, 9-145.56, 9-253, 9-266.4, 9-361, 42.1-80
434	2.1-32.1, 23-38.12
435	22.1-227.1
436	2.1-440.1
437	22.1-350, 22.1-352, 23-7.4:2, 23-14, 23-31, 23-91.20, 23-91.23, 23-231.2—23-231.5
438	2.1-342
439	23-7.4
440	22.1-209.1:7, 22.1-209.1:8, n.
441	59.1-284.16—59.1-284.19
442	22.1-227.1
443	22.1-5
444	22.1-253.13:1
445	22.1-253.13:1
446	22.1-209.1:6
447	22.1-209.1:10
448	22.1-296.2
449	22.1-26
451	23-9.6:1
452	22.1-209, 22.1-253.13:1
453	16.1-228
454	63.1-196.001, 63.1-196.3:1
455	18.2-152.15
456	22.1-199.1, 22.1-212.2:2, 22.1-212.2:3
457	22.1-277.1
458	23-265, 23-266
459	46.2-334, 46.2-335
460	23-9.6:1
461	22.1-253.13:1
462	46.2-334, 46.2-335
463	46.2-340
464	58.1-339.7
465	22.1-5
466	58.1-611.1
469	23-231.15
470	58.1-3, n., 58.1-3983.1, 58.1-3984
471	58.1-609.1
472	58.1-609.7
473	10.1-2211
475	22.1-278.1
481	4.1-100
482	38.2-4307, 38.2-4307.1
483	32.1-122.10:01, 38.2-415, 38.2-1437.1
484	25-233, 56-49
485	2.1-342, 2.1-344, 23-38.75, 23-38.76, 23-38.77, 23-38.80, 23-38.81, 23-38.86, 23-38.87, 58.1-322
486	22.1-302
487	15.2-926.1
488	16.1-278.4, 22.1-199.2, 22.1-253.13:1, 22.1-254, 22.1-254.01, 22.1-254.1, 22.1-254.2, 22.1-256, 22.1-257R 22.1-263, 22.1-271.4
489	29.1-744
490	38.2-1800, 38.2-1814, 38.2-1824
491	38.2-1903
492	22.1-81
493	38.2-514.2, 38.2-1800
494	56-235.8, 59.1-199
495	9-168, 9-170, 9-179, 15.2-1704
496	33.1-13.1
497	62.1-229.1
498	58.1-322

Acts 1999 Chapter	Code 1950 Section
499	23-265, 23-266
501	22.1-355
502	15.2-5601
503	64.1-57.3
504	22.1-32, n.
505	54.1-2012
506	55-248.25:1
507	23-91.23:1
508	16.1-330.1
509	10.1-2129, 10.1-2130, 10.1-2131, 10.1-2132
510	51.1-162, 51.1-207
512	9-6.23, 9-171.1
513	55-248.42:1
514	38.2-2231
515	24.2-307
516	22.1-278.1
518	2.1-342, 2.1-344, 23-38.75, 23-38.76, 23-38.77, 23-38.80, 23-38.81, 23-38.86, 23-38.87, 58.1-322
519	2.1-51.39:3
523	58.1-609.7
526	16.1-260, 22.1-258, 22.1-260, 22.1-261, 22.1-262, 22.1-263
527	64.1-57.3
528	15.2-5601
529	6.1-433, 6.1-435
530	56-484.11
531	25-233, 56-49
532	54.1-1703
533	43-4, 43-32, 43-33
534	18.2-340.16, 18.2-340.33, 18.2-340.34
535	58.1-322
536	29.1-749.2
537	22.1-199.2
538	33.1-221.1:3, 58.1-815.1
540	15.2-6400
541	58.1-3906
542	2.1-548.29, 23-38.19:3—23-38.19:5
543	18.2-285
544	28.2-1210
545	6.1-39.3
546	9-178.2
547	28.2-1204.1
548	2.1-51.12:1, 2.1-51.12:2
549	10.1-2132
550	28.2-701, 28.2-705
551	28.2-102
552	16.1-278.4, 22.1-199.2, 22.1-253.13:1, 22.1-254, 22.1-254.01, 22.1-254.1, 22.1-254.2, 22.1-263, 22.1-271.4, 22.1-256, 22.1-257R
553	28.2-1103, 28.2-1104
554	22.1-18.1
555	10.1-563
557	36-132, n.
558	2.1-1.5, 10.1-2400—10.1-2404R, 10.1-2402, 10.1-2404.1, 10.1-2404.2
559	22.1-201
560	55-79.58, 55-79.58:1, 55-79.62, 55-79.90, 55-374
561	62.1-245, 62.1-247
562	23-9.13:1
563	29.1-529
564	22.1-223, 22.1-224, 22.1-225, 22.1-226
565	23-91.23:1
567	51.1-130, n., 51.1-153
568	51.1-153
569	51.1-153
570	8.01-225, 22.1-274, 22.1-275.1, 54.1-2901, 54.1-3001, 54.1-3005, 54.1-3408
571	58.1-2526
572	30-19.1:8R
573	54.1-2910.1
574	20-124.2
575	54.1-3708
576	2.1-116, 37.1-42.2
577	20-78.1
578	2.1-457.2
579	32.1-14
580	10.1-1408.1, 10.1-1408.3
581	65.2-402
582	20-14.2, 32.1-69.1:1
583	10.1-1454.2
584	10.1-1405, n., 10.1-1406.2, 10.1-1408.1, 10.1-1408.4, 10.1-1410.2, 10.1-1413.2, 10.1-1454.3
585	51.1-124.22, n. 51.1-211—51.1-220,
586	38.2-233, 38.2-1800, 38.2-1814, 38.2-1822, 38.2-1824, 38.2-3725, 38.2-3735, 38.2-3737
587	18.2-308.1
588	58.1-322
589	30-19.9
590	24.2-705
591	51.1-130, n., 51.1-153
592	51.1-130, n., 51.1-153
593	46.2-216.3, 46.2-332, 46.2-343, 46.2-345, 46.2-648.1, 46.2-712
594	55-79.74:1, 55-510
595	22.1-253.13:1
596	51.1-138
597	65.2-402
598	51.1-130, n., 51.1-153
599	51.1-130, n., 51.1-153
600	32.1-272
601	54.1-2957.01, n.
602	65.2-402
603	9-6.14:4.1
604	65.2-402
605	54.1-3452, 54.1-3455
606	9-173.8, 63.1-248.3
607	65.2-402
608	10.1-1454.1
609	54.1-3515
610	6.1-330.60
611	10.1-1408.1, 10.1-1408.3
612	10.1-1454.2
613	10.1-1405, n., 10.1-1406.2, 10.1-1408.1, 10.1-1408.4, 10.1-1410.2, 10.1-1413.2, 10.1-1454.3
614	37.1-207
615	46.2-320
617	58.1-3842
618	18.2-55
619	32.1-31, n.
620	3.1-796.76, 3.1-796.122, 18.2-144, 18.2-403.1, 18.2-403.2, 19.2-8
622	16.1-278.8
623	18.2-38, 18.2-42.1
624	58.1-3980, 58.1-3981
625	18.2-137
626	18.2-457, 18.2-458
627	3.1-796.96, 3.1-796.126:3
628	18.2-308
629	2.1-457.2
630	54.1-3605, 54.1-3609, 54.1-3610, 54.1-3611
631	58.1-535, 58.1-3916, 58.1-3918, 58.1-3981, 58.1-3987, 58.1-3991R
632	32.1-46
633	32.1-176.4, 32.1-176.5
634	20-124.3
635	15.2-1706
636	33.1-1
637	22.1-326.1, 32.1-126.01, 32.1-162.9:1, 54.1-3005, 54.1-3006.2, 63.1-173.2

Acts 1999 Chapter	Code 1950 Section
638	63.1-105
639	2.1-1.6, 2.1-20.4, 9-6.25:1, 54.1-2900, 54.1-2957.4—54.1-2957.6
640	2.1-760, 2.1-768.1
641	4.1-111
643	2.1-20.1, 32.1-137.6, 32.1-137.15, 38.2-3407.9:01, 38.2-3407.10, 38.2-3407.11:1, 38.2-3407.13—38.2-3407.15, 38.2-3418.8, 38.2-3418.9, 38.2-4209, 38.2-4214, 38.2-4312, 38.2-4319, 38.2-4509, 38.2-5804, 38.2-5900—38.2-5905
644	2.1-751, 2.1-753
645	3.1-796.122
646	3.1-796.128:2
647	6.1-2.30—6.1-2.32
648	4.1-227
649	2.1-20.1, 32.1-137.6, 32.1-137.15, 38.2-3407.9:01, 38.2-3407.10, 38.2-3407.11:1, 38.2-3407.13—38.2-3407.15, 38.2-3418.8, 38.2-3418.9, 38.2-4209, 38.2-4214, 38.2-4312, 38.2-4319, 38.2-4509, 38.2-5804, 38.2-5900—38.2-5905
650	22.1-277.01:2
651	54.1-2939
652	8.01-335
653	37.1-195
654	55-510
656	22.1-32
658	18.2-55
659	18.2-374.1:1, 18.2-374.2, 18.2-374.3, 19.2-298.1
661	18.2-247, 54.1-3401
662	19.2-298.1
663	3.1-796.94:1
664	2.1-1.6, 9-6.25:2, 51.1-1200—51.1-1211
665	16.1-228
666	18.2-308
667	44-114
668	16.1-252, 18.2-67.9, 19.2-11.01, 63.1-248.13:1
669	2.1-746, 2.1-751, 2.1-752, 2.1-754, 2.1-755, 2.1-757, 2.1-758, 16.1-286
670	22.1-253.13:3
671	15.2-2019
672	3.1-796.96, 3.1-796.126:3
673	33.1-1
674	58.1-3965, 58.1-3969
676	32.1-46
677	58.1-3980, 58.1-3981
678	3.1-796.128:2
679	18.2-308
680	22.1-199.1
681	28.2-302.8
682	2.1-1.6, 2.1-20.4, 9-6.25:1, 54.1-2900, 54.1-2957.4—54.1-2957.6
683	8.01-471
684	2.1-760, 2.1-768.1
685	19.2-389, 37.1-20.3, 37.1-183.3, 37.1-197.2
686	8.01-6.2
688	6.1-2.13:2
689	22.1-32
690	20-108.2
691	11-45, n., 32.1-276.2—32.1-276.11, n.
692	15.2-3201
693	46.2-882
694	46.2-882
695	22.1-157
696	2.1-343
697	16.1-228, 16.1-241, 18.2-57.2, 19.2-81.3
698	46.2-882
700	19.2-182.7
701	54.1-4300—54.1-4304
702	19.2-11.01
703	2.1-116.05, 2.1-340.1, 2.1-341, 2.1-341.1, 2.1-341.2, 2.1-342, 2.1-342.01 2.1-342.1R, 2.1-342.2, 2.1-343, 2.1-343.1, 2.1-343.2, 2.1-344, 2.1-344.1, 2.1-345R, 2.1-346, 2.1-346.1, 15.2-1722, 19.2-368.3, 23-50.16:32, 32.1-283.1, 52-8.3, 54.1-2517
704	2.1-343.1, n.
705	15.2-3201
706	22.1-277.01:1
707	22.1-277.01
708	11-47.3
709	38.2-510, 38.2-3407.15, 38.2-4214, 38.2-4319, 38.2-4509
710	16.1-309.1
711	8.01-581.15
712	2.1-373
713	2.1-116.07
714	3.1-336.1, 3.1-336.2
715	59.1-480
716	58.1-4007
717	16.1-92
718	15.2-502
719	28.2-245—28.2-247
720	46.2-817
721	16.1-228, 16.1-241, 18.2-57.2, 19.2-81.3
722	18.2-247, 18.2-248, 54.1-3446
723	58.1-602
724	46.2-882
725	24.2-643, 24.2-708
726	2.1-116.05, 2.1-340.1, 2.1-341, 2.1-341.1, 2.1-341.2, 2.1-342, 2.1-342.01, 2.1-342.1R, 2.1-342.2, 2.1-343, 2.1-343.1, 2.1-343.2, 2.1-344, 2.1-344.1, 2.1-345R 2.1-346, 2.1-346.1, 15.2-1722, 19.2-368.3, 23-50.16:32, 32.1-283.1, 52-8.3, 54.1-2517,
727	63.1-198.5
728	32.1-329R
729	46.2-882
730	16.1-69.44, 17.1-327
731	22.1-253.13:3
732	22.1-277.01:1
733	46.2-882
734	18.2-270.1, 18.2-271.3R
735	11-35, 22.1-212.2:2
736	58.1-4007.1
737	63.1-4, 63.1-24, 63.1-331—63.1-335
738	32.1-46
739	38.2-510, 38.2-3407.15, 38.2-4214, 38.2-4319, 38.2-4509
740	63.1-196, 63.1-198.1, 63.1-200, 63.1-201
741	28.2-1205
742	46.2-360
743	18.2-270, 18.2-271.1
744	15.2-3201
745	54.1-2952.1, 54.1-2957.01, 54.1-3301, 54.1-3303
746	19.2-182.7
747	2.1-1.6, 2.1-20.4, 9-6.25:1, 54.1-2900,

Acts 1999 Chapter	Code 1950 Section
	54.1-2957.4—54.1-2957.6
748	22.1-157
749	63.1-55.1, 63.1-55.3
750	54.1-3301, 54.1-3401, 54.1-3434.02
751	3.1-1081, 3.1-1092, 3.1-1093, 3.1-1094, 3.1-1098, 3.1-1099
752	23-165.4
753	22.1-212.2:1
754	3.1-336.1, 3.1-336.2
755	32.1-229, 32.1-232.1, 32.1-235
756	4.1-230
757	22.1-274
758	2.1-20.1:06
759	63.1-133.49
760	58.1-3292, 58.1-3292.1
762	30-19.05, 30-19.1:3, 58.1-608.2, 58.1-609.1, 58.1-609.4, 58.1-609.7, 58.1-609.8, 58.1-609.9, 58.1-609.10, 58.1-623, 58.1-623.1
763	63.1-4, 63.1-24, 63.1-331—63.1-335
764	11-45, n., 32.1-276.2, n., 32.1-276.3, 32.1-276.4 — 32.1-276.7, n., 32.1-276.8, 32.1-276.9 — 32.1-276.11, n., 37.1-98.2
765	2.1-64.34:1
766	34-34
767	15.2-2118
768	56-265.1
769	2.1-807—2.1-811
770	18.2-460
771	18.2-57
772	2.1-328, 26-39, 26-40, 26-40.01, 26-40.2, 26-44, 26-45.1R, 26-45.3—26-45.14, 57-35.14:1, 57-39.22, 64.1-57
773	2.1-807—2.1-811
776	30-19.05, 30-19.1:3, 58.1-608.2, 58.1-609.1, 58.1-609.4, 58.1-609.7, 58.1-609.8, 58.1-609.9, 58.1-609.10, 58.1-623, 58.1-623.1
777	58.1-3123
778	56-1.2
779	54.1-2900, 54.1-2956.9
780	65.2-603
781	32.1-286, 64.1-5.1, 64.1-5.2
782	65.2-524
783	32.1-138, 54.1-3028.1
784	2.1-447.1
785	9-228.1, 9-228.4
786	32.1-27, 32.1-171.2, 32.1-175.01, 32.1-176
787	2.1-51.6:5
788	8.01-241, 8.01-242
789	38.2-3431
791	2.1-64.34:1
792	15.2-2286
793	2.1-342, 3.1-611—3.1-618, 3.1-619R, 3.1-620R, 3.1-621, 3.1-622, 3.1-623, 3.1-624, 3.1-626, 3.1-627, 3.1-628R, 3.1-629, 3.1-630, 3.1-631R, 3.1-632, 3.1-633R, 3.1-634, 3.1-634.1, 3.1-635, 3.1-636, 3.1-637—3.1-646R
794	9-329.6
795	24.2-443.1—24.2-443.4
796	34-34
797	15.2-1517
798	10.1-1406
800	18.2-460
801	19.2-298.1
803	9-313, n., 32.1-70, n.
804	15.2-6400
805	55-515.1
806	38.2-5001, 38.2-5010, 38.2-5013
807	16.1-253.4, 18.2-57.2, 19.2-81.3
808	20-108.2
809	55-511
810	24.2-611
811	15.2-1535
812	32.1-127.1:03
813	9-313, n., 32.1-127, n.
814	37.1-134.21, 54.1-2901, 54.1-2982, 54.1-2984, 54.1-2986, 54.1-2987.1, 54.1-2988, 54.1-2989, 54.1-2990, 54.1-2991
815	38.2-3431
816	2.1-51.6:5
817	54.1-1131, 54.1-1133
818	32.1-325
819	54.1-2820
820	15.2-6400, 15.2-6402, 15.2-6403
821	19.2-128, 19.2-319
822	8.01-273.1, 38.2-5003
823	38.2-5009
824	38.2-5016
825	38.2-5004.1
826	38.2-5015
828	63.1-248.5:1.01
829	8.01-508, 16.1-135, 18.2-308.1, 18.2-308.2, 18.2-308.4, 19.2-80.2, 19.2-119, 19.2-120, 19.2-121, 19.2-123, 19.2-124, 19.2-125, 19.2-126R, 19.2-127, 19.2-132, 19.2-150, 19.2-152.2, 19.2-152.3, 19.2-152.4, 19.2-158, 19.2-186, 19.2-398, 19.2-406, 46.2-936, 53.1-109
830	22.1-253.13:5
831	22.1-295, 22.1-303
832	2.1-20.1:2, 2.1-20.1:3
833	54.1-1131, 54.1-1135
834	54.1-106
835	6.1-5, 6.1-32.31—6.1-32.45
836	20-108.2
837	15.2-6400
838	15.2-2308
839	8.01-4
840	2.1-1.7, 2.1-51.21, 9-6.23, 9-6.25:1, 9-6.25:2, 9-329.1, 9-329.2, 60.2-112R, 63.1-133.44R, 63.1-133.45
841	15.2-2118
842	65.2-307
843	24.2-405
844	19.2-11.01, 19.2-265.01
845	18.2-472.1, 19.2-298.1, 19.2-298.4, 19.2-390.2, 52-8.4, n., 53.1-1
846	8.01-508, 16.1-135, 18.2-308.1, 18.2-308.2, 18.2-308.4, 19.2-80.2, 19.2-119, 19.2-120, 19.2-121, 19.2-123, 19.2-124, 19.2-125, 19.2-126R, 19.2-127, 19.2-132, 19.2-150, 19.2-152.2, 19.2-152.3, 19.2-152.4, 19.2-158, 19.2-186, 19.2-398, 19.2-406, 46.2-936, 53.1-109
847	58.1-609.7

Acts 1999 Chapter	Code 1950 Section
848	3.1-796.93:2
849	2.1-342, 2.1-344, 32.1-283.2
850	9-53, 9-54, 9-55, 9-57.1R, 9-59R
851	24.2-427
852	2.1-342, 2.1-548.53—2.1-548.68, 2.1-548.29:01—2.1-548.29:03R
853	19.2-165.1
854	63.1-26
855	2.1-1.7, 2.1-51.21, 9-6.23, 9-6.25:1, 9-6.25:2, 9-329.1, 9-329.2, 60.2-112R, 63.1-133.44R, 63.1-133.45
856	38.2-3407.11:2, 38.2-4214, 38.2-4319
857	32.1-137.7, 32.1-137.10, 32.1-137.13, 32.1-137.15, 38.2-3407.6:1, 38.2-4214, 38.2-4319
858	9-299, n., 38.2-3418.11, 38.2-4319
860	2.1-1.6, 9-6.25:2, 51.1-1200—51.1-1211,
861	24.2-103
862	58.1-3734
863	54.1-3508
864	24.2-914, 24.2-914.1
865	46.2-874, n.
866	58.1-2606
867	2.1-342, 2.1-344, 32.1-283.3
868	2.1-342, 2.1-344, 32.1-283.2
869	58.1-3967, 58.1-3970.1
870	22.1-175.6—22.1-175.9
871	32.1-164
873	18.2-255.2
874	56-209—56-231.14R, 56-231.15—56-231.52
875	2.1-548.43:1—2.1-548.43:6
876	10.1-1408.5, 10.1-1455
877	65.2-302
878	32.1-325.
879	9-55
880	2.1-1.5, 9-380—9-389, 32.1-354—32.1-365
881	2.1-342, 2.1-548.29:01—2.1-548.29:03R, 2.1-548.53—2.1-548.68
882	15.2-6400, 15.2-6402, 15.2-6403
883	46.2-743, 46.2-749.3, 46.2-749.4, 46.2-749.12—46.2-749.17
884	46.2-833.01
886	8.01-328.1, 18.2-152.2, 18.2-152.4, 18.2-152.12
887	46.2-334
888	54.1-2400.2
889	16.1-277R, 16.1-277.01, 16.1-277.02, 16.1-278.3, 16.1-282, 16.1-282.1, 16.1-283, 63.1-56, 63.1-204
890	63.1-321, 63.1-324, 63.1-325.1
891	2.1-51.18:3, 16.1-273, 18.2-251.01, 19.2-299, 19.2-299.2
892	2.1-20.01:1
893	10.1-1197.3
894	63.1-325
895	54.1-3300, 54.1-3300.1
896	15.2-5102
897	5.1-30.1—5.1-30.10, 62.1-199, 62.1-203
898	33.1-269, 58.1-638
899	32.1-102.1, 32.1-102.1:1, 32.1-102.2, 32.1-102.6, 32.1-102.12,
900	2.1-1.5, 10.1-202, 10.1-1017, 10.1-1018, 10.1-1020, 10.1-1021, 10.1-1022.1, 10.1-2213
901	15.2-905
902	46.2-746.22
903	19.2-299
904	8.01-328.1, 18.2-152.2, 18.2-152.4, 18.2-152.12
905	8.01-328.1, 18.2-152.2, 18.2-152.4, 18.2-152.12
906	2.1-1.5, 10.1-202, 10.1-1017, 10.1-1018, 10.1-1020, 10.1-1021, 10.1-1022.1, 10.1-2213
907	46.2-742.1, 46.2-743, 46.2-746.2R, 46.2-746.2:1, 46.2-746.2:2, 46.2-746.7, 46.2-746.8, 46.2-749.4, 46.2-749.12—46.2-749.26
909	63.1-321, 63.1-324, 63.1-325.1
910	11-40.4, 46.2-1500, 63.1-133.46
911	2.1-457.2
912	32.1-102.3:2, n.
913	2.1-51.18:3, 16.1-273, 18.2-251.01, 19.2-299, 19.2-299.2
914	33.1-46.2
915	46.2-1143
916	15.2-1500, 56-484.7:1—56-484.7:34
917	63.1-325
918	38.2-2232
919	60.2-618
920	32.1-102.1
921	2.1-20.1, 38.2-3418.1:2
922	32.1-102.1, 32.1-102.1:1, 32.1-102.2, 32.1-102.6, 32.1-102.12
923	38.2-3407.16, 38.2-4214, 38.2-4319
924	9-265.1
925	15.2-5102
926	32.1-102.2, 32.1-102.3
927	10.1-1801.1
928	22.1-205
929	51.1-124.3
930	30-19.15, 30-19.16, 30-19.17R
931	36-99.3, n.
932	Va. Const., Art. XI, § 4, n.
933	Va. Const., Art. X, § 7A, n.
934	Va. Const., Art. X, § 7A, n.
936	18.2-391
937	54.1-3215
938	65.2-706
939	56-231.31:1
940	56-231.31:1
941	2.1-1-14.5, n., 2.1-20.1, 9-298, n., 38.2-3412.1, 38.2-3412.1:01, 38.2-4319

Acts 1999 Chapter	Code 1950 Section
942	33.1-56, 33.1-69.2
943	46.2-904
944	22.1-208.01
945	8.01-9, 16.1-77, 18.2-36.1, 18.2-51.4, 18.2-270, 46.2-351—46.2-355R, 46.2-355.1, 46.2-356, 46.2-357, 46.2-360, 46.2-361, 46.2-362, 46.2-389, 46.2-391, 46.2-411, 53.1-21
946	19.2-169.3, 19.2-174.1, 37.1-70.1—37.1-70.19, 37.1-134.21
947	10.1-1406.2, 10.1-1408.1, 10.1-1408.4, 10.1-1410.2, 10.1-1413.2, 10.1-1454.3
948	58.1-346.10—58.1-346.11
949	18.2-270
950	2.1-1.6, 2.1-20.4, 9-6.25:2, 54.1-202, 54.1-300, 54.1-2000, 54.1-2001—54.1-2008
951	53.1-116, 53.1-129
952	16.1-260, 16.1-263, 16.1-305.1
954	8.01-227.1—8.01-227.3
955	8.01-9
956	32.1-127.1:03
957	58.1-3734
958	16.1-356—16.1-361
959	54.1-1103
960	33.1-46.2
961	2.1-548.43:1—2.1-548.43:6
962	2.1-1.5, 9-380—9-389, 32.1-354—32.1-365,
963	18.2-57.3, 19.2-151
964	63.1-174, n., 63.1-175, 63.1-177
965	32.1-324.2
966	13.1-1027
967	22.1-274.02, 32.1-325, 32.1-326.3, 54.1-2603, 54.1-3606
968	58.1-510—58.1-513
969	37.1-1, 37.1-84.1, 37.1-84.3, 37.1-182.3, 37.1-185.1
970	22.1-280.1
971	58.1-400.2, 58.1-401, 58.1-402, 58.1-433.1, 58.1-439.2, 58.1-440.1, 58.1-504, 58.1-2600, 58.1-2601, 58.1-2602, 58.1-2603, 58.1-2604, 58.1-2606, 58.1-2609, 58.1-2610, 58.1-2611, 58.1-2626, 58.1-2627, 58.1-2628, 58.1-2633, 58.1-2660, 58.1-2682, 58.1-2900—58.1-2903, 58.1-3731, 58.1-3814
972	24.2-515, 24.2-544, 24.2-545
974	51.1-124.3, 51.1-142.1
975	55-253—55-268R, 55-277.1—55-277.33, 64.1-57, 64.1-68
976	9-304.1—9-304.6
977	54.1-1103
978	15.2-108
980	2.1-20.1:2, 2.1-20.1:3, 2.1-20.1:6, 51.1-600, 51.1-606,
981	58.1-602
983	58.1-510—58.1-513
984	2.1-20.1:2, 2.1-20.1:3, 2.1-20.1:6, 51.1-600, 51.1-606
985	19.2-169.3, 19.2-174.1, 37.1-70.1—37.1-70.19, 37.1-134.21
986	15.2-1104.1, 58.1-3818
987	8.01-9, 16.1-77, 18.2-36.1, 18.2-51.4, 18.2-270, 46.2-351—46.2-355R, 46.2-355.1, 46.2-356, 46.2-357, 46.2-360, 46.2-361, 46.2-362, 46.2-389, 46.2-391, 46.2-411, 53.1-21
988	22.1-3, 22.1-5
989	2.1-20.1:7
990	53.1-105
991	54.1-1103
992	38.2-2206
993	22.1-291.2, 59.1-475—59.1-477
994	22.1-253.13:1,
995	64.1-57.1
996	18.2-280
997	16.1-356—16.1-361
998	10.1-1119.1, 32.1-324.3, 58.1-346.10, 58.1-346.13
999	46.2-838, 46.2-839
1000	8.01-225, 32.1-111.1, 32.1-111.3, 32.1-111.10, 32.1-111.14:1
1001	54.1-2969
1002	8.01-226.6
1003	17.1-275
1004	38.2-3430.2, 38.2-3430.3, 38.2-3430.8, 38.2-3431, 38.2-3432.3, 38.2-3514.1
1005	22.1-274.02, 32.1-325, 32.1-326.3, 54.1-2603, 54.1-3606
1006	65.2-101
1007	53.1-116, 53.1-129
1008	11-64, 11-65, 11-70
1010	32.1-127.1:03
1011	54.1-3300, 54.1-3300.1
1012	62.1-224, 62.1-225, 62.1-228, 62.1-229
1013	23-174.4
1014	36-106
1015	22.1-253.13:3
1016	30-19.03, 30-19.03:1.1
1018	36-152—36-156
1019	28.2-302.8
1020	18.2-371.2
1021	2.1-373, 11-45, 57-60
1022	10.1-1322.3
1023	15.2-926, 22.1-266
1024	11-45, 32.1-325
1025	21-120
1026	58.1-3231, 58.1-3234, 58.1-3237
1027	22.1-277.01
1028	16.1-241, 20-124.1, 63.1-204, 63.1-220.2, 63.1-220.3, 63.1-225
1029	55-510, 55-510.1
1030	22.1-60.1, 22.1-253.13:5, 22.1-293, 22.1-294, 22.1-295, 22.1-298, 22.1-299.2, 22.1-303, 22.1-303.1, 22.1-305, 22.1-305.1, 23-9.2:3.4
1031	32.1-19.1
1032	22.1-299.2
1034	32.1-351, 32.1-352
1035	22.1-298

Acts 1999 Chapter	Code 1950 Section
1036	18.2-57
1037	22.1-60.1, 22.1-253.13:5, 22.1-293, 22.1-294, 22.1-295, 22.1-298, 22.1-299.2, 22.1-303, 22.1-303.1, 22.1-305, 22.1-305.1, 23-9.2:3.4
1038	32.1-163.5
1039	23-9.2:3.01
1040	58.1-609.7, 58.1-609.10
1041	15.2-2288.1, n.
1042	23-7.4:4

ACTS 2000

Acts 2000 Chapter	Code 1950 Section
1	24.2-544
2	24.2-611
5	50-73.83, 50-73.134
6	29.1-529
7	10.1-2212, 58.1-3607, 58.1-3650.1, n.
8	17.1-400, 17.1-402
10	29.1-109
11	3.1-796.93:1
12	29.1-310.1
13	29.1-521
14	10.1-607
15	3.1-73.5:1
16	3.1-22.19
17	10.1-2500, 32.1-248.01, 62.1-44.17:2, 62.1-44.17:3, 62.1-44.17:4, 62.1-44.19:4 — 62.1-44.19:6, 62.1-44.19:9, 62.1-44.19:10
18	10.1-2212
19	62.1-44.15:3
20	33.1-346
21	10.1-218, 10.1-1018, 10.1-1800, 51.5-55
22	3.1-18.4 — 3.1-18.6, 3.1-18.8
23	10.1-611.1
24	54.1-3938.1
25	2.1-177
26	9-183.2, 9-183.3
27	9-84.09:4
28	55-66.3
29	11-35, 11-41.2:2, 11-41.2:4
30	36-96.7
31	20-21
32	2.1-563.27:2
33	54.1-1115
34	16.1-253.1, 16.1-279.1
35	36-99.01
36	54.1-2310, 54.1-2319, 54.1-2324, 54.1-2333
37	17.1-507
38	62.1-201
39	27-34.2:1
40	9-228.8
41	55-248.42:1
42	54.1-414, 54.1-415R
43	16.1-69.6:1
44	46.2-749.32
45	33.1-62, n.
46	38.2-213, 38.2-1306.2, 38.2-1306.3, 38.2-1307R, 38.2-1312, 38.2-1315, 38.2-1329, 38.2-4123, 38.2-4319, 38.2-4604
47	38.2-4214, 38.2-4319, 38.2-4509.1, 38.2-5513, 38.2-5515
48	46.2-1313
49	33.1-2
50	38.2-4214, 38.2-4319, 38.2-4408, 38.2-4509
51	38.2-216
52	13.1-752, 13.1-768, 13.1-914, 13.1-930, 13.1-1064, 50-73.69
53	13.1-720, 13.1-896
54	46.2-1014
55	6.1-301
56	6.1-112
58	12.1-43, 13.1-1003, 50-73.128, 50-73.131, 50-73.136
59	46.2-1001
60	46.2-803.1
61	63.1-196.001
62	33.1-62, n.
63	46.2-1014
64	2.1-721
65	16.1-340
66	2.1-1.1, 2.1-1.3, 2.1-20.1, 2.1-20.1:02 — 2.1-20.1:04, 2.1-20.1:5, 2.1-20.1:6, 2.1-20.1:06, 2.1-51.27, 2.1-111, 2.1-113.1, 2.1-113.3, 2.1-114.3, 2.1-114.5, 2.1-114.6, n., 2.1-114.7, 2.1-114.7:1, 2.1-116, 2.1-116.03, 2.1-116.07, 2.1-116.14, 2.1-116.21, 2.1-342.01, 2.1-404, 2.1-557, 15.2-1512.1, 15.2-1609.2, 22.1-209.2, 22.1-289.1, 22.1-342.1, 22.1-349, n., 23-50.16:24, 32.1-137.6, 51.1-126.1, 51.1-153, 51.1-205, 51.1-216, 51.1-502.1, 51.1-512.1, 51.1-513.1, 51.1-1101, 51.1-1106, 62.1-129.1
67	2.1-234.11, 2.1-234.13
68	36-106
69	62.1-44.18:3
70	53.1-115.1
71	46.2-639
72	46.2-1222.1
73	32.1-73.5, 32.1-73.6
74	32.1-70.2, 32.1-71, 32.1-71.01
75	46.2-743, 46.2-746.4, 46.2-746.6:1R, 46.2-746.7, 46.2-746.8, 46.2-748.1R, 46.2-749.2:3 — 46.2-749.2:6R, 46.2-749.7:1R, 46.2-749.11R
76	46.2-749.33
77	54.1-2906
78	46.2-749.34
79	8.01-47, 22.1-280.1
80	46.2-749.35
81	46.2-749.36
82	22.1-205
83	54.1-3606.1
84	46.2-1025
85	46.2-749.37
86	22.1-289
87	46.2-209.1
88	33.1-75.3
89	23-231.3
90	2.1-51.6:6
91	58.1-439.2
92	46.2-209.1
93	22.1-129, 22.1-199.1
94	23-38.15, 23-38.16, 23-38.17:1
95	22.1-296.4, 63.1-248.8
96	23-9.13:1
97	33.1-41.1
98	62.1-44.15:3
99	59.1-369
100	8.01-465.4, 8.01-676.1
101	59.1-499 — 59.1-500, 59.1-501.1 — 59.1-509.2, 59.1-501.15, 59.1-502.17, 59.1-503.10, 59.1-504.10, 59.1-505.12, 59.1-506.19, 59.1- 507.11, 59.1-508.17
102	22.1-298
103	62.1-44.15:1.2
104	23-287
105	22.1-354.1 — 22.1-354.5
106	46.2-1573, 46.2-1982, 46.2-1992.75,

Acts 2000 Chapter	Code 1950 Section
	46.2-1993.73
107	46.2-749.19
108	23-14
109	23-288
110	28.2-302.5, 29.1-301
111	46.2-746.4
112	46.2-1001
114	10.1-2211
115	51.5-47, 51.5-48
116	46.2-1530, 46.2-1930, 46.2-1992.23
118	38.2-3411.1
119	62.1-44.15:1.2
120	46.2-920
121	46.2-1025
122	46.2-212.1
123	46.2-1600, 46.2-1608
124	46.2-749.38
125	23-287
126	46.2-726
127	46.2-749.39
128	46.2-1529, 46.2-1929, 46.2-1992.22, 46.2-1993.22
129	46.2-1149
130	63.1-177
131	10.1-1197.3
132	29.1-323, 29.1-327, 29.1-330 — 29.1-335
133	46.2-712
134	32.1-73.5, 32.1-73.6
135	54.1-3408, 54.1-3408.01, 54.1-3421, 54.1-3434, 54.1-3448, 54.1-3450, 54.1-3452
136	38.2-3430.3, 38.2-3432.3
137	10.1-1410
138	10.1-1410
139	32.1-70.2, 32.1-71, 32.1-71.01
140	33.1-369
141	46.2-224
142	28.2-302.5, 29.1-301
143	46.2-749.40
144	46.2-651
145	46.2-746.4:2
146	46.2-749.41
147	4.1-224
148	46.2-746.9
149	2.1-20.1, 38.2-3407.13:1
150	46.2-749.42
151	51.5-9.1
153	9-77.10:2
154	9-77.11
155	38.2-1425, 38.2-1426
156	2.1-51.27:1
157	38.2-3418.12, 38.2-4319
161	64.1-47
162	13.1-619, 13.1-634, 13.1-763, 13.1-819, 13.1-833, 13.1-925, 13.1-1011, 13.1-1015, 50-73.4, 50-73.132
163	16.1-245.1
164	16.1-69.24
165	15.2-2265
166	13.1-521, 13.1-570
167	28.2-630, 28.2-1203, 28.2-1205
168	32.1-17
169	38.2-1019
170	19.2-72
171	38.2-4504
172	30-19.05, 30-19.1:3
173	38.2-102, 38.2-3113.3
174	32.1-122.9:1
175	32.1-122.20 — 32.1-122.22
176	32.1-127, 63.1-174.001
177	32.1-138, 63.1-182.1
178	63.1-175
179	46.2-1705
180	46.2-1508, 46.2-1508.1, 46.2-1519, 46.2-1527.1, 46.2-1531, 46.2-1908, 46.2-1908.1, 46.2-1919, 46.2-1931, 46.2-1992.6, 46.2-1992.6:1, 46.2-1992.17, 46.2-1992.24, 46.2-1993.6, 46.2-1993.6:1, 46.2-1993.17, 46.2-1993.24
181	10.1-1700, 10.1-1801.1
182	10.1-1010
183	56-236.2, 56-261, 56-265.11:1
184	22.1-254
185	16.1-69.24
186	19.2-303.4
187	38.2-510, 38.2-1331, 38.2-1411.2, 38.2-4214, 38.2-4319
188	54.1-3938.1
189	46.2-749.43
190	46.2-743
191	13.1-549, 13.1-549.1, 13.1-1111, 13.1-1112
192	6.1-250, 6.1-267, 6.1-269.1
193	38.2-305
194	13.1-543, 13.1-556, 13.1-1102
195	16.1-309.3
196	23-7.4:2
197	62.1-201
198	37.1-137.2
199	54.1-2910.1
200	32.1-122.20 — 32.1-122.22
201	54.1-2410
202	32.1-122.9:1
203	63.1-175
204	38.2-4504
205	10.1-611.1
206	38.2-1700
207	8.01-273.1, 38.2-5001
208	58.1-13.1
209	22.1-3, 22.1-4.1, 22.1-270
210	63.1-198.2
211	16.1-301
212	16.1-300
213	8.01-581.2
214	20-21
215	24.2-604
216	16.1-358
217	22.1-355, n.
218	20-109
219	20-108.2
221	20-109, 20-110, 20-112
226	46.2-749.44
227	2.1-342.2, 2.1-343
228	58.1-13.1
229	15.2-1113, 15.2-1209
230	21-118.4
231	15.2-928
232	24.2-506, 24.2-521, 24.2-543, 24.2-684.1
233	24.2-920, 24.2-920.1, 24.2-923.1
234	24.2-927
235	46.2-209.1, 46.2-1600, 46.2-1602.1, 46.2-1603
237	2.1-342.01
238	33.1-253, n.
239	2.1-124
240	32.1-122.6:01, 54.1-3011.1, 54.1-3011.2
241	22.1-209.1:5, n.
242	11-45
243	46.2-391
245	8.01-32
246	16.1-340
247	58.1-2111.1, 58.1-2124.1
248	63.1-198.2
249	2.1-51.6:6
250	19.2-390.1
251	8.01-343
252	24.2-506, 24.2-521, 24.2-543, 24.2-684.1
253	22.1-5
254	32.1-122.6:01, 54.1-3011.1, 54.1-3011.2
255	22.1-346.1
256	53.1-68
257	46.2-209.1, 46.2-1600, 46.2-1602.1, 46.2-1603

Acts 2000 Chapter	Code 1950 Section
258	46.2-716
259	46.2-730
260	30-19.1, 30-19.1:1
262	46.2-873.1
263	10.1-109, n.
264	38.2-3407.4:1
265	46.2-1142, 46.2-1142.1
266	55-531
267	46.2-746.8:1
268	24.2-604
269	46.2-328
270	46.2-1222.1
271	32.1-229
272	19.2-11.01
273	22.1-4.2
274	46.2-828.1
275	2.1-177
276	15.2-1505
277	66-28 — 66-30, 66-34, 66-35
278	46.2-1025
279	2.1-234.11, 2.1-234.13
280	24.2-626
281	2.1-563.27:2
282	24.2-613, 24.2-613, 24.2-642
283	63.1-196.3
284	19.2-310.5
285	22.1-217.01, 22.1-281, 22.1-346, 22.1-348
286	18.2-473.1
287	15.2-2118
288	18.2-57
289	15.2-1113.1
290	63.1-238.03, 63.1-238.1, 63.1-238.3
291	53.1-115.1
292	19.2-165.1
293	15.2-1522
294	10.1-218, 10.1-1018, 10.1-1800, 51.5-55
295	18.2-465.1
296	44-123.1, 44-123.2, 44-123.3
297	2.1-786
298	15.2-1702
299	15.2-1414.2
300	15.2-1246
301	65.2-101
302	22.1-354.1 — 22.1-354.5
303	46.2-752
304	24.2-914, 24.2-915, 24.2-919
305	20-60.3, 20-108.2
306	46.2-803.1
307	2.1-373
308	10.1-1413.2
309	44-146.13 — 44-146.17, 44-146.18 — 44-146.22, 44-146.24, 44-146.26 —44-146.28, 44-146.30, 44-146.31, 44-146.34, 44-146.35, 44-146.39
310	33.1-91.1
311	46.2-1176
312	33.1-223.2:4
313	2.1-373
314	2.1-133.7
315	46.2-817
316	58.1-3013
317	2.1-639.14
318	46.2-665, 46.2-667
319	46.2-749.45
320	26-7.1
321	64.1-116, 64.1-118
322	33.1-46.2
323	46.2-924
324	26-17.10
325	4.1-305, 18.2-259.1
326	24.2-905
327	19.2-245.1
328	24.2-437, 24.2-441
329	58.1-3617
331	55-20.1
332	18.2-46.1—18.2-46.3
333	18.2-67.5:2, 18.2-370
334	8.01-390, 8.01-391
335	2.1-361
336	19.2-187
337	16.1-356, 16.1-361
338	19.2-316.2, 19.2-316.3, 53.1-67.7, 53.1-136
339	16.1-302.1, 19.2-265.01
340	46.2-869
341	18.2-270.2
342	46.2-392
343	51.1-155.2
344	51.1-124.12
345	51.1-126.6
346	58.1-609.10
347	58.1-2111
348	18.2-251.3, 54.1-3446, 54.1-3450
349	18.2-186.3
350	18.2-57.01
351	8.01-35.1
352	2.1-361
353	58.1-2111, 58.1-2123
354	46.2-882
355	54.1-3901, 54.1-3902
356	58.1-339.2
357	46.2-882
358	58.1-333, 58.1-430, 63.1-320 — 63.1-325
359	19.2-215.1
360	22.1-277.02:1
361	18.2-10
362	18.2-270.2
363	15.2-1506
364	15.2-958.1
365	46.2-882
366	24.2-643, 24.2-651.1
367	58.1-339.2
368	58.1-400.1, 58.1-2035, 58.1-2670, 58.1-2674.1
369	58.1-1820
370	33.1-89, n.
371	10.1-109, n.
372	3.1-296.12, n.
373	30-16
374	7.1-41
375	58.1-3812
376	20-108.2
378	24.2-700, 24.2-701
379	24.2-545
380	61.1-55
381	4.1-128
382	2.1-41.2, 2.1-116, 2.1-342.01, 2.1-344, 9-6.14:4.1, 11-35, 23-38.75 — 23-38.78, 23-38.80, 23-38.81, 23-38.83, 23-38.84, 58.1-302, 58.1-322
383	58.1-3378
384	20-108.2
385	16.1-251, 16.1-252, 16.1-277.01, 16.1-277.02, 16.1-278.2, 16.1-278.3, 16.1-281 —16.1-283
386	62.1-69.25
387	58.1-322
388	58.1-492
389	58.1-3958
390	27-34.2:1
391	59.1-148.3
392	2.1-21
393	58.1-811
394	58.1-322
395	51.1-602
396	51.1-124.30
397	58.1-339.8
398	15.2-4903
399	58.1-3222
400	2.1-41.2, 2.1-116, 2.1-342.01, 2.1-344, 9-6.14:4.1, 11-35, 23-38.75 — 23-38.78, 23-38.80, 23-38.81, 23-38.83, 23-38.84, 58.1-302, 58.1-322
401	38.2-2125
402	58.1-1820
403	29.1-531
404	53.1-223
405	2.1-380
406	54.1-1129, 54.1-1131
407	46.2-803.1
408	65.2-504
409	58.1-3506

Acts 2000 Chapter	Code 1950 Section
410	58.1-3231
412	17.1-207
413	58.1-3506
414	23-30.28
415	58.1-490
417	11-51.1
418	16.1-272.1
419	58.1-322, 58.1-402, 58.1-323.1, 58.1-323.2R
420	10.1-1408.1
421	24.2-706
422	10.1-1408.1
423	53.1-131, 53.1-131.2, 53.1-132
424	2.1-391
425	58.1-602, 58.1-610, 58.1-610.1
426	9-169
427	58.1-2900, 58.1-2901
428	58.1-339.9
429	58.1-339.2
430	2.1-342.01
431	16.1-299
432	33.1-351, 33.1-370
433	58.1-3916
434	15.2-107.1
435	15.2-4600, n.
436	19.2-163
437	44-146.20
438	60.2-219
439	15.2-4507
440	17.1-227.1, 17.1-252, 17.1-279
441	58.1-3506, 58.1-3609, 58.1-3622
442	58.1-3506
443	15.2-4507
444	17.1-207
445	23-30.28
446	17.1-227.1, 17.1-252, 17.1-279
447	29.1-531
448	19.2-163
449	33.1-351, 33.1-370
450	4.1-128
451	24.2-643, 24.2-651.1
452	33.1-89
453	58.1-3128, 58.1-3921, 58.1-3958
454	2.1-21
455	19.2-368.7
456	62.1-69.25 — 32.1-69.33
458	58.1-3650.848 — 58.1-3650.857, n.
459	63.1-58.2
460	38.2-3411.3, 38.2-4319
461	20-108.2
462	54.1-3601
463	2.1-373.12
464	8.01-38
465	2.1-20.1, 38.2-3418.13, 38.2-4319
466	20-124.3
467	54.1-2952
468	15.2-5201
470	58.1-3819
472	58.1-1101
473	2.1-1.6, 2.1-20.4, 9-6.25:2, 54.1-106, 54.1-2503, 54.1-3500, 54.1-3503, 54.1-3511— 54.1-3515, 54.1-3609— 54.1-3611, 65.2-603
474	58.1-608.3
475	32.1-353.1 — 32.1-353.5
476	22.1-271.2, 22.1-300, 32.1-46
477	32.1-301
478	17.1-513.1
480	32.1-122.7
481	32.1-292.2
482	63.1-248.18
483	2.1-707, 2.1-708, 2.1-710.1—2.1-710.3R, 63.1-133.49, 63.1-133.56— 63.1-133.58
484	32.1-325
485	20-124.6
486	58.1-3650.904, n.
487	58.1-609.1, 58.1-609.7 — 58.1-609.9
489	33.1-18
490	32.1-292.2
491	2.1-707, 2.1-708, 2.1-710.1 — 2.1-710.3R, 63.1-133.49, 63.1-133.56— 63.1-133.58
492	58.1-3650.848 — 58.1-3650.903, n.
493	58.1-608.1, 58.1-609.1, 58.1-609.4, 58.1-609.7—58.1-609.9, 58.1-609.10
494	10.1-1018, 10.1-1020
495	15.2-2317
496	38.2-3411.3, 38.2-4319
497	54.1-2952
498	2.1-1.3, 2.1-1.6, 54.1-3408, 63.1-68, 63.1-69.1, 63.1-70.1, 63.1-73.1
499	9-321
500	2.1-380, 63.1-209, 63.1-248.2 — 63.1-248.4, 63.1-248.2:1, 63.1-248.5:1, 63.1-248.6, 63.1-248.6:01, 63.1-248.6:02, 63.1-248.6:2, 63.1-248.7, 63.1-248.7:1, 63.1-248.10, 63.1-248.13, 63.1-248.18R, 63.1-248.19
501	58.1-461, 58.1-462, 58.1-470
502	51.1-168
503	38.2-4300 — 38.2-4302, 38.2-4307.1, 38.2-4310, 38.2 4310.1, 38.2-4317.1, 38.2-4319
504	22.1-201, 22.1-253.13:1, 22.1-253.13:3
505	58.1-609.10
506	22.1-199.1
507	58.1-3916, 58.1-3918
508	38.2-3407.9:02
509	6.1-363.1
510	24.2-105.2, 24.2-404
511	24.2-914.1, 24.2-915, 24.2-929
512	24.2-114, 24.2-405, 24.2-411
513	24.2-504, 24.2-525
514	24.2-613, 24.2-640
515	58.1-3294
516	58.1-346.3:1
517	2.1-20.1:7
518	51.1-1103, n.
519	9-173.21
520	65.2-503, 65.2-504
521	15.2-4314
522	38.2-1868.1 — 38.2-1872
523	22.1-277.01
524	58.1-345.1
525	58.1-346.15
526	38.2-122, 38.2-122.1, 38.2-122.2, 38.2-233, 38.2-317, 38.2-415, 38.2-1601, 38.2-1800, 38.2-1902, 38.2-2001, 38.2-2003, 38.2-2006.1, 52-36
527	38.2-221.1
528	56-88, 56-232, 56-265.1
529	38.2-231, 38.2-2113, 38.2-2208
530	65.2-300
531	8.01-229
532	38.2-4123, 38.2-4214, 38.2-4319, 38.2-5202.1
533	23-9.13:1

Acts 2000 Chapter	Code 1950 Section
534	2.1-20.1
535	22.1-19
536	3.1-73.5
537	13.1-1015, 50-73.4, 50-73.135
538	22.1-279.3
539	24.2-1014
540	38.2-3503, 38.2-3504, 38.2-4214, 38.2-4319
541	23-295 — 23-298, 9-99.1 — 9-99.4R
542	65.2-604
543	56-88, 56-232, 56-265.1
544	38.2-3432.2
545	38.2-513
546	23-9.13:1
547	22.1-253.13:1
548	38.2-317, 38.2-1903.1
549	6.1-2.21, 6.1-2.23:1, 6.1-2.27, 38.2-1810
550	58.1-345.1
551	2.1-488.4
552	24.2-504, 24.2-525
553	58.1-461, 58.1-462, 58.1-470
554	24.2-105.2, 24.2-404
555	24.2-914.1, 24.2-915, 24.2-929
556	24.2-114, 24.2-405, 24.2-411
557	58.1-3700.1, 58.1-3703
558	8.01-390.1
559	38.2-5200, 38.2-5202, 38.2-5203, 38.2-5207, 38.2-5209, 38.2- 5210
560	52-1, 52-4.3, 52-8.1:1
561	9-170, 36-140.1, 36-140.2
562	16.1-309.5
563	16.1-309.1
564	32.1-137.7, 32.1-138.6
565	37.1-42.1, 37.1-42.2, 51.5-37.1
566	9-329.2, 60.2-318 — 60.2-322
567	23-38.46, 23-38.48, 23-38.49
568	58.1-339.10, 58.1-439.12
569	2.1-812 — 2.1-814
570	22.1-212.2:1, 23-38.10:1
571	2.1-548.43:2 — 2.1-548,43:6
573	60.2-602, 60.2-612
575	46.2-833.01
576	58.1-2403
577	22.1-277.1
578	54.1-2400.4
579	8.01-310, 46.2-692
581	13.1-1010.3, 13.1-1038.1, 13.1-1040.2, 13.1-1046, 50-73.39:1
582	54.1-3812
583	2.1-342.01
584	3.1-722.29 — 3.1-722.43
585	40.1-51.4:4
586	16.1-278.15, 20-103
587	54.1-3005, 54.1-3012.1
588	23-38.46, 23-38.48, 23-38.49
589	2.1-342.01, 51.5-37.2
590	54.1-2987, 54.1-2988, 54.1-2990, 54.1-2992
591	40.1-51.4:4
592	2.1-342.01
593	32.1-323.1
594	2.1-342.01, 51.5-37.2
595	51.5-37
597	22.1-212.2:1, 23-38.10:1
598	54.1-2987, 54.1-2988, 54.1-2990, 54.1-2992
599	2.1-481
600	52-1, 52-4.3, 52-8.1:1
601	16.1-309.5
602	58.1-811, 58.1-1404, 58.1-1501, 58.1-2403
603	16.1-309.1
604	58.1-3506
605	32.1-323.1
606	2.1-812 — 2.1-814
607	58.1-339.10, 58.1-439.12
608	9-329.2, 60.2-318 — 60.2-322
609	51.5-37
610	37.1-42.1, 37.1-42.2, 51.5-37.1
611	22.1-280.1
612	2.1-481
613	15.2-404
614	58.1-2900, 58.1-2901, 58.1-3814
615	2.1-457.2
616	2.1-133.7:1
617	22.1-270
618	2.1-191.5 — 2.1-191.16, 2.1-191.14, 2.1-342.01, 2.1-526.1—2.1-526.9:1R, 2.1-526.11, 2.1-526.11:1R, 8.01-195.9, 8.01-588.1, 15.2-1527, 15.2-1533, 15.2-2702,32.1-27.3, 51.1-1130, 54.1-106
620	2.1-20.1:02
621	11-37
622	Va. Const., Art X, § 7-A, n., 58.1-4022.1
623	22.1-212.2:1, 23-38.10:1
624	38.2-1901, 38.2-1921.1, 65.2-101, 65.2-801, 65.2-803.1
626	58.1-3833, 58.1-3840
627	18.2-152.2
628	11-44, 11-51
629	22.1-1
630	38.2-3407.9
631	22.1-26, 22.1-212.5 — 22.1-212.15
632	2.1-191.5 — 2.1-191.16, 2.1-191.8, 2.1-342.01, 2.1-526.1 — 2.1-526.9:1R, 2.1-526.11, 2.1-526.11:1R, 8.01-195.9, 8.01-588.1, 15.2-1527, 15.2-1533, 15.2-2702, 32.1-127.3, 51.1-1130, 54.1-106
633	2.1-114.5, 2.1-114.5:02, 2.1-526.1, n. 2.1-526.10R
634	22.1-19.1, 22.1-292.1
635	22.1-100.1
636	2.1-457.2
637	11-41, 11-55
638	11-37
639	18.2-340.17
640	8.01-470
641	11-66
642	11-35
643	11-37
644	11-35, 11-37
645	22.1-212.2:1, 23-38.10:1
646	22.1-270
647	11-37, 11-41
648	22.1-277.01:2
649	2.1-20.1:02
650	22.1-291.1
651	22.1-205
652	15.2-2242
653	22.1-253.13:1
654	16.1-253.1, 16.1-279.1
655	55-419, 55-419.1
656	59.1-274
657	2.1-1.1, 2.1-1.3, 2.1-20.1, 2.1-20.1:02 — 2.1-20.1:04, 2.1-20.1:5, 2.1-20.1:6, 2.1-20.1:06, 2.1-51.27, 2.1-111, 2.1-113.1, 2.1-113.3, 2.1-114.3, 2.1-114.5, 2.1-114.7, 2.1-114.7:1, 2.1-116, 2.1-116.03,

Acts 2000 Chapter	Code 1950 Section
	2.1-116.07, 2.1-116.14, 2.1-116.21, 2.1-342.01, 2.1-404, 2.1-557, 15.2-1512.1, 15.2-1609.2, 22.1-209.2, 22.1-342.1, 23-50.16:24, 32.1-137.6, 51.1-126.1, 51.1-153, 51.1-205, 51.1-216, 51.1-502.1, 51.1-512.1, 51.1-513.1, 51.1-1101, 51.1-1106, 62.1-129.1
658	55-13.3
659	22.1-19.1, 22.1-292.1
660	23-38.15, 23-38.16, 23-38.17:1
661	2.1-457.2
662	22.1-253.13:1
663	15.2-2109
664	11-41, 11-55
665	11-37
666	11-35
667	46.2-604
668	19.2-311, 19.2-313 — 19.2-316, 53.1-63
669	38.2-226.3
671	23-14
672	33.1-375.1
674	15.2-915.1
675	23-278, 23-281, 23-284
676	22.1-354.6 — 22.1-354.10
677	22.1-253.13:1
678	59.1-274
680	15.2-6500 — 15.2-6504
681	58.1-815.3, n.
682	18.2-57
683	22.1-296.2
684	22.1-253.13:1
685	46.2-324.1
686	46.2-335
687	2.1-704, 60.2-613
688	2.1-1.6, 2.1-20.4, 9-6.25:1, 9-6.25:2, 13.1-543, 13.1-1102, 54.1-503, 54.1-2900, 54.1-2901, 54.1-2902 — 54.1-2904, 54.1-2908, 54.1-2942 — 54.1-2948R, 54.1-3473 — 54.1-3483
689	22.1-298, 22.1-299, 22.1-299.3, 22.1-303
690	19.2-311, 19.2-313 — 19.2-316, 53.1-63
691	56-235.8, 58.1-400.2, 58.1-403, 58.1-440.1, 58.1-504, 58.1-2626, 58.1-2627.1, 58.1-2660, 58.1-2904 — 58.1-2907, 58.1-3731, 58.1-3814
692	11-37, 11-41
693	22.1-100.1
694	58.1-638
695	59.1-274
696	11-45, 11-47.5
697	2.1-114.5, 2.1-114.5:02, 2.1-526.10R
699	23-9.2:5
700	23-278, 23-281, 23-284
701	54.1-3005, 54.1-3012.1
702	30-90 — 30-93
703	11-35, 11-37
704	2.1-508
705	33.1-253, n.
706	56-235.8, 58.1-400.2, 58.1-403, 58.1-440.1, 58.1-504, 58.1-2626, 58.1-2627.1, 58.1-2660, 58.1-2904 — 58.1-2907, 58.1-2906, 58.1-3731, 58.1-3814, 58.1-2626, n., 58.1-2627.1, n., 58.1-2660, n., 58.1-3731, n., 58.1-3814, 59.1-199
707	58.1-638
708	15.2-1302
709	22.1-304
710	22.1-253.13:1
711	15.2-2242
712	22.1-26, 22.1-212.5, 22.1-212.7, 22.1-212.8, 22.1-212.13, 22.1-212.14
713	Va. Const., Art. X, § 7-A, n., 58.1-4022.1
714	55-12.1 — 55-12.6, 55-13.2, 55-13.3
715	23-9.2:5
716	22.1-199.2
717	58.1-3
718	38.2-1901, 38.2-1921.1, 65.2-101, 65.2-801, 65.2-803.1
719	22.1-212.2:1, 23-38.10:1
720	2.1-1.5, 2.1-20.1, 2.1-20.1:2, 2.1-116, 2.1-342.01, 2.1-344, 23-50.16:1, 23-50.16:3, 23-50.16:4, 23-50.16:5, 23-50.16:7, 23-232, 32.1-85, 32.1-276.3, 51.1-126.1
721	22.1-32
722	51.1-126
723	51.1-126, 51.1-126.3, 51.1-502.2
724	10.1-1700, 15.2-5158
725	38.2-3412.1:01
726	2.1-1.6, 2.1-20.4, 9-6.25:2, 54.1-300, 54.1-700 — 54.1-704, 54.1-704.1, 54.1-704.2, 54.1-705, 54.1-706, 54.1-1200 — 54.1-1207R
727	3.1-796.93:1
728	40.1-51.11
729	33.1-221.1:6, 46.2-749.3, 46.2-819.2, 58.1-609.1, 58.1-2100, n., 58.1-2200, 58.1-2201, 58.1-2289, 58.1-2701, 58.1-2702, 62.1-44.34:13
730	3.1-188.21, 3.1-188.27
732	15.2-2295.1
733	55-210.2 — 55-210.2:2, 55-210.2:2, 55-210.3:01, 55-210.8, 55-210.8:1, 55-210.9 — 55-10.9:2, 55-210.10:1, 55-210.11, 55-210.12, 55-210.13, 55-210.17, 55-210.21, 55-210.22, 55-210.24, 55-210.24:1, 55-210.25, 55-210.26:1, 55-210.27
734	22.1-296.4, 63.1-248.8
735	22.1-253.13:3
736	46.2-1095, 46.2-1156.1
737	58.1-3403, 62.1-145
738	22.1-32
739	22.1-209.1:2
740	15.2-901
741	15.2-301
742	22.1-253.13:3
743	15.2-2403
744	6.1-225.50:1, 6.1-225.50:2
745	55-210.2 — 55-210.2:2, 55-210.3:01, 55-210.8, 55-210.8:1, 55-210.9 — 55-210.9:2, 55-10.10:1, 55-210.11, 55-210.12, 55-210.13, 55-210.17, 55-210.21, 55-210.22, 55-10.24,

Acts 2000 Chapter	Code 1950 Section
	55-210.24:1, 55-210.25, 55-210.26:1, 55-210.27
746	59.1-274
747	10.1-1700, 15.2-5158
748	2.1-504.2
749	15.2-1309
750	22.1-253.13:1, 22.1-253.13:3
751	36-99, 36-97
752	22.1-253.13:3
753	38.2-4301
754	22.1-131
755	57-59, 59.1-9.10
756	58.1-3228, 58.1-3965.1, 58.1-3967
757	15.2-2414 — 15.2-2418
758	33.1-221.1:6, 46.2-749.3, 46.2-819.2, 58.1-609.1, 58.1-2100 — 58.1-147R, 58.1-2200 — 58.1-2290, 58.1-2701, 58.1-2702, 62.1-44.34:13
759	54.1-2105, 54.1-2105.1
760	55-248.3:1, 55-248.4 — 55-248.7, 55-248.9, 55-248.9:1, 55-248.10R, 55-248.10:1, 55-248.11R, 55-248.11:1, 55-248.12, 55-248.13, 55-248.13:2, 55-248.13:3, 55-248.14, 55-248.15, 55-248.15:1, 55-248.16 — 55-248.27, 55-248.28R, 55-248.29R, 55-248.30R, 55-248.31, 55-248.31:01, 55-248.32, 55-248.34, 55-248.35, 55-248.38R, 55-248.38:1, 55-248.39, 55-248.48
761	55-248.15:1
762	33.1-44
763	13.1-543, 13.1-544, 13.1-549, 13.1-1102, 13.1-1103, 13.1-1111, 54.1-411
764	15.2-2286
765	2.1-1.5, 23-38.53:12 — 23-38.53:20
766	46.2-746.4:1R, 46.2-746.4:3, 46.2-746.6:1R, 46.2-746.6:2, 46.2-749.46 — 46.2-749.34
767	18.2-10, 19.2-295.2, 53.1-136, 53.1-157, 53.1-161, 53.1-162, 53.1-164, 53.1-165, 53.1-172, 53.1-174
768	20-124.4
769	19.2-316.1
770	18.2-10, 18.2-11, 18.2-370.2
771	56-484.11:1
772	15.2-1747
773	54.1-2802, 54.1-2803, 54.1-2805, 54.1-2810, 54.1-2814, 54.1-2814.1
774	22.1-296.2
775	19.2-305.1
776	9-390 — 9-395
777	15.2-2110
778	3.1-18.4 — 3.1-18.6, 3.1-18.8
779	56-257
780	4.1-325
781	16.1-244
782	54.1-2956.1, 54.1-2956.5
783	19.2-56
784	18.2-270
785	9-171.1
786	4.1-100, 4.1-201, 4.1-207
787	24.2-226, 24.2-227, 24.2-228.1, 24.2-682
788	54.1-2933.1
789	36-155, 36-157 — 36-170
790	62.1-198, 62.1-199, 62.1-215
791	15.2-1512.2
792	46.2-361
793	16.1-272
794	18.2-308.2:3
795	36-155, 36-157 — 36-170
796	18.2-369
797	19.2-120
798	54.1-2969
799	15.2-2110
800	17.1-255, 17.1-256, 17.1-257R, 17.1-258, 17.1-258.1
801	4.1-240
802	Va. Const., Art. XI, § 4
803	8.01-4
804	63.1-174
805	63.1-248.8
806	16.1-309.3
807	53.1-1, 53.1-25.1
808	63.1-174
809	45.1-392
810	32.1-127, 32.1-127.1, 32.1-127.1:03, 32.1-287, 32.1-289, 32.1-290, 32.1-292.1, 46.2-342, 54.1-2984, 54.1-2986
811	22.1-296.2
812	15.2-1812.1
813	8.01-407, 8.01-413, 16.1-89, 16.1-265, 32.1-127.1:03
814	54.1-2900, 54.1-2901, 54.1-2956.9, 54.1-2956.11
815	15.2-946.1 — 15.2-946.4
816	55-248.4
817	15.2-2286
818	23-76.1
819	18.2-248.1
820	38.2-401
821	8.01-412.2, 8.01-412.4
822	33.1-95.1
823	4.1-216, n., 4.1-223
824	32.1-351, 32.1-351.1, 32.1-351.2, 32.1-352, 32.1-353
825	30-19.1:4, 30-19.1:5R
826	17.1-275
827	19.2-11.01
828	8.01-345
829	15.2-1130, n.
830	16.1-241, 16.1-243, 16.1-262, 17.1-275, 17.1-405, 17.1-410, 20-124.1, 20-158, 20-160, 22.1-3, 63.1-195, 63.1-203, 63.1-204, 63.1-209, 63.1-219.7— 63.1-219.55, 63.1-220—63.1-238.02R
831	18.2-67.4:1
832	18.2-67.4
833	30-19.1:4, 30-19.1:5R
834	46.2-833
835	16.1-278.9
836	16.1-248.1
837	22.1-312
838	19.2-264.4
839	8.01-425.1
840	15.2-1130, n.
841	16.1-69.40:1
842	15.2-912, 18.2-371.3
843	33.1-95.1
844	23-174.4
845	63.1-172, 63.1-174
846	55-79.80:2, 55-513
847	19.2-368.11:1

Acts 2000 Chapter	Code 1950 Section
848	32.1-351, 32.1-351.1, 32.1-351.2, 32.1-352, 32.1-353
849	18.2-152.7:1
850	32.1-102.1
851	15.2-729, 25-46.36, 25-236, 25-238, 25-239, 25-248
852	24.2-908
853	15.2-2400, 15.2-2402, 15.2-2403
854	63.1-248.6
855	32.1-325
856	24.2-544
857	24.2-114, 24.2-417, 24.2-424, 24.2-425R, 24.2-427, 24.2-428
858	22.1-98.1
860	19.2-392.02
861	54.1-3401, 54.1-3408, 54.1-3410.1
862	38.2-3407.10
863	24.2-701
865	22.1-209.2
866	24.2-613
867	22.1-253.13:1, 22.1-253.13:3, 22.1-253.13:5, 22.1-253.13:6
868	32.1-102.3:2, n.
869	2.1-1.5, 33.1-426 — 33.1-429
870	32.1-330.1
871	8.01-226.5:1, 22.1-274.2
872	24.2-908
873	38.2-3407.9:01
874	24.2-1014.1
875	17.1-275.6
876	54.1-3307.2
877	2.1-373.02, 2.1-373.15 — 2.1-373.18
878	54.1-3401, 54.1-3408.02
879	40.1-51.19:3, 40.1-51.19:4.1
880	4.1-105, 58.1-3, 58.1-1009, 58.1-1031, 59.1-200
881	54.1-3408
882	54.1-3303, 54.1-3434.1
883	18.2-371.2
884	24.2-301.1, 24.2-304.1, 24.2-309.1
885	19.2-123, 19.2-143
887	51.1-142
888	2.1-20.1, 32.1-325, 38.2-3418.7:1
889	51.1-1100, 51.1-1103 — 51.1-1105, 51.1-1107, 51.1-1110, 51.1-1112, 51.1-1114, 51.1-1121, 51.1-1123, 51.1-1125, 51.1-1135 — 51.1-1136
890	20-162, 32.1-252
891	55-512, 55-513.1
892	15.2-6400, 15.2-6402, 15.2-6403
893	15.2-2226, 15.2-2229
894	32.1-102.13
895	15.2-1427
896	2.1-373.02, 2.1-373.15 — 2.1-373.18
897	32.1-276.3, 32.1-276.4, 32.1-276.5, 32.1-276.8
898	40.1-51.8, 40.1-51.19:1 — 40.1-51.19:3, 40.1-51.19:4, 40.1-51.19:4.1
899	2.1-548.57
900	2.1-746
901	4.1-105, 58.1-3, 58.1-1009, 58.1-1031—58.1-1037, 59.1-200
902	2.1-1.5, 33.1-426—33.1-429
903	32.1-122.07
905	55-79.39, n., 55-508, n., 55-510, 55-510.1, 55-513, 55-516
906	55-79.74:1, 55-79.75, 55-79.80:2, 55-79.81, 55-79.84
907	32.1-46.1, 32.1-46.2
908	24.2-612, n.
909	2.1-343.1:1, n.
910	2.1-343.1, n.
911	2.1-20.1:2, 2.1-20.1:3, 2.1-116.24, 2.1-384.1, 51.1-124.3, 51.1-124.31, 51.1-142, 51.1-153, 51.1-155.1, 51.1-155.2, 51.1-205, 51.1-206, 51.1-216 — 51.1-218, 51.1-303, 51.1-308, 51.1-502, 51.1-1201
912	32.1-102.3:2, n., 38.2-4900, n.
913	15.2-1628, 15.2-1630, 15.2-1632, 15.2-1633, 15.2-1636.8
914	2.1-757
915	15.2-6400
916	32.1-67
917	2.1-346.2 — 2.1-346.5
918	32.1-71.02
919	55-79.39, n., 55-79.74:1, 55-508, n.
920	32.1-102.1
921	57-60
922	32.1-137.6, 32.1-137.15, 38.2-3407.10, 38.2-3407.11:1, 38.2-3418.9, 38.2-4214, 38.2-4319, 38.2-4509, 38.2-5900 — 38.2-5902, 38.2-5904
923	8.01-413, 32.1-127.1:03
924	9-6.14:4.1, 54.1-2957.01, 54.1-3301, 54.1-3303
925	15.2-2400, 15.2-2402, 15.2-2403
926	32.1-122.6, 32.1-122.6:1, 32.1-122.6:02, 32.1-122.6:03, 32.1-122.9, 32.1-122.10
927	2.1-1.4, 2.1-815 — 2.1-817, 11-45, 32.1-127.1:03
928	8.01-225, 32.1-111.14:1
929	58.1-433.1, 58.1-2626.1
930	8.01-49.1
931	32.1-102.1:1, 32.1-102.3, 32.1-102.6
932	2.1-342.01, 2.1-343.2
933	2.1-342.01, 2.1-717, 2.1-724, 2.1-725
934	38.2-3407.10
935	54.1-3401, 54.1-3408
936	32.1-229
937	2.1-51.14, 2.1-746, 2.1-746.1, 2.1-747, 2.1-748, 2.1-752, 2.1-759, 2.1-759.1, 9-6.25:3
938	24.2-802
939	15.2-1221R, 32.1-111.1
940	46.2-874, n.
941	27-98
942	56-582
943	59.1-162.1
944	56-231.15, 56-231.18, 56.231.20R, 56-231.23 — 56-231.25, 56-231.27, 56-231.28, 56-231.30, 56-231.33, 56-231.34:1, 56-231.38,

Acts 2000 Chapter	Code 1950 Section
	56-231.40, 56-231.43, 56-231.44, 56-231.50:1
945	62.1-44.19:5
946	63.1-325.2
947	2.1-1.1, 2.1-1.3, 2.1-51.27, 2.1-113.1, 2.1-113.3, 2.1-116.01 — 2.1-16.05, 2.1-116.07, 2.1-116.07:1, 2.1-116.09, 2.1-342.01, 15.2-738, 15.2-1507, 17.1-405
951	18.2-85, 27-97, 27-97.2
953	15.2-404
954	16.1-278.7, 16.1-278.8, 16.1-285
956	18.2-36.1, 18.2-51.4, 18.2-270, 18.2-271, 46.2-301, 46.2-357, 46.2-389, 46.2-391, 46.2-394, 46.2-395
957	46.2-874, n.
958	18.2-270, 18.2-270.1, 18.2-271.1, 19.2-299.2, 46.2-341.28, 46.2-391
959	46.2-389, 46.2-391, 46.2-411.1
960	15.2-6400
961	2.1-563.42 — 2.1-563.44
962	8.01-226, 18.2-174.1, 18.2-426
963	15.2-4904
964	56-231.15, 56-231.16, 56-231.30, 56-231.38, 56-231.39
965	15.2-6400
967	32.1-126, 32.1-325.1
968	23-7.4:5
969	53.1-231.1, 53.1-231.2
970	18.2-271.1
971	55-58.2
972	62.1-44.2, 62.1-44.3, 62.1-44.15
973	10.1-559.1, 10.1-559.3 — 10.1-559.5
974	45.1-161.292:30, 45.1-161.292:35
978	16.1-278.8, 16.1-284.1, 16.1-292
980	18.2-270, 18.2-270.1, 18.2-271.1, 19.2-299.2, 46.2-341.28, 46.2-391
981	16.1-278.7, 16.1-278.8, 16.1-285
982	18.2-36.1, 18.2-51.4, 18.2-270, 18.2-271, 46.2-301, 46.2-357, 46.2-389, 46.2-391, 46.2-394, 46.2-395
983	2.1-343.1, n.
984	15.2-4203
985	46.2-389, 46.2-391, 46.2-411.1
986	12.1-13, 12.1-33, 56-483
987	2.1-346.2 — 2.1-346.5
988	16.1-278.7, 16.1-278.8, 16.1-285
989	56-231.15, 56-231.16, 56-231.30, 56-231.38, 56-231.39
990	54.1-409
991	56-576, 56-580 — 56-583, 56-585, 56-587 — 56-590, 56-592.1, 56-593
992	59.1-394.1 — 59.1-394.4
993	3.1-530.10, 3.1-533, 3.1-545.1
994	56-1.2, 56-235.4
995	1-13.32, 2.1-7.4R, 2.1-51.47, 13.1-604, 13.1-804, 13.1-1003, 17.1-258, 50-73.17, 50-73.83, 58.1-9, 59.1-467 — 59.1-469R, 59.1-479 — 59.1-520,
996	59.1-501.1 — 59.1-509.2, 59.1-503.1
997	10.1-1105
998	33.1-90
999	56-231.15, 56-231.18, 56-231.20R, 56-231.23 — 56-231.25, 56-231.27, 56-231.28, 56-231.30, 56-231.33, 56-231.34:1, 56-231.38, 56-231.40, 56-231.43, 56-231.44, 56-231.50:1
1000	18.2-340.20, 18.2-340.33
1001	27-98
1002	59.1-378.1
1004	15.2-2144
1005	8.01-46.1
1006	2.1-1.1, 2.1-1.3, 2.1-51.27, 2.1-113.1, 2.1-113.3, 2.1-116.01 — 2.1-116.05, 2.1-116.07:1, 2.1-116.09, 2.1-342.01, 15.2-738, 15.2-1507, 17.1-405
1007	8.1-105, 8.1-201, 8.2-103, 8.2-210, 8.2-326, 8.2-502, 8.2-716, 8.2A-103, 8.2A-303, 8.2A-307, 8.2A-309, 8.4-208, 8.5A-117.1, 8.6A-102, 8.6A-103, 8.7-503, 8.8A-103, 8.8A-106, 8.8A-110, 8.8A-301, 8.8A-302, 8.8A-510, 8.9-101R, 8.9A-101 — 8.9A-709, 12.1-21.1, 8.9A-101, 12.1-21R
1008	55-510
1009	18.2-373, 18.2-391
1010	3.1-796.96, 3.1-796.120
1011	9-6.14:4.1, 59.1-371, 59.1-380, 59.1-387
1013	65.2-402
1014	23-76.1
1018	65.2-101 — 65.2-603
1019	32.1-267, n., 33.1-23.03:8, 33.1-268, 33.1-269, 33.1-276 — 33.1-278, 33.1-280, 33.1-284
1020	16.1-273, 16.1-278.8, 16.1-278.8:01, 18.2-248 — 18.2-248.1, 18.2-248.5, 18.2-251 — 18.2-252, 18.2-254, 18.2-255, 18.2-255.2, 19.2-123
1021	58.1-322, 58.1-402
1022	22.1-203
1023	44-146.28
1024	19.2-169.3, 19.2-174.1, 37.1-70.1, 37.1-134.21
1025	38.2-3418.10
1026	8.01-397.1
1027	58.1-2403
1028	22.1-26, 22.1-212.5— 22.1-212.15
1029	25-46.3, 25-46.5, 25-46.9, 25-46.11, 25-46.17, 25-46.19 — 25-46.22, 25-46.24, 25-46.25, 25-46.29, 25-46.32, 25-248, 33.1-89, 36-27
1030	2.1-20.1:8
1031	59.1-369, 59.1-385, 59.1-392
1032	62.1-44.3, 62.1-44.5, 62.1-44.15, 62.1-44.15:5, 62.1-44.29
1033	36-132, n.
1034	54.1-2982

Acts 2000 Chapter	Code 1950 Section
1035	9-6.25:1, 62.1-132.11:2
1036	4.1-210, 4.1-231, 4.1-233
1037	4.1-100, 4.1-207, 4.1-219, 4.1-231
1038	38.2-5004.1, 38.2-5009
1039	58.1-322, 58.1-402
1040	18.2-57.3, 18.2-64.2, 18.2-67.4, 19.2-152.4:1, 19.2-299.2, 19.2-303.3, 53.1-82.1, 53.1-82.3, 53.1-150, 53.1-180 — 53.1-182.1, 53.1-182.1:1, 53.1-183 — 53.1-185.3
1041	16.1-273, 16.1-278.8, 16.1-278.8:01, 18.2-248, 18.2-248.01, 18.2-248.1, 18.2-248.5, 18.2-251 — 18.2-252, 18.2-254, 18.2-255, 18.2-255.2, 19.2-123
1042	9-385, 58.1-439.13 — 58.1-439.17
1043	10.1-2500, 32.1-248.01, 62.1-44.17:2, 62.1-44.17:3, 62.1-44.17:4, 62.1-44.19:4 — 62.1-44.19:6, 62.1-44.19:9, 62.1-44.19:10
1044	33.1-23.03:8, 33.1-267, n., 33.1-268, 33.1-269, 33.1-276 — 33.1-278, 33.1-280, 33.1-284
1045	22.1-57.3, 24.2-222, 24.2-222.1, 24.2-223, 24.2-226, 24.2-311, 24.2-503
1046	30-86
1047	4.1-208, 4.1-210, 4.1-231, 4.1-233
1048	2.1-41.3, 2.1-127.1, 3.1-14.1, 8.01-220.1:4
1050	15.2-2309
1051	4.1-210, 4.1-231, 4.1-233
1052	4.1-100, 4.1-207, 4.1-219, 4.1-231
1053	10.1-1018 — 10.1-1021, 10.1-1021.1, 10.1-1024, 10.1-1026
1054	62.1-44.3, 62.1-44.5, 62.1-44.15, 62.1-44.15:5, 62.1-44.29
1055	8.01-126
1056	28.2-1204.2, 28.2-1206, 28.2-1208, 28.2-1213
1057	24.2-802
1058	63.1-196.001
1059	22.1-209.1:4
1060	38.2-3418.10
1061	22.1-253.13:3
1063	22.1-278.3
1064	2.1-342.01, 2.1-344, 2.1-563.35:4 8.01-225, 9-6.25:2, 56-484.8R, 56-484.9R, 56-484.10R, 56-484.11R, 56-484.12 56-484.17, 58.1-3812, 58.1-3813R, 58.1-3813.1, 58.1-3814
1065	18.2-85, 27-97, 27-97.2
1066	58.1-439.2
1067	9-382, 32.1-357, 32.1-358
1068	22.1-298
1069	15.2-4313
1070	24.2-226, 24.2-227, 24.2-228.1, 24.2-682
1071	8.01-226.7

ACTS 2001

Acts 2001 Chapter	Code 1950 Section
1	24.2-304R, 30-19.9
2	18.2-57.02
3	19.2-12
4	19.2-191, 19.2-206, 19.2-208, 19.2-210, 19.2-212, 19.2-213
5	15.2-4903
6	15.2-4903
7	15.2-6403
8	15.2-1535
9	15.2-1414.7
10	15.2-903
13	15.2-2119
14	15.2-1302
15	15.2-6403
16	16.1-69.6:1
17	2.1-1.6, 3.1-4.1, 3.1-73.1, n., 3.1-73.2R, 3.1-73.3, 3.1-73.5, 9-6.25:2
18	15.2-2304
19	46.2-716
20	46.2-726
21	46.2-1188, 46.2-1190
22	32.1-137.13
23	46.2-1519
24	6.1-410
25	18.2-308
26	29.1-521
27	46.2-1188, 46.2-1190
28	28.2-226.2
29	8.01-329
30	37.1-134.10
31	19.2-12
32	38.2-1871
33	9-171.1, 9.1-110
34	38.2-508
35	17.1-415, 17.1-417
36	33.1-223.9
37	58.1-3967
38	26-51
39	51.1-124.23
40	19.2-392.2
41	58.1-3506
42	62.1-44.33
43	2.1-391, 2.2-1501
44	55-248.43
45	2.1-376.1
46	28.2-556
47	55-248.34, 55-248.46, 55-248.46:1, 55-248.48
48	2.1-639.4:2
49	29.1-301
50	58.1-3234
51	28.2-226
52	59.1-310.7— 59.1-310.10, n.
53	10.1-518.1, 10.1-523, 10.1-525, 24.2-506, 24.2-680
54	10.1-530
55	29.1-305
56	46.2-834
57	9-254.1
58	10.1-418
59	17.1-106
60	29.1-521
61	54.1-2957.5, 54.1-2957.6
62	29.1-309.1
63	29.1-339
64	38.2-106
65	36-139.5:1
66	15.2-941
67	2.1-548.59
68	33.1-13.1
69	33.1-8
70	46.2-200
71	46.2-834
72	28.2-1205
73	26-12, 26-17.7
74	16.1-122.4
75	56-265.4:4, 56-481.2
76	56-466.1
77	44-117
78	64.1-122.2
79	26-3
80	46.2-1571
81	55-19

Acts 2001 Chapter	Code 1950 Section
82	46.2-200
83	33.1-13.1
84	58.1-3, 58.1-2712.2
85	64.1-96.11
86	59.1-481, 59.1-494
87	33.1-8
88	4.1-210, n., 4.1-231, n., 4.1-233, n.
89	46.2-1571
90	33.1-190.1
91	58.1-338, n., 58.1-439.7, 58.1-445.1, n.
92	10.1-604
93	29.1-203
94	46.2-1110
95	33.1-72.1, 33.1-75.1
96	4.1-210, n., 4.1-231, n., 4.1-233, n.
97	7.1-40.12
98	8.01-581.1
99	38.2-3407.11
100	2.1-68.1, 9-77.11:03
101	16.1-253.1, 19.2-152.9
102	38.2-3408, 38.2-4221
103	28.2-820
104	33.1-190.1
105	33.1-70.01
106	11-69
107	26-20.1
108	26-10
109	62.1-44.17:1
110	38.2-5901
111	27-23.1
112	29.1-523.1
113	2.1-37.1
114	38.2-5202
115	28.2-302.2, 29.1-328
116	62.1-44.15:1.2
117	4.1-200
118	2.1-127
119	36-105
120	15.2-2117, 15.2-5114
121	15.2-4904
122	19.2-305.4
123	29.1-203
125	23-295.1
126	46.2-844, 46.2-859
127	8.01-9
128	46.2-1220
129	18.2-57
130	33.1-70.01
131	18.2-178
132	23-231.18
133	46.2-411.1
134	7.1-40.12
135	46.2-1572.3
136	46.2-1241
137	5.1-141R, 46.2-2042R
138	63.1-248.7:2
140	16.1-284.1
141	46.2-1220
142	27-6.1, 27-7 — 27-9, 27-10, 27-11, 27-14, 27-15.1, 27-15.2, 27-17, 27-17.1, 27-19, 27-20, 27-23.1 — 27-23.6, 27-23.9
143	46.2-1220
144	46.2-1222.1
145	46.2-880
147	46.2-915.1
148	46.2-342
149	46.2-1568
150	46.2-1572.3
151	46.2-1105, 46.2-1112, 46.2-1113, 46.2-1139
153	2.1-116.9:6
156	46.2-1220
157	46.2-342
160	46.2-411.1
161	63.1-174
162	9-170, 9-173, 9.1-116
163	10.1-2003, 10.1-2004, 10.1-2007, 10.1-2008
164	10.1-1022.1
165	46.2-1572.4, 46.2-1573
166	10.1-1186.4
167	58.1-2259, 58.1-2263, 58.1-2276
168	10.1-1022.1
169	33.1-371.2
170	46.2-932
171	58.1-638
172	10.1-200.2, 10.1-202
173	46.2-1572.4, 46.2-1573
174	10.1-1186.4
175	33.1-386
177	33.1-62, n.
180	46.2-1156
181	18.2-369
182	18.2-271.1
183	19.2-56
184	63.1-105.9
185	53.1-129
186	54.1-2911, 54.1-2940R, 54.1-3605, 54.1-3608R
187	9-316, 30-170
188	32.1-122.6, 32.1-122.6:1, 32.1-122.6:02— 32.1-122.6:03, 32.1-122.6:04, 32.1-122.9, 32.1-122.9:1, 32.1-122.10, 54.1-3011.2
189	23-114, n.
190	2.1-752
191	63.1-55.3
192	46.2-651
193	20-108.2
194	46.2-1527.2, 46.2-1527.5
195	18.2-253
196	53.1-129
197	18.2-60.3
198	54.1-2911, 54.1-2940R, 54.1-3605, 54.1-3608R
199	54.1-2910.1
200	46.2-1088.2
201	19.2-123
203	16.1-223, 19.2-387
204	15.2-2157.1
205	19.2-56
206	2.1-752
208	38.2-3407.4:1R
209	20-79.3
210	9-170, 9.1-102
211	8.01-581.15
212	59.1-479, n.
213	9-362, 9-368
214	19.2-92
215	16.1-223, 19.2-387
216	9-362, 9-368
217	2.1-639.13, 2.1-639.14
218	38.2-2206
219	11-34.1— 11-34.4
220	Sup. Ct. Rule 1:17, n., 17.1-255, n.
221	8.01-328.1
222	8.01-470, 55-237.1, 55-248.38:2
223	64.1-144
224	2.1-64.34:1
225	54.1-3910.1
226	19.2-92
227	2.1-20.3
228	7.1-40.13
229	16.1-218
230	54.1-3922, n., 54.1-3925, n.
231	2.1-344
232	28.2-106
233	28.2-1006
234	28.2-1203
235	54.1-2901
236	63.1-219.50
237	54.1-2901
238	32.1-351
239	38.2-3407.10
240	15.2-2286
241	57-12
242	38.2-3407.11:3
243	54.1-3422
244	54.1-3001
246	15.2-2511.1
247	10.1-104, n., 10.1-109, n.
248	16.1-278.9

Acts 2001 Chapter	Code 1950 Section
249	19.2-13
251	54.1-3001
252	8.01-581.2
253	57-12
254	15.2-1414.7
255	32.1-65
256	16.1-69.9:2, 17.1-509
257	33.1-84.1
258	15.2-924
259	2.1-51.12:4
260	25-248
261	22.1-270
262	22.1-130.1
263	2.1-27.2:01, 22.1-17.4
264	10.1-2128
265	26-12.4, 26-32, 64.1-122.2
266	16.1-278.9
267	10.1-2211
268	54.1-2914
269	22.1-70.2
270	15.2-912, 18.2-371.3
271	55-515.2
272	32.1-353.6
273	33.1-84.1
274	37.1-134.7
275	32.1-73.7
276	38.2-5903
277	33.1-84.1
278	46.2-395
279	10.1-2211
280	65.2-813.2
281	15.2-2202
282	15.2-2303.2
284	10.1-2211
285	33.1-369
286	56-557
287	17.1-207
288	2.1-342.01
289	2.1-304.1:2, 8.9A-109, 8.9A-703
291	32.1-73.7, 32.1-73.7
292	63.1-323, 63.1-325.2, 58.1-333R, 58.1-430R
293	36-55.63, 58.1-336R, 58.1-435
294	58.1-3713.3
295	17.1-302, 17.1-401
296	2.1-304.1:2, 8.9A-109, 8.9A-703
297	58.1-478
298	46.2-870
299	36-55.63, 58.1-336R, 58.1-435
300	63.1-323, 63.1-325.2, 58.1-333R, 58.1-430R
301	2.1-548.49
302	58.1-3816.2
303	58.1-3713.3
304	30-58.3
305	20-125— 20-146R,

Acts 2001 Chapter	Code 1950 Section
	20-146.1— 20-146.38, 63.1-219.37
306	15.2-2110
307	58.1-478
308	6.1-249, 6.1-272.1, 6.1-278, 6.1-285, 6.1-286R, 6.1-288, 6.1-291
309	2.1-37.12:1
310	2.1-548.49
311	3.1-735
312	28.2-109 — 28.2-111
313	15.2-2304
314	36-139.8
315	54.1-3480.1
316	6.1-2.23
317	54.1-3300
318	2.1-37.12:1
319	10.1-1142
320	3.1-73.7
321	63.1-248.8
322	3.1-290
323	11-47
324	11-56.2
326	15.2-2110
327	46.2-665
329	32.1-126.01
330	23-7.4:1, 65.2-102, 65.2-402
332	40.1-51.2:2
333	3.1-735
334	2.1-20.1, 32.1-325, 38.2-3407.4:2
335	38.2-510
336	9-329.1
337	32.1-163.5
338	15.2-2159, 46.2-752
339	54.1-2003
340	23-7.5
341	32.1-276.3, 32.1-276.4, n., 32.1-276.6, 32.1-276.8, 32.1-276.9
342	5.1-152 — 5.1-171
343	58.1-613
345	19.2-392.2
347	56-57
348	8.01-375
349	33.1-12
350	9.1-140, 38.2-1867
351	56-265.32
352	18.2-248, n.
353	27-6.2
354	62.1-44.5
355	33.1-70.1
356	46.2-1304.1
357	18.2-308.1:4
358	18.2-152.5
359	46.2-828, 46.2-1040
360	23-4.01
361	4.1-209

Acts 2001 Chapter	Code 1950 Section
362	58.1-613
363	19.2-368.5, 19.2-368.7
364	16.1-274
365	18.2-472.1, 19.2-298.1
366	33.1-70.1
367	16.1-69.33
368	64.1-123, 64.1-123.1, 64.1-123.3, 64.1-124, 64.1-124.1, 64.1-130, 64.1-132.2, 64.1-151.2— 64.1-151.4
369	64.1-45.2
370	10.1-104, 10.1-200.3, 10.1-202
371	38.2-513R, 38.2-513.1, 38.2-514, 38.2-601, 38.2-602, 38.2-604, 38.2-604.1, 38.2-606, 38.2-612.1, 38.2-612.2, 38.2-613, 52-41
372	6.1-370— 6.1-375, 6.1-377, 6.1-378.4
373	27-6.2
374	19.2-298.1
375	18.2-248, n.
376	64.1-75.1
377	28.2-520
379	18.2-251.4
380	18.2-271.4
381	8.01-581.16, 8.01-581.17
382	33.1-320.2, n.
383	62.1-44.5
384	18.2-308
385	18.2-64.2
386	56-492, 56-495, 56-502
387	38.2-1428
388	9-183.2
389	19.2-295.1
390	15.2-6403
391	15.2-6400, 15.2-6402, 15.2-6403
392	9-84.7, 11-35
393	2.1-116.07:1, 2.1-116.08, 2.2-3007, 17.1-405
394	55-248.13:2, n.
395	11-37, 11-41
396	18.2-271.4
397	38.2-401
398	2.1-1.6, 3.1-4.1, 3.1-73.1, 3.1-73.2R, 3.1-73.3, 3.1-73.5, 9-6.25:2
399	56-265.16:1, 56-265.30
400	15.2-5136
401	54.1-4009, 54.1-4010

Acts 2001 Chapter	Code 1950 Section
402	59.1-21.7
403	18.2-308.1
404	15.2-6400
405	2.1-20.1:9, 2.1-51.31:1, 2.1-51.31:2, 15.2-1512.3
406	15.2-2204
407	3.1-796.96, n., 3.1-796.120, n.
408	32.1-229, 32.1-229.01
409	9-84.7, 11-35
410	18.2-67.9, 19.2-11.01
411	46.2-1135, 46.2-1137
412	11-60
413	38.2-401
414	19.2-258.1, 19.2-349, 19.2-354, 46.2-395, 46.2-416
415	2.1-385.1
416	55-248.3:1
417	46.2-1143
418	33.1-191
419	55-79.74:1, 55-510
420	2.1-116.07:1, 2.1-116.08, 2.2-3006, 2.2-3007, 17.1-405
421	56-576
422	15.2-2314
423	18.2-186.3
424	15.2-5800, n., 15.2-5805, n., 15.2-5806, 15.2-5808, n., 15.2-5814, n., 15.2-5815, n., 15.2-5820, n., 15.2-5821, n.
426	32.1-229, 32.1-229.01
427	2.1-133.8, 9.1-403
428	58.1-3211
429	58.1-609.3
430	18.2-251, 22.1-315
431	22.1-167.3
432	33.1-191
433	46.2-1135, 46.2-1137
434	9-170, 9.1-102
435	62.1-44.3, n., 62.1-44.5, n., 62.1-44.15, n., 62.1-44.15:5, n., 62.1-44.29, n.
436	9-173.21, 9.1-184, 22.1-278.1
437	2.1-754
438	22.1-212.9
439	22.1-215.1
440	9-173.21, 9.1-184, 22.1-278.1
441	15.2-5800, n., 15.2-5805, n., 15.2-5806, 15.2-5808, n., 15.2-5814, n., 15.2-5815, n., 15.2-5820, n., 15.2-5821, n.
443	51.5-44
444	8.01-42.3
445	22.1-178
446	53.1-40.01
447	58.1-3506
448	54.1-3025.1
449	58.1-3257
450	18.2-251, 22.1-315
451	18.2-391
452	22.1-206
453	37.1-84.3
454	32.1-225
455	37.1-62.1
456	22.1-167.3
457	58.1-3211
458	9-170, 9.1-102
459	32.1-49.1, 32.1-50, 32.1-50.1
460	8.01-581.13, 38.2-3412.1, 54.1-3500, 54.1-3505, 54.1-3507, 54.1-3507.1— 54.1-3507.3, 54.1-3509
461	4.1-126, 4.1-210, 4.1-231, 4.1-233
462	58.1-3343, 58.1-3713.5, 58.1-3930, 58.1-3932, 58.1-3959
463	32.1-127
464	62.1-44.3, n., 62.1-44.5, n., 62.1-44.15, n., 62.1-44.15:5, n., 62.1-44.29, n.
465	9-6.14:4.1, 54.1-2952.1, 54.1-3301, 54.1-3303, 54.1-3422
466	32.1-111.4
467	22.1-89.4
468	58.1-609.3
469	22.1-212.9
470	58.1-3133
471	46.2-752
472	22.1-356, 22.1-357
473	16.1-77, 18.2-76
474	16.1-253.4, 19.2-152.8
475	38.2-3408, 38.2-4221
476	58.1-322
477	16.1-77, 18.2-76
478	37.1-67.3, 37.1-134.18
479	37.1-67.3, 37.1-134.18
480	19.2-175
481	17.1-275, 19.2-353.3
482	36-49.1:1
483	2.1-548.29, 2.2-2238, 9-329.2, 15.2-2800, 16.1-287, 22.1-129, 22.1-199.1, 22.1-209.1:8, 22.1-209.1:9, 22.1-213, 22.1-214.2, 22.1-214.3, 22.1-227— 22.1-237, 22.1-228, 22.1-253.13:1, 22.1-253.13:4, n., 22.1-275, 22.1-341— 22.1-343, 22.1-354.2, 23-7.4:2, 23-31, 23-38.19:3, 23-38.19:4, 23-214, 23-215, 23-230, 34-26, 37.1-10.01, 51.5-18, 53.1-32.1, 53.1-41, 53.1-63, 53.1-64, 53.1-67.1, 53.1-197, 54.1-3510, 63.1-105, 63.1-110, 63.1-133.43, 63.1-133.49, 63.1-133.56, 63.1-133.58
484	22.1-199.1, 22.1-253.13:6
485	58.1-3818
486	37.1-179, 37.1-179.1, 37.1-181— 37.1-182.3, 37.1-183.1— 37.1-188.1, 37.1-186.1— 37.1-188.1, 37.1-189.2
487	53.1-40.01
488	16.1-69.40, 47.1-5
489	58.1-3220, 58.1-3220.01, 58.1-3221
490	10.1-563, 10.1-566
491	37.1-62.1
492	62.1-44.15:3
493	62.1-44.18:3
494	16.1-69.35
495	54.1-3932
496	17.1-275
497	17.1-225, 17.1-242
498	15.2-2100 — 15.2-2102
499	16.1-69.40
500	22.1-253.13:4
501	17.1-275, 19.2-353.3
502	6.1-422
503	63.1-55.4
504	6.1-423
505	15.2-1716
506	37.1-179, 37.1-179.1, 37.1-181 — 37.1-182.3, 37.1-183.1 — 37.1-185.1, 37.1-186.1 — 37.1-188.1, 37.1-189.2
507	37.1-67.3, 37.1-134.18
508	6.1-58.1

Acts 2001 Chapter	Code 1950 Section
509	19.2-163
510	6.1-422.1, 6.1-430
511	6.1-413, 6.1-422, 6.1-428
512	6.1-2.23
513	8.01-410, 16.1-93.1, 16.1-276.2, 16.1-276.3, 17.1-513.2
514	8.01-407, n., 8.01-413, n., 16.1-89, n., 16.1-265, n., 32.1-127.1:03, n.
515	32.1-162.8
516	19.2-390
517	13.1-316, 13.1-619, 13.1-634, 13.1-637, 13.1-759, 13.1-763, 13.1-766, 13.1-819, 13.1-833, 13.1-836, 13.1-921, 13.1-925, 13.1-928, 13.1-1011, 13.1-1015, 13.1-1018, 50-73.4, 50-73.7, 50-73.11, 50-73.132, 50-73.135
518	2.1-342.01, 63.1-53, 63.1-209, 63.1-209.1
519	38.2-221.2, 38.2-1301.1, 38.2-1306.1, 38.2-1320.4, 38.2-1320.5, 38.2-1333, 38.2-3127.1, 38.2-4235, 38.2-5508
520	2.1-1.6, 2.1-1.7, 2.1-20.1:01R, 2.1-20.1:02, 2.1-113.1— 2.1-113.3R, 2.1-116.10— 2.1-116.14R, 9-6.25:1, 9-396— 9-399
521	3.1-18.9—3.1-18.12
522	58.1-608.3
523	3.1-530.1, 3.1-530.2, 3.1-530.10, 3.1-530.11, 9-6.14:4.1
524	55-225.3, 55-225.4, 55-248.15:1, 55-248.18, 55-248.27, 55-248.35
525	36-98
526	51.5-31
527	54.1-3101
528	59.1-510— 59.1-518
529	56-484.12, 56-484.17, 58.1-3813.1
530	19.2-11.01
531	2.1-548.29:1
532	43-4.01
533	54.1-2900, 54.1-2901
534	32.1-325
535	58.1-346.16
536	19.2-390
537	8.9A-408, 59.1-475, 59.1-475.1, 59.1-476, 59.1-476.1, 59.1-477, 59.1-477.1
538	15.2-1901
539	59.1-391
540	22.1-304
541	13.1-316, 13.1-619, 13.1-634, 13.1-637, 13.1-759, 13.1-763, 13.1-766, 13.1-819, 13.1-833, 13.1-836, 13.1-921, 13.1-925, 13.1-928, 13.1-1011, 13.1-1015, 13.1-1018, 50-73.4, 50-73.7, 50-73.11, 50-73.132, 50-73.135
543	55-362, 55-369, 55-370, 55-374
544	54.1-111
545	12.1-19, 12.1-20, 12.1-21.1, 12.1-21.2, 13.1-603, 13.1-615, 13.1-615.1, 13.1-616, 13.1-617R, 13.1-658, 13.1-722.2— 13.1-722.7, 13.1-722.8— 13.1-722.14, 13.1-1005, 13.1-1062
546	51.5-31
547	18.2-145.1
548	13.1-1002, 13.1-1014, 13.1-1028, 13.1-1035, 13.1-1038.1, 13.1-1046, 13.1-1067, 54.1-2100
549	19.2-11.01
550	15.2-1129.1
551	8.01-407, n., 8.01-413, n., 16.1-89, n., 16.1-265, n., 32.1-127.1:03, n.
552	19.2-389
553	59.1-510— 59.1-518
554	54.1-3101
555	17.1-402
556	55-79.97, 55-511, 55-512
557	2.1-548.29
558	2.1-20.1, 2.2-2818
559	58.1-346.17
560	58.1-346.18
561	18.2-268.6, 18.2-268.8
562	2.1-764, 2.1-766, 2.2-5304
563	16.1-285.1
564	38.2-2202
565	19.2-390
566	9-400— 9-399
567	8.01-413
568	30-19.3, 30-28.18
569	2.1-442, 10.1-1400, 10.1-1422.5R, 10.1-1422.6
570	27-98
571	58.1-3819
572	18.2-145.1
573	63.1-249, 63.1-274.6
574	62.1-204
575	32.1-163.6
576	56-579
577	2.1-1.7, 2.1-33, 2.1-51.15, 9-6.23, 9-6.25:1, 9-95.5R, 9-95.6R, 9-267 — 9-273R, 9-291.1R, 9-334R, 9-335R, 30-90— 30-93R, 36-132, n.
578	23-14
579	32.1-125.3
580	10.1-1322.3
581	65.2-402
582	19.2-389
583	64.1-45.3
584	30-19.3, 30-28.18
585	58.1-3819
586	58.1-807
587	10.1-1429.1, 10.1-1429.5, 62.1-229.2
588	63.1-248.4:1
589	15.2-1507
590	33.1-23.3
591	19.2-83.1, 22.1-296.2
593	53.1-183
594	4.1-123
595	8.01-420.6
596	46.2-711, 46.2-757— 46.2-768R, 46.2-2000, 46.2-2000.1, 46.2-2002, n., 46.2-2000.2R, 46.2-2000.3, 46.2-2001, 46.2-2001.1—46.2-2001.3, 46.2-2002— 46.2-2004R, 46.2-2005, 46.2-2005.1, 46.2-2006, n., 46.2-2006— 46.2-2010R, 46.2-2011, 46.2-2011.1, 46.2-2011.2— 46.2-2011.32, 46.2-2012— 46.2-2041R, 46.2-2042— 46.1-2050R, 46.2-2051— 46.2-2099.43, 46.2-2100, 46.2-2101, 46.2-2102, 46.2-2108.1— 46.2-2108.6, 46.2-2109, 46.2-2110— 46.2-2114R, 46.2-2114.1— 46.2-2176,

Acts 2001 Chapter	Code 1950 Section
	46.2-2140, 46.2-2176, 46.2-2000.2R, 46.2-2103— 46.2-2108R, 46.2-2200— 46.2-2209R, 46.2-2300— 46.2-2316R, 46.2-2500— 46.2-2519R, 46.2-2600— 46.2-2610R
597	29.1-301
598	26-12.3
599	28.2-209
601	15.2-1507.1
603	22.1-32
605	46.2-752
606	46.2-752
607	22.1-32
609	3.1-621 — 3.1-625, n., 3.1-629, n., 3.1-630, n., 3.1-636.01 — 3.1-636.9
610	15.2-4816 — 15.2-4828
611	33.1-430 — 33.1-446
612	24.2-405, 24.2-406, 24.2-418, 24.2-444
613	24.2-414
614	24.2-305, 24.2-309.1R
615	24.2-424
616	24.2-436— 24.2-439R
617	24.2-707
618	24.2-914, 24.2-915
619	58.1-3833
620	24.2-929, 24.2-930
621	24.2-701, 24.2-706
622	24.2-705, 24.2-705.1, 24.2-705.2, 24.2-710
623	24.2-115.1
624	24.2-707
625	24.2-424, 24.2-428.1
626	24.2-405, 24.2-406, 24.2-418, 24.2-444
627	24.2-422
628	24.2-436— 24.2-439R
629	24.2-443.1
630	24.2-203, 24.2-542, 24.2-543
631	24.2-700, 24.2-701
632	24.2-414
633	24.2-905
634	24.2-427
635	24.2-928, 24.2-929
636	24.2-1004
637	24.2-112
638	24.2-112
639	24.2-802, 24.2-814
640	24.2-629
641	24.2-629, 24.2-802, 24.2-814
642	24.2-112
643	24.2-112
644	18.2-60
645	18.2-259.1, 18.2-271.1, 46.2-320, 46.2-392, 46.2-499
646	24.2-802
647	19.2-299
648	24.2-928, 24.2-929
649	29.1-744
650	9-183.2, 9.1-140
651	22.1-253.13:3
652	62.1-198, 62.1-199
653	18.2-60
654	18.2-268.3, 18.2-268.10, 46.2-341.26:3, 46.2-341.26:10
655	46.2-334.01
656	23-220.01
657	18.2-308
658	37.1-67.3
659	22.1-205, 46.2-330, 46.2-334, 46.2-334.01, n., 46.2-334.02, 46.2-335, 46.2-335.2
660	22.1-290.01, 23-38.10:1, 22.1-212.2:1R
661	62.1-198, 62.1-199
662	54.1-2700, 54.1-2706, 54.1-2709.1 — 54.1-2709.4.
663	2.1-20.1, 2.2-2818, 32.1-325, 38.2-3411.4, 38.2-4319
664	23-9.2:3
665	22.1-205, 46.2-330, 46.2-334, 46.2-334.01, 46.2-334.02, 46.2-335, 46.2-335.2
666	22.1-202
667	22.1-346.1
668	22.1-276
669	22.1-277.2
670	11-4.4
671	32.1-127.1:03, 32.1-122.10:001— 32.1-122.10:005
672	2.1-1.6, 51.1-1200 — 51.1-1202, 51.1-1203, 51.1-1204 — 51.1-1207, 51.1-1208, n., 51.1-1209, n, 51.1-1210, n., 51.1-1211, n.
673	23-9.2:3
674	3.1-796.100, 32.1-48.3
675	11-37
676	63.1-336— 63.1-343
677	22.1-296.2
678	2.1-133.6, 9.1-400
679	51.1-163, 51.1-165, 51.1-165.01
680	30-19.1:7
681	51.1-1300— 51.1-1304
682	51.1-100, n.
683	51.1-162, 51.1-207, 51.1-218
684	51.1-1130
685	51.1-500, 51.1-505.01
686	51.1-124.3, 51.1-142R, 51.1-142.1R, 51.1-142.2, n., 51.1-143R, 51.1-203, n., 51.1-214
687	22.1-346.1
688	8.01-47, 9-6.14:4.1, 16.1-293, 22.1-4.3, 22.1-79.3, 22.1-203.2, 22.1-254, 22.1-266, 22.1-276R, 22.1-276.01, 22.1-276.2, 22.1-277, 22.1-277.01R, 22.1-277.01:1R, 22.1-277.01:2R, 22.1-277.02R, 22.1-277.02:1R, 22.1-277.03R, 22.1-277.04 — 22.1-277.08, 22.1-277.1R, 22.1-277.2, 22.1-277.2:1, 22.1-278 — 22.1-278.3R, 22.1-279.3, 22.1-279.3:1, 22.1-279.5R, 22.1-279.6— 22.1-279.9, 22.1-280.1R, 22.1-280.3R, 22.1-280.4
689	22.1-23, 51.1-155
690	51.1-500, 51.1-505.01
691	51.1-126, 51.1-126.5, 51.1-126.6, 51.1-161
692	51.1-1300 — 51.1-1304
693	51.1-144
694	2.1-20.1:16, 51.1-502.2R, 51.1-1100, 51.1-1116, 51.1-1127, 51.1-1131, 51.1-1135.1
695	51.1-1130
696	51.1-505, 51.1-512, 51.1-512.1
697	51.1-124.3, 51.1-142.2, 51.1-142R, 51.1-142.1R, 51.1-143R, 51.1-203, 51.1-214
698	51.1-126.7
699	51.1-163, 51.1-165, 51.1-165.01

Acts 2001 Chapter	Code 1950 Section
700	22.1-23, 51.1-155
701	63.1-55.02
702	51.1-144
703	15.2-2297, 15.2-2298, 15.2-2303
704	15.2-2243
705	58.1-3231
706	13.1-400.3, 38.2-5105R, 38.2-514 — 38.2-514.2, 38.2-613.1, 38.2-1211, 38.2-1220, 38.2-1300, 38.2-1346, 38.2-1800 — 38.2-1802, 38.2-1803R, 38.2-1804 — 38.2-1806, 38.2-1809, 38.2-1810, 38.2-1812, 38.2-1812.2 — 38.2-1815, 38.2-1815.1, 38.2-1816R, 38.2-1817 — 38.2-1820, 38.2-1821.1, 38.2-1822, 38.2-1824— 38.2-1828, 38.2-1829R, 38.2-1830— 38.2-1834, 38.2-1834.1, 38.2-1836, 38.2-1836.1, 38.2-1837— 38.2-1845, 38.2-1846— 38.2-1857R, 38.2-1858— 38.2-1865R, 38.2-1866, 38.2-1867, 38.2-1868.1, 38.2-1869, 38.2-1870, 38.2-1871, 38.2-1872, 38.2-1874, 38.2-2609, 38.2-3734, 38.2-3919, 38.2-4008, 38.2-4601.1, 38.2-4800— 38.2-4805R, 38.2-4806, 38.2-4807, 38.2-4809, 38.2-4815, 38.2-5702R, 38.2-5703, 58.1-2508, 65.2-803.1
707	38.2-100, 38.2-501
709	2.1-563.40:1
710	2.1-343.2
711	55-66.3
712	18.2-280
713	56-484.16
714	2.1-114.5:03
715	55-79.41, 55-79.75, 55-79.75:1, 55-509, 55-510.1, 55-510.2
716	63.1-55.02
717	6.1-32.12
718	55-20.1, 55-20.2, 55-21
719	24.2-101
720	1-13.39:3
721	60.2-528
722	13.1-501, 13.1-514
723	2.1-1.6, 2.1-20.4, 9-6.25:2, 54.1-300, 54.1-500, 54.1-500.1, 54.1-501, 54.1-516, 54.1-517.1, 54.1-517.2
724	2.1-20.1:07
725	20-107.1, n., 20-109
726	38.2-1005, 38.2-1005.1, 38.2-1005.1:1 — 38.2-1005.1:13
727	3.1-796.96:2
728	38.2-2226
729	36-27, 36-51
730	15.2-4903
731	22.1-253.13:3
732	3.1-385.5, 3.1-385.8
733	15.2-3201
735	32.1-351
736	11-35
737	58.1-2905, 58.1-3814
738	56-580
739	18.2-271, 46.2-391, 46.2-391.01, 46.2-410.1
740	20-109
741	59.1-198
742	40.1-139— 40.1-142
743	6.1-330.60
744	2.1-744.1
745	56-259
746	63.1-55.02
747	24.2-1013, 24.2-1014
748	56-577, 56-580, 56-581.1, 56-582, 56-585, 56-590, 56-596, 58.1-2901, 58.1-2902, 58.1-3814
749	46.2-410.1
750	15.2-901
751	56-259.1
752	56-259
753	11-35
754	18.2-340.33, 18.2-340.38R
755	56-580
756	32.1-351
757	3.1-1111.1, 3.1-1114.1, 9-385.1, 9-389.1
758	56-46.1, 56-265.2:1
759	2.1-744.1, 2.2-2435
760	2.1-114.5:04
761	15.2-2118.1
762	59.1-198, 59.1-501.4, 59.1-501.5, 59.1-501.9, 59.1-502.12, 59.1-505.3
763	59.1-501.2, 59.1-501.3, 59.1-501.4, 59.1-501.5, 59.1-501.9, 59.1-501.10, 59.1-501.12, 59.1-502.9, 59.1-502.12, 59.1-503.10, 59.1-505.3, 59.1-506.5, 59.1-508.16
764	33.1-23.03
765	23-38.53:12, 23-38.53:13, 23-38.53:16— 23-38.53:19
766	19.2-163.7, 19.2-163.8
767	10.1-1408.4, 10.1-1408.5
768	2.1-116.9:7— 2.1-116.9:13
769	58.1-609.3
770	16.1-301
771	1-13.39:2
772	33.1-23.03
773	8.01-229
774	11-35, 11-35.1
775	18.2-186.4
776	18.2-370, 19.2-169.3, n., 37.1-70.1— 37.1-70.19, 37.1-134.21, n.
777	2.1-51.15, 2.2-2679, n., 2.2-2680, n., 9-6.25:1, n., 9-397, 9-404, 9-405, n.
778	63.1-198.1
779	18.2-259.1, 18.2-268.3, 18.2-271.1, 29.1-738.2, 46.2-320, 46.2-391.2, 46.2-392, 46.2-499
780	15.2-944.1
781	8.01-229
782	18.2-186.4
783	4.1-123
784	37.1-183.3, 37.1-197.2
785	30-19.14
786	Const., Art. X, § 6, n.
787	Const., Art. VI, § 1, n.
788	9-6.25:1, 9-406— 9-400
789	24.2-703.1
790	46.2-390.1
791	46.2-1167
792	2.1-816, 2.1-816.1, 2.1-817
793	24.2-701, 24.2-703
794	24.2-906.1, 24.2-915
797	13.1-322
799	24.2-710, 24.2-711
800	46.2-207
801	58.1-3133, 58.1-3912, 58.1-3942
802	58.1-2201
803	46.2-819.1
804	51.1-206, 51.1-216, 51.1-217, 51.1-221,
805	22.1-298, n.
806	2.1-1.6, 2.1-1.7, 2.1-20.1:01R,

Acts 2001 Chapter	Code 1950 Section
	2.1-20.1:02,
	2.1-113.1 — 2.1-113.3R,
	2.1-116.10 — 2.1-116.14R,
	2.2-2409 —2.1-113.3R,
	2.2-2675,
	9-6.25:1,
	9-396 — 9-399
807	9-380, 9-382, 9-383,
	9-384, 9-385
808	46.2-894, 46.2-900,
	46.2-901
809	20-108.1, 20-108.2
810	24.2-914, 24.2-915
811	18.2-308.2
812	46.2-1573.01
813	18.2-340.20,
	18.2-340.33, n.
814	20-49.10
815	2.1-548.01—
	2.1-548.09,
	33.1-400— 33.1-408R
816	55-530
817	46.2-1568.1
818	18.2-55
819	28.2-201.1
820	8.01-47, 9-6.14:4.1,
	16.1-293, 22.1-4.3,
	22.1-79.3, 22.1-203.2,
	22.1-254, 22.1-266,
	22.1-276R, 22.1-276.01,
	22.1-276.2, 22.1-277,
	22.1-277.01R,
	22.1-277.01:1R,
	22.1-277.01:2R,
	22.1-277.02R,
	22.1-277.02:1R,
	22.1-277.03R,
	22.1-277.04— 22.1-277.08,
	22.1-277.1R, 22.1-277.2,
	22.1-277.2:1, 22.1-278R,
	22.1-278.1R, 22.1-278.2R,
	22.1-278.3R 22.1-279.3,
	22.1-279.3:1, 22.1-279.5R,
	22.1-279.6— 22.1-279.9,
	22.1-280.1R, 22.1-280.3R,
	22.1-280.4
821	9-183.1, 9-183.2,
	9-183.3, 9.1-138,
	9.1-139, 9.1-140
822	46.2-1142.1
823	32.1-23
824	2.1-818, 2.1-819
825	8.01-380
827	18.2-251
828	22.1-1
829	58.1-2901, 58.1-3731
831	62.1-44.19:3
832	2.1-1.5, 2.1-41.2,
	2.1-51.40, 9-6.25:3,
	54.1-202, 54.1-300,
	54.1-2000R, 54.1-2001R,

Acts 2001 Chapter	Code 1950 Section
	54.1-2002R, 54.1-2002.1R,
	54.1-2003R, 54.1-2004R,
	54.1-2004.1R, 54.1-2005R,
	54.1-2006R, 54.1-2007R,
	54.1-2008R,
	54.1-4400—54.1-4422,
833	18.2-340.19,
	18.2-340.26,
	18.2-340.26:1
834	15.2-1720, 46.2-100,
	46.2-800, 46.2-839,
	46.2-847, 46.2-849,
	46.2-856, 46.2-857,
	46.2-903, 46.2-904,
	46.2-905, 46.2-906,
	46.2-906.1, 46.2-907,
	46.2-908, 46.2-908.1,
	46.2-932, 46.2-1015,
	46.2-1066, 46.2-1078
835	2.1-27.3:1
836	17.1-126, 17.1-127R,
	17.1-213, 17.1-275,
	26-59, 32.1-267,
	59.1-71, 59.1-72,
	64.1-94
837	16.1-248.1, 16.1-250.1,
	16.1-340, 16.1-341,
	19.2-174.1, 19.2-182.9,
	32.1-48.02, 32.1-48.03,
	32.1-48.04, 37.1-67.3,
	63.1-248.9
838	13.1-322
839	24.2-611
840	18.2-370, 18.2-370.1,
	19.2-298.1
841	22.1-137.1, 22.1-278.1,
	23-9.6:1, 44-146.18
842	2.1-548.01—
	2.1-548.09,
	2.2-1173—2.2-1181,
	33.1-400— 33.1-408R
843	46.2-1573.01
844	2.1-1— 2.1-817R,
	2.2-100— 2.2-5803,
	3.1-1106— 3.1-1114,
	6.1-5.4,
	9-6.14:1—9-395R,
	9.1-100— 9.1-600,
	17.1-900— 17.1-919,
	30-100— 30-142,
	30-145— 30-192,
	37.1-255— 37.1-260,
	42.1-19.1— 42.1-19.4,
	51.1-1400—51.1-1305
845	4.1-126, 4.1-210,
	4.1-231, 4.1-233
846	22.1-200.1
847	9-145.48
848	18.2-55
849	46.2-1568.1
850	24.2-703.1

Acts 2001 Chapter	Code 1950 Section
851	46.2-334
852	46.2-819.1
853	16.1-233— 16.1-237,
	16.1-285,
	16.1-291, 16.1-293,
	63.1-248.3
854	18.2-308.2
855	19.2-368.2, 19.2-368.5,
	19.2-368.8, 19.2-368.10
856	29.1-525.1, 29.1-551
857	46.2-1142.1
858	54.1-2914, 54.1-3473,
	54.1-3474, 54.1-3480,
	54.1-3482, 54.1-3483
859	32.1-325, 32.1-325
860	58.1-609.4,
	58.1-609.7— 58.1-609.10
861	58.1-2901, 58.1-3731
862	18.2-62
863	59.1-284.14,
	59.1-284.14:1, 59.1-284.15,
	59.1-284.15:1
865	22.1-303
866	24.2-706
867	63.1-198.4
868	32.1-162.21—
	32.1-162.22
869	22.1-17.5
870	32.1-162.21—
	32.1-162.22
872	22.1-303
873	19.2-270.4,
	19.2-270.4:1,
	19.2-327.1,
	19.2-327.2— 19.2-327.6
874	19.2-270.4,
	19.2-270.4:1,
	19.2-327.1, 19.2-327.1,
	19.2-327.2— 19.2-327.6
875	19.2-270.4,
	19.2-270.4:1

ACTS 2001, Sp. Sess. I

Acts 2001, Sp. Sess. I Chapter	Code 1950 Section
1	24.2-304R
	34.2-304.01
2	24.2-303R
3	15.2-3226
4	23-182 n.

ACTS 2002

Acts 2002 Chapter	Code 1950 Section
1	12.1-19, n.,
	12.1-20, n.,
	12.1-21.1, n.,
	12.1-21.2, n.,
	13.1-603, n.,
	13.1-615, n.,

Acts 2002 Chapter	Code 1950 Section
	13.1-615.1, n., 13.1-616, n., 13.1-617, n., 13.1-658, n., 13.1-722.2 — 13.1-722.14, n., 13.1-1005, n., 13.1-1062, n.
2	30-28.18, 30-34.14
3	58.1-4028R
4	58.1-2201
6	58.1-3506
7	58.1-2201, 58.1-2208, 58.1-2230, 58.1-2232, 58.1-2251, 58.1-2255, 58.1-2275
8	58.1-3221
9	58.1-3211
13	58.1-611.1
14	58.1-807
15	58.1-1702
16	58.1-3221.1
17	58.1-3812
18	2.2-4510
19	51.5-54 — 51.5-58
20	58.1-3211
21	58.1-3220
23	24.2-703.2
24	24.2-653
25	59.1-148.3
26	30-178 — 30-181, n.
27	15.2-1411
28	58.1-3703
29	58.1-1201
30	24.2-222.1
31	15.2-1132
32	15.2-4509
33	54.1-831.1
34	55-428
35	58.1-22, 58.1-911
36	2.2-3114.1
37	15.2-1505
38	54.1-2910.1
39	29.1-530.1
40	28.2-110, 28.2-111
41	63.1-334
42	3.1-796.96, n., 3.1-796.96:2, n., 3.1-796.120, n.
43	17.1-300
45	63.1-182.1
46	51.5-9.01, 51.5-16 — 51.5-20, 63.1-70.1
47	46.2-649
48	46.2-1220
49	62.1-44.15, n.
50	37.1-3
51	37.1-194
52	32.1-122.9, 32.1-122.9:1
53	3.1-796.96, 3.1-796.96:2, 3.1-796.120
54	19.2-310.2
55	16.1-248.1
56	37.1-179, 37.1-179.1, 51.5-14.1
57	3.1-319, 3.1-329 — 3.1-331
58	64.1-105, n.
59	53.1-191
60	32.1-73.1 — 32.1-73.4R, 46.2-411, 51.5-12.1 — 51.5-12.4
61	46.2-334.01
62	37.1-98
63	58.1-3506
64	58.1-3, 58.1-3133, 58.1-3912, 58.1-3923R, 58.1-3924, 58.1-3934, 58.1-3940, 58.1-3944, 58.1-3946, 58.1-3952, 58.1-3965
65	8.01-294
66	24.2-115, 24.2-611
67	29.1-301, 29.1-302.4, 29.1-311
68	56-484.12, 56-484.17, 58.1-3812
69	65.2-101
70	38.2-323
71	8.9A-525
72	38.2-3723, 38.2-3729
73	38.2-1413
74	22.1-57.3:1
75	30-178, n., 30-179, n., 30-180, n., 30-181, n.
76	38.2-513.1, 38.2-604, 38.2-604.1
77	13.1-544.1, 13.1-544.2, 13.1-551, 13.1-552
79	17.1-802
80	54.1-2970
81	63.1-133.43
82	37.1-256.1
83	32.1-13.1, 32.1-122.01, 32.1-122.02R, 32.1-122.03 — 32.1-122.08
84	23-7.4:4R, 23-9.2:3.01R
85	57-60, 57-63
86	19.2-12
87	2.2-3106, 2.2-3705, 2.2-3711, 2.2-4343, 2.2-4345, 22.1-209.2, 23-14, 32.1-122.6, 32.1-279, 54.1-2961
88	34-26, 34-28
89	33.1-46.2
90	46.2-734.1R, 46.2-738.1R, 46.2-743, 46.2-746.01R, 46.2-746.4, 46.2-746.7, 46.2-746.8, 46.2-746.13R, 46.2-746.15 — 46.2-746.20R, 46.2-747.1R, 46.2-748.2R, 46.2-749.2:8, 46.2-749.2:9R, 46.2-749.2:11, 46.2-749.2:12R, 46.2-749.2:17R, 46.2-749.4:1, 46.2-749.4:3R, 46.2-749.6:1, 46.2-749.6:1.1R, 46.2-749.7:2R
91	19.2-68
92	54.1-2972
93	46.2-613, 46.2-620
94	5.1-1.4, 7.1-10
95	23-9.6:1
96	33.1-206.1
97	23-234
98	46.2-676
99	46.2-1137
100	32.1-35, 32.1-36
101	22.1-253.13:3
102	46.2-941
103	63.1-325
104	4.1-325.1
105	4.1-325, 4.1-325.2
106	59.1-310.7, n., 59.1-310.8, n., 59.1-310.9, n., 59.1-310.10, n.
107	8.01-670, 8.01-670.1
108	46.2-1240
109	46.2-882
110	46.2-205
111	42.1-36
113	33.1-62, n.
114	23-38.53:6
115	46.2-894
118	46.2-221.1
119	64.1-45.2, n.
122	60.2-602
127	24.2-304.1
128	22.1-298
129	23-298
130	19.2-192.1
131	46.2-208
132	46.2-1220
133	46.2-1241
134	46.2-920
135	46.2-342
137	58.1-3221
138	54.1-4300, 54.1-4305

Acts 2002 Chapter	Code 1950 Section
139	58.1-1800, 58.1-3910
140	17.1-279
141	24.2-703.2
142	46.2-1001
143	10.1-515, 10.1-516, 10.1-523, 10.1-525, 10.1-528, 10.1-530
144	58.1-3220
145	38.2-1902, 38.2-1904, 38.2-2001, 38.2-2005, 38.2-3001
146	22.1-36.1
147	38.2-1426, 38.2-1427.2, 38.2-1446, 38.2-4008, 38.2-4111
148	58.1-3506
150	9.1-800 — 9.1-803
151	15.2-2304
153	38.2-4319
154	15.2-2105.1
155	2.2-3705
156	24.2-923
157	29.1-100, 29.1-519, 29.1-523 — 29.1-525, 29.1-549
158	2.2-2502, 23-9.5, 23-14, 23-31, 23-182 — 23-186, 23-188, 23-189, 23-189, 23-191
159	22.1-18
160	22.1-79.3
161	15.2-928
162	2.2-3309.1, 22.1-17.4
163	46.2-921.1
164	22.1-116.1
165	22.1-60
166	22.1-279.8
167	22.1-227.1, 22.1-253.13:3
168	32.1-102.3:2, n.
169	15.2-4903
170	54.1-2722
171	58.1-3211
172	55-58.3
173	58.1-3823
174	29.1-529
175	29.1-328
177	22.1-205, 46.2-490
178	23-276.1 — 23-276.12, 23-265 — 23-276R
179	32.1-102.3:2, n.
180	15.2-2295, 36-99.10:1
181	10.1-2211
182	53.1-127.1
183	58.1-609.6
184	58.1-1833
185	3.1-418, 3.1-419, 3.1-740, 3.1-741
186	6.1-61
187	6.1-71, 6.1-194.58, 6.1-225.49
188	10.1-2211
189	24.2-313
190	24.2-668
191	15.2-961
192	10.1-512
193	15.2-2118
194	21-118
195	18.2-152.4
196	2.2-510.1
197	64.1-118
198	15.2-2403
199	15.2-3306
200	16.1-77
201	54.1-4010
202	15.2-2403
203	32.1-283
204	4.1-209
205	15.2-2308
206	46.2-752
207	8.01-195.6
208	3.1-796.96, 3.1-796.96:2, 3.1-796.120
209	9.1-162
210	33.1-62, n.
211	9.1-202
212	44-93
213	24.2-905
214	46.2-100, 46.2-908.2, 46.2-908.3
215	28.2-302.1, 28.2-302.5
216	24.2-115, 24.2-611
217	59.1-200
218	3.1-394
220	6.1-71, 6.1-194.58, 6.1-225.49, 26-12.3, 26-20
221	22.1-279.8
222	22.1-72
223	46.2-1001
224	32.1-188, 32.1-189
225	10.1-2211
226	15.2-961
227	6.1-71, 6.1-194.58, 6.1-225.49, 26-12.3, 26-20
228	58.1-609.6
229	22.1-279.8
230	15.2-2403
231	22.1-72
232	24.2-905
233	32.1-188
234	46.2-100, 46.2-908.2, 46.2-908.3
235	22.1-279.8
236	10.1-515, 10.1-516, 10.1-523, 10.1-525, 10.1-528, 10.1-530
237	24.2-923
238	22.1-116.1
239	46.2-703
240	53.1-31.1
241	2.2-4007, 2.2-4031
242	2.2-3705
243	63.1-339
244	8.9A-523
245	36-137, 36-139
246	46.2-395
247	2.2-136 — 2.2-138R, 2.2-226.1
248	2.2-426
249	46.2-224
250	17.1-279
251	10.1-411.1
252	24.2-711.1
253	22.1-18
254	15.2-1720, 46.2-100, 46.2-800, 46.2-839, 46.2-847, 46.2-849, 46.2-856, 46.2-857, 46.2-903 — 46.2-908.1, 46.2-932, 46.2-1015, 46.2-1066, 46.2-1078
256	10.1-2211.1
257	2.2-2502, 23-9.5, 23-14, 23-31, 23-182 — 23-186, 23-188, 23-189, 23-191
258	46.2-383
259	58.1-3823
260	2.2-2701, 2.2-2704
261	6.1-225.58, 6.1-225.60R
262	63.1-249.1
263	46.2-1001
264	46.2-1143
265	46.2-1128, 46.2-1139.1, 46.2-1143.1, 58.1-2700.1, 58.1-2701, 58.1-2709
266	46.2-1220
267	59.1-71, 59.1-72R, 59.1-74
268	58.1-17
269	22.1-36.1
270	54.1-2816.1
271	2.2-2905, 37.1-42.2
272	25-46.17, 36-27
273	43-3
274	58.1-3713, n.
275	15.2-2159
276	17.1-249
277	45.1-361.35
278	37.1-194
279	24.2-424
280	2.2-1207
281	2.2-1156
282	18.2-340.16, 18.2-340.20, 18.2-340.33

Acts 2002 Chapter	Code 1950 Section
283	15.2-2801, 15.2-2804
284	3.1-796.96, n., 3.1-796.96:2, n. 3.1-796.120, n.,
285	13.1-603, 13.1-610, 13.1-658, 13.1-664.1, 13.1-686, 13.1-803, 13.1-842, 13.1-846, 13.1-847, 13.1-866
286	27-23.6
288	13.1-1002, 13.1-1008, 13.1-1022, 13.1-1024, 13.1-1025, 13.1-1028, 13.1-1040.1, 13.1-1048
289	46.2-364
290	23-35.9, 32.1-122.6:01, 54.1-3011.2
292	23-231.3
293	10.1-1181.2
294	15.2-1534
295	15.2-2110
296	38.2-1834.1, 38.2-1869
297	2.2-3709, n.
298	63.1-202
299	17.1-208, 17.1-265
300	16.1-278.15
301	65.2-525
302	33.1-23.2
303	33.1-191
304	10.1-1181.2
305	16.1-241.1R, 16.1-276.1R
306	30-154, 54.1-3910
307	51.1-144
308	8.01-399
309	65.2-402
310	19.2-11.01, 19.2-29, 19.2-30, 19.2-32, 19.2-35, 19.2-71, 19.2-82
311	51.1-600, 51.1-601, 51.1-604 — 51.1-606, 51.1-607 — 51.1-613
312	6.1-332.1
313	51.1-162, 51.1-207, 51.1-218, 51.1-505, 51.1-505.01, 51.1-511
314	22.1-274.3
315	54.1-2969
316	38.2-415, n., 52-36, n. — 52-44, n., 58.1-2508, n.
317	36-97, n.
318	17.1-278
319	23-52, n.
320	10.1-603.16 — 10.1-603.20
321	40.1-29
322	46.2-1167, 46.2-1182
323	38.2-1812
324	54.1-2912.1
325	33.1-223.2:5
326	63.1-133.59
327	46.2-924
328	15.2-1717.1
329	32.1-351.2
330	15.2-720.1
331	2.2-4345, n., 32.1-276.2 — 32.1-276.11, n.
332	63.1-174
333	54.1-3012.1
334	38.2-5206
336	53.1-93, 53.1-95.8, 53.1-109
337	15.2-949, 38.2-2217.1, 46.2-695, 46.2-749.10, 46.2-1167, 46.2-1401, 46.2-1404, 46.2-1405, 46.2-1407, 46.2-2000.1, 58.1-3506
338	4.1-305
339	58.1-2901
340	18.2-340.16
341	46.2-921.1
342	8.01-293
343	38.2-3115.1
344	53.1-231.1, 53.1-231.2, n.
345	15.2-1706
346	13.1-554R, 13.1-1119R, 58.1-3732
347	58.1-513
348	56-265.32
349	51.1-1200, n., 51.1-1203, 51.1-1205 — 51.1-1207, 51.1-1210,
350	15.2-1747
351	3.1-796.66, 3.1-796.73, 3.1-796.122
352	4.1-225
353	32.1-268
354	44-93, 44-93.1 — 44-93.5
355	33.1-391.2 — 33.1-391.5
356	15.2-2403
357	19.2-163.2
358	46.2-1095, 46.2-1098
359	16.1-248.1
360	63.1-110
361	2.2-229
362	18.2-308.2
363	58.1-3111
364	58.1-3703.1
365	30-171 — 30-173
366	22.1-26
367	23-2.2
368	23-49.17
370	19.2-389
371	63.1-248.8
372	38.2-5600 — 38.2-5602
374	22.1-60
375	6.1-2.20
376	10.1-1181.2
377	18.2-60.3
378	10.1-1230 — 10.1-1237, 10.1-1429.1 — 10.1-1429.4R
379	47.1-14
380	63.1-196.1
381	2.2-2514
382	2.2-2513, n.
383	8.01-581.13, n., 38.2-3412.1, n., 54.1-3500, n., 54.1-3505, n., 54.1-3507, n., 54.1-3507.1, n., 54.1-3507.2, n., 54.1-3507.3, n., 54.1-3509, n.
384	2.2-2249
385	46.2-501
386	22.1-205
387	54.1-2952
388	22.1-279.3:1
389	38.2-401
390	46.2-1243
391	2.2-4007, 2.2-4015, 63.1-25
393	2.2-3700 — 2.2-3702, 2.2-3705, 2.2-3706, 2.2-3711
394	8.01-251
395	58.1-344.2, 58.1-346.19
396	62.1-44.15
397	16.1-281
398	32.1-122.05
399	55-511, 55-512
400	64.1-105, n.
401	43-34
402	46.2-1088.3
403	59.1-505.3
404	51.1-165.01
405	38.2-2226.1
406	16.1-69.18
407	2.2-4517
408	19.2-298, n., 19.2-310.01, n.
409	30-100, n.
410	2.2-2648, 2.2-2649
411	54.1-3300, 54.1-3408.01, 54.1-3412, 54.1-3420.2
413	58.1-344.2, 58.1-346.20
414	33.1-70.1

Acts 2002 Chapter	Code 1950 Section
415	38.2-3418.4
416	2.2-2705
417	22.1-354.1, 22.1-354.3
418	3.1-796.104:1
419	17.1-256
420	4.1-222
421	22.1-238
422	40.1-61
423	18.2-465.1
424	2.2-226
425	2.2-2651
429	2.2-3708, n.
430	54.1-3505.1
431	46.2-1137
432	46.2-622
433	58.1-3712, 58.1-3713.4
434	54.1-3482
435	51.1-126.8, 51.1-168
436	10.1-104, n.
437	38.2-1903.1
438	2.2-4510
440	32.1-65
441	50-73.11:1R; 50-73.11:2, 50-73.15, 50-73.17, 50-73.54, 50-73.56, 50-73.67, 50-73.70, 50-73.83, 50-73.93, 50-73.132, 50-73.134, 50-73.138
442	2.2-2319
443	58.1-2600
444	58.1-2600, 58.1-2628
445	33.1-149, 33.1-154
446	15.2-2117, 15.2-5114
447	10.1-1181.8 — 10.1-1181.12
448	2.2-4024
449	58.1-3245.12, 58.1-3850
450	46.2-902.1
451	15.2-1132
452	15.2-1231
453	33.1-23.03:001
454	36-55.28
455	2.2-3711, 54.1-2400, 54.1-2409, 54.1-2917
456	38.2-1822
457	32.1-326.3
459	55-79.41, 55-79.83:1, 55-79.97, 55-509, 55-512, 55-514.1
460	58.1-346.2:1, n.
461	36-55.27:1, 36-131, 36-137, 36-139
462	58.1-1833
463	8.01-407, 8.01-413
464	6.1-2.21
465	22.1-354.1, 22.1-354.3
466	51.1-138, 51.1-205, 51.1-216, 51.1-217
467	32.1-297.1
468	24.2-910, 24.2-914, 24.2-915, 24.2-927, 24.2-928
469	65.2-803.1
470	22.1-115
471	54.1-3482
472	38.2-1916.1
473	3.1-106.2, 3.1-106.6, 3.1-126.2:1, 3.1-126.4
474	56-576, n., 56-595, n.
475	58.1-3233
476	58.1-100, n.
477	2.2-1150.1
478	2.2-3106, 2.2-3705, 2.2-3711, 2.2-4343, 2.2-4345, 22.1-209.2, 23-14, 32.1-122.6, 32.1-279, 54.1-2961
479	15.2-1500, 15.2-2160, 56-1, 56-235.5, 56-265.1, 56-265.4:4, 56-458, 56-462, 56-468.1, 56-479.2, 56-484.4, 56-484.7:1, 56-484.7:2, 56-484.7:3R, 56-484.7:4, 58.1-2660, 58.1-3813.1
480	2.2-1503.1
481	2.2-3705, 54.1-2505, 54.1-2519 — 54.1-2525
482	3.1-1106, 3.1-1109.1, 3.1-1110, 3.1-1111
483	10.1-1186.2:1, 56-46.1, 56-580
484	15.2-915
485	17.1-118
486	2.2-1503.1
487	24.2-101, 24.2-622, 24.2-941 — 24.2-944, 24.2-1013, 24.2-1014R
488	3.1-1106, 3.1-1109.1, 3.1-1110, 3.1-1111
489	15.2-1500, 15.2-2160, 56-1, 56-235.5, 56-265.1, 56-265.4:4, 56-458, 56-462, 56-468.1, 56-479.2, 56-484.4, 56-484.7:1, 56-484.7:2, 56-484.7:3R, 56-484.7:4, 58.1-2660, 58.1-3813.1
490	9.1-102
491	2.2-426, 2.2-1120, 2.2-2327, 2.2-2411, 2.2-2511, 2.2-2512R, 2.2-2611 — 2.2-2513R, 2.2-3202, 2.2-3710, 2.2-4343,2.2-5900, 9.1-173, 9.1-175, 9.1-176, 9.1-178 — 9.1-180, 30-193 — 30-195, 30-196, 30-197, 53.1-180 — 53.1-185.3R
492	10.1-1413.2
493	22.1-298
495	25-46.3, 25-46.5, 25-46.9, 25-46.11, 25-46.17, 25-46.19 — 25-46.22, 25-46.24, 25-46.25, 25-46.29, 25-46.32, 25-248, 33.1-89, n., 36-27R
496	62.1-69.25
497	13.1-710, 13.1-711, 13.1-722.1, 13.1-759
498	22.1-18.01
499	2.2-3705, 2.2-3711
500	3.1-796.66, 3.1-796.115, 3.1-796.122, 3.1-796.123R
501	2.2-2261, 2.2-2263, 2.2-2270
502	58.1-2605, n., 58.1-2628 — 58.1-2631, 58.1-2640, 58.1-2901
503	19.2-247
504	2.2-1111
505	46.2-817
506	16.1-77
507	19.2-152.8 — 19.2-152.10
508	16.1-253, 16.1-253.1, 16.1-253.4, 16.1-279.1, 17.1-272
509	55-79.80:2, 55-79.97, 55-511 — 55-513
510	16.1-235
511	16.1-272, 16.1-285.2
512	16.1-281 — 16.1-282.1, 16.1-282.2
513	58.1-2403
514	32.1-126
515	8.01-410, 19.2-269.1
516	55-531, 55-532
517	15.2-2241
518	10.1-1413.2
519	16.1-278.9
520	55-79.78
521	23-38.55, 23-38.56

Acts 2002 Chapter	Code 1950 Section
522	2.2-3705
523	62.1-69.25
525	58.1-3983.1
526	30-193 — 30-195
527	18.2-460
528	22.1-296.3
529	54.1-4300, 54.1-4305
530	15.2-2260
531	55-248.4, 55-248.7:1, 55-248.9
532	58.1-3732.2
533	53.1-120
535	46.2-323, 46.2-335.2
536	18.2-174.1
537	40.1-51.4:5
538	65.2-100, n.
539	25-46.3, 25-46.5, 25-46.9, 25-46.11, 25-46.17, 25-46.19 — 25-46.22, 25-46.24 25.46-25, 25-46.29, 25-46.32, 25-248, 33.1-89, 36-27
540	36-27.2
541	46.2-844, 46.2-859
542	2.2-2261, 2.2-2263, 2.2-2270
544	8.01-410, 19.2-269.1
545	15.2-2308
546	15.2-2309
547	15.2-2286
548	36-19, 36-29
549	54.1-2715
550	58.1-3516
551	15.2-2261.1
552	17.1-300
553	46.2-752
554	22.1-207.1
555	36-99, 36-99.01, 36-103, 36-119.1, 36-137, 36-139
556	2.2-4337
557	37.1-98
558	16.1-249
559	30-189
560	18.2-414.1
561	2.2-1147, 2.2-1147.1, 2.2-2639
562	2.2-2629
563	63.1-325.2
564	58.1-609.4, 58.1-609.7
565	40.1-28.7:1
566	8.9A-516
567	58.1-3822
568	32.1-116.1, 32.1-127.1:03
569	53.1-134 — 53.1-136, 53.1-155
570	33.1-23.02, 56-557, 56-573.1
571	2.2-3705, 56-575.1 — 56-575.16
572	2.2-203, 2.2-510, 2.2-2411, 2.2-2640, 2.2-2646, 2.2-2905, 2.2-3705, 2.2-5302, 37.1-42.1, 37.1-42.2, 51.5-1, 51.5-2, 51.5-36 — 51.5-39R, 51.5-39.1 — 51.5-39.12, 51.5-40, 51.5-46, 63.1-182.1, 63.1-314.8
574	23-77.4
575	33.1-23.3
576	18.2-49.1
577	22.1-253.13:1, n.
578	9.1-139, 9.1-140, 9.1-145, 9.1-149
579	2.2-1121R, 2.2-1303, 2.2-1303.1
580	2.2-1501, 2.2-3707.1
581	23-231.19 — 23-231.23
582	2.2-4343, 23-76.1
583	3.1-796.122
584	30-5
585	2.2-5206, 37.1-189.3, 37.1-197.3
586	23-215
587	19.2-389, 63.1-56.01
588	2.2-511, 15.2-1716.1, 18.2-18, 18.2-31, 18.2-46.4 — 18.2-46.10, 18.2-51.1, 18.2-52.1, 18.2-60, 18.2-85, 19.2-61, 19.2-66, 19.2-70.2, 19.2-120, 19.2-215.1, 19.2-294, 19.2-386.1 — 19.2-386.5, 24.2-233, 52-8.5
589	18.2-423.01
590	58.1-609.4
591	23-9.4, 23-281, 23-282R, 23-284
592	23-91.21, n.
593	56-557, 56-565, 56-573.1
595	2.2-4343, 23-76.1
596	18.2-49.1
597	9.1-139, 9.1-140, 9.1-145, 9.1-149
598	33.1-23.3
599	6.1-2.13:1, 38.2-4614
600	18.2-423.01
601	24.2-802
602	23-77.4
603	Const., Art. VI, § 1, n.
604	19.2-316.2, 19.2-316.3
605	19.2-12, 19.2-13, 54.1-306
606	19.2-389, 63.1-56.01
607	13.1-831, 13.1-887.1, 13.1-888, 13.1-889, 13.1-895, 13.1-898, 13.1-898.1, 13.1-921, 13.1-941R, 13.1-941.01
608	13.1-1010.1, 13.1-1052, 13.1-1065, 13.1-1104
609	56-586.1
610	23-91.21, n.
611	19.2-398
612	23 9.4, 23 281, 23-282R, 23-284
613	3.1-796.122
614	19.2-163.2, 19.2-163.7
615	18.2-29
616	46.2-1095, 46.2-1100
617	30-5
618	2.2-1501, 2.2-3707.1
619	2.2-5206, 37.1-189.3, 37.1-197.3
620	23-231.19 — 23-231.23
621	1-13.19:1, 6.1-343 — 6.1-351R, 13.1-1200 — 13.1-1284, 55-106.4
622	19.2-112
623	2.2-511, 15.2-1716.1, 18.2-18, 18.2-31, 18.2-46.4 — 18.2-46.10, 18.2-51.1, 18.2-52.1, 18.2-60, 18.2-85, 19.2-61, 19.2-66, 19.2-70.2, 19.2-120, 19.2-215.1, 19.2-294, 19.2-386.1 — 19.2-386.5, 24.2-233, 52-8.5
624	8.01-221.1
625	23-215
626	22.1-253.13:1, n.
627	19.2-270.5
628	19.2-306
629	38.2-2233
630	Const., Art. X, § 6, n.
631	8.01-66.1
632	54.1-3411.1
633	2.2-3705, 2.2-4115 — 2.2-4119
634	15.2-2204
635	18.2-29
636	65.2-306
637	17.1-279
638	57-20
639	33.1-23.03
640	32.1-351

Acts 2002 Chapter	Code 1950 Section
641	63.1-248.6:02, 63.1-248.19
642	63.1-248.6:02
643	2.2-4337
644	8.9A-516
645	8.01-195.4, 16.1-77, 16.1-92, 16.1-122
646	58.1-3822
647	24.2-802
648	16.1-278.8, n., 16.1-284.1, n., 16.1-292, n.
650	20-108.2
651	15.2-5900, 15.2-5904, 15.2-5905, n., 15.2-5906, n., 15.2-5907, n., 15.2-5908, 15.2-5911, n., 15.2-5913, n., 15.2-5914, 15.2-5915, n., 15.2-5917, n., 15.2-5918, n., 15.2-5919, n., 15.2-5920, n.
652	24.2-927
653	54.1-1103
654	8.01-413, 8.01-413, n.
655	2.2-3705, 2.2-3711
656	22.1-253.13:3
657	62.1-69.34, n. 62.1-69.36 — 62.1-69.43,
658	32.1-116.1, 32.1-127.1:03
659	40.1-28.7:1
660	46.2-1095, 46.2-1100
662	19.2-301
663	51.1-1103, 51.1-1106, 51.1-1135.2, 51.1-1140
664	16.1-281, 16.1-283
665	19.2-368.4, 19.2-368.5, 19.2-368.8, 19.2-368.11:1
666	54.1-3301, 54.1-3400, n.
667	58.1-1205, 58.1-1206
668	51.1-126.5, 51.1-126.6
669	22.1-32
670	15.2-709.1
671	18.2-187, n., 18.2-187.1, 18.2-190.1 — 18.2-190.4, 18.2-190.5 — 18.2-190.8
672	33.1-351
673	33.1-23.3, 33.1-41.1, 33.1-44
674	15.2-1800.1
675	8.01-581.16, 8.01-581.17
676	2.2-2666.1, 2.2-2666.2, 2.2-2801
677	2.2-4014, 2.2-4015, 2.2-4033, 30-73.1 — 30-73.4
678	33.1-223.2:6
679	30-192
680	15.2-4901, 15.2-4903
681	46.2-2005, 46.2-2080
682	2.2-4337
683	58.1-3.2, 58.1-1008.1, 58.1-1009
684	15.2-1736
686	51.5-805, n.
687	16.1-266
688	8.01-511.1
689	15.2-5900, n., 15.2-5904, n., 15.2-5905, n., 15.2-5906, n., 15.2-5907, n., 15.2-5908, n., 15.2-5911, n., 15.2-5913, n., 15.2-5914, n., 15.2-5915, n., 15.2-5917, n., 15.2-5918, n., 15.2-5919, n., 15.2-5920, n.
690	15.2-928
691	15.2-6402, 15.2-6403, 15.2-6405, 15.2-6409
692	19.2-398
693	65.2-903
694	23-50.16:01
695	18.2-308.2:2
696	32.1-89
697	51.1-1103, 51.1-1106, 51.1-1135.2, 51.1-1140
698	2.2-4024, 54.1-2400, 54.1-2409.3, 54.1-2950.1, 54.1-2956.8, 54.1-2956.11
699	18.2-308
700	16.1-235.1, 16.1-255
701	16.1-305, 19.2-389.1
702	8.01-302R
703	15.2-2242, 15.2-2286, 15.2-2288.1, 36-98
704	16.1-122.2, 16.1-122.3
706	16.1-253.4, 19.2-152.8
707	54.1-3301, 54.1-3400, n.
708	62.1-44.19:11
709	15.2-1736
710	46.2-208, 46.2-1176, 46.2-1178, 46.2-1178.1, 46.2-1178.2, 46.2-1179
711	28.2-1408.1
712	37.1-183.3, 37.1-197.2
713	54.1-3001, 54.1-3018
714	22.1-304
715	2.2-3704, 2.2-3705, 2.2-3706, 2.2-3711
716	64.1-122.2
717	22.1-26.1, 58.1-3703
718	8.01-576.4 — 8.01-576.10, 8.01-576.12, 8.01-581.21 — 8.01-581.23, 8.01-581.24 — 8.01-581.26
719	2.2-614.1, 12.1-17, 17.1-222.1, 24.2-105.2, 29.1-112, 46.2-207, 58.1-13.1R, 58.1-3013R, 60.2-519.2
720	36-105
721	9.1-201, 9.1-205
722	58.1-3.2, 58.1-1008.1, 58.1-1009
723	8.01-399
724	46.2-341.18:1, 46.2-341.20:1, 46.2-341.20:2, 46.2-505
725	15.2-4901, 15.2-4903
726	17.1-100
727	30-133
728	18.2-308
729	16.1-281, 16.1-283
730	15.2-709.1
731	19.2-298.1
732	22.1-253.13:3
733	22.1-32
734	46.2-2005, 46.2-2080
735	16.1-300, 16.1-305
736	37.1-134.7
737	65.2-402
738	24.2-613, 24.2-614, 24.2-640
739	22.1-32
740	54.1-1701, 54.1-2701, 54.1-2901, 54.1-3001, 54.1-3202, 54.1-3301, 54.1-3801
741	16.1-305
742	57-5
743	19.2-243
744	11-33.2
745	38.2-5901, 38.2-5902
747	2.2-3315.1, 2.2-3803, 2.2-4001, 2.2-4007, 2.2-4018, 2.2-4025, 2.2-4345, 15.2-412, 15.2-518, 15.2-527, 15.2-1231, 15.2-1541.1,

Acts 2002 Chapter	Code 1950 Section
	15.2-2811 — 15.2-2817, 16.1-69.53, 16.1-246, 16.1-260, 16.1-278.2, 16.1-278.4, 16.1-278.18, 16.1-281, 16.1-294, 16.1-332, 20-49.9R, 20-64, 20-88.02, 20-108, 20-108.2, 22.1-30, 22.1-287, 24.2-411.2, 32.1-111.14, 32.1-273, 32.1-321.4, 32.1-350, 37.1-98, 37.1-197.1, 46.2-932.1, 51.5-60 — 51.5-105, 51.5-106 — 51.5-114, 53.1-61, 53.1-131, 54.1-2969, 58.1-3, 58.1-439.9, 58.1-3134, 59.1-21.21:1, 63.1-1.1 — 63.1-343R, 63.2-100 — 63.2-2204
748	18.2-268.2
749	19.2-187.02
750	19.2-182.5
751	8.01-424.1
752	46.2-492, 46.2-868.1
753	19.2-310.2, 19.2-310.2:1, 19.2-310.3:1, 19.2-310.4, 19.2-310.5, 19.2-310.7
754	32.1-162.16, 32.1-162.18, 32.1-162.19
755	16.1-278.9, 46.2-307 — 46.2-309
756	53.1-120
757	33.1-46.2
758	15.2-1643
759	18.2-270
760	55-248.21:1
761	55-248.33
762	55-248.38:1
763	8.01-27.2
764	19.2-267.2
765	2.2-1837
766	15.2-6600 — 15.2-6625
767	46.2-105.2, 46.2-308, 46.2-323.1, 46.2-324, 46.2-341.11, 46.2-341.15, 46.2-342, 46.2-345
768	32.1-35, 32.1-36, 32.1-38, 32.1-39, 32.1-42
769	2.2-3706, 9.1-177.1, 19.2-152.4:2
772	43-11
773	19.2-310.2, 19.2-310.2:1, 19.2-310.3:1, 19.2-310.4, 19.2-310.5, 19.2-310.7
774	22.1-208.2:3
775	58.1-608.4, 58.1-623.1
777	58.1-609.6
778	51.1-155
779	15.2-2245
780	2.2-1201
781	51.1-155
782	46.2-492, 46.2-868.1
783	18.2-308.1:4
784	54.1-300, 54.1-2200 — 54.1-2203, 54.1-2206, 54.1-2206.1, 54.1-2206.2, 54.1-2207, 54.1-2208
785	24.2-104, 24.2-419, 24.2-420.1, 24.2-427, 24.2-603.1, 24.2-611, 24.2-700, 24.2-701, 24.2-702.1, 24.2-706, 24.2-707, 24.2-709, 24.2-711, 24.2-713
786	15.2-3201
787	3.1-796.66, 3.1-796.67:2, 3.1-796.68, 3.1-796.73, 3.1-796.96, 3.1-796.96:2, 3.1-796.96:3 — 3.1-796.96:5, 3.1-796.126:7
788	59.1-519 — 59.1-524
789	9.1-101, 19.2-12, 28.2-100, 28.2-106, 28.2-106.1, 28.2-107, 28.2-108, 65.2-402
791	15.2-5509 — 15.2-5515
792	2.2-507.1, 17.1-513.01
794	46.2-694
795	55-70.1
796	57-12
797	54.1-700, 54.1-701, 54.1-703, 54.1-703.1, 54.1-704.1, 54.1-704.2, 54.1-705, 54.1-706
798	2.2-3705
799	33.1-221.1:3, 58.1-815.1
800	53.1-131, 53.1-131.2
801	23-50.16:36
802	15.2-1542
803	37.1-48.2, 37.1-258
805	53.1-131.1
806	18.2-271.1
807	46.2-334.01
809	10.1-104, n., 10.1-109, n.
810	2.2-515.1, 9.1-102, 16.1-228, 16.1-253, 16.1-253.1, 16.1-253.4, 16.1-279.1, 18.2-61, 18.2-164, 18.2-460, 19.2-11.01, 19.2-11.2, 19.2-81.3, 19.2-152.10 — 19.2-152.10, 19.2-305.1, 19.2-387.1, 52-35, 52-45
811	18.2-266, n., 18.2-271, n., 46.2-391.01, 46.2-410.1
812	65.2-804
813	56-232
814	Const., Art. X, § 7-A, 2.2-1124, n., 2.2-2444, n., 2.2-2813, n., 13.1-775.1, n., 15.2-1302, n., 15.2-1636.9, n., 16.1-69.48:1, n., 16.1-69.48:2, n., 16.1-309.7, n., 22.1-100, n., 29.1-700, n., 32.1-351, n., 32.1-360, n., 46.2-216.3, n., 46.2-332, n., 46.2-685, n., 46.2-697.1, n., 51.1-100, n., 56-484.12, n., 58.1-15, n., 58.1-202, n., 58.1-202.1, n., 58.1-301, n., 58.1-605, n., 58.1-606, n., 58.1-612, n., 58.1-615, n., 58.1-624, n., 58.1-635, n., 58.1-638, n., 58.1-801, n., 58.1-3523, n., 62.1-140, n.
816	18.2-52.1
817	18.2-57
818	2.2-515.1, 9.1-102, 16.1-228, 16.1-253, 16.1-253.1, 16.1-253.4, 16.1-279.1, 18.2-61, 18.2-164, 18.2-460, 19.2-11.01, 19.2-11.2, 19.2-81.3, 19.2-152.8 — 19.2-152.10, 19.2-305.1, 19.2-387.1, 52-35
819	24.2-104, 24.2-419, 24.2-420.1, 24.2-427, 24.2-603.1, 24.2-611, 24.2-700, 24.2-701, 24.2-702.1, 24.2-706,

Acts 2002 Chapter	Code 1950 Section
	24.2-707, 24.2-709, 24.2-711, 24.2-713
820	65.2-402.1
821	58.1-1009, 58.1-1033, 58.1-1034
822	10.1-1402.1, 62.1-44.15:6,
823	15.2-2307
824	Const., Art. VI, § 1
825	Const., Art. X, § 6
826	18.2-308
827	2.2-1132, n.
828	52-8.4
829	58.1-4022, 58.1-4022.1
830	2.2-3704 — 2.2-3706, 2.2-3711
831	16.1-69.48:1, 16.1-69.48:3, 17.1-275 — 17.1-175.2, 17.1-275.4 — 17.1-275.6, 17.1-275.7 — 17.1-275.9, 17.1-277R, 17.1-281, 18.2-264.01R, 19.2-11.3, 19.2-303.4, 19.2-354, 19.2-368.18, 53.1-131.1, 53.1-150
832	8.01-600, 15.2-1605.1, 17.1-213, 17.1-219.1, 17.1-232, 17.1-249, 17.1-275, 19.2-187, 19.2-270.4:1, 31-8.1, 32.1-267, 47.1-5, 55-66.4:2, 64.1-94
833	56-234
834	46.2-105.2, 46.2-308, 46.2-323.1, 46.2-324, 46.2-341.11, 46.2-341.15, 46.2-342, 46.2-345
835	32.1-127.1:03, 32.1-127.1:04
836	9.1-101, 9.1-102, 9.1-110, 9.1-184, 15.2-1737, 19.2-13, 22.1-280.2:1
837	22.1-253.13:1
838	2.2-2708.1
839	2.2-1503.2, 2.2-1509, 2.2-1509.1, 2.2-1514
840	15.2-1613.1
841	56-265.15, 56-265.15:1, 56-265.17, 56-265.17:1 — 56-265.17:3, 56-265.18, 56-265.19, 56-265.20:1, 56-265.21, 56-265.22, 56-265.22:1, 56-265.24, 56-265.26:1
842	8.01-216.1 — 8.01-216.19
843	62.1-69.34 — 62.1-69.44
844	63.1-250 — 63.1-250.2, 63.1-250.3:1, 63.1-252.1
845	55-66.3
846	15.2-4816 — 15.2-4828R, 15.2-4829 — 15.2-4840
847	63.1-202.1
848	63.1-202.02
849	46.2-396.1
850	2.2-1705, n.
851	22.1-212.6 — 22.1-212.9, 22.1-212.11, 22.1-212.12, 22.1-212.14 — 22.1-212.15
852	59.1-372
853	33.1-221.1:7, 58.1-540 — 58.1-549, n., 58.1-602, 58.1-604.4, 58.1-604.5, 58.1-605, 58.1-606, 58.1-611.1, 58.1-614, 58.1-626, 58.1-628.1, 58.1-815.1, n., 58.1-3833
856	15.2-974, 27-95, 27-96, 27-96.1, 27-96.2, 27-97, 27-100.1, 59.1-142 — 59.1-148R
857	38.2-5016
858	49-13, 59.1-94
860	16.1-241.3, 32.1-127.1:03, 63.1-248.3, 63.1-248.6:01, 63.1-248.6:02
861	46.2-2000 — 46.2-2001.1, 46.2-2011.4, 46.2-2011.10, 46.2-2011.14 — 46.2-2011.16, 46.2-2011.22, 46.2-2099.20R, 46.2-2099.30, 46.2-2099.31 — 46.2-2099.40R
862	55-66.3
863	8.01-227.4 — 8.01-227.7
864	46.2-742.1, 46.2-742.3, 46.2-743, 46.2-746.2:2, 46.2-746.7, 46.2-746.9, 46.2-749.36:1, 46.2-749.49 — 46.2-749.77
865	18.2-308.1:4
866	58.1-4022, 58.1-4022.1
867	19.2-298.1 — 19.2-298.3, 46.2-323
868	9.1-101, 9.1-102, 9.1-110, 9.1-184, 15.2-1737, 19.2-13, 22.1-280.2:1
869	54.1-700 — 54.1-703, 54.1-704.1 — 54.1-706
870	46.2-2001.3, 46.2-2005, 46.2-2109
871	8.01-689 — 8.01-695
872	46.2-870
873	18.2-271
874	22.1-212.8, 22.1-212.11, 22.1-212.15, 22.1-212.16
875	8.01-407.1
876	15.2-1736
877	2.2-2440 — 2.2-2447, 58.1-609.1
878	25-46.3, 25-238, 33.1-89
879	8.01-44.5
880	18.2-308.2:3
881	20-124.3:1
882	46.2-878.2
883	55-210.31 — 55-210.37
885	19.2-270.5
886	15.2-1512.2
888	2.2-1503.2, 2.2-1509, 2.2-1509.1, 2.2-1514
889	22.1-290.01
890	18.2-323.1
891	22.1-1
892	60.2-602
893	46.2-749.30:1, 46.2-749.78 — 46.2-749.83
894	15.2-100, n.
895	22.1-1, n.
896	32.1-23
897	6.1-249, 6.1-330.55, 6.1-439, 6.1-444, 6.1-444 — 6.1-471, 59.1-200
898	59.1-344 — 59.1-352R, 59.1-352.1 — 59.1-352.10, 59.1-353, 59.1-363

Acts 2002 Chapter	Code 1950 Section
899	2.2-204, n.,
	2.2-211, n.,
	2.2-409, n.,
	2.2-1104, n.,
	2.2-1156, n.,
	2.2-1204, n.,
	2.2-1505, n.,
	2.2-1600, n.,
	2.2-1802, n.,
	2.2-1835, n.,
	2.2-2319, n.,
	2.2-2444, n.,
	2.2-3705, n.,
	2.2-3802, n.,
	2.2-4011, n.,
	2.2-4400, n.,
	2.2-5211, n.,
	3.1-249.34, n.,
	3.1-336.2, n.,
	3.1-361, n.,
	4.1-116, n.,
	10.1-202, n.,
	10.1-1124, n.,
	10.1-1176, n.,
	10.1-1188, n.,
	10.1-1190, n.,
	10.1-2213, n.,
	10.1-2500, n.,
	13.1-775.1, n.,
	15.2-1302, n.,
	15.2-1534, n.,
	15.2-1609.1, n.,
	15.2-1627.1, n.,
	15.2-1628, n.,
	15.2-1629, n.,
	15.2-1630, n.,
	15.2-1631, n.,
	15.2-1636.9, n.,
	15.2-2602, n.,
	15.2-2659, n.,
	15.2-4100, n.,
	16.1-69.48:1, n.,
	16.1-69.48:2, n.,
	16.1-309.2, n.,
	16.1-309.7, n.,
	16.1-322.1, n.,
	17.2-279, n.,
	19.2-169.3, n.,
	19.2-174.1, n.,
	19.2-326, n.,
	19.2-349, n.,
	19.2-399, n.,
	22.1-101.1, n.,
	22.1-205, n.,
	22.1-253.13, n.,
	22.1-290.01, n.,
	23-7.4:1, n.,
	23-7.4:2, n.,
	23-30.27:1, n.,
	23-38.10:1, n.,
	23-38.19:2, n.,
	23-272, n.,
	24.2-108, n.,
	32.1-163, n.,
	32.1-325.1:1, n.,
	32.1-347, n.,
	33.1-75.1, n.,
	35.1-13, n.,
	35.1-14, n.,
	35.1-16, n.,
	35.1-17, n.,
	36-98.1, n.,
	37.1-70.1, n.
	37.1-70.1 —
	37.1-70.19, n.,
	37.1-70.10, n.,
	37.1-134.21, n.,
	45.1-392, n.,
	46.2-216.3, n.,
	46.2-332, n.,
	46.2-685, n.,
	46.2-694, n.,
	46.2-697.1, n.,
	51.1-100, n.,
	51.1-1401, n.,
	51.1-808, n.,
	53.1-105, n.,
	53.1-120, n.,
	53.1-45, n.,
	53.1-67.1, n.,
	53.1-95.2, n.,
	54.1-3916, n.,
	56-232, n.,
	56-234, n.,
	56-484.12, n.,
	58.1-202.2, n.,
	58.1-301, n.,
	58.1-339.4, n.,
	58.1-439.2, n.,
	58.1-462, n.,
	58.1-470, n.,
	58.1-600, n.,
	58.1-602, n.,
	58.1-612, n.,
	58.1-615, n.,
	58.1-624, n.,
	58.1-635, n.,
	58.1-638, n.,
	58.1-801, n.,
	58.1-1605, n.,
	58.1-1803, n.,
	58.1-1804, n.,
	58.1-2510, n.,
	58.1-3523, n.,
	58.1-4200, n.,
	59.1-282.2, n.,
	59.1-282.3, n.,
	59.1-284.14, n.,
	59.1-284.15, n.,
	59.1-364, n.,
	59.1-392, n.,
	60.2-305, n.,
	60.2-315, n.,
	62.1-140, n.

ACTS 2003

Acts 2003 Chapter	Code 1950 Section
1	22.1-271.3, 32.1-45.1
2	58.1-301
3	58.1-322, 58.1-402
5	51.1-1114, 51.1-1125
6	58.1-3292.1
7	51.1-142.2
8	58.1-3118
9	51.1-505
10	58.1-346.8
11	51.1-124.22
12	58.1-3840
13	51.1-1112, 51.1-1123
14	2.2-1503.3
15	51.1-124.4
16	58.1-3970.1
17	2.2-5100—2.2-5102
18	8.01-225
19	33.1-124, 33.1-128
20	24.2-404.2R
21	15.2-2307
23	2.2-1839
24	58.1-202.2, n., 58.1-1840.1
25	15.2-2159
26	53.1-120
27	19.2-390
28	19.2-165.1
29	46.2-100, 46.2-904—46.2-906, 46.2-1081
30	64.1-57
31	16.1-278.15, 20-103
32	46.2-1220
33	18.2-57.3
34	58.1-3511
35	37.1-256, 37.1-256.1
36	58.1-202.1
37	9.1-400
38	18.2-57.3
39	58.1-202.1
40	37.1-256, 37.1-256.1
41	9.1-400
42	64.1-57
43	58.1-3511
44	53.1-120
45	16.1-278.15, 20-103
46	46.2-100, 46.2-904—46.2-906, 46.2-1081
47	33.1-124, 33.1-128
48	15.2-2159
49	2.2-1839
50	24.2-404.2R
52	58.1-202.2, n., 58.1-1840.1

Acts 2003 Chapter	Code 1950 Section
53	15.2-2307
54	63.2-223—63.2-225R, 63.2-226, 63.2-227, 63.2-228R
55	15.2-1308
57	51.5-3—51.5-5, 51.5-5.1R, 51.5-6R, 51.5-9.01R, 51.5-14.01,
58	58.1-322, 58.1-402
59	55-515.1
60	55-248.13:2
61	32.1-102.2
62	18.2-56
63	32.1-122.10:001, 32.1-122.10:002
64	55-248.13:2
66	32.1-325, 32.1-351
67	18.2-56
68	55-248.13:2
70	32.1-122.10:001, 32.1-122.10:002
71	32.1-325, 32.1-351
72	32.1-102.2
73	51.5-3—51.5-5, 51.5-5.1R, 51.5-6R, 51.5-9.01R, 51.5-14.01
74	55-515.1
75	63.2-223—63.2-225R, 63.2-226, 63.2-227, 63.2-228R
77	15.2-1308
78	10.1-1800, 10.1-1801.1, 10.1-1801.2R
79	10.1-105—10.1-107, 10.1-111—10.1-113, 10.1-202, 10.1-218—10.1-225R, 10.1-705, 10.1-707, 10.1-709, 28.2-1100
80	18.2-255.2
81	18.2-130
82	46.2-1001
83	2.2-1161.1, 22.1-16.2, 52-34.1—52-34.3
85	46.2-1001
86	2.2-1161.1, 22.1-16.2, 52-34.1—52-34.3
87	18.2-130
89	10.1-105—10.1-107, 10.1-111—10.1-113, 10.1-202, 10.1-218—10.1-225R, 10.1-705, 10.1-707, 10.1-709, 28.2-1100
90	10.1-1800, 10.1-1801.1, 10.1-1801.2R
91	18.2-255.2
92	29.1-323
93	46.2-1025
94	2.2-2101, 53.1-10, 53.1-45.1, 53.1-45.2—53.1-45.5R
95	29.1-330, 29.1-332, 29.1-333
96	19.2-212
97	8.01-582
98	16.1-266
99	18.2-362, 20-40
100	10.1-109, n.
101	10.1-1418.2, 10.1-1418.3, 10.1-1418.4, 10.1-1418.5, 10.1-1422.3, 58.1-641, 58.1-642
102	16.1-69.35
103	2.2-511, 19.2-11.01
104	16.1-248.1
105	46.2-676
106	59.1-148.3
107	19.2-389.1
108	16.1-300
109	8.01-675.3, 19.2-398, 19.2-400—19.2-406, 19.2-408, 19.2-409
110	18.2-308.2
111	18.2-460
112	18.2-479.1
113	33.1-346
114	18.2-371.2
115	46.2-920, 46.2-1029.2
116	19.2-249
117	29.1-748.1
118	16.1-278.9
119	16.1-301, 16.1-305.1, 16.1-305.2, 16.1-309, 22.1-254, 22.1-277, 22.1-277.2:1, 22.1-288.2
120	29.1-303, 29.1-303.1
121	46.2-1029.1
122	46.2-1222.1
123	29.1-529
124	9.1-138, 9.1-139
125	8.01-32
126	16.1-69.55
127	17.1-255, 17.1-258, 17.1-258.1R
128	10.1-502, 10.1-503
129	16.1-244
130	4.1-352
131	19.2-327.3
132	53.1-136
133	16.1-250.1
134	46.2-832
135	29.1-529
136	9.1-140
137	29.1-352, 29.1-354—29.1-356
138	46.2-1163
139	17.1-803
140	19.2-166
141	17.1-319
142	9.1-176.1
143	16.1-300, 16.1-305
144	16.1-269.6
145	29.1-309.2
146	9.1-177.1, 19.2-299
147	19.2-76.1
148	19.2-226, 19.2-390.01
149	18.2-460
150	16.1-299.1, 19.2-310.2:1—19.2-310.4
151	37.1-71
152	46.2-1023
153	46.2-1020, 46.2-1024
154	53.1-31.1
155	24.2-683
156	58.1-3970.1
158	15.2-6100 — 15.2-6110R
159	15.2-4903
160	56-484.12, 58.1-3812
161	22.1-312
162	22.1-177
163	58.1-301
164	58.1-3221.1
165	22.1-26
166	58.1-442
167	15.2-2110
168	58.1-3965
169	2.2-113
170	58.1-3958
172	56-232
173	15.2-3232
174	2.2-813.1
175	22.1-32
176	42.1-32.7R
177	42.1-80, 42.1-81R
179	58.1-3812
180	58.1-348, 58.1-452
181	58.1-322
182	15.2-953
184	23-9.9:01
185	2.2-4301
186	63.2-2004
187	22.1-313, 22.1-314
189	15.2-2307
190	2.2-1508
191	15.2-2118
192	15.2-2209
193	26-13, 26-15, 26-20
194	26-8, 26-10, 26-10.1
195	8.01-606, 26-4,

Acts 2003 Chapter	Code 1950 Section
	37.1-144, 58.1-1712, 58.1-1714
196	58.1-3983.1
197	2.2-203, 15.2-2901, 15.2-3400, 36-132.1, 36-139
198	15.2-2413
200	15.2-1433
201	26-17.9
202	15.2-634.1
204	15.2-1508
205	17.1-279
207	15.2-906
208	15.2-954.1
209	58.1-322, 58.1-402
210	2.2-2605, n., 2.2-2606, n., 2.2-2607, n., 2.2-2608, n.
211	22.1-23, n., 51.1-155
212	2.2-4014, 2.2-4031, 2.2-4032R, 2.2-4033R, 2.2-4102, 30-34.10:2, 30-146
214	58.1-3940
215	15.2-2110
216	15.2-1104, 15.2-1201.2
217	46.2-1023
218	46.2-395
219	16.1-253.2, 18.2-60.4
220	51.1-155.1, 51.1-505
221	38.2-3432.3
222	38.2-1919
223	19.2-10.1
224	2.2-4007, 2.2-4012, 2.2-4012.1
225	2.2-1120
226	2.2-4310, 2.2-4343
227	62.1-44.38:1
228	20-25
229	16.1-241, 20-124.1, 63.2-1215
231	30-10, 30-34.2:1
232	24.2-112, 24.2-115
233	8.01-27.1
234	8.01-514, 16.1-99
236	51.5-39.2
237	24.2-942, 24.2-943
238	24.2-435
239	2.2-2705
240	10.1-400—10.1-402, 10.1-405, 10.1-406, 10.1-406.1, 10.1-409—10.1-418.1
241	24.2-604.2
242	24.2-914.1
243	38.2-3418.14, 38.2-4319
245	55-66.6
246	15.2-6302
247	24.2-706
248	24.2-904, 24.2-906, 24.2-914, 24.2-920
249	54.1-3007, 54.1-3030—54.1-3040
250	38.2-3418.4
251	8.01-581.20
252	2.2-3003, 2.2-3006
253	32.1-325.02, 37.1-137.5, 55-286.1, 55-286.2, 64.1-57, 64.1-65.1, 64.1-188—64.1-196R, 64.1-196.1—64.1-196.15,
254	64.1-105
255	2.2-4341
256	24.2-923
257	24.2-910.1
258	8.01-217, 20-121.4
259	8.01-470
260	20-109.1
261	18.2-49.1
262	19.2-349
263	51.1-165
264	30-34.4:1, 30-34.6, 30-34.7R
265	64.1-75.1
266	38.2-604, 38.2-604.1, 38.2-612.1
267	51.1-124.12
268	24.2-801, 24.2-801.1, 24.2-802, 24.2-805, 24.2-814
269	6.1-332.1, 11-9.7, 54.1-2989.1
270	30-133
271	24.2-106.1
272	2.2-3801
273	46.2-1054
274	2.2-3705, 2.2-3711
275	2.2-3704
276	33.1-62, n.
277	46.2-880
278	58.1-2403
279	33.1-223.2:7
280	8.01-3, 17.1-318R
281	33.1-12
282	16.1-69.40:1, 46.2-878.2, n.
283	38.2-2206
286	46.2-2099.41
287	56-414
288	33.1-23.3
289	56-560
290	18.2-271.1
291	2.2-3711, 54.1-4400, 54.1-4402, 54.1-4409—54.1-4413, 54.1-4417, 54.1-4423
292	56-575.3, 56-575.16
293	46.2-756
294	2.2-1111
295	46.2-746.2:1R, 46.2-746.8, 46.2-749.12R, 46.2-749.15 — 46.2-749.17R, 46.2-749.19 — 46.2-749.25R, 46.2-749.27R, 46.2-749.30R
297	46.2-600
298	46.2-1569.1
299	46.2-106
300	46.2-809
301	46.2-221
302	33.1-55, 33.1-221.1:2, 33.1-26—33.1-30R
303	33.1-75.1, 33.1-75.3, 33.1-225.1R
304	46.2-1600, 46.2-1605
305	46.2-1231
306	46.2-342
307	2.2-3705
308	46.2-334.01
309	32.1-125.4, 32.1-125.5
310	54.1-2400.02
311	33.1-375.1
312	32.1-315
313	46.2-915.1
314	46.2-652, 46.2-653, 46.2-1112, 46.2-1131, 46.2-1133, 46.2-1135, 46.2-1139—46.2-1144, 46.2-1146—46.2-1149.2, 46.2-1149.3
315	46.2-1143
316	46.2-427
317	33.1-127, 33.1-132
318	33.1-128
319	2.2-3714
320	46.2-216.4
321	33.1-355
322	46.2-2011.6, 46.2-2121
323	46.2-334.01
324	33.1-46.2
325	58.1-2261, 58.1-2262
326	46.2-752
327	2.2-3705
328	58.1-2405
329	4.1-208, 4.1-209
330	2.2-1151.1
331	46.2-1527.1, 46.2-1527.3, 46.2-1527.5, 46.2-1527.9 — 46.2-1527.11
332	2.2-3705, 2.2-3711
333	46.2-330

Acts 2003 Chapter	Code 1950 Section
334	46.2-1993, 46.2-1993.6, 46.2-1993.25, 46.2-1993.64
335	46.2-342
336	46.2-216.5
337	33.1-221.1:3, 58.1-815.1
338	2.2-904
339	2.2-2279, 2.2-2285, 2.2-2287, 2.2-2292, 2.2-2294, 2.2-2295
340	8.9A-406, 8.9A-408, 13.1-603, 13.1-722, 13.1-1001.1, 13.1-1002, 13.1-1003, 13.1-1010.4, 13.1-1012, 13.1-1023.1, 13.1-1067, 13.1-1070, 13.1-1072, 13.1-1073, 50-73.1, 50-73.2, 50-73.48:1, 50-73.48:3, 50-73.48:4, 50-73.84, 50-73.128, 50-73.130, 50-73.144
341	56-484.12, 56-484.17
342	8.3A-602
343	15.2-4903
344	59.1-296, 59.1-296.2:1, 59.1-297, 59.1-297.1, 59.1-297.2, 59.1-298, 59.1-305
345	15.2-4903
346	2.2-3708, n.
347	15.2-4904
348	2.2-2603, 2.2-2604R
349	2.2-2500—2.2-2502R
350	15.2-4903
351	55-428
352	2.2-1303
353	6.1-194.69, 6.1-194.136, 8.1-101—8.1-109R, 8.1-201—8.1-207R, 8.1-208R, 8.2-103, 8.2-202, 8.2-208R, 8.2A-207R, 8.2A-103, 8.2A-501, 8.2A-518, 8.2A-519, 8.2A-527, 8.2A-528, 8.3A-103, 8.4-104, 8.4A-105, 8.4A-106, 8.4A-204, 8.5A-102, 8.5A-103, 8.6A-102, 8.7-102, 8.8A-102, 8.9A-102, 8.10-104, 15.2-4908, 15.2-6612, 55-70.1, 59.1-207.19, 59.1-352.2, 59.1-353, 59.1-481, 59.1-494, 59.1-501.2
354	18.2-187.1, 18.2-190.1—18.2-190.5, 18.2-190.7, 18.2-190.8
355	55-226.2, 55-248.4, 55-248.16, 56-1.2, 56-245.3
356	58.1-3233
357	15.2-4903, 15.2-4904
358	2.2-3705
359	59.1-335.2
360	55-79.81
361	38.2-517
362	2.2-2233.1, 2.2-2515
363	55-248.21, 55-248.31
364	59.1-407—59.1-411, 59.1-414
365	2.2-2513, n.
366	2.2-2440 — 2.2-2447, n.
367	54.1-600, 54.1-607
368	32.1-283, 32.1-285
369	51.1-126, 51.1-126.3
370	13.1-1055, 50-73.57
371	38.2-406
372	58.1-2500, 58.1-2507
373	12.1-43, 13.1-1204, 13.1-1213, 13.1-1214, 13.1-1217, 13.1-1254, 13.1-1260R, 13.1-1261,
374	13.1-815—13.1-816, 13.1-898.2—13.1-898.7
375	62.1-44.17:1
376	58.1-441
377	38.2-3503, 38.2-3504
378	50-73.11, 50-73.54, 50-73.132, 50-73.137:1, 50-73.138
379	13.1-1003, 13.1-1005, 13.1-1011.1
380	40.1-79.01
381	55-58.3
382	60.2-525
383	60.2-204
385	56-265.13:6
386	6.1-411, 6.1-422.1, 6.1-425.1, 6.1-425.2
387	38.2-231, 38.2-2113, 38.2-2208
389	28.2-106.2
390	15.2-2114
391	19.2-390.1
397	8.01-581.14R
399	62.1-44.15:5
400	43-13.2, 43-13.3
401	45.1-161.292:73
402	10.1-549.1
403	15.2-2214, 15.2-2309
404	55-79.75, 55-510.1
405	55-79.75, 55-79.75:1
406	2.2-3802
407	62.1-229.2
408	15.2-2254
409	15.2-1517
410	59.1-21.10, 59.1-21.12, 59.1-21.16:2
411	59.1-437
412	38.2-1800
413	55-79.76
414	46.2-1118
415	38.2-612
416	55-248.6:1
417	36-45
418	46.2-1305
420	3.1-398.1, 3.1-399
421	55-79.83
422	55-508, 55-509, 55-511
423	10.1-560
424	55-248.7
425	55-248.4
426	55-248.9:1
427	8.01-471, 55-248.34R, 55-248.34:1
428	63.2-608, 32.1-328R, 63.2-700—63.2-702R
429	54.1-1115
430	54.1-1115
431	19.2-387
432	19.2-389.1
433	10.1-2600—10.1-2609
434	36-55.28, 36-135
435	2.2-1405
436	2.2-4006, 36-99
437	6.1-334
438	55-248.15:1, 55-248.15:2
439	6.1-330.78:1
440	38.2-3221
442	55-79.41, 55-79.75, 55-79.77, 55-510
443	15.2-5153
444	15.2-3400
445	40.1-51
446	29.1-571—29.1-577
447	54.1-2206
448	15.2-1232.1, 54.1-4009, 54.1-4010, 54.1-4012
449	32.1-162.14R

Acts 2003 Chapter	Code 1950 Section
450	37.1-256—37.1-257
451	2.2-2101, 2.2-2642, 2.2-2643R
452	2.2-208, 2.2-2652—2.2-2654R
453	32.1-11.1
454	2.2-2644—2.2-2647R, 15.2-4217.1
455	8.01-66.2, 8.01-66.5, 8.01-66.7, 8.01-66.8, 43-63.1R
456	54.1-2906
457	2.2-803.1
458	32.1-174.3
459	8.01-390.2, 19.2-188
461	23-276.2, 23-276.5, 23-276.6
462	38.2-3418.13
463	32.1-46.1
464	32.1-127.1:04
465	54.1-3408
466	32.1-276.3, 32.1-276.6
467	20-87.1R, 63.2-100, 63.2-213, 63.2-224, 63.2-608, 63.2-702, 63.2-1205, 63.2-1206, 63.2-1304, 63.2-1602.1, 63.2-1715, 63.2-1717, 63.2-1719, 63.2-1724, 63.2-1738, 63.2-1802, 63.2-1803, 63.2-1902
468	37.1-183.3, 37.1-197.2
469	63.2-1923, 63.2-1924, 63.2-1925, 63.2-1930
470	46.2-1222.1
471	32.1-116.1, 32.1-127.1:03
472	32.1-276.8
473	54.1-2936
474	58.1-3274
475	2.2-3709
476	24.2-541
477	24.2-506, 24.2-521, 24.2-543
478	24.2-701, 24.2-706, 24.2-707
479	3.1-796.98
480	32.1-330
481	32.1-353.1—32.1-353.5, 32.1-353.6R
482	54.1-2961
483	2.2-2648, 2.2-5202, 2.2-5206, 2.2-5207, 2.2-5209
484	32.1-263
485	2.2-2649
486	32.1-102.3:2, n.
487	8.01-581.1
488	38.2-2801
490	54.1-3321, n., 54.1-3322, n.
491	2.2-213.1
492	8.01-581.1
493	15.2-2403
495	54.1-2701
496	54.1-3482
497	54.1-3408
498	2.2-2648
499	2.2-5201
500	32.1-176.5
501	51.5-31
502	63.2-1208
503	51.5-23—51.5-25
504	32.1-262, 32.1-267
505	54.1-2800, 54.1-2803, 54.1-2806, 54.1-2814.1, 54.1-2818.3
506	62.1-234
507	8.01-225.01
508	16.1-251, 63.2-1517
509	54.1-3401, 54.1-3402R, 54.1-3410.2, 54.1-3435.02
510	54.1-2952.1
511	54.1-3410
512	54.1-2956.11
513	32.1-351.1
514	54.1-2901
515	32.1-50.2, 54.1-3408
516	37.1-42.1, 53.1-10
517	32.1-126.01, 32.1-162.9:1
518	15.2-928
519	54.1-2901
520	20-124.2
521	32.1-351
522	15.2-2303.2
523	37.1-64, n.
524	15.2-1102, n.
525	8.01-66.2, 8.01-66.5, 8.01-66.6, 8.01-66.8, 8.01-66.9
526	32.1-162.3, 63.2-1806
527	37.1-137.2
528	37.1-137.5
529	54.1-2957.6
531	22.1-296
532	2.2-406.1
533	33.1-12
534	60.2-604
535	36-45
536	6.1-5, 6.1-58.1, 6.1-58.3
537	32.1-258.1
538	16.1-228
540	32.1-71.02
541	18.2-246.2, 18.2-246.4, 19.2-10.1
542	45.1-161.58, 45.1-161.292:31, 45.1-181, 45.1-184.2, 45.1-235, 45.1-361.29, 45.1-361.33
543	38.2-2114, 38.2-2126, 38.2-2212, 38.2-2234
544	3.1-741.3—3.1-741.5
545	54.1-1805
547	16.1-228
548	32.1-71.02
549	18.2-246.2, 18.2-246.4, 19.2-10.1
550	2.2-4002, n., 45.1-161.58, 45.1-161.292:31, 45.1-181, 45.1-184.2, 45.1-235, 45.1-361.29, 45.1-361.33
551	3.1-741.3—3.1-741.5
552	32.1-258.1
553	38.2-2114, 38.2-2126, 38.2-2212, 38.2-2234
554	54.1-1805
555	60.2-604
556	2.2-406.1
557	22.1-296
558	6.1-5, 6.1-58.1, 6.1-58.3
559	36-45
560	33.1-12
561	62.1-198, 62.1-203, 62.1-209, 62.1-216, 62.1-216.1
562	29.1-101, 29.1-103, 29.1-113
563	8.01-9
564	4.1-132, 4.1-207, 4.1-212, 4.1-238
565	19.2-208
566	15.2-2704
567	50-73.79, 50-73.83, 50-73.93, 50-73.115, 50-73.121, 50-73.131
568	15.2-2314
569	33.1-370.1
570	15.2-2650, 15.2-2651
571	8.01-226.1
572	8.01-15.1
573	18.2-270
574	62.1-229.3
575	36-96.1:1, 36-96.2, 36-96.8, 36-96.20, 54.1-300, 54.1-2342, n., 54.1-2343, 54.1-2344
576	57-48, 57-49, 57-55.3, 57-59, 57-60, 57-61.2
577	15.2-6700—15.2-6704
578	18.2-500
579	16.1-286, 16.1-290
580	2.2-1105

Acts 2003 Chapter	Code 1950 Section
581	58.1-3292.1
582	54.1-204
583	15.2-3400
584	9.1-900—9.1-918, 16.1-272, 18.2-472.1, 19.2-298.1—19.2-298.4R, 19.2-390, 19.2-390.1, 19.2-390.2R, 46.2-323, 53.1-116.1, 53.1-160.1,
585	10.1-2211
587	16.1-260
588	30-34.2:1
589	4.1-209
590	2.2-126
591	18.2-270
592	6.1-112, 13.1-316, 13.1-544.1, 13.1-630, 13.1-762, 13.1-829, 13.1-924, 13.1-1012, 13.1-1104, 13.1-1214, 50-73.2
593	6.1-456, 6.1-459, 6.1-465, 6.1-467
594	4.1-225
595	13.1-504, 13.1-507—13.1-509, 13.1-511, 13.1-512R, 13.1-514, 13.1-523
596	13.1-904
597	13.1-635, 13.1-720, 13.1-722.1, 13.1-764, 13.1-834, 13.1-896, 13.1-926, 13.1-1016, 13.1-1072, 13.1-1221, 50-73.5, 50-73.48:3, 50-73.135
598	13.1-722.10, 13.1-722.12
599	33.1-70.1
600	54.1-700, 54.1-701, 54.1-703, 54.1-703.2, 54.1-704.1—54.1-706
601	2.2-2825, n.
602	54.1-2506.1
603	19.2-152.4:3
604	28.2-200
605	18.2-266.1, 46.2-391.2
606	18.2-251.02
607	16.1-299.1
608	46.2-882
609	60.2-219
610	30-111
611	36-99.6:2
612	2.2-1503
613	19.2-299
614	32.1-164, 62.1-44.3, 62.1-44.18, 62.1-44.19
615	18.2-371.2
616	10.1-531
617	9.1-102, n., 9.1-184, n.
618	2.2-3711
619	18.2-308.1
620	10.1-1400, 10.1-1424.2
621	38.2-1839
622	44-146.18, 44-146.19
623	15.2-1613.1
624	51.1-138, 51.1-202, 51.1-205, 51.1-206
625	20-60.3, 20-107.1
626	51.1-124.22, 51.1-126
627	25.1-204
628	51.1-124.3
629	4.1-207
630	4.1-201
631	4.1-219
632	8.01-53
633	30-168, 30-168.1—30-168.5, 30-169R
634	63.2-1514
635	32.1-229
636	58.1-346.21—58.1-346.23
637	22.1-260
638	40.1-29
639	2.2-4002, 32.1-79—32.1-88R, 54.1-3303, 54.1-3401, 54.1-3408.01, 54.1-3408.03, 54.1-3457
640	54.1-3450, 54.1-3452, 54.1-3454
641	54.1-2901, 32.1-145R, 32.1-146R, 32.1-147R
642	2.2-2669, 2.2-2670, 2.2-2674.1
643	15.2-5431.1—15.2-5431.37
644	2.2-4301, n., 2.2-4303, 2.2-4346, n.
645	38.2-3431
646	2.2-3106
647	32.1-134.01
648	16.1-233, 16.1-235, 16.1-236, 16.1-236.1
649	30-114, 30-116
650	36-99, 36-103, 36-105, 36-114, 36-119.1
651	2.2-4304
652	2.2-2905
653	2.2-2513, n., 2.2-2515, n.
654	38.2-3540.1
655	23-74, 23-75
657	2.2-203, 2.2-1900—2.2-1905R, 2.2-2000—2.2-2004, 2.2-2101, 2.2-2421, 2.2-2422R, 2.2-2435—2.2-2439R, 2.2-2452—2.2-2454, 2.2-2681, 2.2-2682, 2.2-2715—2.2-2719, 23-7.4:1, 58.1-609.1, 58.1-3506
661	2.2-214.1, 32.1-23.1
662	20-155
663	54.1-2820
664	65.2-704—65.2-706
665	16.1-88.03, 55-246.1
667	16.1-88.03, 55-246.1
669	20-155
670	2.2-203, 2.2-1900—2.2-1905R, 2.2-2000—2.2-2004, 2.2-2101, 2.2-2421, 2.2-2422R, 2.2-2435—2.2-2439R, 2.2-2452—2.2-2454, 2.2-2681, 2.2-2682, 2.2-2715—2.2-2719, 23-7.4:1, 58.1-609.1, 58.1-3506
671	65.2-704—65.2-706
673	54.1-2820
674	2.2-214.1, 32.1-23.1
676	59.1-280
677	15.2-2108.2—15.2-2108.16, 56-265.4:4, 56-484.7:1
678	13.1-542.1, 13.1-543, 13.1-544.1, 13.1-544.2, 13.1-1101.1, 13.1-1102, 38.2-231
679	15.2-2656
680	15.2-1904
681	32.1-164.5 — 32.1-164.7
682	59.1-369, 59.1-391, 59.1-395
683	15.2-4908
684	2.2-3310
685	2.2-1201
686	46.2-1085R
687	10.1-418
688	22.1-253.13:4, 22.1-254.2
690	22.1-253.13:1
691	22.1-253.13:3
692	30-34.2
693	22.1-79.3
694	2.2-3100, 2.2-3101, 2.2-3104.2, 2.2-3105, 2.2-3112, 2.2-3114, 2.2-3115, 2.2-3121, 2.2-3126, 2.2-4369
695	2.2-4002, 3.1-398, 35.1-14
697	22.1-199.2, 22.1-253.13:1
698	43-4
699	38.2-508.5

Acts 2003 Chapter	Code 1950 Section
700	23-38.55
701	23-77.3
702	22.1-118
703	2.2-3711
704	2.2-3705
705	59.1-386
706	22.1-304
707	59.1-207.5:1
708	23-4.4
709	32.1-229.01
710	23-9.3:1
711	56-235.5, 56-265.4:4, 56-484.7:1, 56-484.7:2, 56-484.7:4
712	15.2-5152, 15.2-5155
713	22.1-32
714	22.1-253.13:1
715	23-9.6:1
716	15.2-2259
717	38.2-1800, 38.2-1865.1, 38.2-5700—38.2-5707R, 38.2-6000—38.2-6016
719	56-580
720	15.2-2160, 56-265.4:4, 58.1-2660
721	60.2-114
722	59.1-394.1
723	22.1-296.1
724	22.1-79.1
725	2.2-2679, 23-9.6:1
726	24.2-927
727	19.2-390
728	13.1-603, 13.1-610, 13.1-654, 13.1-655, 13.1-657, 13.1-723
729	38.2-602, 38.2-613.2
730	19.2-152.8—19.2-152.10
731	2.2-1201.1, 19.2-389
732	19.2-298.1
733	18.2-111
735	19.2-169.1, 19.2-169.2
736	19.2-294
737	29.1-330, 29.1-332, 29.1-333
738	10.1-1186.5
739	15.2-709.1, 15.2-1505.1, 27-6.2
740	18.2-113
741	10.1-2127
742	15.2-1503.1
743	10.1-1425.26
744	9.1-101, 9.1-113
745	55-66.3
748	59.1-274, 59.1-275
749	2.2-710R, 2.2-718—2.2-720, 37.1-62.1R
750	55-210.4:1, 55-210.4:2, 55-210.12
751	19.2-11.01
752	38.2-4300, 38.2-4302, 38.2-4303, 38.2-4306
753	32.1-27, 32.1-125.01, 54.1-111, 54.1-2400, 54.1-2400.2, 54.1-2400.3, 54.1-2401, 54.1-2408.2, 54.1-2505, 54.1-2506, 54.1-2506.01, 54.1-2906, 54.1-2908, 54.1-2909, 54.1-2911, 54.1-2915, 54.1-3480, 54.1-2921R, 54.1-3218R
754	15.2-1713.1
755	2.2-1829
756	38.2-2204
757	2.2-1829, n., 15.2-1104.1, 30-19.05R, 30-19.1:3, 58.1-3, 58.1-608.2R, 58.1-609.4R, 58.1-609.7—58.1-609.9R, 58.1-609.10, 58.1-609.11, 58.1-610, 58.1-623, 58.1-623.1, 58.1-3510.1, 58.1-3510.3, 58.1-3818
758	15.2-1104.1, 30-19.05R, 30-19.1:3, 58.1-3, 58.1-608.2R, 58.1-609.4R, 58.1-609.7—25.1-609.9R, 58.1-609.10, 58.1-609.11, 58.1-610, 58.1-623, 58.1-623.1, 58.1-3510.1, 58.1-3510.3, 58.1-3818
759	2.2-1829
760	15.2-1713.1
761	38.2-2204
762	32.1-27, 32.1-125.01, 54.1-111, 54.1-2400, 54.1-2400.2, 54.1-2400.3, 54.1-2401, 54.1-2408.2, 54.1-2505, 54.1-2506, 54.1-2506.01, 54.1-2906, 54.1-2908, 54.1-2909, 54.1-2911, 54.1-2915, 54.1-2921R, 54.1-3218R, 54.1-3480
763	59.1-274, 59.1-275
764	19.2-11.01
765	55-210.4:1, 55-210.4:2, 55-210.12
766	2.2-710R, 2.2-718—2.2-720, 37.1-62.1R
767	38.2-4300, 38.2-4302, 38.2-4303, 38.2-4306
768	46.2-208, 46.2-819.1
769	44-102.1
770	3.1-796.96:2, 3.1-796.96:5, 3.1-796.120
771	46.2-334.01
772	19.2-165.1
773	46.2-1220
774	55-50.1
775	45.1-161.311:3—45.1-161.311:8
776	55-96
777	22.1-208.01
778	28.2-515
779	63.2-1225
780	29.1-744.4
781	58.1-2201, 58.1-2204, 58.1-2212, 58.1-2218, 58.1-2221R, 58.1-2225, 58.1-2230, 58.1-2238, 58.1-2242, 58.1-2259, 58.1-2264R
782	2.2-3202
784	18.2-76
785	3.1-796.93:1
786	13.1-546, 13.1-1107
787	3.1-796.122, 18.2-403.2, 33.1-346
788	3.1-796.122
789	2.2-1201, 2.2-2903.1
790	37.1-134.21
791	2.2-3800
792	58.1-3833
793	30-19.1:9
794	32.1-42.1, 54.1-3301, 54.1-3307.3, 54.1-3408
795	56-577, 56-589
796	15.2-1716
797	59.1-352.3
798	3.1-336.1, n., 3.1-336.3—3.1-336.16,
799	38.2-2616
800	8.01-40.2, 59.1-200
801	2.2-3705, 22.1-279.8
802	23-174.4
803	54.1-116
804	3.1-796.104
805	18.2-479.1
806	58.1-611.1
807	58.1-322
808	24.2-542.1
809	36-45
810	57-58
811	15.2-2223
812	10.1-1181.2
813	57-12R
814	2.2-2813
815	24.2-515, 24.2-544
816	8.01-226.5:2, 18.2-371, 18.2-371.1, 40.1-103, 63.2-910.1
817	46.2-105.2, 46.2-328.1, 46.2-341.16:1
818	53.1-116, 53.1-129
819	46.2-105.2, 46.2-328.1, 46.2-341.16:1
820	53.1-116, 53.1-129

Acts 2003 Chapter	Code 1950 Section
821	2.2-2813
822	8.01-226.5:2, 18.2-371, 18.2-371.1, 40.1-103, 63.2-910.1
823	24.2-515, 24.2-544
824	24.2-303.2
825	19.2-194
827	10.1-563, 10.1-566
828	2.2-1837
829	15.2-901, 15.2-904
830	10.1-1454.1, 10.1-1454.2R
831	18.2-23, 18.2-105.2, 18.2-108.01
832	46.2-2100, 46.2-2101
833	18.2-308.2:2
834	10.1-1408.4
835	16.1-228
836	9.1-202, 32.1-111.10
837	58.1-2423
838	46.2-870, 46.2-878.3
839	46.2-878.1
840	19.2-143
841	3.1-796.93:1, 3.1-796.127:1
842	65.2-402.1
843	22.1-277.07
844	46.2-113
845	4.1-305
846	53.1-37, 53.1-132
847	18.2-186.3
848	44-146.22
849	4.1-305
850	53.1-155.1
851	16.1-248.1
852	32.1-111.10
853	46.2-828
854	2.2-2101, 53.1-10, 53.1-45.1, 53.1-45.2—53.1-45.5R
855	55-248.4
856	4.1-111, 4.1-325, 4.1-325.2
857	3.1-796.124, 3.1-796.125
858	3.1-796.106, 3.1-796.106:1, 3.1-796.106:2
859	58.1-609.3, 58.1-3660
860	53.1-131.3
861	22.1-253.13:1
862	17.1-227
865	17.1-279
866	22.1-60
870	33.1-23.3
871	38.2-1833, 38.2-1834
872	15.2-1500, n., 15.2-5100, n.
874	15.2-6400, 15.2-6405
875	15.2-961
876	3.1-796.130, 3.1-796.132, 3.1-796.133
877	33.1-223.2:8, 46.2-947
878	58.1-346.24
879	23-287, 23-288
881	47.1-19
883	16.1-69.48:1
884	2.2-203, 2.2-905, 2.2-2455, 2.2-2456, 2.2-3705, 18.2-340.15, 18.2-340.16, 18.2-340.17R, 18.2-340.18 — 18.2-340.20, 18.2-340.21R, 18.2-340.22 — 18.2-340.26, 18.2-340.29 — 18.21-340.37, 58.1-3, 58.1-4019.1
885	2.2-218, 2.2-220, 2.2-2424, 2.2-2503, 2.2-2506, 2.2-2628, 2.2-2666.1, 2.2-2705, 2.2-2709, 2.2-2710R, 2.2-5601, 3.1-1108, 10.1-1018, 18.2-271.2, 20-108.2, 22.1-337, 22.1-354.1, 30-156, 30-173, 30-182, 30-201—30-209, 30-210—30-217, 32.1-73.7, 51.5-39.2, 56-579, 56-581.1, 56-585, 56-592, 56-592.1, 56-595R, 56-596, 58.1-100, n., 62.1-69.34, 62.1-69.35, 62.1-69.35:1, 62.1-69.35:2, 62.1-69.38, 62.1-69.43, 62.1-69.36, 62.1-69.37, 62.1-69.38, 62.1-69.39, 62.1-69.40, 62.1-69.41, 62.1-69.42, 62.1-69.43, 62.1-69.44
886	19.2-301
887	33.1-23.4
888	2.2-226, 2.2-1508
889	18.2-204.1
890	13.1-601, n., 13.1-801, n., 13.1-1000, n., 58.1-300, n.
891	2.2-3705, 36-105.3
892	54.1-1106, 54.1-1108—54.1-1108.2, 54.1-1130
893	2.2-3705
894	22.1-273.1
895	2.2-1119, 2.2-1303, 2.2-4301, n., 2.2-4304, 53.1-52
896	46.2-668
897	2.2-3701, 2.2-3705, 38.2-5000, n., 38.2-5001, 38.2-5002, 38.2-5002.1, 38.2-5002.2, 38.2-5004—38.2-5005, 38.2-5007—38.2-5009, 38.2-5009.1, 38.2-5015, 38.2-5016, 38.2-5016.1,
899	22.1-279.3:1, 22.1-279.6, 22.1-279.7
900	2.2-1501, 2.2-1509, 2.2-1511, 2.2-2101, 2.2-2683—2.2-2687, 2.2-5510, 2.2-5511
901	36-99
902	22.1-1, n.
903	24.2-304.02
904	56-595
905	55-248.9
906	16.1-69.48:5
907	32.1-127.1:03
908	58.1-1825
910	6.1-5, 6.1-32.30:1—6.1-32.30:7
911	58.1-609.4, 58.1-609.6, 58.1-609.7, 58.1-609.9
912	54.1-2405
913	46.2-341.16:1
914	2.2-3800, 17.1-227, 18.2-186.3, 18.2-186.3:1, 18.2-186.5, 18.2-204.1, 42.1-82
915	19.2-169.3
916	58.1-609.4, 58.1-609.6, 58.1-609.7, 58.1-609.9
917	54.1-2405
918	2.2-3800, 17.1-227, 18.2-186.3, 18.2-186.3:1, 18.2-186.5, 18.2-204.1, 42.1-82
919	19.2-169.3
920	46.2-341.16:1
921	46.2-736.01, 46.2-736.02, 46.2-736.2, 46.2-746.2:2.1, 46.2-746.2:3, 46.2-746.2:4, 46.2-746.4, 46.2-749.5:1, 46.2-749.16:1, 46.2-749.44, 46.2-749.84—46.2-749.90
922	9.1-143, 9.1-150.1—9.1-150.4, 15.2-1737, 19.2-13, 19.2-13
923	46.2-725
924	58.1-4013, 58.1-4020.1

Acts 2003 Chapter	Code 1950 Section
925	46.2-746.7—46.2-746.9, 46.2-749.4, 46.2-749.5:1, 46.2-749.28:1, 46.2-749.73:1, 46.2-749.91—46.2-749.88
926	60.2-602
927	2.2-3800
928	53.1-126, 53.1-133.01:1
929	16.1-278.16, 34-28.1, 63.2-1902, 63.2-1927, 63.2-1929, 63.2-1940.1
930	38.2-2102, 38.2-2107
931	58.1-3131
932	46.2-746.2:3
933	18.2-268.6—18.2-268.8, 18.2-268.11, 46.2-341.26:6—46.2-341.26:8, 46.2-341.26:11
934	9.1-101
935	18.2-374.1:1, 18.2-374.3, 19.2-390.3
936	18.2-268.6—18.2-268.8, 18.2-268.11, 46.2-341.26:6—46.2-341.26:8, 46.2-341.26:11
937	9.1-101
938	18.2-374.1:1, 18.2-374.3, 19.2-390.3
939	58.1-3819
940	2.2-2286, 5.1-2.5, 5.1-34, 5.1-160, 10.1-114, 10.1-201, 10.1-635, 10.1-649, 10.1-1127.1, 10.1-1402, 10.1-1432, 10.1-1446, 15.2-729, 15.2-1901.1, 15.2-1902, 15.2-1904—15.2-1906, 15.2-1907, 15.2-1908—15.2-1916, 15.2-2109, 15.2-2115, 15.2-2140, 15.2-2146, 15.2-3221, 15.2-4518, 15.2-5114, 15.2-5343, 15.2-5367, 15.2-5425, 15.2-5807, 16.1-319, 21-118, 21-248, 22.1-126.1, 22.1-127, 23-50.16:12, 23-288, 23-298, 25-46.1—25-254R, 25.1-100—25.1-106, 25.1-200—25.1-251, 25.1-237, 25.1-300—25.1-318, 25.1-400—25.1-421, 28.2-628, 32.1-193, 33.1-89, 33.1-91, 33.1-95, 33.1-95.1, 33.1-98, 33.1-120, 33.1-121, 33.1-124, 33.1-128, 33.1-132, 33.1-134, 33.1-238, 33.1-422, 33.1-443, 36-27, 36-49.1:1, 45.1-161.320, 55-201.1, 56-49, 56-347, 62.1-98, 62.1-136, 62.1-150
941	30-34.15
942	16.1-278.16, 34-28.1, 63.2-1902, 63.2-1927, 63.2-1929, 63.2-1940.1
943	15.2-915
944	53.1-140, 53.1-142—53.1-145
945	15.2-1408
946	53.1-231.2
947	51.1-142.3
948	22.1-97
949	18.2-308.4
950	36-108
951	22.1-205, 46.2-334
952	3.1-385.1—3.1-385.8R
953	56-556, n.
954	8.01-47, 22.1-279.3:1
955	30-193, n.
956	Const., Art. II, § 1, n.
957	Const., Art. II, § 6, n.
958	Const., Art. II, § 1, n.
959	Const., Art. V, § 16, n.
960	16.1-241
961	18.2-74.2R, 18.2-71.1, 32.1-249
962	16.1-241
963	18.2-71.1, 18.2-74.2R, 32.1-249
964	46.2-1012—46.2-1014
965	46.2-882
966	10.1-563
967	24.2-905.1
968	2.2-3705, 56-573.1, 56-575.16
969	24.2-415
970	2.2-1509.2
971	46.2-111
972	46.2-749.23:1, 46.2-749.92—46.2-749.88
973	28.2-1203
974	2.2-3808
975	54.1-2400.5
976	18.2-282, 18.2-284, 18.2-287.4, 18.2-308.1, 18.2-308.2:01, 18.2-308.2:2, 18.2-308.2:3, 18.2-308.7, 18.2-433.1, 22.1-277.07
977	57-48, 57-49, 57-57, 57-59
978	8.01-225, 32.1-111.14:1R
979	19.2-152.1, 19.2-152.1:1 — 19.2-152.1:7, 38.2-1800, 38.2-1824, 38.2-1865.6 — 38.2-1865.13, 38.2-2411, 38.2-2412, 58.1-3724
980	58.1-322
981	2.2-106, 2.2-225, 2.2-226—2.2-227R, 2.2-1110, 2.2-1119, 2.2-1300—2.2-1304R, 2.2-1303.1—2.2-1304R, 2.2-1700—2.2-1710R, 2.2-2005—2.2-2027, 2.2-2025, 2.2-2247—2.2-2259R, 2.2-2261, 2.2-2403R, 2.2-2423, 2.2-2431, 2.2-2457, 2.2-2458, 2.2-2651, 2.2-3704, 2.2-3708, 2.2-4304, 17.1-279, 19.1-174.1, n., 42.1-80, 53.1-52, 56-484.12, 56-484.13, 56-484.15
982	19.2-305.1
983	16.1-248.3, 32.1-127.1:03
984	24.2-653
985	32.1-261, 63.2-1220
986	63.2-1511, 63.2-1516.1
987	18.2-152.2, 18.2-152.3, 18.2-152.3:1, 18.2-152.4, 18.2-152.6, 18.2-15 2.7, 18.2-152.12, 18.2-152.16, 18.2-376.1
988	2.2-3808.2
989	2.2-3703, 19.2-169.3, n., 19.2-174.1, n., 37.1-70.1—37.1-70.6, 37.1-70.9—37.1-70.16, 37.1-70.17, n., 37.1-103—37.1-104.1, 37.1-134.21, n.
990	56-577, 56-579
991	46.2-205
992	46.2-1240, 46.2-1241
993	9.1-106
994	2.2-4301, 2.2-4321.1
995	54.1-2729.1—54.1-2729.3, 54.1-3401, 54.1-3408
996	54.1-2935
997	46.2-1530, 46.2-1530.1, 46.2-1530.2
998	54.1-2105

Acts 2003 Chapter	Code 1950 Section
999	65.2-101
1000	34-17
1001	17.1-275.5
1002	46.2-1149.4
1003	32.1-212, n., 32.1-222, 32.1-224, 32.1-226, 59.1-200
1004	22.1-253.13:3
1005	9.1-400
1006	2.2-4301, 2.2-4321:1
1007	3.1-796.66, 3.1-796.67:2, 3.1-796.68, 3.1-796.73, 3.1-796.96, 3.1-796.96:2, 3.1-796.96:3, 3.1-796.96:4R, 3.1-796.96:5, 3.1-796.96:6, 3.1-796.96:7
1008	2.2-4343
1009	57-48, 57-49, 57-57, 57-59
1010	18.2-246.6—18.2-246.15, 58.1-1015
1011	8.01-384.1:1, 19.2-164
1012	5.1-152, n.
1013	63.2-1511, 63.2-1516.1
1014	10.1-1010
1015	15.2-408, 15.2-3604, 15.2-3831, 24.2-101, 24.2-106, 24.2-107, 24.2-111, 24.2-114—24.2-116, 24.2-209, 24.2-216, 24.2-226, 24.2-228.1, 24.2-306, 24.2-310, 24.2-404, 24.2-405, 24.2-406, 24.2-416.1, 24.2-423, 24.2-424, 24.2-444, 24.2-501, 24.2-522, 24.2-531, 24.2-533, 24.2-545, 24.2-604, 24.2-610—24.2-612, 24.2-622—24.2-624, 24.2-629, 24.2-635, 24.2-639, 24.2-642, 24.2-643, 24.2-646, 24.2-649, 24.2-651—24.2-653, 24.2-656R, 24.2-659, 24.2-662, 24.2-668, 24.2-669, 24.2-671, 24.2-675, 24.2-707, 24.2-711, 24.2-712, 24.2-1002—24.2-1004, 24.2-1009
1016	18.2-152.2, 18.2-152.3, 18.2-152.3:1, 18.2-152.4, 18.2-152.6, 18.2-1, 52.7, 18.2-152.12, 18.2-152.16, 18.2-376.1
1017	19.2-327.01
1018	2.2-3703, 19.2-169.3, n., 19.2-174.1, n., 37.1-70.1—37.1-70.6, 37.1-70.9—37.1-70.16, 37.1-70.17, n., 37.1-103—37.1-104.1, 37.1-134.21, n.
1019	53.1-126, 53.1-133.01:1
1020	8.01-225, 32.1-111.4, 54.1-3408
1021	2.2-106, 2.2-225, 2.2-226—2.2-227R, 2.2-1110, 2.2-1119, 2.2-1300—2.2-1304R, 2.2-1700—2.2-1710R, 2.2-2005—2.2-2027, 2.2-2247—2.2-2259R, 2.2-2261, 2.2-2403R, 2.2-2423, 2.2-2431, 2.2-2457, 2.2-2458, 2.2-2651, 2.2-3704, 2.2-3708, 2.2-4304, 17.1-279, 42.1-80, 53.1-52, 56-484.12, 56-484.13, 56-484.15
1022	17.1-275.5
1023	46.2-205.1
1024	20-124.2:1
1025	54.1-1101
1026	38.2-2801
1027	54.1-2105
1028	9.1-106
1029	4.1-112.1, 4.1-204, 4.1-207—4.1-209, 4.1-215, 4.1-230, 4.1-231, 4.1-310
1030	4.1-112.1, 4.1-204, 4.1-207—4.1-209, 4.1-215, 4.1-230, 4.1-231, 4.1-310
1031	8.01-654.2, 18.2-10, 19.2-175, 19.2-264.3:1, 19.2-264.3:1.1, 19.2-264.3:1.2, 19.2-264.3:3, 19.2-264.4
1032	30-19.04R, 30-19.1:2R, 58.1-3651
1033	32.1-111.10
1034	56-575.1—56-575.5, 56-575.8, 56-575.9, 56-575.11, 56-575.16
1035	30-192, 30-192.1—30-192.14
1036	15.2-717, 58.1-206, n., 58.1-3256, 58.1-3260, 58.1-3374, 58.1-3378—58.1-3380, 58.1-3384, 58.1-3984, n.
1037	30-192, 30-192.1—30-192.14
1038	30-218—30-208
1039	16.1-69.48:1, 16.1-69.48:2, 17.1-275.1—17.1-275.5, 17.1-275.7—17.1-275.9, 53.1-131.1
1040	8.01-654.2, 18.2-10, 19.2-175, 19.2-264.3:1, 19.2-264.3:1.1, 19.2-264.3:1.2, 19.2-264.3:3, 19.2-264.4
1042	Const, Art. X, § 8, n., 2.2-200, n., 2.2-203, n., 2.2-204, n., 2.2-208, n., 2.2-215, n., 2.2-221, n., 2.2-228, n., 2.2-409, n., 2.2-518, n., 2.2-711, n., 2.2-800, n., 2.2-1100, n., 2.2-1104, n., 2.2-1125, n., 2.2-1147, n., 2.2-1156, n., 2.2-1200, n., 2.2-1204, n., 2.2-1400, n., 2.2-1503, n., 2.2-1505, n., 2.2-1802, n., 2.2-1828, n., 2.2-1829, n., 2.2-1830, n., 2.2-1835, n., 2.2-2200, n., 2.2-2221.1, n., 2.2-2233.1, n., 2.2-2319, n., 2.2-2411, n., 2.2-2417, n., 2.2-2426, n., 2.2-2444, n., 2.2-2617, n., 2.2-2632, n., 2.2-4301, n., 2.2-4309, n.,

Acts 2003 Chapter	Code 1950 Section	Acts 2003 Chapter	Code 1950 Section	Acts 2003 Chapter	Code 1950 Section
	2.2-4011, n.,		22.1-1, n.,		46.2-216.3, R,
	2.2-4400, n.,		22.1-101.1, n.,		46.2-328.1, n.,
	2.2-5200, n.,		22.1-199.2,		46.2-332, n.,
	2.2-5211, n.,		22.1-205, n.,		46.2-333.1,
	3.1-249.34, n.,		22.1-208.2, n.,		46.2-341.16:1, n.,
	3.1-336.2, n.,		22.1-253.13, n.,		46.2-341.24, n.,
	3.1-361, n.,		22.1-254.01,		46.2-341.26:3, n.,
	3.1-425, n.,		22.1-253.13:3,		46.2-685, n.,
	4.1-116, n.,		22.1-290.01, n.,		46.2-694, n.,
	9.1-173, n.,		22.1-346, n.,		46.2-697.1, n.,
	9.1-201, n.,		23-7.4:1, n.,		46.2-1178.1, n.,
	9.1-205, n.,		23-7.4:2, n.,		51.1-100, n.,
	9.1-400, n.,		23-9.2:3.1, n.,		51.1-124.22, n.,
	9.1-402, n.,		23-9.3, n.,		51.1-124.24, n.,
	10.1-202, n.,		23-25.1, n.,		51.1-124.30, n.,
	10.1-1020, n.,		23-30.23, n.,		51.1-124.31, n.,
	10.1-1124, n.,		23-30.28, n.,		51.1-1401, n.,
	10.1-1188, n.,		23-30.27:1, n.,		51.1-808, n.,
	10.1-1190, n.,		23-38.10:1, n.,		51.5-106, n.,
	10.1-2213, n.,		23-38.19:2, n.,		53.1-20, n.,
	10.1-2500, n.,		23-50.4, n.,		53.1-45, n.,
	13.1-775.1, n.,		23-77.4, n.,		53.1-67.1, n.,
	15.2-1302, n.,		23-164.1, n.,		53.1-95.2, n.,
	15.2-1534, n.,		23-164.8, n.,		53.1-105, n.,
	15.2-1609.1, n.,		23-174.1, n.,		53.1-120, n.,
	15.2-1627.1, n.,		23-214, n.,		53.1-131, n.,
	15.2-1628, n.,		23-253.1, n.,		54.1-3916, n.,
	15.2-1629, n.,		23-276.9, n.,		55-297, n.,
	15.2-1630, n.,		23-276.10, n.,		56-232, n.,
	15.2-1631, n.,		23-284, n.,		56-234, n.,
	15.2-1636.9, n.,		23-291, n.,		56-484.12, n.,
	15.2-2602, n.,		24.2-108, n.,		56-575.1, n.,
	15.2-2659, n.,		30-130, n.,		56-592.1, n.,
	15.2-4100, n.,		30-19.03, n.,		58.1-202.2, n.,
	16.1-69.48:1, n.,		32.1-16, n.,		58.1-339.4, n.,
	16.1-69.48:1.01,		32.1-163, n.,		58.1-439.2, n.,
	16.1-69.48:2, n.,		32.1-164, n.,		58.1-461, n.,
	16.1-273, n.,		32.1-176.4, n.,		58.1-462, n.,
	16.1-309.2, n.,		32.1-325, n.,		58.1-470, n.,
	16.1-309.7, n.,		32.1-325.1:1, n.,		58.1-600, n.,
	16.1-322.1, n.,		32.1-347, n.,		58.1-602, n.,
	17.1-275.1 —		32.1-351, n.,		58.1-612, n.,
	17.1-275.4, n.,		33.1-23.1, n.,		58.1-615,
	17.1-275.7 —		33.1-75.1, n.,		58.1-624, n.,
	17.1-275.9, n.,		33.1-206.1, n.,		58.1-635, n.,
	17.1-275.10,		35.1-13, n.,		58.1-638, n.,
	17.1-275.11,		35.1-14, n.,		58.1-801, n.,
	17.2-279, n.,		35.1-16, n.,		58.1-1402, n.,
	17.2-803, n.,		35.1-17, n.,		58.1-1410, n.,
	18.2-36.1, n.,		36-98.1, n.,		58.1-1604,
	18.2-51.4, n.,		36-141, n.,		58.1-1803, n.,
	18.2-266.1, n.,		37.1-70.1 —		58.1-1804, n.,
	18.2-268.3, n.,		37.1-70.19, n.,		58.1-2402, n.,
	18.2-340.31, n.,		37.1-134.21, n.,		58.1-2425, n.,
	19.2-169.3, n.,		37.1-194, n.,		58.1-2510, n.,
	19.2-174.1, n.,		38.2-401,		58.1-3400, n.,
	19.2-316.2, n.,		45.1-392, n.,		58.1-3523, n.,
	19.2-316.3, n.,		46.2-105.2, n.,		58.1-3531, n.,
	19.2-326, n.,		46.2-200, n.,		58.1-4020, n.,
	19.2-349, n.,		46.2-205, n.,		58.1-4200, n.,
	19.2-399, n.,		46.2-214.1,		59.1-282.2, n.,

Acts 2003 Chapter	Code 1950 Section
	59.1-282.3, n., 59.1-284.14, n., 59.1-284.15, n., 59.1-364, n., 59.1-392, n., 60.2-108, n., 60.2-305, n., 60.2-315, n., 62.1-140, n. 63.2-605, n., 63.2-611, n., 63.2-612, n.

ACTS 2004

Acts 2004 Chapter	Code 1950 Section
1	23-164.1, n.
4	58.1-3506
5	58.1-3211
6	58.1-3211
7	58.1-3819
8	58.1-3814, 58.1-3816.2
9	58.1-3824
10	54.1-3510, 54.1-3511R, 54.1-3512R
11	54.1-3600, 54.1-3605, 54.1-3609R, 54.1-3610R
12	44-12R, 44-14, 44-114
13	51.5-72, 51.5-72.1
14	2.2-212, 60.2-113
16	2.2-2640R, 2.2-2641R
17	Va. Const., Art. V, § 16, n.
18	15.2-1213.1
20	24.2-304.02
21	24.2-687
22	15.2-710, 15.2-720.1, 15.2-726
23	52-8.4
24	15.2-2110, 15.2-2118
25	24.2-310
26	24.2-916, 24.2-917, 24.2-923
27	24.2-103, 24.2-109, 24.2-109.1, 24.2-110, 24.2-230, 24.2-234
28	2.2-609
29	3.1-1104R, 3.1-1105R
30	9.1-101, 9.1-400
34	2.2-612, 2.2-2506R, 2.2-2507R
35	15.2-6701, 15.2-6703
36	15.2-6006, 15.2-6011
37	2.2-2101, 2.2-209R, 2.2-210R, 2.2-2600R, 2.2-2601R, 2.2-2602R
38	2.2-2664, 2.2-5302R
40	54.1-2922R, 54.1-2923R, 54.1-3613R
41	59.1-198, 59.1-204
42	15.2-6406
43	58.1-3812
44	65.2-801
46	22.1-298
47	54.1-3321
48	54.1-2715, 54.1-2717, 54.1-2718
49	32.1-127.1:03, 32.1-127.3, 54.1-105, 54.1-106, 54.1-111, 54.1-2400, 54 .1-2400.2, 54.1-2401, 54.1-2403.01, 54.1-2403.1, 54.1-2403.2, 54.1-2408.1, 54.1- 2409, 54.1-2409.1, 54.1-2906, 54.1-2907, 54.1-3000, 54.1-3005, 54.1-3008, 54.1-3 009, 54.1-3016, 54.1-3019, 63.2-1805
50	58.1-3823
51	54.1-3404
53	54.1-2405
54	37.1-226, 37.1-227, 37.1-228, 37.1-229, 37.1-230
55	24.2-943, 24.2-944
56	3.1-1075
57	2.2-204, 3.1-426
58	2.2-216, 2.2-2634, 2.2-2820.1R, 3.1-362R, 10.1-200, 10.1-1118, 10.1-1155, 23-31, 51.5-75
60	58.1-602
61	54.1-2956.1, 54.1-2956.3, 54.1-2956.4, 54.1-2956.5
62	15.2-1208
63	58.1-609.6
64	32.1-125.01, 32.1-127.1:03, 54.1-2400, 54.1-2400.6, 54.1-2400.7, 54.1-2400.8, 54.1-2505, 54.1-2506.01, 54.1-2706, 54.1-2709.2, 54.1-2906R, 54.1-2907R, 54.1-2910.1, 54.1-2915, , 54.1-2919R, 54.1-3009R, 54.1-3010R, 54.1-3216R, 54.1-3480 54.1-3615R
65	2.2-3705, 8.01-413, 32.1-127.1:03, 37.1-230, 38.2-608
66	16.1-266, 16.1-343, 32.1-127.1:03, 37.1-67.3, 37.1-134.9, 37.1-134.12, 37.1-134.21
67	32.1-127.1:03
68	54.1-2922R, 54.1-2923R, 54.1-3613R
69	63.2-1528
70	63.2-100, 63.2-900
71	32.1-102.3, 32.1-102.6
72	32.1-176.4
73	32.1-23.1
74	63.2-1515
75	32.1-102.1
77	58.1-3211
78	58.1-3211
79	51.1-1400
80	51.1-124.22
81	51.1-164
82	19.2-294.2, n., 19.2-310.2, n.
83	51.1-138, 51.1-205, 51.1-216
84	51.1-1401
85	32.1-102.3:2, n., 38.2-4900, n.
86	51.1-602
87	29.1-352, 29.1-355
88	32.1-262, 32.1-267, 32.1-268
89	3.1-6.1, 3.1-1057—3.1-1064R, 3.1-1064.1—3.1-1064.7
90	59.1-198, 59.1-204
91	38.2-4900, n.
92	54.1-2972
93	63.2-1502, 63.2-1516.01
94	62.1-44.15:5
95	32.1-102.3, 32.1-102.6
96	51.1-1112
97	51.1-1113, 51.1-1124
98	51.1-1117, 51.1-1123, 51.1-1133
99	51.1-1114
100	58.1-3975
101	58.1-609.6
102	51.1-505
103	63.2-1527
104	37.1-134.21
105	16.1-260
106	8.01-341.1
107	46.2-1993.67:2
108	46.2-1222.1
109	46.2-341.16:1
110	33.1-12
111	46.2-1500
112	46.2-330
113	63.2-1716
114	63.2-105, 63.2-1503
115	46.2-393
116	8.01-356
118	33.1-23.5:1, 33.1-41.1
121	2.2-1839
122	19.2-66
123	55-222, 55-248.4, 55-248.7:2, 55-248.37
124	32.1-263

Acts 2004 Chapter	Code 1950 Section
125	32.1-325
126	66-3.2
127	54.1-4306
128	18.2-308.1
129	2.2-1100, n.
130	18.2-254
131	54.1-1115
132	36-99.6:3
133	54.1-503
134	2.2-3100.1, 2.2-3101, 2.2-3128—2.2-3131
135	37.1-134.17
136	59.1-148.3
137	54.1-2729
138	36-97, n.
139	32.1-111.6, n.
140	54.1-3434.02
141	8.01-6
142	2.2-212, 2.2-215, 2.2-2628
143	55-362, 55-374, 55-376.1
144	18.2-46
145	2.2-2006, 2.2-4343, 23-77.4
146	23-9.2:7, 23-215
147	44-93.5
149	19.2-62
150	18.2-268.5, 46.2-341.26:5
151	56-235.5:1
152	2.2-609
153	2.2-2640R, 2.2-2641R
154	60.2-113
155	2.2-612, 2.2-2506R, 2.2-2507R
157	15.2-1508.3
158	15.2-6701, 15.2-6703
159	58.1-3814, 58.1-3816.2
160	15.2-1503.1
162	13.1-750, 13.1-912
163	32.1-127.1:03, 40.1-8
164	38.2-401
165	6.1-1.1
166	58.1-3
167	56-484.17
169	37.1-255, 37.1-256, 37.1-256.1, 37.1-257R
170	58.1-439
171	29.1-508.1
172	58.1-3812
173	65.2-801
174	38.2-1230
175	38.2-4300—38.2-4302
176	23-9.5, 23-14, 23-31, 23-91.34, 23-91.35, 23-91.37, 23-91.39—23-91.41, 23-91.43, 23-91.44
177	15.2-6006, 15.2-6011
178	65.2-201
179	22.1-32
180	3.1-14.2
181	3.1-796.104, 3.1-796.104:1, 3.1-796.106
182	38.2-111
183	63.2-2004
184	24.2-405, 24.2-406, 24.2-418
185	38.2-4306, 38.2-4320.1
186	51.1-1103
187	36-55.25, 36-55.26, 36-55.30, 36-55.30:2, 36-55.31, 36-55.33:1, 36-55.34:1, 36-55.37, 36-55.38, 36-55.39
188	54.1-1140—54.1-1143
189	54.1-1101
190	54.1-1103
191	54.1-406
192	54.1-2313.1, 54.1-2316, 54.1-2322
193	55-510
194	46.2-694
195	23-9.5, 23-14, 23-31, 23-91.34, 23-91.35, 23-91.37, 23-91.39—23-91.41, 23-91.43, 23-91.44
196	63.2-100, 63.2-905.1
197	11-34.3
198	8.01-499, 17.1-272
199	22.1-32
200	8.1A-201, 8.2-103, 8.2-104, 8.2-310, 8.2-323, 8.2-401, 8.2-503, 8.2-505, 8.2-506, 8.2-509, 8.2-605, 8.2-705, 8.2A-103, 8.2A-514, 8.2A-526, 8.4-104, 8.4-208, 8.7-102, 8.7-103, 8.7-104, 8.7-105R, 8.7-105.1, 8.7-106, 8.7-202, 8.7-203, 8.7-204, 8.7-205, 8.7-206, 8.7-208, 8.7-209, 8.7-210, 8.7-301, 8.7-302, 8.7-303, 8.7-305, 8.7-307, 8.7-309, 8.7-401, 8.7-402, 8.7-403, 8.7-404, 8.7-501, 8.7-502, 8.7-503, 8.7-504, 8.7-505, 8.7-506, 8.7-507, 8.7-509, 8.7-601, 8.7-602, 8.7-603, 8.8A-103, 8.9A-102, 8.9A-203, 8.9A-207, 8.9A-208, 8.9A-301, 8.9A-310, 8.9A-312, 8.9A-313, 8.9A-314, 8.9A-317, 8.9A-338, 8.9A-601
201	3.1-610.26:1
202	59.1-510, 59.1-511, 59.1-513, 59.1-513.1, 59.1-514
203	8.01-44.6, 18.2-127
204	16.1-278.18, 20-74, 20-108, 20-108.1, 20-112, 63.2-1916
205	24.2-603.1
206	51.1-126.5
207	51.1-139
208	63.2-219
209	51.1-1000, 51.1-1001, 51.1-1002, 51.1-1003, 51.1-1004
210	8.01-293, 15.2-1609.3
211	8.01-499, 17.1-272
212	3.1-6.1, 3.1-666—3.1-684R
213	18.2-340.19, n., 18.2-340.20
214	3.1-618, 3.1-626, 3.1-634, 3.1-634.1, 3.1-635, 3.1-646.01—3.1-646.09R
215	43-32
216	63.2-2002
217	3.1-796.122
218	46.2-330
219	16.1-278.16
220	63.2-105, 63.2-1503
221	20-124.3
222	54.1-516.1
223	58.1-3172.1
224	59.1-510, 59.1-511, 59.1-513, 59.1-513.1, 59.1-514
225	46.2-1222.1
226	55-248.11:2, 55-248.13, 55-248.16
227	35.1-25
228	10.1-1181.2, 10.1-1181.3
229	2.2-3006
230	17.1-276
231	8.01-513
232	55-248.31
233	63.2-1502, 63.2-1516.01
234	15.2-2903
236	38.2-3420
237	2.2-2012
238	2.2-206
239	2.2-2282
240	43-3
241	59.1-443,

Acts 2004 Chapter	Code 1950 Section
	59.1-443.1, 59.1-444
242	55-429, 55-460, 55-462, 55-467, 55-473.1, 55-478, 55-479, 55-484, 55-486
243	37.1-67.5:01
244	62.1-44.38:1, n.
245	16.1-228, 63.2-100
246	32.1-325
247	54.1-2313, 54.1-2324, 54.1-2333, 57-27.3
248	15.2-1718, 52-32
249	10.1-1322, 10.1-1402, 10.1-1402.1, 10.1-1402.1:1, 62.1-44.15:6
250	8.01-581.17
251	22.1-254, 22.1-254.2
252	46.2-833
253	55-60
254	38.2-3100.2
255	16.1-260, 16.1-253.1, n., 16.1-253.4, n., 16.1-260, n., 16.1-279.1, n.
256	22.1-26
262	56-580
263	18.2-433.1
264	19.2-152.1
267	46.2-1157
268	46.2-1077.1
269	29.1-303, 29.1-303.3, 29.1-305
270	52-34.3
271	54.1-3513, 65.2-603
272	15.2-953
273	15.2-1716
274	13.1-616, 13.1-759, 13.1-766.1, 13.1-766.2, 13.1-769.1, 13.1-816, 13.1-921, 13.1-928.2, 13.1-931.1, 13.1-1005, 13.1-1052, 13.1-1060, 13.1-1060.1, 13.1-1064, 13.1-1072, 13.1-1204, 13.1-1242, 13.1-1250.1, 13.1-1254, 50-73.17, 50-73.48:3, 50-73.54, 50-73.57:2, 50-73.57:3, 50-73.69, 50-73.93, 50-73.138
275	18.2-340.33
276	62.1-44.34:15, 62.1-44.34:16
277	28.2-1303
278	2.2-2012
279	2.2-2818
280	29.1-103, 29.1-113
281	55-79.81
282	46.2-1088.4
283	16.1-340, 16.1-341
284	19.2-390
285	38.2-1603
286	2.2-5211
287	62.1-44.33
288	38.2-2125
289	2.2-507.1, 17.1-513.01
290	10.1-104, n.
291	46.2-832
292	15.2-4903
293	62.1-44.15:5
294	40.1-2
295	6.1-453, 6.1-459, 6.1-461
296	30-169.1
297	54.1-307.1
298	19.2-264.5
299	18.2-511
300	38.2-2114
301	32.1-351.2
302	44-146.19
303	13.1-857
304	32.1-126, 63.2-1800
305	63.2-405
306	19.2-194
307	55-248.18
308	19.2-120, 19.2-299
309	16.1-260
310	19.2-295.3
311	19.2-265.1
312	2.2-1208
313	38.2-3220, 38.2-3221, 38.2-3222, 38.2-3229
314	13.1-1011, 13.1-1015
315	38.2-1315.1, 38.2-4123, 38.2-4214, 38.2-4319, 38.2-4509
316	13.1-1065, 13.1-1255, 50-73.70, 50-73.83
317	32.1-170
318	32.1-23.1
319	3.1-6.1, 3.1-1057—3.1-1064R, 3.1-1064.1—3.1-1064.7
320	6.1-62
321	16.1-275
322	4.1-305
323	46.2-1022
324	10.1-1322, 10.1-1402, 10.1-1402.1, 10.1-1402.1:1, 62.1-44.15:6
325	16.1-278.8
326	8.01-6
327	19.2-42R
328	8.01-676.1
329	19.2-163.7
330	16.1-69.33
331	16.1-69.9:3, 17.1-511
332	17.1-918
333	55-510.1
334	10.1-1322.3
335	8.01-407, 8.01-413, 16.1-89, 16.1-265
336	6.1-2.25, 17.1-223
337	19.2-327.01R
338	16.1-88.03, 55-246.1
339	23-4.01
340	58.1-2201, 58.1-2204, 58.1-2216, 58.1-2237, 58.1-2266, 58.1-2271, 58.1-2283
341	16.1-94, 16.1-94, n.
342	16.1-267
343	8.01-129
344	16.1-77
345	8.01-417
346	17.1-302, 17.1-401
347	18.2-308.2:01
348	19.2-265.4
349	46.2-868
350	16.1-69.40:1, 46.2-878.2
351	46.2-322
352	17.1-227
353	46.2-1208
354	18.2-308.2:2
355	18.2-308
356	8.01-676.1
357	38.2-2416, 38.2-2417, 38.2-2418, 38.2-2419
358	40.1-29
359	46.2-892
360	19.2-81.6, 19.2-82, 19.2-120
361	46.2-392
362	8.01-380
363	17.1-900, 17.1-918
364	10.1-1010
365	16.1-88.03, 55-246.1
366	16.1-69.48:5, 16.1-107, 16.1-112
367	26-7.2
368	64.1-145
369	43-34, 46.2-1203, 46.2-1603.1
370	19.2-35, 19.2-36, 19.2-38
371	16.1-69.48:1
372	10.1-603.2, 10.1-603.2:1, 10.1-603.2:2, 10.1-603.3, 10.1-603.4, 10.1-603.4:1, 10.1-603.5, 10.1-603.6, 10.1-603.7, 10.1-603.8, 10.1-603.9, 10.1-603.11, 10.1-603.12, 10.1-603.12:1,

Acts 2004 Chapter	Code 1950 Section
	10.1-603.12:2, 10.1-603.12:3, 10.1-603.12:4, 10.1-603.12:5, 10.1-603.12:6, 10.1-603.12:7, 10.1-603.13, 10.1-603.13:1, 10.1-603.14, 10.1-603.15, 62.1-44.5
373	11-33.3
374	16.1-248.1
375	9.1-116.1, 16.1-69.48:1, 20-15
376	46.2-703
377	18.2-57.3
378	19.2-152.2, 53.1-95.8, 53.1-109
379	4.1-201
380	11-9.1
381	8.01-15.2
382	4.1-230
383	46.2-1166
384	4.1-233
385	2.2-2667, 2.2-2668
386	29.1-527.1
387	8.01-226.8
388	15.2-109
389	24.2-303.2
390	53.1-120
391	24.2-103, 24.2-109, 24.2-109.1, 24.2-110, 24.2-230, 24.2-234
392	2.2-3100.1, 2.2-3101, 2.2-3128—2.2-3131
393	15.2-1208
394	62.1-69.45—62.1-69.52
395	9.1-178
396	18.2-46.1, 18.2-46.3, 18.2-46.3:1, 18.2-46.3:2, 18.2-460, 19.2-215.1
397	9.1-102, 9.1-186—9.1-186.14
398	2.2-3703, 2.2-3705.2, 2.2-3711
399	24.2-687
400	53.1-116
401	19.2-13
402	15.2-923
403	62.1-69.34
404	22.1-253.13:1
405	28.2-1205
406	19.2-120, 19.2-390
407	53.1-166, n., 53.1-167, n, 53.1-172, 53.1-174, 53.1-176.1—53.1-176.3
408	10.1-1300, 10.1-1316.1
409	24.2-629
410	24.2-405, 24.2-406, 24.2-419, 24.2-441, 24.2-442, 24.2-443.2, 24.2-443.3, 24.2-643, 24.2-653, 24.2-668, 24.2-701, 24.2-703, 24.2-706, 24.2-802
411	24.2-919.1
412	19.2-81.6, 19.2-82, 19.2-120
413	10.1-2124
414	9.1-902, 18.2-374.3
415	16.1-247, 16.1-249
416	16.1-260
417	53.1-27
418	16.1-330.1
419	9.1-1000
420	18.2-57
421	29.1-517, 29.1-518
422	29.1-341, 29.1-341.1, 29.1-344, 29.1-349
423	18.2-308
424	24.2-303.2
425	38.2-3407.15
426	2.2-3705.7
427	52-11.4, 52-11.5
428	24.2-404
429	18.2-308.2
430	44-146.17:2
431	10.1-561, 62.1-44.15
432	53.1-120
433	17.1-213
434	8.01-226.8
435	18.2-46.1, 18.2-46.3, 18.2-46.3:1, 18.2-46.3:2, 18.2-460, 19.2-215.1
436	22.1-199.1, 51.1-617, 51.1-618
437	16.1-250, 16.1-250.1R, 16.1-266, 16.1-267
438	15.2-2144
439	16.1-247, 16.1-249
440	18.2-268.5, 19.2-310.3, 46.2-341.26:5
441	24.2-904, 24.2-908
442	10.1-1426
443	15.2-1718
444	9.1-902, 18.2-374.3
445	19.2-310.2:1
446	16.1-305
447	29.1-529
448	18.2-57.2
449	18.2-67.4:1
450	2.2-511, 18.2-186.3, 18.2-186.5, 63.2-1809
451	24.2-303.2, 24.2-304.02
452	16.1-69.9, 16.1-69.9:1, 16.1-69.9:4, 17.1-303, 17.1-400, 17.1-501, 17.1-509, 17.1-512, 19.2-35
453	15.2-1604
455	62.1-44.17:1, 62.1-44.17:1.1
456	22.1-199.4
457	24.2-900, 24.2-901, 24.2-905, 24.2-908, 24.2-921, 24.2-926, 24.2-929, 24.2-943, 24.2-944
458	2.2-4301
459	17.1-805, 18.2-111.1R, 18.2-114R, 18.2-123R,18.2-124, 18.2-161R, 18.2-202R, 18.2-203R, 18.2-211R, 18.2-351R, 18.2-352R, 18.2-353R, 18.2-358R, 18.2-367R, 18.2-374.3, 19.2-299
460	9.1-102, 9.1-143, 9.1-185—9.1-185.18, 16.1-77, 19.2-149, 38.2-1800, 38.2-1824, 38.2-1865.6—38.2-1865.13R, 38.2-2411, 38.2-2412, 38.2-2412.1, 38.2-2412.2, 58.1-3724
461	4.1-305, 18.2-12.1, 18.2-36.1, 18.2-51.1, 18.2-53.1, 18.2-57, 18.2-121, 18.2-154, 18.2-248, 18.2-248.01, 18.2-248.1, 18.2-248.5, 18.2-255, 18.2-255.2, 18.2-270, 18.2-308.1, 18.2-308.2, 18.2-308.2:2, 18.2-308.4, 19.2-120, 30-19.1:4, 46.2-301, 46.2-341.28, 46.2-357, 46.2-391, 53.1-116, 53.1-203
462	8.01-27.3, 8.01-226.9, 8.01-226.10, 15.2-912.2, 15.2-912.3, 15.2-915. 2, 15.2-915.3, 15.2-926, 15.2-926.2, 15.2-1209.1, 15.2-1812.2, 16.1-278.8, 18.2-46.1, 18.2-105R, 18.2-138.1R, 18.2-258, 18.2-287R, 18.2-287.1R, 18.2-308, 29.1-338, 18.2-340.32R, 18.2-389R, 18.2-432R, 18.2-433R, 48-16, 48-17
463	29.1-352, 29.1-355
464	16.1-299
465	22.1-340, 22.1-342, 22.1-343

Acts 2004 Chapter	Code 1950 Section
466	9.1-161, 9.1-162
467	29.1-573
468	16.1-269.6, 16.1-296
469	24.2-911
470	9.1-138, 9.1-139
471	62.1-69.26, 62.1-69.29, 62.1-69.30, 62.1-69.33:1, 62.1-69.33:2
472	22.1-253.13:3
473	22.1-253.13:1, n., 22.1-253.13:3, n.
474	10.1-104.1, 10.1-546.1
475	28.2-527
476	10.1-560
477	15.2-1706
478	46.2-700
479	24.2-304.02
480	24.2-904, 24.2-928, 24.2-929
481	24.2-403
482	2.2-3705.2
484	2.2-1120
485	62.1-44.34:11
486	28.2-302.1, 28.2-302.2:1, 29.1-310.2, 29.1-311
487	4.1-209, 4.1-210, 4.1-230, 4.1-231, 4.1-233
488	2.2-603
489	58.1-3812
492	, 58.1-800, n., 58.1-811, 58.1-3606, 58.1-3800, n.
493	15.2-903
494	58.1-3211
495	60.2-513
496	60.2-612
498	15.2-852
499	23-9.2:4.1
500	22.1-3, 22.1-3.1, 22.1-4.1, 22.1-270, 22.1-271.2
501	23-7.4:2
502	23-9.6:1
503	58.1-3211
504	58.1-2606
506	58.1-608.3
507	15.2-2114
508	15.2-905
509	22.1-253.13:4
510	15.2-710, 15.2-720.1, 15.2-726
512	58.1-301
513	15.2-904
515	58.1-3, 58.1-609.10, 58.1-609.11
516	58.1-3812
517	16.1-260, 19.2-83.1, 22.1-279.3:1
519	23-9.2:4.1
520	23-7.4:2
521	58.1-306
522	58.1-2402, 58.1-2425
523	55-210.21
524	55-210.12
525	60.2-618
526	58.1-3994
527	58.1-3983.1
528	22.1-289.2
529	2.2-1839
530	2.2-3109, 22.1-212.5, 22.1-212.6, 22.1-212.8, 22.1-212.9, 22.1-212.11, 22.1-212.12, 2.2-3109, n.
531	15.2-2300
532	22.1-47.4
533	15.2-1115
534	58.1-3103, 58.1-3983.1
535	55-210.18
536	58.1-3, 58.1-609.10, 58.1-609.11
538	15.2-2307
539	15.2-2204
540	25.1-107
541	15.2-958.2
542	22.1-279.3:1
543	15.2-2304
544	58.1-305, 58.1-306
545	15.2-5114
546	58.1-1803
547	58.1-3528
548	58.1-3916.02
549	15.2-1416
552	15.2-852
553	23-9.14:2
555	58.1-4008, 58.1-4009
556	58.1-3505, 58.1-3506
557	58.1-3400, 58.1-3651
558	16.1-260
559	42.1-15.1
560	22.1-277.07:1
561	15.2-858
562	58.1-9
563	22.1-70.3, 22.1-79, 51.1-155
565	2.2-614.1, 15.2-106
566	58.1-608.3
567	58.1-615
568	58.1-608.3
570	15.2-1414.5
573	16.1-241.2, 16.1-263, 16.1-290.1, 22.1-263, 22.1-279.3
574	22.1-279.6, 22.1-279.9
575	46.2-834
576	58.1-3274
577	15.2-2418, 36-155, 36-156, 36-169
580	57-60
582	58.1-3
583	60.2-528
584	36-99.5:1
585	36-22.1
586	15.2-2108.11
587	46.2-1700, 46.2-1701, 46.2-1701.2, 46.2-1701.3, 46.2-1702, 46.2-1703, 46.2-1705, 46.2-1707
588	8.01-293, 16.1-241, 16.1-264, 17.1-272
589	8.01-216.3
590	58.1-609.6
591	58.1-3506
592	2.2-2407, 40.1-6, 60.2-113
593	2.2-3705.6
594	58.1-3
595	57-3
596	55-66.3
597	6.1-2.25, 6.1-2.27
598	58.1-3825
600	6.1-472, 6.1-473
601	13.1-754, 13.1-916, 13.1-1008, 13.1-1009, 13.1-1019, 13.1-1022, 13.1-1023.1, 13.1-1024, 13.1-1041R, 13.1-1041.1, 13.1-1048, 13.1-1049.1, 13.1-1050.1, 13.1-1059, 13.1-1064, 13.1-1070, 13.1-1239, 13.1-1254, 50-73.46R, 50-73.46:1, 50-73.52:1, 50-73.69, 50-73.83, 50-73.132, 50-73.134, 50-73.137:1, 50-73.137:2
602	54.1-4400, 54.1-4402, 54.1-4403, 54.1-4405.1, 54.1-4407, 54.1-4409, 54.1-4410, 54.1-4412, 54.1-4413, 54.1-4413.1, 54.1-4414
603	15.2-6400, 15.2-6406
604	55-331, 55-332, 55-333R, 55-334, 55-334.1
605	2.2-3705.3
606	58.1-609.6
607	58.1-609.5
608	18.2-341R, 18.2-342R, 18.2-343R, 40.1-28.5R
609	8.01-184.1
610	58.1-3819, 58.1-3822, 58.1-3823, 58.1-3833, 58.1-3842
611	58.1-439.7
612	20-25
613	46.2-1052
614	58.1-339.4
615	55-331, 55-332, 55-333R,55-334, 55-334.1
619	58.1-439
620	18.2-258.2

Acts 2004 Chapter	Code 1950 Section
621	33.1-221.1:1.1
622	46.2-490, 46.2-490.2R, 46.2-490.3, 46.2-490.4, 46.2-490.5, 46.2-490.6, 46.2-490.7, 46.2-490.8, 46.2-490.9, 46.2-490.10, 46.2-490.11
623	33.1-12.1
626	58.1-811
627	8.01-294
628	33.1-62, n.
629	33.1-62, n.
630	58.1-4004, 58.1-4006, 58.1-4007, 58.1-4010, 58.1-4014, 58.1-4020.1
631	2.2-5211
635	58.1-513
636	2.2-1151.1
637	15.2-5158
638	2.2-603, 2.2-2009
639	55-277.4:1
640	15.2-6400, 15.2-6406
644	2.2-1822.1
645	58.1-3967
646	6.1-330.53, 6.1-330.54, 8.01-382
647	8.01-184.1
648	15.2-1518
649	30-19.1:10, 58.1-344.3
650	2.2-608, 2.2-1126R, 2.2-1127R, 2.2-2213, 2.2-2238, 2.2-2242, 2.2-2263, 2.2-2400, 2.2-2407, 2.2-2432, 2.2-2506, 3.1-22.4, 4.1-115, 10.1-1307, 10.1-1802, 10.1-2012, 22.1-171, 23-1.01, 23-30.36, 23-227, 23-253, 23-253.7, 30-34.4:1, 30-34.15, 32.1-14, 40.1-4.1, 46.2-1503.5, 54.1-114, 54.1-4421, 62.1-44.40, 62.1-139,
651	1-13.4:1
652	37.1-137.4
653	46.2-749.43R, 46.2-749.43:1, 46.2-749.101—46.2-749.109,
654	20-107.3
655	33.1-252
656	33.1-370.2
657	63.2-2004
658	46.2-924
659	16.1-69.48:5, 16.1-296, 16.1-296.2
660	46.2-208, n.
661	58.1-2628
662	33.1-391.2, n.
663	46.2-698
665	33.1-252.2
666	2.2-3705.5
667	23-231.15
668	38.2-100, 38.2-316, 38.2-1401, 38.2-1700, 38.2-1800, 38.2-6100—38.2-6113, 58.1-2501
669	54.1-2957.4, 54.1-2957.5, 54.1-2957.6
670	2.2-1124
671	23-276.1, 23-276.2
672	51.1-303
673	63.2-1732
674	2.2-3000, 2.2-3003, 2.2-3005, 2.2-3005.1
675	38.2-3405, 54.1-2963.1
676	2.2-3808.2, 17.1-279
677	33.1-72.1
678	46.2-734
679	33.1-223.2:9
680	20-25
681	18.2-57.4
682	33.1-223.2:10
683	32.1-19.1R
684	2.2-1131.1
685	2.2-3706
686	2.2-435.1—2.2-435.5, 2.2-2670, 37.1-207.1
687	51.1-206
688	18.2-247
689	46.2-752
690	2.2-3703, 2.2-3705R, 2.2-3705.1, 2.2-3705.2, 2.2-3705.3, 2.2-3705.4, 2.2-3705.5, 2.2-3705.6, 2.2-3705.7, 2.2-3705.8, 2.2-3711, 2.2-3714, 2.2-3806, 22.1-279.8, 23-50.16:32, 32.1-283.1, 32.1-283.2, 44-146.18, 44-146.22, 52-8.3, 54.1-2517, 54.1-2523, 56-575.4
691	15.2-2223
692	46.2-604, 46.2-731
693	15.2-2109.2
694	2.2-700, 2.2-703
695	23-41
696	46.2-870
697	2.2-2000, 2.2-2004.1, 2.2-2452, 2.2-2681, 2.2-2715
699	63.2-2002
700	46.2-749.110
701	2.2-203.1, 2.2-2817.1
702	46.2-1222.1
703	54.1-2910.1
704	33.1-46.2
706	2.2-4303, 2.2-4308
707	37.1-70.10
709	1-13.13:1, 1-13.25:1
710	22.1-291.3
711	23-30.28, 23-30.27, n., 23-30.27:1, n
712	15.2-2110, 15.2-2118
714	63.2-1721
715	38.2-3407.10, 38.2-5803
716	58.1-400.3, 58.1-2628, 58.1-2674.1
717	46.2-736.01R, 46.2-736.02R, 46.2-746.2:2.1R, 46.2-746.4:3R, 46.2-749.5:1R, 46.2-746.6:2R, 46.2-746.7, 46.2-746.8, 46.2-746.8:1R, 46.2-746.9, 46.2-749.23:1R, 46.2-749.28:1R, 46.2-749.32—46.2-749.36R, 46.2-749.39R, 46.2-749.41R, 46.2-749.42R, 46.2-749.43R, 46.2-749.47R, 46.2-749.73:1R, 46.2-749.84R, 46.2-749.85R, 46.2-749.87R, 46.2-749.88R, 46.2-749.93R, 46.2-749.95R, 46.2-749.96R, 46.2-749.97R, 46.2-749.98R, 46.2-749.99R, 46.2-749.100R
718	30-19.3
719	46.2-873.1
720	18.2-271.1
721	46.2-750
722	46.2-346
723	46.2-752, 46.2-752
724	46.2-629
725	63.2-2004
726	46.2-1992
727	16.1-69.48:5, 16.1-296, 16.1-296.2
728	51.5-53, 51.5-56
729	2.2-514
730	2.2-3704.1, 2.2-3707, 30-179
731	54.1-2900
732	16.1-278.15, 20-103
733	46.2-335
734	46.2-1188,

Acts 2004 Chapter	Code 1950 Section
	46.2-1189, 46.2-1190, 46.2-1190.1, 46.2-1190.2, 46.2-1190.3, 46.2-1190.4, 46.2-1190.5, 46.2-1190.6, 46.2-1190.7, 46.2-1191, 46.2-1192
735	2.2-3706
736	2.2-3808.3, n.
737	37.1-67.01, 37.1-67.1, 37.1-71
738	18.2-57.2
739	23-31
740	23-9.6:2
741	18.2-67.10
742	8.01-413
743	46.2-833
744	54.1-3200, 54.1-3211, 54.1-3221, 54.1-3222, 54.1-3223, 54.1-3303
745	38.2-2127
746	46.2-100, 46.2-676, 46.2-916.1—46.2-916.3
747	46.2-725, 46.2-736.2, 46.2-742, 46.2-742.1, 46.2-742.1:1, 46.2-742.2, 46.2-745, 46.2-746.3, 46.2-746.7, 46.2-749, 46.2-749.4
748	56-265.1
749	63.2-1603, 63.2-1604, 63.2-1605, 63.2-1606, 63.2-1607R, 63.2-1608, 63.2-1609, 63.2-1610
750	2.2-1131.1
751	38.2-2128
752	22.1-291.3
753	16.1-228, 63.2-100
754	54.1-2711.1, 54.1-2712
755	2.2-203.1, 2.2-2817.1
756	37.1-137.4
757	20-107.3
758	46.2-914
759	18.2-187.2
760	32.1-65
761	38.2-6200, 38.2-6101
762	32.1-127
764	37.1-70.5, 37.1-70.6, 37.1-70.7, 37.1-70.8, 37.1-70.9
765	38.2-1867
766	2.2-3705.3
767	38.2-517
768	2.2-3707, 2.2-3707.01
769	15.2-1727
770	2.2-3705.2, 2.2-3711
771	38.2-3525
772	38.2-3540.1, 38.2-4319
773	2.2-3705.5, 17.1-503, 32.1-42, 32.1-43, 32.1-44, 32.1-45, 32.1-48, 32.1-48.01, 32.1-48.01, 32.1-48.02, 32.1-48.03, 32.1-48.04, 32.1-48.05—32.1-48.17
774	59.1-369
775	46.2-881.1R
776	54.1-1100, n
777	30-73.4
778	55-79.84, 55-516
779	55-79.84, 55-516
780	46.2-2000
781	6.1-32.3, 6.1-32.11, 6.1-32.19, 6.1-32.20
782	15.2-4903
783	33.1-56.1— 33.1-56.5
784	38.2-1800, 38.2-4415R, 59.1-200, 59.1-441.1—59.1-441.6
785	46.2-1088.5
786	55-79.84, 55-516
787	27-98
788	46.2-733, 46.2-1500
789	54.1-1100
790	6.1-363.1R, 6.1-363.2—6.1-363.26, 54.1-3905, 57-60, 59.1-200
791	33.1-23.4
792	33.1-430, 33.1-431, 33.1-433, 33.1-435
793	11-33.2
794	59.1-501.2, 59.1-501.3, 59.1-501.4R, 59.1-501.4:1, 59.1-501.5, 59.1-501.6, 59.1-501.12, 59.1-501.13R, 59.1-501.13:1, 59.1-501.14R, 59.1-501.14:1, 59.1-501.15, 59.1-501.16, 59.1-501.17, 59.1-502.7, 59.1-502.9, 59.1-502.11R, 59.1-503.7, 59.1-503.8R 59.1-504.1, 59.1-504.4, 59.1-504.5, 59.1-504.10
795	46.2-819.2
796	46.2-100, 46.2-730, 46.2-1157
797	46.2-1222
798	59.1-200, 59.1-525—59.1-529
799	15.2-2204, 15.2-2223, 15.2-2283
800	18.2-465.1
801	46.2-301
802	2.2-4002, 3.1-398, 35.1-14
803	33.1-120
804	33.1-132
805	46.2-335
806	15.2-5504
807	33.1-268, 33.1-269, 33.1-277
808	33.1-223.2:11
809	46.2-803.1
810	15.2-2403
811	46.2-208
812	46.2-1530.2
814	63.2-100, 63.2-913
815	63.2-903, 63.2-1200, 63.2-1221, 63.2-1222, 63.2-1817
816	15.2-2110
817	59.1-200, 59.1-525—59.1-529
818	8.01-195.10—8.01-195.12
819	19.2-120, 19.2-299
820	22.1-98.2
821	58.1-609.6
822	2.2-1839, 2.2-1839.1,
823	37.1-179.2
825	10.1-104, n., 10.1-109, n.
826	52-46
827	56-249.6, 56-577, 56-580, 56-582, 56-583, 56-585, 56-589, 56-594
828	58.1-3823
829	56-49.01
830	19.2-37
831	57-27.1
832	2.2-3705.7
833	18.2-52.1
834	9.1-903
835	24.2-659, 24.2-668
836	2.2-2648, 2.2-5201
837	15.2-915, 18.2-308.2:2
838	38.2-1906
839	22.1-98
840	8.01-195.10—8.01-195.12
841	18.2-51.1
842	18.2-90
843	18.2-67.3
844	18.2-386.1,
845	37.1-179.2
846	29.1-301
847	18.2-46.3:1
848	22.1-253.13:1
849	56-484.7:5, 56-484.7:6
850	18.2-55.1
851	36-105, 36-105.1:1
853	54.1-3300, n., 54.1-3300.1, n.
854	54.1-3435.02
855	2.2-2818, 32.1-46,

Acts 2004 Chapter	Code 1950 Section
	32.1-50, 32.1-60, 32.1-64.1, 32.1-138, 32.1-325, 32.1-331.15, 45.1-161.35, 45.1-161.70, 45.1-161.292:43, 46.2-208, 46.2-322, 53.1-22, 54.1-2957.02, 54.1-3812, 59.1-297, 59.1-298, 59.1-310.4, 63.2-1808
856	23-231.20
857	23-14
858	37.1-134.6
859	46.2-865.1, 46.2-867
860	28.2-201
861	56-575.1, n.
862	29.1-521
863	18.2-369
864	18.2-374.3
865	2.2-4310, 2.2-4343, 15.2-965.1
866	17.1-805
867	18.2-46.1
868	22.1-98
869	18.2-359
870	10.1-2009, 10.1-2011
871	58.1-3713
872	2.2-2238, 2.2-2670, 10.1-1413.2, 22.1-199.3R, 22.1-199.3, 22.1-208.2:1.1R, 22.1-208.2:1.1, 22.1-209.1:7R, 22.1-209.1:7, 22.1-209.1:9R, 22.1-209.1:10R, 22.1-291.2R, 22.1-291.2, 22.1-343, 23-38.19:3R, 23-38.19:4, 23-38.19:5, n., 23-38.53:8R, 23-38.53:9R, 23-38.53:10R, 23-38.53:12R, 23-38.53:12, 23-38.53:13, n., 23-38.53:14, n., 23-38.53:15R, 23-38.53:16, 23-38.53:17, n., 23-38.53:18, 23-38.53:19, 23-38.53:20, n., 36-139.8R, 59.1-284.7R, 59.1-284.8R, 59.1-284.9R, 59.1-284.10R, 59.1-284.11R, 59.1-284.12R, 59.1-284.16, 59.1-284.17, 59.1-284.18, 59.1-284.19R, 60.2-318R, 60.2-319R, 60.2-320R, 60.2-321R, 60.2-322R
874	2.2-4303, 2.2-4304
875	22.1-345.1
876	18.2-308
878	54.1-2962.2
879	15.2-3201
881	24.2-504, 24.2-525
882	22.1-212.1:2
883	2.2-511, 18.2-512—18.2-517, 19.2-10.1, 58.1-1017
884	16.1-266, 19.2-159, 19.2-163.01—19.2-163.04, 19.2-163.4:1, 19.2-163.7, 19.2-163.8, 53.1-124
885	18.2-308
886	63.2-1503
887	22.1-98
888	65.2-101, 65.2-500, 65.2-502, 65.2-512
889	23-231.20
890	15.2-1213.1
891	2.2-4310, 2.2-4343, 15.2-965.1
892	28.2-1600—28.2-1623
893	58.1-3713, 58.1-3713.01
894	18.2-287.01
895	30-19.03:1.2
896	38.2-5001, 38.2-5009, 38.2-5020
897	30-193, n.
899	28.2-1205, 28.2-1206, 28.2-1208
900	18.2-308
901	18.2-308
902	58.1-3995
903	18.2-308
904	18.2-308.2:2
905	18.2-308
906	2.2-4303, 2.2-4304
907	20-108.2
908	22.1-279.6
909	8.01-27.4
910	63.2-1732, n., 63.2-1803, n.
911	2.2-4304
912	22.1-345.1
913	4.1-325
914	65.2-309, 65.2-309.1, 65.2-310, 65.2-311
915	46.2-1176, 46.2-1178
916	32.1-164.1:1
917	22.1-25
918	22.1-200.01
919	2.2-518, 2.2-4806
920	22.1-299.3
921	16.1-266, 19.2-159, 19.2-163.01—19.2-163.04, 19.2-163.1R, 19.2-163.2R, 19.2-163.4:1, 19.2-163.6R, 19.2-163.7, 19.2-163.8, 53.1-124
922	18.2-308.2:2
923	15.2-915
924	46.2-819, 46.2-819.1, 46.2-819.3
925	17.1-278
926	18.2-308
927	15.2-975
928	65.2-101
929	59.1-148.1R, 59.1-148.2R
930	15.2-915.4, 15.2-1209, 18.2-299, 22.1-277.07
931	38.2-5001, 38.2-5009, 38.2-5020
932	24.2-303.2, 24.2-304.02
933	15.2-4903
934	15.2-904, 15.2-905
935	30-226—30-231, 23-38.53:21, n.
936	2.2-4304
937	18.2-266, n., 18.2-270, 19.2-294.1, 46.2-391, 46.2-391.2
938	2.2-2720—2.2-2724
939	22.1-19.1, 22.1-200.02, 22.1-202.1, 22.1-209.1:2, 22.1-225, 22.1-253.13:1, 22.1-253.13:2, 22.1-253.13:3, 22.1-253.13:4, 22.1-253.13:5, 22.1-253.13:6, 22.1-253.13:7, 22.1-253.13:8, 22.1-254.2, 22.1-279.3:1, 22.1-279.6, 22.1-292.1
940	2.2-200, 2.2-203.3, 2.2-204
941	65.2-309, 65.2-309.1, 65.2-310, 65.2-311
942	2.2-2233.2
943	Va. Const, Art. X, § 8, n., 2.2-518, n., 2.2-1132, n., 2.2-1155, n., 2.2-1156, n., 2.2-1828, n., 2.2-1829, n., 2.2-1830, n., 2.2-2416, n., 2.2-4802, n., 3.1-919, n., 3.1-925, n.,

Acts 2004 Chapter	Code 1950 Section
	3.1-931, n., 10.1-2128, n., 18.2-340.31, n., 22.1-253.13:1, n., 37.1-179.1, n., 51.5-9.1, n., 53.1-82.3, n., 54.1-3028.1, n., 55-66.6, n., 56-232, n., 56-234, n., 56-575.1, n., 58.1-600, n., 58.1-801, n., 58.1-803, n., 58.1-1402, n., 58.1-1410, n., 58.1-1804, n.
944	36-135
945	54.1-702
946	18.2-270
947	46.2-808, 46.2-838, 46.2-839, 46.2-849, 46.2-905, 46.2-906.1, 46.2-932, 46.2-1015, 46.2-1051
948	18.2-272, 46.2-301, 46.2-329
949	19.2-81
950	18.2-270
951	46.2-391
952	15.2-2241
953	3.1-398.1
954	19.2-120
955	22.1-19.1, 22.1-200.02, 22.1-202.1, 22.1-209.1:2, 22.1-225, 22.1-253.13:1, 22.1-253.13:2, 22.1-253.13:3, 22.1-253.13:4, 22.1-253.13:5, 22.1-253.13:6, 22.1-253.13:7, 22.1-253.13:8, 22.1-254.2, 22.1-279.3:1, 22.1-279.6, 22.1-292.1
956	54.1-603.1
957	18.2-270
958	18.2-270
959	19.2-120
960	46.2-391.2
961	18.2-270.1
962	18.2-270
963	2.2-200, 2.2-203.3, 2.2-204
964	2.2-2720—2.2-2724
965	2.2-4018, 22.1-253.13:3, 22.1-253.13:6, 22.1-253.13:8
966	33.1-447—33.1-463
967	22.1-3, 22.1-5, 22.1-270
968	15.2-906, 15.2-1115, 58.1-3965, 58.1-3970.1
970	2.2-3310.2
971	2.2-2448
972	9.1-102, 16.1-253.2, 16.1-279.1, 19.2-81.4, 63.2-1502
973	46.2-808, 46.2-838, 46.2-839, 46.2-849, 46.2-905, 46.2-906.1, 46.2-932, 46.2-1015, 46.2-1051
974	58.1-807
975	46.2-221.2, 46.2-221.3, 46.2-221.4, 46.2-330, 46.2-331R, 46.2-1521, 54.1-117
976	17.1-705.1
977	60.2-219, 60.2-528, 60.2-618
978	24.2-638, 24.2-642
979	8.01-262
980	9.1-102, 16.1-253.2, 16.1-279.1, 19.2-81.4, 63.2-1502
981	Va. Const., Art. II, § 6, n.
982	Va. Const., Art. V, § 16, n.
983	20-45.3
984	46.2-737, 46.2-742.3R, 46.2-742.4, 46.2-746.2:2.1R, 46.2-746.2:2.2, 46.2-746.2:5, 46.2-746.4, 46.2-746.4:01, 46.2-746.8:2, 46.2-746.9, 46.2-749.28:1R, 46.2-749.28:2, 46.2-749.30:2, 46.2-749.59, 46.2-749.62, 46.2-749.69R, 46.2-749.69:1, 46.2-749.98R, 46.2-749.98:1, 46.2-749.101, 46.2-749.103, 46.2-749.111, 46.2-749.112, 46.2-749.113, 46.2-749.114, 46.2-749.115, 46.2-749.116, 46.2-749.117
985	18.2-268.3, 18.2-268.4
986	56-575.9, 56-575.16
987	35.1-18
988	59.1-296.2:1, 59.1-306
989	2.2-205, 2.2-225, 2.2-2651, 23-231.9, 30-198
990	58.1-812, 58.1-817
991	22.1-319, 22.1-320, 22.1-321, 22.1-322, 22.1-323, 22.1-324, 22.1-325, 22.1-326, 22.1-326.1R, 22.1-328, 22.1-329, 22.1-330, 22.1-331, 22.1-332, 22.1-333R, 22.1-335R, 23-276.1, 23-276.2, 23-276.3, 23-276.4, 23-276.5, 23-276.6, 23-276.10, 23-276.11, 23-276.13, 23-276.14, 23-276.15, 54.1-3029
992	30-232—30-233
993	24.2-602, 24.2-629, 24.2-632, 24.2-633, 24.2-634, 24.2-638, 24.2-639, 24.2-642, 24.2-649, 24.2-659, 24.2-660R, 24.2-1009, 24.2-1010
994	2.2-5512, 2.2-5513
995	18.2-46.9R, 18.2-110R, 18.2-152.16R, 18.2-190.7R, 18.2-246.4R, 18.2-246.13, 18.2-246.14, 18.2-249R, 18.2-253R, 18.2-253.1R, 18.2-253.2R, 18.2-265.4R, 18.2-283.1, 18.2-287.4, 18.2-308, 18.2-308.1:2, 18.2-308.1:3, 18.2-308.1:4, 18.2-308.2, 18.2-308.2:01, 18.2-308.2:1, 18.2-308.4, 18.2-308.5, 18.2-308.7, 18.2-310R, 18.2-336R,

Acts 2004 Chapter	Code 1950 Section
	18.2-374.1:1,
	18.2-374.2R,
	19.2-386.1,
	19.2-386.2,
	19.2-386.3,
	19.2-386.4,
	19.2-386.5,
	19.2-386.15—
	19.2-386.31,
	19.2-386.15,
	59.1-148.4
996	2.2-511, n.,
	18.2-512—18.2-517,
	19.2-10.1, 58.1-1017
997	2.2-1153, 2.2-1156
998	46.2-417
999	18.2-270.01
1000	2.2-508,
	2.2-720, n., 2.2-1503,
	2.2-2423,
	2.2-2424,
	2.2-2434,
	2.2-2453,
	2.2-2457,
	2.2-2626,
	2.2-2666.1,
	2.2-2669,
	2.2-2676,
	2.2-2685,
	2.2-5601,
	2.2-5700.1,
	9.1-108,
	9.1-111,
	10.1-1325,
	10.1-2116R,
	15.2-4503.1,
	15.2-4507,
	15.2-4510,
	15.2-4512,
	15.2-4832,
	15.2-4836,
	17.1-700,
	17.1-701,
	17.1-704,
	17.1-802,
	17.1-901,
	17.1-904,
	22.1-354.6,
	22.1-358,
	22.1-359,
	23-50.16:5,
	23-231.2,
	23-231.3,
	23-231.15,
	23-231.20,
	24.2-300R,
	24.2-301R,
	24.2-301.1R,
	24.2-306,
	30-34.1,
	30-56,
	30-58.3,
	30-112,
	30-145,
	30-156,
	30-158,
	30-171,
	30-173,
	30-174,
	30-175,
	30-178,
	30-179,
	30-182,
	30-183,
	30-186,
	30-187,
	30-188,
	30-189,
	30-192.1,
	30-192.2,
	30-192.8,
	30-192.9,
	30-192.10,
	30-192.12,
	30-193,
	30-198,
	30-202,
	30-203,
	30-219,
	30-220,
	30-240—30-240,
	30-242—30-247,
	30-256,
	30-262,
	30-263—30-250,
	32.1-357,
	37.1-62.1, n.,
	51.1-124.20,
	51.5-39.2,
	58.1-202.2,
	62.1-69.5—
	62.1-69.10R,
	62.1-69.11R—
	62.1-69.13R,
	62.1-69.14R—
	62.1-69.16,
	62.1-69.17R,
	62.1-69.18R—
	62.1-69.20R,
	65.2-1301,
	65.2-1302,
	65.2-1303
1001	55-59.1
1002	4.1-120
1003	33.1-223.2:12
1004	16.1-69.48:1,
	16.1-69.48:3, 17.1-275,
	17.1-275.8, 18.2-251.02,
	18.2-254.1
1005	2.2-2448
1006	24.2-638, 24.2-642
1007	22.1-311, 22.1-312
1008	20-60.3, 20-108.1,
	20-108.2
1009	19.2-12
1010	24.2-602, 24.2-629,
	24.2-632, 24.2-633,
	24.2-634, 24.2-638,
	24.2-639, 24.2-642,
	24.2-649, 24.2-659,
	24.2-660R, 24.2-1009,
	24.2-1010
1011	63.2-1603, 63.2-1604,
	63.2-1605, 63.2-1606,
	63.2-1608, 63.2-1609,
	63.2-1610, 63.2-1607R
1012	18.2-308
1013	18.2-267, 18.2-268.2,
	18.2-268.3, 18.2-268.4,
	18.2-268.5, 18.2-268.8,
	18.2-268.9, 18.2-268.10,
	18.2-272
1014	2.2-3705.5, 8.01-413,
	16.1-266, 16.1-343,
	32.1-127.1:03, 37.1-67.3,
	37.1-134.9, 37.1-134.12,
	37.1-134.21, 37.1-226,
	37.1-227, 37.1-228,
	37.1-229, 37.1-230,
	38.2-608
1015	30-232—30-233,
	30-234, n., 30-235, n.,
	30-236, n., 30-237, n.,
	30-238, n., 30-239, n.
1016	9.1-102, 19.2-81.3,
	19.2-81.4
1017	54.1-2105, n.
1018	28.2-1205, 28.2-1206,
	28.2-1208
1019	51.1-1110
1021	2.2-3705, n.,
	2.2-3705.5, 17.1-503,
	32.1-42, 32.1-43, 32.1-44,
	32.1-45, 32.1-48,
	32.1-48.01, 32.1-48.01,
	32.1-48.02, 32.1-48.03,
	32.1-48.04,
	32.1-48.05—32.1-48.17,
	32.1-48.05, 32.1-116.3,
	32.1-127.1:03, 44-146.16,
	44-146.17
1022	18.2-268.3
1023	18.2-32.2
1024	19.2-327.10—
	19.2-327.14
1025	33.1-223.2:9
1026	18.2-32.2
1027	29.1-103, 29.1-701.1
1028	56-1, 56-49, 56-265.1
1029	3.1-336.2,
	3.1-336.3,
	58.1-1000,
	58.1-1003,

Acts 2004 Chapter — Code 1950 Section

58.1-1009,
58.1-1010,
58.1-1011,
58.1-1013,
58.1-1004,
58.1-1005,
58.1-1014
1030 ....22.1-207.1

ACTS 2004, Sp. Sess. I

Acts 2004, Sp. Sess. I Chapter — Code 1950 Section

1.......... 3.1-1111, 30-133,
58.1-3506, 58.1-3506.1,
58.1-3523, 58.1-3524,
58.1-3912, 58.1-3525 —
58.1-3533, n.,
58.1-3916.01, n.
2..................18.2-268.3
3........32.1-366, 32.1-367,
56-582, n.,
58.1-302,
58.1-321, 58.1-322,
58.1-339.8, 58.1-390R,
58.1-390.1, 58.1-390.2,
58.1-391, 58.1-392,
58.1-393.1, 58.1-394R,
58.1-394.1, 58.1-394.2,
58.1-395, 58.1-402,
58.1-441, 58.1-603,
58.1-604, 58.1-604.1,
58.1-605, 58.1-606,
58.1-609.3, 58.1-611.1,
58.1-614, 58.1-626,
58.1-627R, 58.1-628R,
58.1-628.2, 58.1-638,
58.1-638.1, 58.1-639,
58.1-801, 58.1-803,
58.1-807, 58.1-808,
58.1-1001, 58.1-1009,
58.1-1018, 58.1-1021.01 —
58.1-1021.05, 58.1-1206,
58.1-3833
42.2-200, n., 2.2-203.3, n.,
2.2-204, n., 2.2-212, n.,
2.2-219, n., 2.2-228, n.,
2.2-409, n., 2.2-518, n.,
2.2-800, n., 2.2-803, n.,
2.2-1100, n., 2.2-1104, n.,
2.2-1116, n., 2.2-1125, n.,
2.2-1132, n., 2.2-1149, n.,
2.2-1156, n., 2.2-1204, n.,
2.2-1400, n., 2.2-1501, n.,
2.2-1505, n., 2.2-1802, n.,
2.2-1819, n., 2.2-2005, n.,
2.2-2016, n., 2.2-2022, n.,
2.2-2025, n.,
2.2-2026, n., 2.2-2028, n.,
2.2-2031, n., 2.2-2032, n.,
2.2-2221, n., 2.2-2221.1, n.,

Acts 2004, Sp. Sess. I Chapter — Code 1950 Section

2.2-2318, n., 2.2-2444, n.,
2.2-2457, n., 2.2-2632, n.,
2.2-2670, n., 2.2-2905, n.,
2.2-4011, n., 2.2-4301, n.,
2.2-4309, n., 2.2-4400, n.,
2.2-4806, n., 2.2-5206, n.,
2.2-5209, n., 2.2-5211, n.,
3.1-336.2, n., 3.1-925, n.,
3.1-1107, n., 3.1-1108, n.,
4.1-230, 4.1-231, 5.1-1.2,
n., 5.1-1.6, n., 8.01-195.1,
n., 8.01-384.1:1, n.,
9.1-102, n., 9.1-166, n.,
9.1-168, n., 10.1-202, n.,
10.1-546, n., 10.1-552, n.,
10.1-1020, n., 10.1-1021,
n., 10.1-1124, n.,
10.1-1176, n., 10.1-1188,
n., 10.1-1190, n.,
10.1-2100, n., 10.1-2134,
n., 10.1-2211, n.,
10.1-2213, n., 10.1-2500,
n., 10.1-2501, n.,
10.1-2502, n., 11-35, n.,
12.1-4, n., 13.1-775.1, n.,
15.2-527, n., 15.2-1302, n.,
15.2-1534, n., 15.2-1605,
n., 15.2-1608, n.,
15.2-1609.1, n.,
15.2-1627.1, n., 15.2-1628,
n., 15.2-1629, n.,
15.2-1630, n., 15.2-1631,
n., 15.2-1636.8, n.,
15.2-1636.9, n., 15.2-2602,
n., 15.2-2659, n.,
15.2-4100, n., 16.1-69.6:1,
16.1-266, n., 16.1-273, n.,
16.1-287, n., 16.1-309.2, n.,
16.1-309.7, n., 16.1-322.1,
n., 17.1-278, n., 17.1-279,
n., 17.1-283, n., 17.1-287,
n., 17.1-507, 18.2-152.2, n.,
18.2-340.31, n.,
19.2-163.01, n., 19.2-163.2,
19.2-316.2, n., 19.2-316.3,
n., 19.2-326, n., 19.2-349,
n., 19.2-390.01, n.,
22.1-18.01, n., 22.1-101.1,
n., 22.1-205, n.,
22.1-253.13:1, n.,
22.1-253.13:3, n.,
22.1-253.3:4, n.,
22.1-290.01, n., 23-7.4:1,
n., 23-9.2:3.1, n., 23-9.6:1,
n., 23-9.9, n., 23-30.23, n.,
23-30.27:1, n., 23-30.28, n.,
23-38.12, n., 23-38.14, n.,
23-38.53:21, n., 23-38.77,
n., 23-164.7, n., 23-164.8,
n., 23-174.7, n., 23-215, n.,

Acts 2004, Sp. Sess. I Chapter — Code 1950 Section

23-227, n., 23-231.13, n.,
23-253.1, n., 23-276.10, n.,
23-284, n., 23-291, n.,
24.2-108, n., 28.2-542, n.,
28.2-550, n., 29.1-702, n.,
30-58.3, n., 30-130, n.,
30-158, n., 32.1-16, n.,
32.1-127, n.,
32.1-163, n., 32.1-166.7, n.,
32.1-167, n., 32.1-171.1, n.,
32.1-273.1, n.,
32.1-323, n., 32.1-323.1, n.,
32.1-325, n., 32.1-326.3, n.,
32.1-331.12, n., 32.1-333,
n., 32.1-338, n., 32.1-347,
n., 32.1-351, n., 32.1-352,
n., 32.1-355, n., 32.1-357,
n., 33.1-13, n.,
33.1-23.03:1, n., 33.1-23.1,
n., 33.1-75.1, n.,
33.1-391.3, n., 35.1-13, n.,
35.1-14, n., 35.1-16, n.,
35.1-17, n., 36-132, n.,
36-139, n., 37.1-10, n.,
37.1-70.5, n., 37.1-197, n.,
38.2-3407, n., 38.2-5020.1,
n., 40.1-49.4, n.,
44-146.18:2, n., 44-146.28,
n., 46.2-205, n., 46.2-212.1,
n., 46.2-328.1, n., 46.2-685,
n., 46.2-694, n., 51.1-124.3,
n., 51.1-124.30, n.,
51.1-155.1, n., 51.1-1100,
n., 51.1-1103, n.,
51.1-1401, n., 51.1-1403,
n., 51.5-39.7, n., 51.5-106,
n., 52-1, n., 52-8.1:1, n.,
53.1-5, n., 53.1-10, n.,
53.1-20, n., 53.1-20.1, n.,
53.1-21, n., 53.1-28, n.,
53.1-67.1, n., 53.1-82.3, n.,
53.1-115.1, n., 53.1-120, n.,
53.1-121, n.,
54.1-2400.6, n.,
54.1-3023, n., 54.1-3024,
n., 54.1-3028.1, n.,
54.1-3913, n., 54.1-3916,
n., 54.1-3919, n.,
54.1-3924, n., 55-66.6, n.,
55-297, n., 56-232, n.,
56-234, n., 56-484.12, n.,
56-575.1, n., 58.1-3, n.,
58.1-202.2, n., 58.1-339.4,
n., 58.1-353, n., 58.1-439.2,
n., 58.1-439.12:01,
58.1-461, n., 58.1-462, n.,
58.1-470, n., 58.1-600, n.,
58.1-602, n., 58.1-638, n.,
58.1-638.1, n., 58.1-801, n.,
58.1-803, n., 58.1-815, n.,

Acts 2004, Sp. Sess. I Chapter	Code 1950 Section
	58.1-815.1, n., 58.1-816.1, n., 58.1-1402, n., 58.1-1410, n., 58.1-1803, n., 58.1-1804, n., 58.1-2402, n., 58.1-2425, n., 58.1-2510, n., 58.1-3523, n., 58.1-3524, n., 58.1-3531, n., 58.1-3536, n., 58.1-4022, n., 58.1-4023, n., 59.1-282.2, n., 59.1-282.3, n., 59.1-364, n., 59.1-392, n., 60.2-305, n., 60.2-315, n., 62.1-128, n., 62.1-140, n., 63.2-401, n., 63.2-608, n., 63.2-611, n., 63.2-612, n., 63.2-619, n., 63.2-1509, n., 63.2-1706, n., 63.2-1735, n., 63.2-1907, n., 66-15, n., 66-19, n., 66-20, n.

ACTS 2004, Sp. Sess. II

Acts 2004 Sp. Sess. II Chapter	Code 1950 Section
1	40.1-28.4:1

Table of Sections Amended or Repealed

Sec.
1-4. Amended by Acts 1971, Ex. Sess., c. 14.
1-12. Amended by Acts 1971, Ex. Sess., c. 49; Acts 1981, c. 329.
1-13. Amended by Acts 1950, p. 20.
1-13.2. Amended by Acts 1971, Ex. Sess., c. 49; Acts 1995, c. 155.
1-13.3. Amended by Acts 1987, c. 92.
1-13.3:1. Amended by Acts 1977, c. 93; Acts 1986, c. 166.
1-13.4. Repealed by Acts 1986, c. 155.
1-13.7. Amended by Acts 1997, c. 406.
1-13.11. Repealed by Acts 1981, c. 228.
1-13.19. Amended by Acts 1988, c. 36.
1-13.21. Amended by Acts 1971, Ex. Sess., c. 49.
1-13.22. Amended by Acts 1958, c. 330; Acts 1966, c. 78.
1-13.23:1. Amended by Acts 1986, c. 155.
1-13.25. Amended by Acts 1975, c. 500.
1-13.26. Amended by Acts 1971, Ex. Sess., c. 49.
1-13.27. Amended by Acts 1962, c. 104.
1-13.28:1. Amended by Acts 1989, c. 493.
1-13.29. Amended by Acts 1971, Ex. Sess. c. 49; Acts 1995, c. 155.
1-13.30. Amended by Acts 1966, c. 79; Acts 1986, c. 155.
1-13.32. Amended by Acts 1999, c. 145; Acts 2000, c. 995.
1-13.34. Amended by Acts 1986, c. 155.
1-13.35. Amended by Acts 1960, c. 307; Acts 1962, c. 315; Acts 1964, c. 404; Acts 1966, c. 78.
1-13.36. Amended by Acts 1960, c. 251; Acts 1966, c. 78.
1-13.38. Amended by Acts 1971, Ex. Sess., c. 49.
1-13.39. Repealed by Acts 1983, c. 260.
1-13.39:2. Amended by Acts 2001, c. 771.
1-14. Repealed by Acts 1975, c. 547.
1-15. Amended by Acts 1952, c. 637; Acts 1962, c. 617; Acts 1964, c. 646; Acts 1966, c. 581; Acts 1988, c. 177.
1-17.1. Amended by Acts 1987, c. 56.
1-17.2. Amended by Acts 1987, c. 471; Acts 1988, c. 273.
1-20. Amended by Acts 1972, c. 794.
2-1 to 2-309. Repealed by Acts 1966, c. 677.
2.1-1 to 2.1-819. Repealed by Acts 2001, c. 844.
2.2-106. Amended by Acts 2003, cc. 981, 1021.
2.2-113. Amended by Acts 2003, c. 169.
2.2-126. Amended by Acts 2003, c. 590.
2.2-136 to 2.2-138. Repealed by Acts 2002, c. 247.
2.2-200. Amended by Acts 2004, cc. 940, 963.
2.2-203. Amended by Acts 2002, c. 572; Acts 2003, 197, 657, 670, 884.
2.2-203.1. Amended by Acts 2004, cc. 701, 755.

Sec.
2.2-204. Amended by Acts 2004, cc. 57, 940, 963.
2.2-205. Amended by Acts 2004, c. 989.
2.2-206. Amended by Acts 2004, c. 238.
2.2-208. Amended by Acts 2003, c. 452.
2.2-209, 2.2-210. Repealed by Acts 2004, c. 37.
2.2-212. Amended by Acts 2004, cc. 14, 142.
2.2-215. Amended by Acts 2004, c. 142.
2.2-216. Amended by Acts 2004, c. 58.
2.2-218. Amended by Acts 2003, c. 885.
2.2-220. Amended by Acts 2003, c. 885.
2.2-225. Amended by Acts 2003, cc. 981, 1021; Acts 2004, c. 989.
2.2-226. Repealed by Acts 2003, cc. 888, 981, 1021.
2.2-226.1. Repealed by Acts 2003, cc. 981, 1021.
2.2-227. Repealed by Acts 2003, cc. 981, 1021.
2.2-426. Amended by Acts 2002, cc. 248, 491.
2.2-507.1. Amended by Acts 2004, c. 289.
2.2-508. Amended by Acts 2004, c. 1000.
2.2-510. Amended by Acts 2002, c. 572.
2.2-511. Amended by Acts 2002, cc. 588, 623; Acts 2003, c. 103.
2.2-511. Amended by Acts 2004, cc. 450, 883, 996.
2.2-514. Amended by Acts 2004, c. 729.
2.2-518. Amended by Acts 2004, c. 919.
2.2-603. Amended by Acts 2004, cc. 488, 638.
2.2-608. Amended by Acts 2004, c. 650.
2.2-609. Amended by Acts 2004, cc. 28, 152.
2.2-612. Amended by Acts 2004, cc. 34, 155.
2.2-614.1. Amended by Acts 2004, c. 565.
2.2-700. Amended by Acts 2004, c. 694.
2.2-703. Amended by Acts 2004, c. 694.
2.2-710. Repealed by Acts 2003, cc. 749, 766.
2.2-1105. Amended by Acts 2003, c. 580.
2.2-1110. Amended by Acts 2003, cc. 981, 1021.
2.2-1111. Amended by Acts 2002, c. 504; Acts 2003, c. 294.
2.2-1119. Amended by Acts 2003, cc. 895, 1021.
2.2-1120. Amended by Acts 2002, c. 491; Acts 2003, c. 225; Acts 2004, c. 484.
2.2-1121. Repealed by Acts 2002, c. 579.
2.2-1124. Amended by Acts 2004, c. 670.
2.2-1126, 2.2-1127. Repealed by Acts 2004, c. 650.
2.2-1147. Amended by Acts 2002, c. 561.
2.2-1151.1. Amended by Acts 2004, c. 636.
2.2-1153. Amended by Acts 2004, c. 997.
2.2-1156. Amended by Acts 2002, c. 281; Acts 2004, c. 997.
2.2-1201. Amended by Acts 2002, c. 780; Acts 2003, c. 225.
2.2-1300 to 2.2-1304. Repealed by Acts 2003, cc. 981, 1021.
2.2-1405. Amended by Acts 2003, c. 435.
2.2-1501. Amended by Acts 2002, cc. 580, 618; Acts 2003, c. 900.

Sec.
2.2-1503. Amended by Acts 2003, c. 612; Acts 2004, c. 1000.
2.2-1508. Amended by Acts 2003, cc. 190, 888.
2.2-1509. Amended by Acts 2002, cc. 839, 888; Acts 2003, c. 888.
2.2-1511. Amended by Acts 2003, c. 900.
2.2-1700 to 2.2-1710. Repealed by Acts 2003, cc. 981, 1021.
2.2-1829. Amended by Acts 2003, cc. 755, 759.
2.2-1837. Amended by Acts 2002, c. 765; Acts 2003, c. 828.
2.2-1839. Amended by Acts 2003, cc. 23, 49; Acts 2004, cc. 121, 529, 822.
2.2-1900 to 2.2-1905. Repealed by Acts 2003, cc. 657, 670.
2.2-2000. Amended by Acts 2004, c. 697.
2.2-2006. Amended by Acts 2004, c. 145.
2.2-2009. Amended by Acts 2004, c. 638.
2.2-2012. Amended by Acts 2004, cc. 237, 278.
2.2-2101. Amended by Acts 2003, cc. 94, 451, 657, 670, 854, 900; Acts 2004, c. 37.
2.2-2213. Amended by Acts 2004, c. 650.
2.2-2238. Amended by Acts 2004, cc. 650, 872.
2.2-2242. Amended by Acts 2004, c. 650.
2.2-2247 to 2.2-2259. Repealed by Acts 2003, cc. 981, 1021.
2.2-2261. Amended by Acts 2002, cc. 501, 542; Acts 2003, cc. 981, 1021.
2.2-2263. Amended by Acts 2002, cc. 501, 542; Acts 2004, c. 650.
2.2-2270. Amended by Acts 2002, cc. 501, 542.
2.2-2279. Amended by Acts 2003, c. 339.
2.2-2282. Amended by Acts 2004, c. 239.
2.2-2285. Amended by Acts 2003, c. 339.
2.2-2286. Amended by Acts 2003, c. 940.
2.2-2287. Amended by Acts 2003, c. 339.
2.2-2292. Amended by Acts 2003, c. 339.
2.2-2294. Amended by Acts 2003, c. 339.
2.2-2295. Amended by Acts 2003, c. 339.
2.2-2319. Amended by Acts 2002, c. 442.
2.2-2400. Amended by Acts 2004, c. 650.
2.2-2403. Repealed by Acts 2003, cc. 981, 1021.
2.2-2407. Amended by Acts 2004, cc. 592, 650.
2.2-2411. Amended by Acts 2002, cc. 491, 572.
2.2-2421, 2.2-2422. Repealed by Acts 2003, cc. 657, 670.
2.2-2423. Amended by Acts 2003, cc. 981, 1021; Acts 2004, c. 1000.
2.2-2424. Amended by Acts 2003, c. 885; Acts 2004, c. 1000.
2.2-2431. Amended by Acts 2003, cc 981, 1021.
2.2-2432. Amended by Acts 2004, c. 650.
2.2-2434. Amended by Acts 2004, c. 1000.
2.2-2435 to 2.2-2439. Repealed by Acts 2003, cc. 657, 670.
2.2-2440. Amended by Acts 2002, c. 877.
2.2-2442 to 2.2-2443. Amended by Acts 2002, c. 877.
2.2-2444. Amended by Acts 2002, c. 877; Acts 2003, c. 366.
2.2-2448. Amended by Acts 2004, cc. 971, 1005.

Sec.
2.2-2452. Amended by Acts 2004, c. 697.
2.2-2453. Amended by Acts 2004, c. 1000.
2.2-2457. Amended by Acts 2004, c. 1000.
2.2-2500 to 2.2-2502. Repealed by Acts 2003, c. 349.
2.2-2503. Amended by Acts 2003, c. 885.
2.2-2506. Repealed by Acts 2004, cc. 34, 155.
2.2-2507. Repealed by Acts 2004, c. 34, 155.
2.2-2511, 2.2-2512. Repealed by Acts 2002, c. 491.
2.2-2514. Amended by Acts 2002, c. 381.
2.2-2515. Amended by Acts 2003, c. 362.
2.2-2600. Repealed by Acts 2004, c. 37.
2.2-2601. Repealed by Acts 2004, c. 37.
2.2-2602. Repealed by Acts 2004, c. 37.
2.2-2603, 2.2-2604. Repealed by Acts 2003, c. 348.
2.2-2605 to 2.2.-2608. Repealed by Acts 2003, c. 210.
2.2-2611 to 2.2-2613. Repealed by Acts 2002, c. 491.
2.2-2626. Amended by Acts 2004, c. 1000.
2.2-2628. Amended by Acts 2003, c. 885; Acts 2004, c. 142.
2.2-2629. Amended by Acts 2002, c. 562.
2.2-2634. Amended by Acts 2004, c. 58.
2.2-2639. Amended by Acts 2002, c. 561.
2.2-2640. Repealed by Acts 2004, cc. 16, 153.
2.2-2641. Repealed by Acts 2004, cc. 16, 153.
2.2-2642, 2.2-2643. Repealed by Acts 2003, c. 451.
2.2-2644 to 2.2-2647. Repealed by Acts 2003, c. 454.
2.2-2648. Amended by Acts 2002, c. 410; Acts 2003, cc. 483, 498; Acts 2004, c. 836.
2.2-2649. Amended by Acts 2002, c. 410; Acts 2003, c. 485.
2.2-2650. Repealed by Acts 2003, cc. 502, 806.
2.2-2651. Amended by Acts 2002, c. 425; Acts 2003, cc. 981, 1021; Acts 2004, c. 989.
2.2-2652 to 2.2-2654. Repealed by Acts 2003, c. 452.
2.2-2664. Amended by Acts 2004, c. 38.
2.2-2666.1. Amended by Acts 2003, c. 885; Acts 2004, c. 1000.
2.2-2667. Amended by Acts 2004, c. 385.
2.2-2668. Amended by Acts 2004, c. 385.
2.2-2669. Amended by Acts 2003, c. 642; Acts 2004, c. 1000.
2.2-2670. Amended by Acts 2003, c. 642; Acts 2004, cc. 686, 872.
2.2-2676. Amended by Acts 2004, c. 1000.
2.2-2679. Amended by Acts 2003, c. 725.
2.2-2681. Amended by Acts 2004, c. 697.
2.2-2685. Amended by Acts 2004, c. 1000.
2.2-2701. Amended by Acts 2002, c. 260.
2.2-2704. Amended by Acts 2002, c. 260.
2.2-2705. Amended by Acts 2002, c. 416; Acts 2003, cc. 239, 885.

Sec.
2.2-2709, 2.2-2710. Repealed by Acts 2003, c. 885.
2.2-2715. Amended by Acts 2004, c. 697.
2.2-2801. Amended by Acts 2002, c. 676.
2.2-2813. Amended by Acts 2003, cc. 814, 821.
2.2-2817.1. Amended by Acts 2004, cc. 701, 755.
2.2-2818. Amended by Acts 2004, cc. 279, 855.
2.2-2820.1. Repealed by Acts 2004, c. 58.
2.2-2905. Amended by Acts 2002, cc. 271, 572; Acts 2003, c. 652.
2.2-3000. Amended by Acts 2004, c. 674.
2.2-3003. Amended by Acts 2003, c. 252; Acts 2004, c. 674.
2.2-3005. Amended by Acts 2004, c. 674.
2.2-3006. Amended by Acts 2003, c. 252; Acts 2004, c. 229.
2.2-3100. Amended by Acts 2003, c. 694.
2.2-3101. Amended by Acts 2003, c. 694; Acts 2004, c. 134.
2.2-3105. Amended by Acts 2003, c. 694.
2.2-3106. Amended by Acts 2002, cc. 87, 478; Acts 2003, c. 646.
2.2-3109. Amended by Acts 2004, c. 530.
2.2-3112. Amended by Acts 2003, c. 694.
2.2-3114. Amended by Acts 2003, c. 694.
2.2-3115. Amended by Acts 2003, c. 694.
2.2-3121. Amended by Acts 2003, c. 694.
2.2-3126. Amended by Acts 2003, c. 694.
2.2-3130. Amended by Acts 2004, c. 134.
2.2-3202. Amended by Acts 2002, c. 491; Acts 2003, c. 782.
2.2-3309.1. Amended by Acts 2002, c. 162.
2.2-3310. Amended by Acts 2003, c. 684.
2.2-3700. Amended by Acts 2002, c. 393.
2.2-3701. Amended by Acts 2002, c. 393; Acts 2003, c. 897.
2.2-3702. Amended by Acts 2002, c. 393.
2.2-3703. Amended by Acts 2003, cc. 989, 1018; Acts 2004, cc. 398, 690.
2.2-3704. Amended by Acts 2002, c. 715, 830.
2.2-3705. Repealed by Acts 2004, c. 690.
2.2-3706. Amended by Acts 2002, c. 393, 715, 798, 830; Acts 2004, cc. 685, 735.
2.2-3707. Amended by Acts 2004, cc. 730, 768.
2.2-3708. Amended by Acts 2003, cc. 981, 1021.
2.2-3709. Amended by Acts 2003, c. 475.
2.2-3710. Amended by Acts 2002, c. 491.
2.2-3711. Amended by Acts 2002, c. 87, 393, 455, 478, 499, 655, 715, 830; Acts 2003, cc. 274, 291, 332, 618, 703; Acts 2004, cc. 398, 690, 770.
2.2-3714. Amended by Acts 2003, c. 319; Acts 2004, c. 690.
2.2-3800. Amended by Acts 2003, cc. 791, 914, 918, 927.
2.2-3801. Amended by Acts 2003, c. 272.
2.2-3802. Amended by Acts 2003, c. 406.
2.2-3803. Amended by Acts 2002, c. 747.
2.2-3806. Amended by Acts 2004, c. 690.
2.2-3808. Amended by Acts 2003, c. 974.
2.2-3808.2. Amended by Acts 2004, c. 676.

Sec.
2.2-4001. Amended by Acts 2002, c. 747.
2.2-4002. Amended by Acts 2003, cc. 639, 695; Acts 2004, c. 802.
2.2-4006. Amended by Acts 2003, c. 436.
2.2-4007. Amended by Acts 2002, cc. 241, 391, 747; Acts 2003, c. 224.
2.2-4012. Amended by Acts 2003, c. 224.
2.2-4014. Amended by Acts 2002, c. 677; Acts 2003, c. 212.
2.2-4015. Amended by Acts 2002, cc. 391, 677.
2.2-4018. Amended by Acts 2002, c. 747; Acts 2004, c. 965.
2.2-4024. Amended by Acts 2002, cc. 448, 698.
2.2-4025. Amended by Acts 2002, c. 747.
2.2-4031. Amended by Acts 2002, c. 241; Acts 2003, c. 212.
2.2-4032, 2.2-4033. Repealed by Acts 2003, c. 212.
2.2-4102. Amended by Acts 2003, c. 212.
2.2-4301. Amended by Acts 2003, cc. 185, 895, 994, 1006; Acts 2004, c. 458
2.2-4303. Amended by Acts 2003, cc. 644, 895; Acts 2004, cc. 706, 874, 906.
2.2-4304. Amended by Acts 2003, cc. 651, 895, 981, 1021; Acts 2004, cc. 874, 906, 911, 936.
2.2-4308. Amended by Acts 2004, c. 706.
2.2-4310. Amended by Acts 2003, c. 226; Acts 2004, cc. 865, 891.
2.2-4337. Amended by Acts 2002, cc. 556, 643, 682.
2.2-4341. Amended by Acts 2003, c. 255.
2.2-4343. Amended by Acts 2002, cc. 87, 478, 491, 582, 595; Acts 2003, c. 226, 1008; Acts 2004, cc. 145, 865, 891.
2.2-4345. Amended by Acts 2002, c. 87, 478, 747.
2.2-4369. Amended by Acts 2003, c. 694.
2.2-4510. Amended by Acts 2002, cc. 18, 438.
2.2-4806. Amended by Acts 2004, c. 919.
2.2-5100. Amended by Acts 2003, c. 17.
2.2-5101. Amended by Acts 2003, c. 17.
2.2-5102. Amended by Acts 2003, c. 17.
2.2-5201. Amended by Acts 2003, c. 499; Acts 2004, c. 836.
2.2-5202. Amended by Acts 2003, c. 483.
2.2-5206. Amended by Acts 2002, cc. 585, 619; Acts 2003, c. 483.
2.2-5207. Amended by Acts 2003, c. 483.
2.2-5209. Amended by Acts 2003, c. 483.
2.2-5211. Amended by Acts 2004, cc. 286, 631.
2.2-5302. Repealed by Acts 2004, c. 38.
2.2-5601. Amended by Acts 2003, c. 885; Acts 2004, c. 1000.
2.2-5900. Amended by Acts 2002, c. 491
3-1 to 3-729. Repealed by Acts 1966, c. 702.
3.1-1. Amended by Acts 1971, Ex. Sess., c. 135; Acts 1978, c. 219; Acts 1985, c. 397; Acts 1992, c. 121.
3.1-2. Amended by Acts 1978, c. 219.
3.1-4. Amended by Acts 1972, c. 531; Acts 1994, c. 370.

Sec.
3.1-4.1. Amended by Acts 2001, cc. 17, 398.
3.1-5. Repealed by Acts 1980, c. 728.
3.1-6.1. Amended by Acts 2004, cc. 89, 212, 319.
3.1-7. Repealed by Acts 1966, c. 536.
3.1-8. Amended by Acts 1971, Ex. Sess., c. 34; Acts 1978, c. 219; Acts 1985, c. 397.
3.1-11. Amended by Acts 1978, c. 396.
3.1-14. Amended by Acts 1975, c. 260; Acts 1977, c. 186; Acts 1978, cc. 219, 540; Acts 1982, c. 150; Acts 1993, c. 455; Acts 1994, cc. 261, 370; Acts 1995, c. 10; Acts 1996, c. 996.
3.1-15. Amended by Acts 1972, c. 741; Acts 1978, cc. 219, 702.
3.1-16. Amended by Acts 1978, c. 219.
3.1-17.1. Amended by Acts 1999, c. 346.
3.1-18. Repealed by Acts 1984, c. 734.
3.1-18.1. Amended by Acts 1978, cc. 219, 396.
3.1-18.2. Amended by Acts 1978, c. 219; Acts 1986, c. 30; Acts 1995, c. 703.
3.1-18.3. Amended by Acts 1978, c. 219.
3.1-18.5. Amended by Acts 1982, c. 417; Acts 2000, cc. 22, 778; Acts 2003, c. 384.
3.1-18.6. Amended by Acts 1982, c. 417; Acts 1984, c. 750; Acts 1989, c. 656; Acts 2000, cc. 22, 778.
3.1-18.7. Repealed by Acts 1992, c. 887.
3.1-18.8. Amended by Acts 1982, c. 417; Acts 2000, cc. 22, 778.
3.1-19 to 3.1-22. Repealed by Acts 1972, c. 531.
3.1-22.3. Amended by Acts 1968, c. 85.
3.1-22.4. Amended by Acts 1979, c. 69; Acts 1984, c. 734; Acts 1985, cc. 146, 448; Acts 1992, c. 121; Acts 2004, c. 650
3.1-22.5. Amended by Acts 1970, c. 457; Acts 1976, c. 91; Acts 1994, cc. 577, 649, 740, 743.
3.1-22.8. Amended by Acts 1978, c. 399; Acts 1984, c. 750; Acts 1986, c. 390; Acts 1988, c. 182.
3.1-22.9. Amended by Acts 1984, c. 750; Acts 1986, c. 390.
3.1-22.10. Amended by Acts 1986, c. 390; Acts 1988, c. 182.
3.1-22.11. Amended by Acts 1988, c. 182.
3.1-22.12. Amended by Acts 1986, c. 390.
3.1-22.19. Amended by Acts 2000, c. 16.
3.1-22.22 to 3.1-22.27. Repealed by Acts 1996, c. 729.
3.1-22.28. Amended by Acts 1991, c. 293; Acts 1994, c. 779.
3.1-22.29. Amended by Acts 1994, c. 779.
3.1-22.35. Amended by Acts 1990, c. 100.
3.1-22.49. Amended by Acts 1998, c. 586.
3.1-27.1 to 3.1-27.36. Repealed by Acts 1996, c. 283.
3.1-27.2. Amended by Acts 1983, c. 9.
3.1-27.3. Amended by Acts 1983, c. 9; Acts 1988, c. 477.

Sec.
3.1-27.5. Amended by Acts 1983, c. 9; Acts 1991, c. 190.
3.1-27.6. Amended by Acts 1988, c. 477.
3.1-27.35. Amended by Acts 1984, c. 734; Acts 1985, c. 146; Acts 1988, c. 477.
3.1-27.41. Amended by Acts 1985, c. 357.
3.1-32 to 3.1-39. Repealed by Acts 1985, c. 505.
3.1-40 to 3.1-46.1. Repealed by Acts 1994, c. 433.
3.1-47. Amended by Acts 1975, c. 135.
3.1-48. Amended by Acts 1975, c. 135.
3.1-49. Amended by Acts 1975, c. 135; Acts 1983, c. 379.
3.1-52. Amended by Acts 1975, c. 135.
3.1-73.1. Amended by Acts 2001, cc. 17, 398.
3.1-73.2. Repealed by Acts 2001, cc. 17, 398.
3.1-73.3. Amended by Acts 1989, c. 413; Acts 2001, cc. 17, 398.
3.1-73.4. Repealed by Acts 1989, c. 413.
3.1-73.5. Amended by Acts 2000, c. 536; Acts 2001, cc. 17, 398.
3.1-73.7. Amended by Acts 2001, c. 320.
3.1-74 tp 3.1-106. Repealed by Acts 1994, c. 740.
3.1-106.2. Amended by Acts 2002, c. 473.
3.1-106.6. Amended by Acts 2002, c. 473.
3.1-106.4 to 3.1-106.7. Amended by Acts 1995, c. 104.
3.1-106.9. Amended by Acts 1995, c. 104.
3.1-107 to 3.1-126. Repealed by Acts 1974, c. 647.
3.1-126.2. Repealed by Acts 1994, c. 649.
3.1-126.2:1. Amended by Acts 2002, c. 473.
3.1-126.3 to 3.1-126.11. Amended by Acts 1994, c. 649.
3.1-126.4. Amended by Acts 2002, c. 473.
3.1-126.5. Amended by Acts 1976, c. 91.
3.1-126.7. Amended by Acts 1986, c. 615.
3.1-126.10. Amended by Acts 1986, c. 615.
3.1-126.12. Repealed by Acts 1994, c. 649.
3.1-126.13. Repealed by Acts 1994, c. 649.
3.1-127 to 3.1-134. Repealed by Acts 1972, c. 145.
3.1-135 to 3.1-157. Repealed by Acts 1980, c. 291.
3.1-158 to 3.1-169. Repealed by Acts 1984, c. 367.
3.1-170 to 3.1-176. Repealed by Acts 1984, c. 465.
3.1-178 to 3.1-188. Repealed by Acts 1992, cc. 275, 491.
3.1-188.20. Amended by Acts 1980, c. 291.
3.1-188.21. Amended by Acts 1980, c. 291; Acts 2000, c. 730.
3.1-188.22. Amended by Acts 1980, c. 291.
3.1-188.23. Amended by Acts 1980, c. 291.
3.1-188.25. Amended by Acts 1980, c. 291.
3.1-188.26. Amended by Acts 1980, c. 291.
3.1-188.27. Amended by Acts 1990, c. 370; Acts 2000, c. 730.
3.1-188.29. Amended by Acts 1980, c. 291.
3.1-188.31. Repealed by Acts 1980, c. 291.

Sec.
3.1-188.32. Amended by Acts 1988, c. 552.
3.1-188.36. Amended by Acts 1988, c. 552.
3.1-189 to 3.1-249.26. Repealed by Acts 1989, c. 575.
3.1-249.27. Amended by Acts 1993, c. 773; Acts 1995, c. 103.
3.1-249.28. Amended by Acts 1992, c. 121.
3.1-249.29. Amended by Acts 1991, c. 333.
3.1-249.31. Amended by Acts 1992, c. 114.
3.1-249.33. Amended by Acts 1992, c. 289.
3.1-249.35. Amended by Acts 1993, c. 773.
3.1-249.45. Amended by Acts 1992, c. 114.
3.1-249.46. Amended by Acts 1993, c. 773.
3.1-249.47. Amended by Acts 1993, c. 773.
3.1-249.49. Amended by Acts 1993, c. 773.
3.1-249.51. Amended by Acts 1993, c. 773; Acts 1995, c. 103.
3.1-249.53. Amended by Acts 1993, c. 773; Acts 1995, c. 103.
3.1-249.54. Amended by Acts 1993, c. 773.
3.1-249.55. Amended by Acts 1993, c. 773.
3.1-249.58. Amended by Acts 1993, c. 773.
3.1-249.63=c1 Amended by Acts 1993, c. 773.
3.1-249.64=c1 Amended by Acts 1993, c. 773.
3.1-249.70=c1 Amended by Acts 1993, c. 773.
3.1-249.77. Amended by Acts 1993, c. 773.
3.1-250 to 3.1-261. Repealed by Acts 1984, c. 466.
3.1-263 to 3.1-275.1. Amended by Acts 1994, c. 577.
3.1-276. Amended by Acts 1980, c. 413; Acts 1985, c. 448; Acts 1992, c. 121.
3.1-277. Amended by Acts 1973, c. 401; Acts 1980, c. 413.
3.1-283. Amended by Acts 1980, c. 413.
3.1-287. Amended by Acts 1985, c. 448.
3.1-290. Amended by Acts 1972, c. 98; Acts 1978, c. 540; Acts 1985, c. 448; Acts 2001, c. 322.
3.1-291. Amended by Acts 1978, c. 540.
3.1-292. Amended by Acts 1978, c. 540; Acts 1980, c. 308.
3.1-295. Amended by Acts 1978, c. 540.
3.1-296.1 to 3.1-296.10:1. Repealed by Acts 1984, c. 14.
3.1-296.12, 3.1-296.13. Amended by Acts 1996, c. 266.
3.1-297. Amended by Acts 1978, c. 540.
3.1-308. Amended by Acts 1985, c. 448.
3.1-309. Amended by Acts 1978, c. 540; Acts 1985, c. 448.
3.1-311. Amended by Acts 1973, c. 261; Acts 1992, c. 375.
3.1-315. Amended by Acts 1978, c. 540.
3.1-319. Amended by Acts 1985, c. 448; Acts 2002, c. 57.
3.1-320. Amended by Acts 1978, c. 540; Acts 1985, c. 448; Acts 1994, c. 964.
3.1-321. Amended by Acts 1994, c. 964.
3.1-325. Amended by Acts 1978, c. 540.
3.1-328. Amended by Acts 1970, c. 408; Acts 1974, c. 74; Acts 1980, c. 87; Acts 1990, c. 523.

Sec.
3.1-329. Amended by Acts 2002, c. 57.
3.1-330. Amended by Acts 2002, c. 57.
3.1-331. Amended by Acts 2002, c. 57.
3.1-332. Amended by Acts 1978, c. 540.
3.1-336.2. Amended by Acts 2004, c. 1029.
3.1-336.3. Amended by Acts 2004, c. 1029.
3.1-360.1 to 3.1-360.8. Repealed by Acts 1983, c. 110.
3.1-362. Repealed by Acts 2004, c. 58.
3.1-363. Amended by Acts 1972, c. 741.
3.1-376. Amended by Acts 1997, c. 122.
3.1-378. Repealed by Acts 1997, c. 122.
3.1-382.1. Amended by Acts 1979. c. 358.
3.1-385.1 to 3.1-385.8. Repealed by Acts 2003, c. 952.
3.1-388. Amended by Acts 1986, c. 200.
3.1-394. Amended by Acts 1996, c. 728; Acts 2002, c. 218.
3.1-395. Amended by Acts 1988, c. 110.
3.1-396. Amended by Acts 1996, c. 728.
3.1-398. Amended by Acts 1977, c. 440; Acts 2003, c. 695; Acts 2004, c. 802.
3.1-398.1. Amended by Acts 2003, c. 420; Acts 2004, c. 953.
3.1-399. Amended by Acts 2003, c. 420.
3.1-401. Amended by Acts 1972, c. 741.
3.1-403. Amended by Acts 1972, c. 741.
3.1-410. Amended by Acts 1978, c. 702.
3.1-418. Amended by Acts 2002, c. 185.
3.1-418.1. Amended by Acts 1987, c. 322; Acts 1990, cc. 211, 255, 303; Acts 1998, c. 641.
3.1-419. Amended by Acts 2002, c. 185.
3.1-426. Amended by Acts 1974, c. 467; Acts 1984, c. 444; Acts 1985, c. 397; Acts 2004, c. 57.
3.1-426.1. Amended by Acts 1974, c. 467; Acts 1984, c. 355.
3.1-427. Amended by Acts 1980, c. 728.
3.1-428. Amended by Acts 1979, c. 417.
3.1-436. Repealed by Acts 1974, c. 467.
3.1-437. Amended by Acts 1974, c. 467.
3.1-441. Amended by Acts 1974, c. 467.
3.1-448. Amended by Acts 1996, c. 573; Acts 1996, c. 573.
3.1-450. Amended by Acts 1996, c. 573; Acts 1996, c. 573.
3.1-452. Amended by Acts 1974, c. 467; Acts 1986, c. 408.
3.1-454 to 3.1-457. Repealed by Acts 1974, c. 467.
3.1-462. Repealed by Acts 1974, c. 467.
3.1-463 to 3.1-530. Repealed by Acts 1970, c. 49.
3.1-530.1. Amended by Acts 2001, c. 523.
3.1-530.2. Amended by Acts 2001, c. 523.
3.1-530.10. Amended by Acts 2001, c. 523.
3.1-531. Repealed by Acts 1996, c. 723.
3.1-533. Amended by Acts 1996, c. 723; Acts 2000, c. 993.

Sec.
3.1-539. Amended by Acts 1996, c. 723.
3.1-543. Repealed by Acts 1996, c. 723.
3.1-546 to 3.1-562. Repealed by Acts 1970, c. 48.
3.1-562.6. Amended by Acts 1978, c. 722; Acts 1996, c. 722.
3.1-563. Amended by Acts 1996, c. 724.
3.1-571. Repealed by Acts 1996, c. 724.
3.1-572 to 3.1-581. Repealed by Acts 1988, c. 533.
3.1-582 to 3.1-587. Repealed by Acts 1982, c. 245.
3.1-588 to 3.1-610. Repealed by Acts 1972, c. 499.
3.1-610.1. Amended by Acts 1982, c. 100.
3.1-610.15. Amended by Acts 1982, c. 100.
3.1-610.25. Amended by Acts 1978, c. 267; Acts 1992, c. 121.
3.1-610.26. Amended by Acts 1978, c. 267.
3.1-610.26:1. Amended by Acts 2004, c. 201.
3.1-610.27. Amended by Acts 1978, c. 267.
3.1-610.28. Amended by Acts 1978, c. 267.
3.1-611. Amended by Acts 1999, c. 793.
3.1-612. Amended by Acts 1999, c. 793.
3.1-613. Amended by Acts 1999, c. 793.
3.1-614. Amended by Acts 1999, c. 793.
3.1-615. Amended by Acts 1999, c. 793.
3.1-616. Amended by Acts 1999, c. 793.
3.1-617. Amended by Acts 1999, c. 793.
3.1-618. Amended by Acts 1979, c. 531; Acts 1985, c. 448; Acts 1999, c. 793; Acts 2004, c. 214.
3.1-619, 3.1-620. Repealed by Acts 1999, c. 793.
3.1-621. Amended by Acts 1972, c. 226; Acts 1978, c. 473; Acts 1982, c. 415; Acts 1999, c. 793.
3.1-622 to 3.1-624. Amended by Acts 1999, c. 793.
3.1-626. Amended by Acts 1999, c. 793; Acts 2004, c. 214.
3.1-627. Amended by Acts 1999, c. 793.
3.1-628. Repealed by Acts 1999, c. 793.
3.1-629, 3.1-630. Amended by Acts 1999, c. 793.
3.1-631. Repealed by Acts 1999, c. 793.
3.1-632. Amended by Acts 1974, c. 601; Acts 1982, c. 415; Acts 1999, c. 793.
3.1-633. Repealed by Acts 1999, c. 793.
3.1-634. Amended by Acts 1974, c. 601; Acts 1985, c. 448; Acts 1999, c. 793; Acts 2004, c. 214.
3.1-634.1. Amended by Acts 2004, c. 214.
3.1-635. Amended by Acts 1978, c. 540; Acts 1999, c. 793; Acts 2004, c. 214.
3.1-636. Amended by Acts 1999, c. 793.
3.1-637 to 3.1-646. Repealed by Acts 1999, c. 793.
3.1-646.01 to 3.1-646.09. Repealed by Acts 2004, c. 214.
3.1-647. Amended by Acts 1985, c. 448.
3.1-648. Amended by Acts 1978, c. 540; Acts 1985, c. 448.

Sec.
3.1-649. Amended by Acts 1978, c. 540.
3.1-650. Amended by Acts 1978, c. 540.
3.1-657. Amended by Acts 1973, c. 200; Acts 1983, c. 177; Acts 1995, c. 160.
3.1-660. Amended by Acts 1977, c. 396.
3.1-662. Amended by Acts 1978, c. 540.
3.1-666 to 3.1-684. Repealed by Acts 2004, c. 212.
3.1-684.9. Amended by Acts 1982, c. 603.
3.1-684.10. Amended by Acts 1982, c. 603.
3.1-684.12. Amended by Acts 1982, c. 603; Acts 1990, c. 183.
3.1-684.13. Amended by Acts 1974, c. 297; Acts 1978, c. 540; Acts 1985, c. 448; Acts 1987, c. 476.
3.1-684.14. Amended by Acts 1982, c. 603; Acts 1987, c. 476; Acts 1990, c. 183; Acts 1992, c. 124.
3.1-684.16. Amended by Acts 1977, c. 396.
3.1-684.17. Amended by Acts 1978, c. 540.
3.1-684.32. Amended by Acts 1985, c. 448.
3.1-684.43, 3.1-684.44. Amended by Acts 1992, c. 776.
3.1-684.46. Amended by Acts 1992, c. 776.
3.1-684.53. Amended by Acts 1992, c. 776.
3.1-685. Amended by Acts 1978, c. 396; Acts 1993, c. 115.
3.1-686. Amended by Acts 1993, c. 115.
3.1-687. Amended by Acts 1993, c. 115.
3.1-688. Amended by Acts 1993, c. 115.
3.1-690. Amended by Acts 1993, c. 115.
3.1-692. Amended by Acts 1975, c. 505; Acts 1977, c. 21.
3.1-699.1. Amended by Acts 1985, c. 354.
3.1-701. Amended by Acts 1968, c. 306.
3.1-704. Amended by Acts 1976, c. 164.
3.1-709. Amended by Acts 1979, c. 389.
3.1-712. Amended by Acts 1976, c. 164; Acts 1986, c. 615.
3.1-713. Amended by Acts 1979, c. 389.
3.1-716. Amended by Acts 1968, c. 306; Acts 1979, c. 389.
3.1-718. Amended by Acts 1979, c. 389.
3.1-721. Amended by Acts 1979, c. 389.
3.1-722.1. Amended by Acts 1970, c. 400; Acts 1972, c. 646; Acts 1994, c. 340.
3.1-722.2, 3.1-722.3. Amended by Acts 1994, c. 340.
3.1-722.4. Amended by Acts 1972, c. 646; Acts 1977, c. 21; Acts 1994, c. 340.
3.1-722.5. Amended by Acts 1994, c. 340.
3.1-722.6. Repealed by Acts 1994, c. 340.
3.1-722.7, 3.1-722.8. Amended by Acts 1994, c. 340.
3.1-722.9. Amended by Acts 1970, c. 400; Acts 1972, c. 646; Acts 1994, c. 340.
3.1-722.10. Amended by Acts 1972, c. 646; Acts 1980, c. 277; Acts 1994, c. 340.
3.1-722.11 to 3.1-722.13. Amended by Acts 1994, c. 340.
3.1-722.16. Amended by Acts 1982, c. 187.
3.1-722.19. Amended by Acts 1982, c. 187.

Sec.
3.1-722.20. Amended by Acts 1982, c. 187.
3.1-722.20:1. Amended by Acts 1985, c. 354.
3.1-722.21. Amended by Acts 1982, c. 187.
3.1-722.22. Amended by Acts 1975, c. 531; Acts 1982, c. 187.
3.1-722.23. Amended by Acts 1982, c. 187.
3.1-722.24. Amended by Acts 1975, c. 85; Acts 1982, c. 187.
3.1-723. Amended by Acts 1978, c. 396.
3.1-726. Amended by Acts 1977, c. 299; Acts 1981, c. 130; Acts 1991, c. 294.
3.1-722.27. Amended by Acts 1982, c. 187.
3.1-722.28. Amended by Acts 1982, c. 187.
3.1-731. Amended by Acts 1981, c. 130.
3.1 733. Amended by Acts 1977, c. 395; Acts 1981, c. 130.
3.1-735. Amended by Acts 1993, c. 174; Acts 2001, cc. 311, 333.
3.1-736. Amended by Acts 1977, c. 395.
3.1-737. Amended by Acts 1977, c. 395.
3.1-738. Amended by Acts 1977, c. 395.
3.1-739. Repealed by Acts 1983, c. 71.
3.1-740. Amended by Acts 2002, c. 185.
3.1-741. Amended by Acts 2002, c. 185.
3.1-742. Repealed by Acts 1992, c. 101.
3.1-743. Amended by Acts 1992, c. 101.
3.1-744. Repealed by Acts 1992, c. 101.
3.1-745. Amended by Acts 1992, c. 101.
3.1-746. Amended by Acts 1972, c. 90; Acts 1992, c. 101.
3.1-747, 3.1-748. Amended by Acts 1992, c. 101.
3.1-754. Amended by Acts 1968, c. 49; Acts 1982, c. 284.
3.1-756. Amended by Acts 1968, c. 49.
3.1-758. Amended by Acts 1970, c. 619; Acts 1994, c. 743.
3.1-759. Amended by Acts 1970, c. 619.
3.1-760. Amended by Acts 1970, c. 619.
3.1-761. Amended by Acts 1970, c. 619.
3.1-762. Amended by Acts 1970, c. 619.
3.1-763. Amended by Acts 1970, c. 619.
3.1-763.6. Amended by Acts 1985, c. 448.
3.1-763.7. Amended by Acts 1978, c. 540; Acts 1979, c. 72; Acts 1993, c. 448.
3.1-763.9. Amended by Acts 1979, c. 72; Acts 1982, c. 99.
3.1-763.10. Amended by Acts 1977, c. 396.
3.1-763.11. Amended by Acts 1978, c. 540.
3.1-763.13. Repealed by Acts 1979, c. 72.
3.1-763.15. Amended by Acts 1972, c. 120.
3.1-764. Amended by Acts 1968, c. 142.
3.1-765. Amended by Acts 1968, c. 142.
3.1-767. Amended by Acts 1968, c. 142.
3.1-768. Amended by Acts 1968, c. 142.
3.1-769. Amended by Acts 1968, c. 142.
3.1-770.3. Amended by Acts 1986, c. 615.
3.1-776. Repealed by Acts 1977, c. 598.
3.1-777 to 3.1-796. Repealed by Acts 1980, c. 316.
3.1-796.013. Amended by Acts 1985, c. 448.
3.1-796.1. Amended by Acts 1980, c. 316.

Sec.
3.1-796.2. Amended by Acts 1980, c. 316.
3.1-796.3. Amended by Acts 1980, c. 316.
3.1-796.4. Amended by Acts 1980, c. 316.
3.1-796.5. Amended by Acts 1980, c. 316.
3.1-796.6. Amended by Acts 1980, c. 316; Acts 1982, c. 172.
3.1-796.9. Amended by Acts 1980, c. 316.
3.1-796.11:2. Amended by Acts 1985, c. 448.
3.1-796.11:3. Amended by Acts 1982, c. 172; Acts 1985, c. 173; Acts 1993, c. 809.
3.1-796.11:4. Amended by Acts 1982, c. 172; Acts 1984, c. 550; Acts 1993, c. 809.
3.1-796.11:5. Amended by Acts 1993, c. 809.
3.1-796.11:6. Amended by Acts 1993, c. 809.
3.1-796.11:7. Amended by Acts 1993, c. 809.
3.1-796.11:8. Amended by Acts 1993, c. 809.
3.1-796.11:10. Amended by Acts 1993, c. 809.
3.1-796.13. Amended by Acts 1983, c. 375; Acts 1985, c. 448.
3.1-796.15. Amended by Acts 1983, c. 375; Acts 1985, c. 448.
3.1-796.16 to 3.1-796.20. Amended by Acts 1983, c. 375.
3.1-796.25. Amended by Acts 1983, c. 375; Act 1987, c. 237.
3.1-796.26. Amended by Acts 1978, c. 540; Acts 1983, c. 375; Act 1987, c. 237.
3.1-796.27. Amended by Acts 1985, c. 237.
3.1-796.29. Amended by Acts 1975, c. 283.
3.1-796.30. Amended by Acts 1975, c. 283.
3.1-796.39 to 3.1-796.65. Repealed by Acts 1984, c. 492.
3.1-796.66. Amended by Acts 1988, c. 538; Acts 1991, c. 348; Acts 1993, cc. 174, 959; Acts 1995, c. 610; Acts 1998, c. 817; Acts 2002, cc. 351, 500, 787; Acts 2003, c. 1007.
3.1-796.67:2. Amended by Acts 1998, c. 817; Acts 2002, c. 787; Acts 2003, c. 1007.
3.1-796.68. Amended by Acts 1991, c. 348; Acts 1993, c. 174; Acts 1996, c. 249; Acts 1998, c. 817; Acts 2002, c. 787; Acts 2003, c. 1007.
3.1-796.69. Amended by Acts 1993, c. 174.
3.1-796.70. Amended by Acts 1993, c. 174; Acts 1995, c. 625.
3.1-796.71. Amended by Acts 1993, c. 174.
3.1-796.72. Amended by Acts 1998, c. 817.
3.1-796.73. Amended by Acts 1993, c. 174; Acts 2002, cc. 351, 787; Acts 2003, c. 1007.
3.1-796.74. Amended by Acts 1993, cc. 174, 959.
3.1-796.75. Amended by Acts 1993, c. 174.
3.1-796.76. Amended by Acts 1999, c. 620.
3.1-796.83:1. Amended by Acts 1996, c. 249.
3.1-796.83:2. Amended by Acts 1998, c. 817.
3.1-796.85. Amended by Acts 1988, c. 538; Acts 1993, c. 817.

Sec.
3.1-796.86. Amended by Acts 1991, c. 77; Acts 1993, c. 817.
3.1-796.87. Amended by Acts 1993, c. 817; Acts 1994, c. 108.
3.1-796.88. Amended by Acts 1990, c. 365; Acts 1993, c. 817.
3.1-796.89. Amended by Acts 1993, c. 817.
3.1-796.90. Amended by Acts 1993, c. 817; Acts 1998, c. 394.
3.1-796.91. Amended by Acts 1993, c. 817.
3.1-796.92. Amended by Acts 1990, c. 365; Acts 1993, c. 817; Acts 1998, c. 817.
3.1-796.93:1. Amended by Acts 1994, c. 115; Acts 1997, cc. 582, 892; Acts 1998, c. 817; Acts 2000, cc. 11, 727; Acts 2003, cc. 785, 841.
3.1-796.94. Amended by Acts 1993, c. 959; Acts 1994, cc. 115, 630; Acts 1995, c. 834; Acts 1997, c. 597; Acts 1998, c. 817.
3.1-796.94:1. Amended by Acts 1999, c. 663.
3.1-796.96. Amended by Acts 1993, c. 817; Acts 1994, c. 936; Acts 1995, c. 496; Acts 1997, c. 159; Acts 1998, c. 817; Acts 1999, cc. 627, 672; Acts 2000, c. 1010; Acts 2002, cc. 53, 208, 787; Acts 2003, c. 1007.
3.1-796.96:2. Amended by Acts 2002, cc. 53, 208, 284, 787; Acts 2003, cc. 770, 1007.
3.1-796.96:3, 3.1-796.96:4. Repealed by Acts 2003, c. 1007.
3.1-796.96:5. Amended by Acts 2003, cc. 770, 1007.
3.1-796.97. Amended by Acts 1993, c. 817; Acts 1994, c. 936; Acts 1995, c. 496; Acts 1996, c. 351; Acts 1997, c. 159; Acts 1998, c. 817; Acts 1999, cc. 627, 672; Acts 2000, c. 1010; Acts 2002, cc. 53, 208, 787; Acts 2003, c. 1007.
3.1-796.97:1. Amended by Acts 1992, c. 294; Acts 1994, c. 636; Acts 1996, c. 351; Acts 1998, c. 817.
3.1-796.98. Amended by Acts 1988, c. 538; Acts 1991, c. 380; Acts 2003, c. 479.
3.1-796.100. Amended by Acts 2001, c. 674.
3.1-796.101. Amended by Acts 1993, c. 959; Acts 1998, c. 817.
3.1-796.102. Amended by Acts 1998, c. 817.
3.1-796.104. Amended by Acts 1998, c. 817; Acts 2002, c. 418; Acts 2003, c. 804; Acts 2004, c. 181.
3.1-796.104:1. Amended by Acts 2004, c. 181.
3.1-796.105. Amended by Acts 1991, c. 65; Acts 1993, c. 601; Acts 1997, c. 286; Acts 1998, c. 817.
3.1-796.106. Amended by Acts 1998, c. 817; Acts 2003, c. 858; Acts 2004, c. 181
3.1-796.106:1. Amended by Acts 1999, c. 376.
3.1-796.106:2. Amended by Acts 2003, c. 858.
3.1-796.107. Amended by Acts 1991, c. 451; Acts 1993, c. 174; Acts 1998, c. 817.
3.1-796.108. Amended by Acts 1994, c. 387; Acts 1998, c. 817.
3.1-796.109. Repealed by Acts 1998, c. 817.
3.1-796.110. Amended by Acts 1998, c. 817.
3.1-796.111. Amended by Acts 1998, c. 817.
3.1-796.112. Amended by Acts 1991, c. 121; Acts 1998, c. 817.
3.1-796.113. Amended by Acts 1994, c. 168; Acts 1998, c. 817.
3.1-796.114. Amended by Acts 1998, c. 817.
3.1-796.115. Amended by Acts 1990, c. 322; Acts 1992, c. 123; Acts 1993, c. 119; Acts 1994, c. 387; Acts 1998, c. 817; Acts 1999, c. 113; Acts 2002, c. 500.
3.1-796.116. Amended by Acts 1990, c. 222; Acts 1993, c. 977; Acts 1998, c. 817.
3.1-796.117. Amended by Acts 1993, c. 977; Acts 1998, c. 817.
3.1-796.118. Amended by Acts 1992, c. 461; Acts 1998, c. 817.
3.1-796.119. Amended by Acts 1991, c. 348; Acts 1997, c. 159; Acts 1998, c. 817.
3.1-796.120. Amended by Acts 1993, c. 601; Acts 1996, c. 213; Acts 1997, c. 286; Acts 2000, c. 1010;Acts 2002, cc. 53, 208, 284; Acts 2003, c. 770.
3.1-796.121. Amended by Acts 1993, c. 174; Acts 1998, c. 817.
3.1-796.122. Amended by Acts 1992, c. 177; Acts 1998, c. 817; Acts 1999, cc. 209, 620, 645; Acts 2002, cc. 351, 500, 583, 613; Acts 2003, cc. 787, 788; Acts 2004, c. 217.
3.1-796.123. Repealed by Acts 2002, c. 500.
3.1-796.124. Amended by Acts 1998, c. 817; Acts 1999, c. 113; Acts 2003, c. 857.
3.1-796.125. Amended by Acts 2003, c. 857.
3.1-796.126:1. Amended by Acts 1998, c. 817.
3.1-796.126:3. Amended by Acts 1999, cc. 627, 672.
3.1-796.126:7. Amended by Acts 1998, c. 817; Acts 2002, c. 787.
3.1-796.126:8. Amended by Acts 1998, c. 817.
3.1-796.126:10. Amended by Acts 1998, c. 817.
3.1-796.126:11. Amended by Acts 1998, c. 817.
3.1-796.127. Amended by Acts 1988, c. 537; Acts 1998, c. 817.
3.1-796.128. Amended by Acts 1993, cc. 174, 775, 817; Acts 1998, c. 817.
3.1-796.130. Amended by Acts 2003, c. 876.
3.1-796.132. Amended by Acts 2003, c. 876.
3.1-796.133. Amended by Acts 2003, c. 876.
3.1-797 to 3.1-828. Repealed by Acts 1994, c. 743.
3.1-829 to 3.1-834. Amended by Acts 1994, c. 910.

Sec.
3.1-835. Amended by Acts 1972, c. 741; Acts 1994, c. 743.
3.1-837. Amended by Acts 1994, c. 910.
3.1-839. Amended by Acts 1994, c. 910.
3.1-842, 3.1-843. Amended by Acts 1994, c. 910.
3.1-844=c1 Amended by Acts 1972, c. 741.
3.1-846 to 3.1-866. Repealed by Acts 1968, c. 140.
3.1-867. Amended by Acts 1968, c. 140.
3.1-868. Amended by Acts 1968, c. 140.
3.1-869, 3.1-870. Repealed by Acts 1968, c. 140.
3.1-871. Amended by Acts 1968, c. 140.
3.1-872 to 3.1-884. Repealed by Acts 1966, c. 598.
3.1-884.1 to 3.1-884.16. Repealed by Acts 1970, c. 290.
3.1-884.20. Amended by Acts 1991, c. 344.
3.1-884.30. Amended by Acts 1986, c. 615.
3.1-885 to 3.1-898. Repealed by Acts 1983, c. 294.
3.1-907 to 3.1-917. Repealed by Acts 1979, c. 63.
3.1-919. Amended by Acts 1991, c. 605; Acts 1993, c. 604.
3.1-920. Amended by Acts 1993, c. 604.
3.1-921. Repealed by Acts 1993, c. 604.
3.1-922. Amended by Acts 1993, c. 604.
3.1-923. Amended by Acts 1993, c. 604.
3.1-924. Amended by Acts 1993, c. 604.
3.1-925. Amended by Acts 1993, c. 604.
3.1-926. Amended by Acts 1993, c. 604.
3.1-927. Amended by Acts 1993, c. 604.
3.1-928. Amended by Acts 1993, c. 604.
3.1-932. Amended by Acts 1993, c. 604.
3.1-933. Amended by Acts 1986, c. 615; Acts 1993, c. 604.
3.1-936. Amended by Acts 1991, c. 605; Acts 1993, c. 604.
3.1-937. Amended by Acts 1987, c. 46.
3.1-942. Amended by Acts 1993, c. 604.
3.1-943. Amended by Acts 1993, c. 604.
3.1-944. Amended by Acts 1993, c. 604.
3.1-947. Amended by Acts 1993, c. 604.
3.1-948. Repealed by Acts 1993, c. 604.
3.1-949. Amended by Acts 1993, c. 604.
3.1-949.1. Amended by Acts 1993, c. 604.
3.1-949.2. Amended by Acts 1992, c. 242.
3.1-950. Amended by Acts 1993, c. 604.
3.1-951 to 3.1-954. Repealed by Acts 1993, c. 604.
3.1-955. Repealed by Acts 1993, c. 604.
3.1-956. Amended by Acts 1993, c. 604.
3.1-957. Amended by Acts 1993, c. 604.
3.1-958. Amended by Acts 1993, c. 604.
3.1-962. Repealed by Acts 1993, c. 604.
3.1-962.1. Amended by Acts 1993, c. 604.
3.1-965. Amended by Acts 1993, c. 604.
3.1-966. Repealed by Acts 1991, c. 605.
3.1-967. Amended by Acts 1993, c. 604.
3.1-972. Amended by Acts 1972, c. 824; Acts 1985, c. 24.

Sec.
3.1-991. Amended by Acts 1997, c. 179.
3.1-997. Amended by Acts 1973, c. 199; Acts 1997, c. 179.
3.1-1009. Repealed by Acts 1997, c. 179.
3.1-1021. Amended by Acts 1985, c. 326; Acts 1989, c. 553; Acts 1990, c. 369.
3.1-1022. Amended by Acts 1985, c. 326.
3.1-1025. Amended by Acts 1985, c. 326; Acts 1989, c. 553; Acts 1990, c. 369.
3.1-1027. Amended by Acts 1983, c. 121.
3.1-1030. Amended by Acts 1985, c. 326.
3.1-1033. Amended by Acts 1989, c. 401.
3.1-1042. Amended by Acts 1989, c. 401.
3.1-1043. Amended by Acts 1985, c. 448; Acts 1987, c. 476.
3.1-1044. Amended by Acts 1987, c. 476.
3.1-1050 to 3.1-1056. Repealed by Acts 1996, c. 286.
3.1-1052. Amended by Acts 1986, c. 615.
3.1-1053. Amended by Acts 1993, c. 866.
3.1-1057 to 3.1-1064. Repealed by Acts 2004, cc. 89, 319.
3.1-1075. Amended by Acts 1996, c. 169; Acts 2004, c. 56.
3.1-1081. Amended by Acts 1999, c. 751.
3.1-1092 to 3.1-1094. Amended by Acts 1999, c. 751.
3.1-1098, 3.1-1099. Amended by Acts 1999, c. 751.
3.1-1104, 3.1-1105. Repealed by Acts 2004, c. 29.
3.1-1106. Amended by Acts 2002, cc. 482, 488.
3.1-1108. Amended by Acts 2003, c. 885.
3.1-1110. Amended by Acts 2002, c. 482, 488.
3.1-1111. Amended by Acts 2002, cc. 482, 488; Acts 2004, Sp. Sess. I, c. 1.
4-1 to 4-145. Repealed by Acts 1993, c. 866.
4.1-100. Amended by Acts 1995, cc. 497, 518, 661; Acts 1996, cc. 558, 604; Acts 1997, cc. 124, 425; Acts 1999, cc. 93, 171, 481; Acts 2000, cc. 786, 1037, 1052.
4.1-103. Amended by Acts 1996, c. 558.
4.1-104. Amended by Acts 1996, c. 558.
4.1-105. Amended by Acts 1997, cc. 812, 882; Acts 2000, cc. 880, 901.
4.1-111. Amended by Acts 1997, c. 40; Acts 1998, c. 301; Acts 1999, cc. 98, 641; Acts 2003, c. 856; Acts 2004, Sp. Sess. I, c. 1.
4.1-115. Amended by Acts 2004, c. 650.
4.1-118. Amended by Acts 1994, c. 179.
4.1-119. Amended by Acts 1996, c. 558; Acts 1999, c. 98.
4.1-120. Amended by Acts 2004, c. 1002.
4.1-123. Amended by Acts 2001, cc. 594, 783.
4.1-124. Amended by Acts 1995, c. 177; Acts 1997, c. 126.
4.1-126. Amended by Acts 2001, cc. 461, 845.
4.1-128. Amended by Acts 2000, cc. 381, 450.
4.1-132. Amended by Acts 2003, c. 564.

Sec.
4.1-200. Amended by Acts 1995, cc. 497, 518; Acts 2001, c. 117.
4.1-201. Amended by Acts 1995, cc. 253, 317; Acts 1997, c. 386; Acts 2000, c. 786; Acts 2003, c. 630; Acts 2004, c. 379.
4.1-203. Amended by Acts 1997, c. 37.
4.1-204. Amended by Acts 2003, cc. 1029, 1030.
4.1-206. Amended by Acts 1996, cc. 584, 596; Acts 1998, c. 489; Acts 1999, c. 325.
4.1-207. Amended by Acts 1998, cc. 77, 208; Acts 2000, cc. 786, 1037, 1052; Acts 2003, cc. 564, 629, 1029, 1030.
4.1-208. Amended by Acts 1994, c. 585; Acts 1995, cc. 497, 518, 544, 570; Acts 1996, cc. 443, 604; Acts 1997, cc. 489, 646, 662; Acts 2000, c. 1047; Acts 2003, cc. 329, 1029, 1030.
4.1-209. Amended by Acts 1994, c. 585; Acts 1995, cc. 544, 570; Acts 1996, cc. 443, 604; Acts 1997, c. 489; Acts 2001, c. 361; Acts 2002, c. 204; Acts 2003, cc. 329, 589, 1029, 1030; Acts 2004, c. 487.
4.1-210. Amended by Acts 1998, c. 535; Acts 2000, cc. 1036, 1047, 1051; Acts 2001, cc. 461, 845; Acts 2004, c. 487.
4.1-212. Amended by Acts 1994, cc. 825, 826; Acts 1997, c. 801; Acts 2003, c. 564.
4.1-215. Amended by Acts 1995, cc. 456, 630; Acts 2003, cc. 1029, 1030.
4.1-219. Amended by Acts 2000, cc. 1037, 1052; Acts 2003, c. 631.
4.1-221.1. Amended by Acts 1996, cc. 584, 596.
4.1-222. Amended by Acts 1997, c. 801; Acts 2002, c. 420.
4.1-223. Amended by Acts 2000, c. 823.
4.1-224. Amended by Acts 2000, c. 147.
4.1-225. Amended by Acts 1996, c. 404; Acts 1997, c. 801; Acts 2002, c. 352; Acts 2003, c. 594.
4.1-227. Amended by Acts 1995, cc. 549, 563; Acts 1996, c. 309; Acts 1999, c. 648.
4.1-230. Amended by Acts 1994, c. 825; Acts 1996, cc. 584, 596; Acts 1998, c. 535; Acts 1999, cc. 112, 756; Acts 2003, cc. 1029, 1030; Acts 2004, cc. 382, 487; Acts 2004, Sp. Sess. I, c. 4.
4.1-231. Amended by Acts 1995, cc. 497, 518; Acts 1996, cc. 584, 596, 604; Acts 1998, cc. 489, 535; Acts 1999, c. 325; Acts 2000, cc. 1036, 1037, 1047, 1051, 1052; Acts 2001, cc. 461, 845; Acts 2003, cc. 1029, 1030; Acts 2004, c. 487; Acts 2004, Sp. Sess. I, c. 4.

Sec.
4.1-233. Amended by Acts 2004, cc. 384, 487.
4.1-238. Amended by Acts 2003, c. 564.
4.1-233. Amended by Acts 1995, cc. 497, 518; Acts 1996, cc. 584, 596, 604; Acts 1998, cc. 489, 535; Acts 1999, c. 325; Acts 2000, cc. 1036, 1047, 1051; Acts 2001, cc. 461, 845.
4.1-305. Amended by Acts 1995, c. 374; Acts 1996, cc. 626, 730; Acts 2000, c. 325; Acts 2002, c. 338; Acts 2003, cc. 845, 849; Acts 2004, cc. 322, 461.
4.1-307. Amended by Acts 1997, c. 487.
4.1-309. Amended by Acts 1994, c. 844; Acts 1997, cc. 784, 837.
4.1-310. Amended by Acts 1994, c. 826; Acts 1995, cc. 253, 317; Acts 2003, cc. 1029, 1030.
4.1-320. Amended by Acts 1995, c. 222.
4.1-322. Amended by Acts 1996, c. 717.
4.1-324. Amended by Acts 1998, c. 238.
4.1-325. Amended by Acts 2000, c. 780; Acts 2002, c. 105; Acts 2003, c. 856; Acts 2004, c. 913.
4.1-325.2. Amended by Acts 2003, c. 856.
4.1-338. Amended by Acts 1995, c. 196.
4.1-352. Amended by Acts 2003, c. 130.
4.1-353. Amended by Acts 1997, c. 418.
4.1-401. Amended by Acts 1997, c. 801.
4.1-406. Amended by Acts 1996, c. 3.
4.1-407. Amended by Acts 1997, c. 183.
4.1-500. Amended by Acts 1997, c. 801.
4.1-505. Amended by Acts 1996, c. 3.
4.1-506. Amended by Acts 1997, c. 183.
5-1 to 5-61. Repealed by Acts 1966, c. 576.
5.1-1. Amended by Acts 1970, c. 717; Acts 1975, c. 561; Acts 1979, c. 272; Acts 1980, c. 721; Acts 1988, c. 588.
5.1-1.1. Amended by Acts 1984, c. 720.
5.1-1.4. Amended by Acts 2002, c. 94.
5.1-1.6. Amended by Acts 1991, c. 126; Acts 1992, c. 108.
5.1-2. Repealed by Acts 1979, c. 272.
5.1-2.1. Amended by Acts 1980, c. 750; Acts 1985, c. 448.
5.1-2.2. Amended by Acts 1980, c. 306; Acts 1984, c. 720.
5.1-2.4. Repealed by Acts 1980, c. 728.
5.1-2.5. Amended by Acts 2003, c. 940.
5.1-2.7. Amended by Acts 1982, c. 563.
5.1-2.10. Amended by Acts 1982, c. 563.
5.1-2.16. Amended by Acts 1998, c. 480.
5.1-3. Repealed by Acts 1979, c. 272.
5.1-4. Amended by Acts 1970, c. 717; Acts 1979, c. 272.
5.1-5. Amended by Acts 1970, c. 717; Acts 1974, c. 431; Acts 1979, c. 272; Acts 1980, c. 721.
5.1-6. Repealed by Acts 1988, c. 45.
5.1-7. Amended by Acts 1979, c. 272; Acts 1980, c. 721; Acts 1981, c. 326; Acts

Sec.
1991, c. 126; Acts 1995, cc. 682, 690; Acts 1996, cc. 148, 303.
5.1-7.1. Repealed by Acts 1980, c. 56.
5.1-8. Repealed by Acts 1995, cc. 682, 690.
5.1-9. Amended by Acts 1979, c. 272.
5.1-9.1. Amended by Acts 1970, c. 717; Acts 1979, c. 272; Acts 1980, c. 721.
5.1-9.4. Repealed by Acts 1988, c. 45.
5.1-10. Repealed by Acts 1979, c. 272.
5.1-11. Amended by Acts 1980, c. 721.
5.1-12. Amended by Acts 1980, c. 721; Acts 1988, c. 45; Acts 1991, c. 535.
5.1-15. Amended by Acts 1988, c. 45.
5.1-18. Repealed by Acts 1988, c. 45.
5.1-19. Repealed by Acts 1988, c. 45.
5.1-21.1. Amended by Acts 1979, c. 272.
5.1-22. Amended by Acts 1983, c. 560; Acts 1991, c. 339.
5.1-23. Amended by Acts 1968, c. 737; Acts 1979, c. 394; Acts 1980, c. 721.
5.1-24. Amended by Acts 1979, c. 272.
5.1-25. Amended by Acts 1970, c. 717; Acts 1979, c. 272; Acts 1988, c. 45.
5.1-25.1. Amended by Acts 1979, c. 272; Acts 1981, c. 326; Acts 1989, cc. 202, 255; Acts 1990, c. 384.
5.1-25.2. Amended by Acts 1979, c. 272.
5.1-25.4. Amended by Acts 1979, c. 272.
5.1-26 to 5.1-30. Repealed by Acts 1979, c. 272.
5.1-31. Amended by Acts 1979, c. 272; Acts 1995, c. 453.
5.1-33. Amended by Acts 1971, Ex. Sess., c. 26.
5.1-34. Amended by Acts 2003, c. 940.
5.1-35. Amended by Acts 1989, c. 234.
5.1-36. Amended by Acts 1970, c. 717; Acts 1993, c. 81; Acts 1995, c. 453.
5.1-39. Amended by Acts 1980, c. 721.
5.1-40. Amended by Acts 1979, c. 272.
5.1-41. Amended by Acts 1979, c. 272; Acts 1989, c. 234; Acts 1993, c. 81.
5.1-44. Amended by Acts 1970, c. 717; Acts 1979, c. 272.
5.1-46. Amended by Acts 1979, c. 272; Acts 1988, c. 70.
5.1-47. Amended by Acts 1972, c. 374; Acts 1979, c. 272.
5.1-48. Repealed by Acts 1988, c. 70.
5.1-49. Amended by Acts 1979, c. 272.
5.1-50. Amended by Acts 1979, c. 272.
5.1-51. Reenacted without change by Acts 1970, c. 717; amended by Acts 1974, c. 388; Acts 1979, c. 272; Acts 1997, c. 423; Acts 1998, c. 480.
5.1-52. Amended by Acts 1970, c. 717; Acts 1979, c. 272; Acts 1998, c. 480.
5.1-53. Reenacted without change by Acts 1970, c. 717.
5.1-54. Repealed by Acts 1979, c. 272.
5.1-55. Amended by Acts 1979, c. 272.
5.1-56 to 5.1-76. Repealed by Acts 1980, c. 750.
5.1-77 to 5.1-82. Repealed by Acts 1980, c. 721.

Sec.
5.1-83 to 5.1-88. Repealed by Acts 1970, c. 707.
5.1-88.1. Amended by Acts 1979, c. 272; Acts 1988, c. 588.
5.1-88.2. Amended by Acts 1979, c. 272; Acts 1984, c. 169; Acts 1992, c. 810.
5.1-88.3. Amended by Acts 1979, c. 272.
5.1-88.4. Amended by Acts 1979, c. 272.
5.1-88.5. Repealed by Acts 1988, c. 588.
5.1-89. Amended by Acts 1979, c. 272; Acts 1980, c. 721.
5.1-103 to 5.1-106. Repealed by Acts 1980, c. 721.
5.1-116. Amended by Acts 1975, c. 211.
5.1-118. Amended by Acts 1975, c. 211.
5.1-125. Amended by Acts 1971, Ex. Sess., c. 1.
5.1-136. Amended by Acts 1971, Ex. Sess., c. 17.
5.1-141. Repealed by Acts 2001, c. 137.
5.1-145. Amended by Acts 1979, c. 394; Acts 1980, c. 721.
5.1-160. Amended by Acts 2003, c. 940.
6-1 to 6-585. Repealed by Acts 1966, c. 584.
6.1-1.1. Amended by Acts 1991, c. 127; Acts 2004, c. 165.
6.1-2. Amended by Acts 1974, c. 183; Acts 1987, cc. 556, 558; Acts 1988, c. 303; Acts 1993, cc. 419, 432; Acts 1994, c. 312.
6.1-2.1. Amended by Acts 1976, c. 658; Acts 1978, c. 683; Acts 1983, c. 491; Acts 1996, c. 16.
6.1-2.2 to 6.1-2.4. Repealed by Acts 1975, c. 448.
6.1-2.6. Repealed by Acts 1980, c. 730.
6.1-2.7. Amended by Acts 1979, c. 376; Acts 1987, c. 556; Acts 1989, c. 162.
6.1-2.9. Amended by Acts 1988, c. 155; Acts 1990, c. 7.
6.1-2.9:1. Amended by Acts 1990, c. 7.
6.1-2.9:3. Amended by Acts 1990, c. 7.
6.1-2.9:4. Amended by Acts 1990, c. 3; Acts 1996, c. 16.
6.1-2.10. Amended by Acts 1981, c. 86; Acts 1984, c. 118; Acts 1987, cc. 576, 577; Acts 1990, c. 340; Acts 1991, c. 254; Acts 1996, c. 883; Acts 1999, c. 109.
6.1-2.11. Amended by Acts 1993, c. 530.
6.1-2.12. Amended by Acts 1993, c. 530.
6.1-2.13. Amended by Acts 1987, c. 576; Acts 1992, c. 733; Acts 1996, c. 883.
6.1-2.13:1. Amended by Acts 1999, c. 109; Acts 2002, c. 599.
6.1-2.19. Amended by Acts 1998, cc. 69, 162, 736.
6.1-2.20. Amended by Acts 1998, cc. 69, 598; Acts 2002, c. 375.
6.1-2.21. Amended by Acts 1998, c. 69; Acts 2000, c. 549; Acts 2002, c. 464.
6.1-2.23. Amended by Acts 1998, c. 69; Acts 2001, cc. 316, 512.
6.1-2.25. Amended by Acts 2004, cc. 336, 597.

Sec.
6.1-2.27. Amended by Acts 2000, c. 549; Acts 2004, c. 597.
6.1-4. Amended by Acts 1974, c. 665; Acts 1987, c. 556; Acts 1993, c. 432.
6.1-5. Amended by Acts 1985, c. 544; Acts 1995, c. 301; Acts 1997, c. 801; Acts 1999, c. 835; Acts 2003, cc. 536, 558, 910.
6.1-5.1. Amended by Acts 1975, c. 81; Acts 1987, c. 556; Acts 1997, c. 111.
6.1-5.3. Amended by Acts 1987, c. 556; Acts 1988, c. 2.
6.1-6. Amended by Acts 1987, c. 556.
6.1-6.1. Amended by Acts 1996, c. 218.
6.1-8. Amended by Acts 1993, c. 182.
6.1-12. Amended by Acts 1970, c. 15.
6.1-13. Amended by Acts 1973, c. 454; Acts 1976, c. 658; Acts 1979, c. 57; Acts 1983, c. 193; Acts 1989, Sp. Sess., cc. 4, 7; Acts 1992, c. 460; Acts 1996, c. 26; Acts 1998, c. 18.
6.1-14. Amended by Acts 1980, c. 659.
6.1-16. Amended by Acts 1976, c. 658.
6.1-17. Amended by Acts 1984, c. 172; Acts 1993, c. 432; Acts 1996, c. 26; Acts 1997, c. 801.
6.1-18. Amended by Acts 1988, c. 348; Acts 1993, c. 866.
6.1-19. Amended by Acts 1974, c. 665.
6.1-20. Amended by Acts 1993, c. 432.
6.1-21. Amended by Acts 1992, c. 810; Acts 1993, c. 432; Acts 1994, c. 7.
6.1-22. Amended by Acts 1968, c. 59; Acts 1974, cc. 75, 665.
6.1-23. Amended by Acts 1972, c. 740; Acts 1974, c. 665; Acts 1993, c. 432.
6.1-24. Amended by Acts 1974, c. 665; Acts 1991, c. 252.
6.1-25 to 6.1-30. Repealed by Acts 1983, c. 454.
6.1-30.3. Amended by Acts 1984, c. 299.
6.1-31. Amended by Acts 1972, c. 739; Acts 1974, c. 665; Acts 1978, c. 14.
6.1-31.1. Amended by Acts 1974, c. 665.
6.1-31.2. Amended by Acts 1974, c. 665.
6.1-32. Amended by Acts 1974, c. 665.
6.1-32.2. Amended by Acts 1991, c. 282.
6.1-32.3. Amended by Acts 1991, c. 282; Acts 2004, c. 781.
6.1-32.5. Amended by Acts 1997, c. 801.
6.1-32.6. Amended by Acts 1987, c. 352.
6.1-32.8. Amended by Acts 1991, c. 282.
6.1-32.9. Amended by Acts 1987, c. 352; Acts 1991, c. 282.
6.1-32.11. Amended by Acts 1994, c. 524; Acts 1995, c. 140; Acts 1997, c. 801; Acts 2004, c. 781.
6.1-32.12. Amended by Acts 2001, c. 717.
6.1-32.14. Amended by Acts 1995, c. 140.
6.1-32.14:1. Repealed by Acts 1995, c. 140.
6.1-32.14:2. Amended by Acts 1995, c. 140.
6.1-32.15. Amended by Acts 1994, c. 7.

Sec.
6.1-32.18. Amended by Acts 1994, c. 524; Acts 1995, c. 140.
6.1-32.19. Amended by Acts 1995, c. 140; Acts 2004, c. 781.
6.1-32.20. Amended by Acts 1994, c. 524; Acts 1995, c. 140; Acts 2004, c. 781.
6.1-32.21. Amended by Acts 1997, c. 51.
6.1-32.22. Amended by Acts 1994, c. 105.
6.1-32.23. Amended by Acts 1995, c. 140.
6.1-32.25. Amended by Acts 1994, c. 6.
6.1-32.27. Amended by Acts 1995, c. 140.
6.1-32.28. Amended by Acts 1994, c. 524; Acts 1995, c. 140.
6.1-32.30. Repealed by Acts 1994, c. 7.
6.1-33. Amended by Acts 1993, c. 244; Acts 1996, c. 26.
6.1-39 to 6.1-39.2. Repealed by Acts 1986, c. 505.
6.1-39.3. Amended by Acts 1987, c. 352; Acts 1991, c. 322; Acts 1996, c. 26; Acts 1999, c. 545.
6.1-39.4. Repealed by Acts 1997, c. 141.
6.1-39.5. Amended by Acts 1997, c. 24.
6.1-40. Repealed by Acts 1978, c. 683.
6.1-41. Amended by Acts 1979, c. 59.
6.1-41.1. Amended by Acts 1978, c. 683; Acts 1987, c. 352.
6.1-43. Amended by Acts 1987, c. 423; Acts 1995, c. 301.
6.1-44. Amended by Acts 1970, c. 536; Acts 1987, c. 423.
6.1-45. Amended by Acts 1996, c. 268.
6.1-47. Amended by Acts 1970, c. 95; Acts 1995, c. 63; Acts 1996, cc. 25, 218.
6.1-48, 6.1-48.1. Amended by Acts 1992, c. 552; Acts 1994, c. 105.
6.1-49. Amended by Acts 1979, c. 58.
6.1-50. Amended by Acts 1979, c. 58.
6.1-51. Amended by Acts 1992, c. 136.
6.1-52. Amended by Acts 1981, c. 203.
6.1-54. Amended by Acts 1974, c. 665; Acts 1979, c. 52; Acts 1992, c. 365.
6.1-55. Repealed by Acts 1976, c. 658.
6.1-55.1. Repealed by Acts 1982, c. 328.
6.1-56. Amended by Acts 1976, c. 658; Acts 1979, c. 53; Acts 1992, c. 48; Acts 1995, c. 84.
6.1-57. Amended by Acts 1968, c. 61.
6.1-58.1. Amended by Acts 1978, c. 797; Acts 1988, c. 296; Acts 1993, c. 64; Acts 1997, c. 277; Acts 1999, c. 60; Acts 2001, c. 508; Acts 2003, cc. 536, 558.
6.1-58.2. Amended by Acts 1977, c. 190; Acts 1986, c. 638; Acts 1998, c. 48.
6.1-59. Amended by Acts 1988, c. 296.
6.1-60. Repealed by Acts 1982, c. 185.
6.1-60.1. Amended by Acts 1985, c. 339; Acts 1986, c. 269; Acts 1987, c. 297; Acts 1988, c. 464; Acts 1989, cc. 377, 650; Acts 1992, c. 366; Acts

Sec.

1993, c. 186; Acts 1994, c. 119; Acts 1996, c. 27.

6.1-61. Amended by Acts 1970, c. 42; Acts 1974, c. 557; Acts 1977, cc. 110, 466; Acts 1978, c. 683; Acts 1984, c. 134; Acts 1987, c. 494; Acts 1994, c. 290; Acts 2002, c. 186.

6.1-62. Amended by Acts 1976, c. 658; Acts 1978, c. 683; Acts 1987, c. 351; Acts 1995, c. 82; Acts 1996, c. 13; Acts 2004, c. 320.

6.1-63. Amended by Acts 1968, c. 549; Acts 1972, c. 189; Acts 1976, c. 487; Acts 1978, c. 624; Acts 1979, c. 375; Acts 1981, c. 271; Acts 1982, c. 263; Acts 1984, c. 133; Acts 1988, c. 170; Acts 1991, c. 160; Acts 1992, c. 68; Acts 1994, c. 501.

6.1-64. Amended by Acts 1970, c. 14; Acts 1972, c. 189; Acts 1981, c. 271; Acts 1991, c. 160; Acts 1995, c. 87.

6.1-65.1. Amended by Acts 1994, c. 501.

6.1-66. Amended by Acts 1970, c. 13; Acts 1976, c. 94; Acts 1980, c. 714; Acts 1991, c. 160; Acts 1994, c. 501.

6.1-67. Amended by Acts 1994, c. 7.

6.1-68. Amended by Acts 1974, c. 81; Acts 1976, c. 152; Acts 1989, c. 482; Acts 1994, c. 7.

6.1-68.1. Amended by Acts 1989, c. 482.

6.1-69. Amended by Acts 1976, c. 658; Acts 1981, c. 65.

6.1-70. Amended by Acts 1983, c. 487; Acts 1997, c. 801.

6.1-71. Amended by Acts 1968, c. 379; Acts 1972, c. 191; Acts 1976, c. 228; Acts 1980, c. 462; Acts 1986, c. 334; Acts 1994, c. 7; Acts 1997, c. 278; Acts 2002, c. 187, 220, 227.

6.1-72. Repealed by Acts 1979, c. 407.

6.1-73.1. Repealed by Acts 1988, c. 171.

6.1-76. Repealed by Acts 1991, c. 429.

6.1-77. Repealed by Acts 1979, c. 407.

6.1-78. Amended by Acts 1974, c. 665; Acts 1994, c. 7.

6.1-79. Amended by Acts 1982, c. 112; Acts 1994, c. 7.

6.1-80. Amended by Acts 1982, c. 411; Acts 1989, c. 376; Acts 1993, c. 182; Acts 1994, c. 7; Acts 1996, c. 306.

6.1-81. Amended by Acts 1983, c. 250; Acts 1986, c. 320.

6.1-84. Amended by Acts 1976, c. 658; Acts 1996, c. 80.

6.1-86. Amended by Acts 1976, c. 658.

6.1-87. Amended by Acts 1976, c. 658.

6.1-88. Amended by Acts 1976, c. 658; Acts 1978, c. 14.

6.1-90. Amended by Acts 1976, c. 658; Acts 1992, c. 224.

6.1-92. Amended by Acts 1976, c. 658.

6.1-93. Amended by Acts 1976, c. 658; Acts 1977, c. 257; Acts 1995, c. 561; Acts 1997, c. 407.

6.1-94. Amended by Acts 1972, c. 195; Acts 1973, c. 401; Acts 1974, c. 184; Acts 1997, c. 141; Acts 1998, c. 19. Acts 1976, cc. 554, 658; Acts 1981, c. 520; Acts 1982, c. 455; Acts 1987, c. 172; Acts 1992, c. 283; Acts 1997, c. 141; Acts 1998, c. 19.

6.1-95. Amended by Acts 1984, c. 343.

6.1-97. Repealed by Acts 1984, c. 343.

6.1-98. Repealed by Acts 1994, c. 312.

6.1-100, 6.1-100.1. Amended by Acts 1983, c. 507.

6.1-111. Amended by Acts 1992, c. 136; Acts 1994, c. 7.

6.1-112. Amended by Acts 1972, c. 187; Acts 1992, cc. 24, 136; Acts 2000, c. 56; Acts 2003, c. 592.

6.1-113. Amended by Acts 1987, c. 556; Acts 1992, c. 136; Acts 1994, c. 7.

6.1-114. Amended by Acts 1974, c. 665; Acts 1976, c. 658; Acts 1988, c. 555; Acts 1997, c. 142.

6.1-115 to 6.1-118. Repealed by Acts 1975, c. 589.

6.1-119. Amended by Acts 1991, c. 710.

6.1-121. Repealed by Acts 1981, c. 339.

6.1-122. Amended by Acts 1974, c. 665.

6.1-123. Amended by Acts 1974, c. 665.

6.1-125. Amended by Acts 1974, c. 665; Acts 1976, c. 658.

6.1-125.3. Amended by Acts 1982, c. 302; Acts 1983, c. 531; Acts 1987, c. 296; Acts 1988, cc. 368, 547; Acts 1990, c. 950.

6.1-125.5. Amended by Acts 1981, c. 53.

6.1-125.15. Amended by Acts 1999, c. 125.

6.1-126 to 6.1-193. Repealed by Acts 1972, c. 796.

6.1-194.2. Amended by Acts 1986, c. 500; Acts 1988, c. 536; Acts 1990, c. 3; Acts 1999, c. 77.

6.1-194.3. Amended by Acts 1990, c. 3.

6.1-194.6. Amended by Acts 1987, c. 556; Acts 1988, c. 2.

6.1-194.7. Amended by Acts 1992, c. 693.

6.1-194.12. Amended by Acts 1986, c. 500; Acts 1990, c. 3; Acts 1992, c. 460; Acts 1996, c. 26; Acts 1999, c. 95.

6.1-194.14. Amended by Acts 1986, c. 509; Acts 1992, c. 552; Acts 1994, c. 105.

6.1-194.18. Amended by Acts 1988, c. 555; Acts 1990, c. 3; Acts 1994, c. 319.

6.1-194.20. Amended by Acts 1986, c. 628.

6.1-194.21. Amended by Acts 1995, c. 83; Acts 1996, c. 13.

6.1-194.23. Amended by Acts 1986, c. 500; Acts 1990, c. 3.

6.1-194.32. Amended by Acts 1990, c. 3; Acts 1995, c. 133.

6.1-194.32:1. Amended by Acts 1990, c. 3.

Sec.
6.1-194.33. Amended by Acts 1990, c. 3; Acts 1995, c. 133.
6.1-194.34 to 6.1-194.37. Amended by Acts 1995, c. 133.
6.1-194.39. Amended by Acts 1988, c. 3.
6.1-194.40. Amended by Acts 1991, c. 228.
6.1-194.41. Amended by Acts 1986, cc. 500, 509; Acts 1987, c. 289; Acts 1990, c. 3; Acts 1994, c. 353.
6.1-194.42. Amended by Acts 1994, c. 353.
6.1-194.45. Amended by Acts 1990, c. 3.
6.1-194.46. Amended by Acts 1994, c. 353.
6.1-194.48. Amended by Acts 1990, c. 3.
6.1-194.50. Amended by Acts 1990, c. 3.
6.1-194.53. Amended by Acts 1990, c. 3.
6.1-194.54. Amended by Acts 1986, c. 509.
6.1-194.56. Amended by Acts 1997, c. 801.
6.1-194.58. Amended by Acts 1986, c. 334; Acts 1987, c. 276; Acts 1997, c. 278; Acts 2002, cc. 187, 220, 227.
6.1-194.62. Amended by Acts 1990, c. 3.
6.1-194.69. Amended by Acts 1986, c. 509; Acts 1988, c. 4; Acts 1989, cc. 28, 396, 626; Acts 1990, c. 3; Acts 1992, c. 51; Acts 2003, c. 353.
6.1-194.71. Amended by Acts 1987, c. 335.
6.1-194.72. Amended by Acts 1986, c. 509.
6.1-194.78. Amended by Acts 1996, c. 14; Acts 1997, c. 407.
6.1-194.79. Amended by Acts 1992, c. 224; Acts 1996, c. 80; Acts 1997, c. 50.
6.1-194.83. Amended by Acts 1990, c. 3.
6.1-194.85. Amended by Acts 1986, c. 122; Acts 1987, c. 172; Acts 1988, c. 5; Acts 1992, c. 283; Acts 1998, c. 19.
6.1-194.86. Amended by Acts 1992, c. 136.
6.1-194.87. Amended by Acts 1990, c. 3; Acts 1996, c. 16.
6.1-194.91. Amended by Acts 1986, cc. 500, 509; Acts 1990, c. 3.
6.1-194.93. Amended by Acts 1986, c. 509.
6.1-194.94. Amended by Acts 1990, c. 3.
6.1-194.95. Amended by Acts 1986, c. 509; Acts 1992, c. 136.
6.1-194.96. Amended by Acts 1988, c. 535; Acts 1994, cc. 315, 353.
6.1-194.97. Amended by Acts 1994, c. 353.
6.1-194.98. Amended by Acts 1986, c. 500; Acts 1990, c. 3; Acts 1994, c. 353.
6.1-194.100, 6.1-194.101. Repealed by Acts 1994, c. 353.
6.1-194.103. Amended by Acts 1994, c. 353.
6.1-194.105, 6.1-194.106. Amended by Acts 1994, c. 353.
6.1-194.108. Repealed by Acts 1994, c. 353.
6.1-194.114. Amended by Acts 1996, c. 26.
6.1-194.117. Amended by Acts 1994, c. 105.
6.1-194.131. Amended by Acts 1996, c. 26.
6.1-194.136. Amended by Acts 1994, c. 330; Acts 2003, c. 353.
6.1-194.144. Amended by Acts 1996, c. 14; Acts 1997, c. 407.

Sec.
6.1-194.145. Amended by Acts 1996, c. 80; Acts 1997, c. 50.
6.1-194.149. Amended by Acts 1994, c. 331; Acts 1998, c. 19.
6.1-194.150. Amended by Acts 1994, c. 353.
6.1-195.1 to 6.1-195.76. Repealed by Acts 1985, c. 425.
6.1-195.78. Amended by Acts 1997, c. 801.
6.1-195.80. Amended by Acts 1997, c. 801.
6.1-195.82. Amended by Acts 1993, c. 866.
6.1-195.86. Amended by Acts 1990, c. 3; Acts 1992, c. 810.
6.1-196 to 6.1-225. Repealed by Acts 1990, c. 373.
6.1-225.2. Amended by Acts 1999, c. 63.
6.1-225.6. Amended by Acts 1998, c. 34.
6.1-225.14. Amended by Acts 1999, c. 63.
6.1-225.16. Amended by Acts 1999, c. 63.
6.1-225.19. Amended by Acts 1994, c. 13.
6.1-225.20. Amended by Acts 1995, c. 326.
6.1-225.23. Amended by Acts 1999, c. 63.
6.1-225.27. Amended by Acts 1999, c. 63.
6.1-225.35. Amended by Acts 1995, c. 325.
6.1-225.48. Amended by Acts 1997, c. 801.
6.1-225.49. Amended by Acts 1997, c. 278; Acts 2002, cc. 187, 220, 227.
6.1-225.53. Amended by Acts 1999, c. 63.
6.1-225.57. Amended by Acts 1991, c. 367.
6.1-225.58. Amended by Acts 2002, c. 261.
6.1-225.60. Repealed by Acts 2002, c. 261.
6.1-225.61. Amended by Acts 1993, c. 59.
6.1-226. Repealed by Acts 1968, c. 560; Acts 1982, c. 633.
6.1-226.4. Amended by Acts 1985, c. 365.
6.1-226.6. Amended by Acts 1985, c. 365.
6.1-226.7. Amended by Acts 1976, c. 658; Acts 1985, c. 365.
6.1-226.8. Amended by Acts 1990, c. 3.
6.1-226.9. Amended by Acts 1985, c. 366.
6.1-231. Amended by Acts 1974, c. 176.
6.1-232. Amended by Acts 1974, c. 176; Acts 1978, c. 14; Acts 1996, c. 16.
6.1-234. Amended by Acts 1968, c. 754; Acts 1975, c. 448; Acts 1981, c. 56.
6.1-234.1. Repealed by Acts 1975, c. 448.
6.1-236. Repealed by Acts 1982, c. 633.
6.1-237. Repealed by Acts 1993, c. 419.
6.1-238 to 6.1-242. Repealed by Acts 1993, c. 419.
6.1-244. Amended by Acts 1981, c. 55.
6.1-245. Amended by Acts 1978, c. 14.
6.1-249. Amended by Acts 1968, c. 489; Acts 1974, c. 371; Acts 1986, c. 502; Acts 1995, c. 2; Acts 1998, c. 9; Acts 2001, c. 308; Acts 2002, c. 897.
6.1-250. Amended by Acts 1996, c. 16; Acts 2000, c. 192.
6.1-252. Repealed by Acts 1986, c. 502.
6.1-254. Amended by Acts 1976, c. 658; Acts 1981, c. 452; Acts 1989, c. 239.
6.1-255. Amended by Acts 1989, c. 239.

Sec.
6.1-256. Repealed by Acts 1982, c. 79.
6.1-256.1. Amended by Acts 1995, c. 2.
6.1-259. Amended by Acts 1980, c. 211; Acts 1982, c. 609.
6.1-267. Amended by Acts 1981, c. 452; Acts 2000, c. 192.
6.1-267.1. Amended by Acts 1982, c. 609.
6.1-269. Repealed by Acts 1982, c. 78.
6.1-269.1. Amended by Acts 1988, c. 147; Acts 2000, c. 192.
6.1-271, 6.1-271.1. Repealed by Acts 1995, c. 2.
6.1-272. Repealed by Acts 1974, c. 371.
6.1-272.1. Amended by Acts 2001, c. 308.
6.1-273. Amended by Acts 1975, c. 270; Acts 1987, c. 196.
6.1-274. Amended by Acts 1987, c. 410.
6.1-276. Amended by Acts 1968, c. 489.
6.1-277. Repealed by Acts 1995, c. 2.
6.1-278. Amended by Acts 1978, c. 625; Acts 1981, cc. 37, 38; Acts 1984, c. 296; Acts 1986, c. 502; Acts 1990, c. 751; Acts 1995, c. 2; Acts 2001, c. 308.
6.1-280. Amended by Acts 1968, c. 489; Acts 1974, c. 371.
6.1-282. Amended by Acts 1968, c. 489; Acts 1983, c. 500; Acts 1997, c. 113.
6.1-284. Repealed by Acts 1987, c. 683.
6.1-284.1. Amended by Acts 1995, c. 2.
6.1-285. Amended by Acts 1968, c. 489; Acts 1974, c. 371; Acts 1995, c. 2; Acts 2001, c. 308.
6.1-286. Repealed by Acts 2001, c. 308.
6.1-287. Repealed by Acts 1995, c. 2.
6.1-288. Amended by Acts 1968, c. 489; Acts 1974, c. 371; Acts 1995, c. 2; Acts 2001, c. 308.
6.1-291. Amended by Acts 1968, c. 489; Acts 1974, c. 371; Acts 1995, c. 2; Acts 2001, c. 308.
6.1-293. Amended by Acts 1978, c. 14.
6.1-294. Amended by Acts 1968, c. 489; Acts 1974, c. 371.
6.1-298. Amended by Acts 1976, c. 658; Acts 1998, c. 44.
6.1-299. Repealed by Acts 1983, c. 479.
6.1-300. Amended by Acts 1998, c. 44.
6.1-301. Amended by Acts 1968, c. 489; Acts 2000, c. 55.
6.1-302. Amended by Acts 1993, c. 366.
6.1-303. Amended by Acts 1988, c. 186; Acts 1992, c. 9.
6.1-308. Amended by Acts 1986, c. 502.
6.1-309. Amended by Acts 1976, c. 658; Acts 1986, c. 502.
6.1-311 to 6.1-328. Repealed by Acts 1975, c. 448.
6.1-329. Repealed by Acts 1974, c. 187.
6.1-330, 6.1-330.1. Repealed by Acts 1975, c. 448.
6.1-330.2. Repealed by Acts 1968, c. 324.
6.1-330.3. Repealed by Acts 1975, c. 448.

Sec.
6.1-330.4. Repealed by Acts 1968, c. 324.
6.1-330.5. Repealed by Acts 1975, c. 448.
6.1-330.6 to 6.1-330.44:1. Repealed by Acts 1987, c. 622.
6.1-330.45, 6.1-330.46. Repealed by Acts 1987, c. 622.
6.1-330.47:1. Repealed by Acts 1987, c. 622.
6.1-330.48. Amended by Acts 1996, c. 16.
6.1-330.53. Amended by Acts 2004, c. 646.
6.1-330.54. Amended by Acts 1987, cc. 623, 630; Acts 1991, c. 508; Acts 2004, c. 646.
6.1-330.55. Amended by Acts 1997, c. 180; Acts 2002, c. 897.
6.1-330.60. Amended by Acts 1996, c. 242; Acts 1997, c. 120; Acts 1999, c. 610; Acts 2001, c. 743.
6.1-330.63. Amended by Acts 1987, cc. 639, 714; Acts 1992, Sp. Sess., c. 4; Acts 1997, c. 112.
6.1-330.70. Amended by Acts 1990, c. 3.
6.1-330.71. Amended by Acts 1991, c. 157; Acts 1996, c. 243.
6.1-330.72. Amended by Acts 1993, c. 774; Acts 1995, c. 75; Acts 1996, c. 243; Acts 1998, cc. 69, 89.
6.1-330.76. Amended by Acts 1988, c. 765; Acts 1993, c. 113.
6.1-330.77. Amended by Acts 1988, c. 145; Acts 1990, c. 338; Acts 1999, cc. 62, 373.
6.1-330.78. Amended by Acts 1987, cc. 639, 714; Acts 1992, Sp. Sess., c. 4; Acts 1997, c. 112.
6.1-330.84. Amended by Acts 1990, c. 338; Acts 1991, c. 171.
6.1-330.85. Amended by Acts 1990, c. 338; Acts 1991, c. 171; Acts 1998, c. 89.
6.1-330.86:1. Amended by Acts 1991, c. 171.
6.1-330.89. Amended by Acts 1990, c. 338; Acts 1991, cc. 171, 365.
6.1-331. Amended by Acts 1993, c. 62; Acts 1997, c. 129.
6.1-332.1. Amended by Acts 2002, c. 312; Acts 2003, c. 269.
6.1-333. Amended by Acts 1968, c. 574; Acts 1992, c. 17.
6.1-334. Amended by Acts 2003, c. 437.
6.1-336. Amended by Acts 1997, c. 129.
6.1-338. Amended by Acts 1997, c. 129.
6.1-343 to 6.1-351. Repealed by Acts 2002, c. 621.
6.1-352. Repealed by Acts 1972, c. 113.
6.1-353 to 6.1-360. Repealed by Acts 1972, c. 113.
6.1-361. Repealed by Acts 1970, c. 616.
6.1-362 to 6.1-363. Repealed by Acts 1975, c. 448.
6.1-363.1. Repealed by Acts 2004, c. 790.
6.1-364 to 6.1-369. Repealed by Acts 1976, c. 289.
6.1-369.1 to 6.1-369.10. Repealed by Acts 1989, cc. 651, 655.

Sec.
6.1-370. Amended by Acts 1994, c. 889; Acts 1998, c. 10; Acts 2001, c. 372.
6.1-371. Amended by Acts 1983, c. 156 Acts 1987, c. 283; Acts 1990, c. 259; Acts 1994, c. 889; Acts 2001, c. 372.
6.1-372. Amended by Acts 1987, c. 283; Acts 1990, c. 259; Acts 1992, c. 283; Acts 1994, c. 889; Acts 1996, c. 274; Acts 2001, c. 372.
6.1-373. Amended by Acts 1987, c. 283; Acts 1994, cc. 312, 889; Acts 2001, c. 372.
6.1-374. Amended by Acts 1990, c. 259; Acts 1994, c. 889; Acts 2001, c. 372.
6.1-375. Amended by Acts 1976, c. 531; Acts 1990, c. 259; Acts 1994, c. 889; Acts 2001, c. 372.
6.1-376. Repealed by Acts 1994, c. 889.
6.1-377. Amended by Acts 1994, c. 889; Acts 2001, c. 372.
6.1-378.1. Amended by Acts 1994, c. 889.
6.1-379. Repealed by Acts 1990, c. 259.
6.1-380. Repealed by Acts 1987, c. 283.
6.1-381. Amended by Acts 1983, c. 194; Acts 1985, c. 604; Acts 1993, c. 58; Acts 1996, c. 16.
6.1-382. Amended by Acts 1985, c. 544.
6.1-383. Amended by Acts 1983, cc. 193, 194.
6.1-383.1. Amended by Acts 1985, cc. 544, 604.
6.1-384. Amended by Acts 1983, c. 194.
6.1-387. Amended by Acts 1984, c. 335.
6.1-388. Amended by Acts 1983, c. 194.
6.1-392. Amended by Acts 1985, cc. 509, 544.
6.1-392.1. Amended by Acts 1989, Sp. Sess., cc. 4, 7; Acts 1992, c. 283.
6.1-393. Amended by Acts 1988, c. 115; Acts 1992, c. 283.
6.1-394.1. Amended by Acts 1989, Sp. Sess., cc. 4, 7.
6.1-398. Amended by Acts 1986, c. 257; Acts 1994, cc. 315, 351; Acts 1998, c. 231.
6.1-399. Amended by Acts 1991, c. 282; Acts 1994, c. 351; Acts 1998, c. 231.
6.1-400. Repealed by Acts 1998, c. 231.
6.1-401. Repealed by Acts 1994, c. 351.
6.1-402. Repealed by Acts 1998, c. 231.
6.1-404. Amended by Acts 1994, c. 351.
6.1-405. Repealed by Acts 1998, c. 231.
6.1-406. Amended by Acts 1994, c. 351; Acts 1996, c. 17.
6.1-407. Repealed by Acts 1998, c. 231.
6.1-409. Amended by Acts 1993, c. 183.
6.1-410. Amended by Acts 1990, c. 4; Acts 2001, c. 24.
6.1-411. Amended by Acts 1989, cc. 411, 667; Acts 1992, c. 156; Acts 1995, c. 62; Acts 1996, c. 126; Acts 2003, c. 386.
6.1-412. Amended by Acts 1989, c. 411; Acts 1992, c. 283; Acts 1993, c. 183.

Sec.
6.1-413. Amended by Acts 1989, c. 411; Acts 2001, c. 511.
6.1-415. Amended by Acts 1988, c. 303; Acts 1993, c. 183.
6.1-416. Amended by Acts 1988, c. 303; Acts 1990, c. 8; Acts 1992, c. 283.
6.1-416.1. Amended by Acts 1993, c. 183; Acts 1998, c. 33.
6.1-417. Amended by Acts 1995, c. 62.
6.1-418. Amended by Acts 1996, c. 30.
6.1-420. Amended by Acts 1988, c. 303; Acts 1990, c. 32; Acts 1996, c. 524.
6.1-422. Amended by Acts 1989, c. 667; Acts 1993, c. 183; Acts 1997, c. 228; Acts 2001, cc. 502, 511.
6.1-422.1. Amended by Acts 2003, c. 386.
6.1-423. Amended by Acts 2001, c. 504.
6.1-424. Amended by Acts 1995, c. 62.
6.1-425. Amended by Acts 1993, c. 183.
6.1-428. Amended by Acts 1990, c. 4; Acts 2001, c. 511.
6.1-430. Amended by Acts 2001, c. 510.
6.1-433. Amended by Acts 1999, c. 529.
6.1-435. Amended by Acts 1999, c. 529.
6.1-439. Amended by Acts 2002, c. 897.
6.1-444. Amended by Acts 2002, c. 897.
6.1-453. Amended by Acts 2004, c. 295.
6.1-456. Amended by Acts 2003, c. 593.
6.1-459. Amended by Acts 2003, c. 593; Acts 2004, c. 295.
6.1-461. Amended by Acts 2004, c. 295.
6.1-465. Amended by Acts 2003, c. 593.
6.1-467. Amended by Acts 2003, c. 593.
7-1 to 7-36. Repealed by Acts 1966, c. 102.
7.1-2. Amended by Acts 1972, c. 689.
7.1-8. Repealed by Acts 1983, c. 323.
7.1-10. Amended by Acts 1968, c. 772.
7.1-10.1. Amended by Acts 1998, c. 123; Acts 2002, c. 94.
7.1-13 to 7.1-18. Repealed by Acts 1976, c. 211.
7.1-18.1. Amended by Acts 1981, c. 533.
7.1-20. Amended by Acts 1976, c. 211.
7.1-21. Amended by Acts 1972, c. 597; Acts 1976, c. 211.
7.1-21.1. Amended by Acts 1993, c. 866.
7.1-22. Amended by Acts 1975, c. 449; Acts 1976, c. 211; Acts 1994, c. 23.
7.1-25. Repealed by Acts 1975, c. 411.
7.1-28. Amended by Acts 1994, c. 64; Acts 1998, c. 427.
7.1-29. Amended by Acts 1998, c. 427.
7.1-31.1. Amended by Acts 1995, c. 295.
7.1-35. Amended by Acts 1970, c. 561.
7.1-36. Repealed by Acts 1980, c. 559.
7.1-37. Amended by Acts 1997, c. 576.
7.1-40.2:1. Amended by Acts 1994, c. 220.
7.1-40.8. Amended by Acts 1994, c. 464.
7.1-41. Amended by Acts 2000, c. 374.
8-1 to 8-924. Repealed by Acts 1977, c. 617.
8.01-2. Amended by Acts 1988, c. 37; Acts 1997, c. 921.
8.01-3. Amended by Acts 1979, c. 658; Acts

Sec.

1984, c. 524; Acts 2003, c. 280.

8.01-4. Amended by Acts 1999, c. 839; Acts 2000, c. 803.

8.01-6. Amended by Acts 1990, c. 80; Acts 1996, c. 693; Acts 2004, cc. 141, 326.

8.01-8. Amended by Acts 1998, c. 402.

8.01-9. Amended by Acts 1996, c. 887; Acts cc. 945, 955, 987; Acts 2001, c. 127; Acts 2003, c. 563.

8.01-20. Amended by Acts 1984, c. 703.

8.01-26. Amended by Acts 1991, c. 256.

8.01-27.1. Amended by Acts 1992, c. 238; Acts 1996, c. 334; Acts 2003, c. 233.

8.01-27.2. Amended by Acts 1988, c. 433; Acts 1992, c. 501; Acts 2002, c. 763.

8.01-28. Amended by Acts 1983, c. 136; Acts 1991, cc. 56, 503.

8.01-32. Amended by Acts 2000, c. 245; Acts 2003, c. 125.

8.01-35.1. Amended by Acts 1980, c. 411; Acts 1982, c. 196; Acts 1983, c. 181; Acts 1985, c. 330; Acts 2000, c. 351.

8.01-37.1. Amended by Acts 1985, c. 205.

8.01-38. Amended by Acts 1983, c. 496; Acts 1986, cc. 389, 454; Acts 2000, c. 464.

8.01-40.2. Amended by Acts 2003, c. 800.

8.01-42. Amended by Acts 1977, c. 192.

8.01-43. Amended by Acts 1983, c. 330; Acts 1987, c. 193; Acts 1994, cc. 508, 552; Acts 1996, c. 698.

8.01-44. Amended by Acts 1984, c. 48; Acts 1987, c. 193; Acts 1994, cc. 508, 552; Acts 1996, c. 698.

8.01-44.1. Amended by Acts 1981, c. 40; Acts 1992, c. 603.

8.01-44.5. Amended by Acts 1998, c. 722; Acts 1999, c. 324; Acts 2002, c. 879.

8.01-47. Amended by Acts 1982, c. 259; Acts 1988, c. 159; Acts 1995, c. 759; Acts 2000, c. 79; Acts 2001, cc. 688, 820; Acts 2003, c. 954.

8.01-50. Amended by Acts 1981, c. 115.

8.01-52. Amended by Acts 1977, c. 460; Acts 1982, c. 441.

8.01-53. Amended by Acts 1979, c. 356; Acts 1992, c. 74; Acts 1994, c. 515; Acts 2003, c. 632.

8.01-55. Amended by Acts 1981, c. 286; Acts 1991, c. 97; Acts 1995, c. 366.

8.01-66. Amended by Acts 1979, c. 499; Acts 1986, c. 296; Acts 1987, c. 116; Acts 1989, c. 348.

8.01-66.1. Amended by Acts 1979, c. 521; Acts 1980, c. 437; Acts 1991, c. 155; Acts 1997, c. 401; Acts 2002, c. 631.

8.01-66.2. Amended by Acts 1981, c. 313; Acts 1988, cc. 505, 544; Acts 1995, cc. 470, 550, 669; Acts 2003, cc. 455, 525.

Sec.

8.01-66.5. Amended by Acts 1980, c. 623; Acts 1983, c. 263; Acts 1988, c. 544; Acts 1998, c. 183; Acts 2003, cc. 455, 525.

8.01-66.6. Amended by Acts 1980, c. 623; Acts 2003, c. 525.

8.01-66.7. Amended by Acts 2003, c. 455.

8.01-66.8. Amended by Acts 1980, c. 623; Acts 2003, c. 455, 525.

8.01-66.9. Amended by Acts 1981, c. 562; Acts 1982, c. 491; Acts 1983, c. 263; Acts 1984, c. 767; Acts 1985, c. 580; Acts 1986, c. 238; Acts 1988, c. 544; Acts 1989, c. 624; Acts 1992, c. 104; Acts 2003, c. 525.

8.01-68. Amended by Acts 1997, c. 921.

8.01-69. Amended by Acts 1983, c. 459.

8.01-70. Repealed by Acts 1990, c. 831.

8.01-73. Amended by Acts 1997, c. 540.

8.01-75. Amended by Acts 1980, c. 346.

8.01-76. Amended by Acts 1978, c. 419; Acts 1981, c. 129.

8.01-78. Amended by Acts 983, c. 459.

8.01-81. Amended by Acts 1984, c. 226.

8.01-86. Repealed by Acts 1990, c. 831.

8.01-94. Amended by Acts 1997, c. 801.

8.01-100. Amended by Acts 1978, c. 718.

8.01-103. Amended by Acts 1978, c. 718.

8.01-104. Repealed by Acts 1978, c. 718.

8.01-109. Amended by Acts 1993, c. 311.

8.01-113. Amended by Acts 1984, c. 703.

8.01-114. Amended by Acts 1978, c. 403; Acts 1986, c. 341; Acts 1993, c. 841.

8.01-115. Amended by Acts 1977, c. 230; Acts 1986, c. 341; Acts 1993, c. 841.

8.01-116. Amended by Acts 1993, c. 841.

8.01-117. Amended by Acts 1993, c. 841.

8.01-118. Repealed by Acts 1986, c. 341.

8.01-119. Amended by Acts 1986, c. 341; Acts 1993, c. 841.

8.01-121. Amended by Acts 1987, c. 1; Acts 1993, c. 841.

8.01-126. Amended by Acts 1978, c. 344; Acts 1980, c. 502; Acts 2000, c. 1055.

8.01-129. Amended by Acts 1984, c. 565; Acts 1998, c. 750; Acts 2004, c. 343.

8.01-156. Amended by Acts 1992, c. 454; Acts 1993, c. 16.

8.01-157. Repealed by Acts 1990, c. 831.

8.01-184.1. Amended by Acts 2004, cc. 609, 647.

8.01-195.2. Amended by Acts 1986, cc. 534, 584; Acts 1991, c. 23.

8.01-195.3. Amended by Acts 1982, c. 397; Acts 1986, c. 584; Acts 1988, c. 884; Acts 1989, c. 446; Acts 1993, c. 481; Acts 1998, cc. 203, 820.

8.01-195.4. Amended by Acts 1984, c. 698; Acts 1986, c. 584; Acts 1987, cc. 567, 674; Acts 1989, cc. 121, 337; Acts 1991, c. 23; Acts 1992, cc. 111, 796; Acts 2002, c. 645.

Sec.
8.01-195.5. Amended by Acts 1986, c. 584; Acts 1991, c. 23; Acts 1992, c. 796.
8.01-195.6. Amended by Acts 1984, cc. 638, 698; Acts 1986, c. 584;Acts 1991, c. 23; Acts 1992, c. 796; Acts 2002, c. 207.
8.01-195.7. Amended by Acts 1984, cc. 638, 698; Acts 1985, c. 514; Acts 1986, c. 584; Acts 1988, cc. 778, 801; Acts 1992, c. 796.
8.01-195.8. Amended by Acts 1986, c. 584; Acts 1991, c. 23.
8.01-195.9. Amended by Acts 2000, cc. 618, 632.
8.01-195.10. Amended by Acts 2004, cc. 818, 840.
8.01-195.11. Amended by Acts 2004, cc. 818, 840.
8.01-195.12. Amended by Acts 2004, cc. 818, 840.
8.01-216.3. Amended by Acts 2004, c. 589.
8.01-217. Amended by Acts 1977, c. 457; Acts 1979, cc. 599, 603, 612; Acts 1980, cc. 448, 455; Acts 1981, c. 297; Acts 1983, c. 355; Acts 1985, c. 483; Acts 1991, c. 144; Acts 1993, c. 929; Acts 1996, c. 616; Acts 2003, c. 258.
8.01-220.1:1. Amended by Acts 1988, c. 566.
8.01-225. Amended by Acts 1979, c. 729; Acts 1980, c. 419; Acts 1983, c. 72; Acts 1984, cc. 493, 577; Acts 1987, cc. 260, 382; Acts 1990, c. 898; Acts 1996, c. 899; Acts 1997, cc. 334, 809; Acts 1998, cc. 493, 500; Acts 1999, cc. 570, 1000; Acts 2000, cc. 928, 1064; Acts 2003, cc. 18, 978, 1020.
8.01-225.1. Amended by Acts 1993, c. 702.
8.01-226. Amended by Acts 1992, c. 731; Acts 1996, cc. 646, 660; Acts 2000, c. 962.
8.01-226.1. Amended by Acts 1992, c. 534; Acts 2003, c. 571.
8.01-226.2. Amended by Acts 1997, c. 866.
8.01-226.7. Amended by Acts 2000, c. 1071.
8.01-226.8. Amended by Acts 2004, cc. 387, 434.
8.01-229. Amended by Acts 1978, cc. 65, 767; Acts 1983, cc. 404, 437; Acts 1986, c. 506; Acts 1987, cc. 294, 645; Acts 1988, c. 711; Acts 1989, c. 588; Acts 1990, c. 280; Acts 1991, cc. 693, 722; Acts 1993, c. 844; Acts 1997, c. 801; Acts 2000, c. 531; Acts 2001, cc. 773, 781.
8.01-230. Amended by Acts 1996, c. 328.
8.01-231. Amended by Acts 1988, c. 544.
8.01-236. Amended by Acts 1978, c. 471.
8.01-241. Amended by Acts 1980, c. 499; Acts 1994, c. 547; Acts 1999, c. 788.

Sec.
8.01-242. Amended by Acts 1994, c. 547; Acts 1999, c. 788.
8.01-243. Amended by Acts 1986, cc. 389, 454; Acts 1987, cc. 294, 645, 679.
8.01-243.2. Amended by Acts 1999, c. 47.
8.01-248. Amended by Acts 1995, c. 9.
8.01-249. Amended by Acts 1985, c. 459; Acts 1986, c. 601; Acts 1991, c. 674; Acts 1992, c. 817; Acts 1993, c. 523; Acts 1995, c. 268; Acts 1997, cc. 565, 801.
8.01-250.1. Amended by Acts 1986, c. 458.
8.01-251. Amended by Acts 1983, c. 449; Acts 2002, c. 394.
8.01-259. Amended by Acts 1987, c. 567; Acts 1989, c. 556; Acts 1993, c. 929.
8.01-261. Amended by Acts 1978, c. 334; Acts 1979, c. 331; Acts 1985, c. 433; Acts 1987, c. 567; Acts 1988, c. 766; Acts 1989, c. 556; Acts 1990, c. 831; Acts 1993, cc. 841, 929.
8.01-262. Amended by Acts 1978, c. 414; Acts 1979, c. 331; Acts 1985, c. 213; Acts 1999, c. 73; Acts 2004, c. 979.
8.01-262.1. Amended by Acts 1997, c. 424; Acts 1999, c. 130.
8.01-264. Amended by Acts 1982, c. 601; Acts 1985, cc. 433, 492; Acts 1986, cc. 396, 403.
8.01-265. Amended by Acts 1979, c. 662; Acts 1982, c. 601; Acts 1991, c. 530.
8.01-266. Amended by Acts 1994, c. 32.
8.01-268. Amended by Acts 1988, c. 503.
8.01-269. Amended by Acts 1985, c. 310; Acts 1986, c. 278; Acts 1989, c. 450.
8.01-271.1. Amended by Acts 1998, c. 596.
8.01-272. Amended by Acts 1979, c. 367.
8.01-273.1. Amended by Acts 2000, c. 207.
8.01-274. Amended by Acts 1978, c. 336.
8.01-277. Amended by Acts 1994, c. 37.
8.01-281. Amended by Acts 1981, c. 426; Acts 1983, c. 183.
8.01-285. Amended by Acts 1991, c. 672.
8.01-288. Amended by Acts 1987, c. 594; Acts 1988, c. 583.
8.01-293. Amended by Acts 1981, c. 110; Acts 1986, c. 275; Acts 1996, cc. 501, 608; Acts 1997, c. 820; Acts 2002, c. 342; Acts 2004, cc. 210, 588.
8.01-294. Amended by Acts 1978, c. 831; Acts 2002, c. 65; Acts 2004, c. 627.
8.01-295. Amended by Acts 1982, c. 674.
8.01-296. Amended by Acts 1989, cc. 518, 524; Acts 1990, cc. 729, 767; Acts 1996, c. 538.
8.01-298. Amended by Acts 1979, c. 444.
8.01-299. Amended by Acts 1991, c. 672.
8.01-300. Amended by Acts 1980, c. 732; Acts 1985, c. 416.
8.01-301. Amended by Acts 1991, c. 672.
8.01-302. Repealed by Acts 2002, c. 702.
8.01-306. Amended by Acts 1991, c. 672.

Sec.
8.01-310. Amended by Acts 1987, c. 696; Acts 1992, c. 459; Acts 2000, c. 579.
8.01-313. Amended by Acts 1983, c. 467; Acts 1984, c. 780; Acts 1991, c. 672.
8.01-314. Amended by Acts 1981, c. 495.
8.01-316. Amended by Acts 1982, c. 384; Acts 1983, c. 467; Acts 1996, c. 352; Acts 1999, c. 353.
8.01-317. Amended by Acts 1982, c. 384; Acts 1996, cc. 352, 710.
8.01-319. Amended by Acts 1978, c. 676; Acts 1979, c. 464; Acts 1982, c. 384.
8.01-320. Amended by Acts 1978, c. 90; Acts 1981, c. 6; Acts 1983, c. 402; Acts 1984, c. 18; Acts 1985, c. 177; Acts 1986, c. 263; Acts 1987, c. 594; Acts 1993, c. 929; Acts 1997, c. 754.
8.01-324. Amended by Acts 1983, c. 297; Acts 1989, c. 611; Acts 1992, cc. 392, 537, 719.
8.01-325. Amended by Acts 1996, c. 538.
8.01-327. Amended by Acts 1987, c. 594; Acts 1988, cc. 583, 642.
8.01-327.1. Amended by Acts 1984, c. 93.
8.01-328.1. Amended by Acts 1978, c. 132; Acts 1981, c. 6; Acts 1982, c. 313; Acts 1983, c. 428; Acts 1984, c. 609; Acts 1986, c. 275; Acts 1987, c. 594; Acts 1988, cc. 866, 878; Acts 1992, c. 571; Acts 1999, cc. 886, 904, 905; Acts 2001, c. 221.
8.01-329. Amended by Acts 1979, c. 31; Acts 1986, c. 388; Acts 1987, cc. 449, 450, 459; Acts 1990, c. 741; Acts 1998, c. 259; Acts 2001, c. 29.
8.01-331. Amended by Acts 1983, c. 293; Acts 1990, c. 258; Acts 1993, c. 930.
8.01-334. Repealed by Acts 1983, c. 293.
8.01-335. Amended by Acts 1990, c. 730; Acts 1992, cc. 532, 792, 803, 835; Acts 1994, c. 517; Acts 1997, c. 680; Acts 1999, c. 652.
8.01-337. Amended by Acts 1987, c. 189.
8.01-338. Amended by Acts 1997, c. 801.
8.01-341. Amended by Acts 1977, c. 458; Acts 1978, cc. 176, 340; Acts 1980, c. 535; Acts 1982, c. 315; Acts 1987, c. 256; Acts 1990, c. 758; Acts 1993, c. 572; Acts 1998, c. 83.
8.01-341.1. Amended by Acts 1987, c. 256; Acts 1997, c. 693; Acts 1999, c. 153; Acts 2004, c. 106.
8.01-341.2. Amended by Acts 1987, c. 155.
8.01-342. Amended by Acts 1984, c. 165; Acts 1992, c. 312; Acts 1994, c. 27.
8.01-343. Amended by Acts 1979, c. 269; Acts 1996, c. 332; Acts 1999, c. 221; Acts 2000, c. 251.
8.01-345. Amended by Acts 1977, c. 451; Acts 1978, c. 209; Acts 1979, c. 665; Acts 1983, c. 107; Acts 1984, c. 50; Acts 1989, cc. 616, 632; Acts 1990, c. 758; Acts 2000, c. 828.
8.01-348. Amended by Acts 1983, c. 425.
8.01-350. Repealed by Acts 1977, c. 451.
8.01-351. Amended by Acts 1988, c. 818.
8.01-353. Amended by Acts 1980, c. 452; Acts 1981, c. 150; Acts 1988, c. 350.
8.01-356. Amended by Acts 2004, c. 116.
8.01-357. Amended by Acts 1999, c. 3.
8.01-358. Amended by Acts 1981, c. 280.
8.01-359. Amended by Acts 1985, c. 188.
8.01-360. Amended by Acts 1992, c. 536; Acts 1998, c. 279.
8.01-364. Amended by Acts 1978, c. 415.
8.01-375. Amended by Acts 1986, c. 36; Amended by Acts 1987, c. 70; Acts 2001, c. 348.
8.01-376. Amended by Acts 1978, c. 367.
8.01-378. Amended by Acts 1985, c. 214; Acts 1986, c. 253.
8.01-379.1. Amended by Acts 1993, c. 615.
8.01-380. Amended by Acts c. 404; Acts 1991, c. 19; Acts 2001, c. 825; Acts 2004, c. 362.
8.01-381. Amended by Acts 1992, c. 495.
8.01-382. Amended by Acts 1979, c. 501; Acts 1997, c. 551; Acts 2004, c. 646.
8.01-383.1. Amended by Acts 1994, c. 807; Acts 1998, c. 861.
8.01-384. Amended by Acts 1992, c. 564.
8.01-384.1:1. Amended by Acts 2003, c. 1011.
8.01-389. Amended by Acts 1980, c. 453; Acts 1995, c. 594; Acts 1996, c. 417.
8.01-390. Amended by Acts 1996, c. 668; Acts 2000, c. 334.
8.01-391. Amended by Acts 1978, c. 75; Acts 1979, c. 447; Acts 1989, c. 212; Acts 1990, c. 355; Acts 1991, c. 145; Acts 1992, c. 393; Acts 2000, c. 334.
8.01-397. Amended by Acts 1988, c. 426.
8.01-399. Amended by Acts 1993, c. 556; Acts 1996, cc. 937, 980; Acts 1998, c. 314; Acts 2002, cc. 308, 773.
8.01-400. Amended by Acts 1979, c. 3; Acts 1994, c. 198.
8.01-401.1. Amended by Acts 1994, c. 328.
8.01-402. Amended by Acts 1992, c. 108.
8.01-405. Amended by Acts 1984, c. 536.
8.01-406. Amended by Acts 1978, c. 601.
8.01-407. Amended by Acts 1992, c. 506; Acts 2000, c. 813; Acts 2002, c. 463; Acts 2004, c. 335.
8.01-410. Amended by Acts 1998, c. 596; Acts 2001, c. 513; Acts 2002, cc. 515, 544.
8.01-411. Amended by Acts 1986, c. 599.
8.01-412.2. Amended by Acts 2000, c. 821.
8.01-412.4. Amended by Acts 1993, c. 208; Acts 2000, c. 821.
8.01-412.5. Amended by Acts 1984, c. 95.
8.01-413. Amended by Acts 1977, c. 208; Acts

Sec.
1981, c. 457; Acts 1982, c. 378; Acts 1984, c. 780; Acts 1991, c. 672; Acts 1994, cc. 390, 572; Acts 1995, c. 586; Acts 1997, c. 682; Acts 1998, c. 470; Acts 2000, cc. 813, 923; Acts 2001, c. 567; Acts 2002, cc. 463, 654; Acts 2004, cc. 65, 335, 742, 1014.
8.01-413.01. Amended by Acts 1996, c. 516; Acts 1997, c. 503.
8.01-416. Amended by Acts 1980, c. 183; Acts 1990, c. 724.
8.01-417. Amended by Acts 2004, c. 345.
8.01-418. Amended by Acts 1986, c. 46.
8.01-418.2. Amended by Acts 1995, cc. 770, 818.
8.01-419. Amended by Acts 1986, c. 317; Acts 1996, c. 394.
8.01-420. Amended by Acts 1978, c. 417.
8.01-420.2. Amended by Acts 1992, c. 567.
8.01-420.3. Amended by Acts 1990, c. 77.
8.01-420.4. Amended by Acts 1991, c. 81; Acts 1993, cc. 428, 940.
8.01-421. Amended by Acts 1978, c. 416.
8.01-424. Amended by Acts 1985, c. 499; Acts 1988, c. 409; Acts 1991, cc. 97, 257; Acts 1993, c. 945; Acts 1994, c. 39; Acts 1998, cc. 584, 607, 610.
8.01-425.1. Amended by Acts 2000, c. 839.
8.01-427.1. Repealed by Acts 1978, c. 426.
8.01-428. Amended by Acts 1991, c. 39; Acts 1993, c. 951.
8.01-429. Amended by Acts 1984, c. 703.
8.01-434. Amended by Acts 1986, c. 523.
8.01-438. Amended by Acts 1988, c. 420.
8.01-446. Amended by Acts 1993, c. 412; Acts 1994, c. 538; Acts 1995, c. 434; Acts 1997, c. 579.
8.01-449. Amended by Acts 1982, c. 405; Acts 1985, c. 171; Acts 1988, c. 420; Acts 1996, c. 427; Acts 1997, c. 579.
8.01-450. Amended by Acts 1985, c. 171.
8.01-451. Amended by Acts 1998, c. 639.
8.01-452.1. Amended by Acts 1992, c. 57; Acts 1995, c. 13; Acts 1997, c. 135; Acts 1998, c. 886.
8.01-453. Amended by Acts 1979, c. 192; Acts 1986, c. 276; Acts 1988, c. 420.
8.01-454. Amended by Acts 1988, c. 420.
8.01-457. Amended by Acts 1986, c. 132.
8.01-460. Amended by Acts 1979, c. 496; Acts 1985, c. 529; Acts 1989, c. 8.
8.01-461. Amended by Acts 1982, c. 105.
8.01-465.2. Amended by Acts 1990, c. 738.
8.01-465.4. Amended by Acts 2000, c. 100.
8.01-466. Amended by Acts 1986, c. 341; Acts 1996, cc. 501, 608.
8.01-467. Amended by Acts 1984, c. 94.
8.01-470. Amended by Acts 1991, c. 503; Acts 2000, c. 640; Acts 2001, c. 222; Acts 2003, c. 259.

Sec.
8.01-471. Amended by Acts 1999, c. 683; Acts 2003, c. 427.
8.01-479. Amended by Acts 1984, c. 557.
8.01-480. Amended by Acts 1979, c. 491; Acts 1990, c. 553.
8.01-483. Amended by Acts 1986, c. 341.
8.01-484. Amended by Acts 1988, c. 420.
8.01-498. Amended by Acts 1988, c. 674.
8.01-499. Amended by Acts 2004, cc. 198, 211.
8.01-501, 8.01-502. Amended by Acts 1996, c. 1002.
8.01-502.1. Amended by Acts 1999, c. 48.
8.01-506. Amended by Acts 1978, c. 66; Acts 1979, c. 225; Acts 1985, c. 433; Acts 1987, c. 182; Acts 1991, c. 463.
8.01-506.1. Amended by Acts 1986, c. 249; Acts 1993, c. 267.
8.01-508. Amended by Acts 1983, c. 278; Acts 1985, c. 290; Acts 1986, c. 326; Acts 1999, cc. 829, 846.
8.01-511. Amended by Acts 1977, c. 454; Acts 1978, cc. 321, 506; Acts 1979, cc. 242, 345; Acts 1980, c. 537; Acts 1983, cc. 399, 468; Acts 1984, c. 1; Acts 1985, c. 524; Acts 1991, c. 534; Acts 1996, cc. 501, 608.
8.01-512, 8.01-512.1. Repealed by Acts 1983, c. 399.
8.01-512.2. Amended by Acts 1994, c. 664.
8.01-512.3. Amended by Acts 1994, c. 40; Acts 1995, c. 379; Acts 1996, c. 1051.
8.01-512.4. Amended by Acts 1986, c. 489; Acts 1994, c. 40.
8.01-513. Amended by Acts 1980, c. 514; Acts 1997, c. 395; Acts 1998, cc. 723, 737; Acts 2004, c. 231.
8.01-514. Amended by Acts 1977, c. 454; Acts 1979, c. 36; Acts 2003, c. 234.
8.01-515. Amended by Acts 1979, c. 242; Acts 1983, c. 399.
8.01-516. Repealed by Acts 1983, c. 399.
8.01-516.1. Amended by Acts 1993, c. 385.
8.01-581.17. Amended by Acts 2004, c. 250.
8.01-520. Amended by Acts 1983, c. 399.
8.01-533. Amended by Acts 1986, c. 341; Acts 1993, c. 841.
8.01-534. Amended by Acts 1993, c. 841.
8.01-537. Amended by Acts 1978, c. 418; Acts 1984, c. 646; Acts 1993, c. 841.
8.01-537.1. Amended by Acts 1993, c. 841.
8.01-540. Amended by Acts 1993, c. 841; Acts 1984, c. 646.
8.01-541. Amended by Acts 1993, c. 841.
8.01-543. Amended by Acts 1984, c. 646.
8.01-546. Amended by Acts 1986, c. 341.
8.01-550. Amended by Acts 1984, c. 646.
8.01-551. Amended by Acts 1984, c. 646; Acts 1993, c. 841.
8.01-552. Repealed by Acts 1984, c. 646.
8.01-553. Amended by Acts 1984, c. 646.
8.01-568. Amended by Acts 1984, c. 646.

Sec.

8.01-576.4 to 8.01-576.12. Amended by Acts 2002, c. 718.
8.01-576.9 to 8.01-576.11. Amended by Acts 1994, c. 687.
8.01-577. Amended by Acts 1983, c. 485; Acts 1986, c. 614.
8.01-578 to 8.01-580. Repealed by Acts 1986, c. 614.
8.01-581.09. Amended by Acts 1998, c. 303.
8.01-581.010. Amended by Acts 1998, c. 303.
8.01-581.014. Amended by Acts 1995, c. 342.
8.01-581.015. Amended by Acts 1991, c. 489.
8.01-581.1. Amended by Acts 1981, c. 305; Acts 1986, cc. 227, 511; Acts 1989, c. 146; Acts 1991, cc. 455, 464; Acts 1993, c. 268; Acts 1994, cc. 114, 616, 651; Acts 2001, c. 98; Acts 2003, cc. 487, 492.
8.01-581.2. Amended by Acts 1982, c. 151; Acts 1984, cc. 443, 777; Acts 1986, c. 227; Acts 1989, c. 561; Acts 1993, c. 928; Acts 1994, c. 38; Acts 1995, c. 367; Acts 2000, c. 213; Acts 2001, c. 252.
8.01-581.2:1. Amended by Acts 1993, c. 928.
8.01-581.3. Amended by Acts 1977, c. 202; Acts 1983, c. 208; Acts 1984, c. 777; Acts 1986, c. 227; Acts 1993, c. 928; Acts 1994, c. 384.
8.01-581.3:1. Amended by Acts 1993, c. 928.
8.01-581.4. Amended by Acts 1979, c. 261; Acts 1993, c. 928.
8.01-581.4:1. Amended by Acts 1993, c. 928.
8.01-581.5. Amended by Acts 1993, c. 928; Acts 1979, c. 261; Acts 1984, c. 777; Acts 1993, c. 928.
8.01-581.6. Amended by Acts 1979, c. 261; Acts 1984, c. 777; Acts 1986, c. 227.
8.01-581.7. Amended by Acts 1986, c. 227; Acts 1993, c. 928.
8.01-581.7:1. Amended by Acts 1993, c. 928.
8.01-581.8. Amended by Acts 1978, c. 406; Acts 1993, c. 928.
8.01-581.9. Repealed by Acts 1993, c. 928.
8.01-581.10. Amended by Acts 1984, c. 777.
8.01-581.12. Amended by Acts 1997, c. 801.
8.01-581.12:1. Repealed by Acts 1979, c. 325.
8.01-581.12:2. Amended by Acts 1978, c. 262.
8.01-581.13. Amended by Acts 1983, c. 567; Acts 1984, c. 494; Acts 1987, c. 713; Acts 1992, c. 590; Acts 1993, c. 702; Acts 1995, c. 636; Acts 1996, cc. 937, 980; Acts 1997, cc. 439, 901; Acts 2001, c. 460.
8.01-581.141 Repealed by Acts 2003, c. 397.
8.01-581.15. Amended by Acts 1983, c. 496; Acts 1999, c. 711; Acts 2001, c. 211.
8.01-581.16. Amended by Acts 1981, c. 174; Acts 1987, c. 713; Acts 2001, c. 381; Acts 2002, c. 675.
8.01-581.17. Amended by Acts 1995, c. 500; Acts 1997, c. 292; Acts 2001, c. 381; Acts 2002, c. 675.
8.01-581.18. Amended by Acts 1993, c. 702.
8.01-581.19. Amended by Acts 1987, c. 713; Acts 1993, c. 702; Acts 1996, cc. 937, 980.
8.01-581.19:1. Amended by Acts 1987, c. 713; Acts 1993, c. 702; Acts 1996, cc. 937, 980.
8.01-581.20. Amended by Acts 1980, c. 164; Acts 1989, c. 146; Acts 1992, c. 240; Acts 2003, c. 251.
8.01-581.21. Amended by Acts 2002, c. 718.
8.01-581.22. Amended by Acts 2002, c. 718.
8.01-582. Amended by Acts 1979, c. 498; Acts 1988, c. 553; Acts 1990, c. 414; Acts 1991, c. 635; Acts 1999, c. 198; Acts 2003, c. 97.
8.01-583. Amended by Acts 1988, c. 553; Acts 1990, c. 3.
8.01-585. Amended by Acts 1988, c. 553; Acts 1989, c. 69.
8.01-586. Amended by Acts 1988, c. 553.
8.01-587. Amended by Acts 1988, c. 841.
8.01-588. Amended by Acts 1988, c. 841.
8.01-588.1. Amended by Acts 2000, cc. 618, 632.
8.01-589. Amended by Acts 1979, c. 498; Acts 1988, c. 841.
8.01-600. Amended by Acts 1986, c. 644; Acts 1988, c. 841; Acts 1990, cc. 3, 414; Acts 1991, c. 635; Acts 2002, c. 832.
8.01-600.1. Repealed by Acts 1993, c. 939.
8.01-602. Amended by Acts 1982, c. 155; Acts 1984, c. 121; Acts 1987, c. 708; Acts 1988, c. 841.
8.01-603. Repealed by Acts 1982, c. 155.
8.01-604. Amended by Acts 1981, c. 514; Acts 1982, c. 155.
8.01-605. Amended by Acts 1981, c. 514; Acts 1982, c. 155.
8.01-606. Amended by Acts 1977, c. 462; Acts 1978, c. 525; Acts 1980, c. 544; Acts 1985, c. 216; Acts 1987, c. 378; Acts 1995, c. 405; Acts 1997, c. 801; Acts 2003, c. 195.
8.01-609. Amended by Acts 1981, c. 613; Acts 1992, c. 297.
8.01-615. Amended by Acts 1978, c. 237; Acts 1981, c. 500; Acts 1982, c. 339.
8.01-617. Amended by Acts 1988, c. 553.
8.01-620. Amended by Acts 1995, c. 310.
8.01-621. Repealed by Acts 1987, c. 567.
8.01-626. Amended by Acts 1984, c. 703.
8.01-636. Amended by Acts 1980, c. 705.
8.01-637. Amended by Acts 1980, c. 705.
8.01-638. Repealed by Acts 1987, c. 567.
8.01-645. Amended by Acts 1984, c. 703.
8.01-649. Amended by Acts 1984, c. 703.
8.01-651. Amended by Acts 1984, c. 703.
8.01-654. Amended by Acts 1978, c. 124; Acts

Sec.
1995, c. 503; Acts 1998, c. 577.
8.01-654.1. Amended by Acts 1998, c. 199.
8.01-665. Amended by Acts 1984, c. 703.
8.01-669. Amended by Acts 1984, c. 703.
8.01-670. Amended by Acts 1984, c. 703; Acts 1997, c. 801; Acts 2002, c. 107.
8.01-670.1. Amended by Acts 1984, c. 703.
8.01-671. Amended by Acts 1984, c. 703.
8.01-673. Amended by Acts 1977, c. 449; Acts 1984, c. 703; Acts 1988, c. 324; Acts 1994, c. 64.
8.01-674. Amended by Acts 1984, c. 703.
8.01-675. Repealed by Acts 1984, c. 703.
8.01-675.3. Amended by Acts 1987, c. 710; Acts 2003, c. 109.
8.01-675.4. Amended by Acts 1988, c. 197; Acts 1994, c. 64.
8.01-676. Repealed by Acts 1984, c. 703.
8.01-676.1. Amended by Acts 1986, c. 89; Acts 1987, cc. 460, 684; Acts 1988, c. 883; Acts 1996, c. 77; Acts 2000, c. 100; Acts 2004, cc. 328, 356.
8.01-679. Amended by Acts 1984, c. 703.
8.01-681, 8.01-682. Amended by Acts 1984, c. 703.
8.01-684. Amended by Acts 1984, c. 703.
8.01-685. Amended by Acts 1984, c. 703.
8.01-686, 8.01-687. Repealed by Acts 1984, c. 703.
8.1-101 to 8.1-208. Repealed by Acts 2003, c. 353.
8.1A-201. Amended by Acts 2004, c. 200.
8.2-103. Amended by Acts 2000, c. 1007; Acts 2003, c. 353; Acts 2004, c. 200.
8.2-104. Amended by Acts 2004, c. 200.
8.2-107. Amended by Acts 1973, c. 509.
8.2-202. Amended by Acts 2003, c. 353.
8.2-208. Repealed by Acts 2003, c. 353.
8.2-210. Amended by Acts 2000, c. 1007.
8.2-310. Amended by Acts 1992, c. 493; Acts 2004, c. 200.
8.2-326. Amended by Acts 2000, c. 1007.
8.2-323. Amended by Acts 2004, c. 200.
8.2-401. Amended by Acts 2004, c. 200.
8.2-403. Amended by Acts 1997, c. 121.
8.2-502. Amended by Acts 2000, c. 1007.
8.2-503. Amended by Acts 2004, c. 200.
8.2-505. Amended by Acts 2004, c. 200.
8.2-506. Amended by Acts 2004, c. 200.
8.2-509. Amended by Acts 2004, c. 200.
8.2-511. Amended by Acts 1992, c. 693.
8.2-512. Amended by Acts 1997, c. 343.
8.2-605. Amended by Acts 2004, c. 200.
8.2-705. Amended by Acts 2004, c. 200.
8.2-716. Amended by Acts 1966, c. 392; Acts 2000, c. 1007.
8.2A-103. Amended by Acts 2000, c. 1007; Acts 2003, c. 353; Acts 2004, c. 200.
8.2A-207. Repealed by Acts 2003, c. 353.
8.2A-303. Amended by Acts 2000, c. 1007.
8.2A-307. Amended by Acts 2000, c. 1007.
8.2A-309. Amended by Acts 2000, c. 1007.

Sec.
8.2A-501. Amended by Acts 2003, c. 353.
8.2A-514. Amended by Acts 2004, c. 200.
8.2A-518. Amended by Acts 2003, c. 353.
8.2A-519. Amended by Acts 2003, c. 353.
8.2A-526. Amended by Acts 2004, c. 200.
8.2A-527. Amended by Acts 2003, c. 353.
8.2A-528. Amended by Acts 2003, c. 353.
8.3-101 to 8.3-805. Repealed by Acts 1992, c. 693.
8.3A-103. Amended by Acts 2003, c. 353.
8.3A-308. Amended by Acts 1997, c. 801.
8.3A-602. Amended by Acts 2003, c. 342.
8.4-101. Amended by Acts 1992, c. 693.
8.4-102, 8.4-103. Amended by Acts 1992, c. 693.
8.4-104. Amended by Acts 1976, c. 118; Acts 1992, c. 693; Acts 1996, c. 216; Acts 2003, c. 353; Acts 2004, c. 200.
8.4-105. Amended by Acts 1992, c. 693.
8.4-106. Amended by Acts 1987, c. 180; Acts 1992, c. 693.
8.4-107, 8.4-108. Amended by Acts 1992, c. 693.
8.4-109. Repealed by Acts 1992, c. 693.
8.4-202 to 8.4-204. Amended by Acts 1992, c. 693.
8.4-205. Repealed by Acts 1992, c. 693.
8.4-206. Amended by Acts 1992, c. 693.
8.4-207. Repealed by Acts 1992, c. 693.
8.4-208. Amended by Acts 1992, c. 693; Acts 2004, c. 200.
8.4-209, 8.4-210. Amended by Acts 1992, c. 693.
8.4-211. Repealed by Acts 1992, c. 693.
8.4-212 to 8.4-214. Amended by Acts 1992, c. 693.
8.4-301 to 8.4-303. Amended by Acts 1992, c. 693.
8.4-401 to 8.4-405. Amended by Acts 1992, c. 693.
8.4-406. Amended by Acts 1978, c. 75; Acts 1992, c. 693.
8.4-407. Amended by Acts 1992, c. 693.
8.4A-105. Amended by Acts 2003, c. 353.
8.4A-106. Amended by Acts 2003, c. 353.
8.4A-204. Amended by Acts 2003, c. 353.
8.4-208. Amended by Acts 2000, c. 1007.
8.4-405. Amended by Acts 1997, c. 801.
8.5-101 to 8.5-117. Repealed by Acts 1997, c. 343.
8.5A-102. Amended by Acts 2003, c. 353.
8.5A-103. Amended by Acts 2003, c. 353.
8.6-101 to 8.6-111. Repealed by Acts 1997, c. 121.
8.6A-102. Amended by Acts 2000, c. 1007; Acts 2003, c. 353.
8.6A-103. Amended by Acts 2000, c. 1007.
8.7-102. Amended by Acts 2003, c. 353; Acts 2004, c. 200.
8.7-103. Amended by Acts 2004, c. 200.
8.7-104. Amended by Acts 2004, c. 200.

Sec.
8.7-105. Repealed by Acts 2004, c. 200.
8.7-202 to 8.7-206. Amended by Acts 1974, c. 435; 2004, c. 200.
8.7-207. Amended by Acts 1974, c. 435.
8.7-208 to 8.7-210. Amended by Acts 1974, c. 435; 2004, c. 200.
8.7-301 to 8.7-303. Amended by Acts 2004, c. 200.
8.7-305. Amended by Acts 2004, c. 200.
8.7-307. Amended by Acts 2004, c. 200.
8.7-309. Amended by Acts 2004, c. 200.
8.7-401 to 8.7-404. Amended by Acts 2004, c. 200.
8.7-501 to 8.7-507. Amended by Acts 2000, c. 1007.
8.7-509. Amended by Acts 2004, c. 200.
8.7-601 to 8.7-603. Amended by Acts 2004, c. 200.
8.8-101 to 8.8-408. Repealed by Acts 1996, c. 216.
8.8A-102. Amended by Acts 2003, c. 353.
8.8A-103. Amended by Acts 2000, c. 1007; Acts 2004, c. 200.
8.8A-106. Amended by Acts 2000, c. 1007.
8.8A-110. Amended by Acts 2000, c. 1007.
8.8A-301. Amended by Acts 2000, c. 1007.
8.8A-302. Amended by Acts 2000, c. 1007.
8.8A-510. Amended by Acts 2000, c. 1007.
8.9-101 to 8.9-507. Repealed by Acts 2000, c. 1007.
8.9A-102. Amended by Acts 2003, c. 353; Acts 2004, c. 200.
8.9A-109. Amended by Acts 2001, cc. 289, 296.
8.9A-203. Amended by Acts 2004, c. 200.
8.9A-207. Amended by Acts 2004, c. 200.
8.9A-208. Amended by Acts 2004, c. 200.
8.9A-301. Amended by Acts 2004, c. 200.
8.9A-310. Amended by Acts 2004, c. 200.
8.9A-312. Amended by Acts 2004, c. 200.
8.9A-313. Amended by Acts 2004, c. 200.
8.9A-314. Amended by Acts 2004, c. 200.
8.9A-317. Amended by Acts 2004, c. 200.
8.9A-338. Amended by Acts 2004, c. 200.
8.9A-406. Amended by Acts 2003, c. 340.
8.9A-408. Amended by Acts 2001, c. 537; Acts 2003, c. 340.
8.9A-516. Amended by Acts 2002, cc. 566, 644.
8.9A-523. Amended by Acts 2002, c. 244.
8.9A-525. Amended by Acts 2002, c. 71.
8.9A-601. Amended by Acts 2004, c. 200.
8.9A-703. Amended by Acts 2001, cc. 289, 296.
8.10-104. Amended by Acts 2003, c. 353.
9-1 to 9-410. Repealed by Acts 2001, c. 844.
9.1-101. Amended by Acts 2002, cc. 789, 836, 868; Acts 2003, cc. 744, 934, 937.
9.1-101. Amended by Acts 2004, c. 30.
9.1-102. Amended by Acts 2002, cc. 490, 810, 818, 836, 868; Acts 2004, cc. 460, 972, 980, 1016.
9.1-106. Amended by Acts 2003, cc. 993, 1028.
9.1-108. Amended by Acts 2004, c. 1000.
9.1-110. Amended by Acts 2002, cc. 836, 868.

Sec.
9.1-111. Amended by Acts 2004, c. 1000.
9.1-113. Amended by Acts 2003, c. 744.
9.1-138. Amended by Acts 2003, c. 124; Acts 2004, c. 470.
9.1-139. Amended by Acts 2002, cc. 578, 597; Acts 2003, c. 124; Acts 2004, c. 470.
9.1-140. Amended by Acts 2002, cc. 578, 597; Acts 2003, c. 136.
9.1-143. Amended by Acts 2003, c. 922; Acts 2004, c. 460.
9.1-145. Amended by Acts 2002, cc. 578, 597.
9.1-149. Amended by Acts 2002, cc. 578, 597.
9.1-161. Amended by Acts 2004, c. 466.
9.1-162. Amended by Acts 2002, c. 597; Acts 2004, c. 466.
9.1-173. Amended by Acts 2002, c. 209.
9.1-175. Amended by Acts 2002, c. 491.
9.1-176. Amended by Acts 2002, c. 491.
9.1-177.1. Amended by Acts 2003, c. 146.
9.1-178. Amended by Acts 2002, c. 491;Acts 2004, c. 395..
9.1-179. Amended by Acts 2002, c. 491.
9.1-180. Amended by Acts 2002, c. 491.
9.1-184. Amended by Acts 2002, c. 491.
9.1-184. Amended by Acts 2002, c. 836.
9.1-201. Amended by Acts 2002, c. 868.
9.1-202. Amended by Acts 2002, c. 721; Acts 2003, c. 836.
9.1-400. Amended by Acts 2003, cc. 37, 41, 1005; 2004, c. 30.
9.1-902. Amended by Acts 2004, cc. 414, 444.
9.1-903. Amended by Acts 2004, c. 834.
10-1 to 10-312. Repealed by Acts 1988, c. 891.
10.1-100. Amended by Acts 1989, c. 656.
10.1-101. Amended by Acts 1989, c. 656.
10.1-103. Amended by Acts 1989, c. 656.
10.1-104. Amended by Acts 2001, c. 370.
10.1-104.1. Amended by Acts 2004, c. 474.
10.1-105. Amended by Acts 1989, c. 656; Acts 1991, c. 84; Acts 2003, cc. 79, 89.
10.1-106. Amended by Acts 1991, c. 84; Acts 2003, cc. 79, 89.
10.1-107. Amended by Acts 1991, c. 84; Acts 1998, c. 780; Acts 2003, cc. 79, 89.
10.1-109. Amended by Acts 1991, c. 461.
10.1-110. Amended by Acts 1991, c. 360.
10.1-111. Amended by Acts 2003, cc. 79, 89.
10.1-112. Amended by Acts 1998, c. 168; Acts 2003, cc. 79, 89.
10.1-113. Amended by Acts 2003, cc. 79, 89.
10.1-114. Amended by Acts 2003, c. 940.
10.1-200. Amended by Acts 1998, c. 780; Acts 2004, c. 58.
10.1-201. Amended by Acts 2003, c. 940.
10.1-202. Amended by Acts 1992, c. 426; Acts 1994, c. 391; Acts 1996, cc. 677, 686; Acts 1994, c. 391; Acts 1996, cc. 677, 686; Acts 1999, cc. 900, 906; Acts 2001, cc. 172, 370; Acts 2003, cc. 79, 89.
10.1-204. Amended by Acts 1993, c. 755.

Sec.
10.1-206. Repealed by Acts 1991, c. 84.
10.1-218 to 10.1-225. Repealed by Acts 2003, cc. 79, 89.
10.1-312. Amended by Acts 1996, c. 77.
10.1-400. Amended by Acts 1989, c. 656; Acts 2003, c. 240; Acts 2003, c. 240.
10.1-401 to 10.1-408. Amended by Acts 2003, c. 240.
10.1-409. Amended by Acts 1998, cc. 82, 167; Acts 2003, c. 240.
10.1-410, 10.1-410.1. Amended by Acts 2003, c. 240.
10.1-410.2. Amended by Acts 1994, c. 329; Acts 2003, c. 240.
10.1-411. Amended by Acts 2003, c. 240.
10.1-411.1. Amended by Acts 1991, c. 487; Acts 2002, c. 211; Acts 2003, c. 240.
10.1-412 to 10.1-413.1. Amended by Acts 2003, c. 240.
10.1-413.2. Amended by Acts 1989, c. 656; Acts 2003, c. 240.
10.1-414. Amended by Acts 1992, c. 183; Acts 2003, c. 240.
10.1-415. Amended by Acts 1990, c. 225; Acts 2003, c. 240.
10.1-416. Amended by Acts 1988, cc. 20, 299; Acts 2003, c. 240.
10.1-417. Amended by Acts 1992, c. 341; Acts 2003, c. 240.
10.1-418. Amended by Acts 2001, c. 58; Acts 2003, c. 240.
10.1-418.1. Amended by Acts 2003, c. 240.
10.1-419. Amended by Acts 1989, c. 656.
10.1-502. Amended by Acts 1989, c. 656; Acts 1991, c. 188; Acts 1992, c. 121; Acts 2003, c. 128.
10.1-503. Amended by Acts 2003, c. 128.
10.1-512. Amended by Acts 2002, c. 251.
10.1-515. Amended by Acts 2002, cc. 143, 192.
10.1-516. Amended by Acts 2002, cc. 143, 236.
10.1-523. Amended by Acts 2001, c. 53; Acts 2002, cc. 143, 236.
10.1-525. Amended by Acts 2001, c. 53; Acts 2002, cc. 143, 236.
10.1-528. Amended by Acts 2002, cc. 143, 236.
10.1-530. Amended by Acts 2001, c. 54; Acts 2002, cc. 143, 236.
10.1-531. Amended by Acts 2003, c. 616.
10.1-536. Amended by Acts 1996, c. 493.
10.1-559.1. Amended by Acts 2000, c. 973.
10.1-559.3. Amended by Acts 2000, c. 973.
10.1-559.4. Amended by Acts 2000, c. 973.
10.1-559.5. Amended by Acts 2000, c. 973.
10.1-560. Amended by Acts 1988, cc. 690, 732; Acts 1990, c. 491; Acts 1991, c. 469; Acts 1992, c. 184; Acts 1993, c. 925; Acts 1994, c. 703; Acts 2003, c. 423; Acts 2004, c. 476.
10.1-561. Amended by Acts 1988, c. 732; Acts 1993, c. 925; Acts 2004, c. 431.
10.1-562. Amended by Acts 1988, c. 732; Acts 1992, c. 298; Acts 1993, c. 925.

Sec.
10.1-563. Amended by Acts 1988, cc. 732, 891; Acts 1993, c. 925; Acts 1999, c. 555; Acts 2001, c. 490; Acts 2003, cc. 827, 966.
10.1-564. Amended by Acts 1988, c. 891; Acts 1993, c. 925.
10.1-565. Amended by Acts 1988, cc. 694, 891; Acts 1996, c. 275.
10.1-566. Amended by Acts 1988, cc. 694, 891; Acts 1992, c. 298; Acts 1993, c. 925; Acts 2001, c. 490; Acts 2003, c. 827.
10.1-569. Amended by Acts 1988, c. 694; Acts 1992, c. 298; Acts 1993, c. 925; Acts 1995, c. 832; Acts 1996, c. 518.
10.1-571. Amended by Acts 1996, c. 688.
10.1-572. Amended by Acts 1994, c. 465; Acts 1999, c. 155.
10.1-600. Amended by Acts 1989, cc. 468, 497.
10.1-601. Repealed by Acts 1989, cc. 468, 497.
10.1-602. Amended by Acts 1989, cc. 468, 497.
10.1-603. Amended by Acts 1989, cc. 468, 497.
10.1-603.2. Amended by Acts 1991, c. 84; Acts 1994, cc. 605, 898; Acts 2004, c. 372.
10.1-603.3. Amended by Acts 2004, c. 372.
10.1-603.4. Amended by Acts 1991, c. 84; Acts 2004, c. 372.
10.1-603.5, 10.1-603.6. Amended by Acts 2004, c. 372.
10.1-603.7. Amended by Acts 1991, c. 84; Acts 2004, c. 372.
10.1-603.8. Amended by Acts 1994, cc. 605, 898; Acts 2004, c. 372.
10.1-603.9. Amended by Acts 2004, c. 372.
10.1-603.11. Amended by Acts 2004, c. 372.
10.1-603.12. Amended by Acts 2004, c. 372.
10.1-603.13. Amended by Acts 2004, c. 372.
10.1-603.14 to 10.1-603.16. Amended by Acts 1995, c. 510; Acts 2002, c. 236.
10.1-603.17 to 10.1-603.20. Amended by Acts 2002, c. 320.
10.1-603.18 to 10.1-603.20. Amended by Acts 1995, c. 510.
10.1-603.22. Amended by Acts 1995, c. 510.
10.1-604. Amended by Acts 2001, c. 92.
10.1-607. Amended by Acts 2000, c. 14.
10.1-609. Amended by Acts 1999, c. 110.
10.1-611.1. Amended by Acts 2000, cc. 23, 205.
10.1-617. Amended by Acts 1995, c. 654.
10.1-625. Amended by Acts 1995, c. 654.
10.1-628. Amended by Acts 1995, c. 654.
10.1-630. Amended by Acts 1996, cc. 105, 819.
10.1-631. Amended by Acts 1996, cc. 105, 819.
10.1-634.1. Amended by Acts 1996, c. 983.
10.1-635. Amended by Acts 2003, c. 940.
10.1-649. Amended by Acts 2003, c. 940.
10.1-705. Amended by Acts 2003, cc. 79, 89.
10.1-707. Amended by Acts 1989, cc. 656, 660; Acts 2003, cc. 79, 89.
10.1-709. Amended by Acts 2003, cc. 79, 89.

Sec.
10.1-800 to 10.1-817. Repealed by Acts 1989, c. 656.
10.1-900 to 10.1-906. Repealed by Acts 1989, c. 656.
10.1-1001. Amended by Acts 1989, c. 656.
10.1-1003. Amended by Acts 1989, c. 656.
10.1-1010. Amended by Acts 2000, c. 182; Acts 2003, c. 1014; Acts 2004, c. 364.
10.1-1011. Amended by Acts 1993, c. 390; Acts 1998, c. 487.
10.1-1017. Amended by Acts 1999, cc. 900, 906.
10.1-1018. Amended by Acts 1999, cc. 900, 906; Acts 2000, cc. 21, 294, 494, 1053; Acts 2003, c. 885.
10.1-1019. Amended by Acts 2000, c. 1053.
10.1-1020. Amended by Acts 1999, cc. 900, 906; Acts 2000, cc. 494, 1053.
10.1-1021. Amended by Acts 1999, cc. 900, 906; Acts 2000, c. 1053.
10.1-1022.1. Amended by Acts 2001, cc. 164, 168.
10.1-1024. Amended by Acts 2000, c. 1053.
10.1-1100. Amended by Acts 1993, c. 699.
10.1-1101. Amended by Acts 1995, c. 111.
10.1-1102. Amended by Acts 1990, c. 127; Acts 1992, c. 145.
10.1-1105. Amended by Acts 1989, c. 215; Acts 1993, c. 948; Acts 1997, c. 7; Acts 1998, c. 156; Acts 1999, c. 220; Acts 2000, c. 997.
10.1-1107. Amended by Acts 1999, c. 201.
10.1-1108. Amended by Acts 1995, c. 850.
10.1-1118. Amended by Acts 2004, c. 58.
10.1-1121. Amended by Acts 1989, c. 656.
10.1-1127.1. Amended by Acts 2003, c. 940.
10.1-1135. Amended by Acts 1988, c. 196.
10.1-1142. Amended by Acts 1996, cc. 74, 1008; Acts 2001, c. 319.
10.1-1146. Repealed by Acts 1996, c. 104.
10.1-1152. Amended by Acts 1993, c. 260.
10.1-1155. Amended by Acts 2004, c. 58.
10.1-1163. Amended by Acts 1996, c. 285; Acts 1997, c. 146.
10.1-1164. Amended by Acts 1996, c. 285.
10.1-1167, 10.1-1169. Amended by Acts 1996, c. 285.
10.1-1171. Amended by Acts 1996, c. 733.
10.1-1172. Amended by Acts 1990, c. 196.
10.1-1176. Amended by Acts 1998, c. 420.
10.1-1181.1. Amended by Acts 1998, c. 578.
10.1-1181.2. Amended by Acts 1998, c. 578; Acts 2002, cc. 293, 304, 320; Acts 2003, c. 812; Acts 2004, c. 228.
10.1-1181.3. Amended by Acts 2004, c. 228.
10.1-1182. Amended by Acts 1996, c. 1005.
10.1-1183. Amended by Acts 1999, c. 207.
10.1-1186. Amended by Acts 1996, c. 1005.
10.1-1186.4. Amended by Acts 2001, cc. 166, 174.
10.1-1188. Amended by Acts 1997, c. 268.
10.1-1197.3. Amended by Acts 1999, c. 893; Acts 2000, c. 131.

Sec.
10.1-1200 to 10.1-1212. Repealed by Acts 1992, c. 887.
10.1-1213 to 10.1-1221. Repealed by Acts 1992, cc. 464, 887.
10.1-1300. Amended by Acts 1990, c. 238; Acts 1991, c. 702; Acts 2004, c. 408.
10.1-1302. Amended by Acts 1992, c. 675; Acts 1994, c. 461.
10.1-1303. Amended by Acts 1990, c. 238.
10.1-1305. Amended by Acts 1988, c. 26.
10.1-1307. Amended by Acts 1988, c. 26; Acts 1990, c. 231; Acts 2004, c. 650.
10.1-1307.01. Amended by Acts 1997, c. 612.
10.1-1307.3. Amended by Acts 1995, c. 184.
10.1-1308. Amended by Acts 1988, c. 26; Acts 1993, c. 456; Acts 1997, c. 55.
10.1-1310.1. Amended by Acts 1990, c. 238.
10.1-1311. Amended by Acts 1991, c. 718.
10.1-1316. Amended by Acts 1991, c. 718; Acts 1993, c. 13.
10.1-1318. Amended by Acts 1993, c. 977; Acts 1996, c. 1032.
10.1-1320. Amended by Acts 1993, c. 13; Acts 1995, c. 135.
10.1-1321. Amended by Acts 1994, c. 358.
10.1-1321.1. Amended by Acts 1993, c. 739.
10.1-1322. Amended by Acts 1992, c. 488; Acts 1993, c. 711; Acts 1994, c. 227; Acts 1995, c. 158; Acts 2004, cc. 249, 324, 334.
10.1-1322.2. Amended by Acts 1999, c. 1022.
10.1-1322.3. Amended by Acts 2001, c. 580.
10.1-1325. Amended by Acts 2004, c. 1000.
10.1-1400. Amended by Acts 1988, c. 117; Acts 1990, cc. 499, 781, 919; Acts 1993, cc. 214, 215, 496; Acts 1996, c. 236; Acts 1997, c. 294; Acts 2001, c. 569; Acts 2003, c. 620.
10.1-1401. Amended by Acts 1994, c. 461.
10.1-1402. Amended by Acts 1988, c. 117; Acts 1990, cc. 499, 919; Acts 1991, c. 718; Acts 1992, c. 853; Acts 1993, c. 456; Acts 2003, c. 940; Acts 2004, cc. 249, 324.
10.1-1402.1. Amended by Acts 2004, cc. 249, 324.
10.1-1405. Amended by Acts 1990, c. 919.
10.1-1406. Amended by Acts 1988, c. 627; Acts 1990, cc. 472, 919; Acts 1991, c. 718; Acts 1999, c. 798.
10.1-1407. Repealed by Acts 1988, cc. 696, 891.
10.1-1408. Repealed by Acts 1988, cc. 696, 891.
10.1-1408.1. Amended by Acts 1989, c. 623; Acts 1990, cc. 360, 781, 919; Acts 1992, c. 286; Acts 1993, cc. 214, 469, 476, 496; Acts 1994, c. 614; Acts 1995, c. 442; Acts 1996, c. 236; Acts 1997, c. 875; Acts 1999, cc. 580, 584, 611, 613, 947; Acts 2000, cc. 420, 422.
10.1-1408.2. Amended by Acts 1995, c. 737; Acts 1997, c. 885.

Sec.
10.1-1408.4, 10.1-1408.5. Amended by Acts 2001, c. 767; Acts 2003, c. 834.
10.1-1409. Amended by Acts 1988, c. 569; Acts 1990, c. 919.
10.1-1410. Amended by Acts 1991, c. 702; Acts 1993, c. 837; Acts 1995, c. 739; Acts 2000, cc. 137, 138.
10.1-1411. Amended by Acts 1989, c. 440; Acts 1990, cc. 574, 781; Acts 1991, c. 237; Acts 1995, c. 216; Acts 1997, c. 495.
10.1-1413.2. Amended by Acts 2000, c. 308; Acts 2002, cc. 376, 492; Acts 2004, c. 872.
10.1-1414. Amended by Acts 1995, c. 417.
10.1-1415. Amended by Acts 1989, c. 284; Acts 1995, c. 417.
10.1-1415.1 to 10.1-1416. Amended by Acts 1995, c. 417.
10.1-1418.1. Amended by Acts 1991, c. 718; Acts 1992, c. 286; Acts 1997, c. 353.
10.1-1418.2. Amended by Acts 1997, c. 353; Acts 2003, c. 101.
10.1-1418.3. Amended by Acts 2003, c. 101.
10.1-1422. Amended by Acts 1995, c. 417.
10.1-1422.03. Amended by Acts 1998, c. 86.
10.1-1422.1. Amended by Acts 1993, c. 211.
10.1-1422.3. Amended by Acts 2003, c. 101.
10.1-1422.4. Amended by Acts 1997, c. 627.
10.1-1422.5. Repealed by Acts 2001, c. 569.
10.1-1425.7. Amended by Acts 1996, cc. 589, 599.
10.1-1425.8. Amended by Acts 1993, c. 801; Acts 1994, c. 419; Acts 1995, c. 109; Acts 1996, c. 290; Acts 1994, c. 419; Acts 1995, c. 109; Acts 1996, c. 290.
10.1-1425.10. Amended by Acts 1994, c. 169.
10.1-1425.12. Amended by Acts 1994, c. 169.
10.1-1425.21. Amended by Acts 1995, c. 115.
10.1-1425.23. Amended by Acts 1995, c. 115.
10.1-1426. Amended by Acts 1992, c. 463; Acts 2004, c. 442.
10.1-1427. Amended by Acts 1992, c. 463.
10.1-1428. Amended by Acts 1991, c. 702.
10.1-1429.1 to 10.1-1429.4. Repealed by Acts 2002, c. 378
10.1-1432. Amended by Acts 2003, c. 940.
10.1-1446. Amended by Acts 2003, c. 940.
10.1-1450. Amended by Acts 1992, c. 208; Acts 1997, c. 260.
10.1-1451. Amended by Acts 1988, c. 14.
10.1-1453. Amended by Acts 1995, c. 112.
10.1-1454.1. Amended by Acts 1998, cc. 705, 717; Acts 2003, c. 830.
10.1-1454.2. Repealed by Acts 2003, c. 830.
10.1-1455. Amended by Acts 1990, cc. 12, 781, 912, 919; Acts 1991, c. 718; Acts 1993, c. 23; Acts 1998, c. 837; Acts 1999, c. 876.
10.1-1457. Amended by Acts 1996, c. 1032.

Sec.
10.1-1500. Amended by Acts 1988, c. 390.
10.1-1602. Amended by Acts 1989, c. 226; Acts 1990, c. 210.
10.1-1603. Amended by Acts 1991, c. 706.
10.1-1610. Amended by Acts 1991, c. 706.
10.1-1618. Amended by Acts 1991, c. 706.
10.1-1700. Amended by Acts 1997, c. 130; Acts 2000, cc. 181, 724, 747.
10.1-1704. Amended by Acts 1997, c. 338.
10.1-1800. Amended by Acts 1991, c. 190; Acts 2000, cc. 21, 294; Acts 2003, cc. 78, 90.
10.1-1801.1. Amended by Acts 1999, c. 927; Acts 2000, c. 181.
10.1-1801.2. Repealed by Acts 2003, cc. 78, 90.
10.1-1802. Amended by Acts 2004, c. 650.
10.1-1900, 10.1-1901. Repealed by Acts 1989, c. 659.
10.1-2003, 10.1-2004. Amended by Acts 2001, c. 163.
10.1-2007, 10.1-2008. Amended by Acts 2001, c. 163.
10.1-2009. Amended by Acts 2004, c. 870.
10.1-2011. Amended by Acts 2004, c. 870.
10.1-2012. Amended by Acts 2004, c. 650.
10.1-2103, 10.1-2104. Amended by Acts 1997, c. 266.
10.1-2106. Amended by Acts 1997, c. 266.
10.1-2109. Amended by Acts 1998, cc. 700, 714.
10.1-2117. Amended by Acts 1999, c. 257.
10.1-2124. Amended by Acts 2004, c. 413.
10.1-2127. Amended by Acts 2003, c. 741.
10.1-2128. Amended by Acts 1999, c. 257; Acts 2001, c. 163.
10.1-2129. Amended by Acts 1999, c. 509.
10.1-2130. Amended by Acts 1999, c. 509.
10.1-2131. Amended by Acts 1999, cc. 257, 509.
10.1-2132. Amended by Acts 1999, cc. 257, 509, 549.
10.1-2202. Amended by Acts 1992, cc. 256, 801; Acts 1995, c. 21.
10.1-2203. Amended by Acts 1992, c. 801.
10.1-2204. Amended by Acts 1992, c. 801; Acts 1995, c. 21.
10.1-2205. Amended by Acts 1992, cc. 180, 801.
10.1-2206. Repealed by Acts 1992, c. 801.
10.1-2211. Amended by Acts 1992, c. 640; Acts 1994, c. 78; Acts 1995, c. 176; Acts 1997, cc. 72, 255, 270, 811; Acts 1998, c. 233; Acts 1999, c. 473; Acts 2000, c. 114; Acts 2001, cc. 267, 279, 284; Acts 2002, cc. 181, 188, 378; Acts 2003, c. 585.
10.1-2212. Amended by Acts 1990, c. 817; Acts 1993, c. 264; Acts 1994, cc. 162, 495; Acts 1995, c. 28; Acts 1996, cc. 227, 420; Acts 1998, c. 172; Acts 2000, cc. 7, 18.
10.1-2213. Amended by Acts 1992, cc. 138, 426; Acts 1999, cc. 900, 906.
10.1-2215. Repealed by Acts 1992, c. 592.

Sec.
10.1-2400 to 10.1-2404. Repealed by Acts 1999, c. 558.
10.1-2215, 10.1-2216. Repealed by Acts 1992, c. 592.
10.1-2500. Amended by Acts 1992, c. 812; Acts 1997, cc. 624, 850; Acts 1998, c. 837; Acts 2000, cc. 17, 1043.
10.1-2501. Amended by Acts 1992, c. 887.
10.1-2502. Amended by Acts 1992, c. 887; Acts 1997, cc. 624, 850.
11-1. Amended by Acts 1964, c. 314; Acts 1966, c. 397.
11-2. Amended by Acts 1976, c. 157; Acts 1990, c. 570.
11-2.3. Repealed by Acts 1991, c. 458.
11-3. Amended by Acts 1975, c. 500; Acts 1991, c. 363; Acts 1996, c. 265.
11-4.1. Amended by Acts 1974, c. 430.
11-4.2. Repealed by Acts 1975, c. 448.
11-5 to 11-7. Repealed by Acts 1964, c. 219.
11-8. Amended by Acts 1954, c. 602; Acts 1972, c. 825.
11-9.1. Amended by Acts 1984, c. 101; Acts 1995, c. 369; Acts 1997, c. 921; Acts 2004, c. 380.
11-9.2. Amended by Acts 1988, c. 343; Acts 1998, c. 225.
11-9.6. Amended by Acts 1999, c. 76.
11-14. Amended by Acts 1998, c. 400.
11-17. Repealed by Acts 1982, c. 647.
11-18 to 11-23.5. Repealed by Acts 1982, c. 647.
11-24 to 11-29. Repealed by Acts 1989, c. 684.
11-33.2. Amended by Acts 2004, c. 793.
11-34. Amended by Acts 1990, c. 587.
11-34.3. Amended by Acts 2004, c. 197.
11-35 to 11-80. Repealed by Acts 2001, c. 844.
12-1 to 12-83. Repealed by Acts 1971, Ex. Sess., c. 157.
12.1-4. Amended by Acts 1985, c. 34.
12.1-10. Amended by Acts 1994, c. 181; Acts 1996, c. 77.
12.1-13. Amended by Acts 1992, c. 11; Acts 2000, c. 986.
12.1-15. Amended by Acts 1975, c. 236; Acts 1991, c. 128.
12.1-16. Amended by Acts 1978, c. 14.
12.1-17. Amended by Acts 1986, c. 15; Acts 1995, c. 238; Acts 2002, c. 225.
12.1-18. Amended by Acts 1991, c. 123.
12.1-19. Amended by Acts 1985, cc. 528, 607; Acts 1991, c. 123; Acts 2001, c. 545; Acts 2002, c. 1.
12.1-20. Amended by Acts 1982, c. 564; Acts 1985, c. 522; Acts 1991, c. 123; Acts 2001, c. 545.
12.1-21. Repealed by Acts 2000, c. 1007.
12.1-21.1. Amended by Acts 2001, c. 545.
12.1-22. Repealed by Acts 1991, c. 123.
12.1-23. Amended by Acts 1981, c. 100.
12.1-28. Amended by Acts 1994, c. 15.
12.1-31. Amended by Acts 1978, c. 394; Acts 1980, c. 247.

Sec.
12.1-33. Amended by Acts 2000, c. 986.
12.1-34. Amended by Acts 1991, c. 710.
12.1-39. Amended by Acts 1977, c. 624.
12.1-42. Repealed by Acts 1977, c. 624.
12.1-43. Amended by Acts 1985, c. 522; Acts 2000, c. 58; Acts 2003, c. 373.
13-1 to 13-292. Repealed by Acts 1956, c. 428.
13.1-1 to 13.1-300. Repealed by Acts 1985, c. 522.
13.1-301. Amended by Acts 1986, c. 363; Acts 1992, cc. 155, 653; Acts 1994, c. 217.
13.1-301.1 to 13.1-305. Amended by Acts 1994, c. 217.
13.1-307. Amended by Acts 1994, c. 217.
13.1-308. Amended by Acts 1993, c. 822.
13.1-309, 13.1-309.1. Amended by Acts 1994, c. 217.
13.1-311.1. Amended by Acts 1994, c. 217.
13.1-316. Amended by Acts 1958, c. 564; Acts 2001, cc. 517, 541; Acts 2003, c. 592.
13.1-320. Amended by Acts 1964, c. 220; Acts 1989, c. 576.
13.1-322. Amended by Acts 1975, c. 403; Acts 1981, c. 51; Acts 2001, cc. 797, 838.
13.1-323. Amended by Acts 1989, c. 577.
13.1-333. Repealed by Acts 1989, c. 465.
13.1-336. Amended by Acts 1993, c. 822.
13.1-337. Amended by Acts 1958, c. 564.
13.1-341. Amended by Acts 1982, c. 266.
13.1-400.1. Amended by Acts 1972, c. 684; Acts 1981, c. 10; Acts 1982, cc. 56, 63; Acts 1998, c. 16.
13.1-400.3. Amended by Acts 1998, c. 16; Acts 2001, c. 706.
13.1-400.4. Amended by Acts 1998, c. 16.
13.1-400.5. Amended by Acts 1998, c. 16..
13.1-400.6. Amended by Acts 1971, Ex. Sess., c. 1; Acts 1992, c. 468.
13.1-401 to 13.1-423. Repealed by Acts 1964, c. 219.
13.1-424 to 13.1-433. Repealed by Acts 1996, c. 216.
13.1-425. Amended by Acts 1990, c. 248.
13.1-501. Amended by Acts 1966, c. 186; Acts 1974, cc. 409, 479; Acts 1975, c. 75; Acts 1976, c. 229; Acts 1987, c. 678; Acts 1988, c. 536; Acts 1990, c. 5; Acts 1991, cc. 223, 418; Acts 1992, c. 19; Acts 1997, c. 279; Acts 1998, c. 22; Acts 2001, c. 722.
13.1-503. Amended by Acts 1987, c. 678.
13.1-504. Amended by Acts 1974, cc. 374, 479; Acts 1979, c. 312; Acts 1982, c. 407; Acts 1987, c. 678; Acts 1991, cc. 223, 281, 418; Acts 1997, c. 279; Acts 1998, c. 255; Acts 2003, c. 595.
13.1-505. Amended by Acts 1974, cc. 382, 479; Acts 1980, c. 222; Acts 1981, c. 244; Acts 1984, c. 771; Acts 1987,

Sec.
c. 678; Acts 1990, c. 5; Acts 1991, c. 281; Acts 1992, c. 18; Acts 1997, c. 279.
13.1-505.1. Amended by Acts 1997, c. 279.
13.1-506. Amended by Acts 1974, c. 479; Acts 1981, c. 244; Acts 1987, c. 678; Acts 1997, c. 921.
13.1-507. Amended by Acts 1997, c. 279; Acts 2003, c. 595.
13-1-508. Amended by Acts 1981, c. 168; Acts 1984, c. 771; Acts 1993, c. 179; Acts 2003, c. 595.
13.1-509. Amended by Acts 1984, c. 771; Acts 1990, c. 90; Acts 1994, c. 10; Acts 2003, c. 595.
13.1-510. Amended by Acts 1982, c. 362; Acts 1983, c. 517; Acts 1984, c. 771; Acts 1993, c. 180.
13.1-511. Amended by Acts 1991, c. 223; Acts 2003, c. 595.
13.1-512. Repealed by Acts 2003, c. 595.
13.1-513. Reenacted without change by Acts 1960, c. 71.
13.1-514. Amended by Acts 1966, c. 186; Acts 1970, c. 286; Acts 1972, c. 683; Acts 1974, cc. 86, 380; Acts 1975, cc. 75, 500; Acts 1976, c. 656; Acts 1977, c. 111; Acts 1978, c. 397; Acts 1981, cc. 347, 356, 362; Acts 1982, c. 262; Acts 1983, cc. 231, 516; Acts 1984, cc. 298, 771; Acts 1989, c. 388; Acts 1990, c. 6; Acts 1991, c. 223; Acts 1993, c. 75; Acts 1995, cc. 208, 213, 235; Acts 1996, c. 16; Acts 1997, cc. 279, 538; Acts 1999, c. 92; Acts 2001, c. 722.
13.1-514.1. Amended by Acts 1976, c. 656; Acts 1993; c. 75; Acts 1994, cc. 184, 355; Acts 1995, c. 245; Acts 1997, c. 289; Acts 2003, c. 595.
13.1-515. Amended by Acts 1987, c. 678; Acts 1997, c. 279.
13.1-517. Amended by Acts 1958, c. 564; Acts 1987, c. 678; Acts 1990, c. 263; Acts 1991, c. 672.
13.1-518. Amended by Acts 1979, c. 379; Acts 1987, c. 678; Acts 1992, c. 157.
13.1-518.1. Amended by Acts 1997, c. 279.
13.1-519. Amended by Acts 1971, Ex. Sess., c. 1; Acts 1992, c. 468; Acts 1997, c. 279.
13.1-520. Amended by Acts 1977, c. 484; Acts 1987, c. 678.
13.1-521. Amended by Acts 1987, c. 678; Acts 1990, c. 31; Acts 2000, c. 166.
13.1-522. Amended by Acts 1987, c. 678; Acts 1997, c. 279.
13.1-523. Amended by Acts 2003, c. 595.
13.1-525. Amended by Acts 1984, c. 771; Acts 1992, c. 19.
13.1-528 to 13.1-541. Repealed by Acts 1989, c. 408.

Sec.
13.1-543. Amended by Acts 1972, c. 180; Acts 1980, cc. 701, 757; Acts 1981, c. 217; Acts 1985, c. 576; Acts 1989, c. 665; Acts 1990, cc. 481, 595; Acts 1992, cc. 13, 16; Acts 1994, c. 349; Acts 1999, c. 83; Acts 2000, cc. 194, 688, 763; Acts 2003, c. 678.
13.1-544. Amended by Acts 1981, c. 58; Acts 1989, c. 665; Acts 1994, c. 349; Acts 2000, c. 763.
13.1-544.1. Amended by Acts 1973, c. 136; Acts 1981, c. 58; Acts 2002, c. 719; Acts 2003, cc. 592, 678.
13.1-544.2. Amended by Acts 2002, c. 77; Acts 2003, c. 678.
13.1-545. Repealed by Acts 1988, c. 765.
13.1-545.1. Amended by Acts 1987, c. 425; Acts 1994, c. 349.
13.1-546. Amended by Acts 1994, c. 349; Acts 2003, c. 786.
13.1-547. Amended by Acts 1984, c. 448.
13.1-548. Amended by Acts 1975, c. 543.
13.1-549. Amended by Acts 1972, c. 655; Acts 1980, c. 757; Acts 1998, c. 27; Acts 2000, cc. 191, 763.
13.1-549.1. Amended by Acts 2000, c. 191.
13.1-549.3. Repealed by Acts 1994, c. 349.
13.1-550. Amended by Acts 1980, c. 757; Acts 1999, c. 100.
13.1-551. Amended by Acts 2002, c. 77.
13.1-552. Amended by Acts 1999, c. 100; Acts 2002, c. 77.
13.1-553. Amended by Acts 1978, c. 828; Acts 1982, c. 590; Acts 1995, c. 322.
13.1-554. Repealed by Acts 2002, c. 77.
13.1-556. Amended by Acts 1972, c. 84; Acts 2000, c. 194.
13.1-559. Amended by Acts 1978, c. 670; Acts 1990, c. 420; Acts 1991, c. 475.
13.1-560. Amended by Acts 1978, c. 670.
13.1-561. Amended by Acts 1978, c. 670; Acts 1991, c. 475; Acts 1992, c. 158.
13.1-562. Amended by Acts 1978, c. 670; Acts 1991, c. 475; Acts 1997, c. 921.
13.1-563. Amended by Acts 1978, c. 670; Acts 1991, c. 475.
13.1-565. Amended by Acts 1978, c. 607; Acts 1979, c. 104; Acts 1991, c. 475.
13.1-566. Amended by Acts 1978, c. 670; Acts 1990, c. 263; Acts 1991, c. 672.
13.1-567. Amended by Acts 1979, c. 379.
13.1-568. Amended by Acts 1992, c. 468.
13.1-569. Amended by Acts 1978, c. 670.
13.1-570. Amended by Acts 1990, c. 31; Acts 1991, c. 475; Acts 2000, c. 166.
13.1-572. Amended by Acts 1978, c. 670. Acts 1993, c. 200.
13.1-603. Amended by Acts 1992, cc. 575, 802; Acts 1994, c. 122; Acts 1997, cc. 190, 801; Acts 2001, c. 545; Acts 2002, c. 346; Acts 2003, cc. 340, 728.

Sec.
13.1-604. Amended by Acts 1986, c. 231; Acts 1995, c. 70; Acts 2000, c. 995.
13.1-605. Amended by Acts 1986, c. 231; Acts 1987, c. 183; Acts 1988, c. 405; Acts 1989, c. 152.
13.1-609. Amended by Acts 1988, c. 405; Acts 1993, c. 60.
13.1-610. Amended by Acts 2002, c. 285; Acts 2003, c. 728.
13.1-615. Amended by Acts 1988, c. 405; Acts 1989, c. 152; Acts 1991, c. 309; Acts 1997, c. 216; Acts 2001, c. 545.
13.1-615.1. Amended by Acts 2001, c. 545.
13.1-616. Amended by Acts 1987, c. 183; Acts 1988, c. 405; Acts 1995, c. 368; Acts 2001, c. 545; Acts 2004, c. 274; Acts 2004, c. 274.
13.1-617. Repealed by Acts 2001, c. 545.
13.1-619. Amended by Acts 1986, c. 622; Acts 1993, c. 113; Acts 2000, c. 162; Acts 2001, cc. 517, 541.
13.1-620. Amended by Acts 1990, c. 488; Acts 1991, c. 263; Acts 1993, cc. 61, 265, 419; Acts 1995, c. 281; Acts 1996, c. 16.
13.1-627. Amended by Acts 1993, cc. 61, 143, 419; Acts 1994, c. 452; Acts 1996, cc. 16, 257.
13.1.630. Amended by Acts 1986, c. 232; Acts 2003, c. 592.
13.1-632. Amended by Acts 1995, c. 114.
13.1-633. Amended by Acts 1996, c. 282.
13.1-634. Amended by Acts 1993, c. 113; Acts 2000, c. 162; Acts 2001, cc. 517, 541.
13.1-635. Amended by Acts 1986, c. 622; Acts 1987, c. 183; Acts 1988, c. 405; Acts 2003, c. 597.
13.1-637. Amended by Acts 1986, c. 622; Acts 1991, c. 672; Acts 1995, c. 411; Acts 2001, cc. 517, 541.
13.1-638. Amended by Acts 1990, c. 423.
13.1-639. Amended by Acts 1988, c. 193.
13.1-646. Amended by Acts 1986, c. 74; Acts 1988, c. 442; Acts 1990, c. 423; Acts 1992, c. 472.
13.1-647. Amended by Acts 1986, c. 623; Acts 1990, c. 227.
13.1-654. Amended by Acts 1990, c. 228; Acts 2003, c. 728.
13.1-655. Amended by Acts 2003, c. 728.
13.1-657. Amended by Acts 1999, c. 476; Acts 2003, c. 728.
13.1-658. Amended by Acts 1999, c. 102; Acts 2001, c. 545; Acts 2002, c. 285.
13.1-662. Amended by Acts 1990, c. 267; Acts 1997, c. 801.
13.1-663. Amended by Acts 1991, c. 405.
13.1-664.1. Amended by Acts 2002, c. 285.
13.1-668. Amended by Acts 1986, c. 321.
13.1-671.1. Amended by Acts 1997, c. 226.

Sec.
13.1-672. Repealed by Acts 1992, c. 802.
13.1-672.4. Amended by Acts 1993, c. 233.
13.1-672.5. Amended by Acts 1993, c. 233.
13.1-673. Amended by Acts 1990, c. 337.
13.1-675. Amended by Acts 1991, c. 112.
13.1-677. Amended by Acts 1990, c. 228.
13.1-679. Amended by Acts 1991, c. 124.
13.1-680. Amended by Acts 1991, c. 124.
13.1-682. Amended by Acts 1991, c. 124.
13.1-686. Amended by Acts 2002, c. 285.
13.1-688. Amended by Acts 1992, c. 471.
13.1-692.1. Amended by Acts 1988, c. 561.
13.1-693. Amended by Acts 1994, c. 189.
13.1-695. Amended by Acts 1990, c. 282; Acts 1991, cc. 124, 146.
13.1-700. Repealed by Acts 1987, cc. 59, 257.
13.1-704. Amended by Acts 1987, cc. 59, 257; Acts 1988, c. 561.
13.1-706. Amended by Acts 1989, c. 483; Acts 1990, c. 292.
13.1-708. Amended by Acts 1996, c. 238; Acts 1997, c. 400.
13.1-710. Amended by Acts 2002, c. 285.
13.1-711. Amended by Acts 2002, c. 497.
13.1-712. Repealed by Acts 1988, c. 194.
13.1-716. Amended by Acts 1991, c. 228.
13.1-718. Amended by Acts 1991, c. 109.
13.1-719. Amended by Acts 1990, c. 230.
13.1-720. Amended by Acts 1992, c. 575; Acts 2000, c. 53; Acts 2003, c. 597.
13.1-722. Amended by Acts 1987, c. 191; Acts 1992, c. 575; Acts 1997, c. 190; Acts 2003, c. 340.
13.1-722.1. Amended by Acts 2002, c. 497; Acts 2003, c. 597.
13.1-722.10. Amended by Acts 2003, c. 598.
13.1-722.12. Amended by Acts 2003, c. 598.
13.1-723. Amended by Acts 1994, c. 710.
13.1-724. Amended by Acts 1987, c. 181; Acts 1996, c. 77.
13.1-725. Amended by Acts 1988, c. 442.
13.1-726. Amended by Acts 1988, c. 442.
13.1-727. Amended by Acts 1988, c. 442.
13.1-728. Repealed by Acts 1988, c. 442.
13.1-728.1. Amended by Acts 1990, c. 252.
13.1-728.2. Amended by Acts 1990, c. 252.
13.1-729. Amended by Acts 1992, c. 575.
13.1-730. Amended by Acts 1986, c. 540; Acts 1988, c. 442; Acts 1990, c. 229; Acts 1992, c. 575; Acts 1996, c. 246; Acts 1999, c. 288.
13.1-750. Amended by Acts 1994, c. 291; Acts 2004, c. 162.
13.1-751. Amended by Acts 1986, c. 234.
13.1-752. Amended by Acts 1987, c. 2; Acts 1988, c. 405; Acts 1991, c. 125; Acts 1997, c. 216; Acts 2000, c. 52.
13.1-753. Amended by Acts 1991, c. 310.
13.1-754. Amended by Acts 1986, c. 234; Acts 1988, c. 405; Acts 2004, c. 601.
13.1-756. Repealed by Acts 1988, c. 405.
13.1-757. Amended by Acts 1990, c. 428.

Sec.
13.1-758. Amended by Acts 1986, c. 571; Acts 1990, c. 325; Acts 1991, c. 672.
13.1-759. Amended by Acts 1994, c. 348; Acts 2001, cc. 517, 541; Acts 2002, c. 497; Acts 2004, c. 274.
13.1-760. Amended by Acts 1986, c. 571; Acts 1987, c. 431.
13.1-762. Amended by Acts 1986, cc. 232, 571; Acts 2003, c. 592.
13.1-763. Amended by Acts 1994, c. 348; Acts 2000, c. 162; Acts 2001, cc. 517, 541.
13.1-764. Amended by Acts 1986, c. 622; Acts 2003, c. 597.
13.1-766. Amended by Acts 1986, cc. 571, 622; Acts 1991, c. 672; Acts 2001, cc. 517, 541.
13.1-766.1. Amended by Acts 1990, c. 283; Acts 1992, c. 575; Acts 1997, c. 190; Acts 2004, c. 274.
13.1-767. Amended by Acts 1991, c. 672; Acts 1994, c. 291.
13.1-768. Amended by Acts 1987, c. 2; Acts 1988, c. 405; Acts 1991, c. 125; Acts 1997, c. 216; Acts 2000, c. 52.
13.1-769. Amended by Acts 1991, c. 672; Acts 1995, c. 76.
13.1-769.1. Amended by Acts 1988, c. 405; Acts 2004, c. 274.
13.1-775. Amended by Acts 1986, c. 233; Acts 1987, c. 2; Acts 1997, c. 216.
13.1-775.1. Amended by Acts 1991, c. 311; Acts 1997, c. 216.
13.1-803. Amended by Acts 1997, c. 801; Acts 2002, c. 497.
13.1-804. Amended by Acts 1986, c. 231; Acts 1995, c. 70; Acts 2000, c. 995.
13.1-805. Amended by Acts 1986, c. 231; Acts 1987, c. 183; Acts 1988, c. 405; Acts 1989, c. 152.
13.1-809. Amended by Acts 1988, c. 405; Acts 1993, c. 60.
13.1-815. Amended by Acts 1988, c. 405; Acts 1989, c. 152; Acts 1997, c. 216; Acts 2003, c. 374.
13.1-816. Amended by Acts 1987, c. 183; Acts 1988, c. 405; Acts 1995, c. 368; Acts 2003, c. 374; Acts 2004, c. 274.
13.1-817. Repealed by Acts 1991, c. 123.
13.1-819. Amended by Acts 1986, c. 622; Acts 1993, c. 113; Acts 2000, c. 162; Acts 2001, cc. 517, 541.
13.1-826. Amended by Acts 1996, c. 77.
13.1-829. Amended by Acts 1986, c. 232; Acts 2003, c. 592.
13.1-831. Amended by Acts 1995, c. 114; Acts 2002, c. 285.
13.1-832. Amended by Acts 1996, c. 282.
13.1-833. Amended by Acts 1993, c. 113; Acts 2000, c. 162; Acts 2001, cc. 517, 541

Sec.
13.1-834. Amended by Acts 1986, c. 622; Acts 1987, c. 183; Acts 1988, c. 405; Acts 2003, c. 597.
13.1-836. Amended by Acts 1986, c. 622; Acts 1991, c. 672; Acts 2001, cc. 517, 541.
13.1-842. Amended by Acts 1986, c. 529; Acts 2002, c. 607.
13.1-846. Amended by Acts 2002, c. 285.
13.1-847. Amended by Acts 1999, c. 101; Acts 2002, c. 285.
13.1-851. Amended by Acts 1986, c. 321.
13.1-852.1. Amended by Acts 1997, c. 217.
13.1-857. Amended by Acts 1986, c. 529; Acts 2004, c. 303.
13.1-858. Amended by Acts 1987, c. 140; Acts 1989, c. 419.
13.1-859. Amended by Acts 1991, c. 124.
13.1-860. Amended by Acts 1987, c. 177; Acts 1991, c. 124.
13.1-862. Amended by Acts 1991, c. 124.
13.1-866. Amended by Acts 2002, c. 285.
13.1-868. Amended by Acts 1992, c. 471.
13.1-870.1. Amended by Acts 1988, c. 561; Acts 1989, c. 422.
13.1-872. Amended by Acts 1994, c. 189.
13.1-874. Amended by Acts 1990, c. 282; Acts 1991, c. 124.
13.1-879. Repealed by Acts 1987, cc. 59, 257.
13.1-883. Amended by Acts 1987, cc. 59, 257; Acts 1988, c. 561.
13.1-888. Amended by Acts 2002, c. 285.
13.1-889. Amended by Acts 2002, c. 607.
13.1-895. Amended by Acts 2002, c. 607.
13.1-896. Amended by Acts 2000, c. 53; Acts 2003, c. 597.
13.1-898. Amended by Acts 2002, c. 607.
13.1-898.1. Amended by Acts 2002, c. 607.
13.1-900. Amended by Acts 1991, c. 110.
13.1-904. Amended by Acts 2003, c. 596.
13.1-912. Amended by Acts 1986, c. 529; Acts 2004, c. 162.
13.1-913. Amended by Acts 1986, c. 234.
13.1-914. Amended by Acts 1987, c. 2; Acts 1988, c. 405; Acts 1991, c. 125; Acts 1997, c. 216; Acts 2000, c. 52.
13.1-915. Amended by Acts 1991, c. 310.
13.1-916. Amended by Acts 1986, c. 234; Acts 1988, c. 405; Acts 2004, c. 601.
13.1-918. Repealed by Acts 1988, c. 405.
13.1-920. Amended by Acts 1986, c. 571; Acts 1990, c. 325; Acts 1991, c. 672.
13.1-921. Amended by Acts 1994, c. 348; Acts 2001, cc. 517, 541; Acts 2004, c. 274.
13.1-922. Amended by Acts 1986, c. 571.
13.1-924. Amended by Acts 1986, cc. 232, 571; Acts 1987, c. 431; Acts 2003, c. 592.
13.1-925. Amended by Acts 1994, c. 348; Acts 2000, c. 162; Acts 2001, cc. 517, 541; Acts 2002, c. 607.

Sec.
13.1-1067. Amended by Acts 1992, cc. 574, 575; Acts 1993, c. 113; Acts 1996, c. 282; Acts 1997, c. 190; Acts 2001, c. 548; Acts 2003, c. 340.
13.1-1067.1. Repealed by Acts 1993, c. 113.
13.1-1070. Amended by Acts 1997, c. 190; Acts 2003, c. 340; Acts 2004, c. 601.
13.1-1071. Amended by Acts 1993, c. 113.
13.1-1072. Amended by Acts 1993, c. 113; Acts 1997, c. 190; Acts 2003, cc. 340, 597; Acts 2004, c. 601.
13.1-1073. Amended by Acts 1997, c. 190; Acts 2003, c. 340.
13.1-1102. Amended by Acts 1993, c. 113; Acts 1994, c. 349; Acts 1996, c. 265; Acts 1999, c. 83; Acts 2000, cc. 194, 688, 763; Acts 2003, c. 678.
13.1-1103. Amended by Acts 1994, c. 349; Acts 1997, c. 133; Acts 2000, c. 763.
13.1-1104. Amended by Acts 1996, c. 265; Acts 2002, c. 608; Acts 2003, c. 592.
13.1-1105. Amended by Acts 1996, c. 265.
13.1-1106, 13.1-1107. Amended by Acts 1994, c. 349.
13.1-1107. Amended by Acts 2003, c. 786.
13.1-1110. Amended by Acts 1996, c. 265.
13.1-1111. Amended by Acts 1998, c. 27; Acts 2000, cc. 191, 763.
13.1-1112. Amended by Acts 2000, c. 191.
13.1-1114. Repealed by Acts 1994, c. 349.
13.1-1115. Amended by Acts 1999, c. 100.
13.1-1117. Amended by Acts 1995, c. 168; Acts 1996, c. 265; Acts 1999, c. 100.
13.1-1119. Repealed by Acts 2002, c. 346.
13.1-1121. Amended by Acts 1996, c. 265.
13.1-1204. Amended by Acts 2003, c. 373; Acts 2004, c. 274.
13.1-1213. Amended by Acts 2003, c. 373.
13.1-1214. Amended by Acts 2003, cc. 373, 592.
13.1-1217. Amended by Acts 2003, c. 373.
13.1-1221. Amended by Acts 2003, c. 597.
13.1-1239. Amended by Acts 2004, c. 601.
13.1-1242. Amended by Acts 2004, c. 274.
13.1-1254. Amended by Acts 2003, c. 373; Acts 2004, cc. 274, 601.
13.1-1255. Amended by Acts 2004, c. 316.
13.1-1260. Repealed by Acts 2003, c. 373.
13.1-1261. Amended by Acts 2003, c. 373.
14-1 to 14-197. Repealed by Acts 1964, c. 386.
14.1-1 to 14.1-201. Repealed by Acts 1998, c. 872.
15-1 to 15-969.3. Repealed by Acts 1962, c. 623.
15.1-1 to 15.1-1726. Repealed by Acts 1997, c. 587.
15.2-106. Amended by Acts 1998, c. 502; Acts 2004, c. 565.
15.2-301. Amended by Acts 2000, c. 741.
15.2-404. Amended by Acts 2000, cc. 613, 953.
15.2-408. Amended by Acts 2003, c. 1015.
15.2-412. Amended by Acts 2002, c. 747.
15.2-502. Amended by Acts 1999, c. 718.
15.2-518. Amended by Acts 2002, c. 747.

Sec.
15.2-527. Amended by Acts 2002, c. 747.
15.2-705. Amended by Acts 1998, cc. 345, 369.
15.2-708. Amended by Acts 1999, c. 136.
15.2-709.1. Amended by Acts 2003, c. 739.
15.2-710. Amended by Acts 2004, cc. 22, 510.
15.2-717. Amended by Acts 2003, c. 1036.
15.2-720.1. Amended by Acts 2004, cc. 22, 510.
15.2-726. Amended by Acts 2004, cc. 22, 510.
15.2-729. Amended by Acts 2000, c. 851; Acts 2003, c. 940.
15.2-738. Amended by Acts 2000, cc. 947, 1006.
15.2-852. Amended by Acts 2004, cc. 498, 552.
15.2-858. Amended by Acts 2004, c. 561.
15.2-901. Amended by Acts 1999, c. 174; Acts 2000, c. 740; Acts 2001, c. 750; Acts 2003, c. 829.
15.2-903. Amended by Acts 1998, c. 180; Acts 2001, c. 10; Acts 2004, c. 493.
15.2-904. Amended by Acts 2003, c. 829; Acts 2004, cc. 513, 934.
15.2-905. Amended by Acts 1999, c. 901; Acts 2004, cc. 508, 934.
15.2-906. Amended by Acts 1999, c. 174; Acts 2003, c. 207; Acts 2004, c. 968.
15.2-912. Amended by Acts 2000, c. 842; Acts 2001, c. 270.
15.2-912.2. Amended by Acts 2004, c. 462.
15.2-912.3. Amended by Acts 2004, c. 462.
15.2-915. Amended by Acts 2002, c. 484; Acts 2003, c. 943; Acts 2004, cc. 837, 923.
15.2-915.2. Amended by Acts 2004, c. 462.
15.2-924. Amended by Acts 2001, c. 258.
15.2-923. Amended by Acts 2004, c. 402.
15.2-926. Amended by Acts 1998, c. 865; Acts 1999, c. 1023; Acts 2004, c. 462.
15.2-926.2. Amended by Acts 2004, c. 462.
15.2-928. Amended by Acts 2000, c. 231; Acts 2002, cc. 161, 690; Acts 2003, c. 518.
15.2-941. Amended by Acts 2001, c. 66.
15.2-953. Amended by Acts 1998, c. 376; Acts 1999, c. 430; Acts 2003, c. 182; Acts 2004, c. 272.
15.2-961. Amended by Acts 2002, cc. 191, 226; Acts 2003, c. 875.
15.2-963. Amended by Acts 1998, c. 194.
15.2-965.1. Amended by Acts 2004, cc. 865, 891.
15.2-1104. Amended by Acts 2003, c. 216.
15.2-1104.1. Amended by Acts 2003, cc. 757, 758.
15.2-1113. Amended by Acts 2000, c. 229.
15.2-1115. Amended by Acts 2004, cc. 533, 968.
15.2-1127. Amended by Acts 1999, c. 250.
15.2-1132. Amended by Acts 2002, cc. 31, 451.
15.2-1208. Amended by Acts 2004, cc. 62, 393.
15.2-1209. Amended by Acts 2000, c. 229; Acts 2004, c. 930.
15.2-1209.1. Amended by Acts 2004, c. 462.
15.2-1215. Amended by Acts 1998, cc. 640, 756.
15.2-1221. Repealed by Acts 2000, c. 939.

Sec.
15.2-1231. Amended by Acts 2002, cc. 452, 747.
15.2-1242. Amended by Acts 1999, c. 126.
15.2-1246. Amended by Acts 2000, c. 300.
15.2-1302. Amended by Acts 2000, c. 708; Acts 2001, c. 14.
15.2-1308. Amended by Acts 2003, cc. 55, 77.
15.2-1309. Amended by Acts 2000, c. 749.
15.2-1308. Amended by Acts 2003, cc. 55, 77.
15.2-1408. Amended by Acts 2003, c. 945.
15.2-1411. Amended by Acts 2002, c. 27.
15.2-1412. Amended by Acts 1998, c. 427.
15.2-1414.2. Amended by Acts 2000, c. 299; Acts 2001, cc. 9, 254.
15.2-1414.5. Amended by Acts 2004, c. 570.
15.2-1416. Amended by Acts 2004, c. 549.
15.2-1427. Amended by Acts 1998, c. 823; Acts 2000, c. 895.
15.2-1433. Amended by Acts 2003, c. 200.
15.2-1500. Amended by Acts 1998, c. 906; Acts 1999, c. 916; Acts 2002, cc. 479, 489.
15.2-1503.1. Amended by Acts 2004, c. 160.
15.2-1505. Amended by Acts 1999, c. 375; Acts 2000, c. 276; Acts 2002, c. 37.
15.2-1506. Amended by Acts 2000, c. 363.
15.2-1507. Amended by Acts 2000, cc. 947, 1006; Acts 2001, c. 589.
15.2-1508. Amended by Acts 2003, c. 204.
15.2-1508.3. Amended by Acts 2004, c. 157.
15.2-1512.1. Amended by Acts 1998, c. 256; Acts 2000, cc. 66, 657.
15.2-1512.2. Amended by Acts 2002, c. 886.
15.2-1517. Amended by Acts 1999, c. 797; Acts 2003, c. 409.
15.2-1518. Amended by Acts 1999, c. 151; Acts 2004, c. 648.
15.2-1522. Amended by Acts 2000, c. 293.
15.2-1527. Amended by Acts 2000, cc. 618, 632.
15.2-1533. Amended by Acts 2000, cc. 618, 632.
15.2-1534. Amended by Acts 2002, c. 294.
15.2-1535. Amended by Acts 1998, c. 488; Acts 1999, c. 811; Acts 2001, c. 8.
15.2-1541.1. Amended by Acts 2002, c. 747.
15.2-1542. Amended by Acts 2002, c. 802.
15.2-1604. Amended by Acts 2004, c. 453.
15.2-1605.1. Amended by Acts 1999, c. 283; Acts 2002, c. 832.
15.2-1609.2. Amended by Acts 2000, cc. 66, 657.
15.2-1609.3. Amended by Acts 2004, c. 210.
15.2-1610. Amended by Acts 1998, c. 413.
15.2-1613.1. Amended by Acts 2003, c. 623.
15.2-1627.3. Amended by Acts 1999, c. 9.
15.2-1628. Amended by Acts 2000, c. 913.
15.2-1630. Amended by Acts 2000, c. 913.
15.2-1632. Amended by Acts 2000, c. 913.
15.2-1633. Amended by Acts 2000, c. 913.
15.2-1636.8. Amended by Acts 2000, c. 913.
15.2-1636.20. Amended by Acts 1999, cc. 148, 185.
15.2-1643. Amended by Acts 2002, c. 758.
15.2-1702. Amended by Acts 2000, c. 298.

Sec.
15.2-1704. Amended by Acts 1998, c. 425; Acts 1999, c. 495.
15.2-1706. Amended by Acts 1999, c. 635; Acts 2002, c. 345; Acts 2004, c. 477.
15.2-1716. Amended by Acts 2001, c. 505; Acts 2003, c. 796; Acts 2004, c. 273.
15.2-1717.1. Amended by Acts 2002, c. 328.
15.2-1718. Amended by Acts 2004, cc. 248, 443.
15.2-1720. Amended by Acts 2001, c. 834; Acts 2002, c. 254.
15.2-1722. Amended by Acts 1999, cc. 703, 726.
15.2-1727. Amended by Acts 2004, c. 769.
15.2-1736. Amended by Acts 2002, c. 684, 709, 876.
15.2-1737. Amended by Acts 2002, cc. 836, 868; Acts 2003, c. 922.
15.2-1738. Amended by Acts 1999, c. 278.
15.2-1747. Amended by Acts 2000, c. 772; Acts 2002, c. 350.
15.2-1800. Amended by Acts 1998, c. 696.
15.2-1802. Amended by Acts 1998, c. 198.
15.2-1812. Amended by Acts 1998, c. 752.
15.2-1812.2. Amended by Acts 2004, c. 462.
15.2-1901. Amended by Acts 2001, c. 538.
15.2-1902. Amended by Acts 2003, c. 940.
15.2-1904. Amended by Acts 2003, c. 680, 940.
15.2-1905. Amended by Acts 2003, c. 940.
15.2-2019. Amended by Acts 1999, c. 671.
15.2-2021. Amended by Acts 1999, cc. 409, 417.
15.2-2x100. Amended by Acts 2001, c. 498.
15.2-2101. Amended by Acts 2001, c. 498.
15.2-2102. Amended by Acts 2001, c. 498.
15.2-2108. Amended by Acts 1998, c. 762.
15.2-2108.1. Amended by Acts 1998, cc. 643, 652.
15.2-2108.11. Amended by Acts 2004, c. 586.
15.2-2109. Amended by Acts 2000, c. 663; Acts 2003, c. 940.
15.2-2110. Amended by Acts 2000, cc. 777, 799; Acts 2001, cc. 306, 326; Acts 2002, c. 295; Acts 2003, cc. 167, 215; Acts 2004, cc. 24, 712, 816.
15.2-2114. Amended by Acts 1998, c. 182; Acts 2003, c. 390; Acts 2004, c. 507.
15.2-2115. Amended by Acts 2003, c. 940.
15.2-2117. Amended by Acts 2001, c. 120.
15.2-2118. Amended by Acts 1998, cc. 313, 568; Acts 1999, cc. 311, 767, 841; Acts 2000, c. 287; Acts 2002, c. 193; Acts 2003, c. 191; Acts 2004, cc. 24, 712.
15.2-2119. Amended by Acts 1998, c. 223; Acts 2001, c. 13.
15.2-2140. Amended by Acts 2003, c. 940.
15.2-2143. Amended by Acts 1998, cc. 224, 328.
15.2-2144. Amended by Acts 2000, c. 1004; Acts 2004, c. 438
15.2-2146. Amended by Acts 2003, c. 940.
15.2-2159. Amended by Acts 2001, c. 338; Acts 2002, c. 275; Acts 2003, c. 48.
15.2-2160. Amended by Acts 2003, c. 720.
15.2-2202. Amended by Acts 2001, c. 281.

Sec.
15.2-2204. Amended by Acts 2001, c. 406; Acts 2002, c. 634; Acts 2004, cc. 539, 799.
15.2-2209. Amended by Acts 2003, c. 192.
15.2-2214. Amended by Acts 2003, c. 403.
15.2-2223. Amended by Acts 2003, c. 811; Acts 2004, cc. 691, 799.
15.2-2226. Amended by Acts 2000, c. 893.
15.2-2229. Amended by Acts 2000, c. 893.
15.2-2232. Amended by Acts 1998, c. 683.
15.2-2241. Amended by Acts 2002, c. 517; Acts 2004, c. 952.
15.2-2242. Amended by Acts 2000, cc. 652, 711; Acts 2002, c. 703.
15.2-2243. Amended by Acts 2001, c. 704.
15.2-2244. Amended by Acts 1998, c. 457.
15.2-2245. Amended by Acts 2002, c. 779.
15.2-2247. Amended by Acts 1999, c. 77.
15.2-2254. Amended by Acts 2003, c. 408.
15.2-2257. Amended by Acts 1998, c. 623.
15.2-2259. Amended by Acts 2003, c. 716.
15.2-2260. Amended by Acts 2002, c. 530.
15.2-2265. Amended by Acts 2000, c. 165.
15.2-2283. Amended by Acts 2004, c. 799.
15.2-2286. Amended by Acts 1998, c. 385; Acts 1999, c. 792; Acts 2000, cc. 764, 817; Acts 2001, c. 240; Acts 2002, cc. 547, 703.
15.2-2288.1. Amended by Acts 2002, c. 703.
15.2-2291. Amended by Acts 1998, c. 585.
15.2-2295. Amended by Acts 2002, c. 180.
15.2-2297. Amended by Acts 2001, c. 703.
15.2-2298. Amended by Acts 2001, c. 703.
15.2-2300. Amended by Acts 2004, c. 531.
15.2-2303. Amended by Acts 2001, c. 703.
15.2-2303.2. Amended by Acts 2003, c. 522.
15.2-2304. Amended by Acts 2001, cc. 18, 313; Acts 2002, c. 151; Acts 2004, c. 543.
15.2-2307. Amended by Acts 1998, c. 801; Acts 2002, c. 823; Acts 2003, cc. 21, 53, 189; Acts 2004, c. 538.
15.2-2308. Amended by Acts 1998, cc. 346, 520, 528; Acts 1999, c. 838; Acts 2002, c. 205.
15.2-2309. Amended by Acts 2000, c. 1050; Acts 2002, c. 545; Acts 2003, c. 403.
15.2-2314. Amended by Acts 2001, c. 422; Acts 2003, c. 568.
15.2-2317. Amended by Acts 2000, c. 495.
15.2-2400. Amended by Acts 2000, cc. 853, 925.
15.2-2402. Amended by Acts 2000, cc. 853, 925.
15.2-2403. Amended by Acts 1999, c. 295; Acts 2000, cc. 743, 853, 925; Acts 2002, cc. 198, 202, 230, 356; Acts 2003, c. 493; Acts 2004, c. 810.
15.2-2404. Amended by Acts 1998, cc. 324, 864; Acts 1999, c. 386.
15.2-2413. Amended by Acts 1999, c. 386.
15.2-2418. Amended by Acts 2004, c. 577.
15.2-2650. Amended by Acts 2003, c. 570.

Sec.
15.2-2651. Amended by Acts 2003, c. 570.
15.2-2656. Amended by Acts 2003, c. 679.
15.2-2702. Amended by Acts 2000, cc. 618, 632.
15.2-2704. Amended by Acts 2003, c. 566.
15.2-2800. Amended by Acts 2001, c. 483.
15.2-2801. Amended by Acts 2002, c. 283.
15.2-2804. Amended by Acts 2002, c. 283.
15.2-2901. Amended by Acts 2003, c. 197.
15.2-2903. Amended by Acts 2004, c. 234.
15.2-3201. Amended by Acts 1999, cc. 692, 705, 744; Acts 2001, c. 733; Acts 2002, c. 786; Acts 2004, c. 879.
15.2-3209. Amended by Acts 1999, c. 345.
15.2-3221. Amended by Acts 2003, c. 940.
15.2-3226. Amended by Acts 2001, c. 3.
15.2-3232. Amended by Acts 2003, c. 173.
15.2-3306. Amended by Acts 2002, c. 199.
15.2-3400. Amended by Acts 2003, cc. 197, 444, 583.
15.2-3604. Amended by Acts 2003, c. 1015.
15.2-3831. Amended by Acts 2003, c. 1015.
15.2-4203. Amended by Acts 1998, cc. 668, 686; Acts 2000, c. 984.
15.2-4207. Amended by Acts 1998, cc. 668, 686.
15.2-4208. Amended by Acts 1998, cc. 668, 686.
15.2-4209. Amended by Acts 1998, cc. 668, 686.
15.2-4210. Amended by Acts 1998, cc. 668, 686.
15.2-4305. Amended by Acts 1998, c. 833.
15.2-4307. Amended by Acts 1998, c. 833.
15.2-4308. Amended by Acts 1998, c. 833.
15.2-4309. Amended by Acts 1998, c. 833.
15.2-4313. Amended by Acts 1998, c. 833, Acts 2000, c. 1069.
15.2-4314. Amended by Acts 2000, c. 521.
15.2-4507. Amended by Acts 2000, cc. 439, 443; Acts 2004, c. 1000.
15.2-4509. Amended by Acts 2002, c. 32.
15.2-4510. Amended by Acts 2004, c. 1000.
15.2-4512. Amended by Acts 2004, c. 1000.
15.2-4518. Amended by Acts 2003, c. 940.
15.2-4816 to 15.2-4828. Repealed by Acts 2002, c. 846.
15.2-4832. Amended by Acts 2004, c. 1000.
15.2-4836. Amended by Acts 2004, c. 1000.
15.2-4901. Amended by Acts 2002, c. 680, 725.
15.2-4902. Amended by Acts 1999, c. 379.
15.2-4903. Amended by Acts 1999, c. 157; Acts 2000, c. 398; Acts 2001, cc. 5, 6, 730; Acts 2002, cc. 169, 680, 725; Acts 2003, cc. 159, 343, 345, 350, 357; Acts 2004, cc. 292, 782, 933.
15.2-4904. Amended by Acts 1999, cc. 337, 408, 414; Acts 2000, c. 963; Acts 2001, c. 121; Acts 2003, cc. 347, 357.
15.2-4905. Amended by Acts 1998, c. 728.
15.2-4907. Amended by Acts 1998, c. 728.
15.2-4908. Amended by Acts 2003, cc. 353, 683.
15.2-4917. Amended by Acts 1998, c. 728.
15.2-5002. Amended by Acts 1998, cc. 39, 784.
15.2-5102. Amended by Acts 1999, cc. 896, 925.
15.2-5114. Amended by Acts 2001, c. 120; Acts

Sec.

2002, c. 446; Acts 2003, c. 940; Acts 2004, c. 545.
15.2-5136. Amended by Acts 1998, c. 869; Acts 2001, c. 400.
15.2-5152. Amended by Acts 2003, c. 712.
15.2-5153. Amended by Acts 2003, c. 443.
15.2-5155. Amended by Acts 2003, c. 712.
15.2-5156. Amended by Acts 1998, c. 188.
15.2-5158. Amended by Acts 2000, cc. 724, 747; Acts 2004, c. 637.
15.2-5201. Amended by Acts 2000, c. 468.
15.2-5343. Amended by Acts 2003, c. 940.
15.2-5367. Amended by Acts 2003, c. 940.
15.2-5425. Amended by Acts 2003, c. 940.
15.2-5504. Amended by Acts 2004, c. 806.
15.2-5601. Amended by Acts 1999, cc. 502, 528.
15.2-5806. Amended by Acts 2001, cc. 424, 441.
15.2-5807. Amended by Acts 2003, c. 940.
15.2-5900. Amended by Acts 2002, c. 689.
15.2-5904. Amended by Acts 2002, c. 651.
15.2-5905. Amended by Acts 2002, c. 651.
15.2-5908. Amended by Acts 2002, cc. 651, 689.
15.2-5914. Amended by Acts 2002, cc. 651, 689.
15.2-6100 to 15.2-6110. Repealed by Acts 2003, c. 158.
15.2-6006. Amended by Acts 2004, cc. 36, 177.
15.2-6011. Amended by Acts 2004, cc. 36, 177.
15.2-6302. Amended by Acts 2003, c. 246.
15.2-6400. Amended by Acts 1999, cc. 540, 804, 820, 837, 882; Acts 2000, cc. 892, 915, 960, 965; Acts 2001, cc. 391, 404; Acts 2003, c. 874; Acts 2004, cc. 603, 640.
15.2-6402. Amended by Acts 1999, cc. 820, 882; Acts 2000, c. 892; Acts 2001, c. 391; Acts 2002, c. 691.
15.2-6403. Amended by Acts 1999, cc. 820, 882; Acts 2000, c. 892; Acts 2001, cc. 7, 15, 390, 391; Acts 2002, c. 691.
15.2-6405. Amended by Acts 2002, c. 691; Acts 2003, c. 874.
15.2-6406. Amended by Acts 2004, cc. 42, 603; 640.
15.2-6409. Amended by Acts 2002, c. 691.
15.2-6612. Amended by Acts 2003, c. 353.
15.2-6701. Amended by Acts 2004, cc. 35, 158.
15.2-6703. Amended by Acts 2004, cc. 35, 158.
16-1 to 16-172.84. Repealed by Acts 1956, c. 555.
16.1-1 to 16.1-69. Repealed by Acts 1972, c. 708; Acts 1973, c. 546.
16.1-69.1. Amended by Acts 1973, c. 546.
16.1-69.2. Amended by Acts 1973, c. 546.
16.1-69.3. Amended by Acts 1973, c. 546.
16.1-69.4. Amended by Acts 1973, c. 546.
16.1-69.5. Amended by Acts 1973, c. 546; Acts 1975, c. 334; Acts 1993, c. 929.
16.1-69.6. Amended by Acts 1973, c. 546; Acts 1974, c. 297; Acts 1976, c. 126; Acts 1977, c. 5; Acts 1983, c. 149; Acts 1986, c. 405; Acts 1987, c. 624; Acts 1992, c. 744.

Sec.

16.1-69.6:1. Amended by Acts 1975, c. 41; Acts 1976, c. 56; Acts 1977, c. 5; Acts 1978, c. 2; Acts 1979, c. 7; Acts 1980, c. 93; Acts 1981, c. 26; Acts 1982, c. 4; Acts 1983, c. 1; Acts 1985, c. 44; Acts 1986, c. 75; Acts 1987, c. 16; Acts 1988, c. 22; Acts 1989, c. 44; Acts 1990, c. 112; Acts 1992, c. 91; Acts 1993, cc. 8, 31, 929; Acts 1994, c. 89; Acts 1994, 1st Sp. Sess., cc. 3, 7; Acts 1995, c. 20; Acts 1996, c. 121; Acts 1997, c. 16; Acts 1998, c. 2; Acts 1999, c. 11; Acts 2000, c. 43; Acts 2001, c. 16; Acts 2004, Sp. Sess. I, c. 4.
16.1-69.9:2. Amended by Acts 2001, c. 256.
16.1-69.9:3. Amended by Acts 1999, c. 319.
16.1-69.7. Amended by Acts 1973, c. 546; Acts 1993, c. 979.
16.1-69.8. Amended by Acts 1973, c. 546; Acts 1993, c. 929.
16.1-69.9. Amended by Acts 1973, c. 546; Acts 1975, c. 5; Acts 1976, c. 374; Acts 1977, c. 536; Acts 1980, c. 194; Acts 2004, c. 452.
16.1-69.9:1. Amended by Acts 1975, c. 334; Acts 1993, c. 929; Acts 2004, c. 452.
16.1-69.9:2. Amended by Acts 1980, c. 194.
16.1-69.9:3. Amended by Acts 1975, c. 101; Acts 2004, c. 331.
16.1-69.9:4. Amended by Acts 1993, c. 368; Acts 2004, c. 452.
16.1-69.10. Amended by Acts 1973, c. 546; Acts 1980, c. 194; Acts 1993, c. 929; Acts 1999, c. 319.
16.1-69.11. Amended by Acts 1973, c. 546; Acts 1975, c. 334; Acts 1976, c. 374; Acts 1993, c. 930.
16.1-69.12. Amended by Acts 1973, c. 546; Acts 1980, c. 194; Acts 1993, c. 929.
16.1-69.13. Amended by Acts 1973, c. 546.
16.1-69.14. Amended by Acts 1973, c. 546; Acts 1975, c. 334.
16.1-69.15. Amended by Acts 1973, c. 546.
16.1-69.16. Amended by Acts 1973, c. 546; Acts 1977, c. 25; Acts 1991, c. 403.
16.1-69.17. Amended by Acts 1973, c. 546; Acts 1992, c. 390; Acts 1992, Sp. Sess., cc. 1, 2; Acts 1993, c. 930.
16.1-69.18. Amended by Acts 1973, c. 546; Acts 1974, c. 3; Acts 1975, c. 334; Acts 2002, c. 406.
16.1-69.19. Amended by Acts 1973, c. 546; Acts 1976, c. 374; Acts 1993, c. 312.
16.1-69.20. Repealed by Acts 1973, c. 546.
16.1-69.21. Amended by Acts 1973, c. 546; Acts 1983, c. 128; Acts 1984, c. 570; Acts 1993, c. 929.
16.1-69.22. Amended by Acts 1973, c. 546.
16.1-69.22:1. Amended by Acts 1993, c. 929.
16.1-69.23. Amended by Acts 1973, c. 546.

Sec.
16.1-69.24. Amended by Acts 1973, c. 546; Acts 2000, cc. 164, 185.
16.1-69.25. Amended by Acts 1973, c. 546; Acts 1994, c. 500.
16.1-69.25:1. Amended by Acts 1998, cc. 482, 495.
16.1-69.26. Amended by Acts 1973, c. 546.
16.1-69.27. Amended by Acts 1973, c. 546.
16.1-69.28. Amended by Acts 1973, c. 546; Acts 1997, c. 801.
16.1-69.29. Amended by Acts 1973, c. 546.
16.1-69.30. Amended by Acts 1973, c. 546.
16.1-69.31. Amended by Acts 1973, c. 546.
16.1-69.32. Amended by Acts 1973, c. 546; Acts 1975, c. 334; Acts 1976, c. 306; Acts 1993, c. 930.
16.1-69.33. Amended by Acts 1973, cc. 546, 547; Acts 1974, cc. 333, 484; Acts 1975, c. 334; Acts 1976, cc. 52, 444; Acts 1978, c. 133; Acts 1984, c. 23; Acts 1992, c. 497; Acts 1993, c. 930; Acts 2001, c. 367; Acts 2004, c. 330.
16.1-69.35. Amended by Acts 1973, c. 546; Acts 1976, cc. 307, 444; Acts 1978, c. 200; Acts 1984, c. 570; Acts 1987, c. 703; Acts 1989, c. 264; Acts 1991, cc. 177, 392; Acts 1992, c. 387; Acts 1993, c. 929; Acts 1995, c. 57; Acts 2001, c. 494; Acts 2003, c. 102.
16.1-69.36. Amended by Acts 1973, c. 546.
16.1-69.37. Amended by Acts 1973, c. 546; Acts 1993, c. 929.
16.1-69.38. Amended by Acts 1973, c. 546; Acts 1993, c. 929.
16.1-69.39. Amended by Acts 1973, c. 546; Acts 1975, c. 334; Acts 1993, c. 929.
16.1-69.39:1. Amended by Acts 1980, c. 197.
16.1-69.40. Amended by Acts 1973, c. 546; Acts 1974, c. 671; Acts 1978, c. 463; Acts 1983, c. 135; Acts 1985, c. 99; Acts 1989, c. 229; Acts 2001, cc. 488, 499.
16.1-69.40:1. Amended by Acts 1978, c. 605; Acts 1979, c. 510; Acts 1983, c. 388; Acts 1994, c. 912; Acts 1998, c. 209; Acts 2000, c. 841; Acts 2003, c. 282; Acts 2004, c. 350.
16.1-69.40:2. Amended by Acts 1989, c. 421.
16.1-69.41. Repealed by Acts 1974, c. 3.
16.1-69.42. Amended by Acts 1973, c. 546.
16.1-69.43. Amended by Acts 1973, c. 546.
16.1-69.44. Amended by Acts 1973, c. 546; Acts 1974, c. 612; Acts 1976, cc. 374, 459, 667; Acts 1979, c. 445; Acts 1980, c. 536; Acts 1984, c. 570; Acts 1993, c. 327; Acts 1999, c. 730.
16.1-69.45. Amended by Acts 1973, c. 546; Acts 1975, c. 334; Acts 1976, c. 667; Acts 1980, c. 613.

Sec.
16.1-69.46. Amended by Acts 1973, c. 546.
16.1-69.47. Repealed by Acts 1980, c. 194.
16.1-69.47:1. Amended by Acts 1975, c. 334; Acts 1978, c. 404.
16.1-69.48. Amended by Acts 1973, c. 546; Acts 1976, c. 465; Acts 1977, c. 385; Acts 1978, c. 611; Acts 1993, c. 929.
16.1-69.48:1. Amended by Acts 2002, c. 831; Acts 2003, cc. 883, 1039; Acts 2004, cc. 371, 375, 1004.
16.1-69.48:3. Amended by Acts 2002, c. 831; Acts 2004, c. 1004.
16.1-69.48:5. Amended by Acts 2004, cc. 366, 659, 727.
16.1-69.49. Repealed by Acts 1978, c. 611.
16.1-69.50. Amended by Acts 1973, c. 546; Acts 1993, c. 929.
16.1-69.51. Amended by Acts 1973, c. 546; Acts 1975, c. 334; Acts 1985, c. 133.
16.1-69.52. Repealed by Acts 1983, c. 499.
16.1-69.53. Amended by Acts 2002, c. 747.
16.1-69.55. Amended by Acts 1990, c. 258; Acts 1993, c. 929; Acts 1996, c. 463; Acts 2003, c. 126.
16.1-69.56. Amended by Acts 1987, c. 160.
16.1-69.57. Amended by Acts 1987, c. 160.
16.1-69.58. Amended by Acts 1987, c. 160.
16.1-70.1. Amended by Acts 1973, c. 546; Acts 1974, c. 648; Acts 1977, c. 95.
16.1-75.1. Repealed by Acts 1973, c. 545.
16.1-76. Amended by Acts 1977, c. 624; Acts 1978, c. 421.
16.1-77. Amended by Acts 1968, c. 5; Acts 1973, c. 440; Acts 1978, c. 40; Acts 1981, c. 404; Acts 1983, c. 616; Acts 1987, cc. 87, 93; Acts 1988, c. 799; Acts 1990, cc. 217, 471; Acts 1991, c. 135; Acts 1992, cc. 111, 777; Acts 1995, c. 799; Acts 1997, c. 753; Acts 1998, cc. 482, 495; Acts 1999, cc. 945, 987; Acts 2001, cc. 473, 477; Acts 2002, cc. 200, 506, 645;
16.1-69.48:5. Amended by Acts 2004, cc. 366, 659, 727.
16.1-77.1, 16.1-77.2. Amended by Acts 1983, c. 616.
16.1-79. Amended by Acts 1991, c. 26.
16.1-81. Amended by Acts 1990, c. 762.
16.1-82. Amended by Acts 1981, c. 576; Acts 1990, c. 943.
16.1-83. Amended by Acts 1990, c. 217.
16.1-84. Amended by Acts 1958, c. 210.
16.1-86. Amended by Acts 1980, c. 739; Acts 1990, c. 109.
16.1-86.1. Repealed by Acts 1990, c. 109.
16.1-87. Repealed Acts 1983, c. 499.
16.1-88. Amended by Acts 1973, c. 440; Acts 1991, c. 503.
16.1-88.01. Amended by Acts 1998, cc. 482, 495.
16.1-88.03. Amended by Acts 1992, c. 814; Acts

Sec.

1993, cc. 473, 478; Acts 2003, cc. 665, 667; Acts 2004, cc. 338, 365.

16.1-88.1. Repealed by Acts 1980, c. 183.

16.1-88.2. Amended by Acts 1983, c. 616; Acts 1985, c. 379; Acts 1989, c. 563; Acts 1990, c. 279; Acts 1996, c. 749.

16.1-89. Amended by Acts 1979, c. 668; Acts 1984, c. 500; Acts 1986, c. 160; Acts 2000, c. 813; Acts 2004, c. 335.

16.1-90. Amended by Acts 1960, c. 372.

16.1-91. Repealed by Acts 1984, c. 25.

16.1-92. Amended by Acts 1960, c. 284; Acts 1968, c. 457; Acts 1974, c. 613; Acts 1977, c. 624; Acts 1978, c. 40; Acts 1981, c. 404; Acts 1997, c. 753; Acts 1998, cc. 482, 495; Acts 1999, c. 717; Acts 2002, c. 645.

16.1-94. Amended by Acts 1962, c. 361; Acts 1993, c. 929; Acts 2004, c. 341.

16.1-95. Amended by Acts 1983, c. 499.

16.1-97. Repealed by Acts 1987, c. 98.

16.1-97.1. Amended by Acts 1988, c. 506; Acts 1993, c. 929.

16.1-98. Amended by Acts 1968, c. 260; Acts 1974, c. 666; Acts 1977, c. 624; Acts 1983, c. 499.

16.1-99. Amended by Acts 1979, c. 45; Acts 2003, c. 234.

16.1-100. Amended by Acts 1983, c. 499.

16.1-103. Amended by Acts 1978, c. 66; Acts 1983, c. 499.

16.1-104. Repealed by Acts 1983, c. 499.

16.1-106. Amended by Acts 1977, c. 624; Acts 1990, c. 217; Acts 1993, c. 929; Acts 1997, c. 831.

16.1-107. Amended by Acts 1972, c. 585; Acts 1978, c. 501; Acts 1992, c. 565; 1993, cc. 929, 970; Acts 1996, c. 616; Acts 1998, c. 266; Acts 2004, c. 366.

16.1-108. Amended by Acts 1975, c. 227; Acts 1988, c. 698.

16.1-112. Amended by Acts 1958, c. 211; Acts 1972, c. 585; Acts 1984, c. 108; Acts 1988, c. 698; Acts 2004, c. 366.

16.1-113. Amended by Acts 1980, c. 129; Acts 1984, c. 38; Acts 1988, c. 337.

16.1-114. Repealed by Acts 1983, c. 499.

16.1-114.1. Amended by Acts 1997, c. 753.

16.1-115. Repealed by Acts 1986, c. 45.

16.1-116. Amended by Acts 1962, c. 444; Acts 1983, c. 499.

16.1-118. Amended by Acts 1962, c. 444; Acts 1972, c. 491; Acts 1977, c. 169; Acts 1982, c. 153.

16.1-118.1. Amended by Acts 1973, c. 143; Acts 1977, c. 169; Acts 1982, c. 153.

16.1-119. Amended by Acts 1978, c. 42; Acts 1986, c. 27.

Sec.

16.1-120. Amended by Acts 1978, c. 42; Acts 1983, c. 616.

16.1-122. Amended by Acts 1978, c. 42; Acts 1986, c. 25; Acts 1998, cc. 482, 495; Acts 2001, c. 74; Acts 2002, c. 645.

16.1-122.1. Amended by Acts 1989, c. 451; Acts 1990, c. 564; Acts 1994, c. 576; Acts 1995, c. 589; Acts 1998, cc. 656, 779.

16.1-122.2. Amended by Acts 2002, c. 704.

16.1-122.3. Amended by Acts 1990, c. 564; Acts 2002, c. 704.

16.1-122.4. Amended by Acts 1997, c. 243.

16.1-123. Repealed by Acts 1984, c. 506.

16.1-124, 16.1-125. Repealed by Acts 1984, c. 506.

16.1-127. Amended by Acts 1960, c. 362.

16.1-129. Amended by Acts 1960, c. 373.

16.1-129.1. Repealed by Acts 1990, c. 75.

16.1-129.3. Repealed by Acts 1974, c. 481.

16.1-130. Repealed by Acts 1983, c. 499.

16.1-131. Amended by Acts 1986, c. 160.

16.1-133. Amended by Acts 1973, c. 18; Acts 1974, c. 228; Acts 1979, c. 536; Acts 1982, c. 366; Acts 1983, c. 105; Acts 1990, c. 25; Acts 1993, c. 929.

16.1-133.1. Amended by Acts 1975, c. 298; Acts 1983, c. 21; Acts 1993, c. 930.

16.1-135. Amended by Acts 1981, c. 159; Acts 1999, cc. 829, 846.

16.1-137. Amended by Acts 1958, c. 399.

16.1-138. Repealed by Acts 1983, c. 499.

16.1-139 to 16.1-217. Repealed by Acts 1977, c. 559.

16.1-217.1 to 16.1-217.4. Repealed by Acts 1975, c. 341.

16.1-218. Amended by Acts 1970, c. 559; Acts 1972, c. 518; Acts 1975, c. 334; Acts 1980, c. 447; Acts 1981, c. 231; Acts 2001, c. 229.

16.1-219. Amended by Acts 1970, c. 559; Acts 1989, c. 597; Acts 1990, c. 249; Acts 1993, c. 930.

16.1-220. Amended by Acts 1968, c. 496; Acts 1970, c. 559.

16.1-221. Amended by Acts 1964, c. 9.

16.1-223. Amended by Acts 1978, c. 684; Acts 1988, c. 541; Acts 2001, cc. 203, 213, 853.

16.1-224. Amended by Acts 1978, c. 684; Acts 1988, c. 541; Acts 1993, c. 930.

16.1-225. Amended by Acts 1977, c. 360; Acts 1988, c. 541.

16.1-226. Amended by Acts 1993, c. 929.

16.1-227. Amended by Acts 1990, c. 554; Acts 1991, c. 392; Acts 1996, c. 914.

16.1-228. Amended by Acts 1978, c. 605; Acts 1979, c. 15; Acts 1981, c. 491; Acts 1984, c. 631; Acts 1985, c. 260; Acts 1986, cc. 281, 308; Acts 1987, c. 632; Acts 1988, c. 794; Acts

Sec.

1990, cc. 704, 769, 842; Acts 1991, c. 534; Acts 1992, cc. 742, 830, 886; Acts 1993, cc. 435, 467, 494, 929; Acts 1994, cc. 859, 865, 949; Acts 1996, cc. 755, 914; Acts 1999, cc. 453, 665, 697, 721; Acts 2002, cc. 810, 818; Acts 2004, cc. 245, 753.

16.1-230. Amended by Acts 1993, c. 930.

16.1-232. Amended by Acts 1980, c. 530; Acts 1991, c. 262; Acts 1993, c. 930.

16.1-233. Amended by Acts 1979, c. 700; Acts 1993, c. 930; Acts 1995, cc. 696, 699; Acts 2003, cc. 538, 547, 835; Acts 2003, c. 648.

16.1-234. Amended by Acts 1979, c. 700; Acts 1993, c. 930; Acts 2001, c. 853.

16.1-235. Amended by Acts 1993, c. 930; Acts 2001, c. 853; Acts 2002, c. 510; Acts 2003, c. 648.

16.1-236. Amended by Acts 1993, c. 930; Acts 2001, c. 853; Acts 2003, c. 648.

16.1-237. Amended by Acts 2001, c. 853.

16.1-238. Amended by Acts 1982, c. 636; Acts 1983, c. 358.

16.1-239. Amended by Acts 1982, c. 636; Acts 1983, c. 358.

16.1-240. Amended by Acts 1993, c. 930.

16.1-241. Amended by Acts 1978, c. 648; Acts 1979, cc. 597, 605, 628; Acts 1980, cc. 527, 529; Acts 1981, cc. 454, 475, 488, 491, 501, 502, 510; Acts 1982, c. 46; Acts 1983, c. 280; Acts 1984, cc. 631, 645, 651, 665, 669; Acts 1985, c. 270; Acts 1986, cc. 59, 506; Acts 1987, c. 632; Acts 1988, cc. 797, 906; Acts 1989, c. 368; Acts 1990, cc. 704, 975; Acts 1991, cc. 511, 715; Acts 1993, c. 929; Acts 1994, cc. 575, 719, 813, 859, 949; Acts 1995, cc. 7, 665, 772, 826, 852; Acts 1996, cc. 755, 914; Acts 1997, cc. 690, 708; Acts 1998, c. 829; Acts 1999, cc. 697, 721, 1028; Acts 2000, c. 830; Acts 2003, cc. 229, 960, 962; Acts 2004, c. 588.

16.1-241.1. Repealed by Acts 2002, c. 305.

16.1-241.2. Amended by Acts 1995, c. 852; Acts 1996, c. 771; Acts 2004, c. 573.

16.1-241.3. Amended by Acts 2002, c. 860.

16.1-242. Amended by Acts 1978, c. 740; Acts 1993, c. 929.

16.1-243. Amended by Acts 1985, c. 367; Acts 1987, cc. 598, 608, 620; Act 1989, c. 545; Acts 1993, c. 929; Acts 1995, cc. 772, 826; Acts 1996, c. 866; Acts 2000, c. 830.

16.1-244. Amended by Acts 1978, c. 740; Acts 1984, cc. 657, 669; Acts 1985, c. 183; Acts 1987, c. 36; Acts 1989, c. 509; Acts 1990, c. 600; Acts 1993, c. 929; Acts 2000, c. 781; Acts 2003, c. 129.

Sec.

16.1-245. Amended by Acts 1993, c. 930.

16.1-245.1. Amended by Acts 1993, c. 930; Acts 1996, c. 866; Acts 2000, c. 163.

16.1-246. Amended by Acts 1978, cc. 643, 740; Acts 1979, c. 701; Acts 1981, c. 487; Acts 1982, c. 683; Acts 1985, c. 540; Acts 1990, cc. 635, 642, 743, 744, 975; Acts 1993, c. 930; Acts 2002, c. 747.

16.1-247. Amended by Acts 1978, c. 643; Acts 1979, c. 701; Acts 1984, c. 567; Acts 1993, c. 930; Acts 2004, cc. 415, 439.

16.1-248. Repealed by Acts 1985, c. 260.

16.1-248.1. Amended by Acts 1986, c. 517; Acts 1987, c. 632; Acts 1990, c. 257; Acts 1996, cc. 755, 914; Acts 2000, c. 836; Acts 2001, c. 837; Acts 2002, cc. 55, 359; Acts 2003, cc. 104, 851; Acts 2004, c. 374.

16.1-248.2. Amended by Acts 1996, cc. 755, 914; Acts 1998, c. 434.

16.1-249. Amended by Acts 1979, c. 655; Acts 1983, c. 336; Acts 1985, c. 260; Acts 1988, c. 886; Acts 1989, c. 557; Acts 1993, c. 435; Acts 1994, cc. 859, 904, 949; Acts 1995, cc. 746, 748, 798, 802; Acts 1996, cc. 755, 914; Acts 1998, cc. 576, 830; Acts 2002, c. 558; Acts 2004, cc. 415, 439.

16.1-250. Amended by Acts 1979, c. 338; Acts 1985, c. 260; Acts 1986, c. 542; Acts 1988, c. 220; Acts 1989, c. 549; Acts 1995, c. 451; Acts 2004, c. 437.

16.1-250.1. Amended by Acts 2001, c. 837; Acts 2003, c. 133.

16.1-251. Amended by Acts 1984, c. 499; Acts 1985, c. 584; Acts 1986, c. 308; Acts 1990, c. 769; Acts 2000, c. 385; Acts 2003, c. 508.

16.1-252. Amended by Acts 1984, c. 499; Acts 1985, c. 584; Acts 1986, c. 308; Acts 1990, c. 769; Acts 1994, c. 42; Acts 1995, c. 817; Acts 1997, c. 790; Acts 1999, c. 668; Acts 2000, c. 385.

16.1-253. Amended by Acts 1985, c. 595; Acts 1986, c. 308; Acts 1987, c. 497; Acts 1996, c. 866; Acts 1997, c. 790; Acts 1998, c. 550; Acts 2002, cc. 508, 810, 818.

16.1-253.1. Amended by Acts 1987, c. 497; Acts 1988, c. 165; Acts 1994, c. 907; Acts 1997, c. 603; Acts 1998, c. 684; Acts 2000, cc. 34, 654; Acts 2001, c. 101; Acts 2002, cc. 508, 810, 818.

16.1-253.2. Amended by Acts 1988, c. 501; Acts 1991, cc. 534, 715; Acts 1996, c.

Sec.

866; Acts 2003, c. 219; Acts 2004, cc. 972, 980.

16.1-253.3. Repealed by Acts 1992, c. 886.

16.1-253.4. Amended by Acts 1993, c. 930; Acts 1994, c. 907; Acts 1996, c. 866; Acts 1997, c. 603; Acts 1998, cc. 677, 684; Acts 1999, c. 807; Acts 2001, c. 474; Acts 2002, c. 508, 706, 810, 818.

16.1-254. Amended by Acts 1979, c. 202; Acts 1990, cc. 629, 673; Acts 1993, c. 930.

16.1-255. Amended by Acts 1985, c. 260; Acts 1993, c. 930; Acts 1996, cc. 755, 914; Acts 1997, c. 862; Acts 2002, c. 700.

16.1-256. Amended by Acts 1979, c. 701; Acts 1980, c. 234; Acts 1981, c. 184; Acts 1983, c. 349; Acts 1986, c. 295; Acts 1993, c. 930; Acts 1996, cc. 755, 914.

16.1-258. Amended by Acts 1986, c. 26.

16.1-259. Amended by Acts 1986, c. 95; Acts 1993, c. 930.

16.1-260. Amended by Acts 1979, c. 701; Acts 1982, c. 91; Acts 1983, c. 349; Acts 1985, c. 488; Acts 1986, c. 381; Acts 1987, cc. 203, 632; Acts 1988, cc. 792, 803; Acts 1990, c. 742; Acts 1991, cc. 496, 511, 534; Acts 1993, cc. 929, 981; Acts 1995, cc. 347, 429; Acts 1996, cc. 755, 914; Acts 1997, c. 862; Acts 1999, cc. 54, 526, 952; Acts 2002, c. 747; Acts 2003, c. 587; Acts 2004, cc. 105, 255, 309, 416, 517, 558.

16.1-261. Amended by Acts 1996, cc. 755, 914.

16.1-262. Amended by Acts 1979, c. 615; Acts 1984, c. 631; Acts 1993, c. 929; Acts 1995, cc. 772, 826; Acts 2000, c. 830.

16.1-263. Amended by Acts 1978, c. 613, 740; Acts 1993, c. 929; Acts 1996, cc. 755, 914; Acts 1997, c. 441; Acts 1999, c. 952; Acts 2004, c. 573.

16.1-264. Amended by Acts 1984, c. 594; Acts 1987, c. 632; Acts 1991, c. 62; Acts 1993, c. 929; Acts 2004, c. 588.

16.1-265. Amended by Acts 2000, c. 813; Acts 2004, c. 335.

16.1-266. Amended by Acts 1980, c. 572; Acts 1982, c. 451; Acts 1984, c. 709; Acts 1985, c. 260; Acts 1987, c. 632; Acts 1993, c. 929; Acts 1994, c. 36; Acts 1997, c. 790; Acts 2002, c. 687; Acts 2003, c. 98; Acts 2004, cc. 66, 437, 884, 921, 1014.

16.1-266.1. Amended by Acts 1995, c. 273.

16.1-267. Amended by Acts 1981, c. 213; Acts 1984, c. 709; Acts 1986, c. 425; Acts 1993, cc. 344, 930; Acts 2004, cc. 342, 437.

Sec.

16.1-269. Repealed by Acts 1994, cc. 859, 949.

16.1-269.1. Amended by Acts 1996, cc. 755, 914; Acts 1997, c. 862.

16.1-269.2. Amended by Acts 1999, c. 350.

16.1-269.3, 16.1-269.4. Amended by Acts 1996, cc. 755, 914.

16.1-269.5. Amended by Acts 1995, cc. 746, 798, 802.

16.1-269.6. Amended by Acts 1996, cc. 755, 914; Acts 1997, c. 862; Acts 2003, c. 144; Acts 2004, c. 468.

16.1-270. Amended by Acts 1993, c. 930; Acts 1994, cc. 859, 949.

16.1-271. Amended by Acts 1990, c. 668; Acts 1993, c. 930; Acts 1994, cc. 859, 949.

16.1-272. Amended by Acts 1993, c. 930; Acts 1994, c. 362; Acts 1996, cc. 755, 914; Acts 2000, c. 793; Acts 2002, c. 511; Acts 2003, c. 584.

16.1-273. Amended by Acts 1993, cc. 603, 930; Acts 1998, cc. 783, 840; Acts 1999, cc. 350, 891, 913; Acts 2000, cc. 1020, 1041.

16.1-274. Amended by Acts 1983, c. 174; Acts 1987, c. 5; Acts 1990, c. 752; Acts 1991, cc. 534, 618; Acts 1993, c. 975; Acts 2001, c. 364.

16.1-274.1. Amended by Acts 1996, cc. 755, 914.

16.1-275. Amended by Acts 1978, c. 739; Acts 1982, c. 636; Acts 1983, c. 358; Acts 1984, c. 44; Acts 1988, cc. 47, 826; Acts 1990, c. 975; Acts 1993, c. 930; Acts 1994, cc. 859, 949; Acts 2004, c. 321.

16.1-276. Amended by Acts 1982, c. 636.

16.1-276.1. Repealed by Acts 2002, c. 305.

16.1-277. Repealed by Acts 1999, c. 889.

16.1-277.01. Amended by Acts 2000, c. 385.

16.1-277.02. Amended by Acts 2000, c. 385.

16.1-277.1. Amended by Acts 1988, c. 220; Acts 1993, c. 930; Acts 1999, c. 58.

16.1-278. Amended by Acts 1980, c. 245; Acts 1993, c. 929.

16.1-278.2. Amended by Acts 1993, c. 929; Acts 1994, c. 865; Acts 1997, c. 790; Acts 2000, c. 385; Acts 2002, c. 747.

16.1-278.3. Amended by Acts 1993, c. 929; Acts 1999, c. 889; Acts 2000, c. 385.

16.1-278.4. Amended by Acts 1993, c. 930; Acts 1994, c. 865; Acts 1997, c. 463; Acts 1999, cc. 488, 522; Acts 2002, c. 747.

16.1-278.5. Amended by Acts 1993, c. 930; Acts 1996, c. 45; Acts 1997, c. 210.

16.1-278.6. Amended by Acts 1993, c. 930; Acts 1997, c. 463.

16.1-278.7. Amended by Acts 1993, c. 930; Acts 2000, cc. 954, 981, 988.

16.1-278.8. Amended by Acts 1993, c. 930; Acts

Sec.

1994, cc. 859, 949; Acts 1996, cc. 755, 914; Acts 1997, c. 318; Acts 1999, cc. 350, 622; Acts 2000, cc. 954, 978, 981, 988, 1020, 1041; Acts 2004, cc. 325, 462.

16.1-278.9. Amended by Acts 1992, c. 830; Acts 1993, cc. 482, 866, 972; Acts 1994, c. 338; Acts 2000, c. 835; Acts 2001, cc. 248, 266; Acts 2002, cc. 519, 755; Acts 2003, c. 118.

16.1-278.12. Amended by Acts 1993, c. 929.

16.1-278.13. Amended by Acts 1993, c. 929.

16.1-278.14. Amended by Acts 1992, c. 742; Acts 1993, c. 930; Acts 1996, c. 866.

16.1-278.15. Amended by Acts 1992, cc. 585, 716, 742; Acts 1993, c. 929; Acts 1994, c. 769; Acts 1996, cc. 767, 879, 884; Acts 2000, c. 586; Acts 2002, c. 300; Acts 2003, cc. 31, 45; Acts 2004, c. 732.

16.1-278.16. Amended by Acts 1993, c. 930; Acts 2003, cc. 929, 942; Acts 2004, c. 219.

16.1-278.17. Amended by Acts 1993, c. 930.

16.1-278.18. Amended by Acts 1993, c. 929; Acts 2002, c. 747; Acts 2004, c. 204.

16.1-278.20. Amended by Acts 1994, c. 854.

16.1-279. Repealed by Acts 1991, c. 534.

16.1-279.1. Amended by Acts 1987, c. 497; Acts 1988, cc. 791, 887, 906; Acts 1992, c. 886; Acts 1994, cc. 360, 521, 739, 907; Acts 1996, cc. 866, 900, 945; Acts 1997, c. 603; Acts 1998, c. 684; Acts 2000, cc. 34, 654; Acts 2004, cc. 972, 980.

16.1-280. Amended by Acts 1978, c. 739; Acts 1981, c. 487; Acts 1988, c. 826; Acts 1990, c. 975; Acts 1993, c. 930; Acts 1994, cc. 859, 949.

16.1-281. Amended by Acts 1978, cc. 732, 740; Acts 1982, c. 171; Acts 1984, c. 373; Acts 1985, c. 210; Acts 1991, c. 98; Acts 1993, c. 930; Acts 1994, cc. 604, 865; Acts 1997, c. 790; Acts 1998, c. 550; Acts 2000, c. 385; Acts 2002, cc. 397, 512, 664, 729, 747.

16.1-282. Amended by Acts 1978, c. 740; Acts 1982, c. 171; Acts 1984, c. 71; Acts 1987, c. 250; Acts 1991, c. 98; Acts 1992, c. 869; Acts 1994, cc. 223, 604, 865; Acts 1997, c. 790; Acts 1998, c. 550; Acts 1999, c. 889; Acts 2000, c. 385; Acts 2002, c. 512.

16.1-282.1. Amended by Acts 1998, c. 550; Acts 1999, c. 889; Acts 2000, c. 385; Acts 2002, c. 512.

16.1-283. Amended by Acts 1978, c. 740; Acts 1979, c. 281; Acts 1980, c. 295; Acts 1985, c. 584; Acts 1987, c. 6; Acts 1988, c. 791; Acts 1998, c. 550; Acts 1999, c. 889; Acts 2000, c. 385; Acts 2002, cc. 664, 729.

16.1-284. Amended by Acts 1978, c. 142; Acts 1980, c. 235; Acts 1983, c. 336; Acts 1985, c. 260; Acts 1996, cc. 755, 914.

16.1-284.1. Amended by Acts 1995, cc. 330, 696, 699; Acts 1996, cc. 755, 914; Acts 2000, c. 978; Acts 2001, c. 140.

16.1-285. Amended by Acts 1985, cc. 260, 388; Acts 1996, cc. 755, 914; Acts 2000, cc. 954, 981, 988; Acts 2001, c. 853.

16.1-285.1. Amended by Acts 1989, c. 717; Acts 1992, c. 484; Acts 1994, cc. 859, 949; Acts 1996, cc. 755, 914; Acts 2001, c. 140.

16.1-285.2. Amended by Acts 1995, c. 536; Acts 1996, cc. 755, 914; Acts 2002, c. 511.

16.1-286. Amended by Acts 1978, c. 310; Acts 1982, c. 166; Acts 1987, c. 667; Acts 1991, c. 534; Acts 1992, cc. 732, 837, 880; Acts 1995, cc. 696, 699; Acts 1997, c. 347; Acts 1999, c. 669; Acts 2003, c. 579.

16.1-287. Amended by Acts 1981, c. 487; Acts 2001, c. 483.

16.1-289. Amended by Acts 1993, c. 929; Acts 1996, c. 616.

16.1-290. Amended by Acts 1995, cc. 448, 817; Acts 1996, cc. 755, 914; Acts 2003, c. 579.

16.1-291. Amended by Acts 1991, c. 534; Acts 1992, c. 90; Acts 1993, c. 930; Acts 2001, c. 853.

16.1-292. Amended by Acts 1983, c. 501; Acts 1985, cc. 1, 260; Acts 1987, c. 632; Acts 1988, c. 771; Acts 1990, c. 110; Acts 1991, c. 534; Acts 1993, cc. 632, 929; Acts 1994, c. 21; Acts 2000, c. 978.

16.1-293. Amended by Acts 1980, c. 217; Acts 1981, c. 487; Acts 1985, c. 203; Acts 1988, c. 453; Acts 1993, c. 930; Acts 1996, cc. 755, 914, 916, 1000; Acts 2001, cc. 688, 820, 853.

16.1-294. Amended by Acts 1982, c. 636; Acts 1983, c. 358; Acts 1985, c. 203; Acts 1988, c. 376; Acts 1992, cc. 837, 880; Acts 2002, c. 747.

16.1-296. Amended by Acts 1978, c. 445; Acts 1981, c. 109; Acts 1982, c. 465; Acts 1983, c. 88; Acts 1984, c. 631; Acts 1986, cc. 143, 465; Acts 1989, c. 473; Acts 1991, c. 534; Acts 1993, cc. 929, 930; Acts 1994, c. 673; Acts 1995, c. 517; Acts 1996, c. 866; Acts 1997, cc. 654, 664, 790,

Sec.

862; Acts 1998, c. 550; Acts 2004, cc. 468, 659, 727.

16.1-296.1. Repealed by Acts 1999, c. 161.

16.1-296.2. Amended by Acts 1996, c. 866; Acts 1997, c. 790.

16.1-297. Amended by Acts 1993, c. 929; Acts 1996, c. 828.

16.1-298. Amended by Acts 1984, cc. 631, 703; Acts 1988, c. 771; Acts 1991, c. 534; Acts 1993, c. 929; Acts 1996, cc. 616, 866; Acts 1997, c. 831; Acts 1998, c. 550.

16.1-299. Amended by Acts 1978, c. 383; Acts 1979, c. 267; Acts 1982, c. 514; Acts 1985, c. 211; Acts 1986, c. 264; Acts 1993, cc. 468, 926, 930; Acts 1994, cc. 859, 949; Acts 1996, cc. 755, 914; Acts 1997, c. 657; Acts 2000, c. 431; Acts 2004, c. 464.

16.1-299.1. Amended by Acts 1996, cc. 755, 914; Acts 1998, c. 280; Acts 2003, cc. 150, 607.

16.1-300. Amended by Acts 1978, cc. 738, 740; Acts 1981, c. 487; Acts 1988, c. 541; Acts 1993, c. 929; Acts 1994, c. 19; Acts 2000, c. 212; Acts 2002, c. 735; Acts 2003, cc. 108, 143.

16.1-301. Amended by Acts 1978, c. 740; Acts 1981, c. 175; Acts 1993, cc. 468, 926; Acts 1994, cc. 859, 949; Acts 1995, c. 752; Acts 1996, cc. 755, 914; Acts 1997, c. 430; Acts 2000, c. 211; Acts 2001, c. 770; Acts 2003, c. 119.

16.1-302. Amended by Acts 1978, c. 605; Acts 1979, c. 393; Acts 1983, c. 293; Acts 1993, c. 929; Acts 1996, cc. 755, 914.

16.1-302.1. Amended by Acts 1996, cc. 755, 914; Acts 2000, c. 339.

16.1-303. Amended by Acts 1996, cc. 755, 914.

16.1-304. Repealed by Acts 1983, c. 499.

16.1-305. Amended by Acts 1979, c. 605; Acts 1983, c. 389; Acts 1984, c. 34; Acts 1988, c. 541; Acts 1989, c. 182; Acts 1990, c. 258; Acts 1992, c. 547; Acts 1993, c. 929; Acts 1994, c. 603; Acts 1995, c. 430; Acts 1996, cc. 755, 870, 914; Acts 1998, cc. 278, 521; Acts 2002, cc. 701, 735, 741; Acts 2003, c. 143; Acts 2004, c. 446.

16.1-305.1. Amended by Acts 1994, cc. 835, 913; Acts 1996, cc. 755, 914; Acts 1997, c. 371; Acts 1999, c. 952; Acts 2003, c. 119.

16.1-305.2. Amended by Acts 2003, c. 119.

16.1-306. Amended by Acts 1979, cc. 736, 737; Acts 1989, c. 183; Acts 1993, cc. 468, 589, 926, 929; Acts 1994, cc. 859, 949; Acts 1996, c. 463.

16.1-306.1. Amended by Acts 1994, c. 64.

16.1-307. Amended by Acts 1990, c. 258; Acts 1993, cc. 468, 926, 930; Acts 1996, cc. 755, 914.

16.1-308. Amended by Acts 1996, cc. 755, 914.

16.1-309. Amended by Acts 1978, c. 626; Acts 1979, c. 481; Acts 1989, c. 520; Acts 1993, cc. 645, 889, 930; Acts 1994, cc. 835, 913; Acts 1996, cc. 755, 914; Acts 2003, c. 119.

16.1-309.1. Amended by Acts 1981, c. 307; Acts 1986, c. 506; Acts 1988, c. 749; Acts 1993, c. 297; Acts 1994, cc. 499, 542; Acts 1995, cc. 558, 687, 804; Acts 1997, cc. 434, 452; Acts 1999, c. 710; Acts 2000, cc. 563, 603.

16.1-309.2. Amended by Acts 1996, cc. 671, 682.

16.1-309.3. Amended by Acts 1996, cc. 671, 682; Acts 1997, c. 347; Acts 2000, cc. 195, 806.

16.1-309.4. Amended by Acts 1996, cc. 671, 682, 755, 914.

16.1-309.5. Amended by Acts 2000, cc. 562, 601.

16.1-309.6. Amended by Acts 1996, cc. 671, 682; Acts 1998, c. 54.

16.1-309.7. Amended by Acts 1996, cc. 820, 970.

16.1-309.8. Amended by Acts 1996, cc. 671, 682; Acts 1998, c. 538.

16.1-310 to 16.1-314. Repealed by Acts 1995, cc. 698, 840.

16.1-316. Amended by Acts 1978, cc. 37, 717; Acts 1984, c. 77; Acts 1988, c. 885; Acts 1992, c. 441; Acts 1993, c. 930; Acts 1998, c. 488.

16.1-317. Amended by Acts 1978, cc. 37, 717; Acts 1988, c. 885; Acts 1992, c. 441; Acts 1993, c. 930.

16.1-318. Amended by Acts 1993, c. 833; Acts 1995, cc. 696, 699; Acts 1997, c. 752.

16.1-319. Amended by Acts 2003, c. 940.

16.1-322.1. Amended by Acts 1983, c. 358; Acts 1986, c. 394; Acts 1995, cc. 698, 840.

16.1-322.2. Amended by Acts 1983, c. 358; Acts 1986, c. 394; Acts 1995, cc. 698, 840.

16.1-322.4. Amended by Acts 1995, cc. 698, 840; Acts 1998, c. 856.

16.1-322.5. Amended by Acts 1995, cc. 696, 699; Acts 1992, c. 652.

16.1-322.6, 16.1-322.7. Amended by Acts 1992, c. 652.

16.1-327. Amended by Acts 1979, c. 630.

16.1-328. Amended by Acts 1993, c. 930.

16.1-330.1. Amended by Acts 1996, c. 293; Acts 1999, c. 508; Acts 2004, c. 418.

16.1-331. Amended by Acts 1993, c. 930.

16.1-332. Amended by Acts 2002, c. 747.

Sec.
16.1-334. Amended by Acts 1990, c. 568; Acts 1993, c. 778.
16.1-336. Amended by Acts 1991, c. 159.
16.1-337. Amended by Acts 1992, c. 539.
16.1-338. Amended by Acts 1991, c. 159.
16.1-339. Amended by Acts 1991, c. 159; Acts 1993, c. 930.
16.1-340. Amended by Acts 1991, c. 159; Acts 1992, c. 884; Acts 1993, c. 930; Acts 2000, cc. 65, 246; Acts 2001, c. 837; Acts 2004, c. 283.
16.1-341. Amended by Acts 1991, c. 159; Acts 1992, c. 539; Acts 1993, c. 930; Acts 2001, c. 837; Acts 2004, c. 283.
16.1-342. Amended by Acts 1993, c. 930.
16.1-343. Amended by Acts 1993, c. 344; Acts 2004, cc. 66, 1014.
16.1-344. Amended by Acts 1992, c. 539; Acts 1993, c. 930.
16.1-345. Amended by Acts 1992, c. 539.
16.1-346. Amended by Acts 1991, c. 159.
16.1-346.1. Amended by Acts 1995, c. 304.
16.1-348. Amended by Acts 1993, c. 930.
16.1-356. Amended by Acts 2000, c. 337.
16.1-358. Amended by Acts 2000, c. 216.
16.1-361. Amended by Acts 2000, c. 337.
17-1 to 17-238. Repealed by Acts 1998, c. 872.
17.1-126, 17.1-127. Repealed by Acts 2001, c. 836.
17.1-207. Amended by Acts 2000, cc. 412, 444; Acts 2001, c. 287.
17.1-208. Amended by Acts 2002, c. 299
17.1-213. Amended by Acts 2001, c. 836; Acts 2002, c. 832; Acts 2004, c. 433.
17.1-222.1. Amended by Acts 2002, c. 719.
17.1-223. Amended by Acts 2004, c. 336.
17.1-225. Amended by Acts 2001, c. 497.
17.1-227. Amended by Acts 2003, cc. 862, 914, 918; Acts 2004, c. 352.
17.1-227.1. Amended by Acts 2000, cc. 440, 446.
17.1-232. Amended by Acts 2002, c. 832.
17.1-242. Amended by Acts 2001, c. 497.
17.1-249. Amended by Acts 2002, cc. 276, 832.
17.1-252. Amended by Acts 1999, cc. 133, 163; Acts 2000, cc. 440, 446.
17.1-255. Amended by Acts 2000, c. 800; Acts 2003, c. 127.
17.1-256. Amended by Acts 2000, c. 800; Acts 2002, c. 419; Acts 2003, c. 127.
17.1-257. Repealed by Acts 2000, c. 800.
17.1-258. Amended by Acts 2000, cc. 800, 995; Acts 2003, c. 127.
17.1-258.1. Repealed by Acts 2003, c. 127.
17.1-265. Amended by Acts 2002, c. 299.
17.1-272. Amended by Acts 2004, cc. 198, 211, 588.
17.1-275. Amended by Acts 1999, cc. 9, 1003; Acts 2000, cc. 826, 830; Acts 2001, cc. 481, 496, 501, 836; Acts 2002, cc. 831, 832; Acts 2004, c. 1004.

Sec.
17.1-275.1. Amended by Acts 2002, c. 831; Acts 2003, c. 1039.
17.1-275.2. Amended by Acts 2002, c. 831; Acts 2003, c. 1039.
17.1-275.3. Amended by Acts 2003, c. 1039.
17.1-275.4. Amended by Acts 2002, c. 831; Acts 2003, c. 1039.
17.1-275.5. Amended by Acts 2002, c. 831; Acts 2003, cc. 1001, 1022, 1039.
17.1-275.6. Amended by Acts 2002, c. 831.
17.1-275.7. Amended by Acts 2003, c. 1039.
17.1-275.8. Amended by Acts 2003, c. 1039; Acts 2004, c. 1004.
17.1-275.9. Amended by Acts 2003, c. 1039.
17.1-276. Amended by Acts 2004, c. 230.
17.1-277. Repealed by Acts 2002, c. 831.
17.1-278. Amended by Acts 2002, c. 318; Acts 2004, c. 925.
17.1-279. Amended by Acts 2000, cc. 440, 446; Acts 2002, cc. 140, 250, 637; Acts 2003, c. 205, 865, 981, 1021; Acts 2004, c. 676.
17.1-281. Amended by Acts 1999, c. 9; Acts 2002, c. 831.
17.1-300. Amended by Acts 2002, cc. 43, 552
17.1-302. Amended by Acts 2001, c. 295; Acts 2004, c. 346.
17.1-303. Amended by Acts 2004, c. 452.
17.1-318. Repealed by Acts 2003, c. 280.
17.1-319. Amended by Acts 2003, c. 141.
17.1-327. Amended by Acts 1999, c. 730.
17.1-400. Amended by Acts 2000, c. 8; Acts 2004, c. 452.
17.1-401. Amended by Acts 2001, c. 295; Acts 2004, c. 346.
17.1-402. Amended by Acts 2000, c. 8; Acts 2001, c. 555.
17.1-405. Amended by Acts 2000, cc. 830, 947, 1006; Acts 2001, cc. 393, 420.
17.1-410. Amended by Acts 2000, c. 830.
17.1-415. Amended by Acts 2001, c. 35.
17.1-417. Amended by Acts 2001, c. 35.
17.1-501. Amended by Acts 2004, c. 452.
17.1-503. Amended by Acts 2004, cc. 773, 1021.
17.1-507. Amended by Acts 1999, cc. 10, 319; Acts 2000, c. 37; Acts 2004, Sp. Sess. I, c. 4.
17.1-509. Amended by Acts 2001, c. 256; Acts 2004, c. 452.
17.1-511. Amended by Acts 1999, c. 319; Acts 2004, c. 331.
17.1-512. Amended by Acts 2004, c. 452.
17.1-513.01. Amended by Acts 2004, c. 289.
17.1-700, 17.1-701. Amended by Acts 2004, c. 1000.
17.1-704. Amended by Acts 2004, c. 1000.
17.1-802. Amended by Acts 2002, c. 79; Acts 2004, c. 1000.
17.1-803. Amended by Acts 2003, c. 139.
17.1-805. Amended by Acts 1999, c. 349; Acts 2004, cc. 459, 866.
17.1-900. Amended by Acts 2004, c. 363.

Sec.
17.1-901. Amended by Acts 2004, c. 1000.
17.1-904. Amended by Acts 2004, c. 1000.
17.1-918. Amended by Acts 2004, cc. 332, 363.
18-1 to 18-366. Repealed by Acts 1960, c. 358.
18.1-1 to 18.1-429. Repealed by Acts 1975, cc. 14, 15.
18.2-8. Amended by Acts 1977, c. 585.
18.2-10. Amended by Acts 1977, c. 492; Acts 1990, c. 788; Acts 1991, c. 7; Acts 1994, 2nd Sp. Sess., cc. 1, 2; Acts 1995, c. 427; Acts 2000, cc. 361, 767, 770; Acts 2003, cc. 1031, 1040.
18.2-11. Amended by Acts 1990, c. 788; Acts 2000, c. 770.
18.2-18. Amended by Acts 1977, c. 478; Acts 1997, c. 313; Acts 2002, cc. 588, 623.
18.2-22. Amended by Acts 1983, c. 19.
18.2-23. Amended by Acts 2003, c. 831.
18.2-25. Amended by Acts 1985, c. 280.
18.2-26. Amended by Acts 1994, c. 639.
18.2-29. Amended by Acts 1994, cc. 364, 440; Acts 2002, cc. 615, 635.
18.2-31. Amended by Acts 1976, c. 503; Acts 1977, c. 478; Acts 1979, c. 582; Acts 1980, c. 221; Acts 1981, c. 607; Acts 1982, c. 636; Acts 1983, c. 175; Acts 1985, c. 428; Acts 1988, c. 550; Acts 1989, c. 527; Acts 1990, c. 746; Acts 1991, c. 232; Acts 1995, c. 340; Acts 1996, cc. 876, 959; Acts 1997, cc. 235, 313, 514, 709; Acts 1998, c. 887; Acts 2002, cc. 588, 623.
18.2-32. Amended by Acts 1976, c. 503; Acts 1977, cc. 478, 492; Acts 1981, c. 397; Acts 1993, cc. 463, 490; Acts 1998, c. 281.
18.2-33. Amended by Acts 1999, c. 282.
18.2-36. Amended by Acts 1982, c. 301.
18.2-36.1. Amended by Acts 1992, c. 862; Acts 1994, cc. 635, 682; Acts 1999, cc. 945, 987; Acts 2000, cc. 956, 982; Acts 2004, c. 461.
18.2-38. Amended by Acts 1999, c. 623.
18.2-42.1. Amended by Acts 1999, c. 623.
18.2-43.1. Amended by Acts 1991, c. 506.
18.2-46. Amended by Acts 2004, c. 144.
18.2-46.1. Amended by Acts 2004, cc. 396, 435, 462, 867.
18.2-46.3. Amended by Acts 2004, cc. 396, 435.
18.2-46.9. Repealed by Acts 2004, c. 995.
18.2-47. Amended by Acts 1979, c. 663; Acts 1980, c. 506; Acts 1997, c. 747.
18.2-48. Amended by Acts 1993, c. 317; Acts 1997, c. 747.
18.2-48.1. Amended by Acts 1986, c. 414.
18.2-49.1. Amended by Acts 1989, c. 486; 1994, c. 575; 2002, cc. 576, 596; Acts 2003, c. 261.
18.2-50.1. Repealed by Acts 1992, c. 479.

Sec.
18.2-51.1. Amended by Acts 1985, c. 444; Acts 1994, cc. 205, 427; Acts 1997, cc. 8, 120; Acts 2002, cc. 588, 623, 816; Acts 2004, cc. 461, 841.
18.2-51.2. Amended by Acts 1991, c. 670; Acts 1997, c. 709.
18.2-51.4. Amended by Acts 1999, cc. 945, 987; Acts 2000, cc. 956, 982.
18.2-52. Amended by Acts 1975, c. 604; Acts 1995, c. 439.
18.2-52.1. Amended by Acts 2004, c. 833.
18.2-53.1. Amended by Acts 1976, c. 371; Acts 1980, c. Acts 1982, c. 654; Acts 1992, cc. 191, 726; Acts 1993, cc. 549, 835; Acts 1994, c. 950; Acts 2004, c. 461.
18.2-54.1. Amended by Acts 1983, c. 129.
18.2-55. Amended by Acts 1977, c. 553; Acts 1982, c. 636; Acts 1985, c. 508; Acts 1996, c. 527; Acts 1999, cc. 618, 658; Acts 2001, cc. 818, 848.
18.2-56. Amended by Acts 2003, cc. 62, 67.
18.2-56.1. Amended by Acts 1985, c. 182; Acts 1991, c. 384.
18.2-56.2. Amended by Acts 1994, c. 832.
18.2-57. Amended by Acts 1994, c. 658; Acts 1997, c. 833; Acts 1999, cc. 771, 1036; Acts 2000, cc. 288, 682; Acts 2001, c. 129; Acts 2002, c. 817; Acts 2004, cc. 420, 461.
18.2-57.1. Repealed by Acts 1997, c. 833.
18.2-57.2. Amended by Acts 1992, cc. 526, 886; Acts 1996, c. 866; Acts 1997, c. 603; Acts 1999, cc. 697, 721, 807; Acts 2004, cc. 448, 738.
18.2-57.3. Amended by Acts 2000, c. 1040; Acts 2003, cc. 33, 38; Acts 2004, c. 377.
18.2-58. Amended by Acts 1975, c. 605; Acts 1978, c. 608.
18.2-60. Amended by Acts 1994, c. 265; Acts 1998, cc. 687, 788; Acts 2001, c. 644, 653; Acts 2002, cc. 588, 623.
18.2-60.3. Amended by Acts 1994, cc. 360, 521, 739; Acts 1995, c. 824; Acts 1996, cc. 540, 866; Acts 1998, c. 570; Acts 2001, c. 197; Acts 2002, c. 377.
18.2-60.4. Amended by Acts 2003, c. 219.
18.2-61. Amended by Acts 1975, c. 606; Acts 1981, c. 397; Acts 1982, c. 506; Acts 1986, c. 516; Acts 1994, cc. 339, 772, 794; Acts 1997, c. 330; Acts 1999, c. 367; Acts 2002, cc. 810, 818.
18.2-62. Amended by Acts 1992, cc. 500, 587; Acts 1993, c. 512; Acts 2001, c. 862.
18.2-63. Amended by Acts 1975, c. 606; Acts 1981, c. 397; Acts 1993, c. 852.
18.2-63.1. Amended by Acts 1981, c. 397; Acts 1991, c. 534; Acts 1993, cc. 852, 930.
18.2-64. Repealed by Acts 1981, c. 397.

Sec.
18.2-64.1. Amended by Acts 1981, c. 397.
18.2-64.2. Amended by Acts 2000, c. 1040; Acts 2001, c. 385.
18.2-65. Repealed by Acts 1981, c. 397.
18.2-66. Amended by Acts 1975, c. 606; Acts 1981, c. 397; Acts 1993, c. 418.
18.2-67. Amended by Acts 1975, c. 606; Acts 1981, c. 397; Acts 1987, c. 448.
18.2-67.1. Amended by Acts 1986, c. 516; Acts 1994, cc. 772, 794; Acts 1999, c. 367.
18.2-67.2. Amended by Acts 1982, c. 508; Acts 1986, c. 516; Acts 1988, c. 437; Acts 1993, c. 549; Acts 1994, cc. 772, 794; Acts 1999, c. 367.
18.2-67.2:1. Amended by Acts 1994, cc. 772, 794; Acts 1999, c. 367.
18.2-67.3. Amended by Acts 1993, c. 590; Acts 2004, c. 843.
18.2-67.4. Amended by Acts 1997, c. 643; Acts 1999, c. 294; Acts 2000, cc. 1040, 832.
18.2-67.4:1. Amended by Acts 2004, c. 449.
18.2-67.5. Amended by Acts 1993, c. 549.
18.2-67.5:2. Amended by Acts 2000, c. 333.
18.2-67.8. Amended by Acts 1993, c. 440.
18.2-67.9. Amended by Acts 1999, c. 668; Acts 2001, c. 410.
18.2-67.10. Amended by Acts 1987, c. 227; Acts 1993, c. 549; Acts 1994, c. 568; Acts 2004, c. 741.
18.2-68 to 18.2-70. Repealed by Acts 1994, c. 59.
18.2-74.2. Repealed by Acts 2003, cc. 961, 963.
18.2-76. Amended by Acts 1979, c. 250; Acts 1997, c. 801; Acts 2001, cc. 473, 477; Acts 2003, c. 784.
18.2-77. Amended by Acts 1977, c. 63; Acts 1978, c. 443; Acts 1993, c. 406; Acts 1997, c. 832.
18.2-79. Amended by Acts 1997, c. 832.
18.2-80. Amended by Acts 1981, c. 197.
18.2-81. Amended by Acts 1981, c. 197.
18.2-83. Amended by Acts 1982, c. 502.
18.2-85. Amended by Acts 1976, c. 526; Acts 1977, c. 326; Acts 1990, cc. 644, 647; Acts 1992, c. 540; Acts 2000, cc. 951, 1065; Acts 2002, cc. 588, 623.
18.2-87. Amended by Acts 1988, c. 403.
18.2-90. Amended by Acts 1985, c. 110; Acts 1992, c. 546; Acts 1997, c. 832; Acts 2004, c. 842.
18.2-91. Amended by Acts 1975, c. 602; Acts 1991, c. 710; Acts 1992, c. 486; Acts 1996, c. 1040; Acts 1997, c. 832.
18.2-92. Amended by Acts 1992, c. 486.
18.2-95. Amended by Acts 1975, c. 603; Acts 1980, c. 175; Acts 1991, c. 710; Acts 1992, c. 822; Acts 1998, c. 821.

Sec.
18.2-96. Amended by Acts 1980, c. 175; Acts 1992, c. 822.
18.2-96.1. Amended by Acts 1982, c. 382.
18.2-97. Amended by Acts 1981, c. 197.
18.2-98.1. Repealed by Acts 1984, c. 751.
18.2-102. Amended by Acts 1981, c. 197.
18.2-103. Amended by Acts 1994, c. 706.
18.2-104. Amended by Ac Acts 1994, c. 706ts 1980, c. 174; Acts 1987, c. 178; Acts 1994, c. 706.
18.2-105. Repealed by Acts 2004, c. 462.
18.2-105.2. Amended by Acts 2003, c. 831.
18.2-107. Amended by Acts 1977, c. 107.
18.2-108.1. Amended by Acts 1998, c. 821.
18.2-110. Repealed by Acts 2004, c. 995
18.2-111. Amended by Acts 1979, c. 349; Acts 1994, c. 555; Acts 2003, c. 733.
18.2-111.1. Repealed by Acts 2004, c. 459.
18.2-112. Amended by Acts 1979, c. 585.
18.2-113. Amended by Acts 1996, c. 77; Acts 2003, c. 740.
18.2-114. Repealed by Acts 2004, c. 459.
18.2-115. Amended by Acts 1986, c. 484.
18.2-115.1. Amended by Acts 1993, c. 608.
18.2-118. Amended by Acts 1978, c. 675.
18.2-119. Amended by Acts 1982, c. 169; Acts 1987, cc. 625, 705; Acts 1991, c. 534; Acts 1998, cc. 569, 684.
18.2-121. Amended by Acts 1994, c. 658; Acts 1997, c. 833; Acts 2004, c. 461.
18.2-122. Repealed by Acts 1998, c. 6.
18.2-123. Repealed by Acts 2004, c. 459.
18.2-124. Amended by Acts 2004, c. 459.
18.2-126. Amended by Acts 1995, c. 306.
18.2-127. Amended by Acts 1982, c. 561; Acts 1983, c. 579; Acts 1990, c. 510; Acts 2004, c. 203.
18.2-128. Amended by Acts 1988, c. 497; Acts 1993, c. 961; Acts 1994, c. 326; Acts 1995, cc. 493, 642; Acts 1997, c. 779.
18.2-129. Amended by Acts 1976, c. 76.
18.2-130. Amended by Acts 1992, c. 520; Acts 1999, c. 351; Acts 2003, c. 81.
18.2-134. Amended by Acts 1987, c. 603.
18.2-136. Amended by Acts 1988, c. 593; Acts 1991, cc. 317, 327.
18.2-137. Amended by Acts 1975, c. 598; Acts 1990, c. 933; Acts 1999, c. 625.
18.2-138. Amended by Acts 1990, c. 454.
18.2-138.1. Repealed by Acts 2004, c. 462.
18.2-140. Amended by Acts 1976, c. 757; Acts 1998, c. 81.
18.2-142. Repealed by Acts 1979, c. 252.
18.2-144. Amended by Acts 1977, c. 598; Acts 1978, c. 559; Acts 1999, c. 620.
18.2-144.1. Amended by Acts 1998, c. 8.
18.2-150. Amended by Acts 1981, c. 197.
18.2-152.2. Amended by Acts 1999, cc. 886, 904, 905; Acts 2000, c. 627; Acts 2003, cc. 987, 1016.
18.2-152.16. Repealed by Acts 2004, c. 995.

Sec.

18.2-152.3. Amended by Acts 1985, c. 322; Acts 2003, cc. 987, 1016.

18.2-152.4. Amended by Acts 1985, c. 322; Acts 1990, c. 663; Acts 1998, c. 892; 1999, cc. 886, 904, 905; 2002, c. 195; Acts 2003, cc. 987, 1016.

18.2-152.5. Amended by Acts 1985, c. 398; Acts 2001, c. 358.

18.2-152.6, 18.2-152.7. Amended by Acts 1985, c. 322; Acts 2003, cc. 987, 1016.

18.2-152.7:1 to 18.2-152.9. Amended by Acts 2003, cc. 987, 1016.

18.2-152.10. Amended by Acts 1985, c. 322.

18.2-152.12. Amended by Acts 1985, c. 92; Acts 1999, c. 886, 904, 905; Acts 2003, cc. 987, 1016.

18.2-152.14. Amended by Acts 1985, c. 322.

18.2-152.16. Repealed by Acts 2004, c. 995.

18.2-154. Amended by Acts 1990, c. 426; Acts 2004, c. 461.

18.2-159. Amended by Acts 1993, c. 845.

18.2-160.1. Amended by Acts 1991, c. 241.

18.2-161. Repealed by Acts 2004, c. 459.

18.2-162. Amended by Acts 1980, c. 548; Acts 1981, c. 197; Acts 1985, c. 299; Acts 1992, c. 352.

18.2-162.1. Amended by Acts 1992, c. 352.

18.2-163. Amended by Acts 1976, c. 273; Acts 1978, c. 813; Acts 1992, c. 525.

18.2-164. Amended by Acts 2002, cc. 810, 818.

18.2-165.1. Amended by Acts 1979, c. 500; Acts 1981, c. 197; Acts 1991, c. 502.

18.2-168. Amended by Acts 1976, c. 146.

18.2-174.1. Amended by Acts 2000, c. 962; Acts 2002, c. 536.

18.2-175. Amended by Acts 1979, c. 704; Acts 1991, c. 424.

18.2-178. Amended by Acts 2001, c. 131.

18.2-181. Reenacted without change by Acts 1977, c. 329; amended by Acts 1978, c. 791; Acts 1981, c. 230.

18.2-186. Amended by Acts 1981, c. 197; Acts 1991, c. 546.

18.2-186.1. Repealed by Acts 1981, c. 255.

18.2-186.3. Amended by Acts 2001, c. 423; Acts 2003, cc. 847, 914, 918; Acts 2004, c. 450.

18.2-186.5. Amended by Acts 2004, c. 450.

18.2-187. Repealed by Acts 1978, c. 807.

18.2-187.1. Amended by Acts 1981, c. 197; Acts 1992, c. 525; Acts 1993, c. 439; Acts 2002, c. 671; Acts 2003, c. 354.

18.2-188. Amended by Acts 1977, c. 178; Acts 1981, c. 197; Acts 1993, c. 575.

18.2-189. Amended by Acts 1978, c. 245; Acts 1988, c. 414.

18.2-190.1. Amended by Acts 1998, c. 518; Acts 2002, c. 671.

18.2 190.2. Amended by Acts 1998, c. 518; Acts 2002, c. 671; Acts 2003, c. 354.

18.2-190.3. Amended by Acts 1998, c. 518; Acts 2002, c. 671; Acts 2003, c. 354.

18.2-190.4. Amended by Acts 1998, c. 518; Acts 2002, c. 671; Acts 2003, c. 354.

18.2-190.5. Amended by Acts 2003, c. 354.

18.2-190.7. Repealed by Acts 2004, c. 995.

18.2-190.8. Amended by Acts 2003, c. 354.

18.2-191. Amended by Acts 1977, c. 103; Acts 1980, c. 99; Acts 1985, c. 266; Acts 1991, c. 546.

18.2-192. Amended by Acts 1976, c. 318; Acts 1985, c. 266.

18.2-193. Amended by Acts 1980, c. 99; Acts 1985, c. 266.

18.2-194. Amended by Acts 1985, c. 266.

18.2-195. Amended by Acts 1978, c. 364; Acts 1980, c. 99; Acts 1981, c. 197; Acts 1985, c. 266; Acts 1991, c. 546.

18.2-197. Amended by Acts 1981, c. 197.

18.2-200.1. Amended by Acts 1987, c. 358.

18.2-202. Repealed by Acts 2004, c. 459.

18.2-203. Repealed by Acts 2004, c..

18.2-204.1. Amended by Acts 1979, c. 479; Acts 1981, c. 593; Acts 2003, cc. 889, 914, 918.

18.2-204.2. Amended by Acts 1992, c. 531.

18.2-209. Amended by Acts 1978, c. 359.

18.2-211. Repealed by Acts 2004, c..

18.2-212. Amended by Acts 1976, c. 75; Acts 1982, c. 502.

18.2-213.1. Amended by Acts 1989, c. 570.

18.2-214.1. Amended by Acts 1982, c. 154.

18.2-215. Amended by Acts 1976, c. 305.

18.2-216. Amended by Acts 1975, c. 507.

18.2-219. Repealed by Acts 1992, c. 768.

18.2-221. Amended by Acts 1985, c. 420.

18.2-222. Amended by Acts 1983, c. 290.

18.2-224. Amended by Acts 1983, c. 445; Acts 1988, c. 779; Acts 1992, c. 562.

18.2-242.1. Amended by Acts 1976, c. 641.

18.2-246.2. Amended by Acts 2003, cc. 541, 549.

18.2-246.4. Repealed by Acts 2004, c. 995.

18.2-246.13. Amended by Acts 2004, c. 995.

18.2-246.14. Amended by Acts 2004, c. 995.

18.2-247. Amended by Acts 1979, c. 435; Acts 1982, c. 462; Acts 1984, c. 684; Acts 1992, c. 756; Acts 1999, cc. 661, 722; Acts 2004, c. 688.

18.2-248. Amended by Acts 1976, c. 614; Acts 1977, c. 409; Acts 1978, cc. 177, 779; Acts 1979, c. 435; Acts 1982, c. 462; Acts 1985, c. 569; Acts 1986, c. 453; Acts 1988, c. 355; Acts 1990, c. 82; Acts 1991, c. 13; Acts 1992, cc. 685, 737, 756; Acts 1995, c. 538; Acts 1999, c. 722; Acts 2000, cc. 1020, 1041; Acts 2004, c. 461.

18.2-248.01. Amended by Acts 2000, cc. 1020, 1041; Acts 2004, c. 461.

18.2-248.1. Amended by Acts 1986, c. 467; Acts

Sec.

2000, cc. 819, 1020, 1041; Acts 2004, c. 461.

18.2-248.2. Repealed by Acts 1981, c. 598.

18.2-248.5. Amended by Acts 1988, c. 428; Acts 1989, c. 567; Acts 2000, cc. 1020, 1041; Acts 2004, c. 461.

18.2-248.6, 18.2-248.7. Repealed by Acts 1999, c. 348.

18.2-249. Repealed by Acts 2004, c. 995.

18.2-250. Reenacted without change by Acts 1976, c. 614; amended by Acts 1978, cc. 151, 177, 779; Acts 1979, c. 435; Acts 1980, c. 285; Acts 1991, c. 649; Acts 1998, c. 116.

18.2-250.1. Amended by Acts 1991, c. 649; Acts 1998, c. 116.

18.2-251. Amended by Acts 1976, c. 181; Acts 1979, c. 435; Acts 1983, c. 513; Acts 1991, c. 482; Acts 1992, cc. 58, 833; Acts 1993, c. 410; Acts 1997, c. 380; Acts 1998, cc. 688, 783, 840; Acts 2000, cc. 1020, 1041; Acts 2001, cc. 430, 450, 827.

18.2-251.01. Amended by Acts 1999, cc. 891, 913; Acts 2000, cc. 1020, 1041.

18.2-251.02. Amended by Acts 2003, c. 606; Acts 2004, c. 1004.

18.2-252. Amended by Acts 1979, c. 435; Acts 1998, cc. 783, 840; Acts 2000, cc. 1020, 1041.

18.2-253 to 18.2-253.2. Repealed by Acts 2004, c. 995.

18.2-254. Amended by Acts 1978, c. 640; Acts 1979, cc. 413, 435; Acts 1992, c. 852; Acts 1998, c. 724; Acts 2000, cc. 1020, 1041; Acts 2004, c. 130.

18.2-255. Reenacted without change by Acts 1976, c. 614; amended by Acts 1979, c. 435; Acts 1982, c. 462; Acts 1990, cc. 720, 864, 866; Acts 1992, cc. 708, 724; Acts 2000, cc. 1020, 1041; Acts 2004, c. 461.

18.2-255.2. Amended by Acts 1989, c. 619; Acts 1990, cc. 617, 622; Acts 1991, c. 268; Acts 1991, 1st Sp. Sess., c. 14; Acts 1993, cc. 30, 708, 729; Acts 1999, c. 873; Acts 2000, cc. 1020, 1041; Acts 2003, cc. 80, 91; Acts 2004, c. 461.

18.2-256. Amended by Acts 1978, c. 130.

18.2-257. Amended by Acts 1979, c. 435.

18.2-258. Amended by Acts 1979, c. 435; Acts 1990, c. 948; Acts 1992, cc. 248, 538; Acts 2004, c. 462.

18.2-258.1. Amended by Acts 1979, c. 435; Acts 1992, c. 76; Acts 1997, c. 542.

18.2-259.1. Amended by Acts 1993, c. 920; Acts 1994, cc. 403, 545; Acts 1999, c. 45; Acts 2000, c. 325; Acts 2001, cc. 645, 779.

18.2-261. Amended by Acts 1980, c. 678.

18.2-262. Amended by Acts 1984, c. 667.

Sec.

18.2-264. Amended by Acts 1993, c. 416.

18.2-264.01. Repealed by Acts 2002, c. 831.

18.2-264.1. Repealed by Acts 1994, c. 432.

18.2-265. Repealed by Acts 1979, c. 638.

18.2-265.1, 18.2-265.2. Amended by Acts 1983, c. 535.

18.2-265.3. Amended by Acts 1983, c. 535; Acts 1984, c. 31.

18.2-265.4. Repealed by Acts 2004, c. 995.

18.2-266. Amended by Acts 1977, c. 637; Acts 1984, c. 666; Acts 1986, c. 635; Acts 1987, c. 661; Acts 1992, c. 830; Acts 1994, cc. 359, 363; Acts 1996, c. 439.

18.2-266.1. Amended by Acts 1995, c. 31; Acts 2003, c. 605.

18.2-267. Amended by Acts 1979, c. 717; Acts 1985, cc. 355, 609; Acts 1990, c. 825; Acts 1992, c. 830; Acts 1994, cc. 359, 363; Acts 1996, cc. 154, 952; Acts 2004, c. 1013.

18.2-268. Repealed by Acts 1992, c. 830.

18.2-268.2. Amended by Acts 1993, c. 746; Acts 1994, cc. 359, 363; Acts 1995, c. 23; Acts 2002, c. 748; Acts 2004, c. 1013.

18.2-268.3. Amended by Acts 1994, cc. 359, 363; Acts 1997, c. 691; Acts 2001, cc. 654, 779; Acts 2004, cc. 985, 1013, 1022; Acts 2004, Sp. Sess. I, c. 1.

18.2-268.4. Amended by Acts 1994, cc. 151, 359, 363; Acts 2004, cc. 985, 1013.

18.2-268.5. Amended by Acts 1994, cc. 359, 363; Acts 2004, cc. 150, 440, 1013.

18.2-268.6. Amended by Acts 2001, c. 561; Acts 2003, cc. 933, 936.

18.2-268.7. Amended by Acts 1993, c. 688; Acts 1994, cc. 337, 359, 363; Acts 2003, cc. 933, 936.

18.2-268.8. Amended by Acts 1994, cc. 359, 363; Acts 2001, c. 561; Acts 2003, cc. 933, 936; Acts 2004, c. 1013.

18.2-268.9. Amended by Acts 1994, cc. 359, 363; Acts 1996, cc. 154, 952; Acts 1997, c. 256; Acts 1999, c. 273; Acts 2004, c. 1013.

18.2-268.10. Amended by Acts 1994, cc. 359, 363; Acts 2001, c. 654; Acts 2004, c. 1013.

18.2-268.11. Amended by Acts 2003, cc. 933, 936.

18.2-269. Amended by Acts 1977, c. 638; Acts 1983, c. 504; Acts 1986, c. 635; Acts 1989, cc. 554, 574; Acts 1992, c. 830; Acts 1994, cc. 359, 363.

18.2-270. Amended by Acts 1982, c. 301; Acts 1983, c. 504; Acts 1991, cc. 370, 710; Acts 1992, c. 891; Acts 1993, c. 972; Acts 1997, c. 691; Acts 1999, cc. 743, 945, 949, 987; Acts 2000, cc. 784, 956, 958, 980, 982;

Sec.

Acts 2002, c. 759; Acts 2003, cc. 573, 591; Acts 2004, cc. 461, 937, 946, 950, 957, 958, 962.

18.2-270.1. Amended by Acts 1996, c. 841; Acts 1997, c. 691; Acts 1998, cc. 783, 840; Acts 1999, c. 734; Acts 2000, cc. 958, 980; Acts 2002, c. 806.

18.2-270.2. Amended by Acts 2000, cc. 341, 362.

18.2-270.1. Amended by Acts 2004, c. 961.

18.2-271. Amended by Acts 1982, c. 301; Acts 1983, c. 504; Acts 1984, cc. 623, 673; Acts 1990, c. 949; Acts 1992, cc. 722, 830, 891; Acts 1994, cc. 359, 363; Acts 2000, cc. 956, 982; Acts 2001, c. 739; Acts 2002, c. 759.

18.2-271.1. Amended by Acts 1976, cc. 612, 691; Acts 1977, c. 240; Acts 1978, c. 352; Acts 1979, c. 353; Acts 1980, c. 589; Acts 1981, c. 195; Acts 1982, c. 301; Acts 1983, c. 504; Acts 1984, c. 778; Acts 1986, cc. 552,590; Acts 1987, cc. 465, 663; Acts 1988, cc. 781, 858, 859, 888; Acts 1990, c. 949; Acts 1991, cc. 131, 491; Acts 1992, c. 559; Acts 1993, cc. 527, 919; Acts 1994, cc. 359, 363, 870; Acts 1996, c. 984; Acts 1997, cc. 472, 508; Acts 1998, c. 703; Acts 1999, c. 743; Acts 2000, cc. 958, 970, 980; Acts 2001, cc. 182, 645, 779; Acts 2003, c. 290; Acts 2004, c. 720.

18.2-271.2. Amended by Acts 1988, cc. 781, 859, 888; Acts 1990, cc. 1, 317; Acts 1992, c. 560; Acts 1993, c. 757; Acts 2003, c. 885.

18.2-271.3. Repealed by Acts 1999, c. 734.

18.2-272. Amended by Acts 1988, c. 859; Acts 1991, c. 64; Acts 2004, cc. 948, 1013.

18.2-274 to 18.2-278. Repealed by Acts 1980, c. 759.

18.2-278.1 to 18.2-278.7. Repealed by Acts 1986, c. 492.

18.2-279. Amended by Acts 1992, c. 738.

18.2-280. Amended by Acts 1992, c. 735; Acts 1999, c. 996; Acts 2001, c. 712.

18.2-282. Amended by Acts 1990, cc. 588, 599; Acts 1992, c. 735; Acts 2003, c. 976.

18.2-283.1. Amended by Acts 2004, c. 995.

18.2-284. Amended by Acts 2003, c. 976.

18.2-285. Amended by Acts 1999, c. 543.

18.2-286. Amended by Acts 1993, c. 322; Acts 1994, c. 18.

18.2-287. Repealed by Acts 2004, c. 462.

18.2-287.1. Repealed by Acts 2004, c. 462.

18.2-287.2. Amended by Acts 1997, c. 311.

18.2-287.3. Repealed by Acts 1993, cc. 467, 494.

Sec.

18.2-287.4. Amended by Acts 1992, c. 790; Acts 2003, c. 976; Acts 2004, c. 995.

18.2-295. Amended by Acts 1978, c. 618; Acts 1988, c. 460.

18.2-299. Amended by Acts 1992, c. 580; Acts 2004, c. 930.

18.2-300. Amended by Acts 1978, c. 710; Acts 1992, c. 580.

18.2-301, 18.2-302. Repealed by Acts 1978, c. 710.

18.2-303. Amended by Acts 1992, c. 580.

18.2-303.1. Amended by Acts 1976, c. 351; Acts 1992, c. 580; Acts 1993, c. 449.

18.2-304. Amended by Acts 1992, c. 580.

18.2-305. Repealed by Acts 1976, c. 351.

18.2-306, 18.2-307. Amended by Acts 1992, c. 580.

18.2-308. Amended by Acts 1975, c. 594; Acts 1976, c. 302; Acts 1978, c. 715; Acts 1979, c. 642; Acts 1980, c. 238; Acts 1981, c. 376; Acts 1982, cc. 71, 553; Acts 1983, c. 529; Acts 1984, cc. 360, 720; Acts 1985, c. 427; Acts 1986, cc. 57, 451, 625, 641; Acts 1987, cc. 592, 707; Acts 1988, cc. 359, 793; Acts 1989, cc. 538, 542; Acts 1990, cc. 640, 648, 825; Acts 1991, c. 637; Acts 1992, cc. 510, 705; Acts 1993, cc. 748, 861; Acts 1994, cc. 375, 697; Acts 1995, c. 829; Acts 1997, c. 916; Acts 1998, cc. 662, 670, 846, 847; Acts 1999, cc. 628, 666, 679; Acts 2001, cc. 25, 384; Acts 2002, c. 699, 728, 826; Acts 2004, cc. 355, 423, 462, 876, 885, 900, 901, 903, 905, 926, 995, 1012.

18.2-308.1. Amended by Acts 1986, c. 445; Acts 1988, c. 493; Acts 1990, cc. 635, 744; Acts 1991, c. 579; Acts 1992, cc. 727, 735; Acts 1995, c. 511; Acts 1999, cc. 587, 829, 846; Acts 2001, c. 403; Acts 2003, cc. 619, 976; Acts 2004, cc. 128, 461.

18.2-308.1:2. Amended by Acts 1997, c. 921; Acts 2004, c. 995.

18.2-308.1:3. Amended by Acts 2004, c. 995.

18.2-308.1:4. Amended by Acts 1996, c. 866; Acts 1998, c. 569; Acts 2001, c. 357; Acts 2002, cc. 783, 865; Acts 2004, c. 995.

18.2-308.1:5. Amended by Acts 1995, c. 577.

18.2-308.2. Amended by Acts 1982, c. 515; Acts 1983, c. 233; Acts 1986, cc. 409, 641; Acts 1987, c. 108; Acts 1988, c. 237; Acts 1989, cc. 514, 531; Acts 1993, cc. 468, 926; Acts 1994, cc. 859, 949; Acts 1999, cc. 829, 846; Acts 2001, cc. 811, 854; Acts 2002, c. 362; Acts 2003, c. 110; Acts 2004, cc. 429, 461, 995.

Sec.
18.2-308.2:01. Amended by Acts 2003, c. 976; Acts 2004, cc. 347, 995.
18.2-308.2:1. Amended by Acts 1990, c. 692; Acts 1993, cc. 467, 494; Acts 2004, c. 995.
18.2-308.2:2. Amended by Acts 1990, cc. 594, 692; Acts 1991, cc. 515, 525, 716; Acts 1992, cc. 637, 872; Acts 1993, cc. 451, 461, 486, 493, 674; Acts 1994, c. 624; Acts 1997, c. 341; Acts 1998, c. 844; Acts 2002, c. 695; Acts 2003, cc. 833, 976; Acts 2004, cc. 354, 461, 837, 904, 922.
18.2-308.2:3. Amended by Acts 2002, c. 880; Acts 2003, cc. 833, 976.
18.2-308.3. Amended by Acts 1988, c. 530.
18.2-308.4. Amended by Acts 1990, c. 625; Acts 1992, c. 707; Acts 1993, c. 831; Acts 1999, cc. 829, 846; Acts 2003, c. 949; Acts 2004, cc. 461, 995.
18.2-308.5. Amended by Acts 2004, c. 995.
18.2-308.7. Amended by Acts 2003, c. 976; Acts 2004, c. 995.
18.2-309. Amended by Acts 1992, c. 487; Acts 1993, c. 855.
18.2-310. Repealed by Acts 2004, c. 995.
18.2-311. Amended by Acts 1985, c. 394; Acts 1988, c. 359.
18.2-315. Repealed by Acts 1980, c. 173.
18.2-322.1. Repealed by Acts 1997, c. 391.
18.2-323.1. Amended by Acts 2002, c. 890
18.2-324. Amended by Acts 1997, c. 136.
18.2-325, 18.2-326. Amended by Acts 1992, c. 423.
18.2-328. Amended by Acts 1983, c. 331.
18.2-330. Amended by Acts 1984, c. 625.
18.2-334. Amended by Acts 1992, c. 423.
18.2-334.2. Amended by Acts 1993, c. 513; Acts 1995, c. 837.
18.2-335. Repealed by Acts 1979, c. 420.
18.2-336. Repealed by Acts 2004, c. 995.
18.2-340. Amended by Acts 1991, c. 710.
18.2-340.1 to 18.2-340.14. Repealed by Acts 1995, c. 837.
18.2-340.15. Amended by Acts 2003, c. 884.
18.2-340.16. Amended by Acts 1996, c. 919; Acts 1997, cc. 777, 838; Acts 1998, cc. 57, 398; Acts 1999, c. 534; Acts 2002, cc. 282, 340; Acts 2003, c. 884.
18.2-340.17. Repealed by Acts 2003, c. 884.
18.2-340.18. Amended by Acts 1997, cc. 777, 838; Acts 2003, c. 884.
18.2-340.19. Amended by Acts 1996, c. 919; Acts 1997, cc. 777, 838; Acts 1998, c. 845; Acts 2001, c. 833; Acts 2003, c. 884.
18.2-340.20. Amended by Acts 1996, c. 573; Acts 1997, cc. 777, 838; Acts 2000, c. 1000; Acts 2001, c. 813; Acts 2002, cc. 282; Acts 2003, c. 884; Acts 2004, c. 213.

Sec.
18.2-340.21. Repealed by Acts 2003, c. 884.
18.2-340.23. Amended by Acts 1997, cc. 777, 838; Acts 2003, c. 884.
18.2-340.24. Amended by Acts 1996, c. 919; Acts 2003, c. 884.
18.2-340.25. Amended by Acts 1997, cc. 777, 838; Acts 1999, c. 361; Acts 2003, c. 884.
18.2-340.26. Amended by Acts 1997, cc. 777, 838; Acts 2001, c. 833; Acts 2003, c. 884; Acts 2003, c. 884.
18.2-340.28. Amended by Acts 1997, cc. 777, 838.
18.2-340.29. Amended by Acts 2003, c. 884.
18.2-340.30. Amended by Acts 1997, cc. 777, 838; Acts 1999, c. 360; Acts 2003, c. 884.
18.2-340.31. Amended by Acts 2003, c. 884.
18.2-340.32. Repealed by Acts 2004, c. 462.
18.2-340.33. Amended by Acts 1997, cc. 777, 838; Acts 1998, cc. 57, 398; Acts 1999, c. 534; Acts 2000, c. 1000; Acts 2001, c. 754; Acts 2002, cc. 282; Acts 2003, c. 884; Acts 2004, c. 275.
18.2-340.33.1. Amended by Acts 1997, cc. 777, 838.
18.2-340.34. Amended by Acts 1996, c. 919; Acts 1997, cc. 777, 838; Acts 1999, c. 534; Acts 2003, c. 884.
18.2-340.35. Amended by Acts 2003, c. 884.
18.2-340.36. Amended by Acts 2003, c. 884.
18.2-340.37. Amended by Acts 1996, c. 919; Acts 2003, c. 884.
18.2-340.38. Repealed by Acts 2001, c. 754.
18.2-341 to 18.2-343. Repealed by Acts 2004, c. 608.
18.2-346. Amended by Acts 1980, c. 534; Acts 1993, c. 609.
18.2-348. Amended by Acts 1980, c. 534.
18.2-351 to 18.2-353. Repealed by Acts 2004, c. 459.
18.2-355. Amended by Acts 1980, c. 534; Acts 1997, c. 555.
18.2-356. Amended by Acts 1980, c. 534.
18.2-357. Amended by Acts 1980, c. 534.
18.2-358. Repealed by Acts 2004, c. 459.
18.2-359. Amended by Acts 1976, c. 54; Acts 1978, c. 610; Acts 1981, c. 397; Acts 2004, c. 869.
18.2-360. Amended by Acts 1980, c. 534.
18.2-361. Amended by Acts 1977, c. 285; Acts 1981, c. 397; Acts 1993, c. 450.
18.2-362. Amended by Acts 2003, c. 99.
18.2-366. Amended by Acts 1981, c. 397; Acts 1993, c. 703.
18.2-367. Repealed by Acts 2004, c. 459.
18.2-369. Amended by Acts 1994, c. 620; Acts 2000, c. 796; Acts 2001, c. 181; Acts 2004, c. 863.
18.2-370. Amended by Acts 1979, c. 348; Acts 1981, c. 397; Acts 1986, c. 503;

Sec.

Acts 2000, c. 333; Acts 2001, cc. 776, 840.
18.2-370.1. Amended by Acts 1986, c. 503; Acts 1991, c. 517; Acts 2001, c. 840.
18.2-371. Amended by Acts 1981, cc. 397, 568; Acts 1990, c. 797; Acts 1991, c. 295; Acts 1993, c. 411; Acts 2003, cc. 816, 822.
18.2-371.1. Amended by Acts 1988, c. 228; Acts 1990, c. 638; Acts 1993, c. 628; Acts 2003, cc. 816, 822.
18.2-371.2. Amended by Acts 1991, c. 558; Acts 1993, c. 631; Acts 1994, c. 305; Acts 1995, c. 675; Acts 1996, cc. 509, 517; Acts 1997, cc. 812, 882; Acts 1998, c. 363; Acts 1999, c. 1020; Acts 2000, c. 883; Acts 2003, cc. 114, 615.
18.2-371.3. Amended by Acts 2000, c. 842; Acts 2001, c. 270.
18.2-373. Amended by Acts 1981, c. 293; Acts 1989, c. 546; Acts 2000, c. 1009.
18.2-374.1. Amended by Acts 1983, c. 524; Acts 1986, c. 585; Acts 1992, c. 234; Acts 1995, c. 839.
18.2-374.1:1. Amended by Acts 1993, c. 853; Acts 1994, c. 511; Acts 1999, c. 659; Acts 2003, cc. 935, 938; Acts 2004, c. 995.
18.2-374.2. Repealed by Acts 2004, c. 995.
18.2-374.3. Amended by Acts 1999, c. 659; Acts 2003, cc. 935, 938; Acts 2004, cc. 414, 444, 459, 864.
18.2-380. Amended by Acts 1983, c. 412; Acts 1985, c. 279.
18.2-381. Amended by Acts 1983, c. 412.
18.2-386.1. Amended by Acts 2004, c. 844.
18.2-387. Amended by Acts 1994, c. 398.
18.2-388. Amended by Acts 1979, c. 654; Acts 1982, c. 666; Acts 1983, c. 187; Acts 1990, c. 965.
18.2-389. Repealed by Acts 2004, c. 462.
18.2-390. Amended by Acts 1975, c. 492; Acts 1976, c. 504.
18.2-391. Amended by Acts 1976, c. 504; Acts 1985, c. 506; Acts 1987, c. 356; Acts 1999, c. 936; Acts 2000, c. 1009; Acts 2001, c. 451.
18.2-392 to 18.2-403. Repealed by Acts 1984, c. 492.
18.2-403.1. Amended by Acts 1992, c. 177; Acts 1993, c. 174; Acts 1996, c. 249; Acts 1999, c. 620.
18.2-403.2. Amended by Acts 1992, cc. 174, 177; Acts 1993, c. 174; Acts 1999, c. 620; Acts 2003, c. 787.
18.2-403.3. Amended by Acts 1993, cc. 174, 817.
18.2-414.1. Amended by Acts 2002, c. 560.
18.2-414.2. Amended by Acts 1990, c. 327.
18.2-415. Amended by Acts 1976, c. 244; Acts 1990, c. 627.

Sec.
18.2-423. Amended by Acts 1983, c. 337.
18.2-425.1. Amended by Acts 1986, c. 578.
18.2-426. Amended by Acts 1995, c. 791; Acts 2000, c. 962.
18.2-427. Amended by Acts 1976, c. 312; Acts 1984, c. 592.
18.2-429. Amended by Acts 1989, c. 59; Acts 1995, cc. 410, 478, 791.
18.2-431. Amended by Acts 1982, c. 502.
18.2-432. Repealed by Acts 2004, c. 462.
18.2-433. Repealed by Acts 2004, c. 462.
18.2-433.1. Amended by Acts 2003, c. 976; Acts 2004, c. 263.
18.2-438. Amended by Acts 1978, c. 123.
18.2-444.2. Amended by Acts 1991, c. 501; Acts 1992, c. 318.
18.2-457. Amended by Acts 1999, c. 626.
18.2-458. Amended by Acts 1999, c. 626.
18.2-460. Amended by Acts 1976, c. 269; Acts 1984, c. 571; Acts 1989, c. 506; Acts 1993, c. 747; Acts 1996, c. 718; Acts 1999, cc. 770, 800; Acts 2002, cc. 527, 810, 818; Acts 2003, cc. 111, 149; Acts 2004, cc. 396, 435.
18.2-461. Amended by Acts 1996, cc. 753, 815.
18.2-465.1. Amended by Acts 1985, c. 436; Acts 1988, c. 415; Acts 2000, c. 295; Acts 2002, c. 423; Acts 2004, c. 800.
18.2-472. Amended by Acts 1977, c. 107.
18.2-472.1. Amended by Acts 1999, c. 845; Acts 2001, c. 365; Acts 2003, c. 584.
18.2-473. Amended by Acts 1984, c. 587; Acts 1989, c. 733; Acts 1996, cc. 755, 914.
18.2-473.1. Amended by Acts 2000, c. 286.
18.2-474.1. Amended by Acts 1982, c. 490.
18.2-475, 18.2-476. Amended by Acts 1983, c. 360.
18.2-477. Amended by Acts 1985, c. 555.
18.2-477.1. Amended by Acts 1993, cc. 840, 930; Acts 1994, c. 490; Acts 1997, c. 749.
18.2-478 to 18.2-479. Amended by Acts 1985, c. 555.
18.2-488. Amended by Acts 1975, c. 493.
18.2-499. Amended by Acts 1994, c. 534.
18.2-500. Amended by Acts 2003, c. 578.
18.2-502. Amended by Acts 1986, c. 632.
18.2-503. Amended by Acts 1984, c. 61.
18.2-510. Amended by Acts 1981, c. 578.
19-1 to 19-342. Repealed by Acts 1960, c. 366.
19.1-1 to 19.1-400. Repealed by Acts 1975, c. 495.
19.2-3.1. Amended by Acts 1996, cc. 755, 914.
19.2-6. Amended by Acts 1977, c. 288; Acts 1994, c. 407.
19.2-8. Amended by Acts 1976, cc. 114, 620; Acts 1977, c. 108; Acts 1978, c. 730; Acts 1979, c. 243; Acts 1980, c. 496; Acts 1981, c. 31; Acts 1984,

Sec.
c. 601; Acts 1987, c. 488; Acts 1990, cc. 575, 976; Acts 1992, cc. 177, 435, 650; Acts 1996, c. 484; Acts 1998, c. 566; Acts 1999, c. 620.
19.2-10.1. Amended by Acts 2004, cc. 883, 996.
19.2-11.01. Amended by Acts 1995, c. 687; Acts 1996, c. 546; Acts 1997, c. 691; Acts 1998, c. 485; Acts 1999, cc. 668, 702, 844; Acts 2000, cc. 272, 827; Acts 2001, cc. 410, 530, 549; Acts 2002, cc. 310, 810, 818; Acts 2003, cc. 103, 751, 764.
19.2-11.1. Amended by Acts 1994, cc. 361, 598; Acts 1995, c. 687; Acts 1996, c. 545.
19.2-11.2. Amended by Acts 2002, cc. 810, 818.
19.2-11.3. Amended by Acts 2002, c. 831.
19.2-12. Amended by Acts 1978, c. 697; Acts 1981, cc. 572, 587; Acts 1990, c. 558; Acts 1991, cc. 74, 338; Acts 1994, cc. 375, 569, 626; Acts 1997, c. 34; Acts 2001, cc. 3, 31; Acts 2002, cc. 86, 605, 789; Acts 2004, c. 1009.
19.2-13. Amended by Acts 1976, c. 220; Acts 1982, c. 523; Acts 1989, c. 455; Acts 1996, cc. 850, 956; Acts 2001, c. 249; Acts 2002, cc. 605, 836, 868; Acts 2003, c. 922; Acts 2004, c. 401.
19.2-16. Repealed by Acts 1994, c. 205.
19.2-17. Repealed by Acts 1996, c. 850.
19.2-19. Amended by Acts 1978, c. 500.
19.2-20. Amended by Acts 1978, c. 500; Acts 1979, c. 708.
19.2-21. Amended by Acts 1978, c. 500.
19.2-24. Amended by Acts 1978, c. 500.
19.2-29. Amended by Acts 2002, c. 310.
19.2-30. Amended by Acts 2002, c. 310.
19.2-32. Amended by Acts 2002, c. 310.
19.2-34. Amended by Acts 1976, c. 138; Acts 1977, c. 198; Acts 1981, c. 4; Acts 1992, c. 55.
19.2-35. Amended by Acts 1976, c. 138; Acts 1981, c. 4; Acts 1988, c. 511; Acts 2002, c. 310; Acts 2004, cc. 370, 452.
19.2-36. Amended by Acts 1984, c. 37; Acts 2004, c. 370.
19.2-37. Amended by Acts 1976, c. 138; Acts 1978, cc. 463, 760; Acts 1984, c. 41; Acts 1985, c. 45; Acts 1986, c. 202; Acts 1996, c. 112; Acts 1999, c. 267; Acts 2004, c. 830.
19.2-38. Amended by Acts 1980, c. 505; Acts 2004, c. 370.
19.2-38.1. Amended by Acts 1985, c. 132; Acts 1995, c. 611.
19.2-40. Repealed by Acts 1980, c. 758.
19.2-42. Repealed by Acts 2004, c. 327.

Sec.
19.2-44. Amended by Acts 1976, c. 138; Acts 1995, c. 551.
19.2-44.1. Repealed by Acts 1976, c. 138.
19.2-45. Amended by Acts 1976, c. 471; Acts 1977, c. 332; Acts 1978, cc. 500, 605; Acts 1985, c. 77.
19.2-46. Amended by Acts 1980, c. 139.
19.2-48. Amended by Acts 1980, c. 195.
19.2-48.1. Amended by Acts 1981, c. 5; Acts 1988, c. 510; Acts 1993, c. 930.
19.2-49 to 19.2-51. Repealed by Acts 1980, c. 758.
19.2-52. Amended by Acts 1986, c. 636.
19.2-53. Amended by Acts 1981, c. 559.
19.2-54. Amended by Acts 1976, c. 552; Acts 1977, c. 109; Acts 1979, c. 583; Acts 1980, c. 362: Acts 1981, c. 559.
19.2-56. Amended by Acts 1977, c. 289; Acts 1979, c. 584; Acts 1980, c. 573; Acts 1981, c. 559; Acts 1984, cc. 491, 598; Acts 1988, c. 50; Acts 2000, c. 783; Acts 2001, cc. 183, 205.
19.2-57. Amended by Acts 1976, cc. 142, 552; Acts 1977, c. 109; Acts 1980, c. 573; Acts 1984, c. 491.
19.2-59. Amended by Acts 1976, c. 293; Acts 1978, c. 721; Acts 1997, c. 147.
19.2-59.1. Amended by Acts 1995, c. 112.
19.2-61. Amended by Acts 1988, c. 889; Acts 2002, cc. 588, 623.
19.2-62. Amended by Acts 1988, c. 889; Acts 2004, c. 149.
19.2-63. Amended by Acts 1988, c. 889.
19.2-63.1. Amended by Acts 1988, c. 889.
19.2-66. Amended by Acts 1976, c. 271; Acts 1979, c. 602; Acts 1982, cc. 40, 274; Acts 1988, cc. 855, 889; Acts 2002, cc. 588, 623; Acts 2004, c. 122.
19.2-67. Amended by Acts 1976, c. 231; Acts 1979, c. 602; Acts 1983, c. 536; Acts 1988, c. 889.
19.2-68. Amended by Acts 1976, c. 163; Acts 1977, c. 335; Acts 1979, c. 602; Acts 1980, c. 244; Acts 1988, c. 889; Acts 2002, c. 91.
19.2-69. Amended by Acts 1988, c. 889.
19.2-71. Amended by Acts 1993, c. 930; Acts 1999, c. 266; Acts 2002, c. 310.
19.2-72. Amended by Acts 1991, c. 420; Acts 2000, c. 170.
19.2-73. Amended by Acts 1978, c. 500; Acts 1981, c. 382.
19.2-73.1. Amended by Acts 1991, c. 162; Acts 1993, c. 350.
19.2-74. Amended by Acts 1976, c. 753; Acts 1978, c. 500; Acts 1979, cc. 679, 680; Acts 1980, c. 492; Acts 1981, c. 382; Acts 1982, cc. 485, 500; Acts 1984, c. 24; Acts 1988, c. 455; Acts 1995, c. 471.

Sec.
19.2-74.1. Repealed by Acts 1981, c. 382.
19.2-76. Amended by Acts 1979, c. 661; Acts 1994, c. 933; Acts 1997, c. 10; Acts 1998, c. 615.
19.2-76.1. Amended by Acts 1979, c. 34; Acts 1982, c. 608; Acts 1985, c. 199; Acts 1990, c. 626; Acts 1991, c. 542; Acts 1993, c. 550; Acts 2003, c. 147.
19.2-76.2. Amended by Acts 1978, c. 781; Acts 1983, c. 254; Acts 1984, c. 119.
19.2-76.3. Amended by Acts 1994, c. 642.
19.2-80. Amended by Acts 1979, c. 679; Acts 1986, c. 327; Acts 1997, c. 10.
19.2-81. Amended by Acts 1976, cc. 515, 570; Acts 1977, c. 97; Acts 1979, c. 268; Acts 1982, c. 272; Acts 1983, c. 206; Acts 1984, c. 534; Acts 1985, c. 507; Acts 1988, cc. 353, 744, 752, 853; Acts 1990, cc. 635, 744, 784; Acts 1995, c. 465; Acts 1996, cc. 866, 929, 1015; Acts 1998, c. 684; Acts 2002, cc. 810, 818; Acts 2004, c. 122.
19.2-81.2. Amended by Acts 1979, c. 642; Acts 1984, cc. 720, 779.
19.2-81.3. Amended by Acts 1992, c. 886; Acts 1995, cc. 413, 433; Acts 1996, c. 866; Acts 1997, c. 603; Acts 1998, c. 569; Acts 1999, cc. 697, 721, 807; Acts 2002, cc. 810, 818; Acts 2004, c. 1016.
19.2-81.4. Amended by Acts 2004, cc. 972, 980, 1016.
19.2-81.6. Amended by Acts 2004, cc. 360, 412.
19.2-82. Amended by Acts 1981, c. 382; Acts 1983, c. 564; Acts 1984, c. 766; Acts 1991, c. 41; Acts 2002, c. 310; Acts 2004, cc. 360, 412.
19.2-83. Repealed by Acts 1994, c. 273.
19.2-83.1. Amended by Acts 1996, cc. 958, 960; Acts 1997, c. 721; Acts 2001, c. 591; Acts 2004, c. 517.
19.2-92. Amended by Acts 2001, cc. 214, 226.
19.2-112. Amended by Acts 1999, c. 322; Acts 2002, c. 622.
19.2-114. Amended by Acts 1992, c. 306.
19.2-119. Amended by Acts 1984, c. 703; Acts 1991, c. 581; Acts 1993, c. 636; Acts 1999, cc. 829, 846.
19.2-120. Amended by Acts 1978, c. 755; Acts 1979, c. 649; Acts 1987, c. 390; Acts 1991, c. 581; Acts 1993, c. 636; Acts 1996, c. 973; Acts 1997, cc. 6, 476; Acts 1999, cc. 829, 846; Acts 2000, c. 797; Acts 2002, cc. 588, 623; Acts 2004, cc. 308, 360, 406, 412, 461, 819, 954, 959.
19.2-121. Amended by Acts 1978, c. 755; Acts 1980, c. 190; Acts 1991, c. 581; Acts 1992, c. 576; Acts 1993, c. 636; Acts 1999, cc. 829, 846.

Sec.
19.2-122. Repealed by Acts 1986, c. 327.
19.2-123. Amended by Acts 1978, cc. 500, 755; Acts 1979, c. 518; Acts 1981, c. 528; Acts 1984, c. 707; Acts 1989, c. 369; Acts 1991, cc. 483, 512, 581, 585; Acts 1992, c. 576; Acts 1993, c. 636; Acts 1999, cc. 829, 846; Acts 2000, cc. 885, 1020, 1041; Acts 2001, c. 201.
19.2-124. Amended by Acts 1978, c. 755; Acts 1984, c. 703; Acts 1991, c. 581; Acts 1999, cc. 829, 846.
19.2-125. Amended by Acts 1978, c. 755; Acts 1999, cc. 829, 846.
19.2-126. Repealed by Acts 1999, cc. 829, 846.
19.2-127. Amended by Acts 1999, cc. 829, 846.
19.2-128. Amended by Acts 1981, c. 382; Acts 1982, c. 271; Acts 1999, c. 821.
19.2-130. Amended by Acts 1978, c. 755; Acts 1991, c. 581.
19.2-131. Amended by Acts 1978, c. 755; Acts 1992, c. 576.
19.2-132. Amended by Acts 1978, c. 755; Acts 1989, c. 519; Acts 1991, c. 581; Acts 1999, cc. 829, 846.
19.2-132.1, 19.2-133. Repealed by Acts 1991, c. 581.
19.2-134. Amended by Acts 1991, c. 581; Acts 1992, c. 576.
19.2-135. Amended by Acts 1977, c. 287; Acts 1978, c. 755; Acts 1979, c. 735; Acts 1988, c. 688; Acts 1992, c. 576.
19.2-136. Amended by Acts 1978, c. 755; Acts 1991, c. 581.
19.2-137. Amended by Acts 1991, c. 581.
19.2-138 to 19.2-140. Repealed by Acts 1987, c. 670.
19.2-141. Amended by Acts 1997, c. 801.
19.2-143. Amended by Acts 1978, c. 755: Acts 1979, c. 735; Acts 1987, c. 670; Acts 1988, c. 443; Acts 1990, c. 624; Acts 2000, c. 885; Acts 2003, c. 840.
19.2-144. Amended by Acts 1991, c. 581.
19.2-145. Amended by Acts 1978, c. 755; Acts 1982, c. 153.
19.2-147. Amended by Acts 1994, c. 432.
19.2-148. Amended by Acts 1991, c. 581.
19.2-149. Amended by Acts 1991, c. 581; Acts 2004, c. 460.
19.2-150. Amended by Acts 1978, c. 755; Acts 1999, cc. 829, 846.
19.2-151. Amended by Acts 1997, c. 532; Acts 1999, c. 963.
19.2-152. Amended by Acts 1978, c. 755.
19.2-152.1. Amended by Acts 1988, cc. 473, 475; Acts 1989, c. 569; Acts 1993, c. 423; Acts 1997, c. 455; Acts 2003, c. 979; Acts 2004, c. 264.
19.2-152.1:1 to 19.2-152.1:7. Repealed by Acts 2004, c. 460, eff. 7/01/05.

Sec.
19.2-152.2. Amended by Acts 1999, cc. 829, 846; Acts 2004, c. 378.
19.2-152.8. Amended by Acts 1998, cc. 569, 684; Acts 1999, c. 371; Acts 2001, c. 474; Acts 2002, cc. 507, 706, 810, 818; Acts 2003, c. 730.
19.2-152.9. Amended by Acts 1998, cc. 569, 684; Acts 1999, c. 371; Acts 2001, c. 101; Acts 2002, cc. 507, 810, 818; Acts 2003, c. 730.
19.2-152.10. Amended by Acts 1998, cc. 569, 684; Acts 1999, c. 371; Acts 2002, cc. 507, 810, 818; Acts 2003, c. 730.
19.2-153. Amended by Acts 1984, c. 585; Acts 1985, c. 253.
19.2-155. Amended by Acts 1983, c. 362; Acts 1985, c. 321; Acts 1996, c. 968.
19.2-157. Amended by Acts 1978, c. 362.
19.2-158. Amended by Acts 1998, c. 773; Acts 1999, cc. 829, 846.
19.2-159. Amended by Acts 1976, c. 553; Acts 1978, c. 720; Acts 1984, c. 709; Acts 1984, c. 709; Acts 2004, cc. 884, 921.
19.2-159.1. Amended by Acts 1977, c. 6; Acts 1981, c. 289; Acts 1984, c. 709.
19.2-160. Amended by Acts 1978, c. 365; Acts 1979, c. 468; Acts 1983, c. 97; Acts 1989, c. 385.
19.2-163. Amended by Acts 1976, c. 553; Acts 1980, c. 626: Acts 1981, cc. 472, 486; Acts 1985, c. 525; Acts 1986, c. 425; Acts 1987, c. 638; Acts 1988, cc. 465, 472; Acts 1989, c. 565; Acts 1994, c. 451; Acts 1995, cc. 571, 713; Acts 1997, c. 492; Acts 1998, cc. 440, 451; Acts 2000, cc. 436, 448; Acts 2001, c. 509.
19.2-163.01 to 19.2-163.04. Amended by Acts 2004, cc. 884, 921.
19.2-163.1, 19.2-163.2. Repealed by Acts 2004, cc. 884, 921.
19.2-163.3. Amended by Acts 1975, c. 495; Acts 1978, c. 698; Acts 1979, c. 194; Acts 1990, c. 734; Acts 1992, c. 80.
19.2-163.4. Amended by Acts 1975, cc. 476, 495; Acts 1992, c. 80; Acts 1994, c. 415.
19.2-163.4:1. Amended by Acts 2004, cc. 884, 921.
19.2-163.6. Repealed by Acts 2004, cc. 884, 921.
19.2-163.7. Amended by Acts 1995, c. 503; Acts 2001, c. 766; Acts 2002, c. 614; Acts 2004, cc. 329, 884, 921; Acts 2004, cc. 329, 884, 921.
19.2-163.8. Amended by Acts 2001, c. 766; Acts 2004, cc. 884, 921.
19.2-164. Amended by Acts 1978, c. 601; Acts 1982, c. 444; Acts 1985, c. 396; Acts 1995, c. 546; Acts 1996, c. 402.

Sec.
19.2-164.1. Amended by Acts 1985, c. 396; Acts 1995, c. 546; Acts 1996, c. 402.
198.2-165. Amended by Acts 1983, c. 505; Acts 1984, c. 752; Acts 1994, c. 497; Acts 1999, c. 9.
19.2-165.1. Amended by Acts 1982, c. 507; Acts 1987, c. 330; Acts 1997, c. 322; Acts 1999, c. 853; Acts 2000, c. 292; Acts 2003, cc. 28, 772.
19.2-166. Amended by Acts 2003, c. 140.
19.2-168. Amended by Acts 1986, c. 535.
19.2-168.1. Amended by Acts 1986, c. 535.
19.2-169. Repealed by Acts 1982, c. 653.
19.2-169.1. Amended by Acts 1983, c. 373; Acts 1985, c. 307; Acts 2003, c. 735.
19.2-169.2. Amended by Acts 2003, c. 735.
19.2-169.3. Amended by Acts 1999, cc. 946, 985; Acts 2003, cc. 915, 919, 1018, 1042.
19.2-169.5. Amended by Acts 1986, c. 535; Acts 1987, c. 439; Acts 1996, cc. 937, 980.
19.2-169.6. Amended by Acts 1986, c. 629; Acts 1987, c. 96; Acts 1990, c. 76; Acts 1995, c. 844.
19.2-170 to 19.2-174. Repealed by Acts 1982, c. 653.
19.2-174.1. Amended by Acts 1999, cc. 946, 985; Acts 2001, c. 837.
19.2-175. Amended by Acts 1976, c. 677; Acts 1978, cc. 195, 794; Acts 1979, 516; Acts 1982, c. 653; Acts 1986, c. 535; Acts 1990, c. 697; Acts 1995, c. 645; Acts 2001, c. 480; Acts 2003, cc. 1031, 1040.
19.2-176. Amended by Acts 1982, c. 653; Acts 1986, c. 629; Acts 1990, c. 76.
19.2-177. Repealed by Acts 1988, cc. 787, 873.
19.2-177.1. Amended by Acts 1995, c. 844.
19.2-178. Amended by Acts 1995, c. 645.
19.2-179. Repealed by Acts 1981, c. 310.
19.2-181. Repealed by Acts 1991, c. 427.
19.2-182. Amended by Acts 1991, c. 427.
19.2-182.1. Repealed by Acts 1982, c. 653.
19.2-182.2. Amended by Acts 1993, c. 295; Acts 1996, cc. 937, 980.
19.2-182.3. Amended by Acts 1993, c. 295.
19.2-182.4. Amended by Acts 1993, c. 295.
19.2-182.5. Amended by Acts 1993, c. 295; Acts 1996, cc. 937, 980; Acts 2002, c. 750.
19.2-182.6. Amended by Acts 1993, c. 295.
19.2-182.7. Amended by Acts 1999, cc. 700, 746.
19.2-182.8. Amended by Acts 1993, c. 295; Acts 1996, cc. 937, 980.
19.2-182.9. Amended by Acts 1993, c. 295; Acts 1996, cc. 937, 980; Acts 2001, c. 837.
19.2-182.10. Amended by Acts 1993, c. 295.
19.2-182.12. Amended by Acts 1993, c. 295.
19.2-183. Amended by Acts 1982, c. 513.

Sec.
2002, cc. 588, 623; Acts 2003, c. 736.
19.2-294.1. Amended by Acts 1997, c. 691; Acts 2004, c. 937.
19.2-294.2. Amended by Acts 1994, c. 579.
19.2-295.1. Amended by Acts 1995, c. 567; Acts 1996, c. 664; Acts 2001, c. 389.
19.2-295.2. Amended by Acts 1995, cc. 502, 574; Acts 2000, c. 767.
19.2-295.3. Amended by Acts 2004, c. 310.
19.2-297. Repealed by Acts 1994, c. 706.
19.2-297.1. Amended by Acts 1994, 2nd Sp. Sess., cc. 1, 2; Acts 1995, c. 834; Acts 1996, c. 539.
19.2-298. Amended by Acts 1976, c. 285.
19.2-298.01. Amended by Acts 1996, c. 552; Acts 1997, c. 345; Acts 1998, cc. 200, 353; Acts 1999, cc. 286, 659, 662, 801, 845.
19.2-298.1 to 19.2-298.4. Repealed by Acts 2003, c. 584.
19.2-298.2. Amended by Acts 1997, c. 747; Acts 1998, cc. 785, 834; Acts 2002, c. 867.
19.2-298.3. Amended by Acts 1997, c. 747; Acts 1998, cc. 785, 834; Acts 2002, c. 867.
19.2-298.4. Amended by Acts 1998, cc. 785, 834; Acts 1999, c. 845.
19.2-299. Amended by Acts 1979, c. 286; Acts 1980, c. 733; Acts 1981, c. 263; Acts 1983, c. 541; Acts 1987, c. 676; Acts 1989, c. 169; Acts 1991, cc. 43, 229; Acts 1992, c. 77; Acts 1993, cc. 466, 492; Acts 1994, 2nd Sp. Sess., cc. 1, 2; Acts 1995, cc. 687, 778; Acts 1997, c. 691; Acts 1998, cc. 783, 840; Acts 1999, cc. 891, 903, 913; Acts 2001, c. 647; Acts 2003, cc. 146, 613; Acts 2004, cc. 308, 459, 819.
19.2-299.1. Amended by Acts 1984, c. 282; Acts 1987, c. 676; Acts 1989, c. 374; Acts 1993, cc. 436, 569; Acts 1995, cc. 687, 720; Acts 1996, c. 398.
19.2-299.2. Amended by Acts 1998, c. 783; Acts 1999, cc. 891, 913; Acts 2000, cc. 958, 980, 1040.
19.2-300. Amended by Acts 1990, c. 697.
19.2-301. Amended by Acts 1990, c. 697; Acts 2002, c. 662; Acts 2003, c. 886.
19.2-303. Amended by Acts 1982, cc. 458, 636; Acts 1983, c. 431; Acts 1984, c. 32; Acts 1992, c. 391; Acts 1993, c. 448.
19.2-303.2. Amended by Acts 1999, c. 372.
19.2-303.3. Amended by Acts 1995, cc. 502, 574; Acts 2000, c. 1040.
19.2-303.4. Amended by Acts 2000, c. 186; Acts 2002, c. 831.
19.2-305. Amended by Acts 1977, c. 682; Acts 1978, c. 716; Acts 1984, c. 32; Acts 1995, c. 485.

Sec.
19.2-305.1. Amended by Acts 1978, c. 131; Acts 1981, c. 224; Acts 1984, cc. 32, 269; Acts 1994, c. 197; Acts 1995, cc. 434, 687; Acts 2000, c. 775; Acts 2002, cc. 810, 818; Acts 2003, c. 982.
19.2-305.2. Amended by Acts 1989, c. 386.
19.2-305.3. Repealed by Acts 1997, c. 140.
19.2-305.4. Amended by Acts 2001, c. 122.
19.2-306. Amended by Acts 1978, c. 687; Acts 2002, c. 628.
19.2-307. Amended by Acts 1996, c. 60.
19.2-310. Amended by Acts 1981, c. 529; Acts 1982, cc. 476, 636; Acts 1986, c. 606; Acts 1990, cc. 676, 768.
19.2-310.1. Repealed by Acts 1982, c. 636.
19.2-310.2. Amended by Acts 1993, c. 33; Acts 1996, cc. 154, 952; Acts 1998, c. 280; Acts 2002, cc. 54, 753, 773.
19.2-310.2:1. Amended by Acts 2003, c. 150; Acts 2004, c. 445.
19.2-310.3. Amended by Acts 1997, c. 862; Acts 1998, c. 280; Acts 2003, c. 150; Acts 2004, c. 440.
19.2-310.3:1. Amended by Acts 2003, c. 150.
19.2-310.4. Amended by Acts 1998, c. 280; Acts 2002, cc. 753, 773; Acts 2003, c. 150.
19.2-310.5. Amended by Acts 1998, c. 280; Acts 2000, c. 284.
19.2-310.7. Amended by Acts 2002, cc. 753, 773.
19.2-311. Amended by Acts 1976, c. 498; Acts 1980, c. 531; Acts 1988, c. 38; Acts 1990, c. 701; Acts 1994, cc. 859, 949; Acts 1996, cc. 755, 914; Acts 1997, c. 387; Acts 2000, cc. 668, 690.
19.2-312. Repealed by Acts 1990, c. 701.
19.2-313. Amended by Acts 2000, cc. 668, 690.
19.2-314. Amended by Acts 2000, cc. 668, 690.
19.2-315. Amended by Acts 1984, c. 33; Acts 2000, cc. 668, 690.
19.2-316. Amended by Acts 1990, c. 701; Acts 2000, cc. 668, 690.
19.2-316.1. Amended by Acts 1992, c. 861; Acts 1994, c. 926; Acts 1995, c. 117; Acts 1996, cc. 809, 938; Acts 2000, c. 769.
19.2-316.2. Amended by Acts 1995, cc. 502, 574; Acts 2000, c. 338; Acts 2002, c. 604.
19.2-316.3. Amended by Acts 1995, cc. 502, 574; Acts 2000, c. 338.
19.2-317. Amended by Acts 1984, c. 703; Acts 1997, c. 358.
19.2-317.1. Repealed by Acts 1990, c. 74.
19.2-318. Amended by Acts 1979, c. 649; Acts 1984, c. 703.
19.2-319. Amended by Acts 1979, c. 649; Acts

Sec.

1984, c. 703; Acts 1987, c. 175; Acts 1988, c. 524; Acts 1999, c. 821.

19.2-320. Amended by Acts 1984, c. 703.

19.2-321. Amended by Acts 1976, c. 615; Acts 1984, c. 703.

19.2-322. Repealed by Acts 1984, c. 703.

19.2-323. Amended by Acts 1976, c. 615; Acts 1984, c. 703.

19.2-325. Amended by Acts 1984, c. 703.

19.2-326. Amended by Acts 1980, c. 626; Acts 1984, c. 703.

19.2-327. Amended by Acts 1984, c. 703.

19.2-327.01. Repealed by Acts 2004, c. 337.

19.2-327.3. Amended by Acts 2003, c. 131.

19.2-328. Amended by Acts 1981, c. 386; Acts 1985, c. 321.

19.2-329. Amended by Acts 1977, c. 483.

19.2-334. Amended by Acts 1978, c. 195; Acts 1979, c. 465.

19.2-335. Amended by Acts 1995, c. 485.

19.2-336. Amended by Acts 1978, c. 716; Acts 1995, c. 485.

19.2-338. Amended by Acts 1995, c. 51.

19.2-340. Amended by Acts 1995, c. 438.

19.2-341. Amended by Acts 1983, c. 499.

19.2-345, 19.2-346. Repealed by Acts 1988, c. 509.

19.2-347. Repealed by Acts 1983, c. 499.

19.2-348. Amended by Acts 1983, c. 499; Acts 1992, c. 623.

19.2-349. Amended by Acts 1979, c. 469; Acts 1983, cc. 415, 499; Acts 1988, cc. 742, 750, 770, 852; Acts 1991, c. 202; Acts 1992, c. 623; Acts 1993, c. 269; Acts 1994, cc. 841, 945; Acts 2001, c. 414; Acts 2003, c. 262.

19.2-353.2. Repealed by Acts 1988, cc. 770, 852.

19.2-353.3. Amended by Acts 1988, cc. 770, 852; Acts 1990, c. 899; Acts 1993, c. 930; Acts 1994, cc. 432, 841, 945; Acts 1997, c. 819; Acts 1998, cc. 720, 731; Acts 2001, cc. 481, 501.

19.2-353.4. Repealed by Acts 1988, cc. 770, 852.

19.2-353.5. Amended by Acts 1988, cc. 106, 508; Acts 1995, cc. 375, 566; Acts 1996, c. 226; Acts 2002, cc. 753, 773.

19.2-354. Amended by Acts 1977, c. 585; Acts 1982, c. 244; Acts 1984, c. 32; Acts 1986, c. 230; Acts 1988, cc. 770, 852; Acts 1994, cc. 841, 945; Acts 1995, cc. 380, 441; Acts 1996, c. 273; Acts 1998, c. 831; Acts 1999, c. 9; Acts 2001, c. 414; Acts 2002, c. 831.

19.2-356. Amended by Acts 1987, c. 238.

19.2-358. Amended by Acts 1977, c. 223; Acts 1987, c. 238; Acts 1988, cc. 770, 852; Acts 1992, c. 485; Acts 1994, c. 546.

19.2-360. Amended by Acts 1977, c. 465.

19.2-368. Amended by Acts 1977, c. 215.

19.2-368.2. Amended by Acts 1984, c. 619; Acts 1988, c. 748; Acts 1990, c. 620; Acts 1997, cc. 528, 691; Acts 1998, c. 484; Acts 1999, c. 286; Acts 2001, c. 855.

19.2-368.3. Amended by Acts 1984, c. 619; Acts 1986, c. 422; Acts 1990, c. 551; Acts 1992, c. 547; Acts 1993, c. 930; Acts 1998, c. 484; Acts 1999, cc. 703, 726.

19.2-368.4. Amended by Acts 1978, c. 210; Acts 1981, c. 592; Acts 1984, c. 747; Acts 1985, c. 446; Acts 1986, c. 422; Acts 1988, c. 406; Acts 1990, c. 550; Acts 1996, c. 86; Acts 2002, c. 665.

19.2-368.5. Amended by Acts 1977, c. 215; Acts 1978, c. 122; Acts 1986, c. 457; Acts 1992, c. 681; Acts 1997, c. 801; Acts 1998, c. 484; Acts 2001, cc. 363, 855; Acts 2002, c. 665.

19.2-368.5:1. Amended by Acts 1998, c. 484.

19.2-368.6. Amended by Acts 1977, c. 215; Acts 1993, c. 930; Acts 1994, c. 834; Acts 1997, c. 528; Acts 1998, c. 484.

19.2-368.7. Amended by Acts 1977, c. 215; Acts 1986, c. 457; Acts 1989, c. 335; Acts 2000, c. 455; Acts 2001, c. 363.

19.2-368.8. Amended by Acts 1977, c. 215; Acts 1984, c. 703; Acts 2002, c. 665.

19.2-368.9. Amended by Acts 1977, c. 215; Acts 1985, c. 446.

19.2-368.10. Amended by Acts 1977, c. 215; Acts 1985, c. 446; Acts 2001, c. 855.

19.2-368.11. Repealed by Acts 1986, c. 457.

19.2-368.11:1. Amended by Acts 1988, c. 748; Acts 1989, c. 335; Acts 1990, c. 552; Acts 1992, c. 687; Acts 1996, c. 86; Acts 1998, c. 484; Acts 2000, c. 847; Acts 2002, c. 665.

19.2-368.12. Amended by Acts 1977, c. 215; Acts 1989, c. 335.

19.2-368.13. Repealed by Acts 1984, c. 619.

19.2-368.14. Amended by Acts 1994, c. 834.

19.2-368.15. Amended by Acts 1983, c. 227.

19.2-368.17. Amended by Acts 1986, cc. 457, 472.

19.2-368.18. Amended by Acts 1978, c. 413; Acts 1980, c. 521; Acts 1985, c. 230; Acts 1988, c. 748; Acts 1993, c. 434; Acts 1996, cc. 760, 976; Acts 2002, c. 831.

19.2-368.19 to 19.2-368.21. Amended by Acts 1992, c. 681.

19.2-368.22. Amended by Acts 1992, c. 59.

Sec.
20-41, 20-42. Repealed by Acts 1975, c. 589.
20-44. Repealed by Acts 1975, c. 589.
20-45. Repealed by Acts 1975, c. 644.
20-45.2. Amended by Acts 1997, cc. 354, 365.
20-46, 20-47. Repealed by Acts 1985, c. 421.
20-48. Amended by Acts 1960, c. 363; Acts 1972, c. 823; Acts 1974, cc. 44, 45; Acts 1975, c. 644.
20-49. Amended by Acts 1950, p. 446; Acts 1952, c. 313; Acts 1972, c. 823; Acts 1974, cc. 44, 45; Acts 1975, c. 644; Acts 1980, c. 155; Acts 1991, c. 534; Acts 1993, cc. 778, 929.
20-49.1. Amended by Acts 1990, c. 836; Acts 1992, c. 516; Acts 1997, cc. 792, 896; Acts 1998, c. 884.
20-49.2. Amended by Acts 1989, c. 368; Acts 1993, c. 929.
20-49.3. Amended by Acts 1989, c. 598; Acts 1992, c. 516; Acts 1997, cc. 792, 896.
20-49.4. Amended by Acts 1992, c. 516.
20-49.7. Amended by Acts 1997, cc. 792, 896.
20-49.8. Amended by Acts 1990, c. 615; Acts 1992, c. 867; Acts 1994, c. 869; Acts 1996, c. 491; Acts 1998, c. 592.
20-49.9. Repealed by Acts 2002, c. 747.
20-50 to 20-60. Repealed by Acts 1968, c. 318.
20-60.3. Amended by Acts 1986, c. 594; Acts 1987, cc. 597, 658, 706; Acts 1988, c. 906; Acts 1991, cc. 651, 694; Acts 1992, c. 199; Acts 1993, c. 534; Acts 1994, cc. 764, 795; Acts 1997, cc. 796, 895; Acts 1998, cc. 727, 884; Acts 2000, c. 305; Acts 2003, c. 625; Acts 2004, c. 1008.
20-60.5. Amended by Acts 1986, c. 594; Acts 1986, Sp. Sess., cc. 1, 3; Acts 1987, cc. 609, 658, 706; Acts 1988, c. 906; Acts 1990, c. 836; Acts 1991, cc. 651, 694; Acts 1996, c. 416.
20-60.6. Amended by Acts 1998, c. 884.
20-61. Amended by Acts 1950, p. 613; Acts 1954, c. 481; Acts 1960, c. 275; Acts 1966, c. 360; Acts 1970, c. 284; Acts 1972, cc. 460, 845; Acts 1973, cc. 315, 346; Acts 1974, c. 464; Acts 1975, c. 644; Acts 1976, c. 462.
20-61.1. Repealed by Acts 1988, cc. 866, 878.
20-61.2. Repealed by Acts 1988, cc. 866, 878.
20-61.3. Amended by Acts 1994, c. 869.
20-62. Amended by Acts 1954, c. 481; Acts 1970, c. 630; Acts 1978, c. 377.
20-63. Amended by Acts 1954, c. 481; Acts 1958, c. 637; Acts 1966, cc. 120, 437; Acts 1974, c. 464; Acts 1978, c. 586.
20-64. Amended by Acts 1974, c. 464.
20-65. Amended by Acts 1974, c. 464; Acts 1975, c. 557.

Sec.
20-66. Amended by Acts 1974, c. 464.
20-67. Amended by Acts 1974, c. 464; Acts 1975, c. 644; Acts 1993, c. 930.
20-68. Amended by Acts 1974, c. 464.
20-69. Amended by Acts 1974, c. 464.
20-70. Amended by Acts 1974, c. 464; Acts 1975, c. 644.
20-71. Amended by Acts 1974, c. 464.
20-71.1. Amended by Acts 1974, c. 464; Acts 1975, c. 644; Acts 1993, c. 930.
20-72. Amended by Acts 1952, c. 692; Acts 1974, c. 464.
20-74. Amended by Acts 1975, c. 644; Acts 1987, c. 649; Acts 2004, c. 204.
20-75. Amended by Acts 1975, c. 644.
20-76. Repealed by Acts 1974, c. 464.
20-77. Amended by Acts 1974, c. 464.
20-78. Amended by Acts 1974, c. 464.
20-78.1. Amended by Acts 1978, c. 736; Acts 1980, c. 102; Acts 1987, c. 597; Acts 1991, c. 534; Acts 1999, c. 577.
20-78.2. Amended by Acts 1987, c. 190; Acts 1995, c. 483.
20-79. Amended by Acts 1960, c. 76; Acts 1964, c. 636; Acts 1970, c. 459; Acts 1974, cc. 464, 473; Acts 1975, c. 644; Acts 1976, c. 345; Acts 1977, c. 71; Acts 1988, c. 502; Acts 1993, c. 929; Acts 1994, c. 769.
20-79.1. Amended by Acts 1983, c. 481; Acts 1985, c. 488; Acts 1986, c. 594; Acts 1987, cc. 658, 706; Acts 1988, c. 906; Acts 1990, c. 896; Acts 1991, c. 534; Acts 1997, cc. 648, 663; Acts 1998, c. 727.
20-79.2. Amended by Acts 1990, cc. 836, 896; Acts 1991, c. 534; Acts 1995, c. 714; Acts 1998, c. 727.
20-79.3. Amended by Acts 1991, cc. 651, 694; Acts 1994, c. 767; Acts 1996, c. 416; Acts 1998, c. 727; Acts 2001, c. 209.
20-80. Amended by Acts 1974, c. 464.
20-81. Amended by Acts 1974, c. 464.
20-83. Amended by Acts 1975, c. 644.
20-83.1. Amended by Acts 1974, c. 464.
20-84. Amended by Acts 1974, c. 464.
20-85, 20-86. Repealed by Acts 1988, c. 495.
20-87. Amended by Acts 1974, c. 464; Acts 1975, c. 644; Acts 1988, c. 495.
20-87.1. Repealed by Acts 2003, c. 467.
20-88. Amended by Acts 1952, c. 510; Acts 1954, c. 481; Acts 1962, c. 557; Acts 1968, c. 665; Acts 1970, c. 278; Acts 1974, c. 657; Acts 1975, c. 644; Acts 1982, c. 472; Acts 1984, c. 781; Acts 1993, c. 930.
20-88.01. Repealed by Acts 1992, c. 662.
20-88.02. Amended by Acts 2002, c. 747.
20-88.1 to 20-88.11. Repealed by Acts 1952, c. 516.

Sec.
20-88.12 to 20-88.31. Repealed by Acts 1994, c. 673.
20-88.32. Amended by Acts 1995, c. 484; Acts 1996, cc. 882, 925; Acts 1997, cc. 797, 897; Acts 1998, c. 727.
20-88.36. Amended by Acts 1995, c. 484.
20-88.39. Amended by Acts 1996, cc. 882, 925; Acts 1997, cc. 797, 897.
20-88.41. Amended by Acts 1997, cc. 797, 897.
20-88.47. Amended by Acts 1997, cc. 797, 897.
20-88.48. Amended by Acts 1996, cc. 882, 925; Acts 1997, cc. 797, 897.
20-88.49, 20-88.50. Amended by Acts 1997, cc. 797, 897.
20-88.64. Amended by Acts 1997, cc. 797, 897; Acts 1998, c. 727.
20-88.67. Amended by Acts 1995, c. 484.
20-88.70, 20-88.71. Amended by Acts 1997, cc. 797, 897.
20-88.74. Amended by Acts 1997, c. 69.
20-88.76. Amended by Acts 1997, c. 797.
20-89. Repealed by Acts 1975, c. 644.
20-89.1. Amended by Acts 1976, c. 356.
20-91. Amended by Acts 1952, c. 100; Acts 1960, c. 108; Acts 1962, c. 288; Acts 1964, cc. 363, 648; Acts 1970, c. 311; Acts 1975, c. 644; Acts 1982, c. 308; Acts 1986, c. 397; Acts 1988, c. 404.
20-92. Repealed by Acts 1975, c. 644.
20-93. Amended by Acts 1954, c. 389; reenacted without change by Acts 1975, c. 644.
20-94. Amended by Acts 1975, c. 644.
20-95. Amended by Acts 1975, c. 644.
20-96. Amended by Acts 1975, c. 644; Acts 1977, c. 624; Acts 1979, c. 488; Acts 1987, c. 171; Acts 1989, c. 556; Acts 1993, c. 929.
20-96.1, 20-96.2. Repealed by Acts 1999, c. 161.
20-97. Amended by Acts 1958, c. 169; Acts 1968, c. 455; Acts 1974, c. 278; Acts 1978, c. 412; Acts 1985, c. 304; Acts 1987, c. 35; Acts 1988, c. 448; Acts 1991, c. 259.
20-98. Repealed by Acts 1977, c. 624.
20-99. Amended by Acts 1968, c. 484; Acts 1975, c. 644; Acts 1977, c. 60; Acts 1984, cc. 609, 616; Acts 1987, c. 594; Acts 1991, c. 244; Acts 1992, c. 563.
20-99.1. Repealed by Acts Acts 1988, c. 583.
20-99.1:1. Amended by Acts 1989, c. 562; Acts 1992, c. 563; Acts 1993, c. 929.
20-100. Repealed by Acts 1974, c. 123.
20-101. Repealed by Acts 1975, c. 644.
20-102. Amended by Acts 1975, c. 644.
20-103. Amended by Acts 1975, c. 644; Acts 1982, c. 306; Acts 1983, c. 253; Acts 1991, c. 60; Acts 1994, cc. 518, 769; Acts 1995, c. 674; Acts 1996, cc. 767, 866, 879, 884; Acts 1998, c. 616; Acts 2000, c. 586; Acts 2003, cc. 31, 45; Acts 2004, c. 732.
20-104. Amended by Acts 1950, p. 72; Acts 1975, c. 644; Acts 1996, c. 352.
20-105. Amended by Acts 1974, c. 581.
20-107. Repealed by Acts 1982, c. 309.
20-107.1. Amended by Acts 1984, c. 456; Acts 1988, c. 620; Acts 1994, c. 518; Acts 1998, c. 604; Acts 2003, c. 625.
20-107.2. Amended by Acts 1984, c. 651; Acts 1986, c. 421; Acts 1987, c. 597; Acts 1988, cc. 794, 887; Acts 1991, cc. 60, 545, 588; Acts 1992, cc. 585, 716, 742; Acts 1993, cc. 573, 599, 633; Acts 1994, cc. 719, 769; Acts 1996, c. 331.
20-107.3. Amended by Acts 1984, c. 649; Acts 1985, cc. 4, 442; Acts 1986, cc. 533, 537; Acts 1988, cc. 745, 746, 747, 825, 880; Acts 1989, c. 70; Acts 1990, cc. 636, 764; Acts 1991, cc. 632, 640, 698; Acts 1992, c. 88; Acts 1993, cc. 79, 929; Acts 1996, c. 616; Acts 2004, cc. 654, 757.
20-108. Amended by Acts 1986, c. 537; Acts 1987, c. 649; Acts 1991, c. 438; Acts 2002, c. 747; Acts 2004, c. 204.
20-108.1. Amended by Acts 1988, c. 907; Acts 1989, cc. 528, 599; Acts 1990, c. 567; Acts 1991, cc. 545, 588; Acts 1992, cc. 543, 716, 860; Acts 1993, cc. 520, 534; Acts 1994, c. 764; Acts 1995, c. 261; Acts 1996, c. 491; Acts 1998, cc. 592, 612; Acts 2001, c. 809; Acts 2004, cc. 204, 1008.
20-108.2. Amended by Acts 1989, cc. 528, 578, 579, 599; Acts 1919, cc. 545, 588; Acts 1992, cc. 79, 716, 860; Acts 1995, cc. 1, 481; Acts 1996, cc. 491, 947, 1029; Acts 1998, c. 618; Acts 1999, cc. 690, 808, 836; Acts 2000, cc. 219, 305, 376, 384, 461; Acts 2001, cc. 193, 809; Acts 2002, cc. 650, 747; Acts 2003, c. 885; Acts 2004, cc. 907, 1008.
20-109. Amended by Acts 1972, c. 482; Acts 1975, c. 644; Acts 1977, c. 222; Acts 1978, c. 746; Acts 1987, c. 694; Acts 1994, c. 518; Acts 1998, c. 604; Acts 2000, cc. 218, 221; Acts 2001, cc. 725, 740.
20-109.1. Amended by Acts 1972, c. 482; Acts 1978, c. 746; Acts 1979, c. 659; Acts 1982, c. 312; Acts 1987, c. 424; Acts 1996, c. 331; Acts 2003, c. 260.
20-110. Amended by Acts 1975, c. 644; Acts 2000, c. 221.
20-112. Amended by Acts 1975, c. 644; Acts 1987, c. 649; Acts 1991, c. 698;

Sec.

Acts 2000, c. 221; Acts 2004, c. 204.

20-113. Amended by Acts 1964, c. 273; Acts 1968, c. 483; Acts 1970, c. 761; Acts 1975, c. 644; Acts 1982, c. 298; Acts 1993, c. 929.

20-114. Amended by Acts 1975, c. 644.

20-115. Amended by Acts 1975, c. 644; Acts 1991, c. 698; Acts 1995, c. 428.

20-118. Amended by Acts 1960, c. 399; Acts 1962, c. 290.

20-119. Repealed by Acts 1975, c. 644.

20-120. Amended by Acts 1975, c. 644; Acts 1984, c. 537.

20-121. Amended by Acts 1950, p. 634; Acts 1952, c. 100; Acts 1960, c. 19; Acts 1968, c. 326; Acts 1975, c. 644; Acts 1979, c. 1; Acts 1987, c. 38; Acts 1988, c. 404.

20-121.01. Amended by Acts 1970, c. 538; Acts 1975, c. 644.

20-121.02. Amended by Acts 1984, c. 633; Acts 1986, c. 252; Acts 1988, c. 362; Acts 1989, c. 207.

20-121.4. Amended by Acts 1990, c. 569; Acts 2003, c. 258.

20-122. Amended by Acts 1975, c. 644; Acts 1979, c. 438.

20-123. Repealed by Acts 1964, c. 99.

20-124. Amended by Acts 1990, c. 623.

20-124.1. Amended by Acts 1999, c. 1028; Acts 2000, c. 830; Acts 2003, c. 229.

20-124.2. Amended by Acts 1996, cc. 767, 879, 884; Acts 1999, c. 574; Acts 2003, c. 520.

20-124.3. Amended by Acts 1999, c. 634; Acts 2000, c. 466; Acts 2004, c. 221.

20-124.4. Amended by Acts 2000, c. 768.

20-124.6. Amended by Acts 2000, c. 485.

20-125 to 20-146. Repealed by Acts 2001, c. 305.

20-128. Amended by Acts 1982, c. 483.

20-132. Amended by Acts 1982, c. 519.

20-138. Amended by Acts 1993, c. 930.

20-139. Amended by Acts 1993, c. 930.

20-140. Amended by Acts 1993, c. 930.

20-147 to 20-154. Amended by Acts 1986, c. 201.

20-155. Amended by Acts 1998, c. 638; Acts 2003, cc. 662, 669.

20-158. Amended by Acts 2000, c. 830.

20-160. Amended by Acts 2000, c. 830.

20-162. Amended by Acts 2000, c. 890.

20-164. Amended by Acts 1994, c. 919.

21-1 to 21-112.21. Repealed by Acts 1988, c. 891.

21-113. Amended by Acts 1970, c. 584.

21-116. Amended by Acts 1964, c. 517.

21-116.1. Amended by Acts 1952, c. 202.

21-118. Amended by Acts 1952, c. 113; Acts 1956, c. 588; Acts 1960, c. 36; Acts 1962, c. 497; Acts 1976, cc. 585, 684; Acts 1977, cc. 276, 516; Acts 1981, c. 564; Acts 2002, c. 194; Acts 2003, c. 940.

21-118.4. Reenacted without change by Acts 1964, c. 517; amended by Acts 1970, c. 674; Acts 1975, cc. 251, 490; Acts 1976, c. 684; Acts 1977, c. 516; Acts 1981, cc. 554, 563, 564; Acts 1982, c. 447; Acts 1983, c. 422; Acts 1994, c. 432; Acts 2000, c. 230.

21-118.5. Amended by Acts 1997, c. 12.

21-119. Amended by Acts 1997, c. 261.

21-120. Amended by Acts 1950, cc. 198, 442; Acts 1952, c. 300; Acts 1954, c. 324; Acts 1956, cc. 139, 691; Acts 1958, cc. 454, 521; Acts 1960, c. 561; Acts 1962, c. 554; Acts 1964, c. 344; Acts 1968, c. 678; Acts 1970, cc. 253, 597; Acts 1972, cc. 219, 222; Acts 1977, c. 303; Acts 1981, c. 294; Acts 1984, c. 732; Acts 1989, cc. 51, 394; Acts 1999, c. 1025.

21-121. Amended by Acts 1958, c. 588; Acts 1968, c. 62; Acts 1970, c. 441.

21-121.1. Amended by Acts 1954, c. 68.

21-121.2. Reenacted without change by Acts 1962, c. 26; amended by Acts 1964, c. 243.

21-121.5. Amended by Acts 1977, c. 183.

21-122. Amended by Acts 1964, c. 165.

21-123. Amended by Acts 1976, c. 11.

21-127.1. Amended by Acts 1970, c. 124.

21-133. Amended by Acts 1952, c. 283.

21-134.1. Amended by Acts 1962, c. 335.

21-137. Repealed by Acts 1972, c. 236.

21-140.1. Amended by Acts 1954, c. 68.

21-140.2. Reenacted without change by Acts 1962, c. 26; amended by Acts 1964, c. 243; Acts 1968, c. 62; Acts 1970, c. 441.

21-164. Repealed by Acts 1970, c. 463.

21-168. Amended by Acts 1991, c. 549.

21-176. Amended by Acts 1991, c. 549.

21-243. Amended by Acts 1971, Ex. Sess., c. 1.

21-244. Repealed by Acts 1970, c. 463.

21-248. Amended by Acts 2003, c. 940.

21-254. Amended by Acts 1968, c. 194.

21-291. Repealed by Acts 1960, c. 66. . 21-291.1. Repealed by Acts 1987, c. 57.

21-291.2. Amended by Acts 1962, c. 584; Acts 1964, c. 520; Acts 1974, c. 112; Acts 1976, c. 637; Acts 1977, c. 271; Acts 1989, c. 350; Acts 1998, c. 210.

21-292. Amended by Acts 1954, c. 642; Acts 1966, c. 203.

21-295. Amended by Acts 1997, c. 801.

21-297. Amended by Acts 1954, c. 642.

21-298. Repealed by Acts 1954, c. 642.

Sec.
21-300. Amended by Acts 1954, c. 642.
21-306. Amended by Acts 1954, c. 642.
21-310. Amended by Acts 1997, c. 801.
21-313. Repealed by Acts 1954, c. 642.
21-314. Amended by Acts 1954, c. 642.
21-320. Repealed by Acts 1954, c. 642.
21-334. Amended by Acts 1954, c. 642.
21-337, 21-338. Amended by Acts 1954, c. 642.
21-344. Amended by Acts 1954, c. 642.
21-346 to 21-349. Amended by Acts 1954, c. 642.
21-351 to 21-353. Amended by Acts 1954, c. 642.
21-355 to 21-361. Amended by Acts 1954, c. 642.
21-363 to 21-367. Amended by Acts 1954, c. 642.
21-372. Amended by Acts 1954, c. 642.
21-381 to 21-385. Amended by Acts 1954, c. 642.
21-388, 21-389. Amended by Acts 1954, c. 642.
21-393, 21-394. Amended by Acts 1954, c. 642.
21-396. Amended by Acts 1954, c. 642.
21-398 to 21-400. Amended by Acts 1954, c. 642.
21-402. Amended by Acts 1954, c. 642.
21-405. Amended by Acts 1954, c. 642.
21-408 to 21-418. Amended by Acts 1954, c. 642.
21-420 to 21-424. Amended by Acts 1954, c. 642.
21-426. Amended by Acts 1954, c. 642.
21-427. Amended by Acts 1952, c. 363.
22-1 to 22-363. Repealed by Acts 1980, c. 559.
22.1-1. Amended by Acts 1985, c. 407; Acts 1991, c. 178; Acts 1995, c. 852; Acts 2000, c. 629; Acts 2001, c. 828.
22.1-3. Amended by Acts 1980, c. 576; Acts 1981, cc. 341, 342; Acts 1993, c. 903; Acts 1997, c. 826; Acts 1999, cc. 368, 988; Acts 2000, cc. 209, 830; Acts 2004, cc. 500, 967.
22.1-3.1. Amended by Acts 1991, c. 523; Acts 2004, c. 500.
22.1-4. Repealed by Acts 1991, c. 523.
22.1-4.1. Amended by Acts 2000, c. 209; Acts 2004, c. 500.
22.1-5. Amended by Acts 1981, c. 342; Acts 1993, c. 293; Acts 1994, c. 887; Acts 1999, cc. 394, 443, 465, 988; Acts 2000, c. 253; Acts 2004, c. 500.
22.1-7. Amended by Acts 1985, c. 207; Acts 1994, c. 854.
22.1-15. Repealed by Acts 1980, c. 728.
22.1-17. Amended by Acts 1988, c. 234.
22.1-17.1. Amended by Acts 1996, c. 1000.
22.1-17.4. Amended by Acts 2002, c. 162.
22.1-18. Amended by Acts 1984, c. 157; Acts 2002, cc. 159, 253.
22.1-18.1. Amended by Acts 1999, c. 554.

Sec.
22.1-19. Amended by Acts 1991, c. 178; Acts 1993, cc. 730, 742; Acts 2000, c. 535.
22.1-19.1. Amended by Acts 2004, cc. 939, 955.
22.1-23. Amended by Acts 2001, cc. 689, 700.
22.1-25. Amended by Acts 2004, c. 917.
22.1-26. Amended by Acts 1999, c. 449; Acts 2000, cc. 631, 712, 1028; Acts 2002, c. 366; Acts 2003, c. 165; Acts 2004, c. 256.
22.1-27. Amended by Acts 1989, c. 197.
22.1-29. Amended by Acts 1997, c. 727.
22.1-29.1. Amended by Acts 1987, c. 430.
22.1-30. Amended by Acts 1986, c. 260; Acts 1990, c. 111; Acts 1991, cc. 140, 163; Acts 1993, c. 352; Acts 1994, c. 723; Acts 1995, c. 290; Acts 2002, c. 747.
22.1-32. Amended by Acts 1981, c. 482; Acts 1982, c. 488; Acts 1983, c. 562; Acts 1984, c. 483; Acts 1985, c. 493; Acts 1986, cc. 446, 486; Acts 1987, c. 348; Acts 1988, cc. 567, 582; Acts 1989, cc. 464, 504; Acts 1990, cc. 805, 878; Acts 1991, c. 279; Acts 1992, c. 406; Acts 1993, cc. 658, 783; Acts 1994, cc. 847, 900; Acts 1995, c. 487; Acts 1996, cc. 898, 1041; Acts 1997, cc. 233, 366; Acts 1998, cc. 309, 395, 600, 872; Acts 1999, cc. 423, 656, 689; Acts 2000, cc. 721, 738; Acts 2001, cc. 603, 607; Acts 2002, cc. 669, 733, 739; Acts 2003, cc. 175, 713; Acts 2004, cc. 179, 199.
22.1-36.1. Amended by Acts 1995, c. 316; Acts 2002, cc. 146, 269.
22.1-37. Amended by Acts 1984, c. 131.
22.1-40. Amended by Acts 1981, c. 246.
22.1-42. Amended by Acts 1992, c. 354.
22.1-44. Amended by Acts 1981, c. 246.
22.1-47. Amended by Acts 1981, c. 246.
22.1-47.3. Amended by Acts 1996, c. 185.
22.1-50. Amended by Acts 1991, c. 182; Acts 1992, c. 182.
22.1-57.3. Amended by Acts 1993, c. 878; Acts 1994, c. 723; Acts 1996, c. 873; Acts 2000, c. 1045.
22.1-57.3:1. Amended by Acts 2002, c. 74.
22.1-60. Amended by Acts 1983, c. 145; Acts 1989, c. 550; Acts 1992, c. 164; Acts 1996, c. 759; Acts 2002, c. 165, 374; Acts 2003, c. 866.
22.1-65. Amended by Acts 1990, c. 517.
22.1-67. Amended by Acts 1985, c. 324; Acts 1988, c. 95.
22.1-70.2. Amended by Acts 2001, c. 269.
22.1-71. Amended by Acts 1998, c. 102.
22.1-72. Amended by Acts 1995, c. 74; Acts 2002, cc. 22, 231.
22.1-75. Amended by Acts 1981, c. 246; Acts 1995, c. 56.

Sec.
22.1-76. Amended by Acts 1995, c. 842.
22.1-79. Amended by Acts 1985, c. 8; Acts 1987, c. 402; Acts 1991, cc. 553, 668; Acts 1994, c. 596; Acts 1996, cc. 485, 790, 798; Acts 1997, c. 382; Acts 2004, c. 563.
22.1-79.1. Amended by Acts 1998, c. 702; Acts 2003, c. 724.
22.1-79.3. Amended by Acts 2002, c. 160; Acts 2003, c. 693.
22.1-81. Amended by Acts 1987, c. 205; Acts 1999, cc. 191, 492.
22.1-85. Amended by Acts 1993, c. 287.
22.1-87. Amended by Acts 1981, c. 229; Acts 1993, c. 929.
22.1-88. Amended by Acts 1988, c. 576.
22.1-92. Amended by Acts 1986, c. 282; Acts 1994, cc. 453, 788.
22.1-93. Amended by Acts 1981, c. 541.
22.1-94. Amended by Acts 1989, c. 94.
22.1-97. Amended by Acts 2003, c. 948.
22.1-98. Amended by Acts 1987, c. 65; Acts 1988, c. 112; Acts 1990, c. 213; Acts 2004, cc. 839, 868, 887.
22.1-101. Repealed by Acts 1988, c. 101.
22.1-101.1. Amended by Acts 1992, cc. 837, 880; Acts 1994, c. 854.
22.1-110. Amended by Acts 1987, c. 251.
22.1-115. Amended by Acts 1984, c. 130; Acts 1989, c. 94; Acts 2002, c. 470.
22.1-118. Amended by Acts 1993, cc. 7, 161; Acts 2003, c. 702.
22.1-122. Amended by Acts 1989, c. 179.
22.1-122.1. Amended by Acts 1992, c. 175; Acts 1999, c. 388.
22.1-123. Amended by Acts 1985, c. 194; Acts 1991, c. 386; Acts 1994, c. 55.
22.1-126.1. Amended by Acts 2003, c. 940.
22.1-127. Amended by Acts 1994, c. 786; Acts 2003, c. 940.
22.1-128. Amended by Acts 1983, c. 32; Acts 1987, c. 188.
22.1-129. Amended by Acts 1989, c. 102; Acts 1991, c. 298; Acts 1995, c. 513; Acts 1997, c. 686; Acts 2000, c. 93; Acts 2001, c. 483.
22.1-131. Amended by Acts 2000, c. 754.
22.1-132.1. Amended by Acts 1989, c. 507; Acts 1990, cc. 411, 415, 612, 939; Acts 1991, c. 569; Acts 1992, cc. 204, 336; Acts 1993, cc. 176, 207, 777, 889.
22.1-137. Amended by Acts 1993, c. 212.
22.1-138. Amended by Acts 1993, c. 765.
22.1-140. Amended by Acts 1991, c. 550; Acts 1993, c. 227; Acts 1998, c. 27.
22.1-141. Repealed by Acts 1982, c. 647.
22.1-145. Amended by Acts 1985, c. 139.
22.1-146. Amended by Acts 1988, c. 88; Acts 1991, c. 682; Acts 1994, c. 689; Acts 1997, c. 372.
22.1-147. Amended by Acts 1988, c. 88; Acts 1997, c. 384; Acts 1998, c. 70.
22.1-148. Amended by Acts 1985, c. 226; Acts 1994, c. 689; Acts 1998, Sp. Sess., c. 2.
22.1-154. Amended by Acts 1982, c. 678; Acts 1987, c. 354; Acts 1998, c. 719.
22.1-155. Amended by Acts 1982, c. 678; Acts 1998, c. 719.
22.1-156. Amended by Acts 1998, c. 719.
22.1-157. Amended by Acts 1981, c. 191; Acts 1982, c. 340; Acts 1998, c. 719; Acts 1999, cc. 695, 748.
22.1-158. Amended by Acts 1998, c. 719.
22.1-161.6. Repealed by Acts 1996, cc. 105, 819.
22.1-163. Amended by Acts 1998, cc. 4, 900.
22.1-164. Amended by Acts 1980, c. 728.
22.1-165. Amended by Acts 1990, c. 909.
22.1-166. Amended by Acts 1989, c. 456.
22.1-167. Amended by Acts 1990, c. 909.
22.1-168. Amended by Acts 1990, c. 909.
22.1-168.1. Amended by Acts 1995, cc. 188, 233.
22.1-171. Amended by Acts 1984, c. 734; Acts 1985, c. 146; Acts 2004, c. 650.
22.1-175. Amended by Acts 1988, c. 259.
22.1-175.1. Amended by Acts 1995, c. 762; Acts 1998, Sp. Sess., c. 2; Acts 1999, cc. 354, 391.
22.1-175.2. Amended by Acts 1995, c. 762; Acts 1998, Sp. Sess., c. 2; Acts 1999, cc. 354, 391.
22.1-175.3. Amended by Acts 1995, c. 762; Acts 1998, Sp. Sess., c. 2; Acts 1999, cc. 354, 391.
22.1-175.4. Amended by Acts 1999, cc. 354, 391.
22.1-177. Amended by Acts 1991, c. 191; Acts 2003, c. 162.
22.1-178. Amended by Acts 1992, c. 130; Acts 1993, c. 285; Acts 1994, c. 104; Acts 1998, c. 287; Acts 2001, c. 445.
22.1-179. Repealed by Acts 1992, c. 130.
22.1-199. Amended by Acts 1980, c. 570; Acts 1985, c. 407; Acts 1990, c. 792; Acts 1991, c. 138.
22.1-199.1. Amended by Acts 1996, c. 974; Acts 1997, cc. 357, 394, 617, 686, 923; Acts 1998, c. 828; Acts 1999, cc. 456, 680; Acts 2000, cc. 93, 506; Acts 2001, cc. 483, 484; Acts 2004, c. 436.
22.1-199.2. Amended by Acts 1998, cc. 602, 627, 902; Acts 1999, cc. 488, 537, 552; Acts 2000, c. 716; Acts 2003, c. 697.
22.1-199.3. Amended by Acts 2004, c. 872.
22.1-201. Amended by Acts 1982, c. 354; Acts 1991, c. 178; Acts 1994, c. 693;

Sec.
Acts 1999, c. 559; Acts 2000, c. 504.
22.1-202. Amended by Acts 1996, cc. 122, 124; Acts 1998, c. 128; Acts 2001, c. 666.
22.1-203. Amended by Acts 2000, c. 1022.
22.1-204. Amended by Acts 1991, c. 178.
22.1-205. Amended by Acts 1988, c. 105; Acts 1989, c. 392; Acts 1998, c. 96; Acts 1999, c. 928; Acts 2000, cc. 82, 651; Acts 2001, cc. 659, 665; Acts 2002, cc. 177, 386; Acts 2003, c. 951.
22.1-206. Amended by Acts 2001, c. 452.
22.1-207. Amended by Acts 1991, c. 278.
22.1-207.1. Amended by Acts 1999, c. 422; Acts 2002, c. 554; Acts 2004, c. 1030.
22.1-207.2. Amended by Acts 1991, cc. 139, 526.
22.1-208.01. Amended by Acts 1999, c. 944; Acts 2003, c. 777.
22.1-208.1. Amended by Acts 1991, c. 178; Acts 1995, c. 318.
22.1-208.2:1. Amended by Acts 2004, c. 872.
22.1-209. Amended by Acts 1990, c. 797; Acts 1999, c. 452.
22.1-209.01. Amended by Acts 1995, c. 274.
22.1-209.1:2. Amended by Acts 1994, c. 762; Acts 1995, c. 533; Acts 1996, cc. 755, 914; Acts 2000, c. 739; Acts 2004, cc. 939, 955.
22.1-209.1:4. Repealed by Acts 2000, c. 1059.
22.1-209.1:7. Amended by Acts 2004, c. 872.
22.1-209.1:8. Amended by Acts 2001, c. 483.
22.1-209.1:9. Amended by Acts 2001, c. 483.
22.1-209.1:10. Repealed by Acts 2004, c. 872.
22.1-209.2. Amended by Acts 1992, cc. 209, 439; Acts 1994, c. 854; Acts 2000, cc. 66, 657, 865; Acts 2002, cc. 87, 478.
22.1-211. Amended by Acts 1989, c. 277; Acts 1995, c. 244.
22.1-212. Amended by Acts 1989, c. 277; Acts 1995, c. 244.
22.1-212.1. Amended by Acts 1986, c. 466; Acts 1996, c. 829.
22.1-212.2. Amended by Acts 1998, c. 106.
22.1-212.2:1. Repealed by Acts 2001, c. 660.
22.1-212.2:2. Amended by Acts 1999, cc. 456, 735.
22.1-212.3, 22.1-212.4. Repealed by Acts 1994, c. 789.
22.1-212.5. Amended by Acts 2000, cc. 631, 712, 1028; Acts 2004, c. 530.
22.1-212.6. Amended by Acts 2000, cc. 631, 1028; Acts 2002, c. 851; Acts 2004, c. 530.
22.1-212.7. Amended by Acts 2000, cc. 631, 712, 1028; Acts 2002, c. 851.
22.1-212.8. Amended by Acts 2000, cc. 631, 712, 1028; Acts 2002, cc. 851, 874; Acts 2004, c. 530.
22.1-212.9. Amended by Acts 2000, cc. 631, 1028; Acts 2001, cc. 438, 469; Acts 2002, c. 851; Acts 2004, c. 530.
22.1-212.10. Amended by Acts 2000, cc. 631, 1028.
22.1-212.11. Amended by Acts 2000, cc. 631, 1028; Acts 2002, cc. 851, 874; Acts 2004, c. 530.
22.1-212.12. Amended by Acts 2000, cc. 631, 1028; Acts 2002, c. 851; Acts 2004, c. 530.
22.1-212.13. Amended by Acts 2000, cc. 631, 712, 1028.
22.1-212.14. Amended by Acts 2000, cc. 631, 712, 1028; Acts 2002, c. 851.
22.1-212.15. Amended by Acts 2000, cc. 631, 1028; Acts 2002, cc. 851, 874.
22.1-213. Amended by Acts 1983, c. 538; Acts 1990, c. 444; Acts 1994, c. 854; Acts 2001, c. 483.
22.1-214. Amended by Acts 1981, c. 7; Acts 1982, c. 21; Acts 1985, c. 207; Acts 1990, c. 205; Acts 1991, c. 518; Acts 1993, c. 929; Acts 1994, c. 854; Acts 1997, c. 54.
22.1-214.1. Amended by Acts 1993, c. 929.
22.1-214.2. Amended by Acts 2001, c. 483.
22.1-214.3. Amended by Acts 2001, c. 483.
22.1-215. Amended by Acts 1985, c. 158; Acts 1988, c. 101; Acts 1994, c. 854; Acts 1996, cc. 583, 594.
22.1-216. Amended by Acts 1994, cc. 376, 854; Acts 1996, c. 133.
22.1-217. Amended by Acts 1990, c. 803; Acts 1992, c. 755; Acts 1995, c. 750; Acts 1998, c. 852.
22.1-217.01. Amended by Acts 2000, c. 285.
22.1-218. Amended by Acts 1988, c. 96; Acts 1989, c. 106; Acts 1990, c. 277; Acts 1993, cc. 110, 191; Acts 1996, c. 133.
22.1-218.1. Amended by Acts 1994, c. 854.
22.1-220. Amended by Acts 1989, c. 106; Acts 1994, cc. 376, 854.
22.1-221. Amended by Acts 1983, c. 521; Acts 1994, c. 854; Acts 1996, cc. 123, 247.
22.1-222. Repealed by Acts 1985, c. 421.
22.1-223. Amended by Acts 1999, c. 564.
22.1-224. Amended by Acts 1999, c. 564.
22.1-225. Amended by Acts 1999, c. 564; Acts 2004, cc. 939, 955.
22.1-226. Amended by Acts 1999, c. 564.
22.1-227. Amended by Acts 1992, cc. 673, 897; Acts 2001, c. 483.
22.1-227.01. Amended by Acts 2001, c. 483.
22.1-227.1. Amended by Acts 2001, c. 483; Acts 2002, c. 167.
22.1-228 to 22.1-233. Amended by Acts 2001, c. 483.
22.1-234. Amended by Acts 1991, c. 298; Acts 2001, c. 483.

Sec.

22.1-235 to 22.1-237. Amended by Acts 2001, c. 483.

22.1-238. Amended by Acts 2002, c. 421.

22.1-239. Amended by Acts 1981, c. 190.

22.1-241. Amended by Acts 1995, c. 750.

22.1-251. Amended by Acts 1993, c. 654.

22.1-252. Repealed by Acts 1993, c. 654.

22.1-253.1 to 22.2-253.13. Repealed by Acts 1988, cc. 645, 682.

22.1-253.13:1. Amended by Acts 1990, cc. 797, 820, 839; Acts 1991, c. 304; Acts 1992, cc. 132, 591; Acts 1994, cc. 618, 790; Acts 1996, cc. 163, 522; Acts 1997, cc. 466, 828, 829; Acts 1998, cc. 103, 602, 627, 800, 816, 901, 902; Acts 1999, cc. 377, 444, 445, 452, 461, 488, 552, 595, 994; Acts 2000, cc. 504, 547, 653, 662, 677, 684, 710, 735, 742, 750, 752, 867, 1061; Acts 2001, cc. 483, 731; Acts 2002, c . 656, 837; Amended by Acts 2003, cc. 688, 690, 691, 697, 714, 861, 1004; Acts 2004, cc. 404, 848, 939, 955.

22.1-253.13:2. Amended by Acts 1991, c. 480; Acts 1997, c. 828; Acts 2004, cc. 939, 955.

22.1-253.13:3. Amended by Acts 1990, cc. 820, 839; Acts 1992, c. 591; Acts 1998, cc. 456, 567, 602, 627, 843, 902; Acts 1999, cc. 670, 731, 1015; Acts 2001, c. 651 ; Acts 2004, cc. 472, 939, 955, 965.

22.1-253.13:4. Amended by Acts 1990, cc. 820, 839; Acts 1993, c. 661; Acts 1994, cc. 618, 790; Acts 1997, cc. 828, 835; Acts 1998, cc. 72, 602, 627; Acts 2001, cc. 483, 500; Acts 2004, cc. 509, 939, 955.

22.1-253.13:5. Amended by Acts 1990, cc. 820, 839; Acts 1992, c. 132; Acts 1997, c. 827; Acts 1998, cc. 826, 852; Acts 1999, cc. 830, 1030, 1037; Acts 2004, cc. 939, 955.

22.1-253.13:6. Amended by Acts 1990, cc. 820, 839; Acts 1992, c. 591; Acts 1998, c. 106; Acts 2001, c. 484; Acts 2004, cc. 939, 955, 965.

22.1-253.13:7. Amended by Acts 1990, c. 291; Acts 1992, c. 591; Acts 1998, c. 902; Acts 2004, cc. 939, 955.

22.1-253.13:8. Amended by Acts 1990, cc. 820, 839; Acts 2004, cc. 939, 955, 965.

22.1-254. Amended by Acts 1984, c. 436; Acts 1989, c. 515; Acts 1990, c. 797; Acts 1993, c. 903; Acts 1996, cc. 163, 916, 964; Acts 1997, c. 828; Acts 1999, cc. 488, 552; Acts 2000, c. 184; Acts 2001, cc. 688, 820; Acts 2003, c. 119; Acts 2004, c. 251.

22.1-254.01. Amended by Acts 1997, cc. 466, 828; Acts 1998, cc. 602, 627, 902; Acts 1999, cc. 488, 552.

22.1-254.1. Amended by Acts 1986, c. 215; Acts 1991, c. 306; Acts 1992, c. 131; Acts 1993, c. 992; Acts 1994, c. 854; Acts 1998, c. 435; Acts 1999, cc. 488, 552.

22.1-254.2. Amended by Acts 1997, c. 458; Acts 1999, cc. 488, 552; Acts 2003, c. 688; Acts 2004, cc. 251, 939, 955.

22.1-256, 22.1-257. Repealed by Acts 1999, cc. 488, 552.

22.1-258. Amended by Acts 1985, c. 482; Acts 1990, c. 797; Acts 1996, cc. 891, 916, 964; Acts 1998, c. 620; Acts 1999, c. 526.

22.1-260. Amended by Acts 1987, c. 374; Acts 1988, c. 163; Acts 1999, c. 526; Acts 2003, c. 637.

22.1-261. Amended by Acts 1996, cc. 891, 964; Acts 1999, c. 526.

22.1-262. Amended by Acts 1990, c. 797; Acts 1993, c. 930; Acts 1996, cc. 891, 964; Acts 1999, c. 526.

22.1-263. Amended by Acts 1990, c. 797; Acts 1996, cc. 891, 964; Acts 1999, c. 526; Acts 2004, c. 573.

22.1-265. Amended by Acts 1990, c. 797; Acts 1991, c. 534; Acts 1996, cc. 891, 916, 964.

22.1-266. Amended by Acts 1999, cc. 395, 1023; Acts 2001, cc. 688, 820.

22.1-267. Amended by Acts 1990, c. 797.

22.1-268. Amended by Acts 1993, c. 930.

22.1-270. Amended by Acts 1982, c. 510; Acts 1983, c. 195; Acts 1985, c. 334; Acts 2000, cc. 209, 617, 646; Acts 2001, c. 261; Acts 2004, cc. 500, 967.

22.1-271. Repealed by Acts 1982, c. 510.

22.1-271.1. Amended by Acts 1983, c. 433.

22.1-271.2. Amended by Acts 1983, c. 433; Acts 1988, c. 216; Acts 1989, c. 382; Acts 2000, c. 476; Acts 2004, c. 500.

22.1-271.3. Amended by Acts 1997, c. 685; Acts 2003, c. 1.

22.1-271.4. Amended by Acts 1999, cc. 488, 552.

22.1-273. Amended by Acts 1981, c. 142; Acts 1995, c. 246.

22.1-274. Amended by Acts 1990, c. 797; Acts 1994, c. 712; Acts 1997, c. 597; Acts 1998, c. 871; Acts 1999, cc. 570, 757.

22.1-274.1. Amended by Acts 1988, c. 103.

22.1-275. Amended by Acts 2001, c. 483.

22.1-275.1. Amended by Acts 1992, c. 174; Acts 1999, c. 570.

22.1-276. Repealed by Acts 2001, cc. 688, 820.

22.1-277. Amended by Acts 1984, c. 415; Acts 1997, cc. 585, 608, 734, 830; Acts

Sec.

1998, c. 379; Acts 2001, cc. 688, 820; Acts 2003, c. 119.

22.1-277.01 to 22.1-277.03. Repealed by Acts 2001, cc. 688, 820.

22.1-277.07. Amended by Acts 2003, cc. 843, 976; Acts 2004, c. 930.

22.1-277.1. Repealed by Acts 2001, cc. 688, 820.

22.1-277.2. Amended by Acts 2001, cc. 669, 688, 820.

22.1-277.2:1. Amended by Acts 2003, c. 119.

22.1-278 to 278.3. Repealed by Acts 2001, cc. 688, 820.

22.1-279. Repealed by Acts 1990, c. 797 and Acts 1991, c. 295.

22.1-279.2. Repealed by Acts 1995, c. 533.

22.1-279.3. Amended by Acts 1996, c. 771; Acts 2000, c. 538; Acts 2001, cc. 688, 820; Acts 2004, c. 573.

22.1-279.3:1. Amended by Acts 2002, c. 388; Acts 2003, cc. 899, 954; Acts 2004, cc. 517, 542, 939, 955.

22.1-279.5. Repealed by Acts 2001, cc. 688, 820.

22.1-279.6. Amended by Acts 2003, c. 899; Acts 2004, cc. 574, 908; 939; 955.

22.1-279.7. Amended by Acts 2003, c. 899.

22.1-279.8. Amended by Acts 2002, cc. 166, 221, 229, 235; Acts 2003, c. 801; Acts 2004, c. 690.

22.1-279.9. Amended by Acts 2004, c. 574.

22.1-280. Repealed by Acts 1989, c. 287.

22.1-280.1. Repealed by Acts 2001, cc. 688, 820.

22.1-280.2. Amended by Acts 1994, c. 721.

22.1-280.3. Repealed by Acts 2001, cc. 688, 820.

22.1-281. Amended by Acts 1992, c. 163; Acts 2000, c. 285.

22.1-284. Amended by Acts 1992, cc. 163, 755.

22.1-287. Amended by Acts 1981, c. 535; Acts 1996, c. 1000; Acts 1997, c. 910; Acts 2002, c. 747.

22.1-288. Amended by Acts 1982, c. 258.

22.1-288.2. Amended by Acts 1995, c. 429; Acts 1996, cc. 755, 914; Acts 1998, c. 870; Acts 2003, c. 119.

22.1-289. Amended by Acts 1985, c. 593; Acts 1990, c. 797; Acts 1993, cc. 740, 889; Acts 1994, cc. 808, 835, 913; Acts 1996, c. 1000; Acts 2000, c. 86.

22.1-289.1. Amended by Acts 2000, c. 66.

22.1-290. Amended by Acts 1990, c. 450.

22.1-290.01. Amended by Acts 2002, c. 889.

22.1-290.1. Amended by Acts 1992, c. 132.

22.1-291.1. Amended by Acts 2000, c. 650.

22.1-291.2. Amended by Acts 2004, c. 872.

22.1-292.1. Amended by Acts 2004, cc. 939, 955.

22.1-293. Amended by Acts 1992, c. 132; Acts 1999, cc. 1030, 1037.

Sec.

22.1-294. Amended by Acts 1982, c. 47; Acts 1992, c. 132; Acts 1999, cc. 1030, 1037.

22.1-295. Amended by Acts 1996, c. 186; Acts 1999, cc. 831, 1030, 1037.

22.1-296. Amended by Acts 1998, c. 872; Acts 2003, c. 531, 557.

22.1-296.1. Amended by Acts 1987, c. 359; Acts 1996, c. 960; Acts 1997, c. 103; Acts 2003, c. 723.

22.1-296.2. Amended by Acts 1989, c. 544; Acts 1990, c. 766; Acts 1991, c. 342; Acts 1992, cc. 641, 791; Acts 1993, cc. 210, 458; Acts 1994, cc. 232, 782; Acts 1995, cc. 731, 781, 809; Acts 1996, cc. 396, 467; Acts 1997, cc. 444, 721; Acts 1998, c. 412; Acts 1999, c. 448; Acts 2000, cc. 683, 774, 811; Acts 2001, cc. 591, 677.

22.1-296.3. Amended by Acts 1998, c. 113; Acts 2002, c. 528.

22.1-296.4. Amended by Acts 2000, cc. 95, 734.

22.1-297. Amended by Acts 1980, c. 575.

22.1-298. Amended by Acts 1991, c. 273; Acts 1992, c. 132; Acts 1993, c. 286; Acts 1996, c. 197; Acts 1998, cc. 621, 826, 852; Acts 1999, cc. 429, 1030, 1035, 1037; Acts 2000, cc. 102, 689, 1068; Acts 2002, cc. 128, 493; Acts 2004, c. 46.

22.1-299. Amended by Acts 1992, c. 132; Acts 2000, c. 689.

22.1-299.1. Repealed by Acts 1990, c. 970.

22.1-299.3. Amended by Acts 2004, c. 920.

22.1-300. Amended by Acts 1994, c. 68; Acts 2000, c. 476.

22.1-302. Amended by Acts 1989, c. 92; Acts 1990, c. 388; Acts 1996, c. 986; Acts 1997, c. 689; Acts 1999, c. 486.

22.1-303. Amended by Acts 1985, c. 348; Acts 1989, c. 100; Acts 1999, cc. 831, 1030, 1037; Acts 2000, c. 689; Acts 2001, cc. 865, 872.

22.1-303.1. Amended by Acts 1999, cc. 1030, 1037.

22.1-304. Amended by Acts 1992, c. 132; Acts 1993, c. 294; Acts 1996, c. 840; Acts 2000, c. 709; Acts 2001, c. 540; Acts 2002, c. 714; Acts 2003, c. 706.

22.1-305. Amended by Acts 1999, cc. 1030, 1037.

22.1-305.1. Amended by Acts 1999, cc. 1030, 1037.

22.1-305.2. Amended by Acts 1992, c. 132.

22.1-306. Amended by Acts 1981, c. 646; Acts 1992, c. 679.

22.1-307. Amended by Acts 1993, c. 498; Acts 1996, c. 961.

22.1-308. Amended by Acts 1992, c. 679.

Sec.
22.1-309. Amended by Acts 1985, c. 441; Acts 1992, c. 679.
22.1-311. Amended by Acts 2004, c. 1007..
22.1-312. Amended by Acts 1983, cc. 327, 354; Acts 1984, c. 742; Acts 1988, c. 242; Acts 2000, c. 837; Acts 2003, c. 161; Acts 2004, c. 1007.
22.1-313. Amended by Acts 1983, c. 327; Acts 1992, c. 679; Acts 2003, c. 187.
22.1-314. Amended by Acts 1987, c. 97; Acts 2003, c. 187.
22.1-315. Amended by Acts 1987, c. 328; Acts 1993, c. 498; Acts 1996, c. 960; Acts 1997, c. 721; Acts 2001, cc. 430, 450.
22.1-316. Amended by Acts 1992, c. 132.
22.1-319. Amended by Acts 1988, c. 574; Acts 1993, c. 351; Acts 1996, cc. 691, 832; Acts 2004, c. 991.
22.1-320. Amended by Acts 1988, c. 574; Acts 1993, c. 351; Acts 1996, cc. 691, 832; Acts 2004, c. 991.
22.1-321. Amended by Acts 1988, c. 574; Acts 2004, c. 991.
22.1-322. Amended by Acts 1988, c. 547; Acts 1993, c. 351; Acts 2004, c. 991.
22.1-323. Amended by Acts 1992, c. 666; Acts 1994, c. 258 Acts 2004, c. 991; .
22.1-323.1. Amended by Acts 1994, c. 258.
22.1-324. Amended by Acts 1988, c. 574; Acts 1993, c. 351; Acts 2004, c. 991.
22.1-325. Amended by Acts 2004, c. 991.
22.1-326. Amended by Acts 1996, cc. 691, 832; Acts 2004, c. 991.
22.1-326.1. Repealed by Acts 2004, c. 991.
22.1-327. Amended by Acts 1988, c. 574; Acts 1993, c. 351.
22.1-328. Amended by Acts 1992, c. 666; Acts 1993, c. 351; Acts 2004, c. 991.
22.1-329. Amended by Acts 1988, c. 574; Acts 1996, cc. 691, 832; Acts 2004, c. 991.
22.1-330, 22.1-331. Amended by Acts 2004, c. 991.
22.1-332. Amended by Acts 1988, c. 574; Acts 2004, c. 991.
22.1-333. Repealed by Acts 2004, c. 991.
22.1-335. Repealed by Acts 2004, c. 991.
22.1-337. Amended by Acts 2003, c. 885.
22.1-339. Amended by Acts 1985, cc. 447, 448.
22.1-340. Amended by Acts 1985, c. 447; Acts 1991, c. 79; Acts 2004, c. 465.
22.1-341. Amended by Acts 1985, c. 448; Acts 2001, c. 483.
22.1-342. Amended by Acts 2001, c. 483; Acts 2004, c. 465.
22.1-342.1. Amended by Acts 2000, cc. 66, 657.
22.1-343. Amended by Acts 1984, c. 444; Acts 1985, c. 397; Acts 1987, c. 426; Acts 1989, c. 135; Acts 1992, c. 151; Acts 1995, c. 700; Acts 1996, cc. 703, 726, 1000; Acts 2001, c. 483; Acts 2004, cc. 465, 872.
22.1-344. Amended by Acts 1984, c. 444; Acts 1985, c. 397; Acts 1989, c. 136; Acts 1990, c. 797; Acts 1996, cc. 755, 914, 1000; Acts 1997, c. 894.
22.1-346. Amended by Acts 1998, c. 66 Acts 2000, c. 285.
22.1-346.1. Amended by Acts 2000, c. 255; Acts 2001, cc. 667, 687.
22.1-348. Amended by Acts 1993, c. 2; Acts 1994, c. 259; Acts 1999, cc. 427, 428; Acts 2000, c. 285.
22.1-349. Amended by Acts 1993, c. 2.
22.1-350. Amended by Acts 1994, c. 276; Acts 1999, cc. 424, 437.
22.1-352. Amended by Acts 1999, cc. 424, 437, 1034.
22.1-354.1. Amended by Acts 2002, cc. 417, 465; Acts 2003, c. 885.
22.1-354.2. Amended by Acts 2001, c. 483.
22.1-354.3. Amended by Acts 2002, cc. 417, 465.
22.1-354.6. Amended by Acts 2004, c. 1000..
23-1. Repealed by Acts 1984, c. 734.
23-1.01. Amended by Acts 1985, c. 146 ; Acts 2004, c. 650.
23-1.1. Amended by Acts 1979, c. 630.
23-4.01. Amended by Acts 2001, c. 360; Acts 2004, c. 339.
23-4.1. Amended by Acts 1966, c. 313; Acts 1970, c. 166.
23-4.2. Amended by Acts 1982, c. 210.
23-7. Repealed by Acts 1984, c. 422.
23-7.1. Repealed by Acts 1996, cc. 931, 981.
23-7.1:01. Repealed by Acts 1996, cc. 931, 981.
23-7.2. Repealed by Acts 1996, cc. 931, 981.
23-7.2:1. Repealed by Acts 1996, cc. 931, 981.
23-7.3. Repealed by Acts 1996, cc. 931, 981.
23-7.4. Amended by Acts 1985, cc. 179, 572; Acts 1989, c. 371; Acts 1990, c. 680; Acts 1991, c. 590; Acts 1996, cc. 931, 981; Acts 1999, c. 439.
23-7.4:1. Amended by Acts 1996, cc. 931, 981; Acts 1998, c. 377; Acts 2001, c. 330; Acts 2003, cc. 657, 670.
23-7.4:2. Amended by Acts 1996, cc. 931, 981; Acts 1998, cc. 62, 79; Acts 1999, cc. 424, 437; Acts 2000, c. 196; Acts 2001, c. 483; Acts 2004, cc. 501, 520.
23-7.4:3. Amended by Acts 1996, cc. 931, 981.
23-7.4:4. Repealed by Acts 2002, c. 84.
23-7.5. Amended by Acts 1987, c. 366; Acts 1990, c. 273; Acts 2001, c. 340.
23-8.1. Repealed by Acts 1980, c. 658.
23-8.2. Repealed by Acts 1991, c. 590.
23-8.3, 23-9. Repealed by Acts 1980, c. 658.
23-9.1. Amended by Acts 1958, c. 47; Acts 1986, c. 536.
23-9.1:1. Amended by Acts 1977, c. 341.
23-9.2. Amended by Acts 1981, c. 505.

Sec.
23-9.2:1. Repealed by Acts 1980, c. 229.
23-9.2:2. Repealed by Acts 1972, c. 697.
23.9.2:3. Amended by Acts 1985, c. 520; Acts 1987, c. 109; Acts 1992, c. 630; Acts 1997, c. 827; Acts 1998, cc. 39, 362, 483, 784; Acts 2001, cc. 664, 673.
23-9.2:3.01. Repealed by Acts 2002, c. 84.
23-9.2:3.2. Amended by Acts 1991, c. 590.
23-9.2:4. Amended by Acts 1974, c. 162; Acts 1977, c. 162; Acts 1982, c. 18; Acts 1986, c. 236.
23-9.2:5. Amended by Acts 2000, cc. 699, 715.
23-9.2:6. Repealed by Acts 1990, c. 800.
23-9.3. Amended by Acts 1964, c. 597; Acts 1970, c. 117; Acts 1972, c. 210; Acts 1974, c. 544; Acts 1980, c. 728; Acts 1991, c. 590.
23-9.4. Amended by Acts 1974, c. 544; Acts 1997, cc. 803, 888, 891; Acts 2002, cc. 591, 612.
23-9.5. Amended by Acts 1974, c. 544; Acts 1977, cc. 296, 319, 413; Acts 1979, cc. 2, 136, 145; Acts 1992, c. 103; Acts 2002, cc. 158, 257; Acts 2004, cc. 176, 195.
23-9.6. Repealed by Acts 1974, c. 544.
23-9.6:1. Amended by Acts 1979, c. 619; Acts 1989, c. 105; Acts 1991, c. 590; Acts 1996, c. 215; Acts 1999, cc. 451, 460; Acts 2001, c. 841; Acts 2002, c. 95; Acts 2003, cc. 715, 725; Acts 2004, c. 502.
23-9.6:2. Amended by Acts 2004, c. 740.
23-9.7. Repealed by Acts 1974, c. 544.
23-9.8. Amended by Acts 1997, c. 827.
23-9.9. Amended by Acts 1974, c. 544; Acts 1991, c. 590.
23-9.10. Repealed by Acts 1996, cc. 110, 127.
23-9.10:1. Amended by Acts 1979, c. 28; Acts 1980, c. 728; Acts 1985, c. 448; Acts 1991, cc. 454, 590.
23-9.10:2. Amended by Acts 1980, c. 728; Acts 1985, c. 448.
23-9.10:3. Amended by Acts 1991, c. 590.
23-9.10:4. Amended by Acts 1991, c. 590.
23-9.11, 23-9.12. Repealed by Acts 1974, c. 544.
23-9.13:1. Amended by Acts 1997, c. 827; Acts 1999, c. 562; Acts 2000, cc. 96, 533, 546.
23-9.14. Amended by Acts 1974, c. 544.
23-9.14:1. Amended by Acts 1996, cc. 868, 992.
23-9.15 to 23-9.21. Repealed by Acts 1977, c. 676.
23-10 to 23-13. Repealed by Acts 1971, Ex. Sess., c. 102.
23-14. Amended by Acts 1956, c. 373; Acts 1960, c. 180; Acts 1962, c. 69; Acts 1964, cc. 358, 440, 635; Acts 1966, c. 616; Acts 1972, cc. 550, 861; Acts 1974, c. 317; Acts 1975, c. 396; Acts 1976, c. 189; Acts 1977, cc. 296, 319, 668; Acts 1979, cc. 136, 145; Acts 1987, c. 329; Acts 1992, c. 103; Acts 1999, cc. 424, 437; Acts 2000, cc. 108, 671; Acts 2001, c. 578; Acts 2002, c. 87, 158, 257, 478; Acts 2004, cc. 176, 195, 857.
23-15. Amended by Acts 1964, c. 635; Acts 1996, cc. 672, 689.
23-17. Amended by Acts 1996, cc. 672, 689.
23-18. Amended by Acts 1966, c. 572.
23-19. Amended by Acts 1950, p. 366; Acts 1954, c. 397; Acts 1958, cc. 17, 486; Acts 1959, Ex. Sess., c. 61; Acts 1962, c. 373; Acts 1964, c. 635; Acts 1970, c. 609; Acts 1990, cc. 54, 856; Acts 1996, cc. 636, 656, 672, 689.
23-21. Amended by Acts 1962, c. 373; Acts 1964, c. 635; Acts 1997, c. 308.
23-22. Amended by Acts 1962, c. 373; Acts 1964, c. 635; Acts 1984, c. 734.
23-26. Amended by Acts 1962, c. 373; Acts 1964, c. 635.
23-29. Amended by Acts 1962, c. 577; Acts 1964, c. 90; Acts 1986, c. 597; Acts 1997, c. 310.
23-30.01. Amended by Acts 1970, c. 609; Acts 1981, c. 505.
23-30.02. Amended by Acts 1981, c. 505.
23-30.1 to 23-30.22. Repealed by Acts 1966, c. 685.
23-30.24. Amended by Acts 1986, c. 597; Acts 1996, cc. 672, 689.
23-30.25. Amended by Acts 1980, c. 728; Acts 1986, c. 597.
23-30.26. Amended by Acts 1996, cc. 672, 689; Acts 1996, cc. 672, 689.
23-30.28. Amended by Acts 1986, c. 597; Acts 1994, cc. 191, 218; Acts 1996, cc. 672, 689; Acts 2000, cc. 414, 445; Acts 2004, c. 711.
23-30.29. Amended by Acts 1996, cc. 672, 689.
23-30.29:1 to 23-30.29:3. Amended by Acts 1996, cc. 672, 689.
23-30.31. Amended by Acts 1986, c. 597; Acts 1996, cc. 672, 689.
23-30.36. Amended by Acts 1984, c. 734; Acts 1985, c. 146; Acts 2004, c. 650.
23-30.41. Amended by Acts 1973, c. 205.
23-30.58. Amended by Acts 1973, c. 205.
23-31. Amended by Acts 1952, c. 139; Acts 1964, c. 440; Acts 1966, c. 621; Acts 1974, c. 317; Acts 1975, c. 397; Acts 1976, c. 189; Acts 1977, cc. 296, 319; Acts 1979, cc. 136, 145, 730; Acts 1990, c. 447; Acts 1992, c. 103; Acts 1996, c. 103; Acts 1999, cc. 424, 437; Acts 2001, c. 483; Acts 2002, cc. 158, 257; Acts 2004, cc. 58, 176, 195, 739.
23-32. Amended by Acts 1956, c. 184.

Sec.
23-35.1 to 23-35.8. Repealed by Acts 1994, c. 867.
23-35.9. Amended by Acts 1956, c. 644; Acts 1962, c. 81; Acts 1966, c. 162; Acts 1968, c. 441; Acts 1970, c. 653; Acts 1973, c. 401; Acts 1974, c. 654; Acts 1989, c. 330; Acts 2002, c. 290.
23-35.10. Amended by Acts 1974, c. 654; Acts 1989, c. 330.
23-38.10:1. Amended by Acts 1997, c. 899; Acts 2000, cc. 570, 597, 623, 645, 719; Acts 2001, c. 660.
23-35.11. Amended by Acts 1973, c. 401; Acts 1974, c. 654; Acts 1989, c. 330.
23-35.12. Amended by Acts 1973, c. 401; Acts 1974, c. 654; Acts 1989, c. 330; Acts 1998, c. 483; Acts 1999, c. 434.
23-35.13. Amended by Acts 1973, c. 401; Acts 1974, c. 654; Acts 1989, c. 330.
23-36, 23-36.1. Repealed by Acts 1950, p. 1292.
23-36.2. Amended by Acts 1960, c. 378; Acts 1973, c. 401.
23-37. Repealed by Acts 1979, c. 730.
23-37.1. Amended by Acts 1972, c. 198.
23-38.2. Amended by Acts 1987, c. 413.
23-37.3. Amended by Acts 1972, c. 198.
23-37.4. Amended by Acts 1972, c. 198.
23-37.5. Amended by Acts 1972, c. 198.
23-38.1. Repealed by Acts 1964, Ex. Sess., c. 8.
23-38.5. Amended by Acts 1972, c. 188.
23-38.10:3. Amended by Acts 1991, c. 590.
23-38.10:4. Amended by Acts 1988, c. 544.
23-38.10:5. Repealed by Acts 1991, c. 590.
23-38.10:6. Amended by Acts 1991, c. 590.
23-38.11. Amended by Acts 1975, c. 400; Acts 1980, c. 101.
23-38.12. Amended by Acts 1973, c. 2; Acts 1975, c. 400; Acts 1980, c. 101; Acts 1981, c. 257; Acts 1985, c. 520.
23-38.13. Amended by Acts 1973, c. 2; Acts 1981, c. 257.
23-38.14. Amended by Acts 1975, c. 400; Acts 1980, c. 101.
23-38.15. Amended by Acts 1973, c. 2; Acts 1975, c. 400; Acts 1980, c. 101; Acts 1981, c. 257; Acts 2000, cc. 94, 660.
23-38.16. Amended by Acts 1973, c. 2; Acts 1975, c. 400; Acts 1980, c. 101; Acts 1981, c. 257; Acts 1987, c. 600; Acts 2000, cc. 94, 660.
23-38.17. Amended by Acts 1973, c. 2; Acts 1975, c. 400; Acts 1980, c. 101.
23-38.17:1. Amended by Acts 2000, cc. 94, 660.
23-38.18. Amended by Acts 1973, c. 2; Acts 1985, c. 359; Acts 1995, c. 663.
23-38.19:2. Amended by Acts 1992, c. 311.
23-38.19:3. Amended by Acts 2001, c. 483.

Sec.
23-38.19:4. Amended by Acts 2001, c. 483; Acts 2004, c. 872.
23-38.20 to 23-38.29. Repealed by Acts 1973, cc. 24, 106.
23-38.30 to 23-38.44:4. Repealed by Acts 1998, cc. 39, 784.
23-38.45. Amended by Acts 1975, c. 196; Acts 1988, c. 232.
23-38.46. Amended by Acts 1975, c. 196; Acts 1988, c. 232; Acts 2000, cc. 567, 588.
23-38.47. Amended by Acts 1983, c. 236; Acts 1988, c. 232.
23-38.48. Amended by Acts 2000, cc. 567, 588.
23-38.49. Amended by Acts 1975, c. 196; Acts 1988, c. 232; Acts 2000, cc. 567, 588.
23-38.50. Amended by Acts 1988, c. 232.
23-38.52. Amended by Acts 1996, c. 1009.
23-38.53:2. Amended by Acts 1992, c. 646.
23-38.53:4, 23-38.53:5. Amended by Acts 1994, c. 789.
23-38.53:6. Amended by Acts 1993, c. 832; Acts 1994, c. 789; Acts 2002, c. 114.
23-38.53:7. Repealed by Acts 1994, c. 789.
23-38.53:9. Repealed by Acts 2004, c. 872.
23-38.53:12. Amended by Acts 2001, c. 765; 2004, c. 872.
23-38.53:13, 23-53:14. Amended by Acts 2001, c. 765; 2004, c. 872.
23-38.53:15. Repealed by Acts 2004, c. 872.
23-38.53:16. Amended by Acts 2001, c. 765; 2004, c. 872.
23-38.53:17. Amended by Acts 2001, c. 765.
23-38.53:18, 23-53:19. Amended by Acts 2001, c. 765; 2004, c. 872.
23-38.55. Amended by Acts 1976, c. 19; Acts 1977, c. 281; Acts 2002, c. 521; Acts 2003, c. 700.
23-38.56. Amended by Acts 1977, c. 281; Acts 1982, c. 677; Acts 1984, c. 371; Acts 1988, c. 90; Acts 1989, c. 101; Acts 1999, c. 381; Acts 2002, c. 521.
23-38.57. Repealed by Acts 1977, c. 281.
23-38.58. Amended by Acts 1977, c. 281.
23-38.59. Amended by Acts 1977, c. 281.
23-38.61 to 23-38.69:3. Repealed by Acts 1992, c. 630.
23-38.70. Amended by Acts 1986, c. 77; Acts 1988, c. 94.
23-38.71. Amended by Acts 1988, c. 94; Acts 1992, c. 434.
23-38.72. Amended by Acts 1989, c. 60; Acts 1998, cc. 39, 784.
23-38.73. Amended by Acts 1989, c. 60.
23-38.75. Amended by Acts 1997, cc. 785, 861; Acts 1998, cc. 61, 85; Acts 1999, c. 485, 518; Acts 2000, cc. 382, 400.
23-38.76. Amended by Acts 1997, cc. 785, 861; Acts 1999, cc. 485, 518; Acts 2000, cc. 382, 400.

Sec.
23-38.77. Amended by Acts 1997, cc. 785, 861; Acts 1998, cc. 61, 85; Acts 1999, cc. 485, 518; Acts 2000, cc. 382, 400.
23-38.78. Amended by Acts 1998, c. 373; Acts 2000, cc. 382, 400.
23-38.80. Amended by Acts 1996, c. 508; Acts 1997, cc. 785, 861; Acts 1999, cc. 485, 518; Acts 2000, cc. 382, 400.
23-38.81. Amended by Acts 1995, c. 315; Acts 1997, cc. 785, 861; Acts 1999, cc. 485, 518; Acts 2000, cc. 382, 400.
23-38.82. Repealed by Acts 1997, cc. 785, 861.
23-38.83. Amended by Acts 2000, cc. 382, 400.
23-38.84. Amended by Acts 1995, c. 315; Acts 2000, cc. 382, 400.
23-38.86. Amended by Acts 1999, cc. 485, 518.
23-38.87. Amended by Acts 1999, cc. 485, 518.
23-39. Amended by Acts 1960, c. 180; Acts 1962, c. 69.
23-40. Amended by Acts 1960, c. 180; Acts 1962, cc. 69, 610; Acts 1976, c. 21; Acts 1979, c. 294.
23-41. Amended by Acts 1960, c. 180; Acts 1962, c. 69; Acts 1966, c. 14; Acts 1974, c. 29; Acts 1975, c. 484; Acts 1992, c. 53; Acts 2004, c. 695.
23-42. Amended by Acts 1960, c. 180; Acts 1962, c. 69.
23-43. Repealed by Acts 1975, c. 484.
23-44, 23-45. Amended by Acts 1960, c. 180.
23-47. Amended by Acts 1960, c. 180; Acts 1962, c. 69; Acts 1972, c. 35.
23-48. Repealed by Acts 1960, c. 180.
23-49. Amended by Acts 1960, c. 180; Acts 1962, c. 69; Acts 1972, c. 35.
23-49.1. Amended by Acts 1960, cc. 56, 180; Acts 1962, cc. 69, 610; Acts 1966, cc. 14, 707; Acts 1976, c. 21; Acts 1992, c. 103.
23-49.2 to 23-49.10. Repealed by Acts 1968, c. 93.
23-49.11. Amended by Acts 1966, c. 18; Acts 1974, c. 317.
23-49.12. Amended by Acts 1966, c. 18; Acts 1974, c. 317.
23-49.13. Amended by Acts 1966, c. 18; Acts 1974, c. 317.
23-49.14. Amended by Acts 1966, c. 18; Acts 1970, c. 624; Acts 1980, c. 100.
23-49.15. Amended by Acts 1966, c. 18; Acts 1974, c. 317; Acts 1980, c. 100.
23-49.16. Amended by Acts 1966, c. 18; Acts 1974, c. 317; Acts 1980, c. 100.
23-49.17. Amended by Acts 1966, c. 18; Acts 1974, c. 317; Acts 1980, c. 100; Acts 2002, c. 368.
23-49.18. Amended by Acts 1974, c. 317.
23-49.20. Amended by Acts 1966, c. 18; Acts 1974, c. 317.
23-49.21. Amended by Acts 1968, c. 545; Acts 1974, c. 317.
23-49.22. Repealed by Acts 1968, c. 545.

Sec.
23-49.23, 23-49.24. Amended by Acts 1992, c. 103.
23-49.25. Amended by Acts 1978, c. 376; Acts 1992, c. 103; Acts 1995, c. 40.
23-49.27. Amended by Acts 1992, c. 103.
23-49.28. Amended by Acts 1978, c. 376; Acts 1990, c. 106; Acts 1992, c. 103.
23-49.29. Amended by Acts 1992, c. 103.
23-49.31 to 23-49.33. Amended by Acts 1992, c. 103.
23-50 to 23-50.3. Repealed by Acts 1968, c. 93.
23-50.6. Amended by Acts 1972, c. 51; Acts 1981, c. 225.
23-50.11. Amended by Acts 1996, cc. 905, 1046.
23-50.16:1. Amended by Acts 2000, c. 720.
23-50.16:3. Amended by Acts 2000, c. 720.
23-50.16:4. Amended by Acts 2000, c. 720.
23-50.16:5. Amended by Acts 1998, c. 449; Acts 2000, c. 720; Acts 2004, c. 1000.
23-50.16:7. Amended by Acts 2000, c. 720.
23-50.16:12. Amended by Acts 2003, c. 940.
23-50.16:24. Amended by Acts 1998, c. 449; Acts 2000, cc. 66, 657.
23-50.16:32. Amended by Acts 1998, c. 449; Acts 1999, cc. 703, 726; Acts 2004, c. 690.
23-51. Amended by Acts 1950, p. 1216; reenacted without change by Acts 1966, c. 462; Acts 1986, c. 306.
23-52. Amended by Acts 1950, c. 553.
23-54 to 23-61. Repealed by Acts 1964, c. 97.
23-70. Amended by Acts 1954, c. 343; Acts 1980, c. 559; Acts 1989, Sp. Sess., c. 5.
23-71. Amended by Acts 1954, c. 343; Acts 1980, c. 559.
23-72. Amended by Acts 1980, c. 559; Acts 1989, Sp. Sess., c. 5.
23-74. Amended by Acts 2003, c. 655.
23-75. Amended by Acts 1966, c. 467; Acts 2003, c. 655.
23-76. Amended by Acts 1956, cc. 12, 689.
23-76.1. Amended by Acts 2000, cc. 818, 1014; Acts 2002, cc. 582, 595.
23-77.3. Amended by Acts 2003, c. 701.
23-77.4. Amended by Acts 1996, cc. 933, 995; Acts 2002, cc. 574, 602; Acts 2004, c. 145.
23-81. Amended by Acts 1956, c. 184.
23-86 to 23-91. Repealed by Acts 1972, c. 861.
23-91.1 to 23-91.4. Repealed by Acts 1966, c. 68.
23-91.5 to 23-91.12. Repealed by Acts 1983, c. 63.
23-91.14 to 23-91.17. Repealed by Acts 1972, c. 550.
23-91.20. Amended by Acts 1999, cc. 424, 437.
23-91.23. Amended by Acts 1999, cc. 424, 437.
23-91.26. Amended by Acts 1977, c. 670.
23-91.27. Amended by Acts 1977, c. 670.
23-91.34. Amended by Acts 2004, cc. 176, 195.

Sec.
23-91.35. Amended by Acts 1977, c. 168.
23-91.37. Amended by Acts 2004, cc. 176, 195.
23-91.39. Amended by Acts 2004, cc. 176, 195.
23-91.40. Amended by Acts 2004, c. 195.
23-91.41. Amended by Acts 2004, cc. 176, 195.
23-91.43. Amended by Acts 2004, cc. 176, 195.
23-91.44. Amended by Acts 2004, cc. 176, 195.
23-92. Amended by Acts 1968, c. 719.
23-93. Amended by Acts 1960, c. 187; Acts 1968, c. 719; Acts 1978, c. 453; Acts 1979, c. 17; Acts 1980, c. 648.
23-94. Amended by Acts 1960, c. 187; Acts 1968, c. 719; Acts 1975, c. 111; Acts 1978, c. 453.
23-95. Amended by Acts 1952, c. 213.
23-98. Amended by Acts 1954, c. 154.
23-105. Amended by Acts 1997, c. 788.
23-107. Amended by Acts 1952, c. 482; Acts 1958, c. 569; Acts 1973, c. 83.
23-108. Amended by Acts 1983, c. 385.
23-110. Amended by Acts 1952, c. 272.
23-111. Repealed by Acts 1984, c. 734.
23-114. Amended by Acts 1970, c. 98.
23-115. Amended by Acts 1964, c. 48; Acts 1980, c. 559.
23-116. Amended by Acts 1970, c. 98.
23-117. Amended by Acts 1980, c. 559.
23-118. Amended by Acts 1970, c. 98.
23-122. Amended by Acts 1970, c. 98.
23-123. Repealed by Acts 1981, c. 319.
23-124. Amended by Acts 1970, c. 98.
23-126. Amended by Acts 1970, c. 98.
23-127. Amended by Acts 1970, c. 98.
23-128. Amended by Acts 1970, c. 98.
23-129. Repealed by Acts 1981, c. 319.
23-130. Amended by Acts 1970, c. 98.
23-131. Amended by Acts 1970, c. 98.
23-132. Repealed by Acts 1972, c. 48.
23-133 to 23-135.7. Repealed by Acts 1994, c. 433.
23-135.7:7. Amended by Acts 1984, c. 590; Acts 1985, c. 448; Acts 1996, cc. 589, 599.
23-135.7:9. Amended by Acts 1984, c. 734.
23-135.7:13. Amended by Acts 1984, c. 734; Acts 1985, c. 448.
23-135.7:19. Repealed by Acts 1992, c. 754.
23-135.8. Amended by Acts 1962, c. 78.
23-136. Amended by Acts 1979, c. 147.
23-137. Amended by Acts 1979, c. 147.
23-138. Amended by Acts 1979, c. 147.
23-141.3. Amended by Acts 1985, c. 448.
23-142. Amended by Acts 1973, c. 401.
23-147 to 23-155. Repealed by Acts 1964, c. 50.
23-155.1. Amended by Acts 1979, cc. 136, 145.
23-155.2. Amended by Acts 1979, cc. 136, 145.
23-155.3. Amended by Acts 1979, cc. 136, 145.
23-155.4. Amended by Acts 1976, c. 25.
23-155.6. Amended by Acts 1970, c. 601; Acts 1976, c. 25.
23-155.7. Amended by Acts 1979, cc. 136, 145.
23-155.8. Amended by Acts 1979, cc. 136, 145.
23-155.10. Amended by Acts 1979, cc. 136, 145.
23-156 to 23-164. Repealed by Acts 1977, c. 668.
23-164.1. Amended by Acts 1977, cc. 296, 319.
23-164.2. Amended by Acts 1977, cc. 296, 319.
23-164.3. Amended by Acts 1979, c. 623; Acts 1989, c. 107.
23-164.4. Amended by Acts 1977, cc. 296, 319.
23-164.5. Amended by Acts 1970, c. 601; Acts 1979, c. 623; Acts 1991, c. 96.
23-164.6. Amended by Acts 1977, cc. 296, 319.
23-164.7. Amended by Acts 1977, cc. 296, 319.
23-164.9. Amended by Acts 1977, cc. 296, 319.
23-164.10. Amended by Acts 1977, cc. 296, 319.
23-165. Repealed by Acts 1964, c. 70.
23-165.1. Amended by Acts 1979, c. 147.
23-165.2. Amended by Acts 1979, c. 147.
23-165.3. Amended by Acts 1979, c. 147.
23-165.4. Amended by Acts 1979, c. 147; Acts 1993, c. 697; Acts 1999, c. 752.
23-165.5. Amended by Acts 1979, c. 147; Acts 1993, c. 697.
23-165.6. Amended by Acts 1979, c. 147.
23-165.7. Amended by Acts 1979, c. 147.
23-165.9. Amended by Acts 1979, c. 147.
23-165.10. Amended by Acts 1979, c. 147.
23-166. Amended by Acts 1964, c. 70; Acts 1979, c. 147.
23-167. Amended by Acts 1964, c. 70; Acts 1979, c. 147.
23-168, 23-169. Repealed by Acts 1979, c. 147.
23-170. Amended by Acts 1964, c. 70; Acts 1979, c. 147.
23-171, 23-172. Repealed by Acts 1964, c. 70.
23-173. Repealed by Acts 1979, c. 147.
23-174. Amended by Acts 1979, c. 147.
23-174.1. Amended by Acts 1979, c. 146.
23-174.2. Amended by Acts 1979, c. 146.
23-174.3. Amended by Acts 1979, c. 146.
23-174.4. Amended by Acts 1980, c. 625; Acts 1999, c. 1013; Acts 2000, c. 844; Acts 2003, c. 802.
23-174.5. Amended by Acts 1979, c. 146.
23-174.6. Amended by Acts 1979, c. 146.
23-174.7. Amended by Acts 1979, c. 146.
23-174.8, 23-174.9. Repealed by Acts 1979, c. 146.
23-175 to 23-181. Repealed by Acts 1966, c. 551.
23-181.1 to 23-181.10. Repealed by Acts 1977, c. 668.
23-182. Amended by Acts 2002, cc. 158, 257.
23-183. Amended by Acts 2002, cc. 158, 257.
23-184. Amended by Acts 2002, cc. 158, 257.
23-185. Amended by Acts 1973, c. 55; Acts 1984, c. 772; Acts 2002, cc. 158, 257.
23-186. Amended by Acts 2002, cc. 158, 257.
23-187. Amended by Acts 1970, c. 601.
23-188. Amended by Acts 2002, cc. 158, 257.
23-189. Amended by Acts 2002, cc. 158, 257.
23-191. Amended by Acts 2002, cc. 158, 257.

Sec.
24.2-443. Amended by Acts 1999, c. 154.
24.2-443.1. Amended by Acts 2001, c. 629.
24.2-443.2, 24.2-443.3. Amended by Acts 2004, c. 410.
24.2-444. Amended by Acts 1994, c. 656; Acts 1996, cc. 72, 73; Acts 2001, cc. 612, 626; Acts 2003, c. 1015.
24.2-501. Amended by Acts 2003, c. 1015.
24.2-503. Amended by Acts 2000, c. 1045.
24.2-504. Amended by Acts 2000, cc. 513, 552; Acts 2004, c. 881.
24.2-505. Amended by Acts 1996, c. 270.
24.2-506. Amended by Acts 1998, cc 152, 246; Acts 2000, cc. 232, 252; Acts 2001, c. 53; Acts 2003, c. 477.
24.2-515. Amended by Acts 1999, c. 972; Acts 2003, cc. 815, 823.
24.2-521. Amended by Acts 1998, cc 152, 246; Acts 2000, cc. 232, 252; Acts 2003, c. 477.
24.2-522. Amended by Acts 2003, c. 1015.
24.2-525. Amended by Acts 2000, cc. 513, 552; Acts 2004, c. 881.
24.2-531. Amended by Acts 2003, c. 1015.
24.2-533. Amended by Acts 2003, c. 1015.
24.2-541. Amended by Acts 2003, c. 476.
24.2-542. Amended by Acts 1996, c. 574; Acts 2001, c. 630.
24.2-543. Amended by Acts 1994, c. 149; Acts 1998, cc. 152, 246; Acts 2000, cc. 232, 252; Acts 2001, c. 630; Acts 2003, c. 477.
24.2-544. Amended by Acts 2000, cc. 1, 856; Acts 2003, cc. 815, 823.
24.2-545. Amended by Acts 2000, c. 379; Acts 2003, c. 1015.
24.2-602. Amended by Acts 2004, cc. 993, 1010.
24.2-603.1. Amended by Acts 2004, c. 205.
24.2-604. Amended by Acts 1997, c. 328; Acts 2000, cc. 215, 268; Acts 2003, c. 1015.
24.2-610. Amended by Acts 2003, c. 1015.
24.2-611. Amended by Acts 1994, c. 321; Acts 1999, c. 810; Acts 2000, c. 2; Acts 2001, c. 839; Acts 2002, cc. 66, 216, 785, 819; Acts 2003, c. 1015.
24.2-612. Amended by Acts 2003, c. 1015.
24.2-613. Amended by Acts 2000, cc. 282, 514, 866; Acts 2002, c. 738.
24.2-614. Amended by Acts 1997, c. 209; Acts 2002, c. 738.
24.2-618. Amended by Acts 1997, c. 460.
24.2-620, 24.2-621. Amended by Acts 1997, c. 460.
24.2-622. Amended by Acts 2002, c. 487; Acts 2003, c. 1015.
24.2-623. Amended by Acts 2003, c. 1015.
24.2-624. Amended by Acts 2003, c. 1015.
24.2-626. Amended by Acts 1996, c. 258; Acts 2000, c. 280.
24.2-627. Amended by Acts 1996, c. 271; Acts 1997, cc. 304, 336.

Sec.
24.2-629. Amended by Acts 1994, cc. 287, 742; Acts 2001, cc. 640, 641; Acts 2003, c. 1015; Acts 2004, cc. 409, 993, 1010.
24.2-632. Amended by Acts 1999, c. 219; Acts 2004, cc. 993, 1010.
24.2-633. Amended by Acts 1998, c. 264; Acts 2004, cc. 993, 1010.
24.2-634. Amended by Acts 1998, c. 264; Acts 2004, cc. 993, 1010.
24.2-635. Amended by Acts 2003, c. 1015.
24.2-636. Amended by Acts 1998, c. 187.
24.2-638. Amended by Acts 2004, cc. 978, 993, 1006, 1010.
24.2-639. Amended by Acts 1998, c. 264; Acts 2003, c. 1015; Acts 2004, cc. 993, 1010.
24.2-640. Amended by Acts 1998, c. 797; Acts 2000, c. 514; Acts 2002, c. 738.
24.2-642. Amended by Acts 2000, c. 282; Acts 2003, c. 1015; Acts 2004, cc. 978, 993, 1006, 1010.
24.2-643. Amended by Acts 1995, c. 716; Acts 1996, cc. 72, 73; Acts 1999, c. 725; Acts 2000, cc. 366, 451; Acts 2003, c. 1015; Acts 2004, c. 410.
24.2-644. Amended by Acts 1997, c. 100.
24.2-646. Amended by Acts 2003, c. 1015.
24.2-648. Amended by Acts 1996, c. 5.
24.2-649. Amended by Acts 2003, c. 1015; Acts 2004, cc. 993, 1010.
24.2-651. Amended by Acts 1997, c. 346; Acts 2003, c. 1015.
24.2-651.1. Amended by Acts 2000, cc. 366, 451; Acts 2003, c. 1015.
24.2-652. Amended by Acts 2003, c. 1015.
24.2-653. Amended by Acts 1996, c. 8; Acts 1997, cc. 438, 456; Acts 2002, c. 24; Acts 2003, cc. 984, 1015; Acts 2004, c. 410.
24.2-656. Repealed by Acts 2003, c. 1015.
24.2-656. Amended by Acts 1994, c. 321.
24.2-659. Amended by Acts 1995, c. 197; Acts 2003, c. 1015; Acts 2004, cc. 835, 993, 1010.
24.2-660. Repealed by Acts 2004, cc. 993, 1010.
24.2-662. Amended by Acts 2003, c. 1015.
24.2-668. Amended by Acts 1995, c. 197; Acts 1996, c. 8; Acts 1997, cc. 438, 456; Acts 2002, c. 190; Acts 2003, c. 1015; Acts 2004, cc. 410, 835.
24.2-669. Amended by Acts 1998, c. 270; Acts 2003, c. 1015.
24.2-670. Amended by Acts 1995, c. 197.
24.2-671. Amended by Acts 1996, cc. 8, 223; Acts 2003, c. 1015.
24.2-675. Amended by Acts 1996, cc. 8, 223; Acts 2003, c. 1015.
24.2-680. Amended by Acts 2001, c. 53.
24.2-682. Amended by Acts 2000, cc. 787, 1070.
24.2-683. Amended by Acts 2003, c. 155.

Sec.

24.2-684. Amended by Acts 1994, c. 142; Acts 1996, c. 297.

24.2-684.1. Amended by Acts 2000, cc. 232, 252.

24.2-687. Amended by Acts 2004, cc. 21, 399.

24.2-700. Amended by Acts 1995, c. 157; Acts 1998, c. 254; Acts 2000, c. 378; Acts 2001, c. 631; Acts 2002, cc. 785, 819.

24.2-701. Amended by Acts 1996, c. 295; Acts 1998, c. 254; Acts 2000, cc. 378, 863; Acts 2001, cc. 621, 631, 793; Acts 2002, cc. 785, 819; Acts 2003, c. 478; Acts 2004, c. 410

24.2-702.1. Amended by Acts 2002, cc. 785, 819.

24.2-703. Amended by Acts 2004, c. 410.

24.2-704. Amended by Acts 1996, c. 295.

24.2-705. Amended by Acts 1996, c. 224; Acts 1997, cc. 523, 539; Acts 1999, c. 590; Acts 2001, c. 622.

24.2-705.1. Amended by Acts 2001, c. 622.

24.2-706. Amended by Acts 1994, cc. 633, 656; Acts 1996, c. 253; Acts 2000, c. 421; Acts 2001, cc. 621, 866; Acts 2002, cc. 785, 819; Acts 2003, cc. 247, 478; Acts 2004, c. 410.

24.2-707. Amended by Acts 1996, c. 393; Acts 1997, cc. 429, 450; Acts 2001, cc. 617, 624; Acts 2002, cc. 785, 819; Acts 2003, cc. 478, 1015.

24.2-708. Amended by Acts 1999, c. 725.

24.2-709. Amended by Acts 2002, cc. 785, 819.

24.2-710. Amended by Acts 1997, c. 464; Acts 2001, cc. 622, 799.

24.2-711. Amended by Acts 2001, c. 799; Acts 2002, cc. 785, 819; Acts 2003, c. 1015.

24.2-712. Amended by Acts 1994, cc. 287, 742; Acts 1998, cc. 549, 572; Acts 2003, c. 1015.

24.2-713. Amended by Acts 2002, cc. 785, 819.

24.2-801. Amended by Acts 2003, c. 268.

24.2-802. Amended by Acts 2000, cc. 938, 1057; Acts 2001, cc. 639, 641, 646; Acts 2002, cc. 601, 647; Acts 2003, c. 268; Acts 2004, c. 410.

24.2-803. Amended by Acts 1998, c. 866; Acts 2000, c. 1057.

24.2-805. Amended by Acts 2003, c. 268.

24.2-814. Amended by Acts 2001, cc. 639, 641; Acts 2003, c. 268.

24.2-900. Amended by Acts 2004, c. 457.

24.2-901. Amended by Acts 1994, c. 510; Acts 1996, cc. 405, 1042; Acts 2004, c. 457.

24.2-903. Amended by Acts 1996, c. 405.

24.2-904. Amended by Acts 1996, c. 405; Acts 2003, c. 248; Acts 2004, cc. 441, 480.

24.2-905. Amended by Acts 1996, c. 217; Acts 2000, c. 326; Acts 2001, c. 633; Acts 2002, cc. 213, 232; Acts 2004, c. 457.

24.2-906. Amended by Acts 2003, c. 248.

24.2-908. Amended by Acts 1996, c. 1042; Acts 2000, cc. 852, 872; Acts 2004, cc. 441, 457.

24.2-908.1. Amended by Acts 1996, cc. 586, 601.

24.2-910. Amended by Acts 1996, c. 1042; Acts 2002, c. 468.

24.2-911. Amended by Acts 2004, c. 469.

24.2-914. Amended by Acts 1997, cc. 364, 392; Acts 1999, c. 864; Acts 2000, c. 304; Acts 2001, cc. 618, 810; Acts 2002, c. 468; Acts 2003, c. 248.

24.2-914.1. Amended by Acts 1997, cc. 364, 392; Acts 1998, c. 416; Acts 1999, c. 864; Acts 2000, cc. 511, 555; Acts 2003, c. 242.

24.2-915. Amended by Acts 2000, cc. 304, 511, 555; Acts 2001, cc. 618, 794, 810; Acts 2002, c. 468.

24.2-916, 24.2-917. Amended by Acts 1995, c. 785; Acts 2004, c. 26.

24.2-919. Amended by Acts 1995, c. 785; Acts 1998, c. 382; Acts 2000, c. 304.

24.2-920. Amended by Acts 2000, c. 233; Acts 2003, c. 248.

24.2-921. Amended by Acts 2004, c. 457.

24.2-922. Amended by Acts 1995, c. 785; Acts 1999, c. 120.

24.2-923. Amended by Acts 1995, c. 785; Acts 2002, cc. 156, 237; Acts 2003, c. 256; Acts 2004, c. 26.

24.2-925. Amended by Acts 1994, c. 607.

24.2-926. Amended by Acts 1994, c. 64; Acts 1996, c. 6; Acts 2004, c. 457.

24.2-927. Amended by Acts 2000, c. 234; Acts 2002, cc. 468, 652; Acts 2003, c. 726.

24.2-928. Amended by Acts 1994, c. 903; Acts 1995, c. 785; Acts 1996, cc. 395, 405; Acts 1998, c. 153; Acts 2001, cc. 635, 648; Acts 2002, c. 468; Acts 2004, c. 480.

24.2-929. Amended by Acts 1994, c. 752; Acts 1995, c. 785; Acts 2000, cc. 511, 555; Acts 2001, cc. 620, 635, 648; Acts 2004, cc. 457, 480.

24.2-930. Amended by Acts 2001, c. 620.

24.2-942. Amended by Acts 2003, c. 237.

24.2-943. Amended by Acts 2003, c. 237; Acts 2004, cc. 55, 457.

24.2-944. Amended by Acts 2004, cc. 55, 457.

24.2-1002. Amended by Acts 2003, c. 1015.

24.2-1003. Amended by Acts 2003, c. 1015.

24.2-1004. Amended by Acts 2001, c. 636; Acts 2003, c. 1015.

24.2-1009. Amended by Acts 2003, c. 1015; Acts 2004, cc. 993, 1010.

24.2-1010. Amended by Acts 2004, cc. 993, 1010.

Sec.
24.2-1013. Amended by Acts 2001, c. 747; Acts 2002, c. 487.
24.2-1014. Repealed by Acts 2002, c. 487.
24.2-1019. Amended by Acts 1999, c. 374.
25-1 to 25-46. Repealed by Acts 1962, c. 426.
25-46.1 to 25-254. Repealed by Acts 2003, c. 940.
26-2. Amended by Acts 1966, c. 340; Acts 1974, c. 156; Acts 1987, c. 489; Acts 1997, c. 842.
26-3. Amended by Acts 1966, c. 328; Acts 1997, c. 842; Acts 2001, c. 79.
26-4. Amended by Acts 1964, c. 172; Acts 1976, c. 338; Acts 1980, c. 653; Acts 1994, c. 25; Acts 1997, c. 801; Acts 1998, c. 117; Acts 2003, c. 195.
26-5. Amended by Acts 1997, c. 801.
26-5.2. Amended by Acts 1980, c. 440.
26-6. Amended by Acts 1950, p. 356.
26-7. Amended by Acts 1997, c. 801.
26-7.1. Amended by Acts 1997, c. 801; Acts 2000, c. 320.
26-7.2. Amended by Acts 2004, c. 367.
26-7.4. Amended by Acts 1997, c. 801.
26-8. Amended by Acts 1966, c. 329; Acts 1973, c. 544; Acts 2003, c. 194.
26-8.1. Amended by Acts 1997, c. 842.
26-9. Amended by Acts 1956, c. 59; Acts 1973, c. 544.
26-10. Amended by Acts 1966, c. 326; Acts 1973, c. 544; Acts 2001, c. 108; Acts 2003, c. 194.
26-10.1. Amended by Acts 1964, c. 458; Acts 1966, c. 326; Acts 1973, c. 544; Acts 2003, c. 194.
26-11. Repealed by Acts 1973, c. 544.
26-12. Amended by Acts 1966, c. 337; Acts 1973, c. 544; Acts 1993, c. 581; Acts 1997, c. 842; Acts 1998, c. 610; Acts 2001, c. 73.
26-12.1. Amended by Acts 1972, c. 411; Acts 1993, c. 581; Acts 1997, c. 842.
26-12.3. Amended by Acts 1987, c. 605; Acts 1989, c. 387; Acts 1998, c. 117; Acts 2001, c. 598; Acts 2002, cc. 220, 227.
26-13. Amended by Acts 1956, c. 159; Acts 2003, c. 193.
26-15. Amended by Acts 1966, c. 333; Acts 1980, c. 148; Acts 1996, c. 681; Acts 1997, c. 842; Acts 1998, c. 610; Acts 2003, c. 193.
26-16.1. Repealed by Acts 1962, c. 111.
26-17 to 26-17.2. Repealed by Acts 1993, c. 689.
26-17.3. Amended by Acts 1997, c. 842.
26-17.4. Amended by Acts 1997, cc. 214, 921; Acts 1999, cc. 16, 378.
26-17.7. Amended by Acts 2001, c. 73.
26-17.8. Repealed by Acts 1997, c. 842.
26-17.9. Amended by Acts 1999, c. 74; Acts 2003, c. 201.
26-17.10. Amended by Acts 1997, c. 801; Acts 1999, c. 108; Acts 2000, c. 324.
26-18. Amended by Acts 1995, c. 653; Acts 1997, c. 842; Acts 1999, c. 378.
26-19. Amended by Acts 1999, c. 378.
26-20. Amended by Acts 1962, c. 148; Acts 1976, c. 435; Acts 1999, c. 378; Acts 2002, cc. 220, 227; Acts 2003, c. 193.
26-20.1. Amended by Acts 1972, c. 326; Acts 1975, c. 192; Acts 1980, c. 199; Acts 1981, c. 113; Acts 1983, c. 328; Acts 1984, c. 309; Acts 1993, c. 525; Acts 1998, c. 610; Acts 2001, c. 107.
26-22. Repealed by Acts 1992, c. 395.
26-24. Amended by Acts 1997, cc. 214, 842.
26-27. Amended by Acts 1966, c. 324; Acts 1991, c. 147; Acts 1997, c. 801.
26-30. Amended by Acts 1985, c. 402; Acts 1997, c. 921.
26-31. Amended by Acts 1989, c. 492.
26-32. Amended by Acts 1997, c. 842; Acts 2001, c. 265.
26-33. Amended by Acts 1966, c. 335.
26-35.1. Repealed by Acts 1962, c. 111.
26-36. Repealed by Acts 1994, c. 432.
26-36.1. Repealed by Acts 1997, c. 842.
26-37. Amended by Acts 1950, p. 818; Acts 1962, c. 111; Acts 1977, c. 96; Acts 1997, c. 842.
26-39. Amended by Acts 1997, c. 842; Acts 1999, c. 772.
26-40. Amended by Acts 1952, c. 196; Acts 1954, c. 600; Acts 1956, c. 83; Acts 1958, c. 281; Acts 1960, c. 589; Acts 1970, c. 73; Acts 1971, Ex. Sess., cc. 115, 245; Acts 1973, c. 353; Acts 1974, c. 557; Acts 1982, c. 496; Acts 1984, c. 264; Acts 1985, cc. 362, 399; Acts 1990, c. 3; Acts 1991, c. 697; Acts 1992, c. 810; Acts 1996, c. 508; Acts 1999, c. 772.
26-40.01. Amended by Acts 1996, c. 508; Acts 1999, c. 772.
26-40.2. Amended by Acts Acts 1999, c. 772.
26-44. Amended by Acts 1992, c. 810; Acts 1999, c. 772.
26-44.1. Amended by Acts 1992, c. 684.
26-45. Repealed by Acts 1977, c. 152.
26-45.1. Repealed by Acts 1999, c. 772.
26-45.2. Amended by Acts 1990, c. 3; Acts 1997, c. 801.
26-46. Amended by Acts 1997, c. 801.
26-46.1. Amended by Acts 1977, c. 256; Acts 1981, c. 239; Acts 1997, c. 220.
26-46.2. Amended by Acts 1966, c. 327; Acts 1968, c. 514; Acts 1981, c. 239.
26-48. Amended by Acts 1950, p. 457; Acts 1998, cc. 392, 410.
26-49. Amended by Acts 1964, c. 244; Acts 1970, c. 251; Acts 1992, c. 532;

Sec.

Acts 1993, c. 426; Acts 1998, c. 410.

26-50. Amended by Acts 1972, c. 825; Acts 1990, c. 763; Acts 1997, c. 921.

26-51. Amended by Acts 1998, cc. 392, 410; Acts 2001, c. 38..

26-59. Amended by Acts 1950, p. 724; Acts 1962, c. 576; Acts 1983, c. 467; Acts 1984, c. 39; Acts 1986, cc. 53, 543; Acts 1989, c. 535; Acts 1995, cc. 678, 684; Acts 1996, c. 680; Acts 1997, c. 921; Acts 2001, c. 836.

26-60. Amended by Acts 1968, c. 399; Acts 1983, c. 487; Acts 1997, c. 801.

26-61 to 26-63. Amended by Acts 1997, c. 801.

26-64. Amended by Acts 1968, c. 443; Acts 1972, c. 193.

26-65. Amended by Acts 1974, c. 670.

26-66. Amended by Acts 1968, c. 399; Acts 1997, c. 801.

26-67. Amended by Acts 1997, c. 801.

26-68.1. Amended by Acts 1996, cc. 675, 684.

27-1. Amended by Acts 1966, c. 134; Acts 1977, c. 326; Acts 1995, c. 461.

27-2. Amended by Acts 1966, c. 134; Acts 1968, c. 801; Acts 1995, c. 461.

27-3. Amended by Acts 1966, c. 134; Acts 1995, c. 461.

27-4. Amended by Acts 1970, c. 187; Acts 1991, c. 54; Acts 1995, c. 461.

27-5.1. Repealed by Acts 1986, c. 429.

27-5.2. Repealed by Acts 1988, c. 891.

27-5.4. Repealed by Acts 1988, c. 891.

27-5.5. Amended by Acts 1989, c. 258.

27-6. Repealed by Acts 1970, c. 187.

27-6.1. Amended by Acts 2001, c. 142.

27-6.2. Amended by Acts 2003, c. 739.

27-7. Amended by Acts 1970, c. 187; Acts 1984, c. 595; Acts 2001, c. 142.

27-8. Amended by Acts 1970, c. 187; Acts 2001, c. 142.

27-8.1. Amended by Acts 2001, c. 142.

27-9. Amended by Acts 1970, c. 187; Acts 2001, c. 142.

27-10. Amended by Acts 1970, c. 187; Acts 2001, c. 142.

27-11. Amended by Acts 1970, c. 187; Acts 2001, c. 142.

27-12. Repealed by Acts 1970, c. 187.

27-13. Amended by Acts 1970, c. 187.

27-14. Amended by Acts 1970, c. 187; Acts 2001, c. 142.

27-15. Repealed by Acts 1970, c. 187.

27-15.1. Amended by Acts 1977, c. 326; Acts 1984, c. 644; Acts 2001, c. 142.

27-15.2. Amended by Acts 2001, c. 142.

27-16. Repealed by Acts 1970, c. 187.

27-17. Amended by Acts 1970, c. 187; Acts 2001, c. 142.

27-17.1. Amended by Acts 2001, c. 142.

27-18. Repealed by Acts 1970, c. 187.

Sec.

27-19. Amended by Acts 1970, c. 187; Acts 2001, c. 142.

27-20. Amended by Acts 1970, c. 187; Acts 2001, c. 142.

27-21. Amended by Acts 1970, c. 187.

27-23. Repealed by Acts 1970, c. 187.

27-23.1. Amended by Acts 1972, c. 252; Acts 1977, c. 326; Acts 1978, c. 682; Acts 1985, c. 343; Acts 1993, c. 915; Acts 2001, cc. 111, 142.

27-23.2 to 27-23.5. Amended by Acts 1985, c. 343; Acts 2001, cc. 111, 142.

27-23.6. Amended by Acts 1982, c. 239; Acts 1991, c. 54; Acts 2001, cc. 111, 142; Acts 2002, c. 286.

27-23.7 to 27-23.9. Amended by Acts 2001, cc. 111, 142.

27-24 to 27-29.1. Repealed by Acts 1970, c. 187.

27-30. Amended by Acts 1970, c. 187; Acts 1977, c. 334; Acts 1984, c. 644.

27-31, 27-32. Amended by Acts 1997, c. 436.

27-32. Amended by Acts 1970, c. 187.

27-34. Amended by Acts 1970, c. 187.

27-34.1. Amended by Acts 1979, c. 189.

27-34.2. Amended by Acts 1975, c. 173; Acts 1979, c. 402; Acts 1984, c. 779; Acts 1986, c. 60; Acts 1988, c. 65; Acts 1997, c. 436.

27-34.2:1. Amended by Acts 1979, c. 446; Acts 1984, c. 779; Acts 1986, c. 60; Acts 1988, c. 65; Acts 2000, cc. 39, 390.

27-34.3. Amended by Acts 1988, c. 199.

27-34.4. Amended by Acts 1989, c. 258.

27-36. Amended by Acts 1970, c. 187; Acts 1984, c. 644; Acts 1998, c. 236.

27-38. Repealed by Acts 1950, p. 316.

27-39. Amended by Acts 1970, c. 187; Acts 1973, c. 543; Acts 1976, c. 772; Acts 1977, c. 326.

27-40.1. Amended by Acts 1972, c. 607; Acts 1973, c. 543; Acts 1976, c. 772; Acts 1977, c. 326; Acts 1978, c. 768.

27-40.1:1. Amended by Acts 1976, c. 772; Acts 1977, c. 326.

27-40.2. Amended by Acts 1972, c. 607; Acts 1973, c. 543; Acts 1974, c. 579; Acts 1977, c. 326.

27-40.3. Amended by Acts 1977, c. 326.

27-41. Amended by Acts 1970, c. 187; Acts 1977, c. 326.

27-42. Amended by Acts 1977, c. 326.

27-43. Amended by Acts 1970, c. 187; Acts 1977, c. 326.

27-44. Amended by Acts 1977, c. 326.

27-45. Amended by Acts 1977, c. 326.

27-46. Amended by Acts 1970, c. 187; Acts 1977, c. 326.

27-49. Amended by Acts 1977, c. 326.

27-52. Amended by Acts 1974, c. 41.

27-54.1 to 27-54.5. Repealed by Acts 1988, c. 891.

Sec.
27-55. Amended by Acts 1977, c. 613.
27-56. Amended by Acts 1977, c. 613.
27-58. Amended by Acts 1977, c. 613.
27-59. Amended by Acts 1977, c. 613; Acts 1979, c. 274.
27-60. Amended by Acts 1977, c. 613.
27-61. Amended by Acts 1977, c. 613; Acts 1988, c. 199.
27-63. Repealed by Acts 1988, c. 199.
27-64. Repealed by Acts 1988, c. 199.
27-65. Repealed by Acts 1981, c. 499.
27-66. Repealed by Acts 1977, c. 613.
27-66.1. Repealed by Acts 1989, c. 258.
27-67. Repealed by Acts 1981, c. 499.
27-68. Repealed by Acts 1977, c. 613.
27-69, 27-70. Repealed by Acts 1981, c. 499.
27-70.1. Repealed by Acts 1988, c. 199.
27-70.2. Repealed by Acts 1981, c. 499.
27-71. Repealed by Acts 1977, c. 613.
27-72. Repealed by Acts 1988, c. 199.
27-73. Repealed by Acts 1989, c. 258.
27-73.1. Repealed by Acts 1988, c. 199.
27-74 to 27-77. Repealed by Acts 1977, c. 613.
27-78, 27-78.1. Repealed by Acts 1989, c. 258.
27-79. Repealed by Acts 1988, c. 199.
27-79.1 to 27-79.8. Repealed by Acts 1981, c. 499.
27-79.9. Repealed by Acts 1989, c. 258.
27-80 to 27-84. Repealed by Acts 1988, c. 199.
27-85, 27-85.1. Repealed by Acts 1981, c. 499.
27-85.2. Repealed by Acts 1989, c. 258.
27-85.4. Amended by Acts 1985, c. 58.
27-86 to 27-90. Repealed by Acts 1995, c. 44.
27-91 to 27-93. Repealed by Acts 1981, c. 154.
27-95. Amended by Acts 1988, cc. 340, 549; Acts 1989, c. 258; Acts 2002, c. 856.
27-96. Amended by Acts 1988, c. 340; Acts 2002, c. 856.
27-97. Amended by Acts 1988, cc. 199, 340; Acts 1989, cc. 90, 420; Acts 1990, c. 69; Acts 1991, c. 53; Acts 1997, c. 584; Acts 2000, cc. 951, 1065; Acts 2002, c. 856.
27-98. Amended by Acts 1994, c. 275; Acts 2000, cc. 941, 1001; Acts 2001, c. 570; Acts 2004, c. 787.
27-99. Amended by Acts 1989, c. 258; Acts 1994, c. 275; Acts 1997, c. 584.
28-1 to 28-258. Repealed by Acts 1962, c. 406.
28.1-1 to 28.1-239. Repealed by Acts 1992, c. 836.
28.2-100. Amended by Acts 2002, c. 789.
28.2-102. Amended by Acts 1997, c. 284; Acts 1998, c. 161; Acts 1999, c. 551.
28.2-103. Amended by Acts 1997, c. 845.
28.2-106. Amended by Acts 2001, c. 232; Acts 2002, c. 789.
28.2-107. Amended by Acts 2002, c. 789.
28.2-108. Amended by Acts 2002, c. 789.
28.2-110. Amended by Acts 2002, c. 40.
28.2-111. Amended by Acts 2002, c. 40.

Sec.
28.2-200. Amended by Acts 1994, c. 124; Acts 2003, c. 604.
28.2-201. Amended by Acts 1995, c. 136; Acts 2004, c. 860.
28.2-204.1. Amended by Acts 1998, c. 114.
28.2-208. Amended by Acts 1993, c. 10; Acts 1994, c. 541; Acts 1996, c. 214.
28.2-209. Amended by Acts 2001, c. 599.
28.2-226. Amended by Acts 1993, c. 11; Acts 2001, c. 51.
28.2-226.2. Amended by Acts 2001, c. 28.
28.2-227. Amended by Acts 1993, c. 245; Acts 1994, c. 155.
28.2-240. Repealed by Acts 1993, c. 219.
28.2-241. Amended by Acts 1993, c. 219; Acts 1994, c. 121; Acts 1996, c. 277.
28.2-242. Amended by Acts 1993, c. 237.
28.2-301. Amended by Acts 1993, c. 11.
28.2-301.1. Amended by Acts 1993, c. 241.
28.2-302.1. Amended by Acts 2002, c. 215 Acts 2004, c. 486.
28.2-302.2. Amended by Acts 2001, c. 115.
28.2-302.3. Amended by Acts 1995, c. 169.
28.2-302.5. Amended by Acts 1993, c. 241; Acts 1999, c. 107; Acts 2000, cc. 110, 142; Acts 2002, c. 215.
28.2-302.7. Amended by Acts 1994, c. 559; Acts 1999, c. 106.
28.2-302.7:1. Amended by Acts 1999, c. 106.
28.2-302.8. Amended by Acts 1999, cc. 681, 1019.
28.2-502. Amended by Acts 1993, c. 11.
28.2-503. Amended by Acts 1993, c. 238.
28.2-507. Amended by Acts 1996, c. 842.
28.2-515. Amended by Acts 2003, c. 778.
28.2-520. Amended by Acts 2001, c. 377.
28.2-526. Amended by Acts 1996, c. 434.
28.2-527. Amended by Acts 2004, c. 475.
28.2-528. Amended by Acts 1993, c. 216.
28.2-530. Amended by Acts 1996, c. 434.
28.2-531. Amended by Acts 1994, c. 124.
28.2-532. Amended by Acts 1996, c. 434.
28.2-539. Amended by Acts 1994, c. 120; Acts 1996, c. 483; Acts 1998, c. 98.
28.2-540. Amended by Acts 1993, c. 218;
28.2-550. Amended by Acts 1994, c. 541.
28.2-556. Amended by Acts 2001, c. 46.
28.2-613. Amended by Acts 1996, c. 985; Acts 1997, c. 259.
28.2-628. Amended by Acts 2003, c. 940.
28.2-630. Amended by Acts 2000, c. 167.
28.2-637. Repealed by Acts 1993, c. 217.
28.2-700. Amended by Acts 1995, c. 129; Acts 1996, c. 229.
28.2-701. Amended by Acts 1999, c. 550.
28.2-702. Amended by Acts 1993, c. 11.
28.2-705. Amended by Acts 1995, c. 129; Acts 1998, c. 88; Acts 1999, c. 550.
28.2-707. Amended by Acts 1994, c. 492; Acts 1996, c. 433.
28.2-708. Amended by Acts 1996, cc. 136, 333.
28.2-820. Amended by Acts 2001, c. 103.

Sec.
28.2-1000. Repealed by Acts 1995, c. 283.
28.2-1001. Amended by Acts 1995, c. 257; Acts 1998, c. 216.
28.2-1100. Amended by Acts 2003, cc. 79, 89.
28.2-1200. Amended by Acts 1995, c. 257; Acts 1998, c. 427.
28.2-1201. Amended by Acts 1995, c. 850.
28.2-1203. Amended by Acts 1998, c. 605; Acts 2000, c. 167; Acts 2001, c. 234; Acts 2003, c. 973.
28.2-1205. Amended by Acts 1996, c. 228; Acts 1999, c. 741; Acts 2000, c. 167; Acts 2001, c. 72; Acts 2004, cc. 405, 899, 1018.
28.2-1206. Amended by Acts 2000, c. 1056; Acts 2004, cc. 899, 1018.
28.2-1207. Amended by Acts 1997, c. 845.
28.2-1208. Amended by Acts 1993, c. 644; Acts 2000, c. 1056; Acts 2004, cc. 899, 1018.
28.2-1210. Amended by Acts 1997, c. 258; Acts 1999, c. 544.
28.2-1213. Amended by Acts 2000, c. 1056.
28.2-1301. Amended by Acts 1995, c. 850.
28.2-1302. Amended by Acts 1994, c. 274.
28.2-1303. Amended by Acts 2004, c. 277.
28.2-1306. Amended by Acts 1994, c. 125.
28.2-1307. Amended by Acts 1997, c. 868.
28.2-1308. Amended by Acts 1996, c. 736; Acts 1999, c. 8.
28.2-1400. Amended by Acts 1994, c. 112; Acts 1998, c. 160.
28.2-1401. Amended by Acts 1994, c. 112; Acts 1995, c. 850.
28.2-1403. Amended by Acts 1994, c. 112; Acts 1998, c. 160.
28.2-1405. Amended by Acts 1994, c. 112.
28.2-1406. Amended by Acts 1994, cc. 112, 125.
28.2-1411, 28.2-1412. Amended by Acts 1994, c. 112.
28.2-1415. Amended by Acts 1994, c. 112.
28.2-1500 to 28.2-1514. Amended by Acts 1995, c. 850.
29-1 to 29-248. Repealed by Acts 1987, c. 488.
29.1-100. Amended by Acts 1987, c. 134; Acts 1990, c. 371; Acts 2002, c. 157.
29.1-101. Amended by Acts 1991, c. 70; Acts 1998, c. 320; Acts 2003, c. 562.
29.1-101.3. Amended by Acts 1992, cc. 464, 887; Acts 1996, c. 77.
29.1-101.4 to 29.1-101.9. Amended by Acts 1992, cc. 464, 887.
29.1-103. Amended by Acts 1992, c. 887; Acts 2003, c. 562; Acts 2004, cc. 280, 1027.
29.1-109. Amended by Acts 1999, c. 215; Acts 2000, c. 10.
29.1-110. Amended by Acts 1987, c. 95.
29.1-112. Amended by Acts 2002, c. 719.
29.1-113. Amended by Acts 2004, c. 280.
29.1-200. Amended by Acts 1994, c. 641.
29.1-203. Amended by Acts 2001, cc. 93, 123.

Sec.
29.1-205. Amended by Acts 1988, c. 605.
29.1-217. Amended by Acts 1994, c. 411; Acts 1997, c. 185.
29.1-300.1. Amended by Acts 1988, cc. 179, 384, 474; Acts 1989, c. 204; Acts 1996, cc. 118, 151; Acts 1997, c. 247.
29.1-301. Amended by Acts 1987, cc. 126, 507; Acts 1988, cc. 180, 488; Acts 1992, c. 262; Acts 1996, cc. 118, 151; Acts 1997, c. 267; Acts 2000, cc. 110, 142; Acts 2001, cc. 49, 597; Acts 2002, c. 67; Acts 2004, c. 846.
29.1-302. Amended by Acts 1996, c. 810.
29.1-302.1. Amended by Acts 1988, c. 181; Acts 1989, c. 427; Acts 1996, cc. 7, 109, 810; Acts 1997, c. 247.
29.1-303. Amended by Acts 1988, c. 250; Acts 2003, c. 120; Acts 2004, c. 269.
29.1-303.1. Amended by Acts 2003, c. 120.
29.1-303.3. Amended by Acts 1996, cc. 118, 151; Acts 2004, c. 269.
29.1-304. Amended by Acts 1988, c. 250.
29.1-305. Amended by Acts 1988, c. 250; Acts 2001, c. 55; Acts 2004, c. 269.
29.1-306. Amended by Acts 1988, c. 250; Acts 1994, c. 725; Acts 1996, cc. 102, 825; Acts 1998, c. 144.
29.1-309. Amended by Acts 1988, c. 250; Acts 1995, c. 77.
29.1-310. Amended by Acts 1989, c. 208; Acts 1994, c. 409.
29.1-311. Amended by Acts 1988, c. 250; Acts 1991, c. 242; Acts 2002, c. 67; Acts 2004, c. 486.
29.1-313. Amended by Acts 1987, c. 413.
29.1-317. Amended by Acts 1996, cc. 755, 914.
29.1-318. Amended by Acts 1988, c. 250.
29.1-321. Amended by Acts 1995, c. 77; 1999, c. 255.
29.1-323. Amended by Acts 2000, c. 132; Acts 2003, c. 92.
29.1-327. Amended by Acts 2000, c. 132.
29.1-328. Amended by Acts 1987, c. 95; Acts 1988, c. 161; Acts 2001, c. 115; Acts 2002, c. 175.
29.1-330. Amended by Acts 2000, c. 132; Acts 2003, cc. 95, 737.
29.1-331. Amended by Acts 2000, c. 132.
29.1-332. Amended by Acts 1987, c. 95; Acts 1992, c. 374; Acts 2000, c. 132; Acts 2003, cc. 95, 737.
29.1-333. Amended by Acts 1992, c. 374; Acts 2000, c. 132; Acts 2003, cc. 95, 737.
29.1-334. Amended by Acts 1994, c. 432; Acts 2000, c. 132.
29.1-335. Amended by Acts 1989, c. 421; Acts 1993, c. 839; Acts 2000, c. 132.
29.1-337. Amended by Acts 1989, c. 421.
29.1-338. Amended by Acts 1989, c. 213; Acts 2004, c. 462.
29.1-339. Amended by Acts 2001, c. 63.

Sec.
29.1-341. Amended by Acts 2004, c. 422.
29.1-343. Amended by Acts 1988, c. 250.
29.1-344. Amended by Acts 1989, c. 217; Acts 2004, c. 422.
29.1-344.1. Amended by Acts 1993, c. 209.
29.1-346. Amended by Acts 1987, c. 94.
29.1-349. Amended by Acts 2004, c. 422.
29.1-350. Amended by Acts 1993, c. 209.
29.1-352. Amended by Acts 2003, c. 137; Acts 2004, cc. 87, 463.
29.1-354. Amended by Acts 1989, c. 421; Acts 2003, c. 137.
29.1-355. Amended by Acts 2003, c. 137; Acts 2004, cc. 87, 463.
29.1-356. Amended by Acts 1988, cc. 375, 385; Acts 2003, c. 137.
29.1-401. Amended by Acts 1997, c. 510.
29.1-402. Amended by Acts 1988, c. 250.
29.1-409. Amended by Acts 1988, c. 250.
29.1-413. Amended by Acts 1997, c. 57.
29.1-415. Amended by Acts 1988, c. 250; Acts 1994, c. 194; Acts 1997, c. 57.
29.1-416. Amended by Acts 1988, c. 250; Acts 1997, c. 57.
29.1-417. Amended by Acts 1988, c. 250; Acts 1993, c. 623; Acts 1995, c. 610; Acts 1997, c. 57.
29.1-418. Amended by Acts 1993, c. 623.
29.1-419. Amended by Acts 1997, c. 57.
29.1-422. Amended by Acts 1993, c. 623.
29.1-503. Repealed by Acts 1996, c. 9.
29.1-505. Amended by Acts 1988, c. 19.
29.1-509. Amended by Acts 1988, c. 191; Acts 1989, cc. 26, 500, 505; Acts 1990, cc. 799, 808; Acts 1991, c. 305; Acts 1992, c. 285; Acts 1994, c. 544.
29.1-510. Amended by Acts 1988, c. 158.
29.1-514. Amended by Acts 1993, c. 87.
29.1-517, 29.1-518. Amended by Acts 2004, c. 421.
29.1-519. Amended by Acts 1988, c. 162; Acts 1989, c. 421; Acts 1993, c. 684; Acts 1998, c. 144; Acts 2002, c. 157.
29.1-520. Amended by Acts 1989, c. 421.
29.1-521. Amended by Acts 1988, c. 175; Acts 1989, c. 421; Acts 1990, c. 237; Acts 1994, cc. 244, 436; Acts 1997, c. 249; Acts 1998, c. 415; Acts 2000, c. 13; Acts 2001, cc. 26, 60; Acts 2004, c. 862.
29.1-521.2. Amended by Acts 1994, c. 18.
29.1-523. Amended by Acts 1994, c. 113; Acts 2002, c. 157.
29.1-524. Amended by Acts 2002, c. 157.
29.1-525. Amended by Acts 1988, c. 450; Acts 1994, c. 113; Acts 2002, c. 157.
29.1-526. Amended by Acts 1989, c. 421.
29.1-528. Amended by Acts 1989, c. 421.
29.1-529. Amended by Acts 1987, c. 48; Acts 1991, c. 99; Acts 1993, cc. 204, 273; Acts 1994, c. 571; Acts 1996, c. 314; Acts 1998, c. 179; Acts 1999, c. 563; Acts 2000, c. 6; Acts 2002, c. 174; Acts 2004, c. 447.
29.1-530.1. Amended by Acts 1988, cc. 474, 715; Acts 2002, c. 39; Acts 2003, cc. 123, 135.
29.1-531. Amended by Acts 1994, cc. 413, 848; Acts 2000, cc. 403, 447.
29.1-532. Amended by Acts 1988, c. 487.
29.1-533. Amended by Acts 1988, c. 158.
29.1-534. Amended by Acts 1991, c. 200.
29.1-535. Amended by Acts 1991, c. 200.
29.1-536. Amended by Acts 1994, c. 436; Acts 1999, c. 204.
29.1-544. Amended by Acts 1998, c. 179.
29.1-547. Amended by Acts 1994, c. 848.
29.1-548. Amended by Acts 1988, c. 19.
29.1-549. Amended by Acts 2002, c. 157.
29.1-550. Amended by Acts 1988, c. 19.
29.1-551. Amended by Acts 1994, c. 412; Acts 2001, c. 856.
29.1-552. Amended by Acts 1988, c. 19.
29.1-553. Amended by Acts 1989, c. 203; Acts 1994, c. 848; Acts 1997, c. 172.
29.1-563. Amended by Acts 1990, c. 369.
29.1-566. Amended by Acts 1989, c. 553.
29.1-567. Amended by Acts 1990, c. 123; Acts 1994, c. 848.
29.1-569. Amended by Acts 1999, c. 85.
29.1-573. Amended by Acts 2004, c. 467.
29.1-600. Amended by Acts 1989, c. 424; Acts 1994, c. 753.
29.1-601. Amended by Acts 1992, c. 254.
29.1-603. Amended by Acts 1989, c. 421.
29.1-606. Amended by Acts 1989, c. 421; Acts 1990, c. 408.
29.1-700. Amended by Acts 1998, cc. 84, 443, 512, 514, 515, 533, 537, 563.
29.1-701. Amended by Acts 1987, c. 101.
29.1-702. Amended by Acts 1990, c. 321; Acts 1991, c. 82; Acts 1992, c. 250.
29.1-703. Amended by Acts 1995, c. 241.
29.1-710. Amended by Acts 1995, c. 241.
29.1-711. Amended by Acts 1990, c. 321.
29.1-712. Amended by Acts 1997, c. 877.
29.1-716. Amended by Acts 1997, c. 877.
29.1-717. Amended by Acts 1995, c. 241; Acts 1997, c. 877.
29.1-718. Amended by Acts 1991, c. 82.
29.1-736. Amended by Acts 1998, c. 515.
29.1-737. Amended by Acts 1997, c. 108.
29.1-738. Amended by Acts 1988, c. 176; Acts 1994, c. 587; Acts 1996, cc. 929, 1015; Acts 1997, c. 703.
29.1-738.1. Amended by Acts 1996, c. 631.
29.1-738.2. Amended by Acts 1990, cc. 825, 929; Acts 1992, c. 830; Acts 1995, c. 130; Acts 1996, c. 631; Acts 2001, c. 779.
29.1-738.3. Amended by Acts 1995, c. 130.
29.1-738.4. Amended by Acts 1996, cc. 929, 1015.

Sec.
29.1-739. Amended by Acts 1991, c. 336.
29.1-739.1. Amended by Acts 1994, c. 414.
29.1-742. Amended by Acts 1988, c. 265; Acts 1993, c. 275; Acts 1997, c. 108.
29.1-742.2. Amended by Acts 1999, c. 536.
29.1-743. Repealed by Acts 1997, c. 108.
29.1-744. Amended by Acts 1997, c. 522; Acts 1999, c. 489; Acts 2001, c. 649.
29.1-744.1. Repealed by Acts 1998, c. 537.
29.1-744.2. Repealed by Acts 1998, c. 857.
29.1-747. Repealed by Acts 1998, cc. 84, 443, 512, 514, 515, 537, 563.
29.1-748. Amended by Acts 1998, cc. 443, 537.
29.1-749. Amended by Acts 1998, c. 443..
29.1-801. Amended by Acts 1989, c. 140; Acts 1997, c. 801; Acts 1998, c. 515.
29.1-808. Amended by Acts 1998, c. 515.
29.1-812. Amended by Acts 1989, c. 206; Acts 1992, c. 26.
29.1-813. Amended by Acts 1989, c. 206; Acts 1998, c. 515.
29.1-816. Amended by Acts 1995, c. 376.
29.1-818. Amended by Acts 1998, c. 515.
29.1-824. Amended by Acts 1996, c. 573.
29.1-900. Amended by Acts 1992, c. 887.
30-1. Amended by Acts 1971, Ex. Sess., c. 22.
30-4. Amended by Acts 1997, c. 471.
30-5. Amended by Acts 1952, c. 234; Acts 1960, c. 147; Acts 1973, cc. 242, 322; Acts 1984, c. 703; Acts 1987, c. 192; Acts 2002, cc. 584, 617.
30-6. Amended by Acts 1958, c. 29; Acts 1975, c. 427; Acts 1997, c. 471.
30-7. Amended by Acts 1975, c. 427; Acts 1997, c. 471.
30-10. Amended by Acts 1958, c. 608; Acts 1971, Ex. Sess., c. 155; Acts 2003, c. 231.
30-13. Amended by Acts 1959, Ex. Sess., c. 84; Acts 1969, Ex. Sess., c. 13; Acts 1971, Ex. Sess., c. 71; Acts 1976, c. 170; Acts 1993, c. 399; Acts 1994, c. 623.
30-14. Amended by Acts 1959, Ex. Sess., c. 84; Acts 1970, c. 170; Acts 1994, c. 623.
30-14.2. Amended by Acts 1970, c. 170; Acts 1971, Ex. Sess., c. 1.
30-14.4. Amended by Acts 1972, c. 5.
30-15.1. Amended by Acts 1972, c. 5.
30-16. Amended by Acts 2000, c. 373.
30-18. Repealed by Acts 1972, c. 582.
30-19. Amended by Acts 1971, Ex. Sess., c. 129; Acts 1973, c. 57.
30-19.01, 30-19.02. Repealed by Acts 1984, c. 202.
30-19.03. Amended by Acts 1980, cc. 747, 749; Acts 1995, c. 743; Acts 1999, c. 1016.
30-19.03:1. Amended by Acts 1996, c. 685.
30-19.04. Repealed by Acts 2003, c. 1032.

Sec.
30-19.05. Repealed by Acts 2003, cc. 757, 758 eff. 7/1/04.
30-19.1. Amended by Acts 1969, Ex. Sess., c. 24; Acts 1972, c. 155; Acts 1974, c. 635; Acts 1985, c. 387; Acts 2000, c. 260.
30-19.1:1. Amended by Acts 2000, c. 260.
30-19.1:2. Repealed by Acts 2003, c. 1032.
30-19.1:3. Amended by Acts 1994, c. 222; Acts 1996, c. 606; Acts 1998, c. 812; Acts 1999, cc. 762, 776; Acts 2000, c. 172; Acts 2003, cc. 757, 758.
30-19.1:4. Amended by Acts 1996, c. 972; Acts 2000, cc. 825, 833; Acts 2004, c. 461.
30-19.1:5. Repealed by Acts 2000, cc. 825, 833.
30-19.1:6. Amended by Acts 1996, c. 685.
30-19.1:7. Amended by Acts 2001, c. 680.
30-19.1:8. Repealed by Acts 1999, c. 572.
30-19.2. Amended by Acts 1960, c. 575; Acts 1979, c. 466.
30-19.3. Amended by Acts 1973, c. 488; Acts 1981, c. 196; Acts 1987, c. 124; Acts 2001, cc. 568, 584; Acts 2004, c. 718.
30-19.4. Amended by Acts 1973, c. 512; Acts 1974, c. 356; Acts 1976, c. 735; Acts 1979, c. 475; Acts 1980, c. 151; Acts 1984, c. 161.
30-19.6. Repealed by Acts 1986, c. 156.
30-19.7. Repealed by Acts 1990, c. 485.
30-19.9. Amended by Acts 1999, c. 589; Acts 2001, c. 1.
30-19.14. Amended by Acts 2001, c. 785.
30-19.15. Amended by Acts 1999, c. 930.
30-19.16, 30-19.17. Repealed by Acts 1999, c. 930.
30-20 to 30-28. Repealed by Acts 1964, c. 511.
30-28.01 to 30-28.9:1. Repealed by Acts 1994, cc. 857, 937.
30-28.10. Repealed by Acts 1976, c. 472.
30-28.10:1. Repealed by Acts 1990, c. 485.
30-28.11. Repealed by Acts 1975, c. 232.
30-28.12. Amended by Acts 1970, c. 478; Acts 1973, c. 322.
30-28.13. Amended by Acts 1970, c. 478; Acts 1973, c. 322.
30-28.14. Repealed by Acts 1978, c. 128.
30-28.15. Amended by Acts 1989, c. 412; Acts 1994, c. 64.
30-28.16. Amended by Acts 1973, c. 322; Acts 1977, c. 672; Acts 1979, c. 311; Acts 1980, cc. 687, 723; Acts 1984, c. 202; Acts 1989, c. 412; Acts 1990, c. 485.
30-28.18. Amended by Acts 1976, c. 112; Acts 1988, c. 214; Acts 1989, cc. 412, 512; Acts 2001, cc. 568, 584; Acts 2002, c. 2.
30-28.19. Repealed by Acts 1983, c. 62.
30-28.20. Repealed by Acts 1976, c. 746.
30-29 to 30-34. Repealed by Acts 1980, c. 237.

Sec.
30-34.1. Amended by Acts 2004, c. 1000..
30-34.2. Amended by Acts 1982, c. 243; Acts 2003, c. 692.
30-34.2:1. Amended by Acts 1984, c. 149; Acts 1988, c. 329; Acts 1995, cc. 770, 818; Acts 2003, cc. 231, 588.
30-34.4:1. Amended by Acts 1992, c. 857; Acts 2003, c. 264; Acts 2004, c. 650.
30-34.5. Amended by Acts 1983, c. 108; Acts 1987, c. 128; Acts 1992, c. 857; Acts 1994, c. 64.
30-34.6. Amended by Acts 1987, cc. 123, 128; Acts 1994, c. 64; Acts 2003, c. 264.
30-34.7. Repealed by Acts 2003, c. 264.
30-34.10. Amended by Acts 1987, c. 214.
30-34.10:2. Amended by Acts 1996, c. 338; Acts 2003, c. 212.
30-34.14. Amended by Acts 2002, c. 2.
30-34.15. Amended by Acts 2004, c. 650.
30-35 to 30-41. Repealed by Acts 1958, c. 373.
30-42 to 30-51. Repealed by Acts 1973, c. 267.
30-52 to 30-55. Repealed by Acts 1973, c. 452.
30-56. Amended by Acts 1979, c. 316; Acts 1988, c. 172; Acts 2004, c. 1000.
30-58. Repealed by Acts 1975, c. 324.
30-58.3. Amended by Acts 2004, c. 1000.
30-62. Repealed by Acts 1979, c. 731.
30-66. Amended by Acts 1986, c. 302.
30-67. Amended by Acts 1986, c. 302.
30-70. Amended by Acts 1986, c. 302.
30-71. Amended by Acts 1986, c. 302.
30-73. Repealed by Acts 1986, c. 302.
30-73.4. Amended by Acts 2004, c. 777.
30-74 to 30-77. Repealed by Acts 1984, c. 5.
30-86. Amended by Acts 2000, c. 1046.
30-90 to 30-93. Repealed by Acts 2001, c. 577.
30-111. Amended by Acts 2003, c. 610.
30-112. Amended by Acts 2004, c. 1000..
30-114. Amended by Acts 2003, c. 649.
30-116. Amended by Acts 2003, c. 649.
30-133. Amended by Acts 2002, c. 727; Acts 2003, c. 270; Acts 2004, Sp. Sess. I, c. 1.
30-145. Amended by Acts 2004, c. 1000.
30-146. Amended by Acts 2003, c. 212.
30-154. Amended by Acts 2002, c. 306.
30-156. Amended by Acts 2003, c. 885; Acts 2004, c. 1000.
30-158. Amended by Acts 2004, c. 1000.
30-168. Amended by Acts 2003, c. 633.
30-169. Repealed by Acts 2003, c. 633.
30-171. Amended by Acts 2002, c. 365; Acts 2004, c. 1000.
30-172. Amended by Acts 2002, c. 365.
30-173. Amended by Acts 2002, c. 365; Acts 2003, c. 885; Acts 2004, c. 1000.
30-174. Amended by Acts 2004, c. 1000.
30-175. Amended by Acts 2004, c. 1000.
30-178. Amended by Acts 2004, c. 1000.
30-179. Amended by Acts 2004, cc. 730, 1000.
30-182. Amended by Acts 2003, c. 885; Acts 2004, c. 1000.

Sec.
30-183. Amended by Acts 2004, c. 1000.
30-184. Repealed by Acts 2001, c. 577.
30-186 to 30-188. Amended by Acts 2004, c. 1000.
30-189. Amended by Acts 2002, c. 559; Acts 2004, c. 1000.
30-190. Repealed by Acts 2001, c. 577.
30-192. Amended by Acts 2002, c. 679; Acts 2003, cc. 1035, 1037.
30-192.1. Amended by Acts 2004, c. 1000.
30-192.2. Amended by Acts 2004, c. 1000.
30-192.8 to 30-192.10. Amended by Acts 2004, c. 1000.
30-192.12. Amended by Acts 2004, c. 1000.
30-193. Amended by Acts 2004, c. 1000.
30-198. Amended by Acts 2004, cc. 989, 1000.
30-202, 30-203. Amended by Acts 2004, c. 1000.
30-219, 30-220. Amended by Acts 2004, c. 1000.
30-232 to 30-239. Amended by Acts 2004, cc. 992, 1015.
31-1. Amended by Acts 1999, c. 16.
31-2. Amended by Acts 1989, c. 535; Acts 1999, c. 16.
31-3. Amended by Acts 1999, c. 16.
31-4. Amended by Acts 1989, c. 55; Acts 1999, c. 16.
31-5. Amended by Acts 1954, c. 468; Acts 1999, c. 16.
31-6. Amended by Acts 1954, c. 398; Acts 1995, c. 225; Acts 1999, c. 16.
31-7. Amended by Acts 1999, c. 16.
31-8. Amended by Acts 1989, c. 535; Acts 1993, c. 929; Acts. 1999, c. 16.
31-8.1. Amended by Acts 2002, c. 832.
31-9. Amended by Acts 1972, c. 825; Acts 1973, c. 401; Acts 1999, c. 16.
31-10 to 31-13. Repealed by Acts 1999, c. 16.
31-14. Amended by Acts 1999, c. 16.
31-19 to 31-25. Repealed by Acts 1958, c. 557.
31-26 to 31-36. Repealed by Acts 1988, c. 516.
31-45. Amended by Acts 1989, c. 548; Acts 1990, c. 831.
32-1 to 32-448. Repealed by Acts 1979, c. 711.
32.1-2. Amended by Acts 1995, c. 78.
32.1-5. Amended by Acts 1989, c. 73; Acts 1991, c. 93; Acts 1998, c. 891.
32.1-8. Amended by Acts 1989, c. 73.
32.1-10. Repealed by Acts 1980, c. 728.
32.1-11.1. Amended by Acts 2003, c. 453.
32.1-11.2. Amended by Acts 1993, c. 664; Acts 1994, c. 610.
32.1-11.3, 32.1-11.4. Amended by Acts 1995, c. 78.
32.1-13.1. Amended by Acts 2002, c. 83.
32.1-14. Amended by Acts 1984, c. 734; Acts 1989, c. 73; Acts 1999, c. 579; Acts 2004, c. 650.
32.1-17. Amended by Acts 2000, c. 168.
32.1-19.1. Repealed by Acts 2004, c. 683.

Sec.

32.1-23. Amended by Acts 2001, c. 823; Acts 2002, c. 896.
32.1-23.1. Amended by Acts 2004, cc. 73, 318.
32.1-25. Amended by Acts 1998, c. 772.
32.1-27. Amended by Acts 1980, c. 378; Acts 1989, c. 618; Acts 1999, c. 786; Acts 2003, c. 762.
32.1-27.1. Amended by Acts 1996, cc. 788, 797.
32.1-31. Amended by Acts 1987, c. 206.
32.1-35. Amended by Acts 2002, cc. 100, 768.
32.1-36. Amended by Acts 1981, c. 282; Acts 1988, c. 130; Acts 1989, c. 613; Acts 1995, c. 534; Acts 1997, c. 271; Acts 2002, cc. 100, 768.
32.1-36.1. Amended by Acts 1990, c. 777; Acts 1993, cc. 97, 664.
32.1-37. Amended by Acts 1997, c. 271.
32.1-37.1. Amended by Acts 1993, cc. 957, 993.
32.1-38. Amended by Acts 1988, c. 130; Acts 1990, c. 777; Acts 1997, c. 271; Acts 2002, c. 768.
32.1-39. Amended by Acts 1989, c. 613; Acts 2002, c. 768.
32.1-42. Amended by Acts 2002, c. 768; Acts 2004, cc. 773, 1021.
32.1-43 to 32.1-45. Amended by Acts 1990, c. 958; Acts 2004, cc. 773, 1021.
32.1-45.1. Amended by Acts 1993, c. 315; Acts 1994, cc. 230, 236; Acts 1997, c. 869; Acts 2003, c. 1.
32.1-45.2. Amended by Acts 1994, c. 146; Acts 1997, cc. 722, 804.
32.1-46. Amended by Acts 1980, c. 410; Acts 1989, c. 382; Acts 1991, c. 133; Acts 1992, cc. 127, 166; Acts 1994, c. 62; Acts 1995, cc. 729, 742; Acts 1996, cc. 67, 533; Acts 1999, cc. 632, 676, 738; Acts 2000, c. 476; Acts 2004, c. 855.
32.1-46.1. Amended by Acts 2003, c. 463.
32.1-48. Amended by Acts 2004, cc. 773, 1021.
32.1-48.01. Amended by Acts 2004, cc. 773, 1021.
32.1-48.02 to 32.1-48.04. Amended by Acts 2001, c. 837; Acts 2004, cc. 773, 1021.
32.1-48.05 to 32.1-48.017. Amended by Acts 2004, cc. 773, 1021.
32.1-48.3. Amended by Acts 2001, c. 674.
32.1-50. Amended by Acts 2001, c. 459; Acts 2004, c. 855.
32.1-51, 32.1-52. Repealed by Acts 1990, c. 958.
32.1-57. Amended by Acts 1988, c. 399.
32.1-60. Amended by Acts 1980, c. 184; Acts 1984, c. 140; Acts 1993, c. 364; Acts 2004, c. 855.
32.1-64.1. Amended by Acts 1998, cc. 505, 506, 513; Acts 2004, c. 855.
32.1-64.2. Amended by Acts 1998, cc. 505, 506, 513.
32.1-65. Amended by Acts 1983, c. 582; Acts 1986, c. 172; Acts 1988, c. 97; Acts

Sec.

1992, cc. 747, 873; Acts 2001, c. 255; Acts 2002, c. 440; Acts 2004, c. 760.
32.1-66. Amended by Acts 1986, c. 172; Acts 1988, c. 97.
32.1-67. Amended by Acts 1980, c. 470; Acts 1981, c. 164; Acts 1986, c. 172; Acts 1988, c. 97; Acts 2000, c. 916.
32.1-69.1. Amended by Acts 1986, c. 136; Acts 1988, cc. 459, 843; Acts 1994, c. 854.
32.1-69.25. Amended by Acts 2000, c. 456.
32.1-69.26. Amended by Acts 2000, c. 456.
32.1-69.27. Amended by Acts 2000, c. 456.
32.1-69.28. Amended by Acts 2000, c. 456.
32.1-69.29. Amended by Acts 2000, c. 456.
32.1-69.30. Amended by Acts 2000, c. 456.
32.1-69.31. Amended by Acts 2000, c. 456.
32.1-69.32. Amended by Acts 2000, c. 456.
32.1-69.33. Amended by Acts 2000, c. 456.
32.1-70. Amended by Acts 1988, cc. 447, 459, 843; Acts 1998, c. 315.
32.1-70.1. Repealed by Acts 1998, c. 315.
32.1-71. Amended by Acts 1991, c. 319; Acts 2000, cc. 74, 139; Acts 2003, cc. 540, 548.
32.1-71.1 to 32.1-71.4. Repealed by Acts 1994, c. 109; Acts 2002, c. 60.
32.1-71.1. Amended by Acts 1992, c. 831.
32.1-71.2. Amended by Acts 1991, c. 454; Acts 1992, c. 831.
32.1-71.4. Amended by Acts 1992, c. 831.
32.1-72. Repealed by Acts 1992, cc. 747, 873.
. 32.1-73.1. Repealed by Acts 2002, c. 60.
32.1-73.2. Amended by Acts 1998, c. 703.
32.1-73.7. Amended by Acts 2001, cc. 275, 291; Acts 2003, c. 885.
32.1-74 to 32.1-76. Repealed by Acts 1984, c. 781.
32.1-76.1. Repealed by Acts 1984, c. 629.
32.1-76.2, 32.1-76.3. Repealed by Acts 1984, c. 781.
32.1-77. Amended by Acts 1987, c. 427.
32.1-79 to 32.1-88. Repealed by Acts 2003, c 639.
32.1-89. Amended by Acts 2002, c. 696.
32.1-91. Repealed by Acts 1980, c. 728.
32.1-92. Repealed by Acts 1982, c. 15.
32.1-93 to 32.1-102. Repealed by Acts 1982, c. 388.
32.1-102.1. Amended by Acts 1983, c. 533; Acts 1984, c. 740; Acts 1985, c. 513; Acts 1989, c. 517; Acts 1991, c. 561; Acts 1992, c. 612; Acts 1993, c. 704; Acts 1995, c. 524; Acts 1996, c. 1050; Acts 1997, c. 600; Acts 1998, c. 289; Acts 1999, cc. 899, 920; Acts 2000, cc. 850, 920; Acts 2004, c. 75.
32.1-102.1:1. Amended by Acts 2000, c. 931.
32.1-102.2. Amended by Acts 1991, c. 561; Acts

Sec.
1993, c. 704; Acts 1996, c. 1050; Acts 1999, cc. 899, 922, 926; Acts 2003, cc. 61, 72.
32.1-102.3. Amended by Acts 1984, c. 740; Acts 1993, c. 704; Acts 1999, c. 926; Acts 2000, c. 931; Acts 2004, cc. 71, 95.
32.1-102.3:1. Amended by Acts 1993, cc. 957, 993.
32.1-102.3:2. Amended by Acts 1990, cc. 191, 478, 753, 845; Acts 1991, c. 561; Acts 1992, cc. 612, 682; Acts 1993, cc. 347, 474, 540, 564, 704, 762, 957, 993; Acts 1994, cc. 57, 680, 711, 726, 797; Acts 1995, cc. 505, 632, 641, 695, 753; Acts 1996, cc. 531, 849, 901; Acts 1998, c. 794.
32.1-102.3:2.1. Repealed by Acts 1998, c. 794.
32.1-102.3:3, 32.1-102.3:4. Repealed by Acts 1992, c. 612.
32.1-102.4. Amended by Acts 1991, c. 561; Acts 1992, c. 682; Acts 1993, cc. 668, 704; Acts 1998, c. 794.
32.1-102.6. Amended by Acts 1984, c. 740; Acts 1991, c. 561; Acts 1999, cc. 899, 922; Acts 2000, c. 931; Acts 2004, cc. 71, 95.
32.1-102.7. Repealed by Acts 1984, c. 740.
32.1-102.9. Amended by Acts 1984, c. 740.
32.1-102.11. Amended by Acts 1986, c. 615; Acts 1992, c. 612.
32.1-102.12. Amended by Acts 1999, cc. 899, 922.
32.1-103 to 32.1-111. Repealed by Acts 1984, c. 424.
32.1-111.1. Amended by Acts 1999, c. 1000; Acts 2000, c. 939.
32.1-111.3. Amended by Acts 1997, c. 321; Acts 1998, c. 317; Acts 1999, c. 1000.
32.1-111.4. Amended by Acts 1997, c. 248; Acts 1998, cc. 803, 854; Acts 2001, c. 466; Acts 2003, c. 1020.
32.1-111.5. Amended by Acts 1997, c. 248; Acts 1998, cc. 803, 854.
32.1-111.10. Amended by Acts 1997, c. 446; Acts 1999, c. 1000; Acts 2003, cc. 852, 1033.
32.1-111.14. Amended by Acts 2002, c. 747.
32.1-111.14:1. Repealed by Acts 2003, c. 978
32.1-112 to 32.1-116.01. Repealed by Acts 1996, c. 899.
32.1-116.1. Amended by Acts 2002, cc. 568, 658; Acts 2003, c. 471.
32.1-116.3. Amended by Acts 1989, c. 443; Acts 1993, c. 655; Acts 2004, cc. 773, 1021.
32.1-117 to 32.1-122. Repealed by Acts 1989, cc. 617, 633.
32.1-122.01. Amended by Acts 2002, c. 83.
32.1-122.02. Repealed by Acts 2002, c. 83.
32.1-122.03. Amended by Acts 2002, c. 83.
32.1-122.04. Amended by Acts 2002, c. 83.

Sec.
32.1-122.05. Amended by Acts 2002, cc. 83, 398.
32.1-122.06. Amended by Acts 1990, c. 391; Acts 2002, c. 83.
32.1-122.07. Amended by Acts 2000, c. 903; Acts 2002, c. 83.
32.1-122.08. Amended by Acts 2002, c. 83.
32.1-122.1 to 32.1-122.4. Repealed by Acts 1992, c. 407.
32.1-122.5:1. Amended by Acts 1994, c. 281.
32.1-122.6. Amended by Acts 1991, c. 134; Acts 1994, cc. 281, 867; Acts 2000, c. 926; Acts 2001, c. 188; Acts 2002, cc. 87, 478.
32.1-122.6:01. Amended by Acts 2000, cc. 240, 254, 926; Acts 2001, c. 188; Acts 2002, c. 290.
32.1-122.6:1. Amended by Acts 2000, c. 926; Acts 2001, c. 188.
32.1-122.7. Amended by Acts 1997, c. 329; Acts 2000, c. 480.
32.1-122.9. Amended by Acts 2000, c. 926; Acts 2001, c. 188; Acts 2002, c. 52.
32.1-122.9:1. Amended by Acts 2001, c. 188; Acts 2002, c. 52.
32.1-122.10. Amended by Acts 2000, c. 926; Acts 2001, c. 188.
32.1-122.10:01. Amended by Acts 1998, cc. 744, 891; Acts 1999, c. 483.
32.1-123 to 32.1-125. Amended by Acts 1989, c. 618.
32.1-125.01. Amended by Acts 2004, c. 64.
32.1-125.1. Amended by Acts 1989, c. 618.
32.1-126. Amended by Acts 1989, c. 618; Acts 1996, cc. 940, 999; Acts 2000, c. 967; Acts 2002, c. 514; Acts 2004, c. 304.
32.1-126.01. Amended by Acts 1993, cc. 17, 657; Acts 1999, c. 637; Acts 2001, c. 329; Acts 2003, c. 517.
32.1-126.1. Amended by Acts 1988, c. 723; Acts 1989, c. 398; Acts 1993, c. 660.
32.1-126.3. Amended by Acts 1997, c. 552.
32.1-127. Amended by Acts 1985, c. 335; Acts 1986, c. 135; Acts 1987, c. 224; Acts 1988, cc. 325, 418; Acts 1989, cc. 434, 618; Acts 1992, cc. 334, 428; Acts 1993, c. 335; Acts 1996, cc. 361, 411; Acts 1997, c. 454; Acts 1998, c. 450; Acts 2000, cc. 176, 810; Acts 2001, c. 463; Acts 2003, c. 753; Acts 2004, c. 762.
32.1-127.1. Amended by Acts 2000, c. 810.
32.1-127.1:01. Amended by Acts 1998, c. 470.
32.1-127.1:02. Repealed by Acts 1997, c. 682.
32.1-127.1:03. Amended by Acts 1998, c. 470; Acts 1999, cc. 812, 956, 1010; Acts 2000, cc. 810, 813, 923, 927; Acts 2001, c. 671; Acts 2002, c. 568, 658, 835, 860; Acts 2003, cc. 464, 471, 907; Acts 2004, cc. 49, 64, 65, 66, 67, 163, 773, 1014, 1021.

Sec.
32.1-127.2. Repealed by Acts 1991, c. 94.
32.1-127.3. Amended by Acts 1994, c. 444; Acts 1996, c. 748; Acts 2000, cc. 618, 632; Acts 2004, c. 49.
32.1-132. Amended by Acts 1983, c. 533; Acts 1989, c. 618.
32.1-134.2 to 32.1-134.4. Amended by Acts 1992, c. 452.
32.1-135. Amended by Acts 1989, c. 618.
32.1-135.2. Amended by Acts 1996, cc. 937, 980.
32.1-137. Amended by Acts 1989, c. 618.
32.1-137.6. Amended by Acts 1999, cc. 643, 649; Acts 2000, cc. 66, 657, 922.
32.1-137.7. Amended by Acts 1999, c. 857; Acts 2000, c. 564.
32.1-137.10. Amended by Acts 1999, c. 857.
32.1-137.13. Amended by Acts 1999, c. 857; Acts 2001, c. 22.
32.1-137.15. Amended by Acts 1999, cc. 643, 649, 857; Acts 2000, c. 922.
32.1-138. Amended by Acts 1987, c. 221; Acts 1997, c. 801; Acts 1999, c. 783; Acts 2000, c. 177; Acts 2004, c. 855.
32.1-138.1. Amended by Acts 1993, c. 692.
32.1-138.6. Amended by Acts 2000, c. 564.
32.1-139 to 32.1-144. Repealed by Acts 1993, c. 203.
32.1-145 to 32.1-147. Repealed by Acts 2003, c. 641.
32.1-148 to 32.1-156. Repealed by Acts 1996, c. 899.
32.1-148. Amended by Acts 1987, c. 480.
32.1-149. Amended by Acts 1987, c. 480.
32.1-151. Amended by Acts 1992, c. 412.
32.1-153. Amended by Acts 1987, c. 480; Acts 1992, c. 412.
32.1-157 to 32.1-162. Repealed by Acts 1984, c. 497.
32.1-162.3. Amended by Acts 2003, c. 526.
32.1-162.7. Amended by Acts 1991, c. 695; Acts 1993, cc. 957, 993.
32.1-162.8. Amended by Acts 1991, c. 695; Acts 1995, c. 455; Acts 2001, c. 515.
32.1-162.9. Amended by Acts 1991, c. 695; Acts 1994, c. 902.
32.1-162.9:1. Amended by Acts 1993, cc. 17, 657; Acts 1999, c. 637; Acts 2003, c. 517.
32.1-162.10. Amended by Acts 1991, c. 695.
32.1-162.11. Amended by Acts 1991, c. 695.
32.1-162.12. Amended by Acts 1991, c. 695.
32.1-162.13. Amended by Acts 1991, c. 695.
32.1-162.14. Repealed by Acts 2003, c. 449.
32.1-162.16. Amended by Acts 2002, c. 754.
32.1-162.18. Amended by Acts 1992, c. 603; Acts 2002, c. 754.
32.1-162.19. Amended by Acts 1992, c. 603; Acts 2002, c. 754.
32.1-162.20. Amended by Acts 1992, c. 603.
32.1-163. Amended by Acts 1984, c. 457; Acts 1990, cc. 342, 861, 869; Acts 1994, c. 747.
32.1-163.1. Amended by Acts 1994, c. 747.
32.1-163.5. Amended by Acts 2001, c. 337.
32.1-164. Amended by Acts 1986, c. 401; Acts 1988, c. 203; Acts 1990, cc. 438, 861, 869; Acts 1994, c. 747; Acts 1999, c. 871; Acts 2003, c. 614.
32.1-164.1. Amended by Acts 1980, c. 503; Acts 1984, cc. 457, 548; Acts 1986, c. 615; Acts 1994, c. 747.
32.1-164.1:1. Amended by Acts 1986, c. 331; Acts 1994, c. 747'Acts 2004, c. 916.
32.1-164.2. Amended by Acts 1984, c. 575.
32.1-164.4. Amended by Acts 1986, c. 331.
32.1-164.5. Amended by Acts 2003, c. 681.
32.1-165. Amended by Acts 1984, c. 457.
32.1-166.1. Amended by Acts 1987, c. 47.
32.1-166.4. Amended by Acts 1986, c. 331.
32.1-166.6. Amended by Acts 1986, c. 331; Acts 1994, c. 747.
32.1-166.10. Amended by Acts 1994, c. 747.
32.1-167. Amended by Acts 1997, c. 342.
32.1-169. Amended by Acts 1994, c. 395.
32.1-170. Amended by Acts 1992, c. 804.
32.1-171. Amended by Acts 1992, c. 804; Acts 2004, c. 317.
32.1-172. Amended by Acts 1994, cc. 395, 708.
32.1-174. Amended by Acts 1992, c. 804.
32.1-175. Amended by Acts 1986, c. 615.
32.1-175.01. Amended by Acts 1999, c. 786.
32.1-176. Amended by Acts 1999, c. 786.
32.1-176.4. Amended by Acts 1988, c. 203; Acts 1991, c. 514; Acts 1992, c. 599; Acts 1993, cc. 85, 728, 794; Acts 1994, cc. 141, 747; Acts 1999, c. 633; Acts 1994, cc. 141, 747; Acts 1999, c. 633.
32.1-176.5. Amended by Acts 1988, c. 441; Acts 1989, c. 454; Acts 1990, cc. 544, 547, 661; Acts 1993, c. 794; Acts 1995, c. 220; Acts 1996, c. 202; Acts 1999, c. 633; Acts 2003, c. 500; Acts 2004, c. 72.
32.1-177 to 32.1-186. Repealed by Acts 1986, c. 492.
32.1-188. Amended by Acts 1981, c. 354; Acts 2002, cc. 224, 233.
32.1-189. Amended by Acts 2002, cc. 224, 233.
32.1-193. Amended by Acts 2003, c. 940.
32.1-198. Amended by Acts 1988, c. 60.
32.1-199. Repealed by Acts 1988, c. 60.
32.1-200. Amended by Acts 1988, c. 60.
32.1-203. Amended by Acts 1988, c. 632; Acts 1990, c. 780; Acts 1992, c. 15.
32.1-222. Amended by Acts 2003, c. 1003.
32.1-225. Amended by Acts 1989, c. 130; Acts 2001, c. 454.
32.1-226. Amended by Acts 2003, c. 1003.
32.1-229. Amended by Acts 1987, c. 666; Acts 1988, c. 736; Acts 1989, cc. 275, 283; Acts 1999, c. 755; Acts 2000,

Sec.
cc. 271, 936; Acts 2001, cc. 408, 426; Acts 2003, c. 635.
32.1-229.01. Amended by Acts 1989, cc. 275, 283; Acts 2001, cc. 408, 426; Acts 2003, c. 709.
32.1-233. Amended by Acts 1980, c. 728; Acts 1985, c. 448; Acts 1987, c. 157.
32.1-234. Repealed by Acts 1987, c. 666.
32.1-235. Amended by Acts 1999, c. 755.
32.1-238.1 to 32.1-238.5. Repealed by Acts 1986, c. 492.
32.1-238.6. Repealed by Acts 1983, c. 213.
32.1-238.6:1 to 32.1-238.10. Repealed by Acts 1988, c. 891.
32.1-239. Amended by Acts 1984, c. 433; Acts 1992, c. 203.
32.1-241. Amended by Acts 1982, c. 16; Acts 1992, c. 203; Acts 1995, c. 90.
32.1-242. Repealed by Acts 1995, c. 90.
32.1-243. Amended by Acts 1992, c. 203.
32.1-244. Amended by Acts 1982, c. 16; Acts 1984, c. 433; Acts 1992, c. 203.
32.1-244.1. Repealed by Acts 1992, c. 203.
32.1-245. Amended by Acts 1984, c. 433; Acts 1992, c. 203.
32.1-247. Amended by Acts 1985, c. 372.
32.1-248. Amended by Acts 1981, c. 144.
32.1-249. Amended by Acts 1983, c. 240; Acts 2003, cc. 961, 963.
32.1-250, 32.1-251. Amended by Acts 1983, c. 240.
32.1-252. Amended by Acts 1983, c. 240; Acts 1990, c. 576; Acts 2000, c. 890.
32.1-256. Amended by Acts 1983, c. 240.
32.1-257. Amended by Acts 1983, c. 240; Acts 1984, c. 189, Acts 1991, c. 611; Acts 1994, cc. 796, 919.
32.1-258. Amended by Acts 1983, c. 240; Acts 1993, c. 929.
32.1-259. Amended by Acts 1983, c. 240.
32.1-260. Amended by Acts 1983, c. 240; Acts 1993, c. 929.
32.1-261. Amended by Acts 1983, c. 240; Acts 1984, c. 219; Acts 1991, c. 600; Acts 2003, c. 985.
32.1-261.1. Repealed by Acts 1991, c. 95.
32.1-262. Amended by Acts 1983, c. 240; Acts 1988, c. 431; Acts 2003, c. 504; Acts 2004, c. 88.
32.1-263. Amended by Acts 1983, c. 240; Acts 1993, c. 965; Acts 1997, cc. 794, 898; Acts 2003, c. 484; Acts 2004, c. 124.
32.1-264. Amended by Acts 1983, c. 240; Acts 1987, c. 405.
32.1-267. Amended by Acts 1997, c. 794, 898; Acts 2001, c. 836; Acts 2002, c. 832; Acts 2003, c. 504; Acts 2004, c. 88.
32.1-268. Amended by Acts 1997, c. 794, 898; Acts 2002, c. 353; Acts 2004, c. 88.

Sec.
32.1-269. Amended by Acts 1983, c. 240; Acts 1985, c. 86.
32.1-270. Amended by Acts 1983, c. 240.
32.1-271. Amended by Acts 1983, ch. 240; Acts 1984, c. 189; Acts 1985, c. 313.
32.1-272. Amended by Acts 1983, c. 240; Acts 1994, c. 373; Acts 1997, c. 470; Acts 1999, c. 600.
32.1-273. Amended by Acts 1981, c. 527; Acts 1983, c. 240; Acts 1986, c. 194; Acts 1994, c. 373; Acts 2002, c. 747.
32.1-273.1. Amended by Acts 1994, c. 373.
32.1-274. Amended by Acts 1983, c. 240.
32.1-276. Amended by Acts 1983, c. 240.
32.1-276.3. Amended by Acts 1999, c. 764; Acts 2000, cc. 720, 897; Acts 2001, c. 341; Acts 2003, c. 466.
32.1-276.4. Amended by Acts 2000, c. 897.
32.1-276.5. Amended by Acts 2000, c. 897.
32.1-276.6. Amended by Acts 2001, c. 341; Acts 2003, c. 466.
32.1-276.8. Amended by Acts 1999, c. 764; Acts 2000, c. 897; Acts 2001, c. 341; Acts 2003, c. 472.
32.1-276.9. Amended by Acts 2001, c. 341.
32.1-277. Amended by Acts 1998, c. 217.
32.1-279. Amended by Acts 1991, c. 454; Acts 2002, cc. 87, 478.
32.1-281. Amended by Acts 1998, c. 217.
32.1-283. Amended by Acts 1981, c. 388; Acts 1985, c. 228; Acts 1993, c. 965; Acts 2002, c. 203; Acts 2003, c. 368.
32.1-283.1. Amended by Acts 1995, c. 499; Acts 1999, cc. 703, 726; Acts 2004, c. 690.
32.1-283.2. Amended by Acts 2004, c. 690.
32.1-285. Amended by Acts 1989, c. 66; Acts 1991, c. 644; Acts 1993, c. 965; Acts 2003, c. 368.
32.1-286. Amended by Acts 1997, c. 59; Acts 1999, c. 781.
32.1-287. Amended by Acts 1981, c. 388; Acts 1982, c. 599; Acts 1985, c. 411; Acts 2000, c. 810.
32.1-288. Amended by Acts 1992, c. 128; Acts 1995, c. 532.
32.1-289. Amended by Acts 1990, c. 959; Acts 2000, c. 810.
32.1-289.1. Amended by Acts 1991, c. 600.
32.1-290. Amended by Acts 1990, c. 959; Acts 1997, c. 449; Acts 2000, c. 810.
32.1-290.1. Amended by Acts 1993, c. 986; Acts 1997, c. 609.
32.1-291. Amended by Acts 1990, c. 959.
32.1-292. Repealed by Acts 1990, c. 959.
32.1-292.1. Amended by Acts 1993, c. 986; Acts 2000, c. 810.
32.1-294. Repealed by Acts 1990, c. 959.
32.1-295. Amended by Acts 1993, c. 986.
32.1-297.1. Amended by Acts 1991, c. 37; Acts

Sec.
1997, c. 799; Acts 2002, c. 467.
32.1-301. Amended by Acts 2000, c. 477.
32.1-305 to 32.1-309. Repealed by Acts 1998, c. 867.
32.1-310. Amended by Acts 1982, c. 41; Acts 1993, c. 986.
32.1-311. Repealed by Acts 1982, c. 41.
32.1-313. Amended by Acts 1986, c. 551.
32.1-314. Amended by Acts 1986, c. 551; Acts 1995, c. 491.
32.1-315. Amended by Acts 1986, c. 551; Acts 2003, c. 312.
32.1-316. Amended by Acts 1991, c. 695.
32.1-317. Amended by Acts 1985, c. 153.
32.1-319. Amended by Acts 1984, c. 781.
32.1-320. Amended by Acts 1982, c. 41; Acts 1984, c. 781; Acts 1986, c. 551.
32.1-321.3. Amended by Acts 1996, cc. 941, 991.
32.1-321.4. Amended by Acts 2002, c. 747.
32.1-323.1. Amended by Acts 2000, cc. 593, 605.
32.1-324. Amended by Acts 1986, c. 440; Acts 1989, c. 195; Acts 1992, c. 107.
32.1-324.1. Amended by Acts 1990, c. 383.
32.1-325. Amended by Acts 1985, cc. 519, 532, 535, 564; Acts 1986, cc. 393, 455; Acts 1987, cc. 398, 446, 642; Acts 1988, cc. 99, 215, 504, 790; Acts 1993, cc. 298, 971; Acts 1989, c. 269; Acts 1990, cc. 395, 793; Acts 1996, cc. 155, 201, 511, 788, 796, 946; Acts 1997, cc. 671, 683, 730; Acts 1998, cc. 56, 257, 459, 554, 558, 571, 631, 653, 709, 858, 875; Acts 1999, cc. 818, 878, 967, 1005, 1024; Acts 2000, cc. 484, 855, 888; Acts 2001, cc. 334, 534, 663, 859; Acts 2003, cc. 66, 71; Acts 2004, cc. 125, 246, 855.
32.1-325.02. Amended by Acts 2003, c. 253.
32.1-325.1. Amended by Acts 2000, c. 967.
32.1-325.1:1. Amended by Acts 1994, c. 669; Acts 1999, cc. 1024.
32.1-325.2. Amended by Acts 1994, c. 213; Acts 1996, c. 851.
32.1-325.3. Amended by Acts 1992, c. 107.
32.1-326.3. Amended by Acts 2002, c. 457.
32.1-328. Repealed by Acts 2003, c. 428.
32.1-329. Repealed by Acts 1999, c. 728.
32.1-330. Amended by Acts 1990, c. 716; Acts 2003, c. 480.
32.1-330.1. Amended by Acts 1996, c. 195; Acts 2000, c. 870.
32.1-330.3. Amended by Acts 1998, c. 318.
32.1-331. Repealed by Acts 1989, c. 618.
32.1-331.1 to 32.1-331.11. Repealed by Acts 1992, c. 200.
32.1-331.13. Amended by Acts 1996, c. 515.
32.1-331.15. Amended by Acts 2004, c. 855.
32.1 332 to 32.1 334. Amended by Acts 1994, c. 466; Acts 1995, c. 333.

Sec.
32.1-335. Amended by Acts 1990, cc. 394, 440; Acts 1993, c. 194; Acts 1994, c. 466; Acts 1995, c. 333; Acts 1996, c. 902.
32.1-336. Amended by Acts 1990, cc. 859, 873.
32.1-337. Amended by Acts 1990, cc. 859, 873; Acts 1994, c. 466; Acts 1995, c. 333; Acts 1996, c. 902.
32.1-338. Amended by Acts 1990, cc. 859, 873; Acts 1993, c. 194; Acts 1994, c. 466; Acts 1995, c. 333.
32.1-339. Amended by Acts 1990, cc. 859, 873.
32.1-341. Amended by Acts 1990, cc. 859, 873.
32.1-345, 32.1-346. Amended by Acts 1996, cc. 782, 792.
32.1-347. Amended by Acts 1992, c. 104; Acts 1994, c. 297; Acts 1996, cc. 782, 792.
32.1-350. Amended by Acts 2002, c. 747.
32.1-351. Amended by Acts 1999, c. 1034; Acts 2000, cc. 824, 848; Acts 2001, cc. 238, 735, 756; Acts 2002, c. 640; Acts 2003, cc. 66, 71, 521.
32.1-351.1. Amended by Acts 2003, cc. 513, 481.
32.1-351.2. Amended by Acts 2002, c. 329; Acts 2003, c. 481; Acts 2004, c. 301.
32.1-352. Amended by Acts 2000, cc. 824, 848.
32.1-353. Amended by Acts 2000, cc. 824, 848.
32.1-353.4. Amended by Acts 2003, c. 481.
32.1-353.5. Amended by Acts 2003, c. 481.
32.1-353.6. Repealed by Acts 2003, c. 481.
32.1-357. Amended by Acts 2000, c. 1067; Acts 2004, c. 1000.
32.1-358. Amended by Acts 2000, c. 1067.
32.1-373. Amended by Acts 1988, c. 287.
33-1 to 33-331. Repealed by Acts 1970, c. 322.
33.1-1. Amended by Acts 1974, c. 462; Acts 1984, c. 748; Acts 1985, c. 448; Acts 1986, Sp. Sess., c. 13; Acts 1990, cc. 1, 317; Acts 1995, cc. 195, 223; Acts 1999, cc. 636, 673.
33.1-2. Amended by Acts 1974, c. 462; Acts 1982, c. 487; Acts 1984, c. 748; Acts 1986, Sp. Sess., c. 13; Acts 2000, c. 49.
33.1-3. Amended by Acts 1974, c. 462; Acts 1990, cc. 1, 317; Acts 1995, cc. 195, 223.
33.1-4. Amended by Acts 1974, c. 462; Acts 1995, cc. 195, 223.
33.1-5. Repealed by Acts 1980, c. 728.
33.1-6. Amended by Acts 1974, c. 462.
33.1-8. Amended by Acts 1974, c. 462; Acts 1982, c. 177; Acts 1983, c. 127; Acts 1995, cc. 195, 223; Acts 2001, cc. 69, 87.
33.1-9. Amended by Acts 1974, c. 462.
33.1-10. Amended by Acts 1974, c. 462.
33.1-11. Amended by Acts 1974, c. 462.
33.1-12. Amended by Acts 1974, c. 462; Acts 1977, c. 150; Acts 1978, c. 650;

Sec.

Acts 1986, Sp. Sess., c. 13; Acts 1988, cc. 844, 903; Acts 1992, c. 167; Acts 1995, c. 94; Acts 2001, c. 349; Acts 2003, cc. 281, 533, 560; Acts 2004, c. 110.

33.1-13. Amended by Acts 1974, c. 462; Acts 1978, c. 652; Acts 1986, Sp. Sess., c. 13.

33.1-13.1. Amended by Acts 2001, cc. 68, 83.

33.1-14. Amended by Acts 1974, c. 462.

33.1-16. Amended by Acts 1974, c. 462.

33.1-17. Repealed by Acts 1976, c. 746.

33.1-18. Amended by Acts 1992, c. 44; Acts 2000, c. 489.

33.1-19. Amended by Acts 1974, c. 462.

33.1-20. Repealed by Acts 1979, c. 607.

33.1-22. Amended by Acts 1974, c. 462.

33.1-23.02. Amended by Acts 2002, cc. 302, 570.

33.1-23.03. Amended by Acts 2001, cc. 764, 772; Acts 2002, c. 639.

33.1-23.03:1. Amended by Acts 1988, cc. 844, 903; Acts 1991, cc. 666, 713; Acts 1992, c. 108; Acts 1993, c. 793.

33.1-23.03:2. Amended by Acts 1998, cc. 905, 907.

33.1-23.03:3. Repealed by Acts 1988, cc. 844, 903.

33.1-23.03:4. Amended by Acts 1995, cc. 545, 576; Acts 1997, c. 501.

33.1-23.1. Amended by Acts 1979, c. 84; Acts 1985, c. 42; Acts 1986, c. 572.

33.1-23.1:1. Amended by Acts 1985, c. 42.

33.1-23.2. Amended by Acts 1984, c. 748; Acts 1985, c. 42.

33.1-23.3. Amended by Acts 1985, c. 42; Acts 1987, cc. 523, 536, 545; Acts 1989, c. 303; Acts 1997, c. 494; Acts 2001, c. 590; Acts 2003, cc. 288, 870.

33.1-23.4. Amended by Acts 1978, c. 145; Acts 1985, c. 42; Acts 2004, c. 791.

33.1-23.5:1. Amended by Acts 2004, c. 118.

33.1-24, 33.1-24.1. Repealed by Acts 1977, c. 578.

33.1-26 to 33.1-30. Repealed by Acts 2003, c. 302.

33.1-31. Amended by Acts 1986, c. 498; Acts 1989, c. 656.

33.1-32. Amended by Acts 1986, c. 498; Acts 1989, c. 656.

33.1-38. Repealed by Acts 1977, c. 578.

33.1-39. Amended by Acts 1977, c. 578.

33.1-40. Repealed by Acts 1977, c. 578.

33.1-41. Repealed by Acts 1985, c. 42.

33.1-41.1. Amended by Acts 1991, c. 353; Acts 1992, c. 267; Acts 1994, c. 459; Acts 1996, cc. 149, 821; Acts 1997, c. 49; Acts 1998, c. 441; Acts 2000, c. 97; Acts 2002, c. 673; Acts 2004, c. 118.

Sec.

33.1-43, 33.1-43.1. Repealed by Acts 1985, c. 42.

33.1-44. Amended by Acts 1977, c. 578; Acts 1979, c. 84; Acts 1980, c. 128; Acts 1981, c. 370; Acts 1987, c. 545; Acts 1989, c. 303; Acts 1991, c. 353; Acts 2000, c. 762; Acts 2002, c. 673.

33.1-45. Repealed by Acts 1985, c. 42.

33.1-46. Amended by Acts 1977, c. 578.

33.1-46.1. Amended by Acts 1972, c. 490; Acts 1973, c. 508; Acts 1977, c. 578; Acts 1980, c. 373; Acts 1986, c. 392; Acts 1998, cc. 905, 907.

33.1-46.2. Amended by Acts 1983, c. 339; Acts 1988, c. 637; Acts 1989, c. 573; Acts 1993, cc. 82, 587; Acts 1994, cc. 212, 426, 439; Acts 1995, c. 55; Acts 1996, cc. 34, 187, 191, 695, 921, 1037; Acts 1997, c. 504; Acts 1998, c. 321; Acts 1999, cc. 914, 960; Acts 2000, c. 322; Acts 2002, cc. 89, 757; Acts 2003, c. 324; Acts 2004, c. 704.

33.1-50. Amended by Acts 1982, c. 261.

33.1-55. Amended by Acts 1972, c. 79; Acts 1983, c. 162; Acts 2003, c. 302.

33.1-56. Amended by Acts 1989, c. 46; Acts 1998, c. 219; Acts 1999, c. 942.

33.1-62. Amended by Acts 1974, c. 319; Acts 1984, c. 739; Acts 1989, c. 656.

33.1-63. Amended by Acts 1984, c. 739; Acts 1989, c. 656.

33.1-69.2. Amended by Acts 1999, c. 942.

33.1-70. Repealed by Acts 1977, c. 578.

33.1-70.01. Amended by Acts 1979, c. 64; Acts 1981, c. 240; Acts 1993, c. 802.

33.1-70.1. Amended by Acts 1977, c. 578; Acts 1985, c. 440; Acts 1997, c. 715, 729; Acts 1999, cc. 306, 320; Acts 2001, cc. 355, 366; Acts 2002, c. 414; Acts 2003, c. 599.

33.1-71. Repealed by Acts 1992, c. 94.

33.1-72. Repealed by Acts 1979, c. 321.

33.1-72.1. Amended by Acts 1980, c. 96; Acts 1981, c. 232; Acts 1982, c. 167; Acts 1983, cc. 171, 455; Acts 1984, c. 146; Acts 1987, cc. 156, 207; Acts 1989, c. 274; Acts 1991, c. 250; Acts 1993, c. 71; Acts 1995, c. 416; Acts 1997, c. 740; Acts 1998, cc. 330, 338, 340; Acts 2001, c. 95; Acts 2004, c. 677.

33.1-73 to 33.1-75. Repealed by Acts 1977, c. 578.

33.1-75.1. Amended by Acts 1975, c. 208; Acts 1977, c. 221; Acts 1979, cc. 88, 89; Acts 1980, c. 405; Acts 1983, c. 343; Acts 1984, c. 467; Acts 1985, c. 574; Acts 1987, c. 440; Acts 1988, cc. 31, 84, 562; Acts 1990, c. 561; Acts 1991, c. 250; Acts 1993,

Sec.

c. 71; Acts 1995, c. 416; Acts 1998, cc. 330, 340; Acts 2001, c. 95; Acts 2003, c. 303.

33.1-75.2. Amended by Acts 1982, c. 218.

33.1-75.3. Amended by Acts 1982, c. 218; Acts 1983, cc. 321, 325; Acts 1984, c. 127; Acts 1985, c. 562; Acts 1988, c. 654; Acts 1989, c. 143; Acts 1990, c. 36; Acts 1995, c. 105; Acts 1998, cc. 334, 341, 342; Acts 2000, c. 88; Acts 2003, c. 303.

33.1-76 to 33.1-78.1. Repealed by Acts 1977, c. 578.

33.1-80, 33.1-81. Repealed by Acts 1985, c. 42.

33.1-82. Amended by Acts 1992, c. 108; Acts 1999, c. 318.

33.1-83. Repealed by Acts 1985, c. 42.

33.1-89. Amended by Acts 1976, c. 430; Acts 1993, c. 67; Acts 1999, c. 88; Acts 2000, c. 1029; Acts 2002, c. 878; Acts 2003, c. 940.

33.1-90. Amended by Acts 1972, c. 396; Acts 1973, c. 430; Acts 1983, c. 146; Acts 1988, c. 80; Acts 1992, c. 108; Acts 1997, c. 93; Acts 1998, c. 426; Acts 2000, c. 998.

33.1-90.1. Repealed by Acts 1992, c. 108.

33.1-90.2. Amended by Acts 1992, c. 108.

33.1-91. Amended by Acts 1973, c. 166; Acts 2003, c. 940.

33.1-92. Amended by Acts 1971, Ex. Sess., c. 1.

33.1-95. Amended by Acts 1972, c. 765; Acts 2003, c. 940.

33.1-95.1. Amended by Acts 2003, c. 940.

33.1-96. Amended by Acts 1976, c. 380; Acts 1990, c. 242.

33.1-97. Amended by Acts 1973, c. 508.

33.1-98. Amended by Acts 1972, c. 765; Acts 2003, c. 940.

33.1-99. Repealed by Acts 1972, c. 765.

33.1-101 to 33.1-105. Repealed by Acts 1972, c. 765.

33.1-107 to 33.1-115. Repealed by Acts 1972, c. 765.

33.1-116. Repealed by Acts 1970, c. 40.

33.1-120. Amended by Acts 2003, c. 940; Acts 2004, c. 803.

33.1-121. Amended by Acts 2003, c. 940.

33.1-124. Amended by Acts 1972, c. 765; Acts 1985, c. 594; Acts 1987, c. 641; Acts 1994, c. 584; Acts 2003, cc. 19, 47, 940.

33.1-125. Amended by Acts 1993, c. 35.

33.1-126. Repealed by Acts 1994, c. 432.

33.1-127. Reenacted without change by Acts 1972, c. 765; Acts 1993, c. 35; Acts 2003, c. 317.

33.1-128. Amended by Acts 1981, c. 476; Acts 1994, c. 584; Acts 1997, c. 865; Acts 2003, cc. 19, 47, 318, 940.

33.1-129. Amended by Acts 1993, c. 35.

33.1-132. Amended by Acts 1971, Ex. Sess., c. 141; Acts 1972, c. 765; Acts 1991, c. 520; Acts 2003, cc. 317, 940.

33.1-132.1 to 33.1-132.11. Repealed by Acts 1972, c. 738; Acts 2004, c. 804.

33.1-133. Amended by Acts 1992, c. 714.

33.1-134. Amended by Acts 2003, c. 940.

33.1-141. Amended by Acts 1973, c. 310; Acts 1977, c. 578.

33.1-145. Amended by Acts 1978, c. 187; Acts 1980, c. 39.

33.1-145.1. Amended by Acts 1996, cc. 114, 157.

33.1-147. Amended by Acts 1978, c. 187.

33.1-149. Amended by Acts 2002, c. 445.

33.1-150. Amended by Acts 1978, c. 337; Acts 1981, c. 323.

33.1-151. Amended by Acts 1975, c. 255; Acts 1978, c. 187; Acts 1980, c. 39; Acts 1981, c. 323; Acts 1990, c. 190.

33.1-152. Amended by Acts 1978, c. 187; Acts 1981, c. 323; Acts 1990, c. 190.

33.1-153. Amended by Acts 1981, c. 323.

33.1-154. Amended by Acts 1981, c. 323; Acts 2002, c. 445.

33.1-157. Amended by Acts 1978, c. 616; Acts 1980, c. 39.

33.1-161. Amended by Acts 1978, c. 187.

33.1-162. Amended by Acts 1978, c. 187.

33.1-163. Amended by Acts 1986, c. 12.

33.1-185. Amended by Acts 1973, c. 229; Acts 1977, c. 678; Acts 1978, c. 144; Acts 1982, c. 647; Acts 1992, c. 108.

33.1-186 to 33.1-189. Repealed by Acts 1982, c. 647.

33.1-190. Amended by Acts 1977, c. 678; Acts 1982, c. 647; Acts 1985, c. 130; Acts 1986, Sp. Sess., c. 9.

33.1-190.1. Amended by Acts 2001, cc. 90, 104.

33.1-191. Amended by Acts 1999, c. 405; Acts 2001, cc. 418, 432; Acts 2002, c. 303.

33.1-192.1. Amended by Acts 1982, c. 647.

33.1-206. Amended by Acts 1979, c. 427.

33.1-210.1. Repealed by Acts 1991, c. 251.

33.1-221. Amended by Acts 1978, c. 299; Acts 1980, c. 38; Acts 1989, c. 336; Acts 1996, cc. 85, 128; Acts 1997, c. 89.

33.1-221.1. Repealed by Acts 1997, c. 61.

33.1-221.1:1. Amended by Acts 1992, c. 167; Acts 1996, cc. 590, 598.

33.1-221.1:2. Amended by Acts 2003, c. 302.

33.1-221.1:3. Amended by Acts 1994, cc. 470, 597; Acts 1998, cc. 740, 761; Acts 1999, c. 538; Acts 2002, c. 799; Acts 2003, c. 337.

33.1-221.1:4. Amended by Acts 1995, c. 354.

33.1-221.1:5. Repealed by Acts 1995, c. 354.

33.1-222. Amended by Acts 1982, c. 184; Acts 1984, c. 590.

33.1-223. Amended by Acts 1975, c. 362; Acts 1982, c. 643; Acts 1984, c. 739;

Sec.

Acts 1989, cc. 305, 656; Acts 1990, c. 689; Acts 1992, c. 108; Acts 1996, cc. 101, 131.

33.1-223.1. Amended by Acts 1984, c. 760; Acts 1992, c. 167.

33.1-223.2:1. Amended by Acts 1999, c. 8.

33.1-223.3, 33.1-223.4. Amended by Acts 1994, c. 216.

33.1-223.6 to 33.1-223.8. Amended by Acts 1994, c. 216.

33.1-223.9. Amended by Acts 2001, c. 36.

33.1-225.1. Repealed by Acts 2003, c. 303.

33.1-229. Amended by Acts 1980, c. 441; Acts 1984, c. 198.

33.1-233. Amended by Acts 1977, c. 470.

33.1-238. Amended by Acts 1991, c. 520; Acts 2003, c. 940.

33.1-242. Amended by Acts 1975, c. 445; Acts 1978, c. 305.

33.1-246.1. Repealed by Acts 1982, c. 343.

33.1-251. Amended by Acts 1973, c. 215; Acts 1981, c. 417; Acts 1983, c. 617.

33.1-252. Amended by Acts 1973, c. 215; Acts 1981, c. 417; Acts 1983, c. 617; 1984, cc. 508, 543, 778; Acts 1990, cc. 505, 509, 613; Acts 1992, c. 266; Acts 1993, c. 866; Acts 1994, cc. 65, 771, 874, 927; Acts 1995, c. 572; Acts 1996, c. 138; Acts 1998, c. 565; Acts 2004, c. 655.

33.1-257. Amended by Acts 1995, c. 647.

33.1-263. Repealed by Acts 1995, c. 647.

33.1-267. Amended by Acts 1990, c. 947.

33.1-268. Amended by Acts 1972, c. 2; Acts 1974, cc. 52, 297; Acts 1982, c. 261; Acts 1986, Sp. Sess., c. 13; Acts 1988, cc. 844, 903; Acts 1989, Sp. Sess., cc. 9, 11; Acts 1990, cc. 710, 947; Acts 1991, cc. 666, 713; Acts 1993, cc. 391, 793; Acts 1994, cc. 520, 589; Acts 1995, c. 354; Acts 2000, cc. 1019, 1044; Acts 2004, c. 807.

33.1-269. Amended by Acts 1982, c. 403; Acts 1986, Sp. Sess., c. 13; Acts 1988, cc. 844, 903; Acts 1989, Sp. Sess., cc. 9, 11; Acts 1990, cc. 710, 947; Acts 1991, cc. 666, 713; Acts 1993, cc. 391, 793; Acts 1994, cc. 233, 520, 589, 662; Acts 1995, c. 354; Acts 1996, cc. 23, 143; Acts 1999, c. 898; Acts 2000, cc. 1019, 1044; Acts 2004, c. 807.

33.1-270. Amended by Acts 1986, Sp. Sess., c. 13.

33.1-271. Amended by Acts 1990, c. 947.

33.1-272. Amended by Acts 1991, cc. 666, 713; Acts 1993, c. 793.

33.1-273. Amended by Acts 1990, c. 947.

33.1-276. Amended by Acts 1988, cc. 844, 903; Acts 1989, Sp. Sess., cc. 9, 11; Acts 1990, c. 947; Acts 2000, cc. 1019, 1044.

33.1-277. Amended by Acts 1982, c. 403; Acts 1986, Sp. Sess., c. 13; Acts 1988, cc. 844, 903; Acts 1989, Sp. Sess., cc. 9, 11; Acts 1990, cc. 710, 947; Acts 1991, cc. 666, 713; Acts 1993, cc. 391, 793; Acts 1994, cc. 233, 520, 589, 662; Acts 1995, c. 354; Acts 2000, cc. 1019, 1044; Acts 2004, c. 807.

33.1-278. Amended by Acts 1982, c. 245; Acts 1986, Sp. Sess., c. 13; Acts 1990, c. 947; Acts 2000, cc. 1019, 1044.

33.1-279. Amended by Acts 1990, c. 947.

33.1-279.1. Amended by Acts 1988, cc. 844, 903; Acts 1990, c. 947.

33.1-280. Amended by Acts 2000, cc. 1019, 1044.

33.1-282. Amended by Acts 1990, c. 947.

33.1-283. Amended by Acts 1988, cc. 844, 903; Acts 1990, c. 947.

33.1-284. Amended by Acts 1990, c. 947; Acts 2000, cc. 1019, 1044.

33.1-285. Amended by Acts 1973, c. 215; Acts 1981, c. 417; Acts 1982, c. 242; Acts 1983, c. 617; Acts 1986, Sp. Sess., c. 13; Acts 1988, cc. 844, 903; Acts 1990, c. 947.

33.1-287. Amended by Acts 1986, Sp. Sess., c. 13; Acts 1990, c. 947.

33.1-288 to 33.1-291. Amended by Acts 1990, c. 947.

33.1-293. Amended by Acts 1990, c. 947.

33.1-320.1. Repealed by Acts 1996, cc. 951, 1018.

33.1-320.2. Amended by Acts 1996, cc. 951, 1018.

33.1-335. Amended by Acts 1990, c. 196.

33.1-338. Amended by Acts 1977, c. 206.

33.1-345. Amended by Acts 1972, c. 65; Acts 1980, c. 141; Acts 1981, c. 19; Acts 1988, c. 79; Acts 1997, c. 136.

33.1-346. Amended by Acts 1972, c. 65; Acts 1976, c. 773; Acts 1978, c. 226; Acts 1981, c. 340; Acts 1988, c. 805; Acts 1995, c. 657; Acts 2000, c. 20; Acts 2003, cc. 113, 787.

33.1-346.1. Amended by Acts 1976, c. 773; Acts 1978, c. 226.

33.1-348. Amended by Acts 1973, c. 328.

33.1-349, 33.1-350. Repealed by Acts 1975, c. 589.

33.1-351. Amended by Acts 1976, c. 14; Acts 1980, c. 275; Acts 1984, c. 750; Acts 1993, c. 538; Acts 1996, c. 777; Acts 2000, cc. 432, 449; Acts 2002, c. 672.

33.1-355. Amended by Acts 1971, Ex. Sess., c. 8; Acts 1972, c. 158; Acts 1993, c. 538; Acts 1996, c. 125; Acts 2003, c. 321.

Sec.
33.1-356. Amended by Acts 1979, c. 216; Acts 1993, c. 538.
33.1-358. Amended by Acts 1984, c. 703; Acts 1986, c. 615; Acts 1993, c. 538.
33.1-361. Amended by Acts 1979, c. 216; Acts 1993, c. 538.
33.1-365. Amended by Acts 1979, c. 216.
33.1-366. Amended by Acts 1986, c. 615.
33.1-369. Amended by Acts 1976, c. 14; Acts 1977, c. 219; Acts 1993, c. 538; Acts 1999, c. 290; Acts 2000, c. 140; Acts 2001, c. 285.
33.1-370. Amended by Acts 1976, cc. 14, 29; Acts 1980, c. 275; Acts 1993, c. 538; Acts 2000, cc. 432, 449.
33.1-371. Amended by Acts 1976, c. 14; Acts 1984, c. 745.
33.1-371.1. Amended by Acts 1998, cc. 525, 540.
33.1-373. Amended by Acts 1993, c. 538; Acts 1994, c. 696.
33.1-374. Amended by Acts 1976, c. 14.
33.1-375. Amended by Acts 1976, c. 14.
33.1-375.1. Amended by Acts 1999, c. 195; Acts 2000, c. 672; Acts 2003, c. 311.
33.1-386. Amended by Acts 1982, c. 320; Acts 1991, c. 691; Acts 1994, c. 67; Acts 2001, c. 175.
33.1-387. Amended by Acts 1982, c. 320; Acts 1991, c. 691.
33.1-388. Amended by Acts 1982, c. 320.
33.1-390, 33.1-391. Repealed by Acts 1992, c. 167.
33.1-391.2. Amended by Acts 2002, c. 355.
33.1-391.3. Amended by Acts 2002, c. 355.
33.1-391.4. Amended by Acts 2002, c. 355.
33.1-391.5. Amended by Acts 2002, c. 355.
33.1-392 to 33.1-399. Repealed by Acts 1984, c. 778.
33.1-400 to 33.1-408. Repealed by Acts 2001, cc. 815, 842.
33.1-422. Amended by Acts 2003, c. 940.
33.1-430. Amended by Acts 2004, c. 792.
33.1-431. Amended by Acts 2004, c. 792.
33.1-433. Amended by Acts 2004, c. 792.
33.1-435. Amended by Acts 2004, c. 792.
33.1-443. Amended by Acts 2003, c. 940.
34-1. Amended by Acts 1974, c. 272; Acts 1978, c. 253; Acts 1979, c. 674; Acts 1990, c. 942.
34-3. Amended by Acts 1990, c. 942; Acts 1996, c. 323.
34-4. Amended by Acts 1975, c. 466; Acts 1977, c. 496; Acts 1978, c. 231; Acts 1990, c. 942; Acts 1997, cc. 785, 861.
34-4.1. Amended by Acts 1977, c. 496; Acts 1978, c. 231; Acts 1990, c. 942; Acts 1993, c. 950.
34-5. Reenacted without change by Acts 1956, c. 637; Acts 1986, c. 218; Acts 1990, c. 942; Acts 1991, c. 256; Acts 1993, c. 150.
34-6. Amended by Acts 1998, c. 331.
34-10 to 34-12. Repealed by Acts 1981, c. 580.
34-13. Amended by Acts 1975, c. 466; Acts 1980, c. 167; Acts 1990, c. 942; Acts 1993, c. 150.
34-14. Amended by Acts 1990, c. 942; Acts 1993, c. 150.
34-15, 34-16. Repealed by Acts 1981, c. 580.
34-17. Amended by Acts 1974, c. 272; Acts 1981, c. 580; Acts 1985, c. 521; Acts 1990, c. 942; Acts 2003, c. 1000.
34-18, 34-19. Amended by Acts 1975, c. 466; Acts 1977, c. 496; Acts 1985, c. 521; Acts 1990, c. 942.
34-21. Amended by Acts 1975, c. 466; Acts 1977, c. 496; Acts 1990, c. 942; Acts 1996, c. 330.
34-23. Amended by Acts 1974, c. 272; Acts 1981, c. 580.
34-24. Amended by Acts 1972, c. 825; Acts 1974, c. 272; Acts 1981, c. 580.
34-26. Amended by Acts 1956, c. 637; Acts 1970, c. 428; Acts 1975, c. 466; Acts 1976, c. 150; Acts 1977, cc. 253, 496; Acts 1990, c. 942; Acts 1992, c. 644; Acts 1993, c. 150; Acts 2001, c. 483; Acts 2002, c. 88.
34-27. Amended by Acts 1956, c. 637; Acts 1970, c. 428; Acts 1977, c. 496; Acts 1993, c. 150.
34-28. Amended by Acts 1992, c. 644; Acts 2002, c. 88.
34-28.1. Amended by Acts 1991, c. 256; Acts 1993, c. 150; Acts 1994, c. 35; Acts 2003, cc. 929, 942.
34-29. Amended by Acts 1952, c. 432; Acts 1954, cc. 143, 379; Acts 1958, cc. 217, 417; Acts 1960, c. 498; Acts 1970, c. 428; Acts 1978, c. 564; Acts 1992, c. 674; Acts 1996, c. 330.
34-30. Repealed by Acts 1970, c. 428.
34-31. Amended by Acts 1974, c. 272.
34-32. Amended by Acts 1954, c. 613; Acts 1974, c. 272.
34-34. Amended by Acts 1992, c. 716; Acts 1996, c. 330; Acts 1999, cc. 766, 796.
35-1 to 35-78. Repealed by Acts 1981, c. 468.
35.1-1. Amended by Acts 1995, c. 797.
35.1-8. Repealed by Acts 1989, c. 258.
35.1-9. Amended by Acts 1983, c. 242.
35.1-10. Amended by Acts 1993, c. 336.
35.1-11. Amended by Acts 1993, c. 336.
35.1-14. Amended by Acts 1993, c. 336; Acts 2003, c. 695; Acts 2004, c. 802.
35.1-14.2. Amended by Acts 1998, c. 641.
35.1-18. Amended by Acts 2004, c. 987.
35.1-22. Amended by Acts 1996, cc. 200, 834.

Sec.

35.1-25. Amended by Acts 1982, c. 51; Acts 1993, c. 201; Acts 2004, c. 227.

35.1-26. Amended by Acts 1983, c. 251.

36-3. Amended by Acts 1966, c. 129.

36-4. Amended by Acts 1952, c. 427; Acts 1958, c. 533.

36-4.1. Amended by Acts 1958, c. 171; Acts 1982, c. 395.

36-5. Amended by Acts 1956, c. 643; Acts 1958, c. 116.

36-7. Amended by Acts 1983, c. 68.

36-8, 36-9. Amended by Acts 1956, c. 615.

36-11. Amended by Acts 1956, c. 615; Acts 1958, c. 82; Acts 1966, c. 129; Acts 1978, c. 557.

36-12. Amended by Acts 1972, cc. 466, 782.

36-13. Amended by Acts 1958, c. 82.

36-16. Repealed by Acts 1970, c. 463.

36-17. Amended by Acts 1958, c. 82.

36-19. Amended by Acts 1971, Ex. Sess., c. 153; Acts 1976, c. 510; Acts 1977, c. 136; Acts 1978, c. 679; Acts 1982, c. 596; Acts 1983, c. 27; Acts 1984, cc. 350, 450; Acts 1988, cc. 217, 416; Acts 1995, c. 193; Acts 2002, c. 548.

36-19.3. Repealed by Acts 1960, c. 230.

36-21. Amended by Acts 1975, c. 78.

36-22. Amended by Acts 1958, c. 116; Acts 1972, cc. 466, 782.

36-23. Amended by Acts 1984, c. 350.

36-25. Amended by Acts 1970, c. 405.

36-27. Amended by Acts 1958, c. 518; Acts 1972, cc. 466, 782; Acts 1989, c. 593; Acts 1998, c. 880; Acts 2000, c. 1029; Acts 2001, c. 729; Acts 2002, c. 495; Acts 2003, c. 940.

36-29. Amended by Acts 2002, c. 548.

36-30. Amended by Acts 1972, c. 466; Acts 1980, c. 133.

36-45. Amended by Acts 2003, cc. 417, 535, 559, 809.

36-47. Amended by Acts 1958, c. 82; Acts 1982, c. 330; Acts 1983, c. 347; Acts 1984, c. 350; Acts 1987, c. 433; Acts 1988, c. 217.

36-47.1. Amended by Acts 1962, c. 64; Acts 1974, c. 610.

36-48. Amended by Acts 1975, c. 455; Acts 1988, cc. 572, 591.

36-48.1. Amended by Acts 1978, c. 360.

36-49. Amended by Acts 1962, c. 336; Acts 1972, cc. 466, 782; Acts 1980, c. 133.

36-49.1. Amended by Acts 1966, cc. 81, 418; Acts 1968, c. 312; Acts 1970, cc. 222, 491, 555, 596; Acts 1972, c. 174; Acts 1973, c. 29; Acts 1974, c. 137; Acts 1975, c. 532; Acts 1976, cc. 510; Acts 1980, c. 133; Acts 1988, cc. 572, 591.

36-49.1:1. Amended by Acts 1995, cc. 702, 827; Acts 1996, c. 847; Acts 1997, c. 572; Acts 1998, cc. 690, 898; Acts 1999, cc. 39, 410, 418; Acts 2001, c. 482; Acts 2003, c. 940.

36-50.1. Amended by Acts 1972, c. 733.

36-51. Amended by Acts 2001, c. 729.

36-51.1. Amended by Acts 1966, c. 81.

36-52.1. Amended by Acts 1966, c. 81.

36-53. Amended by Acts 1970, c. 222.

36-55. Amended by Acts 1964, c. 378.

36-55.1 to 36-55.6. Amended by Acts 1973, c. 303; Acts 1975, c. 95.

36-55.7 to 36-55.23. Repealed by Acts 1974, c. 668.

36-55.25. Amended by Acts 1975, c. 536; Acts 1978, c. 508; Acts 1979, c. 374; Acts 1987, c. 254; Acts 2004, c. 187.

36-55.26. Amended by Acts 1975, c. 536; Acts 1987, c. 363; Acts 1988, c. 218; Acts 1996, c. 498; Acts 2004, c. 187.

36-55.27. Amended by Acts 1977, c. 613; Acts 1979, c. 243.

36-55.27:1. Amended by Acts 2002, c. 461.

36-55.28. Amended by Acts 1974, c. 668; Acts 1975, c. 536; Acts 1976, c. 117; Acts 1977, c. 613; Acts 1985, c. 70; Acts 1987, Sp. Sess., c. 1; Acts 1988, c. 226; Acts 1992, c. 754; Acts 1993, c. 857; Acts 2002, c. 454; Acts 2003, c. 434.

36-55.29. Amended by Acts 1995, c. 215..

36-55.30. Amended by Acts 1975, c. 536; Acts 1979, c. 613; Acts 1986, c. 6; Acts 1987, c. 254; Acts 1990, c. 956; Acts 1996, c. 498; Acts 1998, c. 442; Acts 2004, c. 187.

36-55.30:1. Repealed by Acts 1979, c. 374.

36-55.30:2. Amended by Acts 1996, cc. 77, 498; Acts 2004, c. 187.

36-55.30:3. Amended by Acts 1988, c. 364.

36-55.31. Amended by Acts 1975, c. 536; Acts 1979, c. 374; Acts 2004, c. 187.

36-55.31:1. Amended by Acts 1978, c. 631.

36-55.32. Reenacted without change by Acts 1975, c. 536; amended by Acts 1982, c. 152.

36-55.33. Repealed by Acts 1975, c. 536.

36-55.33:1. Amended by Acts 1979, c. 374; Acts 1982, c. 176; Acts 1987, c. 164; Acts 1988, c. 556; Acts 1989, c. 161; Acts 1991, c. 447; Acts 2004, c. 187.

36-55.33:2. Amended by Acts 1996, c. 298.

36-55.34. Repealed by Acts 1975, c. 536.

36-55.34:1. Amended by Acts 1987, c. 164; Acts 1991, c. 447.

36-55.35. Amended by Acts 1975, c. 536; Acts 1982, c. 101; Acts 1996, c. 298.

36-55.36. Amended by Acts 1975, c. 536.

Sec.
36-55.37. Amended by Acts 1974, c. 263; Acts 2004, c. 187.
36-55.37:1. Repealed by Acts 1996, c. 298.
36-55.38. Amended by Acts 1975, c. 536; Acts 1996, c. 498; Acts 2004, c. 187.
36-55.39. Amended by Acts 1975, c. 536; Acts 1978, c. 297; Acts 1982, c. 175; Acts 1990, c. 461; Acts 1996, c. 560; Acts 1997, c. 684; Acts 2004, c. 187.
36-55.40. Amended by Acts 1978, c. 189; Acts 1996, c. 298; Acts 1998, c. 442.
36-55.41. Amended by Acts 1974, c. 263; Acts 1987, c. 451; Acts 1994, c. 378; Acts 1997, c. 41.
36-55.44. Amended by Acts 1975, c. 536; Acts 1982, cc. 231, 235; Acts 1993, c. 224; Acts 1996, c. 77; Acts 1998, c. 442.
36-55.49. Amended by Acts 1975, c. 536.
36-55.51. Amended by Acts 1977, c. 613.
36-55.53 to 36-55.62. Repealed by Acts 1987, c. 306.
36-55.63. Amended by Acts 1990, c. 830; Acts 1992, cc. 325, 347, 754; Acts 1994, c. 611; Acts 1996, cc. 580, 826; Acts 2001, cc. 293, 299.
36-57. Amended by Acts 1973, c. 401.
36-70. Amended by Acts 1986, c. 37.
36-71. Repealed by Acts 1986, c. 37.
36-72. Amended by Acts 1986, c. 37.
36-73. Amended by Acts 1977, c. 613; Acts 1986, c. 37.
36-74. Amended by Acts 1977, c. 613; Acts 1986, c. 37.
36-75. Amended by Acts 1975, c. 250; Acts 1977, c. 613; Acts 1979, c. 489; Acts 1986, c. 37.
36-76. Amended by Acts 1977, c. 613; Acts 1986, c. 37.
36-77. Amended by Acts 1977, c. 613; Acts 1986, c. 37.
36-78. Amended by Acts 1986, c. 37.
36-79. Amended by Acts 1977, c. 613; Acts 1986, c. 37.
36-80. Amended by Acts 1977, c. 613; Acts 1986, c. 37.
36-81. Amended by Acts 1977, c. 613; Acts 1986, c. 37.
36-82. Amended by Acts 197, c. 613; Acts 1986, c. 37.
36-83. Amended by Acts 1986, c. 37.
36-84. Amended by Acts 1977, c. 613; Acts 1986, c. 37.
36-85. Amended by Acts 1977, c. 613; Acts 1986, c. 37.
36-85.1. Amended by Acts 1986, c. 37.
36-85.3. Amended by Acts 1990, c. 593.
36-85.11. Amended by Acts 1988, c. 410; Acts 1990, c. 593.
36-85.16. Amended by Acts 1992, c. 223; Acts 1994, c. 671.

Sec.
36-85.17. Amended by Acts 1992, c. 223; Acts 1995, c. 33.
36-85.18, 36-85.19. Amended by Acts 1992, c. 223; Acts 1994, c. 671.
36-85.20 to 36-85.31. Amended by Acts 1992, c. 223.
36-85.32. Amended by Acts 1992, c. 223; Acts 1994, c. 671.
36-85.33 to 36-85.36. Amended by Acts 1992, c. 223.
36-86 to 36-96. Repealed by Acts 1991, c. 557.
36-96.1:1. Amended by Acts 1992, c. 322; Acts 1996, c. 77; Acts 2003, c. 575.
36-96.2. Amended by Acts 1992, c. 322; Acts 2003, c. 575.
36-96.3. Amended by Acts 1992, c. 322; Acts 1996, c. 327.
36-96.6. Amended by Acts 1998, c. 873.
36-96.7. Amended by Acts 1992, c. 322; Acts 2000, c. 30.
36-96.8. Amended by Acts 2003, c. 575.
36-96.10. Amended by Acts 1998, c. 634.
36-96.11. Amended by Acts 1998, c. 634.
36-96.13. Amended by Acts 1992, c. 322.
36-96.16 to 36-96.18. Amended by Acts 1994, c. 814.
36-96.20. Amended by Acts 1992, c. 84; Acts 2003, c. 575.
36-96.21. Amended by Acts 1996, cc. 173, 369.
36-97. Amended by Acts 1974, cc. 622, 668; Acts 1975, c. 394; Acts 1977, cc. 423, 613; Acts 1978, c. 703; Acts 1986, c. 401; Acts 1993, c. 662; Acts 1994, c. 256; Acts 1998, c. 755; Acts 2000, c. 751.
36-98. Amended by Acts 1977, c. 613: Acts 1979, c. 718; Acts 1980, c. 104; Acts 1982, c. 267; Acts 2001, c. 525; Acts 2002, c. 703.
36-98.01. Amended by Acts 1992, cc. 779, 787.
36-98.1. Amended by Acts 1982, c. 97; Acts 1986, c. 133.
36-99. Amended by Acts 1974, c. 433; Acts 1975, c. 394; Acts 1977, cc. 423, 613; Acts 1978, c. 581; Acts 1982, c. 2; Acts 1982, c. 267; Acts 1998, c. 755; Acts 2000, c. 751; Acts 2002, c. 555; Acts 2003, cc. 436, 650, 901.
36-99.01. Amended by Acts 2002, c. 555.
36-99.1. Repealed by Acts 1994, c. 895.
36-99.3. Amended by Acts 1997, c. 584.
36-99.5. Amended by Acts 1988, c. 183.
36-99.5:1. Amended by Acts 1990, cc. 448, 703; Acts 1992, c. 356; Acts 1993, cc. 957, 993; Acts 2004, c. 584.
36-99.6. Amended by Acts 1992, c. 456; Acts 1994, c. 256.
36-99.6:1. Repealed by Acts 1994, c. 256.
36-99.7. Amended by Acts 1988, c. 723; Acts 1989, c. 398; Acts 1990, c. 823; Acts 1993, c. 660; Acts 1996, c. 742; Acts 1997, c. 166.

Sec.
36-99.10. Repealed by Acts 1994, c. 187.
36-99.10:1. Amended by Acts 2002, c. 180.
36-99.11. Amended by Acts 1997, cc. 783, 904.
36-100. Amended by Acts 1977, c. 613; Acts 1991, c. 49.
36-102. Amended by Acts 1977, c. 613.
36-103. Amended by Acts 1976, c. 638; Acts 1982, c. 267; Acts 1986, c. 32; Acts 2002, c. 555; Acts 2003, c. 650.
36-104. Amended by Acts 1974, c. 298; Acts 1977, c. 613.
36-105. Amended by Acts 1974, c. 433; Acts 1977, cc. 423, 613; Acts 1978, c. 578; Acts 1981, c. 498; Acts 1982, c. 267; Acts 1992, c. 73; Acts 1993, c. 328; Acts 1994, cc. 214, 256, 574; Acts 1995, cc. 85, 523, 702, 827; Acts 1999, cc. 333, 341; Acts 2001, c. 119; Acts 2002, c. 720; Acts 2003, c. 650; Acts 2004, c. 851.
36-105.01. Amended by Acts 1999, cc. 333, 341.
36-106. Amended by Acts 1975, c. 367; Acts 1991, c. 655; Acts 1992, cc. 435, 650; Acts 1993, c. 778; Acts 1994, c. 342; Acts 1995, c. 494; Acts 1998, c. 664; Acts 1999, cc. 251, 362, 392, 1014; Acts 2000, c. 68.
36-107. Amended by Acts 1974, c. 668; Acts 1977, c. 613.
36-108. Amended by Acts 1974, c. 668; Acts 1976, c. 484; Acts 1977, cc. 92, 613; Acts 1993, c. 626; Acts 1997, c. 860.
36-110. Repealed by Acts 1980, c. 728.
36-111. Amended by Acts 1974, c. 668; Acts 1977, c. 613.
36-113. Amended by Acts 1974, c. 668; Acts 1977, c. 613.
36-114. Amended by Acts 1977, c. 423; Acts 1986, cc. 37, 429; Acts 1994, c. 406; Acts 2003, c. 650.
36-115. Amended by Acts 1977, c. 423; Acts 1996, c. 620.
36-116. Repealed by Acts 1977, c. 613.
36-118. Amended by Acts 1977, c. 613; Acts 1986, c. 429.
36-119.1. Amended by Acts 1988, c. 199; Acts 2002, c. 555; Acts 2003, c. 650.
36-120 to 36-130. Repealed by Acts 1977, c. 613.
36-131. Amended by Acts 1992, c. 754; Acts 2002, c. 461.
36-132. Amended by Acts 1984, c. 720; Acts 2000, c. 1033.
36-133. Amended by Acts 1984, c. 720.
36-135. Amended by Acts 1989, c. 258; Acts 1992, c. 754; Acts 1993, c. 139; Acts 1994, c. 53; Acts 1997, c. 860; Acts 2003, c. 434; Acts 2004, c. 944.
36-139.8. Repealed by Acts 2004, c. 872.
36-137. Amended by Acts 1978, c. 751; Acts 1980, c. 107; Acts 1981, c. 309; Acts 1984, c. 720; Acts 1986, c. 427; Acts 1988, c. 687; Acts 1989, c. 279; Acts 1992, c. 754; Acts 1993, c. 814; Acts 2002, cc. 245, 461, 555.
36-138. Repealed by Acts 1980, c. 728.
36-139. Amended by Acts 1978, cc. 737, 751; Acts 1981, cc. 309, 315; Acts 1982, c. 36; Acts 1986, c. 427; Acts 1988, c. 687; Acts 1989, cc. 258, 279; Acts 1992, c. 754; Acts 1994, cc. 44, 140; Acts 1997, c. 611; Acts 1998, c. 693; Acts 2002, cc. 245, 461, 555; Acts 2003, c. 197.
36-139.3. Amended by Acts 1993, cc. 957, 993; Acts 1995, c. 243; Acts 1997, c. 144.
36-139.6. Amended by Acts 1996, cc. 589, 590, 598, 599.
36-140. Repealed by Acts 1995, cc. 732, 796.
36-143. Amended by Acts 1996, c. 77.
36-155. Amended by Acts 2000, cc. 789, 795; Acts 2004, c. 577.
36-156. Amended by Acts 2004, c. 577.
36-158 to 36-168. Amended by Acts 2000, cc. 789, 795.
36-169. Amended by Acts 2000, cc. 789, 795; Acts 2004, c. 577.
37-1 to 37-260. Repealed by Acts 1968, c. 477.
37.1-1. Amended by Acts 1972, cc. 635, 639; Acts 1973, c. 465; Acts 1974, c. 301; Acts 1976, c. 671; Acts 1979, c. 54; 1980, c. 582; Acts 1982, c. 50; Acts 1983, c. 538; Acts 1984, c. 209; Acts 1987, c. 413; Acts 1993, c. 930; Acts 1994, c. 939; Acts 1999, c. 969.
37.1-1.1. Repealed by Acts 1987, c. 413.
37.1-2. Repealed by Acts 1980, c. 582.
37.1-3. Amended by Acts 1980, c. 582; Acts 1993, c. 178; Acts 1998, c. 447; Acts 2002, c. 50.
37.1-5. Amended by Acts 1980, c. 582.
37.1-6. Amended by Acts 1976, c. 671; Acts 1980, c. 582.
37.1-7. Amended by Acts 1974, c. 509.
37.1-8. Repealed by Acts 1980, c. 582.
37.1-9. Repealed by Acts 1980, cc. 582, 728.
37.1-10. Amended by Acts 1976, c. 671; Acts 1979, c. 41; Acts 1980, c. 582; Acts 1984, c. 720; Acts 1985, c. 207.
37.1-10.01. Amended by Acts 2001, c. 483.
37.1-11. Amended by Acts 1980, c. 582.
37.1-12. Amended by Acts 1980, c. 582.
37.1-13. Amended by Acts 1976, c. 671; Acts 1978, c. 770; Acts 1980, c. 582.
37.1-14 to 37.1-18. Repealed by Acts 1978, c. 770.
37.1-19. Amended by Acts 1976, c. 671.
37.1-20. Repealed by Acts 1980, c. 582.

Sec.
37.1-20.1. Amended by Acts 1976, c. 671; Acts 1980, c. 582.
37.1-20.2. Repealed by Acts 1996, cc. 881, 927.
37.1-20.3. Amended by Acts 1999, c. 685.
37.1-21. Repealed by Acts 1980, c. 582.
37.1-22. Amended by Acts 1976, c. 671; Acts 1980, c. 582.
37.1-23. Amended by Acts 1976, c. 671; Acts 1980, c. 582.
37.1-23.1. Amended by Acts 1980, c. 582.
37.1-24. Amended by Acts 1972, c. 639; Acts 1976, c. 671; Acts 1980, c. 582.
37.1-24.01. Amended by Acts 1992, c. 603.
37.1-24.1. Repealed by Acts 1976, cc. 671, 767.
37.1-24.2. Amended by Acts 1980, c. 582.
37.1-25, 37.1-26. Repealed by Acts 1980, c. 582.
37.1-27. Amended by Acts 1976, c. 671; Acts 1980, c. 582; Acts 1984, c. 734.
37.1-28. Amended by Acts 1980, c. 582.
37.1-29. Amended by Acts 1972, c. 639; Acts 1976, c. 671; Acts 1980, c. 582.
37.1-30. Amended by Acts 1972, c. 639; Acts 1976, c. 671; Acts 1980, c. 582.
37.1-31. Amended by Acts 1972, c. 639; Acts 1976, c. 671; Acts 1980, c. 582.
37.1-32. Amended by Acts 1972, c. 639; Acts 1976, c. 671; Acts 1980, c. 582.
37.1-33. Amended by Acts 1972, c. 639; Acts 1976, c. 671; Acts 1980, c. 582; Acts 1996, cc. 196, 853.
37.1-34. Amended by Acts 1972, c. 639; Acts 1976, c. 671; Acts 1980, c. 582.
37.1-34.1. Repealed by Acts 1980, c. 582.
37.1-35. Repealed by Acts 1976, c. 671.
37.1-36. Repealed by Acts 1978, c. 213.
37.1-37. Repealed by Acts 1970, c. 463.
37.1-38. Amended by Acts 1976, c. 671.
37.1-38.1 to 37.1-38.4. Repealed by Acts 1976, c. 671.
37.1-39. Amended by Acts 1976, c. 671; Acts 1980, c. 582.
37.1-40. Amended by Acts 1976, c. 671.
37.1-42. Amended by Acts 1976, c. 671; Acts 1980, c. 582.
37.1-42.1. Amended by Acts 1980, c. 582; Acts 1985, c. 158; Acts 2002, c. 572; Acts 2003, c. 516.
37.1-42.2. Amended by Acts 1980, c. 582; Acts 1999, c. 576; Acts 2002, cc. 271, 572.
37.1-43. Repealed by Acts 1980, c. 582.
37.1-45, 37.1-46. Repealed by Acts 1976, c. 671.
37.1-47. Amended by Acts 1973, c. 115.
37.1-48. Amended by Acts 1976, c. 671; Acts 1984, c. 174.
37.1-49 to 37.1-54. Repealed by Acts 1972, c. 289.
37.1-54.1 to 37.1-57. Repealed by Acts 1976, c. 671.

Sec.
37.1-58. Amended by Acts 1976, c. 671; Acts 1980, c. 582.
37.1-59, 37.1-60. Repealed by Acts 1976, c. 671.
37.1-61. Amended by Acts 1976, c. 671; Acts 1980, c. 582; Acts 1990, c. 975.
37.1-62. Repealed by Acts 1976, c. 671.
37.1-62.1. Repealed by Acts 2003, cc. 749, 766.
37.1-63. Amended by Acts 1976, c. 671.
37.1-64. Amended by Acts 1970, c. 673; Acts 1972, c. 639; Acts 1976, c. 671; Acts 1980, c. 582; Acts 1993, c. 930.
37.1-65. Amended by Acts 1970, c. 46; Acts 1972, cc. 639, 823; Acts 1976, c. 671; Acts 1980, c. 582; Acts 1998, c. 446.
37.1-65.1. Amended by Acts 1979, c. 204; Acts 1980, c. 582; Acts 1984, c. 425.
37.1-66. Repealed by Acts 1970, c. 673.
37.1-67. Repealed by Acts 1974, c. 351.
37.1-67.01. Amended by Acts 1996, c. 893; Acts 1998, c. 611; Acts 2004, c. 737.
37.1-67.1. Amended by Acts 1975, cc. 237, 433; Acts 1976, c. 671; Acts 1980, c. 582; Acts 1981, c. 463; Acts 1986, cc. 478, 629; Acts 1987, c. 96; Acts 1988, c. 98; Acts 1990, cc. 429, 728; Acts 1991, c. 159; Acts 1992, c. 566; Acts 1995, c. 844; Acts 1996, cc. 343, 893; Acts 1998, cc. 37, 594, 611; Acts 2004, c. 737.
37.1-67.2. Repealed by Acts 1995, c. 844.
37.1-67.3. Amended by Acts 1979, c. 426; Acts 1980, cc. 166, 582; Acts 1982, c. 471; Acts 1984, c. 277; Acts 1985, c. 261; Acts 1986, cc. 349, 609; Acts 1988, c. 225; Acts 1990, cc. 59, 60, 728, 798; Acts 1991, c. 636; Acts 1992, c. 752; Acts 1994, cc. 736, 907; Acts 1995, cc. 489, 668, 844; Acts 1996, cc. 343, 893; Acts 1997, cc. 558, 921; Acts 1998, c. 446; Acts 2001, cc. 478, 479, 507, 658, 837; Acts 2004, c. 1014.
37.1-67.4. Amended by Acts 1981, c. 233; Acts 1982, c. 435; Acts 1986, c. 134; Acts 1995, c. 844.
37.1-67.5. Amended by Acts 1979, c. 204.
37.1-67.6. Amended by Acts 1979, c. 204; Acts 1980, c. 176; Acts 1985, c. 106; Acts 1990, c. 274.
37.1-68. Amended by Acts 1972, c. 639; Acts 1976, c. 671.
37.1-69. Repealed by Acts 1970, c. 673.
37.1-70. Amended by Acts 1970, c. 673; Acts 1976, c. 671; Acts 1980, c. 582.
37.1-70.1 to 37.1-70.4. Amended by Acts 2001, c. 776; Acts 2003, cc. 989, 1018.
37.1-70.5 to 37.1-70.10. Amended by Acts 2004, c. 707.
37.1-70.11 to 37.1-70.16. Amended by Acts

Sec.
2001, c. 776; Acts 2003, cc. 989, 1018.
37.1-70.17 to 37.1-70.19. Amended by Acts 2001, c. 776.
37.1-71. Amended by Acts 1970, c. 673; Acts 1971, Ex. Sess., c. 155; Acts 1972, c. 639; Acts 1976, c. 671; Acts 1980, c. 582; Acts 1987, c. 719; Acts 1989, cc. 334, 534; Acts 1990, c. 94; Acts 1992, c. 419; Acts 1995, c. 844; Acts 1996, c. 184; Acts 2003, c. 151; Acts 2004, c. 737.
37.1-72. Amended by Acts 1976, c. 671; Acts 1995, c. 844.
37.1-73. Amended by Acts 1971, Ex. Sess., c. 155; Acts 1972, c. 751; Acts 1976, c. 671; Acts 1979, c. 707.
37.1-74. Amended by Acts 1971, Ex. Sess., c. 155.
37.1-75. Amended by Acts 1971, Ex. Sess., c. 155.
37.1-76. Amended by Acts 1972, c. 639; Acts 1976, c. 671; Acts 1981, c. 242.
37.1-78. Amended by Acts 1971, Ex. Sess., c. 155; Acts 1972, c. 639; Acts 1976, c. 671; Acts 1980, c. 582.
37.1-78.1. Amended by Acts 1976, c. 671; Acts 1986, c. 349.
37.1-79 to 37.1-84. Repealed by Acts 1970, c. 673.
37.1-84.1. Amended by Acts 1976, c. 671; Acts 1989, cc. 459, 591; Acts 1992, c. 603; Acts 1999, c. 969.
37.1-84.2. Amended by Acts 1976, c. 671.
37.1-84.3. Amended by Acts 2001, c. 453.
37.1-85. Amended by Acts 1972, c. 639.
37.1-86. Repealed by Acts 1970, c. 673.
37.1-87. Amended by Acts 1997, c. 801.
37.1-88. Amended by Acts 1974, c. 111; Acts 1976, c. 671; Acts 1995, c. 844.
37.1-89. Amended by Acts 1970, c. 673; Acts 1975, c. 197; Acts 1976, cc. 374, 459, 671; Acts 1977, c. 674; Acts 1979, c. 204; Acts 1982, c. 454; Acts 1989, c. 591; Acts 1991, c. 86; Acts 1995, c. 844; Acts 1996, c. 893; Acts 1997, c. 921; Acts 1998, c. 455.
37.1-90. Amended by Acts 1976, c. 671.
37.1-91. Amended by Acts 1976, c. 671.
37.1-94. Amended by Acts 1972, c. 639.
37.1-95. Amended by Acts 1972, c. 639; Acts 1980, c. 582.
37.1-96. Amended by Acts 1974, c. 366; Acts 1975, c. 568; Acts 1976, c. 680; Acts 1986, c. 154; Acts 1987, c. 413.
37.1-97. Amended by Acts 1972, c. 639; Acts 1974, cc. 44, 45; Acts 1976, c. 671; Acts 1980, c. 582; Acts 1991, c. 534; Acts 1993, c. 930.
37.1-98. Amended by Acts 1972, c. 639; Acts 1976, c. 671; Acts 1977, c. 189; Acts 1980, c. 582; Acts 1985, c. 87; Acts 1986, cc. 256, 309; Acts 1993, cc. 957, 993; Acts 1998, c. 680; Acts 2002, cc. 62, 557.
37.1-98.1. Repealed by Acts 1985, c. 87.
37.1-98.2. Amended by Acts 1999, c. 764.
37.1-99. Amended by Acts 1976, c. 671; Acts 1980, cc. 582, 583.
37.1-101. Amended by Acts 1986, c. 349.
37.1-102. Repealed by Acts 1976, c. 671.
37.1-103. Amended by Acts 1976, c. 671; Acts 2003, cc. 989, 1018.
37.1-104. Amended by Acts 1976, c. 671; Acts 2003, cc. 989, 1018.
37.1-104.1. Amended by Acts 1976, c. 671; Acts 2003, cc. 989, 1018.
37.1-104.2. Amended by Acts 1972, c. 639.
37.1-105. Amended by Acts 1972, c. 342; Acts 1974, c. 667; Acts 1982, c. 50; Acts 1988, c. 713.
37.1-106. Amended by Acts 1970, c. 758; Acts 1976, c. 671.
37.1-107. Amended by Acts 1976, c. 671.
37.1-108. Amended by Acts 1997, c. 801.
37.1-109. Amended by Acts 1971, Ex. Sess., c. 257; Acts 1976, c. 671; Acts 1997, cc. 801, 921.
37.1-110. Amended by Acts 1972, c. 590; Acts 1876, c. 671; Acts 1978, c. 482; Acts 1979, c. 669; Acts 1982, c. 50; Acts 1987, c. 137; Acts 1990, c. 927; Acts 1997, c. 801.
37.1-111. Amended by Acts 1972, c. 382; Acts 1997, c. 801.
37.1-117. Amended by Acts 1972, c. 383; Acts 1976, c. 671.
37.1-118. Amended by Acts 1876, c. 671.
37.1-120. Repealed by Acts 1979, c. 534.
37.1-121. Amended by Acts 1972, c. 639; Acts 1976, c. 671; Acts 1980, c. 582.
37.1-122. Amended by Acts 1972, c. 639; Acts 1979, c. 54; Acts 1980, c. 582.
37.1-123. Amended by Acts 1972, cc. 635, 639; Acts 1974, cc. 44, 45; Acts 1976, c. 671.
37.1-124. Amended by Acts 1972, c. 639; Acts 1980, c. 582.
37.1-125. Amended by Acts 1971, Ex. Sess., c. 155; Acts 1976, c. 671.
37.1-126. Amended by Acts 1972, c. 639; Acts 1976, c. 671.
37.1-127. Repealed by Acts 1976, c. 671.
37.1-128. Repealed by Acts 1976, c. 671.
37.1-128.01, 37.1-128.02. Repealed by Acts 1997, c. 921.
37.1-128.03. Repealed by Acts 1980, c. 582.
37.1-128.04 to 37.1-132.1. Repealed by Acts 1997, c. 921.
37.1-133. Repealed by Acts 1972, c. 173.
37.1-133.1, 37.1-134.1. Repealed by Acts 1997, c. 921.

Sec.
37.1-134.2. Repealed by Acts 1989, c. 591.
37.1-134.3. Repealed by Acts 1997, c. 921.
37.1-134.4. Repealed by Acts 1992, cc. 748, 772.
37.1-134.5. Repealed by Acts 1997, c. 921.
37.1-134.6. Amended by Acts 1998, cc. 582, 787; Acts 2004, c. 858.
37.1-134.7. Amended by Acts 2001, c. 274; Acts 2002, c. 747.
37.1-134.9. Amended by Acts 2004, cc. 66, 1014.
37.1-134.10. Amended by Acts 2001, c. 30.
37.1-134.12. Amended by Acts 2004, c. 66, 1014.
37.1-134.14. Amended by Acts 1998, c. 582.
37.1-134.15. Amended by Acts 1998, c. 582.
37.1-134.17. Amended by Acts 2004, c. 135.
37.1-134.18. Amended by Acts 1998, c. 582; Acts 2001, cc. 478, 479, 507.
37.1-134.19. Amended by Acts 1998, c. 787.
37.1-134.21. Amended by Acts 1999, cc. 814, 946, 985; Acts 2003, c. 790; Acts 2004, cc. 66, 104.
37.1-135. Repealed by Acts 1997, c. 921.
37.1-136. Amended by Acts 1976, c. 671.
37.1-137. Amended by Acts 1971, Ex. Sess., c. 155; Acts 1976, c. 671.
37.1-137.2. Amended by Acts 1998, c. 582; Acts 2003, c. 527.
37.1-137.4. Amended by Acts 2004, cc. 652, 756.
37.1-137.5. Amended by Acts 2003, cc. 253, 528.
37.1-138. Repealed by Acts 1997, c. 921.
37.1-139. Amended by Acts 1980, c. 582.
37.1-140. Repealed by Acts 1976, c. 671.
37.1-141. Amended by Acts 1976, c. 671; Acts 1980, c. 582.
37.1-142. Repealed by Acts 1997, c. 921.
37.1-144. Repealed by by Acts 1997, c. 921.
37.1-145. Amended by Acts 1972, c. 639.
37.1-148. Amended by Acts 1972, c. 639; Acts 1976, c. 671; Acts 1977, c. 326.
37.1-151. Amended by Acts 1972, c. 639.
37.1-151.1. Repealed by Acts 1993, c. 295.
37.1-152. Amended by Acts 1976, c. 671.
37.1-153. Amended by Acts 1972, c. 639; Acts 1976, c. 671.
37.1-155. Amended by Acts 1976, c. 671; Acts 1991, c. 161.
37.1-156 to 37.1-171. Repealed by Acts 1974, c. 296.
37.1-171.1. Repealed by Acts 1981, c. 454.
37.1-179. Amended by Acts 1971, Ex. Sess., c. 182; Acts 1976, c. 671; Acts 1977, cc. 89, 346; Acts 1979, c. 54; Acts 1980, c. 582; Acts 2001, cc. 486, 506; Acts 2002, c. 736.
37.1-179.1. Amended by Acts 2001, cc. 486, 506; Acts 2002, c. 56.
37.1-179.2. Amended by Acts 2004, cc. 823, 845.

Sec.
37.1-180. Repealed by Acts 1980, c. 582.
37.1-181. Amended by Acts 1976, c. 671; Acts 1980, c. 582; Acts 1983, c. 67; Acts 1992, c. 666; Acts 2001, cc. 486, 506.
37.1-182. Amended by Acts 1980, c. 582; Acts 1992, c. 666; Acts 2001, cc. 486, 506.
37.1-182.1. Amended by Acts 2001, cc. 486, 506.
37.1-182.2. Amended by Acts 1996, cc. 38, 54; Acts 2001, cc. 486, 506.
37.1-183. Repealed by Acts 1971, Ex. Sess., c. 181.
37.1-183.1. Amended by Acts 1976, c. 671; Acts 1977, c. 346; Acts 1980, c. 582.
37.1-183.2. Amended by Acts 1990, c. 311.
37.1-183.3. Amended by Acts 2001, cc. 486, 506, 784; Acts 2002, c. 712; Acts 2003, c. 468.
37.1-184. Amended by Acts 1976, c. 671; Acts 1979, c. 54; Acts 2001, cc. 486, 506.
37.1-185. Amended by Acts 1976, c. 671; Acts 1980, c. 582; Acts 1986, c. 104; Acts 2001, cc. 486, 506.
37.1-185.1. Amended by Acts 2001, cc. 486, 506.
37.1-186. Amended by Acts 1976, c. 671; Acts 1980, c. 582; Acts 1984, c. 703; Acts 1986, c. 615.
37.1-186.1. Amended by Acts 1996, cc. 937, 980; Acts 2001, cc. 486, 506.
37.1-187. Amended by Acts 1976, c. 671; Acts 1980, c. 582; Acts 2001, cc. 486, 506.
37.1-188. Amended by Acts 1976, c. 671; Acts 2001, cc. 486, 506.
37.1-188.1. Amended by Acts 2001, cc. 486, 506.
37.1-189. Amended by Acts 1976, c. 671.
37.1-190 to 37.1-193. Repealed by Acts 1976, c. 671.
37.1-194. Amended by Acts 1972, c. 498; Acts 1974, c. 404; Acts 1975, c. 200; Acts 1976, cc. 41, 671; Acts 1977, c. 90; Acts 1980, c. 582; Acts 1982, c. 295; Acts 1984, c. 653; Acts 1998, c. 680; Acts 2002, cc. 51, 278.
37.1-195. Amended by Acts 1970, c. 346; Acts 1972, c. 498; Acts 1973, c. 78; Acts 1976, c. 671; Acts 1978, c. 11; Acts 1980, c. 582; Acts 1988, c. 285; Acts 1989, c. 254; Acts 1994, c. 939; Acts 1996, c. 412; Acts 1997, c. 323; Acts 1998, cc. 667, 680; Acts 1999, c. 653.
37.1-196. Amended by Acts 1970, c. 346; Acts 1972, c. 498; Acts 1977, c. 88; Acts 1979, c. 391; Acts 1980, c. 582; Acts 1998, c. 680.
37.1-196.1. Amended by Acts 1998, c. 680.
37.1-197. Amended by Acts 1970, c. 346; Acts

Sec.
1972, c. 498; Acts 1976, c. 671; Acts 1977, c. 191; Acts 1980, c. 582; Acts 1982, c. 50; Acts 1984, cc. 496, 505; Acts 1986, c. 92; Acts 1987, c. 79; Acts 1995, c. 844; Acts 1998, c. 680.
37.1-197.1. Amended by Acts 1986, c. 609; Acts 1992, c. 837, 880; Acts 1995, c. 844; Acts 1998, c. 680; Acts 2002, c. 747.
37.1-197.2. Amended by Acts 1998, cc. 130, 680, 882; Acts 1999, c. 685; Acts 2001, c. 784; Acts 2002, c. 712; Acts 2003, c. 468.
37.1-198. Amended by Acts 1970, c. 346; Acts 1972, c. 498; Acts 1976, c. 671; Acts 1980, c. 582; Acts 1986, c. 176; Acts 1998, c. 680.
37.1-199. Amended by Acts 1972, c. 629; Acts 1974, c. 273; Acts 1976, c. 671; Acts 1977, cc. 88, 351; Acts 1980, c. 582; Acts 1985, c. 309; Acts 1998, c. 680.
37.1-200. Amended by Acts 1970, c. 346; Acts 1972, c. 629; Acts 1980, c. 582.
37.1-201, 37.1-202. Repealed by Acts 1972, c. 629.
37.1-202.1. Amended by Acts 1984, c. 431; Acts 1998, c. 680.
37.1-203. Amended by Acts 1980, c. 582; Acts 1998, c. 724.
37.1-204. Amended by Acts 1980, c. 582; Acts 1998, c. 724.
37.1-205. Amended by Acts 1977, c. 18; Acts 1980, c. 582; Acts 1998, c. 724.
37.1-205.1. Amended by Acts 1998, c. 724.
37.1-206. Amended by Acts 1980, c. 582; Acts 1998, c. 724.
37.1-207. Amended by Acts 1977, c. 18; Acts 1978, c. 171; Acts 1979, c. 678; Acts 1980, c. 582; Acts 1984, c. 589; Acts 1990, cc. 1, 288, 317; Acts 1998, c. 724; Acts 1999, c. 614.
37.1-208, 37.1-209. Repealed by Acts 1998, c. 724.
37.1-210 to 37.1-213. Repealed by Acts 1980, c. 582.
37.1-214 to 37.1-218. Repealed by Acts 1998, c. 724.
37.1-219. Amended by Acts 1980, c. 582; Acts 1998, c. 724.
37.1-220. Amended by Acts 1977, c. 27; Acts 1980, c. 582; Acts 1998, c. 724.
37.1-221. Amended by Acts 1998, c. 724.
37.1-222. Amended by Acts 1998, c. 724.
37.1-223. Amended by Acts 1980, c. 582; Acts 1998, c. 724.
37.1-225. Amended by Acts 1980, c. 556.
37.1-226. Amended by Acts 1980, c. 556; Acts 2004, cc. 54, 1014.

Sec.
37.1-227. Amended by Acts 1980, c. 556; Acts 2004, cc. 54, 1014.
37.1-228. Amended by Acts 1980, c. 556; Acts 2004, cc. 54, 1014.
37.1-229. Amended by Acts 2004, cc. 54, 1014.
37.1-230. Amended by Acts 1980, c. 556; Acts 2004, cc. 54, 65, 1014.
37.1-234 to 37.1-238. Repealed by Acts 1992, c. 603.
37.1-239 to 37.1-241. Repealed by Acts 1988, c. 127.
37.1-242. Amended by Acts 1998, c. 680.
37.1-243. Amended by Acts 1997, c. 587; Acts 1998, c. 680.
37.1-244. Amended by Acts 1997, c. 587.
37.1-245 to 37.1-248. Amended by Acts 1997, c. 587; Acts 1998, c. 680.
37.1-249. Amended by Acts 1997, c. 587.
37.1-250. Amended by Acts 1997, c. 587; Acts 1998, c. 680.
37.1-253. Amended by Acts 1998, c. 680.
37.1-255. Amended by Acts 2004, c. 169.
37.1-256. Amended by Acts 2003, cc. 35, 40, 450; Acts 2004, c. 169.
37.1-256.1. Amended by Acts 2002, c. 82; Acts 2003, cc. 35, 40, 450; Acts 2004, c. 169.
37.1-257. Repealed by Acts 2004, c. 169.
37.1-258. Amended by Acts 2002, c. 803.
38-1 to 38-564. Repealed by Acts 1952, c. 317.
38.1-1 to 38.1-971. Repealed by Acts 1986, c. 562.
38.2-100. Amended by Acts 2001, c. 707; Acts 2004, c. 668.
38.2-102. Amended by Acts 1992, c. 210.
38.2-106. Amended by Acts 1992, c. 210; Acts 1993, c. 764; Acts 1996, c. 425; Acts 2001, c. 64.
38.2-107. Amended by Acts 1993, c. 764.
38.2-109. Amended by Acts 1997, c. 28.
38.2-111. Amended by Acts 2004, c. 182.
38.2-124. Amended by Acts 1991, c. 4; Acts 1996, c. 276.
38.2-135. Amended by Acts 1994, c. 316; Acts 1995, c. 789.
38.2-136. Amended by Acts 1993, c. 158.
38.2-204, 38.2-205. Repealed by Acts 1991, c. 620.
38.2-203. Amended by Acts 1998, c. 42.
38.2-204. Repealed by Acts 1991, c. 620.
38.2-208. Amended by Acts 1987, c. 353; Acts 1988, c. 554.
38.2-212. Amended by Acts 1992, c. 588.
38.2-226.1. Amended by Acts 1997, cc. 414, 475.
38.2-231. Amended by Acts 1987, c. 697; Acts 1988, c. 189; Acts 1992, c. 160; Acts 1996, c. 237; Acts 1998, c. 142; Acts 2003, cc. 387, 678.
38.2-233. Amended by Acts 1994, c. 306; Acts 1995, c. 167; Acts 1999, c. 586.
38.2-300. Amended by Acts 1988, cc. 333, 523.

Sec.
38.2-301. Amended by Acts 1988, c. 831; Acts 1992, cc. 8, 50; Acts 1993, c. 105.
38.2-302. Amended by Acts 1988, c. 831; Acts 1993, c. 105.
38.2-305. Amended by Acts 1987, c. 519; Acts 1988, c. 333; Acts 1997, c. 688.
38.2-310. Amended by Acts 1990, c. 281.
38.2-316. Amended by Acts 1990, c. 332; Acts 1994, c. 316; Acts 1996, c. 12; Acts 1998, c. 17; Acts 2004, c. 668.
38.2-317. Amended by Acts 1987, c. 519; Acts 1988, c. 523; Acts 1993, c. 985; Acts 1997, c. 26.
38.2-322. Amended by Acts 1997, c. 531.
38.2-400. Amended by Acts 1987, cc. 558, 565, 655; Acts 1994, c. 316.
38.2-401. Amended by Acts 1986, c. 60; Acts 1988, c. 336; Acts 1995, cc. 615, 637; Acts 1997, c. 791; Acts 1998, cc. 166, 877; Acts 2001, cc. 397, 413; Acts 2002, c. 389; Acts 2004, c. 164.
38.2-402. Amended by Acts 1996, c. 22.
38.2-403. Amended by Acts 1994, c. 316.
38.2-406. Amended by Acts 2003, c. 371.
38.2-407. Amended by Acts 1998, c. 15.
38.2-414. Amended by Acts 1993, c. 196.
38.2-415. Amended by Acts 1999, c. 483.
38.2-501. Amended by Acts 1989, c. 653; Acts 1992, c. 7; Acts 2001, c. 707.
38.2-502. Amended by Acts 1990, c. 265.
38.2-508. Amended by Acts 1993, c. 130; Acts 2001, c. 34.
38.2-508.1. Amended by Acts 1991, c. 678.
38.2-510. Amended by Acts 1988, c. 29; Acts 1999, cc. 709, 739; Acts 2001, c. 335.
38.2-512. Amended by Acts 1998, c. 12.
38.2-513. Repealed by Acts 2001, c. 371.
38.2-513.1. Amended by Acts 2002, c. 76.
38.2-514. Amended by Acts 1991, c. 620; Acts 1992, c. 7; Acts 1994, c. 320; Acts 2001, cc. 371, 706.
38.2-514.1. Amended by Acts 2001, c. 706.
38.2-514.2. Amended by Acts 1999, c. 493; Acts 2001, c. 706.
38.2-515. Amended by Acts 1991, c. 356.
38.2-517. Amended by Acts 1999, c. 129; Acts 2003, c. 361; Acts 2004, c. 767.
38.2-601. Amended by Acts 2001, c. 371.
38.2-602. Amended by Acts 2001, c. 371; Acts 2003, c. 729
38.2-604. Amended by Acts 2001, c. 371; Acts 2002, c. 76; Acts 2003, c. 266.
38.2-604.1. Amended by Acts 2002, c. 76; Acts 2003, c. 266.
38.2-606. Amended by Acts 2001, c. 371.
38.2-608. Amended by Acts 2004, cc. 65, 1014.
38.2-612. Amended by Acts 1990, c. 524; Acts 2003, c. 415.
38.2-612.1. Amended by Acts 2003, c. 266.
38.2-613. Amended by Acts 1987, c. 325; Acts 1996, c. 704; Acts 2001, c. 371.
38.2-613.1. Amended by Acts 2001, c. 706.
38.2-616. Amended by Acts 1991, c. 672.
38.2-1000, 38.2-1001. Amended by Acts 1995, c. 69.
38.2-1005. Amended by Acts 2001, c. 726.
38.2-1005.1. Amended by Acts 1996, cc. 801, 831; Acts 2001, c. 726.
38.2-1024. Amended by Acts 1994, c. 316.
38.2-1026. Amended by Acts 1998, c. 60.
38.2-1028. Amended by Acts 1991, c. 261.
38.2-1029. Amended by Acts 1991, c. 261.
38.2-1030. Amended by Acts 1987, c. 520; Acts 1991, c. 261.
38.1-1031. Amended by Acts 1991, c. 261.
38.2-1034. Amended by Acts 1994, c. 503.
38.2-1037. Amended by Acts 1987, c. 520; Acts 1991, c. 261.
38.2-1038. Amended by Acts 1991, c. 261.
38.2-1040. Amended by Acts 1987, c. 431.
38.2-1045. Amended by Acts 1991, c. 261; Acts 1992, c. 14.
38.2-1046. Amended by Acts 1988, c. 298; Acts 1992, c. 20; Acts 1995, c. 60.
38.2-1047. Amended by Acts 1988, c. 298.
38.2-1048. Amended by Acts 1988, c. 298; Acts 1995, c. 60.
38.2-1049. Amended by Acts 1992, c. 14.
38.2-1051. Repealed by Acts 1992, c. 14.
38.2-1206. Amended by Acts 1991, c. 261.
38.2-1207. Amended by Acts 1991, c. 261.
38.2-1211. Amended by Acts 2001, c. 706.
38.2-1213. Amended by Acts 1991, c. 261.
38.2-1220. Amended by Acts 2001, c. 706.
38.2-1222. Amended by Acts 1990, c. 10.
38.2-1223. Amended by Acts 1990, c. 10.
38.2-1224. Amended by Acts 1990, c. 10.
38.2-1225. Amended by Acts 1994, c. 503.
38.2-1230. Amended by Acts 2004, c. 174.
38.2-1300. Amended by Acts 1990, c. 240; Acts 1991, c. 312; Acts 1992, c. 588; Acts 1994, c. 308; Acts 2001, c. 706.
38.2-1301. Amended by Acts 1991, c. 312; Acts 1992, c. 588; Acts 1994, c. 308; Acts 2001, c. 706.
38.2-1301.1. Amended by Acts 2001, c. 519.
38.2-1303. Amended by Acts 1994, c. 316.
38.2-1306. Amended by Acts 1994, c. 308.
38.2-1306.1. Amended by Acts 1994, c. 308; Acts 1996, c. 32; Acts 2001, c. 519.
38.2-1306.2. Amended by Acts 1993, c. 158.
38.2-1307 to 38.2-1309. Repealed by Acts 2000, c. 46.
38.2-1310. Repealed by Acts 1993, c. 158.
38.2-1310.1. Repealed by Acts 2000, c. 46.
38.2-1314. Amended by Acts 1994, c. 503.
38.2-1315. Amended by Acts 1989, c. 236.
38.2-1316. Repealed by Acts 1991, c. 264.
38.2-1316.2. Amended by Acts 1994, c. 647.
38.2-1317. Amended by Acts 1992, c. 588; Acts 1996, c. 47.

Sec.
38.2-1318 to 38.2-1320. Amended by Acts 1992, c. 588.
38.2-1320.1. Amended by Acts 1994, c. 308.
38.2-1320.4, 38.2-1320.5. Amended by Acts 2001, c. 519.
38.2-1321. Amended by Acts 1992, c. 588.
38.2-1322. Amended by Acts 1992, c. 588; Acts 1993, c. 158; Acts 1998, c. 42.
38.2-1323. Amended by Acts 1992, c. 588; Acts 1993, c. 158.
38.2-1329. Amended by Acts 1992, c. 588.
38.2-1330. Amended by Acts 1987, c. 417; Acts 1992, c. 588.
38.2-1331. Amended by Acts 1989, c. 606; Acts 1992, c. 588; Acts 1993, c. 158; Acts 1994, c. 308.
38.2-1332. Amended by Acts 1992, c. 588.
38.2-1333. Amended by Acts 2001, c. 519.
38.2-1341. Amended by Acts 2001, c. 706.
38.2-1346. Amended by Acts 2001, c. 706.
38.2-1400. Amended by Acts 1990, c. 893; Acts 1992, c. 588; Acts 1993, c. 55.
38.2-1401. Amended by Acts 1992, c. 588; Acts 1994, c. 503; Acts 1998, c. 42; Acts 2004, c. 668.
38.2-1403. Amended by Acts 1992, c. 588; Acts 1998, c. 414.
38.2-1405. Amended by Acts 1992, c. 588.
38.2-1407. Amended by Acts 1992, c. 588.
38.2-1411. Repealed by Acts 1992, c. 588.
38.2-1411.1. Amended by Acts 1992, c. 588.
38.2-1413. Amended by Acts 1990, c. 893; Acts 1992, c. 588; Acts 1995, c. 60; Acts 1998, c. 414; Acts 2002, c. 73.
38.2-1414. Amended by Acts 1992, c. 588; Acts 1993, c. 47; Acts 1995, c. 60; Acts 1998, c. 414.
38.2-1415. Amended by Acts 1992, c. 588; Acts 1998, c. 414.
38.2-1416 to 38.2-1418. Amended by Acts 1992, c. 588.
38.2-1421. Amended by Acts 1992, c. 588; Acts 1998, c. 414.
38.2-1422. Amended by Acts 1992, c. 588.
38.2-1423. Amended by Acts 1998, c. 414.
38.2-1426. Amended by Acts 1992, c. 588; Acts 2002, c. 147.
38.2-1427. Amended by Acts 1992, c. 588.
38.2-1427.2. Amended by Acts 2002, c. 147.
38.2-1427.3. Amended by Acts 1993, c. 47; Acts 1995, c. 60.
38.2-1428. Amended by Acts 2001, c. 387.
38.2-1429. Amended by Acts 1992, c. 588.
38.2-1432. Amended by Acts 1990, c. 3; Acts 1995, c. 60; Acts 1996, c. 77.
38.2-1433. Amended by Acts 1998, c. 414.
38.2-1437. Amended by Acts 1992, c. 588.
38.2-1437.1. Amended by Acts 1999, c. 483.
38.2-1440, 38.2-1441. Amended by Acts 1992, c. 588.
38.2-1443. Amended by Acts 1992, c. 588.
38.2-1445. Amended by Acts 1992, c. 588.

Sec.
38.2-1446. Amended by Acts 2002, c. 147.
38.2-1508. Amended by Acts 1992, c. 468.
38.2-1509. Amended by Acts 1996, c. 81.
38.2-1514. Amended by Acts 1996, c. 81.
38.2-1601. Amended by Acts 1987, c. 529; Acts 1993, cc. 77, 774; Acts 1998, c. 230.
38.2-1603. Amended by Acts 1987, c. 529; Acts 1998, c. 230; Acts 2004, c. 285.
38.2-1604. Amended by Acts 1998, c. 230.
38.2-1606. Amended by Acts 1987, cc. 529, 565, 655; Acts 1998, c. 230.
38.2-1608. Amended by Acts 1987, c. 529.
38.2-1609. Amended by Acts 1987, c. 529.
38.2-1610. Amended by Acts 1987, c. 529.
38.2-1611. Amended by Acts 1987, c. 529.
38.2-1611.1. Amended by Acts 1991, c. 371; Acts 1997, c. 160.
38.2-1612. Amended by Acts 1996, c. 245.
38.2-1614. Repealed by Acts 1993, c. 679.
38.2-1616. Amended by Acts 1987, c. 529.
38.2-1618. Amended by Acts 1998, c. 230.
38.2-1620. Amended by Acts 1998, c. 230.
38.2-1621. Amended by Acts 1998, c. 230.
38.2-1622. Amended by Acts 1998, c. 230.
38.2-1700. Amended by Acts 1988, c. 178; Acts 1991, c. 340; Acts 1992, c. 299; Acts 2004, c. 668.
38.2-1704. Amended by Acts 1991, c. 340; Acts 1993, c. 142.
38.2-1705. Amended by Acts 1992, c. 299.
38.2-1709. Amended by Acts 1987, cc. 565, 655; Acts 1991, c. 371; Acts 1997, c. 160.
38.2-1800. Amended by Acts 1987, cc. 520, 521; Acts 1992, c. 586; Acts 1994, cc. 106, 316; Acts 1995, c. 167; Acts 1998, cc. 16, 47, 164; Acts 1999, cc. 86, 490, 493, 586; Acts 2001, c. 706; Acts 2003, cc. 412, 717, 979; Acts 2004, cc. 460, 668, 784
38.2-1800.1. Amended by Acts 2001, c. 706.
38.2-1801. Amended by Acts 1987, c. 521; Acts 1988, c. 229; Acts 1989, c. 543; Acts 1993, c. 145; Acts 2001, c. 706.
38.2-1802. Amended by Acts 1987, c. 521; Acts 1987, cc. 519, 521; Acts 2001, c. 706.
38.2-1803. Repealed by Acts 2001, c. 706.
38.2-1804. Amended by Acts 2001, c. 706.
38.2-1805. Amended by Acts 1987, c. 521; Acts 1990, c. 464; Acts 2001, c. 706.
38.2-1806. Amended by Acts 1987, c. 521; Acts 2001, c. 706.
38.2-1807. Amended by Acts 1987, c. 521; Acts 2001, c. 706.
38.2-1808. Amended by Acts 1987, c. 521; Acts 2001, c. 706.
38.2-1809. Amended by Acts 1987, c. 521; Acts 1990, c. 464; Acts 1991, c. 417; Acts 2001, c. 706.

Sec.

38.2-1810. Amended by Acts 1987, c. 521; Acts 2001, c. 706.

38.2-1811. Repealed by Acts 1991, c. 620.

38.2-1812. Amended by Acts 1987, c. 521; Acts 1999, c. 97; Acts 2001, c. 706; Acts 2002, cc. 323, 456.

38.2-1813. Amended by Acts 1992, c. 49; Acts 1993, c. 145; Acts 2001, c. 706.

38.2-1814. Amended by Acts 1986, c. 364; Acts 1987, c. 521; Acts 1989, c. 435; Acts 1994, c. 106; Acts 1995, c. 167; Acts 1998, cc. 16, 47, 164; Acts 1999, cc. 490, 586; Acts 2001, c. 706.

38.2-1814.1. Amended by Acts 1987, c. 521; Acts 1988, c. 187; Acts 1989, c. 435; Acts 2001, c. 706.

38.2-1815. Amended by Acts 1987, c. 521; Acts 1993, c. 695; Acts 1998, c. 47; Acts 1999, c. 86; Acts 2001, c. 706.

38.2-1816. Repealed by Acts 2001, c. 706.

38.2-1817. Amended by Acts 1987, c. 521; Acts 1989, c. 435; Acts 1990, c. 464; Acts 1999, c. 86; Acts 2001, c. 706.

38.2-1818. Amended by Acts 1987, c. 521; Acts 1997, c. 583; Acts 2001, c. 706.

38.2-1819. Amended by Acts 1987, c. 521; Acts 1989, c. 435; Acts 1994, c. 316; Acts 2001, c. 706.

38.2-1820. Amended by Acts 2001, c. 706.

38.2-1821. Amended by Acts 1987, c. 521.

38.2-1822. Amended by Acts 1987, c. 521; Acts 1989, c. 435; Acts 1991, c. 88; Acts 1994, c. 316; Acts 1997, c. 583; Acts 1999, c. 586; Acts 2001, c. 706; Acts 2002, c. 456.

38.2-1823. Amended by Acts 1987, c. 521.

38.2-1824. Amended by Acts 1987, c. 521; Acts 1988, c. 32; Acts 1991, c. 620; Acts 1994, c. 106; Acts 1995, c. 167; Acts 1998, cc. 16, 47, 164; Acts 1999, cc. 86, 490, 586; Acts 2001, c. 706; Acts 2003, c. 979; Acts 2004, c. 460.

38.2-1825. Amended by Acts 1987, c. 521; Acts 1997, c. 583; Acts 2001, c. 706.

38.2-1826. Amended by Acts 1987, c. 521; Acts 1999, c. 59; Acts 2001, c. 706.

38.2-1827. Amended by Acts 1987, c. 521; Acts 2001, c. 706.

38.2-1828. Amended by Acts 1987, c. 521; Acts 2001, c. 706.

38.2-1829. Repealed by Acts 2001, c. 706.

38.2-1830. Amended by Acts 1987, c. 521; Acts 1989, c. 435; Acts 2001, c. 706.

38.2-1831. Amended by Acts 1987, c. 521; Acts 1996, c. 10; Acts 2001, c. 706.

38.2-1832. Amended by Acts 1987, c. 521.

38.2-1833. Amended by Acts 1987, c. 521; Acts 1988, c. 302; Acts 1994, c. 316; Acts 2001, c. 706; Acts 2003, c. 871.

38.2-1834. Amended by Acts 1987, c. 521; Acts 1988, c. 32; Acts 1994, c. 316; Acts 2001, c. 706; Acts 2002, c. 296; Acts 2003, c. 871.

38.2-1835. Amended by Acts 1987, c. 521; Acts 2001, c. 706.

38.2-1836. Amended by Acts 1987, c. 521; Acts 1988, c. 335; Acts 1989, c. 435; Acts 1990, c. 464; Acts 2001, c. 706.

38.2-1837. Amended by Acts 1987, cc. 521, 678; Acts 1992, c. 574; Acts 2001, c. 706.

38.2-1838. Amended by Acts 1987, c. 678; Acts 1992, c. 574; Acts 1997, c. 583; Acts 2001, c. 706.

38.2-1839. Amended by Acts 1987, cc. 521, 678; Acts 1996, c. 989; Acts 2001, c. 706; Acts 2003, c. 621.

38.2-1840. Amended by Acts 1987, cc. 521, 678; Acts 1994, c. 316; Acts 1999, c. 44; Acts 2001, c. 706.

38.2-1841. Amended by Acts 1987, cc. 521, 678; Acts 1992, c. 574; Acts 1997, c. 583; Acts 1999, c. 44; Acts 2001, c. 706.

38.2-1842. Amended by Acts 1987, cc. 521, 678; Acts 1999, c. 59; Acts 2001, c. 706.

38.2-1843. Amended by Acts 1987, cc. 521, 678; Acts 1996, c. 10; Acts 2001, c. 706.

38.2-1844. Amended by Acts 1987, cc. 521, 678; Acts 2001, c. 706.

38.2-1845. Amended by Acts 1987, cc. 521, 678; Acts 1988, c. 335; Acts 2001, c. 706.

38.2-1846 to 38.2-1857. Repealed by Acts 2001, c. 706.

38.2-1858 to 38.2-1865. Repealed by Acts 2001, c. 706.

38.2-1865.1. Amended by Acts 2003, c. 717.

38.2-1865.6 to 38.2-1865.13. Repealed by Acts 2004, c. 460, eff. 7/1/05

38.2-1866. Amended by Acts 1994, c. 175; Acts 1996, c. 159; Acts 1998, c. 46; Acts 1999, c. 86; Acts 2001, c. 706.

38.2-1867. Amended by Acts 1996, c. 159; Acts 2001, cc. 350, 706; Acts 2004, c. 765.

38.2-1868. Repealed by Acts 1996, c. 159

38.2-1868.1. Amended by Acts 1998, c. 46; Acts 2000, c. 522; Acts 2001, c. 706.

38.2-1869. Amended by Acts 1994, c. 175; Acts 1995, c. 554; Acts 1996, c. 159; Acts 1997, c. 583; Acts 1998, c. 46; Acts 2001, c. 706; Acts 2002, c. 296.

38.2-1870. Amended by Acts 1996, c. 159; Acts 2001, c. 706.

38.2-1871. Amended by Acts 1994, c. 175; Acts 1996, c. 159; Acts 1997, c. 583; Acts 2001, cc. 32, 706.

Sec.
38.2-1872. Amended by Acts 1996, c. 159; Acts 1998, c. 46; Acts 2001, c. 706.
38.2-1874. Amended by Acts 1994, c. 175; Acts 1996, c. 159; Acts 2001, c. 706.
38.2-1901. Amended by Acts 1990, c. 596; Acts 1993, c. 985; Acts 1997, c. 153.
38.2-1902. Amended by Acts 1987, c. 519; Acts 1993, cc. 774, 985; Acts 1995, cc. 744, 803; Acts 2002, c. 145.
38.2-1903. Amended by Acts 1997, c. 153; Acts 1999, c. 491; Acts 2002, c. 437.
38.2-1904. Amended by Acts 1987, c. 697; Acts 1991, c. 104; Acts 1993, c. 985; Acts 1996, c. 250; Acts 2002, c. 145.
38.2-1905. Amended by Acts 1990, cc. 275, 960; Acts 1994, c. 925.
38.2-1905.1, 38.2-1905.2. Repealed by Acts 1997, c. 199.
38.2-1906. Amended by Acts 1987, c. 697; Acts 1990, cc. 596, 597; Acts 1993, c. 985; Acts 1997, c. 199; Acts 2004, c. 838.
38.2-1908. Amended by Acts 1987, c. 697; Acts 1990, c. 596; Acts 1993, c. 985.
38.2-1909. Amended by Acts 1987, c. 697.
38.2-1910. Amended by Acts 1987, c. 697; Acts 1990, cc. 290, 597.
38.2-1912. Amended by Acts 1987, c. 697; Acts 1990, cc. 487, 597; Acts 1993, c. 985.
38.2-1913. Amended by Acts 1990, c. 596; Acts 1993, c. 985.
38.2-1916. Amended by Acts 1990, c. 596; Acts 1993, c. 985.
38.2-1919. Amended by Acts 1993, c. 985; Acts 2003, c. 222.
38.2-1923. Amended by Acts 1990, c. 596.
38.2-2001. Amended by Acts 1993, c. 985; Acts 2002, c. 145.
38.2-2002. Amended by Acts 1993, c. 985.
38.2-2003. Amended by Acts 1987, c. 697; Acts 1988, c. 189.
38.2-2005. Amended by Acts 1987, c. 697; Acts 1996, c. 250; Acts 2002, c. 145.
38.2-2006. Amended by Acts 1987, c. 697.
38.2-2009. Repealed by Acts 1993, c. 985.
38.2-2014. Amended by Acts 1993, c. 985.
38.2-2015. Amended by Acts 1993, c. 985.
38.2-2102. Amended by Acts 2003, c. 930.
38.2-2107. Amended by Acts 2003, c. 930.
38.2-2113. Amended by Acts 1992, c. 160; Acts 2003, c. 387.
38.2-2114. Amended by Acts 1990, c. 293; Acts 1995, c. 3; Acts 1996, c. 237; Acts 1998, c. 142; Acts 2003, cc. 543, 553; Acts 2004, c. 300.
38.2-2119. Amended by Acts 1992, c. 762; Acts 1996, c. 373.
38.2-2121. Amended by Acts 1992, c. 470.
38.2-2125. Amended by Acts 2004, c. 288.
38.2-2201. Amended by Acts 1987, c. 429; Acts 1989, c. 243; Acts 1991, c. 4; Acts 1996, c. 276; Acts 1997, c. 503.
38.2-2202. Amended by Acts 1987, c. 429; Acts 1989, c. 243; Acts 1992, c. 230; Acts 2001, c. 564.
38.2-2204. Amended by Acts 1986, c. 544; Acts 1992, c. 140; Acts 1995, c. 652; Acts 1999, c. 4; Acts 2003, cc. 756, 761.
38.2-2205. Amended by Acts 1987, c. 685; Acts 1992, c. 474.
38.2-2206. Amended by Acts 1987, c. 519; Acts 1988, cc. 565, 578, 585, 586, 594; Acts 1989, c. 621; Acts 1993, c. 381; Acts 1995, cc. 189, 267, 476; Acts 1997, cc. 170, 191; Acts 1999, c. 992; Acts 2001, cc. 218, 564; Acts 2003, c. 283.
38.2-2207. Amended by Acts 1987, c. 519.
38.2-2208. Amended by Acts 1992, c. 160; Acts 2003, c. 387.
38.2-2210. Amended by Acts 1988, cc. 655, 665.
38.2-2212. Amended by Acts 1988, c. 655; Acts 1990, c. 960; Acts 1991, c. 116; Acts 1995, c. 3; Acts 1996, cc. 206, 239; Acts 1998, cc. 141, 142; Acts 2003, cc. 543, 553.
38.2-2217. Amended by Acts 1995, c. 226; Acts 2002, c. 337.
38.2-2217.1. Amended by Acts 1986, c. 612; Acts 1995, c. 744.
38.2-2223. Amended by Acts 1994, c. 316.
38.2-2226. Amended by Acts 1997, c. 377; Acts 2001, c. 728.
38.2-2228, 38.2-2228.1. Repealed by Acts 1996, c. 31.
38.2-2231. Amended by Acts 1999, c. 514.
38.2-2232. Amended by Acts 1999, c. 918.
38.2-2403. Amended by Acts 1988, cc. 529, 548.
38.2-2407. Amended by Acts 1987, c. 519.
38.2-2411. Amended by Acts 2003, c. 979; Acts 2004, c. 460.
38.2-2412. Amended by Acts 2003, c. 979; Acts 2004, c. 460.
38.2-2416 to 38.2-2419. Amended by Acts 2004, c. 357.
38.2-2529. Amended by Acts 1994, c. 316.
38.2-2601. Amended by Acts 1992, c. 21.
38.2-2609. Amended by Acts 2001, c. 706.
38.2-2701. Amended by Acts 1987, c. 520; Acts 1995, c. 119.
38.2-2710. Amended by Acts 1995, c. 60.
38.2-2801. Amended by Acts 2003, cc. 488, 1026.
38.2-2802. Amended by Acts 1987, c. 554.
38.2-2804. Amended by Acts 1987, c. 554; Acts 1988, c. 341.
38.2-2806. Amended by Acts 1987, cc. 519, 520, 554; Acts 1988, c. 341; Acts 1997, c. 160.
38.2-2807. Amended by Acts 1987, cc. 526, 554; Acts 1988, c. 341.

Sec.
1990, c. 301; Acts 1999, c. 276.
38.2-3543.1. Amended by Acts 1998, c. 154.
38.2-3600. Amended by Acts 1992, c. 225; Acts 1996, c. 11.
38.2-3602. Repealed by Acts 1989, c. 151.
38.2-3603. Amended by Acts 1991, c. 120.
38.2-3604. Amended by Acts 1989, c. 151.
38.2-3605. Amended by Acts 1995, c. 522.
38.2-3606. Amended by Acts 1996, c. 11.
38.2-3607. Amended by Acts 1989, c. 646; Acts 1996, c. 11.
38.2-3608. Amended by Acts 1990, c. 268; Acts 1992, c. 225; Acts 1996, c. 11.
38.2-3700 to 38.2-3716. Repealed by Acts 1992, c. 586.
38.2-3723. Amended by Acts 2002, c. 72.
38.2-3725. Amended by Acts 1999, c. 586.
38.2-3727. Amended by Acts 1995, c. 167.
38.2-3729. Amended by Acts 2002, c. 72.
38.2-3734. Amended by Acts 2001, c. 706.
38.2-3735. Amended by Acts 1999, c. 586.
38.2-3737. Amended by Acts 1993, c. 627; Acts 1994, c. 202; Acts 1999, c. 586.
38.2-3812. Amended by Acts 1987, cc. 565, 655.
38.2-3912. Amended by Acts 1987, c. 520.
38.2-3919. Amended by Acts 2001, c. 706.
38.2-4008. Amended by Acts 2002, c. 147.
38.2-4011. Amended by Acts 2002, c. 147.
38.2-4123. Amended by Acts 1987, cc. 565, 655; Acts 1993, c. 158; Acts 1994, c. 308; Acts 2004, c. 315.
38.2-4135. Amended by Acts 1995, c. 321.
38.2-4200. Amended by Acts 1997, c. 801.
38.2-4201. Amended by Acts 1987, c. 647; Acts 1988, c. 185.
38.2-4208. Amended by Acts 1988, c. 185.
38.2-4209. Amended by Acts 1999, cc. 643, 649.
38.2-4209.1. Amended by Acts 1995, c. 467.
38.2-4209.2. Repealed by Acts 1995, c. 467.
38.2-4214. Amended by Acts 1986, c. 550; Acts 1987, cc. 565, 655; Acts 1989, cc. 606, 653; Acts 1990, cc. 301, 393, 439, 531, 795, 802, 826; Acts 1991, c. 369; Acts 1992, c. 800; Acts 1993, cc. 158, 306, 307; Acts 1994, cc. 213, 320, 374, 522; Acts 1995, cc 420, 522; Acts 1996, cc. 550, 776, 967; Acts 1997, cc. 688, 807, 913; Acts 1998, cc. 154, 891, 908; Acts 1999, cc. 643, 649, 709, 739, 856, 857, 923; Acts 2004, c. 315.
38.2-4216. Repealed by Acts 1987, cc. 565, 655.
38.2-4216.1. Amended by Acts 1988, c. 185; Acts 1997, cc. 807, 913.
38.2-4217. Amended by Acts 1987, cc. 565, 655; Acts 1997, cc. 807, 913.
38.2-4221. Amended by Acts 1987, cc. 549, 551, 557; Acts 1988, c. 522; Acts 1989, cc. 7, 201; Acts 1997, c. 203; Acts 1998, c. 146; Acts 2001, cc. 102, 475.
38.2-4222. Amended by Acts 1987, c. 565, 655; Acts 1988, c. 185; Acts 1994, c. 503.
38.2-4223. Amended by Acts 1987, cc. 565, 655.
38.2-4224. Amended by Acts 1999, c. 86.
38.2-4225. Repealed by Acts 1987, cc. 565, 655.
38.2-4226. Amended by Acts 1987, cc. 565, 655.
38.2-4229.1. Amended by Acts 1992, c. 473; Acts 1994, c. 294; Acts 1997, cc. 807, 913.
38.2-4230 to 38.2-4232. Amended by Acts 1992, c. 588.
38.2-4233. Amended by Acts 1993, c. 158.
38.2-4234. Amended by Acts 1992, c. 588.
38.2-4235. Amended by Acts 2001, c. 519.
38.2-4300. Amended by Acts 1986, cc. 76, 528; Acts 1990, c. 224; Acts 1992, cc. 241, 481; Acts 1993, c. 305; Acts 1995, cc. 182, 345; Acts 2003, cc. 752, 767; Acts 2004, c. 175.
38.2-4301. Amended by Acts 1998, c. 891; Acts 2004, c. 175.
38.2-4302. Amended by Acts 1992, c. 481; Acts 1998, cc. 42, 891; Acts 2003, cc. 752, 767; Acts 2004, c. 175.
38.2-4303. Amended by Acts 1990, c. 224; Acts 1992, c. 481; Acts 2003, cc. 752, 767.
38.2-4306. Amended by Acts 1997, cc. 807, 913; Acts 2003, cc. 752, 767; Acts 2004, c. 185.
38.2-4306.1. Amended by Acts 1996, c. 75.
38.2-4307. Amended by Acts 1987, c. 520; Acts 1998, c. 891; Acts 1999, c. 482.
38.2-4307.1. Amended by Acts 1999, c. 482.
38.2-4308. Repealed by Acts 1998, c. 891.
38.2-4309. Amended by Acts 1998, c. 42.
38.2-4310. Amended by Acts 1989, c. 216; Acts 1990, c. 224; Acts 1992, cc. 14, 20.
38.2-4311. Repealed by Acts 1998, c. 891.
38.2-4312. Amended by Acts 1989, c. 221; Acts 1997, c. 297; Acts 1998, c. 891; Acts 1999, cc. 643, 649.
38.2-4312.1. Amended by Acts 1995, cc. 446, 467.
38.2-4312.2. Repealed by Acts 1995, c. 467.
38.2-4313. Amended by Acts 1999, c. 86.
38.2-4315. Amended by Acts 1977, c. 688; Acts 1990, c. 224.
38.2-4316. Amended by Acts 1992, c. 481.
38.2-4317. Amended by Acts 1989, c. 216.
38.2-4317.1. Amended by Acts 1990, c. 224.
38.2-4318. Amended by Acts 1987, c. 519.
38.2-4319. Amended by Acts 1989, cc. 646, 653; Acts 1990, cc. 301, 393, 439, 531, 826; Acts 1991, cc. 103, 369; Acts 1992, cc. 14, 23, 800; Acts 1993, cc. 148, 158, 306, 307; Acts 1997, c. 94, cc. 213, 320, 374, 522, 699; Acts 1995, cc. 80, 420, 522, 537; Acts 1996, c. 22; Acts 1997, cc. 688, 807, 913; Acts 1998, cc. 42, 43, 56, 120, 154, 625, 631, 709, 858, 891,

Sec.

908; Acts 1999, cc. 35, 643, 649, 709, 739, 856, 857, 858, 923, 941; Acts 2001, c. 663; Acts 2002, cc. 153, 599; Acts 2003, c. 243; Acts 2004, cc. 315, 772.

38.2-4400, 38.2-4401. Amended by Acts 1994, c. 224.

38.2-4402. Repealed by Acts 1994, c. 224.

38.2-4404, 38.2-4405. Amended by Acts 1994, c. 224.

38.2-4408. Amended by Acts 1993, c. 158; Acts 1994, c. 224; Acts 2000, c. 50.

38.2-4408.1, 38.2-4409. Amended by Acts 1994, c. 224.

38.2-4411. Amended by Acts 1994, c. 224.

38.2-4415. Repealed by Acts 2004, c. 784.

38.2-4500. Amended by Acts 1997, c. 801.

38.2-4508. Amended by Acts 1987, c. 520; Acts 1994, c. 224.

38.2-4509. Amended by Acts 1989, c. 653; Acts 1993, cc. 158, 307; Acts 1994, c. 224; Acts 1996, c. 776; Acts 1998, cc. 42, 891; Acts 1999, cc. 643, 649, 709, 739; Acts 2004, c. 315.

38.2-4517. Amended by Acts 1987, cc. 565, 655; Acts 1994, c. 503.

38.2-4518. Amended by Acts 1987, cc. 565, 655.

38.2-4521. Amended by Acts 1987, cc. 565, 655.

38.2-4601.1. Amended by Acts 1997, c. 426; Acts 2001, c. 706.

38.2-4608. Amended by Acts 1993, c. 950.

38.2-4609. Amended by Acts 1990, c. 334.

38.2-4610. Repealed by Acts 1986, c. 404.

38.2-4611, 38.2-4612. Repealed by Acts 1986, c. 404.

38.2-4613. Amended by Acts 1986, c. 404.

38.2-4614. Amended by Acts 1987, c. 174; Acts 1993, c. 147; Acts 1996, c. 883; Acts 2002, c. 857.

38.2-4700. Amended by Acts 1996, c. 77.

38.2-4705. Amended by Acts 1994, cc. 8, 123.

38.2-4706. Amended by Acts 1994, c. 123.

38.2-4800. Amended by Acts 1987, c. 519; Acts 1988, c. 828.

38.2-4801 to 38.2-4805. Repealed by Acts 2001, c. 706.

38.2-4806. Amended by Acts 1987, c. 519; Acts 1988, c. 828; Acts 1996, c. 240; Acts 2001, c. 706.

38.2-4807. Amended by Acts 2001, c. 706.

38.2-4809. Amended by Acts 1987, c. 519; Acts 1988, c. 153; Acts 2001, c. 706.

38.2-4811. Amended by Acts 1994, c. 647; Acts 1995, c. 60.

38.2-4812. Amended by Acts 1988, c. 153.

38.2-4815. Amended by Acts 2001, c. 706.

38.2-4900. Amended by Acts 1986, c. 598; Acts 1993, c. 683.

38.2-4902. Amended by Acts 1986, c. 598; Acts 1992, c. 139.

38.2-4904.1. Amended by Acts 1986, c. 598.

38.2-4905. Amended by Acts 1986, c. 598.

Sec.

38.2-4910. Amended by Acts 1992, c. 139.

38.2-4917. Amended by Acts 1986, c. 265.

38.2-5001. Amended by Acts 1989, c. 523; Acts 1990, cc. 234, 534; Acts 1994, c. 872; Acts 1995, c. 302; Acts 1999, c. 806; Acts 2003, c. 897; Acts 2004, cc. 896, 931.

38.2-5002. Amended by Acts 1990, c. 535; Acts 2003, c. 897.

38.2-5003. Amended by Acts 1999, c. 822.

38.2-5004. Amended by Acts 1989, c. 523; Acts 2003, c. 897.

38.2-5004.1. Amended by Acts 2000, c. 1038; Acts 2003, c. 897.

38.2-5005. Amended by Acts 1989, c. 523; Acts 2003, c. 897.

38.2-5006. Amended by Acts 1989, c. 523.

38.2-5007. Amended by Acts 1989, c. 523; Acts 2003, c. 897.

38.2-5008. Amended by Acts 1989, c. 523; Acts 1990, cc. 534, 535; Acts 2003, c. 897.

38.2-5009. Amended by Acts 1989, c. 523; Acts 1990, c. 535; Acts 1999, c. 823; Acts 2000, c. 1038; Acts 2003, c. 897; Acts 2004, cc. 896, 931.

38.2-5010. Amended by Acts 1999, c. 806.

38.2-5011. Amended by Acts 1989, c. 523.

38.2-5013. Amended by Acts 1999, c. 806.

38.2-5015. Amended by Acts 1999, c. 826; Acts 2003, c. 897.

38.2-5016. Amended by Acts 1989, c. 523; Acts 1994, c. 872; Acts 1996, c. 232; Acts 1997, c. 399; Acts 1999, c. 824; Acts 2003, c. 897.

38.2-5017. Amended by Acts 1994, c. 872.

38.2-5018. Amended by Acts 1989, c. 523; Acts 1990, c. 244.

38.2-5019. Repealed by Acts 1989, c. 523.

38.2-5020. Amended by Acts 1989, cc. 361, 463, 523; Acts 1990, c. 498; Acts 1991, c. 486; Acts 1992, cc. 414, 767; Acts 1994, c. 872; Acts 2004, cc. 896, 931.

38.2-5021. Amended by Acts 1989, c. 523.

38.2-5100 to 38.2-5103. Amended by Acts 1992, c. 588.

38.2-5105. Repealed by Acts 2001, c. 706.

38.2-5108, 38.2-5109. Amended by Acts 1992, c. 588.

38.2-5110. Amended by Acts 1995, c. 843.

38.2-5200, 38.2-5201. Amended by Acts 1990, c. 285.

38.2-5202. Amended by Acts 1990, c. 285; Acts 2001, c. 114.

38.2-5202.1 to 38.2-5205. Amended by Acts 1990, c. 285.

38.2-5206. Amended by Acts 1990, c. 286; Acts 2002, c. 334.

38.2-5207, 38.2-5208. Amended by Acts 1990, c. 285.

Sec.
38.2-5300 to 38.2-5309. Repealed by Acts 1998, c. 129.
38.2-5400 to 38.2-5409. Repealed by Acts 1998, c. 891.
38.2-5508. Amended by Acts 2001, c. 519.
38.2-5600. Amended by Acts 2002, c. 372.
38.2-5700 to 38.2-5707. Repealed by Acts 2003, c. 717.
38.2-5601. Amended by Acts 2002, c. 372.
38.2-5602. Amended by Acts 2002, c. 372.
38.2-5701. Amended by Acts 1998, c. 11.
38.2-5702. Amended by Acts 1998, c. 11.
38.2-5703. Amended by Acts 1999, c. 59; Acts 2001, c. 706.
38.2-5802. Amended by Acts 1999, c. 20.
38.2-5803. Amended by Acts 2004, c. 715.
38.2-5804. Amended by Acts 1999, cc. 643, 649.
38.2-5901. Amended by Acts 2001, c. 110; Acts 2002, c. 745.
38.2-5902. Amended by Acts 2002, c. 745.
38.2-5903. Amended by Acts 2001, c. 276.
39-1 to 39-13. Repealed by Acts 1968, c. 639.
39.1-1 to 39.1-25. Repealed by Acts 1973, c. 545.
40-1 to 40-146. Repealed by Acts 1970, c. 321.
40.1-1. Amended by Acts 1972, c. 567; Acts 1973, c. 425; Acts 1979, c. 354; Acts 1984, c. 590; Acts 1985, c. 449; Acts 1995, c. 373.
40.1-2. Amended by Acts 1972, c. 567; Acts 1973, c. 425; Acts 1985, c. 448; Acts 2004, c. 294.
40.1-4. Repealed by Acts 1984, c. 734.
40.1-4.1. Amended by Acts 2004, c. 650.
40.1-5. Amended by Acts 1978, c. 372.
40.1-6. Amended by Acts 1972, c. 567; Acts 1973, c. 425; Acts 1984, cc. 590, 734; Acts 1987, c. 165; Acts 1997, c. 919; Acts 1998, c. 97; Acts 2004, c. 592.
40.1-8. Amended by Acts 2004, c. 163.
40.1-11. Amended by Acts 1984, c. 590.
40.1-11.1. Amended by Acts 1979, c. 472.
40.1-12 to 40.1-21. Repealed by Acts 1978, c. 840.
40.1-22. Amended by Acts 1972, c. 567; Acts 1973, c. 425; Acts 1974, c. 195; Acts 1976, c. 607; Acts 1979, c. 656; Acts 1980, c. 728; Acts 1984, c. 590; Acts 1985, c. 448; Acts 1987, c. 165; Acts 1988, c. 467.
40.1-22.1. Amended by Acts 1997, c. 282.
40.1-23 to 40.1-25.1. Repealed by Acts 1988, c. 340.
40.1-26. Repealed by Acts 1979, c. 631.
40.1-28. Amended by Acts 1973, c. 425; Acts 1982, c. 84.
40.1-28.4. Amended by Acts 1975, c. 70.
40.1-28.5. Repealed by Acts 2004, c. 608.
40.1-28.7. Repealed by Acts 1985, c. 421.
40.1-28.9. Amended by Acts 1976, c. 442; Acts 1977, c. 432; Acts 1993, c. 930.

Sec.
40.1-28.10. Amended by Acts 1976, c. 736; Acts 1978, c. 371; Acts 1980, c. 532; Acts 1991, cc. 547, 596; Acts 1997, c. 544.
40.1-29. Amended by Acts 1972, c. 848; Acts 1977, c. 308; Acts 1979, c. 50; Acts 1989, c. 583; Acts 1991, c. 499; Acts 1993, c. 600; Acts 2002, c. 321; Acts 2004, c. 358.
40.1-30. Amended by Acts 1972, c. 241; Acts 1979, c. 484.
40.1-34 to 40.1-38. Repealed by Acts 1974, c. 272.
40.1-39. Repealed by Acts 1979, c. 354.
40.1-40. Repealed by Acts 1985, c. 449.
40.1-41 to 40.1-43. Repealed by Acts 1979, c. 354.
40.1-44. Repealed by Acts 1973, c. 425.
40.1-44.1. Amended by Acts 1973, c. 425; Acts 1979, c. 406.
40.1-45 to 40.1-48. Repealed by Acts 1979, c. 354.
40.1-49. Repealed by Acts 1973, c. 425.
40.1-49.1. Repealed by Acts 1976, c. 607.
40.1-49.2. Repealed by Acts 1979, c. 354.
40.1-49.3. Amended by Acts 1992, c. 777.
40.1-49.4. Amended by Acts 1982, c. 412; Acts 1989, c. 341; Acts 1991, c. 153; Acts 1992, c. 777.
40.1-49.5. Amended by Acts 1992, c. 777; Acts 1993, c. 526.
40.1-49.6 to 40.1-49.7. Amended by Acts 1992, c. 777.
40.1-50. Repealed by Acts 1985, c. 449.
40.1-51. Amended by Acts 1972, c. 567; Acts 1985, c. 449; Acts 2003, c. 445.
40.1-51.1. Amended by Acts 1973, c. 425; Acts 1976, c. 607; Acts 1979, c. 354; Acts 1995, c. 373.
40.1-51.1:1. Repealed by Acts 1979, c. 354.
40.1-51.2. Amended by Acts 1973, c. 425; Acts 1976, c. 607.
40.1-51.2:2. Amended by Acts 2001, c. 332.
40.1-51.3. Amended by Acts 1979, c. 354.
40.1-51.3:1. Amended by Acts 1994, c. 28.
40.1-51.4. Repealed by Acts 1979, c. 354.
40.1-51.4:1, 40.1-51.4:2. Amended by Acts 1994, c. 28.
40.1-51.4:3. Amended by Acts 1990, c. 368.
40.1-51.4:4. Amended by Acts 1998, c. 140.
40.1-51.5. Amended by Acts 1974, c. 195; Acts 1986, c. 211; Acts 1993, c. 543; Acts 1996, c. 294.
40.1-51.6. Amended by Acts 1973, c. 425; Acts 1985, c. 40.
40.1-51.7. Amended by Acts 1974, c. 195; Acts 1986, c. 211.
40.1-51.8. Amended by Acts 1977, c. 301; Acts 1978, c. 355; Acts 1986, c. 211; Acts 1988, c. 289; Acts 1990, c. 226; Acts 1993, c. 543; Acts 1999, c. 335.

Sec.
40.1-51.9. Amended by Acts 1974, c. 195; Acts 1995, c. 97.
40.1-51.9:1. Amended by Acts 1986, c. 266; Acts 1997, c. 212.
40.1-51.10. Amended by Acts 1974, c. 195; Acts 1976, c. 288; Acts 1986, c. 266; Acts 1988, c. 289; Acts 1992, c. 3; Acts 1993, c. 544; Acts 1995, c. 97; Acts 1997, c. 212.
40.1-51.11. Amended by Acts 1981, c. 39.
40.1-51.11:1. Amended by Acts 1986, c. 266; Acts 1995, c. 212.
40.1-51.12. Amended by Acts 1995, c. 97.
40.1-51.13. Amended by Acts 1990, c. 226.
40.1-51.15. Amended by Acts 1985, c. 40; Acts 1986, c. 266; Acts 1988, c. 289; Acts 1992, c. 3; Acts 1993, c. 544; Acts 1995, c. 97; Acts 1997, c. 212.
40.1-51.16. Amended by Acts 1986, c. 615; Acts 1988, c. 289.
40.1-51.19. Amended by Acts 1990, c. 226.
40.1-51.20. Amended by Acts 1995, cc. 543, 585; Acts 1996, cc. 180, 846.
40.1-51.21. Amended by Acts 1995, cc. 543, 585.
40.1-52. Amended by Acts 1997, c. 761.
40.1-53. Amended by Acts 1974, c. 254.
40.1-61. Amended by Acts 2002, c. 422.
40.1-69. Amended by Acts 1973, c. 425.
40.1-71. Amended by Acts 1979, c. 515.
40.1-76, 40.1-77. Repealed by Acts 1991, c. 443.
40.1-78. Amended by Acts 1991, c. 511.
40.1-79. Repealed by Acts 1991, c. 511.
40.1-79.01. Amended by Acts 1998, c. 30.
40.1-79.1. Amended by Acts 1983, c. 123; Acts 1991, c. 511.
40.1-80. Repealed by Acts 1991, c. 511.
40.1-81. Repealed by Acts 1972, c. 480.
40.1-81.1. Amended by Acts 1982, c. 134; Acts 1991, c. 511.
40.1-82. Repealed by Acts 1979, c. 219.
40.1-83. Repealed by Acts 1991, c. 511.
40.1-84. Amended by Acts 1972, cc. 480, 824; Acts 1974, cc. 283, 525; Acts 1979, c. 219; Acts 1991, c. 511.
40.1-85. Amended by Acts 1982, c. 135; Acts 1991, c. 511.
40.1-86. Repealed by Acts 1979, c. 219.
40.1-87. Amended by Acts 1979, c. 219; Acts 1982, c. 136; Acts 1991, c. 511.
40.1-88. Amended by Acts 1979, c. 219; Acts 1982, c. 670.
40.1-89. Amended by Acts 1982, c. 252; Acts 1991, c. 511.
40.1-90, 40.1-91. Repealed by Acts 1991, c. 511.
40.1-92. Amended by Acts 1979, c. 219; Acts 1991, c. 511.
40.1-93. Amended by Acts 1972, c. 480; Acts 1991, c. 511.
40.1-95. Repealed by Acts 1991, c. 511.
40.1-96. Amended by Acts 1978, c. 596; Acts 1991, c. 511.

Sec.
40.1-97. Repealed by Acts 1972, c. 480.
40.1-98, 40.1-99. Repealed by Acts 1991, c. 511.
40.1-100. Amended by Acts 1972, c. 824; Acts 1973, c. 13; Acts 1979, cc. 219, 348; Acts 1991, c. 511; Acts 1994, c. 156.
40.1-101. Amended by Acts 1973, c. 13; Acts 1979, c. 348; Acts 1991, c. 511.
40.1-103. Amended by Acts 1991, c. 511; Acts 2003, cc. 816, 822.
40.1-104. Amended by Acts 1972, c. 824; Acts 1979, c. 219.
40.1-105. Repealed by Acts 1991, c. 511.
40.1-106 to 40.1-108. Repealed by Acts 1979, c. 219.
40.1-109. Amended by Acts 1972, c. 807; Acts 1973, c. 13; Acts 1979, c. 219; Acts 1982, c. 83; Acts 1991, c. 511.
40.1-110. Repealed by Acts 1979, c. 219.
40.1-111. Repealed by Acts 1991, c. 511.
40.1-112. Amended by Acts 1973, c. 13; Acts 1979, c. 219; Acts 1982, c. 137; Acts 1991, c. 511; Acts 1998, c. 157.
40.1-113. Amended by Acts 1973, c. 425; Acts 1979, c. 348; Acts 1982, c. 416; Acts 1991, c. 511.
40.1-114. Amended by Acts 1979, c. 219.
40.1-117. Amended by Acts 1978, c. 206; Acts 1980, c. 728; Acts 1981, c. 331; Acts 1987, c. 165; Acts 1992, c. 231.
40.1-118. Amended by Acts 1978, c. 206; Acts 1990, c. 614; Acts 1996, cc. 134, 486.
40.1-119. Amended by Acts 1990, c. 614.
40.1-120. Amended by Acts 1978, c. 206; Acts 1990, c. 614.
40.1-122. Amended by Acts 1974, c. 272.
40.1-126. Amended by Acts 1990, c. 614.
40.1-128 to 40.1-134. Repealed by Acts 1991, c. 152.
40.1-135 to 40.1-138. Amended by Acts 1992, c. 798.
41-1 to 41-89. Repealed by Acts 1970, c. 291.
41.1-1. Amended by Acts 1998, c. 427.
41.1-2. Amended by Acts 1998, c. 427.
41.1-3. Amended by Acts 1991, c. 378; Acts 1995, c. 850.
41.1-4. Repealed by Acts 1995, c. 850.
41.1-4.1. Repealed by Acts 1992, c. 836.
41.1-5. Amended by Acts 1991, c. 378; Acts 1995, c. 850; Acts 1998, c. 427.
41.1-6. Amended by Acts 1998, c. 427.
41.1-7. Amended by Acts 1998, c. 427.
41.1-15. Amended by Acts 1982, c. 565; Acts 1998, c. 427.
41.1-16. Amended by Acts 1977, c. 624; Acts 1995, c. 850.
42-1 to 42-67. Repealed by Acts 1970, c. 606.
42.1-1. Amended by Acts 1984, cc. 389, 734; Acts 1986, c. 565; Acts 1987, c.

Sec.
458; Acts 1994, c. 64; Acts 1998, c. 427.
42.1-2. Amended by Acts 1986, c. 565; Acts 1987, c. 458; Acts 1994, c. 64.
42.1-3. Amended by Acts 1986, c. 565.
42.1-3.1. Amended by Acts 1994, c. 64.
42.1-4. Repealed by Acts 1986, c. 565.
42.1-7. Repealed by Acts 1985, c. 397.
42.1-8 to 42.1-11. Amended by Acts 1994, c. 64.
42.1-12. Amended by Acts 1998, c. 427.
42.1-13. Amended by Acts 1984, c. 444; Acts 1985, c. 397; Acts 1986, c. 565; Acts 1994, c. 64; Acts 1996, c. 812; Acts 1998, c. 427.
42.1-14. Amended by Acts 1998, c. 427.
42.1-15. Amended by Acts 1994, c. 64; Acts 1998, c. 427.
42.1-15.1. Amended by Acts 2004, c. 559.
42.1-16. Amended by Acts 1998, c. 427.
42.1-17. Amended by Acts 1994, c. 64.
42.1-18. Amended by Acts 1994, c. 64; Acts 1998, c. 427.
42.1-19. Amended by Acts 1981, c. 234; Acts 1994, c. 64.
42.1-20 to 42.1-28. Repealed by Acts 1976, c. 746.
42.1-29 to 42.1-29.2. Repealed by Acts 1976, c. 746.
42.1-30. Amended by Acts 1998, c. 427.
42.1-31. Amended by Acts 1998, c. 427.
42.1-32.7. Repealed by Acts 2003, c. 176.
42.1-35. Amended by Acts 1974, c. 84; Acts 1985, c. 278; Acts 1998, c. 212.
42.1-36. Amended by Acts 1978, c. 6; Acts 2002, c. 111.
42.1-39. Amended by Acts 1985, c. 278.
42.1-40. Amended by Acts 1986, c. 247.
42.1-41. Amended by Acts 1994, c. 64.
42.1-48. Amended by Acts 1978, c. 565; Acts 1989, c. 85; Acts 1990, c. 48.
42.1-51. Amended by Acts 1988, c. 716; Acts 1994, c. 64.
42.1-52. Amended by Acts 1988, c. 716.
42.1-53. Repealed by Acts 1999, c. 24.
42.1-54. Amended by Acts 1987, c. 458; Acts 1994, c. 64.
42.1-57. Amended by Acts 1972, c. 167.
42.1-60. Amended by Acts 1977, c. 397.
42.1-62. Amended by Acts 1977, c. 397.
42.1-63. Amended by Acts 1977, c. 397.
42.1-64. Amended by Acts 1977, c. 397.
42.1-65. Amended by Acts 1977, c. 397.
42.1-66. Amended by Acts 1977, c. 397.
42.1-67 to 42.1-69. Repealed by Acts 1977, c. 397.
42.1-70. Amended by Acts 1972, c. 343; Acts 1977, c. 397; Acts 1981, c. 48; Acts 1982, c. 607; Acts 1983, cc. 309, 355; Acts 1984, c. 16; Acts 1985, c. 381; Acts 1988, c. 571.
42.1-72. Amended by Acts 1975, c. 318; Acts 1994, c. 64.

Sec.
42.1-73. Amended by Acts 1975, c. 318.
42.1-73.1. Amended by Acts 1986, c. 33.
42.1-77. Amended by Acts 1977, c. 501; Acts 1981, c. 637; Acts 1987, c. 217; Acts 1990, c. 778; Acts 1994, cc. 390, 955; Acts 1998, cc. 427, 470.
42.1-78. Amended by Acts 1979, c. 110; Acts 1990, c. 778; Acts 1994, c. 64.
42.1-79. Amended by Acts 1986, c. 565; Acts 1990, c. 778; Acts 1994, c. 64; Acts 1998, c. 427.
42.1-79.1. Amended by Acts 1994, cc. 64, 955; Acts 1998, c. 427.
42.1-80, 42.1-81. Repealed by Acts 2003, c. 177.
42.1-82. Amended by Acts 1977, c. 501; Acts 1981, c. 637; Acts 1990, c. 778; Acts 1994, cc. 64, 955; Acts 2003, cc. 914, 918.
42.1-83. Amended by Acts 1994, cc. 64, 955.
42.1-85. Amended by Acts 1990, c. 778; Acts 1994, c. 64; Acts 1998, c. 427.
42.1-86. Amended by Acts 1980, c. 365; Acts 1990, c. 778; Acts 1994, c. 64; Acts 1998, c. 427.
42.1-86.1. Amended by Acts 1998, c. 427.
42.1-87. Amended by Acts 1994, cc. 64, 955.
42.1-88. Amended by Acts 1994, c. 64; Acts 1998, c. 427.
42.1-89. Amended by Acts 1998, c. 427.
42.1-91. Amended by Acts 1994, cc. 64, 955.
43-1. Amended by Acts 1977, c. 294; Acts 1992, cc. 779, 787; Acts 1994, c. 382.
43-2. Amended by Acts 1962, c. 152; Acts 1968, c. 568; Acts 1976, c. 213; Acts 1996, c. 513.
43-3. Amended by Acts 1968, c. 568; Acts 1979, cc. 360, 542; Acts 1980, c. 449; Acts 1992, cc. 72, 779, 787; Acts 2002, c. 273; Acts 2004, c. 240.
43-4. Amended by Acts 1968, c. 568; Acts 1976, c. 413; Acts 1980, c. 491; Acts 1992, cc. 779, 787; Acts 1999, c. 533.
43-4.01. Amended by Acts 2001, c. 532.
43-4.1. Amended by Acts 1964, c. 338; Acts 1968, c. 568; Acts 1985, c. 392.
43-5. Amended by Acts 1968, c. 568.
43-6. Repealed by Acts 1968, c. 568.
43-7. Amended by Acts 1984, c. 521.
43-8. Amended by Acts 1968, c. 568.
43-10. Amended by Acts 1968, c. 568; Acts 1984, c. 647.
43-11. Amended by Acts 1968, c. 568; Acts 2002, c. 772.
43-12. Repealed by Acts 1968, c. 568.
43-13. Amended by Acts 1968, c. 568; Acts 1980, c. 390; Acts 1982, c. 391; Acts 1992, c. 713; Acts 1998, c. 754.
43-13.2. Amended by Acts 2003, c. 400.
43-13.3. Amended by Acts 2003, c. 400.
43-14. Repealed by Acts 1968, c. 568.

Sec.
43-14.1. Amended by Acts 1971, Ex. Sess., c. 155.
43-17. Amended by Acts 1956, c. 399.
43-20. Amended by Acts 1968, c. 568; Acts 1980, c. 574.
43-21. Amended by Acts 1968, c. 568.
43-23.1. Amended by Acts 1976, c. 253.
43-27. Repealed by Acts 1964, c. 219.
43-28. Repealed by Acts 1964, c. 219.
43-29. Amended by Acts 1956, c. 80.
43-32. Amended by Acts 1968, c. 320; Acts 1970, c. 56; Acts 1976, c. 77; Acts 1977, c. 382; Acts 1981, c. 453; Acts 1984, c. 396; Acts 1988, c. 120; Acts 1990, c. 665; Acts 1992, c. 403; Acts 1999, c. 533; Acts 2004, c. 215.
43-33. Amended by Acts 1956, c. 558; Acts 1966, c. 458; Acts 1968, c. 395; Acts 1973, c. 492; Acts 1974, c. 166; Acts 1980, c. 598; Acts 1984, c. 396; Acts 1999, c. 533.
43-34. Amended by Acts 1960, c. 571; Acts 1968, c. 605; Acts 1971, Ex. Sess., c. 155; Acts 1978, c. 59; Acts 1980, c. 598; Acts 1987, c. 37; Acts 1988, c. 227; Acts 1992, c. 111; Acts 1993, c. 759; Acts 1998, c. 868; Acts 2002, c. 401; Acts 2004, c. 369.
43-42, 43-43. Amended by Acts 1994, c. 432.
43-44 to 43-61. Repealed by Acts 1964, c. 219.
43-63. Amended by Acts 1964, c. 272; Acts 1973, c. 317.
43-63.1. Repealed by Acts 2003, c. 455.
43-69. Repealed by Acts 1994, c. 432.
43-70. Amended by Acts 1962, c. 166; Acts 1976, c. 388; Acts 1992, c. 532.
43-71. Amended by Acts 1962, c. 166; Acts 1976, c. 390; Acts 1992, c. 532.
44-1. Amended by Acts 1958, c. 393; Acts 1970, c. 662; Acts 1973, c. 401; Acts 1976, c. 399; Acts 1979, c. 647; Acts 1984, c. 765; Acts 1989, c. 414.
44-2. Amended by Acts 1958, c. 393; Acts 1976, c. 399; Acts 1979, c. 647.
44-2.1. Repealed by Acts 1989, c. 414.
44-3. Amended by Acts 1972, c. 823; Acts 1973, c. 401.
44-4. Amended by Acts 1970, c. 662; Acts 1973, c. 401; Acts 1984, c. 765.
44-5. Amended by Acts 1958, c. 393; Acts 1976, c. 399.
44-6. Amended by Acts 1958, c. 393; Acts 1984, c. 765.
44-8. Amended by Acts 1958, c. 393; Acts 1964, c. 227.
44-9. Amended by Acts 1958, c. 393.
44-10. Amended by Acts 1958, c. 393.
44-11. Amended by Acts 1964, c. 227.
44-12. Repealed by Acts 2004, c. 12.

Sec.
44-13. Amended by Acts 1958, c. 393; Acts 1989, c. 414.
44-14. Amended by Acts 2004, c. 12.
44-15. Amended by Acts 1958, c. 393.
44-16. Amended by Acts 1970, c. 662.
44-17. Amended by Acts 1964, c. 227.
44-19. Amended by Acts 1958, c. 393; Acts 1989, c. 414.
44-20. Amended by Acts 1964, c. 227; Acts 1979, c. 504; Acts 1983, c. 74.
44-21. Amended by Acts 1964, c. 227.
44-23. Repealed by Acts 1984, c. 734.
44-24. Amended by Acts 1958, c. 393.
44-25. Amended by Acts 1958, c. 393; Acts 1964, c. 227.
44-26. Amended by Acts 1958, c. 393.
44-27. Amended by Acts 1958, c. 393; Acts 1964, c. 227; Acts 1970, c. 662.
44-28. Amended by Acts 1958, c. 393; Acts 1970, c. 662.
44-29. Amended by Acts 1958, c. 393.
44-30. Amended by Acts 1958, c. 393; Acts 1964, c. 227; Acts 1970, c. 662.
44-31. Amended by Acts 1964, c. 227.
44-32. Amended by Acts 1958, c. 393.
44-32.1. Amended by Acts 1979, c. 647.
44-33. Amended by Acts 1958, c. 393; Acts 1964, c. 227; Acts 1970, c. 662.
44-34. Repealed by Acts 1958, c. 393.
44-35. Amended by Acts 1958, c. 393.
44-36. Amended by Acts 1958, c. 393.
44-37. Amended by Acts 1958, c. 393.
44-38. Amended by Acts 1958, c. 393.
44-39. Amended by Acts 1958, c. 393.
44-40. Amended by Acts 1958, c. 393; Acts 1976, c. 399; Acts 1984, c. 7; Acts 1987, c. 32.
44-41. Amended by Acts 1958, c. 393; Acts 1964, c. 227.
44-41.1. Amended by Acts 1978, c. 342; Acts 1983, c. 65.
44-42. Amended by Acts 1976, c. 399.
44-43. Amended by Acts 1958, c. 393; Acts 1964, c. 227; Acts 1976, c. 399; Acts 1977, c. 74.
44-44. Amended by Acts 1958, c. 393; Acts 1964, c. 227; Acts 1976, c. 399; Acts 1977, c. 74.
44-44.1. Amended by Acts 1987, c. 206.
44-45. Amended by Acts 1958, c. 393; Acts 1964, c. 227; Acts 1976, c. 399; Acts 1977, c. 74.
44-46. Repealed by Acts 1977, c. 74.
44-47. Amended by Acts 1976, c. 399.
44-48. Amended by Acts 1958, c. 393; Acts 1964, c. 227; Acts 1976, c. 399.
44-49. Amended by Acts 1958, c. 393; Acts 1964, c. 227; Acts 1976, c. 399.
44-50. Amended by Acts 1958, c. 393; Acts 1976, c. 399.
44-51. Amended by Acts 1958, c. 393; Acts 1976, c. 399.

Sec.
44-52. Amended by Acts 1976, c. 399.
44-53. Amended by Acts 1976, c. 399; Acts 1977, c. 74.
44-54. Amended by Acts 1958, c. 393.
44-54.2. Amended by Acts 1980, c. 221.
44-54.6. Amended by Acts 1996, c. 70.
44-55. Amended by Acts 1973, c. 401.
44-59. Amended by Acts 1973, c. 401.
44-60. Amended by Acts 1998, c. 52.
44-62. Amended by Acts 1973, c. 401.
44-63. Amended by Acts 1973, c. 401.
44-64. Amended by Acts 1973, c. 401.
44-69. Amended by Acts 1973, c. 401.
44-75. Repealed by Acts 1988, c. 352.
44-75.1. Amended by Acts 1993, c. 932; Acts 1995, c. 49; Acts 1996, cc. 71, 805.
44-75.1:1. Amended by 1996, cc. 153, 566.
44-76. Amended by Acts 1958, c. 393.
44-78. Repealed by Acts 1988, c. 352.
44-79. Repealed by Acts 1988, c. 352.
44-80. Amended by Acts 1964, c. 227; Acts 1989, c. 414.
44-81. Amended by Acts 1958, c. 393; Acts 1989, c. 414; Acts 1993, c. 112.
44-82. Amended by Acts 1958, c. 393; Acts 1973, c. 401.
44-83. Amended by Acts 1958, c. 393; Acts 1988, c. 352.
44-84. Amended by Acts 1958, c. 393.
44-86. Amended by Acts 1958, c. 393.
44-87. Amended by Acts 1958, c. 393; Acts 1984, c. 765.
44-88. Amended by Acts 1984, c. 765.
44-90. Amended by Acts 1958, c. 393.
44-91, 44-92. Repealed by Acts 1958, c. 393.
44-93. Amended by Acts 1958, c. 393; Acts 1964, c. 227; Acts 1966, c. 295; Acts 1968, c. 503; Acts 1983, c. 590; Acts 1984, c. 540; Acts 1985, c. 103; Acts 1986, c. 611; Acts 1989, cc. 474, 414; Acts 1991, c. 653; Acts 2002, cc. 212, 354.
44-93.5. Amended by Acts 2004, c. 147.
44-95. Repealed by Acts 1958, c. 393.
44-96. Amended by Acts 1958, c. 393; Acts 1984, c. 765.
44-97. Amended by Acts 1984, c. 765.
44-97.1. Amended by Acts 1984, c. 765; Acts 1990, c. 790.
44-98. Amended by Acts 1958, c. 393; Acts 1984, c. 765.
44-99. Amended by Acts 1958, c. 393; Acts 1984, c. 765.
44-100. Amended by Acts 1972, c. 416; Acts 1973, c. 401; Acts 1984, c. 765.
44-101. Repealed by Acts 1958, c. 544.
44-102. Amended by Acts 1958, c. 393; Acts 1984, c. 765.
44-104. Amended by Acts 1958, c. 393; Acts 1984, c. 765.
44-105. Repealed by Acts 1958, c. 393.

Sec.
44-106 to 44-108. Amended by Acts 1958, c. 393.
44-111 to 44-113. Amended by Acts 1958, c. 393.
44-114. Amended by Acts 1999, c. 667; Acts 2004, c. 12.
44-114.4. Amended by Acts 1973, c. 401.
44-115. Amended by Acts 1964, c. 227; Acts 1984, c. 765; Acts 1989, c. 414.
44-116. Amended by Acts 1958, c. 393.
44-117. Amended by Acts 1958, c. 393; Acts 1978, c. 384; Acts 2001, c. 77.
44-117.1, 44-118. Repealed by Acts 1958, c. 393.
44-119. Amended by Acts 1958, c. 393; Acts 1983, c. 157.
44-120. Amended by Acts 1958, c. 393.
44-124. Repealed by Acts 1976, c. 266.
44-125 to 44-128. Repealed by Acts 1976, c. 266.
44-134.1. Repealed by Acts 1981, c. 219.
44-135. Repealed by Acts 1976, c. 266.
44-135.1. Amended by Acts 1996, cc. 137, 802.
44-137. Amended by Acts 1976, c. 266.
44-141 to 44-146.1. Repealed by Acts 1973, c. 260.
44-146.2 to 44-146.12. Repealed by Acts 1975, c. 11.
44-146.14. Amended by Acts 1974, c. 4; reenacted without change by Acts 1975, c. 11.
44-146.16. Amended by Acts 1975, c. 4; reenacted without change by Acts 1975, c. 11; amended by Acts 1978, c. 60; Acts 1979, c. 193; Acts 1981, c. 116; Acts 1984, c. 743; Acts 1993, c. 671; Acts 2004, cc. 773, 1021.
44-146.17. Amended by Acts 1974, c. 4; reenacted without change by Acts 1975, c. 11; amended by Acts 1981, c. 116; Acts 1990, c. 95; Acts 1997, c. 893; Acts 2004, cc. 773, 1021.
44-146.18. Amended by Acts 1974, c. 4; Acts 1975, c. 11; Acts 1979, c. 193; Acts 1984, c. 720; Acts 1985, cc. 443, 447; Acts 1997, c. 893; Acts 2001, c. 841; Acts 2003, c. 622; Acts 2004, c. 690.
44-146.18:2. Amended by Acts 1990, cc. 1, 317.
44-146.19. Amended by Acts 1974, c. 4; reenacted without change by Acts 1975, c. 11; amended by Acts 1978, c. 495; Acts 1982, c. 5; Acts 1990, cc. 404, 945; Acts 1990, Acts 1993, cc. 621, 671, 781; Acts 2003, c. 622; Acts 2004, c. 302.
44-146.21. Amended by Acts 1974, c. 4; reenacted without change by Acts 1975, c. 11; amended by Acts 1976, c. 594; Acts 1986, c. 24; Acts 1990, c. 945; Acts 1994, c. 75.
44-146.22. Amended by Acts 1974, c. 4; reen-

Sec.

acted without change by Acts 1975, c. 11; Acts 2003, c. 848; Acts 2004, c. 690.
44-146.23. Amended by Acts 1979, c. 193; Acts 1984, c. 743.
44-146.24. Amended by Acts 1974, c. 4; reenacted without change by Acts 1975, c. 11.
44-146.27. Amended by Acts 1999, cc. 6, 7.
44-146.28. Amended by Acts 1974, c. 4; reenacted without change by Acts 1975, c. 11; Acts 1997, c. 893.
44-146.30. Amended by Acts 1984, c. 745; Acts 1988, c. 30.
44-146.32. Amended by Acts 1984, c. 322; Acts 1988, c. 56.
44-146.36. Amended by Acts 1989, c. 378.
44-146.40. Amended by Acts 1992, cc. 633, 656; Acts 1994, c. 691.
44-147. Amended by Acts 1952, c. 359.
44-149. Amended by Acts 1977, c. 326.
44-151. Amended by Acts 1952, c. 359.
44-152. Amended by Acts 1977, c. 326.
44-156. Amended by Acts 1977, c. 326.
44-157. Amended by Acts 1977, c. 326.
44-160 to 44-203. Repealed by Acts 1950, p. 188.
44-204. Amended by Acts 1964, c. 227; Acts 1986, c. 611.
45-0.1 to 45-157. Repealed by Acts 1966, c. 594.
45.1-1 to 45.1-161. Repealed by Acts 1994, c. 28.
45.1-161.7. Amended by Acts 1997, c. 390.
45.1-161.8. Amended by Acts 1996, c. 774; Acts 1997, c. 390; Acts 1999, c. 256.
45.1-161.10. Amended by Acts 1996, c. 774.
45.1-161.17. Amended by Acts 1999, c. 256.
45.1-161.19, 45.1-161.20. Amended by Acts 1997, c. 390.
45.1-161.22. Repealed by Acts 1997, c. 390.
45.1-161.31. Amended by Acts 1996, c. 774.
45.1-161.32. Amended by Acts 1999, c. 256.
45.1-161.35. Amended by Acts 2004, c. 855.
45.1-161.38. Amended by Acts 1997, c. 274.
45.1-161.42 to 45.1-161.56. Repealed by Acts 1997, c. 390.
45.1-161.57. Amended by Acts 1996, c. 774; Acts 1997, c. 390.
45.1-161.58. Amended by Acts 1999, c. 256; Acts 2003, cc. 542, 550.
45.1-161.59. Amended by Acts 1996, c. 774; Acts 1997, c. 390; Acts 1999, c. 256.
45.1-161.60, 45.1-161-61. Amended by Acts 1997, c. 390.
45.1-161.62. Amended by Acts 1996, c. 774; Acts 1997, c. 390.
45.1-161.63. Amended by Acts 1996, c. 774; Acts 1997, c. 390; Acts 1999, c. 256.
45.1-161.64. Amended by Acts 1995, c. 265; Acts 1996, c. 774; Acts 1997, c. 390; Acts 1999, c. 256.
45.1-161.65. Amended by Acts 1999, c. 256.
45.1-161.66. Amended by Acts 1999, c. 256.
45.1-161.68. Amended by Acts 1996, c. 774.
45.1-161.70. Amended by Acts 1999, c. 256; Acts 2004, c. 855.
45.1-161.73. Amended by Acts 1996, c. 774.
45.1-161.77, 45.1-161.78. Amended by Acts 1997, c. 390; Acts 1999, c. 256.
45.1-161.80. Amended by Acts 1996, c. 774; Acts 1999, c. 256.
45.1-161.81, 45.1-161.82. Amended by Acts 1997, c. 390.
45.1-161.83. Amended by Acts 1997, c. 390; Acts 1999, c. 256.
45.1-161.87. Amended by Acts 1999, c. 256.
45.1-161.88. Amended by Acts 1996, c. 774; Acts 1999, c. 256.
45.1-161.89. Amended by Acts 1996, c. 774; Acts 1997, c. 390.
45.1-161.90. Amended by Acts 1997, c. 390.
45.1-161.91. Amended by Acts 1996, c. 774.
45.1-161.104. Repealed by Acts 1997, c. 390.
45.1-161.108. Amended by Acts 1996, c. 774; Acts 1999, c. 256.
45.1-161.109. Amended by Acts 1999, c. 256.
45.1-161.112, 45.1-161.113. Repealed by Acts 1996, c. 774.
45.1-161.114. Amended by Acts 1999, c. 256.
45.1-161.115, 45.1-161.116. Amended by Acts 1996, c. 774; Acts 1999, c. 256.
45.1-161.117. Amended by Acts 1999, c. 256.
45.1-161.118. Amended by Acts 1999, c. 256.
45.1-161.121. Amended by Acts 1999, c. 156.
45.1-161.122. Amended by Acts 1996, c. 774.
45.1-161.123. Amended by Acts 1996, c. 774; Acts 1999, c. 256.
45.1-161.124. Amended by Acts 1999, c. 256.
45.1-161.128. Amended by Acts 1996, c. 774.
45.1-161.129. Amended by Acts 1999, c. 256.
45.1-161.133. Amended by Acts 1996, c. 774; Acts 1999, c. 256.
45.1-161.134. Amended by Acts 1999, c. 256.
45.1-161.135. Amended by Acts 1996, c. 774; Acts 1999, c. 256.
45.1-161.139. Amended by Acts 1996, c. 774.
45.1-161.140. Amended by Acts 1999, c. 256.
45.1-161.141. Amended by Acts 1996, c. 774; Acts 1999, c. 256.
45.1-161.142. Amended by Acts 1996, c. 774.
45.1-161.143. Amended by Acts 1999, c. 256.
45.1-161.144. Amended by Acts 1996, c. 774; Acts 1999, c. 256.
45.1-161.145. Amended by Acts 1996, c. 774.
45.1-161.147. Amended by Acts 1996, c. 774; Acts 1999, c. 256.
45.1-161.150 to 45.1-161.152. Amended by Acts 1996, c. 774; Acts 1999, c. 256.
45.1-161.155. Amended by Acts 1997, c. 293.
45.1-161.156. Amended by Acts 1996, c. 774.

Sec.
45.1-161.158. Amended by Acts 1999, c. 256.
45.1-161.159. Amended by Acts 1999, c. 256.
45.1-161.160. Amended by Acts 1996, c. 774.
45.1-161.162. Amended by Acts 1996, c. 774; Acts 1999, c. 256.
45.1-161.164. Amended by Acts 1996, c. 774.
45.1-161.165. Amended by Acts 1999, c. 256.
45.1-161.166 to 45.1-161.169. Amended by Acts 1996, c. 774.
45.1-161.170. Amended by Acts 1999, c. 256.
45.1-161.173. Amended by Acts 1999, c. 256.
45.1-161.177. Amended by Acts 1995, c. 569.
45.1-161.179. Amended by Acts 1995, c. 569.
45.1-161.181. Amended by Acts 1996, c. 774; Acts 1999, c. 256.
45.1-161.185. Repealed by Acts 1999, c. 256.
45.1-161.186, 45.1-161.187. Amended by Acts 1996, c. 774; Acts 1999, c. 256.
45.1-161.188. Amended by Acts 1999, c. 256.
45.1-161.189. Amended by Acts 1999, c. 256.
45.1-161.190. Repealed by Acts 1996, c. 774.
45.1-161.191. Amended by Acts 1996, c. 774; Acts 1999, c. 256.
45.1-161.192. Repealed by Acts 1999, c. 256.
45.1-161.193. Amended by Acts 1999, c. 256.
45.1-161.194. Amended by Acts 1999, c. 256.
45.1-161.195, 45.1-161.196. Amended by Acts 1996, c. 774; Acts 1999, c. 256.
45.1-161.197. Amended by Acts 1999, c. 256.
45.1-161.200. Amended by Acts 1996, c. 774.
45.1-161.202. Amended by Acts 1996, c. 774.
45.1-161.203. Amended by Acts 1999, c. 256.
45.1-161.205. Amended by Acts 1996, c. 774.
45.1-161.206. Amended by Acts 1996, c. 774; Acts 1997, c. 422.
45.1-161.207. Amended by Acts 1999, c. 256.
45.1-161.208. Amended by Acts 1996, c. 774.
45.1-161.209. Amended by Acts 1996, c. 774; Acts 1999, c. 256.
45.1-161.210. Amended by Acts 1996, c. 774; Acts 1999, c. 256.
45.1-161.211. Amended by Acts 1999, c. 256.
45.1-161.213. Amended by Acts 1996, c. 774; Acts 1999, c. 256.
45.1-161.214. Amended by Acts 1996, c. 774.
45.1-161.216. Amended by Acts 1996, c. 774.
45.1-161.220 to 45.1-161.222. Amended by Acts 1996, c. 774; Acts 1999, c. 256.
45.1-161.223 to 45.1-161.226. Amended by Acts 1996, c. 774.
45.1-161.227, 45.1-161.228. Amended by Acts 1996, c. 774; Acts 1999, c. 256.
45.1-161.229. Amended by Acts 1996, c. 774.
45.1-161.230. Repealed by Acts 1999, c. 256.
45.1-161.231. Amended by Acts 1996, c. 774; Acts 1999, c. 256.
45.1-161.234. Amended by Acts 1996, c. 774; Acts 1999, c. 256.
45.1-161.235. Amended by Acts 1996, c. 774; Acts 1999, c. 256.

Sec.
45.1-161.249. Amended by Acts 1996, c. 774; Acts 1999, c. 256.
45.1-161.251. Amended by Acts 1999, c. 256.
45.1-161.256 to 45.1-161.258. Amended by Acts 1996, c. 774; Acts 1999, c. 256.
45.1-161.263. Amended by Acts 1999, c. 256.
45.1-161.266. Amended by Acts 1999, c. 256.
45.1-161.269. Amended by Acts 1999, c. 256.
45.1-161.270. Amended by Acts 1996, c. 774; Acts 1999, c. 256.
45.1-161.276. Amended by Acts 1996, c. 774.
45.1-161.279. Amended by Acts 1996, c. 774.
45.1-161.280. Amended by Acts 1996, c. 774; Acts 1999, c. 256.
45.1-161.282. Amended by Acts 1999, c. 256.
45.1-161.285. Amended by Acts 1999, c. 256.
45.1-161.286. Amended by Acts 1996, c. 774.
45.1-161.290. Amendment by Acts 1999, c. 256.
45.1-161.292. Amended by Acts 2003, cc. 542, 401, 550.
45.1-161.292:2. Amended by Acts 1998, c. 695.
45.1-161.292:4. Amended by Acts 1998, c. 695.
45.1-161.292:7. Amended by Acts 1998, c. 695.
45.1-161.292:8. Amended by Acts 1998, c. 695.
45.1-161.292:15. Amended by Acts 1998, c. 695.
45.1-161.292:26. Amended by Acts 1998, c. 695.
45.1-161.292:29. Amended by Acts 1998, c. 695.
45.1-161.292:30. Amended by Acts 1998, c. 695.
45.1-161.292:32. Amended by Acts 1998, c. 695.
45.1-161.292:33. Amended by Acts 1998, c. 695.
45.1-161.292:35. Amended by Acts 1998, c. 695.
45.1-161.292:36. Amended by Acts 1998, c. 695.
45.1-161.292:37. Amended by Acts 1998, c. 695.
45.1-161.292:38. Amended by Acts 1998, c. 695.
45.1-161.292:43. Amended by Acts 2004, c. 855.
45.1-161.292:44. Amended by Acts 1998, c. 695.
45.1-161.292:46. Amended by Acts 1998, c. 695.
45.1-161.292:47. Amended by Acts 1998, c. 695.
45.1-161.292:49. Amended by Acts 1998, c. 695.
45.1-161.292:50. Amended by Acts 1998, c. 695.
45.1-161.292:51. Amended by Acts 1998, c. 695.
45.1-161.292:54. Amended by Acts 1998, c. 695.

Sec.

45.1-161.292:55. Amended by Acts 1998, c. 695.
45.1-161.292:56. Amended by Acts 1998, c. 695.
45.1-161.292:62. Amended by Acts 1998, c. 695.
45.1-161.292:63. Amended by Acts 1998, c. 695.
45.1-161.292:64. Amended by Acts 1998, c. 695.
45.1-161.292:66. Amended by Acts 1998, c. 695.
45.1-161.292:70. Amended by Acts 1998, c. 695.
45.1-161.292:71. Amended by Acts 1998, c. 695.
45.1-161.293. Amended by Acts 1997, c. 390.
45.1-161.294. Amended by Acts 1996, c. 774; Acts 1998, c. 695.
45.1-161.296. Amended by Acts 1997, c. 390; Acts 1998, c. 695.
45.1-161.304. Amended by Acts 1997, c. 390.
45.1-161.305. Amended by Acts 1996, c. 774; Acts 1998, c. 695.
45.1-161.307. Amended by Acts 1997, c. 390; Acts 1998, c. 695.
45.1-161.309 to 45.1-161.311. Amended by Acts 1997, c. 390.
45.1-161.320. Amended by Acts 2003, c. 940.
45.1-162 to 45.1-179. Repealed by Acts 1972, c. 785.
45.1-179.2. Amended by Acts 1984, c. 590.
45.1-179.11. Amended by Acts 1986, c. 615.
45.1-180. Amended by Acts 1972, c. 206; Acts 1974, c. 312; Acts 1977, c. 312; Acts 1984, c. 590.
45.1-180.1. Repealed by Acts 1974, c. 96.
45.1-180.2, 45.1-180.3. Amended by Acts 1984, c. 590.
45.1-181. Amended by Acts 1972, c. 206; Acts 1974, c. 312; Acts 1977, c. 312; Acts 1983, c. 322; Acts 1996, cc. 648, 659; Acts 2003, cc. 542, 550.
45.1-182. Repealed by Acts 1977, c. 312.
45.1-182.1. Amended by Acts 1984, c. 590.
45.1-184.2. Amended by Acts 1996, cc. 648, 659; Acts 2003, cc. 542, 550.
45.1-183. Amended by Acts 1970, c. 245; Acts 1972, c. 206; Acts 1974, c. 312; Acts 1977, c. 312.
45.1-184. Amended by Acts 1974, c. 312; Acts 1977, c. 312.
45.1-185. Amended by Acts 1974, c. 312; Acts 1977, c. 312.
45.1-186. Repealed by Acts 1977, c. 312.
45.1-187. Amended by Acts 1974, c. 312.
45.1-188. Amended by Acts 1974, c. 312.
45.1-189. Repealed by Acts 1977, c. 312.
45.1-190. Repealed by Acts 1974, c. 312.
45.1-191. Amended by Acts 1974, c. 312.
45.1-193. Repealed by Acts 1977, c. 312.
45.1-194. Amended by Acts 1974, c. 312; Acts 1979, c. 302; Acts 1982, c. 117.
45.1-195. Amended by Acts 1974, c. 312; Acts 1977, c. 312; Acts 1979, c. 68; Acts 1980, cc. 677, 728.
45.1-196. Amended by Acts 1986, c. 615.
45.1-197. Amended by Acts 1974, c. 312; Acts 1977, c. 312.
45.1-197.1. Repealed by Acts 1974, c. 96.
45.1-197.2. Repealed by Acts 1984, c. 590.
45.1-197.18. Amended by Acts 1984, c. 590.
45.1-198, 45.1-199. Amended by Acts 1984, c. 590.
45.1-200. Amended by Acts 1977, c. 515; Acts 1984, c. 590.
45.1-200.1. Amended by Acts 1980, c. 364; Acts 1984, c. 590.
45.1-201. Amended by Acts 1974, c. 573; Acts 1984, c. 590.
45.1-202. Amended by Acts 1974, cc. 573, 651; Acts 1984, c. 590.
45.1-203. Amended by Acts 1974, c. 573; Acts 1984, c. 590.
45.1-204. Amended by Acts 1974, c. 573.
45.1-205. Amended by Acts 1974, c. 573.
45.1-206. Amended by Acts 1973, c. 418.
45.1-207. Amended by Acts 1974, c. 573; Acts 1984, c. 590.
45.1-209.1. Amended by Acts 1984, c. 590.
45.1-212. Amended by Acts 1974, c. 651; Acts 1984, c. 590.
45.1-212.1. Repealed by Acts 1984, c. 590.
45.1-213. Amended by Acts 1978, c. 92; Acts 1984, c. 590.
45.1-219. Amended by Acts 1996, c. 774.
45.1-220.3. Amended by Acts 1982, c. 425; Acts 1984, c. 590.
45.1-220.5. Amended by Acts 1984, c. 590.
45.1-221. Amended by Acts 1984, c. 590; Acts 1997, c. 390.
45.1-222. Amended by Acts 1984, c. 590; Acts 1999, c. 256.
45.1-223. Amended by Acts 1984, c. 590.
45.1-228, 45.1-229. Amended by Acts 1984, c. 590.
45.1-224. Amended by Acts 1999, c. 256.
45.1-225. Amended by Acts 1997, c. 390.
45.1-225.1. Amended by Acts 1998, c. 695.
45.1-225.2. Amended by Acts 1998, c. 695.
45.1-230. Amended by Acts 1982, c. 425; Acts 1984, c. 590.
45.1-231. Amended by Acts 1984, c. 590.
45.1-232. Repealed by Acts 1984, c. 590.
45.1-234. Amended by Acts 1980, c. 364; Acts 1983, c. 134; Acts 1984, c. 590.
45.1-235. Amended by Acts 1982, c. 246; Acts 1984, c. 590; Acts 1999, c. 114; Acts 2003, cc. 542, 550.
45.1-236, 45.1-237. Amended by Acts 1984, c. 590.
45.1-239. Amended by Acts 1984, c. 590.
45.1-240. Amended by Acts 1983, c. 92; Acts 1986, c. 615.

Sec.
45.1-241. Amended by Acts 1984, c. 590; Acts 1997, c. 285; Acts 1998, c. 692.
45.1-242. Amended by Acts 1984, c. 590.
45.1-243. Amended by Acts 1984, c. 590; Acts 1993, c. 582; Acts 1996, cc. 409, 410.
45.1-244. Amended by Acts 1984, cc. 323, 590.
45.1-246. Amended by Acts 1980, c. 510; Acts 1993, c. 663.
45.1-247, 45.1-248. Amended by Acts 1984, c. 590.
45.1-249. Amended by Acts 1983, c. 93.
45.1-250. Amended by Acts 1984, c. 590.
45.1-251. Amended by Acts 1983, c. 93; Acts 1984, c. 590; Acts 1986, c. 615.
45.1-252. Amended by Acts 1984, c. 590.
45.1-253. Amended by Acts 1984, c. 590; Acts 1988, c. 295.
45.1-254. Amended by Acts 1986, c. 615.
45.1-255. Repealed by Acts 1984, c. 714.
45.1-255.1. Repealed by Acts 1988, c. 489.
45.1-256. Amended by Acts 1984, cc. 230, 590; Acts 1996, c. 758.
45.1-258. Amended by Acts 1993, c. 582.
45.1-260. Amended by Acts 1984, c. 590.
45.1-261.1. Amended by Acts 1984, c. 590; Acts 1991, c. 495.
45.1-262. Amended by Acts 1984, c. 590.
45.1-270.2. Amended by Acts 1983, c. 131; Acts 1989, c. 432.
45.1-270.3. Amended by Acts 1983, c. 131; Acts 1989, c. 432; Acts 1991, c. 495.
45.1-270.3:1. Repealed by Acts 1991, c. 495.
45.1-270.4. Amended by Acts 1983, c. 131; Acts 1987, c. 468; Acts 1991, c. 495.
45.1-270.4:1. Amended by Acts 1991, c. 495.
45.1-270.5. Amended by Acts 1984, c. 590.
45.1-270.6. Amended by Acts 1987, c. 468.
45.1-270.7. Amended by Acts 1984, c. 590; Acts 1985, c. 448.
45.1-273. Amended by Acts 1984, c. 590.
45.1-279. Amended by Acts 1984, c. 590.
45.1-282. Amended by Acts 1984, c. 590.
45.1-283. Amended by Acts 1983, c. 3.
45.1-286 to 45.1-361. Repealed by Acts 1990, c. 92.
45.1-361.1. Amended by Acts 1990, c. 92; Acts 1992, c. 812; Acts 1993, c. 254.
45.1-361.2, 45.1-361.3. Amended by Acts 1990, c. 92.
45.1-361.9. Amended by Acts 1997, c. 759.
45.1-361.10 to 45.1-361.12. Amended by Acts 1990, c. 92.
45.1-361.13. Amended by Acts 1990, c. 92; Acts 1998, c. 159.
45.1-361.14, 45.1-361.15. Amended by Acts 1990, c. 92.
45.1-361.16. Amended by Acts 1990, c. 92.
45.1-361.17. Amended by Acts 1996, c. 854; Acts 1997, c. 759.
45.1-361.18. Amended by Acts 1990, c. 92.
45.1-361.19. Amended by Acts 1990, c. 92; Acts 1997, c. 759.
45.1-361.20. Amended by Acts 1990, c. 92.
45.1-361.21. Amended by Acts 1990, c. 92; Acts 1995, c. 269; Acts 1996, c. 854.
45.1-361.22. Amended by Acts 1999, c. 122.
45.1-361.23. Amended by Acts 1997, c. 759.
45.1-361.24 to 45.1-361.26. Amended by Acts 1990, c. 92.
45.1-361.27. Amended by Acts 1990, c. 92; Acts 1997, c. 421.
45.1-361.28. Amended by Acts 1990, c. 92.
45.1-361.29. Amended by Acts 1990, c. 92; Acts 1994, c. 957; Acts 1995, c. 269; Acts 1996, c. 854; Acts 1997, cc. 759, 765; Acts 1998, c. 229; Acts 2003, cc. 542, 550.
45.1-361.30. Amended by Acts 1990, c. 92; Acts 1996, c. 854.
45.1-361.33. Amended by Acts 1996, c. 854; Acts 2003, cc. 542, 550.
45.1-361.35. Amended by Acts 1990, c. 92; Acts 1996, c. 854; Acts 1998, c. 228; Acts 2002, c. 277.
45.1-361.36. Amended by Acts 1990, c. 92.
45.1-361.38. Amended by Acts 1992, c. 361.
45.1-361.39. Amended by Acts 1990, c. 92.
45.1-361.41. Amended by Acts 1993, c. 276.
45.1-362 to 45.1-380. Repealed by Acts 1988, c. 295.
45.1-382. Amended by Acts 1984, c. 590.
45.1-390.1. Repealed by Acts 1993, c. 274.
45.1-392. Amended by Acts 1996, cc. 582, 593.
46-1 to 46-553. Repealed by Acts 1958, c. 541.
46.1-1 through 46.1-570. Repealed by Acts 1989, c. 727.
46.2-100. Amended by Acts 1990, cc. 45, 418; Acts 1992, c. 98; Acts 1993, c. 133; Acts 1994, c. 866; Acts 1996, cc. 943, 994; Acts 1997, cc. 9, 186, 486, 783, 904; Acts 1998, c. 888; Acts 1999, cc. 67, 77; Acts 2001, c. 834; Acts 2002, cc. 214, 234, 254; Acts 2003, cc. 29, 46; Acts 2004, cc. 746, 796.
46.2-102. Amended by Acts 1995, c. 132.
46.2-105.1. Amended by Acts 1990, c. 964.
46.2-105.2. Amended by Acts 2002, cc. 767, 834; Acts 2003, cc. 817, 819.
46.2-106. Amended by Acts 1995, cc. 744, 803; Acts 2003, c. 299.
46.2-111. Amended by Acts 2003, c. 971.
46.2-113. Amended by Acts 1992, c. 533; Acts 1997, c. 637; Acts 2003, c. 844.
46.2-200. Amended by Acts 1990, cc. 1, 317; Acts 1995, cc. 744, 803; Acts 1997, c. 283; Acts 2001, cc. 70, 82.
46.2-205. Amended by Acts 1999, c. 308; Acts 2002, c. 110; Acts 2003, c. 991.
46.2-206. Amended by Acts 1997, c. 423.
46.2-207. Amended by Acts 2001, c. 800; Acts 2002, c. 719.

Sec.

46.2-208. Amended by Acts 1991, c. 307; Acts 1993, cc. 48, 348; Acts 1994, cc. 304, 700, 830, 959; Acts 1995, cc. 118, 657, 676, 686; Acts 1998, cc. 147, 802; Acts 1998, Sp. Sess., c. 2; Acts 2002, cc. 131, 710; Acts 2003, c. 768; Acts 2004, cc. 811, 855.

46.2-209. Amended by Acts 1994, c. 959; Acts 1995, c. 118.

46.2-210. Amended by Acts 1994, c. 959.

46.2-212.1. Amended by Acts 1996, cc. 943, 994.

46.2-214. Amended by Acts 1991, c. 167.

46.2-216.1. Amended by Acts 1996, cc. 943, 994.

46.2-216.2. Amended by Acts 1996, cc. 943, 994.

46.2-216.3. Repealed by Acts 2003, c. 1042, cl. 12.

46.2-217. Amended by Acts 1993, c. 533.

46.2-221. Amended by Acts 2003, c. 301.

46.2-223. Amended by Acts 1990, cc. 1, 317; Acts 1998, c. 743.

46.2-224. Amended by Acts 1990, cc. 1, 317; Acts 1992, c. 95; Acts 2002, c. 249.

46.2-301. Amended by Acts 1991, c. 64; Acts 1992, c. 273; Acts 1993, c. 24; Acts 1994, cc. 359, 363; Acts 1997, c. 691; Acts 2004, cc. 461, 801, 948.

46.2-301.1. Amended by Acts 1994, 1st Sp. Sess., c. 10; Acts 1995, cc. 426, 435; Acts 1997, cc. 378, 478, 691.

46.2-302. Amended by Acts 1991, c. 118.

46.2-307. Amended by Acts 1997, c. 486; Acts 2002, c. 755.

46.2-308. Amended by Acts 1994, c. 356; Acts 2002, cc. 767, 834.

46.2-309. Amended by Acts 1993, c. 444; Acts 2002, c. 755.

46.2-314. Amended by Acts 1997, c. 801.

46.2-316. Amended by Acts 1997, c. 691.

46.2-320. Amended by Acts 1995, c. 595; Acts 1996, cc. 785, 1013; Acts 1997, cc. 473, 794, 857, 898; Acts 1999, c. 615; Acts 2001, cc. 645, 779.

46.2-321. Amended by Acts 1990, c. 418.

46.2-322. Amended by Acts 1997, c. 801; Acts 2004, cc. 351, 855.

46.2-323. Amended by Acts 1993, cc. 471, 501; Acts 1994, c. 362; Acts 1998, c. 322; Acts 2002, cc. 535, 867; Acts 2003, c. 584.

46.2-323.1. Amended by Acts 2002, cc. 767, 834.

46.2-324. Amended by Acts 1996, cc. 943, 994; Acts 2002, cc. 767, 834.

46.2-325. Amended by Acts 1995, c. 847; Acts 1997, c. 841.

46.2-329. Amended by Acts 2004, c. 948.

46.2-330. Amended by Acts 1993, cc. 471, 501; Acts 1997, c. 486; Acts 2001, cc. 645, 779; Acts 2003, c. 333; Acts 2004, cc. 112, 218, 975.

Sec.

46.2-331. Repealed by Acts 2004, c. 975.

46.2-332. Amended by Acts 1993, c. 70; Acts 1996, cc. 943, 994; Acts 1997, cc. 104, 493; Acts 1999, c. 593.

46.2-334. Amended by Acts 1991, c. 214; Acts 1993, cc. 471, 501, 930; Acts 1995, c. 535; Acts 1996, cc. 943, 994, 1011, 1022; Acts 1997, c. 841; Acts 1999, cc. 459, 462, 887; Acts 2001, cc. 659, 665, 851; Acts 2003, c. 951.

46.2-334.01. Amended by Acts 1998, cc. 124, 792; Acts 2001, cc. 655, 659, 665; Acts 2002, cc. 61, 807; Acts 2003, cc. 308, 323, 771.

46.2-335. Amended by Acts 1993, cc. 471, 501; Acts 1995, cc. 254, 337, 535, 847; Acts 1996, cc. 892, 894, 918, 943, 994, 1011, 1022, 1035; Acts 1997, c. 841; Acts 1998, c. 322; Acts 1999, cc. 459, 462; Acts 2001, cc. 659, 665; Acts 2004, cc. 733, 805.

46.2-335.2. Amended by Acts 2001, cc. 659, 665; Acts 2002, c. 535.

46.2-336. Amended by Acts 1993, cc. 53, 930; Acts 1998, c. 472.

46.2-338. Repealed by Acts 1989, c. 705.

46.2-340. Amended by Acts 1993, c. 52; Acts 1999, c. 463.

46.2-341. Repealed by Acts 1989, c. 705.

46.2-341.4. Amended by Acts 1990, c. 218; Acts 1993, c. 70; Acts 1998, c. 883.

46.2-341.7. Amended by Acts 1993, c. 70.

46.2-341.11. Amended by Acts 2002, cc. 767, 834.

46.2-341.15. Amended by Acts 2002, c. 767, 834.

46.2-341.16. Amended by Acts 1990, c. 218.

46.2-341.16:1. Amended by Acts 2004, c. 109.

46.2-341.18. Amended by Acts 1992, c. 830; Acts 1997, c. 691.

46.2-341.20. Amended by Acts 1990, c. 218.

46.2-341.21. Amended by Acts 1990, c. 218; Acts 1995, cc. 145, 151.

46.2-341.22. Amended by Acts 1992, c. 830.

46.2-341.24. Amended by Acts 1992, c. 830; Acts 1994, cc. 359, 363.

46.2-341.25. Amended by Acts 1990, cc. 218, 825; Acts 1992, c. 830; Acts 1996, cc. 154, 952.

46.2-341.26. Repealed by Acts 1992, c. 830.

46.2-341.26:2. Amended by Acts 1993, c. 673.

46.2-341.26:3. Amended by Acts 2001, c. 654.

46.2-341.26:5. Amended by Acts 2004, cc. 150, 440.

46.2-341.26:6 through 46.2-341.26:8. Amended by Acts 2003, cc. 933, 936.

46.2-341.26:10. Amended by Acts 2001, c. 654.

46.2-341.26:11. Amended by Acts 2003, cc. 933, 936.

Sec.
46.2-341.27. Amended by Acts 1992, c. 830; Acts 1994, cc. 359, 363.
46.2-341.28. Amended by Acts 1993, c. 673; Acts 1997, c. 691; Acts 2004, c. 461.
46.2-341.31. Amended by Acts 1990, c. 218; Acts 1992, c. 830.
46.2-342. Amended by Acts 1990, c. 159; Acts 1993, cc. 118, 986; Acts 1995, cc. 350, 372; Acts 1997, c. 486; Acts 1998, c. 322; Acts 1999, c. 330; Acts 2001, cc. 148, 157; Acts 2002, cc. 135, 767, 834; Acts 2003, cc. 306, 335.
46.2-343. Amended by Acts 1995, c. 468; Acts 1997, c. 486; Acts 1999, c. 593.
46.2-345. Amended by Acts 1993, cc. 471, 501; Acts 1997, c. 486; Acts 1998, c. 322; Acts 1999, c. 593; Acts 2002, cc. 767, 834.
46.2-346. Amended by Acts 2004, c. 722.
46.2-347. Amended by Acts 1992, c. 531; Acts 1993, c. 866.
46.2-348. Amended by Acts 1993, cc. 471, 501.
46.2-351 to 46.2-355. Repealed by Acts 1999, cc. 945, 987.
46.2-356. Amended by Acts 1995, c. 799; Acts 1999, cc. 945, 987.
46.2-357. Amended by Acts 1990, c. 828; Acts 1993, c. 677; Acts 1994, c. 50; Acts 1995, c. 799; Acts 1997, cc. 5, 344; Acts 1998, c. 298; Acts 1999, cc. 945, 987; Acts 2004, c. 461.
46.2-358. Amended by Acts 1993, c. 617; Acts 1995, c. 799.
46.2-360. Amended by Acts 1990, c. 828; Acts 1993, c. 514; Acts 1994, c. 573; Acts 1995, cc. 486, 799; Acts 1996, c. 374; Acts 1998, c. 749; Acts 1999, cc. 742, 945, 987.
46.2-361. Amended by Acts 1992, c. 568; Acts 1993, cc. 291, 518, 687; Acts 1995, c. 799; Acts 1998, c. 749; Acts 1999, cc. 945, 987.
46.2-362. Amended by Acts 1996, c. 414; Acts 1999, cc. 945, 987.
46.2-364. Amended by Acts 1996, cc. 474, 489; Acts 2002, c. 289. =sn46.2-368. Amended by Acts 1991, c. 374; Acts 1995, c. 85; Acts 1997, c. 553.
46.2-370. Amended by Acts 1992, c. 99.
46.2-373. Amended by Acts 1992, cc. 149, 413.
46.2-380. Amended by Acts 1997, c. 801; Acts 1998, c. 522.
46.2-382. Amended by Acts 1998, c. 147.
46.2-383. Amended by Acts 2002, c. 258.
46.2-384. Amended by Acts 1992, c. 838; Acts 1997, c. 691.
46.2-386. Amended by Acts 1992, c. 838; Acts 1993, c. 930.
46.2-389. Amended by Acts 1990, c. 949; Acts 1992, cc. 109, 891; Acts 1997, cc. 486, 691; Acts 1999, cc. 945, 987.
46.2-390. Amended by Acts 1992, c. 109.
46.2-390.1. Amended by Acts 1993, c. 920; Acts 1997, c. 486; Acts 2001, c. 790.
46.2-391. Amended by Acts 1990, c. 949; Acts 1994, c. 573; Acts 1995, c. 486; Acts 1997, cc. 691, 706; Acts 1999, cc. 945, 987; Acts 2001, c. 739; Acts 2004, cc. 461, 937, 951.
46.2-391.01. Amended by Acts 2002, c. 811.
46.2-391.1. Amended by Acts 1994, cc. 841, 945.
46.2-391.2. Amended by Acts 1996, cc. 865, 1007; Acts 1997, c. 691; Acts 2001, c. 779; Acts 2003, c. 605; Acts 2004, cc. 937, 960.
46.2-391.4. Amended by Acts 1997, c. 691.
46.2-392. Amended by Acts 1996, c. 615; Acts 2001, cc. 645, 779; Acts 2004, c. 361.
46.2-393. Amended by Acts 2004, c. 115.
46.2-394. Amended by Acts 1997, c. 691.
46.2-395. Amended by Acts 1992, c. 891; Acts 1993, c. 24; Acts 1994, cc. 841, 945; Acts 1997, c. 691; Acts 1998, c. 831; Acts 2001, cc. 278, 414; Acts 2002, c. 246; Acts 2003, c. 218.
46.2-400. Amended by Acts 1997, c. 921.
46.2-402. Amended by Acts 1996, cc. 943, 994.
46.2-410.1. Amended by Acts 2002, c. 811.
46.2-411. Amended by Acts 1992, c. 109; Acts 1998, c. 703; Acts 1999, cc. 945, 897; Acts 2001, cc. 133, 160; Acts 2002, c. 60.
46.2-416. Amended by Acts 1993, c. 24; Acts 1994, c. 345; Acts 1996, cc. 943, 994; Acts 2001, c. 414.
46.2-417. Amended by Acts 1992, c. 109; Acts 2004, c. 998.
46.2-427. Amended by Acts 2003, c. 316.
46.2-434. Amended by Acts 1992, c. 109; Acts 1997, c. 486.
46.2-438. Amended by Acts 1997, c. 283.
46.2-440. Amended by Acts 1993, c. 164; Acts 1995, c. 121.
46.2-441. Amended by Acts 1995, c. 121.
46.2-487. Amended by Acts 1994, c. 255.
46.2-489, 46.2-490. Amended by Acts 1995, c. 672.
46.2-490. Amended by Acts 2002, c. 177; Acts 2004, c. 622.
46.2-490.2. Repealed by Acts 2004, c. 622.
46.2-491. Amended by Acts 1995, c. 672.
46.2-492. Amended by Acts 1992, c. 856; Acts 1998, c. 430; Acts 2002, cc. 752, 782.
46.2-495. Amended by Acts 1995, c. 672; Acts 1998, cc. 124, 792.
46.2-496, 46.2-497. Repealed by Acts 1995, c. 672.
46.2-498. Amended by Acts 1995, cc. 226, 672;

Sec.
Acts 1996, cc. 307, 1035; Acts 1998, cc. 124, 792.
46.2-499. Amended by Acts 1994, c. 849; Acts 1995, c. 672; Acts 1996, cc. 943, 994; Acts 2001, cc. 645, 779.
46.2-500. Amended by Acts 1995, c. 672.
46.2-501. Amended by Acts 1995, c. 672; Acts 2002, c. 385.
46.2-502. Amended by Acts 1992, c. 459; Acts 1995, c. 672; Acts 1996, c. 171; Acts 1998, c. 437.
46.2-503. Amended by Acts 1995, c. 672.
46.2-505, 46.2-506. Amended by Acts 1995, c. 672; Acts 2002, c. 724.
46.2-600. Amended by Acts 2003, c. 297.
46.2-604. Amended by Acts 1990, c. 79; Acts 1998, cc. 285, 302; Acts 2004, c. 692.
46.2-605. Amended by Acts 1996, cc. 591, 917.
46.2-606. Amended by Acts 1996, cc. 943, 994.
46.2-613. Amended by Acts 1997, c. 283; Acts 1999, c. 212; Acts 2002, c. 93.
46.2-619. Amended by Acts 1996, c. 761.
46.2-620. Amended by Acts 2002, c. 93.
46.2-622. Amended by Acts 2002, c. 432.
46.2-623. Amended by Acts 1998, Sp. Sess., c. 2.
46.2-626. Repealed by Acts 1996, cc. 591, 917.
46.2-629. Amended by Acts 2004, c. 724.
46.2-640. Amended by Acts 1999, c. 299.
46.2-649. Amended by Acts 1997, c. 283; Acts 2002, c. 47.
46.2-651. Amended by Acts 2001, c. 192.
46.2-652. Amended by Acts 1997, c. 283; Acts 2003, c. 314.
46.2-653. Amended by Acts 1997, c. 283; Acts 1999, c. 77; Acts 2003, c. 314.
46.2-659. Repealed by Acts 1997, c. 283.
46.2-665. Amended by Acts 1994, c. 253; Acts 2001, c. 327.
46.2-666. Amended by Acts 1995, c. 126; Acts 1998, c. 323.
46.2-667. Amended by Acts 1996, c. 55.
46.2-668. Amended by Acts 2003, c. 896.
46.2-674. Amended by Acts 1997, c. 500.
46.2-676. Amended by Acts 1995, c. 670; Acts 1996, c. 920; Acts 1997, cc. 485, 783, 904; Acts 1999, c. 211; Acts 2002, cc. 44, 98; Acts 2003, c. 105; Acts 2004, c. 746.
46.2-681. Repealed by Acts 1999, c. 329.
46.2-687. Amended by Acts 1990, c. 418.
46.2-692. Amended by Acts 1992, c. 631; Acts 1997, c. 486.
46.2-692.1. Amended by Acts 1997, cc. 774, 816.
46.2-694. Amended by Acts 1990, c. 508; Acts 1991, c. 472; Acts 1994, c. 279; Acts 1997, c. 283; Acts 2002, c. 794; Acts 2004, c. 194.
46.2-695. Amended by Acts 2002, c. 337.

Sec.
46.2-696, 46.2-697. Amended by Acts 1997, c. 283.
46.2-697.1. Repealed by Acts 2003, c. 1042, cl. 12.
46.2-698. Amended by Acts 1996, cc. 943, 994; Acts 1997, cc. 774, 816; Acts 2004, c. 663.
46.2-699. Repealed by Acts 1997, c. 283.
46.2-700. Amended by Acts 2004, c. 478.
46.2-701. Amended by Acts 1997, c. 283.
46.2-703. Amended by Acts 1995, cc. 744, 803; Acts 2002, c. 239; Acts 2004, c. 376.
46.2-706. Amended by Acts 1993, c. 127; Acts 1996, cc. 477, 489; Acts 1998, c. 404.
46.2-706.1 to 46.2-707. Amended by Acts 1996, cc. 474, 489.
46.2-708. Amended by Acts 1998, c. 404.
46.2-711. Amended by Acts 1993, c. 290; Acts 1995, c. 46; Acts 1997, cc. 774, 816; Acts 2001, c. 596.
46.2-712. Amended by Acts 1997, c. 283; Acts 1999, c. 593.
46.2-714. Amended by Acts 1997, c. 283.
46.2-716. Amended by Acts 2001, c. 19.
46.2-717. Repealed by Acts 1997, c. 486.
46.2-724. Amended by Acts 1995, c. 46; Acts 1997, cc. 774, 816.
46.2-725. Amended by Acts 1995, c. 747; Acts 1996, cc. 922, 1026; Acts 1997, cc. 774, 816; Acts 2003, c. 923; Acts 2004, c. 747.
46.2-725.1. Repealed by Acts 1995, c. 747.
46.2-726. Amended by Acts 1992, c. 141; Acts 1995, c. 747; Acts 1997, cc. 94, 283; Acts 2000, c. 126; Acts 2001, c. 20.
46.2-728.3. Amended by Acts 1995, c. 747.
46.2-729. Repealed by Acts 1995, c. 747.
46.2-730. Amended by Acts 1999, c. 292; Acts 2000, c. 259; Acts 2004, c. 796.
46.2-731. Amended by Acts 1993, c. 566; Acts 1994, cc. 225, 866; Acts 1995, cc. 776, 805; Acts 1997, cc. 783, 904; Acts 2004, c. 692.
46.2-732. Amended by Acts 1995, c. 747.
46.2-733. Amended by Acts 1998, c. 370; Acts 2004, c. 788.
46.2-734. Amended by Acts 2004, c. 678.
46.2-734.1. Repealed by Acts 2002, c. 90.
46.2-735, 46.2-736. Amended by Acts 1996, c. 1026.
46.2-736.01, 46.2-736.02. Repealed by Acts 2004, c. 717.
46.2-736.2. Amended by Acts 1996, c. 1026; Acts 2003, c. 921; Acts 2004, c. 747.
46.2-737. Amended by Acts 1995, c. 747; Acts 2004, c. 984.
46.2-738. Amended by Acts 1996, cc. 943, 994.
46.2-738.1. Repealed by Acts 2002, c. 90.

Sec.
46.2-739. Amended by Acts 1994, c. 866; Acts 1997, cc. 774, 816.
46.2-740. Amended by Acts 1995, c. 747.
46.2-741. Amended by Acts 1995, c. 747; Acts 1997, cc. 774, 816.
46.2-742. Amended by Acts 1994, c. 914; Acts 1995, c. 747; Acts 1996, cc. 922, 1026; Acts 2004, c. 747.
46.2-742.1. Amended by Acts 1996, c. 1026; Acts 1997, cc. 774, 816; Acts 1999, c. 907; Acts 2002, c. 864; Acts 2004, c. 747.
46.2-742.2. Amended by Acts 1996, c. 1026; Acts 1997, cc. 774, 816; Acts 2004, c. 747.
46.2-742.3. Repealed by Acts 2004, c. 984.
46.2-743. Amended by Acts 1995, c. 747; Acts 1996, c. 1026; Acts 1997, cc. 774, 816; Acts 1999, cc. 883, 907; Acts 2000, cc. 75, 190; Acts 2002, cc. 90, 864.
46.2-744. Amended by Acts 1995, cc. 252, 747.
46.2-745. Amended by Acts 1995, c. 747; Acts 2004, c. 747.
46.2-746. Amended by Acts 1994, c. 127.
46.2-746.01. Repealed by Acts 2002, c. 90.
46.2-746.2. Repealed by Acts 1999, c. 907.
46.2-746.2:1. Repealed by Acts 2003, c. 295.
46.2-746.2:2. Amended by Acts 2002, c. 864.
46.2-746.2:2.1. Repealed by Acts 2004, cc. 717, 984.
46.2-746.3. Amended by Acts 1996, c. 1026; Acts 2004, c. 747.
46.2-746.4. Amended by Acts 1996, c. 1026; Acts 1997, cc. 774, 816; Acts 2000, cc. 75, 111; Acts 2002, c. 90; Acts 2003, c. 921; Acts 2004, c. 747.
46.2-746.4:1. Repealed by Acts 2000, c. 766.
46.2-746.4:3. Repealed by Acts 2004, c. 717.
46.2-746.5. Amended by Acts 1997, cc. 774, 816.
46.2-746.6:1. Repealed by Acts 2000, cc. 75, 766.
46.2-746.6:2. Repealed by Acts 2004, c. 717.
46.2-746.7. Amended by Acts 1996, c. 1026; Acts 1998, c. 175; Acts 1999, c. 907; Acts 2000, c. 75; Acts 2002, cc. 90, 864; Acts 2003, c. 925; Acts 2004, cc. 717, 747.
46.2-746.8. Amended by Acts 1997, cc. 774, 816; Acts 1999, c. 907; Acts 2000, c. 75; Acts 2002, c. 90; Acts 2003, cc. 295, 925; Acts 2004, c. 717.
46.2-746.8:1. Repealed by Acts 2004, c. 717.
46.2-746.9. Amended by Acts 2000, c. 148; Acts 2002, c. 864; Acts 2003, c. 925; Acts 2004, cc. 717, 984.
46.2-746.13. Repealed by Acts 2002, c. 90.
46.2-746.15 to 46.2-746.20. Repealed by Acts 2002, c. 90.
46.2-747.1. Repealed by Acts 2002, c. 90.
46.2-748. Amended by Acts 1996, c. 1026.

Sec.
46.2-748.1. Repealed by Acts 2000, c. 75.
46.2-748.2. Repealed by Acts 2002, c. 90.
46.2-749. Amended by Acts 1990, c. 319; Acts 1995, c. 747; Acts 1996, c. 1026; Acts 2004, c. 747.
46.2-749.1. Amended by Acts 1995, c. 747.
46.2-749.2. Amended by Acts 1995, cc. 747, 749, 823.
46.2-749.2:1. Amended by Acts 1995, c. 747; Acts 1996, c. 922.
46.2-749.2:2. Amended by Acts 1996, cc. 922, 1026; Acts 1997, c. 878.
46.2-749.2:3 to 46.2-749.2:6. Repealed by Acts 2000, c. 75.
46.2-749.2:8, 46.2-749.2:9. Repealed by Acts 2002, c. 90.
46.2-749.2:11, 46.2-749.2:12. Repealed by Acts 2002, c. 90.
46.2-749.2:13. Amended by Acts 1998, c. 763.
46.2-749.2:14. Amended by Acts 1998, cc. 174, 181.
46.2-749.2:1. Repealed by Acts 2002, c. 90.
46.2-749.3. Amended by Acts 1995, c. 134; Acts 1999, c. 883; Acts 2000, cc. 729, 758.
46.2-749.4. Amended by Acts 1995, c. 747; Acts 1996, c. 1026; Acts 1999, cc. 883, 907; Acts 2003, c. 925; Acts 2004, c. 747.
46.2-749.4:1 to 46.2-749.4:3. Repealed by Acts 2002, c. 90.
46.2-749.5:1. Repealed by Acts 2004, c. 717.
46.2-749.6 to 46.2-749.11. Amended by Acts 1995, c. 747.
46.2-749.6:1. Repealed by Acts 2002, c. 90.
46.2-749.7:1. Repealed by Acts 2000, c. 75.
46.2-749.7:2. Repealed by Acts 2002, c. 90.
46.2-749.11. Repealed by Acts 2000, c. 75.
46.2-749.12. Repealed by Acts 2003, c. 295.
46.2-749.15. Repealed by Acts 2003, c. 295.
46.2-749.17. Repealed by Acts 2003, c. 295.
46.2-749.19. Repealed by Acts 2003, c. 295.
46.2-749.23:1. Repealed by Acts 2004, c. 717.
46.2-749.24. Repealed by Acts 2003, c. 295.
46.2-749.27. Repealed by Acts 2003, c. 295.
46.2-749.28:1. Repealed by Acts 2004, cc. 717, 984.
46.2-749.30. Repealed by Acts 2003, c. 295.
46.2-749.32 to 46.2-749.36. Repealed by Acts 2004, c. 717.
46.2-749.39. Repealed by Acts 2004, c. 717.
46.2-749.41. Repealed by Acts 2004, c. 717.
46.2-749.42. Repealed by Acts 2004, c. 717.
6.2-749.43. Repealed by Acts 2004, cc. 653, 717.
46.2-749.44. Amended by Acts 2003, c. 921.
46.2-749.47. Repealed by Acts 2004, c. 717.
46.2-749.59. Amended by Acts 2004, c. 984.
46.2-749.62. Amended by Acts 2004, c. 984.
46.2-749.69. Repealed by Acts 2004, c. 984.
46.2-749.73:1. Repealed by Acts 2004, c. 717.

Sec.
46.2-749.84, 46.2-749.85. Repealed by Acts 2004, c. 717.
46.2-749.87, 46.2-749.88. Repealed by Acts 2004, c. 717.
46.2-749.93. Repealed by Acts 2004, c. 717.
46.2-749.95 to 46.2-749.100. Repealed by Acts 2004, c. 717.
46.2-750. Amended by Acts 1994, 1st Sp. Sess., c. 6; Acts 1995, cc. 432, 747; Acts 1996, cc. 590, 598, 1026; Acts 2004, c. 721.
46.2-751. Amended by Acts 1994, 1st Sp. Sess., c. 6.
46.2-752. Amended by Acts 1990, cc. 181, 187, 188, 455; Acts 1991, c. 622; Acts 1992, cc. 226, 355, 794, 806; Acts 1993, cc. 50, 63, 175, 565; Acts 1994, cc. 528, 962; Acts 1995, cc. 91, 412, 449, 460, 479, 659; Acts 1996, cc. 89, 562; Acts 1997, cc. 246, 499, 854, 905, 911; Acts 1998, c. 649; Acts 1999, c. 236; Acts 2000, c. 303; Acts 2001, cc. 338, 471, 605, 606; Acts 2002, cc. 206, 553; Acts 2003, c. 326; Acts 2004, cc. 689, 723.
46.2-755. Amended by Acts 1997, cc. 283, 496, 853.
46.2-756. Amended by Acts 2003, c. 293.
46.2-757 to 46.2-768. Repealed by Acts 2001, c. 596.
46.2-769. Repealed by Acts 1997, c. 283.
46.2-800. Amended by Acts 1994, c. 176; Acts 2001, c. 834; Acts 2002, c. 254.
46.2-803.1. Amended by Acts 1998, c. 555; Acts 2000, cc. 60, 306, 407; Acts 2004, c. 809.
46.2-808. Amended by Acts 1991, c. 55; Acts 2004, cc. 947, 973.
46.2-809. Amended by Acts 2003, c. 300.
46.2-817. Amended by Acts 1993, c. 796; Acts 1996, cc. 577, 817; Acts 1999, c. 720; Acts 2000, c. 315; Acts 2002, c. 505.
46.2-819. Amended by Acts 1998, c. 802; Acts 2003, c. 768; Acts 2004, c. 924.
46.2-819.1. Amended by Acts 2001, cc. 803, 852; Acts 2004, c. 924.
46.2-819.2. Amended by Acts 2004, c. 795.
46.2-828. Amended by Acts 1994, c. 54; Acts 2001, c. 359; Acts 2003, c. 853.
46.2-829. Amended by Acts 1993, c. 579.
46.2-830. Amended by Acts 1994, c. 280; Acts 1997, c. 881.
46.2-832. Amended by Acts 2003, c. 134; Acts 2004, c. 291.
46.2-833. Amended by Acts 2000, c. 834; Acts 2004, cc. 252, 743.
46.2-833.01. Amended by Acts 1996, c. 392; Acts 1998, cc. 663, 685; Acts 1999, c. 884; Acts 2000, c. 575.
46.2-834. Amended by Acts 1994, c. 469; Acts 2001, cc. 56, 71; Acts 2004, c. 575.
46.2-838. Amended by Acts 1999, c. 999; Acts 2004, cc. 947, 973.
46.2-839. Amended by Acts 1999, c. 999; Acts 2001, c. 834; Acts 2002, c. 254; Acts 2004, cc. 947, 973.
46.2-840. Repealed by Acts 1996, c. 147.
46.2-844. Amended by Acts 1997, cc. 622, 800, 908; Acts 2001, c. 126; Acts 2002, c. 541.
46.2-847. Amended by Acts 2001, c. 834; Acts 2002, c. 254.
46.2-849. Amended by Acts 2001, c. 834; Acts 2002, c. 54; Acts 2004, cc. 947, 973.
46.2-853. Amended by Acts 1991, c. 119.
46.2-856. Amended by Acts 2001, c. 834; Acts 2002, c. 254.
46.2-857. Amended by Acts 2001, c. 834; Acts 2002, c. 254.
46.2-859. Amended by Acts 2001, c. 126; Acts 2002, c. 541.
46.2-862. Amended by Acts 1992, c. 608.
46.2-867. Amended by Acts 1993, c. 866; Acts 2004, c. 859.
46.2-868. Amended by Acts 2004, c. 349.
46.2-869. Amended by Acts 1990, c. 770; Acts 2000, c. 340.
46.2-870. Amended by Acts 1992, c. 598; Acts 1994, c. 423; Acts 1996, c. 1; Acts 1998, cc. 546, 560; Acts 1999, c. 142; Acts 2001, c. 298; Acts 2002, c. 872; Acts 2003, c. 838; Acts 2004, c. 696.
46.2-871. Amended by Acts 1993, c. 278; Acts 1994, c. 676; Acts 1999, c. 166.
46.2-872. Amended by Acts 1995, c. 113; Acts 1996, cc. 36, 87; Acts 1998, c. 439.
46.2-873. Amended by Acts 1990, c. 928; Acts 1994, c. 157; Acts 1997, cc. 629, 781.
46.2-873.1. Amended by Acts 2004, c. 719.
46.2-878. Amended by Acts 1990, c. 779; Acts 1993, c. 98.
46.2-878.1. Amended by Acts 1995, c. 54; Acts 2003, c. 839.
46.2-878.2. Amended by Acts 1999, c. 87; Acts 2002, c. 882; Acts 2004, c. 350.
46.2-880. Amended by Acts 2001, c. 145; Acts 2003, c. 277.
46.2-882. Amended by Acts 1990, cc. 691, 974; Acts 1991, c. 345; Acts 1994, c. 734; Acts 1997, c. 33; Acts 1998, c. 423; Acts 1999, cc. 693, 694, 698, 724, 729, 733; Acts 2000, cc. 354, 357, 365; Acts 2002, c. 109; Acts 2003, cc. 608, 965.
46.2-888. Amended by Acts 1997, c. 431.
46.2-892. Amended by Acts 1998, c. 411; Acts 2004, c. 359.
46.2-894. Amended by Acts 1997, c. 431; Acts 2001, c. 808; Acts 2002, c. 115.
46.2-896. Amended by Acts 1997, c. 431.

Sec.
46.2-900. Amended by Acts 1992, c. 279; Acts 2001, c. 808.
46.2-901. Amended by Acts 2001, c. 808.
46.2-903. Amended by Acts 1994, c. 116; Acts 2001, c. 864; Acts 2002, c. 254.
46.2-904. Amended by Acts 1999, c. 943; Acts 2001, c. 864; Acts 2002, c. 254; Acts 2003, cc. 29, 46.
46.2-905, 46.2-906. Amended by Acts 2001, c. 834; Acts 2002, c. 254; Acts 2003, cc. 29, 46; Acts 2004, cc. 947, 973.
46.2-906.1. Amended by Acts 1994, c. 56; Acts 1995, cc. 42, 671; Acts 2001, c. 834; Acts 2002, c. 254; Acts 2004, cc. 947, 973.
46.2-907, 46.2-908. Amended by Acts 2001, c. 834; Acts 2002, c. 254.
46.2-908. Amended by Acts 2002, c. 254.
46.2-908.1. Amended by Acts 2002, c. 134.
46.2-910. Amended by Acts 1996, c. 690; Acts 1998, c. 789.
46.2-911. Repealed by Acts 1994, c. 51.
46.2-914. Amended by Acts 2004, c. 758.
46.2-915.1. Amended by Acts 1995, c. 670; Acts 2001, c. 147; Acts 2003, c. 313.
46.2-917.2. Amended by Acts 1997, c. 283.
46.2-920. Amended by Acts 1992, cc. 33, 96; Acts 1994, c. 69; Acts 1995, c. 92; Acts 2000, c. 120; Acts 2003, c. 115.
46.2-920.1. Amended by Acts 1990, c. 470.
46.2-924. Amended by Acts 2000, c. 323; Acts 2002, c. 327; Acts 2004, c. 658.
46.2-932. Amended by Acts 2001, cc. 170, 834; Acts 2002, c. 254; Acts 2004, cc. 947, 973.
46.2-933. Amended by Acts 1990, c. 555.
46.2-936. Amended by Acts 1990, c. 218; Acts 1992, c. 830; Acts 1999, cc. 829, 846.
46.2-941. Amended by Acts 1999, cc. 291, 323; Acts 2002, c. 102.
46.2-1001. Amended by Acts 1990, cc. 20, 167; Acts 1991, cc. 284, 416; Acts 1993, c. 409; Acts 1995, cc. 39, 458; Acts 1996, cc. 24, 91, 144, 525; Acts 1997, c. 35; Acts 1999, cc. 68, 279; Acts 2000, cc. 59, 112; Acts 2002, cc. 142, 223, 263; Acts 2003, cc. 82, 85.
46.2-1012. Amended by Acts 1991, c. 165; Acts 2003, c. 964.
46.2-1013. Amended by Acts 2003, c. 964.
46.2-1014. Amended by Acts 2000, cc. 54, 63; Acts 2003, c. 964.
46.2-1014.1. Amended by Acts 1990, c. 955.
46.2-1015. Amended by Acts 2001, c. 834; Acts 2002, c. 254; Acts 2004, cc. 947, 973.
46.2-1017. Amended by Acts 1997, c. 23.
46.2-1020. Amended by Acts 1991, c. 516; Acts 1995, c. 122; Acts 2003, c. 153.

Sec.
46.2-1021. Amended by Acts 1998, c. 419.
46.2-1022. Amended by Acts 1992, c. 96; Acts 1996, cc. 141, 347; Acts 2004, c. 323.
46.2-1023. Amended by Acts 1991, c. 105; Acts 1992, c. 34; Acts 1994, c. 178; Acts 1995, c. 92; Acts 2003, cc. 152, 217.
46.2-1024. Amended by Acts 1992, c. 379; Acts 2003, c. 153.
46.2-1025. Amended by Acts 1991, c. 465; Acts 1992, cc. 93, 410, 805; Acts 1995, c. 727; Acts 1997, c. 149; Acts 1998, cc. 134, 417; Acts 1999, cc. 18, 72, 232; Acts 2000, cc. 84, 121, 278; Acts 2003, c. 93.
46.2-1028. Amended by Acts 1996, c. 403.
46.2-1029.1. Amended by Acts 1994, c. 69; Acts 2003, c. 121.
46.2-1030. Amended by Acts 1992, c. 364; Acts 1997, cc. 25, 589.
46.2-1040. Amended by Acts 2001, c. 359.
46.2-1042. Amended by Acts 1996, c. 92.
46.2-1051. Amended by Acts 2004, cc. 947, 973.
46.2-1052. Amended by Acts 1991, cc. 100, 328; Acts 1993, c. 808; Acts 1994, c. 118; Acts 1997, cc. 744, 880; Acts 1998, c. 133; Acts 1999, c. 75; Acts 2004, c. 613.
46.2-1053. Amended by Acts 1990, c. 161; Acts 1993, cc. 800, 808; Acts 1996, cc. 943, 994.
46.2-1054. Amended by Acts 2003, c. 273.
46.2-1055.1. Amended by Acts 1990, c. 955.
46.2-1061. Amended by Acts 1990, c. 418.
46.2-1063. Amended by Acts 1991, c. 688; Acts 1992, c. 864; Acts 1993, c. 73.
46.2-1066. Amended by Acts 2001, c. 834; Acts 2002, c. 254.
46.2-1072. Amended by Acts 1997, c. 96.
46.2-1073 to 46.2-1075. Amended by Acts 1996, cc. 591, 917.
46.2-1077. Amended by Acts 1994, c. 117.
46.2-1078. Amended by Acts 1993, c. 126; Acts 1997, c. 36; Acts 2001, c. 834; Acts 2002, c. 254.
46.2-1079. Amended by Acts 1992, c. 825; Acts 1998, c. 300.
46.2-1081. Amended by Acts 1996, c. 82; Acts 2003, cc. 29, 46.
46.2-1085. Repealed by Acts 2003, c. 686.
46.2-1090. Amended by Acts 1995, c. 106; Acts 1996, c. 512.
46.2-1090.1. Amended by Acts 1997, c. 65.
46.2-1091. Amended by Acts 1994, c. 104.
46.2-1092. Amended by Acts 1992, c. 553.
46.2-1094. Amended by Acts 1993, c. 591; Acts 1997, c. 793.
46.2-1095. Amended by Acts 1992, cc. 119, 405; Acts 1997, c. 793; Acts 2000, c. 736; Acts 2002, cc. 358, 616, 660.
46.2-1097. Amended by Acts 1996, c. 145.

Sec.
46.2-1098. Amended by Acts 1992, cc. 119, 405; Acts 1993, c. 930.
46.2-1099. Amended by Acts 1992, cc. 119, 405; Acts 1993, c. 181.
46.2-1100. Amended by Acts 2002, cc. 616, 660.
46.2-1102. Amended by Acts 1993, c. 151; Acts 1997, c. 149.
46.2-1105. Amended by Acts 1994, c. 819; Acts 1996, cc. 446, 506; Acts 2001, c. 151.
46.2-1109. Amended by Acts 1994, c. 456; Acts 1997, c. 773.
46.2-1110. Amended by Acts 2001, c. 94.
46.2-1112. Amended by Acts 1993, c. 984; Acts 1994, c. 456; Acts 1995, c. 71; Acts 1997, c. 773; Acts 2001, c. 151; Acts 2003, c. 314.
46.2-1113. Amended by Acts 1993, c. 984; Acts 2001, c. 151.
46.2-1114. Amended by Acts 1994, c. 456.
46.2-1115. Amended by Acts 1996, cc. 39, 146; Acts 1999, c. 77.
46.2-1116. Amended by Acts 1994, c. 456; Acts 1996, c. 340.
46.2-1117. Amended by Acts 1994, c. 456.
46.2-1118. Amended by Acts 2003, c. 414.
46.2-1126. Amended by Acts 1994, c. 456.
46.2-1128. Amended by Acts 1997, c. 283; Acts 2002, c. 265.
46.2-1129. Amended by Acts 1997, c. 283.
46.2-1131. Amended by Acts 1990, c. 418; Acts 2003, c. 314.
46.2-1133. Amended by Acts 2003, c. 314.
46.2-1135. Amended by Acts 1994, c. 922; Acts 1997, c. 479; Acts 2001, cc. 411, 433; Acts 2003, c. 314.
46.2-1137. Amended by Acts 1996, c. 422; Acts 2001, cc. 411, 433; Acts 2002, cc. 99, 431.
46.2-1139. Amended by Acts 1993, c. 68; Acts 1996, cc. 36, 87; Acts 1997, c. 70; Acts 2001, c. 151; Acts 2003, c. 314.
46.2-1139.1. Amended by Acts 2003, c. 314.
46.2-1140. Amended by Acts 1996, cc. 36, 87; Acts 2003, c. 314.
46.2-1141. Amended by Acts 1991, Sp. Sess., c. 17; Acts 1995, c. 146; Acts 1996, cc. 36, 87; Acts 2003, c. 314.
46.2-1142. Amended by Acts 1994, c. 154; Acts 1996, cc. 36, 87; Acts 2000, c. 265; Acts 2003, c. 314.
46.2-1142.1. Amended by Acts 1990, c. 195; Acts 1997, c. 283; Acts 2000, c. 265; Acts 2001, cc. 822, 857; Acts 2003, c. 314.
46.2-1143. Amended by Acts 1996, cc. 36, 87; Acts 1999, c. 915; Acts 2001, c. 417; Acts 2002, c. 264; Acts 2003, c. 314.
46.2-1143.1. Amended by Acts 2002, c. 265; Acts 2003, c. 314.

Sec.
46.2-1144. Amended by Acts 2003, c. 314.
46.2-1146 to 46.2-1149.2. Amended by Acts 2003, c. 314.
46.2-1144 to 46.2-1148. Amended by Acts 1996, cc. 36, 87.
46.2-1149. Amended by Acts 1996, cc. 36, 87; Acts 2000, c. 129.
46.2-1150. Amended by Acts 1991, c. 106.
46.2-1156. Amended by Acts 1992, c. 149; Acts 1997, c. 283; Acts 2001, c. 180.
46.2-1157. Amended by Acts 1991, cc. 107, 717; Acts 1993, c. 134; Acts 1995, c. 670; Acts 1997, c. 283; Acts 2004, cc. 267, 796.
46.2-1163. Amended by Acts 1996, c. 573; Acts 2003, c. 138.
46.2-1164. Amended by Acts 1993, c. 94; Acts 1994, c. 396.
46.2-1166. Amended by Acts 2004, c. 383.
46.2-1167. Amended by Acts 1990, c. 39; Acts 2001, c. 791; Acts 2002, cc. 322, 337.
46.2-1168. Amended by Acts 1990, cc. 418, 496; Acts 1992, c. 597; Acts 1997, c. 283.
46.2-1172. Amended by Acts 1998, c. 299.
46.2-1175. Amended by Acts 1997, c. 283.
46.2-1176. Amended by Acts 1993, cc. 995, 998; Acts 1993, Sp. Sess., c. 2; Acts 1994, c. 838; Acts 1995, cc. 836, 851; Acts 2000, c. 311; Acts 2002, c. 710; Acts 2004, c. 915.
46.2-1177. Amended by Acts 1993, cc. 995, 998; Acts 1993, Sp. Sess., c. 2; Acts 1995, cc. 836, 851.
46.2-1178. Amended by Acts 1993, cc. 995, 998; Acts 1993, Sp. Sess., c. 2; Acts 1994, c. 838; Acts 1995, cc. 836, 851; Acts 1997, c. 507; Acts 2002, c. 710; Acts 2004, c. 915.
46.2-1178.1. Amended by Acts 1996, cc. 35, 100; Acts 2002, c. 710.
46.2-1179. Amended by Acts 1993, cc. 995, 998; Acts 1993, Sp. Sess., c. 2; Acts 1995, cc. 836, 851; Acts 2002, c. 710.
46.2-1179.1. Amended by Acts 1995, c. 141; Acts 1998, cc. 401, 421.
46.2-1180. Amended by Acts 1993, cc. 995, 998; Acts 1993, Sp. Sess., c. 2; Acts 1994, c. 838; Acts 1995, cc. 836, 851.
46.2-1181. Amended by Acts 1993, cc. 995, 998; Acts 1993, Sp. Sess., c. 2; Acts 1995, cc. 836, 851.
46.2-1182. Amended by Acts 1990, c. 522; Acts 1993, cc. 995, 998; Acts 1993, Sp. Sess., c. 2; Acts 1995, cc. 836, 851; Acts 2002, c. 322.
46.2-1183. Amended by Acts 1993, cc. 995, 998; Acts 1993, Sp. Sess., c. 2; Acts

Sec.
1995, cc. 836, 851; Acts 1996, cc. 35, 100.
46.2-1184. Amended by Acts 1993, cc. 995, 998; Acts 1993, Sp. Sess., c. 2.
46.2-1185. Amended by Acts 1991, c. 531; Acts 1993, cc. 995, 998; Acts 1993, Sp. Sess., c. 2.
46.2-1186. Amended by Acts 1993, cc. 995, 998; Acts 1993, Sp. Sess., c. 2.
46.2-1187. Amended by Acts 1991, c. 531; Acts 1993, cc. 995, 998; Acts 1993, Sp. Sess., c. 2.
46.2-1187.2. Amended by Acts 1995, cc. 836, 851.
46.2-1188. Amended by Acts 2001, cc. 21, 27; Acts 2004, c. 734.
46.2-1189. Amended by Acts 2004, c. 734.
46.2-1190. Amended by Acts 1997, c. 559; Acts 2004, c. 734.
46.2-1191. Amended by Acts 1997, cc. 104, 493; Acts 1998, c. 322; Acts 2004, c. 734.
46.2-1192. Amended by Acts 2004, c. 734.
46.2-1200. Amended by Acts 1997, c. 150.
46.2-1200.1. Amended by Acts 1997, c. 150; Acts 1990, c. 725.
46.2-1201, 46.2-1202. Amended by Acts 1997, c. 150.
46.2-1203. Amended by Acts 2004, c. 369.
46.2-1207. Amended by Acts 1990, c. 207.
46.2-1208. Amended by Acts 2004, c. 353.
46.2-1212. Amended by Acts 1992, c. 269.
46.2-1216. Amended by Acts 1990, c. 686.
46.2-1217. Amended by Acts 1993, c. 405; Acts 1999, c. 78.
46.2-1219.1. Amended by Acts 1990, c. 891; Acts 1993, c. 574.
46.2-1220. Amended by Acts 1990, cc. 121, 418; Acts 1991, c. 372; Acts 1992, c. 268; Acts 1993, cc. 86, 125; Acts 1994, cc. 218, 417; Acts 1995, c. 144; Acts 1996, c. 348; Acts 1997, cc. 506, 780, 912; Acts 1998, c. 545; Acts 1999, c. 71; Acts 2001, cc. 128, 141, 143, 156; Acts 2002, cc. 48, 132, 266; Acts 2003, cc. 32, 773.
46.2-1221. Amended by Acts 1991, c. 219; Acts 1994, c. 218; Acts 1995, c. 66.
46.2-1222. Amended by Acts 1990, c. 78; Acts 2004, c. 797.
46.2-1222.1. Amended by Acts 2001, c. 144; Acts 2003, cc. 122, 470; Acts 2004, cc. 108, 225, 702.
46.2-1224. Amended by Acts 1996, c. 770; Acts 1997, c. 19; Acts 1998, cc. 391, 403, 424.
46.2-1225. Amended by Acts 1995, c. 459.
46.2-1231. Amended by Acts 1990, c. 502; Acts 1991, c. 221; Acts 1993, c. 394; Acts 1994, c. 619; Acts 2003, c. 305.
46.2-1231.1. Amended by Acts 1990, c. 604.

Sec.
46.2-1232. Amended by Acts 1990, cc. 502, 573.
46.2-1233. Amended by Acts 1990, cc. 502, 571, 573.
46.2-1233.1. Amended by Acts 1990, c. 266; Acts 1993, c. 598.
46.2-1236. Repealed by Acts 1994, c. 866.
46.2-1237. Repealed by Acts 1997, cc. 783, 904.
46.2-1238. Repealed by Acts 1994, c. 866.
46.2-1240. Amended by Acts 1999, c. 188; Acts 2002, c. 108; Acts 2003, c. 992.
46.2-1241. Amended by Acts 2001, c. 136; Acts 2002, c. 133; Acts 2003, c. 992.
46.2-1243. Amended by Acts 2002, c. 390.
46.2-1302. Amended by Acts 1997, c. 47.
46.2-1304. Amended by Acts 1998, cc. 547, 574.
46.2-1305. Amended by Acts 2003, c. 418.
46.2-1309. Amended by Acts 1995, c. 473.
46.2-1313. Amended by Acts 1991, c. 224; Acts 1993, c. 302; Acts 1994, c. 264; Acts 2000, c. 48.
46.2-1314. Amended by Acts 1993, c. 72.
46.2-1401. Amended by Acts 2002, c. 337.
46.2-1404. Amended by Acts 2002, c. 337.
46.2-1405. Amended by Acts 2002, c. 337.
46.2-1407. Amended by Acts 2002, c. 337.
46.2-1500. Amended by Acts 1992, cc. 148, 572; Acts 1993, c. 124; Acts 1994, c. 888; Acts 1995, cc. 767, 816; Acts 1996, c. 1053; Acts 1997, cc. 801, 848; Acts 1999, cc. 77, 910; Acts 2004, cc. 111, 788.
46.2-1502. Repealed by Acts 1995, cc. 767, 816.
46.2-1503. Amended by Acts 1992, c. 95; Acts 1995, cc. 767, 816.
46.2-1503.3. Amended by Acts 1998, c. 325.
46.2-1503.5. Amended by Acts 2004, c. 650.
46.2-1504 to 46.2-1506. Amended by Acts 1995, cc. 767, 816.
46.2-1507. Amended by Acts 1995, cc. 767, 816.
46.2-1508. Amended by Acts 1993, c. 123; Acts 1997, c. 848; Acts 2000, c. 180.
46.2-1508.1. Amended by Acts 2000, c. 180.
46.2-1509. Amended by Acts 1995, cc. 767, 816.
46.2-1510. Amended by Acts 1995, cc. 767, 816; Acts 1998, c. 418.
46.2-1511 to 46.2-1515. Amended by Acts 1995, cc. 767, 816.
46.2-1516. Amended by Acts 1990, c. 940; Acts 1993, c. 69; Acts 1995, cc. 767, 816.
46.2-1517, 46.2-1518. Amended by Acts 1995, cc. 767, 816.
46.2-1519. Amended by Acts 1992, c. 148; Acts 1993, c. 122; Acts 1995, cc. 767, 816; Acts 2000, c. 180; Acts 2001, c. 23.
46.2-1520. Amended by Acts 1995, cc. 767, 816.
46.2-1521. Amended by Acts 1990, c. 197; Acts 1995, cc. 767, 816; Acts 1997, c. 848; Acts 1998, c. 325; Acts 2004, c. 975.
46.2-1522 to 46.2-1527. Repealed by Acts 1994, c. 478.

Sec.
46.2-1527.1. Amended by Acts 1995, cc. 767, 816; Acts 1998, c. 325; Acts 2000, c. 180; Acts 2003, c. 331.
46.2-1527.2. Amended by Acts 1995, cc. 767, 816; Acts 1998, c. 325; Acts 2001, c. 194.
46.2-1527.3. Amended by Acts 1995, cc. 767, 816; Acts 1998, c. 325; Acts 2003, c. 331.
46.2-1527.4. Amended by Acts 1995, cc. 767, 816.
46.2-1527.5. Amended by Acts 1995, cc. 767, 816; Acts 1998, c. 325; Acts 2001, c. 194; Acts 2003, c. 331.
46.2-1527.6 to 46.2-1528. Amended by Acts 1995, cc. 767, 816.
46.2-1529. Amended by Acts 1991, c. 712; Acts 1995, cc. 767, 816; Acts 2000, c. 128.
46.2-1530. Amended by Acts 1990, c. 900; Acts 1993, c. 586; Acts 1995, cc. 767, 816, 849; Acts 2000, c. 116; Acts 2003, c. 997.
46.2-1530.2. Amended by Acts 2004, c. 812.
46.2-1531. Amended by Acts 1993, c. 289; Acts 2000, c. 180.
46.2-1532. Amended by Acts 1995, cc. 767, 816.
46.2-1532.1. Amended by Acts 1990, c. 786; Acts 1994, c. 72.
46.2-1533. Amended by Acts 1995, cc. 767, 816.
46.2-1535. Amended by Acts 1991, c. 117.
46.2-1536. Amended by Acts 1995, cc. 767, 816.
46.2-1539. Amended by Acts 1995, cc. 767, 816.
46.2-1541. Repealed by Acts 1995, cc. 767, 816.
46.2-1542 to 46.2-1545. Amended by Acts 1995, cc. 767, 814.
46.2-1546. Amended by Acts 1990, c. 197; Acts 1991, c. 712; Acts 1995, cc. 767, 814.
46.2-1547. Amended by Acts 1990, c. 954; Acts 1995, cc. 767, 814.
46.2-1548. Amended by Acts 1990, c. 197; Acts 1991, c. 712; Acts 1995, cc. 767, 814.
46.2-1549. Amended by Acts 1991, c. 712; Acts 1995, cc. 767, 814.
46.2-1549.1. Amended by Acts 1994, 1st Sp. Sess., c. 6.
46.2-1550. Amended by Acts 1991, c. 712; Acts 1993, c. 504; Acts 1995, cc. 767, 814; Acts 1998, c. 827.
46.1-1551. Amended by Acts 1991, c. 712; Acts 1995, cc. 767, 814.
46.1-1552. Amended by Acts 1991, c. 712.
46.2-1552.1. Amended by Acts 1997, c. 283.
46.2-1553 to 46.2-1556. Amended by Acts 1995, cc. 767, 814.
46.2-1558. Amended by Acts 1992, c. 631.
46.2-1566. Amended by Acts 1994, c. 537; Acts 1995, cc. 767, 816.
46.2-1568. Amended by Acts 1995, cc. 767, 816; Acts 2001, c. 149.

Sec.
46.2-1569. Amended by Acts 1990, c. 83; Acts 1992, c. 116; Acts 1994, c. 385; Acts 1995, cc. 767, 816; Acts 1998, c. 682.
46.2-1569.1. Amended by Acts 2003, c. 298.
46.2-1571. Amended by Acts 1990, c. 250; Acts 1991, c. 92; Acts 1992, c. 135; Acts 1993, c. 90; Acts 1994, c. 783; Acts 1995, cc. 421, 477; Acts 1997, c. 484; Acts 1998, c. 681; Acts 2001, cc. 80, 89.
46.2-1572. Amended by Acts 1990, c. 41.
46.2-1572.1. Amended by Acts 1990, c. 329.
46.2-1573. Amended by Acts 1992, c. 115; Acts 1994, c. 702; Acts 1995, cc. 767, 816; Acts 2000, c. 106; Acts 2001, cc. 165, 173.
46.2-1575. Amended by Acts 1990, cc. 197, 954; Acts 1995, cc. 767, 816; Acts 1999, c. 217.
46.2-1576. Amended by Acts 1990, c. 197; Acts 1995, cc. 767, 816; Acts 1996, cc. 639, 658; Acts 1999, c. 217.
46.2-1577. Amended by Acts 1990, c. 197; Acts 1995, cc. 767, 816.
46.2-1578. Amended by Acts 1990, c. 197; Acts 1996, c. 573.
46.2-1581. Amended by Acts 1990, c. 84; Acts 1991, c. 626; Acts 1996, c. 1027; Acts 1998, c. 325.
46.2-1582. Amended by Acts 1995, cc. 767, 816.
46.2-1600. Amended by Acts 1992, c. 148; Acts 1993, c. 376; Acts 2000, cc. 123, 235, 257; Acts 2003, c. 304.
46.2-1601. Amended by Acts 1990, c. 197; Acts 1992, c. 148; Acts 1999, c. 53.
46.2-1602. Amended by Acts 1992, c. 148.
46.2-1602.1. Amended by Acts 1992, c. 148; Acts 1993, c. 376; Acts 2000, cc. 235, 257.
46.2-1603. Amended by Acts 1992, c. 148; Acts 1993, c. 376; Acts 2000, cc. 235, 257.
46.2-1603.1. Amended by Acts 1992, c. 148; Acts 1995, cc. 390, 394; Acts 2004, c. 369.
46.2-1603.2. Amended by Acts 1992, c. 148; Acts 1993, c. 376; Acts 1995, c. 390.
46.2-1604. Amended by Acts 1992, c. 148.
46.2-1605. Amended by Acts 1992, c. 148; Acts 1994, c. 73; Acts 1996, cc. 21, 843; Acts 2003, c. 304.
46.2-1606. Amended by Acts 1992, c. 148.
46.2-1607. Amended by Acts 1992, c. 148.
46.2-1608. Amended by Acts 1992, c. 148; Acts 2000, c. 123.
46.2-1609. Amended by Acts 1992, c. 148.
46.2-1700, 46.2-1701. Amended by Acts 1990, c. 466; Acts 2004, c. 587.
46.2-1702. Amended by Acts 1990, c. 466; Acts 1991, c. 214.

Sec.
46.2-1703. Amended by Acts 1990, c. 466; Acts 1991, c. 214; Acts 2004, c. 587.
46.2-1705. Amended by Acts 2000, c. 179; Acts 2004, c. 587.
46.2-1707. Amended by Acts 2004, c. 587.
46.2-1801 to 46.2-1805. Repealed by Acts 1996, cc. 165, 926.
46.2-1900. Amended by Acts 1995, cc. 1043, 1052; Acts 1997, cc. 801, 848; Acts 1999, c. 77.
46.2-1900.1, 46.2-1900.2. Amended by Acts 1995, cc. 744, 803.
46.2-1901. Amended by Acts 1995, cc. 744, 803.
46.2-1902, 46.2-1903. Repealed by Acts 1995, cc. 744, 803; Acts 1996, cc. 1043, 1052.
46.2-1904 to 46.2-1906. Amended by Acts 1995, cc. 744, 803.
46.2-1907. Amended by Acts 1995, cc. 744, 803; Acts 1996, cc. 1043, 1052.
46.2-1908. Amended by Acts 1995, cc. 744, 803; Acts 1997, c. 848; Acts 2000, c. 180.
46.2-1909 to 46.2-1912. Amended by Acts 1995, cc. 744, 803; Acts 1996, cc. 1043, 1052.
46.2-1913 to 46.2-1915. Amended by Acts 1995, cc. 744, 803.
46.2-1916. Amended by Acts 1996, cc. 1043, 1052.
46.2-1917. Amended by Acts 1995, cc. 744, 803.
46.2-1918. Amended by Acts 1995, cc. 744, 803; Acts 1996, cc. 1043, 1052.
46.2-1919. Amended by Acts 1995, cc. 744, 803; Acts 1996, cc. 1043, 1052; Acts 2000, c. 180.
46.2-1920. Amended by Acts 1995, cc. 744, 803.
46.2-1920.1. Amended by Acts 1995, cc. 744, 803.
46.2-1921. Amended by Acts 1995, cc. 744, 803; Acts 1997, c. 848; Acts 1998, c. 325.
46.2-1922 to 46.2-1926. Amended by Acts 1995, cc. 744, 803.
46.2-1927. Amended by Acts 1995, cc. 744, 803; Acts 1996, cc. 1043, 1052.
46.2-1928. Amended by Acts 1995, cc. 744, 803.
46.2-1929. Amended by Acts 1995, cc. 744, 803; Acts 2000, c. 128.
46.2-1930. Amended by Acts 1996, cc. 1043, 1052; Acts 2000, c. 116.
46.2-1931. Amended by Acts 1996, cc. 1043, 1052; Acts 2000, c. 180.
46.2-1932. Amended by Acts 1995, cc. 744, 803.
46.2-1933. Amended by Acts 1995, cc. 744, 803; Acts 1996, cc. 1043, 1052.
46.2-1934 to 46.2-1941. Amended by Acts 1995, cc. 744, 803.
46.2-1942. Repealed by Acts 1996, cc. 1043, 1052.
46.2-1943 to 46.2-1944. Amended by Acts 1995, cc. 744, 803; Acts 1996, cc. 1043, 1052.
46.2-1945, 46.2-1946. Amended by Acts 1995, cc. 744, 803.
46.2-1947 to 46.2-1950. Amended by Acts 1995, cc. 744, 803; Acts 1996, cc. 1043, 1052.
46.2-1951. Amended by Acts 1996, cc. 1043, 1052.
46.2-1952. Amended by Acts 1996, cc. 1043, 1052; Acts 1998, c. 827.
46.2-1953. Amended by Acts 1996, cc. 1043, 1052.
46.2-1955 to 46.2-1956. Amended by Acts 1996, cc. 1043, 1052.
46.2-1961. Repealed by Acts 1996, cc. 1043, 1052.
46.2-1975 to 46.2-1977. Amended by Acts 1996, cc. 1043, 1052.
46.2-1979. Amended by Acts 1996, cc. 453, 1043, 1052.
46.2-1982. Amended by Acts 2000, c. 106.
46.2-1985. Amended by Acts 1996, cc. 1043, 1052; Acts 1999, c. 217.
46.2-1986. Amended by Acts 1999, c. 217.
46.2-1988. Amended by Acts 1996, cc. 1043, 1052; Acts 1997, c. 88.
46.2-1992. Amended by Acts 1997, cc. 801, 848; Acts 2004, c. 726.
46.2-1992.6. Amended by Acts 1997, c. 848; Acts 2000, c. 180.
46.2-1992.17. Amended by Acts 2000, c. 180.
46.2-1992.19. Amended by Acts 1997, c. 848; Acts 1998, c. 325.
46.2-1992.22. Amended by Acts 2000, c. 128.
46.2-1992.23. Amended by Acts 2000, c. 116.
46.2-1992.24. Amended by Acts 2000, c. 180.
46.2-1992.44. Amended by Acts 1998, c. 827.
46.2-1992.75. Amended by Acts 2000, c. 106.
46.2-1992.79. Amended by Acts 1999, c. 217.
46.2-1992.80. Amended by Acts 1999, c. 217.
46.2-1992.82. Amended by Acts 1997, c. 88.
46.2-1993. Amended by Acts 1997, cc. 801, 848; Acts 2003, c. 334.
46.2-1993.3. Amended by Acts 1997, c. 802.
46.2-1993.6. Amended by Acts 1997, c. 848; Acts 2000, c. 180; Acts 2003, c. 334.
46.2-1993.17. Amended by Acts 2000, c. 180.
46.2-1993.19. Amended by Acts 1997, c. 848.
46.2-1993.22. Amended by Acts 2000, c. 128.
46.2-1993.23. Amended by Acts 2000, c. 116.
46.2-1993.24. Amended by Acts 2000, c. 180.
46.2-1993.25. Amended by Acts 2003, c. 334.
46.2-1993.44. Amended by Acts 1998, c. 827.
46.2-1993.64. Amended by Acts 2003, c. 334.
46.2-1993.67. Amended by Acts 1997, c. 802.
46.2-1993.73. Amended by Acts 2000, c. 106.
46.2-1993.76. Amended by Acts 1999, c. 217.
46.2-1993.77. Amended by Acts 1999, c. 217.
46.2-1993.79. Amended by Acts 1997, c. 88.
46.2-2000. Amended by Acts 1995, cc. 744, 803;

Sec.

Acts 2001, c. 596; Acts 2002, c. 861; Acts 2004, c. 780.

46.2-2000.1. Amended by Acts 2001, c. 596; Acts 2002, c. 337.

46.2-2000.2. Repealed by Acts 2001, c. 596.

46.2-2001. Amended by Acts 1995, cc. 744, 803; Acts 2001, c. 596; Acts 2002, c. 861.

46.2-2001.1. Amended by Acts 2002, c. 861.

46.2-2001.3. Amended by Acts 2002, c. 870.

46.2-2002 to 46.2-2004. Repealed by Acts 2001, c. 596.

46.2-2005. Amended by Acts 1995, cc. 744, 803; Acts 2001, c. 596; Acts 2002, cc. 681, 734, 870.

46.2-2006 to 46.2-2010. Repealed by Acts 2001, c. 596.

46.2-2011. Amended by Acts 1995, cc. 744, 803; Acts 2001, c. 596.

46.2-2011.1. Amended by Acts 1995, cc. 744, 803; Acts 2001, c. 596.

46.2-2011.4. Amended by Acts 2002, c. 861.

46.2-2011.6. Amended by Acts 2003, c. 322.

46.2-2011.10. Amended by Acts 2002, c. 861.

46.2-2011.14. Amended by Acts 2002, c. 861.

46.2-2011.15. Amended by Acts 2002, c. 861.

46.2-2011.16. Amended by Acts 2002, c. 861.

46.2-2011.22. Amended by Acts 2002, c. 861.

46.2-2012 to 46.2-2041. Repealed by Acts 2001, c. 596.

46.2-2042. Repealed by Acts 2001, c. 137.

46.2-2043 to 46.2-2050. Repealed by Acts 2001, c. 596.

46.2-2080. Amended by Acts 2002, cc. 681, 734.

46.2-2099.20. Repealed by Acts 2002, c. 861.

46.2-2099.22 to 46.2-2099.29. Repealed by Acts 2002, c. 861.

46.2-2099.31 to 46.2-2099.40. Repealed by Acts 2002, c. 861.

46.2-2099.41. Amended by Acts 2003, c. 286.

46.2-2100. Amended by Acts 1995, cc. 744, 803; Acts 1997, c. 283; Acts 2001, c. 596; Acts 2003, c. 832.

46.2-2101. Amended by Acts 1995, cc. 744, 803; Acts 2001, c. 596; Acts 2003, c. 832.

46.2-2102. Amended by Acts 2001, c. 596.

46.2-2103 to 46.2-2108. Repealed by Acts 2001, c. 596.

46.2-2109. Amended by Acts 2002, c. 870.

46.2-2110 to 46.2-2114. Repealed by Acts 2001, c. 596.

46.2-2121. Amended by Acts 2003, c. 322.

46.2-2200 to 2209. Repealed by Acts 2001, c. 596.

46.2-2210 to 46.2-2212. Amended by Acts 1995, cc. 744, 803.

46.2-2300 to 46.2-2316. Repealed by Acts 2001, c. 596.

46.2-2400 to 46.2-2409. Repealed by Acts 2001, c. 596.

Sec.

46.2-2500 to 46.2-2519. Repealed by Acts 2001, c. 596.

46.2-2600 to 46.2-2610. Repealed by Acts 2001, c. 596.

46.2-2700 to 46.2-2703. Repealed by Acts 1997, c. 117.

47-1 to 47-7. Repealed by Acts 1980, c. 580.

47.1-4. Amended by Acts 1983, c. 435; Acts 1986, c. 561; Acts 1989, c. 163.

47.1-19. Amended by Acts 1981, c. 311; Acts 1996, c. 219; Acts 2003, c. 881.

47.1-21. Amended by Acts 1989, c. 594.

47.1-23, 47.1-24. Amended by Acts 1983, c. 435.

47.1-30. Amended by Acts 1992, c. 194.

48-5. Amended by Acts 1996, cc. 291, 808.

48-11. Amended by Acts 1996, cc. 291, 808.

49-1. Amended by Acts 1971, Ex. Sess., c. 16; Acts 1980, c. 320; Acts 1988, c. 255.

49-3. Amended by Acts 1968, c. 639; Acts 1983, c. 228; Acts 1986, c. 255; Acts 1988, c. 255; Acts 1992, c. 390.

49-4. Amended by Acts 1968, c. 639; Acts 1970, c. 783; Acts 1986, c. 255.

49-7. Amended by Acts 1986, c. 616.

49-13. Amended by Acts 1984, c. 703; Acts 2002, c. 858.

49-22. Amended by Acts 1984, c. 703.

49-25. Amended by Acts 1979, c. 664.

49-26. Amended by Acts 1979, c. 664.

50-1 to 50-43.12. Repealed by Acts 1996, c. 292.

50-44 to 50-73. Repealed by Acts 1985, c. 607.

50-73.1. Amended by Acts 1987, c. 702; Acts 1990, c. 343; Acts 1992, c. 575; Acts 1997, c. 190; Acts 2003, c. 340.

50-73.2. Amended by Acts 1987, c. 702; Acts 1998, c. 163; Acts 2003, cc. 340, 592.

50-73.4. Amended by Acts 1987, c. 702; Acts 1993, c. 292; Acts 2000, cc. 162, 537; Acts 2001, cc. 517, 541.

50-73.5. Amended by Acts 1987, c. 702; Acts 1991, c. 225; Acts 2003, c. 597.

50-73.7. Amended by Acts 1991, c. 672; Acts 2001, cc. 517, 541.

50-73.8. Amended by Acts 1987, c. 702.

50-73.11. Amended by Acts 1987, c. 702; Acts 1993, c. 292; Acts 2001, cc. 517, 541; Acts 2003, c. 378.

50-73.11:1. Repealed Acts 2002, c. 441.

50-73.11:2. Amended by Acts 2002, c. 441.

50-73.12. Amended by Acts 1987, c. 702; Acts 1990, c. 343; Acts 1993, c. 292.

50-73.13. Amended by Acts 1990, c. 343; Acts 1993, c. 292.

50-73.14. Repealed by Acts 1987, c. 702.

50-73.15. Amended by Acts 1987, c. 702; Acts 1990, c. 343; Acts 1993, c. 292; Acts 2002, c. 441.

50-73.16. Amended by Acts 1987, c. 702.

Sec.
50-73.17. Amended by Acts 1987, c. 702; Acts 1991, c. 434; Acts 1992, c. 575; Acts 1993, c. 292; Acts 1995, cc. 70, 368; Acts 2000, c. 995; Acts 2002, c. 441; Acts 2004, c. 274.
50-73.18, 50-73.19. Amended by Acts 1987, c. 702.
50-73.20. Amended by Acts 1987, c. 702; Acts 1991, c. 434.
50-73.21. Amended by Acts 1987, c. 702.
50-73.22. Repealed by Acts 1987, c. 702.
50-73.23. Amended by Acts 1987, c. 702.
50-73.24. Amended by Acts 1987, c. 702; Acts 1990, c. 343.
50-73.25. Amended by Acts 1987, c. 702.
50-73.28. Amended by Acts 1987, c. 702; Acts 1990, c. 343; Acts 1997, c. 801.
50-73.33 to 50-73.35. Amended by Acts 1987, c. 702.
50-73.36. Amended by Acts 1987, c. 702; Acts 1997, c. 188.
50-73.38. Amended by Acts 1987, c. 702; Acts 1997, c. 188.
50-73.39. Repealed by Acts 1997, c. 188.
50-73.39.1, 50-73.40. Amended by Acts 1987, c. 702.
50-73.43. Amended by Acts 1987, c. 702.
50-73.46. Repealed by Acts 2004, c. 601.
50-73.47. Amended by Acts 1987, c. 702.
50-73.48. Amended by Acts 1997, c. 801.
50-73.48:1. Amended by Acts 1997, c. 190; Acts 2003, c. 340.
50-73.48:3. Amended by Acts 1997, c. 190; Acts 2003, cc. 340, 597; Acts 2004, c. 274.
50-73.48:4. Amended by Acts 1997, c. 190; Acts 2003, c. 340.
50-73.49. Amended by Acts 1987, c. 702; Acts 1996, c. 255.
50-73.50. Amended by Acts 1987, c. 702.
50-73.51. Amended by Acts 1987, c. 702; Acts 1990, c. 343; Acts 1997, c. 188.
50-73.54. Amended by Acts 1987, c. 702; Acts 2002, c. 441; Acts 2003, c. 378; Acts 2004, c. 274.
50-73.56. Amended by Acts 1990, c. 343; Acts 2002, c. 441.
50-73.57. Amended by Acts 1993, c. 292; Acts 2003, c. 370.
50-73.57:2. Amended by Acts 1997, c. 190; Acts 2004, c. 274.
50-73.61. Amended by Acts 1987, c. 305; Acts 1990, c. 343.
50-73.63, 50-73.64. Amended by Acts 1987, c. 702.
50-73.67. Amended by Acts 1987, c. 702; Acts 1991, c. 434; Acts 1995, c. 621; Acts 2002, c. 441.
50-73.68. Amended by Acts 1995, c. 621.
50-73.69. Amended by Acts 1996, c. 255; Acts 1998, c. 163; Acts 2000, c. 52; Acts 2004, cc. 274, 601.

Sec.
50-73.70. Amended by Acts 2002, c. 441; Acts 2004, c. 316.
50-73.75. Amended by Acts 1996, c. 292.
50-73.77. Amended by Acts 1987, c. 702; Acts 1991, c. 434; Acts 1993, c. 292; Acts 1996, c. 292.
50-73.78. Amended by Acts 1996, c. 292; Acts 1998, c. 163.
50-73.79. Amended by Acts 2003, c. 567.
50-73.83. Amended by Acts 1997, c. 188; Acts 2000, cc. 5, 995; Acts 2002, c. 441; Acts 2003, c. 567; Acts 2004, cc. 316, 601.
50-73.84. Amended by Acts 2003, c. 340.
50-73.93. Amended by Acts 2002, c. 441; Acts 2003, c. 567; Acts 2004, c. 274.
50-73.109. Amended by Acts 1997, c. 801.
50-73.115. Amended by Acts 2003, c. 567.
50-73.121. Amended by Acts 2003, c. 567.
50-73.125. Amended by Acts 1997, c. 188.
50-73.128. Amended by Acts 2000, c. 58; Acts 2003, c. 340.
50-73.130. Amended by Acts 1997, cc. 188, 190; Acts 1998, c. 163; Acts 2003, c. 340.
50-73.131. Amended by Acts 2000, c. 58; Acts 2003, c. 567.
50-73.132. Amended by Acts 2000, c. 162; Acts 2001, cc. 517, 541; Acts 2002, c. 441; Acts 2003, c. 378; Acts 2004, c. 601.
50-73.133. Amended by Acts 1998, c. 163.
50-73.134. Amended by Acts 2000, c. 5; Acts 2002, c. 441; Acts 2004, c. 601.
50-73.135. Amended by Acts 2000, c. 537; Acts 2001, cc. 517, 541; Acts 2003, c. 597.
50-73.136. Amended by Acts 2000, c. 58.
50-73.137:1. Amended by Acts 2004, c. 601.
50-73.138. Amended by Acts 2002, c. 441; Acts 2003, c. 378; Acts 2004, c. 274.
50-73.144. Amended by Acts 2003, c. 340.
50-74. Repealed by Acts 1996, c. 292.
50-75 to 50-78. Repealed by Acts 1997, c. 188.
51-1 to 51-180. Repealed by Acts 1990, c. 832.
51.01-3. Amended by Acts 1988, c. 44.
51.01-11. Amended by Acts 1986, c. 112; Acts 1987, c. 49.
51.01-21. Amended by Acts 1987, c. 50.
51.01-28. Amended by Acts 1987, c. 50.
51.01-44, 51.01-45. Amended by Acts 1987, c. 500.
51.1-100 to 51.1-124. Repealed by Acts 1994, cc. 4, 85.
51.1-124.3. Amended by Acts 1996, cc. 711, 731; Acts 1999, cc. 929, 974; Acts 2000, c. 911; Acts 2001, cc. 686, 697; Acts 2003, c. 628.
51.1-124.4. Amended by Acts 2003, c. 15.
51.1-124.12. Amended by Acts 2000, c. 344; Acts 2003, c. 267.
51.1-124.20. Amended by Acts 1995, c. 788;

Sec.

Acts 1997, c. 641; Acts 1998, c. 196; Acts 2004, c. 1000.

51.1-124.22. Amended by Acts 1995, c. 307; Acts 1997, c. 711; Acts 1998, c. 176; Acts 2003, cc. 11, 626; Acts 2004, c. 80.

51.1-124.23. Amended by Acts 1997, c. 78; Acts 2001, c. 39.

51.1-124.26. Amended by Acts 1995, c. 788; Acts 1997, c. 641; Acts 1998, c. 196.

51.1-124.27. Amended by Acts 1997, c. 711.

51.1-124.30. Amended by Acts 1995, c. 788; Acts 2000, c. 396.

51.1-124.31. Amended by Acts 2000, c. 911.

51.1-126. Amended by Acts 1991, cc. 217, 645; Acts 1996, cc. 933, 995; Acts 2000, cc. 722, 723; Acts 2001, c. 691; Acts 2003, cc. 369, 626.

51.1-126.1. Amended by Acts 1993, c. 895; Acts 1996, cc. 905, 933, 995, 1046; Acts 2000, cc. 66, 657, 720.

51.1-126.2. Repealed by Acts 1998, c. 449.

51.1-126.3. Amended by Acts 2000, c. 723; Acts 2003, c. 369.

51.1-126.5. Amended by Acts 1999, c. 111; Acts 2001, c. 691; Acts 2002, c. 668; Acts 2004, c. 206.

51.1-126.6. Amended by Acts 2000, c. 345; Acts 2001, c. 691; Acts 2002, c. 668.

51.1-128. Amended by Acts 1992, c. 811.

51.1-130. Amended by Acts 1994, 1st Sp. Sess., c. 5.

51.1-132. Amended by Acts 1994, c. 883.

51.1-138. Amended by Acts 1991, c. 719; Acts 1999, c. 596; Acts 2002, c. 466; Acts 2003, c. 624; Acts 2004, c. 83.

51.1-139. Amended by Acts 2004, c. 207.

51.1-142, 51.1-142.1. Repealed by Acts 2001, cc. 686, 697.

51.1-142.2. Amended by Acts 2003, c. 7.

51.1-143. Repealed by Acts 2001, cc. 686, 697.

51.1-144. Amended by Acts 1998, c. 660; Acts 2001, cc. 693, 702; Acts 2002, c. 307.

51.1-145. Amended by Acts 1991, c. 719; Acts 1996, c. 1030; Acts 1996, c. 1030.

51.1-146. Amended by Acts 1995, c. 307; Acts 1997, c. 273.

51.1-151. Repealed by Acts 1997, c. 641.

51.1-153. Amended by Acts 1995, cc. 152, 692, 811; Acts 1996, cc. 768, 997; Acts 1999, cc. 111, 567, 568, 569, 591, 592, 598, 599; Acts 2000, cc. 66, 657, 911.

51.1-155. Amended by Acts 1991, c. 719; Acts 1992, c. 826; Acts 1994, 1st Sp. Sess., c. 5; Acts 1995, cc. 152, 692, 811; Acts 1998, cc. 407, 674, 746; Acts 1999, c. 111; Acts 2001, cc. 689, 700; Acts 2002, cc. 778, 781;

Sec.

Acts 2003, c. 211; Acts 2004, c. 563.

51.1-155.1. Amended by Acts 1995, cc. 152, 692, 721, 811; Acts 1996, cc. 662, 924; Acts 1997, c. 711; Acts 1998, c. 746; Acts 2000, c. 911; Acts 2003, c. 220.

51.1-155.2. Amended by Acts 1996, cc. 662, 924; Acts 1998, c. 676; Acts 2000, cc. 343, 911.

51.1-156. Amended by Acts 1992, c. 811; Acts 1995, c. 307.

51.1-157. Amended by Acts 1993, c. 895; Acts 1994, 1st Sp. Sess., c. 5; Acts 1998, c. 674.

51.1-159. Amended by Acts 1998, c. 657.

51.1-161. Amended by Acts 2001, c. 691.

51.1-162. Amended by Acts 1998, c. 407; Acts 1999, cc. 111, 510; Acts 2001, c. 683; Acts 2002, c. 313.

51.1-163. Amended by Acts 1991, c. 302; Acts 1995, c. 307; Acts 2001, cc. 679, 699.

51.1-164. Amended by Acts 2004, c. 81.

51.1-165. Amended by Acts 1992, cc. 518, 548, 811; Acts 1993, c. 548; Acts 1995, cc. 152, 307, 692, 811; Acts 1998, c. 676; Acts 1999, c. 111; Acts 2001, cc. 679, 699; Acts 2003, c. 263.

51.1-165.01. Amended by Acts 2002, c. 404.

51.1-166. Amended by Acts 1991, c. 719; Acts 1996, c. 1030.

51.1-168. Amended by Acts 1995, c. 307; Acts 1998, c. 389; Acts 2000, c. 502; Acts 2002, c. 435.

51.1-202. Amended by Acts 2003, c. 624.

51.1-203. Amended by Acts 2001, cc. 686, 697.

51.1-205. Amended by Acts 1995, cc. 152, 692, 811; Acts 1996, c. 997; Acts 1999, c. 111; Acts 2000, cc. 66, 657, 911; Acts 2002, c. 466; Acts 2003, c. 624; Acts 2004, c. 83.

51.1-206. Amended by Acts 1992, c. 815; Acts 1993, cc. 408, 568; Acts 1994, 1st Sp. Sess., c. 5; Acts 1995, cc. 152, 692, 811; Acts 1998, cc. 674, 676; Acts 2000, c. 911; Acts 2001, c. 804; Acts 2003, c. 624; Acts 2004, c. 687.

51.1-207. Amended by Acts 1998, c. 407; Acts 1999, cc. 111, 510; Acts 2001, c. 683; Acts 2002, c. 313.

51.1-208. Amended by Acts 1991, c. 719.

51.1-216. Amended by Acts 2000, cc. 66, 657, 911; Acts 2001, c. 804; Acts 2002, c. 466; Acts 2004, c. 83.

51.1-217. Amended by Acts 2000, c. 911; Acts 2001, c. 804; Acts 2002, c. 466.

51.1-218. Amended by Acts 2000, c. 911; Acts 2001, c. 683; Acts 2002, c. 313.

51.1-301. Amended by Acts 1993, c. 895.

51.1-303. Amended by Acts 1992, c. 811; Acts

Sec.
1994, cc. 821, 899; Acts 2000, c. 911; Acts 2004, c. 672.
51.1-305. Amended by Acts 1992, c. 694.
51.1-306. Amended by Acts 1994, 1st Sp. Sess., c. 5; Acts 1998, c. 674.
51.1-308. Amended by Acts 1993, c. 895; Acts 1994, 1st Sp. Sess., c. 5; Acts 1999, c. 111; Acts 2000, c. 911.
51.1-402. Amended by Acts 1992, c. 811.
51.1-500. Amended by Acts 2001, cc. 685, 690.
51.1-502. Amended by Acts 1992, c. 530; Acts 2000, c. 911.
51.1-502.1. Amended by Acts 1996, cc. 933, 995; Acts 2000, cc. 66, 657.
51.1-502.2. Repealed by Acts 2001, c. 694.
51.1-504. Amended by Acts 1993, c. 895.
51.1-505. Amended by Acts 1991, c. 700; Acts 1995, cc. 52, 307, 605; Acts 1999, c. 111; Acts 2001, c. 696; Acts 2002, c. 313; Acts 2003, cc. 9, 220; Acts 2004, c. 102.
51.1-505.01. Amended by Acts 2001, cc. 685, 690; Acts 2002, c. 313.
51.1-510. Amended by Acts 1994, c. 883; Acts 1997, c. 273.
51.1-511. Amended by Acts 2002, c. 313.
51.1-512. Amended by Acts 1995, c. 360; Acts 1997, c. 273; Acts 2001, c. 696.
51.1-512.1. Amended by Acts 1997, c. 273; Acts 2000, cc. 66, 657; Acts 2001, c. 696.
51.1-513. Repealed by Acts 1998, c. 774.
51.1-513.1. Amended by Acts 2000, cc. 66, 657.
51.1-514. Amended by Acts 1991, c. 700; Acts 1997, c. 273.
51.1-600. Amended by Acts 1992, c. 276; Acts 1999, cc. 980, 984; Acts 2002, c. 311.
51.1-601. Amended by Acts 1992, c. 276; Acts 2002, c. 311.
51.1-602. Amended by Acts 1992, c. 276; Acts 1997, c. 174; Acts 1998, c. 658; Acts 2000, c. 395; Acts 2004, c. 86.
51.1-603. Amended by Acts 1991, c. 379; Acts 1997, c. 174.
51.1-604, 51.1-605. Amended by Acts 1992, c. 276; Acts 2002, c. 311.
51.1-606. Repealed by Acts 2002, c. 311.
51.1-800. Amended by Acts 1991, c. 381; Acts 1993, c. 866.
51.1-802. Amended by Acts 1991, c. 433; Acts 1992, c. 716.
51.1-803. Amended by Acts 1992, c. 810; Acts 1995, c. 307; Acts 1996, c. 508; Acts 1997, c. 213.
51.1-808. Amended by Acts 1994, c. 523.
51.1-1000. Amended by Acts 1991, c. 612; Acts 2004, c. 209.
51.1-1001. Amended by Acts 2004, c. 209.
51.1-1002. Amended by Acts 2004, c. 209.
51.1-1003. Amended by Acts 1991, cc. 381, 612; Acts 2004, c. 209.
51.1-1100. Amended by Acts 1999, c. 144; Acts 2000, c. 889; Acts 2001, c. 694.
51.1-1101. Amended by Acts 1999, c. 144; Acts 2000, cc. 66, 657.
51.1-1103. Amended by Acts 1999, c. 144; Acts 2000, c. 889; Acts 2002, cc. 663, 697; Acts 2004, c. 186.
51.1-1104. Amended by Acts 1999, c. 144; Acts 2000, c. 889.
51.1-1105. Amended by Acts 1999, c. 144; Acts 2000, c. 889.
51.1-1106. Amended by Acts 2000, cc. 66, 657; Acts 2002, cc. 663, 697.
51.1-1107. Amended by Acts 1999, c. 144; Acts 2000, c. 889.
51.1-1110. Amended by Acts 1999, c. 144; Acts 2000, c. 889; Acts 2004, c. 1019.
51.1-1112. Amended by Acts 1999, c. 144; Acts 2000, c. 889; Acts 2003, c. 13; Acts 2004, c. 96.
51.1-1113. Amended by Acts 1999, c. 144; Acts 2004, c. 97.
51.1-1114. Amended by Acts 1999, c. 144; Acts 2000, c. 889; Acts 2003, c. 5; Acts 2004, c. 99.
51.1-1116. Amended by Acts 1999, c. 144; Acts 2001, c. 694.
51.1-1117. Amended by Acts 1999, c. 144; Acts 2004, c. 98.
51.1-1118. Amended by Acts 1999, c. 144.
51.1-1121. Amended by Acts 1999, c. 144; Acts 2000, c. 889.
51.1-1123. Amended by Acts 1999, c. 144; Acts 2000, c. 889; Acts 2003, c. 13; Acts 2004, c. 98.
51.1-1124. Amended by Acts 1999, c. 144; Acts 2004, c. 97.
51.1-1125. Amended by Acts 1999, c. 144; Acts 2000, c. 889; Acts 2003, c. 5.
51.1-1126. Amended by Acts 1999, c. 144.
51.1-1127. Amended by Acts 1999, c. 144; Acts 2001, c. 694.
51.1-1128. Amended by Acts 1999, c. 144.
51.1-1129. Amended by Acts 1999, c. 144.
51.1-1130. Amended by Acts 2000, cc. 618, 632; Acts 2001, cc. 684, 695.
51.1-1131. Amended by Acts 1999, c. 144; Acts 2001, c. 694.
51.1-1132. Amended by Acts 1999, c. 144.
51.1-1133. Amended by Acts 1999, c. 144; Acts 2004, c. 98.
51.1-1134. Amended by Acts 1999, c. 144.
51.1-1135. Amended by Acts 1999, c. 144; Acts 2000, c. 889.
51.1-1135.1. Amended by Acts 2000, c. 889; Acts 2001, c. 694.
51.1-1136. Amended by Acts 2000, c. 889.
51.1-1140. Amended by Acts 2002, cc. 663, 697.
51.1-1200. Amended by Acts 2001, c. 672.
51.1-1201. Amended by Acts 2000, c. 911; Acts 2001, c. 672.
51.1-1202. Amended by Acts 2001, c. 672.
51.1-1203. Amended by Acts 2002, c. 349.

Sec.
51.1-1204. Amended by Acts 2001, c. 672.
51.1-1205. Amended by Acts 2001, c. 672; Acts 2002, c. 349.
51.1-1206. Amended by Acts 2001, c. 672; Acts 2002, c. 349.
51.1-1207. Amended by Acts 2001, c. 672; Acts 2002, c. 349.
51.1-1210. Amended by Acts 2002, c. 349.
51.1-1400. Amended by Acts 2004, c. 79.
51.1-1401. Amended by Acts 2004, c. 84.
51.1-1404. Repealed by Acts 2004, c. 76.
51.5-1, 51.5-2. Amended by Acts 1990, c. 458; Acts 1991, c. 563; Acts 2002, c. 572.
51.5-3. Amended by Acts 1989, c. 181; Acts 1993, c. 807; Acts 1997, c. 801; Acts 2003, cc. 57, 73.
51.5-4. Amended by Acts 1989, cc. 457, 489; Acts 2003, cc. 57, 73.
51.5-5. Amended by Acts 1992, c. 755; Acts 2003, cc. 57, 73.
51.5-5.1, 51.5-6. Repealed by Acts 2003, cc. 57, 73.
51.5-7. Repealed by Acts 1992, c. 755.
51.5-9.01. Repealed by Acts 2003, cc. 57, 73.
51.5-9.1. Amended by Acts 2000, c. 151.
51.5-11. Amended by Acts 1989, c. 176.
51.5-14. Amended by Acts 1989, c. 176; Acts 1992, c. 755.
51.5-15. Amended by Acts 1992, c. 755.
51.5-16. Amended by Acts 1989, c. 181; Acts 2002, c. 46.
51.5-17. Amended by Acts 2002, c. 46.
51.5-18. Amended by Acts 1989, c. 181; Acts 1992, c. 755; Acts 2001, c. 483; Acts 2002, c. 46.
51.5-19. Amended by Acts 2002, c. 46.
51.5-20. Amended by Acts 2002, c. 46.
51.5-21, 51.5-22. Amended by Acts 1992, c. 755.
51.5-23. Amended by Acts 1992, c. 755; Acts 2003, c. 503.
51.5-24. Amended by Acts 2003, c. 503.
51.5-25. Amended by Acts 2003, c. 503.
51.5-27 to 51.5-29. Amended by Acts 1992, c. 755.
51.5-31. Amended by Acts 1989, c. 133; Acts 1990, c. 458; Acts 1992, c. 627; Acts 2001, cc. 526, 546; Acts 2003, c. 501.
51.5-33. Amended by Acts 1990, c. 458; Acts 1992, c. 627; Acts 1994, c. 34.
51.5-34. Repealed by Acts 1995, c. 34.
51.5-35. Repealed by Acts 1992, c. 627.
51.5-35.1. Amended by Acts 1992, c. 627.
51.5-36 to 51.5-39. Repealed by Acts 2002, c. 572.
51.5-39.2. Amended by Acts 2003, cc. 236, 885; Acts 2004, c. 1000.
51.5-40. Amended by Acts 1990, c. 458; Acts 1992, c. 627; Acts 2002, c. 572.
51.5-44. Amended by Acts 1989, c. 326; Acts 1994, c. 108; Acts 2001, c. 443.
51.5-46. Amended by Acts 1990, c. 458; Acts 1992, c. 627; Acts 2002, c. 572.
51.5-47. Amended by Acts 2000, c. 115.
51.5-48. Amended by Acts 2000, c. 115.
51.5-49. Amended by Acts 1994, c. 76.
51.5-53. Amended by Acts 2004, c. 728.
51.5-54. Amended by Acts 2002, c. 19.
51.5-55. Amended by Acts 1996, c. 930; Acts 2000, cc. 21, 294; Acts 2002, c. 19.
51.5-56. Amended by Acts 2002, c. 19; Acts 2004, c. 728.
51.5-57, 51.5-58. Amended by Acts 2002, c. 19.
51.5-72. Amended by Acts 2004, c. 13.
51.5-75. Amended by Acts 2004, c. 58.
52-1. Amended by Acts 1974, c. 483; Acts 1980, c. 232; Acts 2000, cc. 560, 600.
52-4. Amended by Acts 1980, c. 496; Acts 1986, c. 228; Acts 1988, c. 806; Acts 1989, c. 18.
52-4.1. Repealed by Acts 1968, c. 722.
52-4.2. Amended by Acts 1968, c. 760; Acts 1985, c. 10.
52-4.3. Amended by Acts 1982, c. 431; Acts 1989, c. 168; Acts 2000, cc. 560, 600.
52-4.4. Amended by Acts 1997, c. 341.
52-5. Repealed by Acts 1978, c. 470.
52-6. Amended by Acts 1985, c. 272.
52-7. Amended by Acts 1950, p. 150; Acts 1966, c. 213; Acts 1968, c. 492.
52-8.1. Amended by Acts 1975, c. 650; Acts 1980, c. 232.
52-8.2. Amended by Acts 1991, c. 675.
52-8.3. Amended by Acts 1999, cc. 703, 726; Acts 2004, c. 690.
52-8.4. Amended by Acts 1988, cc. 14, 718; Acts 1990, cc. 24, 870; Acts 1991, cc. 382, 505; Acts 1993, c. 108; Acts 1994, c. 71; Acts 1995, cc. 145, 151, 744, 803; Acts 1996, c. 302; Acts 1997, c. 283; Acts 2002, c. 828; Acts 2004, c. 23.
52-8.5. Amended by Acts 2002, cc. 588, 623.
52-9. Amended by Acts 1980, c. 228; Acts 1981, c. 223; Acts 1984, c. 780.
52-9.1. Amended by Acts 1973, c. 401.
52-11. Amended by Acts 1958, c. 542; Acts 1991, c. 631.
52-11.1. Amended by Acts 1952, c. 493; Acts 1979, c. 123.
52-11.2. Amended by Acts 1970, c. 224; Acts 1971, Ex. Sess., c. 177; Acts 1991, c. 189.
52-14. Amended by Acts 1999, c. 150.
52-20. Amended by Acts 1950, p. 888.
52-21. Amended by Acts 1960, c. 375; Acts 1962, c. 22; Acts 1982, c. 35.
52-23, 52-24. Amended by Acts 1958, c. 611.
52-25.1. Amended by Acts 1994, cc. 394, 502.
52-26. Amended by Acts 1979, c. 83.
52-28. Amended by Acts 1979, c. 83.

Sec.
52-32. Amended by Acts 1986, c. 330; Acts 2004, c. 248.
52-34.3. Amended by Acts 2004, c. 270.
52-35. Amended by Acts 2002, c. 818.
52-36. Amended by Acts 2000, c. 526.
52-41. Amended by Acts 2001, c. 371.
53-1 to 53-343. Repealed by Acts 1982, c. 636.
53.1-1. Amended by Acts 1983, c. 477; Acts 1991, c. 383; Acts 1995, c. 224; Acts 1999, c. 845; Acts 2000, c. 807.
53.1-5. Amended by Acts 1984, c. 720.
53.1-10. Amended by Acts 1994, 2nd Sp. Sess., c. 7; Acts 1995, c. 725; Acts 1997, c. 894; Acts 2003, cc. 94, 516, 854.
53.1-14. Repealed by Acts 1984, c. 734.
53.1-16. Amended by Acts 1986, c. 290; Acts 1992, c. 201; Acts 1997, c. 39.
53.1-17. Amended by Acts 1989, c. 298.
53.1-19. Amended by Acts 1995, c. 846; Acts 1996, c. 234.
53.1-20. Amended by Acts 1990, cc. 676, 768; Acts 1993, c. 502; Acts 1994, cc. 128, 859, 949; Acts 1994, 2nd Sp. Sess., cc. 1, 2; Acts 1997, c. 840.
53.1-20.1. Amended by Acts 1990, cc. 676, 768; Acts 1994, 2nd Sp. Sess., cc. 1, 2; Acts 1997, c. 775.
53.1-21. Amended by Acts 1990, cc. 676, 768; Acts 1999, cc. 945, 987.
53.1-22. Amended by Acts 2004, c. 855.
53.1-23.1. Repealed by Acts 1990, c. 669.
53.1-24. Amended by Acts 1994, c. 64.
53.1-27. Amended by Acts 1996, cc. 28, 230; Acts 2004, c. 417.
53.1-29. Amended by Acts 1984, c. 720; Acts 1996, cc. 804, 838.
53.1-31. Amended by Acts 1984, c. 734.
53.1-31.1. Amended by Acts 2003, c. 154.
53.1-32. Amended by Acts 1992, c. 740; Acts 1993, c. 768; Acts 1995, cc. 766, 821; Acts 1998, c. 798.
53.1-32.1. Amended by Acts 1994, 2nd Sp. Sess., cc. 1, 2; Acts 2001, c. 483.
53.1-36. Amended by Acts 1992, c. 603.
53.1-37. Amended by Acts 1989, c. 652; Acts 2003, c. 846.
53.1-40. Amended by Acts 1997, c. 207.
53.1-40.01. Amended by Acts 2001, cc. 446, 487.
53.1-40.1. Amended by Acts 1997, c. 801.
53.1-40.4. Amended by Acts 1994, c. 211.
53.1-40.8. Amended by Acts 1990, c. 221.
53.1-41. Amended by Acts 2001, c. 483.
53.1-45. Amended by Acts 1983, c. 186; Acts 1993, cc. 464, 488.
53.1-45.1. Amended by Acts 1996, cc. 284, 368; Acts 2003, cc. 94, 854.
53.1-45.2 to 53.1-45.5. Repealed by Acts 2003, cc. 94, 854.
53.1-47. Amended by Acts 1982, cc. 499, 647; Acts 1993, cc. 464, 488.

Sec.
53.1-48. Amended by Acts 1982, c. 499; Acts 1984, c. 720.
53.1-49. Amended by Acts 1982, c. 647.
53.1-52. Amended by Acts 1982, c. 647; Acts 2003, cc. 895, 981, 1021.
53.1-56. Amended by Acts 1989, c. 652.
53.1-59. Amended by Acts 1989, c. 652; Acts 1991, c. 412; Acts 1996, cc. 703, 726.
53.1-60. Amended by Acts 1984, c. 516; Acts 1985, c. 488; Acts 1988, c. 397; Acts 1990, cc. 107, 676, 768; Acts 1994, c. 487.
53.1-61. Amended by Acts 2002, c. 747.
53.1-63. Amended by Acts 1990, c. 701; Acts 2000, cc. 668, 690; Acts 2001, c. 483.
53.1-63.1. Amended by Acts 1996, c. 755.
53.1-64. Amended by Acts 1990, c. 701; Acts 2001, c. 483.
53.1-66. Amended by Acts 1990, c. 701; Acts 1996, cc. 755, 914.
53.1-67. Amended by Acts 1983, c. 606; Acts 1984, c. 313; Acts 1990, c. 701.
53.1-67.1. Amended by Acts 1994, c. 926; Acts 1995, c. 117; Acts 1996, cc. 809, 938; Acts 2001, c. 483.
53.1-67.4. Amended by Acts 1995, cc. 502, 574.
53.1-67.7. Amended by Acts 2000, c. 338.
53.1-68. Amended by Acts 1991, c. 383; Acts 1992, c. 179; Acts 1994, c. 861; Acts 1995, c. 797; Acts 1997, c. 644; Acts 2000, c. 256.
53.1-75. Amended by Acts 1991, c. 383.
53.1-76. Amended by Acts 1985, c. 321.
53.1-78. Amended by Acts 1984, c. 703.
53.1-79. Amended by Acts 1991, c. 383.
53.1-80. Amended by Acts 1983, c. 358; Acts 1989, c. 423; Acts 1993, cc. 387, 787; Acts 1995, c. 305.
53.1-81. Amended by Acts 1983, c. 358; Acts 1989, c. 423; Acts 1993, cc. 387, 787; Acts 1995, c. 305.
53.1-82. Amended by Acts 1983, c. 358; Acts 1989, c. 423; Acts 1991, c. 453; Acts 1993, cc. 387, 787; Acts 1995, c. 305.
53.1-82.1. Amended by Acts 2000, c. 1040.
53.1-82.2. Amended by Acts 1995, c. 305; Acts 1996, c. 835.
53.1-82.3. Amended by Acts 1995, c. 305; Acts 1998, cc. 498, 504; Acts 2000, c. 1040.
53.1-83. Repealed by Acts 1993, cc. 387, 787.
53.1-83.1. Amended by Acts 1992, cc. 333, 573.
53.1-84. Amended by Acts 1983, c. 358.
53.1-85. Amended by Acts 1983, c. 358; Acts 1992, cc. 333, 573.
53.1-88. Amended by Acts 1992, c. 859.
53.1-89. Repealed by Acts 1983, c. 358.
53.1-90. Amended by Acts 1991, c. 383.

Sec.
53.1-91. Amended by Acts 1983, c. 358; Acts 1991, c. 383.
53.1-92. Amended by Acts 1991, c. 383.
53.1-93. Amended by Acts 2002, c. 336.
53.1-94. Amended by Acts 1985, c. 321.
53.1-95. Amended by Acts 1983, c. 358.
53.1-95.2, 53.1-95.3. Amended by Acts 1992, c. 421.
53.1-95.7. Amended by Acts 1994, c. 270.
53.1-95.8. Amended by Acts 1994, cc. 270, 923, 953; Acts 2002, c. 336; Acts 2004, c. 378.
53.1-104. Amended by Acts 1983, c. 358.
53.1-105. Amended by Acts 1999, c. 990.
53.1-106. Amended by Acts 1990, c. 185; Acts 1991, cc. 529, 566, 567, 568; Acts 1992, cc. 212, 628; Acts 1994, cc. 102, 270, 354; Acts 1997, c. 340; Acts 1998, c. 541; Acts 2000, cc. 473, 618, 632.
53.1-108. Amended by Acts 1986, c. 191.
53.1-109. Amended by Acts 1991, c. 383; Acts 1994, cc. 923, 953; Acts 1999, cc. 829, 846; Acts 2002, c. 336; Acts 2004, c. 378.
53.1-110. Amended by Acts 1991, c. 383; Acts 1995, c. 5.
53.1-115. Amended by Acts 1983, c. 358.
53.1-115.1. Amended by Acts 2000, cc. 70, 291.
53.1-116. Amended by Acts 1983, c. 561; Acts 1984, c. 643; Acts 1990, c. 934; Acts 1994, 2nd Sp. Sess., cc. 1, 2; Acts 1996, c. 556; Acts 1998, c. 776; Acts 1999, cc. 951, 1007; Acts 2003, cc. 818, 820; Acts 2004, cc. 400, 461.
53.1-116.1. Amended by Acts 1997, c. 747; Acts 2003, c. 584.
53.1-118. Amended by Acts 1991, c. 383.
53.1-119. Amended by Acts 1995, c. 112.
53.1-120. Amended by Acts 1986, c. 568; Acts 1988, c. 119; Acts 1989, c. 571; Acts 2002, cc. 533, 756; Acts 2003, cc. 26, 44; Acts 2004, cc. 390, 432.
53.1-121. Amended by Acts 1983, c. 358; Acts 1996, c. 288; Acts 1998, cc. 204, 350.
53.1-122, 53.1-123. Amended by Acts 1991, c. 383.
53.1-124. Amended by Acts 1990, c. 934; Acts 1991, cc. 218, 383; Acts 1993, c. 930; Acts 2004, cc. 884, 921.
53.1-125. Amended by Acts 1991, c. 383.
53.1-126. Amended by Acts 1991, c. 383; Acts 2003, cc. 928, 1019.
53.1-127. Amended by Acts 1995, c. 797; Acts 2002, c. 182.
53.1-128. Amended by Acts 1991, c. 580; Acts 1997, cc. 123, 546.
53.1-129. Amended by Acts 1984, c. 43; Acts 1991, c. 580; Acts 1994, c. 269; Acts 1997, cc. 134, 546; Acts 1998, c. 311; Acts 1999, cc. 277, 951, 1007; Acts 2001, cc. 185, 196; Acts 2003, cc. 818, 820.
53.1-130. Amended by Acts 1991, c. 383.
53.1-131. Amended by Acts 1984, c. 516; Acts 1985, c. 301; Acts 1988, c. 397; Acts 1989, c. 586; Acts 1990, cc. 107, 676, 768; Acts 2000, c. 423; Acts 2002, cc. 747, 800.
53.1-131.1. Amended by Acts 1984, c. 490; Acts 1994, c. 901; Acts 1999, c. 9; Acts 2002, cc. 805, 831; Acts 2003, c. 1039.
53.1-131.2. Amended by Acts 1990, c. 209; Acts 1991, cc. 278, 428; Acts 1992, c. 604; Acts 1994, cc. 612, 659, 688, 720, 841, 945; Acts 2000, c. 423; Acts 2002, c. 800.
53.1-132. Amended by Acts 2000, c. 423; Acts 2003, c. 846.
53.1-133.01. Amended by Acts 2003, cc. 928, 1019.
53.1-133.1 to 53.1-133.5. Amended by Acts 1995, c. 756.
53.1-134. Amended by Acts 1984, c. 584; Acts 1997, cc. 795, 883; Acts 2002, c. 569.
53.1-135. Amended by Acts 1988, c. 823; Acts 1992, c. 144; Acts 2002, c. 569.
53.1-136. Amended by Acts 1990, c. 538; Acts 2000, cc. 338, 767; Acts 2002, c. 569; Acts 2003, c. 132.
53.1-137. Amended by Acts 1985, c. 174.
53.1-139. Amended by Acts 1984, c. 734; Acts 1988, c. 823; Acts 1992, c. 144.
53.1-139.1. Repealed by Acts 1992, c. 144.
53.1-140. Amended by Acts 2003, c. 944.
53.1-141. Amended by Acts 1984, c. 514.
53.1-142. Amended by Acts 1984, c. 514; Acts 2003, c. 944.
53.1-143. Amended by Acts 1984, c. 514; Acts 2003, c. 944.
53.1-144. Amended by Acts 2003, c. 944.
53.1-145. Amended by Acts 1992, cc. 188, 740; Acts 1993, c. 930; Acts 1994, c. 935; Acts 1994, 2nd Sp. Sess., cc. 1, 2; Acts 1995, cc. 502, 574; Acts 1997, c. 526; Acts 2003, c. 944.
53.1-150. Amended by Acts 1984, c. 668; Acts 1988, c. 824; Acts 1990, cc. 511, 816; Acts 1992, c. 529; Acts 1993, c. 195; Acts 1994, cc. 613, 638; Acts 1994, 2nd Sp. Sess., cc. 1, 2; Acts 1999, c. 9; Acts 2000, c. 1040; Acts 2002, c. 831.
53.1-151. Amended by Acts 1982, c. 270; Acts 1985, c. 555; Acts 1987, c. 668; Acts 1988, c. 872; Acts 1990, cc. 220, 684; Acts 1991, c. 423; Acts 1993, cc. 485, 491, 907.
53.1-153. Amended by Acts 1983, c. 509.

Sec.
53.1-154. Amended by Acts 1983, c. 243; Acts 1984, c. 655.
53.1-155. Amended by Acts 1987, c. 668; Acts 1992, c. 222; Acts 1995, cc. 687, 778; Acts 2002, c. 569.
53.1-156. Amended by Acts 1987, c. 668.
53.1-157. Amended by Acts 2000, c. 767.
53.1-159. Amended by Acts 1985, c. 175; Acts 1987, c. 668; Acts 1991, c. 410; Acts 1994, c. 894.
53.1-160. Amended by Acts 1984, c. 155; Acts 1989, cc. 525, 652; Acts 1993, c. 189; Acts 1995, c. 687.
53.1-160.1. Amended by Acts 1997, c. 747; Acts 2003, c. 584.
53.1-161. Amended by Acts 1990, cc. 676, 768; Acts 2000, c. 767.
53.1-162. Amended by Acts 2000, c. 767.
53.1-164. Amended by Acts 2000, c. 767.
53.1-165. Amended by Acts 1985, c. 174; Acts 1986, c. 433; Acts 2000, c. 767.
53.1-172. Amended by Acts 2000, c. 767; Acts 2004, c. 407.
53.1-174. Amended by Acts 2000, c. 767; Acts 2004, c. 407.
53.1-180 through 53.1-185.3. Repealed by Acts 2002, c. 491, cl. 2.
53.1-187. Amended by Acts 1984, c. 313; Acts 1994, 2nd Sp. Sess., cc. 1, 2.
53.1-189. Amended by Acts 1984, c. 734; Acts 1994, 2nd Sp. Sess., cc. 1, 2.
53.1-191. Amended by Acts 1984, c. 253; Acts 1994, 2nd Sp. Sess., cc. 1, 2; 2002, c. 59.
53.1-197. Amended by Acts 2001, c. 483.
53.1-199. Amended by Acts 1993, c. 491.
53.1-200. Amended by Acts 1994, c. 582.
53.1-203. Amended by Acts 1985, c. 555; Acts 1988, c. 371; Acts 2004, c. 461.
53.1-218. Amended by Acts 1985, c. 247; Acts 1994, c. 579.
53.1-223. Amended by Acts 1992, c. 398; Acts 2000, c. 404.
53.1-227. Amended by Acts 1997, c. 801.
53.1-231.1. Amended by Acts 2002, c. 344.
53.1-231.2. Amended by Acts 2003, c. 946.
53.1-233. Amended by Acts 1989, c. 541; Acts 1994, c. 921.
53.1-234. Amended by Acts 1989, c. 541; Acts 1994, c. 921; Acts 1996, c. 679.
53.1-237. Repealed by Acts 1989, c. 733.
53.1-261. Amended by Acts 1995, c. 694; Acts 1996, c. 632.
53.1-262. Amended by Acts 1995, c. 694; Acts 1998, c. 818.
53.1-265, 53.1-266. Amended by Acts 1995, c. 694.
54-1 to 54-977. Repealed by Acts 1988, c. 765.
54.1-101. Amended by Acts 1993, c. 499.
54.1-103. Amended by Acts 1990, c. 194; Acts 1993, c. 499.
54.1-104. Amended by Acts 1993, c. 499.

Sec.
54.1-105. Amended by Acts 1992, c. 659; Acts 2004, c. 49.
54.1-106. Amended by Acts 1989, c. 159; Acts 1992, cc. 414, 706; Acts 1995, cc. 509, 531; Acts 1996, c. 748; Acts 1999, c. 834; Acts 2004, c. 49.
54.1-108. Amended by Acts 1993, c. 499.
54.1-109. Amended by Acts 1992, c. 659; Acts 1993, c. 499.
54.1-110. Amended by Acts 1992, c. 659.
54.1-111. Amended by Acts 1993, cc. 129, 499; Acts 1998, c. 470; Acts 2001, c. 544; Acts 2003, cc. 753, 762; Acts 2004, c. 49.
54.1-112. Amended by Acts 1993, c. 499.
54.1-113. Amended by Acts 1993, c. 499.
54.1-114. Amended by Acts 1993, c. 499; Acts 1998, c. 744; Acts 2004, c. 650.
54.1-116. Amended by Acts 2003, c. 803.
54.1-200. Amended by Acts 1993, c. 499.
54.1-202. Amended by Acts 1999, cc. 37, 950; Acts 2001, c. 832.
54.1-204. Amended by Acts 2003, c. 582.
54.1-300. Amended by Acts 1990, cc. 459, 466; Acts 1991, c. 551; Acts 1993, c. 499; Acts 1995, c. 737; Acts 1998, c. 27; Acts 1999, c. 950; Acts 2000, c. 726; Acts 2001, cc. 723, 832; Acts 2002, c. 784; Acts 2003, c. 575.
54.1-301. Amended by Acts 1993, c. 499.
54.1-302. Amended by Acts 1993, c. 499.
54.1-306. Amended by Acts 1989, c. 16; Acts 1991, c. 130; Acts 2002, c. 605.
54.1-307. Amended by Acts 1993, c. 499.
54.1-307.1. Amended by Acts 2004, c. 297.
54.1-309. Amended by Acts 1993, c. 499.
54.1-400. Amended by Acts 1990, c. 512; Acts 1992, cc. 780, 783; Acts 1998, c. 27.
54.1-401. Amended by Acts 1992, cc. 595, 780, 783.
54.1-402. Amended by Acts 1992, cc. 780, 783.
54.1-402.1. Amended by Acts 1994, c. 379.
54.1-403. Amended by Acts 1990, c. 512; Acts 1991, c. 291; Acts 1998, c. 27.
54.1-405. Amended by Acts 1992, c. 613; Acts 1994, c. 29.
54.1-406. Amended by Acts 1992, cc. 780, 783; Acts 1994, c. 784; Acts 1996, c. 329; Acts 2004, c. 191.
54.1-407. Amended by Acts 1998, c. 27.
54.1-409. Amended by Acts 2000, c. 990.
54.1-410. Amended by Acts 1992, cc. 780, 783; Acts 1993, c. 662.
54.1-411. Amended by Acts 1992, c. 574; Acts 2000, c. 763.
54.1-413. Amended by Acts 1991, c. 291.
54.1-414. Amended by Acts 1991, c. 291; Acts 1994, c. 625; Acts 2000, c. 42.
54.1-415. Repealed by Acts 2000, c. 42.
54.1-500. Amended by Acts 1989, c. 397; Acts 1990, cc. 49, 73, 823; Acts 1992, c. 152; Acts 1993, cc. 499, 660; Acts

Sec.

1994, cc. 185, 911; Acts 1996, cc. 76, 176, 180, 846; Acts 1997, c. 885; Acts 1998, c. 739; Acts 2001, c. 723.

54.1-500.1. Amended by Acts 1994, cc. 185, 911; Acts 1996, cc. 180, 846; Acts 1997, c. 885; Acts 2001, c. 723.

54.1-501. Amended by Acts 1989, c. 397; Acts 1990, cc. 49, 73, 823; Acts 1991, c. 45; Acts 1992, c. 477; Acts 1993, cc. 499, 660; Acts 1994, cc. 185, 911; Acts 1995, cc. 543, 585; Acts 1996, cc. 180, 846; Acts 1997, cc. 649, 885; Acts 1998, c. 739; Acts 2001, c. 723.

54.1-502. Amended by Acts 1989, c. 397; Acts 1990, cc. 73, 823; Acts 1993, c. 660.

54.1-503. Amended by Acts 1989, c. 397; Acts 1990, c. 73; Acts 1993, c. 660; Acts 1994, cc. 185, 911; Acts 1995, cc. 543, 585; Acts 1996, cc. 180, 846; Acts 1997, cc. 560, 885; Acts 1998, c. 739; Acts 2004, c. 133.

54.1-504. Amended by Acts 1989, c. 397; Acts 1993, c. 660.

54.1-505. Amended by Acts 1989, c. 397; Acts 1993, c. 660; Acts 1996, cc. 180, 846.

54.1-506. Repealed by Acts 1993, c. 660.

54.1-507. Repealed by Acts 1992, c. 477.

54.1-508, 54.1-509. Repealed by Acts 1993, c. 660.

54.1-510. Repealed by Acts 1988, c. 802.

54.1-511. Repealed by Acts 1993, c. 660.

54.1-512. Amended by Acts 1989, c. 397; Acts 1993, c. 660; Acts 1996, cc. 180, 846; Acts 1998, c. 739.

54.1-513. Repealed by Acts 1998, c. 739.

54.1-514. Amended by Acts 1989, c. 397; Acts 1990, c. 105; Acts 1996, cc. 180, 846.

54.1-515. Amended by Acts 1993, cc. 499, 660.

54.1-516. Amended by Acts 1989, c. 397; Acts 1990, c. 823; Acts 1993, c. 660; Acts 1994, cc. 185, 911; Acts 1996, cc. 180, 846; Acts 1997, c. 885; Acts 1998, c. 739; Acts 2001, c. 723.

54.1-517. Amended by Acts 1989, c. 397; Acts 1990, c. 823; Acts 1993, c. 660; Acts 1994, cc. 185, 911; Acts 1996, cc. 180, 846; Acts 1997, c. 885; Acts 1998, c. 739.

54.1-518 to 54.1-525. Repealed by Acts 1992, c. 282.

54.1-600. Amended by Acts 1991, c. 299; Acts 2003, c. 367.

54.1-601. Amended by Acts 1991, c. 299; Acts 1995, c. 227; Acts 1997, c. 801.

54.1-602. Amended by Acts 1991, c. 299.

54.1-603. Amended by Acts 1991, c. 299; Acts 1996, cc. 438, 822; Acts 1997, c. 281.

Sec.

54.1-604. Repealed by Acts 1991, c. 299.

54.1-606. Amended by Acts 1991, c. 299.

54.1-700. Amended by Acts 2000, c. 726; Acts 2002, cc. 797, 869; Acts 2003, c. 600.

54.1-701. Amended by Acts 2000, c. 726; Acts 2002, cc. 797, 869; Acts 2003, c. 600.

54.1-702. Amended by Acts 2000, c. 726; Acts 2002, c. 869; Acts 2004, c. 945.

54.1-703. Amended by Acts 2000, c. 726; Acts 2002, cc. 797, 869; Acts 2003, c. 600.

54.1-704. Amended by Acts 2000, c. 726.

54.1-704.1. Amended by Acts 2002, cc. 797, 869; Acts 2003, c. 600.

54.1-704.2. Amended by Acts 2002, cc. 797, 869; Acts 2003, c. 600.

54.1-705. Amended by Acts 1993, c. 499; Acts 2000, c. 726; Acts 2002, cc. 797, 869; Acts 2003, c. 600.

54.1-706. Amended by Acts 2000, c. 726; Acts 2002, cc. 797, 869.

54.1-800 to 54.1-827. Repealed by Acts 1998, c. 895.

54.1-902. Amended by Acts 1989, c. 584.

54.1-907. Amended by Acts 1990, c. 72.

54.1-918. Amended by Acts 1992, c. 10.

54.1-1000 to 54.1-1003. Repealed by Acts 1990, c. 466.

54.1-1100. Amended by Acts 1990, c. 911; Acts 1992, cc. 330, 713, 715, 812; Acts 1993, cc. 499, 815; Acts 1994, cc. 601, 754; Acts 1997, c. 885; Acts 1998, c. 754.

54.1-1101. Amended by Acts 1990, c. 911; Acts 1995, c. 581; Acts 1998, c. 754; Acts 2003, c. 1025; Acts 2004, c. 189.

54.1-1102. Amended by Acts 1991, c. 659; Acts 1994, c. 895; Acts 1995, c. 771; Acts 1996, cc. 380, 934, 1006; Acts 1997, c. 885.

54.1-1103. Amended by Acts 1990, c. 911; Acts 1992, c. 713; Acts 1994, cc. 601, 754; Acts 1995, cc. 581, 771; Acts 1997, c. 885; Acts 1998, cc. 271, 754; Acts 1999, cc. 959, 977, 991; Acts 2002, c. 653; Acts 2004, c. 190.

54.1-1105. Repealed by Acts 1991, c. 151.

54.1-1106. Amended by Acts 1990, c. 911; Acts 1992, c. 713; Acts 1994, c. 601; Acts 1996, c. 707; Acts 1998, c. 754; Acts 1999, c. 393; Acts 2003, c. 892.

54.1-1106.1. Amended by Acts 1990, c. 911.

54.1-1107. Repealed by Acts 1990, c. 911.

54.1-1108. Amended by Acts 1990, c. 911; Acts 1994, c. 601; Acts 1996, c. 707; Acts 2003, c. 892.

Sec.
54.1-1108.1. Amended by Acts 1996, c. 707; Acts 2003, c. 892.
54.1-1108.2. Amended by Acts 1997, c. 885; Acts 1998, c. 754; Acts 2003, c. 892.
54.1-1109. Amended by Acts 1990, c. 911; Acts 1995, c. 711; Acts 1996, c. 1014.
54.1-1110. Amended by Acts 1990, c. 911; Acts 1992, c. 243; Acts 1995, c. 711; Acts 1996, c. 380.
54.1-1111. Amended by Acts 1990, c. 911; Acts 1991, c. 151; Acts 1992, c. 713; Acts 1995, c. 771; Acts 1998, c. 754.
54.1-1112. Amended by Acts 1990, c. 911; Acts 1995, c. 771.
54.1-1114. Amended by Acts 1990, c. 911; Acts 1995, c. 771.
54.1-1115. Amended by Acts 1990, c. 911; Acts 1994, c. 79; Acts 1995, c. 771; Acts 1998, c. 691; Acts 2000, c. 33; Acts 2003, cc. 429, 430; Acts 2004, c. 131.
54.1-1116. Repealed by Acts 1993, c. 717.
54.1-1117. Amended by Acts 1994, c. 895.
54.1-1118. Amended by Acts 1990, cc. 437, 911; Acts 1994, c. 895; Acts 1995, cc. 771, 784; Acts 1996, cc. 934, 1006; Acts 1997, c. 885; Acts 1999, c. 55.
54.1-1119. Amended by Acts 1990, cc. 3, 437, 911; Acts 1992, c. 810; Acts 1995, c. 771; Acts 1996, c. 96; Acts 1997, c. 885.
54.1-1120. Amended by Acts 1990, cc. 215, 437, 911; Acts 1995, c. 784; Acts 1996, c. 96; Acts 1997, c. 885; Acts 1999, cc. 55, 261.
54.1-1123. Amended by Acts 1990, cc. 437, 911; Acts 1997, c. 885; Acts 1999, c. 262.
54.1-1125. Amended by Acts 1997, c. 885.
54.1-1126. Amended by Acts 1990, c. 911; Acts 1995, c. 771; Acts 1997, c. 885.
54.1-1127. Amended by Acts 1997, c. 885.
54.1-1128. Amended by Acts 1996, cc. 934, 1006; Acts 1997, c. 403; Acts 1999, c. 343.
54.1-1129. Amended by Acts 1996, cc. 934, 1006; Acts 1997, cc. 403, 885; Acts 1999, c. 343; Acts 2000, c. 406.
54.1-1130. Amended by Acts 1996, cc. 934, 1006; Acts 1997, cc. 403, 885; Acts 1999, c. 343; Acts 2003, c. 892.
54.1-1131. Amended by Acts 1995, c. 581; Acts 1996, cc. 934, 1006; Acts 1997, cc. 403, 885; Acts 1999, cc. 343, 817, 833; Acts 2000, c. 406.
54.1-1132 to 54.1-1135. Amended by Acts 1996, cc. 934, 1006; Acts 1997, cc. 403, 885; Acts 1999, cc. 343, 833.
54.1-1200 to 54.1-1207. Repealed by Acts 2000, c. 726.

Sec.
54.1-1300 to 54.1-1308. Repealed by Acts 1996, cc. 61, 179.
54.1-1404. Amended by Acts 1994, c. 247; Acts 1996, c. 49.
54.1-1501. Amended by Acts 1996, c. 741.
54.1-1502, 54.1-1503. Amended by Acts 1994, c. 26.
54.1-1600 to 54.1-1606. Repealed by Acts 1988, c. 716.
54.1-1701. Amended by Acts 2002, c. 740.
54.1-1703. Amended by Acts 1999, c. 532.
54.1-1706. Amended by Acts 1993, c. 206.
54.1-1800. Amended by Acts 1993, c. 499.
54.1-1805. Amended by Acts 2003, cc. 545, 554.
54.1-1900 to 54.1-1908. Repealed by Acts 1992, c. 578.
54.1-2000 to 54.1-2008. Repealed by Acts 2001, c. 832.
54.1-2009. Amended by Acts 1995, c. 327.
54.1-2010. Amended by Acts 1992, c. 68; Acts 1995, c. 327; Acts 1999, c. 259.
54.1-2011. Amended by Acts 1992, c. 338.
54.1-2012. Amended by Acts 1992, c. 68; Acts 1999, cc. 208, 505.
54.1-2013. Amended by Acts 1992, c. 68; Acts 1993, c. 539.
54.1-2017. Amended by Acts 1999, c. 57.
54.1-2019. Amended by Acts 1993, c. 499.
54.1-2100. Amended by Acts 1996, c. 993; Acts 2001, c. 548.
54.1-2101. Amended by Acts 1992, c. 84; Acts 1996, c. 993; Acts 2001, c. 548.
54.1-2102. Repealed by Acts 1992, c. 84.
54.1-2103. Amended by Acts 1992, c. 84; Acts 1993, cc. 816, 899; Acts 1995, c. 227; Acts 1998, cc. 261, 262.
54.1-2104. Amended by Acts 1992, c. 809.
54.1-2105. Amended by Acts 1989, c. 244; Acts 1991, c. 576; Acts 1992, cc. 65, 446, 624, 717; Acts 1995, c. 125; Acts 1996, cc. 890, 903; Acts 1997, c. 389; Acts 1998, c. 268; Acts 2000, c. 759; Acts 2003, cc. 998, 1027.
54.1-2105.1. Amended by Acts 2000, c. 759.
54.1-2106. Repealed by Acts 1996, c. 993.
54.1-2106.1. Amended by Acts 1998, c. 265; Acts 1999, cc. 82, 105.
54.1-2108. Amended by Acts 1997, c. 82; Acts 1998, c. 29.
54.1-2111. Amended by Acts 1993, c. 499.
54.1-2112. Amended by Acts 1992, c. 348; Acts 1993, c. 499.
54.1-2113. Amended by Acts 1992, cc. 348, 810; Acts 1997, c. 82.
54.1-2114. Amended by Acts 1996, c. 115.
54.1-2138. Amended by Acts 1997, cc. 86, 119.
54.1-2200. Amended by Acts 1993, c. 499; Acts 2002, c. 784.
54.1-2201. Amended by Acts 1993, c. 499; Acts 2002, c. 784.
54.1-2202. Amended by Acts 2002, c. 784.
54.1-2203. Amended by Acts 2002, c. 784.

Sec.
54.1-2205. Amended by Acts 1991, c. 181.
54.1-2206. Amended by Acts 1991, c. 181; Acts 2002, c. 784; Acts 2003, c. 447.
54.1-2207, 54.1-2208. Amended by Acts 2002, c. 784.
54.1-2210. Amended by Acts 1996, cc. 78, 824.
54.1-2211, 54.1-2212. Amended by Acts 1997, c. 885.
54.1-2213. Amended by Acts 1990, c. 3.
54.1-2301. Amended by Acts 1989, c. 97.
54.1-2310. Amended by Acts 1998, cc. 708, 721; Acts 2000, c. 36.
54.1-2311. Amended by Acts 1998, cc. 708, 721.
54.1-2312. Amended by Acts 1998, cc. 708, 721.
54.1-2313. Amended by Acts 1998, cc. 708, 721; Acts 2004, c. 247.
54.1-2314. Amended by Acts 1998, cc. 708, 721.
54.1-2315. Amended by Acts 1998, cc. 708, 721.
54.1-2316. Amended by Acts 1998, cc. 708, 721; Acts 2004, c. 192.
54.1-2317. Amended by Acts 1998, cc. 708, 721.
54.1-2318. Amended by Acts 1998, cc. 708, 721.
54.1-2319. Amended by Acts 1998, cc. 708, 721; Acts 2000, c. 36.
54.1-2320. Amended by Acts 1998, cc. 708, 721.
54.1-2321. Amended by Acts 1998, cc. 708, 721.
54.1-2322. Amended by Acts 1998, cc. 708, 721; Acts 2004, c. 192.
54.1-2323. Amended by Acts 1998, cc. 708, 721.
54.1-2324. Amended by Acts 1998, cc. 708, 721; Acts 2000, c. 36; Acts 2004, c. 247.
54.1-2325. Amended by Acts 1998, cc. 708, 721.
54.1-2326. Amended by Acts 1998, cc. 708, 721.
54.1-2327. Amended by Acts 1998, cc. 708, 721.
54.1-2328. Amended by Acts 1998, cc. 708, 721.
54.1-2329. Amended by Acts 1998, cc. 708, 721.
54.1-2330. Amended by Acts 1998, cc. 708, 721.
54.1-2331. Amended by Acts 1998, cc. 708, 721.
54.1-2332. Amended by Acts 1998, cc. 708, 721.
54.1-2333. Amended by Acts 1998, cc. 708, 721; Acts 2000, c. 36; Acts 2004, c. 247.
54.1-2334. Amended by Acts 1998, cc. 708, 721.
54.1-2335. Amended by Acts 1998, cc. 708, 721.
54.1-2336. Amended by Acts 1998, cc. 708, 721.
54.1-2337. Amended by Acts 1998, cc. 708, 721.
54.1-2338. Amended by Acts 1998, cc. 708, 721.
54.1-2339. Amended by Acts 1998, cc. 708, 721.
54.1-2340. Amended by Acts 1998, cc. 708, 721.
54.1-2341. Amended by Acts 1998, cc. 708, 721.
54.1-2342. Amended by Acts 1998, cc. 708, 721.
54.1-2400. Amended by Acts 1992, cc. 659, 890; Acts 1997, cc. 439, 564; Acts 1998, c. 469; Acts 2002, cc. 455, 698; Acts 2003, cc. 753, 762; Acts 2004, cc. 49, 64.
54.1-2400.1. Amended by Acts 1997, c. 901.
54.1-2400.2. Amended by Acts 1998, c. 744; Acts 1999, c. 888; Acts 2003, cc. 753, 762; Acts 2004, c. 49.
54.1-2400.3. Amended by Acts 1998, c. 744; Acts 2003, cc. 753, 762.
54.1-2401. Amended by Acts 1992, c. 659; Acts 1997, c. 564; Acts 2003, cc. 753, 762; Acts 2004, c. 49.
54.1-2403.01. Amended by Acts 2004, c. 49.
54.1-2403.1. Amended by Acts 2004, c. 49.
54.1-2403.2. Amended by Acts 1998, c. 470; Acts 2004, c. 49.
54.1-2403.3. Amended by Acts 1997, c. 682; Acts 1998, c. 470.
54.1-2405. Amended by Acts 2003, cc. 753, 762, 912, 917; Acts 2004, c. 53.
54.1-2408.1. Amended by Acts 2004, c. 49.
54.1-2409. Amended by Acts 1997, c. 801; Acts 2002, c. 455; Acts 2004, c. 49.
54.1-2409.1. Amended by Acts 2004, c. 49.
54.1-2410. Amended by Acts 2000, c. 201.
54.1-2503. Amended by Acts 1992, cc. 706, 841; Acts 1993, c. 869; Acts 2000, cc. 473, 688.
54.1-2505. Amended by Acts 1997, c. 439; Acts 2002, c. 481; Acts 2004, c. 64.
54.1-2506. Amended by Acts 1993, c. 869; Acts 2003, cc. 753, 762.
54.1-2506.01. Amended by Acts 2004, c. 64.
54.1-2506.1. Amended by Acts 1997, c. 806; Acts 2003, c. 602.
54.1-2510. Amended by Acts 1993, c. 869.
54.1-2517. Amended by Acts 1999, cc. 703, 726; Acts 2004, c. 690.
54.1-2523. Amended by Acts 2004, c. 690.
54.1-2600 to 54.1-2602. Amended by Acts 1992, c. 706.
54.1-2603. Amended by Acts 1999, cc. 967, 1005.
54.1-2700. Amended by Acts 2001, c. 662.
54.1-2701. Amended by Acts 1995, c. 509; Acts 2002, c. 740; Acts 2003, c. 495.
54.1-2702. Amended by Acts 1992, c. 411.
54.1-2706. Amended by Acts 2001, c. 662; Acts 2004, c. 64.
54.1-2708. Amended by Acts 1997, c. 556.
54.1-2708.1. Repealed by Acts 1997, c. 698.
54.1-2709. Amended by Acts 1997, c. 855.
54.1-2709.2. Amended by Acts 2004, c. 64.
54.1-2710. Amended by Acts 1995, cc. 608, 627.
54.1-2712. Amended by Acts 1989, c. 131; Acts 1994, c. 749.
54.1-2712.1. Amended by Acts 1998, c. 326; Acts 2004, c. 754.
54.1-2715. Amended by Acts 2002, c. 549; Acts 2004, c. 48.
54.1-2717, 54.1-2718. Amended by Acts 1992, c. 574; Acts 2004, c. 48.
54.1-2722. Amended by Acts 1990, c. 441; Acts 1997, c. 855; Acts 2002, c. 170.
54.1-2726.1. Amended by Acts 1998, c. 326.
54.1-2729. Amended by Acts 1997, c. 3; Acts 2004, c. 137.
54.1-2729.1. Amended by Acts 2003, c. 995.
54.1-2800. Amended by Acts 1991, c. 539; Acts 1997, c. 116; Acts 1998, cc. 718, 867; Acts 2003, c. 505.
54.1-2802. Amended by Acts 2000, c. 773.

Sec.
54.1-2803. Amended by Acts 2000, c. 773; Acts 2003, c. 505.
54.1-2805. Amended by Acts 2000, c. 773.
54.1-2806. Amended by Acts 1990, c. 363; Acts 1996, c. 142; Acts 2003, c. 505.
54.1-2807. Amended by Acts 1993, c. 965.
54.1-2808. Repealed by Acts 1998, c. 867.
54.1-2810. Amended by Acts 1996, c. 757; Acts 2000, c. 773.
54.1-2813. Amended by Acts 1990, c. 363.
54.1-2814. Amended by Acts 2000, c. 773.
54.1-2814.1. Amended by Acts 2003, c. 505.
54.1-2818.3. Amended by Acts 2003, c. 505.
54.1-2820. Amended by Acts 1991, c. 721; Acts 1992, c. 635; Acts 1998, c. 738; Acts 1999, c. 819; Acts 2003, cc. 663, 673.
54.1-2822. Amended by Acts 1992, c. 337.
54.1-2825. Amended by Acts 1998, c. 718.
54.1-2900. Amended by Acts 1991, c. 643; Acts 1994, c. 803; Acts 1995, c. 777; Acts 1996, cc. 152, 158, 470, 937, 980; Acts 1998, cc. 319, 557, 593; Acts 1999, cc. 639, 682, 747, 779; Acts 2000, cc. 688, 814; Acts 2001, c. 533; Acts 2004, c. 731.
54.1-2901. Amended by Acts 1992, cc. 412, 414; Acts 1994, c. 787; Acts 1995, cc. 509, 777; Acts 1996, cc. 775, 779, 937, 980; Acts 1998, cc. 630, 803, 854; Acts 1999, cc. 570, 814; Acts 2000, cc. 688, 814; Acts 2001, c. 235; Acts 2002, c. 740; Acts 2003, cc. 514, 519, 641.
54.1-2902. Amended by Acts 1996, cc. 937, 980; Acts 2000, c. 688.
54.1-2903. Amended by Acts 1991, c. 102; Acts 1996, cc. 937, 980; Acts 2000, c. 688.
54.1-2904. Amended by Acts 1996, cc. 937, 980; Acts 2000, c. 688.
54.1-2906. Repealed by Acts 2004, c. 64.
54.1-2907. Repealed by Acts 2004, c. 64.
54.1-2908. Amended by Acts 1996, cc. 937, 980; Acts 2000, c. 688; Acts 2003, cc. 753, 762.
54.1-2909. Amended by Acts 1998, c. 744; Acts 2003, cc. 753, 762; Acts 2003, cc. 753, 762.
54.1-2910. Repealed by Acts 1997, c. 698.
54.1-2910.1. Amended by Acts 1999, c. 573; Acts 2000, c. 199; Acts 2001, c. 199; Acts 2002, c. 38; Acts 2004, cc. 64, 703.
54.1-2911. Amended by Acts 2001, cc. 186, 198; Acts 2003, cc. 753, 762.
54.1-2912.1. Amended by Acts 2002, c. 324.
54.1-2913. Amended by Acts 1989, c. 45.
54.1-2914. Amended by Acts 1989, c. 510; Acts 1994, c. 70; Acts 1998, c. 580; Acts 2001, cc. 268, 858.
54.1-2915. Amended by Acts 1993, c. 991; Acts 1997, c. 801; Acts 2003, cc. 753, 762; Acts 2004, c. 64.
54.1-2916. Amended by Acts 1997, c. 801.
54.1-2917. Amended by Acts 1992, c. 659; Acts 1993, c. 991; Acts 1997, c. 801; Acts 2002, c. 455.
54.1-2919. Repealed by Acts 2004, c. 64.
54.1-2920. Amended by Acts 1996, c. 530; Acts 1997, c. 556.
54.1-2921. Repealed by Acts 2003, cc. 753, 762.
54.1-2922. Repealed by Acts 2004, cc. 40, 68.
54.1-2923. Repealed by Acts 2004, cc. 40, 68.
54.1-2925. Amended by Acts 1996, c. 519.
54.1-2926. Amended by Acts 1996, cc. 468, 496.
54.1-2927. Amended by Acts 1992, c. 414; Acts 1993, c. 784.
54.1-2929. Amended by Acts 1996, cc. 937, 980.
54.1-2931. Amended by Acts 1990, c. 818.
54.1-2933.1. Amended by Acts 2000, c. 788.
54.1-2935. Amended by Acts 2003, c. 996.
54.1-2936. Amended by Acts 2003, c. 473.
54.1-2938. Repealed by Acts 1991, c. 102.
54.1-2939. Amended by Acts 1999, c. 651.
54.1-2940. Repealed by Acts 2001, cc. 186, 198.
54.1-2942 to 54.1-2948. Repealed by Acts 2000, c. 688.
54.1-2950. Amended by Acts 1997, c. 806.
54.1-2950.1. Amended by Acts 2002, c. 698.
54.1-2951. Repealed by Acts 1998, c. 319.
54.1-2952. Amended by Acts 1992, c. 793; Acts 1996, c. 779; Acts 2000, cc. 467, 497; Acts 2001, c. 465; Acts 2002, c. 387.
54.1-2952.1. Amended by Acts 1997, c. 806; Acts 1999, c. 745; Acts 2003, c. 510.
54.1-2954. Amended by Acts 1998, c. 557.
54.1-2954.1. Amended by Acts 1998, c. 557.
54.1-2955. Amended by Acts 1990, c. 920; Acts 1998, c. 557.
54.1-2956. Amended by Acts 1990, c. 920;. Acts 1998, c. 557.
54.1-2956.1. Amended by Acts 1998, c. 593; Acts 2000, c. 782; Acts 2004, c. 61.
54.1-2956.3. Amended by Acts 2004, c. 61.
54.1-2956.4. Amended by Acts 1998, c. 593; Acts 2004, c. 61.
54.1-2956.5. Amended by Acts 1998, c. 593; Acts 2000, c. 782; Acts 2004, c. 61.
54.1-2956.6, 54.1-2956.7. Repealed by Acts 1994, c. 803.
54.1-2956.8. Amended by Acts 2002, c. 698.
54.1-2956.9. Amended by Acts 1993, c. 753; Acts 1996, c. 470; Acts 1999, c. 779; Acts 2000, c. 814.
54.1-2956.10. Amended by Acts 1993, c. 753.
54.1-2956.11. Amended by Acts 1993, c. 753; Acts 2000, c. 814; Acts 2002, c. 698; Acts 2003, c. 512.
54.1-2957.01. Amended by Acts 1991, c. 524; Acts 1992, c. 409; Acts 1995, c.

Sec.

506; Acts 1999, c. 745; Acts 2000, c. 924.

54.1-2957.1 to 54.1-2957.3. Repealed by Acts 1996, cc. 152, 158.

54.1-2957.4. Amended by Acts 2004, c. 669.

54.1-2957.5. Amended by Acts 2001, c. 61; Acts 2004, c. 669.

54.1-2957.6. Amended by Acts 2001, c. 61; Acts 2003, c. 529; Acts 2004, c. 669.

54.1-2961. Amended by Acts 1998, c. 614; Acts 2002, c. 87, 478; Acts 2003, c. 482.

54.1-2964. Amended by Acts 1989, c. 282; Acts 1993, c. 869.

54.1-2965. Repealed by Acts 1991, c. 643.

54.1-2969. Amended by Acts 1993, c. 930; Acts 1999, c. 1001; Acts 2000, c. 798; Acts 2002, cc. 315, 747.

54.1-2970. Amended by Acts 1989, c. 591; Acts 1997, c. 801; Acts 2002, c. 80.

54.1-2971.1. Amended by Acts 1995, c. 519.

54.1-2972. Amended by Acts 1996, c. 1028; Acts 1997, cc. 107, 453; Acts 2002, c. 92; Acts 2004, c. 92.

54.1-2973. Amended by Acts 1998, c. 718.

54.1-2976. Amended by Acts 1997, c. 921.

54.1-2981. Amended by Acts 1992, cc. 748, 772.

54.1-2982. Amended by Acts 1991, c. 583; Acts 1992, cc. 412, 748, 772; Acts 1994, c. 956; Acts 1997, c. 609; Acts 1998, cc. 630, 803, 854; Acts 1999, c. 814; Acts 2000, c. 1034.

54.1-2983. Amended by Acts 1992, cc. 748, 772; Acts 1997, c. 801.

54.1-2984. Amended by Acts 1989, c. 592; Acts 1991, c. 583; Acts 1992, cc. 748, 772; Acts 1997, c. 609; Acts 1999, c. 814; Acts 2000, c. 810.

54.1-2985. Amended by Acts 1992, cc. 748, 772.

54.1-2986. Amended by Acts 1992, cc. 748, 772; Acts 1999, c. 814; Acts 2000, c. 810.

54.1-2987. Amended by Acts 1992, cc. 748, 772; Acts 2000, cc. 590, 598.

54.1-2987.1. Amended by Acts 1994, c. 956; Acts 1998, cc. 564, 628, 630, 803, 854; Acts 1999, c. 814.

54.1-2988. Amended by Acts 1992, cc. 412, 748, 772; Acts 1998, cc. 803, 854; Acts 1999, c. 814; Acts 2000, cc. 590, 598.

54.1-2989. Amended by Acts 1992, cc. 412, 748, 772; Acts 1998, cc. 803, 854; Acts 1999, c. 814.

54.1-2990. Amended by Acts 1992, cc. 748, 772; Acts 1999, c. 814; Acts 2000, cc. 590, 598.

54.1-2991. Amended by Acts 1992, cc. 412, 748, 772; Acts 1999, c. 814.

54.1-2992. Amended by Acts 1992, cc. 748, 772; Acts 1997, c. 801; Acts 2000, cc. 590, 598.

54.1-3000. Amended by Acts 1989, cc. 7, 278; Acts 1990, c. 104; Acts 1996, c. 166; Acts 1998, c. 458; Acts 2004, c. 49.

54.1-3001. Amended by Acts 1994, cc. 58, 103; Acts 1996, c. 388; Acts 1999, c. 570; Acts 2001, cc. 244, 251; Acts 2002, cc. 713, 740.

54.1-3002. Amended by Acts 1993, c. 404.

54.1-3005. Amended by Acts 1989, cc. 7, 278; Acts 1990, c. 104; Acts 1994, c. 778; Acts 1996, c. 166; Acts 1998, c. 458; Acts 1999, cc. 570, 637; Acts 2000, cc. 587, 701; Acts 2004, c. 49.

54.1-3007. Amended by Acts 1989, c. 278; Acts 2003, c. 249.

54.1-3008. Amended by Acts 1996, c. 166; Acts 2004, c. 49.

54.1-3009. Repealed by Acts 2004, c. 64.

54.1-3010. Repealed by Acts 2004, c. 64.

54.1-3011.1. Amended by Acts 2000, cc. 240, 254.

54.1-3011.2. Amended by Acts 2000, cc. 240, 254; Acts 2001, c. 188; Acts 2002, c. 290.

54.1-3012.1. Amended by Acts 2002, c. 333.

54.1-3013. Amended by Acts 1989, c. 7.

54.1-3016. Amended by Acts 2004, c. 49.

54.1-3018. Amended by Acts 2002, c. 713.

54.1-3019. Amended by Acts 2004, c. 49.

54.1-3029. Amended by Acts 1997, c. 599; Acts 2004, c. 991.

54.1-3101. Amended by Acts 2001, cc. 527, 554.

54.1-3200. Amended by Acts 1991, c. 290; Acts 1996, cc. 152, 158, 365, 436; Acts 2004, c. 744.

54.1-3202. Amended by Acts 2002, c. 740.

54.1-3207. Amended by Acts 1996, cc. 152, 158.

54.1-3211. Amended by Acts 1996, cc. 365, 436; Acts 2004, c. 744.

54.1-3215. Amended by Acts 1990, c. 307; Acts 1992, c. 574; Acts 1999, c. 937.

54.1-3216. Repealed by Acts 2004, c. 64.

54.1-3217. Repealed by Acts 1997, c. 556.

54.1-3218. Repealed by Acts 2003, cc. 753, 762.

54.1-3220. Amended by Acts 1996, cc. 365, 436.

54.1-3221. Amended by Acts 1992, c. 146; Acts 2004, c. 744.

54.1-3222, 54.1-3223. Amended by Acts 1996, cc. 152, 158; Acts 2004, c. 744.

54.1-3224. Amended by Acts 1996, cc. 152, 158.

54.1-3300. Amended by Acts 1999, cc. 895, 1011; Acts 2001, c. 317; Acts 2002, c. 411.

54.1-3301. Amended by Acts 1989, c. 510; Acts 1998, c. 101; Acts 1999, cc. 745, 750; Acts 2000, c. 924; Acts 2001, c. 465; Acts 2002, cc. 666, 740; Acts 2003, c. 794.

54.1-3302. Amended by Acts 1989, c. 510.

54.1-3303. Amended by Acts 1991, cc. 519, 524; Acts 1992, c. 793; Acts 1996, cc. 152, 158, 408; Acts 1997, c. 806;

Sec.

Acts 1998, c. 101; Acts 1999, c. 745; Acts 2000, cc. 882, 924; Acts 2001, c. 465; Acts 2003, c. 639; Acts 2004, c. 744.

54.1-3304.1. Amended by Acts 1989, c. 510.

54.1-3305. Amended by Acts 1994, c. 283.

54.1-3307. Amended by Acts 1995, c. 529; Acts 1996, cc. 37, 407.

54.1-3307.1. Repealed by Acts 1997, c. 206.

54.1-3312. Amended by Acts 1994, c. 657.

54.1-3313. Amended by Acts 1990, c. 269.

54.1-3316. Amended by Acts 1992, c. 868; Acts 1994, c. 296.

54.1-3317. Repealed by Acts 1997, c. 556.

54.1-3321. Amended by Acts 2004, c. 47.

54.1-3401. Amended by Acts 1991, cc. 519, 524; Acts 1992, cc. 737, 793; Acts 1996, cc. 37, 152, 158, 407, 408; Acts 1997, cc. 20, 677, 806; Acts 1998, c. 470; Acts 1999, cc. 661, 750; Acts 2000, cc. 861, 878, 935; Acts 2003, cc. 509, 639, 995.

54.1-3402. Repealed by Acts 2003, c. 509.

54.1-3404. Amended by Acts 1998, c. 105; Acts 2004, c. 51.

54.1-3405. Amended by Acts 1992, cc. 743, 808.

54.1-3408. Amended by Acts 1990, c. 309; Acts 1991, cc. 141, 519, 524, 532; Acts 1992, cc. 610, 760, 793; Acts 1993, cc. 15, 810, 957, 993; Acts 1994, c. 53; Acts 1995, cc. 88, 529; Acts 1996, cc. 152, 158, 183, 406, 408, 490; Acts 1997, cc. 272, 566, 806, 906; Acts 1998, c. 112; Acts 1999, c. 570; Acts 2000, cc. 135, 498, 861, 881, 935; Acts 2003, cc. 465, 497, 515, 794, 995, 1020.

54.1-3408.01. Amended by Acts 2002, c. 411; Acts 2003, c. 639.

54.1-3408.1. Amended by Acts 1990, c. 681; Acts 1995, c. 277.

54.1-3410, 54.1-3411. Amended by Acts 1996, c. 408; Acts 2003, c. 511.

54.1-3412. Amended by Acts 2002, c. 411.

54.1-3415. Amended by Acts 1998, c. 490.

54.1-3420.2. Amended by Acts 2002, c. 411.

54.1-3421. Amended by Acts 2000, c. 135.

54.1-3422. Amended by Acts 1996, cc. 408, 468, 496; Acts 1998, c. 490; Acts 2001, cc. 243, 465.

54.1-3423. Amended by Acts 1996, cc. 468, 496; Acts 1998, c. 490.

54.1-3424. Amended by Acts 1996, cc. 468, 496; Acts 1998, c. 490.

54.1-3425. Amended by Acts 1990, c. 15.

54.1-3426. Amended by Acts 1996, c. 408.

54.1-3431. Amended by Acts 1990, c. 825.

54.1-3434. Amended by Acts 1994, c. 299; Acts 1998, c. 470; Acts 2000, c. 135.

54.1-3434.01. Amended by Acts 1994, c. 668; Acts 1998, c. 470.

54.1-3434.02. Amended by Acts 2004, c. 140.

Sec.

54.1-3434.1. Amended by Acts 1994, c. 300; Acts 2000, c. 882.

54.1-3435. Amended by Acts 1992, c. 737.

54.1-3435.02. Amended by Acts 2004, c. 854.

54.1-3435.1. Amended by Acts 1994, c. 300.

54.1-3435.2. Amended by Acts 1996, c. 408; Acts 1997, c. 677.

54.1-3436. Repealed by Acts 1992, c. 737.

54.1-3437 to 54.1-3439. Amended by Acts 1996, cc. 37, 407.

54.1-3441. Amended by Acts 1996, cc. 37, 407.

54.1-3443. Amended by Acts 1993, c. 866; Acts 1996, c. 408.

54.1-3446. Amended by Acts 1994, c. 763; Acts 1996, c. 408; Acts 1997, c. 594; Acts 1999, c. 722; Acts 2000, c. 348.

54.1-3448. Amended by Acts 1992, c. 737; Acts 1994, c. 763; Acts 1998, c. 105; Acts 2000, c. 135.

54.1-3450. Amended by Acts 1992, c. 737; Acts 2000, cc. 135, 348; Acts 2003, c. 640.

54.1-3452. Amended by Acts 1992, c. 737; Acts 1994, c. 763; Acts 1998, c. 105; Acts 1999, c. 605; Acts 2000, c. 135; Acts 2003, c. 640.

54.1-3454. Amended by Acts 1992, c. 737; Acts 1994, c. 763; Acts 2003, c. 640.

54.1-3455. Amended by Acts 1999, c. 605.

54.1-3457. Amended by Acts 2003, c. 639.

54.1-3463. Amended by Acts 1996, c. 408.

54.1-3473. Amended by Acts 2001, c. 858.

54.1-3474. Amended by Acts 2000, c. 688; Acts 2001, c. 858.

54.1-3475. Amended by Acts 2000, c. 688.

54.1-3476. Amended by Acts 2000, c. 688.

54.1-3477. Amended by Acts 2000, c. 688.

54.1-3478. Amended by Acts 2000, c. 688.

54.1-3479. Amended by Acts 2000, c. 688.

54.1-3480. Amended by Acts 2000, c. 688; Acts 2001, c. 858; Acts 2003, cc. 753, 762; Acts 2004, c. 64.

54.1-3482. Amended by Acts 2000, c. 688; Acts 2001, c. 858; Acts 2002, cc. 434, 471; Acts 2003, c. 496.

54.1-3483. Amended by Acts 2001, c. 858.

54.1-3500. Amended by Acts 1993, c. 342; Acts 1995, c. 820; Acts 1997, c. 901; Acts 2000, c. 473; Acts 2001, c. 460.

54.1-3501. Amended by Acts 1995, c. 820; Acts 1997, c. 901.

54.1-3503 to 54.1-3504. Amended by Acts 1995, c. 820; Acts 1997, c. 901.

54.1-3503. Amended by Acts 2000, c. 473.

54.1-3505. Amended by Acts 1994, cc. 558, 778; Acts 1995, c. 820; Acts 1997, c. 901; Acts 2001, c. 4.

54.1-3506. Amended by Acts 1995, c. 820; Acts 1997, c. 901.

54.1-3507. Amended by Acts 2001, c. 460.

Sec.
54.1-3508. Amended by Acts 1999, c. 863.
54.1-3510. Amended by Acts 1995, c. 343; Acts 1997, c. 839; Acts 2001, c. 483; Acts 2004, c. 10.
54.1-3511. Repealed by Acts 2004, c. 10.
54.1-3512. Repealed by Acts 2004, c. 10.
54.1-3513. Amended by Acts 2000, c. 473; Acts 2004, c. 271.
54.1-3514. Amended by Acts 2000, c. 473.
54.1-3515. Amended by Acts 1999, c. 609; Acts 2000, c. 473.
54.1-3600. Amended by Acts 1994, c. 778; Acts 1996, cc. 937, 980; Acts 2004, c. 11.
54.1-3601. Amended by Acts 1996, cc. 937, 980; Acts 2000, c. 462.
54.1-3603, 54.1-3604. Amended by Acts 1996, cc. 937, 980.
54.1-3605. Amended by Acts 1993, c. 767; Acts 1994, c. 778; Acts 1996, cc. 937, 980; Acts 1997, c. 556; Acts 1999, c. 630; Acts 2001, cc. 186, 198; Acts 2004, c. 11..
54.1-3606. Amended by Acts 1996, cc. 937, 980; Acts 1999, cc. 967, 1005.
54.1-3607. Repealed by Acts 1996, cc. 937, 980.
54.1-3608. Repealed by Acts 2001, cc. 186, 198.
54.1-3609. Repealed by Acts 2004, c. 11.
54.1-3610. Repealed by Acts 2004, c. 11.
54.1-3611. Amended by Acts 1999, c. 630; Acts 2000, c. 473.
54.1-3612. Repealed by Acts 1997, c. 698.
54.1-3613. Repealed by Acts 2004, cc. 40, 68.
54.1-3614. Amended by Acts 1996, cc. 937, 980.
54.1-3615. Repealed by Acts 2004, c. 64.
54.1-3616. Amended by Acts 1996, cc. 937, 980.
54.1-3705. Amended by Acts 1994, c. 778.
54.1-3710 to 54.1-3716. Repealed by Acts 1994, c. 514.
54.1-3801. Amended by Acts 2002, c. 740.
54.1-3802. Amended by Acts 1995, c. 644.
54.1-3806.1. Amended by Acts 1998, c. 158.
54.1-3808. Repealed by Acts 1997, c. 556.
54.1-3812. Amended by Acts 2004, c. 855.
54.1-3900. Amended by Acts 1991, c. 650; Acts 1994, c. 30; Acts 1998, c. 796.
54.1-3900.01. Amended by Acts 1997, c. 239.
54.1-3901. Amended by Acts 2000, c. 355.
54.1-3902. Amended by Acts 1992, c. 574; Acts 1995, c. 116; Acts 2000, c. 355.
54.1-3904. Amended by Acts 1994, c. 441.
54.1-3905. Amended by Acts 1994, c. 567; Acts 2004, c. 790.
54.1-3908. Amended by Acts 1992, c. 574; Acts 1996, c. 399.
54.1-3909. Amended by Acts 1992, c. 574.
54.1-3910. Amended by Acts 1991, c. 564; Acts 2002, c. 306.
54.1-3912. Amended by Acts 1993, c. 38; Acts 1995, c. 15.
54.1-3916. Amended by Acts 1995, c. 93.
54.1-3919. Amended by Acts 1998, c. 796.
54.1-3922. Amended by Acts 1998, c. 796.

Sec.
54.1-3923. Amended by Acts 1992, c. 734; Acts 1993, c. 262.
54.1-3925. Amended by Acts 1992, c. 734; Acts 1998, c. 71.
54.1-3925.1. Amended by Acts 1998, c. 796.
54.1-3926. Amended by Acts 1995, c. 336; Acts 1998, cc. 119, 796.
54.1-3928. Amended by Acts 1998, c. 796.
54.1-3931. Amended by Acts 1998, c. 796.
54.1-3932. Amended by Acts 2001, c. 495.
54.1-3935. Amended by Acts 1997, c. 238; Acts 1998, cc. 339, 637.
54.1-3936. Amended by Acts 1997, c. 239.
54.1-3936, 54.1-3937. Amended by Acts 1992, c. 574.
54.1-4000. Amended by Acts 1998, c. 848.
54.1-4001. Amended by Acts 1998, c. 848.
54.1-4002. Amended by Acts 1998, c. 848.
54.1-4003. Amended by Acts 1998, c. 848.
54.1-4004. Amended by Acts 1998, c. 848.
54.1-4005. Amended by Acts 1998, c. 848; Acts 1999, c. 327.
54.1-4006, 54.1-4007. Repealed by Acts 1998, c. 848.
54.1-4008. Amended by Acts 1998, c. 848; Acts 1999, c. 327.
54.1-4009. Amended by Acts 1990, c. 783; Acts 1998, c. 848; Acts 2001, c. 401; Acts 2003, c. 448.
54.1-4010. Amended by Acts 1998, c. 848; Acts 2001, c. 401; Acts 2002, c. 201; Acts 2003, c. 448.
54.1-4011. Amended by Acts 1990, c. 783; Acts 1998, c. 848.
54.1-4012. Amended by Acts 1998, c. 848; Acts 1999, c. 327; Acts 2003, c. 448.
54.1-4013. Amended by Acts 1998, c. 848.
54.1-4014. Amended by Acts 1998, c. 848.
54.1-4101. Amended by Acts 1990, c. 783; Acts 1991, c. 174.
54.1-4200. Amended by Acts 1993, c. 477.
54.1-4201. Amended by Acts 1993, cc. 461, 493.
54.1-4300. Amended by Acts 2002, cc. 138, 529.
54.1-4400. Amended by Acts 2003, c. 291; Acts 2004, c. 602.
54.1-4402. Amended by Acts 2003, c. 291; Acts 2004, c. 602.
54.1-4403. Amended by Acts 2004, c. 602.
54.1-4407. Amended by Acts 2004, c. 602.
54.1-4409. Amended by Acts 2003, c. 291; Acts 2004, c. 602.
54.1-4410. Amended by Acts 2003, c. 291; Acts 2004, c. 602.
54.1-4411. Amended by Acts 2003, c. 291.
54.1-4412. Amended by Acts 2003, c. 291; Acts 2004, c. 602.
54.1-4413. Amended by Acts 2003, c. 291; Acts 2004, c. 602.
54.1-4414. Amended by Acts 2004, c. 602.
54.1-4417. Amended by Acts 2003, c. 291.
55-1. Amended by Acts 1993, c. 535.
55-3. Amended by Acts 1973, c. 401.

Sec.
55-6. Amended by Acts 1962, c. 169.
55-7. Amended by Acts 1978, c. 659.
55-9. Amended by Acts 1986, c. 583; Acts 1987, c. 186; Acts 1999, c. 196.
55-13.2. Amended by Acts 2000, c. 714.
55-13.3. Amended by Acts 2000, cc. 658, 714.
55-17.1. Amended by Acts 1975, c. 375; Acts 1993, c. 454.
55-19. Amended by Acts 1958, c. 214; Acts 1980, c. 267; Acts 1989, c. 600; Acts 1990, cc. 425, 927; Acts 1996, c. 397; Acts 1997, c. 801; Acts 1998, c. 214; Acts 2001, c. 81.
55-19.1. Repealed by Acts 1990, c. 927.
55-19.2. Repealed by Acts 1991, c. 415.
55-19.3. Amended by Acts 1990, c. 262; Acts 1991, c. 415.
55-19.4. Amended by Acts 1996, c. 839.
55-19.5. Amended by Acts 1994, c. 692; Acts 1998, c. 735.
55-20. Amended by Acts 1990, c. 831.
55-20.1. Amended by Acts 2000, c. 331; Acts 2001, c. 718.
55-21. Amended by Acts 1999, c. 196; Acts 2001, c. 718.
55-24. Amended by Acts 1952, c. 375; Acts 1960, c. 105.
55-26. Repealed by Acts 1975, c. 547.
55-29. Amended by Acts 1997, c. 801.
55-29.1. Amended by Acts 1971, Ex. Sess., c. 173.
55-29.2. Amended by Acts 1971, Ex. Sess., c. 173.
55-29.3. Amended by Acts 1971, Ex. Sess., c. 173.
55-34.5. Amended by Acts 1995, c. 444.
55-34.13. Amended by Acts 1997, c. 801.
55-35. Amended by Acts 1990, c. 831.
55-36. Amended by Acts 1950, p. 460.
55-37. Amended by Acts 1984, c. 504; Acts 1985, c. 202.
55-40. Repealed by Acts 1990, c. 831.
55-41. Amended by Acts 1977, c. 147; Acts 1990, c. 831; Acts 1991, c. 625; Acts 1992, cc. 617, 647.
55-42. Repealed by Acts 1990, c. 831.
55-43. Amended by Acts 1990, c. 831.
55-44, 55-45. Repealed by Acts 1999, c. 16.
55-46. Amended by Acts 1990, c. 831.
55-47. Repealed by Acts 1992, cc. 617, 647.
55-48. Amended by Acts 1990, cc. 208, 374.
55-50. Amended by Acts 1992, c. 373.
55-52. Amended by Acts 1958, c. 424; Acts 1990, c. 831.
55-57.1. Amended by Acts 1982, c. 365; Acts 1984, c. 573.
55-58. Amended by Acts 1990, c. 374.
55-58.1. Amended by Acts 1962, c. 156; Acts 1966, c. 398; Acts 1974, c. 424; Acts 1998, c. 202.
55-58.2. Amended by Acts 1983, c. 124; Acts 1984, c. 19; Acts 1989, c. 346; Acts 1997, c. 205; Acts 2000, c. 971.
55-58.3. Amended by Acts 2002, c. 172; Acts 2003, cc. 381, 745.
55-59. Amended by Acts 1952, c. 370; Acts 1954, c. 557; Acts 1956, c. 674; Acts 1960, c. 5; Acts 1964, c. 501; Acts 1968, c. 786; Acts 1970, c. 12; Acts 1973, c. 341; Acts 1976, c. 257; Acts 1977, cc. 151, 314, 660; Acts 1979, c. 12; Acts 1980, c. 709; Acts 1981, c. 591; Acts 1992, cc. 87, 193; Acts 1993, c. 426; Acts 1994, c. 551.
55-59.1. Amended by Acts 1992, c. 739; Acts 1993, c. 597; Acts 1994, c. 143; Acts 2004, c. 1001.
55-59.2. Amended by Acts 1990, c. 749; Acts 1992, c. 550.
55-59.4. Amended by Acts 1997, c. 842; Acts 1998, c. 610.
55-60. Amended by Acts 1960, c. 93; Acts 1970, c. 39; Acts 1976, c. 155; Acts 1982, c. 230; Acts 2004, c. 253.
55-62. Amended by Acts 1977, c. 660; Acts 1979, c. 12.
55-63. Amended by Acts 1962, c. 448; Acts 1975, c. 284; Acts 1977, c. 660; Acts 1979, c. 12.
55-64. Amended by Acts 1990 c. 831.
55-65, 55-66. Amended by Acts 1975, c. 284.
55-66.01. Amended by Acts 1995, c. 807; Acts 1997, c. 205.
55-66.1. Repealed by Acts 1992, c. 532.
55-66.1:01. Repealed by Acts 1995, c. 807.
55-66.1:1. Amended by Acts 1999, c. 77.
55-66.3. Amended by Acts 1958, c. 14; Acts 1962, c. 39; Acts 1972, c. 280; Acts 1975, c. 469; Acts 1980, c. 116; Acts 1986, c. 462; Acts 1987, c. 673; Acts 1988, c. 546; Acts 1991, c. 414; Acts 1996, cc. 895, 949; Acts 1997, c. 221; Acts 2000, c. 28; Acts 2001, c. 711; Acts 2002, cc. 845, 862; Acts 2004, c. 596.
55-66.3:1. Amended by Acts 1996, c. 77.
55-66.4. Amended by Acts 1952, c. 469; Acts 1966, c. 505; Acts 1975, c. 469; Acts 1977, c. 141.
55-66.4:1. Amended by Acts 1977, c. 254; Acts 1982, c. 420; Acts 1983, c. 220; Acts 1984, c. 376; Acts 1990, c. 328; Acts 1994, c. 929; Acts 1995, c. 271; Acts 1996, c. 949.
55-66.4:2. Amended by Acts 1997, c. 579; Acts 2002, c. 832.
55-66.5. Amended by Acts 1956, c. 426; Acts 1975, c. 469; Acts 1987, c. 604; Acts 1992, c. 532; Acts 1999, c. 66.
55-66.6. Amended by Acts 1975, c. 469; Acts 1979, c. 648; Acts 1991, c. 414; Acts 1993, c. 39; Acts 2003, c. 245.
55-66.7. Repealed by Acts 1992, c. 651.

Sec.
55-70. Amended by Acts 1968, c. 257.
55-70.1. Amended by Acts 1988, c. 394; Acts 1992, c. 431; Acts 1999, c. 560; Acts 2002, c. 795; Acts 2003, c. 353.
55-79.01. Amended by Acts 1992, c. 438.
55-79.2. Amended by Acts 1966, c. 683; Acts 1972, c. 450.
55-79.3. Amended by Acts 1966, c. 683.
55-79.4, 55-79-7. Amended by Acts 1966, c. 683; Acts 1973, c. 375.
55-79.9. Amended by Acts 1966, c. 683; Acts 1973, c. 374.
55-79.11. Amended by Acts 1966, c. 683.
55-79.13. Amended by Acts 1966, c. 683; Acts 1973, c. 375.
55-79.14. Amended by Acts 1966, c. 683.
55-79.17. Amended by Acts 1972, c. 85.
55-79.28. Amended by Acts 1991, c. 710.
55-79.40. Amended by Acts 1982, c. 545; Acts 1989, c. 63.
55-79.41. Amended by Acts 1975, c. 415; Acts 1981, c. 480; Acts 1982, c. 545; Acts 1991, c. 497; Acts 1996, c. 977; Acts 2001, c. 715; Acts 2003, c. 442.
55-79.42. Amended by Acts 1986, c. 324; Acts 1993, c. 667.
55-79.43. Amended by Acts 1975, c. 415; Acts 1982, c. 663; Acts 1991, c. 497.
55-79.44. Amended by Acts 1975, c. 415; Acts 1982, c. 545; Acts 1998, c. 32.
55-79.46. Amended by Acts 1985, c. 107; Acts 1992, c. 72; Acts 1993, c. 667.
55-79.47. Amended by Acts 1975, c. 415.
55-79.48. Amended by Acts 1980, c. 702; Acts 1984, c. 21; Acts 1990, c. 831.
55-79.49. Amended by Acts 1975, c. 415; Acts 1982, c. 545.
55-79.50. Amended by Acts 1982, cc. 206, 545.
55-79.51. Amended by Acts 1975, c. 415.
55-79.52. Amended by Acts 1975, c. 415; Acts 1998, cc. 32, 454.
55-79.53. Amended by Acts 1975, c. 415; Acts 1993, c. 667; Acts 1996, c. 977.
55-79.54. Amended by Acts 1975, c. 415; Acts 1977, c. 428; Acts 1982, c. 545; Acts 1993, c. 667; Acts 1998, c. 32.
55-79.57. Amended by Acts 1983, c. 230; Acts 1991, c. 497; Acts 1998, c. 32.
55-79.58. Amended by Acts 1975, c. 415; Acts 1984, c. 601; Acts 1991, c. 497; Acts 1999, c. 560.
55-79.58:1. Amended by Acts 1988, c. 15; Acts 1999, c. 560.
55-79.59. Amended by Acts 1991, c. 497.
55-79.61. Amended by Acts 1975, c. 415; Acts 1986, c. 324; Acts 1991, c. 497; Acts 1993, c. 45.
55-79.62. Amended by Act 1999, c. 560.
55-79.63, 55-79.67. Amended by Acts 1975, c. 415.

Sec.
55-79.69, 55-79.70. Amended by Acts 1991, c. 497.
55-79.71. Amended by Acts 1993, c. 667.
55-79.72. Repealed by Acts 1993, c. 667.
55-79.73. Reenacted without change by Acts 1978, c. 332; Acts 1993, c. 667; Acts 1998, c. 32.
55-79.73:1. Amended by Acts 1998, c. 32.
55-79.74. Amended by Acts 1975, c. 415; Acts 1978, c. 332; Acts 1980, c. 738; Acts 1984, c. 601; Acts 1985, c. 83; Acts 1996, c. 977.
55-79.74:1. Amended by Acts 1985, c. 75; Acts 1989, c. 57; Acts 1990, c. 662; Acts 1992, c. 72; Acts 1994, c. 463; Acts 1999, c. 594; Acts 2000, cc. 906, 919; Acts 2001, c. 419.
55-79.74:3. Amended by Acts 1991, c. 497; Acts 1996, c. 977.
55-79.75. Amended by Acts 1978, c. 363; Acts 1989, c. 58; Acts 1990, c. 662; Acts 2000, c. 906; Acts 2001, c. 715; Acts 2003, cc. 404, 405, 442.
55-79.75:1. Amended by Acts 2003, c. 405.
55-79.76. Amended by Acts 2003, c. 413.
55-79.77. Amended by Acts 1980, c. 108; Acts 1991, c. 497; Acts 1993, c. 667; Acts 1998, c. 32; Acts 2003, c. 442.
55-79.78. Amended by Acts 1991, c. 497; Acts 1993, c. 667; Acts 2002, c. 520.
55-79.79. Amended by Acts 1975, c. 415; Acts 1980, c. 386; Acts 1982, c. 545; Acts 1984, c. 347; Acts 1987, c. 395.
55-79.80. Amended by Acts 1975, c. 415; Acts 1981, c. 146; Acts 1982, c. 195; Acts 1991, c. 497; Acts 1993, c. 667; Acts 1996, c. 977.
55-79.80:1. Amended by Acts 1991, c. 497; Acts 1992, c. 72; Acts 1996, c. 977.
55-79.80:2. Amended by Acts 1997, cc. 173, 417; Acts 2000, cc. 846, 906; Acts 2002, c. 509.
55-79.80:3. Amended by Acts 1998, c. 454.
55-79.81. Amended by Acts 2000, c. 906; Acts 2003, c. 360; Acts 2004, c. 596.
55-79.82. Repealed by Acts 1991, c. 497.
55-79.83. Reenacted without change by Acts 1977, c. 428; amended by Acts 1981, c. 180; Acts 1984, cc. 27, 84, 601; Acts 1992, c. 72; Acts 1993, c. 667; Acts 2003, c. 421.
55-79.84. Amended by Acts 1975, c. 415; Acts 1991, c. 497; Acts 1992, c. 72; Acts 1997, cc. 760, 766, 887; Acts 2000, c. 906; Acts 2004, cc. 779, 786.
55-79.84:1. Amended by Acts 1981, c. 480; Acts 1984, c. 601; Acts 1985, c. 107; Acts 1988, c. 15; Acts 1993, cc. 667, 900.
55-79.87. Amended by Acts 1975, c. 415; Acts 1984, c. 427; Acts 1993, c. 667.

Sec.
55-79.88. Amended by Acts 1975, c. 415; Acts 1988, c. 15.
55-79.89. Amended by Acts 1975, c. 415; Acts 1977, c. 428; Acts 1988, c. 16.
55-79.90. Amended by Acts 1977, c. 428; Acts 1986, c. 324; Acts 1996, cc. 281, 888; Acts 1999, c. 560.
55-79.91. Amended by Acts 1988, c. 15.
55-79.92. Amended by Acts 1985, c. 107; Acts 1988, c. 15.
55-79.93. Amended by Acts 1975, c. 415; Acts 1988, c. 15.
55-79.94. Amended by Acts 1975, c. 415; Acts 1980, cc. 727, 738; Acts 1981, cc. 455, 503; Acts 1982, cc. 273, 475, 663; Acts 1983, c. 310; Acts 1984, cc. 321, 601; Acts 1985, c. 69; Acts 1987, c. 412; Acts 1988, c. 723; Acts 1989, c. 398; Acts 1991, c. 497; Acts 1993, c. 634.
55-79.95. Amended by Acts 1977, c. 91; Acts 1982, c. 230.
55-79.97. Amended by Acts 1975, c. 415; Acts 1978, cc. 234, 290; Acts 1983, c. 60; Acts 1984, cc. 29, 103; Acts 1990, c. 662; Acts 1991, c. 497; Acts 1994, c. 172; Acts 1997, c. 222; Acts 1998, cc. 32, 454, 463; Acts 1999, c. 263; Acts 2001, c. 556; Acts 2002, cc. 459, 509.
55-79.98. Amended by Acts 1981, c. 480.
55-79.99. Amended by Acts 1993, c. 198.
55-79.100. Amended by Acts 1975, c. 415.
55-79.102. Amended by Acts 1996, c. 573.
55-81. Amended by Acts 1988, c. 512.
55-83 to 55-86. Repealed by Acts 1964, c. 219.
55-88 to 55-94. Repealed by Acts 1964, c. 219.
55-95. Amended by Acts 1964, c. 314; Acts 1966, c. 399.
55-96. Amended by Acts 1964, cc. 219, 309, 314; Acts 1966, c. 400; Acts 1974, c. 522; Acts 1984, c. 19; Acts 1988, c. 51; Acts 2003, c. 776.
55-96.1. Repealed by Acts 1966, c. 401.
55-98, 55-99. Repealed by Acts 1964, c. 219.
55-101. Amended by Acts 1987, c. 104.
55-106. Amended by Acts 1972, c. 130; Acts 1994, c. 554.
55-106.3. Repealed by Acts 1992, c. 532.
55-106.4. Amended by Acts 2002, c. 621.
55-108. Amended by Acts 1983, c. 291; Acts 1986, c. 346.
55-113. Amended by Acts 1968, c. 639; Acts 1972, c. 130.
55-114.1. Amended by Acts 1995, c. 48.
55-115. Amended by Acts 1964, c. 129; Acts 1972, c. 458; Acts 1995, c. 48.
55-116 to 55-118. Repealed by Acts 1980, c. 580.
55-118.5. Amended by Acts 1997, c. 801.
55-119. Amended by Acts 1959, Ex. Sess., c. 41; Acts 1975, c. 500.

Sec.
55-122. Amended by Acts 1959, Ex. Sess., c. 41; Acts 1975, c. 500; Acts 1984, c. 35; Acts 1989, c. 602.
55-123. Amended by Acts 1964, c. 57; Acts 1976, c. 685; Acts 1984, c. 35; Acts 1989, c. 602; Acts 1995, c. 48.
55-125. Amended by Acts 1952, c. 109; Acts 1956, c. 706; Acts 1958, c. 218; Acts 1962, c. 367; Acts 1966, cc. 137, 492; Acts 1968, c. 4; Acts 1972, c. 631; Acts 1976, c. 685; Acts 1980, c. 143; Acts 1984, c. 35; Acts 1989, c. 602; Acts 1995, c. 48.
55-125.1. Amended by Acts 1972, c. 631; Acts 1976, c. 685; Acts 1984, c. 35; Acts 1989, c. 602; Acts 1995, c. 48.
55-126. Amended by Acts 1976, c. 685; Acts 1984, c. 35; Acts 1989, c. 602; Acts 1995, c. 48.
55-127. Amended by Acts 1964, c. 384; Acts 1966, c. 492; Acts 1968, c. 4; Acts 1972, c. 631; Acts 1976, c. 685; Acts 1984, c. 35; Acts 1989, c. 602; Acts 1995, c. 48.
55-129. Amended by Acts 1976, c. 685; Acts 1984, c. 35; Acts 1989, c. 602; Acts 1995, c. 48.
55-130. Amended by Acts 1960, c. 285; Acts 1972, c. 631; Acts 1976, c. 685; Acts 1984, c. 35; Acts 1989, c. 602; Acts 1995, c. 48.
55-131. Amended by Acts 1952, c. 244; Acts 1966, c. 137; Acts 1972, c. 631; Acts 1976, c. 685; Acts 1984, c. 35; Acts 1989, c. 602; Acts 1995, c. 48.
55-132. Amended by Acts 1976, c. 685; Acts 1984, c. 35; Acts 1989, c. 602; Acts 1995, c. 48.
55-134. Amended by Acts 1952, c. 244; Acts 1972, c. 631; Acts 1976, c. 685; Acts 1984, c. 35; Acts 1989, c. 602; Acts 1995, c. 48.
55-134.1. Amended by Acts 1959, Ex. Sess., c. 92; Acts 1972, c. 631; Acts 1976, c. 685; Acts 1984, c. 35; Acts 1989, c. 602; Acts 1995, c. 48.
55-134.2. Amended by Acts 1989, c. 602; Acts 1995, c. 48.
55-135. Amended by Acts 1976, c. 685; Acts 1984, c. 35; Acts 1989, c. 602; Acts 1995, c. 48.
55-136. Amended by Acts 1956, c. 18; Acts 1962, c. 238; Acts 1964, Ex. Sess., c. 20; Acts 1966, c. 492; Acts 1968, c. 4; Acts 1972, c. 631; Acts 1974, c. 130; Acts 1975, c. 500.
55-137.1. Amended by Acts 1976, c. 685; Acts 1984, c. 35; Acts 1989, c. 602; Acts 1995, c. 48.
55-137.2. Amended by Acts 1976, c. 685; Acts 1984, c. 35; Acts 1989, c. 602; Acts 1995, c. 48.

Sec.
55-138. Amended by Acts 1990, c. 831.
55-139 to 55-139.2. Repealed by Acts 1970, c. 76.
55-141. Amended by Acts 1994, c. 432.
55-142. Repealed by Acts 1988, c. 100.
55-142.01. Amended by Acts 1994, c. 432; Acts 1996, c. 344.
55-142.1. Amended by Acts 1986, c. 299; Acts 1988, cc. 113, 388.
55-142.2 to 55-142.3. Amended by Acts 1988, cc. 113, 388.
55-142.4. Amended by Acts 1988, cc. 113, 388; Acts 1993, c. 43; Acts 1994, c. 432.
55-142.7. Amended by Acts 1988, cc. 113, 388.
55-143 to 55-151. Repealed by Acts 1964, c. 219.
55-152. Repealed by Acts 1973, c. 509.
55-154. Amended by Acts 1956, c. 642; Acts 1964, c. 377; Acts 1968, c. 319; Acts 1970, c. 350; Acts 1972, c. 306; Acts 1973, c. 123; Acts 1974, c. 238; Acts 1977, c. 309; Acts 1980, c. 310; Acts 1981, c. 518; Acts 1984, c. 452.
55-154.1. Repealed by Acts 1990, c. 601.
55-155. Amended by Acts 1977, c. 624.
55-167. Amended by Acts 1994, c. 432.
55-168. Amended by Acts 1982, c. 437; Acts 1996, c. 551.
55-169. Amended by Acts 1977, c. 583; Acts 1982, c. 437; Acts 1998, c. 215.
55-170.1. Amended by Acts 1988, c. 312; Acts 1996, c. 551.
55-171. Amended by Acts 1977, c. 583; Acts 1979, c. 340; Acts 1982, cc. 453, 550; Acts 1984, c. 315; Acts 1990, c. 938; Acts 1996, c. 551.
55-172. Amended by Acts 1977, c. 583; Acts 1982, c. 486; Acts 1984, c. 315; Acts 1988, c. 377; Acts 1996, c. 551.
55-173. Amended by Acts 1977, c. 583; Acts 1984, c. 315; Acts 1990, c. 938; Acts 1996, c. 551.
55-174. Amended by Acts 1977, c. 583.
55-175. Amended by Acts 1977, c. 583; Acts 1984, c. 315; Acts 1988, c. 377; Acts 1990, c. 938.
55-176. Amended by Acts 1983, c. 482; Acts 1990, c. 938.
55-180. Amended by Acts 1977, c. 583; Acts 1982, c. 486; Acts 1984, c. 315.
55-181, 55-182. Amended by Acts 1977, c. 583; Acts 1982, c. 486.
55-182.1. Amended by Acts 1990, c. 938; Acts 1991, c. 684.
55-183. Amended by Acts 1977, c. 583; Acts 1982, c. 486.
55-184. Repealed by Acts 1977, c. 583.
55-184.1. Amended by Acts 1981, c. 514; Acts 1982, c. 486; Acts 1996, cc. 256, 551.

Sec.
55-185. Repealed by Acts 1977, c. 583.
55-186. Amended by Acts 1952, c. 132; Acts 1977, c. 583; Acts 1981, c. 514; Acts 1982, c. 486; Acts 1984, c. 315; Acts 1988, c. 377; Acts 1990, c. 938.
55-186.1. Amended by Acts 1977, c. 583; Acts 1984, c. 315.
55-186.2. Amended by Acts 1982, cc. 486, 565; Acts 1984, c. 315; Acts 1998, c. 427.
55-187. Amended by Acts 1990, c. 938.
55-188. Repealed by Acts 1990, c. 938.
55-189. Amended by Acts 1977, c. 583; Acts 1981, c. 514; Acts 1990, c. 938.
55-190. Amended by Acts 1981, c. 514; Acts 1996, c. 551.
55-190.1. Amended by Acts 1990, c. 938.
55-191. Amended by Acts 1982, c. 486.
55-192. Amended by Acts 1977, c. 583; Acts 1981, c. 514; Acts 1984, c. 315.
55-193. Amended by Acts 1977, c. 583.
55-194. Amended by Acts 1990, c. 938.
55-197. Amended by Acts 1956, c. 15; Acts 1966, c. 251; Acts 1977, c. 583; Acts 1981, c. 514; Acts 1984, c. 315.
55-199. Amended by Acts 1977, c. 488.
55-200. Amended by Acts 1968, c. 626; Acts 1977, c. 583; Acts 1979, c. 340; Acts 1980, c. 213; Acts 1981, c. 514; Acts 1983, c. 482; Acts 1984, c. 315; Acts 1988, c. 377; Acts 1998, c. 427.
55-201.1. Amended by Acts 2003, c. 940.
55-202. Amended by Acts 1968, c. 639.
55-210.2. Amended by Acts 1981, c. 47; Acts 1982, c. 331; Acts 1983, c. 190; Acts 1984, c. 121; Acts 2000, cc. 733, 745.
55-210.2:1. Amended by Acts 1985, c. 294; Acts 2000, cc. 733, 745.
55-210.2:2. Amended by Acts 2000, cc. 733, 745.
55-210.3. Repealed by Acts 1984, c. 121.
55-210.3:01. Amended by Acts 1985, c. 294; Acts 1991, c. 357; Acts 1995, c. 624; Acts 1996, c. 419; Acts 2000, cc. 733, 745.
55-210.3:1. Repealed by Acts 1984, c. 121.
55-210.3:2. Amended by Acts 1985, c. 294.
55-210.4. Repealed by Acts 1984, c. 121.
55-210.4:1. Amended by Acts 2003, cc. 750, 765.
55-210.5. Amended by Acts 1981, c. 47; Acts 1983, c. 190.
55-210.6. Repealed by Acts 1991, c. 357.
55-210.6:1. Amended by Acts 1980, c. 293; Acts 1981, c. 47; Acts 1991, c. 357; Acts 1995, c. 624.
55-210.7. Amended by Acts 1981, c. 47; Acts 1983, c. 190.

Sec.
55-210.8. Amended by Acts 1981, c. 47; Acts 1982, c. 331; Acts 1984, c. 121; Acts 2000, cc. 733, 745.
55-210.8:1. Amended by Acts 1988, cc. 595, 643; Acts 2000, cc. 733, 745.
55-210.9. Amended by Acts 1980, c. 293; Acts 1982, c. 331; Acts 1983, c. 190; Acts 2000, cc. 733, 745.
55-210.9:1. Amended by Acts 1985, c. 294; Acts 2000, cc. 733, 745.
55-210.9:2. Amended by Acts 2000, cc. 733, 745.
55-210.10. Repealed by Acts 1984, c. 121.
55-210.10:1. Amended by Acts 2000, cc. 733, 745.
55-210.10:2. Amended by Acts 1983, c. 190.
55-210.11. Amended by Acts 1981, c. 47; Acts 2000, cc. 733, 745.
55-210.11:1. Repealed by Acts 1984, c. 121.
55-210.12. Amended by Acts 1981, c. 47; Acts 1982, c. 331; Acts 1983, c. 190; Acts 1984, c. 121; Acts 1985, c. 294; Acts 1987, c. 236; Acts 1988, c. 378; Acts 1992, c. 583; Acts 2000, cc. 733, 745; Acts 2003, cc. 750, 765; Acts 2004, c. 524.
55-210.12:1. Repealed by Acts 1983, c. 190.
55-210.13. Amended by Acts 1981, c. 47; Acts 1983, c. 190; Acts 1987, c. 236; Acts 1988, c. 378; Acts 1990, c. 460; Acts 2000, cc. 733, 745.
55-210.14. Repealed by Acts 1988, c. 378.
55-210.15. Amended by Acts 1964, c. 466; Acts 1984, c. 121.
55-210.16. Repealed by Acts 1981, c. 47.
55-210.17. Amended by Acts 2000, cc. 733, 745.
55-210.18. Amended by Acts 1981, c. 47; Acts 1982, c. 331; Acts 1984, c. 121; Acts 1985, c. 294; Acts 1994, c. 83; Acts 2004, c. 535.
55-210.19. Amended by Acts 1981, c. 47; Acts 1984, c. 121; Acts 1985, c. 294.
55-210.21. Amended by Acts 1981, c. 47; Acts 2000, cc. 733, 745; Acts 2004, c. 523.
55-210.22. Amended by Acts 2000, cc. 733, 745.
55-210.24. Amended by Acts 1983, c. 190; Acts 1985, c. 294; Acts 1991, c. 357; Acts 2000, cc. 733, 745.
55-210.24:1. Amended by Acts 1985, c. 294; Acts 1988, c. 378; Acts 2000, cc. 733, 745.
55-210.25. Amended by Acts 1983, c. 190; Acts 1988, c. 643; Acts 1991, c. 357; Acts 2000, cc. 733, 745.
55-210.26. Repealed by Acts 1984, c. 121.
55-210.26:1. Amended by Acts 1988, c. 378; Acts 1992, c. 583; Acts 2000, cc. 733, 745.
55-210.27. Amended by Acts 2000, cc. 733, 745.
55-210.27:1. Amended by Acts 1988, c. 378.
55-210.30. Amendment by Acts 1983, c. 308.

Sec.
55-213. Amended by Acts 1997, c. 801.
55-218.1. Amended by Acts 1987, c. 360.
55-220.1. Amended by Acts 1993, c. 427.
55-222. Amended by Acts 1981, c. 155; Acts 1986, c. 428; Acts 1987, c. 473; Acts 1993, c. 841; Acts 2004, c. 123.
55-222.1. Repealed by Acts 1974, c. 680.
55-226.2. Amended by Acts 2003, c. 355.
55-230. Amended by Acts 1962, c. 10; Acts 1974, c. 458; Acts 1976, c. 177; Acts 1980, c. 555; Acts 1986, c. 341; Acts 1993, c. 841.
55-230.1. Amended by Acts 1993, c. 841.
55-232. Amended by Acts 1970, c. 43; Acts 1975, c. 235; Acts 1977, c. 624; Acts 1980, c. 555; Acts 1986, c. 341.
55-232.1. Repealed by Acts 1993, c. 841.
55-232.2. Amended by Acts 1980, c. 555; Acts 1986, c. 341.
55-237. Amended by Acts 1962, c. 10; Acts 1975, c. 235; Acts 1980, c. 555.
55-243. Amended by Acts 1992, c. 427; Acts 1998, c. 269.
55-246. Amended by Acts 1994, c. 432.
55-246.1. Amended by Acts 1989, c. 612; Acts 1998, c. 452; Acts 2003, cc. 665, 667; Acts 2004, cc. 338, 365.
55-248.3. Amended by Acts 1977, c. 427.
55-248.3:1. Amended by Acts 2001, c. 416.
55-248.4. Amended by Acts 1977, c. 427; Acts 1987, c. 428; Acts 1990, c. 55; Acts 1991, c. 205; Acts 1999, cc. 77, 258, 359, 390; Acts 2000, cc. 760, 816; Acts 2002, c. 531; Acts 2003, cc. 355, 425, 855; Acts 2004, c. 123.
55-248.5. Amended by Acts 1975, c. 314; Acts 1977, c. 427; Acts 1983, c. 244; Acts 1985, c. 314; Acts 1988, cc. 184, 602; Acts 1991, c. 552; Acts 2000, c. 760.
55-248.6. Amended by Acts 1982, c. 260; Acts 1993, c. 754; Acts 1998, c. 260; Acts 2000, c. 760.
55-248.6:1. Amended by Acts 1985, c. 208; Acts 1993, c. 382; Acts 2000, c. 760; Acts 2003, c. 416.
55-248.7. Amended by Acts 1977, c. 427; Acts 1983, c. 39; Acts 1988, c. 68; Acts 2000, c. 760; Acts 2003, c. 424.
55-248.9. Amended by Acts 1977, c. 427; Acts 1987, c. 473; Acts 1991, c. 720; Acts 2000, c. 760; Acts 2002, c. 531; Acts 2003, c. 905.
55-248.9:1. Amended by Acts 2000, c. 760; Acts 2003, c. 426.
55-248.10. Repealed by Acts 2000, c. 760.
55-248.11. Repealed by Acts 2000, c. 760.
55-248.11:1. Amended by Acts 1992, c. 451; Acts 2000, c. 760.

Sec.
55-248.12. Amended by Acts 1983, c. 257; Acts 2000, c. 760.
55-248.13. Amended by Acts 1987, cc. 361, 636; Acts 2000, c. 760; Acts 2004, c. 226.
55-248.13:1. Amended by Acts 1988, c. 500.
55-248.13:2. Amended by Acts 2000, c. 760; Acts 2003, cc. 60, 64, 68.
55-248.14. Amended by Acts 1987, c. 313; Acts 2000, c. 760.
55-248.15. Amended by Acts 2000, c. 760.
55-248.15:1. Amended by Acts 2001, c. 524; Acts 2003, c. 438.
55-248.16. Amended by Acts 1987, c. 428; Acts 1999, c. 80; Acts 2000, c. 760; Acts 2003, c. 355; Acts 2004, c. 226.
55-248.17. Amended by Acts 2000, c. 760.
55-248.18. Amended by Acts 1993, c. 634; Acts 1995, c. 601; Acts 1999, c. 65; Acts 2000, c. 760; Acts 2001, c. 524; Acts 2004, c. 307.
55-248.19. Amended by Acts 2000, c. 760.
55-248.20. Amended by Acts 2000, c. 760.
55-248.21. Amended by Acts 1982, c. 260; Acts 1987, c. 387; Acts 2000, c. 760; Acts 2003, c. 363.
55-248.21:1. Amended by Acts 1978, c. 104; Acts 1982, c. 260; Acts 1983, c. 241; Acts 1986, c. 29; Acts 1988, c. 184; Acts 2000, c. 760; Acts 2002, c. 760.
55-248.22. Amended by Acts 2000, c. 760.
55-248.23. Amended by Acts 1982, c. 260; Acts 2000, c. 760.
55-248.24. Amended by Acts 1982, c. 260; Acts 2000, c. 760.
55-248.25. Amended by Acts 1982, c. 260; Acts 2000, c. 760.
55-248.26. Amended by Acts 2000, c. 760.
55-248.27. Amended by Acts 2000, c. 760; Acts 2001, c. 524.
55-248.28 to 55-248.30. Repealed by Acts 2000, c. 760.
55-248.31. Amended by Acts 1978, c. 378; Acts 1980, c. 502; Acts 1982, c. 260; Acts 1984, c. 78; Acts 1987, c. 387; Acts 1988, c. 62; Acts 1989, c. 301; Acts 1995, c. 580; Acts 2000, c. 760; Acts 2003, c. 363; Acts 2004, c. 232.
55-248.31:01. Amended by Acts 2000, c. 760.
55-248.31:1. Amended by Acts 1995, c. 51.
55-248.32. Amended by Acts 2000, c. 760.
55-248.33. Amended by Acts 2002, c. 761.
55-248.34. Repealed by Acts 2003, c. 427.
55-248.35. Amended by Acts 1981, c. 539; Acts 1988, c. 68; Acts 1989, c. 383; Acts 1996, c. 326; Acts 2000, c. 760; Acts 2001, c. 524.
55-248.36. Amended by Acts 1978, c. 520.
55-248.37. Amended by Acts 1977, c. 427; Acts 1982, c. 260; Acts 2004, c. 123.

Sec.
55-248.38. Repealed by Acts 2000, c. 760.
55-248.38:1. Amended by Acts 1995, c. 228; Acts 1998, c. 461; Acts 2000, c. 760; Acts 2002, c. 762.
55-248.39. Amended by Acts 1983, c. 396; Acts 1985, c. 268; Acts 2000, c. 760.
55-248.41. Amended by Acts 1983, c. 386; Acts 1991, c. 500; Acts 1992, c. 709.
55-248.42. Amended by Acts 1986, c. 586; Acts 1991, c. 500; Acts 1992, c. 709.
55-248.42:1. Amended by Acts 1999, c. 513; Acts 2000, c. 41.
55-248.43. Amended by Acts 1992, c. 709; Acts 2001, c. 44.
55-248.44, 55-248.44:1. Amended by Acts 1992, c. 709.
55-248.45. Amended by Acts 1987, c. 513; Acts 1989, c. 87; Acts 1992, c. 709.
55-248.46. Amended by Acts 1991, c. 185; Acts 1992, c. 709; Acts 2001, c. 47.
55-248.47. Amended by Acts 1986, c. 586; Acts 1992, c. 709.
55-248.48. Amended by Acts 2000, c. 760; Acts 2001, c. 47.
55-248.49. Amended by Acts 1999, c. 77.
55-248.50. Amended by Acts 1991, c. 185; Acts 1992, c. 709.
55-253 to 55-268. Repealed by Acts 1999, c. 975.
55-268.1. Amended by Acts 1995, c. 199; Acts 1997, c. 219.
55-269. Repealed by Acts 1973, c. 355.
55-269.1. Amended by Acts 1981, c. 612; Acts 1990, c. 831.
55-270. Amended by Acts 1981, c. 612.
55-271. Amended by Acts 1973, c. 355; Acts 1981, c. 612; Acts 1990, c. 831.
55-272. Repealed by Acts 1973, c. 355.
55-272.1. Amended by Acts 1981, c. 612.
55-273, 55-274. Amended by Acts 1973, c. 355; Acts 1981, c. 612.
55-275. Repealed by Acts 1990, c. 831.
55-276. Amended by Acts 1960, c. 45; Acts 1997, c. 801.
55-277. Amended by Acts 1973, c. 355; Acts 1981, c. 612; Acts 1990, c. 831.
55-286.1. Amended by Acts 1978, c. 338; Acts 2003, c. 253.
55-287. Amended by Acts 1984, c. 726.
55-288. Repealed by Acts 1984, c. 726.
55-289. Amended by Acts 1984, c. 726.
55-290. Amended by Acts 1984, c. 726; Acts 1992, c. 1.
55-292 to 55-296. Amended by Acts 1984, c. 726.
55-297. Amended by Acts 1966, c. 55; Acts 1968, c. 223; Acts 1977, c. 114.
55-297.2. Repealed by Acts 1987, c. 517.
55-298. Repealed by Acts 1982, c. 280.
55-305. Amended by Acts 1992, c. 483.
55-306. Amended by Acts 1979, c. 486.
55-316. Amended by Acts 1979, c. 486.

Sec.
55-318. Amended by Acts 1985, c. 486.
55-321. Amended by Acts 1985, c. 486.
55-323. Amended by Acts 1979, c. 486.
55-327. Amended by Acts 1979, c. 486.
55-328. Amended by Acts 1979, c. 486.
55-330. Amended by Acts 1979, c. 486.
55-331. Amended by Acts 1993, c. 580; Acts 2004, cc. 604, 615.
55-332. Amended by Acts 1987, c. 105; Acts 2004, cc. 604, 615.
55-333. Repealed by Acts 2004, cc. 604, 615.
55-334. Amended by Acts 2004, cc. 604, 615.
55-334.1. Amended by Acts 2004, cc. 604, 615.
55-337. Amended by Acts 1980, c. 546; Acts 1996, c. 372.
55-338. Amended by Acts 1980, c. 546.
55-339 to 55-340.1. Repealed by Acts 1996, c. 372.
55-342. Amended by Acts 1980, c. 546; Acts 1996, c. 372.
55-344. Amended by Acts 1980, c. 546; Acts 1989, c. 68; Acts 1993, c. 36; Acts 1996, c. 77.
55-345, 55-346. Repealed by Acts 1996, c. 372.
55-347. Amended by Acts 1979, c. 243; Acts 1996, c. 372.
55-348. Repealed by Acts 1996, c. 372.
55-350. Repealed by Acts 1996, c. 372.
55-361. Repealed by Acts 1985, c. 517.
55-361.1. Amended by Acts 1986, c. 359; Acts 1989, c. 637; Acts 1991, c. 704; Acts 1994, c. 580.
55-362. Amended by Acts 1985, c. 517; Acts 1986, c. 359; Acts 1991, c. 704; Acts 1994, c. 580; Acts 1998, c. 460; Acts 2001, c. 543; Acts 2004, c. 143.
55-363. Amended by Acts 1985, c. 517; Acts 1994, c. 580.
55-365. Repealed by Acts 1985, c. 517.
55-366. Amended by Acts 1994, c. 580; Acts 1998, c. 460.
55-367. Amended by Acts 1985, c. 517; Acts 1989, c. 637; Acts 1994, c. 580; Acts 1998, c. 460.
55-368. Amended by Acts 1985, c. 517; Acts 1989, c. 637; Acts 1991, c. 704; Acts 1994, c. 580; Acts 1998, c. 460.
55-369. Amended by Acts 1985, c. 517; Acts 1989, c. 637; Acts 1991, c. 704; Acts 1993, c. 842; Acts 1994, c. 580; Acts 1998, c. 460; Acts 2001, c. 543.
55-370. Amended by Acts 1985, c. 517; Acts 1989, c. 637; Acts 1991, c. 704; Acts 1993, c. 842; Acts 1994, cc. 432, 580; Acts 1998, c. 460.
55-370.1. Amended by Acts 1991, c. 704; Acts 1994, c. 580; Acts 1998, c. 460.
55-371. Amended by Acts 1985, c. 517; Acts 1994, c. 580; Acts 1998, c. 460.

Sec.
55-373. Amended by Acts 1985, c. 517.
55-374. Amended by Acts 1983, c. 59; Acts 1984, c. 455; Acts 1985, c. 517; Acts 1986, c. 359; Acts 1989, c. 637; Acts 1994, c. 580; Acts 1998, c. 460; Acts 1999, c. 560; Acts 2001, c. 543; Acts 2004, c. 143.
55-374.1. Amended by Acts 1984, c. 333; Acts 1985, c. 517; Acts 1991, c. 704; Acts 1994, c. 580; Acts 1996, c. 372; Acts 1998, c. 460.
55-374.2. Amended by Acts 1998, c. 460.
55-375. Amended by Acts 1984, c. 429; Acts 1985, c. 517; Acts 1994, c. 580; Acts 1998, c. 460.
55-376. Amended by Acts 1983, c. 147; Acts 1984, c. 572; Acts 1985, c. 517; Acts 1991, c. 704; Acts 1994, c. 580; Acts 1998, c. 460.
55-377, 55-378. Repealed by Acts 1985, c. 517.
55-379. Repealed by Acts 1994, c. 580.
55-380. Amended by Acts 1985, c. 517; Acts 1989, c. 637; Acts 1994, c. 580; Acts 1998, c. 460.
55-381. Amended by Acts 1991, c. 704.
55-382. Amended by Acts 1985, c. 517; Acts 1998, c. 460.
55-384. Amended by Acts 1989, c. 637.
55-386. Amended by Acts 1983, c. 59; Acts 1985, c. 517; Acts 1994, c. 580; Acts 1998, c. 460.
55-387, 55-388. Amended by Acts 1985, c. 517.
55-389. Amended by Acts 1985, c. 517; Acts 1998, c. 460.
55-390. Amended by Acts 1983, c. 59; Acts 1985, c. 517; Acts 1994, c. 580.
55-391. Repealed by Acts 1985, c. 517.
55-391.1. Amended by Acts 1994, c. 580; Acts 1998, c. 460.
55-392. Repealed by Acts 1985, c. 517.
55-393. Repealed by Acts 1985, c. 517.
55-394. Repealed by Acts 1985, c. 517.
55-394.1. Amended by Acts 1998, c. 460.
55-395. Repealed by Acts 1985, c. 517.
55-396. Amended by Acts 1985, c. 517; Acts 1998, c. 460.
55-400. Amended by Acts 1983, c. 59; Acts 1985, c. 517; Acts 1991, c. 704.
55-401. Amended by Acts 1987, c. 498.
55-403. Amended by Acts 1990, c. 831.
55-405, 55-406. Amended by Acts 1992, c. 521.
55-415. Amended by Acts 1994, c. 475.
55-418. Amended by Acts 1984, c. 717; Acts 1999, c. 149.
55-419. Amended by Acts 1984, cc. 717, 774; Acts 2000, c. 655.
55-425. Amended by Acts 1983, c. 312; Acts 1986, cc. 368, 557.
55-428. Amended by Acts 1988, c. 412; Acts 2002, c. 34; Acts 2003, c. 351.
55-429. Amended by Acts 2004, c. 242.
55-454. Amended by Acts 1983, c. 96.

Sec.
55-460. Amended by Acts 2004, c. 242.
55-462. Amended by Acts 2004, c. 242.
55-462. Amended by Acts 1985, c. 83.
55-463. Amended by Acts 1990, c. 831; Acts 1993, c. 849.
55-467. Amended by Acts 2004, c. 242.
55-478. Amended by Acts 2004, c. 242.
55-479. Amended by Acts 2004, c. 242.
55-484. Amended by Acts 1997, c. 222; Acts 1998, c. 463; Acts 2004, c. 242.
55-486. Amended by Acts 2004, c. 242.
55-487. Amended by Acts 1983, c. 310; Acts 1984, c. 321; Acts 1985, c. 69; Acts 1993, c. 634.
55-492. Amended by Acts 1993, c. 849.
55-508. Amended by Acts 1991, c. 667; Acts 1992, c. 677; Acts 1998, cc. 32, 623; Acts 2003, c. 422.
55-509. Amended by Acts 1991, c. 667; Acts 1996, c. 618; Acts 1998, c. 623; Acts 2001, c. 715; Acts 2002, c. 459; Acts 2003, c. 422.
55-510. Amended by Acts 1991, c. 667; Acts 1992, c. 69, 71; Acts 1993, cc. 365, 827; Acts 1999, cc. 594, 654, 1029; Acts 2000, cc. 905, 1008; Acts 2001, c. 419; Acts 2003, c. 442; Acts 2004, c. 193.
55-510.1. Amended by Acts 2000, c. 905; Acts 2001, c. 419; Acts 2003, c. 404; Acts 2004, c. 333.
55-511. Amended by Acts 1991, c. 667; Acts 1995, c. 573; Acts 1997, c. 887; Acts 1998, c. 32; Acts 1999, c. 809; Acts 2001, c. 556; Acts 2002, cc. 399, 509; Acts 2003, c. 422.
55-512. Amended by Acts 1991, c. 667; Acts 1993, c. 96; Acts 1995, c. 573; Acts 1997, c. 222; Acts 1998, cc. 32, 463; Acts 2000, c. 891; Acts 2001, c. 556; Acts 2002, cc. 399, 459, 509.
55-513. Amended by Acts 1991, c. 667; Acts 1993, c. 956; Acts 1994, c. 368; Acts 1997, cc. 173, 417; Acts 2000, cc. 846, 905; Acts 2002, c. 509.
55-514. Amended by Acts 1991, c. 667; Acts 1992, c. 450; Acts 1998, cc. 32, 751.
55-515. Amended by Acts 1993, c. 956.
55-515.1. Amended by Acts 1998, c. 32; Acts 1999, c. 805; Acts 2003, cc. 59, 74.
55-515.2. Amended by Acts 1998, c. 32; Acts 2001, c. 271.
55-515.6. Amended by Acts 1998, c. 32.
55-516. Amended by Acts 1991, c. 667; Acts 1997, cc. 760, 766, 887; Acts 2000, c. 905; Acts 2004, cc. 778, 779, 786.
55-518. Amended by Acts 1993, c. 824; Acts 1994, cc. 80, 242.
55-519. Amended by Acts 1996, c. 379; Acts 1998, cc. 384, 795.
55-520. Amended by Acts 1993, c. 818.
55-524. Amended by Acts 1993, c. 847.

Sec.
55-525. Amended by Acts 1993, c. 848.
55-527. Amended by Acts 1996, c. 557; Acts 1998, c. 617.
55-530. Amended by Acts 1997, c. 222; Acts 1998, c. 463; Acts 2001, c. 81.
55-531. Amended by Acts 2000, c. 266; Acts 2002, c. 516.
55-532. Amended by Acts 2002, c. 516.
56-1. Amended by Acts 1971, Ex. Sess., c. 23; Acts 1983, c. 438; Acts 1984, c. 382; Acts 2002, cc. 479, 489; Acts 2004, c. 1028.
56-1.2. Amended by Acts 1999, c. 778; Acts 2000, c. 994; Acts 2003, c. 355.
56-4. Repealed by Acts 1954, c. 188.
56-16. Amended by Acts 1994, c. 352.
56-35. Amended by Acts 1971, Ex. Sess., c. 38; Acts 1973, c. 377.
56-36. Amended by Acts 1971, Ex. Sess., c. 38.
56-37. Amended by Acts 1971, Ex. Sess., c. 39.
56-38. Amended by Acts 1971, Ex. Sess., c. 24.
56-39. Repealed by Acts 1995, c. 647.
56-41. Repealed by Acts 1971, Ex. Sess., c. 39.
56-42. Repealed by Acts 1971, Ex. Sess., c. 39.
56-43. Amended by Acts 1971, Ex. Sess., c. 39.
56-44 to 56-46. Repealed by Acts 1996, cc. 114, 157.
56-46.1. Amended by Acts 1973, c. 307; Acts 1974, c. 498; Acts 1973, c. 307; Acts 1974, c. 498; Acts 1983, c. 438; Acts 1984, cc. 287, 562; Acts 1985, c. 282; Acts 1991, cc. 90, 148; Acts 1996, c. 254; Acts 2001, c. 758; Acts 2002, c. 483.
56-47, 56-48. Repealed by Acts 1956, c. 438.
56-49. Amended by Acts 1952, c. 497; Acts 1956, c. 438; Acts 1962, c. 222; Acts 1972, c. 657; Acts 1988, c. 649; Acts 1990, c. 630; Acts 1999, cc. 484, 531; Acts 2003, c. 940; Acts 2004, c. 1028.
56-49.1 to 56-51. Repealed by Acts 1956, c. 438.
56-51.1. Amended by Acts 1954, c. 541; Acts 1956, c. 438.
56-52 to 56-54.1. Repealed by Acts 1956, c. 438.
56-55. Amended by Acts 1984, c. 721; Acts 1987, c. 479.
56-56. Amended by Acts 1958, c. 11.
56-57. Amended by Acts 2001, c. 347.
56-61. Amended by Acts 1980, c. 246.
56-64. Repealed by Acts 1975, c. 500.
56-65.1. Amended by Acts 1976, c. 408; Acts 1987, c. 479; Acts 1995, c. 137.
56-65.2. Repealed by Acts 1976, c. 408.
56-66. Amended by Acts 1987, c. 204.
56-75. Amended by Acts 1956, c. 429.
56-76. Amended by Acts 1984, c. 721; Acts 1987, c. 385; Acts 1996, c. 19.
56-77. Amended by Acts 1996, c. 19; Acts 1998, c. 707.
56-82. Amended by Acts 1998, c. 707.

Sec.
56-88. Amended by Acts 1992, c. 376; Acts 2000, cc. 528, 543.
56-90.1. Amended by Acts 1980, c. 703.
56-93 to 56-99.1. Repealed by Acts 1996, cc. 114, 157.
56-100. Repealed by Acts 1970, c. 618.
56-100.1, 56-101. Repealed by Acts 1996, cc. 114, 157.
56-102.1 to 56-110. Repealed by Acts 1996, cc. 114, 157.
56-112 to 56-116. Repealed by Acts 1996, cc. 114, 157.
56-117, 56-118. Amended by Acts 1996, cc. 114, 157.
56-119. Amended by Acts 1979, c. 477.
56-120, 56-121. Repealed by Acts 1964, c. 219.
56-126, 56-127. Repealed by Acts 1964, c. 219.
56-128. Amended by Acts 1987, c. 185.
56-129. Repealed by Acts 1996, cc. 114, 157.
56-129.1. Amended by Acts 1987, c. 145; Acts 1996, cc. 114, 157.
56-130, 56-131. Amended by Acts 1996, cc. 114, 157.
56-132. Repealed by Acts 1996, cc. 114, 157.
56-133 to 56-135. Repealed by Acts 1956, c. 492.
56-136 to 56-138. Repealed by Acts 1979, c. 405.
56-139. Repealed by Acts 1996, cc. 114, 157.
56-141. Repealed by Acts 1994, c. 314.
56-142 to 56-206. Repealed by Acts 1970, c. 708.
56-207, 56-208. Repealed by Acts 1981, c. 177.
56-209 to 56-231.14. Repealed by Acts 1999, c. 874.
56-231.15. Amended by Acts 2000, cc. 944, 964, 989, 999.
56-231.16. Amended by Acts 2000, cc. 964, 989.
56-231.18. Amended by Acts 2000, cc. 944, 999.
56.231.20. Repealed by Acts 2000, cc. 944, 999.
56-231.23. Amended by Acts 2000, cc. 944, 999.
56-231.24. Amended by Acts 2000, cc. 944, 999.
56-231.25. Amended by Acts 2000, cc. 944, 999.
56-231.27. Amended by Acts 2000, cc. 944, 999.
56-231.28. Amended by Acts 2000, cc. 944, 999.
56-231.30. Amended by Acts 2000, cc. 944, 964, 989, 999.
56-231.33. Amended by Acts 2000, cc. 944, 999.
56-231.34:1. Amended by Acts 2000, cc. 944, 999.
56-231.38. Amended by Acts 2000, cc. 944, 964, 989, 999.
56-231.39. Amended by Acts 2000, cc. 964, 989.
56-231.40. Amended by Acts 2000, cc. 944, 999.
56-231.43. Amended by Acts 2000, cc. 944, 999.
56-231.44. Amended by Acts 2000, cc. 944, 999.
56-231.50:1. Amended by Acts 2000, cc. 944, 999.
56-232. Amended by Acts 1950, pp. 54, 481; Acts 1954, c. 525; Acts 1956, c. 436; Acts 1964, c. 195; Acts 1966, c. 620; Acts 1975, c. 358; Acts 1984, c. 341; Acts 1985, cc. 2, 41; Acts 1990, c. 488; Acts 1999, c. 419; Acts 2000, cc. 528, 543; Acts 2002, c. 813; Acts 2003, c. 172.
56-233. Amended by Acts 1980, c. 249; Acts 1981, c. 385.
56-234. Amended by Acts 1950, p. 55; Acts 1964, c. 195; Acts 1970, c. 258; Acts 1976, c. 290; Acts 1985, cc. 2, 41; Acts 2002, c. 833.
56-234.3. Amended by Acts 1977, c. 261; Acts 1978, c. 700; Acts 1984, cc. 453, 454; Acts 1997, c. 138.
56-235. Amended by Acts 1977, c. 336.
56-235.2. Amended by Acts 1984, c. 312; Acts 1996, c. 156.
56-235.4. Amended by Acts 1989, c. 666; Acts 1990, c. 787; Acts 1995, c. 382; Acts 1997, c. 707; Acts 2000, c. 994.
56-235.5. Amended by Acts 1996, c. 18; Acts 2002, c. 479; Acts 2003, c. 711.
56-235.8. Amended by Acts 2000, cc. 691, 706.
56-236.1. Amended by Acts 1980, c. 259.
56-237. Amended by Acts 1954, c. 298; Acts 1976, c. 763.
56-237.2. Amended by Acts 1995, c. 260.
56-238. Amended by Acts 1980, c. 446.
56-239. Amended by Acts 1971, Ex. Sess., c. 31.
56-240. Amended by Acts 1971, Ex. Sess., c. 31; Acts 1973, c. 262; Acts 1979, c. 249; Acts 1998, c. 63.
56-241. Amended by Acts 1964, c. 195; Acts 1973, c. 262; Acts 1984, c. 721.
56-241.1. Amended by Acts 1985, c. 389; Acts 1996, c. 378.
56-245. Amended by Acts 1973, c. 262; Acts 1977, c. 336.
56-245.2. Amended by Acts 1979, c. 313; Acts Acts 1992, c. 766.
56-245.3. Amended by Acts 1979, c. 313; Acts 1980, c. 741; Acts 1986, c. 11; Acts 1988, c. 231; Acts 1989, c. 188; Acts 1991, c. 573; Acts 1992, c. 766; Acts 2003, c. 355.
56-247. Amended by Acts 1966, c. 552.
56-247.1. Amended by Acts 1977, c. 59; Acts 1980, c. 415.
56-248.1. Amended by Acts 1982, c. 107.
56-249.2, 56-249.3. Amended by Acts 1979, c. 617.
56-249.4. Amended by Acts 1982, c. 107.
56-249.5. Repealed by Acts 1979, c. 492.
56-249.6. Amended by Acts 1979, c. 492; Acts 1980, c. 384; Acts 1982, c. 584; Acts 1984, cc. 716, 725; Acts 1989, c. 666; Acts 2004, c. 827.
56-250. Amended by Acts 1974, c. 478; Acts 1975, c. 358.
56-251, 56-252. Repealed by Acts 1974, c. 478.
56-257. Amended by Acts 1996, c. 278; Acts 2000, c. 779.

Sec.
56-259. Amended by Acts 1964, c. 523; Acts 1968, c. 534; Acts 1972, c. 519; Acts 1979, c. 309; Acts 2001, cc. 745, 752.
56-261. Amended by Acts 2000, c. 183.
56-265.1. Amended by Acts 1954, c. 354; Acts 1970, c. 265; Acts 1981, c. 506; Acts 1988, c. 440; Acts 1990, c. 488; Acts 1991, c. 263; Acts 1992, c. 476; Acts 1994, cc. 652, 852; Acts 1995, c. 643; Acts 1997, cc. 105, 148; Acts 1999, c. 768; Acts 2000, cc. 528, 543; Acts 2002, cc. 479, 481; Acts 2004, cc. 748, 1028.
56-265.2. Amended by Acts 1985, c. 282; Acts 1995, cc. 311, 514; Acts 1998, c. 92.
56-265.2:1. Amended by Acts 2001, c. 758.
56-265.3. Amended by Acts 1968, c. 720; Acts 1973, c. 397; Acts 1986, c. 521; Acts 1988, c. 233.
56-265.4. Amended by Acts 1984, c. 382.
56-265.4:1. Amended by Acts 1978, c. 325.
56-265.4:2. Amended by Acts 1987, c. 337; Acts 1995, c. 36.
56-265.4:3. Amended by Acts 1984, c. 449.
56-265.4:4. Amended by Acts 1995, cc. 22, 35, 187; Acts 2001, c. 75; Acts 2002, cc. 479, 489; Acts 2003, cc. 677, 711, 720.
56-265.4:5. Amended by Acts 1992, c. 476.
56-265.13:3. Amended by Acts 1993, c. 369; 1997, c. 143.
56-265.13:5. Amended by Acts 1994, c. 313.
56-265.13:6. Amended by Acts 1990, cc. 410, 431; Acts 1994, c. 313; Acts 1996, c. 15; Acts 2003, c. 385.
56-265.13:7. Amended by Acts 1992, c. 376; Acts 1994, c. 313; Acts 1996, c. 48.
56-265.15. Amended by Acts 1980, c. 710; Acts 1992, c. 192; Acts 1994, c. 890; Acts 1996, c. 79; Acts 2002, c. 841.
56-265.15:1. Amended by Acts 1996, c. 79; Acts 2002, c. 841.
56-265.16. Repealed by Acts 1989, c. 448.
56-265.16:1. Amended by Acts 1992, c. 192; Acts 1994, c. 890; Acts 2001, c. 399.
56-265.17. Amended by Acts 1989, c. 448; Acts 1992, c. 192; Acts 1994, c. 890; Acts 2002, c. 841.
56-265.18. Amended by Acts 1980, c. 696; Acts 1989, c. 448; Acts 1994, c. 890; Acts 2002, c. 841.
56-265.19. Amended by Acts 1980, c. 696; Acts 1994, c. 890; Acts 1996, c. 79; Acts 2002, c. 841.
56-265.20. Repealed by Acts 1994, c. 890.
56-265.21, 56-265.22. Amended by Acts 1994, c. 890; Acts 2002, c. 841.
56-265.23. Amended by Acts 1994, c. 890.
56-265.24. Amended by Acts 1994, c. 890; Acts 1996, c. 79; Acts 2002, c. 841.

Sec.
56-265.25. Amended by Acts 1980, c. 696; Acts 1989, c. 448; Acts 1996, c. 79.
56-265.26. Repealed by Acts 1994, c. 890.
56-265.30. Amended by Acts 2001, c. 399.
56-265.31. Amended by Acts 1996, c. 79.
56-265.32. Amended by Acts 2001, c. 351; Acts 2002, c. 348.
56-266 to 56-272. Repealed by Acts 1996, cc. 114, 157.
56-273 to 56-291.3:7. Repealed by Acts 1995, cc. 744, 803.
56-291.4 to 56-291.8:1. Repealed by Acts 1980, c. 467.
56-291.9 to 56-291.13. Repealed by Acts 1995, cc. 744, 803.
56-292 to 56-296. Repealed by Acts 1995, cc. 744, 803.
56-296.1 to 56-298. Repealed by Acts 1995, cc. 744, 803.
56-299 to 56-303.1. Repealed by Acts 1995, cc. 744, 803.
56-304 to 56-304.11. Repealed by Acts 1995, cc. 744, 803.
56-304.12 to 56-304.16. Repealed by Acts 1995, cc. 744, 803.
56-305 to 56-323. Repealed by Acts 1995, cc. 744, 803.
56-324 to 56-338. Repealed by Acts 1995, cc. 744, 803.
56-338.1 to 56-338.18. Repealed by Acts 1995, cc. 744, 803.
56-338.19 to 56-338.39. Repealed by Acts 1995, cc. 744, 803.
56-338.40 to 56-338.49. Repealed by Acts 1995, cc. 744, 803.
56-338.50 to 56-338.64. Repealed by Acts 1995, cc. 744, 803.
56-338.65 to 56-338.84. Repealed by Acts 1995, cc. 744, 803.
56-338.85 to 56-338.92. Repealed by Acts 1997, c. 628.
56-338.93 to 56-338.103. Repealed by Acts 1995, cc. 744, 803.
56-338.104 to 56-338.127. Repealed by Acts 1995, cc. 744, 803.
56-339 to 56-344. Repealed by Acts 1956, c. 435.
56-345. Repealed by Acts 1996, cc. 114, 157.
56-345.1. Amended by Acts 1996, cc. 114, 157.
56-346. Amended by Acts 1956, c. 435.
56-347. Amended by Acts 1956, c. 435; Acts 1962, c. 221; Acts 2003, c. 940.
56-348. Repealed by Acts 1996, cc. 114, 157.
56-349 to 56-351. Repealed by Acts 1956, c. 435.
56-354. Amended by Acts 1996, cc. 114, 157.
56-355. Repealed by Acts 1956, c. 435.
56-355.2. Amended by Acts 1996, cc. 114, 157.
56-356 to 56-358. Repealed by Acts 1956, c. 435.
56-359 to 56-361. Repealed by Acts 1996, cc. 114, 157.

Sec.
56-362, 56-363. Amended by Acts 1996, cc. 114, 157.
56-364, 56-365. Repealed by Acts 1996, cc. 114, 157.
56-365.1. Amended by Acts 1996, cc. 114, 157.
56-366. Repealed by Acts 1952, c. 398.
56-366.1. Amended by Acts 1996, cc. 114, 157.
56-366.2. Repealed by Acts 1996, cc. 114, 157.
56-366.3. Amended by Acts 1996, cc. 114, 157.
56-367, 56-368. Repealed by Acts 1952, c. 398.
56-368.1. Amended by Acts 1962, c. 538; Acts 1996, cc. 114, 157.
56-369. Amended by Acts 1952, c. 390; Acts 1996, cc. 114, 157.
56-370. Repealed by Acts 1956, c. 435.
56-371 to 56-382. Repealed by Acts 1996, cc. 114, 157.
56-384 to 56-389. Repealed by Acts 1996, cc. 114, 157.
56-390 to 56-404. Repealed by Acts 1970, c. 731.
56-405. Amended by Acts 1952, c. 99; Acts 1960, c. 544; Acts 1968, c. 226; Acts 1978, c. 214; Acts 1996, cc. 114, 157.
56-405.01. Repealed by Acts 1996, cc. 114, 157.
56-405.02. Amended by Acts 1996, cc. 114, 157.
56-405.1, 56-405.2. Amended by Acts 1996, cc. 114, 157.
56-405.3. Repealed by Acts 1996, cc. 114, 157.
56-406. Repealed by Acts 1977, c. 226.
56-406.1. Amended by Acts 1954, c. 122; Acts 1962, c. 527; Acts 1996, cc. 114, 157.
56-406.2. Amended by Acts 1962, c. 528; Acts 1996, cc. 114, 157.
56-407. Repealed by Acts 1956, c. 164.
56-408. Amended by Acts 1956, c. 164.
56-409, 56-410. Repealed by Acts 1954, c. 122.
56-411. Amended by Acts 1996, cc. 114, 157.
56-412.1. Amended by Acts 1976, c. 89.
56-413. Repealed by Acts 1996, cc. 114, 157.
56-413.01. Amended by Acts 1996, cc. 114, 157.
56-413.1, 56-413.2. Repealed by Acts 1996, cc. 114, 157.
56-414. Amended by Acts 1950, p. 944; Acts 1956, c. 164; Acts 1993, c. 483; Acts 2003, c. 287.
56-416. Amended by Acts 1964, c. 621.
56-417. Repealed by Acts 1996, cc. 114, 157.
56-418. Repealed by Acts 1996, cc. 114, 157.
56-419.1. Repealed by Acts 1996, cc. 114, 157.
56-420 to 56-425. Repealed by Acts 1988, c. 7.
56-426. Repealed by Acts 1984, c. 227.
56-426.1. Repealed Acts 1988, c. 891.
56-427. Repealed by Acts 1996, cc. 114, 157.
56-428. Amended by Acts 1996, cc. 114, 157.
56-429. Amended by Acts 1994, c. 352.
56-433. Amended by Acts 1994, c. 352.
56-436, 56-437. Amended by Acts 1994, c. 352.
56-438. Amended by Acts 1994, cc. 352, 432.

Sec.
56-442 to 56-444. Repealed by Acts 1980, c. 142.
56-445. Repealed by Acts 1996, cc. 114, 157.
56-446. Amended by Acts 1996, cc. 114, 157.
56-447 to 56-451. Repealed by Acts 1996, cc. 114, 157.
56-451.1. Amended by Acts 1996, cc. 114, 157.
56-448. Amended by Acts 1956, c. 607.
56-449. Amended by Acts 1986, c. 188.
56-451.2. Repealed by Acts 1987, c. 495.
56-452, 56-453. Repealed by Acts 1970, c. 243.
56-454 to 56-456. Repealed by Acts 1996, cc. 114, 157.
56-457. Repealed by Acts 1971, Ex. Sess., c. 25.
56-457.1 to 56-457.10. Repealed by Acts 1995, cc. 744, 803.
56-457. Repealed by Acts 1971, Ex. Sess., c. 25.
56-457.8. Amended by Acts 1977, c. 399; Acts 1983, c. 484.
56-457.9. Amended by Acts 1977, c. 550.
56-458. Amended by Acts 1997, cc. 474, 515; Acts 1998, cc. 742, 758; Acts 2002, cc. 479, 489.
56-462. Amended by Acts 1971, Ex. Sess., c. 40; Acts 1997, cc. 474, 515; Acts 1998, cc. 742, 758; Acts 2002, cc. 479, 489.
56-466. Amended by Acts 1976, c. 268.
56-468.1. Amended by Acts 1998, cc. 742, 758; Acts 2002, cc. 479, 489.
56-468.2. Amended by Acts 1998, cc. 742, 758.
56-469. Amended by Acts 1977, c. 624; Acts 1989, c. 537.
56-470. Amended by Acts 1989, c. 537.
56-474. Repealed by Acts 1977, c. 624.
56-475, 56-476.1. Amended by Acts 1989, c. 537.
56-477. Amended by Acts 1989, c. 537.
56-478. Repealed by Acts 1973, c. 376.
56-480. Amended by Acts 1973, c. 378.
56-481.2. Amended by Acts 2001, c. 75.
56-483. Amended by Acts 2000, c. 986.
56-484.2. Amended by Acts 1978, c. 232; Acts 1985, c. 382; Acts 1990, c. 339; Acts 1993, c. 974; Acts 1994, cc. 180, 347; Acts 1995, c. 466; Acts 1996, c. 272.
56-484.4. Amended by Acts 1992, c. 549; Acts 1996, c. 68; Acts 2002, cc. 479, 489.
56-484.5. Amended by Acts 1992, c. 549.
56-484.6. Amended by Acts 1992, c. 549; Acts 1996, c. 68; Acts 2002, cc. 479, 489.
56-484.7. Repealed by Acts 1996, c. 68.
56-484.7:1. Amended by Acts 2002, cc. 479, 489; Acts 2003, cc. 677, 711.
56-484.7:2. Amended by Acts 2002, cc. 479, 489; Acts 2003, cc. 677, 711.
56-484.7:3. Repealed by Acts 2002, cc. 479, 489.
56-484.7:4. Amended by Acts 2003, c. 711.
56-484.8 to 56-484.11. Repealed by cts 2000, c. 1064.

Sec.

56-484.12. Amended by Acts 2001, c. 529; Acts 2002, c. 68; Acts 2003, cc. 160, 341, 981, 1021.

56-484.13. Amended by Acts 2003, cc. 981, 1021.

56-484.15. Amended by Acts 2003, cc. 981, 1021.

56-484.16. Amended by Acts 2001, c. 713.

56-484.17. Amended by Acts 2001, c. 529; Acts 2002, c. 68; Acts 2003, c. 341; Acts 2004, c. 167.

56-485, 56-486. Reenacted without change by Acts 1956, c. 434.

56-487. Reenacted without change by Acts 1956, c. 434; amended by Acts 1996, c. 708.

56-488. Amended by Acts 1956, c. 434.

56-489. Reenacted without change by Acts 1956, c. 434.

56-490. Amended by Acts 1956, c. 434.

56-491. Reenacted without change by Acts 1956, c. 434; amended by Acts 1974, c. 73; Acts 1978, c. 236.

56-492. Reenacted without change by Acts 1956, c. 434; amended by Acts 1974, c. 73; Acts 2001, c. 386.

56-493. Reenacted without change by Acts 1956, c. 434; amended by Acts 1968, c. 100; Acts 1992, c. 6; Acts 1996, c. 708.

56-494. Reenacted without change by Acts 1956, c. 434; amended by Acts 1996, c. 708.

56-495. Amended by Acts 1956, c. 434; Acts 1989, c. 185; Acts 2001, c. 386.

56-496. Reenacted without change by Acts 1956, c. 434; amended by Acts 1979, c. 103.

56-497. Reenacted without change by Acts 1956, c. 434; amended by Acts 1979, c. 129.

56-498, 56-499. Reenacted without change by Acts 1956, c. 434.

56-500. Amended by Acts 1956, c. 434.

56-501. Repealed by Acts 1998, c. 252.

56-501.01. Repealed by Acts 1998, c. 252.

56-502. Reenacted without change by Acts 1956, c. 434; Amended by Acts 1985, c. 405; Acts 1996, c. 708; Acts 1998, c. 252; Acts 2001, c. 386.

56-503. Amended by Acts 1956, c. 434.

56-504 to 56-506. Reenacted without change by Acts 1956, c. 434.

56-507. Amended by Acts 1956, c. 434.

56-508. Reenacted without change by Acts 1956, c. 434.

56-508.1 to 56-508.14. Repealed by Acts 1995, c. 281.

56-527. Amended by Acts 1954, c. 108.

56-531. Amended by Acts 1987, c. 295; Acts 1998, c. 64.

Sec.

56-536. Amended by Acts 1991, c. 272.

56-537. Amended by Acts 1993, c. 732.

56-539. Amended by Acts 1991, c. 272.

56-540. Amended by Acts 1990, c. 180; Acts 1991, c. 272.

56-541 to 56-543. Amended by Acts 1991, c. 272; Acts 1993, c. 732.

56-544. Amended by Acts 1991, c. 272.

56-546. Amended by Acts 1990, c. 180.

56-549. Amended by Acts 1991, c. 272.

56-551. Amended by Acts 1991, c. 272.

56-556 to 56-561. Amended by Acts 1995, c. 647.

56-557. Amended by Acts 2001, c. 286; Acts 2002, cc. 570, 593.

56-560. Amended by Acts 2003, c. 289.

56-562. Repealed by Acts 1995, c. 647.

56-563 to 56-573. Amended by Acts 1995, c. 647.

56-573.1. Amended by Acts 2002, cc. 570, 593; Acts 2003, c. 968.

56-574. Amended by Acts 1995, c. 647.

56-575.1. Amended by Acts 2003, c. 1034.

56-575.2. Amended by Acts 2003, c. 1034.

56-575.3. Amended by Acts 2003, cc. 292, 1034.

56-575.4. Amended by Acts 2003, c. 1034; Acts 2004, c. 690.

56-575.8. Amended by Acts 2003, c. 1034.

56-575.9. Amended by Acts 2003, c. 1034; Acts 2004, c. 986.

56-575.11. Amended by Acts 2003, c. 1034.

56-575.16. Amended by Acts 2003, cc. 292, 968, 1034; Acts 2004, c. 986.

56-576. Amended by Acts 2000, c. 991; Acts 2001, c. 421.

56-577. Amended by Acts 2001, c. 748; Acts 2003, cc. 795, 990; Acts 2004, c. 827.

56-579. Amended by Acts 2001, c. 576; Acts 2003, cc. 885, 990.

56-580. Amended by Acts 2000, c. 991; Acts 2001, cc. 738, 748, 755; Acts 2002, c. 483; Acts 2003, c. 719; Acts 2004, cc. 262, 827.

56-581. Amended by Acts 2000, c. 991.

56-581.1. Amended by Acts 2001, c. 748; Acts 2003, c. 885.

56-582. Amended by Acts 2000, cc. 942, 991; Acts 2001, c. 748; Acts 2004, c. 827.

56-583. Amended by Acts 2000, c. 991; Acts 2004, c. 827.

56-585. Amended by Acts 2000, c. 991; Acts 2001, c. 748; Acts 2003, c. 885; Acts 2004, c. 827.

56-587. Amended by Acts 2000, c. 991.

56-588. Amended by Acts 2000, c. 991.

56-589. Amended by Acts 2000, c. 991; Acts 2003, c. 795; Acts 2004, c. 827.

56-590. Amended by Acts 2000, c. 991; Acts 2001, c. 748.

56-592. Amended by Acts 2003, c. 885.

Sec.
56-592.1. Amended by Acts 2003, c. 885.
56-593. Amended by Acts 2000, c. 991.
56-594. Amended by Acts 2004, c. 827.
56-595. Repealed by Acts 2003, cc. 885, 904.
56-596. Amended by Acts 2003, c. 885.
57-1. Amended by Acts 1985, c. 73.
57-2.01. Amended by Acts 1997, c. 388.
57-3. Amended by Acts 1962, c. 101; Acts 1964, cc. 33, 601; Acts 2004, c. 595.
57-5. Amended by Acts 1950, p. 632; Acts 1972, c. 763; Acts 1981, c. 1; Acts 1990, c. 124; Acts 1993, c. 737; Acts 2002, c. 742.
57-7. Repealed by Acts 1993, c. 370.
57-8. Amended by Acts 1962, c. 516; Acts 1966, c. 216.
57-9. Amended by Acts 1972, c. 825.
57-10, 57-11. Amended by Acts 1962, c. 516.
57-12. Repealed by Acts 2003, c. 813.
57-13, 57-14. Amended by Acts 1962, c. 516.
57-15. Amended by Acts 1962, c. 516; Acts 1974, c. 138; Acts 1983, c. 542; Acts 1993, c. 370; Acts 1998, c. 258.
57-16. Amended by Acts 1962, c. 306; Acts 1966, c. 308.
57-19. Amended by Acts 1954, c. 129; Acts 1956, c. 203.
57-20. Amended by Acts 1956, c. 454; Acts 1964, c. 553; Acts 1986, c. 63; Acts 2002, c. 638.
57-22. Amended by Acts 1997, c. 132.
57-25. Amended by Acts 1997, c. 132.
57-26. Amended by Acts 1952, c. 108; Acts 1954, c. 10; Acts 1960, c. 161; Acts 1994, c. 229.
57-27.1. Amended by Acts 2004, c. 831.
57-33. Repealed by Acts 1995, c. 255.
57-35.1 to 57-35.10. Repealed by Acts 1989, c. 631.
57-35.11 to 57-35.35. Repealed by Acts 1998, cc. 708, 721.
57-36, 57-37. Amended by Acts 1985, c. 95.
57-38.1. Amended by Acts 1970, c. 377.
57-39. Amended by Acts 1968, c. 83.
57-39.1. Amended by Acts 1986, c. 55; Acts 1990, c. 675.
57-39.8 to 57-39.18. Repealed by Acts 1989, c. 631.
57-40 to 57-47. Repealed by Acts 1974, c. 574.
57-48. Amended by Acts 1979, cc. 124, 595, 598; Acts 1983, c. 374; Acts 1984, c. 268; Acts 1988, c. 322; Acts 1990, c. 711; Acts 1996, c. 461; Acts 2003, cc. 576, 977, 1009.
57-49. Amended by Acts 1975, c. 221; Acts 1979, c. 595; Acts 1984, c. 268; Acts 1986, c. 31; Acts 1987, c. 561; Acts 1988, c. 322; Acts 1990, c. 711; Acts 1993, cc. 577, 583; Acts 1995, cc. 170, 205; Acts 2003, cc. 576, 977, 1009.

Sec.
57-50. Amended by Acts 1979, c. 595.
57-51. Amended by Acts 1979, c. 595; Acts 1984, c. 268.
57-52. Amended by Acts 1979, c. 595; Acts 1983, c. 374; Acts 1988, c. 322.
57-53. Amended by Acts 1979, c. 595.
57-54. Amended by Acts 1979, c. 595; Acts 1983, c. 374; Acts 1988, c. 322.
57-55. Repealed by Acts 1980, c. 445.
57-55.1. Repealed by Acts 1990, c. 711.
57-55.3. Amended by Acts 2003, c. 576.
57-56. Amended by Acts 1979, c. 595.
57-57. Amended by Acts 1979, c. 595; Acts 1983, c. 374; Acts 1987, c. 561; Acts 1988, c. 322; Acts 1990, c. 711; Acts 2003, cc. 977, 1009.
57-58. Amended by Acts 2003, c. 810.
57-59. Amended by Acts 1979, c. 595; Acts 1983, c. 374; Acts 1987, c. 561; Acts 1990, c. 711; Acts 1991, c. 710; Acts 1999, c. 81; Acts 2000, c. 755; Acts 2003, cc. 576, 977, 1009.
57-60. Amended by Acts 1975, c. 221; Acts 1979, cc. 55, 595, 598, 626; Acts 1980, c. 559; Acts 1983, c. 374; Acts 1984, c. 268; Acts 1991, c. 184; Acts 1995, c. 312; Acts 1996, c. 461; Acts 1997, c. 162; Acts 1998, cc. 104, 232; Acts 1999, c. 1021; Acts 2000, c. 921; Acts 2002, c. 85; Acts 2003, c. 576; Acts 2004, cc. 580, 790.
57-61. Amended by Acts 1979, c. 595; Acts 1983, c. 374; Acts 1984, c. 268; Acts 1987, c. 561; Acts 1988, c. 322; Acts 1990, c. 711; Acts 1996, c. 461; Acts 1999, c. 40.
57-63. Amended by Acts 1977, c. 401; Acts 1979, cc. 55, 595; Acts 1983, cc. 282, 374; Acts 1985, c. 82; Acts 1998, cc. 104, 232; Acts 2002, c. 85.
57-65. Amended by Acts 1975, c. 221; Acts 1979, c. 595; Acts 1984, c. 268.
57-66. Amended by Acts 1979, c. 595.
57-67. Amended by Acts 1979, c. 595; Acts 1984, c. 703; Acts 1986, c. 615.
57-69. Amended by Acts 1977, c. 401; Acts 1979, c. 595.
58-1 to 58-1166. Repealed by Acts 1984, c. 675.
58.1-1. Amended by Acts 1997, c. 694.
58.1-3. Amended by Acts 1985, c. 78; Acts 1988, c. 544; Acts 1989, cc. 99, 327; Acts 1990, c. 678; Acts 1992, c. 386; Acts 1993, cc. 41, 519; Acts 1994, c. 493; Acts 1995, c. 38; Acts 1996, cc. 614, 784, 793, 919, 988; Acts 1997, cc. 517, 705, 787; Acts 1998, c. 855; Acts 2000, cc. 717, 880, 901; Acts 2001, c. 84; Acts 2002, cc. 64, 747; Acts 2003, cc. 757, 758, 884; Acts 2004, cc. 166, 515, 536, 582, 594.
58.1-9. Amended by Acts 1996, cc. 370, 449,

Sec.
58.1-401. Amended by Acts 1985, c. 221; Acts 1987, c. 484; Acts 1988, cc. 581, 899; Acts 1995, cc. 422, 472; Acts 1999, c. 971.
58.1-402. Amended by Acts 1985, cc. 221, 465; Acts 1987, cc. 9, 484; Acts 1989, cc. 39, 639; Acts 1992, c. 678; Acts 1994, c. 590; Acts 1997, c. 106; Acts 1998, c. 874; Acts 1999, cc. 339, 971; Acts 2000, cc. 419, 1021, 1039; Acts 2003, cc. 3, 58, 209; Acts 2004, Sp. Sess. I, c. 3.
58.1-403. Amended by Acts 1985, c. 221; Acts 1987, c. 614; Acts 1988, c. 899; Acts 1996, c. 77; Acts 2000, cc. 691, 706.
58.1-408. Amended by Acts 1999, cc. 158, 186.
58.1-430. Repealed by Acts 2001, cc. 292, 300.
58.1-431. Amended by Acts 1985, c. 221.
58.1-432. Amended by Acts 1990, c. 416.
58.1-433.1. Amended by Acts 2000, c. 929.
58.1-435. Amended by Acts 1990, c. 830; Acts 1992, cc. 325, 347; Acts 1994, c. 611; Acts 1996, cc. 580, 826; Acts 2001, cc. 293, 299.
58.1-436. Amended by Acts 1996, c. 739.
58.1-437. Repealed by Acts 1992, c. 394.
58.1-438.1. Amended by Acts 1994, cc. 164, 875; Acts 1995, c. 100; Acts 1997, c. 350; Acts 1998, c. 599.
58.1-439. Amended by Acts 1995, c. 365; Acts 1996, c. 874; Acts 1997, cc. 786, 852; Acts 1998, c. 367; Acts 2004, cc. 170, 619.
58.1-439.2. Amended by Acts 1996, c. 1034; Acts 1999, c. 971; Acts 2000, cc. 91, 1066.
58.1-439.7. Amended by Acts 2001, c. 91; Acts 2004, c. 611.
58.1-439.9. Amended by Acts 2002, c. 747.
58.1-440.1. Amended by Acts 2000, cc. 691, 706.
58.1-441. Amended by Acts 1988, c. 444; Acts 2003, c. 376; Acts 2004, Sp. Sess. I, c. 3.
58.1-442. Amended by Acts 1990, c. 619; Acts 2003, c. 166.
58.1-445.1. Repealed by Acts 1998, c. 253.
58.1-450. Amended by Acts 1989, cc. 629, 642; Acts 1991, cc. 316, 331.
58.1-452. Amended by Acts 2003, c. 180.
58.1-453. Amended by Acts 1991, cc. 362, 456.
58.1-455. Amended by Acts 1989, cc. 629, 642; Acts 1991, cc. 316, 331.
58.1-460. Amended by Acts 1987, c. 531; Acts 1991, cc. 362, 456; Acts 1992, c. 519; Acts 1993, c. 54.
58.1-461, 58.1-462. Amended by Acts 1989, c. 289; Acts 1992, cc. 385, 401; Acts 2000, cc. 501, 553.
58.1-470. Amended by Acts 1989, c. 289; Acts 1992, cc. 385, 401; Acts 2000, cc. 501, 553.
58.1-472. Amended by Acts 1988, c. 899; Acts 1991, cc. 362, 456.
58.1-475. Amended by Acts 1991, cc. 316, 331.
58.1-478. Amended by Acts 1987, c. 9; Acts 1998, c. 335; Acts 2001, cc. 297, 307.
58.1-486. Amended by Acts 1992, c. 763.
58.1-490. Amended by Acts 1985, c. 221; Acts 1987, cc. 484, 599; Acts 1988, c. 248; Acts 1997, c. 257; Acts 2000, c. 415.
58.1-491.1. Amended by Acts 1991, c. 361; Acts 1996, c. 401.
58.1-492. Amended by Acts 1985, c. 221; Acts 1987, cc. 484, 599, 611; Acts 1990, c. 335; Acts 1991, cc. 362, 456; Acts 2000, c. 388.
58.1-493. Amended by Acts 1987, c. 484.
58.1-498. Amended by Acts 1996, c. 315.
58.1-499. Amended by Acts 1997, c. 355.
58.1-504. Amended by Acts 1999, c. 971; Acts 2000, cc. 691, 706.
58.1-513. Amended by Acts 2002, c. 347; Acts 2004, c. 635.
58.1-520. Amended by Acts 1986, c. 322; Acts 1988, c. 544; Acts 1989, cc. 77, 245; Acts 1994, c. 197; Acts 1996, cc. 363, 413.
58.1-521. Amended by Acts 1986, c. 322.
58.1-524. Amended by Acts 1996, cc. 363, 413.
58.1-525. Amended by Acts 1986, c. 322.
58.1-526. Amended by Acts 1996, cc. 363, 413; Acts 1997, c. 496.
58.1-527. Amended by Acts 1996, cc. 413, 573.
58.1-528. Amended by Acts 1996, cc. 363, 413.
58.1-530. Amended by Acts 1996, cc. 363, 413.
58.1-531. Amended by Acts 1988, c. 331; Acts 1989, c. 77.
58.1-531.1. Amended by Acts 1989, c. 77.
58.1-535. Amended by Acts 1989, c. 77; Acts 1999, c. 631.
58.1-601. Amended by Acts 1988, c. 457.
58.1-602. Amended by Acts 1985, c. 473; Acts 1986, c. 22; Acts 1988, c. 899; Acts 1989, c. 581; Acts 1995, c. 96; Acts 1999, cc. 138, 187, 723, 981; Acts 2000, c. 425; Acts 2002, c. 853; Acts 2004, c. 60.
58.1-602.1. Repealed by Acts 1995, c. 200.
58.1-603. Amended by Acts 1986, Sp. Sess., c. 12; Acts 2004, Sp. Sess. I, c. 3.
58.1-604. Amended by Acts 1986, Sp. Sess., c. 12; Acts 1995, c. 385; Acts 2004, Sp. Sess. I, c. 3.
58.1-604.1. Amended by Acts 2004, Sp. Sess. I, c. 3.
58.1-605. Amended by Acts 1997, cc. 245, 725; Acts 2002, c. 853; Acts 2004, Sp. Sess. I, c. 3.
58.1-606. Amended by Acts 1999, c. 156; Acts

Sec.

2002, c. 853; Acts 2004, Sp. Sess. I, c. 3.

58.1-608. Repealed by Acts 1993, c. 310.

58.1-608.1. Amended by Acts 1990, c. 349; Acts 1993, c. 647; Acts 1994, c. 728; Acts 1999, cc. 12, 334; Acts 2000, c. 493.

58.1-608.2. Repealed by Acts 2003, cc. 757, 758.

58.1-608.3. Amended by Acts 1996, cc. 105, 819; Acts 1998, cc. 492, 497; Acts 1999, cc. 141, 184; Acts 2000, c. 474; Acts 2001, c. 522; Acts 2004, cc. 506, 566, 568.

58.1-609. Repealed by Acts 1993, c. 310.

58.1-609.1. Amended by Acts 1995, cc. 617, 664; Acts 1998, c. 812; Acts 1999, cc. 401, 471, 762, 776; Acts 2000, cc. 487, 493, 729, 758; Acts 2002, c. 877; Acts 2003, cc. 657, 670.

58.1-609.2. Amended by Acts 1999, c. 229.

58.1-609.3. Amended by Acts 1994, cc. 365, 381; Acts 1995, cc. 101, 204, 719; Acts 1996, c. 816; Acts 1997, c. 834; Acts 2001, cc. 429, 468, 769; Acts 2003, c. 859; Acts 2004, Sp. Sess. I, c. 3.

58.1-609.4. Repealed by Acts 2003, cc. 757, 758.

58.1-609.5. Amended by Acts 1994, c. 595; Acts 1998, c. 481; Acts 2004, c. 607.

58.1-609.6. Amended by Acts 1994, c. 446; Acts 1995, cc. 171, 719; Acts 1997, cc. 307, 717, 822, 824; Acts 1998, cc. 645, 812; Acts 2002, cc. 183, 228, 777; Acts 2003, cc. 911, 916; Acts 2004, cc. 63, 101, 590, 606, 821.

58.1-609.7 to 58.1-609.9. Repealed by Acts 2003, cc. 757, 758

58.1-609.10. Amended by Acts 1995, cc. 617, 719; Acts 1997, cc. 631, 822; Acts 1998, c. 812; Acts 1999, cc. 762, 776, 1040; Acts 2000, cc. 346, 493, 505; Acts 2001, c. 860; Acts 2003, cc. 757, 758; Acts 2004, cc. 515, 536.

58.1-609.11. Amended by Acts 2004, cc. 515, 536.

58.1-610. Amended by Acts 1986, c. 605; Acts 1992, cc. 404, 415; Acts 1993, c. 310; Acts 2000, c. 425; Acts 2003, cc. 757, 758.

58.1-611.1. Amended by.Acts 2002, cc. 13, 853; Acts 2003, c. 806; Acts 2004, Sp. Sess. I, c. 3.

58.1-612. Amended by Acts 1991, cc. 544, 565; Acts 1995, c. 276.

58.1-613. Amended by Acts 2001, cc. 343, 362.

58.1-614. Amended by Acts 1986, Sp. Sess., c. 12; Acts 2002, c. 853; Acts 2004, Sp. Sess. I, c. 3.

Sec.

58.1-615. Amended by Acts 2003, c. 1042, cl. 3; Acts 2004, c. 567.

58.1-618. Amended by Acts 1985, c. 221.

58.1-622. Amended by Acts 1986, Sp. Sess., c. 12; Acts 1989, c. 469.

58.1-623. Amended by Acts 1999, cc. 762, 776; Acts 2003, cc. 757, 758.

58.1-623.1. Amended by Acts 1999, cc. 762, 776; Acts 2002, c. 775; Acts 2003, cc. 757, 758.

58.1-626. Amended by Acts 2002, c. 853; Acts 2004, Sp. Sess. I, c. 3.

58.1-627, 58,1-628. Repealed by Acts 2002, c. 853; Acts 2004, Sp. Sess. I, c. 3.

58.1-629. Amended by Acts 1993, c. 310.

58.1-635. Amended by Acts 1991, cc. 316, 331.

58.1-637. Amended by Acts 1992, c. 763.

58.1-638. Amended by Acts 1986, Sp. Sess., c. 12; Acts 1991, cc. 666, 713; Acts 1992, c. 167; Acts 1993, c. 793; Acts 1995, cc. 539, 542; Acts 1998, cc. 320, 905, 907; Acts 1999, cc. 281, 397, 898; Acts 2000, cc. 694, 707; Acts 2001, c. 171; Acts 2004, Sp. Sess. I, c. 3.

58.1-639. Amended by Acts 2004, Sp. Sess. I, c. 3.

58.1-641. Amended by Acts 2003, c. 101.

58.1-642. Amended by Acts 2003, c. 101.

58.1-643. Repealed by Acts 1993, c. 211.

58.1-700 to 58.1-718. Repealed by Acts 1988, c. 261.

58.1-801. Amended by Acts 2004, Sp. Sess. I, c. 3.

58.1-802. Amended by Acts 1988, c. 200.

58.1-803. Amended by Acts 1998, c. 349; Acts 2004, Sp. Sess. I, c. 3.

58.1-807. Amended by Acts 2001, c. 586; Acts 2002, c. 14; Acts 2004, c. 974; Acts 2004, Sp. Sess. I, c. 3.

58.1-808. Amended by Acts 2004, Sp. Sess. I, c. 3.

58.1-811. Amended by Acts 1985, c. 134; Acts 1988, cc. 429, 738; Acts 1990, c. 289; Acts 1992, cc. 574, 575; Acts 1994, c. 429; Acts 1995, cc. 127, 303; Acts 1998, c. 333; Acts 1999, c. 400; Acts 2000, cc. 393, 602; Acts 2004, cc. 492, 626.

58.1-812. Amended by Acts 1988, cc. 421, 738; Acts 2004, c. 990.

58.1-815.1. Amended by Acts 1994, cc. 470, 597; Acts 1998, cc. 740, 761; Acts 1999, c. 538; Acts 2002, c. 799; Acts 2003, c. 337.

58.1-815.2. Repealed by Acts 1995, c. 354.

58.1-816. Amended by Acts 1990, c. 821; Acts 1993, c. 391.

58.1-905. Amended by Acts 1990, c. 700; Acts 1991, cc. 346, 361; Acts 1996, c. 401.

58.1-906. Amended by Acts 1992, c. 678.

Sec.
58.1-908. Amended by Acts 1987, c. 373.
58.1-911. Amended by Acts 2002, c. 35.
58.1-936. Amended by Acts 1987, c. 484.
58.1-1000. Amended by Acts 2004, c. 1029.
58.1-1001. Amended by Acts 2004, Sp. Sess. I, c. 3.
58.1-1003. Amended by Acts 2004, c. 1029.
58.1-1004. Repealed by Acts 2004, c. 1029.
58.1-1005. Repealed by Acts 2004, c. 1029.
58.1-1008. Amended by Acts 1992, c. 763.
58.1-1009. Amended by Acts 2000, cc. 880, 901; Acts 2002, cc. 683, 722, 821; Acts 2004, c. 1029; Acts 2004, Sp. Sess. I, c. 3.
58.1-1010. Amended by Acts 2004, c. 1029.
58.1-1011. Amended by Acts 2004, c. 1029.
58.1-1013. Amended by Acts 2004, c. 1029.
58.1-1014. Repealed by Acts 2004, c. 1029.
58.1-1015. Amended by Acts 2003, c. 1010.
58.1-1017. Amended by Acts 1992, c. 763; Acts 2004, cc. 883, 996.
58.1-1018. Amended by Acts 2004, Sp. Sess. I, c. 3.
58.1-1033, 58.1-1034. Amended by Acts 2002, c. 821.
58.1-1101. Amended by Acts 1993, c. 866; Acts 1996, c. 622; Acts 1999, c. 396; Acts 2000, c. 472.
58.1-1117. Amended by Acts 1985, c. 221.
58.1-1201. Amended by Acts 1995, c. 301; Acts 2002, c. 29.
58.1-1205. Amended by Acts 1999, c. 84; Acts 2002, c. 667.
58.1-1206. Amended by Acts 2002, c. 667; Acts 2004, Sp. Sess. I, c. 3.
58.1-1213. Amended by Acts 1994, c. 186.
58.1-1401. Amended by Acts 1997, c. 877.
58.1-1402. Amended by Acts 1987, c. 516; Acts 1990, c. 666.
58.1-1404. Amended by Acts 1986, c. 545; Acts 1988, c. 314; Acts 1997, c. 877; Acts 2000, c. 602.
58.1-1405. Amended by Acts 1997, c. 877.
58.1-1408. Amended by Acts 1991, cc. 316, 331.
58.1-1410. Amended by Acts 1994, c. 322; Acts 1997, c. 877.
58.1-1501. Amended by Acts 1995, c. 204; Acts 2000, c. 602.
58.1-1505. Amended by Acts 1995, cc. 204, 723, 786.
58.1-1510. Amended by Acts 1991, cc. 316, 331.
58.1-1604. Amended by Acts 1998, c. 420.
58.1-1605. Amended by Acts 1998, c. 420.
58.1-1609. Amended by Acts 1986, c. 567; Acts 1998, c. 420.
58.1-1610. Amended by Acts 1990, c. 196.
58.1-1614. Amended by Acts 1992, c. 763.
58.1-1618. Amended by Acts 1992, c. 763.
58.1-1702. Amended by Acts 2002, c. 15.
58.1-1710. Amended by Acts 1995, c. 417.
58.1-1712. Amended by Acts 1985, c. 474; Acts 1988, c. 292; Acts 1989, c. 387; Acts 1998, c. 117; Acts 2003, c. 195.
58.1-1714. Amended by Acts 1989, c. 387; Acts 1998, c. 117; Acts 2003, c. 195.
58.1-1717. Amended by Acts 1989, c. 223.
58.1-1720. Amended by Acts 1986, c. 435; Acts 1993, c. 310.
58.1-1724. Amended by Acts 1986, c. 435; Acts 1986, Sp. Sess., cc. 6, 15; Acts 1989, c. 417; Acts 1992, c. 579.
58.1-1800. Amended by Acts 2002, c. 139.
58.1-1803. Amended by Acts 1985, c. 464; Acts 1994, c. 932; Acts 1996, cc. 362, 391; Acts 2004, c. 546.
58.1-1805. Amended by Acts 1985, c. 221; Acts 1989, cc. 629, 642; Acts 1993, c. 384; Acts 1996, c. 634.
58.1-1812. Amended by Acts 1986, c. 39.
58.1-1813. Amended by Acts 1994, c. 800; Acts 1998, c. 432.
58.1-1820. Amended by Acts 2000, cc. 369, 402.
58.1-1822. Amended by Acts 1997, c. 428.
58.1-1823. Amended by Acts 1989, Sp. Sess., cc. 1, 2, 6; Acts 1992, c. 678; Acts 1994, c. 488; Act 1994, 1st Sp. Sess., cc. 2, 5; Acts 1996, cc. 637, 654; Acts 1998, cc. 358, 374.
58.1-1825. Amended by Acts 1985, c. 221; Acts 1991, c. 714; Acts 1998, c. 529; Acts 2003, c. 908.
58.1-1826. Amended by Acts 1985, c. 221.
58.1-1833. Amended by Acts 2002, cc. 184, 462.
58.1-1840. Repealed by Acts 1997, c. 63.
58.1-2021. Amended by Acts 1985, c. 528.
58.1-2035. Amended by Acts 2000, c. 368.
58.1-2100 to 58.1-2147. Repealed by Acts 2000, c. 729.
58.1-2201. Amended by Acts 2001, c. 802; Acts 2002, cc. 4, 7; Acts 2003, c. 781; Acts 2004, c. 340.
58.1-2204. Amended by Acts 2003, c. 781; Acts 2004, c. 340.
58.1-2212. Amended by Acts 2003, c. 781.
58.1-2216. Amended by Acts 2004, c. 340.
58.1-2218. Amended by Acts 2003, c. 781.
58.1-2221. Repealed by Acts 2003, c. 781.
58.1-2225. Amended by Acts 2003, c. 781.
58.1-2230. Amended by Acts 2002, c. 7; Acts 2003, c. 781.
58.1-2232. Amended by Acts 2002, c. 7.
58.1-2237. Amended by Acts 2004, c. 340.
58.1-2238. Amended by Acts 2003, c. 781.
58.1-2242. Amended by Acts 2003, c. 781.
58.1-2251. Amended by Acts 2002, c. 7.
58.1-2255. Amended by Acts 2002, c. 7.
58.1-2259. Amended by Acts 2001, c. 167; Acts 2003, c. 781.
58.1-2261. Amended by Acts 2003, c. 325.
58.1-2262. Amended by Acts 2003, c. 325.
58.1-2263. Amended by Acts 2001, c. 167.
58.1-2264. Repealed by Acts 2003, c. 781.
58.1-2266. Amended by Acts 2004, c. 340.

Sec.
58.1-2271. Amended by Acts 2004, c. 340.
58.1-2275. Amended by Acts 2002, c. 7.
58.1-2276. Amended by Acts 2001, c. 167.
58.1-2283. Amended by Acts 2004, c. 340.
58.1-2300 to 58.1-2311. Repealed by Acts 1986, c. 553.
58.1-2401. Amended by Acts 1986, Sp. Sess., c. 11; Acts 1995, c. 50; Acts 1997, cc. 283, 853; Acts 1999, c. 77.
58.1-2402. Amended by Acts 1985, c. 123; Acts 1986, Sp. Sess., cc. 10, 11; Acts 1988, c. 372; Acts 1992, c. 384; Acts 1993, c. 159; Acts 1994, c. 527; Acts 1996, c. 1047; Acts 1997, cc. 283, 853; Acts 2004, c. 522.
58.1-2403. Amended by Acts 1988, c. 372; Acts 1990, cc. 40, 849; Acts 1995, cc. 27, 247, 786; Acts 1997, c. 283; Acts 1998, c. 322; Acts 1999, c. 77; Acts 2000, cc. 576, 602, 1027; Acts 2002, c. 513; Acts 2003, c. 278.
58.1-2405. Amended by Acts 2003, c. 328.
58.1-2423. Amended by Acts 2003, c. 837.
58.1-2424. Amended by Acts 1990, c. 163.
58.1-2425. Amended by Acts 1986, Sp. Sess., c. 11; Acts 1987, c. 696; Acts 1991, c. 323; Acts 1997, cc. 283, 423, 853; Acts 1998, cc. 905, 907; Acts 1999, c. 77; Acts 2004, c. 522.
58.1-2500. Amended by Acts 1998, c. 365; Acts 2003, c. 372.
58.1-2501. Amended by Acts 1987, cc. 565, 655; Acts 1997, cc. 807, 913; Acts 2004, c. 668.
58.1-2506. Amended by Acts 1997, c. 419.
58.1-2507. Amended by Acts 2003, c. 372.
58.1-2508. Amended by Acts 1985, c. 545; Acts 1992, c. 678; Acts 1996, c. 22; Acts 1997c. 590; Acts 1998, c. 590; Acts 2001, c. 706.
58.1-2520. Amended by Acts 1987, cc. 565, 655.
58.1-2526. Amended by Acts 1985, c. 221; Acts 1999, c. 571.
58.1-2600. Amended by Acts 1988, cc. 730, 899; Acts 1995, c. 507; Acts 1996, c. 381; Acts 1998, c. 897; Acts 1999, c. 971; Acts 2002, c. 443, 444.
58.1-2601. Amended by Acts 1999, c. 971.
58.1-2602. Amended by Acts 1999, c. 971.
58.1-2603. Amended by Acts 1999, c. 971.
58.1-2604. Amended by Acts 1993, c. 529; Acts 1999, c. 971.
58.1-2605. Repealed by Acts 2002, c. 502.
58.1-2606. Amended by Acts 1999, cc. 866, 971; Acts 2004, c. 504.
58.1-2608. Amended by Acts 1988, c. 899.
58.1-2609. Amended by Acts 1999, c. 971.
58.1-2610. Amended by Acts 1999, c. 971.
58.1-2611. Amended by Acts 1999, c. 971.
58.1-2621 to 58.1-2625. Repealed by Acts 1988, c. 899.
58.1-2626. Amended by Acts 1985, c. 31; Acts 1987, cc. 320, 364; Acts 1999, c. 971; Acts 2000, cc. 691, 706.

Sec.
58.1-2626.1. Amended by Acts 1989, c. 429; Acts 2000, c. 929.
58.1-2627. Amended by Acts 1986, c. 243; Acts 1993, c. 522; Acts 1998, c. 197; Acts 1999, c. 971; Acts 2000, cc. 691, 706.
58.1-2628. Amended by Acts 1987, c. 376; Acts 1988, c. 899; Acts 1998, c. 197; Acts 1999, c. 971; Acts 2002, cc. 444, 502; Acts 2004, cc. 661, 716.
58.1-2629. Amended by Acts 1988, c. 899; Acts 2002, c. 502.
58.1-2630. Amended by Acts 2002, c. 502.
58.1-2631. Amended by Acts 1988, c. 899; Acts 2002, c. 502.
58.1-2633. Amended by Acts 1988, c. 899; Acts 1999, c. 971.
58.1-2640. Amended by Acts 1988, c. 899; Acts 2002, c. 502.
58.1-2647, 58.1-2648. Amended by Acts 1988, c. 899.
58.1-2650. Amended by Acts 1988, c. 899.
58.1-2652. Amended by Acts 1985, c. 557.
58.1-2653. Amended by Acts 1985, c. 30; Acts 1992, c. 388.
58.1-2654. Amended by Acts 1990, c. 483.
58.1-2655. Amended by Acts 1985, c. 30; Acts 1992, c. 388.
58.1-2656. Amended by Acts 1993, c. 22.
58.1-2660. Amended by Acts 1988, c. 899; Acts 1990, c. 146; Acts 1996, c. 381; Acts 1999, c. 971; Acts 2000, cc. 691, 706; Acts 2002, cc. 479, 489; Acts 2003, c. 720.
58.1-2662.1. Amended by Acts 1995, c. 751; Acts 1998, c. 897.
58.1-2670. Amended by Acts 1990, c. 146; Acts 2000, c. 368.
58.1-2674.1. Amended by Acts 2004, c. 716.
58.1-2682. Amended by Acts 1999, c. 971.
58.1-2690. Amended by Acts 1995, c. 751.
58.1-2700. Amended by Acts 1995, cc. 744, 803; Acts 1996, c. 575; Acts 1997, c. 283.
58.1-2700.1. Amended by Acts 1996, c. 575; Acts 1997, c. 423; Acts 2002, c. 265.
58.1-2701. Amended by Acts 1986, c. 553; Acts 1986, Sp. Sess., c. 15; Acts 1996, c. 575; Acts 2000, cc. 729, 758; Acts 2002, c. 265.
58.1-2702. Amended by Acts 1988, cc. 514, 725; Acts 1993, c. 40; Acts 1995, cc. 744, 803; Acts 1996, c. 575; Acts 1997, c. 283; Acts 2000, cc. 729, 758.
58.1-2704. Amended by Acts 1990, c. 216; Acts 1992, c. 309.
58.1-2705. Amended by Acts 1995, cc. 744, 803.
58.1-2706. Amended by Acts 1986, c. 553; Acts 1986, Sp. Sess., c. 15; Acts 1988, c.

Sec.
381; Acts 1990, c. 245; Acts 1992, c. 309; Acts 1995, cc. 744, 803; Acts 1996, c. 575; Acts 1999, c. 94.
58.1-2707. Amended by Acts 1986, c. 339; Acts 1992, c. 309; Acts 1993, c. 101; Acts 1995, cc. 744, 803.
58.1-2708. Amended by Acts 1995, cc. 744, 803.
58.1-2709. Amended by Acts 1993, c. 42; Acts 1995, cc. 744, 803; Acts 2002, c. 265.
58.1-2711. Amended by Acts 1990, c. 245; Acts 1995, cc. 744, 803; Acts 1996, c. 575.
58.1-2712. Repealed by Acts 1995, cc. 744, 803.
58.1-2800. Repealed by Acts 1985, c. 470.
58.1-2801 to 58.1-2807. Repealed by Acts 1988, c. 405.
58.1-2808 to 58.1-2811. Repealed by Acts 1986, c. 1.
58.1-2812. Repealed by Acts 1985, c. 470.
58.1-2813. Repealed by Acts 1988, c. 405.
58.1-2900. Amended by Acts 2000, cc. 427, 614.
58.1-2901. Amended by Acts 2000, cc. 427, 614; Acts 2001, cc. 748, 829, 861; Acts 2002, cc. 339, 502.
58.1-2902. Amended by Acts 2001, c. 748.
58.1-2905. Amended by Acts 2001, c. 737.
58.1-2906. Amended by Acts 2000, c. 691.
58.1-3001. Amended by Acts 1988, c. 430; Acts 1989, c. 81; Acts 1994, c. 252.
58.1-3005. Amended by Acts 1988, c. 430; Acts 1989, c. 81; Acts 1994, c. 252.
58.1-3012. Amended by Acts 1996, c. 354.
58.1-3013. Repealed by Acts 2002, c. 719.
58.1-3015. Amended by Acts 1997, c. 921.
58.1-3018. Amended by Acts 1997, cc. 180, 846.
58.1-3103. Amended by Acts 2004, c. 534.
58.1-3109. Amended by Acts 1991, cc. 8, 448.
58.1-3110. Amended by Acts 1986, c. 35; Acts 1987, c. 377.
58.1-3111. Amended by Acts 1990, c. 162; Acts 2002, c. 363.
58.1-3112. Amended by Acts 1996, c. 323.
58.1-3118. Amended by Acts 1997, c. 701; Acts 1999, c. 52; Acts 2003, c. 8.
58.1-3123. Amended by Acts 1999, cc. 90, 777.
58.1-3128. Amended by Acts 1997, c. 496; Acts 1998, c. 648; Acts 1999, c. 192; Acts 2000, c. 453.
58.1-3129. Amended by Acts 1996, c. 323; Acts 1998, c. 427.
58.1-3131. Amended by Acts 2003, c. 931.
58.1-3133. Amended by Acts 2001, cc. 470, 801; Acts 2002, c. 64.
58.1-3134. Amended by Acts 2002, c. 747.
58.1-3149. Amended by Acts 1992, c. 683; Acts 1996, c. 77.
58.1-3150. Amended by Acts 1996, cc. 364, 390.
58.1-3156. Amended by Acts 1988, c. 834.
58.1-3157. Repealed by Acts 1988, c. 834.
58.1-3158. Amended by Acts 1996, cc. 364, 390.
58.1-3172.1. Amended by Acts 2004, c. 223.

Sec.
58.1-3200. Amended by Acts 1985, c. 221.
58.1-3201. Amended by Acts 1985, c. 30.
58.1-3203. Amended by Acts 1992, c. 842; Acts 1996, c. 478.
58.1-3205. Amended by Acts 1998, c. 487.
58.1-3210. Amended by Acts 1993, c. 911.
58.1-3211. Amended by Acts 1987, cc. 525, 546; Acts 1988, cc. 463, 466; Acts 1989, cc. 555, 568; Acts 1990, cc. 479, 486, 504; Acts 1991, c. 63; Acts 1992, cc. 346, 383; Acts 1993, cc. 14, 49, 66, 149; Acts 1997, cc. 704, 710, 872; Acts 1998, c. 361; Acts 1999, c. 205; Acts 2001, cc. 428, 457; Acts 2002, cc. 9, 20, 171; Acts 2004, cc. 5, 6, 77, 78, 494, 503.
58.1-3212. Amended by Acts 1989, c. 568.
58.1-3213. Amended by Acts 1986, c. 214; Acts 1988, c. 334; Acts 1990, c. 158; Acts 1991, c. 286; Acts 1996, c. 480; Acts 1997, c. 710.
58.1-3215. Amended by Acts 1987, cc. 525, 534; Acts 1989, c. 40.
58.1-3219.1. Amended by Acts 1991, cc. 316, 331.
58.1-3220. Amended by Acts 1986, c. 271; Acts 1989, cc. 89, 656; Acts 1994, cc. 424, 435; Acts 1995, c. 673; Acts 2001, c. 489; Acts 2002, cc. 16, 21, 144.
58.1-3220.01. Amended by Acts 2001, c. 489.
58.1-3220.1. Amended by Acts 1994, cc. 424, 435.
58.1-3221. Amended by Acts 1986, c. 271; Acts 1989, c. 89; Acts 1994, cc. 424, 435, 608; Acts 1995, c. 673; Acts 2001, c. 489; Acts 2002, cc. 8, 137.
58.1-3221.1. Amended by Acts 2003, c. 164.
58.1-3222. Amended by Acts 2000, c. 399.
58.1-3226.1. Amended by Acts 1988, c. 277.
58.1-3230. Amended by Acts 1987, c. 550; Acts 1988, c. 695; Acts 1989, cc. 648, 656; Acts 1996, c. 573; Acts 1998, c. 516.
58.1-3231. Amended by Acts 1987, c. 628; Acts 1988, c. 695; Acts 1999, c. 1026; Acts 2000, c. 410; Acts 2001, c. 705.
58.1-3233. Amended by Acts 1987, c. 550; Acts 1988, cc. 462, 695; Acts 1989, c. 656; Acts 1990, c. 695; Acts 1991, cc. 69, 490; Acts 2002, c. 475; Acts 2003, c. 356.
58.1-3234. Amended by Acts 1988, c. 695; Acts 1993, c. 102; Acts 1999, c. 1026.
58.1-3235. Amended by Acts 1994, c. 199.
58.1-3237. Amended by Acts 1985, c. 478; Acts 1988, cc. 422, 695; Acts 1990, c. 841; Acts 1992, Sp. Sess., c. 3; Acts 1998, c. 274; Acts 1999, c. 1026.
58.1-3237.1. Amended by Acts 1992, Sp. Sess., c. 3; Acts 1993, c. 584.

Sec.
58.1-3239. Amended by Acts 1985, c. 448; Acts 1987, c. 550; Acts 1989, c. 656.
58.1-3240. Amended by Acts 1987, c. 550; Acts 1989, c. 656.
58.1-3241. Amended by Acts 1988, c. 695.
58.1-3245. Amended by Acts 1989, c. 418; Acts 1990, c. 296; Acts 1994, c. 667.
58.1-3245.1. Amended by Acts 1990, c. 296; Acts 1999, cc. 162, 190.
58.1-3245.2. Amended by Acts 1990, c. 296; Acts 1994, c. 667.
58.1-3245.4. Amended by Acts 1990, c. 296; Acts 1994, c. 667.
58.1-3245.5. Amended by Acts 1990, c. 296; Acts 1994, c. 667; Acts 1994, c. 667.
58.1-3256. Amended by Acts 2003, c. 1036.
58.1-3259. Amended by Acts 1993, c. 866.
58.1-3260. Amended by Acts 2003, c. 1036.
58.1-3274. Amended by Acts 1987, cc. 318, 362; Acts 2003, c. 474; Acts 2004, c. 576.
58.1-3275. Amended by Acts 1985, c. 221; Acts 1988, c. 896; Acts 1994, c. 210.
58.1-3282. Amended by Acts 1988, c. 280.
58.1-3284.1. Amended by Acts 1993, c. 956.
58.1-3292. Amended by Acts 1999, c. 760.
58.1-3292.1. Amended by Acts 2003, cc. 6, 581.
58.1-3294. Amended by Acts 1990, c. 671; Acts 2000, c. 515.
58.1-3300. Amended by Acts 1985, c. 221.
58.1-3301. Amended by Acts 1995, c. 679.
58.1-3303. Amended by Acts 1990, c. 46.
58.1-3306. Amended by Acts 1998, c. 427.
58.1-3310. Amended by Acts 1997, c. 701.
58.1-3321. Amended by Acts 1990, c. 579.
58.1-3340. Amended by Acts 1994, c. 386; Acts 1995, c. 143.
58.1-3341. Amended by Acts 1994, c. 209.
58.1-3343. Amended by Acts 2001, c. 462.
58.1-3350. Amended by Acts 1985, c. 64.
58.1-3370. Amended by Acts 1991, c. 240.
58.1-3371. Amended by Acts 1995, c. 24.
58.1-3372. Repealed by Acts 1985, c. 62.
58.1-3373. Amended by Acts 1989, c. 390; Acts 1995, c. 24.
58.1-3374. Amended by Acts 1995, c. 24; Acts 2003, c. 1036.
58.1-3376. Amended by Acts 1994, c. 509.
58.1-3378. Amended by Acts 1989, c. 300; Acts 2000, c. 383; Acts 2003, c. 1036.
58.1-3379. Amended by Acts 2003, c. 1036.
58.1-3380. Amended by Acts 2003, c. 1036.
58.1-3381. Amended by Acts 1993, c. 136.
58.1-3384. Amended by Acts 2003, c. 1036.
58.1-3400. Amended by Acts 2004, c. 557.
58.1-3403. Amended by Acts 2000, c. 737.
58.1-3406. Amended by Acts 1990, c. 70.
58.1-3503. Amended by Acts 1985, c. 105; Acts 1987, c. 568; Acts 1991, cc. 253, 255; Acts 1994, c. 827; Acts 1996, c. 529; Acts 1997, cc. 192, 250, 433, 457.
58.1-3504. Amended by Acts 1997, c. 250.
58.1-3505. Amended by Acts 1993, c. 866; Acts 1998, c. 332; Acts 2004, c. 556.
58.1-3506. Amended by Acts 1985, c. 220; Acts 1986, c. 195; Acts 1988, c. 822; Acts 1989, c. 80; Acts 1990, c. 677, 693; Acts 1991, cc. 247, 330, 478; Acts 1992, cc. 642, 680; Acts 1993, c. 100; Acts 1994, cc. 171, 221, 266, 631; Acts 1995, c. 142; Acts 1996, cc. 537, 603, 605; Acts 1997, cc. 244, 250, 433, 457; Acts 1999, cc. 289, 358; Acts 2000, cc. 409, 413, 441, 442, 604; Acts 2001, cc. 41, 447; Acts 2002, cc. 6, 63, 148, 337; Acts 2003, cc. 657, 670; Acts 2004, cc 4, 556, 591.
58.1-3506.2. Amended by Acts 1998, c. 361.
58.1-3507. Amended by Acts 1985, c. 221; Acts 1992, c. 680; Acts 1993, cc. 78, 866; Acts 1999, c. 396; Acts 2000, c. 7.
58.1-3508.1. Amended by Acts 1997, c. 77.
58.1-3509. Amended by Acts 1999, c. 200; Acts 2000, c. 441.
58.1-3510. Amended by Acts 1987, cc. 572, 591; Acts 1989, c. 589; Acts 1990, c. 151; Acts 1997, c. 853.
58.1-3510.1. Amended by Acts 1990, c. 164; Acts 1993, c. 310; Acts 2003, cc. 757, 758.
58.1-3510.3. Amended by Acts 1990, c. 164; Acts 1993, c. 310; Acts 2003, cc. 757, 758.
58.1-3511. Amended by Acts 1985, c. 156; Acts 1994, cc. 961, 962; Acts 1995, c. 449; Acts 1998, c. 894; Acts 2003, cc. 34, 43.
58.1-3516. Amended by Acts 1985, cc. 241, 258; Acts 1986, cc. 51, 541; Acts 1987, cc. 212, 233; Acts 1988, cc. 446, 726; Acts 1989, cc. 29, 36, 329; Acts 1990, c. 330; Acts 1991, cc. 61, 624; Acts 1992, cc. 602, 669; Acts 1993, c. 557; Acts 1996, c. 536; Acts 2002, c. 550.
58.1-3516.1. Amended by Acts 1995, cc. 131, 469.
58.1-3617. Amended by Acts 2000, c. 329.
58.1-3518. Amended by Acts 1990, c. 705; Acts 1995, c. 29.
58.1-3518.1. Amended by Acts 1996, c. 322.
58.1-3520, 58.1-3521. Amended by Acts 1994, c. 152.
58.1-3523. Amended by Acts 1999, c. 189; Acts 2004, Sp. Sess. I, c. 1.
58.1-3524. Amended by Acts 2004, Sp. Sess. I, c. 1.
58.1-3525 to 58.1-3533. Repealed by Acts 2004, Sp. Sess. I, c. 1, eff. 1/1/06.
58.1-3526. Amended by Acts 1999, c. 99.

Sec.
58.1-3528. Amended by Acts 2004, c. 547.
58.1-3603. Amended by Acts 1992, c. 889; Acts 1996, c. 534.
58.1-3604. Amended by Acts 1989, c. 38.
58.1-3605. Amended by Acts 1995, c. 346; Acts 1995, c. 346.
58.1-3606. Amended by Acts 1985, c. 495; Acts 2004, c. 492.
58.1-3607. Amended by Acts 1985, c. 495; Acts 1998, c. 172.
58.1-3609. Amended by Acts 1989, c. 400.
58.1-3617. Amended by Acts 1987, c. 533.
58.1-3619. Amended by Acts 1993, c. 559.
58.1-3650. Amended by Acts 1995, c. 346.
58.1-3650.116. Amended by Acts 1988, c. 658.
58.1-3650.326. Amended by Acts 1992, c. 511.
58.1-3650.804. Amended by Acts 1999, cc. 13, 25, 26, 27, 28, 29, 31.
58.1-3651. Amended by Acts 2004, c. 557.
58.1-3660. Amended by Acts 2003, c. 859.
58.1-3660.1. Amended by Acts 1996, cc. 581, 595.
58.1-3661. Amended by Acts 1988, c. 253; Acts 1990, c. 690; Acts 1998, c. 606.
58.1-3700. Amended by Acts 1991, c. 267; Acts 1993, cc. 93, 934; Acts 1996, cc. 715, 720.
58.1-3700.1. Amended by Acts 1996, cc. 715, 720; Acts 2000, c. 557.
58.1-3701. Amended by Acts 1994, c. 267; Acts 1996, cc. 715, 720.
58.1-3703. Amended by Acts 1985, c. 531; Acts 1987, cc. 617, 618, 715; Acts 1988, cc. 480, 499; Acts 1989, c. 314; Acts 1991, cc. 540, 572; Acts 1993, cc. 65, 326, 918; Acts 1996, cc. 715, 720; Acts 1997, cc. 62, 283, 903; Acts 2000, c. 557.
58.1-3703.1. Amended by Acts 1996, cc. 715, 720; Acts 1997, c. 732.
58.1-3704. Amended by Acts 1999, c. 200.
58.1-3706. Amended by Acts 1985, c. 120; Acts 1989, c. 589; Acts 1992, c. 632; Acts 1993, c. 918; Acts 1996, cc. 77, 715, 720.
58.1-3707. Repealed by Acts 1996, cc. 715, 720.
58.1-3708. Amended by Acts 1996, cc. 715, 720.
58.1-3713. Amended by Acts 1986, c. 58; Acts 1988, c. 784; Acts 1989, cc. 265, 380; Acts 1991, c. 164; Acts 1993, c. 163; Acts 1996, c. 706; Acts 2004, cc. 871, 893.
58.1-3713.01. Amended by Acts 1998, c. 694; Acts 2004, c. 893.
58.1-3713.3. Amended by Acts 2001, cc. 294, 303.
58.1-3714. Amended by Acts 1998, c. 503.
58.1-3715. Amended by Acts 1999, c. 203.
58.1-3724. Amended by Acts 2003, c. 979; Acts 2004, c. 460.
58.1-3725. Repealed by Acts 1996, cc. 715, 720.

Sec.
58.1-3730. Amended by Acts 1991, c. 430; Acts 1996, c. 77.
58.1-3730.1. Amended by Acts 1990, c. 278.
58.1-3731. Amended by Acts 1987, c. 244; Acts 1999, c. 971; Acts 2000, cc. 691, 706; Acts 2001, cc. 829, 861.
58.1-3732. Amended by Acts 1992, c. 632; Acts 1996, cc. 715, 720; Acts 2002, c. 346.
58.1-3732.2. Amended by Acts 2002, c. 532.
58.1-3734. Amended by Acts 1999, cc. 862, 957.
58.1-3801. Amended by Acts 1988, c. 421.
58.1-3803. Amended by Acts 1988, c. 421.
58.1-3809 to 58.1-3811. Repealed by Acts 1985, c. 221.
58.1-3812. Amended by Acts 1986, c. 38; Acts 1994, c. 560; Acts 1995, cc. 553, 590; Acts 1997, c. 252; Acts 1998, c. 337; Acts 2000, cc. 375, 1064; Acts 2002, cc. 17, 68; Acts 2003, cc. 160, 179; Acts 2004, cc. 43, 172, 489, 516.
58.1-3813. Repealed by Acts 2000, c. 1064.
58.1-3813.1. Amended by Acts 2001, c. 529.
58.1-3813. Amended by Acts 1993, cc. 25, 76.
58.1-3814. Amended by Acts 1986, c. 38; Acts 1992, c. 399; Acts 1995, cc. 553, 590; Acts 1998, c. 337; Acts 1999, c. 971; Acts 2000, cc. 614, 691, 706, 1064; Acts 2001, cc. 737, 748; Acts 2004, cc. 8, 159.
58.1-3814.1. Amended by Acts 1990, c. 492.
58.1-3816.2. Amended by Acts 2004, cc. 8, 159.
58.1-3817. Amended by Acts 1989, c. 291; Acts 1997, c. 287.
58.1-3818. Amended by Acts 1995, c. 201; Acts 1997, c. 287; Acts 1998, cc. 150, 532; Acts 1999, c. 986; Acts 2001, c. 485.
58.1-3818.1 to 58.1-3818.7. Amended by Acts 2003, cc. 757, 758.
58.1-3819. Amended by Acts 1985, c. 556; Acts 1992, cc. 263, 834; Acts 1996, c. 833; Acts 1997, cc. 757, 764; Acts 1998, cc. 729, 733; Acts 1999, cc. 233, 234, 241, 253, 260; Acts 2000, c. 470; Acts 2001, cc. 571, 585; Acts 2003, c. 939; Acts 2004, cc. 7, 610.
58.1-3822. Amended by Acts 1993, c. 56; Acts 1996, c. 477; Acts 1999, cc. 228, 242; Acts 2002, cc. 567, 646; Acts 2004, c. 610.
58.1-3823. Amended by Acts 1998, cc. 74, 444; Acts 2002, cc. 173, 259; Acts 2004, cc. 50, 610, 828.
58.1-3833. Amended by Acts 1989, c. 391; Acts 1990, cc. 846, 862; Acts 1992, c. 263; Acts 1993, c. 866; Acts 1999, c. 366; Acts 2000, c. 626; Acts 2001, c. 619; Acts 2002, c. 853; Acts 2003, c. 792; Acts 2004, c. 610; Acts 2004, Sp. Sess. I, c. 3.

Sec.
58.1-3840. Amended by Acts 1986, cc. 545, 605; Acts 1989, cc. 314, 391; Acts 1999, c. 366; Acts 2000, c. 626; Acts 2003, cc. 12, 214.
58.1-3842. Amended by Acts 2004, c. 610.
58.1-3850. Amended by Acts 1996, c. 830; Acts 1997, c. 168; Acts 2002, c. 449.
58.1-3901. Amended by Acts 1990, c. 152.
58.1-3902. Amended by Acts 1999, c. 358.
58.1-3903. Amended by Acts 1991, c. 8.
58.1-3906. Amended by Acts 1999, c. 541.
58.1-3907. Amended by Acts 1995, c. 557; Acts 1996, c. 528.
58.1-3910. Amended by Acts 2002, c. 139.
58.1-3912. Amended by Acts 1985, cc. 406, 543; Acts 1991, c. 187; Acts 1994, c. 207; Acts 1996, c. 323; Acts 1998, Sp. Sess., c. 2; Acts 1999, c. 358; Acts 2001, c. 801; Acts 2002, c. 64.
58.1-3914. Amended by Acts 1995, c. 239; Acts 1996, c. 324.
58.1-3916. Amended by Acts 1986, cc. 206, 353; Acts 1987, cc. 570, 582, 595; Acts 1989, c. 238; Acts 1990, cc. 667, 696, 702; Acts 1991, cc. 471, 484, 493, 509; Acts 1993, c. 91; Acts 1994, c. 932; Acts 1995, c. 395; Acts 1997, cc. 481, 496, 911; Acts 1998, cc. 375, 542, 649; Acts 1999, c. 631; Acts 2000, cc. 433, 507.
58.1-3916.1. Amended by Acts 1986, c. 351.
58.1-3918. Amended by Acts 1999, c. 631; Acts 2000, c. 507.
58.1-3919. Amended by Acts 1986, c. 634; Acts 1996, c. 323; Acts 1998, c. 648.
58.1-3919.1. Amended by Acts 1992, cc. 625, 683.
58.1-3921. Amended by Acts 1995, c. 239; Acts 1997, c. 496; Acts 1999, c. 192; Acts 2000, c. 453.
58.1-3922. Amended by Acts 1997, c. 496.
58.1-3923. Repealed by Acts 2002, c. 64.
58.1-3924. Amended by Acts 1988, c. 699; Acts 1995, c. 239; Acts 1997, c. 496; Acts 2002, c. 64.
58.1-3927. Repealed by Acts 1998, c. 648.
58.1-3928. Repealed by Acts 1997, c. 496.
58.1-3929. Repealed by Acts 1985, c. 131.
58.1-3930. Amended by Acts 1985, c. 131; Acts 2001, c. 462.
58.1-3932. Amended by Acts 2001, c. 462.
58.1-3933. Amended by Acts 1997, c. 496.
58.1-3934. Amended by Acts 1992, cc. 625, 683; Acts 1997, c. 496; Acts 1998, c. 648; Acts 2002, c. 64.
58.1-3937. Repealed by Acts 1998, c. 648.
58.1-3938. Amended by Acts 1985, c. 131.
58.1-3939.1. Repealed by Acts 1998, c. 648.
58.1-3940. Amended by Acts 1994, c. 209; Acts 1996, c. 323; Acts 1998, c. 648; Acts 2002, c. 64.

Sec.
58.1-3941. Amended by Acts 1996, c. 323; Acts 1997, cc. 496, 731.
58.1-3942. Amended by Acts 1990, c. 553; Acts 1996, c. 732; Acts 1997, c. 731; Acts 1999, c. 299; Acts 2001, c. 801.
58.1-3944. Amended by Acts 2002, c. 64.
58.1-3946. Amended by Acts 2002, c. 64.
58.1-3952. Amended by Acts 1991, c. 445; Acts 1994, c. 153; Acts 1997, c. 496; Acts 2002, c. 64.
58.1-3954. Amended by Acts 1993, c. 27.
58.1-3957. Amended by Acts 1990, c. 935.
58.1-3958. Amended by Acts 1991, c. 271; Acts 1994, c. 932; Acts 1995, c. 395; Acts 1997, c. 496; Acts 1998, c. 648; Acts 1999, c. 389; Acts 2000, cc. 389, 453; Acts 2003, c. 170.
58.1-3959. Amended by Acts 2001, c. 462.
58.1-3965. Amended by Acts 1988, c. 306; Acts 1994, c. 884; Acts 1995, c. 547; Acts 1996, cc. 323, 710; Acts 1997, c. 724; Acts 1999, c. 674; Acts 2002, c. 64; Acts 2003, c. 168; Acts 2004, c. 968.
58.1-3966. Amended by Acts 1997, c. 724.
58.1-3967. Amended by Acts 1990, cc. 831, 918; Acts 1992, c. 854; Acts 1993, cc. 51, 372; Acts 1994, cc. 295, 884; Acts 1996, c. 710; Acts 1997, c. 327; Acts 1999, cc. 403, 869; Acts 2000, c. 756; Acts 2001, c. 37; Acts 2004, c. 645.
58.1-3968. Amended by Acts 1985, c. 60; Acts 1991, c. 243.
58.1-3969. Amended by Acts 1997, c. 724; Acts 1999, c. 674.
58.1-3970.1. Amended by Acts 2003, cc. 16, 156; Acts 2004, c. 968.
58.1-3971. Amended by Acts 1994, c. 540.
58.1-3980. Amended by Acts 1989, c. 86; Acts 1991, c. 8; Acts 1992, c. 382; Acts 1995, c. 445; Acts 1998, c. 648; Acts 1999, cc. 123, 624, 677.
58.1-3981. Amended by Acts 1995, c. 108; Acts 1998, c. 529; Acts 1999, cc. 624, 631, 677.
58.1-3983.1. Amended by Acts 2002, c. 525; Acts 2003, c. 196; Acts 2004, cc. 527, 534.
58.1-3984. Amended by Acts 1988, c. 282; Acts 1989, c. 86; Acts 1991, c. 8; Acts 1992, c. 382; Acts 1997, c. 251; Acts 1998, c. 529; Acts 1999, cc. 202, 470; Acts 2003, c. 1036.
58.1-3987. Amended by Acts 1999, c. 631.
58.1-3991. Repealed by Acts 1999, c. 631.
58.1-4004. Amended by Acts 2004, c. 630.
58.1-4006. Amended by Acts 1992, cc. 442, 449; Acts 2004, c. 630.
58.1-4007. Amended by Acts 1988, c. 788; Acts 1989, c. 228; Acts 1990, c. 732;

Sec.
Acts 1999, c. 716; Acts 2004, c. 630.
58.1-4007.1. Amended by Acts 1998, c. 201; Acts 1999, c. 736.
58.1-4008. Amended by Acts 1989, c. 478; Acts 1992, c. 449; Acts 2004, c. 555.
58.1-4009. Amended by Acts 1989, c. 478; Acts 2004, c. 555.
58.1-4010. Amended by Acts 2004, c. 630.
58.1-4012. Amended by Acts 1992, c. 449.
58.1-4013. Amended by Acts 1992, c. 449; Acts 1995, c. 423; Acts 2003, c. 924.
58.1-4014. Amended by Acts 1992, c. 449; Acts 2004, c. 630.
58.1-4015. Amended by Acts 1989, c. 478.
58.1-4017. Amended by Acts 1989, c. 478; Acts 1990, c. 732.
58.1-4019. Amended by Acts 1989, c. 478; Acts 1992, c. 449; Acts 1996, c. 954; Acts 1999, c. 34.
58.1-4019.1. Amended by Acts 1996, cc. 462, 505; Acts 2003, c. 884.
58.1-4020. Amended by Acts 1989, c. 478; Acts 1992, c. 449; Acts 1994, c. 49; Acts 1996, c. 975.
58.1-4020.1. Amended by Acts 2004, c. 630.
58.1-4021. Amended by Acts 1990, cc. 732, 1005; Acts 1990, Sp. Sess., c. 1.
58.1-4022. Amended by Acts 1989, c. 478; Acts 1995, cc. 831, 852; Acts 2002, cc. 829, 866.
58.1-4022.1. Amended by Acts 2002, cc. 829, 866.
58.1-4023. Amended by Acts 1989, c. 478.
58.1-4024. Amended by Acts 1994, c. 48.
58.1-4028. Repealed by Acts 2002, c. 3.
59-1 to 59-235. Repealed by Acts 1968, c. 439.
59.1-1 to 59.1-9. Repealed by Acts 1976, c. 10.
59.1-9.4. Amended by Acts 1979, c. 640.
59.1-9.9. Amended by Acts 1975, c. 289.
59.1-9.10. Amended by Acts 1982, c. 285; Acts 2000, c. 755.
59.1-9.15. Amended by Acts 1982, c. 60; Acts 1988, c. 589.
59.1-10 to 59.1-21. Repealed by Acts 1984, c. 582.
59.1-21.2. Amended by Acts 1972, c. 448; Acts 1975, c. 217; Acts 1986, c. 577.
59.1-21.3. Amended by Acts 1972, c. 448.
59.1-21.4. Amended by Acts 1972, c. 448; Acts 1973, c. 147; Acts 1975, c. 217.
59.1-21.5. Amended by Acts 1972, c. 448; Acts 1973, c. 147.
59.1-21.6. Amended by Acts 1973, c. 147.
59.1-21.7. Amended by Acts 2001, c. 402.
59.1-21.9. Amended by Acts 1990, c. 907.
59.1-21.10. Amended by Acts 1979, c. 306; Acts 1990, c. 907; Acts 2003, c. 410.
59.1-21.11. Amended by Acts 1979, c. 306; Acts 1982, c. 350; Acts 1985, c. 498; Acts 1987, c. 535; Acts 1990, c. 907; Acts 1991, c. 199.

Sec.
59.1-21.12. Amended by Acts 1990, c. 907; Acts 2003, c. 410.
59.1-21.13. Amended by Acts 1979, c. 306; Acts 1990; c. 907.
59.1-21.14. Amended by Acts 1976, c. 645; Acts 1979, c. 306; Acts 1997, c. 801.
59.1-21.15. Amended by Acts 1979, c. 306; Acts 1988, c. 589.
59.1-21.16:2. Amended by Acts 1984, c. 720; Acts 1990, c. 907; Acts 1995, c. 664; Acts 2003, c. 410.
59.1-21.20. Amended by Acts 1977, c. 589.
59.1-21.21. Repealed by Acts 1977, c. 589.
59.1-21.22 to 59.1-21.24. Amended by Acts 1977, c. 589.
59.1-22 to 59.1-41. Repealed by Acts 1974, c. 545.
59.1-41.1 to 59.1-41.4. Amended by Acts 1989, c. 240.
59.1-41.6. Amended by Acts 1989, c. 240.
59.1-42 to 59.1-68.1. Repealed by Acts 1975, c. 589.
59.1-68.2. Amended by Acts 1973, c. 537; Acts 1975, c. 43; Acts 1984, c. 582.
59.1-68.3. Amended by Acts 1975, c. 43; Acts 1976, c. 87.
59.1-68.4. Amended by Acts 1975, c. 43.
59.1-68.5. Amended by Acts 1975, c. 43.
59.1-69. Amended by Acts 1987, c. 702; Acts 1995, c. 168; Acts 1996, c. 904.
59.1-70. Amended by Acts 1976, c. 79; Acts 1981, c. 519; Acts 1984, c. 771; Acts 1987, c. 702; Acts 1991, c. 439; Acts 1995, c. 168.
59.1-71, 59.1-72. Repealed by Acts 2002, c. 267.
59.1-73. Repealed by Acts 1994, c. 432.
59.1-74. Amended by Acts 1975, c. 230; Acts 1983 c. 103; Acts 1992, c. 784; Acts 2002, c. 267.
59.1-75. Amended by Acts 1991, c. 710.
59.1-77. Repealed by Acts 1998, c. 819.
59.1-78. Amended by Acts 1976, c. 104.
59.1-79. Amended by Acts 1977, c. 580.
59.1-80. Amended by Acts 1984, c. 771.
59.1-81. Amended by Acts 1976, c. 104.
59.1-82 to 59.1-84. Amended by Acts 1976, c. 104; Acts 1984, c. 771.
59.1-85 to 59.1-88. Amended by Acts 1976, c. 104.
59.1-88. Amended by Acts 1996, c. 756.
59.1-89. Amended by Acts 1995, c. 242; Acts 1996, c. 756.
59.1-92. Amended by Acts 1971, Ex. Sess., c. 1.
59.1-94. Amended by Acts 2002, c. 858.
59.1-102.1 to 59.1-102.7. Repealed by Acts 1974, c. 233.
59.1-104. Repealed by Acts 1994, c. 432.
59.1-116. Repealed by Acts 1994, c. 432.
59.1-121. Amended by Acts 1972, c. 598.
59.1-124. Amended by Acts 1972, c. 598; Acts 1988, c. 765.

Sec.
59.1-127. Amended by Acts 1972, c. 598; Acts 1988, c. 765.
59.1-130. Amended by Acts 1972, c. 598; Acts 1988, c. 765.
59.1-137. Amended by Acts 1976, c. 250.
59.1-138. Amended by Acts 1972, c. 824.
59.1-142 to 59.1-148. Repealed by Acts 2002, c. 856.
59.1-148.1. Repealed by Acts 2004, c. 929.
59.1-148.2. Repealed by Acts 2004, c. 929.
59.1-148.3. Amended by Acts 1990, c. 359; Acts 1991, c. 389; Acts 1992, cc. 63, 83, 195; Acts 1996, c. 50; Acts 1998, c. 173; Acts 1999, c. 312; Acts 2000, c. 391; Acts 2002, c. 25; Acts 2003, c. 106; Acts 2004, c. 136.
59.1-148.4. Amended by Acts 2004, c. 995.
59.1-149 to 59.1-155. Amended by Acts 1992, c. 885.
59.1-156. Amended by Acts 1992, c. 885; Acts 1996, cc. 638, 1012.
59.1-157. Amended by Acts 1992, c. 885.
59.1-158 to 59.1-161. Repealed by Acts 1992, c. 885.
59.1-163. Amended by Acts 1992, c. 885.
59.1-165. Amended by Acts 1972, c. 741; Acts 1992, c. 885.
59.1-166 to 59.1-167.1. Amended by Acts 1992, c. 885.
59.1-168 to 59.1-176. Repealed by Acts 1972, c. 237.
58.1-177 to 59.1-188.1. Repealed by Acts 1983, c. 209.
59.1-189. Amended by Acts 1990, c. 592.
59.1-198. Amended by Acts 1981, c. 205; Acts 1987, c. 464; Acts 1988, c. 485; Acts 1992, c. 278; Acts 2001, cc. 741, 762; Acts 2004, cc. 41, 90.
59.1-199. Amended by Acts 1987, c. 464; Acts 1994, c. 400; Acts 1995, c. 703; Acts 1996, cc. 61, 77, 179; Acts 1999, c. 494; Acts 2000, cc. 691, 706.
59.1-200. Amended by Acts 1979, c. 304; Acts 1981, c. 205; Acts 1983, c. 173; Acts 1986, c. 432; Acts 1987, cc. 462, 463, 464; Acts 1988, cc. 24, 534; Acts 1990, c. 584; Acts 1991, cc. 300, 605, 608, 630, 654; Acts 1992, cc. 278, 545, 768; Acts 1993, cc. 455, 760; Acts 1994, cc. 261, 400, 655; Acts 1995, c. 10; Acts 1998, c. 848; Acts 2000, cc. 880, 901; Acts 2002, c. 217; Acts 2002, c. 897; Acts 2003, cc. 800, 1003; Acts 2004, cc. 784, 790, 798, 817.
59.1-201. Amended by Acts 1979, c. 493; Acts 1982, c. 13; Acts 1987, c. 464; Acts 1995, c. 703.
59.1-202. Amended by Acts 1981, c. 423; Acts 1982, c. 13; Acts 1988, c. 850.
59.1-203. Amended by Acts 1982, c. 13; Acts 1988, c. 485.
59.1-204. Amended by Acts 1995, cc. 703, 726; Acts 2004, cc. 41, 90.
59.1-204.1. Amended by Acts 1995, cc. 703, 726.
59.1-206. Amended by Acts 1980, c. 171; Acts 1982, c. 13; Acts 1991, c. 156; Acts 1995, c. 703.
59.1-207. Amended by Acts 1995, cc. 703, 726.
59.1-207.2. Amended by Acts 1999, c. 77.
59.1-207.3. Amended by Acts 1995, c. 110.
59.1-207.11. Amended by Acts 1988, c. 603; Acts 1990, c. 772; Acts 1998, c. 671.
59.1-207.12. Amended by Acts 1988, c. 603.
59.1-207.13. Amended by Acts 1987, c. 607; Acts 1988, c. 603; Acts 1990, c. 772; Acts 1998, c. 671.
59.1-207.14. Amended by Acts 1988, c. 603.
59.1-207.15. Amended by Acts 1990, c. 772.
59.1-207.16. Amended by Acts 1990, c. 772; Acts 1999, c. 387.
59.1-207.16:1. Amended by Acts 1998, c. 671.
59.1-207.19. Amended by Acts 2003, c. 353.
59.1-207.38. Amended by Acts 1996, c. 63.
59.1-263. Amended by Acts 1985, c. 242.
59.1-265. Amended by Acts 1996, c. 77.
59.1-270. Amended by Acts 1988, c. 236.
59.1-271. Amended by Acts 1986, c. 492; Acts 1988, c. 236; Acts 1993, c. 699; Acts 1995, c. 792; Acts 1996, c. 77; Acts 1997, c. 517.
59.1-272. Amended by Acts 1988, c. 236; Acts 1992, c. 467.
59.1-273. Amended by Acts 1980, c. 171; Acts 1982, c. 13; Acts 1984, c. 734; Acts 1988, c. 236; Acts 1995, c. 792.
59.1-274. Amended by Acts 1980, c. 171; Acts 1982, c. 13; Acts 1984, cc. 678, 720; Acts 1987, c. 115; Acts 1988, c. 236; Acts 1989, c. 172; Acts 1992, c. 528; Acts 1993, cc. 354, 741, 943, 979; Acts 1995, c. 792; Acts 1997, cc. 379, 808; Acts 1999, cc. 235, 249; Acts 2000, cc. 656, 678, 695, 746; Acts 2003, cc. 748, 763.
59.1-274.1. Amended by Acts 1988, c. 236.
59.1-275. Amended by Acts 1984, c. 720; Acts 1988, c. 236; Acts 1989, c. 172; Acts 2003, cc. 748, 763.
59.1-276, 59.1-277. Amended by Acts 1988, c. 236.
59.1-279. Amended by Acts 1983, c. 572; Acts 1988, cc. 236, 374; Acts 1995, c. 792; Acts 1997, cc. 497, 517, 808.
59.1-280. Amended by Acts 1983, c. 572; Acts 1988, c. 236; Acts 1992, c. 301; Acts 1995, c. 792; Acts 1996, c. 77; Acts 1997, c. 517; Acts 1998, c. 759; Acts 2003, c. 676.

Sec.
59.1-280.1. Amended by Acts 1997, cc. 517, 634, 669; Acts 1998, c. 759.
59.1-280.2. Amended by Acts 1997, c. 517; Acts 1998, c. 759.
59.1-281. Repealed by Acts 1983, c. 572.
59.1-282. Amended by Acts 1988, c. 236; Acts 1995, c. 792.
59.1-282.1. Amended by Acts 1988, c. 236; Acts 1997, cc. 634, 669.
59.1-282.2 to 59.1-282.4. Amended by Acts 1988, c. 236.
59.1-283. Amended by Acts 1988, c. 236; Acts 1995, c. 792; Acts 1997, c. 314.
59.1-284. Amended by Acts 1988, c. 236; Acts 1995, c. 792.
59.1-284.01. Amended by Acts 1995, c. 792.
59.1-284.1. Amended by Acts 1995, c. 128; Acts 1996, cc. 589, 599.
59.1-284.2. Amended by Acts 1995, c. 128.
59.1-284.4. Amended by Acts 1995, c. 128.
59.1-284.5. Repealed by Acts 1995, c. 128.
59.1-284.7 to 59.1-284.12. Repealed by Acts 2004, c. 872.
59.1-284.13. Amended by Acts 1996, c. 642.
59.1-284.14. Amended by Acts 1996, cc. 645, 651; Acts 2001, c. 863.
59.1-284.15. Amended by Acts 2001, c. 863.
59.1-284.16. Amended by Acts 2004, c. 872.
59.1-284.17. Amended by Acts 2004, c. 872.
59.1-284.18. Amended by Acts 2004, c. 872.
59.1-284.19. Repealed by Acts 2004, c. 872.
59.1-285 to 59.1-293. Repealed by Acts 1986, c. 424.
59.1-296. Amended by Acts 1985, c. 585; Acts 1986, c. 187; Acts 1990, cc. 392, 433; Acts 1991, c. 149; Acts 1992, c. 102; Acts 2003, c. 344.
59.1-296.1. Amended by Acts 1988, c. 13; Acts 1990, cc. 392, 433.
59.1-296.2. Amended by Acts 1990, cc. 392, 433.
59.1-296.2:1. Amended by Acts 1993, c. 686; Acts 2003, c. 344; Acts 2004, c. 988.
59.1-296.3. Amended by Acts 1990, cc. 392, 433.
59.1-297, 59.1-298. Amended by Acts 1990, cc. 392, 433; Acts 2003, c. 344; Acts 2004, c. 855.
59.1-299. Amended by Acts 1990, cc. 392, 433; Acts 1992, c. 117.
59.1-305. Amended by Acts 2003, c. 344.
59.1-306. Amended by Acts 1985, c. 585; Acts 1990, cc. 392, 433; Acts 1992, c. 117; Acts 2004, c. 988.
59.1-307. Amended by Acts 1987, c. 547.
59.1-308. Amended by Acts 1985, c. 585; Acts 1990, cc. 392, 433.
59.1-308.1. Amended by Acts 1990, cc. 392, 433.
59.1-310.4. Amended by Acts 2004, c. 855.

Sec.
59.1-313. Amended by Acts 1992, c. 545; Acts 1999, c. 77.
59.1-318. Amended by Acts 1992, c. 545.
59.1-320. Repealed by Acts 1992, c. 545.
59.1-321. Amended by Acts 1996, c. 372.
59.1-323. Amended by Acts 1992, c. 545.
59.1-325. Amended by Acts 1988, c. 58; Acts 1992, c. 545.
59.1-326 to 59.1-329. Amended by Acts 1992, c. 545.
59.1-330. Repealed by Acts 1992, c. 545.
59.1-331, 59.1-332. Amended by Acts 1992, c. 545.
59.1-335. Amended by Acts 1992, c. 545.
59.1-335.2. Amended by Acts 1990, c. 3; Acts 2003, c. 359.
59.1-338. Amended by Acts 1990, c. 344.
59.1-344 to 59.1-352. Repealed by Acts 2002, c. 898.
59.1-347. Amended by Acts 1997, c. 801.
59.1-352.2. Amended by Acts 2003, c. 353.
59.1-352.3. Amended by Acts 2003, c. 797.
59.1-353. Amended by Acts 1997, c. 801; Acts 2002, c. 898; Acts 2003, c. 353.
59.1-361. Amended by Acts 1988, c. 865.
59.1-364. Amended by Acts 1992, c. 820; Acts 1998, c. 619.
59.1-365. Amended by Acts 1991, c. 591; Acts 1992, c. 820; Acts 1996, cc. 319, 915, 1025; Acts 1997, c. 18; Acts 1998, cc. 608, 619.
59.1-368. Amended by Acts 1992, c. 820.
59.1-369. Amended by Acts 1990, c. 271; Acts 1991, c. 591; Acts 1992, c. 820; Acts 1993, c. 430; Acts 1998, cc. 619, 845; Acts 2000, cc. 99, 1031; Acts 2003, c. 682; Acts 2004, c. 774.
59.1-370. Amended by Acts 1998, c. 619.
59.1-371. Amended by Acts 1990, c. 774; Acts 1991, c. 591; Acts 1995, c. 370; Acts 1998, c. 619; Acts 2000, c. 1011.
59.1-372. Amended by Acts 1993, c. 146; Acts 1997, c. 798; Acts 2002, c. 852.
59.1-373. Amended by Acts 1996, c. 573.
59.1-374. Amended by Acts 1998, c. 619.
59.1-375. Amended by Acts 1991, c. 591; Acts 1992, c. 820.
59.1-376. Amended by Acts 1991, c. 591.
59.1-377. Amended by Acts 1991, c. 591; Acts 1992, c. 820.
59.1-378. Amended by Acts 1990, c. 206; Acts 1992, c. 820.
59.1-378.1. Amended by Acts 1996, cc. 663, 750; Acts 2000, c. 1002.
59.1-380. Amended by Acts 1992, c. 820; Acts 1996, cc. 915, 1025; Acts 1997, c. 18; Acts 2000, c. 1011.
59.1-381. Amended by Acts 1992, c. 820.
59.1-382. Amended by Acts 1991, c. 591; Acts 1992, c. 820.

Sec.
59.1-383. Amended by Acts 1991, c. 591; Acts 1992, c. 820; Acts 1996, cc. 915, 1025; Acts 1997, c. 18.
59.1-385. Amended by Acts 1991, c. 591; Acts 1995, cc. 212, 275; Acts 1996, cc. 915, 1025; Acts 1997, c. 18; Acts 2000, c. 1031.
59.1-386. Amended by Acts 2003, c. 705.
59.1-387. Amended by Acts 1991, c. 591; Acts 2000, c. 1011.
59.1-389. Amended by Acts 1991, c. 591; Acts 1998, c. 619; Acts 1999, c. 356.
59.1-390. Amended by Acts 1990, c. 456; Acts 1991, c. 591; Acts 1998, c. 619.
59.1-391. Amended by Acts 1989, c. 145; Acts 1991, c. 591; Acts 1992, c. 820; Acts 1998, c. 619; Acts 2001, c. 539; Acts 2003, c. 682.
59.1-392. Amended by Acts 1991, c. 591; Acts 1992, c. 820; Acts 1995, c. 217; Acts 1998, cc. 608, 619; Acts 2000, c. 1031.
59.1-393. Amended by Acts 1991, c. 591.
59.1-394.1. Amended by Acts 2003, c. 722.
59.1-395. Amended by Acts 2003, c. 682.
59.1-396. Amended by Acts 1992, c. 820.
59.1-400. Amended by Acts 1990, c. 366.
59.1-402. Amended by Acts 1990, c. 351.
59.1-403. Amended by Acts 1996, cc. 915, 1025.
59.1-404. Repealed by Acts 1991, c. 591.
59.1-405. Amended by Acts 1991, c. 591.
59.1-407. Amended by Acts 2003, c. 364.
59.1-408. Amended by Acts 1995, c. 298; Acts 2003, c. 364.
59.1-409. Amended by Acts 2003, c. 364.
59.1-410. Amended by Acts 1993, c. 284; Acts 1995, c. 298; Acts 1996, c. 267; Acts 2003, c. 364.
59.1-411. Amended by Acts 1995, c. 298; Acts 1996, c. 267; Acts 2003, c. 364.
59.1-414. Amended by Acts 2003, c. 364.
59.1-415. Amended by Acts 1991, c. 154.
59.1-417. Amended by Acts 1991, c. 154.
59.1-426. Amended by Acts 1990, cc. 346, 357.
59.1-429. Amended by Acts 1991, c. 630.
59.1-430. Amended by Acts 1991, c. 630; Acts 1992, c. 284.
59.1-431 to 59.1-434. Amended by Acts 1991, c. 630.
59.1-435. Amended by Acts 1996, c. 966.
59.1-436. Amended by Acts 1996, c. 966; Acts 1997, c. 30.
59.1-437. Amended by Acts 1996, c. 966; Acts 2003, c. 411.
59.1-440. Amended by Acts 1996, c. 966.
59.1-443. Amended by Acts 1993, c. 453; Acts 2004, c. 241.
59.1-444. Amended by Acts 1993, c. 453; Acts 2004, c. 241.
59.1-445 to 59.1-447. Amended by Acts 1994, c. 482.
59.1-448. Amended by Acts 1994, c. 482.

Sec.
59.1-449. Amended by Acts 1994, c. 482.
59.1-453. Amended by Acts 1994, c. 482.
59.1-460 to 59.1-466. Amended by Acts 1995, c. 648.
59.1-467 to 59.1-469. Repealed by Acts 2000, c. 995.
59.1-470. Amended by Acts 1998, cc. 67, 242.
59.1-471. Amended by Acts 1998, cc. 67, 242.
59.1-472. Amended by Acts 1998, cc. 67, 242.
59.1-473. Amended by Acts 1998, cc. 67, 242.
59.1-474. Amended by Acts 1998, cc. 67, 242.
59.1-475. Amended by Acts 2001, c. 537.
59.1-476. Amended by Acts 2001, c. 537.
59.1-477. Amended by Acts 2001, c. 537.
59.1-481. Amended by Acts 2001, c. 86; Acts 2003, c. 353.
59.1-494. Amended by Acts 2001, c. 86; Acts 2003, c. 353.
59.1-501.2. Amended by Acts 2001, c. 763; Acts 2003, c. 353; Acts 2004, c. 794.
59.1-501.3. Amended by Acts 2001, c. 763; Acts 2004, c. 794.
59.1-501.4. Amended by Acts 2001, cc. 762, 763; Acts 2004, c. 794.
59.1-501.5. Amended by Acts 2001, cc. 762, 763; Acts 2004, c. 794.
59.1-501.6. Amended by Acts 2004, c. 794.
59.1-501.9. Amended by Acts 2001, cc. 762, 763.
59.1-501.10. Amended by Acts 2001, c. 763.
59.1-501.12. Amended by Acts 2001, c. 763; Acts 2004, c. 794.
59.1-501.13. Repealed by Acts 2004, c. 794.
59.1-501.14. Repealed by Acts 2004, c. 794.
59.1-502.7. Amended by Acts 2004, c. 794.
59.1-502.9. Amended by Acts 2001, c. 763; Acts 2004, c. 794.
59.1-502.11. Repealed by Acts 2004, c. 794.
59.1-502.12. Amended by Acts 2001, cc. 762, 763.
59.1-503.7. Amended by Acts 2004, c. 794.
59.1-503.8. Repealed by Acts 2004, c. 794.
59.1-504.1. Amended by Acts 2004, c. 794.
59.1-504.4. Amended by Acts 2004, c. 794.
59.1-504.5. Amended by Acts 2004, c. 794.
59.1-505.3. Amended by Acts 2001, cc. 762, 763; Acts 2002, c. 403.
59.1-506.5. Amended by Acts 2001, c. 763.
59.1-508.16. Amended by Acts 2001, c. 763.
59.1-510. Amended by Acts 2004, cc. 202, 224.
59.1-511. Amended by Acts 2004, cc. 202, 224.
59.1-513. Amended by Acts 2004, cc. 202, 224.
59.1-513.1. Amended by Acts 2004, cc. 202, 224.
59.1-514. Amended by Acts 2004, cc. 202, 224.
59.1-525 to 59.1-529. Amended by Acts 2004, cc. 798, 817.
60-1 to 60-117. Repealed by Acts 1968, c. 738.
60.1-1 to 60.1-134. Repealed by Acts 1986, c. 480.
60.2-112. Repealed by Acts 1999, cc. 840, 855.

Sec.
60.2-113. Amended by Acts 1999, c. 357; Acts 2004, cc. 14, 154, 592.
60.2-114. Amended by Acts 1988, c. 766; Acts 1993, cc. 246, 806; Acts 1996, c. 220; Acts 1997, c. 385; Acts 1998, cc. 91, 108, 745; Acts 2003, c. 721.
60.2-116. Amended by Acts 1987, c. 113.
60.2-204. Amended by Acts 2003, c. 383.
60.2-212. Amended by Acts 1996, c. 244.
60.2-214. Amended by Acts 1987, c. 113; Acts 1993, c. 250; Acts 1996, c. 745.
60.2-219. Amended by Acts 1987, c. 113; Acts 1988, c. 678; Acts 1989, c. 339; Acts 1992, c. 4; Acts 1997, cc. 171, 189; Acts 2000, c. 438; Acts 2003, c. 609; Acts 2004, c. 977.
60.2-226. Amended by Acts 1992, c. 5.
60.2-229. Amended by Acts 1990, c. 908; Acts 1993, c. 576; Acts 1995, c. 515.
60.2-301. Amended by Acts 1993, c. 249; Acts 1995, c. 515.
60.2-302. Amended by Acts 1993, c. 249.
60.2-314. Amended by Acts 1990, c. 687.
60.2-318 to 60.2-322. Repealed by Acts 2004, c. 872.
60.2-511. Amended by Acts 1997, c. 137.
60.2-512. Amended by Acts 1993, c. 249; Acts 1996, c. 264; Acts 1997, c. 385.
60.2-513. Amended by Acts 1999, c. 79; Acts 2004, c. 495.
60.2-519.2. Amended by Acts 2002, c. 719.
60.2-521. Amended by Acts 1990, c. 687.
60.2-524. Amended by Acts 1989, c. 144; Acts 1994, c. 161.
60.2-525. Amended by Acts 2003, c. 382.
60.2-526. Amended by Acts 1995, c. 323.
60.2-528. Amended by Acts 1989, c. 104; Acts 1991, c. 249; Acts 1991, 1st Sp. Sess., c. 9; Acts 1997, c. 202; Acts 2001, c. 721; Acts 2004, cc. 583, 977.
60.2-531. Amended by Acts 1987, c. 114; Acts 1988, c. 766; Acts 1995, c. 515.
60.2-532. Amended by Acts 1987, c. 114; Acts 1990, c. 908; Acts 1993, c. 249.
60.2-533. Amended by Acts 1993, c. 249; Acts 1996, c. 305; Acts 1997, cc. 530, 674.
60.2-535. Amended by Acts 1995, c. 515; Acts 1997, c. 409.
60.2-536. Amended by Acts 1999, c. 79.
60.2-600. Amended by Acts 1987, c. 331; Acts 1996, c. 107; Acts 1997, c. 385.
60.2-602. Amended by Acts 1988, c. 131; Acts 1990, c. 908; Acts 1996, c. 367; Acts 1997, cc. 530, 674; Acts 2000, c. 573; Acts 2002, cc. 122, 892; Acts 2003, c. 926.
60.2-603. Amended by Acts 1992, c. 482.
60.2-604. Amended by Acts 1987, c. 3; Acts 2003, cc. 534, 555.
60.2-611. Amended by Acts 1993, c. 153.

Sec.
60.2-612. Amended by Acts 1988, c. 521; Acts 1990, c. 908; Acts 1993, c. 249; Acts 1995, c. 436; Acts 2004, c. 496.
60.2-613. Amended by Acts 1995, c. 436; Acts 2000, c. 687.
60.2-614. Amended by Acts 1997, c. 202.
60.2-618. Amended by Acts 1991, c. 296; Acts 1993, c. 249; Acts 1996, cc. 175, 182, 194, 199; Acts 1997, c. 202; Acts 1998, c. 241; Acts 1999, c. 919; Acts 2004, cc. 525, 977.
60.2-619. Amended by Acts 1995, c. 515; Acts 1997, c. 202; Acts 1999, c. 79.
60.2-620. Amended by Acts 1995, c. 515; Acts 1999, c. 79.
60.2-622. Amended by Acts 1995, c. 515; Acts 1996, c. 106.
60.2-623. Amended by Acts 1988, c. 766; Acts 1994, c. 203; Acts 1996, cc. 108, 130; Acts 1997, c. 385; Acts 1998, cc. 91, 745.
60.2-625. Amended by Acts 1987, c. 567; Acts 1988, c. 766; Acts 1996, c. 573.
60.2-633. Amended by Acts 1988, c. 544; Acts 1990, c. 687; Acts 1996, c. 95.
61-1 to 61-160. Repealed by Acts 1968, c. 69.
61.1-7 to 61.1-21. Repealed by Acts 1988, c. 149.
61.1-22 to 61.1-37. Repealed by Acts 1972, c. 447.
61.1-55. Amended by Acts 2000, c. 380.
62-1 to 62-195. Repealed by Acts 1968, c. 659.
62.1-1 to 62.1-4. Repealed by Acts 1992, c. 836.
62.1-5. Repealed by Acts 1987, c. 488.
62.1-9.1. Repealed by Acts 1992, c. 836.
62.1-10, 62.1-11. Amended by Acts 1989, c. 410.
62.1-13.1 to 62.1-13.20. Repealed by Acts 1992, c. 836.
62.1-13.21 to 62.1-13.28. Repealed by Acts 1992, c. 836.
62.1-14 to 62.1-44.1. Repealed by Acts 1970, c. 638.
62.1-44.2. Amended by Acts 1978, c. 827; Acts 2000, c. 972.
62.1-44.3. Amended by Acts 1988, c. 167; Acts 1990, c. 717; Acts 1991, c. 702; Acts 2000, cc. 972, 1032, 1054; Acts 2003, c. 614.
62.1-44.5. Amended by Acts 1990, c. 717; Acts 1996, c. 119; Acts 2000, cc. 1032, 1054; Acts 2001, cc. 354, 383; Acts 2004, c. 372.
62.1-44.9. Amended by Acts 1994, c. 461.
62.1-44.10. Repealed by Acts 1980, c. 728.
62.1-44.12. Amended by Acts 1977, c. 32; Acts 1981, c. 620.
62.1-44.14. Amended by Acts 1981, c. 620; Acts 1984, c. 444; Acts 1985, c. 397; Acts 1992, c. 456.
62.1-44.15. Amended by Acts 1975, c. 335; Acts 1976, c. 621; Acts 1977, c. 32; Acts

Sec.

1978, c. 827; Acts 1984, c. 11; Acts 1985, cc. 249, 397; Acts 1988, cc. 167, 328; Acts 1989, c. 389; Acts 1990, c. 717; Acts 1991, cc. 239, 718; Acts 1994, c. 698; Acts 1998, cc. 805, 863; Acts 2000, cc. 972, 1032, 1054; Acts 2002, cc. 49, 396; Acts 2004, c. 431.

62.1-44.15:1. Amended by Acts 1971, Ex. Sess., c. 245; Acts 1973, c. 179; Acts 1975, c. 279; Acts 1981, c. 262; Acts 2001, c. 116.

62.1-44.15:3. Amended by Acts 1990, c. 14; Acts 1993, c. 606; Acts 1994, cc. 262, 549; Acts 1995, c. 256; Acts 2000, cc. 19, 98; Acts 2001, c. 492.

62.1-44.15:4. Amended by Acts 1996, c. 160; Acts 1997, c. 581.

62.1-44.15:5. Amended by Acts 1990, c. 2; Acts 1996, c. 736; Acts 1999, c. 8; Acts 2000, cc. 1032, 1054; Acts 2003, c. 399; Acts 2004, cc. 94, 293.

62.1-44.15:6. Amended by Acts 1993, cc. 749, 756; Acts 1995, c. 107; Acts 1997, cc. 115, 154; Acts 2002, c. 822; Acts 2004, cc. 249, 324.

62.1-44.17:1. Amended by Acts 1998, cc. 805, 863; Acts 2001, c. 109; Acts 2003, c. 375; Acts 2004, c. 455.

62.1-44.17:2. Amended by Acts 2000, cc. 17, 1043.

62.1-44.17:3. Amended by Acts 2000, cc. 17, 1043.

62.1-44.18. Amended by Acts 1991, c. 194; Acts 2003, c. 614.

62.1-44.18:1. Repealed by Acts 1991, c. 194.

62.1-44.18:3. Amended by Acts 2001, c. 493.

62.1-44.19. Amended by Acts 1976, c. 661; Acts 1991, c. 194; Acts 2003, c. 614.

62.1-44.19:3. Amended by Acts 2001, c. 831.

62.1-44.19:4. Amended by Acts 2000, cc. 17, 1043.

62.1-44.19:5. Amended by Acts 2000, cc. 17, 945, 1043.

62.1-44.19:6. Amended by Acts 2000, cc. 17, 1043.

62.1-44.21. Amended by Acts 1974, c. 237.

62.1-44.23. Amended by Acts 1977, c. 263; Acts 1988, c. 167; Acts 1990, c. 717; Acts 1994, c. 489.

62.1-44.24. Amended by Acts 1984, c. 703; Acts 1986, c. 615.

62.1-44.26. Amended by Acts 1977, c. 291; Acts 1993, c. 897.

62.1-44.29. Amended by Acts 1986, c. 615; Acts 1996, c. 1032; Acts 2000, cc. 1032, 1054.

62.1-44.30. Amended by Acts 1984, c. 703.

62.1-44.31. Amended by Acts 1977, c. 263; Acts 1988, c. 167.

62.1-44.31:11. Amended by Acts 1998, c. 87.

62.1-44.32. Amended by Acts 1974, c. 237; Acts 1977, c. 263; Acts 1980, c. 378; Acts 1981, c. 596; Acts 1989, c. 627; Acts 1990, cc. 13, 717; Acts 1991, c. 718.

62.1-44.33. Amended by Acts 1975, c. 204; Acts 2001, c. 42; Acts 2004, c. 287.

62.1-44.34. Repealed by Acts 1978, c. 816.

62.1-44.34:1 to 62.1-44.34:6. Repealed by Acts 1990, c. 917.

62.1-44.34:7. Repealed by Acts 1989, c. 627.

62.1-44.34:8. Amended by Acts 1989, c. 430; Acts 1992, c. 819; Acts 1996, cc. 737, 979.

62.1-44-34:9. Amended by Acts 1989, c. 430; Acts 1992, c. 819; Acts 1993, c. 231; Acts 1996, c. 737.

62.1-44.34:10. Amended by Acts 1989, cc. 430, 627; Acts 1992, c. 819; Acts 1996, cc. 737, 979.

62.1-44.34:11. Amended by Acts 1989, cc. 430, 627; Acts 1990, cc. 580, 581, 582, 917; Acts 1992, cc. 456, 819; Acts 1993, cc. 20, 375; Acts 1994, cc. 196, 535; Acts 1996, cc. 737, 979; Acts 2004, c. 485.

62.1-44.34:12. Amended by Acts 1989, c. 627; Acts 1990, c. 581; Acts 1992, c. 819; Acts 1993, c. 375; Acts 1996, c. 737; Acts 1998, c. 87.

62.1-44.34:13. Amended by Acts 1992, c. 819; Acts 1993, c. 422; Acts 1995, c. 664; Acts 1996, c. 737; Acts 1998, c. 87.

62.1-44.34:14. Amended by Acts 1992, c. 456; Acts 1994, c. 277; Acts 1996, c. 737.

62.1-44.34:15. Amended by Acts 2004, c. 276.

62.1-44.34:15.1. Amended by Acts 1993, c. 353; Acts 1994, c. 277; Acts 1996, c. 737.

62.1-44.34:16. Amended by Acts 1992, cc. 456, 819; Acts 1993, c. 375; Acts 1994, c. 196; Acts 2004, c. 276.

62.1-44.34:17. Amended by Acts 1992, c. 456; Acts 1994, cc. 277, 460.

62.1-44.34:18. Amended by Acts 1992, c. 456; Acts 1998, cc. 90, 836.

62.1-44.34:19. Amended by Acts 1992, c. 456.

62.1-44.34:20. Amended by Acts 1992, c. 456.

62.1-44.34:21. Amended by Acts 1992, c. 345.

62.1-44.34:23. Amended by Acts 1992, cc. 302, 456; Acts 1993, cc. 18, 231; Acts 1994, c. 416.

62.1-44.34:25. Amended by Acts 1991, c. 66.

62.1-44.35. Repealed by Acts 1984, c. 750.

62.1-44.38. Amended by Acts 1981, c. 633; Acts 1989, c. 219.

62.1-44.40. Amended by Acts 1984, c. 734; Acts 2004, c. 650.

62.1-44.43. Amended by Acts 1973, c. 450.

62.1-44.45 to 62.1-44.82. Repealed by Acts 1974, c. 96.

Sec.
62.1-44.83 to 62.1-44.87. Repealed by Acts 1992, c. 812.
62.1-44.88. Repealed by Acts 1984, c. 734.
62.1-44.89 to 62.1-44.100. Repealed by Acts 1992, c. 812.
62.1-44.101. Repealed by Acts 1986, c. 401.
62.1-44.101:1 to 62.1-44.105. Repealed by Acts 1992, c. 812.
62.1-44.106. Repealed by Acts 1986, c. 615.
62.1-44.107. Repealed by Acts 1992, c. 812.
62.1-44.108 to 62.1-44.112. Repealed by Acts 1988, c. 891.
62.1-45 to 62.1-63. Repealed by Acts 1979, c. 711.
62.1-67. Amended by Acts 1979, c. 114; Acts 1981, c. 308.
62.1-69.1 to 62.1-69.4. Repealed by Acts 1990, c. 179.
62.1-69.5 to 62.1-69.10. Repealed by Acts 2004, c. 1000.
62.1-69.11 to 62.1-69.13. Repealed by Acts 2004, c. 1000.
62.1-69.14 to 62.1-69.16. Repealed by Acts 2004, c. 1000.
62.1-69.17. Repealed by Acts 2004, c. 1000.
62.1-69.18 to 62.1-69.20. Repealed by Acts 2004, c. 1000.
62.1-69.25. Amended by Acts 2000, c. 386; Acts 2002, cc. 496, 523.
62.1-69.26. Amended by Acts 2000, c. 386; Acts 2004, c. 471.
62.1-69.27. Amended by Acts 2000, c. 386.
62.1-69.28. Amended by Acts 2000, c. 386.
62.1-69.29. Amended by Acts 2000, c. 386; Acts 2004, c. 471.
62.1-69.30. Amended by Acts 2000, c. 386; Acts 2004, c. 471.
62.1-69.31. Amended by Acts 2000, c. 386.
62.1-69.32. Amended by Acts 2000, c. 386.
62.1-69.33. Amended by Acts 2000, c. 386.
62.1-69.34. Amended by Acts 2003, c. 885; Acts 2004, c. 403.
62.1-69.35. Amended by Acts 2003, c. 885.
62.1-69.36. Amended by Acts 2003, c. 885.
62.1-69.37. Amended by Acts 2003, c. 885.
62.1-69.38. Amended by Acts 2003, c. 885.
62.1-69.39. Amended by Acts 2003, c. 885.
62.1-69.40. Amended by Acts 2003, c. 885.
62.1-69.41. Amended by Acts 2003, c. 885.
62.1-69.42. Amended by Acts 2003, c. 885.
62.1-69.43. Amended by Acts 2003, c. 885.
62.1-85. Amended by Acts 1982, c. 183.
62.1-104. Amended by Acts 1977, c. 26.
62.1-104.1. Repealed by Acts 1982, c. 583.
62.1-105. Amended by Acts 1976, c. 710; Acts 1982, c. 583.
62.1-106. Amended by Acts 1976, c. 710; Acts 1977, c. 26; Acts 1982, c. 583.
62.1-107. Amended by Acts 1977, c. 26.
62.1-109. Amended by Acts 1977, c. 26.
62.1-111. Amended by Acts 1977, c. 26; Acts 1996, c. 573.

Sec.
62.1-115.1 to 62.1-115.10. Repealed by Acts 1988, c. 891.
62.1-117. Amended by Acts 1997, c. 801.
62.1-128. Amended by Acts 1970, c. 171; Acts 1981, c. 589; Acts 1997, c. 232.
62.1-129. Amended by Acts 1970, c. 171; Acts 1978, c. 655; Acts 1980, c. 728; Acts 1981, c. 589; Acts 1983, cc. 218, 298, 338; Acts 1987, c. 688.
62.1-129.1. Amended by Acts 2000, cc. 66, 657.
62.1-130. Amended by Acts 1981, c. 589.
62.1-131. Amended by Acts 1970, c. 171; Acts 1981, c. 589.
62.1-132. Amended by Acts 1970, c. 171; Acts 1981, c. 589.
62.1-132.1. Amended by Acts 1997, c. 232.
62.1-132.4. Amended by Acts 1997, c. 197.
62.1-132.6. Amended by Acts 1997, cc. 232, 488.
62.1-132.7. Amended by Acts 1997, c. 232.
62.1-132.14. Amended by Acts 1982, c. 168.
62.1-132.20. Amended by Acts 1998, c. 543.
62.1-133. Repealed by Acts 1981, c. 589.
62.1-134. Amended by Acts 1972, c. 423.
62.1-135. Repealed by Acts 1981, c. 589.
62.1-136. Amended by Acts 1981, c. 589.
62.1-137. Repealed by Acts 1981, c. 589.
62.1-139. Amended by Acts 1984, c. 734; Acts 1985, c. 146; Acts 2004, c. 650.
62.1-140. Amended by Acts 1972, c. 423; Acts 1981, cc. 589, 590; Acts 1991, c. 246; Acts 1993, c. 656.
62.1-141. Amended by Acts 1974, c. 148.
62.1-142, 62.1-143. Amended by Acts 1981, c. 590.
62.1-145. Amended by Acts 1974, c. 546; Acts 1990, c. 694; Acts 2000, c. 737.
62.1-147. Amended by Acts 1981, c. 590; Acts 1993, c. 656.
62.1-153, 62.1-154. Repealed by Acts 1988, c. 891.
62.1-160. Amended by Acts 1970, c. 598.
62.1-162. Amended by Acts 1970, c. 598.
62.1-163. Amended by Acts 1990, c. 204.
62.1-164. Amended by Acts 1972, c. 415.
62.1-166 to 62.1-186.24. Repealed by Acts 1987, c. 488.
62.1-193. Amended by Acts 1986, c. 145.
62.1-194. Amended by Acts 1970, c. 486; Acts 1974, c. 603.
62.1-194.1:1. Repealed by Acts 1992, c. 836.
62.1-194.2. Amended by Acts 1988, c. 196.
62.1-195. Repealed by Acts 1990, c. 917.
62.1-195.1. Amended by Acts 1990, c. 967; Acts 1992, cc. 480, 487; Acts 1993, c. 239; Acts 1994, c. 957.
62.1-196. Repealed by Acts 1987, c. 488.
62.1-197. Amended by Acts 1985, c. 67.
62.1-198. Amended by Acts 1989, cc. 533, 551; Acts 1990, c. 506; Acts 1998, c. 399; Acts 2000, c. 790; Acts 2001, cc. 652, 661.

Sec.
62.1-199. Amended by Acts 1985, c. 67; Acts 1986, c. 331; Acts 1987, cc. 117, 133; Acts 1989, cc. 533, 551; Acts 1990, c. 506; Acts 1998, c. 399; Acts 1999, c. 897; Acts 2000, c. 790; Acts 2001, cc. 652, 661.
62.1-200. Amended by Acts 1985, c. 67.
62.1-201. Amended by Acts 1989, cc. 533, 551; Acts 1992, c. 887; Acts 2000, cc. 38, 197.
62.1-202. Amended by Acts 1994, c. 684.
62.1-203. Amended by Acts 1985, c. 67; Acts 1986, c. 415; Acts 1987, cc. 117, 133, 324; Acts 1994, c. 684; Acts 1998, c. 399; Acts 1999, c. 897.
62.1-204. Amended by Acts 1985, c. 67; Acts 1989, cc. 533, 551; Acts 1990, c. 506; Acts 1994, c. 684; Acts 1998, c. 399; Acts 1999, c. 104; Acts 2001, c. 574.
62.1-205. Amended by Acts 1994, c. 684.
62.1-206. Amended by Acts 1985, c. 67; Acts 1986, c. 415; Acts 1998, c. 399.
62.1-207. Amended by Acts 1998, c. 399.
62.1-208. Amended by Acts 1985, c. 67; Acts 1998, c. 399.
62.1-209. Amended by Acts 1986, c. 415; Acts 1997, c. 319; Acts 1998, c. 399.
62.1-210. Amended by Acts 1998, c. 399.
62.1-213. Amended by Acts 1998, c. 399.
62.1-214. Amended by Acts 1998, c. 399.
62.1-215. Amended by Acts 1998, c. 399; Acts 2000, c. 790.
62.1-216. Amended by Acts 1985, c. 67; Acts 1998, c. 399.
62.1-216.1. Amended by Acts 2003, c. 561.
62.1-218. Amended by Acts 1992, cc. 378, 887.
62.1-219. Amended by Acts 1985, c. 67; Acts 1998, c. 399.
62.1-221. Amended by Acts 1985, c. 67; Acts 1994, c. 684; Acts 1996, c. 77.
62.1-224. Amended by Acts 1992, c. 28; Acts 1996, c. 20; Acts 1999, c. 1012.
62.1-225. Amended by Acts 1999, c. 1012.
62.1-226. Amended by Acts 1996, c. 77.
62.1-228. Amended by Acts 1999, c. 1012.
62.1-229. Amended by Acts 1996, c. 20; Acts 1999, c. 1012.
62.1-229.2. Amended by Acts 2003, c. 407.
62.1-234. Amended by Acts 2003, c. 506.
62.1-233, 62.1-234. Amended by Acts 1997, cc. 651, 665.
62.1-235. Amended by Acts 1996, c. 77.
62.1-237 to 62.1-239.1. Amended by Acts 1997, cc. 651, 665.
62.1-241.3. Amended by Acts 1996, c. 77.
62.1-242. Amended by Acts 1992, c. 812.
62.1-243. Amended by Acts 1993, c. 213.
62.1-245. Amended by Acts 1999, c. 561.
62.1-247. Amended by Acts 1999, c. 561.
62.1-252. Amended by Acts 1991, c. 718.
62.1-260. Amended by Acts 1994, cc. 513, 592.

Sec.
62.1-263. Amended by Acts 1994, cc. 513, 592.
63-1 to 63-385. Repealed by Acts 1968, c. 578.
63.1-1.1 to 63.1-343. Repealed by Acts 2002, c. 747.
63.2-100. Amended by Acts 2003, c. 467; Acts 2004, cc. 70, 196, 245, 753, 814.
63.2-100. Amended by Acts 2004, cc. 70, 196, 245, 753, 814.
63.2-105. Amended by Acts 2004, cc. 114, 220.
63.2-213. Amended by Acts 2003, c. 467.
63.2-219. Amended by Acts 2004, c. 208.
63.2-223 to 63.2-225. Repealed by Acts 2003, cc. 54, 75.
63.2-226. Amended by Acts 2003, cc. 54, 75.
63.2-227. Amended by Acts 2003, cc. 54, 75.
63.2-228. Repealed by Acts 2003, cc. 54, 75.
63.2-405. Amended by Acts 2004, c. 305.
63.2-608. Amended by Acts 2003, cc. 428, 467.
63.2-700 to 63.2-702. Repealed by Acts 2003, cc. 428, 467.
63.2-900. Amended by Acts 2004, c. 70.
63.2-903. Amended by Acts 2004, c. 815.
63.2-1200. Amended by Acts 2004, c. 815.
63.2-1205. Amended by Acts 2003, c. 467.
63.2-1206. Amended by Acts 2003, c. 467.
63.2-1208. Amended by Acts 2003, c. 502.
63.2-1215. Amended by Acts 2003, c. 229.
63.2-1220. Amended by Acts 2003, c. 985.
63.2-1221. Amended by Acts 2004, c. 815.
63.2-1222. Amended by Acts 2004, c. 815.
63.2-1225. Amended by Acts 2003, c. 779.
63.2-1502. Amended by Acts 2004, cc. 93, 233, 972, 980.
63.2-1503. Amended by Acts 2004, cc. 114, 220, 886.
63.2-1511. Amended by Acts 2003, cc. 986, 1013.
63.2-1514. Amended by Acts 2003, c. 634.
63.2-1515. Amended by Acts 2004, c. 74.
63.2-1517. Amended by Acts 2003, c. 508.
63.2-1527. Amended by Acts 2004, c. 103.
63.2-1528. Amended by Acts 2004, c. 69. =snS 63.2-1603 to 63.2-1606. Amended by Acts 2004, cc. 749, 1011.
63.2-1607. Repealed by Acts 2004, cc. 749, 1011.
63.2-1608 to 63.2-1610. Amended by Acts 2004, cc. 749, 1011.
63.2-1715. Amended by Acts 2003, c. 467.
63.2-1716. Amended by Acts 2004, c. 113.
63.2-1717. Amended by Acts 2003, c. 467.
63.2-1719. Amended by Acts 2003, c. 467.
63.2-1721. Amended by Acts 2004, c. 714.
63.2-1724. Amended by Acts 2003, c. 467.
63.2-1732. Amended by Acts 2004, c. 673.
63.2-1738. Amended by Acts 2003, c. 467.
63.2-1800. Amended by Acts 2004, c. 304.
63.2-1802. Amended by Acts 2003, c. 467.
63.2-1803. Amended by Acts 2003, c. 467.
63.2-1805. Amended by Acts 2004, c. 49.
63.2-1806. Amended by Acts 2003, c. 526.
63.2-1808. Amended by Acts 2004, c. 855.

Sec.
63.2-1809. Amended by Acts 2004, c. 450.
63.2-1817. Amended by Acts 2004, c. 815.
63.2-1902. Amended by Acts 2003, cc. 467, 929, 942.
63.2-1916. Amended by Acts 2004, c. 204.
63.2-1923. Amended by Acts 2003, c. 469.
63.2-1924. Amended by Acts 2003, c. 469.
63.2-1925. Amended by Acts 2003, c. 469.
63.2-1927. Amended by Acts 2003, cc. 929, 942.
63.2-1929. Amended by Acts 2003, cc. 929, 942.
63.2-1930. Amended by Acts 2003, c. 469.
63.2-2002. Amended by Acts 2004, cc. 216, 699.
63.2-2004. Amended by Acts 2003, c. 186; Acts 2004, cc. 183, 657, 725.
64-1 to 64-176. Repealed by Acts 1968, c. 656.
64.1-1. Amended by Acts 1977, c. 474; Acts 1982, c. 304; Acts 1985, c. 189; Acts 1990, c. 831.
64.1-2. Amended by Acts 1986, c. 305.
64.1-5. Repealed by Acts 1978, c. 647.
64.1-5.1. Amended by Acts 1989, c. 466; Acts 1993, c. 929; Acts 1994, c. 919; Acts 1998, c. 603; Acts 1999, c. 781.
64.1-5.2. Amended by Acts 1989, c. 466; Acts 1991, c. 479; Acts 1999, c. 781.
64.1-6. Repealed by Acts 1978, c. 647.
64.1-7. Repealed by Acts 1978, c. 647.
64.1-7.1. Repealed by Acts 1994, c. 919.
64.1-8. Repealed by Acts 1978, c. 647.
64.1-8.1. Amended by Acts 1994, c. 919.
64.1-9. Repealed by Acts 1970, c. 568.
64.1-11. Amended by Acts 1978, c. 647; Acts 1981, c. 580; Acts 1982, c. 304; Acts 1983, c. 320.
64.1-13. Amended by Acts 1990, c. 831; Acts 1995, c. 211.
64.1-14. Amended by Acts 1990, c. 831.
64.1-15. Repealed by Acts 1970, c. 70.
64.1-16. Amended by Acts 1978, c. 647; Acts 1986, c. 526; Acts 1990, c. 831.
64.1-16.1. Amended by Acts 1992, cc. 617, 647; Acts 1998, c. 234; Acts 1999, c. 38.
64.1-16.2. Amended by Acts 1992, cc. 617, 647.
64.1-16.3. Amended by Acts 1992, c. 795.
64.1-18. Repealed by Acts 1981, c. 469.
64.1-19, 64.1-19.1. Repealed by Acts 1990, c. 831.
64.1-20 to 64.1-44. Repealed by Acts 1990, c. 831.
64.1-45.2. Amended by Acts 2002, c. 119.
64.1-47. Amended by Acts 1972, c. 825; Acts 2000, c. 161.
64.1-48. Amended by Acts 1979, c. 438; Acts 1996, c. 265.
64.1-56. Amended by Acts 1970, c. 567.
64.1-57. Amended by Acts 1970, cc. 65, 296; Acts 1972, c. 788; Acts 1973, c. 94; Acts 1974, c. 659; Acts 1976, c. 419; Acts 1982, cc. 525, 549, 551; Acts 1990, c. 782; Acts 1992, c. 584; Acts 1994, c. 476; Acts 1997, c. 801; Acts 1999, cc. 772, 975; Acts 2003, cc. 30, 42, 253.
64.1-57.1. Amended by Acts 1985, c. 345; Acts 1988, c. 345; Acts 1999, c. 995.
64.1-57.2. Amended by Acts 1983, c. 54; Acts 1999, c. 197.
64.1-58. Repealed by Acts 1985, c. 431.
64.1-59. Amended by Acts 1985, c. 429.
64.1-60. Amended by Acts 1985, c. 431.
64.1-62.1. Amended by Acts 1983, c. 512; Acts 1987, c. 504.
64.1-62.3. Amended by Acts 1995, c. 381.
64.1-63. Repealed by Acts 1985, c. 432.
64.1-64. Repealed by Acts 1985, c. 592.
64.1-65. Repealed by Acts 1985, c. 592.
64.1-65.1. Amended by Acts 2003, c. 253.
64.1-66.1. Repealed by Acts 1994, c. 917.
64.1-67. Repealed by Acts 1985, c. 429.
64.1-67.2. Amended by Acts 1991, c. 432; Acts 1992, c. 832.
64.1-68. Amended by Acts 1999, c. 975.
64.1-69.1. Amended by Acts 1991, c. 441.
64.1-70. Amended by Acts 1972, c. 825.
64.1-71. Amended by Acts 1972, c. 825; Acts 1978, c. 647.
64.1-71.1. Amended by Acts 1987, c. 604.
64.1-73. Amended by Acts 1972, c. 332; Acts 1982, c. 373; Acts 1991, c. 343; Acts 1992, c. 66; Acts 1994, c. 562; Acts 1995, c. 684; Acts 1996, c. 680; Acts 1999, c. 252.
64.1-74. Amended by Acts 1978, c. 481.
64.1-75.1. Amended by Acts 2001, c. 376; Acts 2003, c. 265.
64.1-77. Amended by Acts 1973, c. 217.
64.1-87. Amended by Acts 1981, c. 183.
64.1-87.1. Amended by Acts 1977, c. 333; Acts 1979, c. 322; Acts 1983, c. 83; Acts 1985, c. 429; Acts 1986, c. 524; Acts 1990, c. 64.
64.1-87.2. Amended by Acts 1985, c. 429; Acts 1990, c. 64.
64.1-89. Amended by Acts 1977, c. 624.
64.1-90. Amended by Acts 1972, c. 825; Acts 1996, c. 58.
64.1-92. Amended by Acts 1977, c. 249; Acts 1980, c. 264.
64.1-94. Amended by Acts 1978, c. 366; Acts 1994, c. 64; Acts 2001, c. 836; Acts 2002, c. 832.
64.1-96.2 to 64.1-96.11. Amended by Acts 1995, c. 443.
64.1-96.11. Amended by Acts 2001, c. 85.
64.1-97 to 64.1-104. Repealed by Acts 1994, c. 475.
64.1-105. Amended by Acts 1989, c. 153; Acts 1996, cc. 675, 684; Acts 2003, c. 254.
64.1-105.2. Amended by Acts 1983, c. 139.
64.1-106, 64.1-107. Amended by Acts 1996, cc. 675, 684.

Sec.
64.1-108 to 64.1-110. Amended by Acts 1996, cc. 352, 675, 684.
64.1-112. Amended by Acts 1996, cc. 675, 684.
64.1-114. Amended by Acts 1971, Ex. Sess., c. 156.
64.1-116. Amended by Acts 1979, c. 323; Acts 2000, c. 321.
64.1-118. Amended by Acts 1978, c. 483; Acts 2000, c. 321; Acts 2002, c. 197.
64.1-120. Amended by Acts 1996, c. 317.
64.1-121. Amended by Acts 1970, c. 426; Acts 1974, c. 140; Acts 1977, c. 144; Acts 1994, c. 393; Acts 1996, c. 57.
64.1-122.2. Amended by Acts 2001, cc. 78, 265; Acts 2002, c. 716.
64.1-123. Amended by Acts 1970, c. 244; Acts 1976, c. 433; Acts 1978, c. 346; Acts 1980, c. 462; Acts 1996, c. 549; Acts 2001, c. 368.
64.1-123.1. Amended by Acts 1978, c. 281; Acts 1980, c. 462; Acts 1989, c. 158; Acts 1996, c. 549; Acts 2001, c. 368.
64.1-123.2. Amended by Acts 1994, c. 399.
64.1-123.3. Amended by Acts 1987, c. 288; Acts 1996, c. 549; Acts 2001, c. 368.
64.1-124. Amended by Acts 1970, c. 244; Acts 1980, c. 462; Acts 1996, c. 549; Acts 2001, c. 368.
64.1-124.1. Amended by Acts 1980, c. 462; Acts 1996, c. 549; Acts 2001, c. 368.
64.1-125. Amended by Acts 1980, c. 462.
64.1-126, 64.1-127. Repealed by Acts 1981, c. 580.
64.1-130. Amended by Acts 1970, c. 244; Acts 1988, c. 370; Acts 1996, c. 549; Acts 2001, c. 368.
64.1-131. Amended by Acts 1971, Ex. Sess., c. 155; Acts 1980, c. 438; Acts 1996, c. 317.
64.1-132. Amended by Acts 1971, Ex. Sess., c. 155.
64.1-132.2. Amended by Acts 1996, c. 549; Acts 2001, c. 368.
64.1-133. Repealed by Acts 1998, c. 610.
64.1-134. Amended by Acts 1984, c. 339; Acts 1994, c. 327; Acts 1998, c. 610.
64.1-135. Amended by Acts 1998, c. 610.
64.1-140. Amended by Acts 1970, c. 425.
64.1-144. Amended by Acts 2001, c. 223.
64.1-145. Amended by Acts 1977, c. 624; Acts 2004, c. 368
64.1-149, 64.1-150. Amended by Acts 1996, c. 93.
64.1-151.1. Amended by Acts 1987, c. 222; Acts 1990, c. 831.
64.1-151.2. Amended by Acts 1990, c. 831; Acts 1996, c. 549; Acts 2001, c. 368.
64.1-151.3. Amended by Acts 1990, c. 831; Acts 2001, c. 368.
64.1-151.4. Amended by Acts 1996, c. 549; Acts 2001, c. 368.

Sec.
64.1-154, 64.1-155. Amended by Acts 1981, c. 580.
64.1-157. Amended by Acts 1972, c. 96; Acts 1981, c. 580; Acts 1986, c. 109; Acts 1993, c. 259; Acts 1996, c. 84; Acts 1997, c. 801.
64.1-160. Amended by Acts 1979, c. 559; Acts 1981, c. 98; Acts 1994, c. 917.
64.1-161. Amended by Acts 1979, c. 559; Acts 1986, c. 399; Acts 1994, c. 917; Acts 1997, c. 254.
64.1-162. Amended by Acts 1986, c. 399.
64.1-163. Amended by Acts 1994, c. 917.
64.1-164. Repealed by Acts 1986, c. 399.
64.1-165. Amended by Acts 1994, c. 917.
64.1-166. Amended by Acts 1991, c. 58.
64.1-171. Amended by Acts 1981, c. 484; Acts 1989, c. 492.
64.1-173. Amended by Acts 1989, c. 492.
64.1-179. Amended by Acts 1980, c. 439; Acts 1982, c. 588; Acts 1989, c. 492; Acts 1991, c. 527; Acts 1996, c. 352.
64.1-180.1. Amended by Acts 1997, c. 801.
64.1-184. Amended by Acts 1996, c. 65.
64.1-188 to 64.1-196. Repealed by Acts 2003, c. 253.
64.1-199. Amended by Acts 1990, c. 831.
65-1 to 65-134. Repealed by Acts 1968, c. 660.
65.1-1 to 65.1-163. Repealed by Acts 1991, c. 355.
65.1-512. Amended by Acts 1998, c. 100.
65.2-101. Amended by Acts 1992, c. 12; Acts 1993, cc. 280, 930; Acts 1994, cc. 271, 286, 526; Acts 1995, cc. 4, 168, 272, 288; Acts 1996, cc. 250, 721; Acts 1998, c. 52; Acts 1999, c. 1006; Acts 2000, cc. 301, 624, 718, 1018; Acts 2002, c. 69; Acts 2004, cc. 888, 928.
65.2-102. Amended by Acts 2001, c. 330.
65.2-201. Amended by Acts 2004, c. 178.
65.2-300. Amended by Acts 2000, c. 530.
65.2-301. Amended by Acts 1992, c. 469.
65.2-302. Amended by Acts 1999, c. 877.
65.2-306. Amended by Acts 1994, cc. 600, 804; Acts 2002, c. 636.
65.2-307. Amended by Acts 1999, c. 842.
65.2-309 to 65.2-312. Amended by Acts 1994, cc. 11, 366.
65.2-400. Amended by Acts 1997, c. 405.
65.2-401. Amended by Acts 1997, cc. 15, 405.
65.2-402. Amended by Acts 1994, cc. 791, 960; Acts 1997, c. 714; Acts 1999, cc. 581, 597, 602, 604, 607; Acts 2000, c. 1013; Acts 2001, cc. 330, 581; Acts 2002, cc. 309, 737, 789.
65.2-406. Amended by Acts 1992, c. 475; Acts 1995, c. 324.
65.2-500. Amended by Acts 1997, c. 511; Acts 2004, c. 888.
65.2-502. Amended by Acts 1995, c. 319; Acts

Sec.
1997, c. 511; Acts 2000, c. 1018; Acts 2004, c. 888.
65.2-503. Amended by Acts 1997, c. 511; Acts 2000, c. 520.
65.2-504. Amended by Acts 2000, cc. 408, 520.
65.2-505. Amended by Acts 1996, c. 448.
65.2-510. Amended by Acts 1995, c. 319; Acts 1996, c. 252.
65.2-512. Amended by Acts 1992, cc. 2, 147; Acts 2004, c. 888.
65.2-518. Amended by Acts 1997, c. 511.
65.2-520. Amended by Acts 1998, c. 68.
65.2-524. Amended by Acts 1994, c. 248; Acts 1997, c. 383; Acts 1999, c. 782.
65.2-525. Amended by Acts 1997, c. 921; Acts 1998, c. 94; Acts 2002, c. 301.
65.2-527, 65.2-528. Amended by Acts 1997, c. 801.
65.2-531. Amended by Acts 1997, cc. 796, 895.
65.2-600. Amended by Acts 1997, c. 288.
65.2-603. Amended by Acts 1994, c. 558; Acts 1997, c. 839; Acts 1998, c. 65; Acts 1999, c. 780; Acts 2000, cc. 473, 1018; Acts 2004, c. 271.
65.2-604. Amended by Acts 1994, c. 685; Acts 1998, c. 431; Acts 1999, c. 314; Acts 2000, c. 542.
65.2-607. Amended by Acts 1993, c. 379.
65.2-701. Amended by Acts 1997, c. 801.
65.2-702. Amended by Acts 1993, c. 693.
65.2-703. Amended by Acts 1993, c. 694.
65.2-704. Amended by Acts 1997, c. 225.
65.2-705. Amended by Acts 1994, c. 289; Acts 1998, c. 95.
65.2-706. Amended by Acts 1999, c. 938.
65.2-709. Amended by Acts 1997, c. 296.
65.2-711. Amended by Acts 1996, c. 178.
65.2-712. Amended by Acts 1992, c. 466; Acts 1996, c. 570.
65.2-713. Amended by Acts 1997, c. 158.
65.2-714. Amended by Acts 1994, c. 707; Acts 1995, cc. 214, 266.
65.2-801. Amended by Acts 1992, c. 816; Acts 1996, c. 181; Acts 2000, cc. 624, 718; Acts 2004, cc. 44, 173.
65.2-802. Amended by Acts 1994, cc. 333, 408.

Sec.
65.2-803.1. Amended by Acts 2001, c. 706; Acts 2002, c. 469.
65.2-804. Amended by Acts 1993, c. 725; Acts 2002, c. 812.
65.2-805. Amended by Acts 1993, c. 378.
65.2-813.2. Amended by Acts 2001, c. 280.
65.2-823. Amended by Acts 1993, c. 985.
65.2-900. Amended by Acts 1995, c. 86.
65.2-902. Amended by Acts 1993, c. 378.
65.2-903. Amended by Acts 1993, c. 806; Acts 1996, c. 457; Acts 1997, cc. 796, 895; Acts 2002, c. 693.
65.2-1000. Amended by Acts 1996, c. 56.
65.2-1005. Amended by Acts 1996, c. 56.
65.2-1006. Amended by Acts 1994, c. 947.
65.2-1201. Amended by Acts 1997, c. 99; Acts 1998, c. 388.
65.2-1203. Amended by Acts 1993, c. 624; Acts 1997, c. 131.
65.2-1301 to 65.2-1303. Amended by Acts 2004, c. 1000.
66-1. Amended by Acts 1990, c. 350; Acts 1996, c. 503.
66-2. Amended by Acts 1990, cc. 1, 317.
66-3. Amended by Acts 1993, cc. 460, 487; Acts 1995, c. 701.
66-4. Amended by Acts 1996, c. 503.
66-10. Amended by Acts 1990, c. 679; Acts 1996, cc. 755, 914.
66-11. Amended by Acts 1994, c. 672.
66-13. Amended by Acts 1991, c. 534; Acts 1996, cc. 755, 914; Acts 1997, c. 894.
66-14. Amended by Acts 1992, cc. 837, 880; Acts 1996, cc. 587, 597.
66-15. Amended by Acts 1989, c. 683.
66-17. Amended by Acts 1991, c. 534.
66-20. Amended by Acts 1990, c. 975.
66-24. Amended by Acts 1996, cc. 755, 914.
66-25.1. Amended by Acts 1997, c. 639.
66-28. Amended by Acts 2000, c. 277.
66-29. Amended by Acts 2000, c. 277.
66-30. Amended by Acts 1990, c. 679; Acts 2000, c. 277.
66-34. Amended by Acts 2000, c. 277.
66-35. Amended by Acts 1992, cc. 837, 880; Acts 2000, c. 277.

Tables of Comparable Sections for Certain Repealed and Revised Titles

COMPARABLE SECTIONS OF TITLE 2 AND TITLE 2.1

Former Section	Present Section
2-1	2.1-1
2-2	2.1-2
2-3	2.1-3
2-4	2.1-4
2-4.1	2.1-5
2-4.2	2.1-6
2-4.3	2.1-7
2-4.4	2.1-8
2-5	2.1-9
2-6	2.1-10
2-7	2.1-11
2-8	2.1-12
2-9	2.1-13
2-10	2.1-14
2-11	2.1-15
2-12	2.1-16
2-13	2.1-17
2-14	2.1-18
2-15	2.1-19
2-16	2.1-20
2-17, 2-18	Deleted
2-19	2.1-21
2-20	2.1-22
2-20.1	2.1-23
2-21	2.1-24
2-22	2.1-25
2-22.1	2.1-26
2-22.2	Repealed
2-22.3	2.1-27
2-22.4	2.1-28
2-23	2.1-29
2-24 to 2-26	Deleted
2-27	2.1-30
2-27.1	2.1-31
2-27.2	2.1-32
2-28	Repealed
2-29	2.1-33
2-30	2.1-34
2-31	2.1-35
2-32	2.1-36
2-33	2.1-37
2-34	2.1-38
2-35	2.1-39
2-36	2.1-40
2-36.1	2.1-38.1
2-37	2.1-41
2-38	2.1-42
2-38.1 to 2-38.3	Repealed
2-39	2.1-43
2-40	2.1-44
2-40.1	2.1-45
2-41	2.1-46
2-42	2.1-47
2-42.1	2.1-48
2-54	2.1-49
2-44	2.1-50
2-45	2.1-51
2-45.1	2.1-51.1
2-45.2	2.1-51.2
2-45.3	2.1-51.3
2-45.4	2.1-51.4
2-45.5	2.1-51.5
2-46	2.1-52
2-47	2.1-53
2-48	2.1-54
2-49	2.1-55
2-50	2.1-56
2-51	2.1-57
2-52	2.1-58
2-53	2.1-59
2-54	2.1-60
2-55	2.1-61
2-56	2.1-62
2-57	2.1-63
2-57.01	2.1-65
2-57.02	2.1-64.1
2-57.03	2.1-64.2
2-57.04	2.1-64.3
2-57.05	2.1-64.4
2-57.06	2.1-64.5
2-57.07	2.1-64.6
2-57.08	2.1-64.7
2-57.09	2.1-64.8
2-57.010	2.1-64.9
2-57.011	2.1-64.10
2-57.012	2.1-64.11
2-57.013	2.1-64.12
2-57.014	2.1-64.13
2-57.015	2.1-64.14
2-57.1	2.1-65
2-58	2.1-66
12-59	2.1-67
12-60	2.1-68
12-61	2.1-69
12-62	2.1-70
2-62.1	2.1-71
2-63	2.1-72
2-64	2.1-73
2-64.1	2.1-74
2-64.2	2.1-75
2-64.3	2.1-76
2-64.4	2.1-77
2-64.5	2.1-78
2-64.6	2.1-79
2-64.7	2.1-80
2-64.8	2.1-81
2-65	2.1-82
2-65.1	2.1-82.1
2-66	2.1-83
2-66.1	Repealed
2-66.2	2.1-84
2-67	2.1-85
2-68	2.1-86
2-69	2.1-87
2-70	2.1-88
2-71	2.1-89
2-72	2.1-90
2-73	2.1-91
2-74	2.1-92
2-75	2.1-93
2-75.1	2.1-94
2-75.2	2.1-95
2-76	2.1-96
2-77	2.1-97
2-77.1	2.1-98
2-77.2	2.1-99
2-77.3	2.1-100
2-77.4	2.1-101
2-77.5	2.1-102
2-77.6	2.1-103
2-77.7	2.1-104
2-77.8	2.1-105
2-77.9	2.1-106
2-77.10	2.1-107
2-77.11	2.1-108
2-77.12	2.1-109
2-78	2.1-110
2-79	2.1-111
2-80	2.1-112
2-81	2.1-113
2-82	2.1-114
2-83	2.1-115
2-84	2.1-116
2-85	2.1-117
2-86	2.1-118
2-86.1	2.1-119
2-86.2	2.1-120
2-87	2.1-121
2-88	2.1-122
2-89	2.1-123
2-90	2.1-124
2-90.1	2.1-125
2-91	2.1-126
2-92	2.1-127
2-93	2.1-128
2-93.1	2.1-129

Former Section	Present Section
2-94	2.1-130
2-95	2.1-131
2-96	2.1-132
2-97	2.1-133
2-98 to 2-124.1	Repealed
2-125	2.1-153
2-126	2.1-154
2-127	2.1-155
2-128	2.1-156
2-129	2.1-157
2-130	2.1-158
2-131	2.1-159
2-132	2.1-160
2-133	2.1-161
2-134	2.1-162
2-135	2.1-163
2-135.1	2.1-164
2-136	2.1-165
2-137	2.1-166
2-138	2.1-167
2-139	2.1-168
2-140	2.1-169
2-141	2.1-170
2-142	2.1-171
2-143	2.1-172
2-144	2.1-172.1
2-145	2.1-173
2-146	2.1-174
2-147	2.1-175
2-148	2.1-176
2-149	2.1-177
2-149.1	2.1-178
2-149.2	2.1-179
2-150	2.1-180
2-151	2.1-181
2-152	2.1-182
2-153	2.1-183
2-154	2.1-184
2-154.1	2.1-185
2-155	2.1-186
2-155.1	2.1-187
2-156	2.1-188
2-157	2.1-189
2-158	2.1-190
2-159	2.1-191
2-160	2.1-192
2-160.1	2.1-193
2-161	2.1-194
2-161.1	Repealed
2-162	2.1-195
2-163	2.1-196
2-164	Repealed
2-165	2.1-197
2-166	2.1-198
2-167	2.1-199
2-167.1	2.1-200
2-168	2.1-201
2-169	2.1-202
2-170	2.1-203
2-171	Repealed
2-172	2.1-204
2-173	2.1-205
2-174	2.1-206
2-175	2.1-207
2-176	2.1-208
2-177	2.1-209
2-178	2.1-210
2-179	2.1-211
2-180	2.1-212
2-181	2.1-213
2-182	2.1-214
2-183	Repealed
2-184	2.1-215
2-185	2.1-216
2-186	2.1-217
2-187	2.1-218
2-188	2.1-219
2-189	2.1-220
2-190	2.1-221
2-191	2.1-222
2-192	2.1-223
2-193	2.1-223.1
2-194	2.1-223.2
2-195	Deleted
2-196	2.1-223.3
2-197	2.1-223.4
2-198	2.1-223.5
2-199	2.1-223.6
2-200	2.1-224
2-200.1	2.1-225
2-201	2-.1-226
2-202	2.1-227
2-203	2.1-228
2-204	2.1-229
2-205	2.1-230
2-206	2.1-231
2-207	2.1-232
2-208	2.1-233
2-209	2.1-234
2-210	Deleted
2-211	2.1-235
2-211.1	2.1-236
2-212	2.1-237
2-213	2.1-238
2-214	2.1-239
2-215	2.1-240
2-216	2.1-241
2-217	2.1-242
2-218	Repealed
2-218.1	2.1-243
2-219	2.1-244
2-220	2.1-245
2-221	2.1-246
2-222	2.1-247
2-223	2.1-248
2-224	2.1-249
2-225	2.1-250
2-226	2.1-251
2-227	2.1-252
2-228	2.1-253
2-229	2.1-254
2-230	2.1-255
2-231	2.1-256
2-232	2.1-257
2-233	2.1-258
2-234	2.1-259
2-235	2.1-260
2-236	2.1-261
2-237	2.1-262
2-238	2.1-263
2-239	Repealed
2-239.1	2.1-264
2-240	2.1-265
2-241	Repealed
2-242	2.1-266
2-243	2.1-267
2-244	2.1-268
2-245	2.1-269
2-246	2.1-270
2-247	2.1-271
2-248	2.1-272
2-249	2.1-273
2-250	2.1-274
2-251	2.1-275
2-252	2.1-276
2-253	2.1-277
2-254	2.1-278
2-255	2.1-279
2-256	2.1-280
2-257	2.1-281
2-258	2.1-282
2-259	2.1-283
2-259.1	2.1-284
2-259.2	2.1-285
2-260	2.1-286
2-261	2.1-287
2-262	2.1-288
2-263	2.1-289
2-264	2.1-290
2-265	2.1-291
2-266	2.1-292
2-267	2.1-293
2-268	2.1-294
2-268.1	2.1-295
2-268.2	2.1-296
2-268.3	2.1-297
2-268.4	2.1-298
2-268.5	2.1-299
2-268.6	2.1-300
2-268.7	2.1-301
2-268.8	2.1-302
2-269	2.1-303
2-270	2.1-304
2-271	2.1-305
2-272	Repealed
2-273	2.1-306
2-274	2.1-307
2-275	2.1-308
2-276	2.1-309
2-277	2.1-310
2-278, 2-279	Repealed
2-279.1	2.1-311
2-280	2.1-312

Former Section	Present Section
2-281	2.1-313
2-282	2.1-314
2-283	2.1-315
2-284	2.1-316
2-285	2.1-317
2-286	2.1-318
2-287	2.1-319
2-288	2.1-320
2-289	2.1-321
2-290	2.1-322
2-291	Repealed
2-291.1	2.1-323
2-292, 2-293	Repealed
2-294	2.1-324
2-295	2.1-325
2-296	2.1-326
2-297	2.1-327
2-298	2.1-328
2-299	2.1-329
2-300	2.1-330
2-301	2.1-331
2-302	2.1-332
2-303	2.1-333
2-304	2.1-334
2-305	2.1-335
2-306	2.1-336
2-307	2.1-337
2-308	2.1-338
2-309	2.1-339

COMPARABLE SECTIONS OF TITLES 2.1 AND 2.2 AND OTHER CORRESPONDING SECTIONS

Former Section	Present Section
2.1-1.1	Deleted
2.1-1.2	2.2-600
2.1-1.3	Deleted
2.1-1.4	Deleted
2.1-1.5	Deleted
2.1-1.6	Deleted
2.1-1.7	Deleted
2.1-1.8	Deleted
2.1-1.9	Deleted
2.1-2.1	2.2-608
2.1-2.2	2.2-610
2.1-3	2.2-611 A
2.1-4	2.2-611 B
2.1-7	2.2-614
2.1-7.1	2.2-613
2.1-7.2	2.2-606
2.1-7.3	2.2-612
2.1-8.1	2.2-127
2.1-8.2	2.2-128
2.1-8.3	2.2-129
2.1-8.4	2.2-130
2.1-8.5	2.2-131
2.1-8.6	2.2-132 A
2.1-8.7	2.2-132 B
2.1-8.8	2.2-133
2.1-11.1	2.2-2809
2.1-12	2.2-2810
2.1-15	2.2-2811
2.1-17	2.2-2828
2.1-17.1	2.2-2829
2.1-18	2.2-2830 A
2.1-19	2.2-2830 B
2.1-20	2.2-605
2.1-20.01	2.2-2812
2.1-20.01:1	2.2-603
2.1-20.01:2	2.2-604
2.1-20.1	2.2-2818
2.1-20.1:01	2.2-2650 A-D
2.1-20.1:02	2.2-1204
2.1-20.1:03	2.2-2819
2.1-20.1:04	2.2-1205
2.1-20.1:05	2.2-1206
2.1-20.1:06	2.2-2820
2.1-20.1:07	2.2-2820.1
2.1-20.1:1	2.2-2822
2.1-20.1:2	51.1-1300
2.1-20.1:3	51.1-1301
2.1-20.1:4	51.1-1302
2.1-20.1:5	51.1-1304
2.1-20.1:6	51.1-1305
2.1-20.1:7	51.1-1303
2.1-20.1:8	2.2-2817
2.1-20.1:9	2.2-2817.1
2.1-20.1:16	2.2-2817.2
2.1-20.2	2.2-2813 A
2.1-20.3	2.2-2104 B-D 2.2-2813 B-D
2.1-20.4	Deleted
2.1-20.5	2.2-2814
2.1-20.6	2.2-2815
2.1-20.7	2.2-2816
2.1-20.8	2.2-2823 A
2.1-20.9	2.2-2824
2.1-20.10	2.2-2825
2.1-20.11	2.2-2826
2.1-20.12	2.2-2823 B
2.1-21	2.2-3300
2.1-21.1	2.2-3302
2.1-21.2	2.2-3303
2.1-22	2.2-3301
2.1-23	6.1-5.4
2.1-24	2.2-3304
2.1-24.1	2.2-3315
2.1-24.2	2.2-3305
2.1-25	2.2-3306
2.1-26	2.2-3307
2.1-27	2.2-3308
2.1-27.1	2.2-3317
2.1-27.2	2.2-3309
2.1-27.2:01	2.2-3309.1
2.1-27.3	2.2-3310
2.1-27.3:1	2.2-3310.1
2.1-27.4	2.2-3319
2.1-27.5	2.2-3321
2.1-27.6	2.2-3311
2.1-27.7	2.2-3312
2.1-27.8	2.2-3313
2.1-27.9	2.2-3320
2.1-27.10	2.2-3314
2.1-27.11	2.2-3316
2.1-28	2.2-3318
2.1-29	2.2-3322
2.1-30	2.2-2800
2.1-31	2.2-2802
2.1-32	2.2-2803
2.1-32.1	2.2-2804
2.1-33	2.2-2801
2.1-34	2.2-2805
2.1-35	2.2-2806
2.1-37	2.2-2808
2.1-37.01	2.2-2807
2.1-37.1	17.1-900
2.1-37.2	17.1-906
2.1-37.3	17.1-901
2.1-37.4	17.1-902
2.1-37.5	17.1-902
2.1-37.6	17.1-902
2.1-37.7	17.1-903
2.1-37.8	17.1-904
2.1-37.8:1	17.1-905
2.1-37.9	17.1-907
2.1-37.10	17.1-908
2.1-37.11	17.1-909
2.1-37.12	17.1-910
2.1-37.12:1	17.1-911
2.1-37.12:2	17.1-912
2.1-37.13	17.1-913
2.1-37.14	17.1-914
2.1-37.15	17.1-915
2.1-37.16	17.1-916
2.1-37.17	17.1-917
2.1-37.17:1	17.1-918
2.1-37.18	17.1-919
2.1-38	2.2-100
2.1-38.2	2.2-114
2.1-38.3	2.2-101
2.1-39	2.2-105
2.1-39.1	2.2-104
2.1-40	2.2-102
2.1-41.1	2.2-103 A
2.1-41.2	2.2-106
2.1-41.3	2.2-116

Former Section	Present Section
2.1-42	2.2-110
2.1-42.1	2.2-107
2.1-42.2	2.2-405
2.1-42.3	2.2-406
2.1-43	2.2-108
2.1-44	2.2-109
2.1-45	2.2-126
2.1-46	2.2-123
2.1-47	2.2-120
2.1-48	2.2-121
2.1-49	2.2-111
2.1-50	2.2-112
2.1-51.5:1	2.2-113
2.1-51.6	2.2-119
2.1-51.6:3	2.2-117
2.1-51.6:4	2.2-122
2.1-51.6:5	2.2-115
2.1-51.6:6	2.2-118
2.1-51.7	2.2-200 2.2-215
2.1-51.8:1	2.2-200
2.1-51.8:2	2.2-216
2.1-51.8:3	2.2-217
2.1-51.9	2.2-215
2.1-51.9:1	2.2-2711
2.1-51.10	2.2-201 B
2.1-51.10:1	2.2-201 A
2.1-51.12	2.2-202
2.1-51.12:1	2.2-218
2.1-51.12:2	2.2-219
2.1-51.12:3	2.2-220
2.1-51.12:4	2.2-220.1
2.1-51.13	2.2-200/2.2-212
2.1-51.14	2.2-200/2.2-212
2.1-51.14:1	2.2-214
2.1-51.15	2.2-212
2.1-51.15:1	2.2-213
2.1-51.16	2.2-200 2.2-221
2.1-51.17	2.2-200, 2.2-222
2.1-51.17:01	2.2-224
2.1-51.18	2.2-221
2.1-51.18:3	2.2-223
2.1-51.19	2.2-208
2.1-51.20	2.2-208
2.1-51.21	2.2-208
2.1-51.21:1	2.2-209
2.1-51.21:2	2.2-210
2.1-51.21:3	2.2-2652, 2.2-2653
2.1-51.21:4	2.2-2654
2.1-51.25	2.2-203
2.1-51.26	2.2-200
2.1-51.27	2.2-203
2.1-51.27:1	2.2-2705, 2.2-2708A
2.1-51.27:2	2.2-2706
2.1-51.27:3	2.2-2707
2.1-51.27:4	2.2-2708 B
2.1-51.31	2.2-1502

Former Section	Present Section
2.1-51.31:1	2.2-203.1
2.1-51.31:2	2.2-203.2
2.1-51.32	2.2-211
2.1-51.33	2.2-200, 2.2-211
2.1-51.34	2.2-211
2.1-51.35	2.2-134 B
2.1-51.36	2.2-134 A
2.1-51.37	2.2-135
2.1-51.38	2.2-204
2.1-51.39	2.2-200
2.1-51.39:1	2.2-205
2.1-51.39:2	2.2-204
2.1-51.39:3	2.2-206
2.1-51.40	2.2-204
2.1-51.40:1	2.2-207
2.1-51.41	2.2-200, 2.2-228
2.1-51.42	2.2-200
2.1-51.43	2.2-228
2.1-51.44	2.2-200, 2.2-225
2.1-51.45	2.2-200, 2.2-225
2.1-51.46	2.2-225
2.1-51.47	2.2-226
2.1-51.48	2.2-2651
2.1-51.49	2.2-2403
2.1-51.50	2.2-227
2.1-64.28:1	2.2-2617 A, B, E
2.1-64.28:2	2.2-2617 C, D, F
2.1-64.28:3	2.2-2619
2.1-64.28:4	2.2-2618
2.1-64.32	2.2-1400 A
2.1-64.32:1	2.2-1401
2.1-64.33	2.2-1400 A and C
2.1-64.34	2.2-1402
2.1-64.34:1	2.2-2311
2.1-64.35	2.2-1403
2.1-64.36	2.2-1404 A
2.1-64.37	2.2-1404 B, C, D
2.1-64.38	2.2-1405
2.1-65	2.2-400 A
2.1-66	2.2-401
2.1-67	2.2-400 B
2.1-68	2.2-402
2.1-68.1	2.2-403
2.1-69	2.2-404
2.1-71	Deleted
2.1-71.1	2.2-408
2.1-71.2	2.2-409
2.1-72	2.2-410 A
2.1-73	2.2-410 B
2.1-74	2.2-411
2.1-75	2.2-412
2.1-76	2.2-413
2.1-77	2.2-414 A
2.1-78	2.2-415
2.1-79	2.2-414 B

Former Section	Present Section
2.1-81	2.2-414 C
2.1-81.1	2.2-416
2.1-81.2	2.2-417 A
2.1-81.3	2.2-417 B
2.1-81.4	Deleted
2.1-110	2.2-2900
2.1-111	2.2-2901
2.1-111.1	2.2-2902
2.1-112	2.2-2903
2.1-113	2.2-103 B, 2.2-1200 B
2.1-113.1	2.2-2409 A, B, C
2.1-113.2	2.2-2409 D
2.1-113.3	2.2-2410
2.1-114.1	2.2-2904
2.1-114.2	2.2-103 B
2.1-114.2:1	2.2-124
2.1-114.3	2.2-1200 A
2.1-114.4	2.2-601
2.1-114.5	2.2-1201
2.1-114.5:01	2.2-1203
2.1-114.5:02	2.2-2821
2.1-114.5:03	2.2-2821.1
2.1-114.5:04	2.2-2821.2
2.1-114.6	2.2-1202
2.1-114.7	2.2-602
2.1-114.7:1	2.2-607
2.1-116	2.2-2905
2.1-116.01	2.2-1000
2.1-116.02	2.2-1000
2.1-116.03	2.2-1001
2.1-116.04	2.2-3000 B
2.1-116.05	2.2-3000 A, 2.2-3003
2.1-116.06	2.2-3004
2.1-116.07	2.2-3005
2.1-116.07:1	2.2-3006
2.1-116.08	2.2-3007
2.1-116.09	2.2-3001
2.1-116.012	2.2-3008
2.1-116.013	2.2-3002
2.1-116.1	9.1-500
2.1-116.2	9.1-501
2.1-116.3	9.1-503
2.1-116.4	9.1-502
2.1-116.5	9.1-504 A, B, C
2.1-116.6	9.1-505
2.1-116.7	9.1-504 D
2.1-116.8	9.1-506
2.1-116.9	9.1-507
2.1-116.9:1	9.1-300
2.1-116.9:2	9.1-301
2.1-116.9:3	9.1-303
2.1-116.9:4	9.1-304
2.1-116.9:5	9.1-302
2.1-116.9:6	9.1-600
2.1-116.9:7	9.1-700
2.1-116.9:8	9.1-701
2.1-116.9:9	9.1-702
2.1-116.9:10	9.1-703
2.1-116.9:11	9.1-704

Former Section	Present Section
2.1-116.9:12	9.1-705
2.1-116.9:13	9.1-706
2.1-116.10	2.2-2655 A
2.1-116.11	2.2-2655 B, E
2.1-116.12	2.2-2655 C
2.1-116.13	2.2-2655 D
2.1-116.14	2.2-2656
2.1-116.20	2.2-3200
2.1-116.21	2.2-3201
2.1-116.22	2.2-3202
2.1-116.23	2.2-3203
2.1-116.24	2.2-3204
2.1-116.25	2.2-3205
2.1-116.26	2.2-3206
2.1-117	2.2-500
2.1-118	2.2-505
2.1-120	2.2-506
2.1-121	2.2-507
2.1-121.1	2.2-508
2.1-121.2	2.2-509
2.1-122	2.2-510
2.1-124	2.2-511
2.1-125	2.2-512
2.1-126	2.2-513
2.1-127	2.2-514
2.1-127.1	2.2-515
2.1-128	2.2-516
2.1-130	2.2-501
2.1-131	2.2-502
2.1-132	2.2-503
2.1-133	2.2-504
2.1-133.1	2.2-517 A, B
2.1-133.2	Deleted
2.1-133.3	2.2-517 C
2.1-133.4	2.2-518
2.1-133.5	9.1-400 A
2.1-133.6	9.1-400 B
2.1-133.7	9.1-402
2.1-133.7:1	9.1-401
2.1-133.8	9.1-403
2.1-133.9	9.1-404
2.1-133.10	9.1-405
2.1-133.11	9.1-406
2.1-134 through 2.1-152	Deleted
2.1-153	30-130
2.1-154	30-131
2.1-155	30-133 A, B, E
2.1-155.2	30-142
2.1-155.3	30-138
2.1-156	30-137 A
2.1-160	30-135 A and B, 30-133 C
2.1-161	30-135 C
2.1-163	30-133 C
2.1-164	30-140
2.1-165	30-134 A
2.1-166	30-134 B
2.1-167	30-137 B
2.1-168	30-137 C

Former Section	Present Section
2.1-169	30-136
2.1-170	30-139
2.1-171	30-132 B
2.1-172	30-132 A
2.1-172.1	30-141
2.1-173	2.2-801 A, 2.2-1801 A
2.1-174	2.2-801 B, 2.2-1801 B
2.1-175	2.2-801 C, 2.2-1801 C
2.1-176	2.2-801 D, 2.2-1801 D
2.1-177	2.2-1800
2.1-178	2.2-2415
2.1-179	2.2-2416
2.1-179.2	2.2-2417
2.1-179.3	2.2-2418
2.1-179.4	2.2-2419
2.1-179.5	2.2-2420
2.1-180	2.2-1802
2.1-180.1	2.2-1803
2.1-182	2.2-1804
2.1-183	2.2-1805 A
2.1-184	2.2-1805 B
2.1-185	2.2-1806
2.1-186	2.2-1807
2.1-187	2.2-1808
2.1-188	2.2-1809
2.1-189	2.2-1810
2.1-190	2.2-1811
2.1-190.1	2.2-1812
2.1-191.1	2.2-1828
2.1-191.2	2.2-1829
2.1-191.3	2.2-1830
2.1-191.4	2.2-1831
2.1-191.5	2.2-1832
2.1-191.6	2.2-1833
2.1-191.7	2.2-1834
2.1-191.8	2.2-1835
2.1-191.9	2.2-1838
2.1-191.10	2.2-1836
2.1-191.11	2.2-1837
2.1-191.12	2.2-1839
2.1-191.13	2.2-1840
2.1-191.14	2.2-1841
2.1-191.15	2.2-1842
2.1-191.16	2.2-1843
2.1-192	2.2-800 A
2.1-193	Deleted
2.1-194	2.2-800 B
2.1-195	2.2-802
2.1-196.1	2.2-803
2.1-196.2	2.2-804
2.1-197	2.2-805
2.1-198	2.2-806
2.1-199	2.2-807
2.1-200	2.2-808
2.1-202	2.2-809
2.1-203	Deleted
2.1-204	2.2-810

Former Section	Present Section
2.1-205	2.2-811
2.1-206	2.2-812
2.1-207	2.2-813
2.1-209	2.2-1813
2.1-210	2.2-1814
2.1-211	2.2-1815
2.1-219	2.2-1816
2.1-220	2.2-1817
2.1-223	2.2-1818
2.1-223.1	2.2-814 A
2.1-223.2	2.2-814 B
2.1-223.3	2.2-815 A
2.1-223.4	2.2-815 B
2.1-223.6	2.2-816
2.1-224	2.2-1819
2.1-225	Deleted
2.1-226	2.2-1821
2.1-227	2.2-1822
2.1-228	2.2-1823
2.1-229	2.2-1824
2.1-231	2.2-1825
2.1-232	2.2-1826
2.1-233	2.2-1827
2.1-234.1	2.2-4600 A
2.1-234.2	2.2-4601
2.1-234.3	2.2-4600 B
2.1-234.4	2.2-4603
2.1-234.5	2.2-4408 B
2.1-234.6	2.2-4604
2.1-234.7	2.2-4605
2.1-234.8	2.2-4602
2.1-234.9	2.2-4606
2.1-234.9:1	2.2-4700
2.1-234.9:2	2.2-4701
2.1-234.9:3	2.2-4702
2.1-234.9:4	2.2-4703
2.1-234.9:5	2.2-4704
2.1-234.9:6	2.2-4705 A
2.1-234.9:7	2.2-4705 B
2.1-234.10	2.2-2260 A
2.1-234.11	2.2-2260 B
2.1-234.12	2.2-2261
2.1-234.13	2.2-2263
2.1-234.14	2.2-2264
2.1-234.15	2.2-2265
2.1-234.16	2.2-2266
2.1-234.17	2.2-2267
2.1-234.18	2.2-2268
2.1-234.19	2.2-2269
2.1-234.20	2.2-2270
2.1-234.21	2.2-2273
2.1-234.22	2.2-2274
2.1-234.23	2.2-2271
2.1-234.24	2.2-2278
2.1-234.25	2.2-2262
2.1-234.26	2.2-2272
2.1-234.27	2.2-2275
2.1-234.28	2.2-2276
2.1-234.28:1	2.2-2277
2.1-234.29	2.2-1600
2.1-234.30	2.2-1600

Former Section	Present Section
2.1-234.31	2.2-601
2.1-234.32	2.2-1601
2.1-234.33	2.2-1600
2.1-234.34	2.2-1602
2.1-303	2.2-4900
2.1-304	2.2-4901
2.1-304.1:1	2.2-4902
2.1-304.1:2	2.2-4902.1
2.1-304.2	2.2-2712
2.1-304.3	2.2-2713
2.1-304.4	2.2-2714
2.1-304.5	2.2-4903
2.1-304.6	2.2-4904
2.1-304.7	2.2-4905
2.1-313	2.2-4906
2.1-326.1	2.2-5000
2.1-326.2	2.2-5001
2.1-326.2:1	2.2-5002
2.1-326.3	2.2-5003
2.1-327	2.2-4500
2.1-328	2.2-4501
2.1-328.1	2.2-4502
2.1-328.2	2.2-4503
2.1-328.3	2.2-4504
2.1-328.4	Deleted
2.1-328.5	2.2-4505
2.1-328.6	2.2-4506
2.1-328.7	Deleted
2.1-328.8	2.2-4507
2.1-328.9	2.2-4508
2.1-328.10	2.2-4510
2.1-328.11	2.2-4512
2.1-328.12	2.2-4513
2.1-328.13	2.2-4511
2.1-328.14	2.2-4514
2.1-328.15	2.2-4509
2.1-329.01	2.2-4515
2.1-329.1	2.2-4516
2.1-335.1	2.2-2506
2.1-335.2	2.2-2507
2.1-335.3	2.2-2103
2.1-336	2.2-5600
2.1-337	2.2-5601
2.1-338	2.2-5602
2.1-339	2.2-5603
2.1-339.1	2.2-5700
2.1-339.2	2.2-5701
2.1-339.3	2.2-5702
2.1-339.4	2.2-5800
2.1-339.5	2.2-5801 A, B, C, G
2.1-339.6	2.2-5801 D-F
2.1-339.7	2.2-5802
2.1-339.8	2.2-5803
2.1-340	2.2-3700 A
2.1-340.1	2.2-3700 B
2.1-341	2.2-3701
2.1-341.1	2.2-3702
2.1-341.2	2.2-3703
2.1-342	2.2-3704
2.1-342.01	2.2-3705
2.1-342.2	2.2-3706
2.1-343	2.2-3707
2.1-343.1	2.2-3708
2.1-343.1:1	2.2-3709
2.1-343.2	2.2-3710
2.1-344	2.2-3711
2.1-344.1	2.2-3712
2.1-346	2.2-3713
2.1-346.1	2.2-3714
2.1-346.2	30-178
2.1-346.3	30-179
2.1-346.4	30-180
2.1-346.5	30-181
2.1-359	2.2-4400 A, B
2.1-360	2.2-4401
2.1-361	2.2-4400 C, D
2.1-362	2.2-4402
2.1-363	2.2-4403
2.1-363.1	2.2-4404
2.1-364	2.2-4405
2.1-365	2.2-4406
2.1-366	2.2-4407
2.1-367	2.2-4408
2.1-368	2.2-4409
2.1-369	2.2-4411
2.1-370	2.2-4410
2.1-371	2.2-700
2.1-372	2.2-601
2.1-373	2.2-703
2.1-373.01	2.2-709
2.1-373.02	2.2-2626, 2.2-2627
2.1-373.1	2.2-705
2.1-373.2	2.2-706
2.1-373.2:1	2.2-707
2.1-373.3	2.2-704
2.1-373.6	2.2-702
2.1-373.7	2.2-708
2.1-373.8	2.2-701
2.1-373.9	2.2-710
2.1-373.10	2.2-711 A
2.1-373.11	2.2-711 B
2.1-373.12	2.2-712
2.1-373.13	2.2-2411, 2.2-2412
2.1-373.14	2.2-713
2.1-373.15	2.2-714
2.1-373.16	2.2-715
2.1-373.17	2.2-716
2.1-373.18	2.2-717
2.1-374	2.2-4200 A
2.1-375	2.2-4200 C
2.1-376	2.2-4201
2.1-376.1	2.2-4200 B
2.1-377	2.2-3800 A
2.1-378	2.2-3800 B, C
2.1-379	2.2-3801
2.1-380	2.2-3803 A, B
2.1-380.1	2.2-3804
2.1-381	2.2-3805
2.1-382	2.2-3806
2.1-383	2.2-3807
2.1-384	2.2-3802
2.1-384.1	2.2-3803 C
2.1-385	2.2-3808
2.1-385.1	2.2-3808.1
2.1-386	2.2-3809
2.1-387	2.2-103 C
2.1-388	2.2-1500 A
2.1-389	2.2-1500 B
2.1-391	2.2-1501
2.1-393	2.2-1503
2.1-394	2.2-1504
2.1-394.1	2.2-1505
2.1-394.2	Deleted
2.1-395	2.2-1506
2.1-396	Deleted
2.1-397	Deleted
2.1-397.1	2.2-1507
2.1-398	2.2-1508
2.1-399	2.2-1509 A/E
2.1-399.1	2.2-1509 B, C, D
2.1-399.2	2.2-1510
2.1-400	2.2-1511
2.1-401	Deleted
2.1-402	2.2-1512
2.1-403	Deleted
2.1-404	2.2-1513
2.1-422	2.2-1100 A, C
2.1-423	2.2-1100 B
2.1-424	2.2-1102 A, B
2.1-425	2.2-1100 B, C, 2.2-1101
2.1-425.2	2.2-1102
2.1-426	2.2-1103
2.1-429	2.2-1104 A, D
2.1-429.01	2.2-1105
2.1-429.4	2.2-1106
2.1-430	2.2-1104 E
2.1-432	2.2-1107
2.1-432.1	2.2-1108
2.1-435	2.2-1109
2.1-438	2.2-1115 C
2.1-440	2.2-1110
2.1-440.1	2.2-1121
2.1-441	2.2-1114
2.1-442	2.2-1111
2.1-444	2.2-1115 A
2.1-445.1	2.2-1123
2.1-446	2.2-1112
2.1-447	2.2-1120
2.1-447.1	
2.1-450	2.2-1117
2.1-450.1	2.2-1118
2.1-451	2.2-1119
2.1-453	2.2-1116
2.1-454.1	2.2-1122
2.1-455	2.2-1115 B
2.1-456	2.2-1115 D, E
2.1-457.2	2.2-1124
2.1-457.3	2.2-1125
2.1-464	2.2-1113 B

Former Section	Present Section
2.1-465	2.2-1113 A
2.1-466	2.2-1126 B, C
2.1-467	2.2-1127
2.1-467.1	42.1-19.1
2.1-467.2	2.2-609 B 2.2-1127
2.1-467.3	2.2-1126 A
2.1-467.4	2.2-609 A
2.1-467.5	42.1-19.2
2.1-467.7	42.1-19.3
2.1-467.8	42.1-19.4
2.1-468	2.2-1128
2.1-480	2.2-1129 A
2.1-481	2.2-1129 B, C 2.2-1130
2.1-482	2.2-1131
2.1-483.1	2.2-1132
2.1-483.1:1	2.2-1133
2.1-483.1:2	2.2-1134
2.1-483.2	2.2-1135
2.1-484	2.2-1136
2.1-485	2.2-1137
2.1-486	2.2-2434 B, C
2.1-487	2.2-2434 A
2.1-488	2.2-2434 E
2.1-488.1	2.2-2400 A-D
2.1-488.2:1	2.2-2400 F
2.1-488.3	2.2-2401 B
2.1-488.4	2.2-2402
2.1-488.5	2.2-2401 A
2.1-488.6	2.2-2400 E
2.1-489	2.2-1138 A
2.1-490	2.2-1138 B
2.1-491	2.2-1138 C
2.1-492	2.2-1129 D
2.1-493	2.2-1139
2.1-494	Deleted
2.1-495	2.2-1140
2.1-496	2.2-1141
2.1-497	2.2-1142
2.1-498	2.2-1143
2.1-499	2.2-1144 A
2.1-500	2.2-1144 B
2.1-501	2.2-1145
2.1-502	Deleted
2.1-503	2.2-1146
2.1-504	2.2-1147
2.1-504.1	2.2-1148
2.1-504.2	2.2-1149
2.1-504.3	2.2-1150
2.1-504.4	2.2-1150 D, 2.2-1151
2.1-504.5	2.2-1152
2.1-505	2.2-1153
2.1-508	2.2-1154
2.1-511	2.2-1155
2.1-512	2.2-1156
2.1-512.1	2.2-1157
2.1-513	2.2-1158
2.1-514	2.2-1159 A
2.1-515	2.2-1159 A
2.1-516	2.2-1159 B
2.1-517	2.2-1159 C
2.1-519	2.2-1160
2.1-520	2.2-1159 D
2.1-521	2.2-1159 E
2.1-521.1	2.2-1161
2.1-526.12	2.2-1162
2.1-526.13	2.2-1163
2.1-526.14	2.2-1164
2.1-526.15	2.2-1165
2.1-526.16	2.2-1166
2.1-526.17	Deleted
2.1-526.17:1	2.2-1167
2.1-527	2.2-1168
2.1-528	2.2-1169
2.1-529	2.2-1170
2.1-530	2.2-1171
2.1-531	2.2-1172
2.1-548.01	2.2-1173
2.1-548.02	2.2-1174
2.1-548.03	2.2-1175
2.1-548.04	2.2-1176
2.1-548.05	2.2-1177
2.1-548.06	2.2-1178
2.1-548.07	2.2-1179
2.1-548.08	2.2-1180
2.1-548.09	2.2-1181
2.1-548.26	2.2-2234A
2.1-548.27	2.2-2200
2.1-548.28	2.2-2234 C
2.1-548.29	2.2-2238
2.1-548.29:1	2.2-2238.1
2.1-548.30	2.2-2239
2.1-548.31	2.2-2235
2.1-548.32	2.2-2236
2.1-548.33	2.2-2237 (10)
2.1-548.34	2.2-2237 (11)
2.1-548.35	2.2-2237
2.1-548.36	2.2-2245
2.1-548.37	2.2-2246
2.1-548.38	2.2-2244
2.1-548.39	2.2-2241
2.1-548.40	2.2-2242
2.1-548.41	2.2-2243
2.1-548.42	2.2-2103
2.1-548.43	2.2-2240
2.1-548.43:1	2.2-5100 A
2.1-548.43:2	2.2-5100 B
2.1-548.43:3	2.2-5101
2.1-548.43:4	2.2-5102
2.1-548.43:5	2.2-5103
2.1-548.43:6	2.2-5104
2.1-548.44	2.2-900 A
2.1-548.45	2.2-900 B
2.1-548.46	2.2-901
2.1-548.47	2.2-902 A
2.1-548.48	2.2-902 B
2.1-548.49	2.2-2413 A, B
2.1-548.50	2.2-2413 C, D, E
2.1-548.51	2.2-2414
2.1-548.52	2.2-2103
2.1-548.53	2.2-2315 A
2.1-548.54	2.2-2315 B
2.1-548.55	2.2-2200
2.1-548.56	2.2-2315 C
2.1-548.57	2.2-2316
2.1-548.58	2.2-2317
2.1-548.59	2.2-2318
2.1-548.60	2.2-2319
2.1-548.61	2.2-2320
2.1-548.62	2.2-2321
2.1-548.63	2.2-2325
2.1-548.64	2.2-2324
2.1-548.65	2.2-2322
2.1-548.66	2.2-2323
2.1-548.67	2.2-2326
2.1-548.68	2.2-2327
2.1-554	2.2-3600
2.1-555	2.2-3601
2.1-556	2.2-3602
2.1-557	2.2-3603
2.1-557.1	2.2-3604
2.1-558	2.2-3605
2.1-563.13	2.2-1301
2.1-563.14	2.2-1300 A
2.1-563.15	2.2-1300 B
2.1-563.16	2.2-601, 2.2-1302 2.2-1303 C
2.1-563.17	2.2-1303 A
2.1-563.18	2.2-1303 B, D
2.1-563.19	2.2-1304 A
2.1-563.20	2.2-1304 A
2.1-563.21	2.2-1304 A
2.1-563.22	2.2-1304 B, C
2.1-563.27:1	2.2-2426
2.1-563.27:2	2.2-2427
2.1-563.27:3	2.2-2428
2.1-563.27:4	2.2-2429
2.1-563.27:5	2.2-2430
2.1-563.27:6	2.2-2433
2.1-563.27:7	2.2-2431
2.1-563.27:8	2.2-2432
2.1-563.35:1	2.2-1700 A
2.1-563.35:2	2.2-1700 B
2.1-563.35:3	2.2-1701
2.1-563.35:4	2.2-1710
2.1-563.36	2.2-1705
2.1-563.37	2.2-1706
2.1-563.38	2.2-1707
2.1-563.39	2.2-1708
2.1-563.40	2.2-1709
2.1-563.40:1	2.2-1709.1
2.1-563.41	2.2-2423
2.1-563.42	2.2-136
2.1-563.43	2.2-137
2.1-563.44	2.2-138
2.1-564	2.2-300
2.1-565	2.2-301 A
2.1-566	2.2-301 B, C
2.1-567	2.2-302
2.1-568	2.2-303

Former Section	Present Section
2.1-570	2.2-3400
2.1-571	2.2-3401 A
2.1-572	2.2-3401 B
2.1-573	2.2-3402
2.1-587	2.2-5400 A
2.1-588	2.2-5400 B
2.1-589	2.2-5401
2.1-590	2.2-5402
2.1-591	2.2-5403
2.1-592	2.2-5404
2.1-593	2.2-5405
2.1-594	2.2-5406 D, E
2.1-595	2.2-5406 A, B
2.1-596	2.2-5406 C
2.1-597	2.2-5407
2.1-598	2.2-5408
2.1-639.1	2.2-3100
2.1-639.2	2.2-3101
2.1-639.3	2.2-3102
2.1-639.4	2.2-3103
2.1-639.4:1	2.2-3104
2.1-639.4:2	2.2-3104.1
2.1-639.5	2.2-3105
2.1-639.6	2.2-3106
2.1-639.7	2.2-3107
2.1-639.7:1	2.2-3108
2.1-639.8	2.2-3109
2.1-639.9	2.2-3110
2.1-639.10	2.2-3111
2.1-639.11	2.2-3112
2.1-639.12	2.2-3113
2.1-639.13	2.2-3114
2.1-639.14	2.2-3115
2.1-639.14:1	2.2-3116
2.1-639.15	2.2-3117
2.1-639.15:1	2.2-3118
2.1-639.16	2.2-3119
2.1-639.17	2.2-3120
2.1-639.18	2.2-3121
2.1-639.19	2.2-3122
2.1-639.20	2.2-3123
2.1-639.21	2.2-3124
2.1-639.22	2.2-3125
2.1-639.23	2.2-3126
2.1-639.24	2.2-3127
2.1-639.30	30-100
2.1-639.31	30-101
2.1-639.32	30-102
2.1-639.33	30-103
2.1-639.34	30-104
2.1-639.35	30-105
2.1-639.36	30-106
2.1-639.37	30-107
2.1-639.38	30-108
2.1-639.39	30-109
2.1-639.40	30-110
2.1-639.41	30-111
2.1-639.42	30-112
2.1-639.43	30-112 E
2.1-639.44	30-112 F
2.1-639.45	30-113
2.1-639.46	30-114
2.1-639.47	30-115
2.1-639.48	30-116
2.1-639.49	30-117
2.1-639.50	30-118
2.1-639.51	30-112 G
2.1-639.52	30-119
2.1-639.53	30-120
2.1-639.53:1	30-121
2.1-639.54	30-123
2.1-639.55	30-124
2.1-639.56	30-125
2.1-639.57	30-126
2.1-639.58	30-128
2.1-639.59	30-122
2.1-639.60	30-129
2.1-639.61	30-127
2.1-703.1	2.2-2640, 2.2-2641
2.1-704	2.2-2001
2.1-705	Deleted
2.1-706	2.2-2000
2.1-707	2.2-2003
2.1-708	2.2-601, 2.2-2002
2.1-709	2.2-2004
2.1-710	2.2-2005
2.1-711	2.2-2006
2.1-712	2.2-2007
2.1-713	2.2-2008
2.1-714	2.2-3900 A
2.1-715	2.2-3900 B
2.1-716	2.2-3901
2.1-717	2.2-3902
2.1-718	2.2-2632
2.1-719	2.2-2633
2.1-720	2.2-2634
2.1-721	2.2-2635
2.1-722	2.2-2636
2.1-723	2.2-2637
2.1-724	2.2-2638
2.1-725	2.2-2639
2.1-726	2.2-4801
2.1-727	2.2-4800
2.1-728	2.2-4802
2.1-729	2.2-4803
2.1-730	2.2-4804
2.1-731	Deleted
2.1-732	2.2-4805
2.1-733	2.2-4806
2.1-734	2.2-4807
2.1-735	2.2-4808
2.1-736	Deleted
2.1-737	2.2-1900
2.1-738	2.2-601, 2.2-1901
2.1-739	2.2-1902
2.1-739.1	2.2-2438 A
2.1-739.2	2.2-2438 B-E
2.1-739.3	2.2-2439
2.1-739.4	2.2-2438 F
2.1-740	2.2-1903
2.1-741	2.2-2421 A, B
2.1-742	2.2-2421 C
2.1-743	2.2-2422
2.1-744	2.2-2421 E
2.1-744.1	2.2-2435 A, B, C
2.1-744.2	2.2-2435 D
2.1-744.3	2.2-2436
2.1-744.4	2.2-2437
2.1-744.5	2.2-1904
2.1-744.6	2.2-1905
2.1-745	2.2-5200
2.1-746	2.2-2648
2.1-746.1	2.2-2649
2.1-747	2.2-5201
2.1-748	2.2-5202
2.1-749	2.2-5203
2.1-750	2.2-5204
2.1-751	2.2-5205
2.1-752	2.2-5206
2.1-753	2.2-5207
2.1-754	2.2-5208
2.1-755	2.2-5209
2.1-756	2.2-5210
2.1-757	2.2-5211
2.1-758	2.2-5212
2.1-759	2.2-5213
2.1-759.1	2.2-5214
2.1-760	2.2-5300
2.1-761	2.2-5301
2.1-762	2.2-5302
2.1-763	2.2-5303
2.1-764	2.2-5304
2.1-765	2.2-2664
2.1-766	2.2-5305
2.1-767	2.2-5306
2.1-768	2.2-5307
2.1-768.1	2.2-5308
2.1-769	2.2-5500
2.1-770	2.2-5501
2.1-771	2.2-5502
2.1-772	2.2-5503
2.1-773	2.2-5504
2.1-774	2.2-5505
2.1-775	2.2-5506
2.1-776	2.2-5507
2.1-777	2.2-5508
2.1-778	2.2-5509
2.1-779	2.2-418
2.1-780	2.2-419
2.1-781	2.2-420
2.1-781.1	2.2-421
2.1-782	2.2-422
2.1-783	2.2-423
2.1-784	2.2-424
2.1-785	2.2-425
2.1-786	2.2-426
2.1-787	2.2-427
2.1-787.1	2.2-428
2.1-788	2.2-429
2.1-789	2.2-430

Former Section	Present Section
2.1-790	2.2-431
2.1-791	2.2-432
2.1-792	2.2-433
2.1-793	2.2-434
2.1-794	2.2-435
2.1-795	2.2-615
2.1-796	2.2-616
2.1-797	2.2-617
2.1-798	2.2-618
2.1-799	2.2-619
2.1-804	2.2-2827 A
2.1-805	2.2-2827 B
2.1-806	2.2-2827 C
2.1-807	2.2-3500
2.1-808	2.2-3501
2.1-809	2.2-3502
2.1-810	2.2-3503
2.1-811	2.2-3504
2.1-812	37.1-258
2.1-813	37.1-259
2.1-814	37.1-260
2.1-815	37.1-255
2.1-816	37.1-256
2.1-816.1	37.1-256.1
2.1-817	37.1-257
2.1-818	2.2-5900
2.1-819	2.2-5901

COMPARABLE SECTIONS OF CHAPTER 20.1 OF TITLE 2.2

Former Section	Present Section
2.2-226	2.2-2007, 2.2-2014, 2.2-2015
2.2-226.1	2.2-2009
2.2-1301	2.2-2006
2.2-1303	2.2-2011, 2.2-2012
2.2-1304	2.2-2013
2.2-1701	2.2-2010
2.2-1702	2.2-2022
2.2-1703	2.2-2023
2.2-1704	2.2-2024
2.2-1705	2.2-2025
2.2-1706	2.2-2026
2.2-1707	2.2-2027
2.2-1708	2.2-2028
2.2-1709	2.2-2029
2.2-1709.1	2.2-2030
2.2-1710	2.2-2031
2.2-2248	2.2-2032

COMPARABLE SECTIONS OF TITLE 3 AND TITLE 3.1

Former Section	Present Section
3-1	3.1-1
3-2	3.1-2
3-3	3.1-3
3-4	3.1-4
3-5	3.1-5
3-6	3.1-6
3-6.1	3.1-7
3-7	3.1-8
3-8	3.1-9
3-9	3.1-10
3-10	3.1-11
3-11	3.1-12
3-12	3.1-13
3-13	3.1-14
3-13.1	3.1-15
3-13.2	3.1-16
3-14	3.1-17
3-15	3.1-18
3-16	3.1-739.1
3-16.1	3.1-19
3-16.2	3.1-20
3-16.3	3.1-21
3-16.4	3.1-22
3-16.5	3.1-22.1
3-16.6	3.1-22.2
3-16.7	3.1-22.3
3-16.8	3.1-22.4
3-16.9	3.1-22.5
3-17 to 3-27	Deleted
3-27.1	3.1-23
3-27.2	3.1-24
3-27.3	3.1-25
3-27.4	3.1-26
3-27.5	3.1-27
3-28	3.1-28
3-29	3.1-29
3-30	3.1-30
3-31	3.1-31
3-32	3.1-32
3-33	3.1-33
3-34	3.1-34
3-35	3.1-35
3-36	3.1-36
3-37	3.1-37
3-38	3.1-38
3-39	3.1-39
3-40 to 3-44	Repealed
3-44.1	3.1-40
3-44.2	3.1-41
3-44.3	3.1-42
3-44.4	3.1-43
3-44.5	3.1-44
3-44.6	3.1-45
3-44.7	3.1-46
3-44.8	3.1-46.1
3-45 to 3-52	Deleted
3-52.1	Repealed
3-53 to 3-63	Deleted
3-64 to 3-79	Repealed
3-79.1	3.1-47
3-79.2	3.1-48
3-79.3	3.1-49
3-79.4	3.1-50
3-79.5	3.1-51
3-79.6	3.1-52
3-79.7	3.1-53
3-79.8	3.1-54
3-79.9	3.1-55
3-79.10	3.1-56
3-79.11	3.1-57
3-79.12	3.1-58
3-79.13	3.1-59
3-79.14	3.1-60
3-79.15	3.1-61
3-79.16	3.1-62
3-79.17	3.1-63
3-79.18	3.1-64
3-79.19	3.1-65
3-79.20	3.1-66
3-79.21	3.1-67
3-79.22	3.1-68
3-79.23	3.1-69
3-79.24	3.1-70
3-79.25	3.1-71
3-79.26	3.1-72
3-79.27	3.1-73
3-80 to 3-117	Repealed
3-117.1	3.1-74
3-117.2	3.1-75
3-117.3	3.1-76
3-117.4	3.1-77
3-117.5	3.1-78
3-117.6	3.1-79
3-117.7	3.1-80
3-117.8	3.1-81
3-117.9	3.1-82
3-117.10	3.1-83
3-117.11	3.1-84
3-117.12	3.1-85
3-117.13	3.1-86
3-117.14	3.1-87
3-117.15	3.1-88

Former Section	Present Section
3-117.16	3.1-89
3-117.17	3.1-90
3-117.18	3.1-91
3-117.19	3.1-92
3-117.20	3.1-93
3-117.21	3.1-94
3-117.22	3.1-95
3-117.23	3.1-96
3-117.24	3.1-97
3-117.25	3.1-98
3-117.26	3.1-99
3-117.27	3.1-100
3-117.28	3.1-101
3-117.29	3.1-102
3-117.30	3.1-103
3-117.31	3.1-104
3-117.32	3.1-105
3-117.33	3.1-106
3-118	3.1-107
3-119	3.1-108
3-120	3.1-109
3-121	3.1-110
3-122	3.1-111
3-123	3.1-112
3-124	3.1-113
3-125	3.1-114
3-126	3.1-115
3-127	3.1-116
3-128	3.1-117
3-129	3.1-118
3-130	3.1-119
3-131	3.1-120
3-132	3.1-121
3-133	3.1-122
3-134	3.1-123
3-135	3.1-124
3-136	3.1-125
3-137	3.1-126
3-138	3.1-127
3-139	Repealed
3-139.1	3.1-128
3-139.2	3.1-129
3-139.3	3.1-130
3-139.4	3.1-131
3-139.5	3.1-132
3-140, 3-141	Repealed
3-142	3.1-133
3-143 to 3-150	Repealed
3-150.1	3.1-134
3-151 to 3-178	Repealed
3-178.1	3.1-135
3-178.2	3.1-136
3-178.3	3.1-137
3-178.4	3.1-138
3-178.5	3.1-139
3-178.6	3.1-140
3-178.7	3.1-141
3-178.8	3.1-142
3-178.9	3.1-143
3-178.10	3.1-144
3-178.11	3.1-145

Former Section	Present Section
3-178.12	3.1-146
3-178.13	3.1-147
3-178.14	3.1-148
3-178.15	3.1-149
3-178.16	3.1-150
3-178.17	3.1-151
3-178.18	3.1-152
3-178.19	3.1-153
3-178.20	3.1-154
3-178.21	3.1-155
3-178.22	Deleted
3-178.23	3.1-156
3-178.24	3.1-157
3-179	3.1-158
3-180	3.1-159
3-181	3.1-160
3-182	3.1-161
3-183	3.1-162
3-184	3.1-163
3-185	3.1-164
3-186	3.1-165
3-187	3.1-166
3-188	3.1-167
3-189	3.1-168
3-190	3.1-169
3-191	3.1-170
3-192	3.1-171
3-193	3.1-172
3-194	3.1-173
3-195	3.1-174
3-196	3.1-175
3-197	3.1-176
3-197.1	3.1-177
3-197.2	3.1-178
3-197.3	3.1-179
3-197.4	3.1-180
3-197.5	3.1-181
3-197.6	3.1-182
3-197.7	3.1-183
3-197.8	3.1-184
3-197.9	3.1-185
3-197.10	3.1-186
3-197.11	3.1-187
3-197.12	3.1-188
3-198	3.1-189
3-199	3.1-190
3-200	3.1-191
3-201	3.1-192
3-202	3.1-193
3-203	3.1-194
3-203.1	3.1-195
3-203.2	3.1-196
3-204	3.1-197
3-205	3.1-198
3-206	3.1-199
3-207	3.1-200
3-208	3.1-201
3-208.1	3.1-202
3-208.2	3.1-203
3-208.3	3.1-204
3-208.4	3.1-205

Former Section	Present Section
3-208.5	3.1-206
3-208.6	3.1-207
3-208.7	3.1-208
3-208.8	3.1-209
3-208.8:1	3.1-210
3-208.9	3.1-211
3-208.10	3.1-212
3-208.11	3.1-213
3-208.12	3.1-214
3-208.13	3.1-215
3-208.14	3.1-216
3-208.15	3.1-217
3-208.16	3.1-218
3-208.17	3.1-219
3-208.18	3.1-220
3-208.19	3.1-221
3-208.20	3.1-222
3-208.21	3.1-223
3-208.22	3.1-224
3-208.23	3.1-225
3-208.24	3.1-226
3-208.25	3.1-227
3-208.26	3.1-228
3-208.27	3.1-229
3-208.28	3.1-230
3-208.29	3.1-231
3-208.30	3.1-232
3-208.31	3.1-233
3-208.32	3.1-234
3-208.33	3.1-235
3-208.34	3.1-236
3-208.35	3.1-237
3-208.36	3.1-238
3-208.37	3.1-239
3-208.38	3.1-240
3-208.39	3.1-241
3-208.40	3.1-242
3-208.41	3.1-243
3-208.42	3.1-244
3-208.43	3.1-245
3-208.44	3.1-246
3-208.45	3.1-247
3-208.46	3.1-248
3-208.47	3.1-249
3-208.48	3.1-250
3-208.49	3.1-251
3-208.50	3.1-252
3-208.51	3.1-253
3-208.52	3.1-254
3-208.53	3.1-255
3-208.54	3.1-256
3-208.55	3.1-257
3-208.56	3.1-258
3-208.57	3.1-259
3-208.58	3.1-260
3-208.59	3.1-261
3-209 to 3-219	Repealed
3-219.1	3.1-262
3-219.2	3.1-263
3-219.3	3.1-264
3-219.4	3.1-265

Former Section	Present Section
3-219.5	3.1-266
3-219.6	3.1-267
3-219.7	3.1-268
3-219.8	3.1-269
3-219.9	3.1-270
3-219.9:1	3.1-271
3-219.10	3.1-272
3-219.11	3.1-273
3-219.12	3.1-274
3-219.13	3.1-275
3-219.14	3.1-275.1
3-220	3.1-276
3-221	3.1-277
3-222	3.1-278
3-223	3.1-279
3-224	3.1-280
3-225	3.1-281
3-226	3.1-282
3-227	3.1-283
3-228	3.1-284
3-228.1	3.1-285
3-228.2	3.1-286
3-228.3	3.1-287
3-228.4	3.1-288
3-228.5	3.1-289
3-228.6	3.1-290
3-228.7	3.1-291
3-228.8	3.1-292
3-228.9	3.1-293
3-228.10	3.1-294
3-228.11	3.1-295
3-228.12	3.1-296
3-228.13	3.1-296.1
3-228.14	3.1-296.2
3-228.15	3.1-296.3
3-228.16	3.1-296.4
3-228.17	3.1-296.5
3-228.18	3.1-296.6
3-228.19	3.1-296.7
3-228.20	3.1-296.8
3-228.21	3.1-296.9
3-228.22	3.1-296.10
3-229	3.1-297
3-230	3.1-298
3-231	3.1-299
3-232	3.1-300
3-233	3.1-301
3-234	3.1-302
3-235	3.1-303
3-236	3.1-304
3-237	3.1-305
3-238	3.1-306
3-239	3.1-307
3-239.1	3.1-308
3-239.2	3.1-309
3-239.3	3.1-310
3-239.4	3.1-311
3-239.5	3.1-312
3-239.6	3.1-313
3-239.7	3.1-314
3-239.8	3.1-315

Former Section	Present Section
3-239.9	3.1-316
3-239.10	3.1-317
3-239.11	3.1-318
3-240	3.1-319
3-241	3.1-320
3-242	3.1-321
3-243	3.1-322
3-244	3.1-323
3-245	3.1-324
3-246	3.1-325
3-247	3.1-326
3-248	3.1-327
3-249	3.1-328
3-250	3.1-329
3-251	3.1-330
3-252	3.1-331
3-253	3.1-332
3-254	3.1-333
3-255	3.1-334
3-256	3.1-335
3-257	3.1-336
3-258	3.1-337
3-259	3.1-338
3-260	3.1-339
3-261	3.1-340
3-262	3.1-341
3-263	3.1-342
3-264	3.1-343
3-265	3.1-344
3-266	3.1-345
3-267	3.1-346
3-268	3.1-347
3-269	3.1-348
3-269.1	3.1-348.1
3-269.2	3.1-348.2
3-269.3	3.1-348.3
3-269.4	3.1-348.4
3-269.5	3.1-348.5
3-269.6	3.1-348.6
3-270	3.1-349
3-271	3.1-350
3-272	3.1-351
3-273	3.1-352
3-274	3.1-353
3-275	3.1-354
3-276	3.1-355
3-277	3.1-356
3-278	3.1-357
3-279	3.1-358
3-280	3.1-359
3-280.1	3.1-360
3-281	3.1-361
3-281.1	3.1-362
3-282	3.1-363
3-283	3.1-364
3-284	Repealed
3-285	3.1-365
3-286	3.1-366
3-287	3.1-367
3-288	3.1-368
3-289	3.1-369

Former Section	Present Section
3-290	3.1-370
3-291	3.1-371
3-292	3.1-372
3-293	3.1-373
3-294	3.1-374
3-295	Repealed
3-296	3.1-375
3-297	3.1-376
3-298	3.1-377
3-299	3.1-378
3-300	3.1-379
3-301	3.1-380
3-301.1	3.1-381
3-302	3.1-382
3-303	3.1-383
3-304	3.1-384
3-305	3.1-385
3-306	3.1-386
3-307	3.1-387
3-308	3.1-388
3-309	3.1-389
3-310	3.1-390
3-311	3.1-391
3-312	3.1-392
3-313	3.1-393
3-314	3.1-394
3-315	3.1-395
3-316	3.1-396
3-317	3.1-397
3-318	3.1-398
3-319	3.1-399
3-320	3.1-400
3-321	3.1-401
3-322	Repealed
3-323	3.1-402
3-324	3.1-403
3-325	3.1-404
3-326	3.1-405
3-327	3.1-406
3-328	3.1-407
3-329	3.1-408
3-330	3.1-409
3-331	3.1-410
3-332	3.1-411
3-333	3.1-412
3-334	3.1-413
3-335	3.1-414
3-336	3.1-415
3-337	3.1-416
3-338	3.1-417
3-339	3.1-418
3-340	3.1-419
3-341	3.1-420
3-342	3.1-421
3-343	3.1-422
3-344	3.1-423
3-345	3.1-424
3-346	3.1-425
3-347	3.1-426
3-347.1	3.1-426.1
3-347.2	3.1-426.2

Former Section	Present Section
3-348	3.1-427
3-349	Repealed
3-350	3.1-428
3-351	3.1-429
3-352	3.1-430
3-353	3.1-431
3-354	3.1-432
3-355	3.1-433
3-356	3.1-434
3-357	3.1-435
3-358	3.1-436
3-359	3.1-437
3-359.1	3.1-438
3-360	3.1-439
3-361	3.1-440
3-362	3.1-441
3-363	3.1-442
3-364	3.1-443
3-365	3.1-444
3-366	3.1-445
3-367	3.1-446
3-368	3.1-447
3-369	3.1-448
3-370	3.1-449
3-371	3.1-450
3-372	3.1-451
3-373	3.1-452
3-374	3.1-453
3-375	3.1-454
3-376	3.1-455
3-377	3.1-456
3-378	3.1-457
3-379	3.1-458
3-380	3.1-459
3-381	3.1-460
3-382	3.1-461
3-383	3.1-462
3-384 to 3-400.39	Repealed
3-400.40	3.1-463
3-400.41	3.1-464
3-400.42	3.1-465
3-400.43	3.1-466
3-400.44	3.1-467
3-400.45	3.1-468
3-400.46	3.1-469
3-400.47	3.1-470
3-400.48	3.1-471
3-400.49	3.1-472
3-400.50	3.1-473
3-400.51	3.1-474
3-400.52	3.1-475
3-400.53	3.1-476
3-400.54	3.1-477
3-400.55	3.1-478
3-400.56	3.1-479
3-400.57	3.1-480
3-400.58	3.1-481
3-400.59	3.1-482
3-400.60	3.1-483
3-400.61	3.1-484
3-400.62	3.1-485
3-400.63	3.1-486
3-400.64	3.1-487
3-400.65	3.1-488
3-400.66	3.1-489
3-400.67	3.1-490
3-400.68	3.1-491
3-400.69	3.1-492
3-400.70	3.1-493
3-400.71	3.1-494
3-400.72	3.1-495
3-400.73	3.1-496
3-400.74	3.1-497
3-400.75	3.1-498
3-400.76	3.1-499
3-400.77	3.1-500
3-400.78	3.1-501
3-400.79	3.1-502
3-400.80	3.1-503
3-400.81	3.1-504
3-400.82	3.1-505
3-400.83	3.1-506
3-400.84	3.1-507
3-400.85	3.1-508
3-400.86	3.1-509
3-400.87	3.1-510
3-400.88	3.1-511
3-400.89	3.1-512
3-400.90	3.1-513
3-400.91	3.1-514
3-400.92	3.1-515
3-400.93	3.1-516
3-400.94	3.1-517
3-400.95	3.1-518
3-400.96	3.1-519
3-400.97	3.1-520
3-400.98	3.1-521
3-400.99	3.1-522
3-400.100	3.1-523
3-400.101	3.1-524
3-400.102	3.1-525
3-400.103	3.1-526
3-400.104	3.1-527
3-400.105	3.1-528
3-400.106	3.1-529
3-400.107	3.1-530
3-401	3.1-531
3-402	3.1-532
3-403	3.1-533
3-404	3.1-534
3-405	3.1-535
3-406	3.1-536
3-407	3.1-537
3-408	3.1-538
3-409	3.1-539
3-410	3.1-540
3-411	3.1-541
3-412	3.1-542
3-413	3.1-543
3-414	3.1-544
3-415	3.1-545
3-416 to 3-451	Repealed
3-451.1	3.1-546
3-451.2	3.1-547
3-451.3	3.1-548
3-451.4	3.1-549
3-451.5	3.1-550
3-451.6	3.1-551
3-451.7	3.1-552
3-452.8	3.1-553
3-452.9	3.1-554
3-452.10	3.1-555
3-451.11	Repealed
3-451.11:1	3.1-556
3-451.12	3.1-557
3-451.13	3.1-558
3-451.14	3.1-559
3-451.15	3.1-560
3-451.16	3.1-561
3-451.17	3.1-562
3-452	3.1-563
3-453	3.1-564
3-454	3.1-565
3-455	3.1-566
3-456	3.1-567
3-457	3.1-568
3-458	3.1-569
3-459	3.1-570
3-460	3.1-571
3-461	3.1-572
3-462	3.1-573
3-463	3.1-574
3-464	3.1-575
3-465	3.1-576
3-466	3.1-577
3-467	3.1-578
3-468	3.1-579
3-469	3.1-580
3-470	3.1-581
3-471	3.1-582
3-472	3.1-583
3-473	3.1-584
3-474	3.1-585
3-475	3.1-586
3-476	3.1-587
3-477 to 3-482	Deleted
3-483	3.1-588
3-484	3.1-589
3-485	3.1-590
3-486	3.1-591
3-487	3.1-592
3-488	3.1-593
3-489	3.1-594
3-490	3.1-595
3-491	3.1-596
3-492	3.1-597
3-493	3.1-598
3-494	3.1-599
3-495	3.1-600
3-496	3.1-601
3-497	3.1-602
3-498	3.1-603

Former Section	Present Section
3-499	3.1-604
3-500	3.1-605
3-501	3.1-606
3-502	3.1-607
3-503	3.1-608
3-504	3.1-609
3-505	3.1-610
3-506 to 3-512	Repealed
3-512.1	3.1-611
3-512.2	3.1-612
3-512.3	3.1-613
3-512.4	3.1-614
3-512.5	3.1-615
3-512.6	3.1-616
3-512.7	3.1-617
3-512.8	3.1-618
3-512.9	3.1-619
3-512.10	3.1-620
3-512.11	3.1-621
3-512.12	3.1-622
3-512.13	3.1-623
3-512.14	3.1-624
3-512.15	3.1-625
3-512.16	3.1-626
3-512.17	3.1-627
3-512.18	3.1-628
3-512.19	3.1-629
3-512.20	3.1-630
3-513	3.1-631
3-513.1	3.1-632
3-513.2	3.1-633
3-514	3.1-634
3-515	3.1-635
3-516	3.1-636
3-517	3.1-637
3-518	3.1-638
3-519	3.1-639
3-520	3.1-640
3-521	3.1-641
3-522	3.1-642
3-523	3.1-643
3-523.1	3.1-644
3-524	3.1-645
3-525	3.1-646
3-525.1	3.1-647
3-525.2	3.1-648
3-525.3	3.1-649
3-525.4	3.1-650
3-525.5	3.1-651
3-525.6	3.1-652
3-525.7	3.1-653
3-525.8	3.1-654
3-525.9	3.1-655
3-525.10	3.1-656
3-525.11	3.1-657
3-525.12	3.1-658
3-525.13	3.1-659
3-525.14	3.1-660
3-525.15	3.1-661
3-525.16	3.1-662
3-525.17	3.1-663
3-525.18	3.1-664
3-525.19	3.1-665
3-525.20	3.1-666
3-525.21	3.1-667
3-525.22	3.1-668
3-525.23	3.1-669
3-525.24	3.1-670
3-525.25	3.1-671
3-525.26	3.1-672
3-525.27	3.1-673
3-525.28	3.1-674
3-525.29	3.1-675
3-525.30	3.1-676
3-525.31	3.1-677
3-525.32	3.1-678
3-525.33	3.1-679
3-525.34	3.1-680
3-525.35	3.1-681
3-525.36	3.1-682
3-525.37	3.1-683
3-525.38	3.1-684
3-526	3.1-685
3-527	3.1-686
3-528	3.1-687
3-529	3.1-688
3-530	3.1-689
3-531	3.1-690
3-532	Deleted
3-533	3.1-691
3-534	3.1-692
3-535	3.1-693
3-536	3.1-694
3-537	3.1-695
3-538	3.1-696
3-539	3.1-697
3-540	3.1-698
3-541	3.1-699
3-542	3.1-700
3-543	3.1-701
3-544	3.1-702
3-545	3.1-703
3-546	3.1-704
3-547	3.1-705
3-548	3.1-706
3-549	3.1-707
3-550	3.1-708
3-551	3.1-709
3-552	3.1-710
3-553	3.1-711
3-554	3.1-712
3-555	3.1-713
3-556	3.1-714
3-557	3.1-715
3-558	3.1-716
3-559	3.1-717
3-560	3.1-718
3-561	3.1-719
3-562	3.1-720
3-563	3.1-721
3-564	3.1-722
3-565	3.1-723
3-566	3.1-724
3-567	3.1-725
3-568	3.1-726
3-569	3.1-727
3-570	3.1-728
3-571	3.1-729
3-572	3.1-730
3-573	3.1-731
3-574	3.1-732
3-575	3.1-733
3-576	3.1-734
3-576.1	3.1-735
3-577	3.1-736
3-578	3.1-737
3-579	3.1-738
3-579.1, 3-579.2	Deleted
3-580	3.1-739
3-581	Deleted
3-582	3.1-740
3-583	3.1-741
3-583.1	3.1-742
3-583.2	3.1-743
3-583.3	3.1-744
3-583.4	3.1-745
3-583.5	3.1-746
3-583.6	3.1-747
3-583.7	3.1-748
3-583.8	Deleted
3-584	3.1-749
3-585	3.1-750
3-586	3.1-751
3-587	3.1-752
3-588	Deleted
3-589	3.1-753
3-590	3.1-754
3-591	3.1-755
3-592	3.1-756
3-593	Deleted
3-594	3.1-757
3-594.1	Deleted
3-595 to 3-598	Repealed
3-598.1	3.1-758
3-598.2	3.1-759
3-598.3	3.1-760
3-598.4	3.1-761
3-598.5	3.1-762
3-598.6	3.1-763
3-598.7	3.1-763.1
3-598.8	3.1-763.2
3-598.9	3.1-763.3
3-598.10	3.1-763.4
3-598.11	3.1-763.5
3-598.12	3.1-763.6
3-598.13	3.1-763.7
3-598.14	3.1-763.8
3-598.15	3.1-763.9
3-598.16	3.1-763.10
3-598.17	3.1-763.11
3-598.18	3.1-763.12
3-598.19	3.1-763.13
3-599	3.1-764

Former Section	Present Section
3-600	3.1-765
3-601	3.1-766
3-602	3.1-767
3-603	3.1-768
3-603.1	3.1-769
3-604	3.1-770
3-605	3.1-771
3-606	3.1-772
3-607	3.1-773
3-608	3.1-774
3-609	3.1-775
3-609.1	3.1-776
3-609.2	3.1-777
3-609.3	3.1-778
3-609.4	3.1-779
3-609.5	3.1-780
3-609.6	3.1-781
3-609.7	3.1-782
3-609.8	3.1-783
3-609.9	3.1-784
3-609.10	3.1-785
3-609.11	3.1-786
3-609.12	3.1-787
3-609.13	3.1-788
3-609.14	3.1-789
3-609.15	3.1-790
3-609.16	3.1-791
3-609.17	3.1-792
3-609.18	3.1-793
3-609.19	3.1-794
3-609.20	3.1-795
3-609.21	3.1-796
3-610	3.1-797
3-611	3.1-798
3-612	3.1-799
3-613	3.1-800
3-614	3.1-801
3-615	3.1-802
3-616	3.1-803
3-617	3.1-804
3-618	3.1-805
3-619	3.1-806
3-620	3.1-807
3-621	3.1-808
3-621.1	3.1-809
3-622	3.1-810
3-623	3.1-811
3-624	3.1-812
3-625	Repealed
3-626	3.1-813
3-627	3.1-814
3-628	3.1-815
3-629	3.1-816
3-630	3.1-817
3-630.1	Repealed
3-631	3.1-818
3-632, 3-633	Repealed
3-634	3.1-819
3-634.1	3.1-820
3-634.2	3.1-821
3-635	3.1-822
3-636	3.1-823
3-637	3.1-824
3-638	3.1-825
3-639	3.1-826
3-640	3.1-827
3-641	3.1-828
3-642 to 3-646	Repealed
3-646.1	3.1-829
3-646.1:1	3.1-830
3-646.2	3.1-831
3-646.3	3.1-832
3-646.4	3.1-833
3-646.5	3.1-834
3-646.6	3.1-835
3-646.7	3.1-836
3-646.8	3.1-837
3-646.8:1	3.1-838
3-646.9	3.1-839
3-646.10	3.1-840
3-646.11	3.1-841
3-646.12	3.1-842
3-646.13	3.1-843
3-646.14	3.1-844
3-646.15	3.1-845
3-647	3.1-846
3-648	3.1-847
3-649	3.1-848
3-650	3.1-849
3-651	3.1-850
3-652	3.1-851
3-653	3.1-852
3-654	3.1-853
3-655	3.1-854
3-656	3.1-855
3-657	3.1-856
3-658	3.1-857
3-659	3.1-858
3-660	3.1-859
3-661	3.1-860
3-662	3.1-861
3-663	3.1-862
3-664	3.1-863
3-665	3.1-864
3-666	3.1-865
3-666.1	3.1-866
3-667	3.1-867
3-668	3.1-868
3-669	3.1-869
3-670	3.1-870
3-671	3.1-871
3-672	3.1-872
3-673	3.1-873
3-674	3.1-874
3-675	3.1-875
3-676	3.1-876
3-676.1	3.1-877
3-676.2	3.1-878
3-676.3	3.1-879
3-676.4	3.1-880
3-676.4:1	3.1-881
3-676.4:2	3.1-882
3-676.5	3.1-883
3-676.6	3.1-884
3-676.7	3.1-884.1
3-676.8	3.1-884.2
3-676.9	3.1-884.3
3-676.10	3.1-884.4
3-676.11	3.1-884.5
3-676.12	3.1-884.6
3-676.13	3.1-884.7
3-676.14	3.1-884.8
3-676.15	3.1-884.9
3-676.16	3.1-884.10
3-676.17	3.1-884.11
3-676.18	3.1-884.12
3-676.19	3.1-884.13
3-676.20	3.1-884.14
3-676.21	3.1-884.15
3-676.22	3.1-884.16
3-677 to 3-689	Repealed
3-689.1	3.1-885
3-689.2	3.1-886
3-689.3	3.1-887
3-689.4	3.1-888
3-689.5	3.1-889
3-689.6	3.1-890
3-689.7	3.1-891
3-689.8	3.1-892
3-689.9	3.1-893
3-689.10	3.1-894
3-689.11	3.1-895
3-689.12	3.1-896
3-689.13	3.1-897
3-689.14	3.1-898
3-690	3.1-899
3-691	3.1-900
3-692	3.1-901
3-693	3.1-902
3-694	3.1-903
3-695	3.1-904
3-696	3.1-905
3-697	3.1-906
3-698	3.1-907
3-699	3.1-908
3-700	3.1-909
3-701	3.1-910
3-702	3.1-911
3-703	3.1-912
3-704	3.1-913
3-705	3.1-914
3-706	3.1-915
3-706.1	3.1-916
3-706.2	3.1-917
3-707	3.1-918
3-708	Deleted
3-708.1	3.1-919
3-708.2	3.1-920
3-708.3	3.1-921
3-708.4	3.1-922
3-708.5	3.1-923
3-708.6	3.1-924
3-708.7	3.1-925

Former Section	Present Section
3-708.8	3.1-926
3-708.9	3.1-927
3-708.10	3.1-928
3-708.11	3.1-929
3-708.12	3.1-930
3-708.13	3.1-931
3-708.14	3.1-932
3-708.15	3.1-933
3-708.16	3.1-934
3-708.17	3.1-935
3-708.18	3.1-936
3-708.19	3.1-937
3-708.20	3.1-938
3-708.21	3.1-939
3-708.22	3.1-940
3-708.23	3.1-941
3-708.24	3.1-942
3-708.25	3.1-943
3-708.26	3.1-944
3-708.27	3.1-945
3-708.28	3.1-946
3-708.29	3.1-947
3-708.30	3.1-948
3-708.31	3.1-949
3-708.32	3.1-950
3-708.33	3.1-951
3-708.34	3.1-952
3-708.35	3.1-953
3-708.36	3.1-954
3-708.37	3.1-955
3-708.38	3.1-956
3-708.39	3.1-957
3-708.40	3.1-958
3-708.41	3.1-959
3-708.42	3.1-960
3-708.43	3.1-961
3-708.44	3.1-962
3-708.45	3.1-963
3-708.46	3.1-964
3-708.47	3.1-965
3-708.48	3.1-966
3-708.49	3.1-967
3-708.50	3.1-968
3-708.51, 3-708.52	Deleted
3-708.53	3.1-969
3-709	Deleted
3-709.1	3.1-970
3-709.2	3.1-971
3-709.3	3.1-972
3-709.4	3.1-973
3-709.5	3.1-974
3-709.6	3.1-975
3-709.7	3.1-976
3-709.8	3.1-977
3-709.9	3.1-978
3-709.10	3.1-979
3-709.11	3.1-980
3-709.12	3.1-981
3-709.13	3.1-982
3-709.14	3.1-983
3-709.15	3.1-984
3-709.16	3.1-985
3-709.17	3.1-986
3-709.18	3.1-987
3-709.19	3.1-988
3-709.20	3.1-989
3-709.21	3.1-990
3-709.22, 3-709.23	Deleted
3-710	3.1-991
3-711	3.1-992
3-712	3.1-993
3-713	3.1-994
3-714	3.1-995
3-715	3.1-996
3-716	3.1-997
3-717	3.1-998
3-718	3.1-999
3-719	3.1-1000
3-720	3.1-1001
3-721	3.1-1002
3-722	3.1-1003
3-723	3.1-1004
3-724	3.1-1005
3-725	3.1-1006
3-726	3.1-1007
3-727	3.1-1008
3-728	3.1-1009
3-729	3.1-1010

COMPARABLE SECTIONS OF TITLE 4 AND TITLE 4.1

Former Section	Present Section
4-1	Deleted
4-2	4.1-100
4-3	4.1-101
4-4	4.1-102
4-5	Repealed
4-6	Deleted
4-6.1	Deleted
4-7	4.1-103
4-8	4.1-105
4-9	Deleted
4-10	4.1-109
4-10.1	4.1-108
4-11	4.1-111
4-12	4.1-106
4-13	4.1-115
4-14	4.1-115
4-15	4.1-119
4-15.01	4.1-119
4-15.1	Repealed
4-15.2	Repealed
4-15.3	Repealed
4-16	Deleted
4-17	4.1-110
4-18	4.1-104
4-19	4.1-120
4-20	4.1-107
4-21	4.1-115
4-22	4.1-116
	4.1-117
4-22.1	4.1-118
	4.1-234
	4.1-235
4-23	4.1-116
4-24	Repealed
4-24.1	Repealed
4-25	4.1-206
	4.1-207
	4.1-208
	4.1-209
	4.1-214
	4.1-218
4-25.1	4.1-207
	4.1-214
	4.1-230
4-26	4.1-212
	4.1-229
	4.1-230
4-27	4.1-213
	4.1-214
4-28	Deleted
4-29	4.1-207
4-30	4.1-230
4-31	4.1-222
	4.1-223
	4.1-224
4-32	4.1-215
4-32.1	4.1-215
4-33	4.1-230
	4.1-231
	4.1-232
4-34	4.1-203
	4.1-211
4-34.1	4.1-327
4-35	4.1-232
4-36	4.1-111
4-37	4.1-225
	4.1-227
	4.1-228
4-37.1	4.1-226
4-37.2	4.1-202
4-38	4.1-205
	4.1-233
4-39	Deleted
4-40 to 4-43	Repealed
4-44	4.1-204
4-45	4.1-121
4-45.1	Repealed
4-45.2	Deleted

Former Section	Present Section
4-45.3	Deleted
4-46	4.1-122
4-47	4.1-127
4-48	4.1-200
4-49	Repealed
4-50	4.1-200
4-51	4.1-333
4-52	4.1-322
	4.1-334
4-53	4.1-336
4-54	4.1-337
4-55	4.1-338
4-56	4.1-339
	4.1-340
	4.1-341
	4.1-342
	4.1-343
	4.1-344
	4.1-345
	4.1-346
	4.1-347
	4.1-348
4-57	4.1-300
4-57.1	4.1-301
4-58	4.1-302
4-59	4.1-212
4-60	4.1-324
4-61	4.1-315
4-61.1	4.1-316
4-61.2	4.1-212
	4.1-229
4-62	4.1-304
	4.1-305
4-63	4.1-307
4-64	4.1-326
4-65	4.1-331
4-66	4.1-326
4-67	Repealed
4-68	Deleted
4-69	4.1-320
4-69.1	Repealed
4-69.2	4.1-113
	4.1-329
4-70	4.1-319
4-71	4.1-303
4-72	Repealed
4-72.1	4.1-311
4-73	4.1-306
4-73.1, 4-73.2	Repealed
4-74	4.1-312
4-75	4.1-313
4-76	Deleted
4-77	4.1-212
	4.1-314
4-78	4.1-308
4-78.1	4.1-309
4-79	Repealed
4-79.1	4.1-216
	4.1-328
4-80 to 4-80.2	Repealed
4-81	4.1-317
4-82	4.1-335
4-83	4.1-318
4-84	4.1-310
4-84.1	4.1-130
4-85	4.1-131
4-86	4.1-132
4-87	4.1-323
4-88	4.1-354
4-89	4.1-200
	4.1-201
4-90	4.1-352
4-90.1	4.1-353
4-90.2	Deleted
4-91	4.1-351
4-92	4.1-349
4-93	4.1-321
4-94	4.1-350
4-95	Repealed
4-96	4.1-128
4-96.1, 4-96.2	Expired
4-96.3	4.1-123
4-97	4.1-129
4-98	Deleted
4-98.1	4.1-100
4-98.2	4.1-210
4-98.3	4.1-210
4-98.4	4.1-202
4-98.5	4.1-111
4-98.6	4.1-204
4-98.7	4.1-114
4-98.8	Deleted
4-98.9	4.1-223
4-98.10	4.1-325
4-98.11	4.1-221
4-98.12	4.1-124
4-98.12:1	4.1-125
4-98.12:2	4.1-126
4-98.13	4.1-124
4-98.14	4.1-111
4-98.15	Deleted
4-98.16	4.1-212
	4.1-229
	4.1-230
	4.1-330
4-98.17	4.1-223
4-98.18	4.1-231
4-98.19	4.1-233
4-98.20	4.1-234
4-99 to 4-118.3	Deleted
4-118.4	4.1-500
4-118.5	4.1-502
4-118.6	4.1-503
4-118.6:1	4.1-504
4-118.7	4.1-505
4-118.8	4.1-506
4-118.9	4.1-507
4-118.10	4.1-508
4-118.11	4.1-509
4-118.12	4.1-510
4-118.12:1	4.1-511
4-118.13	4.1-512
4-118.14	4.1-513
4-118.15	4.1-514
4-118.16	4.1-515
4-118.17	Repealed
4-118.18	4.1-501
4-118.19	4.1-516
4-118.20	Deleted
4-118.20:1	4.1-517
4-118.21 to 4-118.41	Repealed
4-118.42	4.1-400
4-118.43	4.1-401
4-118.44	4.1-403
4-118.45	4.1-404
4-118.46	4.1-405
4-118.47	4.1-406
4-118.48	4.1-407
4-118.49	4.1-408
4-118.50	4.1-409
4-118.51	4.1-410
4-118.52	4.1-411
4-118.53	4.1-412
4-118.54	4.1-413
4-118.55	4.1-414
4-118.56	4.1-415
4-118.57	4.1-416
4-118.58	4.1-402
4-118.59	4.1-417
4-118.60	4.1-418
4-118.61	Deleted
4-119 to 4-126	Repealed
4-127	4.1-100
4-128	4.1-236
4-129	4.1-236
4-130	4.1-236
4-131	4.1-239
4-132	4.1-239
4-133	4.1-239
4-134	4.1-204
4-135	4.1-205
4-136	4.1-331
4-137	4.1-204
4-138	4.1-238
4-139	4.1-332
4-140	4.1-332
4-141	4.1-237
4-142	4.1-237
4-143	Deleted
4-144	4.1-112
4-145	4.1-118

COMPARABLE SECTIONS OF TITLE 5 AND TITLE 5.1

Former Section	Present Section	Former Section	Present Section	Former Section	Present Section
5-1	5.1-1	5-18	5.1-29	5-41	5.1-50
5-2	5.1-2	5-19	5.1-30	5-42	5.1-51
5-3	5.1-3	5-20	5.1-31	5-43	5.1-52
5-4	5.1-2, 5.1-4	5-21	5.1-32	5-44	5.1-53
5-5	5.1-5	5-22	5.1-33	5-45	5.1-54
5-6	5.1-6	5-23	5.1-34	5-46	5.1-55
5-7	5.1-7	5-24	5.1-35	5-47	5.1-56
5-8	5.1-8	5-24.1	5.1-36	5-48	5.1-57
5-9	5.1-9	5-24.2	5.1-36.1	5-49	5.1-58
5-9.1	5.1-9.1	5-25	5.1-46	5-50	5.1-59
5-10	5.1-10	5-26	5.1-37	5-51	5.1-60
5-10.1	5.1-13	5-27	5.1-38	5-52	5.1-61
5-10.2	5.1-14	5-28	5.1-39	5-52.1	5.1-62
5-10.3	5.1-15	5-29	5.1-31	5-52.2	5.1-63
5-10.4	5.1-16	5-30	5.1-33	5-52.3	5.1-64
5-10.5	5.1-17	5-31	5.1-34	5-52.4	5.1-65
5-10.6	5.1-18	5-32	Deleted	5-52.5	5.1-66
5-10.7	5.1-19	5-33	5.1-42	5-52.6	5.1-67
5-11	5.1-24	5-34	5.1-41	5-53	5.1-68
5-12	5.1-25	5-35	5.1-43	5-54	5.1-69
5-13	5.1-11	5-36	5.1-44	5-55	5.1-70
5-14	5.1-12	5-37	5.1-23	5-56	5.1-71
5-14.1	5.1-20	5-38	5.1-40	5-57	5.1-72
5-14.2	5.1-21	5-39	5.1-45	5-58	5.1-73
5-14.3	5.1-22	5-39.1	5.1-47	5-59	5.1-74
5-15	5.1-26	5-39.2	5.1-48	5-60	5.1-75
5-16	5.1-27	5-39.3	Deleted	5-61	5.1-76
5-17	5.1-28	5-40	5.1-49	None	5.1-7.1

COMPARABLE SECTIONS OF TITLE 6 AND TITLE 6.1

Former Section	Present Section	Former Section	Present Section	Former Section	Present Section
6-1	6.1-1	6-23.1	6.1-10	6-45	Deleted
6-2	Deleted	6-24	6.1-8	6-46	6.1-54
6-3	6.1-124	6-25	6.1-9	6-47	6.1-55
6-4	6.1-2	6-26	6.1-39	6-48	6.1-56
6-5	6.1-3	6-27	6.1-39	6-49	6.1-57
6-6	6.1-4	6-27.1	6.1-4, 6.1-40	6-49.1	6.1-58
6-7	Deleted	6-27.2	6.1-39	6-50	6.1-59
6-8	6.1-7	6-28	6.1-41	6-51	6.1-60
6-9	6.1-5	6-29	6.1-113	6-52	6.1-69
6-10	6.1-6	6-29.1	6.1-42	6-53	6.1-70
6-11	Deleted	6-30	6.1-12	6-54	6.1-71
6-12, 6-12.1	Repealed	6-31	6.1-13	6-55	6.1-72
6-13	Deleted	6-32	Repealed	6-55.1	6.1-73
6-14	6.1-33	6-33	Deleted	6-56	6.1-74
6-15	Repealed	6-34	6.1-14	6-57	6.1-75
6-15.1	6.1-38	6-35	6.1-15	6-58	6.1-106
6-15.2	6.1-34	6-36	6.1-45	6-59	6.1-107
6-15.3	6.1-37	6-37	6.1-47	6-60	6.1-108
6-16, 6-17	Repealed	6-38	Deleted	6-61	6.1-109
6-18	6.1-35	6-39	6.1-48	6-62	6.1-76
6-19	6.1-36	6-40	6.1-49	6-62.1	6.1-77
6-20	6.1-43	6-41	6.1-50	6-63	Repealed
6-21	6.1-44	6-42	6.1-51	6-64	6.1-78
6-22	Deleted	6-43	6.1-52	6-65	6.1-79
6-23	6.1-11	6-44	6.1-53	6-66	6.1-80

Former Section	Present Section
6-67, 6-68	Repealed
6-69	6.1-105
6-70	6.1-83
6-71 to 6-75	Repealed
6-76	6.1-61
6-77	6.1-62
6-78	6.1-63 to 6.1-65
6-79, 6-79.1	Repealed
6-79.2	6.1-66
6-80	6.1-67
6-81	6.1-110
6-82	6.1-68
6-83 to 6-90	Repealed
6-91	6.1-16
6-92	Deleted
6-93	Repealed
6-94	6.1-17
6-95	6.1-18
6-96	6.1-19
6-97	6.1-20
6-98	6.1-23
6-99	6.1-21
6-100	6.1-22
6-101	6.1-23
6-102	6.1-24
6-103	6.1-32
6-103.1	6.1-31
6-104	6.1-17
6-105	6.1-93
6-106	6.1-84
6-107	6.1-85
6-108	6.1-86
6-109	6.1-87
6-110	6.1-88
6-111	6.1-89
6-112	6.1-90
6-113	6.1-92
6-114	6.1-100
6-115	6.1-101
6-116	6.1-102
6-117	6.1-103
6-118	6.1-104
6-119	6.1-91
6-120, 6-121	Deleted
6-122	6.1-94
6-123	6.1-95
6-124	6.1-96
6-125	6.1-97
6-126	6.1-98
6-127	6.1-99
6-128	6.1-114, 6.1-122
6-129	6.1-115
6-129.1	6.1-116
6-130	6.1-117
6-131	6.1-118
6-132	6.1-119
6-133	6.1-111
6-134	6.1-112
6-135	Deleted
6-136	6.1-120
6-137	6.1-121
6-138	6.1-122
6-139	6.1-123
6-140 to 6-201	Repealed
6-201.1	6.1-126
6-201.2	6.1-127
6-201.3	6.1-128
6-201.4	6.1-129
6-201.5	6.1-130
6-201.6	6.1-131
6-201.7	6.1-132
6-201.8	6.1-133
6-201.9	6.1-134
6-201.10	6.1-135
6-201.11	6.1-136
6-201.12	6.1-137
6-201.13	6.1-138
6-201.14	6.1-140
6-201.15	6.1-141
6-201.16	6.1-142
6-201.17	6.1-143
6-201.18	6.1-144
6-201.19	6.1-145
6-201.20	6.1-146
6-201.21	6.1-148
6-201.22	6.1-149
6-201.22:1	6.1-149.1
6-201.23	6.1-150
6-201.24	6.1-151
6-201.25	6.1-152
6-201.26	6.1-153
6-201.26:1	6.1-154
6-201.27	6.1-155
6-201.28	6.1-156
6-201.29	6.1-157
6-201.29:1	6.1-158
6-201.30	6.1-160
6-201.31	6.1-161
6-201.32	6.1-162
6-201.33	6.1-163
6-201.34	6.1-164
6-201.35	6.1-165
6-201.36	6.1-166
6-201.37	6.1-167
6-201.38	6.1-168
6-201.39	6.1-169
6-201.40	6.1-170
6-201.41	6.1-171
6-201.42	6.1-172
6-201.43	6.1-173
6-201.44	6.1-174
6-201.45	6.1-175
6-201.46	6.1-176
6-201.47	6.1-177
6-201.48	6.1-178
6-201.49	6.1-179
6-201.50	6.1-180
6-201.51	6.1-181
6-201.52	6.1-182
6-201.53	6.1-183
6-201.54	6.1-184
6-201.55	6.1-185
6-201.56	6.1-186
6-201.57	6.1-187
6-201.58	6.1-188
6-201.59	6.1-189
6-201.60	6.1-190
6-201.61	6.1-191
6-201.62	6.1-192
6-201.63	6.1-193
6-202	Deleted
6-203	6.1-224
6-204	6.1-196
6-205	6.1-197
6-206	6.1-222.1
6-207	6.1-198
6-208	6.1-199
6-209	6.1-200
6-210	6.1-201
6-211	6.1-202
6-212	6.1-203
6-213	6.1-204
6-214	6.1-206
6-215	6.1-207
6-216	6.1-208
6-217	6.1-205
6-218	6.1-209
6-219	6.1-210
6-220	6.1-211
6-221	6.1-212
6-222	6.1-213
6-223	6.1-214
6-224	6.1-215
6-225	6.1-216
6-226	6.1-217
6-227	6.1-218
6-228	6.1-219
6-229	6.1-220
6-230	6.1-221
6-231	6.1-222
6-232	6.1-223
6-233	6.1-225
6-234	6.1-226
6-235 to 6-241	Deleted
6-242	6.1-227
6-243	Deleted
6-244	6.1-227
6-245	6.1-228, 6.1-230
6-246 to 6-249	Deleted
6-250	6.1-228, 6.1-234
6-251	6.1-232
6-252	6.1-235
6-253	6.1-234
6-254	6.1-234
6-255	6.1-229, 6.1-231
6-256	6.1-236
6-257	6.1-237
6-258	6.1-238
6-259	6.1-239
6-260	6.1-240
6-261	6.1-241
6-262	6.1-242
6-263	6.1-331

Former Section	Present Section
6-264	6.1-332
6-264.1	6.1-333
6-265	6.1-334
6-266	6.1-335
6-267	6.1-336
6-268	6.1-337
6-269	6.1-338
6-270	6.1-339
6-271	6.1-340
6-272	6.1-341
6-273	6.1-342
6-274	6.1-244
6-275	6.1-245
6-276	6.1-246
6-277	6.1-247
6-278	6.1-248
6-279	6.1-249
6-280	6.1-250
6-281	6.1-251
6-282	6.1-252
6-283	6.1-253
6-284	6.1-254
6-285	6.1-255
6-286	6.1-256
6-287	6.1-257
6-288	6.1-258
6-289	6.1-259
6-290	6.1-260
6-291	6.1-261
6-292	6.1-262
6-293	6.1-263
6-294	6.1-264
6-295	6.1-265
6-296	6.1-266
6-297	6.1-267
6-298	6.1-268
6-299	6.1-269
6-300	6.1-270
6-301	6.1-271
6-302	6.1-272
6-303	6.1-273
6-304	6.1-274

Former Section	Present Section
6-305	6.1-275
6-306	6.1-276
6-307	6.1-277
6-308	6.1-278
6-309	6.1-279
6-310	6.1-280
6-311	6.1-281
6-312	6.1-282
6-313	6.1-283
6-314	6.1-284
6-315	6.1-285
6-316	6.1-286
6-316.1	6.1-287
6-317	6.1-288
6-318	6.1-289
6-319	6.1-290
6-320	6.1-291
6-321	6.1-292
6-322	6.1-293
6-323	6.1-294
6-324	6.1-295
6-325	6.1-296
6-326	6.1-297
6-327	6.1-298
6-328	6.1-299
6-329	6.1-300
6-330	6.1-301
6-331	6.1-302
6-332	6.1-303
6-333	6.1-304
6-334	6.1-305
6-335	6.1-306
6-336	6.1-307
6-337	6.1-308
6-338	6.1-309
6-339	6.1-311
6-340	6.1-312
6-341	6.1-313
6-342	6.1-314
6-343	6.1-315
6-344	6.1-316
6-345	6.1-317

Former Section	Present Section
6-346	6.1-318
6-347	6.1-319
6-348	6.1-320
6-348.1	6.1-321
6-348.2	6.1-322
6-348.3	6.1-323
6-348.4	6.1-324
6-349	6.1-325
6-350	6.1-326
6-351	6.1-327
6-351.1	6.1-328
6-352	6.1-329
6-352.1	6.1-330
6-352.2	6.1-330.1
6-352.3	6.1-330.2
6-352.4	6.1-330.3
6-352.5	6.1-330.4
6-353 to 6-421	Repealed
6-422	Deleted
6-423 to 6-568	Repealed
6-569	Deleted
6-570	6.1-25
6-571	6.1-26
6-572	6.1-27
6-573	6.1-28
6-574	6.1-29
6-575	6.1-30
6-576	Deleted
6-577	6.1-343
6-578	6.1-344
6-579	6.1-345
6-580	6.1-346
6-581	6.1-347
6-582	6.1-348
6-583	6.1-349
6-584	6.1-350
6-585	6.1-351
None	6.1-46
None	6.1-139
None	6.1-233

COMPARABLE SECTIONS OF TITLE 7 AND 7.1

Former Section	Present Section
7-1	7.1-1
7-1.1	7.1-2
7-2	7.1-3
7-3	7.1-4
7-4	7.1-5
7-5	7.1-6
7-6	7.1-7
7-7	7.1-8
7-8	7.1-9
7-9	7.1-10
7-10	7.1-11
7-11 to 7-16	Deleted

Former Section	Present Section
7-17	7.1-13
7-18	7.1-14
7-19	7.1-15
7-20	7.1-16
7-21	7.1-17
7-22	7.1-19
7-23	7.1-20
7-24	7.1-21
7-25	7.1-22
7-25.1	7.1-23
7-25.2	7.1-24
7-25.3	7.1-25

Former Section	Present Section
7-26	7.1-26
7-27	7.1-27
7-28	7.1-28
7-29	7.1-29
7-30	7.1-30
7-31	7.1-31
7-32	7.1-32
7-33	7.1-33
7-33.1	7.1-34
7-34	7.1-35
7-34.1	7.1-36
7-35	7.1-37

Former Section	Present Section
7-36	7.1-38
7-37	7.1-39
None	7.1-12
None	7.1-18
None	7.1-31.1

COMPARABLE SECTIONS OF TITLE 8 AND TITLE 8.01

Former Section	Present Section
8-1 to 8-1.2	8.01-3
8-1.3	8.01-4
8-2	8.01-1
8-3	8.01-4.1
8-4	8.01-4.2
8-4.1	8.01-327.2
8-4.1:1	Deleted
8-4.2	8.01-289
8-4.3	Deleted
8-5	8.01-236
8-5.1	8.01-255.1
8-6	Deleted
8-7	8.01-237
8-8	8.01-229
	8.01-237
8-9	8.01-238
8-10	8.01-239
8-10.1	8.01-240
8-10.2	8.01-240
8-11	8.01-241
8-12	8.01-242
8-13	8.01-229
	8.01-243
	8.01-245
	8.01-246
	8.01-249
8-14	8.01-249
8-15	8.01-229
	8.01-230
	8.01-245
	8.01-249
8-16	8.01-245
8-17	8.01-246
8-18	Deleted
8-19	8.01-253
8-20	8.01-229
8-21	8.01-254
8-22	8.01-252
8-23	8.01-247
8-24	8.01-243
	8.01-248
8-24.1	8.01-249
8-24.2	8.01-250
8-25	8.01-229
8-26	8.01-229
8-27	8.01-232
8-28	8.01-232
8-29 to 8-34	8.01-229
8-35	8.01-231
8-36	8.01-234
8-37	8.01-256
8-38	8.01-261
	8-01.262
	8.01-263
	8.01-265
8-39	8.01-262
8-40	Deleted
8-41	8.01-638
8-42	8.01-261
8-42.1	Repealed
8-43	8.01-286
8-44	8.01-292
	8.01-295
8-45	Repealed
8-46	Repealed
8-46.1	8.01-290
8-47	Deleted
8-47.1	Deleted
8-48	Repealed
8-49	8.01-294
8-50	8.01-295
8-51	8.01-296
8-52	8.01-293
	8.01-325
8-53	8.01-288
8-54	8.01-293
8-55	8.01-297
8-56	8.01-287
8-57	8.01-291
8-58	8.01-298
	8.01-353
8-59	8.01-299
	8.01-300
8-59.1	8.01-304
8-60	8.01-301
8-61	Repealed
8-62	Repealed
8-63	8.01-302
8-64	8.01-303
8-65	Deleted
8-66	8.01-15
	8.01-305
8-66.1	8.01-306
8-67	8.01-305
8-67.1	8.01-307
	8.01-308
	8.01-312
8-67.2	8.01-310
	8.01-312
	8.01-313
8-67.3	8.01-311
8-67.4	8.01-309
	8.01-310
8-67.5	Deleted
8-68	Deleted
8-69	8.01-314
8-70	8.01-315
8-71	8.01-316
8-72	8.01-317
8-73	8.01-318
8-73.1	Deleted
8-74	8.01-320
8-75	Deleted
8-76	8.01-319
8-77	8.01-321
8-78	8.01-322
8-79	Deleted
8-80	8.01-323
8-81	8.01-324
8-81.1	8.01-328
8-81.2	8.01-328.1
8-81.3	8.01-329
8.81.4	Deleted
8-81.5	8.01-330
8-82 to 8-86	Repealed
8-86.1	8.01-3
8-87	8.01-8
8-88	8.01-9
8-88.1	8.01-9
8-89	Deleted
8-90	8.01-10
8-91	Deleted
8-92	8.01-11
8-93	8.01-11
8-93.1	8.01-12
8-94	8.01-13
8-94.1	54-729.15
8-95	8.01-14
8-96	8.01-15
8-96.1	8.01-281
8-97	8.01-6
8-98	Deleted
8-99	8.01-273
8-100	Repealed
8-101	Repealed
8-102	8.01-275
8-103	Repealed
8-104	Repealed
8-105	Deleted
8-106	Deleted
8-107	Repealed
8-108	Repealed
8-109	8.01-275
8-110	Repealed
8-111	Deleted
8-111.1	Deleted

Former Section	Present Section
8-112	Repealed
8-113	Repealed
8-114 to 8-116	8.01-279
8-117	Repealed
8-118	8.01-276
	8.01-277
8-119	Deleted
8-120	8.01-273
8-121	Repealed
8-122	8.01-274
8-122.1	8.01-282
8-123	8.01-283
8-124 to 8-128	Repealed
8-129	8.01-7
8-130	8.01-284
8-131	8.01-280
8-132	Repealed
8-133	Deleted
8-134	8.01-272
8-135	8.01-278
8-135.1	8.01-278
8-136	Repealed
8-137	Repealed
8-138	8.01-270
8-138.1 to 8-139	Deleted
8-140	8.01-276
8-140.1	8.01-227
8-140.2	8.01-227
8-140.3	8.01-427.1
8-141	Deleted
8-142	8.01-268
8-143	8.01-269
8-144	Repealed
8-145	8.01-21
8-146	8.01-22
8-147	8.01-19
8-148	8.01-20
8-149	Deleted
8-150	8.01-16
8-151	Repealed
8-152	8.01-17
8-153	8.01-18
8-154	8.01-335
8-155	8.01-23
8-156	8.01-23
8-157	8.01-265
8-158	Repealed
8-159	Deleted
8-160	8.01-331
8-161	Deleted
8-162	8.01-332
8-163	Deleted
8-164	8.01-334
8-165	8.01-331
8-166	Deleted
8-167	8.01-332
8-168	8.01-334
8-169	8.01-424
8-170	8.01-424
8-171	8.01-425
8-172	Deleted

Former Section	Present Section
8-173	8.01-425
8-174 to	
8-208.1	Repealed
8-208.2	8.01-337
8-208.3	8.01-338
8-208.4	8.01-339
8-208.5	8.01-340
8-208.6	8.01-341
8-208.6:1	8.01-341.1
8-208.7	8.01-342
	8.01-352
8-208.8	8.01-343
8-208.9	8.01-344
8-208.10	8.01-342
	8.01-345
8-208.11	8.01-346
8-208.12	8.01-347
8-208.13	8.01-348
8-208.14	8.01-349
8-208.14:1	8.01-350
8-208.15	8.01-351
8-208.16	8.01-353
8-208.17	8.01-355
8-208.18	8.01-356
8-208.19	8.01-357
8-208.20	Repealed
8-208.21	8.01-336
	8.01-359
8-208.22	8.01-360
8-208.23	8.01-361
8-208.24	8.01-354
8-208.25	8.01-362
8-208.26	8.01-363
8-208.27	8.01-352
	8.01-353
8-208.28	8.01-358
8-208.29	8.01-352
8-208.30	Repealed
8-208.31	Repealed
8-208.32	Deleted
8-208.33	14.1-195.1
8-208.34	14.1-195.2
8-208.35	14.1-195.3
8-208.36	14.1-195.4
8-208.37	14.1-195.5
8-208.38	14.1-195.6
8-209	8.01-374
8-210	Repealed
8-210.1	Repealed
8-210.2	Deleted
8-211	8.01-336
8-211.1	8.01-375
8-212 to	
8-214	8.01-336
8-215	8.01-358
8-216	8.01-376
8-217	8.01-377
8-218	8.01-378
8-219	8.01-379
8-220	8.01-380
8-221	8.01-381

Former Section	Present Section
8-222	Repealed
8-223	8.01-382
8-224	8.01-383
8-225 to 8-226	8.01-384
8-227	8.01-365
8-228	8.01-366
8-229	8.01-367
8-230	8.01-368
8-231	8.01-369
8-232	8.01-370
8-233	8.01-371
8-234	8.01-372
8-235	8.01-373
8-236 to 8-238	8.01-421
8-239	Deleted
8-239.1	16.1-88.01
8-239.2	16.1-88.02
8-240	Deleted
8-240.1	Deleted
8-241	8.01-422
8-242	Repealed
8-243	Repealed
8-244	8.01-233
	8.01-380
8-245	Deleted
8-246	8.01-423
8-247	Deleted
8-248	8.01-607
8-249	8.01-608
	8.01-609
8-250	8.01-610
8-251	8.01-611
8-252	8.01-612
8-253	8.01-613
8-254	8.01-614
8-255	8.01-614
8-256	Deleted
8-257	8.01-615
8-258	8.01-616
8-259	8.01-617
8-260	8.01-618
8-261	8.01-619
8-262	14.1-113.1
	14.1-133.1
8-263	Deleted
8-263.1	8.01-419
8-264	8.01-386
8-265	8.01-390
8-266	8.01-391
8-267	8.01-391
8-267.1	8.01-418
8-268	8.01-391
8-269	8.01-390
8-270	8.01-386
8-271	8.01-389
8-272	8.01-388
8-273	8.01-386
8-274	8.10-387
8-275 to 8-277	8.01-389
8-277.1	8.01-413
8-278 to	

Former Section	Present Section
8.279.2	8.01-391
8-280	8.01-392
8-281	8.01-393
8-282	8.01-394
8-283	8.01-394
8-284	8.01-395
8-285	8.01-396
8-286	8.01-397
8-287	8.01-398
8-288	19.2-271.2
8-289	8.01-398
8-289.1	8.01-399
8-289.2	8.01-400
8-290	8.01-401
8-291	8.01-401
8-292	8.01-403
8-293	8.01-404
8-294	8.01-405
8-295	8.01-406
8-296	8.01-407
8-296.1	8.01-402
8-297	8.01-407
8-298	8.01-408
8-299	8.01-409
8-300	19.2-269.1
8-300.1	8.01-410, 14.1-69.1
8-301 to 8-309	Deleted
8-310	Repealed
8-311 to 8-315	Deleted
8-315.1	8.01-420
8-316	Deleted
8-316.1	8.01-411
8-316.2	8.01-412
8-316.3	8.01-412.1
8-317 to 8-327.2	Deleted
8-328	8.01-414
8-329	8.01-325 8.01-415
8-329.1	20-61.2
8-330 to 8-342	Repealed
8-343	8.01-426
8-344	8.01-427
8-345	Repealed
8-346	Repealed
8-347	Deleted
8-348	8.01-428
8-349	8.01-429
8-350	8.01-383.1
8-351	Repealed
8-352	8.01-430
8-353	Deleted
8-353.1	Repealed
8-354	Deleted
8-355	8.01-431
8-356	8.01-432
8-357	8.01-433
8-358	8.01-434
8-359	8.01-435
8-360	8.01-436
8-361	8.01-437
8-362	8.01-438
8-363	8.01-439
8-364	8.01-440
8-365	14.1-178.1
8-366	8.01-441
8-367	8.01-442
8-368	8.01-443
8-369	8.01-444
8-370	8.01-445
8-371	8.01-445
8-372	8.01-445
8-373	8.01-446
8-374	Deleted
8-375	8.01-447
8-376	8.01-448
8-377	8.01-449
8-378	8.01-450
8-378.1	8.01-451
8-379	8.01-452
8-380	8.01-453
8-381	Deleted
8-382	8.01-454
8-383	8.01-455
8-384	8.01-456
8-385	8.01-457
8-386	8.01-458
8-387	8.01-459
8-388	8.01-460
8-389	8.01-461
8-390	Repealed
8-391	8.01-462
8-392	8.01-463
8-393	8.01-251
8-394	8.01-251
8-395	8.01-464
8-396	8.01-251
8-397	8.01-251
8-398	8.01-465
8-399	8.01-466
8-400	8.01-467
8-401	8.01-468 8.01-469
8-402	8.01-470
8-403	8.01-471
8-404	8.01-472
8-405	8.01-473
8-406	8.01-474
8-407	8.01-475
8-408	8.01-476 8.01-255.2
8-409	Repealed
8-410	8.01-477
8-411	8.01-478
8-412	8.01-479
8-413	8.01-480
8-414	8.01-481
8-415	8.01-482
8-416	8.01-483
8-417	8.01-484
8-418	8.01-485
8-419	8.01-486
8-420	8.01-487
8-421	8.01-488
8-421.1	8.01-489
8-421.2	8.01-490
8-422	8.01-491
8-422.1	8.01-492
8-422.2	8.01-493
8-423	8.01-494
8-424	8.01-495
8-425	8.01-496
8-426	8.01-497
8-427	8.01-498
8-428	Deleted
8-429	8.01-499
8-430	8.01-500
8-431	8.01-501
8-432	8.01-502
8-432.1	8.01-503
8-433	8.01-504
8-434	8.01-505
8-435	8.01-506
8-436	8.01-507
8-437	8.01-507.1
8-438	8.01-508
8-439	8.01-509
8-440	8.01-510
8-441	8.01-511
8-441.1	8.01-512
8-441.2	8.01-513
8-441.3	8.01-523
8-442	8.01-514
8-443	8.01-515
8-444	8.01-516
8-445	8.01-517
8-446	8.01-518
8-447	8.01-519
8-448	8.01-520
8-449	8.01-521
8-449.1	8.01-522
8-449.2	8.01-524
8-449.3	8.01-525
8-450	8.01-526
8-451	8.01-527
8-452	8.01-528
8-453	55-232
8-454	8.01-530
8-455	8.01-531
8-456	Deleted
8-457	16.1-77.1
8-458	8.01-529
8-459	8.01-532
8-460	16.1-91.1
8-461	16.1-91.2
8-462	8.01-670
8-463	8.01-671
8-464	8.01-672
8-465	8.01-676
8-466 to 8-468	Repealed
8-468.1	14.1-112.2
8-469	Repealed

Former Section	Present Section
8-470	Repealed
8-471	Deleted
8-472	Repealed
8-473	8.01-673
8-474	Repealed
8-475	8.01-674
8-476	8.01-675
8-477	8.01-676
8-478	8.01-676
8-479 to 8-480.1	Deleted
8-481	Repealed
8-482 to 8-484	Deleted
8-485	8.01-677
8-486	Deleted
8-487	8.01-678
8-488	Repealed
8-489	8.01-679
8-490	Deleted
8-490.1	Deleted
8-491	8.01-680
8-492	Repealed
8-493	8.01-681
8-494	Repealed
8-495	8.01-682
8-496	8.01-683
8-497	Deleted
8-497.1	8.01-684
8-498	8.01-685
8-499	8.01-686
8-500	8.01-687
8-501	8.01-673
8-502	8.01-688
8-503	8.01-577
8-504	8.01-578
8-505	8.01-579
8-506	8.01-580
8-507	8.01-581
8-508	Repealed
8-509	8.01-27
8-509.1	Repealed
8-510	Deleted
8-511	8.01-28
8-511.1	17-123.1
8-512	11-2.01
8-513	8.01-29
8-514	8.01-30
8-514.1	8.01-31
8-515	Repealed
8-516	Repealed
8-517	8.01-32
8-518	8.01-33
8-519	8.01-533
8-520	8.01-534
8-521	8.01-535
8-522	8.01-261
8-523	8.01-536
8-524	8.01-537
8-524.1	8.01-538
8-525	8.01-539
8-526	8.01-540
8-527	8.01-541
8-528	8.01-537
8-529	8.01-542
8-530	8.01-543
8-531	8.01-544
8-532	8.01-545
8-533	8.01-546
8-534	8.01-547
8-535	8.01-548
8-536	8.01-549
8-537	8.01-550
8-538	8.01-551
8-539	8.01-552
8-540	8.01-553
8-541	8.01-554
8-542	8.01-571
8-543	8.01-555
8-544	8.01-556
8-545	8.01-557
8-546	8.01-558
8-547	8.01-559
8-548	8.01-560
8-549	8.01-561
8-550	8.01-562
8-551	8.01-563
8-552	8.01-564
8-553	8.01-565
8-554	8.01-566
8-555	8.01-567
8-556	8.01-568
8-557	8.01-569
8-558	8.01-570
8-559	8.01-572
8-560	8.01-573
8-561	8.01-574
8-562	8.01-575
8-563	8.01-576
8-564	Deleted
8-565	Repealed
8-566 to 8-577	Deleted
8-577.1	8.01-217
8-578	8.01-184
8-579	8.01-185
8-580	Deleted
8-581	8.01-186
8-581.1	8.01-187
8-582	8.01-188
8-583	8.01-189
8-584	8.01-190
8-585	8.01-191
8-586	8.01-114
8-587	8.01-115
8-588	8.01-116
8-589	8.01-117
8-590	8.01-118
8-591	8.01-119
8-592	8.01-120
8-593	8.01-121
8-594	8.01-122
8-595	8.01-123
8-596	8.01-654
8-596.1	8.01-655
8-597	8.01-656
8-598	8.01-657
8-599	8.01-658
8-600	8.01-659
8-601	8.01-660
8-602	8.01-661
8-603	8.01-662
8-604	Deleted
8-605	8.01-663
8-606	8.01-664
8-607	8.01-665
8-608	8.01-666
8-608.1	8.01-667
8-609	8.01-668
8-610	8.01-620
8-611	8.01-621
8-612	8.01-622
8-613	8.01-623
8-614	8.01-624
8-615	8.01-625
8-616	Deleted
8-617	Deleted
8-618	8.01-626
8-619	8.01-627
8-620	8.01-628
8-621	8.01-629
8-622	8.01-630
8-623	8.01-631
8-624	8.01-632
8-625	8.01-633
8-626	8.01-634
8-627	8.01-34
8-628	Repealed
8-628.1	8.01-25
8-628.2	8.01-417
8-628.3	8.01-35
8-629	8.01-36
8-629.1	8.01-37
8-629.2	8.01-38
8-629.3	8.01-39
8-630	8.01-45
8-631	8.01-46
8-631.1	8.01-47
8-632	8.01-48
8-632.1	8.01-49
8-633	8.01-50 8.01-244
8-634	8.01-50 8.01-244
8-635	8.01-51
8-636	Repealed
8-636.1	8.01-52 8.01-53
8-637	Deleted
8-638	8.01-53 8.01-54
8-639	8.01-55
8-640	8.01-56
8-641	8.01-57
8-642	8.01-58

Former Section	Present Section
8-643	8.01-59
8-644	8.01-60
8-645	8.01-61
8-646	8.01-62
8-646.1	8.01-63
8-646.2	8.01-64
8-646.3 to 8-646.7	Deleted
8-646.8	8.01-65
8-646.9	8.01-66
8-647	8.01-218
8-648	8.01-219
8-649	Deleted
8-650	8.01-40
8-651	8.01-41
8-652	8.01-221
8-653	8.01-222
8-654	8.01-42
8-654.1	8.01-43
8-654.1:1	8.01-44
8-654.2	29-130.2
8-654.3	Repealed
8-654.4	8.01-223
8-654.5	8.01-224
8-654.6	8.01-581.13
8-654.7	8.01-581.14
8-654.8	8.01-581.15
8-654.9	8.01-581.16
8-654.10	8.01-581.17
8-654.11	8.01-581.18
8-655	8.01-96
8-656	8.01-97
8-657	8.01-98
8-658	8.01-99
8-659	8.01-101
8-660	8.01-102
8-661	8.01-100
8-662	8.01-103
8-663	8.01-104
8-664	8.01-105
8-665	8.01-106
8-666	8.01-107
8-667	8.01-108
8-668	Deleted
8-669	8.01-109
8-670	8.01-110
8-671	8.01-111
8-672	8.01-112
8-673	8.01-113
8-674	8.01-74 8.01-261
8-675	8.01-68 8.01-261
8-676	8.01-69 8.01-70
8-677	8.01-68
8-678	8.01-72
8-679	8.01-73
8-680	Deleted
8-681 to 8-683	8.01-68
8-684	8.01-75
8-685	8.01-76
8-686	Deleted
8-687	Deleted
8-688	8.01-71 8.01-261
8-689	8.01-77
8-689.1	8.01-78 8.01-261
8-689.2	8.01-79
8-689.3	8.01-80
8-689.4	Deleted
8-690	8.01-81 8.01-261
8-691	8.01-82
8-692	8.01-83
8-693	8.01-84
8-694	8.01-85
8-695	8.01-86
8-696	8.01-87
8-697	Deleted
8-698	8.01-88
8-699	8.01-89
8-700	8.01-90
8-701	8.01-91
8-701.1	8.01-92
8-702	8.01-93
8-703	16.1-77.2; part in 8.01-261
8-703.1	8.01-94
8-703.2	8.01-95
8-704	8.01-644
8-705	8.01-645
8-706	8.01-646
8-707	8.01-647
8-708	Deleted
8-709	8.01-648
8-710	8.01-649
8-711	8.01-650
8-711.1	8.01-651
8-712	Deleted
8-713	8.01-652
8-714	8.01-653
8-715 to 8-724	Repealed
8-725	8.01-582
8-726	8.01-583
8-727	8.01-584
8-728	8.01-585
8-729	8.01-586
8-730	8.01-587
8-731	8.01-588
8-732	8.01-589
8-733	8.01-590
8-734	Deleted
8-735	8.01-591
8-736	8.01-592
8-737	8.01-593
8-738	8.01-594
8-739	8.01-595
8-740	8.01-596
8-741	8.01-597
8-742	8.01-598
8-743	8.01-599
8-744	8.01-600
8-744.1	8.01-601
8-745	Deleted
8-746	8.01-602
8-747	8.01-603
8-748	8.01-604
8-749	8.01-605
8-750	8.01-606
8-750.1	63.1-88.1
8-751	8.01-606
8-752	8.01-192 8.01-255
8-753	8.01-193
8-754	8.01-194
8-755	Deleted
8-756	8.01-195
8-757	8.01-255
8-758	8.01-196
8-759	Deleted
8-760	8.01-197
8-761	8.01-198
8-762	8.01-199
8-763	8.01-200
8-764	8.01-201
8-765	8.01-202
8-766	8.01-203
8-767	8.01-204
8-768	8.01-205
8-769	8.01-206
8-770	8.01-207
8-771	8.01-208
8-772	8.01-209
8-773	8.01-210
8-774	8.01-211
8-775	8.01-212
8-776	8.01-213
8-777	8.01-214
8-778	8.01-215
8-779	8.01-216
8-780 to 8-788	Repealed
8-789	8.01-124 8.01-261
8-790	Repealed
8-791	8.01-126
8-792	8.01-125
8-793	8.01-128
8-794	8.01-129
8-795	8.01-130
8-796	8.01-131
8-797	8.01-131
8-798	8.01-261
8-799	8.01-132
8-800	8.01-133
8-801	8.01-134
8-802	8.01-135
8-803	8.01-136
8-804	8.01-137
8-805	8.01-138
8-806 to 8-808	Repealed

Former Section	Present Section
8-809	8.01-139
8-810	8.01-140
8-811	8.01-141
8-812	8.01-142
8-813	8.01-143
8-814	8.01-144
8-815	8.01-145
8-816	8.01-146
8-817	8.01-147
8-818	8.01-148
8-819	8.01-149
8-820	8.01-150
8-821	8.01-151
8-822	8.01-152
8-823	8.01-153
8-824	8.01-154
8-825	8.01-155
8-825.1	8.01-156
8-826	8.01-157
8-827	8.01-158
8-828	8.01-159
8-829	8.01-160
8-830	8.01-161
8-831	8.01-162
8-832	8.01-163
8-833	Deleted
8-834	8.01-164
8-835	8.01-165
8-836	8.01-179
	8.01-261
8-837	8.01-180
8-838	8.01-181
8-839	8.01-182
8-840	8.01-183
8-841	Deleted
8-842	8.01-166
8-843	8.01-167
8-844	8.01-168
8-845	8.01-169

Former Section	Present Section
8-846	8.01-170
8-847	8.01-171
8-848	8.01-172
8-849	8.01-173
8-850	8.01-174
8-851 to 8-853	8.01-175
8-854	8.01-176
8-855	8.01-177
8-856	8.01-178
8-857	8.01-636
8-858 to 8-860	8.01-637
8-861	8.01-639
8-862	8.01-640
8-863	8.01-641
8-864	8.01-642
8-865	8.01-643
8-866	Deleted
8-867	Deleted
8-868	Repealed
8-868.1	Deleted
8-868.2	18.2-324.1
	55-298
8-869	55-299
8-870	55-300
8-871	55-301
8-872	55-302
8-873	55-303
8-873.1	55-304
8-873.2	55-305
8-873.3	55-305
8-874 to 8-876	55-306
8-877	55-307
8-878	55-308
8-879	55-309
8-880	55-310
8-881	55-311
8-882	55-312
8-883	55-313
8-884	55-314

Former Section	Present Section
8-885	18.2-121.1
	55-315
8-886	55-316
8-887	55-317
8-888	55-318
8-889	55-319
8-890	55-320
8-891	55-321
8-892	55-322
8-893	55-323
8-894	55-324
8-895	55-325
8-896	55-326
8-897	55-327
8-898	55-328
8-899	55-329
8-900	55-330
8-901 to 8-905	Deleted
8-906	55-331
8-907	55-332
8-908	55-333
8-909	55-334
8-910	55-335
8-911	8.01-581.1
8-912	8.01-581.2
8-913	8.01-581.3
8-914	8.01-581.4
8-915	8.01-581.5
8-916	8.01-581.6
8-917	8.01-581.7
8-918	8.01-581.8
8-919	8.01-581.9
8-920	8.01-581.10
8-921	8.01-581.11
8-922	8.01-581.12
8-923	8.01-581.12:1
8-924	8.01-581.12:2

COMPARABLE SECTIONS OF TITLES 8.1 AND 8.1A

Former Section	Present Section
8.1-101	8.1A-101
8.1-102	8.1A-103, 8.1A-106, 8.1A-302
8.1-103	8.1A-103
8.1-104	8.1A-104
8.1-105	8.1A-301
8.1-106	8.1A-305
8.1-107	8.1A-306
8.1-108	8.1A-105
8.1-109	8.1A-107
8.1-201	8.1A-201, 8.1A-202, 8.1A-203, 8.1A-204, 8.1A-206
8.1-202	8.1A-307
8.1-203	8.1A-304
8.1-204	8.1A-205, 8.1A-302
8.1-205	8.1A-303
8.1-206	Omitted
8.1-207	8.1A-308
8.1-208	8.1A-309
8.1-209	8.1A-310
8.2-208	8.1A-303
8.2A-207	8.1A-303

COMPARABLE SECTIONS OF TITLE 8.3 AND TITLE 8.3A

Former Section	Present Section
8.3-101	8.3A-101
8.3-102	8.3A-103
	8.3A-105
8.3-103	8.3A-102
8.3-104	8.3A-104
8.3-105	8.3A-106

Former Section	Present Section
8.3-106	8.3A-104
8.3-107	8.3A-107
8.3-108	8.3A-108
8.3-109	8.3A-108
8.3-110	8.3A-109
	8.3A-110
8.3-111	8.3A-109
8.3-112	8.3A-104
8.3-113	Deleted
8.3-114	8.3A-113
8.3-115	8.3A-115
8.3-116	8.3A-110
8.3-117	8.3A-110
8.3-118	8.3A-114
	8.3A-116
8.3-119	8.3A-117
8.3-120	8.3A-105.1
8.3-121	8.3A-105.1
8.3-122	8.3A-118
8.3-201	8.3A-203
8.3-202	8.3A-201
	8.3A-203
	8.3A-204
8.3-203	8.3A-204
8.3-204	8.3A-205
8.3-205	8.3A-206
8.3-206	8.3A-206
8.3-207	8.3A-207
8.3-208	8.3A-207
8.3-301	8.3A-301
8.3-302	8.3A-302
8.3-303	8.3A-303
8.3-304	8.3A-302
	8.3A-304
	8.3A-307
8.3-305	8.3A-305
	8.3A-306
8.3-306	8.3A-305
	8.3A-306
8.3-307	8.3A-308
8.3-401	8.3A-402
8.3-402	8.3A-204
8.3-403	8.3A-402
8.3-404	8.3A-303
	8.3A-403
8.3-405	8.3A-404
	8.3A-405
8.3-406	8.3A-405
	8.3A-406
8.3-407	8.3A-407
8.3-408	8.3A-305
8.3-409	8.3A-408
8.3-410	8.3A-409
8.3-411	8.3A-414
8.3-412	8.3A-410
8.3-413	8.3A-412
	8.3A-413
	8.3A-414
8.3-414	8.3A-415
8.3-415	8.3A-419
8.3-416	8.3A-419
8.3-417	8.3A-416
	8.3A-417
8.3-418	8.3A-418
8.3-419	8.3A-420
8.3-501	8.3A-111
	8.3A-503
8.3-502	8.3A-414
	8.3A-415
	8.3A-502
8.3-503	8.3A-415
	8.3A-502
8.3-504	8.3A-501
8.3-505	8.3A-501
8.3-506	Deleted
8.3-507	8.3A-501
8.3-508	8.3A-502
	8.3A-503
8.3-509	8.3A-505
8.3-510	8.3A-505
8.3-511	8.3A-504
8.3-601	8.3A-601
8.3-602	8.3A-601
8.3-603	8.3A-602
8.3-604	8.3A-603
8.3-605	8.3A-604
8.3-606	8.3A-605
8.3-701	Deleted
8.3-801	Deleted
8.3-802	8.3A-310
8.3-803	8.3A-119
8.3-804	8.3A-309
8.3-805	Deleted

COMPARABLE SECTIONS OF TITLES 8.9 AND 8.9A

Former Section	Present Section
8.2-326(3)	8.9A-102
8.2A-303 (3)	8.9A-407
8.2A-307(2)(6) and (c)	8.9A-317
8.2A-307(3)	8.9A-321
8.9-101	8.9A-101
8.9-102	8.9A-109
8.9-103(1)(a), (b); (c) omitted	8.9A-301
8.9-103(1)(d)	8.9A-316
8.9-103(2)(a), (b); (c) omitted	8.9A-303, 9-316
8.9-103(2)(d)	8.9A-337
8.9-103(3)(a), (b); (c) omitted	8.9A-301
8.9-103(3)(d)	8.9A-307
8.9-103(3)(e)	8.9A-316
8.9-103(4)	8.9A-301
8.9-103(5)	8.9A-301
8.9-103(6)	8.9A-304, 9-305, 9-306
8.9-104	8.9A-109
8.9-105	8.9A-102
8.9-106	8.9A-102
8.9-107	8.9A-103
8.9-108	Omitted as no longer needed
8.9-109	8.9A-102
8.9-110	8.9A-108
8.9-111	Deleted as unnecessary
8.9-112	Omitted - see 9A-102(a)(28)
8.9-113	8.9A-110
8.9-114	Omitted - see 9A-103 and 9A-324
8.9-115(1)	8.9A-102, 9A-106
8.9-115(2)	8.9A-203, 9A-308
8.9-115(3)	8.9A-108
8.9-115(4)	8.9A-309, 9A-312, 9A-314
8.9-115(5)	8.9A-327, 9A-328, 9A-329
8.9-115(6)	8.9A-203, 9A-313
8.9-115(e)	8.9A-106
8.9-116	8.9A-206, 9A-309
8.9-201	8.9A-201
8.9-202	8.9A-202
8.9-203(1)-(3)	8.9A-203
8.9-203(4)	8.9A-201
8.9-204	8.9A-204
8.9-205	8.9A-205
8.9-206	8.9A-403
8.9-207	8.9A-207
8.9-208	8.9A-210
8.9-301(1)-(2)	8.9A-317
8.9-301(3)	8.9A-102
8.9-301(4)	8.9A-323
8.9-302(1)	8.9A-309, 9A-310
8.9-302(2)	8.9A-310
8.9-302(3), (4)	8.9A-311
8.9-303	8.9A-308
8.9-304	8.9A-312
8.9-305	8.9A-306, 9A-313
8.9-306	8.9A-315
8.9-307(1)-(2)	8.9A-320
8.9-307(3)	8.9A-323
8.9-308	8.9A-330
8.9-309	8.9A-331
8.9-310	8.9A-333

Former Section	Present Section
8.9-311	8.9A-401
8.9-312(1)	8.9A-322
8.9-312(2) omitted	See Appendix II
8.9-312(3), (4)	8.9A-324
8.9-312(5), (6)	8.9A-322
8.9-312(7)	8.9A-323
8.9-313(1)-(7)	8.9A-334
8.9-313 (8)	8.9A-604
8.9-314	8.9A-335
8.9-315	8.9A-336
8.9-316	8.9A-339
8.9-317	8.9A-402
8.9-318 (1)	8.9A-404
8.9-318(2)	8.9A-405
8.9-318(3), (4)	8.9A-406
8.9-401	8.9A-501
8.9-402(1)	8.9A-504, 9A-502
8.9-402(2)	Omitted as unnecessary
8.9-402(3)	8.9A-521
8.9-402(4)	8.9A-512
8.9-402(5), (6)	8.9A-502
8.9-402(7)	8.9A-503(a)(4), 9A-507
8.9-402(8)	8.9A-506
8.9-403(1)	8.9A-516(a)
8.9-403 (2)	8.9A-515
8.9-403(3)	8.9A-515, 9A-522
8.9-403 (4)	8.9A-519
8.9-403(5)	8.9A-525
8.9-403 (6)	8.9A-515
8.9-403(7)	8.9A-519
8.9-404	8.9A-513
8.9-405	8.9A-514, 9A-519
8.9-406	8.9A-512
8.9-407	8.9A-523
8.9-408	8.9A-505
8.9-501(1), (2)	8.9A-601
8.9-501(3)	8.9A-602, 9A-603
8.9-501(4)	8.9A-604
8.9-501 (5)	8.9A-601
8.9-502	8.9A-607, 9A-608
8.9-503	8.9A-609
8.9-504(1)	8.9A-610, 9A-615
8.9-504(2)	8.9A-615
8.9-504(3)	8.9A-610, 9A-611, 9A-624
8.9-504(4)	8.9A-617
8.9-504(5)	8.9A-618
8.9-505	8.9A-620, 9A-621, 9A-624
8.9-506	8.9A-623, 9A-624
8.9-507	8.9A-625, 9A-627
8.12A-307(4)	8.9A-323

COMPARABLE SECTIONS OF TITLES 9 AND 9.1 AND OTHER CORRESPONDING SECTIONS

Former Section	Present Section
9-6.14:1	2.2-4000 A
9-6.14:2	Deleted
9-6.14:3	2.2-4000 B
9-6.14:4	2.2-4001
9-6.14:4.1	2.2-4002, 2.2-4005, 2.2-4006, 2.2-4011, 2.2-4018, 2.2-4025
9-6.14:5	2.2-4003
9-6.14:5.1	2.2-4004
9-6.14:7.1	2.2-4007
9-6.14:7.2	2.2-4008
9-6.14:8	2.2-4009
9-6.14:8.1	2.2-4010
9-6.14:9	2.2-4011 B, 2.2-4012
9-6.14:9.1	2.2-4013
9-6.14:9.2	2.2-4014
9-6.14:9.3	2.2-4015
9-6.14:9.4	2.2-4016
9-6.14:11	2.2-4019, 2.2-4021
9-6.14:12	2.2-4020, 2.2-4021
9-6.14:13	2.2-4022
9-6.14:14	2.2-4023
9-6.14:14.1	2.2-4024
9-6.14:15	2.2-4025
9-6.14:16	2.2-4025 C, 2.2-4026
9-6.14:17	2.2-4027
9-6.14:18	2.2-4028
9-6.14:19	2.2-4029
9-6.14:21	2.2-4030
9-6.14:22	2.2-4031
9-6.14:23	2.2-4032
9-6.14:24	2.2-4033
9-6.14:25	2.2-4017
9-6.15	2.2-4100 B
9-6.16	2.2-4101
9-6.17	2.2-4102
9-6.18	2.2-4103
9-6.20	2.2-4104
9-6.22	2.2-4100 A
9-6.23	2.2-2101
9-6.24	2.2-2102
New	2.2-2103
9-6.25	2.2-2100
9-6.25:1	Deleted
9-6.25:2	Deleted
9-6.25:3	Deleted
9-13	2.2-2105
9-14	2.2-2106 A
9-15	2.2-2106 B
9-49	2.2-2511 A
9-50	2.2-2512
9-51	2.2-2511 B
9-52	2.2-2511 C
9-52.1	2.2-2512 B
9-53	30-171 A, 30-172
9-54	30-173
9-55	30-171 B, C
9-55.1	30-171 D
9-77.4	30-145 A, B
9-77.5	30-145 C
9-77.6	30-145 D
9-77.7	30-146
9-77.8	30-147
9-77.9	30-148
9-77.10	30-149
9-77.10:1	30-150
9-77.10:2	30-151
9-77.11	30-152
9-77.11:01	30-153
9-77.11:02	30-154
9-77.11:03	30-154.1
9-77.12	30-155
9-84.01:1	2.2-2508
9-84.02	2.2-2508 D-F
9-84.03	2.2-2509 B
9-84.04	2.2-2508 B
9-84.05	2.2-2103
9-84.06	2.2-2509 B
9-84.07	2.2-2510
9-84.08	2.2-2700 A
9-84.09	2.2-2700 B-E
9-84.09:1	2.2-2702
9-84.09:2	2.2-2701
9-84.09:3	2.2-2704
9-84.09:4	2.2-2703
9-84.1	2.2-125 A
9-84.2	2.2-125 B
9-84.3	2.2-125 C
9-84.4	2.2-125 D
9-84.5	2.2-2614 A, B
9-84.6	2.2-2614 C-E
9-84.7	2.2-2615 A
9-84.8	2.2-2615 B
9-84.9	2.2-2103
9-84.10	2.2-2616
9-95.5	2.2-2665 A, B
9-95.6	2.2-2665 C, 2.2-2666
9-116	2.2-2630
9-116.1	2.2-2631

Former Section	Present Section
9-125	30-156 A
9-126	30-156 B-E
9-127	30-158 A 3
9-128	30-158 B
9-129	30-159 B
9-130	30-160
9-131	30-157
9-132	30-158 A 4
9-133	30-161
9-134	30-158 A 1 & 2
9-135	30-164
9-136	30-159 A
9-137	30-162
9-138	30-163
9-138.1	2.2-2628
9-138.2	2.2-2629 A
9-138.3	2.2-2629 B
9-138.4	2.2-2629 C
9-145.1	30-189 A
9-145.2	30-188 A-D
9-145.3	30-188 E
9-145.4	30-189 B
9-145.8	30-187
9-145.9	30-186 A-D
9-145.10	30-186 E, F
9-145.16	2.2-2500 A, F
9-145.17	2.2-2500 B-E
9-145.18	2.2-2502
9-145.19	2.2-2501 B
9-145.20	2.2-2103
9-145.30	2.2-2605 E, 2.2-2606 A
9-145.31	2.2-2605 A-D
9-145.32	2.2-2607
9-145.33	2.2-2606 B
9-145.33:1	2.2-2608
9-145.34	2.2-2103
9-145.35	2.2-2603 A-D
9-145.36	2.2-2603 F
9-145.37	2.2-2604
9-145.39	2.2-2603 E
9-145.39:1	2.2-2609 B, C
9-145.39:2	2.2-2609 A
9-145.39:3	2.2-2610 A
9-145.39:4	2.2-2610 B
9-145.39:5	2.2-2709
9-145.39:6	2.2-2710
9-145.39:7	2.2-2709 E
9-145.39:8	2.2-2710 B
9-145.45	30-192
9-145.47	2.2-2667 A, 2.2-2668
9-145.48	2.2-2667 B-D
9-145.49	2.2-2103
9-145.52	2.2-1702 B
9-145.53	2.2-1702 A
9-145.54	2.2-1703 A
9-145.55	2.2-1703 B
9-145.56	2.2-1704
9-149	2.2-2407 A
9-150	2.2-2407 B, D
9-151	2.2-2408
9-152	2.2-2407 E, F
9-153	9.1-200
9-153.1	9.1-202
9-154	9.1-201
9-155	9.1-203
9-155.1	9.1-204
9-155.2	Deleted
9-167	Deleted
9-168	9.1-108, 9.1-111 9.1-112
9-169	9.1-101
9-170	9.1-102, 9.1-127
9-171	9.1-109
9-171.1	9.1-110
9-172	Deleted
9-173	9.1-116
9-173.1	9.1-164
9-173.2	9.1-163
9-173.3	9.1-104
9-173.6	9.1-151
9-173.7	9.1-152
9-173.8	9.1-153
9-173.9	9.1-155
9-173.10	9.1-154
9-173.11	9.1-156 B
9-173.12	9.1-156 A
9-173.13	9.1-157
9-173.16	9.1-158
9-173.17	9.1-159
9-173.18	9.1-160
9-173.19	9.1-161
9-173.20	9.1-162
9-173.21	9.1-184
9-174	9.1-100 A
9-175	9.1-100 A
9-176	9.1-100 B, 9.1-107
9-177	9.1-107 C
9-178	Deleted
9-178.1	9.1-105
9-178.2	9.1-106
9-179	9.1-113
9-180	9.1-114
9-181	9.1-115
9-182	9.1-141
9-183	9.1-103
9-183.1	9.1-138
9-183.2	9.1-140
9-183.3	9.1-139
9-183.4	9.1-142
9-183.5	9.1-143
9-183.6	9.1-144
9-183.7	9.1-145
9-183.8	9.1-146
9-183.9	9.1-149
9-183.10	9.1-148
9-183.11	9.1-147
9-183.12	9.1-150
9-183.13	9.1-166
9-183.14	9.1-165
9-183.15	9.1-167
9-183.16	9.1-169
9-183.17	9.1-170
9-183.18	9.1-171
9-183.19	9.1-168 A, B, C
9-183.20	9.1-168 D
9-183.21	9.1-172
9-184	9.1-126
9-185	9.1-127 A, B
9-186	9.1-131
9-187	9.1-128 A
9-188	9.1-128 B, C
9-189	9.1-129
9-190	9.1-134
9-191	9.1-130
9-192	9.1-132
9-193	9.1-133
9-194	9.1-135
9-195	9.1-136
9-196	9.1-137
9-196.1	9.1-117
9-196.4	9.1-119
9-196.5	9.1-118 A & C
9-196.6	9.1-118 B
9-196.7	9.1-120
9-196.8	9.1-123
9-196.9	9.1-124
9-196.10	9.1-125
9-196.11	9.1-121
9-196.12	9.1-122
9-197	2.2-2279 A
9-198	2.2-2280 A
9-199	2.2-2279 B
9-200	2.2-2281
9-201	2.2-2280 B
9-202	2.2-2282
9-203	2.2-2283
9-204	2.2-2284
9-205	2.2-2285
9-206	2.2-2286
9-207	2.2-2287
9-208	2.2-2314
9-209	2.2-2288
9-210	2.2-2289
9-211	2.2-2290
9-212	2.2-2291 A
9-213	2.2-2291 B
9-214	Deleted
9-215	2.2-2291 C
9-216	2.2-2292
9-217	2.2-2293
9-218	2.2-2294
9-219	2.2-2295
9-220	2.2-2296
9-221	2.2-2297
9-222	2.2-2298
9-223	2.2-2299
9-224	2.2-2300
9-225	2.2-2301

Former Section	Present Section
9-226	2.2-2302
9-227	2.2-2303
9-228	2.2-2285
9-228.1	2.2-2309 A
9-228.2	2.2-2309 B
9-228.3	2.2-2309 C
9-228.4	2.2-2309 D-F
9-228.5	2.2-2310 A
9-228.6	2.2-2310 B
9-228.7	2.2-2310 C
9-228.8	2.2-2310 D, E
9-229	2.2-2304
9-230	2.2-2305
9-231	2.2-2306
9-232	2.2-2308
9-233	2.2-2313
9-234	2.2-2307
9-235	2.2-2312
9-249.1	2.2-903
9-250	2.2-2218 A
9-251	2.2-2218 B
9-252	2.2-2219
9-253	2.2-2220
9-254	2.2-2221
9-254.1	2.2-2221.1
9-255	2.2-2222
9-256	2.2-2223
9-257	2.2-2224
9-258	2.2-2225
9-259	2.2-2226
9-260	2.2-2227
9-261	2.2-2228
9-262	2.2-2230
9-263	2.2-2232
9-264	2.2-2231
9-265	2.2-2229
9-265.1	2.2-2233
9-266	Deleted
9-266.1	2.2-2201 A
9-266.2	2.2-2201 B
9-266.3	2.2-2202
9-266.4	2.2-2203
9-266.5	2.2-2204
9-266.6	2.2-2205
9-266.7	2.2-2206
9-266.8	2.2-2207
9-266.9	2.2-2208
9-266.10	2.2-2209
9-266.11	2.2-2210
9-266.12	2.2-2211
9-266.13	2.2-2216
9-266.14	2.2-2217
9-266.15	2.2-2215
9-266.16	2.2-2212
9-266.17	2.2-2213
9-266.18	2.2-2214
9-266.19	Deleted
9-267	2.2-2657
9-268	2.2-2658
9-269	2.2-2658 B and C
9-270	2.2-2658 D, 2.2-2659
9-270.1	2.2-2659 C
9-271	2.2-2660
9-272	2.2-2661
9-272.1	2.2-2662
9-273	2.2-2663
9-291.1	30-190, 30-191
9-292	30-174 A
9-293	30-174 B-E
9-294	30-175
9-295	30-176
9-296	30-177
9-297	2.2-2503 A-D
9-298	2.2-2503 E, 2.2-2504
9-299	2.2-2505
9-300	2.2-2503 F
9-301	Deleted
9-302	Deleted
9-303	Deleted
9-304	Deleted
9-304.1	2.2-2611 E
9-304.2	2.2-2611 A-D
9-304.3	2.2-2612
9-304.4	2.2-2613
9-304.5	2.2-2103
9-304.6	2.2-2612 E
9-311	30-168 A
9-312	30-168 B-E
9-313	30-169
9-314	30-168 F
9-315	30-169
9-316	30-170
9-317	2.2-2642 A
9-318	2.2-2642 B
9-319	2.2-2642 C, 2.2-2643
9-320	2.2-2644 A, E
9-321	2.2-2644 B-D
9-322	2.2-2645
9-323	2.2-2646
9-324	2.2-2647
9-325	2.2-2600 A
9-326	2.2-2600 B-D
9-327	2.2-2601
9-328	2.2-2602 A
9-329	2.2-2602 B
9-329.1	2.2-2669, 2.2-2670 C-G, 2.2-2671
9-329.2	2.2-2670 A and B
9-329.3	2.2-2672
9-329.4	2.2-2673
9-329.5	2.2-2671 C
9-329.6	2.2-2674
9-334	30-184 A, 30-185
9-335	30-184 B-E
9-336	30-182 A
9-337	30-182 B-D
9-338	30-183
9-339	30-182 E
9-340	Deleted
9-341	2.2-2620
9-342	2.2-2622
9-343	2.2-2621 A-E
9-344	2.2-2103, 2.2-2622
9-345	2.2-2621 F, 2.2-2622 B
9-346	2.2-2623
9-347	2.2-2624
9-348	2.2-2625
9-349	2.2-2622 D
9-350	2.2-2424
9-351	2.2-2424 B-E
9-352	2.2-2425
9-353	2.2-2103, 2.2-2424 F
9-359	2.2-2247
9-360	2.2-2248
9-361	2.2-2249
9-362	2.2-2250
9-363	2.2-2251
9-364	2.2-2252
9-365	2.2-2253
9-365.1	2.2-2254
9-366	2.2-2258
9-367	2.2-2255
9-368	2.2-2256
9-369	2.2-2259
9-370	2.2-2257
9-371	2.2-2442
9-372	2.2-2441
9-373	2.2-2440
9-374	2.2-2443
9-375	2.2-2444
9-376	2.2-2447
9-377	2.2-2445
9-378	2.2-2446
9-380	3.1-1106
9-381	3.1-1107
9-382	3.1-1108
9-383	3.1-1109, 3.1-1112
9-384	3.1-1110
9-385	3.1-1111
9-385.1	3.1-1111.1
9-386	3.1-1113 B
9-387	3.1-1113 A
9-388	3.1-1109 C
9-389	3.1-1114
9-389.1	3.1-1114.1
9-390	30-165 A
9-391	30-165 B-E
9-392	30-166
9-393	30-165 F
9-394	30-166
9-395	30-167
9-396	2.2-2675

Former Section	Present Section
9-397	2.2-2676
9-398	2.2-2677
9-399	2.2-2678
9-400	2.2-2448
9-401	2.2-2449
9-402	2.2-2450
9-403	2.2-2451
9-404	2.2-2679
9-405	2.2-2680
9-406	2.2-2513
9-407	2.2-2514
9-408	2.2-2515
9-409	2.2-2516
9-410	2.2-2517
9-411	2.2-2518

COMPARABLE SECTIONS OF TITLE 10 AND TITLE 10.1

Former Section	Present Section
9-152.1	10.1-1001
	10.1-1002
9-152.2	10.1-1001
9-152.3 to 9-152.5	10.1-1002
10-1	Repealed
10-2	Repealed
10-3	10.1-105
10-4	10.1-106
10-5	10.1-106
10-6	Repealed
10-7	Deleted
10-8 to 10-10	Repealed
10-11	Deleted
10-12	10.1-107
10-12.1	Repealed
10-12.2	Deleted
10-12.3	Deleted
10-13	2.1-548.8:1
10-14	2.1-548.8:2
10-14.1	2.1-548.8:3
10-14.2	Repealed
10-15 to 10-17.9:1	Deleted
10-17.10	10.1-1300
10-17.11	10.1-1301
10-17.12	10.1-1302
10-17.13	Repealed
10-17.14	10.1-1303
10-17.15	10.1-1304
10-17.16	10.1-1305
	10.1-1307
10-17.17	10.1-1306
10-17.18	10.1-1307
	10.1-1308
10-17.18:1	10.1-1309
10-17.18:2	10.1-1310
10-17.18:3	10.1-1311
10-17.19	10.1-1312
10-17.20	10.1-1313
10-17.21	10.1-1314
10-17.22	10.1-1315
10-17.23	10.1-1316
10-17.23:1	10.1-1317
10-17.23:2	10.1-1318
10-17.23:3 to 10-17.27	Repealed
10-17.28	10.1-1319
10-17.29	10.1-1320
10-17.30	10.1-1321
10-17.30:1	10.1-1322
10-17.107	10.1-1200
10-17.108	10.1-1208
10-17.109	10.1-1209
10-17.110	10.1-1210
10-17.111	10.1-1211
10-17.112	10.1-1212
10-17.113	10.1-108
10-17.114	10.1-109
	10.1-110
	10.1-111
	10.1-112
10-18	Deleted
10-19	Deleted
10-20	Repealed
10-21	10.1-201
10-21.1	Repealed
10-21.2	10.1-202
10-21.3	Repealed
10-21.3:1	10.1-203
	10.1-204
10-21.3:2	10.1-205
10-21.3:3	10.1-200
10-21.3:4	10.1-206
	10.1-104
10-21.3:5	10.1-104
	10.1-200
10-21.3:6	10.1-207
10-21.3:7	10.1-208
10-21.3:8	Deleted
10-31.1	10.1-1100
10-31.2	10.1-1101
10-31.3	10.1-1104
10-31.4	10.1-1105
10-31.5	10.1-1112
10-31.6	Deleted
10-31.7	10.1-1113
10-32	10.1-1106
10-33	10.1-1107
10-34	Deleted
10-34.1	Deleted
10-34.2	10.1-1108
10-35	Deleted
10-36	10.1-1114
10-37	10.1-1115
10-38	Repealed
10-39	10.1-1116
10-40	10.1-1118
10-41	10.1-1119
10-42	10.1-1109
10-43	10.1-1110
10-44	10.1-1111
10-45	Deleted
10-45.1	10.1-1120
10-45.2	10.1-1121
10-45.3	10.1-1122
10-45.4	10.1-1123
10-46	10.1-1124
10-46.1	10.1-1125
10-46.2	10.1-1126
10-47	10.1-1127
10-48	10.1-1128
10-49	10.1-1129
10-50	10.1-1130
10-51	10.1-1131
10-52	10.1-1132
10-53	10.1-1133
10-54	10.1-1134
10-54.1	10.1-1117
10-55	10.1-1135
10-56	10.1-1136
10-57	10.1-1137
10-57.1	10.1-1138
10-58	10.1-1141
10-59	10.1-1139
10-60	10.1-1140
10-61	10.1-1141
10-61.1	Deleted
10-62	10.1-1142
10-63	10.1-1142
10-64	10.1-1144
10-64.1	10.1-1143
10-65	10.1-1145
10-66	10.1-1147
10-67	10.1-1148
10-68	10.1-1151
10-69	10.1-1152
10-70	10.1-1153
10-71	10.1-1154
10-72	10.1-1155
10-73	10.1-1156
10-74	10.1-1157
10-74.1	Deleted
10-74.2	Deleted
10-75	10.1-1162
10-76	10.1-1164
10-76.1	Deleted
10-77	10.1-1165
10-78	10.1-1166
10-79	10.1-1167

Former Section	Present Section
10-79.1	10.1-1168
10-80	Repealed
10-81	10.1-1163
10-81.1	Deleted
10-82	10.1-1163
10-83	10.1-1163
10-83.01	10.1-1169
10-83.1 to 10-83.3	Deleted
10-84	10.1-1102
10-84.1	10.1-1102
10-84.2	10.1-1103
10-85 to 10-90.1	Repealed
10-90.2	Deleted
10-90.3	10.1-1177
10-90.4	10.1-1178
10-90.5	10.1-1179
10-90.6	Deleted
10-90.7	10.1-1180
10-90.8	Repealed
10-90.9	10.1-1181
10-90.10 to 10-90.19	Repealed
10-90.20, 10-90.21	Expired
10-90.22, 10-90.23	Repealed
10-90.24, 10-90.25	Expired
10-90.26	Repealed
10-90.27 through 10-90.29	Expired
10-90.30	Deleted
10-90.31	10.1-1170
10-90.32	10.1-1172
10-90.33 to 10-90.35	10.1-1171
10-90.36	10.1-1173
10-90.37	10.1-1174
10-90.38	10.1-1176
10-90.39	10.1-1175
10-99	Deleted
10-100	10.1-300
10-101	10.1-301
10-102	10.1-302
10-103	10.1-303
	10.1-304
10-104	10.1-305
10-105	10.1-306
10-106	10.1-307
10-107	10.1-308
10-108	10.1-309
10-109	10.1-310
10-110	10.1-311
10-111	Deleted
10-112	Deleted
10-112.1	10.1-312
10-127 to 10-135	Deleted
10-136	10.1-800
10-137	Deleted
10-137.1	10.1-807
10-138	10.1-801

Former Section	Present Section
	10.1-802
	10.1-808
10-138.1	10.1-809
10-138.2	10.1-803
	10.1-804
10-139	10.1-808
10-139.1	Deleted
10-140 to 10-143	Repealed
10-144 to 10-145.1	Deleted
10-145.2	10.1-810
10-145.3 to 1.4.10-145.5	Repealed
10-145.6	10.1-811
10-145.7	Deleted
10-145.8	Deleted
10-145.9	Repealed
10-145.10	Deleted
10-145.11	10.1-812
10-145.12	10.1-813
10-145.13	10.1-814
10-150.1	Deleted
10-150.2	10.1-901
10-150.3	10.1-900
10-150.4	10.1-904
10-150.5	10.1-903
10-150.6	10.1-904
10-150.7	10.1-905
10-150.8	10.1-901
10-150.9	10.1-902
10-150.10	10.1-906
10-150.11	10.1-1002
10-150.12	10.1-1000
10-150.13	10.1-1004
10-150.14	10.1-1005
10-150.15	10.1-1006
10-150.16	10.1-1003
10-150.17	10.1-1007
10-150.18	10.1-1008
10-151	Deleted
10-152	10.1-1701
10-153	10.1-1704
10-154	10.1-1702
10-155	Repealed
10-156	10.1-1700
10-157	10.1-1705
10-158	10.1-1703
10-158.1	Deleted
10-158.2	10.1-1600
10-158.3	10.1-1601
10-158.4	10.1-1602
10-158.5	10.1-1603
10-158.6	10.1-1604
	10.1-1605
	10.1-1606
	10.1-1607
	10.1-1608
	10.1-1609
10-158.7	10.1-1610
10-158.8	10.1-1611

Former Section	Present Section
10-158.9	10.1-1612
10-158.10	10.1-1613
10-158.11	10.1-1614
10-158.12	10.1-1615
10-158.13	10.1-1616
10-158.14	Reserved
10-158.15	10.1-1617
10-158.16	10.1-1618
10-158.17	10.1-1619
10-158.18	10.1-1620
10-158.19	10.1-1621
10-158.20	10.1-1622
10-159 to 10-162	10.1-1800
10-163	10.1-1801
10-164	10.1-1802
10-165	10.1-1803
10-166	10.1-1804
10-167	10.1-401
	10.1-402
	10.1-405
10-168	10.1-400
10-169	10.1-401
10-170	10.1-401
	10.1-406
10-171	10.1-404
10-172	10.1-403
10-173	10.1-405
10-173.1	10.1-416
10-173.2	10.1-411
10-173.3	10.1-410
10-173.4	10.1-409
10-173.5	10.1-418
10-173.6	10.1-414
10-173.7	10.1-417
10-173.8	10.1-415
10-173.9	10.1-413
10-174	10.1-407
10-175	10.1-401
10-176	10.1-412
10-177	10.1-1200
10-178	10.1-1201
10-179	Deleted
10-180	10.1-1201
10-181	10.1-1202
	10.1-1204
10-182	Deleted
10-183	10.1-1203
10-184	Repealed
10-184.1	10.1-1204
10-184.2	10.1-1206
10-185	10.1-1205
10-186	10.1-1207
10-215	Deleted
10-216	10.1-706
10-217	10.1-705
10-218	10.1-707
10-219	10.1-708
10-220	10.1-709
10-221	10.1-710
10-222	10.1-711

Former Section	Present Section
10-223 to 10-251	Deleted
10-252	10.1-101
10-252.1	10.1-102
10-253	10.1-103
10-254	10.1-104
10-255	10.1-805
10-256	10.1-815
10-257	10.1-815
10-257.1	10.1-816
10-258	10.1-805
10-259	10.1-801
10-260	Repealed
10-261	10.1-806 10.1-810
10-262	10.1-817
10-263	Deleted
10-264	10.1-1400
10-265	10.1-1401
10-266	10.1-1402
10-267	10.1-1403
10-268	10.1-1400 10.1-1404
10-269	10.1-1405
10-270	10.1-1406
10-270.1	10.1-1407
10-271	10.1-1408
10-272	10.1-1409
10-273	10.1-1410
10-274	10.1-1411
10-275	10.1-1412
10-276	10.1-1413
10-277	10.1-1415
10-277.1	10.1-1414
10-277.2	Deleted
10-277.3	10.1-1416
10-277.4	10.1-1417
10-277.5	10.1-1418
10-277.6	10.1-1419
10-277.7	10.1-1420
10-277.8	10.1-1421
10-277.9	10.1-1422
10-277.10	Deleted
10-277.11	10.1-1423
10-277.12	10.1-1424
10-277.13	Reserved
10-277.14	10.1-1425
10-278	Reserved
10-279	10.1-1426
10-280	10.1-1427
10-281	10.1-1428
10-282	10.1-1429
10-283	10.1-1430
10-284	10.1-1431
10-285	10.1-1432
10-286	Reserved
10-287	10.1-1434
10-288	10.1-1433
10-289	Reserved
10-290	10.1-1434
10-291	10.1-1435
10-292	10.1-1436
10-293	10.1-1437
10-294	2.1-342 2.1-344 10.1-1438
10-295	10.1-1439
10-296	10.1-1440
10-297	10.1-1441
10-298	10.1-1442
10-299	10.1-1443
10-300	10.1-1444
10-301	10.1-1445
10-302	10.1-1446
10-303	10.1-1447
10-304	10.1-1448
10-304.1	10.1-1449
10-305	10.1-1450
10-306	10.1-1451
10-307	10.1-1452
10-308	10.1-1453
10-309	10.1-1454
10-310	10.1-1455
10-311	10.1-1456
10-312	10.1-1457
21-1	Deleted
21-2	10.1-506
21-3	10.1-500
21-4	10.1-549
21-5	10.1-550
21-5.1	Deleted
21-5.2	10.1-572
21-5.3	10.1-573
21-6	10.1-502
21-7	10.1-503
21-8	10.1-504
21-9	Deleted
21-10	10.1-505
21-11	Repealed
21-11.1	10.1-637
21-11.2	10.1-636
21-11.3	10.1-638
21-11.4	10.1-637
21-11.5	10.1-639
21-11.6	10.1-643
21-11.7	10.1-644
21-11.8	10.1-642
21-11.9	10.1-645
21-11.10	10.1-646
21-11.11	10.1-640
21-11.12	10.1-647
21-11.13	10.1-641
21-11.14	10.1-648
21-11.15	10.1-649
21-11.16	Deleted
21-11.16:1	10.1-704
21-11.17	10.1-700
21-11.18	10.1-701
21-11.19	10.1-702
21-11.20	10.1-703
21-11.21	Deleted
21-11.22	10.1-651
21-11.23	10.1-650
21-11.24	10.1-652
21-11.25	10.1-653
21-11.26	10.1-654
21-11.27	10.1-656
21-11.28	10.1-655
21-11.29	10.1-657
21-12	Repealed
21-12.1	10.1-506
21-12.2	10.1-507
21-13	10.1-508
21-13.1	10.1-509
21-14	10.1-510
21-15	Deleted
21-16	10.1-511
21-17	10.1-512
21-18	10.1-513
21-19	Repealed
21-20	10.1-514
21-21	Repealed
21-22	Repealed
21-23	Deleted
21-24 to 21-26	Repealed
21-27	10.1-515
21-27.1	Deleted
21-27.2	10.1-516
21-28	10.1-517
21-29	10.1-518
21-30	10.1-519
21-31	Repealed
21-31.1	Repealed
21-31.2	10.1-520
21-31.3	10.1-521
21-32	10.1-522
21-33 to 21-36	10.1-523
21-37	10.1-524
21-38	10.1-525
21-39	10.1-526
21-40	10.1-527
21-41	10.1-528
21-42	10.1-529
21-43	10.1-529
21-44	10.1-530
21-45	10.1-530
21-46	10.1-531
21-47	10.1-532
21-48	10.1-533
21-49	10.1-534
21-50	10.1-535
21-51	10.1-536
21-52	10.1-537
21-53	10.1-538
21-54	10.1-539
21-55	10.1-540
21-56	10.1-541
21-57	10.1-542
21-58	10.1-543
21-59	10.1-544
21-60	10.1-545
21-61	10.1-546
21-62	10.1-547

Former Section	Present Section
21-63	10.1-548
21-64	10.1-551
21-65	10.1-552
21-66 to 21-89.2	Deleted
21-89.3	10.1-560
21-89.4	10.1-561
21-89.5	10.1-562
21-89.6	10.1-563
	10.1-564
21-89.7	10.1-565
21-89.8	10.1-566
21-89.9	10.1-567
21-89.10	10.1-568
21-89.11	10.1-569
21-89.12	10.1-570
21-89.13	10.1-571
21-89.14 to 21-105	Deleted
21-106	10.1-553
21-107	10.1-554
21-108	10.1-555
21-109	10.1-556
21-110	10.1-557
21-111	10.1-558
21-112	10.1-559
21-112.1	10.1-614
21-112.2	10.1-615
21-112.3	10.1-616
21-112.4	10.1-617
21-112.4:1	10.1-618
21-112.5	10.1-618
	10.1-619
21-112.6	10.1-620
21-112.7	10.1-621
21-112.8	10.1-622
21-112.9	10.1-623
21-112.10	10.1-624
21-112.11	10.1-625
21-112.12	Repealed
21-112.12:1	10.1-626
21-112.13	10.1-627
21-112.14	10.1-628
21-112.15	10.1-628
21-112.16	10.1-629
21-112.17	10.1-630
21-112.18	10.1-631
21-112.19	10.1-632
21-112.20	10.1-633
21-112.20:1	10.1-634
21-112.21	10.1-635
32.1-238.6	Repealed
32.1-238.6:1	10.1-1500
32.1-238.7	10.1-1501
32.1-238.8	10.1-1502
32.1-238.9	10.1-1503
32.1-238.10	Deleted
62.1-44.108	Deleted
62.1-44.109	10.1-603
62.1-44.110	10.1-600
62.1-44.111	10.1-601
62.1-44.112	10.1-602
62.1-115.1	10.1-604
62.1-115.2	10.1-605
62.1-115.3	10.1-606
62.1-115.4	10.1-607
62.1-115.5	10.1-608
62.1-115.6	10.1-609
62.1-115.7	10.1-610
62.1-115.8	10.1-611
62.1-115.9	10.1-612
62.1-115.10	10.1-613
62.1-153	10.1-1900
62.1-154	10.1-1901

COMPARABLE SECTIONS OF TITLE 11, CHAPTER 7 AND TITLE 2.2

Former Section	Present Section
11-35	2.2-4300,
	2.2-4343
11-36	2.2-4302
11-37	2.2-4301
11-38	Deleted
11-39	2.2-4343 B
11-40	2.2-4304,
	2.2-4343
11-40.2	2.2-4343
11-40.3	2.2-4346
11-40.4	2.2-4343
11-41	2.2-4303,
	2.2-4346
11-41.01	2.2-4313
11-41.02	2.2-4314
11-41.1	2.2-4305
11-41.2	2.2-4306
11-41.2:02	2.2-4307
11-41.2:2	2.2-4308
11-41.2:3	2.2-2404
11-41.2:4	2.2-2405
11-41.2:5	2.2-2406
11-41.4	Deleted
11-42	2.2-4319
11-43	2.2-4331
11-44	2.2-4310 A
11-44.1	2.2-4320
11-45	2.2-4309,
	2.2-4344,
	2.2-4345,
	2.2-4346
11-45.1	2.2-4322
11-46	2.2-4317
11-46.1	2.2-4321
11-46.3	2.2-4332
11-47	2.2-4324
11-47.01	2.2-4323
11-47.1	2.2-4325
11-47.2	2.2-4326
11-47.3	2.2-4327
11-47.4	2.2-4328
11-47.5	2.2-4329
11-48	2.2-4310 B
11-49	2.2-4315
11-50	2.2-4316
11-51	2.2-4311
11-51.1	2.2-4312
11-52	2.2-4342
11-53	2.2-4318
11-54	2.2-4330
11-55	2.2-4309 A, C
11-56	2.2-4333
11-56.1	2.2-4334
11-56.2	2.2-4335
11-57	2.2-4336
11-58	2.2-4337
11-59	2.2-4340
11-60	2.2-4341
11-61	2.2-4338
11-62	2.2-4339
11-62.1	2.2-4347
11-62.2	2.2-4350 A
11-62.3	2.2-4350 B
11-62.4	2.2-4351
11-62.5	2.2-4355
11-62.6	2.2-4353
11-62.7	2.2-4356
11-62.8	2.2-4349
11-62.9	2.2-4348
11-62.10	2.2-4352
11-62.11	2.2-4354
11-63	2.2-4357
11-64	2.2-4358
11-65	2.2-4359
11-66	2.2-4360
11-67	2.2-4361
11-68	2.2-4362
11-69	2.2-4363
11-70	2.2-4364
11-71	2.2-4365
11-71.1	2.2-4366
11-72	2.2-4367
11-73	2.2-4368
11-74	2.2-4369
11-75	2.2-4371
11-76	2.2-4370
11-77	2.2-4371 B
11-78	2.2-4372
11 78.1	2.2-4373
11-79	2.2-4374

Former Section	Present Section
11-79.1	2.2-4375
11-79.2	2.2-4376
11-80	2.2-4377

COMPARABLE SECTIONS OF TITLE 13.1, CHAPTERS 1 AND 2 AND TITLE 13.1, CHAPTERS 9 THROUGH 11

Former Section	Present Section
13.1-1	13.1-601
13.1-2	13.1-603
13.1-2.1	13.1-627
13.1-3.1	13.1-696
	to 13.1-704
13.1-4	13.1-653
13.1-5	13.1-629
13.1-6	13.1-630
13.1-6.1	Repealed
13.1-7	13.1-631
13.1-8	13.1-632
13.1-9	13.1-634
13.1-10	13.1-635
13.1-11	13.1-637
13.1-12	13.1-638
13.1-13	13.1-638
13.1-14	13.1-639
13.1-15	13.1-642
	13.1-643
13.1-17	13.1-643
13.1-18	Repealed
13.1-19	13.1-645
	13.1-707
13.1-20	13.1-647
	13.1-648
13.1-21	13.1-641
13.1-22	13.1-644
13.1-23	13.1-651
13.1-24	13.1-624
	13.1-714
13.1-24.1	13.1-625
13.1-25	13.1-654
	13.1-655
13.1-26	13.1-658
13.1-27	13.1-659
	13.1-687
13.1-28	13.1-657
13.1-29	13.1-660
13.1-30	13.1-661
13.1-31	13.1-666
13.1-32	13.1-662
	13.1-663
	13.1-665
	13.1-669
13.1-33	13.1-668
13.1-34	13.1-670
	13.1-671
13.1-35	13.1-673
	13.1-674
	13.1-683
13.1-36	13.1-675
	13.1-677
13.1-37	13.1-676
	13.1-678
13.1-38	13.1-682
13.1-39	13.1-688
13.1-39.1	13.1-691
13.1-40	13.1-689
13.1-41	13.1-684
	13.1-686
13.1-41.1	13.1-685
13.1-42	13.1-680
	13.1-681
13.1-43	13.1-653
13.1-44	13.1-688
	13.1-690
	13.1-692
13.1-45	13.1-693
	13.1-694
13.1-46	13.1-695
13.1-47	13.1-770
	13.1-771
	13.1-772
	13.1-774
13.1-48	13.1-618
13.1-49	13.1-619
13.1-50	13.1-620
13.1-51	13.1-621
13.1-52	13.1-621
13.1-54	13.1-623
13.1-55	13.1-705
13.1-56	13.1-707
13.1-57	13.1-708
13.1-58	13.1-710
13.1-59	13.1-710
13.1-60	13.1-713
13-1-61	13.1-712
13.1-62	13.1-653
13.1-63	Repealed
13.1-64	Repealed
13.1-65	13.1-652
13.1-66	13.1-652
13.1-67	Repealed
13.1-68	13.1-716
13.1-69	Repealed
13.1-69.1	13.1-717
13.1-70	13.1-718
13.1-71	13.1-722
13.1-72	13.1-720
13.1-73	13.1-720
13.1-74	13.1-721
13.1-75	13.1-730
	13.1-731
	13.1-733
	13.1-734
	13.1-735
	13.1-736
	13.1-737
	13.1-739
	13.1-740
	13.1-741
13.1-76	13.1-719
13.1-76.1	Repealed
13.1-77	13.1-723
	13.1-724
13.1-78	13.1-730
	13.1-731
	13.1-733
	13.1-734
	13.1-735
	13.1-736
	13.1-737
	13.1-739
	13.1-740
	13.1-741
13.1-79	13.1-751
13.1-80	13.1-743
13.1-81	13.1-742
	13.1-743
13.1-82	13.1-743
13.1-83	13.1-745
13.1-84	13.1-745
13.1-85	13.1-744
13.1-86	13.1-744
13.1-87	13.1-743
13.1-88	13.1-743
13.1-89	13.1-750
13.1-90	13.1-743
13.1-91	13.1-752
13.1-92	13.1-754
13.1-93	13.1-753
13.1-93.1	13.1-756
13.1-94	13.1-747
	13.1-748
13.1-95	13.1-748
13.1-96	13.1-748
13.1-97	Repealed
13.1-98	Repealed
13.1-99	13.1-749
13.1-100	Repealed
13.1-101	13.1-755
13.1-102	13.1-757
	13.1-761
13.1-102.1	13.1-757
13.1-102.2	13.1-757
13.1-103	13.1-761

Former Section	Present Section
13.1-104	13.1-762
13.1-105	13.1-762
13.1-106	13.1-759
13.1-107	13.1-759
13.1-108	13.1-761
13.1-109	13.1-763
13.1-110	13.1-764
13.1-111	13.1-766
13.1-112	13.1-760
13.1-113	13.1-760
13.1-114	13.1-762
13.1-115	13.1-767
13.1-115.1	13.1-767
13.1-116	13.1-767
13.1-117	13.1-768
13.1-118	13.1-767
13.1-119	13.1-758
13.1-120	13.1-775
13.1-121	13.1-775
13.1-122	13.1-615
13.1-123	13.1-616
13.1-124	13.1-617
13.1-124.1	13.1-616
13.1-125	13.1-614
13.1-126	13.1-605
13.1-127	13.1-633
13.1-128	13.1-778
13.1-129	13.1-602
13.1-130	13.1-779
13.1-132	Repealed
13.1-133	Repealed
13.1-134	13.1-612
13.1-135	13.1-613
13.1-140	13.1-981
13.1-141	13.1-982
13.1-142	13.1-983
13.1-143	13.1-984
13.1-144	13.1-985
13.1-144.1	13.1-986
13.1-145	13.1-987
13.1-146	13.1-988
13.1-147	13.1-989
13.1-148	13.1-990
13.1-149	13.1-991
13.1-149.1	13.1-992
13.1-150	13.1-993
13.1-151	13.1-994
13.1-152	13.1-995
13.1-153	13.1-996
13.1-154	13.1-997
13.1-155	13.1-998
13.1-156	13.1-776
13.1-157 to 13.1-161	13.1-777
13.1-201	13.1-801
13.1-202	13.1-803
13.1-203	13.1-937
13.1-204	13.1-825
13.1-204.1	13.1-826
13.1-205.1	13.1-876 to 13.1-883
13.1-206	13.1-828
13.1-207	13.1-829
13.1-207.1	13.1-830
13.1-207.2	13.1-831
13.1-208	13.1-833
13.1-209	13.1-834
13.1-210	13.1-836
13.1-211	13.1-837
13.1-212	13.1-823
13.1-212.1	13.1-824
13.1-213	13.1-838
	13.1-839
13.1-214	13.1-842
13.1-215	13.1-843
13.1-216	13.1-841
13.1-217	13.1-846
13.1-218	13.1-851
13.1-219	13.1-849
13.1-220	13.1-853
	13.1-854
	13.1-855
13.1-221	13.1-852
	13.1-857
	13.1-858
	13.1-860
	13.1-861
13.1-222	13.1-862
13.1-223	13.1-868
	13.1-871
13.1-224	13.1-869
13.1-225	13.1-864
13.1-226	13.1-872
13.1-227	13.1-874
13.1-228	13.1-932
13.1-229	13.1-814
13.1-230	13.1-818
13.1-231	13.1-819
13.1-232	13.1-820
13.1-233	13.1-820
13.1-234	13.1-822
13.1-235	13.1-884
13.1-236	13.1-885
	13.1-886
13.1-237	13.1-888
13.1-238	13.1-888
13.1-239	13.1-891
13.1-240	13.1-894
13.1-241	Repealed
13.1-242	13.1-895
13.1-242.1	13.1-898
13.1-243	13.1-896
13.1-244	13.1-896
13.1-245	13.1-897
13.1-246	13.1-899
	13.1-900
13.1-246.1	13.1-901
13.1-248	13.1-902
	13.1-903
13.1-249	13.1-907
13.1-250	13.1-907
13.1-251	13.1-905
13.1-252	13.1-904
13.1-253	13.1-904
13.1-254	13.1-914
13.1-255	13.1-916
13.1-256	13.1-915
13.1-256.1	13.1-918
13.1-257	13.1-909
13.1-258	13.1-910
13.1-259	13.1-910
13.1-260	13.1-909
13.1-261	13.1-909
13.1-262	13.1-911
13.1-263	13.1-911
13.1-264	13.1-917
13.1-265 to 13.1-265.2	13.1-919
13.1-266	13.1-923
13.1-267	13.1-924
13.1-268	13.1-924
13.1-269	13.1-921
13.1-270	13.1-921
13.1-271	13.1-923
13.1-272	13.1-925
13.1-273	13.1-926
13.1-274	13.1-928
13.1-275	13.1-922
13.1-276	13.1-922
13.1-277	13.1-922
	13.1-924
13.1-278	13.1-929
13.1-278.1	13.1-929
13.1-279	13.1-930
13.1-280	13.1-931
13.1-281	13.1-920
13.1-282	13.1-936
13.1-283	13.1-936
13.1-284	13.1-815
13.1-285	13.1-816
13.1-286	13.1-117
13.1-286.1	13.1-116
13.1-287	13.1-813
13.1-288	13.1-805
13.1-289	13.1-832
13.1-290	13.1-937
13.1-290.1	13.1-937
13.1-291	13.1-802
13.1-292	13.1-939
13.1-294	Repealed
13.1-295	13.1-811
13.1-296	13.1-812

COMPARABLE SECTIONS OF TITLE 14 AND TITLE 14.1

Former Section	Present Section
14-1	14.1-1
14-2	14.1-2
14-3	14.1-3
14-4	14.1-4
14-5	14.1-5
14-5.1	14.1-6
14-5.2	14.1-7
14-5.3	14.1-8
14-5.4	14.1-9
14-5.5	14.1-10
14-6	14.1-20
14-7	14.1-21
14-8	Deleted
14-9	14.1-12
14-10	14.1-12
14-11	14.1-13
14-12	14.1-12
14-13	14.1-14
14-14	14.1-12
14-15	14.1-12
14-16	14.1-15
14-17	14.1-13
14-18	14.1-12
14-19	14.1-12
14-20	14.1-12, 14.1-13
14-21	14.1-12, 14.1-13
14-22	14.1-12, 14.1-16
14-23	14.1-12, 14.1-13
14-24	14.1-12
14-25	14.1-12, 14.1-13
14-26	14.1-12
14-27	14.1-1
14-28	Deleted
14-28.1	14.1-17
14-28.2	14.1-17
14-29	Deleted
14-29.1	14.1-18
14-30	14.1-19
14-31	14.1-22
14-32	14.1-23
14-33	14.1-24
14-34	14.1-25
14-35	14.1-26
14-36	14.1-27
14-37	14.1-28
14-38	14.1-29
14-39	14.1-30
14-40	14.1-31
14-41	14.1-32
14-42	Deleted
14-43	14.1-33
14-44	14.1-34
14-45	14.1-35
14-45.1	14.1-36
14-46	Deleted
14-47	14.1-37
14-48	14.1-38
14-49	14.1-39
14-50	14.1-40
14-51	14.1-41
14-52	14.1-42
14-52.1	Deleted
14-53	14.1-43
14-54	14.1-44
14-55	14.1-45
14-56	Deleted
14-56.1	14.1-46, 14.1-46.1
14-57	Deleted
14-58	Deleted
14-59	14.1-47
14-60	14.1-48
14-61	14.1-49
14-62	14.1-50
14-63	14.1-51
14-64	14.1-51
14-65	14.1-52
14-66	14.1-53
14-66.2	14.1-52
14-67	14.1-54
14-68 to 14.1-55	14.1-55
14-69 to 14-69.3	14.1-56
14-70 to 14-70.2	14.1-57
14-71 to 14-71.3	14.1-58
14-72	14.1-59
14-73	14.1-60
14-74	14.1-61
14-75	14.1-62
14-76	14.1-63
14-77	14.1-64
14-77.1	14.1-65
14-78	14.1-66
14-79	14.1-67
14-80	Deleted
14-81	14.1-68
14-82	14.1-69
14-83	14.1-70
14-84	14.1-71
14-85	14.1-72
14-86	14.1-73
14-86.1	14.1-74
14-87	14.1-75
14-88	14.1-76
14-89	14.1-77
14-90	14.1-78
14-91	14.1-79
14-92	14.1-81
14-93	14.1-82
14-94	14.1-83
14-95	14.1-84
14-96	14.1-85
14-97	14.1-86
14-98	14.1-87
14-99	14.1-88
14-100	14.1-89
14-101	14.1-90
14-102	14.1-91
14-103	14.1-92
14-104	14.1-93
14-105	14.1-94
14-106	14.1-95
14-107	14.1-96
14-108	14.1-97
14-109	14.1-98
14-110	14.1-99
14-111	14.1-100
14-112	14.1-101
14-113	14.1-102
14-114	14.1-103
14-115	14.1-104
14-116	14.1-105
14-117	14.1-106
14-118	14.1-107
14-119	14.1-108
14-120	14.1-109
14-121	14.1-110
14-122	14.1-111
14-123	14.1-112
14-124	14.1-113
14-124.1	14.1-114
14-125	14.1-115
14-125.1	14.1-116
14-126	14.1-117
14-127	14.1-118
14-128	14.1-119
14-129	14.1-120
14-130	14.1-121
14-131	14.1-122
14-132	14.1-123
14-132.1	14.1-124
14-133	14.1-125
14-134	14.1-126
14-135	14.1-127
14-136	14.1-128
14-137	Deleted
14-138	14.1-129
14-139	14.1-130
14-140	14.1-131
14-141	14.1-132
14-142	14.1-133
14-143	14.1-134
14-144	14.1-135
14-145	14.1-136
14-146	14.1-137
14-147	14.1-138
14-148	14.1-139
14-149	14.1-140
14-150	14.1-140.1
14-151	14.1-141
14-152	14.1-142
14-153	Deleted
14-154	Deleted
14-155	14.1-143
14-155.1	14.1-144

Former Section	Present Section
14-155.2	14.1-145
14-155.3	14.1-146
14-155.4	Deleted
14-155.5	14.1-147
14-155.6	Deleted
14-155.7	14.1-148
14-155.8	14.1-149
14-155.9	14.1-150
14-155.10	Deleted
14-155.11	14.1-152
14-155.12	14.1-153
14-155.13	14.1-154
14-155.14	14.1-155
14-156	14.1-156
14-157	14.1-157
14-158	14.1-158
14-159	14.1-159
14-160	14.1-160
14-161	14.1-161
14-162	14.1-162
14-163	14.1-163
14-163.1	14.1-164
14-164	Deleted
14-164.1	14.1-165
14-164.2	14.1-166
14-164.3	14.1-167
14-165	14.1-168
14-166	14.1-169
14-167	14.1-170
14-168	14.1-171
14-169	14.1-172
14-170	14.1-173
14-171	14.1-174
14-172	14.1-175
14-173	14.1-176
14-174	14.1-177
14-175	14.1-178
14-176	14.1-179
14-177	14.1-180
14-178	14.1-181
14-179	14.1-182
14-180	14.1-183
14-181	14.1-184
14-182	14.1-185
14-183	14.1-186
14-184	14.1-187
14-185	14.1-188
14-186	14.1-189
14-187	14.1-190
14-188	14.1-191
14-189	14.1-192
14-190	14.1-193
14-191	14.1-194
14-192	14.1-195
14-193	14.1-196
14-194	14.1-197
14-195	14.1-198
14-195.1	14.1-199
14-196	14.1-200
14-197	14.1-201
None	14.1-80

COMPARABLE SECTIONS OF TITLE 14.1 AND OTHER CORRESPONDING SECTIONS

Former Section	Present Section
14.1-1	2.1-20.5
14.1-2	2.1-20.6
14.1-3	2.1-20.7
14.1-3.1	17.1-222.1
14.1-4	2.1-20.7
14.1-5	2.1-20.8
14.1-5.1	2.1-20.9
14.1-5.2	2.1-20.10
14.1-5.3	2.1-20.11
14.1-6	2.1-20.10
14.1-7	15.2-1508.1
14.1-8	15.2-1508.2
14.1-9	2.1-20.12
14.1-10	2.1-20.11
14.1-11.1	15.2-1508.3
14.1-11.2	15.2-1508.4
14.1-11.4	15.2-1605.1
14.1-11.5	15.2-1635.1
14.1-12	2.1-38
14.1-13	2.1-38.3, 12.1-12
14.1-14	2.1-68
14.1-15	2.1-180
14.1-16	37.1-39, 37.1-42.3
14.1-17.1	30-19.11
14.1-18	30-19.12
14.1-18.1	30-19.13
14.1-18.2	30-19.14
14.1-19	30-19.15
14.1-19.1	30-19.16
14.1-20	30-19.17
14.1-21	30-19.18
14.1-22	30-19.19
14.1-23	30-19.20
14.1-29	17.1-324
14.1-30	17.1-325
14.1-31	17.1-329
14.1-32	17.1-326
14.1-33	17.1-523
14.1-35	Repealed
14.1-36	Repealed
14.1-37	17.1-524
14.1-39	Repealed
14.1-39.1	17.1-327
14.1-44.1	Repealed
14.1-44.2	19.2-46.1
14.1-44.2:1	19.2-46.2
14.1-44.3	Repealed
14.1-44.4	19.2-47.1
14.1-44.5	Repealed
14.1-45	15.2-1414.1
14.1-46.01	15.2-1414.2
14.1-46.01:1	15.2-1414.3
14.1-46.1	Repealed
14.1-47	15.2-1414.4
14.1-47.1	15.2-1414.5
14.1-47.2	15.2-1414.6
14.1-47.3	15.2-1414.7
14.1-48	15.2-1636.5
14.1-49	15.2-1636.6
14.1-50	15.2-1636.7
14.1-51	15.2-1636.8
14.1-52	15.2-1636.9
14.1-52.01	15.2-1636.10
14.1-53	15.2-1627.1
14.1-54	15.2-1627.2
14.1-55	15.2-1608.1
14.1-56	15.2-1608.2
14.1-57	15.2-1636.1
14.1-58	15.2-1636.2
14.1-59	15.2-1636.3
14.1-60	15.2-1636.4
14.1-61	15.2-1636.11
14.1-62	15.2-1636.12
14.1-63	15.2-1636.13
14.1-64	15.2-1636.14
14.1-65	15.2-1636.15
14.1-66	15.2-1636.16
14.1-67	15.2-1636.17
14.1-68	15.2-1609.2
14.1-69	15.2-1609.3
14.1-70	15.2-1609.1
14.1-73	15.2-1609.2
14.1-73.1:1	15.2-1609.2
14.1-73.1:2	15.2-1609.2
14.1-73.1:3	15.2-1609.2
14.1-73.2	15.2-1612.1
14.1-74	15.2-1609.2
14.1-75	15.2-1609.4
14.1-76	15.2-1609.5
14.1-77	15.2-1609.6
14.1-78	15.2-1609.9
14.1-79	15.2-1609.7
14.1-80	15.2-1615.1
14.1-82	15.2-1609.8
14.1-83	15.2-1614.1
14.1-84.1	9-183.13
14.1-84.2	9-183.14
14.1-84.3	9-183.15
14.1-84.4	9-183.16
14.1-84.5	9-183.17

Former Section	Present Section
14.1-84.6	9-183.18
14.1-84.6:1	9-183.19
14.1-84.6:2	9-183.20
14.1-84.7	9-183.21
14.1-86	Repealed
14.1-87	17.1-266
14.1-88	15.2-1627.3
14.1-89	15.2-1609.3
14.1-90	17.1-267
14.1-92	Repealed
14.1-93	17.1-272
14.1-94	15.2-1609.3
14.1-95	15.2-1609.3
14.1-95.1	17.1-272
14.1-96	17.1-268
14.1-97	17.1-269
14.1-98	17.1-270
14.1-99	Repealed
14.1-100	Repealed
14.1-101	17.1-271
14.1-102	Repealed
14.1-103	2.1-71.2
14.1-104	30-14.01
14.1-105	17.1-272
14.1-105.1	Deleted
14.1-106	Repealed
14.1-107	Repealed
14.1-108	17.1-274
14.1-110	17.1-274
14.1-111.1	17.1-275
14.1-112	17.1-275
14.1-112.1	Repealed
14.1-118.1	17.1-276
14.1-119	Repealed
14.1-120	17.1-328
14.1-120.1	17.1-418
14.1-121	15.2-1627.3
14.1-122	Repealed
14.1-122.1	17.1-277

Former Section	Present Section
14.1-123	16.1-69.48:1
14.1-124	Repealed
14.1-125	16.1-69.48:2
14.1-125.1	17.1-278
14.1-125.2	17.1-279
14.1-126	Repealed
14.1-130	Repealed
14.1-131	17.1-280
14.1-133	8.01-609.1
14.1-133.1	8.01-618.1
14.1-133.2	17.1-281
14.1-133.3	9-178.1
14.1-133.4	9-178.2
14.1-134.1	16.1-69.48:3
14.1-135.1	17.1-282
14.1-136	17.1-283
14.1-137	Repealed
14.1-138	17.1-283
14.1-139	17.1-283
14.1-140	17.1-284
14.1-140.1	17.1-285
14.1-141	15.2-1636.18
14.1-142	15.2-1636.19
14.1-143.2	17.1-287
14.1-144.1	17.1-288
14.1-146	Repealed
14.1-147	Repealed
14.1-151	Reserved
14.1-155.2	17.1-289
14.1-156	Repealed
14.1-157	Repealed
14.1-158	15.2-1636.6:1
14.1-159	Repealed
14.1-160	Repealed
14.1-161	15.2-1537.1, 17.1-286
14.1-162	17.1-290
14.1-163	17.1-291
14.1-164.1	Repealed
14.1-165	Repealed

Former Section	Present Section
14.1-168	Repealed
14.1-169	Repealed
14.1-170	Repealed
14.1-171	Repealed
14.1-172	Repealed
14.1-173	Repealed
14.1-174	Repealed
14.1-175	Repealed
14.1-176	Repealed
14.1-177	17.1-600
14.1-178	17.1-601
14.1-179	17.1-602
14.1-180	17.1-603
14.1-181	17.1-604
14.1-182	17.1-605
14.1-183	17.1-606
14.1-185	17.1-607
14.1-186	17.1-608
14.1-187	17.1-609
14.1-188	17.1-610
14.1-189	17.1-611
14.1-190	17.1-612
14.1-191	17.1-613
14.1-192	17.1-614
14.1-193	17.1-615
14.1-194	17.1-616
14.1-195	17.1-617
14.1-195.1	17.1-618
14.1-195.2	17.1-619
14.1-195.3	17.1-620
14.1-195.4	17.1-621
14.1-195.5	17.1-622
14.1-195.6	17.1-623
14.1-196	17.1-624
14.1-197	17.1-625
14.1-198	17.1-626
14.1-199	17.1-627
14.1-200	17.1-628
14.1-201	17.1-629

COMPARABLE SECTIONS OF TITLE 15 AND TITLE 15.1

Former Section	Present Section
15-1	15.1-6
15-2	15.1-1
15-3	15.1-508
15-4	15.1-506
15-5	15.1-3
15-5.1	15.1-8
15-6	15.1-14
15-6.1	15.1-516
15-7	15.1-15
15-7.1	15.1-16
15-7.2	15.1-18
15-7.3	15.1-18.1
15-8	15.1-504, 15.1-505, 15.1-510, 15.1-512, 15.1-514, 15.1-515

Former Section	Present Section
15-8.1	15.1-513
15-8.2	15.1-18.2
15-9	15.1-507
15-9.1	15.1-9
15-9.2	15.1-9
15-10	15.1 504, 15.1-522
15-10.1	15.1-19
15-10.1:1	15.1-2
15-10.1:2	15.1-509
15-11	15.1-10
15-12	15.1-10, 15.1-10.1
15-13	15.1-10
15-13.1	15.1-20
15-13.2	15.1-21
15-14	15.1-11
15-15	Repealed

Former Section	Present Section
15-15.1	15.1-22
15-15.2	Repealed
15-15.3	15.1-23
15-16	15.1-24
15-16.1	15.1-25
15-16.2	15.1-26
15-16.3	Deleted
15-16.4	Deleted
15-16.5	15.1-27
15-16.6	15.1-515.1
15-17	15.1-511
15-18	15.1-28
15-18.1	15.1-29
15-19	15.1-17
15-19.1	15.1-30
15-20	15.1-521

Former Section	Present Section
15-20.1	15.1-517
15-20.2	15.1-517
15-20.3	15.1-518
15-20.3:1	15.1-518.1
15-20.4	15.1-519
15-20.5	15.1-520
15-20.6	15.1-31
15-20.8	15.1-37
15-21	Deleted
15-22	Repealed
15-23	Deleted
15-24	15.1-32
15-24.1	Repealed
15-24.2	Repealed
15-24.3	15.1-546.1
15-24.4	15.1-34
15-25	15.1-35
15-25.1	15.1-36
15-26	Deleted
15-26.1	15.1-37 15.1-809.1
15-27 to 15-37	Repealed
15-38	15.1-1026
15-39	15.1-1027
15-40	15.1-1028
15-41	15.1-1029
15-42	15.1-1030
15-42.1	15.1-1031
15-43	15.1-559
15-44	15.1-560
15-45	15.1-561
15-46	15.1-562
15-47	15.1-563
15-48	15.1-564
15-49	15.1-565
15-50	15.1-566
15-51	15.1-567
15-52	15.1-568
15-53	15.1-569
15-54	15.1-570
15-55	15.1-571
15-56	15.1-572
15-57	15.1-573
15-58	15.1-574
15-59	15.1-575
15-60	15.1-576
15-61	15.1-577
15-62	15.1-578
15-63	15.1-579
15-64	15-1-580
15-65	15.1-581
15-65.1	15.1-833
15-65.2	15.1-834
15-65.3	15.1-835
15-65.4	15.1-836
15-66	15.1-966
15-67	15.1-967
15-68	15.1-968
15-69	15.1-969
15-70	15.1-970
15-71	15.1-971
15-72	15.1-972
15-73	15.1-973
15-74	15.1-974
15-75	15.1-975
15-76	15.1-976
15-77	15.1-977
15-77.1	15.1-837
15-77.2	15.1-838
15-77.3	15.1-839
15-77.4	15.1-840
15-77.5	15.1-841
15-77.6	15.1-842
15-77.7	15.1-843
15-77.8	15.1-844
15-77.9	15.1-845
15-77.10	15.1-846
15-77.11	15.1-847
15-77.12	15.1-848
15-77.13	15.1-849
15-77.14	15.1-850
15-77.15	15.1-851
15-77.16	15.1-852
15-77.17	15.1-853
15-77.18	15.1-854
15-77.19	15.1-855
15-77.20	15.1-856
15-77.21	15.1-857
15-77.22	15.1-858
15-77.23	15.1-859
15-77.24	15.1-860
15-77.25	15.1-861
15-77.26	15.1-862
15-77.27	15.1-863
15-77.28	15.1-864
15-77.29	15.1-865
15-77.30	15.1-866
15-77.31	15.1-867
15-77.32	15.1-868
15-77.33	15.1-869
15-77.34	15.1-870
15-77.35	15.1-871
15-77.36	15.1-872
15-77.37	15.1-873
15-77.38	15.1-874
15-77.39	15.1-875
15-77.40	15.1-876
15-77.41	15.1-877
15-77.42	15.1-878
15-77.43	15.1-879
15-77.44	15.1-880
15-77.45	15.1-881
15-77.46	15.1-882
15-77.47	15.1-883
15-77.48	15.1-884
15-77.49	15.1-885
15-77.50	15.1-886
15-77.51	15.1-887
15-77.52	15.1-888
15-77.53	15.1-889
15-77.54	15.1-890
15-77.55	15.1-891
15-77.56	15.1-892
15-77.57	15.1-893
15-77.58	15.1-894
15-77.59	15.1-895
15-77.59:1	15.1-896
15-77.60	15.1-897
15-77.61	15.1-898
15-77.62	15.1-899
15-77.63	15.1-900
15-77.64	15.1-901
15-77.65	15.1-902
15-77.66	15.1-903
15-77.67	15.1-904
15-77.68	15.1-905
15-77.69	15.1-906
15-77.70	15.1-907
15-77.71	15.1-908
15-77.72	15.1-910
15-77.73	15.1-911
15-77.74	15.1-912
15-77.75	15.1-913
15-77.76	15.1-914
15-77.77	15.1-915
15-78	15.1-978
15-79	15.1-979
15-80	15.1-980
15-81	15.1-981
15-82	15.1-982
15-83	15.1-983
15-84	15.1-984
15-85	15.1-985
15-86	15.1-986
15-87	15.1-987
15-88	15.1-988
15-89	15.1-989
15-90	15.1-990
15-91	15.1-991
15-92	15.1-992
15-93	15.1-993
15-94	15.1-994
15-94.1	15.1-995
15-95	15.1-996
15-96	15.1-997
15-97	15.1-998
15-98	15.1-999
15-99	15.1-1000
15-100	15.1-1001
15-101	15.1-1002
15-102	15.1-1003
15-103	15.1-1004
15-104	15.1-1005
15-105	15.1-1006
15-106	15.1-1007
15-107	Deleted
15-108	15.1-1009
15-109	15.1-1010
15-110	15.1-1011
15-111	15.1-1012
15-112	15.1-1013
15-113	15.1-1014
15-114	15.1-1015

Former Section	Present Section
15-115	15.1-1016
15-116	15.1-1017
15-117	15.1-1018
15-118	15.1-1019
15-119	15.1-1020
15-120	15.1-1021
15-121	15.1-1022
15-122	15.1-1023
15-123	15.1-1024
15-124	15.1-1025
15-125 to 15-152.1	Repealed
15-152.2	15.1-1032
15-152.3	15.1-1033
15-152.4	15.1-1034
15-152.5	15.1-1035
15-152.6	15.1-1036
15-152.7	15.1-1037
15-152.8	15.1-1038
15-152.9	15.1-1039
15-152.10	15.1-1040
15-152.11	15.1-1041
15-152.12	15.1-1042
15-152.13	15.1-1043
15-152.14	15.1-1044
15-152.15	15.1-1045
15-152.16	15.1-1046
15-152.17	15.1-1047
15-152.18	15.1-1048
15-152.19	15.1-1049
15-152.20	15.1-1050
15-152.21	15.1-1051
15-152.22	15.1-1052
15-152.23	15.1-1053
15-152.24	15.1-1054
15-152.25	15.1-1055
15-152.26	15.1-1056
15-152.27	15.1-1057
15-152.28	15.1-1058
15-153	15.1-1059
15-154	15.1-1060
15-155	15.1-1061
15-156	15.1-1062
15-157	15.1-1063
15-158	15.1-1064
15-159	15.1-1065
15-160	15.1-1066
15-161	15.1-1067
15-161.1	15.1-1068
15-161.2	15.1-1069
15-161.3	15.1-1070
15-162	15.1-1071
15-163	15.1-1072
15-164	15.1-1073
15-165	15.1-1074
15-166	15.1-1075
15-167	15.1-1076
15-168	15.1-1077
15-169	15.1-1078
15-170	15.1-1079
15-171	15.1-1080
15-172	15.1-1081
15-173	15.1-1082
15-174	15.1-1083
15-175	15.1-1084
15-176	15.1-1085
15-177	15.1-1086
15-178	15.1-1087
15-179	15.1-1088
15-180	15.1-1089
15-181	15.1-1090
15-182	15.1-1091
15-183	15.1-1092
15-184	15.1-1093
15-185	15.1-1094
15-186	15.1-1095
15-187	15.1-1096
15-188	15.1-1097
15-189	15.1-1098
15-190	15.1-1099
15-191	15.1-1100
15-192	15.1-1101
15-193	15.1-1102
15-194	15.1-1103
15-195	15.1-1104
15-196	15.1-1105
15-197	15.1-1106
15-198	15.1-1107
15-199	15.1-1108
15-200	15.1-1109
15-201	15.1-1110
15-202	15.1-1111
15-203	15.1-1112
15-203.1	15.1-1113
15-204	15.1-1114
15-205	15.1-1115
15-206	15.1-1116
15-207	15.1-1117
15-208	15.1-1118
15-209	15.1-1119
15-210	15.1-1120
15-211	15.1-1121
15-212	15.1-1122
15-213	15.1-1123
15-214	15.1-1124
15-215	15.1-1125
15-216	15.1-1126
15-217	15.1-1127
15-218	15.1-1128
15-219	15.1-1129
15-220	15.1-1130
15-221	15.1-1131
15-222	15.1-1132
15-222.1	15.1-1133
15-222.2	15.1-1134
15-222.3	15.1-1135
15-222.4	15.1-1136
15-223	15.1-1137
15-224	15.1-1138
15-225	15.1-1139
15-226	15.1-1140
15-227	15.1-1141
15-228	15.1-1142
15-229	15.1-1143
15-230	15.1-1144
15-231	15.1-1145
15-231.1	15.1-1146
15-231.2	15.1-1147
15-231.3	15.1-1148
15-231.4 to 15-231.4:78	Deleted
15-232	15.1-527
15-233	15.1-528
15-234	15.1-529
15-235	15.1-530
15-236	15.1-531
15-237	15.1-532
15-238	15.1-533
15-239	15.1-534
15-240	15.1-535
15-241	15.1-536
15-242	15.1-537
15-243	15.1-538
15-244	15.1-539
15-245	15.1-540
15-246	15.1-541
15-247	15.1-542
15-248	15.1-543
15-249	15.1-544
15-250	15.1-545
15-251	15.1-546
15-252	Deleted
15-253	15.1-547
15-254	15.1-548
15-255	Repealed
15-256	15.1-549
15-257	15.1-550
15-258	15.1-551
15-259	15.1-552
15-260	15.1-553
15-261	15.1-554
15-262	15.1-555
15-263	15.1-556
15-264	15.1-557
15-265	15.1-558
15-266	15.1-582
15-267	15.1-583
15-268	15.1-584
15-269	15.1-585
15-270	15.1-586
15-271	15.1-587
15-272	15.1-588
15-273	15.1-589
15-274	15.1-590
15-274.1	15.1-591
15-275	15.1-592
15-276	15.1-593
15-277	15.1-594
15-278	15.1-595
15-279	15.1-596
15-280	15.1-597
15-281	15.1-598
15-282	15.1-599

Former Section	Present Section
15-283	15.1-600
15-284	15.1-601
15-285	15.1-602
15-286	15.1-603
15-287	15.1-604
15-288	15.1-605
15-289	15.1-606
15-290	15.1-607
15-291	15.1-608
15-292	15.1-609
15-293	15.1-610
15-294	15.1-611
15-295	15.1-612
15-296	15.1-613
15-297	15.1-614
15-298	15.1-615
15-299	15.1-616
15-300	15.1-617
15-301	15.1-618
15-302	15.1-619
15-303	15.1-620
15-304	15.1-621
15-305	15.1-622
15-306	15.1-623
15-306.1	15.1-624
15-307	15.1-625
15-307.1	15.1-626
15-308	15.1-627
15-309	15.1-628
15-310	15.1-629
15-310.1	15.1-630
15-311	15.1-631
15-312	15.1-632
15-313	15.1-633
15-314	15.1-634
15-315	15.1-635
15-316	15.1-636
15-317	15.1-637
15-318	15.1-638
15-319	15.1-639
15-320	15.1-640
15-321	15.1-641
15-322	15.1-642
15-323	15.1-643
15-324	15.1-644
15-325	15.1-645
15-326	15.1-646
15-327	15.1-647
15-328	15.1-648
15-328.1	15.1-649
15-328.2	15.1-650
15-329	15.1-652
15-330	15.1-653
15-331	15.1-654
15-332	15.1-655
15-333	15.1-656
15-334	15.1-657
15-334.1	15.1-658
15-335	15.1-659
15-336	15.1-660
15-337	15.1-661
15-338	15.1-662
15-339	15.1-663
15-340	15.1-664
15-341	15.1-665
15-342	15.1-666
15-343	15.1-667
15-344	15.1-668
15-345	15.1-669
15-346	15.1-670
15-347	15.1-671
15-348	15.1-672
15-349	15.1-673
15-350	15.1-674
15-350.1	15.1-675
15-350.2	15.1-675.1
15-351	15.1-676
15-352	15.1-677
15-352.1	15.1-678
15-352.2	15.1-679
15-352.3	15.1-680
15-352.4	15.1-681
15-353	15.1-682
15-353.1	15.1-683
15-353.2	15.1-684
15-354	15.1-685
15-354.1	15.1-686
15-354.3	15.1-686.1
15-355	15.1-687
15-355.1	15.1-688
15-356	15.1-689
15-356.1	15.1-690
15-357	15.1-691
15-358	15.1-692
15-359	15.1-693
15-360	15.1-694
15-360.1	15.1-695
15-361	Deleted
15-362	15.1-697
15-363	15.1-698
15-364	15.1-699
15-365	15.1-700
15-366	15.1-701
15-367	15.1-702
15-368	15.1-703
15-369	15.1-704
15-370	15.1-705
15-371	15.1-706
15-371.1	15.1-707
15-372	15.1-708
15-373	15.1-709
15-374	15.1-710
15-375	15.1-711
15-376	15.1-712
15-377	15.1-713
15-378	15.1-714
15-379	15.1-715
15-380	15.1-716
15-381	15.1-717
15-382	15.1-718
15-382.1	15.1-719
15-383	15.1-720
15-384	15.1-721
15-384.10	15.1-722
15-384.11	15.1-723
15-384.12	15.1-724
15-384.13	15.1-725
15-384.14	15.1-726
15-384.15	15.1-727
15-384.16	15.1-728
15-384.17	15.1-729
15-384.18	15.1-730
15-384.19	15.1-731
15-384.20	15.1-732
15-384.21	15.1-733
15-384.22	15.1-734
15-384.23	15.1-735
15-384.24	15.1 736
15-384.25	15.1-737
15-384.26	15.1-738
15-384.27	15.1-739
15-384.28	15.1-740
15-384.29	15.1-741
15-384.30	15.1-742
15-384.31	15.1-743
15-384.32	15.1-744
15-384.33	15.1-745
15-384.34	15.1-746
15-384.35	15.1-747
15-384.36	15.1-748
15-384.37	15.1-749
15-384.38	15.1-750
15-284.39	15.1-751
15-384.40	15.1-752
15-384.41	15.1-753
15-384.42	15.1-754
15-384.43	15.1-755
15-384.44	15.1-756
15-384.45	15.1-757
15-384.46	15.1-758
15-384.47	15.1-759
15-384.47:1	15.1-760
15-384.48	15.1-761
15-384.49	15.1-762
15-384.50	15.1-763
15-384.51	15.1-764
15-384.52	15.1-765
15-384.53	15.1-766
15-384.54	15.1-767
15-384.55	15.1-768
15-384.56	15.1-769
15-384.57	15.1-770
15-384.58	15.1-771
15-384.59	15.1-772
15-384.60	15.1-773
15-384.61	15.1-774
15-384.62	15.1-775
15-384.63	15.1-776
15-384.64	15.1-777
15-384.65	15.1-778
15-384.66	15.1-779
15-384.67	15.1-780
15-384.68	15.1-781

Former Section	Present Section
15-384.69	15.1-782
15-384.70	15.1-783
15-384.71	15.1-784
15-384.72	15.1-785
15-384.73	15.1-786
15-384.74	15.1-787
15-384.75	15.1-788
15-384.76	15.1-789
15-384.77	15.1-790
15-384.78	15.1-791
15-385	15.1-792
15-386	15.1-793
15-387	15.1-794
15-388	15.1-795
15-389	15.1-796
15-390	15.1-797
15-391	15.1-798
15-392	15.1-799
15-393	15.1-800
15-394	15.1-801
15-395	15.1-802
15-396	15.1-803
15-397	15.1-804
15-398	15.1-805
15-399	15.1-806
15-400	15.1-807
15-401	15.1-808
15-402	15.1-809
15-403	15.1-810
15-404	15.1-811
15-405	15.1-812
15-406	15.1-813
15-406.1	15.1-813.1
15-407	15.1-814
15-408	15.1-815
15-409	15.1-816
15-410	15.1-817
15-411	15.1-818
15-412	15.1-819
15-413	15.1-820
15-414	15.1-821
15-415	15.1-822
15-416	15.1-823
15-417	15.1-824
15-418	15.1-825
15-419	15.1-826
15-420	15.1-827
15-421	15.1-828
15-422	15.1-829
15-423	15.1-830
15-424	15.1-831
15-425	15.1-832
15-426	15.1-916
15-426.1	15.1-917
15-427	15.1-918
15-428	15.1-919
15-429	15.1-920
15-430	15.1-921
15-431	15.1-922
15-432	15.1-923
15-433	16.1-924

Former Section	Present Section
15-434	15.1-925
15-435	15.1-926
15-436	15.1-927
15-437	15.1-928
15-438	15.1-929
15-439	15.1-930
15-440	15.1-931
15-441	15.1-932
15-442	15.1-933
15-443	15.1-934
15-444	15.1-935
15-445	15.1-936
15-446	15.1-937
15-447	15.1-938
15-448	15.1-939
15-449	15.1-940
15-450	15.1-941
15-451	15.1-942
15-452	15.1-943
15-453	15.1-944
15-454	15.1-945
15-455	15.1-946
15-456	15.1-947
15-457	15.1-948
15-458	15.1-949
15-459	15.1-950
15-460	15.1-951
15-461	15.1-952
15-462	15.1-953
15-463	15.1-954
15-464	15.1-955
15-465	15.1-956
15-466	15.1-957
15-467	15.1-958
15-468	15.1-959
15-469	15.1-960
15-470	15.1-961
15-471	15.1-962
15-472	15.1-963
15-473	15.1-964
15-474	15.1-965
15-475	15.1-38
15-476	15.1-39
15-477	15.1-40
15-478	15.1-41
15-479	15.1-42
15-480	15.1-43
15-481	15.1-44
15-481.1	15.1-44.1
15-482	15.1-45
15-483	15.1-46
15-484	15.1-47
15-485	15.1-48
15-485.1	15.1-49
15-486	15.1-50
15-487	15.1-51
15-487.1	Deleted
15-488	15.1-52
15-489	Deleted
15-490	15.1-53
15-491	15.1-54

Former Section	Present Section
15-492	15.1-55
15-493	15.1-56
15-494	15.1-57
15-495	15.1-58
15-496	15.1-59
15-497	15.1-60
15-498	15.1-61
15-499	15.1-62
15-500	15.1-63
15-501	15.1-64
15-502	15.1-65
15-503	15.1-66
15-504	15.1-67
15-504.1	15.1-68
15-504.2	15.1-69
15-505	15.1-70
15-506	15.1-71
15-507	15.1-72
15-508	15.1-73
15-508.1	15.1-73.1
15-509	15.1-74
15-510	15.1-75
15-511	15.1-76
15-512	15.1-77
15-513	15.1-78
15-514	15.1-79
15-515	15.1-80
15-516	15.1-81
15-517	15.1-82
15-518	15.1-83
15-519	15.1-84
15-520	15.1-85
15-521	15.1-86
15-522	15.1-87
15-523	15.1-88
15-524	15.1-89
15-525	15.1-90
15-526	Repealed
15-527	15.1-91
15-528	15.1-92
15-529	15.1-93
15-530	15.1-94
15-531	15.1-95
15-532	15.1-96
15-533	15.1-97
15-534	15.1-98
15-535	15.1-99
15-536	15.1-100
15-537	15.1-101
15-538	15.1-102
15-539	15.1-103
15-540	15.1-104
15-541	15.1-105
15-542	15.1-106
15-543	15.1-107
15-544	15.1-108
15-545	15.1-109
15-546	15.1-110
15-547	15.1-111
15-548	15.1-112
15-549	15.1-113

Former Section	Present Section
15-550	Deleted
15-551	15.1-114
15-551.1	15.1-115
15-551.2	15.1-116
15-551.3	15.1-117
15-551.4	15.1-118
15-551.5	15.1-119
15-551.6	15.1-120
15-551.7	15.1-121
15-551.8	15.1-122
15-551.9	15.1-123
15-551.10	15.1-124
15-551.11	15.1-125
15-551.11:1	15.1-126
15-551.12	15.1-127
15-551.13	15.1-128
15-551.14	15.1-129
15-551.15	15.1-130
15-552	15.1-131
15-552.1	15.1-131.1
15-553	15.1-132
15-554	15.1-133
15-555	15.1-134
15-555.1	15.1-135
15-555.2	15.1-136
15-556	15.1-137
15-557	15.1-138
15-558	15.1-139
15-559	15.1-140
15-560	15.1-141
15-560.1	15.1-142
15-561	15.1-143
15-562	15.1-144
15-563	15.1-145
15-564	15.1-146
15-565	15.1-147
15-566	15.1-148
15-567	15.1-149
15-568	15.1-150
15-569	15.1-151
15-570	15.1-152
15-571	15.1-153
15-572	15.1-154
15-573	15.1-155
15-574	15.1-156
15-574.1	15.1-157
15-574.2	15.1-158
15-574.3	15.1-159
15-574.4	15.1-159.1
15-575	15.1-160
15-576	15.1-161
15-577	15.1-162
15-578	15.1-163
15-579	15.1-164
15-580	15.1-165
15-581	15.1-166
15-582	Repealed
15-583	15.1-167
15-584	15.1-168
15-585	15.1-169
15-586 to 15-666.12	Repealed
15-666.13	15.1-170
15-666.14	15.1-171
15-666.15	15.1-172
15-666.16	15.1-173
15-666.17	15.1-174
15-666.18	15.1-175
15-666.18:1	15.1-175.1
15-666.19	15.1-176
15-666.20	15.1-177
15-666.21	15.1-178
15-666.22	15.1-179
15-666.23	15.1-180
15-666.24	15.1-181
15-666.25	15.1-182
15-666.26	15.1-183
15-666.27	15.1-184
15-666.27:1	15.1-184.1
15-666.28	15.1-185
15-666.29	15.1-186
15-666.30	15.1-187
15-666.31	15.1-188
15-666.32	15.1-189
15-666.32:1	15.1-190
15-666.32:2	15.1-191
15-666.32:3	15.1-190.1
15-666.33	15.1-192
15-666.34	15.1-193
15-666.35	15.1-194
15-666.36	15.1-195
15-666.37	15.1-196
15-666.38	15.1-197
15-666.39	15.1-198
15-666.40	15.1-199
15-666.41	15.1-200
15-666.42	15.1-201
15-666.43	15.1-202
15-666.44	15.1-203
15-666.45	15.1-204
15-666.46	15.1-205
15-666.47	15.1-206
15-666.48	15.1-207
15-666.49	15.1-208
15-666.50	15.1-209
15-666.51	15.1-210
15-666.52	15.1-211
15-666.53	15.1-212
15-666.54	15.1-213
15-666.55	15.1-214
15-666.56	15.1-215
15-666.57	15.1-216
15-666.58	15.1-217
15-666.59	15.1-218
15-666.60	15.1-219
15-666.61	15.1-220
15-666.62	15.1-221
15-666.63	15.1-222
15-666.64	15.1-223
15-666.65	15.1-224
15-666.66	15.1-225
15-666.67	15.1-226
15-666.68	15.1-227
15-666.69	15.1-228
15-666.70	15.1-229
15-666.71	15.1-230
15-666.72	15.1-231
15-666.73	15.1-232
15-666.74	15.1-233
15-666.75	15.1-234
15-666.76	15.1-235
15-666.77	15.1-235.1
15-667	15.1-236
15-668	15.1-237
15-668.1	15.1-238
15-668.2	15.1-238 15.1-238.1
15-669	15.1-239
15-670	15.1-240
15-671	15.1-241
15-672	15.1-242
15-673	15.1-243
15-674	15.1-244
15-675	15.1-245
15-676	15.1-246
15-677	15.1-247
15-678	15.1-248
15-678.1	15.1-249
15-679	15.1-250
15-680	15.1-251
15-681	15.1-252
15-682	15.1-253
15-683	15.1-254
15-684	15.1-255
15-685	15.1-256
15-686 to 15-688	15.1-257
15-689	15.1-258
15-690	15.1-259
15-691	15.1-260
15-691.1	15.1-261
15-692	15.1-262
15-692.1	15.1-263
15-692.2	15.1-264
15-592.3	15.1-265
15-693	15.1-266
15-693.1	15.1-267
15-694	15.1-268
15-695	15.1-269
15-696	15.1-270
15-697	15.1-271
15-698	15.1-272
15-699	15.1-273
15-700	15.1-274
15-701	15.1-275
15-702	15.1-276
15-703	15.1-277
15.704	15.1-278
15-705	15.1-279
15-705.1	15.1-280
15-706	15.1-281
15-707	15.1-282

Former Section	Present Section
15-707.1	15.1-283
15-708	15.1-284
15-709	15.1-285
15-709.1	15.1-286
15-710	15.1-287
15-711	15.1-288
15-712	15.1-289
15-713	15.1-290
15-714	15.1-291
15-714.1	15.1-1228
15-714.2	15.1-1229
15-714.3	15.1-1230
15-714.4	15.1-1231
15-714.5	15.1-1232
15-714.6	15.1-1233
15-714.7	15.1-1234
15-714.8	15.1-1235
15-714.9	15.1-1236
15-714.10	15.1-1237
15-714.11	15.1-1238
15-714.12	15.1-1238.1
15-714.13	15.1-1271
15-714.14	15.1-1272
15-714.15	15.1-1273
15-714.16	15.1-1274
15-714.17	15.1-1275
15-714.18	15.1-1276
15-714.19	15.1-1277
15-714.20	15.1-1278
15-714.21	15.1-1279
15-714.22	15.1-1280
15-714.23	15.1-1281
15-714.24	15.1-1282
15-714.25	15.1-1283
15-714.26	15.1-1284
15-714.27	15.1-1285
15-714.28	15.1-1286
15-715	15.1-292
15-716	15.1-293
15-717	15.1-294
15-717.1	15.1-295
15-717.2	15.1-296
15-718	15.1-297
15-719	15.1-298
15-719.1	15.1-299
15-720	15.1-300
15-721	15.1-301
15-722	15.1-302
15-723	15.1-303
15-724	15.1-304
15-725	15.1-305
15-726	15.1-306
15-727	15.1-307
15-728	15.1-308
15-729	15.1-309
15-730	15.1-310
15-731	15.1-311
15-732	15.1-312
15-733	15.1-313
15-734	15.1-314
15-735	15.1-315
15-736	15.1-316
15-737	15.1-317
15-738	15.1-318
15-739	15.1-319
15-739.1	15.1-320
15-739.2	15.1-321
15-739.3	15.1-322
15-739.3:1	15.1-322.1
15-739.4	15.1-323
15-739.5	15.1-324
15-739.6	15.1-325
15-739.7	15.1-326
15-739.8	15.1-327
15-739.9	15.1-328
15-739.10	15.1-329
15-739.11	15.1-330
15-739.12	15.1-331
15-739.13	15.1-332
15-740 to 15-746	Repealed
15-747	15.1-333
15-748	15.1-334
15-749	15.1-335
15-750	15.1-336
15-751	15.1-337
15-752	15.1-338
15-753	15.1-339
15-754	15.1-340
15-754.1	15.1-341
15-754.2	15.1-342
15-754.3	15.1-343
15-754.4	15.1-344
15-754.5	15.1-345
15-754.6	15.1-346
15-754.7	15.1-347
15-754.8	15.1-348
15-755	15.1-349
15-756	15.1-350
15-757	15.1-351
15-758	15.1-352
15-759	15.1-353
15-759.1	15.1-354
15-759.2	15.1-355
15-760	15.1-356
15-761	15.1-357
15-761.1	15.1-358
15-761.2	15.1-359
15-762	15.1-360
15-763	15.1-361
15-764	15.1-362
15-764.1	15.1-1239
15-764.2	15.1-1240
15-764.3	15.1-1241
15-764.4	15.1-1242
15-764.5	15.1-1243
15-764.6	15.1-1244
15-764.7	15.1-1245
15-764.8	15.1-1246
15-764.9	15.1-1247
15-765.10	15.1-1248
15-764.11	15.1-1249
15-764.12	15.1-1250
15-764.13	15.1-1251
15-764.14	15.1-1252
15-764.15	15.1-1253
15-764.16	15.1-1254
15-764.17	15.1-1255
15-764.18	15.1-1256
15-764.19	15.1-1257
15-764.20	15.1-1258
15-764.21	15.1-1259
15-764.22	15.1-1260
15-764.23	15.1-1261
15-764.24	15.1-1262
15-764.25	15.1-1263
15-764.26	15.1-1264
15-764.27	15.1-1265
15-764.28	15.1-1266
15-764.29	15.1-1267
15-764.30	15.1-1268
15-764.31	15.1-1269
15-764.32	15.1-1270
15-765	15.1-363
15-766	15.1-364
15-766.1 to 15-766.3	Repealed
15-767	15.1-368
15-768	15.1-369
15-769	15.1-370
15-770	15.1-371
15-771	15.1-372
15-772	15.1-373
15-773	15.1-374
15-774	15.1-375
15-775	15.1-376
15-776	15.1-377
15-777	15.1-378
15-777.1	15.1-379
15-778	15.1-380
15-779, 15-780	Repealed
15-781	15.1-465, 15.1-466
15-782	15.1-470
15-783	15.1-471
15-784	15.1-473
15-785	15.1-473
15-786	15.1-467
15-787	15.1-468
15-788	15.1-469
15-788.1	15.1-474
15-789	15.1-475
15-790	15.1-476
15-791	15.1-477
15-791.1	Repealed
15-792	15.1-478
15-792.1	Repealed
15-793	15.1-481 to 15.1-483
15-794	15.1-485
15-794.1	15.1-473
15-794.2 to 15-818	Repealed
15-819	15.1-486

Former Section	Present Section
15-820	15.1-488
15-821	15.1-489, 15.1-490
15-822	15.1-493
15-823	Repealed
15-824	15.1-487
15-825	15.1-494
15-826, 15-827	Repealed
15-828	15.1-496
15-829	15.1-496
15-830	15.1-496
15-831	15.1-495
15-832	15.1-496
15-833	15.1-496
15-834	15.1-497
15-835	15.1-497
15-836	15.1-497
15-837	15.1-497
15-838	15.1-497
15-839	15.1-497
15-840	15.1-499
15-841	Repealed
15-842	15.1-498
15-843	15.1-492
15-844	15.1-486
15-845	15.1-488
15-846	15.1-493
15-847	Repealed
15-848	15.1-492
15-849	Repealed
15-850	15.1-494 to 15.1-497
15-850.1	Repealed
15-851	15.1-499
15-852 to 15-854.1	Repealed
15-854.2	15.1-503
15-855 to 15-891	Repealed
15-891.1	15.1-427
15-891.2	15.1-432
15-891.3	15.1-433
15-891.4	15.1-432
15-891.5	Repealed
15-891.6	15.1-432
15-891.7	15.1-434, 15.1-435
15-891.8 to 15-899	Repealed
15-900	15.1-427, 15.1-443
15-901	15.1-437
15-902	Repealed
15-903	15.1-443
15-904	Repealed
15-905	15.1-445
15-906	15.1-446, 15.1-452
15-907	15.1-446
15-908	15.1-448, 15.1-449, 15.1-453
15-909	15.1-456
15-910 to 15-913	Repealed
15-914	Deleted
15-915	Repealed
15-916	15.1-427, 15.1-437
15-917	15.1-445
15-918 to 15-920	15.1-446
15-921	15,1-448, 15.1-452, 15.1-453
15-922	15.1-449, 15.1-455
15-923	15.1-456
15-924 to 15-926.1	Repealed
15-927	15.1-1310
15-928	15.1-1311
15-929	15.1-1312
15-930	15.1-1313
15-931	15.1-1314
15-932	15.1-1315
15-933	15.1-1316
15-934	15.1-1317
15-935	15.1-1318
15-936	15.1-1319
15-937	15.1-1320
15-938	15.1-1321
15-939	15.1-1322
15-940	15.1-1323
15-941	15.1-1324
15-942	15.1-1325
15-943	15.1-1326
15-944	15.1-1327
15-945	15.1-1328
15-946	15.1-1329
15-947	15.1-1330
15-948	15.1-1331
15-949	15.1-1332
15-950	15.1-1333
15-951	15.1-1334
15-952	15.1-1335
15-953	15.1-1336
15-954	15.1-1337
15-955	15.1-1338
15-956	15.1-1339
15-957	15.1-1340
15-958	15.1-1341
15-961	15.1-427
15-961.1	15.1-428
15-961.2	15.1-429
15-961.3	15.1-430
15-961.4	15.1-431
15-962	15.1-432
15-962.1	15.1-433
15-962.2	15.1-434
15-962.3	15.1-435
15-962.4	15.1-436
15-963	15.1-437
15-963.1	15.1-438
15-963.2	15.1-439
15-963.3	15.1-440
15-963.4	15.1-441
15-963.5	15.1-442
15-963.6	15.1-443
15-963.7	15.1-444
15-963.8	15.1-445
15-964	15.1-446
15-964.1	15.1-447
15-964.2	15.1-448
15-964.3	15.1-449
15-964.4	15.1-450
15-964.5	15.1-451
15-964.6	15.1-452
15-964.7	15.1-453
15-964.8	15.1-454
15-964.9	15.1-455
15-964.10	15.1-456
15-964.11	15.1-457
15-965	15.1-458
15-965.1	15.1-459
15-965.2	15.1-460
15-965.3	15.1-461
15-965.4	15.1-462
15-965.5	15.1-463
15-966	15.1-464
15-967	15.1-465
15-967.1	15.1-466
15-967.2	15.1-467
15-967.3	15.1-468
15-967.4	15.1-469
15-967.5	15.1-470
15-967.6	15.1-471
15-967.7	15.1-472
15-967.8	15.1-473
15-967.9	15.1-474
15-967.10	15.1-475
15-967.11	15.1-476
15-967.12	15.1-477
15-967.13	15.1-478
15-967.14	15.1-479
15-967.15	15.1-480
15-967.16	15.1-481
15-967.17	15.1-482
15-967.18	15.1-483
15-967.19	15.1-484
15-967.20	15.1-485
15-968	15.1-486
15-968.1	15.1-487
15-968.2	15.1-488
15-968.3	15.1-489
15-968.4	15.1-490
15-968.5	15.1-491
15-968.6	15.1-492
15-968.7	15.1-493
15-968.8	15.1-494
15-968.9	15.1-495
15-968.10	15.1-496
15-968.11	15.1-497
15-968.12	15.1-498
15-969	15.1-499
15-969.1	15.1-500
15-969.2	15.1-501
15-969.3	15.1-502

COMPARABLE SECTIONS OF TITLE 15.1 AND TITLE 15.2

Former Section	Present Section
15.1-1	15.2-100
15.1-2	Repealed
15.1-3	Repealed
15.1-4	Repealed
15.1-5	Repealed
15.1-5.1	Repealed
15.1-5.2	Repealed
15.1-5.3	Repealed
15.1-5.4	Repealed
15.1-6	15.2-102
15.1-7	15.2-1401
15.1-7.01	15.2-1405
15.1-7.1	15.2-1506
15.1-7.2	15.2-1507
15.1-7.3	15.2-1517
15.1-7.3:1	15.2-1518
15.1-7.4	15.2-1508
15.1-7.5	15.2-1509
15.1-8	15.2-1412
15.1-8.1	15.2-1627
15.1-9	15.2-1632
15.1-9.1	15.2-633
15.1-9.1:01	15.2-1542
15.1-9.1:1	15.2-1542
15.1-9.1:3	15.2-1542
15.1-10	15.2-940
15.1-10.1	15.2-1204
15.1-11	15.2-901, 15.2-1227
15.1-11.01	15.2-1215
15.1-11.02	15.2-929
15.1-11.03	15.2-905
15.1-11.04	15.2-936
15.1-11.1	15.2-904
15.1-11.2	15.2-906
15.1-11.2:1	15.2-907
15.1-11.2:2	15.2-908
15.1-11.2:3	15.2-908.1
15.1-11.3	15.2-909
15.1-11.5	15.2-937
15.1-11.5:01	15.2-938
15.1-11.5:1	15.2-935
15.1-11.5:2	15.2-939
15.1-11.5:3	15.2-928
15.1-11.6	15.2-910
15.1-11.7	15.2-962
15.1-12.1	15.2-1226
15.1-13	15.2-1407
15.1-13.1	15.2-1413
15.1-13.2	Repealed
15.1-14	15.2-967, 15.2-2013, 15.2-2029
15.1-14.1	15.2-960
15.1-14.2	15.2-961
15.1-15	Repealed
15.1-16	15.2-2026
15.1-16.1	15.2-2022
15.1-16.2	Repealed
15.1-17	15.2-1414
15.1-18	15.2-1802
15.1-18.1	15.2-944
15.1-18.1:1	15.2-943
15.1-18.2	15.2-2400 through 15.2-2403
15.1-18.3	15.2-2400, 15.2-2403
15.1-18.4	15.2-941
15.1-19	15.2-1656
15.1-19.1	15.2-1214
15.1-19.2	15.2-1520
15.1-19.2:1	15.2-1521
15.1-19.3	15.2-1605
15.1-19.4	15.2-1502
15.1-19.5	15.2-1502
15.1-20	15.2-1303
15.1-20.1	15.2-1304
15.1-20.2	15.2-1305
15.1-20.3	15.2-1513
15.1-20.4	15.2-1515
15.1-20.5	15.2-1514
15.1-20.6	15.2-1516
15.1-21	15.2-1300
15.1-21.1	15.2-1302
15.1-21.2	15.2-1301
15.1-23	15.2-966
15.1-23.1	15.2-2108
15.1-23.2	15.2-963
15.1-23.3	Repealed
15.1-24	15.2-953
15.1-24.1	15.2-954
15.1-25	15.2-953
15.1-26	15.2-953
15.1-26.01	15.2-955
15.1-26.1	21-134.01
15.1-26.2	15.2-2023
15.1-27	Repealed
15.1-27.1	15.2-973
15.1-27.2	15.2-820
15.1-28	15.2-903
15.1-28.01	15.2-931
15.1-28.02	15.2-932
15.1-28.03	15.2-933
15.1-28.04	15.2-934
15.1-28.1	15.2-930
15.1-28.2	15.2-911
15.1-28.3	15.2-912
15.1-28.4	15.2-902
15.1-28.5	Repealed
15.1-28.5:1	Repealed
15.1-28.6	15.2-942
15.1-28.7	15.2-946
15.1-29	15.2-921
15.1-29.1:1	3.1-796.94
15.1-29.2	15.2-2279
15.1-29.3	15.2-969
15.1-29.4	15.2-106
15.1-29.5	Repealed
15.1-29.6	15.2-957
15.1-29.7	15.2-956
15.1-29.8	15.2-920
15.1-29.9	15.2-922
15.1-29.10	15.2-1216
15.1-29.11	15.2-2024
15.1-29.12	15.2-919
15.1-29.13	15.2-918
15.1-29.14	15.2-107
15.1-29.15	15.2-915
15.1-29.16	15.2-2025
15.1-29.17	15.2-951
15.1-29.18	2.1-111.1, 15.2-1504
15.1-29.20	15.2-917
15.1-29.21	15.2-900
15.1-29.22	15.2-1408
15.1-29.23	15.2-1505
15.1-29.24	15.2-1127
15.1-29.25	15.2-1128
15.1-31	15.2-970
15.1-32	15.2-952
15.1-33	Repealed
15.1-33.1	15.2-2205
15.1-33.2	15.2-1411
15.1-33.3	15.2-1804
15.1-33.4	15.2-926
15.1-34	15.2-103
15.1-35	Repealed
15.1-36	Repealed
15.1-36.2	15.2-964
15.1-37	15.2-2134
15.1-37.1	15.2-2142
15.1-37.1:1	15.2-2135
15.1-37.1:2	15.2-2136
15.1-37.1:3	15.2-2137
15.1-37.1:4	15.2-2138
15.1-37.1:5	15.2-2139
15.1-37.1:6	15.2-2140
15.1-37.1:7	15.2-2141
15.1-37.2	15.2-1129
15.1-37.2:1	15.2-923
15.1-37.3	15.2-1433
15.1-37.3:1	15.2-913
15.1-37.3:2	15.2-913
15.1-37.3:3	15.2-949
15.1-37.3:4	15.2-924
15.1-37.3:5	15.2-948
15.1-37.3:6	15.2-105
15.1-37.3:8	15.2-965
15.1-37.3:9	15.2-958, 15.2-959, 15.2-1228
15.1-37.3:10	Repealed
15.1-37.3:12	15.2-914
15.1-37.3:13	15.2-104
15.1-37.3:14	15.2-1419
15.1-37.4	15.2-1400

Former Section	Present Section
15.1-37.10	15.2-1131
15.1-38	15.2-1522
15.1-39	15.2-1523
15.1-40	15.2-1524
15.1-40.1	15.2-1600
15.1-40.2	15.2-1602
15.1-40.3	Repealed
15.1-41	15.2-1527
15.1-41.1	Repealed
15.1-42	15.2-1528
15.1-42.1	Repealed
15.1-43	Repealed
15.1-43.1	15.2-1529
15.1-44	15.2-1530
15.1-44.1	15.2-1531
15.1-44.2	Repealed
15.1-45	Repealed
15.1-46	15.2-1532
15.1-47	15.2-1533
15.1-48	15.2-1603
15.1-48.1	15.2-1604
15.1-49	15.2-1635
15.1-50.01	Repealed
15.1-50.1	15.2-1628
15.1-50.2	15.2-1633
15.1-50.3	15.2-1629
15.1-50.4	15.2-1534
15.1-50.5	15.2-1535
15.1-51	15.2-1525
15.1-52	15.2-1526
15.1-52.1	15.2-1512.1
15.1-66.3	15.2-1607
15.1-66.4	15.2-1606
15.1-73.4	15.2-852
15.1-74	15.2-1616
15.1-75	15.2-1617
15.1-75.1	15.2-1618
15.1-76	Repealed
15.1-77	Repealed
15.1-78	15.2-1619
15.1-80	Repealed
15.1-81	Repealed
15.1-82	Repealed
15.1-83	15.2-1620
15.1-83.1	15.2-1615
15.1-84	15.2-1621
15.1-84.1	15.2-1614
15.1-85	15.2-1622
15.1-86	15.2-1623
15.1-87	15.2-1624
15.1-88	15.2-1625
15.1-89.1	Repealed
15.1-90	Repealed
15.1-90.2	15.2-1611
15.1-90.3	15.2-1610
15.1-90.4	15.2-1612
15.1-103	15.2-1543
15.1-104	Repealed
15.1-105	15.2-1543
15.1-106	15.2-1234
15.1-107	15.2-1235
15.1-108	15.2-1236
15.1-109	15.2-1237
15.1-110	15.2-1238, 15.2-1239
15.1-112	15.2-1240
15.1-113	15.2-1233
15.1-115	Repealed
15.1-116	Repealed
15.1-117	Repealed
15.1-118	Repealed
15.1-119	Repealed
15.1-120	Repealed
15.1-121	15.2-1203
15.1-122	Repealed
15.1-124	Repealed
15.1-125	Repealed
15.1-126	Repealed
15.1-127	15.2-1231
15.1-128	15.2-1231
15.1-129	15.2-1231
15.1-130	Repealed
15.1-131	15.2-1724, 15.2-1727
15.1-131.1	Repealed
15.1-131.2	Repealed
15.1-131.3	15.2-1726
15.1-131.4	15.2-1729
15.1-131.5	15.2-1730
15.1-131.6	15.2-1711
15.1-131.6:1	15.2-1702
15.1-131.6:2	15.2-1703
15.1-131.7	15.2-1701
15.1-131.8	15.2-1705
15.1-131.8:1	15.2-1706
15.1-131.8:2	15.2-1707
15.1-131.8:3	15.2-1708
15.1-131.8:4	15.2-1709
15.1-131.9	15.2-1718
15.1-131.10	15.2-1728
15.1-131.11	Repealed
15.1-131.12	15.2-1715
15.1-132	Repealed
15.1-132.1	15.2-1716
15.1-132.2	15.2-1130
15.1-133	15.2-1720
15.1-133.01	15.2-1719
15.1-133.01:1	15.2-1721
15.1-133.1	15.2-1712
15.1-134	15.2-1511
15.1-135	Repealed
15.1-135.1	15.2-1722
15.1-137	15.2-1700
15.1-137.1	Repealed
15.1-137.2	15.2-1713
15.1-137.3	15.2-1613
15.1-138	15.2-1704, 15.2-1710
15.1-138.1	Repealed
15.1-139	15.2-1717
15.1-140	Repealed
15.1-140.1	15.2-1714
15.1-142	15.2-1725
15.1-142.1	Repealed
15.1-142.2	15.2-1723
15.1-143	Repealed
15.1-143.1	Repealed
15.1-144	15.2-1737
15.1-145	15.2-1738
15.1-146	15.2-1739
15.1-147	15.2-1740
15.1-149	15.2-1741
15.1-150	15.2-1742
15.1-151	15.2-1743
15.1-152	15.2-1744
15.1-153	15.2-1745
15.1-154	15.2-1746
15.1-155	Repealed
15.1-159.2	15.2-1731
15.1-159.3	15.2-1732
15.1-159.4	15.2-1733
15.1-159.5	15.2-1734
15.1-159.6	15.2-1735
15.1-159.7	15.2-1736
15.1-159.7:1	15.2-1747
15.1-159.7:2	15.2-1748
15.1-159.7:3	15.2-1749
15.1-159.7:4	15.2-1750
15.1-159.7:5	15.2-1751
15.1-159.7:6	15.2-1752
15.1-159.7:7	15.2-1753
15.1-159.8	15.2-2500
15.1-159.9	15.2-2502
15.1-160	15.2-2503
15.1-161	15.2-2504
15.1-161.1	15.2-2505
15.1-162	15.2-2506
15.1-162.1	15.2-2507
15.1-163	15.2-2508
15.1-163.1	Repealed
15.1-164	15.2-2509
15.1-165	Repealed
15.1-166	15.2-2510
15.1-167	15.2-2511
15.1-168	15.2-2513
15.1-169	15.2-2513
15.1-227.1	15.2-2600
15.1-227.2	15.2-2601
15.1-227.3	15.2-2602
15.1-227.6	15.2-2603
15.1-227.7	15.2-2604, 15.2-2605
15.1-227.8	15.2-2606
15.1-227.9	15.2-2607
15.1-227.10	15.2-2608
15.1-227.11	15.2-2609
15.1-227.12	15.2-2610
15.1-227.13	15.2-2611
15.1-227.14	15.2-2612
15.1-227.15	15.2-2613
15.1-227.16	15.2-2614
15.1-227.17	15.2-2615
15.1-227.18	15.2-2616

Former Section	Present Section
15.1-227.19	15.2-2617
15.1-227.20	15.2-2618
15.1-227.21	15.2-2619
15.1-227.22	15.2-2620
15.1-227.23	15.2-2621
15.1-227.24	15.2-2622
15.1-227.24:1	15.2-2623
15.1-227.25	15.2-2624
15.1-227.26	15.2-2625
15.1-227.27	15.2-2626
15.1-227.28	15.2-2627
15.1-227.29	15.2-2628
15.1-227.30	15.2-2629
15.1-227.31	15.2-2630
15.1-227.32	15.2-2631
15.1-227.33	15.2-2632
15.1-227.34	15.2-2633
15.1-227.35	15.2-2634
15.1-227.36	15.2-2635
15.1-227.37	15.2-2636
15.1-227.38	15.2-2637
15.1-227.39	15.2-2638
15.1-227.40	15.2-2639
15.1-227.41	15.2-2640
15.1-227.42	15.2-2641
15.1-227.43	15.2-2642
15.1-227.44	15.2-2643
15.1-227.45	15.2-2644
15.1-227.47	15.2-2645
15.1-227.48	15.2-2646
15.1-227.49	15.2-2647
15.1-227.50	15.2-2648
15.1-227.51	15.2-2649
15.1-227.52	15.2-2650
15.1-227.53	15.2-2651
15.1-227.54	15.2-2652
15.1-227.55	15.2-2653
15.1-227.56	15.2-2654
15.1-227.57	15.2-2655
15.1-227.58	15.2-2656
15.1-227.59	15.2-2657
15.1-227.60	15.2-2658
15.1-227.61	15.2-2659
15.1-227.62	15.2-2660
15.1-227.63	15.2-2661
15.1-227.64	15.2-2662
15.1-227.65	15.2-2663
15.1-227.70	15.2-5800
15.1-227.71	15.2-5801
15.1-227.72	15.2-5802
15.1-227.73	15.2-5803
15.1-227.74	15.2-5804
15.1-227.75	15.2-5805
15.1-227.76	15.2-5806
15.1-227.77	15.2-5807
15.1-227.78	15.2-5808
15.1-227.79	15.2-5809
15.1-227.80	15.2-5810
15.1-227.81	15.2-5811
15.1-227.82	15.2-5812
15.1-227.83	15.2-5813
15.1-227.84	15.2-5814
15.1-227.85	15.2-5815
15.1-227.86	15.2-5816
15.1-227.87	15.2-5817
15.1-227.88	15.2-5818
15.1-227.89	15.2-5819
15.1-227.90	15.2-5820
15.1-227.91	15.2-5821
15.1-236	Repealed
15.1-237	Repealed
15.1-238	15.2-1904, 15.2-1905
15.1-238.1	Repealed
15.1-239	15.2-2404
15.1-240	15.2-2405
15.1-241	15.2-2406
15.1-242	15.2-2407
15.1-243	15.2-2408
15.1-244	15.2-2409
15.1-245	15.2-2410
15.1-246	15.2-2411
15.1-247	15.2-2412
15.1-248	Repealed
15.1-249	Repealed
15.1-249.1	15.2-2413
15.1-250	Repealed
15.1-251	Repealed
15.1-252	Repealed
15.1-253	Repealed
15.1-254	Repealed
15.1-255	Repealed
15.1-256	Repealed
15.1-257	15.2-1638
15.1-258	15.2-1639
15.1-259	15.2-1640
15.1-260	15.2-1641
15.1-261	15.2-1810
15.1-261.1	Repealed
15.1-262	15.2-1800
15.1-263	15.2-1642
15.1-266	Repealed
15.1-267	15.2-1643
15.1-268	15.2-971
15.1-269	Repealed
15.1-270	15.2-1812
15.1-271	Repealed
15.1-272	Repealed
15.1-273	Repealed
15.1-274	15.2-1807
15.1-274.1	Repealed
15.1-275	Repealed
15.1-276	15.2-1900
15.1-277	15.2-1801
15.1-278	15.2-1811
15.1-279	Repealed
15.1-280	Repealed
15.1-281	15.2-945
15.1-282	Repealed
15.1-283	Repealed
15.1-284	Repealed
15.1-285	Repealed
15.1-286	15.2-1803
15.1-288	Repealed
15.1-289	15.2-1805
15.1-290	Repealed
15.1-291	15.2-1809
15.1-291.1	15.2-2800
15.1-291.2	15.2-2801
15.1-291.3	15.2-2802
15.1-291.4	15.2-2803
15.1-291.5	15.2-2804
15.1-291.6	15.2-2805
15.1-291.7	15.2-2806
15.1-291.8	15.2-2807
15.1-291.9	15.2-2808
15.1-291.10	15.2-2809
15.1-291.11	15.2-2810
15.1-292	15.2-2109
15.1-292.01	15.2-2109.1
15.1-292.1	15.2-2110
15.1-292.1:1	15.2-2110
15.1-292.2	15.2-2111
15.1-292.3	15.2-2113
15.1-292.4	15.2-2114
15.1-293	15.2-2115
15.1-293.1	15.2-2116
15.1-294	15.2-2117
15.1-295	15.2-2118
15.1-296	15.2-2120
15.1-297	15.2-2117
15.1-298	15.2-2117
15.1-299	15.2-2121
15.1-300 through 15.1-306	Repealed
15.1-306.1	15.2-2112
15.1-307	15.2-2100
15.1-308	15.2-2101
15.1-309	15.2-2101
15.1-310	15.2-2102
15.1-311	15.2-2103
15.1-312	15.2-2104
15.1-313	Repealed
15.1-314	15.2-2105
15.1-315	15.2-2106
15.1-316	15.2-2107
15.1-317	Repealed
15.1-317.1	15.2-2123
15.1-318	15.2-2124
15.1-319	15.2-2125
15.1-320	15.2-2122
15.1-320.1	Repealed
15.1-321	15.2-2119
15.1-322 through 15.1-325	Repealed
15.1-326	15.2-2126
15.1-327	15.2-2127
15.1-327.1	15.2-2128
15.1-328	15.2-2129
15.1-329	15.2-2130
15.1-330	15.2-2131

Former Section	Present Section
15.1-331	15.2-2132
15.1-332	15.2-2133
15.1-332.1	Repealed
15.1-333	Repealed
15.1-334	15.2-2145
15.1-335	15.2-2146
15.1-337	15.2-2147
15.1-338	15.2-2148
15.1-339	Repealed
15.1-340	15.2-1906
15.1-341	15.2-2149
15.1-342	15.2-2150
15.1-343	15.2-2151
15.1-344	15.2-2152
15.1-345	15.2-2153
15.1-346	15.2-2154
15.1-347	15.2-2155
15.1-348	15.2-2156
15.1-349 through 15.1-360	Repealed
15.1-360.1	15.2-2158
15.1-361	Repealed
15.1-362	Repealed
15.1-362.1	15.2-2159
15.1-363	Repealed
15.1-364	15.2-2006
15.1-364.1	15.2-2007
15.1-364.2	15.2-2007.1
15.1-365	15.2-2278
15.1-366	15.2-2008
15.1-368	Repealed
15.1-369	Repealed
15.1-370	Repealed
15.1-371	Repealed
15.1-372	15.2-2002
15.1-373	15.2-2003
15.1-374	15.2-2005
15.1-375	15.2-2017
15.1-376	15.2-2010
15.1-376.1	15.2-2030
15.1-377	15.2-2011
15.1-377.1	15.2-2012
15.1-378	Repealed
15.1-379	15.2-2019
15.1-380	15.2-2020
15.1-381	15.2-2021
15.1-427	15.2-2200
15.1-427.1	15.2-2210
15.1-428	15.2-2211
15.1-428.1	15.2-2202
15.1-429	15.2-2203
15.1-430	15.2-2201
15.1-431	15.2-2204
15.1-431.1	15.2-2206
15.1-437	15.2-2212
15.1-438	15.2-2213
15.1-439	15.2-2214
15.1-440	15.2-2215
15.1-441	15.2-2216
15.1-442	15.2-2217

Former Section	Present Section
15.1-443	15.2-2218, 15.2-2219
15.1-444	15.2-2221
15.1-445	15.2-2222
15.1-446.1	15.2-2223
15.1-447	15.2-2224
15.1-448	15.2-2225
15.1-449	15.2-2225
15.1-450	15.2-2226
15.1-451	15.2-2227
15.1-452	15.2-2228
15.1-453	15.2-2229
15.1-454	15.2-2230
15.1-455	15.2-2231
15.1-456	15.2-2232
15.1-458	15.2-2233
15.1-459	15.2-2234
15.1-460	15.2-2235
15.1-461	15.2-2236
15.1-462	15.2-2237
15.1-463	15.2-2238
15.1-464	15.2-2239
15.1-465	15.2-2240
15.1-465.1	15.2-2277
15.1-466	15.2-2241 through 15.2-2246
15.1-466.01	15.2-2249
15.1-466.1	15.2-2247
15.1-467	15.2-2248
15.1-468	15.2-2249
15.1-469	15.2-2250
15.1-470	15.2-2251
15.1-471	15.2-2252
15.1-472	15.2-2253
15.1-473	15.2-2254
15.1-474	15.2-2255
15.1-474.1	15.2-2256
15.1-474.2	15.2-2257
15.1-475	15.2-2258 through 15.2-2261
15.1-476	15.2-2262
15.1-477	15.2-2264
15.1-478	15.2-2265
15.1-478.1	15.2-2266
15.1-478.2	15.2-2267
15.1-479	15.2-2268
15.1-480	15.2-2269
15.1-480.1	15.2-2270
15.1-481	15.2-2271
15.1-482	15.2-2272
15.1-482.1	15.2-2273
15.1-483	15.2-2274
15.1-483.1	15.2-2275
15.1-484	Repealed
15.1-485	15.2-2276
15.1-486	15.2-2280, 15.2-2281
15.1-486.1	15.2-2289
15.1-486.3	15.2-2291

Former Section	Present Section
15.1-486.4	15.2-2290
15.1-486.5	15.2-2292
15.1-488	15.2-2282
15.1-489	15.2-2283
15.1-490	15.2-2284
15.1-491	15.2-2286, 15.2-2287, 15.2-2288, 15.2-2303
15.1-491.001	15.2-2303.1
15.1-491.01	15.2-2293
15.1-491.02	15.2-2294
15.1-491.03	15.2-2295
15.1-491.1	15.2-2296
15.1-491.2	15.2-2297
15.1-491.2:1	15.2-2298
15.1-491.3	15.2-2299
15.1-491.4	15.2-2300
15.1-491.5	15.2-2301
15.1-491.6	15.2-2302
15.1-491.8	15.2-2304
15.1-491.9	15.2-2305
15.1-492	15.2-2307
15.1-493	15.2-2285
15.1-494	15.2-2308
15.1-495	15.2-2309
15.1-496	15.2-2310
15.1-496.1	15.2-2311
15.1-496.2	15.2-2312
15.1-496.3	15.2-2313
15.1-497	15.2-2314
15.1-498	15.2-2315
15.1-498.1	15.2-2317
15.1-498.2	15.2-2318, 15.2-2319
15.1-498.3	15.2-2320
15.1-498.4	15.2-2321
15.1-498.5	15.2-2322
15.1-498.6	15.2-2323
15.1-498.7	15.2-2324
15.1-498.8	15.2-2325
15.1-498.9	15.2-2326
15.1-498.10	15.2-2327
15.1-499	15.2-2208
15.1-499.1	15.2-2209
15.1-499.2	15.2-819
15.1-500	Repealed
15.1-501	Repealed
15.1-501.1	15.2-2263
15.1-502.1	15.2-2220
15.1-503	15.2-2316
15.1-503.2	15.2-2306
15.1-503.4	15.2-2207
15.1-503.4:1	15.2-2700
15.1-503.4:2	15.2-2701
15.1-503.4:2.1	15.2-2702
15.1-503.4:3	15.2-2703
15.1-503.4:4	15.2-2704
15.1-503.4:5	15.2-2705
15.1-503.4:6	15.2-2706
15.1-503.4:7	15.2-2707

Former Section	Present Section
15.1-503.4:8	15.2-2708
15.1-503.4:9	15.2-2709
15.1-503.4:10	Repealed
15.1-504	15.2-1426, 15.2-1427
15.1-505	15.2-1429
15.1-506	Repealed
15.1-506.2	15.2-1519
15.1-507	Repealed
15.1-508	15.2-1404
15.1-508.1	15.2-1232
15.1-510	15.2-1200
15.1-510.1	15.2-1217
15.1-510.4	15.2-1217
15.1-510.5:1	15.2-2027
15.1-510.6	15.2-1217
15.1-510.8	Repealed
15.1-511	15.2-972
15.1-511.1	15.2-1205
15.1-512	15.2-1218
15.1-512.1	15.2-2018
15.1-513	15.2-1219
15.1-514	15.2-926
15.1-514.1	15.2-925
15.1-514.2	15.2-1220
15.1-515	15.2-1221
15.1-515.2	15.2-1222
15.1-516	15.2-968
15.1-517	3.1-796.94:1
15.1-517.1	3.1-796.94:2
15.1-518	15.2-1209
15.1-518.1	15.2-1210
15.1-518.2	15.2-916
15.1-519	15.2-1223
15.1-520	Repealed
15.1-522	15.2-1201
15.1-523	15.2-1206
15.1-524	15.2-1207
15.1-525	15.2-1208
15.1-526	Repealed
15.1-526.1	15.2-1224
15.1-526.2	15.2-947
15.1-526.3	15.2-1225
15.1-526.4	15.2-951
15.1-527	Repealed
15.1-527.1	15.2-1212
15.1-527.3	15.2-1213
15.1-528	Repealed
15.1-529	15.2-1410
15.1-530	15.2-1241
15.1-531	Repealed
15.1-532	15.2-1539
15.1-533	15.2-1538
15.1-535	15.2-1421
15.1-536	15.2-1416
15.1-537	15.2-1417
15.1-538	15.2-1418
15.1-539	Repealed
15.1-539.1	15.2-1201.1
15.1-540	15.2-1420
15.1-541	Repealed
15.1-542	15.2-1415
15.1-543	15.2-1242
15.1-544	15.2-1202
15.1-547	15.2-1243
15.1-548	15.2-1229
15.1-549	15.2-1244
15.1-550	15.2-1245
15.1-551	15.2-1245
15.1-552	15.2-1246
15.1-553	15.2-1247
15.1-554	15.2-1248
15.1-555	15.2-1249
15.1-556	15.2-1230
15.1-557	15.2-2512
15.1-558	Repealed
15.1-559	15.2-1644
15.1-560	15.2-1645
15.1-561	15.2-1646
15.1-562	15.2-1647
15.1-563	15.2-1648
15.1-564	15.2-1649
15.1-565	15.2-1650
15.1-566	15.2-1651
15.1-567	15.2-1652
15.1-568	15.2-1653
15.1-569	15.2-1654
15.1-570	15.2-1655
15.1-571	Repealed
15.1-571.1	15.2-1211
15.1-582	Repealed
15.1-583	Repealed
15.1-584	Repealed
15.1-585	Repealed
15.1-586	Repealed
15.1-587	Repealed
15.1-588	15.2-500
15.1-589	15.2-502
15.1-589.1	Repealed
15.1-589.2	Repealed
15.1-589.3	15.2-503
15.1-590	15.2-504
15.1-590.1	15.2-505
15.1-592	15.2-506
15.1-593	15.2-507
15.1-594	15.2-508
15.1-595	15.2-509
15.1-596	15.2-510
15.1-597	15.2-511
15.1-598	15.2-512
15.1-599	15.2-513
15.1-600	15.2-514
15.1-600.1	15.2-515
15.1-601	Repealed
15.1-602	15.2-516
15.1-603	15.2-517
15.1-604	15.2-518
15.1-605	15.2-519 through 15.2-525
15.1-606	15.2-526
15.1-607	15.2-527
15.1-608	15.2-528, 15.2-529, 15.2-530
15.1-609	15.2-531
15.1-609.1	15.2-532
15.1-610	Repealed
15.1-611	15.2-534
15.1-612	15.2-535
15.1-613.1	Repealed
15.1-614	15.2-536
15.1-615	15.2-538
15.1-616	15.2-514
15.1-617	15.2-539
15.1-619	15.2-540
15.1-620	Repealed
15.1-621	15.2-541
15.1-622	15.2-600
15.1-623	15.2-602
15.1-623.1	15.2-603
15.1-624	Repealed
15.1-625	15.2-604
15.1-626	15.2-605
15.1-627	15.2-606
15.1-628	15.2-607
15.1-629	15.2-608
15.1-630	Repealed
15.1-631	15.2-609
15.1-632	15.2-610
15.1-633	15.2-611
15.1-634	15.2-612
15.1-635	15.2-613
15.1-636	Repealed
15.1-637	15.2-614
15.1-638	15.2-615
15.1-639	15.2-616
15.1-640	15.2-617 through 15.2-624
15.1-641	15.2-625
15.1-642	15.2-626
15.1-643	Repealed
15.1-644	15.2-627
15.1-644.1	15.2-628
15.1-645	Repealed
15.1-646	15.2-629
15.1-647	15.2-630
15.1-648	15.2-631
15.1-649	15.2-632
15.1-650	15.2-634
15.1-652	15.2-635
15.1-653	15.2-636
15.1-654	15.2-637
15.1-655	15.2-638
15.1-657	15.2-639
15.1-658	15.2-640
15.1-659	Repealed
15.1-660	15.2-641
15.1-661	Repealed
15.1-662	15.2-537, 15.2-642

Former Section	Present Section
15.1-663 through 15.1-669	Repealed
15.1-674	15.2-702
15.1-675	15.2-703
15.1-675.1	15.2-704
15.1-676	15.2-705
15.1-677	15.2-706
15.1-678	15.2-707
15.1-679	15.2-708
15.1-681	15.2-709
15.1-682	15.2-710
15.1-683	15.2-711
15.1-684	15.2-712
15.1-684.1	15.2-713
15.1-684.2	15.2-714
15.1-685	15.2-715
15.1-686	15.2-716
15.1-686.01	15.2-717
15.1-686.5	15.2-718
15.1-686.6	15.2-719
15.1-686.7	15.2-720
15.1-687	15.2-721
15.1-687.01	15.2-722
15.1-687.1	15.2-723
15.1-687.2	15.2-724
15.1-687.3	15.2-725
15.1-687.4	15.2-726
15.1-687.5	15.2-727
15.1-687.6	15.2-728
15.1-687.7	15.2-729
15.1-687.8	15.2-730
15.1-687.9	15.2-731
15.1-687.10	15.2-732
15.1-687.11	15.2-733
15.1-687.12	15.2-734
15.1-687.13	15.2-735
15.1-687.14	15.2-736
15.1-687.15	15.2-737
15.1-687.16	15.2-738
15.1-687.17	15.2-739
15.1-687.18	15.2-740
15.1-687.19	15.2-741
15.1-687.20	15.2-725
15.1-687.21	15.2-743
15.1-687.22	15.2-744
15.1-687.23	15.2-742
15.1-687.24	15.2-725
15.1-687.25	15.2-702.1
15.1-688	15.2-745
15.1-689	15.2-746
15.1-690	15.2-747
15.1-691	Repealed
15.1-692	15.2-748
15.1-693	Repealed
15.1-694	Repealed
15.1-695	15.2-749
15.1-697	15.2-401
15.1-698	Repealed
15.1-699	15.2-400
15.1-700	15.2-402
15.1-701	15.2-403
15.1-702	15.2-404
15.1-703	15.2-405
15.1-704	15.2-406
15.1-705	15.2-407
15.1-706	15.2-408
15.1-707	15.2-409
15.1-708	15.2-410
15.1-709	15.2-411
15.1-710	15.2-412
15.1-711.1	15.2-413
15.1-712	15.2-414
15.1-714	15.2-415
15.1-715	15.2-416
15.1-716	15.2-417
15.1-718	Repealed
15.1-720	15.2-418
15.1-721 through 15.1-727	Repealed
15.1-728	15.2-800
15.1-729	15.2-802
15.1-730	15.2-803
15.1-730.1	15.2-815
15.1-730.2	15.2-816
15.1-731	15.2-804
15.1-732	15.2-805
15.1-733	15.2-806
15.1-734	15.2-807
15.1-735	15.2-808
15.1-736	15.2-809
15.1-736.1	15.2-810
15.1-737	Repealed
15.1-738	15.2-811
15.1-739	15.2-812
15.1-740	Repealed
15.1-754	Repealed
15.1-755	15.2-813
15.1-756 through 15.1-761	Repealed
15.1-762	15.2-814
15.1-763	15.2-821
15.1-764	15.2-822
15.1-765	15.2-823
15.1-765.1	15.2-824
15.1-765.2	15.2-825
15.1-766	15.2-826 through 15.2-833
15.1-767	15.2-834
15.1-768	15.2-835
15.1-769	15.2-836
15.1-770	15.2-837
15.1-771	15.2-838
15.1-772	15.2-839
15.1-773	15.2-840
15.1-774	15.2-841
15.1-775	15.2-842
15.1-776	15.2-843
15.1-777	15.2-844
15.1-778	15.2-845
15.1-778.1	15.2-846
15.1-779	15.2-847
15.1-781	15.2-848
15.1-782	15.2-849
15.1-783	15.2-850
15.1-783.01	15.2-851
15.1-783.1	15.2-853
15.1-783.2	15.2-854
15.1-784	Repealed
15.1-785	15.2-817
15.1-786	15.2-818
15.1-787	15.2-855
15.1-788	15.2-856
15.1-788.1	15.2-857
15.1-791	15.2-858
15.1-791.1	15.2-4800
15.1-791.2	15.2-4801
15.1-791.3	15.2-4800, 15.2-4802
15.1-791.4	15.2-4803
15.1-791.5	15.2-4804
15.1-791.6	15.2-4805
15.1-791.7	15.2-4806
15.1-791.8	15.2-4807
15.1-791.9	15.2-4808
15.1-791.10	15.2-4809
15.1-791.11	15.2-4810
15.1-791.12	15.2-4811
15.1-791.13	15.2-4812
15.1-791.14	15.2-4813
15.1-791.15	15.2-4814
15.1-791.16	15.2-4815
15.1-792 through 15.1-800	Repealed
15.1-801	15.2-1409
15.1-802 through 15.1-818	Repealed
15.1-819	15.2-1428
15.1-820	Repealed
15.1-821	15.2-1630
15.1-821	15.2-1630
15.1-821.1	15.2-1631
15.1-822	through
15.1-827	Repealed
15.1-827.1	14.1-47.3
15.1-828 through 15.1-832	Repealed
15.1-833	15.2-200
15.1-834	15.2-201
15.1-835	15.2-202
15.1-836	15.2-203
15.1-836.1	15.2-205
15.1-836.1:1	15.2-206
15.1-836.2	15.2-207
15.1-836.3	15.2-208
15.1-837	Repealed

Former Section	Present Section
15.1-838	15.2-1100, 15.2-1101
15.1-839	15.2-1102
15.1-840	15.2-1103
15.1-841	15.2-1104
15.1-842	15.2-950
15.1-843	15.2-1105
15.1-844	15.2-1106
15.1-845	15.2-1107
15.1-846	Repealed
15.1-847	Repealed
15.1-848	15.2-1108
15.1-849	15.2-1510
15.1-850	Repealed
15.1-851	Repealed
15.1-852	Repealed
15.1-853	15.2-1109
15.1-854	15.2-2144
15.1-855	Repealed
15.1-856	15.2-2157
15.1-857	15.2-927
15.1-857.1	Repealed
15.1-858	15.2-1110
15.1-859	Repealed
15.1-860	15.2-1111
15.1-861	Repealed
15.1-862	15.2-1112
15.1-865	15.2-1113
15.1-866	15.2-1114
15.1-867	15.2-1115
15.1-868	15.2-1116
15.1-869	15.2-1117
15.1-870	3.1-796.94:1
15.1-871	Repealed
15.1-872	15.2-1118
15.1-873	Repealed
15.1-874	Repealed
15.1-875	15.2-2143
15.1-876	Repealed
15.1-877	Repealed
15.1-878	Repealed
15.1-880	15.2-971
15.1-881	15.2-1119
15.1-882	15.2-1120
15.1-883	15.2-1121
15.1-884	15.2-1122
15.1-885	15.2-1123
15.1-886	15.2-1808
15.1-887	15.2-1124
15.1-888	Repealed
15.1-889	15.2-2001
15.1-889.1	15.2-2014
15.1-890	15.2-2004
15.1-891	15.2-2028
15.1-892	15.2-2015
15.1-893	15.2-2009
15.1-894	Repealed
15.1-895	15.2-2016
15.1-896	15.2-2000
15.1-897	Repealed
15.1-898	Repealed

Former Section	Present Section
15.1-899	Repealed
15.1-900	Repealed
15.1-901	15.2-1429
15.1-902	15.2-1430
15.1-903	15.2-1431
15.1-904	Repealed
15.1-905	15.2-1432
15.1-906	15.2-1125
15.1-907	15.2-1126
15.1-916 through 15.1-945	Repealed
15.1-945.1	15.2-2900
15.1-945.2	15.2-2901
15.1-945.2:1	15.2-2902
15.1-945.3	15.2-2903
15.1-945.4	15.2-2904
15.1-945.5	15.2-2905
15.1-945.6	15.2-2906
15.1-945.7	15.2-2907
15.1-945.8	15.2-2908
15.1-946 through 15.1-965	Repealed
15.1-965.1	15.2-4000
15.1-965.2	15.2-4001
15.1-965.3	15.2-4002
15.1-965.4	Repealed
15.1-965.5	Repealed
15.1-965.6	15.2-4003
15.1-965.7	Repealed
15.1-965.8	Repealed
15.1-965.9	15.2-4100
15.1-965.10	15.2-4101, 15.2-4102
15.1-965.11	15.2-4101
15.1-965.12	15.2-4103
15.1-965.13	15.2-4104
15.1-965.14	Repealed
15.1-965.15	15.2-4105
15.1-965.16	15.2-4106
15.1-965.17	15.2-4107
15.1-965.18	15.2-4108
15.1-965.19	15.2-4109
15.1-965.20	15.2-4110
15.1-965.21	15.2-4111
15.1-965.22	15.2-4112
15.1-965.22:1	15.2-4113
15.1-965.23	15.2-4114
15.1-965.24	15.2-4115
15.1-965.24:1	15.2-4116
15.1-965.24:2	15.2-4117
15.1-965.25	15.2-4118
15.1-965.26	15.2-4119
15.1-965.27	15.2-4120
15.1-965.28	15.2-3700
15.1-965.29	15.2-3701
15.1-965.30	15.2-3702
15.1-965.31	15.2-3703
15.1-965.32	15.2-3704
15.1-965.33	15.2-3704

Former Section	Present Section
15.1-965.34	15.2-3705
15.1-965.35	15.2-3706
15.1-965.36	15.2-3707
15.1-965.37	15.2-3708
15.1-965.38	15.2-3709
15.1-965.39	15.2-3710
15.1-965.40	15.2-3711
15.1-965.41	15.2-3712
15.1-966	15.2-3600
15.1-966.1	15.2-3601
15.1-967	15.2-3602
15.1-967.2	15.2-3603
15.1-969	15.2-3604
15.1-971	15.2-3605
15.1-977	Repealed
15.1-977.1	15.2-3900
15.1-977.2	15.2-3901
15.1-977.2:1	15.2-3902
15.1-977.3	15.2-3903
15.1-977.4	Repealed
15.1-977.5	15.2-3904
15.1-977.6	15.2-3905
15.1-977.7	Repealed
15.1-977.8	15.2-3906
15.1-977.9	15.2-3907
15.1-977.10	15.2-3908
15.1-977.11	15.2-3909
15.1-977.12	15.2-3910
15.1-977.13	15.2-3911
15.1-977.13:1	15.2-3912
15.1-977.14	15.2-3913
15.1-977.15	15.2-3914
15.1-977.16	15.2-3915
15.1-977.17	15.2-3916
15.1-977.18	15.2-3917
15.1-977.18:1	15.2-3918
15.1-977.19	15.2-3919
15.1-977.19:1	15.2-3300
15.1-977.20	15.2-3301
15.1-977.21	15.2-3302
15.1-977.22	15.2-3303
15.1-977.22:1	15.2-3304
15.1-977.22:2	15.2-3305
15.1-977.23	15.2-3306
15.1-977.24	15.2-3307
15.1-977.25	15.2-3308
15.1-982.1	15.2-3800
15.1-982.2	15.2-3801, 15.2-3802
15.1-982.3	15.2-3803
15.1-982.4	15.2-3804
15.1-982.5	15.2-3805
15.1-982.6	Repealed
15.1-982.7	15.2-3806
15.1-982.8	15.2-3807
15.1-982.9	15.2-3808
15.1-982.10	15.2-3809
15.1-982.11	15.2-3810
15.1-982.12	15.2-3811
15.1-983	15.2-3812
15.1-984	15.2-3813

Former Section	Present Section
15.1-985	15.2-3814
15.1-986	15.2-3815
15.1-987	15.2-3816
15.1-988	15.2-3817
15.1-989	15.2-3818
15.1-990	15.2-3819
15.1-991	15.2-3820
15.1-992	15.2-3821
15.1-993	Repealed
15.1-994.1	15.2-1637, 15.2-3822
15.1-995	15.2-3823
15.1-995.1	Repealed
15.1-996	15.2-3824
15.1-997	15.2-3825
15.1-998	15.2-3826
15.1-999	Repealed
15.1-1000	15.2-3827
15.1-1001	Repealed
15.1-1002	15.2-3828
15.1-1003	15.2-3829
15.1-1004	15.2-3829
15.1-1005	15.2-3830
15.1-1006	15.2-3831
15.1-1007	15.2-3832
15.1-1009	15.2-3833
15.1-1010	15.2-3834
15.1-1011 through 15.1-1025	Repealed
15.1-1026	15.2-3100
15.1-1027	15.2-3101
15.1-1028	15.2-3102
15.1-1029	15.2-3103
15.1-1030	15.2-3104
15.1-1031	15.2-3105
15.1-1031.1	15.2-3106
15.1-1031.2	15.2-3107
15.1-1031.3	15.2-3108
15.1-1031.4	15.2-3109
15.1-1031.5	Repealed
15.1-1032	15.2-3200
15.1-1032.1	Repealed
15.1-1032.2	15.2-3201
15.1-1033	15.2-3202
15.1-1034	15.2-3203
15.1-1035	15.2-3204
15.1-1036	15.2-3205
15.1-1037	15.2-3206
15.1-1038	Repealed
15.1-1039	15.2-3004
15.1-1040	15.2-3207
15.1-1040.1	15.2-3208
15.1-1041	15.2-3209
15.1-1041.1	15.2-3210
15.1-1042	15.2-3211
15.1-1043	15.2-3212
15.1-1044	15.2-3213
15.1-1045	15.2-3214
15.1-1045.1	15.2-3215
15.1-1046	15.2-3216
15.1-1047	15.2-3217
15.1-1047.1	15.2-3219
15.1-1047.2	15.2-3218
15.1-1048	15.2-3220
15.1-1049	15.2-3221
15.1-1050	15.2-3222
15.1-1051	15.2-3223
15.1-1052	15.2-3224
15.1-1053	15.2-3225
15.1-1054	15.2-3226
15.1-1055	15.2-3227
15.1-1055.1	Repealed
15.1-1056	15.2-3228
15.1-1057	15.2-3229
15.1-1058	15.2-3230
15.1-1058.1	15.2-3231
15.1-1058.2	15.2-3232
15.1-1058.3	15.2-3233
15.1-1058.4	15.2-3234
15.1-1058.5	15.2-3235
15.1-1059	15.2-3236
15.1-1060	15.2-3237
15.1-1061	15.2-3238
15.1-1062	15.2-3239
15.1-1063	15.2-3240
15.1-1064	15.2-3241
15.1-1065	15.2-3242
15.1-1066	15.2-3243
15.1-1067	15.2-3244
15.1-1067.1	15.2-3245
15.1-1068	Repealed
15.1-1069	Repealed
15.1-1070	Repealed
15.1-1071	15.2-3501
15.1-1072	15.2-3502
15.1-1073	15.2-3503
15.1-1074	15.2-3504
15.1-1075	15.2-3505
15.1-1076	15.2-3506
15.1-1077	15.2-3507
15.1-1078	15.2-3508
15.1-1079	15.2-3510
15.1-1080	15.2-3512
15.1-1081	15.2-3513
15.1-1082	15.2-3514
15.1-1083	15.2-3515
15.1-1084 through 15.1-1095	Repealed
15.1-1096	15.2-3516
15.1-1097	15.2-3517
15.1-1098	15.2-3518
15.1-1099 through 15.1-1122	Repealed
15.1-1123	15.2-3511
15.1-1124	Repealed
15.1-1125	Repealed
15.1-1126	15.2-3512
15.1-1127	Repealed
15.1-1128	Repealed
15.1-1129	Repealed
15.1-1130.1	15.2-3520
15.1-1130.2	15.2-3521
5.1-1130.3	15.2-3522
15.1-1130.4	15.2-3523
15.1-1130.5	15.2-3524
15.1-1130.6	Repealed
15.1-1130.7	15.2-3525
15.1-1130.8	15.2-3526
15.1-1130.9	15.2-3527
15.1-1130.10	15.2-3528
15.1-1131	15.2-3529
15.1-1131.1	15.2-3530
15.1-1132	15.2-3531
15.1-1133	15.2-3532
15.1-1134	15.2-3533
15.1-1135	15.2-3534
15.1-1135.1	15.2-3535
15.1-1136	15.2-3536
15.1-1137	15.2-3537
15.1-1138	15.2-3538
15.1-1139	15.2-3539
15.1-1140	15.2-3540
15.1-1141	15.2-3541
15.1-1141.1	15.2-3542
15.1-1141.2	15.2-3543
15.1-1142	15.2-3544
15.1-1143	15.2-3545
15.1-1144	15.2-3546
15.1-1145	15.2-3547
15.1-1146.1	15.2-3548
15.1-1146.1:1	15.2-3549
15.1-1146.1:2	Repealed
15.1-1147	15.2-3550
15.1-1149 through 15.1-1164	Repealed
15.1-1167.1	15.2-3400
15.1-1167.2	15.2-3401
15.1-1168	15.2-3000
15.1-1168.1	15.2-3001
15.1-1169	15.2-3002
15.1-1170	15.2-3003
15.1-1227.1	15.2-1306
15.1-1227.2	15.2-1307
15.1-1227.3	15.2-1308
15.1-1227.4	15.2-1309
15.1-1227.5	15.2-1310
15.1-1228	15.2-5700
15.1-1229	15.2-5701
15.1-1230	15.2-5702
15.1-1231	15.2-5703
15.1-1232	15.2-5704
15.1-1232.1	15.2-5705
15.1-1232.2	15.2-5706
15.1-1232.3	15.2-5707
15.1-1233	15.2-5708
15.1-1234	15.2-5709
15.1-1235	15.2-5710
15.1-1236	15.2-5711
15.1-1237	15.2-5712

Former Section	Present Section
15.1-1238	15.2-5713
15.1-1238.1	15.2-5714
15.1-1239	15.2-5100
15.1-1239.1	15.2-5123
15.1-1240	15.2-5101
15.1-1241	15.2-5102, 15.2-5152 through 15.2-5157
15.1-1242	15.2-5103
15.1-1243	15.2-5104
15.1-1244	15.2-5105
15.1-1244.1	15.2-5106
15.1-1245	15.2-5107
15.1-1246	15.2-5108
15.1-1247	15.2-5111
15.1-1248	15.2-5112
15.1-1249	15.2-5113
15.1-1250	15.2-5110, 15.2-5114 through 15.2-5118, 15.2-5124, 15.2-5146, 15.2-5148, 15.2-5149, 15.2-5151
15.1-1250.01	15.2-5121
15.1-1250.02	15.2-5120
15.1-1250.03	15.2-5158
15.1-1250.1	15.2-5122
15.1-1250.2	15.2-5119
15.1-1251	15.2-5150
15.1-1252	15.2-5125
15.1-1253	15.2-5127
15.1-1254	15.2-5128
15.1-1255	15.2-5129
15.1-1256	15.2-5130
15.1-1257	15.2-5131
15.1-1258	15.2-5132
15.1-1259	15.2-5133
15.1-1260	15.2-5136
15.1-1261	15.2-5137
15.1-1262	15.2-5138
15.1-1263	15.2-5139
15.1-1264	15.2-5140
15.1-1265	15.2-5141
15.1-1266	15.2-5142
15.1-1267	15.2-5144
15.1-1268	Repealed
15.1-1269	15.2-5147
15.1-1269.1	15.2-5109
15.1-1269.2	15.2-5145
15.1-1270	Repealed
15.1-1271	15.2-5600
15.1-1272	15.2-5601
15.1-1273	15.2-5602
15.1-1274	15.2-5603
15.1-1275	15.2-5604
15.1-1276	15.2-5605
15.1-1277	15.2-5606
15.1-1278	15.2-5607
15.1-1279	15.2-5608
15.1-1280	15.2-5609
15.1-1281	15.2-5610
15.1-1282	15.2-5611
15.1-1283	15.2-5612
15.1-1284	15.2-5613
15.1-1285	15.2-5614
15.1-1286	15.2-5615
15.1-1286.1	15.2-5616
15.1-1310 through 15.1-1319	Repealed
15.1-1320	15.2-6300
15.1-1321	15.2-6301
15.1-1322	15.2-6302
15.1-1323	15.2-6303
15.1-1324	15.2-6304
15.1-1325	15.2-6305
15.1-1326	15.2-6306
15.1-1327	15.2-6307
15.1-1329	15.2-6308
15.1-1330	15.2-6309
15.1-1331	15.2-6310
15.1-1332	15.2-6311
15.1-1333	15.2-6312
15.1-1334	15.2-6313
15.1-1335	15.2-6314
15.1-1336	15.2-6315
15.1-1337	15.2-6316
15.1-1338	15.2-6317
15.1-1339	15.2-6318
15.1-1339.1	15.2-6319
15.1-1340	15.2-6320
15.1-1341	15.2-6321
15.1-1342	15.2-4500
15.1-1343	15.2-4501
15.1-1344	15.2-4502
15.1-1344.1	15.2-4503
15.1-1345	15.2-4504
15.1-1346	15.2-4505
15.1-1347	15.2-4506
15.1-1348	15.2-4507
15.1-1349	15.2-4508
15.1-1350	15.2-4509
15.1-1351	15.2-4510
15.1-1352	15.2-4511
15.1-1353	15.2-4512
15.1-1355	15.2-4513
15.1-1356	15.2-4514
15.1-1357	15.2-4515
15.1-1357.1	15.2-4516
15.1-1357.2	15.2-4517
15.1-1357.3	15.2-4518
15.1-1358	15.2-4518
15.1-1358.2	15.2-4519
15.1-1358.3	15.2-4520
15.1-1359	15.2-4521
15.1-1360	15.2-4522
15.1-1361	15.2-4523
15.1-1362	15.2-4524
15.1-1363	15.2-4525
15.1-1364	15.2-4526
15.1-1365	15.2-4527
15.1-1366	15.2-4528
15.1-1367	15.2-4529
15.1-1368	15.2-4530
15.1-1369	15.2-4531
15.1-1370	15.2-4532
15.1-1371	15.2-4533
15.1-1372	15.2-4534
15.1-1372.1	15.2-4600
15.1-1372.2	15.2-4602
15.1-1372.2:1	15.2-4601
15.1-1372.3	15.2-4600, 15.2-4603
15.1-1372.4	15.2-4604
15.1-1372.5	15.2-4605
15.1-1372.6	15.2-4606
15.1-1372.7	15.2-4607
15.1-1372.7:1	15.2-4608
15.1-1372.8	15.2-4609
15.1-1372.9	15.2-4610
15.1-1372.10	15.2-4611
15.1-1372.11	15.2-4612
15.1-1372.12	15.2-4613
15.1-1372.13	15.2-4614
15.1-1372.14	15.2-4615
15.1-1372.15	15.2-4616
15.1-1372.16	15.2-4617
15.1-1372.17	15.2-4618
15.1-1372.21	15.2-4700
15.1-1372.22	15.2-4701
15.1-1372.23	15.2-4700, 15.2-4702
15.1-1372.24	15.2-4703
15.1-1372.25	15.2-4704
15.1-1372.26	15.2-4705
15.1-1372.27	15.2-4706
15.1-1372.28	15.2-4707
15.1-1372.29	15.2-4708
15.1-1372.30	15.2-4709
15.1-1372.31	15.2-4710
15.1-1372.32	15.2-4711
15.1-1372.33	15.2-4712
15.1-1372.34	15.2-4713
15.1-1372.35	15.2-4714
15.1-1372.36	15.2-4715
15.1-1372.37	15.2-4716
15.1-1373	15.2-4900
15.1-1374	15.2-4902
15.1-1375	15.2-4901
15.1-1376	15.2-4903
15.1-1377	15.2-4904
15.1-1378	15.2-4905
15.1-1378.1	15.2-4906
15.1-1378.2	15.2-4907
15.1-1379	15.2-4908
15.1-1380	15.2-4909
15.1-1381	15.2-4910
15.1-1382	15.2-4911
15.1-1383	15.2-4912

Former Section	Present Section
15.1-1384	15.2-4913
15.1-1385	15.2-4914
15.1-1386	15.2-4915
15.1-1387	15.2-4916
15.1-1388	15.2-4917
15.1-1389	15.2-4918
15.1-1390	15.2-4919
15.1-1391	15.2-4920
15.1-1392	15.2-4901
15.1-1399.10	15.2-5000
15.1-1399.11	15.2-5001
15.1-1399.12	Repealed
15.1-1399.13	Repealed
15.1-1399.14	15.2-5002
15.1-1399.15	15.2-5003
15.1-1399.16	15.2-5004
15.1-1399.17	15.2-5005
15.1-1399.18	15.2-5501
15.1-1399.19	15.2-5500, 15.2-5505
15.1-1399.20	15.2-5502
15.1-1399.21	15.2-5504
15.1-1399.22	15.2-5503
15.1-1399.23	15.2-5506
15.1-1399.24	15.2-5507
15.1-1399.25	15.2-5508
15.1-1400	15.2-4200
15.1-1401	15.2-4201
15.1-1402	15.2-4202
15.1-1403	15.2-4203
15.1-1403.1	15.2-4204
15.1-1404	15.2-4205
15.1-1404.1	15.2-4206
15.1-1405	15.2-4207
15.1-1405.1	15.2-4208
15.1-1406	15.2-4209
15.1-1407	15.2-4210
15.1-1408	15.2-4211
15.1-1409	15.2-4212
15.1-1410	15.2-4213
15.1-1411	15.2-4214
15.1-1411.1	15.2-4215
15.1-1412	15.2-4216
15.1-1412.1	15.2-4217
15.1-1413	15.2-4218
15.1-1415	15.2-4219
15.1-1416	15.2-4220
15.1-1416.1	15.2-4221
15.1-1450	Repealed
15.1-1451	Repealed
15.1-1452	15.2-4222
15.1-1506	15.2-4300
15.1-1507	15.2-4301
15.1-1508	15.2-4302
15.1-1509	15.2-4303
15.1-1510	15.2-4304
15.1-1511	15.2-4305 through 15.2-4311
15.1-1512	15.2-4312, 15.2-4313
15.1-1513	15.2-4314
15.1-1513.1	15.2-4400
15.1-1513.2	15.2-4401
15.1-1513.3	15.2-4402
15.1-1513.4	15.2-4403
15.1-1513.5	15.2-4404
15.1-1513.6	15.2-4405
15.1-1513.7	15.2-4406
15.1-1513.8	15.2-4407
15.1-1513.9	15.2-4407
15.1-1514	15.2-5200
15.1-1515	15.2-5201
15.1-1516	15.2-5202
15.1-1517	15.2-5203
15.1-1518	15.2-5204
15.1-1519	15.2-5205
15.1-1520	15.2-5206
15.1-1521	15.2-5207
15.1-1522	15.2-5208
15.1-1523	15.2-5209
15.1-1524	15.2-5210
15.1-1525	15.2-5211
15.1-1526	15.2-5212
15.1-1527	15.2-5213
15.1-1528	15.2-5214
15.1-1529	15.2-5215
15.1-1530	15.2-5216
15.1-1531	15.2-5217
15.1-1532	15.2-5218
15.1-1533	15.2-5300
15.1-1534	15.2-5301
15.1-1535	15.2-5302
15.1-1536	15.2-5303
15.1-1537	15.2-5304
15.1-1538	15.2-5305
15.1-1539	15.2-5306
15.1-1540	15.2-5307
15.1-1541	15.2-5308
15.1-1542	15.2-5309
15.1-1543	15.2-5310
15.1-1544	15.2-5311
15.1-1545	15.2-5312
15.1-1546	15.2-5313
15.1-1547	15.2-5314
15.1-1548	15.2-5315
15.1-1549	15.2-5316
15.1-1550	15.2-5317
15.1-1551	15.2-5318
15.1-1552	15.2-5319
15.1-1553	15.2-5320
15.1-1554	15.2-5321
15.1-1555	15.2-5322
15.1-1556	15.2-5323
15.1-1557	15.2-5324
15.1-1558	15.2-5324
15.1-1559	15.2-5325
15.1-1560	15.2-5326
15.1-1561	15.2-5327
15.1-1562	15.2-5328
15.1-1563	15.2-5329
15.1-1564	15.2-5330
15.1-1565	15.2-5331
15.1-1566	15.2-5332
15.1-1567	15.2-5333
15.1-1568	15.2-5334
15.1-1569	15.2-5335
15.1-1570	15.2-5336
15.1-1571	15.2-5337
15.1-1572	15.2-5337
15.1-1573	15.2-5338
15.1-1574	15.2-5339
15.1-1575	15.2-5340
15.1-1576	15.2-5341
15.1-1577	15.2-5342
15.1-1578	15.2-5343
15.1-1579	15.2-5344
15.1-1580	15.2-5345
15.1-1581	15.2-5346
15.1-1582	15.2-5347
15.1-1583	15.2-5348
15.1-1584	15.2-5349
15.1-1585	15.2-5350
15.1-1586	15.2-5351
15.1-1587	15.2-5352
15.1-1588	15.2-5353
15.1-1589	15.2-5354
15.1-1590	15.2-5355
15.1-1591	15.2-5356
15.1-1592	15.2-5357
15.1-1593	15.2-5358
15.1-1594	15.2-5359
15.1-1595	15.2-5360
15.1-1596	15.2-5361
15.1-1597	15.2-5362
15.1-1598	15.2-5363
15.1-1599	15.2-5364
15.1-1600	15.2-5365
15.1-1601	15.2-5366
15.1-1602	15.2-5367
15.1-1603	15.2-5400
15.1-1604	15.2-5401
15.1-1605	15.2-5402
15.1-1606	15.2-5403
15.1-1607	15.2-5404
15.1-1608	15.2-5405
15.1-1609	15.2-5406
15.1-1610	15.2-5407
15.1-1611	15.2-5408
15.1-1612	15.2-5409
15.1-1613	15.2-5410
15.1-1614	15.2-5411
15.1-1615	15.2-5412
15.1-1616	15.2-5413
15.1-1617	15.2-5414
15.1-1618	15.2-5415
15.1-1619	15.2-5416
15.1-1620	15.2-5417
15.1-1621	15.2-5418
15.1-1622	15.2-5419
15.1-1623	15.2-5420
15.1-1624	15.2-5421
15.1-1625	15.2-5422

Former Section	Present Section
15.1-1626	15.2-5423
15.1-1627	15.2-5424
15.1-1628	15.2-5425
15.1-1629	15.2-5426
15.1-1630	15.2-5427
15.1-1631	15.2-5428
15.1-1632	15.2-5429
15.1-1633	15.2-5430
15.1-1634	15.2-5431
15.1-1635	15.2-6000
15.1-1636	15.2-6001
15.1-1637	15.2-6002
15.1-1638	15.2-6003
15.1-1639	15.2-6004
15.1-1640	15.2-6005
15.1-1641	15.2-6006
15.1-1642	15.2-6007
15.1-1643	15.2-6008
15.1-1644	15.2-6009
15.1-1645	15.2-6010
15.1-1646	15.2-6011
15.1-1647	15.2-6012
15.1-1648	15.2-6013
15.1-1649	15.2-6014
15.1-1650	15.2-6015
15.1-1651	15.2-6100
15.1-1652	15.2-6101
15.1-1653	15.2-6102
15.1-1654	15.2-6103
15.1-1655	15.2-6104
15.1-1656	15.2-6105
15.1-1657	15.2-6106
15.1-1658	15.2-6107
15.1-1659	15.2-6108
15.1-1660	15.2-6109
15.1-1661	15.2-6110
15.1-1662	15.2-6200
15.1-1662.1	15.2-6201
15.1-1663	15.2-6202
15.1-1664	15.2-6203
15.1-1665	15.2-6204
15.1-1666	15.2-6205
15.1-1667	15.2-6206
15.1-1668	15.2-6207
15.1-1669	15.2-6208
15.1-1670	15.2-6209
15.1-1671	15.2-6210
15.1-1672	15.2-6211
15.1-1673	15.2-6212
15.1-1674	15.2-6213
15.1-1675	15.2-6214
15.1-1676	37.1-242
15.1-1677	37.1-243
15.1-1678	37.1-244
15.1-1679	37.1-245
15.1-1680	37.1-246
15.1-1681	37.1-247
15.1-1682	37.1-248
15.1-1683	37.1-249
15.1-1684	37.1-250
15.1-1685	37.1-251
15.1-1686	37.1-252
15.1-1687	37.1-253
15.1-1688	15.2-5900
15.1-1689	15.2-5901
15.1-1690	15.2-5902
15.1-1691	15.2-5903
15.1-1692	15.2-5904
15.1-1693	15.2-5905
15.1-1694	15.2-5906
15.1-1695	15.2-5907
15.1-1696	15.2-5908
15.1-1697	15.2-5909
15.1-1698	15.2-5910
15.1-1699	15.2-5911
15.1-1700	15.2-5912
15.1-1701	15.2-5913
15.1-1702	15.2-5914
15.1-1703	15.2-5915
15.1-1704	15.2-5916
15.1-1705	15.2-5917
15.1-1706	15.2-5917
15.1-1707	15.2-5918
15.1-1708	15.2-5919
15.1-1709	15.2-5920
15.1-1710	15.2-6400
15.1-1711	15.2-6401
15.1-1712	15.2-6402
15.1-1713	15.2-6403
15.1-1714	15.2-6404
15.1-1715	15.2-6405
15.1-1716	15.2-6406
15.1-1717	15.2-6407
15.1-1718	15.2-6408
15.1-1719	15.2-6409
15.1-1720	15.2-6410
15.1-1721	15.2-6411
15.1-1722	15.2-6412
15.1-1723	15.2-6413
15.1-1724	15.2-6414
15.1-1725	15.2-6415
15.1-1726	15.2-6416

COMPARABLE SECTIONS OF TITLE 17 AND TITLE 17.1

Former Section	Present Section
17-1	17.1-516
17-2	17.1-101
17-3.1	17.1-102
17-5	17.1-103
17-6	17.1-104
17-7	17.1-105
17-7.01	17.1-106
17-7.1	17.1-107
17-7.2	17.1-108
17-8	17.1-109
17-9	17.1-110
17-10	17.1-111
17-12	Repealed
17-13	17.1-112
17-14	17.1-113
17-14.1	Repealed
17-15	17.1-114
17-16	17.1-115
17-17	17.1-114, 17.1-116
17-18	17.1-116
17-19	17.1-117
17-19.1	17.1-118
17-20	Repealed
17-21	17.1-119
17-22	Repealed
17-23	17.1-120
17-24	17.1-121
17-25	17.1-122
17-26	Repealed
17-27	17.1-123
17-28	17.1-124
17-28.1	17.1-125
17-29	17.1-126
17-30	17.1-127
17-30.1	17.1-128
17-30.3	17.1-129
17-32	17.1-130
17-32.1	17.1-131
17-33	17.1-200
17-34	17.1-201
17-35	17.1-202
17-36	Repealed
17-37	17.1-203
17-38	Repealed
17-39	17.1-204
17-40	17.1-206
17-41	17.1-207
17-42	Repealed
17-43	17.1-208
17-44	17.1-209
17-45	17.1-210
17-46	Repealed
17-46.1	17.1-211
17-47	17.1-212
17-47.4	17.1-213
17-50	17.1-214
17-51	17.1-215
17-52	17.1-216
17-53	17.1-217
17-54	17.1-218
17-55	17.1-219
17-56	17.1-220

Former Section	Present Section
17-57	17.1-221
17-58	17.1-222
17-59	17.1-223
17-59.1	17.1-224
17-59.2	17.1-225
17-59.3	17.1-226
17-60	17.1-227
17-60.1	17.1-228
17-61	17.1-229
17-62	17.1-230
17-63	17.1-231
17-64	17.1-232
17-65	17.1-233
17-66	17.1-234
17-67	17.1-235
17-68	17.1-236
17-69	17.1-237
17-69.1	17.1-238
17-70	17.1-239
17-70.1	17.1-240
17-71	17.1-241
17-72	17.1-242
17-73	17.1-243
17-74	17.1-244
17-75	17.1-245
17-76	17.1-246
17-77	17.1-247
17-78	17.1-248
17-79	17.1-249
17-79.1	17.1-250
17-79.2	17.1-251
17-79.3	17.1-252
17-80	17.1-253
17-81	17.1-253
17-82	17.1-253
17-83	17.1-253
17-83.1	17.1-254
17-83.1:1	17.1-255
17-83.1:2	17.1-256
17-83.1:3	17.1-257
17-83.1:4	17.1-258
17-83.2	17.1-259
17-83.3	17.1-259
17-83.4	17.1-260
17-84	17.1-261
17-85	17.1-262
17-86	17.1-262
17-87	17.1-263
17-88	Repealed
17-89	Repealed
17-90	17.1-264
17-91	17.1-264
17-92	17.1-265
17-93	17.1-300
17-93.1	17.1-303
17-94	17.1-308
17-95	17.1-301
17-95.1	17.1-302
17-96	17.1-309
17-97	17.1-310
17-98	17.1-311
17-99	17.1-304
17-100	17.1-305
17-101	17.1-305
17-102	17.1-306
17-103	17.1-307
17-110	17.1-312
17-110.1	17.1-313
17-110.2	17.1-313
17-111	Repealed
17-111.1	17.1-314
17-111.2	17.1-315
17-111.3	17.1-316
17-111.4	17.1-317
17-111.5	17.1-318
17-111.6	17.1-319
17-111.7	17.1-320
17-112	Repealed
17-113	17.1-321
17-114	17.1-321
17-115	17.1-322
17-116	17.1-323
17-116.01	17.1-400
17-116.01:1	17.1-401
17-116.02	17.1-402
17-116.03	17.1-403
17-116.04	17.1-404
17-116.05	17.1-405
17-116.05:1	17.1-406
17-116.05:2	17.1-407
17-116.05:3	17.1-408
17-116.05:4	Repealed
17-116.05:5	Repealed
17-116.06	17.1-409
17-116.07	17.1-410
17-116.08	17.1-411
17-116.09	17.1-412
17-116.010	17.1-413
17-116.011	17.1-414
17-116.012	17.1-415
17-116.013	17.1-416
17-116.014	17.1-417
17-116.1	17.1-500
17-116.2	17.1-501
17-116.3	17.1-502
17-116.4	17.1-503
17-117	Repealed
17-117.1	Repealed
17-118	17.1-505
17-118.1	Repealed
17-119.1:1	17.1-506
17-119.1:2	17.1-507
17-119.2	17.1-508
17-120	17.1-509
17-121	17.1-510
17-122	17.1-511
17-122.1	17.1-512
17-123	17.1-513
17-123.1	17.1-514
17-124	17.1-515
17-125	Not set out
17-126	Not set out
17-126.1	Not set out
17-126.2	Not set out
17-126.3	Not set out
17-126.4	Not set out
17-126.5	Not set out
17-126.6	Not set out
17-126.7	Repealed
17-127.21	17.1-517
17-128	Repealed
17-129	17.1-518
17-130	17.1-519
17-131	17.1-520
17-132	17.1-521
17-133	17.1-522
17-134	Repealed
17-222	17.1-700
17-223	17.1-701
17-224	17.1-702
17-225	17.1-703
17-226	17.1-704
17-227	17.1-705
17-228	17.1-706
17-229	17.1-707
17-230	17.1-708
17-231	17.1-709
17-232	17.1-800
17-233	17.1-801
17-234	17.1-802
17-235	17.1-803
17-236	17.1-804
17-237	17.1-805
17-238	17.1-806

COMPARABLE SECTIONS OF TITLE 18 AND TITLE 18.1

Former Section	Present Section
18-1	18.1-6
18-2	18.1-7
18-3	18.1-11
18-4	18.1-12
18-5	18.1-13
18-6	18.1-14
18-7	18.1-15
18-7.1	18.1-15.1
18-8	18.1-16

Former Section	Present Section
	to 18.1-20
18-9	19.1-20
18-10	19.1-21
18-11	19.1-22
18-12	19.1-23
18-13	19.1-24
18-14	19.1-25
18-15	19.1-26
18-16	19.1-27
18-17	19.1-28
18-18	19.1-29
18-19	19.1-30
18-20	19.1-31
18-21	19.1-32
18-22	18.1-92
18-23	18.1-93
18-24	18.1-94
18-25	18.1-95
18-26	18.1-96
18-27	18.1-97
18-28	18.1-98
18-29	18.1-99
18-30	18.1-21
18-31	18.1-22
18-32	18.1-23
18-33	18.1-24
18-34	18.1-25
18-35	18.1-26
18-36	18.1-27
	18.1-28
18-37	18.1-29
18-38	18.1-30
	18.1-31
18-39	18.1-32
18-40	18.1-33
18-41	18.1-34
18-42	18.1-35
18-43	18.1-38
	18.1-39
18-44	Deleted
18-45	18.1-40
18-46	Deleted
18-47	Deleted
18-48	18.1-41
18-49	18.1-41
18-50	Repealed 1952
18-51	Deleted
18-52	18.1-42
18-53	18.1-43
18-54	18.1-44
18-55	18.1-45
18-55.1	18.1-46
18-56	18.1-47
18-57	Deleted
18-58	Deleted
18-59	Deleted
18-60	Deleted
18-61	Deleted
18-62	Deleted
18-63	Deleted
18-64	Deleted
18-65	Deleted
18-66	Deleted
18-67	Deleted
18-68	18.1-62
	18.1-63
18-69	18.1-64
18-70	18.1-65
18-70.1	18.1-67
18-71	18.1-70
18-72	18.1-71
18-73	18.1-72
18-74	18.1-73
18-74.1	18.1-74
18-75	18.1-54
18-75.1	18.1-55
18-75.2	18.1-56
18-75.3	18.1-57
18-76	18.1-58
18-77	18.1-59
18-78	18.1-60
18-79	18.1-61
18-80	18.1-68
18-81	18.1-69
18-82	18.1-190
18-82	18.1-191
18-83	18.1-192
18-84	18.1-193
18-85	18.1-195
18-86	18.1-197
18-87	18.1-196
18-88	18.1-198
18-89	Deleted
18-89.1	18.1-203
18-90	Deleted
18-91	18.1-199
18-92	Deleted
18-93	Deleted
18-94	18.1-200
18-95	18.1-201
18-96	18.1-202
18-97	18.1-204
	to 18.1-211
18-98	18.1-212
18-98.1	18.1-213
18-98.2	18.1-214
18-98.3	18.1-215
18-99	18.1-216
18-100	18.1-217
18-101	18.1-218
18-102	18.1-219
18-103	18.1-220
18-104	18.1-221
18-105	18.1-222
18-106	18.1-223
18-107	18.1-224
18-108	18.1-225
18-109	18.1-226
18-110 to	
18-113.1	Deleted
18-114	18.1-237
18-115	18.1-238
18-116	18.1-239
18-117	18.1-240
18-118	18.1-241
18-119	18.1-242
18-120	18.1-243
18-121	18.1-244
18-122	18.1-245
18-123	18.1-246
18-124	18.1-247
18-125	18.1-248
18-126	18.1-249
18-127	18.1-250
18-128	18.1-251
18-129	18.1-252
18-130	18.1-253
18-131	18.1-254
18-132	18.1-255
18-133	18.1-256
18-134	18.1-257
18-135	18.1-258
18-136	18.1-259
18-137	18.1-260
18-138	18.1-261
18-139	18.1-262
18-140	18.1-263
18-141	18.1-264
18-142	18.1-265
18-143	18.1-266
18-144	18.1-267
18-145	18.1-268
18-146	18.1-269
18-146.1	18.1-270
18-147	18.1-271
18-147.1	18.1-272
18-148	18.1-75
18-149	18.1-76
18-150	18.1-77
18-151	18.1-78
18-151.1	18.1-78.1
18-151.2	18.1-78.2
18-151.3	18.1-78.3
18-151.4	18.1-78.4
18-151.5	18.1-78.5
18-152	18.1-79
18-153	18.1-80
18-154	18.1-81
18-155	18.1-82
18-156	18.1-83
18-157	18.1-84
18-158	18.1-85
18-159	18.1-86
18-159	18.1-87
18-160	18.1-88
18-161	18.1-89
18-162	18.1-90
18-163	18.1-91
18-164	18.1-100
18-164	18.1-101
18-165	18.1-102
18-165.1	18.1-103
18-166	18.1-104

Former Section	Present Section
18-167	18.1-105
18-168	18.1-106
18-169	18.1-107
18-170	18.1-108
18-171	18.1-109
18-172	18.1-110
18-173	18.1-111
18-174	18.1-112
18-175	18.1-113
18-176	18.1-114
18-177	18.1-115
18-178	18.1-116
18-179	18.1-117
18-180	18.1-118
18-181	18.1-119
18-182	18.1-120
18-183	18.1-121
18-184	18.1-122
18-185	18.1-123
18-186	18.1-124
18-187	18.1-125
18-187.1	18.1-126
18-187.2	18.1-127
18-187.3	18.1-128
18-188	18.1-129
18-188.1	18.1-130
18-189	18.1-131
18-190	18.1-132
18-191	18.1-133
18-192	18.1-134
18-193	18.1-135
18-194	18.1-136
18-195	18.1-137
18-196	18.1-138
18-197	18.1-139
18-198	18.1-140
18-199	18.1-141
18-200	18.1-142
18-201	18.1-143
18-202	18.1-144
18-203	18.1-145
18-204	18.1-146
18-205	18.1-147
18-206	18.1-148
18-207	18.1-149
18-208	18.1-150
18-209	18.1-151
18-210	18.1-152
18-211	18.1-153
18-212	18.1-154
18-213	18.1-155
18-214	18.1-156
18-214.1	18.1-157
18-215	18.1-158
18-216	18.1-159
18-217	18.1-160
18-218	18.1-161
18-219	18.1-162
18-220	18.1-163
18-220.1	18.1-164
18-220.2	18.1-165
18-220.3	18.1-166
18-220.4	18.1-167
18-220.5	18.1-168
18-221	18.1-169
18-222	18.1-170
18-223	Deleted
18-224	18.1-172
18-225	18.1-173
18-225.1	18.1-174
18-225.2	18.1-173.1
18-226	18.1-175
18-227	18.1-176
18-228	18.1-177
18-229	18.1-178
18-229.01	18.1-179
18-230	18.1-180
18-231	18.1-181
18-231.1	18.1-182
18-231.2	18.1-183
18-232	18.1-184
18-233	18.1-185
18-234	18.1-186
18-235	Deleted
18-236	Repealed 1952
18-237	18.1-273
18-238	18.1-274
18-239	18.1-275
18-239.1	18.1-276
18-239.2	18.1-277
18-240	18.1-278
18-241	18.1-279
18-242	18.1-280
18-243	18.1-281
18-244	18.1-282
18-245	18.1-283
18-246	Deleted
18-247	Deleted
18-248	18.1-284
18-248.1	18.1-285
18-249	18.1-286
18-250	18.1-287
18-251	18.1-288
18-252	18.1-289
18-253	18.1-290
18-254	18.1-291
18-255	18.1-292
18-256	18.1-293
18-257	18.1-294
18-258	18.1-295
18-259	18.1-296
18-260	18.1-297
18-261	18.1-298
18-261.1	18.1-299
18-262	18.1-300
18-263	18.1-301
18-264	18.1-302
18-265	18.1-303
18-266	18.1-304
18-267	18.1-305
18-268	18.1-306
18-269	18.1-307
18-270	18.1-308
18-271	18.1-309
18-272	18.1-310
18-273	18.1-311
18-274	18.1-312
18-275	18.1-313
18-276	18.1-314
18-277	18.1-315
18-278	18.1-316
18-279	18.1-317
18-280	18.1-318
18-281	18.1-319
18-282	18.1-320
18-282.1	18.1-321
18-283	18.1-322
18-284	18.1-323
18-285	18.1-324
18-286	18.1-325
18-287	18.1-326
18-288	18.1-327
18-289	18.1-328
18-290	18.1-329
18-291	18.1-330
18-292	18.1-331
18-293	18.1-332
18-294	18.1-333
18-295	18.1-334
18-296	18.1-335
18-297	18.1-336
18-298	18.1-337
18-299	18.1-338
18-300	18.1-339
18-301	18.1-340
18-301.1	18.1-340.1
18-302	18.1-341
18-302.1	18.1-342
18-303	18.1-343
18-304	18.1-344
18-305	18.1-345
18-305.1	18.1-346
18-306	18.1-347
18-307 to 18-312	Deleted
18-313	18.1-349
18-314	18.1-350
18-315	18.1-351
18-316	18.1-352
18-317	18.1-353
18-318	18.1-354
18-319 to 18-326	Deleted
18-327	18.1-356
18-328	18.1-357
18-329	18.1-358
18-329.1	18.1-358.1
18-329.2	18.1-358.2
18-330	18.1-359
18-331	18.1-360
18-332	18.1-361
18-333	18.1-362
18-334	18.1-363

Former Section	Present Section
18-335	18.1-401
18-335.1	18.1-402
18-335.2	18.1-403
18-336	18.1-404
18-337	18.1-405
18-338	18.1-406
18-339	18.1-407
18-339.1	18.1-408
18-340	18.1-409
18-341	18.1-410
18-341.1	18.1-410
18-342	18.1-411
18-343	Deleted
18-344	18.1-412
18-345	Deleted
18-346	Deleted
18-347	18.1-413
18-348	18.1-414
18-348.1	18.1-415
18-348.2	18.1-416
18-349	18.1-417
18-349.1	18.1-364
18-349.2	18.1-365
18-349.3	18.1-366
18-349.4	18.1-367
18-349.5	18.1-368
18-349.6	18.1-369
18-349.7	18.1-370
18-349.8	18.1-371
18-349.9	18.1-372
18-349.10	18.1-373
18-349.11	18.1-374
18.349.12	18.1-375
18-349.13	18.1-376
18-349.14	18.1-377
18-349.15	18.1-378
18-349.16	18.1-379
18-349.17	18.1-380
18-349.18	18.1-381
18-349.19	18.1-382
18-349.20	18.1-383
18-349.21	18.1-384
18-349.22	18.1-385
18-349.23	18.1-386
18-349.24	18.1-387
18-349.25	18.1-388
18-349.26	18.1-389
18-349.27	18.1-390
18-349.28	18.1-391
18-349.29	18.1-392
18-349.30	18.1-393
18-349.31	18.1-394
18-349.32	18.1-395
18-349.33	18.1-396
18-349.34	18.1-397
18-349.35	18.1-398
18-349.36	18.1-399
18-349.37	18.1-400
18-350	18.1-418
18-351	18.1-419
18-352	18.1-420
18-352.1	18.1-421
18-353	18.1-422
18-354	18.1-423
18-355	18.1-424
18-356	18.1-425
18-357	18.1-426
18-358	18.1-427
18-359	18.1-428
18-360	18.1-429
18-361	18.1-48
18-362	18.1-49
18-363	18.1-50
18-364	18.1-51
18-365	18.1-52
18-366	18.1-53
19-264	18.1-8
19-265	18.1-9
19-266	18.1-10
None	18.1-1
None	18.1-2
None	18.1-3
None	18.1-4
None	18.1-5
None	18.1-36
None	18.1-37
None	18.1-66
None	18.1-187
None	18.1-188
None	18.1-194
None	18.1-227 through 18.1-236.3
None	18.1-348
None	18.1-355

COMPARABLE SECTIONS OF TITLE 18.1 AND TITLE 18.2

Former Section	Present Section
18.1-1	18.2-1
18.1-2	18.2-2
18-1-3	18.2-3
18.1-4	18.2-4
18.1-5	18.2-5, 18.2-6
18.1-6	18.2-8
18.1-7	18.2-7
18.1-8	18.2-16
18.1-9	18.2-12
18.1-10	18.2-17
18.1-11	18.2-18, 18.2-19
18.1-12	18.2-19
18.1-13	18.2-21
18.1-14	18.2-371
18.1-15	Repealed
18.1-15.1	18.2-23
18.1-15.2	Repealed
18.1-15.3	18.2-22
18.1-16	18.2-25
18.1-17	18.2-26
18.1-18	18.2-26
18.1-19	18.2-27
18.1-20	18.2-28
18.1-21	18.2-31, 18.2-32
18.1-22	18.2-32
18.1-23	18.2-32
18.1-24	18.2-35
18.1-25	18.2-36
18.1-26	18.2-37
18.1-27	18.2-38
18.1-28	18.2-39
18.1-29	18.2-40
18.1-30	18.2-41
18.1-31	18.2-42
18.1-32	18.2-43
18.1-33	18.2-44
18.1-34	18.2-45
18.1-35	18.2-46
18.1-36	18.2.47
18.1-37	18.2-47
18.1-38	18.2-48
18.1-39	18.2-49
18.1-40	18.2-50
18.1-41	18.2-68
18.1-42	18.2-69
18.1-43	18.2-70
18.1-44	18.2-61, 18.2-62, 18.2-63, 18.2-64
18.1-45	18.2-66
18.1-46	18.2-65
18.1-47	18.2-67
18.1-48	18.2-274
18.1-49	18.2-275
18.1-50	18.2-275
18.1-51	18.2-276
18.1-52	18.2-277
18.1-53	18.2-278
18.1-54	18.2-266
18.1-54.1	18.2-267
18.1-55	Repealed
18.1-55.1	18.2-268
18.1-56	Repealed
18.1-56.1	Repealed
18.1-57	18.2-269
18.1-58	18.2-270
18.1-59	18.2-271
18.1-60	18.2-272
18.1-61	18.2-273
18.1-62	18.2-71
18.1-62.1	18.2-76
18.1-62.2	Deleted
18.1-62.3	18.2-74.1

Former Section	Present Section
18.1-63	18.2-76.1
18.1-63.1	18.2-75
18.1-64	18.2-54.1
18.1-65	18.2-51
18.1-66	18.2-279
18.1-67	18.2-52
18.1-68	18.2-53
18.1-69	18.2-280
18.1-69.1	18.2-281
18.1-69.2	18.2-282
18.1-70	18.2-312
18.1-70.1	18.2-264
18.1-71	18.2-56
18.1-72	18.2-313
18.1-73	18.2-316
18.1-74	18.2-317
18.1-74.1	18.2-318
18.1-74.1:1	18.2-499
18.1-74.1:2	18.2-500
18.1-74.1:3	18.2-501
18.1-74.2	18.2-314
18.1-75	18.2-77
18.1-76	18.2-80
18.1-77	18.2-78
18.1-78	18.2-79
18.1-78.1	18.2-83
18.1-78.2	18.2-83
18.1-78.3	18.2-83
18.1-78.4	18.2-83
18.1-78.5	18.2-84
18.1-78.6	18.2-85
18.1-79	18.2-81
18.1-80	18.2-80
18.1-80.1	18.2-82
18.1-81	18.2-80
18.1-81.1	Deleted
18.1-82	18.2-86
18.1-83	18.2-87
18.1-84	18.2-88
18.1-85	18.2-80, 18.2-81
18.1-86	18.2-89
18.1-87	18.2-94
18.1-88	18.2-90
18.1-88.1	18.2-92
18.1-89	18.2-91
18.1-90	18.2-93
18.1-91	18.2-58
18.1-92	18.2-168
18.1-93	18.2-169
18.1-94	18.2-170
18.1-95	18.2-171
18.1-96	18.2-172
18.1-97	18.2-173
18.1-98	18.2-207
18.1-99	18.2-208
18.1-100	18.2-95
18.1-101	18.2-96
18.1-102	18.2-97
18.1-103	18.2-110
18.1-104	18.2-98
18.1-105	18.2-98
18.1-106	18.2-99
18.1-107	18.2-108
18.1-107.1	18.2-110
18.1-108	18.2-101
18.1-109	18.2-111
18.1-110	18.2-112
18.1-111	18.2-113
18.1-112	18.2-114
18.1-113	18.2-200
18.1-114	18.2-201
18.1-115	18.2-100
18.1-116	18.2-115
18.1-117	18.2-116
18.1-117.1	18.2-118
18.1-118	18.2-178
18.1-119	18.2-186
18.1-119.1	Repealed
18.1-119.1:1	18.2-187
18.1-119.2	18.2-202
18.1-119.3	18.2-203
18.1-120	18.2-188
18.1-121	18.2-189
18.1-122	18.2-204
18.1-123	18.2-205
18.1-124	18.2-179
18.1-125	18.2-180
18.1-125.1	18.2-152
18.1-125.2	18.2-191
18.1-125.3	18.2-192
18.1-125.4	18.2-193
18.1-125.5	18.2-194
18.1-125.6	18.2-195
18.1-125.7	18.2-196
18.1-125.8	18.2-197
18.1-125.9	18.2-198
18.1-125.10	18.2-199
18.1-126	18.2-103
18.1-126.1	18.2-104
18.1-127	18.2-105
18.1-128	18.2-106
18.1-129 to 18.1-146.1	Repealed
18.1-147	18.2-153
18.1-148	18.2-159
18.1-149	18.2-161
18.1-150	18.2-160
18.1-151	18.2-156
18.1-152	18.2-154, 18.2-279
18.1-153	18.2-155
18.1-154	18.2-158
18.1-155	18.2-157
18.1-156	18.2-164
18.1-157	18.2-165
18.1-158	18.2-162
18.1-158.1	18.2-163
18.1-159	18.2-144
18.1-160	18.2-145
18.1-161	18.2-149
18.1-162	18.2-206
18.1-163	18.2-117
18.1-164	18.2-102
18.1-165	18.2-109
18.1-166	18.2-146
18.1-167	18.2-147
18.1-168	18.1-148
18.1-169	18.2-151
18.1-170	18.2-150
18.1-171	Reserved
18.1-172	18.2-137
18.1-173	18.2-119
18.1-173.1	18.2-120
18.1-173.2	18.2-129
18.1-174	18.2-130
18.1-175	Deleted
18.1-175.1	18.2-142
18.1-176	18.2-143
18.1-177	18.2-138
18.1-178	18.2-140
18.1-179	18.2-141
18.1-180	18.2-139
18.1-181	18.2-125
18.1-182	18.2-128
18.1-183	18.2-121
18.1-184	18.2-59
18.1-185	18.2-190
18.1-186	18.2-190
18.1-187	18.2-365
18.1-188	18.2-344
18.1-189	Reserved
18.1-190	18.2-344, 18.2-365
18.1-191	18.2-366
18.1-192	18.1-367
18.1-193	18.2-345
18.1-194	18.2-346
18.1-195	18.2-347
18.1-196	18.2-347
18.1-197	18.2-348
18.1-198	18.2-349
18.1-199	18.2-350
18.1-200	18.2-351
18.1-200.1	Repealed
18.1-201	18.2-352
18.1-202	18.2-353
18.1-203	Deleted
18.1-204	18.2-355
18.1-205	Deleted
18.1-206	18.2-356
18.1-207	18.2-368
18.1-208	18.2-357
18.1-209	18.2-358
18.1-210	18.2-359
18.1-211	18.2-360
18.1-212	18.2-361
18.1-213 to 18.1-215	18.2-370
18.1-216	18.2-392
18.1-216.1	18.2-392
18.1-217	18.2-397
18.1-218	18.2-398
18.1-219	18.2-399

Former Section	Present Section
18.1-220	18.2-400
18.1-221	18.2-401
18.1-222	Repealed
18.1-223	18.2-402
18.1-224	Repealed
18.1-225	18.2-396
18.1-226	18.2-403
18.1-227	18.2-372
18.1-228	18.2-374
18.1-229	18.2-373
18.1-230	18.2-375
18.1-231	18.2-376
18.1-232	18.2-377
18.1-233	18.2-378
18.1-234	18.2-379
18.1-235	18.2-382
18.1-235.1	18.2-380
18.1-236	18.2-387
18.1-236.1	18.2-381
18.1-236.2	18.2-383
18.1-236.3	18.2-384
18.1-236.4	18.2-385
18.1-236.5	18.2-389
18.1-236.6	18.2-390
18.1-236.7	18.2-391
18.1-237	18.2-388
18.1-238	18.2-427
	18.2-430, 18.2-431
18.1-238.1	18.2-428
18.1-238.2	18.2-429
18.1-238.3	18.2-167
18.1-239	18.2-415
18.1-240	18.2-415
18.1-241	18.2-283
18.1-242	18.2-394
18.1-243	18.2-126
18.1-244	18.2-127
18.1-245	Deleted
18.1-246	18.2-395
18.1-246.1	18.2-386
18.1-247 to 18.1-253	Repealed
18.1-253.1 to 18.1-253.3	18.2-415
18.1-254	Repealed
18.1-254.01	18.2-404
18.1-254.1	18.2-405
	18.2-406
18.1-254.2	18.2-405
18.1-254.3	18.2-406
18.1-254.4	18.2-407
18.1-254.5	Repealed
18.1-254.5:1	18.2-408
18.1-254.6	18.2-409
18.1-254.7	18.2-410
18.1-254.8	18.2-411
	18.2-412
18.1-254.9	18.2-411
	18.2-412
18.1-254.10	18.2-413
18.1-254.11	18.2-414

Former Section	Present Section
18.1-254.12	Deleted
18.1-255	18.2-416
18.1-256	18.2-417
18.1-257	18.2-60
18.1-258	18.2-288
18.1-259	18.2-289
18.1-260	18.2-290
18.1-261	18.2-291
18.1-262	18.2-292
18.1-263	18.2-293
	18.2-293.1
18.1-264	18.2-294
18.1-265	18.2-295
18.1-266	18.2-296
18.1-267	18.2-297
18.1-268	18.2-298
18.1-268.1	18.2-299
18.1-268.2	18.2-300
18.1-268.3	18.2-301
18.1-268.4	18.2-302
18.1-268.5	18.2-303
	18.2-303.1
18.1-268.6	18.2-304
18.1-268.7	18.2-305
18.1-268.8	18.2-306
18.1-268.9	18.2-307
18.1-269	18.2-308
18.1-270	18.2-310
18.1-271	18.2-311
18.1-272	18.2-287
18.1-273 to	
18.1-275	18.2-434
18.1-276	18.2-435
18.1-277	18.2-436
	18.2-437
18.1-278	18.2-438
18.1-279	18.2-439
18.1-280	18.2-445
18.1-281	18.2-440
18.1-282	18.2-441
18.1-282.1	18.2-446
18.1-282.2	18.2-447
18.1-282.3	18.2-448
	18.2-450
18.1-282.4	18.2-449
18.1-283	Deleted
18.1-284	18.2-473
18.1-285	18.2-474
18.1-286	18.2-475
18.1-287	18.2-476
18.1-288	18.2-477
18.1-289	18.2-478
18.1-290	18.2-479
18.1-291	18.2-480
18.1-292	18.2-456
18.1-293	18.2-458
18.1-294	18.2-459
18.1-295	18.2-457
18.1-296	18.2-465
18.1-297	18.2-466
18.1-298	18.2-467

Former Section	Present Section
18.1-299	18.2-468
18.1-300	18.2-469
18.1-301	18.2-463
18.1-302	18.2-464
18.1-303	18.2-462
18.1-304	18.2-470
18.1-305	18.2-471
18.1-306	18.2-472
18.1-307	18.2-471
	18.2-472
18.1-308	18.2-107
18.1-309	18.2-504
18.1-310	18.2-460
18.1-311	18.2-174
18.1-312	18.2-175
18.1-313	18.2-213
18.1-314	Deleted
18.1-315	Deleted
18.1-316	18.2-326
18.1-317	Deleted
18.1-318	18.2-327
18.1-318.1	18.2-328
18.1-319	18.2-329
	18.2-330, 18.2-333
18.1-320	Deleted
18.1-321	18.2-336
18.1-322	18.2-333
18.1-323	18.2-331
	18.2-336
18.1-324	18.2-329
18.1-325	18.2-330
18.1-326	18.2-326
18.1-327	18.2-334
18.1-328	Deleted
18.1-329	18.2-331
18.1-330	18.2-331
18.1-331	18.2-325
18.1-332	18.2-331
18.1-333	18.2-336
18.1-334	18.2-338
18.1-335	Deleted
18.1-336	Deleted
18.1-337	18.2-329
18.1-338	Deleted
18.1-339	18.2-329
18.1-340	18.2-329,
	18.2-335
18.1-340.1	18.2-332
18.1-341	18.2-336
18.1-342	18.2-340
18.1-343	18.2-338
18.1-344	18.2-309
18.1-345	18.2-265
18.1-346	18.2-249
18.1-347	18.2-284
18.1-348	Deleted
18.1-349	Deleted
18.1-349.1	18.2-432
18.1-350 to	
18.1-354	18.2-433
18.1-355	Deleted

Former Section	Present Section
18.1-356 to 18.1-363	Repealed
18.1-363.1	18.2-341
18.1-364	18.2-422
18.1-365	18.2-423
18.1-366	18.2-423
18.1-367	18.2-422 18.2-423
18.1-367.1	18.2-418
18.1-367.2 to 18.1-367.6	18.2-419
18.1-368	18.2-424
18.1-369	18.2-425
18.1-370	18.2-426
18.1-371	18.2-431
18.1-372 to 18.1-380	Deleted
18.1-380.1	18.2-420
18.1-380.2	18.2-421
18.1-381 to 18.1-387	Deleted
18.1-388	18.2-451
18.1-389	18.2-452
18.1-390	18.2-452
18.1-391	18.2-453
18.1-392	18.2-454
18.1-393	18.2-455
18.1-394 to 18.1-400	Deleted
18.1-400.1	18.2-493
18.1-400.2	18.2-494
18.1-400.3	18.2-495
18.1-400.4	18.2-496
18.1-400.5	18.2-497
18.1-400.6	18.2-498
18.1-401	18.2-461
18.1-402	18.2-442
18.1-403	18.2-443
18.1-404	18.2-444
18.1-405	18.2-445
18.1-406	Deleted
18.1-407	18.2-209
18.1-408	18.2-211
18.1-408.1	18.2-503
18.1-409	18.2-210
18.1-410	18.2-176
18.1-411	Repealed
18.1-412	18.2-212
18.1-413	Deleted
18.1-414	18.2-315
18.1-415	18.2-319
18.1-415.1	18.2-320
18.1-416	18.2-321
18.1-417	Deleted
18.1-417.1	18.2-166
18.1-417.2	18.2-502
18.1-418	18.2-481
18.1-419	18.2-482
18.1-420	18.2-483
18.1-421	18.2-484
18.2-422	18.2-485
18.1-423	18.2-486
18.1-424	18.2-487
18.1-425	18.2-488
18.1-426	18.2-489
18.1-427	18.2-490
18.1-428	18.2-491
18.1-429	18.2-492

COMPARABLE SECTIONS OF TITLE 19 AND TITLE 19.1

Former Section	Present Section
18-9	19.1-20
18-10	19.1-21
18-11	19.1-22
18-12	19.1-23
18-13	19.1-24
18-14	19.1-25
18-15	19.1-26
18-16	19.1-27
18-17	19.1-28
18-18	19.1-29
18-19	19.1-30
18-20	19.1-31
18-21	19.1-32
19-1	19.1-6
19-2	19.1-7
19-3	19.2-8
19-4	19.1-9
19-5	19.1-10
19-6	19.1-11
19-7	19.1-12
19-7.1	19.1-13
19-8	19.1-14
19-9	19.1-15
19-10	19.1-16
19-11	19.1-17
19-12	19.1-18
19-13	19.1-19
19-14	19.1-33
19-15	19.1-34
19-16	19.1-35
19-17	19.1-36
19-18	19.1-37
19-19	19.1-38
19-20	19.1-39
19-21	19.1-40
19-21.1	Deleted
19-22	19.1-41
19-23	19.1-42
19-24	19.1-43
19-25	19.1-44
19-26	19.1-45
19-27	19.1-46
19-28	19.1-83
19-29	19.1-84
19-30	19.1-85
19-31	19.1-86
19-32	19.1-87
19-33	19.1-88
19-34	19.1-89
19-35	19.1-47
19-36	19.1-48
19-37	19.1-49
19-38	19.1-50
19-39	19.1-51
19-40	19.1-52
19-41	19.1-53
19-42	19.1-54
19-43	19.1-55
19-44	19.1-56
19-45	19.1-57
19-46	19.1-58
19-47	19.1-59
19-48	19.1-60
19-49	19.1-61
19-50	19.1-62
19-51	19.1-63
19-52	19.1-64
19-53	19.1-65
19-54	19.1-66
19-55	19.1-67
19-56	19.1-68
19-57	19.1-69
19-58	19.1-70
19-59	19.1-71
19-60	19.1-72
19-61	19.1-73
19-62	19.1-74
19-63	19.1-75
19-64	19.1-76
19-65	19.1-77
19-66	19.1-78
19-67	19.1-79
19-68	19.1-80
19-69	19.1-81
19-70	19.1-82
19-71	19.1-90
19-72	19.1-91
19-72.1	19.1-92
19-72.2	19.1-93
19-73	19.1-94
19-74	19.1-95
19-75	19.1-96
19-76	19.1-97
19-77	19.1-98
19-78	19.1-99
19-78.1	19.1-100

Former Section	Present Section
19-79	19.1-101
19-80	19.1-102
19-81	Deleted
19-82	19.1-104
19-83	19.1-105
19-84	19.1-106
19-85	19.1-107
19-86	19.1-108
19-87	19.1-109
19-88	19.1-110
19-89	19.1-111
19-90	19.1-112
19-91	19.1-113
19-92	19.1-114
19-92.1	19.1-115
19-93	19.1-116
19-94	19.1-117
19-94.1	19.1-118
19-95	19.1-119
19-96	19.1-120
19-97	19.1-121
19-98	19.1-122
19-99	19.1-123
19-100	19.1-124
19-101	19.1-125
19-102	19.1-126
19-103	19.1-127
19-104	19.1-128
19-105	19.1-129
19-106	19.1-130
19-107	19.1-131
19-108	19.1-132
19-109	19.1-133
19-110	19.1-134
19-111	19.1-135
19-112	19.1-136
19-113	19.1-137
19-114	19.1-138
19-115	19.1-139
19-116	19.1-140
19-117	19.1-141
19-118	19.1-142
19-119	19.1-143
19-120	19.1-144
19-121	19.1-145
19-121.1	19.1-32.1
19-122	19.1-147
19-123	19.1-148
19-124	19.1-149
19-125	19.1-150
19-126	19.1-151
19-127	19.1-152
19-128	19.1-153
19-129	19.1-154
19-130	19.1-155
19-131	19.1-156
19-132	19.1-157
19-133	19.1-158
19-134	19.1-159
19-135	19.1-160
19-135.1	19.1-161
19-136	19.1-162
19-137	19.1-163
19-137.1	19.1-163.1
19-138	19.1-164
19-139	19.1-165
19-140	19.1-166
19-141	19.1-167
19-142	19.1-168
19-143	19.1-169
19-144	19.1-170
19-145	19.1-171
19-146	19.1-172
19-147	19.1-173
19-148	19.1-174
19-149	19.1-175
19-150	19.1-176
19-151	19.1-177
19-152	19.1-178
19-153	19.1-179
19-154	19.1-180
19-155	19.1-181
19-156	19.1-182
19-157	19.1-183
19-158	19.1-184
19-159	19.1-185
19-160	19.1-186
19-161	19.1-187
19-162	19.1-188
19-163	19.1-189
19-164	19.1-190
19-165	19.1-191
19-166	19.1-192
19-167	Repealed 1952
19-168	19.1-193
19-169	19.1-194
19-170	19.1-195
19-171	19.1-196
19-172	19.1-197
19-173	19.1-198
19-174	19.1-199
19-175	19.1-200
19-176	19.1-201
19-177	19.1-202
19-178	19.1-203
19-179	19.1-204
19-180	19.1-205
19-181	19.1-206
19-182	19.1-207
19-183	19.1-208
19-184	19.1-209
19-185	19.1-210
19-186	19.1-211
19-187	19.1-212
19-188	19.1-213
19-189	19.1-214
19-190	19.1-215
19-191	19.1-216
19-192	19.1-217
19-193	19.1-218
19-193.1	19.1-219
19-194	19.1-220
19-195	19.1-221
19-196	19.1-222
19-197	19.1-223
19-198	19.1-224
19-199	19.1-225
19-200	19.1-226
19-201	19.1-227
19-202	19.1-228
19-203	19.1-229
19-204	19.1-230
19-205	19.1-231
19-206	19.1-232
19-207	19.1-233
19-208	19.1-234
19-209	19.1-235
19-210	19.1-236
19-211	19.1-237
19-212	19.1-238
19-213	19.1-239
19-214	19.1-240
19-214.1	19.1-241
19-215	19.1-242
19-216	19.1-243
19-217	19.1-244
19-218	19.1-245
19-219	19.1-246
19-220	19-1-247
19-221	19.1-248
19-222	19.1-249
19-223	19.1-250
19-224	19.1-251
19-225	19.1-252
19-226	19.1-253
19-227	19.1-254
19-228	19.1-255
19-229	19.1-256
19-230	19.1-257
19-231	19.1-258
19-232	19.1-259
19-233	Deleted
19-234	19.1-260
19-235	19.1-261
19-236	19.1-262
19-237	19.1-263
19-238	19-1-264
19-239	19-1-265
19-240	19-1-266
19-241	19.1-267
19-241.1	19.1-268
19-242	19.1-269
19-243	19.1-270
19-244	19.1-271
19-245	19.1-272
19-246	19.1-273
19-247	19.1-274
19-248	19.1-275
19-249	19.1-276
19-250	Z9.1-277
19-251	19.1-278
19-252	19.1-279
19-253	19.1-280

Former Section	Present Section
19-254	19.1-281
19-255	19.1-282
19-256	19.1-283
19-257	19.1-284
19-258	19.1-285
19-259	19.1-286
19-260	19.1-287
19-261	19.1-288
19-262	19.1-289
19-263	19.1-290
19-264	18.1-8
19-265	18.1-9
19-266	18.1-10
19-267	19.1-291
19-267.1	19.1-292
19-268	19.1-293
19-269	19.1-294
19-269.1	19.1-295
19-270	19.1-296
19-271	19.1-297
19-272	Deleted
19-273	19.1-299
19-273.1	19.1-300
19-274	19.1-301
19-275	19.1-302
19-276	19.1-303
19-277	19.1-304
19-278	19.1-305
19-279	19.1-306
19-280	19.1-306.1
19-281	19.1-307
19-282	Deleted
19-283	19.1-308
19-284	19.1-309

Former Section	Present Section
19-285	19.1-310
19-286	19.1-311
19-287	19.1-312
19-288	19.1-313
19-289	Deleted
19-290	19.1-314
19-291	19.1-315
19-292	19.1-316
19-293	19.1-317
19-294	19.1-318
19-295	19.1-319
19-296	19.1-320
19-297	19.1-321
19-297.1	19.1-322
19-298	19.1-323
19-299	19.1-324
19-300	19.1-325
19-301	19.1-326
19-302	19.1-327
19-303	19.1-328
19-304	19.1-329
19-305	19.1-330
19-306	19.1-331
19-307	19.1-332
19-308	19.1-333
19-309	19.1-334
19-310	19.1-335
19-311 to 19-318	Deleted
19-319	19.1-338
19-320	19.1-339
19-321	19.1-340
19-322	19.1-341
19-323	Deleted

Former Section	Present Section
19-324	19.1-341.1
19-325	19.1-342
19-326	19.1-343
19-327	19.1-344
19-328	19.1-345
19-329	19.1-346
19-330	19.1-347
19-331	19.1-348
19-332	19.1-349
19-333	Deleted
19-334	Deleted
19-335	19.1-350
19-336	19.1-351
19-337	19.1-352
19-338	19.1-353
19-339	19.1-354
19-340	19.1-355
19-341	19.1-356
19-342	19.1-357
None	19.1-1
None	19.1-2
None	19.1-3
None	19.1-4
None	19.1-5
None	19.1-122.1
None	19.1-259.1
None	19.1-290.1
None	19.1-336
None	19.1-337
None	19.1-341.2
None	19.1-358 through 19.1-373

COMPARABLE SECTIONS OF TITLE 19.1 AND TITLE 19.2

Former Section	Present Section
19.1-1	19.2-1
19.1-2	19.2-2
19.1-3	19.2-3
19.1-4	19.2-4
19.1-5	19.2-5
19.1-6	19.2-7
19.1-6.1	19.2-7
19.1-7	19.1-153
19.1-8	19.2-8
19.1-9	19.2-155
19.1-10	19.2-155
19.1-11	19.2-156
19.1-12	Deleted
19.1-13	Deleted
19.1-14	19.2-9
19.1-15	19.2-10
19.1-16	19.2-11
19.1-17	19.2-369
19.1-18	19.2-151
19.1-19	19.2-152
19.1-19.1	Repealed

Former Section	Present Section
19.1-19.1:1	19.2-387
19.1-19.2	19.2-388 19.2-389
19.1-19.3	19.2-390
19.1-19.4	19.2-391
19.1-19.5	Reserved
19.1-19.6	19.2-392
19.1-20	19.2-12, 19.2-18
19.1-21	19.2-20
19.1-22	19.2-21
19.1-23	19.2-24
19.1-24	19.2-25
19.1-25	19.2-25
19.1-26	19.2-19
19.1-27	19.2-19
19.1-28	19.2-13
19.1-29	19.2-15
19.1-29.1	19.2-16
19.1-30	19.2-17
19.1-31	19.2-23
19.1-32	19.2-14

Former Section	Present Section
19.1-32.1	Repealed
19.1-32.2	19.2-163.1
19.1-32.3	19.2-163.2
19.1-32.4	19.2-163.3
19.1-32.5	19.2-163.4
19.1-33 to 19.1-44	32-31.9 et seq.
19.1-45	19.2-188
19.1-46, 19.1-46.1	32-21.9 et seq.
19.1-47	19.2-84
19.1-48	Deleted
19.1-49	19.2-85
19.1-50	19.2-86
19.1-51	19.2-87
19.1-52	19.2-88
19.1-53	19.2-89
19.1-54	19.2-90
19.1-55	19.2-91
19.1-56	19.2-92
19.1-57	19.2-93

Former Section	Present Section
19.1-58	19.2-94
19.1-59	19.2-95
19.1-60	19.2-96
19.1-61	19.2-97
19.1-62	19.2-98
19.1-63	19.2-99
19.1-64	19.2-100
19.1-65	19.2-101
19.1-66	19.2-102
19.1-67	19.2-103
19.1-68	19.2-104
19.1-69	19.2-105
19.1-70	19.2-106
19.1-71	19.2-107
19.1-72	19.2-108
19.1-73	19.2-109
19.1-74	19.2-110
19.1-75	19.2-111
19.1-76	19.2-112
19.1-77	19.2-113
19.1-78	19.2-114
19.1-79	19.2-115
19.1-80	19.2-116
19.1-81	19.2-117
19.1-82	19.2-118
19.1-83	19.2-52
19.1-84	19.2-53
19.1-85	19.2-54
19.1-86	19.2-56
19.1-87	19.2-58
19.1-87.1	19.2-57
19.1-88	19.2-59
19.1-89	19.2-55
19.1-89.1	19.2-61
19.1-89.2	19.2-62
19.1-89.3	19.2-63
19.1-89.4	19.2-64
19.1-89.5	19.2-65
19.1-89.6	19.2-66
19.1-89.7	19.2-67
19.1-89.8	19.2-68
19.1-89.9	19.2-69
19.1-89.10	19.2-70
19.1-90	19.2-71
19.1-91	19.2-72
19.1-92	19.2-75
19.1-92.1	19.2-74
19.1-93	Deleted
19.1-94	19.2-77
19.1-95	19.2-78
19.1-96	Repealed
19.1-97	19.2-79
19.1-98	19.2-76, 19-2-80
19.1-99	19.2-76
19.1-100	19.2-81
19.1-100.1	19.2-82
19.1-100.2	19.2-83
19.1-101	19.2-183
19.1-102	19.2-183
19.1-103	Reserved
19.1-104	19.2-184
19.1-105	19.2-185
19.1-106	19.2-186
19.1-106.1	19.2-187
19.1-107	19.2-189
19.1-108	19.2-190
19.1-109	19.2-122
19.1-109.1	19.2-119
19.1-109.2	19.2-123
19.1-109.3	19.2-124
19.1-109.4	19.2-125
19.1-109.5	19.2-126
19.1-109.6	19.2-127
19.1-109.7	19.2-128
19.1-109.8	19.2-129
19.1-109.9	14.1-128.1
19.1-110	Repealed
19.1-111	Repealed
19.1-111.1	19.2-130
19.1-112	19.2-124
19.1-113 to 19.1-115	Deleted
19.1-116	Repealed
19.1-117	Deleted
19.1-118	19.2-131
19.1-119	19.2-131
19.1-120	19.2-132
19.1-121	19.2-133
19.1-122	Repealed
19.1-122.1	Repealed
19.1-123	19.2-134
19.1-124	Repealed
19.1-125	19.2-135
19.1-126	Repealed
19.1-127	19.2-136
19.1-128	19.2-135
19.1-129	19.2-137
19.1-130	19.2-138
19.1-131	19.2-139
19.1-132	19.2-140
19.1-133	19.2-135
19.1-134	19.2-141
19.1-135	Repealed
19.1-136	19.2-142
19.1-137	19.2-143
19.1-138	Repealed
19.1-139	19.2-144
19.1-140	19.2-145
19.1-141	19.2-146
19.1-142	19.2-147
19.1-143	19.2-148
19.1-144	19.2-149
19.1-145	19.2-150
19-1-146	19.2-73
19.1-147	19.2-193
19.1-148	19.2-193
19.1-149	19.2-206
19.1-150	19.2-195
19.1-151	19.2-196
19.1-152	19.2-197
19.1-153	19.2-198
19.1-154	19.2-199
19.1-155	19.2-200
19.1-156	19.1-201
19.1-157	19.2-202
19.1-158	19.2-203
19.1-159	19.2-204
19.1-160	19.2-205
19.1-161	Repealed
19.1-162	19.2-217
19.1-163	19.2-242
19.1-163.1	19.2-218
19.1-164	19.2-219
19.1-165	19.2-227
19.1-166	19.2-221
19.1-167	19.2-222
19.1-168	19.2-223
19.1-169	19.2-224
19.1-170	19.2-225
19.1-171	Deleted
19.1-172	19.2-226
19.1-173	19.2-228
19.1-174	19.2-229
19.1-175 to 19.1-177	19.2-231
19.1-178	19.2-232
19.1-179	19.2-233
19.1-180	19.2-237
19.1-181	19.2-235
19.1-182	19.2-236
19.1-183	19.2-234
19.1-184	19.2-237
19.1-185	Deleted
19.1-186	19.2-238
19.1-186.1	46.1-347.1
19.1-186.2	46.1-347.2
19.1-187	19.2-239
19.1-188	19.2-241
19.1-189	19.2-240 19.2-241
19.1-190	19.2-241
19.1-191	19.2-243
19.1-192	19.2-257
19.1-193	19.2-258
19.1-194 to 19.1-219	Repealed
19.1-220	19.2-245
19.1-221	19.2-246
19.1-221.1	19.2-247
19.1-222	19.2-249
19.1-223	19.2-248
19.1-224	19.2-251
19.1-225	19.2-252
19.1-226	19.2-253
19.1-227	19.2-167
119.1-227.1	19.2-168
19.1-228	19.2-169
19.1-229	19.2-170
19.1-230	19.2-171
19.1-230.1	19.2-172
19.1-231	19.2-173
19.1-232	19.2-174
19.1-233	19.2-175

Former Section	Present Section
19.1-234	19.2-176
19.1-235	19.2-177
19.1-236	19.2-178
19.1-237	19.2-179
19.1-238	19.2-180
19.1-239	19.2-181
19.1-239.1	19.2-182
19.1-240	19.2-259
19.1-241	Repealed
19.1-241.1	19.2-157
19.1-241.2	19.2-158
19.1-241.3	19.2-159
19.1-241.4	19.2-162
19.1-241.5	19.2-163
19.1-241.6	19.2-161
19.1-241.7	19.2-157
19.1-241.8	19.2-158
19.1-241.9	19.2-160
19.1-241.10	19.2-162
19.1-241.11	19.2-163
19.1-241.12	19.2-161
19.1-242	19.2-255
19.1-243	Deleted
19.1-244	19.2-256
19.1-245	19.2-265
19.1-246	19.2-266
19.1-246.1	19.2-164
19.1-247	19.2-284
19.1-248	19.2-283
19.1-249	19.2-285
19.1-250	19.2-288
19.1-251	18.2-54
19.1-252	19.2-289
19.1-253	19.2-290
19.1-254	19.2-286
19.1-255	19.2-291
19.1-256	19.2-287
19.1-257	19.2-292
19.1-258	19.2-293
19.1-259	19.2-294
19.1-259.1	19.2-294.1
19.1-260	Repealed
19.1-261	Repealed
19.1-262	19.2-267
19.1-263	Deleted
19.1-264	19.2-268
19.1-265	19.2-269
19.1-266	18.2-337
19.1-267	19.2-270, 19.2-271
19.1-268	19.2-271
19.1-269	19.2-272
19.1-270	19.2-273
19.1-271	19.2-274
19.1-272	19.2-275
19.1-273	19.2-276
19.1-274	19.2-277
19.1-275	19.2-278
19.1-276	19.2-279
19.1-277	19.2-280
19.1-278	19.2-281
19.1-279	19.2-282
19.1-280	Deleted
19.1-281	19.2-319
19.1-282	19.2-317
19.1-283	19.2-318
19.1-284	19.2-320
19.1-285	19.2-321
19.1-286	19.2-322
19.1-287	19.2-323
19.1-288	19.2-324
19.1-289	19.2-325
19.1-290	19.2-327
19.1-290.1	Deleted
19.1-291	19.2-295
19.1-292	19.2-295
19.1-293	19.2-297
19.1-294	19.2-308
19.1-295	19.2-309
19.1-295.1	19.2-311
19.1-295.2	19.2-312
19.1-295.3	19.2-313
19.1-295.4	19.2-314
19.1-295.5	19.2-315
19.1-295.6	19.2-316
19.1-296	19.2-310
19.1-297	Repealed
19.1-298	Reserved
19.1-299 to 19.1-307	Repealed
19.1-308	19.2-328
19.1-309 to 19.1-311	Repealed
19.1-312	19.2-329
19.1-313	19.2-330
19.1-314	19.2-331
19.1-315	19.2-332
19.1-316	19.2-333
19.1-317	19.2-334
19.1-318	19.2-334
19.1-319	19.2-335
19.1-320	19.2-336
19.1-321	19.2-337
19.1-322	19.2-338
19.1-323	19.2-339
19.1-324	19.2-340 19.2-341
19.1-325	19.2-342
19.1-326	Deleted
19.1-327	Deleted
19.1-328 to 19.1-334	Repealed
19.1-335	19.2-345
19.1-336	19.2-346
19.1-337	19.2-347
19.1-338 to 19.1-341	Repealed
19.1-341.1	19.2-348
19.1-341.2	19.2-349
19.1-342	9.2-350
19.1-343	Deleted
19.1-344	19.2-351
19.1-345	19.2-352
19.1-346	19.2-353
19.1-347	19.2-353.1
19.1-347.1	19.2-354
19.1-347.2	19.2-355
19.1-347.3	19.2-356
19.1-347.4	19.2-357
19.1-347.5	Repealed
19.1-347.6	19.2-358
19.1-348	19.2-359
19.1-349	19.2-360
19.1-350	19.2-361
19.1-351	19.2-362
19.1-352	19.2-363
19.1-353	19.2-364
19.1-354	19.2-365
19.1-355	19.2-366
19.1-356	19.2-367
19.1-357	19.2-368
19.1-358	19.2-369
19.1-359	19.2-370
19.1-360	19.2-371
19.1-361	19.2-372
19.1-362	19.2-373
19.1-363	19.2-374
19.1-363.1	19.2-375
19.1-363.2	19.2-376
19.1-364	19.2-377
19.1-365	19.2-378
19.1-366	19.2-379
19.1-367	19.2-380
19.1-368	19.2-381
19.1-369	19.2-382
19.1-370	19.2-383
19.1-371	19.2-384
19.1-372	19.2-385
19.1-373	19.2-386
19.1-374	19.2-26
19.1-375	19.2-27
19.1-376	19.2-28
19.1-377	19.2-29
19.1-378	19.2-30
19.1-379	19.2-31
19.1-380	19.2-32
19.1-381	19.2-33
19.1-382	19.2-34
19.1-383	19.2-35
19.1-384	19.2-36
19.1-385	19.2-37
19.1-386	19.2-38
19.1-387	19.2-39
19.1-388	19.2-40
19-1-389	19.2-41
19-1-390	Repealed
19-1-391	19.2-42
19-1-392	19.2-43
19-1-393	19.2-44
19-1-393.1	19.2-44.1
19.1-394	19.2-45
19.1-395	19.2-46
19.1-396	19.2-47

Former Section	Present Section
19.1-397	19.2-48
19.1-398	19.2-49
19.1-399	19.2-50
19.1-400	19.2-51

COMPARABLE SECTIONS OF TITLE 20

Former Section	Present Section
20-146.1	20-125
20-146.2	none
20-146.3	none
20-146.4	20-146
20-146.5	20-135
20-146.6	none
20-146.7	20-128
20-146.8	none
20-146.9	none
20-146.10	20-141
20-146.11	20-142, 20-143
20-146.11 A 4	20-145
20-146.11 D	20-144
20-146.12	20-126
20-146.13	none
20-146.14	20-137
20-146.15	none
20-146.16	20-127
20-146.16 C	20-133
20-146.17	20-129
20-146.18	20-130
20-146.19	20-131
20-146.20	20-132
20-146.21	20-134
20-146.22	none
20-146.23	none
20-146.24	20-138
20-146.25	none
20-146.26	20-139
20-146.27	20-138
20-146.28	20-129
20-146.29	none
20-146.30	none
20-146.31	none
20-143.32	none
20-146.33	20-136

COMPARABLE SECTIONS OF TITLE 22 AND TITLE 22.1

Former Section	Present Section
22-1.1	22.1-2
22-2	22.1-2
22-3 to 22-4	Deleted
22-5	22.1-79 22.1-98
22-6	Deleted
22-7	22.1-26
22-7.1, 22-7.2	Deleted
22-9.1:04	22.1-7
22-10, 22-10.1	Deleted
22-10.2	22.1-275
22-10.3	22.1-213
22-10.4	22.1-214
22-10.5	22.1-215
22-10.6	22.1-216
22-10.7	22.1-217
22-10.8	22.1-218
22-10.9	22.1-219
22-10.10	22.1-220
22-10.11	22.1-221
22-10.12	Deleted
22-10.13	22.1-222
22-11	22.1-8 22.1-9
22-12.1	22.1-9
22-13	22.1-10
22-14	22.1-11
22-15	22.1-12
22-16	Deleted
22-17	22.1-13
22-18	22.1-14
22-19	22.1-16
22-19.01	22.1-17
22-19.1	22.1-18
22-20	22.1-15
22-21	22.1-19
22-21.2	22.1-97
22-21.3	22.1-212
22-21.4	22.1-290
22-22	22.1-21
22-23	Deleted
22-24	22.1-22
22-25	22.1-23
22-26	22.1-23
22-27	22.1-24
22-28	22.1-23
22-29 to 22-29.2	Deleted
22-29.3	22.1-163
22-29.4	22.1-164
22-29.5	22.1-165
22-29.6	22.1-166
22-29.7	22.1-167
22-29.8	22.1-168
22-29.9	22.1-169
22-29.10	22.1-170
22-29.11	22.1-171
22-29.12	22.1-172
22-29.13	22.1-173
22-29.14	22.1-174
22-29.15	22.1-175
22-30.1	22.1-25
22-31	22.1-59
22-32	22.1-60, 22.1-62
22-33	22.1-60, 22.1-61
22-35	22.1-63
22-36	22.1-70
22-36.1	22.1-68
22-37	22.1-62 22.1-67
22-38	22.1-66
22-39	22.1-64
22-40	22.1-65
22-40.1	22.1-209
22-41	Deleted
22-41.1	22.1-339 22.1-340
22-41.2	22.1-339 22.1-341
22-41.3	22.1-342
22-41.4	22.1-342
22-41.5	22.1-343
22-41.6	22.1-344
22-41.7	22.1-345
22-42	22.1-36
22-43	22.1-33
22-44	22.1-49
22-45	22.1-72
22-46	22.1-72
22-47	Deleted
22-48 to 22-48.2	22.1-76
22-49	22.1-69
22-50	Deleted
22-51	22.1-73
22-52	22.1-74
22-53	22.1-77
22-53.1	22.1-20
22-54	22.1-81
22-55	22.1-211

Former Section	Present Section
22-56.1	22.1-82
22-56.1:1	22.1-83
22-56.2	22.1-84
22-56.3	22.1-85
22-57	22.1-87
22-57.1	Deleted
22-57.2	22.1-296
22-58, 22-59	Deleted
22-60	22.1-35
22-61	22.1-36, 22.1-44
22-62	22.1-37
22-63	22.1-71
22-64	22.1-38
22-65	22.1-39
22-66	22.1-31
22-67.2	22.1-32
22-68	22.1-29
22-69	22.1-30
22-70	22.1-75
22-71	22.1-76
22-72	22.1-78, 22.1-79, 22.1-82, 22.1-84, 22.1-89, 22.1-251, 22.1-296, 22.1-315
22-72.1	22.1-176
22-72.2	22.1-80
22-73	22.1-122
22-74	22.1-123
22-75 to 22-78	22.1-122
22-79	22.1-86
22-79.1	22.1-44
22-79.2	Deleted
22-79.3	22.1-44
22-79.4	22.1-42
22-79.5	22.1-43
22-79.6	22.1-46
22-80	22.1-47
22-81, 22-82	Deleted
22-83.1	22.1-47
22-83.2	Deleted
22-89	22.1-50
22-89.1	22.1-51
22-90	22.1-29
22-91	22.1-31
22-92	22.1-30
22-93	Deleted
22-94	22.1-71 22.1-125
22-95	22.1-125
22-96	22.1-78
22-97	22.1-72, 22.1-78, 22.1-79, 22.1-86, 22.1-89 22.1-90, 22.1-122 22.1-127, 22.1-135, 22.1-136, 22.1-140, 22.1-251, 22.1-286, 22.1-315
22-97.1	22.1-176
22-98	22.1-176
22-99, 22-100	Deleted
22-100.1	22.1-52
22-100.3	22.1-53
22-100.3:1	Deleted
22-100.4	22.1-54
22-100.5	Deleted
22-100.6	22.1-55
22-100.7	22.1-56
22-100.7:1, 22-100.8	Deleted
22-100.9	22.1-96
22-100.10	22.1-117
22-100.11	22.1-57
22-100.13	Deleted
22-101	22.1-142 22.1-143
22-102	22.1-145, 22.1-157, 22.1-161
22-103	22.1-143
22-104	22.1-144
22-105	22.1-146
22-106	22.1-147
22-107	22.1-153
22-107.1, 22-107.2	Deleted
22-107.3	22.1-159
22-108	22.1-155
22-109	22.1-156
22-110	22.1-154
22-111	22.1-148
22-112	22.1-149, 22.1-150, 22.1-151, 22.1-152
22-113	22.1-158
22-114	22.1-157
22-115	22.1-160, 22.1-161
22-115.29 to 22-115.35	Deleted
22-116	22.1-88
22-117	Deleted
22-118	22.1-107
22-119	22.1-108
22-119.1	22.1-109
22-120	22.1-91, 22.1-110
11-120.2	Deleted
22-120.3	22.1-92
22-120.4	Deleted
22-120.5	22.1-92
22-126.1	22.1-95
22-127	22.1-89, 22.1-93, 22.1-94
22-128	22.1-102
22.128.1	Deleted
22-130.1	22.1-103
22-130.2	22.1-104
22-130.3	22.1-105
22-130.4	22.1-106
22-132	22.1-116
22-133	22.1-116
22-133.1	22.1-118
22-134	22.1-119
22-135	22.1-120
22-136	22.1-121
22-137	Deleted
22-138	22.1-100
22-140	22.1-99
22-140.1	22.1-113
22-141.2	22.1-114
22-142	22.1-101
22-143	22.1-115
22-144	22.1-111
22-145	22.1-112
22-146, 22-147	Deleted
22-148	22.1-126
22-149	22.1-127
22-150	22.1-128
22-151	22.1-130
22-151.1	22.1-134
22-151.2	22.1-182 22.1-183
22-152	22.1-140
22-153	22.1-140
22-154	Deleted
22-156	22.1-137
22-157	22.1-135
22-158	22.1-136
22-160	Deleted
22-161	22.1-129
22-162, 22-163	Deleted
22-164	22.1-131
22-164.1	22.1-131
22-164.2	22.1-132
22-165	22.1-133, 22.1-202
22-166, 22-166.1	Deleted
22-166.2	22.1-139
22-166.3	Deleted
22-166.6, 22-166.7	Deleted
22-166.8	22.1-141
22-166.9 to 22-166.11	Deleted
22-166.12	22.1-141
22-166.13	Deleted
22-188.50, 22-188.51	Deleted
22-189 to 22-193	Deleted
22-195	Deleted
22-197	22.1-6
22-198	22.1-6
22-199	22.1-6
22-200	22.1-276
22-201	Deleted
22-203	22.1-295
22-204	22.1-298 22.1-299
22-205	22.1-297

Former Section	Present Section
22-205.1	22.1-291
22-205.2	22.1-291
22-208.1	Deleted
22-209	22.1-259
22-210	Deleted
22-212	22.1-124
22-214	Deleted
22-215	22.1-292
22-216, 22-217	Deleted
22-217.1	Deleted
22-217.2	22.1-302
22-217.3	22.1-294
	22.1-303
22-217.4	22.1-304
22-217.4:1	22.1-305
22-217.5	22.1-307
22-217.5:1	22.1-306
22-217.5:2	22.1-308
22-217.6	22.1-309
22-217.6:1	22.1-310
22-217.7	22.1-311
22-217.7:1	22.1-312
22-217.8	22.1-313
22-217.8:01	22.1-314
22-217.8:1	22.1-315
22-217.9	22.1-293
22-218	22.1-3
22-218.1:1	22.1-199
22-218.3	22.1-5
22-218.4	22.1-4
22-219	22.1-5
22-220	22.1-5
	22.1-255
22-220.1	22.1-270
22-222	22.1-210
22-223	22.1-281
22-224	22.1-282
22-225	22.1-283
22-226	22.1-284
22-227	22.1-285
22-228	22.1-281
	22.1-284
22-229	22.1-286
22-230.1	22.1-277
	22.1-278
22-230.2	22.1-277
	22.1-278
22-230.3	22.1-279
22-231.1	22.1-280
22-232	Deleted
22-233	22.1-200
22-234	22.1-201
22-234.1	22.1-203
22-235	22.1-204
22-235.1	22.1-205
22-236.1	22.1-206
22-237	22.1-207
22-238	22.1-208
22-239 to	
22-240.1	Deleted
22-241	22.1-274

Former Section	Present Section
22-242	Deleted
22-243	22.1-207
22-244 to	
22-246	Deleted
22-248	22.1-273
22-249	22.1-272,
	22.1-300, 22.1-301
22-250	22.1-271
22-275.1	22.1-254
22-275.2	Deleted
22-275.3	22.1-256
22-275.4	22.1-257
22-275.4:1	22.1-257
22-275.4:2	Deleted
22-275.6	Deleted
22-275.7	22.1-263
22-275.8	22.1-260
22-275.9	22.1-260
22-275.10	22.1-261
22-275.11	22.1-262
22-275.11:1	22.1-266
22-275.12 to	
22-275.14	Deleted
22-275.15	22.1-259
22-275.16	22.1-258
22-275.17	Deleted
22-275.18	22.1-264
22-275.19	22.1-265
22-275.20	22.1-267
22-275.21	22.1-268
22-275.22	Deleted
22-275.23	22.1-269
22-275.26	22.1-287
22-275.27	22.1-288
22-275.28	22.1-289
22-276	22.1-177
22-276.1	22.1-178,
	22.1-179
22-276.2	22.1-180
22-276.3	22.1-181
22-277	22.1-187
22-279	Deleted
22-280.1	22.1-183
22-280.2	22.1-184
22-282	22.1-185
22-283	Deleted
22-283.1	22.1-186
22-284	22.1-189
22-285	22.1-190
22-287	22.1-191
22-288	22.1-192
22-289	22.1-193
22-290	22.1-194
22-291	22.1-195
22-292	22.1-196
22-293	22.1-197
22-294	22.1-198
22-295	22.1-246
22-296	22.1-238
22-297	22.1-239
22-298	22.1-240

Former Section	Present Section
22-299 to	
22-302	22.1-245
22-303	22.1-241
22-304	22.1-242
22-305	22.1-243
22-306	22.1-244
22-306.1	Deleted
22-307.1	22.1-252
22-308	Deleted
22-309	22.1-247
22-310	22.1-248
22-311	22.1-249
22-312	Deleted
22-313	Deleted
22-314	22.1-253
22-315	22.1-250
22-316 to	
22-318	Deleted
22-318.1	22.1-238
22-319	22.1-227
22-320 to	
22-324	Deleted
22-330	Deleted
22-330.1	2.1-574
	2.1-575
22-330.1:1	2.1-576
22-330.2	2.1-577
22-330.3	Deleted
22-330.4:1	2.1-574
	2.1-578
22-330.4:2	2.1-574
	2.1-579
22-330.4:3	2.1-580
22-330.5	2.1-581
22-330.6:1	2.1-582
22-330.6:2	2.1-583
22-330.7,	
22-330.8	Deleted
22-330.9	2.1-584
22-330.10	2.1-585
22-330.11	2.1-586
22-330.17	22.1-319
22-330.18	22.1-320
22-330.19	22.1-321
22-330.20	22.1-321
	22.1-322
22-330.21	22.1-323
22-330.22	22.1-324
22-330.23	22.1-325
22-330.24	22.1-326
22-330.25	22.1-327
22-330.26	22.1-328
22-330.27	22.1-329
22-330.28	22.1-330
22-330.29,	
22-330.30	Deleted
22-330.31	22.1-331
22-330.32	22.1-332
22-330.33	22.1-333
22-330.34	22.1-334
22-330.35	22.1-335

Former Section	Present Section
22-330.36	22.1-229
22-330.37	22.1-228
	22.1-229
22-330.38	22.1-229
22-330.39	22.1-230
22-330.40	22.1-231
22-330.41	22.1-232
22-330.42	22.1-232
22-330.43	22.1-233
22-330.44	22.1-234
22-330.45	22.1-235
22-330.46	22.1-236
22-330.47	22.1-237
22-344.4 to 22-344.15	Deleted
22-345	22.1-336
22-346	22.1-337
22-347	22.1-338
22-348	22.1-316
22-349	22.1-317
22-350	22.1-318
22-351 to 22-359	Deleted
22-360	22.1-223
22-361	22.1-224
22-362	22.1-225
22-363	22.1-226

COMPARABLE SECTIONS OF TITLE 24 AND TITLE 24.1

Former Section	Present Section
24-1	24.1-2
24-2	24.1-3
24-3	24.1-4
24-4	24.1-5
24-5	24.1-6
24-6	24.1-7
24-7	24.1-8
24-8	24.1-9
24-9	24.1-9
24-10	24.1-10
24-11	24.1-11
24-12	24.1-12
24-13	24.1-13
24-13.1	Deleted
24-14	24.1-14
24-15	24.1-15
24-16	24.1-16
24-17	24.1-41
24-17.1, 24-17.2	Deleted
24-18	24.1-42
24-18.1	Deleted
24-18.2	24.1-42
24-19 to 24-21	Deleted
24-22	24.1-41
24-23	24.1-41
24-23.1	24.1-127
24-23.2 to 24-23.4	24.1-128
24-24	24.1-18
24-25	24.1-19
24-26	24.1-20
24-27	24.1-21
24-28	24.1-22
24-28.1	Deleted
24-29	24.1-29
24-30	24.1-32
24-31	24.1-33
24-32	24.1-29
24-33	24.1-29
24-34	24.1-30
24-35	24.1-34
24-36	24.1-34
24-37	24.1-31
24-38	24.1-31
24-39	Deleted
24-40	24.1-31
24-41	24.1-31
24-42	24.1-29
24-43	24.1-30
24-44	24.1-1
24-45	24.1-36
24-45.1	Deleted
24-46	24.1-37
24-47	24.1-38
24-48	24.1-38
24-49 to 24-51	24.1-39
24-52	24.1-43
24-52.1	24.1-43
24-53	24.1-44
24-54	Deleted
24-55	24.1-43
24-55.1	Deleted
24-56, 24-57	Deleted
24-58	24.1-45
24-59 to 24-60.1	24.1-46
24-61	24.1-43
24-62 to 24-64.1	Deleted
24-65	24.1-43
24-66	24.1-43
24-67	24.1-47
24-67.1	Deleted
24-68	24.1-48
24-69, 24-70	Deleted
24-71 to 24-73	24.1-46
24-74 to 24-76	24.1-49
24-77	Deleted
24-78	24.1-46
24-79, 24-80	Deleted
24-81	24.1-51
24-82	24.1-50
24-82.1	Deleted
24-83	Deleted
24-83.1	24.1-50
24-84	Reserved
24-85	24.1-52
24-86	24.1-53
24-87	24.1-53
24-87.1	Deleted
24-88, 24-89	Deleted
24-90	24.1-46
24-91	24.1-58
24-92	Deleted
24-93	24.1-46
24-94	24.1-46
24-95	24.1-55
24-96	24.1-59
24-97	24.1-60
24-98	24.1-61
24-99	24.1-62
24-100	Deleted
24-101	24.1-46
24-102	24.1-63
24-103	24.1-64
24-104	24.1-65
24-105	24.1-66
24-106	Deleted
24-107	24.1-60
24-108	24.1-61
24-109	24.1-62
24-110	Deleted
24-111	24.1-46
24-112	24.1-67
24-113	24.1-56
24-114	24.1-57
24-115	24.1-68
24-116	24.1-265
24-117	24.1-69
24-118	24.1-54
24-118.1	24.1-43
24-118.2 to 24-118.4	Deleted
24-118.5 to 24-118.7	Repealed
24-118.8 to 24-129.1	Deleted
24-130	24.1-166
24-131	24.1-166
24-132	24.1-167
24-133	24.1-168
24-134	24.1-169
24-134.1	24.1-166
24-135	24.1-166
24-136	24.1-1
24-137	24.1-1
24-138	24.1-163
24-139	24.1-163

Former Section	Present Section
24-140	24.1-164
24-141	24.1-165
24-142	24.1-73
24-143	24.1-74
24-144	24.1-75
24-145	24.1-76
24-146	24.1-77
24-147	24.1-78
24-147.1	24.1-79
24-148	24.1-80
24-149	24.1-81
24-150	24.1-82
24-151	24.1-83
24-152	24.1-84
24-153	24.1-85
24-154	24.1-86
24-155	24.1-87
24-156	Deleted
24-157	24.1-88
24-158	24.1-89
24-159	Deleted
24-160	24.1-90
24-161	24.1-86
24-162	24.1-87
24-163 to 24-166	Deleted
24-167	24.1-86
24-168	24.1-90
24-169	24.1-73
24-170	24.1-91
24-171	24.1-92
24-172	24.1-93
24-173, 24-174	Deleted
24-175	24.1-96
24-176	24.1-95
24-177	24.1-96
24-178	Deleted
24-179 to 24-181	24.1-97
24-182	24.1-98
24-183	Repealed
24-184	24.1-99
24-185	24.1-100
24-186	24.1-101
24-187	24.1-102
24-188	24.1-101
24-189	24.1-103
24-190	24.1-104
24-191	24.1-264
24-192	24.1-104
24-193	24.1-105
24-194	Deleted
24-194.1	Repealed
24-194.2 to 24-194.4	Deleted
24-195	24.1-106
24-196	Deleted
24-197	24.1-108
24-198	24.1-33
24-199	24.1-32
24-200 to 24-206	Deleted
24-207 to 24-209	24.1-107
24-210, 24-211	Deleted
24-212	24.1-266
24-213	24.1-109
24-214	24.1-109
24-215	24.1-111
24-216	24.1-112
24-217	24.1-113
24-218	24.1-114
24-219	24.1-115
24-220	Deleted
24-220.1	24.1-115
24-221	24.1-115
24-222	Deleted
24-223	24.1-116
24-224	24.1-116
24-225	24.1-117
24-226	24.1-119
24-227	24.1-119
24-228	24.1-118
24-229	24.1-117
24-230	24.1-120
24-231	24.1-121
24-232	24.1-143
24-233	Deleted
24-234	24.1-110
24-235	24.1-110
24-236	24.1-269
24-237	24.1-267
24-238	24.1-130
24-239	24.1-270
24-240	24.1-122
24-241	24.1-123
23-242	24.1-124
24-243	24.1-124
24-244	24.1-125
24-245	24.1-129
24-246	24.1-142
24-247	24.1-131
24-248	24.1-126
24-249, 24-250	Deleted
24-251	24.1-132
24-252	24.1-129
24-253	24.1-133
24-254	24.1-133
24-255	24.1-35
24-256	24.1-134
24-257	24.1-135
24-258	24.1-136
24-259	24.1-136
24-260	24.1-137
24-261	24.1-137
24-262	24.1-138
24-263	24.1-139
24-264	24.1-141
24-265	24.1-142
24-266	24.1-140
24-267	24.1-143
24-268	24.1-144
24-269	24.1-145
24-270	24.1-144
24-271	24.1-146
24-272	24.1-146
24-273, 24-274	Deleted
24-275	24.1-147
24-276	24.1-148
24-277	24.1-149
24-277.1	24.1-247
24-277.2	24.1-247
24-277.3	24.1-248
24-277.4	24.1-247
24-278 to 24-280	24.1-150
24-281	Deleted
24-282	24.1-151
24-283	24.1-152
24-284	24.1-153
24-285	24.1-154
24-286	24.1-154
24-287	24.1-155
24-288	Deleted
24-289	24.1-155
24-290	24.1-149
24-290.1	24.1-158
24-290.2	Deleted
24-290.3	24.1-159
24-290.4	24.1-160
24-290.5	24.1-161
24-290.6	24.1-162
24-291	24.1-203
24-292	Deleted
24-293	24.1-204
24-294	24.1-205
24-295	24.1-206
24-296	24.1-209
24-297	24.1-207
24-298	24.1-208
24-299	24.1-209
24-300	24.1-210
24-301	24.1-211
24-302	24.1-212
24-303	24.1-213
24-304	24.1-214
24-305	24.1-215
24-306	24.1-216
24-307	24.1-217
24-308	24.1-218
24-309	24.1-219
24-310	24.1-220
24-311	24.1-221
24-312	24.1-222
24-313	24.1-223
24-314	24.1-224
24-315	24.1-225
24-316, 24-317	Deleted
24-318	24.1-275
24-318.1 to 24-318.8	Deleted
24-319	24.1-227
24-320 to 24-324	24.1-228

Former Section	Present Section
24-325	24.1-133
24-326	Deleted
24-327	24.1-229
24-328	24.1-230
24-329	Deleted
24-330	24.1-231
24-331	Deleted
24-332	24.1-229
24-333	24.1-229
24-334	24.1-232
24-334.1	Deleted
24-335	Deleted
24-336	24.1-233
24-337	24.1-232
24-338	24.1-234
24-338.1	24.1-231
24-339	24.1-231
24-340	24.1-234
24-340.1	24.1-233
24-341	24.1-234
24-342	24.1-234
24-343, 24-344	Deleted
24-345	24.1-274
24-345.1	Deleted
24-345.2	24.1-228
24-345.3	24.1-169
24-345.4	Deleted
24-345.5	24.1-228
24-345.6	24.1-229
24-345.7	24.1-229
24-345.8	24.1-231
24-345.9	Deleted
24-345.10	24.1-18
24-345.11	24.1-19
24-345.12 to	
24-345.15	Deleted
24-346	24.1-1
24-347	24.1-170
24-348	24.1-171
24-349	24.1-174
24-350	24.1-175
24-350.1	Deleted
24-351	24.1-176
24-352	24.1-177
24-353 to	
24-355	Deleted
24-356	24.1-178
24-357, 24-358	Deleted
24-359	24.1-170
24-360	Deleted
24-361	24.1-171
24-362	24.1-194
24-363	24.1-172
24-364	24.1-172
24-364.1	24.1-180
24-365	24.1-197
24-366	24.1-173
24-367	24.1-182
34-368	Deleted
24-369	24.1-183
24-370 to	
24-372	24.1-184
24-373	24.1-185
24-374	24.1-186
24-375	24.1-187
24-376	24.1-188
24-377	24.1-189
24-378	Deleted
24-379	24.1-190
24-380 to	
24-387	Deleted
24-388	24.1-191
24-389	24.1-192
24-390	24.1-193
24-391	24.1-195
24-392	24.1-196
24-393	24.1-238
24-394	24.1-239
24-395	Deleted
24-395.1	24.1-246
24-395.2	Deleted
24-395.3	24.1-244
24-396	Deleted
24-397	24.1-181
24-398 to	
24-400	24.1-198
24-401	24.1-199
24-402, 24-403	Deleted
24-404	24.1-273
24-405	24.1-272
24-406	24.1-276
24-407	Deleted
24-408	24.1-200
24-409 to	
24-418	Deleted
24-419 to	
24-426	24.1-236
24-427 to	
24-429	24.1-237
24-430	24.1-240
24-431	Deleted
24-432	24.1-240
24-433	Deleted
24-434	24.1-241
24-435	24.1-242
24-436	24.1-243
24-437	24.1-244
24-438	24.1-245
24-439 to	
24-448	Deleted
24-449	24.1-281
24-450	24.1-268
24-451	24.1-268
24-452	24.1-272
24-453, 24-454	Deleted
24-455	24.1-280
24-456	24.1-277
None	24.1-23 to 24.1-28
None	24.1-251 to 24.1-261
None	24.1-271
None	24.1-278, 24.1-279

COMPARABLE SECTIONS OF TITLE 24.1 AND TITLE 24.2

Former Section	Present Section
24.1-1	24.2-101
	24.2-682
24.1-2	24.2-206
24.1-3	24.2-207
24.1-4 to	
24.1-5	Repealed
24.1-6	24.2-208
24.1-7	24.2-209
24.1-8	24.2-202
24.1-9	24.2-203
	24.2-204
24.1-10	24.2-205
24.1-11	24.2-215
24.1-12 to	
24.1-12.3	Repealed
24.1-13	24.2-214
24.1-14 to	
24.1-15	Repealed
24.1-16	24.2-216
24.1-17	Repealed
24.1-17.1	Repealed
24.1-17.2	24.2-311
24.1-17.3	24.2-312
24.1-17.4 to	
24.2-17.46	24.2-303
24.1-17.47	Repealed
24.1-17.100 to	
24.1-17.202	24.2-304
24.1-17.203	Repealed
24.1-17.300 to	
24.1-17.313	24.2-302
24.1-17.314	Repealed
24.1-18	24.2-102
	24.2-103
24.1-19	24.2-103
24.1-20	Repealed
24.1-21	24.2-104
24.1-22	24.2-105
	24.2-418

Former Section	Present Section
24.1-22.1	Repealed
24.1-23	24.2-404
	24.2-405
	24.2-406
	24.2-407
24.1-24	Repealed
24.1-25	24.2-408
24.1-26	24.2-409
24.1-26.1	24.2-410
24.1-27	Repealed
24.1-28	24.2-445
24.1-29	24.2-106
	24.2-120
24.1-30	24.2-107
24.1-31	24.2-108
24.1-31.1	24.2-121
24.1-32	24.2-109
	24.2-110
	24.2-115
	24.2-120
	24.2-122
24.1-33	24.2-119
24.1-33.1	24.2-106
24.1-33.2	24.2-110
24.1-34	24.2-109
	24.2-110
24.1-35	Repealed
24.1-35.1	Repealed
24.1-36	24.2-307
	24.2-310
24.1-37	24.2-307
	24.2-310
24.1-38	Repealed
24.1-39	24.2-306
24.1-40	24.2-309
24.1-40.1 to 24.1-40.3	Expired
24.1-40.3:1	Repealed
24.1-40.4 to 24.1-40.6	Expired
24.1-40.7	24.2-305
24.1-40.7:1	24.2-301
24.1-40.8	Repealed
24.1-40.9	Repealed
24.1-40.10	24.2-300
24.1-40.11	24.2-301
24.1-41	24.2-101
	24.2-400
	24.2-401
	24.2-402
	24.2-403
24.1-41.1	24.2-402
24.1-41.2	Repealed
24.1-42	24.1-101
24.1-43	24.2-109
	24.2-110
	24.2-111
	24.2-120
	24.2-411
	24.2-413
24.1-44	24.2-110
24.1-45	24.2-112
24.1-45.1	24.2-113
24.1-45.2	24.2-412
24.1-45.3	24.2-112
24.1-46	24.2-114
	24.2-411
	24.2-427
	24.2-429
	24.2-435
24.1-47	24.2-417
24.1-48	24.2-417
	24.2-418
	24.2-419
	24.2-420
	24.2-426
	24.2-1016
24.1-49	24.2-411
	24.2-412
	24.2-414
	24.2-415
24.1-49.01	24.2-1002
	24.2-1003
24.1-49.1	24.2-421
24.1-50	24.2-416
24.1-51	24.2-423
24.1-52	24.2-424
24.1-53	24.2-425
24.1-54	24.2-114
24.1-55	24.2-652
24.1-55.1	24.2-653
24.1-55.2	24.2-653
24.1-56	24.2-444
24.1-57	24.2-610
24.1-58	24.2-446
24.1-59	24.2-428
	24.2-435
24.1-60	24.2-428
	24.2-429
24.1-61	24.2-429
24.1-62	24.2-430
24.1-63	24.2-431
24.1-64	24.2-432
24.1-65	24.2-433
24.1-66	24.2-434
24.1-67	24.2-422
24.1-68	24.2-114
24.1-69	24.2-447
24.1-70 to 24.1-72	Reserved
24.1-72.1	24.2-436
24.1-72.2	24.2-437
24.1-72.3	24.2-438
24.1-72.4	24.2-439
24.1-72.5 to 24.1-72.11	Repealed
24.1-72.12	24.2-440
24.1-72.13	24.2-441
24.1-72.14	24.2-442
24.1-72.15	24.2-443
24.1-73	24.2-200
24.1-74	24.2-224
24.1-75	24.2-201
24.1-76	24.2-225
	24.2-226
	24.2-227
24.1-76.1	24.2-228
24.1-77	24.2-229
24.1-78	Repealed
24.1-79	24.2-226
24.1-79.1	24.2-230
24.1-79.2	24.2-230
24.1-79.3	24.2-231
24.1-79.4	24.2-232
24.1-79.5	24.2-233
24.1-79.6	24.2-234
24.1-79.7	24.2-235
24.1-79.8	24.2-236
24.1-79.9	24.2-237
24.1-79.10	24.2-238
24.1-80	24.2-210
24.1-81	24.2-210
24.1-82	24.2-211
24.1-83	Repealed
24.1-84	24.2-212
24.1-85	24.2-213
24.1-86	24.2-217
24.1-87	24.2-217
24.1-88	24.2-218
	24.2-219
	24.2-220
	24.2-221
24.1-89	Repealed
24.1-90	24.2-222
24.1-90.1	Repealed
24.1-90.2	Repealed
24.1-91	24.2-601
	24.2-675
24.1-92	24.2-308
	24.2-310
24.1-93	24.2-101
	24.2-600
	24.2-601
24.1-94	Reserved
24.1-95	24.2-100
24.1-96	24.2-600
24.1-96.1	24.2-605
24.1-97	24.2-310
24.1-98	24.2-603
24.1-99	24.2-603
24.1-100	24.2-609
24.1-100.1	24.2-610
24.1-101	24.2-604
24.1-102	24.2-608
24.1-103	24.2-606
24.1-104	24.2-607
24.1-105	24.2-115
24.1-105.1	24.2-117
24.1-106	24.2-115
24.1-107	24.2-116
	24.2-610
24.1-108	24.2-118
24.1-109	24.2-612

Former Section	Present Section
24.1-110	24.2-539
	24.2-540
	24.2-541
24.1-111	24.2-613
	24.2-614
24.1-112	24.2-615
24.1-113	24.2-613
24.1-113.1	24.2-602
24.1-114	24.2-616
24.1-115	24.2-617
24.1-116	24.2-618
24.1-117	24.2-619
24.1-118	24.2-619
24.1-119	24.2-620
24.1-120	24.2-621
24.1-121	24.2-621
24.1-122	24.2-622
24.1-123	24.2-623
24.1-124	24.2-624
24.1-125	24.2-643
24.1-126	24.2-643
24.1-126.1	24.2-643
24.1-127	Repealed
24.1-128	Repealed
24.1-129	24.2-643
	24.2-644
	24.2-649
24.1-130	24.2-645
24.1-131	24.2-646
24.1-132	24.2-649
24.1-132.1	24.2-650
24.1-133	24.2-651
24.1-134	24.2-610
24.1-135	24.2-611
	24.2-656
24.1-136	24.2-654
24.1-137	24.2-655
24.1-138	24.2-661
24.1-139	24.2-662
24.1-140	24.2-663
24.1-141	24.2-664
24.1-142	24.2-665
	24.2-667
24.1-143	24.2-668
24.1-143.1	24.2-666
24.1-144	24.2-668
	24.2-669
24.1-145	24.2-670
24.1-146	24.2-671
24.1-147	24.2-672
24.1-148	24.2-673
24.1-149	24.2-674
24.1-150	24.2-675
24.1-151	24.2-676
24.1-152	24.2-677
24.1-153	24.2-678
24.1-154	24.2-679
24.1-155	24.2-679
	24.2-680
24.1-156	Reserved
24.1-157	Reserved
24.1-158	24.2-542
24.1-159	24.2-543
24.1-160	24.2-614
24.1-161	24.2-644
24.1-162	24.2-203
24.1-162.1	Repealed
24.1-163	24.2-682
	24.2-683
24.1-164	24.2-681
24.1-165	24.2-682
	24.2-684
24.1-165.1	24.2-685
24.1-165.2	15.1-760.1
24.1-166	24.2-505
	24.2-507
	24.2-510
24.1-166.1	Repealed
24.1-167	24.2-500
	24.2-501
	24.2-502
	24.2-503
	24.2-504
24.1-168	24.2-506
24.1-169	24.2-511
24.1-170	24.2-512
24.1-171	24.2-509
	24.2-514
24.1-172	24.2-508
	24.2-509
	24.2-510
24.1-173	24.2-528
24.1-174	24.2-515
	24.2-518
24.1-175	24.2-526
24.1-176	24.2-516
24.1-177	24.2-517
24.1-178	24.2-513
24.1-179	24.2-535
24.1-180	24.2-518
24.1-181	Repealed
24.1-182	24.2-530
24.1-183	24.2-519
	24.2-525
24.1-184	24.2-520
	24.2-522
	24.2-525
24.1-185	24.2-521
24.1-186	24.2-522
24.1-186.1	24.2-522
24.1-187	24.2-527
24.1-188	24.2-529
24.1-189	24.2-531
24.1-190	24.2-533
24.1-191	24.2-532
24.1-192	24.2-534
24.1-193	24.2-532
24.1-194	24.2-536
24.1-195	24.2-537
24.1-196	24.2-538
24.1-197	24.2-539
24.1-198	24.2-523
24.1-199	24.2-524
24.1-200	Repealed
24.1-201	Reserved
24.1-202	Reserved
24.1-202.1 to 24.1-202.10	Repealed
24.1-203	24.2-626
24.1-203.1	24.2-627
24.1-203.2	24.2-627
24.1-204	24.2-628
24.1-205	24.2-628
24.1-206	24.2-630
24.1-206.1	24.2-631
24.1-206.2	Repealed
24.1-206.3	24.2-629
24.1-207	24.2-640
24.1-207.1	24.2-629
24.1-208	24.2-641
24.1-209	24.2-632
	24.2-637
24.1-210	24.2-633
24.1-211	24.2-634
24.1-212	24.2-609
24.1-213	24.2-636
24.1-214	24.2-635
24.1-215	24.2-638
24.1-216	24.2-610
	24.2-639
24.1-217	24.2-644
	24.2-648
24.1-218	24.2-643
24.1-219	24.2-647
24.1-220	24.2-649
24.1-221	24.2-642
24.1-222	24.2-654
	24.2-657
	24.2-667
24.1-222.1	24.2-658
24.1-222.2	24.2-660
24.1-223	24.2-661 et seq.
24.1-224	24.2-659
24.1-225	24.2-625
24.1-226	Reserved
24.1-227	24.2-700
24.1-228	Repealed
24.1-228.1	24.2-701
24.1-228.1:1	24.2-703
24.1-228.1:2	24.2-702
24.1-228.2	24.2-704
24.1-229	24.2-706
	24.2-710
24.1-229.1	24.2-705
24.1-230	24.2-709
24.1-231	24.2-710
	24.2-711
24.1-232	24.2-707
24.1-233	24.2-708
24.1-233.1	24.2-710
	24.2-711
	24.2-712
24.1-234	24.2-710

Former Section	Present Section
	24.2-711
24.1-235	Reserved
24.1-236	Repealed
24.1-236.1	24.2-803
24.1-237	24.2-804
24.1-238	24.2-805
24.1-239	24.2-806
24.1-240	24.2-807
24.1-241	24.2-808
24.1-241.1	24.2-814
24.1-242	24.2-809
24.1-243	24.2-810
24.1-244	24.2-811
24.1-245	24.2-812
24.1-246	24.2-813
24.1-246.1 to 24.1-248	Repealed
24.1-249	24.2-800
	24.2-801
24.1-250	24.2-802
24.1-251	24.2-900
24.1-252	24.2-903
24.1-253	24.2-904
24.1-254	24.2-904
	24.2-905
24.1-254.1	24.2-901
	24.2-908
24.1-254.2	24.2-901
	24.2-909
24.1-254.3	24.2-901
	24.2-913
	24.2-924
	24.2-925
24.1-255	24.2-901
	24.2-902
	24.2-907
	24.2-910
	24.2-911
24.1-256	24.2-906
24.1-257	Repealed
24.1-257.1	24.2-923
	24.2-927
24.1-257.2	24.2-915
	24.2-916
	24.2-917
	24.2-918
	24.2-919
	24.2-920
	24.2-927
24.1-257.3	24.2-912
24.1-258	24.2-914
24.1-258.1	24.2-921
24.1-259	Repealed
24.1-260	24.2-922
24.1-261	24.2-926
24.1-262	24.2-929
24.1-263	24.2-928
24.1-263.1	24.2-930
24.1-264	24.2-1000
24.1-265	24.2-1002
24.1-266	24.2-1001
24.1-267	24.2-1006
24.1-268	24.2-1004
24.1-269	24.2-1011
24.1-270	24.2-1008
24.1-271	24.2-1005
24.1-272	24.2-1007
24.1-273	24.2-1009
24.1-274	24.2-1012
24.1-275	24.2-1009
	24.2-1010
24.1-276	24.2-1013
24.1-277	24.2-1014
24.1-278	24.2-1015
24.1-279	24.2-1016
24.1-280	24.2-1017
24.1-281	24.2-1018
24.1-282	24.2-1019

COMPARABLE SECTIONS OF TITLE 25 AND TITLE 25.1

Former Section	Present Section
25-46.1	Repealed
25-46.2	25.1-200
25-46.2:1	Repealed
25-46.2:2	25.1-106
25-46.3	25.1-100
25-46.3:1	Repealed
25-46.4	25.1-201
25-46.4:1	25.1-202
25-46.5	25.1-204
25-46.6	25.1-103, 25.1-104, 25.1-105
25-46.7	25.1-205, 25.1-206, 25.1-207, 25.1-208
25-46.8	25.1-223, 25.1-224, 25.1-225
25-46.9	25.1-205, 25.1-209, 25.1-213, 25.1-214
25-46.10	25.1-210
25-46.11	25.1-211
25-46.12	25.1-212
25-46.13	25.1-215
25-46.14	25.1-216
25-46.15	25.1-217
25-46.16	25.1-218
25-46.17	25.1-219
25-46.17:1	25.1-221
25-46.18	25.1-222
25-46.19	25.1-220
25-46.20	25.1-226, 25.1-227, 25.1-228, 25.1-229, 25.1-230
25-46.21	25.1-231, 25.1-232, 25.1-233
25-46.21:1	25.1-234
25.1-46.22	25.1-235
25-46.23	25.1-236
25-46.24	25.1-237
25-46.25	25.1-238
25-46.26	25.1-239
25-46.27	25.1-247
25-46.28	25.1-240
25-46.29	25.1-242
25-46.30	25.1-243
25-46.31	25.1-244
25-46.32	25.1-245
25-46.33	25.1-246
25-46.34	25.1-248, 25.1-249, 25.1-250, 25.1-251
25-46.36	Repealed
25-47	15.2-1908
25-48	15.2-1909
25-49	15.2-1910
25-50	15.2-1911
25-51	15.2-1912
25-52	15.2-1913
25-53	15.2-1914
25-54	15.2-1915
25-55	15.2-1916
25-232.01	25.1-101, 15.2-1901.1, 15.2-1907
25-232.1	25.1-203
25-232.2	Repealed
25-233	25.1-102
25-234	Repealed
25-235	Repealed
25-235.1	25.1-404, 25.1-417, 25.1-421
25-236	25.1-401, 25.1-416
25-237	Repealed
25-238	25.1-400
25-239	25.1-406, 25.1-407, 25.1-408
25-240	25.1-409
25-241	25.1-410
25-242	25.1-411
25-243	25.1-412
25-244	25.1-405
25-245	25.1-413
25-246	25.1-403
25-247	25.1-414
25-247.1	25.1-415
25-248	25.1-417
25-249	25.1-418

Former Section	Present Section
25-250	25.1-419
25-251	25.1-420
25-252	25.1-421
25-253	25.1-402
25-254	Repealed

COMPARABLE SECTIONS OF TITLE 28 AND TITLE 28.1

Former Section	Present Section
28-1	28.1-1
28-2	28.1-2
28-3	28.1-3
28-4 to 28-6	Repealed
28-7	28.1-18
28-8, 28-9	Repealed
28-10	28.1-21
28-10.1	28.1-21
28-11	28.1-4
28-12	28.1-5
28-13	28.1-6
28-14	28.1-7
28-15	28.1-8
28-16	28.1-9
28-17	28.1-10
28-18	28.1-11
28-19	28.1-12
28-20	28.1-13
28-21	28.1-14
28-21.1	28.1-94.1
28-22	28.1-15
28-23	28.1-16
28-24	28.1-17
28-25 to 28-28	Repealed
28-29	28.1-22
28-30	28.1-19
28-31	28.1-19
28-32	Repealed
28-33	28.1-37
28-33.1	28.1-38
28-34	28.1-39
28-35	28.1-40
28-36	28.1-42
28-37	Repealed
28-38	28.1-43
28-39	28.1-44
28-40	28.1-45
28-41	28.1-46
28-42	28.1-47
28-43	28.1-48
28-44	Repealed
28-45	28.1-49
28-45.01	28.1-50
28-46	28.1-51
28-46.1	28.1-52
28-47	28.1-53
28-48	Repealed
24-49	28.1-54
28-50 to 28-52.1	Repealed
28-53	28.1-55
28-54	28.1-56
28-55	Repealed
28-56	28.1-193
28-57 to 28.58	Repealed
28-59	28.1-57
28-60	28.1-58
28-61	28.1-59
28-62	28.1-60
28-63	28.1-61
28-64	28.1-62, 28.1-63, 28.1-65
28-65	28.1-62
28-66	28.1-64
28-67	28.1-65
28-68	28.1-67
28-69	28.1-68
28-70	28.1-69
28-71	28.1-70
28-72	28.1-71
28-73	Repealed
28-74	28.1-72.1
28-75	28.1-72
28-76	28.1-73
28-77	28.1-74
28-77.1	28.1-75
28-78	28.1-76
28-79	28.1-77
28-80	28.1-78
28-81 to 28-88.3	Repealed
28-88.4	28.1-80
28-88.5	Repealed
28-89	28-1-81
28-90 to 28-91.1	Repealed
28-92	28.1-82
28-93	28.1-83
28-93.1	28.1-83
28-93.2	28.1-83
28-94 to 28-98	Repealed
28-98.1	28.1-85
28-98.2	Repealed
28-99	28.1-86
28-100	28.1-87
28-101	28.1-88
28-102	Repealed
28-103	28.1-90
28-104	Repealed
28-105	28.1-90
28-106 to 28-108	Repealed
28-109	28.1-95
28-110	28.1-96
28-111	28.1-97
28-112	28.1-98
28-112.1	28.1-99
28-113	28.1-104
28-114	28.1-105
28-115, 28-116	Repealed
28-117	28.1-100
28-118	28.1-101, 28.1-101.1
28-119	28.1-102
28-120	28.1-103
28-121	28.1-106
28-122	28.1-107
28-122.1	28.1-115
28-123	28.1-108
28-124	28.1-109
28-125	28.1-111
28-126	28.1-112
28-127	28.1-113
28-128	28.1-114
28-129 to 28-131	Repealed
28-132	28.1-116
28-133	28.1-117
28-134	28.1-118
28-135	Repealed
28-136	28.1-119
28-137	28.1-120
28-137.1	28.1-93
28-138	28.1-121
28-139	28.1-122
28-140	28.1-123
28-141	28.1-124
28-142	28.1-125
28-143	28.1-126
28-144, 28-145	Repealed
28-146	28.1-127
28-147 to 28-149	Repealed
28-150	28.1-129
28-151	28.1-130
28-152	Repealed
28-153	28.1-135
28-154	28.1-132
28-155	28.1-131
28-156	28.1-132
28-157	28.1-133
28-158	28.1-134
28-159	28.1-175
28-160	28.1-176

Former Section	Present Section
28-161	28.1-177
28-162	28.1-178
28-162.1	28.1-179
28-163, 28-164	Repealed
28-165	28.1-181
28-166	28.1-183
28-167	Repealed
28-168	28.1-180
28-169	Repealed
28-170	28.1-165
28-171	28.1-166
28-172	28.1-167
28-172.1	28.1-168
28-173	28.1-169
28-174	28.1-170
28-175	28.1-171
28-176	Repealed
28-177	28.1-174
28-178	28.1-160
28-179	28.1-161
28-180	28.1-162
28-181	28.1-163
28-182 to 28-186	Repealed
28-187	28.1-118.1
28-188	28.1-136
28-189, 28-190	Repealed
28-190.1	28.1-142
28-191	28.1-137
28-193, 28-194	Repealed
28-195	28.1-139, 28.1-172
28-196, 28-196.1	Repealed
28-196.2	28.1-141
28-197	Repealed
28-198	28.1-143
28-198.1	28.1-173
28-199, 28-200	Repealed
28-201	28.1-144
28-201.1	28.1-145
28-201.2	28.1-146
28-201.3	28.1-147
28-201.4	28.1-148
28-202	Repealed
28-203	28.1-149
28-204	28.1-150
28-204.1	28.1-151
28-204.1:1	28.1-152
28-204.1:2	28.1-153
28-204.2	28.1-154
28-204.3	28.1-155
28-204.4	28.1-156
28-204.5	28.1-157
28-204.6	28.1-158
28-205	28.1-159
28-206	28.1-185
28-207	28.1-184
28-208	28.1-185
28-209	28.1-186
28-210, 28-211	Repealed
28-212	28.1-188
28-213	28.1-189
28-214	28.1-190
28-215	28.1-191
28-216	28.1-192
28-217	28.1-194
28-218	28.1-193
28-218.1	28.1-203
28-218.2	28.1-203.1
28-218.3	28.1-203.1
28-219	28.1-204
28-220	28.1-205
28-221	28.1-206
28-222	28.1-207
28-223	28.1-208
28-224	28.1-209
28-225	28.1-210
28-226	28.1-211
28-227	28.1-212
28-228	28.1-213
28-229	28.1-214
28-230	28.1-215
28-231	28.1-216
28-232	28.1-217
28-233	28.1-218
28-234	28.1-219
28-235	28.1-220
28-236	28.1-221
28-237	28.1-222
28-238	28.1-223
28-239	28.1-224
28-240	28.1-225
28-241	28.1-226
28-242 to 28-247	Repealed
28-248	28.1-195
28-249	28.1-197
28-250	28.1-195
28-250.1	28.1-195
28-251	28.1-198
28-252	28.1-198
28-253	28.1-199
28-254	28.1-202
28-255	28.1-202
28-256 to 28-258	Repealed

COMPARABLE SECTIONS OF TITLE 28.1 AND TITLE 28.2

Former Section	Present Section
28.1-1	28.2-100
	28.2-200
28.1-2	Deleted
28.1-2.1	Deleted
28.1-3	28.2-101
28.1-3.1	28.2-205
28.1-4	28.2-102
	28.2-104
28.1-5	28.2-102
28.1-6	Deleted
28.1-7	Deleted
28.1-8	Deleted
28.1-9	28.2-103
	28.2-104
	28.2-202
28.1-10	28.2-102
28.1-11	28.2-104
28.1-12	28.2-104
28.1-12.1	28.2-105
28.1-13	28.2-104
28.1-14	Deleted
28.1-15	Deleted
28.1-16	28.2-202
28.1-17 to 28.1-20	Repealed
28.1-21	28.2-229
28.1-22	Deleted
28.1-22.1	28.2-206
28.1-22.2	28.2-207
28.1-23	28.2-104
	28.2-201
28.1-23.1	28.2-203
28.1-23.2	28.2-204
28.1-24	28.2-209
28.1-25	28.2-210
28.1-26	28.2-211
	28.2-212
28.1-27	28.2-213
28.1-28	28.2-214
28.1-29	28.2-215
28.1-30	28.2-216
28.1-31	28.2-217
28.1-32	28.2-218
28.1-33	28.2-219
28.1-34	28.2-220
28.1-35	28.2-221
28.1-36	28.2-232
28.1-36.01	28.2-822

Former Section	Present Section
28.1-36.1 to 28.1-36.5	Repealed
28.1-36.6 to 28.1-36.12	Repealed
28.1-37	28.2-222
28.1-38	Repealed
28.1-39	28.2-223
28.1-40	Deleted
28.1-41	28.2-106
28.1-42	28.2-106
28.1-43	28.2-224
28.1-44	28.2-600
	28.2-608
	28.2-633
28.1-45	Deleted
28.1-45.1	28.2-106
28.1-45.2	28.2-106
28.1-46	Repealed
28.1-46.1	28.2-107
28.1-46.2	Deleted
28.1-46.3	Deleted
28.1-46.4	28.2-108
28.1-47	28.2-225
	28.2-229
	28.2-300
28.1-47.1	28.2-227
	28.2-229
28.1-47.2	28.2-208
28.1-48	28.2-201
	28.2-225
	28.2-234
	28.2-301
	28.2-310
28.1-49	Repealed
28.1-49.1	28.2-303
28.1-50	28.2-304
28.1-51	28.2-200
	28.2-305
28.1-51.1	28.2-306
28.1-51.2	Repealed
28.1-52	28.2-307
	28.2-308
28.1-52.1	Expired
28.1-52.2	28.2-302
28.1-53	28.2-309
28.1-54	28.2-238
	28.2-405
28.1-55	28.2-313
28.1-56	28.2-313
28.1-57	Repealed
28.1-57.1	Repealed
28.1-58	28.2-408
28.1-59	28.2-225
	28.2-229
	28.2-402
	28.2-409
28.1-60	28.2-401
28.1-61	28.2-400
28.1-62	28.2-403
28.1-63	28.2-404
28.1 64	28.2-225
	28.2-230
	28.2-407
28.1-65	28.2-410
28.1-65.1	28.2-411
28.1-66	Deleted
28.1-67	28.2-314
28.1-68	28.2-316
28.1-69	Repealed
28.1-69.1	28.2-315
28.1-70	28.2-229
	28.2-315
28.1-71	28.2-317
28.1-72	28.2-318
28.1-72.1	28.2-319
28.1-73	28.2-233
28.1-74	28.2-233
	28.2-234
	28.2-236
28.1-75	Repealed
28.1-76	28.2-234
28.1-77	28.2-235
28.1-78	28.2-226
	28.2-239
28.1-79	28.2-237
28.1-80	28.2-311
28.1-81	28.2-312
28.1-81.1	Repealed
28.1-82	28.2-506
28.1-83	28.2-508
28.1-84	28.2-509
28.1-85	28.2-507
28.1-85.1	Repealed
28.1-86	Repealed
28.1-87	28.2-538
	28.2-539
	28.2-540
28.1-88	28.2-547
28.1-89	28.2-546
28.1-90	28.2-548
28.1-91	Repealed
28.1-92	28.2-543
	28.2-544
28.1-93	28.2-541
	28.2-543
	28.2-544
28.1-94	28.2-542
	28.2-544
28.1-94.1	28.2-542
	28.2-550
28.1-95	28.2-549
28.1-96	28.2-546
28.1-97	28.2-535
28.1-98	28.2-200
28.1-99	Deleted
28.1-100	28.2-551
	28.2-552
28.1-101	28.2-553
	28.2-554
28.1-101.1	Repealed
28.1-101.2	28.2-555
28.1-101.3	Deleted
28.1-101.4	28.2-556
28.1-102	28.2-557
28.1-103	28.2-558
28.1-104	28.2-559
28.1-105	28.2-560
28.1-106	28.2-561
28.1-107	28.2-562
28.1-108	28.2-600
	28.2-601
	28.2-602
28.1-109	28.2-603 through 28.2-622
28.1-109.1	28.2-623
28.1-110	28.2-631
28.1-111	28.2-624
28.1-112	28.2-625
28.1-113	28.2-626
28.1-114	28.2-627
28.1-115	28.2-628
28.1-116	28.2-629
28.1-117	Repealed
28.1-118	28.2-630
28.1-118.1	28.2-633
28.1-119	28.2-504
28.1-119.1	28.2-228
	28.2-234
28.1-120	28.2-226
	28.2-231
	28.2-501
	28.2-502
	28.2-503
	28.2-506
	28.2-536
	28.2-537
28.1-120.1	28.2-201
28.1-121	28.2-500
28.1-122	28.2-634
28.1-123	28.2-635
28.1-124	28.2-511
	28.2-514
28.1-125	28.2-510
28.1-126	Repealed
28.1-127	28.2-510
	28.2-512
	28.2-513
28.1-128	Deleted
28.1-128.01	28.2-520
28.1-128.1	28.2-524
28.1-128.2	28.2-525
28.1-128.3	28.2-524
28.1-128.4	28.2-524
28.1-129	28.2-501
28.1-130	Deleted
28.1-131	28.2-522
28.1-132	28.2-523
28.1-133	28.2-231
	28.2-502
28.1-134	28.2-515
	28.2-516
	28.2-517

Former Section	Present Section
28.1-135	28.2-521
28.1-136	28.2-526
28.1-137	28.2-527
	28.2-528
28.1-138	28.2-529
28.1-139	28.2-530
28.1-139.1	28.2-531
28.1-140	28.2-532
28.1-141	28.2-533
28.1-142	28.2-505
28.1-143	28.2-519
28.1-144	28.2-636
28.1-144.1	Deleted
28.1-145	28.2-637
28.1-146	28.2-518
28.1-147	28.2-638
28.1-148	28.2-200
28.1-149	28.2-639
28.1-150	28.2-640
28.1-151	28.2-641
28.1-152	28.2-642
28.1-153	28.2-643
28.1-154	28.2-644
28.1-155	28.2-645
28.1-156	28.2-646
28.1-157	28.2-647
28.1-158	28.2-648
28.1-159	28.2-649
28.1-160	28.2-534
28.1-161	28.2-650
28.1-162	28.2-632
28.1-163	Deleted
28.1-164	Reserved
28.1-165	28.2-226
	28.2-700
	28.2-702
	28.2-703
	28.2-705
28.1-165.1	28.2-700
	28.2-706
	28.2-707
28.1-166	28.2-707
28.1-167	28.2-708
28.1-168	28.2-713
28.1-169	28.2-700
28.1-170	28.2-709
28.1-171	28.2-234
28.1-172	Repealed
28.1-172.1	28.2-704
28.1-173	Repealed
28.1-173.1	28.2-710
28.1-173.1:1	28.2-711
28.1-173.2	28.2-234
	28.2-712
28.1-173.3	28.2-701
28.1-174	28.2-226
28.1-175	28.2-803

Former Section	Present Section
28.1-175.1	28.2-800
28.1-176	28.2-804
	28.2-805
	28.2-806
28.1-177	28.2-807
	28.2-808
28.1-178	28.2-809
28.1-179	28.2-801
	28.2-810 to
	28.2-820
28.1-180	28.2-801
28.1-181	28.2-821
28.1-182	28.2-823
28.1-183	28.2-802
28.1-183.1	28.2-824
28.1-183.2	28.2-825
28.1-184	Deleted
28.1-185	28.2-900
28.1-185.1	28.2-900
28.1-185.2	28.2-901
28.1-186	28.2-902
28.1-187	28.2-903
28.1-188	Repealed
28.1-188.1	28.2-904
28.1-189	Repealed
28.1-190	28.2-238
28.1-191	28.2-905
28.1-192	28.2-906
28.1-193	28.2-907
28.1-194	Deleted
28.1-195	28.2-1100
28.1-196	28.2-1101
28.1-197	Repealed
28.1-197.1	Repealed
28.1-198	Expired
28.1-199	Repealed
28.1-200	28.2-1102
28.1-201	Reserved
28.1-202	28.2-1000
28.1-203	28.2-1001
28.1-203.1	28.2-1002
28.1-204 to	
28.1-226	Repealed
28.1-227	28.2-1003
28.1-228	28.2-1004
28.1-229	28.2-1005
28.1-230	3.1-684.59
28.1-231	3.1-684.59
28.1-232	3.1-684.60
28.1-233	3.1-684.63
28.1-234	3.1-684.61
28.1-235	3.1-684.62
28.1-236	3.1-684.64
28.1-237	3.1-684.59
28.1-238	3.1-684.63
28.1-239	3.1-684.63
41.1-4.1	28.2-1201
62.1-1	28.2-1200

Former Section	Present Section
62.1-2	28.2-1202
62.1-3	28.2-1203
	28.2-1204
	28.2-1205
	28.2-1206
62.1-3.01	28.2-1207
62.1-3.02	28.2-1207
62.1-3.03	28.2-1209
62.1-3.1	28.2-1211
62.1-4	28.2-1208
62.1-5	Repealed
62.1-9.1	28.2-1213
62.1-13.1	28.2-1301
	28.2-1302
62.1-13.2	28.2-1300
62.1-13.2:1	Repealed
62.1-13.3	28.2-1308
62.1-13.4	28.2-103
	28.2-1301
62.1-13.4:1	Repealed
62.1-13.5	28.2-1302
	28.2-1306
62.1-13.5:1	Repealed
62.1-13.5:2	28.2-1307
62.1-13.5:3	28.2-1309
62.1-13.6	28.2-1303
62.1-13.7	28.2-1304
62.1-13.8	28.2-1303
	28.2-1305
62.1-13.9	28.2-1306
62.1-13.10	28.2-1310
62.1-13.11	28.2-1311
62.1-13.12	28.2-1312
62.1-13.13	28.2-1313
62.1-13.14	28.2-1312
62.1-13.14:1	28.2-1314
62.1-13.15	28.2-1315
62.1-13.16	28.2-1316
62.1-13.16:1	28.2-1317
62.1-13.17	28.2-1301
62.1-13.18	28.2-1318
62.1-13.18:1	28.2-1319
62.1-13.18.2	28.2-1320
62.1-13.19	Deleted
62.1-13.20	Deleted
62.1-13.21	28.2-1400
	28.2-1401
	28.2-1403
62.1-13.22	28.2-1400
62.1-13.23	28.2-1408
62.1-13.24	28.2-1401
62.1-13.25	28.2-1403
62.1-13.25:1	28.2-1409
62.1-13.26	28.2-1406
62.1-13.27	Deleted
62.1-13.27:1	28.2-1420
62.1-13.28	28.2-1402
62.1-194.1:1	28.2-1210

COMPARABLE SECTIONS OF TITLE 29 AND TITLE 29.1

Former Section	Present Section
29-1	Repealed
29-1.1	29.1-109
29-2	29.1-109
29-2.1	29.1-100
29-3	29.1-102
29-4	29.1-102
29-5	Repealed
29-6	29.1-103
29-7	29.1-107
29-8	29.1-102
	29.1-109
29-9	Repealed
29-10	Repealed
29-11	29.1-103
29-11.1	29.1-105
29-11.2	29.1-104
29-12	29.1-106
29-12.1	29.1-610
29-13	29.1-109
29-14 to 29-16	29.1-109
29-17	29.1-102
29-18	29.1-108
29-19	Repealed
29-20	29.1-101
29-21	29.1-110
29-22	29.1-110
29-23	29.1-111
29-23.01	29.1-111
29-23.1	Repealed
29-23.2 to 29-23.10	Repealed
29-24	29.1-200
29-25	Repealed
29-26	Repealed
29-27	29.1-201
29-28	29.1-200
29-29	29.1-202
29-30	29.1-203
29-31	29.1-204
29-32	29.1-205
29-32.1	Repealed
29-32.2	29.1-207
29-33	29.1-208
29-34	29.1-209
29-34.1	29.1-210
29-34.2	Repealed
29-35	29.1-212
29-35.1	29.1-213
29-35.2	29.1-214
29-36 to 29-37	Repealed
29-37.1	29.1-217
29-37.2	29.1-218
29-38	29.1-600
29-39	29.1-601
29-40	29.1-602
29-41	29.1-603
29-42	29.1-604
29-43	Repealed
29-44	29.1-606
29-45	29.1-607
29-46	29.1-608
29-47	29.1-609
29-48	29.1-611
29-49	Repealed
29-50	Repealed
29-51	29.1-300
29-52	29.1-301
29-52.1	Repealed
29-52.2	29.1-302
29-53	Repealed
29-54	29.1-303
29-54.1	29.1-304
29-55	29.1-310
29-55.1	29.1-311
29-55.2	Repealed
29-55.3	29.1-312
29-55.3:1	29.1-314
29-55.3:2	29.1-315
29-55.3:3	29.1-316
29-55.3:4	29.1-317
29-55.4	29.1-318
29-56	29.1-309
29-57	29.1-319
29-57.1	Repealed
29-57.1:1	29.1-313
29-57.2	Repealed
29-58	29.1-319
29-59	29.1-321
29-60	29.1-322
29-61	29.1-323
29-62	Repealed
29-63	29.1-325
29-64	Repealed
29-65	29.1-327
29-66	29.1-328
29-67	Repealed
29-68	29.1-330
29-68.1	29.1-331
29-69	29.1-332
29-70	29.1-333
29-71	29.1-332
29-72	29.1-333
29-73	29.1-333
29-74	29.1-334
29-75	29.1-335
	29.1-336
29-76	29.1-337
	29.1-337.1
29-77	29.1-338
29-77.1	Repealed
29-78	29.1-612
29-79	Repealed
29-80	29.1-339
29-81	29.1-340
29-82	29.1-341
29-83	29.1-342
29-84	29.1-343
29-85	29.1-344
29-86	29.1-345
29-87	29.1-346
29-88	29.1-347
29-89	29.1-348
29-90	29.1-349
	29.1-351.1
29-91	29.1-350
29-92	29.1-351
29-92.1	29.1-352
29-92.2	29.1-353
29-92.3	29.1-354
29-92.4	29.1-355
29-92.5	29.1-356
29-92.6	29.1-357
29-92.7	29.1-358
29-93	29.1-400
29-94	29.1-401
29-95	29.1-402
29-96	Repealed
29-97	Repealed
29-98	29.1-403
29-99	29.1-404
29-100	29.1-405
29-101	29.1-406
29-102	29.1-407
29-103	29.1-412
29-104	29.1-413
29-105	29.1-413
29-106 to 29-108.1	Repealed
29-109	29.1-415
29-110	29.1-416
29-111	Repealed
29-111.1	29.1-417
29-112	Repealed
29-112.1	Repealed
29-113	29.1-418
29-114	Repealed
29-114.1	Repealed
29-114.2	29.1-419
29-115	29.1-420
29-116	29.1-412
29-117	29.1-408
29-118	29.1-409
29-119	29.1-410
29-120	29.1-411
29-121	Repealed
29-122	29.1-305
29-122.1	29.1-306
29-123 to 29-125	Repealed
29-126	29.1-501
29-127	29.1-502
29-128	29.1-503
29-128.1	29.1-504
29-129	29.1-505
29-129.1	29.1-506

Former Section	Present Section
29-130	29.1-507
29-130.1	29.1-508
29-130.2	29.1-509
29-131	Repealed
29-132	29.1-510
29-133	29.1-511
29-134	29.1-512
29-135	29.1-513
29-136	29.1-514
29-136.1	Repealed
29-137	29.1-515
29-138	29.1-516
29-139	29.1-517
29-139.1	29.1-518
29-140	29.1-519
29-140.1	Repealed
29-141	29.1-520
29-142	29.1-520
29-143	29.1-521
29-144	29.1-522
29-144.1	Repealed
29-144.2	29.1-523
29-144.3	29.1-524
29-144.4	29.1-525
29-144.4:1	29.1-523
	29.1-525
29-144.5	29.1-526
29-144.5:1	29.1-527
29-144.6	29.1-528
29-145	Repealed
29-145.1	29.1-529
29-145.2	Repealed
29-146	29.1-530
29-147	Repealed
29-147.1	Repealed
29-148	29.1-531
29-148.1 to 29-150.1	Repealed
29-151	29.1-532
29-152	Repealed
29-153	29.1-533
29-153.1	29.1-534
29-153.2	29.1-535
29-154	29.1-536
29-155	29.1-537
29-155.1	Repealed
29-155.2 to 29-155.4	29.1-539
29-155.5	Repealed
29-156	29.1-540
29-157	29.1-541
29-158	29.1-542
29.158.1	29.1-543
29-158.2	29.1-544
29-158.3	29.1-545
29-159 to 29-160	Repealed
29-161	29.1-546
29-161.1	29.1-547
29-162	29.1-548
29-162.1	29.1-549
29-162.2	29.1-549
29-163	29.1-550
29-163.1	29.1-551
29-163.2	29.1-552
29-164	29.1-553
29-165 to 29-170	Repealed
29-171	29.1-554
29-171.1	Repealed
29-172	29.1-556
29-173	29.1-557
29-174 to 29-180	Repealed
29-181	29.1-561
29-183 to 29-213	Repealed
29-213.1	32.1-48.1
29-213.2	32.1-48.2
29-213.3	32.1-48.3
29-213.4	32.1-48.4
29-213.5 to 29-213.34	Repealed
29-213.35	29.1-569
29-213.36	3.1-796.66
29-213.37	3.1-796.67
29-213.38	3.1-796.68
29-213.39	3.1-796.69
29-213.40	3.1-796.70
29-213.41	3.1-796.71
29-213.42	3.1-796.72
29-213.43	3.1-796.73
29-213.44	3.1-796.74
29-213.45	3.1-796.75
29-213.46	3.1-796.76
29-213.47	3.1-796.77
29-213.48	3.1-796.78
29-213.49	3.1-796.79
29-213.50	3.1-796.80
29-213.51	3.1-796.81
29-213.52	3.1-796.82
29-213.53	3.1-796.83
29-213.54	3.1-796.84
29-213.55	3.1-796.85
29-213.56	3.1-796.86
29-213.57	3.1-796.87
29-213.58	3.1-796.88
29-213.59	3.1-796.89
29-213.60	3.1-796.90
29-213.61	3.1-796.91
29-213.62	3.1-796.92
29-213.63	3.1-796.93
29-213.64	3.1-796.94
29-213.65	3.1-796.95
29-213.66	3.1-796.96
29-213.67	3.1-796.97
29-213.68	3.1-796.98
29-213.68:1	3.1-796.99
29-213.69	3.1-796.100
29-213.70	3.1-796.101
29-213.71	3.1-796.102
29-213.72	3.1-796.103
29-213.73	3.1-796.104
29-213.74	3.1-796.105
29-213.75	3.1-796.106
29-213.76	3.1-796.107
29-213.77	3.1-796.108
29-213.78	3.1-796.109
29-213.79	3.1-796.110
29-213.80	3.1-796.111
29-213.81	3.1-796.112
29-213.82	3.1-796.113
29-213-83	3.1-796.114
29-213.84	3.1-796.115
29-213.85	3.1-796.116
29-213.86	3.1-796.117
29-213.87	3.1-796.118
29-213.88	3.1-796.119
29-213.89	3.1-796.120
29-213.90	3.1-796.121
29-213.91	3.1-796.122
29-213.92	3.1-796.123
29-213.92:1	3.1-796.124
29-213.93	3.1-796.125
29-213.94	3.1-796.126
29-213.95	3.1-796.127
29-213.96	29.1-422
29-213.97	Repealed
29-213.98	Repealed
29-213.99	3.1-796.128
29-213.100	3.1-796.129
29-214 to 29-229	Repealed
29-230	Repealed
29-231	29.1-563
29-232	29.1-564
29-233	29.1-566
29-234	29.1-566
29-235	29.1-567
29-236	29.1-568
29-237	Repealed
29-238 to 29-247	Repealed
29-248	29.1-570

COMPARABLE SECTIONS OF TITLE 32 AND TITLE 32.1

Former Section	Present Section
32-1	32.1-5
32-2	32.1-6
32-3	32.1-7
32-4	32.1-8
32-5	32.1-9
32-6	32.1-12
32-6.1 to 32-6.3	Repealed
32-6.4	32.1-27
32-7	Deleted
32-8	32.1-43
32-8.1	32.1-11
32-8.2	32.1-89
32-8.3	32.1-90
32-8.4	32.1-90
32-8.5	32.1-91
32-8.6	32.1-92
32-9	32.1-164, 32.1-165, 32.1-166
32-9.01	32.1-164.1
32-9.1	32.1-177, 32.1-178, 32.1-179, 32.1-180, 32.1-181, 32.1-182, 32.1-183, 32.1-184, 32.1-185, 32.1-186
32-9.2	32.1-177 32.1-178, 32.1-179, 32.1-180, 32.1-181, 32.1-182, 32.1-183, 32.1-184, 32.1-185, 32.1-186
32-10	32.1-39
32-10.1	32.1-40
32-10.2	32.1-41
32-10.3	32.1-41
32-11	32.1-23
32-11.1	32.1-78
32-12	32.1-13
32-13	32.1-44
32-14	Deleted
32-15	32.1-27
32-16	32.1-35
32-17 to 32-19	Deleted
32-20	32.1-14
32-21	32.1-15
32-22	32.1-10
32-23	32.1-17
32-24	32.1-18
32-25	32.1-17
32-26	32.1-21
32-27	32.1-19
32-28	32.1-20
32-29	Deleted
32-30	32.1-14
32-30.1	32.1-74
32-30.2	32.1-75
32-31	32.1-22
32-31.1 to 32-31.9	Repealed
32-31.10	32.1-278
32-31.11	Deleted
32-31.12	32.1-277 32.1-279
32-31.13	32.1-280
32-31.14	Deleted
32-31.15	32.1-281
32-31.16	32.1-282
32-31.17	32.1-283
32-31.18	32.1-283
32-31.19	32.1-285 32.1-286
32-31.20	32.1-283
32-31.21	32.1-288
32-31.22	32.1-287
32-32 to 32-39	Deleted
32-40	32.1-33
32-40.1	32.1-31
32-40.2	32.1-31
32-40.3	Deleted
32-41	Deleted
32-42	32.1-39
32-43 to 32-47	Deleted
32-47.1 to 32-47.8	32.1-46
32-48	32.1-36 32.1-38
32-49	32.1-37
32-50 to 32-55	Deleted
32-56	32.1-45
32-57	Deleted
32-57.1	32.1-46
32-58 to 32-62	Deleted
32-63	32.1-198, 32.1-199, 32.1-200, 32.1-202
32-63.1	32.1-246
32-63.2	32.1-201
32-64 to 32-68	Deleted
32-69	Repealed
32-70	18.2-510
32-70.1	Repealed
32-71 to 32-80	Deleted
32-81	53-19.22:2
32-82	53-135.2
32-83	Deleted
32-84, 32-85	Repealed
32-85.1	32.1-50 32.1-51
32-85.2	Deleted
32-85.3	32.1-51
32-85.4	32.1-52
32-85.5 to 32-89	Deleted
32-90	32.1-55
32-91	Deleted
32-92	32.1-56
32-93	32.1-57
32-94	32.1-58
32-95 to 32-103	Deleted
32-104	32.1-59
32-104.1	32.1-60, 32.1-72
32-104.2 to 32-104.4	Deleted
32-104.5	32.1-139
32-104.6	32.1-141
32-104.7	32.1-140 32.1-142
32-104.8	32.1-143
32-104.9	32.1-140
32-104.10	Deleted
32-104.11	32.1-140
32-105	32.1-61
32-106	32.1-63
32-107	32.1-62
32-108	Deleted
32-109	32.1-64
32-110 to 32-112	Deleted
32-112.1	32.1-65
32-112.2 to 32-112.4	Deleted
32-112.5	32.1-66
32-112.6	32.1-67
32-112.7, 32-112.8	Deleted
32-112.9	32.1-65
32-112.10 to 32-112.19	Repealed
32-112.20	Deleted
32-112.21	32.1-68
32-112.22	32.1-68
32-112.23	32.1-69
32-113 to 32-116	Deleted
32-117	32.1-212
32-118	32.1-213
32-119	32.1-215
32-120	32.1-216
32-120.1	32.1-217 32.1-218
32-121	Deleted
32-122	32.1-219
32-122.1	32.1-220
32-123, 32-124	Repealed
32-125	32.1-221
32-126	32.1-224
32-127	32.1-225
32-128	Deleted
32-129	32.1-226
32-130	15.1-526.3
32-131	15.1-526.3

Former Section	Present Section
32-132 to 32-136	Deleted
32-137	54-325.2
32-137.01	54-325.2:1
32-137.1	54-325.1
32-138	8.01-66.2
32-139	8.01-66.3
32-139.1	8.01-66.9
32-140	8.01-66.4
32-141	8.01-66.10
32-142	8.01-66.5
32-143	8.01-66.6
32-144	8.01-66.11
32-145	8.01-66.7
32-146	8.01-66.8
32-147 to 32-153	Deleted
32-154	32.1-134
32-155 to 32-164	Deleted
32-165	32.1-77
32-166, 32-167	Deleted
32-167.1	32.1-145
32-167.2	32.1-145
32-167.3	32.1-146
32-167.4 to 32-167.6	Deleted
32-167.7	32.1-147
32-168 to 32-195	Repealed
32-195.1	38.1-810
32-195.2	38.1-811
32-195.3	38.1-812
32-195.3:1	38.1-813
32-195.4	38.1-814
32-195.5	38.1-815
32-195.5:1	38.1-816
32-195.5:2	38.1-817
32-195.6, 32-195.7	Repealed
32-195.8	38.1-818
38-195.8:1	38.1-819
32-195.8:2	38.1-820
32-195.8:3	38.1-821
32-195.9	38.1-822
32-195.10	38.1-823
32.195.10:1	38.1-824
32-195.11	38.1-825
32-195.12	38.1-826
32-195.12:1	Deleted
32-195.13	38.1-827
32-195.14	Repealed
32-195.15	38.1-828
32-195.16	38.1-829
32-195.17	38.1-830
32-195.18	38.1-831
32-195.19	28.1-832
32-195.20	38.1-833
32-195.20:1	38.1-834
32-195.21	38.1-835
32-195.22	38.1-836

Former Section	Present Section
32-195.23	38.1-837
32-195.24	38.1-838
32-195.25	38.1-839
32-195.26	38.1-840
32-195.27	38.1-841
32-195.28	38.1-842
32-195.29	38.1-843
32-195.29:1	Deleted
32-195.30	38.1-844
32-195.31	Repealed
32-195.32	38.1-845
32-195.33	38.1-846
32-195.34	38.1-847
32-195.35	38.1-848
32-195.36	38.1-849
32-195.37	38.1-850
32-195.38	38.1-851
32-195.39	38.1-852
32-195.40	38.1-853
32-195.41	38.1-854
32-195.42	38.1-855
32-195.43	38.1-856
32-195.44	38.1-857
32-195.44:1	Deleted
32-195.45	38.1-858
32-195.46	Repealed
32-195.47	38.1-859
32-195.48	38.1-860
32-195.49	38.1-861
32-195.50	38.1-862
32-196	Deleted
32-197	32.1-103
32-198	32.1-104
32-199	32.1-104
32-200	32.1-105
32-201	32.1-104
	32.1-106
32-202	32.1-106
32-203	32.1-104
32-204	32.1-104
32-205	32.1-106
32-206	Deleted
32-207	32.1-106
32-208	32.1-107
32-209	32.1-108
32-210	32.1-109
32-211	32.1-104
	32.1-110
32-211.1	Deleted
32-211.2	32.1-111
32-211.3	Deleted
32-211.4	Deleted
32-211.5	32.1-93
32-211.6	32.1-94
	32.1-95
32-211.7	32.1-96
32-211.8	32.1-97
32-211.9	32.1-98
32-211.10	Deleted
32-211.11	32.1-99
32-211.12	32.1-100

Former Section	Present Section
32-211.13	32.1-101
32-211.14	Deleted
32-211.15	32.1-102
32-211.16	Deleted
32-211.17	Deleted
32-211.18	32.1-117
32-211.19	32.1-118
32-211.20	32.1-119
32-211.21	32.1-120
32-211.22	32.1-121
32-211.23	32.1-122
32-212	Deleted
32-213	15.1-1533
32-214	15.1-1534
32-215	15.1-1535
32-216	15.1-1536
32-217	15.1-1537
32-218	15.1-1538
32-219	15.1-1539
32-220	15.1-1540
32-221	15.1-1541
32-222	15.1-1542
32-223	15.1-1543
32-224	Repealed
32-225	15.1-1544
32-226	15.1-1545
32-227	15.1-1546
32-228	15.1-1547
32-229	15.1-1548
32-230	15.1-1549
32-231	15.1-1550
32-232	15.1-1551
32-233	15.1-1552
32-234	15.1-1553
32-235	15.1-1554
32-236	15.1-1555
32-237	15.1-1556
32-238	15.1-1557
32-238.1	15.1-1558
32-239	15.1-1559
32-240	15.1-1560
32-240.1	15.1-1561
32-241	15.1-1562
32-242	15.1-1563
32-243	15.1-1564
32-244	15.1-1565
32-245	15.1-1566
32-246	15.1-1567
32-247	15.1-1568
32-248	15.1-1569
32-249	15.1-1570
32-250	15.1-1571
32-251	15.1-1572
32-252	15.1-1573
32-253	15.1-1574
32-254	Repealed
32-255	15.1-1575
32-256	15.1-1576
32-257	15.1-1577
32-258	15.1-1578
32-259	15.1-1579

Former Section	Present Section
32-260	15.1-1580
32-261	15.1-1581
32-262	15.1-1582
32-263	15.1-1583
32-264	15.1-1584
32-265	15.1-1585
32-266	15.1-1586
32-267	15.1-1587
32-268	15.1-1588
32-269	15.1-1589
32-270	15.1-1590
32-271	15.1-1591
32-271.1	15.1-1592
32-271.2	15.1-1593
32-271.3	15.1-1594
32-271.4	15.1-1595
32-271.5	15.1-1596
32-271.6	15.1-1597
32-271.7	15.1-1598
32-271.8	15.1-1599
32-272 to 32-275	Repealed
32-275.1	15.1-1600
32-275.2	15.1-1601
32-275.3	15.1-1602
32-276	15.1-1514
32-276.1	15.1-1515
32-277	15.1-1516
32-278	15.1-1517
32-279	15.1-1518
32-280	15.1-1519
32-281	15.1-1520
32-281.1	15.1-1521
32-282	15.1-1522
32-283	15.1-1523
32-284	15.1-1524
32-285	15.1-1525
32-286	15.1-1526
32-287	15.1-1527
32-288	15.1-1528
32-289	15.1-1529
32-290	Deleted
32-290.1	15.1-1530
32-290.2	15.1-1531
32-290.3	15.1-1532
32-291 to 32-296	Repealed
32-296.1	32.1-138
32-297	Deleted
32-298	32.1-123
	32.1-124
32-299	32.1-125
32-300	32.1-126
32-300.1	32.1-125.1
32-301	32.1-127
	32.1-128
32-301.1	32.1-134.2
32-302	Deleted
32-303	32.1-129
32-304	32.1-130
	32.1-131

Former Section	Present Section
32-305	32.1-126
	32.1-132
32-306	32.1-133
32-307	32.1-135
32-308, 32-309	Deleted
32-310	32.1-136
32-310.1	32.1-148
	32.1-150, 32.1-152
32-310.1:1	32.1-112
32-310.2:1	32.1-114
32-310.2:2	32.1-113
32-310.3	32.1-151
	32.1-152
32-310.4	32.1-151
	32.1-153
32-310.5	Deleted
32-310.6	32.1-149
32-310.7	32.1-155
32-310.7:1	32.1-154
32-310.8	32.1-156
32-310.9	32.1-115
32-310.10	32.1-115
32-310.11	32.1-116
32-311, 32-312	Deleted
32-312.1	32.1-54
32-313 to 32-321	Deleted
32-322 to 32-353.3	Repealed
32-353.4	32.1-249
32-353.5	32.1-250
32-353.6	32.1-250
32-353.7	32.1-251
32-353.8	32.1-252
32-353.9	32.1-253
32-353.10	32.1-254
32-353.11	32.1-255
32-353.12	32.1-256
32-353.13	32.1-256
32-353.14	Deleted
32-353.15	32.1-257
32-353.16	32.1-258
32-353.17	32.1-259
32-353.18	32.1-260
32-353.19	32.1-261
32-353.20	32.1-263
32-353.21	32.1-264
32-353.22	32.1-265
32-353.23	32.1-266
32-353.24	32.1-269
32-353.25	32.1-270
32-353.26	32.1-271
32-353.27	32.1-272
32-353.28	32.1-273
32-353.29	32.1-274
32-353.30	32.1-275
32-353.31	32.1-276
32-353.32	32.1-262
32-353.33	32.1-268
32-353.34	32.1-267

Former Section	Present Section
32-354	Deleted
32-355	32.1-300
32-356	32.1-298
32-357	32.1-299
32-358	32.1-299
32-359	32.1-301
32-360	32.1-299
32-361	32.1-303
32-362	32.1-302
32-363	32.1-299
32-364	32.1-304
32-364.1	Repealed
32-364.2	32.1-297
32-364.2:1	Repealed
32-364.3	32.1-289
32-364.3:1	54-325.7
32-364.4	32.1-290
32-364.4:1	54-325.8
32-364.5	32.1-291
32-364.6	32.1-292
32-364.7	32.1-293
32-364.8	32.1-294
32-364.9	32.1-295
32-364.10, 32-364.11	Deleted
32-365 to 32-378.4	Repealed
32-379	32.1-187
32-379.1	32.1-188
32-380	32.1-189
32-381	32.1-190
32-382	32.1-191
32-383	32.1-192
32-384	32.1-193
32-385	32.1-194
32-386	32.1-195
32-386.1	32.1-196
32-387	32.1-197
32-388	32.1-70
32-389	32.1-71
32-390 to 32-410	Deleted
32-411 to 32-414	Repealed
32-414.1	Deleted
32-414.2	32.1-229
32-414.3	32.1-227
32-414.4	32.1-229
	32-1-230
32-414.4:1	32.1-231
32-414.4:2	32.1-232
32-414.5	32.1-233
32-414.6	32.1-229
32-414.7	32.1-228
	32.1-229
32-414.8, 32-414.9	Deleted
32-414.10	32.1-234
32-414.11	32.1-235
32-414.12	32.1-236
32-414.13	32.1-237

Former Section	Present Section
32-414.14, 32-414.15	Deleted
32-414.16	32.1-229
32-414.17	32.1-238
32-414.18, 32-414.19	Deleted
32-415	32.1-203
32-416	32.1-204, 32.1-205, 32.1-206, 32.1-207, 32.1-208, 32.1-209, 32.1-210
32-417	32.1-211
32-418	32.1-211
32-419	Deleted
32-420	32.1-211
32-421, 32-422	Deleted
32-423	54-325.3
32-424	54-325.4
32-424.1	54-325.5
32-425	Repealed
32-426	Deleted
32-427	54-325.6
32-428	Deleted
32-428.1	32.1-241
32-429	32.1-241
32-430	32.1-239
32-431	32.1-240
32-432	32.1-241
32-433	32.1-242
32-434	32.1-243
32-435	Repealed
32-435.1	32.1-244
32-436, 32-437	Deleted
32-438	32.1-245
32-439	32.1-157
32-440	32.1-158
32-441	32.1-159
32-442	32.1-160
32-443	32.1-161
32-444	32.1-162
32-445 to 32-448	Deleted

COMPARABLE SECTIONS OF TITLE 33 AND TITLE 33.1

Former Section	Present Section
33-1	33.1-1
33-2	33.1-2
33-3	33.1-3
33-3.1	33.1-4
33-4	33.1-5
33-5	33.1-6
33-6	33.1-7
33-7	33.1-8
33-8	Deleted
33-9	33.1-9
33-10	33.1-10
33-11	33.1-252
33-11.1	33.1-11
33-12	33.1-12
33-13	33.1-13
33-14	33.1-14
33-15	Deleted
33-15.1	33.1-16
33-16	33.1-17
33-17	33.1-18
33-18	33.1-19
33-19	33.1-20
33-20	33.1-21
33-21	33.1-22
33-22	33.1-23
33-22.1	33.1-24
33-23	33.1-25
33-23.1	33.1-26
33-23.2	33.1-27
33-23.3	33.1-28
33-23.4	33.1-29
33-23.5	33.1-30
33-24	33.1-31
33-25	33.1-32
33-26	33.1-34
33-27	33.1-35
33-28, 33-29	Deleted
33-30	33.1-36
33-31	33.1-37
33-32	33.1-38
33-33, 33-34	Deleted
33-35	33.1-39
33-35.1	33.1-40
33-35.2	33.1-41
33-35.3	33.1-42
33-35.4	33.1-43
33-35.5	33.1-44
33-35.6	33.1-45
33-35.7	33.1-46
33-35.8	33.1-46.1
33-36	33.1-47
33-36.1	33.1-48
33-36.2	33.1-49
33-36.3	33.1-50
33-36.4	Deleted
33-36.5	33.1-51
33-36.6	33.1-52
33-36.7	33.1-53
33-36.8	33.1-54
33-36.9	33.1-55
33-36.10	33.1-56
33-37	33.1-57
33-38	33.1-58
33-39	33.1-59
33-39.1, 33-40	Deleted
33-40.1	33.1-60
33-41	33.1-61
33-42, 33-43	Deleted
33-43.1	33.1-62
33-43.2	33.1-63
33-43.3	33.1-64
33-43.4	33.1-65
33-43.5	33.1-66
33-44	33.1-67
33-45	33.1-68
33-46	33.1-69
33-47	33.1-70
33-47.1	33.1-71
33-47.2	33.1-72
33-48	33.1-73
33-48.1	33.1-74
33-49	33.1-75
33-49.1	33.1-76
33-49.2	33.1-77
33-50	33.1-78
33-50.1	33.1-79
33-50.2	33.1-80
33-50.3	33.1-81
33-50.4	33.1-82
33-50.5	33.1-83
33-51	33.1-84
33-52	Deleted
33-53	33.1-85
33-54	33.1-86
33-55	33.1-87
33-56	33.1-88
33-57	33.1-89
33-57.1	33.1-90
33-57.2	33.1-94
33-57.3	33.1-95
33-58	33.1-96
33-58.1	33.1-97
33-59	33.1-98
33-59.1	33.1-99
33-60	Repealed
33-60.1	33.1-101
33-60.2	33.1-102
33-60.3	33.1-103
33-61	33.1-104
33-62	Repealed
33-62.1	33.1-105
33-63	Repealed
33-63.1	33.1-107
33-64	33.1-108
33-64.1	33.1-109
33-65	33.1-110
33-65.1	33.1-111
33-66	33.1-112
33-67	33.1-113
33-67.1	33.1-114

Former Section	Present Section
33-67.2	33.1-115
33-67.3	33.1-116
33-68	Deleted
33-69	33.1-117
33-70	Repealed
33-70.1	33.1-119
33-70.2	33.1-120
33-70.3	33.1-121
33-70.4	33.1-122
33-70.5	33.1-123
33-70.6	33.1-124
33-70.7	33.1-125
33-70.8	33.1-126
33-70.9	33.1-127
33-70.10	33.1-128
33-70.11	33.1-129
33-71, 33-72	Deleted
33-73	33.1-130
33-74	Repealed
33-75	33.1-132
33-75.01	33.1-132.1
33-75.02	33.1-132.2
33-73.03	33.1-132.3
33-75.04	33.1-132.4
33-75.05	33.1-132.5
33-75.06	33.1-132.6
33-75.07	33.1-132.7
33-75.08	33.1-132.8
33-75.09	33.1-132.9
33-75.010	33.1-132.10
33-87.011	33.1-132.11
33-75.1	33.1-133
33-75.2	33.1-134
33-75.3	33.1-135
33-75.4	33.1-136
33-75.5	33.1-137
33-75.6	33.1-138
33-75.7	33.1-139
33-75.8	33.1-140
33-75.9	33.1-141
33-75.10	33.1-142
33-75.11	33.1-143
33-76	Repealed
33-76.1	33.1-144
33-76.2	33.1-145
33-76.3	33.1-146
33-76.4	33.1-147
33-76.5	33.1-148
33-76.6	33.1-149
33-76.7	33.1-150
33-76.8	33.1-151
33-76.9	33.1-152
33-76.10	33.1-153
33-76.11	33.1-154
33-76.12	33.1-155
33-76.13	33.1-156
33-76.14	33.1-157
33-76.15	33.1-158
33-76.16	33.1-159
33-76.17	33.1-160
33-76.18	33.1-161
33-76.19	33.1-162
33-76.20	33.1-163
33-76.21	33.1-164
33-76.22	33.1-165
33-76.23	33.1-166
33-76.24	33.1-167
33-77 to 33-81	Repealed
33-82	33.1-168
33-83	33.1-169
33-84	33.1-170
33-85	33.1-171
33-86	33.1-172
33-87	33.1-173
33-88	33.1-174
33-89	33.1-175
33-90	33.1-176
33-91	33.1-177
33-92	33.1-178
33-93	33.1-179
33-94	33.1-180
33-95	33.1-181
33-96	33.1-182
33-97	33.1-183
33-98	33.1-184
33-99	33.1-185
33-100	33.1-186
33-101	33.1-187
33-102	33.1-188
33-103	33.1-189
33-104	33.1-190
33-105	33.1-191
33-106	33.1-192
33-107	Repealed
33-108	Deleted
33-109	33.1-193
33-110	33.1-194
33-111	33.1-195
33-112	33.1-196
33-113 to 33-115	Repealed
33-116	33.1-197
33-116.1	33.1-198
33-117	33.1-199
33-117.1	33.1-200
33-117.2	33.1-91
33-117.3	33.1-92
33-117.4	33.1-93
33-118	33.1-201
33-119	33.1-202
33-120	33.1-203
33-120.1	33.1-204
33-121	33.1-205
33-122	33.1-206
33-123	33.1-207
33-123.1	33.1-208
33-124	33.1-209
33-125	33.1-210
33-126	33.1-211
33-127	33.1-212
33-128	33.1-213
33-129	33.1-214
33-130	33.1-215
33-131	33.1-216
33-132	Deleted
33-133	33.1-217
33-133.1	33.1-218
33-134	33.1-219
33-135	33.1-220
33-136	Repealed
33-136.1	33.1-221
33-136.2	33.1-222
33-136.3	33.1-223
33-137	33.1-224
33-138	33.1-225
33-139	33.1-226
33-140	33.1-228
33-141	33.1-229
33-142	33.1-230
33-143	Deleted
33-144	33.1-231
33-145	33.1-232
33-146	33.1-233
33-147	33.1-234
33-148	33.1-235
33-149	33.1-236
33-150	33.1-237
33-151	33.1-238
33-152	33.1-239
33-153	33.1-240
33-154	33.1-241
33-155	33.1-242
33-155.1	33.1-243
33-156 to 33-158	Repealed
33-159	33.1-244
33-160	33.1-245
33-161	33.1-246
33-162 to 33-170	Deleted
33-171	33.1-247
33-172	33.1-248
33-172.1	33.1-249
33-173	33.1-250
33-173.1	33.1-251
33-174 to 33-191	Deleted
33-191.1	33.1-253
33-192 to 33-208	Deleted
33-209	33.1-254
33-210 to 33-214	Deleted
33-215	33.1-255
33-216	33.1-256
33-217	33.1-257
33-218	33.1-258
33-219	33.1-259
33-220	33.1-260
33-221	33.1-261
33-222	33.1-262
33-223	33.1-263
33-224	33.1-264

Former Section	Present Section
33-225	33.1-265
33-226	33.1-266
33-227	33.1-267
33-228	33.1-268
33-229	33.1-269
33-230	33.1-270
33-231	33.1-271
33-232	33.1-272
33-233	33.1-273
33-234	33.1-274
33-235	33.1-275
33-236	33.1-276
33-237	33.1-277
33-238	33.1-278
33-239	33.1-279
33-240	33.1-280
33-241	33.1-281
33-242	33.1-282
33-243	33.1-283
33-244	33.1-284
33-245	33.1-285
33-246	33.1-286
33-247	33.1-287
33-248	33.1-288
33-250	33.1-290
33-251	33.1-291
33-252	33.1-292
33-253	33.1-293
33-254	33.1-294
33-255	33.1-295
33-255.1	33.1-296
33-255.2	33.1-297
33-255.3	33.1-298
33-255.4	33.1-299
33-255.5	33.1-300
33-255.6	33.1-301
33-255.7	33.1-302
33-255.8	33.1-303
33-255.9	33.1-304
33-255.10	33.1-305
33-255.11	33.1-306
33-255.12	33.1-307
33-255.13	33.1-308
33-255.14	33.1-309
33-255.15	33.1-310
33-255.16	33.1-311
33-255.17	33.1-312
33-255.18	33.1-313
33-255.19	33.1-314
33-255.20	33.1-315
33-255.21	33.1-316
33-255.22	33.1-317
33-255.23	33.1-318
33-255.24 to 33-255.44:9	33.1-319
33-255.44:10	Deleted
33-255.44:11 to 33-255.44:32	33.1-320
33-255.45 to 33-255.66	Repealed
33-256	33.1-321
33-257	33.1-322
33-258	33.1-323
33-259	33.1-324
33-260	33.1-325
33-261	33.1-326
33-262	33.1-327
33-263	33.1-328
33-264	33.1-329
33-265	33.1-330
33-266	33.1-331
33-267	33.1-332
33-268	33.1-333
33-269	33.1-334
33-269.1	33.1-335
33-270	33.1-336
33-271	33.1-337
33-272	33.1-338
33-273	33.1-339
33-274	33.1-340
33-275	33.1-341
33-276	33.1-342
	33-277
	33.1-343
33-278	33.1-344
33-279	33.1-345
33-279.1	33.1-346
33-279.2	33.1-347
33-279.3	33.1-348
33-280	Deleted
33-281 to 33-286	Repealed
33-287	33.1-349
33-288	Deleted
33-288.1	33.1-350
33-289 to 33-296	Repealed
33-297	Deleted
33-298	33.1-351
33-299	33.1-352
33-300	33.1-353
33-301	33.1-354
33-302	33.1-355
33-303	33.1-356
33-304	33.1-357
33-305	33.1-358
33-306	33.1-359
33-307	33.1-360
33-308	33.1-361
33-309	33.1-362
33-310	33.1-363
33-311	33.1-364
33-312	33.1-365
33-313	33.1-366
33-314	33.1-367
33-315	Repealed
33-316	33.1-368
33-317	33.1-369
33-317.1	33.1-370
33-317.2	33.1-371
33-317.3	Repealed
33-318	33.1-372
33-319	33.1-373
33-320	33.1-374
33-321	33.1-375
33-322	33.1-376
33-323	33.1-377
33-324	33.1-378
33-325	33.1-379
33-326	33.1-380
33-327	33.1-381
33-328	33.1-382
33-329	33.1-383
33-330	33.1-384
33-331	33.1-385
None	33.1-33

COMPARABLE SECTIONS OF TITLE 35 AND TITLE 35.1

Former Section	Present Section
35-1	35.1-1
35-2	35.1-27
35-3	Deleted
35-3.1	Deleted
35-4	35.1-5, 35.1-22
35-5	35.1-2
35-6	35.1-22
35-7	35.1-7, 35.1-22
35-8	35.1-13
35-9	35.1-13
35-10	35.1-28 (A) and (F)
35-11	35.1-28 (B) and (E)
35-12	35.1-28 (C)
35-13	35.1-28 (D)
35-14	Deleted
35-15	35.1-22
35-16	35.1-13
35-16.1	35.1-13
35-17	35.1-2
35-18	35.1-13
35-19	Deleted
35-20	35.1-5

Former Section	Present Section
35-21	35.1-7
35-22	35.1-18
35-23	35.1-22
35-24	35.1-4
35-25	35.1-1
35-26	35.1-18, 35.1-21
35-27	35.1-5
35-28	35.1-2, 35.1-14
35-29	Deleted
35-30	35.1-5
35-31	35.1-10
35-32 to 35-37	35.1-14
35-38	35.1-25
35-38.1	35.1-26
35-39	Deleted
35-40	35.1-10
35-41	35.1-7
35-42 to 35-42.8	Deleted
35-43	35.1-1
35-44	35.1-18
35-45	35.1-16
35-46	35.1-16, 35.1-22
35-47	35.1-16, 35.1-22
35-48	35.1-16
35-49	35.1-16
35-50	Deleted
35-51	35.1-22
35-52	35.1-4
35-53	35.1-7
35-54	35.1-1
35-55	35.1-17
35-56	35.1-22
35-57 to 35-78	Deleted

COMPARABLE SECTIONS OF TITLE 37 AND TITLE 37.1

Former Section	Present Section
37-1	37.1-34
37-1.1	37.1-1
37-2	37.1-34
37-3	37.1-35
37-4	37.1-34
37-5	37.1-34
37-6	Repealed
37-6.1	Deleted
37-7	37.1-48
37-8	Deleted
37-9	37.1-36
37-10 to 37-12	Repealed
37-13	37.1-37
37-14	37.1-24
37-15	37.1-148
37-16	37.1-150
37-16.1	Reserved
37-16.2	37.1-38
37-17	37.1-49
37-18	37.1-50
37-19	37.1-51
37-20	37.1-52
37-21	37.1-53
37-22	37.1-54
37-23	37.1-55
37-24	37.1-56
37-25	37.1-57
37-25.1	37.1-58
37-25.2	37.1-59
37-25.3	37.1-60
37-25.4	37.1-61
37-25.5	37.1-62
37-25.6	37.1-62
37-26	37.1-2
37-27	37.1-3
37-28	37.1-4
37-29	37.1-5
37-30	37.1-6
37-31	37.1-7
37-32	37.1-8
37-33	37.1-9
37-34	37.1-10
37-34.1	37.1-11
37-34.2	37.1-12
37-34.2:1	37.1-1
37-34.2:2	37.1-13
37-34.2:3	37.1-14
37-34.2:4	37.1-15
37-34.2:5	37.1-16
37-34.2:6	37.1-17
37-34.2:7	37.1-18
37-34.3	37.1-47
37-35	37.1-19
37-36	37.1-20
37-36.1	37.1-21
37-37	37.1-22
37-38	37.1-23
37-38.1	37.1-24
37-39	37.1-25
37-40	37.1-26
37-41	37.1-25
37-42	Deleted
37-42.1	Deleted
37-43	Repealed
37-44	Deleted
37-45	37.1-27
37-46	37.1-27
37-47	37.1-29
37-48	37.1-30
37-48.1	37.1-28
37-49	37.1-31
37-50	37.1-32
37-51	Deleted
37-52	37.1-37
37-53	37.1-39
37-54	37.1-40
37-55	37.1-41
37-56	37.1-42
37-57	37.1-43
37-58	37.1-44
37-59	37.1-45
37-60	37.1-46
37-61	37.1-67
37-61.1	37.1-64
37-61.2	37.1-88
37-62	Deleted
37-62.1	37.1-80
37-63 to 37-66	Deleted
37-67	37.1-64
37-68 to 37-70	Deleted
37-71	37.1-71
37-71.1	37.1-84
37-71.2	37.1-85
37-71.3	Deleted
37-71.4	37.1-80
37-72	Deleted
37-73	37.1-93
37-74	37.1-94
37-75	37.1-89
37-76	Deleted
37-77	Deleted
37-78	37.1-73
37-79	37.1-71, 37.1-72
37-80	Deleted
37-81	37.1-74
37-82	Repealed
37-83	Deleted
37-84	Deleted
37-85	37.1-75
37-86	Deleted
37-86.1	Deleted
37-86.2	37.1-68
37-87	37.1-78
37-88	Deleted
37-89	Deleted
37-90	37.1-70
37-91	37.1-91
37-91.1	37.1-92
37-91.2	Deleted
37-92	Deleted
37-92.1	37.1-101
37-93	37.1-102
37-94	37.1-98
37-95	37.1-96
37-96	37.1-97
37-97	37.1-76

Former Section	Present Section
37-97.1	37.1-77
37-98	37.1-95
37-99 to 37-109	Deleted
37-110	Repealed
37-110.1	Repealed
37-111	Deleted
37-112	Deleted
37-113	37.1-65
37-114	Deleted
37-115	Deleted
37-116	37.1-71
37-117	Deleted
37-118	Repealed
37-119	Deleted
37-120	37.1-100
37-121	37.1-64
37-121.1 to 37-121.3	Deleted
37-122	37.1-103
37-123	37.1-103, 37.1-104
37-124	37.1-104.1
37-125	37.1-104.2
37-125.1	37.1-105
37-125.2	37.1-106
37-125.3	37.1-107
37-125.4	37.1-108
37-125.5	37.1-109
37-125.6	37.1-110
37-125.7	Repealed
37-125.8	37.1-111
37-125.9	37.1-112
37-125.10	37.1-113
37-125.11	37.1-114
37-125.12	37.1-115
37-125.13	37.1-116
37-125.14	37.1-117
37-125.15	37.1-118
37-126	37.1-120
37-126.1	37.1-48
37-127	Deleted
37-128	37.1-121
37-129	37.1-122
37-130	37.1-119
37-130.1	37.1-123
37-131	37.1-124
37-132	37.1-125
37-132.1 to 37-134	Deleted
37-135	37.1-126
37-135.1	37.1-126
37-136	37.1-127
37-136.1	37.1-128
37-136.2	37.1-129
37-137	37.1-130
37-138	Repealed
37-139	37.1-131
37-139.1	Deleted
37-140	37.1-132
37-141	37.1-134
37-142	Deleted
37-143	Deleted
37-144	37.1-135
37-144.1	37.1-136
37-145	37.1-137
37-146	37.1-138
37-147	37.1-139
37-148	37.1-140
37-149	37.1-141
37-150	37.1-142
37-150.1	37.1-143
37-151	37.1-144
37-152	37.1-145
37-153	37.1-146
37-153.1	37.1-147
37-154 to 37-168	Repealed
37-169	Deleted
37-170	Deleted
37-171 to 37-187	Repealed
37-188	Deleted
37-189	Repealed
37-190	Repealed
37-191	37.1-96
37-192	Deleted
37-193 to 37-204	Repealed
37-204.1	37.1-85
37-205 to 37-209	Repealed
37-210	Deleted
37-211	Deleted
37-212	Repealed
37-213	Deleted
37-214 to 37-215.1	Repealed
37-216	Deleted
37-217 to 37-222	Repealed
37-223	Deleted
37-224 to 37-226	Repealed
37-227	37.1-149
37-228	37.1-151
37-229	37.1-152
37-230	37.1-153
37-230.1	37.1-33
37-230.2	37.1-154
37-231	37.1-156
37-231.1	Deleted
37-232	37.1-157
37-233	37.1-158
37-234	37.1-159
37-235	37.1-160
37-236	37.1-161
37-237	37.1-162
37-238	37.1-163
37-239	37.1-164
37-240	37.1-165
37-241	37.1-166
37-242	37.1-167
37-243	37.1-168
37-244	37.1-169
37-245	37.1-170
37-246	37.1-171
37-247	37.1-172
37-248	37.1-173
37-249	37.1-174
37-250	37.1-175
37-251	37.1-176
37-252	37.1-177
37-253	37.1-178
37-254	37.1-179
37-254.1	37.1-1
37-255	37.1-180
37-256	37.1-181
37-257	37.1-182
37-257.1	37.1-183
37-257.2	Repealed
37-258	37.1-184
37-258.1	37.1-185
37-258.2	37.1-186
37-258.3	37.1-187
37-259	37.1-188
37-260	37.1-189
None	37.1-63
None	37.1-66
None	37.1-69
None	37.1-79
None	37.1-81
None	37.1-82
None	37.1-83
None	37.1-86
None	37.1-87
None	37.1-96
None	37.1-99
None	37.1-133
None	37.1-155
None	37.1-190 to 37.1-202

COMPARABLE SECTIONS OF TITLE 38.1 AND TITLE 38.2

Former Section	Present Section
38.1-1	38.2-100
	38.2-4100
38.1-2	38.2-101
38.1-3	38.2-102
38.1-4	38.2-106
38.1-5	38.2-109
38.1-6	38.2-110
38.1-7	38.2-111
38.1-8	38.2-112
38.1-9	38.2-113
38.1-10	38.2-114
38.1-11	38.2-115
38.1-12	38.2-111
38.1-13	38.2-116
38.1-14	Repealed
38.1-15	38.2-117
38.1-16	38.2-118
38.1-17	38.2-119
38.1-18	38.2-120
	38.2-121
38.1-19	38.2-122
38.1-20	38.2-123
38.1-21	38.2-124
	38.2-125
38.1-22	38.2-126
38.1-22.1	38.2-127
38.1-23	38.2-133
38.1-24	38.2-134
38.1-25	38.2-135
38.1-26	38.2-136
38.1-29	38.2-200
38.1-29.1	38.2-203
38.1-30	38.2-201
38.1-30.1	38.2-202
38.1-31	38.2-204
38.1-31.1	38.2-206
38.1-31.2	38.2-207
38.1-31.3	38.2-513
38.1-32	38.2-208
38.1-32.1	38.2-209
38.1-33	38.2-210
38.1-34	38.2-211
38.1-35	38.2-212
38.1-36	38.2-213
38.1-36.1	38.2-214
38.1-37	38.2-215
38.1-38	38.2-216
38.1-39	38.2-217
38.1-39.1	38.2-230
38.1-40	38.2-218
38.1-41	38.2-221
38.1-42	38.2-225
38.1-42.1	38.2-226
38.1-42.2	38.2-227
38.1-43	Repealed
38.1-43.01	38.2-231
38.1-43.1	38.2-900
38.1-43.2	38.2-901
38.1-43.3	38.2-902
38.1-43.4	38.2-903
38.1-43.5	38.2-904
38.1-43.6	Repealed
38.1-43.7	38.2-3420
38.1-43.8	38.2-3421
38.1-43.9	38.2-3422
38.1-43.10	38.2-3423
38.1-43.11	38.2-3424
38.1-44	38.2-400
38.1-44.1	38.2-401
38.1-45	38.2-403
38.1-46	38.2-404
38.1-47	38.2-405
38.1-48	38.2-406
38.1-48.1	38.2-402
38.1-48.2	38.2-402
	38.2-407
38.1-48.3	38.2-408
38.1-48.4	38.2-409
38.1-48.5	38.2-410
38.1-48.6	38.2-411
38.1-48.7	38.2-412
38.1-48.8	Repealed
38.1-48.9	38.2-413
38.1-48.10	Repealed
38.1-49	38.2-500
38.1-50	38.2-501
38.1-51	Repealed
38.1-52	Repealed
38.1-52.1	38.2-502
38.1-52.2	38.2-503
38.1-52.3	38.2-504
38.1-52.4	38.2-505
38.1-52.5	38.2-506
38.1-52.6	38.2-507
38.1-52.7	38.2-508
38.1-52.8	38.2-509
38.1-52.9	38.2-510
38.1-52.10	38.2-511
38.1-52.11	38.2-512
38.1-52.12	38.2-513
38.1-52.13	38.2-514
38.1-52.14	Repealed
38.1-53	38.2-515
38.1-54 to	
38.1-57.2	Repealed
38.1-57.3	38.2-600
38.1-57.4	38.2-601
38.1-57.5	38.2-602
38.1-57.6	38.2-603
38.1-57.7	38.2-604
38.1-57.8	38.2-605
38.1-57.9	38.2-606
38.1-57.10	38.2-607
38.1-57.11	38.2-608
38.1-57.12	38.2-609
38.1-57.13	38.2-610
38.1-57.14	38.2-611
38.1-57.15	38.2-612
38.1-57.16	38.2-613
38.1-57.17	38.2-614
38.1-57.18	38.2-615
38.1-57.19	38.2-616
38.1-57.20 to	
38.1-57.22	Repealed
38.1-57.24	38.2-617
38.1-57.25	38.2-618
38.1-57.26	38.2-619
38.1-57.27	Repealed
38.1-57.28	38.2-620
38.1-58	38.2-700
38.1-59	38.2-701
38.1-60	38.2-702
38.1-61	38.2-703
38.1-62	38.2-704
38.1-63	Repealed
38.1-64	38.2-801
38.1-65	38.2-802
38.1-66	38.2-803
38.1-67	38.2-804
38.1-68	38.2-805
38.1-69	38.2-806
38.1-70	38.2-807
38.1-70.1	Repealed
38.1-70.2	38.2-809
38.1-70.3	38.2-810
38.1-70.4	38.2-811
38.1-70.9 to	
38.1-70.12	Repealed
38.1-70.13	Repealed
38.1-71	38.2-1000
38.1-72	Repealed
38.1-73	Repealed
38.1-74	38.2-1001
38.1-75	38.2-1002
38.1-76	38.2-1003
38.1-77	38.2-1004
38.1-79	38.2-1005
38.1-80	38.2-1017
38.1-81	38.2-1018
38.1-82	Repealed
38.1-83	38.2-1027
38.1-84	Repealed
38.1-85	38.2-1024
38.1-85.1	Repealed
38.1-86	38.2-1024
38.1-87	38.2-1026
38.1-88	38.2-1028
38.1-89	38.2-1033
38.1-90	38.2-1035
38.1-91	38.2-1032
38.1-92	38.2-1034
38.1-92.1	38.2-1034
38.1-93	38.2-1035
38.1-94	38.2-1029
38.1-95	38.2-1031
38.1-95.1	38.2-1030
38.1-96	38.2-1036

Former Section	Present Section
38.1-97	38.2-1037
38.1-97.1	Repealed
38.1-97.2	38.2-1038
38.1-98	38.2-1025
38.1-98.1	38.2-1039
38.1-99	38.2-1040
38.1-100	38.2-1041
38.1-101	38.2-1042
38.1-102	38.2-1043
38.1-103	38.2-1044
38.1-104 to 38.1-107	Repealed
38.1-108	38.2-1045
38.1-109	Repealed
38.1-110	38.2-1046
38.1-111	38.2-1047
38.1-112	38.2-1048
38.1-113	38.2-1049
38.1-114	38.2-1050
38.1-115	38.2-1051
38.1-116	38.2-1052
38.1-117	38.2-1053
38.1-118	38.2-1054
38.1-119	38.2-1055
38.1-120	38.2-1056
38.1-121	38.2-1057
38.1-122	38.2-1058
38.1-123 to 38.1-125	Repealed
38.1-126	38.2-1500
38.1-127	38.2-1501
38.1-128	38.2-1502
38.1-129	38.2-1501 38.2-1503
38.1-130	38.2-1504
38.1-131	38.2-1505
38.1-131.1	38.2-1506
38.1-132	38.2-1507
38.1-133	38.2-1508
38.1-133.1	38.2-1509
38.1-134	38.2-1510
38.1-135	38.2-1511
38.1-136	38.2-1512
38.1-137	38.2-1513
38.1-138	38.2-1514
38.1-139	38.2-1515
38.1-140	38.2-1516
38.1-141	38.2-1517
38.1-142	38.2-1518
38.1-143	38.2-1519
38.1-144	38.2-1520
38.1-145	38.2-1521
38.1-159	38.2-1300
38.1-160	38.2-1301
38.1-161	38.2-1302
38.1-162	38.2-1303
38.1-163	38.2-1304
38.1-164	38.2-1305
38.1-165	38.2-1306
38.1-165.1	38.2-1810
38.1-166	38.2-1307

Former Section	Present Section
38.1-167	38.2-1308
38.1-168	38.2-1309
38.1-169	38.2-1310
38.1-170	38.2-1311
38.1-171	38.2-1312
38.1-171.1	38.2-1316
38.1-172	38.2-1313
38.1-173	38.2-1314
38.1-173.1	38.2-1315
38.1-173.2	38.2-1315
38.1-174	38.2-1317
38.1-175	38.2-1318
38.1-176	38.2-1319
38.1-177	38.2-1320
38.1-178	38.2-1321
38.1-178.1	38.2-1322
38.1-178.1:1	38.2-1323
38.1-178.1:2	38.2-1322 38.2-1324
38.1-178.1:3	38.2-1325
38.1-178.1:4	38.2-1326
38.1-178.1:5	Repealed
38.1-178.1:6	38.2-1327
38.1-178.1:7	38.2-1328
38.1-178.2	38.2-1329
38.1-178.3	38.2-1330
38.1-178.3:1	38.2-1331
38.1-178.4	38.2-1332
38.1-178.5	38.2-1333
38.1-178.6 to 38.1-178.8	Repealed
38.1-178.9	38.2-1334
38.1-178.11	38.2-1335
38.1-178.12	38.2-1336
38.1-178.13	38.2-1337
38.1-178.14	38.2-1338
38.1-178.15	38.2-1339
38.1-178.16 to 38.1-178.18	Repealed
38.1-178.19	38.2-1340
38.1-179 to 38.1-217	Repealed
38.1-217.1	38.2-1400
38.1-217.2	38.2-1401
38.1-217.3	38.2-1402
38.1-217.4	38.2-1403
38.1-217.5	38.2-1404
38.1-217.6	38.2-1405
38.1-217.7	38.2-1406
38.1-217.8	38.2-1407
38.1-217.9	38.2-1408
38.1-217.10	38.2-1409
38.1-217.11	38.2-1410
38.1-217.12	38.2-1411
38.1-217.13	Repealed
38.1-217.14	Repealed
38.1-217.15	38.2-1412
38.1-217.16	38.2-1413
38.1-217.17	38.2-1414
38.1-217.18	38.2-1415
38.1-217.19	38.2-1416

Former Section	Present Section
38.1-217.20	38.2-1417
38.1-217.21	38.2-1418
38.1-217.22	38.2-1419
38.1-217.23	38.2-1420
38.1-217.24	38.2-1421
38.1-217.25	38.2-1422
38.1-217.26	38.2-1423
38.1-217.27	38.2-1424
38.1-217.28	38.2-1425
38.1-217.29	38.2-1426
38.1-217.30	38.2-1427
38.1-217.31	38.2-1428
38.1-217.32	38.2-1429
38.1-217.33	38.2-1430
38.1-217.34	38.2-1431
38.1-217.35	38.2-1432
38.1-217.36	38.2-1433
38.1-217.37	38.2-1434
38.1-217.38	38.2-1435
38.1-217.39	38.2-1436
38.1-217.40	38.2-1437
38.1-217.41	38.2-1438
38.1-217.42	38.2-1439
38.1-217.43	38.2-1440
38.1-217.44	38.2-1441
38.1-217.45	38.2-1443
38.1-217.46	38.2-1444
38.1-217.47	38.2-1445
38.1-218	38.2-2000
38.1-219	38.2-100
38.1-220	38.2-2001
38.1-221 to 38.1-223	Repealed
38.1-224	38.2-2002
38.1-225 to 38.1-240	Repealed
38.1-241	38.2-2003
38.1-242	38.2-2004
38.1-243 to 38.1-251	Repealed
38.1-252	38.2-2005
38.1-253	38.2-2006
38.1-254	38.2-2007
38.1-255	38.2-2008
38.1-255.1	Repealed
38.1-255.2	38.2-2009
38.1-256 to 38.1-258	Repealed
38.1-259	38.2-2010
38.1-260	38.2-2011
38.1-261	38.2-2012
38.1-262	38.2-2013
38.1-262.1	Repealed
38.1-263	38.2-2014
38.1-264	38.2-2015
38.2-265	38.2-1317
38.1-266	38.2-2016
38.1-267	38.2-2017
38.1-268	38.2-2018
38.1-269	38.2-2019
38.1-270	38.2-2020

Former Section	Present Section
38.1-271	38.2-2021
38.1-272	38.2-2022
38.1-273	38.2-2023
38.1-274	38.2-2024
38.1-275	38.2-2025
38.1-276	38.2-2026
38.1-277	38.2-2027
38.1-278 to	
38.1-279.28	Repealed
38.1-279.29	38.2-1900
38.1-279.30	38.2-100
	38.2-1901
38.1-279.31	38.2-1902
38.1-279.32	38.2-1903
38.1-279.33	38.2-1904
38.1-279.33:1	38.1-1905
38.1-279.34	38.2-1906
38.1-279.35	38.2-1907
38.1-279.36	38.2-1908
38.1-279.37	38.2-1909
38.1-279.38	38.2-1910
38.1-279.39	38.2-1911
38.1-279.40	38.2-1912
38.1-279.41	38.2-1913
38.1-279.42	38.2-1914
38.1-279.43	38.2-1915
38.1-279.44	Repealed
38.1-279.44:1	38.2-1916
38.1-279.44:2	Repealed
38.1-279.44:3	38.2-1917
38.1-279.45	38.2-1918
38.1-279.46	38.2-1919
38.1-279.47	38.2-1920
38.1-279.48	Repealed
38.1-279.48:1	38.2-317
38.1-279.49	38.2-1921
38.1-279.49:1	38.2-2118
38.1-279.50	38.2-1922
38.1-279.51	38.2-1923
38.1-279.52	38.2-1924
38.1-279.53	38.2-1925
38.1-279.54	38.2-1926
38.1-279.55	38.2-1927
38.1-279.56	38.2-1928
38.1-279.57 to	
38.1-291	Repealed
38.1-292	38.2-1801
38.1-293	Repealed
38.1-294	38.2-1808
38.1-295 to	
38.1-327	Repealed
38.1-327.1	38.2-1800
38.1-327.2	38.2-1801
38.1-327.3	38.2-1802
38.1-327.4	38.2-1803
38.1-327.5	38.2-1804
38.1-327.6	38.2-1805
38.1-327.7	38.2-1806
38.1-327.8	38.2-1808
38.1-327.9	38.2-1809
38.1-327.10	38.2-205
	38.2-1811
38.1-327.11	38.2-1812
38.1-327.12	38.2-1813
38.1-327.13	Repealed
38.1-327.14	Repealed
38.1-327.15	38.2-1814
38.1-327.16	38.2-1816
38.1-327.17	38.2-1817
38.1-327.18	Repealed
38.1-327.19	38.2-1818
38.1-327.20	38.2-1819
38.1-327.21	38.2-1820
38.1-327.22	38.2-1821
38.1-327.23	Repealed
38.1-327.24	38.2-1815
38.1-327.25 to	
38.1-327.32	Repealed
38.1-327.33	38.2-1822
38.1-327.34	38.2-1823
38.1-327.35	38.2-1824
38.1-327.36	38.2-1825
38.1-327.37	38.2-1826
38.1-327.38	38.2-1827
38.1-327.39	38.2-1828
38.1-327.40	38.2-1829
38.1-327.41	Repealed
38.1-327.42	38.2-1830
38.1-327.43	38.2-1831
38.1-327.44	38.2-1832
38.1-327.44:1	38.2-1833
38.1-327.44:2	38.2-1834
38.1-327.44:3	28.2-1835
38.1-327.45	38.2-1836
38.1-327.46	38.2-4800
38.1-327.47	38.2-4801
38.1-327.48	38.2-4802
38.1-327.49	38.2-4803
38.1-327.50	38.2-4804
38.1-327.51	38.2-4805
38.1-327.52	38.2-4806
38.1-327.53	38.2-4807
38.1-327.54	38.2-4809
38.1-327.55	38.2-4810
38.1-327.56	38.2-4811
38.1-327.57	38.2-4812
38.1-327.58	38.2-4813
38.1-327.59	38.2-4814
38.1-327.60	38.2-4815
38.1-327.61	Repealed
38.1-327.62	38.2-1837
38.1-327.63	38.2-1838
38.1-327.64	38.2-1839
38.1-327.65	38.2-1840
38.1-327.66	38.2-1841
38.1-327.67	38.2-1842
38.1-327.68	38.2-1843
38.1-327.69	38.2-1844
38.1-327.70	38.2-1845
38.1-327.71	Repealed
38.1-328	38.2-300
38.1-329	38.2-301
38.1-330	38.2-302
38.1-331	38.2-303
38.1-332	38.2-304
38.1-333	38.2-305
38.1-334	38.2-306
38.1-335	38.2-307
38.1-335.1	38.2-308
38.1-335.2	38.2-2120
38.1-336	38.2-309
38.1-337	38.2-310
38.1-338	38.2-311
38.1-339	38.2-312
38.1-340	38.2-313
38.1-341	38.2-314
38.1-342	38.2-315
38.1-342.1	38.2-316
38.1-342.2	38.2-3405
38.1-343	38.2-318
38.1-344	38.2-319
38.1-345	38.2-320
38.1-346	38.2-3406
38.1-346.1	38.2-321
38.1-347	38.2-3400
38.1-347.1	38.2-3408
38.1-347.2	38.2-3407
38.1-348	38.2-3500
38.1-348.1	38.2-3409
38.1-348.2	38.2-3402
38.1-348.3	38.2-3403
38.1-348.4	38.2-3502
38.1-348.5	38.2-3410
38.1-348.6	38.2-3411
38.1-348.7	38.2-3412
38.1-348.8	38.2-3413
38.1-348.9	38.2-3414
38.1-348.10	38.2-3415
38.1-348.10:1	38.2-3416
38.1-348.11	38.2-3537
	38.2-3541
38.1-348.12	Repealed
38.1-348.12:1	38.2-3417
38.1-348.13	38.2-3418
38.1-348.14	38.2-3419
38.1-349	38.2-3503
	38.2-3515
38.1-350	38.2-3504
38.1-351	38.2-3505
38.1-352	38.2-3506
38.1-353	38.2-3507
38.1-354	38.2-3508
38.1-354.1	38.2-3404
38.1-355	38.2-3509
38.1-356	38.2-3510
38.1-356.01	38.2-3542
38.1-356.1	38.2-1807
38.1-357	38.2-3511
38.1-358	38.2-3512
38.1-359	38.2-3513
38.1-360	38.2-3400
38.1-361	Repealed
38.1-361.1	38.2-3514

Former Section	Present Section
38.1-362 to 38.1-362.6	Repealed
38.1-362.7	38.2-3600
38.1-362.8	38.2-3501
38.1-362.8:1	38.2-3601
38.1-362.8:2	38.2-3602
38.1-362.8:3	38.2-3603
38.1-362.9	Repealed
38.1-362.10	Repealed
38.1-362.11	32.8-3516
38.1-362.12	38.2-3517
38.1-362.13	38.2-3518
	38.2-3604
38.1-362.14	38.2-3519
38.1-362.15	38.2-3520
	38.2-3605
38.1-362.16	38.2-3606
38.1-362.17	38.2-3607
38.1-363	38.2-2101
38.1-363.1	38.2-2102
38.1-364	38.2-2103
38.1-365	38.2-2104
38.1-366	38.2-2105
38.1-367	38.2-2104
	38.2-2106
38.1-367.1	38.2-2107
38.1-367.2	38.2-2108
38.1-368	38.2-2109
38.1-369	38.2-2110
38.1-370	38.2-2111
38.1-371	38.2-2112
38.1-371.1	38.2-2113
38.1-371.2	38.2-2114
38.1-372	38.2-2116
38.1-373	38.2-2117
38.1-374	38.2-2119
38.1-375	38.2-2121
38.1-376	38.2-2122
38.1-377	Repealed
38.1-378	38.2-2123
38.1-379	Repealed
38.1-379.1	38.2-3000
38.1-379.2	38.2-3001
38.1-379.3	Repealed
38.1-380	38.2-2200
38.1-380.1	38.2-2201
38.1-380.2	38.2-2202
38.1-380.3	38.2-2203
38.1-381	38.2-2204
	38.2-2205
	38.2-2206
	38.2-2207
38.1-381.1	38.2-2208
38.1-381.2	38.2-2209
38.1-381.3	38.2-2210
38.1-381.4	38.2-2211
38.1-381.5	38.2-2212
38.1-381.6	38.2-2213
38.1-381.7	38.2-2214
38.1-381.8	38.2-2215
38.1-381.9	38.2-2216

Former Section	Present Section
38.1-381.10	38.2-2217
38.1-382	38.2-2218
38.1-382.1	Repealed
38.1-383	38.2-2219
38.1-384	38.2-2220
38.1-385	38.2-2221
38.1-386	38.2-2222
38.1-387	38.2-2223
38.1-387.1	38.2-2224
38.1-388	38.2-2225
38.1-389	Repealed
38.1-389.1	38.2-2226
38.1-389.2	38.2-2227
38.1-389.3	Repealed
38.1-389.3:1	38.2-2228
38.1-389.4	38.2-2300
38.1-390	38.2-3300
38.1-390.1	38.2-3301
38.1-391	38.2-3302
38.1-392	38.2-3303
38.1-393	38.2-3304
38.1-394	38.2-3305
38.1-395	38.2-3306
38.1-396	38.2-3307
38.1-397	Repealed
38.1-397.1	38.2-3308
38.1-398	38.2-3309
38.1-399	38.2-3310
38.1-400	38.2-3311
38.1-401	38.2-3312
38.1-402	38.2-3313
38.1-403	38.2-3314
38.1-404	38.2-3315
38.1-405	38.2-3300
38.1-406	38.2-3316
	38.2-3338
38.1-407	38.2-3317
38.1-408	38.2-3114
38.1-408.1	38.2-3112
38.1-409	38.2-3340
38.1-410	38.2-3341
38.1-410.1	38.2-3342
38.1-411	38.2-3343
38.1-412	38.2-3344
38.1-413	38.2-3345
38.1-414	38.2-3346
38.1-415	38.2-3347
38.1-416	38.2-3348
38.1-417	38.2-3349
38.1-418	38.2-3350
38.1-419	38.2-3351
38.1-420	38.2-3352
38.1-421	38.2-3353
38.1-422	38.2-3354
38.1-424	38.2-3324
38.1-424.1	38.2-3325
38.1-425	38.2-3326
38.1-426	38.2-3327
38.1-426.1	38.2-3328
38.1-427	38.2-3329
38.1-427.1	38.2-3330

Former Section	Present Section
38.1-428	38.2-3331
38.1-428.1	38.2-3332
38.1-428.2	38.2-3333
38.1-428.3	38.2-3334
38.1-428.4	38.2-3331
38.1-429	38.2-3335
38.1-430	38.2-3336
38.1-431	38.2-3100
38.1-432	38.2-3101
38.1-433	38.2-3102
38.1-434	38.2-3103
38.1-435	38.2-3104
38.1-436	38.2-3105
38.1-437	38.2-3106
38.1-438	38.2-3107
38.1-439	38.2-3108
38.1-440	38.2-3109
38.1-441	38.2-3110
38.1-442	38.2-3111
38-1-442.1	38.2-3112
38.1-443	38.2-3113
38.1-443.1	38.2-3115
38.1-444	38.2-3118
38.1-445	38.2-3119
38.1-446	38.2-3120
38.1-447	38.2-3121
38.1-448	38.2-3122
38.1-449	38.2-3123
38.1-450	38.2-3124
38.1-451	38.2-3125
38.1-452	38.2-3126
38.1-453	38.2-3127
38.1-454	38.2-3128
38.1-455	38.2-3129
38.1-456	38.2-3130
	to 38.2-3142
38.1-457	38.2-3143
38.1-458	38.2-3144
38.1-459	38.2-3200
38.1-460	38.2-3201
38.1-461	38.2-3202
38.1-462	38.2-3203
38.1-463	38.2-3204
38.1-464	38.2-3205
38.1-465	38.2-3206
38.1-465.1	38.2-3207
38.1-465.2	38.2-3208
38.1-465.3	38.2-3209
38.1-465.4	38.2-3210
38.1-466	38.2-3211
38.1-466.1	38.2-3212
38.1-467	38.2-3213
38.1-468	38.2-3214
38.1-468.1	38.2-3215
38.1-468.2	38.2-3216
38.1-469	38.2-3217
38.1-470	38.2-3218
38.1-470.1	38.2-3219
	to 38.2-3229
38.1-471	38.2-3319
38.1-471.1	38.2-3318

Former Section	Present Section
	38.2-3321
38.1-472	Repealed
38.1-472.1	38.2-3323
38.1-473 to 38.1-479	Repealed
38.1-480	38.2-3320
38.1-481	Repealed
38.1-482	38.2-3339
38.1-482.1	38.2-3700
	38.2-3716
38.1-482.2	38.2-100
	38.2-103
	38.2-109
	38.2-1800
	38.2-3701
38.1-482.3	Repealed
38.1-482.3:1	38.2-3702
38.1-482.4	38.2-3703
	38.2-3704
38.1-482.4:1	Repealed
38.1-482.4:2	38.2-3705
38.1-482.5	38.2-3706
38.1-482.6	38.2-3707
	38.2-3708
	38.2-3709
38.1-482.7	Repealed
38.1-482.7:1	38.2-3710
38.1-482.8	38.2-3711
38.1-482.9	38.2-3712
38.1-482.10	Repealed
38.1-482.11	38.2-3713
38.1-482.12	38.2-3714
38.1-482.12:1	38.2-3715
38.1-482.13 to 38.1-482.17	Repealed
38.1-482.18	38.2-1700
38.1-482.19	38.2-1701
38.1-482.20	38.2-1702
38.1-482.21	38.2-1703
38.1-482.22	38.2-1704
38.1-482.23	38.2-1705
38.1-482.24	38.2-1706
38.1-482.25	38.2-1707
38.1-482.26	38.2-1708
38.1-482.27	38.2-1709
38.1-482.28	38.2-1710
38.1-482.29	38.2-1711
38.1-482.30	38.2-1712
38.1-482.31	38.2-1713
38.1-482.32	38.2-1714
38.1-482.33	38.2-1715
38.1-483	38.2-3544
38.1-484	38.2-3545
38.1-485	38.2-3546
38.1-486	38.2-3547
38.1-487	38.2-3548
38.1-488	38.2-3549
38.1-489	38.2-1006
38.1-490	38.2-1007
38.1-491	38.2-1008
38.1-492	38.2-1009
38.1-493	38.2-1006
38.1-494	38.2-1010
38.1-495	38.2-1011
38.1-495.1	38.2-1012
38.1-495.2	38.2-1013
38.1-495.3	38.2-1014
38.1-495.4	38.2-1015
38.1-495.5	38.2-1016
38.1-496	38.2-3800
38.1-497	38.2-3801
38.1-498	38.2-3802
38.1-499	38.2-3803
38.1-500	Repealed
38.1-501	Repealed
38.1-502	38.2-3804
38.1-503	38.2-3805
38.1-504	38.2-3806
38.1-505	38.2-3807
38.1-506	38.2-3808
38.1-507	38.2-3809
38.1-508	38.2-3810
38.1-509	Repealed
38.1-510	38.2-3811
38.1-511	38.2-3812
38.1-512	38.2-3813
38.1-513	Repealed
38.1-514	38.2-3814
38.1-515	38.2-3815
38.1-516	38.2-3816
38.1-517	38.2-3817
38.1-518	Repealed
38.1-519	38.2-3818
38.1-520 to 38.1-549	Repealed
38.1-549.1	38.2-3900
38.1-549.2	38.2-3901
38.1-549.3	38.2-3902
38.1-549.4	38.2-3903
38.1-549.5	38.2-3904
38.1-549.6	38.2-3905
38.1-549.7	38.2-3906
38.1-549.8	38.2-3907
38.1-549.9	38.2-3908
38.1-549.10	38.2-3909
38.1-549.11	38.2-3910
38.1-549.12	38.2-3911
38.1-549.13	38.2-3912
38.1-549.14	38.2-3913
38.1-549.15	38.2-3914
38.1-549.16	38.2-3915
38.1-549.17	38.2-3916
38.1-549.18	38.2-3917
38.1-549.19	38.2-3918
38.1-549.20	38.2-3919
38.1-549.21	38.2-3920
38.1-549.22	38.2-3921
38.1-549.23	38.2-3922
38.1-549.24	38.2-3923
38.1-550	38.2-4000
38.1-551	38.2-4001
38.1-552	38.2-4002
38.1-553	38.2-4003
38.1-554	38.2-4004
38.1-555	Repealed
38.1-556	38.2-4005
38.1-556.1	Repealed
38.1-557	Repealed
38.1-558	38.2-4008
38.1-559	Repealed
38.1-560	38.2-4013
38.1-561	38.2-4019
38.1-562	38.2-4020
38.1-563	38.2-4021
38.1-564	Repealed
38.1-565	38.2-4022
38.1-566 to 38.1-638	Repealed
38.1-638.1	38.2-4100
38.1-638.2	38.2-4101
38.1-638.3	38.2-4102
38.1-638.4	38.2-4123
38.1-638.5	38.2-4135
38.1-638.6	38.2-4107
38.1-638.7	38.2-4113
	38.2-4114
38.1-638.8	38.2-4106
38.1-638.9	38.2-4124
38.1-638.10	38.2-4134
38.1-638.11	38.2-4110
38.1-638.12	38.2-4136
38.1-638.13	38.2-4102
38.1-638.14	38.2-4109
38.1-638.15	38.2-4109
38.1-638.16	38.2-4109
38.1-638.17	38.2-4109
38.1-638.18	38.2-4109
38.1-638.19	38.2-4109
38.1-638.20	38.2-4127
38.1-638.21 to 38.1-638.23	38.2-4129
38.1-638.23:1	Repealed
38.1-638.24	38.2-4130
38.1-638.25	38.2-4111
38.1-638.26	38.2-4108
38.1-638.27	38.2-4111
38.1-638.28	38.2-4105
	38.2-4119
38.1-638.29	38.2-4101
	38.2-4116
	38.2-4117
38.1-638.30	38.2-4119
38.1-638.31	38.2-4116
38.1-638.32	38.2-4117
38.1-638.33	38.2-4118
38.1-638.34	38.2-4120
38.1-638.35	38.2-4119
38.1-638.36	38.2-4112
38.1-638.37	38.2-4132
38.1-638.38	38.2-4137
38.1-638.39 to 38.1-638.41	Repealed
38.1-638.42	38.2-4122

Former Section	Present Section
38.1-638.43	38.2-4121
38.1-638.44	38.2-4126
38.1-638.45	38.2-4125
	38.2-4126
38.1-638.46	Repealed
38.1-638.47	38.2-4106
38.1-638.48	38.2-4128
38.1-638.49	38.2-4130
38.1-638.50	38.2-4128
	38.2-4131
38.1-638.51	38.2-4128
38.1-638.52	38.2-4131
38.1-638.53 to 38.1-638.59	38.2-4115
38.1-638.60	38.2-4133
38.1-638.61	Repealed
38.1-639	38.2-2400
38.1-640	38.2-2401
38.1-641	38.2-2403
38.1-642	38-2-2404
38.1-643	38-2-2405
38.1-644	38-2-2406
38.1-644.1	38.2-2407
38.1-644.2	38.2-2408
38.1-645	38.2-2409
38.1-646	38.2-2410
38.1-647	38.2-2411
38.1-648	38.2-2412
38.1-649	38.2-2413
38.1-650	38.2-2414
38.1-651	38.2-2415
38.1-652	Repealed
38.1-653	38.2-2416
38.1-654	38.2-2417
38.1-655	38.2-2418
38.1-656	38.2-2419
38.1-657	38.2-2420
38.1-658	38.2-2500
38.1-659	38.2-2501
	38.2-2503
38.1-660	38.2-2502
	38.2-2503
38.1-661	38.2-2504
38.1-662	38.2-2506
38.1-663 to 38.1-665	Repealed
38.1-666	38.2-2508
38.1-667	38.2-2509
38.1-667.1	38.2-2510
38.1-668	38.2-2511
38.1-669	38.2-2512
38.1-669.1	38.2-2513
38.1-670	38.2-2513
38.1-671	38.2-2514
38.1-672	38.2-2515
38.1-673	38.2-2516
38.1-674	38.2-2527
38.1-675	38.2-2528
38.1-676	38.2-2519
38.1-677	38.2-2518
38.1-678	38.2-2523

Former Section	Present Section
38.1-679	38.2-2518
38.1-680	38.2-2518
38.1-681	38.2-2524
38.1-681.1	38-2-1034
38.1-682	Repealed
38.1-683	38.2-2518
38.1-683.1	38.2-2520
38.1-684	38.2-2521
38.1-685	38.2-2522
38.1-686	Repealed
38.1-687	38.2-2505
38.1-687.1	Repealed
38.1-688	38.2-1200
38.1-689	38.2-1201
38.1-690	38.2-1202
38.1-691	38.2-1203
38.1-692	38.2-1204
38.1-693	38.2-1204
38.1-694	38.2-1205
38.1-695	38.2-1206
38.1-695.1	38.2-1207
38.1-696	38.2-1208
38.1-698	38.2-1209
38.1-699	38.2-1210
38.1-700	38.2-1223
38.1-700.1	38.2-1211
38.1-701	38.2-1224
38.1-702	38.2-1212
38.1-703	38.2-1213
38.1-704	38.2-1214
38.1-705	38.2-1215
38.1-706	38.2-1216
38.1-707	38.2-1217
38.1-708	38.2-1218
38.1-709	38.2-1219
38.1-710	38.2-1220
38.1-711	38.2-1221
38.1-712	38.2-1222
38.1-713	38.2-1225
38.1-714	38.2-1226
38.1-715	38.2-1227
38.1-716	38.2-1212
38.1-717	38.2-1228
38.1-718	38.2-1229
38.1-719	Repealed
38.1-720	38.2-4600
38.1-721	38.2-4601
38.1-722	38.2-4602
38.1-723	38.2-4603
38.1-724	38.2-4604
38.1-725	38.2-4605
38.1-726	38.2-4606
38.1-727	38.2-4607
38.1-728	38.2-4608
38.1-729	38.2-4609
38.1-730	38.2-4610
38.1-731	38.2-4611
38.1-732	38.2-4612
38.1-733	38.2-4613
38.1-733.1	38.2-4614
38.1-734	38.2-4615

Former Section	Present Section
38.1-735	38.2-4700
38.1-736	38.2-4701
38.1-737	38.2-4702
38.1-738	38.2-4703
38.1-739	38.2-4704
38.1-740	Repealed
38.1-740.1	38.2-4705
38.1-740.2	38.2-4706
38.1-741	38.2-4707
38.1-742	38.2-4708
38.1-743	38.2-4709
38.1-744	38.2-4710
38.1-745	38.2-4711
	38.2-4712
38.1-746	38.2-2700
38.1-747	38.2-2701
38.1-748	38.2-2702
	38.2-2704
	38.2-2705
38.1-748.1	38.2-2702
	38.2-2706
38.1-749	38.2-2707
38.1-750	38.2-2708
38.1-751	38.2-2709
38.1-752	38.2-2710
38.1-753	38.2-2711
38.1-754	38.2-2712
38.1-755	Repealed
38.1-755.1	38.2-2713
38.1-756	Repealed
38.1-756.1	Repealed
38.1-757	38.2-1600
38.1-758	38.2-1601
38.1-759	38.2-1602
38.1-760	38.2-1603
38.1-761	38.2-1604
38.1-762	38.2-1605
38.1-763	38.2-1606
38.1-764	38.2-1607
38.1-765	38.2-1606
	38.2-1608
38.1-766	38.2-1609
38.1-767	38.2-1610
38.1-768	38.2-1611
38.1-769	38.2-1612
38.1-770	38.2-1613
38.1-771	38.2-1614
38.1-772	38.2-1615
38.1-773	38.2-1616
38.1-774	38.2-1617
38.1-775	38.2-2800
38.1-776	38.2-2801
38.1-776.1	38.2-2802
38.1-776.2	38.2-2801
38.1-777	38.2-2803
38.1-778	38.2-2804
38.1-779	38.2-2805
38.1-780	38.2-2806
38.1-781	38.2-2807
38.1-782	38.2-2808
38.1-783	38.2-2809

Former Section	Present Section
38.1-784	38.2-2810
38.1-785	38.2-2811
38.1-786	38.2-2812
38.1-787	38.2-2813
38.1-788	38.2-2814
38.1-789	Repealed
38.1-790	Repealed
38.1-791	38.2-4400
38.1-792	38.2-4402
38.1-793	38.2-4402
38.1-793.1	38.2-4403
38.1-794	38.2-4404
38.1-795	38.2-4405
38.1-796	38.2-4406
38.1-797	38.2-4407
38.1-798	38.2-4408
	38.2-4409
38.1-799	38.2-4410
38.1-800	38.2-4411
38.1-801	38.2-4412
38.1-802	38.2-4401
	38.2-4413
	38.2-4416
38.1-803	38.2-4414
38.1-804	38.2-4415
38.1-805	38.2-4417
38.1-806	Repealed
38.1-807	Repealed
38.1-808	Repealed
38.1-809	38.2-4418
38.1-810	38.2-4202
38.1-811	38.2-4203
38.1-812	38.2-4204
38.1-813	Repealed
38.1-813.1	38.2-4200
38.1-813.2	38.2-4206
38.1-813.3	38.2-4207
38.1-813.4	38.2-4208
	38.2-4209
38.1-814	38.2-4210
38.1-815	38.2-4211
38.1-816	38.2-4208
	38.2-4212
	38.2-4213
38.1-817	38.2-4212
38.1-818	38.2-4214
	38.2-4215
38.1-818.1	Repealed
38.1-818.2	38.2-4216
38.1-819	38.2-4217
38.1-820	38.2-4218
38.1-821	38.2-4219
38.1-822	Repealed
38.1-822.1	Repealed
38.1-823	38.2-4200
38.1-824	38.2-4221
38.1-825	38.2-4222
38.1-826	38.2-4223
38.1-827	38.2-4224
38.1-828	38.2-4225
	38.2-4226
38.1-829	38.2-4227
38.1-830 to 38.1-832	Repealed
38.1-833	38.2-4228
38.1-834 to 38.1-862	Repealed
38.1-863	38.2-4300
38.1-864	38.2-4301
38.1-865	38.2-4302
38.1-866	38.2-4303
38.1-867	38.2-4304
38.1-868	38.2-4305
38.1-869	38.2-4306
38.1-870	38.2-4307
38.1-871	Repealed
38.1-872	38.2-4308
38.1-873	38.2-4309
38.1-874	38.2-4310
38.1-875	38.2-4311
38.1-876	38.2-4312
38.1-877	38.2-4313
38.1-878	38.2-4314
38.1-879	38.2-4315
38.1-880	38.2-4316
38.1-881	38.2-4317
38.1-882	Repealed
38.1-883	38.2-4302
	38.2-4318
	38.2-4319
38.1-884 to 38.1-886	Repealed
38.1-887	38.2-4319
38.1-888	Repealed
38.1-889	38.2-4320
38.1-890	38.2-4321
38.1-891	Repealed
38.1-892	38.2-4502
38.1-893	38.2-4503
38.1-894	38.2-4500
38.1-895	38.2-4504
38.1-896	38.2-4505
38.1-897	38.2-4506
	38.2-4507
38.1-898	38.2-4508
38.1-899	38.2-4509
38.1-900	38.2-4510
38.1-901	38.2-4511
38.1-902	38.2-4512
38.1-903	38.2-4513
	38.2-4514
38.1-904	38.2-4515
38.1-905	38.2-4516
38.1-906	38.2-4517
38.1-907	38.2-4518
38.1-908	38.2-4519
38.1-909	38.2-4520
	38.2-4521
38.1-910	38.2-4522
38.1-911 to 38.1-913	Repealed
38.1-914	38.2-4523
38.1-915	Repealed
38.1-916	38.2-1100
38.1-917	38.2-1101
38.1-918	38.2-1102
38.1-919	38.2-1103
38.1-920	38.2-1104
38.1-921	38.2-1105
38.1-922	38.2-1106
38.1-923 to 38.1-925	Repealed
38.1-926	38.2-1107
38.1-927	38.2-1603
38.1-928	38.2-1108
38.1-929	Repealed
38.1-930	38.2-1109
38.1-931	Repealed
38.1-932	38.2-2600
38.1-933	38.2-2601
	38.2-2602
	38.2-2603
38.1-934	38.2-2604
38.1-935	38.2-2605
38.1-936	38.2-2606
38.1-937	38.2-2607
38.1-938	38.2-2608
38.1-939	38.2-2609
38.1-940	38.2-2610
38.1-941	38.2-2611
38.1-942	38.2-2612
38.1-943	38.2-2613
38.1-944	38.2-2600
	38.2-2614
38.1-945	38.2-2602
	38.2-2615
38.1-946 to 38.1-948	Repealed
38.1-949	38.2-1019
38.1-950	38.2-1020
38.1-951	38.2-1021
38.1-952	38.2-1022
38.1-953	38.2-1023
38.1-954	Repealed
38.1-955	38.2-4900
38.1-956	38.2-4901
38.1-957	38.2-4902
38.1-958	38.2-4903
38.1-959	38.2-4904
38.1-960	38.2-4905
38.1-961	38.2-4906
38.1-962	38.2-4907
38.1-963	38.2-4908
38.1-964	38.2-4909
38.1-965	38.2-4910
38.1-966	38.2-4911
38.1-967	38.2-4912
38.1-968	38.2-4913
38.1-969	38.2-4914
38.1-970	38.2-4915
38.1-971	38.2-4916

COMPARABLE SECTIONS OF TITLE 40 AND TITLE 40.1

Former Section	Present Section
40-1	40.1-1
40-1.1	40.1-2
40-1.2	40.1-3
40-2	40.1-4
40-3	40.1-5
40-4	40.1-6
40-5	40.1-7
40-6	40.1-8
40-7	40.1-9
40-8	40.1-10
40-9	40.1-11
40-9.1	40.1-12
40-9.2	40.1-13
40-10 to 40-15	Repealed
40-16	40.1-18
40-17	Repealed
40-18	40.1-20
40-18.1	40.1-12
40-18.2	40.1-13
40-18.3	40.1-14
40-18.4	40.1-15
40-18.5	40.1-16
40-18.6	40.1-17
40-18.7	40.1-18
40-18.8	40.1-19
40-18.9	40.1-20
40-18.10	40.1-21
40-19	40.1-21
40-20	40.1-22
40-20.1	40.1-23
40-20.2	40.1-24
40-20.3	40.1-25
40-21	40.1-26
40-22	40.1-27
40-22.1	40.1-28
40-23	Repealed
40-34	40.1-35
40-35	40.1-36
40-36	40.1-37
40-37	40.1-38
40-38 to 40-43	Repealed
40-44	40.1-39
40-44.1	40.1-40
40-45 to 40-54	Repealed
40-54.1	40.1-41
41-55	40.1-42
40-56	40.1-43
40-57	40.1-44
40-58	40.1-45
40-59, 40-60	Repealed
40-61	40.1-46
40-61.1	40.1-47
40-61.2	40.1-48
40-61.3	40.1-49
40-62	Deleted
40-62.1	40.1-50
49-62.2	40.1-51
40-63	40.1-52
40-64	40.1-53
40-64.1	40.1-54
40-64.2	40.1-54.1
40-64.3	40.1-54.2
40-65	40.1-55
40-66	40.1-56
40-67	40.1-57
40-68	40.1-58
40-69	40.1-59
40-70	40.1-60
40-71	40.1-61
40-72	40.1-62
40-73	40.1-63
40-74	40.1-64
40-74.1	40.1-65
40-74.2	40.1-66
40-74.3	40.1-67
40-74.4	40.1-68
40-74.5	40.1-69
40-75 to 40-95	Repealed
40-95.1	40.1-70
40-95.2	40.1-71
40-95.3	40.1-72
40-95.4	40.1-73
40-95.5	40.1-74
40-95.6	40.1-75
40-95.7	40.1-76
40-95.8	40.1-77
40-96	40.1-78
40-96.1	40.1-79
40-97	40.1-80
40-98	40.1-81
40-98.1	40.1-82
40-99	40.1-83
40-100	40.1-84
40-100.1	40.1-85
40-100.2	40.1-86
40-100.3	40.1-87
40-100.4	40.1-88
40-100.4:1	40.1-89
40-100.5	40.1-90
40-100.6	40.1-91
40-101	40.1-92
40-102	40.1-93
40-103	40.1-94
40-104	40.1-95
40-105	40.1-96
40-106	40.1-97
40-107	40.1-98
40-108	40.1-99
40-109	40.1-100
40-110	40.1-101
40-111	40.1-102
40-112	40.1-103
40-113	40.1-104
40-114	40.1-105
40-115	40.1-106
40-116	40.1-107
40-117	40.1-108
40-118	40.1-109
40-118.1	40.1-110
40-118.2	40.1-111
40-118.3	40.1-112
40-119	40.1-113
40-120	40.1-114
40-121	40.1-115
40-122	40.1-116
40-123	40.1-117
40-124	40.1-118
40-125	40.1-119
40-126	40.1-120
40-127	40.1-121
40-128	40.1-122
40-129	40.1-123
40-130	40.1-124
40-131	40.1-125
40-132	40.1-126
40-133 to 40-146	Deleted
41-1	41.1-1
41-2	41.1-2
41-3 to 41-7	Repealed
41-8	41.1-3
41-8.1	41.1-4
41-8.2	41.1-5
41-8.3	41.1-6
41-9	41.1-7
41-10 to 41-38	Repealed
41-39	41.1-8
41-40 to 41-67	Repealed
41-68	41.1-9
41-69	41.1-10
41-70	41.1-11
41-71	41.1-12
41-72 to 41-74	Deleted
41-75	41.1-13
41-76	41.1-14
41-77	41.1-15
41-78 to 41-83	Repealed
41-84	41.1-16
41-85	41.1-17
41-86	Deleted
41-87	41.1-18
41-88	41.1-19
41-89	41.1-20

COMPARABLE SECTIONS OF TITLE 45 AND TITLE 45.1

Former Section	Present Section
45-0.1	45.1-1
45-9.2	45.1-2
45-1	45.1-3
45-2	45.1-3
45-3	45.1-3
45-4	45.1-4
45-4.1	45.1-5
45-5	45.1-4
45-6	45.1-4
45-7	45.1-21
45-8	45.1-104
45-9	45.1-5
45-10	45.1-27, 45.1-91
45-11	45.1-28
45-12	45.1-5, 45.1-21
45-12.1	Deleted
45-13	Repealed
45-14	45.1-6
45-14.1	45.1-89
45-15	Repealed
45-16	45.1-32
45-17	45.1-105
45-17.1	45.1-22
45-17.2	45.1-23
45-17.3	45.1-24
45-17.4	45.1-25
45-18	45.1-7
45-19	45.1-7
45-20	45.1-7
45-21	45.1-7
45-22	Deleted
45-23	45.1-12
45-24	45.1-8
45-25	45.1-9
45-26	45.1-10
45-27	45.1-11
45-28	45.1-12
45-29	45.1-13
45-30	45.1-15
45-31	45.1-13, 45.1-14
45-32	45.1-18, 45.1-19, 45.1-65
45-33	45.1-20, 45.1-65, 45.1-96
45-33.1	45.1-14
45-34	45.1-16
45-35	45.1-17
45-36, 45-37	Repealed
45-38	45.1-93
45-39	Deleted
45-40	45.1-17
45-41	Deleted
45-42	Deleted
45-43	45.1-90
45-44, 45-45	Repealed
45-45.1	Deleted
45-46 to 45-53	Repealed
45-53.1	45.1-45, 45.1-48
45-53.2	45.1-44
45-53.3	45.1-46
45-53.4	45.1-47
45-53.5	45.1-48
45-53.6	45.1-49
45-53.7	45.1-50
45-53.8	45.1-51
45-54 to 45-60	Repealed
45-60.1	45.1-54
45-60.2	45.1-55
45-60.3	45.1-58, 45.1-63
45-60.4	45.1-56, 45.1-57, 45.1-59, 45.1-60, 45.1-61, 45.1-65, 45.1-77
45-60.5	45.1-62
45-61	45.1-42
45-62 to 45-68	Repealed
45-68.1	45.1-41, 45.1-42, 45.1-65
45-68.2	45.1-40
45-68.3	45.1-41
45-68.4	45.1-21, 45.1-68, 45.1-69
45-69	45.1-21
45-69.1	45.1-73
45-69.2	45.1-74
45-69.3	45.1-72
45-69.4	45.1-70
45-69.5	45.1-71
45-69.6	45.1-101
45-69.7	45.1-35, 45.1-64, 45.1-65
45-70	45.1-97
45-71	45.1-57, 45.1-94
45-71.1	45.1-95
45-72	45.1-26, 45.1-98
45-73	45.1-21
45-74	45.1-5
45-75	45.1-21
45-76	Repealed
45-77	45.1-67
45-77.1	45.1-66
45-78	45.1-21
45-79	45.1-21
45-81	45.1-21
45-82	45.1-75, 45.1-78
45-82.1	45.1-78
45-82.2	45.1-76
45-82.3	45.1-75, 45.1-80
45-82.4	45.1-81
45-82.5	45.1-84
45-82.6	45.1-86
45-82.7	45.1-98
45-83	45.1-21, 45.1-83
45-84	45.1-104
45-85	45.1-30
45-85.1	45.1-87
45-85.2	Deleted
45-85.3	45.1-88
45-85.4	Deleted
45-85.5	45.1-34
45-85.6	45.1-35
45-85.7	45.1-36
45-85.8	45.1-37
45-85.9	45.1-39
45-85.10	Deleted
45-86	45.1-99
45-87	45.1-31
45-88	45.1-29
45-89	45.1-29
45-90	Deleted
45-91	45.1-102
45-92	45.1-103
45-93	45.1-103
45-94 to 45-105	Repealed
45-106	45.1-106
45-107	Repealed
45-107.1	45.1-107
45-108	45.1-108
45-109	45.1-109
45-110	45.1-110
45-111	45.1-111
45-112	45.1-112
45-113	45.1-113
45-114	45.1-114
45-115	45.1-115
45-116	45.1-116
45-117	45.1-117
45-118	45.1-118
45-119	45.1-119
45-120	45.1-120
45-121	45.1-121
45-122	45.1-122
45-123	45.1-123
45-124	45.1-124
45-125	45.1-125
45-126	45.1-126
45-127	45.1-127
45-128	45.1-128
45-129	45.1-129
45-130	45.1-130
45-131	45.1-131
45-132	45.1-132
45-133	45.1-133
45-134	45.1-134
45-135	45.1-135
45-136	45.1-136
45-137	45.1-137
45-138	45.1-138
45-139	45.1-139
45-140	45.1-140
45-141	45.1-141
45-142	45.1-142
45-143	45.1-143
45-144	45.1-144
45-145	45.1-145
45-146	45.1-146
45-147	45.1-147

Former Section	Present Section
45-148	45.1-148
45-149	45.1-149
45-150	45.1-150
45-151	45.1-151
45-152	45.1-152
45-153	45.1-153
45-154	45.1-154
45-155	45.1-155
45-156	45.1-156
45-157	45.1-157
None	45.1-33
None	45.1-38
None	45.1-43
None	45.1-52
None	45.1-53
None	45.1-79
None	45.1-82
None	45.1-85
None	45.1-92
None	45.1-100
None	45.1-158
None	45.1-159
None	45.1-160
None	45.1-161

COMPARABLE SECTIONS OF TITLE 45.1, CHAPTERS 1 THROUGH 14 AND TITLE 45.1, CHAPTERS 14.1 THROUGH 14.8

Former Section	Present Section
45.1-1	Repealed
45.1-1.1	45.1-161.2
45.1-1.2	45.1-161.1
45.1-1.3	45.1-161.3
45.1-1.4	45.1-161.4
45.1-1.5	45.1-161.5
45.1-1.6	Deleted
45.1-1.7	45.1-161.9
45.1-1.8	Repealed
45.1-1.9	45.1-161.6
45.1-1.10	45.1-161.7
45.1-2	45.1-161.8
45.1-3	45.1-161.15, 45.1-161.18, 45.1-161.21
45.1-4	45.1-161.16, 45.1-161.17, 45.1-161.19, 45.1-161.20, 45.1-161.21, 45.1-161.23
45.1-5	45.1-161.80, 45.1-161.81, 45.1-161.88, 45.1-161.91, 45.1-161.219
45.1-5.1	Repealed
45.1-5.2	45.1-161.98
45.1-5.3	45.1-161.99, 45.1-161.100
45.1-6	45.1-161.77
45.1-7	45.1-161.24, 45.1-161.27, 45.1-161.42, 45.1-161.45
45.1-8	45.1-161.31, 45.1-161.49
45.1-9	45.1-161.31, 45.1-161.49
45.1-10	45.1-161.25, 45.1-161.43
45.1-11	45.1-161.26, 45.1-161.44
45.1-12	45.1-161.28, 45.1-161.29, 45.1-161.39, 45.1-161.40, 45.1-161.46, 45.1-161.47, 45.1-161.56
45.1-12.1	45.1-161.30, 45.1-161.48
45.1-13	45.1-161.32, 45.1-161.35, 45.1-161.36, 45.1-161.38, 45.1-161.50, 45.1-161.53, 45.1-161.54
45.1-14	45.1-161.28, 45.1-161.33, 45.1-161.38, 45.1-161.51
45.1-15	45.1-161.38
45.1-16	Deleted
45.1-17	45.1-161.210, 45.1-161.213, 45.1-161.214, 45.1-161.249, 45.1-161.251, 45.1-161.258
45.1-18	Deleted
45.1-19	Deleted
45.1-20	45.1-161.171, 45.1-161.208, 45.1-161.209, 45.1-161.213, 45.1-161.256, 45.1-161.257
45.1-20.1	45.1-161.41, 45.1-161.250
45.1-20.2	Deleted
45.1-21	45.1-161.13, 45.1-161.14, 45.1-161.38, 45.1-161.59, 45.1-161.62, 45.1-161.63, 45.1-161.78 to 45.1-161.80, 45.1-161.79 to 45.1-161.87, 45.1-161.159, 45.1-161.252, 45.1-161.258
45.1-22	45.1-161.57
45.1-22.1	45.1-161.60
45.1-23	45.1-161.58
45.1-24	45.1-161.59
45.1-25	45.1-161.61
45.1-26	45.1-161.12, 45.1-161.259
45.1-27	45.1-161.64
45.1-28	45.1-161.65
45.1-29	Repealed
45.1-30	45.1-161.14
45.1-30.1	45.1-161.233
45.1-31	45.1-161.10
45.1-32	45.1-161.11
45.1-33	Repealed
45.1-33.1	45.1-161.67, 45.1-161.68
45.1-33.2	45.1-161.69
45.1-33.3	45.1-161.70
45.1-33.4	45.1-161.71
45.1-33.5	45.1-161.72
45.1-33.5:1	45.1-161.73
45.1-33.5:2	45.1-161.74
45.1-33.5:3	45.1-161.75
45.1-33.5:4	45.1-161.76
45.1-33.6 through 45.1-33.12	Repealed
45.1-34	45.1-161.236, 45.1-161.240 to 45.1-161.242, 45.1-161.261
45.1-35	45.1-161.231
45.1-36	45.1-161.239, 45.1-161.275, 45.1-161.276
45.1-37	45.1-161.236, 45.1-161.260
45.1-38	45.1-161.237, 45.1-161.272
45.1-39	45.1-161.180, 45.1-161.238, 45.1-161.267

Former Section	Present Section
45.1-40	45.1-161.108 to 45.1-161.113
45.1-41	45.1-161.108, 45.1-161.114, 45.1-161.115, 45.1-161.118, 45.1-161.119
45.1-42	45.1-161.112, 45.1-161.116, 45.1-161.117, 45.1-161.118, 45.1-161.120, 45.1-161.256 to 45.1-161.258
45.1-43	45.1-161.113
45.1-44	45.1-161.126, 45.1-161.180, 45.1-161.284
45.1-45	Deleted
45.1-46	45.1-161.127
45.1-47	45.1-161.128
45.1-48	45.1-161.129, 45.1-161.286
45.1-49	45.1-161.130
45.1-50	45.1-161.131, 45.1-161.285
45.1-51	Repealed
45.1-52	Deleted
45.1-53	Deleted
45.1-53.1	45.1-161.132, 45.1-161.286
45.1-54	45.1-161.211, 45.1-161.216, 45.1-161.217
45.1-54.1	Deleted
45.1-55	45.1-161.211, 45.1-161.218
45.1-56	45.1-161.210, 45.1-161.219, 45.1-161.220
45.1-57	45.1-161.221
45.1-58	45.1-161.222
45.1-59	45.1-161.223, 45.1-161.224
45.1-60	45.1-161.225
45.1-61	45.1-161.226
45.1-62	45.1-161.209, 45.1-161.227, 45.1-161.228
45.1-63	45.1-161.229
45.1-64	45.1-161.230, 45.1-161.297
45.1-65	45.1-161.167, 45.1-161.208, 45.1-161.209, 45.1-161.210, 45.1-161.212, 45.1-161.213, 45.1-161.231, 45.1-161.256, 45.1-161.257
45.1-65.1	45.1-161.232
45.1-65.2	45.1-161.215
45.1-66	45.1-161.234, 45.1-161.278
45.1-67	45.1-161.235, 45.1-161.240
45.1-68	45.1-161.153, 45.1-161.154, 45.1-161.158 to 45.1-161.161
45.1-69	45.1-161.153, 45.1-161.155 to 45.1-161.160
45.1-70	45.1-161.133, 45.1-161.134
45.1-71	45.1-161.135 to 45.1-161.138, 45.1-161.268
45.1-72	45.1-161.140, 45.1-161.141, 45.1-161.161, 45.1-161.268
45.1-73	45.1-161.134, 45.1-161.141 to 45.1-161.148, 45.1-161.268, 45.1-161.270
45.1-74	45.1-161.150 to 45.1-161.152, 45.1-161.268, 45.1-161.298
45.1-75	45.1-161.181, 45.1-161.279
45.1-76	45.1-161.182 to 45.1-161.184, 45.1-161.280
45.1-77	45.1-161.184, 45.1-161.185
45.1-78	45.1-161.186, 45.1-161.187, 45.1-161.196, 45.1-161.280, 45.1-161.282, 45.1-161.299, 45.1-161.300
45.1-79	45.1-161.188, 45.1-161.281
45.1-80	45.1-161.189, 45.1-161.190, 45.1-161.282, 45.1-161.301
45.1-81	45.1-161.191, 45.1-161.282
45.1-82	45.1-161.192
45.1-83	45.1-161.193, 45.1-161.209
45.1-84	45.1-161.194, 45.1-161.283
45.1-85	45.1-161.139, 45.1-161.173, 45.1-161.195, 45.1-161.288
45.1-86	45.1-161.172
45.1-87	45.1-161.123, 45.1-161.278
45.1-88	45.1-161.124, 45.1-161.273
45.1-88.1	45.1-161.125, 45.1-161.274
45.1-89	45.1-161.135, 45.1-161.200 to 45.1-161.205, 45.1-161.243, 45.1-161.258, 45.1-161.265, 45.1-161.266, 45.1-161.303
45.1-89.1	45.1-161.154, 45.1-161.156
45.1-90	45.1-161.205, 45.1-161.206
45.1-91	45.1-161.64
45.1-92	Repealed
45.1-92.1	45.1-161.121, 45.1-161.292, 45.1-161.296, 45.1-161.307
45.1-93	45.1-161.122
45.1-94	45.1-161.162 to 45.1-161.166
45.1-95	45.1-161.162, 45.1-161.166, 45.1-161.168 to 45.1-161.170
45.1-96	45.1-161.171
45.1-97	45.1-161.174
45.1-98	45.1-161.207
45.1-98.1	45.1-161.177
45.1-98.2	45.1-161.179
45.1-98.3	45.1-161.178
45.1-98.4	45.1-161.60
45.1-99	45.1-161.175, 45.1-161.259, 45.1-161.302, 45.1-161.308
45.1-99.1	45.1-161.176, 45.1-161.302
45.1-100	45.1-161.205
45.1-101	45.1-161.197, 45.1-161.198, 45.1-161.262, 45.1-161.264
45.1-101.1	45.1-161.199
45.1-101.2	45.1-161.38, 45.1-161.101, 45.1-161.263
45.1-102	45.1-161.310
45.1-103	45.1-161.311
45.1-104	45.1-161.14, 45.1-161.93, 45.1-161.106, 45.1-161.107,

Former Section	Present Section
	45.1-161.254, 45.1-161.255
45.1-105	45.1-161.66, 45.1-161.86, 45.1-161.94, 45.1-161.95
45.1-106 through 45.1-144	Repealed
45.1-145	45.1-161.312
45.1-146	45.1-161.313
45.1-147	45.1-161.314
45.1-148	45.1-161.315
45.1-149	45.1-161.316
45.1-150	45.1-161.319
45.1-151	45.1-161.320
45.1-152	45.1-161.321
45.1-153	45.1-161.322
45.1-154	45.1-161.318
45.1-155	Deleted
45.1-156	45.1-161.317
45.1-157	Deleted
45.1-158	Deleted
45.1-159	Deleted
45.1-160	Deleted
45.1-161	Deleted

COMPARABLE SECTIONS OF TITLE 46 AND TITLE 46.1

Former Section	Present Section
22-278	46.1-370
22-280	46.1-287
22-281	46.1-288
33-283	46.1-229
44-101	46.1-224
46-1	46.1-1
46-3	18.1-164
46-4	46.1-60
46-5	46.1-2
46-5.1	46.1-3
46-6	46.1-4
46-7	18.1-165, 46.1-5, 46.1-88
46-8	18.1-166
46-9	46.1-82
46-10	46.1-83
46-11	46.1-84
46-12	46.1-85, 46.1-112
46-13	18.1-167
46-14	46.1-6
46-15	46.1-7
46-16	46.1-8
46-17	46.1-9
46-17.1	46.1-10
46-17.2	46.1-11
46-17.3	46.1-12
46-17.4	46.1-13
46-18	46.1-16
46-19	46.1-17
46-20	46.1-18
46-21	46.1-19
46-22	46.1-20
46-22.1	46.1-105
46-23	46.1-22
46-24	46.1-23
46-25	46.1-24
46-26	46.1-25
46-27	46.1-26
46-28	46.1-27
46-29	46.1-28
46-30	46.1-29
46-31	46.1-30
46-32	46.1-31
46-33	46.1-32
46-34	46.1-33
46-35	46.1-34
46-36	46.1-35
46-37	46.1-36
46-38	46.1-37
46-39	46.1-38
46-40	46.1-39
46-41	46.1-40
46-42	46.1-41
46-43	46.1-42
46-44	46.1-43
46-44.1	46.1-44
46-45	46.1-45
46-45.1	46.1-46
46-46	46.1-47
46-47	46.1-48
46-48	46.1-49
46-48.1	46.1-50
46-49	46.1-51
46-50	46.1-52
46-51	46.1-53
46-52	46.1-54
46-53	46.1-55
46-54	46.1-56
46-55	46.1-57
46-56	46.1-58
46-57	46.1-59
46-59	46.1-418
46-60	46.1-61
46-61	46.1-62
46-62	46.1-63
46-63	46.1-64
46-64	46.1-65
46-65	46.1-66
46-66	46.1-15
46-67	46.1-67
46-68	46.1-68
46-69	46.1-69
46-70	46.1-70
46-71	46.1-71
46-72	46.1-72
46-73	46.1-73
46-74	46.1-74
46-75	46.1-75
46-76	46.1-76
46-77	46.1-77
46-78	46.1-78
46-79	46.1-79
46-80	46.1-7
46-81	46.1-80
46-82	46.1-81
46-83	46.1-86
46-84	46.1-87
46-85	46.1-89
46-86	46.1-90
46-87	46.1-91
46-88	46.1-92
46-89	46.1-93
46-90	46.1-94
46-91	46.1-95
46-92	46.1-96
46-94	46.1-97
46-95	46.1-98
46-96	46.1-99
46-97	46.1-101
46-98	46.1-102
46-99	46.1-103
46-99.1	46.1-104
46-100	46.1-100
46-101	46.1-106
46-102	46.1-107
46-103	46.1-108
46-104	46.1-109
46-104.1	46.1-110
46-104.2	46.1-111
46-105	46.1-113
46-105.1	46.1-114, 46.1-115
46-105.2	46.1-116
46-106	46.1-117
46-107	46.1-118
46-108	46.1-119
46-109	46.1-120
46-109.1	46.1-121
46-109.2	46.1-122
46-109.3	46.1-123
46-109.4	46.1-124
46-109.5	46.1-125
46-109.6	46.1-126
46-109.7	46.1-127
46-109.8	46.1-128
46-109.9	46.1-129
46-109.10	46.1-130
46-110	46.1-131

Former Section	Present Section
46-111	46.1-132
46-116	46.1-133
46-117	46.1-134
46-120	46.1-135
46-121	46.1-136
46-122	46.1-137
46-123	46.1-138
46-125	46.1-139
46-126	46.1-140
46-127	46.1-141
46-128	46.1-142
46-129	46.1-143
46-130	46.1-144
46-131	46.1-145
46-132	46.1-146
46-133	46.1-147
46-133.1	46.1-148
46-152	46-275.1
46-154	46.1-149
46-155	46.1-149
	46.1-153
46-156	46.1-149
46-157	46.1-151
46-158	46.1-150
46-158.1	46.1-149
46-159	46.1-149
46-160	46.1-99
46-161	46.1-152
46-162	46.1-154
46-163	46.1-155
46-163.1	46.1-149
46-164	46.1-156
46-165	46.1-157
46-166	46.1-158
46-166.1	46.1-149
46-167	46.1-159
46-168	46.1-160
46-169	46.1-161
46-170	46.1-162
46-174	46.1-163
46-175	46.1-164
46-176	46.1-165
46-178	46.1-166
46-179	46.1-167
46-181	46.1-168
46-182	46.1-169
	46.1-170
46-183	46.1-171
46-183.1	46.1-172
46-183.2	46.1-172
46-184	46.1-173
46-185	46.1-1
46-186	46.1-1
46-187	46.1-174
46-188	46.1-175
46-189	46.1-176
46-190	46.1-177
46-191	46.1-14
46-193	46.1-178
46-194	46.1-179
46-195	46.1-412
	46.1-413
46-195.1	46.1-425
46-196	46.1-414
46-197.2	46.1-424
46-198	46.1-180
46-199	46.1-182
46-200	46.1-180
46-201	46.1-183
46-202	46.1-183
46-203	46.1-184
46-206	46.1-181
46-207.1	46.1-186
46-208	46.1-189
46-209	46.1-190
46-209.1	46.1-190
	46.1-423
46-209.2	46.1-191
46-210	46.1-192
	46.1-422
46-212	46.1-193
46-212.1	46.1-194
46-215	46.1-196
46-215.1	46.1-197
46-216	46.1-199
46-218	46.1-200
46-219	46.1-201
46-219.1	46.1-202
46-220	46.1-203
46-220.1	46.1-204
46-221	46.1-205
46-222	46.1-206
46-223	46.1-207
46-224	46.1-208
46-225	46.1-209
46-226	46.1-210
46-227	46.1-211
46-228	46.1-212
46-229	46.1-213
46-230	46.1-214
46-231	46.1-215
46-233	46.1-216
46-234	46.1-217
46-235	46.1-218
46-236	46.1-219
46-237	46.1-220
46-238	46.1-221
46-239	46.1-222
46-240	46.1-223
46-241	46.1-225
46-241.1	46.1-226
46-242	46.1-227
46-242.1	46.1-228
46-243	46.1-230
	46.1-231
46-244	46.1-231
46-245	46.1-232
46-246	46.1-233
46-247	46.1-234
46-248	46.1-235
46-249	46.1-236
46-249.1	46.1-237
46-249.2	46.1-238
46-249.3	46.1-240
46-249.4	46.1-239
46-250	46.1-241
46-252	46.1-242
46-253	46.1-243
46-254	46.1-244
46-254.1	46.1-245
46-254.2	46.1-246
46-255	46.1-247
46-256	46.1-248
46-256.1	46.1-249
46-257	46.1-250
46-258	46.1-251
46-259	46.1-252
46-259.1	46.1-253
46-259.2	46.1-254
46-260	46.1-255
46-261	46.1-256
46-262	46.1-257
46-263	46.1-258
46-264	46.1-259
46-265	46.1-260
46-266	46.1-261
46-267	46.1-262
46-268	46.1-263
46-269	46.1-264
46-270	46.1-263
	46.1-264
46-271	46.1-265
46-272	46.1-266
46-273	46.1-267
46-275	46.1-268
46-276	46.1-269
46-277	46.1-270
46-278	46.1-271
46-279	46.1-272
46-279.1	46.1-273
46-280	46.1-274
46-281	46.1-275
46-282	46.1-276
46-283	46.1-277
46-284	46.1-278
46-285	46.1-279
46-286	46.1-280
46-287	46.1-281
46-288	46.1-282
46-289	46.1-283
46-290	46.1-284
46-291	46.1-285
46-293	46.1-286
46-294	46.1-289
46-294.1	46.1-290
46-295	46.1-291
46-296	46.1-292
46-297	46.1-293
46-298	46.1-294
46-299	46.1-295
46-300	46.1-296
46-301	46.1-297
46-302	46.1-298

Former Section	Present Section
46-303	46.1-299
46-304	46.1-300
46-305	46.1-301
46-306	46.1-302
46-307	46.1-303
46-308	46.1-304
46-309	46.1-305
46-310	46.1-306
46-310.1	46.1-307
46-311	46.1-308
46-312	46.1-309
46-312.1	46.1-310
46-313	46.1-311
46-314	46.1-312
46-315	46.1-313
46-316	46.1-314
46-317	46.1-315
46-317.1	46.1-316
46-317.2	46.1-317
46-318	46.1-318
46-319	46.1-320
46-320	46.1-321
46-321	46.1-322
	46.1-323
46-322	46.1-324
46-322.1	46.1-325
46-322.2	46.1-326
46-323	46.1-319
46-325	46.1-327
46-326	46.1-328
	46.1-332
46-327	46.1-329
46-328	46.1-330
46-328.1	46.1-331
46-329	46.1-333
46-330	46.1-334
46-331	46.1-335
46-332	46.1-336
46-333	46.1-337
46-333.1	46.1-338
46-334	46.1-339
46-335	46.1-340
46-335.1	46.1-341
46-338.2	46.1-342
46-339	46.1-343
46-500	46.1-513
46-501	46.1-514
46-502	46.1-515
46-503	46.1-516
46-504	46.1-517
46-505	46.1-518
46-506	46.1-519
46-507	46.1-520
46-508	46.1-521
46-509	46.1-522
46-510	46.1-523
46-511	46.1-524
46-512	46.1-525
46-513	46.1-526
46-514	46.1-527
46-515	46.1-528
46-516	46.1-529
46-517	46.1-530
46-518	46.1-531
46-519	46.1-532
46-520	46.1-533
46-521	46.1-534
46-522	46.1-535
46-523	46.1-536
46-524	46.1-537
46-525	46.1-538
46-526	46.1-539
46-527	46.1-540
46-528	46.1-541
46-529	46.1-542
46-530	46.1-543
46-531	46.1-544
46-532	46.1-545
46-533	46.1-546
46-534	46.1-547
46-536	46.1-548
46-538	46.1-549
46-539	46.1-550
46-541	46.1-551
46-542	46.1-552
46-543	46.1-553
46-544	46.1-554
46-545	46.1-555
46-546 to 46-553	13.1-400.1 to 13.1-400.8

COMPARABLE SECTIONS OF TITLE 46.1 AND TITLE 46.2

Former Section	Present Section
46.1-1	46.2-100
46.1-1	46.2-914
46.1-2	46.2-1209
46.1-2	46.2-1210
46.1-2.1	46.2-1211
46.1-3	46.2-1213
46.1-3	46.2-1217
46.1-3.01	46.2-1214
46.1-3.02	46.2-1216
46.1-3.02	46.2-1217
46.1-3.1	46.2-1212
46.1-3.2	46.2-1233
46.1-3.2	46.2-1215
46.1-4	46.2-1073
46.1-5	46.2-616
46.1-6	46.2-102
46.1-7	46.2-104
46.1-8	46.2-103
46.1-9	46.2-110
46.1-10	46.2-109
46.1-11	46.2-1218
46.1-12	46.2-109
46.1-13	Repealed
46.1-14	46.2-108
46.1-15	46.2-105
46.1-15.1	46.2-112
46.1-15.2	46.2-112
46.1-15.3	46.2-112
46.1-16.01	46.2-113
46.1-16.1	46.2-1314
46.1-17	Repealed
46.1-18	46.2-114
46.1-19	46.2-106
46.1-20	46.2-106
46.1-21	46.2-101
46.1-22	Repealed
46.1-23	46.2-201
46.1-24	46.2-202
46.1-25	46.2-200
46.1-26	46.2-203
46.1-26.1	46.2-204
46.1-27	Repealed
46.1-28	46.2-205
46.1-29	Repealed
46.1-30	46.2-205
46.1-31	46.2-208
46.1-31.1	46.2-209
46.1-31.2	46.2-214
46.1-32	46.2-210
46.1-32.1	46.2-211
46.1-33.1	46.2-212
46.1-33.2	46.2-212.1
46.1-34	46.2-213
46.1-34.1	46.2-215
46.1-35	Repealed
46.1-35.1	46.2-207
46.1-36	46.2-216
46.1-37	46.2-217
46.1-38	46.2-218
46.1-39	46.2-219
46.1-40	46.2-220
46.1-40.1	46.2-221
46.1-40.1:1	46.2-221
46.1-40.2	Repealed
46.1-40.3	46.2-222
46.1-40.4	46.2-223
46.1-40.5	46.2-224
46.1-40.6	46.2-224
46.1-41	46.2-600
46.1-41.1	46.2-662
46.1-41.2	46.2-602
46.1-42	46.2-650

Former Section	Present Section
46.1-42.1	46.2-651
46.1-43	46.2-652
46.1-44	46.2-653
46.1-44.1	46.2-723
46.1-44.2	46.2-685
46.1-45	46.2-663
46.1-45	46.2-664
46.1-45	46.2-665
46.1-45	46.2-666
46.1-45	46.2-667
46.1-45	46.2-668
46.1-45	46.2-669
46.1-45	46.2-670
46.1-45	46.2-671
46.1-45	46.2-672
46.1-45	46.2-673
46.1-45	46.2-674
46.1-45.1	46.2-675
46.1-45.2	46.2-676
46.1-45.2	46.2-677
46.1-45.2	46.2-678
46.1-45.2	46.2-679
46.1-45.3	46.2-680
46.1-46	46.2-681
46.1-47	46.2-682
46.1-48	46.2-683
46.1-49	46.2-750
46.1-49.1	46.2-750.1
46.1-50	Repealed
46.1-50.1	Repealed
46.1-51	46.2-621
46.1-52	46.2-623
46.1-52.1	46.2-606
46.1-53	46.2-625
46.1-53.1	46.2-734
46.1-54	46.2-645
46.1-55	46.2-607
46.1-55	46.2-692
46.1-56	46.2-608
46.1-57	46.2-751
46.1-58	46.2-1000
46.1-59	46.2-609
46.1-60	46.2-610
46.1-61	46.2-611
46.1-62	46.2-612
46.1-63	46.2-646
46.1-63.1	46.2-647
46.1-64	46.2-613
46.1-64	46.2-1076
46.1-64.1	46.2-624
46.1-65	46.2-752
46.1-65.1	46.2-753
46.1-65.2	46.2-754
46.1-66	46.2-755
46.1-66.1	46.2-908
46.1-67	46.2-614
46.1-68	46.2-603
46.1-68.1	46.2-622
46.1-69	46.2-636
46.1-70	46.2-637
46.1-71	46.2-638
46.1-72	46.2-639
46.1-73	46.2-640
46.1-74	46.2-641
46.1-75	46.2-642
46.1-76	46.2-643
46.1-77	46.2-644
46.1-78	46.2-627
46.1-79	46.2-604
46.1-80	46.2-618
46.1-81	46.2-626
46.1-82	46.2-1074
46.1-83	46.2-1075
46.1-84	46.2-1072
46.1-85	46.2-605
46.1-86	46.2-620
46.1-87	46.2-628
46.1-88	46.2-617
46.1-89	46.2-630
46.1-89.1	46.2-629
46.1-90	46.2-631
46.1-90.2	46.2-654
46.1-91	46.2-619
46.1-92	46.2-632
46.1-93	46.2-633
46.1-94	46.2-634
46.1-96	46.2-615
46.1-97	46.2-688
46.1-98.1	46.2-635
46.1-99	46.2-711
46.1-100	Repealed
46.1-101	46.2-712
46.1-102	46.2-713
46.1-103	46.2-714
46.1-104	46.2-730
46.1-104.1	46.2-731
46.1-104.2	46.2-732
46.1-105	46.2-738
46.1-105.1	46.2-729
46.1-105.2	46.2-726
46.1-105.3	46.2-735
46.1-105.4	46.2-736
46.1-105.5	46.2-727
46.1-105.6	46.2-737
46.1-105.7	46.2-746
46.1-105.8	46.2-745
46.1-105.9	46.2-744
46.1-105.10	46.2-748
46.1-105.11	46.2-743
46.1-105.12	46.2-648
46.1-105.13	46.2-747
46.1-105.14	46.2-728
46.1-105.15	46.2-742
46.1-105.16	46.2-741
46.1-105.17	46.2-740
46.1-105.18	46.2-749
46.1-106	46.2-715
46.1-107	46.2-716
46.1-108	46.2-717
46.1-109	46.2-718
46.1-110	46.2-719
46.1 110.1	46.2-720
46.1-110.2	46.2-721
46.1-111	46.2-756
46.1-112	46.2-722
46.1-131	46.2-655
46.1-132	46.2-656
46.1-133	46.2-657
46.1-134	46.2-658
46.1-135	46.2-659
46.1-136	46.2-660
46.1-137	46.2-661
46.1-139	46.2-601
46.1-149	46.2-694
46.1-149.1	46.2-739
46.1-150	46.2-695
46.1-151	46.2-107
46.1-152	46.2-687
46.1-153	46.2-696
46.1-153.1	46.2-649
46.1-154	46.2-697
46.1-154.01	46.2-689
46.1-154.1	46.2-690
46.1-154.3	46.2-698
46.1-155	46.2-699
46.1-156	46.2-700
46.1-157	46.2-701
46.1-157.1	46.2-703
46.1-157.2	46.2-686
46.1-158.1	46.2-1076
46.1-159	46.2-704
46.1-160	46.2-724
46.1-161	46.2-100
46.1-162	46.2-733
46.1-163	46.2-702
46.1-166	46.2-691
46.1-167	46.2-206
46.1-167.1	46.2-706
46.1-167.2	46.2-705
46.1-167.3	46.2-707
46.1-167.4	46.2-708
46.1-167.5	46.2-709
46.1-167.6	46.2-710
46.1-167.7	Repealed
46.1-167.8	46.2-483
46.1-167.9	46.2-484
46.1-167.10	46.2-485
46.1-167.11	46.2-486
46.1-167.12	46.2-487
46.1-167.13	46.2-488
46.1-168	46.2-801
46.1-169	46.2-919
46.1-169.1	46.2-917
46.1-169.2	46.2-918
46.1-170	46.2-810
46.1-171	46.2-800
46.1-171.01	46.2-800.1
46.1-171.1	46.2-808
46.1-171.2	46.2-809
46.1-172	46.2-909
46.1-172	46.2-910
46.1 172	46.2-911
46.1-172	46.2-915.2

Former Section	Present Section
46.1-172.01	46.2-912
46.1-172.02	46.2-913
46.1-172.03	46.2-915
46.1-172.04	46.2-915.1
46.1-172.1	46.2-813
46.1-173	46.2-830
46.1-174	46.2-831
46.1-175	46.2-832
46.1-176	46.2-894
46.1-176	46.2-895
46.1-176	46.2-896
46.1-176	46.2-897
46.1-176	46.2-898
46.1-176	46.2-899
46.1-177	46.2-900
46.1-177.1	46.2-901
46.1-178	46.2-936
46.1-178.01	46.2-937
46.1-178.1	46.2-938
46.1-178.2	46.2-939
46.1-179	46.2-940
46.1-179.01	46.2-941
46.1-179.02	46.2-1136
46.1-179.1	46.2-944
46.1-179.2	46.2-945
46.1-179.3	46.2-946
46.1-180	46.2-1300
46.1-180.1	46.2-1301
46.1-180.2	46.2-1302
46.1-180.3	46.2-1303
46.1-181	46.2-1304
46.1-181.1	46.2-1219
46.1-181.2	46.2-1305
46.1-181.3	46.2-1306
46.1-181.4:1	46.2-1237
46.1-181.5	46.2-1307
46.1-182	46.2-1308
46.1-183	46.2-1309
46.1-183.1	46.2-1310
46.1-184	46.2-833
46.1-184	46.2-834
46.1-184	46.2-835
46.1-184	46.2-836
46.1-185	46.2-1311
46.1-186	Repealed
46.1-187	46.2-1312
46.1-188	46.2-1313
46.1-189	46.2-852
46.1-190	46.2-853
46.1-190	46.2-854
46.1-190	46.2-855
46.1-190	46.2-856
46.1-190	46.2-857
46.1-190	46.2-858
46.1-190	46.2-859
46.1-190	46.2-860
46.1-190	46.2-861
46.1-190	46.2-862
46.1-190	46.2-863
46.1-190	46.2-864
46.1-191	46.2-865

Former Section	Present Section
46.1-191.1	46.2-866
46.1-191.2	46.2-867
46.1-192	46.2-868
46.1-192.1	46.2-817
46.1-192.2	46.2-869
46.1-193	46.2-870
46.1-193	46.2-871
46.1-193	46.2-872
46.1-193	46.2-873
46.1-193	46.2-874
46.1-193	46.2-875
46.1-193	46.2-876
46.1-193	46.2-877
46.1-193	46.2-878
46.1-193.1	46.2-942
46.1-194	46.2-879
46.1-195	46.2-880
46.1-196	46.2-881
46.1-198	46.2-882
46.1-198.1	46.2-1079
46.1-198.2	46.2-883
46.1-199	46.2-918
46.1-200	46.2-811
46.1-201	46.2-812
46.1-202	46.2-1077
46.1-202.1	46.2-1078
46.1-203	46.2-802
46.1-204	46.2-806
46.1-204	46.2-807
46.1-205	46.2-803
46.1-206	46.2-804
46.1-206.1	46.2-805
46.1-207	46.2-837
46.1-208	46.2-838
46.1-208.1	46.2-839
46.1-209	46.2-840
46.1-209.1	Repealed
46.1-210	46.2-841
46.1-211	46.2-842
46.1-211.1	46.2-842.1
46.1-212	46.2-843
46.1-212.1	46.2-844
46.1-213	46.2-816
46.1-214	46.2-845
46.1-215	46.2-846
46.1-215.1	46.2-847
46.1-216	46.2-848
46.1-217	46.2-849
46.1-218	46.2-850
46.1-219	Repealed
46.1-220	46.2-851
46.1-221	46.2-820
46.1-221	46.2-821
46.1-221	46.2-822
46.1-221	46.2-823
46.1-221.1	46.2-824
46.1-222	46.2-825
46.1-223	46.2-826
46.1-224	46.2-827
46.1-224.1	46.2-828
46.1-225	46.2-829

Former Section	Present Section
46.1-226	46.2-920
46.1-227	46.2-921
46.1-228	46.2-922
46.1-228.1	46.2-815
46.1-229	46.2-903
46.1-229.01	46.2-904
46.1-229.1	46.2-905
46.1-229.2	46.2-906
46.1-229.2:1	46.2-907
46.1-229.3	46.2-916
46.1-229.4	46.2-819
46.1-230	46.2-923
46.1-231	46.2-924
46.1-231.1	46.2-925
46.1-232	46.2-926
46.1-233	46.2-927
46.1-234	46.2-928
46.1-234	46.2-929
46.1-234.1	46.2-930
46.1-234.2	46.2-931
46.1-235	46.2-932
46.1-237	46.2-933
46.1-240	46.2-934
46.1-241	46.2-935
46.1-242	46.2-814
46.1-243	46.2-884
46.1-244	46.2-885
46.1-245	46.2-886
46.1-246	46.2-887
46.1-247	46.2-821
46.1-248	46.2-888
46.1-248	46.2-889
46.1-248	46.2-890
46.1-248	46.2-891
46.1-249	46.2-892
46.1-250	46.2-893
46.1-250.1	46.2-818
46.1-251	46.2-902
46.1-252	46.2-1220
46.1-252.01	46.2-1230
46.1-252.1	46.2-1220
46.1-252.1	46.2-1221
46.1-252.1:1	46.2-1235
46.1-252.2	46.2-1223
46.1-252.3	46.2-1222
46.1-253	46.2-1220
46.1-254	46.2-1224
46.1-254.1	46.2-1225
46.1-254.1	46.2-1226
46.1-254.1	46.2-1227
46.1-254.1	46.2-1228
46.1-254.1	46.2-1229
46.1-254.2	46.2-1238
46.1-254.3	46.2-1236
46.1-255 to 46.1-257	46.2-111
46.1-258	46.2-1239
46.1-259	46.2-1010
46.1-259.1	Repealed
46.1-260	46.2-1011
46.1-261	46.2-1012

Former Section	Present Section
46.1-262	46.2-1013
46.1-262.1	46.2-1014
46.1-263	46.2-1015
46.1-264	46.2-1016
46.1-264.1	46.2-1081
46.1-265	46.2-1017
46.1-265.1	46.2-1018
46.1-266	46.2-1019
46.1-267	46.2-1020
46.1-267	46.2-1021
46.1-267	46.2-1021.1
46.1-267	46.2-1022
46.1-267	46.2-1023
46.1-267	46.2-1024
46.1-267	46.2-1025
46.1-267	46.2-1026
46.1-267	46.2-1027
46.1-267.1	46.2-1028
46.1-267.2	46.2-1029
46.1-268	46.2-1030
46.1-269	46.2-1031
46.1-270	46.2-1032
46.1-271	46.2-1033
46.1-272	46.2-1034
46.1-273	46.2-1035
46.1-274	46.2-1036
46.1-275	Repealed
46.1-276	46.2-1037
46.1-277	46.2-1066
46.1-278	46.2-1067
46.1-278.1	46.2-1068
46.1-279.01	46.2-1001
46.1-279.1	46.2-1069
46.1-280	46.2-1070
46.1-281	46.2-1071
46.1-282	46.2-1065
46.1-282.1	46.2-1063
46.1-282.2	46.2-1064
46.1-283	46.2-1059
46.1-284	46.2-1060
46.1-285	46.2-1061
46.1-286	46.2-1062
46.1-286.1	46.2-1089
46.1-287	46.2-1090
46.1-287.1	Repealed
46.1-287.2	46.2-1091
46.1-289	46.2-1082
46.1-290	46.2-1083
46.1-291	46.2-1052
46.1-291.01	46.2-1053
46.1-291.1	46.2-1054
46.1-292	46.2-1055
46.1-293	46.2-1056
46.1-293.1	46.2-1057
46.1-294	46.2-1058
46.1-294.1	46.2-1164
46.1-295	46.2-1041
46.1-295.2	46.2-1042
46.1-295.3	46.2-1043
46.1-296	46.2-1044
46.1-296.1	46.2-1045
46.1-297	46.2-1046
46.1-298	46.2-1038
46.1-299	46.2-1039
46.1-299	46.2-1040
46.1-300	46.2-1121
46.1-301	46.2-1049
46.1-301.1	46.2-1048
46.1-302	46.2-1047
46.1-302.1	46.2-1084
46.1-302.2	46.2-1085
46.1-302.3	46.2-1050
46.1-302.4	46.2-1051
46.1-303	46.2-1156
46.1-304	46.2-1155
46.1-305	46.2-1086
46.1-306	46.2-1087
46.1-307	46.2-1088
46.1-308	46.2-1002
46.1-308	46.2-1080
46.1-308.1	46.2-1003
46.1-309	46.2-1004
46.1-309.1	46.2-1092
46.1-309.2	46.2-1094
46.1-310	46.2-1093
46.1-311	46.2-1005
46.1-312	46.2-1006
46.1-313	46.2-1007
46.1-314	46.2-1008
46.1-314.1	46.2-1009
46.1-314.2	46.2-1095
46.1-314.3	46.2-1096
46.1-314.4	46.2-1097
46.1-314.5	46.2-1098
46.1-314.6	46.2-1099
46.1-314.7	46.2-1100
46.1-315	46.2-1157
46.1-315.1	Repealed
46.1-315.2	46.2-1158
46.1-316	46.2-1159
46.1-317	46.2-1160
46.1-317.1	46.2-1161
46.1-317.2	46.2-1162
46.1-318	46.2-1163
46.1-319	46.2-1165
46.1-320	46.2-1166
46.1-321	46.2-1167
46.1-321.1	Repealed
46.1-321.2	46.2-1168
46.1-322	46.2-1169
46.1-323	46.2-1170
46.1-324	46.2-1171
46.1-325	46.2-1172
46.1-326	46.2-1173
46.1-326.1	46.2-1174
46.1-326.1:1	46.2-1175
46.1-326.1:2	46.2-1175.1
46.1-326.2	46.2-1176
46.1-326.3	46.2-1177
46.1-326.4	46.2-1178
46.1-326.5	46.2-1179
46.1-326.6	46.2-1180
46.1-326.7	46.2-1181
46.1-326.8	46.2-1182
46.1-326.9	46.2-1183
46.1-326.10	46.2-1184
46.1-326.11	46.2-1185
46.1-326.12	46.2-1186
46.1-326.13	46.2-1187
46.1-327	46.2-1101
46.1-328	46.2-1105
46.1-328	46.2-1106
46.1-328	46.2-1107
46.1-328	46.2-1108
46.1-328.1	46.2-1109
46.1-329	46.2-1110
46.1-330	46.2-1112
46.1-330	46.2-1113
46.1-330	46.2-1153
46.1-330.1	46.2-1114
46.1-331	46.2-1115
46.1-332	46.2-1102
46.1-333	46.2-1120
46.1-334	46.2-1111
46.1-335	46.2-1116
46.1-335	46.2-1153
46.1-335.1	46.2-1117
46.1-336	46.2-1118
46.1-336.1	46.2-1119
46.1-337	46.2-1154
46.1-338	46.2-1150
46.1-339	46.2-1122
46.1-339	46.2-1123
46.1-339	46.2-1124
46.1-339	46.2-1125
46.1-339	46.2-1126
46.1-339	46.2-1127
46.1-339.01	46.2-1128
46.1-339.02	46.2-1129
46.1-339.1	46.2-1151
46.1-339.2	46.2-1152
46.1-340	46.2-1130
46.1-341	46.2-1131
46.1-341.01	46.2-1132
46.1-341.02	46.2-1133
46.1-341.03	46.2-1134
46.1-342	46.2-1135
46.1-342.1	46.2-1138.1
46.1-343	46.2-1139
46.1-343.1	46.2-1148
46.1-343.2	46.2-1139
46.1-343.3	46.2-1140
46.1-343.3	46.2-1141
46.1-343.3	46.2-1142
46.1-343.3	46.2-1143
46.1-343.3	46.2-1144
46.1-343.3	46.2-1145
46.1-343.3	46.2-1146
46.1-343.3	46.2-1147
46.1-343.4	46.2-1149
46.1-344	46.2-1103
46.1-345	46.2-1104
46.1-346	Repealed

Former Section	Present Section
46.1-347	46.2-1137
46.1-347.1	46.2-943
46.1-347.2	46.2-943
46.1-348	Repealed
46.1-349	46.2-300
46.1-350	46.2-301
46.1-351	46.2-302
46.1-351.1	Repealed
46.1-351.2	Repealed
46.1-352	46.2-303
46.1-352.1	46.2-304
46.1-353	46.2-310
46.1-354	46.2-305
46.1-354.1	46.2-306
46.1-355	46.2-307
46.1-355.1	46.2-308
46.1-356	46.2-309
46.1-357	46.2-334
46.1-357	46.2-335
46.1-357.1	Repealed
46.1-357.2	46.2-311
46.1-357.3	46.2-312
46.1-358	46.2-313
46.1-359	Repealed
46.1-360	46.2-314
46.1-361	46.2-315
46.1-362	46.2-316
46.1-363	46.2-317
46.1-364	46.2-318
46.1-365	46.2-319
46.1-366	46.2-320
46.1-367	46.2-321
46.1-368	46.2-323
46.1-368.1	46.2-324
46.1-369	46.2-325
46.1-370	46.2-339
46.1-370.01	46.2-340
46.1-370.1	46.2-337
46.1-370.2	46.2-341
46.1-371	46.2-326
46.1-372	46.2-327
46.1-372.1	46.2-341.1
46.1-372.2	46.2-341.2
46.1-372.3	46.2-341.3
46.1-372.4	46.2-341.4
46.1-372.5	46.2-341.5
46.1-372.6	46.2-341.6
46.1-372.7	46.2-341.7
46.1-372.8	46.2-341.8
46.1-372.9	46.2-341.9
46.1-372.10	46.2-341.10
46.1-372.11	46.2-341.11
46.1-372.12	46.2-341.12
46.1-372.13	46.2-341.13
46.1-372.14	46.2-341.14
46.1-372.15	46.2-341.15
46.1-372.15:1	46.2-341.16
46.1-372.16	46.2-341.17
46.1-372.17	46.2-341.18
46.1-372.18	46.2-341.19
46.1-372.19	46.2-341.20

Former Section	Present Section
46.1-372.20	46.2-341.21
46.1-372.21	46.2-341.22
46.1-372.22	46.2-341.23
46.1-372.23	46.2-341.24
46.1-372.24	46.2-341.25
46.1-372.25	46.2-341.26
46.1-372.26	46.2-341.27
46.1-372.27	46.2-341.28
46.1-372.28	46.2-341.29
46.1-372.29	46.2-341.30
46.1-372.29:1	46.2-341.31
46.1-372.30	46.2-341.32
46.1-372.31	46.2-341.33
46.1-372.32	46.2-341.34
46.1-373	46.2-328
46.1-374	46.2-338
46.1-375	46.2-342
46.1-375.1	46.2-336
46.1-377	46.2-344
46.1-378	46.2-329
46.1-379	46.2-343
46.1-380.1	46.2-330
46.1-380.2	46.2-332
46.1-381	46.2-333
46.1-382	46.2-331
46.1-383	46.2-322
46.1-383.3	46.2-345
46.1-384	46.2-346
46.1-384.1	46.2-347
46.1-385	46.2-348
46.1-386	46.2-349
46.1-387	46.2-350
46.1-387.1	Repealed
46.1-387.2	46.2-351
46.1-387.2	46.2-359
46.1-387.3	46.2-352
46.1-387.4	46.2-353
46.1-387.5	46.2-354
46.1-387.6	46.2-355
46.1-387.7	46.2-356
46.1-387.8	46.2-357
46.1-387.9	46.2-358
46.1-387.9:1	Repealed
46.1-387.9:2	46.2-360
46.1-387.9:3	46.2-361
46.1-387.10	46.2-362
46.1-387.11	46.2-363
46.1-387.12	Repealed
46.1-388	Repealed
46.1-389	46.2-364
46.1-390	Repealed
46.1-391	46.2-365
46.1-392	46.2-366
46.1-393	46.2-367
46.1-395	46.2-368
46.1-396	46.2-369
46.1-397	46.2-370
46.1-398	Repealed
46.1-399	46.2-371
46.1-400	46.2-372
46.1-401	46.2-870

Former Section	Present Section
46.1-401	46.2-1156
46.1-401	46.2-373
46.1-403	46.2-374
46.1-404	46.2-375
46.1-406	46.2-376
46.1-407	46.2-377
46.1-408	46.2-378
46.1-409	46.2-379
46.1-410	46.2-380
46.1-411	46.2-381
46.1-412	46.2-382
46.1-412.1	46.2-382.1
46.1-413	46.2-383
46.1-413.1	46.2-384
46.1-413.2	46.2-385
46.1-414	46.2-386
46.1-416	46.2-387
46.1-416.1	46.2-388
46.1-417	46.2-389
46.1-417.1	46.2-390
46.1-421	46.2-391
46.1-422	46.2-392
46.1-423	46.2-393
46.1-423.1	Repealed
46.1-423.2	46.2-394
46.1-423.3	46.2-395
46.1-423.4	46.2-396
46.1-424	46.2-397
46.1-425	46.2-398
46.1-426	46.2-399
46.1-427	46.2-400
46.1-429	46.2-401
46.1-430	46.2-402
46.1-431	46.2-403
46.1-432	46.2-404
46.1-433	46.2-405
46.1-434	46.2-406
46.1-435	46.2-407
46.1-436	46.2-408
46.1-436.1	46.2-409
46.1-437	46.2-410
46.1-438	46.2-411
46.1-439	46.2-412
46.1-440	46.2-413
46.1-441	46.2-414
46.1-441.1	46.2-415
46.1-441.2	46.2-416
46.1-442	46.2-417
46.1-443	46.2-418
46.1-444	46.2-419
46.1-445	46.2-420
46.1-446	46.2-421
46.1-447	46.2-422
46.1-448	46.2-423
46.1-451	46.2-424
46.1-452	46.2-425
46.1-454	46.2-426
46.1-459	46.2-427
46.1-460	46.2-428
46.1-461	46.2-429
46.1-462	46.2-430

Former Section	Present Section
46.1-463	46.2-431
46.1-464	46.2-432
46.1-465	46.2-433
46.1-466	46.2-434
46.1-467	46.2-435
46.1-468	46.2-436
46.1-469	46.2-437
46.1-470	46.2-438
46.1-471	46.2-439
46.1-472	46.2-440
46.1-473	46.2-441
46.1-474	46.2-442
46.1-475	46.2-443
46.1-476	46.2-444
46.1-477	46.2-445
46.1-478	46.2-446
46.1-479	46.2-447
46.1-480	46.2-448
46.1-481	46.2-449
46.1-482	46.2-450
46.1-483	46.2-451
46.1-484	46.2-452
46.1-485	46.2-453
46.1-486	46.2-454
46.1-486.1	46.2-455
46.1-487	46.2-456
46.1-488	46.2-457
46.1-489	46.2-458
46.1-490	46.2-459
46.1-491	46.2-460
46.1-492	46.2-461
46.1-493	46.2-462
46.1-495	Repealed
46.1-496	46.2-463
46.1-497	46.2-464
46.1-497.1	46.2-465
46.1-498	46.2-466
46.1-499	46.2-467
46.1-500	46.2-468
46.1-501	46.2-469
46.1-502	46.2-470
46.1-503	46.2-471
46.1-504	46.2-472
46.1-505	46.2-473
46.1-506	46.2-474
46.1-507	46.2-475
46.1-508	46.2-476
46.1-509	46.2-477
46.1-510	46.2-478
46.1-511	46.2-479
46.1-512	46.2-480
46.1-513	46.2-481
46.1-513.2	46.2-482
46.1-514.1	Repealed
46.1-514.2	46.2-489
46.1-514.3	46.2-490
46.1-514.5	46.2-491
46.1-514.6	46.2-492
46.1-514.7	46.2-493
46.1-514.8	46.2-494
46.1-514.9	46.2-495
46.1-514.10	46.2-496
46.1-514.11	46.2-497
46.1-514.12	46.2-498
46.1-514.13	46.2-499
46.1-514.13:1	46.2-500
46.1-514.14	46.2-501
46.1-514.15	46.2-502
46.1-514.16	46.2-503
46.1-514.17	46.2-504
46.1-514.18	46.2-505
46.1-514.19	46.2-506
46.1-514.20	Repealed
46.1-515	Repealed
46.1-516	46.2-1500
46.1-517	46.2-1501
46.1-517.1	46.2-1502
46.1-517.2	46.2-1503
46.1-518	46.2-1504
46.1-519	46.2-1505
46.1-520	46.2-1506
46.1-522	46.2-1507
46.1-523	46.2-1508
46.1-525	46.2-1509
46.1-525.01	46.2-1510
46.1-525.02	46.2-1511
46.1-525.03	46.2-1512
46.1-525.04	46.2-1513
46.1-525.05	46.2-1514
46.1-525.06	46.2-1515
46.1-525.07	46.2-1516
46.1-525.08	46.2-1517
46.1-525.09	46.2-1518
46.1-525.010	46.2-1519
46.1-525.011	46.2-1520
46.1-525.012	46.2-1521
46.1-544.1	46.2-1522
46.1-544.2	46.2-1523
46.1-544.3	46.2-1524
46.1-544.4	46.2-1525
46.1-544.5	46.2-1526
46.1-544.6	46.2-1527
46.1-547.3	46.2-1528
46.1-547.4	46.2-1529
46.1-547.5	46.2-1530
46.1-547.6	46.2-1531
46.1-547.7	46.2-1532
46.1-547.8	46.2-1533
46.1-547.9	46.2-1534
46.1-547.10	46.2-1535
46.1-548	46.2-1536
46.1-549	46.2-1537
46.1-550	46.2-1538
46.1-550.3	46.2-1539
46.1-550.3:1	46.2-1540
46.1-550.3:2	46.2-1541
46.1-550.5:1	46.2-1542
46.1-550.5:1.1	46.2-1543
46.1-550.5:2	46.2-1544
46.1-550.5:3	46.2-1545
46.1-550.5:4	46.2-1546
46.1-550.5:5	46.2-1547
46.1-550.5:6	46.2-1548
46.1-550.5:7	46.2-1549
46.1-550.5:8	46.2-1550
46.1-550.5:8	46.2-1557
46.1-550.5:9	46.2-1551
46.1-550.5:10	46.2-1552
46.1-550.5:11	46.2-1553
46.1-550.5:12	46.2-1554
46.1-550.5:13	46.2-1555
46.1-550.5:14	46.2-1556
46.1-550.5:15	46.2-1557
46.1-550.5:16	46.2-1558
46.1-550.5:17	46.2-1559
46.1-550.5:18	46.2-1560
46.1-550.5:19	46.2-1561
46.1-550.5:20	46.2-1562
46.1-550.5:21	46.2-1563
46.1-550.5:22	46.2-1564
46.1-550.5:23	46.2-1565
46.1-550.5:24	46.2-1566
46.1-550.5:25	46.2-1567
46.1-550.5:26	46.2-1568
46.1-550.5:27	46.2-1569
46.1-550.5:28	Repealed
46.1-550.5:29	46.2-1570
46.1-550.5:30	46.2-1571
46.1-550.5:31	46.2-1572
46.1-550.5:32	46.2-1573
46.1-550.5:33	46.2-1574
46.1-550.5:34	46.2-1575
46.1-550.5:35	46.2-1576
46.1-550.5:36	46.2-1577
46.1-550.5:37	46.2-1578
46.1-550.5:38	46.2-1579
46.1-550.5:39	46.2-1580
46.1-550.5:40	46.2-1581
46.1-550.5:41	46.2-1582
46.1-550.6	46.2-1600
46.1-550.6	46.2-1602
46.1-550.7:1	46.2-1601
46.1-550.8	46.2-1603
46.1-550.9	46.2-1604
46.1-550.10	46.2-1605
46.1-550.11	46.2-1606
46.1-550.12	46.2-1607
46.1-550.13	46.2-1608
46.1-550.14	46.2-1609
46.1-550.15	46.2-1610
46.1-551	46.2-1231
46.1-551	46.2-1232
46.1-551	46.2-1233
46.1-552	46.2-1234
46.1-553	33.1-12
46.1-553.1	33.1-12
46.1-554	33.1-12
46.1-555	46.2-12
46.1-555.1	46.2-1200
46.1-555.2	46.2-1201
46.1-555.3	46.2-1201
46.1-555.4	46.2-1202
46.1-555.5	46.2-1203

Former Section	Present Section
46.1-555.6	46.2-1204
46.1-555.7	46.2-1205
46.1-555.8	46.2-1206
46.1-555.9	46.2-1207
46.1-555.10	46.2-1208
46.1-556	46.2-1400
46.1-557	46.2-1401
46.1-558	46.2-1402
46.1-559	46.2-1403
46.1-560	46.2-1404
46.1-561	46.2-1405
46.1-562	46.2-1406
46.1-563	46.2-1407
46.1-564	Repealed
46.1-565	Repealed
46.1-566	46.2-1188
46.1-567	46.2-1189
46.1-568	46.2-1190
46.1-569	46.2-1191
46.1-570	46.2-1192

COMPARABLE SECTIONS OF TITLE 47 AND TITLE 47.1

Former Section	Present Section
47-1	Repealed
47-2	47.1-3 to
	47.1-5, 47.1-8,
	47.1-10, 47.1-23
47-2.1	47.1-12,
	47.1-13, 47.1-24
47-3	47.1-4,
	47.1-26
47-4	Repealed
47-4.1 to	
47-4.6	47.1-24
47-4.7	47.1-25
47-4.8	47.1-24
47-5	47.1-31
47-6	47.1-32
47-7	47.1-33

COMPARABLE SECTIONS OF TITLE 51 AND TITLE 51.1

Former Section	Present Section
51-1	Repealed
51-2	Repealed
51-2.1	51.1-900
51-3 to	
51-111	Repealed
51-111.1	Deleted
51-111.2	51.1-700
51-111.3	51.1-702
51-111.3	51.1-703
51-111.3:1	Deleted
51-111.4	51.1-704
51-111.5	51.1-705
51-111.6	51.1-706
51-111.7	Deleted
51-111.8	51.1-701
51-111.9	Deleted
51-111.10	51.1-101
	51.1-152
51-111.10:01	51.1-101
	51.1-152
51-111.10:1	Deleted
51-111.10:2	51.1-145
51-111.10:3	Deleted
51-111.11	51.1-100
51-111.12	51.1-145
51-111.13	51.1-144
51-111.14	51.1-108
51-111.15	51.1-102
51-111.16	51.1-105
	51.1-106
51-111.17	51.1-110
51-111.18	51.1-109
	51.1-110
51-111.19	51.1-109
51-111.20	51.1-109
	51.1-110
51-111.21 to	
51-111.22:1	51.1-110
51-111.22:2	51.1-103
51-111.23	51.1-110
51-111.24	51.1-102
	51.1-114
51-111.24:1	51.1-117
	51.1-123
51-111.24:2	51.1-116
51-111.24:3	51.1-118
51-111.24:4	51.1-122
51-111.24:5	51.1-119
51-111.24:6	51.1-121
51-111.24:7	51.1-120
51-111.24:8	51.1-124
51-111.25	51.1-111
51-111.26	51.1-112
51-111.26:1	51.1-102
51-111.26:2	51.1-113
51-111.27	51.1-125
	51.1-503
51-111.28	51.1-126
51-111.28	51.1-127
51-111.28:1	Repealed
51-111.29	51.1-128
51-111.30	51.1-129
51-111.30:1	Repealed
51-111.31	51.1-101
51-111.31	51.1-130
51-111.31	51.1-132
51-111.31	51.1-133
51-111.31	51.1-800
51-111.32	51.1-134
51-111.33	51.1-135
51-111.34	51.1-131
51-111.35	51.1-136
51-111.36	51.1-137
51-111.37	51.1-138
51-111.38	51.1-139
51-111.38:1 to	
51-111.38:3	Repealed
51-111.38:4	Deleted
51-111.38:5	Deleted
51-111.38:6 to	
51-111.38:9	Reserved
51-111.38:10 to	
51-111.38:16	Repealed
51-111.39	51.1-140
51-111.40	51.1-141
51-111.41	51.1-140
51-111.41	51.1-142
51-111.41:1	51.1-142
51-111.41:2	Deleted
51-111.41:3	Deleted
51-111.41:4	51.1-143
51-111.41:4	51.1-203
51-111.42	51.1-140
51-111.43	51.1-128
51-111.44	Deleted
51-111.45	51.1-142
51-111.46	51.1-144
51-111.46	51.1-403
51-111.46:1	51.1-144
51-111.47	51.1-145
51-111.47:01	51.1-145
51-111.47:1	51.1-146
51-111.48	Deleted
51-111.49	51.1-147
51-111.50	51.1-148
51-111.51	51.1-149
51-111.52	51.1-150
51-111.52:1	Repealed

Former Section	Present Section
51-111.52:2	Repealed
51-111.52:3	51.1-151
51-111.52:4	Repealed
51-111.52:5	Repealed
51-111.53	51.1-153
51-111.54	51.1-154
51-111.55	51.1-155
51-111.55	51.1-403
51-111.55:1	51.1-155
51-111.56	51.1-156
51-111.57	51.1-157
51-111.57	51.1-404
51-111.57:1	51.1-157
51-111.58	51.1-161
51-111.58:1	51.1-162
51-111.58:2	51.1-164
51-111.59	51.1-163
51-111.59:1	51.1-158
51-111.60	51.1-165
51-111.60:1	51.1-166
51-111.60:2 to 51-111.60:4	Deleted
51-111.61	51.1-159
51-111.62	Repealed
51-111.63	51.1-160
51-111.64	Deleted
51-111.65	51.1-167
51-111.66	Deleted
51-111.67	51.1-107
51-111.67:1	51.1-501
51-111.67:2	51.1-502
51-111.67:2	51.1-505
51-111.67:3	51.1-504
51-111.67:4	51.1-402
51-111.67:4	51.1-505
51-111.67:5	51.1-506
51-111.67:6	51.1-506
51-111.67:6	51.1-507
51-111.67:7	51.1-514
51-111.67:8	51.1-510
51-111.67:9	51.1-508
51-111.67:10	51.1-511
51-111.67:11	Deleted
51-111.67:12	51.1-509
51-111.67:12.1	51.1-510
51-111.67:12.1	51.1-512
51-111.67:13	Repealed
51-111.67:13.1	51.1-513
51-111.67:14	Deleted
51-111.67:15	51.1-600
51-111.67:16	51.1-601
51-111.67:17	51.1-602
51-111.67:18	51.1-603
51-111.67:19	51.1-604
51-111.67:20	51.1-605
51-111.67:21	Deleted
51-111.68	51.1-110
51-111.68	51.1-401
51-111.68:1	Deleted
51-111.69	51.1-402
51-111.70	51.1-402
51-111.70:1	51.1-402
51-111.70:2	Deleted
51-111.71	51.1-104
51-111.72 to 51-111.74	Deleted
51-112	51.1-801 51.1-802
51-112.1	51.1-803
51-113	51.1-804
51-114	51.1-805
51-114.1	Deleted
51-114.2	51-1-806
51-115	51.1-807
51-116	51.1-808
51-117	51.1-809
51-118	51.1-810
51-119	51.1-815
51-120	51.1-811
51-121	51.1-812
51-122	51.1-813
51-122.1	51.1-814
51-122.2	51.1-815
51-122.3	51.1-816
51-123	Deleted
51-124	51.1-817
51-125	51.1-818
51-126	51.1-819
51-126.1	51.1-819
51-127 to 51-127.8	Deleted
51-127.9	51.1-820
51-127.10 to 51-127.30	51.1-805(2)
51-128 to 51-142	Repealed
51-143	51.1-200
51-144	51.1-201
51-145	51.1-202
51-146	51.1-203
51-147	Deleted
51-148	51.1-204
51-149	51.1-115
51-150	51.1-205
51-151	51.1-206
51-151	51.1-405
51-152 to 51-155	Deleted
51-156	51.1-207
51-156.1	Deleted
51-157	Deleted
51-157.1	51.1-208
51-158	Deleted
51-159	Deleted
51-160	51.1-300
51-161	51.1-301
51-162	51.1-302
51-163	51.1-303
51-163.1	Deleted
51-164	Deleted
51-165	Repealed
51-165.1	51.1-304
51-166	51.1-115
51-167	51.1-305
51-168	51.1-306
51-169	51.1-307
51-170	51.1-308
51-170.1 to 51-175	Deleted
51-176	Repealed
51-176.1	Deleted
51-177	Repealed
51-178	12.1-11.1 14.1-39.1 16.1-69.22:1 17-7.01 65.1-101
51-179	51.1-309
51-180	Repealed

COMPARABLE SECTIONS OF TITLE 51.1, ARTICLES 1, 2, AND 3

Former Section	Present Section
51.1-100	51.1-124.2
51.1-101	51.1-124.3
51.1-102	51.1-124.4
51.1-103	51.1-124.5
51.1-104	51.1-124.6
51.1-105	51.1-124.7
51.1-106	51.1-124.8
51.1-107	51.1-124.9
51.1-108	51.1-124.10
51.1-109	51.1-124.20
51.1-110	51.1-124.22
51.1-111	Repealed
51.1-112	51.1-124.23
51.1-113	Deleted
51.1-114	51.1-124.30
51.1-115	51.1-124.31
51.1-116	51.1-124.32
51.1-117	Deleted
51.1-118	Deleted
51.1-119	Deleted
51.1-120	Deleted

Former Section	Present Section
51.1-121	Deleted
51.1-122	51.1-124.33
51.1-123	51.1-124.34
51.1-124	51.1-124.35

COMPARABLE SECTIONS OF TITLE 53 AND TITLE 53.1

Former Section	Present Section
53-19.5	53.1-1
	53.1-8
53-19.6	53.1-9
53-19.7	53.1-9
53-19.8	53.1-10
53-19.9	53.1-27
53-19.10	53.1-11
53-19.11	53.1-12
53-19.12	53.1-12
53-19.13	Deleted
53-19.14	53.1-10
53-19.14:1	53.1-16
53-19.15	Deleted
53-19.15:1	53.1-250
53-19.16	53.1-13
53-19.17	53.1-21
53-19.18	53.1-1
53-19.18:1	53.1-1
53-19.19	53.1-17
53-19.20	53.1-15
	53.1-18
53-19.21	53.1-14
53-19.22	Deleted
53-19.22:1	53.1-251
53-19.22:2	53.1-34
53-19.23	53.1-1
	53.1-2
53-19.24	53.1-2
53-19.25	53.1-4
53-19.27	Deleted
53-19.28	Deleted
53-19.29 to	
53-19.31	53.1-4
53-19.32	53.1-3
53-19.33	53.1-5
53-19.34	53.1-5
53-19.35	Deleted
53-19.36	53.1-6
53-19.31:1	53.1-7
53-19.37	Deleted
53-19.38	Deleted
53-19.38:1	53.1-31
53-19.39	53.1-5
53-19.40	53.1-150
53-20	Deleted
53-21	Deleted
53-21.1	53.1-20
53-21.2	53.1-40
53-23	53.1-25
53-23.1	53.1-26
53-24	53.1-24
53-25	Deleted
53-26	Deleted
53-33	53.1-32
	53.1-41
53-34	53.1-35
53-37	53.1-28
53-37.1	53.1-37
53-37.2	53.1-38
53-38	53.1-60
53-38.01	53.1-61
53-38.1	53.1-62
53-39	53.1-29
53-40	53.1-23
53-42	Deleted
53-45	Deleted
53-47	53.1-33
53-48	Deleted
53-50	Deleted
53-55	53.1-39
53-57	53.1-41
53-57.1	53.1-36
53-60.1	53.1-30
53-61	Deleted
53-62	53.1-54
53-63	53.1-45
53-64	53.1-45
53-67	53.1-47
53-68	53.1-52
53-69	53.1-48
53-70	53.1-49
53-71	53.1-50
53-72	53.1-51
53-73	53.1-54
53-74	53.1-55
53-75 to	
53-76	Deleted
53-76.1	53.1-19
53-76.2	Deleted
53-76.3	53.1-20
53-79	Deleted
53-84	53.1-21
53-87	Deleted
53-89	53.1-22
53-92	Deleted
53-94	53.1-32
	53.1-34
53-94.1 to	
53-102.1	Deleted
53-103	53.1-21
53-104	Deleted
53-107	Deleted
53-109	53.1-56
53-109.1	53.1-57
53-114 to	
53-120	Deleted
53-122	53.1-58
53-122.1	53.1-59
53-123.1	Deleted
53-128.1	53.1-63
53-128.2	53.1-64
53-128.3	53.1-65
53-128.4	53.1-66
53-128.5	53.1-67
53-128.6	53.1-177
	53.1-178, 53.1-179
53-128.7 to	
53-128.15	Deleted
53-128.16	53.1-180
53-128.17	53.1-181
53-128.18	53.1-182
53-128.19	53.1-183
53-128.20	53.1-184
53-128.21	53.1-185
53-129	53.1-71
53-130	Deleted
53-131	Deleted
53-133	53.1-68
53-133.1	53.1-80
53-133.2	53.1-81
53-133.3	53.1-82
53-133.4	53.1-83
53-134	53.1-69
53-135	53.1-70
53-135.1	53.1-21
53-135.2	53.1-133
53-136	53.1-87
53-137	53.1-72
53-138	53.1-73
53-139	53.1-74
53-140	Deleted
53-141	53.1-75
53-142	53.1-76
53-142.1	53.1-77
53-143	53.1-78
53-144	Deleted
53-145	53.1-79
53-146 to	
53-150	Deleted
53-151	53.1-116
53-152	53.1-117
53-161	53.1-118
53-162	53.1-119
53-163	53.1-128
53-164	Deleted
53-165	53.1-129
53-166	53.1-130
53-166.1	53.1-131
53-166.2	53.1-132

Former Section	Present Section
53-168	Deleted
53-168.1	53.1-120
53-169	53.1-121
53-170	53.1-122
53-171	53.1-123
53-172	53.1-124
53-173	53.1-125
53-174	Deleted
53-175	53.1-126
53-176	Deleted
53-178	53.1-88
53-179	Deleted
53-180	53.1-89
53-181	53.1-90
53-182	53.1-91
53-183	53.1-92
53-183.2	53.1-93
53-183.3	53.1-94
53-184 to 53-187	Deleted
53-188	53.1-95
53-195	53.1-96
53-197	53.1-97
53-198	53.1-98
53-198.1	53.1-99
53-199	53.1-100
53-201	53.1-101
53-202	53.1-102
53-203	Deleted
53-204	53.1-103
53-204.1	53.1-104
53-206	Deleted
53-206.1	53.1-105
	53.1-106
53-206.2	Deleted
53-206.3	53.1-106
	53.1-108
53-206.4	53.1-106
	53.1-107
53-206.5	53.1-106
53-206.6	53.1-109
53-206.7	53.1-110
53-206.8	53.1-111
53-206.9	53.1-112
53-206.10	53.1-113
53-206.11	53.1-114
53-206.12	53.1-115
53-207	53.1-186
53-208	53.1-187
53-209	53.1-188
53-209.1	53.1-198
53-209.2	53.1-199
53-209.3	53.1-200
53-209.4	53.1-201
53-209.5	53.1-202
53-209.6	Deleted
53-210	53.1-193
53-211	53.1-194
53-212	53.1-195
53-213	53.1-196
53-213.1	53.1-197
53-214	53.1-189
53-219	53.1-190
53-220	53.1-191
53-220.1	53.1-42
53-222	53.1-43
53-223	53.1-44
53-224	53.1-41
53-226	Deleted
53-228	53.1-229
53-228.1	53.1-230
53-229	53.1-231
53-230	53.1-134
53-230.1	Deleted
53-231 to 53-233	53.1-134
53-234	53.1-134
	53.1-135
53-235	53.1-135
53-236	Deleted
53-237	Deleted
53-238	53.1-136
53-239	53.1-137
53-240	53.1-138
53-241	53.1-139
53-241.1	53.1-140
53-242	53.1-141
53-243	53.1-142
53-244	53.1-143
53-245	53.1-144
53-246	53.1-147
53-247	53.1-147
53-248	Deleted
53-249	53.1-146
53-250	53.1-145
53-250.1	Deleted
53-251	53.1-151
53-251.1	53.1-152
53-251.2	53.1-153
53-251.3	53.1-159
53-252	53.1-154
53-253	53.1-155
53-254	53.1-154
53-255	53.1-156
53-256	53.1-156
53-257	53.1-157
53-258	53.1-161
53-259	53.1-162
53-260	53.1-163
53-261	53.1-164
53-262	53.1-165
53-264	53.1-158
53-265	53.1-136
	53.1-139
53-265.1	53.1-160
53-266 to 53-271	Deleted
53-272	19.2-303
	53.1-151
	53.1-186
53-277	53.1-148
53-278.5	53.1-149
53-279 to 53-287	Deleted
53-288	53.1-166
53-289	53.1-167
53-290	Deleted
53-290.1	53.1-168
53-290.2	53.1-169
53-290.3	53.1-170
53-290.4	53.1-171
53-290.5	53.1-172
53-290.6	Deleted
53-290.7	53.1-173
53-290.8	53.1-174
53-290.9	53.1-175
53-290.10	53.1-176
53-291	53.1-203
53-294	53.1-204
53-295	53.1-205
53-296	Repealed
53-297 to 53-299.2	Deleted
53-300	53.1-205
53-301	53.1-206
53-302	53.1-207
53-303	53.1-208
53-304	53.1-209
53-304.1	53.1-210
53-304.2	53.1-211
53-304.3	53.1-212
53-304.4	Deleted
53-304.5	53.1-213
53-304.6	53.1-214
53-304.7	53.1-215
53-304.8	Deleted
53-304.9	53.1-216
53-304.10	53.1-217
53-305	53.1-221
53-306	53.1-221
53-307	53.1-222
53-307.1	53.1-223
53-308	53.1-224
53-309	53.1-225
53-310	53.1-225
53-311	53.1-226
53-312	53.1-227
53-312.1	53.1-228
53-313	53.1-218
53-314	53.1-218
53-315	53.1-219
53-315.1	53.1-220
53-316	53.1-232
53-317	53.1-233
53-318	53.1-234
53-319.1	53.1-235
53-322	Deleted
53-323	53.1-236
53-324	53.1-237
53-325	53.1-239
53-326	53.1-240
53-327	53.1-241
53-327.1	53.1-242

Former Section	Present Section
53-328	53.1-243
53-329	53.1-244
53-329.1	53.1-245
53-330	53.1-237
	53.1-238
53-331	53.1-249
53-332	53.1-246
53-333	53.1-247
53-334	53.1-248
53-335	53.1-252
53-336	53.1-253
53-337	53.1-254
53-338	53.1-255
53-339	53.1-256
53-340	53.1-257
53-341	53.1-258
53-342	53.1-259
53-343	53.1-260

COMPARABLE SECTIONS OF §§ 53.1-180 TO 53.1-185.3 AND TITLE 9.1

Former Section	Present Section
53.1-180	9.1-173
53.1-181	9.1-174
53.1-182	9.1-175
53.1-182.1	9.1-176
53.1-182.1:1	9.1-177
53.1-183	9.1-178
53.1-184	9.1-179
53.1-185	9.1-180
53.1-185.1	9.1-181
53.1-185.2	9.1-182
53.1-185.3	9.1-183

COMPARABLE SECTIONS OF TITLE 54 AND TITLE 54.1

Former Section	Present Section
9-16	54.1-805
9-16.1	54.1-802
9-16.2	54.1-801
9-17	54.1-805
9-18	Repealed
9-19	54.1-805
9-20	Repealed
9-21	Repealed
9-22	54.1-806
9-23	54.1-809
9-24	54.1-813
9-25	54.1-810
9-26	Repealed
9-27	54.1-810
9-28	54.1-811
9-29	54.1-807
	54.1-814
9-29.1	54.1-815
9-30	54.1-816
9-31	Repealed
9-32	Repealed
9-33	54.1-822
9-34	54.1-808
9-35	54.1-819
9-36	Deleted
9-37	54.1-817
9-38	54.1-812
9-39	54.1-818
9-40	54.1-823
9-41	54.1-824
9-42	54.1-825
9-43	54.1-826
9-44	Deleted
9-44.1	Deleted
9-44.2	Deleted
9-45	54.1-820
9-45.1	54.1-821
9-46	54.1-805
9-46.1	54.1-800
9-47	54.1-803
9-48	54.1-804
54-1	54.1-101
54-1.1	54.1-102
54-1.2	54.1-102
54-1.2:1	54.1-104
54-1.2:2	54.1-106
54-1.2:3	54.1-114
54-1.3 to 54-1.16	Repealed
54-1.17	54.1-100
54-1.18	54.1-300
54-1.18:1	54.1-107
54-1.19	54.1-109
54-1.20	54.1-111
54-1.21	54.1-204
54-1.22	54.1-202
54-1.22:1	54.1-203
54-1.23	54.1-309
54-1.24	54.1-309
54-1.25	54.1-310
54-1.26	54.1-311
54-1.27	54.1-200
54-1.28	54.1-103
	54.1-201
54-1.28:1	54.1-113
54-1.29	Repealed
54-1.30	54.1-301
54-1.31	54.1-302
54-1.32	54.1-303
54-1.33	54.1-304
54-1.34	54.1-305
54-1.35	Deleted
54-1.36	Repealed
54-1.37	54.1-110
54-1.38	Repealed
54-1.39	54.1-306
54-1.40	54.1-307
54-1.41	54.1-108
54-1.42	54.1-308
54-17	Repealed
54-17.1	54.1-400
	54.1-408
	54.1-409
54-18	Repealed
54-18.1	54.1-403
54-19	54.1-403
54-20	Repealed
54-21	Repealed
54-22	54.1-403
54-23	54.1-403
54-24	Repealed
54-25	54.1-404
54-25.1	54.1-407
54-26	54.1-405
54-26.1	54.1-406
54-26.2	Deleted
54-27 to 54-36	Repealed
54-37	54.1-401
54-37.1	54.1-402
54-37.2	54.1-410
54-37.3	54.1-411
54-38	Deleted
54-39	Repealed
54-40	Repealed
54-41	Deleted
54-42	54.1-3900
54-42.1	54.1-3901
	54.1-3902
54-42.2	54.1-3902
54-42.3	Deleted
54-43	54.1-3903
54-44	54.1-3904
54-44.1	54.1-3905
54-44.2	54.1-3907
54-45	Deleted
54-46	54.1-3906
54-47	54.1-3908
54-48	54.1-3909
54-49	54.1-3910

Former Section	Present Section
54-49.1	54.1-3911
54-50	54.1-3912
54-50.1	54.1-3914
54-51	54.1-3915
54-52	54.1-3913
54-52.1	54.1-3916
54-52.2	54.1-3917
54-52.2:1	54.1-3918
54-52.3	Deleted
54-53	54.1-3919
54-54	54.1-3920
54-55	54.1-3919
54-56	54.1-3921
54-57	Repealed
54-57.1	54.1-3922
54-58	54.1-3923
54-59	54.1-3924
54-60	54.1-3925
54-61	Repealed
54-61.1	Repealed
54-62	54.1-3926
54-62.1	Repealed
54-62.2	Deleted
54-63	54.1-3927
54-64	54.1-3928
54-65	54.1-3929
54-66	54.1-3930
54-67	54.1-3931
54-68	Repealed
54-69	Deleted
54-70	54.1-3932
54-71	54.1-3933
54-72	54.1-3934
54-73	Deleted
54-74	54.1-3935
54-74.01	54.1-3936
54-74.1	54.1-3937
54-75	54.1-3935
54-76	54.1-3938
54-77	Deleted
54-78	54.1-3939
54-79	54.1-3941
54-80	Repealed
54-81	Repealed
54-82	54.1-3944
54-83	54.1-3942
54-83.1	54.1-3943
54-83.1:1	54.1-3939
54-83.1:2	54.1-3939
	54.1-3940
54-83.1:3	54.1-3944
54-83.1:4	54.1-3942
54-83.1:5	54.1-2600
54-83.1:6	Repealed
54-83.1:7	54.1-2601
54-83.1:8	54.1-2602
54-83.1:8.1	54.1-2602
54-83.1:9	Repealed
54-83.1:10	54.1-2602
54-83.1:011	54.1-2603
54-83.1:11 to	

Former Section	Present Section
54-83.1:25	Repealed
54-83.2	54.1-700
54-83.3	Repealed
54-83.4	Repealed
54-83.5	54.1-701
54-83.6 to	
54-83.21	Repealed
54-83.22	54.1-702
54-83.22:1	54.1-703
54-83.22:2	54.1-704
54-83.23 to	
54-83.26	Repealed
54-83.27	54.1-705
54-83.28	Deleted
54-102.24	54.1-2002
54-102.25	54.1-2000
54-102.26	54.1-2002
54-102.27	54.1-2003
54-102.28	54.1-2004
54-102.29	54.1-2005
54-102.30	54.1-2006
54-102.31	54.1-2007
54-102.32	54.1-2008
54-102.33	54.1-2001
54-102.34	Deleted
54-102.35	Deleted
54-112.1	54.1-1201
54-112.2	54.1-1200
54-112.3	54.1-1203
54-112.3:1	54.1-1204
54.112.4	Repealed
54-112.4:1	Repealed
54-112.4:2	54.1-1202
54-112.5	Repealed
54-112.6	Repealed
54-112.7	54.1-1202
54-112.8	54.1-1202
54-112.9 to	
54-112.25	Repealed
54-112.26	54.1-1205
54-112.26:1	54.1-1206
54-112.26:2	54.1-1207
54-112.27	Repealed
54-112.28	Repealed
54-112.29	54.1-1201
54-113	54.1-1100
54-113.1	Expired
54-114	54.1-1102
54-115	54.1-1102
54-115.1 to	
54-118	Repealed
54-119 to	
54-121	54.1-1102
54-122	Repealed
54-123	54.1-1102
54-124	54.1-1102
54-125	54.1-1104
54-126	54.1-1105
54-127	Repealed
54-128	54.1-1103
54-129	Repealed

Former Section	Present Section
54-129.1	54.1-1106
54-129.2	54.1-1107
54-129.3	54.1-1108
54-130	Repealed
54-131	54.1-1109
54-132	Repealed
54-132.1	54.1-1110
54-133	54.1-1114
54-134 to	
54-137	Repealed
54-138	54.1-1111
54-139	54.1-1112
54-140	54.1-1113
54-141	54.1-1101
54-142	54.1-1115
54-143	Repealed
54-144	54.1-1116
54-145	Repealed
54-145.1	Repealed
54-145.2	54.1-1117
54-145.3	Deleted
54-145.3:1	54.1-1118
54-145.3:2	54.1-1119
54-145.3:3	54.1-1120
54-145.3:3.1	54.1-1121
54-145.3:4	54.1-1122
54-145.3:5	54.1-1123
54-145.3:6	54.1-1124
54-145.3:7	54.1-1125
54-145.3:8	54.1-1126
54-145.3:9	54.1-1127
54-145.4	54.1-500
54-145.5	54.1-501
54-145.6	54.1-502
54-145.7	54.1-503
54-145.8	54.1-504
54-145.9	54.1-505
54-145.10	54.1-506
54-145.10:1	54.1-507
54-145.10:2	54.1-508
54-145.10:3	54.1-509
54-145.10:4	54.1-510
54-145.10:5	54.1-511
54-145.10:6	54.1-512
54-145.10:7	54.1-513
54-145.10:8	54.1-514
54-145.10:9	54.1-515
54-145.10:10	54.1-516
54-145.10:11	54.1-517
54-145.11	54.1-1000
54-145.12	54.1-1001
54-145.13	54-1-1002
54-145.14 to	
54-145.19	Repealed
54-145.20	54.1-1003
54-146	54.1-2711
54-147	54.1-2712
54-147.1	54.1-2716
54-147.2	54.1-2719
54-148	Repealed
54-149 to	

Former Section	Present Section
54-151	54.1-2701
54-152	54.1-2715
	54.1-2726
54-153 to 54-155	54.1-2702
54-156	54.1-2704
54-157	54.1-2702
54-158 to 54-160	Deleted
54-161	54.1-2702
54-162	54.1-2702
54-162.1	Repealed
54-163	Deleted
54-164	Repealed
54-165	Deleted
54-166	Deleted
54-167	54.1-2703
54-168 to 54-171	54.1-2709
54-172	54.1-2701
	54.1-2710
54-173	Deleted
54-174	Repealed
54-175	54.1-2709
54-175.1	54.1-2713
	54.1-2725
54-175.2	54.1-2714
54-176	54.1-2705
54-177	Deleted
54-178	Deleted
54-179	Repealed
54-180	Deleted
54-181	Repealed
54-181.1	Deleted
54-182	Repealed
54-183	54.1-2717
54-184	54.1-2718
54-185	Deleted
54-186	54.1-2720
54-187	54.1-2706
54-188	Repealed
54-189	54.1-2707
54-189.1	54.1-2708
54-189.2 to 54-194	Repealed
54-195	Deleted
54-196	Deleted
54-197	54.1-2721
54-198 to 54-200.02	Deleted
54-200.1	54.1-2700
54-200.2	54.1-2722
54-200.3	Deleted
54-200.4	54.1-2722
54-200.5	Deleted
54-200.6	54.1-2724
54-200.7 to 54-22.9	54.1-2722
54-200.10	Deleted
54-200.11	54.1-2722
54-200.12	Deleted

Former Section	Present Section
54-200.13	Deleted
54-200.14	54.1-2727
54-200.15	Deleted
54-200.16	Repealed
54-200.16:1	Deleted
54-200.17	Repealed
54-200.18	54.1-2728
54-200.19	Deleted
54-200.20	54.1-2723
54-200.21	Deleted
54-200.22	Deleted
54-200.23	54.1-2701
54-260.64	54.1-2802
54-260.65	54.1-2802
54-260.66	Deleted
54-260.67	54.1-2800
	54.1-2801
54-260.68	54.1-2802
54-260.69	54.1-2803
54-260.70	54.1-2801
	54.1-2804
	54.1-2813
	54.1-2814
54-260.70:1	54.1-2815
54-260.70:2	54.1-2816
54-260.70:3	Deleted
54-260.71	54.1-2818
54-260.71:1	54.1-2812
54-260.72	54.1-2817
54-260.73	54.1-2810
	54.1-2811
54-260.73:1	54.1-2805
54-260.74	54.1-2806
	54.1-2807
	54.1-2808
54-260.74:1	54.1-2819
54-260.75	54.1-2809
54-261	Deleted
54-262	54.1-1602
54-263	Repealed
54-264	54.1-1603
54-265 to 54-268	Repealed
54-268.1	54.1-1604
54-269	Repealed
54-270	Repealed
54-271	54.1-1600
	54.1-1606
54-271.1	54.1-1605
54-272	54.1-1601
54-273	54.1-2900
	54.1-2901
54-274	54.1-2901
	54.1-2902
	54.1-2943
	54.1-2957
54-274.1	54.1-2965
54-275	54.1-2903
54-275.1	54.1-2941
54-275.2	54.1-2939
54-276 to	

Former Section	Present Section
54-276.4	54.1-2901
54-276.5	54.1-2901
	54.1-2927
54-276.6	54.1-2901
54-276.7	54.1-2961
54-276.7:1	54.1-2960
54-276.7:2	54.1-2959
54-276.8	Deleted
54-276.9	Repealed
54-276.9:1	54.1-2966
54-276.10	54.1-2967
54-276.11	54.1-2968
54-276.12	Repealed
54-277	Repealed
54-278	54.1-2962
54-278.1	Repealed
54-278.2	54.1-2963
54-278.3	54.1-2964
54-278.4	18.2-502.1
54-279	54.1-2938
54-280	Repealed
54-280.1	Repealed
54-281	54.1-2929
54-281.1	54.1-2942
54-281.2	54.1-2943
54-281.3	54.1-2929
54-281.4	54.1-2952
54-281.5	54.1-2952
54-281.6	54.1-2951
54-281.7	54.1-2950
54-281.8	54.1-2953
54-281.9	54.1-2953
54-281.10	54.1-2954
54-281.11	54.1-2955
54-281.12	54.1-2956
54-281.13	54.1-2956
54-282	54.1-2911
54-283	54.1-2911
54-284	54.1-2912
54-285	Deleted
54-286	Deleted
54-287	54.1-2911
54-288	Deleted
54-289 to 54-290.2	54.1-2911
54-291	Deleted
54-291.1	54.1-2924
54-292 to 54-295	Deleted
54-295.1	54.1-2944
54-295.2	54.1-2944
54-295.3	54.1-2945
54-295.4	Deleted
54-295.5	Deleted
54-295.6	54.1-2946
54-296	Deleted
54-297	54.1-2931
54-298 to 54-300.1	Repealed
54-300.2	54.1-2913
54-300.3	54.1-2913

Former Section	Present Section
54-301 to	
54-303	Repealed
54-304	54.1-2913
54-305	54.1-2930
54-306	Repealed
54-306.01	Expired
54-306.1	Repealed
54-306.1:1	54.1-2933
54-306.1:2	54.1-2958
54-306.2	54.1-2934
54-306.3	54.1-2935
54-306.4 to	
54-308.4	Repealed
54-308.5	54.1-2947
54-308.6	54.1-2942
	54.1-2943
	54.1-2948
54.308.7	Deleted
54-309	54.1-2932
	54.1-2942
54-309.1	54.1-2940
54.310	54.1-2927
	54.1-2943
54-310.1	Repealed
54-311	54.1-2928
54-311.1	54.1-2936
54-311.2	54.1-2936
54-311.3	54.1-2937
54-312	Deleted
54-313 to	
54-315	Repealed
54-315.1	54.1-2904
54-315.2	54.1-2905
54-315.3	Deleted
54-315.4	Deleted
54-316	54.1-2915
54-317	54.1-2914
	54.1-2915
54-317.1	54.1-2916
54-317.2	Repealed
54-317.3	54.1-2907
54-317.4	54.1-2908
54-317.4:1	54.1-2909
54-315.5	54.1-2910
54-318	Repealed
54-318.1	54.1-2919
54-318.2	54.1-2926
54-318.3	54.1-2920
54-318.4	54.1-2925
54-319	Repealed
54-319.1	Repealed
54-320	Deleted
54-321	54.1-2921
54-321.1	54.1-2918
54-321.2	54.1-2917
54-321.2:1	54.1-2923
54-321.3 to	
54-321.8	54.1-2922
54-322	Deleted
54-323	Deleted
54-324	Repealed
54-325	Deleted
54-325.1	54.1-2906
54-325.2	54.1-2969
54-325.2:1	54.1-2970
54-325.2:2	54.1-2971
54-325.3 to	
54-325.6	Repealed
54-325.7	54.1-2972
54-325.8	54.1-2973
54-325.8:1	54.1-2981
54-325.8:2	54.1-2982
54-325.8:3	54.1-2983
54-325.8:4	54.1-2984
54-325.8:5	54.1-2985
54-325.8:6	54.1-2986
54-325.8:7	54.1-2987
54-325.8:8	54.1-2988
54-325.8:9	54.1-2989
54-325.8:10	54.1-2990
54-325.8:11	54.1-2991
54-325.8:12	54.1-2992
54-325.8:13	Deleted
54-325.9	54.1-2974
54-325.10	54.1-2975
54-325.11	54.1-2976
54-325.12	54.1-2977
54-325.13	54.1-2978
54-325.14	54.1-2979
54-325.15	54.1-2980
54-367.1	Deleted
54-367.2	54.1-3000
54-367.3	54.1-3002
54-367.4	54.1-3002
54-367.4:1	54.1-3004
54-367.5	Deleted
54-367.6	Deleted
54-367.7	Repealed
54-367.8	Deleted
54-367.9	54.1-3003
54-367.10	54.1-3002
54.367.11	54.1-3005
	54.1-3006
54-367.11:1	54.1-3012
54-367.12	54.1-3002
54-367.13	54.1-3017
54-367.14	54.1-3018
54-367.15	Repealed
54-367.16	Repealed
54-367.17	54.1-3016
54-367.18	Repealed
54-367.19	54.1-3020
54-367.20	54.1-3021
54-367.21	Repealed
54-367.22	Repealed
54-367.23	54.1-3019
54-367.24	Repealed
54-367.25	54.1-3011
54-367.26	Deleted
54-367.27	54.1-3013
54-367.28	54.1-3014
54-367.29	54.1-3013
54-367.30	54.1-3015
54-367.31	Repealed
54-367.32	54.1-3007
54-367.33	Repealed
54-367.33:1	54.1-3009
54-367.33:2	54.1-3010
54-367.34	Repealed
54-367.35	54.1-3008
54-367.35:1	Deleted
54-367.36	54.1-3001
54-367.37	Repealed
54-368	54.1-3200
	54.1-3201
54-369	54.1-3202
54-370	54.1-3207
54-371	54.1-3207
54-372	54.1-3208
54-373	Deleted
54-374	Deleted
54-375	54.1-3207
54-375.1	Repealed
54-376	Deleted
54-377	54.1-3209
54-377.1	Deleted
54-378	54.1-3210
54-379	Repealed
54-380	54.1-3211
54-381	54.1-3211
54-382	54.1-3211
	54.1-3212
54-383	54.1-3213
54-384	54.1-3214
54-385	Repealed
54-386	54.1-3203
54-386.1	54.1-3220
54-386.2	54.1-3221
54-387	Repealed
54-388	54.1-3205
	54.1-3215
	54.1-3216
54-388.1	54.1-3217
54-389	Repealed
54-390	Repealed
54-391	54.1-3218
54-392	Repealed
54-393	54.1-3213
54-394	54.1-3213
54-394.1	54.1-3219
54-395	Deleted
54-396	54.1-3204
54-397	Deleted
54-397.1	54.1-3205
54-398	Deleted
54-398.01	Deleted
54-398.02	54.1-3206
54-398.1	54.1-1701
54-398.2	54.1-1700
54-398.3	54.1-1701
	54.1-1704
54-398.4	Repealed
54-398.4:1	54.1-1702

Former Section	Present Section
54-398.5	54.1-1703
54-398.6 to 54-398.8	Repealed
54-398.9	Deleted
54-398.10	54.1-1702
54-398.11 to 54-398.26	Repealed
54-398.27	54.1-1705
54-398.28	Repealed
54-524.1	54.1-3400
54-524.2	54.1-3300
	54.1-3401
54-524.3	Deleted
54-524.4	54.1-3403
54-524.5	54.1-3305
54-524.6	54.1-3305
54-524.7	54.1-3306
54-524.8 to 54-524.10	Deleted
54-524.11	54.1-3305
54-524.12	Deleted
54-524.13	54.1-3305
54-524.14	Deleted
54-524.15	Deleted
54-524.16	54.1-3307
54-524.17	Deleted
54-524.18	54.1-3307
54-524.19	54.1-3308
54-524.20	Repealed
54-524.21	54.1-3312
54-524.22	Repealed
54-524.22:1	54.1-3316
54-524.22:2	54.1-3317
54-524.23	54.1-3311
54-524.24	Deleted
54-524.25	54.1-3311
54-524.26	54.1-3313
54-524.27	Deleted
54-524.28	54.1-3318
54-524.29	Deleted
54-524.30	54.1-3314
54-524.31	54.1-3434
54-524.32	Deleted
54-524.33	Deleted
54-524.34	Repealed
54-524.34:1	54.1-3304
54-524.35	54.1-3315
54-524.36	54.1-3437
54-524.37	54.1-3438
54-524.38	54.1-3430
54-524.39	54.1-3430
54-524.40	54.1-3439
54-524.41	54.1-3440
54-524.41:1	54.1-3441
54-524.41:2	54.1-3442
54-524.42	Repealed
54-524.43	Repealed
54-524.44	54.1-3435
54-524.45	54.1-3436
54-524.46	54.1-3429
54-524.47	54.1-3402
54-524.47:1	54.1-3425
54-524.47:2	54.1-3422
54-524.47:3	54.1-3423
54-524.47:4	54.1-3424
54-524.48	54.1-3310
54-524.49	54.1-3433
54-524.50	Repealed
54-524.50:1	54.1-3303
54-524.51	54.1-3432
54-524.52	Repealed
54-524.53	54.1-3301
	54.1-3302
54-524.54	54.1-3301
54-524.55	Repealed
54-524.56	54.1-3404
54-524.57	54.1-3405
54-524.58	54.1-3406
54-524.58:1	54.1-3413
54-524.58:2	54.1-3420
54-524.59	54.1-3415
54-524.59:1	54.1-3407
54-524.60	54.1-3414
54-524.61	54.1-3417
54-524.62	54.1-3418
54-524.63	Repealed
54-524.64	Repealed
54-524.65	54.1-3408
54-524.66	54.1-3409
54-524.67	54.1-3410
54-524.67:1	54.1-3426
54-524.67:2	54.1-3427
54-524.67:3	54.1-3419
54-524.68	54.1-3411
54-524.69	54.1-3412
54-524.70 to 54-524.74	Repealed
54-524.75	54.1-3416
54-524.76	Repealed
54-524.77	Repealed
54-524.77:1	54.1-3431
54-524.78 to 54-524.84	Repealed
54-524.84:1	54.1-3443
54-524.84:2	54.1-3444
54-524.84:3	54.1-3445
54-524.84:4	54.1-3446
54-524.84:5	54.1-3447
54-524.84:6	54.1-3448
54-524.84:7	54.1-3449
54-524.84:8	54.1-3450
54-524.84:9	54.1-3451
54-524.84:10	54.1-3452
54-524.84:11	54.1-3453
54-524.84:12	54.1-3454
54-524.84:13	54.1-3455
54-524.84:14	54.1-3456
54-524.85	54.1-3457
54-524.86	Deleted
54-524.87	54.1-3458
54-524.88	54.1-3459
54-524.89	Deleted
54-524.90	Repealed
54-524.91	54.1-3460
54-524.92	54.1-3461
54-524.93	54.1-3462
54-524.94	54.1-3463
54-524.95	54.1-3421
54-524.96	54.1-3464
54-524.97	54.1-3465
54-524.98	Deleted
54-524.99	54.1-3309
54-524.100	54.1-3428
54-524.101 to 54-524.108	Repealed
54-524.109	Not Set Out
54-524.109:1	54.1-3466
54-524.109:2	54.1-3467
54-524.109:3	54.1-3468
54-524.109:4	54.1-3469
54-524.109:5	54.1-3470
54-524.109:6	Deleted
54-524.109:7	54.1-3471
54-524.109:8	54.1-3472
54-524.110	54.1-1500
54-524.111	54.1-1501
	54.1-1504
54-524.112	54.1-1501
54-524.113	54.1-1502
54-524.114	54.1-1503
54-524.115	Repealed
54-524.116	54.1-1502
54-524.117 to 54-524.119	Repealed
54-525	54.1-900
54-526	Repealed
54-527	54.1-901
54-528	54.1-901
54-529	54.1-902
54-530	54.1-901
54-531	54.1-901
54-532	Deleted
54-533	54.1-903
54-534	54.1-903
54-535	54.1-904
54-536	54.1-905
54-537	54.1-906
54-538	54.1-906
54-539	54.1-907
54-540	54.1-907
54-541	54.1-908
54-542	54.1-909
54-543	54.1-909
54-544	54.1-910
54-545	Repealed
54-546	Deleted
54-547	54.1-911
54-548	54.1-912
54-549	54.1-913
54-550	54.1-914
54-551	Deleted
54-552	Deleted
54-553	Deleted

Former Section	Present Section
54-554	54.1-915
54-555	54.1-905
54-556	54.1-909
54-557	Deleted
54-558	54.1-916
54-559	Deleted
54-560	Deleted
54-561	54.1-917
54-562	54.1-918
54-563	54.1-919
54-564	54.1-920
54-565	54.1-921
54-566	54.1-922
54-567	Deleted
54-568	Deleted
54-569	54.1-923
54-570	Deleted
54-571	54.1-924
54-572	54.1-925
54-573	54.1-926
54-573.1	54.1-2301
54-573.2	54.1-2300
54-573.3	54.1-2301
54-573.4 to 54-573.17	Repealed
54-573.18	54.1-2302
54-729.27	54.1-1900
54-729.28	54.1-1901
54-729.29	54.1-1902
54-729.30	54.1-1903 54.1-1904
54-729.31	54.1-1905
54-729.32	54.1-1906
54-729.33	54.1-1907
54-729.34	54.1-1908
54-730	54.1-2100
54-731	54.1-2101
54-731.1	54.1-2102
54-731.2	Repealed
54-731.3	54.1-2109
54-732	54.1-2107
54-733	54.1-2110
54-734	54.1-2103
54-735	Repealed
54-736	Repealed
54-737 to 54-739	54.1-2104
54-740	54.1-2105
54-741 to 54-743	Repealed
54-744	54.1-2104
54-745	Deleted
54-746	Deleted
54-747	Repealed
54-748	Repealed
54-749	54.1-2106
54-750 to 54-764.4	Repealed
54-764.5	54.1-2108
54-765	Repealed
54-765.1	Deleted
54-765.2	54.1-2112
54-765.3	54.1-2113
54-765.4	54.1-2114
54-765.4:1	54.1-2115
54-765.5	54.1-2116
54-765.6	54.1-2117
54-765.7	54.1-2118
54-765.8	54.1-2119
54-765.9	54.1-2120
54-766	Deleted
54-770 to 54-772	Repealed
54-773	54.1-2111
54-774	54.1-2111
54-775	Repealed
54-776	54.1-3802
54-777	54.1-3802
54-777.1	54.1-3803
54-778	Repealed
54-779 to 54-782	Deleted
54-783	54.1-3802
54-784	54.1-3802
54-784.01	Repealed
54-784.02	Deleted
54-784.03	54.1-3804
54-784.04	Deleted
54-784.1	Repealed
54-785	Repealed
54-786	54.1-3800 54.1-3801
54-786.1	Repealed
54-786.2	54.1-3805
54-786.3	54.1-3806
54-786.4	54.1-3807
54-786.5	54.1-3808
54-786.6	54.1-3809
54-786.7	Deleted
54-786.8	54.1-3810
54-787 to 54-791	Repealed
54-824.1	Deleted
54-824.2	54.1-600
54-824.3	54.1-601
54-824.4	54.1-602
54-824.5	Repealed
54-824.6	Repealed
54-824.7	54.1-602
54-824.8	Repealed
54-824.9	Repealed
54-824.9:1	54.1-603
54-824.9:2	54.1-604
54-824.9:3	54.1-602
54-824.10 to 54-824.14	Repealed
54-824.15	54.1-605
54-824.16	Repealed
54-824.17	54.1-604
54-824.18	Repealed
54-824.19	54.1-606
54-824.20	Repealed
54-824.21 to 54-835	Deleted
54-836	Repealed
54-840	54.1-4000
54-841	54.1-4001
54-842	54.1-4001
54-843	54.1-4002
54-844	Repealed
54-845	54.1-4003
54-846	54.1-4004
54-847	54.1-4005
54-848	54.1-4006
54-849	54.1-4007
54-850	54.1-4008
54-851	54.1-4009
54-852	54.1-4011
54-853	54.1-4010
54-854	54.1-4011
54-855	54.1-4012
54-856	54.1-4013
54-857	54.1-4014
54-858	54.1-4014
54-859	Deleted
54-859.15	54.1-4100
54-859.16	54.1-4101
54-859.17	54.1-4102
54-859.18	54.1-4103
54-859.19	54.1-4104
54-859.20	54.1-4105
54-859.21	54.1-4106
54-859.22	54.1-4107
54-859.23	54.1-4108
54-859.24	54.1-4109
54-859.25	54.1-4110
54-859.26	54.1-4111
54-859.27	54.1-4109
54-859.28	54.1-4109
54-872.16	54.1-1300 54.1-1301
54-872.17	54.1-1303
54-872.18	54.1-1302
54-872.19	54.1-1305
54-872.20	54.1-1304
54-872.21	54.1-1306
54-872.22	54.1-1307
54-872.23	Repealed
54-872.23:1	54.1-1302
54-872.24	54.1-1308
54-872.25 to 54-899	Deleted
54-900	54.1-3100
54-901	54.1-3103
54-901.1	54.1-3102
54-902	Repealed
54-903	54.1-3101
54-903.1	54.1-3101
54-904 to 54-906.1	Repealed
54-907	54.1-3101
54-908 to 54-915	Repealed

Former Section	Present Section
54-916	54.1-1800
54-917	54.1-1802
54-918	54.1-1801
54-919	Deleted
54-920	54.1-1803
54-921	54.1-1804
54-922	54.1-1805
54-923	Deleted
54-924	54.1-3500
54-925 to 54-927	Repealed
54-928	Deleted
54-929	54.1-3505
	54.1-3605
	54.1-3705
54-930	Repealed
54-931	54.1-3505
	54.1-3605
	54-1.3705
54-932	54.1-3500
54-933	54.1-3503
54-933.1	Deleted
54-933.2	54.1-3504
54-934	Repealed
54-934.1	Repealed
54-935	Deleted
54-935.1	54.1-3506
54-936	54.1-3600

Former Section	Present Section
54-937	54.1-3603
54-937.1	54.1-3604
54-938	54.1-3607
54-939	54.1-3608
54-939.1	54.1-3606
54-940	Reserved
54-941	54.1-3700
54-942	54.1-3703
54-942.1	54.1-3704
54-943	54.1-3707
54-943.1	54.1-3706
54-944	54.1-3501
	54.1-3601
	54.1-3701
54-945	54.1-3502
	54.1-3602
	54.1-3702
54-946	Deleted
54-947	Reserved
54-948	Repealed
54-949	Deleted
54-950	54.1-2500
54-950.1	54.1-2501
54-950.2	54.1-2503
54-950.2:1	Deleted
54-950.3	54.1-2402
54-951	54.1-2507
54-952	Repealed

Former Section	Present Section
54-953	54.1-2508
54-954	54.1-2509
54-954.1	54.1-2504
54-955	54.1-2505
54-955.1	54.1-2510
54-956	Repealed
54-957	Repealed
54-958	Deleted
54-959	Deleted
54-959.1	54.1-2403
54-960	54.1-2506
54-960.1	54.1-2502
54-961	54.1-2401
54-962	54.1-1400
54-963	54.1-1402
54-964	54.1-1403
54-965	54.1-1403
54-966	54.1-1404
54-967	54.1-1405
54-968	54.1-1401
54-969	54.1-2200
54-970	54.1-2201
54-971	54.1-2208
54-972	54.1-2202
54-973	54.1-2203
54-974	54.1-2204
54-975	54.1-2205
54-976	54.1-2206
54-977	54.1-2207

COMPARABLE SECTIONS OF TITLE 56, CHAPTERS 12, 12.1, 12.3, 12.4, 12.7, 12.8 AND 14.1 AND TITLE 46.2, CHAPTERS 20 THROUGH 26

Former Section	Present Section
56-273	46.2-2000
56-274	46.2-2000.1
56-274.1	46.2-2000.2
56-275	Deleted
56-275.01	Deleted
56-275.1	Deleted
56-276	46.2-2001
56-277	46.2-2002
56-277.1	46.2-2003
56-278	46.2-2004
56-279	46.2-2005
56-279.1	46.2-2006
56-280	46.2-2007
56-281	46.2-2008
56-281.1	46.2-2009
56-281.2	46.2-2010
56-282	46.2-2011
56-282.1	Deleted
56-283	Deleted
56-284	Deleted
56-285	Repealed
56-286	46.2-2012
56-287 through 56-291	Deleted
56-291.1	46.2-2013

Former Section	Present Section
56-291.2	46.2-2014
56-291.3	46.2-2015
56-291.3:1	46.2-2016
56-291.3:2	46.2-2017
56-291.3:3	46.2-2018
56-291.3:4	46.2-2019
56-291.3:5	46.2-2020
56-291.3:6	Deleted
56-291.3:7	46.2-2020.1
56-291.4 through 56-291.8:1	Repealed
56-291.9 through 56-291.13	Deleted
56-292	46.2-2021
56-293	46.2-2022
56-293.1	46.2-2023
56-294	46.2-2024
56-295	46.2-2025
56-296	46.2-2026
56-296.1	Repealed
56-297	Deleted
56-298	46.2-2027
56-299	46.2-2028
56-299.1	46.2-2029

Former Section	Present Section
56-300	46.2-2030
56-301 through 56-303	Deleted
56-303.1	46.2-2032
56-304 through 56-304.13	Deleted
56-304.14	Repealed
56-304.15	Deleted
56-304.16	Deleted
56-305	46.2-2031
56-306	Deleted
56-307	Deleted
56-308	46.2-2033
56-309	46.2-2034
56-310 through 56-315	Deleted
56-316	46.2-2035
56-317	46.2-2036
56-318	46.2-2037
56-319	46.2-2038
56-320	46.2-2039
56-321	Deleted
56-322	Deleted

Former Section	Present Section
56-323	46.2-2040
56-324	Deleted
56-324.1	46.2-2041
56-325	46.2-2042
56-326 through 56-328	Repealed
56-329	46.2-2043
56-330	46.2-2044
56-331	46.2-2045
56-332	Deleted
56-333	46.2-2046
56-334	Deleted
56-335	46.2-2047
56-336	Repealed
56-337	46.2-2048
56-337.1	46.2-2049
56-337.2	Deleted
56-338	46.2-2050
56-338.1	46.2-2100
56-338.2	46.2-2101
56-338.3	46.2-2102
56-338.4	46.2-2103
56-338.5	46.2-2104
56-338.6	46.2-2105
56-338.7	46.2-2106
56-338.8	46.2-2107
56-338.9	Repealed
56-338.10	46.2-2108
56-338.11	46.2-2109
56-338.12	46.2-2110
56-338.13	Deleted
56-338.14	46.2-2111
56-338.15	46.2-2112
56-338.16	46.2-2113
56-338.17	46.2-2114
56-338.18	46-2-2114
56-338.40	46.2-2200
56-338.41	46.2-2201
56-338.41:1	46.2-2202
56-338.42	46.2-2203
56-338.43	46.2-2204
56-338.44	46.2-2205
56-338.45	46.2-2206
56-338.46	46.2-2207
56-338.47	46.2-2208
56-338.48	46.2-2209
56-338.49	Deleted
56-338.50	46.2-2300
56-338.51	46.2-2301
56-338.52	46.2-2302
56-338.53	46.2-2303
56-338.54	46.2-2304
56-338.55	46.2-2305
56-338.56	46.2-2306
56-338.57	46.2-2307
56-338.58	46.2-2308
56-338.59	46.2-2309
56-338.60	46.2-2310
56-338.61	Deleted
56-338.62	46.2-2311
56-338.63	46.2-2312
56-338.64	Deleted
56-338.93	46.2-2400
56-338.94	46.2-2401
56-338.95	46.2-2402
56-338.96	46.2-2403
56-338.97	46.2-2404
56-338.98	46.2-2405
56-338.99	46.2-2406
56-338.100	46.2-2407
56-338.101	46.2-2408
56-338.102	46.2-2409
56-338.103	Deleted
56-338.104	46.2-2500
56-338.105	46.2-2501
56-338.106	46.2-2502
56-338.107	46.2-2503
56-338.108	46.2-2504
56-338.109	46.2-2505
56-338.110	46.2-2506
56-338.111	46.2-2507
56-338.111:1	46.2-2508
56-338.112	46.2-2509
56-338.113	46.2-2510
56-338.114	46.2-2511
56-338.115	46.2-2512
56-338.116	46.2-2513
56-338.117	Deleted
56-338.118	46.2-2514
56-338.119	46.2-2515
56-338.120	46.2-2516
56-338.121	46.2-2517
56-338.122	46.2-2518
56-338.123	46.2-2519
56-338.124 through 56-338.127	Deleted
56-457.1	46.2-2600
56-457.2	46.2-2601
56-457.3	46.2-2602
56-457.4	46.2-2603
56-457.5	46.2-2604
56-457.6	46.2-2605
56-457.7	46.2-2606
56-457.8	46.2-2607
56-457.8:1	46.2-2608
56-457.8:2	46.2-2609
56-457.9	Deleted
56-457.10	46.2-2610

COMPARABLE SECTIONS OF TITLE 58 AND TITLE 58.1

Former Section	Present Section
58-1	58.1-1
58-2	58.1-1
58-3	58.1-1
58-3.1	58.1-1
58-4	58.1-1
58-4.1	58.1-8
58-4.2	58.1-9
58-5	58.1-1
58-6	58.1-1
58-7	58.1-1
58-8	58.1-1
58-9	58.1-3000
58-10	58.1-100
58-11	Repealed
58-12	58.1-3606 58.1-3607 58.1-3608
58-12.1	58.1-3600
58-12.2	58.1-3610
58-12.3	58.1-3611
58-12.4	58.1-3650.1
58-12.5	58.1-3612
58-12.6	Repealed
58-12.7	58.1-3650.2
58-12.8	58.1-3650.3
58-12.9	58.1-3613
58-12.10	58.1-3650.4
58-12.11	58.1-3650.5
58-12.12	58.1-3650.6
58-12.13	58.1-3650.7
58-12.14	58.1-3650.8
58-12.15	58.1-3650.9
58-12.16	58.1-3650.10
58-12.17	Repealed
58-12.18	58.1-3650.11
58-12.19	58.1-3650.12
58-12.20	58.1-3614
58-12.21	58.1-3615
58-12.22	58.1-3616
58-12.23	58.1-3650.13
58-12.24	58.1-3617
58-12.25	58.1-3618
58-12.26	58.1-3650.14
58-12.27	58.1-3650.15
58-12.28	58.1-3650.16
58-12.29	58.1-3650.17
58-12.30	58.1-3650.18
58-12.31	58.1-3650.19
58-12.32	58.1-3650.20
58-12.33	58.1-3650.21
58-12.34	58.1-3650.22
58-12.35	58.1-3650.23
58-12.36	58.1-3650.24
58-12.37	58.1-3650.25

Former Section	Present Section
58-12.38	58.1-3650.26
58-12.39	58.1-3650.27
58-12.40	58.1-3650.28
58-12.41	58.1-3650.29
58-12.42	58.1-3650.30
58-12.43	58.1-3650.31
58-12.44	58.1-3650.32
58-12.45	58.1-3650.33
58-12.46	58.1-3650.34
58-12.47	58.1-3650.35
58-12.48	58.1-3650.36
58-12.49	58.1-3650.37
58-12.50	58.1-3650.38
58-12.51	58.1-3650.39
58-12.52	58.1-3650.40
58-12.53	58.1-3650.41
58-12.54	58.1-3650.42
58-12.55	58.1-3650.43
58-12.56	58.1-3650.44
58-12.57	58.1-3650.45
58-12.58	58.1-3650.46
58-12.59	58.1-3650.47
58-12.60	58.1-3650.48
58-12.61	58.1-3650.49
58-12.62	58.1-3650.50
58-12.63	58.1-3650.51
58-12.64	58.1-3650.52
58-12.65	58.1-3650.53
58-12.66	58.1-3650.54
58-12.67	58.1-3650.55
58-12.68	58.1-3650.56
58-12.69	58.1-3650.57
58-12.70	58.1-3650.58
58-12.71	58.1-3650.59
58-12.72	58.1-3650.60
58-12.73	58.1-3650.61
58-12.74	58.1-3650.62
58-12.75	58.1-3650.63
58-12.76	58.1-3650.64
58-12.77	58.1-3650.65
58-12.78	58.1-3650.66
58-12.79	58.1-3620
58-12.80	58.1-3650.67
58-12.81	58.1-3650.68
58-12.82	58.1-3650.69
58-12.83	58.1-3650.70
58-12.84	58.1-3650.71
58-12.85	58.1-3650.72
58-12.86	58.1-3617
58-12.87	58.1-3650.73
58-12.88	58.1-3650.74
58-12.89	58.1-3650.75
58-12.90	58.1-3650.76
58-12.91	58.1-3650.77
58-12.92	58.1-3650.78
58-12.93	58.1-3619
58-12.94	58.1-3650.79
58-12.95	58.1-3650.80
58-12.96	58.1-3650.81
58-12.97	58.1-3650.82
58-12.98	58.1-3650.83
58-12.99	58.1-3650.84
58-12.100	58.1-3650.85
58-12.101	58.1-3650.86
58-12.102	58.1-3650.87
58-12.103	58.1-3650.88
58-12.104	58.1-3650.89
58-12.105	58.1-3650.90
58-12.106	58.1-3650.91
58-12.107	58.1-3650.92
58-12.108	58.1-3650.93
58.12.109	58.1-3650.94
58-12.110	58.1-3650.95
58-12.111	58.1-3650.96
58-12.112	58.1-3650.97
58-12.113	58.1-3650.98
58-12.114	58.1-3650.99
58-12.115	58.1-3650.100
58-12.116	58.1-3650.101
58-12.117	58.1-3650.102
58-12.118	58.1-3650.103
58-12.119	58.1-3650.104
58-12.120	58.1-3650.105
58-12.121	58.1-3650.106
58-12.122	58.1-3650.107
58-12.123	58.1-3650.108
58-12.124	58.1-3650.109
58-12.125	58.1-3650.110
58-12.126	58.1-3650.111
58-12.127	58.1-3650.112
58-12.128	58.1-3650.113
58-12.129	58.1-3650.114
58-12.130	58.1-3650.115
58-12.131	58.1-3650.116
58-12.132	58.1-3650.117
58-12.133	58.1-3650.118
58-12.134	58.1-3650.119
58-12.135	58.1-3650.120
58-12.136	58.1-3650.121
58-12.137	58.1-3650.122
58-12.138	58.1-3650.123
58-12.139	58.1-3650.124
58-12.140	58.1-3650.125
58-12.141	58.1-3650.126
58-12.142	58.1-3650.127
58-12.143	58.1-3650.128
58-12.144	58.1-3650.129
58-12.145	58.1-3650.130
58-12.146	58.1-3650.131
58-12.147	58.1-3650.132
58-12.148	58.1-3650.133
58-12.149	58.1-3650.134
58-12.150	58.1-3650.135
58-12.151	58.1-3650.136
58-12.152	58.1-3650.137
58-12.153	58.1-3650.138
58-12.154	58.1-3650.139
58-12.155	58.1-3650.140
58-12.156	58.1-3650.141
58-12.157	58.1-3650.142
58-12.158	58.1-3650.143
58-12.159	58.1-3650.144
58-12.160	58.1-3650.145
58-12.161	58.1-3650.146
58-12.162	58.1-3650.147
58-12.163	58.1-3650.148
58-12.164	58.1-3650.149
58-12.165	58.1-3650.150
58-12.166	58.1-3650.151
58-12.167	58.1-3650.152
58-12.168	58.1-3650.153
58-12.169	58.1-3650.154
58-12.170	58.1-3650.155
58-12.171	58.1-3650.156
58-12.172	58.1-3650.157
58-12.173	58.1-3650.158
58-12.174	58.1-3650.159
58-12.175	58.1-3650.160
58-12.176	58.1-3650.161
58-12.177	58.1-3650.162
58-12.178	58.1-3650.163
58-12.179	58.1-3650.164
58-12.180	58.1-3650.165
58-12.181	58.1-3650.166
58-12.182	58.1-3650.167
58-12.183	58.1-3650.168
58-12.184	58.1-3650.169
58-12.185	58.1-3650.170
58-12.186	58.1-3650.171
58-12.187	58.1-3650.172
58-13	58.1-3602
58-14	58.1-3603
58-14.1	58.1-3604
58-14.2	58.1-3605
58-15	Repealed
58-16	58.1-3603
58-16.1	58.1-3601
58-16.2	58.1-3400
	58.1-3401
	58.1-3402
	58.1-3403
	58.1-3404
	58.1-3407
58-16.2:1	58.1-3405
58-16.2:2	58.1-3406
58-16.3	58.1-3660
58-16.4	58.1-3661
58-16.5	58.1-3662
58-19	58.1-3663
58-19.6	Repealed
58-19.7	58.1-520
58-19.8	58.1-521
58-19.9	58.1-522
58-19.10	58.1-523
58-19.11	58.1-524
58-19.12	58.1-525
58-19.13	58.1-526
58-19.14	58.1-527
58-19.15	58.1-528
58-19.16	58.1-529
58-19.17	58.1-530
58-19.18	58.1-531
58-19.19	58.1-532

Former Section	Present Section
58-19.20	58.1-533
58-19.21	58.1-534
58-20	58.1-3015
58-21	Repealed
58-22	58.1-3016
58-23	58.1-5
58-24	58.1-6
58-25	58.1-7
58-26	58.1-13
58-26.1	58.1-12
58-27	58.1-11
58-27.1	58.1-2
58-27.2	58.1-3014
58-27.3	58.1-10
58-27.4	58.1-4
58-28	58.1-200
58-29	58.1-201
58-30	58.1-213
58-31	58.1-215
58-32	58.1-212
58-33	58.1-202
58-33.1	58.1-206
58-33.2	58.1-207
58-33.3	58.1-208
58-33.4	58.1-202
58-34	Repealed
58-35	58.1-216
58-36	58.1-216
58-37	58.1-217
58-38	58.1-218
58-39	58.1-219
58-40	58.1-111
58-41	58.1-1805
	58.1-2021
58-42	58.1-1805
	58.1-2021
58-43	58.1-1805
	58.1-2021
58-44	58.1-1806
	58.1-1807
	58.1-2022
	58.1-2023
58-44.1	58.1-1813
	58.1-1814
	58.1-1815
58-44.2	58.1-16
58-45	58.1-105
58-45.1	58.1-101
58-46	58.1-3
58-46.1	Repealed
58-46.2	58.1-3.1
58-46.3	58.1-209
58-47	58.1-210
58-48	58.1-211
58-48.1	58.1-106
58-48.2	58.1-107
58-48.3	58.1-108
58-48.4	58.1-109
58-48.5	58.1-110
58-48.6	58.1-203
58-48.7	58.1-204
58-48.8	58.1-205
58-52	58.1-1725
58-53	58.1-1726
58-54	58.1-801
58-54.1	58.1-802
	58.1-811
58-55	58.1-803
58-55.1	58.1-804
	58.1-811
58-56	58.1-805
58-57	58.1-806
58-58	58.1-807
	58.1-811
58-59	58.1-808
58-60	58.1-809
58-61	58.1-810
	58.1-811
58-62	Repealed
58-63	58.1-812
58-64	58.1-311
58-64.1	58.1-811
58-65	58.1-812
	58.1-813
58-65.1	58.1-814
	58.1-3800
	58.1-3801
	58.1-3802
	58.1-3803
	58.1-3804
58-66	58.1-1712
	58.1-1713
58-66.1	58.1-1714
58-67	58.1-1713
58-67.1	58.1-1718
	58.1-3806
	58.1-3807
	58.1-3808
58-68	58.1-1715
58-69	58.1-1716
58-70	58.1-1717
58-71	58.1-3809
58-72	58.1-3809
58-73	58.1-3809
58-75	58.1-3810
58-76	58.1-3811
58-76.1	58.1-3819
58-76.2	58.1-3820
58-151.01	58.1-301
58-151.02	58.1-302
	58.1-303
58-151.03	58.1-320
	58.1-321
	58.1-360
	58.1-390
	58.1-400
	58.1-401
58-151.04	58.1-300
58-151.011	58.1-320
58-151.012	58.1-324
	58.1-326
58-151.013	58.1-302
	58.1-322
	58.1-324
	58.1-325
	58.1-402
58-151.013:1	58.1-323
58-151.014	58.1-391
58-151.014:1	58.1-330
58-151.014:2	58.1-331
	58.1-431
58-151.015	58.1-332
58-151.016	58.1-321
58-151.021	58.1-360
	58.1-420
58-151.022	58.1-361
58-151.023	58.1-302
	58.1-361
58-151.024	58.1-362
58-151.025	58.1-363
58-151.026	58.1-370
58-151.027	58.1-371
58-151.031	58.1-400
58-151.032	58.1-402
58-151.032:1	58.1-403
58-151.032:2	58.1-403
58-151.032:3	Repealed
58-151.032:4	58.1-333
	58.1-430
58-151.033	58.1-405
58-151.034	58.1-302
58-151.035	58.1-406
58-151.037	58.1-407
58-151.041	58.1-408
58-151.042	58.1-409
58-151.043	58.1-410
58-151.044	58.1-411
58-151.045	58.1-412
58-151.046	58.1-413
58-151.047	58.1-414
58-151.048	58.1-415
58-151.049	58.1-416
58-151.050	58.1-417
58-151.050:1	58.1-418
58-151.050:2	58.1-419
58-151.050:3	58.1-420
58-151.051	58.1-421
58-151.061	58.1-340
	58.1-380
	58.1-440
58-151.062	58.1-341
	58.1-381
	58.1-441
58-151.063	58.1-342
58-151.064	58.1-343
	58.1-382
58-151.065	58.1-306
58-151.066	Repealed
58-151.067	58.1-344
58-151.067:1	58.1-393
58-151.068	58.1-305
58-151.069	Repealed
58-151.070	58.1-307

Former Section	Present Section
58-151.071	58.1-308
58-151.072	58.1-309
58-151.072:1	58.1-345
58-151.072:2	58.1-346
58-151.073	58.1-347
58-151.074	58.1-348
58-151.075	58.1-349
58-151.076	58.1-350
58-151.077	58.1-314
	58.1-351
	58.1-352
	58.1-353
58-151.078	58.1-392
	58.1-441
58-151.079	58.1-442
58-151.079:1	58.1-443
58-151.080	58.1-444
58-151.081	58.1-302
58-151.082	58.1-445
58-151.083	58.1-446
58-151.084	58.1-392
	58.1-447
58-151.085	58.1-448
58-151.086	58.1-449
58-151.087	58.1-450
58-151.088	58.1-451
58-151.089	58.1-452
58-151.090	58.1-453
58-151.091	58.1-454
58-151.093	58.1-455
58-151.094 to 58-151.096	Repealed
58-151.097	58.1-310
58-151.099	58.1-354
58-151.0102	Repealed
58-151.0103	58.1-311
58-151.0104	58.1-312
58-151.0105	58.1-313
58-151.0106	58.1-314
58-151.0111	58.1-315
58-151.1	58.1-460
58-151.2	58.1-461
58-151.3	58.1-462
58-151.4	58.1-463
58-151.5	58.1-464
58-151.6	58.1-465
58-151.7	58.1-466
58-151.8	58.1-467
58-151.8:1	58.1-468
58-151.9	58.1-469
58-151.10	58.1-484
58-151.11	58.1-470
58-151.12	58.1-471
58-151.13	58.1-472
	58.1-473
	58.1-474
	58.1-475
	58.1-476
	58.1-477
58-151.13:1	58.1-12
58-151.14	58.1-478

Former Section	Present Section
58-151.15	58.1-485
58-151.16	58.1-479
58-151.17	58.1-480
58-151.18	58.1-481
58-151.19	58.1-482
58-151.20	58.1-483
58-151.21	58.1-490
58-151.22	58.1-491
58-151.23	58.1-492
58-151.24	58.1-493
58-151.25	58.1-494
58-151.26	58.1-495
58-151.27	58.1-496
58-151.28	58.1-497
58-151.29	Deleted
58-151.30	58.1-498
58-151.31	58.1-499
58-151.33 to 58-151.35	Repealed
58-151.36	58.1-500
58-151.37	58.1-501
58-151.38	58.1-502
58-151.39	58.1-503
58-151.40	58.1-504
58-151.41	Repealed
58-152 to 58-238	Repealed
58-238.1	58.1-900
58-238.2	58.1-901
58-238.3	58.1-902
58-238.4	58.1-903
58-238.5	58.1-904
58-238.6	58.1-905
58-238.7	58.1-906
58-238.8	58.1-907
58-238.9	58.1-908
58-238.10	58.1-909
58-238.11	58.1-910
58-238.12	58.1-911
58-238.14	Repealed
58-238.15	58.1-912
58-238.16	Repealed
58-238.17	58.1-913
58-238.18	58.1-913
58-238.19	58.1-914
58-238.20	58.1-915
58-238.21	58.1-916
58-238.22	58.1-917
58-238.23	58.1-918
58-238.24	58.1-919
58-238.25	58.1-920
58-238.26	58.1-921
58-238.27	58.1-922
58-238.28	58.1-923
58-238.29	58.1-924
58-238.30	58.1-925
58-238.31	58.1-924
58-238.32	58.1-926
58-238.33	58.1-927
58-238.34	58.1-928
58-238.35	58.1-929

Former Section	Present Section
58-238.36	58.1-930
58-238.37	58.1-935
	58.1-936
	58.1-937
	58.1-938
58-238.38	58.1-931
	58.1-932
	58.1-933
	58.1-934
58-239	58.1-3700
58-240	Repealed
58-266.1	58.1-3509
	58.1-3510
	58.1-3701
	58.1-3702
	58.1-3703
	58.1-3704
	58.1-3706
	58.1-3711
	58.1-3720
	58.1-3732
	58.1-3733
	58.1-3734
58-266.1:1	58.1-3712
58-266.1:2	58.1-3713
58-266.1:3	58.1-3713.1
58-266.4	58.1-3707
	58.1-3709
58-266.5	58.1-3705
	58.1-3708
58-266.5:1	58.1-3710
58-266.6	58.1-3735
58-266.7	58.1-3728
58-266.8	58.1-3717
	58.1-3719
58-266.9	58.1-3729
58-266.10	58.1-3730
58-299	58.1-3715
58-302	Repealed
58-302.1	58.1-3714
58-302.2 to 58-303.1	Repealed
58-340	58.1-3717
58-354	58.1-3718
	58.1-3719
58-356	Repealed
58-357	58.1-3722
58-359	58.1-3721
58-360	58.1-3723
58-361.1	Repealed
58-371.2	58.1-3724
58-374	58.1-3725
58-377.1	58.1-3726
58-393.1	58.1-3727
58-404.02	58.1-1700
	58.1-1701
	58.1-1702
	58.1-1703
	58.1-1704
58-404.1	58.1-3817
58-404.2	58.1-3818

Former Section	Present Section
58-405	58.1-1100
	58.1-1101
	58.1-3507
58-412.1	58.1-1102
58-412.2	58.1-1102
58-413	58.1-1103
58-414	58.1-1106
58-415	58.1-1106
58-416	58.1-1104
58-417	58.1-1105
58-421	Repealed
58-422	Repealed
58-423	58.1-1107
58-424	58.1-1108
58-425	58.1-1109
58-426	58.1-216
58-427	58.1-1110
58-428	58.1-1108
	58.1-4
58-429	58.1-1110
58-430	58.1-1110
58-431	58.1-1110
58-432	58.1-1111
58-433	58.1-1111
58-434	58.1-1112
58-435	58.1-1114
58-436	58.1-1115
58-437	58.1-1111
58-438	58.1-1113
58-439	Repealed
58-440	58.1-1118
58-441	58.1-1108
	58.1-1116
	58.1-1117
58-441.1	58.1-600
58-441.2	58.1-602
58-441.3	58.1-602
58-441.4	58.1-603
58-441.5	58.1-604
58-441.6	58.1-602
	58.1-608
58-441.7	58.1-608
58-441.8	58.1-611
58-441.9	58.1-604
58-441.10	58.1-607
58-441.11	58.1-608
58-441.12	58.1-612
58-441.13	Repealed
58-441.14	58.1-627
58-441.15	58.1-610
58-441.16	58.1-613
58-441.17	58.1-623
58-441.18	58.1-625
58-441.19	58.1-626
58-441.20	58.1-615
58-441.21	58.1-616
58-441.22	58.1-619
58-441.23	58.1-620
58-441.24	58.1-621
58-441.25	58.1-622
58-441.26	58.1-617

Former Section	Present Section
58-441.27	58.1-635
58-441.28	58.1-618
58-441.29	58.1-633
58-441.30	58.1-629
58-441.31	58.1-630
58-441.32	58.1-631
58-441.33	58.1-624
58-441.34	58.1-614
58-441.35	58.1-637
	58.1-12
58-441.36	58.1-632
58-441.38	58.1-634
58-441.39	58.1-636
58-441.40	58.1-601
58-441.42	58.1-213
58-441.44	58.1-214
	58.1-215
58-441.45 to 58-441.47	Repealed
58-441.48	58.1-638
58-441.49	58.1-3716
	58.1-605
58-441.49:1	58.1-606
58-441.49:2	58.1-605
58-441.49:3	58.1-609
58-441.50	Repealed
58-441.51	58.1-628
58-442	58.1-2800
58-443	58.1-2801
58-444	58.1-2802
58-445	58.1-2803
58-450	58.1-2804
58-451	58.1-2805
58-454	58.1-2806
58-455	58.1-2807
58-456	58.1-2808
58-458	58.1-2809
58-459	58.1-2810
58-460	58.1-2811
58-462	58.1-2812
58-463	58.1-2813
58-464	58.1-2814
58-485.01	58.1-1201
58-485.02	58.1-1201
58-485.03	58.1-1217
58-485.04	58.1-1202
58-485.05	58.1-1203
58-485.06	58.1-1204
58-485.07	58.1-1205
58-485.08	58.1-1206
58-485.09	58.1-1208
58-485.010	58.1-1209
58-485.011	58.1-1210
58-485.012	58.1-1211
58-485.013	58.1-1207
58-485.014	58.1-1212
58-485.015	58.1-1213
58-485.016	58.1-1214
58-485.017	58.1-1215
58-485.018	58.1-1216
58-486	58.1-2500

Former Section	Present Section
58-487	58.1-2504
58-488	58.1-1205
58-489	58.1-2503
	58.1-2504
58-490	58.1-2501
58-491	58.1-2501
58-492	58.1-2501
58-493	58.1-2502
58-494	58.1-2502
58-495	58.1-2509
58-497	58.1-2506
58-498	58.1-2507
58-499	58.1-2508
58-500	58.1-2508
58-501	58.1-2501
58-502	58.1-2500
58-502.1	58.1-2300
	58.1-2500
58-502.2	58.1-2500
	58.1-2520
	58.1-2522
58-502.3	58.1-2521
	58.1-2522
58-502.4	58.1-2523
	58.1-2524
	58.1-2525
58-502.5	58.1-2526
58-502.6	58.1-2527
	58.1-2528
58-502.7	58.1-2529
58-502.8	Repealed
58-502.9	58.1-2530
58-502.10	Repealed
58-503	58.1-2600
58-503.1	58.1-2600
58-503.2	58.1-2600
	58.1-2620
58-504	58.1-2629
58-505	58.1-2629
58-506	58.1-2630
58-507	58.1-2631
58-508	58.1-2600
58-509	58.1-2632
58-510	58.1-2601
58-511	58.1-2602
58-512	58.1-2603
58-512.1	58.1-2604
58-514	58.1-2610
58-514.1	58.1-2611
58-514.2	58.1-2606
58-514.2:1	58.1-2605
58-514.2:2	58.1-2607
58-514.2:3	58.1-2609
58-514.3	58.1-2600
58-514.4	58.1-2600
	58.1-2640
	58.1-2642
58-514.5	58.1-2641
	58.1-2642
58-514.6	58.1-2643
	58.1-2644

Former Section	Present Section
	58.1-2645
	58.1-2646
58-514.7	58.1-2647
58-514.8	58.1-2648
	58.1-2649
58-514.9	58.1-2650
58-514.10	Repealed
58-514.11	Repealed
58-514.12	58.1-2651
58-515	58.1-2652
58-518	58.1-2690
58-519	58.1-2608
58-522	58.1-2607
58-523	58.1-2690
58-524	58.1-2653
58-525	58.1-2653
58-528	58.1-2653
58-529	58.1-2655
58-530	58.1-2652
	58.1-2657
58-531	Repealed
58-532	58.1-2656
58-536	58.1-2612
58-537	58.1-2611
58-538	58.1-2657
58-539	58.1-2610
58-541.1	58.1-2659
58-556	58.1-2600
	58.1-2653
58-557	58.1-2653
58-558	58.1-2655
58-559	58.1-2657
58-560	58.1-2652
58-561	58.1-2611
58-562	Repealed
58-578	58.1-2690
	58.1-3731
58-579	58.1-2621
	58.1-2622
58-580	58.1-2623
	58.1-2624
	58.1-2625
58-581	58.1-2628
58-582	58.1-2633
58-583	58.1-2634
58-584	58.1-2634
58-586	58.1-2635
58-587	58.1-2611
58-587.1	58.1-3812
58-587.2	58.1-3813
58-588	58.1-2627.1
58-590	58.1-2627.1
58-591	58.1-2635
58-592	58.1-2634
58-593	58.1-2690
58-596	58.1-2690
58-597	58.1-2627.1
58-599	58.1-2612
58-601	58.1-2611
58-602	58.1-2690
58-603	58.1-2626
	58.1-2627
	58.1-3731
58-605	58.1-2606
58-606	58.1-2690
58-607 to 58-609	58.1-2628
58-610	58.1-2633
58-611	58.1-2634
58-612	58.1-2634
58-613	58.1-2635
58-614	58.1-2611
58-615	58.1-2612
58-617.1	Repealed
58-617.2	58.1-3814
58-618	58.1-2654
58-619	58.1-2654
58-620	58.1-2655
58-621	58.1-2657
58-622	58.1-2652
58-623	58.1-2658
58-624	58.1-2657
58-625	58.1-2610
58-626	58.1-2611
58-626.1	58.1-2600
58-627	58.1-2600
	58.1-2700
	58.1-2702
58-628	58.1-2701
58-629	58.1-2706
58-629.1	58.1-2707
58-629.2	58.1-2710
58-630	58.1-2703
58-631	58.1-2701
58-632	58.1-2704
58-633	58.1-2702
	58.1-2705
58-633.1	Deleted
58-634	58.1-2708
58-634.1	58.1-2711
58-635	58.1-2709
58-636	58.1-2709
58-637	58.1-2701
58-660 to 58-663	58.1-2660
58-664	58.1-2660
	58.1-2661
	58.1-2662
58-665	58.1-2660
58-666	58.1-2660
58-667	58.1-2660
	58.1-2663
58-668	58.1-2663
58-669	58.1-2664
58-670	58.1-2665
58-672	58.1-2670
58-673	58.1-2671
58-674	58.1-2672
58-675	58.1-2673
58-678	58.1-2674
58-679	58.1-2675
58-680	58.1-2676
58-681	58.1-2657
	58.1-2680
58-682	58.1-2681
58-683	58.1-2682
58-684	58.1-2680
58-685	58.1-2683
58-685.10	58.1-2400
58-685.11	58.1-2401
58-685.12	58.1-2402
58-685.12:1	58.1-2402
58-685.13	58.1-2401
	58.1-2403
58-685.13:1	58.1-2403
58-685.13:2	58.1-2401
58-685.14	58.1-2404
58-685.15	58.1-2405
58-685.16	58.1-2421
58-685.17	58.1-2406
58-685.17:1	58.1-2407
	58.1-2408
	58.1-2409
	58.1-2410
58-685.17:2	58.1-2411
58-685.17:3	58.1-2412
58-685.17:4	58.1-2415
58-685.17:5	58.1-2416
58-685.17:6	58.1-2417
58-685.17:7	58.1-2413
58-685.17:8	58.1-2414
58-685.18	58.1-2420
58-685.19	58.1-2423
58-685.20	58.1-2424
58-685.21	58.1-2422
58-685.22	58.1-2426
58-685.23	58.1-2425
58-685.24	58.1-2419
58-685.25	58.1-2418
58-685.26	Repealed
58-685.27	58.1-1500
58-685.28	58.1-1501
58-685.29	58.1-1502
58-685.29:1	58.1-1510
58-685.30	58.1-1501
	58.1-1502
	58.1-1503
	58.1-1506
	58.1-1507
	58.1-1510
58-685.31	58.1-1505
58-685.32	58.1-1502
	58.1-1505
	58.1-1506
58-685.33	58.1-1503
58-685.36	58.1-1508
58-685.37	58.1-1504
58-685.38	58.1-1509
58-685.39	58.1-1400
58-685.40	58.1-1401
58-685.41	58.1-1402
58-685.42	58.1-1408
58-685.43	58.1-1406

Former Section	Present Section
58-685.44	58.1-1402
	58.1-1403
	58.1-1404
	58.1-1405
	58.1-1408
58-685.45	58.1-1404
58-685.46	58.1-1404
	58.1-1405
58-685.47	58.1-1403
58-685.48	58.1-1407
58-685.49	58.1-1409
58-685.50	58.1-1410
58-686	58.1-2100
58-687	58.1-2101
58-688	58.1-2103
58-689	58.1-2147
58-690	58.1-2104
58-691	58.1-2142
58-691.1	58.1-2142
	58.1-2143
58-692	58.1-2142
58-692.1	58.1-2102
58-693 to 58-696	58.1-2135
58-697	58.1-2137
58-698 to 58-701	58.1-2135
58-702	58.1-2136
58-703	58-1-2135
58-704	58.1-2136
58-705	58.1-2138
	58.1-2140
58-706	58.1-2138
58-707	58.1-2138
	58.1-2140
58-708	58.1-2139
58-709	58.1-2140
58-710	58.1-2140
58-711	58.1-2105
	58.1-2129
58-712	58.1-2106
	58.1-2111
58-712.1	58.1-2106
58-713	58.1-2107
	58.1-2128
58-713.1	58.1-2107
58-714	58.1-2104
	58.1-2129
58-715	58.1-2111
58-716	58.1-2112
58-717	58.1-2111
	58.1-2113
58-718	Repealed
58-719	58.1-2111
58-720	58.1-2112
58-721	58.1-2144
58-722	58.1-2132
58-723	58.1-2108
58-724	58.1-2133
58-725	58.1-2134
58-726	58.1-2131

Former Section	Present Section
58-727	58.1-2109
58-728	58.1-2110
58-729	58.1-2141
58-730	58.1-2146
58-730.1	58.1-2146
58-730.2	58.1-2135
58-730.3	58.1-2113
	58.1-2146
58-730.4	58.1-2130
58-730.5	58.1-1719
	58.1-1720
	58.1-1721
	58.1-1722
	58.1-1723
	58.1-1724
58-730.6	58.1-1723
58-730.7	58.1-2300
58-730.8	58.1-2302
58-730.9	58.1-2303
	58.1-2310
58-730.10	58.1-2304
58-730.11	58.1-2301
58-730.12	58.1-2305
58-730.13	58.1-2306
58-730.14	58.1-2307
58-730.15	58.1-2308
58-730.16	58.1-2309
58-730.17	58.1-2311
58-731	58.1-2100
58-732	58.1-2101
58-733	58.1-2146
58-734 to 58-735	58.1-2135
58-735.1	58.1-2138
58-735.2	58.1-2139
58-735.3	58.1-2136
58-735.4	58.1-2136
58-736	58.1-2137
58-737 to 58-739.1	58.1-2135
58-739.3	58.1-2133
58-740 to 58-741.1	58.1-2135
58-742	58.1.2140
58-743	58.1-2141
58-744	58.1-2116
	58.1-2118
	58.1-2129
	58.1-2130
58-744.1	58.1-2117
58-746	58.1-2119
	58.1-2128
58-747	58.1-2131
58-748	58.1-2120
58-748.2	58.1-2144
	58.1-2145
58-749	58.1-2144
58-749.1	58.1-2115
58-749.2	58.1-2115
58-750	58.1-2132
58-751	58.1-2133

Former Section	Present Section
58-752	58.1-2134
58-753	58.1-2121
58-753.1	58.1-2122
58-753.1:1	58.1-2123
58-753.1:2	58.1-2124
58-753.1:3	58.1-2125
58-753.2	58.1-2102
58-753.4	58.1-2130
58-754	58.1-2147
58-754.1	58.1-2142
58-755	58.1-2142
58-756	58.1-2103
58-757	58.1-2146
58-757.01	58.1-2114
	58.1-2126
58-757.1	58.1-1001
	58.1-1002
	58.1-1003
58.1-757.1:1	Repealed
58-757.2	58.1-1003
	58.1-1008
58-757.3	58.1-1004
58-757.4	58.1-1005
	58.1-1007
58-757.5	58.1-1006
58-757.6	58.1-1007
58-757.7	58.1-1008
58-757.8	58.1-1009
58-757.9	58.1-1010
58-757.10	58.1-1000
	58.1-1009
	58.1-1011
58-757.11	58.1-1012
58-757.12	58.1-1013
58-757.13	58.1-1014
58-757.14	58.1-1015
58-757.15	58.1-1016
58-757.16	Deleted
58-757.17	58.1-1017
58-757.18	58.1-1000
58-757.19	58.1-1018
58-757.20	58.1-1019
58-757.21	58.1-1020
58-757.22	58.1-1021
58-757.23	58.1-1022
58-757.24 to 58-757.26	Repealed
58-757.27	58.1-3830
58-757.28	58.1-3831
58-757.29	58.1-3832
58-758	58.1-3200
58-758.1	58.1-3203
58-759	58.1-3320
58-760	58.1-3201
	58.1-3202
58-760.1	58.1-3210
	58.1-3211
	58.1-3212
	58.1-3213
	58.1-3214
	58.1-3215

Former Section	Present Section
	58.1-3216
	58.1-3217
	58.1-3218
58-760.2	58.1-3220
58-760.3	58.1-3221
58-761	58.1-3204
58-761.1	58.1-3223
58-762	58.1-3340
58-763	58.1-3351
58-764	58.1-3354
58-764.1	58.1-3355
58-766.3	58.1-3520
58-767	58.1-3341
58-768	Repealed
58-768.1	58.1-3345
58-769	58.1-3260
58-769.1	58.1-3261
58-769.2	58.1-3253
	58.1-3270
58-769.3	58.1-3271
58-769.3:1	58.1-3274
58-769.3:2	58.1-3294
58-769.4	58.1-3229
58-769.5	58.1-3230
58-769.6	58.1-3231
58-769.6:1	58.1-3232
58-769.7	58.1-3233
58-769.8	58.1-3234
58-769.8:1	58.1-3235
58-769.9	58.1-3236
58-769.10	58.1-3237
58-769.10:1	58.1-3238
58-769.11	58.1-3239
58-769.12	58.1-3240
58-769.13	58.1-3241
58-769.14	58.1-3242
58-769.15	58.1-3243
58-769.15:1	58.1-3244
58-769.16	Repealed
58-770	58.1-3343
58-770.1	58.1-3288
58-771	58.1-3342
58-772	Repealed
58-772.1	58.1-3285
58-773	58.1-3290
58-773.1	58.1-3282
58-773.2	58.1-3283
58-774	58.1-3286
58-774.2	58.1-3287
58-776	58.1-3250
58-776.1	58.1-3251
58-776.2	58.1-3272
58-776.3	58.1-3271
58-776.4	Repealed
58-778	58.1-3252
58-778.1	58.1-3253
58-784.3	58.1-3254
58-784.5	58.1-3255
58-785	58.1-3258
58-785.1	58.1-3321
58-786	58.1-3275
58-788	58.1-3271
58-789	58.1-3276
58-790	58.1-3280
58-791	58.1-3300
58-792	58.1-3257
58-792.01	58.1-3330
58-792.02	58.1-3331
58-793	58.1-3277
58-794	58.1-3278
58-795	58.1-3256
58-795.2	58.1-3259
58-796	58.1-3281
58-797	58.1-3303
58-798	58.1-3304
58-799	58.1-3305
58-800	58.1-3306
58-801	Repealed
58-802	58.1-3308
58-803	58.1-3309
58-804	58.1-3284
	58.1-3301
58-805	58.1-3302
58-806	58.1-3310
58-807	58.1-3311
58-808	58.1-3312
58-809	58.1-3313
58-810	58.1-3281
58-811	58.1-3291
58-811.1	58.1-3292
58-811.2	58.1-3222
58-812	58.1-3291
58-813	58.1-3293
58-814	58.1-3352
58-815	58.1-3353
58-816	58.1-3314
58-817	58.1-3315
58-817.1	58.1-3332
58-818	58.1-3360
58-819	58.1-3361
58-820	58.1-3362
58-821	58.1-3363
58-822	58.1-3360
	58.1-3362
58-823	58.1-3360.1
58-824	58.1-3360.2
58-825	58.1-3224
58-826	58.1-3225
58-827	58.1-3226
58-828	58.1-3227
58-829	58.1-3500
	58.1-3503
58-829.1	58.1-3504
58-829.1:1	58.1-3505
58-829.2:1	58.1-3506
58-829.3	58.1-3503
	58.1-3506
	58.1-3521
58-829.5	58.1-3503
	58.1-3506
58-829.6 to 58-829.9	58.1-3506
58-830	58.1-3500
58-831	58.1-3507
58-831.01	58.1-3506
58-831.1	58.1-3501
58-831.2	58.1-3502
58-832	58.1-3509
58-833	58.1-3510
58-834	58.1-3511
58-834.1	58.1-3512
58-834.2	58.1-3513
58-834.3	58.1-3514
58-835	58.1-3515
58-835.1	58.1-3516
58-836	58.1-3517
58-837	58.1-3518
58-838	58.1-3519
58-838.1	58.1-1601
58-838.2	58.1-1602
58-838.3	Repealed
58-838.4	58.1-1603
58-838.5:2	58.1-1604
	58.1-1605
58-838.6	58.1-1608
58-838.7:1	58.1-1609
	58.1-1610
	58.1-1611
58-838.8	58.1-1606
	58.1-1607
	58.1-1612
58-838.9	58.1-1613
58-838.10	58.1-1617
58-838.11	58.1-1618
58-838.12	58.1-1618
58-838.13	58.1-1620
58-838.14	58.1-1619
58-838.15	58.1-1615
58-838.16	58.1-1621
58-838.17	58.1-1622
58-838.18	58.1-1616
58-838.19	58.1-1608
58-838.20	58.1-1620
58-838.21	58.1-3508
58-839	58.1-3001
58-840	58.1-3002
58-841	58.1-3003
58-842	58.1-3004
58-843	Repealed
58-844	58.1-3005
58-845	Repealed
58-846	58.1-3006
58-846.1	58.1-3007
58-847	58.1-3916
58-847.1	58.1-3916.1
58-848	58.1-3917
58-849	58.1-3917
58-850	Repealed
58-851	58.1-3007
58-851.1	Repealed
58-851.2	58.1-3008
	58.1-3009
58-851.3	Repealed

Former Section	Present Section
58-851.4	58.1-3815
58-851.5	58.1-3816
58-851.5:1	58.1-3816.1
58-851.6	58.1-3010
58-851.7	58.1-3011
58-851.8	58.1-3012
58-852	Repealed
58-853	58.1-3101
58-854	58.1-3102
58-855	58.1-3103
58-856	58.1-3104
58-857	58.1-3105
58-858	58.1-3114
58-859	58.1-3107
58-860	58.1-3110
58-861	58.1-3108
58-862	58.1-3108
58-863	58.1-3901
58-863.1	58.1-3902
58-863.2	Repealed
58-864	58.1-3103
58-865	58.1-3109
58-866 to	
58-868	Repealed
58-869	58.1-20
58-870	58.1-21
58-871	58.1-22
58-872	58.1-23
58-873	58.1-24
58-874	58.1-3109
	58.1-3110
58-875	58.1-3111
58-876	58.1-3112
58-877	58.1-3112
58-878	58.1-3113
58-879	58.1-3114
58-881	58.1-3115
58-882	58.1-3116
58-883	58.1-3117
58-884	58.1-3118
58-885	58.1-3119
58-886	Repealed
58-887	58.1-3120
58-888	58.1-3120
58-889	58.1-3121
58-890	58.1-3106
58-891	58.1-3106
58-892	58.1-3122
58-893	58.1-3122
58-894	Repealed
58-895	58.1-3370
58-897	58.1-3371
58-897.1	58.1-3372
58-898.1	58.1-3373
58-899	58.1-3374
58-900	58.1-3375
58-901	58.1-3376
58-902	58.1-3377
58-903	58.1-3378
58-904	58.1-3379
58-905	58.1-3380
58-906	58.1-3381
58-907	58.1-3382
58-908	58.1-3383
58-909	58.1-3384
58-910	58.1-3385
58-911	58.1-3386
58-912	58.1-3387
58-913	58.1-3388
58-914	Repealed
58-915	58.1-3389
58-916	58.1-3124
58-917	58.1-3125
58-918	58.1-3126
58-919	58.1-3127
58-919.1	58.1-3129
58-919.2	58.1-3129
58-919.3	58.1-3130
58-920	58.1-3131
58-921	58.1-3132
58-922	58.1-3133
58-923	58.1-3134
58-924	58.1-3135
58-924.1	58.1-3136
58-925	58.1-3137
58-926	58.1-3138
58-927	58.1-3139
58-928	58.1-3140
58-929	58.1-3141
58-930	58.1-3142
58-931	Repealed
58-932	58.1-3144
58-933	58.1-3145
58-934	58.1-3146
58-935	58.1-3147
58-936	58.1-3148
58-937	58.1-3148
58-938	Repealed
58-939	58.1-3149
58-940	58.1-3151
58-941	58.1-3152
58-942	58.1-3153
58-943	58.1-3154
58-943.1	58.1-3155
58-943.2	58.1-3156
58-943.3	58.1-3157
58-944	58.1-3158
	2.1-359
58-945 to	
58-947	2.1-359
58-948	58.1-3150
58-949	58.1-3160
58-950	58.1-3161
58-951	58.1-3162
58-952	58.1-3163
58-953	58.1-3164
58-954	58.1-3165
58-955	Repealed
58-956	58.1-3166
58-957	Repealed
58-958	58.1-1800
	58.1-3127
	58.1-3910
58-959	58.1-3914
58-960	58.1-3912
58-961	58.1-3913
58-962	58.1-3911
58-963	58.1-3915
58-963.1	Repealed
58-964	58.1-3918
58-965	58.1-3919
58-966	58.1-3920
58-967	58.1-3940
58-968	Repealed
58-969	58.1-3173
58-970	58.1-3174
58-971	58.1-3175
58-972	58.1-3176
58-973	58.1-3168
58-974	58.1-3169
58-975	Repealed
58-976	58.1-3171
58-977	58.1-3172
58-978	58.1-1800
	58.1-3921
58-979	58.1-1800
	58.1-3922
58-980	58.1-3923
58-981	Repealed
58-982	58.1-3926
58-983	58.1-3924
	58.1-3929
58-985	58.1-3930
58-986	Repealed
58-986.1	58.1-3932
58-987	58.1-3129
58-988	58.1-1801
58-989	58.1-3927
58-990	58.1-3928
	58.1-3933
58-991	58.1-3934
58-996	58.1-1802
58-997	58.1-1803
58-998	Repealed
58-999	58.1-3935
58-1000	58.1-3936
58-1000.1	58.1-3937
58-1000.2	58.1-3938
58-1001	58.1-3941
58-1002	Repealed
58-1003	58.1-3947
58-1004	58.1-3948
58-1005	Repealed
58-1006	58.1-3943
58-1007	58.1-3945
58-1008	58.1-3946
58-1009	58.1-3942
58-1010	58.1-1804
	58.1-2020
	58.1-3952
58-1010.1	58.1-1809
58-1011	Repealed
58-1012	Repealed

Former Section	Present Section
58-1013	58.1-3944
58-1014	58.1-1806
	58.1-2022
	58.1-3953
58-1016	58.1-1806
	58.1-2022
	58.1-3954
58-1017	58.1-1807
	58.1-2023
	58.1-3955
58-1018	58.1-1808
	58.1-2024
	58.1-3956
58-1019	58.1-3940
58-1020	58.1-3957
58-1020.1	58.1-3958
58-1021	58.1-3940
58-1021.1	58.1-14
58-1022	Repealed
58-1023	58.1-3340
58-1024	58.1-3344
58-1025	58.1-3959
58-1026	Repealed
58-1026.1	58.1-3960
58-1117.1	58.1-3965
58-1117.2	58.1-3966
58-1117.3	58.1-3967
58-1117.4	58.1-3968
58-1117.5	58.1-3969
58-1117.6	58.1-3970
58-1117.7	58.1-3971
58-1117.8	Repealed
58-1117.9	58.1-3973
58-1117.10	58.1-3974
58-1117.11	Repealed
58-1117.20	58.1-1820
58-1118	58.1-1821
58-1118.1	58.1-1823
58-1119	58.1-1822
58-1119.1	58.1-1824
58-1122	58.1-2030
58-1123	58.1-2031
58-1124	58.1-2032
58-1125	Repealed
58-1126	58.1-2033
58-1127	58.1-2035
58-1128	Repealed
58-1129	58.1-2034
58-1130	58.1-1825
58-1132	58.1-1827
58-1133	Repealed
58-1134	58.1-1826
58-1136	58.1-1830
58-1137	Repealed
58-1138	58.1-1828
58-1139	58.1-1829
58-1140	Repealed
58-1140.1	58.1-1833
58-1141	58.1-3980
58-1142	58.1-3981
58-1143	58.1-3982
58-1144	58.1-3983
58-1145	58.1-3984
58-1145.1	58.1-3985
58-1146	58.1-3984
58-1147	58.1-3986
58-1148	58.1-3987
58-1149	58.1-3984
58-1150	58.1-3988
58-1151	58.1-3989
58-1152	Repealed
58-1152.1	58.1-3990
58-1152.2	58.1-3991
58-1153	58.1-3984
58-1154	58.1-3984
58-1155	58.1-3984
58-1156	Repealed
58-1157	58.1-1829
58-1158	58.1-1831
	58.1-3993
58-1159	58.1-1832
58-1160	58.1-1812
58-1160.1	58.1-15
58-1161	58.1-1812
58-1162	58.1-1812
58-1162.1	58.1-220
58-1164	58.1-3903
58-1165	58.1-3904
58-1166	58.1-3905

COMPARABLE SECTIONS OF TITLE 59 AND TITLE 59.1

Former Section	Present Section
18.1-129	59.1-42
18.1-130	59.1-43
18.1-131	59.1-44
18.1-131.1	59.1-45
18.1-131.2	59.1-46
18.1-131.3	59.1-47
18.1-131.4	59.1-48
18.1-131.5	59.1-49
18.1-131.6	59.1-50
18.1-131.7	59.1-51
18.1-131.8	59.1-52
18.1-132	59.1-53
18.1-133	59.1-54
18.1-134	59.1-55
18.1-135	59.1-56
18.1-136	59.1-57
18.1-137	59.1-58
18.1-138	59.1-59
18.1-139	59.1-60
18.1-140	59.1-61
18.1-141	59.1-62
18.1-142	59.1-63
18.1-143	59.1-64
18.1-144	59.1-65
18.1-145	59.1-66
18.1-146	59.1-67
18.1-146.1	59.1-68
59-1 to 59-8	Deleted
59-8.1	59.1-1
59-8.2	59.1-2
59-8.3	59.1-3
59-8.4	59.1-4
59-8.5	59.1-5
59-8.6	59.1-6
59-8.7	59.1-7
59-8.8	59.1-8
59-8.9	59.1-9
59-9	59.1-10
59-10	59.1-11
59-11	59.1-12
59-12	59.1-13
59-13	59.1-14
59-14	59.1-15
59-15	59.1-16
59-16	59.1-17
59-17	59.1-18
59-18	59.1-19
59-19	59.1-20
59-19.1	59.1-21
59-20	59.1-22
59-21	59.1-23
59-21.1	Repealed
59-22	59.1-24
59-23	59.1-25
59-24	59.1-26
59-25	59.1-27
59-26	59.1-28
59-27	59.1-29
59-28	59.1-30
59-29	59.1-31
59-30	Repealed
59-31	59.1-32
59-32	59.1-33
59-33	59.1-34
59-34	59.1-35
59-35	59.1-36
59-36	59.1-37
59-37	59.1-38
59-38	59.1-39
59-39	59.1-40
59-40	59.1-41
59-41	59.1-149
59-42	59.1-150
59-43	59.1-151
59-44	59.1-152

Former Section	Present Section
59-45	59.1-153
59-46	59.1-154
59-47	59.1-155
59-48	59.1-156
59-49	Deleted
59-50	59.1-157
59-51	59.1-158
59-52	59.1-159
59-53	59.1-160
59-54	59.1-161
59-55	59.1-162
59-56	59.1-163
59-57	59.1-164
59-58	59.1-165
59-59	59.1-166
59-60	59.1-167
59-61	Repealed
59-61.1	59.1-177
59-61.2	59.1-178
59-61.3	59.1-179
59-61.4	59.1-180
59-61.5	59.1-181
59-61.6	59.1-182
59-61.7	59.1-183
59-61.8	59.1-184
59-61.9	59.1-185
59-61.10	59.1-186
59-61.11	59.1-187
59-61.12	59.1-188
59-62 to 59-140.1	Repealed
59-141	15.1-523
59-142	15.1-524
59-143	Deleted
59-144	15.1-525
59-145	59.1-117
59-146	59.1-118
59-147	59.1-119
59-148	59.1-120
59-149	59.1-121
59-150	59.1-122
59-151	59.1-123
59-152	59.1-124
59-153	59.1-125
59-154	59.1-126
59-155	59.1-127
59-155.1	59.1-128
59-155.2	59.1-129
59-155.3	59.1-130
59-156	59.1-131
59-157	59.1-132
59-158	59.1-133
59-159	59.1-134
59-160	59.1-135
59-161	59.1-136
59-162	59.1-189
59-163	59.1-190
59-164	59.1-191
59-165	59.1-192
59-166	59.1-193
59-167	59.1-194
59-168	59.1-195
59-169	59.1-69
59-170	59.1-70
59-171	59.1-71
59-172	59.1-72
59-173	59.1-73
59-174	59.1-74
59-175	59.1-75
59-176	59.1-76
59-177 to 59-189	Repealed
59-189.2	59.1-77
59-189.3	59.1-78
59-189.4	59.1-79
59-189.5	59.1-80
59-189.6	59.1-81
59-189.7	59.1-82
59-189.8	59.1-83
59-189.9	59.1-84
59-189.10	59.1-85
59-189.11	59.1-86
59-189.12	59.1-87
59-189.13	59.1-88
59-189.14	59.1-89
59-189.15	59.1-90
59-189.16	59.1-91
59-189.17	59.1-92
59-190	59.1-93
59-191	59.1-94
59-192	59.1-95
59-193	59.1-96
59-194	59.1-97
59-195	59.1-98
59-196	59.1-99
59-197	59.1-100
59-198	59.1-101
59-199	59.1-102
59-200	59.1-103
59-201	59.1-104
59-202	59.1-105
59-203	59.1-106
59-204	59.1-107
59-205	59.1-108
59-206	59.1-109
59-207	59.1-110
59-208	59.1-111
59-209	59.1-112
59-210	59.1-113
59-211	59.1-114
59-212	59.1-115
59-213	59.1-116
59-214	59.1-142
59-214.1	59.1-143
59-215	59.1-144
59-216	59.1-145
59-217	59.1-146
59-218	59.1-147
59-219	59.1-148
59-220, 59-221	Repealed
59-222	59.1-137
59-223	59.1-138
59-224	59.1-139
59-225	59.1-140
59-226	59.1-141
59-227	59.1-168
59-228	59.1-169
59-229	59.1-170
59-230	59.1-171
59-231	59.1-172
59-232	59.1-173
59-233	59.1-174
59-234	59.1-175
59-235	59.1-176
None	59.1-68.1

COMPARABLE SECTIONS OF TITLE 60 AND TITLE 60.1

Former Section	Present Section
60-1	60.1-1
60-2	60.1-2
60-3	60.1-3
60-4	60.1-4
60-5	60.1-5
60-6	Repealed
60-6.1	60.1-6
60-7	60.1-7
60-8	Repealed
60-8.1	60.1-8
60-9	60.1-9
60-10	60.1-10
60-11	60.1-11
60-12	60.1-12
60-13	60.1-13
60-14	60.1-14
60-15	60.1-15
60-16	60.1-16
60-17	60.1-17
60-17.1	60.1-18
60-17.2	60.1-19
60-17.3	60.1-20
60-18	60.1-21
60-19	60.1-22
60-20	60.1-23
60-21	60.1-24
60-21.1	60.1-25

Former Section	Present Section
60-22	60.1-26
60-23	60.1-27
60-24	60.1-28
60-25	60.1-29
60-25.1	60.1-30
60-26	60.1-31
60-27	60.1-32
60-28	60.1-33
60-29	60.1-34
60-30	60.1-35
60-31	60.1-36
60-32	60.1-37
60-33	60.1-38
60-34	60.1-39
60-35	60.1-40
60-36	60.1-41
60-37	60.1-42
60-38	60.1-43
60-39	60.1-44
60-40	60.1-45
60-41	60.1-46
60-42	60.1-47
60-43	60.1-48
60-44	60.1-49
60-45	Repealed
60-45.1	60.1-50
60-45.2	60.1-51
60-46	60.1-52
60-46.1	60.1-53
60-46.2	60.1-54
60-46.3	60.1-55
60-46.4	60.1-56
60-46.5	60.1-57
60-47	60.1-58
60-47.1	60.1-59
60-48	60.1-60
60-49	60.1-61

Former Section	Present Section
60-50	60.1-62
60-51	60.1-63
60-52	60.1-64
60-53	60.1-65
60-54	60.1-66
60-55	60.1-67
60-56	60.1-68
60-57	60.1-69
60-58	60.1-70
60-59	60.1-71
60-60	60.1-72
60-61	60.1-73
60-62	60.1-74
60-62.1	60.1-74.1
60-63	60.1-75
60-64	60.1-76
60-65	60.1-77
60-66	60.1-78
60-67	60.1-79
60-68	60.1-80
60-69	60.1-81
60-70	60.1-82
60-71	60.1-83
60-72	60.1-84
60-73	60.1-85
60-73.1	60.1-86
60-74	60.1-87
60-75	60.1-88
60-76	60.1-89
60-76.1	60.1-90
60-76.2	60.1-91
60-77	60.1-92
60-77.1	60.1-93
60-78	60.1-94
60-79	60.1-95
60-80	60.1-96
60-81	60.1-97
60-82	60.1-98

Former Section	Present Section
60-83	60.1-99
60-84	60.1-100
60-85	60.1-101
60-86	60.1-102
60-87	60.1-103
60-88	60.1-104
60-89	60.1-105
60-90	60.1-106
60-91	60.1-107
60-92	60.1-108
60-93	60.1-109
60-94	60.1-110
60-94.1	60.1-111
60-95	60.1-112
60-96	60.1-113
60-97	60.1-114
60-98	60.1-115
60-99	60.1-116
60-100	60.1-117
60-101	60.1-118
60-102	60.1-119
60-103	60.1-120
60-104	60.1-121
60-105	60.1-122
60-106	60.1-123
60-107	60.1-124
60-108	60.1-125
60-109	60.1-126
60-110	60-1-127
60-111	60.1-128
60-112	60.1-129
60-113	60.1-130
60-114	60.1-131
60-115	60.1-132
60-116	60.1-133
60-117	60.1-134

COMPARABLE SECTIONS OF TITLE 60.1 AND TITLE 60.2

Former Section	Present Section
60.1-1	60.2-100
60.1-2	60.2-200
60.1-3	60.2-201
60.1-4	60.2-202
60.1-5	60.2-203
60.1-6	60.2-204
60.1-7	60.2-205
60.1-8	60.2-206
60.1-9	60.2-207
60.1-10	60.2-208
60.1-11	60.2-209
60.1-12	60.2-210
60.1-13	60.2-211
60.1-14	60.2-212
	60.2-213
	60.2-214
	60.2-215
	60.2-216

Former Section	Present Section
	60.2-217
	60.2-218
	60.2-219
60.1-14.1	60.2-220
60.1-14.2	60.2-221
60.1-15	60.2-222
60.1-16	60.2-223
60.1-17	60.2-224
60.1-18 to 60.1-20	Repealed
60.1-21	60.2-225
60.1-22	60.2-231
60.1-22.1	60.2-101
60.1-23	60.2-226
60.1-24	60.2-227
60.1-25	60.2-228
60.1-26	60.2-229
60.1-27	60.2-230

Former Section	Present Section
60.1-28	60.2-102
60.1-29	60.2-103
60.1-30	60.2-104
60.1-31	60.2-108
60.1-32	60.2-109
60.1-33	60.2-110
60.1-34	60.2-111
60.1-35	Repealed
60.1-36	60.2-105
60.1-37	Repealed
60.1-38	60.2-112
60.1-39	60.2-113
60.1-40	60.2-114
60.1-40.1	60.2-525
60.1-41	60.2-626
60.1-42	60.2-627
60.1-43	60.2-628
60.1-44	60.2-115

Former Section	Present Section
60.1-45	60.2-116
60.1-46	60.2-601
60.1-47	60.2-602
60.1-48	60.2-603
60.1-48.1	60.2-604
60.1-49	60.2-605
60.1-50	60.2-606
60.1-51	60.2-607
60.1-51.1	Repealed
60.1-51.2	60.2-610
	60.2-611
60.1-52	60.2-612
60.1-52.1	60.2-613
60.1-52.2	60.2-614
60.1-52.3	60.2-615
60.1-52.4	Repealed
60.1-52.4:1	60.2-616
60.1-52.5	Repealed
60.1-52.5:1	60.2-617
60.1-52.6	60.2-608
60.1-53 to 60.1-57	Repealed
60.1-58	60.2-618
60.1-59	60.2-609
60.1-60	60.2-106
60.1-61	60.2-619
60.1-62	60.2-620
60.1-63	60.2-621
60.1-64	60.2-622
60.1-65	60.2-623
60.1-65.1	60.2-623.1
60.1-66	60.2-624
60.1-67	Repealed
60.1-67.1	60.2-625
60.1-68	60.2-629
60.1-68.1	60.2-630
60.1-69	60.2-631
60.1-70	60.2-500
60.1-71	60.2-500
60.1-72	60.2-511
60.1-73	60.2-512
60.1-74	60.2-513
60.1-74.1	60.2-514
60.1-75	60.2-515
60.1-76	60.2-117
60.1-77	60.2-516
60.1-78	60.2-517
60.1-79	60.2-526
60.1-79.1	60.2-527
60.1-80	60.2-528
60.1-81	60.2-529
60.1-82	60.2-530
60.1-83	Repealed
60.1-84	Repealed
60.1-84.1	60.2-531
60.1 84.2	60.2-532
60.1-85	Repealed
60.1-85.1	60.2-533
60.1-86	Repealed
60.1-86.1	Repealed
60.1-87	60.2-534
60.1-88	Repealed
60.1-88.01	60.2-535
60.1-88.1	60.2-536
60.1-89	60.2-501
	60.2-502
	60.2-503
	60.2-504
	60.2-505
60.1-89.1	60.2-506
60.1-89.2	60.2-507
60.1-90	60.2-537
60.1-91	60.2-538
60.1-92	60.2-519
60.1-93	60.2-520
60.1-94	60.2-521
60.1-95	60.2-522
60.1-96	60.2-523
60.1-97	60.2-524
60.1-98	60.2-508
60.1-99	60.2-509
60.1-100	60.2-510
60.1-101	60.2-400
60.1-102	Repealed
60.1-103	60.2-400
60.1-104	60.2-310
60.1-105	60.2-400
60.1-106	60.2-300
60.1-107	60.2-301
60.1-108	60.2-302
60.1-109	60.2-303
60.1-110	60.2-304
60.1-111	60.2-305
60.1-112	60.2-306
60.1-113	60.2-307
60.1-114	60.2-308
60.1-115	60.2-311
60.1-116	60.2-309
60.1-117	60.2-312
60.1-118	60.2-313
60.1-119	60.2-314
60.1-120	60.2-315
60.1-121	60.2-316
60.1-122	60.2-317
60.1-123	60.2-107
60.1-124	60.2-122
60.1-124.1	60.2-123
60.1-125	60.2-600
60.1-126	60.2-118
60.1-127	60.2-119
60.1-128	60.2-120
60.1-129	60.2-632
60.1-130	60.2-518
60.1-131	60.2-121
60.1-132	60.2-633
60.1-133	60.2-634
60.1-134	60.2-635

COMPARABLE SECTIONS OF TITLE 61 AND TITLE 61.1

Former Section	Present Section
61-1 to 61-52	Repealed
61-53	61.1-1
61-54	61.1-2
61-55	61.1-3
61-56	61.1-4
61-57	61.1-5
61-58	61.1-6
61-59	61.1-7
61-60	61.1-8
61-61	61.1-9
61-62	61.1-10
61-63	61.1-11
61-64	61.1-12
61-65	61.1-13
61-66	61.1-14
61-67, 61-68	Deleted
61-69	61.1-15
61-70	61.1-16
61-71	61.1-17
61-72	61.1-18
61-73, 61-74	Deleted
61-75	61.1-19
61-76	61.1-20
61-77	61.1-21
61-78	Deleted
61-79	61.1-22
61-80	61.1-23
61-81	61.1-24
61-82	61.1-25
61-83	61.1-26
61-84	61.1-27
61-85	61.1-28
61-86	61.1-29
61-87	61.1-30
61-88	61.1-31
61-89	61.1-32
61-90	61.1-33
61-91	61.1-34
61-92	61.1-35
61-93	61.1-36
61-94	61.1-37
61-95	61.1-38
61-96 to 61-107	Deleted
61-108	61.1-39
61-109	61.1-40
61-110	61.1-41
61-111	61.1-42
61 112	61.1-43

Former Section	Present Section
61-113 to 61-135	Deleted
61-136	61.1-44
61-137	61.1-45
61-138 to 61-140	Deleted
61-141	61.1-46
61-142 to 61-145	Deleted
61-146	61.1-47
61-147	61.1-48
61-148	61.1-49
61-149	61.1-50
61-150	61.1-51
61-151	61.1-52
61-152	61.1-53
61-153	61.1-54
61-154	61.1-55
61-155	61.1-56
61-156	61.1-57
61-157	61.1-58
61-158	61.1-59
61-159	61.1-60
61-160	61.1-61

COMPARABLE SECTIONS OF TITLE 62 AND TITLE 62.1

Former Section	Present Section
62-1	62.1-1, 62.1-5
62-2	62.1-2
62-2.1	62.1-3
62-3	62.1-4
62-3.1	Deleted
62-4	62.1-6
62-5	62.1-7
62-6	62.1-8
62-7	62.1-9
62-8, 62-9	Deleted
62-9.1	62.1-10
62-9.2	62.1-11
62-9.3	62.1-12
62-9.4	62.1-13
62-10	62.1-14
62-11	62.1-15
62-12	62.1-16
62-13	62.1-17
62-14	62.1-18
62-14.1	Deleted
62-15	62.1-19
62-16	62.1-20
62-17	62.1-21
62-18	62.1-22
62-19	62.1-23
62-20	62.1-24
62-21	62.1-25
62-22	62.1-26
62-23	62.1-27
66-24	62.1-26
62-25	62.1-29
62-26	62.1-28
62-27	62.1-32
62-28	62.1-29
62-29	62.1-35
62-30	62.1-34
62-31	Repealed
62-32	62.1-36
62-33	62.1-37
62-34	62.1-38
62-35	62.1-39
62-36	62.1-40
62-37	62.1-41
62-38	62.1-42
62-39	62.1-31
62-40	62.1-33
62-41	62.1-43
62-42	62.1-44
62-43 to 62-45	Deleted
62-46	62.1-45
62-47	62.1-46
62-47.1	62.1-47
62-48	62.1-48
62-49	62.1-49
62-50	62.1-50
62-51	62.1-51
62-52	62.1-52
62-53	62.1-53
62-53.1	62.1-54
62-54	62.1-55
62-55	62.1-56
62-56	62.1-57
62-57	62.1-58
62-58	62.1-59
62-59	62.1-60
62-60	62.1-61
62-60.1	62.1-62
62-61	62.1-63
62-62	62.1-64
62-63	62.1-65
62-64	62.1-66
62-65	62.1-67
62-66	62.1-68
62-67	62.1-69
62-67.1	62.1-70
62-67.2	62.1-71
62-67.3	62.1-72
62-67.4	62.1-73
62-67.5	62.1-74
62-67.6	62.1-75
62-67.7	62.1-76
62-67.8	62.1-77
62-67.9	62.1-78
62-67.10	62.1-79
62-68	62.1-80
62-69	62.1-81
62-70	62.1-82
62-71	62.1-83
62-72	62.1-84
62-73	62.1-85
62-74	62.1-86
62-75	62.1-87
62-76	62.1-88
62-77	62.1-89
62-78	62.1-90
62-79	62.1-91
62-80	Deleted
62-81	62.1-92
62-82	62.1-93
62-83	62.1-94
62-84	62.1-95
62-85	62.1-96
62-86	62.1-97
62-87	62.1-98
62-88	62.1-99
62-89	62.1-100
62-90, 62-91	Deleted
62-92	62.1-101
62-93	62.1-102
62-94	62.1-103
62-94.1	62.1-104
62-94.2	62.1-105
62-94.3	62.1-106
62-94.4	62.1-107
62-94.5	62.1-108
62-94.6	62.1-109
62-94.7	62.1-110
62-94.8	62.1-111
62-94.9	62.1-112
62-94.10	62.1-113
62-94.11	62.1-114
62-94.12	62.1-115
62-95	62.1-116
62-96	62.1-117
62-97	62.1-118
62-98	62.1-119
62-99	62.1-120
62-100	62.1-121
62-101	62.1-122
62-102	62.1-123
62-103	62.1-124
62-104	62.1-125
62-105	62.1-126
62-106	62.1-127
62-106.1	62.1-128
62-106.2	62.1-129
62-106.3	62.1-130
62-106.4	62.1-131
62-106.5	62.1-132
62-106.6	62.1-133
62-106.7	62.1-134
62-106.8	62.1-135
62-106.8:1	62.1-136
62-106.8:2	62.1-137

Former Section	Present Section
62-106.9	62.1-138
62-106.10	Deleted
62-106.11	62.1-139
62-106.12	62.1-140
62-106.13	62.1-141
62-106.14	62.1-142
62-106.15	62.1-143
62-106.16	62.1-144
62-106.17	62.1-145
62-106.18	62.1-146
62-106.19	62.1-147
62-107 to 62-117	Repealed
62-117.1	62.1-148
62-117.2	62.1-149
62-117.3	62.1-150
62-117.4	62.1-151
62-117.5	62.1-152
62-117.6	62.1-153
62-117.7	62.1-154
62-117.8	62.1-155
62-117.9	62.1-156
62-117.10	62.1-157
62-117.11	62.1-158
62-118	62.1-159
62-119	62.1-160
62-120	62.1-161
62-121	62.1-162
62-122, 62-123	Deleted
62-124	62.1-163
62-125 to 62-138	Deleted
62-139	62.1-164
62-140	62.1-165
62-141 to 62-147	Deleted
62-148 to 62-157	Repealed
62-158 to 62-174	Deleted
62-174.1	62.1-166
62-174.2	62.1-167
62-174.3	62.1-168
62-174.4	62.1-169
62-174.5	62.1-170
62-174.5:1	62.1-171
62-174.6	62.1-172
62-174.7	62.1-173
62-174.8	62.1-174
62-174.9	62.1-175
62-174.10	62.1-176
62-174.11	62.1-177
62-174.12	62.1-178
62-174.13	62.1-179
62-174.13:1	Reserved
62-174.13:2	62.1-180
62-174.14	62.1-181
62-174.15	62.1-182
62-174.16	62.1-183
62-174.17	62.1-184
62-174.18	62.1-185
62-174.19	62.1-186
62-175	62.1-187
62-176	62.1-188
62-177	62.1-189
62-178	62.1-190
62-179	62.1-191
62-180	62.1-192
62-181	62.1-193
62-182	62.1-194
62-183	62.1-194
62-183.1 to 62-187	Deleted
62-187.1	62.1-194.2
62-188, 62-189	Deleted
62-190	62.1-194.3
62-191	Deleted
62-192, 62-193	Repealed
62-194	62.1-195
62-195	62.1-196
None	62.1-30
None	62.1-44.1
None	62.1-194.1

COMPARABLE SECTIONS OF TITLE 63 AND TITLE 63.1

Former Section	Present Section
32-291	63.1-134
32-292	63.1-135
32-293	63.1-136
32-293.1	63.1-137
32-293.2	63.1-138
32-294	63.1-139
32-295	63.1-140
32-296	Repealed
63-1	63.1-1
63-2	63.1-2
63-3	63.1-3
63-4	Deleted
63-5	63.1-4
63-5.1	Repealed
63-5.2	63.1-5
63-5.3	63.1-5.1
63-6	63.1-6
63-7	63.1-7
63-8	63.1-8
63-9	63.1-9
63-10	63.1-10
63-11	63.1-11
63-12	63.1-12
63-13	63.1-13
63-14	63.1-14
63-15	63.1-15
63-16	63.1-16
63-17	63.1-17
63-18	63.1-18
63-19	63.1-19
63-20	63.1-20
63-21	63.1-21
63-22	63.1-22
63-23	63.1-23
63-24	63.1-24
63-25	63.1-25
63-26	63.1-26
63-27	63.1-27
63-28	63.1-28
63-29 to 63-32	Repealed
63-33	63.1-28.1
63-34	Deleted
63-35	63.1-29
63-36	63.1-30
63-37	Deleted
63-38	63.1-31
63-39	63.1-32
63-40	63.1-33
63-41	63.1-34
63-42	63.1-33
63-43	63.1-35
63-44	63.1-36
63-45	Deleted
63-46	63.1-37
63-47 to 63-49	Repealed
63-50	Deleted
63-51	63.1-38, 63.1-44
63-52	63.1-40
63-52.1	Repealed
63-53	63.1-42
63-53.1	63.1-43
63-54	63.1-40
63-55	63.1-42
63-56	63.1-39, 63.1-40, 63.1-42
63-57	63.1-45
63-58	63.1-46
63-59	63.1-47
63-60	63.1-41
63-61	63.1-48
63-62	63.1-48
63-63	Repealed
63-64	63.1-48
63-65	63.1-49
63-66	63.1-50
63-66.1	63.1-51
63-67 to 63-67.2	63.1-52
63-67.3	Repealed
63-68	63.1-53
63-69	63.1-54
63-69.1 to 63-69.3	Repealed
63-70, 63-71	Deleted
63-72	63.1-57.1
63-72.1	63.1-55
63-73	63.1-56

Former Section	Present Section
63-73.1	63.1-57
63-74	63.1-58
63-75	63.1-59
63-75.1	63.1-59
63-76	63.1-60
63-77	63.1-60
63-78	63.1-61
63-79	63.1-62
63-80	63.1-63
63-81	63.1-64
63-81.1	63.1-65
63-82	63.1-66
63-83, 63-84	Deleted
63-85	63.1-67
63-86	Deleted
63-87	63.1-67.1
63-88	Deleted
63-89	63.1-67.2
63-90	Deleted
63-91	63.1-67.3
63-92 to 63-95	Deleted
63-96	63-1-67.4
63-97	63.1-67.5
63-98	63.1-67.6
63-99	63.1-67.7
63-100	63.1-86
63-101	63.1-87
63-102	63.1-88
63-103	63.1-89
63-104	63.1-90
63-105	63.1-91
63-106	63.1-92
63-106.1	63.1-97
63-107	63.1-92
63-108	63.1-94
63-109	63.1-93
63-110	63.1-96
63-110.1	63.1-96.1
63-111	63.1-93
63-112	63.1-95
63-113	Deleted
63-114	63.1-99
63-115	63.1-100
63-116	63.1-107
63-117	63.1-108
63-118	63.1-109
63-119	63.1-110
63-120	Deleted
63-121	63.1-114
63-122	63.1-115
63-123	63.1-113
63-124	63.1-112
63-125	63.1-127
63-126	63.1-120
63-127	63.1-128
63-127.1	63.1-130
63-128	63.1-130
63-129	63.1-133
63-130	63.1-121
63-131	63.1-116
63-132	63.1-117
63-133	63.1-118
63-134	63.1-119
63-135	63.1-122
63-136	63.1-123
63-137	63.1-124
63-138	63.1-131
63-138.1	63.1-132
63-139	63.1-125
63-140	63.1-126
63-140.1	Deleted
63-140.2	63.1-101
63-140.2:1	63.1-102
63-140.3	63.1-107
63-140.4	63.1-108
63-140.5	63.1-111
	63.1-114
63-140.6	63.1-115
63-140.7	63.1-120
63-140.8	63.1-116
63-140.9	63.1-117
63-140.10	63.1-118
63-140.11	63.1-119
63-140.12	63.1-122
63-140.13	63.1-123
63-140.14	63.1-124
63-140.15	63.1-53
	63.1-126
63-140.16	Deleted
63-141	63.1-105
63-142	63.1-107
63-143	63.1-108
63-144	63.1-109
63-145	63.1-110
63-146	Deleted
63-147	63.1-114
63-148	63.1-115
63-149	63.1-113
	63.1-114
63-149.1	63.1-112
63-150	63.1-120
63-151	63.1-127
63-152	63.1-121
63-153	63.1-116
63-154	63.1-117
63-155	63.1-118
63-156	63.1-119
63-157	63.1-122
63-158	63.1-123
63-159	63.1-124
63-160	63.1-125
63-161	63.1-126
63-162	63.1-68
63-163	63.1-69
63-164	63.1-70
63-165	63.1-71
63-165.1	63.1-71.1
63-166	63.1-72
63-167	63.1-73
63-167.1	63.1-74
63-167.2	63.1-74.1
63-168	63.1-75
63-169	63.1-76
63-170	63.1-77
63-171	63.1-78
63-172	63.1-79
63-173	63.1-80
63-174	63.1-81
63-175	63.1-82
63-176	63.1-83
63-177	63.1-84
63-178	63.1-85
63-179	63.1-103
63-180	63.1-107
63-181	63.1-108
63-182	63.1-109
63-183	63.1-110
63-184	Deleted
63-185	63.1-114
63-186	63.1-115
63-187	63.1-113
	63.1-114
63-188	63.1-112
63-189	63.1-127
63-190	63.1-120
63-191	63.1-128
63-192	63.1-130
63-193	63.1-133
63-194	63.1-121
63-195	63.1-116
63-196	63.1-117
63-197	63.1-118
63-198	63.1-119
63-199	63.1-122
63-200	63.1-123
63-201	63.1-124
63-202	63.1-131
63-202.1	63.1-132
63-203	63.1-125
63-204	63.1-126
63-204.1	63.1-142
63-204.2	63.1-143
63-204.3	63.1-144
63-204.4	63.1-145
63-204.5	63.1-146
63-204.6	63.1-147
63-204.7	63.1-148
63-204.8	63.1-149
63-204.9	63.1-150
63-204.10	63.1-151
63-204.11	63.1-152
63-204.12	63.1-153
63-204.13	63.1-154
63-204.14	63.1-155
63-204.15	63.1-156
63-204.16	63.1-157
63-204.17	63.1-158
63-204.18	63.1-159
63-204.19	63.1-160
63-204.20	63.1-161
63-204.21	63.1-162
63-204.22	63.1-163
63-204.23	63.1-164

Former Section	Present Section
63-204.24	63.1-165
63-204.25	63.1-166
63-204.26	63.1-167
63-204.27	63.1-168
63-204.28	63.1-169
63-204.29	63.1-170
63-204.30	63.1-171
63-205	63.1-106
63-206	63.1-107
63-207	63.1-108
63-208	63.1-109
63-209	63.1-110
63-210	Deleted
63-211	63.1-115
63-212	63.1-108
63-213	63.1-120
63-214	63.1-113
	63.1-114
63-215	63.1-112
63-216	63.1-116
63-217	63.1-124
63-218, 63-218.1	Repealed
63-219	63.1-125
63-220	63.1-126
63-220.1	63.1-98
63-221	Deleted
63-222	63.1-172
63-222.1	63.1-173
63-223	63.1-174
63-223.1	63.1-175
63-223.2	63.1-176
63-224	63.1-177
63-224.1	63.1-178
63-224.2	63.1-179
63-224.3	63.1-180
63-224.4	63.1-181
63-225, 63-226	Repealed
63-227	63.1-182
63-228	63.1-183
63-229	63.1-183
63-230, 63-231	Deleted
63-232	63.1-195
63-233	63.1-196
63-234	63.1-197
63-235	63.1-198
63-236	63.1-199
63-237	63.1-200
63-238	63.1-201
63-239	63.1-202
63-240	63.1-203
63-241	63.1-204
63-242	63.1-205
63-243	63.1-206
63-244	63.1-207
63-245	63.1-208
63-246	63.1-209
63-247	63.1-210
63-248	63.1-211
63-249	63.1-212
63-250	63.1-213
63-251	63.1-214
63-252	63.1-215
63-253	63.1-216
63-254	63.1-217
63-255	63.1-218
63-256	63.1-219
63-257 to 63-290	Repealed
63-291	63.1-239
63-291.1	63.1-246
63-292	63.1-243
63-293	63.1-240
63-293.1	63.1-241
63-293.2	63.1-242
63-294 to 63-307	Repealed
63-307.1	16.1-217.1
63-307.2	16.1-217.2
63-307.3	16.1-217.3
63-307.4	16.1-217.4
63-308	63.1-184
63-309	63.1-185
63-310	63.1-186
63-311	63.1-187
63-312	63.1-188
63-313	Deleted
63-314	63.1-189
63-315	63.1-190
63-316	63.1-191
63-317	63.1-192
63-318	63.1-193
63-318.1	63.1-194
63-319 to 63-346	Deleted
63-347	63.1-220
63-348	63.1-221
63-348.1	63.1-222
63-349	63.1-223
63-350	63.1-224
63-351	63.1-220
	63.1-225
63-352	63.1-226
63-353	63.1-227
63-354	63.1-228
63-355	63.1-229
63-356	63.1-230
63-356.1	63.1-231
63-356.2	63.1-232
63-357	63.1-233
63-358	63.1-234
63-359	Repealed
63-359.1	63.1-235
63-360	63.1-236
63-361	63.1-237
63-362	Repealed
63-363	63.1-238
63-364	Deleted
63-365	Deleted
63-366 to 63-369	63.1-245
63-369.1	63.1-248
63-370	Deleted
63-371	63.1-247
63-372, 63-373	Repealed
63-373.1	Deleted
63-374 to 63-380	Deleted
63-381	63.1-244
63-382	Repealed
63-383	Deleted
63-384	63.1-244
63-385	Deleted
None	63.1-104

COMPARABLE SECTIONS OF TITLE 63.1 AND TITLE 63.2

Former Section	Present Section
63.1-1.1	63.2-200
63.1-1.1:01	Deleted
63.1-1.1:1	63.2-101
63.1-2	63.2-201
63.1-3	63.2-202
63.1-4	63.2-203
63.1-5.1	63.2-412
63.1-6	Deleted
63.1-7	63.2-209
63.1-8	63.2-210
63.1-9	63.2-211
63.1-10	63.2-212
63.1-11	63.2-213
63.1-12	63.2-214
63.1-14	63.2-215
63.1-15	63.2-215
63.1-16	63.2-215
63.1-18	63.2-215
63.1-19	63.2-215
63.1-20	63.2-215
63.1-21	63.2-215
63.1-22	63.2-215
63.1-23	63.2-215
63.1-24	63.2-216
63.1-25	63.2-217
63.1-25.01	63.2-218
63.1-25.1	63.2-800
63.1-25.2	63.2-801
63.1-25.3	Deleted
63.1-26	63.2-219

Former Section	Present Section
63.1-27	63.2-220
63.1-28.1	63.2-221
63.1-31	63.2-203
63.1-32	63.2-204
63.1-33	63.2-205
63.1-34	63.2-102
63.1-34	63.2-104
63.1-35	63.2-206
63.1-36	63.2-207
63.1-37	63.2-208
63.1-38	63.2-300
63.1-38.1	Deleted
63.1-39	63.2-301
63.1-40	63.2-302
63.1-41	63.2-303
63.1-43	63.2-304
63.1-43.1	63.2-305
63.1-44	63.2-306
63.1-44.1	63.2-307
63.1-45	63.2-308
63.1-46	63.2-309
63.1-47	63.2-310
63.1-47.1	63.2-311
63.1-48	63.2-312
63.1-49	Deleted
63.1-50	63.2-313
63.1-51	63.2-314
63.1-52	63.2-315
63.1-53	63.2-102
63.1-54	63.2-316
63.1-54.1	63.2-317
63.1-54.2	63.2-318
63.1-55	63.2-319
63.1-55	63.2-410
63.1-55.01	63.2-1600
63.1-55.02	63.2-1604
63.1-55.1	63.2-1605
63.1-55.1:1	63.2-1601
63.1-55.2	63.2-100
63.1-55.2	63.2-1603
63.1-55.3	63.2-1606
63.1-55.4	63.2-104
63.1-55.4	63.2-1607
63.1-55.5	63.2-1608
63.1-55.6	63.2-1609
63.1-55.7	63.2-1610
63.1-55.8	63.2-100
63.1-55.8	63.2-905
63.1-56	63.2-900
63.1-56	63.2-903
63.1-56	63.2-1105
63.1-56.1	63.2-411
63.1-56.2	63.2-907
63.1-56.3	63.2-911
63.1-57	63.2-320
63.1-57.1	63.2-321
63.1-58	63.2-322
63.1-58.1	63.2-323
63.1-58.2	63.2-526
63.1-59	63.2-324
63.1-59.1	Deleted

Former Section	Present Section
63.1-60	63.2-325
63.1-61	63.2-326
63.1-62	63.2-327
63.1-63	Deleted
63.1-64	63.2-328
63.1-65	63.2-329
63.1-66	63.2-330
63.1-67	63.2-331
63.1-67.1	63.2-332
63.1-67.2	63.2-901
63.1-67.3	63.2-333
63.1-67.4	Deleted
63.1-67.5	63.2-334
63.1-67.6	63.2-335
63.1-67.7	63.2-336
63.1-68	51.5-61
63.1-68	51.5-64
63.1-68.1	51.5-62
63.1-69	51.5-61
63.1-69	51.5-64
63.1-69.1	51.5-60
63.1-70	Deleted
63.1-70.1	51.5-71
63.1-71	51.5-68
63.1-71.1	51.5-69
63.1-72	51.5-76
63.1-73	51.5-72
63.1-73.1	51.5-73
63.1-74	51.5-63
63.1-74	51.5-66
63.1-74.1	51.5-74
63.1-75	51.5-75
63.1-75.1	51.5-60
63.1-75.1	51.5-100
63.1-77	Deleted
63.1-79	51.5-70
63.1-80	Deleted
63.1-81	51.5-77
63.1-83	51.5-66
63.1-83.1	51.5-67
63.1-84	Deleted
63.1-85	51.5-65
63.1-85.1:1	51.5-106
63.1-85.1:2	51.5-108
63.1-85.1:3	51.5-107
63.1-85.2	51.5-109
63.1-85.2:1	51.5-110
63.1-85.3:1	51.5-111
63.1-85.4	51.5-112
63.1-85.4:1	51.5-113
63.1-85.7	51.5-114
63.1-86	Deleted
63.1-86.1	63.2-600
63.1-87	63.2-100
63.1-88	63.2-506
63.1-88.1	63.2-507
63.1-89	63.2-508
63.1-89.1	63.2-803
63.1-90	63.2-509
63.1-90.1	63.2-510
63.1-91	63.2-400

Former Section	Present Section
63.1-92	63.2-401
63.1-92.1	63.2-402
63.1-93	63.2-403
63.1-95	63.2-404
63.1-96	Deleted
63.1-96.1	63.2-615
63.1-97.1	63.2-405
63.1-98	63.2-406
63.1-99.1	Deleted
63.1-105	63.2-602
63.1-105	63.2-614
63.1-105.1	63.2-602
63.1-105.2	63.2-603
63.1-105.3	63.2-617
63.1-105.4	63.2-606
63.1-105.5	63.2-1912
63.1-105.6	63.2-607
63.1-105.7	63.2-604
63.1-105.8	63.2-605
63.1-105.9	63.2-620
63.1-106	63.2-802
63.1-107	63.2-501
63.1-107.1	63.2-502
63.1-108	63.2-503
63.1-109	63.2-504
63.1-110	63.2-505
63.1-110.1	63.2-804
63.1-112	63.2-513
63.1-113	63.2-514
63.1-114	63.2-515
63.1-115	63.2-516
63.1-116	63.2-517
63.1-117	63.2-518
63.1-119	63.2-519
63.1-120	63.2-520
63.1-121	63.2-521
63.1-122	63.2-407
63.1-122	63.2-408
63.1-123	63.2-219
63.1-123	63.2-408
63.1-124	63.2-522
63.1-124.1	63.2-523
63.1-124.2	63.2-524
63.1-124.3	63.2-525
63.1-125	63.2-106
63.1-126	51.5-69
63.1-126	63.2-102
63.1-126	63.2-104
63.1-127	63.2-511
63.1-127.2	63.2-512
63.1-133.1	63.2-409
63.1-133.7	Deleted
63.1-133.8	Deleted
63.1-133.9	Deleted
63.1-133.10	Deleted
63.1-133.11	Deleted
63.1-133.12	Deleted
63.1-133.12:1	Deleted
63.1-133.13	Deleted
63.1-133.14	Deleted
63.1-133.15	Deleted

Former Section	Present Section
63.1-133.16	Deleted
63.1-133.17	Deleted
63.1-133.18	Deleted
63.1-133.19	Deleted
63.1-133.20	Deleted
63.1-133.21	Deleted
63.1-133.22	Deleted
63.1-133.23	Deleted
63.1-133.24	Deleted
63.1-133.25	Deleted
63.1-133.26	Deleted
63.1-133.27	Deleted
63.1-133.28	Deleted
63.1-133.29	Deleted
63.1-133.30	Deleted
63.1-133.31	Deleted
63.1-133.32	Deleted
63.1-133.33	Deleted
63.1-133.34	Deleted
63.1-133.35	Deleted
63.1-133.36	Deleted
63.1-133.37	Deleted
63.1-133.38	Deleted
63.1-133.39	Deleted
63.1-133.40	Deleted
63.1-133.41	63.2-601
63.1-133.42	63.2-500
63.1-133.43	63.2-609
63.1-133.45	63.2-610
63.1-133.46	63.2-611
63.1-133.47	63.2-614
63.1-133.48	63.2-609
63.1-133.49	63.2-608
63.1-133.50	63.2-612
63.1-133.51	63.2-613
63.1-133.52	63.2-616
63.1-133.53	63.2-618
63.1-133.54	63.2-619
63.1-133.55	Deleted
63.1-133.56	63.2-700
63.1-133.57	63.2-701
63.1-133.58	63.2-702
63.1-142	51.5-60
63.1-143	51.5-78
63.1-144	51.5-79
63.1-145	51.5-80
63.1-146	51.5-81
63.1-147	51.5-82
63.1-148	51.5-83
63.1-149	51.5-84
63.1-150	51.5-85
63.1-151	51.5-86
63.1-152	51.5-84
63.1-153	51.5-87
63.1-154	51.5-88
63.1-155	51.5-89
63.1-156	51.5-90
63.1-157	51.5-91
63.1-158	51.5-92
63.1-159	51.5-93
63.1-160	51.5-94

Former Section	Present Section
63.1-161	51.5-95
63.1-162	51.5-96
63.1-163	51.5-97
63.1-164	51.5-98
63.1-165	51.5-99
63.1-166	51.5-60
63.1-167	51.5-101
63.1-168	51.5-102
63.1-169	51.5-103
63.1-170	51.5-104
63.1-171	51.5-105
63.1-171.3	46.2-932.1
63.1-171.5	2.2-3315.1
63.1-172	63.2-100
63.1-172	63.2-1803
63.1-173.2	63.2-1720
63.1-173.3	63.2-1804
63.1-174	63.2-1732
63.1-174	63.2-1802
63.1-174	63.2-1803
63.1-174.001	63.2-1805
63.1-174.01	63.2-1700
63.1-174.1	63.2-1705
63.1-174.2	63.2-1806
63.1-174.3	63.2-1807
63.1-175	63.2-1701
63.1-175	63.2-1800
63.1-176	63.2-1702
63.1-177	63.2-1706
63.1-177	63.2-1801
63.1-177.1	63.2-1730
63.1-177.2	63.2-1729
63.1-178	63.2-1707
63.1-178.1	63.2-1736
63.1-179.1	63.2-1709
63.1-180	63.2-1710
63.1-181	63.2-1711
63.1-182	63.2-1712
63.1-182	63.2-1714
63.1-182.1	63.2-1808
63.1-194.1	63.2-100
63.1-194.2	63.2-1733
63.1-194.3	63.2-1700
63.1-194.4	63.2-1705
63.1-194.5	63.2-1701
63.1-194.6	63.2-1702
63.1-194.7	63.2-1706
63.1-194.8	63.2-1707
63.1-194.9	63.2-1709
63.1-194.10	63.2-1710
63.1-194.11	63.2-1711
63.1-194.12	63.2-1712
63.1-194.12	63.2-1714
63.1-194.13	63.2-1720
63.1-195	63.2-100
63.1-196	63.2-1701
63.1-196	63.2-1703
63.1-196.001	63.2-100
63.1-196.001	63.2-1715
63.1-196.002	63.2-1809
63.1-196.01	63.2-1810

Former Section	Present Section
63.1-196.01:1	Deleted
63.1-196.04	63.2-1704
63.1-196.1	63.2-1701
63.1-196.1	63.2-1706
63.1-196.3	63.2-1716
63.1-196.3:1	63.2-1717
63.1-196.4	63.2-1737
63.1-196.5	63.2-1700
63.1-197	63.2-1701A
63.1-197	63.2-1702
63.1-198	63.2-1702
63.1-198	63.2-1721
63.1-198	63.2-1722
63.1-198.01	63.2-1811
63.1-198.03	63.2-1728
63.1-198.03:1	63.2-1731
63.1-198.04	63.2-1718
63.1-198.1	63.2-1719
63.1-198.1	63.2-1720
63.1-198.1	63.2-1721
63.1-198.2	63.2-1724
63.1-198.3	63.2-1727
63.1-198.4	63.2-1723
63.1-198.5	63.2-1725
63.1-199	63.2-1707
63.1-199	63.2-1721
63.1-200	63.2-1812
63.1-201	63.2-1707
63.1-201.1	63.2-1713
63.1-202	63.2-1734
63.1-202.1	63.2-1735
63.1-203	63.2-1708
63.1-203	63.2-1818
63.1-204	63.2-903
63.1-204	63.2-1817
63.1-204.1	63.2-912
63.1-204.2	63.2-909
63.1-204.3	63.2-910
63.1-205	63.2-904
63.1-205	63.2-1819
63.1-206	63.2-902
63.1-206.1	63.2-908
63.1-207	63.2-1104
63.1-207.1	63.2-1105
63.1-209	63.2-104
63.1-209.1	63.2-105
63.1-210	63.2-1706
63.1-210.1	63.2-1813
63.1-211	63.2-904
63.1-211.2	63.2-1814
63.1-211.3	63.2-1709
63.1-212	63.2-1709
63.1-213	63.2-1710
63.1-214	63.2-1711
63.1-215	63.2-1712
63.1-216	63.2-1714
63.1-217	63.2-203
63.1-218	63.2-1815
63.1-219	63.2-1816
63.1-219.1	63.2-1100
63.1-219.2	63.2-1000

Former Section	Present Section
63.1-219.3	63.2-1101
63.1-219.4	63.2-1102
63.1-219.5	63.2-1103
63.1-219.7	63.2-100
63.1-219.8	63.2-1200
63.1-219.9	63.2-1201
63.1-219.10	63.2-1202
63.1-219.11	63.2-1203
63.1-219.12	63.2-1204
63.1-219.13	63.2-1205
63.1-219.14	63.2-1206
63.1-219.15	63.2-1207
63.1-219.16	63.2-1209
63.1-219.17	63.2-1210
63.1-219.18	63.2-1211
63.1-219.19	63.2-1212
63.1-219.20	63.2-1213
63.1-219.21	63.2-1214
63.1-219.22	63.2-1215
63.1-219.23	63.2-1216
63.1-219.24	63.2-1217
63.1-219.25	63.2-1218
63.1-219.26	63.2-1219
63.1-219.27	63.2-1220
63.1-219.28	63.2-1221
63.1-219.29	63.2-1222
63.1-219.30	63.2-1223
63.1-219.31	63.2-1224
63.1-219.32	63.2-1225
63.1-219.33	63.2-1226
63.1-219.34	63.2-1227
63.1-219.35	63.2-1208
63.1-219.35	63.2-1228
63.1-219.36	63.2-1229
63.1-219.37	63.2-1230
63.1-219.38	63.2-1231
63.1-219.39	63.2-1232
63.1-219.40	63.2-1233
63.1-219.41	63.2-1234
63.1-219.42	63.2-1235
63.1-219.43	63.2-1236
63.1-219.44	63.2-1237
63.1-219.45	63.2-1208
63.1-219.45	63.2-1238
63.1-219.46	63.2-1239
63.1-219.47	63.2-1240
63.1-219.48	63.2-1241
63.1-219.49	63.2-1208
63.1-219.49	63.2-1242
63.1-219.50	63.2-1243
63.1-219.51	63.2-1208
63.1-219.51	63.2-1244
63.1-219.52	63.2-1245
63.1-219.53	63.2-1246
63.1-219.54	63.2-1247
63.1-219.55	63.2-1248
63.1-238.03	63.2-1300
63.1-238.1	63.2-100
63.1-238.1	63.2-1300
63.1-238.2	63.2-1301
63.1-238.3	63.2-1302
63.1-238.4	63.2-1303
63.1-238.5	63.2-217
63.1-238.6	63.2-1400
63.1-238.7	63.2-1401
63.1-238.8	63.2-1402
63.1-238.9	63.2-1403
63.1-238.10	63.2-1404
63.1-238.11	63.2-1405
63.1-248.1	63.2-1500
63.1-248.2	63.2-100
63.1-248.2	63.2-1501
63.1-248.2	63.2-1508
63.1-248.2:1	63.2-1504
63.1-248.3	63.2-1509
63.1-248.4	63.2-1510
64.1-248.4:1	63.2-1511
63.1-248.5	63.2-1512
63.1-248.5:1	63.2-1514
63.1-248.5:1.01	63.2-1513
63.1-248.6	63.2-1503
63.1-248.6:01	63.2-1505
63.1-248.6:02	63.2-1506
63.1-248.6:1	63.2-1526
63.1-248.6:2	63.2-1516
63.1-248.7	63.2-1502
63.1-248.7:1	63.2-1527
63.1-248.7:2	63.2-1726
63.1-248.8	63.2-1515
63.1-248.9	63.2-1517
63.1-248.10	63.2-1518
63.1-248.11	63.2-1519
63.1-248.13	63.2-1520
63.1-248.13:1	63.2-1521
63.1-248.13:2	63.2-1522
63.1-248.13:3	63.2-1523
63.1-248.14	63.2-1524
63.1-248.15	63.2-1525
63.1-248.16	63.2-1528
63.1-248.17	63.2-1507
63.1-248.19	63.2-1529
63.1-249	63.2-1901
63.1-249.1	63.2-1907
63.1-249.1	63.2-1950
63.1-250	63.2-100
63.1-250	63.2-1900
63.1-250.1	63.2-1903
63.1-250.1:1	63.2-1951
63.1-250.1:2	63.2-1913
63.1-250.1:3	63.2-1905
63.1-250.2	63.2-1904
63.1-250.2:1	63.2-1917
63.1-250.3	63.2-1924
63.1-250.4	63.2-1936
63.1-251	63.2-1908
63.1-251.1	63.2-1953
63.1-251.2	63.2-1954
63.1-251.3	63.2-1910
63.1-251.4	63.2-1955
63.1-252.1	63.2-1916
63.1-252.2	63.2-1921
63.1-254	63.2-1927
63.1-255	63.2-1928
63.1-256	63.2-1929
63.1-257	63.2-1925
63.1-258	63.2-1930
63.1-258.1	63.2-1923
63.1-258.2	63.2-1926
63.1-258.3	63.2-1915
63.1-259	63.2-1956
63.1-260.1	63.2-1931
63.1-260.3	63.2-1932
63.1-261	63.2-1933
63.1-262	63.2-1934
63.1-263	63.2-1935
63.1-263.1	63.2-1937
63.1-264	63.2-1922
63.1-264.1	63.2-1920
63.1-264.2	63.2-1918
63.1-265	63.2-1938
63.1-266	63.2-1939
63.1-267	63.2-1952
63.1-267.1	63.2-1942
63.1-268.1	63.2-1943
63.1-269	63.2-1957
63.1-270	63.2-1958
63.1-271	63.2-1944
63.1-272	63.2-1945
63.1-273	63.2-1909
63.1-274	Deleted
63.1-274.1	63.2-1953
63.1-274.2	63.2-1911
63.1-274.3	63.2-1906
63.1-274.4	63.2-1949
63.1-274.5	63.2-1919
63.1-274.6	63.2-103
63.1-274.6	63.2-1902
63.1-274.6	63.2-1940
63.1-274.7	63.2-1959
63.1-274.8	63.2-1947
63.1-274.9	63.2-1948
63.1-274.10	63.2-1960
63.1-274.11	63.2-1946
63.1-291	15.2-2811
63.1-292	15.2-2812
63.1-293	15.2-2813
63.1-294	15.2-2814
63.1-296	15.2-2815
63.1-297	15.2-2816
63.1-298	15.2-2817
63.1-314.1	63.2-222
63.1-314.2	63.2-223
63.1-314.3	63.2-224
63.1-314.4	63.2-225
63.1-314.5	63.2-226
63.1-314.6	63.2-227
63.1-314.8	63.2-228
63.1-315	63.2-1611
63.1-316	Deleted
63.1-317	63.2-1612
63.1-317.1	63.2-1613
63.1-318	63.2-1614
63.1-319	63.2-1615

Former Section	Present Section
63.1-320	Deleted
63.1-321	63.2-2000
63.1-322	63.2-2001
63.1-323	63.2-2002
63.1-324	63.2-2003
63.1-325	63.2-2004
63.1-325.1	63.2-2005
63.1-325.2	63.2-2006
63.1-326	63.2-2100
63.1-327	63.2-2101
63.1-328	63.2-2101
63.1-329	63.2-2102
63.1-330	63.2-2103
63.1-331	63.2-2200
63.1-332	63.2-2201
63.1-333	63.2-2202
63.1-334	63.2-2203
63.1-335	63.2-2204
63.1-336	63.2-805
63.1-337	63.2-805
63.1-338	63.2-805
63.1-339	63.2-805
63.1-340	63.2-805
63.1-341	63.2-805
63.1-342	63.2-805
63.1-343	63.2-805
20-49.9	63.2-1914

COMPARABLE SECTIONS OF TITLE 64 AND TITLE 64.1

Former Section	Present Section
64-1	64.1-1
64-2	64.1-2
64-3	64.1-3
64-4	64.1-4
64-5	64.1-5
64-6	64.1-6
64-7	64.1-7
64-8	64.1-8
64-9	64.1-9
64-10	64.1-10
64-11	64.1-11
64-12	64.1-12
64-13	64.1-13
64-14	64.1-14
64-15	64.1-15
64-16	64.1-16
64-17	64.1-17
64-18	64.1-18
64-19	Deleted
64-20	64.1-19
64-21	64.1-20
64-22	64.1-21
64-23	64.1-22
64-24	64.1-23
64-25	64.1-24
64-26	64.1-25
64-27	64.1-19
64-28	64.1-26
64-29	64.1-27
64-30	64.1-28
64-31	64.1-29
64-32	64.1-30
64-33	64.1-31
64-34	64.1-32
64-35	64.1-23
64-36	64.1-33
64-37	64.1-34
64-38	64.1-35
64-38.1	64.1-36
64-39	64.1-37
64-40	64.1-38
64-41	64.1-39
64-42	64.1-40
64-43	64.1-41
64-44	64.1-42
64-45	64.1-43
64-46	64.1-44
64-47	64.1-45
64-48	64.1-46
64-49	64.1-47
64-50	64.1-48
64-51	64.1-49
64-52	64.1-50
64-53	64.1-51
64-54	64.1-51
64-55	64.1-53
64-56	64.1-54
64-57	64.1-55
64-57.1	64.1-56
64-57.2	64.1-57
64-58	Repealed
64-59	64.1-58
64-60	64.1-60
64-61	64.1-61
64-62	64.1-62
64-63	64.1-63
64-64	64.1-64
64-65	64.1-65
64-66	64.1-66
64-67	64.1-67
64-68	64.1-68
64-68.1	64.1-69
64-69	64.1-70
64-70	64.1-71
64-71	64.1-72
64-71.1	64.1-73
64-71.2	64.1-74
64-72	64.1-75
64-72.1	64.1-76
64-73	64.1-77
64-74	64.1-78
64-75	64.1-79
64-76	64.1-80
64-77	64.1-81
64-78	64.1-82
64-79	64.1-83
64-80	64.1-84
64-81	64.1-85
64-82	64.1-86
64-83	64.1-87
64-84	64.1-88
64-85	64.1-89
64-86	64.1-90
64-87	64.1-91
64-88	64.1-92
64-89	64.1-93
64-90	64.1-94
64-91	64.1-95
64-92	64.1-96
64-93	64.1-97
64-94	64.1-98
64-95	64.1-99
64-96	64.1-100
64-97	64.1-101
64-98	64.1-102
64-99	64.1-103
64-100	64.1-104
64-101	64.1-105
64-102	64.1-106
64-103	64.1-107
64-104	64.1-108
64-105	64.1-109
64-106	64.1-110
64-107	64.1-111
64-108	64.1-112
64-109	64.1-113
64-110	64.1-114
64-111	64.1-115
64-112	64.1-116
64-113	64.1-117
64-114	64.1-118
64-115	64.1-119
64-116	64.1-120
64-117	64.1-121
64-118	64.1-122
64-119	64.1-123
64-119.1	64.1-124
64-119.2	64.1-125
64-120	64.1-126
64-121	64.1-127
64-121.1	64.1-128
64-122	64.1-129
64-123	64.1-130
64-124	64.1-131

Former Section	Present Section
64-125	64.1-132
64-126	64.1-133
64-127	64.1-134
64-127.1	64.1-135
64-128	64.1-136
64-129	64.1-137
64-130	64.1-138
64-131	64.1-139
64-131.1	64.1-140
64-131.2	64.1-141
64-132	64.1-142
64-133	64.1-143
64-134	64.1-144
64-135	64.1-145
64-136	64.1-146
64-137	64.1-147
64-138	64.1-148
64-139	64.1-149
64-140	64.1-150
64-141	64.1-151
64-142	64.1-152
64-143	64.1-153
64-144	64.1-154
64-145	64.1-155
64-146	64.1-156
64-147	64.1-157
64-148	64.1-158
64-149	64.1-159
64-150	64.1-160
64-151	64.1-161
64-152	64.1-162
64-153	64.1-163
64-154	64.1-164
64-155	64.1-165
64-156	64.1-166
64-157	64.1-167
64-158	64.1-168
64-159	64.1-169
64-160	64.1-170
64-161	64.1-171
64-162	64.1-172
64-163	64.1-173
64-164	64.1-174
64-165	64.1-175
64-166	64.1-176
64-167	64.1-177
64-168	64.1-178
64-169	64.1-179
64-170	64.1-180
64-171	64.1-181
64-172	64.1-182
64-173	64.1-183
64-173.1	64.1-184
64-174	64.1-185
64-175	64.1-186
64-176	64.1-187
None	64.1-59

COMPARABLE SECTIONS OF TITLE 65 AND TITLE 65.1

Former Section	Present Section
65-1	65.1-1
65-2	65.1-2
65-3	65.1-3
65-4	65.1-4, 65.1-6
65-5	65.1-5
65-6	65.1-6
65-7	65.1-7
65-7.1	65.1-8
65-8	65.1-9
65-9	65.1-10
65-10	65.1-11
65-10.1	65.1-13
65-11	65.1-14
65-12	65.1-15
65-13	65.1-16
65-14	65.1-11, 65.1-12
65-15	65.1-17
65-16	65.1-18
65-17	65.1-19
65-18	65.1-20
65-18.1	65.1-21
65-19	65.1-22
65-20	65.1-23
65-21	65.1-24
65-22	65.1-25
65-23	65.1-26
65-24	65.1-27
65-25	65.1-28
65-26	65.1-29
65-27	65.1-30
65-28	65.1-31
65-29	65.1-32
65-30	65.1-33
65-31	65.1-34
65-32	65.1-35
65-33	65.1-36
65-34	65.1-37
65-35	65.1-38
65-36	65.1-39
65-37	65.1-40
65-38	65.1-41
65-39	65.1-42
65-39.1	65.1-43
65-40	65.1-44
65-41	65.1-45
65-42	65.1-46
65-43	Repealed
65-43.1	65.1-47
65-44	65.1-48
65-45	Repealed
65-46	65.1-49
65-47	65.1-50
65-48	65.1-51
65-49	65.1-52
65-50	65.1-53
65-51	65.1-54
65-52	65.1-55
65-53	65.1-56
65-54	65.1-57
65-55	65.1-58
65-56	65.1-59
65-57	65.1-60
65-58	65.1-61
65-59	65.1-62
65-60	65.1-63
65-61	65.1-64
65-62	65.1-65
65-63	65.1-66
65-64	65.1-67
65-65	65.1-65
65-66	65.1-69
65-67	65.1-70
65-68	65.1-71
65-69	65.1-72
65-70	65.1-73
65-71	65.1-74
65-72	65.1-75
65-73	65.1-76
65-74	65.1-78
65-76	65.1-79
65-77	65.1-80
65-78	65.1-81
65-79	65.1-82
65-80	65.1-83
65-81	65.1-84
65-82	65.1-85
65-83	65.1-86
65-84	65.1-87
65-85	65.1-88
65-86	65.1-89
65-87	65.1-90
65-88	65.1-91
65-89	65.1-92
65-90	65.1-93
65-91	65.1-94
65-91.1	65.1-95
65-92	65.1-96
65-93	65.1-97
65-94	65.1-98
65-95	65.1-99
65-96	65.1-100
65-97	65.1-101
65-98	65.1-102
65-99	65.1-103
65-100	65.1-104

Former Section	Present Section
65-101	65.1-105
65-102	65.1-106
65-103	65.1-107
65-104	65.1-108
65-105	65.1-109
65-106	65.1-110
65-107	65.1-111
65-108	65.1-112
65-109	65.1-113
65-110	65.1-114
65-111	65.1-115
65-112	65.1-116
65-113	65.1-117
65-114	65.1-118
65-114.1	65.1-119
65-114.2	65.1-120
65-114.3	65.1-121
65-114.4	65.1-122
65-114.5	65.1-123
65-115	65.1-124
65-116	65.1-125
65-117	65.1-126
65-118	65.1-127
65-119	65.1-128
65-120	65.1-129
65-121	65.1-130
65-122	65.1-131
65-123	65.1-132
65-124	65.1-133
65-125	65.1-134
65-126	65.1-135
65-127	65.1-136
65-128	65.1-137
65-129 to 65-134	Deleted

COMPARABLE SECTIONS OF TITLE 65.1 AND TITLE 65.2

Former Section	Present Section
65.1-1	65.2-100
65.1-2 to 65.1-4.1	65.2-101 65.2-402
65.1-4.1:1 to 65.1-8	65.2-101
65.1-9	Repealed
65.1-10	65.2-200
65.1-10.1	Repealed
65.1-11	65.2-201
65.1-12	65.2-203
65.1-13	65.2-203
65.1-14	Repealed
65.1-15 to 65.1-17	65.2-204
65.1-18	65.2-201
65.1-19 to 65.1-21	65.2-202
65.1-22	65.2-201
65.1-23	65.2-300
65.1-23.1	65.2-301
65.1-24	Repealed
65.1-25	65.2-300
65.1-26	65.2-300
65.1-27	65.2-101
65.1-28	65.2-101
65.1-29 to 65.1-31	65.2-302
65.1-32	65.2-303
65.1-33	65.2-304
65.1-34	65.2-303
65.1-35	65.2-305
65.1-36	Repealed
65.1-37	65.2-300
65.1-38	65.2-306
65.1-39	Repealed
65.1-40	65.2-307
65.1-40.1	65.2-308
65.1-41	65.2-309
65.1-42	65.2-310
65.1-43	65.2-311
65.1-44	65.2-300
65.1-45	65.2-701
65.1-46	65.2-400
65.1-46.1	65.2-401
65.1-47	Repealed
65.1-47.1	65.2-402
65.1-48	Repealed
65.1-49	65.2-403
65.1-50	65.2-404
65.1-51	65.2-405
65.1-52	65.2-406
65.1-53	65.2-407
65.1-54	65.2-500
65.1-55	65.2-502
65.1-55.1	65.2-708
65.1-56	65.2-501 65.2-503
65.1-56.1	65.2-504
65.1-57	Repealed
65.1-58	65.2-505
65.1-59	65.2-506
65.1-60	65.2-507
65.1-61	65.2-508
65.1-62	65.2-509
65.1-63	65.2-510
65.1-64	65.2-511
65.1-65	65.2-512
65.1-65.1	65.2-513
65.1-65.2	65.2-514
65.1-66	65.2-515
65.1-67	65.2-516
65.1-68	65.2-512
65.1-69	65.2-517
65.1-70	65.2-512
65.1-71	65.2-518
65.1-71.1	65.2-519
65.1-72	65.2-520
65.1-73	65.2-521
65.1-74	65.2-522
65.1-75	65.2-523
65.1-75.1	65.2-524
65.1-76	65.2-525
65.1-77	65.2-526
65.1-78	65.2-527
65.1-79	65.2-528
65.1-80	65.2-529
65.1-81	65.2-530
65.1-82	65.2-531
65.1-83	Repealed
65.1-84	Repealed
65.1-85	65.2-600
65.1-86	65.2-600
65.1-87	65.2-601
65.1-87.1	65.2-602
65.1-88	65.2-603
65.1-88.1	65.2-604
65.1-88.2	Repealed
65.1-89	65.2-605
65.1-90	65.2-606
65.1-91	65.2-607
65.1-92	65.2-700
65.1-93	65.2-701
65.1-94	65.2-702
65.1-95	65.2-703
65.1-96	65.2-704
65.1-97	65.2-705
65.1-98	65.2-706
65.1-98.1	65.2-707
65.1-99	65.2-708
65.1-99.1	65.2-709
65.1-100	Repealed
65.1-100.1	65.2-710
65.1-100.2	65.2-711
65.1-100.3	65.2-712
65.1-101	65.2-713
65.1-102	65.2-714
65.1-103	65.2-800
65.1-104	Repealed
65.1-104.1	65.2-801
65.1-104.2	65.2-802
65.1-104.3	65.2-803
65.1-105	65.2-804
65.1-106	65.2-805
65.1-106.1	65.2-806
65.1-107	65.2-807
65.1-108	65.2-808
65.1-109	65.2-809
65.1-110	65.2-810

Former Section	Present Section
65.1-111	65.2-811
65.1-112	65.2-812
65.1-113	65.2-813
65.1-113.1	65.2-814
65.1-113.2	65.2-815
65.1-114	65.2-816
65.1-115	Repealed
65.1-116	Repealed
65.1-117	65.2-817
65.1-117.1	65.2-818
65.1-118	65.2-819
65.1-119	65.2-820
65.1-120	65.2-821
65.1-121	65.2-822
65.1-122	65.2-823
65.1-123	65.2-824
65.1-124	65.2-900
65.1-125	Repealed
65.1-126	65.2-901
65.1-127	65.2-902
65.1-128	65.2-903
65.1-129	65.2-1000
65.1-130	65.2-1001
65.1-131	65.2-1002
65.1-132	65.2-1003
65.1-133	65.2-1004
65.1-134	65.2-1005
65.1-135	65.2-1006
65.1-136	65.2-1007
65.1-137	65.2-1008
65.1-138	65.2-1100
65.1-139	65.2-1101
65.1-140	65.2-1102
65.1-141	Repealed
65.1-141.1	65.2-1103
65.1-142	Repealed
65.1-142.1	65.2-1104
65.1-143	Repealed
65.1-144	65.2-1105
65.1-145	65.2-1106
65.1-146	65.2-1200
65.1-147	65.2-1201
65.1-148	65.2-1202
65.1-149	65.2-1203
65.1-150	65.2-1204
65.1-151	65.2-1205
65.1-152	65.2-1206
65.1-153	65.2-1300
65.1-154	65.2-1301
65.1-155	65.2-1302
65.1-156	65.2-1303
65.1-157	65.2-1304
65.1-158	65.2-1305
65.1-159	65.2-1306
65.1-160	65.2-1307
65.1-161	65.2-1308
65.1-162	65.2-1309
65.1-163	65.2-1310

CODE OF VIRGINIA

1950

2013 Cumulative Supplement

ANNOTATED

Prepared under the Supervision of

The Virginia Code Commission

BY

The Editorial Staff of the Publishers

VOLUME 10

2004 REPLACEMENT

Includes all acts adopted at the 2013 Regular Session
and 2013 Special Session I
of the General Assembly

Place in Pocket of Corresponding Volume of Main Set.
This Supersedes Previous Supplement, Which
May Be Retained for Reference Purposes.

LexisNexis®

701 East Water Street, Charlottesville, VA 22902-5389

5046030

ISBN 978-0-327-11171-9 (set)
ISBN 978-0-8205-8604-5 (Vol. 10)

www.lexisnexis.com

Customer Service: 1-800-833-9844

(Pub.49005)

USER'S GUIDE

In order to assist both the legal profession and the lay person in obtaining the maximum benefit from the Code of Virginia, a User's Guide has been included in Volume 1. This guide contains comments and information on the many features found within the Code of Virginia intended to increase the usefulness of this set of laws to the user. See Volume 1 for the complete User's Guide.

Suggestions, comments, or questions about the Code of Virginia or this Cumulative Supplement are welcome. You may call us toll free at (800) 833-9844, fax us toll free at (800) 643-1280, email us at customer.support@lexisnexis.com, or write Code of Virginia Editor, LexisNexis, 701 East Water Street, Charlottesville, Virginia 22902-5389.

For an online bookstore, technical and customer support, and other company information, visit our Internet home page at **http://www.lexisnexis.com**.

TABLE OF TITLES

TABLE OF TITLES

IN ADDITION, THIS PUBLICATION CONTAINS

TABLE OF CONTENTS

VOLUME 10

TABLE OF ACTS CODIFIED SUBSEQUENT TO 1948

ACTS 2005

ACTS 2005 Chapter	Code 1950 Section
1	60.2-604
2	25.1-108, 25.1-108, n.
3	45.1-161.8, 45.1-161.12, 45.1-161.14, 45.1-161.20, 45.1-161.21, 45.1-161.33, 45.1-161.37, 45.1-161.63, 45.1-61.64, 45.1-161.80, 45.1-161.83, 45.1-161.97, 45.1-161.109, 45.1-161.115—45.1-116.118, 45.1-161.120R, 45.1-161.122, 45.1-161.124, 45.1-161.126, 45.1-161.135, 45.1-161.147, 45.1-161.154, 45.1-161.156, 45.1-161.163, 45.1-161.165, 45.1-161.172, 45.1-161.175, 45.1-161.176, 45.1-161.186, 45.1-161.194, 45.1-161.195, 45.1-161.198, 45.1-161.200, 45.1-161.207—45.1-161.210, 45.1-161.212, 45.1-161.213R, 45.1-161.216, 45.1-161.218, 45.1-161.219, 45.1-161.225, 45.1-161.228, 45.1-161.229, 45.1-161.233:1, 45.1-161.236, 45.1-161.256, 45.1-161.257, 45.1-161.260, 45.1-161.264, 45.1-161.265, 45.1-161.270, 45.1-161.273, 45.1-161.276, 45.1-161.277, 45.1-161.278, 45.1-161.280, 45.1-161.282, 45.1-161.287, 45.1-161.288, 45.1-221R, 45.1-221.1, 45.1-223R, 45.1-222, 45.1-224, 45.1-224.1, 45.1-225R, 45.1-246
4	3.1-336.2
5	58.1-301
6	44-146.19
7	37.1-179.1, n.
8	29.1-306, 29.1-306.1, 29.1-519
9	24.2-923, 24.2-929
11	Const., Art. 8, § 2, n., 22.1-253.13:1, n.
12	23-41
13	Const., Art. 8, § 2, n., 22.1-253.13:1, n.
14	19.2-305.4
15	23-7.5
16	63.2-301
17	2.2-3709, n.
18	47.1-19
19	32.1-357, 32.1-364
20	58.1-3826
21	58.1-2670
22	56-265.1
23	60.2-602
25	10.1-107, 33.1-223
26	58.1-301
27	58.1-322
28	58.1-1000, 58.1-1003, 58.1-1006, 58.1-1007, 58.1-1008, 58.1-1010, 58.1-1011, 58.1-1017, 58.1-1021
29	58.1-322, n.
30	2.2-4510
31	63.2-2201
33	22.1-208.2:4
34	22.1-4.3
35	56-5.1R, 56-257.2, 56-257.3R
36	15.2-1646
37	32.1-283.4
38	38.2-1057
39	32.1-127.1:03
40	15.2-743
41	2.2-215, 10.1-603.2, n., 10.1-1186.5, 10.1-1194, 10.1-2101, 10.1-2103, n., 10.1-2105R, 10.1-2106, 10.1-2125, 10.1-2129, 28.2-1103
42	58.1-609.11
43	37.1-225—37.1-233R
44	60.2-528
45	16.1-69.29, 17.1-516
46	58.1-609.1
47	18.2-204.3, 60.2-500, 60.2-536.1—60.2-536.5, 60.2-622
48	58.1-302, 58.1-348.1, 58.1-348.2
49	28.2-1205.1, 62.1-44.15:5.01
50	38.2-5004, 38.2-5006
51	16.1-345.1, 37.1-67.7, 37.2-804.1, 37.2-913, 37.2-1109
52	38.2-5004, 38.2-5006
53	63.2-1735, n.
54	54.1-3005
55	54.1-2506.1
57	51.1-512
58	58.1-334, 58.1-432
59	58.1-3941, 58.1-3942
60	32.1-271
61	2.2-2628, 2.2-2629
62	26-40.01
63	6.1-245, 6.1-254, 6.1-256.1, 6.1-258.1
64	37.1-179.1, n.
65	10.1-104.4
66	10.1-1308
67	58.1-322
68	54.1-3411.1
69	65.2-805, 65.2-806
70	54.1-3305
71	58.1-1021.01—58.1-1021.04, 58.1-1021.04:1—58.1-1021.04:5
72	15.2-107
73	10.1-529.1
75	37.1-197, 37.1-198, 37.1-248.1, 37.2-504, 37.2-508,

ACTS 2005 Chapter	Code 1950 Section
	37.2-608
76	58.1-3819
77	63.2-1514
78	62.1-44.17:1.1
79	19.2-305.4
80	10.1-603.19, 10.1-606.1
81	2.2-2690—2.2-2695
82	63.2-2006
84	15.2-743
85	10.1-2202, 10.1-2208.1, 10.1-2208.2
86	10.1-2213
87	10.1-116, 15.2-1736
88	10.1-117, 19.2-81
89	58.1-609.11
90	2.2-426
91	18.2-204.3, 60.2-500, 60.2-536.1—60.2-536.5, 60.2-622
92	2.2-213.1
93	58.1-811
94	10.1-215
95	38.2-1906
96	22.1-277.06
97	54.1-3433
98	43-32
99	32.1-102.1, n., 32.1-102.3, n., 32.1-102.3:2, n.
100	58.1-344, 58.1-393.1, 58.1-453 3, n.
101	32.1-127.1:03
102	2.2-4006, 2.2-4021, 10.1-107, 10.1-502, 10.1-566.1, 10.1-603.4, 10.1-603.12:2
103	58.1-3703
104	28.2-1303
105	60.2-119, 60.2-528
106	15.2-5800, 15.2-5805, 15.2-5806, 15.2-5808, 15.2-5814, 15.2-5815, 15.2-5822, 15.2-5823, 58.1-3818, 58.1-3840
107	10.1-560, 10.1-561
108	58.1-3507
109	2.2-1822.1
110	8.01-400.2, 16.1-356, 16.1-361, 60.2-219
111	37.1-225—37.1-233R
112	32.1-111.10
113	54.1-2901, 54.1-3408
114	16.1-69.29, 17.1-516
115	54.1-3434.1—54.1-3434.4
116	58.1-609.1
117	10.1-610
118	55-210.21
119	54.1-3446, 54.1-3448, 54.1-3450
121	58.1-602
122	58.1-602
123	28.2-1000.1
124	28.2-226.1, 28.2-302.1
125	60.2-603
127	29.1-339.1R, 29.1-339.2
128	10.1-619
129	10.1-562
130	10.1-1454.1
131	46.2-894
132	19.2-120
133	10.1-1455
134	54.1-106.1
135	16.1-69.55
136	16.1-88.03
137	46.2-896
138	8.01-127.1
139	8.01-251, 8.01-252R
140	46.2-711, 46.2-892
141	8.01-27.4
142	8.01-44.4
143	18.2-154, 18.2-279
144	8.01-195.4, 16.1-92
145	29.1-336
146	51.1-165, 51.1-205, 51.1-206
147	51.1-505
148	15.2-1716
149	19.2-389
150	18.2-216
151	40.1-79.1, 40.1-100
152	46.2-393
153	2.2-221.1
154	16.1-287
155	53.1-232, n.
156	58.1-3822
157	18.2-194
158	65.2-803.1
160	18.2-287.4
161	51.1-145
162	51.1-165
163	54.1-2912, 54.1-2914, 54.1-2915, 54.1-2916R, 54.1-2951.3
164	52-47
165	2.2-3705.7, 44-146.18
166	18.2-196.1
167	29.1-530.1
168	59.1-148.3
169	2.2-3114
170	29.1-521, 29.1-553
171	18.2-431.1
172	29.1-530.3
173	17.1-619, 17.1-623
174	18.2-248
175	19.2-389
176	19.2-163.02
177	32.1-127, n.
178	22.1-264.1
179	46.2-1166
180	10.1-1428
181	2.2-3705.5, 16.1-338, 20-124.6, 54.1-2969
182	32.1-111.14
183	17.1-501
184	2.2-1839, 54.1-3900.01, 54.1-3936
185	18.2-67.3, 18.2-361, 18.2-370, 18.2-370.1
186	54.1-2982, 54.1-2984
187	19.2-390, 19.2-390.02
188	19.2-299
189	16.1-69.6:1
190	17.1-507
191	28.2-101
192	38.2-324
193	54.1-4201.1
194	15.2-2307.1
195	8.01-341.1
196	51.1-803
197	32.1-164.5, 62.1-44.19:3
198	28.2-302.8
199	2.2-212, n.
200	54.1-3410.2
201	37.1-84.3, 37.2-204
203	8.01-251, 8.01-252R
204	18.2-85
205	44-146.19
206	58.1-3812
207	16.1-69.35
208	46.2-819.2
209	46.2-1029.1
210	46.2-1077
211	8.01-417
212	2.2-1839, 54.1-3900.01, 54.1-3936
213	8.01-249
214	58.1-3211
215	58.1-3211
216	58.1-202
217	19.2-392.02
218	58.1-3284.1
219	19.2-299
221	9.1-1200
222	32.1-127, n.
223	65.2-103
224	58.1-3211
225	29.1-733.1
226	29.1-530.3
227	2.2-3705.5, 16.1-338, 20-124.6, 54.1-2969
228	16.1-69.6:1
229	19.2-390, 19.2-390.02
230	19.2-163.01
231	17.1-507
232	10.1-1454.1

ACTS 2005 Chapter	Code 1950 Section
233	29.1-739.2
234	8.01-44.4
235	2.2-212, n.
236	2.2-507, 10.1-501
237	17.1-314
238	3.1-249.28
239	46.2-873.1
240	6.1-119.1, 6.1-194.93:1, 6.1-225.65, 59.1-92.22
242	2.2-3306
243	58.1-2259
244	46.2-749.2:10
245	46.2-300, 46.2-309R, 46.2-324.1
246	58.1-2403
248	2.2-2666.1, 46.2-744.1, 46.2-749.109R, 46.2-749.109:1, 46.2-749.118—46.2-749.122
250	59.1-204
251	38.2-1903.1
252	54.1-1123
255	8.01-220.1:1, 13.1-1002, 13.1-1005, 13.1-1010.3, 13.1-1014, 13.1-1014.1, 13.1-1015, 13.1-1022, 13.1-1023, 13.1-1038.1, 13.1-1064, 58.1-513
257	15.2-1408
258	2.2-3705.6, 2.2-3711, 15.2-2108.18, 15.2-2160, 56-265.4:4
259	46.2-323, 46.2-342, 46.2-345
260	46.2-328.1, 46.2-345
261	26-17.9
262	46.2-1112
263	6.1-63, 6.1-66
264	46.2-743
265	15.2-1132
266	46.2-870
267	46.2-870
268	46.2-870
269	59.1-200, 59.1-530—59.1-532
270	33.1-253, n.
271	58.1-3506
273	46.2-742.5, 46.2-742.6, 46.2-743, 46.2-746.2:3.1, 46.2-746.2:6, 46.2-746.23, 46.2-749.2:10, 46.2-749.4, 46.2-749.49R, 46.2-749.49:1, 46.2-749.56R, 46.2-749.56:1, 46.2-749.130—46.2-749.135
274	58.1-2403
275	55-418
276	46.2-1240, 46.2-1241
277	26-17.9
278	55-226.2
280	43-33
281	46.2-345
282	3.1-249.28
283	46.2-621.1
284	34-34
285	55-248.7:2
286	34-29
287	54.1-828
288	51.1-305
289	15.2-1408
290	38.2-231, 38.2-2200
291	33.1-348
292	51.1-142.2
293	46.2-1224
294	46.2-725, 46.2-749.4:4
296	59.1-514
298	33.1-252
299	15.2-5431.3
300	46.2-736.1, 46.2-737
301	46.2-712
302	46.2-330
303	59.1-200, 59.1-530—59.1-532
304	3.1-796.94
305	46.2-603, 46.2-623
307	3.1-796.84
308	12.1-21.1
309	15.2-1215
310	46.2-100, 46.2-874
311	15.2-1907.1, 25.1-109
312	46.2-301.1
313	15.2-2114
314	6.1-371
315	6.1-363.2, 6.1-363.4, 6.1-363.7
316	57-60
317	46.2-752
318	15.2-1132
320	6.1-11
321	46.2-1511
322	30-85—30-88
323	33.1-221.1:1.1, 33.1-391.3:1, 58.1-2425
324	10.1-1101, n.
325	58.1-3506
326	3.1-1089—3.1-1091
327	15.2-953
328	58.1-2403, n.
329	57-48—57-50
330	15.2-1129.1
331	22.1-60.1, 22.1-212.2:2, 22.1-253.13:1—22.1-253.13:3, 22.1-253.13:5, 22.1-253.13:6, 22.1-253.13:8, 22.1-294
332	56-46.1, n.
333	8.01-428
334	16.1-293.1
335	38.2-3430.3
336	32.1-73.7, 37.1-24.001, 37.2-312.1
337	15.2-1610, 15.2-1612
338	15.2-2275
339	24.2-416.6, 24.2-1002.01
340	24.2-310
341	36-97, 36-98.1
342	33.1-75.3
343	22.1-3.4, 22.1-289, 63.2-900
344	18.2-308
345	22.1-253.13:4
346	16.1-340—16.1-342, 16.1-345, 16.1-346.1
347	19.2-392
348	54.1-1100, 54.1-1101, 54.1-1103, 54.1-1106, 54.1-1108.1
349	38.2-3407.15
350	22.1-200
351	10.1-2135—10.1-2139
352	2.2-3707, 2.2-3707.01, 2.2-3708
353	55-79.75, 55-510.1
354	65.2-101
355	58.1-602, 58.1-604.6, 58.1-621
356	8.01-359, 19.2-262
357	58.1-3506, 58.1-3508.2
358	22.1-16.3, 22.1-323.2, 37.1-189.1, 37.2-408, 63.2-1737, 66-24
359	54.1-402, 54.1-404, 54.1-406
360	2.2-2318
361	4.1-230
363	37.1-185, 37.1-189.1, 37.2-408,37.2-418
364	16.1-309.1
365	9.1-138
366	15.2-1716
367	34-17

ACTS 2005 Chapter	Code 1950 Section
368	65.2-101
369	24.2-943, 24.2-944
370	24.2-622
371	24.2-929, 24.2-930
372	19.2-12
373	17.1-275
374	65.2-101
375	18.2-386.1
376	18.2-36.2, 46.2-208, 46.2-382
377	22.1-254.1
378	24.2-404
379	13.1-630, 13.1-754, 13.1-762, 13.1-829, 13.1-916, 13.1-924, 13.1-1012, 13.1-1214, 50-73.2
380	24.2-106, 24.2-108, 24.2-114
381	46.2-1015
382	51.1-1403
383	54.1-201, 54.1-202, 54.1-306, 54.1-307.1
384	24.2-101, 24.2-906.1, 24.2-922
385	2.2-1100
386	2.2-1201
387	40.1-51.10
389	17.1-113, 17.1-114, 17.1-121
390	15.2-1812
391	32.1-212, 32.1-215, 32.1-225
392	59.1-284.14:1, 59.1-284.15:1
394	2.2-4303, 2.2-4304
395	56-265.19
396	32.1-164.5, 62.1-44.19:3
397	2.2-3118.1
398	54.1-111
399	38.2-3407.14
400	26-8
402	54.1-2411, 54.1-2413
403	54.1-3320
404	32.1-102.6
405	16.1-293.1
406	18.2-67.3
407	59.1-436
408	18.2-462
409	53.1-129
410	2.2-3705.2
411	2.2-3705.6, 2.2-3711
412	24.2-416.6, 24.2-1002.01
413	2.2-2903, 15.2-1509
414	58.1-339.9
415	55-79.97, 55-512
416	55-248.46
417	59.1-480
418	15.2-955
419	51.1-1112, 51.1-1113, 51.1-1123, 51.1-1124
420	18.2-308
421	2.2-203.1, 2.2-2817.1
422	18.2-387.1
423	8.01-4.3, 18.2-434
424	18.2-308
425	19.2-73
426	8.01-225
427	16.1-266
428	19.2-169.5
429	65.2-104
430	36-85.16
431	2.2-5100, 2.2-5101, 2.2-5102.1—2.2-5104
432	51.1-1403
433	65.2-406
434	32.1-73.7, 37.1-24.001, 37.2-312.1
435	19.2-81
436	55-426, 55-471.1, 55-478, 55-484
437	54.1-2105.2
438	18.2-346.1
439	2.2-2220
440	54.1-402, 54.1-404, 54.1-406
441	18.2-308
442	36-97, n.
443	46.2-208
444	32.1-35.1
445	46.2-684.1
446	22.1-129
447	23-276.1—23-276.8, 23-276.11
448	32.1-272
449	58.1-2402
450	22.1-60.1, 22.1-212.2:2, 22.1-253.13:1—22.1-253.13:3, 22.1-253.13:5, 22.1-253.13:6, 22.1-253.13:8, 22.1-294
451	5.1-88.2
452	15.2-1610, 15.2-1612
453	33.1-223
454	2.2-3311.1
455	6.1-330.54
456	46.2-1500, 46.2-1572
457	10.1-2300, 10.1-2301
458	37.1-67.3, 37.2-817
459	32.1-164.5, 62.1-44.19:3
460	32.1-164.5
461	22.1-208.01, 22.1-279.3:1, 22.1-279.6
462	8.01-220.1:2
463	63.2-505.1
464	60.2-618
465	15.2-904
466	15.2-2223
468	54.1-2910.01
469	32.1-164.1:1
470	10.1-2213.1
471	22.1-16.3, 22.1-323.2, 37.1-189.1, 37.2-408, 63.2-1737, 66-24
472	63.2-608, 65.2-101, 65.2-500, 65.2-502, 65.2-512
473	51.1-1135.1
474	2.2-3601, 2.2-3602, 2.2-3605, 32.1-48.016, 44-146.23
475	54.1-3401
476	2.2-203.2:1
477	54.1-2813, 54.1-2816, 54.1-2817
478	62.1-44.15:01
479	15.2-1716.1
480	55-210.38
481	22.1-276.3, 22.1-292.2
482	8.01-581.1
483	2.2-2902.1
484	22.1-208.01, 22.1-279.3:1, 22.1-279.6
485	37.1-185, 37.1-189.1, 37.2-408, 37.2-418
486	22.1-296
487	58.1-611.1
488	46.2-931
489	22.1-32
490	44-146.18
491	33.1-12.01
492	2.2-1837, 24.2-121
494	30-133
496	24.2-643
497	3.1-22.38—3.1-22.51R, 3.1-22.53—3.1-22.77
498	19.2-13
499	8.01-379.3
500	20-121.03
501	58.1-3916
502	58.1-3219.1
503	2.2-2818, 6.1-2.9:8, 38.2-5600, 38.2-5600R, 38.2-5601, 38.2-5602, 38.2-5602.1, 38.2-5603R
504	56-557—56-561, 56-563—56-566, 56-566.1, 56-566.2, 56-567, 56-567.1, 56-568—56-572, 56-573.1
505	54.1-2703, 54.1-2704,

ACTS 2005 Chapter	Code 1950 Section
	54.1-2706, 54.1-2709, 54.1-2710R, 54.1-2712, 54.1-2712.1, 54.1-2713, 54.1-2715, 54.1-2718, 54.1-2720, 54.1-2722, 54.1-2723R, 54.1-2726, 54.1-2726.1, 54.1-2728, 54.1-2729
506	32.1-111.10
507	18.2-285
508	2.2-3705.7, 17.1-913
509	15.2-2295
510	55-518, 55-519, 55-519.1, 55-520, 55-521, 55-524
511	55-248.12:1
512	19.2-316.2
513	46.2-324.1, 46.2-341.4, 46.2-341.12, 46.2-341.18, 46.2-341.18:1, 46.2-341.20, 46.2-341.20:2, 46.2-341.20:3, 46.2-341.21, 46.2-433
514	15.2-2204
515	15.2-2406
516	28.2-106.1
517	62.1-73, 62.1-77.1R
518	32.1-134.01
519	18.2-254.1
520	22.1-279.6
521	58.1-611.1
528	22.1-279.3:1
530	23-4.3:1
531	15.2-951
532	23-2.3
533	29.1-521
534	29.1-521
535	51.1-1400
536	22.1-32
537	33.1-223.2:14
539	24.2-643
540	55-186.3
541	46.2-931
542	46.2-1110
543	46.2-1110
544	15.2-917
546	46.2-749.131—46.2-749.120
547	15.2-5152, 15.2-5153, 15.2-5158
548	2.2-1837, 24.2-121
550	23-231.3
551	28.2-826
552	15.2-2303.3
554	46.2-749.69:1
555	57-27.1, n.
556	46.2-1143
557	1-510, 7.1-40.7:1
558	46.2-1561
559	33.1-223.2:15
561	58.1-3219.1
562	56-557—56-561, 56-563—56-566, 56-566.1, 56-566.2, 56-567, 56-567.1, 56-568—56-573.1
563	46.2-1088.5
564	15.2-1209
565	46.2-414
566	2.2-5512, n., 2.2-5513, n.
567	15.2-2121, 15.2-2242
568	2.2-3711, 24.2-625.1
569	24.2-649
571	6.1-444, 6.1-445, 6.1-459
572	2.2-2818, 6.1-2.9:8, 38.2-5600R, 38.2-5601, 38.2-5602, 38.2-5602.1, 38.2-5603R
573	18.2-479
574	46.2-1025
575	15.2-4905
576	63.2-505.2
577	2.2-4115, n.
578	18.2-308.2:2
579	8.01-217
580	19.2-316.2
581	62.1-145
582	46.2-1158.1
583	46.2-920, 46.2-1023
584	32.1-351
585	19.2-143
586	9.1-901—9.1-903
587	54.1-2703, 54.1-2704, 54.1-2706, 54.1-2709, 54.1-2710R, 54.1-2712, 54.1-2712.1, 54.1-2713, 54.1-2715, 54.1-2718, 54.1-2720, 54.1-2722, 54.1-2723R, 54.1-2726, 54.1-2726.1, 54.1-2728, 54.1-2729
588	3.1-22.38—3.1-22.51R, 3.1-22.53—3.1-22.77
589	46.2-388
590	16.1-269.2, 16.1-272
591	19.2-305.1
592	15.2-1416.1
593	32.1-164.5, 62.1-44.19:3
594	9.1-108
595	40.1-29
596	17.1-802
597	8.01-420.4
598	18.2-182
599	54.1-1500, 54.1-1504
600	18.2-308.2
601	2.2-3705.3
602	18.2-254.1
603	9.1-902, 9.1-905, 9.1-907, 9.1-913
604	19.2-316.3
605	22.1-23, n., 22.1-70.3, n., 22.1-79, n., 51.1-155
606	22.1-23, n., 22.1-70.3, n., 22.1-79, n., 51.1-155
607	22.1-70.3, n., 22.1-79, n., 51.1-155, n.
608	22.1-70.3, n., 22.1-79, n., 51.1-155, n.
609	22.1-23, n., 51.1-155, n.
610	2.2-703, 54.1-2503, 54.1-3005, 54.1-3007, 54.1-3041—54.1-3043, 54.1-3100—54.1-3102, 54.1-3103, 54.1-3103.1, 54.1-3408, 63.2-1702, 63.2-1707, 63.2-1709, 63.2-1709.1, 63.2-1709.2, 63.2-1721, 63.2-1732, 63.2-1803, 63.2-1803.1, 63.2-1805
611	2.2-2514
612	53.1-1.1
614	15.2-1812.2
616	18.2-266, 18.2-268.2, 18.2-268.10, 18.2-269, 29.1-738, 29.1-738.2, 29.1-738.3, 46.2-341.24, 46.2-341.26:2, 46.2-341.26:10,

ACTS 2005 Chapter	Code 1950 Section
	46.2-341.27
618	56-575.1
619	2.2-4007, 2.2-4007.1, 2.2-4027
620	2.2-1501, 2.2-1502.1
621	33.1-221.1:3, 58.1-815.1
622	19.2-266.2, 19.2-398
624	2.2-2285, 59.1-284.1—59.1-284.6R
625	15.2-2286, 15.2-2311, 15.2-2314
628	46.2-1167
630	15.2-5307
631	9.1-902, 9.1-908, 9.1-910, 16.1-69.48:1, 17.1-275.1, 17.1-275.2, 17.1-275.7, 17.1-805, 18.2-61, 18.2-67.1, 18.2-67.2, 18.2-67.2:1R, 19.2-218.1, 19.2-218.2, 19.2-299, 19.2-303.4, 19.2-335, 19.2-336
632	32.1-111.3
633	2.2-720, 3.1-14, 3.1-73.5, 3.1-249.29, 4.1-115, 5.1-30.9, 10.1-1018, 10.1-1018.1, 10.1-1021, 10.1-1322, 15.2-5912, 17.1-100, 22.1-209.1:3, 23-1.01, 23-9.2:3.1, 23-38.84, 23-101R, 23-102R, 30-19.8:1, 30-34.15, 30-84, 59.1-369, 62.1-222, 63.2-1529
635	38.2-231
636	2.2-2459—2.2-2461
637	2.2-3705.5, n., 54.1-2505, n., 54.1-2519, 54.1-2520, 54.1-2521, n., 54.1-2522, n., 54.1-2523, 54.1-2523.1, 54.1-2524, n., 54.1-2525, n., 54.1-3434.1
638	63.2-1612
639	53.1-40.7
640	2.2-2818, 59.1-200, 59.1-443.2, 59.1-444
642	8.01-413, 32.1-127.1:03, 54.1-111
643	32.1-46, 32.1-46.01
644	26-1.2, 26-8.1
645	33.1-70.01, 33.1-75.1, 33.1-198, 46.2-1104, 58.1-3713
646	4.1-126
647	16.1-248.1
648	66-25.1:1—66-25.1:4
649	8.01-20.1, 8.01-50.1, 8.01-52.1, 8.01-399, 8.01-581.1, 8.01-581.20:1, 16.1-83.1, 38.2-2228.2, 54.1-2912.3
650	19.2-243
651	4.1-119
652	4.1-209
653	16.1-281, 63.2-900, 63.2-906
655	33.1-267, n.
656	38.2-301
657	53.1-136
658	24.2-304.02
661	18.2-62
662	54.1-2952
665	46.2-345
666	15.2-5114
667	15.2-4303
668	55-508
669	46.2-1077.01
670	6.1-330.63
671	15.2-6203, 15.2-6209
672	9.1-108
676	24.2-919.1, 24.2-929
677	15.2-2286, 15.2-2311, 15.2-2314
678	2.2-3705.5, n., 54.1-2505, n., 54.1-2519, 54.1-2520, 54.1-2521, n., 54.1-2522, n., 54.1-2523, 54.1-2523.1, 54.1-2524, n., 54.1-2525, n., 54.1-3434.1
679	32.1-267, 32.1-268, 32.1-268.1
681	1-13.23:1, 1-237, 3.1-358, 3.1-389, 8.01-2, 8.01-23, 8.01-33, 8.01-270R, 8.01-272, 8.01-282, 8.01-283, 8.01-284R, 8.01-331, 8.01-336, 8.01-426, 8.01-670, 9.1-406, 15.2-4119, 16.1-296, 17.1-124, 17.1-131, 17.1-213, 17.1-240, 17.1-249, 17.1-275, 17.1-278, 17.1-279, 17.1-513, 17.1-520, 18.2-500, 18.2-507, 19.2-385, 19.2-386.13, 20-96, 26-21, 26-29, 31-8.1, 40.1-49.4, 43-62, 51.5-46, 53.1-70, 55-19, 55-277, 56-521, 56-522, 57-9, 57-16, 58.1-1727, 64.1-106, 64.1-179
682	2.2-4007, 2.2-4007.1, 2.2-4027
683	16.1-301, 19.2-368.5, 19.2-368.5:2, 19.2-368.10, 19.2-368.11:1
684	32.1-46, 32.1-46.01
685	63.2-1612
686	32.1-111.3
687	2.2-2514
688	29.1-530.4
689	4.1-126
690	8.01-367
691	54.1-2342
692	8.01-20.1, 8.01-50.1, 8.01-52.1, 8.01-399, 8.01-581.1, 8.01-581.20:1, 16.1-83.1, 38.2-2228.2, 54.1-2912.3
694	19.2-266.2, 19.2-398
695	2.2-2664, 2.2-5300, 2.2-5304, 2.2-5304.1, 2.2-5305
696	23-286.1, 23-286.2
697	8.01-413, 32.1-127.1:03, 54.1-111

TABLE OF ACTS CODIFIED SUBSEQUENT TO 1948

ACTS 2005 Chapter	Code 1950 Section
698	38.2-301
699	15.2-2223
700	59.1-365, 59.1-369, 59.1-370, 59.1-387, 59.1-390
701	15.2-2110
702	15.2-903
703	2.2-2720, 2.2-2723
704	10.1-2117, 10.1-2128, 10.1-2129, 10.1-2131, 10.1-2132
705	10.1-1187.1—10.1-1187.7
706	10.1-1309, 10.1-1316, 10.1-1455, 62.1-44.14, 62.1-44.15, 62.1-44.32, 62.1-44.34:20
707	10.1-2117, 10.1-2128, 10.1-2129, 10.1-2131, 10.1-2132
708	62.1-44.19:12—62.1-44.19:19
709	10.1-2117, 10.1-2128, 10.1-2129, 10.1-2131, 10.1-2132
710	62.1-44.19:12—62.1-44.19:19
711	54.1-3205
712	2.2-711, 2.2-712, 37.1-134.14:1, 37.1-134.19, 37.2-1010, 37.2-1015
713	2.2-2696, 37.1-207
714	15.2-1507, 63.2-219
715	32.1-23.1
716	2.2-2696, 2.2-2697, 2.2-2905, 2.2-3705.5, 8.01-2, 16.1-241, 16.1-278.11, 16.1-339, 16.1-346.1, 16.1-348, 18.2-254, 18.2-255.2, 19.2-169.6, 19.2-177.1, 19.2-182.3, 19.2-182.9, 22.1-281, 33.1-234, 37.1-1—37.1-260R, 37.2-100, 37.2-200—37.2-204, 37.2-300—37.2-314, 37.2-315, 37.2-317—37.2-319, 37.2-400—37.2-402, 37.2-403—37.2-422, 37.2-423—37.2-425, 37.2-426—37.2-431, 37.2-432—37.2-440, 37.2-500—37.2-511, 37.2-600—37.2-614, 37.2-700—37.2-714, 37.2-715—37.2-721, 37.2-800—37.2-804, 37.2-805, 37.2-806, 37.2-807, 37.2-808—37.2-813, 37.2-814—37.2-828, 37.2-829—37.2-836, 37.2-837—37.2-843, 37.2-844—37.2-847, 37.2-900—37.2-918, 37.2-1000—37.2-1018, 37.2-1019—37.2-1029, 37.2-1100—37.2-1108, 53.1-40.1, 53.1-40.2, 53.1-40.8, 53.1-40.9, 53.1-77, 54.1-2400.1, 54.1-2986, 58.1-3607, 63.2-1602, 63.2-1801, 63.2-1805
717	32.1-65—32.1-67.1
718	37.1-179, 37.2-403, 51.5-14.1
719	54.1-2902, n., 54.1-2957.7—54.1-2957.13
720	54.1-3205
721	32.1-65, 32.1-66, 32.1-67, 32.1-67.1
722	63.2-901.1, 63.2-1721
723	63.2-1720
724	63.2-1805
725	37.1-179, 37.2-403, 51.5-14.1
726	8.01-506, 8.01-506.2
727	62.1-198, 62.1-199
728	51.1-168
729	51.1-124.30
730	15.2-2118
731	2.2-2725—2.2-2731, 30-192.7, 30-192.8—30-192.14R
732	9.1-700—9.1-704
733	58.1-3245.4:1
734	6.1-2.23:2
735	55-225.5, 55-248.18:1
736	8.01-184.1
737	2.2-2238.1, n.
738	17.1-279
739	2.2-2818, 38.2-3407.13:2
740	15.2-1411
741	22.1-200.02R, 22.1-200.03, 22.1-208.2:3R, 23-9.2:3.5
742	55-248.21:1
743	40.1-51.2:2
744	17.1-258.2—17.1-258.5, 55-108, 55-142.13
745	24.2-910.1, 24.2-929
746	18.2-152.6, 18.2-152.7, 18.2-152.8, 18.2-152.9R, 18.2-152.10R, 18.2-152.12, 19.2-8, 19.2-249.2
747	18.2-152.3, 18.2-152.5, 18.2 152.5:1
748	24.2-524
749	55-66.14
751	37.1-134.21, 37.2-1100, 37.2-1101, 37.2-1102, 37.2-1106, 37.2-1108
753	22.1-253.13:3, 23-9.8:1, 23-38.53:21—23-38.53:24R, 30-226—30-231R, 30-231.1—30-231.10
754	20-88.32, 20-88.33, 20-88.34, 20-88.35, 20-88.36, 20-88.39, 20-88.40, 20-88.41, 20-88.42, 20-88.43, 20-88.43:1, 20-88.43:2, 20-88.44, 20-88.46, 20-88.47, 20-88.48, 20-88.50, 20-88.51, 20-88.53, 20-88.54, 20-88.56, 20-88.57, 20-88.59, 20-88.60, 20-88.62, 20-88.63, 20-88.64, 20-88.64:1, 20-88.64:2, 20-88.64:5, 20-88.65, 20-88.67, 20-88.69, 20-88.70, 20-88.72, 20-88.75, 20-88.76, 20-88.77, 20-88.77:3, 20-88.78, 20-88.80, 20-88.81
755	15.2-750
756	2.2-2639
757	18.2-267, 18.2-268.2, 18.2-268.3, 18.2-268.4, 18.2-268.5, 18.2-268.8, 18.2-268.9, 18.2-268.10, 18.2-272,

ACTS 2005 Chapter	Code 1950 Section
	46.2-391.2, 46.2-391.4
758	2.2-720, 2.2-2452, 2.2-2503, 2.2-2514, 2.2-2621, 2.2-2628, 2.2-2705, 3.1-1108, 10.1-1018, 18.2-271.2, 19.2-163.02, 20-108.2, 22.1-337, 22.1-346.1, 23-38.53:21—23-38.53:24R, 23-287, 23-297, 30-73.2, 30-168.1, 30-172, 30-208, 30-212, 30-226—30-231R, 53.1-176.3
759	18.2-248
760	18.2-152.5:1
761	18.2-152.2, 18.2-152.3, 18.2-152.4—18.2-152.7, 18.2-152.8, 18.2-152.9R, 18.2-152.10R, 18.2-152.12, 19.2-8, 19.2-249.2
762	18.2-370
763	2.2-3808.2
764	18.2-46.1, 18.2-46.3:3, 19.2-11.2, 48-7, 48-8, 48-9
765	6.1-43, 6.1-44.17, 6.1-44.19, 6.1-100.1, 6.1-194.88, 6.1-194.150, 13.1-603—13.1-604.1, 13.1-607—13.1-611, 13.1-614, 13.1-615, 13.1-616, 13.1-619, 13.1-627, 13.1-628, 13.1-630—13.1-633, 13.1-636, 13.1-638, 13.1-639, 13.1-641, 13.1-642, 13.1-646, 13.1-647, 13.1-649, 13.1-651—13.1-653, 13.1-654—13.1-658, 13.1-660, 13.1-660.1, 13.1-662, 13.1-663, 13.1-664.1, 13.1-665, 13.1-669, 13.1-670, 13.1-671.1, 13.1-672.3, 13.1-672.4, 13.1-673, 13.1-675, 13.1-677, 13.1-679, 13.1-680, 13.1-685, 13.1-686, 13.1-688, 13.1-689, 13.1-691, 13.1-691.1, 13.1-692, 13.1-693, 13.1-695, 13.1-696, 13.1-697, 13.1-699, 13.1-700.1—13.1-704, 13.1-706—13.1-708, 13.1-710, 13.1-711, 13.1-713—13.1-715, 13.1-715.1, 13.1-716—13.1-721, 13.1-721.1, 13.1-722R, 13.1-722.1R, 13.1-722.13, 13.1-723, 13.1-724, 13.1-725, 13.1-727, 13.1-728.1—13.1-728.9, 13.1-729—13.1-734, 13.1-735R, 13.1-735.1, 13.1-736R, 13.1-737—13.1-741, 13.1-742, 13.1-743, 13.1-746, 13.1-746.1—13.1-746.3, 13.1-747, 13.1-748, 13.1-749, 13.1-749.1, 13.1-750, 13.1-752, 13.1-757, 13.1-758, 13.1-762, 13.1-765, 13.1-767—13.1-769.1, 13.1-770—13.1-772, 13.1-773.1, 13.1-774—13.1-775.1, 13.1-776, 13.1-898.1, 13.1-1070, 13.1-1276, 38.2-1000, 38.2-1017, 50-73.48:1, 50-73.128
766	46.2-633
767	63.2-1511
768	10.1-1602
769	62.1-198, 62.1-199
770	2.2-2639
771	38.2-2204
772	57-7.1—57-11, 57-13—57-15, 57-16, 57-16.1, 57-17, 57-21, 57-32
773	23-7.4:1
774	2.2-2101, 23-14, 23-231.24—23-231.29
775	15.2-904, 15.2-905
776	15.2-912.2, n., 18.2-340.33, 18.2-340.34:1
777	54.1-3307
778	32.1-111.2
779	8.01-128
780	6.1-2.23:2
781	33.1-19.1
782	58.1-2259
783	23-7.4:1
784	4.1-209, 4.1-215, 4.1-231, 4.1-233
785	8.01-226.5:1, 22.1-274.2
786	2.2-2101, 22.1-212.17—22.1-212.22
787	42.1-77, 42.1-79, 42.1-79.1R, 42.1-82, 42.1-83, 42.1-84R, 42.1-86, 42.1-86.1, 42.1-87
789	40.1-51.2:2
790	24.2-118.1
791	8.01-156
792	54.1-1128, 54.1-1129, 54.1-1129.1, 54.1-1130
793	51.1-126, 51.1-155
795	3.1-18.13—3.1-18.25
796	18.2-248
797	2.2-2238.1
798	2.2-3808.2
799	2.2-2101, 23-14, 23-231.24—23-231.29
800	8.01-184.1
801	8.01-413.02, 19.2-187.02
802	30-19.4
803	2.2-106, 2.2-107
804	46.2-873.1
805	55-248.37
806	63.2-1511
807	55-248.24
808	55-248.31
809	8.01-398, 19.2-271.2
810	16.1-278.8
811	16.1-88.2
812	18.2-152.2, 18.2-152.4
813	18.2-46.1, 18.2-46.3:3, 19.2-11.2, 48-7, 48-8, 48-9
814	15.2-2157
815	2.2-4363
816	58.1-346.23
817	2.2-1111
818	23-9.2:3, 23-9.2:3.02, 23-9.6:1, 23-9.14:2
819	15.2-4203
820	24.2-115, 24.2-120
821	26-17.7
822	15.2-1800
823	40.1-28.1—40.1-28.4:1R
824	24.2-653, 24.2-671
825	55-225.5, 55-248.18:1
826	15.2-912.2, n., 18.2-340.33, 18.2-340.34:1
827	18.2-152.2, 18.2-152.3, 18.2-152.4, 18.2-152.5, 18.2-152.5:1, 18.2-152.6, 18.2-152.7, 18.2-152.8,

ACTS 2005 Chapter	Code 1950 Section
	18.2-152.9R, 18.2-152.10R, 18.2-152.12, 19.2-8, 19.2-249.2
828	46.2-323, 46.2-342, 46.2-345
829	54.1-700—54.1-703, 54.1-703.3, 54.1-704.1—54.1-706
830	18.2-308.1
831	24.2-918
833	18.2-308.2
834	22.1-253.13:3, 23-9.8:1, 23-38.53:21—23-38.53:24R, 30-226—30-231R, 30-231.1—30-231.10
835	15.2-2511.1
836	8.01-654, 19.2-321.1, 19.2-321.2
837	18.2-152.3, 18.2-152.5, 18.2-152.5:1
839	1-10—1-17.2R, 1-13.24R, 1-18—1-21R, 1-200—1-257, 1-300—1-313, 1-400—1-408, 1-500—1-512, 2.2-122, 2.2-604, 2.2-2200, 2.2-3901, 3.1-383, 3.1-411, 3.1-412, 7.1-1—7.1-40.7R, 7.1-10.1—7.1-40.7R, 7.1-40.8—7.1-43R, 8.01-227.2, 15.2-715, 15.2-2000, 15.2-6301, 16.1-69.35, 16.1-241, 17.1-207, 17.1-207, 18.2-246.6, 18.2-308, 19.2-5, 19.2-95, 21-119, 22.1-208.01, 22.1-212.1, 28.2-1205, 30-13, 30-14, 30-15.1:1, 30-28.18, 32.1-229.01, 32.1-325.1:1, 33.1-12, 33.1-320.2 (Compacts volume), 34-32, 43-35, 43-36, 46.2-728.3, 52-10, 54.1-3401, 55-161, 55-531, 56-123, 56-124, 56-265.10, 56-435, 58.1-3732.4, 59.1-21.10, 59.1-443.1, 62.1-44.114
840	18.2-267, 18.2-268.2—18.2-268.10, 18.2-272, 46.2-391.2, 46.2-391.4
842	15.2-6626—15.2-6651
843	16.1-269.2, 16.1-273, 16.1-299.2R, 18.2-55.1, 52-8.6
845	18.2-266
846	58.1-510, n.
847	33.1-221.1:8,
848	38.2-4608
849	46.2-633
850	3.1-928, 3.1-969.10, 3.1-969.12
851	40.1-29
853	58.1-609.12
854	15.2-2404
855	15.2-2303.2
856	58.1-1000, 58.1-1012
857	2.2-2639
858	2.2-2328—2.2-2335
859	18.2-308.2:2, 54.1-4201
860	2.2-2702, 29.1-101, 30-19.1:10R, 58.1-345—58.1-346R, 58.1-346.1:1R, 58.1-346.2:1R, 58.1-344.3, 58.1-346.3:1R, 58.1-346.4:1—58.1-346.24R, 58.1-546
861	59.1-200, 59.1-533—59.1-534
862	46.2-819.1
863	58.1-3, 58.1-439, 58.1-3245.6, 58.1-3245.8, 58.1-3245.12, 59.1-272—59.1-278R, 59.1-279, 59.1-279.1R, 59.1-280, 59.1-280.1, 59.1-282.1, 59.1-282.2, 59.1-280.2R, 59.1-282R, 59.1-282.3—59.1-284R, 59.1-284.01, 59.1-284.17, 59.1-538—59.1-541
864	3.1-618, 3.1-626, 3.1-636.1—3.1-636.12
865	56-575.1—56-575.3, 56-575.3:1, 56-575.4, 56-575.5, 56-575.7—56-575.9, 56-575.9:1, 56-575.10—56-575.13, 56-575.16
866	8.01-285, 8.01-286.1, 8.01-296, 8.01-299, 8.01-301, 8.01-303—8.01-306, 8.01-320
867	32.1-325.03, 63.2-503.1
868	2.2-1104, 2.2-2101, 2.2-3802, 4.1-352, 9.1-102, 9.1-117—9.1-125R, 9.1-501, 9.1-1100, 9.1-1101, 9.1-1102, 9.1-1103, 9.1-1104, 9.1-1105, 9.1-1106, 9.1-1107, 9.1-1108, 9.1-1109, 9.1-1110, 9.1-1111, 9.1-1112, 9.1-1113, 18.2-267, 18.2-268.1, 18.2-268.6, 18.2-268.7, 18.2-268.8, 18.2-268.9, 19.2-187, 19.2-187.01, 19.2-187.2, 19.2-188.1, 19.2-270.4:1, 19.2-310.2, 19.2-310.2:1, 19.2-310.3, 19.2-310.3:1, 19.2-310.4, 19.2-310.5, 19.2-310.6, 19.2-310.7, 19.2-327.1, 19.2-327.3, 19.2-327.4, 19.2-386.23, 19.2-386.27, 19.2-387, 19.2-389.1, 46.2-341.25, 46.2-341.26:1, 46.2-341.26:6, 46.2-341.26:7, 46.2-341.26:9, 54.1-3404, 54.1-3431
869	15.2-6300, 15.2-6300.1, 15.2-6301, 15.2-6302, 15.2-6304, 15.2-6306, 15.2-6308, 15.2-6308.1, 15.2-6314.1, 15.2-6319, 15.2-6322
870	3.1-336.2
871	38.2-3525
872	38.2-2114
873	55-317
875	3.1-618, 3.1-626, 3.1-636.1—3.1-636.12
876	32.1-325.03, 63.2-503.1
877	25.1-203
878	25.1-204, 25.1-245
879	15.2-1411

TABLE OF ACTS CODIFIED SUBSEQUENT TO 1948

ACTS 2005 Chapter	Code 1950 Section
880	16.1-278.18, 20-78.2, 63.2-1960
881	2.2-1104, 2.2-2101, 2.2-3802, 4.1-352, 9.1-102, 9.1-117—9.1-125R, 9.1-501, 9.1-1100—9.1-1113, 18.2-267, 18.2-268.1, 18.2-268.6, 18.2-268.7, 18.2-268.8, 18.2-268.9, 19.2-187, 19.2-187.01, 19.2-187.2, 19.2-188.1, 19.2-270.4:1, 19.2-310.2, 19.2-310.2:1, 19.2-310.3, 19.2-310.3:1, 19.2-310.4, 19.2-310.5, 19.2-310.6, 19.2-310.7, 19.2-327.1, 19.2-327.3, 19.2-327.4, 19.2-386.23, 19.2-386.27, 19.2-387, 19.2-389.1, 46.2-341.25, 46.2-341.26:1, 46.2-341.26:6, 46.2-341.26:7, 46.2-341.26:9, 54.1-3404, 54.1-3431
882	3.1-14.3
883	19.2-386.8, 55-248.31
884	58.1-3, 58.1-439, 58.1-3245.6, 58.1-3245.8, 58.1-3245.12, 59.1-272—59.1-278R, 59.1-279, 59.1-279.1R, 59.1-280, 59.1-280.1, 59.1-280.2R, 59.1-282R, 59.1-282.1, 59.1-282.2, 59.1-282.3—59.1-284R, 59.1-284.01, 59.1-284.17, 59.1-538—59.1-541, 59.1-547
885	8.01-607, 25.1-241, 56-522, 58.1-3969
886	46.2-411
887	15.2-6300, 15.2-6300.1, 15.2-6301, 15.2-6302, 15.2-6304, 15.2-6306, 15.2-6308, 15.2-6308.1, 15.2-6314.1, 15.2-6319, 15.2-6322
888	2.2-2002, 2.2-2002.1
889	2.2-2702, 29.1-101, 30-19.1:10R, 58.1-344.3, 58.1-345R, 58.1-345.1R, 58.1-346R, 58.1-346.1:1R, 58.1-346.2:1R, 58.1-346.3:1R, 58.1-346.4:1—58.1-346.24R, 58.1-546
890	16.1-241, 20-124.1, 63.2-903, 63.2-1202, 63.2-1222, 63.2-1233
891	22.1-298
892	60.2-212
894	2.2-4324
895	4.1-305, 4.1-306, 16.1-278.9
898	4.1-306
899	3.1-336.2:1, 3.1-336.2:2, 32.1-366, 58.1-439.15:01
900	2.2-2235
901	3.1-336.2:1, 3.1-336.2:2, 32.1-366, 58.1-439.15:01
902	51.1-130, 51.1-700—51.1-705, 51.1-707
903	22.1-298, 23-9.2:3.4
904	22.1-279.8
905	32.1-288, 54.1-2807
906	46.2-1568
907	9.1-400, 44-93.1
908	46.2-746.2:2.2R, 46.2-746.2:5R, 46.2-746.4:01R, 46.2-746.7, 46.2-746.9, 46.2-746.8:2R, 46.2-749.28:2R, 46.2-749.30:1R, 46.2-749.30:2R, 46.2-749.36:1R, 46.2-749.43:1R, 46.2-749.44R, 46.2-749.49R, 46.2-749.50—46.2-749.53R, 46.2-749.55R, 46.2-749.56R, 46.2-749.57R, 46.2-749.59R, 46.2-749.63R, 46.2-749.64R, 46.2-749.65R, 46.2-749.67R, 46.2-749.70—46.2-749.72R, 46.2-749.74—46.2-749.77R, 46.2-749.79R, 46.2-749.82R, 46.2-749.83R, 46.2-749.98:1R, 46.2-749.101R, 46.2-749.104R, 46.2-749.106R, 46.2-749.107R, 46.2-749.109R, 46.2-749.113R, 46.2-749.114R, 46.2-749.116R, 46.2-749.117R
909	8.01-15.2, 8.01-428
910	9.1-400, 44-93.1
911	4.1-100, 4.1-206, 4.1-231, 4.1-233
912	15.2-2119
913	46.2-1077
914	9.1-101, 19.2-389, 19.2-389.1, 37.1-70.1, 37.1-70.2, 37.1-70.4, 37.1-70.5, 37.1-70.6, 37.1-70.9, 37.1-70.10, 37.1-70.13, 37.1-70.20, 37.2-900, 37.2-901, 37.2-903, 37.2-904, 37.2-908, 37.2-909, 37.2-912, 37.2-919
915	58.1-3819, 58.1-3833
916	18.2-313.2, 29.1-574
917	54.1-2902, n., 54.1-2957.7—54.1-2957.13
918	60.2-602
919	33.1-12
920	10.1-1408.4, 10.1-1408.5
921	32.1-111.4
922	58.1-3912
923	18.2-248, 18.2-248.02
924	2.2-703, 54.1-2503, 54.1-3005, 54.1-3007, 54.1-3041—54.1-3043, 54.1-3100—54.1-3103, 54.1-3102, 54.1-3103.1, 54.1-3408, 63.2-1702, 63.2-1707, 63.2-1709, 63.2-1709.1, 63.2-1709.2, 63.2-1721, 63.2-1732, 63.2-1803, 63.2-1803.1, 63.2-1805
925	58.1-1009, 58.1-1021.03

ACTS 2005 Chapter	Code 1950 Section
926	32.1-11.5, 54.1-2901, 54.1-2957.01
927	58.1-3703.1, 58.1-3983.1
928	2.2-4343.1, 8.01-225.1, 9.1-914, 15.2-820, 15.2-4901, 15.2-4902, 15.2-5214, 15.2-5343, 16.1-319, 18.2-280, 18.2-282, 18.2-308.1, 19.2-389, 22.1-7, 22.1-180, 22.1-212.5, 22.1-212.8, 22.1-218, 22.1-271.1, 22.1-296.3, 23-50.16:12, 46.2-100, 46.2-694, 46.2-917, 46.2-918, 54.1-3482, 57-16.1, 58.1-811, 58.1-2259, 58.1-3606, 58.1-3617
929	46.2-743
930	2.2-2101, 2.2-2648
931	18.2-465.1
932	54.1-2400.8
933	2.2-1124, 2.2-1132, 2.2-1149, 2.2-1150, 2.2-1153, 2.2-1404.1, 2.2-1509, n., 2.2-1514, 2.2-2007, 2.2-2518—2.2-2523, 2.2-2901, 2.2-5004, 2.2-5005, 23-9.2:3.03, 23-9.6:1, 23-9.6:1.01, 23-38.88—23-38.121, 23-38.112, 30-133.1, 36-98.1, 51.1-124.3, 51.1-505, 51.1-506
934	19.2-61, 19.2-66, 19.2-68, 19.2-70.2
935	26-5.1R, 26-5.2, 26-30, 26-49R, 26-51, 26-53R, 26-54R, 26-55R, 26-64R, 26-65R, 26-66, 37.1-110, 37.2-718, 38.2-3120R, 55-7, 55-7.1R, 55-7.2R, 55-19R, 55-19.3R, 55-19.4R, 55-27R, 55-28R, 55-29R, 55-29.1R, 55-29.2R, 55-29.3R, 55-29.4R, 55-29.5R, 55-29.6R, 55-30R, 55-31R, 55-31.1R, 55-32R, 55-33R, 55-34R, 55-60, 55-277.4, 55-541.01—55-551.06, 55-544.14, 55-547.03, 55-551.06, 64.1-73, 64.1-67.2R, 64.1-73
937	15.2-2265
938	2.2-106, 2.2-107
939	2.2-2010, 2.2-2032R
940	58.1-511, 58.1-512
941	18.2-248, 18.2-248.02
942	56-484.12, 56-484.14, 56-484.16, 56-484.17
943	18.2-268.4, 46.2-398
944	60.2-114.01
945	2.2-1124, 2.2-1132, 2.2-1149, 2.2-1150, 2.2-1153, 2.2-1404.1, 2.2-1509, n., 2.2-1514, 2.2-2007, 2.2-2518—2.2-2523, 2.2-2901, 2.2-5004, 2.2-5005, 23-9.2:3.03, 23-9.6:1, 23-9.6:1.01, 23-38.88—23-38.121, 30-133.1, 36-98.1, 51.1-124.3, 51.1-505, 51.1-506
946	Const., Art. 1, § 15-A, n.
947	Const., Art. 10, 6, n.
948	Const., Art. 10, 6, n.
949	Const., Art. 1, § 15-A, n.
950	Const., Art. 4, § 14, n.
951	2.2-200, n., 2.2-203.3, n., 2.2-204, n., 2.2-212, n., 2.2-219, n., 2.2-221, n., 2.2-228, n., 2.2-409, n., 2.2-518, n., 2.2-712, n., 2.2-800, n., 2.2-803, n., 2.2-900, n., 2.2-902, n., 2.2-1100, n., 2.2-1101, n., 2.2-1104, n., 2.2-1116, n., 2.2-1124, n., 2.2-1125, n., 2.2-1132, n., 2.2-1149, n., 2.2-1156, n., 2.2-1202, n., 2.2-1204, n., 2.2-1400, n., 2.2-1501, n., 2.2-1505, n., 2.2-1802, n., 2.2-1819, n., 2.2-1829, n., 2.2-2005, n., 2.2-2026, n., 2.2-2028, n., 2.2-2031, n., 2.2-2221, n., 2.2-2221.1, n., 2.2-2318, n., 2.2-2444, n., 2.2-2457, n., 2.2-2632, n., 2.2-2670, n., 2.2-2723, n., 2.2-2905, n., 2.2-3204, n., 2.2-4000—2.2-4032, n., 2.2-4301, n., 2.2-4309, n., 2.2-4400, n., 2.2-4806, n., 2.2-5206, n., 2.2-5209, n., 2.2-5211, n., 3.1-336.2, n., 3.1-336.10, n., 3.1-336.13, n., 3.1-336.14, n., 3.1-336.15, n., 3.1-925, n., 3.1-1107, n., 3.1-1108, n., 4.1-230, 4.1-231, 5.1-1.2, n., 5.1-1.6, n., 8.01-195.1, n., 8.01-384.1:1, n., 9.1-102, n., 9.1-166, n., 9.1-168, n., 9.1-176, n., 9.1-182, n., 9.1-200, n., 10.1-202, n., 10.1-401, n., 10.1-411.1, n., 10.1-546, n., 10.1-552, n., 10.1-1020, n., 10.1-1021, n., 10.1-1124, n., 10.1-1176, n., 10.1-1188, n., 10.1-1190, n., 10.1-1422.01, n., 10.1-2100, n., 10.1-2134, n., 10.1-2202.1, n., 10.1-2211, n., 10.1-2213, n., 10.1-2500, n., 10.1-2501, n., 10.1-2502, n., 11-35, n., 12.1-4, n., 13.1-775.1, n., 15.2-407, n., 15.2-516, n., 15.2-519, n., 15.2-527, n., 15.2-539, n., 15.2-614, n., 15.2-617, n., 15.2-638, n., 15.2-710, n., 15.2-811, n., 15.2-826, n., 15.2-847, n., 15.2-1302, n., 15.2-1534, n., 15.2-1605, n., 15.2-1608, n., 15.2-1609.1, n., 15.2-1609.2, n., 15.2-1609.7, n., 15.2-1612.1, n., 15.2-1627.1, n., 15.2-1628, n., 15.2-1629, n., 15.2-1630, n., 15.2-1631, n., 15.2-1634, n., 15.2-1635, n., 15.2-1636.8, n., 15.2-1636.9, n., 15.2-2503, n.,

ACTS 2005 Chapter	Code 1950 Section
	15.2-2504, n.,
	15.2-2602, n.,
	15.2-2659, n.,
	15.2-4100, n.,
	16.1-69.6:1, 16.1-266, n.,
	16.1-273, n., 16.1-287, n.,
	16.1-309.2, n.,
	16.1-309.5, n.,
	16.1-309.7, n.,
	16.1-322.1, n.,
	17.1-278, n., 17.1-279, n.,
	17.1-283, n., 17.1-287, n.,
	17.1-507, 18.2-152.2, n.,
	18.2-340.31, n.,
	19.2-163.01, n., 19.2-163.2,
	19.2-295.2, n.,
	19.2-298.01, n.,
	19.2-306, n., 19.2-316.2, n.,
	19.2-316.3, n., 19.2-326, n.,
	19.2-349, n.,
	19.2-390.01, n.,
	22.1-18.01, n.,
	22.1-101.1, n.,
	22.1-205, n.,
	22.1-253.13, n.,
	22.1-253.13:1, n.,
	22.1-290.01, n.,
	22.1-346—22.1-349, n.,
	23-7.4:1, n.,
	23-7.4:2, n., 23-9.2:3.03, n.,
	23-9.2:3.1, n., 23-9.6:1, n.,
	23-9.9, n., 23-30.23, n.,
	23-30.27:1, n., 23-30.28, n.,
	23-38.12, n., 23-38.14, n.,
	23-38.53:21, n.,
	23-38.77, n.,
	23-164.7, n., 23-164.8, n.,
	23-174.7, n., 23-215, n.,
	23-220.01, n., 23-227, n.,
	23-231.8—23-231.12, n.,
	23-231.13, n., 23-253.1, n.,
	23-276.10, n., 23-284, n.,
	23-291, n., 24.2-108, n.,
	28.2-542, n., 28.2-550, n.,
	29.1-702, n., 30-58.3, n.,
	30-130, n., 30-158, n.,
	32.1-11.2, n., 32.1-16, n.,
	32.1-19.1, n., 32.1-127, n.,
	32.1-163, n., 32.1-171.1, n.,
	32.1-176, n., 32.1-273.1, n.,
	32.1-313, n., 32.1-323, n.,
	32.1-323.1, n., 32.1-325, n.,
	32.1-325.1, n.,
	32.1-325.1:1, n.,
	32.1-326.3, n.,
	32.1-330.1, n.,
	32.1-331.12, n.,
	32.1-331.15, n.,
	32.1-333, n., 32.1-338, n.,
	32.1-347, n., 32.1-351, n.,

ACTS 2005 Chapter	Code 1950 Section
	32.1-352, n., 32.1-355, n.,
	32.1-357, n., 33.1-13, n.,
	33.1-23.03:1, n.,
	33.1-23.03:2, n.,
	33.1-23.1, n., 33.1-23.3, n.,
	33.1-41.1, n., 33.1-72.1, n.,
	33.1-75.1, n.,
	33.1-391.3, n.,
	33.1-391.5, n., 35.1-13, n.,
	35.1-14, n., 35.1-16, n.,
	35.1-17, n., 36-132, n.,
	36-139, n., 36-153, n.,
	37.1-10, n., 37.1-70.1, n.,
	37.1-70.5, n., 37.1-70.7, n.,
	37.1-70.8, n., 37.1-70.9, n.,
	37.1-197, n., 37.2-203, n.,
	37.2-316, n., 37.2-504, n.,
	37.2-904, n., 38.2-3407, n.,
	38.2-5020.1, n.,
	40.1-49.4, n.,
	44-146.18:2, n.,
	44-146.28, n.,
	46.2-205, n., 46.2-212.1, n.,
	46.2-328.1, n., 46.2-685, n.,
	46.2-694, n., 51.1-124.3, n.,
	51.1-124.30, n., 51.1-142.2,
	51.1-155.1, n., 51.1-203, n.,
	51.1-214, n., 51.1-303, n.,
	51.1-1100, n.,
	51.1-1103, n.,
	51.1-1112, n.,
	51.1-1401, n.,
	51.1-1403, n., 51.5-39.7, n.,
	51.5-106, n., 52-1, n.,
	52-8.1:1, n., 52-12, n.,
	53.1-5, n., 53.1-10, n.,
	53.1-20, n., 53.1-20.1, n.,
	53.1-21, n., 53.1-28, n.,
	53.1-67.1, n., 53.1-82.3, n.,
	53.1-106.1, n.,
	53.1-115.1, n.,
	53.1-120, n., 53.1-121, n.,
	53.1-131, n., 53.1-165, n.,
	53.1-179, n.,
	54.1-2400.6, n.,
	54.1-2906, n.,
	54.1-3023, n.,
	54.1-3024, n.,
	54.1-3028.1, n.,
	54.1-3913, n.,
	54.1-3916, n.,
	54.1-3919, n.,
	54.1-3924, n.,
	55-66.6, n., 55-297, n.,
	56-232, n., 56-234, n.,
	56-484.12, n., 56-575.1, n.,
	58.1-3, n., 58.1-202.2, n.,
	58.1-339.4, n., 58.1-353, n.,
	58.1-439.2, n.,
	58.1-439.12:01,

ACTS 2005 Chapter	Code 1950 Section
	58.1-461, n., 58.1-462, n.,
	58.1-470, n., 58.1-600, n.,
	58.1-602, n., 58.1-638, n.,
	58.1-638.1, n., 58.1-801, n.,
	58.1-803, n., 58.1-815, n.,
	58.1-815.1, n.,
	58.1-816.1, n.,
	58.1-1402, n.,
	58.1-1410, n.,
	58.1-1803, n.,
	58.1-1804, n.,
	58.1-1840.1, n.,
	58.1-2402, n.,
	58.1-2425, n.,
	58.1-2510, n.,
	58.1-3523, n.,
	58.1-3523—58.1-3536, n.,
	58.1-3912, n.,
	58.1-4022, n.,
	58.1-4023, n.,
	58.1-4102, n.,
	59.1-282.2, n.,
	59.1-282.3, n.,
	59.1-284.1—59.1-284.6, n.,
	59.1-364, n., 59.1-392, n.,
	60.2-305, n., 60.2-315, n.,
	62.1-128, n., 62.1-140, n.,
	62.1-241.12, n.,
	63.2-222, n.,
	63.2-401, n., 63.2-501, n.,
	63.2-602, n., 63.2-608, n.,
	63.2-611, n., 63.2-612, n.,
	63.2-619, n. 63.2-1509, n.,
	63.2-1706, n.,
	63.2-1735, n.,
	63.2-1907, n., 66-15, n.,
	66-19, n., 66-20, n.

ACTS 2006

ACTS 2006 Chapter	Code 1950 Section
4	10.1-418.3
5	28.2-201
6	10.1-1422, 10.1-1422.01, 10.1-1422.03, 10.1-1422.05, 58.1-1709
7	10.1-1411
8	29.1-314
9	15.2-852, 15.2-2289, 55-79.43
10	15.2-2403
11	15.2-2114
12	29.1-103.1
13	10.1-1152
16	10.1-1402, 46.2-635
18	62.1-44.38:1
19	10.1-1410.3
20	29.1-521, 29.1-530

ACTS 2006 Chapter	Code 1950 Section
21	10.1-560, 10.1-561, 10.1-603.2, 10.1-603.4
22	10.1-1602
23	29.1-746
24	29.1-103.2
25	2.2-3705.3, 22.1-19.1, 22.1-253.13:3
26	22.1-98
27	22.1-292.1, 22.1-292.2, 22.1-298R, 22.1-298.1, 22.1-298.2, 22.1-349, 23-9.2:3.4R, 23-9.2:3.6
29	22.1-57.3, 22.1-75
30	10.1-604, 10.1-605.1, 10.1-606.1, 10.1-607.1, 10.1-609, 10.1-609.2, 10.1-610.1, 10.1-612.1, 10.1-613, 10.1-613.1—10.1-613.5
31	3.1-336.4, 3.1-336.8, 58.1-3
32	10.1-2202, 10.1-2204, 10.1-2205, 10.1-2206.1, 10.1-2206.2
33	28.2-539, 28.2-546, 28.2-548
34	16.1-69.6:1
35	17.1-507
36	18.2-10
37	29.1-314
38	22.1-253.13:3
39	10.1-104, n., 10.1-109, n.
40	10.1-1411
41	22.1-199.2, 22.1-254.01
42	22.1-18.01
43	22.1-279.8
44	10.1-418.3
45	3.1-1108, 10.1-1018
46	32.1-50
47	22.1-289
48	23-276.12
50	23-38.53:1—23-38.53:3R
51	23-38.70R, 23-38.71R
52	22.1-70.2
53	22.1-3.2
54	2.2-5510
55	8.01-511, 8.01-512.3
56	54.1-2800, 54.1-2803, 54.1-2806, 54.1-2813, 54.1-2817
57	2.2-1147.2, 15.2-1800
58	9.1-202, 38.2-401
59	2.2-609, 42.1-92—42.1-97, 42.1-17R, 42.1-19—42.1-19.4R
60	17.1-213, 42.1-76.1, 42.1-77—42.1-79, 42.1-82, 42.1-83R, 42.1-85—42.1-87, 42.1-90.1, 42.1-91R
61	54.1-2105
62	10.1-1408.1
63	58.1-301
64	58.1-1003, 58.1-1003.1
65	51.1-138
66	51.1-605, 51.1-1304
67	58.1-3819
68	Const., Art. 4, § 14, n.
69	29.1-102, 29.1-108, 29.1-109
70	29.1-309.3
71	10.1-1308
72	Const., Art. 1, § 15-A, n.
73	2.2-3705.6, 15.2-2108R, 15.2-2108.19—15.2-2108.32, 15.2-2160, 56-265.4:4, 56-466.1, 56-502
74	15.2-934
75	54.1-2729.2, 54.1-2729.3, 54.1-3408
76	2.2-3705.6, 15.2-2108R, 15.2-2108.19—15.2-2108.31, 15.2-2160, 56-265.4:4, 56-466.1, 56-502
77	2.2-2233.2, 23-4.3, 23-4.4, 23-9.10:4R
78	58.1-3713, 58.1-3713.01
79	2.2-205.1
80	2.2-205.1
81	33.1-382—33.1-385R
82	18.2-270
83	24.2-511, 24.2-527
84	63.2-304
85	46.2-221.2
86	46.2-1023
87	4.1-306
88	19.2-12
89	16.1-250
90	22.1-202.1
91	55-237.1
92	23-9.3:1
93	2.2-2818.1
94	4.1-209
95	2.2-3705.3, 22.1-19.1, 22.1-253.13:3
96	22.1-98
97	54.1-2604
98	53.1-41
99	19.2-299
100	2.2-4304
101	18.2-268.9
102	15.2-2159
103	44-102.2, 58.1-344.3
104	53.1-203
105	57-27.1, n.
106	4.1-119, 4.1-201
107	19.2-386.23
108	53.1-28
109	2.2-3304.1
110	51.5-25.1
113	30-170
114	19.2-175
115	33.1-75.3
116	16.1-107
117	22.1-253.13:3
118	15.2-953
119	58.1-3703.1
120	24.2-228.1
121	23-9.2:3
122	46.2-1020
123	44-117
124	2.2-1100, n., 2.2-2005, n., 2.2-5005, n.
125	22.1-79.1, n.
126	15.2-702.1R, 15.2-1414.4R, 22.1-32, 22.1-47.4
127	8.01-391.1
128	1-510
129	8.01-156, 55-237.1, 55-248.38:2
130	22.1-18.01
131	22.1-253.13:3
132	53.1-28
134	24.2-904, 24.2-947.1, n.
135	63.2-104.1, 63.2-1612
137	2.2-2817.1
138	44-146.19
139	46.2-881
140	44-146.17
141	16.1-122.2, 16.1-122.3
142	63.2-703
143	22.1-264.1
144	16.1-69.35, 17.1-105
145	22.1-79.3
146	22.1-279.3:1
147	33.1-221
148	46.2-752
149	63.2-1605
150	2.2-203, 2.2-221, 2.2-2681, 2.2-2715
151	8.01-277
153	4.1-209
154	62.1-44.19:7
155	54.1-2400.2
156	2.2-3311
157	30-155
158	63.2-304

ACTS 2006 Chapter	Code 1950 Section
159	2.2-3803, 58.1-3, 58.1-202
160	23-231.25
161	22.1-202.1
162	58.1-301
163	10.1-1402, 46.2-635
164	27-94, n.
165	2.2-2725, 2.2-2726, 2.2-2729, 2.2-2731R
166	32.1-292.2, 32.1-297.1
167	54.1-2521
168	22.1-329, 37.2-418, 37.2-419.1, 63.2-1737, 66-24
169	51.5-25.1
170	19.2-175
171	10.1-603.2— 10.1-603.3, 10.1-603.14
172	46.2-1527.1, 46.2-1527.2, 46.2-1527.5
173	Const., Art. 10, § 6, n.
174	22.1-79.1, n.
175	18.2-254.1
176	54.1-2715
177	24.2-655
178	30-170
179	15.2-6800—15.2-6809
180	57-27.1, n.
181	58.1-3703.1
182	19.2-310.2:1
183	22.1-3.2
184	54.1-2400.2
185	59.1-148.3
186	33.1-288, 33.1-319R
187	53.1-67.4
188	22.1-3
189	17.1-278
190	54.1-3005
191	22.1-295.1
192	12.1-21.2
193	19.2-8
194	32.1-111.4
195	54.1-3408.01
196	2.2-3802
197	33.1-12
198	54.1-3902
199	19.2-182.10
200	58.1-3506, 58.1-3916
202	46.2-653
203	9.1-102.
204	62.1-44.117, 62.1-44.118
205	24.2-101, 24.2-403, 24.2-544
206	2.2-4301
207	4.1-305
208	46.2-703, 46.2-2011.6, 46.2-2053, 46.2-2121, 46.2-2143
209	38.2-3115
210	46.2-1112
211	18.2-340.25
212	15.2-3400
213	46.2-870
214	58.1-322, 58.1-402
215	29.1-521
216	58.1-3843
217	58.1-609.10
218	17.1-415
219	15.2-5101
220	62.1-132.12:1
221	58.1-3241
222	33.1-391.3:1
223	22.1-167.1
225	19.2-182.10
226	46.2-341.16
227	10.1-1020
228	10.1-1142
229	58.1-1003, 58.1-1003.1
230	54.1-3902
231	58.1-3506, 58.1-3916
232	46.2-1112
233	9.1-102
234	58.1-311, 58.1-311.1, 58.1-312, 58.1-1823
235	24.2-109.1
236	10.1-2117, 10.1-2128, 10.1-2129, 10.1-2131
237	11-4.5
238	58.1-439.1
239	22.1-110
240	24.2-304.02
241	19.2-11.01
242	24.2-649, 24.2-704, 24.2-1012
243	24.2-404
244	15.2-2307
246	25.1-108
247	55-519
248	15.2-2209
249	15.2-2288.2
250	18.2-415
251	2.2-115, 2.2-2238.1
252	51.1-512
253	24.2-228.1
254	2.2-106, 2.2-200, 15.2-1510.1
255	58.1-3330
256	4.1-209, 4.1-325, 4.1-325.2
257	19.2-389
258	60.2-602
259	16.1-309.1
260	20-107.3
261	24.2-304.02
262	18.2-46.1
264	15.2-2309
265	65.2-801
266	2.2-2666.3
267	8.01-226.11
270	18.2-57
271	18.2-204.1
272	30-19.12
273	6.1-64
274	4.1-200
275	15.2-901
276	46.2-940
277	19.2-389
278	8.01-232
279	38.2-209
280	64.1-132.2
281	55-20.2
282	16.1-290
283	24.2-653.1, 24.2-708, 24.2-711
284	18.2-67.4
285	19.2-3.1, 19.2-54
286	15.2-1736
287	15.2-852
288	9.1-116.1, 16.1-69.48:1
289	9.1-177.1
290	19.2-13
291	45.1-161.202
292	24.2-803, 24.2-804
294	19.2-187
295	22.1-288.1, 52-31.1
296	19.2-123, 19.2-143, 38.2-2416
297	24.2-705, 24.2-709, 24.2-710, 24.2-712
298	18.2-186.3:1, 18.2-186.5
299	15.2-1127
300	18.2-54.1
301	46.2-862
302	24.2-687
303	55-248.45:1
304	15.2-2286
305	16.1-69.48
306	8.01-343, 17.1-105
307	51.1-1302
308	16.1-253.1, 16.1-279.1
309	16.1-309.1
310	2.2-3117
312	6.1-2.27:1
313	18.2-59
314	18.2-270
316	19.2-143
317	15.2-852, 15.2-2289, 55-79.43
318	17.1-275, 55-218.1
319	18.2-46.1
320	38.2-1315.1
321	18.2-178, 18.2-186
322	38.2-401
324	15.2-4902, 15.2-6402

TABLE OF ACTS CODIFIED SUBSEQUENT TO 1948

ACTS 2006 Chapter	Code 1950 Section
325	18.2-255.2
326	2.2-221
327	9.1-1101, 9.1-1110
328	2.2-2666.3
329	38.2-1022
330	13.1-639, 13.1-675, 13.1-690.1, 13.1-706
331	58.1-609.2, 58.1-609.10
332	19.2-163
333	58.1-3969
334	24.2-919, 24.2-947.9, n.
335	22.1-223, 22.1-254, 22.1-254.2
336	51.1 1403
337	23-218
338	58.1-609.10
339	32.1-122.10:001—32.1-122.10:005, n., 32.1-127.1:03, n.
340	2.2-803
341	18.2-254.1
342	58.1-1826
343	19.2-182.8, 19.2-182.9
344	2.2-212, 51.5-56, 51.5-59
345	2.2-604.1
346	54.1-3401, 54.1-3414, 54.1-3415, 54.1-3450, 54.1-3452, 54.1-3454
347	2.2-720
348	46.2-865.1
349	22.1-292.1, 22.1-292.2, 22.1-298R, 22.1-298.1, 22.1-298.2, 22.1-349, 23-9.2:3.4R, 23-9.2:3.6
350	8.01-44.7
351	64.1-105, 64.1-105.1R, 64.1-105.2R, 64.1-106, 64.1-106.1, 64.1-107, 64.1-108, 64.1-109R, 64.1-110—64.1-115
352	58.1-4007.2
353	32.1-164.5
354	15.2-4504, 15.2-4529, 58.1-1720
355	58.1-3303
356	58.1-3219.2R
357	17.1-304
358	19.2-182.4
359	19.2-349
360	63.2-900, 63.2-900.1
361	58.1-609.2, 58.1-609.10
362	59.1-526
363	13.1-718, 13.1-719.1, 13.1-720
364	32.1-46
365	20-79.3
366	2.2-213.2
367	54.1-2409
368	32.1-122.10:001—32.1-122.10:005, n.
369	19.2-182.8
370	19.2-182.8, 19.2-182.9
371	20-108
372	58.1-3919.1, 58.1-3934
373	22.1-289.1, 22.1-295, 22.1-303
374	16.1-88.03
375	58.1-3660
376	58.1-3819
377	58.1-3823
378	32.1-122.07, 32.1-125.3
379	23-9.2:3.02, 23-9.6:1, 23-9.14:2
380	2.2-212, 51.5-56, 51.5-59
381	2.2-720
382	22.1-290.01, n., 22.1-298, n., 23-9.2:3.6, n., 23-9.13:1, n.
383	56-16.2
384	63.2-1205.1
385	58.1-609.3
386	63.2-703
387	19.2-82.1
388	51.1-138
389	30-225R
390	18.2-272
391	24.2-417.1
392	3.1-396.1, 18.2-236R
393	58.1-485.1
394	15.2-2403
395	33.1-23.03:0001
396	2.2-2818, 22.1-178, 32.1-46, 32.1-50, 32.1-60, 32.1-138, 32.1-325, 45.1-161.70, 45.1-161.292:43, 46.2-208, 46.2-322, 54.1-3812, 59.1-297, 59.1-298, 63.2-1716, 63.2-1808
397	54.1-3434.1
398	38.2-3407.10
399	6.1-474—6.1-479, 59.1-200
400	58.1-3506
401	16.1-340, 16.1-341
402	8.01-419.1
403	51.1-161
404	51.1-1112, 51.1-1123
405	51.1-1112, 51.1-1123
406	51.1-800
407	58.1-641
408	2.2-4321.1
409	58.1-1013, 58.1-1017
410	38.2-1800
411	56-232, 56-265.1
412	8.01-581.13, 8.01-581.16, 8.01-581.17, 8.01-581.19, 32.1-111.3, 32.1-116.1
413	2.2-2503, 30-58.1
414	19.2-368.5, 19.2-368.20, 19.2-368.21
415	25.1-205.1
416	46.2-871
417	33.1-12
418	46.2-756
419	33.1-223.2:16
420	33.1-13.01
421	15.2-2242
422	6.1-58.3, 6.1-409
423	11-4.5
424	36-105
425	32.1-325
426	32.1-276.4, 32.1-276.5
427	38.2-3551—38.2-3555, 38.2-4214, 38.2-4319, 38.2-4509
428	32.1-351
429	19.2-163.01, 19.2-163.02
430	2.2-3711
431	2.2-2618, 16.1-300, 53.1-10, 66-3.2
432	32.1-126.4, 54.1-3303, 54.1-3408
433	32.1-127.1:03
434	33.1-190
435	8.01-695, 8.01-696, 8.01-697
436	19.2-303
437	46.2-742.5R, 46.2-743, 46.2-744.1R, 46.2-746.2:3.1R, 46.2-746.23R, 46.2-749.56:1R, 46.2-749.90—46.2-749.92R, 46.2-749.94R, 46.2-749.109:1R, 46.2-749.118R, 46.2-749.120R, 46.2-749.121R, 46.2-749.126—46.2-749.128R, 46.2-749.131—46.2-749.133R
438	24.2-701, 24.2-703, 24.2-706, 24.2-707
440	58.1-339.3
441	46.2-1500, 46.2-1537

ACTS 2006 Chapter	Code 1950 Section
442	2.2-4002, 3.1-741.6
443	3.1-741.7
444	46.2-613
445	18.2-204.2
446	15.2-2314
447	19.2-188.1
448	38.2-4300, 38.2-4307.1, 38.2-5800
449	46.2-2099.1
450	15.2-2297, 15.2-2298, 15.2-2303
451	59.1-529.1
452	25.1-408
453	59.1-204
454	54.1-1102
455	18.2-186.3
456	15.2-2244.1
457	18.2-164
458	44-146.15
459	58.1-3916
460	15.2-906
461	15.2-2260
462	27-14, 40.1-79.1
463	18.2-390, 18.2-391
464	2.2-4303
465	30-266—30-274
466	10.1-563
467	2.2-3705.6
468	2.2-1124, 15.2-951
469	18.2-152.17
470	56-594
471	37.2-1002
472	46.2-613
473	33.1-221
474	2.2-1201, 2.2-3707.1, 2.2-3801, 17.1-276, 22.1-70.2, 24.2-105.1, 24.2-914.1, 24.2-946.1, n., 42.1-36.1, 58.1-609.5, 58.1-3122.2
475	54.1-1102
476	30-225R
477	10.1-1454.1
478	10.1-1408.1, n.
479	44-102.2, 58.1-344.3
480	33.1-190
481	15.2-735.1
482	15.2-1129.1
483	19.2-303
484	18.2-204.2
485	3.1-396.1, 18.2-236R
486	37.2-821
487	46.2-819.2
488	16.1-69.6:1
489	10.1-2211
490	3.1-18.6
491	55-248.9:1
492	24.2-646.1
493	2.2-1124, 15.2-951
494	54.1-2957.01
495	53.1-120
496	18.2-186.3
497	58.1-3713, 58.1-3713.01
498	45.1-361.21, 45.1-361.22
499	2.2-3711
500	2.2-2618, 16.1-300, 53.1-10, 66-3.2
501	19.2-163.01, 19.2-163.02
502	19.2-389.1
503	3.1-796.70
504	19.2-120
505	13.1-830, 13.1-1013, 13.1-1215, 50-73.3
507	28.2-1203
508	33.1-23.03:0001
509	58.1-3330
510	2.2-4303, 2.2-4308
512	33.1-371.1
513	51.1-155
514	15.2-2242, 15.2-2286, 55-519
515	46.2-755
516	3.1-22.8, 15.2-6501, 62.1-67
517	58.1-2606
518	2.2-3705.4, 2.2-3711, 30-231.01, 30-231.1—30-231.3, 30-231.8
519	58.1-602, 58.1-609.3
522	46.2-725, n.
524	58.1-609.3
526	22.1-253.13:4, n.
527	15.2-2222.1, 15.2-2223
528	54.1-3013.1
529	15.2-919, 46.2-100, 46.2-808, 46.2-904—46.2-907, 46.2-908.1, 46.2-911.1, 46.2-914, 46.2-932, 46.2-1047, 46.2-1049
530	63.2-1509
531	23-9.2:3.02
533	15.2-2242, 15.2-2286, 55-519
534	46.2-1128, 46.2-1129
535	9.1-407
536	46.2-1530.2
537	23-9.6:1, 23-9.14:3—23-9.14:7
538	15.2-919, 46.2-100, 46.2-808, 46.2-904—46.2-907, 46.2-908.1, 46.2-911.1, 46.2-914, 46.2-932, 46.2-1047, 46.2-1049
539	42.1-15.1
540	46.2-100
541	58.1-602, 58.1-609.3
543	33.1-371.1
544	33.1-13.01
545	46.2-1558.1, 46.2-1964.1, 46.2-1992.56:1, 46.2-1993.55:1
546	33.1-70.1
547	46.2-878.2
548	33.1-210.2
549	46.2-716
550	46.2-725, 46.2-742.6, n., 46.2-743, n., 46.2-746.2:6, n., 46.2-749.119, n., 46.2-749.122—46.2-749.125, n., 46.2-749.129, n., 46.2-749.134, n., 46.2-749.135, n.
551	9.1-1101, 9.1-1110
552	37.2-1001
553	53.1-223
554	38.2-231
555	54.1-2819
556	3.1-22.8, 15.2-6501, 62.1-67
557	23-38.53:25—23-38.53:28
558	63.2-901.1
559	58.1-609.12
560	2.2-3711
561	23-4.3:1
562	22.1-254.1
563	15.2-2222.1, 15.2-2223
564	15.2-2223, 15.2-2224
565	15.2-2239
566	33.1-72.2
567	22.1-254.1
568	58.1-602, 58.1-3833, 58.1-3840
569	2.2-4308.1
570	58.1-322, 58.1-339.11
571	16.1-131.1, 19.2-398
572	58.1-3219.4
573	15.2-2316.1, 15.2-2316.2
574	56-235.6
575	8.01-501, 8.01-514
576	56-264.2
577	38.2-1329, 38.2-1330, 38.2-1330.1
578	19.2-266.2
579	58.1-611.2, 58.1-625, 58.1-626
580	2.2-1839, n., 2.2-1839.1, n.

ACTS 2006 Chapter	Code 1950 Section
581	58.1-608.3
582	2.2-1120
583	15.2-2303.2
584	22.1-253.13:4
585	58.1-3211
586	25.1-100, 25.1-209, 25.1-213, 25.2-214, 25.1-219, 25.1-220, 25.1-226R, 25.1-227R, 25.1-228, 25.1-229, 25.1-235, 25.1-318, 36-27, 62.1-98
587	33.1-228.1
589	38.2-1868.1, 38.2-1869
590	2.2-3803, 58.1-3, 58.1-202
591	56-264.2
593	58.1-611.2, 58.1-625, 58.1-626
594	58.1-2200, n., 58.1-2201, 58.1-2211, 58.1-2215, 58.1-2241, 58.1-2246, 58.1-2247, 58.1-2272, 58.1-2273, 58.1-2280
595	2.2-3707.1
596	2.2-1502.1
597	15.2-1512.4, 15.2-2511.2
598	58.1-4006, 58.1-4007, 58.1-4009, 58.1-4014, 58.1-4014.1, 58.1-4018, 58.1-4018.1, 58.1-4021
599	58.1-322, 58.1-339.11
600	33.1-46.2
601	19.2-270.1:1
602	58.1-602, 58.1-3833, 58.1-3840
603	46.2-1207
604	58.1-2403
605	2.2-4308.1
607	30-275—30-277
608	58.1-608.3
609	46.2-2157, 46.2-2158, 46.2-2161, 46.2-2163, 46.2-2170, 46.2-2173
611	58.1-3703.1, 58.1-3983.1
615	46.2-1072.1, 46.2-1605, 46.2-1610
616	58.1-3967, 58.1-3975
617	58.1-322
618	58.1-609.3
620	46.2-1163, 46.2-1167
621	44-93
622	51.1-1400
623	16.1-69.48:2, 17.1-132, 17.1-275, 17.1-328, 17.1-329, 17.1-418
624	8.3A-118.1, 8.3A-311
625	20-27
626	54.1-3320
627	54.1-2105, 54.1-2130—54.1-2134, 54.1-2138, 54.1-2138.1, 54.1-2141, 54.1-2145
628	55-248.31
629	65.2-101
630	10.1-2211
631	54.1-113, 54.1-2505
632	2.2-4006, 54.1-3307
633	6.1-6.1
634	38.2-2600—38.2-2602, 38.2-2604, 38.2-2605, 38.2-2613, 38.2-2615, 38.2-2617—38.2-2628
635	51.1-142.2
636	32.1-69.3
637	51.1-124.4
638	8.01-581.1, 8.01-581.13, 38.2-602, 38.2-3412.1
639	51.1-126.5, 51.1-126.6
640	51.1-505
641	51.1-1139
642	58.1-3851
643	54.1-409
644	15.2-912.2, 18.2-340.15, 18.2-340.16, 18.2-340.18—18.2-340.20, 18.2-340.23—18.2-340.31, 18.2-340.33, 18.2-340.34, 18.2-340.37, 19.2-389
645	15.2-2118
646	55-79.40, 55-79.74:3, 55-79.79, 55-79.90
647	2.2-3808.2, 17.1-279
648	10.1-603.16—10.1-603.18, 10.1-603.18:1, 10.1-603.18:2, 10.1-603.19, 10.1-603.20, 10.1-603.21R, 10.1-603.22R, 10.1-603.22:1—10.1-603.22:4, 10.1-603.23, 10.1-606.1, 38.2-401.1, 58.1-2508, 62.1-203
649	13.1-553
651	32.1-288.1
652	45.1-393, 45.1-394
653	55-370, 55-370.01, 55-373—55-374.1, 55-375, 55-376.2, 55-383, 55-394.1
654	63.2-1225, 63.2-1226, 63.2-1232
656	2.2-4343, 37.2-512, 37.2-615
657	31-46
658	2.2-4345, 15.2-5201, 15.2-5202, 15.2-5204, 15.2-5205, 15.2-5219, 15.2-5301, 15.2-5307, 15.2-5339, 15.2-5340.1, 15.2-5340.2
659	13.1-615, 13.1-815, 13.1-1065, 13.1-1255, 50-73.70
660	65.2-502
661	30-196
662	30-28.16, 30-34.14
663	13.1-603, 13.1-609, 13.1-716, 13.1-718, 13.1-754, 13.1-766.1, 13.1-809, 13.1-916, 13.1-928.1
665	20-124.2
666	55-544.08
667	8.01-471, 55-248.9:1, 55-248.15:2, 55-248.21:1, 55-248.34:1
668	59.1-547
669	15.2-903
670	15.2-2241
671	51.5-116—51.5-118, 51.5-119, n.
672	13.1-543, 13.1-544, 13.1-549, 13.1-549.1, 13.1-550, 54.1-4412
673	15.2-5214, 15.2-5343, 16.1-319, 23-50.16:12
674	3.1-336.3, 3.1-336.8, 3.1-336.9:1, 3.1-336.10
675	16.1-274
676	18.2-374.1:2
677	16.1-260
678	8.01-581.17
679	15.2-1716
680	19.2-159
681	37.2-900.1
682	16.1-309.1
683	54.1-404.2
684	8.01-581.18, 8.01-581.18:1
685	54.1-3703
686	54.1-3005, 54.1-3408
687	15.2-2212, 15.2-4904, 28.2-1303
688	58.1-3295
689	24.2-659, 24.2-669, 24.2-671, 24.2-802
691	56-1, 56-1.3, 56-484.12:1, 56-484.12:2, 58.1-3813.1

ACTS 2006 Chapter	Code 1950 Section
692	18.2-371.3
693	36-96.2
694	2.2-4337
695	2.2-509.1, 4.1-105
696	2.2-435.1—2.2-435.5R, 2.2-435.1, n., 2.2-435.6, 2.2-435.7, 2.2-2669, 2.2-2670, 2.2-2674.1
697	18.2-248, 18.2-248.1
698	37.2-910, 37.2-912, 53.1-145
699	32.1-69.1, 32.1-69.2
700	15.2-1215
701	32.1-126.01, 32.1-162.9:1, 63.2-1720
702	2.2-4020.1, 2.2-4021
703	22.1-277.07
704	15.2-917
705	55-519
706	55-518
707	2.2-2101, 51.1-1201
708	19.2-159, 19.2-163.03
709	18.2-57
710	3.1-796.137—3.1-796.139
711	36-55.64
713	2.2-1839
714	4.1-100, 4.1-302.1, 4.1-324
715	13.1-543, 13.1-544, 13.1-549, 13.1-549.1, 13.1-550, 54.1-4412
716	32.1-46
717	55-248.31
718	16.1-69.48:2, 17.1-132, 17.1-275, 17.1-328, 17.1-329, 17.1-418
719	2.2-4006, 36-100
720	20-60.3, 63.2-1916
721	36-139
722	15.2-903
723	54.1-1122, 54.1-2114
724	37.2-1000, 64.1-118
725	63.2-1715
726	55-79.92
728	46.2-916.2
729	46.2-1177, 46.2-1180, 46.2-1183
730	37.2-910, 37.2-912, 53.1-145
731	4.1-210
732	18.2-374.1:2
733	18.2-10
734	20-121.03
735	32.1-69.3
736	15.2-851.1
737	4.1-206, 4.1-231, 4.1-233
738	17.1-507
739	56-484.12—56-484.15, 56-484.17
740	4.1-200
741	51.5-116—51.5-119
743	15.2-2159
744	32.1-126.01, 32.1-162.9:1, 63.2-1720, 63.2-1721, 63.2-1724, 63.2-1725
745	55-142.10—55-142.12, 55-142.14, 55-142.15
746	36-106
747	10.1-2202.3
748	13.1-1003, 13.1-1005, 13.1-1010, 13.1-1011, 13.1-1011.1, 13.1-1014, 13.1-1014.1, 13.1-1038.1, 13.1-1048, 13.1-1050, 13.1-1062
749	15.2-2118
750	54.1-2901, 54.1-2957, 54.1-2957.03
751	2.2-435.1—2.2-435.5R, 2.2-435.6, 2.2-435.7, 2.2-2669, 2.2-2670, 2.2-2674.1
752	4.1-126
753	6.1-330.64
754	6.1-225.20
755	6.1-225.45
756	51.1-608
757	8.01-375
758	15.2-6403
759	18.2-248, 18.2-248.1
760	24.2-103
762	38.2-1356, 38.2-1363
763	58.1-3700.1, 58.1-3706
764	32.1-126.01, 32.1-162.9:1, 63.2-1720
765	10.1-603.16—10.1-603.20, 10.1-603.21R, 10.1-603.22R, 10.1-603.22:1—10.1-603.22:4, 10.1-603.23, 10.1-606.1, 38.2-401.1, 58.1-2508, 62.1-203
766	19.2-386.2
767	55-519
768	3.1-336.8, 58.1-1000, 58.1-1001, 58.1-1003, 58.1-1003.2, 58.1-1021.01
769	24.2-942, 24.2-955.1, n.
770	24.2-901, 24.2-945.1
771	24.2-901, 24.2-907.1, 24.2-908, 24.2-908.2, 24.2-910.2—24.2-910.4, 24.2-922, 24.2-930.1, 24.2-945.1, 24.2-947.3:1, 24.2-948.2, 24.2-949.2, 24.2-949.9:1, 24.2-953.5
772	24.2-901, 24.2-910, 24.2-945.1, 24.2-945.2
773	24.2-905, 24.2-908, 24.2-947.2, n., 24.2-949.4, n.
774	56-446.1
775	23-38.88
776	32.1-102.3:2, n.
777	38.2-5016, 38.2-5016.1
778	51.1-1114, 51.1-1123, 51.1-1125
779	2.2-3114, 2.2-3117, 2.2-3118, 30-110, 30-111
780	8.01-225, 15.2-2108R, 15.2-2108.1:1, 51.5-115, 56-458, 56-462, 56-468.1, 56-484.4—56-484.6R, 56-484.12, 56-484.17, 56-484.18, 58.1-3, 58.1-645—58.1-662, 58.1-1730, 58.1-3812R, 58.1-3813.1R, 58.1-3815, 58.1-3816.2, 58.1-3818.1—58.1-3818.7R
781	2.2-5211.1, 22.1-323.2, 37.2-408, 63.2-1737, 66-24
782	33.1-49.1, 33.1-49.1
783	23-7.4, 23-7.4:2
784	36-2—36-4.1, 36-9.1, 36-19, 36-19.2, 36-27, 36-39R, 36-48—36-49.1:1, 36-50—36-52.1, 36-52.3, 36-53, 36-55.30:2, 36-60, 58.1-3245.1
785	20-108.1, 20-108.2
786	59.1-475, 59.1-477.1

ACTS 2006 Chapter	Code 1950 Section
787	2.2-419, 2.2-3103, 2.2-3117, 19.2-8, 24.2-101, 24.2-405, 24.2-503.1R, 24.2-622, 24.2-676, 24.2-680, 24.2-900—24.2-903.1R, 24.2-904—24.2-907R, 24.2-908—24.2-913R, 24.2-914—24.2-928R, 24.2-929, 24.2-930R, 24.2-940R, 24.2-941—24.2-944R, 24.2-945—24.2-953.4, 24.2-954, 24.2-955—24.2-959.1, 24.2-1013R, 24.2-1014.1R, 30-103, 30-111, 30-127
788	58.1-433.1, 58.1-439.2
789	24.2-922, 24.2-948.2, 24.2-928, 24.2-929, 24.2-946.3, n., 24.2-953.3, n., 24.2-953.4, n.
790	22.1-296.1
791	24.2-943, 24.2-944, 24.2-955.3, n.
792	53.1-131, 53.1-131.1
793	23-7.4:1
794	15.2-2288.3
795	55-50.2
796	63.2-1727
797	23-7.4, 23-7.4:2
798	20-108.1, 20-108.2
799	24.2-905, 24.2-908, 24.2-947.2, n., 24.2-949.4, n.
800	24.2-901, 24.2-945.1
801	63.2-1509
802	24.2-943, 24.2-944, 24.2-953.3, n.
803	58.1-433.1, 58.1-439.2
804	63.2-1727
805	24.2-901, 24.2-907.1, 24.2-908, 24.2-908.2, 24.2-910.2, 24.2-910.3, 24.2-910.4, 24.2-922, 24.2-930.1, 24.2-945.1, 24.2-947.3:1, 24.2-948.2, 24.2-949.2, 24.2-949.9:1, 24.2-949.9:2, 24.2-949.9:3, 24.2-953.5
806	23-7.4, 23-7.4:3, n.
807	56-446.1
808	2.2-2101, 23-14, 23-231.30—23-231.36
809	46.2-1571
810	23-105—23-107, 23-107.1, 23-107.2
811	56-580
812	30-205
813	2.2-109.01, 2.2-2831, 2.2-3202
814	23-276.4
815	6.1-232.2, 6.1-232.3
816	32.1-102.3:2, n.
817	58.1-3230
818	46.2-1571
819	56-580
820	55-248.38:3
822	32.1-50
823	54.1-2721, 54.1-2727
824	9.1-400
825	16.1-277.01, 17.1-275, 63.2-1200—63.2-1202, 63.2-1205, 63.2-1208, 63.2-1210, 63.2-1213, 63.2-1222, 63.2-1223, 63.2-1225—63.2-1228, 63.2-1231—63.2-1234, 63.2-1237, 63.2-1241, 63.2-1242.1—63.2-1242.3, 63.2-1243, 63.2-1249—63.2-1253
826	4.1-132, 4.1-201, 4.1-201.1, 4.1-206, 4.1-209, 4.1-212, 4.1-221.1, 4.1-325, 4.1-325.2
827	33.1-23.05, 33.1-72.1, 33.1-75.1R, 33.1-75.3
828	Const., Art. 1, § 15-A, n.
829	18.2-57
830	46.2-1051
831	2.2-1401—2.2-1404, 2.2-1405, 2.2-3705.6, 2.2-4310, 15.2-965.1, 18.2-213.1
832	15.2-2317
833	33.1-12
834	22.1-199.2, 22.1-254.01
835	46.2-1542
836	3.1-796.86, 3.1-796.87, 3.1-796.87:1, 3.1-796.88—3.1-796.90, 3.1-796.97
837	3.1-796.93:1, 3.1-796.93:3, 3.1-796.117R
838	12.1-6, 65.2-200
839	2.2-3106, 2.2-3110
840	22.1-32
841	51.1-1114, 51.1-1123, 51.1-1125
842	2.2-2101, 23-14, 23-231.30—23-231.36
843	2.2-419, 2.2-420, 2.2-426
844	18.2-46.1, 18.2-282.1
845	4.1-112.1, 4.1-207, 4.1-208, 4.1-209, 4.1-231
846	46.2-208, 46.2-214
847	15.2-928
848	63.2-1200—63.2-1202, 63.2-1205, 63.2-1208, 63.2-1210, 63.2-1213, 63.2-1222, 63.2-1223, 63.2-1227, 63.2-1228, 63.2-1231—63.2-1234, 63.2-1237, 63.2-1241, 63.2-1242.1—63.2-1242.3, 63.2-1243
849	63.2-1254—63.2-1259
850	33.1-464
851	38.2-2212, 38.2-2213.1, 46.2-1088.6, 46.2-1532.2
852	46.2-725, n., 46.2-749.78
853	18.2-48, 18.2-61, 18.2-67.1, 18.2-67.2, 18.2-370.4, 19.2-303
854	2.2-713
855	8.01-226.7
856	33.1-221.1:1.2
857	2.2-3706, 2.2-3802, 9.1-102, 9.1-902—9.1-910, 9.1-913, 9.1-914, 9.1-918, 9.1-921, 16.1-249.1, 16.1-278.7:01, 16.1-278.7:02, 18.2-370.2, 18.2-370.3, 18.2-370.4, 18.2-472.1, 19.2-295.2:1, 19.2-390.1, 22.1-79, 22.1-79.3, 23-2.2:1, 46.2-323, 46.2-324, 46.2-330, 46.2-345, 46.2-348, 53.1-23.2, 53.1-115.1, 53.1-116.1, 53.1-116.1:01, 53.1-121, 53.1-160.1
858	54.1-2722, 54.1-3408
859	33.1-56.4, 33.1-252, 46.2-208, 46.2-819.1, 46.2-819.3

ACTS 2006 Chapter	Code 1950 Section
860	2.2-304—2.2-306, 2.2-2101, 2.2-2666.1
861	2.2-2609, 15.2-6202, 15.2-6203, 15.2-6209, 15.2-6210, 15.2-6214, 16.1-69.6, 17.1-500, 17.1-506, 22.1-354.1, 55-288.1
862	19.2-266.2
863	19.2-169.3, 19.2-299, 37.2-900, 37.2-903—37.2-908, 37.2-910, 37.2-912, 37.2-919, 37.2-920, 53.1-136, 53.1-145, 63.2-105
864	3.1-796.93:1, 3.1-796.93:3, 3.1-796.117R
865	18.2-248.8
866	38.2-1318, 38.2-4306, 38.2-4319, 38.2-5803, 38.2-5804
867	10.1-1327, 10.1-1328
868	16.1-228, 63.2-100
869	20-60.3, 63.2-1916
870	46.2-1307.1
871	46.2-105.1
872	15.2-2303.2
873	33.1-46.2, 46.2-749.3
874	43-32, 43-34, 46.2-100, 46.2-649.1, 46.2-1028, 46.2-1070, 46.2-1150, 46.2-1209, 46.2-1217, 46.2-1224, 46.2-1231, 46.2-1232, 46.2-1233.1, 46.2-1233.2, 46.2-2100, 46.2-2800—46.2-2828
875	9.1-902, 18.2-67.5:1
876	16.1-131.1, 19.2-398
877	8.01-581.18
878	9.1-402
879	Const., Art. 8, § 2, n., 22.1-253.13:1, n.,
881	54.1-2928.1
882	15.2-2298, 15.2-2303.2
883	9.1-174, 19.2-303.3
885	63.2-1721
886	15.2-915.3, 18.2-308
888	46.2-1532.2
889	38.2-2212, 38.2-2213.1, 46.2-1088.6, 46.2-1532.2
890	2.2-115
891	43-32, 43-34, 46.2-100, 46.2-649.1, 46.2-1028, 46.2-1070, 46.2-1150, 46.2-1209, 46.2-1217, 46.2-1224, 46.2-1231, 46.2-1232, 46.2-1233.1, 46.2-1233.2, 46.2-2100, 46.2-2800—46.2-2828
892	2.2-419, 2.2-3103, 2.2-3117, 19.2-8, 24.2-101, 24.2-405, 24.2-503.1R, 24.2-622, 24.2-676, 24.2-680, 24.2-900—24.2-930R, 24.2-940R, 24.2-941R, 24.2-942R, 24.2-943, 24.2-944R, 24.2-945—24.2-953.4, 24.2-954, 24.2-955—24.2-959.1, 24.2-1013R, 24.2-1014.1R, 30-103, 30-111, 30-127
893	18.2-248.8
894	2.2-2524—2.2-2529
895	18.2-46.1, 18.2-282.1
896	46.2-100, 46.2-616, 46.2-619, 46.2-623, 46.2-629, 46.2-637, 46.2-638, 46.2-644.1—46.2-644.3, 46.2-679.1, 46.2-679.2, 46.2-915.1, 46.2-1051, 46.2-1993, 46.2-1993.35, 46.2-1993.39, 46.2-1993.55, 58.1-3503, 58.1-3504, 58.1-3523
897	46.2-1542
898	3.1-796.93:1, 3.1-796.93:3, 3.1-796.117R
899	2.2-2233.2, 23-4.3, 23-4.4, 23-9.10:4R
900	30-275—30-277
901	2.2-304—2.2-306, 2.2-2101, 2.2-2666.1
902	2.2-109.01, 2.2-2831, 2.2-3202
903	15.2-2242, 15.2-2286, 15.2-2286.1, 36-98
904	Const., Art. 8, § 2, n., 22.1-253.13:1, n.
905	33.1-464
906	32.1-69.1, 32.1-69.2
907	17.1-279, n., 55-66.3, 55-66.5, 55-66.8—55-66.13
908	33.1-46.2, 33.1-46.2, 46.2-749.3
909	42.1-86.1
910	2.2-302.1
911	22.1-254.1
912	6.1-61, 8.01-513, 13.1-1002, 13.1-1005, 13.1-1009, 13.1-1010.1, 13.1-1010.3, 13.1-1014, 13.1-1014.1, 13.1-1019, 13.1-1038, 13.1-1038.1, 13.1-1039, 13.1-1040.2, 13.1-1041.1, 13.1-1049.2, 13.1-1049.3, 13.1-1057, 13.1-1067, 13.1-1074—13.1-1080, 15.2-5800, 50-73.46:1, 50-73.52:2, 50-73.52:3, 50-73.79, 50-73.108, 50-73.117, 50-73.137:3, 50-73.137:4, 56-1, 58.1-2201
913	18.2-471.1
914	2.2-3706, 2.2-3802, 9.1-102, 9.1-902—9.1-910, 9.1-913, 9.1-914, 9.1-918, 9.1-921, 16.1-249.1, 16.1-278.7:01, 16.1-278.7:02, 18.2-48, 18.2-61, 18.2-67.1, 18.2-67.2, 18.2-370.2, 18.2-370.3, 18.2-370.4, 18.2-472.1, 19.2-169.3, 19.2-295.2:1, 19.2-299, 19.2-303, 19.2-390.1, 22.1-79, 22.1-79.3, 23-2.2:1, 37.2-900, 37.2-900.1, 37.2-903—37.2-908, 37.2-910, 37.2-912, 37.2-919, 37.2-920, 46.2-323, 46.2-324, 46.2-330, 46.2-345, 46.2-348, 53.1-23.2, 53.1-115.1, 53.1-116.1, 53.1-116.1:01, 53.1-121, 53.1-136, 53.1-145, 53.1-160.1, 63.2-105
915	29.1-102, 29.1-108, 29.1-109
916	19.2-299
917	33.1-465
918	46.2-725, n.
919	38.2-5010, 38.2-5013
920	10.1-1327, 10.1-1328
921	2.2-1401—2.2-1404, 2.2-1405, 2.2-3705.6, 2.2-4310, 15.2-965.1, 18.2-213.1

ACTS 2006 Chapter	Code 1950 Section
922	33.1-23.03:1, 33.1-23.03:9, 56-557, 56-558, 56-560, 56-563, 56-564, 56-566, 56-567.1, 56-573.1, 58.1-811, 58.1-3203, 58.1-3606.1, 58.1-3703
923	63.2-1809.1
924	15.2-2001, 33.1-12
925	2.2-4336, 2.2-4337
926	24.2-404, 24.2-410.1, 24.2-427, 46.2-208.1
927	15.2-1903
928	46.2-833
929	15.2-5401, 15.2-5402, 15.2-5403, 15.2-5405, 15.2-5405.1, 15.2-5406, 15.2-5406.1, 15.2-5406.2, 15.2-5409, 15.2-5423, 15.2-5423.1, 56-1, 56-580
930	46.2-882
931	9.1-902, 18.2-472.1
932	22.1-254.1
935	18.2-371, 18.2-371.1, 40.1-103
936	2.2-3705.6, 56-573.1, 56-573.1:1, 56-575.16, 56-575.17
937	33.1-23.1
938	24.2-901, 24.2-910
939	2.2-1132, 23-135.7:6, 45.1-390, 56-249.6, 58.1-322, 58.1-3660, 67-100—67-102, 67-200—67-203, 67-300, 67-400—67-403, 67-500, 67-501, 67-600—67-604, 67-700, 67-701, 67-800, 67-801, 67-900—67-903, 67-1000—67-1003
940	24.2-404, 24.2-410.1, 24.2-427, 46.2-208.1
941	15.2-5401—15.2-5403, 15.2-5405—15.2-5406.2, 15.2-5409, 15.2-5423, 15.2-5423.1, 56-1, 56-580
942	2.2-229
944	Const., Art. 1, § 15-A, n.
945	Const., Art. 4, § 14, n.
946	Const., Art. 10, § 6, n.
947	Const., Art. 1, § 15-A, n.

ACTS 2006, Sp. Sess. I

ACTS 2006, Sp. Sess. I Chapter	Code 1950 Section
1	2.2-3705.6, 56-573.1:1
3	2.2-204, n. 2.2-219, n. 2.2-221.1, n. 2.2-228, n. 2.2-409, n., 2.2-518, n., 2.2-800, n. 2.2-803, n., 2.2-1104, n. 2.2-1149, n. 2.2-1155, n. 2.2-1156, n. 2.2-1505, n. 2.2-1802, n. 2.2-1819, n. 2.2-1829, n. 2.2-2005, n. 2.2-2221, n. 2.2-2221.1, n., 2.2-2318, n., 2.2-2444, n., 2.2-2457, n., 2.2-2670, n., 2.2-2723, n., 2.2-2905, n., 2.2-4000, n., 2.2-4011, n., 2.2-4401, n., 2.2-4300, n., 2.2-4301, n., 2.2-4400, n., 2.2-4806, n., 2.2-5206, n., 2.2-5209, n., 2.2-5211, n., 3.1-336.1, n., 3.1-336.2, n., 3.1-336.3, n., 3.1-361, n., 3.1-1107, n., 4.1-235, n., 5.1-1.2, n., 8.01-195.1, n., 8.01-384.1:1, n., 9.1-102, n., 9.1-165, n., 9.1-166, n., 9.1-168, n., 10.1-202, n., 10.1-552, n., 10.1-1124, n., 10.1-1176, n., 10.1-1188, n.,

ACTS 2006,	
	10.1-1190, n., 10.1-2128, n., 10.1-2202.1, n., 10.1-2211, n., 10.1-2213, n., 10.1-2213.1, n., 10.1-2500, n., 13.1-775.1, n., 15.2-1302, n., 15.2-1605, n., 15.2-1608, n., 15.2-1609.1, n., 15.2-1609.2, n., 15.2-1609.7, n., 15.2-1612.1, n., 15.2-1627.1, n., 15.2-1628, n., 15.2-1629, n., 15.2-1630, n., 15.2-1631, n., 15.2-1634, n., 15.2-1636.8, n., 15.2-2222.1, n., 15.2-4100, n., 16.1-266, n., 16.1-273, n., 16.1-287, n., 16.1-309.2, n., 16.1-309.7, n., 16.1-322.1, n., 17.1-278, n., 17.1-279, n., 17.2-283, n., 17.1-287, n., 17.1-327, n., 18.2-340.31, n., 19.2-163, n., 19.2-163.01, n., 19.2-295.2:1, n., 19.2-298.01, n., 19.2-326, n., 19.2-349, n., 22.1-18.01, n., 22.1-101.1, n., 22.1-205, n., 22.1-253.13:1, n., 22.1-290.01, n., 23-7.4:1, n., 23-7.4:2, n., 23-9.2:3.03, n., 23-9.2:3.1, n., 23-9.6:1, n., 23-9.9, n., 23-30.23, n., 23-30.28, n., 23-38.3, n., 23-38.12, n., 23-38.14, n., 23-38.77, n.,

ACTS 2006,
23-164.8, n.,
23-215, n.,
23-220.01, n.,
23-227, n.,
23-231.13, n.,
23-253.1, n.,
23-276.10, n.,
28.2-542, n.,
28.2-550, n.,
30-58.3, n.,
30-266, n.,
32.1-16, n.,
32.1-50, n.,
32.1-122.7, n.,
32.1-163, n.,
32.1-171.1, n.,
32.1-273.1, n.,
32.1-323, n.,
32.1-325.1, n.,
32.1-325.1:1, n.,
32.1-330.1, n.,
32.1-331.12, n.,
32.1-347, n.,
32.1-352, n.,
32.1-355, n.,
33.1-23.1, n.,
33.1-23.03:2, n.,
33.1-23.3, n.,
33.1-23.5:1, n.,
33.1-41.1, n.,
33.1-391.5, n.,
35.1-13, n.,
35.1-14, n.,
35.1-16, n.,
35.1-17, n.,
36-139, n.,
37.2-203, n.,
37.2-316, n.,
37.2-319, n.,
37.2-500, n.,
37.2-504, n.,
37.2-808, n.,
37.2-900, n.,
37.2-904, n.,
40.1-49.4, n.,
44-146.28, n.,
45.1-393, n.,
45.1-394, n.,
46.2-205, n.,
46.2-212.1, n.,
46.2-685, n.,
46.2-694, n.,
46.2-710, n.,
51.1-124.3, n.,
51.1-142.2, n.,
51.1-155.1, n.,
51.1-203, n.,
51.1-214, n.,
51.1-303, n.,
51.1-1100, n.,

ACTS 2006,
51.1-1103, n.,
51.1-1400, n.,
51.1-1401, n.,
51.1-1403, n.,
51.5-39.7, n.,
51.5-106, n.,
52-1, n.,
52-8.1:1, n.,
52-12, n.,
52-28, n.,
53.1-20, n.,
53.1-20.1, n.,
53.1-45, n.,
53.1-67.1, n.,
53.1-82.3, n.,
53.1-120, n.,
54.1-3913, n.,
54.1-3916, n.,
54.1-3919, n.,
54.1-3924, n.,
55-66.6, n.,
55-297, n.,
56-232, n.,
56-234, n.,
56-484.12, n.,
58.1-202.2, n.,
58.1-339.4, n.,
58.1-353, n.,
58.1-439.2, n.,
58.1-600, n.,
58.1-602, n.,
58.1-608.3, n.,
58.1-638, n.,
58.1-638.1, n.,
58.1-609.11, n.,
58.1-801, n.,
58.1-803, n.,
58.1-815.1, n.,
58.1-816.1, n.,
58.1-1402, n.,
58.1-1410, n.,
58.1-1803, n.,
58.1-2402, n.,
58.1-2425, n.,
58.1-2510, n.,
58.1-3523, n.,
58.1-3524, n.,
58.1-4022, n.,
59.1-282.1, n.,
59.1-282.2, n.,
59.1-284.13, n.,
59.1-364, n.,
59.1-392, n.,
60.2-305, n.,
60.2-315, n.,
62.1-128, n.,
62.1-140, n.,
63.2-401, n.,
63.2-605, n.,
63.2-611, n.,

ACTS 2006,
63.2-612, n.,
63.2-619, n.,
63.2-1706, n.,
63.2-1735, n.,
63.2-1907, n.,
66-15, n.,
66-20, n.,
4 .... 58.1-511, n.,
58.1-512,
58.1-512.1,
58.1-513,
58.1-901
5 .... 58.1-511, n.,
58.1-512,
58.1-512.1,
58.1-513,
58.1-901
6 ....46.2-1110
7 ....33.1-13.01
8 ....33.1-12
9 ....33.1-23.02
10 .... 2.2-1502.1, n.,
15.2-1302, n.,
22.1-101.1, n.,
22.1-205, n.,
22.1-253.13:1, n.,
51.1-1401, n.,
56-232, n.,
56-234, n.

ACTS 2007

ACTS 2007 Chapter	Code 1950 Section
1	6.1-39.3, 6.1-44.2, 6.1-44.8, 6.1-232.2, 6.1-232.3R
2	32.1-102.3:2, n., 38.2-4900, n.
4	32.1-11.4R
5	32.1-102.13R
7	37.2-808, 37.2-810
8	32.1-102.3:2, n., 38.2-4900, n.
9	54.1-3482, 54.1-3482.1
10	2.2-212
11	63.2-1904
12	19.2-389
13	32.1-116.1, 32.1-116.1:1
14	54.1-3450
15	32.1-111.3
16	54.1-2952.1
17	54.1-3408
18	54.1-3482, 54.1-3482.1
19	32.1-283
20	54.1-2709
22	54.1-2408.1
23	10.1-1408.1, 10.1-1408.3R,

ACTS 2007 Chapter	Code 1950 Section
	10.1-1454.3R
24	62.1-194
25	28.2-1203
26	62.1-194.1
27	62.1-44.19:15
28	28.2-603, 28.2-603.1, 28.2-603.2
29	62.1-44.19:11
30	28.2-302.2, 28.2-302.2:1, 28.2-302.7:1
31	22.1-290.01
32	22.1-207.1
33	22.1-214
34	22.1-253.13:4
35	29.1-103
36	28.2-526
37	10.1-1027
38	29.1-348
39	29.1-328
40	29.1-303.3, 29.1-310.1
41	2.2-4002, 2.2-4103, 28.2-1000.2
42	22.1-5
43	22.1-23, 32.1-19
44	22.1-279.8
45	22.1-26, 22.1-118
46	23-9.2:3.02
47	23-9.2:3.5
48	22.1-287
49	22.1-3.1, 23-2.1:2
51	10.1-562
52	22.1-214
53	22.1-32
55	22.1-23, 32.1-19
56	22.1-253.13:4
57	58.1-3713
58	58.1-609.6
59	58.1-301
60	58.1-3211
61	3.1-22.30—3.1-22.37R, 58.1-3825, 59.1-392
62	2.2-813.2
63	22.1-343
64	51.1-1133, 51.1-1400
65	51.1-124.32
67	2.2-4501
68	58.1-339.7
69	58.1-344.3
70	58.1-344.3
71	22.1-344.1
72	22.1-341
73	44-102.2
74	46.2-1307
75	46.2-1157, 46.2-1163
76	23-7.4:2
77	10.1-1020
78	46.2-819.1, 46.2-819.3
79	46.2-208
80	2.2-229
81	62.1-198, 62.1-199
82	23-276.1
84	58.1-609.10
85	58.1-3732
86	58.1-3819
87	3.1-1029, 9.1-101, 9.1-400, 9.1-500, 9.1-801, 18.2-51.1, 18.2-283.1, 18.2-287.01, 18.2-308, 29.1-200, 29.1-201, 29.1-204, 29.1-205, 29.1-207, 29.1-208, 29.1-212, 29.1-213, 29.1-217, 29.1-218, 29.1-300.2, 29.1-337, 29.1-349, 29.1-355, 29.1-516, 29.1-517, 29.1-521.3, 29.1-530, 29.1-539, 29.1-548, 29.1-552, 29.1 -553, 29.1-556, 29.1-739—29.1-739.2, 29.1-745, 51.1-212, 65.2-402.1
88	58.1-3506, 58.1-3916
89	51.1-124.3, 51.1-142.2
90	9.1-403, 51.1-1132
91	46.2-1095, 46.2-1100
92	32.1-287R, 32.1-289R, 32.1-289.1R, 32.1-290R, 32.1-291R, 32.1-291.1—32.1-291.25, 32.1-292.1R, 32.1-292.2, 32.1-293R, 32.1-295R, 46.2-342, 54.1-2982, 54.1-2984, 57-48
94	19.2-11.01, 53.1-133.02, 53.1-160
95	53.1-96
96	9.1-202
97	44-146.19
98	46.2-871
99	4.1-112.1R, 4.1-204, 4.1-209.1, 4.1-212.1, 4.1-215, 4.1-230, 4.1-231, 4.1-310
100	22.1-57.3, 22.1-75
101	4.1-100, 4.1-206, 4.1-231, 4.1-233
102	23-7.4:2
103	4.1-222, 4.1-225
104	22.1-177
105	8.01-265
106	53.1-96
107	4.1-210, 4.1-231, 4.1-233
108	23-7.4
109	19.2-11.01, 53.1-133.02, 53.1-160
110	46.2-1077
111	46.2-915
112	23-7.4:2
113	17.1-205, 17.1-328
114	2.2-2428
115	23-276.1
116	23-7.4:1
117	2.2-2329
118	22.1-212.5:1
119	9.1-914, 32.1-127, 63.2-1732
120	32.1-138, 63.2-1808
121	22.1-146, 22.1-148, 22.1-151, 22.1-153, 22.1-154—22.1-157R, 22.1-161
122	19.2-45
123	Const., Art. 8, § 2, n., 22.1-253.13:1, n., 22.1-299.3, n.
124	2.2 3300, n.
125	22.1-344.1
126	4.1-210
127	44-11.1
128	8.01-470
129	44-146.19
130	52-34.3
131	16.1-108
132	2.2-3300, n.
133	2.2-3706, 2.2-3711, 4.1-305, 9.1-173—9.1-183, 9.1-185.4, 9.1-186.4, 16.1-305, 18.2-55, 18.2-57.3, 18.2-64.2,

ACTS 2007 Chapter	Code 1950 Section
	18.2-67.4, 18.2-251, 18.2-251.01, 18.2-252, 18.2-254, 18.2-254.1, 19.2-80.2, 19.2-152.2—19.2-152.7, 19.2-299.2, 19.2-303.3, 19.2-389.1, 19.2-390.01, 30-19.1:4
134	19.2-120, 19.2-386.31
135	52-26
136	23-4.2:1
137	46.2-1157, 46.2-1163
138	44-146.19
139	46.2-920.2
140	4.1-128
142	22.1-343
143	65.2-402
144	62.1-44.15
145	18.2-136
146	33.1-23.2
148	10.1-1307.3
149	22.1-343
150	15.2-1517
151	24.2-946.1, 24.2-947.1, 24.2-947.5, 24.2-947.9
152	15.2-2118
153	33.1-23.4
154	2.2-4317
156	46.2-208, 46.2-214
157	38.2-800, 38.2-4811, 38.2-4812
158	10.1-113
159	58.1-3507
160	18.2-340.16, 18.2-340.26:2
161	23-7.4:1
162	33.1-386
163	32.1-138, 63.2-1808
164	9.1-914, 32.1-127, 63.2-1732
165	13.1-603, 13.1-607, 13.1-610, 13.1-610.1, 13.1-654, 13.1-656, 13.1-657, 13.1-666, 13.1-669, 13.1-672.1, 13.1-672.1, 13.1-672.6, 13.1-677, 13.1-679, 13.1-682, 13.1-704, 13.1-711, 13.1-718, 13.1-729, 13.1-729, 13.1-730, 13.1-732—13.1-734, 13.1-735.1, 13.1-737,

ACTS 2007 Chapter	Code 1950 Section
	13.1-738, 13.1-741.1, 13.1-746, 13.1-746.1, 13.1-747, 13.1-748, 13.1-749.1
166	24.2-303.2
167	44-93.2—44-93.5
168	29.1-738.2
170	28.2-603, 28.2-603.1, 28.2-603.2
171	24.2-709.1
172	46.2-725, n., 46.2-746.8
175	24.2-231
176	58.1-609.1, 58.1-625, 58.1-626
177	46.2-1130.1
178	33.1-23.2
179	8.01-380
180	46.2-490
181	46.2-725, n., 46.2-746.8
182	8.01-226.8
183	8.01-324
184	46.2-725, n.
186	38.2-301
187	46.2-1307, 46.2-1307.1
188	46.2-208
189	46.2-891, 46.2-920.1
190	46.2-325, 46.2-328, 46.2-332, 46.2-337, 46.2-1190.2
191	58.1-3507
192	2.2-2905
194	18.2-271.1
195	23-52, n.
196	18.2-340.26:1
197	55-548.10
198	52-34.1
199	8.01-407
200	46.2-819.1, 46.2-819.3
201	46.2-725, n.
202	15.2-2259, 15.2-2260, 15.2-2269
203	15.2-1209.1
204	10.1-562
205	16.1-253.1, 20-103
206	5.1-88.7
207	5.1-88.2
209	46.2-100, 46.2-808, 46.2-905—46.2-906.1, 46.2-908.1, 46.2-932
210	15.2-2403
211	15.2-976
212	19.2-54
213	46.2-752
214	44-93.2—44-93.5
215	55-14.1
216	55-541.05, 55-545.01,

ACTS 2007 Chapter	Code 1950 Section
	55-545.03, 55-545.06
217	2.2-514
218	55-546.04
219	2.2-229
220	18.2-460
221	16.1-271
222	46.2-870
223	46.2-332
224	19.2-12
225	46.2-629
226	18.2-340.33, 18.2-340.34:1
227	47.1-19
228	9.1-112
229	15.2-2403
230	46.2-752
231	46.2-882
232	2.2-3806
233	13.1-1002, 13.1-1020, 13.1-1123, 58.1-811
234	22.1-253.13:1, 22.1-253.13:3—22.1-253.13:7
235	46.2-725, n.
236	15.2-1129.1
237	62.1-132, n.
238	46.2-2062
239	12.1-21.1
241	60.2-315
242	59.1-548
245	22.1-296.1
246	24.2-945.1, 24.2-949.2
247	36-11
248	2.2-507, 2.2-510
249	46.2-221.2
250	8.01-195.3, 8.01-226.6R, 8.01-227.1—8.01-227.3R, 8.01-418.3R, 15.2-108R
251	15.2-1129.1
252	55-248.21:1
253	51.1-600, 51.1-601, 51.1-601.1
254	55-548.13
255	8.01-226.7
256	15.2-922.1, 15.2-1118R
257	15.2-1510.1
258	18.2-272
259	19.2-295, 19.2-298.01, 19.2-303
260	15.2-2404
261	59.1-466.1—

ACTS 2007 Chapter	Code 1950 Section
	59.1-466.4
262	15.2-1129.2
263	46.2-1219.2
264	18.2-340.16,
	18.2-340.34
265	54.1-2105.1,
	55-517—55-222,
	55-524, 55-525
266	55-79.87
267	55-362, 55-370,
	55-370.01, 55-374,
	55-376.3, 55-376.4
268	15.2-502
269	2.2-409,
	47.1-2, n.,
	47.1-3—47.1-5,
	47.1-7,
	47.1-8—47.1-11,
	47.1-11.1,
	47.1-12—47.1-14,
	47.1-15,
	47.1-16—47.1-20,
	47.1-21—47.1-23,
	47.1-25, 47.1-29.1,
	47.1-30,
	47.1-31—47.1-33R
270	3.1-796.87:1
272	15.2-915.3,
	18.2-308
273	55-248.31
276	2.2-2007
277	16.1-323,
	16.1-323.1,
	16.1-324—16.1-330R
278	22.1-205
279	15.2-2266
280	15.2-1129.1
281	24.2-709.1
282	18.2-460.
283	15.2-4904
284	16.1-241, 18.2-370.5
285	24.2-668, 24.2-802
286	24.2-946.1,
	24.2-947.1,
	24.2-947.5,
	24.2-947.9
287	59.1-548
288	15.2-542
290	36-106
291	36-105
292	15.2-953
295	4.1-100, 4.1-210,
	4.1-231, 4.1-233
296	46.2-755
297	15.2-2507
298	3.1-763.5:1,
	3.1-763.5:2,
	3.1-763.5:8
300	2.2-3707,
	2.2-3707.1,
	2.2-4031
301	55-414
302	34-34
304	33.1-223.2:17
305	33.1-23.1
306	20-111.1
307	31-37, 31-50
308	64.1-16.1,
	64.1-16.2
309	2.2-507.2
310	46.2-1307
311	24.2-101, 24.2-107,
	24.2-442,
	24.2-443.3,
	24.2-444
312	63.2 805
313	24.2-1005.1
314	58.1-3523
315	24.2-701
316	2.2-4007.04
317	33.1-46.2
318	24.2-107,
	24.2-405, 24.2-406,
	24.2-407.1,
	24.2-411.1,
	24.2-411.2,
	24.2-416.5, 24.2-427,
	24.2-444, 24.2-533,
	24.2-706,
	24.2-1002.1
320	32.1-19
321	15.2-2303.2
322	58.1-3506
324	15.2-2298
325	46.2-100,
	46.2-602.1,
	46.2-625
326	54.1-909
327	46.2-395
328	58.1-3221.2
331	24.2-945.2
332	54.1-1101
333	15.2-1511.1
334	54.1-2206.2
335	33.1-13.02
336	2.2-2903
337	33.1-12
338	15.2-4904
339	62.1-132, n.
340	24.2-105.1
341	64.1-157.1
342	36-19.2
343	32.1-19
344	58.1-3330
345	32.1-354,
	32.1-356, 32.1-359,
	32.1-360, 32.1-361.1
346	38.2-5902,
	38.2-5905
347	18.2-340.34:1
349	10.1-2211.1
350	24.2-102
351	22.1-253.13:4
352	3.1-14.4
353	58.1-3330
354	58.1-3221.2
355	33.1-13.02
356	65.2-520
357	58.1-3210,
	58.1-3211.1,
	58.1-3213,
	58.1-3215
358	2.2-2428
359	58.1-322
360	38.2-5501,
	38.2-5503
361	19.2-389
362	2.2-409
363	15.2-2316.1,
	15.2-2316.2
364	9.1-500
365	65.2-402.1
366	46.2-100,
	46.2-808, 46.2-905,
	46.2-906, 46.2-906.1,
	46.2-908.1,
	46.2-932
367	8.01-380
368	8.01-195.6,
	8.01-222R,
	15.2-209
369	16.1-69.55
370	16.1-241,
	18.2-370.5
371	19.2-163.01
372	17.1-205,
	17.1-328
373	19.2-45
374	2.2-3705.6,
	2.2-3711,
	56-573.1:1
375	24.2-651
376	46.2-1231.1
377	53.1-120
378	56-529, n.
379	18.2-51.5,
	19.2-187.02
380	19.2-13
381	19.2-368.11:1
382	33.1-70.3
383	19.2-164
384	2.2-5101
385	11-9.6, 37.2-1018
386	19.2-120, 19.2-386.31
387	16.1-323,
	16.1-323.1,
	16.1-324—16.1-330R
388	19.2-295.1
389	9.1-126
390	32.1-164.5,

ACTS 2007 Chapter	Code 1950 Section
	62.1-44.19:3
391	1-510
392	53.1-10
393	46.2-100,
	46.2-602.1,
	46.2-625
394	53.1-261,
	53.1-263
395	54.1-2400.2
396	16.1-253.4
397	32.1-162.1,
	32.1-162.3,
	32.1-162.5,
	63.2-1806
398	32.1-102.3:5
399	2.2-212
400	37.2-815
401	30-200.1
402	30-19.10
403	32.1-176.5:2
404	35.1-14.2
406	2.2-3705.7
407	32.1-351
408	18.2-308
409	2.2-511,
	18.2-46.5
410	15.2-2316.1,
	15.2-2316.2
411	32.1-283.1
412	19.2-72
413	32.1-162.19
414	19.2-409
415	2.2-2666.1
416	19.2-56
417	15.2-1629,
	15.2-1631
418	18.2-374.1
419	19.2-265.6
420	15.2-2241.1
421	46.2-1090
422	46.2-341.18:2
423	19.2-11.01,
	40.1-28.7:2
424	54.1-1140,
	54.1-1141,
	54.1-1142,
	54.1-1142.1,
	54.1-1143
425	16.1-88.2
426	60.2-512
427	56-484.14,
	56-484.19, 56-484.20,
	56-484.21, 56-484.22,
	56-484.23, 56-484.24,
	56-484.25
428	38.2-3525
429	46.2-1149.5
430	18.2-511.1
431	22.1-296.1
432	46.2-392

ACTS 2007 Chapter	Code 1950 Section
434	2.2-4343,
	23-76.1
435	33.1-391.5
436	18.2-323.02
437	18.2-147.2
438	2.2-3703
439	2.2-3704
440	19.2-301
441	18.2-186.3
442	30-19.3
443	8.01-35.1
444	3.1-22.28
445	55-79.95
446	63.2-1208
447	46.2-208,
	46.2-214
448	32.1-164.1:01
449	38.2-1839
450	8.01-187,
	8.01-345,
	8.01-346,
	25.1-229
451	17.1-223
452	4.1-201.1
453	18.2-59
454	4.1-100,
	4.1-128
455	18.2-308
456	48-17.1
457	13.1-514
458	13.1-504
459	30-239
460	16.1-272
461	18.2-160.2
462	19.2-124
463	9.1-902,
	18.2-67.4:2
464	16.1-109,
	16.1-296
465	19.2-327.5,
	19.2-327.13,
	19.2-392.2
466	51.1-137.1
467	18.2-424,
	18.2-425R,
	18.2-426
468	16.1-69.55
469	4.1-126
470	42.1-36.1
471	23-155.4
472	15.2-5204
473	51.5-25.1
474	32.1-353.1—
	32.1-353.3,
	32.1-353.4,
	32.1-353.5R
475	65.2-101
476	22.1-176.1
477	33.1-23.03:9, n.,
	33.1-23.03:10,

ACTS 2007 Chapter	Code 1950 Section
	56-556, n.
478	19.2-295.1
479	63.2-100
481	19.2-13
482	38.2-1704
483	18.2-152.4
484	18.2-97.1
485	19.2-182.1,
	19.2-182.2,
	19.2-182.5—19.2-182.7,
	19.2-182.10
486	15.2-1718.1,
	52-34.4—52-34.6
487	46.2-1222.2
488	38.2-1306.1,
	38.2-1320.5, 38.2-4319
489	8.01-20.1,
	8.01-50.1, 16.1-83.1
490	1-405, n.
491	23-7.4
492	46.2-730
493	46.2-328.1
494	4.1-216.1,
	4.1-328, 4.1-329
495	19.2-389, 63.2-1505
496	46.2-316
497	32.1-127.1:03
498	8.01-335
499	18.2-46.1
500	16.1-336,
	16.1-339, 16.1-341,
	16.1-345.1, 16.1-348,
	37.2-803, 37.2-804
501	46.2-804
502	32.1-102.1,
	32.1-102.2
503	19.2-11.2
504	43-5, 43-8,
	43-10
505	43-4
506	18.2-67.5:3
507	2.2-5510
508	53.1-221
509	18.2-308.2:2
510	16.1-273,
	16.1-278.7
511	16.1-300
512	2.2-3708
513	37.2-406
514	32.1-164,
	32.1-248.3
515	32.1-164.1:01
516	32.1-127
517	26-40.01,
	26-45.13,
	31-48, 55-34.7
518	18.2-186,
	18.2-195.2
519	18.2-57.02,
	18.2-283.1,

ACTS 2007 Chapter	Code 1950 Section
	18.2-287.01, 18.2-308.1, 18.2-308.2, 19.2-386.28, 19.2-386.29
520	11-9.1, 11-9.6, 37.2-1018
521	18.2-477.2
522	2.2-5407
523	46.2-1143
524	58.1-312
525	30-287—30-283
526	37.2-809
527	58.1-321, 58.1-322
528	9.1-176.1, 16.1-237, 16.1-299.1, 19.2-303, 19.2-303.3, 19.2-310.2, 53.1-145
529	58.1-439.7
530	8.01-581.17
532	46.2-300
533	8.01-328.1
534	2.2-212
535	32.1-325.2
536	32.1-325
537	56-235.2
538	64.1-49.1
539	63.2-1805
540	46.2-1130.1
541	18.2-340.30
543	58.1-321, 58.1-322
544	46.2-870
545	35.1-14.2
546	4.1-119
547	18.2-59
548	2.2-3703, 2.2-3808.1, 2.2-3808.2R, 8.01-449, 17.1-208, 17.1-275, 17.1-279, 17.1-292—17.1-294, 20-121.03
549	19.2-124
550	18.2-340.30:1
551	19.2-349
552	19.2-267
553	18.2-271.1
554	28.2-106.1
555	22.1-287
556	51.5-25.1
557	20-79.3
558	4.1-100, 4.1-207, 4.1-231
559	54.1-909
560	2.2-3713
561	2.2-4007.04
562	18.2-369
563	3.1-106.4:1, 15.2-924.1
565	19.2-182.2, 19.2-182.5, 19.2-182.6, 19.2-182.7, 19.2-182.10, 19.2-182.11
566	2.2-3711
567	17.1-124
568	63.2-608, 63.2-609, 63.2-611, 63.2-612
569	8.01-216.3, 8.01-216.5, 8.01-216.6, 8.01-216.9, 32.1-312, 32.1-313
570	37.2-502
571	19.2-163.03
572	19.2-389, 63.2-1601.1
573	63.2-1726
574	55-299
575	59.1-310.1, 59.1-310.3, 59.1-310.5
576	2.2-5102.1
577	30-133
578	15.2-958.2
579	38.2-1016.1, 38.2-4319
581	2.2-212
582	15.2-542
583	42.1-36.1
584	2.2-2622
586	58.1-3713
587	58.1-3211
588	63.2-2200, 63.2-2201, 63.2-2203
589	46.2-221.2
590	2.2-409, 47.1-2, 47.1-3, 47.1-4, 47.1-5, 47.1-7, 47.1-8, 47.1-9, 47.1-10, 47.1-11, 47.1-11.1, 47.1-12, 47.1-13, 47.1-14, 47.1-15, 47.1-16, 47.1-17, 47.1-18, 47.1-19, 47.1-20, 47.1-21, 47.1-22, 47.1-23, 47.1-25, 47.1-29.1, 47.1-30, 47.1-31—47.1-33R
591	53.1-33
592	15.2-953
593	58.1-439.7
594	63.2-1809.1
595	2.2-507, 10.1-119
596	58.1-3819
597	63.2-100
598	8.01-404
599	2.2-515.1, 2.2-515.2
600	63.2-1900, 63.2-1903, 63.2-1904, 63.2-1916
601	58.1-344.3
602	55-79.94
603	8.01-324
604	58.1-609.6
605	2.2-2903
606	63.2-901.1, 63.2-903, 63.2-1201, 63.2-1202, 63.2-1212, 63.2-1213, 63.2-1222, 63.2-1223, 63.2-1226, 63.2-1229, 63.2-1233, 63.2-1241
608	58.1-611.3, 58.1-625, 58.1-626
609	58.1-3506, 58.1-3916
610	58.1-1505
611	15.2-2288.3
612	15.2-1133, 23-155.05
613	2.2-3112, 15.2-1415
614	30-151, 30-152
615	29.1-735.2, 29.1-748
616	65.2-402
617	63.2-901.1
618	54.1-402.2
619	56-1
620	30-111
621	6.1-5, 54.1-2820, 54.1-2822
622	24.2-952.7
623	63.2-901.1, 63.2-903, 63.2-1201, 63.2-1202, 63.2-1212, 63.2-1213, 63.2-1222, 63.2-1223, 63.2-1226, 63.2-1229, 63.2-1233, 63.2-1241
624	2.2-1150
625	29.1-735.3

ACTS 2007 Chapter	Code 1950 Section
626	2.2-3703,
	2.2-3808.1,
	2.2-3808.2R,
	8.01-449,
	17.1-208, 17.1-275,
	17.1-279,
	17.1-292—17.1-294,
	20-121.03
627	30-111
628	60.2-602
629	13.1-553,
	13.1-1118
630	2.2-1111,
	2.2-2012,
	2.2-2622,
	23-9.9:01
631	12.1-43,
	50-73.1, 50-73.4,
	50-73.5, 50-73.7,
	50-73.10:1,
	50-73.11,
	50-73.11:2R,
	50-73.11:3,
	50-73.11:4,
	50-73.12,
	50-73.13,
	50-73.15, 50-73.17,
	50-73.48:1,
	50-73.48:3,
	50-73.49, 50-73.53,
	50-73.54,
	50-73.55R,
	50-73.67,
	50-73.77, 50-73.78,
	50-73.79, 50-73.83,
	50-73.84, 50-73.93,
	50-73.101,
	50-73.125R,
	50-73.127,
	50-73.128, 50-73.129,
	50-73.131, 50-73.132,
	50-73.133, 50-73.134
632	10.1-104
633	62.1-44.15
634	55-222,
	55-248.4,
	55-248.13,
	55-248.15:1,
	55-248.15:2
636	58.1-322
637	2.2-220,
	10.1-202,
	10.1-642,
	10.1-1193,
	10.1-2127,
	10.1-2134,
	62.1-44.118
638	60.2-512
639	13.1-1002,
	13.1-1020,
	13.1-1123,
	58.1-811
640	3.1-796.85
641	15.2-953
642	29.1-528
643	29.1-519
644	29.1-339.2
645	40.1-100
646	10.1-1152,
	10.1-1154R, 10.1-1155R
	10.1-1156,
	17.1-275
647	9.1-201,
	9.1-206—9.1-208,
	27-61, 27-97,
	27-97.2, 27-99,
	36-139,
	36-139.2—36-139.4R,
	38.2-401
648	15.2-2146,
	32.1-167,
	32.1-174.4
649	56-575.1,
	62.1-198,
	62.1-199
650	10.1-411
652	2.2-3705.7,
	53.1-233,
	53.1-234
653	18.2-369
654	2.2-115
655	62.1-44.19:5
656	62.1-44.15:5.02
657	15.2-2288.3
658	18.2-136
659	10.1-1408.5,
	62.1-44.3,
	62.1-44.15:5R,
	62.1-44.15:20,
	62.1-44.15:21,
	62.1-44.15:22,
	62.1-44.15:23,
	62.1-44.29
660	2.2-3705.7
661	16.1-253.4
662	54.1-3315R,
	54.1-3316,
	54.1-3322R,
	54.1-3434.3,
	54.1-3435.1,
	54.1-3435.3,
	54.1-3435.5R
663	62.1-198,
	62.1-199
664	29.1-509
665	55-79.94
666	51.5-11
667	40.1-113
668	13.1-559,
	13.1-560,
	13.1-561,
	13.1-562,
	13.1-572
669	46.2-725, n.
670	15.2-1133,
	23-155.05
671	3.1-969.7,
	3.1-969.10,
	3.1-969.12
672	24.2-604
673	10.1-1020
674	15.2-958.2
675	55-79.73:1,
	55-79.75,
	55-510
676	15.2-5368—
	15.2-5386
677	63.2-1808.1
678	54.1-2959
679	18.2-51.5,
	19.2-187.02
680	19.2-163.3
681	2.2-4327
683	59.1-296
684	45.1-394
685	1-510
686	18.2-270.1
689	10.1-1107
691	32.1-46.1
692	24.2-653
693	2.2-2240.1,
	2.2-3705.6
694	37.2-1023
695	15.2-2305
696	55-79.74:01,
	55-79.81,
	55-79.93:1, n.,
	55-79.97,
	55-511, 55-512,
	55-514.2, 55-516.1, n.
697	2.2-4343
698	58.1-609.11
699	32.1-42.1,
	32.1-48.06,
	32.1-48.09,
	32.1-48.010,
	32.1-48.012,
	32.1-48.013,
	32.1-48.013:1,
	32.1-48.014,
	32.1-48.015,
	54.1-3408
700	51.1-124.36
701	2.2-1124,
	2.2-2007
702	54.1-2722,
	54.1-3408
703	38.2-1825
704	58.1-609.11
705	23-9.2:8

ACTS 2007 Chapter	Code 1950 Section
706	2.2-904.1
707	1-406, n., 15.2-6304, n., 15.2-6304.1
708	9.1-185, 9.1-185.8
709	58.1-609.11
710	15.2-1544—15.2-1549
711	51.1-124.36
712	55-79.74:01, 55-79.81, 55-79.93:1, n., 55-79.97, 55-511, 55-512, 55-514.2, 55-516.1, n.
713	15.2-2305
714	2.2-306
715	46.2-731, 46.2-739, 46.2-1240, 46.2-1241
716	2.2-2817.1
717	23-7.4:1
718	9.1-901, 9.1-902, 9.1-903, 9.1-907, 9.1-908, 9.1-910, 18.2-63
719	15.2-1628, n., 15.2-1630, n., 15.2-1632, n., 15.2-1633, n., 15.2-1636.8, n.
720	8.01-187, 8.01-345, 8.01-346, 25.1-229
721	18.2-97.1
722	4.1-201.1
723	15.2-1718.1, 52-34.4—52-34.6
724	15.2-1704, 15.2-1727
726	4.1-119
727	23-155.4
728	44-11.1
729	2.2-306, 5.1-158, 44-146.17, 44-146.28
730	Const., Art. 8, § 2, n., 22.1-253.13:1, n., 22.1-299.3, n.
731	16.1-278.9
732	29.1-735.2, 29.1-748, 2.2-4014, n.
734	1-211.1
735	64.1-157
736	18.2-186.4
737	2.2-3705.7, 53.1-233, 53.1-234
738	46.2-1144.1, 46.2-1149.3
739	2.2-3705.7, 2.2-3711
740	1-406, n., 15.2-6304, 15.2-6304.1
741	9.1-201, 9.1-206, 9.1-207, 9.1-208, 27-61, 27-97, 27-97.2, 27-99, 36-139, 36-139.2—36-139.4R, 38.2-401
742	2.2-306, 5.1-158, 44-146.17, 44-146.28
743	3.1-796.122
744	9.1-901
745	16.1-253.2, 19.2-120
746	58.1-113
747	2.2-701
748	58.1-802
750	58.1-1803, 58.1-1821
751	58.1-602, 58.1-609.3
752	55-542.06
753	58.1-472
754	54.1-3807, 54.1-3813
755	33.1-94
756	56-46.1
757	59.1-365, 59.1-369, 59.1-376.1
758	58.1-609.10
759	9.1-902, 9.1-903, 9.1-904, 9.1-912, 18.2-374.1, 18.2-374.1:1, 18.2-374.1:2R, 18.2-374.3
760	36-106
761	15.2-2202, 15.2-2204, 15.2-2223, 15.2-2224, 56-46.1
762	38.2-111, 38.2-113
763	36-49.1:1
764	30-278—30-281, 56-575.1, 56-575.3:1, 56-575.4, 56-575.16, 56-575.18
765	58.1-339.7
767	58.1-3819
768	58.1-802
769	2.2-2006, 2.2-2009
770	58.1-478.1
771	13.1-616, 13.1-633R, 13.1-781, 13.1-816, 13.1-832R, 13.1-945, 13.1-1067, 13.1-1204, 13.1-1285, 50-73.17, 50-73.76:1, 50-73.83, 50-73.130R, 50-73.150
773	2.2-1839
774	15.2-2146, 32.1-167, 32.1-174.4
775	2.2-2009
776	56-46.1
777	46.2-334.01
778	36-55.63, 58.1-435
779	2.2-2316, 2.2-2317, 2.2-2318
780	32.1-11.6, 54.1-2403.01
781	19.2-169.1, 19.2-169.2, 19.2-169.3
782	58.1-301
783	32.1-42.1, 32.1-48.06, 32.1-48.09, 32.1-48.010, 32.1-48.012, 32.1-48.013, 32.1-48.013:1, 32.1-48.014, 32.1-48.015, 54.1-3408
784	55-519
785	19.2-182.6
786	36-27.2
787	2.2-2001, 2.2-4310
788	63.2-2002
789	67-900, 67-901, 67-902, 67-903, n., 67-1000, 67-1001, 67-1002, 67-1003
790	18.2-340.33
791	54.1-2113
792	15.2-2222.1
793	32.1-19

ACTS 2007 Chapter	Code 1950 Section
794	24.2-625.1,
	24.2-629
796	58.1-486.1,
	58.1-486.2
797	32.1-19
798	8.01-223.2
799	4.1-112.1R,
	4.1-204, 4.1-209.1,
	4.1-212.1, 4.1-215,
	4.1-230, 4.1-231,
	4.1-310
800	17.1-266
801	15.2-2232
802	19.2-10.2
803	30-58.4
804	54.1-1106,
	54.1-4400—54.1-4408,
	54.1-4409R,
	54.1-4409.1,
	54.1-4409.2, 54.1-4410R,
	54.1-4411, 54.1-4412R,
	54.1-4412.1, 54.1-4413R,
	54.1-4413.1R,
	54.1-4413.2—54.1-4413.5,
	54.1-4414,
	54.1-4415,
	54.1-4416, 54.1-4417R,
	54.1-4418, 54.1-4419R,
	54.1-4420,
	54.1-4421,
	54.1-4423
805	59.1-41.6
806	3.1-14.5
807	54.1-3913.1
808	63.2-1231
809	54.1-2100,
	54.1-2105,
	54.1-2105.01—
	54.1-2105.04,
	54.1-2105.1,
	54.1-2344
810	13.1-615,
	13.1-615.1,
	13.1-616,
	13.1-815,
	13.1-815.1,
	13.1-1005,
	13.1-1065,
	13.1-1252,
	13.1-1255,
	50-73.67,
	50-73.70
811	58.1-648
813	4.1-123,
	4.1-126,
	4.1-208, 4.1-209,
	4.1-210, 4.1-309,
	10.1-1408.5,
	15.2-912.1, 15.2-930,
	15.2-931, 15.2-958.1,
	15.2-961, 15.2-1124,
	15.2-1131, 15.2-1220,
	15.2-1508.4, 15.2-1638,
	15.2-2007.1, 15.2-2109,
	15.2-2157.1, 15.2-2204,
	15.2-2220, 15.2-2242,
	15.2-2263, 15.2-2291,
	15.2-2303.1, 15.2-2308,
	15.2-2403, 15.2-2404,
	15.2-2406, 15.2-3830,
	15.2-4402, 15.2-4407,
	15.2-5114, 15.2-5115,
	15.2-5136, 15.2-5204,
	15.2-5307, 16.1-118.1,
	16.1-309.3, 17.1-273,
	18.2-287.4, 19.2-250,
	21-118.2, 21-119,
	22.1-118, 22.1-129,
	24.2-112, 27-23.1,
	29.1-514, 29.1-748.1,
	29.1-749.2, 33.1-41.1,
	33.1-44, 33.1-225,
	44-146.40, 46.2-752,
	46.2-873, 46.2-874.1,
	46.2-924, 46.2-932,
	46.2-1094, 46.2-1216,
	46.2-1304, 46.2-2080,
	46.2-2099.21,
	46.2-2099.41,
	56-15, 56-265.1,
	58.1-540, 58.1-811,
	58.1-3237.1, 58.1-3257,
	58.1-3292.1, 58.1-3381,
	58.1-3506.2, 58.1-3818,
	58.1-3818, 59.1-148.3,
	59.1-284.13,
	59.1-284.14, 59.1-284.15
814	19.2-10.2
815	58.1-3523
816	40.1-28.9
817	58.1-609.1,
	58.1-625, 58.1-626
818	44-117
819	51.1-138, 51.1-206
820	4.1-119, 4.1-201
821	15.2-2286
822	32.1-11.6,
	54.1-2403.01
823	9.1-902, 9.1-903,
	9.1-904, 9.1-912,
	18.2-374.1,
	18.2-374.1:1,
	18.2-374.1:2R,
	18.2-374.3,
824	19.2-327.5,
	19.2-327.13,
	19.2-392.2
825	56-46.1
826	46.2-1527.3,
	46.2-1527.5
827	46.2-1569
828	46.2-1521
829	19.2-175
830	46.2-1571
831	24.2-945.1,
	24.2-945.2
832	40.1-28.9
833	15.2-1420,
	15.2-1421
834	58.1-3732
835	15.2-2403
836	15.2-968.1
837	46.2-1569
842	Const., Art. 10, § 6, n.
843	Const., Art. 10, § 6, n.
844	18.2-31
845	18.2-31
846	18.2-31
847	2.2-204, n.
	2.2-219, n.
	2.2-221.1, n.
	2.2-228, n.
	2.2-409, n.,
	2.2-518, n.,
	2.2-800, n.
	2.2-803, n.,
	2.2-1104, n.
	2.2-1149, n.
	2.2-1155, n.
	2.2-1156, n.
	2.2-1505, n.
	2.2-1802, n.
	2.2-1819, n.
	2.2-1829, n.
	2.2-2005, n.
	2.2-2221, n.
	2.2-2221.1, n.,
	2.2-2318, n.,
	2.2-2444, n.,
	2.2-2457, n.,
	2.2-2670, n.,
	2.2-2723, n.,
	2.2-2905, n.,
	2.2-4000, n.,
	2.2-4011, n.,
	2.2-4401, n.,
	2.2-4300, n.,
	2.2-4301, n.,
	2.2-4400, n.,
	2.2-4806, n.,
	2.2-5206, n.,
	2.2-5209, n.,
	2.2-5211, n.,
	3.1-336.1, n.,
	3.1-336.2, n.,
	3.1-336.3, n.,
	3.1-361, n.,
	3.1-1107, n.,
	4.1-235, n.,
	5.1-1.2, n.,

ACTS 2007 Chapter	Code 1950 Section
	8.01-195.1, n.,
	8.01-384.1:1, n.,
	9.1-102, n.,
	9.1-165, n.,
	9.1-166, n.,
	9.1-168, n.,
	10.1-202, n.,
	10.1-552, n.,
	10.1-1124, n.,
	10.1-1176, n.,
	10.1-1188, n.,
	10.1-1190, n.,
	10.1-2128, n.,
	10.1-2202.1, n.,
	10.1-2211, n.,
	10.1-2213, n.,
	10.1-2213.1, n.,
	10.1-2500, n.,
	13.1-775.1, n.,
	15.2-1302, n.,
	15.2-1605, n.,
	15.2-1608, n.,
	15.2-1609.1, n.,
	15.2-1609.2, n.,
	15.2-1609.7, n.,
	15.2-1612.1, n.,
	15.2-1627.1, n.,
	15.2-1628, n.,
	15.2-1629, n.,
	15.2-1630, n.,
	15.2-1631, n.,
	15.2-1634, n.,
	15.2-1636.8, n.,
	15.2-2222.1, n.,
	15.2-4100, n.,
	16.1-266, n.,
	16.1-273, n.,
	16.1-287, n.,
	16.1-309.2, n.,
	16.1-309.7, n.,
	16.1-322.1, n.,
	17.1-278, n.,
	17.1-279, n.,
	17.2-283, n.,
	17.1-287, n.,
	17.1-327, n.,
	18.2-340.31, n.,
	19.2-163, n.,
	19.2-163.01, n.,
	19.2-295.2:1, n.,
	19.2-298.01, n.,
	19.2-326, n.,
	19.2-349, n.,
	22.1-18.01, n.,
	22.1-101.1, n.,
	22.1-205, n.,
	22.1-253.13:1, n.,
	22.1-290.01, n.,
	23-7.4:1, n.,
	23-7.4:2, n.,
	23-9.2:3.03, n.,
	23-9.2:3.1, n.,
	23-9.6:1, n.,
	23-9.9, n.,
	23-30.23, n.,
	23-30.28, n.,
	23-38.3, n.,
	23-38.12, n.,
	23-38.14, n.,
	23-38.77, n.,
	23-164.8, n.,
	23-215, n.,
	23-220.01, n.,
	23-227, n.,
	23-231.13, n.,
	23-253.1, n.,
	23-276.10, n.,
	28.2-542, n.,
	28.2-550, n.,
	30-58.3, n.,
	30-266, n.,
	32.1-16, n.,
	32.1-50, n.,
	32.1-122.7, n.,
	32.1-163, n.,
	32.1-171.1, n.,
	32.1-273.1, n.,
	32.1-323, n.,
	32.1-324.3, n.,
	32.1-325.1, n.,
	32.1-325.1:1, n.,
	32.1-330.1, n.,
	32.1-331.12, n.,
	32.1-347, n.,
	32.1-352, n.,
	32.1-355, n.,
	33.1-23.1, n.,
	33.1-23.03:2, n.,
	33.1-23.3, n.,
	33.1-23.5:1, n.,
	33.1-41.1, n.,
	33.1-221.1:8, n.,
	33.1-391.5, n.,
	35.1-13, n.,
	35.1-14, n.,
	35.1-16, n.,
	35.1-17, n.,
	36-139, n.,
	37.2-203, n.,
	37.2-316, n.,
	37.2-319, n.,
	37.2-500, n.,
	37.2-504, n.,
	37.2-808, n.,
	37.2-900, n.,
	37.2-904, n.,
	40.1-49.4, n.,
	44-146.28, n.,
	45.1-393, n.,
	45.1-394, n.,
	46.2-205, n.,
	46.2-212.1, n.,
	46.2-685, n.,
	46.2-694, n.,
	46.2-710, n.,
	51.1-124.3, n.,
	51.1-142.2, n.,
	51.1-155.1, n.,
	51.1-203, n.,
	51.1-214, n.,
	51.1-303, n.,
	51.1-1100, n.,
	51.1-1103, n.,
	51.1-1400, n.,
	51.1-1401, n.,
	51.1-1403, n.,
	51.5-39.7, n.,
	51.5-106, n.,
	52-1, n.,
	52-8.1:1, n.,
	52-12, n.,
	52-28, n.,
	53.1-20, n.,
	53.1-20.1, n.,
	53.1-45, n.,
	53.1-67.1, n.,
	53.1-80, n.,
	53.1-82.3, n.,
	53.1-120, n.,
	54.1-3408, n.,
	54.1-3913, n.,
	54.1-3916, n.,
	54.1-3919, n.,
	54.1-3924, n.,
	55-66.6, n.,
	55-297, n.,
	56-232, n.,
	56-234, n.,
	56-484.12, n.,
	58.1-202.2, n.,
	58.1-339.4, n.,
	58.1-353, n.,
	58.1-439.2, n.,
	58.1-600, n.,
	58.1-602, n.,
	58.1-608.3, n.,
	58.1-638, n.,
	58.1-638.1, n.,
	58.1-609.11, n.,
	58.1-801, n.,
	58.1-803, n.,
	58.1-815.1, n.,
	58.1-816.1, n.,
	58.1-1402, n.,
	58.1-1410, n.,
	58.1-1803, n.,
	58.1-2402, n.,
	58.1-2425, n.,
	58.1-2510, n.,
	58.1-3523, n.,

ACTS 2007 Chapter	Code 1950 Section
	58.1-3524, n., 58.1-4022, n., 59.1-282.1, n., 59.1-282.2, n., 59.1-284.13, n., 59.1-364, n., 59.1-392, n., 60.2-305, n., 60.2-315, n., 62.1-44.19:3, n., 62.1-44.19:3.1, n., 62.1-128, n., 62.1-140, n., 63.2-401, n., 63.2-605, n., 63.2-611, n., 63.2-612, n., 63.2-619, n., 63.2-1706, n., 63.2-1735, n., 63.2-1907, n., 66-15, n., 66-20, n.,
848	46.2-819.4
849	2.2-2101, 2.2-2530, 2.2-2531
850	23-38.10:8—23-38.10:13
851	10.1-1186.01
853	54.1-829, 54.1-831.01
854	55-79.75:2, 55-79.90, 55-79.97, 55-513.1
856	15.2-2244.1
857	2.2-2698, 2.2-2699, 2.2-2698, 2.2-2699
858	32.1-46
859	22.1-253.13:4
860	46.2-920
861	54.1-2900, 54.1-2910.1, 54.1-2910.2, 54.1-2912.3
863	33.1-13, 33.1-198, 33.1-198.1, 33.1-199
864	15.2-5516—15.2-5522
865	46.2-752
866	51.1-1401
867	58.1-3921
868	32.1-283, 32.1-283.4
869	8.01-127R, 8.01-127.1R, 16.1-69.55, 16.1-77.1, 16.1-77.2, 16.1-88.2, 16.1-92R, 16.1-107, 16.1-114.1, 16.1-122, 55-32
870	2.2-4002, 3.1-14.01, 4.1-203, 4.1-207, 4.1-207.1, 4.1-208, 4.1-223, 4.1-231
871	63.2-901.1
872	8.01-512.4, 20-108.1
873	2.2-4001, 2.2-4003, 2.2-4006, 2.2-4007, 2.2-4007.01—2.2-4007.07, 2.2-4009, 2.2-4011, 2.2-4012, 2.2-4012.1, 2.2-4013, 2.2-4014, 2.2-4015, 2.2-4027, 2.2-4031, 3.1-398, 28.2-1507, 32.1-325, 35.1-14, 59.1-153, 62.1-44.15, 62.1-246, 63.2-217
874	54.1-2344
876	19.2-169.3, 37.2-900, 37.2-901, 37.2-902, 37.2-903, 37.2-904, 37.2-905, 37.2-905.1, 37.2-905.2, 37.2-906, 37.2-907, 37.2-908, 37.2-910, 37.2-912
877	56-580, 56-594
878	15.2-2283.1
879	28.2-1200.1
880	15.2-2157.1
881	32.1-164.2—32.1-164.7R, 62.1-44.19:3, 62.1-44.19:3.1—62.1-44.19:3.4
882	1-219.1, 15.2-1800, 15.2-1814, 15.2-1900R, 25.1-108
883	19.2-327.5, 19.2-327.13, 19.2-392.2
885	28.2-1001, 28.2-1007
886	15.2-2118
887	54.1-2409.4
888	56-233.1, 56-234.2, 56-235.2, 56-235.6, 56-249.6, 56-576, 56-577, 56-578, 56-579, 56-580, 56-581, 56-581.1R, 56-582, 56-583R, 56-584, 56-585, 56-585.1, 56-585.2, 56-585.3, 56-587, 56-589, 56-590, 56-594
889	17.1-406, 57-2.02
890	18.2-67.7
891	2.2-2699, 2.2-2699.1, 2.2-2699.2
892	32.1-163, 32.1-164, 32.1-164.8, 54.1-300, 54.1-2300, 54.1-2301, 54.1-2302
893	8.01-227.8—8.01-227.10
894	45.1-161.31, 45.1-161.32, 45.1-161.35, 45.1-161.37, 45.1-161.39, 45.1-161.64, 45.1-161.76, 45.1-161.78, 45.1-161.87, 45.1-161.257
895	25.1-245, 25.1-417.1
896	2.2-1514, 10.1-1188, 15.2-2223.1, 15.2-2317—15.2-2327, 15.2-2328, 15.2-2829, 15.2-2403, 15.2-2403.1, 15.2-4830, n., 15.2-4838.1, 15.2-4839, 15.2-4840, 30-282—30-286, 33.1-3, 33.1-13, 33.1-19.1, 33.1-23.03, 33.1-23.03:8, 33.1-23.4:01, 33.1-223.2:12, 33.1-268, 33.1-269, 33.1-277, 33.1-391.5, n., 33.1-391.6—33.1-391.15, 46.2-206.1, 46.2-694, 46.2-694, 46.2-694.1, 46.2-697, 46.2-702.1, 46.2-755.1, 46.2-755.2, 46.2-1135, 46.2-1167.1, 58.1-540, n., 58.1-605, 58.1-606, 58.1-625.1, 58.1-802.1, 58.1-811, 58.1-815.4, 58.1-1724.2—

ACTS 2007 Chapter	Code 1950 Section
	58.1-1724.7, 58.1-2217, 58.1-2249, 58.1-2289, 58.1-2402.1, 58.1-2403, 58.1-2425, 58.1-2531, 58.1-2701, 58.1-2706, 58.1-3221.3, 58.1-3825.1
897	16.1-336, 16.1-339, 16.1-341, 16.1-345.1, 16.1-348, 37.2-803, 37.2-804
898	6.1-2.21
899	23-38.10:8—23-38.10:13
900	10.1-1186.01
901	1-219.1, 15.2-1800, 15.2-1814, 15.2-1900R, 25.1-108
902	44-146.18
903	15.2-968.1
904	67-600, 67-602
905	19.2-327.5, 19.2-327.13, 19.2-392.2
906	29.1-103
907	32.1-291.1—32.1-291.25, 32.1-287R, 32.1-289R, 32.1-290R, 32.1-291R, 32.1-292.1R, 32.1-292.2, 32.1-293R, 32.1-295R, 46.2-342, 54.1-2982, 54.1-2984, 57-48
908	46.2-920
909	16.1-278.17:1
910	55-79.75:2, 55-79.90, 55-79.97, 55-513.1
911	44-102.2
914	45.1-161.31, 45.1-161.32, 45.1-161.35, 45.1-161.37, 45.1-161.39, 45.1-161.64, 45.1-161.76, 45.1-161.78, 45.1-161.87, 45.1-161.257
915	2.2-2101, 2.2-2628, 2.2-2629.1, 2.2-2629.2
916	2.2-4001, 2.2-4003, 2.2-4006, 2.2-4007, 2.2-4007.01—2.2-4007.07, 2.2-4007.02, 2.2-4007.03, 2.2-4007.04, 2.2-4007.05, 2.2-4007.06, 2.2-4007.07, 2.2-4007.1, 2.2-4009, 2.2-4011, 2.2-4012, 2.2-4012.1, 2.2-4013, 2.2-4014, 2.2-4015, 2.2-4027, 2.2-4031, 3.1-398, 28.2-1507, 32.1-325, 35.1-14, 59.1-153, 62.1-44.15, 62.1-246, 63.2-217
917	59.1-123, 59.1-129, 59.1-136.1—59.1-136.7
918	46.2-891, 46.2-920.1
919	22.1-253.13:4
920	15.2-2157.1
921	51.1-1401
922	32.1-46
923	16.1-253.2, 19.2-120
924	10.1-2117, 15.2-2157, 32.1-163, 32.1-164, 54.1-300, 54.1-2300, 54.1-2301, 54.1-2302
925	6.1-225.27, 13.1-801—13.1-804, 13.1-804.1, 13.1-806—13.1-810, 13.1-810.1, 13.1-811, 13.1-812, 13.1-813, 13.1-815, 13.1-815.1, 13.1-816, 13.1-819, 13.1-820, 13.1-822—13.1-831, 13.1-833—13.1-844, 13.1-844.1, 13.1-845, 13.1-846, 13.1-847, 13.1-847.1, 13.1-848, 13.1-849, 13.1-850, 13.1-852, 13.1-852.1, 13.1-852.2, 13.1-853, 13.1-854, 13.1-855, 13.1-857—13.1-862, 13.1-864—13.1-871, 13.1-871.1, 13.1-872, 13.1-874, 13.1-875, 13.1-876, 13.1-878, 13.1-879.1—13.1-883, 13.1-885, 13.1-886, 13.1-887.1, 13.1-888, 13.1-889, 13.1-890R, 13.1-891, 13.1-892, 13.1-893, 13.1-893.1, 13.1-894—13.1-897, 13.1-897.1, 13.1-898R, 13.1-898.1R, 13.1-898.2—13.1-900, 13.1-902, 13.1-904, 13.1-906, 13.1-907, 13.1-908, 13.1-908.1, 13.1-908.2, 13.1-908.3, 13.1-909—13.1-917, 13.1-919—13.1-928.1, 13.1-929—13.1-934, 13.1-935.1, 13.1-936, 13.1-936.1, 13.1-939, 55-532, 13.1-898.1R
926	1-219.1, 15.2-1800, 15.2-1814, 15.2-1900R, 25.1-108
927	32.1-164.5, 62.1-44.19:3
928	33.1-13, 33.1-198, 33.1-198.1, 33.1-199
929	32.1-164.2—32.1-164.7R, 62.1-44.19:3, 62.1-44.19:3.1—62.1-44.19:3.4
930	54.1-2409.4
931	55-50.1
932	2.2-4002, 3.1-14.01, 4.1-203, 4.1-207, 4.1-207.1, 4.1-208, 4.1-223, 4.1-231
933	56-233.1, 56-234.2, 56-235.2, 56-235.6, 56-249.6, 56-576, 56-577, 56-578, 56-579, 56-580, 56-581, 56-581.1R, 56-582, 56-583R, 56-584, 56-585, 56-585.1, 56-585.2, 56-585.3, 56-587, 56-589, 56-590, 56-594
934	46.2-600
935	46.2-1095, 46.2-1100
937	15.2-2286
938	19.2-163
939	24.2-625.2, 24.2-626, 24.2-626.1, 24.2-802
941	15.2-6400, 15.2-6407, 15.2-6900

ACTS 2007 Chapter	Code 1950 Section
942	58.1-322
943	24.2-625.2, 24.2-626, 24.2-626.1, 24.2-802
944	19.2-243
945	2.2-3701, 2.2-3708, 2.2-3708.1, 23-38.95, 23-50.16:32
946	19.2-163
947	15.2-6400, 15.2-6407, 15.2-6900
948	58.1-3321

ACTS 2008

ACTS 2008 Chapter	Code 1950 Section
1	58.1-301
2	58.1-301
3	62.1-198, 62.1-199
7	2.2-4401
8	3.1-796.77, 3.2-6505
9	3.1-796.66, 3.2-6500
10	62.1-193.1, 62.1-193.2
12	10.1-1425.26
13	10.1-603.14:1
14	10.1-418.4, 10.1-418.5
15	10.1-2109
16	2.2-3705.7, 3.1-796.87:1, 3.2-6529
17	29.1-529
18	29.1-300.1, 29.1-300.4
19	10.1-1115
20	28.2-1400, 28.2-1403
21	3.1-741.4
22	10.1-109
23	10.1-563
24	62.1-198, 62.1-199
25	58.1-662
26	58.1-3506
27	51.1-142.2
28	51.1-205
29	51.1-608
30	58.1-3822
31	29.1-520
32	58.1-641
33	46.2-1144.1
34	54.1-3002
35	54.1-2971R
36	54.1-2957.10
37	54.1-2506
38	2.2-2649
39	2.2-2648, 2.2-5206, 2.2-5208
40	51.5-12.3
41	32.1-227, 32.1-228, 32.1-228.1, 32.1-229, 32.1-229.01, 32.1-229.1, 32.1-229.2, 32.1-229.3, 32.1-232.1, 32.1-233, 32.1-234.1, 32.1-235, 32.1-238
42	32.1-11
43	63.2-1509
45	10.1-1188
46	22.1-209.2
47	22.1-16.4
48	22.1-290.01
49	22.1-26
50	2.2-2523R
51	22.1-299
52	2.2-4344
53	17.1-209
54	17.1-402
55	23-70
56	23-14
57	49-3
58	38.2-231, 38.2-2114, 38.2-2212
59	54.1-3446
60	8.01-268
61	32.1-111.9
62	32.1-176.5:2
63	2.2-2233.1
64	54.1-2900, 54.1-2956.1, 54.1-2956.4, 54.1-2956.5
66	32.1-111.3
67	54.1-2301
68	54.1-400, 54.1-402
69	18.2-308
70	2.2-2221.01
71	2.2-3705.6, 32.1-276.5:1
72	32.1-162.3, n., 32.1-162.5, n.
73	16.1-253, 16.1-253.1, 16.1-253.4, 16.1-279.1, 19.2-152.8, 19.2-152.9, 19.2-152.10, 19.2-390
74	54.1-3448
75	18.2-308
76	9.1-922
77	54.1-2971R
78	2.2-4303
79	18.2-248, 54.1-3434.1, 54.1-3434.2, 54.1-3434.4
80	18.2-308
81	32.1-11
82	32.1-290.1R, 32.1-291.21, 32.1-292.2, 46.2-342,
83	37.2-311
84	54.1-2712, 54.1-2729.01
85	54.1-3408
86	63.2-527
87	24.2-625.2
88	24.2-611
89	54.1-2900, 54.1-2956.1, 54.1-2956.4, 54.1-2956.5
90	55-210.3:01
91	13.1-607, 13.1-614, 13.1-657, 13.1-708, 13.1-741.1, 13.1-746—13.1-746.2, 13.1-770, 13.1-771, 13.1-807, 13.1-813
92	6.1-2.21
93	38.2-1423
94	58.1-3506
95	38.2-1039
96	59.1-293.1—59.1-293.9
97	58.1-344.3
98	60.2-113
100	60.2-507.1
101	13.1-1204, 13.1-1210, 13.1-1216, 13.1-1217, 13.1-1234—13.1-1236, 13.1-1238, 13.1-1238.1, 13.1-1238.2, 13.1-1239, 13.1-1241, 13.1-1242, 13.1-1243R, 13.1-1245, 13.1-1246.1—13.1-1246.3, 13.1-1250, 13.1-1254, 13.1-1261
102	2.2-3705.6, 32.1-276.5:1
103	2.2-4518
104	38.2-3407.9:03
106	24.2-706
107	24.2-659, 24.2-682
108	13.1-1005, 13.1-1009, 13.1-1014, 13.1-1014.1, 13.1-1046—13.1-1048, 13.1-1050, 13.1-1050.1R, 13.1-1050.2—13.1-1050.4, 13.1-1052, 13.1-1053R, 13.1-1055, 13.1-1056.1—13.1-1056.3, 13.1-1060, 13.1-1064, 13.1-1070, 13.1-1072
109	65.2-102
110	24.2-653
111	38.2-517
112	24.2-309.2
113	24.2-310, 24.2-601
114	46.2-742.6R, 46.2-749.122—46.2-749.125R, 46.2-749.129R, 46.2-749.134, 46.2-749.135R

ACTS 2008 Chapter	Code 1950 Section
115	16.1-69.33, 16.1-218, 17.1-700, 17.1-706, 19.2-163.02
116	63.2-1201
117	17.1-223, 47.1-5, 47.1-8, 47.1-9, 47.1-13, 47.1-13.1, 47.1-14, 47.1-16, 47.1-28, 55-106.2
118	15.2-1518, 32.1-111.1, 32.1-116.1:1, 32.1-116.3
119	55-218.1
120	46.2-931
121	8.01-225.01, 8.01-225.02, 8.01-581.1, 38.2-324, 44-146.16, 44-146.17, 44-146.18:1, 44-146.23, 59.1-526
122	19.2-159
123	63.2-1735
124	19.2-267
125	8.01-581.20
126	19.2-319
127	3.1-796.66, 3.2-6500
128	19.2-152.9
129	19.2-123
130	46.2-702.2
131	22.1-115
132	63.2-612
133	63.2-913, 63.2-1220.1
134	4.1-120
135	4.1-104
136	8.01-271.1, 16.1-260, 16.1-278.15, 54.1-3900, 63.2-1901
137	32.1-263
138	58.1-609.6
139	16.1-336, 16.1-339
140	16.1-341
141	22.1-290.01
142	17.1-209
143	58.1-3506
144	58.1-3211
145	38.2-5008.1, 38.2-5010, n., 38.2-5013, n.
146	19.2-319
147	19.2-54, 19.2-57
148	58.1-662
149	58.1-322, 58.1-402
150	22.1-227.1
151	22.1-209.2
152	24.2-945.1, 24.2-947.4, 24.2-949.5, 24.2-949.9:2, 24.2-950.1, 24.2-950.4, 24.2-950.5R
153	58.1-3822
154	19.2-159
155	23-70
156	17.1-402
157	8.01-225.01, 8.01-225.02, 8.01-581.1, 38.2-324, 44-146.16, 44-146.17, 44-146.18:1, 44-146.23, 59.1-526
158	58.1-641
159	46.2-730
160	29.1-521
161	29.1-521
162	8.01-226.12
163	46.2-752
164	16.1-241, 20-49.2
165	46.2-873.2
166	46.2-1581
167	33.1-56.1, 33.1-56.3
168	46.2-1508.2
169	8.01-581.1, 8.01-581.20
170	2.2-2648, 2.2-5206, 2.2-5208
171	43-34, 46.2-623, 46.2-1200.2
172	4.1-210
173	62.1-44.15:23
174	18.2-66R, 18.2-371, 20-48
175	8.01-243, 8.01-244
176	3.1-336.8:1, 3.2-4209.1
177	53.1-32.2
178	46.2-653
179	4.1-209
180	19.2-83.2, 19.2-294.2, 53.1-218
181	46.2-1022, 46.2-1023
182	46.2-694
183	19.2-54, 19.2-57
184	2.2-4343, 2.2-4515, 3.1-1109.1, 3.2-3104, 15.2-5205, 15.2-5340.1, 15.2-5374, 23-76.1, 32.1-361.1, 51.5-63, 55-268.1—55-268.10R, 55-268.11—55-268.20
185	4.1-225
186	4.1-209
187	63.2-905.1
188	63.2-912
189	46.2-1052
190	46.2-341.4, 46.2-341.15, 46.2-341.18, 46.2-341.18:01, 46.2-341.20:2, 46.2-341.20:3, 46.2-341.21, 46.2-505
191	32.1-45.1
192	4.1-209
193	46.2-1220
194	4.1-207, 4.1-219
195	33.1-70.1
196	46.2-916.2
198	4.1-100, 4.1-206, 4.1-231, 4.1-233
201	16.1-241, 20-49.2
202	37.2-808
203	19.2-165.1, 19.2-368.3, 19.2-368.11:1
204	8.01-268
205	8.01-581.1, 8.01-581.20
206	18.2-66R, 18.2-371, 20-48
208	58.1-3215
209	38.2-3525
210	58.1-3818.01
211	58.1-322, 58.1-402
212	38.2-4806
213	38.2-1820, 38.2-1822, 38.2-1836, 38.2-1838, 38.2-1845, 38.2-1857.2, 38.2-1857.5, 38.2-1857.9, 38.2-1865.1, 38.2-1865.4
214	38.2-4303
215	38.2-3407
216	38.2-1401, 38.2-1443.1, 38.2-3100.2
217	58.1-9
218	18.2-472.1
219	8.01-382
220	9.1-903
221	38.2-231, 38.2-2114, 38.2-2212
222	60.2-113
224	34-6
225	10.1-1188
226	8.01-241, 8.01-241.1
227	45.1-361.29
228	58.1-461, n., 58.1-462, n., 58.1-470, n.
229	8.01-225
230	58.1-3819
231	58.1-3211
232	38.2-6300,

TABLE OF ACTS CODIFIED SUBSEQUENT TO 1948

ACTS 2008 Chapter	Code 1950 Section
	38.2-6301
233	2.2-3701, 2.2-3708, 2.2-3714
234	46.2-919.1
235	46.2-931
236	23-231.15
237	22.1-212.22
238	62.1-198, 62.1-199
239	2.2-3117
240	2.2-1501, n., 2.2-1509, n., 2.2-1511, n., 2.2-2101, n., 2.2-2683, n., 2.2-2684, n., 2.2-2685, n., 2.2-2686, n., 2.2-2687, n., 2.2-2688, n., 2.2-2689, n., 2.2-5510, n., 2.2-5511, n.
241	63.2-900, 63.2-902
242	23-298
243	2.2-2674.01
244	62.1-44.15:21
245	51.1-124.22, 51.1-602, 51.1-608, 51.1-618
246	16.1-253, 16.1-253.1, 16.1-253.4, 16.1-279.1, 19.2-152.8, 19.2-152.9, 19.2-152.10, 19.2-390
247	60.2-507.1
248	38.2-4610.1, 38.2-4610.1:1
249	38.2-1317.1, 38.2-1317.2
250	38.2-1814.1
251	19.2-165.1, 19.2-368.3, 19.2-368.11:1
253	55-532
254	10.1-1124
255	3.1-965, 3.2-5645
256	59.1-284.20—59.1-284.22
257	3.1-610.19R, 3.2-4412
258	10.1-1308.1
259	62.1-198, 62.1-199
260	29.1-529
262	1-510
263	37.2-837
264	54.1-2712, 54.1-2729.01
265	13.1-543, 13.1-549, 13.1-549.1, 13.1-550, 13.1-1102
266	2.2-3705.6
267	38.2-5008, 38.2-5009, 38.2-5016, 38.2-5020, 38.2-5021
268	63.2-1509
269	2.2-435.7, 2.2-2669
272	56-576
273	56-575.1
274	33.1-13, n., 33.1-198, n., 33.1-198.1, n., 33.1-199, n.
275	45.1-254
276	10.1-1184, 10.1-1185, 10.1-1301, 10.1-1302, 10.1-1304, 10.1-1322, 10.1-1322.01, 10.1-1401, 62.1-44.8, 62.1-44.9, 62.1-44.15:02, 62.1-44.26
277	2.2-2648, 2.2-2649, 2.2-5206, 2.2-5210, 37.2-308, 63.2-226
278	10.1-2128
279	29.1-301
280	33.1-56.1, 33.1-56.3
281	54.1-2952
282	10.1-1322.4
284	15.2-1610
285	32.1-69.3
287	32.1-283
288	58.1-3221.2
289	24.2-945.1, 24.2-947.4, 24.2-949.5, 24.2-949.9:2, 24.2-950.1, 24.2-950.4, 24.2-950.5R
290	15.2-1129.1
291	33.1-223.2:18
292	32.1-102.3
293	2.2-2695R
294	54.1-1115, 59.1-200
295	2.2-4501
296	56-560
297	15.2-2286
298	58.1-3211, 58.1-3211.1
299	2.2-2220
300	24.2-706
301	54.1-2983, 54.1-2985, 54.1-2994—54.1-2996
302	58.1-4006, 58.1-4007
303	6.1-2.27:1, 38.2-1834.1
304	46.2-602.2, 46.2-1548, 46.2-1549, 46.2-1550, 58.1-2403
305	9.1-108.1
306	2.2-2732, 2.2-2733
308	63.2-900, 63.2-902
309	18.2-308
310	46.2-931
313	58.1-344.3
314	2.2-4806, 2.2-4809
315	32.1-127.1:03
317	15.2-2286
318	15.2-2309
319	54.1-2106.1
320	54.1-3434, 54.1-3434.2, 54.1-3435, 54.1-3435.01, 54.1-3435.2, 54.1-3435.4, 54.1-3439
321	2.2-4007.02, n.
324	62.1-132.12
325	62.1-129.1
328	9.1-102
329	55-248.45
330	54.1-2969
331	37.2-809
332	15.2-2118
333	15.2-961.1
334	58.1-3211
335	15.2-1511.01
336	10.1-418.4, 10.1-418.5
338	9.1-922
339	32.1-45.1
340	15.2-2244
341	8.01-226.12
343	15.2-2286
345	3.1-796.96, 3.2-6546, 18.2-510
347	15.2-3201
348	59.1-293.1—59.1-293.9
349	16.1-69.45, 16.1-69.46
350	36-85.16, 36-85.18, 36-85.20
351	22.1-253.13:4
352	18.2-340.33
353	15.2-2503, 22.1-93
354	51.1-510
355	15.2-2404
356	2.2-1151
357	38.2-1833
358	54.1-111
359	24.2-945
360	3.1-796.93:1,

ACTS 2008 Chapter	Code 1950 Section
	3.2-6540
361	2.2-703,
	2.2-703.1
362	19.2-316.2
363	19.2-130
364	22.1-254.1
365	22.1-151,
	22.1-161
366	24.2-101.1
367	32.1-37
368	2.2-216
369	28.2-1208,
	45.1-161.5,
	45.1-383
370	2.2-1133
371	2.2-4301
372	19.2-168
373	54.1-3012.1
374	2.2-2817.1
375	2.2-2817.1
376	55-362, 55-369,
	55-382, 55-383, 55-396
377	15.2-2307
378	15.2-2311
379	24.2-404,
	24.2-444, 24.2-706
380	24.2-947.9,
	24.2-948
381	15.2-1806, 15.2-1809.1
382	24.2-427
383	37.2-416,
	37.2-506
384	19.2-316.3
385	24.2-659,
	24.2-682
386	24.2-701
387	2.2-203,
	2.2-905R, 2.2-906R,
	2.2-2455, 2.2-2456,
	2.2-3705.3, 2.2-3705.6,
	18.2-340.15, 18.2-340.16,
	18.2-340.25, 19.2-389,
	58.1-3, 58.1-4019.1
388	2.2-435.7,
	2.2-2669
389	15.2-2123
390	57-27.1
391	2.2-708
392	55-70.1
393	24.2-625.2
394	24.2-310,
	24.2-601
395	24.2-300, n.
396	54.1-2816.1
397	16.1-252,
	16.1-281, 63.2-900.2
398	22.1-16.4
399	23-185
400	6.1-2.13:3
401	58.1-3221.2

ACTS 2008 Chapter	Code 1950 Section
402	53.1-32.2
403	2.2-1204
404	22.1-93
405	10.1-603.4
406	19.2-169.3
407	37.2-416,
	37.2-506
408	18.2-308.2:01,
	18.2-308.2:1
409	30-293—30-300
410	27-6.1,
	27-13, 27-14,
	27-15.1, 27-20,
	27-34, 27-85.4
411	15.2-2307
412	32.1-37
413	23-9.2:11
414	46.2-2800
415	19.2-83.2,
	19.2-294.2, 53.1-218
416	29.1-300.1,
	29.1-300.4
417	22.1-207.1
418	45.1-394
419	2.2-708
420	2.2-2818,
	38.2-3418.1:1R
422	22.1-254.02
423	24.2-603,
	24.2-712
424	24.2-414,
	24.2-416, 24.2-611
425	24.2-700,
	24.2-701
426	15.2-2260, 15.2-2261
427	46.2-725, n.
428	15.2-2118
429	54.1-3411.1
430	22.1-238,
	22.1-239,
	22.1-240R,
	22.1-241—22.1-243,
	22.1-244—22.1-251R,
	22.1-253R
431	51.5-44
432	46.2-725, n.
433	32.1-283
434	15.2-4832
436	46.2-725, n.
437	15.2-1724,
	15.2-1726, 15.2-1728,
	30-34.2:1
438	9.1-185.4
439	63.2-214.1
441	23-9.2:3
442	33.1-62, n.
443	46.2-1088
444	2.2-225.1
445	2.2-2285,
	15.2-5000—15.2-5004,

ACTS 2008 Chapter	Code 1950 Section
	36-137, 36-139
446	2.2-214.2—
	2.2-214.4
447	46.2-919.1
448	63.2-1900, n.
449	58.1-339.10
450	23-9.2:9—
	23-9.2:11, 44-146.18
451	46.2-925
452	15.2-5138.1
453	4.1-212
454	33.1-13, n.,
	33.1-198, n.,
	33.1-198.1, n.,
	33.1-199, n.
455	22.1-199.5
456	46.2-916.3
457	46.2-752
459	3.1-398.1,
	3.2-5130
460	9.1-101,
	18.2-57, 19.2-81,
	46.2-217
461	58.1-344.3
462	58.1-3851
463	58.1-439.24,
	63.2-2006
464	18.2-308
465	23-165.4
466	32.1-227,
	32.1-228, 32.1-228.1,
	32.1-229, 32.1-229.01,
	32.1-229.1, 32.1-229.2,
	32.1-229.3, 32.1-232.1,
	32.1-233, 32.1-234.1,
	32.1-235, 32.1-238
467	2.2-2001,
	2.2-2004, 2.2-2452,
	2.2-2681, 2.2-2682,
	2.2-2715, 2.2-2716
468	33.1-223.2:19
469	19.2-120.1
470	46.2-808.1,
	46.2-1217, 46.2-2810,
	46.2-2814, 46.2-2814.1
471	33.1-223.2:20
472	33.1-190
473	10.1-1188
474	19.2-291.1,
	22.1-253.13:7,
	22.1-298.1, 22.1-313,
	63.2-1503
475	16.1-228,
	16.1-281—16.1-282.2,
	63.2-100,
	63.2-904—63.2-906,
	63.2-1819
476	56-585.1,
	56-597—56-599
477	23-165.4

ACTS 2008 Chapter	Code 1950 Section
478	2.2-3104.1
479	54.1-2910.1
480	59.1-444.1, 59.1-444.2
481	33.1-465R
482	58.1-439.12:02
483	16.1-228, 16.1-281—16.1-282.2, 63.2-100, 63.2-904—63.2-906, 63.2-1819
484	58.1-605, 58.1-606
485	59.1-200.1, 59.1-201, 59.1-203, 59.1-205—59.1-207
486	2.2-2715, 2.2-2716
487	46.2-330
488	58.1-605, 58.1-606, 58.1-622
489	8.01-27.1, 8.01-27.2, 8.01-129, 8.01-296, 55-225, 55-225.3, 55-248.4, 55-248.6, 55-248.6:1, 55-248.9:1, 55-248.13, 55-248.15:2, 55-248.16, 55-248.18, 55-248.31, 55-248.34:1
490	54.1-3813
491	10.1-603.17, 10.1-603.19:1, 10.1-606.1R, 10.1-606.2—10.1-606.4, 15.2-2224, 15.2-2235, 15.2-2241, 15.2-2243.1, 15.2-2258, 15.2-2283, 15.2-2284, 15.2-2295.2, 55-519
492	60.2-633
493	46.2-335
494	63.2-1231
495	23-9.2:3
496	59.1-444.1, 59.1-444.2
497	2.2-3104.1
498	63.2-1704.1—63.2-1704.3
499	27-98
500	10.1-2128
501	32.1-102.2:1
502	46.2-214.2
503	46.2-930
504	62.1-198, 62.1-199
506	51.5-44
507	63.2-2203
508	6.1-363.14
509	13.1-545.1, 13.1-555, 13.1-607, 13.1-615.1, 13.1-716, 13.1-807, 13.1-815.1, 13.1-894, 13.1-1106, 13.1-1121
510	3.1-796.115, 3.2-6569
511	33.1-46.2
512	19.2-9.1
513	4.1-100, 4.1-111, 4.1-204, 4.1-227, 4.1-324, 4.1-325
514	6.1-2.10
515	32.1-163.6
516	38.2-517
517	16.1-272, 53.1-202.2, 53.1-202.3
518	56-245.1:2
519	16.1-306
520	38.2-5008, 38.2-5009, 38.2-5016, 38.2-5020, 38.2-5021
521	2.2-2001, 2.2-4310
522	56-233.1
523	13.1-1057, 13.1-1247, 50-73.59
524	59.1-435
525	46.2-914
526	23-9.2:9, 44-146.18
527	2.2-2233.1
528	10.1-1186.2:1
529	62.1-132.12
530	3.1-18.10, 3.2-201
531	2.2-2732, 2.2-2733
532	2.2-3100, 15.2-2287.1
533	23-9.2:10
534	45.1-361.19, 45.1-361.30
535	29.1-739.2
536	19.2-163.01, 19.2-163.01:1
537	51.1-155.2
538	19.2-263.3
539	2.2-3705.5, 32.1-283.5, 63.2-1606
540	58.1-3253, 58.1-3258, 58.1-3258.1, 58.1-3258.2, 58.1-3271, 58.1-3275, 58.1-3276
541	10.1-1425.27—10.1-1425.38
542	15.2-5114
543	3.1-796.113, 3.1-796.122, 3.1-796.124, 3.1-796.125R, 3.2-6570, 3.2-6571, 3.2-6572, 18.2-403.2
544	24.2-613
545	58.1-609.6
547	24.2-949.6, 24.2-953.1
548	2.2-620
549	58.1-3.3, 58.1-394.3, 58.1-1820, 58.1-1821, 58.1-1822, 58.1-1825, 58.1-1826
550	58.1-3924
551	3.1-383, 3.1-796.93:1, 3.1-796.116, 3.1-796.126:10, 3.2-6540, 3.2-6552, 3.2-6583, 8.01-126, 8.01-537, 8.01-540, 15.2-1704, 15.2-1710, 16.1-135, 19.2-5, 19.2-30R, 19.2-34—19.2-39, 19.2-38.1, 19.2-41R, 19.2-43, 19.2-44, 19.2-45—19.2-46.1, 19.2-48, 19.2-48.1, 19.2-77, 19.2-81.3, 19.2-119, 19.2-152.4:3, 20-70, 20-84, 27-32—27-32.2, 27-37.1, 37.2-808, 37.2-809, 37.2-1103, 37.2-1104, 43-29, 46.2-104, 49-6, 55-205, 55-230, 59.1-98, 59.1-106
552	40.1-100
553	22.1-254.1
554	58.1-609.1

ACTS 2008 Chapter	Code 1950 Section
555	22.1-296.1, 22.1-296.4, 22.1-307, 63.2-1505
556	55-210.3:01
557	10.1-1184, 10.1-1185, 10.1-1301, 10.1-1302, 10.1-1304, 10.1-1322, 10.1-1322.01, 10.1-1401, 62.1-44.8, 62.1-44.9, 62.1-44.15:02, 62.1-44.26
558	58.1-609.3
559	24.2-653
561	2.2-3705.4
562	59.1-443.2
563	32.1-116.1, 51.5-11R
564	63.2-612
565	24.2-669, 24.2-671.1
566	18.2-186.6
567	32.1-111.3
568	2.2-1207, 2.2-1208, 51.1-513.2—51.1-513.4
569	58.1-609.10
571	23-2.1:3
572	10.1-1186.01
573	18.2-340.26
575	2.2-4007.02, n.
576	2.2-1201
577	2.2-507, 10.1-501
578	18.2-108
579	18.2-10, 18.2-370.2
580	15.2-958
581	15.2-2286
582	15.2-908
583	15.2-2208
584	2.2-2001.1, 37.2-304, 51.5-14
585	58.1-439.18—58.1-439.24, 63.2-2000, 63.2-2001R, 63.2-2002, 63.2-2003—63.2-2006R
586	50-73.12, 50-73.13R, 50-73.15, 50-73.17, 50-73.48:3, 50-73.49—50-73.51, 50-73.52:4—50-73.52:7, 50-73.57, 50-73.57:2, 50-73.58:1—50-73.58:3, 50-73.69, 50-73.77
587	46.2-1224.1
588	13.1-753, 13.1-769, 13.1-915, 13.1-931, 13.1-1046, 13.1-1056, 13.1-1234, 13.1-1246, 50-73.49, 50-73.58
589	22.1-98.2
590	19.2-368.2
591	46.2-221.2, 46.2-221.4, 46.2-752, 58.1-341, 58.1-3916
592	9.1-902
593	15.2-2286
595	18.2-172.2
596	19.2-120
597	62.1-129.2
598	2.2-4311.1
599	55-50.3
600	9.1-102, 9.1-1300, 9.1-1301, 19.2-81.4R
601	15.2-2291
602	33.1-23.03:10, 56-565
603	56-597—56-599
605	62.1-198, 62.1-199
606	46.2-725, n.
608	33.1-23.05
609	4.1-119
610	2.2-2221.01
611	2.2-2220
612	15.2-953
613	62.1-198, 62.1-199
614	46.2-742
615	22.1-238, 22.1-239, 22.1-240R, 22.1-241—22.1-243, 22.1-244—22.1-251R, 22.1-253R
617	55-248.16, 55-248.18
618	18.2-248, 54.1-3434.1, 54.1-3434.2, 54.1-3434.4
619	15.2-4904
620	46.2-725, n.
621	62.1-129.1
622	62.1-129.2
623	53.1-129
624	23-4.3:2
625	2.2-2705
626	2.2-3711
627	55-471
628	55-453
629	4.1-324, 4.1-325
630	59.1-284.20—59.1-284.22
631	54.1-1129
632	15.2-953
633	2.2-3705.6, 2.2-3711
634	46.2-725, n.
635	15.2-2201
636	16.1-299
637	2.2-519, 2.2-4806, 30-133
638	9.1-138—9.1-140, 9.1-140.1, 9.1-143
639	56-600—56-602
640	55-225.3, 55-225.4, 55-225.6—55-225.9, 55-248.4, 55-248.6, 55-248.11:2, 55-248.13, 55-248.16, 55-248.18:2
641	32.1-37.2, 32.1-45.2, 54.1-2403.01
642	58.1-2606
643	2.2-1514, 10.1-2128, 10.1-2128.1, 10.1-2129, 10.1-2132, 10.1-2134
644	19.2-194, 19.2-207, 19.2-212, 19.2-215.4
645	15.2-6016—15.2-6024
646	10.1-1422.6
647	46.2-808.1, 46.2-1217, 46.2-2810, 46.2-2814, 46.2-2814.1
648	15.2-6016—15.2-6024
649	2.2-515.1, n., 2.2-515.2
650	24.2-947.7, 24.2-948.2
651	56-585.2, 67-202, 67-202.1
652	46.2-755.1, n., 46.2-755.2, n., 46.2-1167.1, n., 58.1-605, n., 58.1-606, n., 58.1-802.1, n., 58.1-2402.1, n., 58.1-3825.1, n.
653	2.2-2666.3, n.
654	2.2-2101, 2.2-2532—2.2-2535
655	10.1-1618, n.
656	33.1-23.03:1, n., 46.2-206.1R,

ACTS 2008 Chapter	Code 1950 Section
	46.2-395, n., 46.2-411, n.
657	33.1-23.03:1, n.,
	46.2-206.1R,
	46.2-395, n., 46.2-411, n.
659	2.2-2101,
	2.2-2532—2.2-2536
660	32.1-111.5,
	32.1-111.8
661	22.1-253.13:1
662	63.2-1234
663	22.1-238,
	22.1-239,
	22.1-240R,
	22.1-241—22.1-243,
	22.1-244—22.1-251R,
	22.1-253R
664	32.1-102.1
665	2.2-3705.4
666	64.1-157
667	56-575.17
668	2.2-3705.3, 2.2-3711
669	22.1-212.22
670	23-38.12, n.,
	23-38.15, n.
671	32.1-245
672	2.2-4002,
	54.1-3314.1
674	54.1-2901,
	54.1-3001, 54.1-3202,
	54.1-3301, 54.1-3801
676	2.2-1150.1,
	2.2-1150.2, 2.2-1151
677	30-28.16
678	16.1-281—16.1-282.1
679	2.2-2674.01
680	30-231.3, 30-231.8
681	18.2-513
682	24.2-802
684	46.2-300
685	47.1-15
686	3.1-106.4:2, 3.2-3602.1
688	8.01-226.8, 33.1-12.2
689	2.2-203,
	2.2-905, 2.2-906R,
	2.2-2455, 2.2-2456,
	2.2-3705.3, 2.2-3705.6,
	18.2-340.15, 18.2-340.16,
	18.2-340.25, 19.2-389,
	58.1-3, 58.1-4019.1
690	2.2-1150.1,
	2.2-1150.2, 2.2-1151
691	3.1-383,
	3.1-796.93:1,
	3.1-796.116,
	3.1-796.126:10,
	3.2-6540,
	3.2-6552,
	3.2-6583, 8.01-126,
	8.01-537, 8.01-540,
	15.2-1704, 15.2-1710,
	16.1-135, 19.2-5,
	19.2-30R,
	19.2-34—19.2-39,
	19.2-41R,
	19.2-43, 19.2-44,
	19.2-45—19.2-46.1,
	19.2-48, 19.2-48.1,
	19.2-77, 19.2-81.3,
	19.2-119, 19.2-152.4:3,
	20-70, 20-84,
	27-32—27-32.2,
	27-37.1, 37.2-808,
	37.2-809, 37.2-1103,
	37.2-1104, 43-29,
	46.2-104, 49-6,
	55-205, 55-230,
	59.1-98, 59.1-106
692	17.1-278
694	54.1-3408
695	58.1-3211,
	58.1-3211.1
696	54.1-2983,
	54.1-2985,
	54.1-2994—54.1-2996
697	20-108.2
698	2.2-214.2—2.2-214.4
699	20-104
700	63.2-913,
	63.2-1220.1
701	2.2-1514,
	10.1-2128,
	10.1-2128.1, 10.1-2129,
	10.1-2132, 10.1-2134
702	2.2-4311.1
703	24.2-629
704	19.2-215.1
705	22.1-98.2
706	16.1-106.1,
	16.1-107, 16.1-298
707	3.1-796.113,
	3.1-796.122,
	3.1-796.124,
	3.1-796.125R,
	3.2-6570,
	3.2-6571,
	3.2-6572,
	18.2-403.2
708	46.2-725, n.
710	2.2-2523R
711	15.2-961.1
712	30-279, 30-280
713	49-3
714	46.2-1098
715	46.2-1242
716	46.2-1143
717	15.2-2244
718	15.2-2201,
	15.2-2241, 15.2-2260,
	15.2-2269
719	60.2-618
720	15.2-2286
721	2.2-3705.2, 2.2-3711
722	46.2-1158.1
723	23-7.4, 23-7.4:2
725	60.2-602
726	18.2-370.3
727	15.2-2209
728	37.2-809
729	18.2-266.1
730	15.2-5152, n.
731	56-575.1
732	18.2-386.1
733	15.2-2303
735	46.2-325,
	46.2-335, 46.2-341.14
736	2.2-3705.6
737	19.2-81, 46.2-888
738	18.2-112.1
739	2.2-3705.7
740	30-293—30-300
741	54.1-2131, 54.1-2133
742	18.2-308
743	2.2-3705.6, 2.2-3711
744	2.2-2279,
	2.2-2285, 2.2-2290
745	2.2-2699.1
746	52-28.1
747	9.1-902
748	19.2-9.1
749	16.1-69.55, 17.1-213
750	20-124.7—20-124.10
751	18.2-308.1:3,
	19.2-169.2, 37.2-814,
	37.2-819
752	18.2-308.2
753	46.2-602.2,
	46.2-1548, 46.2-1549,
	46.2-1550, 58.1-2403
754	2.2-2001.1,
	37.2-304, 51.5-14
755	18.2-112.1
756	18.2-62
757	19.2-316.3
758	2.2-3705.3,
	3.1-336.4, 3.1-336.5,
	3.1-336.5:1, 3.1-336.7,
	3.1-336.7:1, 3.1-336.8,
	3.1-336.10, 3.1-336.13:1,
	3.1-336.15:1, 3.2-4205,
	3.2-4206, 3.2-4206.1,
	3.2-4208, 3.2-4208.1,
	3.2-4209, 3.2-4212,
	3.2-4215.1,
	3.2-4217.1
759	59.1-92.2,
	59.1-92.12, 59.1-92.13
760	19.2-163
761	19.2-316.2
762	19.2-299.2
763	53.1-31.2

ACTS 2008 Chapter	Code 1950 Section
764	58.1-609.3
765	4.1-230
766	15.2-1511.01
767	2.2-2001, 2.2-4310
768	2.2-2001, 2.2-2004, 2.2-2452, 2.2-2681, 2.2-2682, 2.2-2715, 2.2-2716
769	19.2-8
770	13.1-753, 13.1-769, 13.1-915, 13.1-931, 13.1-1046, 13.1-1056, 13.1-1234, 13.1-1246, 50-73.49, 50-73.58
771	9.1-102, 9.1-1300, 9.1-1301, 19.2-81.4R
772	9.1-902, 18.2-370.6
773	46.2-817
774	16.1-336, 16.1-339
775	37.2-808
776	16.1-341
777	15.2-2286
779	19.2-169.6, 19.2-176, 19.2-177.1, 37.2-808, 37.2-809, 37.2-813, 37.2-815—37.2-817, 53.1-40.2
780	37.2-817
781	18.2-370.5
782	16.1-337, 19.2-169.6, 32.1-127.1:03, 37.2-804.2, 37.2-808, 37.2-809, 37.2-817
783	16.1-338—16.1-341
784	37.2-808
785	58.1-3
786	8.01-389
787	2.2-2235
788	18.2-308.1:1, 18.2-308.1:3, 19.2-169.2, 37.2-814, 37.2-819
789	2.2-3701, 2.2-3708, 2.2-3714
790	15.2-2305
791	18.2-239, 59.1-200
792	52-48, 52-49
793	37.2-808, 37.2-809, 37.2-817
794	4.1-225, 4.1-226, 4.1-325
795	19.2-13
796	19.2-169.3
797	18.2-198.1
798	16.1-309.1
799	15.2-2232, n.
800	59.1-92.2, 59.1-92.12, 59.1-92.13
801	18.2-186.6
802	32.1-102.3:2, n.
803	15.2-5370
804	16.1-69.45, 16.1-69.46
805	19.2-270.4
806	37.2-818
807	16.1-339, 16.1-341, 16.1-343
808	16.1-338—16.1-341
809	20-124.3:1R
810	19.2-182.7—19.2-182.9
811	46.2-817
812	19.2-130
813	17.1-107
814	17.1-223, 47.1-5, 47.1-8, 47.1-9, 47.1-13, 47.1-13.1, 47.1-14, 47.1-16, 47.1-28, 55-106.2
815	19.2-163.01, 19.2-163.01:1
816	1-210
817	64.1-157
818	46.2-921.1
819	8.01-417
820	59.1-443.2
822	55-401—55-406, 55-411, 55-414
823	8.01-446, 8.01-446.1, 8.01-449, 17.1-223, 17.1-225, 17.1-226, 17.1-227.1, 17.1-228, 17.1-244, 17.1-249, 17.1-258.3, 17.1-258.3:1, 17.1-258.4, 17.1-276, 17.1-295
824	23-38.90
825	24.2-945.2, 24.2-955, 24.2-955.2
826	22.1-253.13:1, n., Const., Art. 8, § 2, n.
827	19.2-291.1, 22.1-253.13:7, 22.1-298.1, 22.1-313, 63.2-1503
828	37.2-809
829	23-38.90
830	55-401—55-406, 55-411, 55-414
831	22.1-253.13:1, n., Const., Art. 8, § 2, n.
833	8.01-446, 8.01-446.1, 8.01-449, 17.1-223, 17.1-225, 17.1-226, 17.1-227.1, 17.1-228, 17.1-244, 17.1-249, 17.1-258.3, 17.1-258.3:1, 17.1-258.4, 17.1-276, 17.1-295
834	19.2-120.1
835	10.1-1141
836	46.2-2801, 46.2-2809, 46.2-2812, 46.2-2814, 46.2-2819, 46.2-2820, 46.2-2824
837	59.1-21.15:1
838	33.1-23.03:10, 56-565
839	58.1-3823
840	2.2-3801, 2.2-3808, 2.2-3809, 16.1-77
841	56-542
842	18.2-239, 59.1-200
843	2.2-3801, 2.2-3808, 2.2-3809, 16.1-77
844	56-542
845	8.01-271.1, 16.1-260, 16.1-278.15, 54.1-3900, 63.2-1901
846	53.1-153
848	46.2-755.2
849	6.1-453.1, 6.1-459—6.1-461, 6.1-467, 6.1-469, 6.1-469.1
850	16.1-337, 19.2-169.6, 19.2-176, 19.2-177.1, 32.1-127.1:03, 37.2-800, 37.2-804.2, 37.2-808, 37.2-809, 37.2-813, 37.2-814, 37.2-815, 37.2-816, 37.2-817, 37.2-817.1, 37.2-817.2, 37.2-817.3, 37.2-817.4, 37.2-818, 37.2-821, 53.1-40.2
851	54.1-2105.1, 54.1-2130, 54.1-2345—54.1-2354, 55-79.41, 55-79.58, 55-79.58:1, 55-79.74, 55-79.79, 55-79.81, 55-79.84:1, 55-79.86, 55-79.89, 55-79.93:1, 55-79.95, 55-79.97, 55-79.97:1, 55-79.97:2, 55-79.97:3, 55-362, 55-362.1, 55-374.1, 55-374.2, 55-375, 55-392.1, 55-484, 55-487, 55-496, 55-504.1, 55-508, 55-509, 55-509.2, 55-509.3,

ACTS 2008 Chapter	Code 1950 Section
	55-509.4—55-509.10,
	55-510,
	55-511R, 55-512R,
	55-513, 55-513.1,
	55-514, 55-514.2,
	55-516.1, 55-528,
	55-529, 55-530,
	55-530.1
852	3.1-796.66,
	3.1-796.71:1,
	3.1-796.77:1—3.1-796.77:6,
	3.1-796.104, 3.1-796.122:1,
	3.2-6500, n.,
	3.2-6507.1—3.2-6507.6,
	3.2-6511.1, 3.2-6555,
	3.2-6570.1,
	58.1-3109
853	56-484.19, 56-484.23
854	18.2-308.1:1,
	18.2-308.2:2
855	15.2-2259,
	15.2-2260
856	23-276.1,
	23-276.10, 23-276.12
857	32.1-102.3:1,
	32.1-102.3:1.1
858	18.2-248.03
859	22.1-203.3
860	2.2-203.3,
	3.1-1 to 3.1-1114.1R,
	3.2-100 to 3.2-6590,
	10.1-217.1—10.1-217.6,
	10.1-559.1—10.1-559.11R,
	15.2-902
861	46.2-395
862	18.2-270.1
863	6.1-409, 6.1-414,
	6.1-423.1, 6.1-423.2,
	6.1-425, 6.1-428,
	6.1-430, 19.2-389,
	30-261
864	46.2-1122, n.,
	46.2-1139, n.,
	46.2-1144.1, n.,
	46.2-1149.3, n.
865	24.2-416.2, 24.2-418.1
866	46.2-214.3, 46.2-330
867	56-235.9
868	63.2-1201, 63.2-1201.1
869	18.2-308.1:1,
	18.2-308.2:2
870	16.1-337, 19.2-169.6,
	19.2-176, 19.2-177.1,
	32.1-127.1:03, 37.2-800,
	37.2-804.2, 37.2-808,
	37.2-809, 37.2-813,
	37.2-814, 37.2-815,
	37.2-816, 37.2-817,
	37.2-817.1—37.2-817.4,
	37.2-818, 37.2-821,
	53.1-40.2
871	54.1-2105.1,
	54.1-2130,
	54.1-2345—54.1-2354,
	55-79.41, 55-79.58,
	55-79.58:1, 55-79.74,
	55-79.79, 55-79.81,
	55-79.84:1, 55-79.86,
	55-79.89, 55-79.93:1,
	55-79.95, 55-79.97,
	55-79.97:1, 55-79.97:2,
	55-79.97:3, 55-362,
	55-362.1, 55-374.1,
	55-374.2, 55-375,
	55-392.1, 55-484,
	55-487, 55-496,
	55-504.1, 55-508,
	55-509, 55-509.2,
	55-509.3,
	55-509.4—55-509.10,
	55-510, 55-511R,
	55-512R, 55-513,
	55-513.1, 55-514,
	55-514.2, 55-516.1,
	55-528, 55-529,
	55-530, 55-530.1
872	2.2-2715, 2.2-2716
873	22.1-323.2,
	37.2-408, 37.2-408.1,
	63.2-1737, 66-24
874	18.2-248.03
875	4.1-100, 4.1-209,
	4.1-324, 4.1-325
876	6.1-453.1,
	6.1-459—6.1-461,
	6.1-467, 6.1-469,
	6.1-469.1, 6.1-453.1
877	9.1-902, 9.1-908,
	9.1-910
878	55-59.1:1
879	2.2-204, n.,
	2.2-219, n.,
	2.2-221.1, n.,
	2.2-228, n.,
	2.2-409, n.,
	2.2-518, n.,
	2.2-800, n.,
	2.2-803, n.,
	2.2-1104, n.,
	2.2-1149, n.,
	2.2-1155, n.,
	2.2-1156, n.,
	2.2-1204, n.,
	2.2-1502.1, n.,
	2.2-1505, n.,
	2.2-1508, n.,
	2.2-1802, n.,
	2.2-1819, n.,
	2.2-1829, n.,
	2.2-2005, n.,
	2.2-2031, n.,
	2.2-2221, n.,
	2.2-2221.1, n.,
	2.2-2318, n.,
	2.2-2402, n.,
	2.2-2457, n.,
	2.2-2458, n.,
	2.2-2670, n.,
	2.2-2675, n.,
	2.2-2723, n.,
	2.2-2818, n.,
	2.2-4000, n.,
	2.2-4011, n.,
	2.2-4300, n.,
	2.2-4301, n.,
	2.2-4400, n.,
	2.2-4401, n.,
	2.2-4803, n.,
	2.2-4806, n.,
	2.2-5206, n.,
	2.2-5209, n.,
	2.2-5211, n.,
	3.1-336.1, n.,
	3.1-336.2, n.,
	3.1-336.3, n.,
	3.1-361, n.,
	3.2-4201, n.,
	4.1-116, n.,
	5.1-1.6, n.,
	8.01-195.1, n.,
	8.01-384.1:1, n.,
	9.1-102, n.,
	9.1-165, n.,
	9.1-166, n.,
	9.1-168, n.,
	10.1-202, n.,
	10.1-552, n.,
	10.1-1124, n.,
	10.1-1176, n.,
	10.1-1188, n.,
	10.1-1190, n.,
	10.1-2128, n.,
	10.1-2202.1, n.,
	10.1-2211, n.,
	10.1-2213, n.,
	10.1-2213.1, n.,
	10.1-2500, n.,
	13.1-775.1, n.,
	15.2-1302, n.,
	15.2-1605, n.,
	15.2-1608, n.,
	15.2-1609.1, n.,
	15.2-1609.2, n.,
	15.2-1609.7, n.,
	15.2-1612.1, n.,
	15.2-1627.1, n.,
	15.2-1628, n.,
	15.2-1629, n.,
	15.2-1630, n.,
	15.2-1631, n.,

ACTS 2008 Chapter	Code 1950 Section
	15.2-1634, n.,
	15.2-1636.8, n.,
	15.2-4100, n.,
	16.1-266, n.,
	16.1-273, n.,
	16.1-287, n.,
	16.1-309.2, n.,
	16.1-309.7, n.,
	16.1-322.1, n.,
	17.1-278, n.,
	17.1-279, n.,
	17.1-283, n.,
	17.1-287, n.,
	17.1-327, n.,
	18.2-308, n.,
	18.2-308.2:2, n.,
	18.2-340.31, n.,
	19.2-152.4, n.,
	19.2-163, n.,
	19.2-163.01, n.,
	19.2-298.01, n.,
	19.2-316.3, n.,
	19.2-326, n.,
	19.2-349, n.,
	19.2-368.11:1, n.,
	19.2-386.14, n.,
	19.2-389, n.,
	22.1-18.01, n.,
	22.1-101.1, n.,
	22.1-205, n.,
	22.1-253.13:1, n.,
	22.1-290.01, n.,
	23-7.4:1, n.,
	23-7.4:2, n.,
	23-9.2:3.03, n.,
	23-9.2:3.1, n.,
	23-9.6:1, n.,
	23-9.9, n.,
	23-30.23, n.,
	23-30.28, n.,
	23-38.3, n.,
	23-38.12, n.,
	23-38.14, n.,
	23-38.77, n.,
	23-164.8, n.,
	23-215, n.,
	23-220.01, n.,
	23-227, n.,
	23-253.1, n.,
	23-276.10, n.,
	28.2-245, n.,
	28.2-542, n.,
	28.2-550, n.,
	30-58.3, n.,
	30-266, n.,
	32.1-50, n.,
	32.1-163, n.,
	32.1-171.1, n.,
	32.1-273.1, n.,
	32.1-323, n.,
	32.1-325.1, n.,
	32.1-325.1:1, n.,
	32.1-330.1, n.,
	32.1-331.12, n.,
	32.1-347, n.,
	32.1-352, n.,
	33.1-23.03:2, n.,
	33.1-23.03:8, n.,
	33.1-23.1, n.,
	33.1-23.3, n.,
	33.1-23.5:1, n.,
	33.1-41.1, n.,
	33.1-75.3, n.,
	35.1-13, n.,
	35.1-14, n.,
	35.1-16, n.,
	35.1-17, n.,
	36-139, n.,
	37.2-203, n.,
	37.2-319, n.,
	37.2-500, n.,
	37.2-504, n.,
	37.2-808, n.,
	37.2-900, n.,
	37.2-904, n.,
	38.2-401, n.,
	40.1-49.4, n.,
	44-146.28, n.,
	46.2-205, n.,
	46.2-212.1, n.,
	46.2-342, n.,
	46.2-694, n.,
	46.2-710, n.,
	46.2-1167, n.,
	51.1-124.3, n.,
	51.1-124.30, n.,
	51.1-142.2, n.,
	51.1-155.1, n.,
	51.1-203, n.,
	51.1-214, n.,
	51.1-303, n.,
	51.1-1100, n.,
	51.1-1103, n.,
	51.1-1401, n.,
	51.1-1403, n.,
	51.5-39.7, n.,
	51.5-106, n.,
	52-1, n.,
	52-4.3, n.,
	52-8.1:1, n.,
	52-12, n.,
	52-28, n.,
	53.1-5, n.,
	53.1-20, n.,
	53.1-20.1, n.,
	53.1-45, n.,
	53.1-67.1, n.,
	53.1-68, n.,
	53.1-80, n.,
	53.1-82.3, n.,
	53.1-120, n.,
	54.1-3041, n.,
	54.1-3913, n.,
	54.1-3916, n.,
	54.1-3919, n.,
	54.1-3924, n.,
	55-66.6, n.,
	55-297, n.,
	56-232, n.,
	56-234, n.,
	56-484.12, n.,
	56-484.13, n.,
	58.1-339.4, n.,
	58.1-353, n.,
	58.1-439.2, n.,
	58.1-600, n.,
	58.1-602, n.,
	58.1-608.3, n.,
	58.1-638, n.,
	58.1-638.1, n.,
	58.1-801, n.,
	58.1-803, n.,
	58.1-815.1, n.,
	58.1-816.1, n.,
	58.1-1402, n.,
	58.1-1410, n.,
	58.1-1803, n.,
	58.1-2402, n.,
	58.1-2425, n.,
	58.1-2510, n.,
	58.1-3221.3, n.,
	58.1-3523, n.,
	58.1-3524, n.,
	58.1-4022, n.,
	59.1-282.1, n.,
	59.1-282.2, n.,
	59.1-284.13, n.,
	59.1-364, n.,
	59.1-392, n.,
	60.2-305, n.,
	60.2-315, n.,
	62.1-44.15, n.,
	62.1-128, n.,
	62.1-140, n.,
	63.2-222, n.,
	63.2-401, n.,
	63.2-605, n.,
	63.2-611, n.,
	63.2-612, n.,
	63.2-619, n.,
	63.2-1706, n.,
	63.2-1735, n.,
	63.2-1907, n.,
	66-15, n.,
	66-20, n.,
880	24.2-101, 24.2-700, 24.2-701, 24.2-703.1, 24.2-703.2, 24.2-704, 24.2-705, 24.2-705.1

ACTS 2008 Chapter	Code 1950 Section
881	67-700, 67-701
882	30-301—30-308
883	30-201, 30-202, 30-205, 30-208R, 30-209, 56-576, 56-579, 56-582, 56-592, 56-592.1, 56-596, 58.1-3814, 67-101, 67-202
884	19.2-123

ACTS 2008, Sp. Sess. I

ACTS 2008, Sp. Sess. I Chapter	Code 1950 Section
1	2.2-1503.2R, 2.2-1509.1, 2.2-1514, 2.2-1515—2.2-1520, 2.2-2260, 23-30.28
2	2.2-1503.2R, 2.2-1509.1, 2.2-1514, 2.2-1515—2.2-1520, 2.2-2260, 23-30.28

ACTS 2008, Sp. Sess. II

ACTS 2008, Sp. Sess. II Chapter	Code 1950 Section
3	33.1-69
4	46.2-743
5	33.1-12
6	33.1-221.1:8, n.
7	46.2-633
8	15.2-2404
9	54.1-1141, n.
11	60.2-611

ACTS 2009

ACTS 2009 Chapter	Code 1950 Section
1	46.2-373
2	58.1-301
3	58.1-301
4	58.1-344.3
6	51.1-138
7	58.1-608.3
8	29.1-529
9	28.2-226.2, 28.2-227—28.2-228.1, 28.2-241, 28.2-301, 28.2-302, 28.2-302.2, 28.2-302.2:1, 28.2-302.6—28.2-302.10:1, 28.2-315, 28.2-402, 28.2-502, 28.2-504, 28.2-702, 29.1-300.4, 29.1-302—29.1-305, 29.1-306, 29.1-307, 29.1-309—29.1-310, 29.1-310.2—29.1-312, 29.1-318, 29.1-339.2, 29.1-343
10	58.1-439.18, 58.1-439.20
11	29.1-530.1
12	58.1-512
13	58.1-3819
14	62.1-198, 62.1-199
15	58.1-339.7
16	58.1-3825.2
17	58.1-3852
18	10.1-603.3
19	45.1-394
20	4.1-325
21	19.2-182.9, 37.2-808, 37.2-815—37.2-817, 37.2-819
22	51.1-162, 51.1-165.1, 51.1-207, 51.1-218
23	51.1-1401
24	58.1-202, 58.1-609.11, 58.1-609.12
25	58.1-3374
26	32.1-368, 32.1-369, 58.1-344.3
27	10.1-1400
28	28.2-307
29	63.2-1704
30	58.1-3321
31	58.1-3819
32	63.2-1529R
33	51.1-900R
34	58.1-331R, 58.1-431R, 58.1-439.3R, 58.1-439.7, 58.1-439.8R, 58.1-490
35	58.1-20R
36	58.1-609.10
37	58.1-390.2, 58.1-400.1, 58.1-400.3
38	62.1-132.20
39	53.1-10
40	58.1-3506
41	58.1-344.3
42	62.1-44.19:3, 62.1-44.19:3.4
43	10.1-1107
44	58.1-3506
45	29.1-315.1
46	2.2-1518, n.
47	58.1-608.3
48	54.1-3408
50	29.1-304
51	2.2-720
52	33.1-23.3
53	10.1-2211
54	46.2-334.01
55	23-9.6:1
56	23-9.6:1
58	22.1-296.4
59	32.1-176.3, 32.1-176.5
60	46.2-1930, 46.2-1930.1, 46.2-1930.2, 46.2-1992.23, 46.2-1992.23:1, 46.2-1992.23:2, 46.2-1993.23, 46.2-1993.23:1, 46.2-1993.23:2
61	63.2-617
62	2.2-2001
63	46.2-2809, 46.2-2826
64	2.2-4403—2.2-4405
65	33.1-250R
66	2.2-3309.1, 2.2-3310, 22.1-17.4
67	32.1-102.1
68	46.2-916.2
69	55-509.10
70	22.1-277
71	18.2-272
72	23-80R
73	33.1-221.1:1.1
74	46.2-873.1
75	2.2-1124
76	17.1-276
77	46.2-328
78	36-4, 36-4.1
79	46.2-1012
80	16.1-281, 16.1-282
81	22.1-243
82	2.2-2203
83	54.1-2900, 54.1-2956.8:1, 54.1-2956.8:2
84	22.1-212.1:1
85	2.2-4007.2
86	2.2-203.1, 2.2-2007, 2.2-2024, 2.2-2651R
87	2.2-2010
88	54.1-2103
89	54.1-2708.2

ACTS 2009 Chapter	Code 1950 Section
90	2.2-2690—2.2-2694R
91	51.1-138
92	46.2-1129.1
93	58.1-608.3
94	19.2-3.1
95	58.1-812
96	32.1-45.1
97	32.1-163.6
98	16.1-277.01, 16.1-277.02, 16.1-278.3, 16.1-283.1, 63.2-1228.1, 63.2-1228.2
99	54.1-2722
100	54.1-3434.02
101	54.1-3301
102	46.2-341.18:01
103	28.2-104
104	22.1-90
105	32.1-176.4
106	58.1-609.11
107	3.2-4104, 3.2-6543
108	44-121R
109	54.1-3411.1
110	32.1-46.02, 54.1-3408
111	37.2-400
112	16.1-345, 37.2-808, 37.2-810, 37.2-817.2, 37.2-829, 37.2-830R
113	33.1-62, n.
114	54.1-3411.1
115	46.2-1157
116	58.1-3819
117	46.2-2812, 46.2-2814, 46.2-2819, 46.2-2820, 46.2-2824
118	46.2-1044
119	22.1-213.1
120	33.1-223.2:21
121	18.2-340.16, 18.2-340.23, 18.2-340.24
122	4.1-111
123	2.2-4303
124	63.2-906, 63.2-910
125	63.2-1903, 63.2-1931
127	63.2-805
128	32.1-5
129	15.2-3201
131	15.2-2419—15.2-2429
132	37.2-815
133	54.1-3041, n., 54.1-3042, n., 54.1-3043, n., 54.1-3408, n.
134	2.2-2458, 2.2-2458.1
135	4.1-227
136	2.2-2002, 2.2-2002.1
137	55-248.25:1
138	16.1-305
139	19.2-327.2, 19.2-327.3, 19.2-327.5
140	6.1-2.21:1, 6.1-2.22
141	36-85.28, 36-85.31, 36-85.32
142	59.1-369, 59.1-376.1R
144	2.2-220.2
145	1-510
148	13.1-559, 13.1-560, 13.1-563, 13.1-565, 13.1-566
149	54.1-3423, 54.1-3425R, 54.1-3801
150	65.2-804
151	2.2-5100
152	58.1-390.2, 58.1-400.1, 58.1-400.3
153	15.2-2820—15.2-2833, 15.2-2800—15.2-2810R, 18.2-511.1, n.
154	15.2-2820—15.2-2833, 15.2-2800—15.2-2810R, 18.2-511.1
157	24.2-228.1
158	54.1-2523, 54.1-2523.2, 54.1-2526
159	23-290.1
160	47.1-6.1, 47.1-7, 47.1-16, 59.1-489, n.
162	54.1-2523, 54.1-2523.2, 54.1-2526
163	8.01-241
164	46.2-2812, 46.2-2814, 46.2-2819, 46.2-2820, 46.2-2824
166	54.1-703.3
167	13.1-1046, 13.1-1050.3, 13.1-1056, 13.1-1056.2, 13.1-1234, 13.1-1238.2, 13.1-1246, 13.1-1246.2, 50-73.49, 50-73.52:6, 50-73.58, 50-73.58:2
169	54.1-3423, 54.1-3425R, 54.1-3801
170	28.2-709
171	46.2-632, 46.2-1603
172	9.1-1100, n.
173	46.2-1569, 46.2-1571, 46.2-1573
174	2.2-5100
175	32.1-102.1—32.1-102.3:1, 32.1-102.3:2, 32.1-102.3:5, 32.1-102.4, 32.1-102.6, 32.1-102.10, 32.1-102.12, 32.1-122.06, 32.1-276.5
176	46.2-1569, 46.2-1571, 46.2-1573
180	2.2-203.2R, 2.2-225.1, 2.2-2817.1
181	1-219.1, n., 15.2-907.1, 36-3, 36-49.1:1, 36-105, 48-5, 58.1-3965, 58.1-3969
182	8.01-27.1
183	46.2-1224
184	36-105, 54.1-1102, 54.1-1134, 54.1-1140, 54.1-1142, 54.1-1142.1, 54.1-1142.2, 54.1-1143
185	46.2-633.1
186	46.2-1232
187	22.1-360, 22.1-361
188	46.2-1143, 46.2-1144.1, n., 46.2-1149.3, n.
189	6.1-422, 6.1-431
190	23-9.2:3.7
192	19.2-298
193	15.2-2241
194	15.2-2241, 15.2-2260
195	22.1-79.3
196	15.2-2209.1
197	6.1-74
198	15.2-958.2
199	15.2-4904
200	15.2-4904
201	13.1-1078, 13.1-1116
203	59.1-200.1
204	6.1-430, 6.1-430.1
205	18.2-254.1
206	15.2-2309
207	59.1-280, 59.1-548, 59.1-549, 59.1-282.1, 59.1-282.2R

ACTS 2009 Chapter	Code 1950 Section
208	22.1-277.2:1
209	10.1-546.1, 10.1-2128.1
210	2.2-208, 2.2-2101, 22.1-346, 22.1-346.1R, 22.1-346.2, 22.1-348, 22.1-349
211	37.2-801, 37.2-805.1, 37.2-1009, 54.1-2982, 54.1-2983, 54.1-2983.1—54.1-2983.3, 54.1-2984, 54.1-2985, 54.1-2985.1, 54.1-2986, 54.1-2986.1, 54.1-2986.2, 54.1-2987—54.1-2989, 54.1-2990—54.1-2992
212	8.01-390.1
213	2.2-3815, 2.2-3816
214	15.2-2263
215	38.2-231, 38.2-325, 38.2-2113, 38.2-3114, 38.2-2208, 38.2-2212
216	13.1-615, 13.1-630, 13.1-716, 13.1-720, 13.1-815, 13.1-829, 13.1-893.1, 13.1-896, 15.2-5109
217	8.9A-503
218	40.1-100
219	65.2-1201
220	32.1-163.6, 32.1-164, n.
221	55-453
222	22.1-279.8, 23-9.2:9, 32.1-111.3, 32.1-111.11, 44-146.18, 44-146.19
223	2.2-3705.7, 2.2-3711
224	11-7.1
225	9.1-140
226	38.2-3407.1
227	1-510
228	32.1-323.2
229	18.2-270
230	24.2-702.1
231	24.2-948.4, 24.2-949.9, 24.2-950.9, 24.2-951.9, 24.2-952.7
233	44-146.23
235	18.2-308
236	18.2-308.2
237	2.2-3705.3
238	4.1-210, n.
239	18.2-268.3
240	19.2-305
241	46.2-1163
242	18.2-460
243	2.2-2233.1
244	56-249.6
245	15.2-1716
246	2.2-2260, 2.2-2261, 2.2-2263, 2.2-3705.6, 30-309—30-312, 62.1-198, 62.1-199
247	2.2-2818, 2.2-2818.2
248	4.1-305
249	19.2-390
250	64.1-130
251	54.1-1141, n.
252	15.2-1215
253	6.1-2.7:1
254	55-66.3
255	18.2-272
256	6.1-2.26, 6.1-2.27
257	18.2-57
258	63.2-1716
259	30-275
260	16.1-277.01, 16.1-277.02, 16.1-278.3, 16.1-283.1, 63.2-1228.1, 63.2-1228.2
261	6.1-422, 6.1-431
262	54.1-2103, 55-526
263	10.1-546.1, 10.1-2128.1
264	58.1-3295
265	2.2-1839
266	37.2-804
267	2.2-5101
268	37.2-801, 37.2-805.1, 37.2-1009, 54.1-2982, 54.1-2983, 54.1-2983.1—54.1-2983.3, 54.1-2984, 54.1-2985, 54.1-2985.1, 54.1-2986, 54.1-2986.1, 54.1-2986.2, 54.1-2987—54.1-2989, 54.1-2990—54.1-2992
269	22.1-279.8, 23-9.2:9, 32.1-111.3, 32.1-111.11, 44-146.18, 44-146.19
270	8.01-413
271	59.1-280, 59.1-282.1, 59.1-282.2R, 59.1-548, 59.1-549
272	59.1-200.1
273	6.1-431.1—6.1-431.21
274	2.2-2648
275	2.2-2649
276	16.1-305.2, 66-25.2:1
277	18.2-423.2
278	19.2-8.1
279	4.1-227
280	15.2-2506, 22.1-93
281	18.2-254.1
282	51.1-138
283	15.2-2244
284	19.2-163
285	15.2-2703, 65.2-801, 65.2-1203
286	16.1-301
287	54.1-3935
288	18.2-308.6R
289	59.1-148.3
290	15.2-2306
291	19.2-45, 19.2-71, 19.2-72
292	4.1-209.1
293	45.1-361.43, 45.1-361.44
294	18.2-254.1
295	18.2-271.1
296	32.1-163.6, 32.1-164, n.
297	10.1-1152
299	38.2-3301.1
300	15.2-1129.1
301	2.2-2533
302	15.2-2403, 15.2-2403.2
303	32.1-323.2
304	2.2-5211
305	29.1-529
306	15.2-1512.2
307	55-59.1
308	16.1-305
309	10.1-560, 13.1-543, 13.1-549, 13.1-553, 13.1-1102, 13.1-1111, 15.2-851, 15.2-2263, 54.1-400, 54.1-401, 54.1-402.2, 54.1-403, 54.1-404.2, 54.1-405, 54.1-409—54.1-411, 54.1-2201
310	24.2-702.1
311	2.2-2260, 2.2-2261, 2.2-2263, 2.2-3705.6, 30-309—30-312, 30-310—30-312, 62.1-198, 62.1-199
312	17.1-294
313	18.2-57.3
314	18.2-186.3
315	15.2-2302
316	2.2-6000
317	2.2-2818, 2.2-2818.2
318	24.2-405, 24.2-406, 24.2-418, 24.2-444
319	15.2-908
320	19.2-327.2, 19.2-327.3, 19.2-327.5
321	15.2-969, 18.2-152.2, 59.1-200, 59.1-336

ACTS 2009 Chapter	Code 1950 Section
322	4.1-210, 4.1-320
323	9.1-1109
324	62.1-204
325	2.2-225, 2.2-225.1, 2.2-2218—2.2-2221, 2.2-2233.1, 2.2-2513—2.2-2517R, 2.2-3705.6, 2.2-3711, 23-4.4
326	2.2-3705.3
327	15.2-2223.1
328	54.1-703.3
329	28.2-1105—28.2-1107
330	56-265.4:4
331	56-463
332	8.01-512.4, 34-4.2
333	65.2-603.1
335	15.2-2404
336	15.2-2703, 65.2-801, 65.2-1203
337	62.1-44.33
338	58.1-609.10
339	2.2-703
340	2.2-3009—2.2-3014, 2.2-3705.3
341	19.2-152.8—19.2-152.10
342	54.1-2400.2
343	16.1-253.1, 16.1-279.1
344	19.2-45, 19.2-71, 19.2-72
345	24.2-706
346	6.1-370—6.1-374, 6.1-374.1, 6.1-374.2, 6.1-375, 6.1-377, 6.1-378, 6.1-378.2—6.1-378.4, 6.1-378.5—6.1-378.8
347	18.2-57.3
348	10.1-1402.02
349	10.1-104.3
350	58.1-3660.1
351	62.1-225
352	38.2-221.3
353	54.1-1706, 54.1-3202, 54.1-3204, 54.1-3301
354	3.2-6542
355	29.1-200
356	6.1-2.7:1
357	38.2-2217
358	54.1-300, 54.1-500—54.1-501, 54.1-516, 54.1-517.3—54.1-517.5
359	59.1-198, 59.1-200
361	62.1-44.19:14, n., 62.1-44.19:18, n.
362	51.1-142.2, 51.1-156, 51.1-162, 51.1-505
363	15.2-2288.01
364	10.1-603.8:1
365	10.1-1425.39
366	46.2-752
367	58.1-3713
368	2.2-2715
370	10.1-523
371	28.2-201
372	8.01-694
373	11-33.2
374	2.2-2235, 2.2-2238
375	9.1-138, 9.1-141, 9.1-143
376	15.2-969, 18.2-152.2, 59.1-200, 59.1-336
377	3.2-6540
378	19.2-70.3
379	18.2-374.1:1
380	18.2-186.3
381	19.2-368.5
382	54.1-2506.1, 54.1-3012.1
383	37.2-808
384	28.2-229
385	16.1-260
386	24.2-800
387	8.01-512.4, 34-4
388	8.01-512.4, 34-4.1
389	3.2-201
390	46.2-301
391	28.2-1408.2
392	10.1-104
393	9.1-403
394	32.1-102.3:2, n.
395	33.1-223.2:22
396	24.2-115.1, 24.2-604
399	11-34.3
400	15.2-1535, 37.2-603
401	56-585.3
402	15.2-977, 15.2-5101, 15.2-5114
403	24.2-110
404	2.2-2708, n.
405	24.2-700, 24.2-701, 24.2-706
406	59.1-444.2
407	24.2-103
408	15.2-2403, 15.2-2403.2
409	10.1-1422, 10.1-1422.01, 10.1-1422.05R
410	15.2-4838.1
411	67-101, 67-102
412	59.1-148.3
413	15.2-2316.1, 15.2-2316.2
414	8.01-52.1, 8.01-581.20:1
415	58.1-3833, 58.1-3840
416	15.2-2288.3
417	65.2-402.1
418	2.2-3705.2
419	46.2-216.1, 46.2-216.2R, 46.2-706.1, 58.1-2261
420	15.2-5139
421	55-66.3
422	46.2-931
423	2.2-5101
424	2.2-2696, 2.2-2905, 32.1-354—32.1-356, 32.1-359—32.1-361.1
425	32.1-137.01
426	58.1-402
427	2.2-2329
428	2.2-4118
429	15.2-6601
430	23-7.4:5
431	22.1-279.6
432	46.2-930
433	37.2-1007
434	23-9.3:1
435	15.2-3201
437	22.1-207.1
439	46.2-323, 46.2-334.001
440	22.1-132.2
441	22.1-212.8, 22.1-212.11
442	38.2-2114
443	8.01-487
444	30-231.01—30-231.3, 30-231.8
445	63.2-1530
446	15.2-901
447	23-7.4:6
448	22.1-238, n.
449	64.1-5.1
450	13.1-1002, 13.1-1015, 13.1-1016, 13.1-1018.1, 13.1-1055, 13.1-1065
451	22.1-207.2
452	6.1-423.1, 6.1-423.2R
453	6.1-431.1—6.1-431.21
454	8.01-419
455	16.1-336—16.1-339, 16.1-339.1, 16.1-340—16.1-342, 16.1-344, 16.1-345, 16.1-345.1, 16.1-345.2—16.1-345.5, 37.2-808, 37.2-809

ACTS 2009 Chapter	Code 1950 Section
456	46.2-1139
457	2.2-2821.2
459	22.1-79
460	15.2-4904
461	15.2-1736
462	15.2-908
463	22.1-253.13:3, n., 22.1-253.13:4, n.
464	15.2-5368, 15.2-5386
465	15.2-2244
467	62.1-73
468	22.1-214
469	15.2-2223.1, n.
470	23-7.4:2
471	15.2-7000—15.2-7021, 33.1-23.03:1, 33.1-287—33.1-288, 33.1-320R,
472	2.2-3705.5, 2.2-3711, 2.2-4002, 8.01-581.13, 54.1-113, 54.1-2400, 54.1-2400.2, 54.1-2505, 54.1-2515—54.1-2517, 54.1-2523, 54.1-2709.4
473	15.2-5101, 15.2-5108, 15.2-5114, 15.2-5115, 15.2-5125, 15.2-5132, 15.2-5133, 15.2-5136, 15.2-5141, 15.2-5142, 15.2-5147, 15.2-5148, 15.2-5152—15.2-5155, 15.2-5158, 15.2-5159
475	15.2-908
476	33.1-35, 33.1-84.1
477	55-277.4:1, 55-277.18, 55-277.29
478	32.1-45.1, 32.1-116.3
479	2.2-213.3, 54.1-3303, n.
480	58.1-3510, 58.1-3510.1—58.1-3510.3R, 58.1-3510.4—58.1-3510.7
481	15.2-926
482	22.1-291.1
483	15.2-4116
485	2.2-2699.1
486	4.1-225
488	22.1-253.13:1, n.
489	2.2-3310.3
490	22.1-253.13:4
491	19.2-215.1
492	24.2-404.3
494	24.2-604, 24.2-638
495	2.2-4301
496	58.1-339.7
497	58.1-3819
498	10.1-1402.02

ACTS 2009 Chapter	Code 1950 Section
499	58.1-608.3
501	58.1-3901
502	58.1-439.20
503	58.1-1834
504	46.2-916.2
505	32.1-271
506	54.1-2722, 54.1-3408
507	54.1-2900, 54.1-2956.8:1, 54.1-2956.8:2
508	58.1-322, 58.1-402
509	4.1-325
510	58.1-512
511	58.1-3321
512	58.1-3221.2
513	58.1-3819
514	46.2-1157
515	65.2-402
516	51.5-33
517	37.2-400
518	15.2-2263
519	2.2-2405
521	32.1-368, 32.1-369, 58.1-344.3
522	24.2-612
523	46.2-1158.1
524	58.1-3819
525	45.1-394
526	58.1-609.11
528	58.1-3508.3
529	58.1-3252
530	58.1-2250
531	58.1-1731—58.1-1733
532	58.1-1718.1, 58.1-1719, 58.1-1720, 58.1-1721R, 58.1-1722, 58.1-1723R
534	54.1-2400, 54.1-3029.1
535	46.2-1222.1
536	2.2-1508
537	2.2-1503
538	63.2-1606
540	56-529, 56-530
541	10.1-416
542	30-277R
543	62.1-198, 62.1-199
544	46.2-1232
545	38.2-2217
546	15.2-2288.3
547	63.2-617
548	2.2-2529
549	54.1-2987.1
550	2.2-608
551	1-219.1, n., 15.2-907.1, 36-3, 36-49.1:1, 36-105, 48-5, 58.1-3965, 58.1-3969,
552	32.1-45.1, 32.1-116.3

ACTS 2009 Chapter	Code 1950 Section
553	2.2-720
554	2.2-2696, 2.2-2905, 32.1-354—32.1-356, 32.1-359—32.1-361.1
555	16.1-336—16.1-339, 16.1-339.1, 16.1-340—16.2-342, 16.1-344, 16.1-345, 16.1-345.1, 16.1-345.2—16.1-345.5, 37.2-808, 37.2-809
556	15.2-4838.1
557	54.1-300, 54.1-2349, 54.1-2351, 54.1-2352, 55-79.2, 55-79.93:1, 55-399, 55-399.1, 55-504.1, 55-509.6, 55-516.1, 55-530.1
558	58.1-402
559	65.2-603.1
560	10.1-202.2
561	54.1-2722
562	2.2-4301
563	46.2-703
564	2.2-4301, 33.1-391.3
565	2.2-2279, 2.2-2280, 2.2-2289, 2.2-2291, 2.2-2292
566	13.1-521
567	58.1-2510
568	2.2-1839
569	2.2-2235, 2.2-2238
571	58.1-520, 58.1-530
572	10.1-1181.2
573	2.2-3802
574	58.1-811
575	67-600, 67-601, 67-602, 67-603, 67-604
576	46.2-2809, 46.2-2826
578	32.1-332— 32.1-342R, 32.1-351.1,
579	36-85.28, 36-85.31, 36-85.32
580	9.1-403
581	2.2-4300, n., 33.1-1, n., 56-535, n., 56-556, n.
582	8.01-328.1, 20-97
583	22.1-207.1
584	42.1-64
585	3.2-206
586	36-105, 54.1-1102, 54.1-1134, 54.1-1140, 54.1-1142, 54.1-1142.1, 54.1-1142.2, 54.1-1143
587	13.1-696, 13.1-875
588	64.1-57.3
589	2.2-2905
591	18.2-98

ACTS 2009 Chapter	Code 1950 Section
592	17.1-524R
593	55-82, 55-82.1
594	17.1-275, 19.2-353.3
595	46.2-1023
596	2.2-2905, 23-232
597	15.2-4904
598	23-231.15
599	10.1-1801.1
600	10.1-2140
601	62.1-69.29
602	38.2-1300
603	23-7.4:5
604	58.1-3852
605	15.2-2225, 15.2-2226
606	32.1-127.1:03, 37.2-804.2
607	37.2-808
608	37.2-803
609	15.2-1736
610	8.9A-503
611	58.1-1840.1
612	2.2-1130, 2.2-1131.1, 2.2-1136, 2.2-1146, 2.2-1153, 2.2-1154, 2.2-1156, 2.2-1157, 10.1-1122, 36-139.1
613	56-484.13, 56-484.15
614	2.2-2031
615	22.1-238, n.
616	15.2-6400
617	42.1-65, 42.1-70
618	19.2-392.2
619	2.2-220.2
620	4.1-119
621	53.1-10
622	8.01-506
623	19.2-3.1
624	2.2-4007.2
626	2.2-3704, 2.2-3704.1
627	10.1-1322.01, 62.1-44.15:02
628	2.2-3707
629	10.1-523
631	15.2-3201
632	62.1-198, 62.1-199
633	2.2-2699.1
634	2.2-3713, 8.01-644
635	33.1-72.1
636	15.2-2288.4
637	15.2-1129.1
638	33.1-464R
639	24.2-115
640	19.2-188
641	55-519
642	38.2-3723
643	38.2-233, 38.2-3724, 38.2-3729, 38.2-3735, 38.2-3737
644	38.2-1903.1

ACTS 2009 Chapter	Code 1950 Section
645	15.2-7022—15.2-7035
646	54.1-2957.03, 54.1-2957.9
647	37.2-814
648	29.1-103, 29.1-530.5, 29.1-530.5
649	15.2-1535
650	59.1-149, 59.1-151, 59.1-153, 59.1-155, 59.1-156, 59.1-163
651	32.1-127.1:03, 37.2-804.2
652	32.1-276.6
653	38.2-3100.3
655	15.2-5113
656	46.2-931
657	59.1-136.1
660	18.2-266.1
661	46.2-1078.1
662	18.2-47, 18.2-513
663	16.1-77, 36-105.1:1, 55-225.10, 55-248.13, 55-248.13:3, 55-248.15:2, 55-248.16, 55-248.18, 55-248.18:2, 55-248.32, 55-248.37
664	18.2-189, 43-32, 43-34, 46.2-208, 46.2-617, 46.2-633, 46.2-640, 46.2-644.01—46.2-644.03, 46.2-1200, 46.2-1202, 46.2-1202.1, 46.2-1204R, 46.2-1206, 46.2-1208R, 46.2-1600, 46.2-1601, 54.1-601, 55-417—55-419
665	55-510
666	16.1-81.1
667	19.2-389, 54.1-204, 54.1-2106.1, n.
668	18.2-371.4
669	19.2-82
670	2.2-229, 15.2-2232, 33.1-12, 33.1-23.03
671	58.1-3660
672	58.1-3901
673	63.2-1605
676	33.1-46.2
677	58.1-3221.3
678	63.2-914
679	46.2-743, 46.2-749.5
680	58.1-662
681	59.1-155.1
682	58.1-3967

ACTS 2009 Chapter	Code 1950 Section
683	58.1-662
684	20-124.3
686	58.1-812
687	54.1-2400.02, 54.1-3005
688	8.01-424
689	10.1-109, n.
690	2.2-229, 15.2-2232, 33.1-12, 33.1-23.03
691	46.2-633.1
692	58.1-3510, 58.1-3510.1—58.1-3510.3R, 58.1-3510.4—58.1-3510.7,
693	33.1-23.3
695	10.1-2132, 32.1-164
697	16.1-345, 37.2-808, 37.2-810, 37.2-817.2, 37.2-829, 37.2-830R
698	40.1-28.7:3
699	18.2-425.1R, 59.1-200, 59.1-518.1—58.1-518.4
700	59.1-198, 59.1-200
701	8.01-411—8.01-412.1R, 8.01-412.8—8.01-412.15
703	15.2-2114
704	62.1-44.19:14, n., 62.1-44.19:18, n.
705	63.2-100
706	20-60.3, 63.2-1916
707	30-170
708	37.2-801
709	10.1-603.4
710	32.1-176.4
711	32.1-102.4
712	2.2-2648
713	20-60.3, 20-103, 20-107.2, 20-108.1, 20-108.2, 20-124.2, 63.2-1900, 63.2-1902, 63.2-1903, 63.2-1916, 63.2-1924.1, 63.2-1954.1
714	8.01-399
715	9.1-102, 9.1-187—9.1-190
716	50-73.83, 50-73.132, 50-73.134, 50-73.135, 50-73.136, 50-73.137:1, 50-73.138
717	38.2-1329
718	15.2-978
719	2.2-703
720	15.2-6018, 15.2-6021
721	15.2-2286
722	46.2-931
723	17.1-276
725	19.2-56

ACTS 2009 Chapter	Code 1950 Section
726	4.1-305, 16.1-237, 16.1-260, 18.2-57.2
727	6.1-430, 6.1-430.1
728	40.1-29
729	16.1-106, 16.1-296
730	58.1-439.1
731	15.2-2316.1, 15.2-2316.2
732	16.1-253, 16.1-253.1, 16.1-253.4, 16.1-279.1, 19.2-152.8, 19.2-152.9, 19.2-152.10
733	2.2-614.2
734	15.2-2308
735	15.2-915
736	15.2-1507
737	2.2-4343, 23-44.1, 23-50.10:01, 23-122.1
738	15.2-1129.1
739	10.1-1618, n.
740	16.1-69.55, 16.1-300, 16.1-305, 37.2-900, 37.2-901, 37.2-902, 37.2-903, 37.2-904, 37.2-905, 37.2-905.1, 37.2-905.2, 37.2-906, 37.2-907, 37.2-908, 37.2-909, 37.2-911, 37.2-912, 37.2-913, 37.2-914, 37.2-918, 53.1-32
741	19.2-354
742	15.2-5102.1
743	46.2-916.3
744	56-585.2
745	56-235.1:1
746	1-222.1, 56-1, 56-88, 56-232, 56-265.1, 56-594.1
747	32.1-164
748	56-576
749	15.2-2109.3
750	18.2-248
751	24.2-626
752	10.1-1307.02
753	58.1-439
754	56-575.1
755	46.2-725, n., 46.2-749.49:1R
756	3.2-6521, 3.2-6536, 16.1-69.48:1, 17.1-275.7, 46.2-104, 46.2-752, 46.2-1157
757	2.2-1509.3, 2.2-2008
758	2.2-1115.1, 30-133
759	24.2-626
760	18.2-160.1
761	54.1-1706, 54.1-3202, 54.1-3204, 54.1-3301
762	56-575.1, 56-575.17, 56-575.18
763	13.1-1002, 13.1-1011, 13.1-1023, 13.1-1035, 13.1-1036, 13.1-1040.1, 13.1-1049.1, 13.1-1049.3, 13.1-1117
764	46.2-301
765	2.2-3705.6, 2.2-3711
766	28.2-1208
767	2.2-4343, 23-44.1, 23-50.10:01, 23-122.1
768	67-101, 67-102
769	2.2-614.2
770	58.1-3286, 58.1-3712
772	15.2-915
773	15.2-958.3
774	Const., Art. 10, § 8, n.
775	Const., Art. 10, § 6-A, n.
776	Const., Art. 10, § 6, n.
777	Const., Art. 10, § 6-A, n.
778	Const., Art. 10, § 6, n.
779	18.2-308
780	18.2-308
781	2.2-204, n.,
	2.2-219, n.,
	2.2-221.1, n.,
	2.2-228, n.,
	2.2-409, n.,
	2.2-518, n.,
	2.2-800, n.,
	2.2-803, n.,
	2.2-1149, n.,
	2.2-1155, n.,
	2.2-1156, n.,
	2.2-1204, n.,
	2.2-1502.1, n.,
	2.2-1505, n.,
	2.2-1508, n.,
	2.2-1802, n.,
	2.2-1819, n.,
	2.2-1829, n.,
	2.2-2005, n.,
	2.2-2031, n.,
	2.2-2221, n.,
	2.2-2221.1, n.,
	2.2-2233, n.,
	2.2-2318, n.,
	2.2-2402, n.,
	2.2-2457, n.,
	2.2-2458, n.,
	2.2-2670, n.,
	2.2-2675, n.,
	2.2-2723, n.,
	2.2-2813, n.,
	2.2-2818, n.,
	2.2-3204, n.,
	2.2-3205, n.,
	2.2-4000, n.,
	2.2-4011, n.,
	2.2-4401, n.,
	2.2-4300, n.,
	2.2-4301, n.,
	2.2-4400, n.,
	2.2-4401, n.,
	2.2-4800, n.,
	2.2-4803, n.,
	2.2-4805, n.,
	2.2-5206, n.,
	2.2-5209, n.,
	2.2-5211, n.,
	3.2-4200, n.,
	3.2-4204, n.,
	3.2-4201, n.,
	4.1-116, n.,
	5.1-1.26, n.,
	8.01-195.1, n.,
	8.01-384.1:1, n.,
	9.1-102, n.,
	9.1-165, n.,
	9.1-166, n.,
	9.1-168, n.,
	9.1-1100, n.,
	10.1-202, n.,
	10.1-552, n.,
	10.1-564, n.,
	10.1-603.19, n.,
	10.1-1124, n.,
	10.1-1176, n.,
	10.1-1188, n.,
	10.1-1190, n.,
	10.1-1422.01, n.,
	10.1-2128, n.,
	10.1-2128.1, n.,
	10.1-2129, n.,
	10.1-2132, n.,
	10.1-2202.1, n.,
	10.1-2211, n.,
	10.1-2213, n.,
	10.1-2213.1, n.,
	10.1-2500, n.,
	13.1-775.1, n.,
	15.2-540, n.,
	15.2-639, n.,
	15.2-848, n.,
	15.2-1302, n.,
	15.2-1605, n.,
	15.2-1608, n.,
	15.2-1634, n.,
	15.2-1636.8, n.,
	15.2-4100, n.,
	15.2-4526, n.,
	16.1-273, n.,
	16.1-287, n.,
	16.1-309.2, n.,

ACTS 2009 Chapter	Code 1950 Section
	16.1-309.7, n.,
	16.1-322.1, n.,
	17.1-279, n.,
	17.2-283, n.,
	17.1-327, n.,
	18.2-308, n.,
	18.2-308.2:2, n.,
	18.2-340.31, n.,
	19.2-152.4, n.,
	19.2-163, n.,
	19.2-163.01, n.,
	19.2-298.01, n.,
	19.2-316.3, n.,
	19.2-326, n.,
	19.2-349, n.,
	19.2-368.11:1, n.,
	19.2-386.14, n.,
	22.1-18.01, n.,
	22.1-100.1, n.,
	22.1-101.1, n.,
	22.1-175.5, n.,
	22.1-205, n.,
	22.1-253.13:1, n.,
	22.1-290.01, n.,
	23-7.4:1, n.,
	23-7.4:2, n.,
	23-9.2:3.03, n.,
	23-9.2:3.1, n.,
	23-9.6:1, n.,
	23-30.23, n.,
	23-30.28, n.,
	23-38.3, n.,
	23-38.12, n.,
	23-38.14, n.,
	23-38.77, n.,
	23-164.8, n.,
	23-215, n.,
	23-220.01, n.,
	23-227, n.,
	23-253.1, n.,
	23-276.10, n.,
	28.2-245, n.,
	28.2-542, n.,
	28.2-550, n.,
	30-19.1:4, n.,
	30-58.3, n.,
	30-232 to 30-239, n.,
	30-266, n.,
	30-267 to 30-276, n.,
	32.1-50, n.,
	32.1-163, n.,
	32.1-171.1, n.,
	32.1-218, n.,
	32.1-273.1, n.,
	32.1-323, n.,
	32.1-325.1, n.,
	32.1-325.1:1, n.,
	32.1-330.1, n.,
	32.1-331.12, n.,
	32.1-343, n.,
	32.1-347, n.,
	32.1-352, n.,
	33.1-23.03:2, n.,
	33.1-23.1, n.,
	33.1-23.3, n.,
	33.1-23.5:1, n.,
	33.1-41.1, n.,
	33.1-75.3, n.,
	35.1-13, n.,
	35.1-14, n.,
	35.1-16, n.,
	35.1-17, n.,
	36-139, n.,
	37.2-203, n.,
	37.2-316, n.,
	37.2-319, n.,
	37.2-500, n.,
	37.2-504, n.,
	37.2-605, n.,
	37.2-808, n.,
	37.2-900, n.,
	37.2-904, n.,
	38.2-401, n.,
	40.1-49.4, n.,
	44-146.28, n.,
	46.2-205, n.,
	46.2-212.1, n.,
	46.2-342, n.,
	46.2-694, n.,
	46.2-710, n.,
	46.2-1167, n.,
	51.1-124.3, n.,
	51.1-124.30, n.,
	51.1-142.2, n.,
	51.1-155.1, n.,
	51.1-203, n.,
	51.1-214, n.,
	51.1-303, n.,
	51.1-1100, n.,
	51.1-1103, n.,
	51.1-1109, n.,
	51.1-1110, n.,
	51.1-1111, n.,
	51.1-1112, n.,
	51.1-1122, n.,
	51.1-1123, n.,
	51.1-1401, n.,
	51.1-1403, n.,
	51.5-39.7, n.,
	51.5-47, n.,
	51.5-48, n.,
	51.5-106, n.,
	52-1, n.,
	52-4.3, n.,
	52-8.1:1, n.,
	52-12, n.,
	52-28, n.,
	53.1-5, n.,
	53.1-20, n.,
	53.1-45, n.,
	53.1-47, n.,
	53.1-67.1, n.,
	53.1-68, n.,
	53.1-80, n.,
	54.1-2700, n.,
	54.1-3041, n.,
	54.1-3913, n.,
	55-66.6, n.,
	55-297, n.,
	56-232, n.,
	56-234, n.,
	56-484.12, n.,
	56-484.13, n.,
	58.1-339.4, n.,
	58.1-353, n.,
	58.1-439.2, n.,
	58.1-520, n.,
	58.1-530, n.,
	58.1-600, n.,
	58.1-602, n.,
	58.1-608.3, n.,
	58.1-615.1,
	58.1-638, n.,
	58.1-638.1, n.,
	58.1-801, n.,
	58.1-803, n.,
	58.1-1402, n.,
	58.1-1410, n.,
	58.1-1803, n.,
	58.1-2402, n.,
	58.1-2425, n.,
	58.1-2510, n.,
	58.1-3221.3, n.,
	58.1-3523, n.,
	58.1-3524, n.,
	58.1-4022, n.,
	59.1-282.1, n.,
	59.1-284.13, n.,
	59.1-364, n.,
	59.1-392, n.,
	60.2-305, n.,
	60.2-315, n.,
	62.1-44.15, n.,
	62.1-128, n.,
	62.1-140, n.,
	63.2-401, n.,
	63.2-605, n.,
	63.2-611, n.,
	63.2-612, n.,
	63.2-619, n.,
	63.2-1706, n.,
	63.2-1735, n.,
	63.2-1907, n.,
	66-15, n.,
	66-20, n.,
782	15.2-2307
783	46.2-1530, 46.2-1542
784	6.1-330.78
785	22.1-205
786	15.2-2157

TABLE OF ACTS CODIFIED SUBSEQUENT TO 1948

ACTS 2009 Chapter	Code 1950 Section
787	58.1-520, 58.1-530
788	56-235.5
789	60.2-602, 60.2-610, 60.2-611
790	8.01-343
791	2.2-2822
792	22.1-209.1:2
793	17.1-279, 17.1-502
794	56-265.1, 56-265.4:6
795	46.2-908.1, 46.2-914
796	32.1-102.4, 38.2-3406.1, 38.2-3406.2, 38.2-3541.1, 38.2-4214, 38.2-4319
797	2.2-518, 2.2-4023, 2.2-4801, 2.2-4805, 2.2-4806, 8.01-220.2, 8.01-382, 17.1-276, 58.1-202, n.
798	59.1-284.23
799	15.2-958.4
800	58.1-3230
802	22.1-209.1:2, 22.1-225, 22.1-253.13:1
803	15.2-979
804	56-594
805	63.2-1201, 63.2-1202, 63.2-1203, 63.2-1204, 63.2-1209, 63.2-1212, 63.2-1221, 63.2-1222, 63.2-1225, 63.2-1230, 63.2-1233, 63.2-1250
806	2.2-4024, 46.2-2800, 46.2-2801, 46.2-2805, 46.2-2806, 46.2-2809, 46.2-2810R, 46.2-2814, 46.2-2816, 46.2-2818R, 46.2-2821, 46.2-2824R, 46.2-2825, 46.2-2825.1, 46.2-2825.2, 46.2-2825.3, 46.2-2825.4, 46.2-2827
807	56-15, 56-17, 56-259, 67-1100—67-1110
808	10.1-1197.5, n., 56-46.1, 56-580
809	24.2-649
810	2.2-225, 2.2-225.1, 2.2-2513—2.2-2517R, 2.2-2218, 2.2-2219, 2.2-2220, 2.2-2221, 2.2-2233.1, 2.2-3705.6, 2.2-3711, 23-4.4
811	54.1-2818.4
812	2.2-1115.1, 30-133
813	2.2-212, 2.2-213, 2.2-214, 2.2-223, 2.2-507, 2.2-704, 2.2-705, 2.2-1839, 2.2-2001.1, 2.2-2411, 2.2-2648, 2.2-2664, 2.2-2691, 2.2-2692, 2.2-2694, 2.2-2696, 2.2-2818, 2.2-2905, 2.2-3705.5, 2.2-4344, 2.2-5201, 2.2-5206, 2.2-5300, 4.1-305, 9.1-111, 9.1-901, 15.2-2291, 15.2-5386, 16.1-275, 16.1-278.8, 16.1-278.8:01, 16.1-280, 16.1-293.1, 16.1-336, 16.1-345, 16.1-356, 16.1-357, 16.1-361, 18.2-73, 18.2-74, 18.2-251, 18.2-251.01, 18.2-252, 18.2-254, 18.2-254.1, 18.2-258.1, 18.2-271.2, 18.2-308.1:1, 18.2-308.2:2, 19.2-169.1, 19.2-169.2, 19.2-169.3, 19.2-169.5, 19.2-175, 19.2-182.2, 19.2-182.13, 19.2-182.16, 19.2-264.3:1, 19.2-264.3:1.1, 19.2-264.3:1.2, 19.2-301, 19.2-302, 19.2-389, 19.2-390, 20-88, 22.1-7, 22.1-205, 22.1-209.2, 22.1-214.2, 22.1-214.3, 22.1-215, 22.1-217.1, 22.1-272.1, 23-38.2, 25.1-100, 29.1-313, 32.1-45.1, 32.1-64.1, 32.1-73.7, 32.1-102.1, 32.1-122.5, 32.1-124, 32.1-125.1, 32.1-127.1:03, 32.1-127.1:04, 32.1-135.2, 32.1-276.3, 32.1-276.8, 32.1-283, 32.1-283.1, 32.1-283.5, 32.1-325, 32.1-351.2, 37.2-100, 37.2-200, 37.2-300, 37.2-316, 37.2-317, 37.2-318, 37.2-319, 37.2-423, 37.2-716, 37.2-900, 37.2-900.1, 37.2-909, 37.2-912, 37.2-919, 37.2-1101, 38.2-3412.1, 38.2-3418.5, 46.2-400, 46.2-401, 46.2-1229, 51.5-1, 51.5-2, 51.5-14, 51.5-14.1, 51.5-31, 51.5-39.2, 51.5-39.7, 51.5-39.12, 53.1-32, 53.1-40.2, 53.1-136, 53.1-145, 54.1-2715, 54.1-2726, 54.1-2970, 54.1-2987.1, 54.1-3408, 54.1-3408.01, 54.1-3437.1, 54.1-3506, 56-484.19, 57-2.02, 57-60, 63.2-100, 63.2-1503, 63.2-1528, 63.2-1709, 63.2-1726, 63.2-1735, 63.2-1805
814	17.1-281
816	12.1-12, n.
817	15.2-1627.4
818	2.2-2699.3, 2.2-2699.4
819	54.1-500, 54.1-500.1, 54.1-501, 54.1-503, 54.1-512, 54.1-516, 54.1-517
821	58.1-408, 58.1-422
822	58.1-3221.3
824	56-231.15, n., 56-576, 56-585.1, 56-585.3
825	22.1-253.13:3
826	2.2-2005, 2.2-2033, 2.2-2034, 2.2-2457, 2.2-2458
827	2.2-3705.7, 2.2-3711, 23-9.2:3.03, 23-38.76, 23-38.77, 23-38.79, 23-38.79:1, 23-38.80, 23-38.87, 23-38.87:1, 23-38.88
829	32.1-163, 32.1-164.1:2,

ACTS 2009 Chapter	Code 1950 Section
	32.1-166.6
833	58.1-609.10
834	32.1-292.2,
	32.1-297.1,
	46.2-342, 58.1-344.3
835	46.2-916.3
836	58.1-608.3
837	54.1-3041, n.,
	54.1-3042, 54.1-3408, n.
838	19.2-182.9, 37.2-808,
	37.2-815, 37.2-816,
	37.2-817, 37.2-819
839	38.2-3418.15,
	38.2-4319
840	2.2-212, 2.2-213,
	2.2-214, 2.2-223,
	2.2-507, 2.2-704,
	2.2-705, 2.2-1839,
	2.2-2001.1, 2.2-2411,
	2.2-2648, 2.2-2664,
	2.2-2691, 2.2-2692,
	2.2-2694, 2.2-2696,
	2.2-2818, 2.2-2905,
	2.2-3705.5, 2.2-4344,
	2.2-5201, 2.2-5206,
	2.2-5300,
	4.1-305, 9.1-111,
	9.1-901, 15.2-2291,
	15.2-5386, 16.1-275,
	16.1-278.8,
	16.1-278.8:01,
	16.1-280, 16.1-293.1,
	16.1-336, 16.1-345,
	16.1-356, 16.1-357,
	16.1-361, 18.2-73,
	18.2-74, 18.2-251,
	18.2-251.01, 18.2-252,
	18.2-254, 18.2-254.1,
	18.2-258.1,
	18.2-271.2,
	18.2-308.1:1,
	18.2-308.2:2,
	19.2-169.1, 19.2-169.2,
	19.2-169.3, 19.2-169.5,
	19.2-175, 19.2-182.2,
	19.2-182.13, 19.2-182.16,
	19.2-264.3:1,
	19.2-264.3:1.1,
	19.2-264.3:1.2,
	19.2-301, 19.2-302,
	19.2-389, 19.2-390,
	20-88, 22.1-7,
	22.1-205,
	22.1-209.2,
	22.1-214.2,
	22.1-214.3,
	22.1-215,
	22.1-217.1,
	22.1-272.1, 23-38.2,
	25.1-100, 29.1-313,
	32.1-45.1, 32.1-64.1,
	32.1-73.7, 32.1-102.1,
	32.1-122.5, 32.1-124,
	32.1-125.1,
	32.1-127.1:03,
	32.1-127.1:04,
	32.1-135.2,
	32.1-276.3,
	32.1-276.8,
	32.1-283, 32.1-283.1,
	32.1-283.5, 32.1-325,
	32.1-351.2, 37.2-100,
	37.2-200, 37.2-300,
	37.2-316, 37.2-317,
	37.2-318, 37.2-319,
	37.2-423, 37.2-716,
	37.2-900, 37.2-900.1,
	37.2-909, 37.2-912,
	37.2-919, 37.2-1101,
	38.2-3412.1,
	38.2-3418.5,
	46.2-400, 46.2-401,
	46.2-1229, 51.5-1,
	51.5-2, 51.5-14,
	51.5-14.1, 51.5-31,
	51.5-39.2, 51.5-39.7,
	51.5-39.12,
	53.1-32, 53.1-40.2,
	53.1-136, 53.1-145,
	54.1-2715, 54.1-2726,
	54.1-2970, 54.1-2987.1,
	54.1-3408,
	54.1-3408.01, 54.1-3437.1,
	54.1-3506, 56-484.19,
	57-2.02, 57-60,
	63.2-100, 63.2-1503,
	63.2-1528, 63.2-1709,
	63.2-1726, 63.2-1735,
	63.2-1805
841	2.2-2822
842	53.1-131.3
843	46.2-752
845	2.2-3705.7, 2.2-3711,
	23-9.2:3.03,
	23-38.76, 23-38.77,
	23-38.79, 23-38.79:1,
	23-38.80, 23-38.87,
	23-38.87:1, 23-38.88
846	15.2-2157
847	2.2-511, 3.2-4212,
	3.2-4219,
	18.2-246.11,
	18.2-246.13,
	18.2-246.15, 18.2-513,
	18.2-514, 19.2-245.01,
	58.1-1008.2
848	19.2-108
849	2.2-3800, 2.2-3801,
	2.2-3808
850	59.1-284.23
851	58.1-439.18,
	58.1-439.20, 58.1-439.21,
	58.1-439.22, 58.1-439.24,
	63.2-2002R
852	2.2-2699.3, 2.2-2699.4
853	2.2-2233.1, 2.2-2515,
	2.2-2516, 58.1-339.4
854	10.1-1197.5—
	10.1-1197.11,
	56-46.1, 56-580
855	10.1-1307.02
856	10.1-107, 10.1-202
857	17.1-281
858	17.1-279, 17.1-502
859	2.2-2101,
	22.1-212.17—
	22.1-212.22R,
	30-313—30-314
860	6.1-330.78
861	15.2-5146
862	2.2-3109
863	15.2-4207
864	15.2-4830, n.,
	33.1-23.03,
	33.1-23.03:1, n.,
	33.1-391.6—
	33.1-391.15R,
	46.2-755.1R,
	46.2-755.2R,
	46.2-1167.1R,
	58.1-625.1R,
	58.1-802.1R,
	58.1-811,
	58.1-1724.5R,
	58.1-1724.6R,
	58.1-1724.7R,
	58.1-2402.1R,
	58.1-2403, 58.1-2425,
	58.1-3221.3
865	24.2-101, 24.2-115,
	24.2-115.1, 24.2-404,
	24.2-418, 24.2-604,
	24.2-1004
866	67-701
867	2.2-3800, 2.2-3801,
	2.2-3808
868	24.2-235, 24.2-238
869	2.2-1400, 2.2-1401,
	2.2-1402, 2.2-1403,
	2.2-1404, 2.2-1404.1,
	2.2-3705.6, 2.2-4310,
	15.2-965.1, 18.2-213.1
870	24.2-101, 24.2-115,
	24.2-115.1, 24.2-404,
	24.2-418, 24.2-604,
	24.2-1004
871	15.2-4830, n.,
	33.1-23.03,
	33.1-23.03:1, n.,
	33.1-391.6— 33.1-391.15R,

ACTS 2009 Chapter	Code 1950 Section
	46.2-755.1R, 46.2-755.2R, 46.2-1167.1R, 58.1-625.1R, 58.1-802.1R, 58.1-811, 58.1-1724.3R, 58.1-1724.5R, 58.1-1724.6R, 58.1-1724.7R, 58.1-2402.1R, 58.1-2403, 58.1-2425, 58.1-3221.3
872	46.2-323, 46.2-323.01, 46.2-328.1, 46.2-330, 46.2-341.12, 46.2-341.15, 46.2-342, 46.2-343, 46.2-344, 46.2-345
873	24.2-700, 24.2-701, 24.2-706
874	24.2-101, 24.2-115, 24.2-115.1, 24.2-404, 24.2-418, 24.2-604, 24.2-1004
876	24.2-235, 24.2-238
877	32.1-102.4, 38.2-3406.1, 38.2-3406.2, 38.2-4214
878	60.2-528, 60.2-618
879	23-7.1:02

ACTS 2009, Sp. Sess. I

ACTS 2009, Sp. Sess. I Chapter	Code 1950 Section
1	9.1-907, 9.1-1101, 16.1-277.1, 18.2-268.7, 18.2-268.9, 18.2-472.1, 19.2-187, 19.2-187.1, 19.2-243, 46.2-341.26:7, 46.2-341.26:9
4	9.1-907, 9.1-1101, 16.1-277.1, 18.2-268.7, 18.2-268.9, 18.2-472.1, 19.2-187, 19.2-187.1, 19.2-243, 46.2-341.26:7, 46.2-341.26:9

ACTS 2010

ACTS 2010 Chapter	Code 1950 Section
1	56-235.4, n., 56-238
2	56-235.4, n., 56-238
3	29.1-330
4	10.1-1425.26
5	29.1-529
6	29.1-310
7	3.2-1904, 3.2-1905, 3.2-1907
8	10.1-1157
9	29.1-344, 29.1-345
10	29.1-521
11	62.1-44.19:18
12	28.2-227
13	10.1-603.18, 10.1-603.19, 10.1-613.5
14	3.2-1506
15	46.2-208
16	54.1-2983, 54.1-2995
17	33.1-19
18	46.2-311, 46.2-312
19	46.2-873.1
20	33.1-128
21	38.2-3541.1
22	33.1-185, 33.1-190
23	46.2-1216
24	46.2-1116
25	32.1-292.2, 46.2-324, 46.2-342, 46.2-416, 46.2-606
26	46.2-870
27	28.2-603
28	37.2-500, 37.2-601, 54.1-3420.2, 54.1-3423
29	10.1-114.1
30	58.1-1802.1
32	2.2-2712
33	2.2-4518
34	58.1-3
35	58.1-1013, 58.1-1017
36	58.1-9, 58.1-478, 58.1-615
37	3.2-1904, 3.2-1905, 3.2-1907
38	22.1-253.13:9
39	23-231.15
40	22.1-132.2
41	10.1-605.2
42	62.1-198, 62.1-199
43	29.1-509
45	33.1-223.2:23
46	54.1-2972
47	46.2-1240, 46.2-1257R, 46.2-1259
48	46.2-873.1
49	22.1-79.1
50	33.1-185, 33.1-190
51	33.1-19
52	46.2-857
53	33.1-128
54	32.1-102.3:6
55	32.1-292.2, 46.2-324, 46.2-342, 46.2-416, 46.2-606
56	46.2-870
57	32.1-138
58	2.2-2001.1
59	55-530
60	22.1-253.13:3, n., 22.1-253.13:4, n.
61	22.1-70.2, 22.1-139R, 22.1-199.2, 22.1-209.1:2, 22.1-212.15, 22.1-226R
62	54.1-1100, 54.1-1103
63	36-105, 36-114
64	2.2-2452, 2.2-2681, 2.2-2715
65	2.2-4002, 2.2-4006, 10.1-1308.1, 28.2-103, 28.2-1307, 36-100
66	36-137
67	23-276.1
68	23-9.6:1
69	32.1-69.4, 54.1-2403.02
70	54.1-3481
71	37.2-502
72	22.1-16, n.
73	32.1-47.1
74	54.1-3303
75	2.2-2666.3
76	22.1-253.13:3
77	36-73, 36-82.1
78	2.2-115
79	2.2-113
80	22.1-253.13:4
81	54.1-1140—54.1-1142, 54.1-1143
82	54.1-1111
83	54.1-1102
84	2.2-2001
85	22.1-243
86	35.1-25
87	36-106
88	22.1-79.1
89	22.1-253.13:4
90	54.1-3320
91	54.1-403, 54.1-404.1R, 54.1-406, 54.1-603, 54.1-702, 54.1-2012, 54.1-2013, 54.1-2104, 54.1-2206, 54.1-2210, 54.1-2313, 54.1-2344
92	55-248.1R
93	22.1-302
94	36-106
95	22.1-57.3, 22.1-57.3:1.1
96	1-210
97	22.1-241
98	67-301
99	54.1-411
100	54.1-4110
101	2.2-2235, 2.2-2316, 2.2-2685, 23-253.1, 30-233
102	27-98

ACTS 2010 Chapter	Code 1950 Section
103	22.1-253.13:9
104	23-9.2:9
105	36-98.1
106	38.2-3430.1:1
107	38.2-3430.1:1
108	38.2-3430.1:1
110	46.2-857
111	33.1-46.2
112	46.2-916.3
113	58.1-638
114	4.1-315
115	4.1-119
116	58.1-3824.1
117	15.2-2160, 15.2-7200—15.2-7226
119	58.1-610
120	58.1-486.2, 58.1-486.3
121	15.2-2222.1
122	15.2-5000
124	53.1-228
125	46.2-752
126	30-282, n., 56-556, n.
127	46.2-1025
128	53.1-56
129	46.2-328.1
130	33.1-221.1:8, n.
131	46.2-752
132	53.1-129
133	33.1-46.2
134	33.1-223.4
135	46.2-100, 46.2-600, 46.2-636.1, 46.2-638
136	2.2-106, 2.2-225, 2.2-1115.1, 2.2-1509.3, 2.2-2005—2.2-2009, 2.2-2012, 2.2-2013, 2.2-2015, 2.2-2017, n., 2.2-2019—2.2-2021, 2.2-2023, 2.2-2033, 2.2-2034R, 2.2-2457—2.2-2458.1R, 2.2-2699.5—2.2-2699.7, 23-38.111, 23-77.4, 30-133, n.
137	10.1-603.3, n.
139	10.1-418.6
141	15.2-958.3
142	56-603, 56-604
143	59.1-198
144	28.2-227
145	2.2-106, 2.2-225, 2.2-1115.1, 2.2-1509.3, 2.2-2005—2.2-2009, 2.2-2012, 2.2-2013, 2.2-2015, 2.2-2017, n., 2.2-2019—2.2-2021, 2.2-2023, 2.2-2033, 2.2-2034R, 2.2-2457—2.2-2458.1R, 2.2-2699.5—2.2-2699.7, 23-38.111, 23-77.4, 30-133
146	6.1-409, 6.1-410, 6.2-1600, 6.2-1601
148	22.1-360, 22.1-361
149	15.2-2241
151	58.1-9, 58.1-478, 58.1-615
152	59.1-165
153	28.2-106.1
154	15.2-716, 15.2-716.1, 58.1-3255
155	38.2-3406.1
157	2.2-2818, 38.2-3407.7, 38.2-4209.1, 38.2-4312.1
158	65.2-101
159	65.2-715
160	65.2-704—65.2-706
161	15.2-901
162	22.1-253.13:4
163	22.1-253.13:4
164	58.1-439.18
165	55-509.4, 55-509.7
166	55-79.75:2, 55-513.1
167	36-85.28, 36-85.31, n.
168	53.1-128
169	4.1-309.1
170	4.1-119
171	13.1-803, 13.1-804, 13.1-810, 13.1-813, 13.1-823, 13.1-842, 13.1-844.2, 13.1-845, 13.1-847, 13.1-847.1, 13.1-855, 13.1-866, 13.1-878, 13.1-883, 13.1-939
172	2.2-220.3
174	62.1-44.38:2
175	15.2-968.1, 46.2-208
176	20-108.1
177	25.1-235
178	2.2-4002, 2.2-4103, 28.2-1000.2
179	32.1-46.02, 54.1-3408
180	55-221.1, 55-248.4
181	16.1-77, 54.1-2108.1
182	3.2-6521
183	18.2-56.1, 18.2-135, 29.1-338, 29.1-521.2, 29.1-523, 29.1-523.1, 29.1-525, 29.1-525.1, 29.1-530.3
184	29.1-501
185	32.1-127.1:03, 54.1-3408.2
186	34-14
187	32.1-122.7, 32.1-122.7:1, 32.1-122.7:2, 32.1-122.21, n.,
188	54.1-3005
189	15.2-1503.1, 15.2-4517.1, 19.2-389
190	24.2-115
191	58.1-1021.01, 58.1-1021.02, 58.1-1021.02:1, 58.1-1021.03
192	63.2-900, n.
193	54.1-3420.1
195	58.1-3700.1, 58.1-3732.5
196	8.01-581.17
197	26-17.7
198	15.2-2122
199	15.2-716, 15.2-716.1, 58.1-3255
200	58.1-3916, n.
202	15.2-1132
203	1-219.1, n., 15.2-1800, n., 15.2-1814, n., 15.2-1900, n., 25.1-108, n.
204	24.2-613, 24.2-640
205	56-265.15, 56-265.19:1, 56-265.32
206	54.1-411
207	54.1-1140—54.1-1142, 54.1-1143
208	55-530
210	15.2-2160, 15.2-7200—15.2-7226
211	38.2-3724, 38.2-3735
212	15.2-2403
213	24.2-706
214	24.2-627
215	24.2-506, 24.2-521
216	15.2-2244
222	38.2-3418.16, 38.2-4319
223	9.1-177.1, 19.2-299
224	9.1-102
225	38.2-3430.2
226	38.2-218
227	38.2-3323
228	58.1-1823
229	58.1-513
230	6.1-225.30:1, 6.2-1347.1
231	10.1-418.7
232	10.1-418.8
233	62.1-44.15:20
234	38.2-1907

ACTS 2010 Chapter	Code 1950 Section
235	38.2-2617—38.2-2619
236	55-66.3
237	10.1-2202.4
238	64.1-62.4
239	15.2-2316.2
240	3.2-6566, 19.2-71, 19.2-72
241	15.2-2311, 15.2-2314
242	46.2-2059.1
243	20-108.2, 63.2-1900, 63.2-1954.1R
244	24.2-700, 24.2-701
245	54.1-2901, 54.1-3001, 54.1-3408
246	58.1-512
247	4.1-235
248	58.1-513
249	10.1-605
250	63.2-602
251	29.1-302.1
252	32.1-46.02, 54.1-3408
253	44-93.3
254	22.1-253.13:1, n.
255	58.1-3500, 58.1-3510.4, 58.1-3510.6, 58.1-3704, 58.1-3706
256	56-412.3
257	63.2-905.1
258	18.2-254.1
259	2.2-2721
260	54.1-201.1
261	53.1-32
262	18.2-422
263	23-276.1
264	58.1-3221.4, 58.1-3506
265	58.1-512
266	58.1-1717.1, 58.1-1718, 58.1-3805
267	16.1-107
268	24.2-946
269	6.1-71R, 6.1-125.10, 6.1-125.11, 6.1-194.58R, 6.1-225.49R, 6.1-225.50, 6.2-613, 6.2-614, 6.2-895R, 6.2-1175R, 6.2-1366R, 6.2-1367, 51.1-164R, 51.1-511, 64.1-123R, 64.1-123.1R, 64.1-123.3—64.1-125R, 64.1-132.1—64.1-132.4, 64.1-132.5, 64.1-132.6
270	10.1-605, 10.1-607.1, 10.1-609
271	63.2-1300—63.2-1303
272	38.2-3540.2, 38.2-4319
273	19.2-390, 53.1-149, 53.1-162
274	65.2-715
275	10.1-562
276	63.2-1232
277	60.2-113.1
278	65.2-101
279	10.1-1618, n.
280	54.1-201.1
281	38.2-1815, 38.2-1825, 38.2-1869
282	65.2-804
283	58.1-3700.1, 58.1-3732.5
284	46.2-1500, 46.2-1569, 46.2-1571, 46.2-1572.3, 46.2-1573, 46.2-1573.02
285	58.1-662
286	2.2-1150.1
287	44-102.2, n.
288	62.1-44.19:14, 62.1-44.19:15
289	46.2-921.1
290	10.1-411.2
291	10.1-2208, 10.1-2213
292	46.2-1500, 46.2-1530
293	46.2-665, 46.2-666, 46.2-670
294	4.1-200
295	58.1-3500, 58.1-3510.4, 58.1-3510.6, 58.1-3704, 58.1-3706
296	15.2-2292.1
297	24.2-946.2
298	18.2-59
299	2.2-3713
300	2.2-3705.7
301	2.2-3110
302	8.01-407
303	16.1-131.1
304	2.2-3110
305	32.1-312, 32.1-314—32.1-317, 32.1-321.3, 32.1-321.4, 32.1-325
306	63.2-1241, 63.2-1242.2, 63.2-1242.3
308	10.1-418.6
309	2.2-3707
310	2.2-3705.6, 2.2-3711
311	36-11
312	19.2-130.1
313	22.1-253.13:4
314	19.2-163.01, 19.2-163.01:1
315	15.2-2307
316	24.2-706
317	4.1-209, 4.1-209.1, 4.1-231, 13.1-313
318	46.2-1500, 46.2-1569, 46.2-1571, 46.2-1572.3, 46.2-1573, 46.2-1573.02
319	19.2-70.3
320	56-247.1
321	58.1-512
322	56-479.3
323	24.2-959, 24.2-959.1
324	54.1-2806, 54.1-2825
326	56-577
327	60.2-633
328	59.1-547, 59.1-549
329	2.2-2505
330	37.2-815, 37.2-817—37.2-817.4
331	16.1-277.01, 16.1-277.02, 16.1-278.3, 16.1-283.1, 63.2-1220.2—63.2-1220.4, 63.2-1228.1—63.2-1228.2R
332	46.2-800.2
333	15.2-1719
334	63.2-1514
335	38.2-1874
336	2.2-902, 2.2-904.2
337	38.2-323R
338	15.2-6304, 15.2-6304.1R, 15.2-7300—15.2-7315
339	2.2-2699.1, 2.2-2699.2
340	19.2-169.6, 19.2-174.1, 19.2-175, 19.2-176R, 19.2-177.1R, 19.2-178, 19.2-389, 32.1-127.1:03, 37.2-803, 37.2-804, 37.2-809, 37.2-811
341	43-1, 43-4.01
342	2.2-2528, 2.2-2529
343	6.1-118.1, 8.01-66, 8.01-66.2, 8.01-416, 8.01-504, 8.01-682, 15.2-1716, 16.1-105, 17.1-605, 17.1-626.1, 19.2-69, 21-186, 38.2-807, 43-3, 43-24, 46.2-364
344	18.2-51.1
345	29.1-301
346	2.2-2648
347	24.2-103, 24.2-115
348	24.2-653.1, 24.2-708
349	15.2-412
350	8.01-420.7
351	46.2-749.3
352	17.1-218, 17.1-229, 19.2-270.4, 19.2-310, 20-32R, 43-17.1, 55-66.6
353	54.1-106
354	8.01-417
355	37.2-313.1

ACTS 2010 Chapter	Code 1950 Section
356	24.2-626
357	2.2-2818, 38.2-3407.7, 38.2-4209.1, 38.2-4312.1
358	Const., Art. 10, § 6-A, n.
359	46.2-1530, 46.2-1930, 46.2-1992.23, 46.2-1993.23
360	15.2-5000
361	46.2-1143
362	4.1-235
363	58.1-439
364	18.2-46.3:3
365	58.1-662
366	19.2-270.4
367	16.1-300, 16.1 309.1, 52-8.6
368	54.1-3481
369	2.2-2718
370	10.1-603.3, n.
371	38.2-2617—38.2-2619
372	6.1-225.30:1, 6.2-1347.1
373	54.1-2105, 54.1-2111.1
374	38.2-3323
375	19.2-130.1
376	65.2-804
377	54.1-2818.1
378	46.2-931
379	58.1-202
380	54.1-2825
381	15.2-6304
382	2.2-4305
383	54.1-2807, 54.1-2807.01
384	58.1-512
385	58.1-662
386	15.2-3207, 15.2-3525, 15.2-3806, 15.2-3906, 15.2-4105, 22.1-261, 22.1-281—22.1-286R, 37.2-713, 58.1-605, 58.1-638
387	18.2-308
388	30-209
389	37.2-903
390	33.1-46.2, 46.2-749.3
391	44-102.2, n.
392	15.2-2404
393	22.1-212.9, 22.1-212.10
394	62.1-69.34
395	32.1-137.13—32.1-137.15
396	15.2-1215
397	56-577
398	22.1-253.13:3, n., 22.1-253.13:4, n.
399	18.2-31

ACTS 2010 Chapter	Code 1950 Section
401	33.1-70.3
402	16.1-241, 18.2-370.5
403	15.2-901
404	19.2-124, 19.2-132
405	54.1-2708.3
406	19.2-169.6, 19.2-174.1, 19.2-175, 19.2-176R, 19.2-177.1R, 19.2-178, 19.2-389, 32.1-127.1:03, 37.2-803, 37.2-804, 37.2-809, 37.2-811
407	2.2-4103
408	32.1-102.3:6
409	55-525.1—55-525.7
410	30-19.03, 30-19.03:1R, 30-19.03:1.1R, 30-19.1, 30-19.1:1R, 30-19.1:3R, 30-19.1:6R, 30-19.1:7, 36-132.1,
411	2.2-212, 2.2-213.4, 2.2-703, 2.2-703.1, 2.2-708, 2.2-709R, 2.2-712, 2.2-714, 2.2-720, 2.2-2412, 2.2-2626, 2.2-2627, 2.2-5510
412	60.2-602
413	30-145
414	54.1-2400, 54.1-2408, 54.1-2409
415	32.1-162.9:1
416	32.1-276.2, 32.1-276.4
417	55-59.4, 58.1-3340
418	30-111
419	58.1-439.12:03
420	18.2-422
421	59.1-335.5, 59.1-335.7
422	2.2-1503, 2.2-1513
423	54.1-3448, 54.1-3450, 54.1-3452, 54.1-3454
424	46.2-341.18
425	16.1-279.1, 19.2-152.10
426	17.1-315, n.
427	30-116
428	18.2-31
429	18.2-340.16, 18.2-340.19, 18.2-340.27, 18.2-340.30:1R, 18.2-340.33
430	8.01-449, 17.1-258.3, 17.1-258.3:1, 17.1-258.3:2, 17.1-276, 17.1-279, 17.1-293
431	24.2-226, 24.2-228, 24.2-682
432	55-79.71:1, 55-515.3
433	18.2-308

ACTS 2010 Chapter	Code 1950 Section
434	13.1-635, 13.1-636, 13.1-764, 13.1-765, 13.1-834, 13.1-835, 13.1-926, 13.1-927, 13.1-1016, 13.1-1017, 13.1-1221, 13.1-1222, 50-73.6, 50-73.135
435	8.01-417
436	15.2-412
437	8.01-6.3
438	19.2-215.3
439	59.1-296—59.1-296.2:1, 59.1-297—59.1-298, 59.1-306
440	2.2-4301
441	58.1-1718.1
442	45.1-361.22, 45.1-361.22:1
443	2.2-2818, 38.2-3407.5
445	18.2-160.1
446	18.2-271.1
447	22.1-214
448	24.2-604, 24.2-639, 24.2-653, 24.2-655
449	24.2-209, 24.2-216, 24.2-226, 24.2-442, 24.2-443.3, 24.2-507, 24.2-510, 24.2-516, 24.2-522, 24.2-524, 24.2-527, 24.2-536—24.2-538, 24.2-612, 24.2-702.1, 24.2-703, 24.2-706, 24.2-709
450	30-279, 30-280
451	17.1-114, 17.1-330, 17.1-331
452	24.2-405, 24.2-407.1
453	55-79.75:2, 55-513.1
454	19.2-270.4
455	6.1-125.15:1, 6.2-619, 11-9.1—11-9.7R, 26-72—26-116, 37.2-1009, 37.2-1018R, 37.2-1020, 37.2-1023, 55-34.7, 55-544.01, 55-544.02, 55-546.02
456	2.2-3705.4, 19.2-389, 19.2-389.1, 23-9.2:10, 32.1-127.1:03
457	54.1-2343, 54.1-2344
458	2.2-1111, 45.1-394, n.
459	46.2-1500, 46.2-1530
460	15.2-6304, 15.2-6304.1R, 15.2-7300—15.2-7315,

ACTS 2010 Chapter	Code 1950 Section
461	37.2-815, 37.2-817—37.2-817.4
463	46.2-800.2
464	19.2-188.3
465	15.2-2223.1
466	56-484.12, 56-484.17, 56-484.17:1
467	17.1-315, n.
468	16.1-279.1, 19.2-152.10
469	58.1-439
470	2.2-115
471	58.1-1013, 58.1-1017
472	16.1-300, 16.1-309.1, 52-8.6
473	19.2-70.3
474	30-111
475	18.2-31
477	6.1-249, 6.1-330.55, 6.1-330.78, 6.1-480—6.1-507, 6.2-303, 6.2-312, 6.2-1501, 6.2-2200—6.2-2228, 59.1-200
478	23-9.2:9
479	10.1-2202.4
480	2.2-4002
481	4.1-111, 4.1-325
482	59.1-284.24
483	22.1-271.5
484	28.2-302.1:1, 28.2-302.7
485	33.1-46.2
486	8.01-407
487	2.2-2240.2
488	32.1-122.7, 32.1-122.7:1, 32.1-122.7:2, 32.1-122.21R
489	18.2-152.2, 18.2-152.3:1, 18.2-152.12
490	Const., Art. 10, § 6, n.
492	38.2-2206
493	46.2-398.1
494	8.01-676.1
495	15.2-1206R, 15.2-1207
496	8.01-195.10
497	33.1-375.1
498	33.1-69.001
499	58.1-3523
500	28.2-106.1
501	15.2-980
502	19.2-310.5
503	38.2-3541
504	38.2-3541.2, 38.2-4214, 38.2-4319
505	58.1-3819
506	20-107.3
507	67-1200—67-1211
508	54.1-2020—54.1-2023
509	15.2-953
510	38.2-1442, 38.2-1700—38.2-1715
511	54.1-2347—54.1-2349
512	29.1-528.1
513	12.1-19
514	56-603, 56-604
515	38.2-3406.1, 38.2-4319
516	15.2-1747
517	4.1-119
518	55-519
519	46.2-301, 46.2-301.1
520	36-55.63, 58.1-435, 58.1-439.12:04
521	18.2-271
522	16.1-278.9
523	15.2-1736
524	2.2-3705.4, 19.2-389, 19.2-389.1, 23-9.2:10, 32.1-127.1:03
525	22.1-279.3:1
526	16.1-309.1
527	23-9.6:1
528	15.2-2223.1
529	18.2-152.12
530	19.2-13
531	15.2-6415
532	13.1-553
533	24.2-626
534	2.2-2004
535	58.1-341, n.
536	2.2-2240.2
537	22.1-212.23—22.1-212.27, 22.1-253.13:2
538	24.2-706
539	24.2-705.1
540	54.1-4010
541	46.2-335
542	24.2-507, 24.2-510, 24.2-682
543	30-309, 30-310, 30-312
544	37.2-821
545	27-15.2
546	24.2-955.3
547	53.1-105
548	53.1-131.3
549	15.2-2303.1:1
550	6.1-330.54, 6.2-302, 8.01-128, 16.1-79.1, 34-5, 55-226.2, 55-246.1, 55-248.4, 55-248.7:2, 55-248.9:1, 55-248.15:1, 55-248.15:2, 55-248.38:3
551	63.2-214.2, 63.2-900, 63.2-1231, 63.2-1700, 63.2-1737
552	58.1-3258.1, 58.1-3259, 58.1-3295, 58.1-3331, 58.1-3374, 58.1-3379
553	2.2-3705.1
554	2.2-2001
555	17.1-275.5, 19.2-183, 19.2-187.1
556	15.2-967.1
557	8.01-195.10—8.01-195.12
558	2.2-1112, 19.2-270.7
559	19.2-264.3:1
560	16.1-69.11:1
561	4.1-209, 4.1-209.1, 4.1-231, 13.1-313
562	59.1-284.24
563	15.2-1503.1, 15.2-4517.1, 19.2-389
564	65.2-704—65.2-706
565	18.2-427
566	56-484.12, 56-484.17, 56-484.17:1
567	2.2-4303
568	9.1-408
569	16.1-278.9
570	16.1-278.9
572	18.2-340.19
573	2.2-435.7
574	54.1-3812.1
575	15.2-5370, 15.2-5371
576	18.2-308
577	15.2-906.1
578	54.1-1802R, 54.1-1802.1, 54.1-1806
579	30-231.01—30-231.5, 30-231.8
580	2.2-115
581	56-234.5
582	19.2-70.3
583	38.2-3407.17, 38.2-4214, 38.2-4319, 38.2-4509
584	2.2-5403
585	64.1-134
586	18.2-308
587	27-95, 27-97, 27-97.2
588	Const., Art. 10, § 6-A, n.
589	46.2-931
590	59.1-148.3
591	37.2-821
592	19.2-124, 19.2-132
593	46.2-335
594	35.1-25

ACTS 2010 Chapter	Code 1950 Section
595	38.2-5604
596	16.1-69.11:1
597	22.1-258, 22.1-261
598	23-9.2:3.8
599	58.1-439.12:03
600	15.2-953
601	24.2-710
602	18.2-308
603	63.2-1706, 63.2-1728
604	22.1-253.13:3, n., 22.1-253.13:4, n.
605	22.1-254, 22.1-254.2, 22.1-271.4
606	Const., Art. 10, § 8, n.
607	67-300
608	36-55.63, 58.1-435, 58.1-439.12:04
609	16.1-131.1
610	46.2-1993, 46.2-1993.67
611	2.2-115
612	54.1-405
613	15.2-2303.1:1
614	46.2-1118
615	54.1-2349, 54.1-2351
616	53.1-41
617	57-36
619	20-61
620	54.1-2343, 54.1-2344
621	9.1-101, 15.2-632
622	16.1-79.1
623	32.1-102.3, n., 32.1-102.3:2, n.
624	24.2-228, 24.2-229.1
625	54.1-1800—54.1-1805
626	29.1-521.1
627	2.2-3704, 2.2-3706
628	2.2-2721
629	15.2-3207, 15.2-3525, 15.2-3806, 15.2-3906, 15.2-4105, 22.1-261, 22.1-281—22.1-286R, 37.2-713, 58.1-605, 58.1-638
630	2.2-2218, 2.2-2221, 2.2-3711
631	15.2-2118
632	6.1-125.15:1, 6.2-619, 11-9.1—11-9.7R, 26-72—26-116, 26-72, 37.2-1009, 37.2-1018R, 37.2-1020, 37.2-1023, 55-34.7, 55-544.01, 55-544.02, 55-546.02
633	40.1-11.2
634	2.2-4311.2
635	58.1-9
637	54.1-2105, 54.1-2111.1

ACTS 2010 Chapter	Code 1950 Section
639	24.2-310
640	2.2-4400—2.2-4411
641	15.2-901
642	38.2-3430.2
643	27-95, 27-97, 27-97.2
644	62.1-229.3, 62.1-229.4
645	24.2-209, 24.2-216, 24.2-226, 24.2-442, 24.2-443.3, 24.2-507, 24.2-510, 24.2-516, 24.2-522, 24.2-524, 24.2-527, 24.2-536—24.2-538, 24.2-612, 24.2-702.1, 24.2-703, 24.2-706, 24.2-709
646	32.1-102.6
648	58.1-3703
649	15.2-914
650	22.1-212.9, 22.1-212.10
651	26-17.7
652	19.2-76.1
653	15.2-4405, 58.1-3233
654	9.1-401.1, 51.1-1121
655	46.2-817
656	18.2-472.1, 19.2-187, 19.2-187.1
657	54.1-4010
658	19.2-264.4
660	58.1-3824.1
661	46.2-1094, 46.2-1095
662	2.2-703.2
663	22.1-205
664	63.2-1530
665	6.1-409, 6.2-1600
666	22.1-348
667	30-319—30-325
668	15.2-1245—15.2-1247
669	12.1-20, 12.1-21.1, 12.1-21.2
670	2.2-3117, 30-111
671	30-133
672	2.2-3705.2
673	8.01-502.1, 8.01-512.4
674	2.2-4400—2.2-4411
675	12.1-19.1, 12.1-43, 50-73.1, 50-73.4, 50-73.5, 50-73.8, 50-73.11, 50-73.12, 50-73.15, 50-73.54, 50-73.77, 50-73.83
676	2.2-3119
677	18.2-308
678	Const., Art. 10, § 6, n.
679	2.2-212, n., 2.2-225, n.
680	57-60

ACTS 2010 Chapter	Code 1950 Section
681	67-1200—67-1211
682	18.2-271.1, 46.2-320, 53.1-131.2
683	16.1-248.1
684	2.2-1514, 10.1-2128, 10.1-2129, 10.1-2133
685	17.1-275.12
686	10.1-603.8:1
687	38.2-3406.1, 38.2-4319
688	32.1-102.3:2, n.
689	10.1-1307.03
690	58.1-344.3
691	10.1-1238—10.1-1250
692	51.5-39.5
693	38.2-3412.1, 38.2-3412.1:01
694	2.2-4343, 23-91.29:1
695	67-600, 67-602
696	24.2-947.6—24.2-947.8, 24.2-948R, 24.2-948.1, 24.2-953.1
697	2.2-904.1
698	15.2-2307
699	2.2-5800—2.2-5803R
700	18.2-308
701	58.1-1003
702	19.2-10.1
703	13.1-1004, 13.1-1050.2, 13.1-1056.1, 13.1-1062, 13.1-1063R
704	38.2-4229.2
705	15.2-2308
706	2.2-3701
707	24.2-101, 24.2-310, 24.2-604
708	15.2-106
709	18.2-308
710	19.2-386.16
711	18.2-340.20
712	20-160, 20-161, 20-162, 20-165
713	8.2-317.1, 59.1-200
714	15.2-981
715	8.01-401.2:1, 54.1-2900
716	30-309, 30-310, 30-312
717	8.01-271.01, 16.1-243, 17.1-124, 17.1-224, 17.1-258.3, 17.1-258.4, 17.1-258.6
718	22.1-207.4
719	2.2-904.1
720	19.2-70.3
721	19.2-70.3
722	58.1-439.12:05

ACTS 2010 Chapter	Code 1950 Section
723	22.1-32
724	15.2-2430—15.2-2440, 62.1-198, 62.1-199
725	8.01-401.2:1, 54.1-2900
726	63.2-1530
727	58.1-439.12:05
728	2.2-4002, n., 2.2-4103, n., 28.2-1000.2
729	62.1-69.34
730	45.1-361.21:1
731	10.1-1618, n.
732	2.2-3104.01, 2.2-4376.1, 56-573.3, 56-575.17:1
733	33.1-223.2:24
734	38.2-3407.17, 38.2-4214, 38.2-4319, 38.2-4509
735	2.2-115, 2.2-5102.1
736	2.2-4304
737	51.1-124.3, 51.1-126, 51.1-142.2, 51.1-144, 51.1-153, 51.1-155, 51.1-166, 51.1-301, 51.1-303
738	51.1-124.3, 51.1-126, 51.1-142.2, 51.1-144, 51.1-153, 51.1-155, 51.1-166, 51.1-301, 51.1-303
739	16.1-249, 16.1-269.5, 16.1-269.6
740	18.2-308
741	18.2-308
742	16.1-260, 16.1-293
743	54.1-2413
744	Const., Art. 10, § 8, n.
745	51.1-138
746	9.1-106
747	8.3A-118.1
748	56-235.5:1
749	2.2-3808
750	51.1-1103, 51.1-1110, 51.1-1111, 51.1-1112, 51.1-1122, 51.1-1123
751	51.1-505, 51.1-512
752	51.1-166
753	13.1-615, 13.1-752, 13.1-768, 13.1-775, 13.1-775.1, 13.1-815, 13.1-914, 13.1-930, 13.1-936, 13.1-936.1
754	18.2-308
755	54.1-1111
756	67-300
757	17.1-114, 17.1-330
758	51.1-161
759	2.2-3119
760	8.01-271.01, 16.1-243, 17.1-124, 17.1-224, 17.1-258.3, 17.1-258.4, 17.1-258.6
761	3.2-5904
762	45.1-361.21:1
763	22.1-129
764	54.1-831
765	8.01-353.1
766	15.2-2241
767	18.2-186.4, 18.2-186.4:1
768	2.2-115, 2.2-5102.1
769	24.2-103, 24.2-115
770	Const., Art. 10, § 6, n.
771	Const., Art. 10, § 6-A, n.
772	Const., Art. 10, § 8, n.
773	Const., Art. 10, § 6-A, n.
774	Const., Art. 10, § 8, n.
775	Const., Art. 10, § 6, n.
776	46.2-725, n.
777	33.1-375.1, 56-265.15, 56-265.15:1
778	8.01-389, 15.2-1704, 15.2-1724, 16.1-280, 16.1-335, 16.1-335, 16.1-336, 16.1-336.1, 16.1-337, 16.1-338, 16.1-339, 16.1-340, 16.1-340.1, 16.1-340.2, 16.1-340.3, 16.1-340.4, 16.1-341, 16.1-342, 16.1-343, 16.1-344, 16.1-345, 16.1-345.1, 16.1-345.2, 16.1-345.3, 16.1-345.4, 16.1-345.5, 16.1-345.6, 16.1-346, 16.1-346.1, 16.1-347, 19.2-13, 32.1-127.1:03, 37.2-808, 37.2-809, 37.2-812R, 37.2-813, 54.1-2400.1
779	9.1-301
780	19.2-368.3
781	18.2-308.1:1, 18.2-308.1:3, 18.2-308.2
782	13.1-603, 13.1-604, 13.1-610, 13.1-614, 13.1-624, 13.1-635, 13.1-646, 13.1-656, 13.1-657, 13.1-658, 13.1-660, 13.1-660.2, 13.1-661, 13.1-663, 13.1-664.1, 13.1-669.1, 13.1-672.1, 13.1-675, 13.1-681R, 13.1-686, 13.1-689, 13.1-699, 13.1-704, 13.1-714, 13.1-718, 13.1-720, 13.1-721.1, 13.1-725, 13.1-730, 13.1-733, 13.1-734, 13.1-770, 13.1-771, 13.1-772, 13.1-773, 13.1-774, 13.1-779
783	10.1-1328
784	58.1-609.3, 58.1-609.10
785	32.1-325
787	2.2-2101, 2.2-2101, 2.2-2462, 2.2-2463, 2.2-2464
788	15.2-980
789	19.2-264.3:1.3, 19.2-264.3:4
790	32.1-162.2, 32.1-162.3, 32.1-162.4, 32.1-162.8, 32.1-162.9, n., 32.1-162.9:1, 32.1-162.10, 32.1-162.13, 32.1-162.15, 32.1-325
791	58.1-3295
792	2.2-713, 54.1-2982, 54.1-2983.2, 54.1-2983.3, 54.1-2984, 54.1-2986, 54.1-2986.2, 54.1-2987.1, 54.1-2988
793	55-243, 55-248.34:1
794	6.1-1—6.1-479R, 6.2-100—6.2-2100, 6.2-2300—6.2-2505, 8.4-105, 11-30—11-34R, 17.1-626.1, 19.2-10.1, 26-7.5, 36-55.33:1, 36-96.20, 55-525.8—55-525.32, 57-60, 59.1-21.19—59.1-21.28R, 59.1-207.19
795	24.2-418
796	15.2-2291
797	2.2-2723
798	15.2-6023, 15.2-6023.1
799	8.01-353
800	19.2-3.1, 19.2-187.1
801	2.2-212, 2.2-213.4, 2.2-703, 2.2-703.1, 2.2-708, 2.2-709R, 2.2-712, 2.2-714, 2.2-720, 2.2-2412, 2.2-2626, 2.2-2627, 2.2-5510

ACTS 2010 Chapter	Code 1950 Section
802	58.1-322, 58.1-402
803	2.2-435.8
804	58.1-1021.01, 58.1-1021.02, 58.1-1021.02:1, 58.1-1021.03
805	59.1-117, 59.1-120, 59.1-121, 59.1-124, 59.1-136.1
808	2.2-3705.6, 2.2-3711
809	45.1-161.39, 45.1-161.87, 45.1-161.276, 45.1-161.284
810	18.2-32.3
811	44-102.1
812	24.2-114, 24.2-407, 24.2-418, 24.2-531, 24.2-533R, 24.2-611, 24.2-706, 24.2-710
813	46.2-208, 46.2-819.5
814	22.1-16, n.
815	28.2-110, 28.2-111, 62.1-132.11:2
816	23-299—23-299.10
817	22.1-212.23—22.1-212.27
818	38.2-3430.1:1
820	36-156.1, 36-156.2, 36-156.1, 36-156.2, 62.1-198, 62.1-199
821	15.2-2229
822	29.1-302.01
823	54.1-2811.1
824	58.1-3295
825	8.01-389, 15.2-1704, 15.2-1724, 16.1-280, 16.1-335, 16.1-335, 16.1-336, 16.1-336.1, 16.1-337, 16.1-338, 16.1-339, 16.1-340, 16.1-340.1, 16.1-340.2, 16.1-340.3, 16.1-340.4, 16.1-341, 16.1-342, 16.1-343, 16.1-344, 16.1-345, 16.1-345.1, 16.1-345.2, 16.1-345.3, 16.1-345.4, 16.1-345.5, 16.1-345.6, 16.1-346, 16.1-346.1, 16.1-347, 19.2-13, 32.1-127.1:03, 37.2-808, 37.2-809, 37.2-812R, 37.2-813, 54.1-2400.1
826	58.1-609.3, 58.1-609.10
827	8.01-316
828	2.2-212, n.
829	46.2-301.1
830	58.1-322, 58.1-402
831	6.1-409, 6.1-410, 6.1-431.13, 6.2-1600, 6.2-1601, 6.2-1712
832	33.1-375.1, 56-265.15, 56-265.15:1
833	2.2-2723
834	3.2-6521, 3.2-6522, 3.2-6525, 3.2-6562.1, 18.2-313.1, 54.1-3812
835	8.01-187, 25.1-100, 25.1-209, 25.1-213, 25.1-214, 25.1-219, 25.1-220, 25.1-227.1, 25.1-227.2, 25.1-235, 25.1-318, 62.1-98
836	2.2-2699.1, 2.2-2699.2
837	18.2-160.1
838	54.1-2957.14, 54.1-2957.15
839	46.2-819.1, 46.2-819.3:1
840	19.2-73, 19.2-74, 19.2-81
841	18.2-308
843	9.1-903
844	19.2-11.4, 53.1-30
845	19.2-303.5
846	23-300—23-303
847	15.2-2291
849	58.1-3221.4, 58.1-3506
850	56-585.2
851	18.2-32.3
852	32.1-127.1:05
853	10.1-603.12:3
855	63.2-1224
856	53.1-116.1:02
857	45.1-161.39, 45.1-161.87, 45.1-161.276, 45.1-161.284
858	9.1-902, 9.1-907, 9.1-908, 37.2-921, 53.1-116.1, 53.1-160.1
859	22.1-204.1
860	2.2-3300, 15.2-1812
861	44-102.1
862	19.2-120, 19.2-389
863	18.2-308
864	59.1-148.3
865	46.2-208, 46.2-819.5
866	58.1-609.10
867	10.1-1328
868	3.2-5508—3.2-5516
869	2.2-2233.2, 2.2-2235, 2.2-2236, 2.2-2240, 2.2-2414, 2.2-2423, 10.1-1237, 13.1-985, 15.2-6003, 15.2-6203, 33.1-221.1:1
871	23-299—23-299.10
872	58.1-301, 58.1-615.1R
873	46.2-1608, 46.2-1608.1
874	2.2-204, n., 2.2-219, n., 2.2-221.1, n., 2.2-228, n., 2.2-409, n., 2.2-518, n., 2.2-800, n., 2.2-803, n., 2.2-1104, n., 2.2-1149, n., 2.2-1155, n., 2.2-1156, n., 2.2-1204, n., 2.2-1502.1, n., 2.2-1505, n., 2.2-1508, n., 2.2-1802, n., 2.2-1819, n., 2.2-1829, n., 2.2-2005, n., 2.2-2031, n., 2.2-2221, n., 2.2-2221.1, n., 2.2-2318, n., 2.2-2402, n., 2.2-2670, n., 2.2-2675, n., 2.2-2723, n., 2.2-2818, n., 2.2-3204, n., 2.2-3205, n., 2.2-4000, n., 2.2-4011, n., 2.2-4300, n., 2.2-4301, n., 2.2-4400, n., 2.2-4800, n., 2.2-4806, n., 2.2-5206, n., 2.2-5209, n., 2.2-5211, n., 3.2-3100, n., 3.2-4200, n., 3.2-4201, n., 3.2-4204, n., 3.2-5100, n., 3.2-5600, n., 3.2-5702, n., 4.1-116, n., 5.1-1.6, n., 8.01-195.1, n., 8.01-195.3, n.,

ACTS 2010 Chapter	Code 1950 Section
	8.01-384.1:1, n.,
	9.1-102, n.,
	9.1-165, n.,
	9.1-166, n.,
	9.1-168, n.,
	9.1-1109, n.,
	10.1-202, n.,
	10.1-552, n.,
	10.1-564, n.,
	10.1-1124, n.,
	10.1-1176, n.,
	10.1-1188, n.,
	10.1-1190, n.,
	10.1-2128, n.,
	10.1-2128.1, n.,
	10.1-2129, n.,
	10.1-2131, n.,
	10.1-2202.1, n.,
	10.1-2211, n.,
	10.1-2213, n.,
	10.1-2213.1, n.,
	10.1-2500, n.,
	13.1-775.1, n.,
	15.2-1302, n.,
	15.2-1605, n.,
	15.2-1608, n.,
	15.2-1609.1, n.,
	15.2-1609.2, n.,
	15.2-1609.7, n.,
	15.2-1612.1, n.,
	15.2-1627.3,
	15.2-1634, n.,
	15.2-1636.8, n.,
	15.2-1643, n.,
	15.2-2602, n.,
	15.2-2659, n.,
	15.2-4100, n.,
	15.2-4518.3, n.,
	15.2-4526, n.,
	16.1-69.48:1,
	16.1-69.48:2,
	16.1-273, n.,
	16.1-287, n.,
	16.1-309.2, n.,
	16.1-309.7, n.,
	16.1-322.1, n.,
	17.1-132, n.,
	17.1-275,
	17.1-278, n.,
	17.1-279, n.,
	17.2-283, n.,
	17.2-286, n.,
	17.1-287, n.,
	17.1-327, n.,
	18.2-308, n.,
	18.2-308.2:2, n.,
	18.2-325,
	18.2-325.1,
	18.2-340.31, n.,
	19.2-152.4, n.,
	19.2-163, n.,
	19.2-163.01, n.,
	19.2-298.01, n.,
	19.2-326, n.,
	19.2-349, n.,
	19.2-368.11:1, n.,
	19.2-386.14, n.,
	19.2-389, n.,
	22.1-18.01, n.,
	22.1-100.1, n.,
	22.1-205, n.,
	22.1-253.13:1, n.,
	22.1-290.01, n.,
	23-7.4:1, n.,
	23-7.4:2, n.,
	23-9.2:3.03, n.,
	23-9.2:3.1, n.,
	23-9.6:1, n.,
	23-9.9, n.,
	23-38.12, n.,
	23-38.14, n.,
	23-30.23, n.,
	23-30.28, n.,
	23-38.3, n.,
	23-38.77, n.,
	23-164.8, n.,
	23-215, n.,
	23-220.01, n.,
	23-227, n.,
	23-253.1, n.,
	23-276.10, n.,
	23-284, n.,
	24.2-108, n.,
	24.2-668, n.,
	24.2-712, n.,
	24.2-947.5, n.,
	24.2-946.3, n.,
	24.2-953.4, n.,
	28.2-245, n.,
	28.2-542, n.,
	28.2-550, n.,
	30-19.1:4, n.,
	30-58.3, n.,
	30-266, n.,
	32.1-50, n.,
	32.1-163, n.,
	32.1-171.1, n.,
	32.1-273.1, n.,
	32.1-323, n.,
	32.1-325.1, n.,
	32.1-325.1:1, n.,
	32.1-330.1, n.,
	32.1-331.12, n.,
	32.1-351, n.,
	32.1-352, n.,
	32.1-354, n.,
	32.1-360, n.,
	32.1-361.1, n.,
	32.1-366, n.,
	33.1-23.03:2, n.,
	33.1-23.03:8, n.,
	33.1-23.1, n.,
	33.1-23.3, n.,
	33.1-23.5:1, n.,
	33.1-41.1, n.,
	33.1-221.1:1.1, n.,
	33.1-221.1:1.2, n.,
	33.1-75.3, n.,
	35.1-13, n.,
	35.1-14, n.,
	35.1-16, n.,
	35.1-17, n.,
	36-139, n.,
	37.2-203, n.,
	37.2-316, n.,
	37.2-319, n.,
	37.2-500, n.,
	37.2-504, n.,
	37.2-605, n.,
	37.2-808, n.,
	37.2-900, n.,
	37.2-904, n.,
	38.2-401, n.,
	40.1-49.4, n.,
	40.1-117, n.,
	44-146.28, n.,
	45.1-161.58, n.,
	45.1-161.292:31, n.,
	45.1-361.29, n.,
	46.2-205, n.,
	46.2-212.1, n.,
	46.2-214.2, n.,
	46.2-342, n.,
	46.2-694, n.,
	46.2-710, n.,
	46.2-878.3,
	46.2-1167, n.,
	51.1-124.3, n.,
	51.1-124.30, n.,
	51.1-142.2, n.,
	51.1-144, n.,
	51.1-155.1, n.,
	51.1-203, n.,
	51.1-214, n.,
	51.1-303, n.,
	51.1-1100, n.,
	51.1-1103, n.,
	51.1-1109, n.,
	51.1-1111, n.,
	51.1-1112, n.,
	51.1-1122, n.,
	51.1-1123, n.,
	51.1-1401, n.,
	51.1-1403, n.,
	51.5-39.7, n.,
	51.5-47, n.,
	51.5-48, n.,
	51.5-106, n.,
	52-1, n.,
	52-4.3, n.,

ACTS 2010 Chapter	Code 1950 Section
	52-8.1:1, n.,
	52-12, n.,
	52-28, n.,
	53.1-5, n.,
	53.1-20, n.,
	53.1-45, n.,
	53.1-47, n.,
	53.1-67.1, n.,
	53.1-68, n.,
	53.1-80, n.,
	53.1-120, n.,
	53.1-131, n.,
	53.1-135, n.,
	54.1-3913, n.,
	54.1-3916, n.,
	54.1-3919, n.,
	54.1-3924, n.,
	55-66.6, n.,
	55-210.13, n.,
	55-297, n.,
	56-232, n.,
	56-234, n.,
	56-484.12, n.,
	56-484.13, n.,
	58.1-301,
	58.1-339.4, n.,
	58.1-353, n.,
	58.1-439.2, n.,
	58.1-600, n.,
	58.1-602, n.,
	58.1-608.3, n.,
	58.1-615.1R,
	58.1-638, n.,
	58.1-638.1, n.,
	58.1-662, n.,
	58.1-801, n.,
	58.1-803, n.,
	58.1-815.1, n.,
	58.1-816.1, n.,
	58.1-1402, n.,
	58.1-1410, n.,
	58.1-2402, n.,
	58.1-2425, n.,
	58.1-2510, n.,
	58.1-3176, n.,
	58.1-3221.3, n.,
	58.1-3403, n.,
	58.1-3524, n.,
	58.1-3912, n.,
	58.1-4022, n.,
	59.1-282.1, n.,
	59.1-282.2, n.,
	59.1-284.13, n.,
	59.1-364, n.,
	59.1-392, n.,
	60.2-229, n.,
	60.2-305, n.,
	60.2-315, n.,
	62.1-128, n.,
	62.1-140, n.,

ACTS 2010 Chapter	Code 1950 Section
	62.1-4415, n.,
	63.2-222, n.,
	63.2-401, n.,
	63.2-605, n.,
	63.2-611, n.,
	63.2-612, n.,
	63.2-619, n.,
	63.2-1706, n.,
	63.2-1735, n.,
	63.2-1907, n.,
	66-15, n.,
	66-20, n.,
875	3.2-6503, 3.2-6574
876	30-112, 30-113, 30-113.1, 30-114, 30-116, 30-118
877	18.2-325, 18.2-325.1

ACTS 2011

ACTS 2011 Chapter	Code 1950 Section
1	46.2-2059.1
2	58.1-301
3	24.2-515.1, n.
4	63.2-600, 63.2-601.1
5	63.2-100, 63.2-901.1
6	4.1-231
7	51.5-12R, 51.5-23, 51.5-25.1
8	4.1-200
9	63.2-900
10	58.1-3371, 58.1-3373, 58.1-3374
12	58.1-3237.1
13	58.1-3534, n.
14	8.01-195.4, 16.1-77, 43-34, 46.2-644.03
15	8.01-581.17
16	60.2-602
17	2.2-2801, 67-1202
18	23-38.79:1, 23-38.84
19	32.1-102.3:2, n.
20	32.1-102.3:2, n.
21	46.2-742.1:1R, 46.2-749.16:1R, 46.2-749.61R, 46.2-749.108R, 46.2-749.112R
22	27-15.3
23	2.2-4343
24	2.2-4301
25	58.1-3703
26	23-38.79:1, 23-38.84
27	23-9.6:2
29	46.2-873.1
30	51.1-1135.2
31	4.1-306
32	19.2-187.1
33	46.2-725, n.
34	54.1-2131—54.1-2135, 55-225.11, 55-248.12:2, 55-519.2, 58.1-3284.2
35	2.2-2818.1
36	10.1-1425.8, n., 33.1-1, 33.1-8, 33.1-13.03, 33.1-34, 33.1-35, 33.1-148, 33.1-149, 33.1-150, 33.1-154, 33.1-155, 33.1-13.01, 33.1-13.02R, 46.2-206, n., 46.2-302, n., 46.2-373, n., 46.2-675, n., 46.2-819.1, n., 46.2-819.3:1, n., 46.2-819.5, n., 46.2-873.1, n., 46.2-877, n., 46.2-878, n., 46.2-881, n., 46.2-883, n., 46.2-930, n., 46.2-932, n., 46.2-1104, n., 46.2-1109, n., 46.2-1110, n., 46.2-1112, n., 46.2-1144.1, n., 46.2-1145, n., 46.2-1223, n., 46.2-1307, n., 46.2-1307.1, n.
37	32.1-122.20, 32.1-122.22R
38	23-7.4
39	16.1-293
40	53.1-56
41	15.2-1535, 51.5-5.01, 51.5-47—51.5-52R
42	37.2-902, 37.2-904, 37.2-907, 37.2-910, 37.2-913
43	15.2-2903, n.
44	23-7.4
45	2.2-2818.1
46	54.1-2131—54.1-2135, 55-225.11, 55-248.12:2, 55-519.2, 58.1-3284.2
47	29.1-563, 29.1-568
48	53.1-56
49	58.1-439.12:06, 58.1-439.15
50	54.1-2506
51	15.2-1535, 51.5-3, 51.5-5.01, 51.5-47—51.5-52R
52	62.1-44.15
53	44-146.28
54	46.2-411
55	22.1-253.13:2
56	46.2-725.2
57	46.2-330, 46.2-332, 46.2-692.2

ACTS 2011 Chapter	Code 1950 Section
58	16.1-107
59	19.2-92
60	33.1-94
61	46.2-608, 46.2-609
62	46.2-217, 46.2-388, 46.2-613.1— 46.2-613.5, 46.2-703, 46.2-1133, 46.2-1134, 46.2-1136, 46.2-1137, 46.2-1139
63	17.1-218R
64	33.1-221.1:1
65	4.1-230
66	19.2-310.5
67	6.2-1001, 6.2-1014
68	46.2-916.3
69	44-146.28
70	46.2-330, 46.2-332, 46.2-692.2
71	46.2-411
72	44-41.1
73	46.2-217, 46.2-388, 46.2-613.1—46.2-613.5, 46.2-703, 46.2-1133, 46.2-1134, 46.2-1136, 46.2-1137, 46.2-1139
74	22.1-253.13:2
75	5.1-7
76	8.01-128, 16.1-77
77	55-58.3
78	24.2-228
79	54.1-410.1
80	59.1-126
81	8.01-385
82	55-520, 55-525.12, 55-525.13
83	19.2-386.3
84	38.2-5009
85	10.1-1700
86	33.1-221.1:1.1, 33.1-391.3:1R
87	62.1-44.15:6
88	54.1-2818.1
89	2.2-2004.1R, 2.2-3711
90	32.1-111.9
91	46.2-870, n., 46.2-873, n., 46.2-873.1, n., 46.2-873.2, n., 46.2-874, n., 46.2-874.1, n., 46.2-875, n.
92	32.1-102.1
93	29.1-534
94	32.1-273
95	3.2-201
96	10.1-414
97	2.2-515.1, n., 2.2-515.2

ACTS 2011 Chapter	Code 1950 Section
98	3.2-109
99	16.1-300
100	33.1-221.1:8, n.
101	62.1-44.15
102	33.1-62, n.
103	46.2-733
104	33.1-12, 33.1-21R, 33.1-23, 33.1-23.03,
105	29.1-733.1
106	22.1-361
107	38.2-2206
108	44-41.1
109	32.1-271
110	2.2-3705.5, 32.1-310, 32.1-320, 32.1-321.01
111	2.2-3705.2, 2.2-3711
112	19.2-130.1
113	31-8, 31-15—31-18R
115	46.2-725, 46.2-725, n.
117	25.1-100, 25.1-108, 25.1-204, 25.1-400, 25.1-410, 25.1-411, 25.1-414, 25.1-417
118	19.2-8, 36-106
119	22.1-253.13:9
120	56-484.12
121	54.1-2900
122	2.2-800, n.
123	2.2-423, 2.2-3118, 47.1-5.1
124	54.1-3434.03, 54.1-3434.1
125	22.1-271.2, 22.1-271.4, 32.1-46
126	15.2-6319
127	15.2-107.2
128	46.2-100
129	33.1-152.1
130	32.1-102.3:2, n.
131	46.2-1143
132	58.1-439.22
133	2.2-3713
134	18.2-266.1
135	15.2-2295
136	10.1-414
137	58.1-3295
138	2.2-225, 2.2-2031, 56-484.12, 56-484.13, 56-484.14
139	63.2-1734
140	46.2-916.3
141	15.2-2244.2
143	19.2-8, 36-106
145	22.1-253.13:9
146	58.1-3221.1
147	2.2-2004.1R, 2.2-3711
148	32.1-273
149	62.1-44.15:6

ACTS 2011 Chapter	Code 1950 Section
150	32.1-102.1
151	29.1-733.1
152	10.1-1425.8, n., 33.1-1, 33.1-8, 33.1-13.01, 33.1-13.02R, 33.1-13.03, 33.1-34, 33.1-35, 33.1-148, 33.1-149, 33.1-150, 33.1-154, 33.1-155, 46.2-206, n., 46.2-302, n., 46.2-373, n., 46.2-675, n.
153	24.2-626
154	16.1-281, 22.1-3.4, 63.2-900.3
155	32.1-102.3:1, 32.1-102.3:1.1
156	63.2-100, 63.2-901.1
157	23-9.2:3.8
158	3.2-1301—3.2-1306
159	10.1-1700
160	3.2-201
162	56-484.17
163	12.1-10
164	33.1-12, 33.1-21R, 33.1-23, 33.1-23.03
165	58.1-609.1, 58.1-2201
166	51.5-12R, 51.5-23, 51.5-25.1
167	32.1-102.3:2, n.
169	16.1-300
170	63.2-900
171	19.2-310.5
172	2.2-515.1, n., 2.2-515.2
173	15.2-2303.1:1
174	32.1-102.3:2, n.
175	2.2-3705.5, 32.1-310, 32.1-320, 32.1-321.01
176	58.1-439.1
177	2.2-423, 2.2-3118, 47.1-5.1
178	15.2-6319
179	29.1-534
180	15.2-1418
181	32.1-102.3:5
182	46.2-875
183	58.1-609.3
184	58.1-3331, 58.1-3379, 58.1-3984
185	3.2-109
186	38.2-102
187	54.1-2900
188	58.1-3703
189	10.1-2129
190	25.1-100, 25.1-108, 25.1-204, 25.1-400, 25.1-410, 25.1-411, 25.1-414, 25.1-417
191	18.2-97.1, 18.2-136,

ACTS 2011 Chapter	Code 1950 Section
	29.1-419
192	58.1-3842
193	19.2-63.1
194	38.2-3117.1—38.2-3117.4
195	18.2-119
196	19.2-54
197	24.2-416.3
198	38.2-1401, 38.2-1407, 38.2-1428, 38.2-1501, 38.2-1522
199	15.2-5102
200	58.1-3294
201	46.2-1222.1
202	59.1-549
204	18.2-260.1
205	19.2-71, 19.2-72
206	24.2-226
207	10.1-1012
208	52-36
209	22.1-253.13:4
210	15.2-1627
211	65.2-402.1
212	58.1-512
213	10.1-502
214	58.1-339.12
216	22.1-79.1, 22.1-92, 22.1-93, 22.1-199.1, 22.1-208.1—22.1-208.2:1R, 22.1-208.2:2R, 22.1-209.01—22.1-209.1:1R, 22.1-209.1:6R, 22.1-212.2, 22.1-212.2:2, 22.1-212.2:3R, 22.1-217.01, 22.1-274.01R, 22.1-291R
217	28.2-709
218	36-55.35
219	19.2-54
220	62.1-44.33
221	28.2-507
222	38.2-1800, 38.2-1875—38.2-1880
223	19.2-71, 19.2-72
224	36-55.35
225	24.2-416.3
226	58.1-339.12
227	38.2-3117.1—38.2-3117.4
228	10.1-502
229	65.2-105
230	18.2-57
231	18.2-308
232	58.1-3331, 58.1-3379, 58.1-3984
233	18.2-57
234	18.2-308
235	18.2-308.2:2
236	56-46.1, 56-585.1, 67-101
237	15.2-2201, 15.2-2306
238	4.1-234
239	56-594
240	6.2-817
241	2.2-4001, 2.2-4007.1
242	2.2-3701
243	56-46.1
245	10.1-2128.1, 62.1-44.118
246	18.2-427
247	19.2-310.2
248	22.1-19.1, 22.1-253.13:3, 22.1-292.1
249	16.1-340, 37.2-808
250	51.1-155.1
251	15.2-914
252	45.1-254
253	28.2-1308, 33.1-223.2:1, 62.1-44.15:23
254	59.1-544
255	15.2-106
257	57-27.1
258	63.2-200, n.
259	2.2-2812
260	53.1-43.1
261	22.1-79.3
262	54.1-3420.1
263	9.1-138, 9.1-140
264	55-510.3
265	4.1-213
266	2.2-2699.6, 2.2-2699.7
267	15.2-1300.1
268	46.2-1025
269	59.1-366, n.
270	62.1-198, 62.1-199
271	46.2-398
272	15.2-2209.1
273	29.1-302.02
274	58.1-608.3
275	46.2-1077
276	10.1-409
278	19.2-321.1, 19.2-321.2
279	46.2-1608.2
280	46.2-864
281	62.1-44.19:7
282	17.1-805, 18.2-308.1
283	16.1-69.48:1, 17.1-275.7, 46.2-700, 46.2-908.3, 46.2-1157, 46.2-1158.01, 46.2-1158.02, 46.2-1158.1, 46.2-1161R
284	53.1-43.1
285	18.2-472.1, 19.2-188.3
286	58.1-609.3
287	28.2-302.2:1, 29.1-310.2
288	4.1-213
289	54.1-2722
290	45.1-254
291	10.1-1327, n., 10.1-1328, n.
292	54.1-3408
294	58.1-433.1
295	58.1-1822
296	58.1-512
297	3.2-4206.1, 3.2-4211
298	13.1-400.10
299	4.1-234
300	15.2-1613.1
301	6.2-1700
302	30-19.03:1.2
303	60.2-610, 60.2-611
304	65.2-105
305	2.2-6000R
306	38.2-1715
307	6.2-2000
308	56-575.3
310	59.1-544
311	10.1-1402, n., 46.2-635, n.
312	58.1-439.18
313	2.2-2699.6, 2.2-2699.7
314	28.2-603
315	2.2-4001, 2.2-4007.1
316	3.2-5130
317	58.1-439.20
318	54.1-3420.1
320	59.1-549
321	46.2-208
322	62.1-44.19:7
323	10.1-605, 10.1-605.1
324	58.1-3965.2
325	46.2-859
326	46.2-859
327	2.2-3714
329	38.2-3420
330	2.2-2002.1
331	46.2-1102
332	2.2-1110, 2.2-4301, 2.2-4303, 23-38.90, 23-38.110, 56-573.1:1, 56-575.17
333	24.2-684.1
334	54.1-2346, 54.1-2347, 54.1-2349, 54.1-2353, 55-79.74:1, 55-79.97, 55-79.97:1, 55-509, 55-509.3, 55-509.6, 55-509.7
335	25.1-417
336	19.2-76.1
337	15.2-3548

ACTS 2011 Chapter	Code 1950 Section
339	15.2-1609.1
340	15.2-2118
341	3.2-102, n., 3.2-3600, 3.2-3602, 3.2-3602.1, 3.2-3607, 3.2-3607.1, 3.2-3607.2, 3.2-3611, 10.1-104.2, 10.1-104.5, 10.1-603.7, 15.2-924.1R
342	54.1-117
343	2.2-4324
344	15.2-4302—15.2-4305, 15.2-4307, 15.2-4308R, 15.2-4309, 15.2-4310, 15.2-4314
345	23-288, 23-290.1R
346	22.1-205
347	19.2-76.1
349	15.2-3548
350	15.2-1609.1
351	20-108, 20-124.8, 20-124.9
352	58.1-339.3
353	3.2-102, n., 3.2-3600, 3.2-3602, 3.2-3602.1, 3.2-3607, 3.2-3607.1, 3.2-3607.2, 3.2-3611, 10.1-104.2, 10.1-104.5, 10.1-603.7, 15.2-924.1R
354	55-545.05
355	15.2-4302—15.2-4305, 15.2-4307, 15.2-4308R, 15.2-4309, 15.2-4310, 15.2-4314
356	23-288, 23-290.1R
357	54.1-117
358	2.2-2002.1
359	2.2-1837
360	58.1-610
361	55-79.74:1, 55-510
362	19.2-392.2
363	63.2-1715
364	58.1-662
365	58.1-339.7
367	56-585.1
368	58.1-9
369	8.1A-204, 8.1A-301, 8.2-403, 8.6A-101—8.6A-110R 59.1-352.7, 59.1-481, 59.1-501.3,
370	58.1-439.18, 58.1-439.21
371	56-585.1
372	16.1-77, 55-79.80:2, 55-513
373	18.2-308.1:4
374	18.2-57
375	53.1-5, 53.1-7R
376	23-7.4:2
377	58.1-512
378	16.1-77, 55-79.80:2, 55-513
379	13.1-1042
380	56-585.1
381	15.2-2903
382	56-585.1
383	58.1-3919.1
384	4.1-225, 9.1-176.1, 15.2-907, 16.1-260, 16.1-278.8:01, 18.2-248.1:1, 18.2-251, 18.2-255, 18.2-255.1, n., 18.2-255.2, 18.2-258, 18.2-258.02, 18.2-258.1, 18.2-308, 18.2-308.1:5, 18.2-308.4, 18.2-474.1, 19.2-83.1, 19.2-187, 19.2-386.22—19.2-386.25, 22.1-277.08, 22.1-279.3:1, 24.2-233, 53.1-145, 53.1-203, 54.1-3446
385	58.1-3819
386	32.1-102.3:2, n.
387	22.1-79.1
388	22.1-227.1
389	8.01-341.1
390	54.1-2951.1, 54.1-2954.1, 54.1-2956.1, 54.1-2956.8:2, 54.1-3017, 54.1-3020, 54.1-3023
391	22.1-253.13:3, n., 22.1-253.13:4, n.
392	19.2-70.3
393	10.1-1308, 10.1-1308.01
394	32.1-164.1:1, 32.1-164.1:3
395	32.1-102.3, n., 32.1-102.3:2, n.
396	46.2-328.1
397	2.2-2648
398	53.1-33.1
399	18.2-374.1:1
400	10.1-603.8, 33.1-23.3, 33.1-70.1, 33.1-70.2
401	18.2-204.1, 18.2-204.2
402	18.2-308.1:4
403	19.2-66, 19.2-70
405	33.1-221.1:1.1, 46.2-711, 46.2-755, 58.1-604.1, 58.1-1734—58.1-1741, 58.1-2401—58.1-2404, 58.1-2407, n., 58.1-2411, 58.1-2412, n., 58.1-2419—58.1-2421, 58.1-2424, 58.1-2425, 58.1-3510
406	32.1-127
407	46.2-1527.1, 46.2-1527.2, 46.2-1527.5
408	56-1, 56-1.2, 56-1.2:1, 56-232.2:1, 56-234, n., 56-235.2, n.
409	58.1-439.12:07
410	4.1-225, 9.1-176.1, 15.2-907, 16.1-260, 16.1-278.8:01, 18.2-248.1:1, 18.2-251, 18.2-255—18.2-255.2, 18.2-258, 18.2-258.02, 18.2-258.1, 18.2-258.1, 18.2-308, 18.2-308.1:5, 18.2-308.4, 18.2-474.1, 19.2-83.1, 19.2-187, 19.2-386.22—19.2-386.25, 22.1-277.08, 22.1-279.3:1, 24.2-233, 53.1-145, 53.1-203, 54.1-3446
411	22.1-253.13:3, n., 22.1-253.13:4, n.
412	32.1-127
413	2.2-2648
414	19.2-66, 19.2-70
415	53.1-33.1
416	18.2-374.1:1
417	58.1-439.12:07
418	6.2-2201, 6.2-2215, 6.2-2225
419	23-38.12
420	10.1-1402.1:1
421	23-38.12
422	46.2-725, n.
423	58.1-3219.4, 58.1-3220
424	46.2-2005, 46.2-2080
426	63.2-609
427	24.2-442, 24.2-443.3, 24.2-612, 24.2-643, 24.2-701, 24.2-702.1, 24.2-703, 24.2-703, 24.2-706
428	33.1-220R
429	56-51.1R
430	33.1-221.1:4R, 33.1-221.1:6R
431	58.1-3910
432	19.2-389
433	32.1-123
434	17.1-276, 33.1-41.1, 33.1-70.01, 33.1-330

ACTS 2011 Chapter	Code 1950 Section
435	6.2-1603, 6.2-1607, 6.2-1608, 6.2-1700, 6.2-1712, n., 6.2-1721
436	46.2-742
438	15.2-936, 15.2-2407, 21-118.4, 58.1-3210, n., 58.1-3211R, 58.1-3211.1—58.1-3213, 58.1-3213.1, n., 58.1-3214, n., 58.1-3215, 58.1-3216, n., 58.1-3217, n., 58.1-3218R
440	62.1-44.19:15
441	46.2-322
442	16.1-293
443	58.1-1505
444	32.1-314
445	16.1-69.55, 16.1-228, 16.1-253.1, 16.1-253.4, 16.1-279.1, 17.1-213, 17.1-272, 18.2-60.4, 19.2-81.3, 19.2-120, 19.2-152.7:1, 19.2-152.8—19.2-152.10
446	37.2-901, 37.2-906, 37.2-907, 37.2-910
447	24.2-626
448	37.2-901, 37.2-906, 37.2-907, 37.2-910
449	19.2-389
450	19.2-120
451	28.2-1207
452	15.2-2114
453	10.1-603.12:1
455	24.2-219
456	32.1-11.5
457	15.2-2204, 15.2-2301, 15.2-2311
458	24.2-442, 24.2-443.3, 24.2-612, 24.2-643, 24.2-701, 24.2-702.1, 24.2-703, 24.2-706
459	29.1-516.1
460	58.1-3219.4, 58.1-3220
461	54.1-2105.01, 54.1-2105.03, 54.1-2105.1, 54.1-2130, 54.1-2131, 54.1-2133, 54.1-2135, 54.1-2137, 54.1-2139, 54.1-2139.1—54.1-2139.3, 54.1-2142.1, 54.1-2146, 55-519
462	23-9.2:3.8
463	54.1-2400.6
464	2.2-4006, 2.2-4007.01
465	35.1-26
466	58.1-609.2, 58.1-1707
467	52-48
468	54.1-2952.2
469	46.2-916.2, 46.2-916.3
470	8.01-353.1, 19.2-310, 38.2-2419
471	46.2-833
473	37.2-304
475	58.1-3910
476	33.1-223.2:21
477	46.2-339, 46.2-341.9, 46.2-341.10, 46.2-341.18:3
479	32.1-314
480	16.1-69.55, 16.1-228, 16.1-253.1, 16.1-253.4, 16.1-279.1, 17.1-213, 17.1-272, 18.2-60.4, 19.2-81.3, 19.2-120, 19.2-152.7:1, 19.2-152.8—19.2-152.10
481	24.2-626
482	16.1-264
483	51.1-124.13, 51.1-153, 51.1-205, 51.1-216, 51.1-305
485	58.1-3131
486	32.1-261, 63.2-1200.1, 63.2-1202, 63.2-1210, 63.2-1220
487	46.2-1200
489	2.2-1204
490	54.1-2910.3
491	53.1-116
492	58.1-1505
493	17.1-276, 33.1-41.1, 33.1-70.01, 33.1-330
494	19.2-8
495	2.2-2813
496	15.2-936, 15.2-2407, 21-118.4, 58.1-3211R, 58.1-3211.1—58.1-3213, 58.1-3213.1, n., 58.1-3214, n., 58.1-3215, 58.1-3218R 58.1-3210, n., 58.1-3215, n., 58.1-3216, n., 58.1-3217, n.
497	32.1-111.5
498	38.2-1857.1, 38.2-1857.2, 38.2-1857.4—38.2-1857.7, 38.2-1857.9, 38.2-4805.1, 38.2-4805.2, 38.2-4806, 38.2-4807, 38.2-4809— 38.2-4811
499	32.1-127.1:03
500	56-247.1
501	30-170
502	32.1-174.1
503	2.2-224.1
504	19.2-215.1
505	10.1-104.6
506	32.1-325.02, n.
509	15.2-2118
510	19.2-81
511	16.1-69.48:1.02, 17.1-275.11:1
512	15.2-2241
513	65.2-406, 65.2-504
514	15.2-5370
515	15.2-4507
517	2.2-3119
518	24.2-410, 26-30, 26-59, 37.2-1001, 37.2-1014, 37.2-1031—37.2-1052
519	15.2-2286.1
520	24.2-684.1
521	2.2-2101, 2.2-2532, n., 2.2-2734—2.2-2737
522	24.2-802
523	10.1-603.8:1
524	10.1-2128.2, 62.1-44.19:15, 62.1-44.19:18
525	2.2-1149
526	54.1-2709.5
528	24.2-404, 46.2-208.1
529	15.2-2119, 15.2-5139
530	55-225.10
531	63.2-601.2
532	53.1-127.2
533	15.2-2118
534	57-60
535	2.2-3705.5, 32.1-321.01
536	2.2-3705.2, 2.2-3711
537	42.1-62
538	2.2-4345
539	2.2-115
540	2.2-2699.1
541	2.2-3705.6, 2.2-3711
542	15.2-901
543	10.1-2211
544	2.2-4341
545	23-9.2:3.8
546	36-98.3
548	2.2-2101, 2.2-2532, n., 2.2-2734—2.2-2737
549	15.2-2286.1
551	66-25.1
552	3.2-3600, 3.2-3601, 3.2-3602.1, 3.2-3605—3.2-3613,

ACTS 2011 Chapter	Code 1950 Section
	3.2-3615, 3.2-3619—3.2-3621, 3.2-3623R, 3.2-3624, 3.2-3625,
553	19.2-8
554	33.1-23.03:01, 33.1-223.2:25
555	2.2-4301
556	52-48
557	17.1-293
559	4.1-201
560	4.1-124
561	15.2-2223.1
562	15.2-1815—15.2-1817
563	58.1-423
564	3.2-3600, 3.2-3601, 3.2-3602.1, 3.2-3605— 3.2-3613, 3.2-3615, 3.2-3619, 3.2-3620, 3.2-3621, 3.2-3623R, 3.2-3624, 3.2-3625
565	17.1-275.1— 17.1-275.4, 17.1-275.7—17.1-275.9
566	1-206, 2.2-401.1, 2.2-601.1, 2.2-4347, n., 3.2-101.1, 4.1-101.1, 6.2-101.1, 9.1-101.1, 9.1-1100.1, 10.1-500.1, 10.1-603.2:01, 10.1-603.16:1, 10.1-1100.1, 10.1-1182.1, 10.1-1300.1, 10.1-1400.1, 23-276.1:1, 24.2-101.01, 28.2-521, 32.1-3.1, 33.1-13.04, 35.1-1.1, 36-85.16:1, 37.2-101, 38.2-100.1, 40.1-2.01, 45.1-161.1:1, 46.2-100.1, 53.1-1.01, 54.1-101.1, 58.1-105.1, 59.1-313.1, 62.1-44.3:1, 62.1-255.1, 63.2-100.1, 65.2-101.1, 66-10.01
567	32.1-288
568	30-282, n., 56-556, n.
569	32.1-288
570	24.2-515, 24.2-544, 24.2-545
571	58.1-3221.5
572	2.2-2666.1, 9.1-400, 9.1-801, 23-7.4:1, 44-1, 44-2, 44-5, 44-6, 44-16, 44-19, 44-21, 44-27, 44-32.1, 44-36, 44-40.1, 44-42, 44-43R, 44-44, 44-45, 44-46.1, 44-48, 44-52R, 44-54.4, 44-54.6, 44-54.8—44-54.12, 44-75.2, 44-80—44-83, 44-88, 44-93.2— 44-93.4, 44-96, 44-97.1—44-100, 44-102, 44-102.1, 44-104, 44-110, 44-115, 44-116R, 44-120, 46.2-743, 65.2-101, 65.2-103
573	2.2-4308.2, 2.2-4317
574	2.2-115
575	19.2-305.1
577	55-79.97:1, 55-509.6
579	9.1-102
580	15.2-2119, 15.2-5139
581	58.1-3221.5
583	2.2-4308.2, 2.2-4317
584	24.2-515, 24.2-544, 24.2-545
585	55-79.97:1, 55-509.6
586	2.2-2666.1, 9.1-400, 9.1-801, 23-7.4:1, 44-1, 44-2, 44-5, 44-6, 44-16, 44-19, 44-21, 44-27, 44-32.1, 44-36, 44-40.1, 44-42, 44-43R, 44-44, 44-45, 44-46.1—44-48, 44-52R, 44-54.4, 44-54.6, 44-54.8—44-54.12, 44-75.2, 44-80—44-83, 44-88, 44-93.2—44-93.4, 44-96, 44-97.1—44-100, 44-102, 44-102.1, 44-104, 44-110, 44-115, 44-116R, 44-120, 46.2-743, 65.2-101, 65.2-103
587	2.2-115
588	19.2-305.1
589	56-559
590	15.2-2606, 24.2-687
591	2.2-3104.02
592	18.2-271.1
594	2.2-1134R, 2.2-2404—2.2-2406R, 2.2-2407R, 2.2-2408R, 2.2-2667R, 2.2-2668R, 2.2-2732R, 2.2-2733R, 2.2-4303, 2.2-4308, 2.2-4323, 3.2-2800, 3.2-2805, 3.2-2801—3.2-2804R, 3.2-2806, 3.2-2807R, 9.1-108, 9.1-112, 9.1-802R, 9.1-803R, 10.1-419, 15.2-6500—15.2-6504R, 33.1-21.1:1.1, 33.1-391.3:1R, 44-146.35, 44-146.38, 44-146.39R, 44-146.40, 60.2-113, 62.1-44.34:26, 62.1-132.11:2R
595	2.2-3005.1
596	55-225.12— 55-225.14
597	58.1-3131
599	22.1-57.2, 24.2-228.1, 24.2-507, 24.2-510, 24.2-685
600	33.1-296—33.1-317R, 33.1-318R
601	28.2-642, n.
602	24.2-652
603	10.1-2211
604	2.2-3704
605	54.1-2346, 54.1-2347, 54.1-2353, 55-79.74:1, 55-79.89, 55-79.90, 55-79.98, 55-79.99, 55-391.1, 55-396, 55-399
606	58.1-3819
607	30-170
608	30-313, n., 30-314, n., 30-315, n., 30-316, n., 30-317, n., 30-318, n.
609	54.1-3103.1, 63.2-1803
610	54.1-3434
611	2.2-1178
612	2.2-4303
613	32.1-263, 54.1-2972
614	30-133.2
615	59.1-198, 59.1-200
616	62.1-199, 62.1-203, 62.1-209, 62.1-216.1
617	8.01-243
618	38.2-1903.1
619	18.2-186.5
620	46.2-1110
621	32.1-134.02
622	16.1-308, 19.2-389.1
623	9.1-185.8
624	2.2-3104.01,

ACTS 2011 Chapter	Code 1950 Section
	2.2-4376.1, 56-573.3, 56-575.17:1
625	17.1-293
626	4.1-209, 4.1-231, 4.1-233
627	28.2-526
628	59.1-148.3
629	46.2-920
630	56-484.17
631	46.2-725, n.
632	54.1-2901
633	30-282, n., 56-556, n.
634	22.1-207.1:1
635	9.1-102
636	38.2-1903.1
637	10.1-603.19, 10.1-604.1, 10.1-605.3, 10.1-606.4
638	9.1-1101, 19.2-310.5
639	33.1-221.1:1.1, 46.2-711, 46.2-755, 58.1-604.1, 58.1-1734—58.1-1741, 58.1-2401—58.1-2404, 58.1-2407, n., 58.1-2411, 58.1-2412, n., 58.1-2419—58.1-2421, 58.1-2424, 58.1-2425, 58.1-3510, n.,
641	8.01-243
642	15.2-5137
643	19.2-81
644	16.1-248.1
645	19.2-187, 19.2-187.01
646	58.1-3851.1
647	15.2-2222.1
648	18.2-370.5
649	58.1-640
650	46.2-1573
651	8.01-216.2, 8.01-216.8
652	46.2-624
653	15.2-5114
654	24.2-709
655	20-107.3
656	65.2-603
657	37.2-416, 37.2-506
658	15.2-2239
659	2.2-1136, 2.2-1153, 2.2-1156
660	15.2-1815—15.2-1817
661	55-17.1
663	58.1-604.2, 58.1-613
664	15.2-1613.1
665	65.2-101
666	22.1-253.13:3
667	33.1-223.2:17
668	32.1-127.1:03
669	52-34.7—52-34.9
670	32.1-127
671	1-510
672	58.1-512
674	58.1-604.2, 58.1-613
675	2.2-1136, 2.2-1153, 2.2-1156
676	8.01-216.2, 8.01-216.3, 8.01-216.8—8.01-216.10, 8.01-216.17
677	58.1-3823
678	46.2-624
679	64.1-62.4
680	58.1-202.3
681	2.2-1134R, 2.2-2404— 2.2-2406R, 2.2-2407, 2.2-2408R, 2.2-2667, 2.2-2668R, 2.2-2732, 2.2-2733R, 2.2-4303, 2.2-4308, 2.2-4323, 3.2-2800, 3.2-2801—3.2-2804R, 3.2-2805, 3.2-2806, 3.2-2807R, 9.1-108, 9.1-112, 9.1-802, 9.1-803R, 10.1-419, 15.2-6500—15.2-6504R, 33.1-221.1:1.1, 33.1-391.3:1R, 44-146.35, 44-146.39R, 44-146.38, 44-146.40, 60.2-113, 62.1-44.34:26, 62.1-132.11:2R
682	38.2-1705
683	18.2-266.1
684	18.2-56.1
685	58.1-3702
686	30-232, 30-236
687	20-103
688	58.1-3970.1
689	17.1-293
690	36-55.25, 36-55.26, 36-55.30
691	2.2-233, 2.2-306, 2.2-1503, 2.2-2261, 2.2-2282, 2.2-2400, 2.2-2404, 2.2-2413, 2.2-2666.1, 2.2-2669, 2.2-2696, 2.2-2699.1, 2.2-2699.5, 3.2-1301, 3.2-1401, 3.2-1501, 3.2-1601, 3.2-1700, 3.2-1801, 3.2-1901, 3.2-2101, 3.2-2201, 3.2-2301, 3.2-2401, 3.2-2501, 3.2-3001, 3.2-4022, 9.1-108, 9.1-202, 10.1-1102, 10.1-1800, 10.1-2136, 22.1-164, 22.1-337, 22.1-346.2, 23-30.25, 23-253.1, 54.1-2950.1, 54.1-2956, 54.1-2956.8, 54.1-2956.11, 54.1-2957.5, 63.2-1735
692	15.2-2209.2
693	8.01-220.1:1, 13.1-870.1, 13.1-870.2
694	16.1-69.40:1, 16.1-69.40:2
695	15.2-901
696	10.1-109, n.
697	2.2-1516— 2.2-1518
698	13.1-782—13.1-791
699	15.2-2202
700	54.1-3448
701	55-48
702	8.01-195.4, 16.1-77, 43-34, 46.2-644.03
703	54.1-3906
704	8.01-220.1:1, 13.1-870.1, 13.1-870.2
705	51.1-309
706	55-70.2
707	17.1-275
708	8.01-341.1
709	54.1-3925
710	8.01-277.1
711	15.2-2209.2
712	54.1-3017.1
713	4.1-119
714	2.2-233, 2.2-306, 2.2-1503, 2.2-2261, 2.2-2282, 2.2-2400, 2.2-2404, 2.2-2413, 2.2-2666.1, 2.2-2669, 2.2-2696, 2.2-2699.1, 2.2-2699.5, 3.2-1301, 3.2-1401, 3.2-1501, 3.2-1601, 3.2-1700, 3.2-1801, 3.2-1901, 3.2-2101, 3.2-2201, 3.2-2301, 3.2-2401, 3.2-2501, 3.2-3001, 3.2-4022, 9.1-108, 9.1-202, 10.1-1102, 10.1-1800, 10.1-2136, 22.1-164, 22.1-337, 22.1-346.2, 23-30.25, 23-253.1, 54.1-2950.1, 54.1-2956, 54.1-2956.8, 54.1-2956.11, 54.1-2957.5, 63.2-1735
715	17.1-258.3:2, 17.1-293, 17.1-294, 17.1-502

ACTS 2011 Chapter	Code 1950 Section
716	2.2-2336—2.2-2350, 15.2-7300—15.2-7315R
717	2.2-4330
718	2.2-1516—2.2-1518
719	9.1-102
720	10.1-563
721	10.1-563
722	51.1-142.2, 51.1-513.2, 51.1-513.3, 51.1-1116, 51.1-1117, 51.1-1128, 51.1-1134, 51.1-1401, 51.1-1405
724	37.2-319
725	2.2-1829
726	22.1-79.3, 32.1-73.8
727	53.1-126
728	4.1-111, 4.1-232, 4.1-320
729	37.2-319
730	16.1-281—16.1-282.1, 63.2-906
731	47.1-2, 47.1-7, 47.1-12, 47.1-13, 47.1-14, 47.1-15
732	18.2-326, 59.1-369, 59.1-392
733	28.2-1200.1
734	28.2-1200.1
735	33.1-46.2
736	46.2-819.1, 46.2-819.3, 46.2-819.3:1, 46.2-819.6, 46.2-819.7
737	2.2-613
738	56-1, 56-88.1, 56-234, 56-235.1, 56-236, 56-237—56-238, 56-240, 56-247.1—56-248.1, 56-249.2, 56-481.1, 56-482.1, 56-465.4:3R, 56-469—56-477R, 56-478.1R, 56-481R
739	2.2-225, 2.2-1509.3, 2.2-2006—2.2-2008, 2.2-2012, 2.2-2015, 2.2-2017, 2.2-2018R, 2.2-2018.1, 2.2-2019R, 2.2-2020, 2.2-2021, 58.1-1840.1
740	56-1, 56-88.1, 56-234, 56-235.1, 56-236, 56-237—56-238, 56-240, 56-241, 56-247.1—56-248.1, 56-249.2, 56-265.4:3R, 56-469—56-477R, 56-478.1R, 56-481R, 56-481.1, 56-482.1,
741	2.2-613
742	58.1-439.12:06
743	54.1-1128
744	54.1-1128
745	58.1-439.12:06, n., 58.1-439.12:08
746	47.1-30
747	51.1-124.9
748	60.2-604
749	59.1-284.23
750	67-103
751	60.2-604
752	30-326—30-329
753	8.01-581.17
754	3.2-6500, 3.2-6503.1, 3.2-6569
755	2.2-122
756	Const., Art. I, § 11, n.
757	Const., Art. IV, § 6, n.
758	8.01-581.15
759	8.01-581.15
760	46.2-725, n.
761	34-26
762	22.1-207.5, 23-9.2:3.9
763	18.2-359
764	24.2-106
765	30-28.16
766	8.01-293, 15.2-922, 16.1-79.1, 36-99.5, 55-225.4, 55-248.6:1, 55-248.15:2, 55-248.16, 55-248.18, 55-248.24, 55-248.38:3, 58.1-486.2
767	53.1-128
768	29.1-113
769	58.1-3219.5, 58.1-3219.6
770	15.2-958.5
771	10.1-1197.5, n., 10.1-1197.8, n., 56-265.2, n., 56-580, n., 56-585.1, n.
772	2.2-2001, 2.2-2001.1, 9.1-173.1
773	46.2-320
774	46.2-1569
775	18.2-308.1:1, 18.2-308.1:2, 18.2-308.1:3, 18.2-308.2:1
776	22.1-57.3, 22.1-57.3:1.2
777	54.1-2200, 54.1-2201, 54.1-2202, 54.1-2203, 54.1-2204, n., 54.1-2205, 54.1-2206, 54.1-2207, 54.1-2208
779	55-225.9, 55-248.18:2
780	2.2-200, 2.2-221, 2.2-230—2.2-233, 2.2-304—2.2-306R, 2.2-2004, 2.2-2101, 2.2-2338, 2.2-2666.1, 2.2-2666.2, 2.2-2666.3, 2.2-2705, 2.2-2715, 2.2-2732R, 2.2-2733R, 9.1-1200R, 15.2-7302, 58.1-344.3
781	2.2-3705.6, 10.1-104.7—10.1-104.7
782	23-7.4
783	2.2-3713
784	32.1-261
785	18.2-48, 18.2-67.7, 18.2-356
786	46.2-1550.3
787	46.2-844
788	32.1-137.6, 32.1-137.7, 32.1-137.9, 32.1-137.13, 32.1-137.14, 32.1-137.15, 32.1-137.16, 38.2-3556—38.2-3571, 38.2-4214, 38.2-4319, 38.2-4509, 38.2-5900, 38.2-5901R, 38.2-5902R, 38.2-5903R, 38.2-5905R
789	2.2-1839, 2.2-4336, 2.2-4337
790	33.1-223.2:21
791	46.2-1503, 46.2-1510, 46.2-1519, 46.2-1529, 46.2-1530, 46.2-1910, 46.2-1919, 46.2-1929, 46.2-1930, 46.2-1992.8, 46.2-1992.17, 46.2-1992.22, 46.2-1992.23, 46.2-1993.8, 46.2-1993.17, 46.2-1993.22, 46.2-1993.23
792	54.1-2310, 54.1-2312, 54.1-2312.1
793	46.2-1144.1, n., 46.2-1149.3, n.
794	54.1-3709, 54.1-3709, n.
795	2.2-2715, 2.2-2716

ACTS 2011 Chapter	Code 1950 Section
796	18.2-370.5
798	2.2-211, 2.2-307—2.2-322, 2.2-1600—2.2-1602, n., 2.2-3010, 2.2-3014, 2.2-3705.3, 2.2-3705.6, 2.2-3706, 2.2-3802, 2.2-4344, 30-138, 32.1-127.1:03, 32.1-283, 37.2-423—37.2-425, n., 53.1-16, n., 58.1-202.2, 66-3.1, n.
799	19.2-123, 19.2-303
800	2.2-4031, 58.1-204, 58.1-205
801	59.1-92.2, 59.1-92.12, 59.1-92.13
802	19.2-136, 19.2-143
803	55-70.1
804	32.1-170
805	29.1-103
806	67-1300—67-1305
807	54.1-2409.4
808	54.1-2912.3
809	5.1-1
810	24.2-611
811	54.1-2901
812	32.1-127.1:03, 54.1-2525
813	2.2-1176
814	58.1-3851.1
815	2.2-1111, 45.1-392, n., 45.1-393, n., 45.1-394, 59.1-284.25—59.1-284.27
816	2.2-2220, 2.2-2220.1, 2.2-2221, 2.2-2221.2, 2.2-2233.1, 2.2-2233.2R, 2.2-3711
817	58.1-2510
818	19.2-386.16, 19.2-386.32, 52-33
819	29.1-328
820	58.1-439.12:06
821	9.1-102, 9.1-127R, 9.1-150, 9.1-158R, 9.1-159R, 9.1-160R, 9.1-163, 9.1-164R, 9.1-176
822	46.2-915.1
823	38.2-3500, n., 38.2-3551, n.
824	46.2-1200, 46.2-1603.1, 46.2-1605, 46.2-1609
825	16.1-260
826	45.1-161.21, 45.1-161.64, 45.1-161.74, 45.1-161.77, 45.1-161.85, 45.1-161.109, 45.1-161.122, 45.1-161.133, 45.1-161.154, 45.1-161.166, 45.1-161.175, 45.1-161.186, 45.1-161.188, 45.1-161.193, 45.1-161.216, 45.1-161.250, 45.1-161.259, 45.1-161.288, 45.1-161.289, 45.1-161.290, 45.1-161.291
827	2.2-300—2.2-303, 2.2-3705.7
828	23-9.2:3.02, 23-9.2:3.03R, 23-9.6:1, 23-9.6:1.01, n., 23-9.6:1.01, 23-38.87:10—23-38.87:21, 23-38.88, 23-38.90, 23-38.91, 23-38.93
829	62.1-44.15:5.01, 62.1-44.15:20
830	33.1-23.05, 33.1-23.4:01, 33.1-23.6— 33.1-23.26, 33.1-221.1:1.3, 33.1-267, n., 33.1-268, 33.1-269, 33.1-276, 33.1-277, 33.1-280
831	58.1-439.12:06
832	15.2-915.4
833	15.2-958.5
834	47.1-2, 47.1-7, 47.1-12—47.1-15
835	34-26
836	59.1-116.1, 59.1-117—59.1-123, 59.1-125
837	19.2-123, 19.2-303
838	46.2-844
839	67-1300—67-1305
840	58.1-3219.5, 58.1-3219.6
841	29.1-103
842	62.1-44.15:5.01, 62.1-44.15:20
843	32.1-170
844	32.1-127.1:03, 54.1-2525
845	2.2-608
846	3.2-4207
847	2.2-2001, 2.2-2001.1, 9.1-173.1
848	30-145
849	54.1-2409.4
850	32.1-352, 38.2-1026, 38.2-1611.1, 38.2-1709, 38.2-4809, 38.2-4809.1, 38.2-4816, 58.1-435, 58.1-2500, 58.1-2503, 58.1-2504, 58.1-2505, 58.1-2506, 58.1-2507, 58.1-2508, 58.1-2510, 58.1-2520, 58.1-2521, 58.1-2522, 58.1-2525, 58.1-2526, 58.1-2528, 58.1-2531, 58.1-2532, 58.1-2533, 59.1-280
851	58.1-322, 58.1-339R, 58.1-339.9, 58.1-402, 58.1-433.1, 58.1-439.2, 58.1-490, 58.1-610, 58.1-3260, 58.1-3607, 58.1-3938
852	19.2-386.16, 19.2-386.32, 52-33
854	9.1-102, 9.1-127R, 9.1-150, 9.1-158—9.1-160R, 9.1-163R, 9.1-164R 9.1-176
855	18.2-370.5
856	46.2-1569
857	63.2-600, 63.2-601.1
858	2.2-200, 2.2-221, 2.2-230, 2.2-230, 2.2-231, 2.2-232, 2.2-233, 2.2-304R, 2.2-305R, 2.2-306R, 2.2-2004, 2.2-2101, 2.2-2338, , 2.2-2666.1, 2.2-2666.2, 2.2-2666.3, 2.2-2705, 2.2-2715, 2.2-2732R, 2.2-2733R, 9.1-1200R, 15.2-7302, 58.1-344.3
859	54.1-2200—54.1-2203, 54.1-2205, 54.1-2206—54.1-2208
860	23-7.4
861	58.1-439.12:06
862	45.1-161.21, 45.1-161.64, 45.1-161.74, 45.1-161.77, 45.1-161.85, 45.1-161.109, 45.1-161.122, 45.1-161.133, 45.1-161.154, 45.1-161.166, 45.1-161.175, 45.1-161.186, 45.1-161.188, 45.1-161.193,

ACTS 2011 Chapter — Code 1950 Section

45.1-161.216,
45.1-161.250,
45.1-161.259,
45.1-161.288,
45.1-161.289,
45.1-161.290,
45.1-161.291
863 .... 58.1-2510
864 . 2.2-1111, 45.1-392, n.,
45.1-393, n., 45.1-394,
59.1-284.25—59.1-284.27
865 .. 54.1-1144—54.1-1146
866 ....58.1-301
867 ...... 2.2-300—2.2-303,
2.2-3705.7
868 ....33.1-23.05,
33.1-23.4:01,
33.1-23.6—33.1-23.26,
33.1-221.1:1.3, 33.1 -268,
33.1-269, 33.1-276,
33.1-277, 33.1-280,
33.1-267, n.
869 .... 23-9.2:3.02,
23-9.2:3.03R, 23-9.6:1,
23-9.6:1.01,
23-38.87:10—23-38.87:21,
23-38.88, 23-38.90,
23-38.91, 23-38.93
870 ....15.2-2222.1, n.,
15.2-2223, n., 33.1-13, n.,
33.1-70.3, n., 33.1-198, n.,
33.1-198.1, n., 33.1-199, n.
871 .... 2.2-211,
2.2-307—2.2-322,
2.2-1600, n., 2.2-1601, n.,
2.2-1602, n., 2.2-3010,
2.2-3014, 2.2-3705.3,
2.2-3705.6, 2.2-3706,
2.2-3802, 2.2-4344,
30-138, 32.1-127.1:03,
32.1-283, 37.2-423, n.,
37.2-424, n., 37.2-425, n.,
53.1-16, n., 58.1-202.2,
66-3.1, n.
872 ....58.1-439.12:06
873 .... 2.2-614.3, 2.2-614.3
874 ...2.2-2220, 2.2-2220.1,
2.2-2221, 2.2-2221.2,
2.2-2233.1, 2.2-2233.2R,
2.2-3711
875 .... 58.1-3245.12,
58.1-3508.4, 58.1-3853
876 .... 38.2-3418.17,
38.2-4319
877 .... 58.1-3245.12,
58.1-3508.4, 58.1-3853
878 .... 38.2-3418.17,
38.2-4319
879 . 18.2-325, 18.2-325.1R
880 ...2.2-3204, 51.1-142.2,
51.1-155.1, 51.1-155.2,
51.1-162, 51.1-512.1, 5
1.1-1112, 51.1-1123,
51.1-1128
881 .... 33.1-46.2,
46.2-208.2, 46.2-341.12,
46.2-341.20, 46.2-668,
46.2-696R,
46.2-711, 46.2-755,
46.2-2000, 46.2-2000.1,
46.2-2001.3, 46.2-2005,
46.2-2011.4, 46.2-2011.8,
46.2-2011.27, 46.2-2075,
46.2-2084R,
46.2-2096, 46.2-2097R,
46.2-2097.1R, 46.2-2099.4,
46.2-2099.5, 46.2-2099.6R,
46.2-2099.44,
46.2-2100, 46.2-2108.2,
46.2-2108.4—46.2-2108.6,
46.2-2109, 46.2-2115,
46.2-2116,
46.2-2118—46.2-2120,
46.2-2122—46.2-2124,
46.2-2132, 46.2-2133,
46.2-2135—46.2-2137,
46.2-2143,
46.2-2144, 46.2-2146,
46.2-2147, 46.2-2150,
46.2-2151, 46.2-2155,
46.2-2156, 58.1-2259,
58.1-2402, 58.1-2426,
58.1-2701
882 ....38.2-508.5,
38.2-3406.1,
38.2-3406.2, 38.2-3407.11,
38.2-3411.1, 38.2-3418.5,
38.2-3432.3, 38.2-3438,
38.2-3439—38.2-3446,
38.2-3500, 38.2-3525,
38.2-4214, 38.2-4216.1,
38.2-4312.3, 38.2-4319
883 .... 62.1-44.34:15.1
884 .... 62.1-44.34:15.1
885 ....15.2-2223.2,
28.2-104.1, 28.2-1100
886 ....3.2-6500,
3.2-6503.1, 3.2-6569
887 .... 18.2-325,
18.2-325.1R
888 .... 15.2-2222.1
889 ... 33.1-46.2, 33.1-46.2,
46.2-208.2,
46.2-341.12,
46.2-341.20, 46.2-668,
46.2-696R, 46.2-711,
46.2-755, 46.2-2000,
46.2-2000.1, 46.2-2001.3,
46.2-2005, 46.2-2011.4,
46.2-2011.8, 46.2-2011.27,
46.2-2075, 46.2-2084R,
46.2-2096, 46.2-2097R,
46.2-2097.1R, 46.2-2099.4,
46.2-2099.5, 46.2-2099.6R,
46.2-2099.44, 46.2-2100,
46.2-2108.2, 46.2-2108.4,
46.2-2108.5, 46.2-2108.6,
46.2-2109, 46.2-2115,
46.2-2116,
46.2-2118, 46.2-2119,
46.2-2120, 46.2-2122,
46.2-2123, 46.2-2124,
46.2-2132, 46.2-2133,
46.2-2135, 46.2-2136,
46.2-2137, 46.2-2143,
46.2-2144, 46.2-2146,
46.2-2147, 46.2-2150,
46.2-2151, 46.2-2155,
46.2-2156, 58.1-2259,
58.1-2402, 58.1-2426,
58.1-2701
890 ....2.2-204, n.,
2.2-219, n.,
2.2-221.1, n.,
2.2-228, n.,
2.2-409, n.,
2.2-518, n.,
2.2-800, n.,
2.2-803, n.,
2.2-804, n.,
2.2-1104, n.,
2.2-1149, n.,
2.2-1155, n.,
2.2-1156, n.,
2.2-1204, n.,
2.2-1502.1, n.,
2.2-1505, n.,
2.2-1508, n.,
2.2-1514,
2.2-1802, n.,
2.2-1819, n.,
2.2-1829, n.,
2.2-2005, n.,
2.2-2031, n.,
2.2-2221, n.,
2.2-2221.1, n.,
2.2-2233.1, n.,
2.2-2318, n.,
2.2-2402, n.,
2.2-2670, n.,
2.2-2675, n.,
2.2-2723, n.,
2.2-2818, n.,
2.2-3204, n.,
2.2-3205, n.,
2.2-4000, n.,
2.2-4011, n.,
2.2-4300, n.,
2.2-4301, n.,

ACTS 2011 Chapter	Code 1950 Section
	2.2-4400, n.,
	2.2-4401,
	2.2-4800, n.,
	2.2-4806, n.,
	2.2-5206, n.,
	2.2-5209, n.,
	2.2-5211, n.,
	3.2-3100, n.,
	3.2-4200, n.,
	3.2-4201, n.,
	3.2-4204, n.,
	3.2-5100, n.,
	3.2-5600, n.,
	3.2-5702, n.,
	4.1-116, n.,
	5.1-1.6, n.,
	8.01-195.1, n.,
	8.01-195.3, n.,
	8.01-384.1:1, n.,
	9.1-102, n.,
	9.1-165, n.,
	9.1-166, n.,
	9.1-168, n.,
	9.1-400, n.,
	9.1-1109, n.,
	10.1-202, n.,
	10.1-552, n.,
	10.1-564, n.,
	10.1-1124, n.,
	10.1-1176, n.,
	10.1-1188, n.,
	10.1-1190, n.,
	10.1-2128, n.,
	10.1-2128.1, n.,
	10.1-2129, n.,
	10.1-2131, n.,
	10.1-2202.1, n.,
	10.1-2211, n.,
	10.1-2213, n.,
	10.1-2213.1, n.,
	10.1-2500, n.,
	13.1-775.1, n.,
	15.2-1302, n.,
	15.2-1605, n.,
	15.2-1608, n.,
	15.2-1609.1, n.,
	15.2-1609.2, n.,
	15.2-1609.7, n.,
	15.2-1612.1, n.,
	15.2-1627.3,
	15.2-1634, n.,
	15.2-1636.8, n.,
	15.2-1643, n.,
	15.2-2602, n.,
	15.2-2659, n.,
	15.2-4100, n.,
	15.2-4526, n.,
	16.1-69.48:1,
	16.1-69.48:2,
	16.1-266,
	16.1-273, n.,
	16.1-287, n.,
	16.1-309.2, n.,
	16.1-309.6, n.,
	16.1-309.7, n.,
	16.1-322.1, n.,
	17.1-132, n.,
	17.1-275,
	17.1-278, n.,
	17.1-279, n.,
	17.2-283, n.,
	17.2-286, n.,
	17.1-287, n.,
	17.1-327, n.,
	18.2-271.1, n.,
	18.2-308, n.,
	18.2-308.2:2, n.,
	18.2-340.31, n.,
	19.2-152.4, n.,
	19.2-163, n.,
	19.2-163.01, n.,
	19.2-298.01, n.,
	19.2-316.3,
	19.2-326, n.,
	19.2-349, n.,
	19.2-368.11:1, n.,
	19.2-386.14, n.,
	22.1-18.01, n.,
	22.1-101.1, n.,
	22.1-175.5,
	22.1-205, n.,
	22.1-253.13:1, n.,
	22.1-290.01, n.,
	23-7.4:1, n.,
	23-7.4:2, n.,
	23-9.2:3.03, n.,
	23-9.2:3.1, n.,
	23-9.6:1, n.,
	23-9.9, n.,
	23-30.23, n.,
	23-30.28, n.,
	23-38.3, n.,
	23-38.12, n.,
	23-38.14, n.,
	23-38.77, n.,
	23-164.8, n.,
	23-215, n.,
	23-220.01, n.,
	23-227, n.,
	23-253.1, n.,
	23-276.10, n.,
	23-284, n.,
	24.2-108, n.,
	24.2-668, n.,
	24.2-712, n.,
	24.2-946.3, n.,
	24.2-946.4, n.,
	24.2-947.5, n.,
	28.2-245, n.,
	28.2-542, n.,
	28.2-550, n.,
	30-19.1:4, n.,
	30-58.3, n.,
	30-232,
	30-266, n.,
	30-267—30-276,
	30-301—30-308,
	32.1-50, n.,
	32.1-163, n.,
	32.1-171.1, n.,
	32.1-273.1, n.,
	32.1-323, n.,
	32.1-325.1, n.,
	32.1-325.1:1, n.,
	32.1-330.1, n.,
	32.1-331.12, n.,
	32.1-351, n.,
	32.1-352, n.,
	32.1-354, n.,
	32.1-360, n.,
	32.1-361.1, n.,
	32.1-366, n.,
	33.1-23.03:2, n.,
	33.1-23.03:8, n.,
	33.1-23.1, n.,
	33.1-23.3, n.,
	33.1-23.5:1, n.,
	33.1-23.6, n.,
	33.1-41.1, n.,
	33.1-75.3, n.,
	33.1-221.1:1, n.,
	33.1-221.1:1.1, n.,
	33.1-221.1:1.2, n.,
	35.1-13, n.,
	35.1-14, n.,
	35.1-16, n.,
	35.1-17, n.,
	36-139, n.,
	37.2-203, n.,
	37.2-316, n.,
	37.2-319, n.,
	37.2-500, n.,
	37.2-504, n.,
	37.2-605, n.,
	37.2-808, n.,
	37.2-900, n.,
	38.2-401, n.,
	40.1-49.4, n.,
	40.1-29, n.,
	44-146.28, n.,
	45.1-161.58, n.,
	45.1-161.292:31, n.,
	45.1-361.29, n.,
	46.2-205, n.,
	46.2-214.2, n.,
	46.2-342, n.,
	46.2-694, n.,
	46.2-694.1,
	46.2-697,
	46.2-702.1,

ACTS 2011 Chapter	Code 1950 Section
	46.2-878.3,
	46.2-1135,
	46.2-1167, n.,
	51.1-124.3, n.,
	51.1-124.30, n.,
	51.1-142.2, n.,
	51.1-144, n.,
	51.1-155.1, n.,
	51.1-203, n.,
	51.1-214, n.,
	51.1-303, n.,
	51.1-1100, n.,
	51.1-1103, n.,
	51.1-1109, n.,
	51.1-1111, n.,
	51.1-1112, n.,
	51.1-1122, n.,
	51.1-1123, n.,
	51.1-1401, n.,
	51.1-1403, n.,
	51.5-39.7, n.,
	51.5-106, n.,
	52-1, n.,
	52-4.3, n.,
	52-8.1:1, n.,
	52-12, n.,
	52-28, n.,
	53.1-5, n.,
	53.1-20, n.,
	53.1-45, n.,
	53.1-47, n.,
	53.1-67.1, n.,
	53.1-68, n.,
	53.1-80, n.,
	53.1-120, n.,
	53.1-131, n.,
	53.1-135, n.,
	54.1-3913, n.,
	54.1-3916, n.,
	54.1-3919, n.,
	54.1-3924, n.,
	55-66.6, n.,
	55-297, n.,
	56-232, n.,
	56-234, n.,
	56-484.12, n.,
	58.1-202.2, n.,
	58.1-214, n.,
	58.1-301,
	58.1-339.4, n.,
	58.1-353, n.,
	58.1-439.2, n.,
	58.1-600, n.,
	58.1-602, n.,
	58.1-608.3, n.,
	58.1-638, n.,
	58.1-638.1, n.,
	58.1-662, n.,
	58.1-801, n.,
	58.1-803, n.,

ACTS 2011 Chapter	Code 1950 Section
	58.1-815.1, n.,
	58.1-815.4, n.,
	58.1-816.1, n.,
	58.1-1402, n.,
	58.1-1410, n.,
	58.1-1803,
	58.1-2217, n.,
	58.1-2249 n.,
	58.1-2289, n.,
	58.1-2425, n.,
	58.1-2510, n.,
	58.1-2701, n.,
	58.1-3176, n.,
	58.1-3221.3, n.,
	58.1-3403, n.,
	58.1-3524, n.,
	58.1-3912, n.,
	58.1-4022, n.,
	59.1-284.13, n.,
	59.1-364, n.,
	59.1-392, n.,
	60.2-229, n.,
	60.2-305, n.,
	60.2-315, n.,
	62.1-44.15, n.,
	62.1-128, n.,
	62.1-140, n.,
	63.2-222, n.,
	63.2-401, n.,
	63.2-605, n.,
	63.2-611, n.,
	63.2-612, n.,
	63.2-619, n.,
	63.2-1706, n.,
	63.2-1735, n.,
	63.2-1907, n.,
	66-15, n.,
	66-20, n.,

ACTS 2011, Sp. Sess. I

ACTS 2011, Sp. Sess. I Chapter	Code 1950 Section
1	24.2-303.1R, 24.2-303.2R, 24.2-303.3, 24.2-304.01R, 24.2-304.02R, 24.2-304.03

ACTS 2012

ACTS 2012 Chapter	Code 1950 Section
1	2.2-508, 24.2-302.1R, 24.2-302.2
2	58.1-301, 58.1-322
3	54.1-2900, 54.1-2957.16, 54.1-2957.17
4	58.1-3814
5	19.2-54
6	32.1-229
7	46.2-857
8	8.01-630, 8.01-631, 8.01-676.1
9	46.2-916.2
10	46.2-1527.1, 46.2-1527.2
11	46.2-103
12	46.2-341.9
13	46.2-1516, 46.2-1916, 46.2-1993.14
14	10.1-109, n.
15	54.1-2400.01:1
16	32.1-271
17	46.2-1245
18	23-9.2:9
19	33.1-221.1:1
20	54.1-2709, 54.1-2711.1, 54.1-2712, 54.1-2713, 54.1-2714, 54.1-2714.1R, 54.1-2725
21	54.1-2521, 54.1-2523—54.1-2523.2
22	46.2-217, 46.2-341.16, 46.2-613.1, 46.2-613.4, 46.2-703, 46.2-725.2, 46.2-2000, 46.2-2001, 46.2-2001.3, 46.2-2011.4, 46.2-2011.8, 46.2-2011.11, 46.2-2099.2R, 46.2-2099.3R, 46.2-2099.7—46.2-2099.10R, 46.2-2099.12R, 46.2-2099.13—46.2-2099.16R, 46.2-2116R, 46.2-2119R, 46.2-2123R, 46.2-2155, 58.1-2402, 58.1-2403, 58.1-2700.1, 58.1-2700.2, 58.1-2712.1
23	8.01-512.4
24	54.1-2808.1, 54.1-2808.2
25	56-484.17
26	46.2-828
27	46.2-920.1
28	5.1-40
29	22.1-3
30	46.2-336
31	8.01-435
32	46.2-112
33	2.2-2452
35	46.2-2067
36	56-484.13
37	18.2-308.2:2
38	19.2-368.2
39	20-113
40	19.2-389
41	33.1-223.2:26

ACTS 2012 Chapter	Code 1950 Section
42	44-146.15
43	8.01-606
44	6.2-1323
45	55-37
46	56-576, 56-585.2
47	2.2-2235
48	58.1-1003.3
49	54.1-2013, n.
50	60.2-623
51	56-605—56-608
52	6.2-1700, 6.2-1701, 6.2-1701.1, 6.2-1709, 6.2-1711, 6.2-1715, 6.2-1719, 6.2-1720
53	6.2-1600, 6.2-1602
54	56-46.1, 56-265.2
55	2.2-2013
56	2.2-1001, 2.2-3003, 2.2-3004, 2.2-3006, 51.1-124.13
57	26-81, 64.2-1608
58	8.01-682
59	6.2-872
60	2.2-2818
61	64.1-150, 64.2-524
62	16.1-69.45
63	13.1-630, 13.1-762, 13.1-829, 13.1-924, 13.1-1012, 13.1-1054, 13.1-1214, 13.1-1244, 50-73.2, 50-73.24, 50-73.78
64	46.2-1600, 46.2-1602.2
65	60.2-500
66	59.1-293.2
67	56-585.2
68	58.1-1003.3
69	29.1-520
70	10.1-611
71	54.1-2521, 54.1-2523—54.1-2523.2
72	20-106
73	58.1-3851.1
74	17.1-223
75	58.1-3219.5
76	17.1-706
77	8.01-630, 8.01-631, 8.01-676.1
78	20-99, 20-99.2
79	8.01-512.4
80	23-231.15
81	54.1-2952
82	63.2-1104
83	22.1-19, n., 22.1-253.13:3, n.
84	20-99, 20-99.2
85	51.1-205
86	58.1-408, 58.1-422.1
87	58.1-3970.1
88	58.1-3131
89	58.1-3832
90	9.1-402.1
91	58.1-3245.12, 58.1-3853
92	58.1-339.2
93	58.1-439
94	16.1-284.1
95	58.1-609.1
96	58.1-322, 58.1-402
97	58.1-3506
98	8.01-341.1
99	2.2-1105
100	46.2-336
101	10.1-1114
102	54.1-2722
103	22.1-3
104	46.2-1216
105	46.2-2067
106	22.1-304
107	3.2-6540, 3.2-6542
108	46.2-920.1
109	45.1-161.64, 45.1-161.252
110	54.1-2900
111	46.2-217, 46.2-341.16, 46.2-613.1, 46.2-613.4, 46.2-703, 46.2-725.2, 46.2-2000, 46.2-2001, 46.2-2001.3, 46.2-2011.4, 46.2-2011.8, 46.2-2011.11, 46.2-2099.2R, 46.2-2099.3R, 46.2-2099.7—46.2-2099.10R, 46.2-2099.12R, 46.2-2099.13—46.2-2099.16R, 46.2-2116R, 46.2-2119R, 46.2-2123R, 46.2-2155, 58.1-2402, 58.1-2403, 58.1-2700.1, 58.1-2700.2, 58.1-2712.1
112	23-9.2:9
113	63.2-1530
114	62.1-201
115	37.2-1101, 37.2-1102
116	54.1-2709, 54.1-2711.1, 54.1-2712, 54.1-2713, 54.1-2714, 54.1-2714.1R, 54.1-2725
117	54.1-3001
118	8.01-435
119	46.2-618, 46.2-654.1, 46.2-1527.1, 46.2-1527.2, 46.2-1527.5
120	54.1-2808.1, 54.1-2808.2
121	37.2-906, 37.2-915
122	46.2-112
123	32.1-102.12R
124	54.1-2400.01:1
125	32.1-229
126	19.2-386.14
127	8.01-511
128	63.2-800
129	8.01-511
130	13.1-604.1, 13.1-616, 13.1-722.2, 13.1-722.4, 13.1-722.11, 13.1-767, 13.1-816, 13.1-888, 13.1-898.2, 13.1-898.4, 13.1-929, 13.1-1005, 13.1-1056, 13.1-1075, 13.1-1077, 13.1-1204, 13.1-1246, 13.1-1266, 13.1-1268, 50-73.17, 50-73.58
131	18.2-76
132	18.2-308
133	18.2-429
134	19.2-295.1
135	46.2-619
136	54.1-2972
137	32.1-324
138	37.2-709.1
139	32.1-162.9
140	9.1-102
141	18.2-270.1, 18.2-271.1
142	23-9.2:3.02, 23-9.6:1
143	18.2-186.4:1
144	20-107.3
145	33.1-351, 33.1-360—33.1-362
146	19.2-152.8
147	32.1-46.01, 32.1-46.1, 32.1-64.1, 32.1-64.2, 32.1-65, 32.1-67, 32.1-67.1
148	19.2-271.4
149	46.2-1232
150	46.2-1216
151	46.2-706, 46.2-708
152	16.1-279.1, 17.1-513, 19.2-152.10
153	46.2-341.9, 46.2-341.10, 46.2-341.18:3
154	10.1-2209, n.
155	4.1-212, 8.2A-103, 8.9A-102,

ACTS 2012 Chapter	Code 1950 Section
	8.9A-105, 8.9A-307,
	8.9A-311, 8.9A-316,
	8.9A-317, 8.9A-326,
	8.9A-406, 8.9A-408,
	8.9A-502, 8.9A-503,
	8.9A-507, 8.9A-515,
	8.9A-516, 8.9A-518,
	8.9A-521.1, 8.9A-526,
	8.9A-527, 8.9A-607,
	8.9A-801—8.9A-809,
156	38.2-4123,
	38.2-5500, 38.2-5501,
	38.2-5503
157	6.2-872
158	44-146.15
159	9.1-102
160	18.2-265.6—
	18.2-265.18
161	60.2-500
162	2.2-2452
163	24.2-947.4:1
164	2.2-223R,
	9.1-201— 9.1-204,
	16.1-235.1, 16.1-238,
	16.1-240, 16.1-274,
	16.1-275, 66-10,
	66-11R, 66-23
165	56-484.17
166	24.2-506,
	24.2-521, 24.2-543
167	23-9.2:3.7
168	54.1-2900
169	23-9.2:3.7
170	22.1-212.26, 23-299.8
171	33.1-223.2:21
172	22.1-19, n.,
	22.1-253.13:3, n.
173	54.1-3410.2
174	46.2-665,
	46.2-666, 46.2-670
175	18.2-308,
	15.2-915.3R
176	23-299,
	23-299.2, 23-299.4,
	23-299.9
177	46.2-100,
	46.2-602.3, 46.2-625,
	46.2-1001.1, 46.2-1048,
	46.2-1049, 46.2-1158
178	54.1-3001
179	33.1-210.2
180	32.1-137.02,
	37.2-505
181	22.1-271.2
182	22.1-227.1, n.
183	22.1-253.13:3
184	32.1-164.1
186	15.2-2404
187	6.2-1700,
	6.2-1701, 6.2-1701.1,
	6.2-1709, 6.2-1711,
	6.2-1715, 6.2-1719,
	6.2-1720
188	6.2-1600,
	6.2-1602
189	6.2-1605,
	6.2-1608, 19.2-389
191	15.2-1517
192	15.2-2223.1
195	59.1-293.2
196	2.2-5100
197	10.1-1107,
	10.1-1156
199	2.2-1176.1
200	56-576, 56-585.2
201	2.2-2818
202	56-605—56-608
203	4.1-210,
	4.1-231, 4.1-233
204	2.2-4329.1
206	8.01-367
207	46.2-873.1
208	38.2-4900,
	38.2-4902, 38.2-4904,
	38.2-4905,
	38.2-4918—38.2-4923,
	38.2-4924—38.2-4932,
	38.2-4906—38.2-4909R,
	38.2-4911R,
	38.2-4913—38.2-4916R
209	30-34.2:2
210	56-576,
	56-600
211	15.2-915.5
212	22.1-90.1
213	32.1-263,
	54.1-2900, 54.1-2901,
	54.1-2957, 54.1-2957.01,
	54.1-3000, 54.1-3005,
	54.1-3301, 54.1-3401
214	22.1-129.1
215	46.2-205.2,
	46.2-324.1, 46.2-325,
	46.2-330, 46.2-335,
	46.2-345, 46.2-692,
	46.2-752.1, 46.2-1550.2,
	46.2-1558, 46.2-1954,
	46.2-1964, 46.2-1992.46,
	46.2-1992.56,
	46.2-1993.46,
	46.2-1993.55
216	46.2-1176,
	46.2-1177.1, 46.2-1178,
	46.2-1178.1,
	46.2-1180—46.2-1182,
	46.2-1182.2
217	58.1-1718.1,
	58.1-1719,
	58.1-1720,
	58.1-1722,
	58.1-1724,
	58.1-1724.1,
	58.1-1724.2,
	58.1-1724.4,
	58.1-2291—58.1-2299.20
218	59.1-148.3
219	18.2-248,
	18.2-248.04
220	1-219.1, n.,
	15.2-907.2
222	46.2-205.2,
	46.2-324.1, 46.2-325,
	46.2-330, 46.2-335,
	46.2-345, 46.2-692,
	46.2-752.1, 46.2-1550.2,
	46.2-1558, 46.2-1954,
	46.2-1964, 46.2-1992.46,
	46.2-1992.56,
	46.2-1993.46,
	46.2-1993.55
223	2.2-2648
225	58.1-1718.1, n.,
	58.1-1719, n.,
	58.1-1720, n.,
	58.1-1722, n.,
	58.1-1724, n.,
	58.1-1724.1, n.,
	58.1-1724.2—
	58.1-1724.4R,
	58.1-2291—
	58.1-2299.20
226	29.1-520
227	29.1-344
228	28.2-305
229	2.2-3802
230	10.1-611
231	29.1-112, n.
232	58.1-513
233	29.1-702
234	17.1-258.3:1,
	17.1-276, 17.1-293,
	17.1-294, 17.1-502
235	38.2-2129
236	3.2-6540, 3.2-6542
237	4.1-210,
	4.1-231, 4.1-233
238	36-55.30
239	15.2-5003
240	63.2-501
241	45.1-161.64,
	45.1-161.252
242	62.1-201
243	9.1-902
244	29.1-302.02
245	4.1-120
246	37.2-906, 37.2-915
247	29.1-100, 29.1-529
248	10.1-1107,
	10.1-1156
249	10.1-566

ACTS 2012 Chapter	Code 1950 Section
250	4.1-305
251	8.01-511
252	18.2-248.8, n., 18.2-265.6—18.2-265.18
253	16.1-247
254	58.1-3916, n.
256	58.1-322, 58.1-402
257	18.2-308.2:2
258	58.1-3832
259	2.2-2235
260	4.1-305
261	16.1-279.1, 17.1-513, 19.2-152.10
262	16.1-300
263	58.1-3219.5
264	38.2-305
265	30-19.1:11
266	2.2-2903
267	58.1-3508.5
268	2.2-3802
269	2.2-2903
270	65.2-524
271	2.2-402
272	58.1-3505
273	38.2-515, 38.2-518
274	56-585.2
275	58.1-609.6
276	58.1-609.1
277	38.2-515, 38.2-518
278	10.1-1241
279	27-32.2
280	46.2-1600, 46.2-1602.2
281	9.1-184
282	23-234
283	1-219.1, 2.2-3124, 3.2-4212, 3.2-5139, 4.1-336, 4.1-340—4.1-345R, 4.1-347R, 6.2-1003, 6.2-1085, 18.2-270, 18.2-340, 19.2-369—19.2-386R, 19.2-386.1, 19.2-386.2, 19.2-386.2:1, 19.2-386.3—19.2-386.5, 19.2-386.14, 19.2-386.16, 19.2-386.19, 19.2-386.26, 19.2-386.29—19.2-386.32, 19.2-386.33, 19.2-386.34, 22.1-142, 28.2-319, 28.2-407, 28.2-821, 28.2-900, 29.1-407, 29.1-521.2, 29.1-523.1, 29.1-524, 29.1-549, 30-126, 46.2-867, 46.2-1087, 46.2-1605, 58.1-2274
284	56-46.1, 56-265.2
285	2.2-2013
286	46.2-1245
287	2.2-2903
288	58.1-3506
290	58.1-3819
291	18.2-308
292	58.1-332.2
293	38.2-325
294	38.2-1866, 38.2-1868.1, 38.2-1869, 38.2-1872—38.2-1874
295	18.2-283.1
296	42.1-15.1
297	3.2-4000, 3.2-4008, 3.2-4015
298	24.2-953
299	58.1-3212
300	37.2-805, 37.2-817
301	32.1-102.3:2, n., 32.1-102.3:5R, 32.1-102.3:6R
302	5.1-7.3
303	38.2-4900, 38.2-4902, 38.2-4904, 38.2-4905, 38.2-4906—38.2-4909R, 38.2-4911R, 38.2-4913—38.2-4916R, 38.2-4918—38.2-4923, 38.2-4924—38.2-4932
304	15.2-2286, 58.1-3700
305	58.1-322
307	2.2-804
308	54.1-1103
309	58.1-439.2
311	15.2-901
312	60.2-602
313	57-49
316	60.2-512
317	22.1-16.5, 63.2-214.3
318	15.2-2286, 58.1-3700
320	19.2-271.4
321	29.1-302
322	2.2-712
323	63.2-1200.1
324	2.2-5002.1
325	55-79.87
326	4.1-113.1
327	58.1-439.12:07
328	24.2-120, 24.2-306, 24.2-415, 24.2-517, 24.2-709.1
329	30-283
330	27-32.2
331	2.2-2002.1
332	40.1-51.8
335	58.1-301
336	32.1-127.1:01, 54.1-2403.2
337	15.2-4904
338	55-226.2, 56-245.2, 56-245.3
339	46.2-924
340	58.1-3819.1
341	58.1-439.12:07
342	2.2-2002.1
343	15.2-1627.4
344	4.1-119
345	2.2-3101
346	38.2-2129
347	23-2.1:3
348	56-585.2
349	2.2-1001, 2.2-3003, 2.2-3004, 2.2-3006, 51.1-124.13
351	59.1-21.10, 59.1-21.16:2
352	15.2-4904
353	24.2-419, 24.2-440—24.2-443R, 24.2-443.1—24.2-443.4R, 24.2-444, 24.2-451—24.2-470, 24.2-612, 24.2-700, 24.2-701, 24.2-702.1, 24.2-703, 24.2-709
354	15.2-2118
355	54.1-2322
356	32.1-271
357	24.2-304.1
358	20-124.3
359	2.2-4329.1
360	53.1-48
361	54.1-2508
362	58.1-1000, 58.1-1017.1, 58.1-1037
363	58.1-2204, 58.1-2208, 58.1-2263, 58.1-2274
364	18.2-46.1
365	22.1-298.1
366	2.2-1837
367	32.1-325, 63.2-501.1
368	36-156.1
369	18.2-374.1:1
370	22.1-16.5, 63.2-214.3
371	38.2-2130
372	2.2-2220.1
373	19.2-386.14
374	9.1-400
375	54.1-4424
376	4.1-111, 4.1-201
377	15.2-4507
378	37.2-1101, 37.2-1102
379	46.2-743
380	29.1-302
381	22.1-212.8:1
382	23-2.1:3
383	32.1-126.01, 32.1-162.9:1, 37.2-314,

TABLE OF ACTS CODIFIED SUBSEQUENT TO 1948

ACTS 2012 Chapter	Code 1950 Section
	37.2-408.1, 63.2-1719, 63.2-1726
384	46.2-221.2
385	46.2-221.4
386	19.2-389, 19.2-389.1, 32.1-127.1:03
387	63.2-800
388	54.1-2013, n.
389	15.2-1802
391	63.2-1509
393	24.2-706
394	30-5
395	58.1-3, 58.1-3.2
396	15.2-802
397	46.2-878.1
398	5.1-22
399	54.1-2900
400	15.2-2311
401	15.2-2301
402	32.1-116.1, 32.1-127.1:03
403	15.2-901
404	15.2-2404
405	54.1-2011, 54.1-2012, 54.1-2020, 54.1-2021, 54.1-2021.1, 54.1-2022, 54.1-2023
406	55-370
407	2.2-5100
408	19.2-136, 19.2-143, 46.2-114, 46.2-1308
409	8.01-511
411	58.1-609.6
412	3.2-4415, 3.2-4416
413	38.2-1815
414	15.2-2288.5
415	15.2-2302
416	54.1-102
417	51.1-1110, 51.1-1114, 51.1-1121, 51.1-1125, 51.1-1127
418	22.1-279.8, 23-9.2:9, 32.1-111.3, 32.1-111.11, 44-146.18, 44-146.19
419	15.2-4402, 15.2-4407
420	17.1-275, 19.2-353.3
421	16.1-300
423	51.1-138
424	16.1-241, 16.1-243, 63.2-1202, 63.2-1220.01, 63.2-1222, 63.2-1241, 63.2-1250, 63.2-1251
425	63.2-1203
427	58.1-422
428	2.2-3712
429	2.2-3112, 2.2-3115, 2.2-3117, 2.2-3120
430	15.2-901
431	15.2-901
432	63.2-905.2
433	9.1-184
434	2.2-110, 2.2-608, 30-34.15
435	56-585.1
436	2.2-2337, 2.2-2339, 2.2-2339.1, 2.2-2340, 2.2-2341.1, 2.2-2349.1
437	36-56—36-64R, 36-65—36-69R
440	2.2-2698
441	15.2-2118
443	46.2-652, 46.2-652.1, 46.2-685, 46.2-1128, 46.2-1129, 46.2-1139, 46.2-1140, 46.2-1140.1, 46.2-1141—46.2-1144.1, 46.2-1144.2, 46.2-1145, 46.2-1147—46.2-1149.1, 46.2-1149.3—46.2-1149.5
445	58.1-439, 59.1-547
447	38.2-1800
448	23-9.2:3
449	59.1-136.1
450	23-234
451	37.2-817
454	22.1-253.13:4, 22.1-254
455	15.2-2288
456	2.2-223R, 9.1-201—9.1-204, 16.1-235.1, 16.1-238, 16.1-240, 16.1-274, 16.1-275, 66-10, 66-11R, 66-23
458	9.1-400
463	2.2-713, 37.2-1020
464	55-248.7
465	15.2-2302
466	3.2-303—3.2-309
467	19.2-120
468	15.2-2241
469	17.1-276
470	33.1-223.2:27
471	46.2-706, 46.2-708
472	58.1-1000, 58.1-1017.1, 58.1-1037
473	3.2-4415, 3.2-4416
474	46.2-1209, 46.2-1211, 46.2-1212, 46.2-1213, 46.2-1215
475	58.1-439
476	2.2-701, 2.2-705, 2.2-1124, 2.2-1204, 2.2-1207, 2.2-1839, 2.2-2411, 2.2-2525, 2.2-2649, 2.2-3705.3, 2.2-3705.5, 2.2-3711, 2.2-4002, 15.2-964, 15.2-2291, 16.1-241, 16.1-269.1, 16.1-278.11, 16.1-280, 16.1-283, 16.1-336, 16.1-361, 18.2-369, 19.2-123, 19.2-182.2, 19.2-182.3, 19.2-182.8, 19.2-182.9, 19.2-218.1, 19.2-316, 19.2-389, 22.1-3, 22.1-7, 22.1-213, 22.1-214.2, 22.1-214.3, 22.1-217.1, 22.1-253.13:2, 22.1-319, 23-38.2, 25.1-100, 29.1-313, 32.1-59, 32.1-65, 32.1-102.1, 32.1-127.01, 32.1-283, 32.1-323.2, 32.1-331.13, 36-96.6, 37.2-100, 37.2-200, 37.2-203, 37.2-204, 37.2-303—37.2-306, 37.2-312, 37.2-314—37.2-316, 37.2-318, 37.2-319, 37.2-400, 37.2-401, 37.2-403, 37.2-406, 37.2-408, 37.2-408.1, 37.2-409, 37.2-411, 37.2-416, 37.2-419, 37.2-420, 37.2-427, 37.2-428, 37.2-430, 37.2-500, 37.2-501, 37.2-505, 37.2-506, 37.2-508, 37.2-509, 37.2-511, 37.2-512, 37.2-600, 37.2-601, 37.2-602, 37.2-605, 37.2-608, 37.2-609, 37.2-612, 37.2-613, 37.2-615, 37.2-700—37.2-706, 37.2-709, 37.2-710—37.2-715, 37.2-717—37.2-721, 37.2-802, 37.2-806, 37.2-837—37.2-840, 37.2-843, 37.2-1028, 37.2-1101, 38.2-3323, 38.2-3409, 40.1-28.9, 46.2-314, 46.2-400, 46.2-401, 51.1-513.3, 51.5-3, 51.5-30, 51.5-39.7, 51.5-39.8, 51.5-39.12, 51.5-39.13, 51.5-40.1, 51.5-134,

ACTS 2012 Chapter	Code 1950 Section
	51.5-140, 51.5-169, 53.1-40.3, 53.1-40.5, 53.1-40.7, 53.1-216, 54.1-701, 54.1-2970, 54.1-2982, 58.1-638, 58.1-3214, 60.2-213, 63.2-1000, 63.2-1105, 63.2-1602, 63.2-1603, 63.2-1801, 63.2-1805, 63.2-1808.1, 64.1-62.3, 64.1-157.1, 64.2-415, 64.2-531, 64.2-2000, 64.2-2027, 66-18—66-20
477	58.1-609.6
478	15.2-2288.5
479	2.2-3705.5, 8.01-216.8, 8.01-216.10, 32.1-127.1:03, 32.1-320
480	58.1-301
481	54.1-2349, 55-79.93, 55-79.93:1, 55-79.93:2, 55-394.1, 55-394.2, 55-504.1, 55-516.1, 55-530
482	2.2-2337, 2.2-2339, 2.2-2339.1, 2.2-2340, 2.2-2341.1, 2.2-2349.1
483	51.5-55
484	10.1-1152
485	21-118.4
486	24.2-120, 24.2-306, 24.2-415, 24.2-517, 24.2-709.1
488	24.2-310
489	24.2-116
491	24.2-418
492	32.1-102.1, 32.1-102.3:2
493	20-111.1
494	36-105
495	30-293, n., 30-294, n., 30-295, n., 30-296, n., 30-297, n., 30-298, n., 30-299, n., 30-300, n.
496	58.1-3916, n.
497	54.1-2816.1
498	15.2-4901
499	8.01-390.1
500	15.2-4217
501	37.2-817
502	2.2-2449, 2.2-2630, 2.2-2631, 2.2-2698, 10.1-2002, 32.1-111.10, 67-1202
503	55-225.15, 55-248.7
504	16.1-241.3, 63.2-1509
505	58.1-803
506	15.2-2293.2
507	2.2-701, 2.2-705, 2.2-1124, 2.2-1204, 2.2-1207, 2.2-1839, 2.2-2411, 2.2-2525, 2.2-2649, 2.2-3705.3, 2.2-3705.5, 2.2-3711, 2.2-4002, 15.2-964, 15.2-2291, 16.1-241, 16.1-269.1, 16.1-278.11, 16.1-280, 16.1-283, 16.1-336, 16.1-361, 18.2-369, 19.2-123, 19.2-182.2, 19.2-182.3, 19.2-182.8, 19.2-182.9, 19.2-218.1, 19.2-316, 19.2-389, 22.1-3, 22.1-7, 22.1-213, 22.1-214.2, 22.1-214.3, 22.1-217.1, 22.1-253.13:2, 22.1-319, 23-38.2, 25.1-100, 29.1-313, 32.1-59, 32.1-65, 32.1-102.1, 32.1-127.01, 32.1-283, 32.1-323.2, 32.1-331.13, 36-96.6, 37.2-100, 37.2-200, 37.2-203, 37.2-204, 37.2-303—37.2-306, 37.2-312, 37.2-314—37.2-316, 37.2-318, 37.2-319, 37.2-400, 37.2-401, 37.2-403, 37.2-406, 37.2-408, 37.2-408.1, 37.2-409, 37.2-411, 37.2-416, 37.2-419, 37.2-420, 37.2-427, 37.2-428, 37.2-430, 37.2-500, 37.2-501, 37.2-504—37.2-506, 37.2-508, 37.2-509, 37.2-511, 37.2-512, 37.2-600, 37.2-601, 37.2-602, 37.2-605, 37.2-608, 37.2-609, 37.2-612, 37.2-613, 37.2-615, 37.2-700—37.2-706, 37.2-709, 37.2-710—37.2-715, 37.2-717—37.2-721, 37.2-802, 37.2-806, 37.2-837—37.2-840, 37.2-843, 37.2-1028, 37.2-1101, 38.2-3323, 38.2-3409, 40.1-28.9, 46.2-314, 46.2-400, 46.2-401, 51.1-513.3, 51.5-3, 51.5-30, 51.5-39.7, 51.5-39.8, 51.5-39.12, 51.5-39.13, 51.5-40.1, 51.5-134, 51.5-140, 51.5-169, 53.1-40.3, 53.1-40.5, 53.1-40.7, 53.1-216, 54.1-701, 54.1-2970, 54.1-2982, 58.1-638, 58.1-3214, 60.2-213, 63.2-1000, 63.2-1105, 63.2-1602, 63.2-1603, 63.2-1801, 63.2-1805, 63.2-1808.1, 64.1-62.3, 64.1-157.1, 64.2-415, 64.2-531, 64.2-2000, 64.2-2027, 66-18—66-20
508	15.2-2209.1, 15.2-2303.1:1, 15.2-2241, n.
509	2.2-703.1, 51.5-136
510	22.1-7.1
511	18.2-515
512	15.2-2316.2
513	58.1-802
515	15.2-1517
516	15.2-1129.1
517	15.2-1716.2
518	15.2-2223.1
519	24.2-956, 24.2-956.1
520	55-79.54, 55-79.61
521	15.2-2303.2
522	54.1-309, 54.1-500.1, 54.1-602, 54.1-831.01, 54.1-1102, 54.1-2012, 54.1-2313, 54.1-2348
523	43-3
524	54.1-118
525	24.2-949.6
526	8.01-44.4
527	24.2-946.2
528	2.2-2699.3
529	2.2-1403
530	63.2-501
531	2.2-1176.1
533	Const., Art. IV, § 6, n.
534	10.1-2211
535	58.1-3221.3, n.
536	58.1-3295.1
537	15.2-3201
538	24.2-506, 24.2-521, 24.2-543
539	38.2-1316.1, 38.2-1316.2, 38.2-1316.3R, 38.2-1316.4,

ACTS 2012 Chapter	Code 1950 Section
	38.2-1316.5, 38.2-1316.6R, 38.2-1316.8
540	54.1-3452
541	54.1-3454
542	52-38
543	65.2-714
544	67-101
545	56-466.1
546	22.1-79.3
547	22.1-254.1
548	15.2-2204
549	5.1-155
550	15.2-2311
552	54.1-1117
553	15.2-2230.1
554	15.2-2201
555	64.2-745.1, 64.2-745.2, 64.2-747, 55-545.03:2, 55-545.03:3, 55-545.05
557	15.2-915.3R, 18.2-308
558	55-17.1
559	64.2-778.1, 55-548.16:1
560	6.2-1323
561	38.2-2130
562	64.2-770, 55-548.08
563	2.2-507
564	Const., Art. I, § 11, n.
565	20-23
566	47.1-2, 47.1-2, 47.1-9, 47.1-30
568	63.2-900.1, 63.2-901.1
569	46.2-1143
570	18.2-270.1, 18.2-271.1
571	30-319, n., 30-320, n., 30-321, n., 30-322, n., 30-323, n., 30-324, n., 30-325, n.
572	58.1-3851.1
573	9.1-400
574	62.1-44.15
575	18.2-61, 18.2-67.1, 18.2-67.2
576	9.1-402.1
577	18.2-51.6
578	58.1-301, 58.1-322
579	28.2-302.2:1, 29.1-310.2
580	23-299, 23-299.2, 23-299.4, 23-299.9
581	10.1-1322, 10.1-1408.1, 62.1-44.15
582	58.1-3814
583	2.2-1401, 2.2-1403
584	38.2-402, 38.2-403, 38.2-406, 38.2-407—38.2-411R
585	15.2-1104, 15.2-1201.2
586	54.1-4005
587	22.1-254.1
588	65.2-201, 65.2-704, 65.2-705
589	38.2-3420
590	58.1-612
591	30-330—30-334
592	24.2-653
593	22.1-190
594	2.2-4002, 58.1-3219.7
595	28.2-101, 29.1-109
596	58.1-439.22
597	58.1-609.1, n., 58.1-625, n., 58.1-626, n., 58.1-611.3, n., 58.1-625, n., 58.1-626, n.
598	10.1-204
599	23-70, 23-71
600	2.2-2818.01
601	17.1-100, n.
602	18.2-51.6
603	29.1-100
604	54.1-119
605	18.2-61, 18.2-67.1, 18.2-67.2
606	15.2-2311
607	27-98, 36-105
608	6.2-1001, 6.2-1014, 6.2-1067
610	58.1-3970.1
612	24.2-701
613	58.1-609.3
614	2.2-4519, 26-1—26-116R, 31-1—31-59R, 37.2-1000—37.2-1030R, 37.2-1031—37.2-1052R, 55-34.1—55-34.19R, 55-268.11—55-268.20R, 55-277.1—55-277.33R, 55-278—55-286.2R, 55-401—55-415R, 55-541.01—55-551.06R, 64.1-01—64.1-206.8R, 64.2-100—64.2-2704
615	19.2-349, 19.2-354, 46.2-395, 46.2-416
616	15.2-1716.2
617	2.2-3705.2
618	4.1-113.1
619	4.1-208
620	15.2-2118
621	10.1-1114
622	3.2-303—3.2-309
623	46.2-617, 58.1-3942
624	18.2-374.4
625	15.2-1627.4
626	1-219.1
627	58.1-3969, 58.1-3971, 58.1-3974
628	62.1-44.15:20
629	3.2-3108
630	40.1-11.3
631	62.1-44.15:23
632	2.2-1111, 2.2-1118, 2.2-4301, 2.2-4344
634	38.2-3407.18, 38.2-4214, 38.2-4319
635	27-98
636	19.2-56.2
637	16.1-241, 16.1-253.2, 16.1-253.4, 16.1-260, 19.2-152.8, 19.2-152.11
638	46.2-2101, 46.2-2143, 46.2-2143.1
639	58.1-339.2
640	16.1-241.3, 63.2-1509
641	38.2-3407.18, 38.2-4214, 38.2-4319
642	22.1-253.13:4, 22.1-254
643	4.1-203.1
644	54.1-3014
645	24.2-708
646	32.1-325, 32.1-351
647	65.2-1201, n.
649	58.1-439.2
650	46.2-603, 46.2-603.1, 46.2-623, 46.2-629, 46.2-1542, 46.2-1561
651	58.1-3511
652	24.2-1004
653	58.1-3230
654	65.2-101
655	58.1-609.3

ACTS 2012 Chapter	Code 1950 Section
656	37.2-505
657	2.2-904.03
658	23-9.2:3
659	30-330—30-335
660	51.1-603, 51.1-603.1
661	63.2-1530
662	24.2-411.1
664	24.2-406
665	58.1-3712, n., 58.1-3712.1, n., 58.1-3713.3, 58.1-3713.4, n.
666	58.1-408, 58.1-422.1
667	24.2-1004
668	19.2-169.3, 37.2-903, 37.2-904
669	2.2-904.03
670	30-19.3
671	55-509.1:1, 55-509.2, 55-509.1:1
672	56-484.17
673	38.2-102
674	56-466.1
675	8.01-195.11
676	18.2-160.1
677	54.1-2301
678	58.1-608.3
679	19.2-56.2
680	2.2-1182, 2.2-1183
681	33.1-46.2, 46.2-749.3
682	23-281
683	23-281
684	Const., Art. I, § 11, n.
685	2.2-4321.2
686	24.2-404, 24.2-427
687	22.1-304
688	8.01-3, 30-146, n., 30-147, n., 30-153R, Sup. Ct. R. 2:102
689	32.1-325, 32.1-351
690	63.2-1709.3
691	57-39.1:1
692	32.1-297.1
693	2.2-3705.6, 32.1-276.2, 32.1-276.4, 32.1-276.7:1, 32.1-276.9:1
694	23-9.2:3.04
695	45.1-181, 55-154.2
696	51.1-140R, 51.1-142.2, 51.1-161, 51.1-207, 51.1-218, 51.1-505, 51.1-512
697	23-9.2:8
698	63.2-1509
699	25.1-100, 25.1-230.1
700	29.1-744.3
701	51.1-124.3, 51.1-126, 51.1-126.5, 51.1-126.6, 51.1-135, 51.1-142.2, 51.1-145, 51.1-153, 51.1-155, 51.1-157, 51.1-166, 51.1-169, 51.1-302, 51.1-306, 51.1-308, 51.1-601.1, 51.1-603.1, 51.1-611, 51.1-1100, 51.1-1131.1, 51.1-1150—51.1-1183, 51.1-1400—51.1-1403, 51.1-1405
702	22.1-212.6, 22.1-212.7, 22.1-212.10, 22.1-212.12—22.1-212.14
703	22.1-208.01
704	54.1-2301
705	55-225.1, 55-225.8
706	13.1-603, 13.1-654, 13.1-655, 13.1-657, 13.1-661, 13.1-674, 13.1-711, 13.1-732, 13.1-734, 13.1-737, 13.1-749.1, 13.1-803, 13.1-838, 13.1-839, 13.1-944.1—13.1-944.7, 13.1-1023, 13.1-1047.1
707	58.1-3295.1
708	8.01-3, 30-146, n., 30-147, n., 30-153R, Sup. Ct. R. 2:102
709	2.2-3705.6, 32.1-276.2, 32.1-276.4, 32.1-276.5:1, 32.1-276.7:1, 32.1-276.9:1
710	18.2-248
711	63.2-900.3
712	5.1-155
713	8.01-227.11—8.01-227.23
714	17.1-275, 17.1-275.5, 19.2-336, 19.2-353.3
715	63.2-1709.3
716	23-9.2:3
717	56-585.2
718	64.2-747, 64.2-1025, 55-277.26, 55-545.05
719	25.1-100, 25.1-230.1
720	22.1-212.6, 22.1-212.7, 22.1-212.10, 22.1-212.12—22.1-212.14
721	23-9.2:8
722	58.1-3712, n., 58.1-3712.1, n., 58.1-3713, n., 58.1-3713.3, 58.1-3713.4, n.
723	24.2-643, 24.2-651.1
725	8.01-50
726	2.2-3705.7
727	2.2-208, n., 22.1-325, n.
728	63.2-1509
729	2.2-1514, 15.2-2223, 33.1-12, 33.1-23.05, 33.1-23.1, 33.1-49.1, 58.1-2201, 58.1-2249
730	32.1-123, n.
731	58.1-439.18—58.1-439.21, 58.1-439.24, 58.1-439.25—58.1-439.28
732	2.2-4321.2
733	2.2-1514, 15.2-2223, 33.1-12, 33.1-23.05, 33.1-23.1, 33.1-49.1, 58.1-2201, 58.1-2249
734	38.2-812—38.2-815, 38.2-1824, 38.2-1845.1—38.2-1845.23
735	38.2-812—38.2-815, 38.2-1824, 38.2-1845.1—38.2-1845.23
736	Const., Art. I, § 11, n.
737	Const., Art. IV, § 6, n.
738	Const., Art. I, § 11, n.
739	33.1-373, 33.1-375.1
740	63.2-1509
741	30-236, 30-239R

ACTS 2012 Chapter	Code 1950 Section
742	58.1-3284.3
743	33.1-46.2, 46.2-749.3
744	22.1-253.13:3, n., 22.1-253.13:4, n.
746	2.2-2648
747	36-135
748	10.1-603.4:1, 10.1-603.8:1, 10.1-603.15:1—10.1-603.15:5, 62.1-44.19:15, n., 62.1-44.19:18, 62.1-44.19:20
749	19.2-340.1
750	54.1-2105, 54.1-2105.03, 54.1-2106.1, 54.1-2106.2, 54.1-2110.1, 54.1-2130—54.1-2134, 54.1-2137, 54.1-2138, 54.1-2138.1, 54.1-2139, 54.1-2139.01, 54.1-2139.1, 54.1-2139.2R, 54.1-2139.3R, 54.1-2141
751	55-362, 55-376.5, 55-380, 55-380.1, 55-394.3, 55-394.4, 55-396, 55-397, 55-400
753	2.2-1105
754	24.2-604
755	22.1-298.3
756	1-219.1, 2.2-3124, 3.2-4212, 3.2-5139, 4.1-336, 4.1-340—4.1-345R, 4.1-347R, 6.2-1003, 6.2-1085, 18.2-270, 18.2-340, 19.2-369—19.2-386R 19.2-386.1—19.2-386.5, 19.2-386.2:1, 19.2-386.14, 19.2-386.16, 19.2-386.19, 19.2-386.26, 19.2-386.29—19.2-386.32, 19.2-386.33, 19.2-386.34, 22.1-142, 28.2-319, 28.2-407, 28.2-821, 28.2-900, 29.1-407, 29.1-521.2, 29.1-523.1, 29.1-524, 29.1-549, 30-126, 46.2-867, 46.2-1087, 46.2-1605, 58.1-2274
757	15.2-915
758	55-79.53, 55-79.73, 55-515
759	24.2-310
760	4.1-111, 4.1-112.2, 4.1-320, 33.1-371.1, 33.1-375, 33.1-377.1, 33.1-377R, 33.1-377.1,
761	1-219.1, n., 15.2-907.2
762	18.2-248.1:1, 54.1-3446
763	29.1-300.2
764	54.1-3029
765	15.2-2159
766	15.2-2119, 15.2-5139
767	18.2-488.1, 18.2-490
768	33.1-13.03:1
769	54.1-201, 54.1-831, 54.1-1802.1
770	15.2-2222.1
771	2.2-3101
772	16.1-269.1
773	63.2-1104
774	2.2-904.01, 2.2-904.2R
775	2.2-900, 2.2-902, 2.2-903.1, 2.2-904, 2.2-904.02, 2.2-904.1, 2.2-904.2R
776	9.1-101, 9.1-187, 18.2-308, 18.2-308.2:2, 19.2-81, 19.2-81.3, 23-7.4:1, 52-34.7, 65.2-402, 65.2-402.1
777	30-336—30-338
778	32.1-11.7
779	2.2-2201—2.2-2204, 2.2-2203.1—2.2-2203.4, 2.2-2213, 2.2-2215, 33.1-23.03:2, 33.1-23.7, 58.1-423, 58.1-638
780	17.1-275, 17.1-276
781	10.1-104.2
782	58.1-3219.5, 58.1-3219.8, 58.1-3360, 58.1-3360.1, 58.1-3360.2
783	2.2-1839, n., 2.2-4317, n., 2.2-4336, n., 2.2-4337
784	2.2-5700, 2.2-5700.1, 2.2-5701, 2.2-5702
785	10.1-560—10.1-566.1, 10.1-566.2, 10.1-567—10.1-571, 10.1-572R, 10.1-573R, 10.1-603.2:1—10.1-603.4:1, 10.1-603.4:2, 10.1-603.5—10.1-603.8:1, 10.1-603.9R, 10.1-603.11—10.1-603.12:4, 10.1-603.12:6, 10.1-603.12:7, 10.1-603.13, 10.1-603.14—10.1-603.15, 10.1-659, 10.1-2101, 10.1-2102R, 10.1-2104.1, 10.1-2106, 10.1-2107, 10.1-2112R, 10.1-2129, 62.1-195.1,
786	22.1-16, n., 22.1-253.13:1, n.
787	8.01-225, 22.1-274.2, 54.1-3408
788	8.01-126, 54.1-517.4, 55-225.8, 55-225.10, 55-225.12, 55-225.13, 55-225.14, 55-243, 55-248.4, 55-248.7:2, 55-248.34:1
789	58.1-608.3
790	15.2-2306
791	24.2-311
792	2.2-614.2:1
793	2.2-1182, 2.2-1183
794	22.1-253.13:1, 22.1-253.13:9, 23-9.2:3.02
795	2.2-4007.02, 2.2-4009
796	3.2-3607, 10.1-104.2:1
797	54.1-2349, 55-79.93, 55-79.93:1, 55-79.93:2, 55-394.1, 55-394.2, 55-504.1, 55-516.1, 55-530
798	15.2-2303.1:1, 15.2-2303.3
799	33.1-12.01, n.
800	19.2-169.3, 37.2-903, 37.2-904
801	19.2-169.6
802	8.01-391, 8.01-431, 15.2-1412, 17.1-209R, 17.1-213, 20-14.2R, 20-25, 27-42, 32.1-69.1:1, 38.2-2411R
803	2.2-118R, 2.2-203, 2.2-203.2:1, 2.2-203.2:2, 2.2-212, 2.2-214, 2.2-215, 2.2-221, 2.2-230, 2.2-435.8, 2.2-517, 2.2-520—2.2-524, 2.2-700—2.2-720R, 2.2-800, n., 2.2-1000R, 2.2-1001R, 2.2-1111,

ACTS 2012 Chapter	Code 1950 Section
	2.2-1122, 2.2-1137,
	2.2-1200, n., 2.2-1201,
	2.2-1202.1, 2.2-1204,
	2.2-1501.1, 2.2-1507,
	2.2-2001, 2.2-2001.1,
	2.2-2004, 2.2-2006,
	2.2-2012, 2.2-2101,
	2.2-2328—2.2-2335R,
	2.2-2411,
	2.2-2413R, 2.2-2414R,
	2.2-2426—2.2-2434R,
	2.2-2465—2.2-2469,
	2.2-2528,
	2.2-2620— 2.2-2625R,
	2.2-2626R, 2.2-2627R,
	2.2-2628—2.2-2629.2R,
	2.2-2632—2.2-2639R,
	2.2-2666.3,
	2.2-2674.01,
	2.2-2675—2.2-2678R,
	2.2-2696,
	2.2-2705—2.2-2708.1R,
	2.2-2711R, 2.2-2818, n.,
	2.2-3000, 2.2-3003,
	2.2-3004, 2.2-3005,
	2.2-3005.1, 2.2-3501,
	2.2-3705.2, 2.2-3705.3,
	2.2-3705.5, 2.2-3711,
	2.2-3902, 2.2-3903,
	2.2-4002, 2.2-4006,
	2.2-4024, 2.2-4117,
	2.2-4118R, 2.2-4343,
	2.2-4345, 2.2-5510,
	3.2-102, 3.2-109,
	3.2-111, 3.2-114,
	3.2-1100, 3.2-1102,
	3.2-1800, 3.2-1802,
	3.2-1803, 3.2-1804,
	3.2-1805, 3.2-1806,
	3.2-1807, 3.2-1808,
	3.2-1810, 3.2-1812,
	3.2-1813, 3.2-1815,
	3.2-1816—3.2-1822,
	3.2-2400, 3.2-2401,
	3.2-2402, 3.2-2403,
	3.2-2404, 3.2-2405,
	3.2-2406, 3.2-2407,
	3.2-2407.1, 3.2-2408,
	3.2-2409, 3.2-2410,
	3.2-2500—3.2-2510R,
	3.2-3900,
	3.2-3901—3.2-3903R,
	3.2-3905R,
	3.2-4100—3.2-4111R,
	4.1-103.02, 4.1-207.1,
	4.1-223, 8.01-66.9,
	8.01-418.2, 8.01-581.23,
	9.1-102, 9.1-108,
	10.1-104,
	10.1-107,
	10.1-217.1—10.1-217.6R,
	10.1-400, 10.1-406R,
	10.1-1102, 10.1-1103,
	10.1-1172R, 10.1-1183,
	10.1-1186,
	10.1-2135—10.1-2140R,
	15.2-738, 15.2-1507,
	15.2-1535, 15.2-1604,
	15.2-2159, 15.2-2232,
	16.1-287, 16.1-293,
	19.2-389, 22.1-17.1,
	22.1-19, 22.1-20.1,
	22.1-209.1:2,
	22.1-289,
	22.1-339—22.1-345.1R,
	23-9.9:01, 23-50.16:24,
	30-34.2:1, 30-182,
	30-193, 30-198,
	30-326, 32.1-23.1,
	32.1-89, 32.1-102.1,
	32.1-116.1, 32.1-127.1:04,
	32.1-283.5, 32.1-330.3,
	37.2-304, 37.2-312.1,
	37.2-504, 37.2-505,
	37.2-605, 37.2-1000,
	37.2-1010, 37.2-1015,
	40.1-51.4:4, 44-123.3,
	45.1-186.1, 45.1-194,
	45.1-195R, 45.1-196R,
	45.1-161.292:2,
	45.1-161.292:11,
	45.1-161.292:15,
	45.1-161.292:16R,
	45.1-161.292:18R,
	45.1-161.292:19,
	45.1-161.292:20,
	45.1-161.292:21,
	45.1-161.292:22,
	45.1-161.292:23R,
	45.1-161.292:24,
	45.1-161.292:25,
	45.1-161.292:26,
	45.1-161.292:27,
	45.1-161.292:28,
	45.1-161.292:29,
	45.1-161.292:71,
	45.1-186.1,
	45.1-194, 45.1-195R,
	45.1-196R,
	46.2-116—46.2-119,
	46.2-221, 46.12-224R,
	46.2-411, 46.2-1206,
	46.2-1217,
	46.2-2800—46.2-2828R,
	51.1-124.22,
	51.1-124.27, 51.1-1101,
	51.5-1, 51.5-2R,
	51.5-3—51.5-5.01R,
	51.5-8—51.5-10.1R,
	51.5-12.1—51.5-12.4R,
	51.5-13—51.5-14.1R,
	51.5-15—51.5-22R,
	51.5-23—51.5-30R,
	51.5-31, 51.5-33,
	51.5-39.2, 51.5-39.7,
	51.5-39.10,
	51.5-40.1,
	51.5-41,
	51.5-44,
	51.5-115—51.5-181, 53.1-5,
	53.1-10, 53.1-32,
	53.1-32.1, 53.1-41,
	53.1-63.1, 54.1-300,
	54.1-500, 54.1-500.1,
	54.1-501,
	54.1-516,
	54.1-517.3—54.1-517.5R,
	54.1-700, 54.1-701,
	54.1-703, 54.1-704.1,
	54.1-704.2, 54.1-705,
	54.1-706, 54.1-703.2R,
	54.1-1400—54.1-1405R,
	54.1-1500, 54.1-1500.1,
	54.1-1500.2, 54.1-1502R,
	54.1-1503R,
	54.1-1506—54.1-1509,
	54.1-1700—54.1-1706R,
	54.1-2200, 54.1-2200.1,
	54.1-2200.2, 54.1-2202R,
	54.1-2208.1—54.1-2208.4,
	54.1-3005, 54.1-3408,
	57-60,
	58.1-344.3, 58.1-439.11,
	59.1-203, 59.1-207.3,
	59.1- 207.34, 59.1-207.39,
	59.1-207.44, 59.1-429,
	59.1-432, 59.1-473,
	63.2-100, 63.2-215,
	63.2-217, 63.2-313,
	63.2-315, 63.2-401,
	63.2-405, 63.2-800R,
	63.2-1528R, 63.2-1600,
	63.2-1601, 63.2-1602,
	63.2-1602.1R,
	63.2-1603, n.,
	63.2-1604R, 63.2-1605,
	63.2-1606, 63.2-1700,
	63.2-1706, 63.2-1734,
	63.2-1735R, 63.2-1810,
	63.2-2100, 63.2-2102,
	64.2-2000, 64.2-2010,
	64.2-2015, 66-3, 66-10,
	66-13, 66-13.1, 66-25.1,
	66-25.1:2, 66-25.4
804	15.2-108.1
805	2.2-1124,
	2.2-4303, 2.2-4343,
	5.1-40, 15.2-968.1,
	15.2-1643, 15.2-2223.1,
	22.1-18.1, 22.1-92,

ACTS 2012 Chapter	Code 1950 Section
	22.1-129, 22.1-275.1, 37.2-504, 37.2-508, 42.1-36.1, 51.5-89
806	58.1-3219.5
807	2.2-2462R, 2.2-2463, 2.2-2464
808	10.1-603.4:1, 10.1-603.8:1, 10.1-603.15:1—10.1-603.15:5, 62.1-44.19:13, 62.1-44.19:15, 62.1-44.19:18, 62.1-44.19:20
809	15.2-1725.1
810	55-82.1, 55-82.2
811	51.1-153, 51.1-155
812	46.2-1232
813	32.1-137.02, 37.2-505
814	15.2-2403.3
815	63.2-1509
816	18.2-248.1:1, 54.1-3446
817	2.2-2201, 2.2-2202, 2.2-2203, 2.2-2203.1—2.2-2203.4, 2.2-2204, 2.2-2213, 2.2-2215, 33.1-23.03:2, 33.1-23.7, 58.1-423, 58.1-638
818	4.1-111, 4.1-112.2, 4.1-320, 33.1-371.1, 33.1-375, 33.1-377R, 33.1-377.1
819	10.1-572R, 10.1-560, 10.1-561, 10.1-561.1, 10.1-562, 10.1-563, 10.1-564, 10.1-565, 10.1-566, 10.1-566.1, 10.1-566.2, 10.1-567, 10.1-568, 10.1-569, 10.1-569.1, 10.1-570, 10.1-571, 10.1-573R, 10.1-603.2, 10.1-603.2:1, 10.1-603.2:2, 10.1-603.3, 10.1-603.4, 10.1-603.4:1, 10.1-603.4:2, 10.1-603.5, 10.1-603.6, 10.1-603.7, 10.1-603.8, 10.1-603.8:1, 10.1-603.9R, 10.1-603.11, 10.1-603.12, 10.1-603.12:1, 10.1-603.12:2, 10.1-603.12:3, 10.1-603.12:4, 10.1-603.12:6, 10.1-603.12:7, 10.1-603.13, 10.1-603.14, 10.1-603.14:1, 10.1-603.15, 10.1-659, 10.1-2101, 10.1-2102R, 10.1-2104.1, 10.1-2106, 10.1-2107, 10.1-2112R, 10.1-2129, 62.1-195.1
820	58.1-803
821	56-576, 56-600
822	51.1-144
823	51.1-124.3, 51.1-126, 51.1-126.5, 51.1-126.6, 51.1-135, 51.1-142.2, 51.1-145, 51.1-153, 51.1-155, 51.1-157, 51.1-166, 51.1-169, 51.1-302, 51.1-306, 51.1-308, 51.1-601.1, 51.1-603.1, 51.1-611, 51.1-1100, 51.1-1131.1, 51.1-1150—51.1-1183, 51.1-1400, 51.1-1401, 51.1-1402, 51.1-1403, 51.1-1405
824	46.2-1176, 46.2-1177.1, 46.2-1178, 46.2-1178.1, 46.2-1180, 46.2-1181, 46.2-1182, 46.2-1182.2
825	33.1-13.03:1
826	24.2-604
827	9.1-102, 9.1-112, 15.2-1731, 16.1-253.4, 19.2-81.3, 19.2-152.8, 53.1-31.1
828	46.2-885
829	46.2-320, 46.2-320.1, 46.2-320.2, 53.1-127.3—53.1-127.5, 63.2-1941
830	58.1-608.3
831	58.1-605
832	15.2-1902
833	8.01-225, 22.1-274.2, 54.1-3408
834	10.1-1411
835	2.2-118R, 2.2-203, 2.2-203.2:1, 2.2-203.2:2, 2.2-212, 2.2-214, 2.2-215, 2.2-221, 2.2-230, 2.2-435.8, 2.2-517, 2.2-520—2.2-524, 2.2-700—2.2-720R, 2.2-800, n., 2.2-1000R, 2.2-1001R, 2.2-1111, 2.2-1122, 2.2-1137, 2.2-1200, n., 2.2-1201, 2.2-1202.1, 2.2-1204, 2.2-1501.1, 2.2-1507, 2.2-2001, 2.2-2001.1, 2.2-2004, 2.2-2006, 2.2-2012, 2.2-2101, 2.2-2328—2.2-2335R, 2.2-2411, 2.2-2413R, 2.2-2414R, 2.2-2426—2.2-2434R, 2.2-2465—2.2-2469, 2.2-2528, 2.2-2620—2.2-2625R, 2.2-2626R, 2.2-2627R, 2.2-2628—2.2-2629.2R, 2.2-2632—2.2-2639R, 2.2-2666.3, 2.2-2674.01, 2.2-2675—2.2-2678R, 2.2-2696, 2.2-2705—2.2-2708.1R, 2.2-2711R, 2.2-2818, n., 2.2-3000, 2.2-3003, 2.2-3004, 2.2-3005, 2.2-3005.1, 2.2-3501, 2.2-3705.2, 2.2-3705.3, 2.2-3705.5, 2.2-3711, 2.2-3902, 2.2-3903, 2.2-4002, 2.2-4006, 2.2-4024, 2.2-4117, 2.2-4118R, 2.2-4343, 2.2-4345, 2.2-5510, 3.2-102, 3.2-109, 3.2-111, 3.2-114, 3.2-1100, 3.2-1102, 3.2-1800, 3.2-1802, 3.2-1803, 3.2-1804, 3.2-1805, 3.2-1806, 3.2-1807, 3.2-1808, 3.2-1810, 3.2-1812, 3.2-1813, 3.2-1815, 3.2-1816—3.2-1822, 3.2-2400, 3.2-2401, 3.2-2402, 3.2-2403, 3.2-2404, 3.2-2405, 3.2-2406, 3.2-2407, 3.2-2407.1, 3.2-2408, 3.2-2409, 3.2-2410, 3.2-2500—3.2-2510R, 3.2-3900, 3.2-3901—3.2-3903R, 3.2-3905R, 3.2-4100—3.2-4111R, 4.1-103.02, 4.1-207.1, 4.1-223, 8.01-66.9, 8.01-418.2, 8.01-581.23, 9.1-102, 9.1-108, 10.1-104, 10.1-107, 10.1-217.1—10.1-217.6R, 10.1-400, 10.1-406R,

ACTS 2012 Chapter	Code 1950 Section
	10.1-1102, 10.1-1103,
	10.1-1172R, 10.1-1183,
	10.1-1186,
	10.1-2135—10.1-2140R,
	15.2-738, 15.2-1507,
	15.2-1535, 15.2-1604,
	15.2-2159, 15.2-2232,
	16.1-287, 16.1-293,
	19.2-389, 22.1-17.1,
	22.1-19, 22.1-20.1,
	22.1-209.1:2,
	22.1-289,
	22.1-339—22.1-345.1R,
	23-9.9:01, 23-50.16:24,
	30-34.2:1, 30-182,
	30-193, 30-198,
	30-326, 32.1-23.1,
	32.1-89, 32.1-102.1,
	32.1-116.1, 32.1-127.1:04,
	32.1-283.5, 32.1-330.3,
	37.2-304, 37.2-312.1,
	37.2-504, 37.2-505,
	37.2-605, 37.2-1000,
	37.2-1010, 37.2-1015,
	40.1-51.4:4, 44-123.3,
	45.1-186.1, 45.1-194,
	45.1-195R, 45.1-196R,
	45.1-161.292:2,
	45.1-161.292:11,
	45.1-161.292:15,
	45.1-161.292:16R,
	45.1-161.292:18R,
	45.1-161.292:19,
	45.1-161.292:20,
	45.1-161.292:21,
	45.1-161.292:22,
	45.1-161.292:23R,
	45.1-161.292:24,
	45.1-161.292:25,
	45.1-161.292:26,
	45.1-161.292:27,
	45.1-161.292:28,
	45.1-161.292:29,
	45.1-161.292:71,
	45.1-186.1,
	45.1-194, 45.1-195R,
	45.1-196R,
	46.2-116—46.2-119,
	46.2-221, 46.12-224R,
	46.2-411, 46.2-1206,
	46.2-1217,
	46.2-2800—46.2-2828R,
	51.1-124.22,
	51.1-124.27, 51.1-1101,
	51.5-1, 51.5-2R,
	51.5-3—51.5-5.01R,
	51.5-8—51.5-10.1R,
	51.5-12.1—51.5-12.4R,
	51.5-13—51.5-14.1R,
	51.5-15—51.5-22R,

ACTS 2012 Chapter	Code 1950 Section
	51.5-23—51.5-30R,
	51.5-31, 51.5-33,
	51.5-39.2, 51.5-39.7,
	51.5-39.10,
	51.5-40.1,
	51.5-41,
	51.5-44,
	51.5-115—51.5-181, 53.1-5,
	53.1-10, 53.1-32,
	53.1-32.1, 53.1-41,
	53.1-63.1, 54.1-300,
	54.1-500, 54.1-500.1,
	54.1-501,
	54.1-516,
	54.1-517.3—54.1-517.5R,
	54.1-700, 54.1-701,
	54.1-703, 54.1-704.1,
	54.1-704.2, 54.1-705,
	54.1-706, 54.1-703.2R,
	54.1-1400—54.1-1405R,
	54.1-1500, 54.1-1500.1,
	54.1-1500.2, 54.1-1502R,
	54.1-1503R,
	54.1-1506—54.1-1509,
	54.1-1700—54.1-1706R,
	54.1-2200, 54.1-2200.1,
	54.1-2200.2, 54.1-2202R,
	54.1-2208.1—54.1-2208.4,
	54.1-3005, 54.1-3408,
	57-60,
	58.1-344.3, 58.1-439.11,
	59.1-203, 59.1-207.3,
	59.1- 207.34, 59.1-207.39,
	59.1-207.44, 59.1-429,
	59.1-432, 59.1-473,
	62.1-44.5, 62.1-229.4,
	63.2-100, 63.2-215,
	63.2-217, 63.2-313,
	63.2-315, 63.2-401,
	63.2-405, 63.2-800R,
	63.2-1528R, 63.2-1600,
	63.2-1601, 63.2-1602,
	63.2-1602.1R,
	63.2-1603, n.,
	63.2-1604R, 63.2-1605,
	63.2-1606, 63.2-1700,
	63.2-1706, 63.2-1734,
	63.2-1735R, 63.2-1810,
	63.2-2100, 63.2-2102,
	64.2-2000, 64.2-2010,
	64.2-2015, 66-3, 66-10,
	66-13, 66-13.1, 66-25.1,
	66-25.1:2, 66-25.4
836	2.2-1124,
	2.2-4303, 2.2-4343,
	5.1-40, 15.2-968.1,
	15.2-1643, 15.2-2223.1,
	22.1-18.1, 22.1-92,
	22.1-129, 22.1-275.1,
	37.2-504, 37.2-508,

ACTS 2012 Chapter	Code 1950 Section
	42.1-36.1, 51.5-89
837	58.1-439.20
838	24.2-643,
	24.2-651, 24.2-651.1,
	24.2-653, 24.2-701
839	24.2-643,
	24.2-651, 24.2-651.1,
	24.2-653, 24.2-701
840	58.1-1802.1
841	65.2-105
842	58.1-439.18,
	58.1-439.19, 58.1-439.20,
	58.1-439.21, 58.1-439.22,
	n., 58.1-439.24,
	58.1-439.25, 58.1-439.26,
	58.1-439.27, 58.1-439.28
844	18.2-248
845	22.1-253.13:1
846	10.1-1188,
	58.1-439.12:06,
	58.1-439.12:09,
	58.1-439.12:10, 62.1-129,
	62.1-132.3:1, 62.1-132.6,
	62.1-139
847	2.2-510,
	37.2-304, 37.2-709,
	51.5-39.1—51.5-39.12R,
	51.5-39.13, 51.5-40
848	33.1-223.2:26
849	10.1-1188,
	58.1-439.12:06,
	58.1-439.12:09,
	58.1-439.12:10, 62.1-129,
	62.1-132.3:1, 62.1-132.6,
	62.1-139

ACTS 2012

ACTS 2012, Sp. Sess. I Chapter	Code 1950 Section
1	30-209
3	2.2-409, n.,
	2.2-1104, n.,
	2.2-1149, n.,
	2.2-1156, n.,
	2.2-1502.1, n.,
	2.2-1505, n.,
	2.2-1508, n.,
	2.2-1802, n.,
	2.2-2233.1, n.,
	2.2-2402, n.,
	2.2-3205, n.,
	2.2-3800, n.,
	2.2-4400, n.,
	8.01-195.3, n.,
	9.1-165, n.,
	10.1-202, n.,
	10.1-552, n.,
	10.1-564, n.,
	10.1-603.19, n.,
	13.1-775.1, n.,

ACTS 2012, Sp. Sess. I Chapter	Code 1950 Section
	10.1-1176, n.,
	10.1-1322, n.,
	10.1-1422.3, n.,
	10.1-2128, n.,
	10.1-2128.1, n.,
	10.1-2129, n.,
	10.1-2131, n.,
	10.1-2132, n.,
	10.1-2211, n.,
	10.1-2211.1, n.,
	10.1-2213, n.,
	10.1-2213.1, n.,
	10.1-2500, n.,
	13.1-775.1, n.,
	15.2-540, n.,
	15.2-639, n.,
	15.2-848, n.,
	15.2-1605, n.,
	15.2-4518, n.,
	15.2-4526, n.,
	16.1-69.48, n.,
	16.1-69.6:1, n.,
	16.1-273, n.,
	16.1-309.2, n.,
	16.1-309.6, n.,
	16.1-309.7, n.,
	16.1-322.1, n.,
	17.1-279, n.,
	17.1-285, n.,
	17.1-286, n.,
	17.1-287, n.,
	17.1-507, n.,
	18.2-254.1, n.,
	18.2-340.31, n.,
	19.2-163, n.,
	19.2-303.5, n.,
	19.2-326, n.,
	19.2-386.14, n.,
	22.1-79.1, n.,
	22.1-175.5, n.,
	22.1-253.13:3, n.,
	23-7.4:1, n.,
	23-7.4:2, n.,
	23-38.11, n.,
	24.2-108, n.,
	30-19.1:4, n.,
	30-232—30-238, n.,
	30-266 through 30-274, n.,
	30-275, n., 30-276, n.,
	30-293—30-300, n.,
	30-313—30-318, n.,
	32.1-50, n.,
	32.1-163, n.,
	32.1-273.1, n.,
	32.1-323.2, n.,
	32.1-325.1, n.,
	32.1-325.1:1, n.,
	32.1-331.12, n.,
	32.1-354, n.,
	32.1-360, n.,

ACTS 2012, Sp. Sess. I Chapter	Code 1950 Section
	32.1-361.1, n.,
	32.1-366, n.,
	33.1-23.1, n.,
	33.1-221.1:1.1, n.,
	37.2-319, n.,
	38.2-401, n.,
	38.2-415, n.,
	40.1-49.4, n.,
	45.1-161.58, n.,
	45.1-161.292:31, n.,
	45.1-361.2, n.,
	46.2-342, n.,
	46.2-411, n.,
	46.2-694, n.,
	46.2-1167, n.,
	51.1-1401, n.,
	51.1-1403, n.,
	51.5-39.7, n.,
	51.5-135, n.,
	52-8.1:1, n.,
	52-4.3, n.,
	53.1-20, n.,
	53.1-45, n.,
	53.1-47, n.,
	53.1-67.1, n.,
	53.1-120, n.,
	53.1-131, n.,
	55-297, n.,
	55-66.6, n.,
	55-210.13, n.,
	56-232, n.,
	56-234, n.,
	56-484.12, n.,
	58.1-202.2, n.,
	58.1-214, n.,
	58.1-478, n.,
	58.1-608.3, n.,
	58.1-609.12, n.,
	58.1-622, n.,
	58.1-638, n.,
	58.1-642, n.,
	58.1-645, n.,
	58.1-656, n.,
	58.1-662, n.,
	58.1-801, n.,
	58.1-803, n.,
	58.1-1021.03, n.,
	58.1-1410, n.,
	58.1-1730, n.,
	58.1-1741, n.,
	58.1-3176, n.,
	58.1-3403, n.,
	58.1-3524, n.,
	58.1-3700, n.,
	58.1-3912, n.,
	58.1-4022, n.,
	59.1-392, n.,
	59.1-479, n.,
	59.1-547, n.,
	59.1-548, n.,

ACTS 2012, Sp. Sess. I Chapter	Code 1950 Section
	62.1-132.3:2,
	62.1-140, n.,
	63.2-1300, n.

ACTS 2013

ACTS 2013 Chapter	Code 1950 Section
1	2.2-2649
2	56-585.1, 56-585.2
3	4.1-509.1
4	58.1-301
5	2.2-5211, 2.2-5212, 63.2-100, 63.2-905, 63.2-905.1
6	3.2-1905
7	6.2-1367
9	38.2-1878
10	58.1-609.3
11	38.2-4504
12	38.2-2107
13	38.2-231
14	65.2-204
15	40.1-92, 40.1-93, 40.1-96
16	6.2-1300, 6.2-1376
17	13.1-1003, 13.1-1007, 13.1-1009, 13.1-1010.1, 13.1-1014, 13.1-1014.1, 13.1-1050, 13.1-1050.2, 13.1-1050.4, 13.1-1056, 13.1-1056.1, 13.1-1056.3, 13.1-1057, 13.1-1062, 13.1-1074, 13.1-1077
18	50-73.11, 50-73.15, 50-73.52:5, 50-73.58, 50-73.58:1, 50-73.59, 50-73.67, 50-73.68R, 50-73.131, 50-73.132, 50-73.134—50-73.136
19	58.1-3819
20	6.2-1700, 6.2-1701
21	12.1-17
22	58.1-344.3
23	58.1-439.12:04
24	3.2-113—3.2-115R, 15.2-963, 57-48, 57-55.2, 57-55.3, 59.1-298, 59.1-326, 59.1-328
25	13.1-1202—13.1-1204, 13.1-1214, 13.1-1238, 13.1-1238.1, 13.1-1239, 13.1-1246, 13.1-1246.1, 13.1-1246.3, 13.1-1247, 13.1-1249, 13.1-1252, 13.1-1253R
26	56-235.5:1
27	38.2-305

TABLE OF ACTS CODIFIED SUBSEQUENT TO 1948

ACTS 2013 Chapter	Code 1950 Section
28	58.1-344.2, 58.1-344.4
29	38.2-4809, 38.2-4809.1, 58.1-3, 58.1-2504, 58.1-2505, 58.1-2507, 58.1-2525—58.1-2527
30	6.2-600R
32	6.2-947—6.2-950
34	2.2-2001.2
35	4.1-126
36	18.2-334.2, 18.2-340.16, 18.2-340.19, 18.2-340.22, 18.2-340.28, 18.2-340.28:1, 18.2-340.33, 18.2-340.34:2, 58.1-3732.1
37	66-1
38	28.2-226, 28.2-228, 28.2-511, 28.2-538, 28.2-541, 28.2-542, 28.2-546, 28.2-548—28.2-550, 28.2-539, 28.2-540R, 28.2-543, 28.2-544R
39	58.1-3506
40	3.2-1905
41	62.1-44.19:12, n.
42	10.1-2211
43	10.1-200.1
44	22.1-294
45	28.2-1205.2
47	10.1-571, 45.1-198R, 45.1-234, 45.1-261.1, 45.1-361.2,
48	29.1-735.2
49	23-219.1
50	28.2-232
51	15.2-5136
52	22.1-212.9
53	22.1-299.4
54	2.2-3705.6, 10.1-1458
55	28.2-302.10:1
56	22.1-227.1
57	67-1400—67-1406
58	3.2-6540, 3.2-6540.1, 3.2-6570
59	2.2-4002, 2.2-4103, n., 28.2-204.1, 28.2-400.1—28.2-400.6, 28.2-402, 28.2-403, 28.2-1000.2
60	19.2-188.1
61	8.01-397
62	59.1-148.3
63	8.01-27.1, 8.01-27.2, 8.01-126, 8.01-471
64	46.2-916.2
65	8.01-20.1, 8.01-50.1, 16.1-83.1
66	15.2-1752
67	6.2-107
68	64.2-601
69	9.1-141
70	6.2-618
71	8.01-262
72	32.1-111.5, 63.2-1509, 63.2-1606
73	16.1-106, 16.1-298
74	17.1-258.3
75	38.2-2201
76	8.01-420
77	17.1-208, 17.1-258.3—17.1-258.4, 17.1-276, 17.1-292, 17.1-293, 17.1-295
78	16.1-88.2
79	2.2-2618
80	46.2-380
81	20-99
82	46.2-752
83	19.2-215.1
84	58.1-1735
85	33.1-56.3
86	47.1-4, 47.1-23
87	37.2-809
88	58.1-322
89	64.2-108.1
90	58.1-609.5
91	53.1-127.1
92	6.2-1300, 6.2-1376
93	38.2-232
94	12.1-10
95	6.2-1367
96	63.2-1726
97	16.1-106, 16.1-298
98	6.2-875
99	15.2-1752
100	20-99
101	33.1-56.3
102	6.2-600R
103	8.01-262
104	46.2-380
105	19.2-13
107	4.1-100, 4.1-207
108	54.1-2810
109	22.1-294
110	55-225.2, 55-248.26, 55-248.40
111	46.2-1190.2
113	8.01-301, 8.01-310, 8.01-312, 8.01-329
114	54.1-3408
115	54.1-2408.3
116	54.1-1106, 54.1-1108, 54.1-1108.2
117	4.1-100, 4.1-207
118	46.2-1104, 46.2-1129.1, 46.2-1139, 46.2-1148
119	2.2-3708.1
120	33.1-223.2:21
121	33.1-23.5:2R
122	19.2-13
123	22.1-253.13:1, 22.1-253.13:2
124	10.1-1114
125	3.2-5701, 3.2-5701.1
126	6.2-875
127	33.1-348, 33.1-351
128	46.2-100, 46.2-804, 46.2-805, 46.2-807, 46.2-821, 46.2-822, 46.2-826, 46.2-830, 46.2-831—46.2-833, 46.2-834—46.2-836, 46.2-846
129	10.1-571, 45.1-198R, 45.1-234, 45.1-261.1, 45.1-361.2
130	16.1-252, 16.1-253, 16.1-277.02, 16.1-278.2, 16.1-278.3, 16.1-281—16.1-282.1
131	2.2-2828R
132	54.1-3408
133	64.2-2020
135	18.2-308, 18.2-308.03
136	32.1-352, 38.2-508, 38.2-3432.3, 38.2-3444, 38.2-4216.1R, 38.2-4229.1, 58.1-2501
137	46.2-1241
138	53.1-133.10
139	23-7.4
140	30-73.3
141	2.2-4338
142	6.2-107
143	53.1-10, 66-3
144	38.2-5004, 54.1-2409.3, 54.1-2904, 54.1-2905R, 54.1-2913R, 54.1-2913.1, 54.1-2915, 54.1-2917R, 54.1-2924R, 54.1-2928R 54.1-2930—54.1-2933, 54.1-2935, 54.1-2939, 54.1-2949, 54.1-2950, 54.1-2951.1, 54.1-2953, 54.1-2957.4
145	16.1-88.2
146	38.2-236
147	2.2-2466, n., 2.2-2468, n.

ACTS 2013 Chapter	Code 1950 Section
148	6.2-947—6.2-950
149	15.2-2200, 15.2-2201, 15.2-2204, 15.2-2211
150	44-114
151	2.2-231
152	2.2-2529
154	19.2-266.3
155	2.2-904.1
156	33.1-346, 33.1-346.1R
157	22.1-253.13:1, 22.1-253.13:2
158	22.1-253.13:2
159	2.2-2669, 2.2-2670
160	63.2-621
161	2.2-2699.5
162	53.1-160
163	38.2-4809, 38.2-4809.1, 58.1-3, 58.1-2504, 58.1-2505, 58.1-2507, 58.1-2525—58.1-2527
164	53.1-40.10
165	19.2-389, 46.2-311, 46.2-324.1, 46.2-341.4, 46.2-341.7—46.2-341.9, 46.2-341.10, 46.2-341.12, 46.2-341.14, 46.2-341.14:1—46.2-341.14:10, 46.2-341.15, 46.2-341.16, 46.2-341.20, 46.2-341.20:4, 46.2-341.20:5, 46.2-348, 46.2-1076, 46.2-2001.1, 46.2-2001.3, 46.2-2005, 46.2-2011.9, 46.2-2011.11, 46.2-2011.23, 46.2-2011.24, 46.2-2099.19, 46.2-2108.4, 46.2-2122, 46.2-2132, 46.2-2133, 46.2-2176
166	23-7.4, 23-7.4:2
167	2.2-1501, n., 2.2-1509, n., 2.2-1511, n., 2.2-2101, n., 2.2-2683, n., 2.2-2684, n., 2.2-2685, n., 2.2-2686, n., 2.2-2687, n., 2.2-2688, n., 2.2-2689, n., 2.2-5510, n., 2.2-5511, n.
169	65.2-105
170	19.2-327.1, 19.2-327.2, 19.2-327.3, 19.2-327.5, 19.2-327.10—19.2-327.13
171	40.1-51.8
172	15.2-2402.1
173	62.1-69.25, 62.1-69.29, 62.1-69.30
174	65.2-301.1
175	60.2-618
176	19.2-389, 32.1-111.5
177	46.2-725, n.
178	15.2-2292.1
179	37.2-805, 37.2-817
180	19.2-327.3, 19.2-327.5, 19.2-327.11, 19.2-327.13
181	63.2-1726
182	63.2-1702, 63.2-1707
183	8.01-225, 54.1-3408
184	32.1-162.9, 32.1-162.11
185	15.2-958.6
186	4.1-126
187	16.1-69.55
188	35.1-25, 35.1-26
189	15.2-901
190	54.1-2344
191	54.1-3408
192	54.1-3300, 54.1-3300.1
193	17.1-223
195	33.1-56.1
196	28.2-1205.2
197	58.1-3374, 58.1-3378—58.1-3381
198	44-114
199	2.2-3705.7
200	58.1-3819
201	54.1-3503
202	32.1-164.9
203	38.2-1800, 38.2-1881—38.2-1886
204	65.2-1306
205	6.2-890
206	2.2-904.1
207	19.2-72, 19.2-76
208	58.1-3713.3
209	53.1-160
210	32.1-352, 38.2-508, 38.2-3432.3, 38.2-3444, 38.2-4216.1, n., 38.2-4229.1, 58.1-2501
211	33.1-391.4, 33.1-391.5
212	38.2-1822
213	15.2-2200, 15.2-2201, 15.2-2204, 15.2-2211
214	53.1-10, 66-3
215	54.1-2963.2
216	46.2-602.3
217	8.01-219.1
218	53.1-31.3
219	65.2-106
221	2.2-2342
222	33.1-223
223	58.1-609.2
224	22.1-253.13:2
225	22.1-212.9
226	46.2-649, 46.2-1190, 46.2-1190.3, 46.2-1190.5, 46.2-1192
227	2.2-2699.5
228	22.1-318.1, 22.1-318.2
229	23-276.1, 23-276.8, 23-276.16
230	58.1-3
231	2.2-300—2.2-303
232	66-4
233	54.1-3450
234	2.2-2001, 2.2-2001.3, 2.2-2004, 2.2-2465, 2.2-2466, 2.2-4002, 58.1-34 4.3, 2.2-2467—2.2-2469R
235	53.1-40.10
236	2.2-2669, 2.2-2670
237	6.2-1902
239	15.2-2511
240	54.1-2700, 54.1-2722
241	46.2-1203
242	46.2-1120
243	23-7.4, 23-7.4:2
244	46.2-600, 46.2-626.1
245	2.2-2529
246	15.2-982, 55-519.3
247	46.2-1516, 46.2-1531, 46.2-1916, 46.2-1931, 46.2-1992.14, 46.2-1992.24, 46.2-1993.14,

ACTS 2013 Chapter	Code 1950 Section
	46.2-1993.24
248	15.2-961
249	58.1-3295
250	15.2-1726
251	54.1-2313, n.
252	54.1-3408
253	15.2-1127
254	15.2-1129.1
255	32.1-122.6:1
256	55-79.83,
	55-513.3
257	38.2-231,
	38.2-325,
	38.2-2113,
	38.2-2114, 38.2-2208,
	38.2-2212
258	37.2-910
259	55-369, 55-370
260	46.2-1571
261	19.2-389,
	63.2-1725
262	54.1-4009,
	54.1-4010, 54.1-4101
263	8.01-389,
	8.01-446,
	17.1-247R, 17.1-275,
	17.1-275.5, 17.1-295,
	46.2-383, 55-137.1,
	63.2-1245
264	54.1-3500,
	54.1-3505, 54.1-3506
266	4.1-215
267	8.01-225, 54.1-3408
268	56-594
269	58.1-3237
271	58.1-3506
272	46.2-325
273	8.01-66.5, 8.01-66.6,
	19.2-305.1, 19.2-368.15
274	8.01-380
275	55-79.75, 55-510
276	20-108.1
277	15.2-2242, n.
278	22.1-32
279	55-225.8, 55-248.5
280	64.2-109, 64.2-110
281	56-235.10
282	32.1-229
283	8.01-576.10,
	8.01-581.22
284	56-607
285	3.2-5130
286	3.2-6521
287	33.1-351, n.,
	58.1-3503, 58.1-3506
288	22.1-277.07
289	58.1-318
290	33.1-223.2:29
291	22.1-295.1
292	8.01-249
293	43-3—43-4.01,
	43-5, 43-8, 43-10
294	58.1-439.6
295	18.2-248.1:1,
	54.1-3446
297	54.1-4425
298	54.1-1103
299	58.1-3912
300	8.01-225
301	22.1-253.13:7
302	23-7.4:2
303	46.2-878
304	40.1-11.3
305	15.2-6009,
	45.1-161.62,
	45.1-361.5,
	45.1-361.38,
	46.2-1143,
	58.1-3343,
	58.1-3712,
	58.1-3713,
	58.1-3713.01,
	58.1-3713.1R,
	58.1-3713.2R,
	58.1-3713.3,
	58.1-3713.5R,
	58.1-3740—
	58.1-3745,
	58.1-3930,
	58.1-3932,
	58.1-3959,
	45.1-161.62, n,
	46.2-1143, n.,
	58.1-3712, n.,
	58.1-3713.3, n.,
	58.1-3740, n.
306	58.1-3713
307	15.2-1705,
	15.2-1707
308	56-585.2
310	55-513.2
311	58.1-1009
312	46.2-348,
	46.2-828.2,
	46.2-2900—
	46.2-2910
313	2.2-1501, n.,
	2.2-1509, n.,
	2.2-1511, n.,
	2.2-2101, n.,
	2.2-2683, n.,
	2.2-2684, n.,
	2.2-2685, n.,
	2.2-2686, n.,
	2.2-2687, n.,
	2.2-2688, n.,
	2.2-2689, n.,
	2.2-5510, n.,
	2.2-5511, n.
314	19.2-215.1
317	35.1-25, 35.1-26
318	46.2-615, 46.2-633.2
319	58.1-3819
320	32.1-127,
	63.2-1805, 63.2-1808
321	37.2-809
323	55-12.4,
	55-13.3
324	64.2-776
325	58.1-611.3
326	46.2-502
327	55-369, 55-370
328	54.1-3408
329	60.2-114, 63.2-1946
331	32.1-111.5,
	63.2-1509, 63.2-1606
332	30-282
334	58.1-3965
336	8.01-225,
	22.1-274.2, 54.1-3408
337	46.2-646
338	9.1-151, 16.1-283.2
340	63.2-1505
341	10.1-418.3
342	58.1-3200, n.,
	58.1-3230, n.
343	54.1-1118,
	54.1-1120—54.1-1122,
	54.1-1125, 54.1-1126R
344	28.2-302.10:1
345	29.1-516
346	29.1-529
347	15.2-973, 46.2-662
348	10.1-1183
349	29.1-517, 29.1-530
350	18.2-334.2,
	18.2-340.16,
	18.2-340.19,
	18.2-340.22,
	18.2-340.28,
	18.2-340.28:1,
	18.2-340.33,
	18.2-340.34:2,
	58.1-3732.1
351	29.1-303.1, 29.1-311
352	10.1-411.3
353	54.1-2022
354	46.2-1149
355	15.2-1127
356	27-14
357	55-79.97,
	55-509.5, 55-509.10,
	55-519, 67-701
358	56-594
359	54.1-3408
360	46.2-725, n.
361	15.2-2119.2
362	16.1-293,
	63.2-100, 63.2-905.1

ACTS 2013 Chapter	Code 1950 Section
363	15.2-4116
364	15.2-905
365	54.1-2408.2
366	8.01-380
367	46.2-600,
	46.2-626.1
369	64.2-109,
	64.2-110
370	32.1-286
371	37.2-808,
	37.2-810
372	2.2-2101,
	2.2-2462—2.2-2464R
373	32.1-288
374	58.1-439.12:04
376	51.5-152
377	16.1-69.55
378	58.1-3819
379	8.01-401.1
380	6.2-1700,
	6.2-1701
381	3.2-4209,
	58.1-1003, 58.1-1008,
	58.1-1008.1, 58.1-1009,
	58.1-1021.02:1
382	56-594
383	8.01-576.10,
	8.01-581.22
384	58.1-3200, n.,
	58.1-3230, n.
385	46.2-1120
386	15.2-1129.1
387	8.4A-108
388	33.1-12
389	58.1-1009
390	58.1-811,
	64.2-531,
	64.2-621—64.2-638
391	58.1-3713.3
392	15.2-2511
393	58.1-3506
394	67-1400—67-1406
395	54.1-2312.1,
	54.1-2312.2
396	54.1-3931
397	46.2-334.01
398	54.1-201
400	46.2-100,
	46.2-804, 46.2-805,
	46.2-807, 46.2-821,
	46.2-822, 46.2-826,
	46.2-830,
	46.2-831—46.2-833,
	46.2-834—46.2-836,
	46.2-846
401	2.2-300—2.2-303
402	58.1-344.2,
	58.1-344.4
403	56-585.2
405	15.2-1127
406	56-235.10
407	19.2-389,
	32.1-111.5
408	19.2-124,
	19.2-132
409	24.2-106
410	18.2-174
411	9.1-140
412	54.1-3401,
	54.1-3408.04,
	54.1-3434.1,
	54.1-3457,
	54.1-3408.04, n.
414	59.1-116.1,
	59.1-117, 59.1-121,
	59.1-123, 59.1-136.1,
	59.1-136.3, 59.1-136.5,
	59.1-136.6
415	18.2-270,
	18.2-271, 46.2-391
416	18.2-308.1,
	63.2-1734
417	18.2-346
419	18.2-178.1
420	18.2-186.3
422	17.1-295, 17.1-502
423	18.2-370, 18.2-374.3
424	17.1-805
425	24.2-404
426	18.2-248
427	15.2-3226, n.
428	15.2-1724
430	46.2-1043.1
431	15.2-1612,
	18.2-174, 18.2-174.1
433	32.1-102.3:2
434	18.2-60.5
435	24.2-404.4
436	54.1-2602,
	54.1-2604
437	63.2-915
438	23-38.90
439	2.2-2614
440	22.1-299.4
441	54.1-2970.1
442	63.2-1606.1
443	24.2-522,
	24.2-527, 24.2-545
444	24.2-115.1
445	65.2-708
446	24.2-406
447	2.2-2735
448	19.2-66,
	19.2-68
449	53.1-127.2
450	18.2-308.2:2
451	37.2-405.1
452	18.2-178.1
454	18.2-213.2
456	51.1-153,
	51.1-155, 51.1-169
457	33.1-373
458	65.2-301.1
459	19.2-215.1
460	32.1-102.4
461	24.2-107,
	24.2-115
462	24.2-115.1
463	51.1-124.30,
	51.1-126.6, 51.1-144,
	51.1-145, 51.1-166,
	51.1-306, 51.1-601.1,
	51.1-603.1, 51.1-609,
	51.1-610, 51.1-1100,
	51.1-1103, 51.1-1155,
	51.1-1156, 51.1-1163,
	51.1-1164, 51.1-1173
464	63.2-1606.1
465	24.2-416.3,
	24.2-416.6, 24.2-418,
	24.2-1002.01
466	18.2-186.3
467	18.2-346
468	15.2-1705,
	15.2-1707
469	24.2-663
470	18.2-370, 18.2-374.3
471	15.2-3226, n.,
	15.2-3400, n.
472	15.2-1726
473	38.2-4509
474	19.2-124, 19.2-132
475	2.2-3101
476	4.1-119, 4.1-206
477	46.2-348,
	46.2-828.2,
	46.2-2900—46.2-2910
478	46.2-743
479	4.1-210,
	4.1-231, 4.1-233
480	23-287
481	2.2-3705.7
482	2.2-204,
	2.2-205.1,
	2.2-435.8,
	2.2-900, n.,
	2.2-903.1, n.,
	2.2-904.1, n.,
	2.2-1400, n.,
	2.2-1603—
	2.2-1617,
	2.2-2238.1,
	2.2-2282,
	2.2-2284,
	2.2-2311,
	2.2-3705.6, 2.2-4301,
	2.2-4302.1,
	2.2-4310,
	3.2-201,
	10.1-1425.7,

ACTS 2013 Chapter	Code 1950 Section
	11-7.1, 15.2-965.1, 15.2-4904, 18.2-213.1, 23-9.6:1.01, 23-38.88, 23-135.7:7, 33.1-221, 36-139.6, 46.2-749.69:1, 58.1-439.6, 59.1-284.22, 63.2-601, 63.2-610
483	24.2-304.1
484	40.1-54.3
485	2.2-1175, 2.2-1179, 2.2-1180
486	54.1-201
487	15.2-2119.2
489	54.1-2108.1
490	15.2-901
491	19.2-389, 24.2-114, 24.2-409
492	55-79.97, 55-509.5
493	2.2-1110, 2.2-1115.1
494	56-576
495	40.1-28.7:4
496	2.2-4331
497	38.2-1800, 38.2-1887—38.2-1890
498	22.1-178, 22.1-253.13:1, 22.1-253.13:4, 22.1-274, 22.1-274.4, 22.1-298.1, 22.1-299.3
499	54.1-2142.1
500	22.1-227.1
501	24.2-709.1, 24.2-711, 24.2-712
502	2.2-4303
503	24.2-653
504	54.1-3401, 54.1-3435.2
505	32.1-162.9
506	63.2-1505
507	46.2-924
508	15.2-901
509	15.2-2209.1, n., 15.2-2241, n., 15.2-2261
510	15.2-2303.2
512	35.1-25, 35.1-26
513	15.2-2302
514	59.1-544
515	32.1-102.3:2, 32.1-102.3:7, 32.1-102.3:8, 32.1-138.2, n. 32.1-276.5,
516	15.2-2295.1
517	32.1-111.13
518	2.2-4301
520	24.2-416.7, 24.2-423, 24.2-424
521	24.2-543, 24.2-545
522	20-108.1
523	64.2-719, 64.2-2001, 64.2-2002, 64.2-2007, 64.2-2008, 64.2-2022, 64.2-2023
524	15.2-2402.1
525	24.2-103, 24.2-107
526	36-105.4
529	36-106
530	22.1-178, 22.1-253.13:1, 22.1-253.13:4, 22.1-274, 22.1-274.4, 22.1-298.1, 22.1-299.3
531	55-225.16, 55-248.21:2
532	54.1-2970.1
533	54.1-3707.1
534	32.1-252, 32.1-270, 32.1-272, 32.1-273, 32.1-276
535	24.2-701
536	18.2-118
537	24.2-711.1
538	32.1-320
539	22.1-253.13:3
540	2.2-4301, 2.2-4302.2
541	15.2-2303.2
542	24.2-101, 24.2-102, 24.2-103, 24.2-404.1, 24.2-411.2, 24.2-455, 24.2-464, 24.2-502, 24.2-644, 24.2-713, 24.2-946.4, 24.2-953.3, 24.2-953.4, 64.2-2014
543	2.2-4301, 2.2-4302.2
544	54.1-3401, 54.1-3408.04, 54.1-3434.1, 54.1-3457
545	63.2-1702, 63.2-1707
546	54.1-2206.2
547	2.2-115, 2.2-621, 2.2-903.1, 2.2-2319, 2.2-2320, 2.2-5103, 3.2-305, 3.2-3108
548	58.1-3373
549	62.1-132.3:2
550	24.2-543, 24.2-545
551	8.01-36, 8.01-243
553	22.1-5.1
554	2.2-3705.7
555	2.2-1839
556	42.1-33, n.
557	32.1-11.7, 55-225.17, 55-248.12:3, 55-519.4
558	4.1-126
559	18.2-308, 18.2-308.03
560	56-573.1:1
561	15.2-2223
562	4.1-304
563	55-222, 55-243, 55-246.1, 55-248.4, 55-248.6:1, 55-248.7, 55-248.15:1, 55-248.15:2, 55-248.31, 55-248.34:1, 55-248.37, 55-248.38:1, 55-248.38:2
564	16.1-293, 63.2-100, 63.2-905.1
566	23-231.1:1
567	58.1-1017.1
568	58.1-608.3
569	33.1-12
570	58.1-1017
571	2.2-309.1, 2.2-316, 2.2-510, n., 2.2-2905, n., 2.2-2411, 2.2-2664, 2.2-2905, 2.2-3705.3, 2.2-3711, 2.2-5300, 22.1-253.13:3, 37.2-304, 37.2-709, 51.5-1, 51.5-39.1, 51.5-39.13, 51.5-46, 63.2-1808
572	2.2-1202.1, 2.2-2905, n., 2.2-3014, 2.2-3705.3, 2.2-3802
573	18.2-46.1
574	2.2-3705.6, 2.2-3705.7
575	8.01-220.1:2, 22.1-208.01, 22.1-276.01,

ACTS 2013 Chapter	Code 1950 Section
	22.1-279.6, 22.1-291.4
576	2.2-2001.2
577	23-2.01—23-2.05, 23-9.14:1, 23-38.95R
578	15.2-1301
579	46.2-334.01
580	2.2-3711
581	15.2-1901, 15.2-2200, n.
582	19.2-389, 46.2-311, 46.2-324.1, 46.2-341.4, 46.2-341.7—46.2-341.9, 46.2-341.10, 46.2-341.12, 46.2-341.14, 46.2-341.14:1—46.2-341.14:10, 46.2-341.15, 46.2-341.16, 46.2-341.20, 46.2-341.20:4, 46.2-341.20:5, 46.2-348, 46.2-1076, 46.2-2001.1, 46.2-2001.3, 46.2-2005, 46.2-2011.9, 46.2-2011.11, 46.2-2011.23, 46.2-2011.24, 46.2-2099.19, 46.2-2108.4, 46.2-2122, 46.2-2132, 46.2-2133, 46.2-2176
583	2.2-2012, 2.2-3104.01, 2.2-3106, 2.2-3109, 2.2-4301, 2.2-4302.1, 2.2-4302.2, 2.2-4303, 2.2-4343, 2.2-4359, 11-34.3, 23-38.110, 30-105, 33.1-391.3, 56-573.1, 56-575.16
584	22.1-253.13:3
585	2.2-507, 5.1-49, 15.2-2223, 22.1-205, 28.2-555, 33.1-7, 33.1-11, 33.1-12, 33.1-13.05, 33.1-23.03:7, 33.1-23.5:3, 33.1-61, 33.1-89.3, 33.1-183.1, 33.1-190.4, 33.1-195, 33.1-196, 33.1-201, 33.1-207, 33.1-208, 33.1-229, 33.1-293, 33.1-342, 33.1-343, 33.1-370, 36-98.1, 46.2-462, n., 46.2-804, 46.2-806, 46.2-830, 46.2-831, 46.2-847, 46.2-878.2, 46.2-889, 46.2-924, 46.2-1041, 46.2-1046, 46.2-1107—46.2-1109, 46.2-1112, 46.2-1114, 46.2-1116, 46.2-1117, 53.1-56, 53.1-57, 56-258, 56-462, 67-1101, 67-1103
586	23-38.76
587	22.1-253.13:1
588	2.2-507, 22.1-79, 22.1-253.13:5, 22.1-293—22.1-295, 22.1-298.1, 22.1-299, 22.1-299.3R, 22.1-302, 22.1-303, 22.1-304—22.1-305.1, 22.1-306, 22.1-307, 22.1-309, 22.1-311, 22.1-310R, 22.1-312R, 22.1-313, 22.1-314
589	15.2-4507, 15.2-4512
590	54.1-3503
591	10.1-603.7
592	46.2-1233.1
593	10.1-104.2, 10.1-104.2:1, 10.1-505, 10.1-546.1
594	15.2-1726
595	38.2-3455, 38.2-3456
596	4.1-207
597	63.2-1000, n.
598	46.2-417, 46.2-427
599	55-79.74, 55-79.79
600	2.2-3705.2
601	4.1-126
602	18.2-64.2
603	33.1-95.2
604	4.1-201, 4.1-215
605	23-9.3
606	23-219.1
607	15.2-4209
608	22.1-280.2:2
609	22.1-137.2, 22.1-279.8
610	8.01-20.1, 8.01-50.1, 16.1-83.1
611	33.1-95.2
612	15.2-1301
614	19.2-123, 19.2-390
615	18.2-459
616	27-14
617	8.01-225, 22.1-274.2, 54.1-3408
618	15.2-6009, 45.1-161.62, 45.1-361.5, 45.1-361.38, 46.2-1143, 58.1-3343, 58.1-3712, 58.1-3713, 58.1-3713.01, 58.1-3713.1R, 58.1-3713.2R, 58.1-3713.3, 58.1-3713.5R, 58.1-3740, n., 58.1-3741, n., 58.1-3742, n., 58.1-3743, n., 58.1-3744, n., 58.1-3745, n., 58.1-3930, n., 58.1-3932, n., 58.1-3740—58.1-3745, 58.1-3930, 58.1-3932, 58.1-3959,
619	2.2-4027
620	24.2-701
621	18.2-345R
622	56-573.1:1
623	58.1-1017.1
624	58.1-1017
625	18.2-246.13—18.2-246.15, 19.2-245.01
626	18.2-513
627	19.2-386.21
629	2.2-4011
630	46.2-1571
631	58.1-344.3
633	4.1-126
634	46.2-1178
635	28.2-1001
636	8.01-44.5
637	8.01-397
638	18.2-174
639	33.1-23.4:01, 33.1-269, 58.1-638, 58.1-815.4
640	22.1-19, n.
641	22.1-5
642	4.1-203
643	22.1-18
644	22.1-25, 22.1-302

ACTS 2013 Chapter	Code 1950 Section
645	18.2-46.1
646	2.2-507, 5.1-49, 15.2-2223, 22.1-205, 28.2-555, 33.1-7, 33.1-11, 33.1-12, 33.1-13.05, 33.1-23.03:7, 33.1-23.5:3, 33.1-61, 33.1-89.3, 33.1-183.1, 33.1-190.4, 33.1-195, 33.1-196, 33.1-201, 33.1-207, 33.1-208, 33.1-229, 33.1-293, 33.1-342, 33.1-343, 33.1-370, 36-98.1, 46.2-804, 46.2-806, 46.2-830, 46.2-831, 46.2-847, 46.2-878.2, 46.2-889, 46.2-924, 46.2-1041, 46.2-1046, 46.2-1107—46.2-1109, 46.2-1112, 46.2-1114, 46.2-1116, 46.2-1117, 53.1-56, 53.1-57, 56-258, 56-462, 67-1101, 67-1103
647	17.1-805
648	2.2-3104
649	23-38.76
650	2.2-507, 22.1-79, 22.1-253.13:5, 22.1-293—22.1-295, 22.1-298.1, 22.1-299, 22.1-299.3R, 22.1-302, 22.1-303, 22.1-304—22.1-305.1, 22.1-306, 22.1-307, 22.1-309, 22.1-310R, 22.1-311, 22.1-312R, 22.1-313, 22.1-314,
651	16.1-284.1
652	33.1-351, n., 58.1-3503, 58.1-3506
653	38.2-3411, 38.2-4319
654	58.1-3818.02
655	18.2-270, 18.2-271, 46.2-391
656	15.2-2223
657	58.1-319
658	10.1-104.2, 10.1-104.2:1, 10.1-505, 10.1-546.1
659	18.2-308, 18.2-308.02
660	15.2-5369, 15.2-5374, 15.2-5376
661	4.1-225, 4.1-226, 4.1-325, 4.1-325.2

ACTS 2013 Chapter	Code 1950 Section
662	18.2-308.2:2
663	46.2-725, n.
664	19.2-66, 19.2-68
665	8.01-47
666	51.1-153, 51.1-155, 51.1-169
667	30-313, n., 30-314, n., 30-315, n., 30-316, n., 30-317, n., 30-318
668	1-240.1
669	22.1-5
670	32.1-16, 32.1-137.2, 38.2-316.1, 38.2-326, 38.2-4214, 38.2-4319, 38.2-4509
671	54.1-2974
672	22.1-19, n.
673	46.2-208, 46.2-212.2, 46.2-328, 46.2-337, 46.2-345.1, 46.2-646.1, 46.2-707, 46.2-752.1, 46.2-1183.1
674	32.1-12, n.
675	19.2-324.1
676	9.1-184
677	58.1-3237.1
678	1-240.1
679	32.1-16, 32.1-137.2, 38.2-316.1, 38.2-326, 38.2-4214, 38.2-4319, 38.2-4509
680	24.2-414.1, 24.2-416.4
681	46.2-924
682	32.1-12, n.
683	60.2-633
684	24.2-101, 24.2-424, 24.2-506, 24.2-543, 24.2-612
685	9.1-151, 16.1-283.2
686	24.2-404, 24.2-427, 46.2-328.1
687	2.2-1204, 15.2-1512.1, 23-284
688	28.2-1001
689	8.01-36, 8.01-243
690	2.2-1202.1, 2.2-3014, 2.2-3705.3, 2.2-3802
691	22.1-318.1, 22.1-318.2
692	22.1-19, n.
693	58.1-301
694	2.2-3708, 2.2-3708.1, 30-179
695	2.2-3706, 2.2-3711, 15.2-1713.1
696	23-9.2:12
697	22.1-227.1, n.
698	18.2-57

ACTS 2013 Chapter	Code 1950 Section
699	15.2-2159
700	8.01-27.5
701	23-9.2:12
702	1-510
703	24.2-643, 24.2-701
704	22.1-217.02
705	10.1-413.3
706	29.1-416.1
707	18.2-48.1, 18.2-57, 18.2-431.1, 18.2-473.1—18.2-476, 18.2-477.2
708	53.1-136
709	2.2-2503R, 2.2-2818, 30-58.1, 30-339—30-346, 38.2-3431
710	9.1-184, 22.1-79.4, 23-9.2:10
711	18.2-57
712	55-225.8, 55-248.5
713	58.1-439.20, 58.1-439.24—58.1-439.28
714	23-9.2:8
715	22.1-273.2
716	58.1-439.20, 58.1-439.24—58.1-439.28
717	2.2-309, 2.2-309.1—2.2-309.4, 2.2-310, 2.2-311, 2.2-313, 2.2-314—2.2-316R, 2.2-317R, 2.2-318R, 2.2-319R, 2.2-320R, 2.2-321R, 2.2-322R, 2.2-1202.1, 2.2-3705.3, 2.2-3802
718	22.1-47.3, n.
719	23-7.4:1
720	63.2-1104
721	56-597, n., 56-599, n.
722	2.2-2828R
723	2.2-309, 2.2-309.1—2.2-309.4, 2.2-310, 2.2-311, 2.2-313, 2.2-1202.1, 2.2-3705.3, 2.2-3802, 2.2-314—2.2-316R, 2.2-317, 2.2-318R, 2.2-319, 2.2-320R, 2.2-321R, 2.2-322R
724	58.1-608.3
725	24.2-404, 24.2-411.1, 24.2-643, 24.2-701
726	22.1-253.13:5, n.
727	Const., Art. 10, § 6A, n.
728	22.1-253.13:3

ACTS 2013 Chapter	Code 1950 Section
729	22.1-17.01
731	54.1-2301, 54.1-2301
732	3.2-6540,
	3.2-6540.1, 3.2-6570
733	63.2-621
734	15.2-906
735	23-9.2:8
737	33.1-371.1
738	54.1-1133, n.
739	54.1-2523,
	54.1-2523.1
740	60.2-637
741	33.1-12
742	62.1-44.15:21,
	62.1-44.15:23.1
743	18.2-248.02
744	58.1-439.12:10
745	29.1-344,
	29.1-344.2, 29.1-345,
	29.1-345.1, 29.1-347,
	29.1-349
746	16.1-260,
	17.1-406,
	18.2-57.3,
	18.2-287.01,
	18.2-307.1,
	18.2-308,
	18.2-308.01—
	18.2-308.015,
	18.2-311,
	19.2-83.1,
	19.2-120.1,
	19.2-386.27,
	19.2-386.28,
	24.2-643
747	15.2-250
748	18.2-57
749	15.2-979
750	9.1-902
751	32.1-137.6, n.,
	32.1-137.7, n.,
	32.1-137.9, n.,
	32.1-137.13, n.,
	32.1-137.14, n.,
	32.1-137.15, n.,
	32.1-137.16, n.,
	38.2-508.1,
	38.2-508.5, n.,
	38.2-3406.1,
	38.2-3406.2, n.,
	38.2-3407.11, n.,
	38.2-3411.1, n.,
	38.2-3407.12,
	38.2-3412.1,
	38.2-3412.1:01,
	38.2-3417,
	38.2-3418.5, n.,
	38.2-3418.8,
	38.2-3430.3,
	38.2-3431,
	38.2-3432.1,
	38.2-3432.2,
	38.2-3432.3, n.,
	38.2-3433, n.,
	38.2-3436,
	38.2-3438—
	38.2-3440,
	38.2-3441, n.,
	38.2-3442,
	38.2-3443, n.,
	38.2-3444, n.,
	38.2-3445, n.,
	38.2-3446, n.,
	38.2-3447—
	38.2-3454,
	38.2-3500, n.,
	38.2-3501,
	38.2-3503, 38.2-3520,
	38.2-3521.1,
	38.2-3522.1,
	38.2-3523.4,
	38.2-3525, n.,
	38.2-3540.2,
	38.2-3551,
	38.2-3556, n.,
	38.2-3557, n.,
	38.2-3558, n.,
	38.2-3559, n.,
	38.2-3560, n.,
	38.2-3561,
	n.,
	38.2-3562, n.,
	38.2-3563, n.,
	38.2-3564, n.,
	38.2-3565, n.,
	38.2-3566, n.,
	38.2-3567, n.,
	38.2-3568, n.,
	38.2-3569, n.,
	38.2-3570, n.,
	38.2-3571, n.,
	38.2-4109,
	38.2-4214,
	38.2-4216.1, n.,
	38.2-4306, n.,
	38.2-4312.3, n.,
	38.2-4319, n.,
	38.2-4306, 38.2-4509, n.,
	38.2-4319,
	38.2-5900, n.,
	38.2-5901, n.,
	38.2-5902, n.,
	38.2-5903, n.,
	38.2-5905, n.
752	46.2-868, 46.2-1078.1
754	36-137, 36-139,
	36-141—36-145,
	36-147—36-150,
	54.1-2113, 55-530.1,
	58.1-344.3
755	15.2-836, n.,
	52-34.3, n., 52-34.6, n.,
	52-34.9, n.
756	2.2-4006,
	3.2-409,
	3.2-410,
	3.2-3602,
	10.1-104.1,
	10.1-502,
	10.1-504,
	10.1-506, n.,
	10.1-560—
	10.1-571R,
	10.1-603.1—
	10.1-603.15:5R,
	10.1-603.10—
	10.1-603.15R,
	10.1-603.15:1—
	10.1-603.15:5R,
	10.1-659,
	10.1-2100—
	10.1-2115R,
	10.1-2123,
	15.2-1129.2,
	15.2-2114,
	15.2-2295.1,
	15.2-2403.3,
	33.1-70.1,
	36-55.64,
	58.1-3660.1,
	58.1-3851,
	62.1-44.5,
	62.1-44.9,
	62.1-44.14,
	62.1-44.15,
	62.1-44.15:24,
	62.1-44.15:28, n.,
	62.1-44.15:36, n.,
	62.1-44.15:51, n.,
	62.1-44.15:67, n.,
	62.1-44.15:79—
	62.1-44.15:79,
	62.1-44.19:13,
	62.1-44.19:15,
	62.1-44.19:20,
	62.1-44.19:21—
	62.1-44.19:23,
	62.1-44.23,
	62.1-44.32,
	62.1-44.44,
	62.1-73,
	62.1-195.1,
	62.1-229.4
757	8.9A-516, 12.1-21.1
758	3.2-3607.2,
	10.1-1188, 15.2-1123
759	18.2-60.3,
	18.2-308.1:4
760	2.2-4002,
	2.2-4103, n.,

ACTS 2013 Chapter	Code 1950 Section
	28.2-204.1,
	28.2-400.1—
	28.2-400.6,
	28.2-402,
	28.2-403,
	28.2-1000.2,
	2.2-4002, n.,
	2.2-4103, n.
761	16.1-253.2,
	18.2-46.3:3,
	18.2-60.4,
	18.2-61,
	18.2-67.1, 18.2-67.2,
	18.2-154,
	18.2-308.2:2,
	18.2-374.1,
	18.2-374.1:1
762	2.2-4343,
	33.1-1,
	62.1-129,
	62.1-132.1,
	62.1-132.3,
	62.1-132.4,
	62.1-132.6,
	62.1-132.19,
	62.1-132.20,
	62.1-139,
	62.1-147.1:1,
	62.1-129, n.,
	62.1-132.1, n.,
	62.1-132.3, n.,
	62.1-132.4, n.,
	62.1-132.6, n.,
	62.1-132.19, n.,
	62.1-132.20, n.,
	62.1-139, n.,
	62.1-147.1:1, n.
763	2.2-122
764	25.1-204,
	25.1-305,
	25.1-417,
	33.1-89,
	33.1-120
765	54.1-2408.1,
	54.1-3401,
	54.1-3410.2,
	54.1-3434.1,
	54.1-3434.2
766	2.2-1509.2, n.,
	5.1-152, n.,
	15.2-4838.01,
	15.2-4838.1,
	33.1-23.03:1, n.,
	33.1-23.03:8,
	33.1-23.5:1,
	33.1-23.5:4,
	33.1-221.1:2, n.,
	33.1-221.1:1.3,
	58.1-300,
	58.1-520,
	58.1-540—
	58.1-549R,
	58.1-601,
	58.1-602,
	58.1-603,
	58.1-603.1,
	58.1-604,
	58.1-604.01,
	58.1-604.1,
	58.1-605,
	58.1-606,
	58.1-608.3,
	58.1-609.13, n.,
	58.1-611.1, n.,
	58.1-612, 58.1-614,
	58.1-615,
	58.1-625,
	58.1-635,
	58.1-638,
	58.1-638.2,
	58.1-638.3,
	58.1-639,
	58.1-802.2,
	58.1-811,
	58.1-1742,
	58.1-2201,
	58.1-2217,
	58.1-2249,
	58.1-2251,
	58.1-2259,
	58.1-2289,
	58.1-2290, n.,
	58.1-2290.1,
	58.1-2295,
	58.1-2299.20,
	58.1-2401,
	58.1-2402,
	58.1-2425,
	58.1-2701,
	58.1-2706
767	15.2-5900, n.,
	15.2-5921—15.2-5927
768	24.2-104
769	16.1-301
770	15.2-906
771	60.2-528.1,
	60.2-618, 60.2-619,
	60.2-636
772	13.1-1039
773	15.2-3108
774	16.1-253.2,
	18.2-46.3:3, 18.2-60.4,
	18.2-61, 18.2-67.1,
	18.2-67.2, 18.2-154,
	18.2-308.2:2, 18.2-374.1,
	18.2-374.1:1
775	15.2-1726
776	46.2-665,
	46.2-666, 46.2-670
777	46.2-674
778	22.1-177
779	22.1-3
780	2.2-4002
781	9.1-902
782	18.2-48.1,
	18.2-57, 18.2-431.1,
	18.2-473.1—18.2-476,
	18.2-477.2
783	15.2-919,
	15.2-1720, 46.2-100,
	46.2-328, 46.2-337,
	46.2-600, 46.2-613,
	46.2-629, 46.2-662,
	46.2-694, 46.2-694,
	46.2-705, 46.2-711,
	46.2-714, 46.2-715,
	46.2-720, 46.2-721,
	46.2-904, 46.2-905,
	46.2-907, 46.2-908.1,
	46.2-908.3, 46.2-914,
	46.2-915, 46.2-915.2,
	46.2-1047, 58.1-602,
	58.1-2403, 58.1-3503,
	58.1-3504, 58.1-3523
784	64.2-432, 64.2-747
785	18.2-248.1:1,
	54.1-3446
786	22.1-217.02
787	8.2A-104,
	19.2-81,
	29.1-712, n.,
	29.1-713, n.,
	29.1-714, n.,
	29.1-715, n.,
	29.1-716, n.,
	29.1-717, n.,
	29.1-717.1, n.,
	29.1-717.2, n.,
	29.1-717.3, n.,
	29.1-718, n.,
	29.1-719, n.,
	29.1-720, n.,
	29.1-721, n.,
	29.1-722, n.,
	29.1-723, n.,
	29.1-724, n.,
	29.1-725, n.,
	29.1-726, n.,
	29.1-727, n.,
	29.1-728, n.,
	29.1-729, n.,
	29.1-730, n., 29.1-731, n.,
	29.1-732, n.,
	29.1-733, n.,
	29.1-733.1, n.,
	29.1-733.2—
	29.1-733.29,
	29.1-738,
	29.1-801,
	58.1-1404

ACTS 2013 Chapter	Code 1950 Section
	29.1-733.2, n.,
	29.1-738, n.,
	29.1-801, n.,
	58.1-1404, n.
789	46.2-208,
	46.2-212.2, 46.2-328,
	46.2-337, 46.2-646.1,
	46.2-707, 46.2-752.1,
	46.2-1183.1
790	46.2-868,
	46.2-1078.1
791	38.2-3455,
	38.2-3456
792	29.1-417
793	2.2-4006,
	3.2-409,
	3.2-410,
	3.2-3602,
	10.1-104.1,
	10.1-502,
	10.1-504,
	10.1-506, n.,
	10.1-560—
	10.1-571R,
	10.1-603.1—
	10.1-603.15:5R,
	10.1-603.10—
	10.1-603.15R,
	10.1-603.15:1—
	10.1-603.15:5R,
	10.1-659,
	10.1-2100—
	10.1-2115R,
	10.1-2123,
	15.2-1129.2,
	15.2-2114,
	15.2-2295.1,
	15.2-2403.3,
	33.1-70.1,
	36-55.64,
	58.1-3660.1,
	58.1-3851,
	62.1-44.5,
	62.1-44.9,
	62.1-44.14,
	62.1-44.15,
	62.1-44.15:24,
	62.1-44.15:28, n.,
	62.1-44.15:36, n.,
	62.1-44.15:51, n.,
	62.1-44.15:67, n.,
	62.1-44.15:79—
	62.1-44.15:79,
	62.1-44.19:13,
	62.1-44.19:15,
	62.1-44.19:20,
	62.1-44.19:21—
	62.1-44.19:23,
	62.1-44.23,
	62.1-44.32,
	62.1-44.44,
	62.1-73,
	62.1-195.1,
	62.1-229.4
794	2.2-4343,
	33.1-1, 62.1-129,
	62.1-132.1,
	62.1-132.3, 62.1-132.4,
	62.1-132.6, 62.1-132.19,
	62.1-132.20, 62.1-139,
	62.1-147.1:1
796	15.2-836, n.,
	52-34.3, n., 52-34.6, n.,
	52-34.9, n.
797	18.2-308.2:1,
	18.2-308.2:2
798	2.2-1509.4,
	58.1-512
799	32.1-263
800	22.1-279.3:1
801	58.1-322
802	58.1-439.20
804	58.1-3902
805	2.2-2101,
	2.2-2101, 22.1-7.1,
	22.1-25,
	22.1-27.1—22.1-17.6,
	23-14, n.
806	2.2-409, n.,
	2.2-1104, n.,
	2.2-1149, n.,
	2.2-1156, n.,
	2.2-1502.1, n.,
	2.2-1505, n.,
	2.2-1508, n.,
	2.2-1802, n.,
	2.2-2233.1, n.,
	2.2-2402, n.,
	2.2-3205, n.,
	2.2-3800, n.,
	2.2-4400, n.,
	8.01-195.3, n.,
	9.1-165, n.,
	10.1-202, n.,
	10.1-552, n.,
	10.1-564, n.,
	10.1-603.19, n.,
	10.1-1176, n.,
	10.1-1322, n.,
	10.1-1422.3, n.,
	10.1-2128, n.,
	10.1-2128.1, n.,
	10.1-2129, n.,
	10.1-2131, n.,
	10.1-2132, n.,
	10.1-2211, n.,
	10.1-2211.1, n.,
	10.1-2213, n.,
	10.1-2213.1, n.,
	10.1-2500, n.,
	13.1-775.1, n.,
	15.2-540, n.,
	15.2-639, n.,
	15.2-848, n.,
	15.2-1605, n.,
	15.2-4518, n.,
	15.2-4526, n.,
	16.1-69.48, n.,
	16.1-69.6:1, n.,
	16.1-273, n.,
	16.1-309.2, n.,
	16.1-309.6, n.,
	16.1-309.7, n.,
	16.1-322.1, n.,
	17.1-279, n.,
	17.1-285, n.,
	17.1-286, n.,
	17.1-287, n.,
	17.1-507,
	18.2-254.1, n.,
	18.2-340.31, n.,
	19.2-163, n.,
	19.2-303.5, n.,
	19.2-326, n.,
	19.2-386.14, n.,
	22.1-79.1, n.,
	22.1-175.5, n.,
	22.1-253.13:3, n.,
	23-7.4:1, n.,
	23-7.4:2, n.,
	23-38.11, n.,
	24.2-108, n.,
	30-19.1:4, n.,
	30-232—30-238, n.,
	30-266—30-274, n.,
	30-275, n., 30-276, n.,
	30-293—30-300, n.,
	30-310,
	30-313—30-318, n.,
	30-347,
	32.1-50, n.,
	32.1-163, n.,
	32.1-273.1, n.,
	32.1-323.2, n.,
	32.1-325.1, n.,
	32.1-325.1:1, n.,
	32.1-331.12, n.,
	32.1-354, n.,
	32.1-360, n.,
	32.1-361.1, n.,
	32.1-366, n.,
	33.1-23.1, n.,
	33.1-221.1:1.1, n.,
	37.2-319, n.,
	38.2-401, n.,
	38.2-415, n.,
	40.1-49.4, n.,
	45.1-161.58, n.,
	45.1-161.292:31, n.,
	45.1-361.2, n.,

ACTS 2013 Chapter	Code 1950 Section
	46.2-342, n.,
	46.2-411, n.,
	46.2-694, n.,
	46.2-1167, n.,
	51.1-1401, n.,
	51.1-1403, n.,
	51.5-39.7, n.,
	51.5-135, n.,
	52-8.1:1, n.,
	52-4.3, n.,
	53.1-20, n.,
	53.1-45, n.,
	53.1-47, n.,
	53.1-67.1, n.,
	53.1-120, n.,
	53.1-131, n.,
	55-297, n.,
	55-66.6, n.,
	55-210.13, n.,
	56-232, n.,
	56-234, n.,
	56-484.12, n.,
	58.1-202.2, n.,
	58.1-214, n.,
	58.1-478, n.,
	58.1-608.3, n.,
	58.1-609.12, n.,
	58.1-622, n.,
	58.1-638, n.,
	58.1-642, n.,
	58.1-645, n.,
	58.1-656, n.,
	58.1-662, n.,
	58.1-801, n., 58.1-803, n.,
	58.1-1021.03, n.,
	58.1-1410, n.,
	58.1-1730, n.,
	58.1-1741, n.,
	58.1-3176, n.,
	58.1-3403, n.,
	58.1-3524, n.,
	58.1-3700, n.,
	58.1-3912, n.,
	58.1-4022, n.,
	59.1-392, n.,
	59.1-479, n.,
	59.1-547, n.,
	59.1-548, n.,
	62.1-132.3:2,
	62.1-140, n.,
	63.2-1300, n.
	62.1-132.3:2

ACTS 2013, Sp. Sess. I

ACTS 2013, Sp. Sess. I Chapter	Code 1950 Section
1	33.1-23.5:1

TABLE OF SECTIONS AMENDED OR REPEALED

Section
1-10 to 1-21. Repealed by Acts 2005, c. 839.
1-13.23:1. Amended by Acts 2005, c. 681.
1-206. Amended by Acts 2011, c. 566.
1-210. Amended by Acts 2008, c. 816; 2010, c. 96.
1-219.1. Amended by Acts 2012, cc. 283, 756.
1-237. Amended by Acts 2005, c. 681.
1-510. Amended by Acts 2005, c. 557; 2006, c. 128; 2007, cc. 391, 685; 2008, c. 262; 2009, cc. 145, 227; 2011, c. 671; 2013, c. 702.
2.2-106. Amended by Acts 2005, cc. 803, 938; 2006, c. 254; 2010, cc. 136, 145.
2.2-107. Amended by Acts 2005, cc. 803, 938.
2.2-110. Amended by Acts 2012, c. 434.
2.2-113. Amended by Acts 2010, c. 79.
2.2-115. Amended by Acts 2006, cc. 251, 890; 2007, c. 654; 2010, cc. 78, 470, 580, 611, 735, 768; 2011, cc. 539, 574, 587; 2013, c. 547.
2.2-118. Repealed by Acts 2012, c. 835.
2.2-122. Amended by Acts 2005, c. 839; 2011, c. 755; 2013, c. 763.
2.2-200. Amended by Acts 2006, c. 254; 2011, cc. 780, 858.
2.2-203. Amended by Acts 2006, c. 150; 2008, cc. 387, 689; 2012, cc. 803, 835.
2.2-203.1. Amended by Acts 2005, c. 421; 2009, c. 86.
2.2-203.2. Repealed by Acts 2009, c. 180.
2.2-203.2:1. Amended by Acts 2012, cc. 803, 835.
2.2-203.3. Amended by Acts 2008, c. 860.
2.2-204. Amended by Acts 2013, c. 482.
2.2-205.1. Amended by Acts 2013, c. 482.
2.2-208. Amended by Acts 2009, c. 210.
2.2-211. Amended by Acts 2011, cc. 798, 871.
2.2-212. Amended by Acts 2006, cc. 344, 380; 2007, cc. 10, 399, 534, 581; 2009, cc. 813, 840; 2010, cc. 411, 801; 2012, cc. 803, 835.
2.2-213. Amended by Acts 2009, cc. 813, 840.
2.2-214. Amended by Acts 2009, cc. 813, 840; 2012, cc. 803, 835.
2.2-215. Amended by Acts 2005, c. 41; 2012, cc. 803, 835.
2.2-216. Amended by Acts 2008, c. 368.
2.2-220. Amended by Acts 2007, c. 637.
2.2-221. Amended by Acts 2006, cc. 150, 326; 2011, cc. 780, 858; 2012, cc. 803, 835.
2.2-223. Amended by Acts 2009, cc. 813, 840; Repealed by Acts 2012, cc. 164, 456.
2.2-225. Amended by Acts 2009, cc. 325, 810; 2010, cc. 136, 145; 2011, cc. 138, 739.

Section
2.2-225.1. Amended by Acts 2009, cc. 180, 325, 810.
2.2-229. Amended by Acts 2006, c. 942; 2007, cc. 80, 219; 2009, cc. 670, 690.
2.2-230. Amended by Acts 2012, cc. 803, 835.
2.2-231. Amended by Acts 2013, c. 151.
2.2-233. Amended by Acts 2011, cc. 691, 714.
2.2-300 to 2.2-303. Amended by Acts 2011, cc. 827, 867; 2013, cc. 231, 401.
2.2-304 to 2.2-306. Repealed by Acts 2011, cc. 780, 858.
2.2-309. Amended by Acts 2013, cc. 717, 723.
2.2-310, 2.2-311. Amended by Acts 2013, cc. 717, 723.
2.2-313. Amended by Acts 2013, cc. 717, 723.
2.2-314 to 2.2-316. Repealed by Acts 2013, cc. 717, 723.
2.2-316. Amended by Acts 2013, c. 571.
2.2-317, 2.2-318. Repealed by Acts 2013, cc. 717, 723.
2.2-319, 2.2-320. Repealed by Acts 2013, cc. 717, 723.
2.2-321. Repealed by Acts 2013, cc. 717, 723.
2.2-322. Repealed by Acts 2013, cc. 717, 723.
2.2-402. Amended by Acts 2012, c. 271.
2.2-409. Amended by Acts 2007, cc. 269, 362, 590.
2.2-419. Amended by Acts 2006, cc. 787, 843, 892.
2.2-420. Amended by Acts 2006, c. 843.
2.2-423. Amended by Acts 2011, cc. 123, 177.
2.2-426. Amended by Acts 2005, c. 90; 2006, c. 843.
2.2-435.1 to 2.2-435.5. Repealed by Acts 2006, cc. 696, 751.
2.2-435.7. Amended by Acts 2008, cc. 269, 388; 2010, c. 573.
2.2-435.8. Amended by Acts 2012, cc. 803, 835; 2013, c. 482.
2.2-507. Amended by Acts 2005, c. 236; 2007, cc. 248, 595; 2008, c. 577; 2009, cc. 813, 840; 2012, c. 563; 2013, cc. 585, 588, 646, 650.
2.2-508. Amended by Acts 2012, c. 1.
2.2-510. Amended by Acts 2007, c. 248; 2012, c. 847.
2.2-511. Amended by Acts 2007, c. 409; 2009, c. 847.
2.2-514. Amended by Acts 2007, c. 217.
2.2-515.1. Amended by Acts 2007, c. 599.
2.2-515.2. Amended by Acts 2008, c. 649; 2011, cc. 97, 172.
2.2-511. Amended by Acts 2009, c. 847.
2.2-517. Amended by Acts 2012, cc. 803, 835.
2.2-518. Amended by Acts 2009, c. 797.
2.2-520 to 2.2-523. Amended by Acts 2012, cc. 803, 835.
2.2-604. Amended by Acts 2005, c. 839.

Section
2.2-608. Amended by Acts 2009, c. 550; 2011, c. 845; 2012, c. 434.
2.2-609. Amended by Acts 2006, c. 59.
2.2-613. Amended by Acts 2011, cc. 737, 741.
2.2-700 to 2.2-720. Repealed by Acts 2012, cc. 803, 835.
2.2-803. Amended by Acts 2006, c. 340.
2.2-804. Amended by Acts 2012, c. 307.
2.2-900 to 2.2-904.1. Repealed by Acts 2013, c. 482.
2.2-904.2. Repealed by Acts 2012, cc. 774, 775.
2.2-905, 2.2-906. Repealed by Acts 2008, cc. 387, 689.
2.2-1000. Repealed by Acts 2012, cc. 803, 835.
2.2-1001. Amended by Acts 2012, cc. 56, 349; repealed by Acts 2012, cc. 803, 835.
2.2-1100. Amended by Acts 2005, c. 385.
2.2-1104. Amended by Acts 2005, cc. 868, 881.
2.2-1105. Amended by Acts 2012, cc. 99, 753.
2.2-1110. Amended by Acts 2011, c. 332; 2013, c. 493.
2.2-1111. Amended by Acts 2005, c. 817; 2007, c. 630; 2010, c. 458; 2011, cc. 815, 864; 2012, cc. 632, 803, 835.
2.2-1112. Amended by Acts 2010, c. 558.
2.2-1115.1. Amended by Acts 2010, cc. 136, 145; 2013, c. 493.
2.2-1118. Amended by Acts 2012, c. 632.
2.2-1120. Amended by Acts 2006, c. 582.
2.2-1122. Amended by Acts 2012, cc. 803, 835.
2.2-1124. Amended by Acts 2005, cc. 933, 945; 2006, cc. 468, 493; 2007, c. 701; 2009, c. 75; 2012, cc. 476, 507, 805, 836.
2.2-1130. Amended by Acts 2009, c. 612.
2.2-1131.1. Amended by Acts 2009, c. 612.
2.2-1132. Amended by Acts 2005, cc. 933, 945; 2006, c. 939.
2.2-1133. Amended by Acts 2008, c. 370.
2.2-1134. Repealed by Acts 2011, cc. 594, 681.
2.2-1136. Amended by Acts 2009, c. 612; 2011, cc. 659, 675.
2.2-1137. Amended by Acts 2009, c. 612; 2012, cc. 803, 835.
2.2-1146. Amended by Acts 2009, c. 612.
2.2-1149. Amended by Acts 2005, cc. 933, 945; 2011, c. 525.
2.2-1150. Amended by Acts 2005, cc. 933, 945; 2007, c. 624.
2.2-1150.1. Amended by Acts 2008, cc. 676, 690; 2010, c. 286.
2.2-1151. Amended by Acts 2008, cc. 356, 676, 690.
2.2-1153. Amended by Acts 2005, cc. 933, 945; 2009, c. 612; 2011, cc. 659, 675.
2.2-1154. Amended by Acts 2009, c. 612.
2.2-1156. Amended by Acts 2009, c. 612; 2011, cc. 659, 675.
2.2-1157. Amended by Acts 2009, c. 612.

Section
2.2-1175. Amended by Acts 2013, c. 485.
2.2-1176. Amended by Acts 2011, c. 813.
2.2-1178. Amended by Acts 2011, c. 611.
2.2-1179, 2.2-1180. Amended by Acts 2013, c. 485.
2.2-1201. Amended by Acts 2005, c. 386; 2006, c. 474; 2008, c. 576; 2012, cc. 803, 835.
2.2-1202.1. Amended by Acts 2013, cc. 572, 690, 717, 723.
2.2-1204. Amended by Acts 2011, c. 489; 2012, cc. 476, 507, 803, 835; 2013, c. 687.
2.2-1207. Amended by Acts 2008, c. 568; 2012, cc. 476, 507.
2.2-1208. Amended by Acts 2008, c. 568.
2.2-1400 to 2.2-1405. Repealed by Acts 2013, c. 482.
2.2-1501. Amended by Acts 2005, c. 620.
2.2-1502.1. Amended by Acts 2006, c. 596.
2.2-1503. Amended by Acts 2009, c. 537; 2010, c. 422; 2011, cc. 691, 714.
2.2-1507. Amended by Acts 2012, cc. 803, 835.
2.2-1508. Amended by Acts 2009, c. 536; 2013, c. 806.
2.2-1509. Amended by Acts 2013, c. 806.
2.2-1509.3. Amended by Acts 2010, cc. 136, 145; 2011, c. 739.
2.2-1513. Amended by Acts 2010, c. 422.
2.2-1514. Amended by Acts 2005, cc. 933, 945; 2007, c. 896; 2008, cc. 643, 701; 2010 c. 684; 2012, cc. 729, 733.
2.2-1516 to 2.2-1518. Amended by Acts 2011, cc. 697, 718.
2.2-1600 to 2.2-1602. Repealed by Acts 2011, cc. 798, 871.
2.2-1822.1. Amended by Acts 2005, c. 109.
2.2-1829. Amended by Acts 2011, c. 725.
2.2-1837. Amended by Acts 2005, cc. 492, 548; 2011, c. 359; 2012, c. 366.
2.2-1839. Amended by Acts 2005, cc. 184, 212; 2006, c. 713; 2007, c. 773; 2009, cc. 265, 568, 813, 840; 2011, c. 789; 2012, cc. 476, 507; 2013, c. 555.
2.2-2001. Amended by Acts 2007, c. 787; 2008, cc. 467, 521, 767, 768; 2009, c. 62; 2010, cc. 84, 554; 2011, cc. 772, 847; 2012, cc. 803, 835; 2013, c. 234.
2.2-2001.1. Amended by Acts 2009, c. 813, 840; 2010 c. 58; 2011, cc. 772, 847; 2012, cc. 803, 835.
2.2-2002. Amended by Acts 2005, c. 888; 2009, c. 136.
2.2-2002.1. Amended by Acts 2009, c. 136; 2011, cc. 330, 358; 2012, cc. 331, 342.
2.2-2004. Amended by Acts 2008, cc. 467, 768; 2010 c. 534; 2011, cc. 780, 858; 2012, cc. 803, 835; 2013, c. 234.
2.2-2004.1. Repealed by Acts 2011, cc. 89, 147.

Section

2.2-2005. Amended by Acts 2009, c. 826; 2010 cc. 136, 145.

2.2-2006. Amended by Acts 2007, c. 769; 2010 cc. 136, 145; 2011, c. 739; 2012, cc. 803, 835.

2.2-2007. Amended by Acts 2005, cc. 933, 945; 2007, cc. 276, 701; 2009, c. 86; 2010 cc. 136, 145; 2011, c. 739.

2.2-2008. Amended by Acts 2009, c. 757; 2010 cc. 136, 145; 2011, c. 739.

2.2-2009. Amended by Acts 2007, cc. 769, 775; 2010 cc. 136, 145.

2.2-2010. Amended by Acts 2005, c. 939; 2009, c. 87.

2.2-2012. Amended by Acts 2007, c. 630; 2010 cc. 136, 145; 2011, c. 739; 2012, cc. 803, 835; 2013, c. 583.

2.2-2013. Amended by Acts 2010 cc. 136, 145; 2012, cc. 55, 285.

2.2-2015. Amended by Acts 2010 cc. 136, 145; 2011, c. 739.

2.2-2017. Amended by Acts 2011, c. 739.

2.2-2018, 2.2-2019. Repealed by Acts 2011, c. 739.

2.2-2020. Amended by Acts 2010 cc. 136, 145; 2011, c. 739.

2.2-2021. Amended by Acts 2010 cc. 136, 145; 2011, c. 739.

2.2-2023. Amended by Acts 2010 cc. 136, 145.

2.2-2024. Amended by Acts 2009, c. 86.

2.2-2031. Amended by Acts 2009, c. 614; 2011, c. 138.

2.2-2032. Repealed by Acts 2005, c. 939.

2.2-2033, 2.2-2034. Repealed by Acts 2010, cc. 136, 145.

2.2-2101. Amended by Acts 2005, cc. 774, 786, 799, 868, 881, 930; 2006, cc. 707, 808, 842, 860, 901; 2007, cc. 849, 915; 2008, cc. 654, 659; 2009, cc. 210, 859; 2010 c. 787; 2011, cc. 521, 548, 780, 858; 2012, cc. 803, 835; 2013, cc. 372, 805.

2.2-2200. Amended by Acts 2005, c. 839.

2.2-2201 to 2.2-2204. Amended by Acts 2012, cc. 779, 817.

2.2-2203. Amended by Acts 2009, c. 82.

2.2-2213. Amended by Acts 2012, cc. 779, 817.

2.2-2215. Amended by Acts 2012, cc. 779, 817.

2.2-2218. Amended by Acts 2009, cc. 325, 810; 2010 c. 630.

2.2-2219. Amended by Acts 2009, cc. 325, 810.

2.2-2220. Amended by Acts 2005, c. 439; 2008, cc. 299, 611; 2009, cc. 325, 810; 2011, cc. 816, 874.

2.2-2220.1. Amended by Acts 2012, c. 372.

2.2-2221. Amended by Acts 2009, cc. 325, 810; 2010 c. 630; 2011, cc. 816, 874.

2.2-2233.1. Amended by Acts 2008, cc. 63, 527; 2009, cc. 243, 325, 810, 853; 2011, cc. 816, 874.

Section

2.2-2033.2. Repealed by Acts 2011, cc. 816, 874.

2.2-2235. Amended by Acts 2005, c. 900; 2008, c. 787; 2009, cc. 374, 569; 2010 cc. 101, 869; 2012, cc. 47, 259.

2.2-2236. Amended by Acts 2010, c. 869.

2.2-2238. Amended by Acts 2009, cc. 374, 569.

2.2-2238.1. Amended by Acts 2005, cc. 737, 797; 2006, c. 251; 2013, c. 482.

2.2-2240. Amended by Acts 2010, c. 869.

2.2-2260. Amended by Acts 2009, cc. 246, 311.

2.2-2261. Amended by Acts 2009, cc. 246, 311; 2011, cc. 691, 714.

2.2-2263. Amended by Acts 2009, cc. 246, 311.

2.2-2279. Amended by Acts 2008, c. 744; 2009, c. 565.

2.2-2280. Amended by Acts 2009, c. 565.

2.2-2282. Amended by Acts 2011, cc. 691, 714; 2013, c. 482.

2.2-2284. Amended by Acts 2013, c. 482.

2.2-2285. Amended by Acts 2005, c. 624; 2008, cc. 445, 744.

2.2-2289. Amended by Acts 2009, c. 565.

2.2-2290. Amended by Acts 2008, c. 744.

2.2-2291, 2.2-2292. Amended by Acts 2009, c. 565.

2.2-2311. Amended by Acts 2013, c. 482.

2.2-2316. Amended by Acts 2007, c. 779; 2010 c. 101.

2.2-2317. Amended by Acts 2007, c. 779.

2.2-2318. Amended by Acts 2005, c. 360; 2007, c. 779.

2.2-2319, 2.2-2320. Amended by Acts 2013, c. 547.

2.2-2335. Repealed by Acts 2012, cc. 803, 835.

2.2-2337. Amended by Acts 2012, cc. 436, 482.

2.2-2338. Amended by Acts 2011, cc. 780, 858.

2.2-2339, 2.2-2340. Amended by Acts 2012, cc. 436, 482.

2.2-2342. Amended by Acts 2013, c. 221.

2.2-2400. Amended by Acts 2011, cc. 691, 714.

2.2-2404 to 2.2-2408. Repealed by Acts 2011, cc. 594, 681.

2.2-2411. Amended by Acts 2009, cc. 813, 840; 2012, cc. 476, 507, 803, 835.

2.2-2412. Amended by Acts 2010, cc. 411, 801.

2.2-2413, 2.2-2414. Repealed by Acts 2012, cc. 803, 835.

2.2-2423. Amended by Acts 2010, c. 869.

2.2-2426 to 2.2-2434. Repealed by Acts 2012, cc. 803, 835.

2.2-2449. Amended by Acts 2012, c. 502.

2.2-2452. Amended by Acts 2005, c. 758; 2008, cc. 467, 768; 2010, c. 64; 2012, cc. 33, 162.

2.2-2455. Amended by Acts 2008, cc. 387, 689.

2.2-2456. Amended by Acts 2008, cc. 387, 689.

2.2-2457 to 2.2-2458.1. Repealed by Acts 2010, cc. 136, 145.

2.2-2462 to 2.2-2464. Repealed by Acts 2013, c. 372.

Section
2.2-2463, 2.2-2464. Amended by Acts 2012, c. 807.
2.2-2465, 2.2-2466. Amended by Acts 2012, cc. 803, 835; 2013, c. 234.
2.2-2467 to 2.2-2469. Repealed by Acts 2013, c. 234.
2.2-2503. Repealed by Acts 2013, c. 709.
2.2-2505. Amended by Acts 2010, c. 329.
2.2-2513 to 2.2-2517. Repealed by Acts 2009, cc. 325, 810.
2.2-2523. Repealed by Acts 2008, cc. 50, 710.
2.2-2525. Amended by Acts 2012, cc. 476, 507.
2.2-2528. Amended by Acts 2010, c. 342; 2012, cc. 803, 835.
2.2-2529. Amended by Acts 2009, c. 548; 2010, c. 342; 2013, cc. 152, 245.
2.2-2630, 2.2-2631. Amended by Acts 2012, c. 502.
2.2-2533. Amended by Acts 2009, c. 301.
2.2-2609. Amended by Acts 2006, c. 861.
2.2-2614. Amended by Acts 2013, c. 439.
2.2-2618. Amended by Acts 2006, cc. 431, 500; 2013, c. 79.
2.2-2620 to 2.2-2639. Repealed by Acts 2012, cc. 803, 835.
2.2-2648. Amended by Acts 2005, c. 930; 2008, cc. 39, 170, 277; 2009, cc. 274, 712, 813, 840; 2010, c. 346; 2011, cc. 397, 413; 2012, cc. 223, 746.
2.2-2649. Amended by Acts 2008, cc. 38, 277; 2009, c. 275; 2012, cc. 476, 507; 2013, c. 1.
2.2-2651. Repealed by Acts 2009, c. 86.
2.2-2664. Amended by Acts 2005, c. 695; 2009, cc. 813, 840; 2013, c. 571.
2.2-2666.1. Amended by Acts 2005, c. 248; 2006, cc. 860, 901; 2007, c. 415; 2011, cc. 572, 586, 691, 714, 780, 858.
2.2-2666.2. Amended by Acts 2011, cc. 780, 858.
2.2-2666.3. Amended by Acts 2010, c. 75; 2011, cc. 780, 858; 2012, cc. 803, 835.
2.2-2667, 2.2-2668. Repealed by Acts 2011, cc. 594, 681.
2.2-2669. Amended by Acts 2006, cc. 696, 751; 2008, cc. 269, 388; 2011, cc. 691, 714; 2013, cc. 159, 236.
2.2-2670. Amended by Acts 2006, cc. 696, 751; 2013, cc. 159, 236.
2.2-2674.01. Amended by Acts 2012, cc. 803, 835.
2.2-2674.1. Amended by Acts 2006, cc. 696, 751.
2.2-2675 to 2.2-2678. Repealed by Acts 2012, cc. 803, 835.
2.2-2676, 2.2-2677. Amended by Acts 2012, cc. 803, 835.
2.2-2681. Amended by Acts 2006, c. 150; 2008, cc. 467, 768; 2010, c. 64.

Section
2.2-2682. Amended by Acts 2008, cc. 467, 768.
2.2-2685. Amended by Acts 2010, c. 101.
2.2-2690 to 2.2-2694. Repealed by Acts 2009, c. 90.
2.2-2695. Repealed by Acts 2008, c. 293.
2.2-2696. Amended by Acts 2005, c. 713; 2009, cc. 424, 554, 813, 840; 2011, cc. 691, 714; 2012, cc. 803, 835.
2.2-2698. Amended by Acts 2012, cc. 803, 835.
2.2-2699.1. Amended by Acts 2008, c. 745; 2009, cc. 485, 633; 2010, cc. 339, 836; 2011, cc. 540, 691, 714.
2.2-2699.2. Amended by Acts 2010, cc. 339, 836.
2.2-2699.3. Amended by Acts 2012, c. 528.
2.2-2699.5. Amended by Acts 2011, cc. 691, 714.; 2013, cc. 161, 227.
2.2-2699.6, 2.2-2699.7. Amended by Acts 2011, cc. 266, 313.
2.2-2702. Amended by Acts 2005, cc. 860, 889.
2.2-2705 to 2.2-2708.1. Repealed by Acts 2012, cc. 803, 835.
2.2-2711. Repealed by Acts 2012, cc. 803, 835.
2.2-2712. Amended by 2010, c. 32.
2.2-2715. Amended by Acts 2006, c. 150; 2008, cc. 467, 486, 768, 872; 2009, c. 368; 2010, c. 64; 2011, cc. 780, 795, 858.
2.2-2716. Amended by Acts 2008, cc. 467, 486, 768, 852; 2011, c. 795.
2.2-2718. Amended by Acts 2008, c. 420; 2009, cc. 247, 317, 813, 840; 2010, c. 369.
2.2-2720. Amended by Acts 2005, c. 703.
2.2-2721. Amended by Acts 2010, cc. 259, 628.
2.2-2723. Amended by Acts 2005, c. 703; 2010, cc. 797, 833.
2.2-2725. Amended by Acts 2006, c. 165.
2.2-2726. Amended by Acts 2006, c. 165.
2.2-2729. Amended by Acts 2006, c. 165.
2.2-2731. Repealed by Acts 2006, c. 165.
2.2-2732, 2.2-2733. Repealed by Acts 2011, cc. 594, 681, 780, 858.
2.2-2801. Amended by Acts 2011, c. 17.
2.2-2812. Amended by Acts 2011, c. 259.
2.2-2813. Amended by Acts 2011, c. 495.
2.2-2817.1. Amended by Acts 2005, c. 421; 2006, c. 137; 2007, c. 716; 2008, cc. 374, 375; 2009, c. 180.
2.2-2818. Amended by Acts 2005, cc. 503, 572, 640, 739; 2006, c. 396; 2010, cc. 357, 443; 2012, cc. 60, 2012; 2013, c. 709.
2.2-2818.1. Amended by Acts 2011, cc. 35, 45.
2.2-2821.2. Amended by Acts 2009, c. 457.
2.2-2822. Amended by Acts 2009, cc. 791, 841.
2.2-2828. Repealed by Acts 2013, cc. 131, 722.
2.2-2901. Amended by Acts 2005, cc. 933, 945.
2.2-2903. Amended by Acts 2005, c. 413; 2007, cc. 336, 605; 2012, cc. 266, 269, 287.
2.2-2905. Amended by Acts 2005, c. 716; 2007,

Section
c. 192; 2009, cc. 424, 554, 589, 596, 813, 840; 2013, c. 571.
2.2-3000. Amended by Acts 2012, cc. 803, 835.
2.2-3003, 2.2-3004. Amended by Acts 2012, cc. 56, 349, 803, 835.
2.2-3005. Amended by Acts 2012, cc. 803, 835.
2.2-3005.1. Amended by Acts 2011, c. 595; 2012, cc. 803, 835.
2.2-3006. Amended by Acts 2012, cc. 56, 349.
2.2-3010. Amended by Acts 2011, cc. 798, 871.
2.2-3014. Amended by Acts 2011, cc. 798, 871; 2013, cc. 572, 690.
2.2-3100. Amended by Acts 2008, c. 532.
2.2-3101. Amended by Acts 2012, cc. 345, 771; 2013, c. 475.
2.2-3103. Amended by Acts 2006, cc. 787, 892.
2.2-3104. Amended by Acts 2013, c. 648.
2.2-3104.01. Amended by Acts 2011, c. 624; 2013, c. 583.
2.2-3104.1. Amended by Acts 2008, cc. 478, 497.
2.2-3106. Amended by Acts 2006, c. 839; 2013, c. 583.
2.2-3109. Amended by Acts 2009, c. 862; 2013, c. 583.
2.2-3110. Amended by Acts 2006, c. 839; 2010, cc. 301, 304.
2.2-3112. Amended by Acts 2007, c. 613; 2012, c. 429.
2.2-3114. Amended by Acts 2005, c. 169; 2006, c. 779.
2.2-3115. Amended by Acts 2012, c. 429.
2.2-3117. Amended by Acts 2006, cc. 310, 779, 787, 892; 2008, c. 239; 2010, c. 670; 2012, c. 429.
2.2-3118. Amended by Acts 2006, c. 779; 2011, cc. 123, 177.
2.2-3119. Amended by Acts 2010, cc. 676, 759; 2011, c. 517.
2.2-3120. Amended by Acts 2012, c. 429.
2.2-3124. Amended by Acts 2012, cc. 283, 756.
2.2-3202. Amended by Acts 2006, cc. 813, 902.
2.2-3204. Amended by Acts 2011, c. 880.
2.2-3300. Amended by Acts 2010, c. 860.
2.2-3306. Amended by Acts 2005, c. 242.
2.2-3309.1. Amended by Acts 2009, c. 66.
2.2-3310. Amended by Acts 2009, c. 66.
2.2-3311. Amended by Acts 2006, c. 156.
2.2-3501. Amended by Acts 2012, cc. 803, 835.
2.2-3601. Amended by Acts 2005, c. 474.
2.2-3602. Amended by Acts 2005, c. 474.
2.2-3605. Amended by Acts 2005, c. 474.
2.2-3701. Amended by Acts 2007, c. 945; 2008, cc. 233, 789; 2010, c. 706; 2011, c. 242.
2.2-3703. Amended by Acts 2007, cc. 438, 548, 626.
2.2-3704. Amended by Acts 2007, c. 439; 2009, c. 626; 2010, c. 627; 2011, c. 604.
2.2-3704.1. Amended by Acts 2009, c. 626.

Section
2.2-3705.1. Amended by Acts 2010, c. 553.
2.2-3705.2. Amended by Acts 2005, c. 410; 2008, c. 721; 2009, c. 418; 2010, c. 672; 2011, cc. 111, 536; 2012, cc. 617, 803, 835; 2013, c. 600.
2.2-3705.3. Amended by Acts 2005, c. 601; 2006, cc. 25, 95; 2008, cc. 387, 668, 689, 758; 2009, cc. 237, 326, 340; 2011, cc. 798, 871; 2012, cc. 476, 507, 803, 835; 2013, cc. 571, 572, 690, 717, 723.
2.2-3705.4. Amended by Acts 2006, c. 518; 2008, cc. 561, 665; 2010, cc. 456, 524.
2.2-3705.5. Amended by Acts 2005, cc. 181, 227, 716; 2008, c. 539; 2009, c. 472, 813, 840; 2011, cc. 110, 175, 535; 2012, cc. 476, 479, 803, 835.
2.2-3705.6. Amended by Acts 2005, cc. 258, 411; 2006, cc. 73, 76, 467, 831, 921, 936; 2006 Sp. Sess. I, c. 1; 2007, cc. 374, 693; 2008, cc. 71, 102, 266, 387, 633, 689, 736, 743; 2009, cc. 246, 311, 325, 765, 810, 869; 2010, cc. 310, 808; 2011, cc. 541, 781, 798, 871; 2012, cc. 693, 709; 2013, cc. 54, 482, 574.
2.2-3705.7. Amended by Acts 2005, cc. 165, 508; 2007, cc. 406, 652, 660, 737, 739; 2008, cc. 13, 739; 2009, cc. 223, 827, 845; 2010, c. 300; 2011, cc. 827, 867; 2012, c. 726; 2013, cc. 199, 481, 554, 574.
2.2-3706. Amended by Acts 2006, cc. 857, 914; 2007, c. 133; 2010, c. 627; 2011, cc. 798, 871; 2013, c. 695.
2.2-3707. Amended by Acts 2005, c. 352; 2007, c. 300; 2009, c. 628; 2010, c. 309.
2.2-3707.01. Amended by Acts 2005, c. 352.
2.2-3707.1. Amended by Acts 2006, cc. 474, 595; 2007, c. 300.
2.2-3708. Amended by Acts 2005, c. 352; 2007, cc. 512, 945; 2008, cc. 233, 789; 2013, c. 694.
2.2-3708.1. Amended by Acts 2013, cc. 119, 694.
2.2-3711. Amended by Acts 2005, cc. 258, 411, 568; 2006, cc. 430, 499, 518, 560; 2007, cc. 133, 374, 566, 739; 2008, cc. 626, 633, 668, 721, 743; 2009, cc. 223, 325, 472, 765, 810, 827, 845; 2010, cc. 310, 630, 808; 2011, cc. 89, 111, 147, 536, 541, 816, 874; 2012, cc. 476, 507, 803, 835; 2013, cc. 571, 580, 695.
2.2-3712. Amended by Acts 2012, c. 428.
2.2-3713. Amended by Acts 2007, c. 560; 2009, c. 634; 2010 c. 299; 2011, cc. 133, 783.
2.2-3714. Amended by Acts 2007, cc. 233, 789; 2011, c. 327.

Section

2.2-3800. Amended by Acts 2009, cc. 849, 867.
2.2-3801. Amended by Acts 2006, c. 474; 2008, cc. 840, 843; 2009, cc. 849, 867.
2.2-3802. Amended by Acts 2005, cc. 868, 881; 2006, cc. 196, 857, 914; 2009, c. 573; 2011, cc. 798, 871; 2012, cc. 229, 268; 2013, cc. 572, 690, 717, 723.
2.2-3803. Amended by Acts 2006, cc. 159, 590.
2.2-3806. Amended by Acts 2007, c. 232.
2.2-3808. Amended by 2008, cc. 840, 843; 2009, cc. 849, 867; 2010 c. 749.
2.2-3808.1. Amended by Acts 2007, cc. 548, 626.
2.2-3808.2. Repealed by Acts 2007, cc. 548, 626.
2.2-3809. Amended by 2008, cc. 840, 843.
2.2-3901. Amended by Acts 2005, c. 839.
2,2-3902. Amended by Acts 2012, cc. 803, 835.
2.2-4001. Amended by Acts 2007, cc. 873, 916; 2011, cc. 241, 315.
2.2-4002. Amended by Acts 2006, c. 442; 2007, cc. 41, 870, 932; 2008, c. 672; 2009, c. 472; 2010 cc. 65, 178, 480; 2012, cc. 476, 507, 594, 803, 835; 2013, cc. 59, 234, 760, 780.
2.2-4003. Amended by Acts 2007, cc. 873, 916.
2.2-4006. Amended by Acts 2005, c. 102; 2006, cc. 632, 719; 2007, cc. 873, 916; 2010 c. 65; 2011, c. 464; 2012, cc. 803, 835; 2013, cc. 756, 793.
2.2-4007. Amended by Acts 2005, cc. 619, 682; 2007, cc. 316, 561, 873, 916.
2.2-4007.01. Amended by Acts 2011, c. 464.
2.2-4007.02. Amended by Acts 2012, c. 795.
2.2-4007.04. Amended by Acts 2007, cc. 316, 561.
2.2-4007.1. Amended by Acts 2007, cc. 873, 916; 2011, cc. 241, 315.
2.2-4009. Amended by Acts 2007, cc. 873, 916; 2012, c. 795.
2.2-4011. Amended by Acts 2007, cc. 873, 916; 2013, c. 629.
2.2-4012. Amended by Acts 2007, cc. 873, 916.
2.2-4012.1. Amended by Acts 2007, cc. 873, 916.
2.2-4013 to 2.2-4015. Amended by Acts 2007, cc. 873, 916.
2.2-4021. Amended by Acts 2005, c. 102; 2006, c. 702.
2.2-4023. Amended by Acts 2009, c. 797.
2.2-4024. Amended by Acts 2009, c. 806; 2012, cc. 803, 835.
2.2-4027. Amended by Acts 2005, cc. 619, 682; 2007, cc. 873, 916; 2013, c. 619.
2.2-4031. Amended by Acts 2007, cc. 300, 873, 916; 2011, c. 800.
2.2-4103. Amended by Acts 2007, c. 41; 2010 cc. 178, 407.
2.2-4117. Amended by Acts 2012, cc. 803, 835.

Section

2.2-4118. Repealed by Acts 2012, cc. 803, 835.
2.2-4301. Amended by Acts 2006, c. 206; 2008, c. 371; 2009, cc. 495, 562, 564; 2010, c. 440; 2011, cc. 24, 332, 555; 2012, c. 632; 2013, cc. 482, 518, 540, 543, 583.
2.2-4302.1. Amended by Acts 2013, c. 482.
2.2-4302.2. Amended by Acts 2013, cc. 540, 543.
2.2-4303. Amended by Acts 2005, c. 394; 2006, cc. 464, 510; 2008, c. 78; 2009, c. 123; 2010, c. 567; 2011, cc. 332, 594, 612, 681; 2012, cc. 805, 836; 2013, c. 482; 2013, cc. 502, 583.
2.2-4304. Amended by Acts 2005, c. 394; 2006, c. 100; 2010, c. 736.
2.2-4305. Amended by Acts 2010, c. 382.
2.2-4308. Amended by Acts 2006, c. 510; 2011, cc. 594, 681.
2.2-4310. Amended by Acts 2006, cc. 831, 921; 2007, c. 787; 2008, cc. 521, 767; 2009, c. 869; 2013, c. 482.
2.2-4317. Amended by 2007, c. 154; 2011, cc. 573, 583.
2.2-4321.1. Amended by Acts 2006, c. 408.
2.2-4323. Amended by Acts 2011, cc. 594, 681
2.2-4324. Amended by Acts 2005, c. 894; 2011, c. 343.
2.2-4327. Amended by Acts 2007, c. 681.
2.2-4330. Amended by Acts 2011, c. 717.
2.2-4331. Amended by Acts 2013, c. 496.
2.2-4336. Amended by Acts 2006, c. 925; 2011, c. 789.
2.2-4337. Amended by Acts 2006, cc. 694, 925; 2011, c. 789; 2012, c. 783.
2.2-4338. Amended by Acts 2013, c. 141.
2.2-4341. Amended by Acts 2011, c. 544.
2.2-4343. Amended by Acts 2006, c. 656; Acts 2007, cc. 434, 697; 2008, c. 184; 2009, cc. 737, 767; 2010, c. 694; 2011, c. 23; 2012, cc. 803, 805, 835, 836; 2013, cc. 583, 762, 794.
2.2-4343.1. Amended by Acts 2005, c. 928.
2.2-4344. Amended by Acts 2008, c. 52; 2009, cc. 813, 840; 2011, cc. 798, 871; 2012, c. 632.
2.2-4345. Amended by Acts 2006, c. 658; 2011, c. 538; 2012, cc. 803, 835.
2.2-4359

l Amended by Acts 2013, c. 583.
2.2-4363. Amended by Acts 2005, c. 815.
2.2-4376.1. Amended by Acts 2011, c. 624.
2.2-4400. Amended by Acts 2010, cc. 640, 674.
2.2-4401. Amended by Acts 2008, c. 7; 2010, cc. 640, 674.
2.2-4402. Amended by Acts 2010, cc. 640, 674.
2.2-4403. Amended by Acts 2009, c. 64; 2010, cc. 640, 674.
2.2-4404. Amended by Acts 2009, c. 64; 2010, cc. 640, 674.

Section
2.2-4405. Amended by Acts 2009, c. 64; 2010, cc. 640, 674.
2.2-4406. Amended by Acts 2010, cc. 640, 674.
2.2-4407. Amended by Acts 2010, cc. 640, 674.
2.2-4408. Amended by Acts 2010, cc. 640, 674.
2.2-4409. Amended by Acts 2010, cc. 640, 674.
2.2-4410. Amended by Acts 2010, cc. 640, 674.
2.2-4411. Amended by Acts 2010, cc. 640, 674.
2.2-4501. Amended by Acts 2007, c. 67; 2008, c. 295.
2.2-4510. Amended by Acts 2005, c. 30.
2.2-4515. Amended by Acts 2008, c. 184.
2.2-4518. Amended by Acts 2010, c. 33.
2.2-4801. Amended by Acts 2009, c. 797.
2.2-4805, 2.2-4806. Amended by Acts 2009, c. 797.
2.2-4806. Amended by Acts 2008, cc. 314, 637.
2.2-5100. Amended by Acts 2005, c. 431; 2009, cc. 151, 174; 2012, cc. 196, 407.
2.2-5101. Amended by Acts 2005, c. 431; 2007, c. 384; 2009, cc. 267, 423.
2.2-5102.1. Amended by Acts 2007, c. 576; 2010, cc. 735, 768; 2013, c. 547.
2.2-5103. Amended by Acts 2005, c. 431.
2.2-5104. Amended by Acts 2005, c. 431.
2.2-5201. Amended by Acts 2009, cc. 813, 840.
2.2-5206. Amended by Acts 2008, cc. 39, 170, 277; 2009, cc. 813, 840.
2.2-5208. Amended by Acts 2008, cc. 39, 170.
2.2-5210. Amended by Acts 2008, c. 277.
2.2-5211. Amended by Acts 2009, c. 304; 2013, c. 5.
2.2-5212. Amended by Acts 2013, c. 5.
2.2-5300. Amended by Acts 2005, c. 695; 2009, cc. 813, 840; 2013, c. 571.
2.2-5304. Amended by Acts 2005, c. 695.
2.2-5305. Amended by Acts 2005, c. 695.
2.2-5403. Amended by Acts 2010, c. 584.
2.2-5407. Amended by Acts 2007, c. 522.
2.2-5510. Amended by Acts 2006, c. 54; 2007, c. 507; 2010, cc. 411, 801; 2012, 803, 835.
2.2-5800 through 2.2-5803. Repealed by Acts 2010, c. 699.
2.2-6000. Repealed by Acts 2011, c. 305.
3.1-1 through 3.1-1114.1. Repealed by Acts 2008, c. 860.
3.2-102. Amended by Acts 2012, cc. 803, 835.
3.2-113 to 3.2-115. Repealed by Acts 2013, c. 24.
3.2-109. Amended by Acts 2011, cc. 98, 185; 2012, cc. 803, 835.
3.2-111. Amended by Acts 2012, cc. 803, 835.
3.2-114. Amended by Acts 2012, cc. 803, 835.
3.2-201. Amended by Acts 2009, c. 389; 2011, cc. 95, 160; 2013, c. 482.
3.2-206. Amended by Acts 2009, c. 585.
3.2-305. Amended by Acts 2013, c. 547.
3.2-409. Amended by Acts 2013, cc. 756, 793.
3.2-410. Amended by Acts 2013, cc. 756, 793.

Section
3.2-1100. Amended by Acts 2012, cc. 803, 835.
3.2-1102. Amended by Acts 2012, cc. 803, 835.
3.2-1301. Amended by Acts 2011, cc. 158, 691, 714.
3.2-1302 to 3.2-1306. Amended by Acts 2011, c. 158.
3.2-1401. Amended by Acts 2011, cc. 691, 714.
3.2-1501. Amended by Acts 2011, cc. 691, 714.
3.2-1506. Amended by Acts 2010, c. 14.
3.2-1601. Amended by Acts 2011, cc. 691, 714.
3.2-1700. Amended by Acts 2011, cc. 691, 714.
3.2-1800. Amended by Acts 2012, cc. 803, 835.
3.2-1801. Amended by Acts 2011, cc. 691, 714.
3.2-1802 to 3.2-1808. Amended by Acts 2012, cc. 803, 835.
3.2-1810. Amended by Acts 2012, cc. 803, 835.
3.2-1812, 3.2-1813. Amended by Acts 2012, cc. 803, 835.
3.2-1815 to 3.2-1821. Amended by Acts 2012, cc. 803, 835.
3.2-1901. Amended by Acts 2011, cc. 691, 714.
3.2-1904. Amended by Acts 2010, cc. 7, 37.
3.2-1905. Amended by Acts 2010, cc. 7, 37; 2013, cc. 6, 40.
3.2-1907. Amended by Acts 2010, cc. 7, 37.
3.2-2101. Amended by Acts 2011, cc. 691, 714.
3.2-2201. Amended by Acts 2011, cc. 691, 714.
3.2-2301. Amended by Acts 2011, cc. 691, 714.
3.2-2400. Amended by Acts 2012, cc. 803, 835.
3.2-2401. Amended by Acts 2011, cc. 691, 714; 2012, cc. 803, 835.
3.2-2402 to 2410. Amended by Acts 2012, cc. 803, 835.
3.2-2500 to 3.2-2510. Repealed by Acts 2012, cc. 803, 835.
3.2-2800. Amended by Acts 2011, cc. 594, 681.
3.2-2801 to 3.2-2804. Repealed by Acts 2011, cc. 594, 681.
3.2-2805, 3.2-2806. Amended by Acts 2011, cc. 594, 681.
3.2-2807. Repealed by Acts 2011, cc. 594, 681.
3.2-3001. Amended by Acts 2011, cc. 691, 714.
3.2-3108. Amended by Acts 2012, c. 629; 2013, c. 547.
3.2-3600. Amended by Acts 2011, cc. 341, 353, 552, 564.
3.2-3601. Amended by Acts 2011, cc. 552, 564.
3.2-3602. Amended by Acts 2011, cc. 341, 353; 2013, cc. 756, 793.
3.2-3602.1. Amended by Acts 2011, cc. 341, 353, 552, 564.
3.2-3605, 3.2-3606. Amended by Acts 2011, cc. 552, 564.
3.2-3607. Amended by Acts 2011, cc. 341, 353, 552, 564.
3.2-3607.1. Amended by Acts 2011, cc. 341, 353.
3.2-3607.2. Amended by Acts 2011, cc. 341, 353; 2013, c. 758.
3.2-3607. Amended by Acts 2011, cc. 341, 353, 552, 564; 2012, c. 796.

Section
3.2-3608 to 3.2-3610. Amended by Acts 2011, cc. 552, 564.
3.2-3611. Amended by Acts 2011, cc. 341, 353, 552, 564.
3.2-3612, 3.2-3613. Amended by Acts 2011, cc. 552, 564.
3.2-3615. Amended by Acts 2011, cc. 552, 564.
3.2-3619 to 3.2-3621. Amended by Acts 2011, cc. 552, 564.
3.2-3623. Repealed by Acts 2011, cc. 552, 564.
3.2-3624, 3.2-3625. Amended by Acts 2011, cc. 552, 564.
3.2-3900. Amended by Acts 2012, cc. 803, 835.
3.2-3901 to 3.2-3903. Repealed by Acts 2012, cc. 803, 835.
3.2-3905. Repealed by Acts 2012, cc. 803, 835.
3.2-4000. Amended by Acts 2012, c. 297.
3.2-4008. Amended by Acts 2012, c. 297.
3.2-4015. Amended by Acts 2012, c. 297.
3.2-4022. Amended by Acts 2011, cc. 691, 714.
3.2-4101 to 3.2-4111. Repealed by Acts 2012, cc. 803, 835.
3.2-4206.1. Amended by Acts 2011, c. 297.
3.2-4207. Amended by Acts 2011, c. 846.
3.2-4209. Amended by Acts 2013, c. 285.
3.2-4211. Amended by Acts 2011, c. 297.
3.2-4212. Amended by Acts 2009, c. 847; 2012, cc. 283, 756.
3.2-5130. Amended by Acts 2011, c. 316; 2013, c. 285.
3.2-5139. Amended by Acts 2012, cc. 283, 756.
3.2-5701. Amended by Acts 2013, c. 125.
3.2-5904. Amended by Acts 2010, c. 761.
3.2-6500. Amended by Acts 2011, cc. 754, 886.
3.2-6503. Amended by Acts 2010, c. 875.
3.2-6521. Amended by Acts 2009, c. 756; 2010, cc. 182, 834; 2013, c. 286.
3.2-6522. Amended by Acts 2010, c. 834.
3.2-6525. Amended by Acts 2010, c. 834.
3.2-6536. Amended by Acts 2009, c. 756.
3.2-6540. Amended by Acts 2009, c. 377; 2012, cc. 107, 236; 2013, cc. 58, 732.
3.2-6542. Amended by Acts 2009, c. 354; 2012, cc. 107, 236.
3.2-6543. Amended by Acts 2009, c. 107.
3.2-6566. Amended by Acts 2010, c. 240.
3.2-6569. Amended by Acts 2011, cc. 754, 886.
3.2-6570. Amended by Acts 2013, cc. 58, 732.
3.2-6574. Amended by Acts 2010, c. 875.
4.1-100. Amended by Acts 2005, c. 911; 2006, c. 714; 2007, cc. 101, 295, 454, 558; 2008, cc. 198, 513, 875; 2013, cc. 107, 117.
4.1-104. Amended by Acts 2008, c. 135.
4.1-105. Amended by Acts 2006, c. 695.
4.1-111. Amended by Acts 2008, c. 513; 2009, c. 122; 2010, c. 481; 2011, c. 728; 2012, cc. 376, 760, 818.
4.1-112.1. Repealed by Acts 2007, cc. 99, 799.
4.1-115. Amended by Acts 2005, c. 633.

Section
4.1-119. Amended by Acts 2005, c. 651; 2006, c. 106; 2007, cc. 546, 726, 820; 2008, c. 609; 2009, c. 620; 2010, cc. 115, 170, 517; 2011, c. 713; 2012, c. 344; 2013, c. 476.
4.1-120. Amended by Acts 2008, c. 134; 2012, c. 245.
4.1-123. Amended by Acts 2007, c. 813.
4.1-124. Amended by Acts 2011, c. 560.
4.1-126. Amended by Acts 2005, cc. 646, 689; 2006, c. 752; 2007, cc. 469, 813; 2013, cc. 35, 186, 558, 601, 633.
4.1-128. Amended by Acts 2007, cc. 140, 454.
4.1-132. Amended by Acts 2006, c. 826.
4.1-200. Amended by Acts 2006, cc. 274, 740; 2010, c. 294; 2011, c. 8.
4.1-201. Amended by Acts 2006, cc. 106, 826; 2007, c. 820; 2011, c. 559; 2012, c. 376; 2013, c. 604.
4.1-201.1. Amended by Acts 2007, cc. 452, 722.
4.1-203. Amended by Acts 2007, cc. 870, 932; 2013, c. 642.
4.1-204. Amended by Acts 2007, cc. 99, 799; 2008, c. 513.
4.1-206. Amended by Acts 2005, c. 911; 2006, cc. 737, 826; 2007, c. 101; 2008, c. 198; 2013, c. 476.
4.1-207. Amended by Acts 2006, c. 845; 2007, cc. 558, 870, 932; 2008, c. 194; 2013, cc. 107, 117, 596.
4.1-207.1. Amended by Acts 2012, cc. 803, 835.
4.1-208. Amended by Acts 2006, c. 845; 2007, cc. 813, 870, 932; 2012, c. 619.
4.1-209. Amended by Acts 2005, cc. 652, 784; 2006, cc. 94, 153, 256, 826, 845; 2007, c. 813; 2008, cc. 179, 186, 192, 875; 2010, cc. 317, 561; 2011, c. 626.
4.1-209.1. Amended by Acts 2009, c. 292; 2010, cc. 317, 561.
4.1-210. Amended by Acts 2006, c. 731; 2007, cc. 107, 126, 295, 813; 2008, c. 172; 2009, c. 322; 2012, cc. 203, 237; 2013, c. 479.
4.1-212. Amended by Acts 2006, c. 826; 2008, c. 453; 2012, c. 155.
4.1-213. Amended by Acts 2011, cc. 265, 288.
4.1-215. Amended by Acts 2005, c. 784; 2007, cc. 99, 799; 2013, cc. 266, 604.
4.1-219. Amended by Acts 2008, c. 194.
4.1-221.1. Amended by Acts 2006, c. 826.
4.1-222. Amended by Acts 2007, c. 103.
4.1-223. Amended by Acts 2007, cc. 870, 932; 2012, cc. 803, 835.
4.1-225. Amended by Acts 2007, c. 103; 2008, cc. 185, 794; 2009, c. 486; 2011, cc. 384, 410; 2013, c. 661.
4.1-226. Amended by Acts 2008, c. 794; 2013, c. 661.
4.1-227. Amended by Acts 2008, c. 513; 2009, cc. 135, 279.

Section
4.1-230. Amended by Acts 2005, cc. 361, 951; 2007, cc. 99, 799; 2008, c. 765; 2011, c. 65.
4.1-231. Amended by Acts 2005, cc. 784, 911, 951; 2006, cc. 737, 845; 2007, cc. 99, 101, 107, 295, 558, 799, 870, 932; 2008, c. 198; 2010, cc. 317, 561; 2011, cc. 6, 626; 2012, cc. 203, 237; 2013, c. 479.
4.1-232. Amended by Acts 2011, c. 728.
4.1-233. Amended by Acts 2005, cc. 784, 911; 2006, c. 737; 2007, cc. 101, 107, 295; 2008, c. 198; 2011, c. 626; 2012, cc. 203, 237; 2013, c. 479.
4.1-234. Amended by Acts 2011, cc. 238, 299.
4.1-235. Amended by Acts 2010, cc. 247, 362.
4.1-304. Amended by Acts 2013, c. 562.
4.1-305. Amended by Acts 2005, c. 895; 2006, c. 207; 2007, c. 133; 2009, cc. 248, 726, 813, 840; 2012, cc. 250, 260.
4.1-306. Amended by Acts 2005, cc. 895, 898; 2006, c. 87; 2011, c. 31.
4.1-309. Amended by Acts 2007, c. 813.
4.1-310. Amended by Acts 2007, cc. 99, 799.
4.1-315. Amended by Acts 2010, c. 114.
4.1-320. Amended by Acts 2009, c. 322; 2011, c. 728; 2012, cc. 760, 818.
4.1-324. Amended by Acts 2006, c. 714; 2008, cc. 513, 629, 875.
4.1-325. Amended by Acts 2006, cc. 256, 826; 2008, cc. 513, 629, 794, 875; 2009, cc. 20, 509; 2010, c. 481; 2013, c. 661.
4.1-325.2. Amended by Acts 2006, cc. 256, 826; 2013, c. 661.
4.1-328, 4.1-329. Amended by Acts 2007, c. 494.
4.1-336. Amended by Acts 2012, cc. 283, 756.
4.1-352. Amended by Acts 2005, cc. 868, 881.
4.1-340 to 4.1-347. Repealed by Acts 2012, cc. 283, 756.
5.1-1. Amended by Acts 2011, c. 809.
5.1-7. Amended by Acts 2011, c. 75.
5.1-22. Amended by Acts 2012, c. 398.
5.1-30.9. Amended by Acts 2005, c. 633.
5.1-40. Amended by Acts 2012, cc. 28, 805, 836.
5.1-49. Amended by Acts 2013, cc. 585, 646.
5.1-88.2. Amended by Acts 2005, c. 451; 2007, c. 207.
5.1-88.7. Amended by Acts 2007, c. 206.
5.1-155. Amended by Acts 2012, cc. 549, 712.
5.1-158. Amended by Acts 2007, cc. 729, 742.
6.1-1 through 6.1-479. Repealed by Acts 2010, c. 794.
6.2-302. Amended by Acts 2010, c. 550.
6.2-303. Amended by Acts 2010, c. 477.
6.2-312. Amended by Acts 2010, c. 477.
6.2-600. Repealed by Acts 2013, cc. 30, 102.
6.2-613. Amended by Acts 2010, c. 269.
6.2-614. Amended by Acts 2010, c. 269.

Section
6.2-618. Amended by Acts 2013, c. 70.
6.2-619. Amended by Acts 2010, cc. 455, 632.
6.2-817. Amended by Acts 2011, c. 240.
6.2-872. Amended by Acts 2012, cc. 59, 157.
6.2-875. Amended by Acts 2013, cc. 98, 126.
6.2-895. Repealed by Acts 2010, c. 269.
6.2-890. Amended by Acts 2013, c. 205.
6.2-1001. Amended by Acts 2011, c. 67; 2012, c. 608.
6.2-1003. Amended by Acts 2012, cc. 283, 756.
6.2-1014. Amended by Acts 2011, c. 67; 2012, c. 608.
6.2-1067. Amended by Acts 2012, c. 608.
6.2-1085. Amended by Acts 2012, cc. 283, 756.
6.2-1175. Repealed by Acts 2010, c. 269.
6.2-1300. Amended by Acts 2013, cc. 16, 92.
6.2-1366. Repealed by Acts 2010, c. 269.
6.2-1323. Amended by Acts 2012, cc. 44, 560.
6.2-1367. Amended by Acts 2010, c. 269; 2013, cc. 7, 95.
6.2-1376. Amended by Acts 2013, cc. 16, 92.
6.2-1501. Amended by Acts 2010, c. 477.
6.2-1600. Amended by Acts 2010, cc. 146, 665, 831; 2012, cc. 53, 188.
6.2-1601. Amended by Acts 2010, cc. 146, 831.
6.2-1602. Amended by Acts 2012, cc. 53, 188.
6.2-1603. Amended by Acts 2011, c. 435.
6.2-1605. Amended by Acts 2012, c. 189.
6.2-1607. Amended by Acts 2011, c. 435.
6.2-1608. Amended by Acts 2011, c. 435; 2012. c. 189.
6.2-1700. Amended by Acts 2011, cc. 301, 435; 2012, cc. 52, 187; 2013, cc. 20, 380.
6.2-1701. Amended by Acts 2012, cc. 52, 187.
6.2-1709. Amended by Acts 2012, cc. 52, 187.
6.2-1711. Amended by Acts 2012, cc. 52, 187.
6.2-1712. Repealed by Acts 2011, c. 735.
6.2-1715. Amended by Acts 2012, cc. 52, 187.
6.2-1719, 6.2-1720. Amended by Acts 2012, cc. 52, 187.
6.2-1902. Amended by Acts 2013, c. 237.
6.2-2000. Amended by Acts 2011, c. 307.
6.2-2201. Amended by Acts 2011, c. 418.
6.2-2215. Amended by Acts 2011, c. 418.
6.2-2225. Amended by Acts 2011, c. 418.
7.1-1 to 7.1-43. Repealed by Acts 2005, c. 839.
8.01-2. Amended by Acts 2005, cc. 681, 716.
8.01-3. Amended by Acts 2012, cc. 688, 708.
8.01-15.2. Amended by Acts 2005, c. 909.
8.01-20.1. Amended by Acts 2007, c. 489; 2013, cc. 65, 610.
8.01-23. Amended by Acts 2005, c. 681.
8.01-27.1. Amended by Acts 2008, c. 489; 2009, c. 182; 2013, c. 63.
8.01-27.2. Amended by Acts 2008, c. 489.
8.01-27.4. Amended by Acts 2005, c. 141.
8.01-33. Amended by Acts 2005, c. 681.
8.01-35.1. Amended by Acts 2007, c. 443.
8.01-36. Amended by Acts 2013, cc. 551, 689.
8.01-44.4. Amended by Acts 2005, cc. 142, 234; 2012, c. 526.

Section
8.01-44.5. Amended by Acts 2013, c. 636.
8.01-47. Amended by Acts 2013, c. 665.
8.01-50. Amended by Acts 2012, c. 725.
8.01-50.1. Amended by Acts 2007, c. 489; 2013, cc. 65, 610.
8.01-52.1. Amended by Acts 2009, c. 414.
8.01-66.5, 8.01-66.6. Amended by Acts 2013, c. 273.
8.01-66. Amended by Acts 2010, c. 343.
8.01-66.2. Amended by Acts 2010, c. 343.
8.01-66.9. Amended by Acts 2012, cc. 803, 835.
8.01-126. Amended by Acts 2008, cc. 551, 691; 2012, c, 788; 2013, c. 63.
8.01-127, 8.01-127.1. Repealed by Acts 2007, c. 869.
8.01-128. Amended by Acts 2005, c. 779; 2010, c. 550; 2011, c. 76.
8.01-129. Amended by Acts 2008, c. 489.
8.01-156. Amended by Acts 2005, c. 791; 2006, c. 129.
8.01-184.1. Amended by Acts 2005, cc. 736, 800.
8.01-187. Amended by Acts 2007, cc. 450, 720; 2010, c. 835.
8.01-195.3. Amended by Acts 2007, c. 250.
8.01-195.4. Amended by Acts 2005, c. 144; 2011, cc. 14, 702.
8.01-195.6. Amended by Acts 2007, c. 368.
8.01-195.10. Amended by Acts 2010, cc. 496, 557.
8.01-195.11. Amended by Acts 2010, c. 557; 2012, c. 675.
8.01-195.12. Amended by Acts 2010, c. 557.
8.01-216.2. Amended by Acts 2011, cc. 651, 676.
8.01-216.3. Amended by Acts 2007, c. 569; 2011, c. 676.
8.01-216.5, 8.01-216.6. Amended by Acts 2007, c. 569.
8.01-216.8. Amended by Acts 2011, cc. 651, 676; 2012, c. 479.
8.01-216.9. Amended by Acts 2007, c. 569; 2011, c. 676.
8.01-216.10. Amended by Acts 2011, c. 676; 2012, c. 479.
8.01-216.17. Amended by Acts 2011, c. 676.
8.01-217. Amended by Acts 2005, c. 579.
8.01-220.1:1. Amended by Acts 2005, c. 255; 2011, cc. 693, 704.
8.01-220.1:2. Amended by Acts 2005, c. 462; 2013, c. 575.
8.01-220.2. Amended by Acts 2009, c. 797.
8.01-222. Repealed by Acts 2007, c. 368.
8.01-225. Amended by Acts 2005, c. 426; 2006, c. 780; 2008, c. 229; 2012, cc. 787, 833; 2013, cc. 183, 267, 300, 336, 617.
8.01-225.01. Amended by Acts 2008, cc. 121, 157.
8.01-225.1. Amended by Acts 2005, c. 928.

Section
8.01-226.5:1. Amended by Acts 2005, c. 785.
8.01-226.6. Repealed by Acts 2007, c. 250.
8.01-226.7. Amended by Acts 2006, c. 855; 2007, c. 225.
8.01-226.8. Amended by Acts 2007, c. 182; 2008, c. 688.
8.01-227.1 to 8.01-227.3. Repealed by Acts 2007, c. 250.
8.01-232. Amended by Acts 2006, c. 278.
8.01-241. Amended by Acts 2008, c. 226; 2009, c. 163.
8.01-241.1. Amended by Acts 2008, c. 226.
8.01-243. Amended by Acts 2008, c. 175; 2011, cc. 617, 641; 2013, cc. 551, 689.
8.01-244. Amended by Acts 2008, c. 175.
8.01-249. Amended by Acts 2005, c. 213; 2013, c. 292.
8.01-251. Amended by Acts 2005, cc. 139, 203.
8.01-252. Repealed by Acts 2005, cc. 139, 203.
8.01-262. Amended by Acts 2013, cc. 71, 103.
8.01-265. Amended by Acts 2007, c. 105.
8.01-268. Amended by Acts 2008, cc. 60, 204.
8.01-270. Repealed by Acts 2005, c. 681.
8.01-271.1. Amended by Acts 2008, cc. 136, 845.
8.01-272. Amended by Acts 2005, c. 681.
8.01-277. Amended by Acts 2006, c. 151.
8.01-282. Amended by Acts 2005, c. 681.
8.01-283. Amended by Acts 2005, c. 681.
8.01-284. Repealed by Acts 2005, c. 681.
8.01-285. Amended by Acts 2005, c. 866.
8.01-293. Amended by Acts 2011, c. 766.
8.01-296. Amended by Acts 2005, c. 866; 2008, c. 489.
8.01-299. Amended by Acts 2005, c. 866.
8.01-301. Amended by Acts 2005, c. 866.
8.01-303. Amended by Acts 2005, c. 866; 2013, c. 113.
8.01-304. Amended by Acts 2005, c. 866.
8.01-305. Amended by Acts 2005, c. 866.
8.01-306. Amended by Acts 2005, c. 866.
8.01-310. Amended by Acts 2013, c. 113.
8.01-312. Amended by Acts 2013, c. 113.
8.01-316. Amended by Acts 2010, c. 827.
8.01-320. Amended by Acts 2005, c. 866.
8.01-324. Amended by Acts 2007, cc. 183, 603.
8.01-328.1. Amended by Acts 2007, c. 533; 2009, c. 582.
8.01-329. Amended by Acts 2013, c. 113.
8.01-331. Amended by Acts 2005, c. 681.
8.01-335. Amended by Acts 2007, c. 498.
8.01-336. Amended by Acts 2005, c. 681.
8.01-341.1. Amended by Acts 2005, c. 195; 2011, cc. 389, 708; 2012, c. 98.
8.01-343. Amended by Acts 2006, c. 306; 2009, c. 790.
8.01-345. Amended by Acts 2007, cc. 450, 720.
8.01-346. Amended by Acts 2007, cc. 450, 720.
8.01-353. Amended by Acts 2010, c. 799.
8.01-353.1. Amended by Acts 2011, c. 470.

Section
8.01-359. Amended by Acts 2005, c. 356.
8.01-367. Amended by Acts 2005, c. 690; 2012, c. 206.
8.01-375. Amended by Acts 2006, c. 757.
8.01-380. Amended by Acts 2007, cc. 179, 367; 2013, cc. 274, 366.
8.01-382. Amended by Acts 2008, c. 219; 2009, c. 797.
8.01-385. Amended by Acts 2011, c. 81.
8.01-389. Amended by Acts 2008, c. 786; 2010, cc. 778, 825; 2013, c. 263.
8.01-390.1. Amended by Acts 2009, c. 212; 2012, c. 499.
8.01-391. Amended by Act 2012, c. 802.
8.01-397. Amended by Acts 2013, cc. 61, 637.
8.01-398. Amended by Acts 2005, c. 809.
8.01-399. Amended by Acts 2005, cc. 649, 692; 2009, c. 714.
8.01-400.2. Amended by Acts 2005, c. 110.
8.01-401.1. Amended by Acts 2013, c. 379.
8.01-404. Amended by Acts 2007, c. 598.
8.01-407. Amended by Acts 2007, c. 199; 2010, cc. 302, 486.
8.01-411 to 8.01-412.1. Repealed by Acts 2009, c. 701.
8.01-413. Amended by Acts 2005, cc. 642, 697; 2009, c. 270.
8.01-416. Amended by Acts 2010, c. 343.
8.01-417. Amended by Acts 2005, c. 211; 2008, c. 819; 2010, cc. 343, 435.
8.01-418.2. Amended by Acts 2012, cc. 803, 835.
8.01-418.3. Repealed by Acts 2007, c. 250.
8.01-419. Amended by Acts 2009, c. 454.
8.01-419.1. Amended by Acts 2006, c. 402.
8.01-420. Amended by Acts 2013, c. 76.
8.01-420.4. Amended by Acts 2005, c. 597.
8.01-424. Amended by Acts 2009, c. 688.
8.01-426. Amended by Acts 2005, c. 681.
8.01-428. Amended by Acts 2005, cc. 333, 909.
8.01-431. Amended by Acts 2012, c. 802.
8.01-435. Amended by Acts 2012, cc. 31, 118.
8.01-446. Amended by Acts 2008, cc. 823, 833; 2013, c. 263.
8.01-446.1. Amended by Acts 2008, cc. 823, 833.
8.01-449. Amended by Acts 2007, cc. 548, 626; 2008, cc. 823, 833; 2010, c. 430.
8.01-470. Amended by Acts 2007, c. 128.
8.01-471. Amended by Acts 2006, c. 667; 2013, c. 63.
8.01-487. Amended by Acts 2009, c. 443.
8.01-501. Amended by Acts 2006, c. 575.
8.01-502.1. Amended by Acts 2010, c. 673.
8.01-504. Amended by Acts 2010, c. 343.
8.01-506. Amended by Acts 2005, c. 726; 2009, c. 622.
8.01-511. Amended by Acts 2006, c. 55; 2012, cc. 127, 129, 251, 409.
8.01-512.3. Amended by Acts 2006, c. 55.

Section
8.01-512.4. Amended by Acts 2007, c. 872; 2009, cc. 332, 387, 388; 2010, c. 673; 2012, cc. 23, 79.
8.01-513. Amended by Acts 2006, c. 912.
8.01-514. Amended by Acts 2006, c. 575.
8.01-537. Amended by Acts 2008, cc. 551, 691.
8.01-540. Amended by Acts 2008, cc. 551, 691.
8.01-576.10. Amended by Acts 2013, cc. 283, 383.
8.01-581.1. Amended by Acts 2005, cc. 482, 649, 692; 2006, c. 638; 2008, cc. 121, 157, 169, 205.
8.01-581.13. Amended by Acts 2006, cc. 412, 638; 2009, c. 472.
8.01-581.15. Amended by Acts 2011, cc. 758, 759.
8.01-581.16. Amended by Acts 2006, c. 412.
8.01-581.17. Amended by Acts 2006, cc. 412, 678; 2007, c. 530; 2010, c. 196; 2011, cc. 15, 753.
8.01-581.18. Amended by Acts 2006, cc. 684, 877.
8.01-581.19. Amended by Acts 2006, c. 412.
8.01-581.20. Amended by Acts 2008, cc. 125, 169, 205.
8.01-581.20:1. Amended by Acts 2009, c. 414.
8.01-581.22. Amended by Acts 2013, cc. 283, 383.
8.01-581.23. Amended by Acts 2012, cc. 803, 835.
8.01-606. Amended by Acts 2012, c. 43.
8.01-607. Amended by Acts 2005, c. 885.
8.01-630, 8.01-631. Amended by Acts 2012, cc. 8, 77.
8.01-644. Amended by Acts 2009, c. 634.
8.01-654. Amended by Acts 2005, c. 836.
8.01-670. Amended by Acts 2005, c. 681.
8.01-676.1. Amended by Acts 2010, c. 494; 2012, cc. 8, 77.
8.01-682. Amended by Acts 2010, c. 343; 2012, c. 58.
8.01-694. Amended by Acts 2009, c. 372.
8.01-695. Amended by Acts 2006, c. 435.
8.1A-204. Amended by Acts 2011, c. 369.
8.1A-301. Amended by Acts 2011, c. 369.
8.2-403. Amended by Acts 2011, c. 369.
8.2A-103. Amended by Acts 2012, c. 155.
8.2A-104. Amended by Acts 2013, c. 787.
8.3A-118.1. Amended by Acts 2010, c. 747.
8.3A-311. Amended by Acts 2006, c. 624.
8.4-105. Amended by Acts 2010, c. 794.
8.4A-108. Amended by Acts 2013, c. 387.
8.6A-101 to 8.6A-110. Repealed by Acts 2011, c. 369.
8.9A-102. Amended by Acts 2012, c. 155.
8.9A-105. Amended by Acts 2012, c. 155.
8.9A-307. Amended by Acts 2012, c. 155.
8.9A-311. Amended by Acts 2012, c. 155.
8.9A-316, 8.9A-317. Amended by Acts 2012, c. 155.

Section
8.9A-326. Amended by Acts 2012, c. 155.
8.9A-406. Amended by Acts 2012, c. 155.
8.9A-408. Amended by Acts 2012, c. 155.
8.9A-502. Amended by Acts 2012, c. 155.
8.9A-503. Amended by Acts 2009, cc 217, 610; 2012, c. 155.
8.9A-507. Amended by Acts 2012, c. 155.
8.9A-515. Amended by Acts 2012, c. 155.
8.9A-516. Amended by Acts 2012, c. 155; 2013, c. 757.
8.9A-518. Amended by Acts 2012, c. 155.
8.9A-526, 8.9A-527. Amended by Acts 2012, c. 155.
8.9A-607. Amended by Acts 2012, c. 155.
8.9A-802. Amended by Acts 2012, c. 155.
8.9A-806, 8.9A-807. Amended by Acts 2012, c. 155.
9.1-101. Amended by Acts 2005, c. 914; 2007, c. 87; 2008, c. 460; 2010, c. 621; 2012, c. 776.
9.1-102. Amended by Acts 2005, cc. 868, 881; 2006, cc. 203, 233, 857, 914; 2008, cc. 328, 600, 771; 2009, c. 715; 2010, c. 224; 2011, cc. 579, 635, 719, 821, 854; 2012, cc. 140, 159, 803, 827, 835.
9.1-106. Amended by Acts 2010, c. 746.
9.1-108. Amended by Acts 2005, cc. 594, 672; 2011, cc. 594, 681, 691, 714; 2012, cc. 803, 835.
9.1-111. Amended by Acts 2009, cc. 813, 840
9.1-112. Amended by Acts 2007, c. 228; 2011, cc. 594, 681; 2012, c. 827.
9.1-116.1. Amended by Acts 2006, c. 288.
9.1-117 to 9.1-125. Repealed by Acts 2005, cc. 868, 881.
9.1-126. Amended by Acts 2007, c. 389.
9.1-127. Repealed by Acts 2011, cc. 821, 854.
9.1-138. Amended by Acts 2005, c. 365; 2008, c. 638; 2009, c. 375; 2011, c. 263.
9.1-139. Amended by Acts 2008, c. 638.
9.1-140. Amended by Acts 2008, c. 638; 2009, c. 225; 2011, c. 263; 2013, c. 411.
9.1-141. Amended by Acts 2009, c. 375; 2013, c. 69.
9.1-143. Amended by Acts 2008, c. 638; 2009, c. 375.
9.1-150. Amended by Acts 2011, cc. 821, 854.
9.1-151. Amended by Acts 2013, cc. 38, 685.
9.1-158 to 9.1-160. Repealed by Acts 2011, cc. 821, 854.
9.1-163, 9.1-164. Repealed by Acts 2011, cc. 821, 854.
9.1-173. Amended by Acts 2007, c. 133.
9.1-174. Amended by Acts 2006, c. 883; 2007, c. 133.
9.1-175. Amended by Acts 2007, c. 133.
9.1-176. Amended by Acts 2007, c. 133; 2011, cc. 821, 854.
9.1-176.1. Amended by Acts 2007, cc. 133, 528; 2011, cc. 384, 410.

Section
9.1-177. Amended by Acts 2007, c. 133.
9.1-177.1. Amended by Acts 2006, c. 289; 2007, c. 133; 2010, c. 223.
9.1-178 to 9.1-183. Amended by Acts 2007, c. 133.
9.1-184. Amended by Acts 2012, cc. 281, 433; 2013, cc. 676, 710.
9.1-185. Amended by Acts 2007, c. 708.
9.1-185.4. Amended by Acts 2007, c. 133; 2008, c. 438.
9.1-185.8. Amended by Acts 2007, c. 708; 2011, c. 623.
9.1-186.4. Amended by Acts 2007, c. 133.
9.1-187. Amended by Acts 2012, c. 776.
9.1-201. Amended by Acts 2007, cc. 647, 741; 2012, cc. 164, 456.
9.1-202. Amended by Acts 2006, c. 58; 2007, c. 96; 2011, cc. 691, 714; 2012, cc. 164, 456.
9.1-203, 9.1-204. Amended by Acts 2012, cc. 164, 456
9.1-301. Amended by Acts 2010, c. 779.
9.1-400. Amended by Acts 2005, cc. 907, 910; 2006, c. 824; 2007, c. 87; 2011, cc. 572, 586; 2012, cc. 374, 458, 573.
9.1-402. Amended by Acts 2006, c. 878.
9.1-403. Amended by Acts 2007, c. 90; 2009, cc. 393, 580.
9.1-406. Amended by Acts 2005, c. 681.
9.1-500. Amended by Acts 2007, cc. 87, 364.
9.1-501. Amended by Acts 2005, cc. 868, 881.
9.1-700. Amended by Acts 2005, c. 732.
9.1-701. Amended by Acts 2005, c. 732.
9.1-702. Amended by Acts 2005, c. 732.
9.1-703. Amended by Acts 2005, c. 732.
9.1-704. Amended by Acts 2005, c. 732.
9.1-801. Amended by Acts 2007, c. 87; 2011, cc. 572, 586.
9.1-802, 9.1-803. Repealed by Acts 2011, cc. 594, 681.
9.1-901. Amended by Acts 2005, c. 586; 2007, cc. 718, 744; 2009, cc. 813, 840.
9.1-902. Amended by Acts 2005, cc. 586, 603, 631; 2006, cc. 857, 875, 914, 931; 2007, c. 463, 718, 759, 823; 2008, cc. 592, 747, 772, 877; 2010, c. 858; 2012, c. 243; 2013, cc. 750, 781.
9.1-903. Amended by Acts 2005, c. 586; 2006, cc. 857, 914; 2007, cc. 718, 759, 823; 2008, c. 220; 2010, c. 843.
9.1-904. Amended by Acts 2006, cc. 857, 914; 2007, cc. 759, 823.
9.1-905. Amended by Acts 2005, c. 603; 2006, cc. 857, 914.
9.1-906. Amended by Acts 2006, cc. 857, 914.
9.1-907. Amended by Acts 2005, c. 603; 2006, cc. 857, 914; 2007, c. 718; 2010, c. 858.
9.1-908. Amended by Acts 2005, c. 631; 2006, cc. 857, 914; 2007, c. 718; 2008, c. 877; 2010, c. 858.

Section
9.1-909. Amended by Acts 2006, cc. 857, 914.
9.1-910. Amended by Acts 2005, c. 631; 2006, cc. 857, 914; 2007, c. 718; 2008, c. 877.
9.1-912. Amended by Acts 2007, cc. 759, 823.
9.1-913. Amended by Acts 2005, c. 603; 2006, cc. 857, 914.
9.1-914. Amended by Acts 2005, c. 928; 2006, cc. 857, 914; 2007, cc. 119, 164.
9.1-918. Amended by Acts 2006, cc. 857, 914.
9.1-1101. Amended by Acts 2006, cc. 327, 551; 2011, c. 638.
9.1-1109. Amended by Acts 2009, c. 323.
9.1-1110. Amended by Acts 2006, cc. 327, 551.
9.1-1200. Repealed by Acts 2011, cc. 780, 858.
10.1-104. Amended by Acts 2007, c. 632; 2009, c. 392; 2012, cc. 803, 835.
10.1-104.1. Amended by Acts 2013, cc. 756, 793.
10.1-104.2. Amended by Acts 2011, cc. 341, 353; 2012, c. 781; 2013, cc. 593, 658.
10.1-104.2:1. Amended by Acts 2013, cc. 593, 658.
10.1-104.3. Amended by Acts 2009, c. 349.
10.1-107. Amended by Acts 2005, cc. 25, 102; 2009, c. 856; 2012, cc. 803, 835.
10.1-109. Amended by Acts 2008, c. 22.
10.1-113. Amended by Acts 2007, c. 158.
10.1-116. Amended by Acts 2005, c. 87.
10.1-117. Amended by Acts 2005, c. 88.
10.1-200.1. Amended by Acts 2013, c. 43.
10.1-202. Amended by Acts 2007, c. 637; 2009, c. 856.
10.1-204. Amended by Acts 2012, c. 598.
10.1-215. Amended by Acts 2005, c. 94.
10.1-217.1 to 10.1-217.6. Repealed by Acts 2012, cc. 803, 835.
10.1-400. Amended by Acts 2012, cc. 803, 835.
10.1-406. Repealed by Acts 2012, cc. 803, 835.
10.1-409. Amended by Acts 2011, c. 276.
10.1-411. Amended by Acts 2007, c. 650.
10.1-414. Amended by Acts 2011, cc. 96, 136.
10.1-416. Amended by Acts 2009, c. 541.
10.1-418.3. Amended by Acts 2013, c. 341.
10.1-419. Amended by Acts 2011, cc. 594, 681.
10.1-501. Amended by Acts 2005, c. 236; 2008, c. 577.
10.1-502. Amended by Acts 2005, c. 102; 2011, cc. 213, 228; 2013, cc. 756, 793.
10.1-504. Amended by Acts 2013, cc. 756, 793.
10.1-505. Amended by Acts 2013, cc. 593, 658.
10.1-523. Amended by Acts 2009, cc. 370, 629.
10.1-546.1. Amended by Acts 2009, cc. 209, 263; 2013, cc. 593, 658.
10.1-559.1 to 10.1-559.11. Repealed by Acts 2008, c. 860, cl. 9.
10.1-560 to 10.1-571. Repealed by Acts 2013, cc. 756, 793.
10.1-572, 10.1-573. Repealed by Acts 2012, cc. 785, 819.

Section
10.1-603.1 to 10.1-603.15:5. Repealed by Acts 2013, cc. 756, 793.
10.1-603.16. Amended by Acts 2006, cc. 648, 765; 2011, c. 637.
10.1-603.17. Amended by Acts 2006, cc. 648, 765; 2008, c. 491.
10.1-603.18. Amended by Acts 2006, cc. 648, 765; 2010, c. 13.
10.1-603.19. Amended by Acts 2005, c. 80; 2006, cc. 648, 765; 2010, c. 13; 2011, c. 637.
10.1-603.21. Repealed by Acts 2006, cc. 648, 765.
10.1-603.22. Repealed by Acts 2006, c. 648, 765.
10.1-604. Amended by Acts 2006, c. 30.
10.1-605. Amended by Acts 2010, cc. 249, 270; 2011, c. 323.
10.1-605.1. Amended by Acts 2011, c. 323.
10.1-606.1. Repealed by Acts 2008, c. 491.
10.1-606.4. Amended by Acts 2011, c. 637.
10.1-607.1. Amended by Acts 2010, c. 270.
10.1-609. Amended by Acts 2006, c. 30; 2010, c. 270.
10.1-610. Amended by Acts 2005, c. 117.
10.1-611. Amended by Acts 2012, cc. 70, 230.
10.1-613. Amended by Acts 2006, c. 30.
10.1-613.5. Amended by Acts 2010, c. 13.
10.1-619. Amended by Acts 2005, c. 128.
10.1-603.20. Amended by Acts 2006, cc. 648, 765.
10.1-603.23. Amended by Acts 2006, cc. 648, 765.
10.1-642. Amended by Acts 2007, c. 637.
10.1-659. Amended by Acts 2012, cc. 785, 819; 2013, cc. 756, 793.
10.1-1012. Amended by Acts 2011, c. 207.
10.1-1018. Amended by Acts 2005, cc. 633, 758; 2006, c. 45.
10.1-1020. Amended by Acts 2006, c. 227; 2007, cc. 77, 673.
10.1-1021. Amended by Acts 2005, c. 633.
10.1-1102. Amended by Acts 2011, cc. 691, 714; 2012, cc. 803, 835.
10.1-1103. Amended by Acts 2012, cc. 803, 835.
10.1-1107. Amended by Acts 2007, c. 689; 2009, c. 43; 2012, cc. 197, 248.
10.1-1114. Amended by Acts 2012, cc. 101, 621; 2013, c. 124.
10.1-1115. Amended by Acts 2008, c. 19.
10.1-1122. Amended by Acts 2009, c. 612.
10.1-1124. Amended by Acts 2008, c. 254.
10.1-1141. Amended by Acts 2008, c. 835.
10.1-1142. Amended by Acts 2006, c. 228.
10.1-1152. Amended by Acts 2006, c. 13; 2007, c. 646; 2009, c. 297; 2012, c. 484.
10.1-1154, 10.1-1155. Repealed by Acts 2007, c. 646.
10.1-1156. Amended by Acts 2007, c. 646; 2012, cc. 197, 248.

Section

10.1-1157. Amended by Acts 2010, c. 8.
10.1-1172. Repealed by Acts. 2012, cc. 803, 835.
10.1-1181.2. Amended by Acts 2009, c. 572.
10.1-1183. Amended by Acts 2012, cc. 803, 835; 2013, c. 348.
10.1-1184. Amended by Acts 2008, cc. 276, 557.
10.1-1185. Amended by Acts 2008, cc. 276, 557.
10.1-1186. Amended by Acts 2012, cc. 803, 835.
10.1-1186.01. Amended by Acts 2008, c. 572.
10.1-1186.2:1. Amended by Acts 2008, c. 528.
10.1-1186.5. Amended by Acts 2005, c. 41.
10.1-1188. Amended by Acts 2007, c. 637; 2008, cc. 45, 225, 473; 2012, cc. 846, 849; 2013, c. 758.
10.1-1193. Amended by Acts 2007, c. 637.
10.1-1194. Amended by Acts 2005, c. 41.
10.1-1237. Amended by Acts 2010, c. 869.
10.1-1241. Amended by Acts 2012, c. 278.
10.1-1301. Amended by Acts 2008, cc. 276, 557.
10.1-1302. Amended by Acts 2008, cc. 276, 557.
10.1-1304. Amended by Acts 2008, cc. 276, 557.
10.1-1307.3. Amended by Acts 2007, c. 148.
10.1-1308. Amended by Acts 2005, c. 66; 2006, c. 71; 2011, c. 393.
10.1-1308.1. Amended by Acts 2010, c. 65.
10.1-1309. Amended by Acts 2005, c. 706.
10.1-1316. Amended by Acts 2005, c. 706.
10.1-1322. Amended by Acts 2005, c. 633; 2008, cc. 276, 557; 2012, c. 581.
10.1-1322.01. Amended by Acts 2009, c. 627.
10.1-1322.4. Amended by Acts 2008, c. 282.
10.1-1328. Amended by Acts 2010, cc. 783. 867.
10.1-1400. Amended by Acts 2009, c. 27.
10.1-1401. Amended by Acts 2008, cc. 276, 557.
10.1-1402. Amended by Acts 2006, cc. 16, 163.
10.1-1402.1:1. Amended by Acts 2011, c. 420.
10.1-1408.1. Amended by Acts 2006, c. 62; 2007, c. 23; 2012, c. 581.
10.1-1408.3. Repealed by Acts 2007, c. 23.
10.1-1408.4. Amended by Acts 2005, c. 920.
10.1-1408.5. Amended by Acts 2005, c. 920; 2007, cc. 659, 813.
10.1-1411. Amended by Acts 2006, cc. 7, 40; 2012, c. 834.
10.1-1422. Amended by Acts 2006, c. 6; 2009, c. 409.
10.1-1422.01. Amended by Acts 2006, c. 6; 2009, c. 409.
10.1-1422.03. Amended by Acts 2006, c. 6.
10.1-1422.05. Repealed by Acts 2009, c. 409.
10.1-1422.6. Amended by Acts 2008, c. 646.
10.1-1425.7. Amended by Acts 2013, c. 482.
10.1-1425.26. Amended by Acts 2008, c. 12; 2010, c. 4.
10.1-1428. Amended by Acts 2005, c. 180.
10.1-1454.1. Amended by Acts 2005, cc. 130, 232; 2006, c. 477.
10.1-1454.3. Repealed by Acts 2007, c. 23.
10.1-1455. Amended by Acts 2005, cc. 133, 706.
10.1-1602. Amended by Acts 2005, c. 768; 2006, c. 22.

Section

10.1-1700. Amended by Acts 2011, cc. 85, 159.
10.1-1800. Amended by Acts 2011, cc. 691, 714.
10.1-1801.1. Amended by Acts 2009, c. 599.
10.1-2002. Amended by Acts 2012, c. 502.
10.1-2100 to 10.1-2115. Repealed by Acts 2013, cc. 756, 793.
10.1-2117. Amended by Acts 2005, cc. 704, 707, 709; 2006, c. 236; 2007, c. 924.
10.1-2125. Amended by Acts 2005, c. 41.
10.1-2123. Amended by Acts 2013, cc. 756, 793.
10.1-2127. Amended by Acts 2007, c. 637.
10.1-2128. Amended by Acts 2005, cc. 704, 707, 709; 2006, c. 236; 2008, cc. 278, 500, 643, 701; 2010, c. 684.
10.1-2128.1. Amended by Acts 2009, cc. 209, 263; 2011, c. 245.
10.1-2129. Amended by Acts 2005, cc. 41, 704, 707, 709; 2006, c. 236; 2008, cc. 643, 701; 2010, c. 684; 2011, c. 189; 2012, 785, 819.
10.1-2131. Amended by Acts 2005, cc. 704, 707, 709; 2006, c. 236.
10.1-2132. Amended by Acts 2005, cc. 704, 707, 709; 2008, cc. 643, 701; 2009, c. 695.
10.1-2133. Amended by Acts 2010, c. 684.
10.1-2134. Amended by Acts 2007, c. 637; 2008, cc. 643, 701.
10.1-2135 to 2140. Repealed by Acts 2012, cc. 803, 835.
10.1-2136. Amended by Acts 2011, cc. 691, 714.
10.1-2202. Amended by Acts 2005, c. 85; 2006, c. 32.
10.1-2204. Amended by Acts 2006, c. 32.
10.1-2205. Amended by Acts 2006, c. 32.
10.1-2206.1. Amended by Acts 2006, c. 32.
10.1-2206.2. Amended by Acts 2006, c. 32.
10.1-2208. Amended by Acts 2010, c. 291.
10.1-2211. Amended by Acts 2006, cc. 489, 630; 2009, c. 53; 2011, cc. 543, 603; 2012, c. 534; 2013, c. 42.
10.1-2211.1. Amended by Acts 2007, c. 349.
10.1-2213. Amended by Acts 2005, c. 86; 2010, c. 291.
10.1-2300. Amended by Acts 2005, c. 457.
10.1-2301. Amended by Acts 2005, c. 457.
11-7.1. Amended by Acts 2013, c. 482.
11-9.1 through 11-9.7. Repealed by Acts 2010, cc. 455, 632.
11-30 through 11-34. Repealed by Acts 2010, c. 794.
11-33.2. Amended by Acts 2009, c. 373.
11-34.3. Amended by Acts 2009, c. 399; 2013, c. 583.
12.1-6. Amended by Acts 2006, c. 838.
12.1-10. Amended by Acts 2011, c. 163; 2013, c. 94.
12.1-17. Amended by Acts 2013, c. 21.
12.1-19. Amended by Acts 2010, c. 513.
12.1-19.1. Amended by Acts 2010, c. 675.

Section
12.1-20. Amended by Acts 2010, c. 669
12.1-21.1. Amended by Acts 2005, c. 308; 2007, c. 239; 2010, c. 669; 2013, c. 757.
12.1-21.2. Amended by Acts 2006, c. 192; 2010, c. 669.
12.1-43. Amended by Acts 2007, c. 631; 2010, c. 675.
13.1-313. Amended by Acts 2010, cc. 317, 561.
13.1-504. Amended by Acts 2007, c. 458.
13.1-514. Amended by Acts 2007, c. 457.
13.1-521. Amended by Acts 2009, c. 566.
13.1-543. Amended by Acts 2006, cc. 672, 715; 2008, c. 265; 2009, c. 309.
13.1-544. Amended by Acts 2006, cc. 672, 715.
13.1-545.1. Amended by Acts 2008, c. 509.
13.1-549. Amended by Acts 2006, cc. 672, 715; 2008, c. 509; 2009, c. 309.
13.1-549.1. Amended by Acts 2006, cc. 672, 715; 2008, c. 265.
13.1-550. Amended by Acts 2006, cc. 672, 715; 2008, c. 265.
13.1-553. Amended by Acts 2006, c. 649; 2007, c. 629; 2009, c. 309; 2010, c. 532.
13.1-555. Amended by Acts 2008, c. 509.
13.1-559. Amended by Acts 2007, c. 668; 2009, c. 148.
13.1-560. Amended by Acts 2007, c. 668; 2009, c. 148.
13.1-561, 13.1-562. Amended by Acts 2007, c. 668.
13.1-563. Amended by Acts 2009, c. 148.
13.1-565. Amended by Acts 2009, c. 148.
13.1-566. Amended by Acts 2009, c. 148.
13.1-572. Amended by Acts 2007, c. 668.
13.1-603. Amended by Acts 2005, c. 765; 2006, c. 663; 2007, c. 165; 2010, c. 782.
13.1-604. Amended by Acts 2005, c. 765; 2010, c. 782.
13.1-604.1. Amended by Acts 2005, c. 765; 2012, c. 130.
13.1-607. Amended by Acts 2005, c. 765; 2007, c. 165; 2008, cc. 91, 509.
13.1-608. Amended by Acts 2005, c. 765.
13.1-609. Amended by Acts 2005, c. 765; 2006, c. 663.
13.1-610. Amended by Acts 2005, c. 765; 2007, c. 165; 2010, c. 782.
13.1-611. Amended by Acts 2005, c. 765.
13.1-614. Amended by Acts 2005, c. 765; 2008, c. 91; 2010, c. 782.
13.1-615. Amended by Acts 2005, c. 765; 2006, c. 659; 2007, c. 810; 2009, c. 216; 2010, c. 753.
13.1-615.1. Amended by Acts 2007, c. 810; 2008, c. 509.
13.1-616. Amended by Acts 2005, c. 765; 2007, cc. 771, 810; 2012, c. 130.
13.1-624. Amended by Acts 2010, c. 782.
13.1-627. Amended by Acts 2005, c. 765.
13.1-628. Amended by Acts 2005, c. 765.

Section
13.1-630. Amended by Acts 2005, cc. 379, 765; 2009, c. 216; 2012, c. 63.
13.1-631. Amended by Acts 2005, c. 765.
13.1-632. Amended by Acts 2005, c. 765.
13.1-633. Repealed by Acts 2007, c. 771.
13.1-635. Amended by Acts 2010, cc. 434, 782.
13.1-636. Amended by Acts 2005, c. 765; 2010, c. 434.
13.1-638. Amended by Acts 2005, c. 765.
13.1-639. Amended by Acts 2005, c. 765; 2006, c. 330.
13.1-641. Amended by Acts 2005, c. 765.
13.1-642. Amended by Acts 2005, c. 765.
13.1-646. Amended by Acts 2005, c. 765; 2010, c. 782.
13.1-647. Amended by Acts 2005, c. 765.
13.1-649. Amended by Acts 2005, c. 765.
13.1-651. Amended by Acts 2005, c. 765.
13.1-652. Amended by Acts 2005, c. 765.
13.1-653. Amended by Acts 2005, c. 765.
13.1-654. Amended by Acts 2005, c. 765; 2007, c. 165; 2012, c. 706.
13.1-655. Amended by Acts 2005, c. 765; 2012, c. 706.
13.1-656. Amended by Acts 2005, c. 765; 2007, c. 165; 2010, c. 782.
13.1-657. Amended by Acts 2005, c. 765; 2007, c. 165; 2008, c. 91; 2010, c. 782; 2012, c. 706.
13.1-658. Amended by Acts 2005, c. 765; 2010, c. 782.
13.1-660. Amended by Acts 2005, c. 765; 2010, c. 782.
13.1-661. Amended by Acts 2010, c. 782; 2012, c. 706.
13.1-662. Amended by Acts 2005, c. 765.
13.1-663. Amended by Acts 2005, c. 765; 2010, c. 782.
13.1-664.1. Amended by Acts 2005, c. 765; 2010, c. 782.
13.1-665. Amended by Acts 2005, c. 765.
13.1-666. Amended by Acts 2007, c. 165.
13.1-669. Amended by Acts 2005, c. 765; 2007, c. 165.
13.1-670. Amended by Acts 2005, c. 765.
13.1-671.1. Amended by Acts 2005, c. 765.
13.1-672.1. Amended by Acts 2007, c. 165; 2010, c. 782.
13.1-672.3. Amended by Acts 2005, c. 765.
13.1-672.4. Amended by Acts 2005, c. 765.
13.1-673. Amended by Acts 2005, c. 765.
13.1-674. Amended by Acts 2012, c. 706.
13.1-675. Amended by Acts 2005, c. 765; 2006, c. 330; 2010, c. 782.
13.1-677. Amended by Acts 2005, c. 765; 2007, c. 165.
13.1-679. Amended by Acts 2005, c. 765; 2007, c. 165.
13.1-680. Amended by Acts 2005, c. 765.
13.1-681. Repealed by Acts 2010, c. 782.

Section
13.1-682. Amended by Acts 2007, c. 165.
13.1-685. Amended by Acts 2005, c. 765.
13.1-686. Amended by Acts 2005, c. 765; 2010, c. 782.
13.1-688. Amended by Acts 2005, c. 765.
13.1-689. Amended by Acts 2005, c. 765; 2010, c. 782.
13.1-691. Amended by Acts 2005, c. 765.
13.1-692. Amended by Acts 2005, c. 765.
13.1-693. Amended by Acts 2005, c. 765.
13.1-695. Amended by Acts 2005, c. 765.
13.1-696. Amended by Acts 2005, c. 765; 2009, c. 587.
13.1-697. Amended by Acts 2005, c. 765.
13.1-699. Amended by Acts 2005, c. 765; 2010, c. 782.
13.1-700.1. Amended by Acts 2005, c. 765.
13.1-701. Amended by Acts 2005, c. 765.
13.1-702. Amended by Acts 2005, c. 765.
13.1-703. Amended by Acts 2005, c. 765.
13.1-704. Amended by Acts 2005, c. 765; 2007, c. 165; 2010, c. 782.
13.1-706. Amended by Acts 2005, c. 765; 2006, c. 330.
13.1-707. Amended by Acts 2005, c. 765.
13.1-708. Amended by Acts 2005, c. 765; 2008, c. 91.
13.1-710. Amended by Acts 2005, c. 765.
13.1-711. Amended by Acts 2005, c. 765; 2007, c. 165; 2012, c. 706.
13.1-713. Amended by Acts 2005, c. 765.
13.1-714. Amended by Acts 2005, c. 765; 2010, c. 782.
13.1-715. Amended by Acts 2005, c. 765.
13.1-715.1. Amended by Acts 2005, c. 765.
13.1-716. Amended by Acts 2005, c. 765; 2006, c. 663; 2008, c. 509; 2009, c. 216.
13.1-717. Amended by Acts 2005, c. 765.
13.1-718. Amended by Acts 2005, c. 765; 2006, cc. 363, 663; 2007, c. 165; 2010, c. 782.
13.1-719. Amended by Acts 2005, c. 765.
13.1-720. Amended by Acts 2005, c. 765; 2006, c. 363; 2009, c. 216; 2010, c. 782.
13.1-721. Amended by Acts 2005, c. 765.
13.1-721.1. Amended by Acts 2010, c. 782.
13.1-722, 13.1-722.1. Repealed by Acts 2005, c. 765.
13.1-722.2. Amended by Acts 2012, c. 130.
13.1-722.4. Amended by Acts 2012, c. 130.
13.1-722.11. Amended by Acts 2012, c. 130.
13.1-722.13. Amended by Acts 2005, c. 765.
13.1-723. Amended by Acts 2005, c. 765.
13.1-723. Amended by Acts 2005, c. 765.
13.1-724. Amended by Acts 2005, c. 765.
13.1-725. Amended by Acts 2005, c. 765; 2010, c. 782.
13.1-727. Amended by Acts 2005, c. 765.
13.1-728.1. Amended by Acts 2005, c. 765.
13.1-728.2. Amended by Acts 2005, c. 765.

Section
13.1-728.3. Amended by Acts 2005, c. 765.
13.1-728.4. Amended by Acts 2005, c. 765.
13.1-728.5. Amended by Acts 2005, c. 765.
13.1-728.6. Amended by Acts 2005, c. 765.
13.1-728.7. Amended by Acts 2005, c. 765.
13.1-728.8. Amended by Acts 2005, c. 765.
13.1-728.9. Amended by Acts 2005, c. 765.
13.1-729. Amended by Acts 2005, c. 765; 2007, c. 165.
13.1-730. Amended by Acts 2005, c. 765; 2007, c. 165; 2010, c. 782.
13.1-731. Amended by Acts 2005, c. 765.
13.1-732. Amended by Acts 2005, c. 765; 2007, c. 165; 2012, c. 706.
13.1-733. Amended by Acts 2005, c. 765; 2007, c. 165; 2010, c. 782.
13.1-734. Amended by Acts 2005, c. 765; 2007, c. 165; 2010, c. 782; 2012, c. 706.
13.1-735. Repealed by Acts 2005, c. 765.
13.1-735.1. Amended by Acts 2007, c. 165.
13.1-736. Repealed by Acts 2005, c. 765.
13.1-737. Amended by Acts 2005, c. 765; 2007, c. 165; 2012, c. 706.
13.1-738. Amended by Acts 2005, c. 765; 2007, c. 165.
13.1-739. Amended by Acts 2005, c. 765.
13.1-740. Amended by Acts 2005, c. 765.
13.1-741. Amended by Acts 2005, c. 765.
13.1-741.1. Amended by Acts 2008, c. 91.
13.1-742. Amended by Acts 2005, c. 765.
13.1-743. Amended by Acts 2005, c. 765.
13.1-746. Amended by Acts 2005, c. 765; 2007, c. 165; 2008, c. 91.
13.1-746.1. Amended by 2007, c. 165; 2008, c. 91.
13.1-746.2. Amended by 2008, c. 91.
13.1-747. Amended by Acts 2005, c. 765; 2007, c. 165.
13.1-748. Amended by Acts 2005, c. 765; 2007, c. 165.
13.1-749. Amended by Acts 2005, c. 765.
13.1-749.1. Amended by 2007, c. 165; 2012, c. 706.
13.1-750. Amended by Acts 2005, c. 765.
13.1-752. Amended by Acts 2005, c. 765; 2010, c. 753.
13.1-753. Amended by 2008, cc. 588, 770.
13.1-754. Amended by Acts 2005, c. 379; 2006, c. 663.
13.1-757. Amended by Acts 2005, c. 765.
13.1-758. Amended by Acts 2005, c. 765.
13.1-762. Amended by Acts 2005, cc. 379, 765; 2012, c. 63.
13.1-764. Amended by Acts 2010, c. 434.
13.1-765. Amended by Acts 2005, c. 765; 2010, c. 434.
13.1-766.1. Amended by Acts 2006, c. 663.
13.1-767. Amended by Acts 2005, c. 765; 2012, c. 130.
13.1-768. Amended by Acts 2005, c. 765; 2010, c. 753.

Section
13.1-769. Amended by Acts 2005, c. 765; 2008, cc. 588, 770.
13.1-769.1. Amended by Acts 2005, c. 765.
13.1-770. Amended by Acts 2005, c. 765; 2008, c. 91; 2010, c. 782.
13.1-771. Amended by Acts 2005, c. 765; 2008, c. 91; 2010, c. 782.
13.1-772. Amended by Acts 2005, c. 765; 2010, c. 782.
13.1-773. Amended by Acts 2010, c. 782.
13.1-774. Amended by Acts 2005, c. 765; 2010, c. 782.
13.1-775. Amended by Acts 2005, c. 765; 2010, c. 753.
13.1-775.1. Amended by Acts 2005, c. 765; 2010, c. 753.
13.1-776. Amended by Acts 2005, c. 765.
13.1-779. Amended by Acts 2010, c. 782.
13.1-801 to 13.1-804. Amended by Acts 2007, c. 925.
13.1-802. Amended by Acts 2007, c. 925.
13.1-803. Amended by Acts 2007, c. 925; 2010, c. 171; 2012, c. 706.
13.1-804. Amended by Acts 2010, c. 171.
13.1-806. Amended by Acts 2007, c. 925.
13.1-807. Amended by Acts 2007, c. 925; 2008, cc. 91, 509.
13.1-808. Amended by Acts 2007, c. 925.
13.1-809. Amended by Acts 2006, c. 663; 2007, c. 925.
13.1-810. Amended by Acts 2007, c. 925; 2010, c. 171.
13.1-811. Amended by Acts 2007, c. 925.
13.1-812. Amended by Acts 2007, c. 925.
13.1-813. Amended by Acts 2007, c. 925; 2008, c. 91; 2010, c. 171.
13.1-815. Amended by Acts 2006, c. 659; 2007, cc. 810, 925; 2009, c. 216; 2010, c. 753.
13.1-815.1. Amended by Acts 2007, cc. 810, 925; 2008, c. 509.
13.1-816. Amended by Acts 2007, cc. 771, 925; 2012, c. 130.
13.1-819, 13.1-820. Amended by Acts 2007, c. 925.
13.1-822. Amended by Acts 2007, c. 925.
13.1-823. Amended by Acts 2007, c. 925; 2010, c. 171.
13.1-824. Amended by Acts 2007, c. 925.
13.1-825. Amended by Acts 2007, c. 925.
13.1-826. Amended by Acts 2007, c. 925.
13.1-827. Amended by Acts 2007, c. 925.
13.1-828. Amended by Acts 2007, c. 925.
13.1-829. Amended by Acts 2005, c. 379; 2007, c. 925; 2009, c. 216; 2012, c. 63.
13.1-830. Amended by Acts 2006, c. 505; 2007, c. 925.
13.1-831. Amended by Acts 2007, c. 925.
13.1-832. Repealed by Acts 2007, c. 771.
13.1-833. Amended by Acts 2007, c. 925.

Section
13.1-834. Amended by Acts 2007, c. 925; 2010 c. 434.
13.1-835. Amended by Acts 2007, c. 925; 2010 c. 434.
13.1-836. Amended by Acts 2007, c. 925.
13.1-837. Amended by Acts 2007, c. 925.
13.1-838. Amended by Acts 2007, c. 925; 2012, c. 706.
13.1-839. Amended by Acts 2007, c. 925; 2012, c. 706.
13.1-840. Amended by Acts 2007, c. 925.
13.1-841. Amended by Acts 2007, c. 925.
13.1-842. Amended by Acts 2007, c. 925; 2010 c. 171.
13.1-843. Amended by Acts 2007, c. 925.
13.1-844. Amended by Acts 2007, c. 925.
13.1-845. Amended by Acts 2007, c. 925; 2010 c. 171.
13.1-846. Amended by Acts 2007, c. 925.
13.1-847. Amended by Acts 2007, c. 925; 2010 c. 171.
13.1-847.1. Amended by Acts 2010 c. 171.
13.1-848. Amended by Acts 2007, c. 925.
13.1-849. Amended by Acts 2007, c. 925.
13.1-850. Amended by Acts 2007, c. 925.
13.1-852. Amended by Acts 2007, c. 925.
13.1-853. Amended by Acts 2007, c. 925.
13.1-854. Amended by Acts 2007, c. 925.
13.1-855. Amended by Acts 2007, c. 925; 2010 c. 171.
13.1-857 to 13.1-862. Amended by Acts 2007, c. 925.
13.1-864. Amended by Acts 2007, c. 925.
13.1-865. Amended by Acts 2007, c. 925.
13.1-866. Amended by Acts 2007, c. 925; 2010 c. 171.
13.1-867. Amended by Acts 2007, c. 925.
13.1-868. Amended by Acts 2007, c. 925.
13.1-869. Amended by Acts 2007, c. 925.
13.1-870. Amended by Acts 2007, c. 925.
13.1-870.1. Amended by Acts 2011, cc. 693, 704.
13.1-870.2. Amended by Acts 2011, cc. 693, 704.
13.1-871. Amended by Acts 2007, c. 925.
13.1-872. Amended by Acts 2007, c. 925.
13.1-874. Amended by Acts 2007, c. 925.
13.1-875. Amended by Acts 2007, c. 925; 2009, c. 587.
13.1-876. Amended by Acts 2007, c. 925.
13.1-878. Amended by Acts 2007, c. 925; 2010 c. 171.
13.1-879.1. Amended by Acts 2007, c. 925.
13.1-880. Amended by Acts 2007, c. 925.
13.1-881. Amended by Acts 2007, c. 925.
13.1-882. Amended by Acts 2007, c. 925.
13.1-883. Amended by Acts 2007, c. 925; 2010 c. 171.
13.1-885, 13.1-886. Amended by Acts 2007, c. 925.

Section
13.1-887.1. Amended by Acts 2007, c. 925.
13.1-888. Amended by Acts Acts 2007, c. 925; 2012, c. 130.
13.1-889. Amended by Acts 2007, c. 925.
13.1-890. Repealed by Acts 2007, c. 925.
13.1-891 to 13.1-893. Amended by Acts 2007, c. 925.
13.1-893.1. Amended by Acts 2009, c. 216.
13.1-894. Amended by Acts 2007, c. 925; 2008, c. 509.
13.1-895. Amended by Acts 2007, c. 925.
13.1-896. Amended by Acts 2009, c. 216.
13.1-897. Amended by Acts 2007, c. 925.
13.1-898, 13.1-898.1. Repealed by Acts 2007, c. 925.
13.1-898.1. Amended by Acts 2005, c. 765.
13.1-898.2. Amended by Acts 2007, c. 925; 2012, c. 130.
13.1-898.3. Amended by Acts 2007, c. 925.
13.1-898.4. Amended by Acts 2007, c. 925; 2012, 130.
13.1-898.5 to 13.1-898.7. Amended by Acts 2007, c. 925.
13.1-899, 13.1-900. Amended by Acts 2007, c. 925.
13.1-902. Amended by Acts 2007, c. 925.
13.1-904. Amended by Acts 2007, c. 925.
13.1-906. Amended by Acts 2007, c. 925.
13.1-907. Amended by Acts 2007, c. 925.
13.1-908. Amended by Acts 2007, c. 925.
13.1-909. Amended by Acts 2007, c. 925.
13.1-910. Amended by Acts 2007, c. 925.
13.1-911. Amended by Acts 2007, c. 925.
13.1-912. Amended by Acts 2007, c. 925.
13.1-913. Amended by Acts 2007, c. 925.
13.1-914. Amended by Acts 2007, c. 925; 2010, c. 753.
13.1-915. Amended by Acts 2007, c. 925; 2008, cc. 588, 770.
13.1-916. Amended by Acts 2005, c. 379; 2006, c. 663; 2007, c. 925.
13.1-917. Amended by Acts 2007, c. 925.
13.1-919. Amended by Acts 2007, c. 925.
13.1-920. Amended by Acts 2007, c. 925.
13.1-921. Amended by Acts 2007, c. 925.
13.1-922. Amended by Acts 2007, c. 925.
13.1-923. Amended by Acts 2007, c. 925.
13.1-924. Amended by Acts 2005, c. 379; 2007, c. 925; 2012, c. 63.
13.1-925. Amended by Acts 2007, c. 925.
13.1-926. Amended by Acts 2007, c. 925; 2010 c. 434.
13.1-927. Amended by Acts 2007, c. 925; 2010 c. 434.
13.1-928. Amended by Acts 2007, c. 925.
13.1-928.1. Amended by Acts 2006, c. 663.
13.1-929. Amended by Acts 2007, c. 925; 2012, c. 130.
13.1-930. Amended by Acts 2007, c. 925; 2010 c. 753.

Section
13.1-931. Amended by Acts 2007, c. 925; 2008, c. 770.
13.1-932 to 13.1-934. Amended by Acts 2007, c. 925.
13.1-936. Amended by Acts 2007, c. 925; 2010 c. 753.
13.1-936.1. Amended by Acts 2007, c. 925; 2010 c. 753.
13.1-939. Amended by Acts 2007, c. 925; 2010 c. 171.
13.1-985. Amended by Acts 2010 c. 869.
13.1-1002. Amended by Acts 2005, c. 255; 2006, c. 912; 2007, cc. 233, 639; 2009, cc. 450, 763.
13.1-1003. Amended by Acts 2006, c. 748; 2013, c. 17.
13.1-1004. Amended by Acts 2010 c. 703.
13.1-1005. Amended by Acts 2005, c. 255; 2006, cc. 748, 912; 2007, c. 810; 2008, c. 108; 2012, c. 130.
13.1-1007. Amended by Acts 2013, c. 17.
13.1-1009. Amended by Acts 2006, c. 912; 2008, c. 108; 2013, c. 17.
13.1-1010. Amended by Acts 2006, c. 748.
13.1-1010.1. Amended by Acts 2006, c. 912; 2013, c. 17.
13.1-1010.3. Amended by Acts 2005, c. 255; 2006, c. 912.
13.1-1011. Amended by Acts 2006, c. 748; 2009, c. 763.
13.1-1011.1. Amended by Acts 2006, c. 748.
13.1-1012. Amended by Acts 2005, c. 379; 2012, c. 63.
13.1-1013. Amended by Acts 2006, c. 505.
13.1-1014. Amended by Acts 2005, c. 255; 2006, cc. 748, 912; 2008, c. 108; 2013, c. 17.
13.1-1014.1. Amended by Acts 2006, cc. 748, 912; 2008, c. 108; 2013, c. 17.
13.1-1015. Amended by Acts 2005, c. 255.
13.1-1016. Amended by Acts 2009, c. 450; 2010 c. 434.
13.1-1017. Amended by 2010 c. 434.
13.1-1019. Amended by Acts 2006, c. 912.
13.1-1020. Amended by Acts 2007, cc. 233, 639.
13.1-1022. Amended by Acts 2005, c. 255.
13.1-1023. Amended by Acts 2005, c. 255; 2009, c. 763; 2012, c. 706.
13.1-1035. Amended by Acts 2009, c. 763.
13.1-1036. Amended by Acts 2009, c. 763.
13.1-1038. Amended by Acts 2006, c. 912.
13.1-1038.1. Amended by Acts 2005, c. 255; 2006, cc. 748, 912.
13.1-1039. Amended by Acts 2006, c. 912; 2013, c. 17.
13.1-1040.1. Amended by Acts 2009, c. 763.
13.1-1040.2. Amended by Acts 2006, c. 912.
13.1-1041.1. Amended by Acts 2006, c. 912.
13.1-1042. Amended by Acts 2011, c. 379.
13.1-1046. Amended by Acts 2008, cc. 108, 588, 770; 2009, c. 167.

Section
13.1-1047. Amended by Acts 2008, c. 108.
13.1-1048. Amended by Acts 2006, c. 748; 2008, c. 108.
13.1-1049.1. Amended by Acts 2009, c. 763.
13.1-1049.3. Amended by Acts 2009, c. 763.
13.1-1050. Amended by Acts 2006, c. 748; 2008, c. 108; 2013, c. 17.
13.1-1050.1. Repealed by Acts 2008, c. 108.
13.1-1050.2. Amended by Acts 2010, c. 703; 2013, c. 17.
13.1-1050.3. Amended by Acts 2009, c. 167.
13.1-1050.4. Amended by Acts 2013, c. 17.
13.1-1051. Amended by Acts 2008, c. 108.
13.1-1052. Amended by Acts 2008, c. 108.
13.1-1053. Repealed by Acts 2008, c. 108.
13.1-1054. Amended by Acts 2012, c. 63.
13.1-1055. Amended by Acts 2008, c. 108; 2009, c. 450.
13.1-1056. Amended by Acts 2008, cc. 588, 770; 2009, c. 167; 2012, c. 130; 2013, c. 17.
13.1-1056.1. Amended by Acts 2010, c. 703; 2013, c. 17.
13.1-1056.2. Amended by Acts 2009, c. 167.
13.1-1056.3. Amended by Acts 2013, c. 17.
13.1-1057. Amended by Acts 2006, c. 912; 2008, c. 523; 2013, c. 17.
13.1-1060. Amended by Acts 2008, c. 108.
13.1-1062. Amended by Acts 2006, c. 748; 2010, c. 703; 2013, c. 17.
13.1-1064. Amended by Acts 2005, c. 255; 2008, c. 108.
13.1-1065. Amended by Acts 2006, c. 659; 2007, c. 810; 2009, c. 450.
13.1-1067. Amended by Acts 2006, c. 912; 2007, c. 771.
13.1-1069. Repealed by Acts 2005, c. 839.
13.1-1070. Amended by Acts 2005, c. 765; 2008, c. 108.
13.1-1072. Amended by Acts 2008, c. 108.
13.1-1074. Amended by Acts 2013, c. 17.
13.1-1075. Amended by Acts 2012, c. 130.
13.1-1077. Amended by Acts 2012, c. 130; 2013, c. 17.
13.1-1078. Amended by Acts 2009, c. 201.
13.1-1102. Amended by Acts 2008, c. 265; 2009, c. 309.
13.1-1106. Amended by Acts 2008, c. 509.
13.1-1111. Amended by Acts 2009, c. 309.
13.1-1116. Amended by Acts 2009, c. 201.
13.1-1117. Amended by Acts 2009, c. 763.
13.1-1118. Amended by Acts 2007, c. 629.
13.1-1121. Amended by Acts 2008, c. 209.
13.1-1123. Amended by Acts 2007, cc. 233, 639.
13.1-1202, 13.1-12043. Amended by Acts 2013, c. 25.
13.1-1204. Amended by Acts 2007, c. 771; 2008, c. 101; 2012, c. 130; 2013, c. 25.
13.1-1210. Amended by Acts 2008, c. 101.
13.1-1214. Amended by Acts 2005, c. 379; 2012, c. 63; 2013, c. 25.

Section
13.1-1215. Amended by Acts 2006, c. 505.
13.1-1216. Amended by Acts 2008, c. 101.
13.1-1217. Amended by Acts 2008, c. 101.
13.1-1221. Amended by Acts 2010, c. 434.
13.1-1222. Amended by Acts 2010, c. 434.
13.1-1234. Amended by Acts 2008, cc. 101, 588, 770; 2009, c. 167.
13.1-1235. Amended by Acts 2008, c. 101.
13.1-1236. Amended by Acts 2008, c. 101.
13.1-1238. Amended by Acts 2008, c. 101; 2013, c. 25.
13.1-1238.1. Amended by Acts 2013, c.25.
13.1-1238.2. Amended by Acts 2009, c. 167.
13.1-1239. Amended by Acts 2008, c. 101; 2013, c. 25.
13.1-1241. Amended by Acts 2008, c. 101.
13.1-1242. Amended by Acts 2008, c. 101.
13.1-1243. Repealed by Acts 2008, c. 101.
13.1-1244. Amended by Acts 2012, c. 63.
13.1-1245. Amended by Acts 2008, c. 101.
13.1-1246. Amended by Acts 2008, cc. 588, 770; 2009, c. 167; 2012, c. 130; 2013, c. 25.
13.1-1246.1. Amended by Acts 2013, c. 25.
13.1-1246.2. Amended by Acts 2009, c. 167.
13.1-1246.3. Amended by Acts 2013, c. 25.
13.1-1247. Amended by Acts 2008, c. 523; 2013, c. 25.
13.1-1249. Amended by Acts 2013, c. 25.
13.1-1250. Amended by Acts 2008, c. 101.
13.1-1252. Amended by Acts 2007, c. 810; 2013, c. 25.
13.1-1253. Repealed by Acts 2013, c. 25.
13.1-1254. Amended by Acts 2008, c. 101.
13.1-1255. Amended by Acts 2006, c. 659; 2007, c. 810.
13.1-1261. Amended by Acts 2008, c. 101.
13.1-1266. Amended by Acts 2012, c. 130.
13.1-1268. Amended by Acts 2012, c. 130.
13.1-1276. Amended by Acts 2005, c. 765.
15.2-106. Amended by Acts 2010, c. 708; 2011, c. 255.
15.2-107. Amended by Acts 2005, c. 72.
15.2-108. Repealed by Acts 2007, c. 250.
15.2-412. Amended by Acts 2010, cc. 349, 436.
15.2-502. Amended by Acts 2007, c. 268.
15.2-632. Amended by Acts 2010, c. 621.
15.2-702.1. Repealed by Acts 2006, c. 126.
15.2-715. Amended by Acts 2005, c. 839.
15.2-716. Amended by Acts 2010, cc. 154, 199.
15.2-738. Amended by Acts 2012, cc. 803, 835.
15.2-743. Amended by Acts 2005, cc. 40, 84.
15.2-802. Amended by Acts 2012, c. 396.
15.2-820. Amended by Acts 2005, c. 928.
15.2-851. Amended by Acts 2009, c. 309.
15.2-852. Amended by Acts 2006, cc. 9, 287, 317.
15.2-901. Amended by Acts 2006, c. 275; 2009, c. 446; 2010, cc. 161, 403, 641; 2011, cc. 542, 695; 2012, cc. 311,

Section

403, 430, 431; 2013, cc. 189, 490, 508.
15.2-902. Amended by Acts 2008, c. 877.
15.2-903. Amended by Acts 2005, c. 702; 2006, cc. 669, 722.
15.2-904. Amended by Acts 2005, cc. 465, 775.
15.2-905. Amended by Acts 2005, c. 775; 2013, c. 364.
15.2-906. Amended by Acts 2006, c. 460; 2013, cc. 734, 770.
15.2-907. Amended by Acts 2011, cc. 384, 410.
15.2-908. Amended by Acts 2006, c. 582; 2008, c. 877; 2009, cc. 319, 462, 475.
15.2-912.1. Amended by Acts 2007, c. 813.
15.2-912.2. Amended by Acts 2006, c. 644.
15.2-914. Amended by Acts 2010, c. 649; 2011, c. 251.
15.2-915. Amended by Acts 2009, cc. 735, 772; 2012, c. 757.
15.2-915.3. Amended by Acts 2006, c. 886; 2007, c. 272.
15.1-915.3. Repealed by Acts 2012, cc. 175, 557.
15.2-915.4. Amended by Acts 2011, c. 832.
15.2-917. Amended by Acts 2005, c. 544; 2006, c. 704.
15.2-919. Amended by Acts 2006, cc. 529, 538; 2013, c. 783.
15.2-922. Amended by Acts 2011, c. 766.
15.2-924.1. Repealed by Acts 2011, cc. 341, 353.
15.2-926. Amended by Acts 2009, c. 481.
15.2-928. Amended by Acts 2006, c. 847.
15.2-930, 15.2-931. Amended by Acts 2007, c. 813.
15.2-934. Amended by Acts 2006, c. 74.
15.2-936. Amended by Acts 2011, cc. 438, 496.
15.2-951. Amended by Acts 2005, c. 531; 2006, cc. 468, 493.
15.2-953. Amended by Acts 2005, c. 327; 2006, c. 118; 2007, cc. 292, 592, 641; 2008, cc. 612, 632; 2010, cc. 509, 600.
15.2-955. Amended by Acts 2005, c. 418.
15.2-958. Amended by Acts 2008, c. 580.
15.2-961. Amended by Acts 2013, c. 248.
15.2-963. Amended by Acts 2013, c. 24.
15.2-964. Amended by Acts 2012, cc. 476, 507.
15.2-965.1. Amended by Acts 2006, cc. 831, 921; 2009, c. 869; 2013, c. 482.
15.2-968.1. Amended by Acts 2010, c. 175; 2012, cc. 805, 836.
15.2-969. Amended by Acts 2009, cc. 321, 376.
15.2-973. Amended by Acts 2013, c. 347.
15.2-979. Amended by Acts 2013, c. 749.
15.2-1104. Amended by Acts 2012, c. 585.
15.2-1118. Repealed by Acts 2007, c. 256.
15.2-1123. Amended by Acts 2013, c. 758.
15.2-1124. Amended by Acts 2007, c. 813.
15.2-1127. Amended by Acts 2006, c. 299; 2013, cc. 253, 355, 405.

Section

15.2-1129.1. Amended by Acts 2005, c. 330; 2006, c. 482; 2007, cc. 236, 251, 280; 2008, c. 290; 2009, cc. 300, 637, 738; 2012, c. 516; 2013, cc. 254, 386.
15.2-1129.2. Amended by Acts 2013, cc. 756, 793.
15.2-1131. Amended by Acts 2007, c. 813.
15.2-1132. Amended by Acts 2005, cc. 265, 318; 2010, c. 202.
15.2-1201.2. Amended by Acts 2012, c. 585.
15.2-1206. Repealed by Acts 2010, c. 495.
15.2-1207. Amended by Acts 2010, c. 495.
15.2-1209. Amended by Acts 2005, c. 564.
15.2-1209.1. Amended by Acts 2007, c. 203.
15.2-1215. Amended by Acts 2005, c. 309; 2006, c. 700; 2009, c. 252; 2010, c. 396.
15.2-1220. Amended by Acts 2007, c. 813.
15.2-1245. Amended by Acts 2010, c. 668.
15.2-1246. Amended by Acts 2010, c. 668.
15.2-1247. Amended by Acts 2010, c. 668.
15.2-1301. Amended by Acts 2013, cc. 578, 612.
15.2-1408. Amended by Acts 2005, cc. 257, 289.
15.2-1411. Amended by Acts 2005, cc. 740, 879.
15.2-1412. Amended by Acts 2012, c. 802.
15.2-1414.4. Repealed by Acts 2006, c. 126.
15.2-1415. Amended by Acts 2007, c. 613.
15.2-1418. Amended by Acts 2011, c. 180.
15.2-1420, 15.2-1421. Amended by Acts 2007, c. 833.
15.2-1503.1. Amended by Acts 2010, cc. 189, 563.
15.2-1507. Amended by Acts 2005, c. 714; 2009, c. 736; 2012, cc. 803, 835.
15.2-1508.4. Amended by Acts 2007, c. 813.
15.2-1509. Amended by Acts 2005, c. 413.
15.2-1510.1. Amended by Acts 2007, c. 257.
15.2-1512.1. Amended by Acts 2013, c. 687
15.2-1512.2. Amended by Acts 2009, c. 306.
15.2-1517. Amended by Acts 2007, c. 150; 2012, cc. 191, 515.
15.2-1518. Amended by Acts 2008, c. 118.
15.2-1535. Amended by Acts 2009, cc. 400, 649; 2011, cc. 41, 51; 2012, cc. 803, 835.
15.2-1604. Amended by Acts 2012, cc. 803, 835.
15.2-1609.1. Amended by Acts 2011, cc. 339, 350.
15.2-1610. Amended by Acts 2005, cc. 337, 452; 2008, c. 551.
15.2-1612. Amended by Acts 2005, cc. 337, 452; 2013, c. 431.
15.2-1613.1. Amended by Acts 2011, cc. 300, 664.
15.2-1627. Amended by Acts 2011, c. 210.
15.2-1627.3. Amended by Acts 2010, c. 874; 2011, c. 890.
15.2-1627.4. Amended by Acts 2012, cc. 343, 625.
15.2-1629. Amended by Acts 2007, c. 417.
15.2-1631. Amended by Acts 2007, c. 417.

Section
15.2-1638. Amended by Acts 2007, c. 813.
15.2-1643. Amended by Acts 2012, cc. 805, 836.
15.2-1646. Amended by Acts 2005, c. 36.
15.2-1704. Amended by Acts 2007, c. 724; 2008, cc. 551, 691; 2010, cc. 778, 825.
15.2-1705. Amended by Acts 2013, cc. 307, 468.
15.2-1707. Amended by Acts 2013, cc. 307, 468.
15.2-1710. Amended by Acts 2008, cc. 551, 691.
15.2-1713.1. Amended by Acts 2013, c. 695.
15.2-1716. Amended by Acts 2005, cc. 148, 366; 2006, c. 679; 2009, c. 245; 2010, c. 343.
15.2-1716.1. Amended by Acts 2005, c. 479.
15.2-1719. Amended by Acts 2010, c. 333.
15.2-1720. Amended by Acts 2013, c. 783.
15.2-1724. Amended by Acts 2008, c. 437; 2010, cc. 778, 825; 2013, c. 428.
15.2-1726. Amended by Acts 2008, c. 437; 2013, cc. 250, 472, 594, 775.
15.2-1727. Amended by Acts 2007, c. 714.
15.2-1728. Amended by Acts 2008, c. 437.
15.2-1731. Amended by Acts 2012, c. 827.
15.2-1736. Amended by Acts 2005, c. 87; 2006, c. 286; 2009, cc. 461, 609; 2010, c. 523.
15.2-1747. Amended by Acts 2010, c. 516.
15.2-1752. Amended by Acts 2013, cc. 66, 99.
15.2-1800. Amended by Acts 2005, c. 822; 2006, c. 57; 2007, cc. 882, 901, 926.
15.2-1802. Amended by Acts 2012, c. 389.
15.2-1806. Amended by Acts 2008, c. 381.
15.2-1812. Amended by Acts 2005, c. 390; 2010, c. 860.
15.2-1812.2. Amended by Acts 2005, c. 614.
15.2-1814. Amended by Acts 2007, cc. 882, 901, 926.
15.2-1900. Repealed by Acts 2007, cc. 882, 901, 926.
15.2-1901. Amended by Acts 2013, c. 581.
15.2-1902. Amended by Acts 2012, c. 832.
15.2-1903. Amended by Acts 2006, c. 927.
15.2-2000. Amended by Acts 2005, c. 839.
15.2-2001. Amended by Acts 2006, c. 924.
15.2-2007.1. Amended by Acts 2007, c. 813.
15.2-2108. Repealed by Acts 2006, cc. 73, 76, 780.
15.2-2109. Amended by Acts 2007, c. 813.
15.2-2110. Amended by Acts 2005, c. 701.
15.2-2114. Amended by Acts 2005, c. 313; 2006, c. 11; 2009, c. 703; 2011, c. 452; 2013, cc. 756, 793.
15.2-2118. Amended by Acts 2005, c. 730; 2006, cc. 645, 749; 2007, cc. 152, 886; 2008, cc. 332, 428; 2010, c. 631; 2011, cc. 340, 509, 533; 2012, cc. 354, 441, 620.
15.2-2119. Amended by Acts 2005, c. 912; 2011, cc. 529, 580; 2012, c. 766.
15.2-2121. Amended by Acts 2005, c. 567.
15.2-2122. Amended by Acts 2010, c. 198.

Section
15.2-2123. Amended by Acts 2008, c. 389.
15.2-2146. Amended by Acts 2007, cc. 648, 774.
15.2-2157. Amended by Acts 2005, c. 814; 2007, c. 924; 2009, cc. 786, 846.
15.2-2157.1. Amended by Acts 2007, cc. 813, 880, 920.
15.2-2159. Amended by Acts 2006, cc. 102, 743; 2012, cc. 765, 803, 835; 2013, c. 699.
15.2-2160. Amended by Acts 2005, c. 258; 2006, cc. 73, 76; 2010, cc. 117, 210.
15.2-2200. Amended by Acts 2013, cc. 149, 213.
15.2-2201. Amended by Acts 2008, cc. 635, 718; 2011, c. 237; 2012, 554; 2013, cc. 149, 213.
15.2-2202. Amended by Acts 2007, c. 761; 2011, c. 699.
15.2-2204. Amended by Acts 2005, c. 514; 2007, cc. 761, 813; 2011, c. 457; 2012, c. 548; 2013, cc. 149, 213.
15.2-2208. Amended by Acts 2008, c. 583.
15.2-2209. Amended by Acts 2006, c. 248; 2008, c. 727.
15.2-2209.1. Amended by Acts 2011, c. 272; 2012, c. 508.
15.2-2211. Amended by Acts 2013, cc. 149, 213.
15.2-2212. Amended by Acts 2006, c. 687.
15.2-2220. Amended by Acts 2007, c. 813.
15.2-2222.1. Amended by Acts 2007, c. 792; 2010, c. 121; 2011, cc. 647, 888; 2012, c. 770.
15.2-2223. Amended by Acts 2005, cc. 466, 699; 2006, cc. 527, 563, 564; 2007, c. 761; 2012, cc. 729, 733; 2013, cc. 561, 585, 646, 656.
15.2-2223.1. Amended by Acts 2009, c. 327; 2010, cc. 465, 528; 2011, c. 561; 2012, cc. 192, 518, 805, 836.
15.2-2224. Amended by Acts 2006, c. 564; 2007, c. 761; 2008, c. 491.
15.2-2225. Amended by Acts 2009, c. 605.
15.2-2226. Amended by Acts 2009, c. 605.
15.2-2229. Amended by Acts 2010, c. 821.
15.2-2230.1. Amended by Acts 2012, c. 553.
15.2-2232. Amended by Acts 2007, c. 801; 2009, cc. 670, 690; 2012, cc. 803, 835.
15.2-2235. Amended by Acts 2008, c. 491.
15.2-2239. Amended by Acts 2006, c. 565; 2011, c. 658.
15.2-2241. Amended by Acts 2006, c. 670; 2008, cc. 491, 718; 2009, cc. 193, 194; 2010, cc. 149, 766; 2011, c. 512; 2012, c. 468.
15.2-2242. Amended by Acts 2005, c. 567; 2006, cc. 421, 514, 533, 903; 2007, c. 813.
15.2-2244. Amended by Acts 2008, cc. 340, 717; 2009, cc. 283, 465; 2010, c. 216.
15.2-2244.1. Amended by Acts 2007, c. 856.
15.2-2258. Amended by Acts 2008, c. 491.
15.2-2259. Amended by Acts 2007, c. 202; 2008, c. 855.

Section
15.2-2260. Amended by Acts 2006, c. 461; 2007, c. 202; 2008, cc. 426, 718, 855; 2009, c. 194.
15.2-2261. Amended by Acts 2008, c. 426; 2013, c. 509.
15.2-2263. Amended by Acts 2007, c. 813; 2009, cc. 214, 309, 518.
15.2-2265. Amended by Acts 2005, c. 937.
15.2-2266. Amended by Acts 2007, c. 279.
15.2-2269. Amended by Acts 2007, c. 202; 2008, c. 718.
15.2-2275. Amended by Acts 2005, c. 338.
15.2-2283. Amended by Acts 2005, c. 491.
15.2-2284. Amended by Acts 2005, c. 491.
15.2-2286. Amended by Acts 2005, cc. 625, 677; 2006, cc. 304, 514, 533, 903; 2007, cc. 821, 937; 2008, cc. 297, 317, 343, 581, 593, 720, 777; 2009, c. 721; 2012, cc. 304, 318.
15.2-2286.1. Amended by Acts 2011, cc. 519, 549.
15.2-2288. Amended by Acts 2012, c. 455.
15.2-2288.3. Amended by Acts 2007, cc. 611, 657; 2009, cc. 416, 546.
15.2-2289. Amended by Acts 2006, cc. 9, 317.
15.2-2291. Amended by Acts 2007, c. 813; 2008, c. 601; 2009, cc. 813, 840; 2010, cc. 796, 847; 2012, cc. 476, 507.
15.2-2292.1. Amended by Acts 2013, c. 178.
15.2-2295. Amended by Acts 2005, c. 509; 2011, c. 135.
15.2-2295.1. Amended by Acts 2013, cc. 516, 756, 793.
15.2-2297. Amended by Acts 2006, c. 450.
15.2-2298. Amended by Acts 2006, cc. 450, 882; 2007, c. 324.
15.2-2301. Amended by Acts 2011, c. 457; 2012, c. 401.
15.2-2302. Amended by Acts 2009, c. 315; 2012, cc. 415, 465; 2012, c. 521; 2013, c. 513.
15.2-2303. Amended by Acts 2006, c. 450; 2008, c. 733; 2012, c. 798.
15.2-2303.1. Amended by Acts 2007, c. 813.
15.2-2303.1:1. Amended by Acts 2011, c. 173; 2012, cc. 508, 798.
15.2-2303.2. Amended by Acts 2005, c. 855; 2006, cc. 583, 872, 882; 2007, c. 321; 2013, cc. 510, 541.
15.2-2303.3. Amended by Acts 2013, cc. 756, 793.
15.2-2305. Amended by Acts 2007, cc. 695, 713; 2008, c. 790.
15.2-2306. Amended by Acts 2009, c. 290; 2011, c. 237; 2012, c. 790.
15.2-2307. Amended by Acts 2006, c. 244; 2008, cc. 377, 411; 2009, c. 782; 2010, cc. 315, 698.
15.2-2308. Amended by Acts 2007, c. 813; 2009, c. 734; 2010, c. 705.

Section
15.2-2309. Amended by Acts 2006, c. 264; 2008, c. 318; 2009, c. 206.
15.2-2311. Amended by Acts 2005, cc. 625, 677; 2008, c. 378; 2010, c. 241; 2011, c. 457; 2012, cc. 400, 550, 606.
15.2-2314. Amended by Acts 2005, cc. 625, 677; 2006, c. 446; 2010, c. 241.
15.2-2316.1. Amended by Acts 2007, cc. 363, 410; 2009, cc. 413, 731.
15.2-2316.2. Amended by Acts 2007, cc. 363, 410; 2009, cc. 413, 731; 2010, c. 239; 2012, c. 512.
15.2-2317. Amended by Acts 2006, c. 832; 2007, c. 896.
15.2-2318 to 15.2-2327. Amended by Acts 2007, c. 896.
15.2-2403. Amended by Acts 2006, cc. 10, 394; 2007, cc. 210, 229, 813, 835, 896; 2009, c. 302, 408; 2010, c. 212.
15.2-2404. Amended by Acts 2005, c. 854; 2007, cc. 260, 813; 2008, c. 355; 2008, Sp. Sess. II, c. 8; 2009, c. 335; 2010, c. 392; 2012, cc. 186, 404.
15.2-2406. Amended by Acts 2005, c. 515; 2007, c. 813.
15.2-2407. Amended by Acts 2011, cc. 438, 496.
15.2-2503. Amended by Acts 2008, c. 353; 2013, c. 747.
15.2-2506. Amended by Acts 2009, c. 280.
15.2-2507. Amended by Acts 2007, c. 297.
15.2-2511. Amended by Acts 2013, cc. 239, 392.
15.2-2511.1. Amended by Acts 2005, c. 835.
15.2-2606. Amended by Acts 2011, c. 590.
15.2-2703. Amended by Acts 2009, cc. 285, 336.
15.2-2800 to 15.2-2810. Repealed by Acts 2009, cc. 153, 154.
15.2-2903. Amended by Acts 2011, c. 381.
15.2-3108. Amended by Acts 2013, c. 773.
15.2-3201. Amended by Acts 2008, c. 347; 2009, cc. 129, 435, 631; 2012, c. 537.
15.2-3207. Amended by Acts 2010, cc. 386, 629.
15.2-3400. Amended by Acts 2006, c. 212.
15.2-3525. Amended by Acts 2010, cc. 386, 629.
15.2-3548. Amended by Acts 2011, cc. 337, 349.
15.2-3806. Amended by Acts 2010, cc. 386, 629.
15.2-3830. Amended by Acts 2007, c. 813.
15.2-3906. Amended by Acts 2010, cc. 386, 629.
15.2-4105. Amended by Acts 2010, cc. 386, 629.
15.2-4116. Amended by Acts 2009, c. 483; 2013, c. 363.
15.2-4119. Amended by Acts 2005, c. 681.
15.2-4203. Amended by Acts 2005, cc. 819, 667.
15.2-4207. Amended by Acts 2009, c. 863.
15.2-4209. Amended by Acts 2013, c. 607.
15.2-4217. Amended by Acts 2012, c. 500.
15.2-4302. Amended by Acts 2011, cc. 344, 355.
15.2-4303. Amended by Acts 2011, cc. 344, 355.
15.2-4304. Amended by Acts 2011, cc. 344, 355.
15.2-4305. Amended by Acts 2011, cc. 344, 355.
15.2-4307. Amended by Acts 2011, cc. 344, 355.

Section
15.2-4308. Repealed by Acts 2011, cc. 344, 355.
15.2-4309. Amended by Acts 2011, cc. 344, 355.
15.2-4310. Amended by Acts 2011, cc. 344, 355.
15.2-4314. Amended by Acts 2011, cc. 344, 355.
15.2-4402. Amended by Acts 2007, c. 813; 2012, c. 419.
15.2-4405. Amended by Acts 2010, c. 653.
15.2-4407. Amended by Acts 2007, c. 813; 2012, c. 419.
15.2-4504. Amended by Acts 2006, c. 354.
15.2-4507. Amended by Acts 2011, c. 515; 2012, c. 377; 2013, c. 589.
15.2-4512. Amended by Acts 2013, c. 589.
15.2-4529. Amended by Acts 2006, c. 354.
15.2-4832. Amended by Acts 2008, c. 434.
15.2-4838.1. Amended by Acts 2009, cc. 410, 556; 2013, c. 766.
15.2-4839, 15.2-4840. Amended by Acts 2007, c. 896.
15.2-4901. Amended by Acts 2005, c. 928; 2012, c. 498.
15.2-4902. Amended by Acts 2005, c. 928; 2006, c. 324.
15.2-4904. Amended by Acts 2006, c. 687; 2007, cc. 283, 338; 2008, c. 619; 2009, cc. 199, 200, 460, 597; 2012, cc. 337, 352; 2013, c. 482.
15.2-4905. Amended by Acts 2005, c. 575.
15.2-5000. Amended by Acts 2008, c. 445; 2010, cc. 122, 360.
15.2-5001. Amended by Acts 2008, c. 445.
15.2-5002. Amended by Acts 2008, c. 445.
15.2-5003. Amended by Acts 2008, c. 445; 2012, c. 239.
15.2-5004. Amended by Acts 2008, c. 445.
15.2-5101. Amended by Acts 2006, c. 219; 2009, cc. 402, 473.
15.2-5102. Amended by Acts 2011, c. 199.
15.2-5108. Amended by Acts 2009, c. 473.
15.2-5109. Amended by Acts 2009, c. 216.
15.2-5113. Amended by Acts 2009, c. 655.
15.2-5114. Amended by Acts 2005, c. 666; 2007, c. 813; 2008, c. 542; 2009, cc. 402, 473; 2011, c. 653.
15.2-5115. Amended by Acts 2007, c. 813; 2009, c. 473.
15.2-5125. Amended by Acts 2009, c. 473.
15.2-5132. Amended by Acts 2009, c. 473.
15.2-5133. Amended by Acts 2009, c. 473.
15.2-5136. Amended by Acts 2007, c. 813; 2009, c. 473; 2013, c. 51.
15.2-5137. Amended by Acts 2011, c. 642.
15.2-5139. Amended by Acts 2009, c. 420; 2011, cc. 529, 580; 2012, c. 766.
15.2-5141. Amended by Acts 2009, c. 473.
15.2-5142. Amended by Acts 2009, c. 473.
15.2-5146. Amended by Acts 2009, c. 861.
15.2-5147. Amended by Acts 2009, c. 473.
15.2-5148. Amended by Acts 2009, c. 473.
15.2-5152. Amended by Acts 2005, c. 547; 2009, c. 473.

Section
15.2-5153. Amended by Acts 2005, c. 547; 2009, c. 473.
15.2-5154. Amended by Acts 2009, c. 473.
15.2-5155. Amended by Acts 2009, c. 473.
15.2-5158. Amended by Acts 2005, c. 547; 2009, c. 473.
15.2-5201. Amended by Acts 2006, c. 658.
15.2-5202. Amended by Acts 2006, c. 658.
15.2-5204. Amended by Acts 2006, c. 658; 2007, cc. 472, 813.
15.2-5205. Amended by Acts 2006, c. 658; 2008, c. 184.
15.2-5214. Amended by Acts 2005, c. 928; 2006, c. 673.
15.2-5301. Amended by Acts 2006, c. 658.
15.2-5307. Amended by Acts 2005, c. 630; 2006, c. 658; 2007, c. 813.
15.2-5339. Amended by Acts 2006, c. 658.
15.2-5340.1. Amended by Acts 2008, c. 184.
15.2-5343. Amended by Acts 2005, c. 928; 2006, c. 673.
15.2-5368. Amended by Acts 2009, c. 464.
15.2-5369. Amended by Acts 2013, c. 660.
15.2-5370. Amended by Acts 2008, c. 803; 2010, c. 575; 2011, c. 514.
15.2-5371. Amended by Acts 2010, c. 575.
15.2-5374. Amended by Acts 2008, c. 184; 2013, c. 660.
15.2-5376. Amended by Acts 2013, c. 660.
15.2-5386. Amended by Acts 2009, cc. 464, 813, 840.
15.2-5401 to 15.2-5403. Amended by Acts 2006, cc. 929, 941.
15.2-5405. Amended by Acts 2006, cc. 929, 941.
15.2-5406. Amended by Acts 2006, cc. 929, 941.
15.2-5409. Amended by Acts 2006, cc. 929, 941.
15.2-5423. Amended by Acts 2006, cc. 929, 941.
15.2-5431.3. Amended by Acts 2005, c. 299.
15.2-5800. Amended by Acts 2005, c. 106; 2006, c. 912.
15.2-5805. Amended by Acts 2005, c. 106.
15.2-5806. Amended by Acts 2005, c. 106.
15.2-5808. Amended by Acts 2005, c. 106.
15.2-5814. Amended by Acts 2005, c. 106.
15.2-5815. Amended by Acts 2005, c. 106.
15.2-5912. Amended by Acts 2005, c. 633.
15.2-6003. Amended by Acts 2010, c. 869.
15.2-6009. Amended by Acts 2013, cc. 305, 618.
15.2-6018. Amended by Acts 2009, c. 720.
15.2-6021. Amended by Acts 2009, c. 720.
15.2-6023. Amended by Acts 2010, c. 798.
15.2-6202. Amended by Acts 2006, c. 861.
15.2-6203. Amended by Acts 2005, c. 671; 2006, c. 861; 2010, c. 869.
15.2-6209. Amended by Acts 2005, c. 671; 2006, c. 861.
15.2-6210. Amended by Acts 2006, c. 861.
15.2-6214. Amended by Acts 2006, c. 861.
15.2-6300. Amended by Acts 2005, cc. 869, 887.
15.2-6301. Amended by Acts 2005, cc. 839, 869, 887.

Section
15.2-6302. Amended by Acts 2005, cc. 869, 887.
15.2-6304. Amended by Acts 2005, cc. 869, 887; 2007, cc. 707, 740; 2010, cc. 338, 381, 460.
15.2-6304.1. Repealed by Acts 2010, cc. 338, 460.
15.2-6306. Amended by Acts 2005, cc. 869, 887.
15.2-6308. Amended by Acts 2005, cc. 869, 887.
15.2-6319. Amended by Acts 2005, cc. 869, 887; 2011, cc. 126, 178.
15.2-6400. Amended by Acts 2007, cc. 941, 947; 2009, c. 616.
15.2-6402. Amended by Acts 2006, c. 324.
15.2-6403. Amended by Acts 2006, c. 758.
15.2-6407. Amended by Acts 2007, cc. 941, 947.
15.2-6415. Amended by Acts 2010, c. 531.
15.2-6500 to 15.2-6504. Repealed by Acts 2011, cc. 594, 681.
15.2-6601. Amended by Acts 2009, c. 429.
15.2-7300 to 15.2-7315. Repealed by Acts 2011, c. 716.
16.1-69.6. Amended by Acts 2006, c. 861.
16.1-69.6:1. Amended by Acts 2005, cc. 189, 228, 951; 2006, cc. 34, 488.
16.1-69.29. Amended by Acts 2005, cc. 45, 114.
16.1-69.33. Amended by Acts 2008, c. 115.
16.1-69.35. Amended by Acts 2005, cc. 207, 839.
16.1-69.40:1. Amended by Acts 2011, c. 694.
16.1-69.40:2. Amended by Acts 2011, c. 694.
16.1-69.45. Amended by Acts 2008, cc. 349, 804; 2012, c. 62.
16.1-69.46. Amended by Acts 2008, cc. 349, 804.
16.1-69.48. Amended by Acts 2006, c. 305.
16.1-69.48:1. Amended by Acts 2005, c. 631; 2009, c. 756; 2010, c. 874; 2011, cc. 283, 890.
16.1-69.48:2. Amended by Acts 2006, cc. 623, 718; 2010, c. 874; 2011, c. 890.
16.1-69.55. Amended by Acts 2005, c. 135; 2007, cc. 369, 468, 869; 2008, c. 749; 2009, c. 740; 2011, cc. 445, 480; 2013, cc. 187, 377.
16.1-69.77. Amended by Acts 2008, cc. 840, 843.
16.1-77. Amended by Acts 2009, c. 663; 2010, c. 181; 2011, cc. 14, 76, 372, 378, 702.
16.1-77.1, 16.1-77.2. Amended by Acts 2007, c. 869.
16.1-79.1. Amended by Acts 2011, c. 766.
16.1-83.1. Amended by Acts 2007, c. 489; 2013, cc. 65, 610.
16.1-88.03. Amended by Acts 2005, c. 136; 2006, c. 374.
16.1-88.2. Amended by Acts 2005, c. 811; 2007, cc. 425, 869; 2013, cc. 78, 145.
16.1-92. Repealed by Acts 2007, c. 869.
16.1-105. Amended by Acts 2010, c. 343.
16.1-106. Amended by Acts 2009, c. 729; 2013, cc. 73, 97.

Section
16.1-107. Amended by Acts 2006, c. 116; 2007, c. 869; 2008, c. 706; 2010, c. 267; 2011, c. 58.
16.1-108. Amended by Acts 2007, c. 131.
16.1-109. Amended by Acts 2007, c. 464.
16.1-114.1. Amended by Acts 2007, c. 869.
16.1-118.1. Amended by Acts 2007, c. 813.
16.1-122. Amended by Acts 2007, c. 869.
16.1-122.2. Amended by Acts 2006, c. 141.
16.1-122.3. Amended by Acts 2006, c. 141.
16.1-131.1. Amended by Acts 2010, cc. 303, 609.
16.1-135. Amended by Acts 2008, cc. 551, 691.
16.1-218. Amended by Acts 2008, c. 115.
16.1-228. Amended by Acts 2006, c. 868; 2008, cc. 475, 483; 2011, cc. 445, 480.
16.1-235.1. Amended by Acts 2012, cc. 164, 456.
16.1-237. Amended by Acts 2007, c. 528; 2009, c. 726.
16.1-238. Amended by Acts 2012, cc. 164, 456.
16.1-241. Amended by Acts 2005, cc. 716, 839, 890; 2007, cc. 284, 370; 2008, cc. 164, 201; 2010, c. 402; 2012, cc. 424, 476, 507, 637.
16.1-241.3. Amended by Acts 2012, cc. 504, 640.
16.1-243. Amended by Acts 2010, cc. 717, 760; 2012, c. 424.
16.1-247. Amended by Acts 2012, c. 253.
16.1-248.1. Amended by Acts 2005, c. 647; 2010, c. 683; 2011, c. 644.
16.1-249. Amended by Acts 2010, c. 739.
16.1-250. Amended by Acts 2006, c. 89.
16.1-252. Amended by Acts 2008, c. 397; 2013, c. 130.
16.1-253. Amended by Acts 2008, cc. 73, 246; 2009, c. 732; 2013, c. 130.
16.1-253.1. Amended by Acts 2006, c. 308; 2007, c. 205; 2008, cc. 73, 246; 2009, cc. 343, 732; 2011, cc. 445, 480.
16.1-253.2. Amended by Acts 2007, cc. 745, 923; 2012, c. 637; 2013, cc. 761, 774.
16.1-253.4. Amended by Acts 2007, cc. 396, 661; 2008, cc. 73, 246; 2009, c. 732; 2011, cc. 445, 480; 2012, cc. 637, 827.
16.1-260. Amended by Acts 2006, c. 677; 2008, cc. 136, 845; 2009, cc. 385, 726; 2010, c. 742; 2011, cc. 384, 410, 825; 2012, c. 637; 2013, c. 746.
16.1-264. Amended by Acts 2011, c. 482.
16.1-266. Amended by Acts 2005, c. 427.
16.1-269.1. Amended by Acts 2012, cc. 476, 507, 772,
16.1-269.2. Amended by Acts 2005, cc. 590, 843.
16.1-269.5. Amended by Acts 2010, c. 739.

Section
16.1-269.6. Amended by Acts 2010, c. 739.
16.1-271. Amended by Acts 2007, c. 221.
16.1-272. Amended by Acts 2005, c. 590; 2007, c. 460; 2008, c. 517.
16.1-273. Amended by Acts 2005, c. 843; 2007, c. 510.
16.1-274. Amended by Acts 2006, c. 675; 2012, cc. 164, 456.
16.1-275. Amended by Acts 2009, cc. 813, 840; 2012, cc. 164, 456.
16.1-277.01. Amended by Acts 2006, c. 825; 2009, cc. 98, 260; 2010, c. 331.
16.1-277.02. Amended by Acts 2009, cc. 98, 260; 2010, c. 331; 2013, c. 130.
16.1-278.2. Amended by Acts 2013, c. 130.
16.1-278.3. Amended by Acts 2009, cc. 98, 260; 2010, c. 331; 2013, c. 130.
16.1-278.7. Amended by Acts 2007, c. 510.
16.1-278.8. Amended by Acts 2005, c. 810; 2009, cc. 813, 840.
16.1-278.8:01. Amended by Acts 2009, cc. 813, 840; 2011, cc. 384, 410.
16.1-278.9. Amended by Acts 2005, c. 895; 2007, c. 731; 2010, cc. 522, 569, 570.
16.1-278.11. Amended by Acts 2005, c. 716; 2012, cc. 476, 507.
16.1-278.15. Amended by Acts 2008, cc. 136, 845.
16.1-278.18. Amended by Acts 2005, c. 880.
16.1-279.1. Amended by Acts 2006, c. 308; 2008, cc. 73, 246; 2009, cc. 343, 732; 2010, cc. 425, 468; 2011, cc. 445, 480.
16.1-280. Amended by Acts 2009, cc. 813, 840; 2010, cc. 778, 825; 2012, cc. 476, 507.
16.1-281. Amended by Acts 2005, c. 653; 2008, cc. 397, 475, 483, 678; 2009, c. 80; 2011, cc. 154, 730; 2013, c. 130.
16.1-282. Amended by Acts 2008, cc. 475, 483, 678; 2009, c. 80; 2011, c. 730; 2013, c. 130.
16.1-282.1. Amended by Acts 2008, cc. 475, 483, 678; 2011, c. 730; 2013, c. 130.
16.1-282.2. Amended by Acts 2008, cc. 475, 483; 2013, c. 130.
16.1-283. Amended by Acts 2012, cc. 476, 507.
16.1-283.1. Amended by Acts 2010, c. 331.
16.1-284.1. Amended by Acts 2012, c. 94; 2013, c. 651.
16.1-287. Amended by Acts 2005, c. 154; 2012, cc. 803, 835.
16.1-290. Amended by Acts 2006, c. 282.
16.1-293. Amended by Acts 2010, c. 742; 2011, cc. 39, 442; 2012, cc. 803, 835; 2013, cc. 362, 564.
16.1-293.1. Amended by Acts 2009, cc. 813, 840.
16.1-296. Amended by Acts 2005, c. 681; 2007, c. 464; 2009, c. 729.

Section
16.1-298. Amended by Acts 2008, c. 706; 2013, cc. 73, 97.
16.1-299. Amended by Acts 2008, c. 636.
16.1-299.1. Amended by Acts 2007, c. 528.
16.1-299.2. Repealed by Acts 2005, c. 843.
16.1-300. Amended by Acts 2006, cc. 431, 500; 2007, c. 511; 2009, c. 740; 2010, cc. 367, 472; 2011, cc. 99, 169; 2012, cc. 262, 421.
16.1-301. Amended by Acts 2005, c. 683; 2009, c. 286; 2013, c. 769.
16.1-305. Amended by Acts 2007, c. 133; 2009, cc. 138, 308, 740.
16.1-305.2. Amended by Acts 2009, c. 276.
16.1-306. Amended by Acts 2008, c. 519.
16.1-308. Amended by Acts 2011, c. 622.
16.1-309.1. Amended by Acts 2005, c. 364; 2006, cc. 259, 309, 682; 2008, c. 798; 2010, cc. 367, 472, 526.
16.1-309.3. Amended by Acts 2007, c. 813.
16.1-319. Amended by Acts 2005, c. 928; 2006, c. 673.
16.1-323. Amended by Acts 2007, cc. 277, 387.
16.1-324 to 16.1-330. Repealed by Acts 2007, cc. 277, 387.
16.1-335. Amended by Acts 2010, cc. 778, 825.
16.1-336. Amended by Acts 2007, cc. 500, 897; 2008, cc. 139, 774; 2009, cc. 455, 555, 813, 840; 2010, cc. 778, 825.
16.1-337. Amended by Acts 2008, cc. 782, 850, 870; 2009, cc. 455, 555; 2010, cc. 778, 825.
16.1-338. Amended by Acts 2005, cc. 181, 227; 2008, cc. 783, 808; 2009, cc. 455, 555; 2010, cc. 778, 825.
16.1-336. Amended by Acts 2012, cc. 476, 507.
16.1-339. Amended by Acts 2005, c. 716; 2007, cc. 500, 897; 2008, cc. 139, 774, 783, 807, 808; 2009, cc. 455, 555; 2010, cc. 778, 825.
16.1-340. Amended by Acts 2005, c. 346; 2006, c. 401; 2008, cc. 783, 808; 2009, cc. 455, 555; 2010, cc. 778, 825; 2011, c. 249.
16.1-341. Amended by Acts 2005, c. 346; 2006, c. 401; 2007, cc. 500, 897; 2008, cc. 140, 776, 783, 807, 808; 2009, cc. 455, 555; 2010, cc. 778, 825.
16.1-342. Amended by Acts 2005, c. 346; 2009, cc. 455, 555; 2010, cc. 778, 825.
16.1-343. Amended by Acts 2008, c. 807; 2010, cc. 778, 825.
16.1-344. Amended by Acts 2009, cc. 455, 555; 2010, cc. 778, 825.
16.1-345. Amended by Acts 2005, c. 346; 2009, cc. 112, 455, 555, 697, 813, 840; 2010, cc. 778, 825.
16.1-345.1. Amended by Acts 2007, cc. 500, 897; 2009, cc. 455, 555; 2010, cc. 778, 825.

Section

16.1-345.2. Amended by Acts 2010, cc. 778, 825.
16.1-345.3. Amended by Acts 2010, cc. 778, 825.
16.1-345.4. Amended by Acts 2010, cc. 778, 825.
16.1-345.5. Amended by Acts 2010, cc. 778, 825.
16.1-346. Amended by Acts 2010, cc. 778, 825.
16.1-346.1. Amended by Acts 2005, cc. 346, 716; 2010, cc. 778, 825.
16.1-347. Amended by Acts 2010, cc. 778, 825.
16.1-348. Amended by Acts 2005, c. 716; 2007, cc. 500, 897.
16.1-356. Amended by Acts 2005, c. 110; 2009, cc. 813, 840.
16.1-357. Amended by Acts 2009, cc. 813, 840.
16.1-361. Amended by Acts 2005, c. 110; 2009, cc. 813, 840; 2012, cc. 476, 507.
17.1-100. Amended by Acts 2005, c. 633.
17.1-105. Amended by Acts 2006, cc. 144, 306.
17.1-107. Amended by Acts 2008, c. 813.
17.1-113. Amended by Acts 2005, c. 389.
17.1-114. Amended by Acts 2005, c. 389; 2010, cc. 451, 757.
17.1-121. Amended by Acts 2005, c. 389.
17.1-124. Amended by Acts 2005, c. 681; 2007, c. 567; 2010, cc. 717, 760.
17.1-131. Amended by Acts 2005, c. 681.
17.1-207. Amended by Acts 2005, c. 839.
17.1-208. Amended by Acts 2007, cc. 548, 626; 2013, c. 77.
17.1-209. Amended by Acts 2008, cc. 53, 142.
17.1-209. Repealed by Acts 2012, c. 802.
17.1-213. Amended by Acts 2005, c. 681; 2006, c. 60; 2008, c. 749; 2011, cc. 445, 480; 2012, c. 802.
17.1-218. Repealed by Acts 2011, c. 63.
17.1-223. Amended by Acts 2007, c. 451; 2008, cc. 117, 814, 823, 833; 2012, c. 74; 2013, c. 193.
17.1-224. Amended by Acts 2010, cc. 717, 760.
17.1-225. Amended by Acts 2008, cc. 823, 833.
17.1-226. Amended by Acts 2008, cc. 823, 833.
17.1-227.1. Amended by Acts 2008, cc. 823, 833.
17.1-228. Amended by Acts 2008, cc. 823, 833.
17.1-229. Amended by Acts 2010, c. 352.
17.1-240. Amended by Acts 2005, c. 681.
17.1-244. Amended by Acts 2008, cc. 823, 833.
17.1-247. Repealed by Acts 2013, c. 263.
17.1-249. Amended by Acts 2005, c. 681; 2008, cc. 823, 833.
17.1-258.3. Amended by Acts 2008, cc. 823, 833; 2010, cc. 430, 717, 760; 2013, cc. 74, 77.
17.1-258.3:1. Amended by Acts 2010, c. 430; 2012, c. 234; 2013, cc. 74, 77.
17.1-258.3:2. Amended by Acts 2011, c. 715; 2013, cc. 74, 77.

Section

17.1-258.4. Amended by Acts 2008, cc. 823, 833; 2010, cc. 717, 760; 2013, cc. 74, 77.
17.1-266. Amended by Acts 2007, c. 800.
17.1-272. Amended by Acts 2011, cc. 445, 480.
17.1-273. Amended by Acts 2007, c. 813.
17.1-275. Amended by Acts 2005, cc. 373, 681; 2006, cc. 318, 623, 718, 825; 2007, cc. 548, 626, 646; 2009, c. 594; 2010, c. 874; 2011, cc. 707, 890; 2012, cc. 420, 714, 780; 2013, c. 263.
17.1-275.1. Amended by Acts 2005, c. 631; 2011, c. 565.
17.1-275.2. Amended by Acts 2005, c. 631; 2011, c. 565.
17.1-275.3. Amended by Acts 2011, c. 565.
17.1-275.4. Amended by Acts 2011, c. 565.
17.1-275.5. Amended by Acts 2010, c. 555; 2012, c. 714; 2013, c. 263.
17.1-276. Amended by Acts 2012, cc. 234, 469, 780.
17.1-275.7. Amended by Acts 2005, c. 631; 2009, c. 756; 2011, cc. 283, 565.
17.1-275.8. Amended by Acts 2011, c. 565.
17.1-275.9. Amended by Acts 2011, c. 565.
17.1-276. Amended by Acts 2006, c. 474; 2008, cc. 823, 833; 2009, cc. 76, 723, 797; 2010, c. 430; 2011, cc. 434, 493; 2013, c. 77.
17.1-278. Amended by Acts 2005, c. 681; 2006, c. 189; 2008, c. 692.
17.1-279. Amended by Acts 2005, cc. 681, 738; 2006, c. 647; 2007, cc. 548, 626; 2009, c. 793, 858; 2010, c. 430.
17.1-281. Amended by Acts 2009, cc. 814, 857.
17.1-292. Amended by Acts 2013, c. 77.
17.1-293. Amended by Acts 2010, c. 430; 2011, cc. 557, 625, 689, 715; 2012, c. 234; 2013, c. 77.
17.1-294. Amended by Acts 2009, c. 312; 2011, c. 715; 2012, c. 234.
17.1-295. Amended by Acts 2013, cc. 77, 263, 422.
17.1-304. Amended by Acts 2006, c. 357.
17.1-314. Amended by Acts 2005, c. 237.
17.1-328. Amended by Acts 2006, cc. 623, 718; 2007, cc. 113, 372.
17.1-329. Amended by Acts 2006, cc. 623, 718.
17.1-402. Amended by Acts 2008, cc. 54, 156.
17.1-406. Amended by Acts 2007, c. 889; 2013, c. 746.
17.1-415. Amended by Acts 2006, c. 218.
17.1-418. Amended by Acts 2006, cc. 623, 718.
17.1-500. Amended by Acts 2006, c. 861.
17.1-501. Amended by Acts 2005, c. 183.
17.1-502. Amended by Acts 2009, cc. 793, 858; 2011, c. 715; 2012, c. 234; 2013, c. 422.
17.1-506. Amended by Acts 2006, c. 861.

Section
17.1-507. Amended by Acts 2005, cc. 190, 231, 951; 2006, cc. 35, 738; 2013, c. 806.
17.1-513. Amended by Acts 2005, c. 681; 2012, cc. 152, 261.
17.1-516. Amended by Acts 2005, cc. 45, 114.
17.1-520. Amended by Acts 2005, c. 681.
17.1-524. Repealed by Acts 2009, c. 592.
17.1-605. Amended by Acts 2010, c. 343.
17.1-619. Amended by Acts 2005, c. 173.
17.1-623. Amended by Acts 2005, c. 173.
17.1-626.1. Amended by Acts 2010, c. 343.
17.1-700. Amended by Acts 2008, c. 115.
17.1-706. Amended by Acts 2008, c. 115; 2012, c. 76.
17.1-802. Amended by Acts 2005, c. 596.
17.1-805. Amended by Acts 2005, c. 631; 2011, c. 282; 2013, cc. 424, 647.
17.1-913. Amended by Acts 2005, c. 508.
18.2-5. Repealed by Acts 2005, c. 839.
18.2-10. Amended by Acts 2006, cc. 36, 733; 2008, c. 579.
18.2-31. Amended by Acts 2007, cc. 844, 845, 846; 2010, cc. 399, 428, 475.
18.2-46.1. Amended by Acts 2005, cc. 764, 813; 2006, cc. 262, 319, 844, 895; 2007. c. 499; 2012, c. 364; 2013, cc. 573, 645.
18.2-46.3:3. Amended by Acts 2010, c. 364; 2013, cc. 761, 774. .
18.2-46.5. Amended by Acts 2007, c. 409.
18.2-47. Amended by Acts 2009, c. 662.
18.2-48. Amended by Acts 2006, cc. 853, 914; 2011, c. 785.
18.2-48.1. Amended by Acts 2013, cc. 707, 782.
18.2-51.1. Amended by Acts 2007, c. 87; 2010, c. 344.
18.2-54.1. Amended by Acts 2006, c. 300.
18.2-55. Amended by Acts 2007, c. 133.
18.2-55.1. Amended by Acts 2005, c. 843.
18.2-56.1. Amended by Acts 2010, c. 183; 2011, c. 684.
18.2-57. Amended by Acts 2006, cc. 709, 829; 2008, c. 460; 2009, c. 257; 2011, cc. 230, 233, 374; 2013, cc. 698, 707, 711, 748, 782.
18.2-57.02. Amended by Acts 2007, c. 519.
18.2-57.2. Amended by Acts 2009, c. 726.
18.2-57.3. Amended by Acts 2007, c. 133; 2009, cc. 313, 347; 2013, c. 746.
18.2-59. Amended by Acts 2006, c. 313; 2007, cc. 453, 547; 2010, c. 298.
18.2-60.3. Amended by Acts 2013, c. 759.
18.2-60.4. Amended by Acts 2011, cc. 445, 480; 2013, cc. 761, 774.
18.2-61. Amended by Acts 2005, c. 631; 2006, cc. 853, 914; 2012, cc. 575, 605; 2013, cc. 761, 774.
18.2-62. Amended by Acts 2005, c. 661; 2008, c. 756.
18.2-63. Amended by Acts 2007, c. 718.

Section
18.2-64.2. Amended by Acts 2007, c. 133.
18.2-66. Repealed by Acts 2008, cc. 174, 206.
18.2-67.1. Amended by Acts 2005, c. 631; 2006, cc. 853, 914; 2012, cc. 575, 605; 2013, cc. 761, 774.
18.2-67.2. Amended by Acts 2005, c. 631; 2006, cc. 853, 914; 2012, cc. 575, 605; 2013, cc. 602, 761, 774.
18.2-67.2:1. Repealed by Acts 2005, c. 631.
18.2-67.3. Amended by Acts 2005, cc. 185, 406.
18.2-67.4. Amended by Acts 2006, c. 284; 2007, c. 133.
18.2-67.5:1. Amended by Acts 2006, c. 875.
18.2-67.5:3. Amended by Acts 2007, c. 506.
18.2-67.7. Amended by Acts 2007, c. 890; 2011, c. 785.
18.2-73. Amended by Acts 2009, cc. 813, 840.
18.2-74. Amended by Acts 2009, cc. 813, 840.
18.2-76. Amended by Acts 2012, c. 131.
18.2-85. Amended by Acts 2005, c. 204.
18.2-97.1. Amended by Acts 2011, c. 191.
18.2-98. Amended by Acts 2009, c. 591.
18.2-108. Amended by Acts 2008, c. 578.
18.2-118. Amended by Acts 2013, c. 536.
18.2-119. Amended by Acts 2011, c. 195.
18.2-135. Amended by Acts 2010, c. 183.
18.2-136. Amended by Acts 2007, cc. 145, 658; 2011, c. 191.
18.2-147.2. Amended by Acts 2007, c. 437.
18.2-152.2. Amended by Acts 2005, cc. 761, 812, 827; 2009, cc. 321, 376; 2010, c. 489.
18.2-152.3. Amended by Acts 2005, cc. 747, 761, 827, 837.
18.2-152.3:1. Amended by Acts 2010, c. 489.
18.2-152.4. Amended by Acts 2005, cc. 761, 812, 827; 2007, c. 483.
18.2-152.5. Amended by Acts 2005, cc. 747, 761, 827, 837.
18.2-152.6. Amended by Acts 2005, cc. 746, 761, 827.
18.2-152.7. Amended by Acts 2005, cc. 746, 761, 827.
18.2-152.8. Amended by Acts 2005, cc. 746, 761, 827.
18.2-152.9. Repealed by Acts 2005, cc. 746, 761, 827.
18.2-152.10. Repealed by Acts 2005, cc. 746, 761, 827.
18.2-152.12. Amended by Acts 2005, cc. 746, 761, 827; 2010, cc. 489, 529.
18.2-154. Amended by Acts 2005, c. 143; 2013, cc. 761, 774.
18.2-160.1. Amended by Acts 2009, c. 760; 2010, cc. 445, 837; 2012, c. 676.
18.2-164. Amended by Acts 2006, c. 457.
18.2-174. Amended by Acts 2013, cc. 410, 431, 638.
18.2-174.1. Amended by Acts 2013, c. 431.
18.2-182. Amended by Acts 2005, c. 598.

Section
18.2-186. Amended by Acts 2006, c. 321; 2007, c. 518.
18.2-186.3. Amended by Acts 2006, cc. 455, 496; 2007, c. 441; 2009, cc. 314, 380; 2013, cc. 420, 466.
18.2-186.3:1. Amended by Acts 2006, c. 298.
18.2-186.4. Amended by Acts 2007, c. 736; 2010, c. 767.
18.2-186.4:1. Amended by Acts 2012, c. 143.
18.2-186.5. Amended by Acts 2006, c. 298; 2011, c. 619.
18.2-189. Amended by Acts 2009, c. 664.
18.2-194. Amended by Acts 2005, c. 157.
18.2-195.2. Amended by Acts 2007, c. 518.
18.2-198.1. Amended by Acts 2008, c. 797.
18.2-204.1. Amended by Acts 2006, c. 271; 2011, c. 401.
18.2-204.2. Amended by Acts 2006, cc. 445, 484; 2011, c. 401.
18.2-213.1. Amended by Acts 2006, cc. 831, 921; 2009, c. 869; 2013, c. 482.
18.2-216. Amended by Acts 2005, c. 150.
18.2-236. Repealed by Acts 2006, cc. 392, 485.
18.2-239. Amended by Acts 2008, cc. 791, 842.
18.2-246.6. Amended by Acts 2005, c. 839.
18.2-246.11. Amended by Acts 2009, c. 847.
18.2-246.13. Amended by Acts 2009, c. 847; 2013, c. 625.
18.2-246.14. Amended by Acts 2013, c. 625.
18.2-246.15. Amended by Acts 2009, c. 847; 2013, c. 625.
18.2-248. Amended by Acts 2005, cc. 174, 759, 796, 923, 941; 2006, cc. 697, 759; 2008, cc. 79, 618; 2009, c. 750; 2012, cc. 219, 710; 2012, c. 844; 2013, c. 426.
18.2-248.02. Amended by Acts 2013, c. 743.
18.2-248.1. Amended by Acts 2006, cc. 697, 759.
18.2-248.1:1. Amended by Acts 2012, cc. 762, 816.
18.2-251. Amended by Acts 2007, c. 133; 2009, cc. 813, 840; 2011, cc. 384, 410.
18.2-251.01. Amended by Acts 2007, c. 133; 2009, cc. 813, 840.
18.2-252. Amended by Acts 2007, c. 133; 2009, cc. 813, 840.
18.2-254. Amended by Acts 2005, c. 716; 2007, c. 133; 2009, cc. 813, 840.
18.2-254.1. Amended by Acts 2005, cc. 519, 602; 2006, cc. 175, 341; 2007, c. 133; 2009, cc. 205, 281, 294, 813, 840; 2010, c. 258.
18.2-255. Amended by Acts 2011, cc. 384, 410.
18.2-255.1. Amended by Acts 2011, cc. 384, 410.
18.2-255.2. Amended by Acts 2005, c. 716; 2006, c. 325; 2011, cc. 384, 410.
18.2-258. Amended by Acts 2011, cc. 384, 410.
18.2-258.02. Amended by Acts 2011, cc. 384, 410.

Section
18.2-258.1. Amended by Acts 2009, cc. 813, 840; 2011, cc. 384, 410.
18.2-260.1. Amended by Acts 2011, c. 204.
18.2-266. Amended by Acts 2005, cc. 616, 845.
18.2-266.1. Amended by Acts 2008, c. 729; 2009, c. 660; 2011, cc. 134, 683.
18.2-267. Amended by Acts 2005, cc. 757, 840, 868, 881.
18.2-268.1. Amended by Acts 2005, cc. 868, 881.
18.2-268.2. Amended by Acts 2005, cc. 616, 757, 840.
18.2-268.3. Amended by Acts 2005, cc. 757, 840; 2009, c. 239.
18.2-268.4. Amended by Acts 2005, cc. 757, 840, 943.
18.2-268.5. Amended by Acts 2005, cc. 757, 840.
18.2-268.6. Amended by Acts 2005, cc. 868, 881.
18.2-268.7. Amended by Acts 2005, cc. 868, 881.
18.2-268.8. Amended by Acts 2005, cc. 757, 840, 868, 881.
18.2-268.9. Amended by Acts 2005, cc. 757, 840, 868, 881; 2006, c. 101.
18.2-268.10. Amended by Acts 2005, cc. 616, 757, 840.
18.2-269. Amended by Acts 2005, c. 616.
18.2-270. Amended by Acts 2006, cc. 82, 314; 2009, c. 229; 2012, cc. 283, 756; 2013, cc. 415, 655.
18.2-270.1. Amended by Acts 2007, c. 686; 2008, c. 862; 2012, cc. 141, 570.
18.2-271. Amended by Acts 2010, c. 521; 2013, cc. 415, 655.
18.2-271.1. Amended by Acts 2007, cc. 194, 553; 2009, c. 295; 2010, cc. 446, 682; 2011, c. 592; 2012, cc. 141, 570.
18.2-271.2. Amended by Acts 2005, c. 758; 2009, cc. 813, 840.
18.2-272. Amended by Acts 2005, cc. 757, 840; 2006, c. 390; 2007, c. 258; 2009, cc. 71, 255.
18.2-279. Amended by Acts 2005, c. 143.
18.2-280. Amended by Acts 2005, c. 928.
18.2-282. Amended by Acts 2005, c. 928.
18.2-283.1. Amended by Acts 2007, cc. 87, 519; 2012, c. 295.
18.2-285. Amended by Acts 2005, c. 507.
18.2-287.01. Amended by Acts 2007, cc. 87, 519; 2013, c. 746.
18.2-287.4. Amended by Acts 2005, c. 160; 2007, c. 813.
18.2-308. Amended by Acts 2005, cc. 344, 420, 424, 441, 839; 2006, c. 886; 2007, cc. 87, 272, 408, 455; 2008, cc. 69, 75, 80, 309, 464, 742; 2009, cc. 235, 779, 780; 2010, cc. 387, 433,

Section

576, 586, 602, 677, 700, 709, 740, 741, 754, 841, 863; 2011, cc. 231, 234, 384, 410; 2012, 132, 175, 291, 557, 776; 2013, cc. 135, 559, 659, 746.

18.2-308.1. Amended by Acts 2005, cc. 830, 928; 2007, c. 519; 2011, c. 282; 2013, c. 416.

18.2-308.1:1. Amended by Acts 2008, cc. 788, 854, 869; 2009, cc. 813, 840; 2010, c. 781; 2011, c. 775.

18.2-308.1:2. Amended by Acts 2011, c. 775.

18.2-308.1:3. Amended by Acts 2008, cc. 751, 788; 2010, c. 781; 2011, c. 775.

18.2-308.1:4. Amended by Acts 2011, cc. 373, 402; 2013, c. 759.

18.2-308.1:5. Amended by Acts 2011, cc. 384, 410.

18.2-308.2. Amended by Acts 2005, cc. 600, 833; 2007, c. 519; 2008, c. 752; 2009, c. 236; 2010, c. 781.

18.2-308.2:01. Amended by Acts 2008, c. 408.

18.2-308.2:1. Amended by Acts 2008, c. 408; 2011, c. 775; 2013, c. 797.

18.2-308.2:2. Amended by Acts 2005, cc. 578, 859; 2007, c. 509; 2008, cc. 854, 869; 2009, cc. 813, 840; 2011, c. 235; 2012, cc. 37, 257, 776; 2013, cc. 450, 662, 761, 774, 797.

18.2-308.4. Amended by Acts 2011, cc. 384, 410.

18.2-308.6. Repealed by Acts 2009, c. 288.

18.2-311. Amended by Acts 2013, c. 746.

18.2-313.1. Amended by Acts 2010, c. 834.

18.2-325. Amended by Acts 2010, c. 877; 2011, cc. 879, 887.

18.2-325.1. Repealed by Acts 2011, cc. 879, 887.

18.2-326. Amended by Acts 2011, c. 732.

18.2-334.2. Amended by Acts 2013, cc. 36, 350.

18.2-340. Amended by Acts 2012, cc. 283, 756.

18.2-340.15. Amended by Acts 2006, c. 644; 2008, cc. 387, 689.

18.2-340.16. Amended by Acts 2006, c. 644; 2007, cc. 160, 264; 2008, cc. 387, 689; 2009, c. 121; 2010, c. 429; 2013, cc. 36, 350.

18.2-340.18. Amended by Acts 2006, c. 644.

18.2-340.19. Amended by Acts 2006, c. 644; 2010, cc. 429, 572; 2013, c. 36, 350.

18.2-340.20. Amended by Acts 2006, c. 644; 2010, c. 711.

18.2-340.22. Amended by Acts 2013, cc. 36, 350.

18.2-340.23. Amended by Acts 2006, c. 644; 2009, c. 121.

18.2-340.24. Amended by Acts 2006, c. 644; 2009, c. 121.

18.2-340.25. Amended by Acts 2006, cc. 211, 644; 2008, cc. 387, 689.

18.2-340.26. Amended by Acts 2006, c. 644; 2008, c. 573.

Section

18.2-340.26:1. Amended by Acts 2006, c. 644; 2007, c. 196.

18.2-340.27. Amended by Acts 2006, c. 644; 2010, c. 429.

18.2-340.28. Amended by Acts 2006, c. 644; 2013, cc. 36, 350.

18.2-340.29. Amended by Acts 2006, c. 644.

18.2-340.30. Amended by Acts 2006, c. 644; 2007, c. 541.

18.2-340.30:1. Repealed by Acts 2010, c. 429.

18.2-340.31. Amended by Acts 2006, c. 644.

18.2-340.33. Amended by Acts 2005, cc. 776, 826; 2006, c. 644; 2007, cc. 226, 790; 2008, c. 352; 2010, c. 429; 2013, cc. 36, 350.

18.2-340.34. Amended by Acts 2006, c. 644; 2007, c. 264.

18.2-340.34:1. Amended by Acts 2007, cc. 226, 347.

18.2-340.37. Amended by Acts 2006, c. 644.

18.2-345. Repealed by Acts 2013, c. 621.

18.2-346. Amended by Acts 2013, cc. 417, 467.

18.2-346.1. Amended by Acts 2005, c. 438.

18.2-356. Amended by Acts 2011, c. 785.

18.2-359. Amended by Acts 2011, c. 763.

18.2-361. Amended by Acts 2005, c. 185.

18.2-369. Amended by Acts 2007, cc. 562, 653; 2012, cc. 476, 507.

18.2-370. Amended by Acts 2005, cc. 185, 762; 2013, cc. 423, 470.

18.2-370.1. Amended by Acts 2005, c. 185.

18.2-370.2. Amended by Acts 2006, cc. 857, 914; 2008, c. 579.

18.2-370.3. Amended by Acts 2008, c. 726.

18.2-370.5. Amended by Acts 2008, c. 781; 2010, c. 402; 2011, cc. 648, 796, 855.

18.2-371. Amended by Acts 2006, c. 935; 2008, cc. 174, 206.

18.2-371.1. Amended by Acts 2006, c. 935; 2013, cc. 761, 774.

18.2-371.3. Amended by Acts 2006, c. 692.

18.2-374.1. Amended by Acts 2007, cc. 418, 759, 823.

18.2-374.1:1. Amended by Acts 2007, cc. 759, 823; 2009, c. 379; 2011, cc. 399, 416; 2012, c. 369; 2013, cc. 761, 774.

18.2-374.1:2. Repealed by Acts 2007, cc. 759, 823.

18.2-374.3. Amended by Acts 2007, cc. 759, 823; 2013, cc. 423, 470.

18.2-386.1. Amended by Acts 2005, c. 375; 2008, c. 732.

18.2-390. Amended by Acts 2006, c. 463.

18.2-391. Amended by Acts 2006, c. 463.

18.2-403.2. Amended by Acts 2008, cc. 543, 707.

18.2-415. Amended by Acts 2006, c. 250.

18.2-422. Amended by Acts 2010, cc. 262, 420.

Section

18.2-424, 18.2-425. Repealed by Acts 2007, c. 467.

18.2-425.1. Repealed by Acts 2009, c. 699.

18.2-426. Amended by Acts 2007, c. 467.

18.2-427. Amended by Acts 2010, c. 565; 2011, c. 246.

18.2-429. Amended by Acts 2012, c. 133.

18.2-431.1. Amended by Acts 2013, cc. 707, 782.

18.2-434. Amended by Acts 2005, c. 423.

18.2-459. Amended by Acts 2013, c. 615.

18.2-460. Amended by Acts 2007, cc. 220, 282; 2009, c. 242.

18.2-462. Amended by Acts 2005, c. 408.

18.2-465.1. Amended by Acts 2005, c. 931.

18.2-472.1. Amended by Acts 2006, cc. 857, 914, 931; 2008, c. 218; 2010, c. 656; 2011, c. 285.

18.2-473.1 to 18.2-474. Amended by Acts 2013, cc. 707, 782.

18.2-474.1. Amended by Acts 2011, cc. 384, 410; 2013, cc. 707, 782.

18.2-475, 18.2-476. Amended by Acts 2013, cc. 707, 782.

18.2-477.2. Amended by Acts 2007, c. 521; 2013, cc. 707, 782.

18.2-479. Amended by Acts 2005, c. 573.

18.2-490. Amended by Acts 2012, c. 490.

18.2-500. Amended by Acts 2005, c. 681.

18.2-507. Amended by Acts 2005, c. 681.

18.2-510. Amended by Acts 2008, c. 345.

18.2-511.1. Amended by Acts 2009, cc. 153, 154.

18.2-513. Amended by Acts 2008, c. 681; 2009, cc. 662, 847; 2013, c. 626.

18.2-514. Amended by Acts 2009, c. 847.

18.2-515. Amended by Acts 2012, c. 511.

19.2-3.1. Amended by Acts 2006, c. 285; 2009, cc. 94, 623; 2010, c. 800.

19.2-5. Amended by Acts 2005, c. 839; 2008, cc. 551, 691.

19.2-8. Amended by Acts 2005, cc. 746, 761, 827; 2006, cc. 193, 787, 892; 2008, c. 769; 2011, cc. 118, 143, 494, 553.

19.2-9.1. Amended by Acts 2008, cc. 512, 748.

19.2-10.1. Amended by Acts 2010, cc. 702, 794.

19.2-11.01. Amended by Acts 2006, c. 241; 2007, cc. 94, 109, 423.

19.2-11.2. Amended by Acts 2005, cc. 764, 813; 2007, c. 503.

19.2-11.4. Amended by Acts 2010, c. 844.

19.2-12. Amended by Acts 2005, c. 372; 2006, c. 88; 2007, c. 224.

19.2-13. Amended by Acts 2005, c. 498; 2006, c. 290; 2007, cc. 380, 481; 2008, c. 795; 2010, cc. 530, 778, 825; 2013, cc. 105, 122.

19.2-30. Repealed by Acts 2008, cc. 551, 691.

19.2-34. Amended by Acts 2008, cc. 551, 691.

19.2-35. Amended by Acts 2008, cc. 551, 691.

Section

19.2-36. Amended by Acts 2008, cc. 551, 691.

19.2-37. Amended by Acts 2008, cc. 551, 691.

19.2-38. Amended by Acts 2008, cc. 551, 691.

19.2-38.1. Amended by Acts 2008, cc. 551, 691.

19.2-39. Amended by Acts 2008, cc. 551, 691.

19.2-41. Repealed by Acts 2008, cc. 551, 691.

19.2-43. Amended by Acts 2008, cc. 551, 691.

19.2-44. Amended by Acts 2008, cc. 551, 691.

19.2-45. Amended by Amended by Acts 2007, cc. 122, 373; 2008, cc. 551, 691; 2009, cc. 291, 344.

19.2-46. Amended by Acts 2008, cc. 551, 691.

19.2-46.1. Amended by Acts 2008, cc. 551, 691.

19.2-48. Amended by Acts 2008, cc. 551, 691.

19.2-48.1. Amended by Acts 2008, cc. 551, 691

19.2-54. Amended by Acts 2006, c. 285; 2007, c. 212; 2008, cc. 147, 183; 2011, cc. 196, 219; 2012, c. 5.

19.2-56. Amended by Acts 2007, c. 416; 2009, c. 725.

19.2-57. Amended by Acts 2008, cc. 147, 183.

19.2-61. Amended by Acts 2005, c. 934.

19.2-63.1. Amended by Acts 2011, c. 193.

19.2-66. Amended by Acts 2005, c. 934; 2011, cc. 403, 414; 2013, cc. 448, 664.

19.2-68. Amended by Acts 2005, c. 934; 2013, cc. 448, 664.

19.2-69. Amended by Acts 2010, c. 343.

19.2-70. Amended by Acts 2011, cc. 403, 414.

19.2-70.2. Amended by Acts 2005, c. 934.

19.2-70.3. Amended by Acts 2009, c. 378; 2010, cc. 319, 473, 582, 720, 721; 2011, c. 392.

19.2-71. Amended by Acts 2009, cc. 291, 344; 2010, c. 240; 2011, cc. 205, 223.

19.2-72. Amended by Acts 2007, c. 412; 2009, cc. 291, 344; 2010, c. 240; 2011, cc. 205, 223; 2013, c. 207.

19.2-73. Amended by Acts 2005, c. 425; 2010, c. 840.

19.2-74. Amended by Acts 2010, c. 840.

19.2-76. Amended by Acts 2013, c. 207.

19.2-76.1. Amended by Acts 2010, c. 652; 2011, cc. 336, 347.

19.2-77. Amended by Acts 2008, cc. 551, 691.

19.2-80.2. Amended by Acts 2007, c. 133.

19.2-81. Amended by Acts 2005, cc. 88, 435; 2008, cc. 460, 737; 2010, c. 840; 2011, cc. 510, 643; 2012, c. 776; 2013, c. 787.

19.2-81.3. Amended by Acts 2008, cc. 551, 691; 2011, cc. 445, 480; 2012, cc. 776, 827.

19.2-81.4. Repealed by Acts 2008, cc. 600, 771.

19.2-82. Amended by Acts 2009, c. 669.

19.2-83.1. Amended by Acts 2011, cc. 384, 410; 2013, c. 746.

19.2-92. Amended by Acts 2011, c. 59.

19.2-95. Amended by Acts 2005, c. 839.

19.2-108. Amended by Acts 2009, c. 848.

Section

19.2-119. Amended by Acts 2008, cc. 551, 691.

19.2-120. Amended by Acts 2005, c. 132; 2006, c. 504; 2007, cc. 134, 386, 745, 923; 2008, c. 596; 2010, c. 862; 2011, cc. 445, 450, 480; 2012, c. 467.

19.2-120.1. Amended by Acts 2013, c. 746.

19.2-123. Amended by Acts 2006, c. 296; 2008, cc. 129, 884; 2011, cc. 799, 837; 2012, cc. 476, 507; 2013, c. 614.

19.2-124. Amended by Acts 2007, cc. 462, 549; 2010, cc. 404, 592; 2013, cc. 408, 474.

19.2-130. Amended by Acts 2008, cc. 363, 812.

19.2-130.1. Amended by Acts 2011, c. 112.

19.2-132. Amended by Acts 2010, cc. 404, 592; 2013, cc. 408, 474.

19.2-136. Amended by Acts 2011, c. 802; 2012, c. 408.

19.2-143. Amended by Acts 2005, c. 585; 2006, cc. 296, 316; 2011, c. 802; 2012, c. 408.

19.2-152.2 to 19.2-152.7. Amended by Acts 2007, c. 133.

19.2-152.4:3. Amended by Acts 2008, cc. 551, 691.

19.2-152.7:1. Amended by Acts 2011, cc. 445, 480.

19.2-152.8. Amended by Acts 2008, cc. 73, 246; 2009, cc. 341, 732; 2011, cc. 445, 480; 2012, cc. 146, 637, 827.

19.2-152.9. Amended by Acts 2008, cc. 73, 128, 246; 2009, cc. 341, 732; 2011, cc. 445, 480; 2012, cc. 152, 261.

19.2-152.10. Amended by Acts 2008, cc. 73, 246; 2009, cc. 341, 732; 2010, cc. 425, 468; 2011, cc. 445, 480.

19.2-159. Amended by Acts 2006, c. 708; 2008, cc. 122, 154.

19.2-163. Amended by Acts 2006, c. 332; 2007, cc. 938, 946; 2008, c. 760; 2009, c. 284.

19.2-163.01. Amended by Acts 2005, c. 230; 2006, cc. 429, 501; 2007, c. 371; 2008, cc. 536, 815; 2010, c. 314.

19.2-163.01:1. Amended by Acts 2010, c. 314.

19.2-163.02. Amended by Acts 2005, cc. 176, 758; 2006, cc. 429, 501; 2008, c. 115.

19.2-163.03. Amended by Acts 2006, c. 708; 2007, c. 571.

19.2-163.2. Amended by Acts 2005, c. 951.

19.2-164. Amended by Acts 2007, c. 383.

19.2-165.2. Amended by Acts 2008, cc. 203, 251.

19.2-168. Amended by Acts 2008, c. 372.

19.2-169.1. Amended by Acts 2007, c. 781; 2009, cc. 813, 840.

19.2-169.2. Amended by Acts 2007, c. 781; 2008, cc. 751, 788; 2009, cc. 813, 840.

Section

19.2-169.3. Amended by Acts 2006, cc. 863, 914; 2007, cc. 781, 876; 2008, cc. 406, 796; 2009, cc. 813, 840; 2012, cc. 668, 800.

19.2-169.5. Amended by Acts 2005, c. 428; 2009, cc. 813, 840.

19.2-169.6. Amended by Acts 2005, c. 716; 2008, cc. 779, 782, 850, 870; 2010, cc. 340, 406; 2012, c. 801.

19.2-174.1. Amended by Acts 2010, cc. 340, 406.

19.2-175. Amended by Acts 2006, c. 170; 2007, c. 829; 2009, cc. 813, 840; 2010, cc. 340, 406.

19.2-176. Repealed by Acts 2010, cc. 340, 406.

19.2-177.1. Repealed by Acts 2010, cc. 340, 406.

19.2-178. Amended by Acts 2010, cc. 340, 406.

19.2-182.2. Amended by Acts 2007, cc. 485, 565; 2009, cc. 813, 840; 2012, cc. 476, 507.

19.2-182.3. Amended by Acts 2005, c. 716; 2012, cc. 476, 507.

19.2-182.4. Amended by Acts 2006, c. 358.

19.2-182.5. Amended by Acts 2007, cc. 485, 565.

19.2-182.6. Amended by Acts 2007, cc. 485, 565, 785.

19.2-182.7. Amended by Acts 2007, cc. 485, 565; 2008, c. 810.

19.2-182.8. Amended by Acts 2006, cc. 343, 369, 370; 2008, c. 810; 2012, cc. 476, 507.

19.2-182.9. Amended by Acts 2005, c. 716; 2006, cc. 343, 370; 2008, c. 810; 2009, cc. 21, 838; 2012, cc. 476, 507.

19.2-182.10. Amended by Acts 2006, cc. 199, 225; 2007, cc. 485, 565.

19.2-182.11. Amended by Acts 2007, cc. 485, 565.

19.2-182.13. Amended by Acts 2009, cc. 813, 840.

19.2-182.16. Amended by Acts 2009, cc. 813, 840.

19.2-183. Amended by Acts 2010, c. 555.

19.2-187. Amended by Acts 2005, cc. 868, 881; 2006, c. 294; 2010, c. 656; 2011, cc. 384, 410, 645.

19.2-187.01. Amended by Acts 2005, cc. 868, 881; 2011, c. 645.

19.2-187.02. Amended by Acts 2005, c. 801; 2007, cc. 379, 679.

19.2-187.1. Amended by Acts 2010, cc. 555, 656, 800; 2011, c. 32.

19.2-187.2. Amended by Acts 2005, cc. 868, 881.

19.2-188. Amended by Acts 2009, c. 640.

19.2-188.1. Amended by Acts 2005, cc. 868, 881; 2006, c. 447; 2013, c. 60.

Section
19.2-188.3. Amended by Acts 2011, c. 285.
19.2-194. Amended by Acts 2008, c. 644.
19.2-207. Amended by Acts 2008, c. 644.
19.2-212. Amended by Acts 2008, c. 644.
19.2-215.1. Amended by Acts 2008, c. 704; 2009, c. 491; 2011, c. 504; 2013, cc. 83, 314, 459.
19.2-215.3. Amended by Acts 2010, c. 438.
19.2-215.4. Amended by Acts 2008, c. 644.
19.2-218.1. Amended by Acts 2005, c. 631; 2012, cc. 476, 507.
19.2-218.2. Amended by Acts 2005, c. 631.
19.2-243. Amended by Acts 2005, c. 650; 2007, c. 944.
19.2-245.01. Amended by Acts 2013, c. 625.
19.2-250. Amended by Acts 2007, c. 813.
19.2-262. Amended by Acts 2005, c. 356.
19.2-264.3:1. Amended by Acts 2009, cc. 813, 840; 2010, c. 559.
19.2-264.3:1.1. Amended by Acts 2009, cc. 813, 840.
19.2-264.3:1.2. Amended by Acts 2009, cc. 813, 840.
19.2-264.4. Amended by Acts 2010, c. 658.
19.2-266.2. Amended by Acts 2005, cc. 622, 694; 2006, cc. 578, 862.
19.2-267. Amended by Acts 2007, c. 552; 2008, c. 124.
19.2-270.4. Amended by Acts 2008, c. 805; 2010, cc. 352, 366, 454.
19.2-270.4:1. Amended by Acts 2005, cc. 868, 881.
19.2-271.2. Amended by Acts 2005, c. 809.
19.2-294.2. Amended by Acts 2008, cc. 180, 415.
19.2-295. Amended by Acts 2007, c. 259.
19.2-295.1. Amended by Acts 2007, cc. 388, 478; 2012, cc. 134.
19.2-298. Amended by Acts 2009, c. 192.
19.2-298.01. Amended by Acts 2007, c. 259.
19.2-299. Amended by Acts 2005, cc. 188, 219, 631; 2006, cc. 99, 863, 914, 916; 2010, c. 223.
19.2-299.2. Amended by Acts 2007, c. 133; 2008, c. 762.
19.2-301. Amended by Acts 2007, c. 440; 2009, cc. 813, 840.
19.2-302. Amended by Acts 2009, cc. 813, 840.
19.2-303. Amended by Acts 2006, cc. 436, 483, 853, 914; 2007, cc. 259, 528; 2011, cc. 799, 837.
19.2-303.3. Amended by Acts 2006, c. 883; 2007, cc. 133, 528.
19.2-303.4. Amended by Acts 2005, c. 631.
19.2-305. Amended by Acts 2009, c. 240.
19.2-305.1. Amended by Acts 2005, c. 591; 2011, cc. 575, 588; 2013, c. 273.
19.2-305.4. Amended by Acts 2005, cc. 14, 79.
19.2-310. Amended by Acts 2010, c. 352; 2011, c. 470.

Section
19.2-310.2. Amended by Acts 2005, cc. 868, 881; 2006, c. 182; 2007, c. 528; 2011, c. 247.
19.2-310.2:1. Amended by Acts 2005, cc. 868, 881.
19.2-310.3. Amended by Acts 2005, cc. 868, 881.
19.2-310.3:1. Amended by Acts 2005, cc. 868, 881.
19.2-310.4. Amended by Acts 2005, cc. 868, 881.
19.2-310.5. Amended by Acts 2005, cc. 868, 881; 2010, c. 502; 2011, cc. 66, 171, 638.
19.2-310.6. Amended by Acts 2005, cc. 868, 881.
19.2-310.7. Amended by Acts 2005, cc. 868, 881.
19.2-316. Amended by Acts 2012, cc. 476, 507.
19.2-316.2. Amended by Acts 2005, cc. 512, 580; 2008, cc. 362, 761.
19.2-316.3. Amended by Acts 2005, c. 604; 2008, cc. 384, 757.
19.2-319. Amended by Acts 2008, cc. 126, 146.
19.2-321.1. Amended by Acts 2011, c. 278.
19.2-321.2. Amended by Acts 2011, c. 278.
19.2-327.1. Amended by Acts 2005, cc. 868, 881; 2013, c. 170.
19.2-327.2. Amended by Acts 2009, cc. 139, 320; 2013, c. 170.
19.2-327.3. Amended by Acts 2005, cc. 868, 881; 2009, cc. 139, 320; 2013, cc. 170, 180.
19.2-327.4. Amended by Acts 2005, cc. 868, 881.
19.2-327.5. Amended by Acts 2007, cc. 465, 824, 883, 905; 2009, cc. 139, 320; 2013, cc. 170, 180.
19.2-327.10. Amended by Acts 2013, c. 170.
19.2-327.11. Amended by Acts 2013, cc. 170, 180.
19.2-327.12. Amended by Acts 2013, c. 170.
19.2-327.13. Amended by Acts 2013, cc. 170, 180.
19.2-327.13. Amended by Acts 2007, cc. 465, 824, 883, 905; 2013, cc. 170, 180.
19.2-335. Amended by Acts 2005, c. 631.
19.2-336. Amended by Acts 2005, c. 631.
19.2-349. Amended by Acts 2006, c. 359; 2007, c. 551; 2012, c. 615.
19.2-353.3. Amended by Acts 2009, c. 594; 2012, cc. 420, 714.
19.2-354. Amended by 2009, c. 741; 2012, c. 615.
19.2-368.2. Amended by Acts 2008, c. 590; 2012, c. 38.
19.2-368.3. Amended by Acts 2008, cc. 203, 251; 2010, c. 780.
19.2-368.5. Amended by Acts 2005, c. 683; 2006, c. 414; 2009, c. 381.

Section
19.2-368.10. Amended by Acts 2005, c. 683.
19.2-368.11:1. Amended by Acts 2005, c. 683; 2007, c. 381; 2008, cc. 203, 251.
19.2-368.15. Amended by Acts 2013, c. 273.
19.2-368.20. Amended by Acts 2006, c. 414.
19.2-368.21. Amended by Acts 2006, c. 414; 2013, c. 627.
19.2-369 to 19.2-386. Repealed by Acts 2012, cc. 283, 756.
19.2-386.1. Amended by Acts 2012, cc. 283, 756.
19.2-386.2. Amended by Acts 2006, c. 766; 2012, cc. 283, 756.
19.2-386.3. Amended by Acts 2011, c. 83; 2012, cc. 283, 756.
19.2-386.4. Amended by Acts 2012, cc. 283, 756.
19.2-386.5. Amended by Acts 2012, cc. 283, 756.
19.2-386.8. Amended by Acts 2005, c. 883.
19.2-386.12. Amended by Acts 2005, c. 681.
19.2-386.13. Amended by Acts 2005, c. 868.
19.2-386.14. Amended by Acts 2012, cc. 126, 283, 373, 756.
19.2-386.16. Amended by Acts 2010, c. 710; 2011, cc. 818, 852.
19.2-386.19. Amended by Acts 2012, cc. 283, 756.
19.2-386.22. Amended by Acts 2011, cc. 384, 410.
19.2-386.23. Amended by Acts 2005, c. 881; 2006, c. 107; 2011, cc. 384, 410.
19.2-386.24. Amended by Acts 2011, cc. 384, 410.
19.2-386.25. Amended by Acts 2011, cc. 384, 410.
19.2-386.26. Amended by Acts 2012, cc. 283, 756.
19.2-386.27. Amended by Acts 2005, cc. 868, 881; 2013, c. 746.
19.2-386.28. Amended by Acts 2007, c. 519; 2013, c. 746.
19.2-386.29. Amended by Acts 2007, c. 519; 2012, cc. 283, 756.
19.2-386.30. Amended by Acts 2012, cc. 283, 756.
19.2-386.31. Amended by Acts 2007, cc. 134, 386; 2012, cc. 283, 756.
19.2-386.32. Amended by Acts 2012, cc. 283, 756.
19.2-387. Amended by Acts 2005, cc. 868, 881.
19.2-389. Amended by Acts 2005, cc. 149, 175, 914, 928; 2006, cc. 257, 277, 644; 2007, cc. 12, 361, 495, 572; 2008, cc. 387, 689, 863; 2009, cc. 667, 813, 840; 2010, cc. 189, 340, 406, 456, 524, 563, 862; 2011, cc. 432, 449; 2012, cc. 40, 189, 386, 476, 507, 803, 835; 2013, cc. 165, 176, 261, 407, 491, 582.

Section
19.2-389.1. Amended by Acts 2005, cc. 868, 881, 914; 2006, c. 644; 2007, c. 133; 2010, cc. 456, 524; 2011, c. 622; 2012, c. 386.
19.2-390. Amended by Acts 2005, cc. 187, 229; 2008, cc. 73, 246; 2009, cc. 249, 813, 840; 2010, c. 273; 2013, c. 614.
19.2-390.01. Amended by Acts 2007, c. 133.
19.2-390.1. Amended by Acts 2006, cc. 857, 914.
19.2-392. Amended by Acts 2005, c. 347.
19.2-392.02. Amended by Acts 2005, c. 217.
19.2-392.2. Amended by Acts 2007, cc. 465, 824, 883, 905; 2009, c. 618; 2011, c. 362.
19.2-398. Amended by Acts 2005, cc. 622, 694; 2006, cc. 571, 876.
19.2-409. Amended by Acts 2007, c. 414.
20-14.2. Repealed by Acts 2012, c. 802.
20-23. Amended by Acts 2012, c. 565.
20-25. Amended by Acts 2012, c. 802.
20-27. Amended by Acts 2006, c. 625.
20-32. Repealed by Acts 2010, c. 352.
20-48. Amended by Acts 2008, cc. 174, 206.
20-49.2. Amended by Acts 2008, cc. 164, 201.
20-60.3. Amended by Acts 2006, cc. 720, 869; 2009, cc. 706, 713.
20-61. Amended by Acts 2010, c. 619.
20-70. Amended by Acts 2008, cc. 551, 691.
20-78.2. Amended by Acts 2005, c. 880.
20-79.3. Amended by Acts 2006, c. 365; 2007, c. 557.
20-84. Amended by Acts 2008, cc. 551, 691.
20-88. Amended by Acts 2009, cc. 813, 840.
20-88.32. Amended by Acts 2005, c. 754.
20-88.33. Amended by Acts 2005, c. 754.
20-88.34. Amended by Acts 2005, c. 754.
20-88.35. Amended by Acts 2005, c. 754.
20-88.36. Amended by Acts 2005, c. 754.
20-88.39. Amended by Acts 2005, c. 754.
20-88.40. Amended by Acts 2005, c. 754.
20-88.41. Amended by Acts 2005, c. 754.
20-88.42. Amended by Acts 2005, c. 754.
20-88.43. Amended by Acts 2005, c. 754.
20-88.44. Amended by Acts 2005, c. 754.
20-88.46. Amended by Acts 2005, c. 754.
20-88.47. Amended by Acts 2005, c. 754.
20-88.48. Amended by Acts 2005, c. 754.
20-88.50. Amended by Acts 2005, c. 754.
20-88.51. Amended by Acts 2005, c. 754.
20-88.53. Amended by Acts 2005, c. 754.
20-88.54. Amended by Acts 2005, c. 754.
20-88.56. Amended by Acts 2005, c. 754.
20-88.57. Amended by Acts 2005, c. 754.
20-88.59. Amended by Acts 2005, c. 754.
20-88.60. Amended by Acts 2005, c. 754.
20-88.62. Amended by Acts 2005, c. 754.
20-88.63. Amended by Acts 2005, c. 754.
20-88.64. Amended by Acts 2005, c. 754.

Section
20-88.64:1. Amended by Acts 2005, c. 754.
20-88.64:2. Amended by Acts 2005, c. 754.
20-88.64:5. Amended by Acts 2005, c. 754.
20-88.65. Amended by Acts 2005, c. 754.
20-88.67. Amended by Acts 2005, c. 754.
20-88.69. Amended by Acts 2005, c. 754.
20-88.70. Amended by Acts 2005, c. 754.
20-88.72. Amended by Acts 2005, c. 754.
20-88.75. Amended by Acts 2005, c. 754.
20-88.76. Amended by Acts 2005, c. 754.
20-88.77. Amended by Acts 2005, c. 754.
20-88.80. Amended by Acts 2005, c. 754.
20-88.81. Amended by Acts 2005, c. 754.
20-96. Amended by Acts 2005, c. 681.
20-97. Amended by Acts 2009, c. 582.
20-99. Amended by Acts 2012, cc. 78, 84; 2013, cc. 81, 100.
20-99.2. Amended by Acts 2012, cc. 78, 84.
20-103. Amended by Acts 2007, c. 205; 2009, c. 713; 2011, c. 687.
20-104. Amended by Acts 2008, c. 699.
20-106. Amended by Acts 2012, c. 72.
20-107.2. Amended by Acts 2009, c. 713.
20-107.3. Amended by Acts 2006, c. 260; 2010, c. 506; 2011, c. 655; 2012, c. 144.
20-108. Amended by Acts 2006, c. 371; 2011, c. 351.
20-108.1. Amended by Acts 2006, cc. 785, 798; 2007, c. 872; 2009, c. 713; 2010, c. 176; 2013, cc. 276, 522.
20-108.2. Amended by Acts 2005, c. 758; 2006, cc. 785, 798; 2008, c. 697; 2009, c. 713; 2010, c. 243.
20-111.1. Amended by Acts 2007, c. 306; 2012, c. 493.
20-113. Amended by Acts 2012, c. 39.
20-121.03. Amended by Acts 2006, c. 734; 2007, cc. 548, 626.
20-124.1. Amended by Acts 2005, c. 890.
20-124.2. Amended by Acts 2006, c. 665; 2009, c. 713.
20-124.3. Amended by Acts 2009, c. 684; 2012, c. 358.
20-124.3:1. Repealed by Acts 2008, c. 809.
20-124.6. Amended by Acts 2005, cc. 181, 227.
20-124.8. Amended by Acts 2011, c. 351.
20-124.9. Amended by Acts 2011, c. 351.
20-160. Amended by Acts 2010, c. 712.
20-161. Amended by Acts 2010, c. 712.
20-162. Amended by Acts 2010, c. 712.
20-165. Amended by Acts 2010, c. 712.
21-118.2. Amended by Acts 2007, c. 813.
21-118.4. Amended by Acts 2011, cc. 438, 496; 2012, c. 485.
21-119. Amended by Acts 2005, c. 839; Acts 2007, c. 813.
21-186. Amended by Acts 2010, c. 343.
21-291.2. Amended by Acts 2008, c. 54.
22.1-3. Amended by Acts 2006, c. 188; 2012, cc. 29, 103, 476, 507; 2013, c. 779.

Section
22.1-3.1. Amended by Acts 2007, c. 49.
22.1-3.2. Amended by Acts 2006, cc. 53, 183.
22.1-3.4. Amended by Acts 2011, c. 154.
22.1-4.3. Amended by Acts 2005, c. 34.
22.1-5. Amended by Acts 2007, c. 42; 2013, cc. 641, 669.
22.1-7. Amended by Acts 2005, c. 928; 2009, cc. 813, 840; 2012, cc. 476, 507.
22.1-7.1. Amended by Acts 2013, c. 805; 2013, c. 805.
22.1-17.1. Amended by Acts 2012, cc. 803, 835.
22.1-17.4. Amended by Acts 2009, c. 66.
22.1-18. Amended by Acts 2013, c. 643.
22.1-18.01. Amended by Acts 2006, cc. 42, 130.
22.1-18.1. Amended by Acts 2012, cc. 805, 836.
22.1-19. Amended by Acts 2012, cc. 803, 835.
22.1-19.1. Amended by Acts 2006, cc. 25, 95; 2011, c. 248.
22.1-23. Amended by Acts 2007, cc. 43, 55.
22.1-25. Amended by Acts 2013, c. 805.
22.1-26. Amended by Acts 2007, c. 45; 2006, c. 49.
22.1-32. Amended by Acts 2005, cc. 489, 536; 2006, cc. 126, 840; 2007, c. 53; 2010, c. 723; 2013, c. 278.
22.1-47.4. Amended by Acts 2006, c. 126.
22.1-57.2. Amended by Acts 2011, c. 599.
22.1-57.3. Amended by Acts 2006, c. 29; 2007, c. 100; 2010, c. 95; 2011, c. 776.
22.1-60.1. Amended by Acts 2005, cc. 331, 450.
22.1-70.2. Amended by Acts 2006, cc. 52, 474; 2010, c. 61.
22.1-75. Amended by Acts 2006, c. 29; 2007, c. 100.
22.1-79. Amended by Acts 2006, cc. 857, 914; 2009, c. 459; 2013, cc. 588, 650.
22.1-79.1. Amended by Acts 2010, cc. 49, 88; 2011, cc. 216, 387.
22.1-79.3. Amended by Acts 2006, cc. 145, 857, 914; 2009, c. 195; 2011, cc. 261, 726; 2012, c. 546.
22.1-90. Amended by Acts 2009, c. 104.
22.1-92. Amended by Acts 2011, c. 216; 2012, cc. 805, 836.
22.1-93. Amended by Acts 2008, cc. 353, 404; 2009, c. 280; 2011, c. 216.
22.1-98. Amended by Acts 2006, cc. 26, 96.
22.1-98.2. Amended by Acts 2008, cc. 589, 705.
22.1-110. Amended by Acts 2006, c. 239.
22.1-115. Amended by Acts 2008, c. 131.
22.1-118. Amended by Acts 2007, cc. 45, 813.
22.1-129. Amended by Acts 2005, c. 446; 2007, c. 813; 2010, c. 763; 2012, cc. 805, 836.
22.1-132.2. Amended by Acts 2010, c. 40.
22.1-139. Repealed by Acts 2010, c. 61.
22.1-142. Amended by Acts 2012, cc. 283, 756.
22.1-146. Amended by Acts 2007, c. 121.
22.1-148. Amended by Acts 2007, c. 121.
22.1-151. Amended by Acts 2007, c. 121; 2008, c. 365.

Section
22.1-153. Amended by Acts 2007, c. 121.
22.1-154 to 22.1-157. Repealed by Acts 2007, c. 121.
22.1-161. Amended by Acts 2007, c. 121; 2008, c. 365.
22.1-164. Amended by Acts 2011, cc. 691, 714.
22.1-167.1. Amended by Acts 2006, c. 223.
22.1-177. Amended by Acts 2007, c. 104; 2013, c. 778.
22.1-178. Amended by Acts 2006, c. 396; 2013, cc. 498, 530.
22.1-180. Amended by Acts 2005, c. 928.
22.1-190. Amended by Acts 2012, c. 593.
22.1-199.1. Amended by Acts 2011, c. 216.
22.1-199.2. Amended by Acts 2006, cc. 41, 834; 2010, c. 61.
22.1-200. Amended by Acts 2005, c. 350.
22.1-200.02. Repealed by Acts 2005, c. 741.
22.1-202.1. Amended by Acts 2006, cc. 90, 161.
22.1-205. Amended by Acts 2007, c. 278; 2009, cc. 785, 813, 840; 2010, c. 663; 2011, c. 346; 2013, cc. 585, 646.
22.1-207.1. Amended by Acts 2007, c. 32; 2008, c. 417; 2009, cc. 437, 583.
22.1-207.2. Amended by Acts 2009, c. 451.
22.1-208.01. Amended by Acts 2005, cc. 461, 484, 839; 2012, c. 702; 2013, c. 575.
22.1-208.1 to 22.1-208.2:2. Repealed by Acts 2011, c. 216.
22.1-208.2:3. Repealed by Acts 2005, c. 741.
22.1-209.01. Repealed by Acts 2011, c. 216.
22.1-209.1. Repealed by Acts 2011, c. 216.
22.1-209.1:1. Repealed by Acts 2011, c. 216.
22.1-209.1:2. Amended by Acts 2009, cc. 792, 802, 2010, c. 61; 2012, cc. 803, 835.
22.1-209.1:3. Amended by Acts 2005, c. 633.
22.1-209.1:6. Repealed by Acts 2011, c. 216.
22.1-209.2. Amended by Acts 2008, cc. 46, 151; 2009, cc. 813, 840.
22.1-212.1. Amended by Acts 2005, c. 839.
22.1-212.1:1. Amended by Acts 2009, c. 84.
22.1-212.2. Amended by Acts 2011, c. 216.
22.1-212.2:2. Amended by Acts 2005, cc. 331, 450; 2011, c. 216.
22.1-212.2:3. Repealed by Acts 2011, c. 216.
22.1-212.5. Amended by Acts 2005, c. 928.
22.1-212.6, 22.1-212.7. Amended by Acts 2012, cc. 702, 720.
22.1-212.8. Amended by Acts 2005, c. 928; 2009, c. 441.
22.1-212.9. Amended by Acts 2010, cc. 393, 650; 2013, cc. 52, 225.
22.1-212.10. Amended by Acts 2010, cc. 393, 650; 2012, cc. 702, 720.
22.1-212.11. Amended by Acts 2009, c. 441.
22.1-212.12 to 22.1-212.14. Amended by Acts 2012, cc. 702, 720.
22.1-212.15. Amended by Acts 2010, c. 61.
22.1-212.17 to 22.1-212.21. Repealed by Acts 2009, c. 859.

Section
22.1-212.22. Amended by Acts 2008, cc. 237, 669. Repealed by Acts 2009, c. 859.
22.1-212.26. Amended by Acts 2012, c. 170.
22.1-213. Amended by Acts 2012, cc. 476, 507.
22.1-214. Amended by Acts 2007, cc. 33, 52; 2009, c. 468; 2010, c. 447.
22.1-214.2, 22.1-214.3. Amended by Acts 2009, cc. 813, 840; 2012, cc. 702, 720.
22.1-215. Amended by Acts 2009, cc. 813, 840; 2012, cc. 702, 720.
22.1-217.01. Amended by Acts 2011, c. 216.
22.1-217.1. Amended by Acts 2009, cc. 813, 840; 2012, cc. 702, 720.
22.1-218. Amended by Acts 2005, c. 928.
22.1-223. Amended by Acts 2006, c. 335.
22.1-225. Amended by Acts 2009, c. 802.
22.1-226. Repealed by Acts 2010, c. 61.
22.1-227.1. Amended by Acts 2008, c. 150; 2011, c. 388; 2013, cc. 56, 500.
22.1-238. Amended by Acts 2008, cc. 615, 663.
22.1-238. Amended by Acts 2008, cc. 430, 615, 663.
22.1-240. Repealed by Acts 2008, cc. 430, 615, 663.
22.1-241. Amended by Acts 2008, cc. 430, 615, 663; 2010, c. 97.
22.1-242. Amended by Acts 2008, cc. 430, 615, 663.
22.1-243. Amended by Acts 2008, cc. 430, 615, 663; 2009, c. 81; 2010, c. 85.
22.1-244 to 22.1-22.1-253. Repealed by Acts 2008, cc. 430, 615, 663.
22.1-253.13:1. Amended by Acts 2005, cc. 331, 450; 2007, c. 234; 2008, c. 661; 2009, c. 802; 2012, cc. 794, 845; 2013, cc. 123, 157, 798, 530.
22.1-253.13:2. Amended by Acts 2005, cc. 331, 450; 2010, cc. 537, 817; 2011, cc. 55, 74; 2012, cc. 476, 507; 2013, cc. 123, 157, 158, 224.
22.1-253.13:3. Amended by Acts 2005, cc. 331, 450, 753, 834; 2006, cc. 25, 38, 95, 117, 131; 2007, c. 234; 2009, c. 825; 2010, c. 76; 2011, cc. 248, 666; 2012, c. 183; 2013, cc. 539, 571, 584, 728.
22.1-253.13:4. Amended by Acts 2005, c. 345; 2006, c. 584; 2007, cc. 34, 56, 234, 351, 859, 919; 2008, c. 351; 2009, c. 490; 2010, cc. 80, 89, 162, 163, 313; 2011, c. 209; 2012, cc. 454, 642; 2013, cc. 498, 530.
22.1-253.13:5. Amended by Acts 2005, cc. 331, 450; 2007, c. 234; 2013, cc. 588, 650.
22.1-253.13:6. Amended by Acts 2005, cc. 331, 450; 2007, c. 234.
22.1-253.13:7. Amended by Acts 2007, c. 234; 2008, cc. 474, 827; 2013, c. 301.
22.1-253.13:8. Amended by Acts 2005, cc. 331, 450.

Section
22.1-253.13:9. Amended by Acts 2011, cc. 119, 145; 2012, c. 794.
22.1-254. Amended by Acts 2006, c. 335; 2010, c. 605; 2012, cc. 454, 642.
22.1-254.01. Amended by Acts 2006, cc. 41, 834.
22.1-254.1. Amended by Acts 2005, c. 377; 2006, cc. 562, 567, 911, 932; 2008, cc. 364, 553; 2012, cc. 547, 587.
22.1-254.2. Amended by Acts 2006, c. 335; 2010, c. 605.
22.1-258. Amended by Acts 2010, c. 597.
22.1-261. Amended by Acts 2010, cc. 386, 597, 629.
22.1-264.1. Amended by Acts 2006, c. 143.
22.1-271.1. Amended by Acts 2005, c. 928.
22.1-271.2. Amended by Acts 2011, c. 125; 2012, c. 181.
22.1-271.4. Amended by Acts 2010, c. 605; 2011, c. 125.
22.1-272.1. Amended by Acts 2009, cc. 813, 840.
22.1-274. Amended by Acts 2013, cc. 498, 530.
22.1-274.01. Repealed by Acts 2011, c. 216.
22.1-274.2. Amended by Acts 2005, c. 785; 2012, cc. 803, 835.
22.1-275.1. Amended by Acts 2012, cc. 805, 836.
22.1-276.01. Amended by Acts 2013, c. 575.
22.1-277. Amended by Acts 2009, c. 70.
22.1-277.06. Amended by Acts 2005, c. 96.
22.1-277.07. Amended by Acts 2006, c. 703; 2013, c. 288.
22.1-277.08. Amended by Acts 2011, cc. 384, 410.
22.1-277.2:1. Amended by Acts 2009, c. 208.
22.1-279.3:1. Amended by Acts 2005, cc. 484, 528; 2006, c. 146; 2010, c. 525; 2011, cc. 384, 410; 2013, c. 800.
22.1-279.6. Amended by Acts 2005, cc. 461, 484, 520; 2009, c. 431; 2013, c. 575.
22.1-279.8. Amended by Acts 2005, c. 904; 2006, c. 43; 2007, c. 44; 2009, cc. 222, 269; 2012, c. 418; 2013, c. 609.
22.1-281 through 22.1-286. Repealed by Acts 2010, cc. 386, 629.
22.1-287. Amended by Acts 2007, cc. 48, 555.
22.1-288.1. Amended by Acts 2006, c. 295.
22.1-289. Amended by Acts 2005, c. 343; 2006, c. 47; 2012, cc. 803, 835.
22.1-289.1. Amended by Acts 2006, c. 373.
22.1-290.01. Amended by Acts 2007, c. 31; 2008, cc. 48, 141.
22.1-291. Repealed by Acts 2011, c. 216.
22.1-291.1. Amended by Acts 2009, c. 482.
22.1-292.1. Amended by Acts 2006, cc. 27, 349; 2011, c. 248.
22.1-292.2. Amended by Acts 2006, cc. 27, 349.

Section
22.1-293. Amended by Acts 2013, cc. 588, 650.
22.1-294. Amended by Acts 2005, cc. 331, 450; 2013, cc. 44, 109, 588, 650.
22.1-295. Amended by Acts 2006, c. 373; 2013, cc. 588, 650.
22.1-295.1. Amended by Acts 2006, c. 191; 2013, c. 291.
22.1-296. Amended by Acts 2005, c. 486.
22.1-296.1. Amended by Acts 2006, c. 790; 2007, cc. 245, 431; 2008, c. 555.
22.1-296.4. Amended by Acts 2008, c. 555; 2009, c. 58.
22.1-298. Repealed by Acts 2006, cc. 27, 349.
22.1-298.1. Amended by Acts 2008, cc. 474, 827; 2012, c. 365; 2013, cc. 498, 530, 588, 650.
22.1-299. Amended by Acts 2008, c. 51; 2013, cc. 588, 650.
22.1-299.3. Repealed by Acts 2013, cc. 588, 650.
22.1-302. Amended by Acts 2010, c. 93; 2013, cc. 588, 644, 650.
22.1-303. Amended by Acts 2006, c. 373; 2013, cc. 588, 650.
22.1-304. Amended by Acts 2012, cc. 106, 687; 2013, cc. 588, 650.
22.1-305.1. Amended by Acts 2013, cc. 588, 650.
22.1-306, 22.1-307. Amended by Acts 2013, cc. 588, 650.
22.1-307. Amended by Acts 2008, c. 555.
22.1-309. Amended by Acts 2013, cc. 588, 650.
22.1-310r. Repealed by Acts 2013, cc. 588, 650.
22.1-311. Amended by Acts 2013, cc. 588, 650.
22.1-312. Repealed by Acts 2013, cc. 588, 650.
22.1-313. Amended by Acts 2008, cc. 474, 827; 2013, cc. 588, 650.
22.1-314. Amended by Acts 2013, cc. 588, 650.
22.1-319. Amended by Acts 2012, cc. 476, 507.
22.1-323.2. Amended by Acts 2005, c. 471; 2006, c. 781; 2008, c. 873.
22.1-329. Amended by Acts 2006, c. 168.
22.1-337. Amended by Acts 2005, c. 758; 2011, cc. 691, 714.
22.1-339 to 22.1-345.1. Repealed by Acts 2012, cc. 803, 835.
22.1-341. Amended by Acts 2007, c. 72.
22.1-343. Amended by Acts 2007, cc. 63, 142, 149.
22.1-344.1. Amended by Acts 2007, cc. 71, 125.
22.1-346. Amended by Acts 2009, c. 210.
22.1-346.1. Repealed by Acts 2009, c. 210.
22.1-346.2. Amended by Acts 2011, cc. 691, 714.
22.1-347. Repealed by Acts 2009, c. 210.
22.1-348. Amended by Acts 2009, c. 210; 2010, c. 666.
22.1-349. Amended by Acts 2006, cc. 27, 349; 2009, c. 210.
22.1-354.1. Amended by Acts 2006, c. 861.

Section
22.1-360. Amended by Acts 2010, c. 148.
22.1-361. Amended by Acts 2010, c. 148; 2011, c. 106.
23-1.01. Amended by Acts 2005, c. 633.
23-2.1:3. Amended by Acts 2012, cc. 347, 382.
23-4.3. Amended by Acts 2006, cc. 77, 899.
23-4.3:1. Amended by Acts 2006, c. 561.
23-4.4. Amended by Acts 2006, cc. 77, 899; 2009, cc. 325, 810.
23-7.1:02. Amended by Acts 2009, c. 879.
23-7.4. Amended by Acts 2006, cc. 783, 797, 806; 2007, cc. 108, 491; 2008, c. 723; 2011, cc. 38, 44, 782, 860; 2013, cc. 139, 166, 243.
23-7.4:1. Amended by Acts 2005, cc. 773, 783; 2006, c. 793; 2007, cc. 116, 161, 717; 2011, cc. 572, 586; 2012, c. 776; 2013, c. 719.
23-7.4:2. Amended by Acts 2006, cc. 783, 797; 2007, cc. 76, 102, 112; 2008, c. 723; 2009, c. 470; 2011, c. 376; 2013, cc. 166, 243, 302.
23-7.4:5. Amended by Acts 2009, cc. 430, 603.
23-7.5. Amended by Acts 2005, c. 15.
23-9.2:3. Amended by Acts 2005, c. 818; 2006, c. 121; 2008, cc. 441, 495; 2012, cc. 448, 658, 716.
23-9.2:3.02. Amended by Acts 2006, cc. 379, 531; 2007, c. 46; 2011, cc. 828, 869; 2012, cc. 142, 794.
23-9.2:3.03. Repealed by Acts 2011, cc. 828, 869.
23-9.2:3.1. Amended by Acts 2005, c. 633; 2006, c. 92.
23-9.2:3.4. Amended by Acts 2005, c. 903.
23-9.2:3.5. Amended by Acts 2007, c. 47.
23-9.2:3.4. Repealed by Acts 2006, cc. 27, 349.
23-9.2:3.7. Amended by Acts 2012, cc. 167, 169.
23-9.2:3.8. Amended by Acts 2011, cc. 157, 462, 545.
23-9.2:8. Amended by Acts 2012, cc. 697, 721; 2013, cc. 714, 735.
23-9.2:9. Amended by Acts 2009, cc. 222, 269; 2010, cc. 104, 478; 2012, 18, 112, 418.
23-9.2:10. Amended by Acts 2010, cc. 456, 524; 2013, c. 710.
23-9.3. Amended by Acts 2013, c. 605.
23-9.3:1. Amended by Acts 2009, c. 434.
23-9.6:1. Amended by Acts 2005, cc. 818, 933, 945; 2006, cc. 379, 537; 2009, cc. 55, 56; 2010, cc. 68, 527; 2011, cc. 828, 869; 2012, c. 142.
23-9.6:1.01. Amended by Acts 2011, cc. 828, 869; 2013, c. 482.
23-9.6:2. Amended by Acts 2011, c. 27.
23-9.9:01. Amended by Acts 2007, c. 630; 2012, cc. 803, 835.
23-9.10:4. Repealed by Acts 2006, cc. 77, 899.
23-9.14:1. Amended by Acts 2013, c. 577.

Section
23-9.14:2. Amended by Acts 2005, c. 818; 2006, c. 379.
23-14. Amended by Acts 2005, cc. 774, 799; 2006, cc. 808, 842; 2008, c. 56; 2013, c. 805.
23-30.25. Amended by Acts 2011, cc. 691, 714.
23-38.2. Amended by Acts 2009, cc. 813, 840; 2012, cc. 476, 507.
23-38.12. Amended by Acts 2011, cc. 419, 421.
23-38.53:1 to 23-38.53:3. Repealed by Acts 2005, c. 50.
23-38.53:21 to 23-38.53:24. Repealed by Acts 2005, cc. 753. 834.
23-38.70. Repealed by Acts 2006, c. 51.
23-38.71. Repealed by Acts 2006, c. 51.
23-38.76. Amended by Acts 2009, cc. 827, 845; 2013, cc. 586, 649.
23-38.77. Amended by Acts 2009, cc. 827, 845.
23-38.79. Amended by Acts 2009, cc. 827, 845.
23-38.79:1. Amended by Acts 2011, cc. 18, 26.
23-38.80. Amended by Acts 2009, cc. 827, 845.
23-38.84. Amended by Acts 2005, c. 633; 2011, cc. 18, 26.
23-38.87. Amended by Acts 2009, cc. 827, 845.
23-38.88. Amended by Acts 2006, c. 775; 2009, cc. 827, 845; 2011, cc. 828, 869; 2013, c. 482.
23-38.90. Amended by Acts 2008, cc. 824, 829; 2011, cc. 332, 828, 869; 2013, c. 438.
23-38.91. Amended by Acts 2011, cc. 828, 869.
23-38.93. Amended by Acts 2011, cc. 828, 869.
23-38.95. Repealed by Acts 2013, c. 577.
23-38.110. Amended by Acts 2011, c. 332; 2013, c. 583.
23-38.111. Amended by Acts 2010, cc. 136, 145.
23-41. Amended by Acts 2005, c. 12.
23-50.16:12. Amended by Acts 2005, c. 928; 2006, c. 673.
23-50.16:24. Amended by Acts 2012, cc. 803, 835.
23-50.16:32. Amended by Acts 2007, c. 945.
23-70. Amended by Acts 2008, cc. 55, 155; 2012, c. 599.
23-71. Amended by Acts 2012, c. 599.
23-76.1. Amended by Acts 2007, c. 434; 2008, c. 184.
23-77.4. Amended by Acts 2010, cc. 136, 145.
23-80. Repealed by Acts 2009, c. 72.
23-101, 23-102. Repealed by Acts 2005, c. 633.
23-105. Amended by Acts 2006, c. 810.
23-106. Amended by Acts 2006, c. 810.
23-107. Amended by Acts 2006, c. 810.
23-135.7:6. Amended by Acts 2006, c. 939.
23-135.7:7. Amended by Acts 2013, c. 482.
23-155.4. Amended by Acts 2007, cc. 471, 727.
23-165.4. Amended by Acts 2008, cc. 465, 477.
23-185. Amended by Acts 2008, c. 399.
23-218. Amended by Acts 2006, c. 337.
23-231.3. Amended by Acts 2005, c. 550.

Section
23-231.15. Amended by Acts 2008, c. 236; 2009, c. 598; 2010, c. 39; 2012, c. 80.
23-231.25. Amended by Acts 2006, c. 160.
23-232. Amended by Acts 2009, c. 596.
23-234. Amended by Acts 2012, cc. 282, 450.
23-253.1. Amended by Acts 2011, cc. 691, 714.
23-253.3. Amended by Acts 2010, c. 101.
23-276.1. Amended by Acts 2005, c. 447; 2007, cc. 82, 115; 2008, c. 856; 2010, cc. 67, 263; 2013, c. 229.
23-276.2. Amended by Acts 2005, c. 447.
23-276.3. Amended by Acts 2005, c. 447.
23-276.4. Amended by Acts 2005, c. 447; 2006, c. 814.
23-276.5. Amended by Acts 2005, c. 447.
23-276.6. Amended by Acts 2005, c. 447.
23-276.7. Amended by Acts 2005, c. 447.
23-276.8. Amended by Acts 2005, c. 447; 2013, c. 229.
23-276.10. Amended by Acts 2008, c. 856.
23-276.11. Amended by Acts 2005, c. 447.
23-276.12. Amended by Acts 2006, c. 48; 2008, c. 856.
23-281. Amended by Acts 2012, cc. 682, 683.
23-284. Amended by Acts 2013, c. 687.
23-287. Amended by Acts 2005, c. 758; 2013, c. 480.
23-288. Amended by Acts 2011, cc. 345, 356.
23-290.1. Repealed by Acts 2011, cc. 345, 356.
23-297. Amended by Acts 2005, c. 758.
23-298. Amended by Acts 2008, c. 242.
23-299. Amended by Acts 2012, cc. 176, 580.
23-299.2. Amended by Acts 2012, cc. 176, 580.
23-299.4. Amended by Acts 2012, cc. 176, 580.
23-299.8. Amended by Acts 2012, cc. 176, 580.
23-299.9. Amended by Acts 2012, cc. 176, 580.
23-310. Amended by Acts 2008, cc. 113, 394.
24.2-101. Amended by Acts 2005, c. 384; 2006, cc. 205, 787, 892; 2007, c. 311; 2008, c. 880; 2009, cc. 865, 870, 874; 2010, c. 707; 2013, cc. 542, 684.
24.2-102. Amended by Acts 2007, c. 350; 2013, c. 542.
24.2-103. Amended by Acts 2006, c. 760; 2009, c. 407; 2010, cc. 347, 769; 2013, cc. 525, 542.
24.2-104. Amended by Acts 2013, c. 768.
24.2-105.1. Amended by Acts 2006, c. 474; 2007, c. 340.
24.2-106. Amended by Acts 2005, c. 380; 2011, c. 764; 2013, c. 409.
24.2-107. Amended by Acts 2007, cc. 311, 318; 2013, cc. 461, 525.
24.2-108. Amended by Acts 2005, c. 380.
24.2-109.1. Amended by Acts 2006, c. 235.
24.2-110. Amended by Acts 2009, c. 403.
24.2-112. Amended by Acts 2007, c. 813.
24.2-114. Amended by Acts 2005, c. 380; 2010, c. 812; 2013, c. 491.

Section
24.2-115. Amended by Acts 2005, c. 820; 2009, cc. 639, 865, 870, 874; 2010, cc. 190, 347, 769; 2013, c. 461.
24.2-115.1. Amended by Acts 2009, cc. 396, 865, 870, 874; 2013, cc. 444, 462.
24.2-116. Amended by Acts 2012, c. 489.
24.2-120. Amended by Acts 2005, c. 820; 2012, cc. 328, 486.
24.2-121. Amended by Acts 2005, cc. 492, 548.
24.2-209. Amended by Acts 2010, cc. 449, 645.
24.2-216. Amended by Acts 2010, cc. 449, 645.
24.2-219. Amended by Acts 2011, c. 455.
24.2-226. Amended by Acts 2010, cc. 431, 449, 645; 2011, c. 206.
24.2-228. Amended by Acts 2010, cc. 431, 624; 2011, c. 78.
24.2-228.1. Amended by Acts 2006, cc. 120, 253; 2009, c. 157; 2011, c. 599.
24.2-231. Amended by Acts 2007, c. 175.
24.2-233. Amended by Acts 2011, cc. 384, 410.
24.2-235. Amended by Acts 2009, cc. 868, 876.
24.2-238. Amended by Acts 2009, cc. 868, 876.
24.2-302.1. Repealed by Acts 2012, c. 1.
24.2-303.1, 24.2-303.2. Repealed by Acts 2011, Sp. I, c. 1.
24.2-304.01, 24.2-304.02. Repealed by Acts 2011, Sp. I, c. 1.
24.2-304.1. Amended by Acts 2012, c. 357; 2013, c. 483.
24.2-306. Amended by Acts 2012, cc. 328, 486.
24.2-310. Amended by Acts 2005, c. 340; 2008, cc. 113, 394; 2010, cc. 639, 707; 2012, cc. 488, 759.
24.2-311. Amended by Acts 2012, c. 791.
24.2-403. Amended by Acts 2006, c. 205.
24.2-404. Amended by Acts 2005, c. 378; 2006, cc. 243, 926, 940; 2008, c. 379; 2009, cc. 865, 870, 874; 2011, c. 528; 2012, c. 686; 2013, cc. 425, 686, 725.
24.2-404.1. Amended by Acts 2013, c. 542.
24.2-405. Amended by Acts 2006, cc. 787, 892; 2007, c. 318; 2009, c. 318; 2010, c. 452.
24.2-406. Amended by Acts 2007, c. 318; 2009, c. 318; 2012, c. 664; 2013, c. 446.
24.2-407. Amended by Acts 2010, c. 812.
24.2-407.1. Amended by Acts 2007, c. 318; 2010, c. 452.
24.2-409. Amended by Acts 2013, c. 491.
24.2-410. Amended by Acts 2011, c. 518.
24.2-411.1. Amended by Acts 2007, c. 318; 2012, c. 662; 2013, c. 725.
24.2-411.2. Amended by Acts 2007, c. 318; 2013, c. 542.
24.2-414. Amended by Acts 2008, c. 424.
24.2-415. Amended by Acts 2012, cc. 328, 486.
24.2-416. Amended by Acts 2008, c. 424.
24.2-416.2. Amended by Acts 2008, c. 865.
24.2-416.3. Amended by Acts 2011, cc. 197, 225; 2013, c. 465.

Section

24.2-416.4. Amended by Acts 2013, c. 680.
24.2-416.5. Amended by Acts 2007, c. 318.
24.2-416.6. Amended by Acts 2013, c. 465.
24.2-417.1. Amended by Acts 2006, c. 391.
24.2-418. Amended by Acts 2009, cc. 318, 865, 870, 874; 2010, cc. 795, 812; 2012, c. 491; 2013, c. 465.
24.2-419. Amended by Acts 2012, c. 353.
24.2-423. Amended by Acts 2013, c. 520.
24.2-424. Amended by Acts 2013, cc. 520, 684.
24.2-427. Amended by Acts 2006, cc. 926, 940; 2007, c. 318; 2008, c. 382; 2012, c. 686; 2013, c. 686.
24.2-440 to 24.2-443.4. Repealed by Acts 2012, c. 353.
24.2-442. Amended by Acts 2007, c. 311; 2010, cc. 449, 645; 2011, cc. 427, 458.
24.2-443.3. Amended by Acts 2007, c. 311; 2010, cc. 449, 645; 2011, cc. 427, 458.
24.2-444. Amended by Acts 2007, cc. 311, 318; 2008, c. 379; 2009, c. 318; 2012, c. 353.
24.2-455. Amended by Acts 2013, c. 542.
24.2-464. Amended by Acts 2013, c. 542.
24.2-502. Amended by Acts 2013, c. 542.
24.2-503.1. Repealed by Acts 2006, cc. 787, 892.
24.2-506. Amended by Acts 2010, c. 215; 2012, cc. 166, 538; 2013, c. 684.
24.2-507. Amended by Acts 2010, cc. 449, 542, 645; 2011, c. 599.
24.2-510. Amended by Acts 2010, cc. 449, 542, 645; 2011, 599.
24.2-511. Amended by Acts 2006, c. 83.
24.2-515. Amended by Acts 2011, cc. 570, 584.
24.2-516. Amended by Acts 2010, cc. 449, 645.
24.2-517. Amended by Acts 2012, cc. 328, 486.
24.2-521. Amended by Acts 2010, c. 215; 2012, cc. 166, 538.
24.2-522. Amended by Acts 2010, cc. 449, 645; 2013, c. 443.
24.2-524. Amended by Acts 2005, c. 748; 2010, cc. 449, 645.
24.2-527. Amended by Acts 2006, c. 83; 2010, cc. 449, 645; 2013, c. 443.
24.2-531. Amended by Acts 2010, c. 812.
24.2-533. Repealed by Acts 2010, c. 812.
24.2-536. Amended by Acts 2010, cc. 449, 645.
24.2-537. Amended by Acts 2010, cc. 449, 645.
24.2-538. Amended by Acts 2010, cc. 449, 645.
24.2-543. Amended by Acts 2012, cc. 166, 538; 2013, cc. 521, 550, 684.
24.2-544. Amended by Acts 2006, c. 205; 2011, cc. 570, 584.
24.2-545. Amended by Acts 2011, cc. 570, 584; 2013, cc. 443, 521, 550.
24.2-601. Amended by Acts 2008, cc. 113, 394.
24.2-603. Amended by Acts 2008, c. 423.
24.2-604. Amended by Acts 2007, c. 672; 2009, cc. 396, 494, 865, 870, 874; 2010, cc. 448, 707; 2012, cc. 754, 826.
24.2-611. Amended by Acts 2008, cc. 88, 424; 2010, c. 812; 2011, c. 810.
24.2-612. Amended by Acts 2009, c. 522; 2010, cc. 449, 645; 2011, cc. 427, 458; 2012, c. 353.
24.2-613. Amended by Acts 2008, c. 544; 2010, c. 204.
24.2-622. Amended by Acts 2005, c. 370; 2006, c. 892.
24.2-625.1. Amended by Acts 2007, c. 794.
24.2-625.2. Amended by Acts 2008, cc. 87, 393.
24.2-626. Amended by Acts 2007, cc. 939, 943; 2009, cc. 751, 759; 2010, cc. 356, 533; 2011, cc. 153, 447, 481.
24.2-627. Amended by Acts 2010, c. 214.
24.2-629. Amended by Acts 2007, c. 794; 2008, c. 703.
24.2-638. Amended by Acts 2009, c. 494.
24.2-639. Amended by Acts 2010, c. 448.
24.2-640. Amended by Acts 2010, c. 204.
24.2-643. Amended by Acts 2005, cc. 496, 539; 2011, cc. 427, 458; 2012, cc. 723, 838, 839; 2013, cc. 703, 725, 746.
24.2-644. Amended by Acts 2013, c. 542.
24.2-649. Amended by Acts 2005, c. 569; 2006, c. 242; 2009, c. 809.
24.2-651. Amended by Acts 2007, c. 375; 2012, cc. 838, 839.
24.2-651.1. Amended by Acts 2012, c. 723; 2012, cc. 838, 839.
24.2-652. Amended by Acts 2011, c. 602.
24.2-653. Amended by Acts 2005, c. 824; 2007, c. 692; 2008, cc. 110, 559; 2010, c. 448; 2012, cc. 592, 838, 839; 2013, c. 503.
24.2-653.1. Amended by Acts 2010, c. 348.
24.2-655. Amended by Acts 2006, c. 177; 2010, c. 448.
24.2-659. Amended by Acts 2006, c. 689; 2008, cc. 107, 385.
24.2-663. Amended by Acts 2013, c. 469.
24.2-668. Amended by Acts 2007, c. 285.
24.2-669. Amended by Acts 2006, c. 689; 2008, c. 565.
24.2-671. Amended by Acts 2005, c. 824; 2006, c. 689.
24.2-676. Amended by Acts 2006, c. 892.
24.2-680. Amended by Acts 2006, cc. 787, 892.
24.2-682. Amended by Acts 2008, cc. 107, 385; 2010, cc. 431, 542.
24.2-684.1. Amended by Acts 2011, cc. 333, 520.
24.2-685. Amended by Acts 2011, c. 599.
24.2-687. Amended by Acts 2006, c. 302; 2011, c. 590.
24.2-700. Amended by Acts 2008, cc. 425, 880; 2009, cc. 405, 873; 2010, c. 244; 2012, c. 353.

Section
24.2-701. Amended by Acts 2006, c. 438; 2007, c. 315; 2008, cc. 386, 425, 880; 2009, cc. 405, 873; 2010, c. 244; 2011, cc. 427, 458; 2012, cc. 353, 612, 838, 839; 2013, cc. 535, 620, 703, 725.
24.2-702.1. Amended by Acts 2009, cc. 230, 310; 2010, cc. 449, 645; 2011, cc. 427, 458; 2012, c. 353.
24.2-703. Amended by Acts 2006, c. 438; 2010, cc. 449, 645; 2011, cc. 427, 458; 2012, c. 353.
24.2-703.1. Amended by Acts 2008, c. 880.
24.2-703.2. Amended by Acts 2008, c. 880.
24.2-704. Amended by Acts 2006, c. 242; 2008, c. 880.
24.2-705. Amended by Acts 2006, c. 297; 2008, c. 880.
24.2-705.1. Amended by Acts 2008, c. 880; 2010, c. 539.
24.2-706. Amended by Acts 2006, c. 438; 2007, c. 318; 2008, cc. 106, 300, 379; 2009, cc. 345, 405, 873; 2010, cc. 213, 316, 449, 538, 645, 812; 2011, cc. 427, 458; 2012, c. 353.
24.2-707. Amended by Acts 2006, c. 438.
24.2-708. Amended by Acts 2006, c. 283; 2010, c. 348; 2012, c. 645.
24.2-709. Amended by Acts 2006, c. 297; 2010, cc. 449, 645; 2011, c. 654; 2012, c. 353.
24.2-709.1. Amended by Acts 2012, cc. 328, 486; 2013, c. 501.
24.2-710. Amended by Acts 2006, c. 297; 2010, cc. 601, 812.
24.2-711. Amended by Acts 2006, c. 283; 2013, c. 501.
24.2-711.1. Amended by Acts 2013, c. 537.
24.2-712. Amended by Acts 2006, c. 297; 2008, c. 423; 2013, c. 501.
24.2-713. Amended by Acts 2013, c. 542.
24.2-800. Amended by Acts 2009, c. 386.
24.2-802. Amended by Acts 2006, c. 689; 2007, cc. 285, 939, 943; 2008, c. 682; 2011, c. 522.
24.2-803. Amended by Acts 2006, c. 292.
24.2-804. Amended by Acts 2006, c. 292.
24.2-900 to 24.2-930. Repealed by Acts 2006, cc. 787, 892.
24.2-940. Repealed by Acts 2006, cc. 787, 892.
24.2-941 to 24.2-944. Repealed by Acts 2006, cc. 787, 892.
24.2-945. Amended by Acts 2008, c. 359.
24.2-945.1. Amended by Acts 2007, cc. 246, 831; 2008, cc. 152, 289.
24.2-945.2. Amended by Acts 2007, cc. 331, 831; 2008, c. 825.
24.2-946. Amended by Acts 2010, c. 268.
24.2-946.1. Amended by Acts 2007, cc. 151, 286.

Section
24.2-946.2. Amended by Acts 2010, c. 297; 2012, c. 527.
24.2-947.1. Amended by Acts 2007, cc. 151, 286.
24.2-947.4. Amended by Acts 2008, cc. 152, 289, 650; 2013, c. 542.
24.2-947.5. Amended by Acts 2007, cc. 151, 286.
24.2-947.6. Amended by Acts 2010, c. 696.
24.2-947.7. Amended by Acts 2010, c. 696.
24.2-947.8. Amended by Acts 2010, c. 696.
24.2-947.9. Amended by Acts 2007, cc. 151, 286; 2008, c. 380.
24.2-948. Repealed by Acts 2010 c. 696.
24.2-948.1. Amended by Acts 2010, c. 696.
24.2-948.2. Amended by Acts 2008, c. 650.
24.2-948.4. Amended by Acts 2009, c. 231.
24.2-949.2. Amended by Acts 2007, c. 246.
24.2-949.5. Amended by Acts 2008, cc. 152, 289.
24.2-949.6. Amended by Acts 2008, c. 547; 2012, c. 949.6.
24.2-949.9. Amended by Acts 2009, c. 231.
24.2-949.9:2. Amended by Acts 2008, cc. 152, 289.
24.2-950.1. Amended by Acts 2008, cc. 152, 289.
24.2-950.4. Amended by Acts 2008, cc. 152, 289.
24.2-950.5. Repealed by Acts 2008, cc. 152, 289.
24.2-950.9. Amended by Acts 2009, c. 231.
24.2-951.9. Amended by Acts 2009, c. 231.
24.2-952.7. Amended by Acts 2009, c. 231.
24.2-953. Amended by Acts 2012, c. 298.
24.2-953.1. Amended by Acts 2008, c. 547; 2010, c. 696.
24.2-953.3, 24.2-953.4. Amended by Acts 2013, c. 542.
24.2-955. Amended by Acts 2008, c. 825.
24.2-955.2. Amended by Acts 2008, c. 825.
24.2-955.3. Amended by Acts 2010, c. 546.
24.2-956. Amended by Acts 2012, c. 519.
24.2-956.1. Amended by Acts 2012, c. 519.
24.2-959. Amended by Acts 2010, c. 323.
24.2-959.1. Amended by Acts 2010, c. 323.
24.2-1002.01. Amended by Acts 2005, cc. 339, 412; 2013, c. 465.
24.2-1002.1. Amended by Acts 2007, c. 318.
24.2-1004. Amended by Acts 2009, cc. 865, 870, 874; 2012, cc. 652, 667.
24.2-1012. Amended by Acts 2006, c. 242.
24.2-1013. Repealed by Acts 2006, cc. 787, 892.
24.2-1014.1. Repealed by Acts 2006, cc. 787, 892.
25.1-100. Amended by Acts 2006, c. 586; 2009, cc. 813, 840; 2010,c. 835; 2011, cc. 117, 190; 2012, 476, 507, 699, 719.
25.1-108. Amended by Acts 2006, c. 246; 2007, cc. 882, 901, 926; 2011, cc. 117, 190.

Section
25.1-203. Amended by Acts 2005, c. 877.
25.1-204. Amended by Acts 2005, c. 878; 2011, cc. 117, 190; 2013, c. 764.
25.1-209. Amended by Acts 2006, c. 586; 2010, c. 835.
25.1-213. Amended by Acts 2006, c. 586; 2010, c. 835.
25.1-214. Amended by Acts 2006, c. 586; 2010, c. 835.
25.1-219. Amended by Acts 2006, c. 586; 2010, c. 835.
25.1-220. Amended by Acts 2006, c. 586; 2010, c. 835.
25.1-226. Repealed by Acts 2006, c. 586.
25.1-227. Repealed by Acts 2006, c. 586.
25.1-228. Amended by Acts 2006, c. 586.
25.1-229. Amended by Acts 2006, c. 586; 2007, cc. 450, 720.
25.1-235. Amended by Acts 2006, c. 586; 2010, cc. 177, 835.
25.1-241. Amended by Acts 2005, c. 885.
25.1-245. Amended by Acts 2005, c. 878; 2007, c. 895.
25.1-305. Amended by Acts 2013, c. 764.
25.1-318. Amended by Acts 2006, c. 586; 2010, c. 835.
25.1-400. Amended by Acts 2011, cc. 117, 190.
25.1-408. Amended by Acts 2006, c. 452.
25.1-410. Amended by Acts 2011, cc. 117, 190.
25.1-411. Amended by Acts 2011, cc. 117, 190.
25.1-414. Amended by Acts 2011, cc. 117, 190.
25.1-417. Amended by Acts 2011, cc. 117, 190, 335; 2013, c. 764.
26-1 to 26-116. Repealed by Acts 2012, c. 614.
27-6.1. Amended by Acts 2008, c. 410.
27-13. Amended by Acts 2008, c. 410.
27-14. Amended by Acts 2006, c. 462; 2008, c. 410; 2013, cc. 356, 616.
27-15.1. Amended by Acts 2008, c. 410.
27-15.2. Amended by Acts 2010, c. 545.
27-20. Amended by Acts 2008, c. 410.
27-23.1. Amended by Acts 2007, c. 813.
27-32. Amended by Acts 2008, cc. 551, 691.
27-32.1. Amended by Acts 2008, cc. 551, 691.
27-32.2. Amended by Acts 2008, cc. 551, 691; 2012, cc. 279, 330.
27-34. Amended by Acts 2008, c. 410.
27-37.1. Amended by Acts 2008, cc. 551, 691.
27-42. Amended by Acts 2012, c. 802.
27-61. Amended by Acts 2007, cc. 647, 741.
27-85.4. Amended by Acts 2008, c. 410.
27-95. Amended by Acts 2010, cc. 587, 643.
27-97. Amended by Acts 2007, cc. 647, 741; 2010, cc. 587, 643.
27-97.2. Amended by Acts 2007, cc. 647, 741; 2010, cc. 587, 643.
27-98. Amended by Acts 2008, c. 499; 2010, c. 102; 2012, cc. 607, 635.
27-99. Amended by Acts 2007, cc. 647, 741.
28.2-101. Amended by Acts 2005, c. 191; 2012, c. 595.

Section
28.2-103. Amended by Acts 2010, c. 65.
28.2-104. Amended by Acts 2009, c. 103.
28.2-106.1. Amended by Acts 2005, c. 516; 2007, c. 554; 2010, cc. 153, 500.
28.2-110. Amended by Acts 2010, c. 815.
28.2-111. Amended by Acts 2010, c. 815.
28.2-201. Amended by Acts 2006, c. 5; 2009, c. 371.
28.2-204.1. Amended by Acts 2013, cc. 59, 760.
28.2-226. Amended by Acts 2013, c. 38.
28.2-226.1. Amended by Acts 2005, c. 124.
28.2-226.2. Amended by Acts 2009, c. 9.
28.2-227. Amended by Acts 2009, c. 9; 2010, cc. 12, 144.
28.2-228. Amended by Acts 2009, c. 9; 2013, c. 38.
28.2-228.1. Amended by Acts 2009, c. 9.
28.2-229. Amended by Acts 2009, c. 384.
28.2-232. Amended by Acts 2013, c. 50.
28.2-241. Amended by Acts 2009, c. 9.
28.2-301. Amended by Acts 2009, c. 9.
28.2-302. Amended by Acts 2009, c. 9.
28.2-302.1. Amended by Acts 2005, c. 124.
28.2-302.2. Amended by Acts 2007, c. 30; 2009, c. 9.
28.2-302.2:1. Amended by Acts 2007, c. 30; 2009, c. 9; 2011, c. 287; 2012, c. 579.
28.2-302.6. Amended by Acts 2009, c. 9.
28.2-302.7. Amended by Acts 2009, c. 9; 2010, c. 484.
28.2-302.7:1. Amended by Acts 2007, c. 30; 2009, c. 9.
28.2-302.8. Amended by Acts 2005, c. 198; 2009, c. 9.
28.2-302.9. Amended by Acts 2009, c. 9.
28.2-302.10. Amended by Acts 2009, c. 9.
28.2-302.10:1. Amended by Acts 2009, c. 9; 2013, cc. 55, 344.
28.2-305. Amended by Acts 2012, c. 228.
28.2-307. Amended by Acts 2009, c. 28.
28.2-315. Amended by Acts 2009, c. 9.
28.2-319. Amended by Acts 2012, cc. 283, 756.
28.2-402. Amended by Acts 2009, c. 9; 2013, cc. 59, 760.
28.2-403. Amended by Acts 2013, cc. 59, 760.
28.2-407. Amended by Acts 2012, cc. 283, 756.
28.2-502. Amended by Acts 2009, c. 9.
28.2-504. Amended by Acts 2009, c. 9.
28.2-507. Amended by Acts 2011, c. 221.
28.2-511. Amended by Acts 2013, c. 38.
28.2-521. Amended by Acts 2011, c. 566.
28.2-526. Amended by Acts 2007, c. 36; 2011, c. 627.
28.2-539. Amended by Acts 2006, c. 33; 2013, c. 38.
28.2-540. Repealed by Acts 2013, c. 38.
28.2-541, 28.2-542. Amended by Acts 2013, c. 38.
28.2-543, 28.2-544. Repealed by Acts 2013, c. 38.

Section
28.2-546. Amended by Acts 2006, c. 33; 2013, c. 38.
28.2-548. Amended by Acts 2006, c. 33; 2013, c. 38.
28.2-549, 28.2-550. Amended by Acts 2013, c. 38.
28.2-555. Amended by Acts 2013, cc. 585, 646.
28.2-603. Amended by Acts 2007, cc. 28, 170; 2010, c. 27; 2011, c. 314.
28.2-702. Amended by Acts 2009, c. 9.
28.2-709. Amended by Acts 2009, c. 170; 2011, c. 217.
28.2-821. Amended by Acts 2012, cc. 283, 756.
28.2-900. Amended by Acts 2012, cc. 283, 756.
28.2-1000.2. Amended by Acts 2010, c. 178; 2013, c. 59.
28.2-1001. Amended by Acts 2007, c. 885.
28.2-1000.2. Repealed by Acts 2013, cc. 59, 760.
28.2-1001. Amended by Acts 2013, cc. 635, 688.
28.2-1100. Amended by Acts 2011, c. 885.
28.2-1103. Amended by Acts 2005, c. 41.
28.2-1200.1. Amended by Acts 2011, cc. 733, 734.
28.2-1203. Amended by Acts 2006, c. 507; 2007, c. 25.
28.2-1205. Amended by Acts 2005, c. 839.
28.2-1207. Amended by Acts 2011, c. 451.
28.2-1208. Amended by Acts 2008, c. 369; 2009, c. 766.
28.2-1303. Amended by Acts 2005, c. 104; 2006, c. 687.
28.2-1307. Amended by Acts 2010, c. 65.
28.2-1308. Amended by Acts 2011, c. 253.
28.2-1400. Amended by Acts 2008, c. 20.
28.2-1403. Amended by Acts 2008, c. 20.
28.2-1507. Amended by Acts 2007, cc. 873, 916.
29.1-100. Amended by Acts 2012, cc. 247, 603.
29.1-101. Amended by Acts 2005, cc. 860, 889.
29.1-102. Amended by Acts 2006, cc. 69, 915.
29.1-103. Amended by Acts 2007, cc. 35, 906; 2009, c. 648; 2011, cc. 805, 841.
29.1-108. Amended by Acts 2006, cc. 69, 915.
29.1-109. Amended by Acts 2006, cc. 69, 915; 2012, c. 595.
29.1-113. Amended by Acts 2011, c. 768.
29.1-200. Amended by Acts 2007, c. 87; 2009, c. 355.
29.1-201. Amended by Acts 2007, c. 87.
29.1-204. Amended by Acts 2007, c. 87.
29.1-205. Amended by Acts 2007, c. 87.
29.1-207. Amended by Acts 2007, c. 87.
29.1-208. Amended by Acts 2007, c. 87.
29.1-212. Amended by Acts 2007, c. 87.
29.1-213. Amended by Acts 2007, c. 87.
29.1-217. Amended by Acts 2007, c. 87.
29.1-218. Amended by Acts 2007, c. 87.
29.1-300.1. Amended by Acts 2008, cc. 18, 416.
29.1-300.2. Amended by Acts 2007, c. 87; 2012, c. 763.

Section
29.1-300.4. Amended by Acts 2009, c. 9.
29.1-301. Amended by Acts 2008, c. 279; 2010, c. 345.
29.1-302. Amended by Acts 2009, c. 9; 2012, cc. 321, 380.
29.1-302.02. Amended by Acts 2012, c. 244.
29.1-302.1. Amended by Acts 2009, c. 9; 2010, c. 251.
29.1-302.2. Amended by Acts 2009, c. 9.
29.1-302.3. Amended by Acts 2009, c. 9.
29.1-302.4. Amended by Acts 2009, c. 9.
29.1-303. Amended by Acts 2009, c. 9.
29.1-303.1. Amended by Acts 2009, c. 9; 2013, c. 351.
29.1-303.2. Amended by Acts 2009, c. 9.
29.1-303.3. Amended by Acts 2007, c. 40; 2009, c. 9.
29.1-304. Amended by Acts 2009, cc. 9, 50.
29.1-305. Amended by Acts 2009, c. 9.
29.1-306. Amended by Acts 2005, c. 8; 2009, c. 9.
29.1-307. Amended by Acts 2009, c. 9.
29.1-309. Amended by Acts 2009, c. 9.
29.1-309.1. Amended by Acts 2009, c. 9.
29.1-309.2. Amended by Acts 2009, c. 9.
29.1-309.3. Amended by Acts 2009, c. 9.
29.1-310. Amended by Acts 2009, c. 9; 2010, c. 6.
29.1-310.1. Amended by Acts 2007, c. 40.
29.1-310.2. Amended by Acts 2009, c. 9; 2011, c. 287; 2012, c. 579.
29.1-311. Amended by Acts 2009, c. 9; 2013, c. 351.
29.1-312. Amended by Acts 2008, c. 11; 2009, c. 5.
29.1-313. Amended by Acts 2009, cc. 813, 840; 2012, cc. 476, 507.
29.1-314. Amended by Acts 2006, cc. 8, 37.
29.1-318. Amended by Acts 2009, c. 9.
29.1-328. Amended by Acts 2007, c. 39; 2011, c. 819.
29.1-330. Amended by Acts 2010, c. 3.
29.1-336. Amended by Acts 2005, c. 145.
29.1-337. Amended by Acts 2007, c. 87.
29.1-338. Amended by Acts 2010, c. 183.
29.1-339.1. Repealed by Acts 2005, c. 127.
29.1-339.2. Amended by Acts 2007, c. 644; 2009, c. 9.
29.1-343. Amended by Acts 2009, c. 9.
29.1-344. Amended by Acts 2010, c. 9; 2012, c. 227; 2013, c. 745.
29.1-345. Amended by Acts 2010, c. 9; 2013, c. 745.
29.1-347. Amended by Acts 2013, c. 745.
29.1-348. Amended by Acts 2007, c. 38.
29.1-349. Amended by Acts 2007, c. 87; 2013, c. 745.
29.1-355. Amended by Acts 2007, c. 87.
29.1-407. Amended by Acts 2012, cc. 283, 756.
29.1-417. Amended by Acts 2013, c. 792.

Section
29.1-419. Amended by Acts 2011, c. 191.
29.1-501. Amended by Acts 2010, c. 184.
29.1-509. Amended by Acts 2007, c. 664; 2010, c. 43.
29.1-514. Amended by Acts 2007, c. 813.
29.1-516. Amended by Acts 2007, c. 87; 2013, c. 345.
29.1-517. Amended by Acts 2007, c. 87; 2013, c. 349.
29.1-519. Amended by Acts 2005, c. 8; 2007, c. 643.
29.1-520. Amended by Acts 2008, c. 31; 2012, cc. 69, 226.
29.1-521. Amended by Acts 2005, cc. 170, 533, 534; 2006, cc. 20, 521; 2008, cc. 160, 161; 2010, c. 10.
29.1-521.1. Amended by Acts 2010, c. 626.
29.1-521.2. Amended by Acts 2010, c. 183; 2012, cc. 283, 756.
29.1-521.3. Amended by Acts 2007, c. 87.
29.1-523. Amended by Acts 2010, c. 183.
29.1-523.1. Amended by Acts 2010, c. 183; 2012, cc. 283, 756.
29.1-524. Amended by Acts 2012, cc. 283, 756.
29.1-525. Amended by Acts 2010, c. 183.
29.1-525.1. Amended by Acts 2010, c. 183.
29.1-528. Amended by Acts 2007, c. 642.
29.1-529. Amended by Acts 2008, cc. 17, 260; 2009, cc. 8, 305; 2010, c. 5; 2012, c. 247; 2013, c. 346.
29.1-530. Amended by Acts 2006, c. 20; 2007, c. 87; 2013, c. 349.
29.1-530.1. Amended by Acts 2005, c. 167; 2009, c. 11.
29.1-530.3. Amended by Acts 2010, c. 183.
29.1-534. Amended by Acts 2011, cc. 93, 179.
29.1-539. Amended by Acts 2007, c. 87.
29.1-549. Amended by Acts 2012, cc. 283, 756.
29.1-552. Amended by Acts 2007, c. 87.
29.1-553. Amended by Acts 2005, c. 170; 2007, c. 87.
29.1-556. Amended by Acts 2007, c. 87.
29.1-563. Amended by Acts 2011, c. 47.
29.1-568. Amended by Acts 2011, c. 47.
29.1-574. Amended by Acts 2005, c. 916.
29.1-702. Amended by Acts 2012, c. 233.
29.1-712 to 29.1-733.1. Repealed by Acts 2013, c. 787.
29.1-735.2. Amended by Acts 2013, c. 48.
29.1-738. Amended by Acts 2005, c. 616; 2013, c. 787.
29.1-738.2. Amended by Acts 2005, c. 616; 2007, c. 168.
29.1-738.3. Amended by Acts 2005, c. 616.
29.1-739. Amended by Acts 2007, c. 87.
29.1-739.1. Amended by Acts 2007, c. 87.
29.1-739.2. Amended by Acts 2007, c. 87; 2008, c. 535.
29.1-744.3. Amended by Acts 2012, c. 700.
29.1-745. Amended by Acts 2007, c. 87.

Section
29.1-746. Amended by Acts 2006, c. 23.
29.1-748. Amended by Acts 2007, cc. 615, 732.
29.1-748.1. Amended by Acts 2007, c. 813.
29.1-749.2. Amended by Acts 2007, c. 813.
29.1-801. Amended by Acts 2013, c. 787.
30-5. Amended by Acts 2012, c. 349.
30-13. Amended by Acts 2005, c. 839.
30-14. Amended by Acts 2005, c. 839.
30-19.03. Amended by Acts 2010, c. 410.
30-19.03:1, 30-19.03:1.1. Repealed by Acts 2010, c. 410.
30-19.03:1.2. Amended by Acts 2011, c. 302.
30-19.1, 30-19.1:1. Repealed by Acts 2010, c. 410.
30-19.1:3. Repealed by Acts 2010, c. 410.
30-19.1:4. Amended by Acts 2007, c. 133.
30-19.1:6. Repealed by Acts 2010, c. 410.
30-19.1:7. Amended by Acts 2010, c. 410.
30-19.1:10. Repealed by Acts 2005, cc. 860, 889.
30-19.3. Amended by Acts 2007, c. 442; 2012, c. 670.
30-19.4. Amended by Acts 2005, c. 802.
30-19.10. Amended by Acts 2007, c. 402.
30-19.12. Amended by Acts 2006, c. 272.
30-28.16. Amended by Acts 2006, c. 662; 2008, c. 677; 2011, c. 765.
30-28.18. Amended by Acts 2005, c. 839.
30-34.2:1. Amended by Acts 2008, c. 437; 2012, cc. 803, 835.
30-34.14. Amended by Acts 2006, c. 662.
30-34.15. Amended by Acts 2005, c. 633; 2012, c. 434.
30-58.1. Amended by Acts 2006, c. 413; 2013, c. 709.
30-73.2. Amended by Acts 2005, c. 758.
30-73.3. Amended by Acts 2013, c. 140.
30-84. Amended by Acts 2005, c. 633.
30-85. Amended by Acts 2005, c. 322.
30-86. Amended by Acts 2005, c. 322.
30-87. Amended by Acts 2005, c. 322.
30-88. Amended by Acts 2005, c. 322.
30-103. Amended by Acts 2006, cc. 787, 892.
30-105. Amended by Acts 2013, c. 583.
30-110. Amended by Acts 2006, c. 779.
30-111. Amended by Acts 2006, cc. 779, 787, 892; 2007, cc. 620, 627; 2010, cc. 418, 474, 670.
30-116. Amended by Acts 2010, c. 427.
30-126. Amended by Acts 2012, cc. 283, 756.
30-127. Amended by Acts 2006, cc. 787, 892.
30-133. Amended by Acts 2005, c. 494; 2007, c. 577; 2008, c. 637; 2009, cc. 758, 812; 2010, cc. 145, 671.
30-138. Amended by Acts 2011, cc. 798, 871.
30-145. Amended by Acts 2010, c. 413; 2011, c. 848.
30-151. Amended by Acts 2007, c. 614.
30-152. Amended by Acts 2007, c. 614.
30-153. Repealed by Acts 2012, cc. 688, 708.

Section
30-155. Amended by Acts 2006, c. 157.
30-168.1. Amended by Acts 2005, c. 758.
30-170. Amended by Acts 2006, cc. 113, 178; 2009, c. 707; 2011, cc. 501, 607.
30-172. Amended by Acts 2005, c. 758.
30-179. Amended by Acts 2013, c. 694.
30-182. Amended by Acts 2012, cc. 803, 835.
30-192.7. Amended by Acts 2005, c. 731.
30-192.8, 30-192.9. Repealed by Acts 2005, c. 731.
30-192.10 to 30-192.14. Repealed by Acts 2005, c. 731.
30-193. Amended by Acts 2012, cc. 803, 835.
30-198. Amended by Acts 2012, cc. 803, 835.
30-196. Amended by Acts 2006, c. 661.
30-201. Amended by Acts 2008, c. 883.
30-202. Amended by Acts 2008, c. 883.
30-205. Amended by Acts 2006, c. 812; 2008, c. 883.
30-208. Repealed by Acts 2008, c. 883.
30-209. Amended by Acts 2008, c. 883; 2010, c. 388; 2012, Sp. Sess. I, c. 1.
30-212. Amended by Acts 2005, c. 758.
30-225. Repealed by Acts 2006, cc. 389, 476.
30-226 to 30-231. Repealed by Acts 2005, cc. 753, 834.
30-231.01. Amended by Acts 2009, c. 444; 2010, c. 579.
30-231.1. Amended by Acts 2006, c. 518; 2009, c. 444; 2010, c. 579.
30-231.2. Amended by Acts 2006, c. 518; 2009, c. 444; 2010, c. 579.
30-231.3. Amended by Acts 2006, c. 518; 2008, c. 680; 2009, c. 444; 2010, c. 579.
30-231.4. Amended by Acts 2010, c. 579.
30-231.5. Amended by Acts 2010, c. 579.
30-231.8. Amended by Acts 2006, c. 518; 2008, c. 680; 2009, c. 444; 2010, c. 579.
30-232. Amended by Acts 2011, c. 686.
30-233. Amended by Acts 2010, c. 101.
30-236. Amended by Acts 2011, c. 686; 2012, c. 741.
30-239. Repealed by Acts 2012, c. 741.
30-261. Amended by Acts 2008, c. 863.
30-275. Amended by Acts 2009, c. 259.
30-277. Repealed by Acts 2009, c. 542.
30-279. Amended by Acts 2008, c. 712; 2010, c. 450.
30-280. Amended by Acts 2008, c. 712; 2010, c. 450.
30-282. Amended by Acts 2013, c. 332.
30-283. Amended by Acts 2012, c. 239.
30-309. Amended by Acts 2010, cc. 543, 716.
30-310. Amended by Acts 2010, cc. 543, 716; 2013, c. 806.
30-312. Amended by Acts 2010, cc. 543, 716.
30-318. Amended by Acts 2013, c. 667.
30-326. Amended by Acts 2012, cc. 803, 835.
31-1 to 31-59. Repealed by Acts 2012, c. 614.
32.1-5. Amended by Acts 2009, c. 128.

Section
32.1-11. Amended by Acts 2008, cc. 42, 81.
32.1-11.4. Repealed by Acts 2007, c. 4.
32.1-11.5. Amended by Acts 2011, c. 456.
32.1-11.7. Amended by Acts 2013, c. 557.
32.1-16. Amended by Acts 2013, cc. 670, 679.
32.1-19. Amended by Acts 2007, cc. 43, 55, 320, 343, 793, 797.
32.1-23.1. Amended by Acts 2005, c. 715; 2012, cc. 803, 835.
32.1-37. Amended by Acts 2008, cc. 367, 412, 641.
32.1-42.1. Amended by Acts 2007, cc. 699, 783.
32.1-45.1. Amended by Acts 2008, cc. 191, 339; 2009, cc. 96, 478, 552, 813, 840.
32.1-45.2. Amended by Acts 2008, c. 641.
32.1-46. Amended by Acts 2005, cc. 643, 684; 2006, cc. 364, 396, 716; 2007, cc. 858, 922; 2011, c. 125.
32.1-46.01. Amended by Acts 2012, c. 147.
32.1-46.02. Amended by Acts 2010, cc. 179, 252.
32.1-46.1. Amended by Acts 2007, c. 691; 2012, c. 147.
32.1-48.016. Amended by Acts 2005, c. 474.
32.1-48.06. Amended by Acts 2007, cc. 699, 783.
32.1-48.09. Amended by Acts 2007, cc. 699, 783.
32.1-48.010. Amended by Acts 2007, cc. 699, 783.
32.1-48.012. Amended by Acts 2007, cc. 699, 783.
32.1-48.013. Amended by Acts 2007, cc. 699, 783.
32.1-48.014. Amended by Acts 2007, cc. 699, 783.
32.1-48.015. Amended by Acts 2007, cc. 699, 783.
32.1-50. Amended by Acts 2006, cc. 46, 396, 822.
32.1-59. Amended by Acts 2012, cc. 476, 507.
32.1-60. Amended by Acts 2006, c. 396.
32.1-64.1. Amended by Acts 2009, cc. 813, 840; 2012, c. 147.
32.1-64.2. Amended by Acts 2012, c. 147.
32.1-65. Amended by Acts 2005, cc. 717, 721; 2012, cc. 147, 476, 507.
32.1-66. Amended by Acts 2005, cc. 717, 721.
32.1-67. Amended by Acts 2005, cc. 717, 721; 2012, c. 147.
32.1-67.1. Amended by Acts 2005, cc. 717, 721; 2012, c. 147.
32.1-69.1. Amended by Acts 2006, cc. 699, 906.
32.1-69.1:1. Amended by Acts 2012, c. 802.
32.1-69.2. Amended by Acts 2006, cc. 699, 906.
32.1-69.3. Amended by Acts 2008, c. 285.
32.1-73.7. Amended by Acts 2005, cc. 336, 434; 2009, cc. 813, 840.
32.1-89. Amended by Acts 2012, cc. 803, 835.
32.1-102.1. Amended by Acts 2007, c. 502;

Section
2008, c. 664; 2009, cc. 67, 175, 813, 840; 2011, cc. 92, 150; 2012, 476, 492, 507, 803, 835.
32.1-102.1:1. Amended by Acts 2009, c. 175.
32.1-102.2. Amended by Acts 2007, c. 502; 2009, c. 175.
32.1-102.2:1. Amended by Acts 2009, c. 175.
32.1-102.3. Amended by Acts 2008, c. 292; 2009, c. 175.
32.1-102.3:1. Amended by Acts 2008, c. 857; 2009, c. 175; 2011, c. 155.
32.1-102.3:1.1. Amended by Acts 2011, c. 155.
32.1-102.3:2. Amended by Acts 2009, c. 175; 2012, c. 492; 2013, cc. 433, 515.
32.1-102.3:5, 32.1-102.3:6. Repealed by Acts 2012, c. 301.
32.1-102.4. Amended by Acts 2009, cc. 175, 711, 796, 877; 2013, c. 460.
32.1-102.6. Amended by Acts 2005, c. 404; 2009, c. 175; 2010, c. 646.
32.1-102.10. Amended by Acts 2009, c. 175.
32.1-102.12. Repealed by Acts 2012, c. 123.
32.1-102.13. Repealed by Acts 2007, c. 5.
32.1-111.1. Amended by Acts 2008, c. 118.
32.1-111.2. Amended by Acts 2005, c. 778.
32.1-111.3. Amended by Acts 2005, cc. 632, 686; 2006, c. 412; 2007, c. 15; 2008, cc. 66, 567; 2009, cc. 222, 269; 2012, c. 418.
32.1-111.4. Amended by Acts 2005, c. 921; 2006, c. 194.
32.1-111.5. Amended by Acts 2008, c. 660; 2011, c. 497; 2013, cc. 72, 176.
32.1-111.8. Amended by Acts 2008, c. 660.
32.1-111.9. Amended by Acts 2008, c. 61; 2011, c. 90.
32.1-111.10. Amended by Acts 2005, cc. 112, 506; 2012, c. 502.
32.1-111.11. Amended by Acts 2009, cc. 222, 269; 2012, c. 418.
32.1-111.13. Amended by Acts 2013, c. 517.
32.1-111.14. Amended by Acts 2005, c. 182.
32.1-116.1. Amended by Acts 2006, c. 412; 2007, c. 13; 2008, c. 563; 2012, cc. 402, 803, 835.
32.1-116.3. Amended by Acts 2008, c. 118; 2009, cc. 478, 552.
32.1-122.06. Amended by Acts 2009, c. 175.
32.1-122.07. Amended by Acts 2006, c. 378.
32.1-122.5. Amended by Acts 2009, cc. 813, 840.
32.1-122.6:1. Amended by Acts 2013, c. 255.
32.1-122.7. Amended by Acts 2010, cc. 187, 488.
32.1-122.20. Amended by Acts 2011, c. 37.
32.1-122.21. Repealed by Acts 2010, c. 488.
32.1-122.22. Repealed by Acts 2011, c. 37.
32.1-123. Amended by Acts 2011, c. 433.
32.1-124. Amended by Acts 2009, cc. 813, 840.
32.1-125.1. Amended by Acts 2009, cc. 813, 840.

Section
32.1-125.3. Amended by Acts 2006, c. 378.
32.1-126.01. Amended by Acts 2006, cc. 701, 744, 764; 2012, c. 383.
32.1-127. Amended by Acts 2007, cc. 119, 164, 516; 2011, cc. 406, 412, 670; 2013, c. 320.
32.1-127.01. Amended by Acts 2012, cc. 476, 507.
32.1-127.1:01. Amended by Acts 2012, c. 336.
32.1-127.1:03. Amended by Acts 2005, cc. 39, 101, 642, 697; 2006, c. 433; 2007, c. 497; 2008, cc. 315, 782, 850, 870; 2009, cc. 606, 651, 813, 840; 2010, cc. 185, 340, 406, 456, 524, 778, 825; 2011, cc. 499, 668, 798, 812, 844, 871; 2012, cc. 386, 402, 479.
32.1-127.1:04. Amended by Acts 2009, cc. 813, 840; 2012, cc. 803, 835.
32.1-134.01. Amended by Acts 2005, c. 518.
32.1-135.2. Amended by Acts 2009, cc. 813, 840; 2013, cc. 670, 679.
32.1-137.6. Amended by Acts 2011, c. 788.
32.1-137.7. Amended by Acts 2011, c. 788.
32.1-137.9. Amended by Acts 2011, c. 788.
32.1-137.13. Amended by Acts 2010, c. 395; 2011, c. 788.
32.1-137.14. Amended by Acts 2010, c. 395; 2011, c. 788.
32.1-137.15. Amended by Acts 2010, c. 395; 2011, c. 788.
32.1-137.16. Amended by Acts 2011, c. 788.
32.1-138. Amended by Acts 2006, c. 396; 2007, cc. 120, 163; 2010, c. 57.
32.1-162.1. Amended by Acts 2007, c. 397.
32.1-162.2. Amended by Acts 2010, c. 790.
32.1-162.3. Amended by Acts 2007, c. 397; 2010, c. 790.
32.1-162.4. Amended by Acts 2010, c. 790.
32.1-162.5. Amended by Acts 2007, c. 397.
32.1-162.8. Amended by Acts 2010, c. 790.
32.1-162.9. Amended by Acts 2012, c. 139; 2013, cc. 184, 505.
32.1-162.9:1. Amended by Acts 2006, cc. 701, 744, 764; 2010, cc. 415, 790; 2012, c. 383.
32.1-162.10. Amended by Acts 2010, c. 790.
32.1-162.11. Amended by Acts 2013, c. 184.
32.1-162.13. Amended by Acts 2010, c. 790.
32.1-162.15. Amended by Acts 2010, c. 790.
32.1-162.19. Amended by Acts 2007, c. 413.
32.1-163. Amended by Acts 2007, cc. 892, 924; 2009, c. 829.
32.1-163.6. Amended by Acts 2009, c. 97, 220, 296.
32.1-164. Amended by Acts 2007, cc. 514, 892, 924; 2009, 695, 747.
32.1-164.1. Amended by Acts 2012, c. 184.
32.1-164.1:01. Amended by Acts 2007, cc. 448, 515.
32.1-164.1:1. Amended by Acts 2005, c. 469; 2011, c. 394.

Section
32.1-164.2 to 32.1-164.7. Repealed by Acts 2007, cc. 881, 929.
32.1-164.5. Amended by Acts 2005, cc. 197, 396, 459, 460, 593; 2006, c. 353; 2007, cc. 390, 927.
32.1-166.6. Amended by Acts 2009, c. 829.
32.1-167. Amended by Acts 2007, cc. 648, 774.
32.1-170. Amended by Acts 2011, cc. 804, 843.
32.1-174.1. Amended by Acts 2011, c. 502.
32.1-176.3. Amended by Acts 2009, c. 59.
32.1-176.4. Amended by Acts 2009, cc. 105, 710.
32.1-176.5. Amended by Acts 2009, c. 59.
32.1-176.5:2. Amended by Acts 2008, c. 62.
32.1-212. Amended by Acts 2005, c. 391.
32.1-215. Amended by Acts 2005, c. 391.
32.1-225. Amended by Acts 2005, c. 391.
32.1-227. Amended by Acts 2008, cc. 41, 466.
32.1-228. Amended by Acts 2008, cc. 41, 466.
32.1-229. Amended by Acts 2008, cc. 41, 466; 2012, cc. 6, 125; 2013. c. 282.
32.1-229.01. Amended by Acts 2005, c. 839; 2008, cc. 41, 466.
32.1-229.1. Amended by Acts 2008, cc. 41, 466.
32.1-229.2. Amended by Acts 2008, cc. 41, 466.
32.1-232.1. Amended by Acts 2008, cc. 41, 466.
32.1-233. Amended by Acts 2008, cc. 41, 466.
32.1-235. Amended by Acts 2008, cc. 41, 466.
32.1-238. Amended by Acts 2008, cc. 41, 466.
32.1-245. Amended by Acts 2008, c. 671.
32.1-252. Amended by Acts 2013, c. 534.
32.1-261. Amended by Acts 2011, cc. 486, 784.
32.1-263. Amended by Acts 2008, cc. 137; 2011, c. 613; 2012, c. 213; 2013, c. 799.
32.1-267. Amended by Acts 2005, c. 679.
32.1-268. Amended by Acts 2005, c. 679.
32.1-270. Amended by Acts 2013, c. 534.
32.1-271. Amended by Acts 2005, c. 60; 2009, c. 505; 2011, c. 109; 2012, cc. 16, 356.
32.1-272. Amended by Acts 2005, c. 448; 2013, c. 534.
32.1-273. Amended by Acts 2011, cc. 94, 148; 2013, c. 534.
32.1-276. Amended by Acts 2013, c. 534.
32.1-276.2. Amended by Acts 2010, c. 416; 2012, cc. 693, 709.
32.1-276.3. Amended by Acts 2009, cc. 813, 840.
32.1-276.4. Amended by Acts 2006, c. 426; 2010, c. 416; 2012, cc. 693. 709.
32.1-276.5. Amended by Acts 2006, c. 426; 2009, c. 175; 2013, c. 515.
32.1-276.6. Amended by Acts 2009, c. 652.
32.1-276.8. Amended by Acts 2009, cc. 813, 840.
32.1-283. Amended by Acts 2007, cc. 19, 868; 2008, cc. 287, 433; 2009, cc. 813, 840; 2011, cc. 798, 871; 2012, cc. 476, 507.
32.1-283.1. Amended by Acts 2007, c. 411; 2009, cc. 813, 840.

Section
32.1-283.4. Amended by Acts 2007, c. 868.
32.1-283.5. Amended by Acts 2009, cc. 813, 840; 2012, cc. 803, 835.
32.1-286. Amended by Acts 2013, c. 370.
32.1-287. Repealed by Acts 2007, cc. 92, 907.
32.1-288. Amended by Acts 2005, c. 905; 2011, cc. 567, 569; 2013, c. 373.
32.1-289. Repealed by Acts 2007, cc. 92, 907.
32.1-289.1. Repealed by Acts 2007, c. 92.
32.1-290. Repealed by Acts 2007, cc. 92, 907.
32.1-290.1. Repealed by Acts 2008, c. 82.
32.1-291. Repealed by Acts 2007, cc. 92, 907.
32.1-291.21. Amended by Acts 2008, c. 82.
32.1-292.1. Repealed by Acts 2007, cc. 92, 907.
32.1-292.2. Amended by Acts 2006, c. 166; 2007, c. 92, 907; 2008, c. 82; 2009, c. 834; 2010, cc. 25, 55.
32.1-293. Repealed by Acts 2007, cc. 92, 907.
32.1-295. Repealed by Acts 2007, cc. 92, 907.
32.1-297.1. Amended by Acts 2006, c. 166; 2009, c. 834; 2012, c. 692.
32.1-310. Amended by Acts 2011, cc. 110, 175.
32.1-312. Amended by Acts 2007, c. 569; 2010, c. 305.
32.1-313. Amended by Acts 2007, c. 569.
32.1-314. Amended by Acts 2010, c. 305; 2011, cc. 444, 479.
32.1-315. Amended by Acts 2010, c. 305.
32.1-316. Amended by Acts 2010, c. 305.
32.1-317. Amended by Acts 2010, c. 305.
32.1-320. Amended by Acts 2011, cc. 110, 175; 2012, c. 320; 2013, c. 538.
32.1-321.3. Amended by Acts 2010, c. 305.
32.1-321.4. Amended by Acts 2010, c. 305.
32.1-263. Amended by Acts 2013, c. 799.
32.1-323.2. Amended by Acts 2012, cc. 476, 507.
32.1-324. Amended by Acts 2012, c. 137.
32.1-325. Amended by Acts 2006, cc. 396, 425; 2007, cc. 536, 873, 916; 2009, cc. 813, 840; 2010, cc. 305, 785, 790; 2012, cc. 367, 646, 689.
32.1-325.1. Amended by Acts 2009, c. 578.
32.1-325.1:1. Amended by Acts 2005, c. 839.
32.1-325.2. Amended by Acts 2007, c. 535; 2009, cc. 813, 840.
32.1-330.3. Amended by Acts 2012, cc. 803, 835.
32.1-331.13. Amended by Acts 2012, cc. 476, 507.
32.1-332 to 32.1-342. Repealed by Acts 2009, c. 578.
32.1-351. Amended by Acts 2005, c. 584; 2006, c. 428; 2007, c. 407; 2012, cc. 646, 689.
32.1-351.1. Amended by Acts 2009, c. 578.
32.1-351.2. Amended by Acts 2009, cc. 813, 840.
32.1-352. Amended by Acts 2011, c. 850; 2013, cc. 136, 210.

Section
32.1-353.1. Amended by Acts 2007, c. 474.
32.1-353.2. Amended by Acts 2007, c. 474.
32.1-353.3. Amended by Acts 2007, c. 474.
32.1-353.4, 32.1-353.5. Repealed by Acts 2007, c. 474.
32.1-354. Amended by Acts 2007, c. 345; 2009, cc. 424, 554.
32.1-355. Amended by Acts 2009, cc. 424, 554.
32.1-356. Amended by Acts 2007, c. 345; 2009, cc. 424, 554.
32.1-357. Amended by Acts 2005, c. 19.
32.1-359. Amended by Acts 2007, c. 345; 2009, cc. 424, 554.
32.1-360. Amended by Acts 2007, c. 345; 2009, cc. 424, 554.
32.1-361. Amended by Acts 2009, cc. 424, 554.
32.1-361.1. Amended by Acts 2008, c. 184; 2009, cc. 424, 554.
32.1-364. Amended by Acts 2005, c. 19.
32.1-366. Amended by Acts 2005, cc. 899, 901.
33.1-1. Amended by Acts 2011, cc. 36, 152; 2013, cc. 762, 794.
33.1-3. Amended by Acts 2007, c. 896.
33.1-7. Amended by Acts 2013, cc. 585, 646.
33.1-8. Amended by Acts 2011, cc. 36, 152.
33.1-11. Amended by Acts 2013, cc. 585, 646.
33.1-12. Amended by Acts 2005, cc. 839, 919; 2006, cc. 197, 417, 833; 2007, c. 337; 2008, Sp. Sess. II, c. 5; 2009, cc. 670, 690; 2011, cc. 104, 164; 2012, cc. 729, 733; 2013, cc. 388, 569, 585, 646, 741.
33.1-13. Amended by Acts 2007, cc. 863, 896, 928.
33.1-13.01, 33.1-13.02. Repealed by Acts 2011, cc. 36, 152.
33.1-19. Amended by Acts 2010, cc. 17, 51.
33.1-19.1. Amended by Acts 2007, c. 896.
33.1-21. Repealed by Acts 2011, cc. 104, 164.
33.1-23. Amended by Acts 2011, cc. 104, 164.
33.1-23.03. Amended by Acts 2007, c. 896; 2009, cc. 670, 690, 864, 871; 2011, cc. 104, 164.
33.1-23.03:01. Amended by Acts 2011, c. 554.
33.1-23.05. Amended by Acts 2011, cc. 830, 868.
33.1-23.03:1. Amended by Acts 2006, c. 922; 2008, cc. 602, 838; 2009, c. 471.
33.1-23.03:2. Amended by Acts 2012, cc. 779, 817.
33.1-23.03:7. Amended by Acts 2013, cc. 585, 646.
33.1-23.03:8. Amended by Acts 2007, c. 896; 2013, c. 766.
33.1-23.05. Amended by Acts 2008, c. 608; 2011, cc. 830, 868; 2012, cc. 729, 733.
33.1-23.1. Amended by Acts 2006, c. 937; 2007, c. 305; 2012, cc. 729, 733.
33.1-23.2. Amended by Acts 2007, cc. 146, 178.

Section
33.1-23.3. Amended by Acts 2009, cc. 52, 693; 2011, c. 400.
33.1-23.4. Amended by Acts 2007, c. 153.
33.1-23.4:01. Amended by Acts 2011, cc. 830, 868; 2013, c. 639.
33.1-23.5:1. Amended by Acts 2013, c. 766; 2013, Sp. Sess. I , c. 1.
33.1-23.5:2. Repealed by Acts 2013, c. 121.
33.1-23.7. Amended by Acts 2012, cc. 779, 817.
33.1-34. Amended by Acts 2011, cc. 36, 152.
33.1-35. Amended by Acts 2009, c. 476; 2011, cc. 36, 152.
33.1-41.1. Amended by Acts 2007, c. 813; 2011, cc. 434, 493.
33.1-44. Amended by Acts 2007, c. 813.
33.1-46.2. Amended by Acts 2006, cc. 600, 873, 908; 2007, c. 317; 2008, c. 511; 2009, c. 676; 2010, cc. 111, 133, 390, 485; 2011, cc. 735, 881, 889; 2012, cc. 681, 743.
33.1-49.1. Amended by Acts 2012, cc. 729, 733.
33.1-56.1. Amended by Acts 2008, cc. 167, 280; 2013, c. 195.
33.1-56.3. Amended by Acts 2008, cc. 167, 280; 2013, cc. 85, 101.
33.1-56.4. Amended by Acts 2006, c. 859.
33.1-61. Amended by Acts 2013, cc. 585, 646.
33.1-69. Amended by Acts 2009, Sp. Sess. II, c. 3.
33.1-70.01. Amended by Acts 2005, c. 645; 2011, cc. 434, 493.
33.1-70.1. Amended by Acts 2006, c. 546; 2008, c. 195; 2011, c. 400; 2013, cc. 756, 793.
33.1-70.2. Amended by Acts 2011, c. 400.
33.1-70.3. Amended by Acts 2010, c. 401.
33.1-72.1. Amended by Acts 2006, c. 827; 2009, c. 635.
33.1-75.1. Repealed by Acts 2006, c. 827.
33.1-75.3. Amended by Acts 2005, c. 342; 2006, cc. 115, 827.
33.1-84.1. Amended by Acts 2009, c. 476.
33.1-89. Amended by Acts 2013, c. 764.
33.1-94. Amended by Acts 2007, c. 755; 2011, c. 60.
33.1-120. Amended by Acts 2013, c. 764.
33.1-128. Amended by Acts 2010, cc. 20, 53.
33.1-148. Amended by Acts 2011, cc. 36, 152.
33.1-149. Amended by Acts 2011, cc. 36, 152.
33.1-150. Amended by Acts 2011, cc. 36, 152.
33.1-152.1. Amended by Acts 2011, c. 129.
33.1-154. Amended by Acts 2011, cc. 36, 152.
33.1-155. Amended by Acts 2011, cc. 36, 152.
33.1-183.1. Amended by Acts 2013, cc. 585, 646.
33.1-185. Amended by Acts 2010, cc. 20, 50.
33.1-190. Amended by Acts 2006, cc. 434, 480; 2008, c. 472; 2010, cc. 22, 50.
33.1-195, 33.1-196. Amended by Acts 2013, cc. 585, 646.

Section
33.1-198. Amended by Acts 2005, c. 645; 2007, cc. 863, 928.
33.1-199. Amended by Acts 2007, cc. 863, 928.
33.1-201. Amended by Acts 2013, cc. 585, 646.
33.1-207, 33.1-208. Amended by Acts 2013, cc. 585, 646.
33.1-210.2. Amended by Acts 2006, c. 548; 2012, c. 179.
33.1-220. Repealed by Acts 2011, c. 428.
33.1-221. Amended by Acts 2006, c. 147; 2013, c. 482.
33.1-221.1:1. Amended by Acts 2011, c. 64; 2012, c. 19.
33.1-221.1:1.1. Amended by Acts 2005, c. 323; 2009, c. 73; 2010, c. 869; 2011, cc. 86, 405, 594, 639, 681.
33.1-221.1:3. Amended by Acts 2005, c. 621; 2013, c. 766.
33.1-221:4. Repealed by Acts 2011, c. 430.
33.1-221:6. Repealed by Acts 2011, c. 430.
33.1-223. Amended by Acts 2005, cc. 25, 453; 2013, c. 222.
33.1-223.2:1. Amended by Acts 2007, c. 896; 2011, c. 253.
33.1-223.2:17. Amended by Acts 2011, c. 667.
33.1-223.2:21. Amended by Acts 2011, cc. 476, 790; 2012, c. 171; 2013, c. 120.
33.1-223.2:26. Amended by Acts 2012, c. 848.
33.1-223.4. Amended by Acts 2010, c. 134.
33.1-225. Amended by Acts 2007, c. 813.
33.1-229. Amended by Acts 2013, cc. 585, 646.
33.1-234. Amended by Acts 2005, c. 716.
33.1-250. Repealed by Acts 2009, c. 65.
33.1-252. Amended by Acts 2005, c. 298; 2006, c. 859.
33.1-268. Amended by Acts 2007, c. 896; 2011, cc. 830, 868.
33.1-269. Amended by Acts 2007, c. 896; 2011, cc. 830, 868; 2013, c. 639.
33.1-276. Amended by Acts 2011, cc. 830, 868.
33.1-277. Amended by Acts 2007, c. 896; 2011, cc. 830, 868.
33.1-280. Amended by Acts 2011, cc. 830, 868.
33.1-287. Amended by Acts 2009, c. 471.
33.1-288. Amended by Acts 2006, c. 186; 2009, c. 471.
33.1-293. Amended by Acts 2013, cc. 585, 646.
33.1-296 to 33.1-318. Repealed by Acts 2011, c. 600.
33.1-319. Repealed by Acts 2006, c. 186.
33.1-320. Repealed by Acts 2009, c. 471.
33.1-320.2. Amended by Acts 2005, c. 839 (Compacts volume).
33.1-330. Amended by Acts 2011, cc. 434, 493.
33.1-342. Amended by Acts 2013, cc. 585, 646.
33.1-343. Amended by Acts 2013, cc. 585, 646.
33.1-346. Amended by Acts 2013, c. 156.
33.1-346.1. Repealed by Acts 2013, c. 156.
33.1-348. Amended by Acts 2005, c. 291; 2013, c. 127.

Section
33.1-351. Amended by Acts 2012, c. 145; 2013, c. 127.
33.1-360. Amended by Acts 2012, c. 145.
33.1-361. Amended by Acts 2012, c. 145.
33.1-362. Amended by Acts 2012, c. 145.
33.1-370. Amended by Acts 2013, cc. 585, 646.
33.1-371.1. Amended by Acts 2006, cc. 512, 543; 2012, cc. 760, 818; 2013, c. 737.
33.1-373. Amended by Acts 2012, c. 739; 2013, c. 457.
33.1-375. Amended by Acts 2012, cc. 760, 818.
33.1-375.1. Amended by Acts 2010, cc. 497, 777, 832; 2012, c. 739.
33.1-377. Repealed by Acts 2012, cc. 760, 818.
33.1-382 to 33.1-385. Repealed by Acts 2006, c. 81.
33.1-386. Amended by Acts 2007, c. 162.
33.1-391.3. Amended by Acts 2009, c. 564; 2013, c. 583.
33.1-391.3:1. Repealed by Acts 2011, cc. 86, 594, 681.
33.1-391.4. Amended by Acts 2013, c. 211.
33.1-391.5. Amended by Acts 2007, c. 435; 2009, c. 146; 2013, c. 211.
33.1-391.6 to 33.1-391.15. Repealed by Acts 2009, cc. 864, 871.
33.1-464. Repealed by Acts 2009, c. 638.
33.1-465. Repealed by Acts 2008, c. 481.
34-4. Amended by Acts 2009, c. 387.
34-4.1. Amended by Acts 2009, c. 388.
34-5. Amended by Acts 2010, c. 550.
34-6. Amended by Acts 2008, c. 224.
34-14. Amended by Acts 2010, c. 186.
34-17. Amended by Acts 2005, c. 367.
34-26. Amended by Acts 2011, cc. 761, 835.
34-29. Amended by Acts 2005, c. 286.
34-32. Amended by Acts 2005, c. 839.
34-34. Amended by Acts 2005, c. 284; 2007, c. 302.
35.1-14. Amended by Acts 2007, cc. 873, 916.
35.1-14.2. Amended by Acts 2007, cc. 404, 545.
35.1-25. Amended by Acts 2010, cc. 86, 594; 2013, cc. 188, 317, 512.
35.1-26. Amended by Acts 2011, c. 465; 2013, c. 188, 317, 512.
36-2. Amended by Acts 2006, c. 784.
36-3. Amended by Acts 2006, c. 784; 2009, cc. 181, 551.
36-4. Amended by Acts 2006, c. 784; 2009, c. 78.
36-4.1. Amended by Acts 2006, c. 784; 2009, c. 78.
36-11. Amended by Acts 2007, c. 247; 2010, c. 311.
36-19. Amended by Acts 2006, c. 784.
36-19.2. Amended by Acts 2006, c. 784; 2007, c. 342.
36-27. Amended by Acts 2006, cc. 586, 784.
36-27.2. Amended by Acts 2007, c. 786.

Section
36-39. Repealed by Acts 2006, c. 784.
36-48. Amended by Acts 2006, c. 784.
36-48.1. Amended by Acts 2006, c. 784.
36-49. Amended by Acts 2006, c. 784.
36-49.1. Amended by Acts 2006, c. 784.
36-49.1:1. Amended by Acts 2006, c. 784; 2007, c. 763; 2009, cc. 181, 551.
36-50. Amended by Acts 2006, c. 784.
36-50.1. Amended by Acts 2006, c. 784.
36-51. Amended by Acts 2006, c. 784.
36-51.1. Amended by Acts 2006, c. 784.
36-52. Amended by Acts 2006, c. 784.
36-52.1. Amended by Acts 2006, c. 784.
36-52.3. Amended by Acts 2006, c. 784.
36-53. Amended by Acts 2006, c. 784.
36-55.25. Amended by Acts 2011, c. 690.
36-55.26. Amended by Acts 2011, c. 690.
36-55.30. Amended by Acts 2011, c. 690.
36-55.30:2. Amended by Acts 2006, c. 784.
36-55.33:1. Amended by Acts 2010, c. 794.
36-55.35. Amended by Acts 2011, cc. 218, 224.
36-55.63. Amended by Acts 2007, c. 778; 2010, cc. 520, 608.
36-55.64. Amended by Acts 2013, cc. 756, 793.
36-56 to 36-69. Repealed by Acts 2012, c. 437.
36-73. Amended by Acts 2010, c. 77.
36-82.1. Amended by Acts 2010, c. 77.
36-85.16. Amended by Acts 2005, c. 430; 2008, c. 350.
36-85.18. Amended by Acts 2008, c. 350.
36-85.20. Amended by Acts 2008, c. 350.
36-85.28. Amended by Acts 2009, cc. 141, 579; 2010, c. 167.
36-55.30. Amended by Acts 2012, c. 238.
36-85.31. Amended by Acts 2009, cc. 141, 579.
36-85.32. Amended by Acts 2009, cc. 141, 579.
36-96.2. Amended by Acts 2006, c. 693.
36-96.6. Amended by Acts 2012, cc. 476, 507.
36-96.20. Amended by Acts 2010, c. 794.
36-97. Amended by Acts 2005, c. 341.
36-98. Amended by Acts 2006, c. 903.
36-98.1. Amended by Acts 2005, cc. 341, 933, 945; 2010, c. 105; 2013, cc. 585, 646.
36-98.3. Amended by Acts 2011, c. 546.
36-99.5. Amended by Acts 2011, c. 766.
36-100. Amended by Acts 2006, c. 719; 2010, c. 65.
36-105. Amended by Acts 2006, c. 424; 2007, c. 291; 2009, cc. 181, 184, 551, 586; 2010, c. 63; 2012, cc. 494, 607.
36-105.1:1. Amended by Acts 2009, c. 663.
36-106. Amended by Acts 2006, c. 746; 2007, cc. 290, 760; 2010, cc. 87, 94; 2011, cc. 118, 143; 2013, c. 529.
36-114. Amended by Acts 2010, c. 63.
36-132.1. Amended by Acts 2010, c. 410.
36-135. Amended by Acts 2012, c. 747.
36-137. Amended by Acts 2008, c. 445; 2010, c. 66; 2013, c. 754.

Section
36-139. Amended by Acts 2006, c. 721; 2007, cc. 647, 741; 2008, c. 445; 2013, c. 754.
36-139.1. Amended by Acts 2009, c. 612.
36-139.2 to 36-139.4. Repealed by Acts 2007, cc. 647, 741.
36-139.6. Amended by Acts 2013, c. 482.
36-141 to 36-145. Amended by Acts 2013, c. 754.
36-147 to 36-150. Amended by Acts 2013, c. 754.
36-156.1. Amended by Acts 2012, c. 368.
37.1-1 to 37.1-260. Repealed by Acts 2005, c. 716.
37.2-100. Amended by Acts 2009, cc. 813, 840; 2012, cc. 476, 507.
37.2-200. Amended by Acts 2009, cc. 813, 840; 2012, cc. 476, 507.
37.2-203. Amended by Acts 2012, cc. 476, 507.
37.2-204. Amended by Acts 2005, c. 201; 2012, cc. 476, 507.
37.2-300. Amended by Acts 2009, cc. 813, 840.
37.2-303. Amended by Acts 2012, cc. 476, 507.
37.2-304. Amended by Acts 2008, cc. 584, 754; 2011, c. 473; 2012, cc. 476, 507; 2012, c. 847; 2013, c. 571.
37.2-305, 37.2-306. Amended by Acts 2012, cc. 476, 507.
37.2-308. Amended by Acts 2008, c. 277.
37.2-311. Amended by Acts 2008, c. 83.
37.2-312. Amended by Acts 2012, cc. 476, 507.
37.2-312.1. Amended by Acts 2012, cc. 803, 835.
37.2-314. Amended by Acts 2012, cc. 383, 476, 507.
37.2-315. Amended by Acts 2012, cc. 476, 507.
37.2-316. Amended by Acts 2009, cc. 813, 840; 2012, cc. 476, 507.
37.2-317. Amended by Acts 2009, cc. 813, 840.
37.2-318. Amended by Acts 2009, cc. 813, 840; 2012, cc. 476, 507.
37.2-319. Amended by Acts 2009, cc. 813, 840; 2011, cc. 724, 729; 2012, cc. 476, 507.
37.2-400. Amended by Acts 2009, cc. 111, 517; 2012, cc. 476, 507.
37.2-401. Amended by Acts 2012, cc. 476, 507.
37.2-403. Amended by Acts 2005, cc. 718, 725.
37.2-406. Amended by Acts 2007, c. 513; 2012, cc. 476, 507.
37.2-408. Amended by Acts 2005, cc. 358, 363, 471, 485; 2006, c. 781; 2008, c. 873; 2012, cc. 476, 507.
37.2-408.1. Amended by Acts 2012, cc. 383, 476, 507.
37.2-409. Amended by Acts 2012, cc. 476, 507.
37.2-411. Amended by Acts 2012, cc. 476, 507.
37.2-416. Amended by Acts 2008, cc. 383, 407; 2011, c. 657; 2012, cc. 476, 507.
37.2-418. Amended by Acts 2005, cc. 363, 485; 2006, c. 168.

Section
37.2-419. Amended by Acts 2012, cc. 476, 507.
37.2-420. Amended by Acts 2012, cc. 476, 507.
37.2-423. Amended by Acts 2009, cc. 813, 840.
37.2-423 to 37.2-425. Repealed by Acts 2011, cc. 798, 871.
37.2-427, 37.2-428. Amended by Acts 2012, cc. 476, 507.
37.2-430. Amended by Acts 2012, cc. 476, 507.
37.2-432 to 37.2-440. Repealed by Acts 2005, cc. 43, 111.
37.2-500. Amended by Acts 2010, c. 28; 2012, cc. 476, 507.
37.2-501. Amended by Acts 2012, cc. 476, 507.
37.2-502. Amended by Acts 2007, c. 570; 2010, c. 71.
37.2-504. Amended by Acts 2005, c. 75; 2012, cc. 476, 507, 803, 805, 835, 836.
37.2-505. Amended by Acts 2012, cc. 180, 476, 507, 656, 803, 813, 835.
37.2-506. Amended by Acts 2008, cc. 383, 407; 2011, c. 657; 2012, cc. 476, 507.
37.2-508. Amended by Acts 2005, c. 75; 2012, cc. 476, 507, 805, 836.
37.2-509. Amended by Acts 2012, cc. 476, 507.
37.2-511, 37.2-512. Amended by Acts 2012, cc. 476, 507.
37.2-600. Amended by Acts 2012, cc. 476, 507.
37.2-601. Amended by Acts 2010, c. 28; 2012, cc. 476, 507.
37.2-602. Amended by Acts 2012, cc. 476, 507.
37.2-603. Amended by Acts 2009, c. 400.
37.2-605. Amended by Acts 2012, cc. 476, 507, 803, 835.
37.2-608. Amended by Acts 2005, c. 75; 2012, cc. 476, 507.
37.2-609. Amended by Acts 2012, cc. 476, 507.
37.2-612, 37.2-613. Amended by Acts 2012, cc. 476, 507.
37.2-615. Amended by Acts 2012, cc. 476, 507.
37.2-700 to 37.2-706. Amended by Acts 2012, cc. 476, 507.
37.2-709. Amended by Acts 2012, cc. 476, 507, 847; 2013, c. 571.
37.2-710 to 37.2-712. Amended by Acts 2012, cc. 476, 507.
37.2-713. Amended by Acts 2010, cc. 386, 629.
37.2-714 to 37.2-715. Amended by Acts 2012, cc. 476, 507.
37.2-716. Amended by Acts 2009, cc. 813, 840.
37.2-717. Amended by Acts 2012, cc. 476, 507.
37.2-718. Amended by Acts 2005, c. 935.
37.2-719 to 37.2-721. Amended by Acts 2012, cc. 476, 507.
37.2-800. Amended by Acts 2008, cc. 850, 870.
37.2-801. Amended by Acts 2009, cc. 211, 268, 708.
37.2-802. Amended by Acts 2012, cc. 476, 507.
37.2-803. Amended by Acts 2007, cc. 500, 897; 2009, c. 608; 2010, cc. 340, 406.
37.2-804. Amended by Acts 2007, cc. 500, 897; 2009, c. 266; 2010, cc. 340, 406.

Section
37.2-804.1. Amended by Acts 2005, c. 51.
37.2-804.2. Amended by Acts 2009, cc. 606, 651.
37.2-805. Amended by Acts 2012, c. 300; 2013, c. 179.
37.2-806. Amended by Acts 2012, cc. 476, 507.
37.2-808. Amended by Acts 2007, c. 7; 2008, cc. 202, 551, 691, 775, 779, 782, 784, 793, 850, 870; 2009, cc. 21, 112, 383, 455, 555, 607, 697, 838; 2010, cc. 778, 825; 2011, c. 249; 2013, c. 371.
37.2-809. Amended by Acts 2007, c. 526; 2008, cc. 331, 551, 691, 728, 779, 782, 793, 828, 850, 870; 2009, cc. 455, 555; 2010, cc. 340, 406, 778, 825; 2013, cc. 87, 321.
37.2-810. Amended by Acts 2007, c. 7; 2009, cc. 112, 697; 2013, c. 371.
37.2-811. Amended by Acts 2010, cc. 340, 406.
37.2-812. Repealed by Acts 2010, cc. 778, 825.
37.2-813. Amended by Acts 2008, cc. 779, 850, 870; 2010, cc. 778, 825.
37.2-814. Amended by Acts 2008, cc. 751, 788, 850, 870; 2009, c. 647.
37.2-815. Amended by Acts 2007, c. 400; 2008, cc. 779, 850, 870; 2009, cc. 21, 132, 838; 2010, cc. 330, 461.
37.2-816. Amended by Acts 2008, cc. 779, 850, 870; 2009, cc. 21, 838.
37.2-817. Amended by Acts 2005, c. 458; 2008, cc. 779, 780, 782, 793, 850, 870; 2009, cc. 21, 838; 2010, cc. 330, 461; 2012, cc. 300, 451, 501; 2013, c. 179.
37.2-817.1. Amended by Acts 2010, cc. 330, 461.
37.2-817.2. Amended by Acts 2009, cc. 112, 697; 2010, cc. 330, 461.
37.2-817.3. Amended by Acts 2010, cc. 330, 461.
37.2-817.4. Amended by Acts 2010, cc. 330, 461.
37.2-818. Amended by Acts 2008, cc. 806, 850, 870.
37.2-819. Amended by Acts 2008, cc. 751, 788; 2009, cc. 21, 838.
37.2-821. Amended by Acts 2006, c. 486; 2008, cc. 850, 870; 2010, cc. 544, 591.
37.2-829. Amended by Acts 2009, cc. 112, 697.
37.2-830. Repealed by Acts 2009, cc. 112, 697.
37.2-837. Amended by Acts 2008, c. 263; 2012, cc. 476, 507.
37.2-838 to 37.2-840. Amended by Acts 2012, cc. 476, 507.
37.2-843. Amended by Acts 2012, cc. 476, 507.
37.2-900. Amended by Acts 2005, c. 914; 2006, cc. 863, 914; 2007, c. 876; 2009, cc. 740, 813, 840.
37.2-900.1. Amended by Acts 2009, cc. 813, 840.

Section
37.2-901. Amended by Acts 2005, c. 914; 2007, c. 876; 2009, c. 740; 2011, cc. 446, 448.
37.2-902. Amended by Acts 2007, c. 876; 2009, c. 740; 2011, c. 42.
37.2-903. Amended by Acts 2005, c. 914; 2006, cc. 863, 914; 2007, c. 876; 2009, c. 740; 2010, c. 389; 2012, cc. 668, 800.
37.2-904. Amended by Acts 2005, c. 914; 2006, cc. 863, 914; 2007, c. 876; 2009, c. 740; 2011, c. 42; 2012, cc. 668, 800.
37.2-905. Amended by Acts 2006, cc. 863, 914; 2007, c. 876; 2009, c. 740.
37.2-905.1. Amended by Acts 2009, c. 740.
37.2-905.2. Amended by Acts 2009, c. 740.
37.2-906. Amended by Acts 2006, cc. 863, 914; 2007, c. 876; 2009, c. 740; 2011, cc. 446, 448; 2012, cc. 121, 246.
37.2-907. Amended by Acts 2006, cc. 863, 914; 2007, c. 876; 2009, c. 740; 2011, cc. 42, 446, 448.
37.2-908. Amended by Acts 2005, c. 914; 2006, cc. 863, 914; 2007, c. 876; 2009, c. 740.
37.2-909. Amended by Acts 2005, c. 914; 2007, c. 876; 2009, cc. 740, 813, 840.
37.2-910. Amended by Acts 2006, cc. 698, 730, 863, 914; 2007, c. 876; 2011, cc. 42, 446, 448; 2013, c. 258.
37.2-911. Amended by Acts 2009, c. 740.
37.2-912. Amended by Acts 2005, c. 914; 2006, cc. 698, 730, 863, 914; 2007, c. 876; 2009, cc. 740, 813, 840.
37.2-913. Amended by Acts 2005, c. 51; 2009, c. 740; 2011, c. 42.
37.2-914. Amended by Acts 2009, c. 740.
37.2-915. Amended by Acts 2012, cc. 121, 246.
37.2-918. Amended by Acts 2009, c. 740.
37.2-919. Amended by Acts 2005, c. 914; 2006, cc. 863, 914; 2009, cc. 813, 840.
37.2-1000 to 37.2-1030. Repealed by Acts 2012, c. 614.
37.2-1031 to 37.2-1052. Repealed by Acts 2012, c. 614.
37.2-1100. Amended by Acts 2005, c. 751.
37.2-1101. Amended by Acts 2005, c. 751; 2009, cc. 813, 840; 2012, cc. 115, 378, 476, 507.
37.2-1102. Amended by Acts 2005, c. 751; 2012, cc. 115, 378.
37.2-1103. Amended by Acts 2008, cc. 551, 691.
37.2-1104. Amended by Acts 2008, cc. 551, 691.
37.2-1106. Amended by Acts 2005, c. 751.
37.2-1108. Amended by Acts 2005, c. 751.
37.2-1109. Amended by Acts 2005, c. 751.
38.2-102. Amended by Acts 2011, c. 186; 2012, c. 673.
38.2-111. Amended by Acts 2007, c. 762.
38.2-113. Amended by Acts 2007, c. 762.

Section
38.2-209. Amended by Acts 2006, c. 279.
38.2-218. Amended by Acts 2010, c. 226.
38.2-231. Amended by Acts 2005, cc. 290, 635; 2006, c. 554; 2008, cc. 58, 221; 2009, c. 215; 2013, cc. 13, 257.
38.2-232. Amended by Acts 2013, c. 93.
38.2-233. Amended by Acts 2009, c. 643.
38.2-301. Amended by Acts 2005, cc. 656, 698; 2007, c. 186.
38.2-305. Amended by Acts 2012, c. 264; 2013, c. 27.
38.2-323. Repealed by Acts 2010, c. 337.
38.2-324. Amended by Acts 2008, cc. 121, 157.
38.2-325. Amended by Acts 2012, c. 293; 2013, c. 257.
38.2-401. Amended by Acts 2006, cc. 58, 322; 2007, cc. 647, 741.
38.2-401.1. Amended by Acts 2006, cc. 648, 765.
38.2-402, 38.2-403. Amended by Acts 2012, c. 584.
38.2-406. Amended by Acts 2012, c. 584.
38.2-407 to 38.2-411. Repealed by Acts 2012, c. 584.
38.2-508. Amended by Acts 2013, cc. 136, 210.
38.2-508.1. Amended by Acts 2013, c. 751.
38.2-508.5. Amended by Acts 2011, c. 882.
38.2-515. Amended by Acts 2012, cc. 273, 277.
38.2-517. Amended by Acts 2008, cc. 111, 516.
38.2-602. Amended by Acts 2006, c. 638.
38.2-800. Amended by Acts 2007, c. 157.
38.2-807. Amended by Acts 2010, c. 343.
38.2-1000. Amended by Acts 2005, c. 765.
38.2-1017. Amended by Acts 2005, c. 765.
38.2-1022. Amended by Acts 2006, c. 329.
38.2-1026. Amended by Acts 2011, c. 850.
38.2-1039. Amended by Acts 2008, c. 95.
38.2-1057. Amended by Acts 2005, c. 38.
38.2-1300. Amended by Acts 2009, c. 602.
38.2-1306.1. Amended by Acts 2007, c. 488.
38.2-1315.1. Amended by Acts 2006, c. 320.
38.2-1316.1. Amended by Acts 2012, c. 539.
38.2-1316.2. Amended by Acts 2012, c. 539.
38.2-1316.3. Repealed by Acts 2012, c. 539.
38.2-1316.4. Amended by Acts 2012, c. 539.
38.2-1316.5, 38.2-1316.6. Repealed by Acts 2012, c. 539.
38.2-1316.8. Amended by Acts 2012, c. 539.
38.2-1317.1. Amended by Acts 2008, c. 249.
38.2-1318. Amended by Acts 2006, c. 866.
38.2-1320.5. Amended by Acts 2007, c. 488.
38.2-1329. Amended by Acts 2006, c. 577; 2009, c. 717.
38.2-1330. Amended by Acts 2006, c. 577.
38.2-1356. Amended by Acts 2006, c. 762.
38.2-1363. Amended by Acts 2006, c. 762.
38.2-1401. Amended by Acts 2008, c. 216.
38.2-1401. Amended by Acts 2008, c. 216; 2011, c. 198.
38.2-1407. Amended by Acts 2011, c. 198.

Section
38.2-1423. Amended by Acts 2008, c. 93.
38.2-1428. Amended by Acts 2011, c. 198.
38.2-1442. Amended by Acts 2010, c. 510.
38.2-1443.1. Amended by Acts 2008, c. 216.
38.2-1501. Amended by Acts 2011, c. 198.
38.2-1611.1. Amended by Acts 2011, c. 850.
38.2-1700. Amended by Acts 2010, c. 510.
38.2-1701. Amended by Acts 2010, c. 510.
38.2-1702. Amended by Acts 2010, c. 510.
38.2-1703. Amended by Acts 2010, c. 510.
38.2-1704. Amended by Acts 2007, c. 482; 2010, c. 510.
38.2-1705. Amended by Acts 2010, c. 510; 2011, c. 682.
38.2-1706. Amended by Acts 2010, c. 510.
38.2-1707. Amended by Acts 2010, c. 510.
38.2-1708. Amended by Acts 2010, c. 510.
38.2-1709. Amended by Acts 2010, c. 510; 2011, c. 850.
38.2-1710. Amended by Acts 2010, c. 510.
38.2-1711. Amended by Acts 2010, c. 510.
38.2-1712. Amended by Acts 2010, c. 510.
38.2-1713. Amended by Acts 2010, c. 510.
38.2-1714. Amended by Acts 2010, c. 510.
38.2-1715. Amended by Acts 2010, c. 510; 2011, c. 306.
38.2-1800. Amended by Acts 2006, c. 410; 2011, c. 222; 2012, c. 447; 2013, cc. 203, 497.
38.2-1814.1. Amended by Acts 2008, c. 250.
38.2-1815. Amended by Acts 2010, c. 281; 2012, c. 413.
38.2-1820. Amended by Acts 2008, c. 213.
38.2-1822. Amended by Acts 2007, c. 703; 2008, c. 213; 2013, c. 212.
38.2-1824. Amended by Acts 2012, cc. 734, 735.
38.2-1825. Amended by Acts 2010, c. 281.
38.2-1833. Amended by Acts 2008, c. 357.
38.2-1834.1. Amended by Acts 2008, c. 303.
38.2-1836. Amended by Acts 2008, c. 213.
38.2-1838. Amended by Acts 2008, c. 213.
38.2-1839. Amended by Acts 2007, c. 449.
38.2-1845. Amended by Acts 2008, c. 213.
38.2-1857.1. Amended by Acts 2011, c. 498.
38.2-1857.2. Amended by Acts 2008, c. 213; 2011, c. 498.
38.2-1857.4. Amended by Acts 2011, c. 498.
38.2-1857.5. Amended by Acts 2008, c. 213; 2011, c. 498.
38.2-1857.6. Amended by Acts 2011, c. 498.
38.2-1857.7. Amended by Acts 2011, c. 498.
38.2-1857.9. Amended by Acts 2008, c. 213; 2011, c. 498.
38.2-1865.1. Amended by Acts 2008, c. 213.
38.2-1865.4. Amended by Acts 2008, c. 213.
38.2-1866. Amended by Acts 2012, c. 294.
38.2-1868.1. Amended by Acts 2006, c. 589; 2012, c. 294.
38.2-1869. Amended by Acts 2006, c. 589; 2010, c. 281; 2012, c. 294.

Section
38.2-1872 to 38.2-1874. Amended by Acts 2012, c. 294.
38.2-1874. Amended by Acts 2010, c. 335.
38.2-1878. Amended by Acts 2013, c. 9.
38.2-1903.1. Amended by Acts 2005, c. 251; 2009, c. 644; 2011, cc. 618, 636.
38.2-1906. Amended by Acts 2005, c. 95.
38.2-1907. Amended by Acts 2010, c. 234.
38.2-2107. Amended by Acts 2013, c. 12.
38.2-2113. Amended by Acts 2009, c. 215; 2013, c. 257.
38.2-2114. Amended by Acts 2005, c. 872; 2008, cc. 58, 221; 2009, cc. 215, 442; 2013, c. 257.
38.2-2200. Amended by Acts 2005, c. 290.
38.2-2201. Amended by Acts 2013, c. 75.
38.2-2204. Amended by Acts 2005, c. 771.
38.2-2206. Amended by Acts 2010, c. 492; 2011, c. 107.
38.2-2208. Amended by Acts 2009, c. 215; 2013, c. 257.
38.2-2212. Amended by Acts 2006, cc. 851, 889; 2008, cc. 58, 221; 2009, c. 215; 2013, c. 257.
38.2-2217. Amended by Acts 2009, cc. 357, 545.
38.2-2411. Repealed by Acts 2012, c. 802.
38.2-2416. Amended by Acts 2006, c. 296.
38.2-2419. Amended by Acts 2011, c. 470.
38.2-2600. Amended by Acts 2006, c. 634.
38.2-2601. Amended by Acts 2006, c. 634.
38.2-2602. Amended by Acts 2006, c. 634.
38.2-2604. Amended by Acts 2006, c. 634.
38.2-2605. Amended by Acts 2006, c. 634.
38.2-2613. Amended by Acts 2006, c. 634.
38.2-2615. Amended by Acts 2006, c. 634.
38.2-2617. Amended by Acts 2010, cc. 235, 371.
38.2-2618. Amended by Acts 2010, cc. 235, 371.
38.2-2619. Amended by Acts 2010, cc. 235, 371.
38.2-3100.2. Amended by Acts 2008, c. 216.
38.2-3115. Amended by Acts 2006, c. 209.
38.2-3120. Repealed by Acts 2005, c. 935.
38.2-3323. Amended by Acts 2010, cc. 227, 374; 2012, cc. 476, 507.
38.2-3406.1. Amended by Acts 2010, cc. 155, 515, 687; 2011, c. 882.
38.2-3406.2. Amended by Acts 2011, c. 882.
38.2-3407. Amended by Acts 2008, c. 215.
38.2-3407.1. Amended by Acts 2009, c. 226.
38.2-3407.5. Amended by Acts 2010, c. 443.
38.2-3406.1. Amended by Acts 2013, c. 751.
38.2-3407.7. Amended by Acts 2010, cc. 157, 357.
38.2-3407.10. Amended by Acts 2006, c. 398.
38.2-3407.11. Amended by Acts 2011, c. 882.
38.2-3407.12. Amended by Acts 2013, c. 751.
38.2-3407.14. Amended by Acts 2005, c. 399.
38.2-3407.15. Amended by Acts 2005, c. 349.
38.2-3409. Amended by Acts 2012, cc. 476, 507.
38.2-3411. Amended by Acts 2013, c. 653.
38.2-3411.1. Amended by Acts 2011, c. 882.

Section

38.2-3412.1. Amended by Acts 2006, c. 638; 2009, cc. 813, 840; 2010, c. 693; 2013, c. 751.

38.2-3412.1:01. Amended by Acts 2010, c. 693; 2013, c. 751.

38.2-3417. Amended by Acts 2013, c. 751.

38.2-3418.1:1. Repealed by Acts 2008, c. 420.

38.2-3418.5. Amended by Acts 2009, cc. 813, 840; 2011, c. 882.

38.2-3418.8. Amended by Acts 2013, c. 751.

38.2-3420. Amended by Acts 2011, c. 329; 2012, c. 589.

38.2-3430.2. Amended by Acts 2010, cc. 225, 642.

38.2-3430.3. Amended by Acts 2005, c. 335; 2013, c. 751.

38.2-3431 Amended by Acts 2013, cc. 709, 751.

38.2-3432.1, 38.2-3432.2. Amended by Acts 2013, c. 751.

38.2-3432.3. Amended by Acts 2011, c. 882; 2013, cc. 136, 210.

38.2-3433. Repealed by Acts 2013, c. 751.

38.2-3436. Amended by Acts 2013, c. 751.

38.2-3438 to 38.2-3440. Amended by Acts 2013, c. 751.

38.2-3442. Amended by Acts 2013, c. 751.

38.2-3444. Amended by Acts 2013, cc. 136, 210.

38.2-3500. Amended by Acts 2011, c. 882.

38.2-3501. Amended by Acts 2013, c. 751.

38.2-3503. Amended by Acts 2013, c. 751.

38.2-3520. Amended by Acts 2013, c. 751.

38.2-3521.1. Amended by Acts 2013, c. 751.

38.2-3522.1. Amended by Acts 2013, c. 751.

38.2-3523.4. Amended by Acts 2013, c. 751.

38.2-3525. Amended by Acts 2005, c. 871; 2007, c. 428; 2008, c. 209; 2011, c. 882.

38.2-3540.2. Amended by Acts 2013, c. 751.

38.2-3541. Amended by Acts 2010, c. 503.

38.2-3541.1. Amended by Acts 2010, c. 21.

38.2-3551. Amended by Acts 2013, c. 751.

38.2-3723. Amended by Acts 2009, c. 642.

38.2-3724. Amended by Acts 2009, c. 643; 2010, c. 211.

38.2-3729. Amended by Acts 2009, c. 643.

38.2-3735. Amended by Acts 2009, c. 643; 2010, c. 211.

38.2-3737. Amended by Acts 2009, c. 643.

38.2-4109. Amended by Acts 2013, c. 751.

38.2-4123. Amended by Acts 2012, c. 156.

38.2-4209.1. Amended by Acts 2010, cc. 157, 357.

38.2-4214. Amended by Acts 2006, c. 427; 2009, cc. 796, 877; 2010, cc. 504, 583, 734; 2011, cc. 788, 882; 2012, cc. 634, 641; 2013, cc. 670, 679, 751.

38.2-4216.1. Repealed by Acts 2013, cc. 136, 210.

38.2-4229.1. Amended by Acts 2013, cc. 136, 210.

38.2-4300. Amended by Acts 2006, c. 448.

Section

38.2-4303. Amended by Acts 2008, c. 214.

38.2-4306. Amended by Acts 2006, c. 866; 2013, c. 751.

38.2-4307.1. Amended by Acts 2006, c. 448.

38.2-4312.1. Amended by Acts 2010, cc. 157, 357.

38.2-4312.3. Amended by Acts 2011, c. 882.

38.2-4319. Amended by Acts 2006, cc. 427, 866; 2007, cc. 488, 579; 2009, cc. 796, 839; 2010, cc. 222, 272, 504, 515, 583, 687, 734; 2011, cc. 788, 876, 878, 882; 2012, cc. 634, 641; 2013, cc. 653, 670, 679, 751.

38.2-4504. Amended by Acts 2013, c. 11.

38.2-4509. Amended by Acts 2006, c. 427; 2010, cc. 583, 734; 2011, c. 788; 2013, cc. 473, 670, 679.

38.2-4608. Amended by Acts 2005, c. 848.

38.2-4610.1. Amended by Acts 2008, c. 248.

38.2-4806. Amended by Acts 2008, c. 212; 2011, c. 498.

38.2-4807. Amended by Acts 2011, c. 498.

38.2-4809. Amended by Acts 2011, cc. 498, 850; 2013, cc. 29, 163.

38.2-4809.1. Amended by Acts 2013, cc. 29, 163.

38.2-4810. Amended by Acts 2011, c. 498.

38.2-4811. Amended by Acts 2007, c. 157; 2011, c. 498.

38.2-4812. Amended by Acts 2007, c. 157.

38.2-4900. Amended by Acts 2012, cc. 208, 303.

38.2-4902. Amended by Acts 2012, cc. 208, 303.

38.2-4904. Amended by Acts 2012, cc. 208, 303.

38.2-4905. Amended by Acts 2012, cc. 208, 303.

38.2-4906 to 38.2-4911. Repealed by Acts 2012, cc. 208, 303.

38.2-4913 to 38.2-4916. Repealed by Acts 2012, cc. 208, 303.

38.2-5004. Amended by Acts 2005, cc. 50, 52; 2013, c. 144.

38.2-5006. Amended by Acts 2005, cc. 50, 52.

38.2-5008. Amended by Acts 2008, cc. 267, 520.

38.2-5009. Amended by Acts 2008, cc. 267, 520; 2011, c. 84.

38.2-5010. Amended by Acts 2006, c. 919.

38.2-5013. Amended by Acts 2006, c. 919.

38.2-5016. Amended by Acts 2006, c. 777; 2008, cc. 267, 520.

38.2-5016.1. Amended by Acts 2006, c. 777.

38.2-5020. Amended by Acts 2008, cc. 267, 520.

38.2-5021. Amended by Acts 2008, cc. 267, 520.

38.2-5500. Amended by Acts 2012, c. 156.

38.2-5501. Amended by Acts 2007, c. 360; 2012, c. 156.

38.2-5503. Amended by Acts 2007, c. 360; 2012, c. 156.

38.2-5600. Repealed by Acts 2005, cc. 503, 572.

38.2-5601. Amended by Acts 2005, c. 503.

38.2-5601. Amended by Acts 2005, c. 572.

38.2-5602. Amended by Acts 2005, cc. 503, 572.

Section
38.2-5603. Repealed by Acts 2005, cc. 503, 572.
38.2-5800. Amended by Acts 2006, c. 448.
38.2-5803. Amended by Acts 2006, c. 866.
38.2-5804. Amended by Acts 2006, c. 866.
38.2-5900. Amended by Acts 2011, c. 788.
38.2-5901 to 38.2-5903. Repealed by Acts 2011, c. 788.
38.2-5905. Repealed by Acts 2011, c. 788.
40.1-11.3. Amended by Acts 2013, c. 304.
40.1-28.1 to 40.1-28.4:1. Repealed by Acts 2005, c. 823.
40.1-28.9. Amended by Acts 2007, cc. 816, 832; 2012, cc. 476, 507.
40.1-29. Amended by Acts 2005, cc. 595, 851; 2009, c. 728.
40.1-49.4. Amended by Acts 2005, c. 681.
40.1-51.2:2. Amended by Acts 2005, cc. 743, 789.
40.1-51.4:4. Amended by Acts 2012, cc. 803, 835.
40.1-51.8. Amended by Acts 2012, c. 332; 2013, c. 171.
40.1-51.10. Amended by Acts 2005, c. 387.
40.1-79.1. Amended by Acts 2005, c. 151; 2006, c. 462.
40.1-92, 40.1-93. Amended by Acts 2013, c. 15.
40.1-96. Amended by Acts 2013, c. 15.
40.1-100. Amended by Acts 2005, c. 151; 2007, c. 645; 2008, c. 552; 2009, c. 218.
40.1-103. Amended by Acts 2006, c. 935.
40.1-113. Amended by Acts 2007, c. 667.
42.1-15.1. Amended by Acts 2006, c. 539; 2012, c. 296.
42.1-17. Repealed by Acts 2006, c. 59.
42.1-19 to 42.1-19.4. Repealed by Acts 2006, c. 59.
42.1-36.1. Amended by Acts 2006, c. 474; 2007, cc. 470, 583; 2012, cc. 805, 836.
42.1-62. Amended by Acts 2011, c. 537.
42.1-64. Amended by Acts 2009, c. 584.
42.1-65. Amended by Acts 2009, c. 617.
42.1-70. Amended by Acts 2009, c. 617.
42.1-77. Amended by Acts 2005, c. 787; 2006, c. 60.
42.1-78. Amended by Acts 2006, c. 60.
42.1-79. Amended by Acts 2005, c. 787; 2006, c. 60.
42.1-79.1. Repealed by Acts 2005, c. 787.
42.1-82. Amended by Acts 2005, c. 787; 2006, c. 60.
42.1-83. Repealed by Acts 2006, c. 60.
42.1-84. Repealed by Acts 2005, c. 787.
42.1-85. Amended by Acts 2006, c. 60.
42.1-86. Amended by Acts 2005, c. 787; 2006, c. 60.
42.1-86.1. Amended by Acts 2005, c. 787; 2006, cc. 60, 909.
42.1-87. Amended by Acts 2005, c. 787; 2006, c. 60.
42.1-91. Repealed by Acts 2006, c. 60.

Section
43-1. Amended by Acts 2010, c. 341.
43-3. Amended by Acts 2010, c. 343; 2012, c. 523; 2013, c. 293.
43-4. Amended by Acts 2007, c. 505; 2013, c. 293.
43-4.01. Amended by Acts 2010, c. 341; 2013, c. 293.
43-5. Amended by Acts 2007, c. 504; 2013, c. 293.
43-8. Amended by Acts 2007, c. 504; 2013, c. 293.
43-10. Amended by Acts 2007, c. 504; 2013, c. 293.
43-17.1. Amended by Acts 2010, c. 352.
43-24. Amended by Acts 2010, c. 343.
43-29. Amended by Acts 2008, cc. 551, 691.
43-32. Amended by Acts 2005, c. 98; 2006, cc. 874, 891; 2009, c. 664.
43-33. Amended by Acts 2005, c. 280.
43-34. Amended by Acts 2006, cc. 874, 891; 2008, c. 171; 2009, c. 664; 2011, cc. 14, 702.
43-35. Amended by Acts 2005, c. 839.
43-36. Amended by Acts 2005, c. 839.
43-62. Amended by Acts 2005, c. 681.
44-1. Amended by Acts 2011, cc. 572, 586.
44-2. Amended by Acts 2011, cc. 572, 586.
44-5. Amended by Acts 2011, cc. 572, 586.
44-6. Amended by Acts 2011, cc. 572, 586.
44-16. Amended by Acts 2011, cc. 572, 586.
44-19. Amended by Acts 2011, cc. 572, 586.
44-21. Amended by Acts 2011, cc. 572, 586.
44-27. Amended by Acts 2011, cc. 572, 586.
44-32.1. Amended by Acts 2011, cc. 572, 586.
44-36. Amended by Acts 2011, cc. 572, 586.
44-40.1. Amended by Acts 2011, cc. 572, 586.
44-41.1. Amended by Acts 2011, cc. 72, 108.
44-42. Amended by Acts 2011, cc. 572, 586.
44-43. Repealed by Acts 2011, cc. 572, 586.
44-44. Amended by Acts 2011, cc. 572, 586.
44-45. Amended by Acts 2011, cc. 572, 586.
44-46.1. Amended by Acts 2011, cc. 572, 586.
44-47. Amended by Acts 2011, cc. 572, 586.
44-48. Amended by Acts 2011, cc. 572, 586.
44-52. Repealed by Acts 2011, cc. 572, 586.
44-54.4. Amended by Acts 2011, cc. 572, 586.
44-54.6. Amended by Acts 2011, cc. 572, 586.
44-54.8. Amended by Acts 2011, cc. 572, 586.
44-54.9. Amended by Acts 2011, cc. 572, 586.
44-54.10. Amended by Acts 2011, cc. 572, 586.
44-54.11. Amended by Acts 2011, cc. 572, 586.
44-54.12. Amended by Acts 2011, cc. 572, 586.
44-75.2. Amended by Acts 2011, cc. 572, 586.
44-80. Amended by Acts 2011, cc. 572, 586.
44-81. Amended by Acts 2011, cc. 572, 586.
44-82. Amended by Acts 2011, cc. 572, 586.
44-83. Amended by Acts 2011, cc. 572, 586.
44-88. Amended by Acts 2011, cc. 572, 586.
44-93. Amended by Acts 2006, c. 621.
44-93.1. Amended by Acts 2005, cc. 907, 910.

Section
44-93.2. Amended by Acts 2007, cc. 167, 214; 2011, cc. 572, 586.
44-93.3. Amended by Acts 2007, cc. 167, 214; 2010, c. 253; 2011, cc. 572, 586.
44-93.4. Amended by Acts 2007, cc. 167, 214; 2011, cc. 572, 586.
44-93.5. Amended by Acts 2007, cc. 167, 214.
44-96. Amended by Acts 2011, cc. 572, 586.
44-97.1. Amended by Acts 2011, cc. 572, 586.
44-98. Amended by Acts 2011, cc. 572, 586.
44-99. Amended by Acts 2011, cc. 572, 586.
44-100. Amended by Acts 2011, cc. 572, 586.
44-102. Amended by Acts 2011, cc. 572, 586.
44-102.1. Amended by Acts 2010, cc. 811, 861; 2011, cc. 572, 586.
44-102.2. Amended by Acts 2007, cc. 73, 911.
44-104. Amended by Acts 2011, cc. 572, 586.
44-110. Amended by Acts 2011, cc. 572, 586.
44-115. Amended by Acts 2011, cc. 572, 586.
44-116. Repealed by Acts 2011, cc. 572, 586.
44-117. Amended by Acts 2006, c. 123; 2007, c. 818.
44-120. Amended by Acts 2011, cc. 572, 586.
44-121. Repealed by Acts 2009, c. 108.
44-123.3. Amended by Acts 2012, cc. 803, 835.
44-146.15. Amended by Acts 2006, c. 458; 2012, cc. 42, 158.
44-146.16. Amended by Acts 2008, cc. 121, 157.
44-146.17. Amended by Acts 2006, c. 140; 2007, cc. 729, 742; 2008, cc. 121, 157.
44-146.18. Amended by Acts 2005, cc. 165, 490; 2007, c. 902; 2008, cc. 450, 526; 2009, cc. 222, 269; 2012, c. 418.
44-146.18:1. Amended by Acts 2008, cc. 121, 157.
44-146.19. Amended by Acts 2005, cc. 6, 205; 2006, c. 138; 2007, cc. 97, 129, 138; 2009, cc. 222, 269; 2012, c. 418.
44-146.23. Amended by Acts 2005, c. 474; 2008, cc. 121, 157; 2009, c. 233.
44-146.28. Amended by Acts 2007, cc. 729, 742; 2011, cc. 53, 69.
44-146.35. Amended by Acts 2011, cc. 594, 681.
44-146.38. Amended by Acts 2011, cc. 594, 681.
44-146.39. Repealed by Acts 2011, cc. 594, 681.
44-146.40. Amended by Acts 2007, c. 813; 2011, cc. 594, 681.
45.1-161.5. Amended by Acts 2008, c. 369
45.1-161.8. Amended by Acts 2005, c. 3.
45.1-161.12. Amended by Acts 2005, c. 3.
45.1-161.14. Amended by Acts 2005, c. 3.
45.1-161.20. Amended by Acts 2005, c. 3.
45.1-161.21. Amended by Acts 2005, c. 3; 2011, cc. 826, 862.
45.1-161.31. Amended by Acts 2007, cc. 894, 914.
45.1-161.32. Amended by Acts 2007, cc. 894, 914.
45.1-161.33. Amended by Acts 2005, c. 3.
45.1-161.35. Amended by Acts 2007, cc. 894, 914.

Section
45.1-161.37. Amended by Acts 2005, c. 3; 2007, cc. 894, 914.
45.1-161.39. Amended by Acts 2007, cc. 894, 914; 2010, cc. 809, 857.
45.1-161.62. Amended by Acts 2013, cc. 305, 618.
45.1-161.63. Amended by Acts 2005, c. 3.
45.1-161.64. Amended by Acts 2005, c. 3; 2007, cc. 894, 914; 2011, cc. 826, 862; 2012, cc. 109, 241.
45.1-161.70. Amended by Acts 2006, c. 396.
45.1-161.74. Amended by Acts 2011, cc. 826, 862.
45.1-161.76. Amended by Acts 2007, cc. 894, 914.
45.1-161.77. Amended by Acts 2011, cc. 826, 862.
45.1-161.78. Amended by Acts 2007, cc. 894, 914.
45.1-161.80. Amended by Acts 2005, c. 3.
45.1-161.83. Amended by Acts 2005, c. 3.
45.1-161.85. Amended by Acts 2011, cc. 826, 862.
45.1-161.87. Amended by Acts 2007, cc. 894, 914; 2010, cc. 809, 857.
45.1-161.97. Amended by Acts 2005, c. 3.
45.1-161.109. Amended by Acts 2005, c. 3; 2011, cc. 826, 862.
45.1-161.115. Amended by Acts 2005, c. 3.
45.1-161.116. Amended by Acts 2005, c. 3.
45.1-161.117. Amended by Acts 2005, c. 3.
45.1-161.118. Amended by Acts 2005, c. 3.
45.1-161.120. Repealed by Acts 2005, c. 3.
45.1-161.122. Amended by Acts 2005, c. 3; 2011, cc. 826, 862.
45.1-161.124. Amended by Acts 2005, c. 3.
45.1-161.126. Amended by Acts 2005, c. 3.
45.1-161.133. Amended by Acts 2011, cc. 826, 862.
45.1-161.135. Amended by Acts 2005, c. 3.
45.1-161.147. Amended by Acts 2005, c. 3.
45.1-161.154. Amended by Acts 2005, c. 3; 2011, cc. 826, 862.
45.1-161.156. Amended by Acts 2005, c. 3.
45.1-161.163. Amended by Acts 2005, c. 3.
45.1-161.165. Amended by Acts 2005, c. 3.
45.1-161.166. Amended by Acts 2011, cc. 826, 862.
45.1-161.172. Amended by Acts 2005, c. 3.
45.1-161.175. Amended by Acts 2005, c. 3; 2011, cc. 826, 862.
45.1-161.176. Amended by Acts 2005, c. 3.
45.1-161.186. Amended by Acts 2005, c. 3; 2011, cc. 826, 862.
45.1-161.188. Amended by Acts 2011, cc. 826, 862.
45.1-161.193. Amended by Acts 2011, cc. 826, 862.
45.1-161.194. Amended by Acts 2005, c. 3.
45.1-161.195. Amended by Acts 2005, c. 3.

Section
45.1-161.198. Amended by Acts 2005, c. 3.
45.1-161.200. Amended by Acts 2005, c. 3.
45.1-161.202. Amended by Acts 2006, c. 291.
45.1-161.207. Amended by Acts 2005, c. 3.
45.1-161.208. Amended by Acts 2005, c. 3.
45.1-161.209. Amended by Acts 2005, c. 3.
45.1-161.210. Amended by Acts 2005, c. 3.
45.1-161.212. Amended by Acts 2005, c. 3.
45.1-161.213. Repealed by Acts 2005, c. 3.
45.1-161.216. Amended by Acts 2005, c. 3; 2011, cc. 826, 862.
45.1-161.218. Amended by Acts 2005, c. 3.
45.1-161.219. Amended by Acts 2005, c. 3.
45.1-161.225. Amended by Acts 2005, c. 3.
45.1-161.228. Amended by Acts 2005, c. 3.
45.1-161.229. Amended by Acts 2005, c. 3.
45.1-161.236. Amended by Acts 2005, c. 3.
45.1-161.250. Amended by Acts 2011, cc. 826, 862.
45.1-161.252. Amended by Acts 2012, cc. 109, 241.
45.1-161.256. Amended by Acts 2005, c. 3.
45.1-161.257. Amended by Acts 2005, c. 3; 2007, cc. 894, 914.
45.1-161.259. Amended by Acts 2011, cc. 826, 862.
45.1-161.260. Amended by Acts 2005, c. 3.
45.1-161.264. Amended by Acts 2005, c. 3.
45.1-161.265. Amended by Acts 2005, c. 3.
45.1-161.270. Amended by Acts 2005, c. 3.
45.1-161.273. Amended by Acts 2005, c. 3.
45.1-161.276. Amended by Acts 2005, c. 3; 2010, cc. 809, 857.
45.1-161.277. Amended by Acts 2005, c. 3.
45.1-161.278. Amended by Acts 2005, c. 3.
45.1-161.280. Amended by Acts 2005, c. 3.
45.1-161.282. Amended by Acts 2005, c. 3.
45.1-161.284. Amended by Acts 2010, cc. 809, 857.
45.1-161.287. Amended by Acts 2005, c. 3.
45.1-161.288. Amended by Acts 2005, c. 3; 2011, cc. 826, 862.
45.1-161.289. Amended by Acts 2011, cc. 826, 862.
45.1-161.290. Amended by Acts 2011, cc. 826, 862.
45.1-161.291. Amended by Acts 2011, cc. 826, 862.
45.1-161.292:2. Amended by Acts 2012, cc. 803, 835.
45.1-161.292:11. Amended by Acts 2012, cc. 803, 835.
45.1-161.292:15, 45.1-161.292:16. Repealed by Acts 2012, cc. 803, 835.
45.1-161.292:18. Repealed by Acts 2012, cc. 803, 835.
45.1-161.292:19 to 45.1-161.292:22. Amended by Acts 2012, cc. 803, 835.
45.1-161.292:23. Repealed by Acts 2012, cc. 803, 835.

Section
45.1-161.292:24 to 45.1-161.292:29. Amended by Acts 2012, cc. 803, 835.
45.1-161.292:43. Amended by Acts 2006, c. 396.
45.1-161.292:71. Amended by Acts 2012, cc. 803, 835.
45.1-181. Amended by Acts 2012, c. 695.
45.1-186.1. Amended by Acts 2012, cc. 803, 835.
45.1-194. Amended by Acts 2012, cc. 803, 835.
45.1-195, 45.1-196. Repealed by Acts 2012, cc. 803, 835.
45.1-198. Repealed by Acts 2013, cc. 47, 129.
45.1-221. Repealed by Acts 2005, c. 3.
45.1-222. Amended by Acts 2005, c. 3.
45.1-223. Repealed by Acts 2005, c. 3.
45.1-224. Amended by Acts 2005, c. 3.
45.1-224. Repealed by Acts 2012, cc. 803, 835.
45.1-225. Repealed by Acts 2005, c. 3.
45.1-234. Amended by Acts 2013, cc. 47, 129.
45.1-246. Amended by Acts 2005, c. 3.
45.1-254. Amended by Acts 2008, c. 275; 2011, cc. 252, 290.
45.1-261.1. Amended by Acts 2013, cc. 47, 129.
45.1-361.2. Amended by Acts 2013, cc. 47, 129.
45.1-361.5. Amended by Acts 2013, cc. 305, 618.
45.1-361.19. Amended by Acts 2008, c. 534.
45.1-361.29. Amended by Acts 2008, c. 227.
45.1-361.30. Amended by Acts 2008, c. 534.
45.1-361.21. Amended by Acts 2006, c. 498.
45.1-361.22. Amended by Acts 2006, c. 498; 2010, c. 442.
45.1-361.38. Amended by Acts 2013, cc. 305, 618.
45.1-361.43. Amended by Acts 2009, c. 293.
45.1-361.44. Amended by Acts 2009, c. 293.
45.1-383. Amended by Acts 2008, c. 369.
45.1-390. Amended by Acts 2006, c. 939.
45.1-392. Repealed by Acts 2011, cc. 815, 864.
45.1-393. Repealed by Acts 2011, cc. 815, 864, effective July 1, 2017.
45.1-394. Amended by Acts 2007, c. 684; 2008, c. 369; 2009, cc. 19, 525; 2011, cc. 815, 864.
45.1-394. Repealed by Acts 2011, cc. 815, 864, effective July 1, 2017.
46.2-100. Amended by Acts 2005, cc. 310, 928; 2006, cc. 529, 538, 540, 874, 891, 896; 2007, cc. 209, 325, 366, 393; 2010, c. 135; 2011, c. 128; 2012, c. 177; 2013, cc. 128, 400, 783.
46.2-103. Amended by Acts 2012, c. 11.
46.2-104. Amended by Acts 2008, cc. 551, 691; 2009, c. 756.
46.2-105.1. Amended by Acts 2006, c. 871.
46.2-112. Amended by Acts 2012, cc. 32, 122.
46.2-114. Amended by Acts 2012, c. 408.
46.2-206.1. Repealed by Acts 2008, c. 657.
46.2-208. Amended by Acts 2005, cc. 376, 443;

Section
2006, cc. 396, 846, 859; 2007, cc. 79, 156, 188, 447; 2009, c. 664; 2010, cc. 15, 175, 813, 865; 2011, c. 321; 2013, cc. 673, 789.
46.2-208.1. Amended by Acts 2006, cc. 926, 940; 2011, c. 528.
46.2-214. Amended by Acts 2006, c. 846; 2007, cc. 156, 447.
46.2-216.1. Amended by Acts 2009, c. 419.
46.2-216.2. Repealed by Acts 2009, c. 419.
46.2-217. Amended by Acts 2006, c. 85; 2007, cc. 249, 589; 2008, c. 460; 2011, cc. 62, 73; 2012, cc. 22, 111.
46.2-221. Amended by Acts 2012, cc. 803, 835.
46.2-221.2. Amended by Acts 2008, c. 591; 2012, c. 384.
46.2-221.4. Amended by Acts 2008, c. 591; 2012, c. 385.
46.2-300. Amended by Acts 2005, c. 245; 2007, c. 532; 2008, c. 684.
46.2-301. Amended by Acts 2009, cc. 390, 764; 2010, c. 519.
46.2-301.1. Amended by Acts 2005, c. 312; 2010, cc. 519, 829.
46.2-309. Repealed by Acts 2005, c. 245.
46.2-311. Amended by Acts 2010, c. 18; 2013, cc. 165, 582.
46.2-312. Amended by Acts 2010, c. 18.
46.2-314. Amended by Acts 2012, cc. 476, 507.
46.2-316. Amended by Acts 2007, c. 496.
46.2-320. Amended by Acts 2010, c. 682; 2011, c. 773; 2012, c. 829.
46.2-322. Amended by Acts 2006, c. 396; 2011, c. 441.
46.2-323. Amended by Acts 2005, cc. 259, 828; 2006, cc. 857, 914; 2009, cc. 439, 872.
46.2-324. Amended by Acts 2006, cc. 857, 914; 2010, cc. 25, 55.
46.2-324.1. Amended by Acts 2005, cc. 245, 513; 2012, cc. 215, 222; 2013, cc. 165, 582.
46.2-325. Amended by Acts 2007, c. 190; 2008, c. 735; 2012, cc. 215, 222; 2013, c. 272.
46.2-328. Amended by Acts 2007, c. 190; 2009, c. 77; 2013, cc. 673, 783, 789.
46.2-328.1. Amended by Acts 2005, c. 260; 2007, c. 493; 2009, c. 872; 2010, c. 129; 2011, c. 396; 2013, c. 686.
46.2-330. Amended by Acts 2005, c. 302; 2006, cc. 857, 914; 2008, cc. 487, 866; 2009, c. 872; 2011, cc. 57, 70; 2012, cc. 215, 222.
46.2-332. Amended by Acts 2007, cc. 190, 223; 2011, cc. 57, 70.
46.2-334.01. Amended by Acts 2007, c. 777; 2009, c. 54; 2013, cc. 397, 579.
46.2-335. Amended by Acts 2008, cc. 493, 735; 2010, cc. 541, 593; 2012, cc. 215, 222.

Section
46.2-336. Amended by Acts 2012, cc. 30, 100.
46.2-337. Amended by Acts 2007, c. 190; 2013, cc. 673, 783, 789.
46.2-339. Amended by Acts 2011, c. 477.
46.2-341.4. Amended by Acts 2005, c. 513; 2008, c. 190; 2013, cc. 165, 582.
46.2-341.7, 46.2-341.8. Amended by Acts 2013, cc. 165, 582.
46.2-341.9. Amended by Acts 2011, c. 477; 2012, cc. 12, 153; 2013, cc. 165, 582.
46.2-341.10. Amended by Acts 2011, c. 477; 2012, c. 153; 2013, cc. 165, 582.
46.2-341.12. Amended by Acts 2005, c. 513; 2009, c. 872; 2011, cc. 881, 889; 2013, cc. 165, 582.
46.2-341.14. Amended by Acts 2008, c. 735; 2013, cc. 165, 582.
46.2-341.15. Amended by Acts 2008, c. 190; 2009, c. 872; 2013, cc. 165, 582.
46.2-341.16. Amended by Acts 2006, c. 226; 2012, cc. 22, 111; 2013, cc. 165, 582.
46.2-341.18. Amended by Acts 2005, c. 513; 2008, c. 190; 2010, c. 424.
46.2-341.18:01. Amended by Acts 2009, c. 102.
46.2-341.18:1. Amended by Acts 2005, c. 513.
46.2-341.18:3. Amended by Acts 2012, c. 153.
46.2-341.20. Amended by Acts 2005, c. 513; 2011, cc. 881, 889; 2013, cc. 165, 582.
46.2-341.20:2. Amended by Acts 2005, c. 513; 2008, c. 190.
46.2-341.20:2. Amended by Acts 2008, c. 190.
46.2-341.21. Amended by Acts 2005, c. 513; 2008, c. 190.
46.2-341.24. Amended by Acts 2005, c. 616.
46.2-341.25. Amended by Acts 2005, cc. 868, 881.
46.2-341.26:1. Amended by Acts 2005, cc. 868, 881.
46.2-341.26:2. Amended by Acts 2005, c. 616.
46.2-341.26:6. Amended by Acts 2005, cc. 868, 881.
46.2-341.26:7. Amended by Acts 2005, cc. 868, 881.
46.2-341.26:9. Amended by Acts 2005, cc. 868, 881.
46.2-341.26:10. Amended by Acts 2005, c. 616.
46.2-341.27. Amended by Acts 2005, c. 616.
46.2-342. Amended by Acts 2005, cc. 259, 828; 2007, cc. 92, 907; 2008, c. 82; 2009, cc. 834, 872; 2010, cc. 25, 55.
46.2-343. Amended by Acts 2009, c. 872.
46.2-344. Amended by Acts 2009, c. 872.
46.2-345. Amended by Acts 2005, cc. 259, 260, 281, 665, 828; 2006, cc. 857, 914; 2009, c. 872; 2012, cc. 215, 222.
46.2-348. Amended by Acts 2006, cc. 857, 914; 2013, cc. 165, 312, 477, 582.

Section
46.2-364. Amended by Acts 2010, c. 343.
46.2-373. Amended by Acts 2009, c. 1.
46.2-380. Amended by Acts 2013, cc. 80, 104.
46.2-382. Amended by Acts 2005, c. 376.
46.2-383. Amended by Acts 2013, c. 263.
46.2-388. Amended by Acts 2005, c. 589; 2011, cc. 62, 73.
46.2-391. Amended by Acts 2013, cc. 415, 655.
46.2-391.2. Amended by Acts 2005, cc. 757, 840.
46.2-391.4. Amended by Acts 2005, cc. 757, 840.
46.2-392. Amended by Acts 2007, c. 432.
46.2-393. Amended by Acts 2005, c. 152.
46.2-395. Amended by Acts 2007, c. 327; 2008, c. 861; 2012, c. 615.
46.2-398. Amended by Acts 2005, c. 943; 2011, c. 271.
46.2-400. Amended by Acts 2009, cc. 813, 840; 2012, cc. 476, 507.
46.2-401. Amended by Acts 2009, cc. 813, 840; 2012, cc. 476, 507.
46.2-411. Amended by Acts 2005, c. 886; 2011, cc. 54, 71; 2012, cc. 803, 835.
46.2-414. Amended by Acts 2005, c. 565.
46.2-416. Amended by Acts 2010, cc. 25, 55; 2012, c. 615.
46.2-417. Amended by Acts 2013, c. 598.
46.2-427. Amended by Acts 2013, c. 598.
46.2-433. Amended by Acts 2005, c. 513.
46.2-490. Amended by Acts 2007, c. 180.
46.2-502. Amended by Acts 2013, c. 326.
46.2-505. Amended by Acts 2008, c. 190.
46.2-600. Amended by Acts 2007, c. 934; 2010, c. 135; 2013, cc. 244, 367, 783.
46.2-602.3. Amended by Acts 2013, c. 216.
46.2-603. Amended by Acts 2005, c. 305; 2012, c. 650.
46.2-606. Amended by Acts 2010, cc. 25, 55.
46.2-608. Amended by Acts 2011, c. 61.
46.2-609. Amended by Acts 2011, c. 61.
46.2-613. Amended by Acts 2006, cc. 444, 472; 2013, c. 783.
46.2-613.1. Amended by Acts 2012, cc. 22, 111.
46.2-613.4. Amended by Acts 2012, cc. 22, 111.
46.2-615. Amended by Acts 2013, c. 318.
46.2-616. Amended by Acts 2006, c. 896.
46.2-617. Amended by Acts 2009, c. 664; 2012, c. 623.
46.2-618. Amended by Acts 2012, c. 119.
46.2-619. Amended by Acts 2006, c. 896; 2012, c. 135.
46.2-623. Amended by Acts 2005, c. 305; 2006, c. 896; 2008, c. 171; 2012, c. 650.
46.2-624. Amended by Acts 2011, cc. 652, 678.
46.2-625. Amended by Acts 2007, cc. 325, 393; 2012, c. 177.
46.2-629. Amended by Acts 2006, c. 896; 2007, c. 225; 2012, c. 650; 2013, c. 783.
46.2-632. Amended by Acts 2009, c. 171.

Section
46.2-633. Amended by Acts 2005, cc. 766, 849; 2008, Sp. Sess. II, c. 7; 2009, c. 664.
46.2-635. Amended by Acts 2006, cc. 16, 163.
46.2-637. Amended by Acts 2006, c. 896.
46.2-638. Amended by Acts 2006, c. 896; 2010, c. 135.
46.2-640. Amended by Acts 2009, c. 664.
46.2-644.03. Amended by Acts 2011, cc. 14, 702.
46.2-646. Amended by Acts 2013, c. 337.
46.2-649. Amended by Acts 2013, c. 226.
46.2-649.1. Amended by Acts 2006, cc. 874, 891.
46.2-629. Amended by Acts 2012, c. 650.
46.2-652. Amended by Acts 2012, c. 443.
46.2-653. Amended by Acts 2006, c. 202; 2008, c. 178.
46.2-662. Amended by Acts 2013, cc. 347, 783.
46.2-665. Amended by Acts 2010, c. 293; 2012, c. 174; 2013, c. 776.
46.2-666. Amended by Acts 2010, c. 293; 2012, c. 174.
46.2-668. Amended by Acts 2011, cc. 881, 889.
46.2-670. Amended by Acts 2010, c. 293; 2012, c. 174; 2013, c. 776.
46.2-674. Amended by Acts 2013, c. 777.
46.2-685. Amended by Acts 2012, c. 443.
46.2-692. Amended by Acts 2012, cc. 215, 222.
46.2-694. Amended by Acts 2005, c. 928; 2007, c. 896; 2008, c. 182; 2013, c. 783.
46.2-694.1. Amended by Acts 2007, c. 896.
46.2-696. Repealed by Acts 2011, cc. 881, 889.
46.2-697. Amended by Acts 2007, c. 896.
46.2-700. Amended by Acts 2011, c. 283.
46.2-703. Amended by Acts 2006, c. 208; 2009, c. 563; 2011, cc. 62, 73; 2012, cc. 22, 111.
46.2-705. Amended by Acts 2013, c. 783.
46.2-706. Amended by Acts 2012, cc. 151, 471.
46.2-706.1. Amended by Acts 2009, c. 419.
46.2-707. Amended by Acts 2013, cc. 673, 789.
46.2-708. Amended by Acts 2012, cc. 151, 471.
46.2-711. Amended by Acts 2005, c. 140; 2011, cc. 405, 639, 881, 889; 2013, c. 783.
46.2-712. Amended by Acts 2005, c. 301.
46.2-714, 46.2-715. Amended by Acts 2013, c. 783.
46.2-716. Amended by Acts 2006, c. 549.
46.2-720, 46.2-721. Amended by Acts 2013, c. 783.
46.2-725. Amended by Acts 2005, c. 294; 2006, c. 550; 2011, c. 115.
46.2-725.2. Amended by Acts 2012, cc. 22, 111.
46.2-728.3. Amended by Acts 2005, c. 839.
46.2-730. Amended by Acts 2007, c. 492; 2008, c. 159.
46.2-731. Amended by Acts 2007, c. 715.
46.2-733. Amended by Acts 2011, c. 103.
46.2-736.1. Amended by Acts 2005, c. 300.

Section
46.2-737. Amended by Acts 2005, c. 300.
46.2-739. Amended by Acts 2007, c. 715.
46.2-742. Amended by Acts 2008, c. 614; 2011, c. 436.
46.2-743. Amended by Acts 2012, c. 379; 2013, c. 478.
46.2-742.1:1. Repealed by Acts 2011, c. 21.
46.2-742.5. Repealed by Acts 2006, c. 437.
46.2-742.6. Repealed by Acts 2008, c. 114.
46.2-743. Amended by Acts 2005, cc. 264, 273, 929; 2006, c. 437; 2008, Sp. Sess. II, c. 4; 2009, c. 679; 2011, cc. 572, 586.
46.2-744.1. Repealed by Acts 2006, c. 437.
46.2-746.2:2.2. Repealed by Acts 2005, c. 908.
46.2-746.2:3.1. Repealed by Acts 2006, c. 437.
46.2-746.2:5. Repealed by Acts 2005, c. 908.
46.2-746.4:01. Repealed by Acts 2005, c. 908.
46.2-746.7. Amended by Acts 2005, c. 908.
46.2-746.8. Amended by Acts 2007, cc. 172, 181.
46.2-746.8:2. Repealed by Acts 2005, c. 908.
46.2-746.9. Amended by Acts 2005, c. 908.
46.2-746.23. Repealed by Acts 2006, c. 437.
46.2-749.2:10. Amended by Acts 2005, cc. 244, 273.
46.2-749.3. Amended by Acts 2006, cc. 873, 908; 2010, cc. 351, 390; 2012, cc. 681, 743.
46.2-749.4. Amended by Acts 2005, c. 273.
46.2-749.5. Amended by Acts 2009, c. 679.
46.2-749.16:1. Repealed by Acts 2011, c. 21.
46.2-749.28:2. Repealed by Acts 2005, c. 908.
46.2-749.30:1. Repealed by Acts 2005, c. 908.
46.2-749.30:2. Repealed by Acts 2005, c. 908.
46.2-749.36:1. Repealed by Acts 2005, c. 908.
46.2-749.43:1. Repealed by Acts 2005, c. 908.
46.2-749.44. Repealed by Acts 2005, c. 908.
46.2-749.49. Repealed by Acts 2005, cc. 273, 908.
46.2-749.49:1. Repealed by Acts 2009, c. 755.
46.2-749.50 to 46.2-749.53. Repealed by Acts 2005, c. 908.
46.2-749.55. Repealed by Acts 2005, c. 908.
46.2-749.56. Repealed by Acts 2005, cc. 273, 908.
46.2-749.56:1. Repealed by Acts 2006, c. 437.
46.2-749.57. Repealed by Acts 2005, c. 908.
46.2-749.59. Repealed by Acts 2005, c. 908.
46.2-749.61. Repealed by Acts 2011, c. 21.
46.2-749.63. Repealed by Acts 2005, c. 908.
46.2-749.64. Repealed by Acts 2005, c. 908.
46.2-749.65. Repealed by Acts 2005, c. 908.
46.2-749.67. Repealed by Acts 2005, c. 908.
46.2-749.69:1. Amended by Acts 2005, c. 554; 2013, c. 482.
46.2-749.70 to 46.2-749.72. Repealed by Acts 2005, c. 908.
46.2-749.74 to 46.2-749.77. Repealed by Acts 2005, c. 908.

Section
46.2-749.78. Amended by Acts 2006, c. 852.
46.2-749.79. Repealed by Acts 2005, c. 908.
46.2-749.82. Repealed by Acts 2005, c. 908.
46.2-749.83. Repealed by Acts 2005, c. 908.
46.2-749.90 to 46.2-749.92. Repealed by Acts 2006, c. 437.
46.2-749.94. Repealed by Acts 2006, c. 437.
46.2-749.98:1. Repealed by Acts 2005, c. 908.
46.2-749.101. Repealed by Acts 2005, c. 908.
46.2-749.104. Repealed by Acts 2005, c. 908.
46.2-749.106. Repealed by Acts 2005, c. 908.
46.2-749.107. Repealed by Acts 2005, c. 908.
46.2-749.108. Repealed by Acts 2011, c. 21.
46.2-749.109. Repealed by Acts 2005, cc. 248, 908.
46.2-749.109:1. Repealed by Acts 2006, c. 437.
46.2-749.112. Repealed by Acts 2011, c. 21.
46.2-749.113, 46.2-749.114. Repealed by Acts 2005, c. 908.
46.2-749.116, 46.2-749.117. Repealed by Acts 2005, c. 908.
46.2-749.118. Repealed by Acts 2006, c. 437.
46.2-749.120, 46.2-121. Repealed by Acts 2006, c. 437.
46.2-749.122 to 46.2-749.125. Repealed by Acts 2008, c. 114.
46.2-749.126 to 46.2-128. Repealed by Acts 2006, c. 437.
46.2-749.129. Repealed by Acts 2008, c. 114.
46.2-749.131 to 46.2-133. Repealed by Acts 2006, c. 437.
46.2-749.134, 46.2-749.135. Repealed by Acts 2008, c. 114.
46.2-752. Amended by Acts 2005, c. 317; 2006, c. 148; 2007, cc. 213, 230, 813, 865; 2008, cc. 163, 457, 591; 2009, cc. 366, 756, 843; 2010, cc. 125, 131; 2013, c. 82.
46.2-752.1. Amended by Acts 2013, cc. 673, 789.
46.2-755. Amended by Acts 2006, c. 515; 2007, c. 296; 2011, cc. 405, 639, 881, 889.
46.2-755.1, 46.2-755.2. Repealed by Acts 2009, cc. 864, 871.
46.2-755.2. Amended by Acts 2008, c. 848.
46.2-756. Amended by Acts 2006, c. 418.
46.2-804. Amended by Acts 2007, c. 501; 2013, cc. 128, 400, 585, 646.
46.2-805. Amended by Acts 2013, cc. 128, 400.
46.2-806. Amended by Acts 2013, cc. 585, 646.
46.2-807. Amended by Acts 2013, cc. 128, 400.
46.2-808. Amended by Acts 2006, cc. 529, 538; 2007, cc. 209, 366.
46.2-808.1. Amended by Acts 2008, cc. 470, 647.
46.2-817. Amended by Acts 2008, cc. 773, 811; 2010, c. 655.
46.2-819.1. Amended by Acts 2005, c. 862; 2006, c. 859; 2007, cc. 78, 200; 2010, c. 839; 2011, c. 736.

Section
46.2-819.2. Amended by Acts 2005, c. 208; 2006, c. 487.
46.2-819.3. Amended by Acts 2006, c. 859; 2007, cc. 78, 200; 2011, c. 736.
46.2-819.3:1. Amended by Acts 2011, c. 736.
46.2-821, 46.2-822. Amended by Acts 2013, cc. 128, 400.
46.2-826. Amended by Acts 2013, cc. 128, 400.
46.2-828. Amended by Acts 2012, c. 26.
46.2-830. Amended by Acts 2013, cc. 128, 400, 585, 646.
46.2-831. Amended by Acts 2013, cc. 128, 400, 585, 646.
46.2-832. Amended by Acts 2013, cc. 128, 400.
46.2-833. Amended by Acts 2006, c. 928; 2011, c. 471; 2013, cc. 128, 400.
46.2-834 to 46.2-836. Amended by Acts 2013, cc. 128, 400.
46.2-844. Amended by Acts 2011, cc. 787, 838.
46.2-846. Amended by Acts 2013, cc. 128, 400.
46.2-847. Amended by Acts 2013, cc. 585, 646.
46.2-857. Amended by Acts 2010, cc. 52, 110; 2012, c. 7.
46.2-859. Amended by Acts 2011, cc. 325, 326.
46.2-862. Amended by Acts 2006, c. 301.
46.2-864. Amended by Acts 2011, c. 280.
46.2-865.1. Amended by Acts 2006, c. 348.
46.2-867. Amended by Acts 2012, cc. 283, 756.
46.2-868. Amended by Acts 2013, cc. 752, 790.
46.2-870. Amended by Acts 2005, cc. 266, 267, 268; 2006, c. 213; 2007, cc. 222, 544; 2010, cc. 26, 56.
46.2-871. Amended by Acts 2006, c. 416; 2007, c. 98.
46.2-873. Amended by Acts 2007, c. 813.
46.2-873.1. Amended by Acts 2005, cc. 239, 804; 2009, c. 74; 2010, cc. 19, 48; 2011, c. 29; 2012, c. 207.
46.2-874. Amended by Acts 2005, c. 310.
46.2-874.1. Amended by Acts 2007, c. 813.
46.2-875. Amended by Acts 2011, c. 182.
46.2-878. Amended by Acts 2013, c. 303.
46.2-878.1. Amended by Acts 2012, c. 397.
46.2-878.2. Amended by Acts 2006, c. 547; 2013, cc. 585, 646.
46.2-878.3. Amended by Acts 2010, c. 874; 2011, c. 890.
46.2-881. Amended by Acts 2006, c. 139.
46.2-882. Amended by Acts 2006, c. 930; 2007, c. 231.
46.2-885. Amended by Acts 2012, c. 828.
46.2-888. Amended by Acts 2008, c. 737.
46.2-889. Amended by Acts 2013, cc. 585, 646.
46.2-891. Amended by Acts 2007, cc. 189, 918.
46.2-892. Amended by Acts 2005, c. 140.
46.2-894. Amended by Acts 2005, c. 131.
46.2-896. Amended by Acts 2005, c. 137.
46.2-904. Amended by Acts 2006, c. 538; 2013, c. 783.
46.2-905. Amended by Acts 2006, cc. 529, 538; 2007, cc. 209, 366; 2013, c. 783.

Section
46.2-906. Amended by Acts 2006, cc. 529, 538; 2007, cc. 209, 366.
46.2-906.1. Amended by Acts 2006, cc. 529, 538; 2007, cc. 209, 366.
46.2-907. Amended by Acts 2006, cc. 529, 538; 2013, c. 783.
46.2-908.1. Amended by Acts 2006, cc. 529, 538; 2007, cc. 209, 366; 2009, c. 795; 2013, c. 783.
46.2-908.3. Amended by Acts 2011, c. 283; 2013, c. 783.
46.2-914. Amended by Acts 2006, cc. 529, 538; 2008, c. 525; 2009, c. 795; 2013, c. 783.
46.2-915. Amended by Acts 2007, c. 111; 2013, c. 783.
46.2-915.1. Amended by Acts 2006, c. 896; 2011, c. 822.
46.2-915.2. Amended by Acts 2013, c. 783.
46.2-916.2. Amended by Acts 2006, c. 728; 2008, c. 196; 2009, cc. 68, 504; 2011, c. 469; 2012, c. 9; 2013, c. 64.
46.2-916.3. Amended by Acts 2008, c. 456; 2009, cc. 743, 835; 2010, c. 112; 2011, cc. 68, 140, 469.
46.2-917. Amended by Acts 2005, c. 928.
46.2-918. Amended by Acts 2005, c. 928.
46.2-920. Amended by Acts 2005, c. 583; 2007, cc. 860, 908; 2011, c. 629.
46.2-920.1. Amended by Acts 2007, cc. 189, 918; 2012, cc. 27, 108.
46.2-921.1. Amended by Acts 2008, c. 818; 2010, c. 289.
46.2-924. Amended by Acts 2007, c. 813; 2012, c. 339; 2013, cc. 507, 585, 646, 581.
46.2-925. Amended by Acts 2008, c. 451.
46.2-930. Amended by Acts 2008, c. 503; 2009, c. 432.
46.2-931. Amended by Acts 2005, cc. 488, 541; 2008, cc. 120, 235, 310; 2009, cc. 422, 656, 722; 2010, cc. 378, 589.
46.2-932. Amended by Acts 2006, cc. 529, 538; 2007, cc. 209, 366, 813.
46.2-940. Amended by Acts 2006, c. 276.
46.2-1012. Amended by Acts 2009, c. 79.
46.2-1015. Amended by Acts 2005, c. 381.
46.2-1020. Amended by Acts 2006, c. 122.
46.2-1022. Amended by Acts 2008, c. 181.
46.2-1023. Amended by Acts 2005, c. 583; 2006, c. 86; 2008, c. 189; 2009, c. 595.
46.2-1025. Amended by Acts 2005, c. 574; 2010, c. 127; 2011, c. 268.
46.2-1028. Amended by Acts 2006, cc. 874, 891.
46.2-1029.1. Amended by Acts 2005, c. 209.
46.2-1041. Amended by Acts 2013, cc. 585, 646.
46.2-1044. Amended by Acts 2009, c. 118.
46.2-1046. Amended by Acts 2013, cc. 585, 646.
46.2-1047. Amended by Acts 2006, cc. 529, 538; 2013, c. 783.
46.2-1048. Amended by Acts 2012, c. 177.

Section
46.2-1049. Amended by Acts 2006, cc. 529, 538; 2012, c. 177.
46.2-1051. Amended by Acts 2006, cc. 830, 896.
46.2-1070. Amended by Acts 2006, cc. 874, 891.
46.2-1072.1. Amended by Acts 2006, c. 615.
46.2-1076. Amended by Acts 2013, cc. 165, 582.
46.2-1077. Amended by Acts 2005, cc. 210, 913; 2007, c. 110; 2011, c. 275.
46.2-1078.1. Amended by Acts 2013, cc. 752, 790.
46.2-1087. Amended by Acts 2012, cc. 283, 756.
46.2-1088. Amended by Acts 2008, c. 443.
46.2-1088.5. Amended by Acts 2005, c. 563.
46.2-1090. Amended by Acts 2007, c. 421.
46.2-1094. Amended by Acts 2007, c. 813; 2010, c. 661.
46.2-1095 Amended by Acts 2007, cc. 91, 935; 2010, c. 661.
46.2-1098. Amended by Acts 2008, c. 714.
46.2-1100. Amended by Acts 2007, cc. 91, 935.
46.2-1102. Amended by Acts 2011, c. 331.
46.2-1104. Amended by Acts 2005, c. 645; 2013, c. 118.
46.2-1107 to 46.2-1109. Amended by Acts 2013, cc. 585, 646.
46.2-1110. Amended by Acts 2005, cc. 542, 543; 2011, c. 620.
46.2-1112. Amended by Acts 2005, c. 262; 2006, cc. 210, 232; 2013, cc. 585, 646.
46.2-1114. Amended by Acts 2013, cc. 585, 646.
46.2-1116. Amended by Acts 2010, c. 24; 2013, cc. 585, 646.
46.2-1117. Amended by Acts 2013, cc. 585, 646.
46.2-1118. Amended by Acts 2010, c. 614.
46.2-1120. Amended by Acts 2013, cc. 242, 385.
46.2-1128. Amended by Acts 2006, c. 534; 2012, c. 443.
46.2-1129. Amended by Acts 2006, c. 534; 2012, c. 443.
46.2-1129.1. Amended by Acts 2013, c. 118.
46.2-1133. Amended by Acts 2011, cc. 62, 73.
46.2-1134. Amended by Acts 2011, cc. 62, 73.
46.2-1135. Amended by Acts 2007, c. 896.
46.2-1136. Amended by Acts 2011, cc. 62, 73.
46.2-1137. Amended by Acts 2011, cc. 62, 73.
46.2-1139. Amended by Acts 2009, c. 456; 2011, cc. 62, 73; 2012, c. 443; 2013, c. 118.
46.2-1140 to 46.2-1142.1. Amended by Acts 2012, c. 443.
46.2-1143. Amended by Acts 2005, c. 556; 2007, c. 523; 2008, c. 716; 2009, c. 188; 2010, c. 361; 2011, c. 131; 2012, c. 443; 2013, cc. 305, 618.
46.2-1143.1, 46.2-1144. Amended by Acts 2012, c. 443.
46.2-1144.1. Amended by Acts 2008, c. 33.
46.2-1145. Amended by Acts 2012, c. 443.
46.2-1147. Amended by Acts 2012, c. 443.
46.2-1148. Amended by Acts 2012, c. 443; 2013, c. 118.

Section
46.2-1149. Amended by Acts 2012, c. 443; 2013, c. 354.
46.2-1149.1. Amended by Acts 2012, c. 443.
46.2-1149.3. Amended by Acts 2007, c. 738; 2012, c. 443.
46.2-1149.4, 46.2-1149.5. Amended by Acts 2012, c. 443.
46.2-1150. Amended by Acts 2006, cc. 874, 891.
46.2-1157. Amended by Acts 2007, cc. 75, 137; 2009, cc. 115, 514, 756; 2011, c. 283.
46.2-1158. Amended by Acts 2012, c. 177.
46.2-1158.1. Amended by Acts 2008, c. 722; 2009, c. 523; 2011, c. 283.
46.2-1161. Repealed by Acts 2011, c. 283.
46.2-1163. Amended by Acts 2006, c. 620; 2007, cc. 75, 137; 2009, c. 241.
46.2-1166. Amended by Acts 2005, c. 179.
46.2-1167. Amended by Acts 2005, c. 628; 2006, c. 620.
46.2-1167.1. Repealed by Acts 2009, cc. 864, 871.
46.2-1176. Amended by Acts 2012, cc. 216, 824.
46.2-1177. Amended by Acts 2006, c. 729.
46.2-1178. Amended by Acts 2012, cc. 216, 824; 2013, c. 634.
46.2-1178.1. Amended by Acts 2012, cc. 216, 824.
46.2-1180. Amended by Acts 2006, c. 729; 2012, cc. 216, 824.
46.2-1181, 46.2-1182. Amended by Acts 2012, cc. 216, 824.
46.2-1182.2. Amended by Acts 2012, cc. 216, 824.
46.2-1183. Amended by Acts 2006, c. 729.
46.2-1190. Amended by Acts 2013, c. 226.
46.2-1190.2. Amended by Acts 2007, c. 190; 2013, c. 111.
46.2-1190.3. Amended by Acts 2013, c. 226.
46.2-1190.5. Amended by Acts 2013, c. 226.
46.2-1192. Amended by Acts 2013, c. 226.
46.2-1200. Amended by Acts 2009, c. 664; 2011, cc. 487, 824.
46.2-1202. Amended by Acts 2009, c. 664.
46.2-1203. Amended by Acts 2013, c. 241.
46.2-1204. Repealed by Acts 2009, c. 664.
46.2-1206. Amended by Acts 2009, c. 664; 2012, cc. 803, 835.
46.2-1207. Amended by Acts 2006, c. 603.
46.2-1208. Repealed by Acts 2009, c. 664.
46.2-1209. Amended by Acts 2006, cc. 874, 891; 2012, c. 474.
46.2-1211, 46.2-1212. Amended by Acts 2012, c. 474.
46.2-1213. Amended by Acts 2012, c. 474.
46.2-1215. Amended by Acts 2012, c. 474.
46.2-1216. Amended by Acts 2007, c. 813; 2010, c. 23; 2012, cc. 104, 156.
46.2-1217. Amended by Acts 2006, cc. 874, 891; 2008, cc. 470, 647; 2012, cc. 803, 835.

Section
46.2-1220. Amended by Acts 2008, c. 193.
46.2-1222.1. Amended by Acts 2009, c. 535; 2011, c. 201.
46.2-1224. Repealed by Acts 2009, c. 806; 2009, c. 183.
46.2-1224.1. Amended by Acts 2008, c. 587.
46.2-1229. Amended by Acts 2009, cc. 813, 840.
46.2-1231. Amended by Acts 2006, cc. 874, 891.
46.2-1231.1. Amended by Acts 2007, c. 376.
46.2-1232. Amended by Acts 2006, cc. 874, 891; 2009, cc. 186, 544; 2012, cc. 149, 812.
46.2-1233.1. Amended by Acts 2006, cc. 874, 891; 2013, c. 592.
46.2-1233.2. Amended by Acts 2006, cc. 874, 891.
46.2-1240. Amended by Acts 2005, c. 276; 2007, c. 715; 2010, c. 47.
46.2-1241. Amended by Acts 2005, c. 276; 2007, c. 715; 2013, c. 137.
46.2-1242. Amended by Acts 2008, c. 715.
46.2-1245. Amended by Acts 2012, cc. 17, 286.
46.2-1257. Repealed by Acts 2010, c. 47.
46.2-1259. Amended by Acts 2010, c. 47.
46.2-1304. Amended by Acts 2007, c. 813.
46.2-1307. Amended by Acts 2007, cc. 74, 187, 310.
46.2-1307.1. Amended by Acts 2007, c. 187.
46.2-1308. Amended by Acts 2012, c. 408.
46.2-1500. Amended by Acts 2005, c. 456; 2006, c. 441; 2010, cc. 284, 292, 318, 459.
46.2-1503. Amended by Acts 2011, c. 791.
46.2-1510. Amended by Acts 2011, c. 791.
46.2-1511. Amended by Acts 2005, c. 321.
46.2-1516. Amended by Acts 2012, c. 13; 2013, c. 247.
46.2-1519. Amended by Acts 2011, c. 791.
46.2-1521. Amended by Acts 2007, c. 828.
46.2-1527.1. Amended by Acts 2006, c. 172; 2011, c. 407; 2012, cc. 10, 119.
46.2-1527.2. Amended by Acts 2006, c. 172; 2011, c. 407; 2012, cc. 10, 119.
46.2-1527.3. Amended by Acts 2007, c. 826.
46.2-1527.5. Amended by Acts 2006, c. 172; 2007, c. 826; 2011, c. 407; 2012, c. 119.
46.2-1529. Amended by Acts 2011, c. 791.
46.2-1530. Amended by Acts 2009, c. 783; 2010, cc. 292, 359, 459; 2011, c. 791.
46.2-1530.2. Amended by Acts 2006, c. 536.
46.2-1531. Amended by Acts 2013, c. 247.
46.2-1537. Amended by Acts 2006, c. 441.
46.2-1542. Amended by Acts 2006, cc. 835, 897; 2009, c. 783; 2012, c. 650.
46.2-1548. Amended by Acts 2008, cc. 304, 753.
46.2-1549. Amended by Acts 2008, cc. 304, 753.
46.2-1550. Amended by Acts 2008, cc. 304, 753.
46.2-1550.2. Amended by Acts 2012, cc. 215, 222.
46.2-1558. Amended by Acts 2012, cc. 215, 222.

Section
46.2-1561. Amended by Acts 2005, c. 558; 2012, c. 650.
46.2-1568. Amended by Acts 2005, c. 906.
46.2-1569. Amended by Acts 2007, cc. 827, 837; 2009, cc. 173, 176; 2010, cc. 284, 318; 2011, cc. 774, 856.
46.2-1571. Amended by Acts 2006, cc. 809, 818; 2007, c. 830; 2009, cc. 173, 176; 2010, cc. 284, 318; 2013, cc. 260, 630.
46.2-1572. Amended by Acts 2005, c. 456.
46.2-1572.3. Amended by Acts 2010, cc. 284, 318.
46.2-1573. Amended by Acts 2009, cc. 173, 176; 2010, cc. 284, 318; 2011, c. 650.
46.2-1581. Amended by Acts 2008, c. 166.
46.2-1600. Amended by Acts 2009, c. 664; 2012, cc. 64, 280.
46.2-1601. Amended by Acts 2009, c. 664.
46.2-1603. Amended by Acts 2009, c. 171.
46.2-1603.1. Amended by Acts 2011, c. 824.
46.2-1605. Amended by Acts 2006, c. 615; 2011, c. 824; 2012, cc. 283, 756.
46.2-1608. Amended by Acts 2010, c. 873.
46.2-1609. Amended by Acts 2011, c. 824.
46.2-1610. Amended by Acts 2006, c. 615.
46.2-1910. Amended by Acts 2011, c. 791.
46.2-1916. Amended by Acts 2012, c. 13; 2013, c. 247.
46.2-1919. Amended by Acts 2011, c. 791.
46.2-1929. Amended by Acts 2011, c. 791.
46.2-1930. Amended by Acts 2009, c. 60; 2010, c. 359; 2011, c. 791.
46.2-1931. Amended by Acts 2013, c. 247.
46.2-1954. Amended by Acts 2012, cc. 215, 222.
46.2-1964. Amended by Acts 2012, cc. 215, 222.
46.2-1992.8. Amended by Acts 2011, c. 791.
46.2-1992.14. Amended by Acts 2013, c. 247.
46.2-1992.17. Amended by Acts 2011, c. 791.
46.2-1992.22. Amended by Acts 2011, c. 791.
46.2-1992.23. Amended by Acts 2009, c. 60; 2010, c. 359; 2011, c. 791.
46.2-1992.24. Amended by Acts 2013, c. 247.
46.2-1992.46. Amended by Acts 2012, cc. 215, 222.
46.2-1992.56. Amended by Acts 2012, cc. 215, 222.
46.2-1993. Amended by Acts 2006, c. 896; 2010, c. 610.
46.2-1993.8. Amended by Acts 2011, c. 791.
46.2-1993.14. Amended by Acts 2012, c. 13; 2013, c. 247.
46.2-1993.17. Amended by Acts 2011, c. 791.
46.2-1993.22. Amended by Acts 2011, c. 791.
46.2-1993.23. Amended by Acts 2009, c. 60; 2010, c. 359; 2011, c. 791.
46.2-1993.24. Amended by Acts 2013, c. 247.
46.2-1993.35. Amended by Acts 2006, c. 896.
46.2-1993.39. Amended by Acts 2006, c. 896.
46.2-1993.46. Amended by Acts 2012, cc. 215, 222.

Section

46.2-1993.55. Amended by Acts 2006, c. 896; 2012, cc. 215, 222.
46.2-1993.67. Amended by Acts 2010, c. 610.
46.2-2000. Amended by Acts 2011, cc. 881, 889; 2012, cc. 22, 111.
46.2-2000.1. Amended by Acts 2011, cc. 881, 889; 2013, cc. 165, 582.
46.2-2001. Amended by Acts 2012, cc. 22, 111.
46.2-2001.3. Amended by Acts 2011, cc. 881, 889; 2012, cc. 22, 111; 2013, cc. 165, 582.
46.2-2005. Amended by Acts 2011, cc. 424, 881, 889; 2013, cc. 165, 582.
46.2-2011.4. Amended by Acts 2011, cc. 881, 889; 2012, cc. 22, 111.
46.2-2011.6. Amended by Acts 2006, c. 208.
46.2-2011.8. Amended by Acts 2011, cc. 881, 889; 2012, cc. 22, 111.
46.2-2011.9. Amended by Acts 2013, cc. 165, 582.
46.2-2011.11. Amended by Acts 2012, cc. 22, 111; 2013, cc. 165, 582.
46.2-2011.23, 46.2-2011.24. Amended by Acts 2013, cc. 165, 582.
46.2-2011.27. Amended by Acts 2011, cc. 881, 889.
46.2-2053. Amended by Acts 2006, c. 208.
46.2-2059.1. Amended by Acts 2011, c. 1.
46.2-2062. Amended by Acts 2007, c. 238.
46.2-2067. Amended by Acts 2012, cc. 22, 111.
46.2-2075. Amended by Acts 2011, cc. 881, 889.
46.2-2080. Amended by Acts 2007, c. 813; 2011, c. 424.
46.2-2084. Repealed by Acts 2011, cc. 881, 889.
46.2-2096. Amended by Acts 2011, cc. 881, 889.
46.2-2097. Repealed by Acts 2011, cc. 881, 889.
46.2-2097.1. Repealed by Acts 2011, cc. 881, 889.
46.2-2099.1. Amended by Acts 2006, c. 449.
46.2-2099.2, 46.2-2099.3. Repealed by Acts 2012, cc. 22, 111.
46.2-2099.4. Amended by Acts 2011, cc. 881, 889.
46.2-2099.5. Amended by Acts 2011, cc. 881, 889.
46.2-2099.6. Repealed by Acts 2011, cc. 881, 889.
46.2-2099.7 to 46.2-2099.10. Repealed by Acts 2012, cc. 22, 111.
46.2-2099.12 to 46.2-2099.16. Repealed by Acts 2012, cc. 22, 111.
46.2-2099.19. Amended by Acts 2013, cc. 165, 582.
46.2-2099.21. Amended by Acts 2007, c. 813.
46.2-2099.41. Amended by Acts 2007, c. 813.
46.2-2100. Amended by Acts 2006, cc. 874, 891; 2011, cc. 881, 889.
46.2-2101. Amended by Acts 2012, c. 638.
46.2-2108.2. Amended by Acts 2011, cc. 881, 889.

Section

46.2-2108.4. Amended by Acts 2011, cc. 881, 889; 2013, cc. 165, 582.
46.2-2108.5. Amended by Acts 2011, cc. 881, 889.
46.2-2108.6. Amended by Acts 2011, cc. 881, 889.
46.2-2109. Amended by Acts 2011, cc. 881, 889.
46.2-2115. Amended by Acts 2011, cc. 881, 889.
46.2-2116. Repealed by Acts 2012, cc. 22, 111.
46.2-2118. Amended by Acts 2011, cc. 881, 889.
46.2-2119. Repealed by Acts 2012, cc. 22, 111.
46.2-2120. Amended by Acts 2011, cc. 881, 889.
46.2-2121. Amended by Acts 2006, c. 208.
46.2-2122. Amended by Acts 2011, cc. 881, 889; 2013, cc. 165, 582.
46.2-2123. Repealed by Acts 2012, cc. 22, 111.
46.2-2124. Amended by Acts 2011, cc. 881, 889.
46.2-2132. Amended by Acts 2011, cc. 881, 889; 2013, cc. 165, 582.
46.2-2133. Amended by Acts 2011, cc. 881, 889; 2013, cc. 165, 582.
46.2-2135. Amended by Acts 2011, cc. 881, 889.
46.2-2136. Amended by Acts 2011, cc. 881, 889.
46.2-2137. Amended by Acts 2011, cc. 881, 889.
46.2-2143. Amended by Acts 2006, c. 208; 2011, cc. 881, 889; 2012, c. 638.
46.2-2144. Amended by Acts 2011, cc. 881, 889.
46.2-2146. Amended by Acts 2011, cc. 881, 889.
46.2-2147. Amended by Acts 2011, cc. 881, 889.
46.2-2150. Amended by Acts 2011, cc. 881, 889.
46.2-2151. Amended by Acts 2011, cc. 881, 889.
46.2-2155. Amended by Acts 2011, cc. 881, 889; 2012, cc. 22, 111.
46.2-2156. Amended by Acts 2011, cc. 881, 889.
46.2-2157. Amended by Acts 2006, c. 609.
46.2-2158. Amended by Acts 2006, c. 609.
46.2-2161. Amended by Acts 2006, c. 609.
46.2-2163. Amended by Acts 2006, c. 609.
46.2-2170. Amended by Acts 2006, c. 609.
46.2-2173. Amended by Acts 2006, c. 609.
46.2-2176. Amended by Acts 2013, cc. 165, 582.
46.2-2800. Amended by Acts 2008, c. 414; 2009, c. 806.
46.2-2801. Amended by Acts 2008, c. 836; 2009, c. 806.
46.2-2805. Amended by Acts 2009, c. 806.
46.2-2806. Amended by Acts 2009, c. 806.
46.2-2809. Amended by Acts 2008, c. 836; 2009, cc. 63, 576, 806.
46.2-2810. Repealed by Acts 2008, c. 806.
46.2-2812. Amended by Acts 2008, c. 836; 2009, cc. 117, 164.
46.2-2814. Amended by Acts 2008, cc. 470, 647, 836; 2009, cc. 117, 164, 806.
46.2-2816. Amended by Acts 2009, c. 806.
46.2-2818. Repealed by Acts 2008, c. 806.
46.2-2819. Amended by Acts 2008, c. 836; 2009, cc. 117, 164.
46.2-2820. Amended by Acts 2008, c. 836; 2009, cc. 117, 164.

Section
46.2-2821. Amended by Acts 2009, c. 806.
46.2-2824. Amended by Acts 2008, c. 836; 2009, cc. 117, 164; Repealed by Acts 2009, c. 806.
46.2-2825. Amended by Acts 2009, c. 806.
46.2-2826. Amended by Acts 2009, cc. 63, 576.
46.2-2827. Amended by Acts 2009, c. 806.
47.1-2. Amended by Acts 2007, cc. 269, 590; 2011, cc. 731, 834; 2012, c. 566.
47.1-3. Amended by Acts 2007, cc. 269, 590.
47.1-4. Amended by Acts 2007, cc. 269, 590; 2013, c. 86.
47.1-5. Amended by Acts 2007, cc. 269, 590; 2008, cc. 117, 814.
47.1-7. Amended by Acts 2009, c. 160; 2011, cc. 731, 834.
47.1-8. Amended by Acts 2007, cc. 269, 590; 2008, cc. 117, 814.
47.1-9. Amended by Acts 2007, cc. 269, 590; 2008, cc. 117, 814; 2012, c. 566.
47.1-10. Amended by Acts 2007, cc. 269, 590.
47.1-11. Amended by Acts 2007, cc. 269, 590.
47.1-12. Amended by Acts 2007, cc. 269, 590; 2011, cc. 731, 834.
47.1-13. Amended by Acts 2007, cc. 269, 590; 2008, cc. 117, 814; 2011, cc. 731, 834.
47.1-14. Amended by Acts 2007, cc. 269, 590; 2008, cc. 117, 814; 2011, cc. 731, 834.
47.1-15. Amended by Acts 2007, cc. 269, 590; 2008, c. 685; 2011, cc. 731, 834.
47.1-16. Amended by Acts 2007, cc. 269, 590; 2008, cc. 117, 814; 2009, c. 160.
47.1-17. Amended by Acts 2007, cc. 269, 590.
47.1-18. Amended by Acts 2007, cc. 269, 590.
47.1-19. Amended by Acts 2005, c. 18; Acts 2007, cc. 269, 590.
47.1-20. Amended by Acts 2007, cc. 269, 590.
47.1-21. Amended by Acts 2007, cc. 269, 590.
47.1-22. Amended by Acts 2007, cc. 269, 590.
47.1-23. Amended by Acts 2007, cc. 269, 590; 2013, c. 86.
47.1-25. Amended by Acts 2007, cc. 269, 590.
47.1-28. Amended by Acts 2008, cc. 117, 814
47.1-30. Amended by Acts 2007, cc. 269, 590; 2011, c. 746; 2012, c. 566.
47.1-31 to 47.1-33. Repealed by Acts 2007, cc. 269, 590.
48-5. Amended by Acts 2009, cc. 181, 551.
48-7. Amended by Acts 2005, cc. 764, 813.
48-8. Amended by Acts 2005, cc. 764, 813.
48-9. Amended by Acts 2005, cc. 764, 813.
49-3. Amended by Acts 2008, cc. 57, 713.
49-6. Amended by Acts 2008, cc. 551, 691.
50-73.1. Amended by Acts 2007, c. 631; 2010, c. 675.
50-73.2. Amended by Acts 2005, c. 379; 2012, c. 63.
50-73.3. Amended by Acts 2006, c. 505.

Section
50-73.4. Amended by Acts 2007, c. 631; 2010, c. 675.
50-73.5. Amended by Acts 2007, c. 631; 2010, c. 675.
50-73.6. Amended by Acts 2010, c. 434.
50-73.7. Amended by Acts 2007, c. 631.
50-73.8. Amended by Acts 2010, c. 675.
50-73.11. Amended by Acts 2007, c. 631; 2010, c. 675; 2013, c. 86.
50-73.11:2. Repealed by Acts 2007, c. 631.
50-73.12. Amended by Acts 2007, c. 631; 2008, c. 586; 2010, c. 675.
50-73.13. Amended by Acts 2008, c. 586.
50-73.15. Amended by Acts 2007, c. 631; 2008, c. 586; 2010, c. 675; 2013, c. 86.
50-73.17. Amended by Acts 2007, c. 771; 2008, c. 586; 2012, c. 130.
50-73.24. Amended by Acts 2012, c. 63.
50-73.46:1. Amended by Acts 2006, c. 912.
50-73.48:1. Amended by Acts 2005, c. 765; 2007, c. 631.
50-73.48:3. Amended by Acts 2007, c. 631; 2008, c. 586.
50-73.49. Amended by Acts 2007, c. 631; 2008, cc. 586, 588, 770; 2009, c. 167.
50-73.50. Amended by Acts 2008, c. 586.
50-73.51. Amended by Acts 2008, c. 586.
50-73.52:5. Amended by Acts 2013, c. 18.
50-73.52:6. Amended by Acts 2009, c. 167.
50-73.53. Amended by Acts 2007, c. 631.
50-73.54. Amended by Acts 2007, c. 631; 2010, c. 675.
50-73.55. Repealed by Acts 2007, c. 631.
50-73.57. Amended by Acts 2008, c. 586.
50-73.57:2. Amended by Acts 2008, c. 586.
50-73.58. Amended by Acts 2008, cc. 588, 770; 2009, c. 167; 2012, c. 130; 2013, c. 18.
50-73.58:1. Amended by Acts 2013, c. 18.
50-73.58:2. Amended by Acts 2009, c. 167.
50-73.59. Amended by Acts 2008, c. 523; 2013, c. 18.
50-73.67. Amended by Acts 2007, cc. 631, 810; 2013, c. 18.
50-73.69. Amended by Acts 2008, c. 586; 2013, c. 18.
50-73.70. Amended by Acts 2006, c. 659; 2007, c. 810.
50-73.77. Amended by Acts 2007, c. 631; 2008, c. 586; 2010, c. 675.
50-73.78. Amended by Acts 2007, c. 631; 2012, c. 63.
50-73.79. Amended by Acts 2006, c. 912; 2007, c. 631.
50-73.83. Amended by Acts 2007, cc. 631, 771; 2009, c. 716; 2010, c. 675.
50-73.84. Amended by Acts 2007, c. 631.
50-73.93. Amended by Acts 2007, c. 631.
50-73.101. Amended by Acts 2007, c. 631.
50-73.108. Amended by Acts 2006, c. 912.

Section
50-73.117. Amended by Acts 2006, c. 912.
51.1-124.3. Amended by Acts 2012, c. 701.
50-73.125. Repealed by Acts 2007, c. 631.
50-73.127. Amended by Acts 2007, c. 631.
50-73.128. Amended by Acts 2005, c. 765; 2007, c. 631.
50-73.129. Amended by Acts 2007, c. 631.
50-73.130. Repealed by Acts 2007, c. 771.
50-73.131. Amended by Acts 2007, c. 631; 2013, c. 18.
50-73.132. Amended by Acts 2007, c. 631; 2009, c. 716; 2013, c. 18.
50-73.133. Amended by Acts 2007, c. 631.
50-73.134. Amended by Acts 2007, c. 631; 2009, c. 716; 2013, c. 18.
50-73.135. Amended by Acts 2009, c. 716; 2010, c. 434; 2013, c. 18.
50-73.136. Amended by Acts 2009, c. 716; 2013, c. 18.
50-73.137:1. Amended by Acts 2009, c. 716.
50-73.138. Amended by Acts 2009, c. 716.
51.1-124.3. Amended by Acts 2005, cc. 933, 945; 2007, c. 89; 2010, cc. 737, 738; 2012, c. 823.
51.1-124.4. Amended by Acts 2006, c. 637.
51.1-124.9. Amended by Acts 2011, c. 747.
51.1-124.13. Amended by Acts 2012, cc. 56, 349.
51.1-124.22. Amended by Acts 2008, c. 245; 2012, cc. 803, 835.
51.1-124.27. Amended by Acts 2012, cc. 803, 835.
51.1-124.30. Amended by Acts 2005, c. 729; 2013, c. 463.
51.1-124.32. Amended by Acts 2007, c. 65.
51.1-124.36. Amended by Acts 2007, cc. 700, 711.
51.1-126. Amended by Acts 2005, c. 793; 2010, cc. 737, 738; 2012, cc. 701, 823.
51.1-126.5. Amended by Acts 2006, c. 639; 2012, cc. 701, 823.
51.1-126.6. Amended by Acts 2006, c. 639; 2012, cc. 701, 823; 2013, c. 463.
51.1-130. Amended by Acts 2005, c. 902.
51.1-135. Amended by Acts 2012, cc. 701, 823.
51.1-138. Amended by Acts 2006, cc. 65, 388; 2007, c. 819; 2009, cc. 6, 91, 282; 2010, c. 745; 2012, c. 423.
51.1-140. Repealed by Acts 2012, c. 696.
51.1-142.2. Amended by Acts 2005, c. 292; 2006, c. 635; 2007, c. 89; 2008, c. 27; 2009, c. 362; 2010, cc. 737, 738; 2011, cc. 722, 880; 2012, cc. 696, 701, 823.
51.1-144. Amended by Acts 2010, cc. 737, 738; 2012, c. 822; 2013, c. 463.
51.1-145. Amended by Acts 2005, c. 161; 2012, cc. 701, 823; 2013, c. 463.
51.1-153. Amended by Acts 2010, cc. 737, 738; 2011, c. 483; 2012, cc. 701, 811, 823; 2013, cc. 456, 666.

Section
51.1-155. Amended by Acts 2005, cc. 605, 606, 793; 2006, c. 513; 2010, cc. 737, 738; 2012, cc. 701, 811, 823; 2013, cc. 456, 666.
51.1-155.1. Amended by Acts 2011, cc. 250, 880.
51.1-155.2. Amended by Acts 2008, c. 537; 2011, c. 880.
51.1-156. Amended by Acts 2009, c. 362.
51.1-157. Amended by Acts 2012, cc. 701, 823.
51.1-161. Amended by Acts 2006, c. 403; 2010, c. 758; 2012, c. 161.
51.1-162. Amended by Acts 2009, cc. 22, 362; 2011, c. 880.
51.1-164. Repealed by Acts 2010, c. 269.
51.1-165. Amended by Acts 2005, cc. 146, 162.
51.1-165.1. Amended by Acts 2009, c. 22.
51.1-166. Amended by Acts 2010, cc. 737, 738, 752; 2012, cc. 701, 823; 2013, c. 463.
51.1-168. Amended by Acts 2005, c. 728.
51.1-169. Amended by Acts 2013, cc. 456, 666.
51.1-205. Amended by Acts 2005, c. 146; 2008, c. 28; 2011, c. 483; 2012, c. 85.
51.1-206. Amended by Acts 2005, c. 146; 2007, c. 819.
51.1-207. Amended by Acts 2009, c. 22; 2012, c. 696.
51.1-212. Amended by Acts 2007, c. 87.
51.1-216. Amended by Acts 2011, c. 483.
51.1-218. Amended by Acts 2009, c. 22; 2012, c. 696.
51.1-301. Amended by Acts 2010, cc. 737, 738.
51.1-302. Amended by Acts 2012, cc. 701, 823.
51.1-303. Amended by Acts 2010, cc. 737, 738.
51.1-305. Amended by Acts 2005, c. 288; 2011, c. 483.
51.1-306. Amended by Acts 2012, cc. 701, 823; 2013, c. 463.
51.1-308. Amended by Acts 2012, cc. 701, 823.
51.1-309. Amended by Acts 2011, c. 705.
51.1-505. Amended by Acts 2005, cc. 147, 933, 945; 2006, c. 640; 2009, c. 362; 2010, c. 751; 2012, c. 696.
51.1-506. Amended by Acts 2005, cc. 933, 945.
51.1-510. Amended by Acts 2008, c. 354.
51.1-511. Amended by Acts 2010, c. 269.
51.1-512. Amended by Acts 2005, c. 57; 2006, c. 252; 2010, c. 751; 2012, c. 696.
51.1-512.1. Amended by Acts 2011, c. 880.
51.1-513.2. Amended by Acts 2011, c. 722.
51.1-513.3. Amended by Acts 2011, c. 722; 2012, cc. 476, 507.
51.1-600. Amended by Acts 2007, c. 253.
51.1-601. Amended by Acts 2007, c. 253.
51.1-601.1. Amended by Acts 2012, cc. 701, 823; 2013, c. 463.
51.1-602. Amended by Acts 2008, c. 245.
51.1-603. Amended by Acts 2012, c. 660.
51.1-603.1. Amended by Acts 2012, cc. 660, 701, 823; 2013, c. 463.

Section
51.1-605. Amended by Acts 2006, c. 66.
51.1-608. Amended by Acts 2006, c. 756; 2008, cc. 29, 245.
51.1-609, 51.1-610. Amended by Acts 2013, c. 463.
51.1-611. Amended by Acts 2012, cc. 701, 823.
51.1-618. Amended by Acts 2008, c. 245.
51.1-700. Amended by Acts 2005, c. 902.
51.1-701. Amended by Acts 2005, c. 902.
51.1-702. Amended by Acts 2005, c. 902.
51.1-703. Amended by Acts 2005, c. 902.
51.1-704. Amended by Acts 2005, c. 902.
51.1-705. Amended by Acts 2005, c. 902.
51.1-800. Amended by Acts 2006, c. 406.
51.1-803. Amended by Acts 2005, c. 196.
51.1-900. Repealed by Acts 2009, c. 33.
51.1-1100. Amended by Acts 2012, cc. 701, 823; 2013, c. 463.
51.1-1101. Amended by Acts 2012, cc. 803, 835.
51.1-1103. Amended by Acts 2010, c. 750; 2013, c. 463.
51.1-1110. Amended by Acts 2010, c. 750; 2012, c. 417.
51.1-1111. Amended by Acts 2010, c. 750.
51.1-1112. Amended by Acts 2005, c. 419; 2006, cc. 404, 405; 2010, c. 750; 2011, c. 880.
51.1-1113. Amended by Acts 2005, c. 419.
51.1-1114. Amended by Acts 2006, cc. 778, 841; 2012, c. 417.
51.1-1116. Amended by Acts 2011, c. 722.
51.1-1117. Amended by Acts 2011, c. 722.
51.1-1121. Amended by Acts 2010, c. 654; 2012, c. 417.
51.1-1122. Amended by Acts 2010, c. 750.
51.1-1123. Amended by Acts 2005, c. 419; 2006, cc. 404, 405, 778, 841; 2010, c. 750; 2011, c. 880.
51.1-1124. Amended by Acts 2005, c. 419.
51.1-1125. Amended by Acts 2006, cc. 778, 841; 2012, c. 417.
51.1-1127. Amended by Acts 2012, c. 417.
51.1-1128. Amended by Acts 2011, cc. 722, 880.
51.1-1132. Amended by Acts 2007, c. 90.
51.1-1133. Amended by Acts 2007, c. 64.
51.1-1134. Amended by Acts 2011, c. 722.
51.1-1135.1. Amended by Acts 2005, c. 473.
51.1-1135.2. Amended by Acts 2011, c. 30.
51.1-1139. Amended by Acts 2006, c. 641.
51.1-1155, 51.1-1156. Amended by Acts 2013, c. 463.
51.1-1163, 51.1-1164. Amended by Acts 2013, c. 463.
51.1-1171. Amended by Acts 2012, c. 823.
51.1-1173. Amended by Acts 2013, c. 463.
51.1-1201. Amended by Acts 2006, c. 707.
51.1-1302. Amended by Acts 2006, c. 307.
51.1-1304. Amended by Acts 2006, c. 66.
51.1-1400. Amended by Acts 2005, c. 535; 2006, c. 622; 2007, c. 64; 2012, cc. 701, 823.

Section
51.1-1401. Amended by Acts 2007, cc. 866, 921; 2009, c. 23; 2011, c. 722; 2012, cc. 701, 823.
51.1-1402. Amended by Acts 2012, cc. 701, 823.
51.1-1403. Amended by Acts 2005, cc. 382, 432; 2006, c. 336; 2012, cc. 701, 823.
51.1-1405. Amended by Acts 2011, c. 722; 2012, cc. 701, 823.
51.5-1. Amended by Acts 2009, cc. 813, 840; 2012, cc. 803, 835; 2013, c. 571.
51.5-2. Amended by Acts 2009, cc. 813, 840.
51.5-2 to 51.5-5.01. Repealed by Acts 2012, cc. 803, 835.
51.5-8, 51.5-9.01. Repealed by Acts 2012, cc. 803, 835.
51.5-9.1 to 51.5-10.1. Repealed by Acts 2012, cc. 803, 835.
51.5-11. Repealed by Acts 2008, c. 563.
51.5-12. Repealed by Acts 2011, cc. 7, 166.
51.5-12.1 to 51.5-30. Repealed by Acts 2012, cc. 803, 835.
51.5-31. Amended by Acts 2009, cc. 813, 840; 2012, cc. 803, 835.
51.5-33. Amended by Acts 2009, c. 516; 2012, cc. 803, 835.
51.5-39.1 to 51.5-39.12. Repealed by Acts 2012, c. 847, effective July 1, 2014.
51.5-39.1. Amended by Acts 2013, c. 571.
51.5-39.2. Amended by Acts 2009, cc. 813, 840; 2012, cc. 803, 835.
51.5-39.5. Amended by Acts 2010, c. 692.
51.5-39.7. Amended by Acts 2009, cc. 813, 840; 2012, cc. 476, 507, 803, 835.
51.5-39.8. Amended by Acts 2012, cc. 476, 507.
51.5-39.10. Amended by Acts 2012, cc. 803, 835.
51.5-39.12. Amended by Acts 2009, cc. 813, 840; 2012, cc. 476, 507.
51.5-39.13. Amended by Acts 2013, c. 571.
51.5-40. Repealed by Acts 2012, c. 847.
51.5-41. Amended by Acts 2012, cc. 803, 835.
51.5-44. Amended by Acts 2008, cc. 431, 506; 2012, cc. 803, 835.
51.5-46. Amended by Acts 2005, c. 681; 2013, c. 571.
51.5-47 to 51.5-52. Repealed by Acts 2011, cc. 41, 51.
51.5-55. Amended by Acts 2012, c. 483.
51.5-56. Amended by Acts 2006, cc. 344, 380.
51.5-59. Amended by Acts 2006, cc. 344, 380.
51.5-63. Amended by Acts 2008, c. 184.
51.5-89. Amended by Acts 2012, cc. 805, 836.
51.5-116 to 51.5-149. Amended by Acts 2012, cc. 803, 835.
51.5-150. Amended by Acts 2012, cc. 322, 803, 835.
51.5-151. Amended by Acts 2012, cc. 463, 803, 835.
51.5-152. Amended by Acts 2013, c. 376.
51.5-153 to 51.5-180. Amended by Acts 2012, cc. 803, 835.

Section
52-8.6. Amended by Acts 2010, cc. 367, 472.
52-10. Amended by Acts 2005, c. 839.
52-26. Amended by Acts 2007, c. 135.
52-31.1. Amended by Acts 2006, c. 295; 2012, c. 827.
52-33. Amended by Acts 2011, cc. 818, 852.
52-34.1. Amended by Acts 2007, c. 198.
52-34.3. Amended by Acts 2007, c. 130.
52-34.7. Amended by Acts 2012, c. 776.
52-36. Amended by Acts 2011, c. 208.
52-38. Amended by Acts 2012, c. 542.
52-48. Amended by Acts 2011, cc. 467, 556.
53.1-5. Amended by Acts 2011, c. 375; 2012, cc. 803, 835.
53.1-7. Repealed by Acts 2011, c. 375.
53.1-10. Amended by Acts 2006, cc. 431, 500; 2007, c. 392; 2009, cc. 39, 621; 2012, cc. 803, 835; 2013, cc. 143, 214.
53.1-16. Repealed by Acts 2011, cc. 798, 871.
53.1-28. Amended by Acts 2006, cc. 108, 132.
53.1-30. Amended by Acts 2010, c. 844.
53.1-32. Amended by Acts 2009, cc. 740, 813, 840; 2010, c. 261; 2012, cc. 803, 835.
53.1-32.1. Amended by Acts 2012, cc. 803, 835.
53.1-33. Amended by Acts 2007, c. 591.
53.1-40.1. Amended by Acts 2005, c. 716.
53.1-40.2. Amended by Acts 2005, c. 716; 2008, cc. 779, 850, 870; 2009, cc. 813, 840.
53.1-40.3. Amended by Acts 2012, cc. 476, 507.
53.1-40.5. Amended by Acts 2012, cc. 476, 507.
53.1-40.7. Amended by Acts 2005, c. 639; 2012, cc. 476, 507.
53.1-40.8. Amended by Acts 2005, c. 716.
53.1-40.9. Amended by Acts 2005, c. 716.
53.1-40.10. Amended by Acts 2013, cc. 164, 235.
53.1-41. Amended by Acts 2006, c. 98; 2010, c. 616; 2012, cc. 803, 835.
53.1-48. Amended by Acts 2012, c. 360.
53.1-56. Amended by Acts 2010, c. 128; 2011, cc. 40, 48; 2013, cc. 585, 646.
53.1-57. Amended by Acts 2013, cc. 585, 646.
53.1-63.1. Amended by Acts 2012, cc. 803, 835.
53.1-67.4. Amended by Acts 2006, c. 187.
53.1-70. Amended by Acts 2005, c. 681.
53.1-77. Amended by Acts 2005, c. 716.
53.1-96. Amended by Acts 2007, cc. 95, 106.
53.1-105. Amended by Acts 2010, c. 547.
53.1-115.1. Amended by Acts 2006, cc. 857, 914.
53.1-116. Amended by Acts 2011, c. 491.
53.1-116.1. Amended by Acts 2006, cc. 857, 914; 2010, c. 858.
53.1-120. Amended by Acts 2006, c. 495; 2007, c. 377.
53.1-121. Amended by Acts 2006, cc. 857, 914.
53.1-126. Amended by Acts 2011, c. 727.

Section
53.1-127.1. Amended by Acts 2013, c. 91.
53.1-127.2. Amended by Acts 2013, c. 449.
53.1-128. Amended by Acts 2010, c. 168; 2011, c. 767.
53.1-129. Amended by Acts 2005, c. 409; 2008, c. 623; 2010, c. 132.
53.1-131. Amended by Acts 2006, c. 792.
53.1-131.1. Amended by Acts 2006, c. 792.
53.1-131.2. Amended by Acts 2010, c. 682.
53.1-131.3. Amended by Acts 2009, c. 842; 2010, c. 548.
53.1-133.02. Amended by Acts 2007, cc. 94, 109.
53.1-136. Amended by Acts 2005, c. 657; 2006, cc. 863, 914, 2009, cc. 813, 840; 2013, c. 708.
53.1-145. Amended by Acts 2006, cc. 698, 730, 863, 914; 2007, c. 528; 2009, cc. 813, 840; 2011, cc. 384, 410.
53.1-149. Amended by Acts 2010, c. 273.
53.1-159. Amended by Acts 2008, c. 846.
53.1-160. Amended by Acts 2007, cc. 94, 109; 2013, cc. 162, 209.
53.1-160.1. Amended by Acts 2006, cc. 857, 914; 2010, c. 858.
53.1-162. Amended by Acts 2010, c. 273.
53.1-176.3. Amended by Acts 2005, c. 758.
53.1-202.2. Amended by Acts 2008, c. 517.
53.1-202.3. Amended by Acts 2008, c. 517.
53.1-203. Amended by Acts 2006, c. 104; 2011, cc. 384, 410.
53.1-216. Amended by Acts 2012, cc. 476, 507.
53.1-218. Amended by Acts 2008, cc. 180, 415.
53.1-221. Amended by Acts 2007, c. 508.
53.1-223. Amended by Acts 2006, c. 553.
53.1-228. Amended by Acts 2010, c. 124.
53.1-233. Amended by Acts 2007, cc. 652, 737.
53.1-234. Amended by Acts 2007, cc. 652, 737.
53.1-261. Amended by Acts 2007, c. 394.
53.1-263. Amended by Acts 2007, c. 394.
54.1-102. Amended by Acts 2012, c. 416.
54.1-106. Amended by Acts 2010, c. 353.
54.1-111. Amended by Acts 2005, cc. 398, 642, 697; 2008, c. 358.
54.1-113. Amended by Acts 2006, c. 631; 2009, c. 472.
54.1-117. Amended by Acts 2011, cc. 342, 357.
54.1-201. Amended by Acts 2005, c. 383; 2012, c. 769; 2013, cc. 398, 486.
54.1-202. Amended by Acts 2005, c. 383.
54.1-204. Amended by Acts 2009, c. 667.
54.1-300. Amended by Acts 2007, cc. 892, 924; 2009, cc. 358, 557; 2012, cc. 803, 835.
54.1-306. Amended by Acts 2005, c. 383.
54.1-307.1. Amended by Acts 2005, c. 383.
54.1-309. Amended by Acts 2012, c. 522.
54.1-400. Amended by Acts 2008, c. 68; 2009, c. 309.
54.1-401. Amended by Acts 2009, c. 309.

Section
54.1-402. Amended by Acts 2005, cc. 359, 440; 2008, c. 294.
54.1-402.2. Amended by Acts 2009, c. 309.
54.1-403. Amended by Acts 2009, c. 309; 2010, c. 91.
54.1-404. Amended by Acts 2005, cc. 359, 440.
54.1-404.1. Repealed by Acts 2010, c. 91.
54.1-404.2. Amended by Acts 2009, c. 309.
54.1-405. Amended by Acts 2009, c. 309; 2010, c. 612.
54.1-406. Amended by Acts 2005, cc. 359, 440; 2010, c. 91.
54.1-409. Amended by Acts 2006, c. 643; 2009, c. 309.
54.1-410. Amended by Acts 2009, c. 309.
54.1-411. Amended by Acts 2009, c. 309; 2010, cc. 99, 206.
54.1-500. Amended by Acts 2009, cc. 358, 819; 2012, cc. 803, 835.
54.1-500.1. Amended by Acts 2009, cc. 358, 819; 2012, cc. 522, 803, 835.
54.1-501. Amended by Acts 2009, cc. 358, 819; 2012, cc. 803, 835.
54.1-503. Amended by Acts 2009, c. 819.
54.1-512. Amended by Acts 2009, c. 819.
54.1-516. Amended by Acts 2009, cc. 358, 819; 2012, cc. 803, 835.
54.1-517. Amended by Acts 2009, c. 819.
54.1-517.3. Repealed by Acts 2012, cc. 803, 835.
54.1-517.4. Repealed by Acts 2012, cc. 803, 835.
54.1-517.5. Repealed by Acts 2012, cc. 803, 835.
54.1-601. Amended by Acts 2009, c. 664.
54.1-602. Amended by Acts 2012, c. 522.
54.1-603. Amended by Acts 2010, c. 91.
54.1-700. Amended by Acts 2005, c. 829; 2012, cc. 803, 835.
54.1-701. Amended by Acts 2005, c. 829; 2012, cc. 476, 507, 803, 835.
54.1-702. Amended by Acts 2005, c. 829; 2010, c. 91.
54.1-703. Amended by Acts 2005, c. 829; 2012, cc. 803, 835.
54.1-703.2. Repealed by Acts 2012, cc. 803, 835.
54.1-703.3. Amended by Acts 2009, cc. 166, 328.
54.1-704.1. Amended by Acts 2005, c. 829; 2012, cc. 803, 835.
54.1-704.2. Amended by Acts 2005, c. 829; 2012, cc. 803, 835.
54.1-705. Amended by Acts 2005, c. 829; 2012, cc. 803, 835.
54.1-706. Amended by Acts 2005, c. 829; 2012, cc. 803, 835.
54.1-828. Amended by Acts 2005, c. 287.
54.1-829. Amended by Acts 2007, c. 853.
54.1-831. Amended by Acts 2010, c. 764; 2012, c. 769.

Section
54.1-831.01. Amended by Acts 2012, c. 522.
54.1-909. Amended by Acts 2007, cc. 326, 559.
54.1-1100. Amended by Acts 2005, c. 348; 2010, c. 62.
54.1-1101. Amended by Acts 2005, c. 348; 2007, c. 332.
54.1-1102. Amended by Acts 2006, cc. 454, 475; 2009, cc. 184, 586; 2010, c. 83; 2012, c. 522.
54.1-1103. Amended by Acts 2005, c. 348; 2010, c. 62; 2012, c. 308; 2013, c. 298.
54.1-1106. Amended by Acts 2005, c. 348; 2007, c. 804; 2013, c. 116.
54.1-1108. Amended by Acts 2013, c. 116.
54.1-1108.1. Amended by Acts 2005, c. 348.
54.1-1108.2. Amended by Acts 2013, c. 116.
54.1-1111. Amended by Acts 2010, cc. 82, 755.
54.1-1117. Amended by Acts 2012, c. 552.
54.1-1118. Amended by Acts 2013, c. 343.
54.1-1120, 54.1-1121. Amended by Acts 2013, c. 343.
54.1-1122. Amended by Acts 2006, c. 723; 2013, c. 343.
54.1-1123. Amended by Acts 2005, c. 252.
54.1-1125. Amended by Acts 2013, c. 343.
54.1-1126. Repealed by Acts 2013, c. 343.
54.1-1128. Amended by Acts 2005, c. 792; 2011, cc. 743, 744.
54.1-1129. Amended by Acts 2005, c. 792; 2008, c. 631.
54.1-1130. Amended by Acts 2005, c. 792.
54.1-1134. Amended by Acts 2009, cc. 184, 586.
54.1-1140. Amended by Acts 2007, c. 424; 2009, cc. 184, 586; 2010, cc. 81, 207.
54.1-1141. Amended by Acts 2007, c. 424; 2010, cc. 81, 207.
54.1-1142. Amended by Acts 2007, c. 424; 2009, cc. 184, 586; 2010, cc. 81, 207.
54.1-1142.1. Amended by Acts 2009, cc. 184, 586.
54.1-1143. Amended by Acts 2007, c. 424; 2009, cc. 184, 586; 2010, cc. 81, 207.
54.1-1400 to 54.1-1405. Repealed by Acts 2012, cc. 803, 835.
54.1-1500. Amended by Acts 2005, c. 599; 2012, cc. 803, 835.
54.1-1502, 54.1-1503. Repealed by Acts 2012, cc. 803, 835.
54.1-1504. Amended by Acts 2005, c. 599.
54.1-1507, 54.1-1508. Amended by Acts 2012, cc. 803, 835.
54.1-1700 to 54.1-1706. Repealed by Acts 2012, cc. 803, 835.
54.1-1800. Amended by Acts 2010, c. 625.
54.1-1801. Amended by Acts 2010, c. 625.
54.1-1802. Repealed by Acts 2010, c. 578.
54.1-1802.1. Amended by Acts 2010, c. 625; 2012, c. 769.
54.1-1803. Amended by Acts 2010, c. 625.
54.1-1804. Amended by Acts 2010, c. 625.

Section
54.1-1805. Amended by Acts 2010, c. 625.
54.1-1806. Amended by Acts 2010, c. 578.
54.1-2011. Amended by Acts 2012, c. 405.
54.1-2012. Amended by Acts 2010, c. 91; 2012, cc. 405, 522.
54.1-2013. Amended by Acts 2010, c. 91.
54.1-2020, 54.1-2021. Amended by Acts 2012, c. 405.
54.1-2022. Amended by Acts 2012, c. 405; Acts 2013, c. 353.
54.1-2023. Amended by Acts 2012, c. 405.
54.1-2100. Amended by Acts 2007, c. 809.
54.1-2103. Amended by Acts 2009, cc. 88, 262.
54.1-2104. Amended by Acts 2010, c. 91.
54.1-2105. Amended by Acts 2006, cc. 61, 627; 2007, c. 809; 2010, cc. 373, 637; 2012, c. 750.
54.1-2105.01. Amended by Acts 2011, c. 461.
54.1-2105.03. Amended by Acts 2011, c. 461; 2012, c. 750.
54.1-2105.1. Amended by Acts 2007, cc. 265, 809; 2008, cc. 851, 871; 2011, c. 461.
54.1-2106.1. Amended by Acts 2008, c. 319; 2012, c. 750.
54.1-2108.1. Amended by Acts 2013, c. 489.
54.1-2113. Amended by Acts 2007, c. 791; 2013, c. 754.
54.1-2114. Amended by Acts 2006, c. 723.
54.1-2130. Amended by Acts 2006, c. 627; 2008, cc. 851, 871; 2011, c. 461; 2012, c. 750.
54.1-2131. Amended by Acts 2006, c. 627; 2008, c. 741; 2011, cc. 34, 46, 461; 2012, c. 750.
54.1-2132. Amended by Acts 2006, c. 627; 2011, cc. 34, 46; 2012, c. 750.
54.1-2133. Amended by Acts 2006, c. 627; 2008, c. 741; 2011, cc. 34, 46, 461; 2012, c. 750.
54.1-2134. Amended by Acts 2006, c. 627; 2011, cc. 34, 46; 2012, c. 750.
54.1-2135. Amended by Acts 2011, cc. 34, 46, 461.
54.1-2137. Amended by Acts 2011, c. 461; 2012, c. 750.
54.1-2138. Amended by Acts 2006, c. 627; 2012, c. 750.
54.1-2138.1. Amended by Acts 2012, c. 750.
54.1-2139. Amended by Acts 2011, c. 461; 2012, c. 750.
54.1-2139.1. Amended by Acts 2012, c. 750.
54.1-2139.2, 54.1-2139.3. Repealed by Acts 2012, c. 750.
54.1-2141. Amended by Acts 2006, c. 627; 2012, c. 750.
54.1-2142.1. Amended by Acts 2013, c. 499.
54.1-2200. Amended by Acts 2011, cc. 777, 859; 2012, cc. 803, 835.
54.1-2201. Amended by Acts 2009, c. 309; 2011, cc. 777, 859.

Section
54.1-2202. Repealed by Acts 2012, cc. 803, 835.
54.1-2203. Amended by Acts 2011, cc. 777, 859.
54.1-2204. Repealed by Acts 2011, cc. 777, 859.
54.1-2205. Amended by Acts 2011, cc. 777, 859.
54.1-2206. Amended by Acts 2010, c. 91; 2011, cc. 777, 859.
54.1-2206.2. Amended by Acts 2007, c. 334; 2013, c. 546.
54.1-2207. Amended by Acts 2011, cc. 777, 859.
54.1-2208. Amended by Acts 2011, cc. 777, 859.
54.1-2208.2. Amended by Acts 2012, cc. 803, 835.
54.1-2208.3. Amended by Acts 2012, cc. 803, 835.
54.1-2210. Amended by Acts 2010, c. 91.
54.1-2300. Amended by Acts 2007, cc. 892, 924.
54.1-2301. Amended by Acts 2007, cc. 892, 924; 2008, c. 67; 2012, cc. 677, 704; 2013, c. 731.
54.1-2301.1. Amended by Acts 2008, c. 641.
54.1-2302. Amended by Acts 2007, cc. 892, 924.
54.1-2310. Amended by Acts 2011, c. 792.
54.1-2312. Amended by Acts 2011, c. 792.
54.1-2312.1. Amended by Acts 2013, c. 395.
54.1-2313. Amended by Acts 2010, c. 91; 2012, c. 522.
54.1-2322. Amended by Acts 2012, c. 355.
54.1-2342. Amended by Acts 2005, c. 691; 2013, c. 190.
54.1-2343. Amended by Acts 2010, cc. 457, 620.
54.1-2344. Amended by Acts 2007, cc. 809, 874; 2010, cc. 91, 457, 620.
54.1-2346. Amended by Acts 2011, cc. 334, 605.
54.1-2347. Amended by Acts 2010, c. 511; 2011, cc. 334, 605.
54.1-2348. Amended by Acts 2010, c. 511; 2012, c. 522.
54.1-2349. Amended by Acts 2009, c. 557; 2010, cc. 511; 615; 2011, c. 334; 2012, cc. 481, 797.
54.1-2351. Amended by Acts 2009, c. 557; 2010, 615.
54.1-2352. Amended by Acts 2009, c. 557.
54.1-2353. Amended by Acts 2011, cc. 334, 605.
54.1-2400. Amended by Acts 2009, cc. 472, 534; 2010, c. 414.
54.1-2400.02. Amended by Acts 2009, c. 687.
54.1-2400.1. Amended by Acts 2005, c. 716; 2010, cc. 778, 825.
54.1-2400.2. Amended by Acts 2006, cc. 155, 184; 2007, c. 395; 2009, cc. 342, 472.
54.1-2400.6. Amended by Acts 2011, c. 463.
54.1-2400.8. Amended by Acts 2005, c. 932.
54.1-2403.01. Amended by Acts 2007, cc. 780, 822.
54.1-2403.2. Amended by Acts 2012, c. 336.
54.1-2408. Amended by Acts 2010, c. 414.
54.1-2408.1. Amended by Acts 2007, c. 22; 2013, c. 765.

Section
54.1-2408.2. Amended by Acts 2013, c. 365.
54.1-2409.3. Amended by Acts 2013, c. 144.
54.1-2409. Amended by Acts 2006, c. 367; 2010, c. 414.
54.1-2409.3. Amended by Acts 2013, c. 144.
54.1-2409.4. Amended by Acts 2011, cc. 807, 849.
54.1-2411. Amended by Acts 2005, c. 402.
54.1-2413. Amended by Acts 2005, c. 402; 2010, c. 743.
54.1-2503. Amended by Acts 2005, cc. 610, 924.
54.1-2505. Amended by Acts 2006, c. 631; 2009, c. 472.
54.1-2506. Amended by Acts 2008, c. 37; 2011, c. 50.
54.1-2506.1. Amended by Acts 2005, c. 55; 2009, c. 382.
54.1-2508. Amended by Acts 2012, c. 361.
54.1-2515. Amended by Acts 2009, c. 472.
54.1-2516. Amended by Acts 2009, c. 472.
54.1-2517. Amended by Acts 2009, c. 472.
54.1-2519. Amended by Acts 2005, cc. 637, 678.
54.1-2520. Amended by Acts 2005, cc. 637, 678.
54.1-2521. Amended by Acts 2006, c. 167; 2012, cc. 21, 71.
54.1-2523. Amended by Acts 2005, cc. 637, 678; 2009, cc. 158, 162, 472; 2012, cc. 21, 71; 2013, c. 739.
54.1-2523.1. Amended by Acts 2012, cc. 21, 71; 2013, c. 739.
54.1-2523.2. Amended by Acts 2012, cc. 21, 71.
54.1-2602. Amended by Acts 2013, c. 436.
54.1-2604. Amended by Acts 2013, c. 436.
54.1-2700. Amended by Acts 2013, c. 240.
54.1-2709. Amended by Acts 2012, cc. 20, 116.
54.1-2711.1. Amended by Acts 2012, cc. 20, 116.
54.1-2712. Amended by Acts 2012, cc. 20, 116.
54.1-2713, 54.1-2714. Amended by Acts 2012, cc. 20, 116.
54.1-2722. Amended by Acts 2012, c. 120; 2013, c. 240.
54.1-2525. Amended by Acts 2011, cc. 812, 844; 2012, c. 116.
54.1-2703. Amended by Acts 2005, c. 587.
54.1-2704. Amended by Acts 2005, cc. 505, 587.
54.1-2706. Amended by Acts 2005, cc. 505, 587.
54.1-2709. Amended by Acts 2005, cc. 505, 587; 2007, c. 20.
54.1-2709.4. Amended by Acts 2009, c. 472.
54.1-2710. Repealed by Acts 2005, cc. 505, 587.
54.1-2712. Amended by Acts 2005, cc. 505, 587; 2008, cc. 84, 264.
54.1-2712.1. Amended by Acts 2005, cc. 505, 587.
54.1-2713. Amended by Acts 2005, cc. 505, 587.
54.1-2714.1. Repealed by Acts 2012, cc. 20, 116.
54.1-2715. Amended by Acts 2005, cc. 505, 587; 2006, c. 176; 2009, cc. 813, 840.
54.1-2718. Amended by Acts 2005, cc. 505, 587.

Section
54.1-2720. Amended by Acts 2005, cc. 505, 587.
54.1-2721. Amended by Acts 2006, c. 823.
54.1-2722. Amended by Acts 2005, cc. 505, 587; 2006, c. 858; 2007, c. 702; 2009, cc. 99, 506, 561; 2011, c. 289.
54.1-2723. Repealed by Acts 2005, cc. 505, 587.
54.1-2725. Amended by Acts 2012, cc. 20, 116.
54.1-2726. Amended by Acts 2005, cc. 505, 587; 2009, cc. 813, 840.
54.1-2726.1. Amended by Acts 2005, cc. 505, 587.
54.1-2727. Amended by Acts 2006, c. 823.
54.1-2728. Amended by Acts 2005, cc. 505, 587.
54.1-2729. Amended by Acts 2005, cc. 505, 587.
54.1-2729.2. Amended by Acts 2006, c. 75.
54.1-2729.3. Amended by Acts 2006, c. 75.
54.1-2800. Amended by Acts 2006, c. 56.
54.1-2803. Amended by Acts 2006, c. 56.
54.1-2806. Amended by Acts 2006, c. 56; 2010, c. 324.
54.1-2807. Amended by Acts 2005, c. 905; 2010, c. 383.
54.1-2808.1. Amended by Acts 2012, cc. 24, 120.
54.1-2810. Amended by Acts 2013, c. 108.
54.1-2813. Amended by Acts 2005, c. 477; 2006, c. 56.
54.1-2816. Amended by Acts 2005, c. 477.
54.1-2816.1. Amended by Acts 2008, c. 396; 2012, c. 497.
54.1-2817. Amended by Acts 2005, c. 477; 2006, c. 56.
54.1-2818.1. Amended by Acts 2010, c. 377; 2011, c. 88.
54.1-2819. Amended by Acts 2006, c. 555.
54.1-2820. Amended by Acts 2007, c. 621.
54.1-2822. Amended by Acts 2007, c. 621.
54.1-2825. Amended by Acts 2010, cc. 324, 380.
54.1-2900. Amended by Acts 2007, c. 861; 2008, cc. 64, 89; 2009, cc. 83, 507; 2010, cc. 715, 725; 2011, cc. 121, 187; 2012, cc. 3, 110, 168, 213, 399.
54.1-2901. Amended by Acts 2005, cc. 113, 926; 2006, c. 750; 2008, c. 674; 2010, c. 245; 2011, cc. 632, 811; 2012, c. 213.
54.1-2904. Amended by Acts 2013, c. 144.
54.1-2905. Repealed by Acts 2013, c. 144.
54.1-2910.1. Amended by Acts 2007, c. 861; 2008, c. 479.
54.1-2912. Amended by Acts 2005, c. 163.
54.1-2912.3. Amended by Acts 2007, c. 861; 2011, c. 808.
54.1-2913. Repealed by Acts 2013, c. 144.
54.1-2913.1. Amended by Acts 2013, c. 144.
54.1-2914. Amended by Acts 2005, c. 163.
54.1-2915. Amended by Acts 2005, c. 163; 2013, c. 144.
54.1-2916. Repealed by Acts 2005, c. 163.
54.1-2917. Repealed by Acts 2013, c. 144.

Section
54.1-2924. Repealed by Acts 2013, c. 144.
54.1-2928. Repealed by Acts 2013, c. 144.
54.1-2930 to 54.1-2933. Amended by Acts 2013, c. 144.
54.1-2935. Amended by Acts 2013, c. 144.
54.1-2939. Amended by Acts 2013, c. 144.
54.1-2949, 54.1-2950. Amended by Acts 2013, c. 144.
54.1-2950.1. Amended by Acts 2011, cc. 691, 714.
54.1-2951.1. Amended by Acts 2011, c. 390; 2013, c. 144.
54.1-2951.3. Amended by Acts 2005, c. 163.
54.1-2952. Amended by Acts 2005, c. 662; 2008, c. 281; 2012, c. 81.
54.1-2952.1. Amended by Acts 2007, c. 16.
54.1-2953. Amended by Acts 2013, c. 144.
54.1-2954.1. Amended by Acts 2011, c. 390.
54.1-2956. Amended by Acts 2011, cc. 691, 714.
54.1-2956.1. Amended by Acts 2008, cc. 64, 89; 2011, c. 390.
54.1-2956.4. Amended by Acts 2008, c. 89.
54.1-2956.5. Amended by Acts 2008, cc. 64, 89.
54.1-2956.8. Amended by Acts 2011, cc. 691, 714.
54.1-2956.8:1. Amended by Acts 2009, cc. 83, 507.
54.1-2956.8:2. Amended by Acts 2009, cc. 83, 507; 2011, c. 390.
54.1-2956.11. Amended by Acts 2011, c. 691, 714.
54.1-2957. Amended by Acts 2006, c. 750; 2012, c. 213.
54.1-2957.01. Amended by Acts 2005, c. 926; 2006, c. 494; 2012, c. 213.
54.1-2957.03. Amended by Acts 2009, c. 646.
54.1-2957.4. Amended by Acts 2013, c. 144.
54.1-2957.5. Amended by Acts 2011, cc. 691, 714.
54.1-2957.9. Amended by Acts 2009, c. 646.
54.1-2957.10. Amended by Acts 2008, c. 36.
54.1-2959. Amended by Acts 2007, c. 678.
54.1-2969. Amended by Acts 2005, cc. 181, 227; 2008, c. 330.
54.1-2970. Amended by Acts 2009, cc. 813, 840; 2012, cc. 476, 507.
54.1-2971. Repealed by Acts 2008, cc. 35, 77.
54.1-2972. Amended by Acts 2010, c. 46; 2011, c. 613; 2012, c. 136.
54.1-2974. Amended by Acts 2013, c. 671.
54.1-2982. Amended by Acts 2005, c. 186; 2007, cc. 92, 907; 2009, cc. 211, 268; 2010, c. 792; 2012, cc. 476, 507.
54.1-2983. Amended by Acts 2008, cc. 301, 696; 2009, cc. 211, 268; 2010, c. 16.
54.1-2983.2. Amended by Acts 2010, c. 792.
54.1-2983.3. Amended by Acts 2010, c. 792.
54.1-2984. Amended by Acts 2005, cc. 186; 2007, cc. 92, 907; 2009, cc. 211, 268; 2010, c. 792.

Section
54.1-2985. Amended by Acts 2008, c. 301, 696; 2009, cc. 211, 268.
54.1-2986. Amended by Acts 2005, c. 716; 2009, cc. 211, 268; 2010, c. 792.
54.1-2986.2. Amended by Acts 2010, c. 792.
54.1-2987. Amended by Acts 2009, cc. 211, 268.
54.1-2987.1. Amended by Acts 2009, cc. 211, 268, 549, 813, 840; 2010, c. 792.
54.1-2988. Amended by Acts 2009, cc. 211, 268; 2010, c. 792.
54.1-2989. Amended by Acts 2009, cc. 211, 268.
54.1-2990. Amended by Acts 2009, cc. 211, 268.
54.1-2991. Amended by Acts 2009, cc. 211, 268.
54.1-2992. Amended by Acts 2009, cc. 211, 268.
54.1-2995. Amended by Acts 2010, c. 16.
54.1-3000. Amended by Acts 2012, c. 213.
54.1-3001. Amended by Acts 2008, c. 674; 2010, c. 245; 2012, cc. 117, 178.
54.1-3002. Amended by Acts 2008, c. 34.
54.1-3005. Amended by Acts 2005, cc. 54, 610, 924; 2006, cc. 190, 686; 2009, c. 687; 2010, c. 188; 2012, cc. 213, 803, 835.
54.1-3007. Amended by Acts 2005, cc. 610, 924.
54.1-3012.1. Amended by Acts 2008, c. 373; 2009, c. 382.
54.1-3014. Amended by Acts 2012, c. 644.
54.1-3017. Amended by Acts 2011, c. 390.
54.1-3020. Amended by Acts 2011, c. 390.
54.1-3023. Amended by Acts 2011, c. 390.
54.1-3029. Amended by Acts 2012, c. 764.
54.1-3042. Amended by Acts 2009, cc. 133, 837.
54.1-3100. Amended by Acts 2005, cc. 610, 924.
54.1-3101. Amended by Acts 2005, cc. 924, 610.
54.1-3102. Amended by Acts 2005, c. 924.
54.1-3103. Amended by Acts 2005, cc. 610, 924.
54.1-3103.1. Amended by Acts 2011, c. 609.
54.1-3202. Amended by Acts 2008, c. 674; 2009, cc. 353, 761.
54.1-3204. Amended by Acts 2009, cc. 353, 761.
54.1-3205. Amended by Acts 2005, cc. 711, 720.
54.1-3300, 54.1-3300.1. Amended by Acts 2013, c. 192.
54.1-3301. Amended by Acts 2008, c. 674; 2009, cc. 101, 353, 761; 2012, c. 213.
54.1-3303. Amended by Acts 2006, c. 432; 2010, c. 74.
54.1-3305. Amended by Acts 2005, c. 70.
54.1-3307. Amended by Acts 2005, c. 777; 2006, c. 632.
54.1-3314. Amended by Acts 2008, c. 672.
54.1-3315. Repealed by Acts 2007, c. 662.
54.1-3316. Amended by Acts 2007, c. 662.
54.1-3320. Amended by Acts 2005, c. 403; 2006, c. 626; 2010, c. 90.
54.1-3322. Repealed by Acts 2007, c. 662.
54.1-3401. Amended by Acts 2005, cc. 475, 839; 2006, c. 346; 2012, c. 213; 2013, cc. 412, 504, 544, 765.
54.1-3404. Amended by Acts 2005, cc. 868, 881.

Section
54.1-3408. Amended by Acts 2005, cc. 113, 610, 924; 2006, cc. 75, 432, 686, 858; 2007, c. 17, 699, 702, 783; 2008, cc. 85, 694; 2009, cc. 48, 110, 506, 813, 840; 2010, cc. 179, 245, 252; 2011, c. 292.
54.1-3408. Amended by Acts 2012, cc. 787, 803, 833, 835; 2013, cc. 114, 132, 183, 191, 252, 267, 328, 336, 359, 617.
54.1-3408.01. Amended by Acts 2006, c. 195; 2009, cc. 813, 840.
54.1-3410.2. Amended by Acts 2005, c. 200; 2012, c. 173; 2013, c. 765.
54.1-3411.1. Amended by Acts 2005, c. 68; 2008, c. 429; 2009, cc. 109, 114.
54.1-3414. Amended by Acts 2006, c. 346.
54.1-3415. Amended by Acts 2006, c. 346.
54.1-3420.1. Amended by Acts 2010, c. 193; 2011, cc. 262, 318.
54.1-3420.2. Amended by Acts 2010, c. 28.
54.1-3423. Amended by Acts 2009, cc. 149, 169; 2010, c. 28.
54.1-3425. Repealed by Acts 2009, cc. 149, 169.
54.1-3431. Amended by Acts 2005, cc. 868, 881.
54.1-3433. Amended by Acts 2005, c. 97.
54.1-3434. Amended by Acts 2008, c. 320; 2011, c. 610.
54.1-3434.02. Amended by Acts 2009, c. 100.
54.1-3434.1. Amended by Acts 2005, cc. 115, 637, 678; 2006, c. 397; 2008, cc. 79, 618; 2011, c. 124; 2013, cc. 412, 544, 765.
54.1-3434.2. Amended by Acts 2005, c. 115; 2008, cc. 79, 320, 618; 2013, c. 765.
54.1-3434.3. Amended by Acts 2005, c. 115; 2007, c. 662.
54.1-3434.4. Amended by Acts 2005, c. 115; 2008, cc. 79, 618.
54.1-3435. Amended by Acts 2008, c. 320.
54.1-3435.01. Amended by Acts 2008, c. 320.
54.1-3435.1. Amended by Acts 2007, c. 662.
54.1-3435.2. Amended by Acts 2008, c. 320; 2013, c. 504.
54.1-3435.3. Amended by Acts 2007, c. 662.
54.1-3435.4. Amended by Acts 2008, c. 320.
54.1-3435.5. Repealed by Acts 2007, c. 662.
54.1-3437.1. Amended by Acts 2009, cc. 813, 840.
54.1-3439. Amended by Acts 2008, c. 320.
54.1-3446. Amended by Acts 2005, c. 119; 2008, c. 59; 2011, cc. 384, 410; 2012, cc. 762, 816; 2013, cc. 295, 785.
54.1-3448. Amended by Acts 2005, c. 119; 2008, c. 59; 2010, c. 423; 2011, c. 700.
54.1-3450. Amended by Acts 2005, c. 119; 2006, c. 346; 2007, c. 14; 2010, c. 423; 2013, c. 233.
54.1-3452. Amended by Acts 2006, c. 346; 2010, c. 423; 2012, c. 540.
54.1-3454. Amended by Acts 2006, c. 346; 2010, c. 423; 2012, c. 541.

Section
54.1-3457. Amended by Acts 2013, cc. 412, 544.
54.1-3481. Amended by Acts 2010, cc. 70, 368.
54.1-3482. Amended by Acts 2005, c. 928; 2007, cc. 9, 18.
54.1-3500. Amended by Acts 2013, c. 264.
54.1-3503. Amended by Acts 2013, cc. 201, 590.
54.1-3505. Amended by Acts 2013, c. 264.
54.1-3506. Amended by Acts 2009, cc. 813, 840; 2013, c. 264.
54.1-3703. Amended by Acts 2006, c. 685.
54.1-3801. Amended by Acts 2008, c. 674; 2009, cc. 149, 169.
54.1-3807. Amended by Acts 2007, c. 754.
54.1-3812. Amended by Acts 2006, c. 396; 2010, c. 834.
54.1-3813. Amended by Acts 2008, c. 490.
54.1-3900. Amended by Acts 2008, cc. 136, 845.
54.1-3900.01. Amended by Acts 2005, cc. 184, 212.
54.1-3902. Amended by Acts 2006, cc. 198, 230.
54.1-3906. Amended by Acts 2011, c. 703.
54.1-3913.1. Amended by Acts 2007, c. 807.
54.1-3925. Amended by Acts 2011, c. 709.
54.1-3931. Amended by Acts 2013, c. 396.
54.1-3935. Amended by Acts 2009, c. 287.
54.1-3936. Amended by Acts 2005, cc. 184, 212.
54.1-4005. Amended by Acts 2012, c. 586.
54.1-4009. Amended by Acts 2013, c. 262.
54.1-4010. Amended by Acts 2010, cc. 540, 657; 2013, c. 262.
54.1-4101. Amended by Acts 2013, c. 262.
54.1-4104. Amended by Acts 2012, c. 532
54.1-4110. Amended by Acts 2010, c. 100.
54.1-4201. Amended by Acts 2005, c. 859.
54.1-4201.1. Amended by Acts 2005, c. 193.
54.1-4400. Amended by Acts 2007, c. 804.
54.1-4401. Amended by Acts 2007, c. 804.
54.1-4402. Amended by Acts 2007, c. 804.
54.1-4403. Amended by Acts 2007, c. 804.
54.1-4404. Amended by Acts 2007, c. 804.
54.1-4405. Amended by Acts 2007, c. 804.
54.1-4405.1. Amended by Acts 2007, c. 804.
54.1-4406. Amended by Acts 2007, c. 804.
54.1-4407. Amended by Acts 2007, c. 804.
54.1-4408. Amended by Acts 2007, c. 804.
54.1-4409. Repealed by Acts 2007, c. 804.
54.1-4410. Repealed by Acts 2007, c. 804.
54.1-4411. Amended by Acts 2007, c. 804.
54.1-4412. Repealed by Acts 2007, c. 804.
54.1-4413, 54.1-4413.1. Repealed by Acts 2007, c. 804.
54.1-4414. Amended by Acts 2007, c. 804.
54.1-4415. Amended by Acts 2007, c. 804.
54.1-4416. Amended by Acts 2007, c. 804.
54.1-4417. Repealed by Acts 2007, c. 804.
54.1-4418. Amended by Acts 2007, c. 804.
54.1-4419. Repealed by Acts 2007, c. 804.
54.1-4420. Amended by Acts 2007, c. 804.
54.1-4421. Amended by Acts 2007, c. 804.
54.1-4423. Amended by Acts 2007, c. 804.

Section
55-7. Amended by Acts 2005, c. 935.
55-7.1. Repealed by Acts 2005, c. 935.
55-7.2. Repealed by Acts 2005, c. 935.
55-12.4. Amended by Acts 2013, c. 323.
55-13.3. Amended by Acts 2013, c. 323.
55-17.1. Amended by Acts 2011, c. 661; 2012, c. 558.
55-19. Repealed by Acts 2005, c. 935.
55-19.3. Repealed by Acts 2005, c. 935.
55-19.4. Repealed by Acts 2005, c. 935.
55-20.2. Amended by Acts 2006, c. 281.
55-27 to 55-34. Repealed by Acts 2005, c. 935.
55-34.1 to 55-34.19. Repealed by Acts 2012, c. 614.
55-37. Amended by Acts 2012, c. 45.
55-48. Amended by Acts 2011, c. 701.
55-50.1. Amended by Acts 2007, c. 931.
55-58.3. Amended by Acts 2011, c. 77.
55-59.1. Amended by Acts 2009, c. 307.
55-59.4. Amended by Acts 2010, c. 417.
55-60. Amended by Acts 2005, c. 935.
55-66.3. Amended by Acts 2006, c. 907; 2009, cc. 254, 421; 2010, c. 236.
55-66.5. Amended by Acts 2006, c. 907.
55-66.6. Amended by Acts 2010, c. 352.
55-70.1. Amended by Acts 2008, c. 392; 2011, c. 803.
55-79.2. Amended by Acts 2009, c. 557.
55-79.40. Amended by Acts 2006, c. 646.
55-79.41. Amended by Acts 2008, cc. 851, 871.
55-79.43. Amended by Acts 2006, cc. 9, 317.
55-79.53. Amended by Acts 2012, c. 758.
55-79.54. Amended by Acts 2012, c. 520.
55-79.58, 55-79.58:1. Amended by Acts 2008, cc. 851, 871.
55-79.61. Amended by Acts 2012, c. 520.
55-79.73. Amended by Acts 2012, c. 758.
55-79.73:1. Amended by Acts 2007, c. 675.
55-79.74. Amended by Acts 2008, cc. 851, 871; 2013, c. 599.
55-79.74:1. Amended by Acts 2011, cc. 334, 361, 605.
55-79.74:3. Amended by Acts 2006, c. 646.
55-79.75. Amended by Acts 2005, c. 353; 2007, c. 675; 2013, c. 275.
55-79.75:2. Amended by Acts 2010, cc. 166, 453.
55-79.79. Amended by Acts 2006, c. 646; 2008, cc. 851, 871; 2013, c. 599.
55-79.80:2. Amended by Acts 2011, cc. 372, 378.
55-79.81. Amended by Acts 2007, cc. 696, 712; 2008, cc. 851, 871.
55-79.83. Amended by Acts 2013, c. 256.
55-79.84:1. Amended by Acts 2008, cc. 851, 871.
55-79.86. Amended by Acts 2008, cc. 851, 871.
55-79.87. Amended by Acts 2007, c. 266; 2012, c. 325.
55-79.89. Amended by Acts 2008, cc. 851, 871; 2011, c. 605.

Section
55-79.90. Amended by Acts 2006, c. 646; 2007, cc. 854, 910; 2011, c. 605.
55-79.92. Amended by Acts 2006, c. 726.
55-79.93. Amended by Acts 2012, cc. 481, 797.
55-79.93:1. Amended by Acts 2008, cc. 851, 871; 2009, c. 557; 2012, cc. 481, 797.
55-79.94. Amended by Acts 2007, cc. 602, 665.
55-79.95. Amended by Acts 2007, c. 445; 2008, cc. 851, 871.
55-79.97. Amended by Acts 2005, c. 415; 2007, cc. 696, 712, 854, 910; 2008, cc. 851, 871; 2011, c. 334; 2013, cc. 357, 492.
55-79.97:1. Amended by Acts 2011, cc. 334, 577, 585.
55-79.98. Amended by Acts 2011, c. 605.
55-79.99. Amended by Acts 2011, c. 605.
55.82. Amended by Acts 2009, c. 593.
55-82.1. Amended by Acts 2012, c. 810.
55-106.2. Amended by Acts 2008, cc. 117, 814.
55-108. Amended by Acts 2005, c. 744.
55-137.1. Amended by Acts 2013, c. 263.
55-154.2. Amended by Acts 2012, c. 695.
55-161. Amended by Acts 2005, c. 839.
55-205. Amended by Acts 2008, cc. 511, 691.
55-210.3:01. Amended by Acts 2008, cc. 90, 556.
55-210.21. Amended by Acts 2005, c. 118.
55-218.1. Amended by Acts 2006, c. 318; 2008, c. 119.
55-222. Amended by Acts 2007, c. 634; 2013, c. 563.
55-225. Amended by Acts 2008, c. 489.
55-225.1. Amended by Acts 2012, c. 705.
55-225.2. Amended by Acts 2013, c. 110.
55-225.3. Amended by Acts 2008, cc. 489, 640.
55-225.4. Amended by Acts 2008, c. 640; 2011, c. 766.
55-225.8. Amended by Acts 2012, cc. 705, 788; 2013, cc. 279, 712.
55-225.9. Amended by Acts 2011, c. 779.
55-225.10. Amended by Acts 2011, c. 530; 2012, c. 788.
55-225.12, 55-225.13. Amended by Acts 2012, c. 788.
55-225.14. Amended by Acts 2012, c. 788.
55-226.2. Amended by Acts 2005, c. 278; 2010, c. 550; 2012, c. 338.
55-230. Amended by Acts 2008, cc. 551, 691.
55-232. Amended by Acts 2007, c. 869.
55-237.1. Amended by Acts 2006, cc. 91, 129.
55-243. Amended by Acts 2010, c. 793; 2012, c. 788; 2013, c. 563.
55-246.1. Amended by Acts 2010, c. 550; 2013, c. 563.
55-248.1. Repealed by Acts 2010, c. 92.
55-248.4. Amended by Acts 2007, c. 634; 2008, cc. 489, 640; 2010, cc. 180, 550; 2012, c. 788; 2013, c. 563.

Section
55-248.5. Amended by Acts 2013, cc. 279, 712.
55-248.6. Amended by Acts 2008, cc. 489, 640.
55-248.6:1. Amended by Acts 2008, c. 489; 2011, c. 766; 2013, c. 563.
55-248.7. Amended by Acts 2012, cc. 464, 503.
55-248.7:2. Amended by Acts 2005, c. 285; 2010, c. 550; 2012, c. 788.
55-248.9:1. Amended by Acts 2006, cc. 491, 667; 2008, c. 489; 2010, c. 550.
55-248.11:2. Amended by Acts 2008, c. 640.
55-248.13. Amended by Acts 2007, c. 634; 2008, cc. 489, 640; 2009, c. 663.
55-248.13:3. Amended by Acts 2009, c. 663.
55-248.15:1. Amended by Acts 2007, c. 634; 2010, c. 550; 2013, c. 563.
55-248.15:2. Amended by Acts 2006, c. 667; 2007, c. 634; 2008, c. 489; 2009, c. 663; 2010, c. 550; 2011, c. 766; 2013, c. 563.
55-248.16. Amended by Acts 2008, cc. 489, 617, 640; 2009, c. 663; 2011, c. 766.
55-248.18. Amended by Acts 2008, cc. 489, 617; 2009, c. 663; 2011, c. 766.
55-248.18:2. Amended by Acts 2009, c. 663; 2011, c. 779.
55-248.21:1. Amended by Acts 2005, c. 742; 2006, c. 667; 2007, c. 252.
55-248.24. Amended by Acts 2005, c. 807; 2011, c. 766.
55-248.25.1. Amended by Acts 2009, c. 137.
55-248.26. Amended by Acts 2013, c. 110.
55-248.31. Amended by Acts 2005, cc. 808, 883; 2006, cc. 628, 717; 2007, c. 273; 2008, c. 489; 2013, c. 563.
55-248.32. Amended by Acts 2009, c. 663.
55-248.34:1. Amended by Acts 2006, c. 667; 2008, c. 489; 2010, c. 793; 2012, c. 788; 2013, c. 563.
55-248.37. Amended by Acts 2005, c. 805; 2009, c. 663; 2013, c. 563.
55-248.38:1. Amended by Acts 2013, c. 563.
55-248.38:2. Amended by Acts 2006, c. 129; 2013, c. 563.
55-248.38:3. Amended by Acts 2010, c. 550; 2011, c. 766.
55-248.40. Amended by Acts 2013, c. 110.
55-248.45. Amended by Acts 2008, c. 329.
55-248.45:1. Amended by Acts 2006, c. 303.
55-248.46. Amended by Acts 2005, c. 416.
55-268.1 to 55-268.10. Repealed by Acts 2008, c. 184.
55-268.11 to 55-268.20. Repealed by Acts 2012, c. 614.
55-277. Amended by Acts 2005, c. 681.
55-277.1 to 55-277.33. Repealed by Acts 2012, c. 614.
55-278 to 55-286.2. Repealed by Acts 2012, c. 614.
55-288.1. Amended by Acts 2006, c. 861.
55-299. Amended by Acts 2007, c. 574.

Section
55-317. Amended by Acts 2005, c. 873.
55-362. Amended by Acts 2007, c. 267; 2008, cc. 376, 851, 871; 2012, c. 751.
55-362.1. Amended by Acts 2008, cc. 851, 871.
55-369. Amended by Acts 2008, c. 376; 2013, cc. 259, 327.
55-370. Amended by Acts 2006, c. 653; 2007, c. 267; 2012, c. 460; 2013, cc. 259, 327.
55-370.01. Amended by Acts 2007, c. 267.
55-373. Amended by Acts 2006, c. 653.
55-374. Amended by Acts 2006, c. 653; 2007, c. 267.
55-374.1. Amended by Acts 2006, c. 653; 2008, cc. 851, 871.
55-374.2. Amended by Acts 2008, cc. 851, 871.
55-375. Amended by Acts 2006, c. 653; 2008, cc. 851, 871.
55-380. Amended by Acts 2012, c. 751
55-382. Amended by Acts 2008, c. 376.
55-383. Amended by Acts 2006, c. 653; 2008, c. 376.
55-391.1. Amended by Acts 2011, c. 605.
55-392.1. Amended by Acts 2008, cc. 851, 871.
55-394.1. Amended by Acts 2006, c. 653; 2012, cc. 481, 797.
55-396. Amended by Acts 2008, c. 376; 2011, c. 605; 2012, c. 751.
55-397. Amended by Acts 2012, c. 751.
55-399. Amended by Acts 2009, c. 557; 2011, c. 605.
55-399.1. Amended by Acts 2009, c. 557.
55-401 to 55-415. Repealed by Acts 2012, c. 614.
55-417. Amended by Acts 2009, c. 664.
55-418. Amended by Acts 2005, c. 275; 2009, c. 664.
55-419. Amended by Acts 2009, c. 664.
55-426. Amended by Acts 2005, c. 436.
55-453. Amended by Acts 2008, cc. 822, 830; 2009, c. 221.
55-471. Amended by Acts 2008, c. 627.
55-478. Amended by Acts 2005, c. 436.
55-484. Amended by Acts 2005, c. 436; 2008, cc. 851, 871.
55-487. Amended by Acts 2008, cc. 851, 871.
55-496. Amended by Acts 2008, cc. 851, 871.
55-504.1. Amended by Acts 2008, cc. 851, 871; 2009, c. 557; 2012, cc. 481, 797.
55-508. Amended by 2008, cc. 851, 871.
55-509. Amended by 2008, cc. 851, 871; 2011, c. 334.
55-509.2. Amended by Acts 2008, cc. 851, 871; 2012, c. 671.
55-509.3. Amended by Acts 2011, c. 334.
55-509.4. Amended by Acts 2010, c. 165.
55-509.5. Amended by Acts 2013, cc. 357, 492.
55-509.6. Amended by Acts 2009, c. 557; 2011, cc. 334, 577, 585.
55-509.7. Amended by Acts 2010, c. 165; 2011, c. 334.

Section
55-509.10. Amended by Acts 2009, c. 69; 2013, c. 275.
55-510. Amended by Acts 2007, c. 675; 2008, cc. 851, 871; 2009, c. 665; 2011, c. 361.
55-510.1. Amended by Acts 2005, c. 353.
55-511, 55-512. Repealed by Acts 2008, cc. 851, 871.
55-513. Amended by Acts 2008, cc. 851, 871; 2011, cc. 372, 378.
55-513.1. Amended by Acts 2007, cc. 854, 910; 2008, cc. 851, 871; 2010, cc. 166, 453.
55-514. Amended by Acts 2008, cc. 851, 871.
55-514.2. Amended by Acts 2008, cc. 851, 871.
55-515. Amended by Acts 2012, c. 758.
55-516.1. Amended by Acts 2008, cc. 851, 871; 2009, c. 557; 2012, cc. 481, 797.
55-517. Amended by Acts 2007, c. 265.
55-518. Amended by Acts 2005, c. 510; 2006, c. 706; 2007, c. 265.
55-519. Amended by Acts 2005, c. 510; 2006, cc. 247, 514, 533, 705, 767; 2007, cc. 265, 784; 2008, c. 491; 2009, c. 641; 2010, c. 518; 2011, c. 461; 2013, c. 357.
55-519.1. Amended by Acts 2007, c. 265.
55-520. Amended by Acts 2005, c. 510; 2007, c. 265; 2011, c. 82.
55-521. Amended by Acts 2005, c. 510; 2007, c. 265.
55-522. Amended by Acts 2007, c. 265.
55-524. Amended by Acts 2005, c. 510; 2007, c. 265.
55-525. Amended by Acts 2007, c. 265.
55-525.12. Amended by Acts 2011, c. 82.
55-525.13. Amended by Acts 2011, c. 82.
55-526. Amended by Acts 2009, c. 262.
55-528. Amended by Acts 2008, cc. 851, 871.
55-529. Amended by Acts 2008, cc. 851, 871.
55-530. Amended by Acts 2008, cc. 851, 871; 2010, cc. 59, 208; 2012, cc. 481, 797.
55-530.1. Amended by Acts 2009, c. 557; 2013, c. 754.
55-531. Amended by Acts 2005, c. 839.
55-532. Amended by Acts 2007, c. 925; 2008, c. 253.
55-541.01 to 55-541.06. Repealed by Acts 2012, c. 614.
55-542.06. Amended by Acts 2007, c. 752.
55-544.01. Amended by Acts 2010, cc. 455, 632.
55-544.02. Amended by Acts 2010, cc. 455, 632.
55-544.08. Amended by Acts 2006, c. 666.
55-545.01. Amended by Acts 2007, c. 216.
55-545.03. Amended by Acts 2007, c. 216.
55-545.05. Amended by Acts 2011, c. 354; 2012, cc. 555, 718.
55-545.06. Amended by Acts 2007, c. 216.
55-546.02. Amended by Acts 2010, cc. 455, 632.
55-546.04. Amended by Acts 2007, c. 218.

Section
55-548.08. Amended by Acts 2012, c. 562.
55-548.10. Amended by Acts 2007, c. 197.
55-548.13. Amended by Acts 2007, c. 254.
56-1. Amended by Acts 2006, cc. 691, 912, 929, 941; 2007, c. 619; 2009, c. 746; 2011, cc. 408, 738, 740.
56-1.2. Amended by Acts 2011, c. 408.
56-5.1. Repealed by Acts 2005, c. 35.
56-15. Amended by Acts 2007, c. 813; 2009, c. 807.
56-17. Amended by Acts 2009, c. 807.
56-46.1. Amended by Acts 2007, cc. 756, 761, 776, 825; 2009, cc. 808, 854; 2011, cc. 236, 243; 2012, cc. 54, 284.
56-51.1. Repealed by Acts 2011, c. 429.
56-88. Amended by Acts 2009, c. 746.
56-88.1. Amended by Acts 2011, cc. 738, 740.
56-123. Amended by Acts 2005, c. 839.
56-124. Amended by Acts 2005, c. 839.
56-232. Amended by Acts 2006, c. 411; 2009, c. 746.
56-233.1. Amended by Acts 2007, cc. 888, 933; 2008, c. 522.
56-234. Amended by Acts 2011, cc. 738, 740.
56-234.2. Amended by Acts 2007, cc. 888, 933.
56-234.5. Amended by Acts 2010, c. 581.
56-235.1. Amended by Acts 2011, cc. 738, 740.
56-235.2. Amended by Acts 2007, cc. 537, 888, 933.
56-235.5. Amended by Acts 2009, c. 788.
56-235.5:1. Amended by Acts 2010, c. 748; 2013, c. 26.
56-235.6. Amended by Acts 2006, c. 574; 2007, cc. 888, 933.
56-236. Amended by Acts 2011, cc. 738, 740.
56-237. Amended by Acts 2011, cc. 738, 740.
56-237.1. Amended by Acts 2011, cc. 738, 740.
56-237.2. Amended by Acts 2011, cc. 738, 740.
56-238. Amended by Acts 2010, cc. 1, 2; 2011, cc. 738, 740.
56-240. Amended by Acts 2011, cc. 738, 740.
56-241. Amended by Acts 2011, cc. 738, 740.
56-245.2. Amended by Acts 2012, c. 338.
56-245.3. Amended by Acts 2012, c. 338.
56-247.1. Amended by Acts 2010, c. 320; 2011, cc. 500, 738, 740.
56-248. Amended by Acts 2011, cc. 738, 740.
56-248.1. Amended by Acts 2011, cc. 738, 740.
56-249.2. Amended by Acts 2011, cc. 738, 740.
56-249.6. Amended by Acts 2006, c. 939; 2007, cc. 888, 933; 2009, c. 244.
56-257.2. Amended by Acts 2005, c. 35.
56-257.3. Repealed by Acts 2005, c. 35.
56-258. Amended by Acts 2013, cc. 585, 646.
56-259. Amended by Acts 2009, c. 807.
56-265.1. Amended by Acts 2005, c. 22; 2006, c. 411; 2007, c. 813; 2009, cc. 746, 794.
56-265.2. Amended by Acts 2012, cc. 54, 284.
56-265.4:3. Repealed by Acts 2011, cc. 738, 740.

Section
56-265.4:4. Amended by Acts 2005, c. 258; 2006, cc. 73, 76; 2009, c. 330.
56-265.10. Amended by Acts 2005, c. 839.
56-265.15. Amended by Acts 2010, cc. 205, 777, 832.
56-265.15:1. Amended by Acts 2010, cc. 777, 832.
56-265.19. Amended by Acts 2005, c. 395.
56-265.32. Amended by Acts 2010, c. 205.
56-435. Amended by Acts 2005, c. 839.
56-458. Amended by Acts 2006, c. 780.
56-462. Amended by Acts 2006, c. 780; 2013, cc. 585, 646.
56-463. Amended by Acts 2009, c. 331.
56-466.1. Amended by Acts 2006, cc. 73, 76; 2012, cc. 545, 674.
56-468.1. Amended by Acts 2006, c. 780.
56-469 to 56-477. Repealed by Acts 2011, cc. 738, 740.
56-478.1. Repealed by Acts 2011, cc. 738, 740.
56-481. Repealed by Acts 2011, cc. 738, 740.
56-481.1. Amended by Acts 2011, cc. 738, 740.
56-482.1. Amended by Acts 2011, cc. 738, 740.
56-484.4 to 56-484.6. Repealed by Acts 2006, c. 780.
56-484.12. Amended by Acts 2005, c. 942; 2006, cc. 739, 780; 2010, cc. 466, 566; 2011, cc. 120, 138.
56-484.13. Amended by Acts 2006, c. 739; 2009, c. 613; 2011, c. 138; 2012, c. 36.
56-484.14. Amended by Acts 2005, c. 942; 2006, c. 739; 2007, c. 427; 2011, c. 138.
56-484.15. Amended by Acts 2006, c. 739; 2009, c. 613.
56-484.16. Amended by Acts 2005, c. 942.
56-484.17. Amended by Acts 2005, c. 942; 2006, cc. 739, 780; 2010, cc. 466, 566; 2011, cc. 162, 630; 2012, cc. 25, 165, 672.
56-484.18. Amended by Acts 2006, c. 780.
56-484.19. Amended by Acts 2008, c. 853; 2009, cc. 813, 840.
56-484.23. Amended by Acts 2008, c. 853.
56-502. Amended by Acts 2006, cc. 73, 76.
55-511, 55-512. Repealed by Acts 2008, c. 851.
56-521. Amended by Acts 2005, c. 681.
56-522. Amended by Acts 2005, cc. 681, 885.
56-542. Amended by Acts 2008, cc. 841, 844.
56-557. Amended by Acts 2005, cc. 504, 562; 2006, c. 922.
56-558. Amended by Acts 2005, cc. 504, 562; 2006, c. 922.
56-559. Amended by Acts 2005, cc. 504, 562; 2011, c. 589.
56-560. Amended by Acts 2005, cc. 504, 562; 2006, c. 922; 2008, c. 296.
56-561. Amended by Acts 2005, cc. 504, 562.
56-563. Amended by Acts 2005, cc. 504, 562; 2006, c. 922.
56-564. Amended by Acts 2005, cc. 504, 562; 2006, c. 922.

Section
56-565. Amended by Acts 2005, cc. 504, 562; 2008, cc. 602, 838.
56-566. Amended by Acts 2005, cc. 504, 562; 2006, c. 922.
56-567. Amended by Acts 2005, cc. 504, 562.
56-567.1. Amended by Acts 2006, c. 922.
56-568. Amended by Acts 2005, cc. 504, 562.
56-569. Amended by Acts 2005, cc. 504, 562.
56-570. Amended by Acts 2005, cc. 504, 562.
56-571. Amended by Acts 2005, cc. 504, 562.
56-572. Amended by Acts 2005, cc. 504, 562.
56-573.1. Amended by Acts 2005, cc. 504, 562; 2006, cc. 922, 936; 2013, c. 583.
56-573.1:1. Amended by Acts 2007, c. 374; 2011, c. 332; 2013, cc. 560, 622.
56-573.3. Amended by Acts 2011, c. 624.
56-573.3:1. Amended by Acts 2006, Sp. Sess. I, c. 1.
56-575.1. Amended by Acts 2005, cc. 618, 865; 2007, cc. 649, 764; 2008, cc. 273, 731; 2009, cc. 754, 762.
56-575.2. Amended by Acts 2005, c. 865.
56-575.3. Amended by Acts 2005, c. 865; 2011, c. 308.
56-575.3:1. Amended by Acts 2007, c. 764.
56-575.4. Amended by Acts 2005, c. 865; 2007, c. 764.
56-575.5. Amended by Acts 2005, c. 865.
56-575.7. Amended by Acts 2005, c. 865.
56-575.8. Amended by Acts 2005, c. 865.
56-575.10. Amended by Acts 2005, c. 865.
56-575.11. Amended by Acts 2005, c. 865.
56-575.12. Amended by Acts 2005, c. 865.
56-575.13. Amended by Acts 2005, c. 865.
56-575.16. Amended by Acts 2005, cc. 865, 936; 2007, c. 764; 2013, c. 583.
56-575.17. Amended by Acts 2008, c. 667; 2009, c. 762; 2011, c. 332.
56-575.17:1. Amended by Acts 2011, c. 624.
56-575.18. Amended by Acts 2009, c. 762.
56-576. Amended by Acts 2007, cc. 888, 933; 2008, cc. 272, 883; 2009, cc. 748, 824; 2012, cc. 46, 200, 210, 821; 2013, c. 494.
56-577. Amended by Acts 2007, cc. 888, 933; 2010, cc. 326, 397.
56-578. Amended by Acts 2007, cc. 888, 933.
56-579. Amended by Acts 2007, cc. 888, 933; 2008, c. 883.
56-580. Amended by Acts 2006, cc. 811, 819, 929, 940; 2007, cc. 877, 888, 933; 2009, cc. 808, 854.
56-581. Amended by Acts 2007, cc. 888, 933.
56-581.1. Repealed by Acts 2007, cc. 888, 933.
56-582. Amended by Acts 2007, cc. 888, 933; 2008, c. 883.
56-583. Repealed by Acts 2007, cc. 888, 933.
56-584. Amended by Acts 2007, cc. 888, 933.
56-585. Amended by Acts 2007, cc. 888, 933.
56-585.1. Amended by Acts 2008, c. 476; 2009,

Section

c. 824; 2011, cc. 236, 367, 371, 380, 382; 2012, c. 435; 2013, c. 2.

56-585.2. Amended by Acts 2008, c. 651; 2009, c. 744; 2010, c. 850; 2012, cc. 46, 67, 200, 274, 348, 717; 2013, cc. 2, 308, 403.

56-585.3. Amended by Acts 2009, cc. 401, 824.

56-587. Amended by Acts 2007, cc. 888, 933.

56-589. Amended by Acts 2007, cc. 888, 933.

56-590. Amended by Acts 2007, cc. 888, 933.

56-592. Amended by Acts 2008, c. 883.

56-592.1. Amended by Acts 2008, c. 883.

56-594. Amended by Acts 2006, c. 470; 2007, cc. 877, 888, 933; 2009, c. 804; 2011, c. 239; 2013, c. 268.

56-596. Amended by Acts 2008, c. 883.

56-600. Amended by Acts 2012, cc. 210, 821.

56-607. Amended by Acts 2013, c. 284.

57-2.02. Amended by Acts 2009, cc. 813, 840.

57-7.1. Amended by Acts 2005, c. 772.

57-8. Amended by Acts 2005, c. 772.

57-9. Amended by Acts 2005, cc. 681, 772.

57-10. Amended by Acts 2005, c. 772.

57-11. Amended by Acts 2005, c. 772.

57-13. Amended by Acts 2005, c. 772.

57-14. Amended by Acts 2005, c. 772.

57-15. Amended by Acts 2005, c. 772.

57-16. Amended by Acts 2005, cc. 681, 772.

57-17. Amended by Acts 2005, c. 772.

57-21. Amended by Acts 2005, c. 772.

57-27.1. Amended by Acts 2008, c. 390; 2011, c. 257.

57-32. Amended by Acts 2005, c. 772.

57-36. Amended by Acts 2010, c. 617.

57-39.1:1. Amended by Acts 2012, c. 691.

57-48. Amended by Acts 2005, c. 329; 2007, cc. 92, 907; 2013, c. 24.

57-49. Amended by Acts 2005, c. 329; 2012, c. 313.

57-50. Amended by Acts 2005, c. 329.

57-55.2. Amended by Acts 2013, c. 24.

57-55.3. Amended by Acts 2013, c. 24.

57-60. Amended by Acts 2005, c. 316; 2009, cc. 813, 840; 2010, cc. 680, 794; 2011, c. 534; 2012, cc. 803, 835.

58.1-3. Amended by Acts 2005, cc. 863, 884; 2006, cc. 31, 159, 590, 780; 2008, cc. 387, 689, 785; 2010, c. 34; 2012, c. 395; 2013, cc. 29, 163, 230.

58.1-3.2. Amended by Acts 2012, c. 395.

58.1-9. Amended by Acts 2008, c. 217; 2010, cc. 36, 151, 635; 2011, c. 368.

58.1-20. Repealed by Acts 2009, c. 35.

58.1-202. Amended by Acts 2005, c. 216; 2006, cc. 159, 590; 2009, c. 24; 2010, c. 379.

58.1-202.2. Amended by Acts 2011, cc. 798, 871.

58.1-204. Amended by Acts 2011, c. 800.

58.1-205. Amended by Acts 2011, c. 800.

Section

58.1-300. Amended by Acts 2013, c. 766.

58.1-301. Amended by Acts 2005, cc. 5, 26; 2006, cc. 63, 162; 2007, cc. 59, 782; 2008, cc. 1, 2; 2009, cc. 2, 3, 781; 2010, cc. 872, 874; 2011, cc. 2, 866, 890; 2012, cc. 2, 335, 480, 578; 2013, cc. 4, 693.

58.1-302. Amended by Acts 2005, c. 48.

58.1-311. Amended by Acts 2006, c. 234.

58.1-312. Amended by Acts 2006, c. 234; 2007, c. 524.

58.1-321. Amended by Acts 2007, cc. 527, 543.

58.1-322. Amended by Acts 2005, cc. 27, 67; 2006, cc. 214, 570, 599, 617, 939; 2007, cc. 359, 527, 543, 636, 942; 2008, cc. 149, 211; 2009, c. 508; 2010, cc. 802, 830; 2011, c. 851; 2012, cc. 2, 96, 256, 305, 578; 2013, cc. 88, 801.

58.1-331. Repealed by Acts 2009, c. 34.

58.1-334. Amended by Acts 2005, c. 58.

58.1-339. Repealed by Acts 2011, c. 851.

58.1-339.2. Amended by Acts 2012, cc. 92, 639.

58.1-339.3. Amended by Acts 2006, c. 440; 2011, c. 352.

58.1-339.4. Amended by Acts 2009, c. 853.

58.1-339.7. Amended by Acts 2007, cc. 68, 765; 2009, cc. 15, 496; 2011, c. 365.

58.1-339.9. Amended by Acts 2005, c. 414; 2011, c. 851.

58.1-339.10. Amended by Acts 2008, c. 449.

58.1-339.11. Repealed by Acts 2013, c. 801.

58.1-341. Amended by Acts 2008, c. 591.

58.1-344. Amended by Acts 2005, c. 100.

58.1-344.2. Amended by Acts 2013, cc. 28, 402.

58.1-344.3. Amended by Acts 2005, cc. 860, 889; 2006, cc. 103, 479; 2007, cc. 69, 70, 601; 2008, cc. 97, 313, 461; 2009, cc. 4, 26, 41, 521, 834; 2010, c. 690; 2011, cc. 780, 858; 2012, cc. 803, 835; 2013, cc. 22, 234, 631, 754.

58.1-345. Repealed by Acts 2005, cc. 860, 889.

58.1-345.1. Repealed by Acts 2005, cc. 860, 889.

58.1-346. Repealed by Acts 2005, cc. 860, 889.

58.1-346.1:1. Repealed by Acts 2005, cc. 860, 889.

58.1-346.2:1. Repealed by Acts 2005, cc. 860, 889.

58.1-346.3:1. Repealed by Acts 2005, cc. 860, 889.

58.1-346.4:1 to 58.1-346.24. Repealed by Acts 2005, cc. 860, 889.

58.1-390.2. Amended by Acts 2009, cc. 37, 152.

58.1-393.1. Amended by Acts 2005, c. 100.

58.1-400.1. Amended by Acts 2009, cc. 37, 152.

58.1-400.3. Amended by Acts 2009, cc. 37, 152.

58.1-402. Amended by Acts 2006, c. 214; 2008, cc. 149, 211; 2009, cc. 426, 508,

Section

558; 2010, cc. 802, 830; 2011, c. 851; 2012, cc. 96, 256.

58.1-408. Amended by Acts 2009, c. 821.

58.1-422. Amended by Acts 2012, c. 427.

58.1-423. Amended by Acts 2012, cc. 779, 817.

58.1-431. Repealed by Acts 2009, c. 34.

58.1-432. Amended by Acts 2005, c. 58.

58.1-433.1. Amended by Acts 2006, cc. 788, 803; 2011, cc. 294, 851.

58.1-435. Amended by Acts 2007, c. 778; 2010, cc. 520, 608; 2011, c. 850.

58.1-439. Amended by Acts 2005, cc. 863, 884; 2009, c. 753; 2010, cc. 363, 469; 2012, cc. 93, 445, 475.

58.1-439.1. Amended by Acts 2006, c. 238; 2009, c. 730; 2011, c. 176.

58.1-439.2. Amended by Acts 2006, cc. 788, 803; 2011, c. 851; 2012, cc. 309, 649.

58.1-439.3. Repealed by Acts 2009, c. 34.

58.1-439.6. Amended by Acts 2013, cc. 294, 482.

58.1-439.7. Amended by Acts 2007, cc. 529, 593; 2009, c. 34.

58.1-439.8. Repealed by Acts 2009, c. 34.

58.1-439.11. Amended by Acts 2012, cc. 803, 835.

58.1-439.12:01. Amended by Acts 2005, c. 951.

58.1-439.12:04. Amended by Acts 2013, cc. 23, 374.

58.1-439.12:06. Repealed by Acts 2012, cc. 846, 849.

58.1-439.12:07. Amended by Acts 2012, cc. 327, 341.

58.1-439.12:09. Repealed by Acts 2012, cc. 846, 849.

58.1-439.12:10. Repealed by Acts 2012, cc. 846, 849.

58.1-439.12:10. Amended by Acts 2013, c. 744.

58.1-439.15. Amended by Acts 2011, c. 49.

58.1-439.18. Amended by Acts 2009, cc. 10, 851; 2010, c. 164; 2011, cc. 312, 370; 2012, cc. 731, 842.

58.1-439.19. Amended by Acts 2012, cc. 731, 842.

58.1-439.20. Amended by Acts 2009, cc. 10, 502, 851; 2011, c. 317; 2012, cc. 731, 837, 842; 2013, cc. 713, 716, 802.

58.1-439.21. Amended by Acts 2009, c. 851; 2011, c. 370; 2012, cc. 731, 842.

58.1-439.22. Amended by Acts 2009, c. 851; 2011, c. 132; 2012, c. 596.

58.1-439.24. Amended by Acts 2008, c. 463; 2009, c. 851; 2012, cc. 731, 842; 2013, cc. 713, 716.

58.1-439.25 to 58.1-439.28. Amended by Acts 2012, c. 842; 2013, cc. 713, 716.

58.1-453. Amended by Acts 2005, c. 100.

58.1-472. Amended by Acts 2007, c. 753.

Section

58.1-478. Amended by Acts 2010, cc. 36, 151.

58.1-486.2. Amended by Acts 2010, c. 120; 2011, c. 766.

58.1-490. Amended by Acts 2009, c. 34; 2011, c. 851.

58.1-511. Amended by Acts 2005, c. 940.

58.1-512. Amended by Acts 2005, c. 940; 2009, cc. 12, 510; 2010, cc. 246, 265, 321, 384; 2011, cc. 212, 296, 377, 672; 2013, c. 798.

58.1-513. Amended by Acts 2005, c. 255; 2010, cc. 229, 248; 2012, c. 232.

58.1-520. Amended by Acts 2009, cc. 571, 787; 2013, c. 766.

58.1-530. Amended by Acts 2009, cc. 571, 787.

58.1-540 to 58.1-549. Repealed by Acts 2013, c. 766.

58.1-601, 58.1-602. Amended by Acts 2013, c. 766.

58.1-602. Amended by Acts 2005, cc. 121, 122, 355; 2006, c. 519, 541, 568, 602; 2007, c. 751; 2013, cc. 766, 783.

58.1-603. Amended by Acts 2013, c. 766.

58.1-604. Amended by Acts 2013, c. 766.

58.1-604.1. Amended by Acts 2011, cc. 405, 639; 2013, c. 766.

58.1-604.2. Amended by Acts 2011, cc. 663, 674.

58.1-605. Amended by Acts 2007, c. 896; 2008, cc. 484, 488; 2010, cc. 386, 629; 2012, c. 831; 2013, c. 766.

58.1-606. Amended by Acts 2007, c. 896; 2008, cc. 484, 488; 2013, c. 766.

58.1-608.3. Amended by Acts 2006, cc. 581, 608; 2009, cc. 7, 47, 93, 499, 836; 2011, c. 274; 2012, cc. 678, 789, 830; 2013, cc. 568, 724, 766.

58.1-609.1. Amended by Acts 2005, cc. 46, 116; 2007, cc. 176, 817; 2008, c. 554; 2011, c. 165; 2012, cc. 95, 276.

58.1-609.2. Amended by Acts 2006, cc. 331, 361; 2011, c. 466; 2013, c. 223.

58.1-609.3. Amended by Acts 2006, cc. 385, 519, 524, 541, 618; 2007, c. 751; 2008, cc. 558, 764; 2010, cc. 784, 826; 2011, cc. 183, 286; 2012, cc. 613, 655; 2013, c. 10.

58.1-609.5. Amended by Acts 2006, c. 474.

58.1-609.6. Amended by Acts 2007, cc. 58, 604; 2008, cc. 138, 545; 2012, cc. 275, 411, 477; 2013, c. 90.

58.1-609.10. Amended by Acts 2006, cc. 217, 331, 338, 361; 2007, cc. 84, 758; 2008, c. 569; 2009, cc. 36, 338, 833; 2010, cc. 784, 826, 866.

58.1-609.11. Amended by Acts 2005, cc. 42, 89; 2007, cc. 698, 704, 709; 2009, cc. 24, 106, 526.

58.1-609.12. Amended by Acts 2006, c. 559; 2009, c. 24; 2012, c. 590.

Section
58.1-609.13. Repealed by Acts 2013, c. 766.
58.1-610. Amended by Acts 2010, c. 119; 2011, cc. 360, 851.
58.1-611.1. Amended by Acts 2005, cc. 487, 521.
58.1-611.3. Amended by Acts 2013, c. 325.
58.1-612. Amended by Acts 2013, c. 766.
58.1-613. Amended by Acts 2011, cc. 663, 674.
58.1-614. Amended by Acts 2013, c. 766.
58.1-615. Amended by Acts 2005, c. 951; 2010, cc. 36, 151; 2013, c. 766.
58.1-615.1. Repealed by Acts 2009, c. 781; 2010, cc. 872, 874, 890.
58.1-621. Amended by Acts 2005, c. 355.
58.1-622. Amended by Acts 2008, c. 488.
58.1-625. Amended by Acts 2006, cc. 579, 593; 2007, cc. 176, 608, 817; 2013, c. 766.
58.1-625.1. Repealed by Acts 2009, cc. 864, 871.
58.1-626. Amended by Acts 2006, cc. 579, 593; 2007, cc. 176, 608, 817.
58.1-635. Amended by Acts 2013, c. 766.
58.1-638. Amended by Acts 2010, cc. 113, 386, 629; 2012, cc. 476, 507, 779, 817; 2013, cc. 639, 766.
58.1-639. Amended by Acts 2013, c. 766.
58.1-640. Amended by Acts 2011, c. 649.
58.1-641. Amended by Acts 2006, c. 407; 2006, c. 407; 2008, cc. 32, 158.
58.1-648. Amended by Acts 2007, c. 811.
58.1-662. Amended by Acts 2008, cc. 25, 148; 2009, cc. 680, 683; 2010, cc. 285, 365, 385; 2011, c. 364.
58.1-802. Amended by Acts 2007, cc. 748, 768; 2012, c. 513.
58.1-802.1. Repealed by Acts 2009, cc. 864, 871.
58.1-803. Amended by Acts 2012, cc. 505, 820.
58.1-811. Amended by Acts 2005, cc. 93, 928; 2006, c. 922; 2007, cc. 233, 639, 813, 896; 2009, cc. 574, 864, 871; 2013, cc. 390, 766.
58.1-812. Amended by Acts 2009, cc. 95, 686.
58.1-815.1. Amended by Acts 2005, c. 621.
58.1-815.4. Amended by Acts 2013, c. 639.
58.1-1000. Amended by Acts 2005, cc. 28, 856; 2006, c. 768; 2012, cc. 362, 472.
58.1-1001. Amended by Acts 2006, c. 768.
58.1-1003. Amended by Acts 2005, c. 28; 2006, cc. 64, 229, 768; 2010, c. 701; 2013, c. 381.
58.1-1006. Amended by Acts 2005, c. 28.
58.1-1007. Amended by Acts 2005, c. 28.
58.1-1008. Amended by Acts 2005, c. 28; 2013, c. 381.
58.1-1008.1. Amended by Acts 2013, c. 381.
58.1-1009. Amended by Acts 2005, c. 925; 2013, cc. 311, 381, 389.
58.1-1010. Amended by Acts 2005, c. 28.

Section
58.1-1011. Amended by Acts 2005, c. 28.
58.1-1012. Amended by Acts 2005, c. 856.
58.1-1013. Amended by Acts 2006, c. 409; 2010, cc. 35, 471.
58.1-1017. Amended by Acts 2005, c. 28; 2006, c. 409; 2010, cc. 35, 471; 2013, cc. 570, 624.
58.1-1017.1. Amended by Acts 2013, cc. 567, 623.
58.1-1021. Amended by Acts 2005, c. 28.
58.1-1021.01. Amended by Acts 2005, c. 71; 2006, c. 768, 2010, cc. 191, 804.
58.1-1021.02. Amended by Acts 2005, c. 71; 2010, cc. 191, 804.
58.1-1021.03. Amended by Acts 2005, cc. 71, 925; 2010, cc. 191, 804.
58.1-1021.02:1. Amended by Acts 2013, c. 381.
58.1-1021.04. Amended by Acts 2005, c. 71.
58.1-1037. Amended by Acts 2012, cc. 362, 472.
58.1-1404. Amended by Acts 2013, c. 787.
58.1-1505. Amended by Acts 2007, c. 610; 2011, cc. 443, 492.
58.1-1707. Amended by Acts 2011, c. 466.
58.1-1709. Amended by Acts 2006, c. 6.
58.1-1718. Amended by Acts 2010, c. 266.
58.1-1718.1. Amended by Acts 2010, c. 441.
58.1-1719. Amended by Acts 2009, c. 532.
58.1-1720. Amended by Acts 2006, c. 354; 2009, c. 532.
58.1-1721. Repealed by Acts 2009, c. 532.
58.1-1722. Amended by Acts 2009, c. 532.
58.1-1723. Repealed by Acts 2009, c. 532.
58.1-1724.3. Repealed by Acts 2009, cc. 864, 871.
58.1-1724.5. Repealed by Acts 2009, cc. 864, 871.
58.1-1724.6. Repealed by Acts 2009, cc. 864, 871.
58.1-1724.7. Repealed by Acts 2009, cc. 864, 871.
58.1-1727. Amended by Acts 2005, c. 681.
58.1-1735. Amended by Acts 2013, c. 84.
58.1-1802.1. Amended by Acts 2010, c. 30; 2012, c. 840.
58.1-1803. Amended by Acts 2007, c. 750.
58.1-1820. Amended by Acts 2008, c. 549.
58.1-1821. Amended by Acts 2007, c. 750; 2008, c. 549.
58.1-1822. Amended by Acts 2008, c. 549; 2011, c. 295.
58.1-1823. Amended by Acts 2006, c. 234; 2010, c. 228.
58.1-1825. Amended by Acts 2008, c. 549.
58.1-1826. Amended by Acts 2008, c. 549.
58.1-1826. Amended by Acts 2006, c. 342.
58.1-1834. Amended by Acts 2009, c. 503.
58.1-1840.1. Amended by Acts 2009, 611; 2011, c. 739.
58.1-2201. Amended by Acts 2006, cc. 594, 912; 2011, c. 165; 2012, cc. 729, 733; 2013, c. 766.

Section
58.1-2204. Amended by Acts 2012, c. 363.
58.1-2208. Amended by Acts 2012, c. 363.
58.1-2211. Amended by Acts 2006, c. 594.
58.1-2215. Amended by Acts 2006, c. 594.
58.1-2217. Amended by Acts 2007, c. 896; 2013, c. 766.
58.1-2241. Amended by Acts 2006, c. 594.
58.1-2246. Amended by Acts 2006, c. 594.
58.1-2247. Amended by Acts 2006, c. 594.
58.1-2249. Amended by Acts 2007, c. 896; 2012, cc. 729, 733; 2013, c. 766.
58.1-2250. Amended by Acts 2009, c. 530.
58.1-2251. Amended by Acts 2013, c. 766.
58.1-2259. Amended by Acts 2005, cc. 243, 782, 928; 2011, cc. 881, 889; 2012, cc. 803, 835; 2013, c. 766.
58.1-2261. Amended by Acts 2009, c. 419.
58.1-2272. Amended by Acts 2006, c. 594.
58.1-2273. Amended by Acts 2006, c. 594.
58.1-2274. Amended by Acts 2012, cc. 283, 363, 756.
58.1-2280. Amended by Acts 2006, c. 594.
58.1-2289. Repealed by Acts 2013, c. 766.
58.1-2290. Repealed by Acts 2013, c. 766.
58.1-2295. Amended by Acts 2013, c. 766.
58.1-2299.20. Amended by Acts 2013, c. 766.
58.1-2401. Amended by Acts 2011, cc. 405, 639; 2013, c. 766.
58.1-2402. Amended by Acts 2005, c. 449; 2011, cc. 405, 639, 881, 889; 2012, cc. 22, 111; 2013, c. 766.
58.1-2402.1. Repealed by Acts 2009, cc. 864, 871.
58.1-2403. Amended by Acts 2005, cc. 246, 274; 2006, c. 604; 2007, c. 896; 2008, cc. 304, 753; 2009, cc. 864, 871; 2011, cc. 405, 639; 2012, cc. 22, 111; 2013, c. 783.
58.1-2404. Amended by Acts 2011, cc. 405, 639.
58.1-2407 to 58.1-2410. Repealed by Acts 2011, cc. 405, 639.
58.1-2411. Amended by Acts 2011, cc. 405, 639.
58.1-2412 to 58.1-2417. Repealed by Acts 2011, cc. 405, 639.
58.1-2419. Amended by Acts 2011, cc. 405, 639.
58.1-2420. Amended by Acts 2011, cc. 405, 639.
58.1-2421. Amended by Acts 2011, cc. 405, 639.
58.1-2424. Amended by Acts 2011, cc. 405, 639.
58.1-2425. Amended by Acts 2005, c. 323; 2007, c. 896; 2009, cc. 864, 871; 2011, cc. 405, 639; 2013, c. 766.
58.1-2426. Amended by Acts 2011, cc. 881, 889.
58.1-2500. Amended by Acts 2011, c. 850.
58.1-2501. Amended by Acts 2013, cc. 136, 210.
58.1-2503 to 58.1-2507. Amended by Acts 2011, c. 850.
58.1-2504, 58.1-2505. Amended by Acts 2013, cc. 29, 163.
58.1-2507. Amended by Acts 2013, cc. 29, 163.
58.1-2508. Amended by Acts 2006, cc. 648, 765; 2011, c. 850.

Section
58.1-2510. Amended by Acts 2009, c. 567; 2011, cc. 817, 850, 863.
58.1-2520 to 58.1-2522. Amended by Acts 2011, c. 850.
58.1-2525, 58.1-2526. Amended by Acts 2011, c. 850; 2013, cc. 29, 163.
58.1-2527. Amended by 2013, cc. 29, 163.
58.1-2528. Amended by Acts 2011, c. 850.
58.1-2531. Amended by Acts 2011, c. 850.
58.1-2606. Amended by Acts 2006, c. 517; 2008, c. 642.
58.1-2670. Amended by Acts 2005, c. 21.
58.1-2700.1. Amended by Acts 2012, cc. 22, 111.
58.1-2700.2. Amended by Acts 2012, cc. 22, 111.
58.1-2701. Repealed by Acts 2013, c. 766.
58.1-2706. Amended by Acts 2007, c. 896; 2013, c. 766.
58.1-2712.1. Amended by Acts 2012, cc. 22, 111.
58.1-3109. Amended by Acts 2008, c. 852.
58.1-3122.2. Amended by Acts 2006, c. 474.
58.1-3131. Amended by Acts 2011, cc. 485, 597; 2012, c. 88.
58.1-3203. Amended by Acts 2006, c. 922.
58.1-3210. Amended by Acts 2007, c. 357.
58.1-3211. Repealed by Acts 2011, cc. 438, 496.
58.1-3211.1. Amended by Acts 2008, cc. 298, 695; 2011, cc. 438, 496.
58.1-3212. Amended by Acts 2011, cc. 438, 496; 2012, c. 299.
58.1-3213. Amended by Acts 2007, c. 357; 2011, cc. 438, 496.
58.1-3214. Amended by Acts 2012, cc. 476, 507.
58.1-3215. Amended by Acts 2007, c. 357; 2008, c. 208; 2011, cc. 438, 496.
58.1-3218. Repealed by Acts 2011, cc. 438, 496.
58.1-3219.1. Amended by Acts 2005, cc. 502, 561.
58.1-3219.2. Repealed by Acts 2006, c. 356.
58.1-3219.4. Amended by Acts 2011, cc. 423, 460.
58.1-3219.5. Amended by Acts 2012, cc. 75, 263, 782, 806.
58.1-3220. Amended by Acts 2011, cc. 423, 460.
58.1-3221.1. Amended by Acts 2011, c. 146.
58.1-3221.2. Amended by Acts 2008, cc. 288, 401; 2009, c. 512.
58.1-3221.3. Amended by Acts 2009, cc. 677, 822, 864, 871.
58.1-3230. Amended by Acts 2006, c. 817; 2009, c. 800; 2012, c. 653.
58.1-3233. Amended by Acts 2010, c. 653.
58.1-3237. Amended by Acts 2013, c. 269.
58.1-3237.1. Amended by Acts 2007, c. 813; 2011, c. 12; 2013, c. 677.
58.1-3241. Amended by Acts 2006, c. 221.
58.1-3245.1. Amended by Acts 2006, c. 784.
58.1-3245.4:1. Amended by Acts 2005, c. 733.

Section
58.1-3245.6. Amended by Acts 2005, cc. 863, 884.
58.1-3245.8. Amended by Acts 2005, cc. 863, 884.
58.1-3245.12. Amended by Acts 2005, cc. 863, 884; 2011, cc. 875, 877; 2012, c. 91.
58.1-3252. Amended by Acts 2009, c. 529.
58.1-3253. Amended by Acts 2008, c. 540.
58.1-3255. Amended by Acts 2010, cc. 154, 199.
58.1-3257. Amended by Acts 2007, c. 813.
58.1-3258. Amended by Acts 2008, c. 540.
58.1-3258.1. Amended by Acts 2010, c. 552.
58.1-3259. Amended by Acts 2010, c. 552.
58.1-3260. Amended by Acts 2011, c. 851.
58.1-3271. Amended by Acts 2008, c. 540.
58.1-3275. Amended by Acts 2008, c. 540.
58.1-3276. Amended by Acts 2008, c. 540.
58.1-3284.1. Amended by Acts 2005, c. 218.
58.1-3286. Amended by Acts 2009, c. 770.
58.1-3292.1. Amended by Acts 2007, c. 813.
58.1-3294. Amended by Acts 2011, c. 200.
58.1-3295. Amended by Acts 2009, c. 264; 2010, cc. 552, 791, 824; 2011, c. 137; 2013, c. 249.
58.1-3303. Amended by Acts 2006, c. 355.
58.1-3321. Amended by Acts 2007, c. 948; 2009, cc. 30, 511.
58.1-3330. Amended by Acts 2006, cc. 255, 509; 2007, cc. 344, 353.
58.1-3331. Amended by Acts 2010, c. 552; 2011, cc. 184, 232.
58.1-3340. Amended by Acts 2010, c. 417.
58.1-3343. Amended by Acts 2013, cc. 305, 618.
58.1-3360. Amended by Acts 2012, c. 782.
58.1-3360.1. Amended by Acts 2012, c. 782.
58.1-3360.2. Amended by Acts 2012, c. 782.
58.1-3371. Amended by Acts 2011, c. 10.
58.1-3373. Amended by Acts 2011, c. 10; 2013, c. 548.
58.1-3374. Amended by Acts 2009, c. 25; 2010, c. 552; 2011, c. 10; 2013, c. 197.
58.1-3378. Amended by Acts 2013, c. 197.
58.1-3379. Amended by Acts 2010, c. 552; 2011, cc. 184, 232; 2013, c. 197.
58.1-3380. Amended by Acts 2013, c. 197.
58.1-3381. Amended by Acts 2007, c. 813; 2013, c. 197.
58.1-3500. Amended by Acts 2010, cc. 255, 295.
58.1-3503. Amended by Acts 2006, c. 896; 2013, cc. 287, 652, 783.
58.1-3504. Amended by Acts 2006, c. 896; 2013, c. 783.
58.1-3505. Amended by Acts 2012, c. 272.
58.1-3506. Amended by Acts 2005, cc. 271, 325, 357; 2006, cc. 200, 231, 400; 2007, cc. 88, 322, 609; 2008, cc. 26, 94, 143; 2009, cc. 40, 44; 2010, cc. 264, 849; 2012, cc. 97, 288; 2013, cc. 39, 271, 287, 393, 652.
58.1-3506.2. Amended by Acts 2007, c. 813.

Section
58.1-3510. Amended by Acts 2009, cc. 480, 692; 2011, cc. 405, 639.
58.1-3510.1. Repealed by Acts 2009, cc. 480, 692.
58.1-3510.2. Repealed by Acts 2009, cc. 480, 692.
58.1-3510.3. Repealed by Acts 2009, cc. 480, 692.
58.1-3510.4. Amended by Acts 2010, cc. 255, 295.
58.1-3510.6. Amended by Acts 2010, cc. 255, 295.
58.1-3511. Amended by Acts 2012, c. 651.
58.1-3523. Amended by Acts 2006, c. 896; 2007, cc. 314, 815; 2010, c. 499; 2013, c. 783.
58.1-3606. Amended by Acts 2005, c. 928.
58.1-3607. Amended by Acts 2005, c. 716; 2011, c. 851.
58.1-3617. Amended by Acts 2005, c. 928.
58.1-3660. Amended by Acts 2006, cc. 375, 939; 2009, c. 671.
58.1-3660.1. Amended by Acts 2009, c. 350; 2013, cc. 756, 793.
58.1-3700. Amended by Acts 2012, cc. 304, 318.
58.1-3700.1. Amended by Acts 2006, c. 763; 2010, cc. 195, 283.
58.1-3702. Amended by Acts 2011, c. 685.
58.1-3703. Amended by Acts 2005, c. 103; 2006, c. 922; 2010, c. 648; 2011, cc. 25, 188.
58.1-3703.1. Amended by Acts 2005, c. 927; 2006, cc. 119, 181, 611.
58.1-3704. Amended by Acts 2010, cc. 255, 295.
58.1-3706. Amended by Acts 2006, c. 763; 2010, cc. 255, 295.
58.1-3712. Amended by Acts 2009, c. 770; 2013, cc, 305, 618.
58.1-3713. Amended by Acts 2005, c. 645; 2006, cc. 78, 497; 2007, cc. 57, 586; 2009, c. 367; 2013, cc. 305, 306, 618.
58.1-3713.01. Amended by Acts 2006, cc. 78, 497; 2013, cc. 305, 618.
58.1-3713.1, 58.1-3713.2. Repealed by Acts 2013, cc. 305, 618.
58.1-3713.3. Amended by Acts 2012, cc. 665, 722; 2013, cc. 208, 305, 391, 618.
58.1-3713.5. Repealed by Acts 2013, cc. 305, 618.
58.1-3732. Amended by Acts 2007, cc. 85, 834.
58.1-3732.1. Amended by Acts 2013, cc. 36, 350.
58.1-3732.4. Amended by Acts 2005, c. 839.
58.1-3805. Amended by Acts 2010, c. 266.
58.1-3812. Repealed by Acts 2006, c. 780.
58.1-3813.1. Repealed by Acts 2006, c. 780.
58.1-3814. Amended by Acts 2008, c. 883; 2012, cc. 4, 582.
58.1-3815. Amended by Acts 2006, c. 780.
58.1-3816.2. Amended by Acts 2006, c. 780.

Section
58.1-3818. Amended by Acts 2005, c. 106; 2007, c. 813.
58.1-3818.1 to 58.1-3818.7. Repealed by Acts 2006, c. 780.
58.1-3819. Amended by Acts 2005, cc. 76, 915; 2006, cc. 67, 376; 2007, cc. 86, 596, 767; 2008, c. 230; 2009, cc. 13, 31, 116, 497, 513, 524; 2010, c. 505; 2011, cc. 385, 606; 2012, c. 290; 2013, cc. 19, 200, 319, 378.
58.1-3822. Amended by Acts 2005, c. 156; 2008, cc. 30, 153.
58.1-3823. Amended by Acts 2006, c. 377; 2008, c. 839; 2011, c. 677.
58.1-3825. Amended by Acts 2007, c. 61.
58.1-3832. Amended by Acts 2012, cc. 89, 258.
58.1-3833. Amended by Acts 2005, c. 915; 2006, cc. 568, 602; 2009, c. 415.
58.1-3840. Amended by Acts 2005, c. 106; 2006, cc. 568, 602; 2009, c. 415.
58.1-3842. Amended by Acts 2011, c. 192.
58.1-3851. Amended by Acts 2008, c. 462; 2013, cc. 756, 793.
58.1-3851.1. Amended by Acts 2012, cc. 73, 572.
58.1-3853. Amended by Acts 2012, c. 91.
58.1-3901. Amended by Acts 2009, cc. 501, 672.
58.1-3902. Amended by Acts 2013, c. 804.
58.1-3910. Amended by Acts 2011, cc. 431, 475.
58.1-3912. Amended by Acts 2005, c. 922; 2013, c. 299.
58.1-3916. Amended by Acts 2005, c. 501; 2006, cc. 200, 231, 459; Acts 2007, cc. 88, 609; 2008, c. 591.
58.1-3919.1. Amended by Acts 2006, c. 372; 2011, c. 383.
58.1-3921. Amended by Acts 2007, c. 867.
58.1-3930. Amended by Acts 2013, cc. 305, 618.
58.1-3932. Amended by Acts 2013, cc. 305, 618.
58.1-3934. Amended by Acts 2006, c. 372; 2008, c. 550.
58.1-3938. Amended by Acts 2011, c. 851.
58.1-3941. Amended by Acts 2005, c. 59.
58.1-3942. Amended by Acts 2005, c. 59; 2012, c. 623.
58.1-3959. Amended by Acts 2013, cc. 305, 618.
58.1-3965. Amended by Acts 2009, cc. 181, 551; 2013, c. 334.
58.1-3967. Amended by Acts 2006, c. 616; 2009, c. 682.
58.1-3969. Amended by Acts 2005, c. 885; 2006, c. 333; 2009, cc. 181, 551; 2012, c. 627.
58.1-3970.1. Amended by Acts 2011, c. 688; 2012, cc. 87, 610.
58.1-3971. Amended by Acts 2012, c. 627.
58.1-3974. Amended by Acts 2012, c. 627.
58.1-3975. Amended by Acts 2006, c. 616.
58.1-3983.1. Amended by Acts 2005, c. 927; 2006, c. 611.

Section
58.1-3984. Amended by Acts 2011, cc. 184, 232.
58.1-4006. Amended by Acts 2006, c. 598; 2008, c. 302.
58.1-4007. Amended by Acts 2006, c. 598; 2008, c. 302.
58.1-4009. Amended by Acts 2006, c. 598.
58.1-4014. Amended by Acts 2006, c. 598.
58.1-4018. Amended by Acts 2006, c. 598.
58.1-4019.1. Amended by Acts 2008, cc. 387, 689.
58.1-4021. Amended by Acts 2006, c. 598.
59.1-21.10. Amended by Acts 2005, c. 839; 2012, c. 351.
59.1-21.16:2. Amended by Acts 2012, c. 351.
59.1-21.19 through 59.1-21.28. Repealed by Acts 2010, c. 794.
59.1-41.6. Amended by Acts 2007, c. 805.
59.1-92.2. Amended by Acts 2008, cc. 759, 800; 2011, c. 801.
59.1-92.12, 59.1-92.13. Amended by Acts 2008, cc. 759, 800; 2011, c. 801.
59.1-98. Amended by Acts 2008, cc. 551, 691.
59.1-106. Amended by Acts 2008, cc. 551, 691.
59.1-116.1. Amended by Acts 2013, c. 414.
59.1-117. Amended by Acts 2010, c. 805; 2011, c. 836; 2013, c. 414.
59.1-118, 59.1-119. Amended by Acts 2011, c. 836.
59.1-120. Amended by Acts 2010, c. 805; 2011, c. 836.
59.1-121. Amended by Acts 2010, c. 805; 2011, c. 836; 2013, c. 414.
59.1-122. Amended by Acts 2011, c. 836; 2013, c. 414.
59.1-123. Amended by Acts 2007, c. 917; 2011, c. 836.
59.1-124. Amended by Acts 2010, c. 805.
59.1-125, 59.1-126. Amended by Acts 2011, c. 836.
59.1-129. Amended by Acts 2007, c. 917.
59.1-136.1. Amended by Acts 2009, c. 657; 2010, c. 805; 2012, c. 449; 2013, c. 414.
59.1-136.3. Amended by Acts 2013, c. 414.
59.1-136.5, 59.1-136.6. Amended by Acts 2013, c. 414.
59.1-148.3. Amended by Acts 2005, c. 168; 2006, c. 185; 2007, c. 813; 2009, cc. 289, 412; 2010, cc. 590, 864; 2011, c. 628; 2012, c. 218; 2013, c. 62.
59.1-149. Amended by Acts 2009, c. 650.
59.1-151. Amended by Acts 2009, c. 650.
59.1-153. Amended by Acts 2007, cc. 873, 916; 2009, c. 650.
59.1-155. Amended by Acts 2009, c. 650.
59.1-156. Amended by Acts 2009, c. 650.
59.1-163. Amended by Acts 2009, c. 650.
59.1-165. Amended by Acts 2010, c. 152.
59.1-198. Amended by Acts 2009, cc. 359, 700; 2010, c. 143; 2011, c. 615.

Section
59.1-200. Amended by Acts 2005, cc. 269, 303, 640, 861; 2006, c. 399; 2008, cc. 294, 791, 842; 2009, cc. 321, 359, 376, 699, 700; 2010, cc. 477, 713; 2011, c. 615.
59.1-200.1. Amended by Acts 2009, cc. 203, 272.
59.1-201. Amended by Acts 2008, c. 485.
59.1-203. Amended by Acts 2008, c. 485; 2012, cc. 803, 835.
59.1-204. Amended by Acts 2005, c. 250; 2006, c. 453.
59.1-205. Amended by Acts 2008, c. 485.
59.1-206. Amended by Acts 2008, c. 485.
59.1-207. Amended by Acts 2008, c. 485.
59.1-207.3. Amended by Acts 2012, cc. 803, 835.
59.1-207.19. Amended by Acts 2010, c. 794.
59.1-207.34. Amended by Acts 2012, cc. 803, 835.
59.1-207.39. Amended by Acts 2012, cc. 803, 835.
59.1-207.44. Amended by Acts 2012, cc. 803, 835.
59.1-272 to 59.1-278. Repealed by Acts 2005, cc. 863, 884.
59.1-279. Amended by Acts 2005, cc. 863, 884.
59.1-279.1. Repealed by Acts 2005, cc. 863, 884.
59.1-280. Amended by Acts 2005, cc. 863, 884; 2009, cc. 207, 271; 2011, c. 850.
59.1-280.1. Amended by Acts 2005, cc. 863, 884.
59.1-280.2. Repealed by Acts 2005, c. 884.
59.1-282. Repealed by Acts 2005, cc. 863, 884.
59.1-282.1, 59.1-282.2. Repealed by Acts 2009, cc. 207, 271.
59.1-282.3 to 59.1-284. Repealed by Acts 2005, cc. 863, 884.
59.1-284.01. Amended by Acts 2005, cc. 863, 884.
59.1-284.1 to 59.1-284.6. Repealed by Acts 2005, c. 624.
59.1-284.13. Amended by Acts 2007, c. 813.
59.1-284.14. Amended by Acts 2007, c. 813.
59.1-284.14:1. Amended by Acts 2005, c. 392.
59.1-284.15. Amended by Acts 2007, c. 813.
59.1-284.15:1. Amended by Acts 2005, c. 392.
59.1-284.17. Amended by Acts 2005, cc. 863, 884.
59.1-284.22. Amended by Acts 2013, c. 482.
59.1-284.23. Amended by Acts 2011, c. 749.
59.1-293.2. Amended by Acts 2012, cc. 66, 195.
59.1-296. Amended by Acts 2007, c. 683; 2010, c. 439.
59.1-296.1. Amended by Acts 2010, c. 439.
59.1-296.2. Amended by Acts 2010, c. 439.
59.1-296.2:1. Amended by Acts 2010, c. 439.
59.1-297. Amended by Acts 2006, c. 396; 2010, c. 439.

Section
59.1-297.1. Amended by Acts 2010, c. 439.
59.1-297.2. Amended by Acts 2010, c. 439.
59.1-298. Amended by Acts 2006, c. 396; 2010, c. 439; 2013, c. 24.
59.1-306. Amended by Acts 2010, c. 439.
59.1-310.1. Amended by Acts 2007, c. 575.
59.1-310.3. Amended by Acts 2007, c. 575.
59.1-310.5. Amended by Acts 2007, c. 575.
59.1-326. Amended by Acts 2013, c. 24.
59.1-328. Amended by Acts 2013, c. 24.
59.1-335.5. Amended by Acts 2010, c. 421.
59.1-335.7. Amended by Acts 2010, c. 421.
59.1-336. Amended by Acts 2009, cc. 321, 376.
59.1-352.7. Amended by Acts 2011, c. 369.
59.1-365. Amended by Acts 2005, c. 700; 2007, c. 757.
59.1-369. Amended by Acts 2005, cc. 633, 700; 2007, c. 757; 2009, c. 142; 2011, c. 732.
59.1-370. Amended by Acts 2005, c. 700.
59.1-376.1. Repealed by Acts 2009, c. 142.
59.1-387. Amended by Acts 2005, c. 700.
59.1-390. Amended by Acts 2005, c. 700.
59.1-392. Amended by Acts 2007, c. 61; 2011, c. 732.
59.1-429. Amended by Acts 2012, cc. 803, 835.
59.1-432. Amended by Acts 2012, cc. 803, 835.
59.1-435. Amended by Acts 2008, c. 524.
59.1-436. Amended by Acts 2005, c. 407.
59.1-443.1. Amended by Acts 2005, c. 839; 2008, cc. 562, 820.
59.1-444. Amended by Acts 2005, c. 640.
59.1-444.2. Amended by Acts 2009, c. 406.
59.1-473. Amended by Acts 2012, cc. 803, 835.
59.1-475. Amended by Acts 2006, c. 786.
59.1-477.1. Amended by Acts 2006, c. 786.
59.1-480. Amended by Acts 2005, c. 417.
59.1-481. Amended by Acts 2011, c. 369.
59.1-501.3. Amended by Acts 2011, c. 369.
59.1-514. Amended by Acts 2005, c. 296.
59.1-526. Amended by Acts 2006, c. 362; 2008, cc. 121, 157.
59.1-544. Amended by Acts 2011, cc. 254, 310; 2013, c. 514.
59.1-547. Amended by Acts 2006, c. 668; 2010, c. 328; 2012, c. 445.
59.1-548. Amended by Acts 2007, cc. 242, 287; 2009, cc. 207, 271.
59.1-549. Amended by Acts 2009, cc. 207, 271; 2010, c. 328; 2011, cc. 202, 320.
60.2-113. Amended by Acts 2008, c. 222; 2011, cc. 594, 681.
60.2-114. Amended by Acts 2013, c. 329.
60.2-119. Amended by Acts 2005, c. 105.
60.2-212. Amended by Acts 2005, c. 892.
60.2-213. Amended by Acts 2012, cc. 476, 507.
60.2-219. Amended by Acts 2005, c. 110.
60.2-315. Amended by Acts 2007, c. 241.
60.2-500. Amended by Acts 2005, cc. 47, 91; 2012, cc. 65, 161.

Section
60.2-512. Amended by Acts 2007, cc. 426, 638; 2012, c. 316.
60.2-528. Amended by Acts 2005, cc. 44, 105; 2009, c. 878.
60.2-602. Amended by Acts 2005, cc. 23, 918; 2006, c. 258; 2007, c. 628; 2008, c. 725; 2009, c. 789; 2010, c. 412; 2011, c. 16; 2012, c. 312.
60.2-603. Amended by Acts 2005, c. 125.
60.2-604. Amended by Acts 2005, c. 1; 2011, c. 748, 751.
60.2-610. Amended by Acts 2009, c. 789; 2011, c. 303.
60.2-611. Amended by Acts 2008, Sp. Sess. II, c. 11; 2009, c. 789; 2011, c. 303.
60.2-618. Amended by Acts 2005, c. 464; 2008, c. 719; 2009, c. 878; 2013, cc. 175, 771.
60.2-619. Amended by Acts 2013, c. 771.
60.2-622. Amended by Acts 2005, cc. 47, 91.
60.2-623. Amended by Acts 2012, c. 50.
60.2-633. Amended by Acts 2008, c. 492; 2010, c. 327; 2013, c. 683.
62.1-44.3. Amended by Acts 2007, c. 659.
62.1-44.5. Amended by Acts 2012, cc. 803, 835; 2013, cc. 756, 793.
62.1-44.8. Amended by Acts 2008, cc. 276, 557.
62.1-44.9. Amended by Acts 2008, cc. 276, 557; 2013, cc. 756, 793.
62.1-44.14. Amended by Acts 2005, c. 706; 2013, cc. 756, 793.
62.1-44.15. Amended by Acts 2005, c. 706; 2007, cc. 144, 633, 873, 916; 2011, cc. 52, 101; 2012, cc. 574, 581; 2013, cc. 756, 793.
62.1-44.15:01. Amended by Acts 2005, c. 478.
62.1-44.15:02. Amended by Acts 2009, c. 627.
62.1-44.15:5. Repealed by Acts 2007, c. 659.
62.1-44.15:5.01. Amended by Acts 2011, cc. 829, 842.
62.1-44.15:6. Amended by Acts 2011, cc. 87, 149.
62.1-44.15:20. Amended by Acts 2010, c. 233; 2011, cc. 829, 842; 2012, c. 628.
62.1-44.15:21. Amended by Acts 2008, c. 244; 2013, c. 742.
62.1-44.15:23. Amended by Acts 2008, c. 173; 2011, c. 253; 2012, c. 631.
62.1-44.17:1.1. Amended by Acts 2005, c. 78.
62.1-44.19:3. Amended by Acts 2005, cc. 197, 396, 459, 593; 2007, cc. 390, 881, 927, 929; 2009, c. 42.
62.1-44.19:3.4. Amended by Acts 2009, c. 42.
62.1-44.19:5. Amended by Acts 2007, c. 655.
62.1-44.19:7. Amended by Acts 2006, c. 154; 2011, cc. 281, 322.
62.1-44.19:11. Amended by Acts 2007, c. 29.
62.1-44.19:13. Amended by Acts 2012, cc. 748, 808; 2013, cc. 756, 793.
62.1-44.19:14. Amended by Acts 2010, c. 288.

Section
62.1-44.19:15. Amended by Acts 2007, c. 27; 2010, c. 288; 2011, cc. 440, 524; 2012, cc. 748, 808; 2013, cc. 756, 793.
62.1-44.19:18. Amended by Acts 2010, c. 11; 2011, c. 524; 2012, cc. 748, 808.
62.1-44.19:20. Amended by 2013, cc. 756, 793.
62.1-44.19:23. Amended by 2013, cc. 756, 793.
62.1-44.26. Amended by Acts 2008, cc. 276, 557.
62.1-44.29. Amended by Acts 2007, c. 659.
62.1-44.32. Amended by Acts 2005, c. 706; 2013, cc. 756, 793.
62.1-44.33. Amended by Acts 2009, c. 337; 2011, c. 220.
62.1-44.34:15.1. Amended by Acts 2011, cc. 883, 884.
62.1-44.34:20. Amended by Acts 2005, c. 706.
62.1-44.34:26. Amended by Acts 2011, cc. 594, 681.
62.1-44.38:1. Amended by Acts 2006, c. 18.
62.1-44.44. Amended by Acts 2013, cc. 756, 793.
62.1-44.114. Amended by Acts 2005, c. 839.
62.1-44.118. Amended by Acts 2007, c. 637; 2011, c. 245.
62.1-67. Amended by Acts 2006, cc. 516, 566.
62.1-69.25. Amended by Acts 2013, c. 173.
62.1-69.29. Amended by Acts 2009, c. 601; 2013, c. 173.
62.1-69.30. Amended by Acts 2013, c. 173.
62.1-69.34. Amended by Acts 2010, cc. 394, 729.
62.1-73. Amended by Acts 2005, c. 517; 2009, c. 467; 2013, cc. 756, 793.
62.1-77.1. Repealed by Acts 2005, c. 517.
62.1-98. Amended by Acts 2006, c. 586; 2010, c. 835.
62.1-129. Amended by Acts 2012, cc. 846, 849; 2013, cc. 762, 794.
62.1-129.1. Amended by Acts 2008, cc. 325, 621.
62.1-132.1. Amended by Acts 2013, cc. 762, 794.
62.1-132.3. Amended by Acts 2013, cc. 762, 794.
62.1-132.3:1. Amended by Acts 2012, cc. 846, 849.
62.1-132.3:2. Amended by Acts 2013, cc. 549, 806.
62.1-132.4. Amended by Acts 2013, cc. 762, 794.
62.1-132.6. Amended by Acts 2012, cc. 846, 849; 2013, cc. 762, 794.
62.1-132.11:2. Repealed by Acts 2011, cc. 594, 681.
62.1-132.12. Amended by Acts 2008, cc. 324, 529.
62.1-132.19, 62.1-132.20. Amended by Acts 2013, cc. 762, 794.

Section
62.1-132.20. Amended by Acts 2009, c. 38.
62.1-139. Amended by Acts 2012, cc. 846, 849; 2013, cc. 762, 794.
62.1-145. Amended by Acts 2005, c. 581.
62.1-193.1. Amended by Acts 2008, c. 10.
62.1-193.2. Amended by Acts 2008, c. 10.
62.1-194. Amended by Acts 2007, c. 24.
62.1-194.1. Amended by Acts 2007, c. 26.
62.1-195.1. Amended by Acts 2012, cc. 785, 819; 2013, cc. 756, 793.
62.1-198. Amended by Acts 2005, cc. 727, 769; 2007, cc. 81, 649, 663; 2008, cc. 3, 24, 238, 259, 504, 605, 613; 2009, cc. 14, 246, 311, 543, 632; 2010, cc. 42, 724, 820; 2011, c. 270.
62.1-199. Amended by Acts 2005, cc. 727, 769; 2007, cc. 81, 649, 663; 2008, cc. 2, 24, 238, 259, 504, 605, 613; 2009, cc. 14, 246, 311, 543, 632; 2010, cc. 42, 724, 820; 2011, cc. 270, 616.
62.1-203. Amended by Acts 2006, cc. 648, 765; 2011, c. 616.
62.1-201. Amended by Acts 2012, cc. 114, 242.
62.1-204. Amended by Acts 2009, c. 324.
62.1-209. Amended by Acts 2011, c. 616.
62.1-216.1. Amended by Acts 2011, c. 616.
62.1-222. Amended by Acts 2005, c. 633.
62.1-225. Amended by Acts 2009, c. 351.
62.1-229.3. Amended by Acts 2010, c. 644.
62.1-229.4. Amended by Acts 2012, cc. 803, 835; 2013, cc. 756, 793.
62.1-246. Amended by Acts 2007, cc. 873, 916.
63.2-100. Amended by Acts 2006, c. 868; 2007, cc. 479, 597; 2008, cc. 475, 483; 2009, cc. 705, 813, 840; 2011, cc. 5, 156; 2012, cc. 803, 835; 2013, cc. 5, 362, 564.
63.2-105. Amended by Acts 2006, cc. 863, 914; 2012, c. 841.
63.2-215. Amended by Acts 2012, cc. 803, 835.
63.2-217. Amended by Acts 2007, cc. 873, 916.
63.2-219. Amended by Acts 2005, c. 714.
63.2-226. Amended by Acts 2008, c. 277.
63.2-301. Amended by Acts 2005, c. 16.
63.2-304. Amended by Acts 2006, cc. 84, 158.
63.2-313. Amended by Acts 2012, cc. 803, 835.
63.2-315. Amended by Acts 2012, cc. 803, 835.
63.2-401. Amended by Acts 2012, cc. 803, 835.
63.2-405. Amended by Acts 2012, cc. 803, 835.
63.2-501. Amended by Acts 2012, cc. 240, 530.
63.2-600. Amended by Acts 2011, cc. 4, 857.
63.2-601. Amended by Acts 2013, c. 482.
63.2-602. Amended by Acts 2010, c. 250.
63.2-608. Amended by Acts 2005, c. 472; 2007, c. 568.
63.2-609. Amended by Acts 2007, c. 568; 2011, c. 426.
63.2-610. Amended by Acts 2013, c. 482.
63.2-611. Amended by Acts 2007, c. 568.
63.2-612. Amended by Acts 2007, c. 568; 2008, cc. 132, 564.

Section
63.2-617. Amended by Acts 2009, cc. 61, 547.
63.2-703. Amended by Acts 2006, cc. 142, 386.
63.2-800. Repealed by Acts 2012, cc. 803, 835.
63.2-805. Amended by Acts 2007, c. 312; 2009, c. 127.
63.2-900. Amended by Acts 2005, cc. 343, 653; 2006, c. 360; 2008, cc. 241, 308; 2010, c. 551; 2011, cc. 9, 170.
63.2-900.1. Amended by Acts 2012, c. 568.
63.2-900.3. Amended by Acts 2012, c. 711.
63.2-901.1. Amended by Acts 2005, c. 722; 2006, c. 558; 2007, cc. 606, 617, 623, 871; 2011, cc. 5, 156; 2012, c. 568.
63.2-902. Amended by Acts 2008, cc. 241, 308.
63.2-903. Amended by Acts 2005, c. 890; 2007, cc. 606, 623.
63.2-904 Amended by Acts 2008, cc. 475, 483.
63.2-905. Amended by Acts 2008, cc. 475, 483; 2013, c. 5.
63.2-905.1. Amended by Acts 2008, cc. 187, 475, 483; 2010, c. 257; 2013, cc. 5, 362, 564.
63.2-906. Amended by Acts 2005, c. 653; 2008, cc. 475, 483; 2009, c. 124; 2011, c. 730.
63.2-910. Amended by Acts 2009, c. 124.
63.2-912. Amended by Acts 2008, c. 188.
63.2-1000. Amended by Acts 2012, cc. 476, 507.
63.2-1104. Amended by Acts 2012, cc. 82, 773; 2013, c. 720.
63.2-1105. Amended by Acts 2012, cc. 476, 507.
63.2-1200. Amended by Acts 2006, cc. 825, 848.
63.2-1200.1. Amended by Acts 2012, c. 323.
63.2-1201. Amended by Acts 2006, cc. 825, 848; 2007, cc. 606, 623; 2008, cc. 116, 868; 2009, c. 805.
63.2-1202. Amended by Acts 2005, c. 890; 2006, cc. 825, 848; 2007, cc. 606, 623; 2009, c. 805; 2011, c. 486; 2012, c. 424.
63.2-1203. Amended by Acts 2009, c. 805; 2012, c. 425.
63.2-1204. Amended by Acts 2009, c. 805.
63.2-1205. Amended by Acts 2006, cc. 825, 848.
63.2-1208. Amended by Acts 2006, cc. 825, 848; 2007, c. 446.
63.2-1209. Amended by Acts 2009, c. 805.
63.2-1210. Amended by Acts 2006, cc. 825, 848; 2011, c. 486.
63.2-1212. Amended by Acts 2007, cc. 606, 623; 2009, c. 805.
63.2-1213. Amended by Acts 2006, cc. 825, 848; 2007, cc. 606, 623.
63.2-1220. Amended by Acts 2011, c. 486.
63.2-1221. Amended by Acts 2009, c. 805.
63.2-1222. Amended by Acts 2005, c. 890; 2006, cc. 825, 848; 2007, cc. 606, 623; 2009, c. 805; 2012, c. 424.
63.2-1223. Amended by Acts 2006, cc. 825, 848; 2007, cc. 606, 623.

Section
63.2-1224. Amended by Acts 2010, c. 855.
63.2-1225. Amended by Acts 2006, cc. 825, 848; 2009, c. 805.
63.2-1226. Amended by Acts 2006, cc. 825, 848; 2007, cc. 606, 623.
63.2-1227. Amended by Acts 2006, cc. 825, 848.
63.2-1228. Amended by Acts 2006, cc. 825, 848.
63.2-1228.1, 63.2-1228.2. Repealed by Acts 2010, c. 331.
63.2-1229. Amended by Acts 2007, cc. 606, 623.
63.2-1230. Amended by Acts 2009, c. 805.
63.2-1231. Amended by Acts 2006, cc. 825, 848; 2007, c. 808; 2008, c. 494; 2010, c. 551.
63.2-1232. Amended by Acts 2006, cc. 654, 825, 848; 2010, c. 276.
63.2-1233. Amended by Acts 2005, c. 890; 2006, cc. 825, 848; 2007, cc. 606, 623; 2009, c. 805.
63.2-1234. Amended by Acts 2006, cc. 825, 848; 2008, c. 662.
63.2-1237. Amended by Acts 2006, cc. 825, 848.
63.2-1241. Amended by Acts 2006, cc. 825, 848; 2007, cc. 606, 623; 2010, c. 306; 2012, c. 424.
63.2-1242.2. Amended by Acts 2010, c. 306.
63.2-1242.3. Amended by Acts 2010, c. 306.
63.2-1243. Amended by Acts 2006, cc. 825, 848.
63.2-1245. Amended by Acts 2013, c. 263.
63.2-1250. Amended by Acts 2009, c. 805; 2012, c. 424.
63.2-1251. Amended by Acts 2012, c. 424.
63.2-1300. Amended by Acts 2010, c. 271.
63.2-1301. Amended by Acts 2010, c. 271.
63.2-1302. Amended by Acts 2010, c. 271.
63.2-1303. Amended by Acts 2010, c. 271.
63.2-1503. Amended by Acts 2008, cc. 474, 827; 2009, cc. 813, 840.
63.2-1505. Amended by Acts 2007, c. 495; 2008, c. 555; 2013, cc. 340, 506.
63.2-1509. Amended by Acts 2006, cc. 530, 801; 2008, cc. 43, 268; 2012, cc. 391, 504, 640, 698, 728, 740, 815; 2013, cc. 72, 331.
63.2-1511. Amended by Acts 2005, cc. 767, 806.
63.2-1514. Amended by Acts 2005, c. 77; 2010, c. 334.
63.2-1528. Repealed by Acts 2012, cc. 803, 835.
63.2-1529. Repealed by Acts 2009, c. 32.
63.2-1530. Amended by Acts 2010, cc. 664, 726; 2012, cc. 113, 661.
63.2-1600. Amended by Acts 2012, cc. 803, 835.
63.2-1601. Amended by Acts 2012, cc. 803, 835.
63.2-1602. Amended by Acts 2005, c. 716; 2012, cc. 476, 507, 803, 835.
63.2-1602.1. Repealed by Acts 2012, cc. 803, 835.
63.2-1603. Amended by Acts 2012, cc. 476, 507.
63.2-1604. Repealed by Acts 2012, cc. 803, 835.
63.2-1605. Amended by Acts 2006, c. 149; 2009, c. 673; 2012, cc. 803, 835.

Section
63.2-1606. Amended by Acts 2008, c. 539; 2009, c. 538; 2012, cc. 803, 835; 2013, cc. 72, 331.
63.2-1612. Amended by Acts 2005, cc. 638, 685; 2006, c. 135.
63.2-1700. Amended by Acts 2010, c. 551; 2012, cc. 803, 835.
63.2-1702. Amended by Acts 2005, cc. 610, 924; 2013, cc. 182, 545.
63.2-1704. Amended by Acts 2009, c. 29.
63.2-1706. Amended by Acts 2010, c. 603; 2012, cc. 803, 835.
63.2-1707. Amended by Acts 2005, cc. 610, 924; 2013, cc. 182, 545.
63.2-1709. Amended by Acts 2005, cc. 610, 924; 2009, cc. 813, 840.
63.2-1715. Amended by Acts 2006, c. 725; 2011, c. 363.
63.2-1716. Amended by Acts 2006, c. 396; 2009, c. 258.
63.2-1719. Amended by Acts 2012, c. 383.
63.2-1720. Amended by Acts 2005, c. 723; 2006, cc. 701, 744, 764.
63.2-1721. Amended by Acts 2005, cc. 610, 722, 924; 2006, cc. 744, 885.
63.2-1724. Amended by Acts 2006, c. 744.
63.2-1725. Amended by Acts 2006, c. 744; 2013, c. 261.
63.2-1726. Amended by Acts 2007, c. 573; 2009, cc. 813, 840; 2012, c. 383; 2013, cc. 96, 181.
63.2-1727. Amended by Acts 2006, cc. 796, 804.
63.2-1728. Amended by Acts 2010, c. 603.
63.2-1732. Amended by Acts 2005, cc. 610, 924; 2007, cc. 119, 164.
63.2-1734. Amended by Acts 2011, c. 139; 2012, cc. 803, 835; 2013, c. 416.
63.2-1735. Repealed by Acts 2012, cc. 803, 835.
63.2-1737. Amended by Acts 2005, cc. 358, 471; 2006, cc. 168, 781; 2008, c. 873; 2010, c. 551.
63.2-1801. Amended by Acts 2005, c. 716; 2012, cc. 476, 507.
63.2-1803. Amended by Acts 2005, cc. 610, 924; 2011, c. 609.
63.2-1805. Amended by Acts 2005, cc. 610, 716, 724, 924; 2007, c. 539; 2009, cc. 813, 840; 2012, cc. 476, 507; 2013, c. 320.
63.2-1806. Amended by Acts 2007, c. 397.
63.2-1808. Amended by Acts 2006, c. 396; 2007, cc. 120, 163; 2013, cc. 320, 571.
63.2-1808.1. Amended by Acts 2012, c. 476, 507.
63.2-1809.1. Amended by Acts 2007, c. 594.
63.2-1810. Amended by Acts 2012, cc. 803, 835.
63.2-1819. Amended by Acts 2008, cc. 475, 483.
63.2-1900. Amended by Acts 2007, c. 600; 2009, c. 713; 2010, c. 243.
63.2-1901. Amended by Acts 2008, c. 845.

Section
63.2-1902. Amended by Acts 2009, c. 713.
63.2-1903. Amended by Acts 2007, c. 600; 2009, cc. 125, 713.
63.2-1904. Amended by Acts 2007, cc. 11, 600.
63.2-1916. Amended by Acts 2006, cc. 720, 869; 2007, c. 600; 2009, cc. 706, 713.
63.2-1924.1. Amended by Acts 2009, c. 713.
63.2-1931. Amended by Acts 2009, c. 125.
63.2-1941. Amended by Acts 2012, c. 829.
63.2-1946. Amended by Acts 2013, c. 329.
63.2-1954.1. Repealed by Acts 2010, c. 243.
63.2-1960. Amended by Acts 2005, c. 880.
63.2-2000, 63.2-2001. Repealed by Acts 2008, c. 585.
63.2-2002. Repealed by Acts 2009, c. 851.
63.2-2003 to 63.2-2006. Repealed by Acts 2008, c. 585.
63.2-2006. Amended by Acts 2005, c. 82; 2008, c. 463.
63.2-2100. Amended by Acts 2012, cc. 803, 835.
63.2-2102. Amended by Acts 2012, cc. 803, 835.
63.2-2200. Amended by Acts 2007, c. 588.
63.2-2201. Amended by Acts 2005, c. 31; 2007, c. 588.
63.2-2203. Amended by Acts 2007, c. 588; 2008, c. 507.
64.1-01 to 64.1-206.8. Repealed by Acts 2012, c. 614.
64.2-432. Amended by Acts 2013, c. 784.
64.2-531. Amended by Acts 2013, c. 390.
64.2-601. Amended by Acts 2013, c. 68.
64.2-719. Amended by Acts 2013, c. 523.
64.2-747. Amended by Acts 2013, c. 784.
64.2-776. Amended by Acts 2013, c. 324.
64.2-2001, 64.2-2002. Amended by Acts 2013, c. 523.
64.2-2007, 64.2-2008. Amended by Acts 2013, c. 523.
64.2-2014. Amended by Acts 2013, c. 542.
64.2-2020. Amended by Acts 2013, c. 133.
64.2-2022, 64.2-2023. Amended by Acts 2013, c. 523.
65.2-101. Amended by Acts 2005, cc. 354, 368, 374, 472; 2006, c. 629; 2007, c. 475; 2010, cc. 158, 278; 2011, cc. 572, 586, 665; 2012, c. 654.
65.2-102. Amended by Acts 2008, c. 109.
65.2-103. Amended by Acts 2011, cc. 572, 586.
65.2-105. Amended by Acts 2013, c. 169.
65.2-200. Amended by Acts 2006, c. 838.
65.2-201. Amended by Acts 2012, c. 588.
65.2-202. Amended by Acts 2008, c. 651.
65.2-204. Amended by Acts 2013, c. 14.
65.2-402. Amended by Acts 2007, cc. 143, 616; 2009, c. 515; 2012, c. 776.
65.2-402.1. Amended by Acts 2007, cc. 87, 365; 2009, c. 417; 2011, c. 211; 2012, c. 776.
65.2-406. Amended by Acts 2005, c. 433; 2011, c. 513.

Section
65.2-500. Amended by Acts 2005, c. 472.
65.2-502. Amended by Acts 2005, c. 472; 2006, c. 660.
65.2-504. Amended by Acts 2011, c. 513.
65.2-512. Amended by Acts 2005, c. 472.
65.2-520. Amended by Acts 2007, c. 356.
65.2-524. Amended by Acts 2012, c. 270.
65.2-603. Amended by Acts 2011, c. 656.
65.2-704. Amended by Acts 2010, cc. 160, 564; 2012, c. 588.
65.2-705. Amended by Acts 2010, cc. 160, 564; 2012, c. 588.
65.2-706. Amended by Acts 2010, cc. 160, 564.
65.2-708. Amended by Acts 2013, c. 445.
65.2-714. Amended by Acts 2012, c. 543.
65.2-715. Amended by Acts 2010, cc. 159, 274.
65.2-801. Amended by Acts 2006, c. 265; 2009, cc. 285, 336.
65.2-803.1. Amended by Acts 2005, c. 158.
65.2-804. Amended by Acts 2009, c. 150; 2010, cc. 282, 376.
65.2-805. Amended by Acts 2005, c. 69.
65.2-806. Amended by Acts 2005, c. 69.
65.2-1201. Amended by Acts 2009, c. 219.
65.2-1203. Amended by Acts 2009, cc. 285, 336.
65.2-1306. Amended by Acts 2013, c. 204.
66-3. Amended by Acts 2012, cc. 803, 835; 2013, cc. 143, 214.
66-3.1. Repealed by Acts 2011, cc. 798, 871.
66-3.2. Amended by Acts 2006, cc. 431, 500.
66-4. Amended by Acts 2013, cc. 37, 232.
66-10. Amended by Acts 2012, cc. 164, 456, 803, 835.
66-11. Repealed by Acts 2012, cc. 164, 456.
66-13. Amended by Acts 2012, cc. 803, 835.
66-19. Amended by Acts 2012, cc. 476, 507.
66-20. Amended by Acts 2012, cc. 476, 507.
66-23. Amended by Acts 2012, cc. 164, 456.
66-24. Amended by Acts 2005, cc. 358, 471; 2006, cc. 168, 781; 2008, c. 873.
66-25.1. Amended by Acts 2011, c. 551; 2012, cc. 803, 835.
66-25.1:2. Amended by Acts 2012, cc. 803, 835.
66-25.4. Amended by Acts 2012, cc. 803, 835.
67-101. Amended by Acts 2008, c. 883; 2009, cc. 411, 768; 2011, c. 236; 2012, c. 544.
67-102. Amended by Acts 2009, cc. 411, 768.
67-202. Amended by Acts 2008, c. 883.
67-300. Amended by Acts 2010, cc. 607, 756.
67-600. Amended by Acts 2007, c. 904; 2009, c. 575; 2010, c. 695.
67-601. Amended by Acts 2009, c. 575.
67-602. Amended by Acts 2007, c. 904; 2009, c. 575; 2010, c. 695.
67-603. Amended by Acts 2009, c. 575.
67-604. Amended by Acts 2009, c. 575.
67-700. Amended by Acts 2008, c. 881.
67-701. Amended by Acts 2008, c. 881; 2009, c. 866; 2013, c. 357.
67-900. Amended by Acts 2007, c. 789.

Section
67-901. Amended by Acts 2007, c. 789.
67-902. Amended by Acts 2007, c. 789.
67-1000. Amended by Acts 2007, c. 789.
67-1001. Amended by Acts 2007, c. 789.
67-1002. Amended by Acts 2007, c. 789.

Section
67-1003. Amended by Acts 2007, c. 789.
67-1101. Amended by Acts 2013, cc. 585, 646.
67-1103. Amended by Acts 2013, cc. 585, 646.
67-1202. Amended by Acts 2011, c. 17; 2012, c. 502.

TABLES OF COMPARABLE SECTIONS FOR CERTAIN REPEALED AND REVISED TITLES

COMPARABLE SECTIONS OF CHAPTER 2 TO 2.1 OF TITLE 1

Former Section	Present Section
1-10	1-200
1-11	1-201
1-12	1-214, 30-14
1-13	1-202
1-13.1	1-222
1-13.1:1	1-205
1-13.2	1-208
1-13.3	1-210
1-13.3:1	1-210
1-13.4:1	1-209
1-13.5	Repealed
1-13.5:1	1-212
1-13.6	Repealed
1-13.7	1-216, 2.2-3901
1-13.8	Repealed
1-13.9	1-217
1-13.9:1	1-244
1-13.10	Repealed
1-13.10:1	1-235
1-13.12	1-219
1-13.13	1-223
1-13.13:1	1-225
1-13.14	1-226
1-13.15	1-227
1-13.16	1-228
1-13.17	1-248
1-13.18	Repealed
1-13.19	1-230
1-13.19:1	1-231
1-13.20	1-233
1-13.21	1-234
1-13.22	1-235
1-13.23	Repealed
1-13.23:1	1-237
1-13.24	Repealed
1-13.25	1-241
1-13.25:1	1-242
1-13.26	1-245
1-13.27	1-210
1-13.27:1	Repealed
1-13.27:2	1-249
1-13.27:3	Repealed
1-13.28	1-250
1-13.28:1	1-252
1-13.28:2	1-252
1-13.29	1-254
1-13.30	Repealed
1-13.31	1-255
1-13.32	1-257
1-13.33	1-223
1-13.34	1-246
1-13.35	1-236
1-13.35:1	1-229
1-13.36	1-236
1-13.37	Repealed
1-13.38	Repealed
1-13.39:1	Repealed
1-13.39:2	1-220
1-13.39:3	1-238
1-13.40	1-251
1-13.41	1-211
1-13.42	1-203,
	1-204,
	1-207,
	1-232
1-15	1-253
1-15.1	1-206
1-15.2	1-256
1-16	1-239
1-17	1-240
1-17.1	1-243
1-17.2	1-213, 2.2-604

COMPARABLE SECTIONS OF TITLE 3.1 AND TITLE 3.2

Former Section	Present Section
3.1-1	3.2-108
3.1-2	3.2-109
3.1-3	3.2-109
3.1-4	3.2-110
	3.2-5900
3.1-4.1	3.2-110
	3.2-1101
3.1-5	Repealed
3.1-6	Deleted
3.1-6.1	3.2-1100
3.1-7	Repealed
3.1-8	3.2-101
	3.2-102
3.1-9	Deleted
3.1-10	3.2-102
3.1-11 to	
3.1-13	Deleted
3.1-14	3.2-102 A
	3.2-103
	3.2-5900
3.1-14.01	3.2-102 B
3.1-14.1	3.2-104
3.1-14.2	3.2-101 B
3.1-14.3	3.2-14.4
3.1-14.4	3.2-102 B
3.1-15	3.2-107
3.1-16	3.2-107 B
	3.2-107 C
3.1-17	Deleted
3.1-17.1	3.2-105
3.1-18	Repealed
3.1-18.1	3.2-112
3.1-18.2	3.2-113
3.1-18.3	3.2-114
3.1-18.4	Deleted
3.1-18.5	3.2-205
3.1-18.6	3.2-206
3.1-18.7	Repealed
3.1-18.8	3.2-204
3.1-18.9	3.2-200
3.1-18.10	3.2-201
3.1-18.11	3.2-202
3.1-18.12	3.2-203
3.1-18.13 to	
3.1-18.25	Not in effect
3.1-19 to	
3.1-22	Repealed
3.1-22.1,	
3.1-22.2	Deleted
3.1-22.3	3.2-2900
3.1-22.4	3.2-2901
	3.2-2902
	3.2-2903
	3.2-2904 A
	3.2-2904 B
3.1-22.5	3.2-2905
3.1-22.6	Deleted
3.1-22.7	10.1-217.1
3.1-22.8	10.1-217.2
3.1-22.9	10.1-217.3
3.1-22.10	10.1-217.4
3.1-22.11	10.1-217.5
3.1-22.12	10.1-217.6
3.1-22.13,	
3.1-22.14	Deleted
3.1-22.15	3.2-503
3.1-22.16	3.2-501
3.1-22.17	3.2-500
3.1-22.18	3.2-504

Former Section	Present Section
3.1-22.19	3.2-505
3.1-22.20	3.2-506
3.1-22.21	3.2-502
3.1-22.22 to	
3.1-22.27	Repealed
3.1-22.28	3.2-300
	3.2-301
3.1-22.29	3.2-300
	3.2-302
3.1-22.30 to	
3.1-22.37	Repealed
3.1-22.38 to	
3.1-22.51	Repealed
3.1-22.52	Expired
3.1-22.53	Deleted
3.1-22.54	3.2-1700
3.1-22.55	3.2-1701
3.1-22.56	3.2-1702
3.1-22.57	3.2-1703
3.1-22.58	3.2-1704
3.1-22.59	3.2-112
3.1-22.60	3.2-1705
3.1-22.61	3.2-1706
3.1-22.62	3.2-1707
3.1-22.63	3.2-1708
3.1-22.64	3.2-1709
3.1-22.65	3.2-1710
3.1-22.66	3.2-1711
3.1-22.67	3.2-1712
3.1-22.68	3.2-1713
3.1-22.69	3.2-1714
3.1-22.70	3.2-1715
3.1-22.71	3.2-1716
3.1-22.72	3.2-1717
3.1-22.73	3.2-1718
3.1-22.74	3.2-1719
3.1-22.75	3.2-1720
3.1-22.76	3.2-1721
3.1-22.77	3.2-1722
3.1-23	3.2-600
3.1-24	3.2-601
3.1-25	3.2-602
3.1-26	3.2-603
3.1-27	3.2-604
3.1-27.1 to	
3.1-27.36	Repealed
3.1-27.37 to	
3.1-27.50	Deleted
3.1-28	3.2-3400 A
3.1-29	3.2-3400 B
3.1-30	3.2-3401
3.1-31	3.2-3402
3.1-32 to	
3.1-39	Repealed
3.1-40 to	
3.1-46.1	Repealed
3.1-47 to	
3.1-73.1	Deleted
3.1-73.2	Repealed
3.1-73.3	3.2-3500

Former Section	Present Section
3.1-73.4	Repealed
3.1-73.5	3.2-3501
3.1-73.5:1	3.2-3502
3.1-73.6	3.2-2600
3.1-73.7	3.2-2601
3.1-73.8	3.2-2602
	3.2-2603 B-C
3.1-74 to	
3.1-106	Repealed
3.1-106.1	Deleted
3.1-106.2	3.2-3600
3.1-106.3	Deleted
3.1-106.4	3.2-3601
3.1-106.4:1	3.2-3602
3.1-106.5	3.2-3611
3.1-106.6	3.2-3605
	3.2-3606 A-E
	3.2-3607 A-F
	3.2-3608 A-C
3.1-106.7	3.2-3618
3.1-106.8	3.2-3609
	3.2-3621 B
3.1-106.9	3.2-3610
3.1-106.10	3.2-3612
3.1-106.11	3.2-3613
3.1-106.12	3.2-3614
3.1-106.13	3.2-3615
3.1-106.14	3.2-3616
3.1-106.15	3.2-3619
3.1-106.16	3.2-3620
3.1-106.17	3.2-3623
	3.2-3622 A-B
3.1-106.18	3.2-3621
3.1-106.19	3.2-3603
3.1-106.20	3.2-3604
3.1-106.21	Deleted
3.1-106.22	3.2-3617
3.1-107 to	
3.1-126	Repealed
3.1-126.1	Deleted
3.1-126.2	Repealed
3.1-126.2:1	3.2-3700
3.1-126.2:2	Deleted
3.1-126.3	3.2-3706
3.1-126.4	3.2-3702
	3.2-3703 A-B
	3.2-3704 A-C
3.1-126.5	3.2-3705
3.1-126.6	3.2-3707
3.1-126.7	3.2-3708
3.1-126.8	3.2-3709
	3.2-3713
3.1-126.9	3.2-3711
3.1-126.10	3.2-3712
3.1-126.11	3.2-3715
3.1-126.12	Repealed
3.1-126.12:1	3.2-3701
3.1-126.12:2	3.2-3714
3.1-126.12:3	3.2-3710
3.1-126.13	Repealed

Former Section	Present Section
3.1-127 to	
3.1-134	Repealed
3.1-135 to	
3.1-157	Repealed
3.1-158 to	
3.1-169	Repealed
3.1-170 to	
3.1-176	Repealed
3.1-177,	
3.1-177.1	15.2-902
3.1-178 to	
3.1-188	Repealed
3.1-188.1	3.2-715
3.1-188.2	3.2-716
3.1-188.3	3.2-714
3.1-188.4	3.2-717
3.1-188.5	3.2-718
3.1-188.6	3.2-719
3.1-188.7	3.2-720
3.1-188.8	3.2-721
3.1-188.9	3.2-722
3.1-188.10	3.2-723
3.1-188.11	3.2-724
3.1-188.12	3.2-725
3.1-188.13	3.2-726
3.1-188.14	3.2-727
3.1-188.15	3.2-728
3.1-188.16	3.2-729
3.1-188.17	3.2-730
3.1-188.18	3.2-714
3.1-188.19	3.2-731
3.1-188.20	3.2-700
3.1-188.21	3.2-701
3.1-188.22	3.2-702
3.1-188.23	3.2-703
3.1-188.24	3.2-704
3.1-188.25	3.2-705
3.1-188.26	3.2-706
3.1-188.27	3.2-707
3.1-188.27:1	3.2-708
3.1-188.28	3.2-709
3.1-188.29	3.2-710
3.1-188.30	3.2-711
3.1-188.31	Repealed
3.1-188.31:1	3.2-712
3.1-188.31:2	3.2-713
3.1-188.32	3.1-3800
3.1-188.33	Deleted
3.1-188.34	3.2-3801
3.1-188.35	Deleted
3.1-188.36	3.2-3803
	3.2-3810 A
3.1-188.37	3.2-3803 C
	3.2-3806 A
	3.2-3807
3.1-188.38	3.2-3804
3.1-188.39	3.2-3808
3.1-188.40	3.2-3809
3.1-188.41	3.2-3805
3.1-188.42	3.2-3802

Former Section	Present Section
3.1-188.43	3.2-3801 A
3.1-188.44	3.2-3806 C
3.1-188.45	Deleted
3.1-188.46	3.2-3806
	3.2-3810 B
3.1-188.47	3.2-3810
3.1-188.48	3.2-3801 B
3.1-188.49	3.2-3811
3.1-189 to	
3.1-249.26	Repealed
3.1-249.27	3.2-3900
	3.2-3938
3.1-249.28	3.2-3902
3.1-249.29	3.2-3904
3.1-249.30	3.2-3906
3.1-249.31	3.2-3906
3.1-249.32	3.2-3910
3.1-249.33	3.2-3907
3.1-249.34	3.2-3912
3.1-249.35	3.2-3914
3.1-249.36	3.2-3915
3.1-249.37	3.2-3916
3.1-249.38	3.2-3917
3.1-249.39	3.2-3918
3.1-249.40	3.2-3919
3.1-249.41	3.2-3920
3.1-249.42	3.2-3921
3.1-249.43	3.2-3921
3.1-249.44	3.2-3922
3.1-249.45	3.2-3923
3.1-249.46	3.2-3924
3.1-249.47	3.2-3925
3.1-249.48	3.2-3926
3.1-249.49	3.2-3927
3.1-249.50	3.2-3928
3.1-249.51	3.2-3929
3.1-249.52	3.2-3930
3.1-249.53	3.2-3931
3.1-249.54	3.2-3932
3.1-249.55	3.2-3933
3.1-249.56	3.2-3911
	3.2-3909
3.1-249.57	3.2-3934
3.1-249.58	3.2-3942
3.1-249.59	3.2-3935
3.1-249.60	3.2-3936
3.1-249.61	3.2-3937
3.1-249.62	3.2-3904
3.1-249.63	3.2-3917
	3.2-3939
	3.2-3940 A-B, E
3.1-249.64	3.2-3939 B-D
3.1-249.65	3.2-3939 E
3.1-249.66	3.2-3939 F
3.1-249.67	3.2-3939 G
3.1-249.68	3.2-3908
3.1-249.69	3.2-3939 H
3.1-249.70	3.2-3943
	3.2-3947
3.1-249.71	3.2-3946 A
3.1-249.72	3.2-3946 B
3.1-249.73	3.2-3946 C
3.1-249.74	3.2-3941
3.1-249.75	3.2-3913
3.1-249.76	3.2-3940 C-D
3.1-249.77	3.2-3944
3.1-249.78	3.2-3945
3.1-250 to	
3.1-261	Repealed
3.1-262	Deleted
3.1-263	3.2-4000
3.1-264	3.2-4008
3.1-265	3.2-4015
3.1-266	3.2-4006
3.1-267	3.2-4016
3.1-268	3.2-4017
3.1-269	3.2-4001
3.1-270	3.2-4003
	3.2-4011
	3.2-4012
3.1-271	3.2-4001
3.1-271.1	3.2-4002
3.1-272	3.2-4013
3.1-273	3.2-4014
	3.2-4020
3.1-274	3.2-4018
3.1-275	3.2-4007
3.1-275.1	3.2-4009
3.1-275.2	3.2-4005
3.1-275.3	3.2-4010
3.1-275.4	3.2-4008 K
3.1-275.5	3.2-4001
3.1-275.6	3.2-4019
3.1-275.7	3.2-4004
3.1-276	3.2-4021
	3.2-4022
3.1-277	3.2-4024
3.1-278	3.2-4023
3.1-279	3.2-4022
3.1-280	3.2-4025
3.1-281	3.2-4024
3.1-282	3.2-4024
3.1-283	3.2-4024
	3.2-4026
3.1-284	3.2-4027
3.1-285, 3.1-286	Deleted
3.1-287	3.2-4100
3.1-288	3.2-4105
3.1-289	3.2-4104
3.1-290	3.2-4102
	3.2-4104
3.1-291	Deleted
3.1-292	3.2-4107
	3.2-4108
3.1-293	3.2-4109
3.1-294	3.2-4106
3.1-295	3.2-4110
	3.2-4111
3.1-296	Deleted
3.1-296.1 to	
3.1-296.10:1	Repealed
3.1-296.11	Deleted
3.1-296.12	3.2-800
3.1-296.13	3.2-801
3.1-296.14	3.2-802
3.1-296.15	3.2-803
3.1-296.16	3.2-804
3.1-296.17	3.2-805
3.1-296.18	3.2-809
3.1-296.19	3.2-806
3.1-296.20	3.2-807
3.1-296.21	3.2-808
3.1-297 to	
3.1-307	Deleted
3.1-308	3.2-2500
3.1-309	3.2-2501
	3.2-2502
	3.2-2503
	3.2-2504
3.1-310	3.2-2504
3.1-311	3.2-2505
3.1-312	3.2-2507
3.1-313	3.2-2508
3.1-314	3.2-2509
3.1-315	3.2-2506
3.1-316	3.2-2506
3.1-317	3.2-2510
3.1-318	3.2-1103
3.1-319	3.2-2400
3.1-320	3.2-2401
3.1-321	3.2-2401
3.1-322	3.2-2403
	3.2-2404 A
3.1-323	3.2-2404
3.1-324	3.2-2405
3.1-325	3.2-2405 B
	3.2-2405 C
	3.2-2405 F
3.1-326	3.2-2405 D
3.1-327	3.2-2405 E
3.1-328	3.2-2406
3.1-329	3.2-2408
3.1-330	3.2-2409
3.1-331	3.2-2410
3.1-332	3.2-2407
3.1-333	3.2-2407
3.1-334	3.2-2411
3.1-335	3.2-1103
3.1-336	Deleted
3.1-336.1	3.2-4200
3.1-336.2	3.2-4201
3.1-336.2:1	3.2-4202
3.1-336.2:2	3.2-4203
3.1-336.3	3.2-4204
3.1-336.4	3.2-4205
3.1-336.5	3.2-4206
3.1-336.6	3.2-4207
3.1-336.7	3.2-4208
3.1-336.8	3.2-4209
3.1-336.9	3.2-4210

Former Section	Present Section
3.1-336.9:1	3.2-4211
3.1-336.10	3.2-4212
3.1-336.11	3.2-4213
3.1-336.12	3.2-4214
3.1-336.13	3.2-4215
3.1-336.14	3.2-4216
3.1-336.15	3.2-4217
3.1-336.16	3.2-4218
3.1-337	3.2-4300
3.1-338	3.2-4302
3.1-339	3.2-4303
3.1-340	3.2-4304
3.1-341	3.2-4306
3.1-342	3.2-4307
3.1-343	3.2-4308
3.1-344	3.2-4305
3.1-345	3.2-4301
3.1-346	3.2-4309
3.1-347	3.2-4310
3.1-348	3.2-4311
3.1-348.1	3.2-4322
3.1-348.2	3.2-4323
3.1-348.3	3.2-4324
3.1-348.4	3.2-4325
3.1-348.5	3.2-4326
3.1-348.6	3.2-4327
3.1-349	3.2-4312
3.1-350	3.2-4313
3.1-351	3.2-4314
3.1-352	3.2-4320
3.1-353	3.2-4315
3.1-354	3.2-4316
3.1-355	Deleted
3.1-356	3.2-4317
3.1-357	3.2-4321
3.1-358	3.2-4318 A
3.1-359	3.2-4318 B
3.1-360	3.2-4319
3.1-360.1 to 3.1-360.8	Repealed
3.1-361	Deleted
3.1-362	Repealed
3.1-363	3.2-5104
3.1-364	3.2-5103
3.1-365	3.2-5105
3.1-366	3.2-5106 A
3.1-367	3.2-5106 B
3.1-368	3.2-5111
3.1-369	3.2-5106 C
3.1-370	3.2-5110
3.1-371	3.2-5112
3.1-372	3.2-5107 A
3.1-373	3.2-5107 A
3.1-374	3.2-5107 B
3.1-375	3.2-5108
3.1-376	3.2-5115
3.1-377	3.2-5113
3.1-378	Repealed
3.1-379	3.2-5114
3.1-380	3.2-5109

Former Section	Present Section
3.1-381	3.2-5117
3.1-382	3.2-5118
3.1-382.1	3.2-5116
3.1-383, 3.1-384	Deleted
3.1-385	3.2-5119
3.1-385.1 to 3.1-385.8	Repealed
3.1-386	Deleted
3.1-387	3.2-5120
	3.2-5123 A-B
3.1-388	3.2-5126 A
3.1-388.1	3.2-5127
3.1-389	3.2-5126 E
3.1-390	3.2-5126 B-D
3.1-391	3.2-5134
3.1-392	3.2-5128 A-B
3.1-393	3.2-5128 C
3.1-394	3.2-5101
3.1-395	3.2-5122
3.1-396	3.2-5123
3.1-397	3.2-5125
3.1-398	3.2-5121
3.1-398.1	3.2-5130
3.1-399	3.2-5102
3.1-400	Deleted
3.1-401	3.2-5141
3.1-402	3.2-5100 A
3.1-403	3.2-5100 B
3.1-404	3.2-5100 C
3.1-405	3.2-5131
3.1-406	3.2-5132
3.1-407	3.2-5133
3.1-408	3.2-5135 A
3.1-409	3.2-5135 B
3.1-410	3.2-5135 C
3.1-411	3.2-5137
3.1-412	3.2-5138
3.1-413	3.2-5139
3.1-414	3.2-5140
3.1-415	3.2-5141
3.1-416	3.2-5142
3.1-417	3.2-5136
3.1-418	3.2-5145
3.1-418.1	3.2-5144
3.1-419	3.2-5143
3.1-420	3.2-5200
3.1-421	3.2-5204
3.1-422 to 3.1-424	Deleted
3.1-425	3.2-3200
3.1-426	3.2-3201
3.1-426.1	3.2-3202
3.1-426.2	3.2-3203
3.1-427, 3.1-428	Deleted
3.1-429	3.2-3203
3.1-430	3.2-3204
3.1-431	3.2-3205
3.1-432	3.2-3206
3.1-433	3.2-3206 A
3.1-434	3.2-3206 B

Former Section	Present Section
3.1-435	3.2-3206 C
3.1-436	Repealed
3.1-437	3.2-3208
3.1-437.1	3.2-3209
3.1-438	3.2-3210
3.1-439	3.2-3212
3.1-440	3.2-3211
3.1-441	3.2-3207
3.1-442	Deleted
3.1-443	3.2-3213
3.1-444	3.2-3214
3.1-445	3.2-3215
3.1-446	3.2-3216
3.1-447	Deleted
3.1-448	3.2-3217 A
3.1-449	Deleted
3.1-450	3.2-3217 B
	3.2-3217 C
3.1-451	3.2-3218
3.1-452	3.2-3219
3.1-453	3.2-3220
3.1-454 to 3.1-457	Repealed
3.1-458	3.2-3221
3.1-459	3.2-3222
3.1-460	3.2-3224
3.1-461	3.2-3223
3.1-462	Repealed
3.1-461.1	3.2-3300
3.1-461.2	3.2-3301
3.1-461.3	3.2-3302
3.1-461.4	3.2-3303
3.1-463 to 3.1-530	Repealed
3.1-530.1	3.2-5206
3.1-530.2	Deleted
3.1-530.3	3.2-5207
3.1-530.4	3.2-5208
3.1-530.5	3.2-5202
3.1-530.6	3.2-5203
3.1-530.7	Deleted
3.1-530.8	3.2-5205
3.1-530.9	3.2-5209
3.1-530.10	3.2-5210
3.1-530.11	3.2-5211
3.1-531	Repealed
3.1-531.1	3.2-5219
3.1-532	3.2-5220
3.1-533	3.2-5221
3.1-534	3.2-5222
3.1-535	3.2-5223
3.1-535.1	3.2-5224
3.1-536	3.2-5225
3.1-537	3.2-5226
3.1-538	3.2-5227
3.1-539	3.2-5228
3.1-540	3.2-5229
3.1-541	3.2-5230
3.1-542	3.2-5231
3.1-543	Repealed

Former Section	Present Section
3.1-544	3.2-5232
3.1-545	3.2-5218
3.1-545.1	3.2-5233
3.1-546 to 3.1-562	Repealed
3.1-562.1	3.2-5212
3.1-562.2	3.2-5201
3.1-562.3	3.2-5213
3.1-562.4	
3.1-562.5	Deleted
3.1-562.6	3.2-5214
3.1-562.7	Deleted
3.1-562.8	3.2-5215
3.1-562.9	3.2-5216
3.1-562.10	3.2-5217
3.1-563 to 3.1-570	Deleted
3.1-571	Repealed
3.1-572 to 3.1-581	Repealed
3.1-582 to 3.1-587	Repealed
3.1-588 to 3.1-610	Repealed
3.1-610.1	3.2-4400
	3.2-4408
	3.2-4411
3.1-610.2	3.2-4402
3.1-610.3	3.2-4402
3.1-610.4	Deleted
3.1-610.5	3.2-4410
3.1-610.6	3.2-4410 E
3.1-610.7	3.2-4409
3.1-610.8	3.2-4404
3.1-610.9	3.2-4401
3.1-610.10	3.2-4403
3.1-610.11	3.2-4410 D
3.1-610.12	3.2-4408
3.1-610.13	3.2-4408
3.1-610.14	3.2-4406
3.1-610.15	3.2-4405
3.1-610.16	Deleted
3.1-610.17	3.2-4407
3.1-610.18	3.2-4411
3.1-610.19	3.2-4412
3.1-610.20	3.2-4413
3.1-610.21	3.2-4414
3.1-610.22	Deleted
3.1-610.23	3.2-2800
3.1-610.24	3.2-2801
3.1-610.25	3.2-2801
	3.2-2802
	3.2-2803
	3.2-2805
3.1-610.26	3.2-2804
3.1-610.26:1	3.2-2805
3.1-610.27	3.2-2806
3.1-610.28	3.2-2806
	3.2-2807
3.1-611	3.2-4500
3.1-612	3.2-4502
3.1-613	3.2-4503
3.1-614	3.2-4504
3.1-615	3.2-4501
3.1-616	3.2-4505
3.1-617	3.2-4506
3.1-618	3.2-1200
3.1-619, 3.1-620	Repealed
3.1-621 to 3.1-625	Repealed
3.1-626	3.2-1206
3.1-627	3.2-1206
3.1-628	Repealed
3.1-629, 3.1-630	Repealed
3.1-631	Repealed
3.1-632	3.2-1205
3.1-633	Repealed
3.1-634	3.2-1201 A
	3.2-1202
	3.2-1203
3.1-634.1	3.2-1201 B
	3.2-1202
3.1-635	3.2-1204
3.1-636	3.2-1207
3.1-636.1	3.2-1208
3.1-636.2	3.2-112
3.1-636.3	3.2-1209
3.1-636.4	3.2-1210
3.1-636.5	3.2-1211
3.1-636.6	3.2-1212
3.1-636.7	3.2-1213
3.1-636.8	3.2-1214
3.1-636.9	3.2-1215
3.1-636.10	3.2-1102
3.1-636.11	3.2-1216
3.1-636.12	3.2-1217
3.1-637 to 3.1-646	Repealed
3.1-646.01 to 3.1-646.09	Repealed
3.1-646.1 to 3.1-646.3	Deleted
3.1-647	3.2-1900
3.1-648	3.2-1901
3.1-649	3.2-1901
	3.2-1902
3.1-650	3.2-1903
	3.2-1904 F
3.1-651	3.2-1903 B
3.1-652	3.2-1904
3.1-653	3.2-1904 B
3.1-654	3.2-1904 C
3.1-655	3.2-1904 D
3.1-656	3.2-1904 E
3.1-657	3.2-1905
3.1-658	3.2-1907
3.1-659	3.2-1908
3.1-660	3.2-1102
3.1-661	3.2-1102
3.1-662	3.2-1906
3.1-663	3.2-1906
3.1-664	3.2-1909
3.1-665	3.2-1910
3.1-666 to 3.1-684	Repealed
3.1-684.1	Deleted
3.1-684.2	3.2-2300
3.1-684.3	Deleted
3.1-684.4	3.2-2306
3.1-684.5	3.2-2308
3.1-684.6	3.2-112
3.1-684.7	3.2-2306
3.1-684.8	3.2-2306
3.1-684.9	3.2-2309
3.1-684.10	3.2-2309
3.1-684.11	3.2-2305
3.1-684.12	3.2-2307
3.1-684.13	3.2-2300
	3.2-2301
	3.2-2302
	3.2-2303
	3.2-2304
	3.2-2310
3.1-684.14	3.2-2300
	3.2-2312
3.1-684.15	3.2-2313
3.1-684.16	3.2-1102
3.1-684.17	3.2-2311
3.1-684.18	3.2-2311
3.1-684.19	3.2-2314
3.1-684.20	Deleted
3.1-684.21	3.2-1800
3.1-684.22	Deleted
3.1-684.23	3.2-1806
3.1-684.24	3.2-1808
3.1-684.25	3.2-112
3.1-684.26	3.2-112
	3.2-1806 B
3.1-684.27	3.2-1806 C
	3.2-1806 D
3.1-684.28	3.2-1809
3.1-684.29	Deleted
3.1-684.30	3.2-1805
3.1-684.31	3.2-1807
3.1-684.32	3.2-1801
	3.2-1802
	3.2-1803
	3.2-1804
3.1-684.33	3.2-1811
3.1-684.34	3.2-1813
3.1-684.35	3.2-1812
3.1-684.36	3.2-1804 C
	3.2-1810
3.1-684.37	3.2-1810
3.1-684.38	3.2-1814
3.1-684.39	3.2-1800
3.1-684.40	3.2-1815
3.1-684.41	3.2-2200
3.1-684.42	Deleted
3.1-684.43	3.2-2206

Former Section	Present Section
3.1-684.44	3.2-2208
3.1-684.45	3.2-112
3.1-684.46	3.2-2206 B
3.1-684.47	3.2-2206 A
	3.2-2206 C
	3.2-2206 D
3.1-684.48	3.2-2209
3.1-684.49	Deleted
3.1-684.50	3.2-2205
3.1-684.51	3.2-2207
3.1-684.52	3.2-2201
	3.2-2202
	3.2-2203
	3.2-2204
	3.2-2210
3.1-684.53	3.2-2200
	3.2-2212
3.1-684.54	3.2-2213
3.1-684.55	3.2-1102
	3.2-2212
3.1-684.56	3.2-2211
3.1-684.57	3.2-2211
3.1-684.58	3.2-2214
3.1-684.59	3.2-2700
	3.2-2701
	3.2-2702
3.1-684.60	3.2-2703
3.1-684.61	3.2-2704
3.1-684.62	3.2-2704 C
3.1-684.63	3.2-2705
3.1-684.64	3.2-2704 D
3.1-685	3.2-4700
	3.2-4701
3.1-686	3.2-4702
3.1-687	3.2-4705
3.1-688	3.2-4706
	3.2-4707
3.1-689	3.2-4703
3.1-690	3.2-4702
3.1-690.1	3.2-4704
3.1-690.2	3.2-4708
3.1-691	Deleted
3.1-692	3.2-4709
	3.2-4710
3.1-693	3.2-4736
3.1-694	3.2-4711
3.1-695	3.2-4711 C-D
3.1-696	3.2-4712
3.1-697	3.2-4713
3.1-698	3.2-4714
3.1-699	3.2-4716
3.1-699.1	3.2-4717
3.1-700	3.2-4718
3.1-700.1	3.2-4719
3.1-701	3.2-4720
3.1-702	3.2-4721
3.1-703	3.2-4722
3.1-704	3.2-4722 B
3.1-705	3.2-4723
3.1-706	3.2-4723

Former Section	Present Section
3.1-707	3.2-4726
3.1-708	3.2-4727
3.1-709	3.2-4724
3.1-710	3.2-4725
3.1-711	3.2-4715
3.1-712	3.2-4728
3.1-713	3.2-4729
3.1-714	3.2-4730
3.1-715	3.2-4731
3.1-716	3.2-4732
3.1-717	3.2-4733
3.1-718	3.2-4737
3.1-719	3.2-4734
3.1-720	3.2-4735
3.1-721,	
3.1-722	Deleted
3.1-722.1	3.2-4738
3.1-722.1:1	Deleted
3.1-722.2	3.2-4739 E
	3.2-4750
3.1-722.3	3.2-4739
3.1-722.4	3.2-4740
3.1-722.5	3.2-4741
3.1-722.5:1	3.2-4742
3.1-722.6	Repealed
3.1-722.6:1	3.2-4739
3.1-722.7	3.2-4743
3.1-722.8	3.2-4744
3.1-722.9	3.2-4746
3.1-722.10	3.2-4747
3.1-722.11	3.2-4749
	3.2-4751
3.1-722.12	3.2-4748
3.1-722.13	Deleted
3.1-722.14	3.2-4745
3.1-722.15	3.2-4752
3.1-722.16	3.2-4753
3.1-722.17	3.2-4754 A
3.1-722.18	3.2-4754 B
3.1-722.19	3.2-4755 A
3.1-722.20	3.2-4756
3.1-722.20:1	3.2-4757
3.1-722.21	3.2-4755 B
3.1-722.22	3.2-4758
3.1-722.23	3.2-4759
3.1-722.24	3.2-4760
3.1-722.25	3.2-4761
3.1-722.26	3.2-4762
3.1-722.27	Deleted
3.1-722.28	3.2-4763
3.1-722.29	3.2-4764
3.1-722.30	3.2-4765 A
3.1-722.31	3.2-4765
3.1-722.32	3.2-4765 B
3.1-722.33	3.2-4766
3.1-722.34	Deleted
3.1-722.35	3.2-4767
3.1-722.36	3.2-4768
3.1-722.37	3.2-4769
3.1-722.38	3.2-4770

Former Section	Present Section
3.1-722.39	3.2-4771
3.1-722.40	3.2-4772
3.1-722.41	3.2-4773
3.1-722.42	3.2-4774
3.1-722.43	3.2-4775
3.1-723	3.2-5901
3.1-724	3.2-6001
3.1-725	3.2-5903
3.1-726	3.2-6002
3.1-727	3.2-6003
3.1-728	3.2-6007
3.1-729	3.2-6006
3.1-730	3.2-6004
3.1-731	3.2-6000
3.1-732	3.2-6005
3.1-733	3.2-6018
3.1-734	3.2-6008
	3.2-6010
3.1-735	3.2-5902
3.1-736	3.2-6011
3.1-737	3.2-6012
3.1-738	3.2-6013
3.1-738.1	3.2-6014
3.1-739	Repealed
3.1-739.1	3.2-6015
3.1-740	3.2-6019
3.1-741	Deleted
3.1-741.1	3.2-5900
3.1-741.2	3.2-106
3.1-741.3	3.2-5900
3.1-741.4, 3.1-741.5	Deleted
3.1-741.6	3.2-6023
3.1-741.7	3.2-5905
3.1-742	Repealed
3.1-742.1	3.2-6024
3.1-743	3.2-6025
3.1-744	Repealed
3.1-745	3.2-6026
3.1-745.1	3.2-6027
3.1-745.2	Deleted
3.1-746	3.2-6028
3.1-747	3.2-6029
3.1-748	Deleted
3.1-748.1	3.2-6030
3.1-749	3.2-6008
3.1-750	3.2-6020
3.1-751	3.2-6008
	3.2-6009
3.1-752, 3.1-753	Deleted
3.1-754	3.2-6021
3.1-755	3.2-6016
3.1-756	3.2-6017
3.1-757	Deleted
3.1-758	3.2-6031
3.1-759	3.2-6032
3.1-760 to	
3.1-762	Deleted
3.1-762.1	3.2-6033
3.1-763	3.2-6034
3.1-763.1	Deleted

Former Section	Present Section
3.1-763.2	3.2-6008
3.1-763.3	3.2-6022
3.1-763.4	
3.1-763.5	Deleted
3.1-763.5:1	3.2-6035
3.1-763.5:2	3.2-6036
3.1-763.5:3	3.2-6037
3.1-763.5:4	3.2-6038
3.1-763.5:5	3.2-6039
3.1-763.5:6	3.2-6040
3.1-763.5:7	3.2-6041
3.1-763.5:8	3.2-6042
3.1-763.6	3.2-2000
3.1-763.7	3.2-2001
	3.2-2002
	3.2-2003
	3.2-2004
3.1-763.8	3.2-2004
3.1-763.9	3.2-2006
	3.2-2007
	3.2-2008
3.1-763.10	3.2-1102
3.1-763.11	3.2-2005
3.1-763.12	3.2-2009
3.1-763.13	Repealed
3.1-763.14	3.2-5300
3.1-763.15	3.2-5301
3.1-763.16	3.2-5302
3.1-763.17	3.2-5304
3.1-764	3.2-5303
3.1-765	3.2-5305
3.1-766	3.2-5306 B
3.1-767	3.2-5302 C
3.1-768	3.2-5306
3.1-769	3.2-5307
3.1-769.1	3.2-5308
3.1-769.2	3.2-5309
3.1-769.3	3.2-5310
3.1-769.4	3.2-5311
3.1-770	3.2-5312
3.1-770.1	3.2-5313
3.1-770.2	3.2-5314
3.1-770.3	3.2-5315
3.1-771 to	
3.1-775	Deleted
3.1-776	Repealed
3.1-777 to	
3.1-796	Repealed
3.1-796.01	Deleted
3.1-796.02 to	
3.1-796.020	Deleted
3.1-796.1 to	
3.1-796.11	Deleted
3.1-796.11:1	Deleted
3.1-796.11:2	3.2-1601
	3.2-1602
	3.2-1603
	3.2-1604
3.1-796.11:3	3.2-1606
3.1-796.11:4	3.2-1600
	3.2-1607
3.1-796.11 :5	3.2-1608
3.1-796.11:6	3.2-1609
3.1-796.11:7	Deleted
3.1-796.11 :8	3.2-1605
3.1-796.11:9	3.2-1605
3.1-796.11:10	3.2-1610
3.1-796.12	Deleted
3.1-796.13	3.2-1300
3.1-796.14	3.2-1304
	3.2-1304
3.1-796.15	3.2-1301
3.1-796.16	Deleted
3.1-796.17	3.2-112
3.1-796.18 to	
3.1-796.20	Deleted
3.1-796.21	3.2-1301
3.1-796.22	3.2-1302
	3.2-1303
	3.2-1304
	3.2-1304 D
3.1-796.23	3.2-1304
3.1-796.24	3.2-1100 B
	3.2-1304 E
3.1-796.25	3.2-1306 A
3.1-796.26	3.2-1300
	3.2-1305
	3.2-1306
	3.2-1307
3.1-796.27	3.2-1102
	3.2-1308
3.1-796.28	3.2-1103
3.1-796.29	3.2-6100
3.1-796.30	3.2-6102
3.1-796.31	3.2-6107
3.1-796.32	3.2-6103
3.1-796.33	3.2-6104
3.1-796.34	3.2-6105
3.1-796.35	3.2-6106
3.1-796.36	3.2-6101
3.1-796.37	3.2-6108
3.1-796.38	3.2-6109
3.1-796.39 to	
3.1-796.65	Repealed
3.1-796.66	3.2-5900
	3.2-6500
3.1-796.67	3.2-6501
3.1-796.67:1	3.2-5904
3.1-796.67:2	3.2-6502
3.1-796.68	3.2-6503
3.1-796.69	3.2-6508
3.1-796.70	3.2-6510
3.1-796.71	3.2-6511
3.1-796.72	3.2-6509
3.1-796.73	3.2-6504
3.1-796.74	3.2-6506
3.1-796.75	3.2-6520
3.1-796.76	3.2-6507
3.1-796.77	3.2-6505
3.1-796.78	3.2-6512
3.1-796.79	3.2-6513
3.1-796.80	3.2-6514
3.1-796.81	3.2-6515
3.1-796.82	3.2-6516
3.1-796.83	3.2-6517
3.1-796.83:1	3.2-6518
3.1-796.83:2	3.2-6519
3.1-796.84	3.2-6537
3.1-796.85	3.2-6524
3.1-796.86	3.2-6527
3.1-796.87	3.2-6528
3.1-796.87:1	3.2-6529
3.1-796.88	3.2-6530
3.1-796.89	3.2-6533
3.1-796.90	3.2-6526
3.1-796.91	3.2-6532
3.1-796.92	3.2-6531
3.1-796.93	3.2-6538
3.1-796.93:1	3.2-6540
3.1-796.93:2	3.2-6541
3.1-796.93:3	3.2-6542
3.1-796.94	3.2-6543
3.1-796.94:1	3.2-6544
3.1-796.94:2	3.2-6545
3.1-796.95	3.2-6539
3.1-796.96	3.2-6546
3.1-796.96:1	3.2-6547
3.1-796.96:2	3.2-6548
3.1-796.96:3,	
3.1-796.96:4	Repealed
3.1-796.96:5	3.2-6549
3.1-796.96:6	3.2-6550
3.1-796.96:7	3.2-6551
3.1-796.97	3.2-6521 B
	3.2-6526 B
3.1-796.97:1	3.2-6521 A
3.1-796.98	3.2-6522
3.1-796.99	3.2-6523
3.1-796.100	3.2-6525
3.1-796.101	3.2-6434
3.1-796.102	3.2-6435
3.1-796.103	3.2-6436
3.1-796.104	3.2-6555
3.1-796.104:1	3.2-6556
3.1-796.105	3.2-6557
3.1-796.106	3.2-6558
3.1-796.106:1	3.2-6561
3.1-796.106:2	3.2-6559
3.1-796.107	3.2-6564
3.1-796.108	3.2-6565
3.1-796.109	Repealed
3.1-796.110	3.2-6560
3.1-796.111	3.2-6566
3.1-796.112	3.2-6567
3.1-796.113	3.2-6568
3.1-796.114	3.2-6563
3.1-796.115	3.2-6569
3.1-796.116	3.2-6552
3.1-796.117	Repealed
3.1-796.118	3.2-6553

Former Section	Present Section
3.1-796.119	3.2-6562
3.1-796.120	Deleted
3.1-796.121	3.2-6554
3.1-796.122	3.2-6570
3.1-796.123	Repealed
3.1-796.124	3.2-6571
3.1-796.125	3.2-6572
3.1-796.126	3.2-6573
3.1-796.126:1	3.2-6574
3.1-796.126:2	3.2-6575
3.1-796.126:3	3.2-6576
3.1-796.126:4	3.2-6577
3.1-796.126:5	3.2-6578
3.1-796.126:6	3.2-6579
3.1-796.126:7	3.2-6580
3.1-796.126:8	3.2-6581
3.1-796.126:9	3.2-6582
3.1-796.126:10	3.2-6583
3.1-796.126:11	3.2-6584
3.1-796.127	3.2-6585
3.1-796.127:1	3.2-6586
3.1-796.128	3.2-6587
3.1-796.128.1	3.2-6588
3.1-796.128.2	3.2-6589
3.1-796.129	3.2-6590
3.1-796.130	3.2-6200
3.1-796.131	3.2-6201
3.1-796.132	3.2-6202
3.1-796.133	3.2-6203
3.1-796.134	3.2-6300
3.1-796.135	3.2-6301
3.1-796.136	3.2-6302
3.1-796.137	3.2-6400
3.1-796.138	3.2-6401
3.1-796.139	3.2-6402
3.1-797 to 3.1-828	Repealed
3.1-828.1	Deleted
3.1-828.2	3.2-4800
3.1-828.3	Deleted
3.1-828.4	3.2-4801
3.1-828.5	3.2-4806
3.1-828.6	3.2-4803
3.1-828.7	3.2-4804 3.2-4805 3.2-4816
3.1-828.8	3.2-4809
3.1-828.9	3.2-4807
3.1-828.10	3.2-4808
3.1-828.11	3.2-4810
3.1-828.12	3.2-4812
3.1-828.13	3.2-4811 3.2-4815 3.2-4817
3.1-828.14	3.2-4813
3.1-828.15	Deleted
3.1-828.16	3.2-4802
3.1-828.17	3.2.4814
3.1-829	3.2-4900 3.2-4907

Former Section	Present Section
3.1-830	Deleted
3.1-831	3.2-4906
3.1-832	3.2-4907
3.1-833	3.2-4908
3.1-834	3.2-4902
3.1-835	3.2-4909
3.1-836	3.2-4903
3.1-837	3.2-4912
3.1-838	3.2-4910
3.1-839	Deleted
3.1-840	3.2-4911
3.1-841	3.2-4901
3.1-842	3.2-4904
3.1-843	3.2-4905
3.1-844	3.2-4913
3.1-845	3.2-4914
3.1-846 to 3.1-866	Repealed
3.1-867	3.2-5419
3.1-868	3.2-5420
3.1-869	
3.1-870	Repealed
3.1-871	3.2-5421
3.1-872 to 3.1-876	Repealed
3.1-877 to 3.1-884	Repealed
3.1-884.1 to 3.1-884.16	Repealed
3.1-884.17	Deleted
3.1-884.18	3.2-5400 3.2-5401 3.2-5402
3.1-884.19	3.2-5403
3.1-884.20	3.2-5404
3.1-884.21	3.2-5405
3.1-884.21:1	3.2-5406
3.1-884.21:2	Deleted
3.1-884.22	3.2-5407
3.1-884.23	3.2-5408
3.1-884.24	3.2-5409
3.1-884.25	3.2-5410
3.1-884.26	3.2-5411
3.1-884.27	3.2-5412
3.1-884.28	3.2-5413
3.1-884.29	3.2-5414
3.1-884.30	3.2-5405 B
3.1-884.31	3.2-5415
3.1-884.32	3.2-5416
3.1-884.33	3.2-5417
3.1-884.34	3.2-5418
3.1-884.35	Deleted
3.1-884.36	Deleted
3.1-885 to 3.1-898	Repealed
3.1-899	3.2-5501
3.1-900	3.2-5500
3.1-901	3.2-5502
3.1-902	3.2-5503
3.1-903	3.2-5504

Former Section	Present Section
3.1-904	3.2-5505
3.1-905	3.2-5506
3.1-906	3.2-5507
3.1-907 to 3.1-917	Repealed
3.1-918	3.2-5000
3.1-919	3.2-5600
3.1-920	3.2-5603
3.1-921	Repealed
3.1-922	3.2-5604
3.1-923	3.2-5605
3.1-924	3.2-5601
3.1-924.1	3.2-5602
3.1-925	3.2-5606
3.1-926	3.2-5607
3.1-927	3.2-5608
3.1-928	3.2-5609
3.1-929	3.2-5610
3.1-930	Deleted
3.1-931	3.2-5629
3.1-932	3.2-5611
3.1-933	3.2-5612
3.1-934	3.2-5613
3.1-935	3.2-5614
3.1-936	Deleted
3.1-937	3.2-5615
3.1-938	3.2-5616
3.1-939	3.2-5617
3.1-940	3.2-5618
3.1-941	3.2-5619
3.1-941.1	3.2-5620
3.1-942	3.2-5621
3.1-943	3.2-5622
3.1-944	3.2-5623
3.1-945	3.2-5624
3.1-946	3.2-5625
3.1-947	3.2-5626
3.1-948	Repealed
3.1-949	3.2-5631
3.1-949.01	3.2-5632
3.1-949.1	3.2-5627
3.1-949.2	3.2-5628
3.1-949.3	3.2-5630
3.1-949.4	3.2-5633
3.1-950	3.2-5634
3.1-951 to 3.1-954	Repealed
3.1-954.1	3.2-5635
3.1-955	Repealed
3.1-956	3.2-5641
3.1-957	3.2-5642
3.1-958	3.2-5636
3.1-959	3.2-5637
3.1-960	3.2-5638
3.1-961	3.2-5639
3.1-962	Repealed
3.1-962.1	3.2-5640
3.1-963	3.2-5643
3.1-964	3.2-5644
3.1-965	3.2-5645
3.1-966	Repealed

Former Section	Present Section
3.1-966.1	3.2-5646
3.1-966.2	3.2-5647
3.1-967	3.2-5648
3.1-968	
3.1-969	Deleted
3.1-969.1	3.2-5700
3.1-969.2	3.2-5701
3.1-969.3	3.2-5702
3.1-969.4	3.2-5703
3.1-969.5	3.2-5704
3.1-969.6	3.2-5705
3.1-969.7	3.2-5706
3.1-969.8	3.2-5707
3.1-969.9	3.2-5708
3.1-969.10	3.2-5709
3.1-969.11	3.2-5710
3.1-969.12	3.2-5711
3.1-969.13	3.2-5712
3.1-969.14	3.2-5713
3.1-969.15	3.2-5714
3.1-970	3.2-5800
3.1-971	3.2-5801
3.1-972	3.2-5802
3.1-973	3.2-5803
3.1-974	3.2-5804
3.1-975	3.2-5805
3.1-976	3.2-5806
3.1-977	3.2-5807
3.1-978	3.2-5808
3.1-979	3.2-5809
3.1-980	3.2-5810
3.1-981	3.2-5811
3.1-982	3.2-5812
3.1-983	3.2-5813
3.1-984	3.2-5814
3.1-985	3.2-5815
3.1-986	3.2-5800
	3.2-5816
3.1-987	3.2-5817
3.1-988	3.2-5818
3.1-989	3.2-5819
3.1-990	3.2-5820
3.1-991	3.2-4600
3.1-992	3.2-4607
3.1-993	3.2-4608
3.1-994	3.2-4602
3.1-995	3.2-4603
3.1-996	Deleted
3.1-997	3.2-4601
3.1-998	3.2-4609
3.1-999	3.2-4603C
3.1-1000	3.2-4604
3.1-1001	3.2-4605
3.1-1002	3.2-4610
3.1-1003	3.2-4606
3.1-1004	3.2-4611
3.1-1005	3.2-4612
3.1-1006	Deleted
3.1-1007	3.2-4613
3.1-1008	Deleted

Former Section	Present Section
3.1-1009	Repealed
3.1-1010	
3.1-1011	Deleted
3.1-1012	3.2-900
3.1-1013	3.2-901
3.1-1014	3.2-901 C
3.1-1015	3.2-901 D
3.1-1016 to	
3.1-1018	Deleted
3.1-1019	3.2-901 E
3.1-1020	Deleted
3.1-1021	3.2-1000
3.1-1022	3.2-1001
	3.2-1004
3.1-1023	3.2-1003
3.1-1024	3.2-1001
	3.2-1003
3.1-1025	3.2-1002
	3.2-1005
3.1-1026	3.2-1006
3.1-1027	3.2-1007
3.1-1027.1	3.2-1008
3.1-1028	3.2-1009
3.1-1029	3.2-1010
3.1-1030	3.2-1011
3.1-1031	Deleted
3.1-1032	3.2-1400
3.1-1033	Deleted
3.1-1034	3.2-1406
3.1-1035	3.2-1408
3.1-1036	3.2-112
3.1-1037	3.2-1406 B
3.1-1038	3.2-1406 C
	3.2-1406 D
3.1-1039	3.2-1406
	3.2-1409
3.1-1040	Deleted
3.1-1041	3.2-1405
3.1-1042	3.2-1407
3.1-1043	3.2-1400
	3.2-1401
	3.2-1402
	3.2-1403
	3.2-1404
	3.2-1410
3.1-1044	3.2-1400
	3.2-1412
3.1-1045	3.2-1413
3.1-1046	3.2-1102
	3.2-1412
3.1-1047	3.2-1411
3.1-1048	3.2-1411
3.1-1049	3.2-1414
3.1-1050 to	
3.1-1056	Repealed
3.1-1057 to	
3.1-1064	Repealed
3.1-1064.1	3.2-3000
3.1-1064.2	3.2-3001
3.1-1064.3	3.2-3001 B

Former Section	Present Section
	3.2-3001 C
	3.2-3002
	3.2-3003 A
3.1-1064.4	3.2-3003
3.1-1064.5	3.2-3004
3.1-1064.6	3.2-3005
3.1-1064.7	3.2-3006
3.1-1065	3.2-2100
3.1-1066	3.2-2104 B
3.1-1067	3.2-2108
3.1-1068	3.2-112
3.1-1069	3.2-2106
3.1-1070	3.2-2106
3.1-1071	3.2-2109
3.1-1072	3.2-2105
3.1-1073	3.2-2107
3.1-1074	3.2-2101
	3.2-2104 A
3.1-1075	3.2-2101
	3.2-2102
	3.2-2103
	3.2-2110
3.1-1076	3.2-2111
3.1-1077	3.2-2112 A
3.1-1078	3.2-2112
	3.2-2113
3.1-1079	3.2-2114
3.1-1080	Expired
3.1-1081	3.2-1500
3.1-1082,	
3.1-1083	Deleted
3.1-1084	3.2-112
3.1-1085	3.2-1506
3.1-1086	3.2-1508
3.1-1087	3.2-1506 C
	3.2-1506 D
3.1-1088	Deleted
3.1-1089	3.2-1505
3.1-1090	3.2-1509
3.1-1091	3.2-1507
3.1-1092	3.2-1510
3.1-1093	3.2-1501
3.1-1094	3.2-1502
3.1-1095	3.2-1503
	3.2-1504 A
3.1-1096	3.2-1504 B
3.1-1097	3.2-1504 C
3.1-1098	3.2-1512
3.1-1099	3.2-1513
3.1-1100	Deleted
3.1-1101	3.2-1511
3.1-1102	3.2-1102
3.1-1103	3.2-1514
3.1-1104,	
3.1-1105	Repealed
3.1-1106	3.2-3100
3.1-1107	3.2-3101
3.1-1108	3.2-3102
3.1-1109	3.2-3103
3.1-1109.1	3.2-3104

Former Section	Present Section
3.1-1110	3.2-3105
3.1-1111	3.2-3106
3.1-1111.1	3.2-3107
3.1-1112	3.2-3108
3.1-1113	3.2-3109
3.1-1114	3.2-3110
3.1-1114.1	3.2-3111

COMPARABLE SECTIONS OF TITLE 6.1 AND TITLE 6.2

Former Section	Present Section
6.1-1	6.2-100
6.1-1.1	6.2-101
6.1-2	6.2-102
6.1-2.1	6.2-100
	6.2-103
6.1-2.2 to 6.1-2.4	6.2-416
6.1-2.6.	Repealed
6.1-2.6:1	6.2-412
6.1-2.7	6.2-104
6.1-2.7:1	6.2-105
6.1-2.8	6.2-414
6.1-2.9	6.2-407
6.1-2.9:1	6.2-413
6.1-2.9:2	6.2-600
6.1-2.9:3, 6.1-2.9:4	6.2-601
6.1-2.9:5	6.2-406
6.1-2.9:6	6.2-415
6.1-2.9:7	6.2-602
6.1-2.9:8	6.2-603
6.1-2.10	55-525.8
6.1-2.11	55-525.9
6.1-2.12	55-525.10
6.1-2.13	55-525.11
6.1-2.13:1	55-525.12
6.1-2.13:2	55-525.13
6.1-2.13:3	55-525.14
6.1-2.14	55-525.9
6.1-2.15	55-525.15
6.1-2.16 to 6.1-2.18	6.2-807
	6.2-1113
6.1-2.19	55-525.17
	55-525.18
6.1-2.20	55-525.16
6.1-2.21	55-525.19
	55-525.20
	55-525.21
6.1-2.21:1	55-525.22
6.1-2.22	55-525.23
6.1-2.23	55-525.24
6.1-2.23:1	55-525.25
6.1-2.23:2	55-525.26
6.1-2.24	55-525.27
6.1-2.25	55-525.28
	55-525.29
	55-525.30
6.1-2.26	55-525.30
6.1-2.27	55-525.31
6.1-2.27:1	55-525.32
6.1-2.28	Deleted
6.1-2.29	Deleted
6.1-2.30	55-525.17
6.1-2.31	Deleted
6.1-2.32	55-525.16
	55-525.18
6.1-3	Deleted
6.1-4	6.2-800
	6.2-801
6.1-5	6.2-803
	6.2-1001
6.1-5.1	6.2-804
6.1-5.2	6.2-805
6.1-5.3	6.2-310
6.1-5.4	6.2-806
6.1-6	6.2-808
6.1-6.1	6.2-809
	6.2-800
6.1-7	6.2-810
	6.2-802
6.1-8	6.2-811
6.1-9	6.2-812
6.1-10	6.2-813
6.1-11	6.2-814 A
6.1-11.1	6.2-814 B
6.1-11.2	6.2-800
	6.2-814 A 13
6.1-12	6.2-815
	6.2-1002
6.1-13	6.2-816
6.1-14	6.2-817
6.1-15	6.2-818
6.1-16	6.2-819
6.1-17	6.2-820
	6.2-1002
	26-7.5
6.1-18	6.2-1003
6.1-19	6.2-1004
6.1-20	6.2-821
	6.2-1024
6.1-21	6.2-1005
6.1-22	6.2-1006
6.1-23	6.2-1007
6.1-24	6.2-1008
6.1-25 to 6.1-30	Repealed
6.1-30.1 to 6.1-30.3	6.2-1009
6.1-31	6.2-1010
6.1-31.1, 6.1-31.2	6.2-1011
6.1-32	6.2-1012
6.1-32.1	Deleted
6.1-32.2	6.2-1000
	6.2-1047
6.1-32.3	6.2-1048
6.1-32.4	6.2-1050
6.1-32.5	6.2-1001
	6.2-1049
	6.2-1054
6.1-32.6	6.2-1055
6.1-32.7	6.2-1056
6.1-32.8	6.2-1057
6.1-32.9	6.2-1058
	6.2-1059
6.1-32.10	6.2-1060
6.1-32.11	6.2-1000
	6.2-1013
6.1-32.12	6.2-1000
6.1-32.13	6.2-1014
6.1-32.14	6.2-1015
6.1-32.14:1	Repealed
6.1-32.14:2	6.2-1020
6.1-32.15, 6.1-32.16	6.2-1018
6.1-32.17	6.2-1016
6.1-32.18	6.2-1017
6.1-32.18:1	6.2-1019
6.1-32.18:2	6.2-1021
6.1-32.18:3	6.2-1022
6.1-32.19	6.2-1023
6.1-32.20	6.2-1024
6.1-32.21	6.2-1028
6.1-32.22	6.2-1029
6.1-32.23	6.2-1031
6.1-32.24	6.2-1032
6.1-32.25	6.2-1033
6.1-32.26	6.2-1034
6.1-32.27	6.2-1035
6.1-32.28	6.2-1036
6.1-32.29	6.2-1037
6.1-32.30	Repealed
6.1-32.30:1	6.2-1074
6.1-32.30:2	6.2-1075
6.1-32.30:3	6.2-1076
6.1-32.30:4	6.2-1077
6.1-32.30:5	6.2-1078
6.1-32.30:6	6.2-1079
6.1-32.30:7	6.2-1074
	6.2-1080
6.1-32.31	Deleted
6.1-32.32	6.2-1065
6.1-32.33	6.2-1066

Former Section	Present Section
6.1-32.34	6.2-1067
6.1-32.35	6.2-1067
6.1-32.36, 6.1-32.37	6.2-1068
6.1-32.38	6.2-1069
6.1-32.39	6.2-1070
6.1-32.40	6.2-1071
6.1-32.41	6.2-1072
6.1-32.42	6.2-1068
6.1-32.43	6.2-1073
6.1-32.44	6.2-1068
6.1-32.45	Deleted
6.1-33	6.2-823 A
6.1-34	6.2-824
6.1-35	6.2-825
6.1-36	6.2-826
6.1-37	6.2-827
6.1-38	6.2-823 B
6.1-39 to 6.1-39.2	Repealed
6.1-39.3	6.2-831
6.1-39.4.	Repealed
6.1-39.4:1	6.2-832
6.1-39.5	6.2-833
6.1-40	Repealed
6.1-41	6.2-834
6.1-41.1	6.2-814 A 14
6.1-42	6.2-835
6.1-43, 6.1-44	6.2-822
6.1-44.1	Deleted
6.1-44.2	6.2-836
6.1-44.3	6.2-837
6.1-44.4	6.2-838
6.1-44.5	6.2-839
6.1-44.6	6.2-840
6.1-44.7	6.2-841
6.1-44.8	6.2-842
6.1-44.9	6.2-843
6.1-44.10	6.2-844
6.1-44.11	6.2-845
6.1-44.12	6.2-846
6.1-44.13	6.2-847
6.1-44.14	6.2-848
6.1-44.15	Deleted
6.1-44.16	6.2-849
6.1-44.17	6.2-850
6.1-44.18	6.2-851
6.1-44.19	6.2-852
6.1-44.20	6.2-853
6.1-44.21	6.2-854
6.1-44.22	6.2-855
	6.2-856
6.1-44.23	6.2-857
6.1-44.24	6.2-858
6.1-44.25	6.2-859
6.1-45	6.2-860
6.1-46	6.2-861
6.1-47	6.2-862
6.1-48	6.2-863
6.1-48.1	6.2-864
6.1-49, 6.1-50	6.2-865
6.1-51	6.2-865
6.1-51.1	6.2-1025
	6.2-1026
	6.2-1043
	6.2-1044
6.1-52	6.2-866
6.1-53	6.2-867
	6.2-1030
6.1-54	6.2-868
	6.2-1027
	6.2-1053
6.1-55, 6.1-55.1	Repealed
6.1-56	6.2-869
6.1-57	6.2-870
6.1-58	6.2-871
6.1-58.1	6.2-885
	6.2-886
6.1-58.2	6.2-887
6.1-58.3	6.2-888
6.1-59	6.2-872
6.1-59.1	6.2-873
6.1-60.	Repealed
6.1-60.1	6.2-874
6.1-61	6.2-875
6.1-62	6.2-876
6.1-62.1	6.2-877
6.1-63	6.2-878
6.1-64	6.2-880
6.1-65	6.2-878
	6.2-879
6.1-65.1	6.2-881
6.1-66	6.2-879
6.1-67	6.2-882
6.1-68	6.2-883
6.1-68.1	6.2-884
6.1-69	6.2-889
6.1-70	6.2-893
6.1-70.1	6.2-894
6.1-71	6.2-895
6.1-72 to 6.1-73.1.	Repealed
6.1-74	6.2-896
6.1-75	6.2-897
6.1-76, 6.1-77	Repealed
6.1-78	6.2-890
6.1-79	6.2-890
6.1-80	6.2-890
6.1-81	6.2-891
6.1-82	Deleted
6.1-83	6.2-892
6.1-84	6.2-898
6.1-85	6.2-899
6.1-86	6.2-900
6.1-87	6.2-901
6.1-88	6.2-902
6.1-89	6.2-903
6.1-90	6.2-904
6.1-91	6.2-905
6.1-92	6.2-906
6.1-93	6.2-907
6.1-94	6.2-908
6.1-95	6.2-909
6.1-96	6.2-910
6.1-97, 6.1-98	Repealed
6.1-99	6.2-911
6.1-100	6.2-912
	6.2-913
6.1-100.1	6.2-914
6.1-101	6.2-915
6.1-102	6.2-916
	6.2-1038
6.1-103	6.2-917
6.1-104	6.2-918
6.1-105	6.2-919
6.1-106	6.2-920
6.1-107	6.2-921
6.1-108	6.2-922
6.1-109	6.2-923
6.1-110	6.2-924
6.1-110.1	6.2-925
6.1-110.2	6.2-926
6.1-110.3	6.2-927
6.1-110.4	6.2-928
6.1-110.5	6.2-929
6.1-110.6	6.2-930
6.1-110.7	6.2-931
6.1-110.8	6.2-932
6.1-110.9	6.2-933
6.1-110.10	6.2-934
6.1-110.11	6.2-935
6.1-110.12	6.2-936
6.1-110.13	6.2-937
6.1-111	6.2-938
	6.2-1039
6.1-112	6.2-939
	6.2-1040
6.1-113	6.2-831
	6.2-834
6.1-114	6.2-907
	6.2-901
	6.2-1041
	6.2- 1061
6.1-115 to 6.1-118	Repealed
6.1-118.1	17.1-626.1
6.1-119	6.2-940
	6.2-1042
6.1-119.1	6.2-941
	6.2-1043
6.1-120	6.2-942
6.1-121	Repealed
6.1-122	6.2-943
	6.2-1044
	6.2-1062
6.1-123	6.2-944
	6.2-1045
	6.2-1063
6.1-124	6.2-945

Former Section	Present Section
6.1-125	6.2-946
	6.2-1046
	6.2-1064
6.1-125.1	6.2-604
6.1-125.2	6.2-605
6.1-125.3	6.2-606
6.1-125.4	6.2-607
6.1-125.5	6.2-608
6.1-125.6	6.2-609
6.1-125.7	6.2-610
6.1-125.8	6.2-611
6.1-125.9	6.2-612
6.1-125.10	6.2-613
6.1-125.11	6.2-614
6.1-125.12	6.2-615
6.1-125.13	6.2-616
6.1-125.14	6.2-617
6.1-125.15	6.2-618
6.1-125.15:1	6.2-619
6.1-125.16	6.2-620
6.1-126 to	
6.1-193.	Repealed
6.1-194, 6.1-194.1	Deleted
6.1-194.2	6.2-1100
6.1-194.3	6.2-1108
6.1-194.4	6.2-1110
6.1-194.5	6.2-1111
6.1-194.6	6.2-310
6.1-194.7	6.2-1112
	8.4-105
6.1-194.8	6.2-1114
6.1-194.9	6.2-1115
6.1-194.10	6.2-1116
6.1-194.11	6.2-1117
6.1-194.12	6.2-1118
6.1-194.13	6.2-1119
6.1-194.14	6.2-1121
6.1-194.15	6.2-1122
6.1-194.16	6.2-1123
6.1-194.17	6.2-1124
6.1-194.18	6.2-1125
6.1-194.19	6.2-1126
6.1-194.20	6.2-1127
6.1-194.21	6.2-1128
6.1-194.22	6.2-1129
6.1-194.23	6.2-1130
6.1-194.24	6.2-1131
6.1-194.25	6.2-1132
6.1-194.26	6.2-1133
6.1-194.27	6.2-1134
6.1-194.28	6.2-1135
6.1-194.29	6.2-1136
6.1-194.30	6.2-1137
6.1-194.31	6.2-1138
6.1-194.32	6.2-1139
6.1-194.32:1	6.2-1140
6.1-194.33,	
6.1-194.34	6.2-828
	6.2-1141
6.1-194.35 to	
6.1-194.37	6.2-1142
6.1-194.38	6.2-830
	6.2-1144
6.1-194.39	6.2-1145
6.1-194.40	6.2-1100
	6.2-1146
6.1-194.41	6.2-1149
6.1-194.42	6.2-1150
6.1-194.43	6.2-1151
6.1-194.44	6.2-1152
6.1-194.45	6.2-1153
6.1-194.46	6.2-1154
6.1-194.47	6.2-1155
6.1-194.48	6.2-1156
6.1-194.49	6.2-1166
6.1-194.50	6.2-1167
6.1-194.51	6.2-1168
6.1-194.52	6.2-1169
6.1-194.53	6.2-1170
6.1-194.54	6.2-1171
6.1-194.55	6.2-1172
6.1-194.56	6.2-1173
6.1-194.57	6.2-1174
6.1-194.58	6.2-1175
6.1-194.59	6.2-1176
6.1-194.60	6.2-1177
6.1-194.61	6.2-1178
6.1-194.62	6.2-1179
6.1-194.63	6.2-1180
6.1-194.64	6.2-1181
6.1-194.65	6.2-1182
6.1-194.66	6.2-1183
6.1-194.67	6.2-1184
6.1-194.68	6.2-1185
6.1-194.69	6.2-1186
6.1-194.70	6.2-1188
6.1-194.71	6.2-1189
6.1-194.72	6.2-1190
6.1-194.73	6.2-1191
6.1-194.74 to	
6.1-194.76	6.2-1192
6.1-194.77	6.2-1193
6.1-194.78	6.2-1194
6.1-194.79	6.2-1195
6.1-194.80	6.2-1196
6.1-194.81	6.2-1197
6.1-194.82	6.2-1198
6.1-194.83	6.2-1199
6.1-194.84	6.2-1200
6.1-194.84:1	6.2-1201
6.1-194.85	6.2-1202
6.1-194.86	6.2-1203
6.1-194.87	6.2-1100
	6.2-1147
	6.2-1192
	6.2-1204
6.1-194.88	6.2-1205
6.1-194.89,	
6.1-194.90	6.2-1101
6.1-194.91	6.2-1102
	6.2-1108
6.1-194.92	6.2-1109
6.1-194.93	6.2-1104
6.1-194.93:1	6.2-1105
6.1-194.94	6.2-1107
6.1-194.95	6.2-1103
	6.2-1106
6.1-194.96	6.2-1148
6.1-194.97	6.2-1157
6.1-194.98	6.2-1158
6.1-194.99	6.2-1159
6.1-194.100,	
6.1-194.101	Repealed
6.1-194.102	6.2-1161
6.1-194.103	6.2-1162
6.1-194.104	6.2-1161
6.1-194.105	6.2-1160
6.1-194.106	6.2-1165
6.1-194.107	6.2-1163
6.1-194.108	Repealed
6.1-194.109	Deleted
6.1-194.110	6.2-1100
6.1-194.111	6.2-1115
6.1-194.112	6.2-1116
6.1-194.113	6.2-1117
6.1-194.114	6.2-1118
6.1-194.115	6.2-1119
6.1-194.116	6.2-1120
6.1-194.117	6.2-1121
6.1-194.118	6.2-1122
6.1-194.119	6.2-1133
6.1-194.120	6.2-1134
6.1-194.121	6.2-1135
6.1-194.122	6.2-1136
6.1-194.123	6.2-1137
6.1-194.123:1	6.2-1139
6.1-194.124,	
6.1-194.125	6.2-1141
6.1-194.126 to	
6.1-194.128	6.2-1142
6.1-194.129	6.2-829
	6.2-1143
	6.2-1144
6.1-194.130	6.2-1145
6.1-194.131	6.2-1100
	6.2-1146
6.1-194.132	6.2-1164
6.1-194.133	6.2-1166
6.1-194.134	6.2-1167
6.1-194.135	6.2-1170
6.1-194.136	6.2-1186
	6.2-1187
6.1-194.137	6.2-1188
6.1-194.138	6.2-1099
6.1-194.139	6.2-1191
6.1-194.140 to	
6.1-194.142	6.2-1192
6.1-194.143	6.2-1193
6.1-194.144	6.2-1194
6.1-194.145	6.2-1195

Former Section	Present Section
6.1-194.146	6.2-1196
6.1-194.147	6.2-1197
6.1-194.148	6.2-1198
6.1-194.149	6.2-1202
6.1-194.150	6.2-1205
6.1-194.151	6.2-1180
	6.2-1181
	6.2-1182
	6.2-1183
6.1-194.152	6.2-1147
6.1-194.153, 6.1-194.154	6.2-1101
6.1-195	Deleted
6.1-195.1 to 6.1-195.76	Repealed
6.1-195.77	Deleted
6.1-195.78	6.2-1081
6.1-195.79	6.2-1082
6.1-195.80	6.2-1083
6.1-195.81	6.2-1084
6.1-195.82	6.2-1085
6.1-195.83	6.2-1086
6.1-195.84	6.2-1087
6.1-195.85	6.2-1088
6.1-195.86	6.2-1089
6.1-195.87	6.2-1090
6.1-195.88	6.2-1091
6.1-195.89	6.2-1092
6.1-195.90	6.2-1093
6.1-195.91	6.2-1094
6.1-195.92	6.2-1095
6.1-195.93	6.2-1096
6.1-195.94	6.2-1097
6.1-195.95	6.2-1098
6.1-196 to 6.1-225.1	Repealed
6.1-225.2	6.2-1300
	6.2-1301
6.1-225.3	6.2-1303
	6.2-1308
6.1-225.3:1	6.2-1303
6.1-225.4	6.2-1309
6.1-225.5	6.2-1310
6.1-225.6	6.2-1311
6.1-225.7	6.2-1312
6.1-225.8	6.2-1313
6.1-225.9	6.2-1314
	6.2-1315
6.1-225.10	6.2-1317
6.1-225.11	6.2-1318
6.1-225.12	6.2-1319
6.1-225.13	6.2-1320
6.1-225.14	6.2-1321
6.1-225.15	6.2-1322
6.1-225.16	6.2-1323
6.1-225.17	6.2-1324
6.1-225.18	6.2-1325
6.1-225.19	6.2-1306
6.1-225.20	6.2-1326
6.1-225.21	6.2-1302

Former Section	Present Section
6.1-225.22	6.2-1303
6.1-225.23	6.2-1327
6.1-225.23:1	6.2-1328
6.1-225.24	6.2-1329
6.1-225.25	6.2-1330
6.1-225.26	6.2-1332
6.1-225.27	6.2-1344
6.1-225.28	6.2-1345
6.1-225.29	6.2-1346
6.1-225.30	6.2-1347
6.1-225.30:1	6.2-1347.1
6.1-225.31	6.2-1348
6.1-225.32	6.2-1349
6.1-225.33	6.2-1350
6.1-225.34	6.2-1351
6.1-225.35	6.2-1352
6.1-225.36	6.2-1353
6.1-225.37	6.2-1354
6.1-225.38	6.2-1355
6.1-225.39	6.2-1356
6.1-225.40	6.2-1357
6.1-225.41	6.2-1358
6.1-225.42	6.2-1359
6.1-225.43	6.2-1360
6.1-225.44	6.2-1361
6.1-225.45	6.2-1362
6.1-225.46	6.2-1363
6.1-225.47	6.2-1364
6.1-225.48	6.2-1365
6.1-225.49	6.2-1366
6.1-225.50	6.2-1367
6.1-225.50:1	6.2-1368
6.1-225.50:2	6.2-1369
6.1-225.51	6.2-1370
6.1-225.52	6.2-1371
6.1-225.53	6.2-1372
6.1-225.54	6.2-1373
6.1-225.55	6.2-1374
6.1-225.56	6.2-1375
6.1-225.57	6.2-1376
6.1-225.58	6.2-1377
6.1-225.59	6.2-1378
6.1-225.60	Repealed
6.1-225.61	6.2-1379
6.1-225.61:1	6.2-1380
6.1-225.62	6.2-1316
6.1-225.63	6.2-1304
6.1-225.64	6.2-1305
6.1-225.65	6.2-1307
6.1-226, 6.1-226.1	Repealed
6.1-226.2	6.2-1331
6.1-226.3	6.2-1333
6.1-226.4	6.2-1334
6.1-226.5	6.2-1335
6.1-226.6	6.2-1336
6.1-226.7	6.2-1337
6.1-226.8	6.2-1338
6.1-226.9	6.2-1339
6.1-226.10	6.2-1340

Former Section	Present Section
6.1-226.11	6.2-1341
6.1-226.12	6.2-1342
6.1-226.13	6.2-1343
6.1-226.14	Deleted
6.1-227	6.2-1401
	6.2-1402
6.1-227.1	6.2-1404
6.1-228	6.2-1405
6.1-229	6.2-1406
6.1-230	6.2-1405
6.1-231	6.2-1406
6.1-232	6.2-1407
6.1-232	6.2-1407
6.1-232.2, 6.1-232.3	Repealed
6.1-233	6.2-1408
6.1-234	6.2-1410
6.1-234.1	Repealed
6.1-235	6.2-1403
6.1-236, 6.1-237	Repealed
6.1-237.1	6.2-1411
6.1-237.2	6.2-1412
6.1-237.3	6.2-1413
6.1-237.4	6.2-1414
6.1-237.5	6.2-1415
6.1-237.6	6.2-1416
6.1-237.7	6.2-1417
6.1-237.8	6.2-1418
6.1-237.9	6.2-1419
6.1-237.10	6.2-1420
6.1-237.11	6.2-1421
6.1-238 to 6.1-242	Repealed
6.1-243	Omitted
6.1-244	Deleted
6.1-245	6.2-1500
6.1-246 to 6.1-248	Deleted
6.1-249	6.2-1501 A and B
6.1-250	6.2-1502
	6.2-1503
6.1-251	6.2-1501 C
6.1-252	Repealed
6.1-253	6.2-1504
6.1-254	6.2-1505
6.1-255	6.2-1506
6.1-256	Repealed
6.1-256.1	6.2-1507
	6.2-1508
6.1-257	6.2-1507
6.1-258	6.2-1509
6.1-258.1	6.2-1510
6.1-259	6.2-1509
6.1-260	6.2-1511
6.1-261	6.2-1512
6.1-262	6.2-1513
6.1-263	6.2-1514
6.1-264	6.2-1515
6.1-265	6.2-1516
6.1-266	6.2-1517

Former Section	Present Section
6.1-267,	
6.1-267.1	6.2-1518
6.1-268	6.2-1517
6.1-269	Repealed
6.1-269.1	6.2-1519
6.1-270	Deleted
6.1-271 to	
6.1-272	Repealed
6.1-272.1	6.2-1520
6.1-273	6.2-1521
6.1-274 to	
6.1-276	6.2-1522
6.1-277	Repealed
6.1-278	6.2-1523
6.1-279 to	
6.1-283	6.2-1524
6.1-284	Repealed
6.1-284.1,	
6.1-285	6.2-1524
6.1-286,	
6.1-287	Repealed
6.1-288	6.2-1525
6.1-289	6.2-1526
	6.2-1527
	6.2-1528
6.1-290	6.2-1526
6.1-291	6.2-1529
6.1-292,	
6.1-293	Deleted
6.1-294 to	
6.1-297	6.2-1530
6.1-298	6.2-1531
6.1-299	Repealed
6.1-299.1	6.2-1532
6.1-300	6.2-1533
6.1-301	6.2-1534
6.1-302	6.2-1535
	6.2-1536
6.1-303	6.2-1537
6.1-304	6.2-1537 F
6.1-305	6.2-1538
6.1-306	6.2-1539
6.1-307	Deleted
6.1-308	6.2-1540
	6.2-1541
6.1-309	6.2-1542
	6.2-1543
6.1-310	Deleted
6.1-311 to	
6.1-330.46	Repealed
6.1-330.47	Deleted
6.1-330.47:1	Repealed
6.1-330.48	Deleted
6.1-330.49	6.2-300
6.1-330.50	6.2-200
6.1-330.51	6.2-201
6.1-330.52	6.2-202
	6.2-203
	6.2-204
6.1-330.53	6.2-301

Former Section	Present Section
6.1-330.54	6.2-302
6.1-330.55	6.2-303
6.1-330.56	6.2-304
6.1-330.57	6.2-305
6.1-330.58	6.2-306
6.1-330.59	6.2-307
	6.2-327 I
	6.2-328 G
6.1-330.60	6.2-309
	6.2-314
	6.2-323
6.1-330.61	6.2-316
6.1-330.62	6.2-315
6.1-330.63	6.2-313
	6.2-432
	6.2-433
	6.2- 434
6.1-330.64	6.2-318
	6.2-1302
6.1-330.65	6.2-322
6.1-330.66	6.2-324
6.1-330.66:1	Deleted
6.1-330.67	6.2-319
6.1-330.68	6.2-320
6.1-330.69	6.2-325
	6.2-300
	6.2-408
	6.2-409
	6.2-421
6.1-330.70	6.2-326
	6.2-410
6.1-330.71	6.2-327
	6.2-300
6.1-330.72	6.2-328
	6.2-411
6.1-330.73	Deleted; see
	6.2-327
	6.2-328
	6.2-423
6.1-330.74	6.2-329
6.1-330.75	6.2-317
6.1-330.76	6.2-308
6.1-330.77	6.2-311
6.1-330.77:1	6.2-301 C
6.1-330.78	6.2-312
	6.2-432
	6.2-435
6.1-330.78:1	6.2-321
6.1-330.79	6.2-436
6.1-330.80	6.2-400
6.1-330.81	6.2-421
6.1-330.82	6.2-418
6.1-330.83	6.2-422
6.1-330.84	6.2-1409
6.1-330.85	6.2-423
6.1-330.85:1	6.2-402
6.1-330.86	6.2-403
6.1-330.86:1	6.2-404
6.1-330.87	6.2-420
6.1-330.88	6.2-417

Former Section	Present Section
6.1-330.89	6.2-401
6.1-330.90	6.2-437
6.1-331	6.2-2305
6.1-332	6.2-2301
6.1-332.1	6.2-2302
	6.2-2303
	6.2-2304
6.1-333	6.2-2204
6.1-334	6.2-2306
6.1-335	6.2-2307
6.1-336	6.2-2308
6.1-337	6.2-2309
6.1-338	6.2-2310
6.1-339	6.2-2311
6.1-340	6.2-2313
6.1-341	6.2-2314
6.1-342	6.2-2312
6.1-343 to	
6.1-363	Repealed
6.1-363.2	6.2-2000
6.1-363.3	6.2-2001
	6.2-2022
6.1-363.4	6.2-2002
6.1-363.5	6.2-2003
6.1-363.6	6.2-2004
6.1-363.7	6.2-2005
	6.2-2000
6.1-363.8	6.2-2006
6.1-363.9	6.2-2007
6.1-363.10	6.2-2008
6.1-363.11	6.2-2009
6.1-363.12	6.2-2010
6.1-363.13	6.2-2011
6.1-363.14	6.2-2012
6.1-363.15	6.2-2013
6.1-363.16	6.2-2014
6.1-363.17	6.2-2015
6.1-363.18	6.2-2016
6.1-363.19	6.2-2017
6.1-363.20	6.2-2018
6.1-363.21	6.2-2019
6.1-363.22	6.2-2020
6.1-363.23	6.2-2021
6.1-363.24	6.2-2023
6.1-363.25	6.2-2024
6.1-363.26	6.2-2025
6.1-364 to	
6.1-369.10	Repealed
6.1-370	6.2-1900
6.1-371	6.2-1901
	6.2-1902
6.1-372	6.2-1903
	6.2-1904
6.1-373	6.2-1903
	6.2-1905
6.1-374	6.2-1906
	6.2-1907
6.1-374.1	6.2-1908
6.1-374.2	6.2-1909
6.1-375	6.2-1910

COMPARABLE SECTIONS FOR CERTAIN REPEALED AND REVISED TITLES

Former Section	Present Section
	6.2-1921
6.1-376	Repealed
6.1-377	6.2-1901
	6.2-1911
6.1-378	6.2-1912
6.1-378.1	6.2-1913
6.1-378.2	6.2-1914
6.1-378.3	6.2-1915
6.1-378.4	6.2-1920
6.1-378.5	6.2-1916
6.1-378.6	6.2-1917
6.1-378.7	6.2-1918
6.1-378.8	6.2-1919
6.1-379, 6.1-380	Repealed
6.1-381	6.2-700
	6.2-701
6.1-382	6.2-702
6.1-383	6.2-703
6.1-383.1	6.2-704
6.1-383.2	6.2-705
6.1-384	6.2-707
6.1-385	6.2-708
6.1-386	6.2-709
6.1-387	6.2-710
	6.2-705
6.1-388	6.2-711
6.1-389 to 6.1-397	Deleted
6.1-398	6.2-700
6.1-399	6.2-704
6.1-399.1	6.2-712
6.1-400 to 6.1-402	Repealed
6.1-403	6.2-713
6.1-404	6.2-714
	6.2-706
6.1-405	Repealed
6.1-406	6.2-715
6.1-407	Repealed
6.1-408	Deleted
6.1-409	6.2-1600
6.1-410	6.2-1601
6.1-411	6.2-1602
6.1-412	6.2-1603
6.1-413	6.2-1604
6.1-414	6.2-1605
6.1-415	6.2-1606
6.1-416	6.2-1607
6.1-416.1	6.2-1608
6.1-417	6.2-1609
6.1-418	6.2-1610
6.1-419	6.2-1611
6.1-420	6.2-1612
6.1-421	6.2-1613
6.1-422	6.2-1614
	6.2-1615
	6.2-1616
	6.2-1617
6.1-422.1	6.2-1614
	6.2-1628
6.1-423	6.2-1618
6.1-423.1, 6.1-423.2	Repealed
6.1-424	6.2-1614
6.1-425	6.2-1619
6.1-425.1	6.2-1620
6.1-425.2	6.2-1621
6.1-426	6.2-1622
6.1-427	6.2-1623
6.1-428	6.2-1624
6.1-429	6.2-1625
6.1-430	6.2-1626
6.1-430.1	6.2-1629
6.1-431	6.2-1627
6.1-431.1	6.2-1700
6.1-431.2	6.2-1701
6.1-431.3	6.2-1702
6.1-431.4	6.2-1703
6.1-431.5	6.2-1704
6.1-431.6	6.2-1705
6.1-431.7	6.2-1706
6.1-431.8	6.2-1707
6.1-431.9	6.2-1708
6.1-431.10	6.2-1709
6.1-431.11	6.2-1710
6.1-431.12	6.2-1711
6.1-431.13	6.2-1712
6.1-431.14	6.2-1713
6.1-431.15	6.2-1714
6.1-431.16	6.2-1715
6.1-431.17	6.2-1716
6.1-431.18	6.2-1717
6.1-431.19	6.2-1718
6.1-431.20	6.2-1719
6.1-431.21	6.2-1720
6.1-432	6.2-2100
6.1-433	6.2-2101
6.1-434	6.2-2102
6.1-435	6.2-2103
6.1-436	6.2-2104
6.1-437	6.2-2105
6.1-438	6.2-2106
6.1-439	6.2-2107
6.1-440	6.2-2108
6.1-441	6.2-2109
6.1-442	6.2-2110
6.1-443	6.2-2111
6.1-444	6.2-1800
6.1-445	6.2-1801
6.1-446	6.2-1802
6.1-447	6.2-1803
6.1-448	6.2-1804
6.1-449	6.2-1805
6.1-450	6.2-1806
6.1-451	6.2-1807
6.1-452	6.2-1808
6.1-453	6.2-1809
6.1-453.1	6.2-1810
6.1-454	6.2-1811
6.1-455	6.2-1812
6.1-456	6.2-1813
6.1-457	6.2-1814
6.1-458	6.2-1815
6.1-459	6.2-1816
6.1-460	6.2-1817
6.1-461	6.2-1818
6.1-462	6.2-1819
6.1-463	6.2-1820
6.1-464	6.2-1821
6.1-465	6.2-1822
6.1-466	6.2-1823
6.1-467	6.2-1824
6.1-468	6.2-1825
6.1-469	6.2-1826
6.1-469.1	6.2-1827
6.1-470	6.2-1828
6.1-471	6.2-1829
6.1-472	Deleted
6.1-473	6.2-2400
	6.2-2401
	6.2-2402
6.1-474	6.2-2500
6.1-475	6.2-2501
6.1-476	6.2-2501
	6.2-2502
6.1-477	6.2-2503
6.1-478	6.2-2504
6.1-479	6.2-2505
11-30	6.2-424
11-31	6.2-425
11-32	6.2-426
11-33	6.2-427
11-33.1	6.2-428
11-33.2	6.2-429
11-33.3	6.2-430
11-34	6.2-431

COMPARABLE SECTIONS OF TITLE 7.1 TO CHAPTERS 3.1, 4 AND 5 OF TITLE 1

Former Section	Present Section
7.1-1	1-300, 1-301
7.1-2	1-302
7.1-3	1-303

COMPARABLE SECTIONS FOR CERTAIN REPEALED AND REVISED TITLES

Former Section	Present Section
7.1-4	1-304
7.1-4.1	1-305
7.1-5	1-306
7.1-6	1-307
7.1-7	1-308
7.1-7.1	1-309
7.1-7.2	1-310
7.1-9	1-311
7.1-10	1-312
7.1-10.1	1-313
7.1-12	Repealed
7.1-18.1	1-400
7.1-19	1-402
7.1-20	1-403

Former Section	Present Section
7.1-21	1-401
7.1-21.1	1-404
7.1-22	1-405
7.1-23	1-406
7.1-24	1-407
7.1-25.1	1-408
7.1-26	1-500
7.1-27	1-501
7.1-28	1-502
7.1-29	Repealed
7.1-30	1-503
7.1-31	1-504
7.1-31.1	1-505
7.1-32	1-506

Former Section	Present Section
7.1-33	1-507
7.1-34	1-508
7.1-35	1-509
7.1-37	1-510
7.1-38	1-510
7.1-39	1-510
7.1-40	1-510
7.1-40.1 through 7.1-40.13	1-510
7.1-41	30-15.1:1
7.1-42	1-511
7.1-43	1-512
30-19.93	1-247

COMPARABLE SECTIONS OF TITLE 10, ARTICLE 4 OF CHAPTER 5, ARTICLES 1.1 AND 1.1:1 OF CHAPTER 6, AND CHAPTER 21, AND ARTICLES 2.3, 2.4, 2.5 AND 4.02 OF TITLE 62.1, CHAPTER 3.1

Former Section	Present Section
10.1-560	62.1-44.15:51
10.1-561	62.1-44.15:52
10.1-561.1	62.1-44.15:53
10.1-562	62.1-44.15:54
10.1-563	62.1-44.15:55
10.1-564	62.1-44.15:56
10.1-565	62.1-44.15:57
10.1-566	62.1-44.15:58
10.1-566.1	62.1-44.15:59
10.1-566.2	62.1-44.15:60
10.1-567	62.1-44.15:61
10.1-568	62.1-44.15:62
10.1-569	62.1-44.15:63
10.1-569.1	62.1-44.15:64
10.1-570	62.1-44.15:65
10.1-571	62.1-44.15:66
10.1-603.2	62.1-44.15:24
10.1-603.2:1	62.1-44.15:25
10.1-603.2:2	62.1-44.15:26
10.1-603.3	62.1-44.15:27

Former Section	Present Section
10.1-603.4	62.1-44.15:28
10.1-603.4:1	62.1-44.15:29
10.1-603.4:2	62.1-44.15:30
10.1-603.5	62.1-44.15:31
10.1-603.6	62.1-44.15:32
10.1-603.7	62.1-44.15:33
10.1-603.8	62.1-44.15:34
10.1-603.8:1	62.1-44.15:35
10.1-603.10	62.1-44.15:36
10.1-603.11	62.1-44.15:37
10.1-603.12	62.1-44.15:38
10.1-603.12:1	62.1-44.15:39
10.1-603.12:2	62.1-44.15:40
10.1-603.12:3	62.1-44.15:41
10.1-603.12:4	62.1-44.15:42
10.1-603.12:5	62.1-44.15:43
10.1-603.12:6	62.1-44.15:44
10.1-603.12:7	62.1-44.15:45
10.1-603.13	62.1-44.15:46
10.1-603.13:1	62.1-44.15:47

Former Section	Present Section
10.1-603.14	62.1-44.15:48
10.1-603.14:1	62.1-44.15:49
10.1-603.15	62.1-44.15:50
10.1-603.15:3	62.1-44.19:21
10.1-603.15:4	62.1-44.19:22
10.1-603.15:5	62.1-44.19:23
10.1-2100	62.1-44.15:67
10.1-2101	62.1-44.15:68
10.1-2103	62.1-44.15:69
10.1-2104	62.1-44.15:70
10.1-2104.1	62.1-44.15:71
10.1-2107	62.1-44.15:72
10.1-2108	62.1-44.15:73
10.1-2109	62.1-44.15:74
10.1-2110	62.1-44.15:75
10.1-2111	62.1-44.15:76
10.1-2113	62.1-44.15:77
10.1-2114	62.1-44.15:78
10.1-2115	62.1-44.15:79

COMPARABLE SECTIONS OF TITLE 24.2, FORMER CHAPTERS 9, 9.1 AND 9.2

Former Section	Present Section
24.2-900	24.2-945
24.2-901	24.2-945.1
24.2-903	24.2-946
24.2-904	24.2-947.1
	24.2-947.3
	24.2-947.5
24.2-905	24.2-947.2
24.2-905.1	24.2-947.2
24.2-906	24.2-947.3
24.2-906.1	24.2-948.1
24.2-907	24.2-947.2
24.2-908	24.2-947.1
	24.2-947.2

Former Section	Present Section
	24.2-949.2
24.2-908.1	24.2-949.3
24.2-909	24.2-949.1
24.2-910	24.2-945.2
24.2-910.1	24.2-951
24.2-911	24.2-950.1
24.2-912	24.2-950.5
24.2-913	24.2-952
24.2-914	24.2-947.4
24.2-914.1	24.2-946.1
24.2-915	24.2-947.5
24.2-916	24.2-947.6
	24.2-951.4

Former Section	Present Section
24.2-917	24.2-947.7
24.2-918	24.2-947.8
	24.2-951.6
24.2-919	24.2-947.9
24.2-919.1	24.2-948
24.2-920	24.2-948.4
24.2-920.1	24.2-946.5
24.2-921	24.2-948.4
	24.2-949.9
24.2-922	24.2-948.2
24.2-923	24.2-949.6
	24.2-949.7
	24.2-950.6

Former Section	Present Section
	24.2-950.7
24.2-923.1	24.2-946.5
24.2-924	24.2-952.4
24.2-925	24.2-952.7
24.2-926	24.2-946.2
24.2-927	24.2-946.4
	24.2-946.5
24.2-928	24.2-946.3
24.2-929	24.2-953
	24.2-953.3
	24.2-953.4
24.2-930	24.2-953.1
	24.2-953.2
	24.2-953.3
	24.2-953.4
24.2-940	24.2-954
24.2-941	24.2-955
24.2-942	24.2-955.1
24.2-943	24.2-956
24.2-944	24.2-957
	24.2-958

COMPARABLE SECTIONS OF TITLE 26 AND 64.2

Former Section	Present Section
26-1	64.2-1412
26-1.1	64.2-1403
26-1.2	64.2-1409
26-2	64.2-1204
26-3	64.2-1410
26-4	64.2-1411
26-5	64.2-1415
26-5.1	Repealed
26-5.2	64.2-1416
26-6	64.2-1417
26-7	64.2-1418
26-7.1	64.2-1419
26-7.2	64.2-1420
26-7.3	64.2-1421
26-7.4	64.2-1422
26-7.5	64.2-1414
26-8	64.2-1200
26-8.1	64.2-1203
26-9	64.2-1221
26-10	64.2-1201
26-10.1	64.2-1202
26-11	Repealed
26-12	64.2-1300
26-12.1	64.2-1308
26-12.2	64.2-1301
26-12.3	64.2-1302
26-12.4	64.2-1303
26-13	64.2-1215
26-14	64.2-1205
26-15	64.2-1309
26-16	64.2-1310
26-16.1	Repealed
26-17 through 26-17.2	Repealed
26-17.3	64.2-1206, 64.2-1308
26-17.4	64.2-1305
26-17.5	64.2-1304
26-17.6	64.2-1306
26-17.7	64.2-1307
26-17.8	Repealed
26-17.9	64.2-1311
26-17.10	64.2-1312
26-18	64.2-1216
26-19	64.2-1217
26-20	64.2-1313
26-20.1	64.2-1314
26-21	64.2-1315
26-22	Repealed
26-23	64.2-1218
26-24	64.2-1219
26-25	64.2-1316
26-26	64.2-1220
26-27	64.2-1222
26-28	64.2-1207
26-29	64.2-1209
26-30	64.2-1208
26-31	64.2-1210
26-32	64.2-1211
26-33	64.2-1212
26-34	64.2-1213
26-35	64.2-1214
26-35.1	Repealed
26-36	Repealed
26-36.1	Repealed
26-37	64.2-1317
26-38	64.2-1500
26-39	64.2-1501
26-40	2.2-4519
26-40.01	64.2-1502
26-40.1	64.2-1503
26-40.2	64.2-1504
26-41	2.2-4519
26-42	2.2-4519
26-43	2.2-4519
26-44	2.2-4519, 64.2-1505
26-44.1	64.2-1506
26-45	Repealed
26-45.1	Repealed
26-45.2	64.2-1413
26-45.3	64.2-781
26-45.4	64.2-782
26-45.5	64.2-783
26-45.6	64.2-784
26-45.7	64.2-785
26-45.8	64.2-786
26-45.9	64.2-787
26-45.10	64.2-788
26-45.11	64.2-789
26-45.12	64.2-790
26-45.13	64.2-780
26-45.14	64.2-791
26-46	64.2-1424
26-46.1	64.2-1400
26-46.2	64.2-1401
26-46.3	64.2-1401, 64.2-1402
26-47	64.2-1404
26-48	64.2-1405
26-49	Repealed
26-50	64.2-1406
26-51	64.2-1407
26-52	64.2-1408
26-53 through 26-55	Repealed
26-56	64.2-1425
26-57	Deleted
26-58	64.2-1423
26-59	64.2-1426
26-60	64.2-1427
26-61	64.2-1428
26-62	64.2-1429
26-63	64.2-1430
26-64, 26-65	Repealed
26-66	64.2-1431
26-67	64.2-1432
26-68	64.2-2400
26-68.1	64.2-2401
26-69	64.2-2402
26-70	64.2-2403
26-71	64.2-2404
26-72	Deleted
26-73	64.2-1600
26-74	64.2-1601
26-75	64.2-1602
26-76	64.2-1603
26-77	64.2-1604
26-78	64.2-1605
26-79	64.2-1606
26-80	64.2-1607
26-81	64.2-1608
26-82	64.2-1609
26-83	64.2-1610
26-84	64.2-1611
26-85	64.2-1612
26-86	64.2-1613
26-87	64.2-1614
26-88	64.2-1615
26-89	64.2-1616

Former Section	Present Section
26-90	64.2-1617
26-91	64.2-1618
26-92	64.2-1619
26-93	64.2-1620
26-94	64.2-1621
26-95	64.2-1622
26-96	64.2-1623
26-97	64.2-1624
26-98	64.2-1625
26-99	64.2-1626
26-100	64.2-1627
26-101	64.2-1628
26-102	64.2-1629
26-103	64.2-1630
26-104	64.2-1631
26-105	64.2-1632
26-106	64.2-1633
26-107	64.2-1634
26-108	64.2-1635
26-109	64.2-1636
26-110	64.2-1637
26-111	64.2-1638
26-112	Deleted
26-113	64.2-1639
26-114	64.2-1640
26-115	64.2-1641
26-116	64.2-1642

COMPARABLE SECTIONS OF TITLE 31 AND 64.2

Former Section	Present Section
31-1	64.2-1700
31-2	64.2-1701
31-3	64.2-1701
31-4	64.2-1702
31-5	64.2-1703
31-6	64.2-1704
31-6.1	64.2-1705
31-7	64.2-1706
31-8	64.2-1800
31-8.1	64.2-1801
31-8.2	64.2-1802
31-9	64.2-1803
31-10 through 31-13.	Repealed
31-14	64.2-1804
31-14.1	64.2-1805
31-15 through 31-18.	Repealed
31-18.1	64.2-1806
31-19 through 31-25	Repealed
31-26 through 31-36	Repealed
31-37	64.2-1900
31-38	64.2-1901
31-39	64.2-1902
31-40	64.2-1903
31-41	64.2-1904
31-42	64.2-1905
31-43	64.2-1906
31-44	64.2-1907
31-45	64.2-1908
31-46	64.2-1909
31-47	64.2-1910
31-48	64.2-1911
31-49	64.2-1912
31-50	64.2-1913
31-51	64.2-1914
31-52	64.2-1915
31-53	64.2-1916
31-54	64.2-1917
31-55	64.2-1918
31-56	64.2-1919
31-57	64.2-1920
31-58	64.2-1921
31-59	64.2-1922

COMPARABLE SECTIONS OF TITLE 37.1 TO 37.2

Former Section	Present Section
37.1-1	37.2-100
37.1-1.2	Deleted
37.1-3	37.2-200A
37.1-4	37.2-200B
37.1-5	37.2-200C
37.1-6	37.2-200D
37.1-7	37.2-200D
37.1-10	37.2-203
37.1-10.01	37.2-312
37.1-10.1	37.2-201
37.1-11	37.2-700A
37.1-12	37.2-700B
37.1-13	37.2-701
37.1-19	37.2-202
37.1-20.1	37.2-313
37.1-20.3	37.2-314
37.1-22	37.2-305
37.1-23	Deleted
37.1-23.1	Deleted
37.1-24	37.2-306
37.1-24.01	37.2-402
37.1-24.2	37.2-702
37.1-27	37.2-703
37.1-28	37.2-704
37.1-29	37.2-705A
37.1-30	37.2-705B
37.1-31	37.2-705C
37.1-32	37.2-705D
37.1-33	37.2-706
37.1-34	37.2-203
37.1-38	37.2-307
37.1-39	37.2-300
37.1-40	37.2-301
37.1-41	37.2-302
37.1-42	37.2-303
37.1-42.1	37.2-304
37.1-42.2	37.2-707, 37.2-709
37.1-42.3	37.2-708
37.1-44	Deleted
37.1-47	Deleted
37.1-48	37.2-840
37.1-48.1	37.2-315
37.1-48.2	37.2-316
37.1-58	Deleted
37.1-58.1	Deleted
37.1-61	Deleted
37.1-63	37.2-800
37.1-64	37.2-801
37.1-65	37.2-805
37.1-65.1	37.2-806
37.1-65.2	37.2-807
37.1-65.3	Deleted
37.1-67.01	37.2-808
37.1-67.1	37.2-809 through 37.2-813
37.1-67.3	37.2-814 through 37.2-819
37.1-67.4	37.2-809, 37.2-820
37.1-67.5	37.2-802
37.1-67.5:01	37.2-802
37.1-67.6	37.2-821
37.1-68	37.2-823
37.1-70	37.2-823
37.1-70.1	37.2-900
37.1-70.2	37.2-901
37.1-70.3	37.2-902
37.1-70.4	37.2-903
37.1-70.5	37.2-904

Former Section	Present Section
37.1-70.6	37.2-905
37.1-70.7	37.2-906
37.1-70.8	37.2-907
37.1-70.9	37.2-908
37.1-70.10	37.2-909
37.1-70.11	37.2-910
37.1-70.12	37.2-911
37.1-70.13	37.2-912
37.1-70.14	37.2-913
37.1-70.15	37.2-914
37.1-70.16	37.2-915
37.1-70.17	37.2-916
37.1-70.18	37.2-917
37.1-70.19	37.2-918
37.1-71	37.2-829
37.1-72	37.2-830
37.1-73	37.2-831
37.1-74	37.2-832
37.1-75	37.2-833
37.1-76	37.2-834
37.1-77	37.2-835
37.1-78	37.2-836
37.1-78.1	37.2-840
37.1-84.1	37.2-400, 37.2-401
37.1-84.1:1	37.2-712
37.1-84.2	37.2-824
37.1-84.3	37.2-204
37.1-85	37.2-822
37.1-87	37.2-825
37.1-88	37.2-803
37.1-89	37.2-804
37.1-90	Deleted
37.1-91	37.2-826
37.1-92	37.2-827
37.1-93	37.2-841
37.1-94	37.2-842
37.1-95	37.2-828
37.1-96	37.2-713
37.1-97	37.2-714
37.1-98	37.2-837
37.1-98.2	37.2-710, 37.2-711, 37.2-839
37.1-99	37.2-838, 37.2-840
37.1-100	Deleted
37.1-101	37.2-843
37.1-103	37.2-844
37.1-104	37.2-845
37.1-104.1	37.2-846
37.1-104.2	37.2-847
37.1-105	37.2-715
37.1-106	37.2-716
37.1-107	Deleted
37.1-108	37.2-717A
37.1-109	37.2-717B
37.1-110	37.2-718A,B
37.1-111	37.2-718C
37.1-112	37.2-718D
37.1-113	37.2-718E
37.1-114	37.2-718F
37.1-115	37.2-718G
37.1-116	37.2-720
37.1-117	37.2-721
37.1-118	37.2-719
37.1-119	Deleted
37.1-121	Deleted
37.1-122	Deleted
37.1-123	Deleted
37.1-124	Deleted
37.1-125	Deleted
37.1-126	Deleted
37.1-134.6	37.2-1000
37.1-134.7	37.2-1001
37.1-134.8	37.2-1002
37.1-134.9	37.2-1003
37.1-134.10	37.2-1004
37.1-134.11	37.2-1005
37.1-134.12	37.2-1006
37.1-134.13	37.2-1007
37.1-134.13:1	37.2-1008
37.1-134.14	37.2-1009
37.1-134.14:1	37.2-1010
37.1-134.15	37.2-1011
37.1-134.16	37.2-1012
37.1-134.17	37.2-1013
37.1-134.18	37.2-1014
37.1-134.19	37.2-1015
37.1-134.20	37.2-1016
37.1-134.21	37.2-1100 through 37.2-1108
37.1-134.22	37.2-1018
37.1-136	37.2-1019
37.1-137	37.2-1015
37.1-137.1	37.2-1020
37.1-137.2	37.2-1021
37.1-137.3	37.2-1022
37.1-137.4	37.2-1023
37.1-137.5	37.2-1024
37.1-139	37.2-1025
37.1-141	37.2-1026
37.1-143	37.2-1017
37.1-144	37.2-1027
37.1-146	37.2-1028
37.1-147	37.2-1029
37.1-148	37.2-426
37.1-149	Deleted
37.1-150	37.2-427
37.1-151	37.2-428
37.1-152	37.2-429
37.1-153	37.2-430
37.1-154	37.2-431
37.1-155	Deleted
37.1-172	Deleted
37.1-173	Deleted
37.1-174	Deleted
37.1-175	Deleted
37.1-176	Deleted
37.1-177	Deleted
37.1-178	Deleted
37.1-179	37.2-403
37.1-179.1	37.2-404
37.1-179.2	37.2-406
37.1-181	37.2-410
37.1-182	37.2-411
37.1-182.1	37.2-407
37.1-182.2	Deleted
37.1-182.3	37.2-412
37.1-183.1	37.2-405
37.1-183.2	37.2-415
37.1-183.3	37.2-416
37.1-184	37.2-413
37.1-185	37.2-418
37.1-185.1	37.2-419
37.1-186	37.2-418
37.1-186.1	37.2-420
37.1-187	37.2-417
37.1-188	37.2-414
37.1-188.1	37.2-421
37.1-189	37.2-422
37.1-189.1	37.2-408
37.1-189.2	37.2-409
37.1-189.3	37.2-308
37.1-194	37.2-500
37.1-194.1	37.2-100
37.1-195	37.2-501
37.1-196	37.2-502
37.1-196.1	37.2-503
37.1-197	37.2-504
37.1-197.1	37.2-505
37.1-197.2	37.2-506, 37.2-607
37.1-197.3	37.2-507, 37.2-605
37.1-198	37.2-508
37.1-199	37.2-509
37.1-200	37.2-510
37.1-202.1	37.2-511, 37.2-612
37.1-203	37.2-100
37.1-204	37.2-309
37.1-205	37.2-310
37.1-205.1	37.2-310
37.1-206	37.2-311
37.1-207	2.2-2690
37.1-207.1	2.2-2691
37.1-219A	Deleted
37.1-219B	37.2-310(12)
37.1-219C	37.2-310(13)
37.1-219D	37.2-309
37.1-220 through 37.1-224	Deleted
37.1-225	37.2-432
37.1-226	37.2-433
37.1-227	37.2-434
37.1-228	37.2-435
37.1-229	37.2-436
37.1-230	37.2-437

COMPARABLE SECTIONS FOR CERTAIN REPEALED AND REVISED TITLES

Former Section	Present Section
37.1-231	37.2-438
37.1-232	37.2-439
37.1-233	37.2-440
37.1-242	37.2-601
37.1-243	37.2-100, 37.2-600
37.1-244	37.2-601
37.1-245	37.2-602
37.1-246	37.2-603
37.1-247	37.2-604
37.1-248	37.2-605, 37.2-606, 37.2-612
37.1-248.1	37.2-608
37.1-249	37.2-609
37.1-250	37.2-610
37.1-251	37.2-611
37.1-252	37.2-613
37.1-253	37.2-614
37.1-255	37.2-423
37.1-256	37.2-424
37.1-256.1	37.2-425
37.1-258	37.2-317
37.1-259	37.2-318
37.1-260	37.2-319

COMPARABLE SECTIONS OF TITLE 37.2 AND 64.2

Former Section	Present Section
37.2-100	64.2-2000
37.2-1001	64.2-2001
37.2-1002	64.2-2002
37.2-1003	64.2-2003
37.2-1004	64.2-2004
37.2-1005	64.2-2005
37.2-1006	64.2-2006
37.2-1007	64.2-2007
37.2-1008	64.2-2008
37.2-1009	64.2-2009
37.2-1010	64.2-2010
37.2-1011	64.2-2011
37.2-1012	64.2-2012
37.2-1013	64.2-2013
37.2-1014	64.2-2014
37.2-1015	64.2-2015
37.2-1016	64.2-2016
37.2-1017	64.2-2017
37.2-1018	Repealed
37.2-1019	64.2-2018
37.2-1020	64.2-2019
37.2-1021	64.2-2020
37.2-1022	64.2-2021
37.2-1023	64.2-2022
37.2-1024	64.2-2023
37.2-1025	64.2-2024
37.2-1026	64.2-2025
37.2-1027	64.2-2026
37.2-1028	64.2-2027
37.2-1029	64.2-2028
37.2-1030	64.2-20
37.2-1031	Deleted
37.2-1032	64.2-2100
37.2-1033	64.2-2101
37.2-1034	64.2-2102
37.2-1035	64.2-2103
37.2-1036	64.2-2104
37.2-1037	64.2-2105
37.2-1038	64.2-2106
37.2-1039	64.2-2107
37.2-1040	64.2-2108
37.2-1041	64.2-2109
37.2-1042	64.2-2110
37.2-1043	64.2-2111
37.2-1044	64.2-2112
37.2-1045.	64.2-2113
37.2-1046	64.2-2114
37.2-1047	64.2-2115
37.2-1048	64.2-2116
37.2-1049	64.2-2117
37.2-1050	64.2-2118
37.2-1051	64.2-2119
37.2-1052	64.2-2120

COMPARABLE SECTIONS OF TITLE 55 AND 64.2

Former Section	Present Section
55-34.1	64.2-900
55-34.2	64.2-901
55-34.3	64.2-902
55-34.4	64.2-903
55-34.5	64.2-904
55-34.6	64.2-905
55-34.7	64.2-906
55-34.8	64.2-907
55-34.9	64.2-908
55-34.10	64.2-909
55-34.11	64.2-910
55-34.12	64.2-911
55-34.13	64.2-912
55-34.14	64.2-913
55-34.15	64.2-914
55-34.16	64.2-915
55-34.17	64.2-916
55-34.18	64.2-917
55-34.19	64.2-918
55-268.11	Deleted
55-268.12	64.2-1100
55-268.13	64.2-1101
55-268.14	64.2-1102
55-268.15	64.2-1103
55-268.16	64.2-1104
55-268.17	64.2-1105
55-268.18	64.2-1106
55-268.19	64.2-1107
55-268.20	64.2-1108
55-277.1	Deleted
55-277.2	64.2-1000
55-277.3	64.2-1001
55-277.4	64.2-1002
55-277.4:1	64.2-1003
55-277.5	64.2-1004
55-277.6	64.2-1005
55-277.7	64.2-1006
55-277.8	64.2-1007
55-277.9	64.2-1008
55-277.10	64.2-1009
55-277.11	64.2-1010
55-277.12	64.2-1011
55-277.13	64.2-1012
55-277.14	64.2-1013
55-277.15	64.2-1014
55-277.16	64.2-1015
55-277.17	64.2-1016
55-277.18	64.2-1017
55-277.19	64.2-1018
55-277.20	64.2-1019
55-277.21	64.2-1020
55-277.22	64.2-1021
55-277.23	64.2-1022
55-277.24	64.2-1023
55-277.25	64.2-1024
55-277.26	64.2-1025
55-277.27	64.2-1026
55-277.28	64.2-1027
55-277.29	64.2-1028
55-277.30	64.2-1029
55-277.31	64.2-1030
55-277.32	64.2-1031
55-277.33	64.2-1032
55-278	64.2-2700
55-279	64.2-2701
55-280	64.2-2702
55-281	Deleted
55-282	64.2-2704
55-283	64.2-2703

Former Section	Present Section
55-284	64.2-2703
55-285	64.2-2703
55-286	64.2-2703
55-286.1	64.2-2704
55-286.2	64.2-2704
55-401	64.2-2500
55-402	64.2-2501
55-403	64.2-2502
55-404	64.2-2502
55-405	64.2-2503
55-406	64.2-2503
55-407	64.2-2504
55-408	64.2-2505
55-409	64.2-2506
55-410	64.2-2507
55-411	64.2-2508
55-412	64.2-2509
55-413	64.2-2510
55-414	64.2-2511
55-415	64.2-2511
55-541.01	Deleted
55-541.02	64.2-700
55-541.03	64.2-701
55-541.04	64.2-702
55-541.05	64.2-703
55-541.06	64.2-704
55-541.07	64.2-705
55-541.08	64.2-706
55-541.09	64.2-707
55-541.10	64.2-708
55-541.11	64.2-709
55-542.01	64.2-710
55-542.02	64.2-711
55-542.03, 55-542.04	Deleted
55-542.05	64.2-712
55-542.06	64.2-713
55-543.01	64.2-714
55-543.02	64.2-715
55-543.03	64.2-716
55-543.04	64.2-717
55-543.05	64.2-718
55-544.01	64.2-719
55-544.02	64.2-720
55-544.03	64.2-721
55-544.04.	64.2-722
55-544.05	64.2-723
55-544.06	64.2-724
55-544.07	64.2-725
55-544.08	64.2-726
55-544.09	64.2-727
55-544.10	64.2-728
55-544.11	64.2-729
55-544.12	64.2-730
55-544.13	64.2-731
55-544.14	64.2-732
55-544.15	64.2-733
55-544.16	64.2-734
55-544.17	64.2-735
55-544.18	64.2-736
55-544.19	64.2-737
55-544.20	64.2-738
55-544.21	64.2-739
55-544.22	64.2-740
55-544.23	64.2-741
55-545.01	64.2-742
55-545.02	64.2-743
55-545.03	64.2-744
55-545.03:1	64.2-745
55-545.04	64.2-746
55-545.05	64.2-747
55-545.06	64.2-748
55-545.07	64.2-749
55-546.01	64.2-750
55-546.02	64.2-751
55-546.03	64.2-752
55-546.04	64.2-753
55-547.01	64.2-754
55-547.02	64.2-755
55-547.03	64.2-756
55-547.04	64.2-757
55-547.05	64.2-758
55-547.06	64.2-759
55-547.07	64.2-760
55-547.08	64.2-761
55-547.09	64.2-762
55-548.01	64.2-763
55-548.02	64.2-764
55-548.03	64.2-765
55-548.04	64.2-766
55-548.05	64.2-767
55-548.06	64.2-768
55-548.07	64.2-769
55-548.08	64.2-770
55-548.09	64.2-771
55-548.10	64.2-772
55-548.11	64.2-773
55-548.12	64.2-774
55-548.13	64.2-775
55-548.14	64.2-776
55-548.15	64.2-777
55-548.16	64.2-778
55-548.17	64.2-779
55-550.01	64.2-792
55-550.02	64.2-793
55-550.03	64.2-794
55-550.04	64.2-795
55-550.05	64.2-796
55-550.06	64.2-797
55-550.07	64.2-798
55-550.08	64.2-799
55-550.09	64.2-800
55-550.10	64.2-801
55-550.11	64.2-802
55-550.12	64.2-803
55-550.13	64.2-804
55-551.01	64.2-805
55-551.02	64.2-806
55-551.03	64.2-807
55-551.04, 55-551.05	Deleted
55-551.06	64.2-808

COMPARABLE SECTIONS OF TITLE 64.1 AND 64.2

Former Section	Present Section
64.1-01	64.2-100
64.1-1	64.2-200
64.1-2	64.2-202
64.1-3	64.2-202
64.1-4	64.2-203
64.1-5	Repealed
64.1-5.1	64.2-102
64.1-5.2	64.2-103
64.1-6	Repealed
64.1-6.1	64.2-203
64.1-7	Repealed
64.1-7.1	Repealed
64.1-8	Repealed
64.1-8.1	64.2-204
64.1-9	Repealed
64.1-10	64.2-205
64.1-11	64.2-201
64.1-12	64.2-201
64.1-13	64.2-302
64.1-14	64.2-303
64.1-15	Repealed
64.1-16	64.2-304
64.1-16.1	64.2-300, 64.2-305
64.1-16.2	64.2-300, 64.2-306
64.1-16.3	64.2-308
64.1-16.4	64.2-307
64.1-17	64.2-206
64.1-18	Repealed
64.1-19, 64.1-19.1	Repealed
64.1-19.2	64.2-301
64.1-20 through 64.1-44	Repealed
64.1-45	64.2-100
64.1-45.1	64.2-400
64.1-45.2	64.2-104

Former Section	Present Section
64.1-45.3	64.2-620
64.1-46	64.2-401
64.1-47	64.2-401
64.1-48	64.2-402
64.1-49	64.2-403
64.1-49.1	64.2-404
64.1-50	64.2-406
64.1-51	64.2-405
64.1-52	Deleted
64.1-53	64.2-407, 64.2-408
64.1-54	64.2-408
64.1-55	Deleted
64.1-56	64.2-409
64.1-57	64.2-105
64.1-57.1	64.2-106
64.1-57.2	64.2-107
64.1-57.3	64.2-108
64.1-58	Repealed
64.1-58.1	64.2-410
64.1-59	64.2-412
64.1-60	64.2-411
64.1-61	64.2-413
64.1-62	64.2-414
64.1-62.1	64.2-430
64.1-62.2	64.2-431
64.1-62.3	64.2-415
64.1-62.4	64.2-432
64.1-63.	Repealed
64.1-63.1	64.2-417
64.1-64	Repealed
64.1-64.1	64.2-418
64.1-65	Repealed
64.1-65.1	64.2-416
64.1-66	64.2-415
64.1-66.1	Repealed
64.1-66.2	64.2-421
64.1-67	Repealed
64.1-67.1	64.2-423
64.1-67.2	Repealed
64.1-68	64.2-425
64.1-69	64.2-424
64.1-69.1	64.2-422
64.1-70	64.2-419
64.1-71	64.2-420
64.1-71.1	64.2-101
64.1-72	64.2-414
64.1-73	64.2-426
64.1-73.1	64.2-427
64.1-74	64.2-428
64.1-74.1	64.2-429
64.1-75	64.2-443
64.1-75.1	64.2-454
64.1-76	64.2-443
64.1-77	64.2-444
64.1-78	64.2-445
64.1-79	64.2-446
64.1-80	64.2-446
64.1-81	64.2-449
64.1-82	64.2-446
64.1-83	64.2-446
64.1-84	64.2-448
64.1-85	64.2-446
64.1-86	64.2-449
64.1-87	64.2-447
64.1-87.1	64.2-452
64.1-87.2	64.2-453
64.1-88	64.2-448
64.1-89	64.2-448
64.1-90	64.2-448
64.1-91	64.2-449
64.1-92	64.2-450
64.1-93	64.2-451
64.1-94	64.2-455
64.1-95	64.2-456
64.1-96	64.2-457
64.1-96.1	64.2-458
64.1-96.2	64.2-433
64.1-96.3	64.2-434
64.1-96.4	64.2-435
64.1-96.5	64.2-436
64.1-96.6	64.2-437
64.1-96.7	64.2-438
64.1-96.8	64.2-439
64.1-96.9	64.2-440
64.1-96.10	64.2-441
64.1-96.11	64.2-442
64.1-97 through 64.1-104	Repealed
64.1-104.1	64.2-2200
64.1-104.2	64.2-2201
64.1-104.3	64.2-2202
64.1-104.4	64.2-2203
64.1-104.5	64.2-2204
64.1-104.6	64.2-2205
64.1-104.7	64.2-2206
64.1-104.8	64.2-2207
64.1-104.9	64.2-2208
64.1-105	64.2-2300
64.1-105.1, 64.1-105.2	Repealed
64.1-106	64.2-2301
64.1-106.1	64.2-2302
64.1-107	64.2-2303
64.1-108	64.2-2304
64.1-109.	Repealed
64.1-110	64.2-2304
64.1-111	64.2-2305
64.1-112	64.2-2306
64.1-113	64.2-2307
64.1-114	64.2-2308
64.1-115	64.2-2309
64.1-116	64.2-500
64.1-117	64.2-501
64.1-118	64.2-502
64.1-119	64.2-502, 64.2-503
64.1-120	64.2-504
64.1-121	64.2-505
64.1-122	64.2-506
64.1-122.1	64.2-507
64.1-122.2	64.2-508
64.1-123 through 64.1-123.1	Repealed
64.1-123.2	64.2-606
64.1-123.3 through 64.1-125	Repealed
64.1-126, 64.1-127	Repealed
64.1-128	64.2-607
64.1-129	64.2-608
64.1-130	64.2-609
64.1-131	64.2-610
64.1-132	64.2-611
64.1-132.1	64.2-600
64.1-132.2	64.2-601
64.1-132.3	64.2-602
64.1-132.4	64.2-603
64.1-132.5	64.2-604
64.1-132.6	64.2-605
64.1-133.	Repealed
64.1-134	64.2-509
64.1-135	64.2-510
64.1-136	64.2-511
64.1-136.1	64.2-512
64.1-137	64.2-513
64.1-138	Deleted
64.1-139	64.2-514
64.1-140	64.2-515
64.1-141	64.2-516
64.1-142	64.2-517
64.1-143	64.2-518
64.1-144	64.2-519
64.1-145	64.2-520
64.1-146	64.2-521
64.1-147	64.2-521
64.1-148	64.2-523
64.1-149	64.2-524
64.1-150	64.2-524
64.1-151	64.2-522
64.1-151.1	64.2-309
64.1-151.2	64.2-310
64.1-151.3	64.2-311
64.1-151.4	64.2-309, 64.2-312
64.1-151.5	64.2-313
64.1-151.6	64.2-314
64.1-152	64.2-525
64.1-153	64.2-526
64.1-154	64.2-526
64.1-155	64.2-526
64.1-156	64.2-527
64.1-157	64.2-528
64.1-157.1	64.2-531
64.1-158	64.2-529
64.1-159	64.2-530
64.1-160	64.2-539
64.1-161	64.2-540
64.1-162	64.2-541
64.1-163	64.2-542

Former Section	Present Section
64.1-164	Repealed
64.1-165	64.2-543
64.1-165.1	64.2-544
64.1-166	64.2-545
64.1-167	64.2-546
64.1-168	64.2-547
64.1-169	64.2-548
64.1-170	64.2-548, 64.2-549
64.1-171	64.2-550
64.1-172	64.2-550, 64.2-551
64.1-173	64.2-552
64.1-174	64.2-553
64.1-175	64.2-553
64.1-176	64.2-553
64.1-177	64.2-554
64.1-178	64.2-555
64.1-179	64.2-556
64.1-180	64.2-557
64.1-180.1	64.2-558
64.1-181	64.2-532
64.1-182	64.2-533
64.1-183	64.2-534
64.1-184	64.2-535
64.1-185	64.2-536
64.1-186	64.2-537
64.1-187	64.2-538
64.1-188 through 64.1-196	Repealed
64.1-196.1	64.2-2600
64.1-196.2	64.2-2601
64.1-196.3	64.2-2602
64.1-196.4	64.2-2603
64.1-196.5	64.2-2604
64.1-196.6	64.2-2605
64.1-196.7	64.2-2606
64.1-196.8	64.2-2607
64.1-196.9	64.2-2608
64.1-196.10	64.2-2609
64.1-196.11	64.2-2610
64.1-196.12	64.2-2611
64.1-196.13	64.2-2612
64.1-196.14	64.2-2613
64.1-196.15	64.2-2614
64.1-197	64.2-315
64.1-198	64.2-316
64.1-199	64.2-317
64.1-200	64.2-318
64.1-201	64.2-319
64.1-202	64.2-320
64.1-203	64.2-321
64.1-204	64.2-322
64.1-205	64.2-323
64.1-206	64.2-324
64.1-206.1	64.2-612
64.1-206.2	64.2-613
64.1-206.3	64.2-614
64.1-206.4	64.2-615
64.1-206.5	64.2-616
64.1-206.6	64.2-617
64.1-206.7	64.2-618
64.1-206.8	64.2-619